Architectural Graphic Standards

THE AMERICAN INSTITUTE OF ARCHITECTS

PRESENTING THE

SIXTH EDITION

OF THE LATE AUTHORS

CHARLES G. RAMSEY

AND

HAROLD R. SLEEPER

The American Institute of Architects proudly presents this new edition of Architectural Graphic Standards. Many individuals and members have contributed generously to the preparation of its plates. To them the Institute extends its thanks.

It can be stated without qualification that this standard refernce work should be in every architect's office. The very fact that it has been published in five previous editions is testimony to its usefulness. In this time of technological transformation, The American Institute of Architects is in-increasingly obligated to provide authoritative practice aids. Six years in preparation, this book with painstaking research helps to meet that responsibility. We sincerely hope that you find it useful.

Rex Whitaker Allen, FAIA
President
The American Institute of Architects

JOHN WILEY & SONS, INC.

ARCHITECTURAL GRAPHIC STANDARDS

CHAIRMAN, EDITORIAL ADVISORY COMMITTEE
HAROLD D. HAUF, FAIA

EDITOR,
JOSEPH N. BOAZ, AIA

NEW YORK   LONDON   SYDNEY   TORONTO

Project Director and Technical Editor, Walker G. Stone

Coordinating Editor for Production and Operations, Charles Fouhy, AIA

Coordinating Editor for Manuscript, Douglas S. Stenhouse, AIA

Chief, Architectural Draftsmen, David E. Miller

Designer, Format of Architectural Plates, Joe N. Boaz, AIA

Designers, Cover and Title Page, Robert Goff and Walker G. Stone

Supervisors of Manufacturing, Dennis M. Hudson and Jeramiah McCarthy

ARCHITECTURAL GRAPHIC STANDARDS

Copyright © 1970 by John Wiley & Sons, Inc.
Copyright © 1932, 1936, 1941, 1951, 1956, by Charles George Ramsey and Harold Reese Sleeper

Library of Congress Catalog Card Number 79-136970

ISBN 0-471-70780-5

Printed in the United States of America

10 9 8 7 6

FOREWORD

Architectural Graphic Standards was initially authored in 1932 by Charles George Ramsey, AIA, and Harold Reeve Sleeper, FAIA. Since then, this encyclopedia has served as a major reference guide serving architects, engineers, designers, builders, decorators, homeowners, draftsmen, and students. Keeping with the high standards and traditions of the late authors, the Sixth Edition represents the optimum judgment on current standards and practice and is the joint effort of The American Institute of Architects and John Wiley & Sons, Inc. Because of its breadth of scope the book reflects a contribution from the entire profession of architects.

The Sixth Edition is entirely new in organization and format but carries on the philosophy of earlier editions. It remains a source book and standards guide, and not a book of experimental, exotic or sophisticated techniques. It illustrates proven and current practice. The book will be exceptionally valuable to its users for establishing the general parameters of design in the early stages of a project. Although it includes overall design guidelines, it does not attempt to influence the technique of building construction since this process is the province of the practitioner. Throughout, an effort has been made to present materials free of bias in design either in a traditional or contemporary sense.

The reader will note that in organizing the Sixth Edition the authors supported a 16-part organizational sequence upon which the Uniform System for Construction Specifications, Data Filing and Cost Accounting* was to be based. It was anticipated, however, that Architectural Graphic Standards' fundamental emphasis upon the graphic presentation of construction details would require a degree of departure from the evolving Uniform System. Deviations did develop and are indicated by differences between chapter titles in Architectural Graphic Standards and corresponding division titles in the Uniform System (see statement on Table of Contents page). Essentially, the 16-part idea is utilized to make the Sixth Edition easier to use for those familiar with the System. For others, it can serve as an introduction to the logic and convenience of a standardized sequence for information within the building industry.

The user of Architectural Graphic Standards can be assured that every page has been subject to careful review and analysis and represents the best effort possible within the constraint of space and time. Some readers will also regret the omission of certain plates—for example, the beautiful sketch of a Georgian Town Clock, and its replacement by an equally elegant Clock and Carillon Tower to meet present day needs and usage. However, in some cases, we have retained material from earlier editions since it would be nearly impossible to find such material outside of the Library of Congress if it were needed in a work of archeological restoration or alteration. Such examples can be found in the fireplace section.

In summary, the Editorial Advisory Committee, editor, coordinating editors, and project directors have attempted to provide the user of Architectural Graphic Standards with the basic information needed for day to day actual practice; by indicating guidelines for construction applicable to the entire architectural spectrum, ranging from the humble shed to the complex curtain wall high rise building. We have not thrown away the past, nor have we endeavored to fill the book with the complicated and specialized world of technology which is coming in the next decade.

WALKER G. STONE
Vice President
John Wiley & Sons, Inc.

New York, N.Y.
June 30, 1970

* Copyright © 1966, American Institute of Architects
Associated General Contractors of America, Inc.
The Construction Specifications Institute, Inc.
Council of Mechanical Specialty Contracting Industries, Inc.

PREFACE

For generations of architects, engineers, draftsmen and builders, Architectural Graphic Standards will need no introduction. It has been their drafting room companion since 1932 when the 233-page First Edition, authored by Charles George Ramsey, AIA, and Harold Reeve Sleeper, FAIA, was published by Wiley. In the subsequent four editions, including the Fifth published in 1956, these authors revised, modernized, added new pages and dropped obsolete ones until the Fifth Edition contained 758 pages, and the work was established as the architects' and building industry's reference bible. With every edition, the task of updating required more and more time for research, analysis, and plate development and this activity became in essence Harold R. Sleeper's career and his major contribution to the architectural profession. During Sleeper's last years, and after work on the Sixth Edition had begun, he invited his publisher to carry on this work. He also expressed the hope that The American Institute of Architects would assume authorship and carry on his, Ramsey's, and his publisher's graphic standards philosophy for the benefit of future generations of practitioners.

In 1962, Walker G. Stone, an Architectural Engineering graduate of the University of Illinois, with a position at that time as Editor-in-Chief, Professional Publications, and later Vice President of Wiley, began discussion with William H. Scheick, Executive Director of the AIA, with the objective of carrying out Sleeper's expressed wish. The AIA responded favorably since a new edition of Architectural Graphic Standards, reflecting the rapidly changing techniques of contemporary building, was in keeping with the Institute's goal of serving its membership and the building industry with authoritative practice aids. In 1963, Wiley and the AIA jointly established an Advisory Board on Architectural Graphic Standards to advise both parties on the feasibility, contents and format of the project. The members of the ten man board were Walker G. Stone, Wiley, New York, New York; John C. Anderson, AIA, Minneapolis, Minnesota; Joseph N. Boaz, AIA, Atlanta, Georgia; Harold D. Hauf, FAIA, Los Angeles, California; Dean F. Hilfinger, FAIA, Bloomington, Illinois; Gershon Meckler, PE, Toledo, Ohio; Edwin T. Pairo, AIA, Washington, D.C.; F. Spencer Roach, AIA, Philadelphia, Pennsylvania; Harry E. Rodman, FAIA, Troy, New York, and Jack Train, FAIA, Chicago, Illinois.

Thus in July, 1964, on the basis of the Advisory Board's report, Wiley and the AIA agreed as publisher and author to produce this Sixth Edition. Joseph N. Boaz, AIA, former Professor of Architecture, School of Design, North Carolina State University and now with the architectural firm of Toombs, Amisano and Wells, Atlanta,

Georgia, accepted the invitation to become its editor. His leave of absence was arranged through the willing support of the Dean of the School of Design, Henry Kamphoefner, FAIA. He immediately took up residence in New York City where the project became headquartered in space provided by Wiley.

The Advisory Board's recommendations had made it clear that the new edition would be a completely new book, not simply a revision. To assist the Editor in determining content, organization and format, a smaller Editorial Advisory Committee succeeded the earlier ten man board. The committee was composed of the following: Harold D. Hauf, FAIA, then with the architectural firm of Charles Luckman Associates of Los Angeles and later Professor of Architecture at the University of Southern California; Louis DeMoll, FAIA, partner of the Ballinger Company, Architects and Engineers of Philadelphia, Pennsylvania; Dean D. Kenneth Sargent, FAIA, School of Architecture, Syracuse University; and ex officio committee members Walker G. Stone, Project Director for Wiley, and myself, bearing project management responsibility for the AIA.

In the initial 14 months, Editor Boaz devoted full time to the project at Wiley's office in New York City and for the year and a half following his September, 1965, return to his teaching duties in North Carolina, he was able to continue direction of the work on a part-time basis. During the period February, 1965, to February, 1966, he was ably assisted by William Tashlick, AIA, Assistant to the Editor, now with the Rouse Co., Columbia, Maryland, and Wiley's architectural drafting staff, headed up by Chief Draftsman David Edward Miller, an architectural student of Rensselaer Polytechnic Institute. During this 20-month period, Editor Boaz undertook the staggering task of determining the detailed contents of the book, its organization, the graphic design of typical pages, including typography, and the meticulous research and assembly of definitive data sources and technical files for each subject. He worked closely with many authors of technical references, with trade associations, and with scholars with specialized knowledge. At the same time, he and his assistant supervised the Wiley drafting staff in the production of approximately 200 pages of the finished book.

The Editorial Advisory Committee, after several review sessions, concluded that the revision as initially planned would not meet the standards of the AIA in a period of rapidly changing technology unless the participation of many specially qualified members of the Institute were obtained.

In the new approach adopted by the Editorial Advisory

Committee, 94 architectural and engineering firms were selected for their special interest and experience in the subjects assigned. The coordination of this selection process and the work of these firms was part of my own AIA management responsibilities. Beginning in 1968, I was assisted in this task by a new Coordinating Editor for Manuscript, Douglas S. Stenhouse, AIA, Washington, D.C. These firms, with the careful guidance of Editor Boaz and the Editorial Advisory Committee chaired by Harold Hauf, FAIA, contributed over 475 plates of this book. Their contributions are acknowledged on each of the pages they prepared.

In order for these firms, scattered all over the nation, to produce pages of technical excellence, a highly complex coordinating procedure was devised. Editor Boaz transmitted a data file for each subject ranging in size from one to thirteen pages. His transmittal included his own Editor's remarks, instructions for graphic make up of pages, sample completed pages and tracing paper forms. To assist him in this highly complex task, the AIA and Wiley employed Charles Fouhy, AIA, as Coordinating Editor for Production and Operations at Wiley's offices in New York. Charles Fouhy managed the complicated flow of pages and communications among all concerned and then supervised the preparation and accuracy of the final inked drawings prepared by Wiley's architectural drafting staff and the J. and R. Technical Services, Inc., New York, New York. They are to be commended for their adherence to the highest publishing standards.

Each of the contributing firms submitted a preliminary drawing for review by the Editorial Advisory Committee, followed by a final submission for editorial approval. Although the technical judgment of the individuals in firms who prepared the plates was given heaviest weighting, every page received review and critique at both stages by one member of the Committee, by Editor Boaz, and by Chairman Hauf, who resolved any ambiguities in the critiques and indicated final approval. The review was meticulous and often resulted in returns to the contributors for revision. It was a long and difficult task but it is believed that the results herein attest to a conscientious, scholarly, and thorough effort by all participants.

A parallel development in 1967 was the enlargement of the Editorial Advisory Committee which was then made a part of the regular national AIA Committee Structure. The new members were Bernard B. Rothschild, FAIA, of Finch, Alexander, Barnes, Rothschild and Paschal, Atlanta, Georgia, and Robert E. Walters, AIA, of Caudill, Rowlett and Scott, Houston, Texas. In 1968 the Committee was further augmented by the addition of Andrew Bustard, AIA, Havertown, Pennsylvania; Gordon Comb, AIA, St. Paul, Minnesota; and Jay S. Pettit, Jr., AIA, Detroit, Michigan.

Throughout this long history, the ultimate responsibility has been patiently borne by the successive Presi-

dents of the AIA, the Board of Directors and, particularly, the Chairmen of the Commission on Professional Practice. They are listed as follows:

	President	Chairman, Commission on Professional Practice
1964	Arthur G. Odell, Jr., FAIA Charlotte, North Carolina	Daniel Schwartzman, FAIA New York, New York
1965	Morris Ketchum, Jr., FAIA New York, New York	Dean F. Hilfinger, FAIA Bloomington, Illinois
1966	Charles M Nes, Jr., FAIA Baltimore, Maryland	Victor C. Gilbertson, FAIA Minneapolis, Minnesota
1967	Robert L. Durham, FAIA Seattle, Washington	Bernard B. Rothschild, FAIA Atlanta, Georgia
1968	George E. Kassabaum, FAIA St. Louis, Missouri	Jack D. Train, FAIA Chicago, Illinois
1969- 1970	Rex W. Allen, FAIA San Francisco, California	Joseph H. Flad, FAIA Madison, Wisconsin

When Victor Gilbertson completed his term on the AIA Board in 1966, he was asked to continue his policy direction on behalf of the Board, in recognition of the complexity of the project and the confusion caused by annual changes in assignment of responsibility. He deserves a note of thanks.

Those of us who have been associated with this project from its beginning feel strongly that two men of the AIA deserve particular thanks and recognition for their interest, patience and enthusiastic support. They are William H. Scheick, FAIA, Executive Director of the AIA from 1960-1969, and Morris Ketchum, Jr., FAIA, whose strong position of leadership reinforced the AIA and the project staff when problems of finance, staff, and the complexity of the project were discouraging.

Additionally, William L. Slayton, Executive Vice President of the AIA since December 1969, has enthusiastically supported the project.

So the efforts of hundreds of people, mostly volunteers, were combined to finally produce a document of technical excellence. Here, also, we wish to acknowledge the vitally important assistance of hundreds of organizations and individuals whose contributions have provided the data sources utilized by plate contributors. Their names are listed following the text. Without their technical output, this work would not have been possible.

Most important to any author is the encouragement and professional guidance of his publisher. Walker G. Stone, Vice President of Wiley, who has been deeply involved with Architectural Graphic Standards, played a continuous and decisive role in this entire project. For this, The American Institute of Architects extends its thanks.

It has been my privilege to work with all of these devoted and generous contributors from the inception of the AIA's authorship of Architectural Graphic Standards. The patience and fortitude of all participants has been an inspiration to me. They deserve the appreciation of the entire building industry.

ELLIOTT CARROLL, FAIA
Deputy Executive Vice President
The American Institute of Architects

July 16, 1970

TABLE OF CONTENTS

ARCHITECTURAL GRAPHIC STANDARDS AND THE UNIFORM SYSTEM

Within the limits of Architectural Graphic Standards' fundamental emphasis on graphic presentation of design and construction information, the contents of this edition are arranged in Chapters substantially paralleling the sixteen Divisions of the Uniform System for Construction Specifications, Data Filing and Cost Accounting.

GENERAL PLANNING AND DESIGN DATA

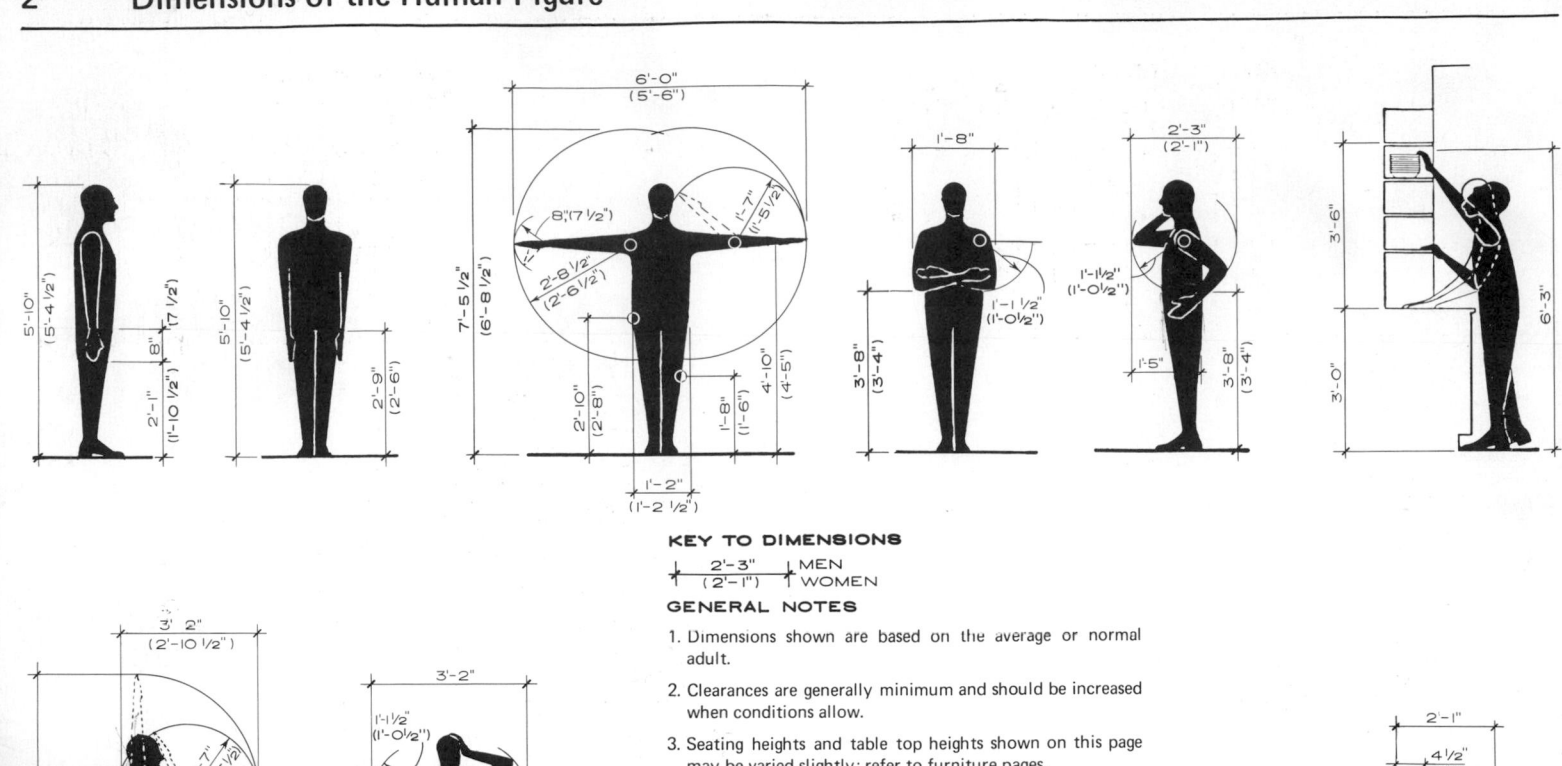

KEY TO DIMENSIONS

2'-3"
(2'-1") — MEN / WOMEN

GENERAL NOTES

1. Dimensions shown are based on the average or normal adult.

2. Clearances are generally minimum and should be increased when conditions allow.

3. Seating heights and table top heights shown on this page may be varied slightly; refer to furniture pages.

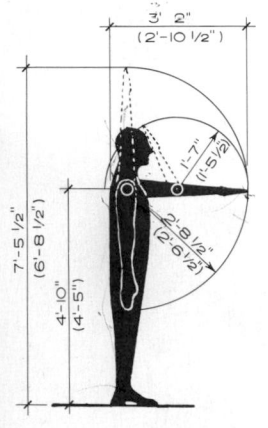

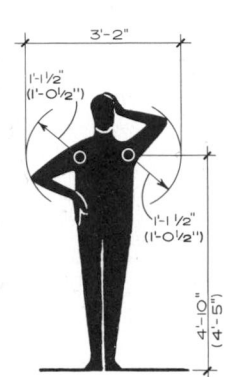

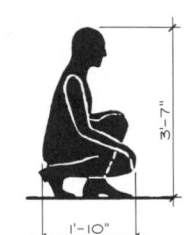

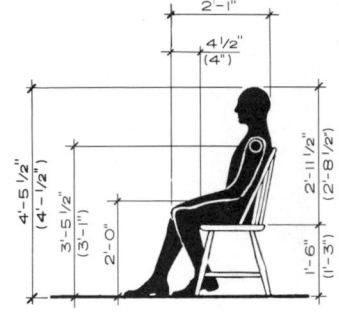

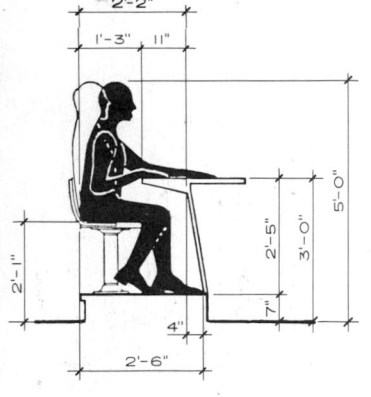

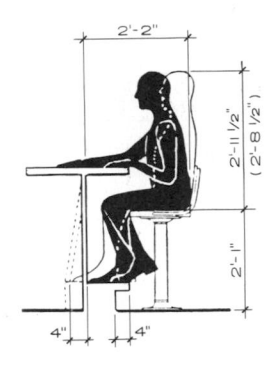

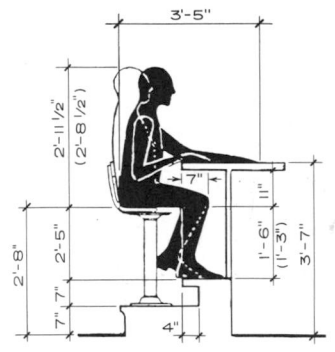

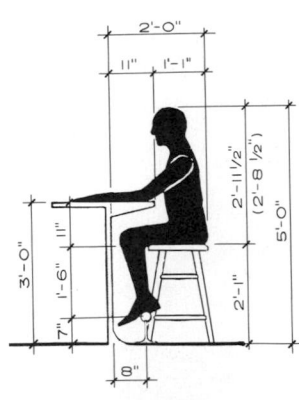

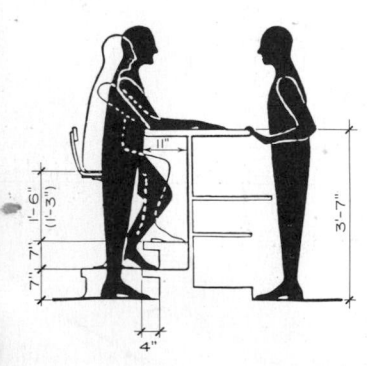

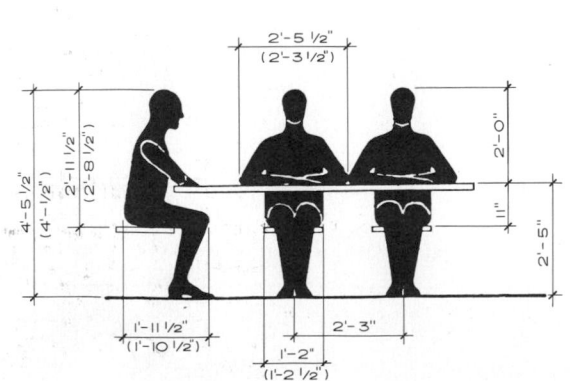

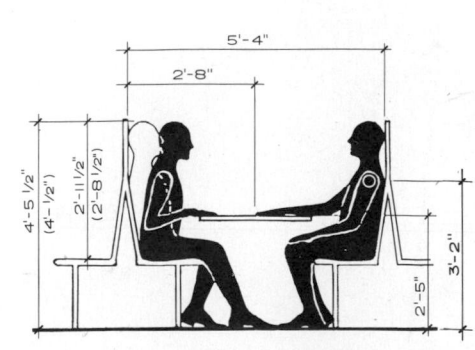

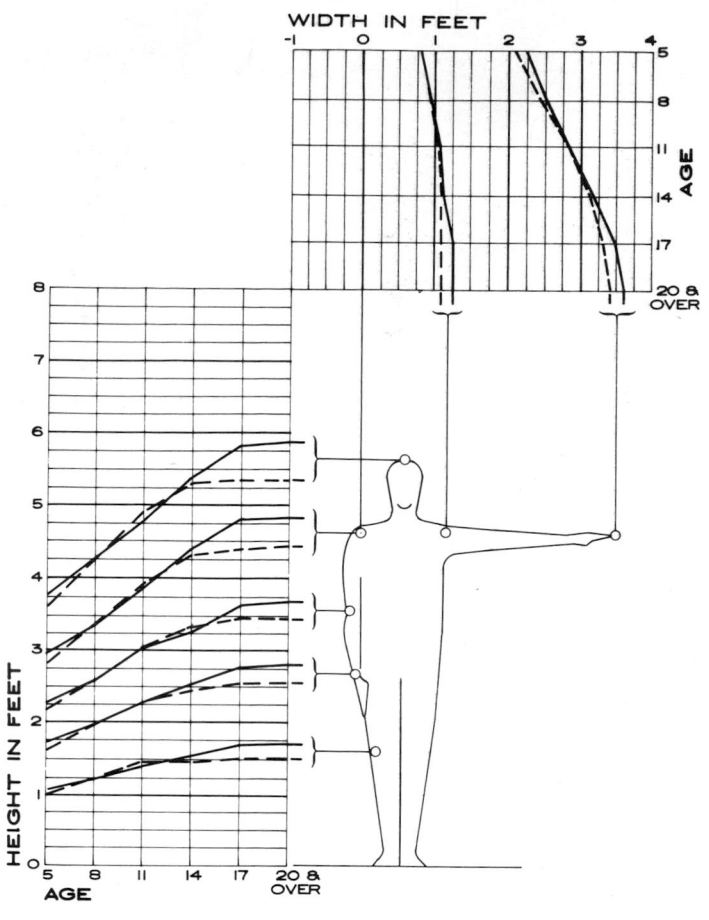

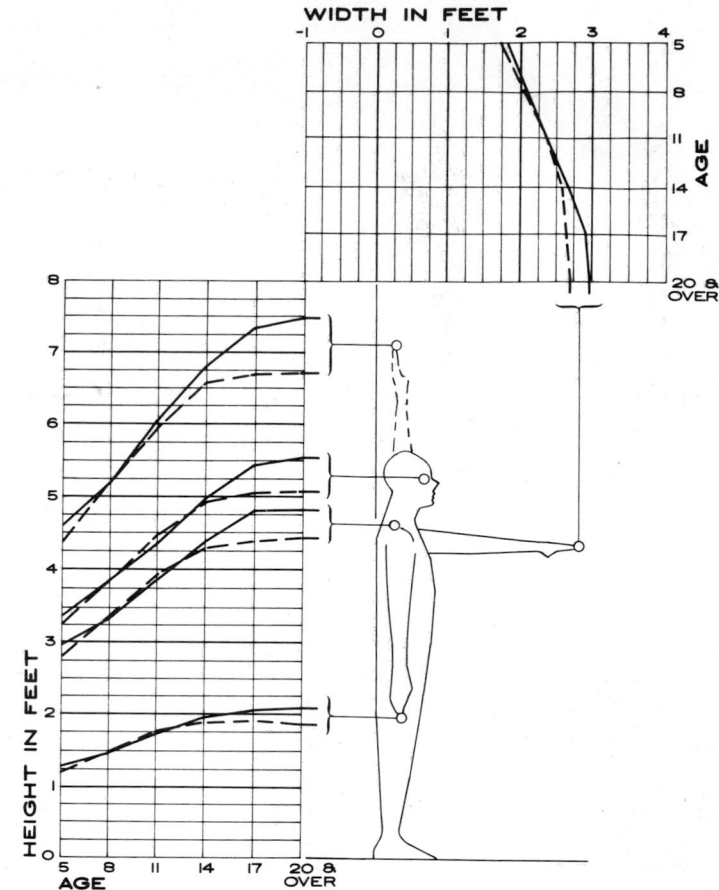

LEGEND
MALE ————
FEMALE — — — —

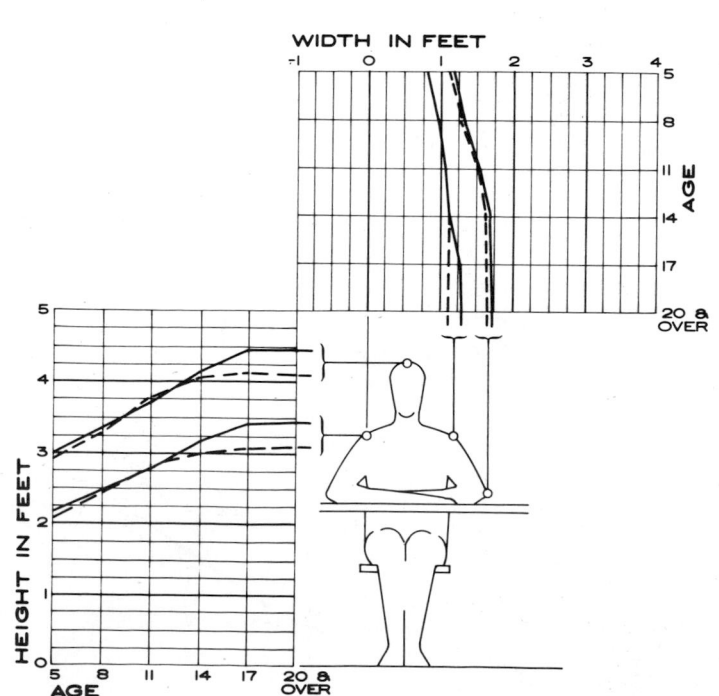

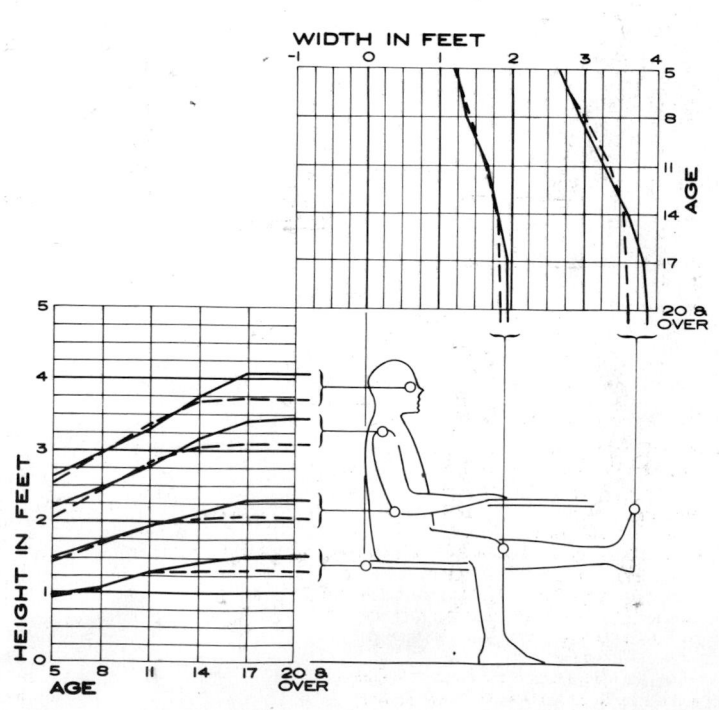

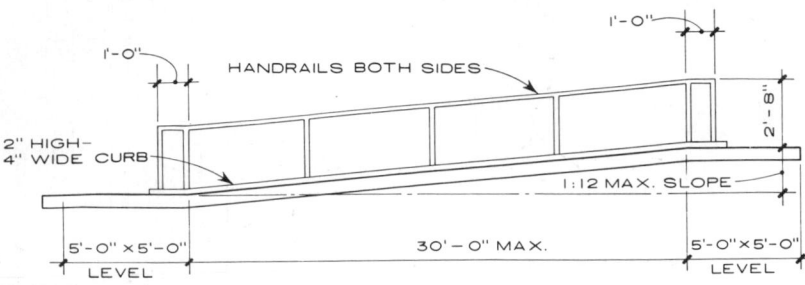

RAMPS

NOTE:

Avoid ramps if possible.
Ramp surface should be non-slip.
Ramp should be minimum 36″ wide clear.

ACCESS

Access from main entrance sidewalk through the entrance to the elevator, and from the elevator to all of building planned for occupancy should be free of steps.

Exterior and interior thresholds should be flush, if not possible — maximum height 1″.

Revolving doors not usable.

If double doors used — one leaf must have 2′-6″ clear opening.

Door closers must be adjustable for both speed and effort.

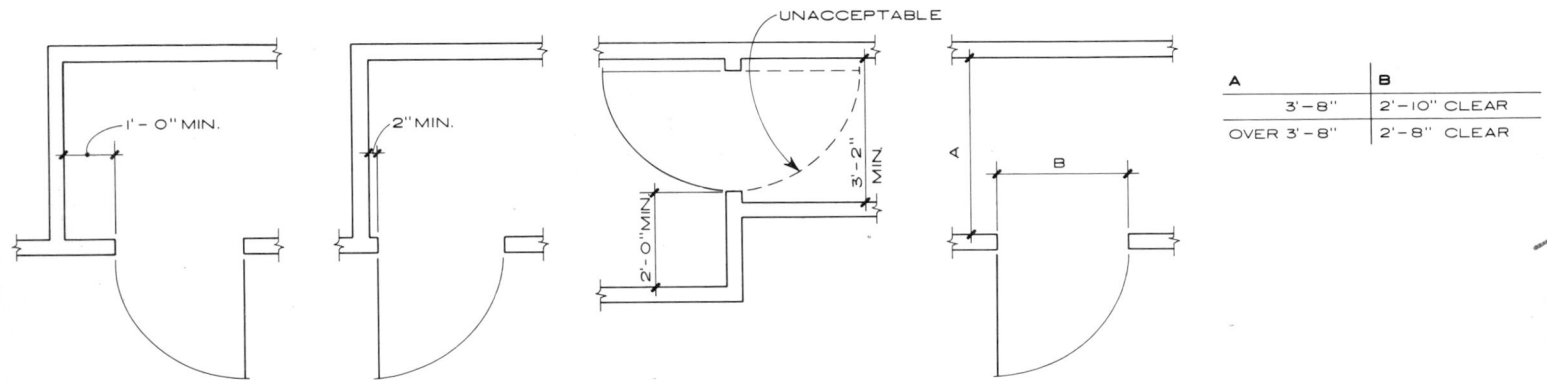

A	B
3′-8″	2′-10″ CLEAR
OVER 3′-8″	2′-8″ CLEAR

RESTRICTED SPACE PLANNING

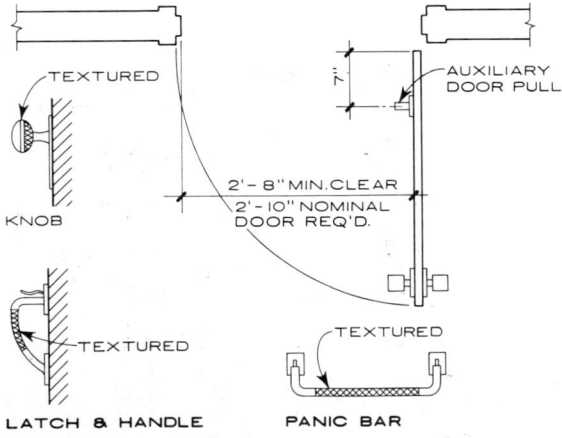

DOORS & HARDWARE

NOTE:

Provide 32″ clear width when door is at 90°.
Plan door swings to open into larger spaces.
Auxilary door handle 7″ from hinge edge as shown is recommended.
Door knob height and auxilary door handle height maximum 36″.
Floor should be level on each side of door for distance of 5′-0″ from door in direction it swings and 3′-0″ from door in opposite direction it swings.
Hardware identification for blind — integral or applied textured surfaces as shown above.

Wm. Baltzer Fox, AIA; Noakes Associates, Architects; Washington, D. C.

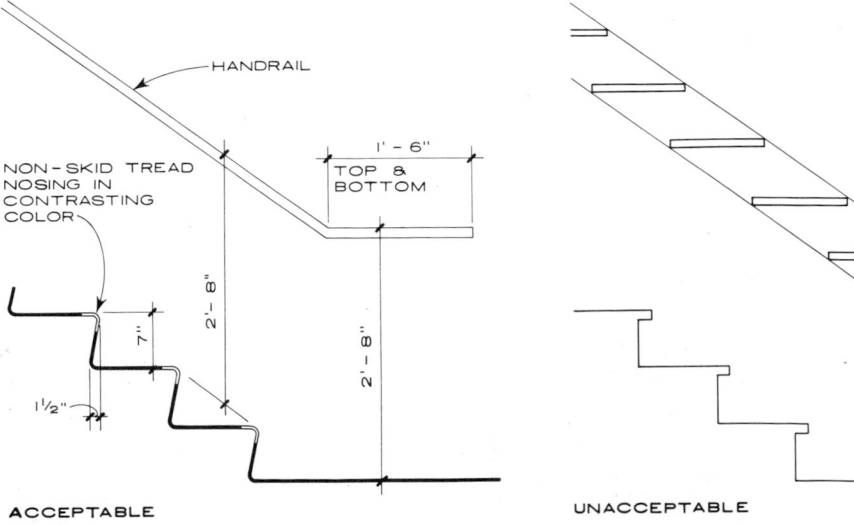

STAIRS

NOTE:

Individuals with restrictions in the knee, ankle, or hip, with artificial legs or leg braces cannot use steps noted as unacceptable, without great difficulty and hazard.
Steps noted as acceptable can be used with minimum difficulty by the above mentioned individuals.

THE HANDICAPPED

Where capable of movement may be classified as:

1. Confined to wheelchairs.

2. Walk with difficulty (braces or crutches).

3. Blind or see with difficulty.

4. Deaf or hear poorly.

5. Badly coordinated or subject to palsy.

6. Infirm from age.

IDENTIFICATION FOR BLIND

1. Room identification—raised letters or numbers 4'– 6" to 5'– 6" to side of door.

2. Hazardous openings—integral or applied textured surfaces on hardware.

3. Audible signals—to provide warning.

4. Flooring materials—direct and locate blind occupants of building.

IDENTIFICATION FOR DEAF

1. Visible signals as warning.

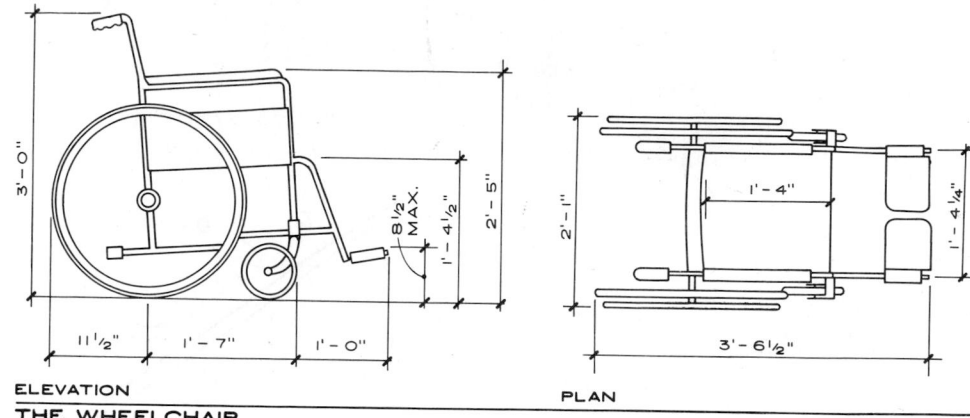

ELEVATION   **PLAN**

THE WHEELCHAIR
NOTE:

All information shown here is predicated on requirements of a wheelchair and therefore will be adequate for any other means of ambulation.

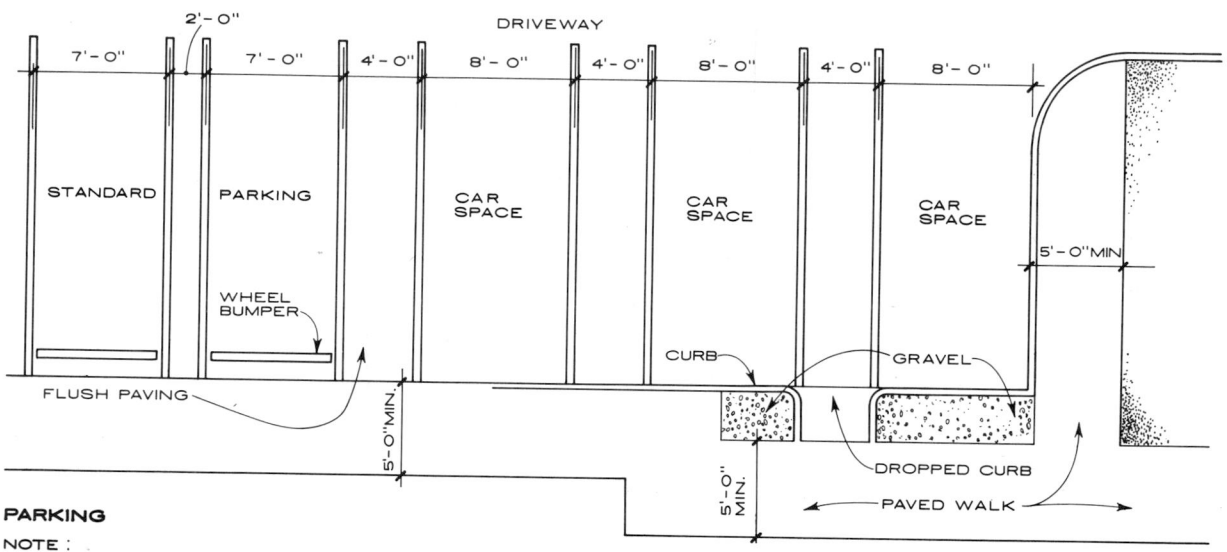

PARKING
NOTE :

Spaces should be clearly marked: "for use by the handicapped."

Locate close to building entrance.

Avoid travel behind parked cars.

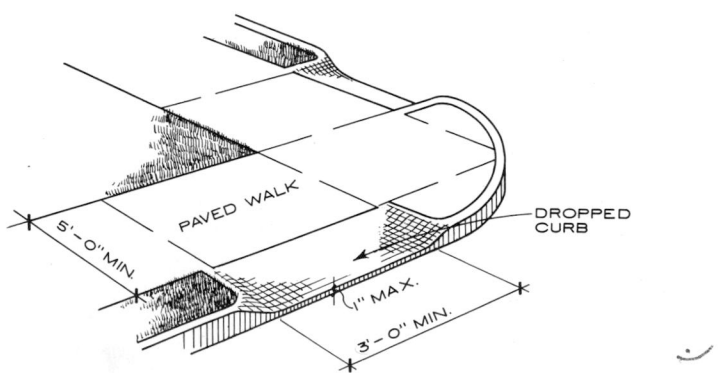

SIDEWALKS & CURBS
NOTE :

Minimum 5'– 0" wide sidewalk.

Sidewalk gradient not to exceed 1:20.

Provide dropped curbs at intersections.

Do not locate dropped curbs on curves.

Wm. Baltzer Fox, AIA; Noakes Associates, Architects; Washington, D. C.

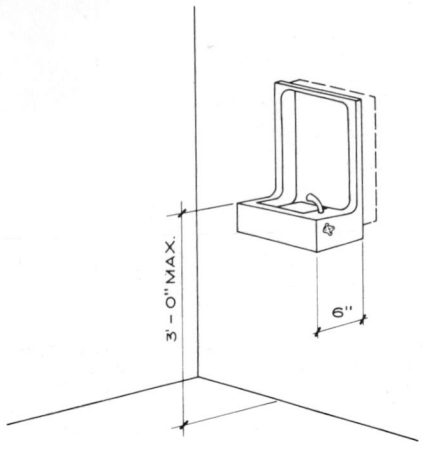

DRINKING FOUNTAINS

NOTE:

If recessed unit in alcove, control and spout should project minimum of 2″ beyond adjacent walls. Controls and spout at front of unit, and water should spout parallel to front face.

Provide hand only or hand-foot control.

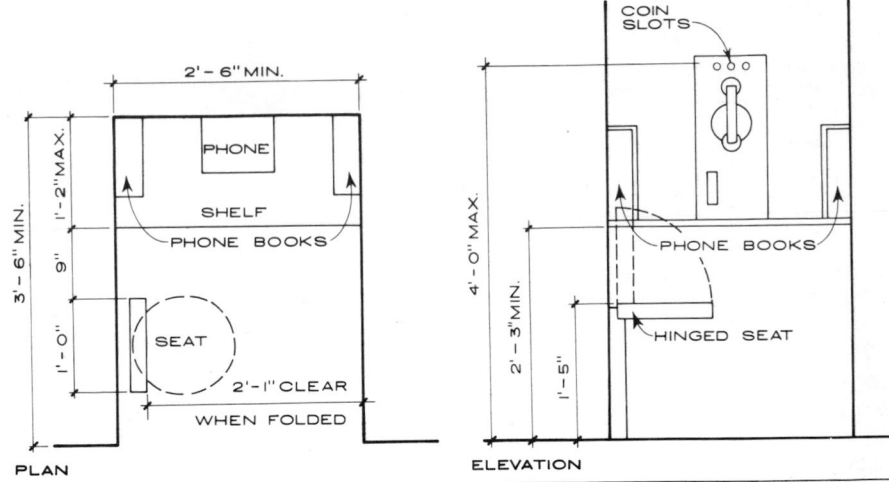

PLAN   ELEVATION

PUBLIC TELEPHONES

NOTE:

Folding seat must be easily operable. Add to depth of booth, as required, for doors if they are necessary. Doors must not project into 3′ — 6″ clearance.

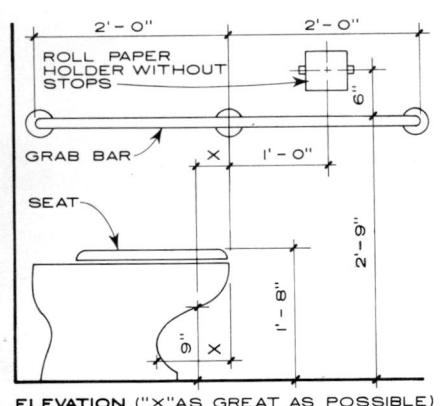

ELEVATION ("X"AS GREAT AS POSSIBLE)

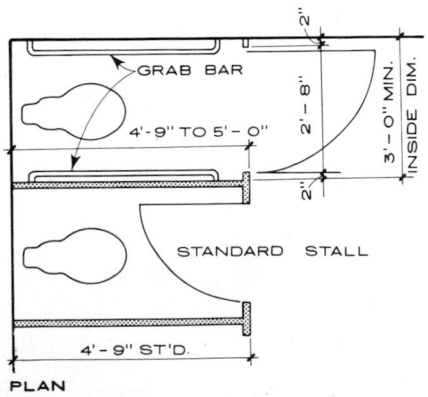

PUBLIC TOILETS

NOTE:

Provide one toilet stall for handicapped in all public toilet rooms. Stall to be one farthest from toilet room entrance.

Urinals may be floor or wall mounted with projection of 1′ — 6″ from wall and lip at 1′ — 5″ above floor. Urinal flush valve at max. of 4′ — 0″ above floor.

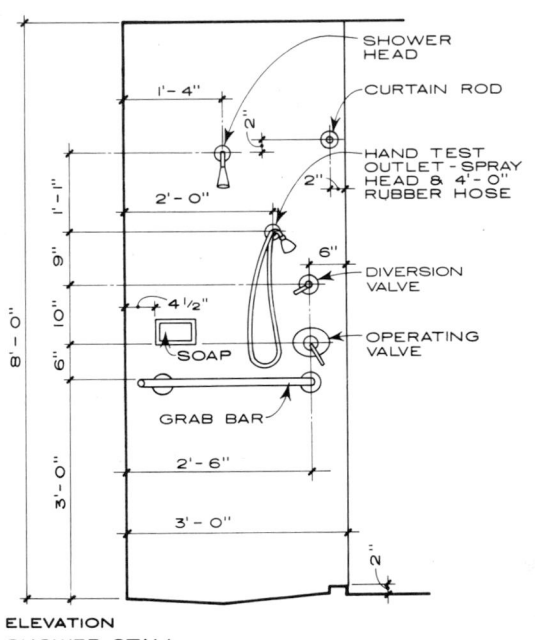

**ELEVATION
SHOWER STALL**

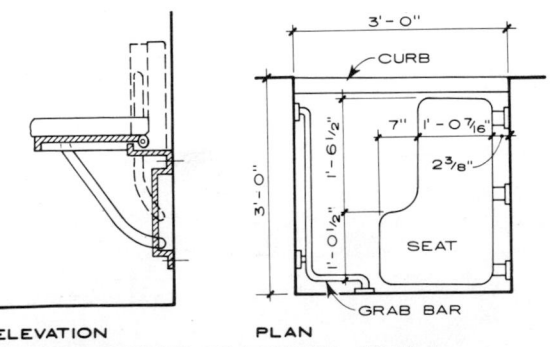

ELEVATION   PLAN

FOLDING SHOWER SEAT MODEL NO. UI-1

SHOWER

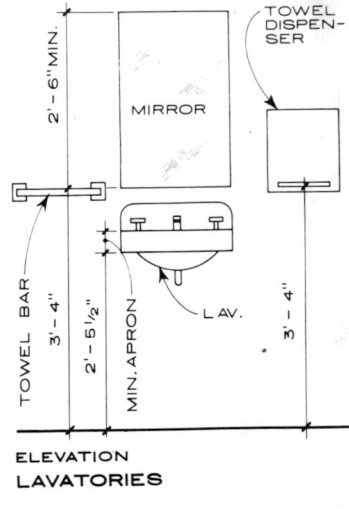

**ELEVATION
LAVATORIES**

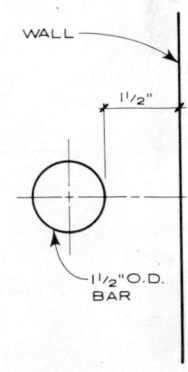

GRAB BAR

Wm. Baltzer Fox, AIA; Noakes Associates, Architects; Washington, D. C.

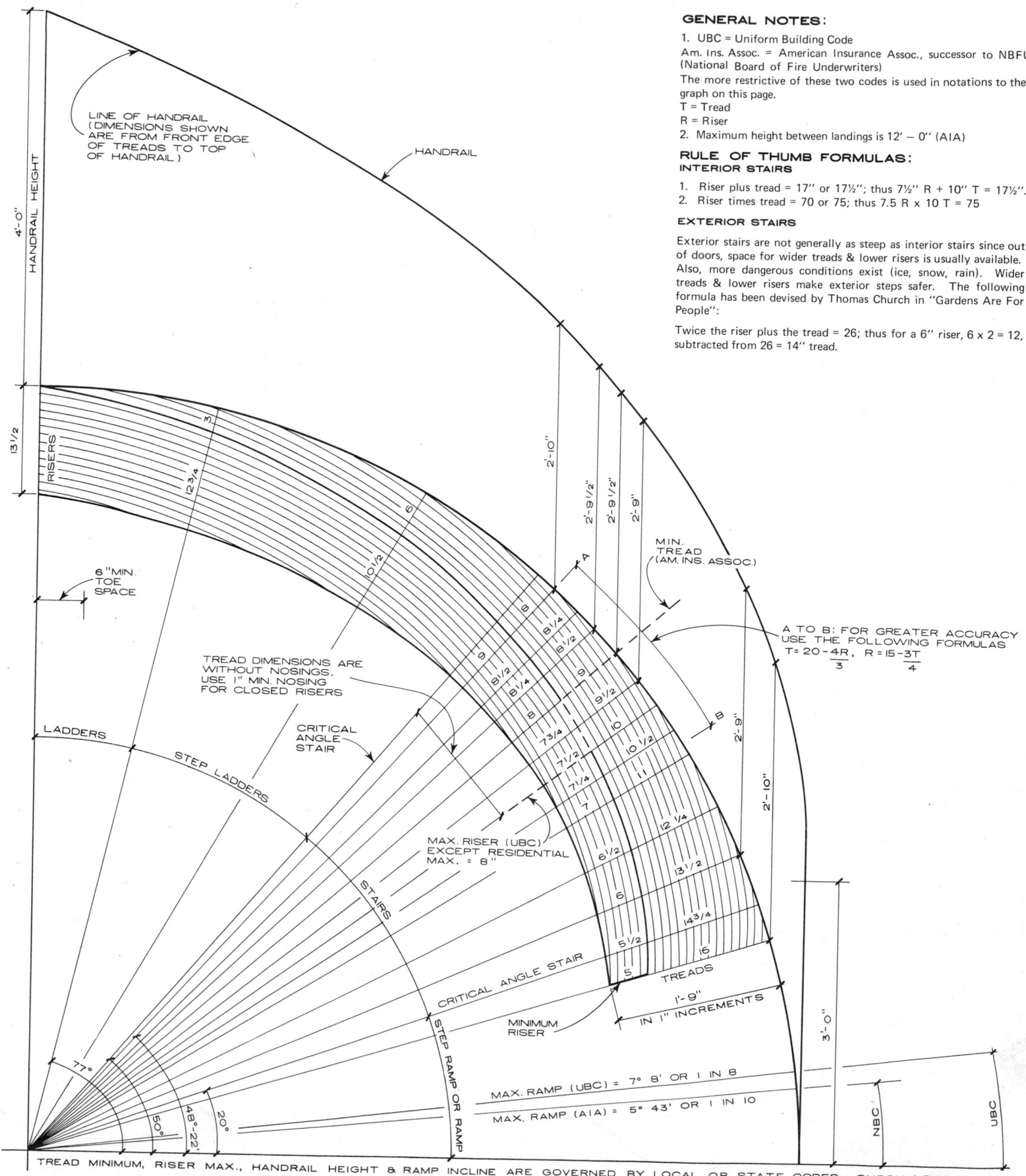

GENERAL NOTES:

1. UBC = Uniform Building Code
Am. Ins. Assoc. = American Insurance Assoc., successor to NBFU (National Board of Fire Underwriters)
The more restrictive of these two codes is used in notations to the graph on this page.
T = Tread
R = Riser
2. Maximum height between landings is 12' – 0'' (AIA)

RULE OF THUMB FORMULAS:
INTERIOR STAIRS

1. Riser plus tread = 17'' or 17½''; thus 7½'' R + 10'' T = 17½''.
2. Riser times tread = 70 or 75; thus 7.5 R x 10 T = 75

EXTERIOR STAIRS

Exterior stairs are not generally as steep as interior stairs since out of doors, space for wider treads & lower risers is usually available. Also, more dangerous conditions exist (ice, snow, rain). Wider treads & lower risers make exterior steps safer. The following formula has been devised by Thomas Church in "Gardens Are For People":

Twice the riser plus the tread = 26; thus for a 6'' riser, 6 x 2 = 12, subtracted from 26 = 14'' tread.

A TO B: FOR GREATER ACCURACY USE THE FOLLOWING FORMULAS $T = \frac{20 - 4R}{3}$, $R = \frac{15 - 3T}{4}$

LINE OF HANDRAIL (DIMENSIONS SHOWN ARE FROM FRONT EDGE OF TREADS TO TOP OF HANDRAIL)

HANDRAIL

HANDRAIL HEIGHT

4'-0''

13½

RISERS

6" MIN. TOE SPACE

MIN. TREAD (AM. INS. ASSOC.)

LADDERS

TREAD DIMENSIONS ARE WITHOUT NOSINGS. USE 1" MIN. NOSING FOR CLOSED RISERS

STEP LADDERS

CRITICAL ANGLE STAIR

MAX. RISER (UBC) EXCEPT RESIDENTIAL MAX. = 8"

STAIRS

CRITICAL ANGLE STAIR

MINIMUM RISER

TREADS

1'-9'' IN 1'' INCREMENTS

STEP RAMP OR RAMP

77°

50°

48°-22'

20°

MAX. RAMP (UBC) = 7° 8' OR 1 IN 8

MAX. RAMP (AIA) = 5° 43' OR 1 IN 10

2'-10''

2'-9½''

2'-9½''

2'-9''

2'-9''

2'-10''

3'-0''

NBC

UBC

TREAD MINIMUM, RISER MAX., HANDRAIL HEIGHT & RAMP INCLINE ARE GOVERNED BY LOCAL OR STATE CODES. CHECK LOCAL CODE.

TREADS AND RISERS
SCALE: 3/4"=1'-0"

Paul Vaughan, AIA; Charleston, West Virginia

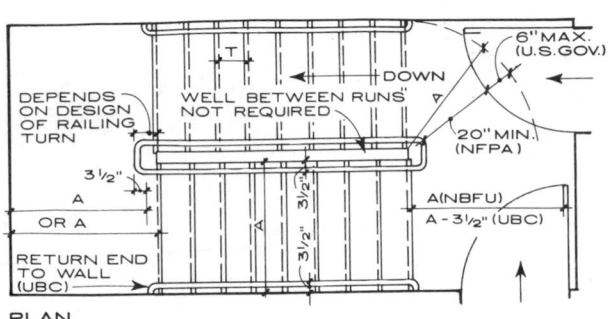
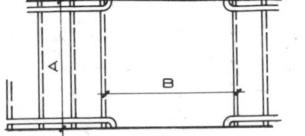
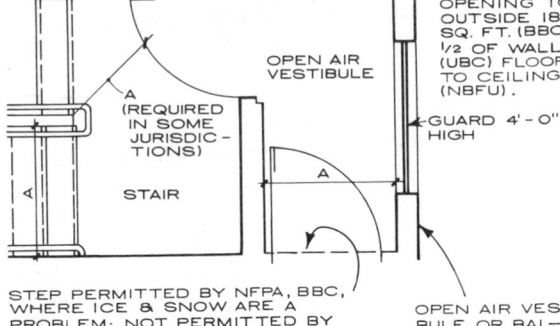

STRAIGHT RUN LANDING
B = A UP TO 4' - 0" (UBC, NBFU)
B = 44" MIN. (NFPA)

6" MAX. (U.S. GOV.)
DOWN
20" MIN. (NFPA)
WELL BETWEEN RUNS NOT REQUIRED
DEPENDS ON DESIGN OF RAILING TURN
A OR A
RETURN END TO WALL (UBC)
A (NBFU)
A - 3½" (UBC)

PLAN

OPENING TO OUTSIDE 18 SQ. FT. (BBC) ½ OF WALL (UBC) FLOOR TO CEILING (NBFU).
OPEN AIR VESTIBULE
GUARD 4'-0" HIGH
A (REQUIRED IN SOME JURISDICTIONS)
STAIR

STEP PERMITTED BY NFPA, BBC, WHERE ICE & SNOW ARE A PROBLEM; NOT PERMITTED BY NBFU, UBC.

OPEN AIR VESTIBULE OR BALCONY TO OPEN TO PUBLIC WAY OR COURT AT LEAST 10' WIDE & 200 SQ. FT. (BBC) OR 20' WIDE & 1000 SQ. FT. (NFPA) OR 10' WIDE & 100 SQ FT. (NBFU), OR TO AIR ON AN ACCESSIBLE FACE OF BUILDING (UBC).

STAIR   BALCONY
A
GUARD 4'-0" HIGH
STEP-SEE NOTE ABOVE

OPEN AIR VESTIBULE & BALCONY

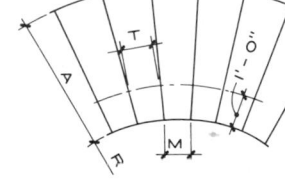

1" OVERHANG DESIRABLE, REQUIRED BY NFPA IF T IS NOT MORE THAN 10"

EXIT LIGHT
BARRIER TO PREVENT UNKNOWING CONTINUED TRAVEL TO BASEMENT
EXIT TO EXTERIOR
GROUND LEVEL LANDING
LANDING
30'-34'
VERTICAL RISE 8'-0" MAX. (NFPA CLASS A, NBFU FOR PUBLIC ASSEMBLY AREAS). 12'-0" OTHERWISE IS COMMON.
HEADROOM 6'-8"
LANDING
STAIR FROM BASEMENT
BASEMENT FLOOR

ALL CODES PROHIBIT USABLE ENCLOSED SPACE AND ANY USE OF OPEN SPACE UNDER STAIR IN ANY REQUIRED EXIT ENCLOSURE.

SECTION
ENCLOSED STAIR DIMENSIONS

R = 2 A MIN. (UBC)
R = 25' - 0" MIN. (NFPA)

CURVED STAIRS

Winders and curved stairs are permitted by most codes for residences and for monumental stairs between 2 floors if not required exit stairways, T is req'd tread, and M = 6".

UBC permits curved stair as required stair if inside radius is 2 times width and M is 10".

NFPA permits curved stair if requirements are met including enclosures, min. tread width, and inside radius is at least 25'-0". Many other codes prohibit use as required stairs.

TO DETERMINE REQUIRED WIDTH "A"

Determine occupancy load from tables of allowed area per person for various occupancies for floor under consideration. (UBC requires adding occupancy load from floor under consideration + 50% of occupancy load from floor next above + 25% of occupancy load from second floor above.)

One unit of width = 22"

NUMBER OF PERSONS PER UNIT OF WIDTH FOR VARIOUS TYPES OF OCCUPANCY

	NFPA	NBFU	BBC
PLACES OF ASSEMBLY	100	60	60
EDUCATIONAL, MERCANTILE, OFFICE, INDUSTRIAL	60	60	50
RESIDENTIAL	45	30	25
INSTITUTIONAL	22	30	25

UBC "A" IN FT. = no. of persons divided by 50.

MINIMUM WIDTHS:

All codes set 44" as the minimum except for residential or light occupancy, service access, or private use, usually 36" for less than 50 persons. (NBFU says 42" for less than 40 persons; BBC says 36" for 40 or less below grade or 75 above.)

NOTE:
Widest "A", determined as above, must extend to discharge at ground level.

Foster C. Parriott; James M. Hunter & Associates; Boulder, Colorado

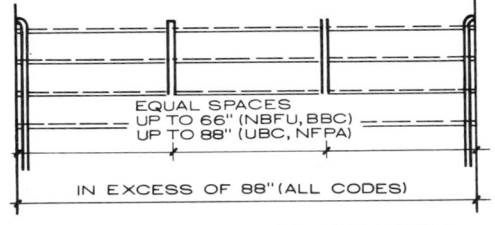

EQUAL SPACES UP TO 66" (NBFU, BBC)
UP TO 88" (UBC, NFPA)

IN EXCESS OF 88" (ALL CODES)

INTERMEDIATE RAILS FOR WIDE STAIRS

TREAD AND RISER

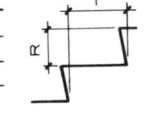

CODES	MIN. "T"	MAX. "R"
NFPA, UBC	10"	7½"
BBC	9½"	7½"
NBFU	9½"	7¾"

Variations for residential and existing buildings.

Maximum variation in "R" for any run is 3/16".

SEE STAIR CHART DESIGN.

NOTE:
The minimum number of risers in any run of stairs is 3 (NFPA).

SMOKEPROOF ENCLOSURES
(FIRE TOWERS, SMOKEPROOF TOWERS, ETC.)

One required for buildings of more than 6 stories (NBFU and BBC) or 5 stories (UBC).

Some local codes have deleted the requirement for smokeproof enclosures.

CONSTRUCTION REQUIREMENTS

Requirements of the codes cited vary, but typically stairs and stair enclosures for buildings of 4 or more stories are required to be of 2 hour incombustible construction, 3 stories and less, 1 hour.

Smokeproof enclosures and stairs therein must be of 2 hour construction.

These requirements are relaxed in varying ways for residential occupancies.

BUILDING CODES CITED

NFPA—National Fire Protection Association
NBFU—National Board of Fire Underwriters, now American Insurance Association
BBC—Basic Building Code, Building Officials Conference of America
UBC—Uniform Building Code, International Conference of Building Officials

THE BUILDING CODE IN FORCE

in any jurisdiction should always be consulted to determine exact requirements, as it governs in all points of conflict.

DEFINITIONS

MEANS OF EGRESS are simply systems for vacating a building. They are vertical and/or horizontal methods of conveying people with reasonable safety to a place of refuge outside at ground level and are composed of three basic elements. The terminology of each component is important.

EXIT ACCESS is that portion of a means of egress which leads to an exit entrance.

An EXIT is that portion of a means of egress which is separated from the area of the building from which escape is to be made, by walls, ceilings and doors or other means of specified fire resistance.

An EXIT DISCHARGE is that portion of a means of egress between the termination of the exit and a place of refuge outside the building at ground level.

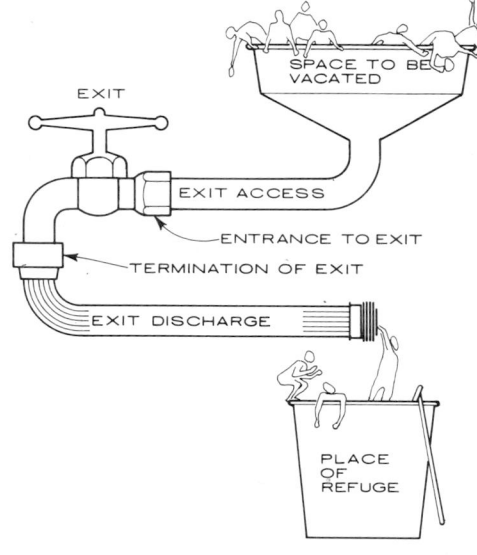

PROPER DESIGN CRITERIA
GENERAL NOTE

The criteria indicated hereinafter are generally accepted throughout the United States but should be checked against requirements of specific code accepted by local authorities having jurisdiction.

FIRE-RATINGS

Fire-ratings are expressed as an approved time of exposure to fire and related damage. Ratings are determined by specific tests upon various construction assemblies conducted by approved laboratories. One hour fire-rated floor, wall and ceiling construction is required for protection of exits in buildings three stories or less in height; two hour construction, for those four stories or more.

UNIT OF MEASUREMENT

The unit of measurement for exits is a certain increment of width, usually 22 inches, which has been determined as the "average" shoulder width of a man.

NUMBER OF EXITS

The basic requirements of means of egress are proper design, construction and method of compartmentation. Fundamentally, every building and space within must have a certain minimum number of exits depending upon the number of occupants and the nature of its use.

LOCATION OF EXITS

Exits should be located as remote from each other as possible; however, their exact placement is generally left to the discretion of local authorities so as to permit some freedom in design. Exits must be placed so that they do not create deadended passageways, unless it can be demonstrated that by so doing, a hazard is not created.

Douglas S. Stenhouse, AIA; Washington, D. C.

DESIGN CRITERIA (CONT'D)
TRAVEL DISTANCE

The appropriateness and maximum capacity per unit and the maximum distance one must travel to reach an exit may vary depending on the use of the building, the fire hazard and physical ability and alertness of its occupants to proceed with reasonable safety to a place of refuge outside the building at ground level. Travel distance is calculated differently depending on the use of the space.

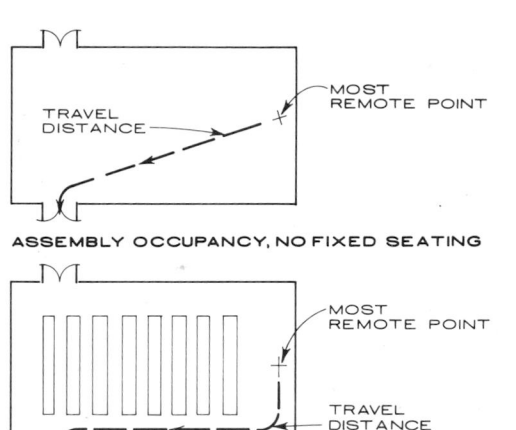

ASSEMBLY OCCUPANCY, NO FIXED SEATING

ASSEMBLY OCCUPANCY, FIXED SEATING

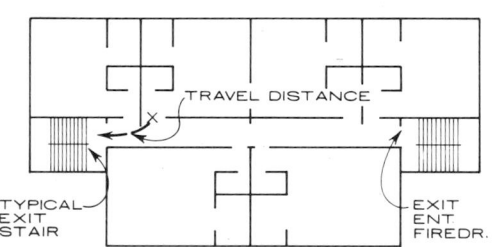

APARTMENT OCCUPANCY

Measures travel distance from door that leads from space to exit.

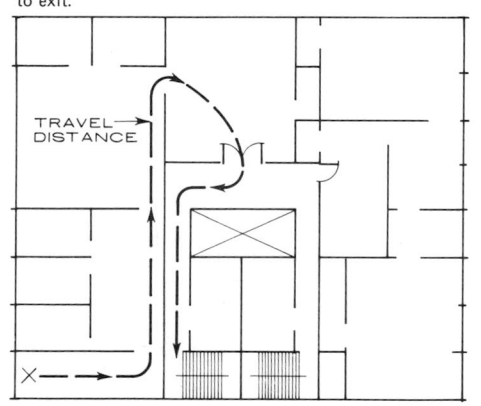

OFFICE OCCUPANCY

The allowable travel distance is usually greater, though measured from the most remote place in any office area.

ALTERATIONS

Non-conforming structures are usually given special consideration to encourage improvement in required means of egress, construction assemblies and flamespread ratings. Variances may be permitted for surface coverings, in opening sizes and arrangement of exits depending on the type of occupancy, degree to which the Owner may be handicapped by strict interpretation of the local code, and the desire of local authorities to accept something that can be demonstrated as a considerable improvement.

DESIGN CRITERIA (CONT'D)
CUMULATIVE REQUIREMENTS FOR MULTISTORYED BUILDINGS

Though some codes require that the cumulative total be considered and that the width of an exit at any one floor reflect the increased load from floors above, generally for multistoried single occupancy buildings in most cities, exit requirements are not cumulative.

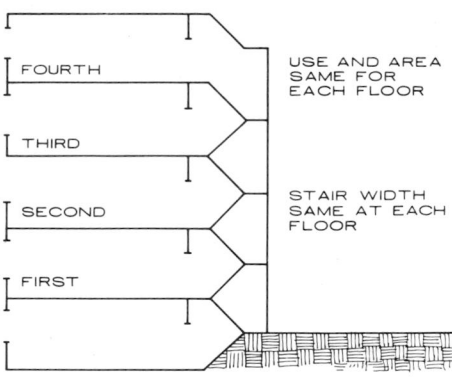

COMMON MEANS OF EGRESS

Common means of egress are generally adequate for different types of occupancies used simultaneously by different groups of people in the same building if they are designed to accommodate both groups at the same time. If the same people use different occupancies at different times, exit units for each aren't cumulative.

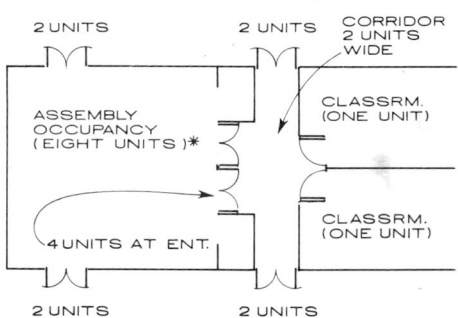

＊ Used at different times by same people who use classrooms. If different people, increase corridor, exit doors.

UNOBSTRUCTED PATH OF TRAVEL

An unobstructed path free from any projections in the path of travel must be maintained to all exits. Good general illumination and judicious use of color and materials also helps to produce a safe means of egress.

SMOKEPROOF TOWERS

Smokeproof Towers are enclosed exterior stairs separated yet accessible to a building from an open vestibule or balcony so that smoke from the building can not enter the stair itself. (Refer to Stair Dimension page for design data).

ENCLOSED AND UNCLOSED INTERIOR STAIRS

There are two types of ENCLOSED INTERIOR STAIRS (Class A & B) differing in minimum allowable width, riser height, tread width and length of run (see Stair Dimension page). UNENCLOSED INTERIOR STAIRS between balconies and main assembly floors or adjacent floors in educational occupancies may qualify (see local code) as required means of egress for balcony or floor if not connected with other required means of egress.

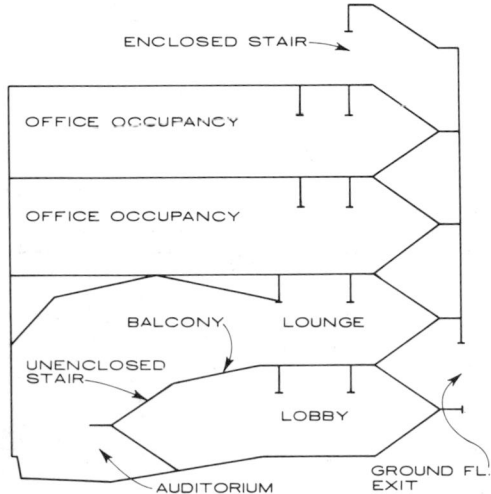

HORIZONTAL EXITS

Horizontal Exits may be utilized to meet one half of total required capacity of exits for separate or connected buildings except in the case of institutional occupancies where two-thirds of the required capacity is permitted. They are means, on approximately the same level, of getting from one space to another which can qualify as a place of refuge. It may be an approved fire-rated self-closing door by which occupants pass through or around a firewall or other fire barrier into another portion of the same building which affords a temporary place of refuge until they can be moved in a safe and orderly manner through a vertical exit to the ground level below and a permanent place of refuge outside the building.

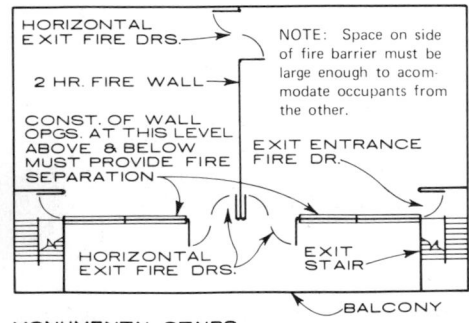

MONUMENTAL STAIRS

Enclosed, unenclosed, interior or exterior monumental stairs may be used to satisfy exit requirements or as other types of means of egress if the specifications for stairs with respect to riser and tread proportions, protection from snow, ice and fire within the building are satisfied. Curved stairs or other variations from the usual may also be accepted. (See Stair page).

Douglas S. Stenhouse, AIA; Washington, D. C.

PASSAGEWAYS

Passageways, for example, halls, balconies, ramps, corridors, lobbies, tunnels, etc., either inside or outside a building, must be wide enough to accommodate the aggregate of all means of egress discharging through them. Walking surfaces should be level with small differences taken up by ramps, large ones, by stairs.

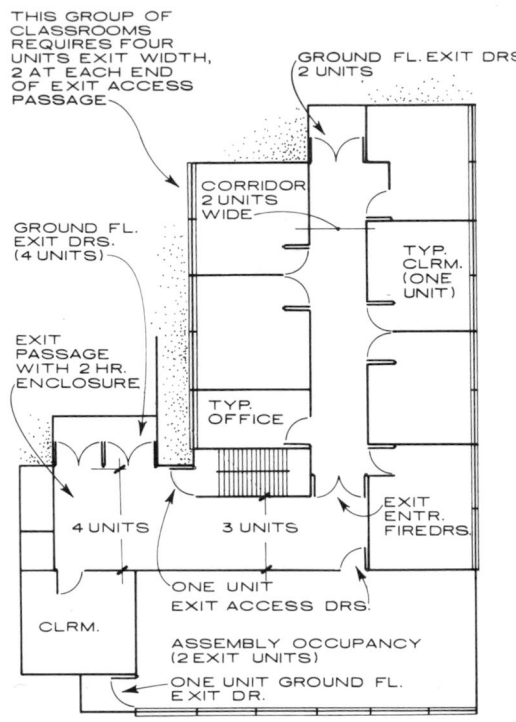

COMPUTATION OF REQUIRED WIDTHS FOR MEANS OF EGRESS

1. $\text{ACTUAL OCCUPANT LOAD} = \dfrac{\text{FLOOR AREA}}{\text{USE FACTOR}}$

2. $\text{UNITS OF EXIT WIDTHS REQ.} = \dfrac{\text{OCCUPANT LOAD}}{\text{ALLOWABLE CAPACITY PER UNIT}}$

The Use Factor is expressed in square feet and represents the floor area permitted per person for the particular occupancy (consult your local code). The Allowable Capacity will vary with the type of exit used. Since exit units are usually expressed in increments of 22 inches and since the capacity varies with type of exit used, number, size and disposition of each exit will vary. Consult your local code for allowable capacities for various types of exits and other approved means of egress.

SLIDE ESCAPES

Slide Escapes are sometimes permitted in high hazard industrial occupancies to satisfy one unit but never more than 25% of the required exits in lieu of fire escapes and ladders.

UNENCLOSED EXTERIOR STAIRS

Unenclosed Exterior Stairs may be accepted as required exits under the same conditions as an interior stair if protected from accumulation of snow and ice in climates subject to same and if so arranged as to avoid any handicap to the use of the stair by persons having a fear of high places and if protected from fire within the building itself (see Fire Escape page).

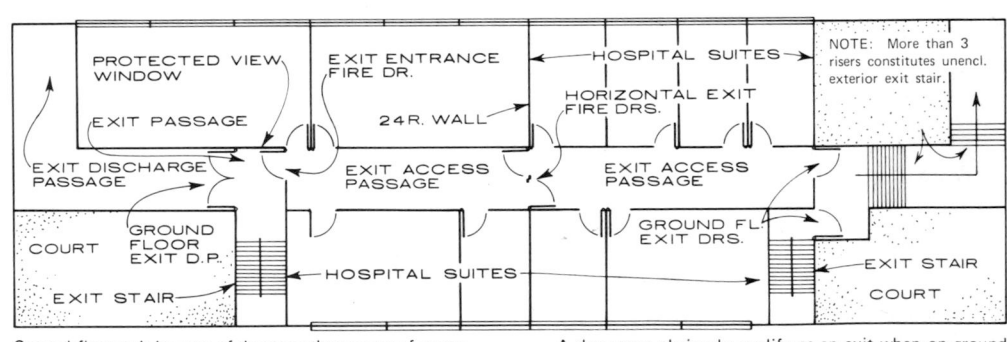

Ground floor exit by way of door or other means of egress leads directly (by means of exit discharge), to place of refuge outside bldg.

A door may obviously qualify as an exit when on ground floor but not unless it complies with strict definition of specific means of egress.

GROUND FLOOR EXITS AND DOORS

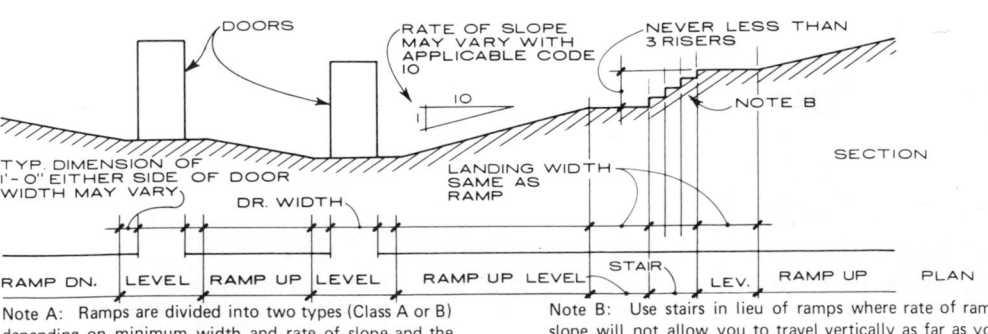

Note A: Ramps are divided into two types (Class A or B) depending on minimum width and rate of slope and the capacity per unit of width.

Note B: Use stairs in lieu of ramps where rate of ramp slope will not allow you to travel vertically as far as you might wish.

RAMPS

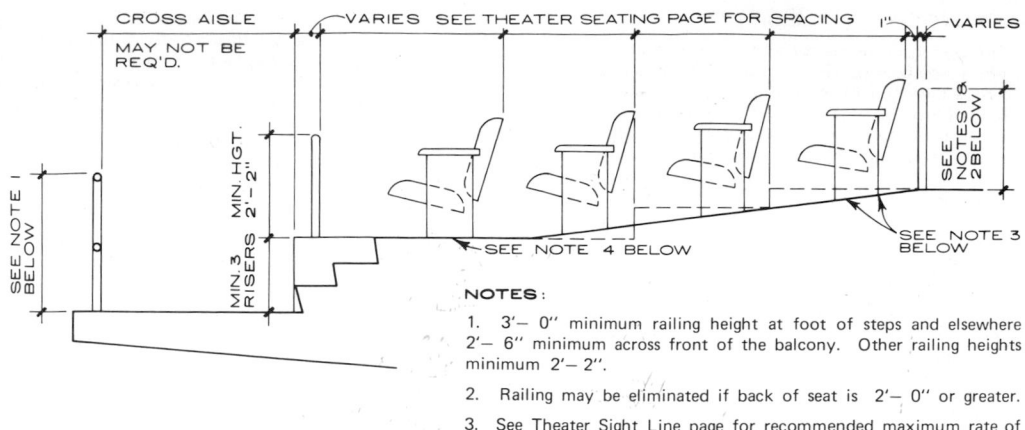

CROSS AISLE — MAY NOT BE REQ'D.

VARIES   SEE THEATER SEATING PAGE FOR SPACING

1"   VARIES

SEE NOTES 1&2 BELOW

MIN. HGT. 2'-2"

SEE NOTE 1 BELOW

MIN. 3 RISERS

SEE NOTE 4 BELOW

SEE NOTE 3 BELOW

NOTES:

1.   3'-0" minimum railing height at foot of steps and elsewhere 2'-6" minimum across front of the balcony. Other railing heights minimum 2'-2".

2.   Railing may be eliminated if back of seat is 2'-0" or greater.

3.   See Theater Sight Line page for recommended maximum rate of slope; greater slopes must be accommodated by equal risers, full aisle width.

4.   In most cases seats must be anchored to the floor (consult your local code).

SECTION THROUGH TYPICAL BALCONY OF PUBLIC ASSEMBLY OCCUPANCY

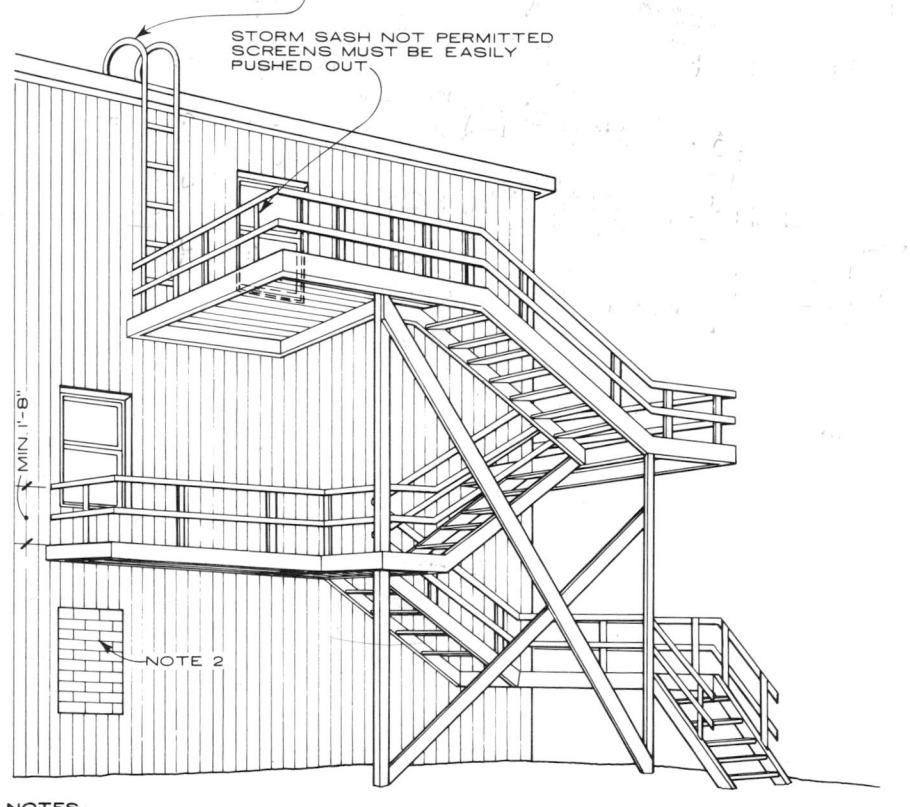

LADDER TO ROOF IF ROOF DOES NOT SLOPE MORE THAN 2 IN 12

STORM SASH NOT PERMITTED SCREENS MUST BE EASILY PUSHED OUT

MIN 1'-8"

NOTE 2

NOTES:

1 — An unenclosed exterior stair may sometimes be permitted when no other practical means of providing exits for older, nonconforming buildings can be found. Fire escapes as such must provide a safe, continuous, protected, unobstructed path of travel to the ground or other approved place of refuge.

2 — Brick up all existing openings below runs of stairs, bridges or landings.

3 — Fire escapes may be parallel or perpendicular to a building with respect to landings, bridges or stair runs.

4 — If circumstances warrant and officials having jurisdiction approve, a fire escape may be used to provide indirect access to the roof of an adjacent building in lieu of direct access to a place of refuge at the ground level below.

FIRE ESCAPES

Douglas S. Stenhouse, AIA; Washington, D. C.

DEFINITION OF PLACE OF PUBLIC ASSEMBLY

A place of Public Assembly is generally recognized as any space that will accommodate 100 or more persons. The number of exits required is proportional to the capacity and may vary somewhat depending on the type of exit used.

MEANS OF EGRESS FOR PUBLIC ASSEMBLY OCCUPANCIES

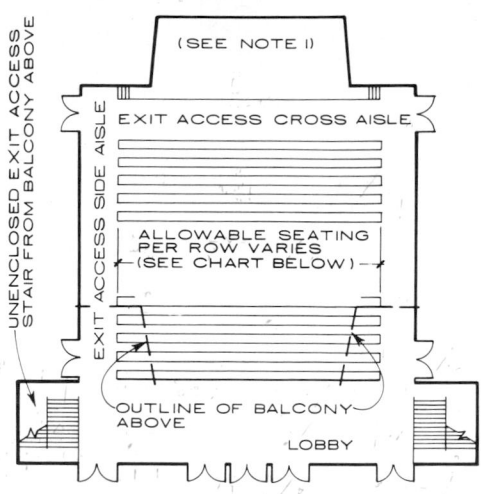

(SEE NOTE 1)

UNENCLOSED EXIT ACCESS STAIR FROM BALCONY ABOVE

EXIT ACCESS CROSS AISLE

EXIT ACCESS SIDE AISLE

ALLOWABLE SEATING PER ROW VARIES (SEE CHART BELOW)

OUTLINE OF BALCONY ABOVE

LOBBY

RELATION OF MAX. SEATING PER ROW TO CLEAR PASSAGE FOR CONTINENTAL SEATING

NUMBER OF SEATS PER ROW	CLEAR PASSAGE
18 OR LESS	18 INCHES
35 — 19	20 INCHES
45 — 36	21 INCHES
46 OR MORE	22 INCHES

NOTES:

1   Stages or enclosed platforms have special fire protection requirements.

2   Main entrances must accommodate one half the required number of exit units.

3   Provide one 3 unit exit door each side for each five rows (see exceptions and variations on Theater Seating page).

4   Maintain constant width for exit access cross aisle equal to widest aisle served plus 50% of all other exit access aisles.

5   Aisles must terminate in cross aisles, foyer, or at an exit and should increase in width in the direction of required exits proportional to number of persons they are required to handle.

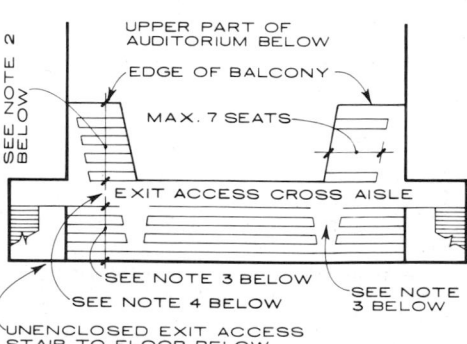

SEE NOTE 2

UPPER PART OF AUDITORIUM BELOW

EDGE OF BALCONY

MAX. 7 SEATS

EXIT ACCESS CROSS AISLE

SEE NOTE 3 BELOW

SEE NOTE 4 BELOW

SEE NOTE 3 BELOW

UNENCLOSED EXIT ACCESS STAIR TO FLOOR BELOW

NOTES:

1 — Furthest distance of travel must not exceed allowable travel distance (see local code).

2 — Maximum length 20'-0"; minimum width 3'-0" or 2'-6" if serving less than 60 persons. Increase 1 1/2" for each five feet of length.

3 — Minimum width 3'-6". Increase 1 1/2" for each 5 feet of length (see Theater Seating page).

BALCONY FLOOR PLAN
(CONVENTIONAL SEATING)

OBJECTIVE AND METHODS

The objective is to maintain fire compartmentation of a structure by minimizing the effects of vertical openings in a horizontal surface or series of surfaces forming a sandwich, or of horizontal openings in a vertical surface that might be intended perhaps to limit the area of spaces on the same level.

Openings may be relatively small as in the case of those for pipes, ducts, chutes and doors, or they may be larger as for escalators passing between floors or interior courtyards such as those at the Regency Hyatt Hotel in Atlanta or the Ford Foundation in New York. Enclosures for vertical openings through horizontal surfaces or horizontal openings through vertical surfaces must be constructed of certain material assemblies which are accepted by local authorities having jurisdiction over the project. (Note that Underwriters' Laboratories, Inc., publish regular reports of tests conducted on various construction assemblies. Their recommendations are accepted by most codes.)

Just as enclosures must meet certain requirements, so must openings into them incorporate accepted devices such as dampers to assist in maintaining the desirable compartmentation.

FIREDOOR TYPES & APPLICATIONS

Firedoors maintain the integrity of openings through walls which have been designed to maintain fire compartmentation within a building. They should be selected on the basis of their use and the class of opening rather than upon the basis of the fire resistance of the wall in which they occur, since testing labs use different methods of evaluation resulting in hourly fire resistance labeled ratings that may not mean the same for one lab as for another. Fire doors are "labeled" or classed with respect to the openings in which they are placed. In setting up "door" or "opening" schedules, selection of frame, hardware, size, and finish should be considered as an integral affair.

Class A openings occur in fire walls and are principally used to maintain horizontal compartmentation. Doors for these openings have a fire rating of 3 hours and are installed in pairs with one door on each side of the opening. Class B openings are used to maintain fire compartmentation in vertical communication enclosures such as stairs or elevators. In the case of the latter, though desirable, few authorities require Class B elevator doors. The Class B door has 1 $1/2$ hour ratings. Class C openings are in corridors and room partitions and hold a $3/4$ hour rating, while

Class D, E and F openings occur in exterior walls, the former where openings are subject to severe fire exposure ($3/4$ hr) and the latter two in moderate to light fire exposure conditions ($1/2$ hr rating). Where labeled doors are required, frames also must be labeled, since the opening is considered as an integral unit. (Refer to page on hollow metal frames and to local code for specific data.)

In order to maintain fire compartmentation, it is important that the field installation of a door and its frame, type of hardware, louvers, and glazing be done in strict accord with label requirements. Don't accept labeled construction in lieu of a labeled door.

UTILITY SHAFTS

Utility shafts shall be provided with protected enclosures for walls, bottoms of shafts not terminating at grade or tops of shafts terminating below roofs. Access doors listed by approved testing labs shall be installed in all openings, incombustible material around all pipes penetrating the enclosure.

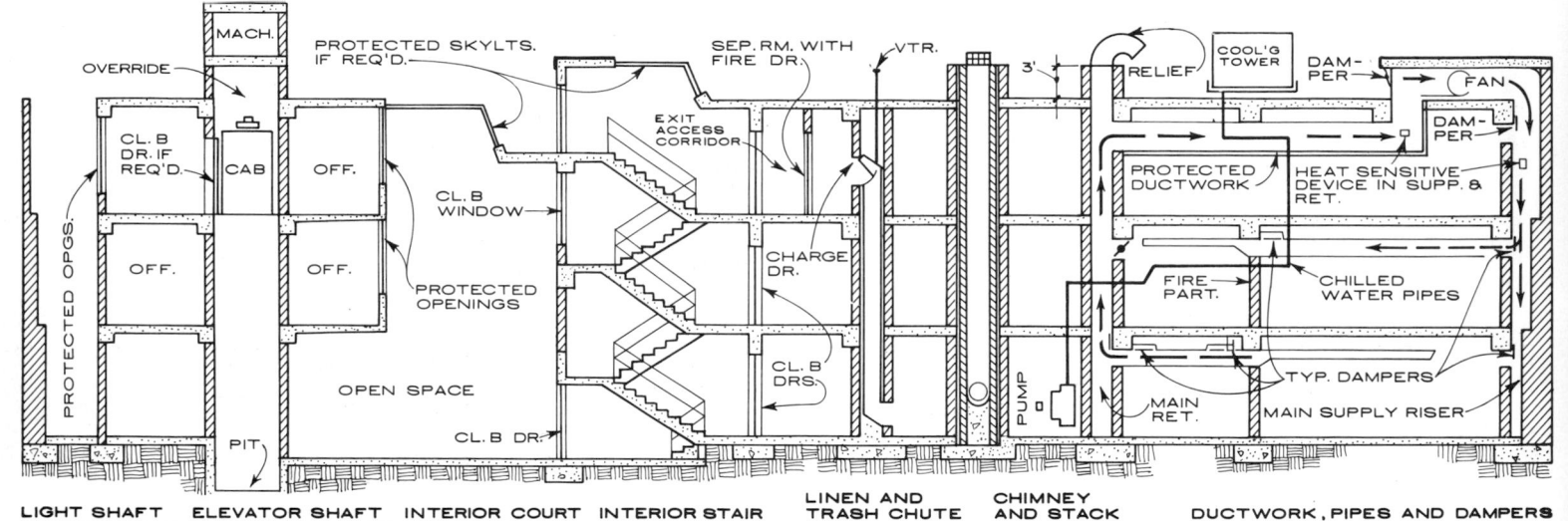

LIGHT SHAFT   ELEVATOR SHAFT   INTERIOR COURT   INTERIOR STAIR   LINEN AND TRASH CHUTE   CHIMNEY AND STACK   DUCTWORK, PIPES AND DAMPERS

TYPES OF ENCLOSURES FOR VERTICAL AND HORIZONTAL OPENINGS

NOTE: 1. Shading and hatching are not intended to indicate any particular materials but only to clarify and make the sections more readable.

2. Some codes will not permit large vertical "open spaces" or interior courtyards. Other codes are extremely oblique in the way they allow or do not allow such spaces which are not directly compatible with codes. Check their acceptability with local authorities responsible for enforcement of codes.

FIRE DAMPERS

Fire dampers for ducts in air-conditioning systems are located to automatically seal off the circulation of air through a portion of the system and therefore isolate heat and smoke thru compartmentation. The fire damper is usually held open by a fusible link which melts at a certain temperature and causes the damper to close by gravity. There are many types of dampers manufactured, single and multiple blade types, which have been tested by approved labs.

Fire dampers are required (see illustration at right) (1) where ducts pass through fire partitions that serve to restrict the spread of fire but which do not qualify as fire walls, (2) where branch ducts are taken off supply or return risers and are 20 sq. in. or more in diameter, aluminum or constructed of Class 1 materials, (3) where a duct pierces a fire-resistive ceiling, (4) where a duct penetrates a vertical opening and is 20 sq. in. or more in diameter, aluminum or constructed of Class 1 materials, (5) where a duct 20 sq. in. or more in diameter, aluminum or constructed of Class 1 materials penetrates a fire-resistive floor or where a protected enclosure is not built around a main supply or return riser of a system at one storey of a building serving only the storeys above and below, and (6) where a fresh air intake passes through an exterior wall.

Douglas S. Stenhouse, AIA; Washington, D. C.

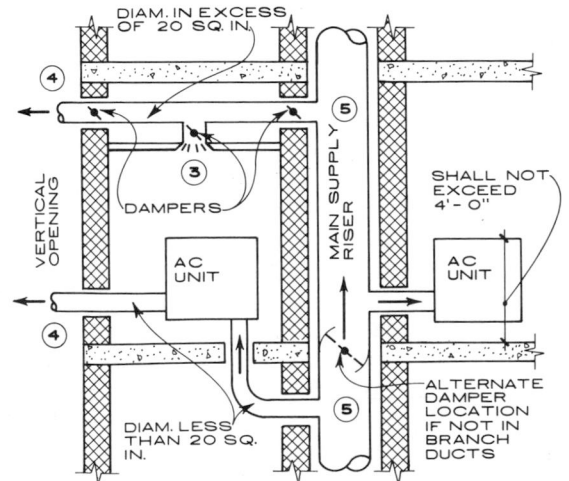

FIRE DAMPERS

Fire dampers are permitted, though undesirable, in fire walls if automatically closing fire doors are installed, one on each side. They are not required where ducts pass through non-fire walls or in one-storey exhaust systems.

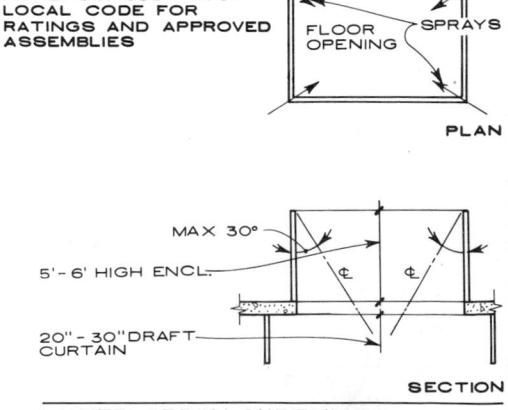

WATER SPRAY CURTAINS

Water spray curtains are used for the protection of openings in walls and floors through which conveyors or escalators pass and where fire doors are impractical. Protection is accomplished through the pressure effect and cooling action of the water spray directed from nozzles overcoming drafts caused by temperature and height differential between opening above and floor below.

SPACE DIMENSIONS

Room sizes, general: Minimum room sizes and or number of occupants permitted in rooms are generally governed by State or Local Codes and or lending agency standards (FHA). Space use, function, esthetics, number of occupants, economics, furniture arrangement and traffic flow should be given primary consideration in sizing rooms. Minimum room dimension is generally 7'−0''.

RESIDENTIAL OCCUPANCIES

The adjacent chart summarizes the requirements of the various model codes for residential occupancies:

RESIDENTIAL OCCUPANCY DESCRIPTION	Minimum Residential Room Size ††††			
	UBC	NBC	BBC	SBC
Living Room	120 sq. ft.	Habitable	Habitable	Habitable
Living and Cooking	150 sq. ft.	Rooms	Rooms	Rooms
Living and Sleeping	150 sq. ft.	70 sq. ft.	400 cu. ft.	125 sq. ft.
Bedroom	90 sq. ft.†		Per	Per
Efficiency or Bachelor Apartment	220 sq. ft.††		Person	Person
Kitchen	50 sq. ft.	60 sq. ft. †††		
Kitchen and Dining		90 sq. ft.		

† Add 50 sq. ft. for each occupant over 2.
†† Add 100 sq. ft. for each occupant over 2.
††† Kitchen without bedroom 50 sq. ft.
†††† UBC = Uniform Building Code.
　　　NBC = National Building Code.
　　　BBC = Basic Building Code.
　　　SBC = Southern Building Code.

LOBBIES

Lobby sizes should be determined by the anticipated use and number of occupants. The adjacent chart may guide preliminary assumptions:

LOBBY DESCRIPTION	PRELIMINARY ASSUMPTION WIDTH OR AREA
Elevator one side	6'−0'' minimum width
	9'−0'' ample
Elevator two side	10'−0'' minimum width
	12'−0'' ample
Theater Foyer	3 sq. ft. per person
Waiting Room	1 1/2 sq. ft. per person

CORRIDORS

Since corridors are primary means of emergency egress from buildings, State and Local Codes have established minimum width. Normal circulation dictates greater widths. Traffic load, door swings, length of corridor and type of illumination should be considered in determining corridor width. The adjacent chart may guide preliminary assumptions:

CORRIDOR DESCRIPTION		PRELIMINARY ASSUMPTION CORRIDOR WIDTH
Residential:	Bedroom Hall	3'−0'' to 5'−0''
	Service Hall	3'−0'' minimum
	Dormitories	5'−0'' to 7'−0''
Office Buildings		5'−0'' to 7'−0''
School Buildings		8'−0'' to 12'−0''
Hospital		8'−0'' minimum non ambulatory

STAIRWAYS

Exit stairway width is generally determined by code minimum. Some codes have the same minimum width requirement for stairs and corridors, others require stair minimums greater than corridor minimums, while others have corridor minimums greater than stair minimums. Be sure to check the local code authorities having jurisdiction.

VARIOUS OCCUPANCIES

Preliminary room size assumption may be determined by the number of occupants. The adjacent chart summarizes the requirements of the various model codes for various occupancies:

VARIOUS OCCUPANCIES DESCRIPTION		Required Square Feet Per Person ††††			
		UBC	NBC	BBC	SBC
Assembly Areas:	Fixed Seats	7	6	6	6
	Movable Seats	15	15	15	15
Educational:		−	40	40	−
	Classrooms	20	−	−	40
	Shops	50	−	−	100
Institutional		−	150	150	125
Mercantile:	Ground floor	30	30	30	30
	Basement	20	30	30	30
	Upper floor	50	60	60	60
Office		100	100	100	100

CEILING HEIGHTS

Minimum heights are governed by code. Generally accepted residential ceiling height is 8'−0'', however many codes permit 7'−6'' ceiling height in habitable rooms and 7'−0'' in corridors. Room function (gymnasium, or bedroom), width, type of illumination, type of structure, attic or plenum requirements, duct and pipe ways should be given primary consideration in determining ceiling heights. The adjacent chart may guide preliminary assumptions:

SPACE WIDTH	PRELIMINARY ASSUMPTION CEILING HEIGHT
7' to 10'	7'−6'' to 9'−0''
10' to 16'	8'−0'' to 9'−6''
16' to 24'	8'−6'' to 10'−0''

Raymond Ziegler, FAIA; Allison, Rible, Robinson & Ziegler; Los Angeles, California

GENERAL NOTE:
Various methods listed below are applicable to different purposes, e.g. preliminary cost analysis, rental income appraisal, estimation of financial value for loan requirements, and design.

1. CALCULATION OF GROSS BLDG. AREA OR "ARCHITECTURAL AREA"
Total sq. ft. of basic areas of the several floors of a building including basements, mezzanine & intermediate floored tiers and penthouses of headroom height, added to total percentages of partial areas.

a. SUGGESTED STANDARDS FOR BASIC AREA
To calculate floor areas, include the full square foot area of spaces on all floors enclosed within the face of exterior wall surfaces of the building with the addition of dormers, bays, and chimneys, including tunnels 6'–0" wide w/slab.

b. PERCENTAGE OF PARTIAL AREAS

Garage	2/3 of area
Carport	1/2 of area
Unenclosed porch	1/2 of area
Enclosed porch	2/3 of area
Unfinished basement	1/2 of area
Covered walkways (paved)	1/2 of area
Open area under bldg. (paved)	1/2 of area
Canopies	1/4 of area
Two story room	1½ of area
Penthouse (headroom height)	2/3 of area
Tunnels under 6'–0" wide w/slab	1/2 of "

c. EXCLUDE THE FOLLOWING:
Unfinished attics (finished attics are included where headroom is 5'–0" or over), crawl spaces and terraces, pipe trenches, roof overhangs, chimneys.

2. BREAKDOWN OF GROSS BLDG. AREA (SIMILAR TO G.S.A. STANDARDS)
a. NET ASSIGNABLE AREA OR "NET USABLE SPACE".
(Include interior columns or necessary projections)
b. CIRCULATION AREA
(1.) Horizontal—corridors, lobbies, ent. tunnels, & bridges.
(2.) Vertical—stairs, elev. shafts, & towers.
c. MECHANICAL AREA
(1.) Boiler rm. elec. vault, etc.
(2.) Cooling towers, enclosed shafts, duct-space.
(3.) Toilets & restroom lounge area.
d. CONSTRUCTION AREA (STRUCTURE, WALL THICKNESSES, ETC.)
e. PARTIAL AREAS (SEE 1.b.)

3. EXPLANATION OF FAMILIAR TERMS:
a. "GROSS INSIDE SPACE" equals net assignable area, plus horizontal circulation plus mechanical area.
b. "NET RENTABLE SPACE" equals net assignable plus horiz. circulation & mechanical services pertaining directly to rentable area.
c. "TOTAL NET AREA" (GSA standards) equals net assignable plus horizontal circulation area.
d. "BLDG. EFFICIENCY" equals percentage of net assignable in relation to "gross inside space."

4. STANDARD OF THE FEDERAL HOUSING ADMINISTRATION
Include areas of floors above basement, measured from outside surfaces of exterior walls; include bays, dormers, utility rooms, vestibules, hall & closets.
Do not include garage or finished attic spaces.
In a half story measure from outside surfaces of exterior walls or partitions enclosing the areas, except do not include areas where ceiling height is less than 5'–0".
Do not deduct for stairwells, interior light shafts, chimneys, fireplaces, thickness of partitions, or thickness of enclosing walls.
Porches, attached terraces, balconies and projecting fireplaces or chimneys, outside the exterior walls, are not included.

DEFINITIONS:
Half story: If finished as living area, must be 50% or greater than 50% of the calculated area of floor below.
Full story: Completely finished for living area, enclosed by exterior walls with a ceiling height 5'–0" min. at exterior walls.
Attic: Unfinished or partially finished as living area when the calculated area is less than 50% of floor below.

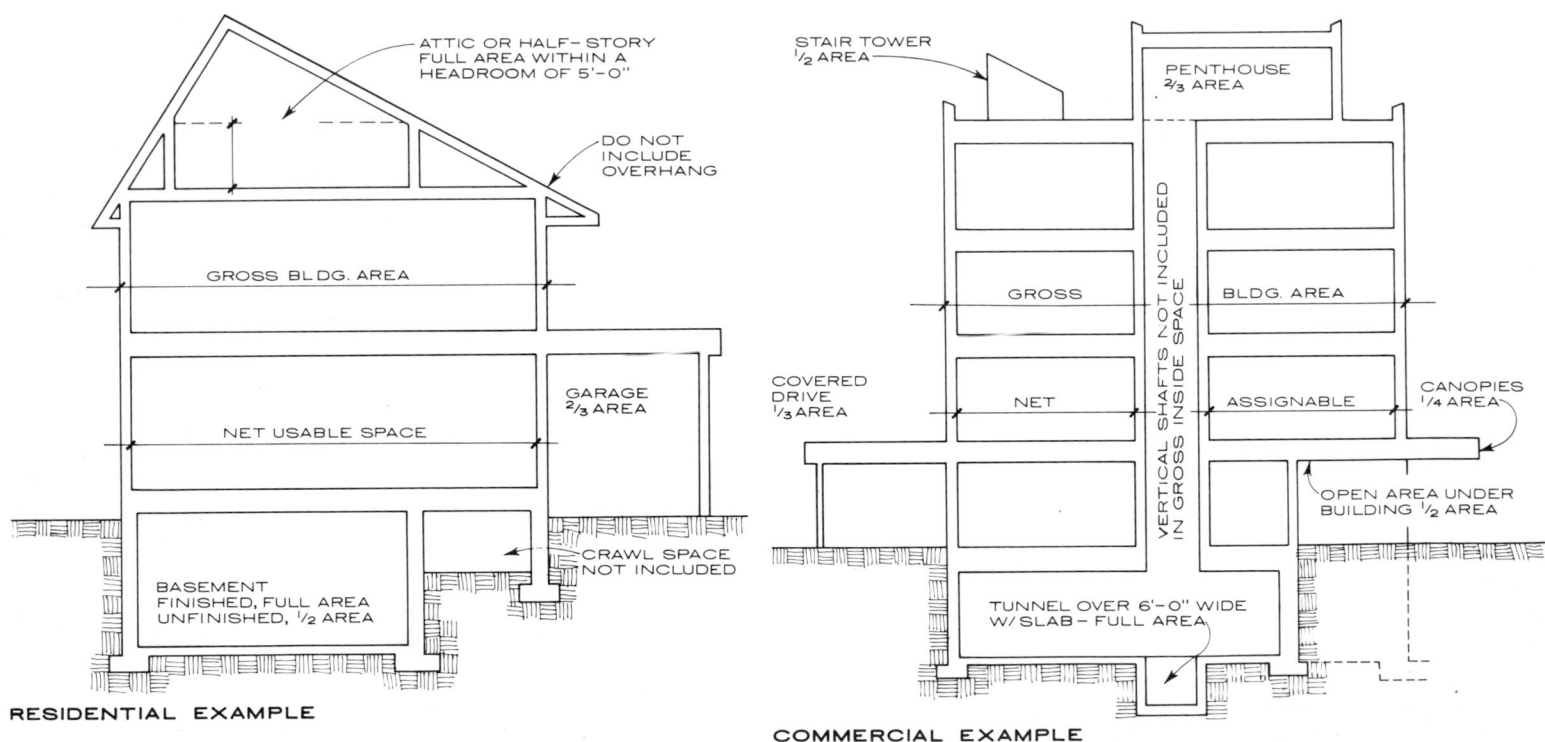

RESIDENTIAL EXAMPLE

COMMERCIAL EXAMPLE

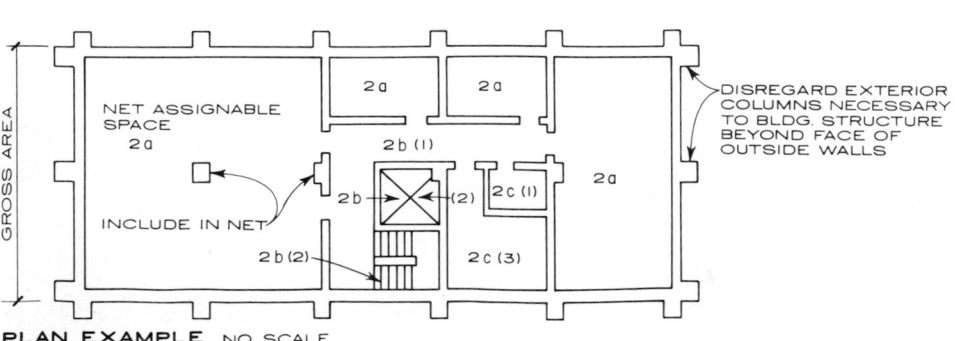

PLAN EXAMPLE NO SCALE

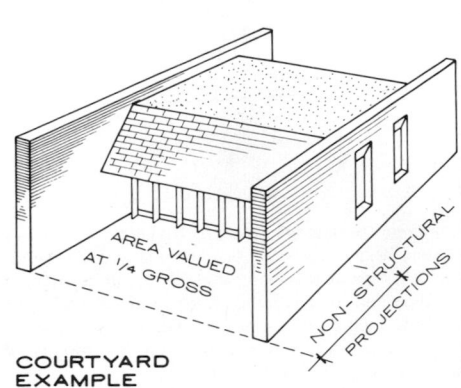

COURTYARD EXAMPLE

Noel M. Knudson; Hammel, Green and Abrahamson, Inc.; St. Paul, Minnesota

ARCHITECTURAL VOLUME OF BUILDINGS

The ARCHITECTURAL VOLUME (cube or cubage) of a building is the sum of the products of the areas defined on previous page (using the area of a single story for multi-story portions having the same area on each floor) and the height from the underside of the lowest floor construction system to the average height of the surface of the finished roof above for the various parts of the building.

From AIA Document D101, 1967

CUBAGE includes the following volumes, taken in full:

The cubic content of the actual space enclosed within the outer surfaces of the exterior or outer walls and contained between the outside of the roof and the bottom of the lowest floor; bays, oriels, dormers; penthouses; chimneys; walk through tunnels; tanks, vaults, pits and trenches, if made of building construction materials (not simple earth excavations); enclosed porches and balconies, including screened areas.

The CUBAGE includes the following volumes in part:

a) Two-thirds ($^2/_3$) volume for:
Non-enclosed porches, if recessed into the building and not having enclosing sash or screens.

b) One-half ($^1/_2$) volume for:
Non-enclosed porches built as an extension to the building, without enclosing sash or screens.

Areaways and pipe tunnels.

Patio areas that have building walls extended on two sides, roof over and paved surfacing.

The CUBAGE does not include the following features:

The cubage of outside steps, terraces, courts, garden walls; light shafts; parapets, cornices, roof overhangs; footings, deep foundations, piling, caissons, special foundations and similar features. Note: In making cubic foot cost analysis, as a matter of information and reference, it is recommended that cost items such as piling, caissons, deep foundations, unusual step construction and other non-typical features be listed as factors having an effect on the unit cost without being included in the cubage.

CUBIC FOOT COST

The CUBIC FOOT COST equals the net cost divided by the total cubage.

The NET COST in usual practice includes the following:

The building construction, including built-in cabinets and furniture, all finishes and hardware; mechanical work, including plumbing, heating, air conditioning and controls; electrical work, lighting fixtures, sound and signal systems; elevators; sprinklers; equipment provided for the operation of the building.

The NET COST usually excludes the following:

Furniture and furnishings, such as ranges, laundry and kitchen equipment, clocks, lockers, files; organs; draperies, shades, blinds, awnings; non-built in furniture; roads, walks, terraces, and other site development; landscaping; sewage disposal system; power plant; wells or other water supply; utilities to the building. Also fees for Architects, Engineers and specialty consultants.

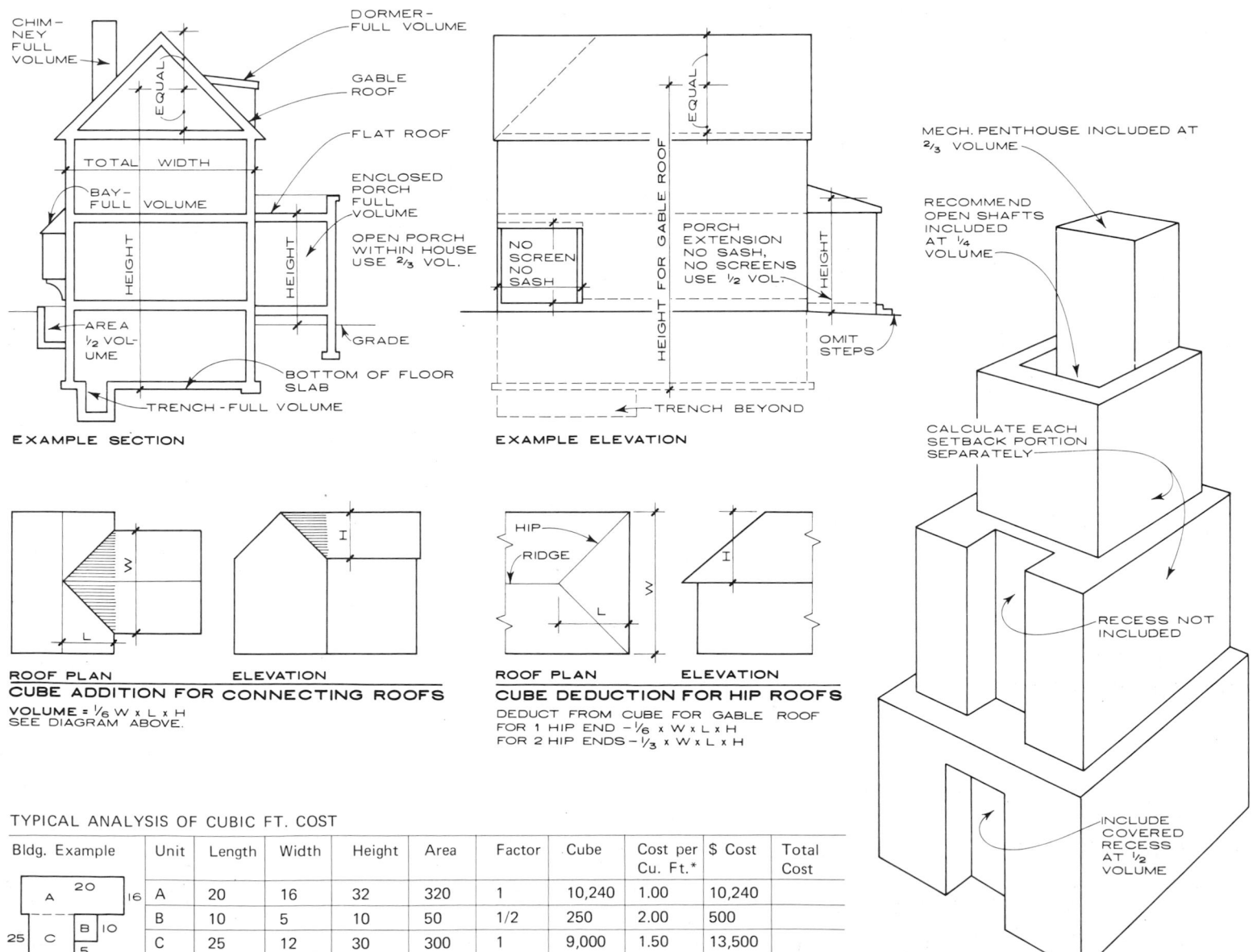

EXAMPLE SECTION

EXAMPLE ELEVATION

CUBE ADDITION FOR CONNECTING ROOFS
VOLUME = $^1/_6$ W x L x H
SEE DIAGRAM ABOVE.

CUBE DEDUCTION FOR HIP ROOFS
DEDUCT FROM CUBE FOR GABLE ROOF
FOR 1 HIP END − $^1/_6$ x W x L x H
FOR 2 HIP ENDS − $^1/_3$ x W x L x H

CONSIDERATIONS IN DETERMINING CUBAGE OF MULTI-STORY BUILDING

TYPICAL ANALYSIS OF CUBIC FT. COST

Bldg. Example	Unit	Length	Width	Height	Area	Factor	Cube	Cost per Cu. Ft.*	$ Cost	Total Cost
	A	20	16	32	320	1	10,240	1.00	10,240	
	B	10	5	10	50	1/2	250	2.00	500	
	C	25	12	30	300	1	9,000	1.50	13,500	
										$24,240

* DETERMINE VARYING UNIT COST DIFFERENCE

Noel M. Knudson; Hammel, Green and Abrahamson, Inc.; St. Paul, Minnesota

PRINCIPLES OF FALLOUT PROTECTION

TIME

Radiation intensity decreases 10 fold for every 7 fold increase in time.

DISTANCE

The farther fallout travels, the more radiation decays before falling to earth.

MATERIAL

Shielding is accomplished by the weight of material used as a barrier.

PROTECTION FACTOR – PF

A factor used to express the relation between the amount of fallout gamma radiation that would be received by an unprotected person and the amount that would be received by one in a shelter. For example, an occupant of a shelter with a Pf of 40 would be exposed to a dose of $1/40$ (or $2\frac{1}{2}\%$) of the rate to which he would be exposed if his location were unprotected.

MINIMUM REQUIREMENTS FOR PUBLIC SHELTERS – OFFICE OF CIVIL DEFENSE

Protection factor 40
Area per person . . . . 10 S.F.
Volume per person . . . . 65 C.F.
Fresh air per person . . . . 3 C.F.M.
Means of egress 2
Number people per egress 200
Volume of storage per person
    (with water drum) . . . . 1.5 C.F.
Volume of storage per person
    (without water drum) . . . . 9 C.F.
Number of people per toilet 50
Light in sleeping areas (at floor) . . . . 2 F.C.
Light in activity areas (at floor) . . . . 5 F.C.
Light in administrative and medical
    areas (at desk) . . . . 20 F.C.

Accessible trapped water in plumbing system is taken into account when determining the amount of water to be stored.

Toilets are not required by the Office of Civil Defense but if included should be based on this figure.

NOTES

The Office of Civil Defense requires that Protection Factors for all public fallout shelters be certified by an architect or engineer qualified as a Fallout Shelter Analyst.

Public shelters are stocked with emergency supplies which include food, water, medical supplies, sanitary kits, etc.

Public fallout shelters are identified by a black and yellow sign.

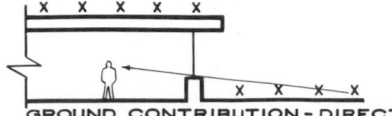

GROUND CONTRIBUTION – DIRECT
Some radiation comes directly from ground surface.

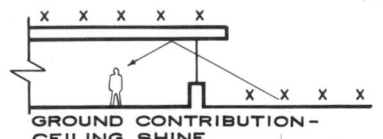

GROUND CONTRIBUTION – CEILING SHINE
Some radiation is reflected by the ceiling or other horizontal plane.

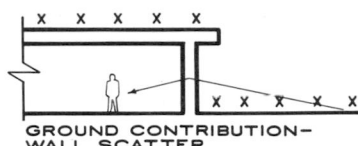

GROUND CONTRIBUTION – WALL SCATTER
Some radiation is deflected by the wall.

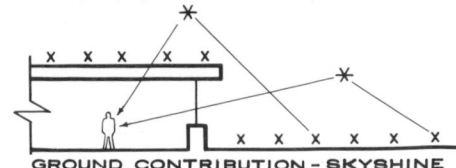

GROUND CONTRIBUTION – SKYSHINE
Some radiation is reflected from particles in the air.

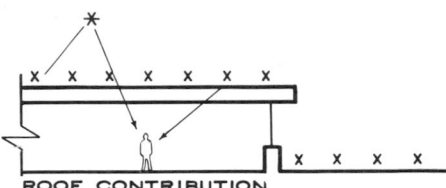

ROOF CONTRIBUTION
Some radiation comes directly from the roof surface.

RADIATION TYPES AND SOURCES

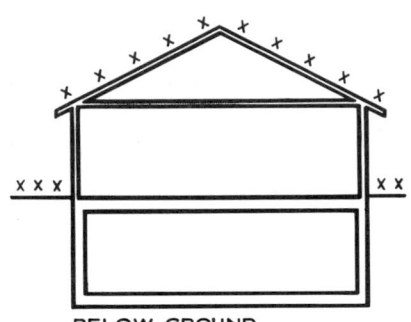

BELOW GROUND AREA = 1000 S.F.

WT. OF FLOOR-PSF	CONSTRUCTION OF FLOOR	Pf
20	wood frame	20
50	4" concrete	50
125	10" concrete	220
225	18" concrete	2000

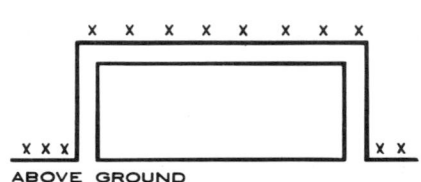

ABOVE GROUND AREA = 1000 S.F.

WT. OF WALL-PSF	WEIGHT OF ROOF-PSF			
	50	100	200	300
50	4	5	5	5
100	7	12	15	15
200	14	40	115	145
300	15	55	345	910

APPROXIMATE Pf VALUES FOR SMALL STRUCTURES

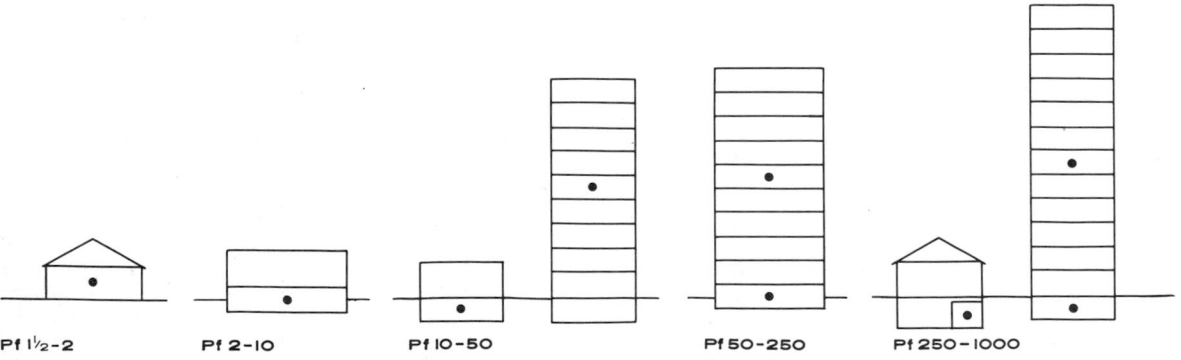

Pf 1½–2
Above ground areas of low buildings including residences, stores, light industrial types of structure.

Pf 2–10
Small buildings having partly exposed basements (or first floor of heavy wall structures).

Pf 10–50
Central areas of some upper floors in a multistory building with light floor and wall construction. Basement in a 1 or 2 story building.

Pf 50–250
Center of some upper floors, basement, in heavy multistory type building.

Pf 250–1000
Central portions of some upper floors in high-rise buildings (more than 10 stories) and basement in a multistory structure with heavy floor and wall construction.

Pf VARIATION AT DIFFERENT FLOORS

10
50
100
200
250
200
100
50
1000

APPROXIMATE Pf VALUES FOR VARIOUS BUILDING TYPES & LOCATIONS IN BUILDING

Robert Berne, AIA; Chief Architect, U. S. Office of Civil Defense; Washington, D. C.

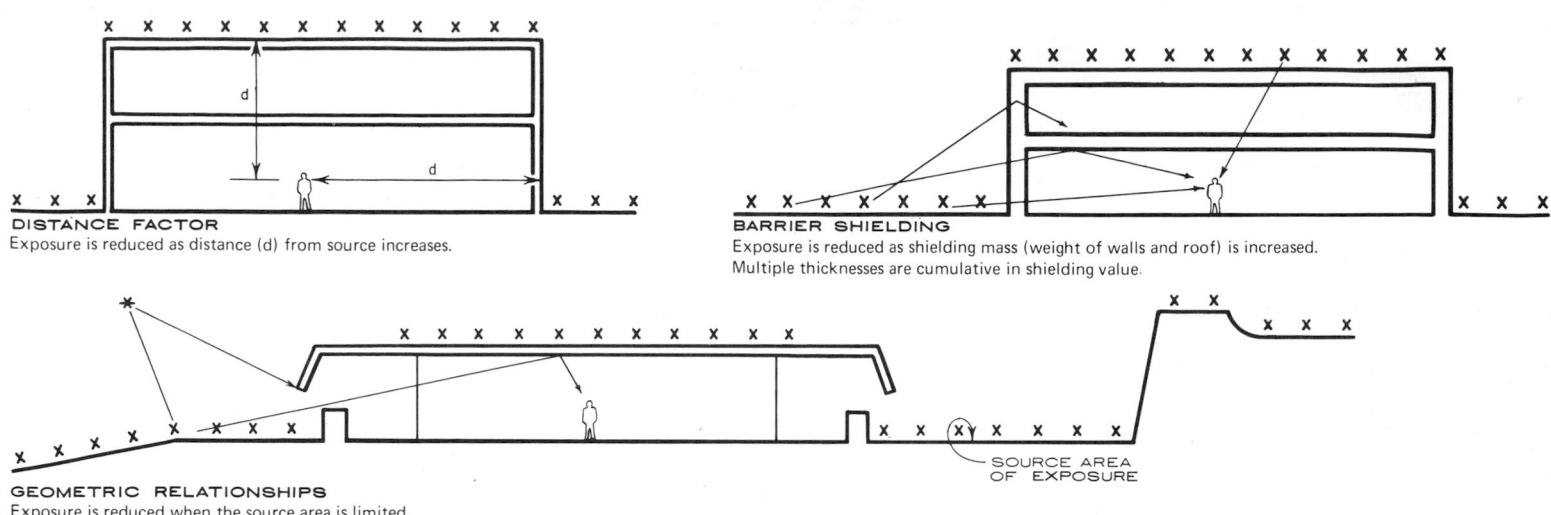

DISTANCE FACTOR
Exposure is reduced as distance (d) from source increases.

BARRIER SHIELDING
Exposure is reduced as shielding mass (weight of walls and roof) is increased. Multiple thicknesses are cumulative in shielding value.

SOURCE AREA OF EXPOSURE

GEOMETRIC RELATIONSHIPS
Exposure is reduced when the source area is limited.

TECHNIQUES OF EXPOSURE CONTROL

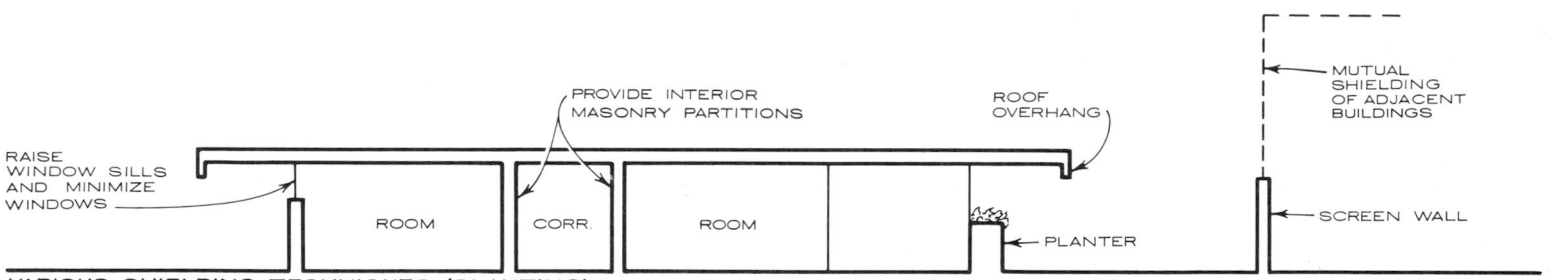

PROVIDE INTERIOR MASONRY PARTITIONS

ROOF OVERHANG

MUTUAL SHIELDING OF ADJACENT BUILDINGS

RAISE WINDOW SILLS AND MINIMIZE WINDOWS

ROOM   CORR.   ROOM

PLANTER

SCREEN WALL

VARIOUS SHIELDING TECHNIQUES (SLANTING)

DEFINITION OF "SLANTING"

"Slanting" is defined as the incorporation, at little or no increase in cost or reduction in efficiency, of certain architectural and engineering features into all new structures to protect personnel from fallout gamma radiation in the event of an emergency. The slanting features may provide immediate improvement or may be of such nature as to facilitate later conversion of the structure for protective purposes. Thus, "Slanting" adds the protective function to the other criteria normally considered in the design of structures.

"SLANTING" IN DESIGN

Increase sill heights

Offset entrances

Stagger doors and windows

Use masonry partitions

Use smaller window areas

Fill hollow blocks with sand

Use screen walls

Use roof fill

Use planter boxes

Roof overhangs

Increase weight of walls

Depress building in ground

Use shields for openings

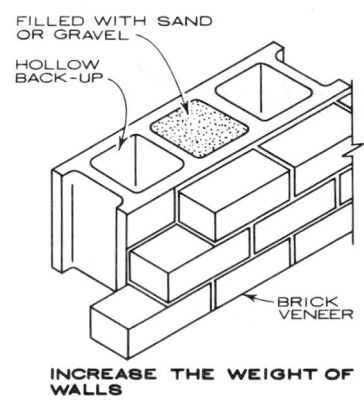

FILLED WITH SAND OR GRAVEL

HOLLOW BACK-UP

BRICK VENEER

INCREASE THE WEIGHT OF WALLS

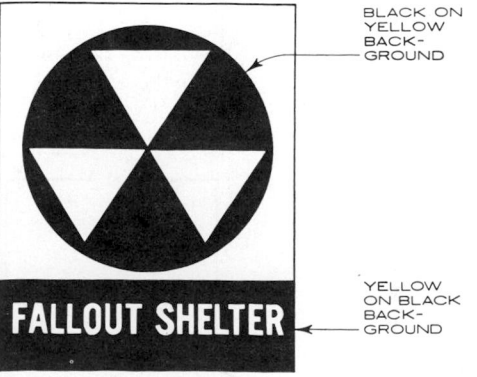

BLACK ON YELLOW BACKGROUND

FALLOUT SHELTER

YELLOW ON BLACK BACKGROUND

PUBLIC SHELTER SIGN

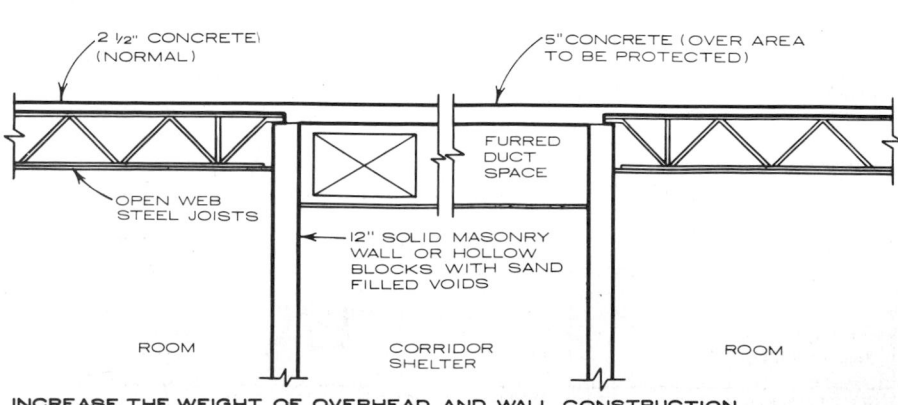

2 1/2" CONCRETE (NORMAL)

5" CONCRETE (OVER AREA TO BE PROTECTED)

FURRED DUCT SPACE

OPEN WEB STEEL JOISTS

12" SOLID MASONRY WALL OR HOLLOW BLOCKS WITH SAND FILLED VOIDS

ROOM   CORRIDOR SHELTER   ROOM

INCREASE THE WEIGHT OF OVERHEAD AND WALL CONSTRUCTION

Robert Berne, AIA; Chief Architect, U. S. Office of Civil Defense; Washington, D. C.

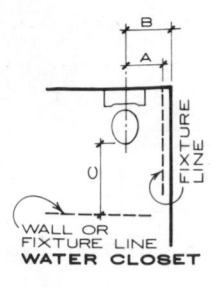
WATER CLOSET

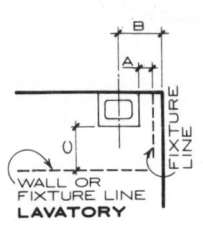
LAVATORY

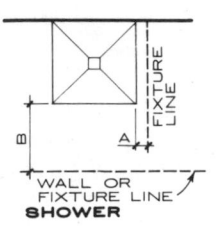
SHOWER

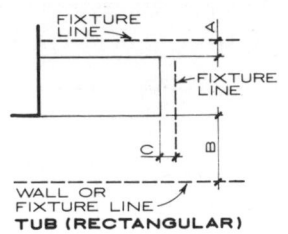
TUB (RECTANGULAR)

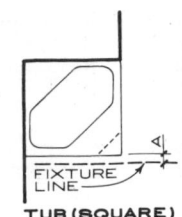
TUB (SQUARE)

FIXTURE CLEARANCES

FIXTURE	A MINIMUM	A LIBERAL	B MINIMUM	B LIBERAL	C MINIMUM	C LIBERAL
WATER CLOSET	12"	18"	15"	22"	wall — 18" fixt. — 18"	wall — 36" fixt. — 34"
LAVATORY	2"	6"	14"	22"	18"	30"
SHOWER	2"	8"	18"	34"		
TUB (RECT.)	2"	8"	wall — 20" fixt. — 18"	wall — 34" fixt. — 30"	2"	8"
TUB (SQ.)	2"	4"				

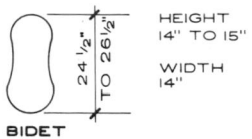
BIDET   HEIGHT 14" TO 15"   WIDTH 14"   24½" TO 26½"

TYPICAL ARRANGEMENTS

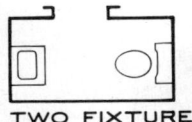 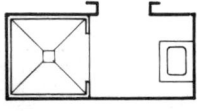 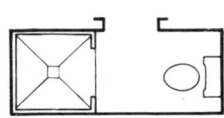 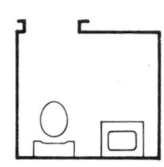

TWO FIXTURE

NOTE :
ROOM DIMENSION MAY BE
DETERMINED BY APPLICATION
OF FIXTURE CLEARANCES
TABULATED ABOVE

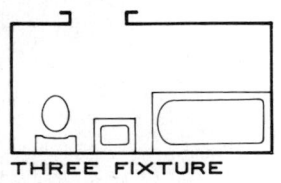 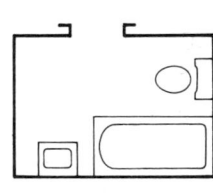 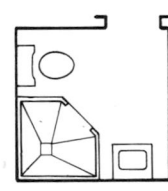 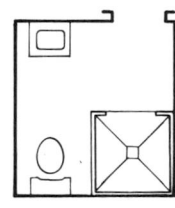 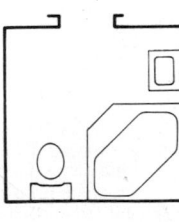

THREE FIXTURE

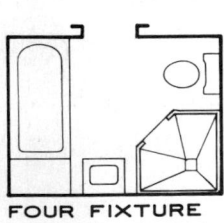 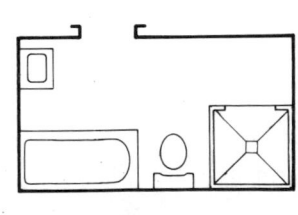 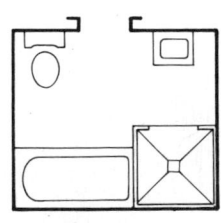 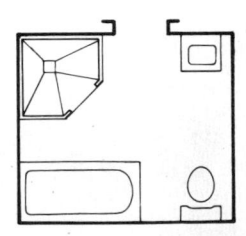 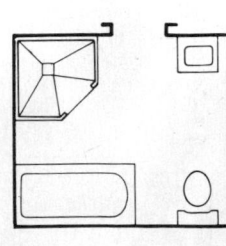

FOUR FIXTURE

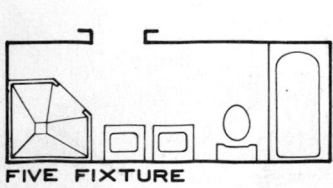 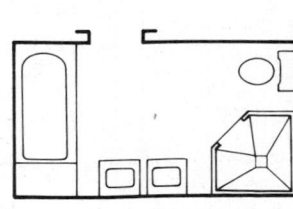 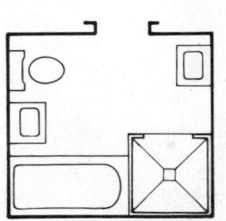 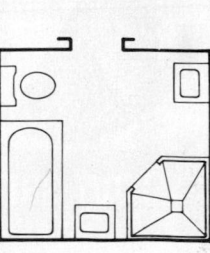

FIVE FIXTURE

THREE FIXTURE: NOTE: SEE FIRST PAGE OF THIS SERIES FOR "MINIMUM" AND "LIBERAL" FIXTURE DIMENSIONS.

LIMITED	LIBERAL	MINIMUM

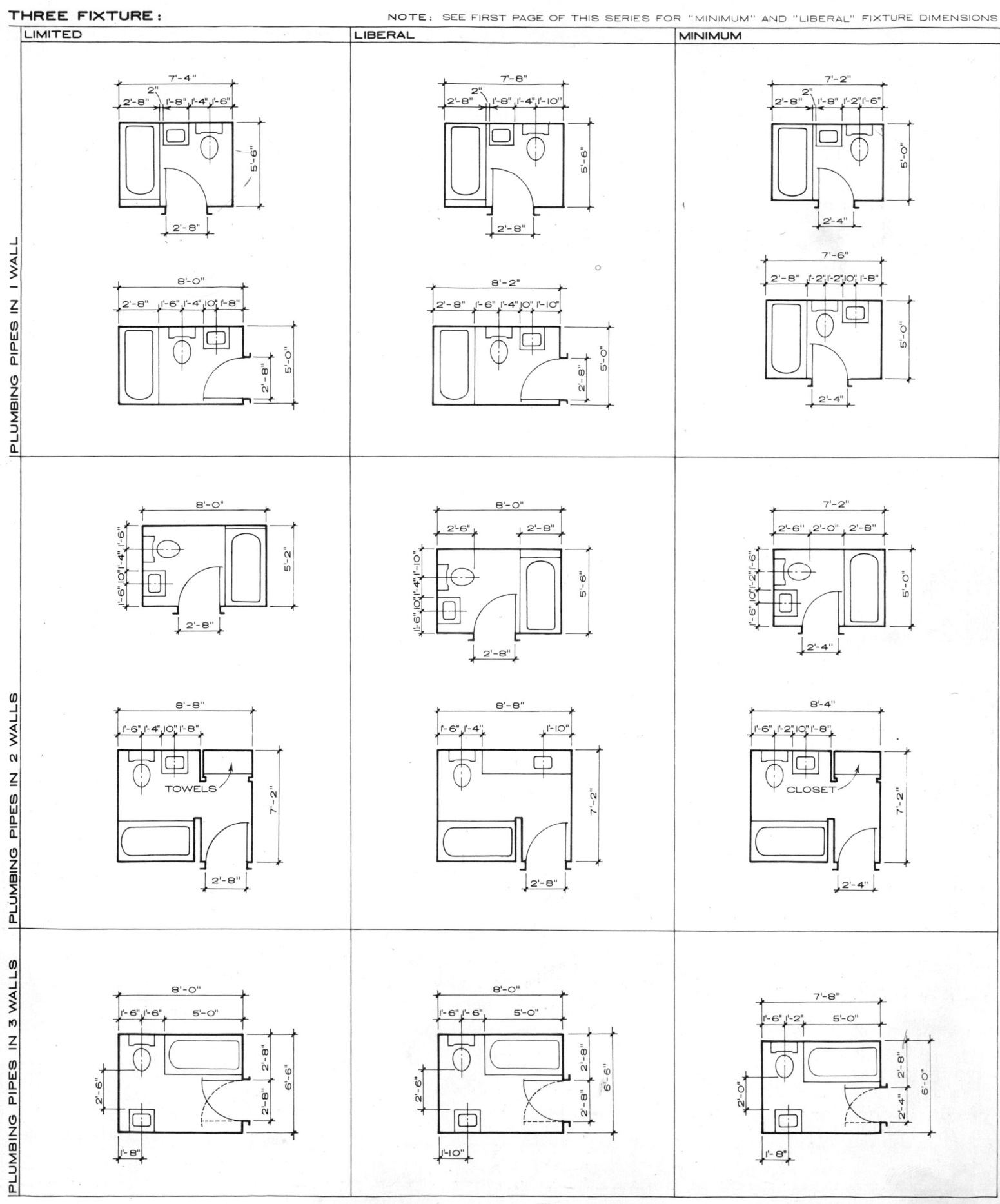

THREE FIXTURE

PLUMBING PIPES IN 3 WALLS

LIMITED	LIBERAL - FOR HOSPITALS, THE HANDICAPPED OR THE AGED, ETC.	MINIMUM

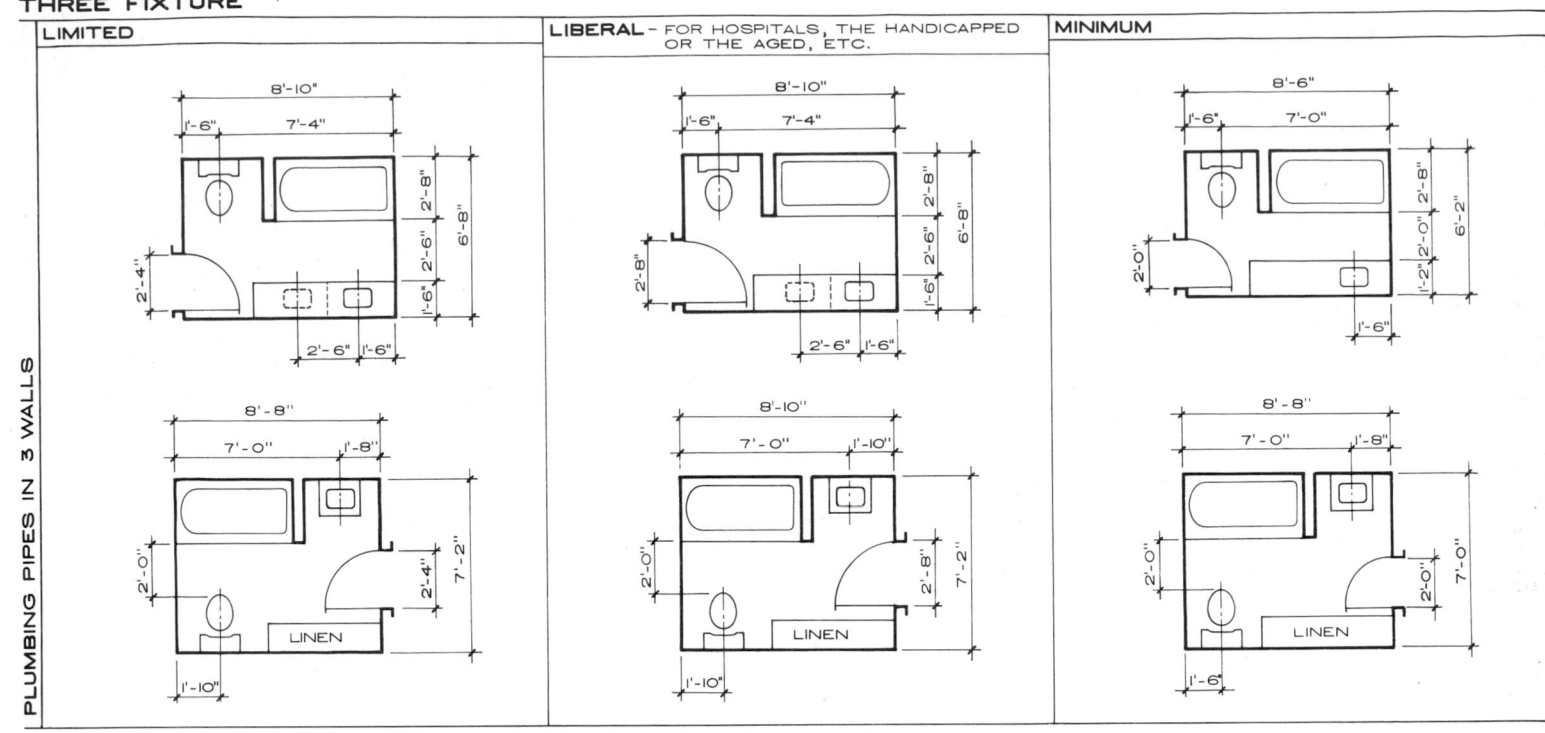

FOUR FIXTURE

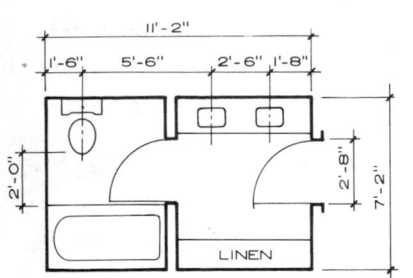

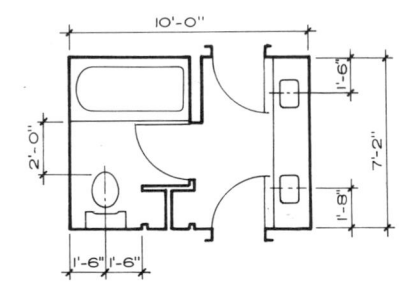

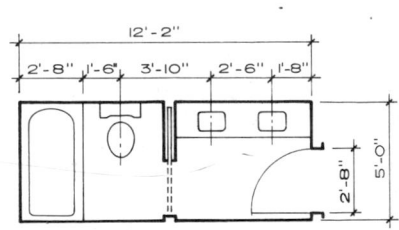

FIVE FIXTURE

NOTE: MULTIPLE ACCESS BATHROOMS ARE HIGHLY QUESTIONABLE FROM POINT OF VIEW OF PRIVACY; FOR SPECIAL OCCUPANCY, USUALLY.

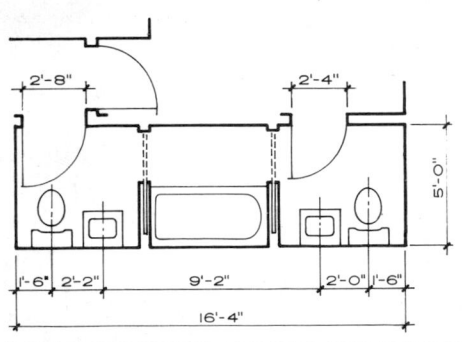

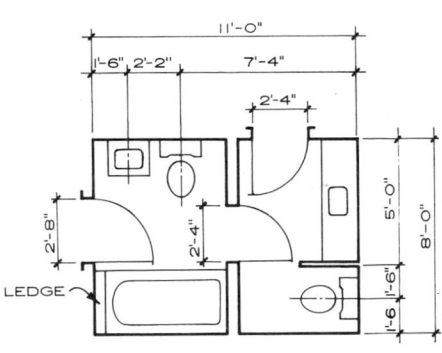

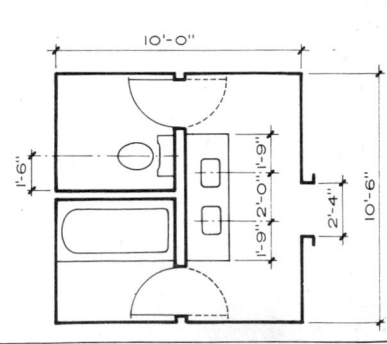

BATHROOMS WITH SHOWER STALLS

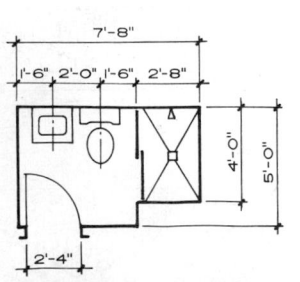

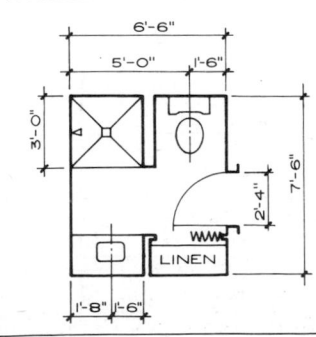

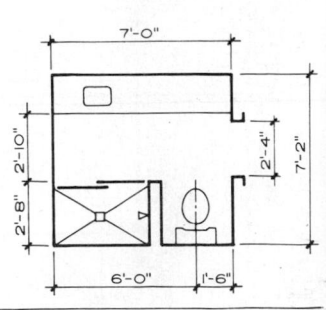

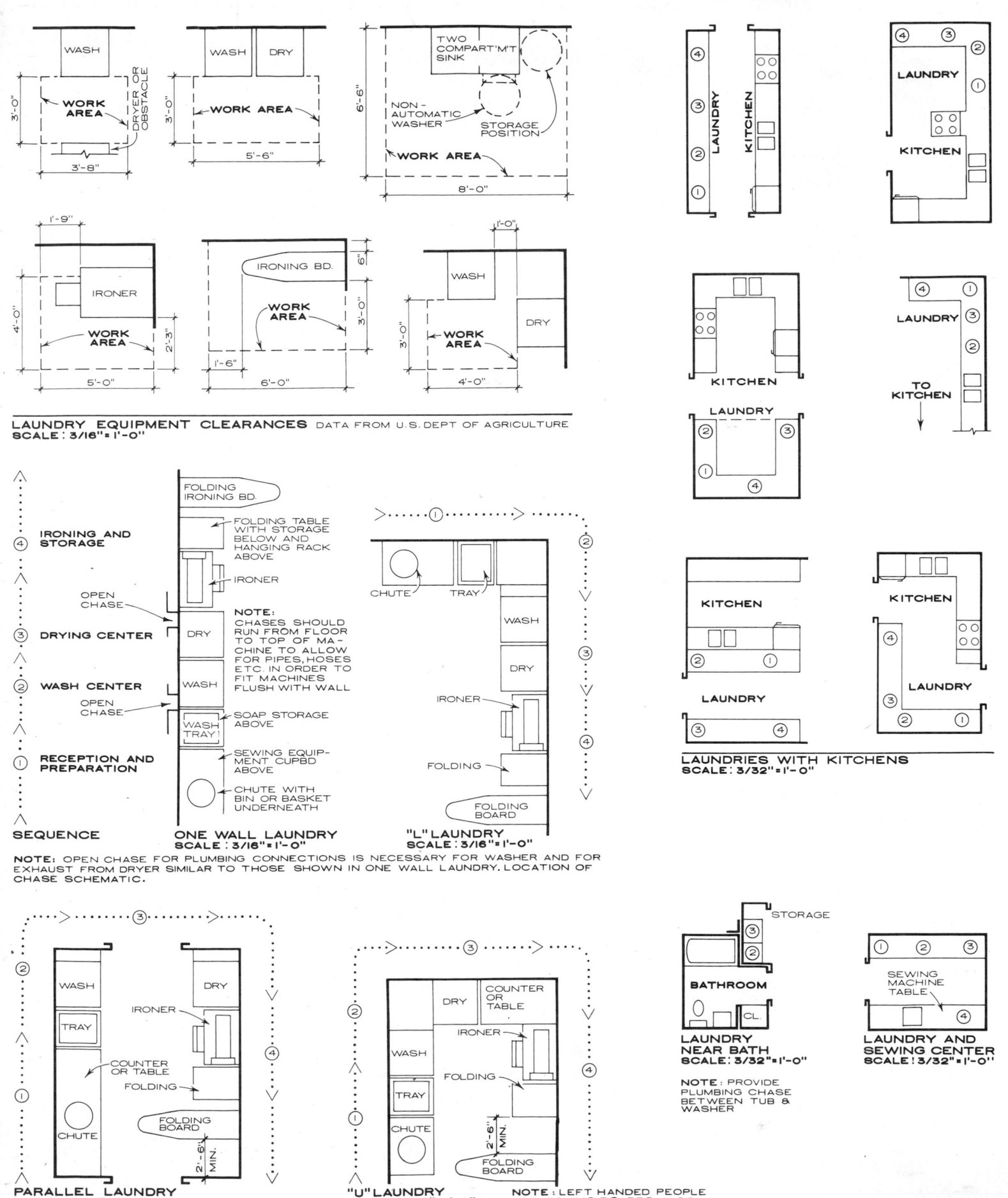

LAUNDRY EQUIPMENT CLEARANCES DATA FROM U.S. DEPT OF AGRICULTURE
SCALE: 3/16"=1'-0"

SEQUENCE

④ IRONING AND STORAGE

③ DRYING CENTER

② WASH CENTER

① RECEPTION AND PREPARATION

ONE WALL LAUNDRY
SCALE: 3/16"=1'-0"

NOTE:
CHASES SHOULD RUN FROM FLOOR TO TOP OF MACHINE TO ALLOW FOR PIPES, HOSES ETC. IN ORDER TO FIT MACHINES FLUSH WITH WALL

"L" LAUNDRY
SCALE: 3/16"=1'-0"

NOTE: OPEN CHASE FOR PLUMBING CONNECTIONS IS NECESSARY FOR WASHER AND FOR EXHAUST FROM DRYER SIMILAR TO THOSE SHOWN IN ONE WALL LAUNDRY. LOCATION OF CHASE SCHEMATIC.

LAUNDRIES WITH KITCHENS
SCALE: 3/32"=1'-0"

PARALLEL LAUNDRY
SCALE: 3/16"=1'-0"

"U" LAUNDRY
SCALE: 3/16"=1'-0"

NOTE: LEFT HANDED PEOPLE USE IRONING BOARDS ALSO

LAUNDRY NEAR BATH
SCALE: 3/32"=1'-0"

NOTE: PROVIDE PLUMBING CHASE BETWEEN TUB & WASHER

LAUNDRY AND SEWING CENTER
SCALE: 3/32"=1'-0"

R. E. Powe, Jr.; Hugh N. Jacobsen, AIA; Washington, D. C.

KITCHEN SPACE PLANNING

The layouts shown here, together with their general area requirements, are based on studies of furniture appliances, storage, and clearances for the average residential kitchen. They have been developed to accomodate storage, work, and required floor areas for various functions, but the location of appliances and their order should be determined by individual preferences, check clearances, traffic flow, and appliance functions rather than total square footage in determining kitchen size during early planning stages.

To simplify comparison of the various room types, basic sizes of furniture, appliances, and clearances have been standardized. However, the appliances shown in the kitchenettes are the more compact units available from some manufacturers (see Equip. pgs.) In all cases, the depth of the counter is assumed as 24'', the depth of base storage units as 20'', and the depth of wall storage units as 12''. Their widths vary in relation to their location.

A useful rule-of-thumb to determine storage area requirements for residential kitchens is: Provide a minimum of 18 square feet of space for basic storage with an additional 6 square feet for each person usually served.

The letters A, B, and C shown below refer to the "work centers" described on another page. The asterisks(*) indicate the best locations for a wall oven if such an oven is used.

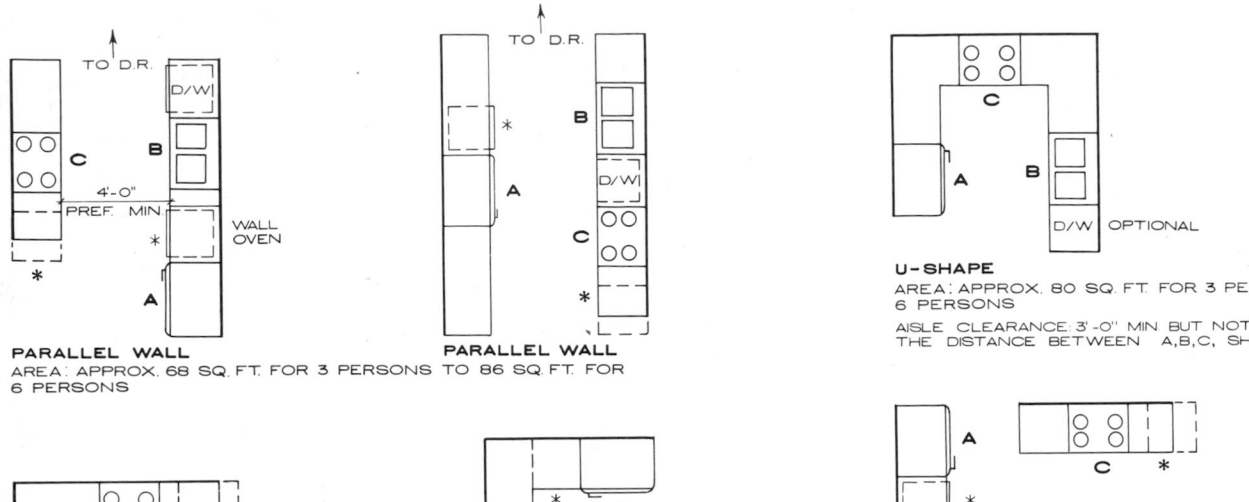

PARALLEL WALL
AREA: APPROX. 68 SQ. FT. FOR 3 PERSONS TO 86 SQ. FT. FOR 6 PERSONS

PARALLEL WALL

U-SHAPE
AREA: APPROX. 80 SQ. FT. FOR 3 PERSONS TO 92 SQ. FT. FOR 6 PERSONS

AISLE CLEARANCE 3'-0" MIN BUT NOT DESIRABLE 4'-0" IS ADEQUATE. THE DISTANCE BETWEEN A,B,C, SHOULD AVERAGE 15" TO 20" MAX.

U-SHAPE

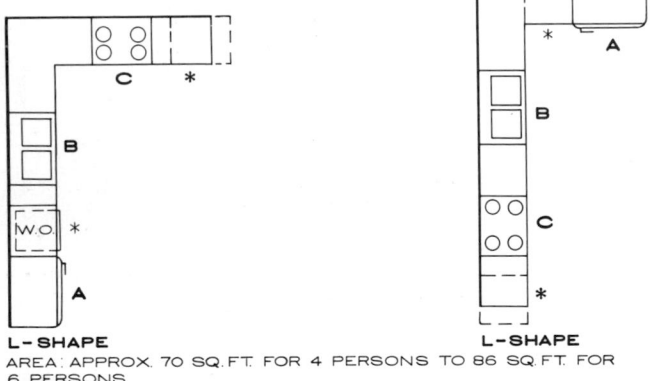

L-SHAPE
AREA: APPROX. 70 SQ. FT. FOR 4 PERSONS TO 86 SQ. FT. FOR 6 PERSONS

L-SHAPE

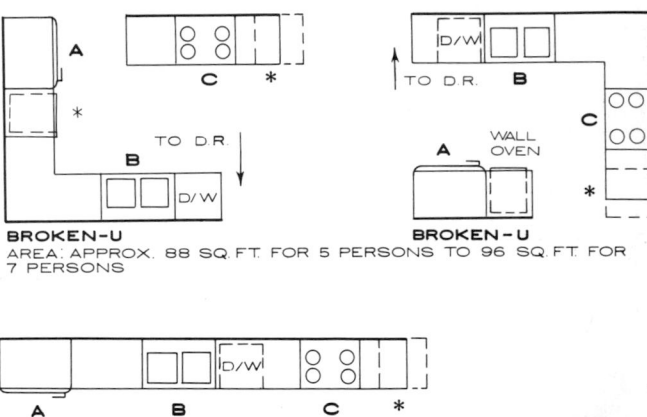

BROKEN-U
AREA: APPROX. 88 SQ. FT. FOR 5 PERSONS TO 96 SQ. FT. FOR 7 PERSONS

BROKEN-U

SINGLE WALL
AREA: APPROX. 93 SQ. FT. FOR 3 PERSONS TO 111 SQ. FT. FOR 6 PERSONS

RESIDENTIAL KITCHEN ARRANGEMENTS

NOTE: SMALL KITCHENS USUALLY HAVE UP TO 10 RUUNNING FEET OF COUNTER & EQUIPMENT; AVERAGE KITCHEN HAS UP TO 20 FEET OF COUNTER & EQUIPMENT

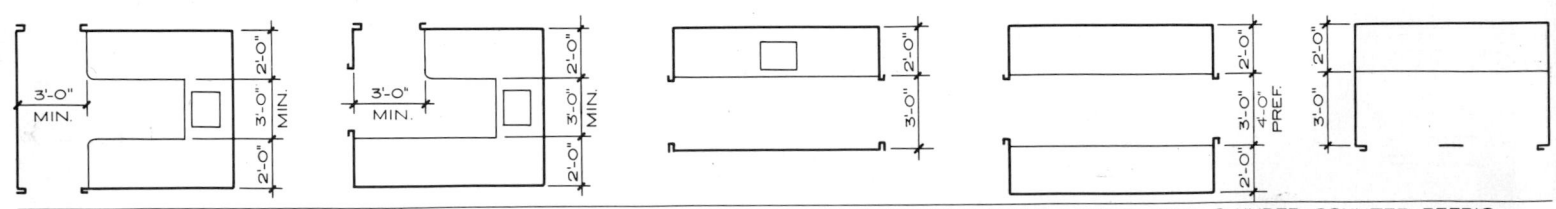

PANTRY TYPES USUAL EQUIPMENT INCLUDES DRAWER & CABINET SPACE FOR GLASSWARE, CHINA, LINENS; SINK & UNDER-COUNTER REFRIG

ABBREVIATIONS:
D/W = DISHWASHER
W. O. = WALL OVEN
D. R. = DINING ROOM

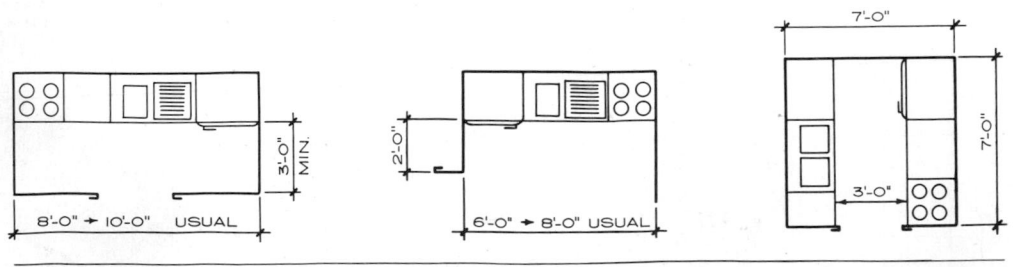

KITCHENETTES

GENERAL NOTES

1. For equipment not shown, such as covered ranges and under-counter refrigerators see manufacturers' literature.

2. Consult local building codes for kitchenette requirements.

R. E. Powe, Jr.; Hugh N. Jacobsen, AIA; Washington, D. C.

KITCHEN WORK CENTERS:

A residential kitchen may be considered in terms of three interconnected work centers, A, B and C, as shown below. Each encompasses a distinct phase of kitchen activity, and storage should be provided for those items most used in connection with each center.

The functions of the "sink center" are most common to the other two; it is recommended, therefore, that its location, if possible, be convenient to each of them (usually between them). The "refrigerator center" is best located near the entry, and the "range center" near the dining area.

CABINETS SHOULD PROJECT FLUSH OVER REFRIGERATOR.

FASCIA TO CLOSE OFF TOP OF CABINETS MAY BE PROVIDED.

FASCIA (OR BULKHEAD) SPACE MAY BE USED FOR EXTRA CABINETS FOR RARELY USED ITEMS.

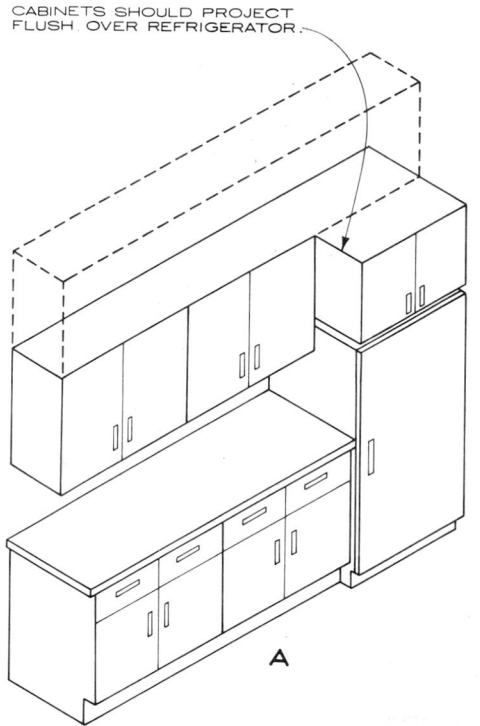

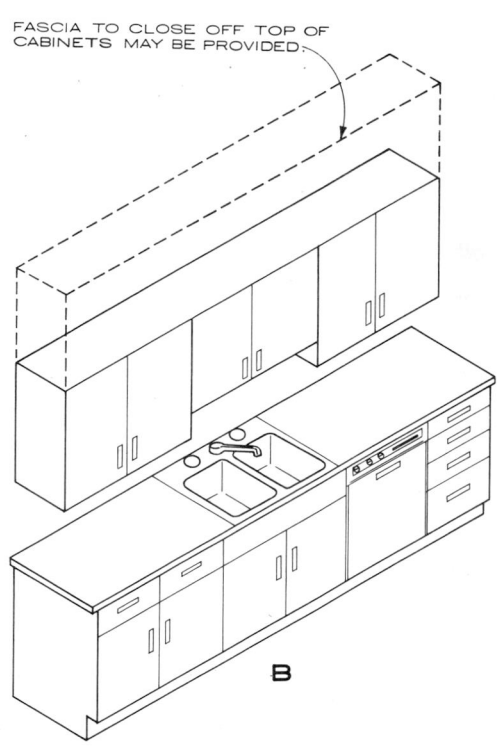

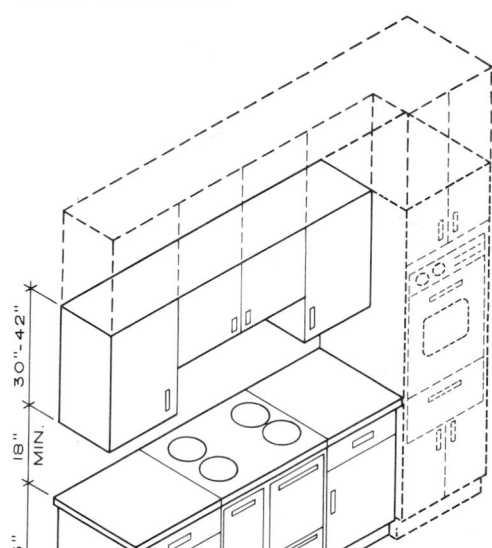

REFRIGERATOR CENTER
(RECEIVING AND FOOD PREPARATION)

Provide storage for mixer and mixing bowls; other utensils: sifter, grater, salad molds, cake and pie tins, occasional dishes, condiments, staples, canned goods, brooms and extra storage for miscellaneous items.

SINK CENTER
(FOOD PREPARATION, CLEANING AND CLEAN-UP)

Provide storage for everyday dishes, glassware, pots and pans, cutlery, silver, pitchers and shakers, vegetable bins, linen, towel rack, wastebasket, cleaning materials and utensils, garbage can or disposal, and dishdrain. Some codes require louvres or other venting provision in the doors under enclosed sinks.

RANGE CENTER
(COOKING AND SERVING)

Provide storage for pots, potholders, frying pans, roaster, cooking utensils, grease container, seasoning, canned goods, bread bin, bread board, toaster, plate warmer, platters, serving dishes and trays.

CLEARANCES AND COUNTER WIDTHS:

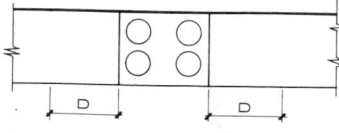

D = 18" to 24"
D = counter distance on either side of a cooking facility.

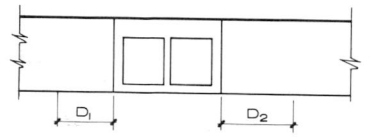

D₁ = 18" to 36"
D₂ = 24" to 36"
Provide work space on both sides of sink. If dishwasher is used allow at least 24" to the right or left.

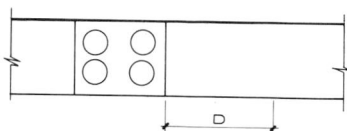

D = 36" to 42"
D = counter space between range and nearest piece of equipment.

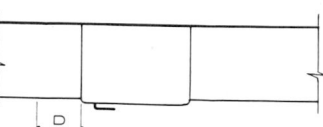

D = 15" minimum
Provide room at latch side of refrigerator for loading and unloading.

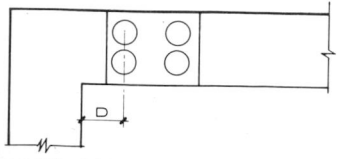

D = 14" minimum
D = clearance between the center of the front unit (or burner) and the turn of the counter.

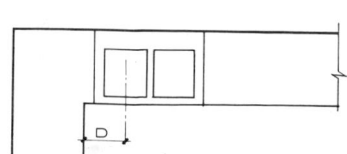

D = 14" minimum
D = clearance between the center of the sink bowl and the turn of the counter.

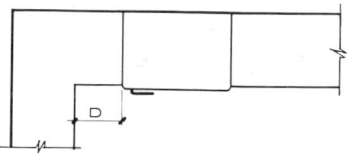

D = 16" minimum
D = clearance between latch side of refrigerator door and turn of the counter.

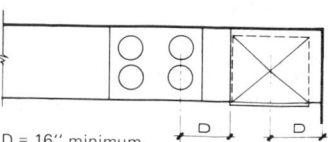

D = 16" minimum
D = clearance between center of front burner and nearest piece of high equipment or nearest wall; or between the center of a wall oven and an adjoining wall.

R. E. Powe, Jr.; Hugh N. Jacobsen, AIA; Washington, D. C.

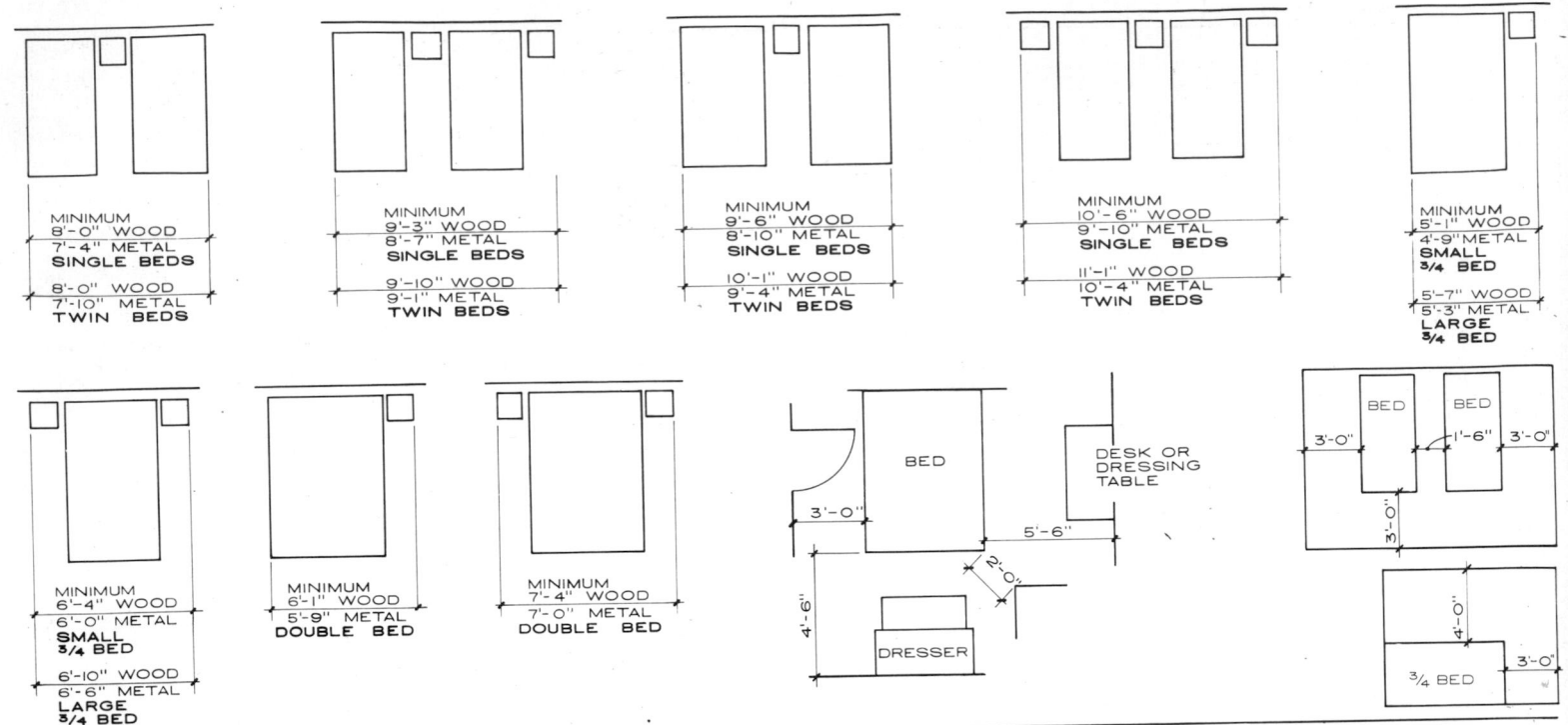

WALL SPACE REQUIREMENTS FOR BED & NIGHT TABLE ARRANGEMENTS

The average person requires 8 linear feet of drawer space for clothing. Clearances required for the pulling out of drawers and for access and entry into room must be taken into consideration. The bedroom clearances shown are recommended for passage and are desirable for bedmaking. The diagrams below show a relationship of square foot areas required when planning bedrooms with clothes storage. Sitting, writing, and makeup areas are not included. These must be included if required.

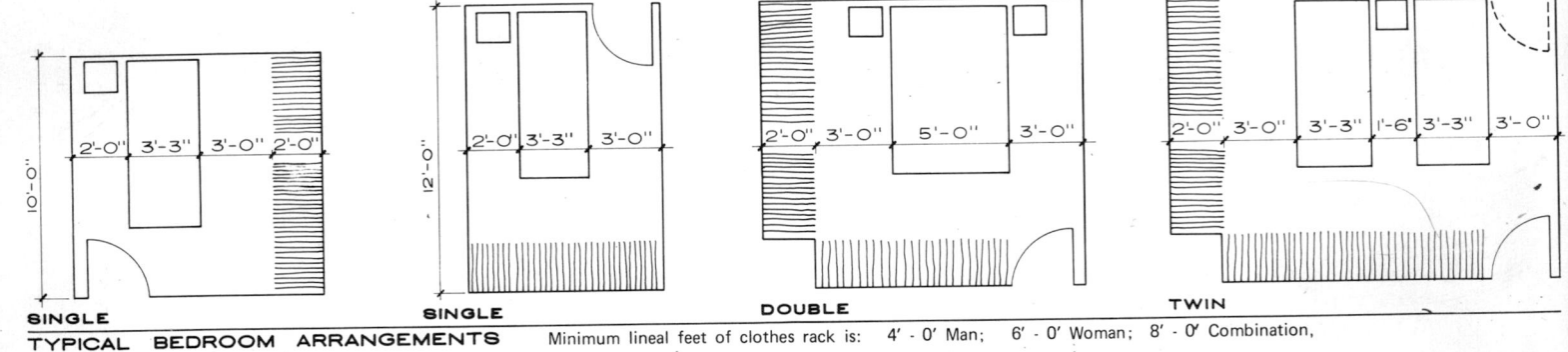

TYPICAL BEDROOM ARRANGEMENTS   Minimum lineal feet of clothes rack is: 4' - 0' Man; 6' - 0' Woman; 8' - 0' Combination,

LIVING ROOM FURNITURE CLEARANCES

Mitchell Scott; Hugh N. Jacobsen, AIA; Washington, D. C.

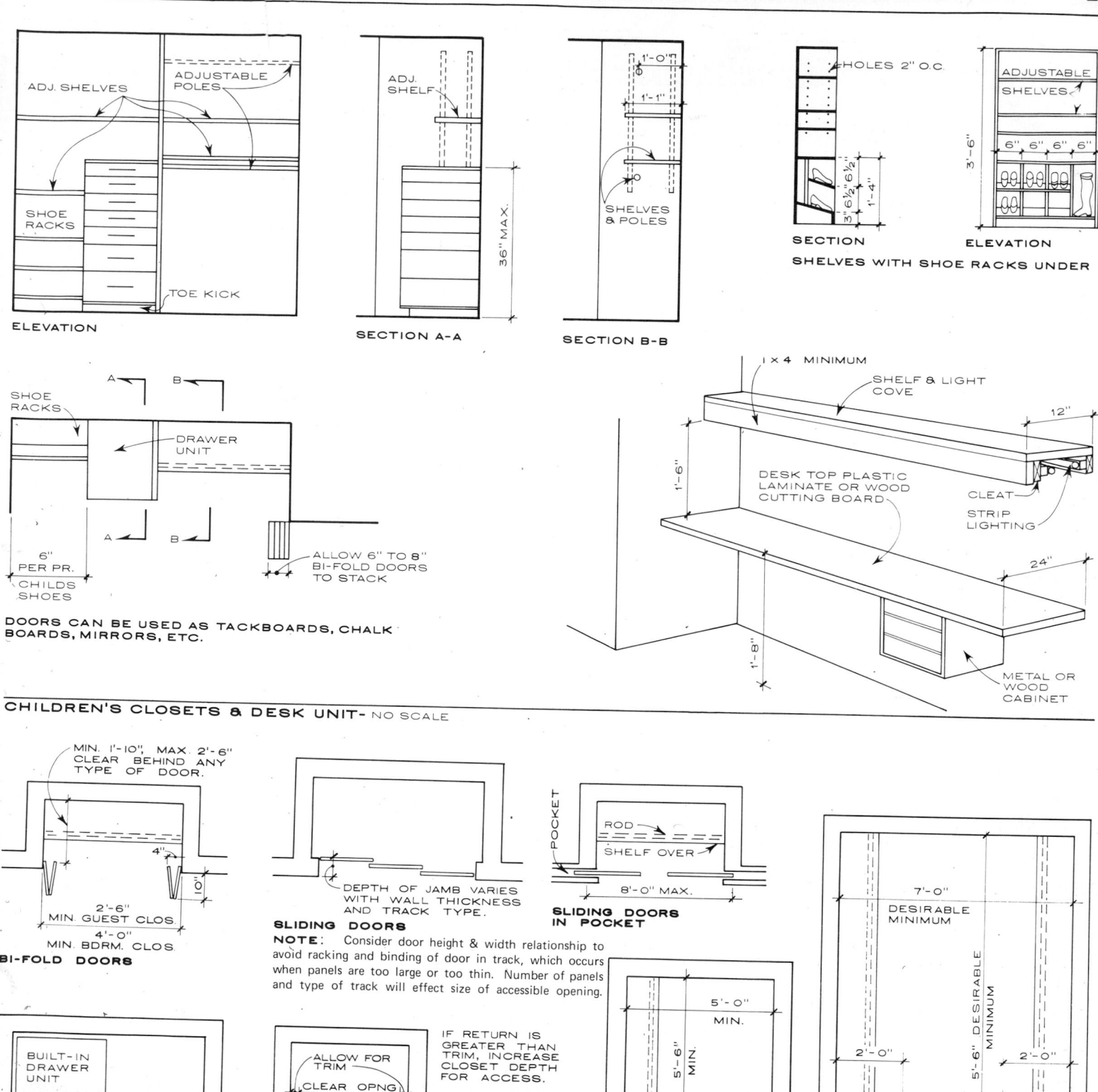

ELEVATION

SECTION A-A

SECTION B-B

SHELVES WITH SHOE RACKS UNDER

DOORS CAN BE USED AS TACKBOARDS, CHALK BOARDS, MIRRORS, ETC.

CHILDREN'S CLOSETS & DESK UNIT- NO SCALE

BI-FOLD DOORS

SLIDING DOORS

NOTE: Consider door height & width relationship to avoid racking and binding of door in track, which occurs when panels are too large or too thin. Number of panels and type of track will effect size of accessible opening.

SLIDING DOORS IN POCKET

HINGED DOORS

HINGED DOOR

WALK-IN

WALK-IN

HINGED DOORS NOTE: CLEAR OPENINGS ARE DIMINISHED BY DOOR THICKNESS WHEN OPEN.

ADULTS CLOSETS- NO SCALE

RECOMMENDATIONS AND ADVANTAGES IN DESIGNING CLOSETS FOR ADULTS AND CHILDREN

Recommended:

No closet bi-fold door should exceed 2'-0" panel. Largest door stock in pocket and sliding door is 4'-10".

All doors should allow easy access to top shelves.

All closets should have two shelves.

E. Powe, Jr.; Hugh N. Jacobsen, AIA; Washington, D. C.

Advantages:

Bi-fold doors allow 66 2/3% minimum of closet to be opened at once.

Pocket slides — 100%

Sliding doors — 50% max. (varies with no. of tracks and doors.)

Hinged doors — 90%

TYPICAL LAYOUTS

This and the following page show schematic drawings of various kitchen areas. The drawings are intended to show efficient functional relationships of the main equipment and do not attempt to present design solutions to kitchen.

Type, quantity and layout of equipment will vary with anticipated patronage and menu. For example, large kitchens may need more items, such as ranges and kettles, than are shown under "Cooking Sections." Small kitchens may combine in a cooking area functions shown separately below, such as cooking and baking.

WORK AISLES

If no thru-traffic, minimum width is 3'-0''.

With 2 parallel work tables, minimum aisle width is 3'—6'', preferably 4'—0'' to 4'—6''.

SCALE –ALL DRAWINGS : 1/8" = 1'-0"

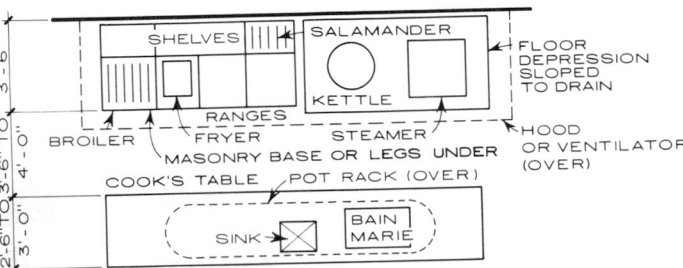

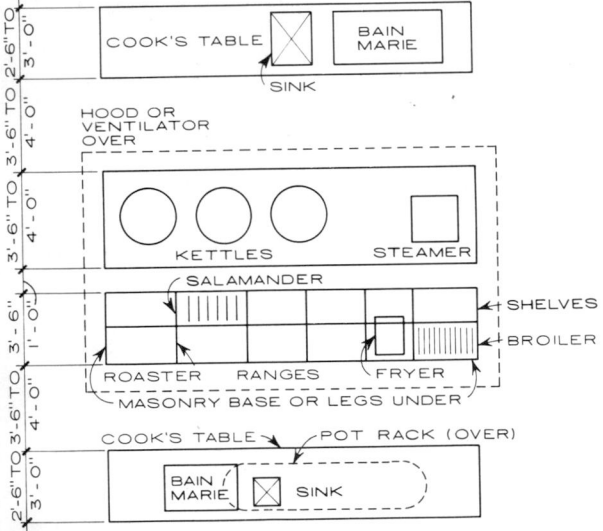

COOKING AREA AGAINST WALL

COOKING AREA: ISLAND TYPE

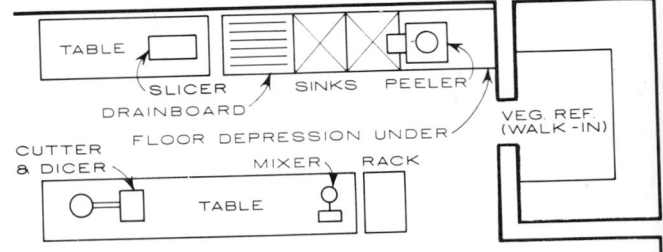

VEGETABLE & SALAD PREPARATION

May also have portable racks, cold cabinets, plate dispensers, etc.

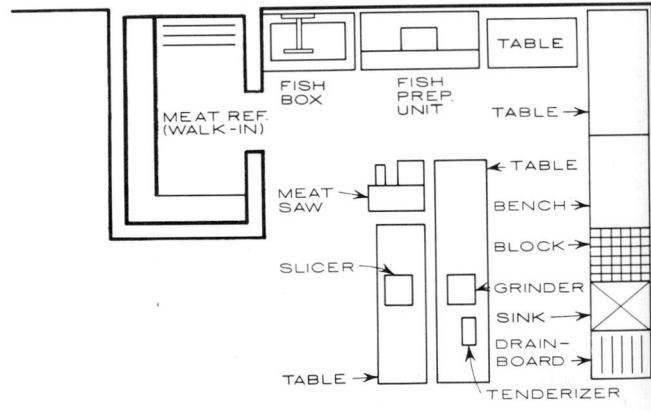

MEAT & FISH PREPARATION

This arrangement is typical in places where meat and fish are prepared on prem

Because of the availability of frozen and precut meat and fish this arrange may be modified.

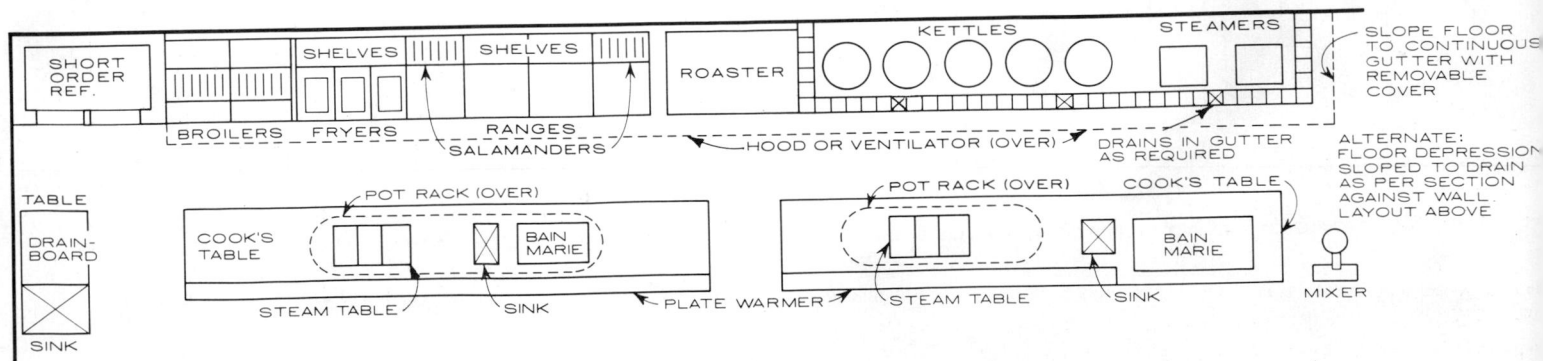

COOKING AREA FOR LARGE DINING ESTABLISHMENTS

Anthony J. Amendola, AIA; Forest Hills, New York

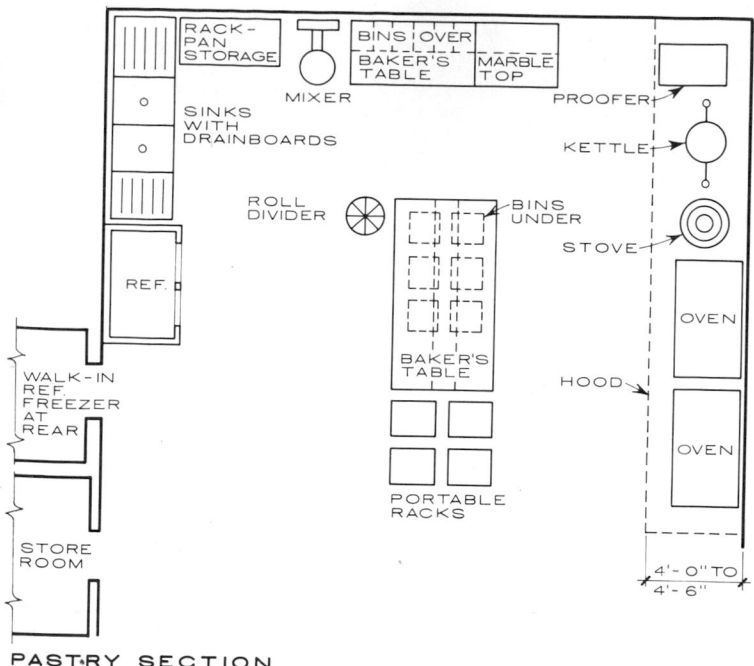

PASTRY SECTION

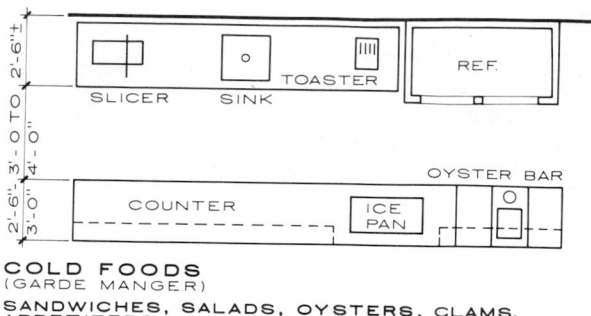

COLD FOODS
(GARDE MANGER)

SANDWICHES, SALADS, OYSTERS, CLAMS, APPETIZERS

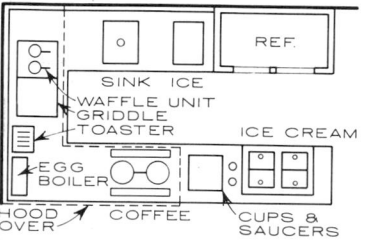

PANTRY
BREAKFASTS, DESSERTS, LIQUIDS

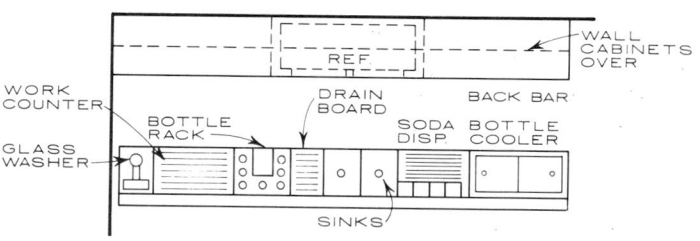

SERVICE BAR
LIQUOR, WINES, SOFT DRINKS

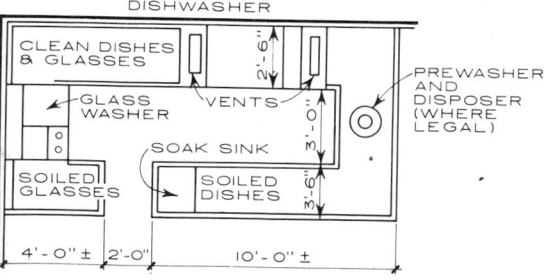

TYPICAL DISHWASHING LAYOUT

GENERAL NOTES:

Many designs can be adopted.

Arrangements influenced by size of establishment and shape of space available.

Arrangements for washing glasses, silver and trays are quite similar and may be designed within dishwashing area.

Many types of machines are available for all types of operations.

Flight type (straight line conveyor) and continuous oval shaped conveyor systems are available.

Anthony J. Amendola, AIA; Forest Hills, New York

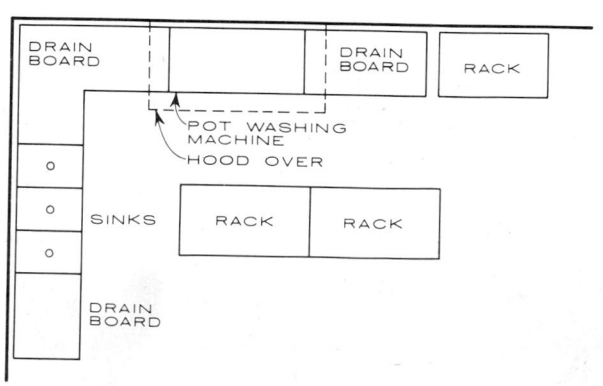

POT WASHING
NOTE: MACHINE MAY BE OMITTED

GENERAL NOTES:

Fast food service is that type provided by luncheonettes, soda fountains, and dinettes (serving simple meals), which provide counter service and by short-order sections of main kitchens.

Counter service operations may have a separate kitchen with food preparation, cooking, and dish-washing areas.

The basic installations for counter service are:
1. Back-bar
2. Front counter
3. Island
4. Combinations of above

KEY TO EQUIPMENT

1. Broiler
2. Open top range
3. Fry top range
4. Deep fryer - heavy duty unit
5. Sink
6. Refrigerator
7. Cooks table with steam table inset
8. Griddle - counter type
9. Deep fryer - counter type
10. Steam table
11. Sandwich unit - refrigerator under
12. Toaster
13. Service counter
14. Soda fountain - ice cream
15. Sinks with glass rinse, disposal chute and drainboard
16. Counter work top
17. Drink mixers
18. Coffee urns
19. Griddle with broiler under
20. Salad - dessert case
21. Water and ice
22. Coffee servers
23. Milk dispensers
24. Cold pan desserts
25. Display case - overhead
26. Ice cream
27. Service counter - hot foods, sandwiches and salads

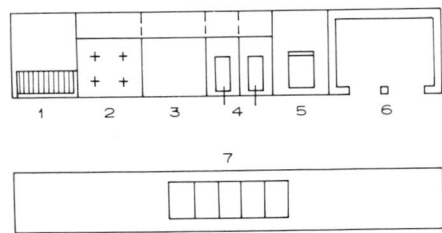

UNIT A

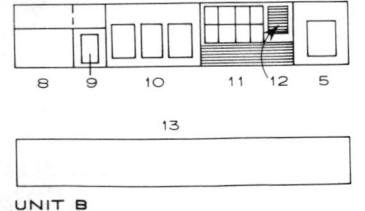

UNIT B

SHORT-ORDER KITCHEN

A short-order section in a main kitchen does the same type of cooking as behind-the-counter installations but usually has heavy equipment larger than that used in counters.

Unit B provides simpler service than unit A.

SCALE ALL DRAWINGS: 1/8"= 1'-0"

Anthony J. Amendola, AIA; Forest Hills, New York

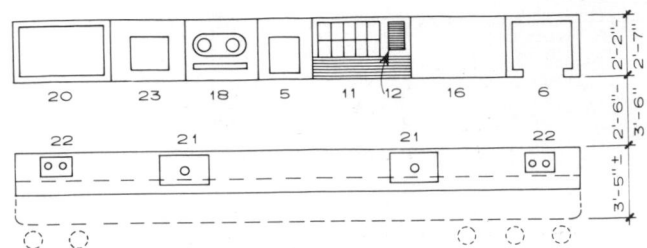

NOTE:
Dimensions of counter and work aisles are typical for all details shown.

BACK-BAR INSTALLATION (SMALL)

Usually for a small operation with minimum menu and rapid customer turn-over.
Has short counter; therefore usually uses straight counter rather than bay.

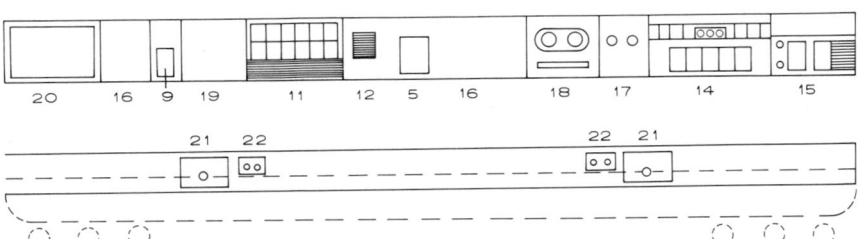

BACK-BAR INSTALLATION (LARGE)

May have entire cooking unit in back-bar installation.
Lengthy counter requires duplication of coffee-making facilities.
Bay counter seating may be used also.

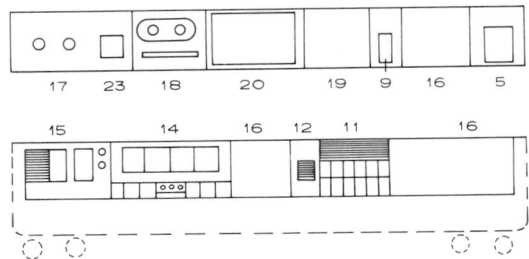

COMBINED FRONT COUNTER AND BACK-BAR INSTALLATION

Usually for operations with limited area and staff, and a larger menu.
May serve booths from waitress stand at end of counter.

BOOTHS

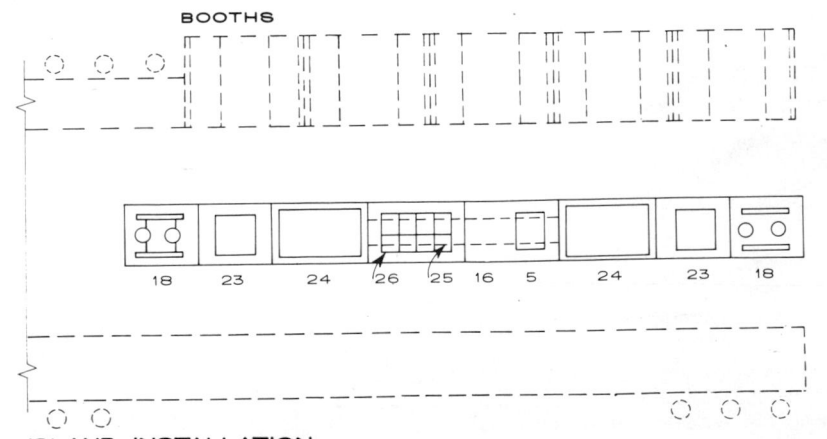

ISLAND INSTALLATION

May have straight or bay counter seating;
also allows for direct booth service by counter waiters.

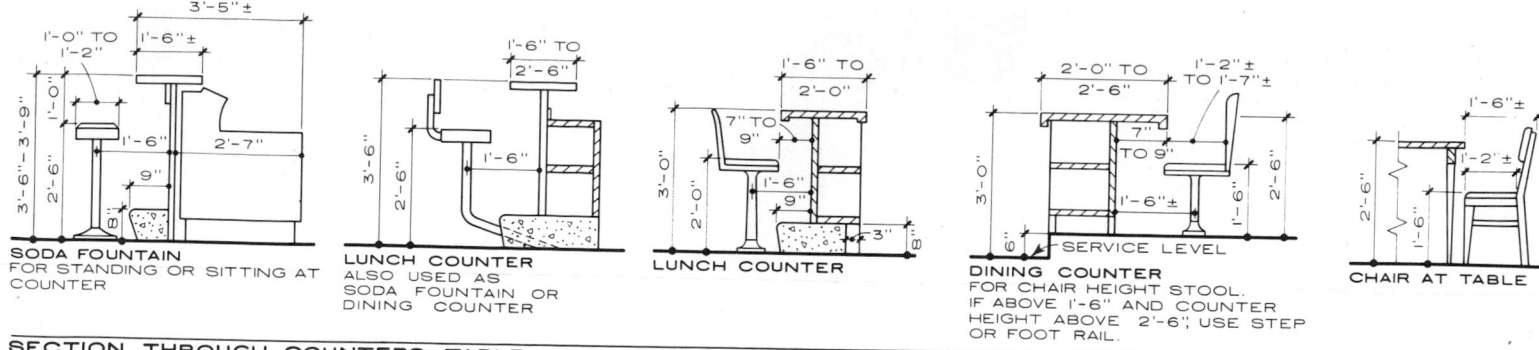

SODA FOUNTAIN
FOR STANDING OR SITTING AT
COUNTER

LUNCH COUNTER
ALSO USED AS
SODA FOUNTAIN OR
DINING COUNTER

LUNCH COUNTER

DINING COUNTER
FOR CHAIR HEIGHT STOOL.
IF ABOVE 1'-6" AND COUNTER
HEIGHT ABOVE 2'-6", USE STEP
OR FOOT RAIL.

CHAIR AT TABLE

SECTION THROUGH COUNTERS, TABLE, AND SEAT
SCALE : 1/4"= 1'-0"

KEY TO DIMENSIONS

A. Work aisles;

Minimum width with one waitress is 2' – 3''. With two
or more waitresses working in one area, increase width
to 2' – 6'' to 3' – 0''.

B. All seats are 2' – 0'' to 2' – 2'' o.c.; depends on style
and size of seat.

C. Minimum width is 2' – 3''. Recom. width is 3' – 0''.

D. Back-bar width depends on the type of equipment used.
With only small counter appliances, 1' – 6'' to 1' – 8''
may be adequate.
With reach-in refrigerator or heavy equipment; 2' – 0''
to 2' – 9'' will be required.

E. Distance from counter to counter, with multiple bays,
is 5' – 0'' to 5' – 6''.

F. Front counter width varies with the type of service provided, 1' – 6'' to 2' – 6''.

G. 1' – 3'' to 1' – 6''.

H. 3' – 0'' – 4' – 0''.

I. 1' – 3'' ±

NOTE:

Dimensions of work aisles, seating spacing, etc., do not
vary with different types of counter arrangements.

See furniture pages for chair & table sizes.

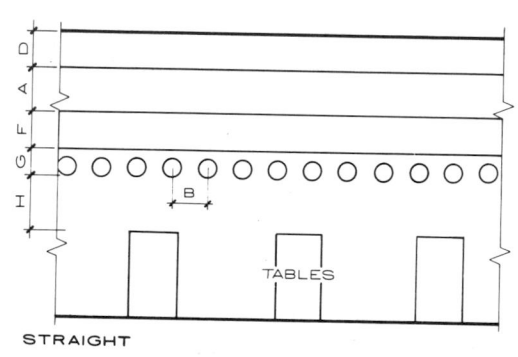

STRAIGHT

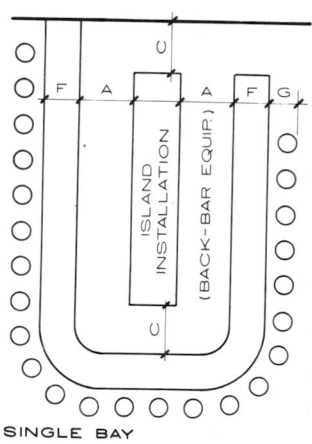

SINGLE BAY

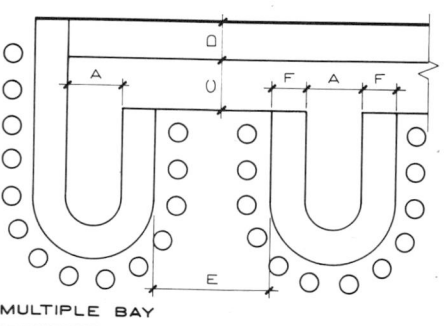

MULTIPLE BAY

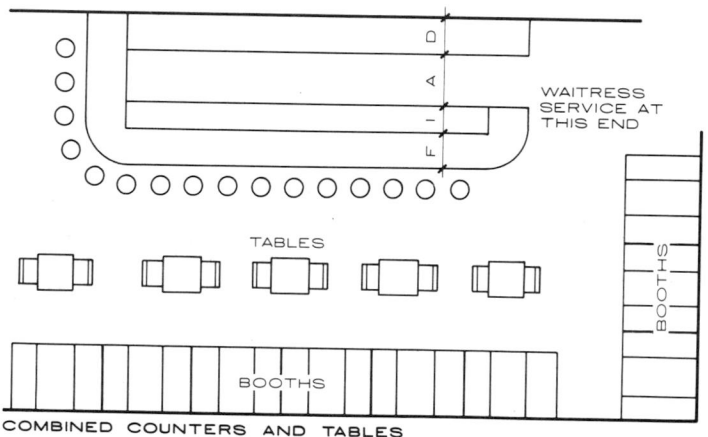

WAITRESS
SERVICE AT
THIS END

TABLES

BOOTHS

BOOTHS

COMBINED COUNTERS AND TABLES

TYPICAL COUNTER ARRANGEMENTS
SCALE : 3/32"= 1'-0"

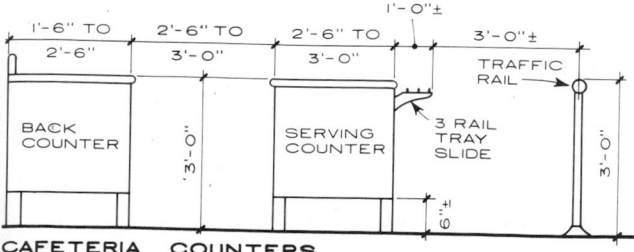

BACK
COUNTER

SERVING
COUNTER

3 RAIL
TRAY
SLIDE

TRAFFIC
RAIL

CAFETERIA COUNTERS
SCALE : 1/4"= 1'-0"

NOTE: COUNTERS MAY ALSO BE SET ON MASONRY BASES

Anthony J. Amendola, AIA; Forest Hills, New York

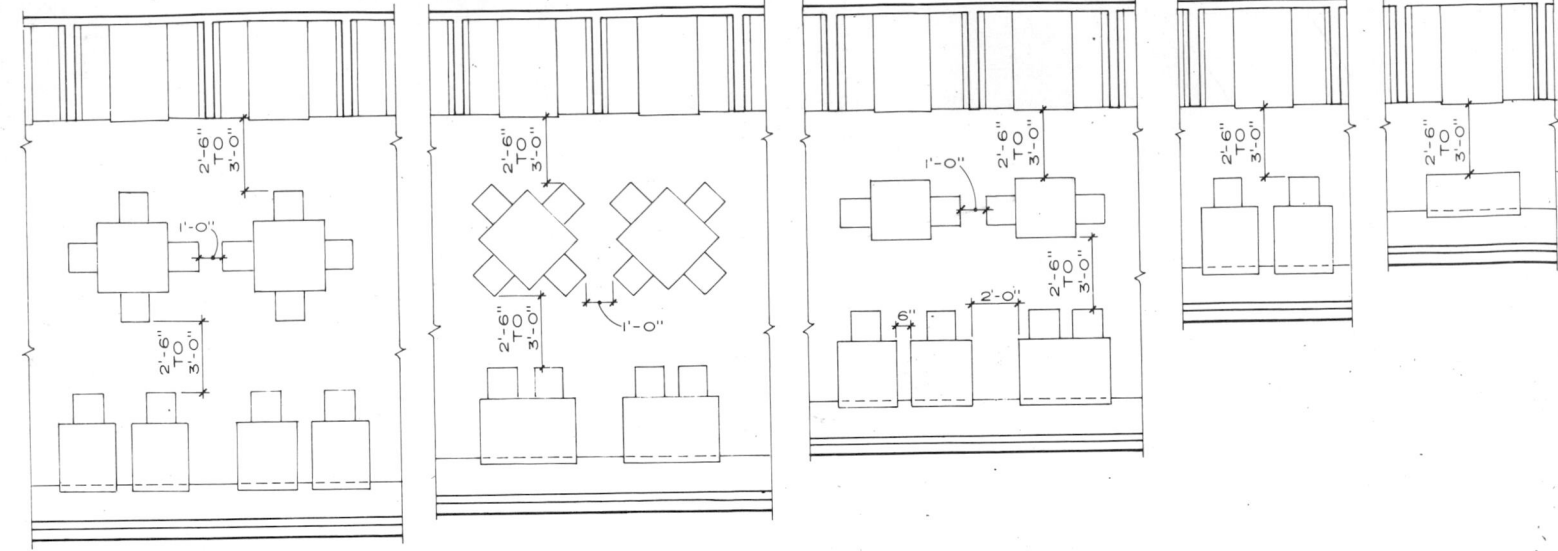

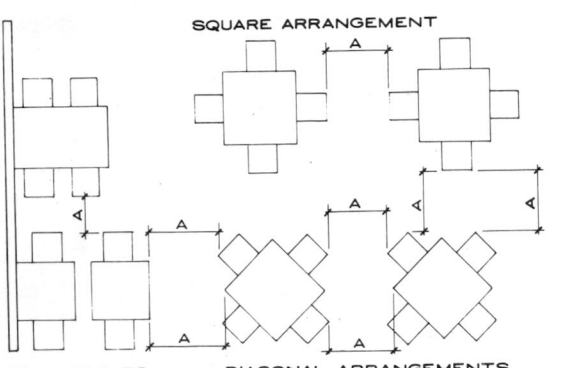

SQUARE ARRANGEMENT

WALL TABLES   DIAGONAL ARRANGEMENTS

TYPICAL SEATING ARRANGEMENTS

CLEARANCES

A = 6" MINIMUM (NO PASSAGE)

A = 1'-6" LIMITED PASSAGE

A = 2'-6" TO 3'-0" SERVICE AISLE

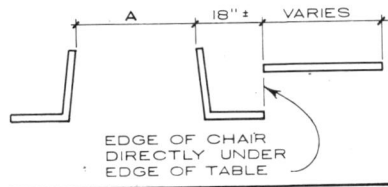

ELEVATION SHOWING RELATION OF CHAIR TO TABLE WHEN A PERSON IS SEATED

EDGE OF CHAIR DIRECTLY UNDER EDGE OF TABLE

TYPE OF ROOM	MAX.	MIN.
BANQUET	10-11	7
TEA ROOM	12-14	10
DINING ROOM / RESTAURANT	14-15	10-12
CAFETERIA	15	12
LUNCHRMS: COUNTER AND CHAIR - TABLE TYPES INCL. COUNTERS, CHAIRS TABLES	20	16

SEATING ALLOWANCES

These figures are rule-of-thumb for square feet per-person (non-standardized), and are to be used only for making an approximation of seating capacities.

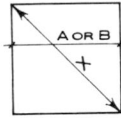

SQUARE

PERSONS	A or B	X
2	1'-8" to 2'-6"	2'-5" to 3'-6"
4	2'-6" to 3'-0"	3'-6" to 4'-3"

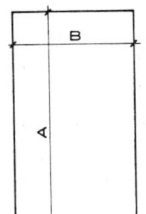

RECTANGLE

PERSONS	A	B
2 (ON ONE SIDE)	3'-6" to 4'-0"	2'-0"
2	2'-0" to 2'-6"	2'-0" to 2'-6"
4	3'-6" to 4'-0"	2'-0"
6	5'-0" to 8'-0"	2'-0" to 3'-0"

Tables wider than 2'-6" will seat one at each end.

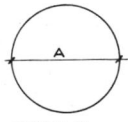

CIRCLE

PERSONS	A
2	2'-0"
3	2'-6"
4	3'-0"

Round tables are usually recommended only for seating 5 persons or more.

"A" dim. depends on the perimeter, (1'-10" — 1'-2" per person), necessary to seat required number. For cocktails, 1'-6" is sufficient.

TABLES

Minimum sizes are satisfactory for drink service; larger sizes for food. Tables with wide spread bases are more practical than four legged tables.

Anthony J. Amendola, AIA; Forest Hills, New York

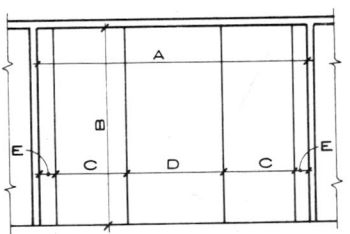

PLAN

A With sloping seat back: 5'-4" to 6'-2". Without sloping seat back: 5'-4" to 6'-2".

B One person per side: 2'-0" to 2'-6". Two persons per side: 3'-6" to 4'-6". Recommended max. for serving and cleaning 4'-0".

C 1'-6" ±

D 2'-0" to 2'-6".

E 2" to 6"

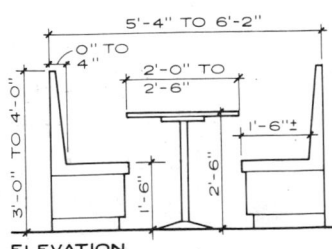

ELEVATION

BOOTHS

Local regulations determine actual booth sizes. Tables are often two inches shorter than seats, and may have rounded ends. Circular booths have overall diameter of 6'-4" ±.

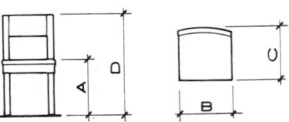

TYPES	A	B	C	D
STRAIGHT	1'-5" to 1'-6½"	1'-2" to 1'-4"	1'-2" to 1'-4"	2'-8" to 3'-0"
ARM	1'-5" to 1'-6"	1'-7" to 2'-0"	1'-3" to 2'-0"	2'-0" to 3'-6"
TAVERN	1'-5"	1'-5" to 1'-8"	1'-3" to 1'-6"	2'-4" to 2'-6"
DINING ROOM	1'-6"	1'-6" to 1'-9"	1'-8" to 1'-10"	2'-10" to 3'-3"

CHAIR AND CHAIR DIMENSIONS

Chair rail heights are determined by dimension D.

NOTE:
DIMENSIONS SHOWN ARE NOT NECESSARILY DRAWN TO SCALE

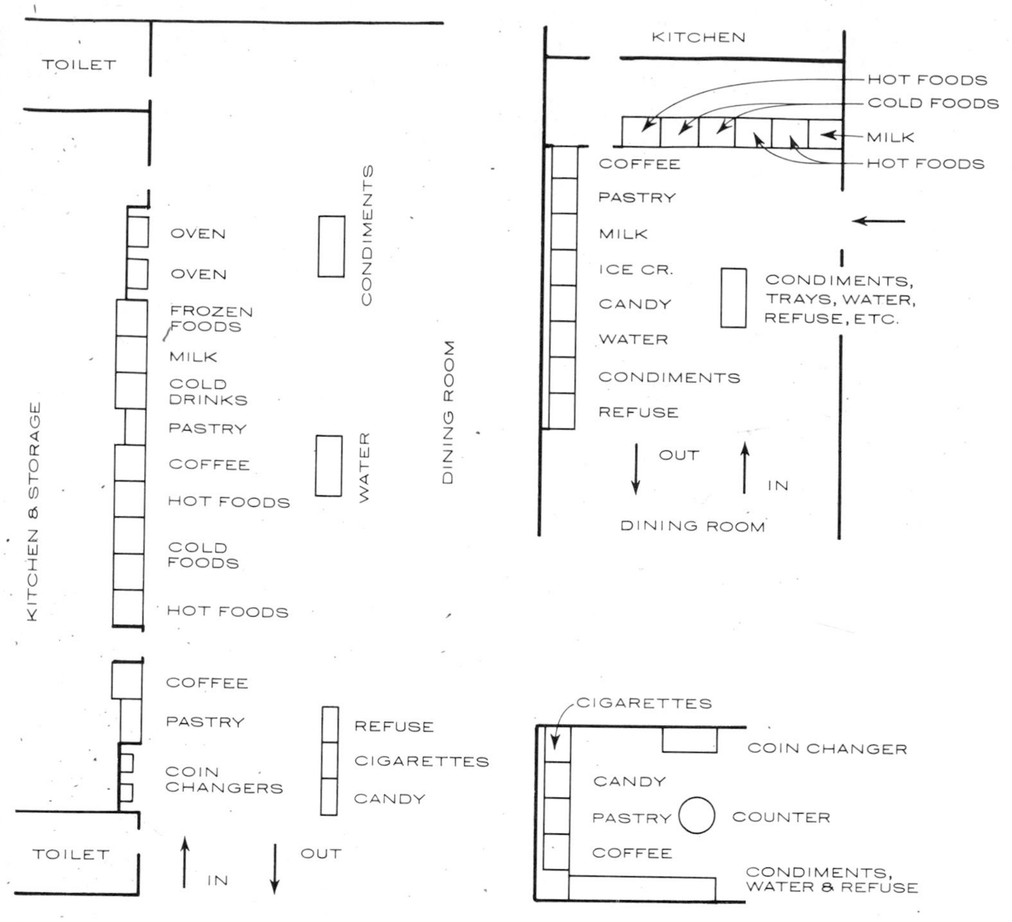

TYPICAL VENDING CAFETERIA PLANS
SCALE: 1/16" = 1'-0"

INSTITUTIONAL OR COMMERCIAL CAFETERIAS WITH KITCHEN

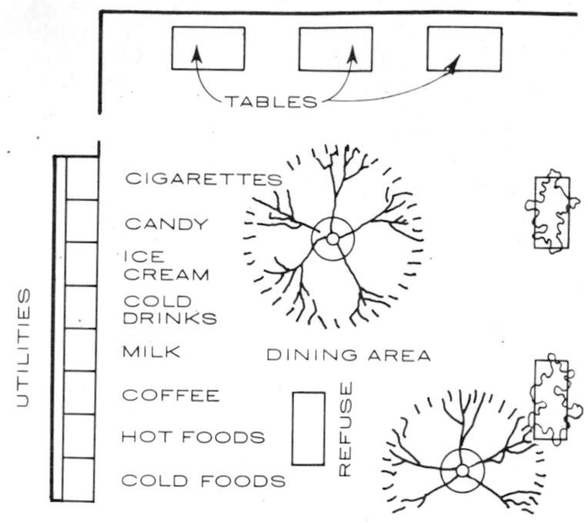

TOILET

KITCHEN & STORAGE

OVEN
OVEN
FROZEN FOODS
MILK
COLD DRINKS
PASTRY
COFFEE
HOT FOODS
COLD FOODS
HOT FOODS

CONDIMENTS
WATER
DINING ROOM

COFFEE
PASTRY
COIN CHANGERS
TOILET — IN — OUT

REFUSE
CIGARETTES
CANDY

KITCHEN

HOT FOODS
COLD FOODS
MILK
HOT FOODS

COFFEE
PASTRY
MILK
ICE CR.
CANDY
WATER
CONDIMENTS
REFUSE
OUT — DINING ROOM — IN

CONDIMENTS, TRAYS, WATER, REFUSE, ETC.

CIGARETTES
CANDY
PASTRY
COFFEE

COIN CHANGER
COUNTER
CONDIMENTS, WATER & REFUSE

SHOPPING PLAZA CAFETERIA

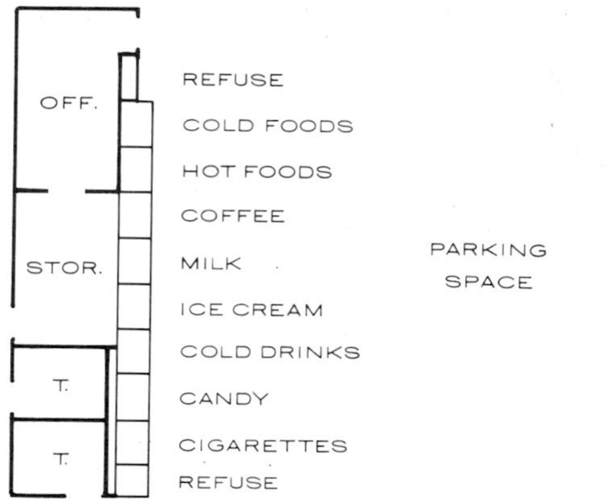

TABLES
UTILITIES

CIGARETTES
CANDY
ICE CREAM
COLD DRINKS
MILK
COFFEE
HOT FOODS
COLD FOODS

DINING AREA
REFUSE

ROADSIDE CAFETERIA

OFF.
STOR.
T.
T.

REFUSE
COLD FOODS
HOT FOODS
COFFEE
MILK
ICE CREAM
COLD DRINKS
CANDY
CIGARETTES
REFUSE

PARKING SPACE

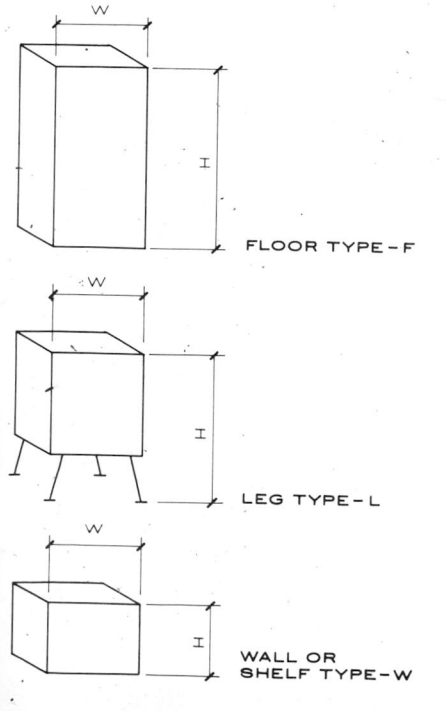

FLOOR TYPE – F

LEG TYPE – L

WALL OR SHELF TYPE – W

NOTE: No hot water required.
Waste disposal—into bucket, where required.
Ventilation space at rear—up to 8".
Service access—generally from front; also at top for some cigarette units.

C. K. Hirzel; New York, New York;
Howard Vermilya, AIA; Lawrenceville, New Jersey

VENDING MACHINE DATA

MERCHANDISE		TYPE		TYPICAL			APPROX. RANGE				ELECT.	WATER
				W	D	H		W	D	H	LBS.*		
FOODS	HOT BEVERAGES	F	small	24	21	63	min.	24	21	63	275	R	V
			large	35 1/2	29 1/2	79	max.	35 1/2	30 1/4	79 1/2	680		
		L	small	25 1/2	14 3/4	66	min.	25 1/2	14 3/4	66	213		
		W	large	30	28	68	max.	30	28	68	385		
			typical	14	14	23					68		
	COLD BEVERAGES	F	small	24	28 1/2	63	min.	24	21 1/2	63	445	R	V
			large	35 1/2	29 1/2	79	max.	35 1/2	34 1/4	80	875		
	COLD FOODS	F	small	35 1/2	21 1/2	79	min.	35 1/2	21 1/2	79	640	R	V
			large	35 1/2	31 1/2	79	max.	35 1/2	31 1/2	79	985		
	HOT FOODS	F	small	39	16 1/4	63	min.	35 1/2	16 1/4	63	350	R	V
			large	35 1/2	31 1/2	79	max.	39	31 1/2	79	800		
	COLD & HOT FOODS	F	small	40	24	72	min.	35 1/2	24	72	657	R	V
			large	35 1/2	31 1/2	79	max.	40	31 1/2	79	880		
	CONFECTIONS & PASTRY	F	small	31 3/4	13 1/4	63	min.	31 3/4	13 1/4	63	250	V	O
		L	large	41	22	79	max.	41	22	79	580		
			typical	35 3/4	12	58					298		
OTHER	CIGARETTES	F	small	39	13 1/4	63	min.	31 3/4	13 1/4	63	232	R	O
			large	38	17	79	max.	39	17	79	438		
		L	small	30	17	66	min.	30	12	48 1/2	283		
			large	34	20	49 3/4	max.	37 1/4	22 3/4	66	350		
	MISC.	L	small	31	31	63	min.	31	31	72	380	R	O
			large	40	24	79	max.	40	31	79	657		
	COIN CHANGER	W	small	14 1/2	9 3/4	24	min.	14 1/2	9 1/2	24	65	R	O
			large	24 3/4	9 1/2	25 1/4	max.	24 3/4	9 3/4	25 1/4	137		

* Net Weight   R—Required   V—Optional, or Varies   O—Not required.   Cold water only.

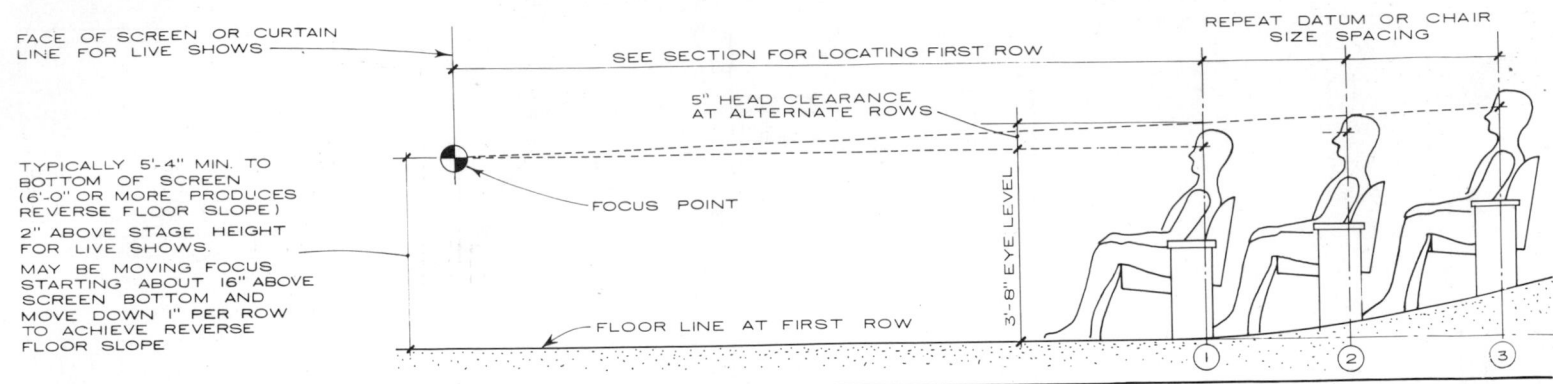

FACE OF SCREEN OR CURTAIN LINE FOR LIVE SHOWS

SEE SECTION FOR LOCATING FIRST ROW

REPEAT DATUM OR CHAIR SIZE SPACING

5" HEAD CLEARANCE AT ALTERNATE ROWS

TYPICALLY 5'-4" MIN. TO BOTTOM OF SCREEN (6'-0" OR MORE PRODUCES REVERSE FLOOR SLOPE)
2" ABOVE STAGE HEIGHT FOR LIVE SHOWS.
MAY BE MOVING FOCUS STARTING ABOUT 16" ABOVE SCREEN BOTTOM AND MOVE DOWN 1" PER ROW TO ACHIEVE REVERSE FLOOR SLOPE

FOCUS POINT

FLOOR LINE AT FIRST ROW

3'-8" EYE LEVEL

DETERMINING THE MAIN FLOOR SLOPE DIAGRAM

SCALE USUALLY ¼"= 1'-0" HORIZ., ¼", ¾", 1½" = 1'-0" VERTICAL

Balcony sight lines similar but start from rear row forward, maintaining uniform terrace heights to front of balcony or cross aisle.

Stagger seats in plan to allow unobstructed view between alternate rows of spectators so that min. ²/₃ width of screen or acting area is in view.

Floor curve varies only with first row location & focus height. Not affected by row spacing. Several diagrams should be made using different initial assumptions to determine the best combination of overall relationships.

Raise first row of seating behind cross aisle to clear head of people using aisle.

See local code for maximum aisle slopes permitted:
B.O.C.A. & B.B.C. allow 1:7 (1¾"/ft.).
U.B.C. allows 1:8
N.B.C., N.F.P.A., S.S.B.C. allow 1:10
Slopes greater than above must be in equal aisle risers full aisle width, usually allowed only in galleries & balconies.

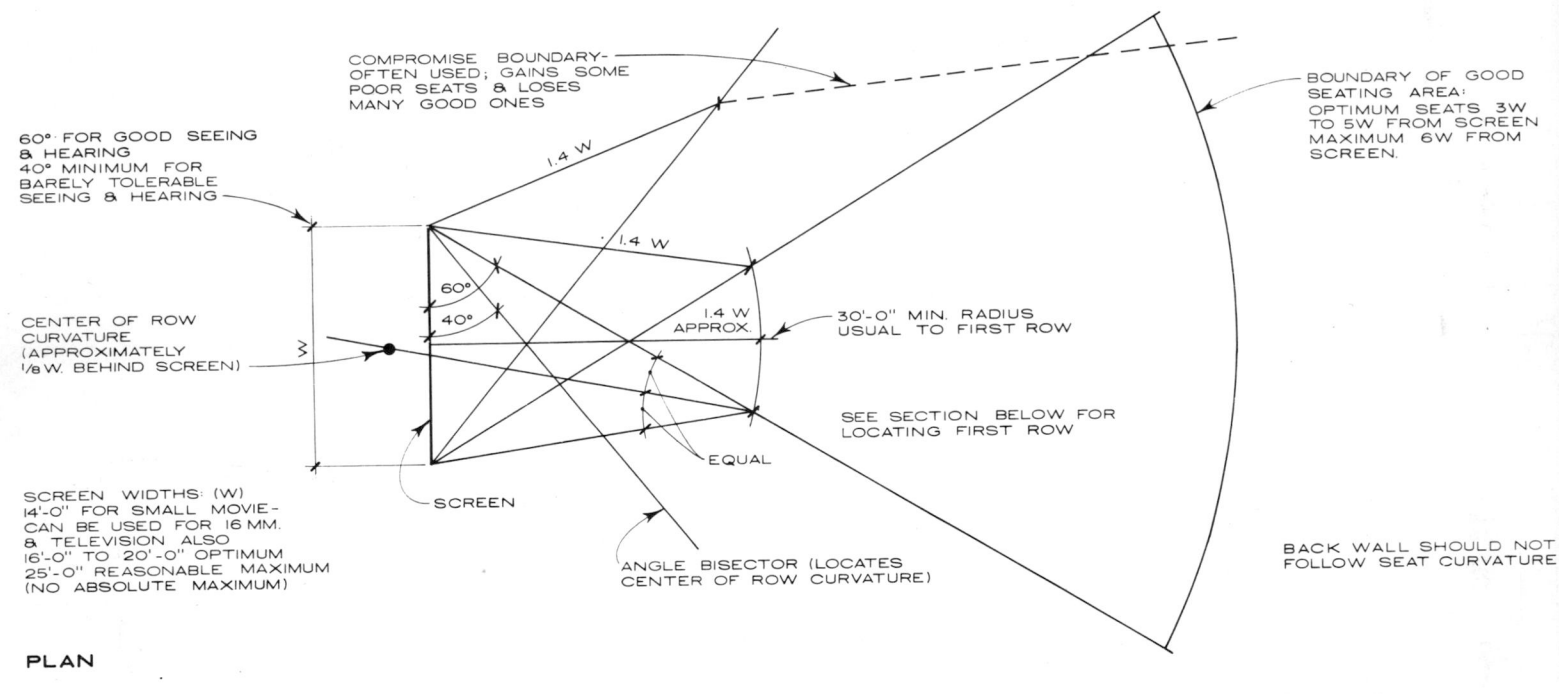

COMPROMISE BOUNDARY- OFTEN USED; GAINS SOME POOR SEATS & LOSES MANY GOOD ONES

BOUNDARY OF GOOD SEATING AREA: OPTIMUM SEATS 3W TO 5W FROM SCREEN MAXIMUM 6W FROM SCREEN.

60° FOR GOOD SEEING & HEARING
40° MINIMUM FOR BARELY TOLERABLE SEEING & HEARING

1.4 W

1.4 W

1.4 W APPROX.

30'-0" MIN. RADIUS USUAL TO FIRST ROW

CENTER OF ROW CURVATURE (APPROXIMATELY ⅛ W. BEHIND SCREEN)

60°
40°

SEE SECTION BELOW FOR LOCATING FIRST ROW

EQUAL

SCREEN

SCREEN WIDTHS: (W)
14'-0" FOR SMALL MOVIE- CAN BE USED FOR 16 MM. & TELEVISION ALSO
16'-0" TO 20'-0" OPTIMUM
25'-0" REASONABLE MAXIMUM (NO ABSOLUTE MAXIMUM)

ANGLE BISECTOR (LOCATES CENTER OF ROW CURVATURE)

BACK WALL SHOULD NOT FOLLOW SEAT CURVATURE

PLAN

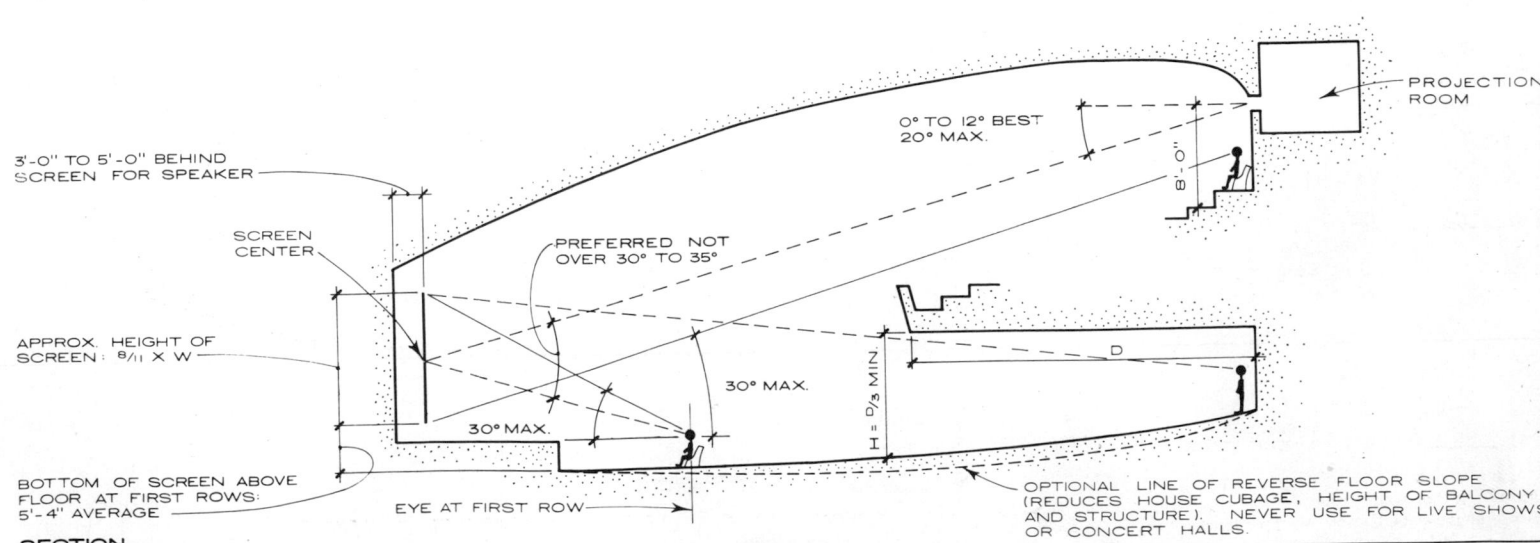

PROJECTION ROOM

0° TO 12° BEST 20° MAX.

8'-0"

3'-0" TO 5'-0" BEHIND SCREEN FOR SPEAKER

SCREEN CENTER

PREFERRED NOT OVER 30° TO 35°

APPROX. HEIGHT OF SCREEN: ⁸/₁₁ X W

D

30° MAX.

H = D/3 MIN.

30° MAX.

BOTTOM OF SCREEN ABOVE FLOOR AT FIRST ROWS: 5'-4" AVERAGE

EYE AT FIRST ROW

OPTIONAL LINE OF REVERSE FLOOR SLOPE (REDUCES HOUSE CUBAGE, HEIGHT OF BALCONY AND STRUCTURE). NEVER USE FOR LIVE SHOWS OR CONCERT HALLS.

SECTION

SCREEN SHOWS

TOTAL NET VOLUME = 125-150 CU. FT. PER SEAT

Warren Anderson; The Perkins and Will Partnership; Chicago, Illinois

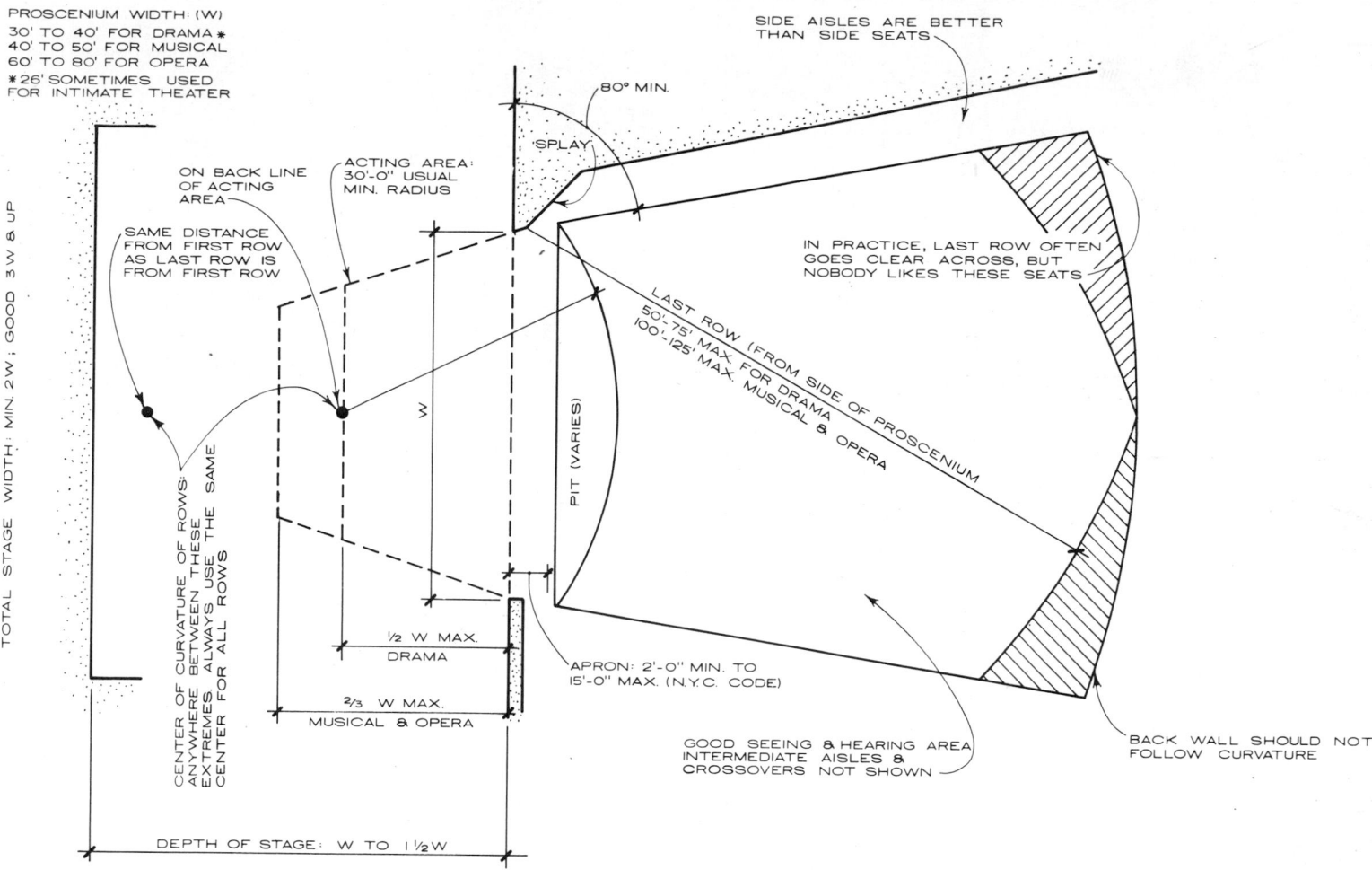

PROSCENIUM WIDTH: (W)
30' TO 40' FOR DRAMA*
40' TO 50' FOR MUSICAL
60' TO 80' FOR OPERA
*26' SOMETIMES USED
FOR INTIMATE THEATER

SIDE AISLES ARE BETTER
THAN SIDE SEATS

80° MIN.

SPLAY

ON BACK LINE
OF ACTING
AREA

ACTING AREA:
30'-0" USUAL
MIN. RADIUS

SAME DISTANCE
FROM FIRST ROW
AS LAST ROW IS
FROM FIRST ROW

IN PRACTICE, LAST ROW OFTEN
GOES CLEAR ACROSS, BUT
NOBODY LIKES THESE SEATS

TOTAL STAGE WIDTH: MIN. 2W; GOOD 3W & UP

LAST ROW (FROM SIDE OF PROSCENIUM
50-75' MAX FOR DRAMA
100-125' MAX. MUSICAL & OPERA

W

PIT (VARIES)

CENTER OF CURVATURE OF ROWS:
ANYWHERE BETWEEN THESE
EXTREMES. ALWAYS USE THE SAME
CENTER FOR ALL ROWS

½ W MAX.
DRAMA

⅔ W MAX.
MUSICAL & OPERA

APRON: 2'-0" MIN. TO
15'-0" MAX. (N.Y.C. CODE)

GOOD SEEING & HEARING AREA
INTERMEDIATE AISLES &
CROSSOVERS NOT SHOWN

BACK WALL SHOULD NOT
FOLLOW CURVATURE

DEPTH OF STAGE: W TO 1½W

PLAN

SOUNDBOARD FOR CONCERT HALL. PLATFORM
IN ROOM INSTEAD OF STAGE BEHIND PROSCENIUM.
SIGHT LINES SAME AS OTHER LIVE SHOWS.

LIGHT SLOT

45°

WORKING HEIGHT OF CURTAIN:
(PROSCENIUM USUALLY HIGHER)
15' TO 20' FOR DRAMA
20' TO 30' FOR MUSICAL & OPERA

I

D

H = D/2 MIN.

30°
MAX.

30° MAX.

10'-0" TO
15'-0"

3'-4" TYPICAL
3'-6" MAX.

TRAPS

ORCHESTRA PIT: 10 SQ. FT. PER MUSICIAN PLUS
100 TO 200 SQ. FT. WHERE PIT USED,
FIRST ROW WILL BE SUFFICIENT DISTANCE
FROM STAGE

SECTION

LIVE SHOWS (DRAMA, MUSICAL, OPERA, BALLET)
TOTAL NET VOLUME (EXCLUDING STAGE) = 150 - 200 CU. FT. PER SEAT

Warren Anderson; The Perkins and Will Partnership; Chicago, Illinois

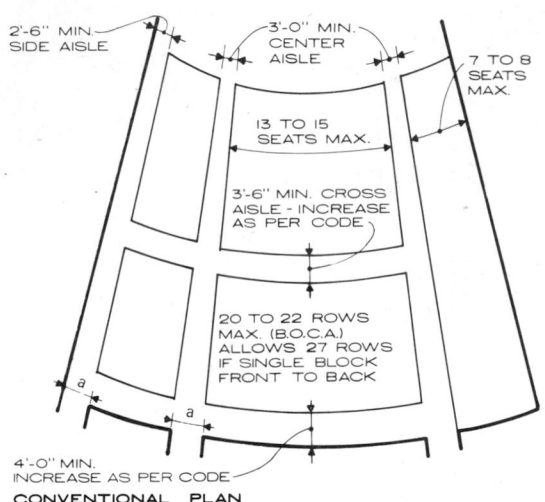

2'-6" MIN. SIDE AISLE

3'-0" MIN. CENTER AISLE

7 TO 8 SEATS MAX.

13 TO 15 SEATS MAX.

3'-6" MIN. CROSS AISLE - INCREASE AS PER CODE

20 TO 22 ROWS MAX. (B.O.C.A.) ALLOWS 27 ROWS IF SINGLE BLOCK FRONT TO BACK

a

a

4'-0" MIN. INCREASE AS PER CODE

CONVENTIONAL PLAN

DESIGN CONSIDERATIONS:

Area: allow min. 6 to generous 8 sq. ft. per seat floor area in conventional seating layout — allow min. 8 to generous 10 sq. ft. per seat floor area in continental seating layout. Area includes all aisles, side wall areas for duct work and acoustical baffles and forestage to curtain line — for preliminary assumptions only.

Aisles: consult local code: begin with usual min. widths shown and increase at rate of $1/4''$ per ft. (B.B.C. and B.O.C.A.), $1 1/2''$ per 5'–0" (N.F.P.A., U.B.C. and S.S.B.C.) or 22" per 100 persons (N.B.C.) to determine "a".

Exits: consult local code: generally 100 ft. max. from any point on floor to nearest exit: often increased to 133 or 150 ft. if sprinklers provided, or principal entry at grade, or aisle exit route assumed. Number of exits based on occupancy requirements per local code.
Codes specify seating as back to back.

Max. floor slope - see page on Theater Sightlines.

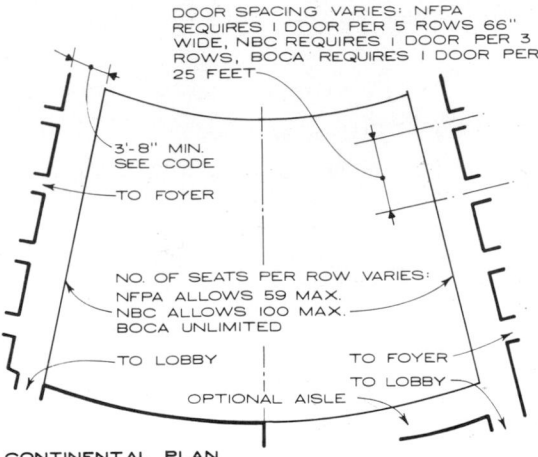

DOOR SPACING VARIES: NFPA REQUIRES 1 DOOR PER 5 ROWS 66" WIDE, NBC REQUIRES 1 DOOR PER 3 ROWS, BOCA REQUIRES 1 DOOR PER 25 FEET

3'-8" MIN. SEE CODE

TO FOYER

NO. OF SEATS PER ROW VARIES: NFPA ALLOWS 59 MAX. NBC ALLOWS 100 MAX. BOCA UNLIMITED

TO LOBBY

TO FOYER

TO LOBBY

OPTIONAL AISLE

CONTINENTAL PLAN

Note: Many codes do not permit continental seating.

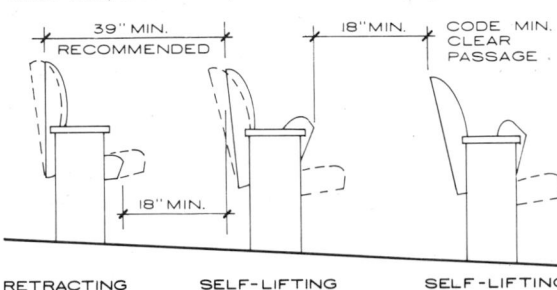

39" MIN. RECOMMENDED

18" MIN.

CODE MIN. CLEAR PASSAGE

18" MIN.

RETRACTING SEAT   **SELF-LIFTING & RETRACTING**   **SELF-LIFTING**

CONTINENTAL SEAT SPACING

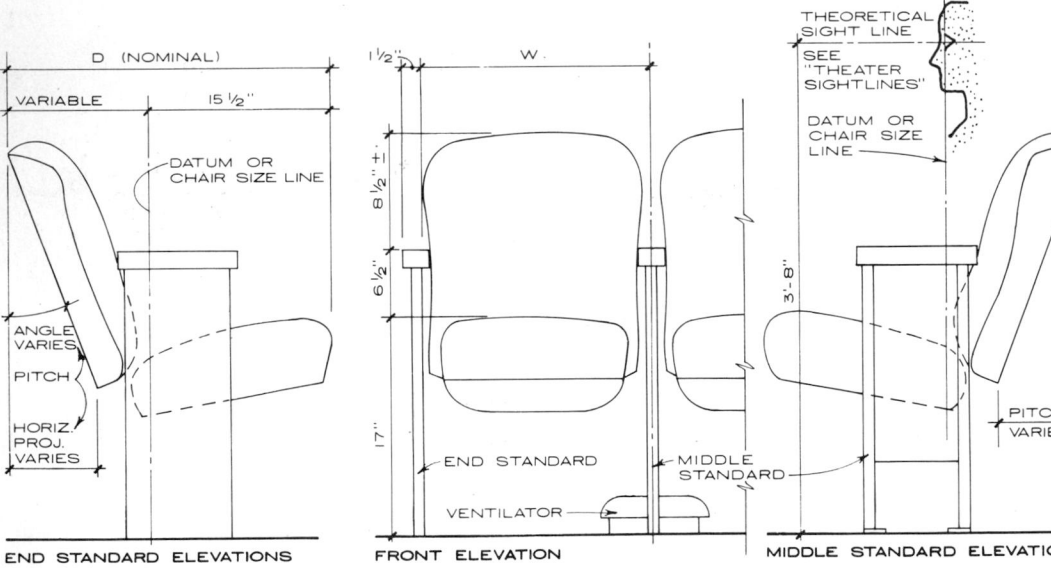

45" MIN EASY PASSAGE BY SEATED VIEWER

30" TO 33" CODE MIN 34" MIN. RECOM.

DATUM LINES DRAWN ON PLAN

MODESTY SCREEN

CONVENTIONAL SEATING

D (NOMINAL)

VARIABLE   **15 1/2"**

DATUM OR CHAIR SIZE LINE

ANGLE VARIES

PITCH

HORIZ. PROJ. VARIES

END STANDARD ELEVATIONS

1 1/2"   **W**

8 1/2" ±

6 1/2"

17"

END STANDARD

MIDDLE STANDARD

VENTILATOR

FRONT ELEVATION

THEORETICAL SIGHT LINE

SEE "THEATER SIGHTLINES"

DATUM OR CHAIR SIZE LINE

3'-8"

PITCH VARIES

MIDDLE STANDARD ELEVATION

1" RECOMMENDED FROM WALL OR RAIL FOR STANDEE

BACK WALLS

1" MIN. CLEARANCE

15" MAX. (2 AISLE RISERS)

RISERS

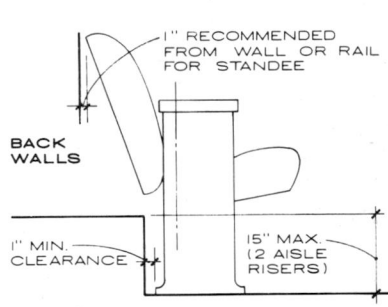

1" RECOMMENDED

12" MAX. FOR 45° ANGLE (SEAT TO WALL) AND 8 1/4" PITCH BACK

SIDE WALLS

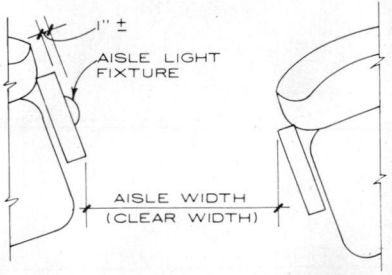

1" ±

AISLE LIGHT FIXTURE

AISLE WIDTH (CLEAR WIDTH)

AISLES

CLEARANCES

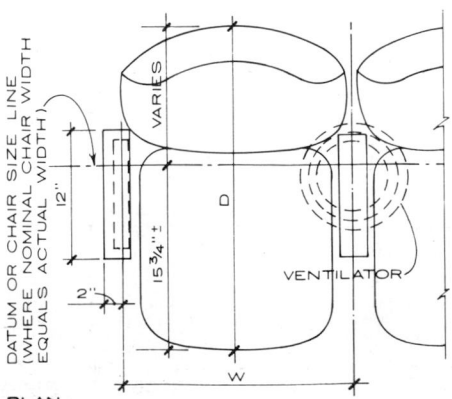

12"

15 3/4" ±

2"

DATUM OR CHAIR SIZE LINE (WHERE NOMINAL CHAIR WIDTH EQUALS ACTUAL WIDTH)

VARIES

D

W

VENTILATOR

PLAN

AVAILABLE SIZES

W	D
18"	26 7/8"
19"	27 1/4"
20"	27 5/8"
21"	28"
22"	28 3/8"
23"	28 3/4"
24"	29 1/8"

18" width not recommended — 19" width recommended only for ends of rows — 20" to 22" usual for all locations.

Optional finishes: fully upholstered, and molded plywood.

Optional equipment: folding tablet arms, folding writing shelf, riser mounted standards, pedestal mounting using continuous beam support or cantilevered standards — verify row spacings with mfr. Folding and portable seating usually not allowed in theater work.

Pitches: measured either by angle or horiz. projection. $8 1/4''$ usual max. — $6 3/4''$, $7 1/2''$ standard — $5 1/4''$ usual min.

TYPICAL SEAT DIMENSIONS

Warren Anderson; The Perkins and Will Partnership; Chicago, Illinois

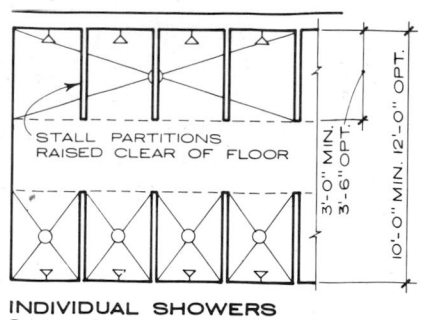

INDIVIDUAL SHOWERS 2 WALLS

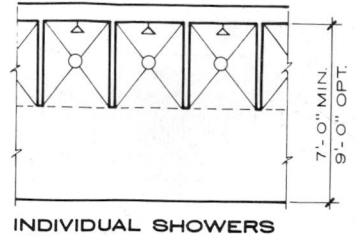

INDIVIDUAL SHOWERS 1 WALL

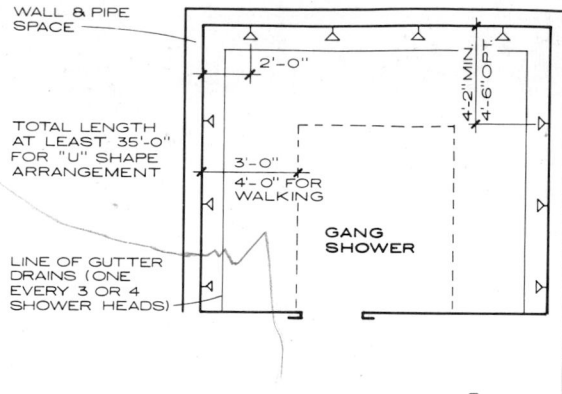

WALL & PIPE SPACE

TOTAL LENGTH AT LEAST 35'-0" FOR "U" SHAPE ARRANGEMENT

LINE OF GUTTER DRAINS (ONE EVERY 3 OR 4 SHOWER HEADS)

3'-0" / 4'-0" FOR WALKING

GANG SHOWER

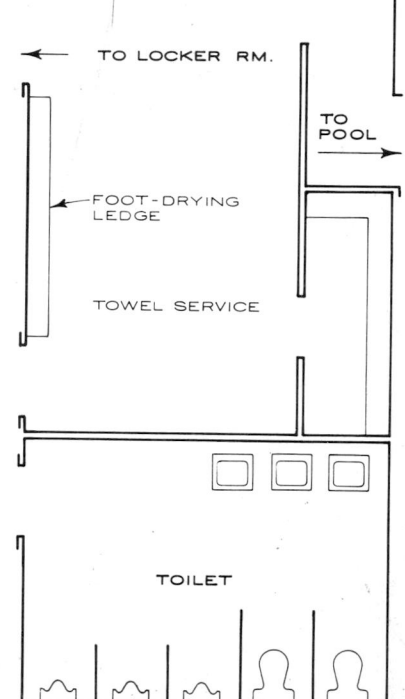

TO LOCKER RM.

TO POOL

FOOT-DRYING LEDGE

TOWEL SERVICE

TOILET

BOYS' LOCKER AND SHOWER FACILITIES

RECOMMENDED TOILET FIXTURES FOR GYM LOCKER SUITES

FIXTURE	NO. OF FIXTURES - BY PROPORTION	MINIMUM
TOILETS	Girls – 1 to 30 Individuals	3
	Boys – 1 to 50 Individuals	2
URINALS	Boys – 1 to 25 Individuals	2
LAVATORIES	Girls – 1 to 20 Individuals	3
	Boys – 1 to 20 Individuals	3

AUXILIARY ROOMS FOR GYM LOCKER SUITES

TOWELLING ROOM	
TOWEL SERVICE ROOM	Area varies with material to be stored (room may also be used to distribute uniforms)
EQUIPMENT DRYING ROOM	Depends on drying time and No. of uniforms. This room requires special heating and ventilating.

RECOMMENDATIONS FOR SHOWERING FACILITIES

BUILDING TYPE	NUMBER OF SHOWERS	TYPE
SCHOOL GYNASIUMS	Girls – 40% of peak period load + 1 to 3 individual showers	Gang and individual
	Boys – 30% of peak period load can be reduced by 1/3 for walkaround type	Gang and walkaround
BATHHOUSES	Women – 1 shower for each 250 women using pool.	Individual
	Men – 1 shower for each 250 men using pool.	Gang
COMMUNITY RECREATION BUILDINGS	Minimum for women – 6 gang + 4 individual	Gang and individual
	Minimum of 12 for men	Gang

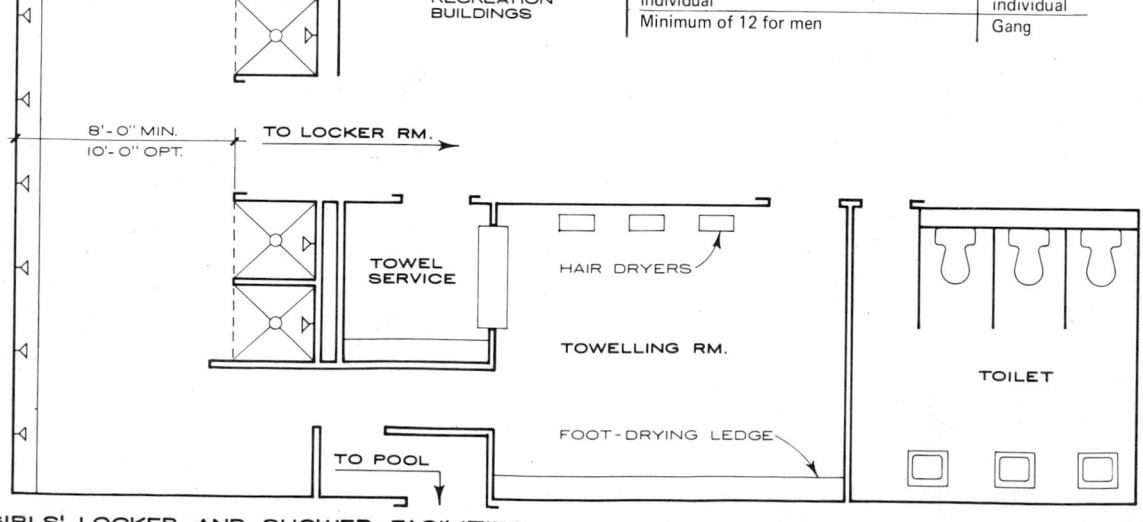

GIRLS' LOCKER AND SHOWER FACILITIES
(SHOWING GANG SHOWERS AND INDIVIDUAL SHOWERS)

Reed B. Fuller; Stetson–Spina Associates; Palm Beach, Florida

NOTES:

1. Both individual and master temperature control for gang showers. Individual temperature control usually provided for individual shower.

2. Minimum gutter drain spacing equals 10'– 0".

3. Height of shower head from floor:
Men   6'– 1"
Women   5'– 9"
Children   5'– 0"

4. See other page in this series for locker planning.

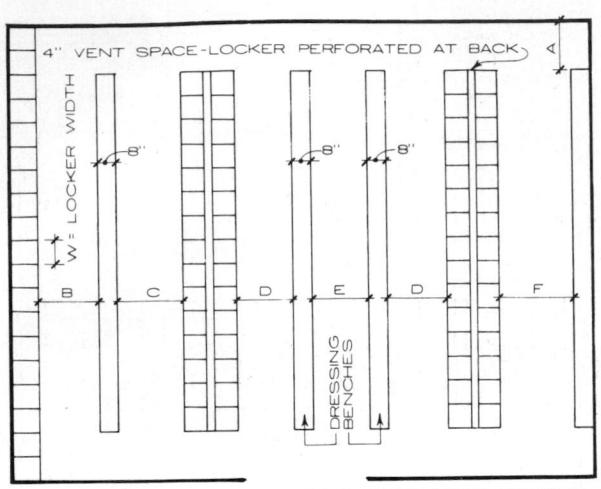

MINIMUM AISLE SPACE FOR DRESSING ROOMS

	SCHOOLS	AVERAGE TRAFFIC
A	2'-0"	2'-0"
B	3'-6"	3'-4"
C	3'-0"	2'-10"
D	3'-0"	2'-10"
E	2'-6"	1'-8"
F	3'-0"	4'-0"

<u>Rule of thumb area for locker rooms</u> (school gymnasiums and community recreation buildings) 14 sq. ft. per person (peak period load) exclusive of locker space.

LOCKER ROOM FACILITIES

Stationary benches

Mirrors for both boys and girls.

Shelves below mirrors for girls.

Full—length mirror for girls.

Drinking fountain

Bulletin board

Lighting located so that aisles and passages are well illuminated.

Windows located with regard to height and arrangement of lockers.

Adequate ventilation for all storage lockers.

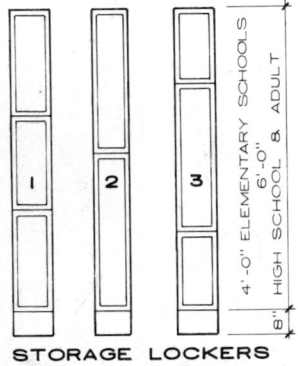

STORAGE LOCKERS

RECOMMENDED LOCKERS FOR GYMNASIUM CLOTHING STORAGE:

1. 7 1/2" wide x 12" deep x 24" high.
2. 6" wide x 12" deep x 36" high.
3. 7 1/2" wide x 12" deep x 18" high.

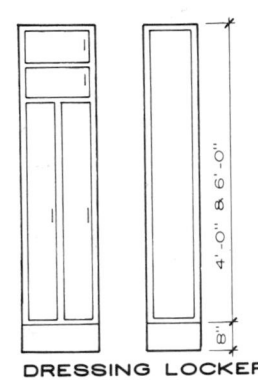

DRESSING LOCKERS

RECOMMENDED DRESSING LOCKER SIZES:

12" wide x 12" deep x 48" high.

12" wide x 12" deep x 12" high.

NO. OF LOCKERS REQUIRED FOR SCHOOL GYMNASIUMS:

One dressing locker per student (peak period load) + 10% to allow for variation in class sizes and scheduling.

One storage locker per student enrolled + 10% to allow for expansion.

GYMNASIUM DRESSING ROOMS & LOCKERS

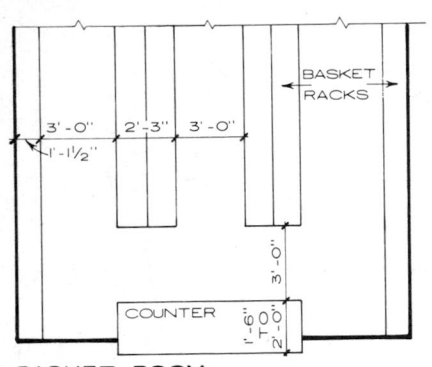

BASKET ROOM

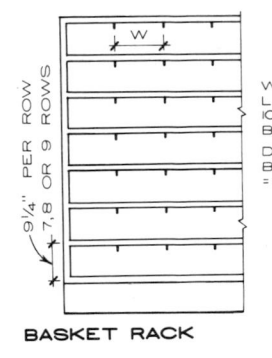

BASKET RACK

W=1'-1" FOR LARGE BASKETS, 10" FOR SMALL BASKETS.

DEPTH OF BASKETS = 1'-1 1/2"

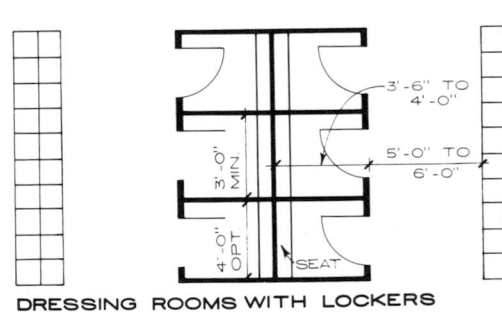

DRESSING ROOMS WITH LOCKERS

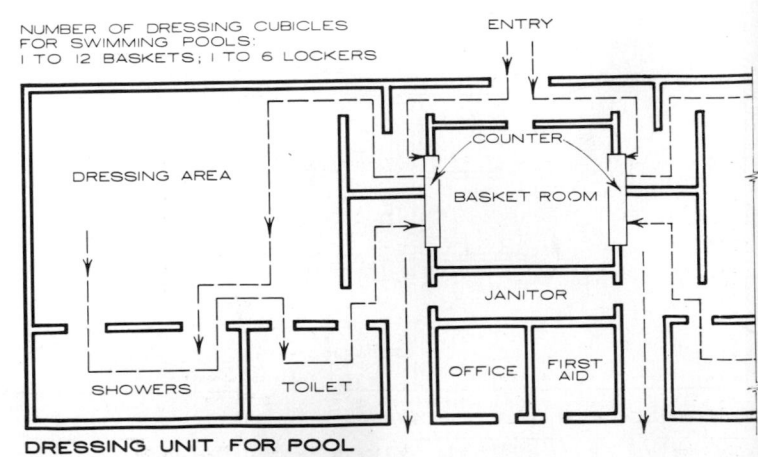

NUMBER OF DRESSING CUBICLES FOR SWIMMING POOLS: 1 TO 12 BASKETS; 1 TO 6 LOCKERS

DRESSING UNITS FOR COMMUNITY USE

SHOWER ROOMS

TOWELLING ROOMS

DRESSING AREAS

DRESSING UNIT FOR POOL

Reed B. Fuller; Stetson—Spina Associates; Palm Beach, Florida

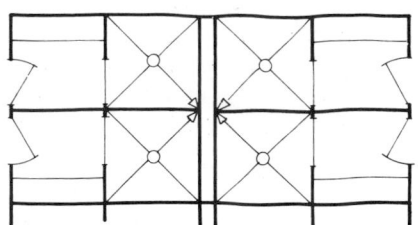

1:1 RATIO (DRESSING RM. TO SHOWER)
(PLANNING ALLOWANCE 22-32 SQ. FT. PER DRESSING ROOM)

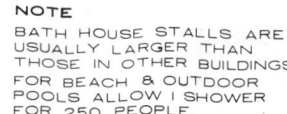

NOTE
BATH HOUSE STALLS ARE USUALLY LARGER THAN THOSE IN OTHER BUILDINGS. FOR BEACH & OUTDOOR POOLS ALLOW 1 SHOWER FOR 250 PEOPLE.

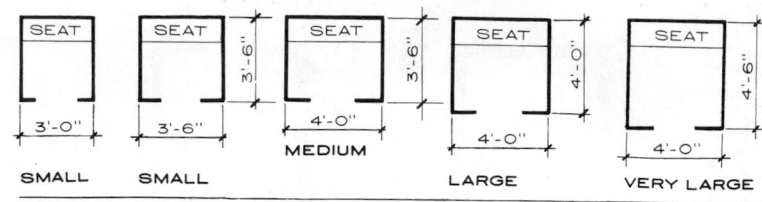

DRESSING ROOM SIZES
SCALE 1/8"=1'-0"

SMALL   SMALL   MEDIUM   LARGE   VERY LARGE

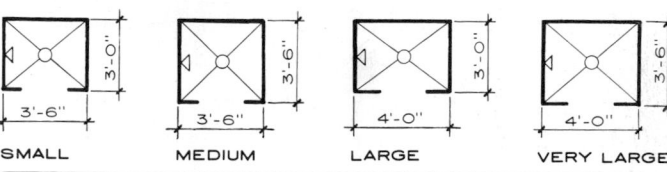

SHOWER STALL SIZES

SMALL   MEDIUM   LARGE   VERY LARGE

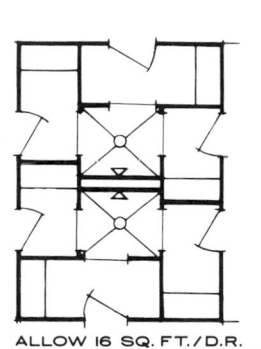

ALLOW 22 SQ. FT./D.R.
TOTAL AREA = 88 SQ. FT.
2:1 RATIO

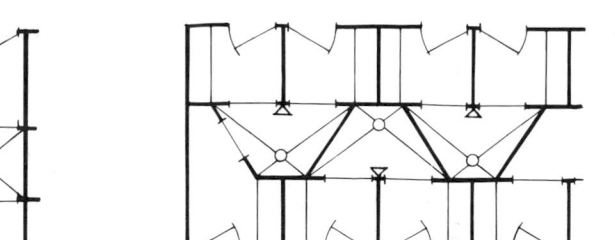

3:1 RATIO   **2:1 RATIO**

ALLOW 16 SQ. FT./D.R.
TOTAL AREA = 96 SQ. FT.
3:1 RATIO

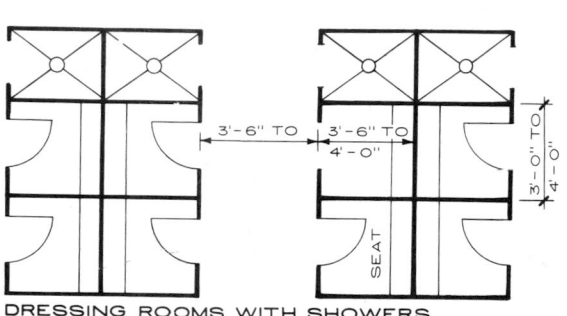

DRESSING ROOMS WITH SHOWERS

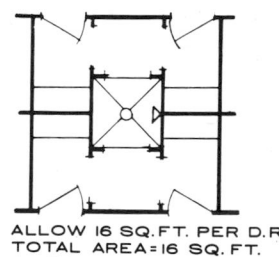

ALLOW 16 SQ. FT. PER D.R.
TOTAL AREA = 16 SQ. FT.
4:1 RATIO

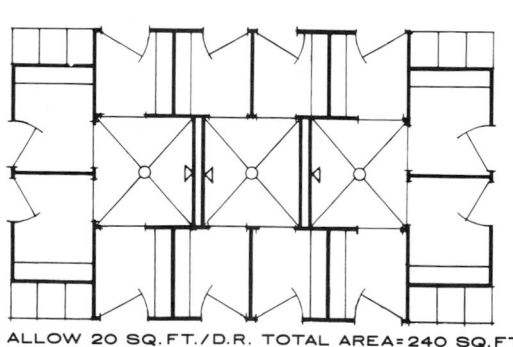

ALLOW 20 SQ. FT./D.R. TOTAL AREA=240 SQ. FT.
4:1 RATIO (12 D.R., 12 LOCKERS, 3 SHOWERS)

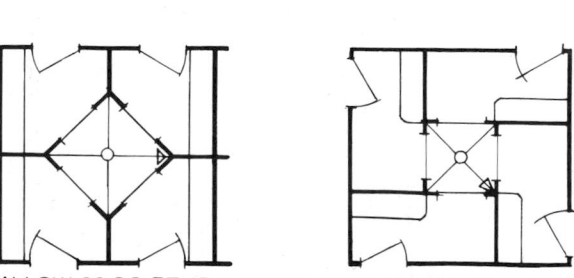

ALLOW 20 SQ.FT./D.R. TOTAL AREA = 81 SQ. FT.
4:1 RATIO

COMBINATION SHOWERS AND DRESSING ROOMS

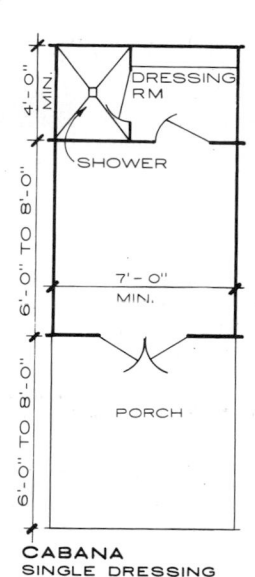

CABANA
SINGLE DRESSING ROOM

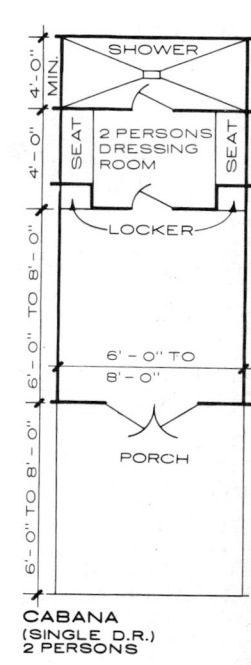

CABANA
(SINGLE D.R.)
2 PERSONS

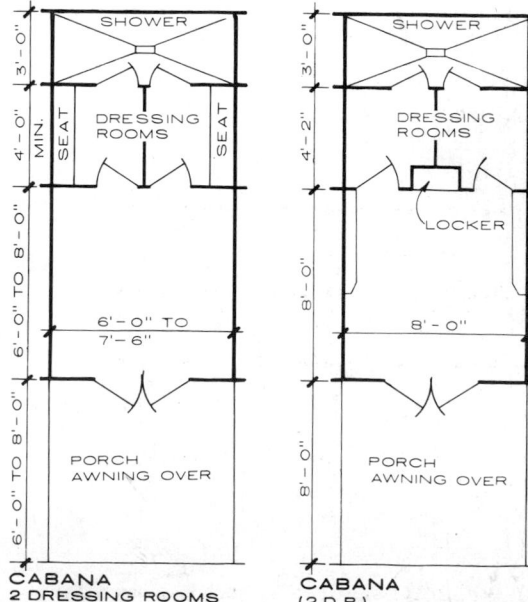

CABANA
2 DRESSING ROOMS

CABANA
(2 D.R.)

Reed B. Fuller; Stetson–Spina Associates; Palm Beach, Florida

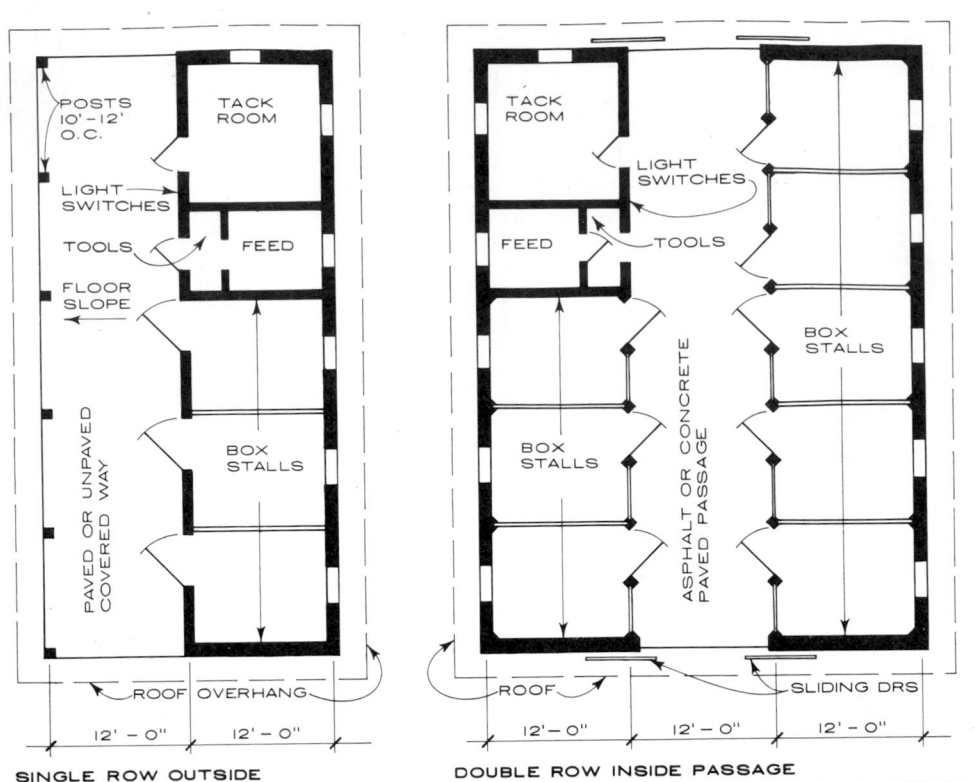

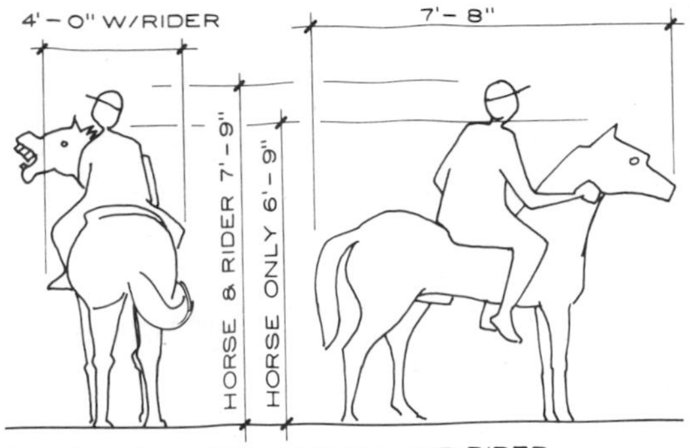

CLEARANCES FOR HORSE AND RIDER

4'-0" W/RIDER   7'-8"

HORSE & RIDER 7'-9"
HORSE ONLY 6'-9"

SINGLE ROW OUTSIDE

POSTS 10'-12' O.C.
TACK ROOM
LIGHT SWITCHES
TOOLS   FEED
FLOOR SLOPE
PAVED OR UNPAVED COVERED WAY
BOX STALLS
ROOF OVERHANG
12'-0"   12'-0"

DOUBLE ROW INSIDE PASSAGE

TACK ROOM
LIGHT SWITCHES
FEED   TOOLS
BOX STALLS
ASPHALT OR CONCRETE PAVED PASSAGE
BOX STALLS
ROOF
SLIDING DRS
12'-0"   12'-0"   12'-0"

ARRANGEMENTS OF STALLS, TACK AND FEED RMS – SCALE 1/16" = 1'-0"

NOTES:

Double row outside arrangements with stalls back to back are sometimes used at fairgrounds. Woven wire screening between stalls is omitted in racing stables, and wood is carried to full partition height. Combination protected incandescent lighting and heat lamps, frostproof hose bib and water supply are recommended where weather conditions warrant same. Passage lighting should be strip flourescent type (40 footcandles). Windows shown are glass jalousie type with fixed inside screen (plus woven wire guard for box stalls). Hardware for stalls should be heavy-duty galvanized, surface-applied type, "T" strap hinges and slide bolts for stall doors. Provide conventional heavy-duty hardware with locks for tack, feed and tool rooms. If exterior walls of stalls are masonry, furr out and finish interior surfaces with hardwood. Passages are sized to accept machinery. A tack room serves forty stalls.

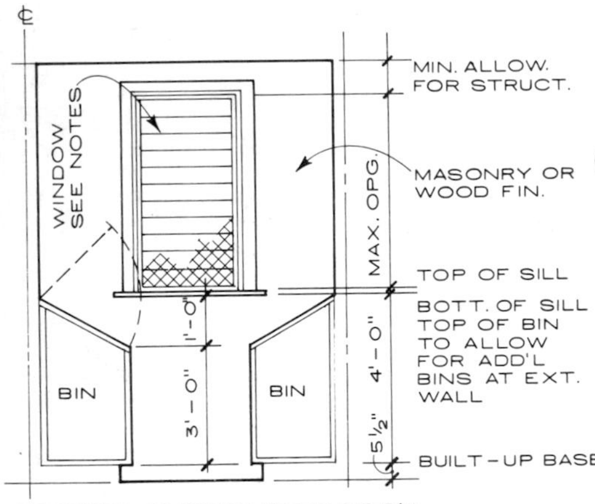

SECTION - ELEV. OF FEED ROOM

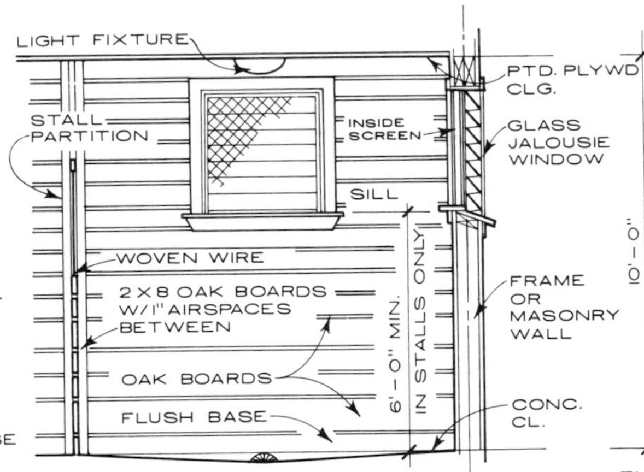

WINDOW SEE NOTES
BIN   BIN
MIN. ALLOW. FOR STRUCT.
MASONRY OR WOOD FIN.
TOP OF SILL
BOTT. OF SILL TOP OF BIN TO ALLOW FOR ADD'L BINS AT EXT. WALL
BUILT-UP BASE
MAX. OPG.
1'-0"   3'-0"   4'-0"   5 1/2"

SECT. - ELEV. STALL EXT. WALL

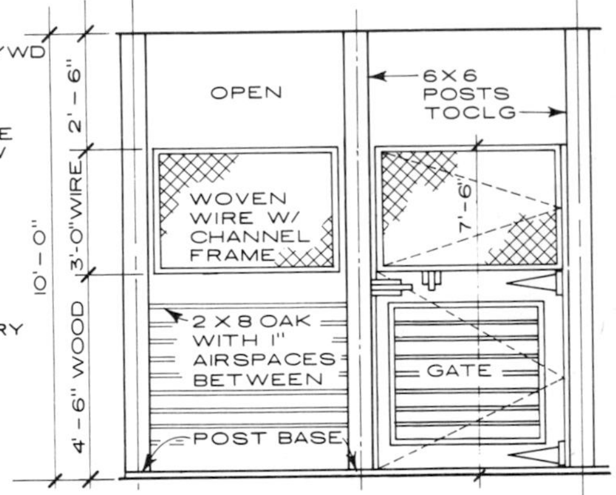

LIGHT FIXTURE
STALL PARTITION
INSIDE SCREEN
SILL
WOVEN WIRE
2 x 8 OAK BOARDS W/1" AIRSPACES BETWEEN
OAK BOARDS
FLUSH BASE
PTD. PLYWD CLG.
GLASS JALOUSIE WINDOW
FRAME OR MASONRY WALL
CONC. CL.
6'-0" MIN. IN STALLS ONLY

ELEVATION OF BOX STALL

OPEN
6 x 6 POSTS TO CLG
WOVEN WIRE W/ CHANNEL FRAME
2 x 8 OAK WITH 1" AIRSPACES BETWEEN
POST BASE
GATE
3'-0" WIRE   2'-6"
4'-6" WOOD   10'-0"   7'-6"

PLAN OF FEED & TOOL ROOMS

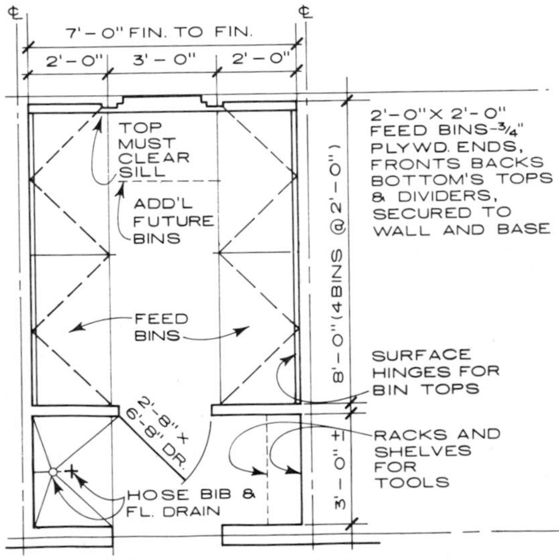

7'-0" FIN. TO FIN.
2'-0"   3'-0"   2'-0"
TOP MUST CLEAR SILL
ADD'L FUTURE BINS
FEED BINS
2'-8" x 6'-8" DR.
HOSE BIB & FL. DRAIN
8'-0" (4 BINS @ 2'-0")
2'-0" x 2'-0" FEED BINS-3/4" PLYWD. ENDS, FRONTS BACKS BOTTOM'S TOPS & DIVIDERS, SECURED TO WALL AND BASE
SURFACE HINGES FOR BIN TOPS
RACKS AND SHELVES FOR TOOLS
3'-0"

PLAN OF TACK ROOM

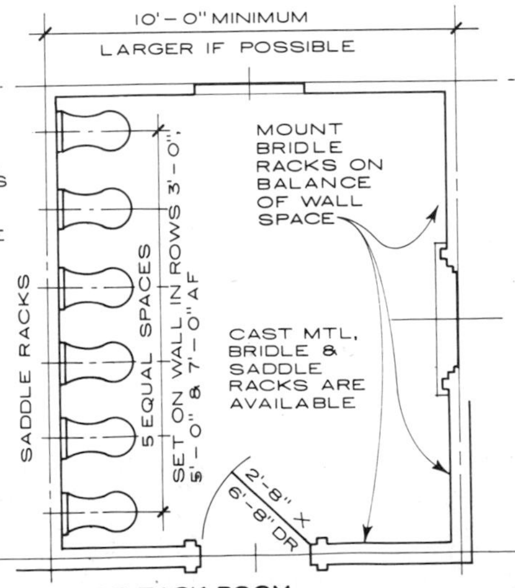

10'-0" MINIMUM
LARGER IF POSSIBLE
SADDLE RACKS
5 EQUAL SPACES
SET ON WALL IN ROWS 3'-0" 5'-0" & 7'-0" AF
MOUNT BRIDLE RACKS ON BALANCE OF WALL SPACE
CAST MTL. BRIDLE & SADDLE RACKS ARE AVAILABLE
2'-8" x 6'-8" DR.

PLAN OF BOX STALL

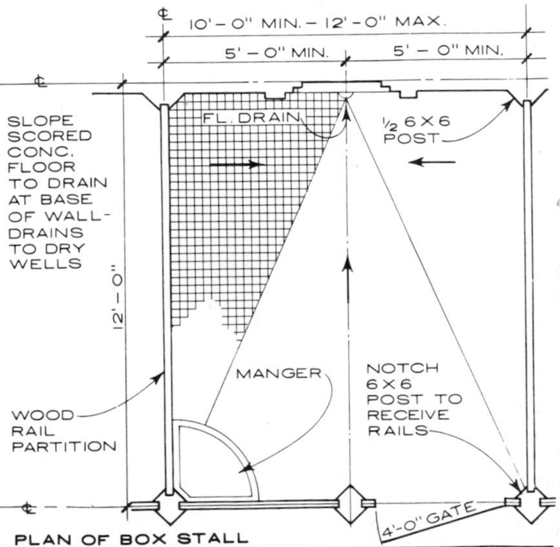

10'-0" MIN. - 12'-0" MAX.
5'-0" MIN.   5'-0" MIN.
FL. DRAIN
SLOPE SCORED CONC. FLOOR TO DRAIN AT BASE OF WALL-DRAINS TO DRY WELLS
1/2 6 x 6 POST
MANGER
NOTCH 6 x 6 POST TO RECEIVE RAILS
WOOD RAIL PARTITION
4'-0" GATE
12'-0"

DETAILS OF FEED, TOOL, TACK ROOMS AND BOX STABLE

SCALE 3/16" = 1'-0"

Douglas S. Stenhouse, AIA; Washington, D. C.

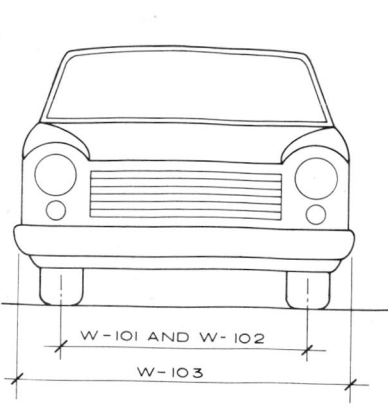

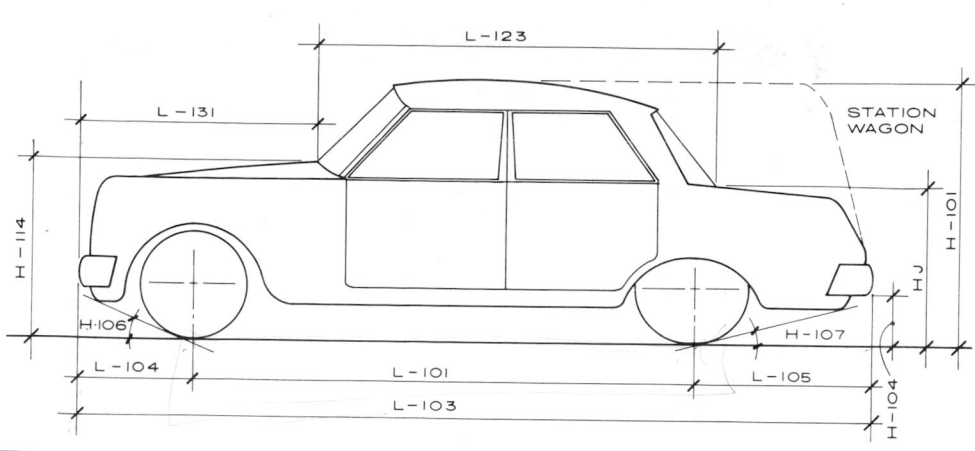

AMERICAN AUTOMOBILE DIMENSIONS – COMPOSITE ELEVATIONS OF AUTOMOBILE DEVISED BY AGS STAFF (STANDARD DIMENSIONS OF AUTOMOBILE MANUFACTURERS ASSOC. INC.)

NOTES :

1 – Foreign cars not included (except Volkswagen, see below).
2 – Dimensions are for 1968 models.
3 – Dimensions cover: sedans, coupes and stationwagons.

OVERALL DIMENSIONS	MINIMUM		MAXIMUM	
W–103 Overall width	Corvette	5'–9 1/4''	Buick	6'–8''
H–101 Overall height	Corvette	3'–11 3/4''	Jeep	5'–3 13/16''
L–101 Wheelbase	Corvette	8'–2''	Cadillac	11'–0''
L–103 Overall length	AMC AMX	14'–10 1/4''	Cadillac	19'–0 1/4''
H–156 Ground clearance	Pontiac	0'–3 11/16''	Jeep	0'–7 11/16''

ANGLES, RAMPS & DIAMS.	MINIMUM		MAXIMUM	
H–106 Angle of approach (degrees)	Cadillac	19.2°	Jeep	39.0°
H–107 Angle of departure (degrees)	Mercury	10.8°	Javelin	23.8°
H–147 Ramp breakover angle (degrees)	Tempest	9.0°	Jeep	24.0°
Wall to wall turning diam. (ft.)	Jeep	37'–8''	Oldsmobile	49'–7''

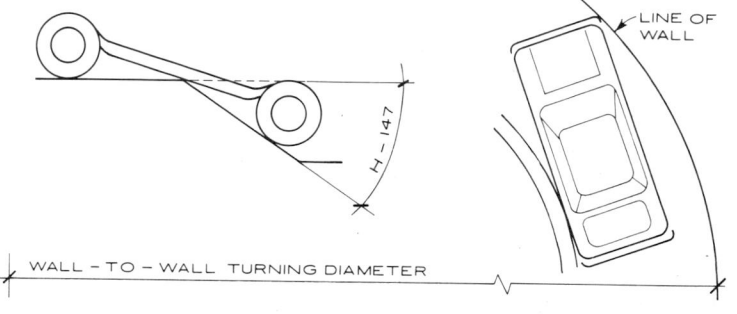

WALL – TO – WALL TURNING DIAMETER

REAR OF CAR DIMENSIONS	MINIMUM		MAXIMUM	
HJ Deck at rear window to grnd.	Firebird	2'–9 13/16''	Checker	3'–10 1/2''
L–105 Overhang rear	Camaro	3'–4''	Imperial	5'–4''
W–102 Tread width - distance between ₵ of tires at ground	Rambler	4'–7''	Pontiac	5'–4''
H–104 Bottom of rear bumper to ground	AMC Ambassador	0'–9 11/16''	Camaro	0'–17''
H–153 Rear axle differential to ground	Buick	0'–5''	Chrysler	0'–7 1/2''

FRONT OF CAR DIMENSIONS	MINIMUM		MAXIMUM	
H–114 Hood at rear to ground	Corvette	2'–2 1/2''	Checker	3'–10 1/2''
L–104 Overhang front	Jeep	2'–4 3/4''	Eldorado	3'–8''
L–131 Front of car to base of windshield	Jeep	4'–4 3/4''	Toronado	6'–0''
W–101 Tread width - distance between ₵ of tires at ground	Rambler	4'–8''	Toronado	6'–3 1/2''
L–123 Upper structure	Corvette	4'–7 1/2''	Rebel	11'–11 3/16''

VOLKSWAGEN SEDAN

DIMENSIONS – SEDAN

Overall height	4'–11''
Overall length	13'–3''
Wheelbase	7'–10 1/2''
Front tread width	4'–3 1/2''
Rear tread width	4'–5''
Overall width	5'–1''

VOLKSWAGEN MICROBUS

DIMENSIONS – MICROBUS

Overall height	6'–5''
Overall length	14'–6''
Wheelbase	7'–10 1/2''
Front tread width	4'–6 1/2''
Rear tread width	4'–8''
Overall width	5'–9 1/2''

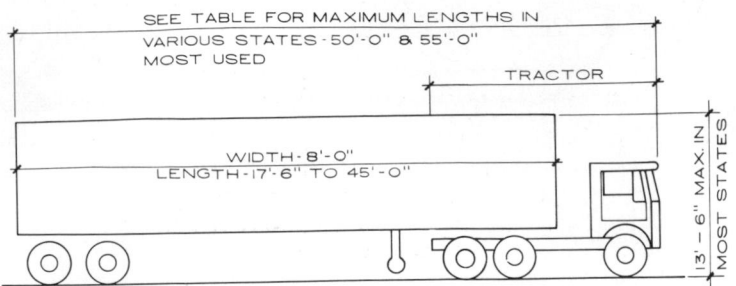

SEMITRAILER & TRUCK TRACTOR

Turning radius of tractors and semitrailer depends on turning radius of tractor (50'–0" practical minimum for long combinations).

MAX. LENGTH	STATES
50'–0"	Oregon, Washington D.C.
55'–0"	Ala., Ark., Conn., Del., Fla., Ga., Haw., Ill., Ind., Iowa, Kans., Ky., Mass., Md., Me., Mich., Minn., Miss., Mo., N.C., N.H., N.J., N.Y., Ohio, Okla., Pa., R.I., S.C., Tenn., Texas, Va., Vt., W. Va., Wisc.
60'–0"	Alaska, Calif., Idaho, La., Mont., N.D., Neb., Utah, Wash.
65'–0"	Ariz., Colo., N.H., S.D., Wyom.
70'–0"	Nev.

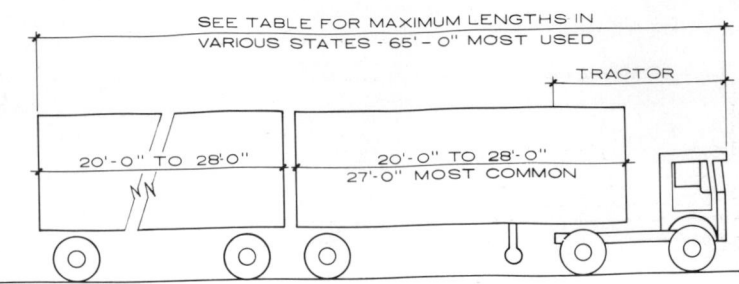

FULL TRAILER, SEMITRAILER & TRUCK TRACTOR

NOT PERMITTED IN THE FOLLOWING STATES

Ala., Conn., Fla., La., Mass., Me., Minn., N.C., N.Y., Pa., R.I., S.C., Tenn., Va., Vt., W. Va., Washington D.C., Wisc.

MAXIMUM LENGTH	STATES
55'–0"	Ga., Miss., N.H., N.J.
60'–0"	Iowa
65'–0"	Alaska, Ariz., Ark., Calif., Colo., Del., Haw., Idaho, Ill., Ind., Kans., Ky., Md., Mich., Mo., Mont., N.D., N.M., Neb., Ohio, Okla., Ore., S.D., Texas, Utah, Wash., Wyom.
70'–0"	Nev.

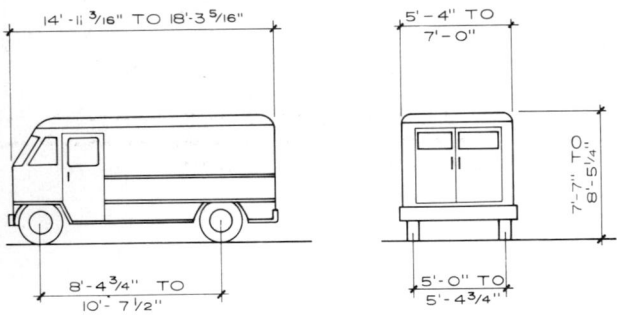

DELIVERY TRUCK

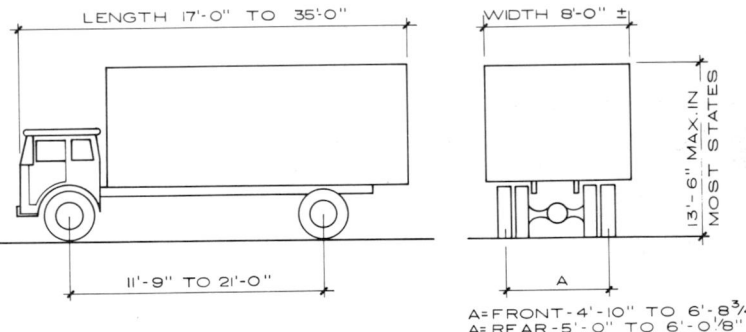

VAN TYPE TRUCK

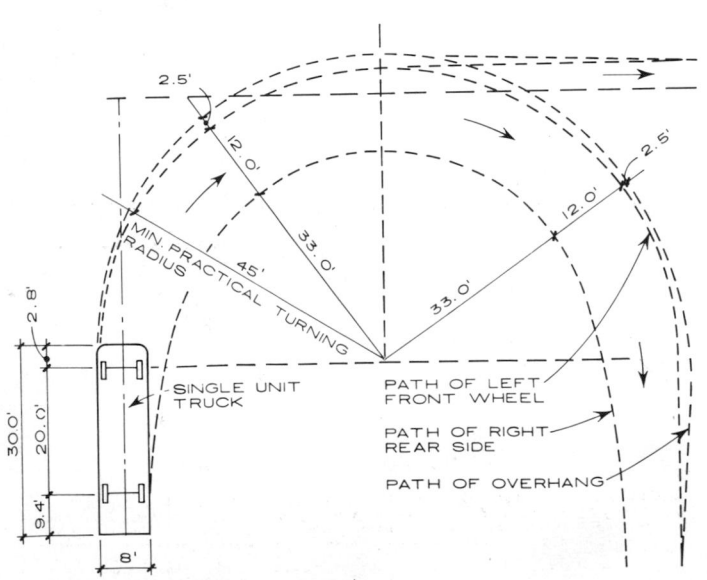

SINGLE UNIT TRUCK MINIMUM PRACTICAL TURNING RADIUS

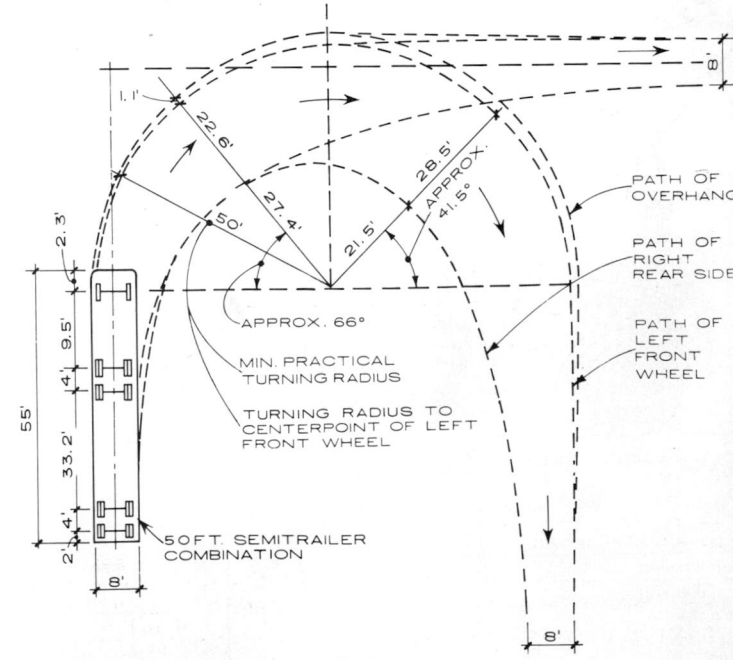

SEMITRAILER COMBINATION MINIMUM PRACTICAL TURNING RADIUS

V. Peruchietti; Giffels & Rossetti, Inc.; Detroit, Michigan
The Operations Council, American Trucking Associations, Inc.; Washington, D. C.

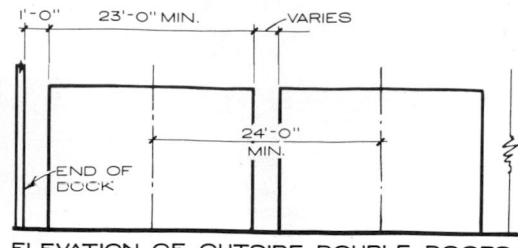

ELEVATION OF OUTSIDE DOUBLE DOORS

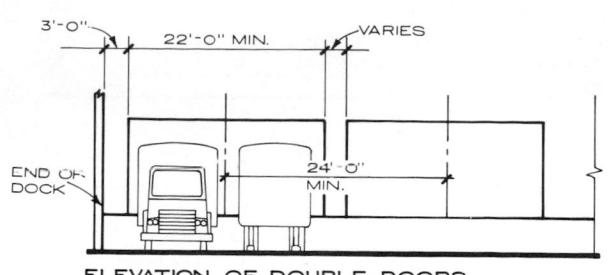

ELEVATION OF DOUBLE DOORS

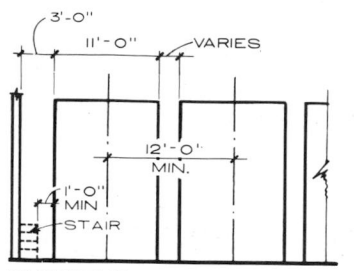

ELEVATION OF OUTSIDE
SINGLE DOORS
NOTE STAIR AT INSIDE DOCK

	A	B	C
	55'—0"	55'—0"	60'—0"
	30'—0"	30'—0"	35'—0"
	25'—0"	25'—0"	30'—0"

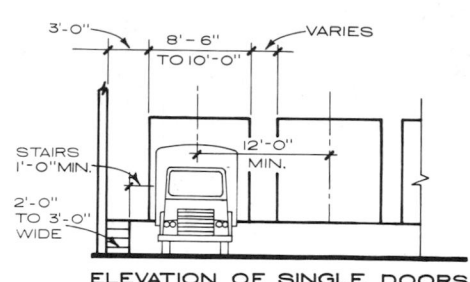

ELEVATION OF SINGLE DOORS

	A	D
	55'—0"	110'—0"
	30'—0"	60'—0"
	25'—0"	50'—0"

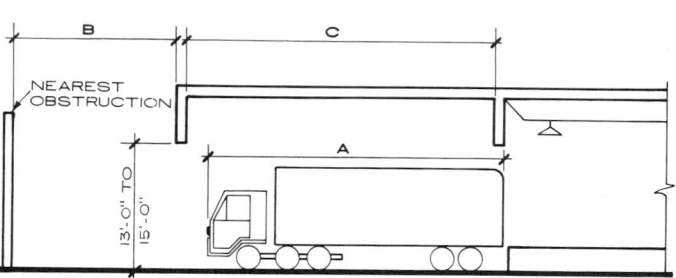

SECTION THROUGH CLOSED MOTOR CARRIER DOCK

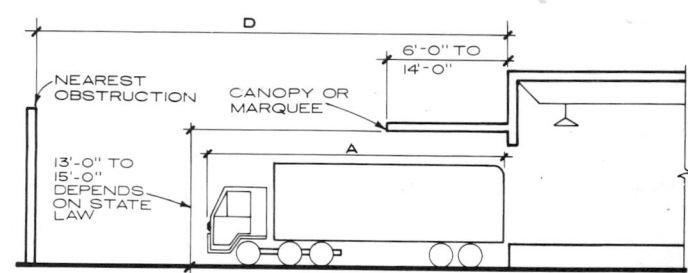

SECTION THROUGH OPEN CARRIER DOOR

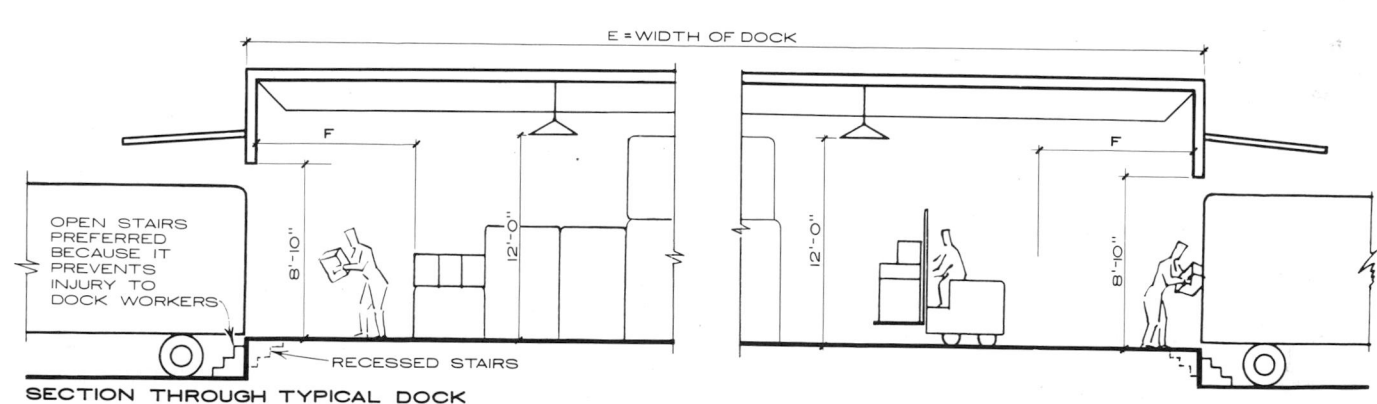

SECTION THROUGH TYPICAL DOCK

GENERAL NOTES:

1. Maintain a minimum space of 1'—0" between first door opening and either the end of the building or the stairway.

2. The slope of the pavement is to be the minimum required for drainage.

3. Dock dimensions shown are the same for all types of motor carrier docks.

4. Check local codes and laws.

SIZE OF VEHICLE	PLATFORM HEIGHT
55'—0"	4'—4"±
30'—0"	4'—0"±
25'—0"	3'—8"±

	2 WHEEL HAND TRUCK OPERATION	FORK LIFT TRUCK OPERATION	4 WHEELED HAND TRUCK OPERATION	DRAG LINE OPER	AUTOMATIC SPUR TYPE DRAG LINE
F	6'—0"	10'—0"	10'—0"	10'—0"	10'—0"
E	50'—0"	60'—0"	70'—0"	80'—0"	120'—0" 140'—0"

Giffels & Rossetti, Inc.; Detroit, Michigan

The Operations Council, American Trucking Associations, Inc.; Washington, D. C.

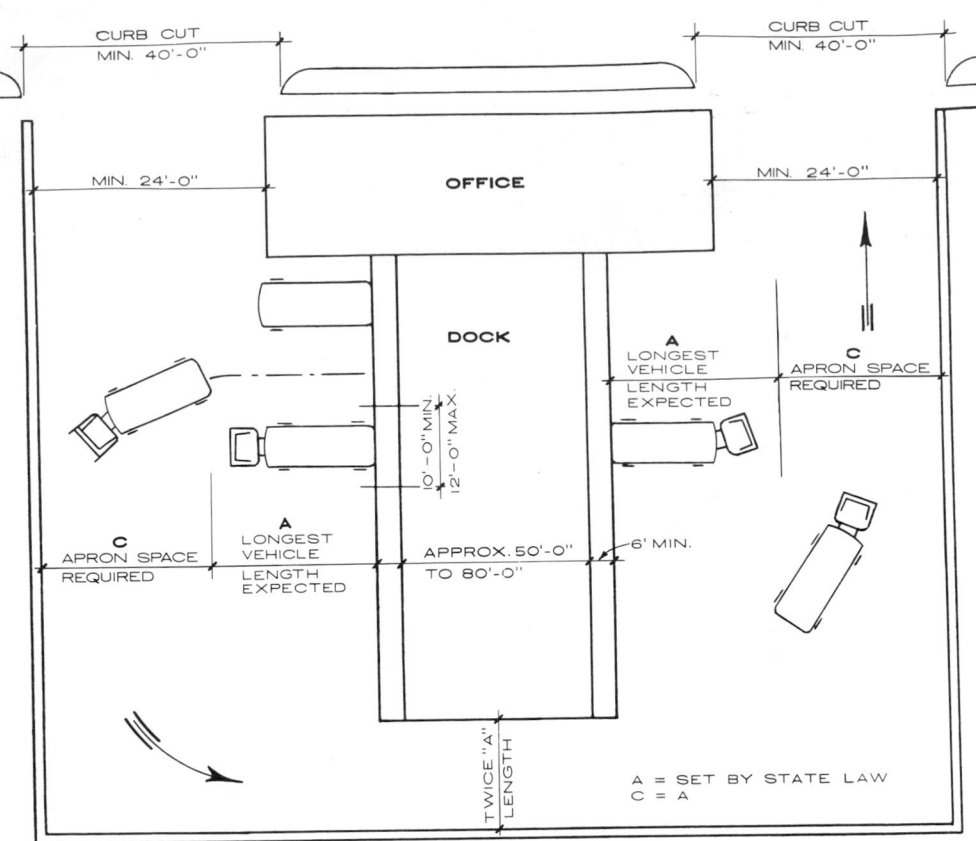

PLAN OF TYPICAL DOCK SHOWING REQUIRED CLEARANCE

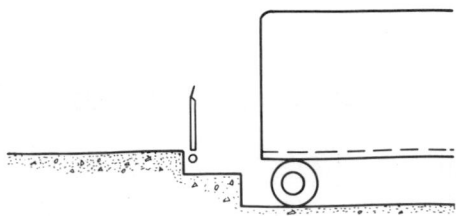

STEP – DOWN DOCK BOARD
CARRIER DOORS CAN BE OPENED AND
CLOSED AT DOCK, 6'- 0" WIDTH, AND MECH
OPERATED

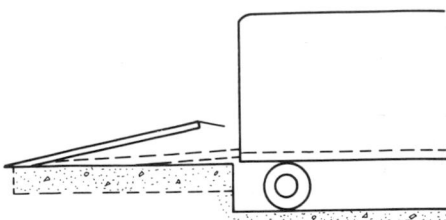

ADJUST – A – LIP DOCKBOARD
AUTOMATICALLY EXTENDING AND RETRACT
RETRACTING, HINGED TIP 6 WAY ADJUSTABLE
AND HAS 7'- 0" WIDTH.

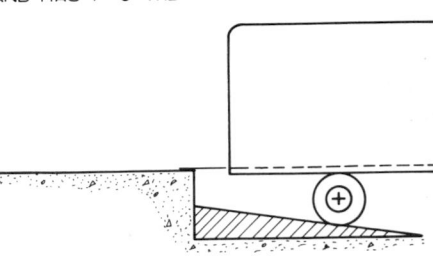

**LOADING LEVEL OF TRUCK MAY BE
RAISED BY MOVABLE INCLINE**

**SECTIONS – LOADING DOCK
LEVELING DEVICES**
1 TO 2 NEEDED PER TERMINAL

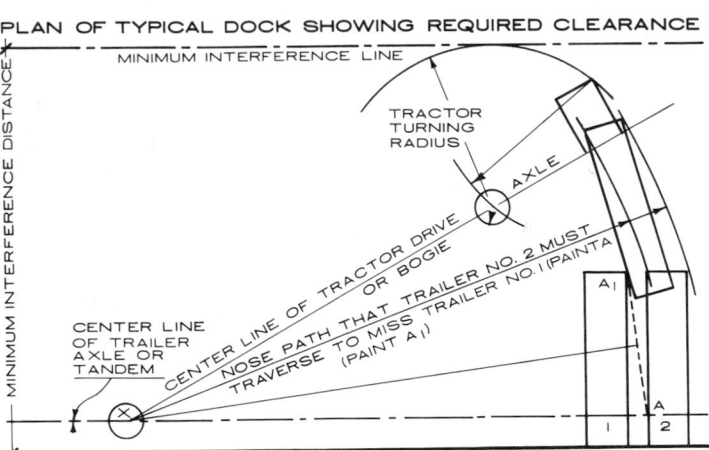

DETERMINING THE MINIMUM APRON SPACE REQUIREMENT

1. Draw to scale trailers up against the loaddock at expected minimum spacings. (Use measurements of longest and widest trailer expected at dock with rearmost axle or tandem position.

2. Extend trailer #2 axle or tandem centerline in direction of turn.

3. Draw chord AA, from that point on the side of trailer #2 where the axle or tandem center line intersects the side of the body, to the nose corner of the adjacent trailer (#1). This is a chord of the curve through which point trailer #2 must traverse to miss trailer #1.

4. Bisect chord AA, and extend a perpendicular line until it intersects the extension of trailer #2 axle or tandem center line at point X. This is the point about which all points on trailer #2 must rotate to miss striking trailer #1.

5. With the compass point on X, swing trailer #2's nose around until point A reaches A₁. Sketch trailer #2 into its position as shown.

6. Through the location of the kingpin, extend a line back through point X, this line then represents the

center line of the tractor drive, axle or bogie. From this drive axle center line, draw the tractor with the greatest turning radius in its proper position with respect to trailer #2 in its second position.

7. With the compass point on the tractor front bumber (opposite side from the direction of the turn) scribe an arc equal to the turning radius of the tractor so that it intersects the center line of the tractor drive axle at point Y.

8. With the compass set at the turning radius of the tractor, place the point at Y and scribe an arc that represents the curve through which the bumber will travel.

For the result, measure the distance from the dock to a point on the curve which represents the greatest distance from the dock.

NOTE: Distances may be decreased by increasing the min. spacing between trailers or by using a saw-toothed loading platform. An additional allowance over and beyond the main, interference distance be provided to allow for a proper safety margin.

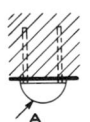 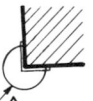 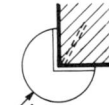

 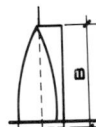 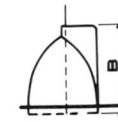

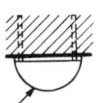 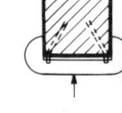

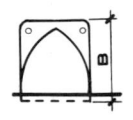 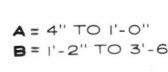 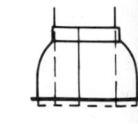

A = 4" TO 1'-0"
B = 1'-2" TO 3'-6"

NOTE:

Usually made of cast iron 3" minimum thickness and used to protect door jambs, walls and corner. May be combined with corner and wall guards.

WHEEL GUARDS

Giffels & Rossetti, Inc.; Detroit, Michigan

The Operations Council, American Trucking Associations, Inc.; Washington, D. C.

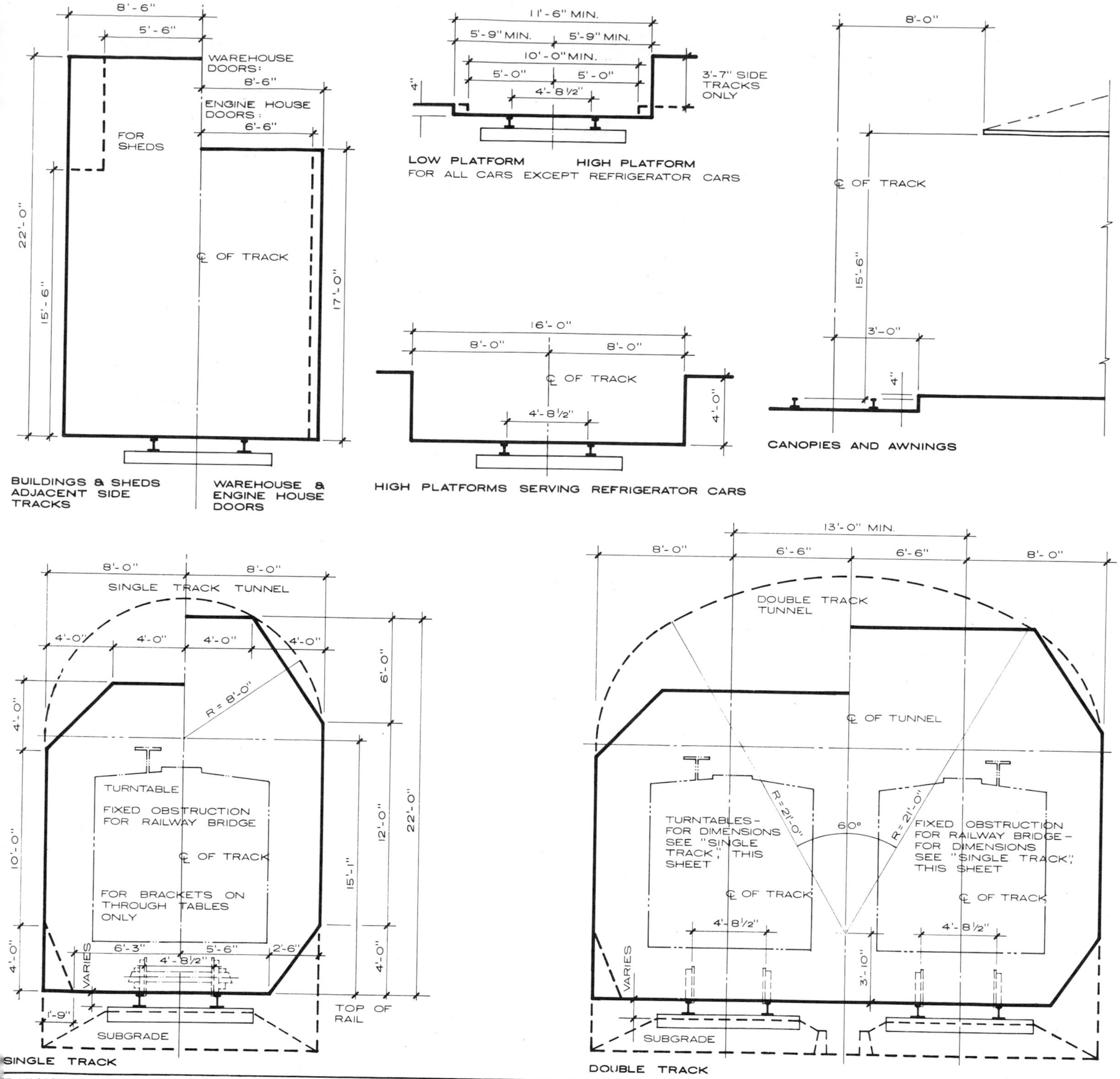

BUILDINGS & SHEDS ADJACENT SIDE TRACKS

8'-6"
5'-6"
22'-0"
15'-6"
FOR SHEDS
WAREHOUSE DOORS: 8'-6"
ENGINE HOUSE DOORS: 6'-6"
℄ OF TRACK
17'-0"

WAREHOUSE & ENGINE HOUSE DOORS

11'-6" MIN.
5'-9" MIN.   5'-9" MIN.
10'-0" MIN.
5'-0"   5'-0"
4'-8½"
4"
3'-7" SIDE TRACKS ONLY

LOW PLATFORM   HIGH PLATFORM
FOR ALL CARS EXCEPT REFRIGERATOR CARS

16'-0"
8'-0"   8'-0"
℄ OF TRACK
4'-8½"
4'-0"

HIGH PLATFORMS SERVING REFRIGERATOR CARS

8'-0"
℄ OF TRACK
15'-6"
3'-0"
4"

CANOPIES AND AWNINGS

SINGLE TRACK TUNNEL

8'-0"   8'-0"
4'-0" 4'-0" 4'-0" 4'-0"
4'-0"
6'-0"
R = 8'-0"
TURNTABLE
FIXED OBSTRUCTION FOR RAILWAY BRIDGE
℄ OF TRACK
FOR BRACKETS ON THROUGH TABLES ONLY
10'-0"
22'-0"
12'-0"
15'-1"
4'-0"
6'-3"   5'-6"   2'-6"
4'-8½"
4'-0"
VARIES
1'-9"
SUBGRADE
TOP OF RAIL

SINGLE TRACK

DOUBLE TRACK TUNNEL

13'-0" MIN.
8'-0"   6'-6"   6'-6"   8'-0"
℄ OF TUNNEL
R = 21'-0"   60°   R = 21'-0"
TURNTABLES— FOR DIMENSIONS SEE "SINGLE TRACK" THIS SHEET
FIXED OBSTRUCTION FOR RAILWAY BRIDGE— FOR DIMENSIONS SEE "SINGLE TRACK" THIS SHEET
℄ OF TRACK   ℄ OF TRACK
4'-8½"   4'-8½"
3'-10"
VARIES
SUBGRADE

DOUBLE TRACK

RAILWAY CLEARANCES   SCALE: 1/8" = 1'-0"

GENERAL NOTES:

1. 4'-8½" gauge is from inside to inside of rail heads.

2. On curved track the clearance shall be increased to allow for overhanging and tilting of a car 85'-0" long x 16'-0" high.

3. The super-elevation of the outer rail shall be in accordance with recommended practice of the American Railway Engineering Association, (see chart, "Legal Requirements — Clearances").

4. 16'-0" min. required to clear highest cars and locomotives.

B. J. Baldwin; Giffels & Rossetti, Inc.; Detroit, Michigan

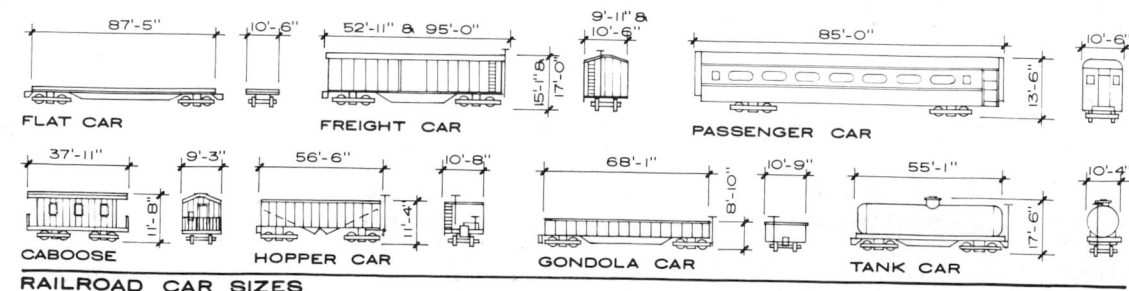

RAILROAD CAR SIZES

FLAT CAR   87'-5"   10'-6"
FREIGHT CAR   52'-11" & 95'-0"   9'-11" & 10'-6"   15'-1½" & 17'-0"
PASSENGER CAR   85'-0"   13'-6"   10'-6"
CABOOSE   37'-11"   9'-3"   11'-8"
HOPPER CAR   56'-6"   10'-8"   11'-4"
GONDOLA CAR   68'-1"   10'-9"   8'-10"
TANK CAR   55'-1"   10'-4"   17'-6"

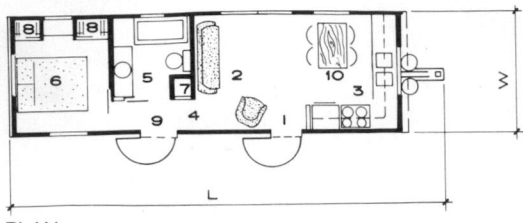

PLAN

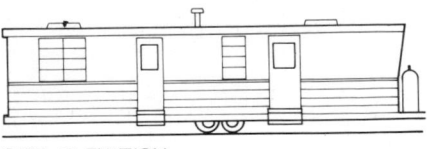

SIDE ELEVATION

TYPICAL ONE BEDROOM UNIT

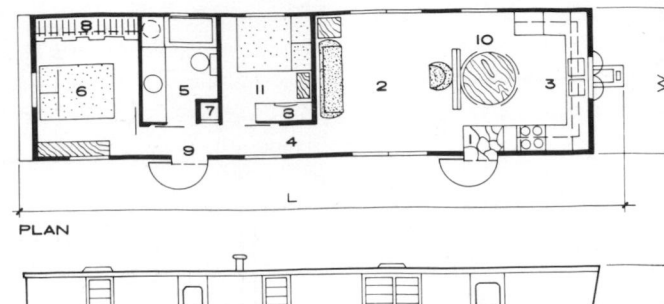

PLAN

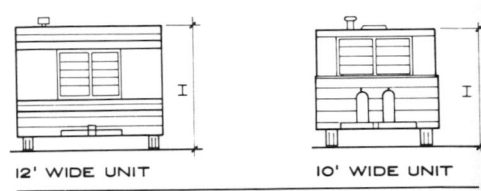

SIDE ELEVATION

TYPICAL TWO BEDROOM UNIT

FRONT ELEVATIONS

12' WIDE UNIT   10' WIDE UNIT

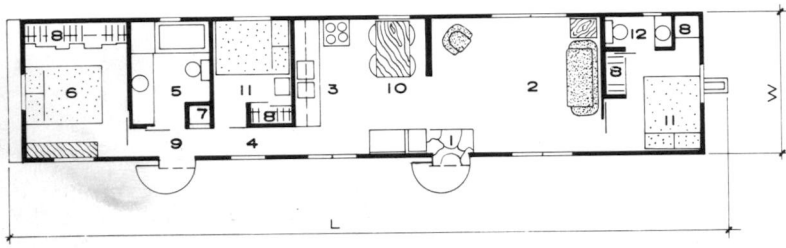

PLAN

SIDE ELEVATION

TYPICAL THREE BEDROOM UNIT

SCHEDULE OF ROOMS FOR ALL PLANS

1. Entrance
2. Living
3. Kitchen
4. Corridor
5. Bath
6. Master Bedroom
7. Furnace
8. Closet-Storage
9. Rear Entrance
10. Dining
11. Bedroom
12. Lavatory

GENERAL DIMENSIONS

W	L	H
10'	36'	9'
10'	43'	9'
10'	46'	9'
10'	50'	9'
10'	55'	9'
10'	60'	9'
10'	65'	9'
12'	36'	9'
12'	43'	9'
12'	46'	9'
12'	50'	9'
12'	55'	9'
12'	60'	9'
12'	65'	9'

ASSOCIATED REFERENCE MATERIAL AND PUBLICATIONS ON MOBILE HOMES

I. MOBILE HOME HIGHWAY MOVEMENT HANDBOOK

Legal lengths and widths, where and how to obtain permits, costs of permits, special rules for movement of oversize mobile homes.

2. THE LAW OF MOBILE HOMES

Comprehensive coverage of statutes, ordinances and court decisions relating to mobile homes. Problems of taxation, zoning, regulations of mobile homes and parks, park operators' rights, liabilities and licensing fully covered. Presents the opinions of certain attorneys general of the states concerning their respective mobile home statutes.

STANDARDS

I. U.S.A. STANDARD A119.1– FOR MOBILE HOMES

Defines the installation and material requirements for the plumbing, heating and electrical systems in mobile homes.

2. MOBILE HOME MINIMUM BODY & FRAME DESIGN & CONSTRUCTION STANDARDS

Defines the minimum design and performance criteria for the complete mobile home structure and its associated running gear.

3. WHAT MOBILE HOME STANDARDS MEAN TO YOU

Explains the significance of U.S.A. Standards A119.1 for the plumbing, heating and electrical installations in mobile homes and how they act to protect the health, welfare and safety of the owner.

NOTE:

Publications mentioned above, and other publications, are available from Mobile Home Manufacturers Association, Chicago, Illinois.

C. T. Skinner; Giffels & Rossetti, Inc.; Detroit, Michigan

TYPICAL CONSTRUCTION AND STANDARD FEATURES

1. Heavy duty I beam steel frame
2. 2 x 4 & 2 x 8 stringer with 1 x 4 cross stringers form floor section
3. Floor glued and screwed to floor stringers
4. 16'–0' x 8" wood beam construction over door and window areas
5. 3" sidewall framing studs are mortised and glued
6. 6" truss-type bows unitized by heavy duty timbers
7. Galvanized steel roofs with taped sidewall
8. Color bonded aluminum siding—metal straps tie sidewall to floor
9. Interior plywood is glued and screwed to sidewall studs for moisture protection and unitized construction strength
10. 1/2" insulation board ceiling
11. Heavy duty fiber glass insulation with vapor barrier
12. Asphalt impregnated insulation board, type bottom seal
13. Gun type furnace with silent flow, one-piece metal duct heat system
14. Inlaid linoleum or patterned tile on floors
15. Awning type windows
16. Kitchen cabinets, fixtures and appliances
17. Bathroom fixtures
18. Electrical fixtures
19. Furniture in all rooms

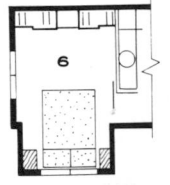

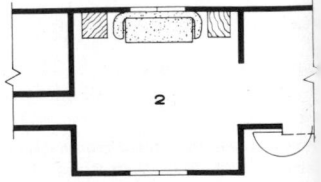

SPECIAL OPTIONS

Tip-out rooms of varying size are available in most models for either living room or rear bedroom or both. This applies to ten and twelve foot wide models.

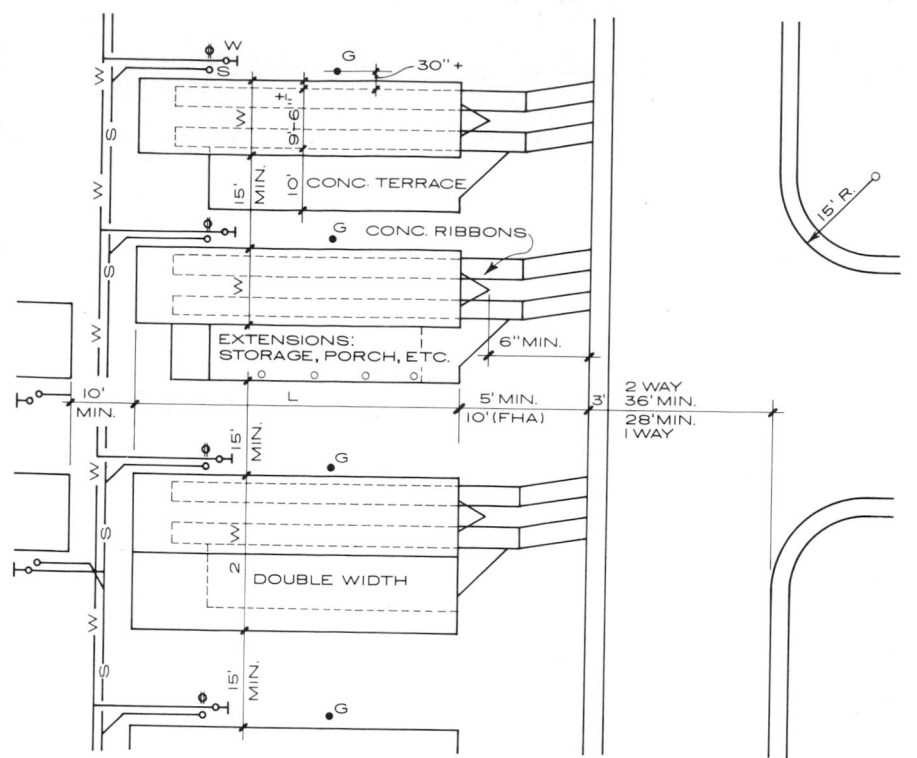

PLAN (NOT TO SCALE)

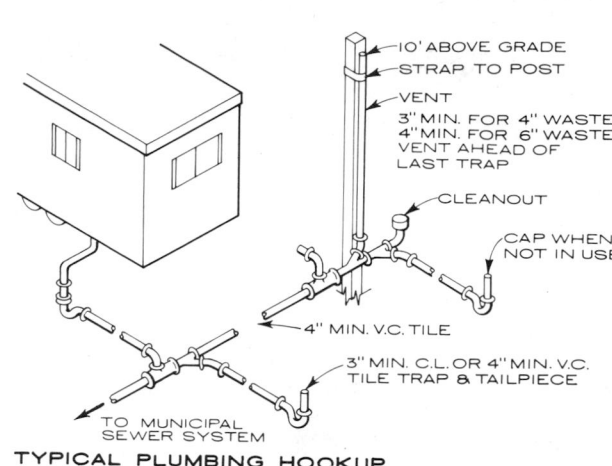

TYPICAL PLUMBING HOOKUP

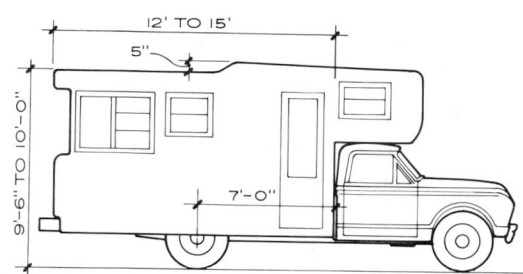

CHASSIS MOUNTED CAMPER
For trucks of 157″ — 159″ wheelbase, dual rear wheels. Side door, rear lounge.

Widths: 7′– 6″, 8′– 0″.

NOTES

Data given here are from a widely used zoning ordinance. FHA Minimum Property Standards are somewhat more restrictive in some respects. Local regulations should be consulted.

W = width. 10′ or 12′ standard. Some 14′ models on market. Many states restrict width for highway transport.

L = length. From 46′ to 60′. A 68′ model available.

Utility lines: W = water, S = sewer, G = gas,
  = electric outlet.

Water service—400 gallons/day/unit.

Gas service—metered. Connected only after inspection and approval. Individual storage tanks outside unit, rigidly connected, at least 5′ from any door.

Electrical service—metered, 110—220V., underground distribution recommended, required by some codes.

SERVICE BUILDINGS

For independent mobile homes—provide 1 lavatory and 1 flush toilet each for males and females for emergency use.

For dependent mobile homes—10 units or less:
Male: 1 w.c., 1 urinal, 1 lavatory, 1 shower.
Female: 2 w.c., 1 lavatory, 1 shower.
Same for each additional 10 units or less.
Location: 15′ to 200′ from dependent units.

Construction—permanent, heated, sound retardant wall separating male and female sides, well ventilated.

Many parks provide coin-operated laundry facilities for occupants, whether of dependent or independent units.

WEIGHT OF MOBILE HOME: 15 – 20 TONS.

CLASSIFICATION OF MOBILE HOMES

Independent—equipped with flush toilet and tub or shower.

Dependent—not so equipped.

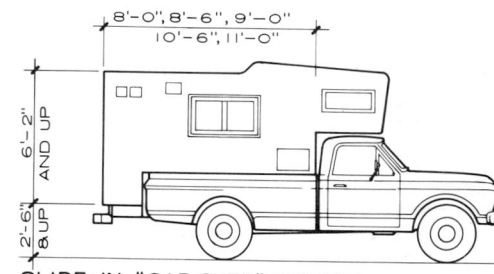

SLIDE-IN, "CAB OVER" CAMPER
Made to fit 6 1/2′, 8′, 9′ pickup beds.
Widths vary. 6′– 9″, 7′– 6″, 8′– 0″ typical.

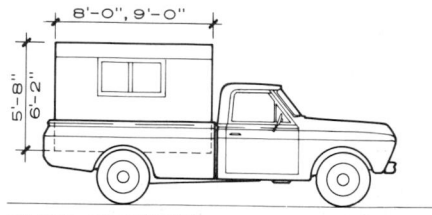

SLIDE-IN CAMPER
Made to fit most standard pickup beds.
Widths: 6′– 4″, 7′– 6″.

REQUIREMENTS FOR MOBILE HOME PARKS

LENGTH OF CAR AND TRAILER

Maximum permissible length of motor vehicle and trailer together varies from 50′ to 65′, according to the various state statutes.

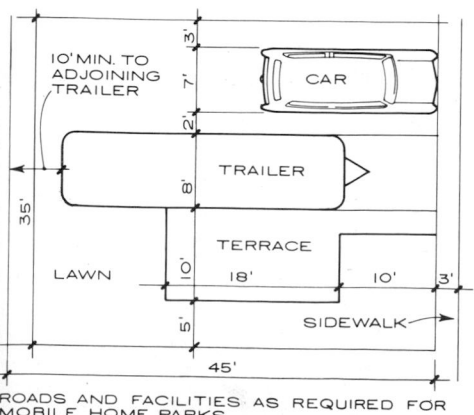

ROADS AND FACILITIES AS REQUIRED FOR MOBILE HOME PARKS

TOURING TRAILER PARK LOT

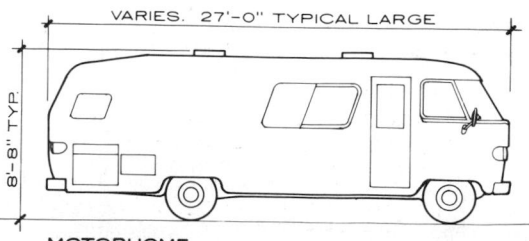

MOTORHOME
Sizes and designs vary. Typical width 8′– 0″ clear.

CAMPERS

Foster C. Parriott; James M. Hunter & Associates; Boulder, Colorado

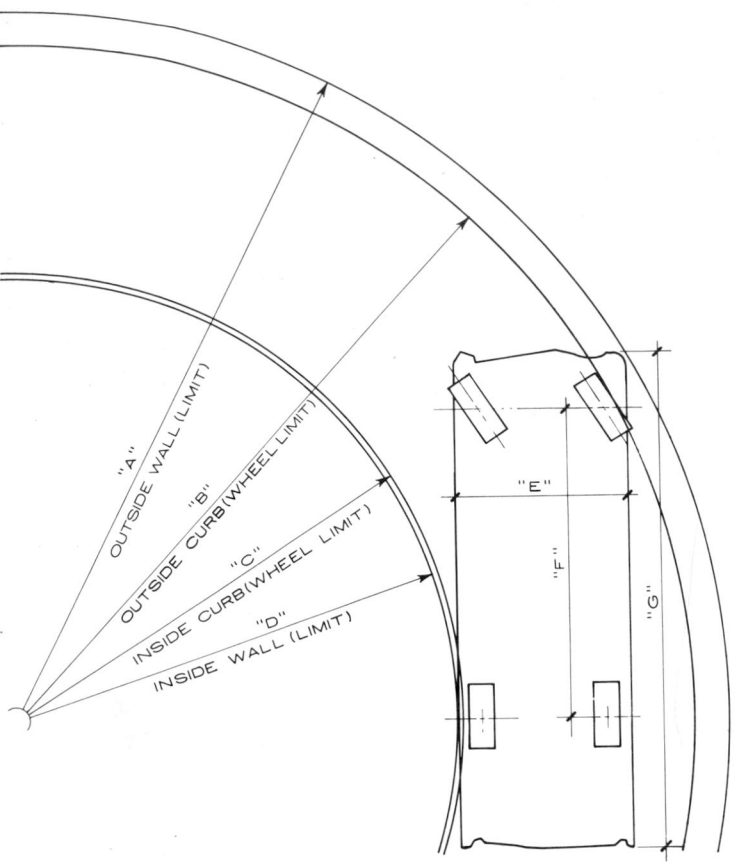

AMBULANCES AND HEARSES
DIMENSIONS & TURNING RADII

MAKE OF CAR	"A"	"B"	"C"	"D"	"E"	"F"	"G"
Cadillac	30'–0''	28'–6''	18'–11 1/2''	18'–9''	6'–11''	13'–0''	20'–10 1/4''
Dodge	23'–4''	21'–9''	13'–4 1/2''	12'–10 3/4''	6'–8''		18'–4''

AIRPORT LIMOUSINE

Checker	28'–3''				6'–4''	15'–9''	22'–5 3/4''

Racing handlebars narrower and underslung.

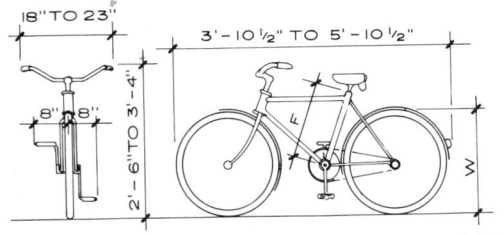

FRAME SIZE "W"	FRAME SIZE "F"
16''	12''
20''	13''
24''	16'' boys 15'' girls
26''	18'', 19'', 21'', 23''
27''	19'', 21'', 23''

CHILDREN'S, STANDARD, TOURIST, RACING BICYCLES

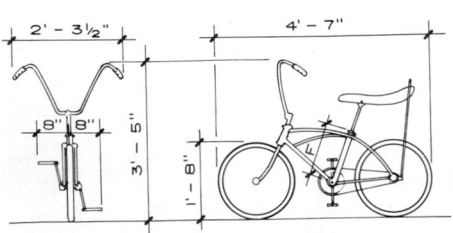

YOUTH'S SPORT W/"HIGHRISE" HANDLEBARS
FRAME SIZE (F) 13 1/2'', 14 1/2''

BICYCLE SIZES

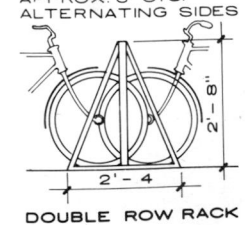

UPRIGHTS & BICYCLES APPROX. 6'' O.C. ALTERNATING SIDES

DOUBLE ROW RACK   **SINGLE ROW RACK**

BICYCLE RACK

GOLF CARTS GASOLINE OR ELECTRIC POWER

3 WHEELS		4 WHEELS
46 3/4''	Overall Height	47 1/8''
10 3/4''	Floorboard Height	11 1/4''
27 3/4''	Seat Height	28 1/4''
102''	Length	102''
47''	Width	47''
68''	Wheel Base	68 3/4''
—	Front Wheel Tread	34''
34 5/8''	Rear Wheel Tread	34 5/8''
4 5/8''	Ground Clearance	4 5/8''
19'–6''	Clearance Circle	24'–0''

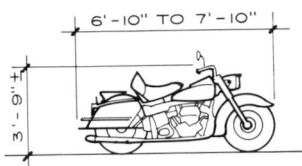

WIDTH AT HANDLEBAR 2'–7'' TO 3'–3''

When parked on stand motorcycle leans about 10°. Large vehicle requires about 3'–8'' of space.

HEAVYWEIGHTS WEIGH FROM ABOUT 400 LBS. TO 661 LBS.

HEAVYWEIGHT MOTORCYCLES

Consult manufacturers information for width of motorcycle and sidecar.

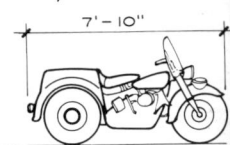

POLICE TRICYCLE
WIDTH AT BOX 4'–0''±

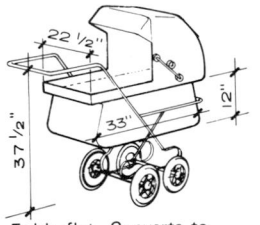

Folds flat. Converts to stroller. Body makes car bed;
BABY CARRIAGE

Handlebar width 23'' and up.
Weight about 230 lbs. to about 300 lbs.

LIGHTWEIGHT MOTORCYCLE

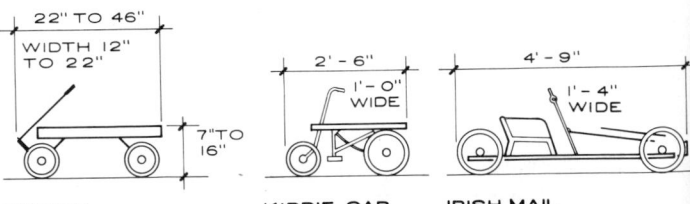

WAGON   **KIDDIE CAR**   **IRISH MAIL**

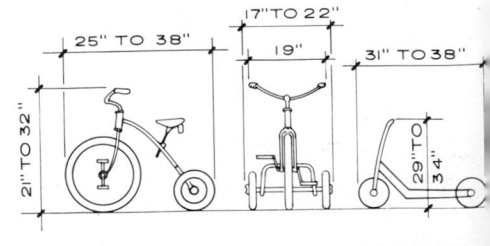

TRICYCLE   **SCOOTER**

Foster C. Parriott; James M. Hunter & Associates; Boulder, Colorado

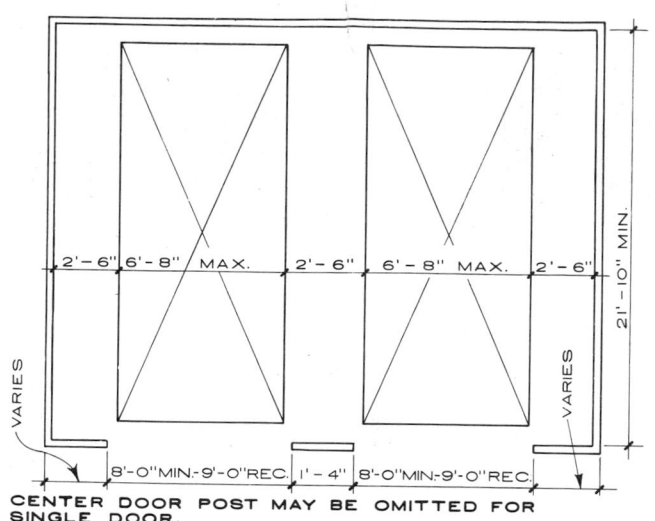

CENTER DOOR POST MAY BE OMITTED FOR SINGLE DOOR.
TWO CAR GARAGE

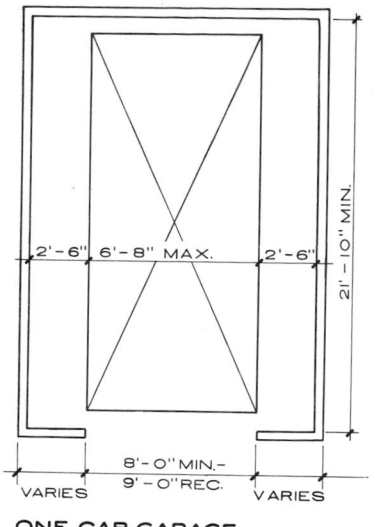

ONE CAR GARAGE

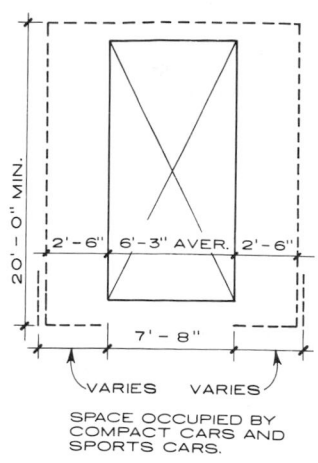

SPACE OCCUPIED BY COMPACT CARS AND SPORTS CARS.

NOTE: Garages may be enlarged to provide for work areas, photo labs, laundry rooms etc.

JAMB CLEARANCE – WIDTH OF DR.
SINGLE DOOR

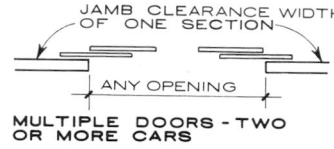

MULTIPLE DOORS – TWO OR MORE CARS

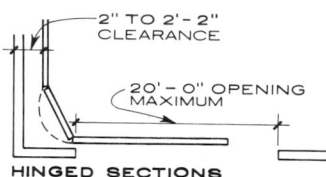

HINGED SECTIONS

NOTE:
6 1/2″ to 9″ necessary from top of opening to ceiling (all sliding doors).
SLIDING DOORS

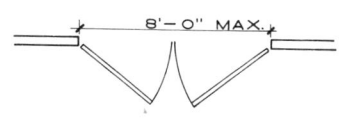

DOUBLE OR TRIPLE HINGED

MULTIPLE HINGED DOOR FOR TWO OR MORE CARS

OFFSET HINGE – MULTI-LEAVE

NOTE: For multiple and offset hinged doors, swinging to one or both sides, hinged in or out and used for 2 or more cars: 6 1/2″ to 11″ necessary from top of opening to ceiling.
HINGED DOORS

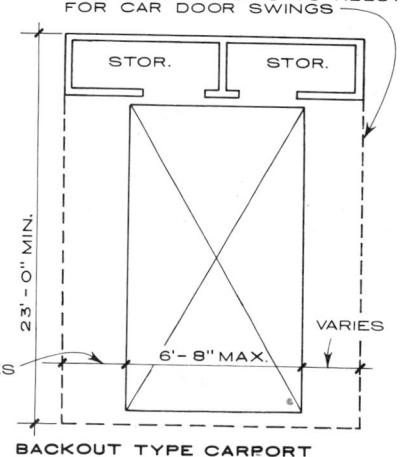

LOCATE SUPPORTS TO ALLOW FOR CAR DOOR SWINGS

BACKOUT TYPE CARPORT

WIDTHS OF COMMONLY USED HINGED DOORS

A. 8′-0″ opening 2 door—4′-0″, 3 door—2′-8″, 4 door—2′-0″
B. 8′-6″ opening 2 door—4′-3″, 3 door—2′-10″, 4 door—2′-1 1/2″
C. 9′-0″ opening 2 door—4′-6″, 3 door—3′-0″, 4 door—2′-3″

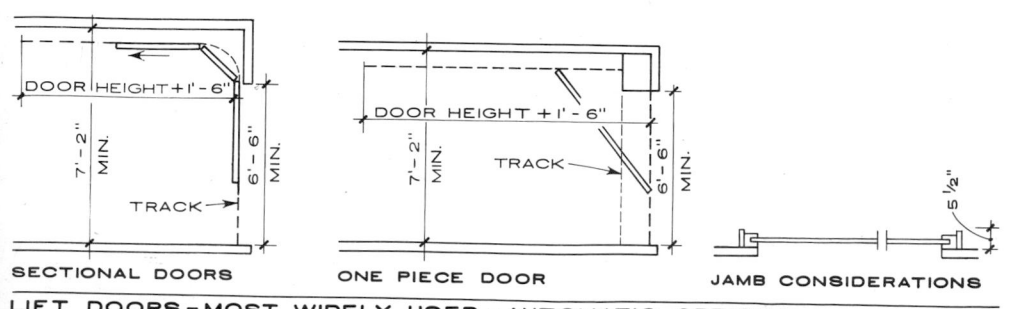

SECTIONAL DOORS   **ONE PIECE DOOR**   **JAMB CONSIDERATIONS**
LIFT DOORS – MOST WIDELY USED – AUTOMATIC OPTIONAL

NOTE:

Heights: 6′-6″, 6′-10″, 7′-0″, 7′-6″ and 8′-0″.
Lift doors generally 4′-0″ sections high, sometimes 2′-0″ or 3′-0″

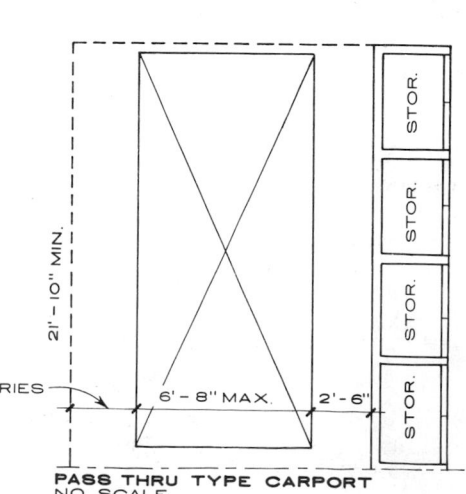

PASS THRU TYPE CARPORT
NO SCALE

R. E. Powe, Jr.; Hugh N. Jacobsen, AIA; Washington, D. C.

GENERAL NOTES:

Types and sizes shown are for easy driving at moderate rate.
See page on car sizes for turning radii of cars. "R" = This radius.
Overall sizes are shown in terms of radii for preliminary assumptions.
Any decrease in radii will decrease speed of driving.

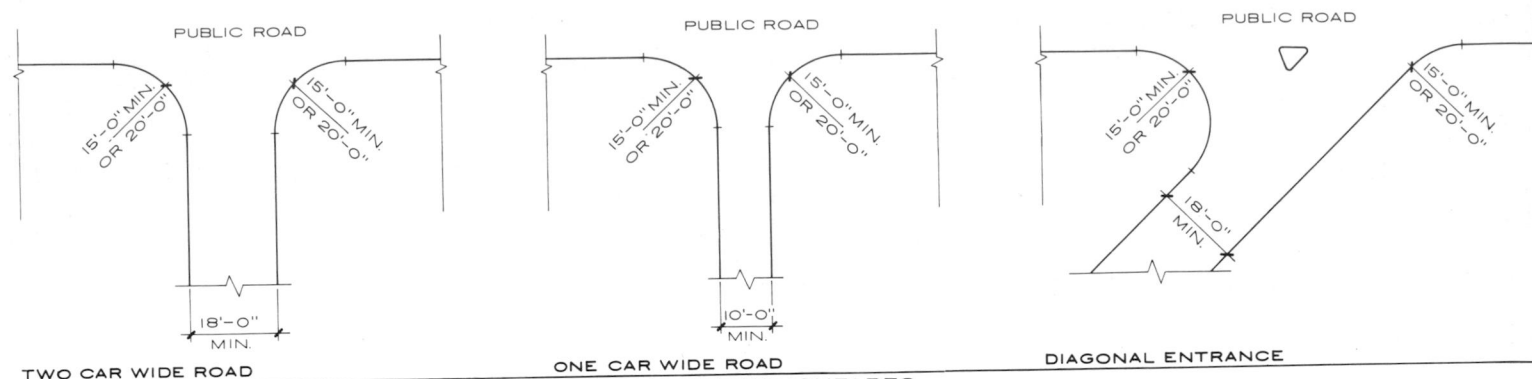

PUBLIC ROAD   PUBLIC ROAD   PUBLIC ROAD

15'-0" MIN. OR 20'-0"   15'-0" MIN. OR 20'-0"   15'-0" MIN. OR 20'-0"   15'-0" MIN. OR 20'-0"   15'-0" MIN. OR 20'-0"   15'-0" MIN OR 20'-0"

18'-0" MIN.

18'-0" MIN.   10'-0" MIN.

TWO CAR WIDE ROAD   **ONE CAR WIDE ROAD**   **DIAGONAL ENTRANCE**

PRIVATE ENTRANCE ROADS INTERSECTING PUBLIC THOROUGHFARES
SCALE: 1" = 40'-0"

Construction point locations are found by intersecting solid arrows; dotted arrows are radii from these points for curves.

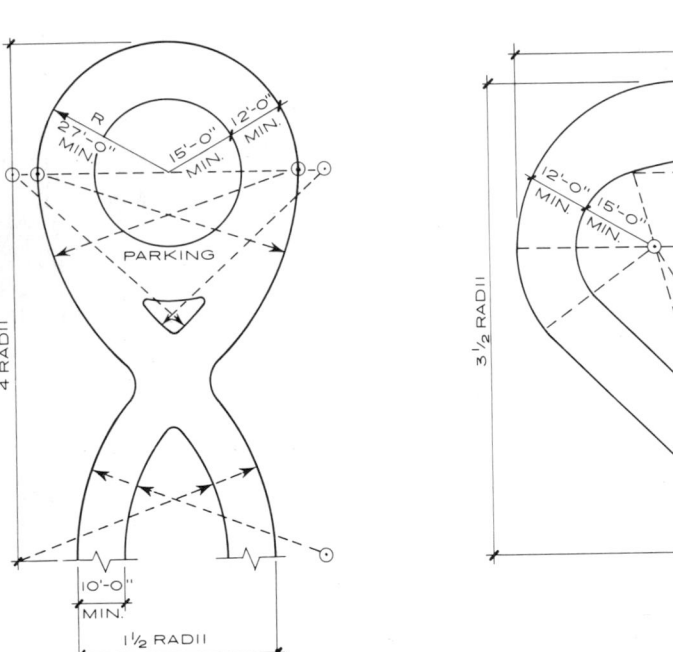

NO LANDING–CROSSOVER
LANDING MAY BE HAD BY BACKING ONLY

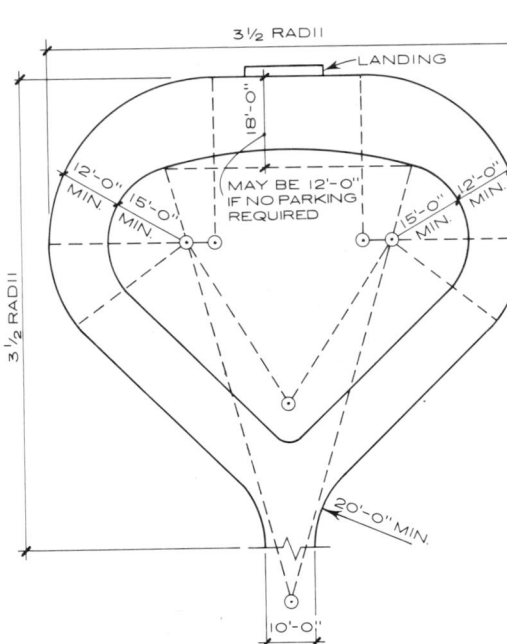

LANDING OPPOSITE APPROACH

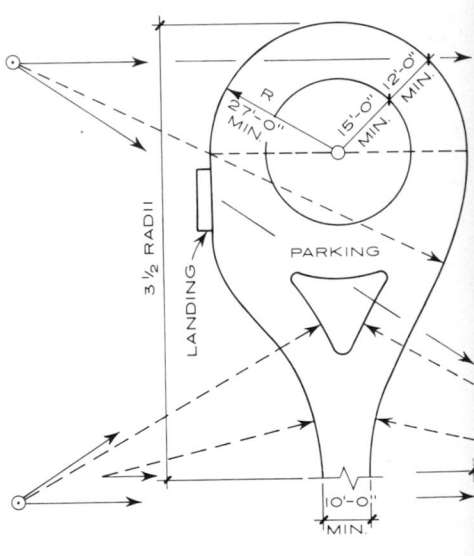

LANDING ON SIDE
LANDING AT THE END BY BACKING ONLY

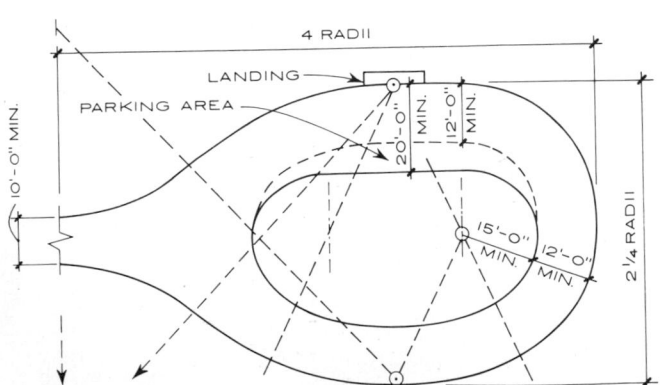

LANDING ON ONE SIDE OF APPROACH
TURNAROUNDS–ONE CAR WIDTH–DOUBLE ROAD WIDTH FOR TWO CARS

LANDING ON LINE OF APPROACH

PRIVATE ROADS, DRIVES & TURNAROUNDS
SCALE: 1" = 40'-0"

GENERAL NOTES:

All turns require 1'– 6'' clearance beyond road line shown.

These turns are for easy driving with average size car.

Larger radii will permit faster and easier driving.

Smaller radii should be used for small cars only.

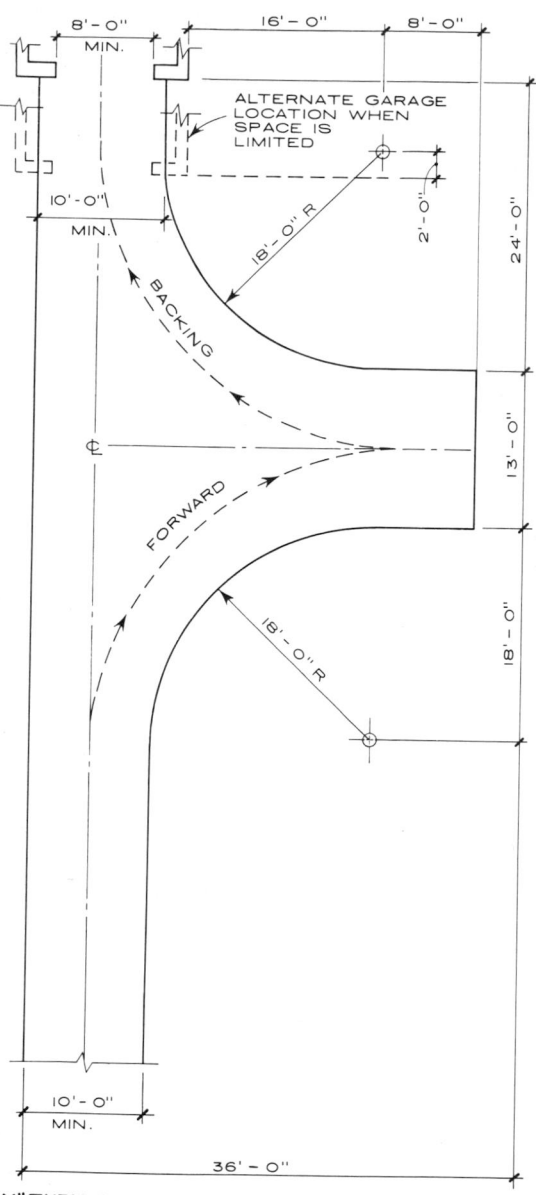

"Y" TURN FOR BACKING IN
SCALE: 1/16" = 1'– 0"

Dotted line shows route going in.

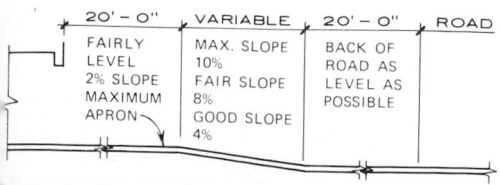

RECOMMENDED SLOPES GARAGE TO ROAD
SCALE: 1/32" = 1'– 0"

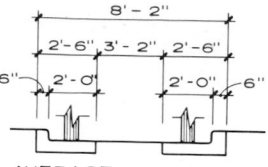

AVERAGE

Do not use curbs on narrower runways as trucks often have 5'– 10'' to 6'– 0'' wheel gauge.

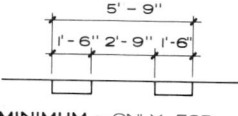

MINIMUM - ONLY FOR WOLKSWAGENS, ETC.

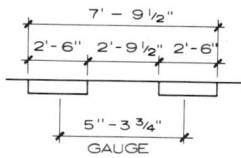

MAXIMUM

CONCRETE RUNWAYS TO GARAGES

SCALE: 1/8" = 1'– 0"

Widen for all turns.

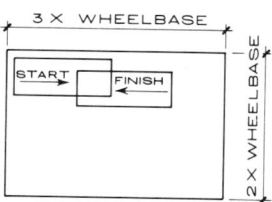

MINIMUM TURNING SPACE BACKING THREE TIMES

Used only when req'd by space limitations.
Wheelbase:
Minimum 7'– 10 1/2'' (Volkswagens, etc.)
Maximum 11'– 1''
Normally under 10'– 6''

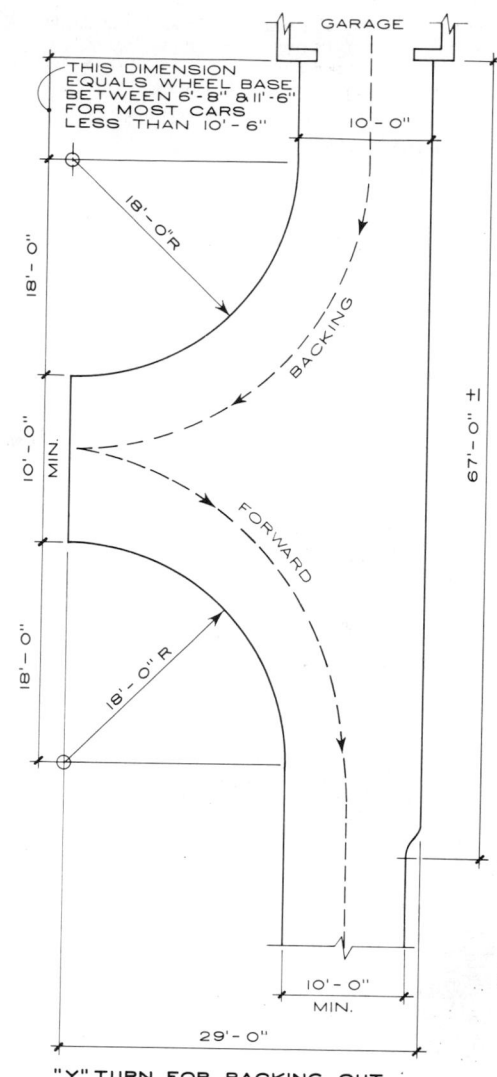

"Y" TURN FOR BACKING OUT
SCALE: 1/16" = 1'– 0"

Dotted line shows route going out.

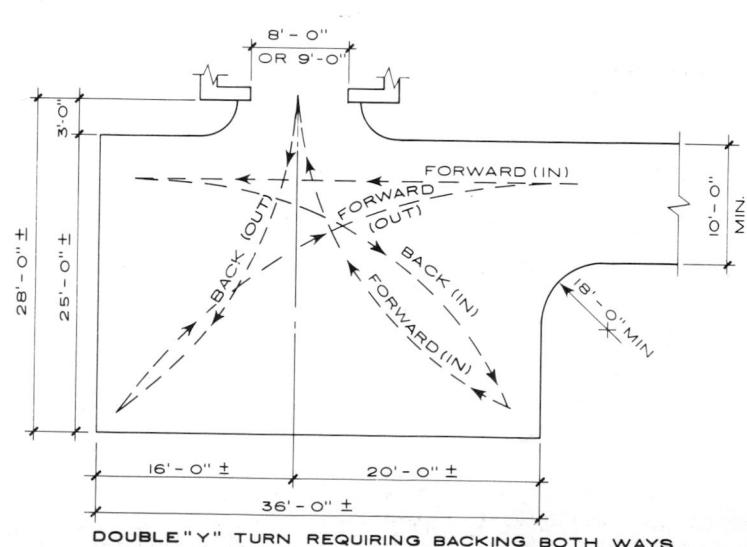

DOUBLE "Y" TURN REQUIRING BACKING BOTH WAYS
SCALE: 1/16" = 1'– 0"

Exact size depends on car. This is for average car.
Employed only where space limitations demand its use.

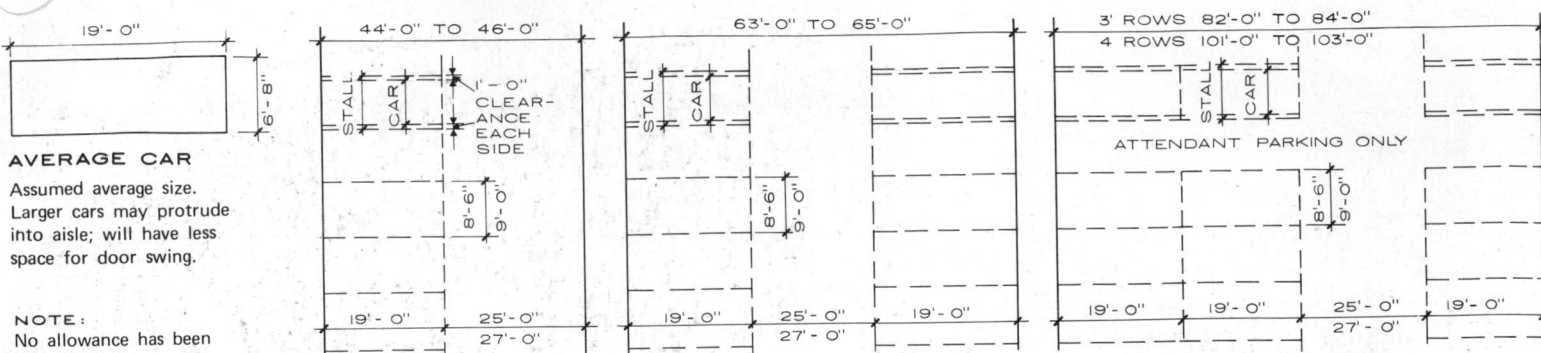

ONE ROW

TWO ROWS

THREE AND FOUR ROWS

ATTENDANT PARKING ONLY

AVERAGE CAR

Assumed average size.
Larger cars may protrude
into aisle; will have less
space for door swing.

NOTE:
No allowance has been
made for columns on
this page. Allow 1'-0" ±

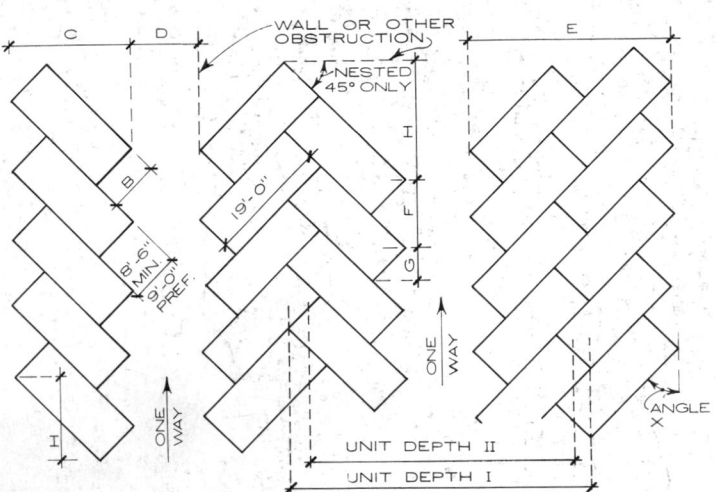

STALL AND AISLE DIAGRAM

WALL OR OTHER OBSTRUCTION

NESTED 45° ONLY

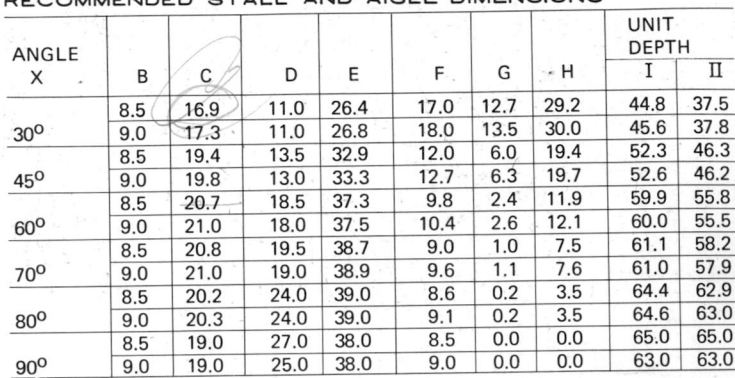

RECOMMENDED STALL AND AISLE DIMENSIONS

ANGLE X	B	C	D	E	F	G	H	UNIT DEPTH I	II
	8.5	16.9	11.0	26.4	17.0	12.7	29.2	44.8	37.5
30°	9.0	17.3	11.0	26.8	18.0	13.5	30.0	45.6	37.8
	8.5	19.4	13.5	32.9	12.0	6.0	19.4	52.3	46.3
45°	9.0	19.8	13.0	33.3	12.7	6.3	19.7	52.6	46.2
	8.5	20.7	18.5	37.3	9.8	2.4	11.9	59.9	55.8
60°	9.0	21.0	18.0	37.5	10.4	2.6	12.1	60.0	55.5
	8.5	20.8	19.5	38.7	9.0	1.0	7.5	61.1	58.2
70°	9.0	21.0	19.0	38.9	9.6	1.1	7.6	61.0	57.9
	8.5	20.2	24.0	39.0	8.6	0.2	3.5	64.4	62.9
80°	9.0	20.3	24.0	39.0	9.1	0.2	3.5	64.6	63.0
	8.5	19.0	27.0	38.0	8.5	0.0	0.0	65.0	65.0
90°	9.0	19.0	25.0	38.0	9.0	0.0	0.0	63.0	63.0

NOTE: Even number of spaces, "N" in length of curb,

$$"L" = N = \frac{L - H + C}{F} \quad \text{Stall length} = 19'-0"$$

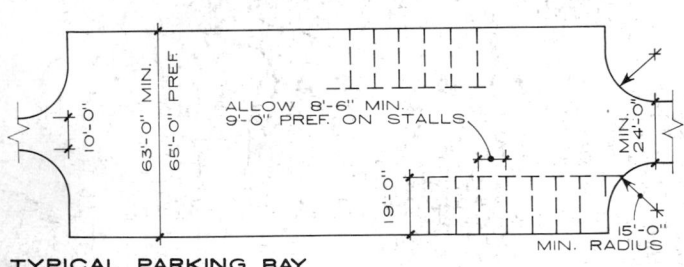

TYPICAL PARKING BAY
90° PARKING EACH SIDE

ALLOW 8'-6" MIN.
9'-0" PREF. ON STALLS

MIN. RADIUS

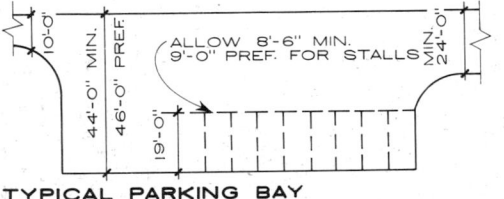

TYPICAL PARKING BAY
90° PARKING ONE SIDE

ALLOW 8'-6" MIN. 9'-0" PREF. FOR STALLS

NOTE: Provide extra width for walks along side
parking bay to compensate for bumper overhang.

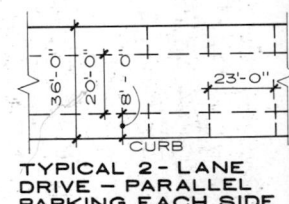

TYPICAL 2-LANE
DRIVE – PARALLEL
PARKING EACH SIDE

CURB

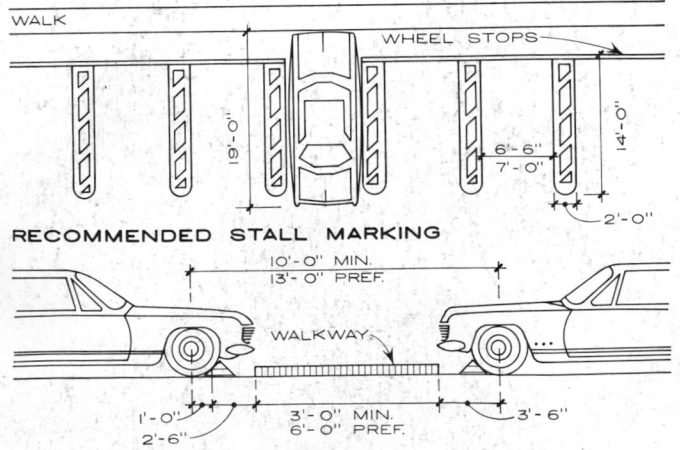

WALK   WHEEL STOPS

RECOMMENDED STALL MARKING

WALKWAY

PEDESTRIAN WALKWAY

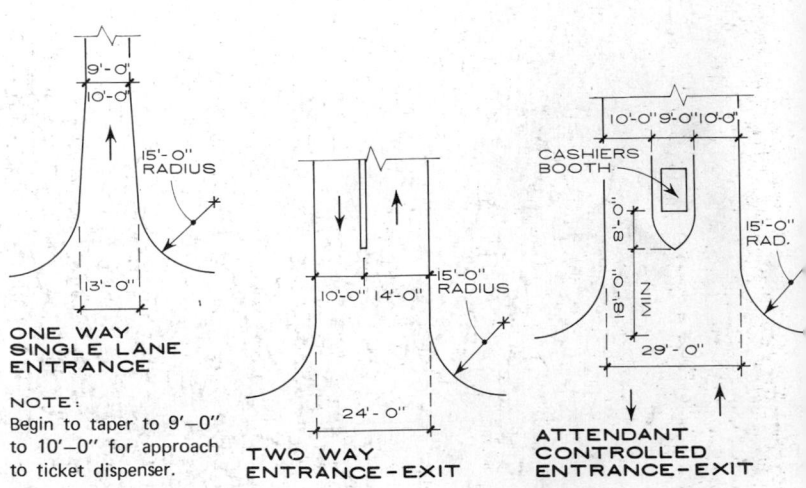

ONE WAY
SINGLE LANE
ENTRANCE

15'-0" RADIUS

NOTE:
Begin to taper to 9'-0"
to 10'-0" for approach
to ticket dispenser.

TWO WAY
ENTRANCE – EXIT

15'-0" RADIUS

CASHIERS BOOTH

15'-0" RAD.

ATTENDANT
CONTROLLED
ENTRANCE – EXIT

Lyles, Bissett, Carlisle & Wolff; Columbia, South Carolina
Wilbur Smith and Associates; Washington, D. C.

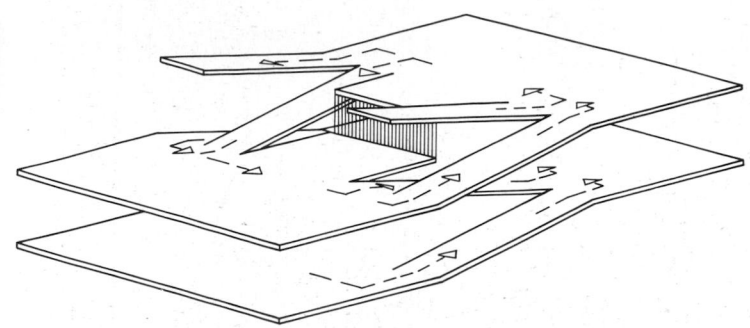

STAGGERED FLOORS-ONE-WAY CIRCULATION

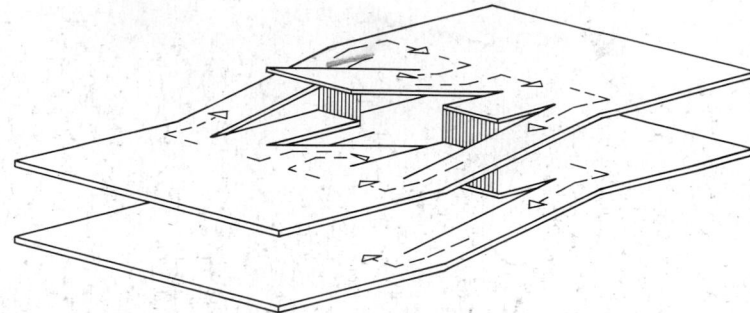

STAGGERED FLOORS-TWO-WAY CENTER RAMP

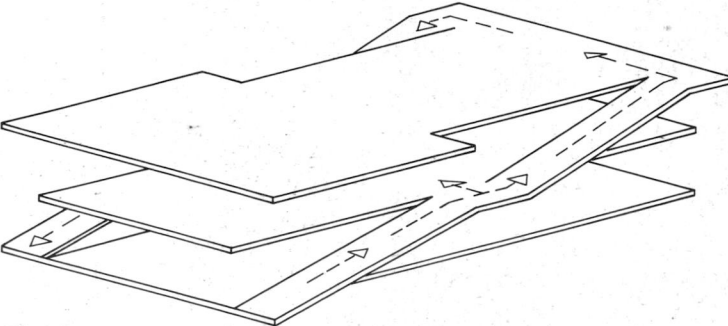

FLAT FLOORS-STRAIGHT, ONE-WAY RAMPS

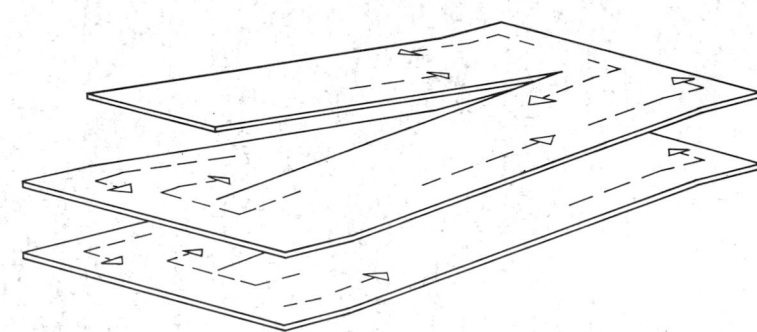

SLOPING FLOORS - TWO-WAY CIRCULATION

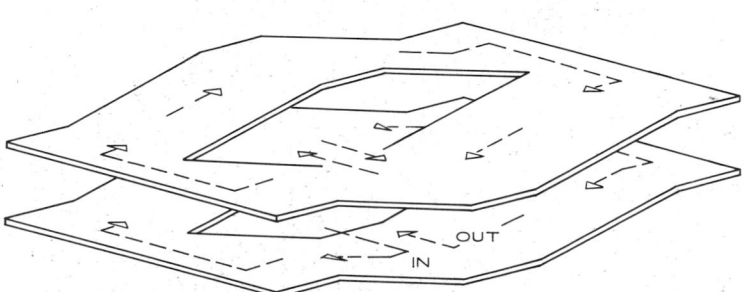

SLOPING FLOORS - ONE WAY CIRCULATION

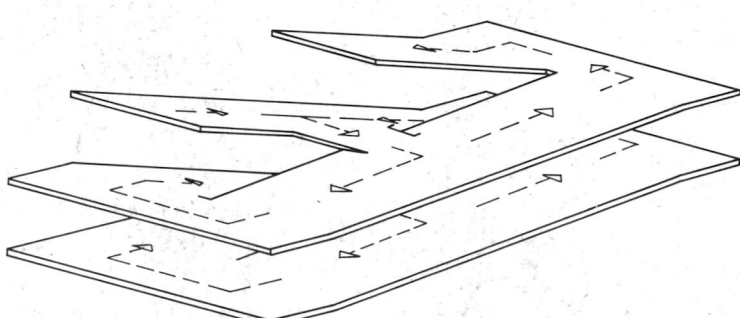

SLOPING FLOORS-CROSS CONNECTED ONE-WAY CIRCULATION

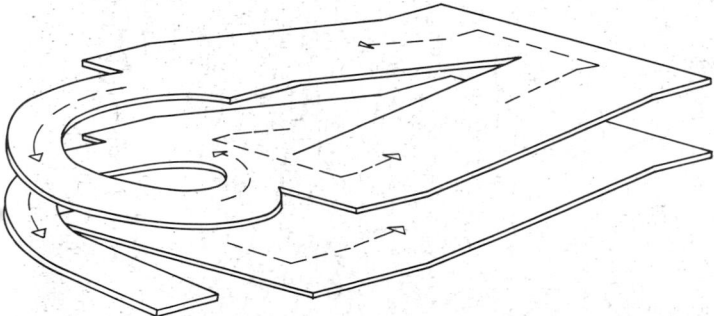

SLOPING FLOOR WITH EXPRESS HELICAL DOWN-RAMP

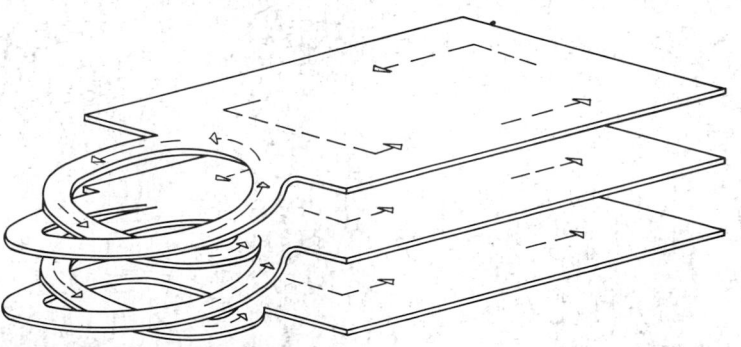

CONCENTRIC OPPOSED PLANE HELICAL RAMPS

TWO INTERTWINED HELICAL DOWN RAMPS SPIRALING IN THE SAME DIRECTION

Lyles, Bissett, Carlisle & Wolff; Columbia, South Carolina
Wilbur Smith and Associates; Washington, D. C.

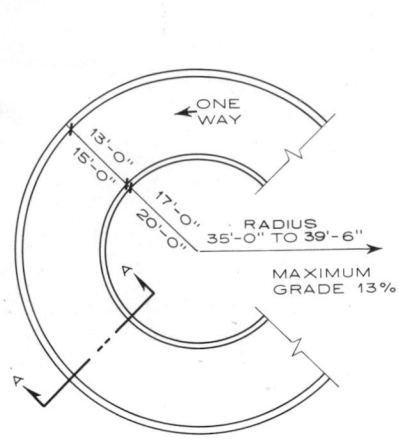

ONE WAY DOWN RAMP

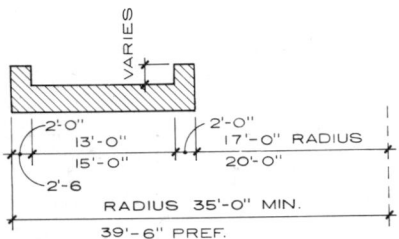

SECTION A-A

NOTE:

RAMP GRADE:

15—17% maximum on short ramps—staggered floor garage.

10—13% straight or helical ramps—used purely for travel—7 — 8% preferred

3—5% ramps in sloping floor garages, 3% preferred

RAMPS

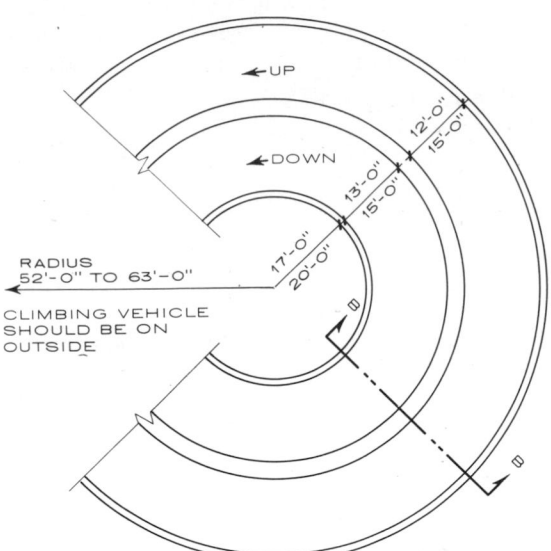

OPPOSITE CIRCULAR RAMPS

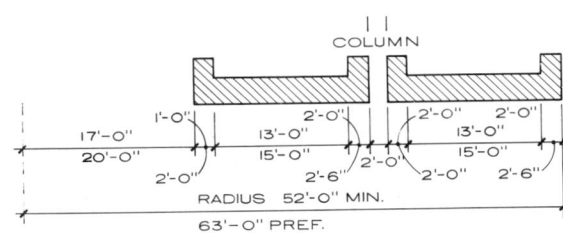

SECTION B-B

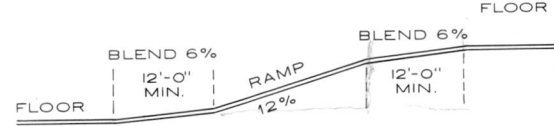

NOTE: Change in grade should be equal to 1/2 ramp grade.

RAMP GRADES

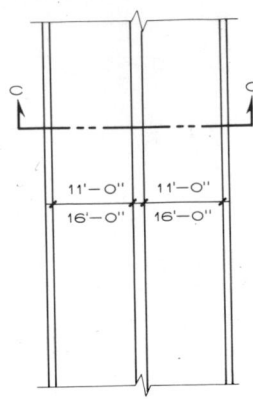

NOTE:

11'—0" width for straight approach
16'—0" width for sharp turn approach

STRAIGHT RAMP

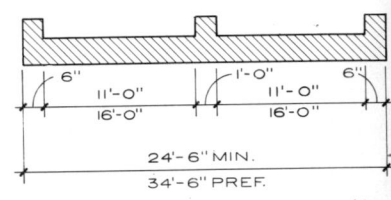

SECTION C-C

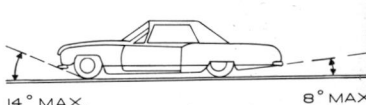

14° MAX.   8° MAX.

ANGLE OF APPROACH   ANGLE OF DEPARTURE

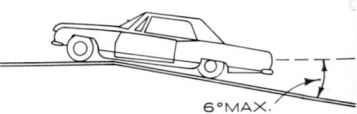

6° MAX.

BREAKOVER ANGLE

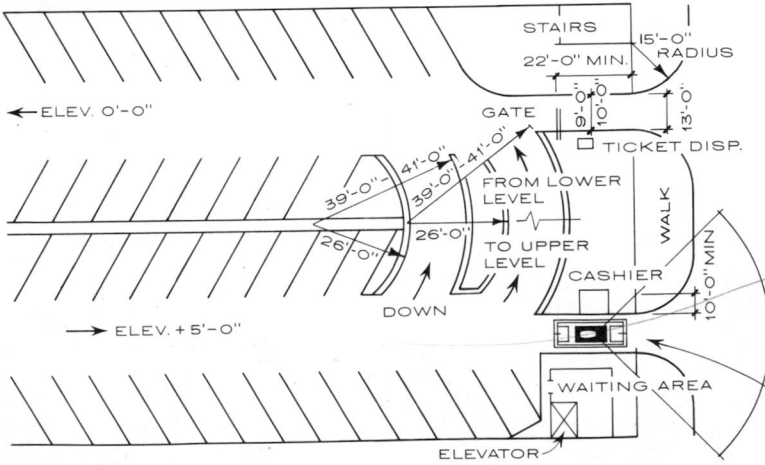

NOTES:

Design Features:
Floor to floor height = 10' — 0".
Floor to clear height: 7' — 0" min.
Area per car space = 350 to 400 sq. ft.
Column spacing:

A. of 30 ft., establishes 73° angle parking, 8' — 11" x 19' — 0" stalls, 21' — 0" aisles.

B. of 31' — 0" x 28' — 0", establishes 90° angle of parking, 9' — 0" x 19' — 0" stalls, 22' — 0" aisles.

C. equal to unit depth (clear span construction). Is highly desirable, as the flexible design allows for future changes in auto dimensions.

MOTORIST-PEDESTRIAN CONE OF VISION SHOULD BE UNOBSTRUCTED

NOTES:

As a general rule allow at least:

1 outbound lane for every 200 spaces
1 inbound lane for every 300 to 500 spaces
2 exits to every garage
1 elevator up to 250 spaces
2 elevators up to 500 spaces
3 — 4 elevators up to 1000 spaces

Establish down-ramp on inside; up-ramp outside.
Establish counter-clockwise circulation whenever possible.
Locate elevators, customer waiting area, and exits as close to customer's destination as possible.
Establish all elevators, stairs, and door openings away from traffic lanes.

INTERIOR GARAGE DESIGN FEATURES

Lyles, Bissett, Carlisle & Wolff; Columbia, South Carolina
Wilbur Smith and Associates; Washington, D. C.

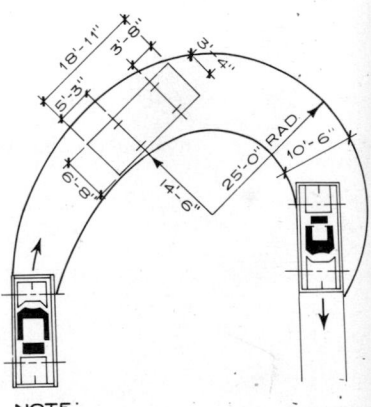

NOTE:

Turning radii and vehicle dimensions for large '69 passenger car for checking garage and lot dimensions.

VEHICLE TURNING RADII

STORAGE FOR SAILBOAT EQUIPMENT
Mast, spars, sheets, sails, halyards, etc. should be stored in a heated space.

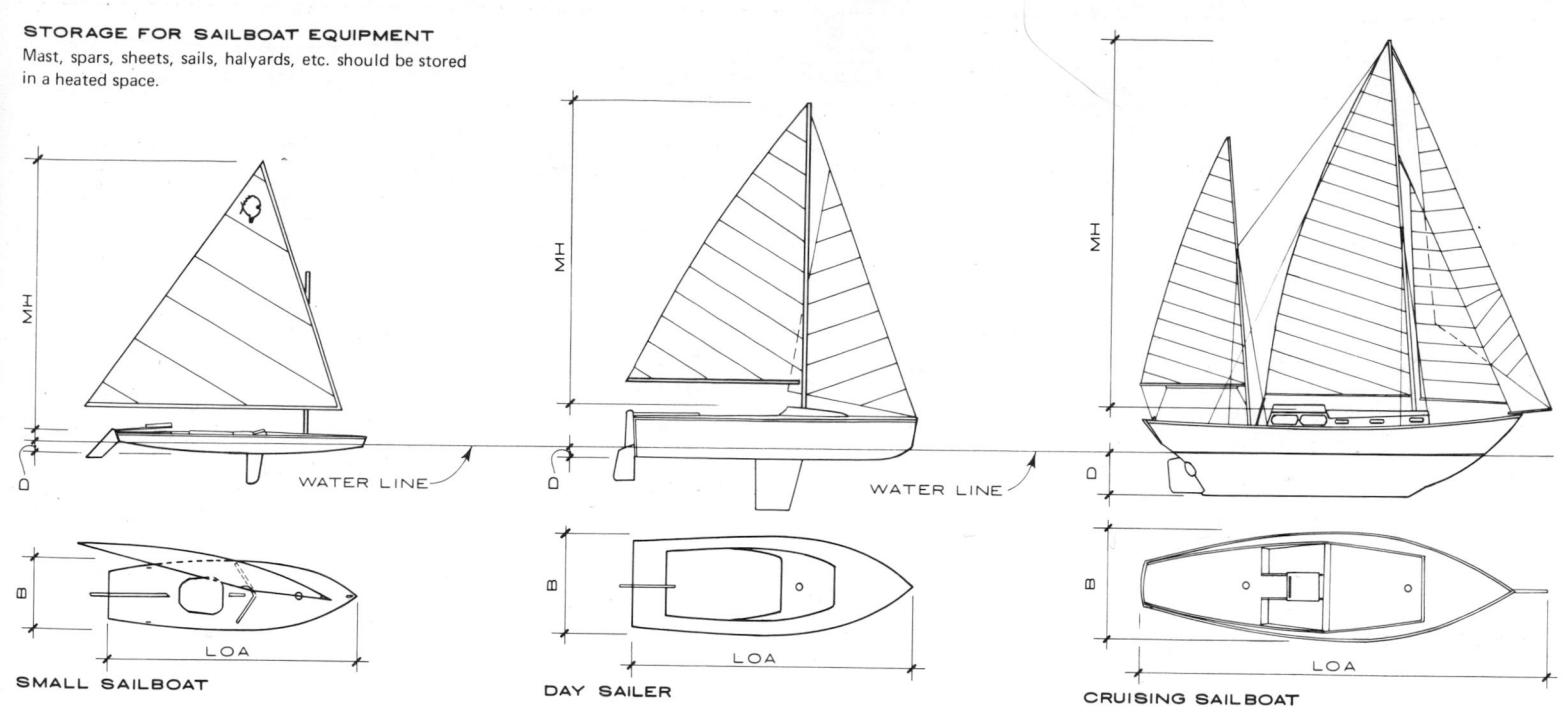

SMALL SAILBOAT   DAY SAILER   CRUISING SAILBOAT

TYPES AND SIZES OF TYPICAL SAILBOATS

LOA=LENGTH OVERALL, B=BEAM, MH=MAST HEIGHT, D=DRAFT.

CLASSIFICATION AND NAME		LENGTH OVERALL	BEAM	MAST HEIGHT	DRAFT	WEIGHT (LBS.)
SMALL SAILBOAT	SEVEN ELEVEN	7'−11''	4'−2''	13'−0''	0'−4''	89
	ROOSTER	9'−7''	3'−10''	8'−0''	0'−5''	100
	SPRITE	10'−2''	4'−9''	15'−10''	0'−3''	150
	SUNFISH	13'−9''	4'−0''	9'−1 1/2''	0'−4''	139
DAY SAILER	WINDMILL	15'−6''	4'−8''	17'−10''	0'−6''	198
	HIGHLANDER	20'−0''	6'−8''	27'−0''	0'−8''	830
	Y-FLYER	18'−2''	5'−9''	23'−0''	0'−6''	500
	LIGHTNING	19'−0''	6'−6''	26'−0''	0'−6''	700
CRUISING SAILBOAT	FIREBIRD	19'−5''	6'−7''	23'−8''	1'−4''	1,060
	CAL 25	25'−0''	8'−0''	29'−9''	4'−0''	4,000
	PRIVATEER	31'−3''	8'−0''	31'−6''	3'−6''	6,340
	ISLANDER 55	54'−8''	14'−0''	53'−0''	5'−9''	38,000

TABLE OF DIMENSIONS FOR SLIPS AND CATWALKS TO BE USED WITH DIAGRAM I

LENGTH GROUP FOR BOAT	BEAM TO BE PROVIDED FOR	MIN. CLEAR WIDTH OF SLIP	GROSS SLIP WIDTH TYPE "A"	GROSS SLIP WIDTH TYPE "B"	GROSS SLIP WIDTH TYPE "C"	1ST CATWALK SPAN LENGTH "D"	2ND CATWALK SPAN LENGTH "E"	3RD CATWALK SPAN LENGTH "F"	DISTANCE "G" TO ANCHOR PILE
Up to 14'	6'−7''	8'−10''	10'−9''	10'−6''	11'−2''	12'−0''			17'−0''
Over 14' to 16'	7'−4''	9'−8''	11'−7''	11'−4''	12'−0''	12'−0''			19'−0''
Over 16' to 18'	8'−0''	10'−5''	12'−4''	12'−1''	12'−9''	14'−0''			21'−0''
Over 18' to 20'	8'−7''	11'−1''	13'−0''	12'−9''	13'−5''	8'−0''	8'−0''		23'−0''
Over 20' to 22'	9'−3''	11'−9''	13'−8''	13'−5''	14'−1''	10'−0''	8'−0''		25'−0''
Over 22' to 25'	10'−3''	13'−1''	15'−0''	14'−9''	15'−5''	10'−0''	8'−0''		28'−0''
Over 25' to 30'	11'−3''	14'−3''	16'−2''	15'−11''	16'−7''	10'−0''	10'−0''		33'−0''
Over 30' to 35'	12'−3''	15'−8''	17'−7''	17'−4''	18'−0''	12'−0''	10'−0''		38'−0''
Over 35' to 40'	13'−3''	16'−11''	18'−10''	18'−7''	19'−3''	12'−0''	12'−0''		43'−0''
Over 40' to 45'	14'−1''	17'−11''	19'−10''	19'−7''	20'−3''	14'−0''	12'−0''		48'−0''
Over 45' to 50'	14'−11''	19'−0''	20'−11''	20'−8''	21'−4''	9'−0''	9'−0''	10'−0''	53'−0''
Over 50' to 60'	16'−6''	21'−0''	22'−11''	22'−8''	23'−4''	11'−0''	11'−0''	12'−0''	63'−0''
Over 60' to 70'	18'−1''	23'−0''	26'−8''	24'−8''	25'−4''	11'−0''	11'−0''	12'−0''	73'−0''
Over 70' to 80'	19'−9''	24'−11''	28'−7''	26'−7''	26'−3''	11'−0''	11'−0''	12'−0''	83'−0''

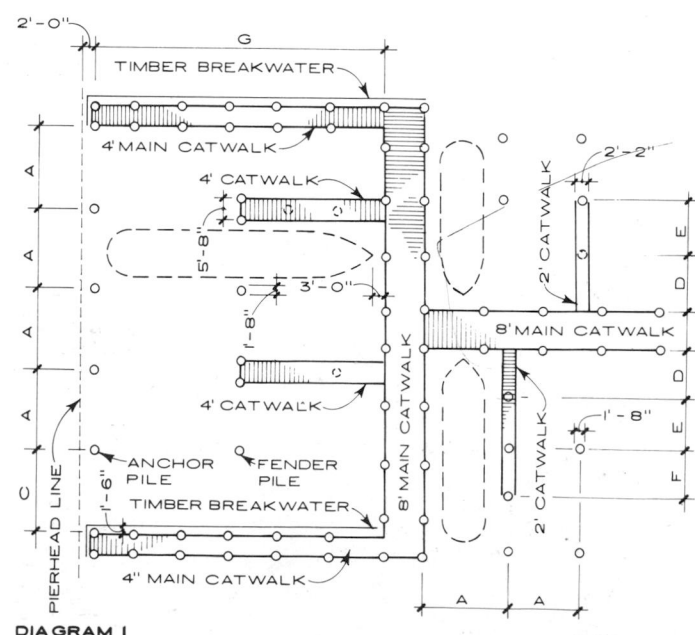

DIAGRAM I

Fred Sahli & George Simms; Neil R. Greene, AIA; Silver Spring, Maryland
William H. Ostermayer; The Ballinger Company; Philadelphia, Pennsylvania

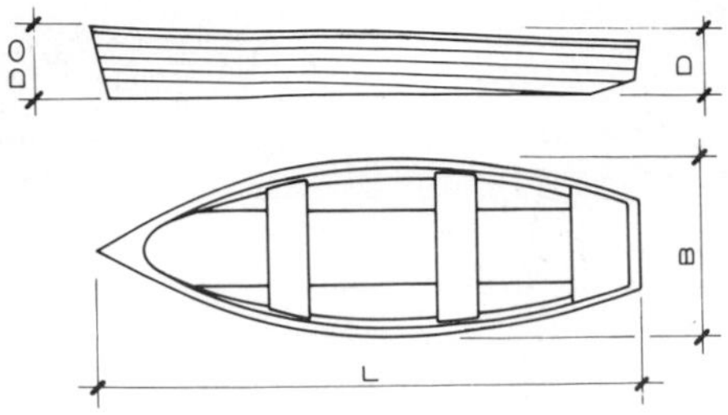

DO
D
B
L

ROW BOATS

DO
D
B
L

DINGY OR TENDER

DO
D
B
L

DORIES

WASHBOX OR GUNRAIL 4"H
D
30" OR 32" OUTRIGGER
B
L

RACING SHELL OR GIG RACING

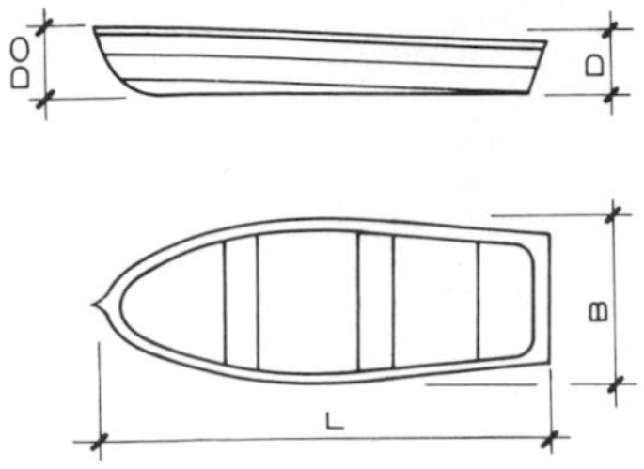

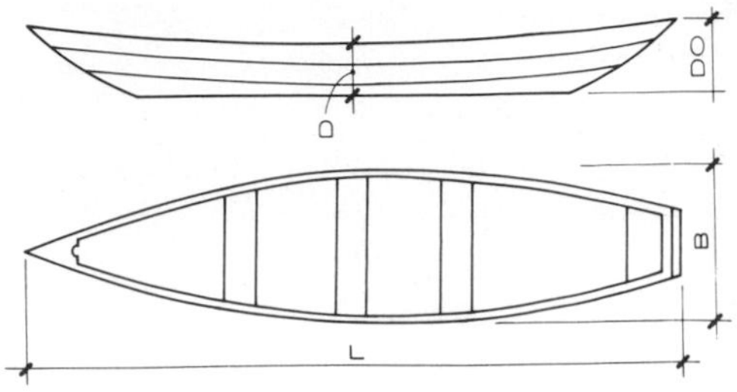

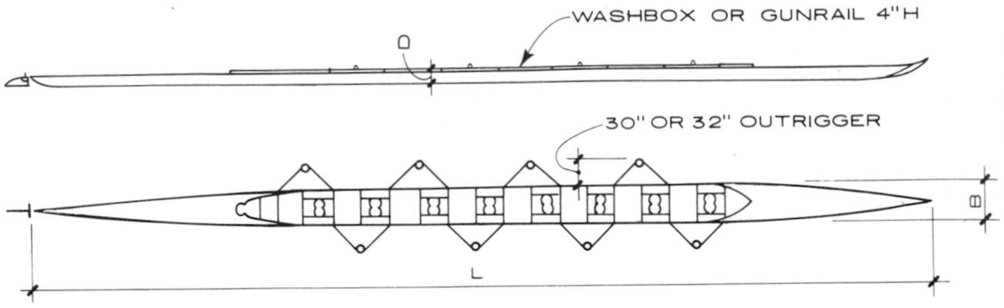

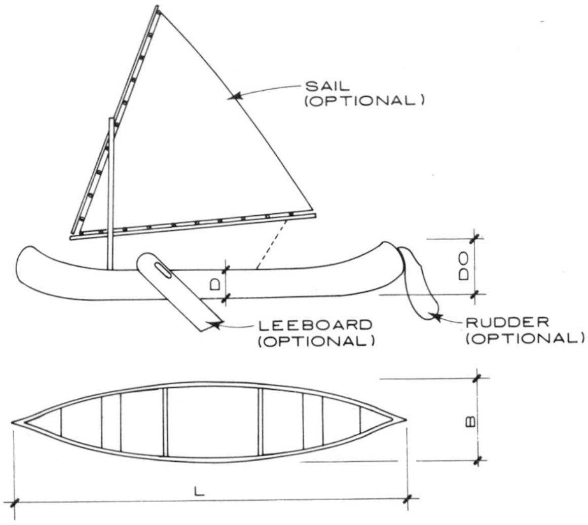

SAIL (OPTIONAL)
DO
D
LEEBOARD (OPTIONAL)
RUDDER (OPTIONAL)
B
L

CANOES

NOTE :

In many cases all boats shown above, except racing shells and gigs, may be fitted with sails.

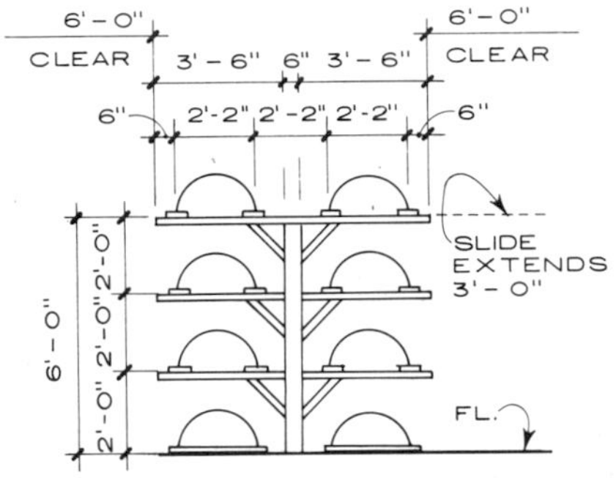

6'-0" CLEAR
3'-6"
6"
3'-6"
6'-0" CLEAR
6"
2'-2"
2'-2"
2'-2"
6"
SLIDE EXTENDS 3'-0"
6'-0"
2'-0"
2'-0"
2'-0"
2'-0"
FL.

RACKS

RACK SPACING

Single and double	–	2 racks 8'–0" apart
Four-Oared	–	3 racks 8'–0" apart
Eight-Oared	–	3 racks 18'–0" apart
		or
		4 racks 12'–0" apart

Racks are 6'–0" high for daily use, higher for long term storage.

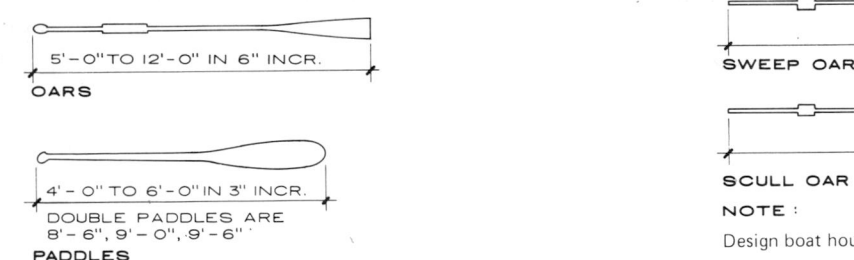

5'-0" TO 12'-0" IN 6" INCR.

OARS

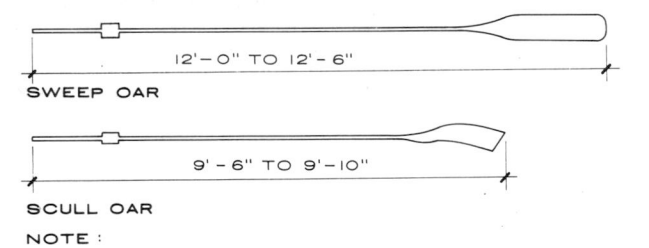

4'-0" TO 6'-0" IN 3" INCR.

DOUBLE PADDLES ARE 8'-6", 9'-0", 9'-6"

PADDLES

12'-0" TO 12'-6"

SWEEP OAR

9'-6" TO 9'-10"

SCULL OAR

NOTE :

Design boat house with ceiling height to allow receiving oars on end.

TYPES & SIZES OF TYPICAL SMALL BOATS

LOA = LENGTH OVERALL   B = BEAM   D = DEPTH   DO = DEPTH OVERALL

	CLASSIFICATION & TYPE	LENGTH OVERALL	BEAM	DEPTH	DEPTH OVERALL	WEIGHT (LBS.)
	ROW BOATS (MANY TYPES AND DESIGNS)	6'–5" to 18'–0"	3'–11" to 5'–5"	1'–2" to 1'–8"	2'–0"±	59 # to 270 #
	DINGY OR TENDER	6'–1" to 14'–0"	2'–10" to 5'–5"	1'–6" to 1'–8"	1'– 6" to 1'– 8"	40 # to 155 #
DORY	LIFE SAVING	18'–0"±	4'–6"±	1'–8"±	1'–11"±	275// ±
DORY	FISHERMAN	12'–0" to 16'–0"	3'–6" to 5'–8"	1'– 6" to 1'– 8"	1'– 6" to 1'– 10"	64 # to 320 #
CANOE	ONE MAN	9'–0" to 15'–0"	2'–10 1/2" to 3'–0"	11" to 1'–0 1/2"	2'–0" to 2'–4"	44 # to 85 #
CANOE	STANDARD	16'–0" to 18'–0"	2'–4" to 3'–1"	1'–0" to 1'–1"	2'–0" to 2'–4"	70 # ±
CANOE	SAFETY	16'–0" to 18'–0"	3'–5" to 3'–7"	1'–0" to 1'–1"	2'–0" to 2'–4"	70 # ±
CANOE	GUIDES	18'–0" to 20'–0"	3'–0" to 3'–3"	1'–1" to 1'–1 1/2"	2'–0" to 2'–4"	80 # ±
CANOE	11 PADDLE WAR	25'–0"	3'–8"	1'–2 1/2"	2'–3"	180 #
CANOE	21 PADDLE WAR	34'–0"	3'–8"	1'–3"	2'– 3"	225
RACING SHELL & GIG ROWING	SINGLE RACING	2'–1" to 2'–3"	1'–0"	6 1/2"	10 1/2"	30 #
RACING SHELL & GIG ROWING	DOUBLE RACING	2'–7" to 2'–11"	1'–4"	7"	11"	60 #
RACING SHELL & GIG ROWING	FOUR - OARED	3'–2" to 3'–11"	1'–9"	8 1/2"	12 1/2"	120 #
RACING SHELL & GIG ROWING	8 - OARED SHELL	4'–8" to 5'–3"	2'–0" to 2'–4"	10" to 1'–4"	1'–2" to 1'–8"	270 #
RACING SHELL & GIG ROWING	PRACTICE GIGS	Gigs in all classes, same depth but shorter and wider than shells.				

George Simms; Neil R. Greene, AIA; Silver Spring, Maryland
William H. Ostermayer; The Ballinger Company; Philadelphia, Pennsylvania

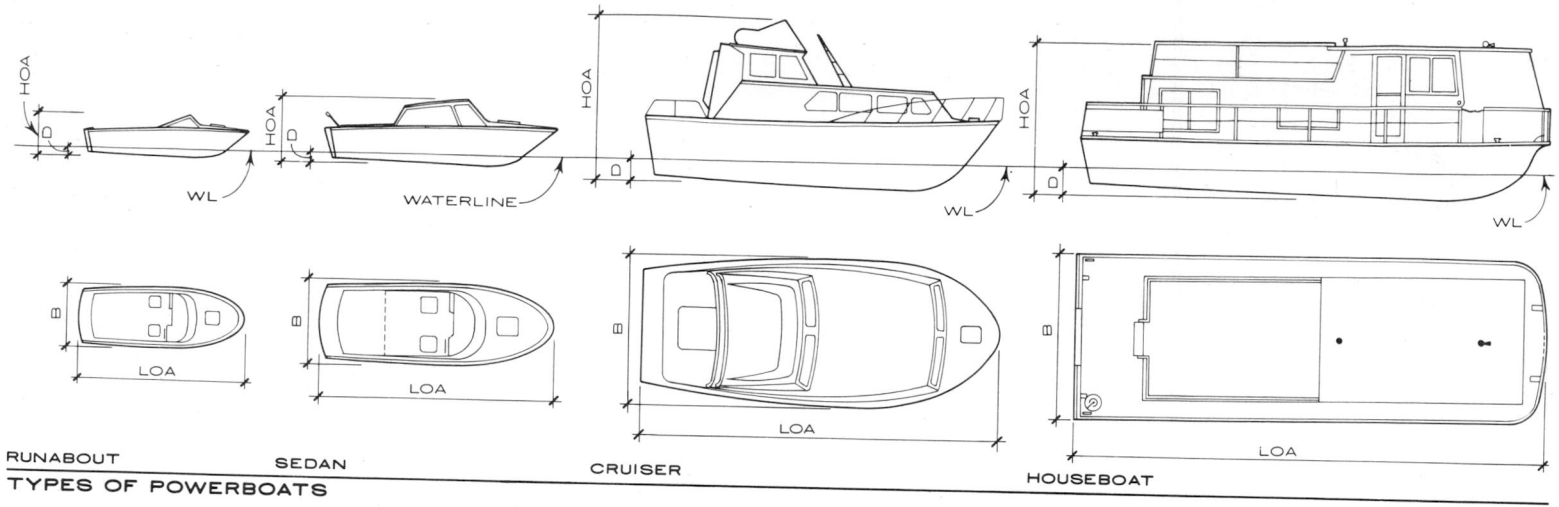

RUNABOUT   SEDAN   CRUISER   HOUSEBOAT
TYPES OF POWERBOATS

TYPES AND SIZES OF TYPICAL POWERBOATS

LOA = LENGTH OVERALL   B = BEAM   HOA = HEIGHT OVERALL   D = DRAFT

CLASSIFICATION AND NAME		LENGTH OVERALL	BEAM	HEIGHT OVERALL	DRAFT	WEIGHT (LBS)
RUNABOUT	SEA ROCKET	9'–8''	4'–8''	1'–9''	0'–4''	210
	MONARCH 1230	12'–0''	3'–9''	1'–2''	0'–3''	80
	PIRANNA I	14'–0''	5'–6''	2'–4''	0'–6''	375
	OPEN FISHERMAN	19'–8''	7'–6''	4'–5''	0'–11''	1200
SEDAN	CAPRICE 197	18'–2''	7'–5''	3'–5''	0'–10''	2400
	NORSEMAN 19	19'–0''	7'–4''	4'–1''	1'–3''	1560
	COMMODORE 486	23'–0''	8'–0''	5'–0''	1'–0''	2970
	SEAMASTER 27	26'–9''	9'–10''	9'–0''	1'–8''	7200
CRUISER	EXPRESS CRUISER	28'–3''	10'–10''	10'–10''	–	6000
	CONSTELLATION	36'–0''	12'–0''	12'–7''	2'–8''	14870
	38' MOTOR YACHT	37'–10''	14'–2''	11'–6''	2'–6''	22400
	SEA VOYAGER	42'–5''	14'–10''	11'–0''	3'–2''	25000
HOUSE-BOAT	GYPSY	20'–1''	7'–11''	7'–4''	0'–9''	2000
	CRIS–CRAFT 33	33'–3''	12'–0''	12'–11''	2'–5''	10000
	RIVER QUEEN 40	40'–0''	12'–0''	10'–6''	2'–0''	16000
	SPORTSMAN	50'–0''	12'–6''	10'–0''	0'–10''	19000

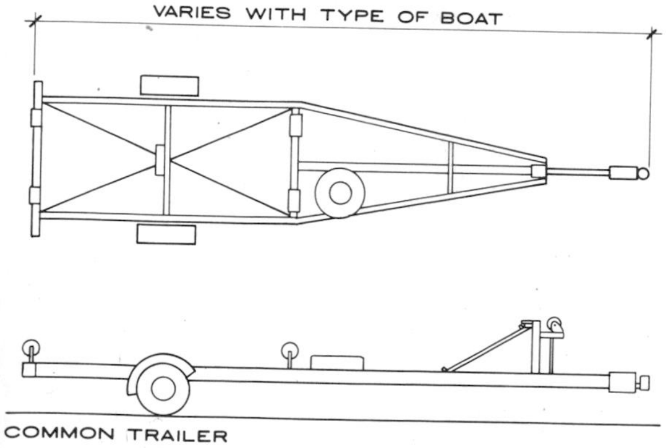

VARIES WITH TYPE OF BOAT

COMMON TRAILER

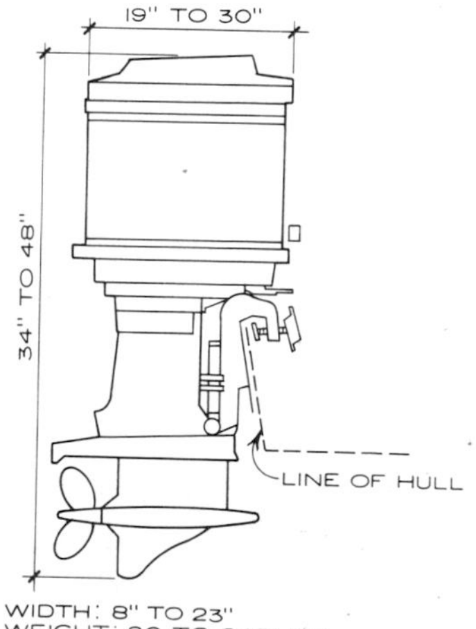

19'' TO 30''

34'' TO 48''

LINE OF HULL

WIDTH: 8'' TO 23''
WEIGHT: 20 TO 245 LBS.
OUTBOARD

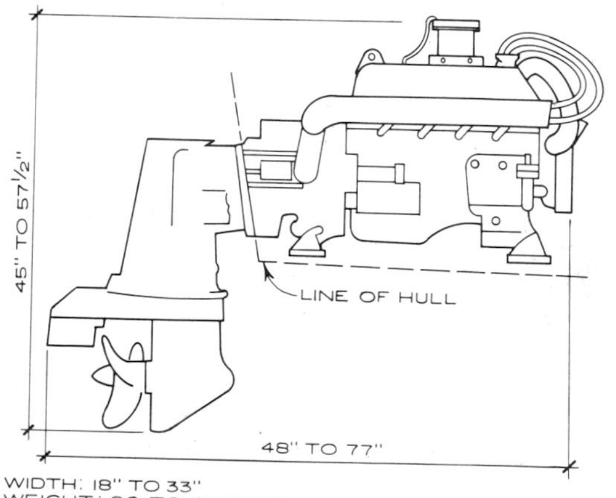

45'' TO 57½''

LINE OF HULL

48'' TO 77''

WIDTH: 18'' TO 33''
WEIGHT: 20 TO 245 LBS.
STERNDRIVE

FLAT   ROUND   VEE   TRI-HULL   CATHEDRAL VEE   TRIMARAN   CATAMARAN
TYPICAL HULL TYPES

Fred Sahli & George Simms; Neil R. Greene, AIA; Silver Spring, Maryland

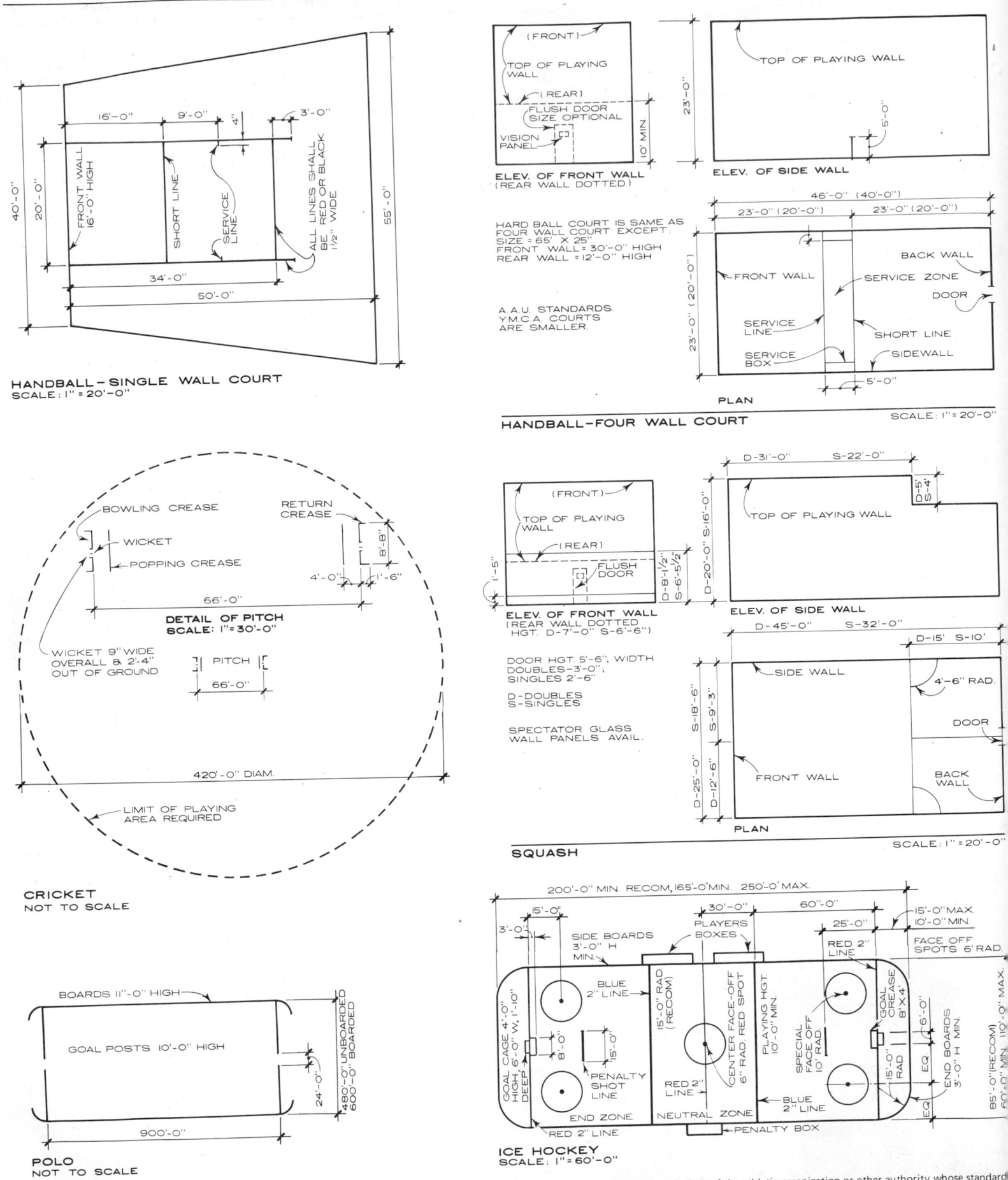

HANDBALL — SINGLE WALL COURT
SCALE: 1" = 20'-0"

ELEV. OF FRONT WALL
(REAR WALL DOTTED)

ELEV. OF SIDE WALL

HARD BALL COURT IS SAME AS
FOUR WALL COURT EXCEPT:
SIZE = 65" X 25"
FRONT WALL = 30'-0" HIGH
REAR WALL = 12'-0" HIGH

A.A.U. STANDARDS.
Y.M.C.A. COURTS
ARE SMALLER.

PLAN

HANDBALL — FOUR WALL COURT   SCALE: 1" = 20'-0"

DETAIL OF PITCH
SCALE: 1" = 30'-0"

WICKET 9" WIDE
OVERALL & 2'-4"
OUT OF GROUND

CRICKET
NOT TO SCALE

ELEV. OF FRONT WALL
(REAR WALL DOTTED
HGT. D-7'-0" S-6'-6")

ELEV. OF SIDE WALL

DOOR HGT. 5'-6", WIDTH
DOUBLES — 3'-0";
SINGLES 2'-6"

D — DOUBLES
S — SINGLES

SPECTATOR GLASS
WALL PANELS AVAIL.

PLAN

SQUASH   SCALE: 1" = 20'-0"

BOARDS 11'-0" HIGH
GOAL POSTS 10'-0" HIGH

POLO
NOT TO SCALE

ICE HOCKEY
SCALE: 1" = 60'-0"

NOTE: This information is for preliminary planning and design only. For final layouts and design investigate current rules and regulations of the athletic organization or other authority whose standard
will govern.

Charles F. D. Egbert, AIA; Architect; Washington, D. C.

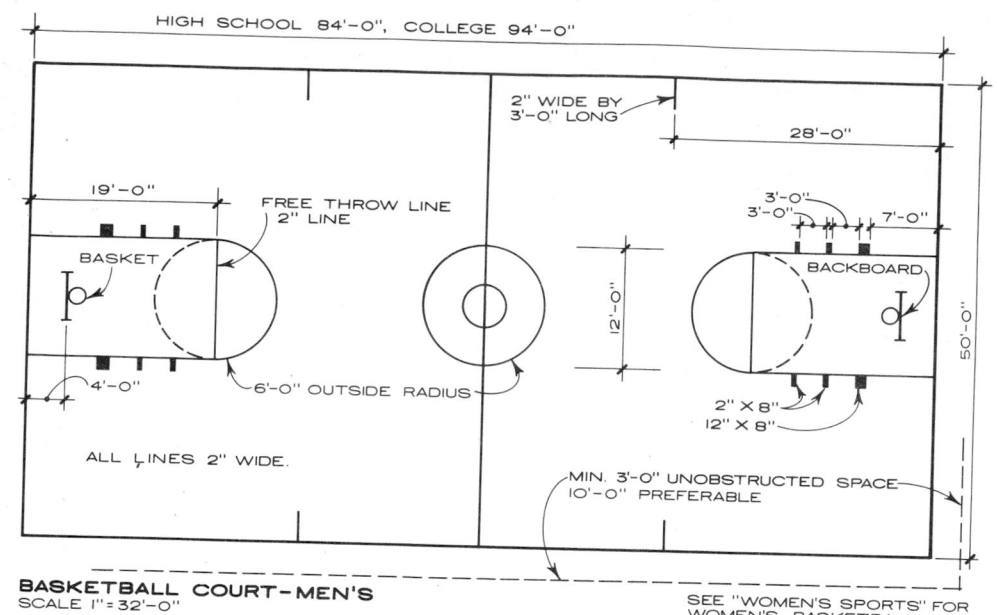

BASKETBALL COURT – MEN'S
SCALE 1"=32'-0"

HIGH SCHOOL 84'-0", COLLEGE 94'-0"

19'-0"

FREE THROW LINE 2" LINE

BASKET

4'-0"

6'-0" OUTSIDE RADIUS

ALL LINES 2" WIDE.

2" WIDE BY 3'-0" LONG

28'-0"

3'-0"
3'-0"
7'-0"

BACKBOARD

12'-0"

50'-0"

2" X 8"
12" X 8"

MIN. 3'-0" UNOBSTRUCTED SPACE
10'-0" PREFERABLE

SEE "WOMEN'S SPORTS" FOR WOMEN'S BASKETBALL

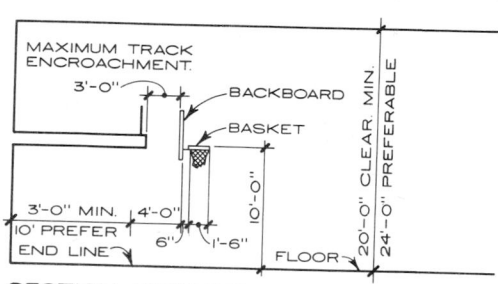

BACKBOARD DETAIL   NO SCALE
BOTH TYPES LEGAL FOR COLLEGE & H.S.

RECTANGULAR BACKBOARD (DOTTED)

MODIFIED BACKGROUND (SOLID)

6'-0"
4'-6"
4'-0"
18" DIAM. RING
2'-5"
3"
2'-11"

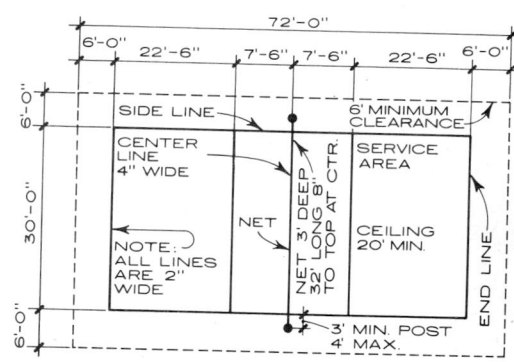

SECTION SHOWING BASKET & ENCROACHMENTS
SCALE 1" = 16'

MAXIMUM TRACK ENCROACHMENT.
3'-0"
BACKBOARD
BASKET
20'-0" CLEAR MIN.
24'-0" PREFERABLE
3'-0" MIN.
10' PREFER END LINE
4'-0"
6"
1'-6"
FLOOR

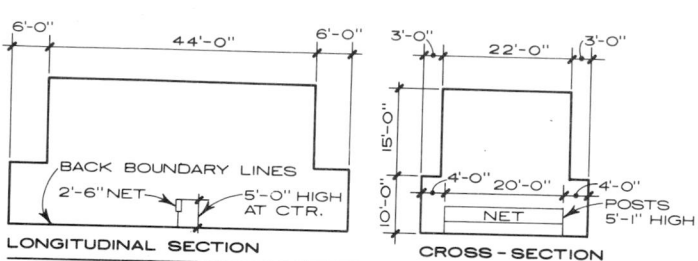

LONGITUDINAL SECTION   CROSS-SECTION
ENCROACHMENTS

6'-0"
44'-0"
6'-0"
3'-0"
22'-0"
3'-0"

BACK BOUNDARY LINES
2'-6" NET
5'-0" HIGH AT CTR.
15'-0"
10'-0"
4'-0" 20'-0" 4'-0"
NET
POSTS 5'-1" HIGH

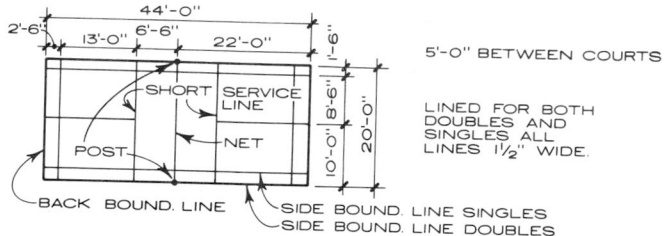

BADMINTON – MEN & WOMEN   SCALE 1"=32'-0"

44'-0"
2'-6"
13'-0" 6'-6"
22'-0"
1'-6"
SHORT SERVICE LINE
NET
POST
10'-0" 8'-6" 20'-0"
BACK BOUND. LINE
SIDE BOUND. LINE SINGLES
SIDE BOUND. LINE DOUBLES

5'-0" BETWEEN COURTS

LINED FOR BOTH DOUBLES AND SINGLES ALL LINES 1½" WIDE.

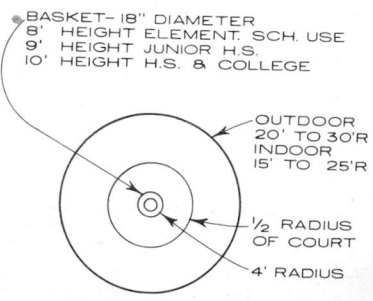

VOLLEY BALL
SCALE 1"=32'-0"

72'-0"
6'-0" 22'-6" 7'-6" 7'-6" 22'-6" 6'-0"
6'-0"
SIDE LINE
6' MINIMUM CLEARANCE
CENTER LINE 4" WIDE
SERVICE AREA
30'-0"
NET
CEILING 20' MIN.
NOTE: ALL LINES ARE 2" WIDE
NET 3' DEEP 32' LONG 8' TO TOP AT CTR.
END LINE
6'-0"
3' MIN. POST 4' MAX.

NOTE:
U.S. Volley Ball Association dimensions for unofficial games. Court may be varied to suit players. (for children and the less agile). Min. clearance 3'-0". See page on womens sports.

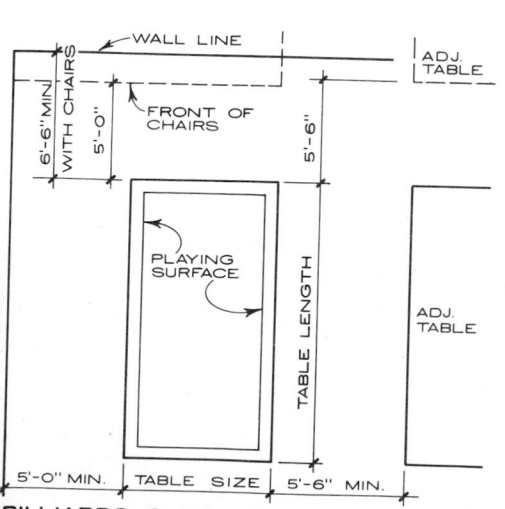

BILLIARDS & POCKET BILLIARDS (POOL)
NO SCALE

WALL LINE
ADJ. TABLE
FRONT OF CHAIRS
6'-6" MIN WITH CHAIRS
5'-0"
5'-6"
PLAYING SURFACE
TABLE LENGTH
ADJ. TABLE
5'-0" MIN. TABLE SIZE 5'-6" MIN.

DIMENSIONS FOR BILLIARDS & POCKET BILLIARDS

TYPE OF TABLE	PLAYING SURFACE		TABLE SIZE	
	W.	L.	W.	L.
ENGLISH (SNOOKER)	6'-0"	12'-0"	6'-9"	12'-9"
STANDARD POOL OR BILL.	5'-0"	10'-0"	5'-9"	10'-0"
STANDARD POOL OR BILL.	4'-6"	9'-0"	5'-3"	9'-9"
STANDARD POOL OR BILL.	4'-0"	8'-0"	4'-9"	8'-9"
JUNIOR POOL	3'-6"	7'-0"	4'-3"	7'-9"
JUNIOR POOL	3'-0"	6'-0"	3'-9"	6'-9"

TABLE HEIGHT 2'-6" ±

GOAL-HI COURT
SCALE 1"=32"

BASKET – 18" DIAMETER
8' HEIGHT ELEMENT. SCH. USE
9' HEIGHT JUNIOR H.S.
10' HEIGHT H.S. & COLLEGE

OUTDOOR 20' TO 30'R
INDOOR 15' TO 25'R
½ RADIUS OF COURT
4' RADIUS

NOTE: This information is for preliminary planning and design only. For final layouts and design investigate current rules and regulations of the athletic organization or other authority whose standards will govern.

Charles F. D. Egbert, AIA; Architect; Washington, D. C.

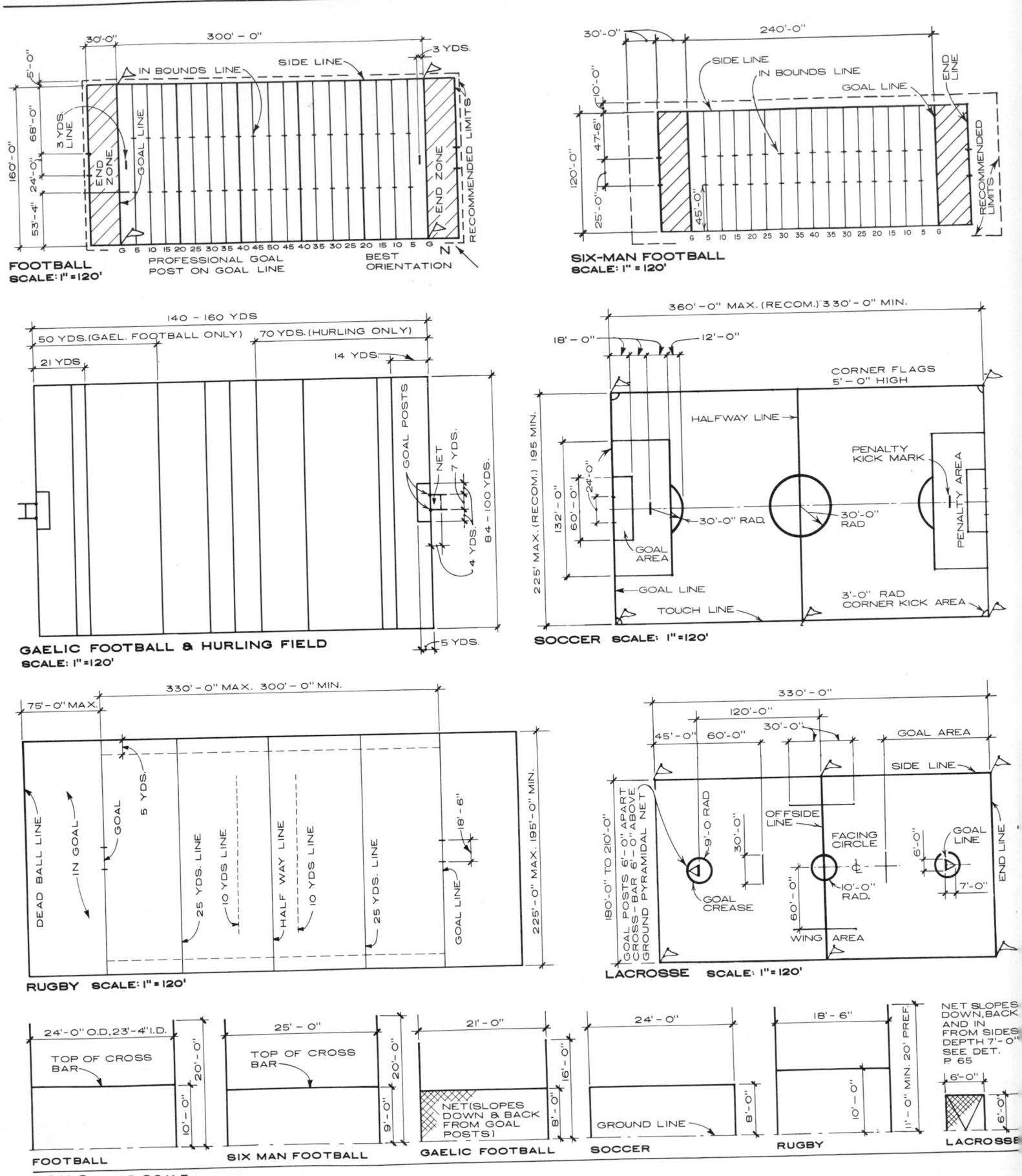

FOOTBALL
SCALE: I" = 120'

PROFESSIONAL GOAL
POST ON GOAL LINE

BEST
ORIENTATION

SIX-MAN FOOTBALL
SCALE: I" = 120'

GAELIC FOOTBALL & HURLING FIELD
SCALE: I" = 120'

SOCCER SCALE: I" = 120'

RUGBY SCALE: I" = 120'

LACROSSE SCALE: I" = 120'

GOALS — NO SCALE

FOOTBALL   SIX MAN FOOTBALL   GAELIC FOOTBALL   SOCCER   RUGBY   LACROSSE

NOTE:

This information is for preliminary planning and design only. For final layouts and design investigate current rules and regulations of the athletic organization or other authority whose standards will govern.

Charles F. D. Egbert, AIA; Architect; Washington, D. C.

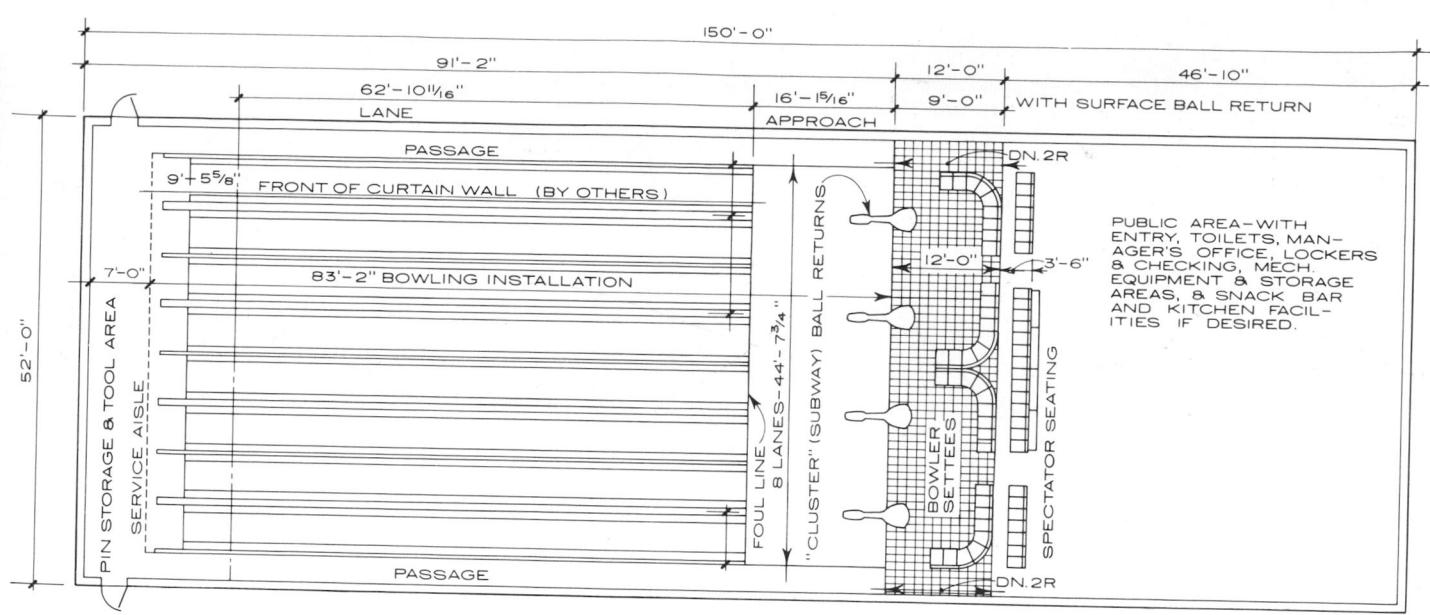

TYPICAL 8 LANE INSTALLATION LAYOUT – SUBSURFACE BALL RETURN
NO SCALE

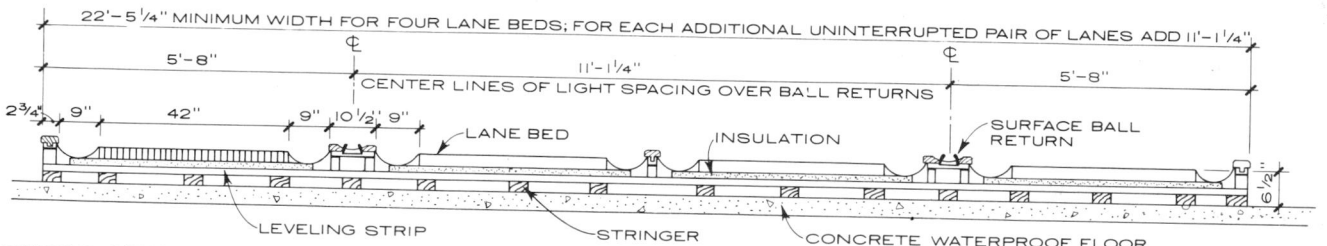

CROSS SECTION – STRINGER FOUNDATION – SURFACE BALL RETURN
NO SCALE

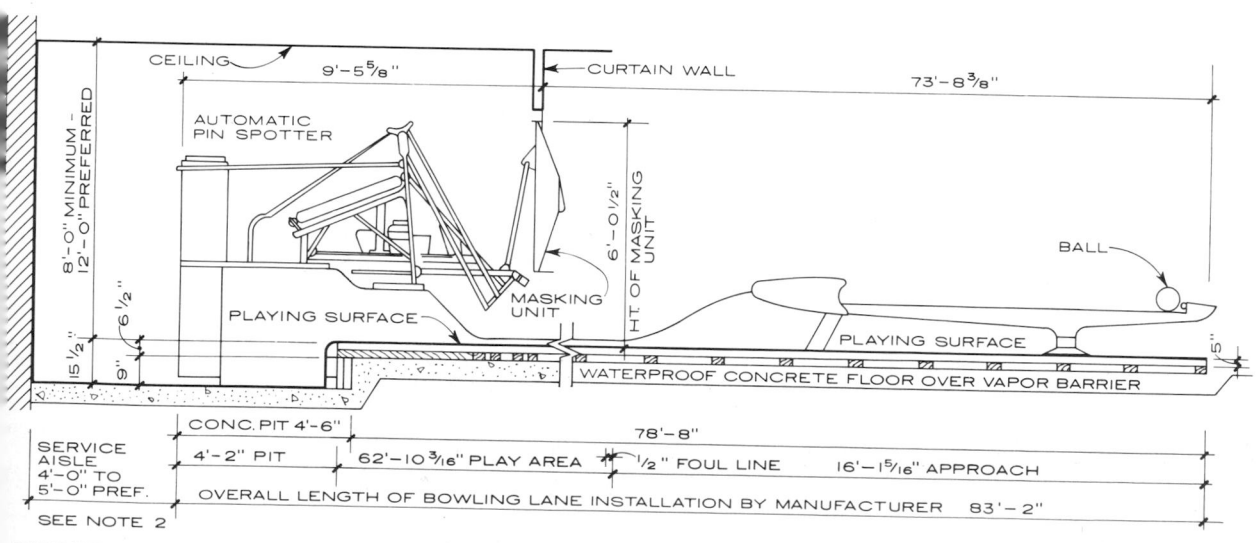

NOTES:

1. Subsurface ball returns also available.

2. Min service aisle width at 6'–6" above concrete floor is 4'–0".

LONGITUDINAL SECTION – STRINGER FOUNDATION – SURFACE BALL RETURN
NO SCALE

NOTE:

This information is for preliminary planning and design only. For final layout and design investigate current rules and regulations of the athletic organization or other authority whose standards will govern.

Charles F. D. Egbert, AIA; Architect; Washington, D. C.

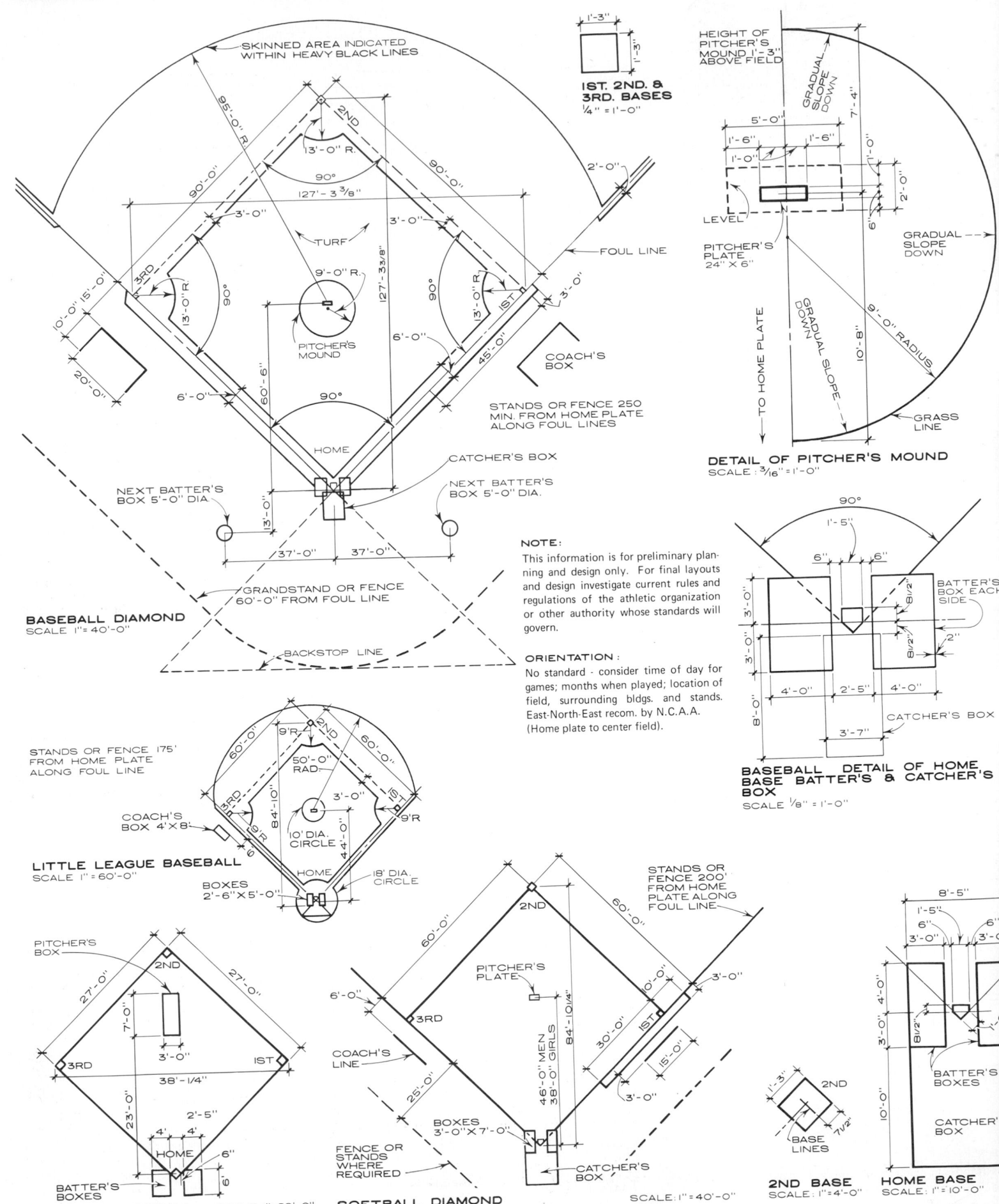

1ST. 2ND. & 3RD. BASES
1/4" = 1'-0"

DETAIL OF PITCHER'S MOUND
SCALE : 3/16" = 1'-0"

SKINNED AREA INDICATED WITHIN HEAVY BLACK LINES

FOUL LINE

STANDS OR FENCE 250 MIN. FROM HOME PLATE ALONG FOUL LINES

COACH'S BOX

PITCHER'S MOUND

TURF

2ND

HOME

CATCHER'S BOX

NEXT BATTER'S BOX 5'-0" DIA.

NEXT BATTER'S BOX 5'-0" DIA.

GRANDSTAND OR FENCE 60'-0" FROM FOUL LINE

BASEBALL DIAMOND
SCALE 1" = 40'-0"

BACKSTOP LINE

NOTE:
This information is for preliminary planning and design only. For final layouts and design investigate current rules and regulations of the athletic organization or other authority whose standards will govern.

ORIENTATION :
No standard - consider time of day for games; months when played; location of field, surrounding bldgs. and stands. East-North-East recom. by N.C.A.A. (Home plate to center field).

BASEBALL DETAIL OF HOME BASE BATTER'S & CATCHER'S BOX
SCALE 1/8" = 1'-0"

BATTER'S BOX EACH SIDE

CATCHER'S BOX

STANDS OR FENCE 175' FROM HOME PLATE ALONG FOUL LINE

COACH'S BOX 4'X8'

LITTLE LEAGUE BASEBALL
SCALE 1" = 60'-0"

BOXES 2'-6"X5'-0"

18' DIA. CIRCLE

10' DIA. CIRCLE

PITCHER'S BOX

2ND

3RD

1ST

HOME

BATTER'S BOXES

INDOOR BASEBALL   SCALE: 1"=20'-0"

STANDS OR FENCE 200' FROM HOME PLATE ALONG FOUL LINE

PITCHER'S PLATE

2ND

3RD

1ST

COACH'S LINE

BOXES 3'-0"X7'-0"

FENCE OR STANDS WHERE REQUIRED

CATCHER'S BOX

SOFTBALL DIAMOND   SCALE:1"=40'-0"

2ND BASE
SCALE:1"=4'-0"

BASE LINES

BATTER'S BOXES

CATCHER'S BOX

HOME BASE
SCALE 1"=10'-0"

Charles F. D. Egbert, AIA; Architect; Washington, D. C.

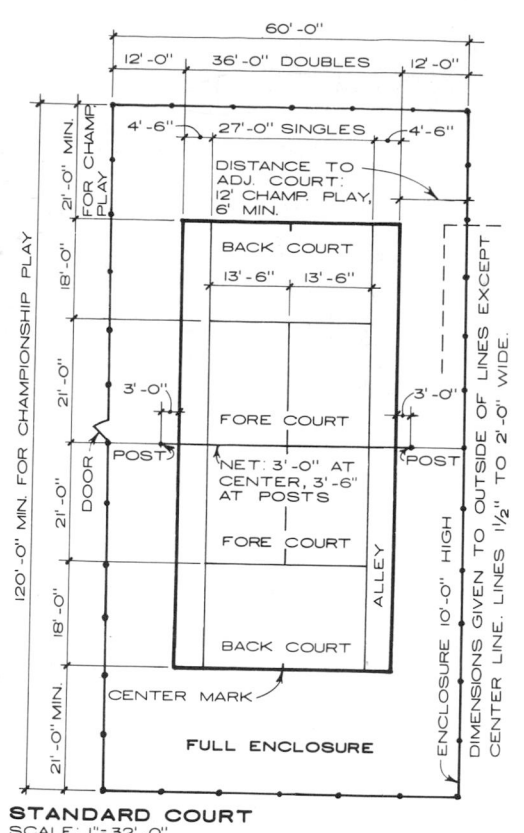

STANDARD COURT
SCALE: 1"= 32'-0"

ORIENTATION:

For the Northern states, North-Northeast and South-Southwest is best.

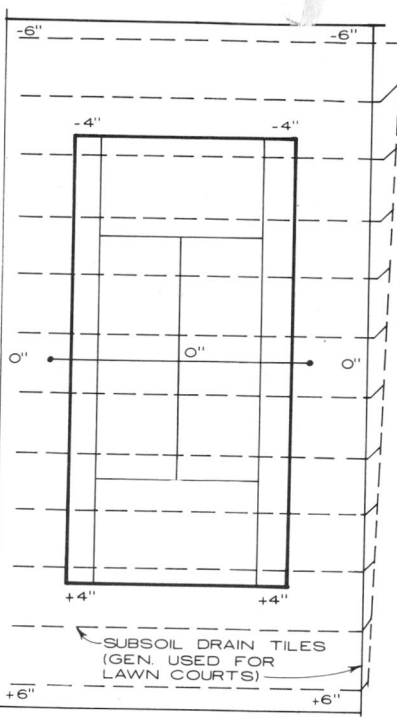

PARTIAL ENCLOSURES
SCALE: 1"- 32'-0"

DRAINAGE PLAN (2 OR MORE COURTS)
SCALE: 1"= 32'-0"

NOTE:

Surface drainage-Pitch 1" per 10'— 0". Pitch side to side for single court: pitch end to end for 2 or more courts. Need for drainage system depends on soil conditions.

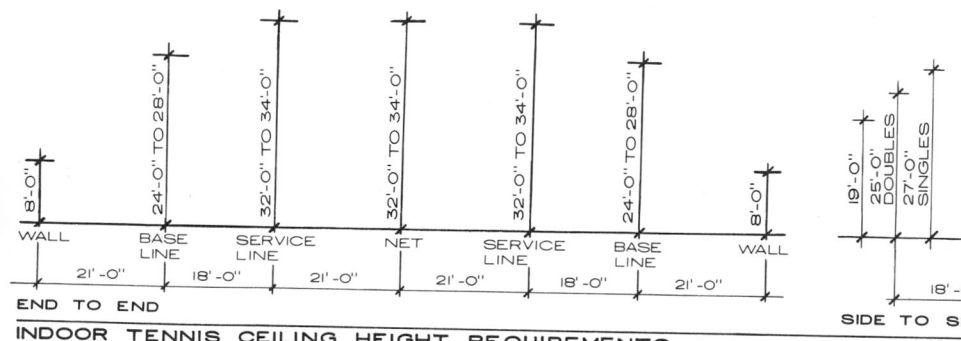

INDOOR TENNIS CEILING HEIGHT REQUIREMENTS

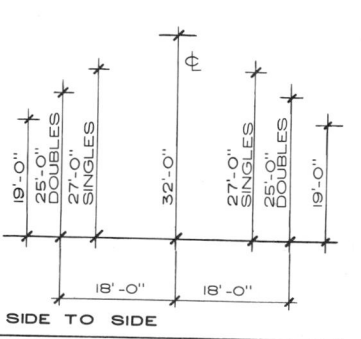

NOTE:

This information is for preliminary planning and design only. For final layouts and design investigate current rules and regulations of the athletic organization or other authority whose standards will govern.

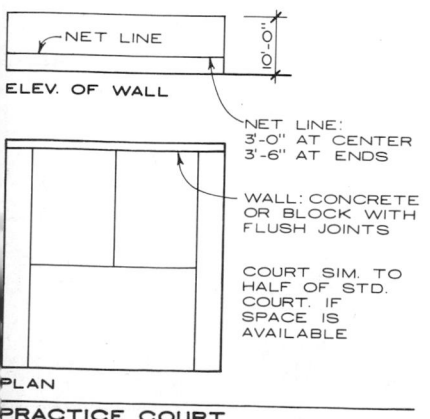

PRACTICE COURT
SCALE: 1"= 32'-0"

Charles F. D. Egbert, AIA; Architect; Washington, D. C.

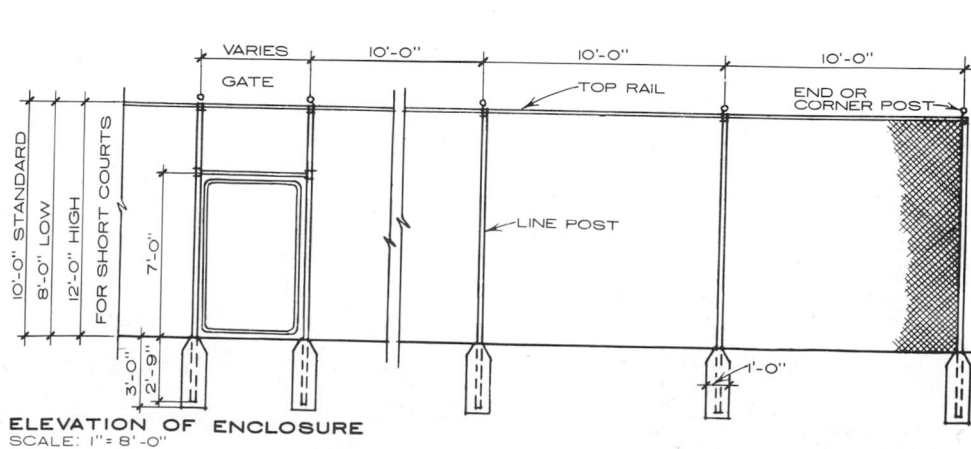

ELEVATION OF ENCLOSURE
SCALE: 1"= 8'-0"

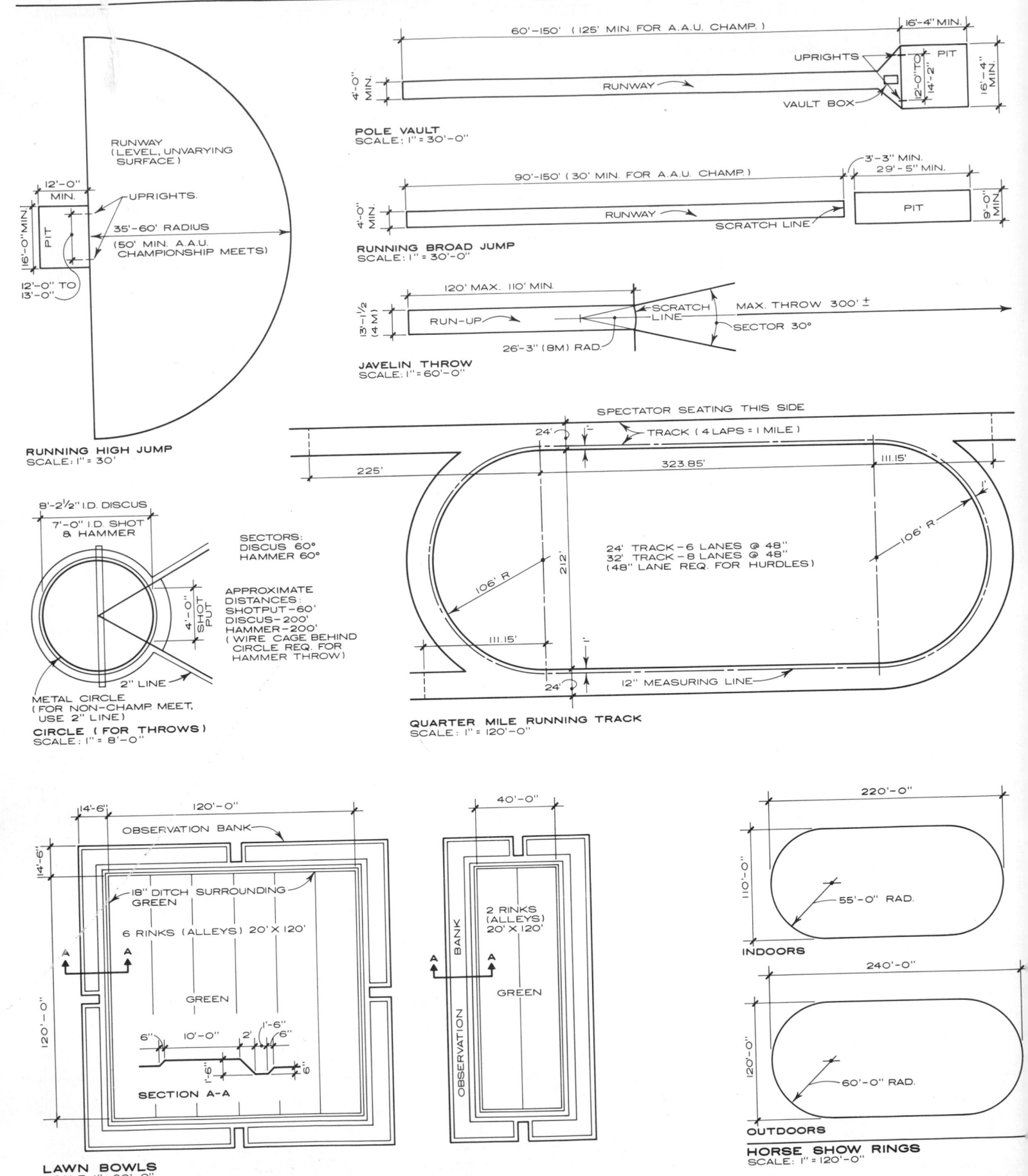

RUNNING HIGH JUMP
SCALE: 1" = 30'

POLE VAULT
SCALE: 1" = 30'-0"

RUNNING BROAD JUMP
SCALE: 1" = 30'-0"

JAVELIN THROW
SCALE: 1" = 60'-0"

CIRCLE (FOR THROWS)
SCALE: 1" = 8'-0"

QUARTER MILE RUNNING TRACK
SCALE: 1" = 120'-0"

LAWN BOWLS
SCALE: 1" = 60'-0"

HORSE SHOW RINGS
SCALE: 1" = 120'-0"

NOTE: This information is for preliminary planning and design only. For final layouts and design investigate current rules and regulations of the athletic organization or other authority whose standard will govern.

Charles F. D. Egbert, AIA; Architect; Washington, D. C.

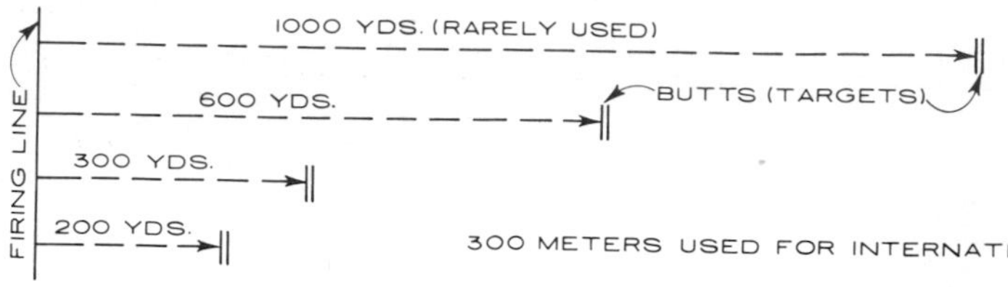

1000 YDS. (RARELY USED)

600 YDS.

BUTTS (TARGETS)

300 YDS.

FIRING LINE

200 YDS.

300 METERS USED FOR INTERNATIONAL TOURNAMENTS

STAGGERED BUTT RIFLE RANGE

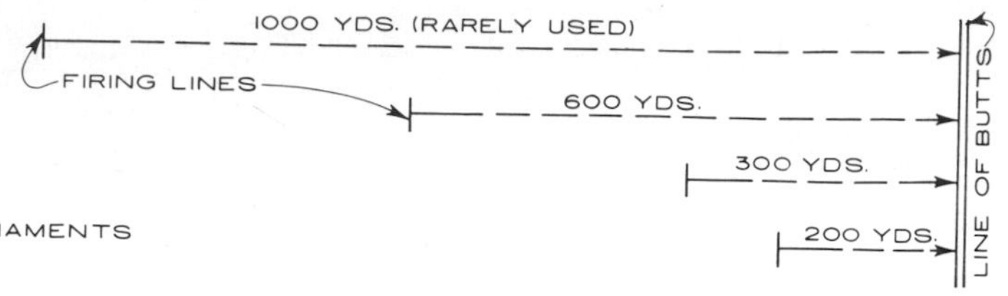

1000 YDS. (RARELY USED)

FIRING LINES

600 YDS.

300 YDS.

200 YDS.

LINE OF BUTTS

BUTT – IN – LINE RIFLE RANGE

OUTDOOR RIFLE & PISTOL RANGES   NO SCALE

NOTES :

1. Orientation: North—South
2. Earth berm 12' – 0" high, ideal for maximum safety.

3. Small bore ranges: 50 & 100 yds. and 50 & 100 meters.
4. Pistol ranges: 25 & 50 yds. and 25 & 50 meters.

5. Spacing of targets:
   Pistol   4' – 0" O.C. Min.
   Small bore rifle 5' – 0" O.C. Min.
   High power rifle 8' – 0" O.C. Min.

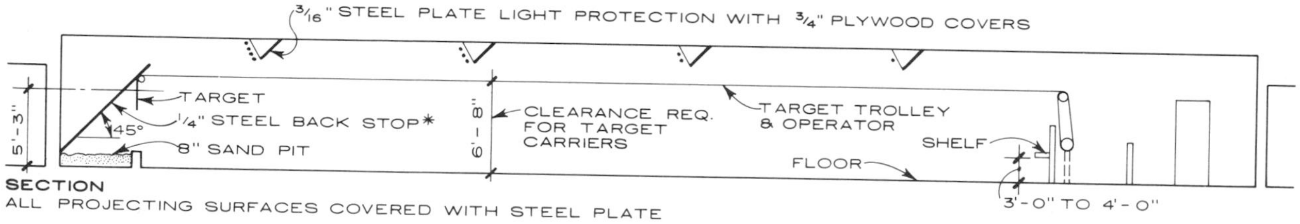

³⁄₁₆" STEEL PLATE LIGHT PROTECTION WITH ¾" PLYWOOD COVERS

TARGET

¼" STEEL BACK STOP*

45°

8" SAND PIT

5' – 3"

CLEARANCE REQ. FOR TARGET CARRIERS

TARGET TROLLEY & OPERATOR

SHELF

FLOOR

6' – 8"

3' – 0" TO 4' – 0"

SECTION
ALL PROJECTING SURFACES COVERED WITH STEEL PLATE

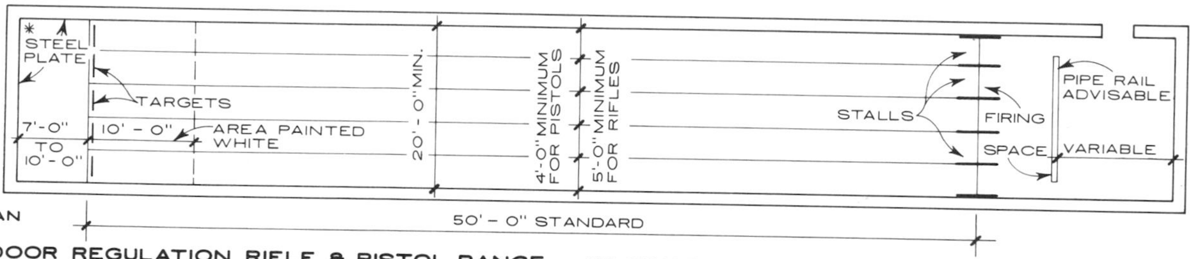

STEEL PLATE

TARGETS

7' – 0" TO 10' – 0"

10' – 0"

AREA PAINTED WHITE

20' – 0" MIN.

4' – 0" MINIMUM FOR PISTOLS

5' – 0" MINIMUM FOR RIFLES

STALLS

FIRING

SPACE VARIABLE

PIPE RAIL ADVISABLE

PLAN   50' – 0" STANDARD

INDOOR REGULATION RIFLE & PISTOL RANGE   NO SCALE
* "MULTI – BAFFLE" & "ESCALATOR" TYPE BULLET TRAPS AVAILABLE & LESS HAZARDOUS THAN PLATE & PIT TYPE SHOWN

DESIGN PROBLEMS

1. Safety
   a. Trap safety.
   b. Firing line safety- use stalls.
   c. Spectator safety.
   d. Ricochet protection.
   e. Safety from spilled powder explosion.
2. Ventilation.
3. Noise.
4. Lighting.

The use of range design consultants is advisable.

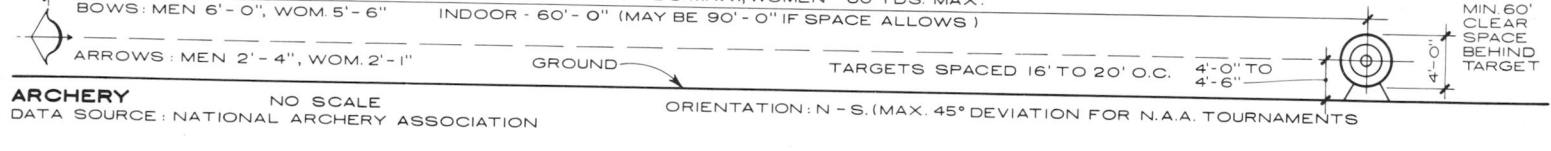

OUTDOOR – MEN - 100 YDS. MAX., WOMEN - 60 YDS. MAX.

BOWS: MEN 6' – 0", WOM. 5' – 6"

INDOOR - 60' – 0" (MAY BE 90' – 0" IF SPACE ALLOWS)

ARROWS : MEN 2' – 4", WOM. 2' – 1"   GROUND

TARGETS SPACED 16' TO 20' O.C.   4' – 0" TO 4' – 6"

MIN. 60' CLEAR SPACE BEHIND TARGET

ARCHERY   NO SCALE
DATA SOURCE : NATIONAL ARCHERY ASSOCIATION

ORIENTATION : N - S. (MAX. 45° DEVIATION FOR N.A.A. TOURNAMENTS

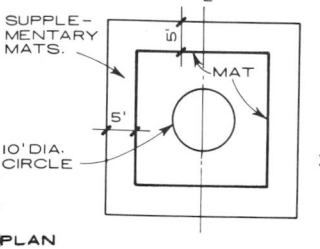

SUPPLE- MENTARY MATS.

MAT

5'

5'

10' DIA. CIRCLE

NOTES :

1. Rope and raised platform illegal (NCAA Rules).

2. Raised platform legal in other rules but not recommended.

PLAN

MAT SIZES

INTERCOLLEGIATE COMPETITION: 24' x 24' minimum & standard.

INTERNAT'L COMPETITION: 6M x 6M. (19' – 8 1/4") min. 1.10M raised platform.

OLYMPIC COMPETITION: 8M x 8M. (26' – 3") minimum.

28' diam. mat also available.

WRESTLING   1/32" = 1' - 0"
DATA SOURCE : N.C.A.A.

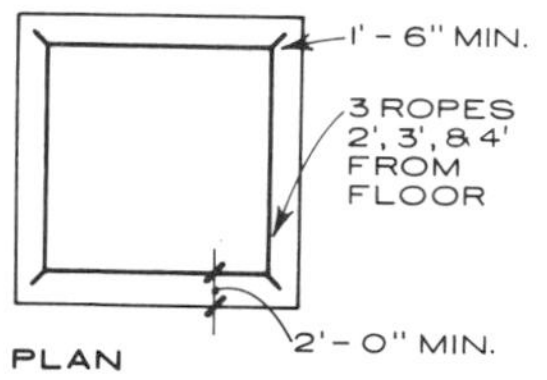

1' – 6" MIN.

3 ROPES 2', 3', & 4' FROM FLOOR

2' – 0" MIN.

PLAN

IF RING IS ON FLOOR EXTEND PADS 2' – 0" BEYOND ROPES.

PLATFORM MAX. 4' – 0" ABOVE FLOOR.

RING SIZES

MIN. 16' x 16'
MAX. 24' x 24'

BOXING   1/32" = 1' - 0"
DATA SOURCE A.A.U.

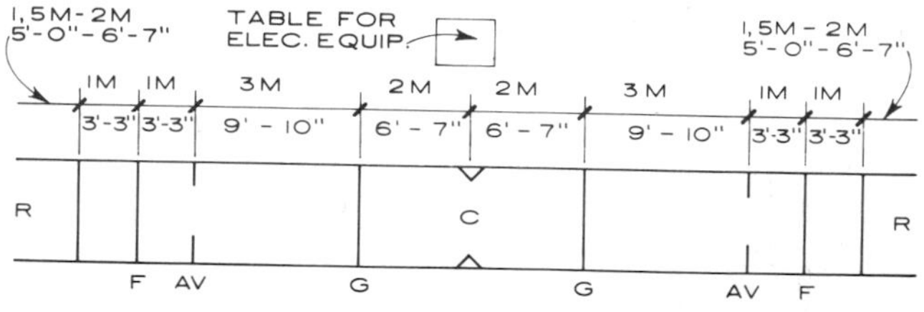

1,5M - 2M 5' – 0" – 6' – 7"

TABLE FOR ELEC. EQUIP.

1,5M - 2M 5' – 0" – 6' – 7"

1M 1M 3M 2M 2M 3M 1M 1M

3' – 3" 3' – 3" 9' – 10" 6' – 7" 6' – 7" 9' – 10" 3' – 3" 3' – 3"

R   C   R

F AV   G   G   AV F

REGULATION PISTE (STRIP) FOR ALL 3 WEAPONS

G— ON GUARD LINE   R— EXTENSION OF PISTE
C— CENTRE (LINE)
AV— WARNING LINE (ALL WEAPONS)
F— REAR LIMIT. FOIL 12M (39' – 4"), EPEE 24M (78' – 8") SABRE 14M (46' – 0")

WIDTH OF PISTE: 1.8M (5' – 11") TO 2M (6' – 7")
WEAPON SIZES: FOIL & EPEE 110CM (43 1/4")
          SABRE 105CM (41 3/8")

FENCING   1/16" = 1' - 0"
DATA SOURCE : AMATEUR FENCERS LEAGUE OF AMERICA
M = METERS CM = CENTIMETERS

NOTE : This information is for preliminary planning and design only. For final layout and design investigate current rules and regulations of the athletic organization or other authority whose authority will govern.

Charles F. D. Egbert, AIA; Architect; Washington, D. C.

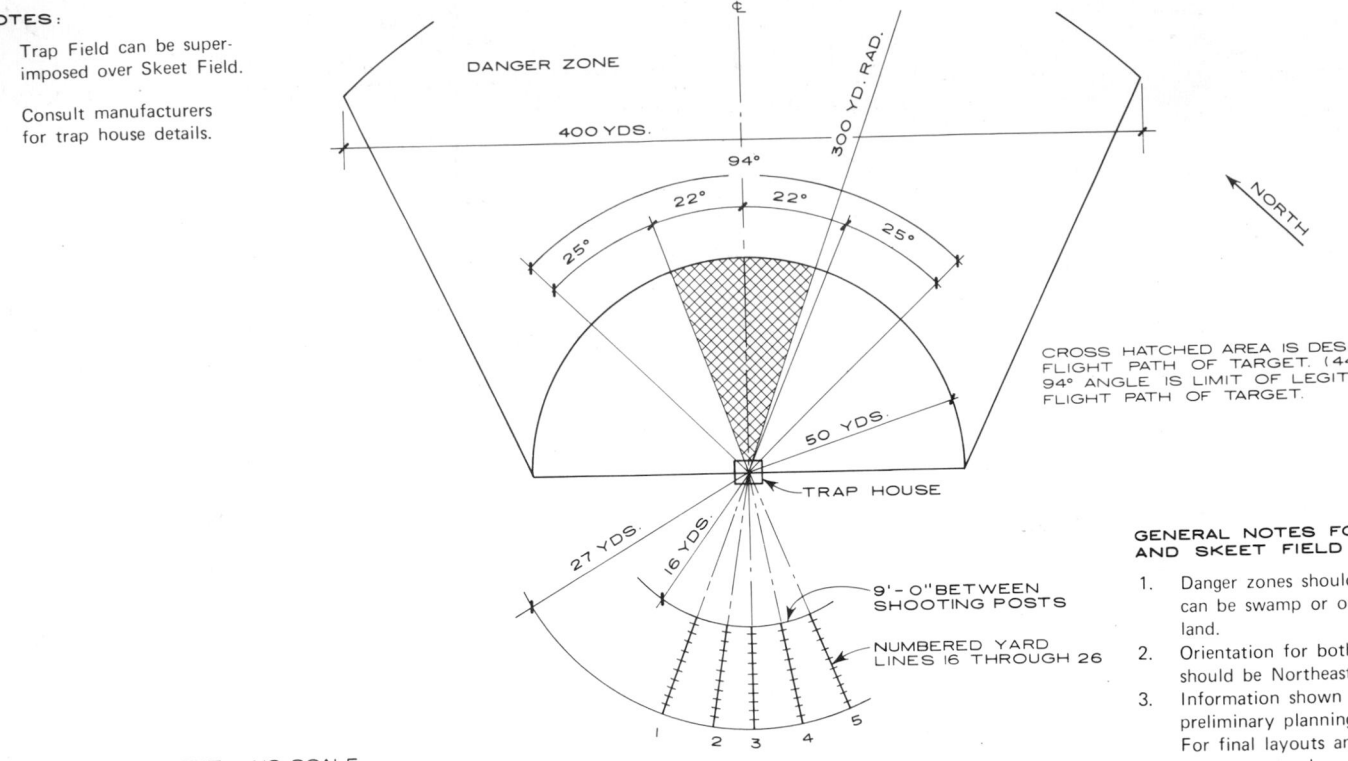

NOTES:

1. Trap Field can be super-imposed over Skeet Field.

2. Consult manufacturers for trap house details.

DANGER ZONE

400 YDS.

300 YD. RAD.

94°

22° 22°

25° 25°

NORTH

CROSS HATCHED AREA IS DESIRABLE FLIGHT PATH OF TARGET. (44°) 94° ANGLE IS LIMIT OF LEGITMATE FLIGHT PATH OF TARGET.

50 YDS.

TRAP HOUSE

27 YDS.

16 YDS.

9'-0" BETWEEN SHOOTING POSTS

NUMBERED YARD LINES 16 THROUGH 26

1   2   3   4   5

TRAP FIELD LAYOUT   NO SCALE
Data reference: Amateur Trapshooting Association

GENERAL NOTES FOR TRAP FIELD AND SKEET FIELD LAYOUTS

1. Danger zones should be cleared, but can be swamp or other types of waste-land.

2. Orientation for both types of fields should be Northeast, as indicated.

3. Information shown on this page is for preliminary planning and design only. For final layouts and design investigate current rules and regulations of the organization or other authority where standards will govern.

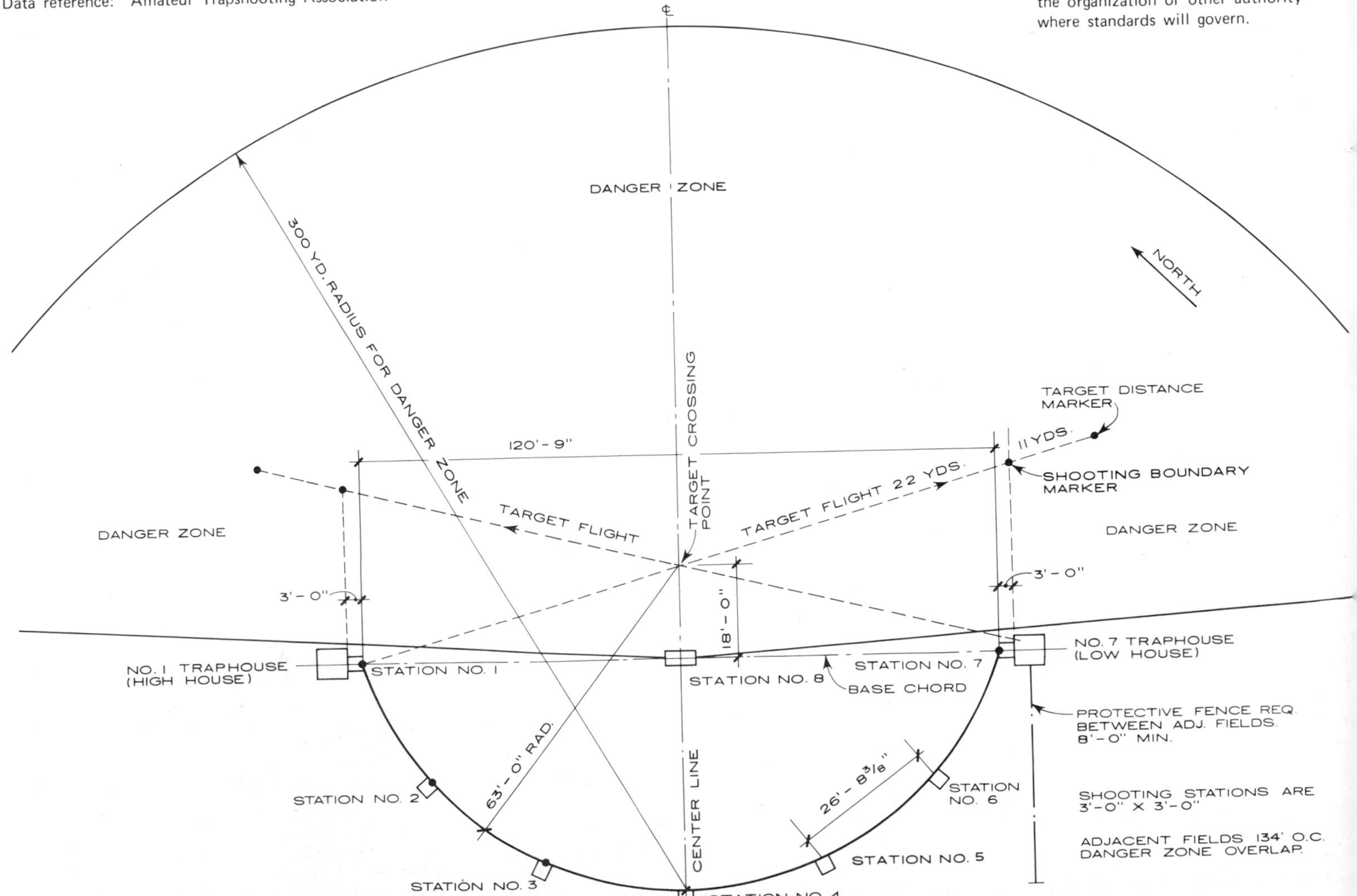

DANGER ZONE

300 Y.D. RADIUS FOR DANGER ZONE

NORTH

DANGER ZONE

TARGET CROSSING POINT

120'-9"

TARGET FLIGHT

TARGET FLIGHT 22 YDS.

11 YDS.

TARGET DISTANCE MARKER

SHOOTING BOUNDARY MARKER

DANGER ZONE

3'-0"

3'-0"

18'-0"

NO. 1 TRAPHOUSE (HIGH HOUSE)

STATION NO. 1

STATION NO. 8

BASE CHORD

STATION NO. 7

NO. 7 TRAPHOUSE (LOW HOUSE)

CENTER LINE

63'-0" RAD.

STATION NO. 2

STATION NO. 3

STATION NO. 4

STATION NO. 5

26'-8³/₈"

STATION NO. 6

PROTECTIVE FENCE REQ. BETWEEN ADJ. FIELDS. 8'-0" MIN.

SHOOTING STATIONS ARE 3'-0" X 3'-0"

ADJACENT FIELDS 134' O.C. DANGER ZONE OVERLAP.

SKEET FIELD LAYOUT   NO SCALE
Data reference: National Skeet Shooting Association

Charles F. D. Egbert, AIA; Architect; Washington, D. C.

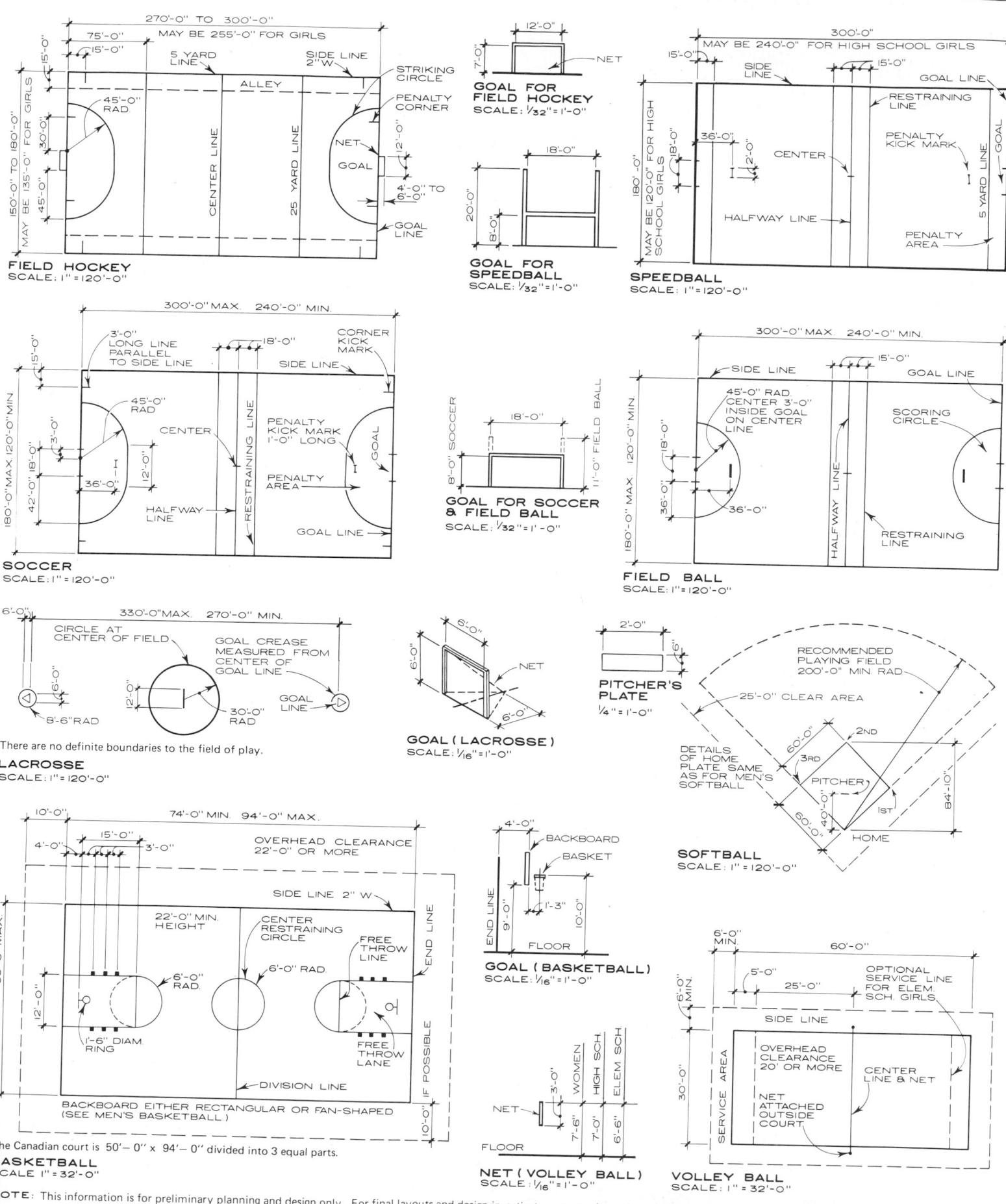

FIELD HOCKEY
SCALE: 1" = 120'-0"

GOAL FOR FIELD HOCKEY
SCALE: 1/32" = 1'-0"

GOAL FOR SPEEDBALL
SCALE: 1/32" = 1'-0"

SPEEDBALL
SCALE: 1" = 120'-0"

SOCCER
SCALE: 1" = 120'-0"

GOAL FOR SOCCER & FIELD BALL
SCALE: 1/32" = 1'-0"

FIELD BALL
SCALE: 1" = 120'-0"

There are no definite boundaries to the field of play.

LACROSSE
SCALE: 1" = 120'-0"

GOAL (LACROSSE)
SCALE: 1/16" = 1'-0"

PITCHER'S PLATE
1/4" = 1'-0"

SOFTBALL
SCALE: 1" = 120'-0"

BACKBOARD EITHER RECTANGULAR OR FAN-SHAPED (SEE MEN'S BASKETBALL.)

The Canadian court is 50'-0" x 94'-0" divided into 3 equal parts.

BASKETBALL
SCALE: 1" = 32'-0"

GOAL (BASKETBALL)
SCALE: 1/16" = 1'-0"

NET (VOLLEY BALL)
SCALE: 1/16" = 1'-0"

VOLLEY BALL
SCALE: 1" = 32'-0"

NOTE: This information is for preliminary planning and design only. For final layouts and design investigate current rules and regulations of the athletic organization or other authority whose standards will govern.

Charles F. D. Egbert, AIA; Architect; Washington, D. C.

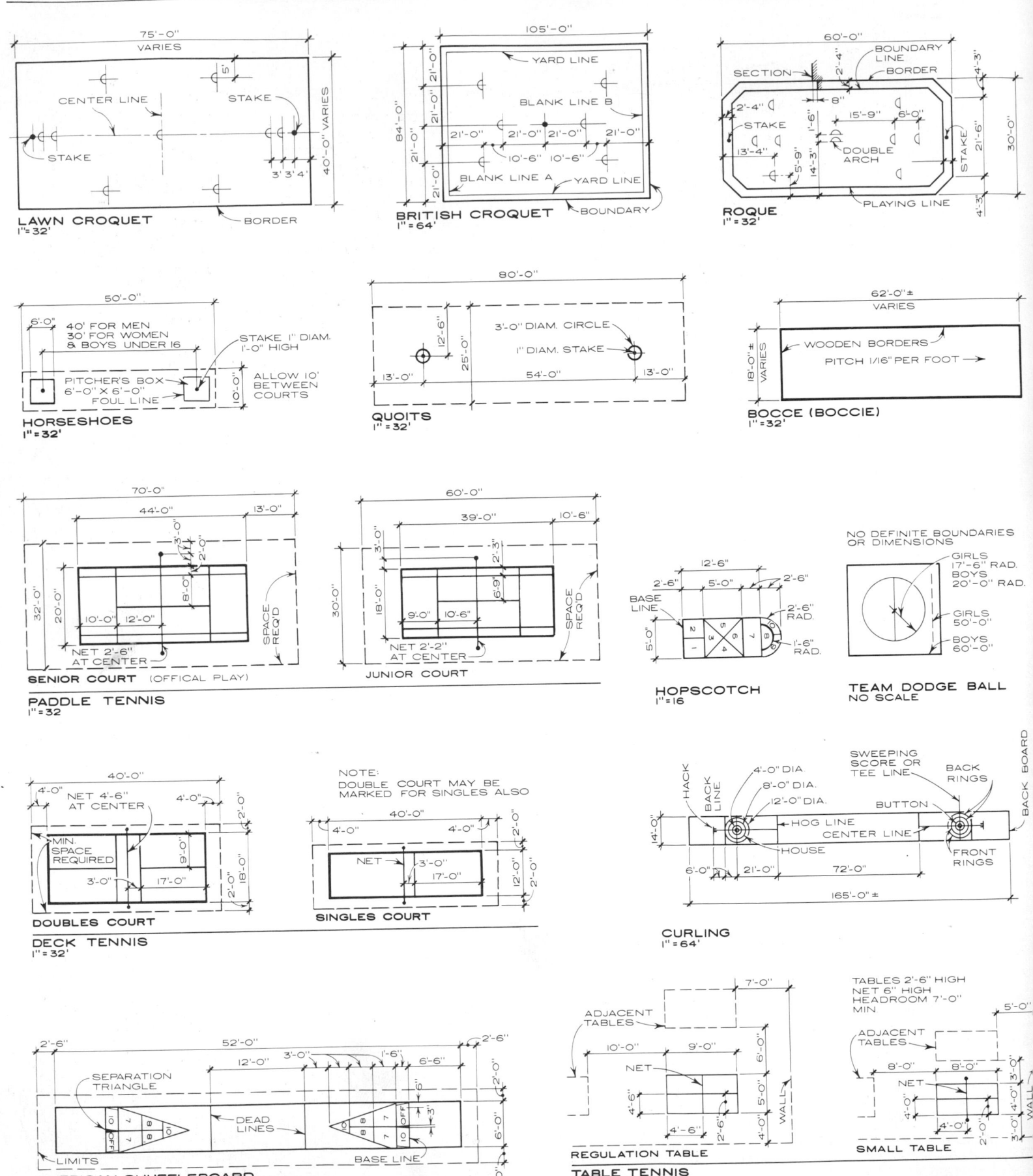

LAWN CROQUET
1" = 32'

BRITISH CROQUET
1" = 64'

ROQUE
1" = 32'

HORSESHOES
1" = 32'

QUOITS
1" = 32'

BOCCE (BOCCIE)
1" = 32'

PADDLE TENNIS
1" = 32
SENIOR COURT (OFFICAL PLAY)
JUNIOR COURT

HOPSCOTCH
1" = 16

TEAM DODGE BALL
NO SCALE

DECK TENNIS
1" = 32'
DOUBLES COURT
SINGLES COURT

CURLING
1" = 64'

AMERICAN SHUFFLEBOARD
1" = 16'

TABLE TENNIS
1" = 6'
REGULATION TABLE
SMALL TABLE

NOTE: This information is for preliminary planning and design only. For final layouts and design investigate current rules and regulations of the athletic organization or other authority whose standard will govern.

Charles F. D. Egbert, AIA; Architect; Washington, D. C.

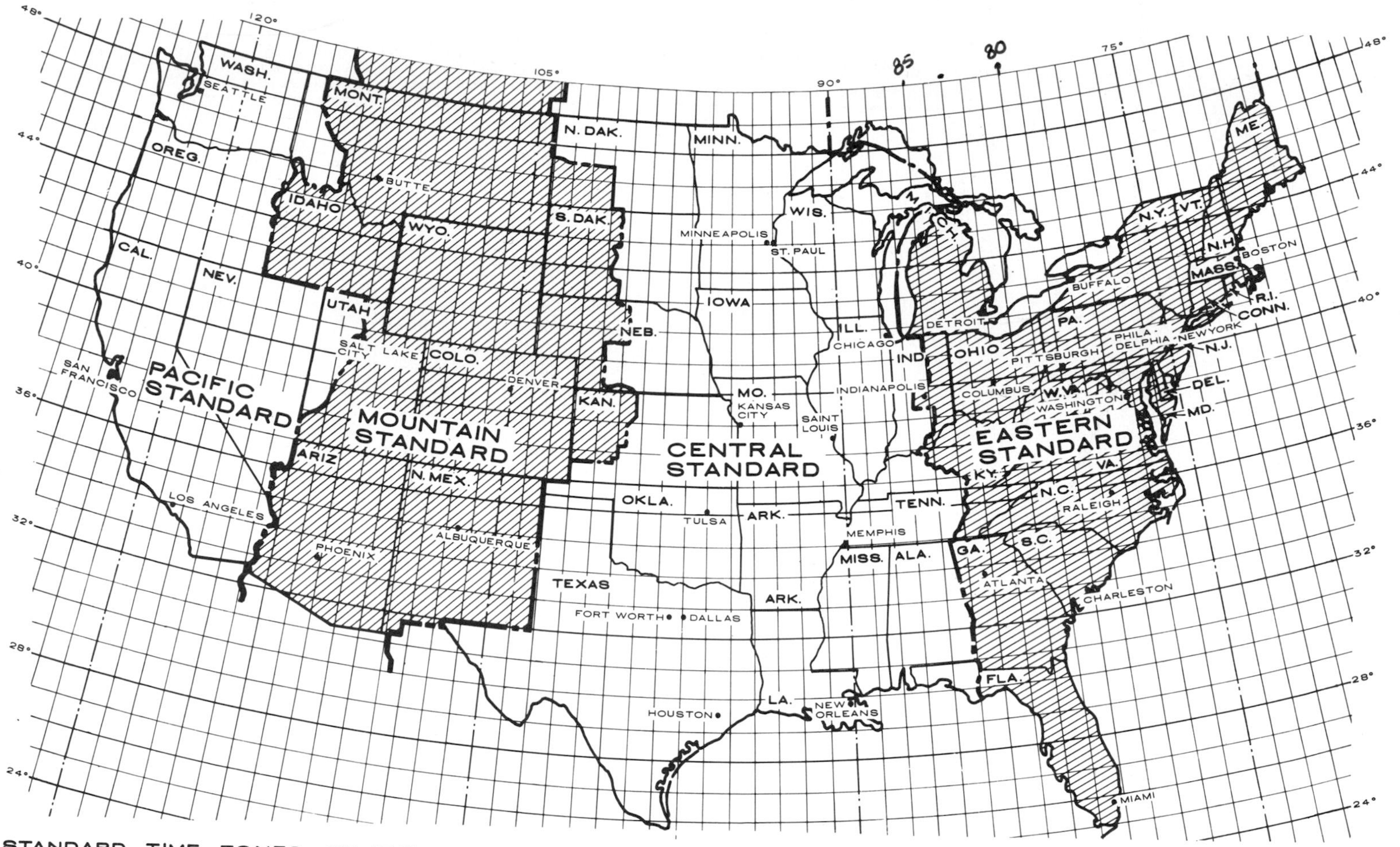

STANDARD TIME ZONES OF THE UNITED STATES

SUN TIME

Explanation of map.

LATITUDES: Curved horizontal lines. LONGITUDES: straight vertical lines.

TIME ZONES: Alternating vertical gray and white bands. Central longitudes of time zones are: Eastern Standard Time at 75°; Central S. T. at 90°; Mountain S. T. at 105°; Pacific S. T. at 120°. If conversion to SUN TIME is desired for site location then: 1) If Daylight Savings Time is in effect subtract one hour from local time. 2) Subtract 4 minutes for every degree of longitude if site is west of central longitude or add 4 mins. for every degree of longitude if site is east of it. 3) Correct time variations for day and months; add or subtract minutes as follows:

JAN 21	−11.4	APR 21	+1.2	JULY 21	−6.2	OCT 21	+15.3
FEB 21	−13.8	MAY 21	+3.6	AUG 21	−3.1	NOV 21	−14.1
MAR 21	− 7.4	JUNE 21	−1.5	SEPT 21	+6.8	DEC 21	+2.0

EXAMPLE: Calculate sun time at site for Columbus, Ohio at 12 noon local time on June 21st.

STEP 1. As in June, Daylight Savings Time is in effect, subtract one hour from local time to 11:00 o'clock.

STEP 2. Locate Columbus on map. The longitude is 83°. This is in the Eastern Time Zone with the central longitude of 75°. As Columbus is 8 degrees west of the central longitude: subtract 8X4 minutes or 32 minutes from 11:00 o'clock, changing the time to 10:28 o'clock.

STEP 3. To correct time variation for June 21st, subtract 1.5 minutes. The result indicates 10 hours, 26 minutes and 30 seconds; which will be the sun time at 12 noon, local time.

SHADOW CONSTRUCTION WITH TRUE SUN ANGLES

Required information: angle of orientation in relation to north—south axis, bearing angle (∠ B) and altitude angle (∠ A) of the sun at the desired time (Fig. 1).

STEP 1. Lay out building axis, true south and bearing ∠ B of sun in plan. (Fig. 2).

STEP 2. Lay out altitude ∠ A upon bearing ∠ B. Construct any perpendicular to ∠ B. From the intersection of this perpendicular and ∠ B project a line perpendicular to elevation plane (building orientation). Measure distance "x" along this line from elevation plane. Connect the point at distance "x" from elevation plane to center to construct sun elevation D. (Fig. 2).

STEP 3. Use sun plan ∠ B + C and sun elevation ∠ D to construct shadows in plan and elevation in conventional way. (Fig. 3).

The figures illustrate shadow projection for a building in Columbus, Ohio (40° N. Latitude) on February 21 at 2 P.M. The sun's altitude ∠ A is 32°, the bearing ∠ B is 35 ½° West.

Methods for calculating the sun's altitudes and bearings are described on pages on Solar Angles and Solar Position Calculation.

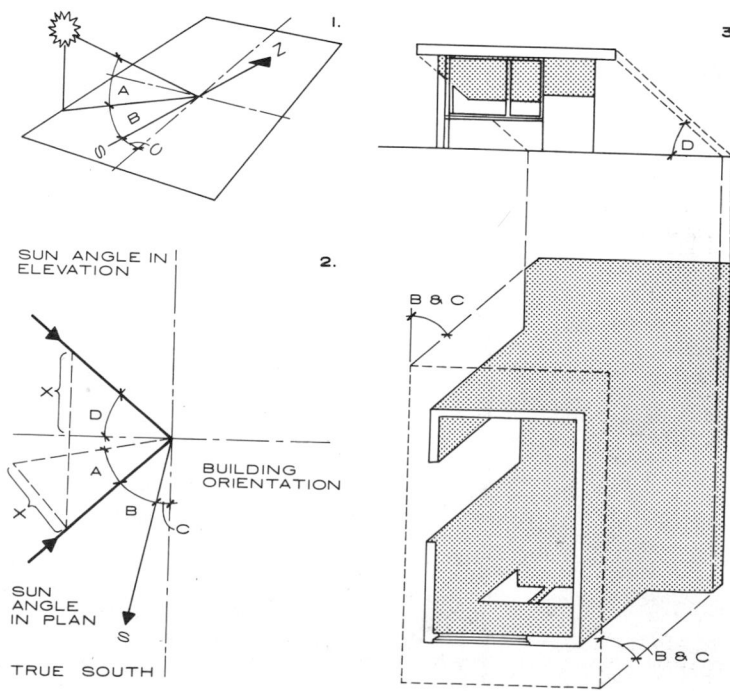

SUN ANGLE IN ELEVATION

BUILDING ORIENTATION

SUN ANGLE IN PLAN

TRUE SOUTH

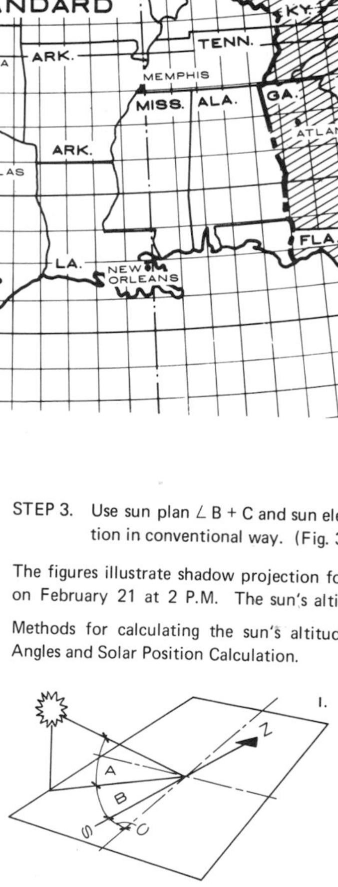

Victor Olgyay, AIA; Associate Professor; School of Architecture, Princeton University; Princeton, New Jersey

DIAGRAM		A — EXCLUDES DIRECT SUN RAYS	B — RE-RADIATES HEAT	C — CONTROLS SKY GLARE	D — CONTROLS GROUND GLARE & HEAT	E — EFFECTIVE ORIENTATION	F — RESTRICTS VIEW	G — HINDERS FREE AIR MOVEMENT	H — CONTROLS WINTER RAYS	I — MAINTENANCE (NOT CLEANING)
1. OVERHANG	Length of overhang calculated to eliminate summer sun.	Seasonal	No	No	No	South	No	Yes	Yes	Minimum unless otherwise noted
2. VERTICAL SCREEN (WITH OVERHANG)	Length of louver calculated to eliminate summer sun. Length of louver for sky glare dependent on amount of control desired on exterior conditions and occupants normal eye level.	Optional: Completely or seasonal.	Minimal	Yes	Some—amount varies with design.	Any direction. depends on design.	Yes—If opaque blade in louver. No—if tinted glass blade.	Slight	Depends on design	High for louver.
3. VERTICAL SCREEN (WITHOUT OVERHANG)	Length of louver or glass panel calculated to eliminate summer sun. Length of louver for sky glare dependent on amount of control desired on exterior conditions and occupants normal eye level.	Optional: Completely or seasonal.	Minimal	Yes	Some—amount varies with design.	Any direction. depends on design.	Yes—If opaque blade in louver. No—if tinted glass blade.	No—if louvers. Yes—if glass panel unless vent slats are provided.	Depends on design	Low for glazing
4. ADJUSTABLE EXTERIOR HORIZONTAL LOUVERS	Louvers can be adjusted to control direct rays of sun.	Optional	Minimal	No	Yes	Any direction. South is least restrictive to view.	Yes	No	Depends on design	Varies—depending on scale and materials used.
5A. OVERHANG VERTICALLY LOUVERED	Length of overhang calculated to eliminate summer sun.	Seasonal	No	Yes	No	South	No	No	Yes	Varies—depends on material used.
5B. OVERHANG ANGLE LOUVERED	Length of overhang and pitch of louvers calculated to eliminate summer sun and permit winter rays full penetration.	Seasonal	No	No	No	No	No	No	Yes—with louvers as shown, can permit maximum winter sun if desired.	Varies—depends on material used.
6. EXTERIOR VERTICAL LOUVERED	If fixed louvers can be set so as to eliminate low angle sun rays for predetermined orientation. If operable, maximum control any orientation but with various amount of view interference.	Optional: Completely or seasonal depending on orientation or other factors.	Minimal	Some	Some	East or west, south with adequate overhang.	Yes	No	Depends on design	Moderate
		As desired.	Minimal	Can be good see J	Some	Any	Yes	No	Yes	High
7. OPTIC. GLAZING (GLASS, PLASTIC, COATED GLASS)	Heat absorbing glazing controls solar heat gain. Heat absorbing and low transmission glazing controls heat gain and sky glare. Sandwich of glass and fixed louvers can control direct sun rays and sky glare and admits greater amounts of useful daylight.	No—reduces—depending on glazing material.	Can be substantial unless double glazing used.	Yes—ideal if darker sheets used in upper portion of window.	Yes	Any	No	See K	Yes—more than others	Low
		Seasonal	Low to minimal.	Yes	Same	Any	Yes	See K	Less than 7A	Low

J. Stanley Sharp, AIA; Handren, Sharp and Associates; New York, New York

J	K	L
EFFECT ON INTERIOR LIGHTING	**CAUTIONS**	**VARIATIONS**
Harsh without ideal exterior conditions, or with no glare control in glass or interior control devices.	Tends to trap warm air. High sash if open may let heat into building.	Overhang with light & heat transmission glass. Overhang with open framing with removable material (fabric, fiber glass). Trellis with plant material—permits entry of winter sun. Fixed awning—similar characteristics, except maintenance is high. Operable awning—also similar, plus lower sun angle control (west), restricts view when down.
Good	Check clearance for operating sash and window cleaning.	Addition of vertical member may be used to cut off low angle oblique rays. Adjustable vertical blinds or awnings afford good control for low sun, or glare from beach or water, without permanent restriction of view. Maintenance is high.
Good	Check clearance for operating sash and window cleaning.	Addition of vertical member may be used to cut off low angle oblique rays. Adjustable vertical blinds or awnings afford good control for low sun, or glare from beach or water, without permanent restriction of view. Maintenance is high.
Good—could be used for darkening device.		Exterior operating shutters have similar characteristics, and can be opened when not required but with loss of sky glare control.
Diffused reflected light from louvers improves quality of daylighting by reducing contrast between interior ceiling and bright sky.		Egg crate overhang instead of louvers to control oblique sun rays. Adjustable louvered awnings (questionable in cold climates) require high maintenance.
Diffused reflected light from louvers improves quality of daylighting by reducing contrast between interior ceiling and bright sky.		Egg crate overhang instead of louvers to control oblique sun rays. Adjustable louvered awnings (questionable in cold climates) require high maintenance.
Varies depending on position in room.	Check clearance for operating sash and window cleaning.	Narrow windows with adequate side reveals or projecting blades have similar sun and glare control.
Good—if a limited view is acceptable.		When used with adequate overhang on south will eliminate all sun in summer months.
Good (see C) w/high levels of artificial light, interior visual comfort is improved as reduces contrast between work surfaces and window area. Good—combine w/7A for ideal sky glare control w/a restricting eye level view.	Open sash may defeat sun & glare control, but is appropriate for a/c buildings. Replacement delay is probable.	Allow only storm sash to be tinted to eliminate problem noted under B.
	Open sash may defeat sun & glare control, but is appropriate for a/c buildings.	Louvered screen placed in front of glazing would control sun but restricts view, maintenance factor if movable, and sky glare control is lost.

J. Stanley Sharp, AIA; Handren, Sharp and Associates; New York, New York

GENERAL NOTES:

Uncontrolled glare, generated by the sun's rays, can become uncomfortable in winter; in summer, this glare plus solar heat can be intolerable. Glare can be effectively controlled by either interior or exterior devices, but solar heat gain is best controlled by interception outside the building. Tinted glass and/or interior devices such as shades, horizontal blinds, vertical blinds, as well as various screening methods may be used to control sky glare and glare from the direct rays of the sun. However, they do little to reduce interior air temperature because the sun rays have been allowed to enter the room. Do not use any form of translucent glass where sun will fall directly on it because this will produce glare similar to the dirty windshield of a car. Objectionable glare (i.e., a brightness ratio in excess of 10:1 between peripheral vision and the immediate area of vision) can occur at any orientation, including north, through indirect sources, by reflection from various surfaces. For example, light from a slightly overcast sky or from patches of white clouds can be 30 to 300 times greater than the light reflected from a well-lighted work surface. Provisions for shielding these secondary sources are particularly important to good vision when occupants of a space must remain in relatively fixed positions.

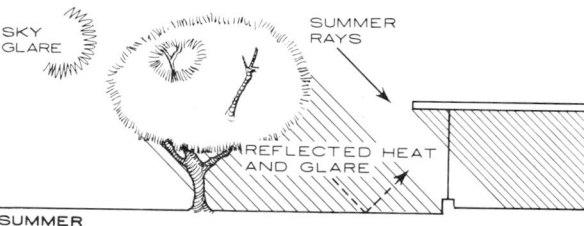

SUMMER
SUN AND GLARE AND HEAT CONTROLLED; I.E. EXCLUDED

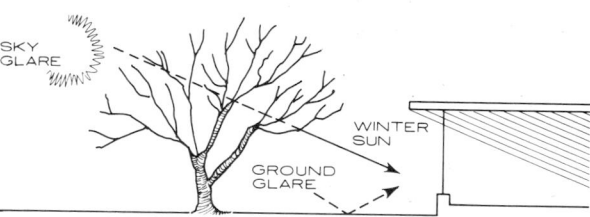

WINTER
SUN ACCEPTED-GLARE CAN BE A PROBLEM (SNOW IN PARTICULAR). CLOSELY SPACED LIMBS CAN CONTROL SKY GLARE.

SOUTH EXPOSURE

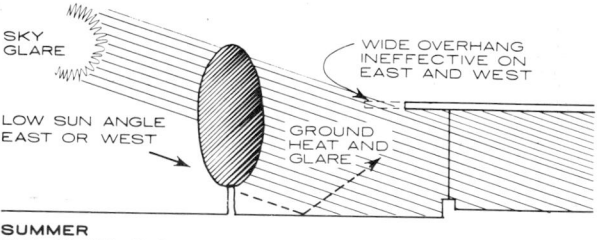

SUMMER
SUN GLARE AND HEAT CONTROLLED

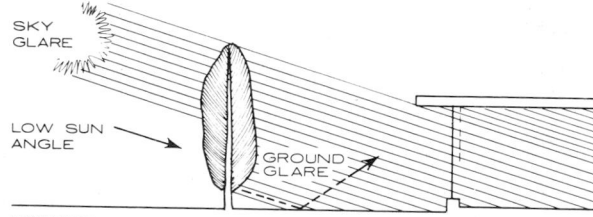

WINTER
LOW SUN ANGLE NOW ACCEPTED; GLARE CONTROLLED BY DENSE BRANCH STRUCTURE; HEAT CAN BE REASONABLY CONTROLLED AS DESIRED BY INSIDE DEVICES (SHADES, BLINDS, OR DRAPES).

EAST AND WEST EXPOSURE

APPLICATIONS IN CONJUNCTION WITH PLANTING

EXAMPLES OF HOW BASIC CONTROL DEVICES CAN BE USED IN CONJUNCTION WITH NATURAL FEATURES TO ACHIEVE GOOD SEASONAL RESULTS

NOTE:

For more positive sky glare control in winter and summer, coniferous trees should be used.

SOLAR ANGLES

The position of the sun in relation to specific geographic locations, seasons, and times of day can be determined by several different methods. Model measurements, by means of sun machines or shade dials, have the advantage of direct visual observations. Tabulative and calculative methods have the advantage of exactness. However, graphic projection methods are usually preferred by architects as they are easily understood and can be correlated to both radiant energy and shading calculations.

SUN PATH DIAGRAMS

The most practical graphic projection is the Sun Path Diagram method. Such diagrams depict the path of the sun within the sky-vault as projected onto a horizontal plane. The horizon is represented as a circle with the observation point in the center. The sun's position at any date and hour can be determined from the diagram in terms of its altitude (α) and bearing angle (β). (See figure on right). The graphs are constructed in equidistant projection. The altitude angles are represented at 10° intervals by equally spaced concentric circles; they range from 0° at the outer circle (horizon) to 90° at the center point. These intervals are graduated along the south meridian. Bearing angles are represented at 10° intervals by equally spaced radii; they range from 0° at the south meridian to 180° at the north meridian. These intervals are graduated along the periphery. The sun's bearing will be to the east during morning hours, and to the west during afternoon hours.   (CONTINUED)

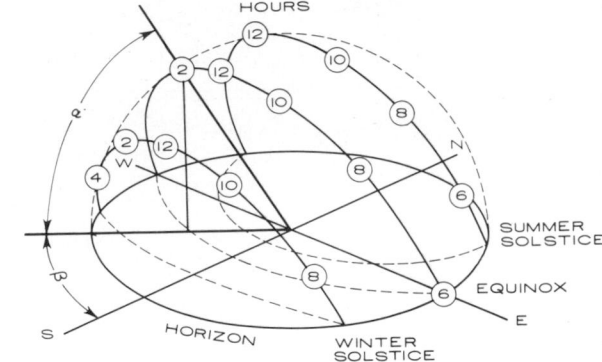

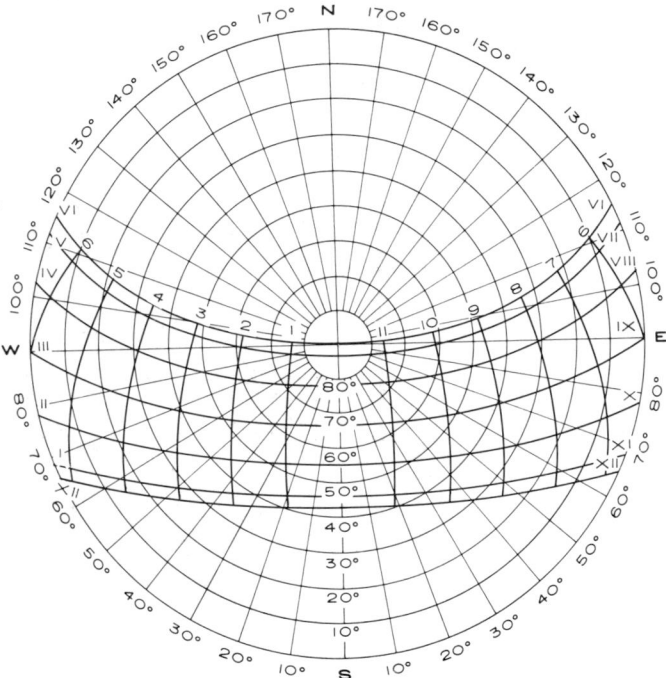

24°N LATITUDE

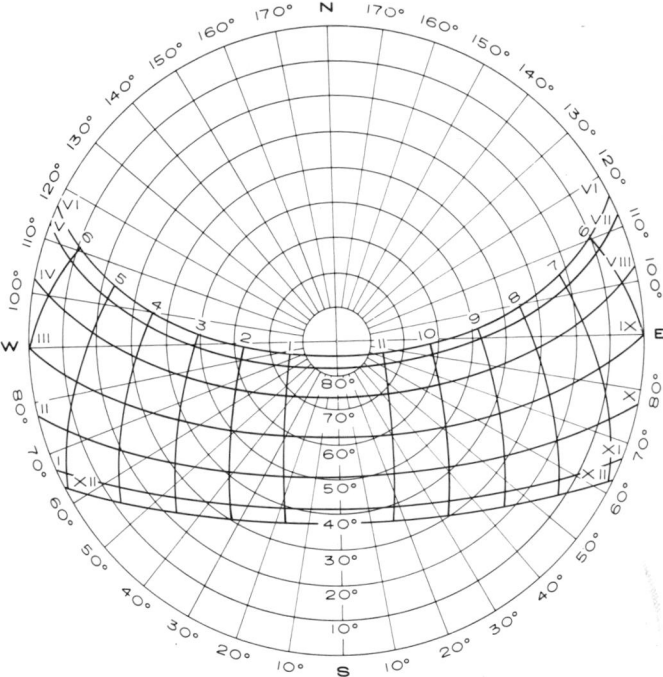

28° N LATITUDE

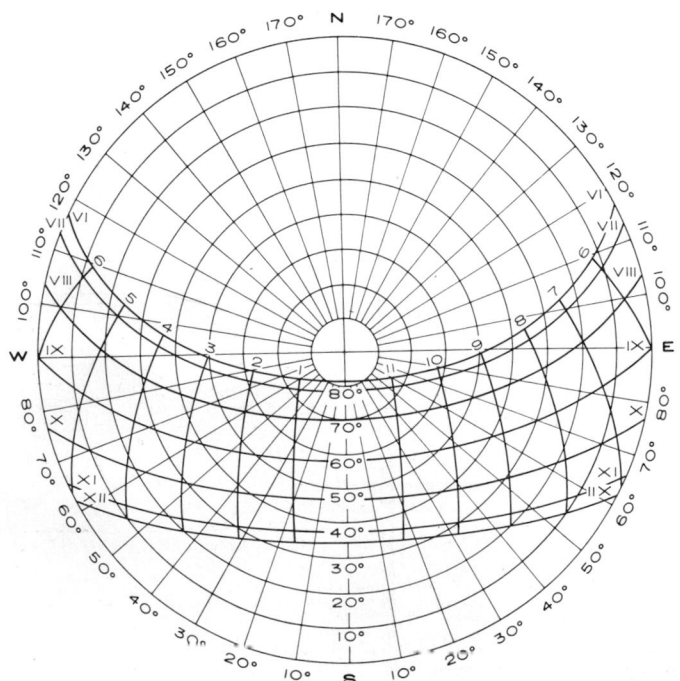

32°N LATITUDE

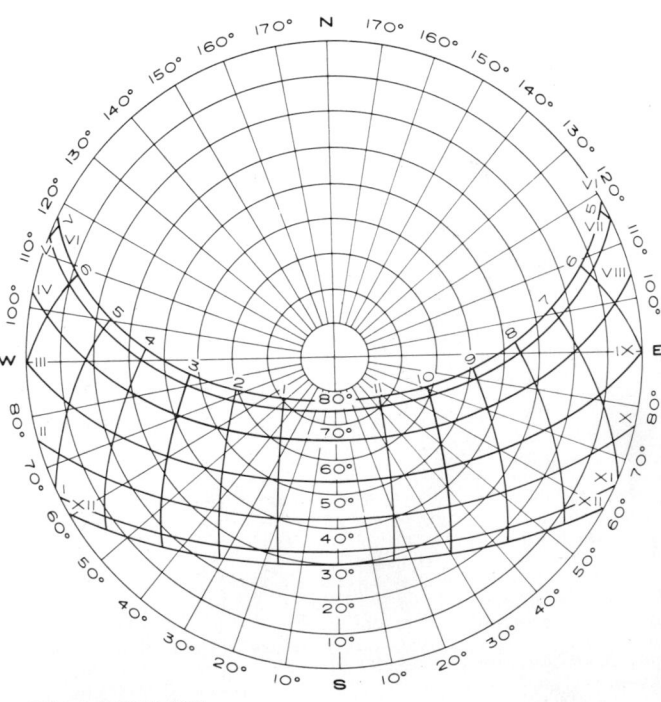

36°N LATITUDE

Victor Olgyay, AIA; Associate Professor; School of Architecture, Princeton University; Princeton, New Jersey

SUN PATH DIAGRAMS (CONTINUED)

The earth's axis is inclined 23°27′ to its orbit around the sun and rotates 15 degrees hourly. Thus, from all points on the earth, the sun appears to move across the skyvault on various parallel circular paths with maximum declinations of ± 23°27′. The declination of the sun's path changes in a cycle between the extremes of the summer solstice and winter solstice. Thus, the sun follows the same path on two corresponding dates each year. Due to irregularities between the calendar year and the astronomical data, here a unified calibration is adapted. The differences as they do not exceed 41′, are negligible for architectural purposes.

DECLINATION OF THE SUN

Date	Declination	Corresp. Date	Declination	Unified Calibr.
June 21	+23°27′			+23°27′
May 21	+20°09′	July 21	+20°31′	+20°20′
Apr. 21	+11°48′	Aug. 21	+12°12′	+12°00′
Mar. 21	+ 0°10′	Sep. 21	+ 0°47′	+ 0°28′
Feb. 21	−10°37′	Oct. 21	−10°38′	−10°38′
Jan. 21	−19°57′	Nov. 21	−19°53′	−19°55′
Dec. 21	−23°27′			−23°27′

The elliptical curves in the diagrams represent the horizontal projections of the sun's path. They are given on the 21st day of each month. Roman numerals designate the months. A cross grid of curves graduate the hours indicated in arabic numerals. Eight sun path diagrams are shown at 4° intervals from 24° N to 52° N latitude.

EXAMPLE

Find the sun's position in Columbus, Ohio on February 21st 2 P.M.:

STEP 1. Locate Columbus on the map. The latitude is 40° N.

STEP 2. In the 40° sun path diagram select the February path (marked with II), and locate the 2 hour line. Where the two lines cross is the position of the sun.

STEP 3. Read the altitude on the concentric circles (32°) and the bearing angle along the outer circle (35°30′W).

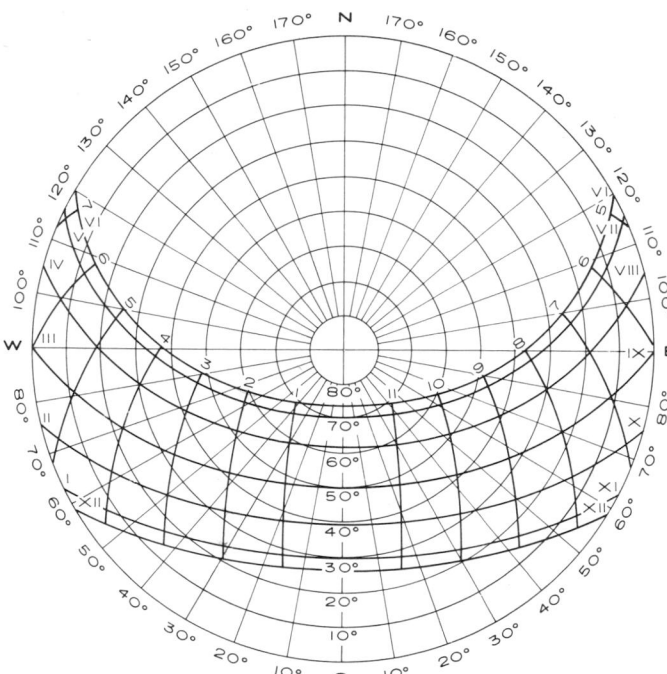

40°N LATITUDE

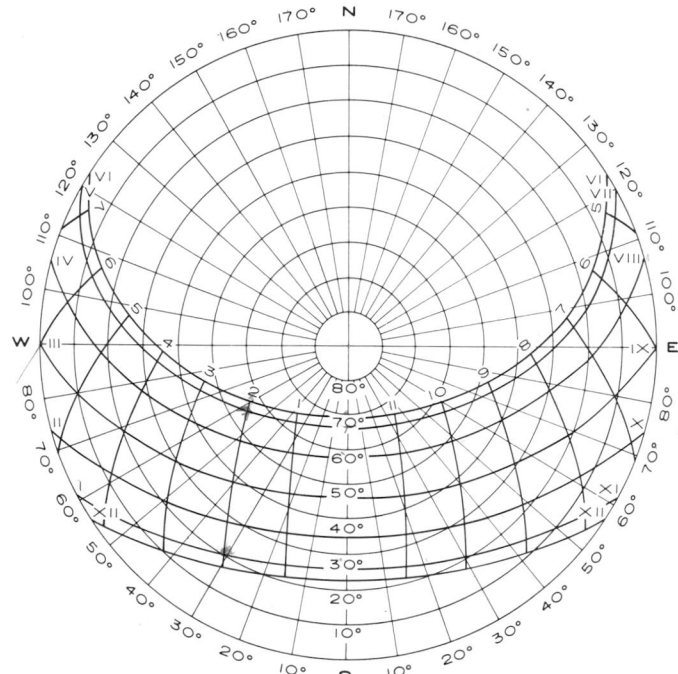

44°N LATITUDE

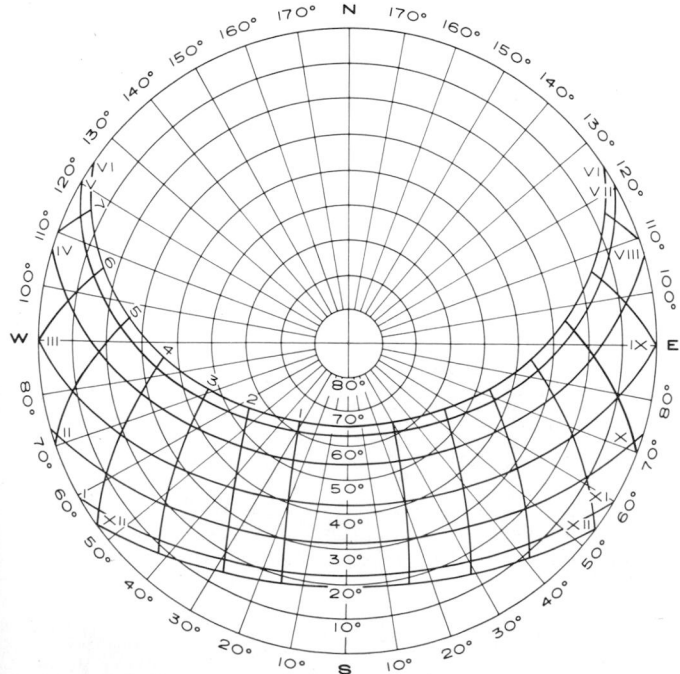

48°N LATITUDE

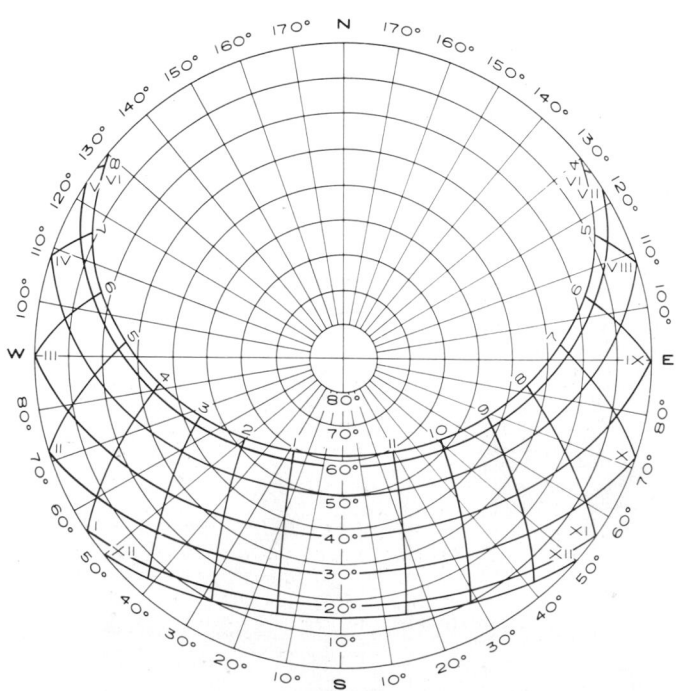

52°N LATITUDE

Victor Olgyay, AIA; Associate Professor; School of Architecture, Princeton University; Princeton, New Jersey

CALCULATION OF SOLAR POSITION

One can calculate accurately the solar position to any locale and time by relating the spherical triangle formed by the observer's celestial meridian, the meridian of the sun, and the great circle passing through zenith and the sun. The following formulas can be used to find the altitude and bearing angles:

(1) $\sin A = \sin d \sin l + \cos d \cos l \cos t$

(2) $\cos B = \dfrac{\sin d \cos l - \cos d \sin l \cos t}{\cos A}$

where: A = altitude of the sun in degrees, measured from the horizontal.

      d = declination of the sun (see page on solar angles) at the desired date. (North declinations are conventionally positive; south declinations negative.)

      l = latitude of the locale; conventionally negative in the southern hemisphere.

      t = hour angle of the sun in degrees, measured counterclockwise from north towards east. At solar noon it is zero and changes 15° per hour.

      B = bearing angle of the sun in degrees; here measured clockwise from north towards east.

CALCULATION OF SOLAR RADIATION

To evaluate the importance of solar shading one has to know the amount of solar energy falling on the exposed surface. As the primary protection of the shading devices is from the direct solar radiation, only these energy calculations are described here.

The magnitude of solar radiation depends, first of all, on the sun's altitude. The tabulated values indicate direct radiation energies received under clear atmospheric conditions at normal incidence (ID):

Solar altitude in degrees:

5	10	15	20	25	30	35	40	45	50	60	70	80	90
67	123	166	197	218	235	248	258	266	273	283	289	292	294

Btu/sq. ft./hour

The energy received on a surface depends also on the cosine of the angle of incidence. As this is a spacial angle, it is conventional on vertical surfaces to substitute it with the functions of the altitude ($\angle A$) and the azimuth ($\angle a$) angles related to the normal of the surface in question. Thus, the direct radiation on vertical surfaces (R) can be defined as:

$$R = I_D \times \cos A \cos a$$

For horizontal surfaces the received direct radiation energy will be:

$$R = I_D \times \sin A$$

In the following tables calculated values of solar position in degrees, and direct radiation energies in Btu/sq. ft./hour values are shown at different orientations. The tables indicate from 24°N to 46°N latitude at 4 degree intervals.

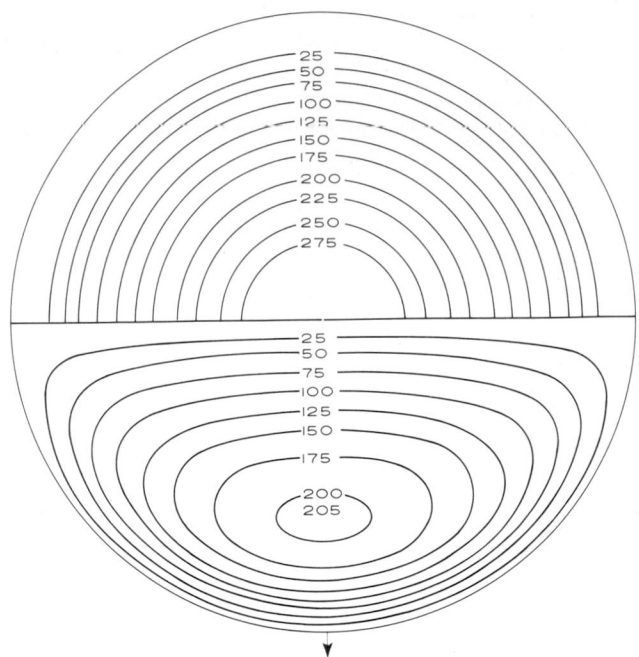

RADIATION CALCULATOR

Radiation calculations can be performed by graphical means. The upper half of the above shown direct radiation calculator charts the energies falling on a horizontal plain under clear sky conditions. The equi-intensity radiation lines are indicated at 25 Btu/sq. ft./hour intervals. The lower half circle shows the amount of direct radiation falling on a vertical surface. The calculator can be used at any latitude and at any orientation. The calculator is in the same scale and projection as the sun-path diagrams on pages on solar angles. Transfer calculator diagram to a transparent overlay, and superimpose it on a sun-path diagram in the desired orientation: the radiation values can be read directly.

26° N. LATITUDE

JUNE 22

AM →		ALT.	BEAR.	BTU/sq.ft./hour						HOR.
				S	SE	E	NE	N	SW	
6 a.m.	6 p.m.	10.05	111.30		49	113	111	44		22
7	5	22.82	105.97		93	185	168	53		81
8	4	35.93	101.15		113	199	168	39		147
9	3	49.24	96.45		111	176	139	20		206
10	2	62.69	88.83	3	94	131	90			253
11	1	76.15	82.61	9	55	69	43			282
12		87.45	0.00	13	9				9	293
PM →		α	β	S	SW	W	NW	N	SE	HOR.

MARCH 21, SEPT. 24

AM →		ALT.	BEAR.	BTU/sq.ft./hour						HOR.
				S	SW	W	NW	N	SE	
6 a.m.	6 p.m.	0.00	90.00							
7	5	13.45	83.30	17	117	147	92			36
8	4	26.70	75.80	49	172	194	102			101
9	3	39.46	66.33	80	185	182	72			163
10	2	51.11	52.79	104	171	137	23			213
11	1	60.25	31.44	120	137	73			33	246
12		64.00	0.00	125	88				88	257
PM →		α	β	S	SE	E	NE	N	SW	HOR.

DECEMBER 22

AM →		ALT.	BEAR.	BTU/sq.ft./hour						HOR.
				S	SE	E	NE	N	SW	
7 a.m.	5 p.m.	2.23	62.48	14	29	27	9			1
8	4	13.76	54.88	87	149	123	26			37
9	3	24.12	45.30	138	196	139	1			88
10	2	32.66	33.01	171	199	111			42	131
11	1	38.46	17.65	190	177	61			92	159
12		45.55	0.00	197	139				139	168
PM →		α	β	S	SW	W	NW	N	SE	HOR.

30° N. LATITUDE

JUNE 22

AM →		ALT.	BEAR.	BTU/sq.ft./hour						HOR.
				S	SE	E	NE	N	SW	
6 a.m.	6 p.m.	11.48	110.59		55	124	121	47		27
7	5	23.87	104.30		100	189	168	48		86
8	4	36.60	98.24		121	200	162	29		150
9	3	49.53	91.79		121	177	129	6		207
10	2	62.50	83.46	15	103	131	82			252
11	1	75.11	67.48	29	69	69	29			281
12		83.45	0.00	33	24				24	291
PM →		α	β	S	SW	W	NW	N	SE	HOR.

MARCH 21, SEPT. 24

AM →		ALT.	BEAR.	BTU/sq.ft./hour						HOR.
				S	SE	E	NE	N	SW	
6 a.m.	6 p.m.	0.00	90.00							
7	5	12.95	82.37	19	115	143	88			33
8	4	25.66	73.90	55	174	191	96			95
9	3	37.76	63.44	90	190	179	63			155
10	2	48.59	49.11	117	179	136	13			203
11	1	56.77	28.19	135	147	72			44	234
12		60.00	0.00	142	100				100	245
PM →		α	β	S	SW	W	NW	N	SE	HOR.

DECEMBER 22

AM →		ALT.	BEAR.	BTU/sq.ft./hour						HOR.
				S	SE	E	NE	N	NW	
7 a.m.	5 p.m.	0.38	62.40	2	5	5	2			
8	4	11.44	54.15	78	131	108	21			27
9	3	21.27	44.12	135	189	131			3	73
10	2	29.28	31.73	173	197	107			47	114
11	1	34.64	16.77	195	179	59			96	140
12		36.55	0.00	202	143				143	150
PM →		α	β	S	SW	W	NW	N	SE	HOR.

Victor Olgyay, AIA; Associate Professor; School of Architecture, Princeton University; Princeton, New Jersey

34° N. LATITUDE

JUNE 22

AM		ALT.	BEAR.	S	SE	E	NE	N	SW	HOR.
5 a.m.	7 p.m.	1.47	117.57		6	17	19	9		1
6	6	12.86	109.78		61	135	130	49		33
7	5	24.80	102.54		106	192	166	43		91
8	4	37.07	95.28		129	200	155	19		152
9	3	49.49	87.10	9	131	177	119			207
10	2	61.79	76.00	32	115	130	69			250
11	1	73.17	55.11	48	83	69	15			278
12		79.45	0.00	53	38				38	287
PM		α	β	S	SW	W	NW	N	SE	HOR.

MARCH 21, SEPT. 24

AM		ALT.	BEAR.	S	SE	E	NE	N	SW	HOR.
6 a.m.	6 p.m.	0.00	90.00							
7	5	12.39	81.48	21	113	139	83			31
8	4	24.49	72.11	60	175	187	90			89
9	3	35.89	60.79	99	195	177	55			146
10	2	45.89	45.92	129	186	134	3			192
11	1	53.21	25.60	149	156	71			55	221
12		56.00	0.00	156	110				110	231
PM		α	β	S	SW	W	NW	N	SE	HOR.

DECEMBER 22

AM		ALT.	BEAR.	S	SE	E	NE	N	SW	HOR.
8 a.m.	4 p.m.	9.08	53.57	66	110	90	17			18
9	3	18.38	43.12	129	177	121			6	59
10	2	25.86	30.65	171	193	101			49	96
11	1	30.81	16.05	196	178	56			99	121
12		32.55	0.00	204	144				144	130
PM		α	β	S	SW	W	NW	N	SE	HOR.

38° N. LATITUDE

JUNE 22

AM		ALT.	BEAR.	S	SE	E	NE	N	SW	HOR.
5 a.m.	7 p.m.	3.32	118.42		13	39	42	20		3
6	6	14.18	108.87		68	146	138	50		39
7	5	25.60	100.70		112	195	164	37		95
8	4	37.33	92.25		136	201	148	8		153
9	3	49.13	82.47	23	141	176	108			206
10	2	60.58	69.06	50	127	130	57			246
11	1	70.61	45.67	67	96	69	1			273
12		75.45	0.00	73	52				52	281
PM		α	β	S	SW	W	NW	N	SE	HOR.

MARCH 21, SEPT. 24

AM		ALT.	BEAR.	S	SE	E	NE	N	SW	HOR.
6 a.m.	6 p.m.	0.00	90.00							
7	5	11.77	80.63	22	110	134	79			28
8	4	23.20	70.43	65	175	182	83			83
9	3	33.86	58.38	107	198	173	47			137
10	2	43.03	42.16	140	192	131			6	179
11	1	49.57	23.52	162	164	71			65	207
12		52.00	0.00	169	120				120	217
PM		α	β	S	SW	W	NW	N	SE	HOR.

DECEMBER 22

AM		ALT.	BEAR.	S	SE	E	NE	N	SW	HOR.
8 a.m.	4 p.m.	6.69	53.12	51	84	68	12			10
9	3	15.44	42.30	120	162	109			8	45
10	2	22.40	29.75	166	185	95			50	79
11	1	26.96	15.45	193	174	53			99	102
12		28.55	0.00	202	143				143	110
PM		α	β	S	SW	W	NW	N	SE	HOR.

42° N. LATITUDE

JUNE 22

AM		ALT.	BEAR.	S	SE	E	NE	N	SW	HOR.
5 a.m.	7 p.m.	5.15	117.16		21	61	65	31		6
6	6	15.44	107.87		74	155	145	50		45
7	5	26.28	98.78		118	197	161	30		98
8	4	37.38	89.19	3	144	201	140			153
9	3	48.45	77.96	37	151	176	98			203
10	2	58.95	62.79	67	138	129	44			242
11	1	67.64	38.62	85	109	68			12	266
12		71.45	0.00	92	65				65	274
PM		α	β	S	SW	W	NW	N	SE	HOR.

MARCH 21, SEPT. 24

AM		ALT.	BEAR.	S	SE	E	NE	N	SW	HOR.
6 a.m.	6 p.m.	0.00	90.00							
7	5	11.09	79.84	23	107	128	74			25
8	4	21.81	68.88	68	174	177	77			76
9	3	31.70	57.81	113	200	169	40			126
10	2	40.06	40.79	150	197	129			15	166
11	1	45.88	21.82	173	171	69			73	192
12		48.00	0.00	181	128				128	201
PM		α	β	S	SW	W	NW	N	SE	HOR.

DECEMBER 22

AM		ALT.	BEAR.	S	SE	E	NE	N	SW	HOR.
8 a.m.	4 p.m.	4.28	52.82	35	57	46	8			4
9	3	12.46	41.63	105	141	94			8	31
10	2	18.91	29.01	157	173	87			50	62
11	1	23.09	14.96	187	167	50			97	82
12		24.55	0.00	197	139				139	90
PM		α	β	S	SW	W	NW	N	SE	HOR.

46° N. LATITUDE

JUNE 22

AM		ALT.	BEAR.	S	SE	E	NE	N	SW	HOR.
5 a.m.	7 p.m.	6.97	116.78		28	79	84	40		11
6	6	16.63	106.77		80	162	149	49		50
7	5	26.82	96.80		124	199	157	24		101
8	4	37.22	86.15	14	151	201	132			153
9	3	47.47	73.66	51	160	175	87			199
10	2	56.95	57.25	83	149	128	32			235
11	1	64.40	33.33	103	121	68			25	258
12		67.45	0.00	110	78				78	265
PM		α	β	S	SW	W	NW	N	SE	HOR.

MARCH 21, SEPT. 24

AM		ALT.	BEAR.	S	SE	E	NE	N	SW	HOR.
6 a.m.	6 p.m.	0.00	90.00							
7	5	10.36	79.09	23	103	122	70			23
8	4	20.32	67.45	71	172	172	71			69
9	3	29.42	54.27	119	200	165	33			114
10	2	36.98	38.75	157	200	126			22	152
11	1	42.14	20.43	182	176	68			81	175
12		44.00	0.00	190	134				134	184
PM		α	β	S	SW	W	NW	N	SE	HOR.

DECEMBER 22

AM		ALT.	BEAR.	S	SE	E	NE	N	SW	HOR.
8 a.m.	4 p.m.	1.86	52.65	15	25	20	3			1
9	3	9.46	41.12	87	115	76			8	19
10	2	15.41	28.41	143	156	77			46	45
11	1	19.23	14.56	176	156	46			92	63
12		20.55	0.00	187	132				132	70
PM		α	β	S	SW	W	NW	N	SE	HOR.

Victor Olgyay, AIA; Associate Professor; School of Architecture, Princeton University; Princeton, New Jersey

SHADING DEVICES

The effect of shading devices can be plotted in the same manner as the sun-path was projected. The diagrams show which part of the sky vault will be obstructed by the devices and are projections of the surface covered on the sky vault as seen from an observation point at the center of the diagram. These projections also represent those parts of the sky vault from which no sunlight will reach the observation point; if the sun passes through such an area the observation point will be shaded.

SHADING MASKS

Any building element will define a characteristic form in these projection diagrams, known as "shading masks." Masks of horizontal devices (overhangs) will create a segmental pattern; vertical intercepting elements (fins) produce a radial pattern; shading devices with horizontal and vertical members (eggcrate type) will make a combinative pattern. A shading mask can be drawn for any shading device, even for very complex ones, by geometric plotting. As the shading masks are geometric projections they are independent of latitude and exposed directions, therefore they can be used in any location and at any orientation. By overlaying a shading mask in the proper orientation on the sun-path diagram, one can read off the times when the sun rays will be intercepted. Masks can be drawn for full shade (100% mask) when the observation point is at the lowest point of the surface needing shading; or for 50% shading when the observation point is placed at the halfway mark on the surface. It is customary to design a shading device in such a way that as soon as shading is needed on a surface the masking angle should exceed 50%. Solar calculations should be used to check the specific loads. Basic shading devices are shown below, with their obstruction effect on the sky vault and with their projected shading masks.

SHADING MASK PROTRACTOR

The half of the protractor showing segmental lines is used to plot lines parallel and normal to the observed vertical surface. The half showing bearing and altitude lines is used to plot shading masks of vertical fins or any other obstruction objects. The protractor is in the same projection and scale as the sun-path diagrams (see pages on solar angles); therefore it is useful to transfer the protractor to a transparent overlay to read the obstruction effect.

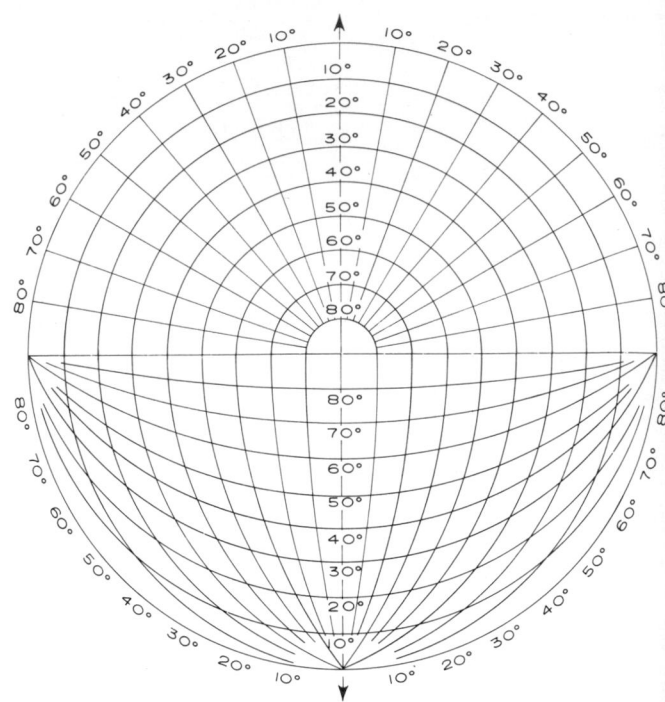

SHADING MASK PROTRACTOR

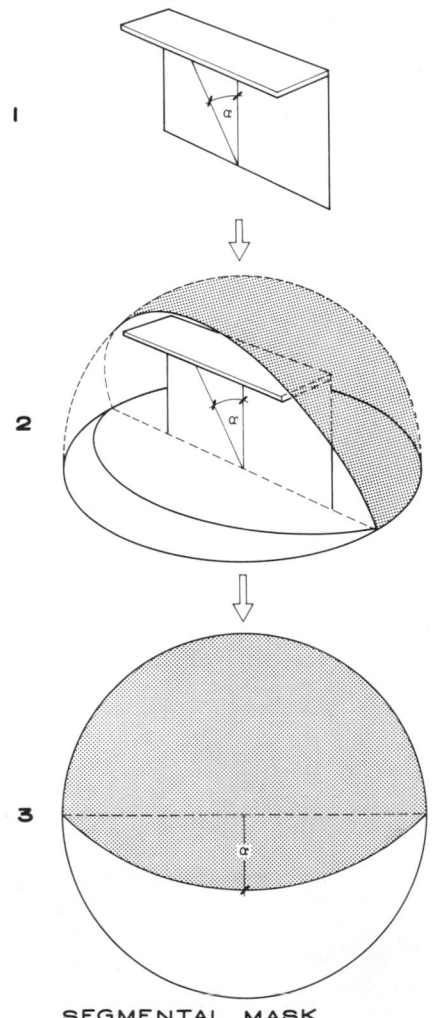

HORIZONTAL

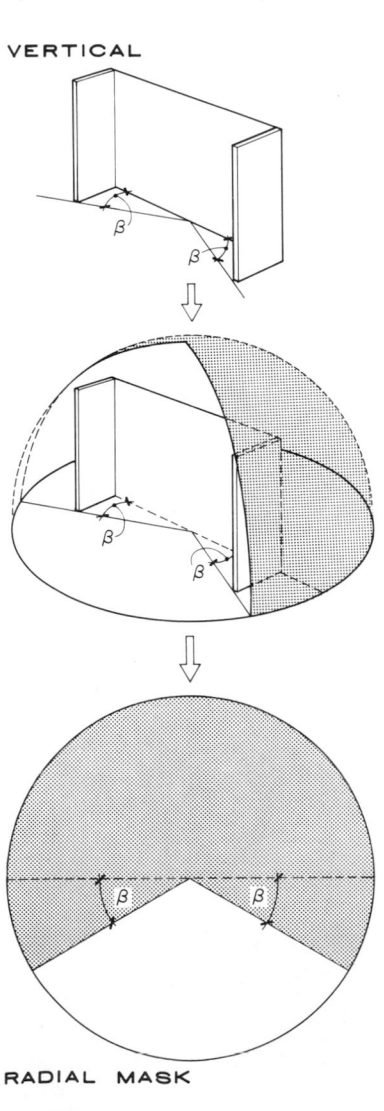

VERTICAL

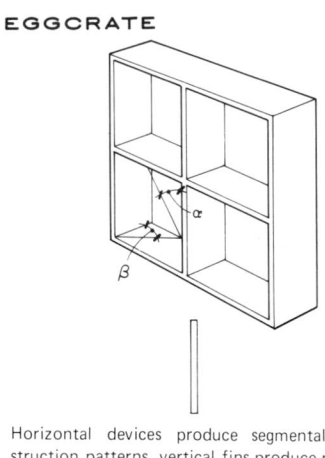

EGGCRATE

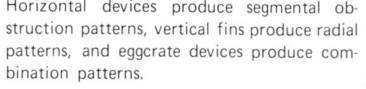

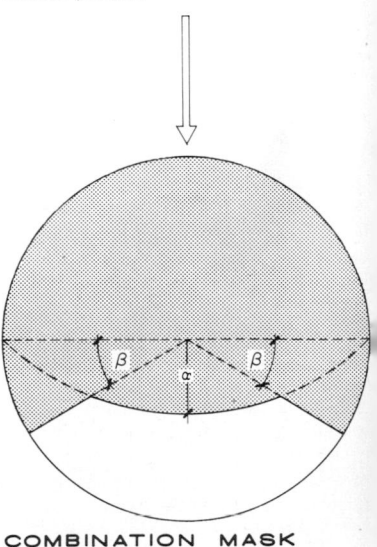

Horizontal devices produce segmental obstruction patterns, vertical fins produce radial patterns, and eggcrate devices produce combination patterns.

SEGMENTAL MASK

RADIAL MASK

COMBINATION MASK

Victor Olgyay, AIA; Associate Professor; School of Architecture, Princeton University; Princeton, New Jersey

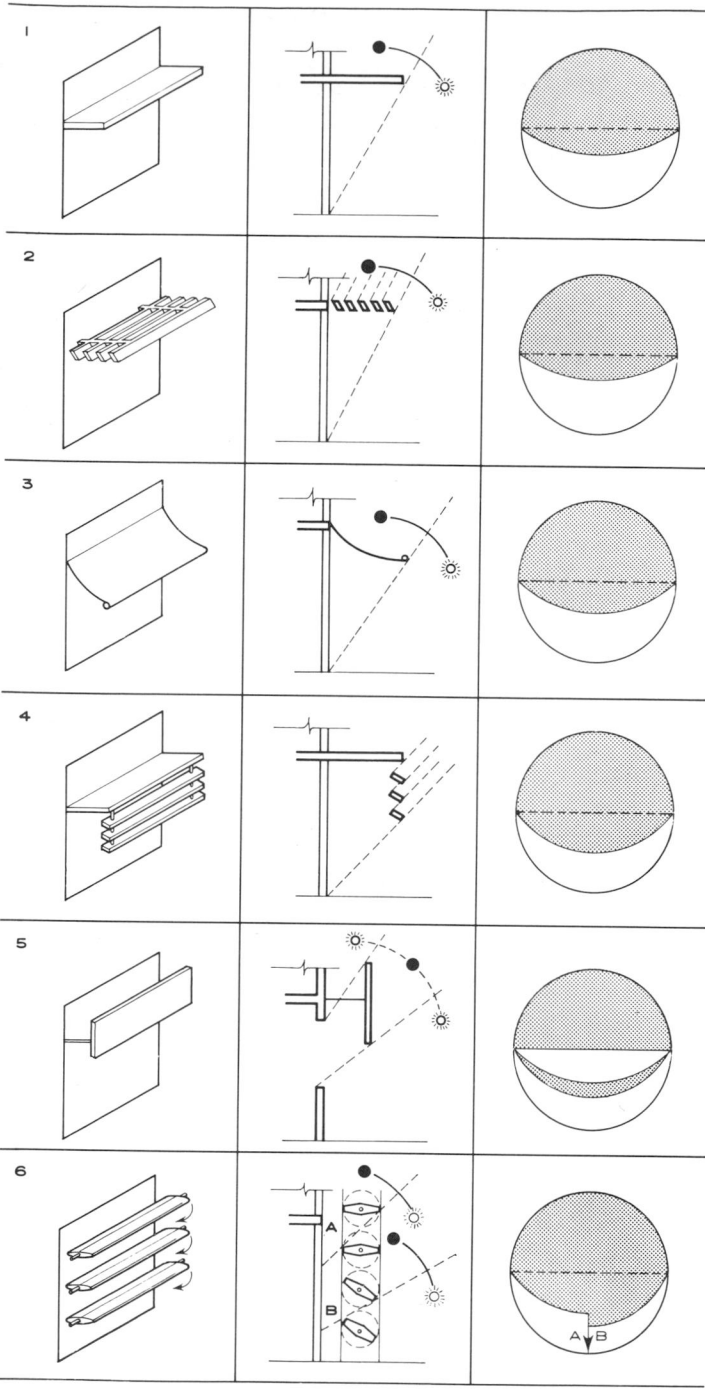

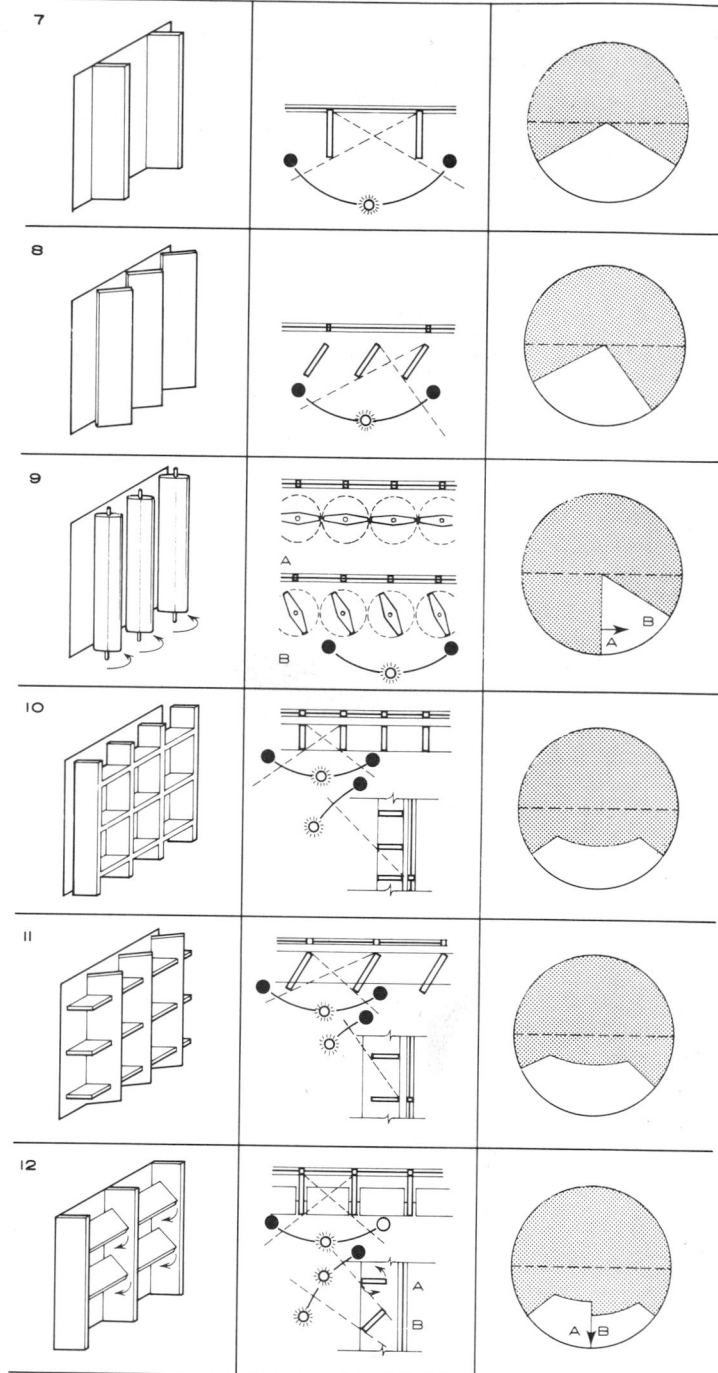

EXAMPLES OF VARIOUS TYPES OF SHADING DEVICES

The illustrations show a number of basic types of devices, classified as horizontal, vertical, and eggcrate types. The dash lines shown in the section diagram in each case indicate the sun angle at the time of 100% shading. The shading mask for each device is also shown, the extent of 100% shading being indicated by the gray area.

General rules can be deduced for the types of shading devices to be used for different orientations. Southerly orientations call for shading devices with segmental mask characteristics, and horizontal devices work in these directions efficiently. For easterly and westerly orientations vertical devices serve well, having radial shading masks. If slanted, they should incline toward the north, to give more protection from the southern positions of the sun. The eggcrate type of shading device works well on walls facing southeast, and is particularly effective for southwest orientations. Because of this type's high shading ratio and low winter head admission; its best use is in hot climate regions. For north walls, fixed vertical devices are recommended; however, their use is needed only for large glass surfaces, or in hot regions. At low latitudes on both south and north exposures eggcrate devices work efficiently.

Whether the shading devices be fixed or movable, the same recommendations apply in respect to the different orientations. The movable types can be most efficiently utilized where the sun's altitude and bearing angles change rapidly: on the east, southeast, and especially, because of the afternoon heat, on the southwest and west.

Victor Olgyay, AIA; Associate Professor; School of Architecture, Princeton University; Princeton, New Jersey

HORIZONTAL TYPES 1. Horizontal overhangs are most efficient toward south, or around southern orientations. Their mask characteristics are segmental. 2. Louvers parallel to wall have the advantage of permitting air circulation near the elevation. Slanted louvers will have the same characteristics as solid overhangs, and can be made retractable. 4. When protection is needed for low sun angles, louvers hung from solid horizontal overhangs are efficient. 5. A solid, or perforated screen strip parallel to wall cuts out the lower rays of the sun. 6. Movable horizontal louvers change their segmental mask characteristics according to their positioning.

VERTICAL TYPES 7. Vertical fins serve well toward the near east and near west orientations. Their mask characteristics are radial. 8. Vertical fins oblique to wall will result in asymmetrical mask. Separation from wall will prevent heat transmission. 9. Movable fins can shade the whole wall, or open up in different directions according to the sun's position.

EGGCRATE TYPES 10. Eggcrate types are combinations of horizontal and vertical types, and their masks are superimposed diagrams of the two masks. 11. Solid eggcrate with slanting vertical fins results in asymmetrical mask. 12. Eggcrate device with movable horizontal elements shows flexible mask characteristics. Because of their high shading ratio, eggcrates are efficient in hot climates.

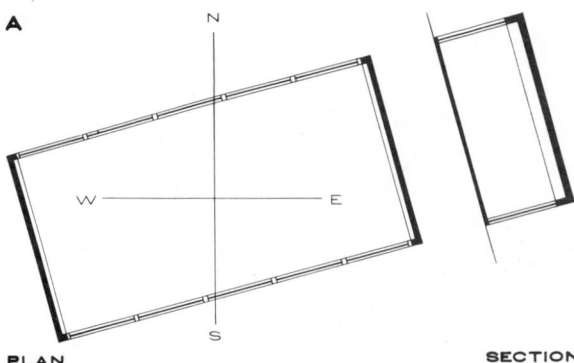

PLAN   **SECTION**

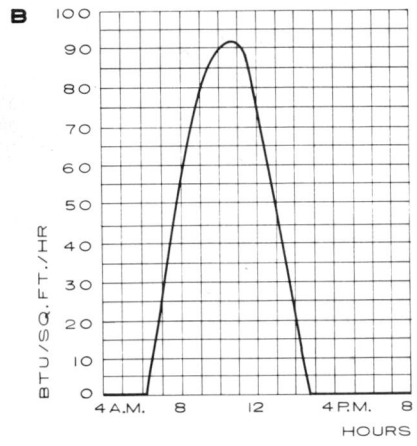

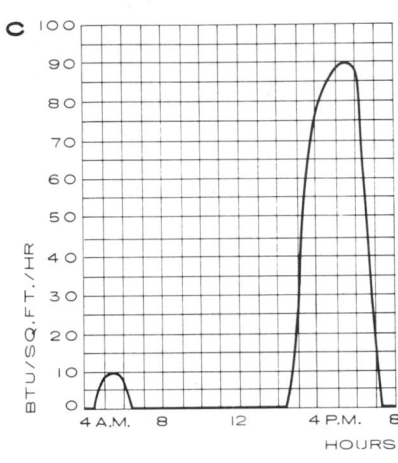

EXAMPLE OF SHADING DEVICE CALCULATION

The structure in the example is located in New York, N.Y. Two sides of the building (here called north and south) are fully glazed. The two other sides are closed.

STEP 1. Position structure to true orientation (see page on orientation). The long axis of the building lies 15° north of east (see Figure A).

STEP 2. To evaluate the need for solar control, the amount of solar energy falling on the exposed glass surfaces should be calculated. New York lies nearest to the 40°N latitude. The most penetrating sun angles occur at June 21st. Superimpose over the 40° sun-path diagram (see page on solar angles) the radiation calculator (see page on solar energy calculation), and turning the calculator 15° east of south, read along the June 21st sun-path the hourly radiation impacts. Figure B shows the Btu/sq. ft./hour sun energy values falling on the south side. One can see from it that this surface receives an eight hour insolation, with energies over 90 Btu/sq. ft./hour around 11 a.m. Figure C shows the sun energies impinging on the north side. One can see from it that the early morning impact is negligible, but around 6 p.m. a considerable amount of energy falls on the surface. Conclusion: both exposed sides should be protected by shading devices.

STEP 3. To determine the times when shading is needed: during cool times of the year (called "underheated period") the warming effect of the sun is desirable. During the warm times (called "overheated period") shading is needed to approach comfort conditions. For practical use the 70° temperature can be accepted as a dividing line between these two conditions.

Figure D illustrates the New York (40°N latitude) sun-path diagram on which are charted all conditions throughout the year when the temperatures equal or exceed 70°F. In these overheated times, illustrated with the shaded area on the graph, shading will be needed.

STEP 4. Construction of shading mask: lay the "shading mask protractor" (see page on shading devices) over the overheated period diagram in the proper orientation; as figure E illustrates. Here the contours of the overheated period are shown by the dotted line. From the shading mask lines one can see that towards the south, devices with segmental character (overhang types) will cover conveniently the overheated period. At the north side the application of devices having radial mask patterns (fin types) will be effective.

In the figure in darker tone is shown the 100% shading effect; when the total wall surface is in shadow. In lighter tone is shown the 50% shading effect; when only half of the surface will be in shade.

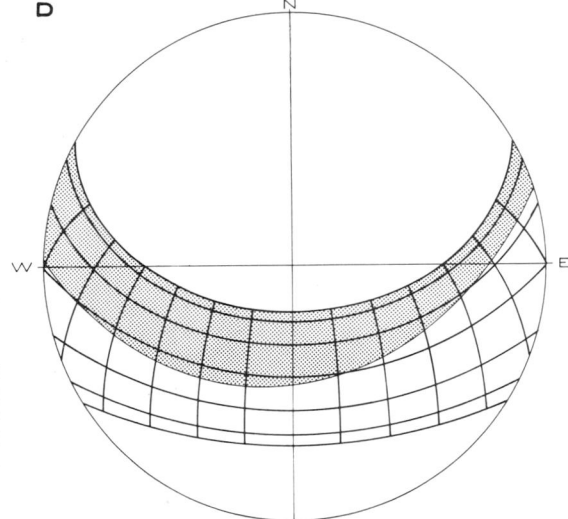

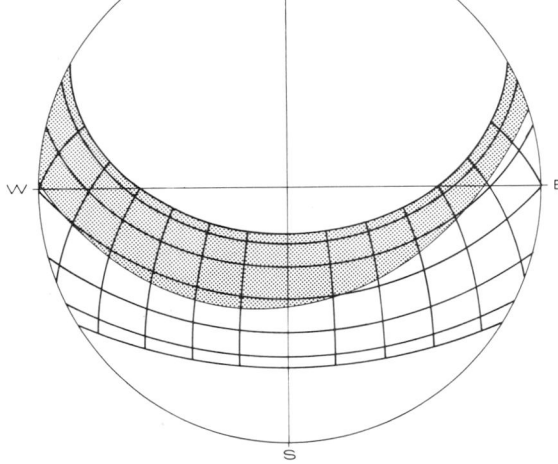

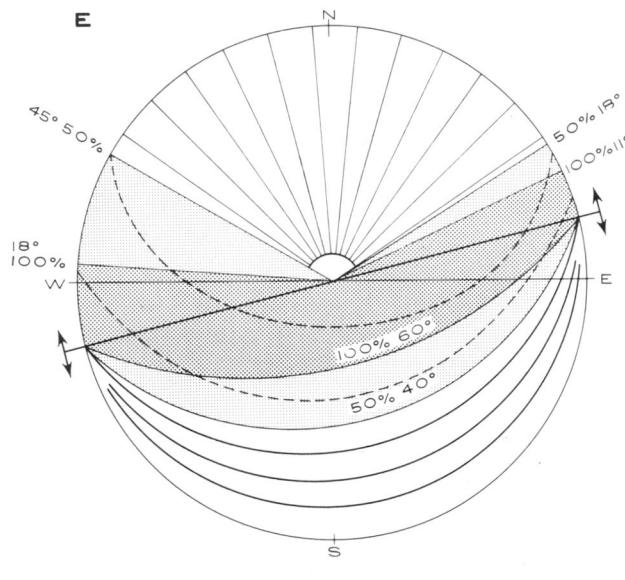

STEP 5. Design of shading devices from shading masks; the mask defines the type and the angles of the devices only, and possibilities remain for various design arrangements. In the example at the north side vertical fins will serve effectively. As the required angles in the shading mask are different towards the west (18° for 100% and 45° for 50% shading effect) as for the easterly direction (11° for 100% and 18° for 50% shading effect); the device shall be oblique to the wall surface. Figure F illustrates an application for the north side. The necessary shading angle is measured in the plan from the middle of the shading fins; the full shade giving angles are measured from the inside corners os of the shading elements.

On the south side one could apply a 60° solid overhang. However, this might be too long to cantilever. Instead, the solution here is a combination of horizontal and vertical elements, which corresponds to the same shading mask (see page on Shading Devices). In the section the 50% shading effect is measured from the middle of the glass pane; the 100% shading effect, from the bottom. The horizontal part of the shading device could be solid; however, it is constructed here with louver elements to secure ventilation. The critical angle for the louvers is 73 ½°, to correspond to the sun's highest altitude angle at this latitude. (See section in Figure F).

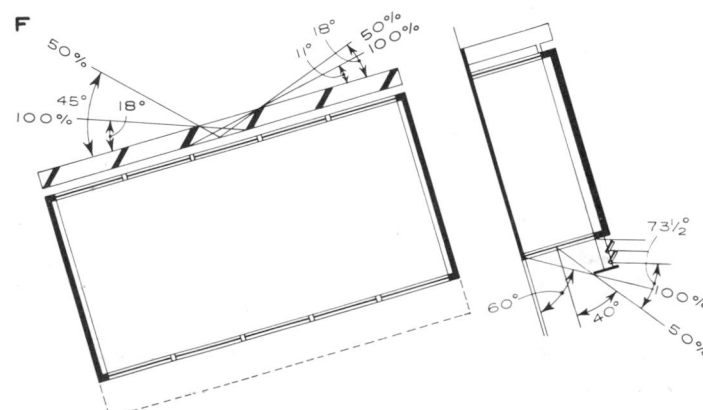

Victor Olgyay, AIA; Associate Professor; School of Architecture, Princeton University; Princeton, New Jersey

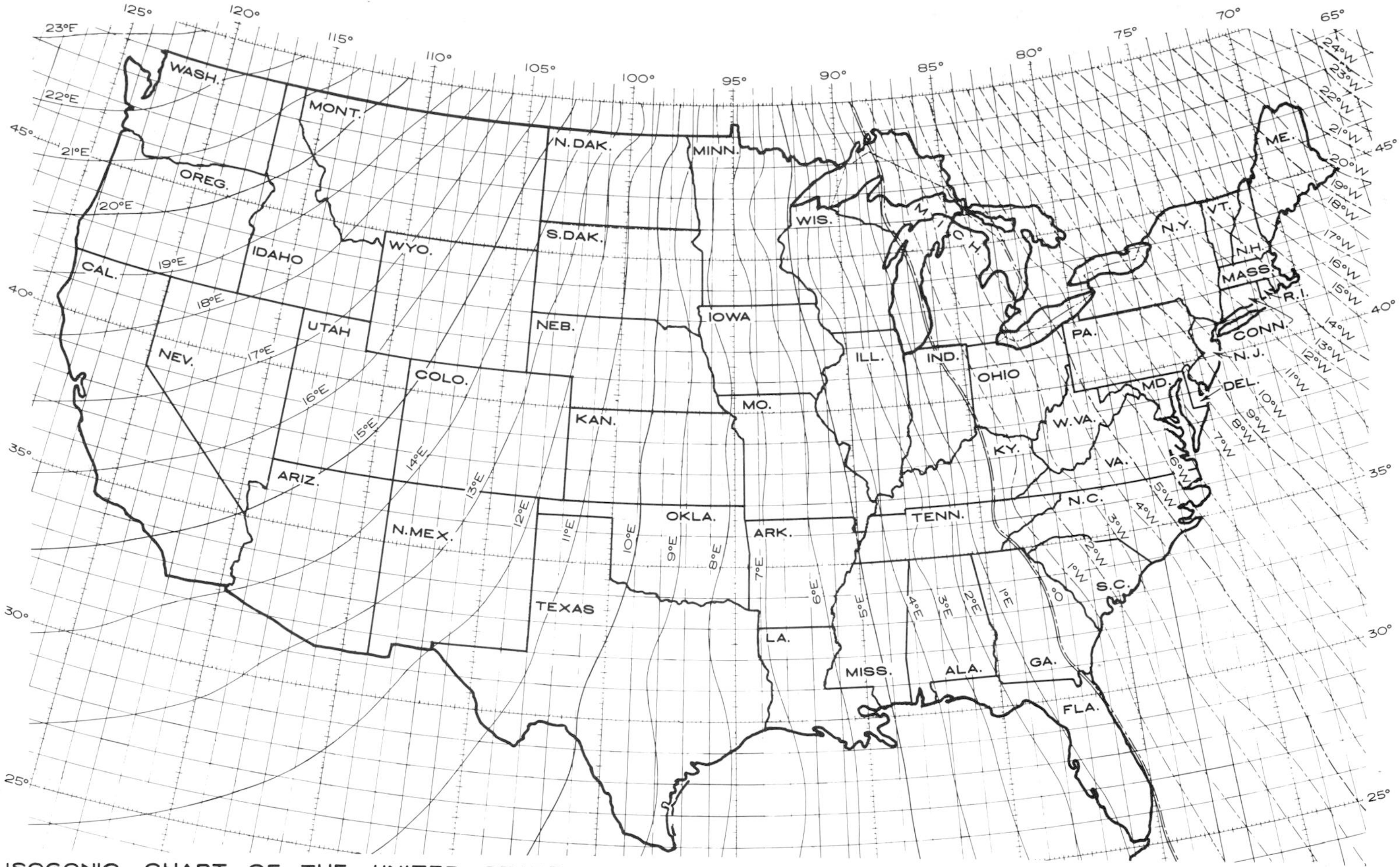

ISOGONIC CHART OF THE UNITED STATES
FROM U.S. DEPARTMENT OF COMMERCE, COAST & GEODETIC SURVEY 1965

ORIENTATION PRINCIPLES

Orientation in architecture encompasses a large segment of different considerations. The expression "total orientation" refers both to the physiological and psychological aspects of the problem.

At the physiological side the factors which affect our senses and have to be taken into consideration are: the thermal impacts—the sun, wind, and temperature effects acting through our skin envelope; the visible impacts—the different illumination and brightness levels affecting our visual senses; the sonic aspects—the noise impacts and noise levels of the surroundings influencing our hearing organs. In addition, our respiratory organs are affected by the smoke, smell, and dust of the environs.

On the psychological side, the view and the privacy are aspects in orientation which quite often override the physical considerations.

Above all, as a building is only a mosaic unit in the pattern of a town organization, the spatial effects, the social intimacy, and its relation to the urban representative directions—aesthetic, political, or social—all play a part in positioning a building.

THERMAL FORCES INFLUENCING ORIENTATION

The climatic factors such as wind, solar radiation, and air temperature play the most eminent role in orientation. The position of a structure in northern latitudes, where the air temperature is generally cool, should be oriented to receive the maximum amount of sunshine without wind exposure. In southerly latitudes, however, the opposite will be desirable; the building should be turned on its axis to avoid the sun's unwanted radiation and to face the cooling breezes instead.

At right the figure shows these regional requirements diagrammatically.

Adaptation for wind orientation is not of great importance in low buildings, where the use of windbreaks and the arrangement of openings in the high and low pressure areas can help to ameliorate the airflow situation. However, for high buildings, where the surrounding terrain has little effect on the upper stories, careful consideration has to be given to wind orientation.

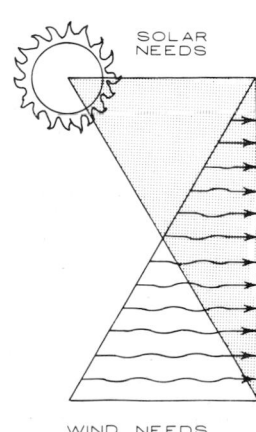

SOLAR NEEDS

WIND NEEDS

COMPASS ORIENTATION

The above map is the isogonic chart of the United States. The wavy lines from top to bottom show the compass deviations from the true north. At the lines marked E the compass will point east of true north; at those marked W the compass will point west of true north. According to the location, correction should be done from the compass north to find the true north.

EXAMPLE: On a site in Wichita, Kansas, find the true north.

STEP 1.   Find the compass orientation on the site.

STEP 2.   Locate Wichita on the map. The nearest compass deviation is the 10°E line.

STEP 3.   Adjust the orientation correction to true north.
The graphical example illustrates a building which lies 25° east with its axis from the compass orientation.

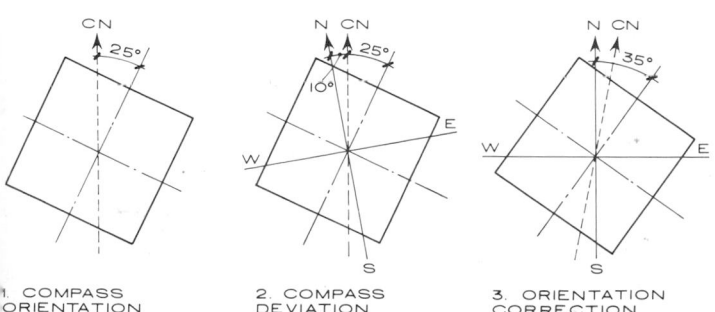

1. COMPASS ORIENTATION

2. COMPASS DEVIATION

3. ORIENTATION CORRECTION

Victor Olgyay, AIA; Associate Professor; School of Architecture, Princeton University; Princeton, New Jersey

To visualize the thermal impacts on differently exposed surfaces four locations are shown approximately at the 24°, 32°, 40° and 44° latitudes. The forces are indicated on average clear winter and summer days. The air temperature variation is indicated by the outside concentric circles. Each additional line represents a 2°F difference from the lowest daily temperature. The direction of the impact is indicated according to the sun's direction as temperatures occur. (Note the low temperatures at the east side, and the high ones in westerly directions.)

The total (direct and diffuse) radiation impact on the various sides of the building is indicated with arrows. Each arrow represents 250 Btu/sq. ft./day radiation. At the bottom of the page the radiations are expressed in numerical values.

The values show that in the upper latitudes the south side of a building receives nearly twice as much radiation in winter as in summer. This effect is even more pronounced at the lower latitudes, where the ratio is about one to four. Also, in the upper latitudes, the east and west sides receive about 2 1/2 times more radiation in summer than in winter. This ratio is not as large in the lower latitudes; but it is noteworthy that in summer these sides receive two to three times as much radiation as the south elevation. In the summer the west exposure is more disadvantageous than the east exposure, as the afternoon high temperatures combine with the radiation effects. In all latitudes the north side receives only a small amount of radiation, and this comes mainly in the summer. In the low latitudes, in the summer, the north side receives nearly twice the impact of the south side. The amount of radiation received on a horizontal roof surface exceeds all other sides.

Experimental observations were conducted on the thermal behavior of building orientation at Princeton University's Architectural Laboratory. Below are shown the summer results of structures exposed to the cardinal directions. Note the unequal heat distribution and high heat impact of the west exposure compared to the east orientation. The southern direction gives a pleasantly low heat volume, slightly higher, however, than the north exposure.

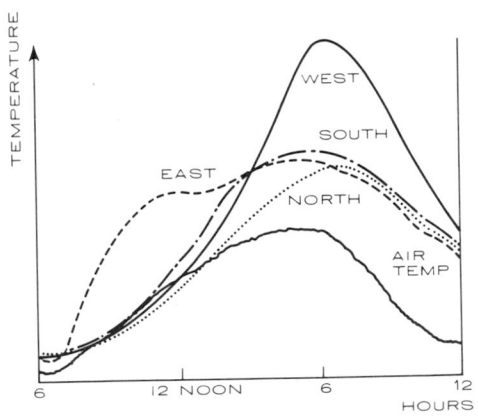

ROOM TEMPERATURE IN DIFFERENTLY ORIENTED HOUSES

JANUARY   JULY

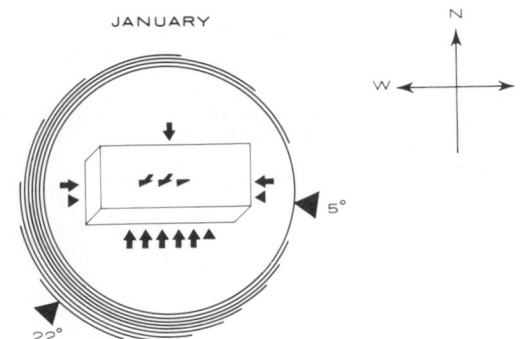

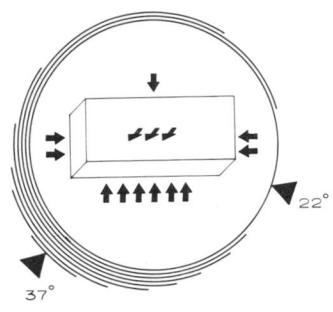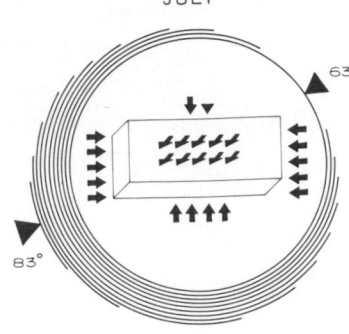

MINNEAPOLIS, MINN.

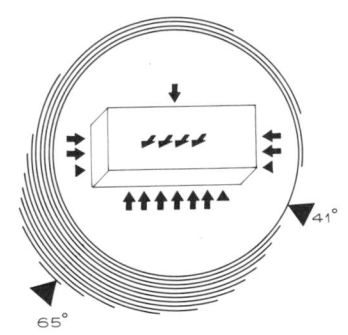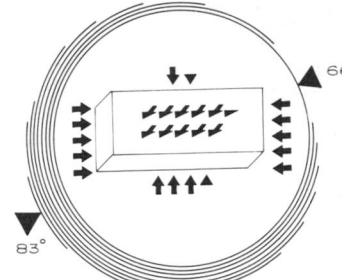

NEW YORK AREA

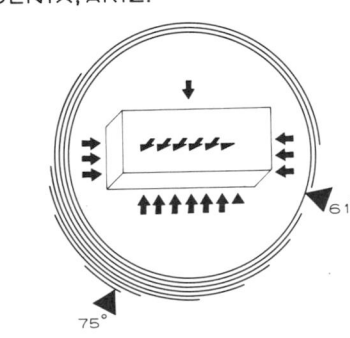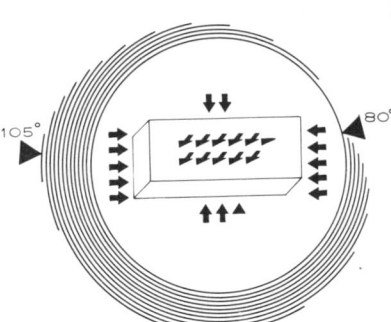

PHOENIX, ARIZ.

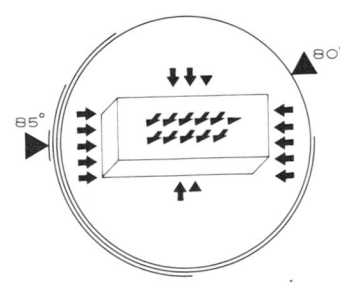

MIAMI, FLA.

On orientation the following conclusions can be drawn:

1. The optimum orientation will lie near the south; however, will differ in the various regions, and will depend on the daily temperature distribution.

2. In all regions an orientation eastward from south gives a better yearly performance and a more equal daily heat distribution. Westerly directions perform more poorly with unbalanced heat impacts.

3. The thermal orientation exposure has to be correlated with the local wind directions.

Victor Olgyay, AIA; Associate Professor; School of Architecture, Princeton University; Princeton, New Jersey

		EAST	SOUTH	WEST	NORTH	HORIZONTAL
44° LATITUDE	WINTER	416	1374	416	83	654
	SUMMER	1314	979	1314	432	2536
40° LATITUDE	WINTER	517	1489	517	119	787
	SUMMER	1277	839	1277	430	2619
32° LATITUDE	WINTER	620	1606	620	140	954
	SUMMER	1207	563	1207	452	2596
24° LATITUDE	WINTER	734	1620	734	152	1414
	SUMMER	1193	344	1193	616	2568

RESIDENTIAL SITE STANDARDS

(FHA) — 1965 ED. (SUMMARY)

Source: F.H.A. minimum property standards for one and two living units.

DESIGN

The dwelling together with any accessory buildings may be located anywhere on the lot provided:

A. No part of the front or accessory structures extend into the minimum front, rear or side yard space required.

B. The maximum F.H.A. lot coverage is not exceeded.

C. At least one of the front, rear, or side yard areas is of such size and so planned as to permit usable and reasonable private yard space for laundrydrying, gardening landscaping, outdoor living, and similar functions.

SITE CONDITIONS

The property shall be free of those hazards which may affect the health and safety of the occupants, or the structural soundness of the improvements, or which may impair the customary use and enjoyment of the property by typical occupants. These hazards may be subsidence, flood, erosion, or others.

LOT COVERAGE

Maximum area of plot which may be used for building area:

A. Detached dwelling: one family - 30%

B. Detached dwelling: two family - 35%

C. Semi-detached or end row dwelling, one or two families 35%

D. Row dwelling, one or two families - 45%

E. Note: The building area includes the total ground area of each building and accessory building, but does not include the area of uncovered entrance platforms, terraces and steps.

YARD DIMENSIONS

A. Front and rear yards: minimum distance from front or rear building line to property line, at any point, 15 feet, except garage or carport to rear property line, 5 feet minimum.

B. Side yards (the criteria providing the larger dimension shall govern).
1. Detached dwelling; minimum distance from side building line to property line, at any point, 5 feet except:
   a) Where established controls assure at least 10 feet between adjacent structures, 3 feet minimum.
   b) Where garages or carports are adjacent to each other, 3 feet minimum.
2. Semi-detached or end row dwelling; minimum distance from side building line to property line, at any point, 8 feet.

C. Sum of side yard: (detached dwelling)
1. Sum of side yard dimensions on subject plot, measured along front building line:
   a) width of plot 70 feet or less - 10 feet
   b) width of plot over 70 feet - 15% of width
2. Criteria considered only to nearest foot.

D. Other Conditions:
1. Side yard with driveway or planned for future driveway - 8 feet clear of obstruction.
2. Where adjacent structures have roof overhangs, distance between edge of overhangs, 6 feet minimum, except that when both structures are garages, the minimum distance between edges of overhang may be reduced to 4 feet.

DISTANCE BETWEEN BUILDINGS ON SAME PLOT

A. Minimum distance between dwelling and another dwelling on same plot, at any point - 10 feet.

B. Minimum distance between dwelling and an accessory building, at any point, 10 feet, except:
1. Where no required windows are located in opposing walls - 5 feet minimum.
2. Minor passageways (10 feet maximum length) no windows in opposing walls, 3 feet minimum.

Thomas Johnson; Sasaki, Dawson, DeMay Associates, Inc.; Watertown, Massachusetts

COURT YARD

A. Outer courts (enclosed on 3 sides)
1. Minimum distance between required window and another window in same living unit, opposite each other across a court - 10 feet.
2. Minimum distance between any window and wall of another living unit, measure across court - 10 feet.
3. Distance between opposite building walls in other cases, 5 feet minimum.

B. Inner courts
1. Minimum area of inner court - 100 sq. ft.
2. Minimum dimensions of inner courts same as outer courts.

ACCESS

A. Access to the property
1. Each property, other than those in planned unit developments, shall be provided with vehicular access to the property by abutting public or private streets. Private streets shall be protected by permanent easements.
2. The width and construction of the required street and provisions for its continued maintenance shall provide safe and suitable vehicular access to and from the property at all times.

B. Access to rear yard
1. Each dwelling shall be provided with a means of access to the rear yard.
2. For a row type dwelling, the access shall be by means of an alley, easement, open passage through the dwelling, or other acceptable means.

C. Access to living unit
1. A means of access to each living unit shall be provided without passing through any other living unit.
2. Acceptable means of access to the rear yard shall be provided for each living unit without passing through any other living unit.

FINISH GRADE IN RELATIONSHIP TO HABITABLE SPACE

The average finish grade elevation at exterior walls shall not be more than 48 inches above finish floor of a habitable room. This does not apply to basement recreation rooms not intended for year round occupancy, bathrooms, storage, or utility rooms etc.

PLOT PLAN

Drawings for F.H.A. individual applications shall be submitted in duplicate and provide at least the following information.

A. Scale 1" = 20' or $1/16" = 1'- 0"$ minimum.

B. Lot and Block number.

C. Dimensions of plot and north point.

D. Dimensions of front, rear and side yards.

E. Location and dimension of garage, carport, and other accessory buildings.

F. Location of walks, driveways and approaches.

G. Location of steps, terraces, porches, fences, and retaining walls.

H. Location and dimensions of easements and established setback requirements.

I. Elevations at the following points:
1. First floor of dwelling, and floor of garage, carport and other accessory buildings.
2. Finish curb or crown of street at points of extension of lot lines.
3. Finish grade elevation at each principle corner of structure.

J. The following additional elevations, as applicable, shall be submitted if the topography or the design of the structure is such that special grading, drainage, or foundations may be necessary. Examples are irregular or steeply sloping sites, filled areas on sites; or multi-level structure designs.
1. Finish and existing grade elevations at each corner of plot.
2. Existing grade at each principle corner of dwelling.
3. Finish grade at both sides of abrupt changes of grade such as retaining walls, sloping, etc.
4. Other elevations necessary to show grading and drainage.

K. Indication of lot grading type and approximate locations of swales.

L. Individual water supply and sewage disposal information (including all details).

LOCAL BUILDING CODES:

The minimum F.H.A. standards do not relieve the builder of his responsibility for compliance with local ordinances, codes and regulations including established requirements of a health authority having jurisdiction.

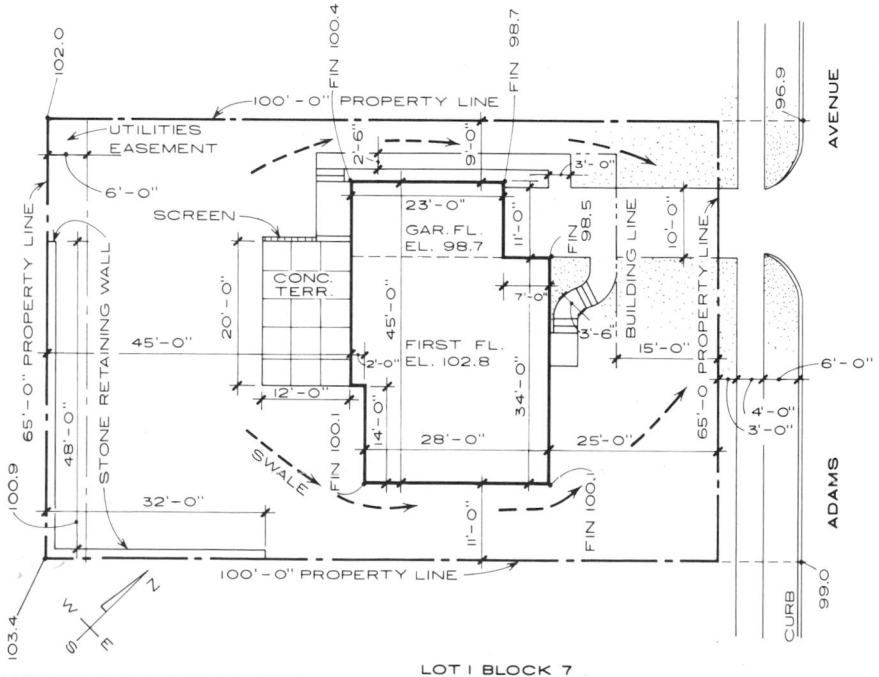

LOT GRADING TYPE "A"
(ALL DRAINAGE TO STREET)

LOT I BLOCK 7
CHESTNUT HILL - BRAINARD, COLUMBIA
SCALE: 1" = ___

EXAMPLE PLOT PLAN No. I

SITE LAYOUT

A. The house should relate harmoniously to the lot.

B. Observe legal setback restrictions.

C. Plan the use of space around the house.

D. Consider climate orientation—sun, wind, rain, snow, heat, shade.

E. Try to preserve existing trees and topography.

F. Plan access to house.

GRADING AND DRAINAGE

A. Drain away from the house on all sides.

B. Keep drainage swales inconspicuous.

C. Set house above, and drain to street.

D. Prevent drainage from conflicting with outdoor use areas.

E. All grades should have a minimum slope of 1% and a maximum slope of 8%.

SITE DEVELOPMENT

A. Open house with windows to the outdoor living area.

B. Consider special features such as pools or patios.

C. Plant for privacy, shade, wind screen, views, and decoration.

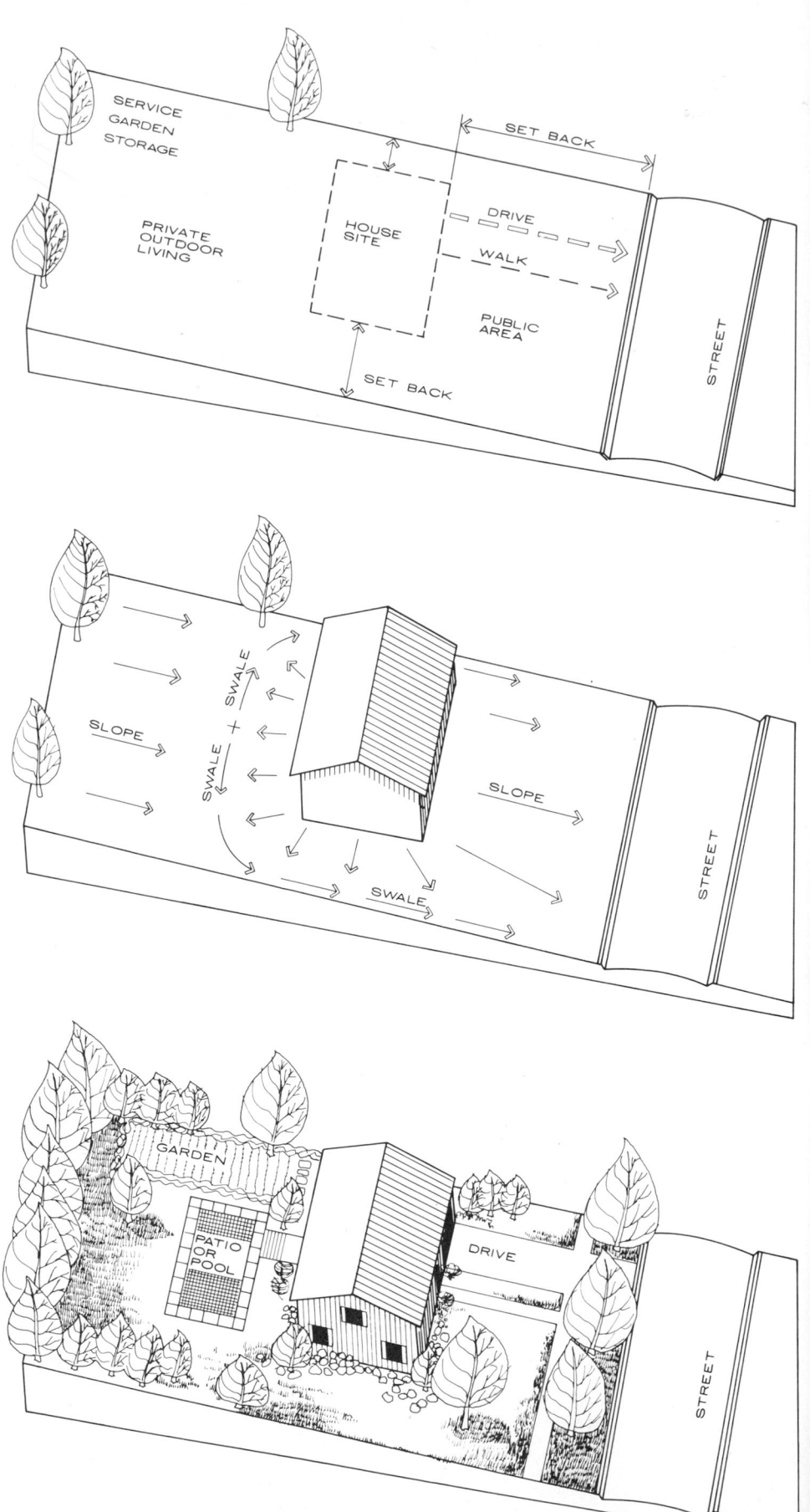

Thomas Johnson; Sasaki, Dawson, DeMay Associates, Inc.; Watertown, Massachusetts

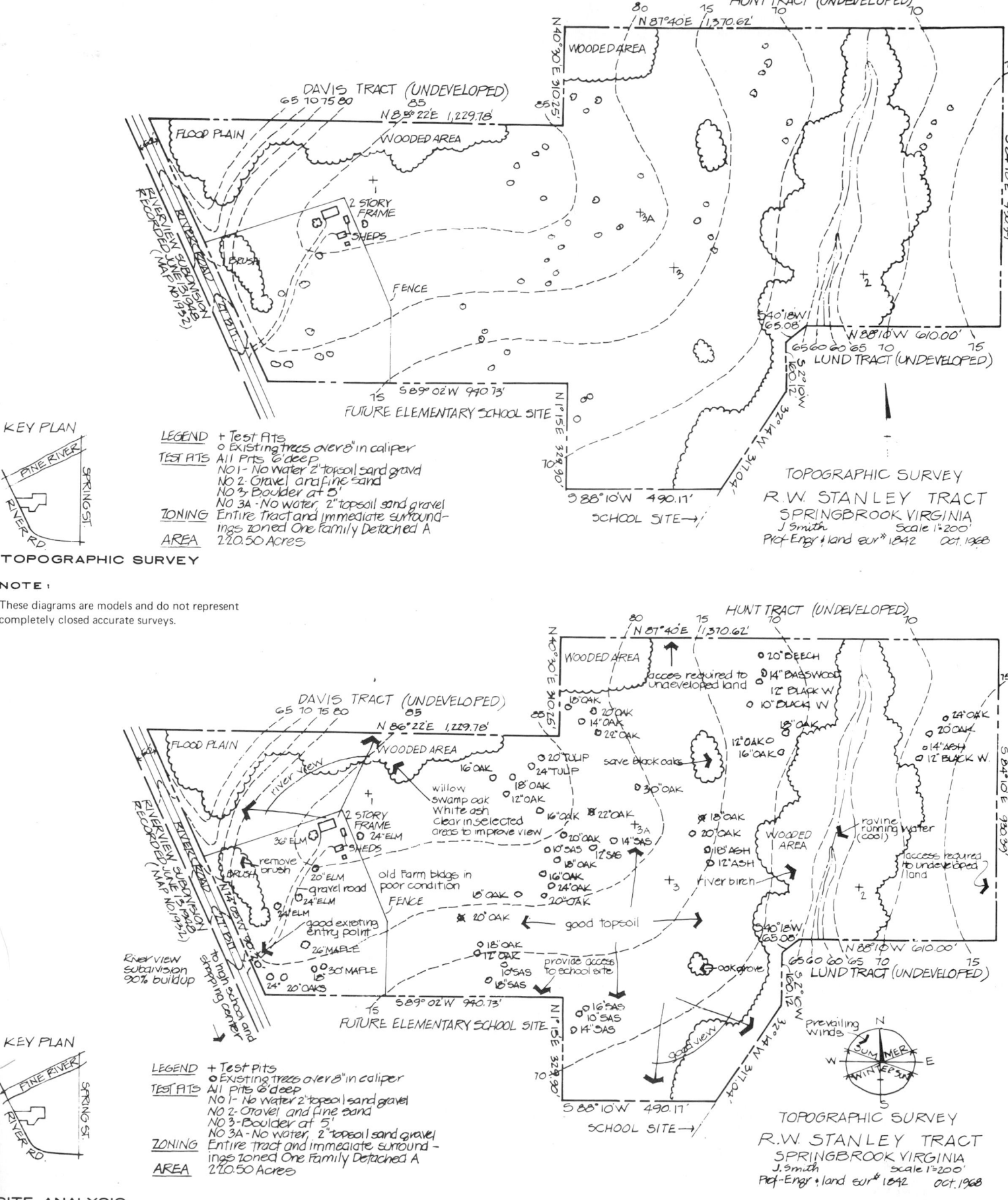

TOPOGRAPHIC SURVEY

NOTE:

These diagrams are models and do not represent completely closed accurate surveys.

SITE ANALYSIS

Grossman and Greenan, Landscape Architects; Washington, D. C.

INTRODUCTION:

In developing a subdivision plan, it is important to recognize the myriad factors affecting a given project. It is up to the site planner to analyze and appropriately weigh the social, economic, engineering and aesthetic considerations and synthesize these factors into a balanced solution within the context of existing local zoning regulations.

ZONING

Having selected a site, the site planner must turn his attention to the prevailing zoning ordinance since this will be a principal determinant of the site's use and development. Zoning is an attempt by local authorities to legally regulate the use of land. Restrictions are placed on such factors as density of population, coverage of lots, and size and bulk of structures. Although local zoning regulations often favor a lot by lot subdivision of land, in some areas these regulations have been amended to permit cluster zoning or planned unit development. In a planned unit development, the site planner correlates the physical components of a subdivision (namely, amount of floor area, open space, livability space, recreation space and car storage of a property) with the size of the site. (See standards for subdivision planning.) The system used to measure these components is called the land use intensity ratio space. Thus, land use intensity measures dwelling units per acre while density bases its measurements on people per acre.

SITE FACTORS

Before the site planner can make a physical evaluation of the site, he must have an accurate survey of existing conditions. This may be accomplished by personally inspecting the site and graphically recording pertinent information on a topographic survey which, in most cases, is used as a base map.

A typical topographic survey includes the following information:

1. Boundary lines: bearings and distances.

2. Easements: location, width and purpose.

3. Streets on and adjacent to the tract:

    a. name and right-of-way width and location.

    b. type, width and elevation of surfacing.

    c. any legally established center-line elevations.

    d. walks, curbs, gutters, culverts, etc.

4. Utilities on and adjacent to the tract:

    a. location, size and invert elevation of sanitary, storm and/or combined sewers.

    b. location and size of water mains.

    c. location of gas lines, fire hydrants, electric and telephone poles and street lights.

    d. direction and distance to, and size of nearest water mains and sewers; show invert elevation of sewers. (This is necessary only if water mains and sewers are not on or adjacent to the tract.)

5. Ground elevations on the tract:

    a. For land that slopes more than approximately 2%, show spot elevations at all breaks in grade, along all drainage channels or swales and at selected points not more than 100 ft. apart in all directions.

    b. For land that slopes more than approximately 2%, show contours with an interval of not more than 5 ft. where ground slope is regular and such information is sufficient for planning purposes; or show contours with an interval of not more than 2 ft. where necessary because of irregular land or need for more detailed data for preparing plans and construction drawings.

6. Subsurface conditions on the tract:

    a. location and results of test made to ascertain

Grossman and Greenan, Landscape Architects; Washington, D. C.

subsurface soil, rock and ground water conditions.

    b. depth to ground water unless test pits are dry at a depth of 5 ft.

    c. location of percolation test if individual sewage disposal systems proposed.

7. Other conditions on the tract: water courses marshes, rock outcrop, wooded areas, isolated trees one ft. or more in diameter, houses, barns, shacks and other significant features.

8. Other conditions on adjacent land:

    a. approximate direction and gradient of ground slope, including any embankments or retaining walls.

    b. location of buildings, railroads, power lines, towers, and other nearby nonresidential land uses.

    c. approximate area of off-site water shed drainage into tract.

    d. owners of adjacent unplatted land.

    e. For adjacent platted land, refer to subdivision plat by name, recording date and number and showing approximate per cent built up, typical lot size and dwelling type.

9. Zoning on and adjacent to the tract.

10. Proposed public improvements: highways or other major improvements planned by public authorities for future construction on or near the tract.

11. General information including: scale, north arrow, datum, benchmark and date of survey.

ADDITIONAL INFORMATION

To supplement and interpret the topographic survey, the site planner, in diagrammatic form, sketches on the survey map the following additional information:

1. Location and direction of best views, poor views and objectionable views.

2. Location of off-site nuisances with their bearings and approximate distances.

3. Location of logical points of ingress or egress.

4. Routes of surface water runoff.

5. Notes on flood, undrained or swampy conditions.

6. An analysis of the micro-climate.

7. A sun and wind diagram.

8. An indication of trees that should be saved, if possible, and trees that should be removed.

9. Notes on other natural features such as rock outcrop, erosion problems, natural springs, ground cover, topsoil, etc.

I. SINGLE FAMILY

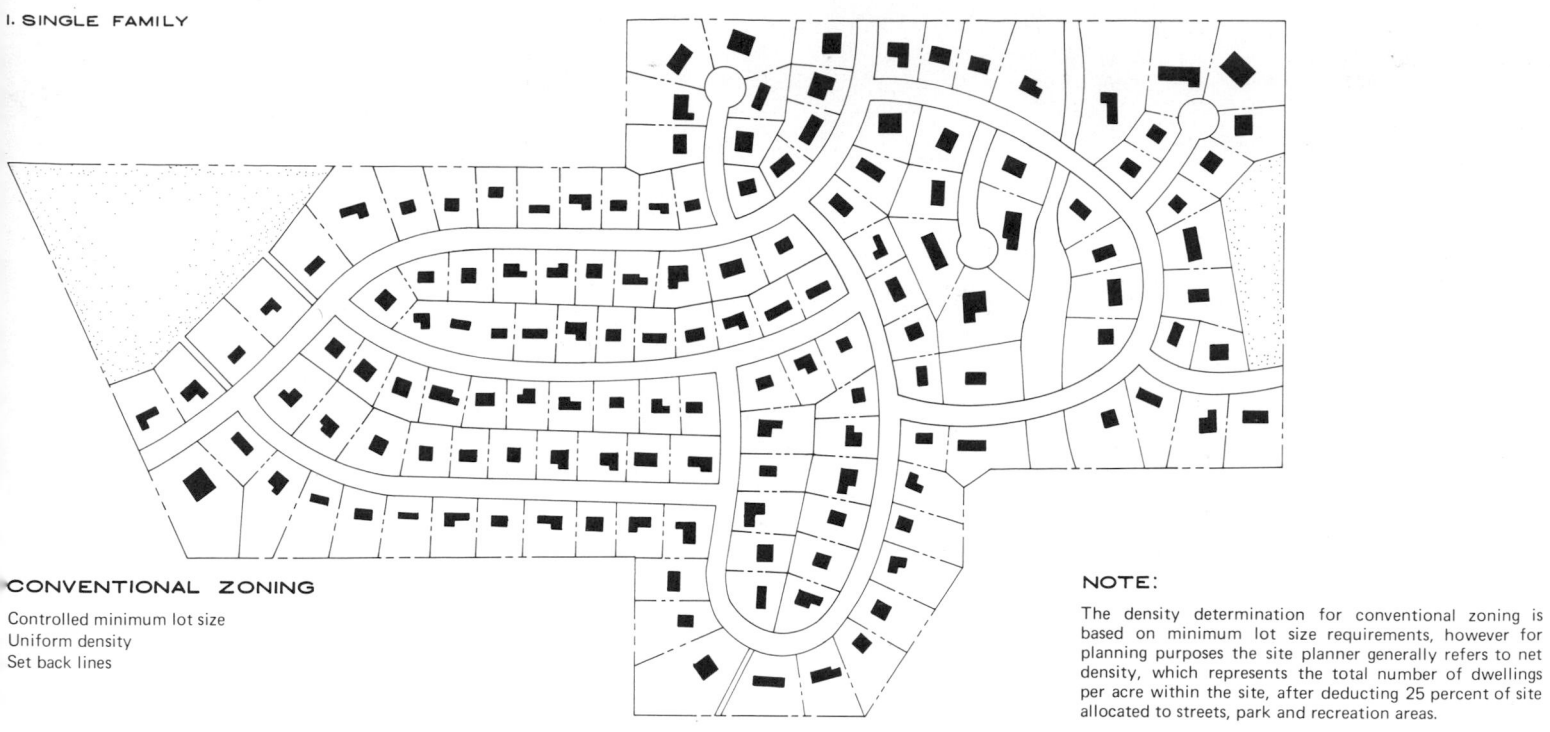

CONVENTIONAL ZONING

Controlled minimum lot size
Uniform density
Set back lines

NOTE:

The density determination for conventional zoning is based on minimum lot size requirements, however for planning purposes the site planner generally refers to net density, which represents the total number of dwellings per acre within the site, after deducting 25 percent of site allocated to streets, park and recreation areas.

I. SHOPPING
2. MULTIFAMILY
3. SINGLE FAMILY

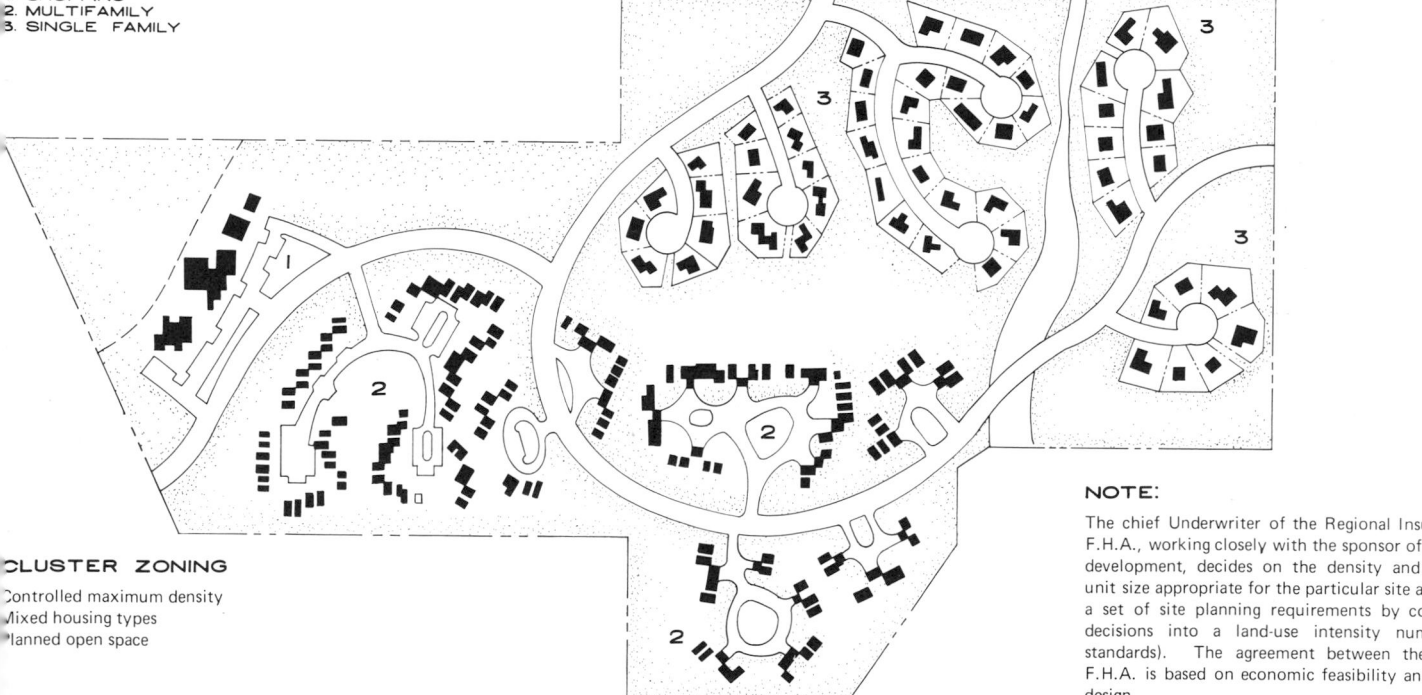

CLUSTER ZONING

Controlled maximum density
Mixed housing types
Planned open space

NOTE:

The chief Underwriter of the Regional Insuring Office of F.H.A., working closely with the sponsor of a planned-unit development, decides on the density and average living unit size appropriate for the particular site and then selects a set of site planning requirements by converting these decisions into a land-use intensity number (see site standards). The agreement between the sponsor and F.H.A. is based on economic feasibility and flexibility of design.

ADVANTAGES OF PLANNED UNIT DEVELOPMENT (CLUSTER ZONING)

Although conventional zoning for the lot by lot type of subdivision is still the standard practice in suburbia, the amenities offered by the planned unit development (cluster zoning) are becoming more apparent. The use of extensive areas of common open space makes possible a fitting of development to the land far more effective than in subdivisions where the objective is to obtain the maximum number of individual lots as possible. Following is a list of apparent positive objectives gained from the wise employment of the planned unit development theory of subdivision design.

1. With smaller individual lots, excess land particles can be massed together to provide larger and more useful community recreational space.

2. With the use of connecting community open spaces and fewer through traffic streets, children are better protected from vehicular traffic.

3. With larger amounts of open space, the natural character of the site can be preserved.

4. With the use of clustering, row housing and multi-story

housing lower priced units with ample open space can be provided.

5. With the shorter networks of streets and utilities, construction costs can be reduced.

6. With more common open space, social intercourse in a community becomes more prevalent.

Grossman and Greenan, Landscape Architects; Washington, D. C.

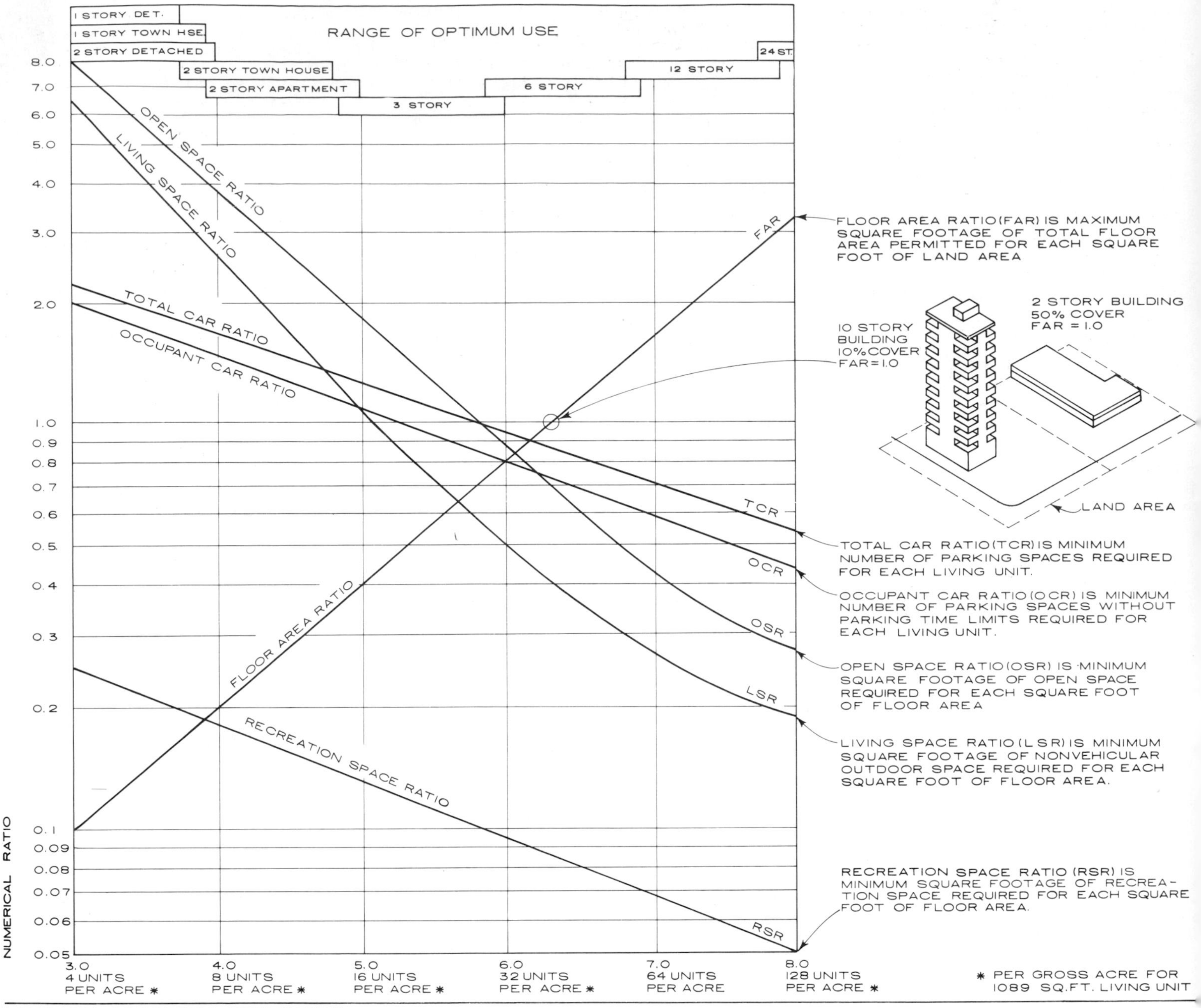

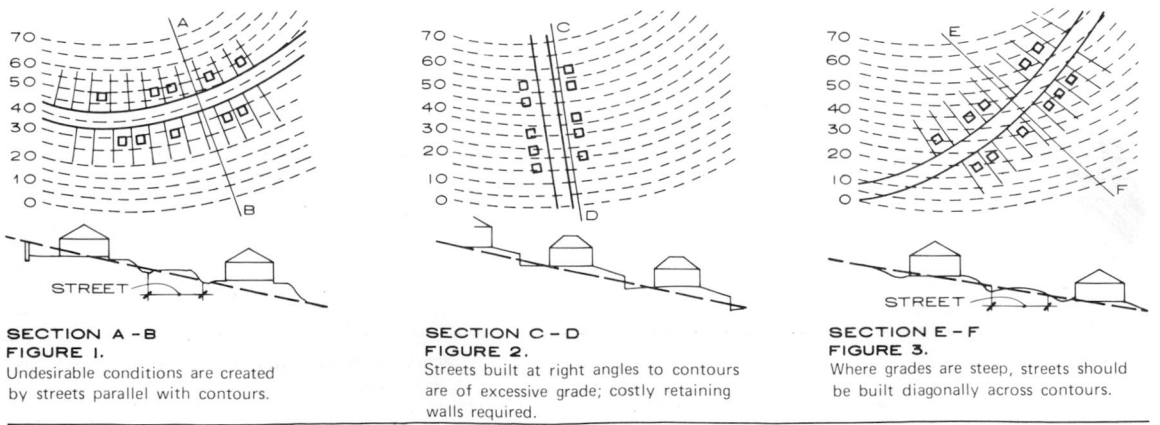

LAND-USE INTENSITY STANDARDS

Chart labels and annotations:

RANGE OF OPTIMUM USE

1 STORY DET.
1 STORY TOWN HSE
2 STORY DETACHED
2 STORY TOWN HOUSE
2 STORY APARTMENT
3 STORY
6 STORY
12 STORY
24 ST.

OPEN SPACE RATIO
LIVING SPACE RATIO
TOTAL CAR RATIO
OCCUPANT CAR RATIO
FLOOR AREA RATIO
RECREATION SPACE RATIO

FAR
TCR
OCR
OSR
LSR
RSR

NUMERICAL RATIO

FLOOR AREA RATIO (FAR) IS MAXIMUM SQUARE FOOTAGE OF TOTAL FLOOR AREA PERMITTED FOR EACH SQUARE FOOT OF LAND AREA

10 STORY BUILDING 10% COVER FAR = 1.0

2 STORY BUILDING 50% COVER FAR = 1.0

LAND AREA

TOTAL CAR RATIO (TCR) IS MINIMUM NUMBER OF PARKING SPACES REQUIRED FOR EACH LIVING UNIT.

OCCUPANT CAR RATIO (OCR) IS MINIMUM NUMBER OF PARKING SPACES WITHOUT PARKING TIME LIMITS REQUIRED FOR EACH LIVING UNIT.

OPEN SPACE RATIO (OSR) IS MINIMUM SQUARE FOOTAGE OF OPEN SPACE REQUIRED FOR EACH SQUARE FOOT OF FLOOR AREA

LIVING SPACE RATIO (LSR) IS MINIMUM SQUARE FOOTAGE OF NONVEHICULAR OUTDOOR SPACE REQUIRED FOR EACH SQUARE FOOT OF FLOOR AREA.

RECREATION SPACE RATIO (RSR) IS MINIMUM SQUARE FOOTAGE OF RECREATION SPACE REQUIRED FOR EACH SQUARE FOOT OF FLOOR AREA.

3.0 / 4 UNITS PER ACRE *
4.0 / 8 UNITS PER ACRE *
5.0 / 16 UNITS PER ACRE *
6.0 / 32 UNITS PER ACRE *
7.0 / 64 UNITS PER ACRE
8.0 / 128 UNITS PER ACRE *

* PER GROSS ACRE FOR 1089 SQ. FT. LIVING UNIT

SECTION A - B
FIGURE 1.
Undesirable conditions are created by streets parallel with contours.

SECTION C - D
FIGURE 2.
Streets built at right angles to contours are of excessive grade; costly retaining walls required.

SECTION E - F
FIGURE 3.
Where grades are steep, streets should be built diagonally across contours.

STREET

STREET LAYOUT ON SLOPES

Grossman and Greenan, Landscape Architects; Washington, D. C.

FINAL DEVELOPMENT PLANS

After the layout of the subdivision is determined from preliminary sketches, final development plans must be prepared. Final development plans show the final design for the location of streets, residential lots and other features in a proposed development. The following checklist is for selective use as appropriate for each development. For example, the data may be combined on fewer drawings, such as a single grading and drainage plan. All drawings should show the name and location of the development, the date of preparation or revision and when appropriate, the scale, north point, datum and approval of local authorities.

NEIGHBORHOOD GRADING PLAN

1. Subdivision layout: data from the accepted preliminary subdivision plan; include existing topography, street names, and lot numbers.

2. Proposed grading by contours or by spot elevations.

NEIGHBORHOOD DRAINAGE PLAN

1. Subdivision data as in 1, above.

2. Storm sewer plan, profiles, design criteria and specifications.

3. Plans for disposal of subsurface water as needed.

4. Details and specifications for inlets, manholes, catch basins, headwalls and surface drainage channels.

5. Adjacent contributory drainage area: if adjacent land drains into, or is diverted around the development, show data on size of adjacent drainage area, and slope of land. For any proposed diversion systems, show design flow computations and details.

6. Plans, profiles, cross-section and details of off-site outfall drainage to a point where backwater will not affect subdivision.

7. Data on necessary easements.

UTILITY PLANS

1. Water supply and sewage disposal. Public: exhibits which will enable the insuring office to determine that continuous satisfactory service will be provided. Community: complete construction plans and specifications, and details of the proposed maintenance organization.

2. Street lighting: type and location.

STREET PLANS

1. Plan and profile of each street.

2. Cross-section of each street type.

3. Details and specifications for pavement base and surfacing, curbs, etc.

OTHER NEIGHBORHOOD IMPROVEMENT PLANS

1. Protective screening
   Fences and walls: plan, details and specifications. Planting: plan for typical 100 ft. length of screen planting: quantities, sizes, species and specifications. (See pages on plant materials)

2. Alleys, cross-walks, entranceways, parks, etc.: plans, details and specifications.

MASTER PLOT PLANS, TYPICAL PLOT PLANS AND LOT GRADING PLAN

The preceding plans do not apply where land development is for individual custom building. They do apply when the individual housing units are to be sited by the site planner. (See pages on Residential Site Standards).

THE SUBDIVISION PLAT

A subdivision plat, when properly prepared and filed in the public land records, establishes a legal description of the streets, residential lots and other sites in a residential development. The following checklist of information to be shown on a subdivision plat should be used when and as indicated by local F.H.A. office.

1. Right-of-way lines of streets, easements and other rights-of-way, and property lines of residential lots and other sites with accurate dimensions, bearings and curve data.

2. Name and right-of-way width of each street or other right-of-way.

3. Location, dimensions and purpose of any easements.

4. Number to identify each lot or site.

5. Purpose for which sites, other than residential lots, are dedicated or reserved.

6. Minimum building setback line on all lots and other sites.

7. Location and description of monuments.

8. Names of record owners of adjoining unplatted land.

9. Reference to recorded subdivision plats of adjoining platted land by record name, date and number.

10. Certification by surveyor or engineer.

11. Statement by owner dedicating streets, rights-of-way and any sites for public use.

12. Approval by local authorities.

13. Title, scale, north arrow and date.

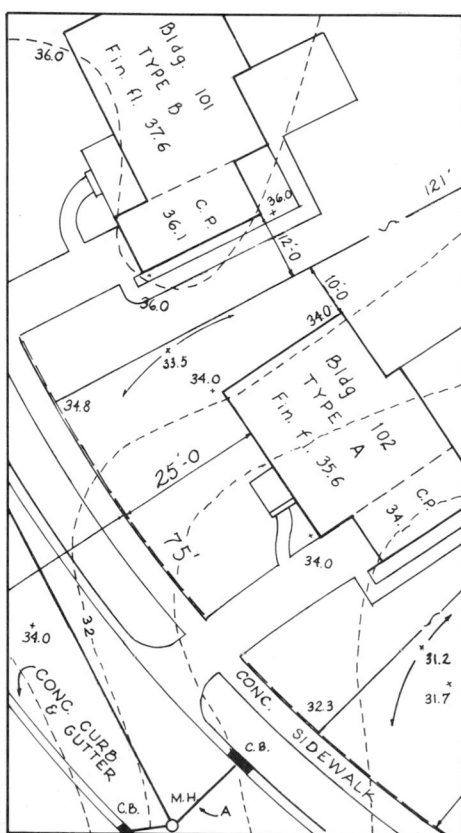

Composite Development Plan in which the neighborhood grading plan, neighborhood drainage plan, master plot plan and master lot grading plan are prepared as a single combined drawing.

Grossman and Greenan, Landscape Architects; Washington, D. C.

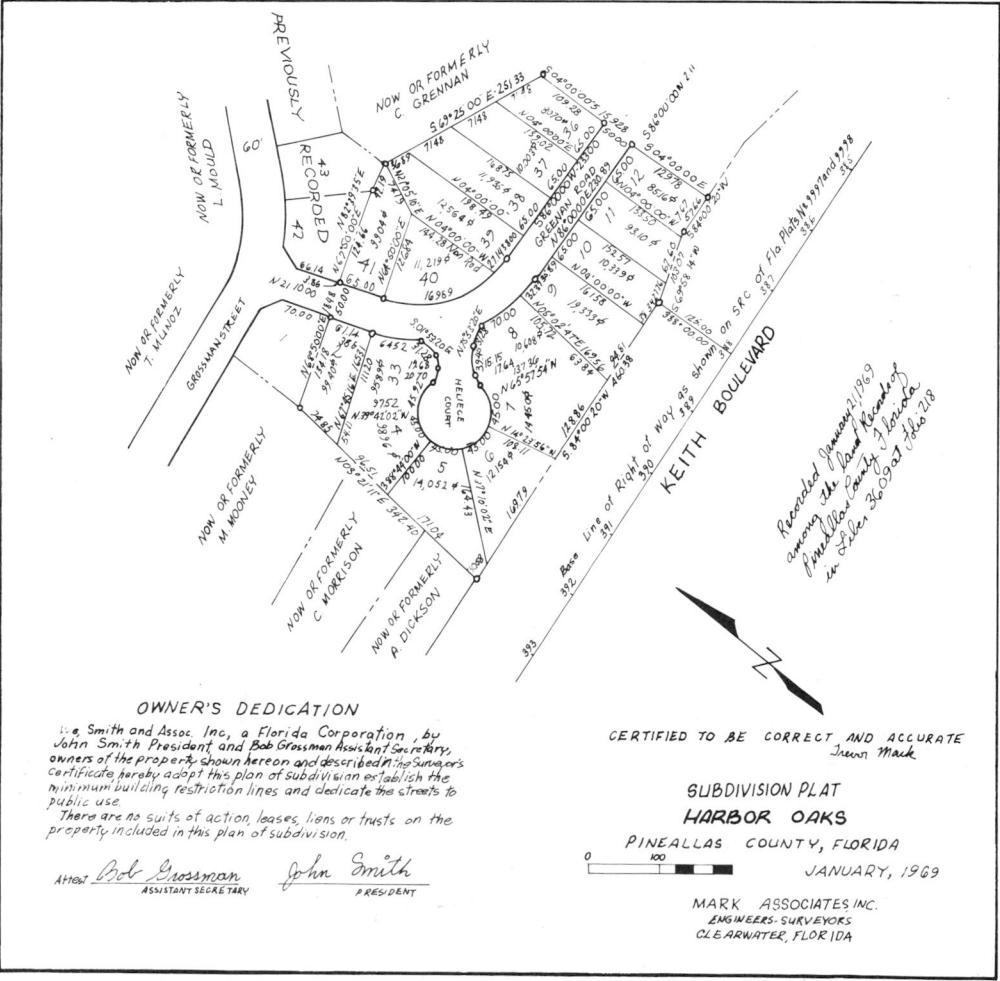

This drawing illustrates information which should be shown on a subdivision plat. It is not intended as illustrative of required design standards or drafting technique.

This diagram is a model and does not represent a completely closed accurate survey.

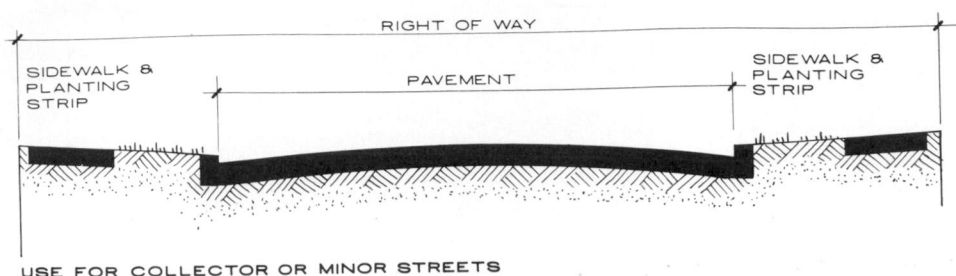

USE FOR COLLECTOR OR MINOR STREETS

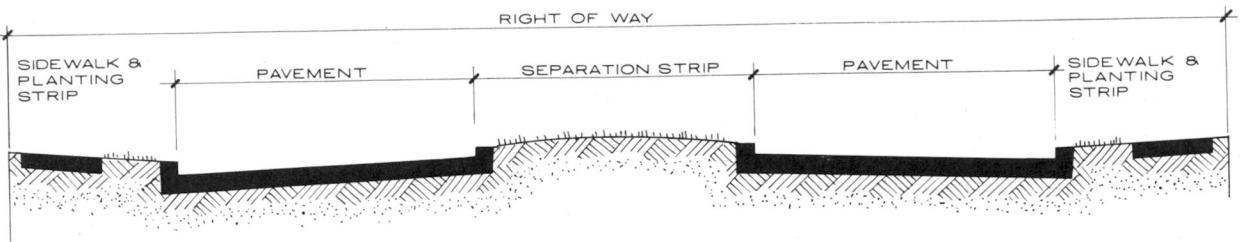

DIVIDED STREET

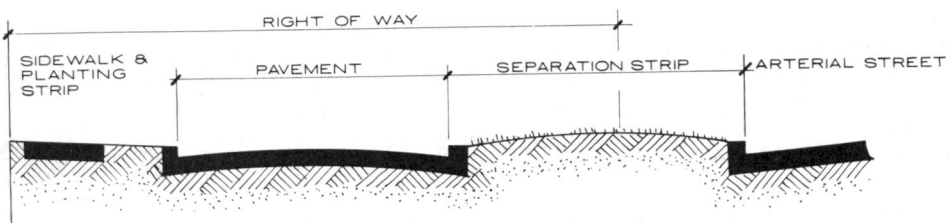

MARGINAL ACCESS STREET

Grossman and Greenan, Landscape Architects; Washington, D. C.

NOTES:

Dimension as specified elsewhere

With rolled curbs, pavement width is measured from the faces of the curbs at a point 6 inches from backs of the curbs.

Pavement crown: for cement concrete 1/8 inch per 1 ft., for bituminous surface 1/4 inch per 1 ft., unless otherwise specified.

Pavement edging details as specified elsewhere

Sidewalk locations as specified elsewhere

Slope sidewalks and planting strips 1/4 inch per 1 ft. to the pavement unless otherwise specified

STREET TYPES

Arterial — Major street for community wide use
Collector — Secondary street for traffic originating in the neighborhood
Minor — Local residential street affords principal means of vehicular access to properties
Marginal — Service street for properties fronting on an arterial street

GRADING

Planning and execution of grading involve certain basic steps pertaining to street layout, block grading and lot grading. The objective is to establish the street grades, floor elevations and lot grades in proper relation to each other and to existing topography, considering property protection, appeal and use.

STREET GRADES

Street grades should be established during the planning stage to provide proper relation between the streets and the first floor elevations of the house and to permit convenient and economical access to and drainage of lots. Proper establishment of street grades is necessary for the drainage design for both lots and streets and for the determination of the proper depth for the underground utilities. Street gradients should be sufficient for the runoff of storm water but not so steep as to be hazardous to traffic.

DRAINAGE

To prevent flooding of the streets and abutting properties, catch basins should be provided at all low points, at street intersections and at intermediate locations as necessary to prevent overloading of the street gutters. Catch basins should be connected to collections mains of adequate size with outfalls approved by the civil authorities having jurisdiction.

TREES

Existing trees on a development site should be saved whenever possible. Proposed trees should be selected for adaptability to local climate and soil conditions, for resistance to disease and insect pests, for healthy foliage that withstands dust and smoke and for a root system that will not damage nearby utility lines and paved areas. Street trees should have open growth, high branching and an ultimate size proportionate to the surroundings.

TYPICAL STREET IMPROVEMENT STANDARDS

STANDARD A FOR APARTMENTS AND ROW HOUSES
STANDARD B FOR TYPICAL ONE-FAMILY DETACHED HOUSES
STANDARD C FOR COUNTRY HOUSES

A	B	C	STREETS
X	X	X	1. Arterial streets: widths of row, pavement and sidewalk as determined after consultation with local authorities and FHA.
X	X		2a. Collector streets: 80' r.o.w., two 22' pavements, 5' sidewalk 1' from property line.
X	X		2b. Collector streets: 80' r.o.w., 44' pavement, 5' sidewalks 1' from property line.
		X	2c. Collector streets: 60' r.o.w., 36' pavement, 4' sidewalks 1' from property line.
		X	2d. Collector streets: 60' r.o.w., 24' pavement, applicable only where typical lot is larger than one-half acre.
X			3a. Minor streets: 50' r.o.w., 36' pavement, 5' sidewalks 1' from property line.
	X		3b. Minor streets: 50' r.o.w., 30' pavement, 4' sidewalks 1' from property line.
		X	3c. Minor streets: 50' r.o.w., 22' pavement
X	X		4a. *Marginal access street: 40' r.o.w., 20' pavement, 4' sidewalks
X	X		4b. *Marginal access street: 40' r.o.w., 26' pavement, 4' sidewalks
X	X	X	5a. Streets along development boundaries: widths of r.o.w., pavement and sidewalks as determined after consultation with local authorities and the F.H.A.
X	X	X	5b. Streets connecting development with existing improved streets system: widths of r.o.w., pavement and sidewalks as determined after consultation with local authorities and F.H.A.
X	X	X	6. Street trees 3" caliper 40' to 50' apart

*4a. for one way marginal access street
*4b. for two way marginal access street   r.o.w. = right of way

FOUNDATIONS AND SITEWORK

SOIL BORING PROGRAMING
(CONSULT FOUNDATION ENGINEER QUALIFIED IN SOIL MECHANICS)

A. PRELIMINARY INVESTIGATION FOR SITE SELECTION:

1. Topographic or aerial map.
2. Geologic survey maps.
3. Case history of site development.
4. Soil information from existing soil borings.
5. Case history of foundations of adjacent buildings.
6. Drill minimum 2 holes, one down to 25 ft. depth & the other to hard strata. Perform standard penetration test (SPT) & note ground water level at each hole.

B. FINAL INVESTIGATION OF SOIL AFTER STRUCTURE IS ORIENTED AT THE SITE:

1. Drill a minimum of 4 SPT holes, one at each corner of building. Reference all holes to benchmark elevation.
2. Determine ground water level, PH and electro-resistivity of soil.
3. Take undisturbed soil samples & perform laboratory tests as required.

LABORATORY TESTS TO BE PERFORMED FOR VARYING TYPES OF SOILS

	SANDS & SILTS	SANDY CLAYS	CLAYS
DRY DENSITY	YES	YES	YES
MOISTURE CONTENT	YES	YES	YES
ATTERBERG LIMITS	NO	YES	YES
PERMEABILTY	YES	YES	NO
MECHANICAL ANALYSIS	YES	YES	YES
CONSOLIDATION	NO	YES	YES
UNCONFINED COMPRESSION	NO	YES	YES
DIRECT SHEAR	YES	NO	NO
TRIAXIAL	YES	YES	YES
VANE SHEAR	NO	NO	YES
RELATIVE DENSITY	YES	NO	NO

SOIL TYPES & VARIOUS PROPERTIES OF EACH

DIVISION	SYMBOLS			SOIL DESCRIPTION	VALUE AS A FOUNDATION MATERIAL	FROST ACTION	DRAINAGE
	LETTER	HATCHING	COLOR				
GRAVEL AND GRAVELLY SOILS	GW		Red	Well graded Gravel, or Gravel-Sand mixture, little or no Fines	Excellent	None	Excellent
	GP		Red	Poorly graded Gravel, or Gravel-Sand mixtures, little or no Fines	Good	None	Excellent
	GM		Yellow	Silty Gravels, Gravel-Sand-Silt mixtures	Good	Slight	Poor
	GC		Yellow	Clayey-Gravels, Gravel-Clay-Sand Mixtures	Good	Slight	Poor
SAND AND SANDY SOILS	SW		Red	Well-graded Sands, or Gravelly Sands, little or no Fines	Good	None	Excellent
	SP		Red	Poorly Graded Sands, or Gravelly Sands, little or no Fines	Fair	None	Excellent
	SM		Yellow	Silty Sands, Sand-Silt mixtures	Fair	Slight	Fair
	SC		Yellow	Clayey Sands, Sand-Clay mixtures	Fair	Medium	Poor
SILTS AND CLAYS LL < 50	ML		Green	Inorganic Silts & Very Fine Sands, Rock Flour, Silty or Clayey Fine Sands, or Clayey Silts with slight plasticity	Fair	Very High	Poor
	CL		Green	Inorganic Silts of low to medium plasticity, Gravelly Sands, Silty Clays, Lean Clays	Fair	Very High	Impervious
	OL		Green	Organic Silt-Clays of low plasticity	Poor	High	Impervious
SILTS AND CLAYS LL > 50	MH		Blue	Inorganic Silts, Micaceous or Diatomaceous Fine Sandy or Silty Soils, Elastic Silts	Poor	Very High	Poor
	CH		Blue	Inorganic Clays of high plasticity, Fat Clays	Very Poor	Medium	Impervious
	OH		Blue	Organic Clays of medium to high plasticity, Organic Silts	Very Poor	Medium	Impervious
HIGHLY ORGANIC SOILS	Pt		Orange	Peat & Other Highly Organic Soils	Not Suitable	Slight	Poor

1. Consult soil engineers and local building codes for allowable soil bearing capacities.

2. L. L. indicates liquid limit.

Smith, Hinchman & Grylls Associates, Inc.; Detroit, Michigan

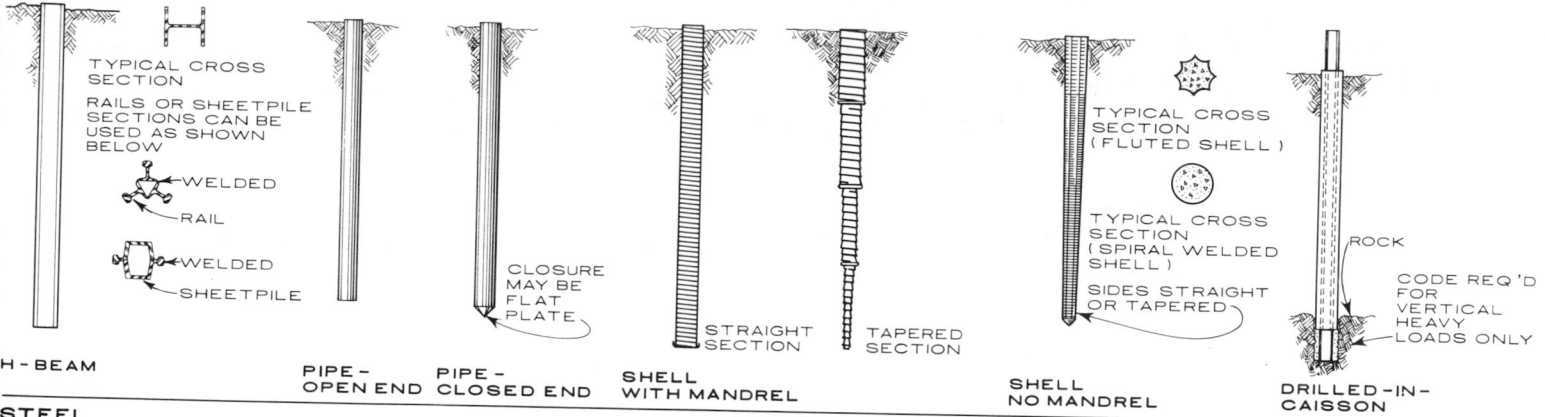

STEEL

NOTE: A mandrel is a member inserted into a hollow pile to reinforce the pile shell while it is driven into the ground.

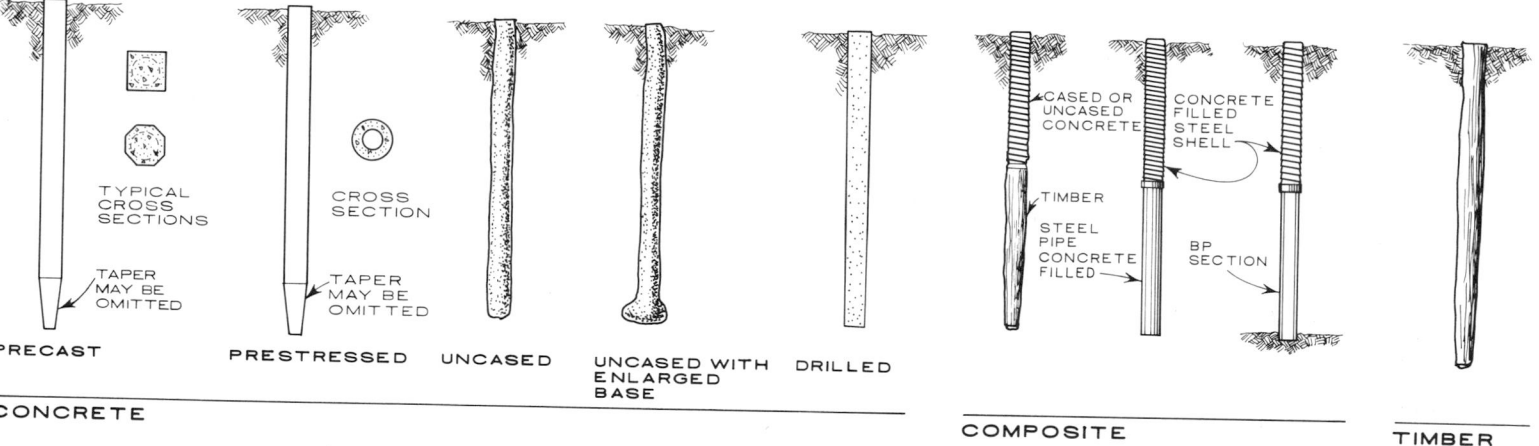

CONCRETE   **COMPOSITE**   **TIMBER**

PILE DATA

PILE TYPE	MAXIMUM LENGTH (FT.)	OPTIMUM LENGTH (FT.)	DIAMETER (IN.)	MAXIMUM LOAD CAPACITY (TONS)	OPTIMUM LOAD RANGE (TONS)	USUAL SPACING
TIMBER *	110	30 – 60	5 – 10 Tip; 12 – 20 Butt	30	15 – 25	2' – 6'' to 3' – 0''
STEEL						
H – BEAM	200	40 – 100		200	40 – 120	3' – 0''
PIPE – OPEN END CONCRETE FILLED	200	40 – 120	10 – 22	200	80 – 120	2' – 6'' to 3' – 6''
PIPE – CLOSED END CONCRETE FILLED	150	30 – 80	10 – 18	100	50 – 70	2' – 6'' to 3' – 0''
SHELL – MANDREL CONCRETE FILLED						
STRAIGHT SECTIONS	100	40 – 60	8 – 18	75	30 – 60	3' – 0''
TAPERED SECTIONS	40	15 – 35	8 – 23	60	30 – 45	3' – 0''
SHELL – NO MANDREL CONCRETE FILLED	150	30 – 80	8 – 18	80	50 – 70	3' – 0''
DRILLED – IN – CAISSON	200	50 – 120	24, 30	2,000	500 – 1,500	6' – 0''
CONCRETE						
PRECAST	100	40 – 50	10 – 24	100	40 – 60	3' – 0''
PRESTRESSED	200	60 – 100	10 – 54	200	50 – 150	3' – 0'' to 8' – 0''
UNCASED	60	25 – 40	14 – 20	75	30 – 60	3' – 0''
UNCASED – ENLARGED BASE	60	25 – 40	14 – 20	150	40 – 100	6' – 0''
DRILLED (CAISSONS)	200	40 – 100	16 – 84	500	60 – 200	4' – 0'' to 10' – 0''
COMPOSITE						
CONCRETE – TIMBER	150	60 – 100	5 – 10 Tip; 12 – 20 Butt	30	15 – 25	2' – 6'' to 3' – 0''
CONCRETE – PIPE	180	60 – 120	10 – 23	150	30 – 80	3' – 0''
CONCRETE – H – BEAM	180	60 – 120	10 – 23	150	30 – 80	3' – 0''

NOTE:

*Timber pile must be treated with wood preservative when any portion is above permanent ground water table.

Applicable Material Specifications — Concrete: ACL 318; Timber: ASTM D25; Pipe: ASTM A252; Structural Sections: ASTM A36

V. DeSimone; Mueser, Rutledge, Wentworth & Johnston; New York, New York

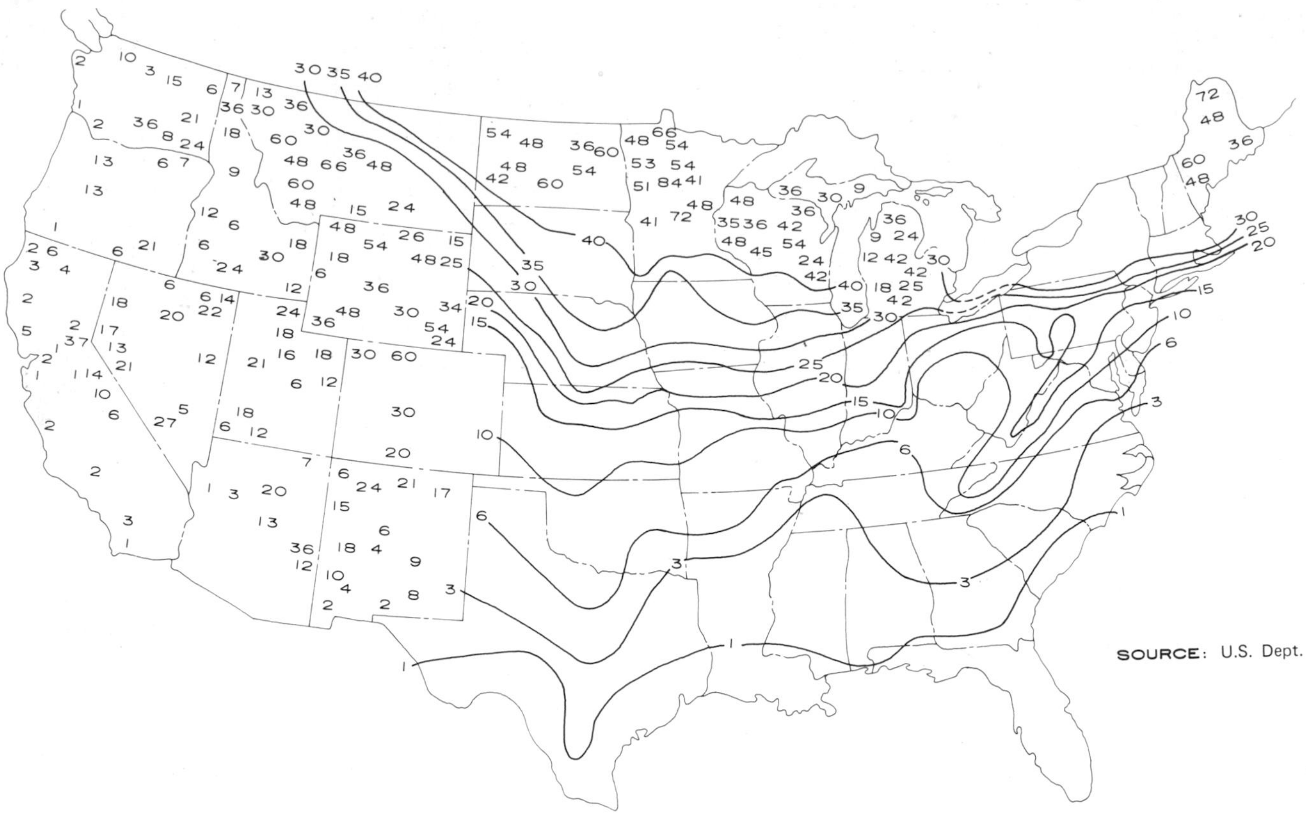

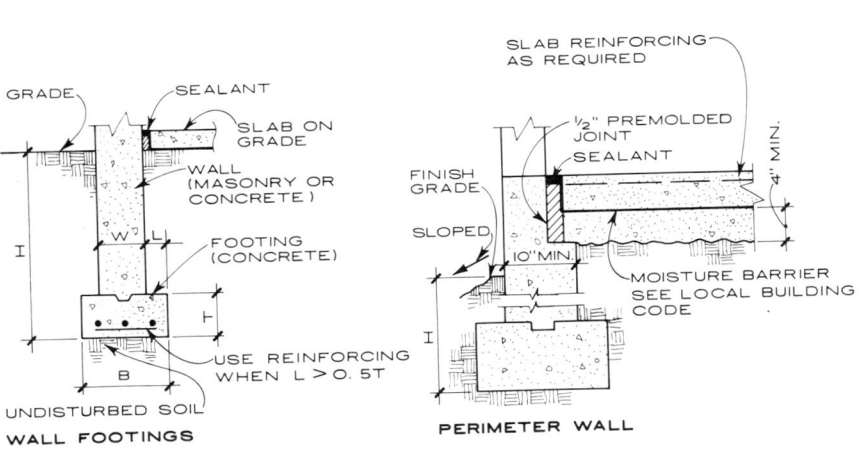

AVERAGE DEPTH OF FROST PENETRATION – H INCHES

SOURCE: U.S. Dept. of Commerce Weather Bureau

WALL FOOTINGS

PERIMETER WALL

GRADE BEAM AND COLLAPSIBLE FORM

TYPICAL GRADE BEAMS

NOTES:

A. Use temperature reinforcing only when face of grade beam is exposed over 18" to weather.

B. Use main reinforcing only when finish grade is below 24" and/or finish floor surcharge load so dictates.

C. When finish grade is below finish floor, design grade beam for vertical and horizontal forces.

D. Use collapsible form when soil under beam is expansive or fat clay (CH). This provides a void which allows for periodic heaving of the soil due to increased moisture content, without lifting the grade beam.

E. Use top & bottom reinforcing for all grade beams.

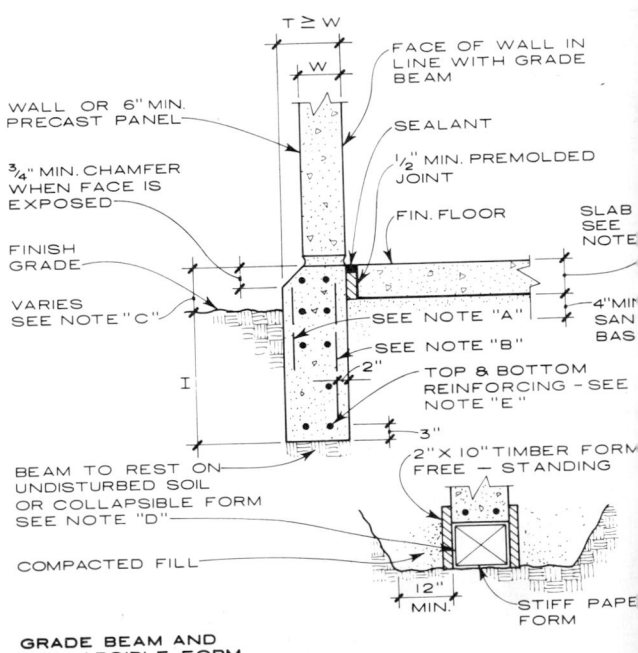

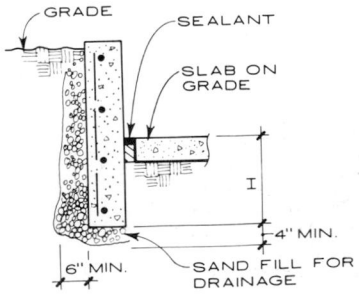

AREA WALLS

GENERAL NOTES:

1. Adjoining ground to slope away from foundation in all directions and underlying soil to be preferably sand or gravel to reduce to a minimum heaving due to frost action.

2. It is good practice for foundations to extend 12" below frost line; consult local codes.

Smith, Hinchman & Grylls Associates, Inc.; Detroit, Michigan

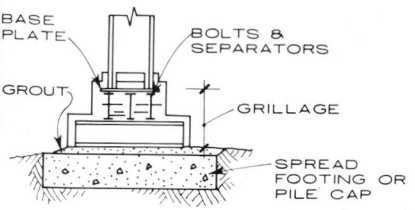

STEEL GRILLAGE FOUNDATION

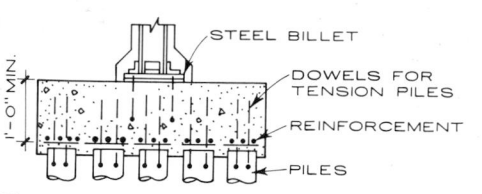

PILE FOUNDATION

WALL

2 OR 3T

FOOTING

$\frac{a}{2}$ = ANGLE OF REPOSE

UNDISTURBED SOIL (SAND OR CLAY)

STEPPING OF CONTINUOUS FOOTINGS

max. steepness: 2 horizontal to 1 vertical, or 1/2 angle of repose of supporting soil.

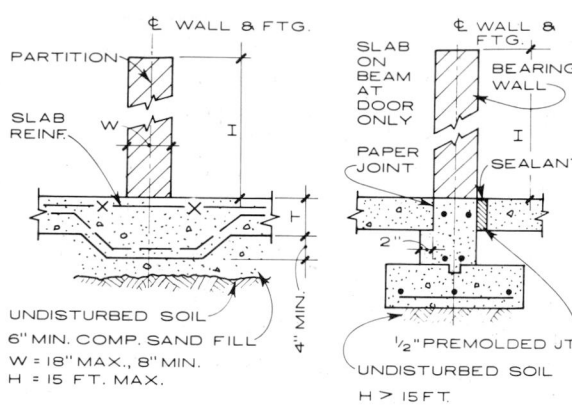

Ç WALL & FTG.

PARTITION

SLAB REINF.

Ç WALL & FTG.

SLAB ON BEAM AT DOOR ONLY

BEARING WALL

PAPER JOINT

SEALANT

UNDISTURBED SOIL
6" MIN. COMP. SAND FILL
W = 18" MAX., 8" MIN.
H = 15 FT. MAX.

2"

1/2" PREMOLDED JT.

UNDISTURBED SOIL
H > 15FT

NOTE: REINFORCE FOOTING AS REQUIRED

PARTITION AND INTERIOR BEARING WALL FOOTINGS

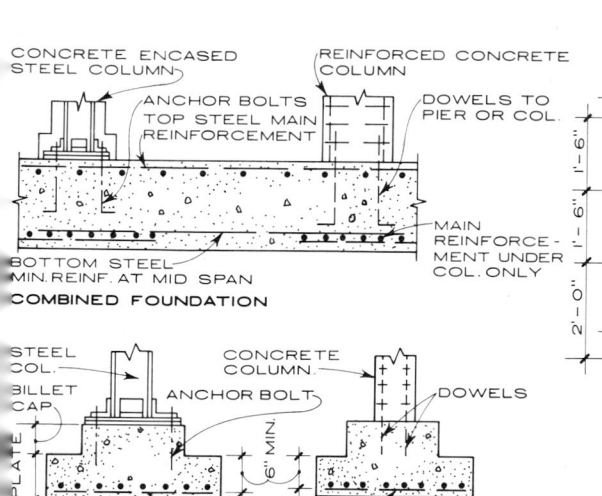

CONCRETE ENCASED STEEL COLUMN

REINFORCED CONCRETE COLUMN

ANCHOR BOLTS
TOP STEEL MAIN REINFORCEMENT

DOWELS TO PIER OR COL.

MAIN REINFORCEMENT UNDER COL. ONLY

BOTTOM STEEL
MIN. REINF. AT MID SPAN

COMBINED FOUNDATION

STEEL COL.

CONCRETE COLUMN

BILLET CAP

ANCHOR BOLT

DOWELS

REINFORCEMENT

STEEL COLUMN   **REINFORCED CONC.**

COLUMNS ON SPREAD FOOTINGS

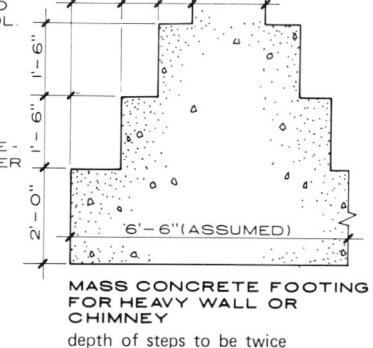

1'-0"   9"   9"   1'-6"

6'-6" (ASSUMED)

MASS CONCRETE FOOTING FOR HEAVY WALL OR CHIMNEY

depth of steps to be twice their projection

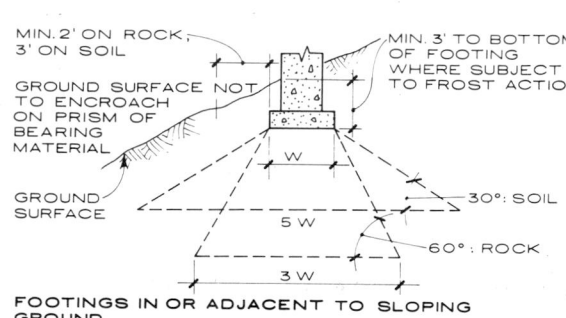

MIN. 2' ON ROCK,
3' ON SOIL

MIN. 3' TO BOTTOM OF FOOTING WHERE SUBJECT TO FROST ACTION

GROUND SURFACE NOT TO ENCROACH ON PRISM OF BEARING MATERIAL

GROUND SURFACE

W

5 W

3 W

30°: SOIL

60°: ROCK

FOOTINGS IN OR ADJACENT TO SLOPING GROUND

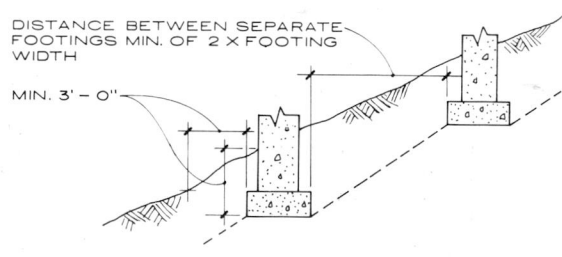
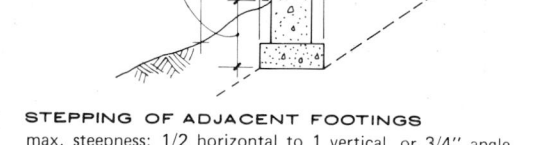

DISTANCE BETWEEN SEPARATE FOOTINGS MIN. OF 2 × FOOTING WIDTH

MIN. 3'-0"

STEPPING OF ADJACENT FOOTINGS

max. steepness: 1/2 horizontal to 1 vertical, or 3/4" angle of repose of supporting soil.

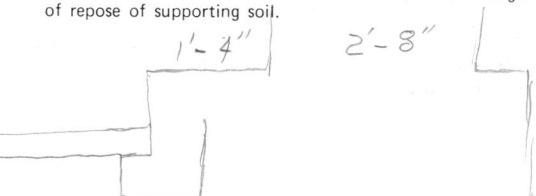

1'-4"   2'-8"

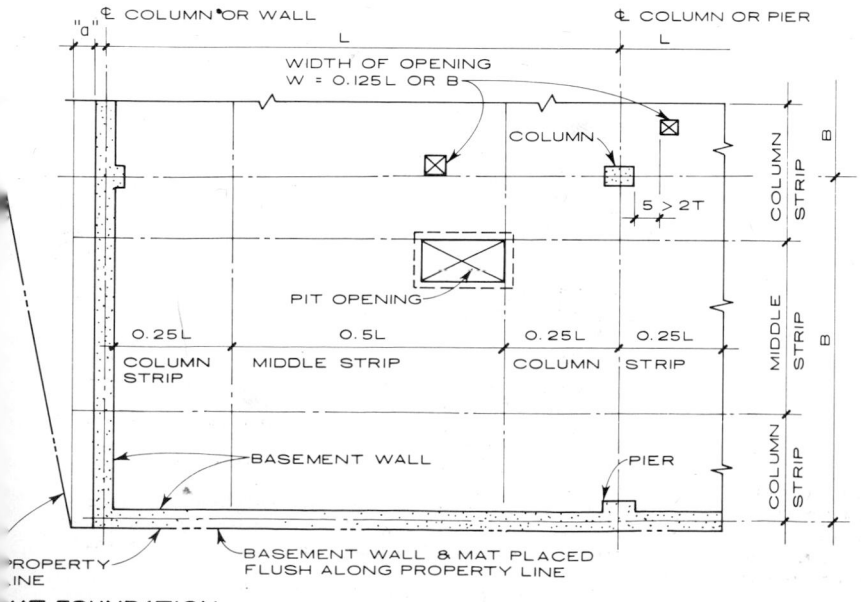

Ç COLUMN OR WALL

Ç COLUMN OR PIER

"a"

L

L

WIDTH OF OPENING
W = 0.125L OR B

COLUMN

COLUMN STRIP

B

5 > 2T

COLUMN

PIT OPENING

MIDDLE STRIP

B

0.25L   0.5L   0.25L   0.25L

COLUMN STRIP   MIDDLE STRIP   COLUMN STRIP

COLUMN STRIP

BASEMENT WALL

PIER

PROPERTY LINE

BASEMENT WALL & MAT PLACED FLUSH ALONG PROPERTY LINE

MAT FOUNDATION

NOTES FOR MAT FOUNDATIONS:

1. Column spacing should be L = 1.33 B max.
2. Place pit (if necessary) at middle strip.
3. Adjust distance "a" to get an even pressure under mat within the allowable soil pressure.
4. Provide membrane waterproofing under mat when mat is less than 12" thick and the ground water level is above the mat.
5. Provide water stops in mat and in walls at construction joints.
6. Mat thickness, t = 0.0278 L inches max.

Smith, Hinchman & Grylls Associates, Inc.; Detroit, Michigan

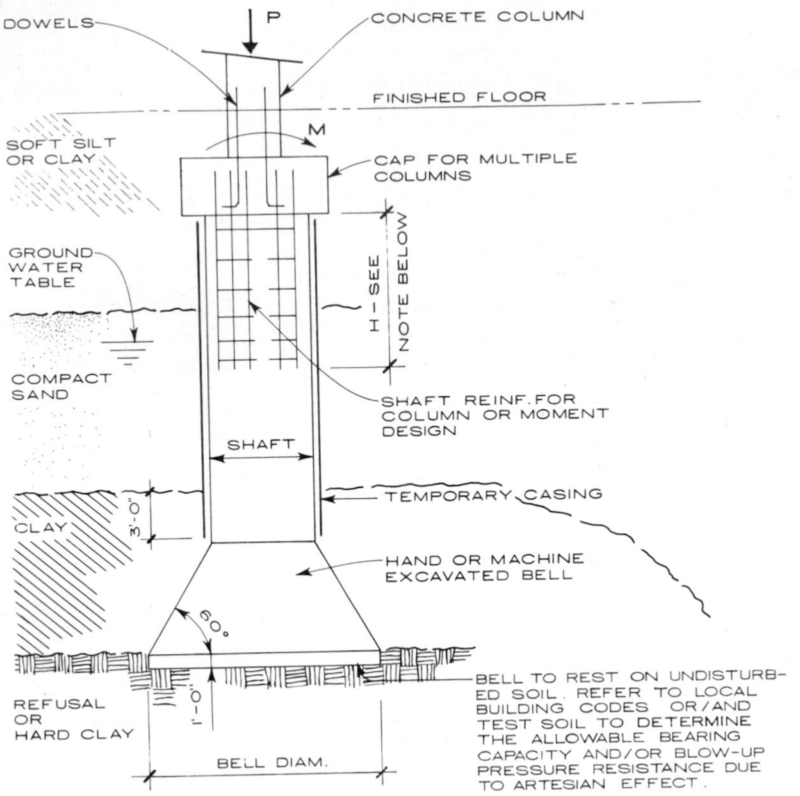

DOWELS — | P | — CONCRETE COLUMN

FINISHED FLOOR

M

SOFT SILT OR CLAY

CAP FOR MULTIPLE COLUMNS

GROUND WATER TABLE

H — SEE NOTE BELOW

COMPACT SAND

SHAFT REINF. FOR COLUMN OR MOMENT DESIGN

SHAFT

TEMPORARY CASING

CLAY

3'-0"

HAND OR MACHINE EXCAVATED BELL

60°

1'-0"

REFUSAL OR HARD CLAY

BELL TO REST ON UNDISTURB-ED SOIL. REFER TO LOCAL BUILDING CODES OR/AND TEST SOIL TO DETERMINE THE ALLOWABLE BEARING CAPACITY AND/OR BLOW-UP PRESSURE RESISTANCE DUE TO ARTESIAN EFFECT.

BELL DIAM.

BELL FOUNDATION

P

M — STEEL COLUMN

FINISHED FLOOR

MINIMUM 2" CONCRETE COVER OVER STEEL COLUMN & BASE PLATE

CAP FOR MULTIPLE COLUMNS

ANCHOR BOLTS

TIES OR SPIRAL

SHAFT REINF. FOR COLUMN OR MOMENT DESIGN

SHAFT

HAND OR MACHINE EXCAVATED SOCKET

TEMPORARY CASING

SOCKET — CHECK WITH FOUNDATION ENGINEER FOR DEPTH

SOCKET PIER INTO ROCK TO TRANSMIT HIGH COMPRESSION OR TENSION LOADS INTO ROCK BY BOND

ROCK

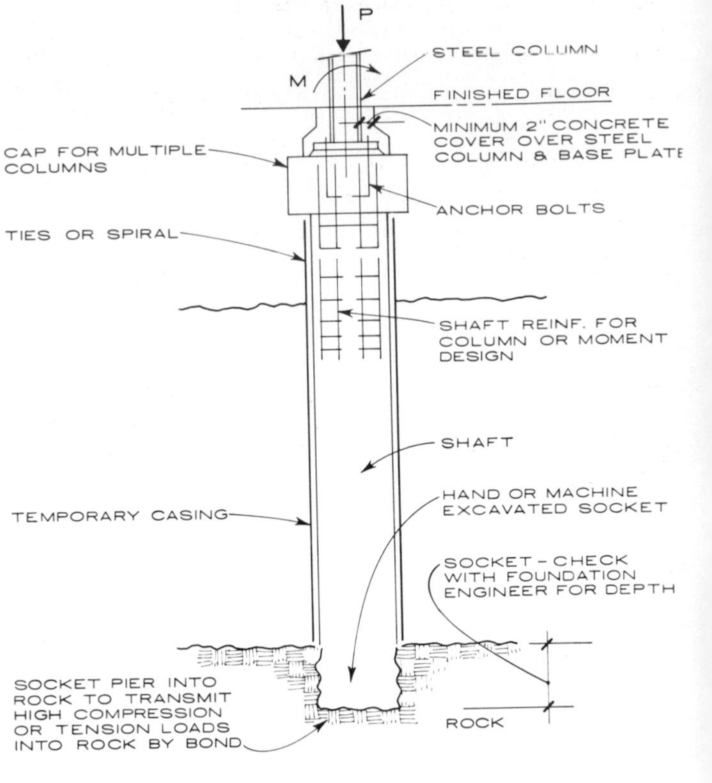

SOCKET FOUNDATION

DEEP FOUNDATIONS; DRILLED – IN – PIERS

NOTE :

1. Use temporary casing to seal-off inflow of water or sand into excavation. Delete casing when shaft is in stiff clay.

2. Grout bottom of shaft against artesian water or sulphur gas intrusion into the excavation.

3. Determine max. bearing capacity of pier by the unconfined compression strength of the soil, and verify it by load tests.

4. H is a function of the passive resistance of the soil, generated by the moment applied to the caisson cap.

5. Caissons may be used under grade beams or concrete walls.

—I— —I— —I—

PLAN OF LAGGING

PLAN OF INTERLOCKING SHEET PILE

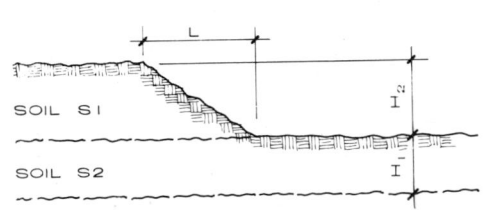

L

SOIL S1

$\frac{1}{2}$

SOIL S2

I

SOIL S3

OPEN EXCAVATION

EMBANKMENT STABILITY (CONSULT FOUNDATION ENGINEER)

NOTE :

When ground water level is above H_1 use well-point prior to excavating and as long as the hole is kept open if the soils below excavation level are permeable.

SOIL TYPES			L/H_o	REMARKS
S1	S2	S3		
Fill	Rock		>1.5	Check Sliding of S1
S. Clay	H. Clay	Rock	>1.0	Check Sliding of S1
Sand	S. Clay	H. Clay	>1.5	Check Lateral Displace. of S2
Sand	Sand	H. Clay	>1.5	
H. Clay	S. Clay	Sand	<1.0	Check Lateral Displace. of S2

S = SOFT, H = HARD

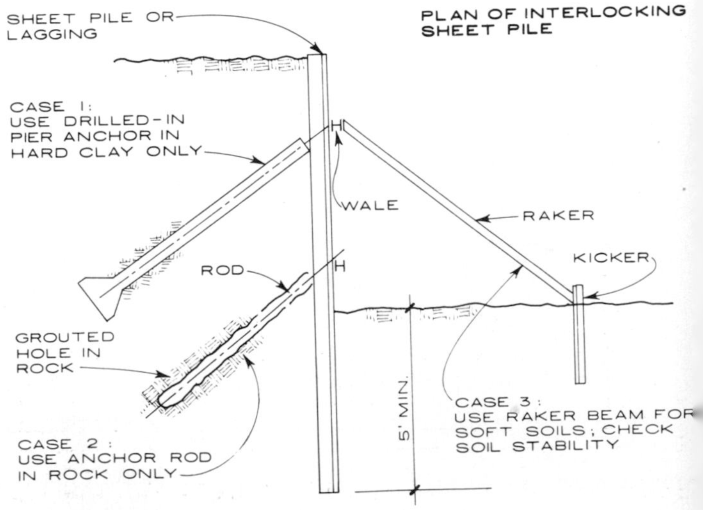

Smith, Hinchman & Grylls Associates, Inc.; Detroit, Michigan

SHEET PILE OR LAGGING

CASE 1: USE DRILLED–IN PIER ANCHOR IN HARD CLAY ONLY

WALE

RAKER

ROD

H

KICKER

GROUTED HOLE IN ROCK

5' MIN

CASE 2: USE ANCHOR ROD IN ROCK ONLY

CASE 3: USE RAKER BEAM FOR SOFT SOILS; CHECK SOIL STABILITY

BRACED EXCAVATION

CONCRETE CRIB RETAINING WALLS

Continuous back wall anchorage types may be erected with a long radius and fishtail types with a short radius. Adverse soil conditions require wall to have extra sill units or foundation. Preliminary wall proportions: 6'– 0" high x 4'– 0" deep; 11'– 6" high x 6'– 0" deep. Walls up to 6'– 0" high may be erected plumb. Continuous back wall anchorage type with exposed "H" type headers is most commonly available.

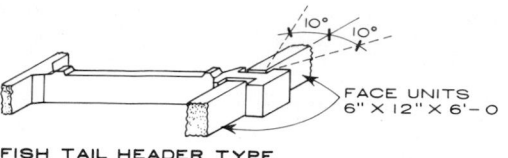

FISH TAIL HEADER TYPE

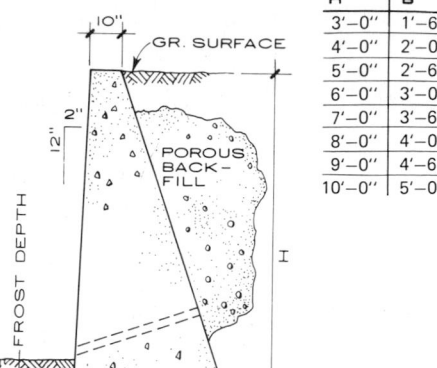

H	B
3'–0"	1'–6"
4'–0"	2'–0"
5'–0"	2'–6"
6'–0"	3'–0"
7'–0"	3'–6"
8'–0"	4'–0"
9'–0"	4'–6"
10'–0"	5'–0"

MASS CONCRETE RETAINING WALL WITHOUT SURCHARGE

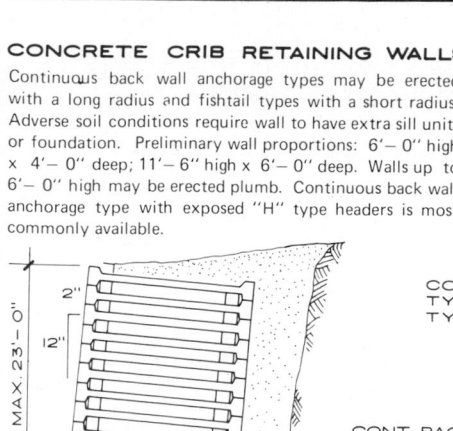

SECTION

PARTIAL ISOMETRIC VIEWS

PLAN DETAIL

*Passive earth pressure is developed at lower grade to reduce heel tension to zero and to resist sliding and overturning; therefore low grade must be protected. Place base below frost. Dimensions are preliminary.

Soil pressure at toe equals .2h in tips per square foot. Dimensions are preliminary only.

Provide control, i.e. contraction, joints in concrete retaining walls about every 25 feet and keyed expansion joints about every fourth contraction joint.
Dowels: 1" x 2'– 0" plain bars @ 12" O.C.
Filler: Premolded joint filler.
Parting strip: 16 ga. galvanized sheet steel coated to prevent bond and wire tied to rebars @ 12" O.C.

RETAINING WALL EXPANSION JOINT

RETAINING WALL CONTROL JOINT

CONCRETE OUTLINES FOR "L" TYPE RETAINING WALLS

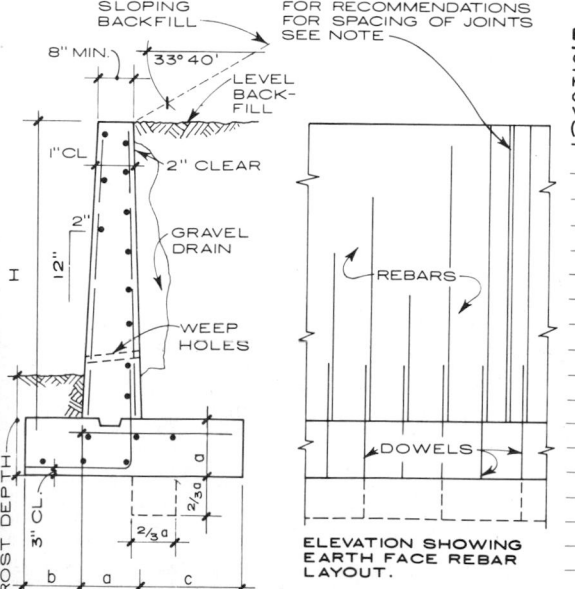

ELEVATION SHOWING EARTH FACE REBAR LAYOUT.

BACKFILL SLOPING Φ = 33°– 40'

CONCRETE OUTLINES

HEIGHT OF WALL=h (ft)	B (ft)	a (ft)	b (ft)	c (ft)	*BASE PRESS. AT TOE (psf)
3	2'–6"	0'–11"	0'–7"	1'–0"	1,072
4	3'–2"	1'–0"	0'–9"	1'–5"	1,421
5	3'–10"	1'–1"	1'–0"	1'–9"	1,699
6	4'–6"	1'–2"	1'–3"	2'–1"	1,990
7	5'–3"	1'–3"	1'–6"	2'–6"	2,238
8	5'–11"	1'–4"	1'–9"	2'–10"	2,512
9	6'–8"	1'–5"	2'–0"	3'–3"	2,753
10	7'–5"	1'–6"	2'–3"	3'–8"	3,018
11	8'–1"	1'–7"	2'–6"	4'–0"	3,298
12	8'–10"	1'–8"	2'–9"	4'–5"	3,536
13	9'–6"	1'–9"	3'–0"	4'–9"	3,805
14	10'–3"	1'–10"	3'–3"	5'–2"	4,058
15	11'–0"	1'–11"	3'–6"	5'–7"	4,310
16	11'–10"	2'–0"	3'–10"	6'–0"	4,477
17	12'–7"	2'–1"	4'–1"	6'–5"	4,719
18	13'–4"	2'–2"	4'–4"	6'–10"	4,959
19	14'–2"	2'–3"	4'–7"	7'–3"	5,104
20	15'–0"	2'–4"	5'–0"	7'–8"	5,300

BACKFILL LEVEL–NO SURCHARGE

CONCRETE OUTLINES

HEIGHT OF WALL=h (ft)	B (ft)	a (ft)	b (ft)	c (ft)	*BASE PRESS. AT TOE (psf)
3	1'–9"	0'–10½"	0'–4"	0'–6½"	885
4	2'–2"	0'–11"	0'–5"	0'–10"	1,136
5	2'–8"	0'–11"	0'–5"	1'–4"	1,361
6	3'–3"	1'–0"	0'–8"	1'–7"	1,415
7	3'–10"	1'–0"	1'–0"	1'–10"	1,398
8	4'–3"	1'–1"	1'–1"	2'–1"	1,643
9	4'–9"	1'–1"	1'–1"	2'–7"	1,851
10	5'–4"	1'–2"	1'–4"	2'–10"	1,944
11	5'–10"	1'–2"	1'–6"	3'–2"	2,051
12	6'–6"	1'–4"	1'–8"	3'–7"	2,129
13	7'–0"	1'–4"	1'–8"	4'–0"	2,403
14	7'–8"	1'–4"	2'–1"	4'–3"	2,332
15	8'–1"	1'–5"	2'–1"	4'–7"	2,608
16	8'–6"	1'–5"	2'–2"	4'–11"	2,799
17	9'–0"	1'–6"	2'–3"	5'–3"	3,008
18	9'–6"	1'–7"	2'–4"	5'–7"	3,207
19	10'–2"	1'–7"	2'–6"	6'–1"	3,264
20	10'–5"	1'–8"	2'–6"	6'–3"	3,119

Lug shown dashed may be required to prevent sliding in high walls & those on moist clay

CONCRETE OUTLINES FOR "T" TYPE RETAINING WALL WITH LEVEL AND SLOPING BACKFILL

EQUIVALENT FLUID PRESSURE = 28.7 LBS / FT.³

* BASE PRESS. = BASE PRESSURE

rvin Bruce Schafer; Peoria, Illinois

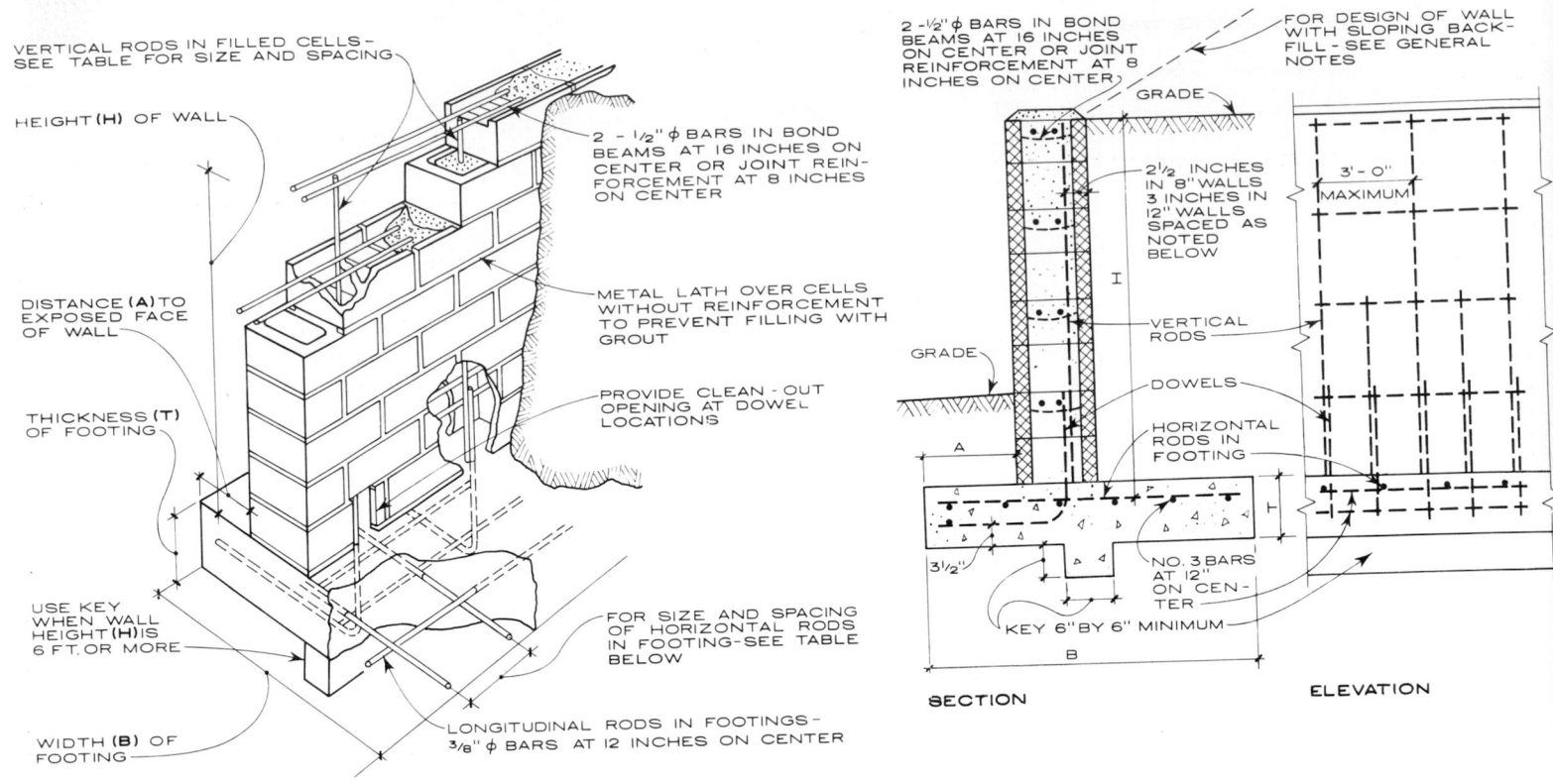

VERTICAL RODS IN FILLED CELLS—
SEE TABLE FOR SIZE AND SPACING

HEIGHT (H) OF WALL

DISTANCE (A) TO
EXPOSED FACE
OF WALL

THICKNESS (T)
OF FOOTING

USE KEY
WHEN WALL
HEIGHT (H) IS
6 FT. OR MORE

WIDTH (B) OF
FOOTING

2 - 1/2" φ BARS IN BOND
BEAMS AT 16 INCHES ON
CENTER OR JOINT REIN-
FORCEMENT AT 8 INCHES
ON CENTER

METAL LATH OVER CELLS
WITHOUT REINFORCEMENT
TO PREVENT FILLING WITH
GROUT

PROVIDE CLEAN - OUT
OPENING AT DOWEL
LOCATIONS

FOR SIZE AND SPACING
OF HORIZONTAL RODS
IN FOOTING-SEE TABLE
BELOW

LONGITUDINAL RODS IN FOOTINGS—
3/8" φ BARS AT 12 INCHES ON CENTER

2 -1/2" φ BARS IN BOND
BEAMS AT 16 INCHES
ON CENTER OR JOINT
REINFORCEMENT AT 8
INCHES ON CENTER

FOR DESIGN OF WALL
WITH SLOPING BACK-
FILL - SEE GENERAL
NOTES

GRADE

2 1/2 INCHES
IN 8" WALLS
3 INCHES IN
12" WALLS
SPACED AS
NOTED
BELOW

VERTICAL
RODS

GRADE

DOWELS

HORIZONTAL
RODS IN
FOOTING

NO. 3 BARS
AT 12"
ON CEN-
TER

KEY 6" BY 6" MINIMUM

3 1/2"

3'- 0"
MAXIMUM

SECTION

ELEVATION

TYPICAL DETAILS OF CANTILEVER RETAINING WALL

DIMENSIONS AND REINFORCEMENT

WALL	H	B	T	A	VERTICAL RODS IN THE WALL	HORIZONTAL RODS IN FOOTING
8 INCH THICKNESS	3'-4"	2'-4"	9"	8"	3/8" @ 32"	3/8" @ 27"
	4'-0"	2'-9"	9"	10"	1/2" @ 32"	3/8" @ 27"
	4'-8"	3'-3"	10"	12"	5/8" @ 32"	3/8" @ 27"
	5'-4"	3'-8"	10"	14"	1/2" @ 16"	1/2" @ 30"
	6'-0"	4'-2"	12"	15"	1/2" @ 24"	1/2" @ 25"
12 INCH THICKNESS	6'-8"	4'-6"	12"	16"	3/4" @ 24"	1/2" @ 22"
	7'-4"	4'-10"	12"	18"	7/8" @ 32"	5/8" @ 26"
	8'-0"	5'-4"	12"	20"	7/8" @ 24"	5/8" @ 21"
	8'-8"	5'-10"	14"	22"	7/8" @ 16"	3/4" @ 26"
	9'-4"	6'-4"	14"	24"	1" @ 8"	3/4" @ 21"

Vertical reinforcement is usually secured in place after the masonry work has been completed and before grouting. Accurately position and tie at vertical intervals not exceeding 160 bar diameters. Place wire loop extending into core in mortar joints as wall is laid up. Loosen before mortar sets. After inserting bar, pull wire loop and bar to proper position and secure wire by tying free ends. Control joints should be designed to resist shear and other lateral forces while permitting longitudinal movement.

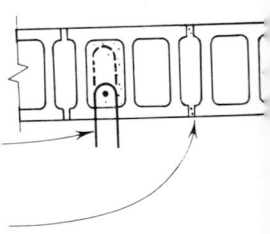

**PLAN DETAIL AT
VERTICAL ROD
AND CONTROL JOINT**

GENERAL NOTES

Concrete masonry units for retaining wall construction shall comply with the requirements of "Specifications For Hollow Load Bearing Concrete Masonry Units," ASTM C90—64T.

Concrete for footings should be mixed in the following approximate proportions: 1 part portland cement, 2 3/4 parts of sand and 4 parts of gravel. Gravel should be well graded and not exceed 1 1/2 inches in size. Amount of water used for each bag of cement should not exceed 5 1/2 gallons unless the sand is very dry.

Mortar and grout should comply with the requirements of "Specifications For Mortar and Grout For Reinforced Masonry," ASTM C476—63. Use fine grout where grout space is less than three inches in least dimension. Use coarse grout where the least dimension of the grout space is three inches or more. Aggregates for grout shall conform to ASTM Standard Specifications C404—61.

Steel reinforcement should be clean, free from harmful rust, and should comply with applicable ASTM standards for deformed bars and steel wire.

Designs herein are based upon an assumed soil weight (vertical pressure) of 100 pounds per cubic foot. Horizontal pressure is based upon an equivalent fluid weight for the soil of 45 pounds per cubic foot.

Walls shown are designed with a safety factor against overturning of not less than 2 and a safety factor against horizontal sliding of not less than 1.5. Designs are based on the following standards: Footings (AC1 318—63) and walls (ASA 41.2—1960). Computations in the table for

wall heights are based on level backfill. One method of providing for additional loads due to sloping backfill surface loads is to consider them as an additional depth soil, that is an extra load of 300 pounds per square f can be treated as 3 extra feet of soil weighing 100 pou per square foot.

Allow 24 hours for masonry to set up before grouti Pour grout in 4 foot layers, an hour between each po Break long walls into panels of 20 to 30 feet in len with vertical control joints. Allow 7 days for finished w to set up before backfilling. Prevent water from accumu ting behind wall by means of 4 inch diameter weep h at a 5 to 10 foot spacing (with screen and graded stone by a continuous drain with felt covered open joints combination with waterproofing.

Robert S. Dame, R. A.; Kensington, Maryland

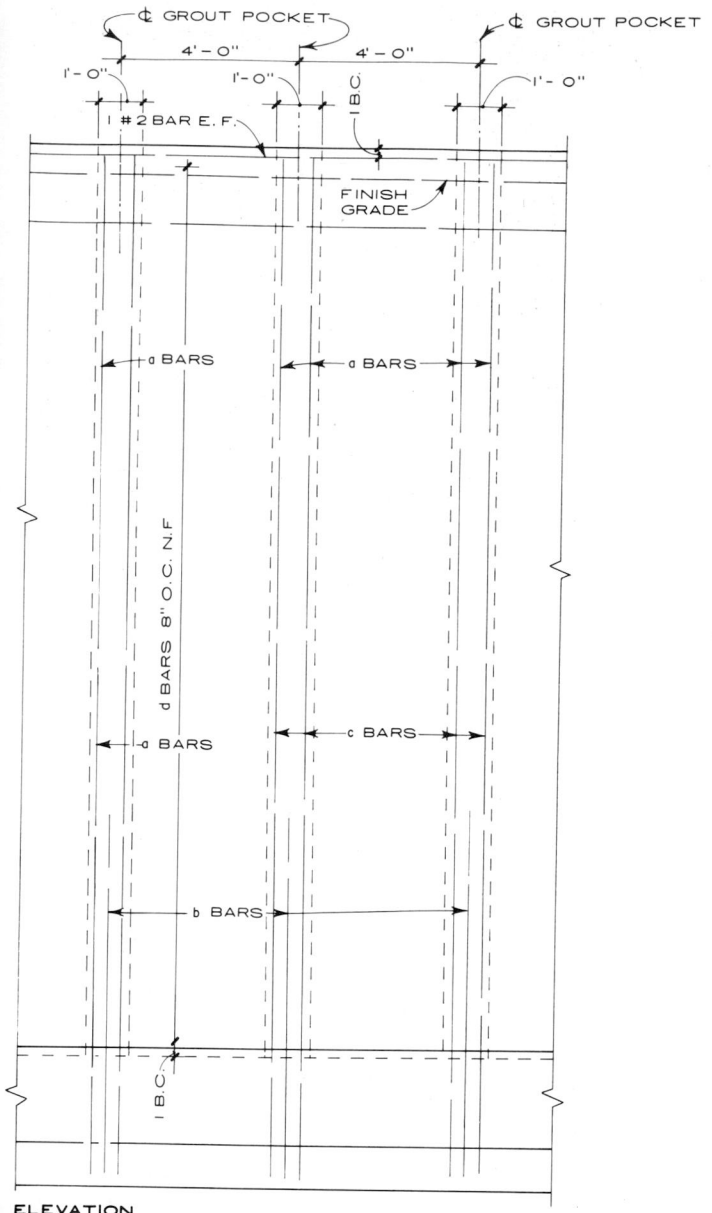

ELEVATION

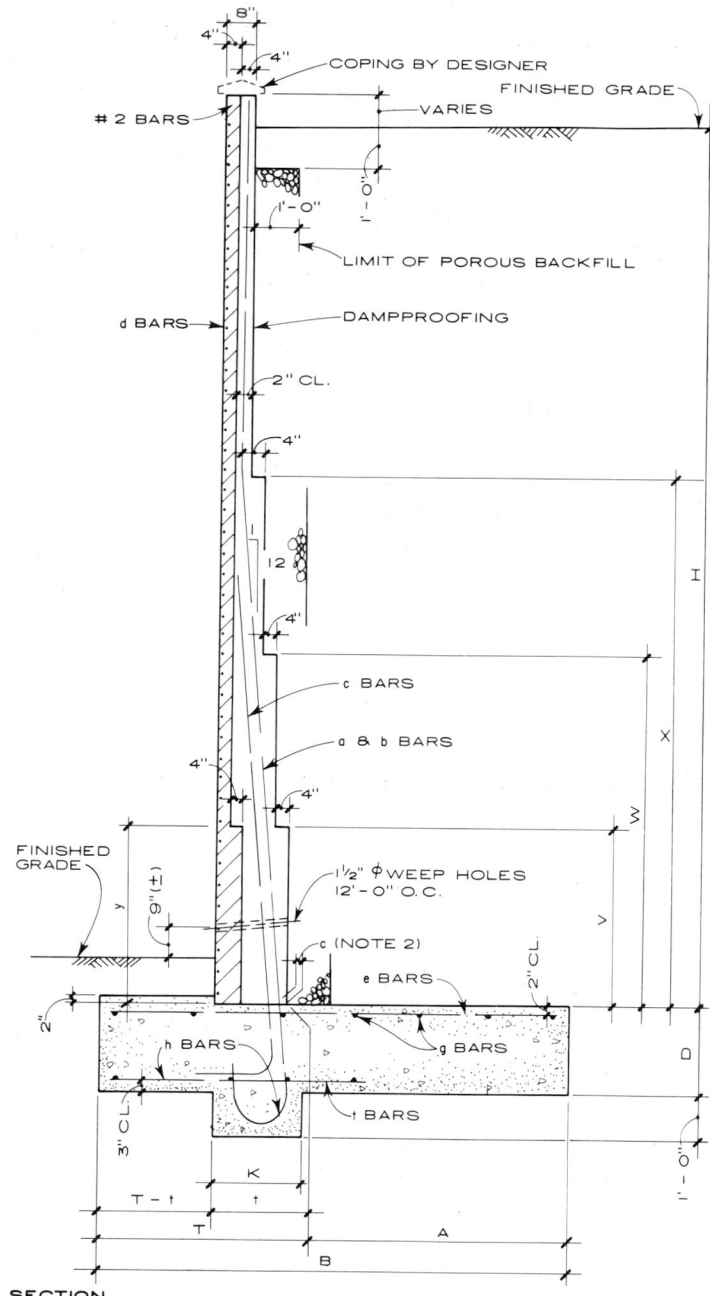

SECTION

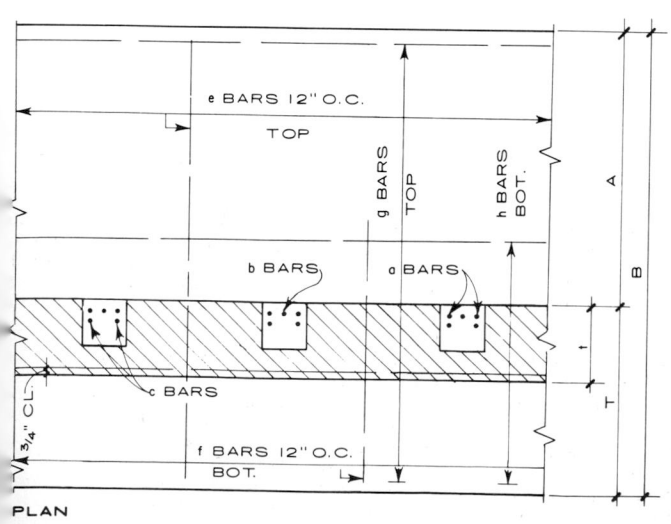

PLAN

DESIGN DETAILS

Structural Clay Products Institute; McLean, Virginia

ABBREVIATIONS:

N.F. = NEAR FACE
E.F. = EACH FACE
B.C. = BRICK COURSE (STANDARD 3 COURSES PER 8 INCHES)
C.L. = CLEAR
BOT. = BOTTOM
O.C. = ON CENTER

NOTE:

See following page for explanation of dimension symbols and design tables.

GROUTED REINFORCED BRICK MASONRY CANTILEVER RETAINING WALLS

STEM Dimensions							Loads		FOOTING Dimensions					Loads		
H ft.	t in.	C in.	V ft.	W ft.	X ft.	Y ft.	V kips per 4 ft.	⋀ ft.-kips per 4 ft.	B	T	A	D	K	P kips per ft.	⋀ or ft. kips per ft.	Toe pressure kips per sq. ft.
6	8	2					2.06	4.13	3'–6"	1'–3"	2'–3"	1'–0"		0.70	1.63	1.33
7	8	2					2.80	6.55	4'–0"	1'–3"	2'–9"	1'–0"		0.92	2.45	1.54
8	8	2					3.66	9.78	4'–6"	1'–3"	3'–3"	1'–0"		1.16	3.48	1.74
9	12	5			1		4.63	13.92	5'–0"	1'–6"	3'–6"	1'–0"		1.43	4.76	2.00
10	12	4			2		5.72	19.10	5'–6"	1'–9"	3'–9"	1'–0"		1.73	6.35	2.11
11	12	3			3		6.92	25.42	6'–0"	2'–0"	4'–0"	1'–3"	1'–3"	2.14	8.75	2.31
12	12	2			4		8.24	33.00	6'–6"	2'–3"	4'–3"	1'–3"	1'–3"	2.52	11.10	2.37
13	16	5	1		5		9.67	41.96	7'–0"	2'–6"	4'–6"	1'–3"	1'–3"	2.90	13.80	2.62
14	16	4	2		6		11.21	52.41	7'–6"	2'–9"	4'–9"	1'–6"	1'–6"	3.43	17.70	2.82
15	16	3	3		7		12.87	64.46	8'–0"	3'–0"	5'–0"	1'–6"	1'–6"	3.89	21.40	2.87
16	16	2	4		8		14.64	78.23	8'–6"	3'–3"	5'–3"	1'–6"	1'–6"	4.51	26.70	3.04
17	20	5	1	5	9	1	16.53	93.84	9'–0"	3'–6"	5'–6"	1'–9"	1'–9"	5.03	31.40	3.32
18	20	4	2	6	10	2	18.53	111.39	9'–6"	3'–9"	5'–9"	1'–9"	1'–9"	5.72	38.20	3.49
19	20	3	3	7	11	3	20.65	131.01	10'–0"	4'–0"	6'–0"	1'–9"	1'–9"	6.30	44.10	3.52
20	20	2	4	8	12	4	22.88	152.80	10'–6"	4'–3"	6'–3"	2'–0"	2'–0"	6.92	50.80	3.65

REINFORCEMENT

Bars	a (2 per pocket)		b (1 per pocket)		c (2 per pocket)		d		e		f		g		h	
H ft.	Bar Size	Extension Above Top of Footing	Bar Size	Extension Above Top of Footing	Bar Size	Extension Above Top of Footing	Bar Size	No. of Bars	Bar Size	Length of Bar	Bar Size	Length of Bar	Bar Size	No. of Bars	Bar Size	No. of Bars
6	#5	Full Height of Pocket					#2	10	#3	3'–2"	#3	2'–3"	#3	4	#3	3
7	#6						#2	11	#4	3'–8"	#3	2'–3"	#3	4	#3	3
8	#6		#6	3'–0"			#2	13	#4	4'–2"	#3	2'–3"	#3	4	#3	3
9	#7		#6	3'–0"			#2	14	#5	4'–8"	#3	2'–6"	#3	4	#3	3
10	#7		#7	4'–0"			#2	16	#5	5'–2"	#3	2'–9"	#3	5	#3	4
11	#8		#7	4'–0"			#2	17	#6	5'–8"	#3	3'–0"	#3	5	#3	5
12	#8		#8	5'–0"			#2	19	#6	6'–2"	#3	3'–3"	#3	5	#3	5
13	#8		#8	6'–0"			#2	20	#7	6'–8"	#4	3'–9"	#4	5	#4	5
14	#9		#10	6'–0"			#2	22	#7	7'–2"	#4	4'–0"	#4	6	#4	5
15	#10		#9	5'–0"			#2	23	#7	7'–8"	#4	4'–3"	#4	6	#4	5
16	#10		#11	6'–6"			#2	25	#8	8'–2"	#5	4'–9"	#4	6	#4	5
17	#10		#8	4'–0"	#8	7'–0"	#2	26	#8	8'–8"	#5	5'–0"	#4	6	#4	5
18	#10		#9	4'–0"	#9	8'–0"	#2	28	#8	9'–2"	#5	5'–3"	#4	7	#4	6
19	#10		#9	4'–0"	#10	9'–0"	#2	29	#9	9'–8"	#6	6'–0"	#4	7	#4	6
20	#10		#11	5'–6"	#10	10'–0"	#2	31	#9	10'–2"	#6	6'–3"	#4	7	#4	6

NOTE:

1. The "c" dimension shown on the drawing and given in Table is the grout cover over the a and b bars at top of footing elevation.

2. The key on the bottom of the footing which resists sliding may be eliminated for walls with an H dimension of 10' and less.

3. In case the dimensions v, w, x and y shown in Table cannot be obtained with the brick used for the construction, the v, w and x dimensions should be increased and the y dimension decreased the distance required for the brick to course out.

Structural Clay Products Institute; McLean, Virginia

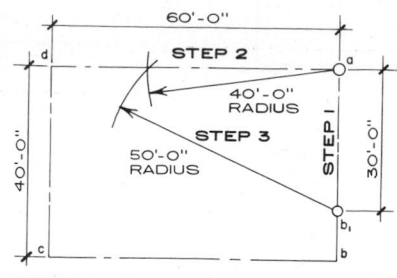

BUILDING DIAGRAM

STEP I
SQUARE BUILDING LINES WITH TAPE

1. "a" may be any corner of
   the building.
   "ab" may be along any side
   of the building.
2. See diagram.
3. See diagram.
4. Assume building is 40'−0"
   x 60'−0". Extend lines
   to full length of walls and
   mark corners with stakes.

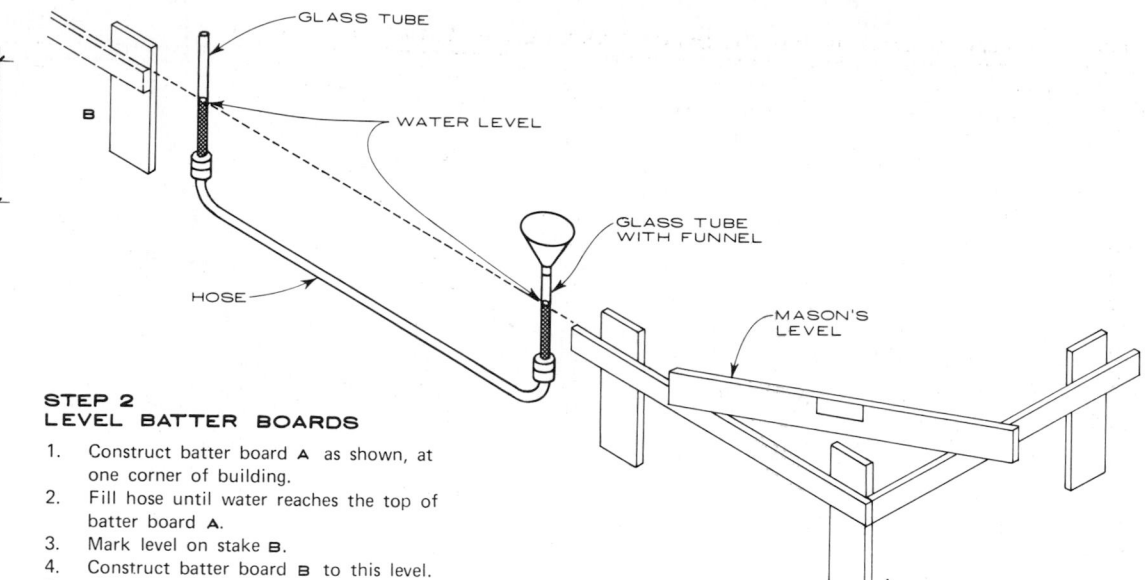

STEP 2
LEVEL BATTER BOARDS

1. Construct batter board **A** as shown, at
   one corner of building.
2. Fill hose until water reaches the top of
   batter board **A**.
3. Mark level on stake **B**.
4. Construct batter board **B** to this level.
5. Repeat for other corners.

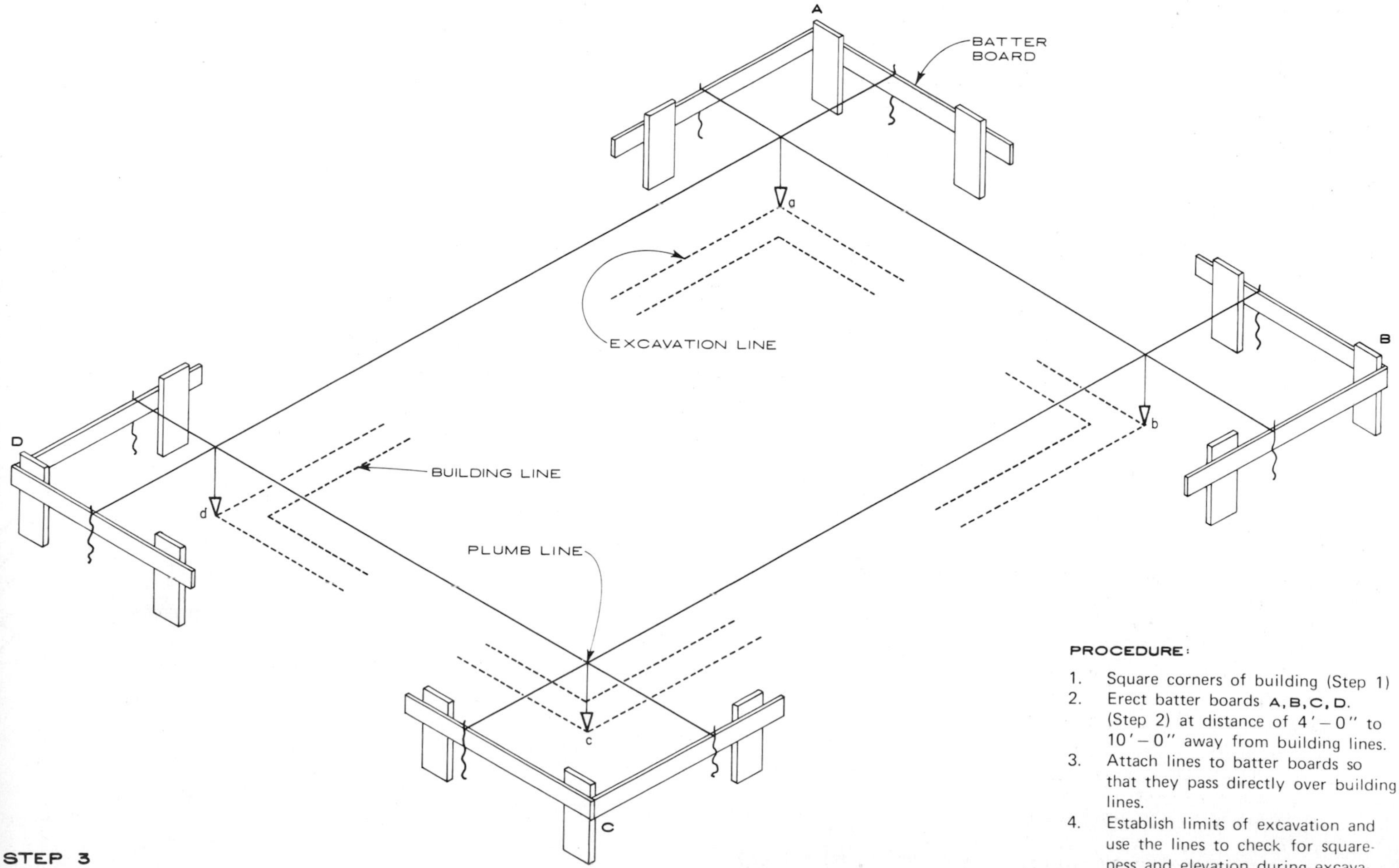

STEP 3
BUILDING LAYOUT

PROCEDURE:

1. Square corners of building (Step 1)
2. Erect batter boards **A,B,C,D**.
   (Step 2) at distance of 4'−0" to
   10'−0" away from building lines.
3. Attach lines to batter boards so
   that they pass directly over building
   lines.
4. Establish limits of excavation and
   use the lines to check for squareness and elevation during excavation and construction.

LENGTH:

House sewer may be 50'– 0'' to 100'– 0'' long. Run as directly as possible. If over 300'– 0'' long, place manhole at center. Longer runs are desirable.

MATERIALS:

Piping may be salt glazed clay bell and spigot, tile pipe, asbestos cement or concrete bell and spigot. If near well, or any other water supply, use cast iron.

Where trees or shrubs may cause root stoppage in clay pipe, use cast iron.

Use bituminous joints or rubber ring type joints for clay, concrete or asbestos cement pipe; use lead for cast iron pipe.

SIZE:

4'' diameter for small installations; 6'' is better in all cases.

GRADE:

In northern latitudes, start sewer approximately 3'– 0'' below grade. In southern latitudes, sewer may start just below grade.

PITCH:

Pitch 4'' sewer $\frac{1}{4}$'' per foot minimum. Pitch 6'' sewer $\frac{1}{8}$'' per foot minimum.

LENGTH:

10'– 0'' for small system, for large systems allow 40'– 0'' to 50'– 0'' minimum.

MATERIAL

Same as for house sewer.

SIZE:

6'' unless very small system where 4'' is acceptable.

PITCH:

$\frac{1}{8}$'' per foot minimum. Maintain uniform pitch.

NOTES:

A distribution (absorption) field for the disposal of effluent or the filtering of effluent is required for the 3 types of disposal methods shown.

Pitch for closed joints: 5'' per 100'– 0''.

Pitch for open joints: 3'' to 4'' per 100'– 0''.

For selection of disposal method, see details and tables on the following pages.

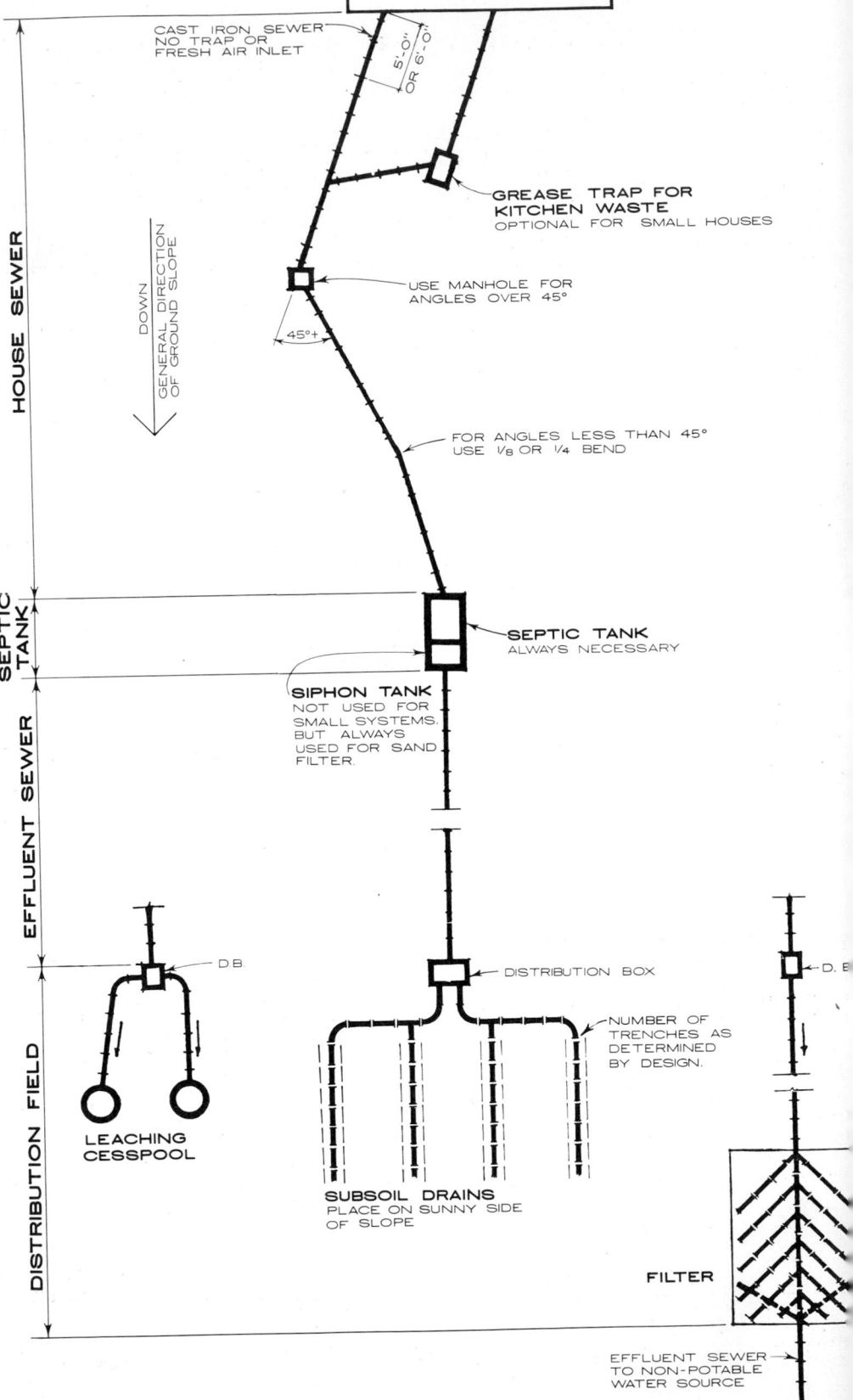

KEY DIAGRAM OF SEWAGE DISPOSAL SYSTEM
For selection of specific system of disposal see following pages.

CRITERIA FOR SELECTION OF TYPE OF DISTRIBUTION OF THE EFFLUENT

	LEACHING CESSPOOL One or more may be used as needed.	SUBSOIL DISPOSAL DRAINS Type 5.1 includes, in addition, collection tile under the distributing tile.	SAND FILTER Rectangular circular or narrow trench types. Open or closed type.
TERRAIN SLOPE OR GRADE	Applicable to any slope.	For level or slight slope.	Applicable to any slope, except filter area to be approximately level.
POROSITY OF SOIL	Soil adjacent to cesspools must be fairly porous below intake. Above may be impervious.	Top 1'-6" to 2'-0" must be fairly porous unless type 5.1 is used, and this may be used with impervious soil.	Soil may be impervious.
GROUND WATER	Water level must be at least 8'-0" below grade at cesspools. Never less than 2'-0" below bottom of cesspools.	Water level 4'-0" below bottom of trench.	Water level approximately 4'-0" below bottom of filter bed.
ORIENTATION AND LOCATION	Not important. Small area required, not less than 15'-0" from building.	If possible place field on southern slope; drains run parallel to contours. Requires large area.	Open type requires placing to leeward and away from buildings; on sunny site. Closed type requires more area than open. Small area required.
FINAL DISPOSAL OF EFFLUENT	No provision necessary.	No provision necessary, except for type 5.1 it is desirable.	Means for final disposal necessary in water course that will not pollute any potable water supply.
MAINTENANCE	Cleaned approximately every 2 years.	Cleaned only when absorbtion ceases. May be years if septic is kept in condition.	When filtering ceases remove and replace top 2".
INITIAL COST	Usually lowest cost.	More expensive than cesspools. type 5.1 is more expensive.	More expensive. Only used where other types are not possible. Open type cheaper than closed.

DESIGN OF SEWAGE DISPOSAL SYSTEMS

EXPLANATION OF TABLES BELOW

"No. of persons served" in first column refers to "Residential Work". To use tables for other types of buildings multiply this "No. of Persons Served" by the appropriate conversion factor listed in the table directly below.

TYPE OF BUILDING	GALS. OF SEWAGE PER PERSON	CONVERSION FACTORS
Residential	50	1.0 (Unity)
Camps	25	.5
Summer Cottages, small farms	40	.8
Day Schools, factories (no kitchens or showers)	15 to 25	.3 to .25
Day Schools, factories with kitchens and showers	30 to 50	.6 to .5
Institutions except hospitals	100	2.0
Hospitals	150 to 250	3.0 to 5.0

METHOD OF RELATIVE ABSORPTION DETERMINATION

Dig or bore 8" to 12" Dia. hole to a depth of 6" below bottom of proposed trench or cesspool. Presoak hole & allow to drain away. Fill hole to depth of 6" and record time it takes water to drop 1". Repeat minimum three times until 1" drop for two successive tests give approximately equal results. Last test will be stabilized absorption rate.

MINUTES REQ'D FOR WATER TO DROP 1 INCH	RELATIVE ABSORPTION	DISPOSAL METHOD RECOMMENDED
0 to 5	Rapid	Cesspool or Drains
6 to 10	Medium	Cesspool or Drains
11 to 15	Slow	Cesspool or Drains
16 to 29	Semi-impervious	Dr'ns-Collect & Filter
30 & Over	Impervious	Filter

SEPTIC AND SIPHON TANKS

NO. OF PERSONS SERVED	SEPTIC TANK					SIPHON TANK			SIPHON		CONCRETE THICKNESS		
	GALS. WORKING CAPACITY	LENGTH	WIDTH	AIR SPACE	LIQUID DEPTH	* NOT ESSENTIAL FOR THESE SIZES			SIZE	DRAWING DEPTH	WALLS	TOP	BOTTOM
						LENGTH	WIDTH	DEPTH					
1–7	750	7'-6"	3'-6"	1'-3"	4'-0"	3'-6"	3'-6"	3'-0"	3"	1'-1"	6"	4"	6"
8–10	1000	8'-0"	4'-0"	1'-3"	4'-4"	4'-0"	4'-0"	3'-0"	3"	1'-1"	6"	4"	6"
11–15	1500	9'-6"	5'-8"	1'-3"	4'-6"	4'-8"	4'-8"	3'-6"	4"	1'-5"	8"	5"	8"

Capacity of above septic tanks is based on 100 gallons flow of sewage per person for 24 hours, and is for residential work. To design tanks of larger sizes refer to local regulations. Length of tanks should be approximately twice width. Minimum depth 4'-0". When purchasing a prefabricated septic tank, require manufacturers guarantee that the tank will treat the gals. capacity as above calculated within a 24 hour period.

If garbage destructor is used & discharges into septic tank, increase capacity for additional sludge up to 50%.

LEACHING CESSPOOL DISPOSAL

NO. OF PERSONS SERVED	FOR RAPID ABSORPTION			FOR MEDIUM ABSORPTION			FOR SLOW ABSORPTION		
	NO. OF CESS-POOLS	DIA.	DEPTH	NO. OF CESS-POOLS	DIA.	DEPTH	NO. OF CESS-POOLS	DIA.	DEPTH
1–7	1	8'-0"	8'-0"	2	6'-0"	7'-0"	2	8'-0"	7'-0"
8–10	2	6'-0"	7'-0"	2	8'-0"	7'-0"	2	8'-0"	10'-0"
11–15	2	8'-0"	8'-0"	2	10'-0"	8'-0"	3	10'-0"	8'-0"

Capacity of above cesspools based on 100 gals. flow of sewage per 24 hours, and is for residential work. Total absorptive area = Area of walls (below inlet) + area of bottom.
Total absorptive area = $2\pi R \times$ height $+ \pi R^2$

SUBSOIL DISPOSAL DRAINS — 4"

NO. OF PERSONS SERVED	LINEAL FEET		
	ABSORPTION		
	RAPID	MED.	SLOW
1–7	160	150	195
8–10	210	200	260
11–15	320	300	390

Assuming 2' wide absorption trench for rapid absorption soil. 3' wide absorption trench bottom for medium and slow absorption soil.

SAND FILTERS

NO. OF PERSONS SERVED	AREA REQU'D IN SQ. FT.	
	OPEN	CLOSED
1–7	250	655
8–10	335	870
11–15	500	1310

These areas are based on 1.15 gal./sq.ft. per day for closed and 3 gal./sq.ft. per day for open.

W. Papin; Giffels & Rossetti, Inc.; Detroit, Michigan

SCALE: 1/4" = 1'-0"

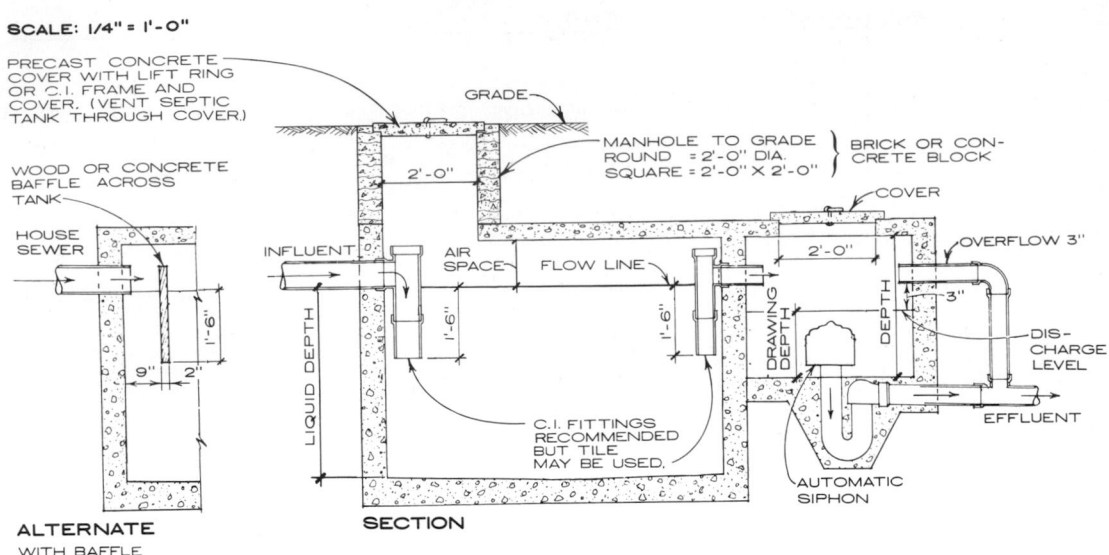

PRECAST CONCRETE COVER WITH LIFT RING OR C.I. FRAME AND COVER. (VENT SEPTIC TANK THROUGH COVER.)

WOOD OR CONCRETE BAFFLE ACROSS TANK

HOUSE SEWER

GRADE

MANHOLE TO GRADE ROUND = 2'-0" DIA. SQUARE = 2'-0" X 2'-0"

BRICK OR CONCRETE BLOCK

COVER

2'-0"

INFLUENT

AIR SPACE

FLOW LINE

OVERFLOW 3"

LIQUID DEPTH

DRAWING DEPTH

DEPTH

DISCHARGE LEVEL

EFFLUENT

C.I. FITTINGS RECOMMENDED BUT TILE MAY BE USED.

AUTOMATIC SIPHON

ALTERNATE
WITH BAFFLE AT INLET

SECTION

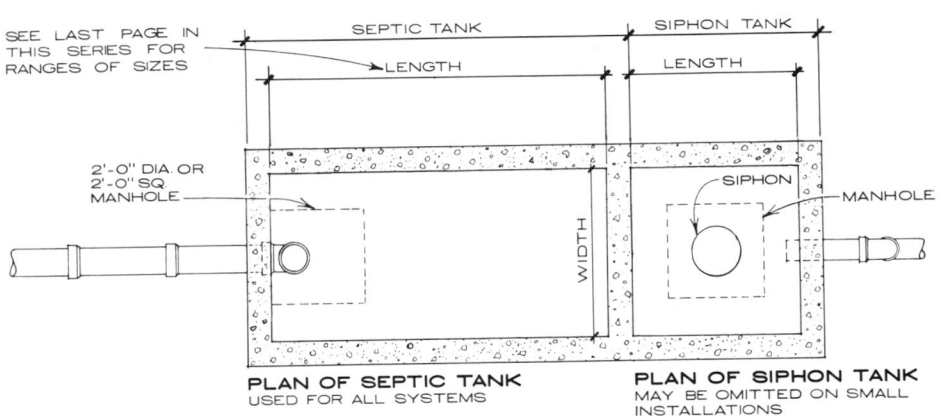

SEE LAST PAGE IN THIS SERIES FOR RANGES OF SIZES

SEPTIC TANK

LENGTH

SIPHON TANK

LENGTH

2'-0" DIA. OR 2'-0" SQ. MANHOLE

WIDTH

SIPHON

MANHOLE

PLAN OF SEPTIC TANK
USED FOR ALL SYSTEMS

PLAN OF SIPHON TANK
MAY BE OMITTED ON SMALL INSTALLATIONS

PLAN

Precast concrete cylindrical tank with adjoining siphon tank of similar shape and construction are commonly used; other features follow above drawings.

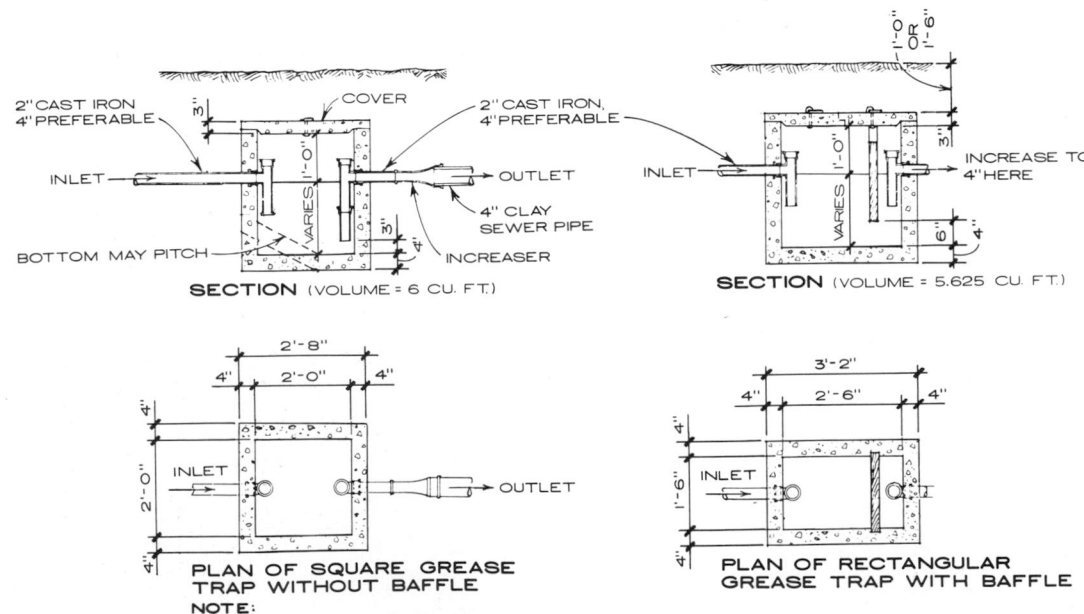

2" CAST IRON 4" PREFERABLE

COVER

2" CAST IRON, 4" PREFERABLE

INLET

VARIES 1'-0"

OUTLET

4" CLAY SEWER PIPE

BOTTOM MAY PITCH

INCREASER

SECTION (VOLUME = 6 CU. FT.)

INLET

1'-0" OR 1'-6"

VARIES 1'-0"

INCREASE TO 4" HERE

SECTION (VOLUME = 5.625 CU. FT.)

2'-8"
2'-0"
4"

INLET

OUTLET

PLAN OF SQUARE GREASE TRAP WITHOUT BAFFLE

3'-2"
2'-6"
4"

INLET

PLAN OF RECTANGULAR GREASE TRAP WITH BAFFLE

NOTE:
1. Grease traps may be omitted in small systems.
2. C. I. connections are shown, but may be clay tile for economy.
3. Grease traps may be built of 8" brick walls.

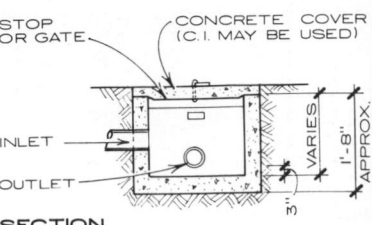

STOP OR GATE

CONCRETE COVER (C.I. MAY BE USED)

INLET

OUTLET

VARIES 1'-8" APPROX.

SECTION

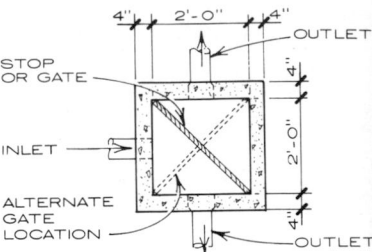

STOP OR GATE

4" 2'-0" 4"

OUTLET

INLET

ALTERNATE GATE LOCATION

OUTLET

PLAN OF DISTRIBUTION BOX WITH 2 OUTLETS

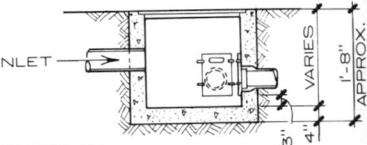

INLET

VARIES 1'-8" APPROX.

SECTION

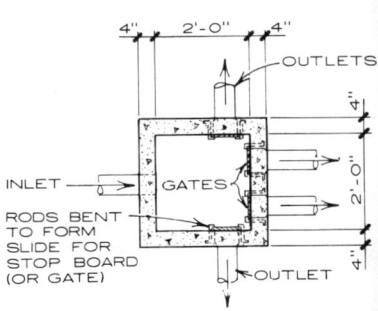

4" 2'-0" 4"

OUTLETS

INLET

GATES

RODS BENT TO FORM SLIDE FOR STOP BOARD (OR GATE)

OUTLET

PLAN OF DISTRIBUTION BOX WITH 3 OR 4 OUTLETS

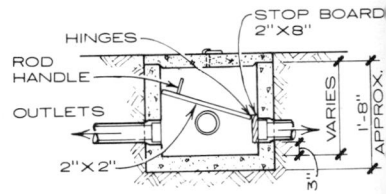

STOP BOARD 2" X 8"

HINGES

ROD HANDLE

OUTLETS

2" X 2"

VARIES 1'-8" APPROX.

SECTION

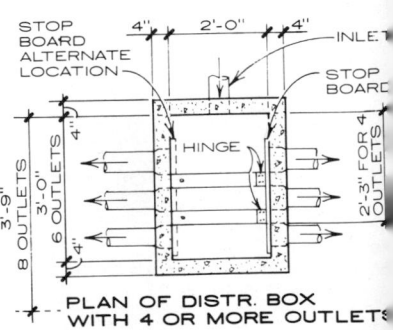

STOP BOARD ALTERNATE LOCATION

4" 2'-0" 4"

INLET

STOP BOARD

HINGE

OUTLETS

3'-9" 8 OUTLETS 3'-0" 6 OUTLETS 2'-3" FOR 4

PLAN OF DISTR. BOX WITH 4 OR MORE OUTLETS

NOTE:
All outlets must be set exactly level. Stop boards which must always be included for filter bed systems, and are recommended for all but very small systems, are used to provide a rest period for part of the disposal field.

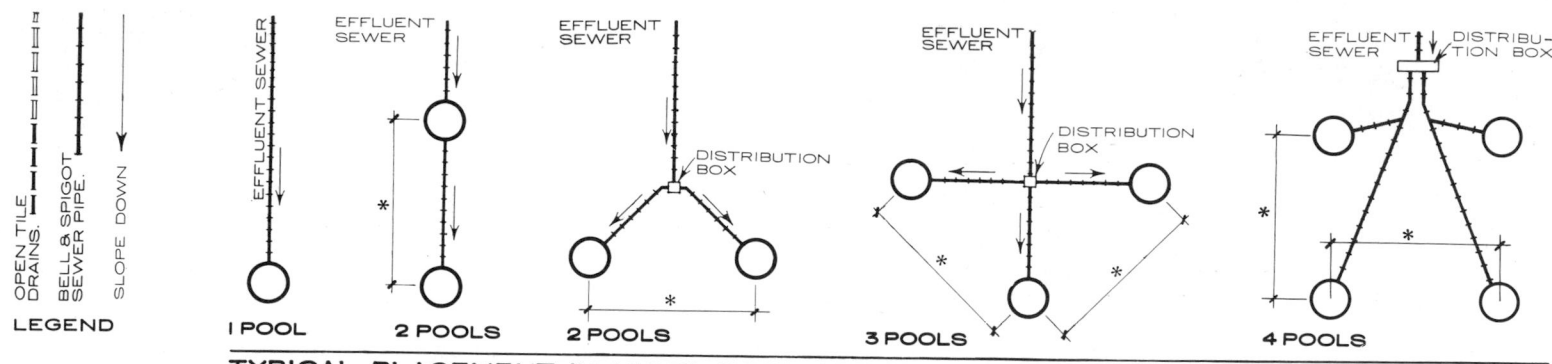

TYPICAL PLACEMENT IN MULTI-POOL ARRANGEMENTS

(Keep cesspools on downgrade and at least 100' away from any water supply.) *Minimum distance between pools = to 3 times the largest pool dimension.

LEGEND — OPEN TILE DRAINS. / BELL & SPIGOT SEWER PIPE. / SLOPE DOWN

1 POOL — EFFLUENT SEWER

2 POOLS — EFFLUENT SEWER

2 POOLS — EFFLUENT SEWER / DISTRIBUTION BOX

3 POOLS — EFFLUENT SEWER / DISTRIBUTION BOX

4 POOLS — EFFLUENT SEWER / DISTRIBUTION BOX

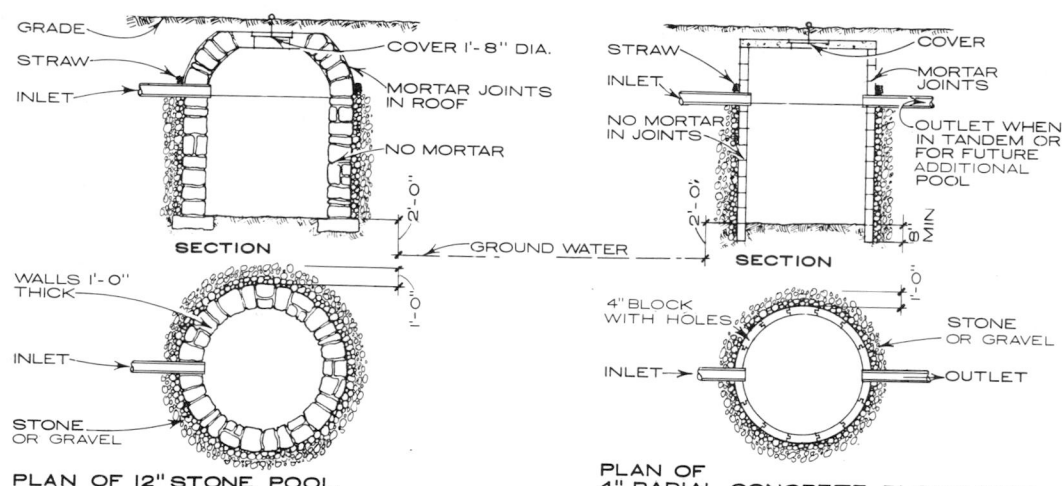

GRADE / STRAW / INLET / COVER 1'-8" DIA. / MORTAR JOINTS IN ROOF / NO MORTAR / 2'-0" / GROUND WATER

SECTION

WALLS 1'-0" THICK / INLET / STONE OR GRAVEL / 1'-0"

PLAN OF 12" STONE POOL

STRAW / INLET / NO MORTAR IN JOINTS / COVER / MORTAR JOINTS / OUTLET WHEN IN TANDEM OR FOR FUTURE ADDITIONAL POOL / 2'-0" / 6" MIN / 1'-0"

SECTION

4" BLOCK WITH HOLES / INLET / STONE OR GRAVEL / OUTLET / 1'-0"

PLAN OF 4" RADIAL CONCRETE BLOCK POOL

REINF CONC. COVER WITH LIFTING RING / PRECAST REINF CONC / GRADE / INLET / OUTLET / 2'-0" / 1'-0" / 4" / 7'-6" DIAM. / 4" / 1'-0" / SLOTS FOR LEACHING / STONE OR GRAVEL

SECTION

PRECAST CONCRETE LEACHING POOL

TYPES OF LEACHING CESSPOOLS

SCALE = 1/8"=1'-0"
Cesspool tops are interchangeable.

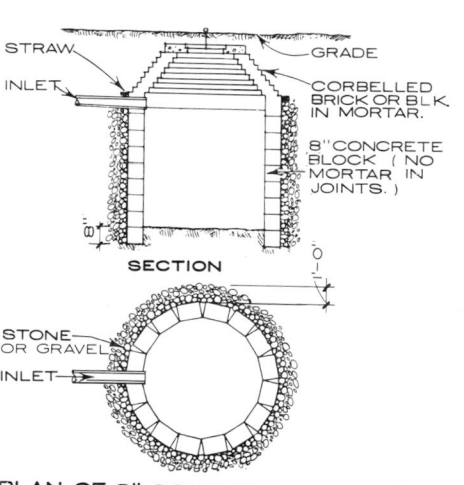

STRAW / INLET / GRADE / CORBELLED BRICK OR BLK IN MORTAR. / 8" CONCRETE BLOCK (NO MORTAR IN JOINTS.) / 8" / 1'-0"

SECTION

STONE OR GRAVEL / INLET

PLAN OF 8" CONCRETE BLOCK POOL

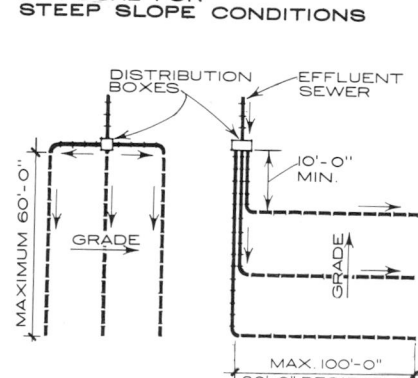

PITCH OF LATERAL

DISPOSAL FOR STEEP SLOPE CONDITIONS

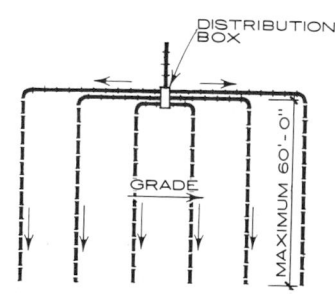

DISTRIBUTION BOXES / EFFLUENT SEWER / MAXIMUM 60'-0" / GRADE / 10'-0" MIN. / GRADE / MAX. 100'-0" / 60'-0" DESIRABLE

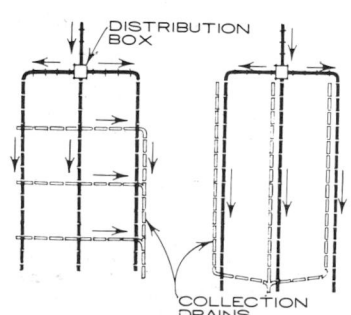

DISTRIBUTION BOX / GRADE / MAXIMUM 60'-0"

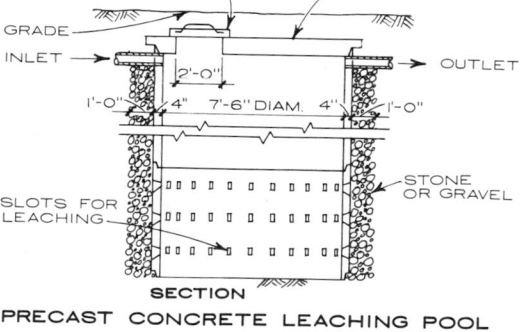

FINE CINDERS OR GRAVEL / EARTH / 1'-9" average / 2'-1" MAXIMUM / 1'-0" AVE. / 4" MAX. / COARSE CINDERS OR GRAVEL. / TILE WITH 1/4" OPEN JOINTS. / JOINTS 2/3 COVERED WITH 4" STRIP OF TAR PAPER WIRED ON. / 1'-0" MIN.

DRAIN TILE TRENCH
SCALE : 3/8"=1'-0"
Uniform pitch = 0.5% (0.3% when dosing siphon is used)

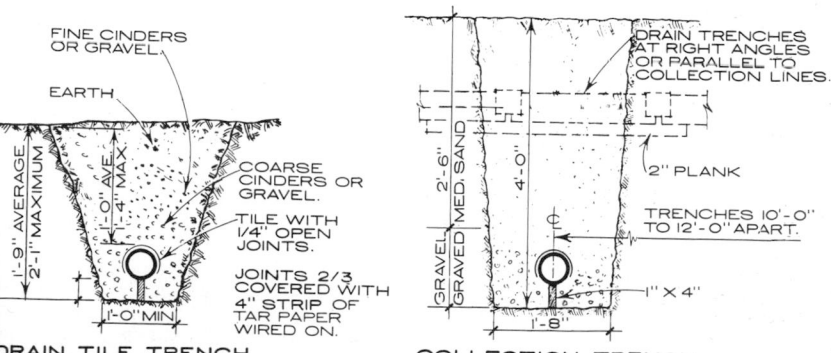

DRAIN TRENCHES AT RIGHT ANGLES OR PARALLEL TO COLLECTION LINES. / 2'-6" / 4'-0" / GRAVEL / GRAVEL MED. SAND / 2" PLANK / TRENCHES 10'-0" TO 12'-0" APART. / 1" X 4" / 1'-8"

COLLECTION TRENCH

NOTE:
SEE LAST PAGE IN THIS SERIES FOR SIZES & DIMENSIONS.

DISTRIBUTION BOX / COLLECTION DRAINS

SUB-SOIL DISPOSAL FIELD DRAINS

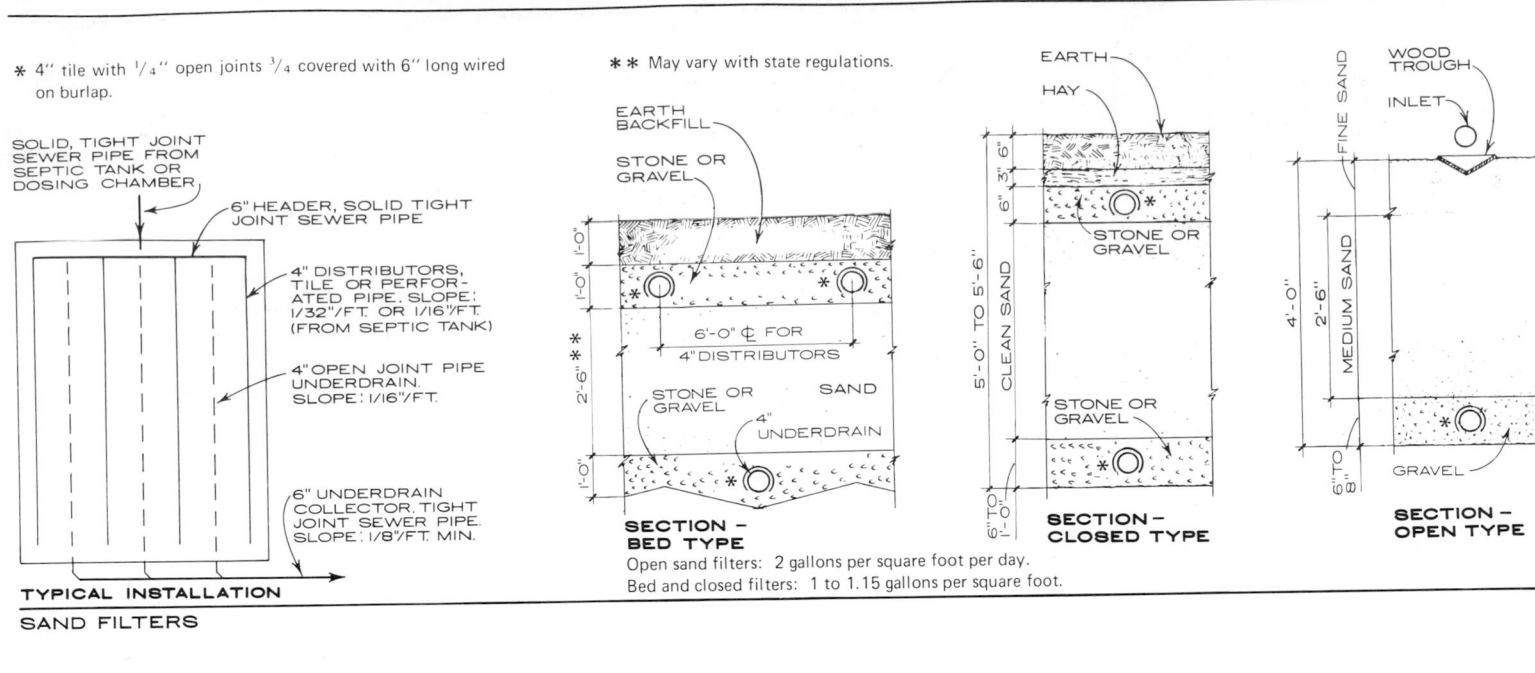

* 4" tile with 1/4" open joints 3/4 covered with 6" long wired on burlap.

** May vary with state regulations.

SOLID, TIGHT JOINT SEWER PIPE FROM SEPTIC TANK OR DOSING CHAMBER

6" HEADER, SOLID TIGHT JOINT SEWER PIPE

4" DISTRIBUTORS, TILE OR PERFORATED PIPE. SLOPE: 1/32"/FT. OR 1/16"/FT. (FROM SEPTIC TANK)

4" OPEN JOINT PIPE UNDERDRAIN. SLOPE: 1/16"/FT.

6" UNDERDRAIN COLLECTOR. TIGHT JOINT SEWER PIPE. SLOPE: 1/8"/FT. MIN.

TYPICAL INSTALLATION

SAND FILTERS

EARTH BACKFILL
STONE OR GRAVEL
6'-0" ℄ FOR 4" DISTRIBUTORS
STONE OR GRAVEL   SAND
4" UNDERDRAIN

SECTION – BED TYPE

Open sand filters: 2 gallons per square foot per day.
Bed and closed filters: 1 to 1.15 gallons per square foot.

EARTH
HAY
STONE OR GRAVEL
CLEAN SAND
STONE OR GRAVEL

SECTION – CLOSED TYPE

EARTH
WOOD TROUGH
FINE SAND
INLET
MEDIUM SAND
GRAVEL

SECTION – OPEN TYPE

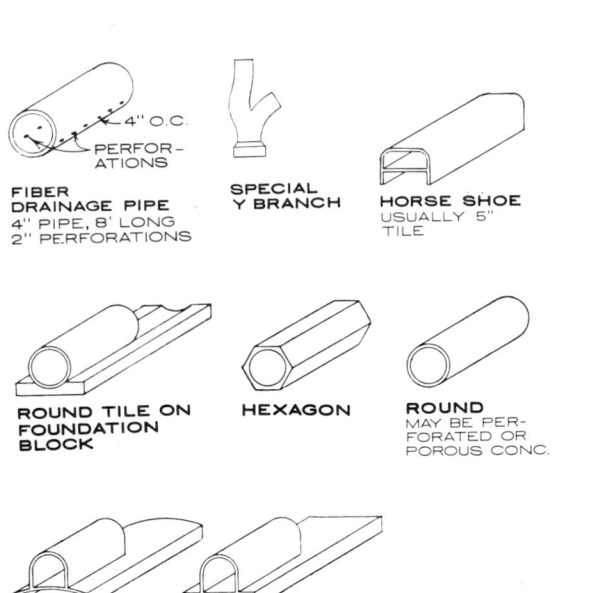

4" O.C. PERFORATIONS

FIBER DRAINAGE PIPE
4" PIPE, 8' LONG
2" PERFORATIONS

SPECIAL Y BRANCH

HORSE SHOE
USUALLY 5" TILE

ROUND TILE ON FOUNDATION BLOCK

HEXAGON

ROUND
MAY BE PERFORATED OR POROUS CONC.

U-TILE ON HOLLOW FOUNDATION BLOCKS

DRAINAGE TILES AND PIPES
Available in 2 foot lengths — inside diameter usually 4".

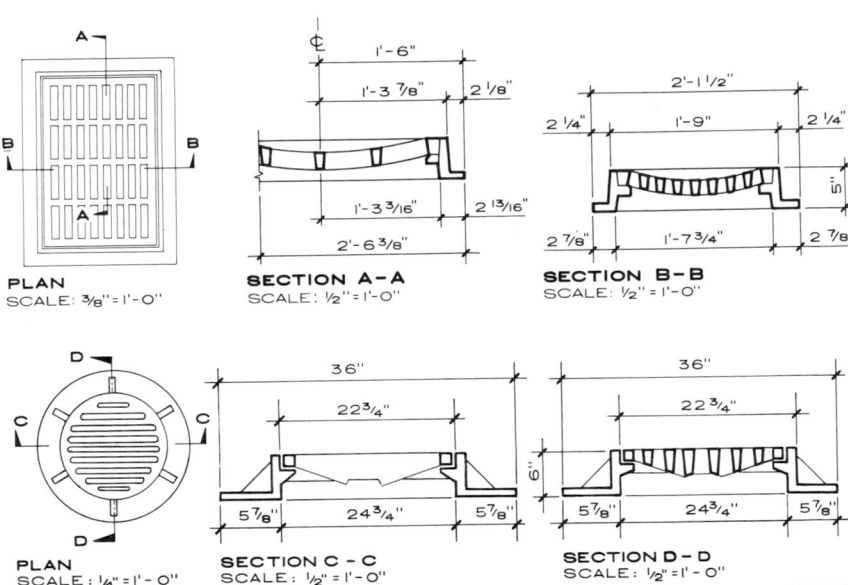

PLAN
SCALE: 3/8" = 1'-0"

SECTION A-A
SCALE: 1/2" = 1'-0"

SECTION B-B
SCALE: 1/2" = 1'-0"

PLAN
SCALE: 1/4" = 1'-0"

SECTION C-C
SCALE: 1/2" = 1'-0"

SECTION D-D
SCALE: 1/2" = 1'-0"

TYPICAL INLET FRAMES AND GRATES

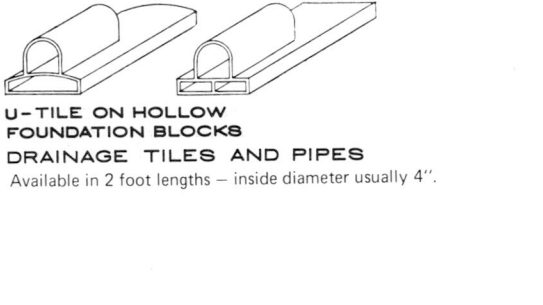

TIED ON AND COVERING 2/3 OF TILE

BURLAP OR TAR PAPER SCREENING

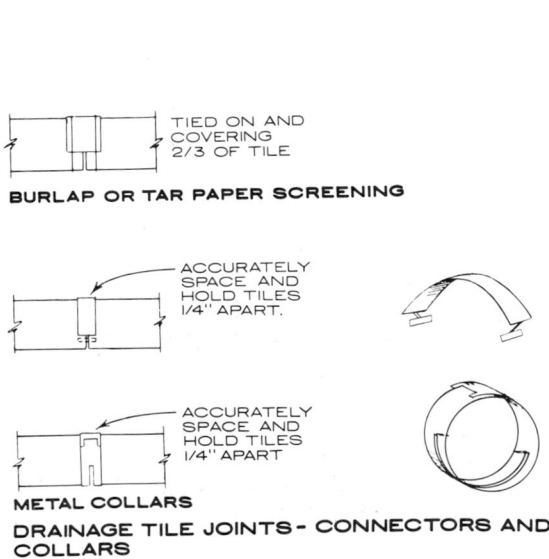

ACCURATELY SPACE AND HOLD TILES 1/4" APART.

ACCURATELY SPACE AND HOLD TILES 1/4" APART

METAL COLLARS

DRAINAGE TILE JOINTS - CONNECTORS AND COLLARS

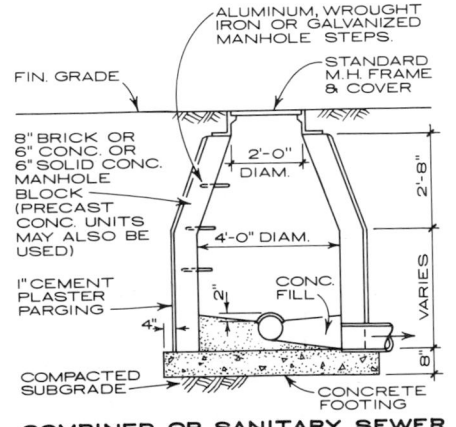

ALUMINUM, WROUGHT IRON OR GALVANIZED MANHOLE STEPS.

FIN. GRADE

STANDARD M.H. FRAME & COVER

8" BRICK OR 6" CONC. OR 6" SOLID CONC. MANHOLE BLOCK (PRECAST CONC. UNITS MAY ALSO BE USED)

1" CEMENT PLASTER PARGING

CONC. FILL

COMPACTED SUBGRADE

CONCRETE FOOTING

COMBINED OR SANITARY SEWER MANHOLE
SCALE: 3/8" = 1'-0"

NOTE:
1. Maximum depth   12'-0" below finished grade.
2. For storm drain manhole, concrete fill, flow channel and parging may be omitted.

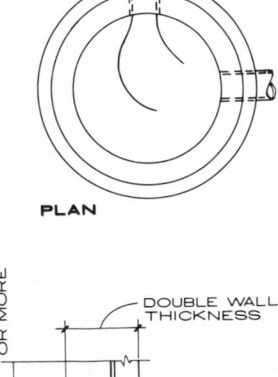

PLAN

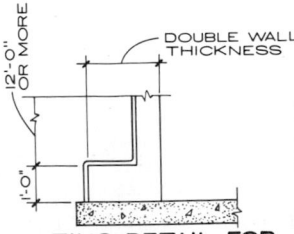

DOUBLE WALL THICKNESS

FOOTING DETAIL FOR DEEP MANHOLES

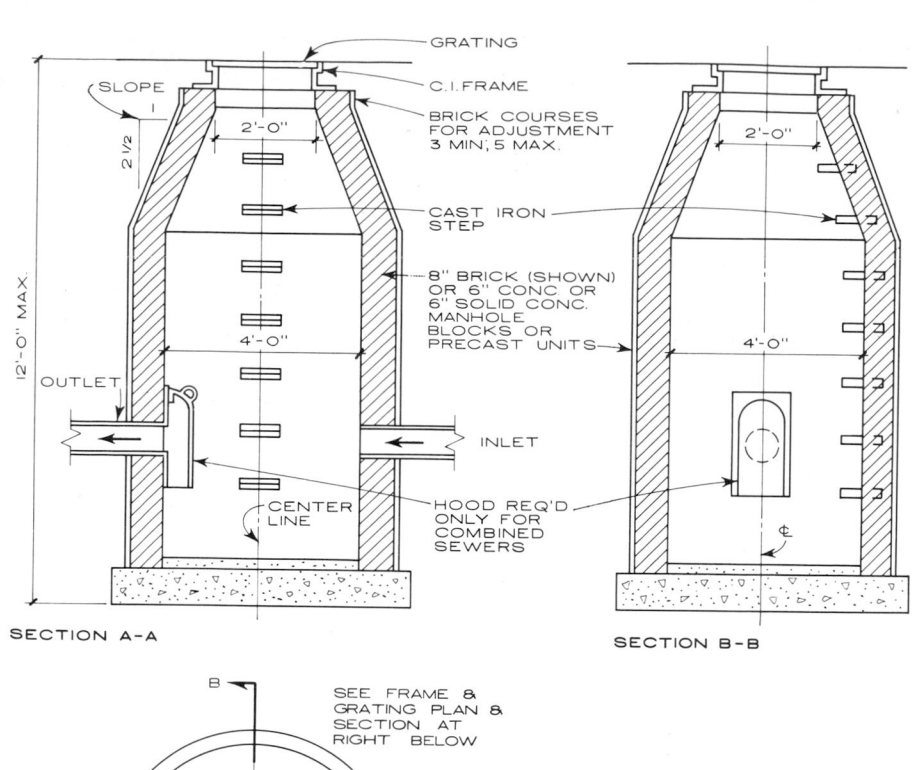

SECTION A-A

SECTION B-B

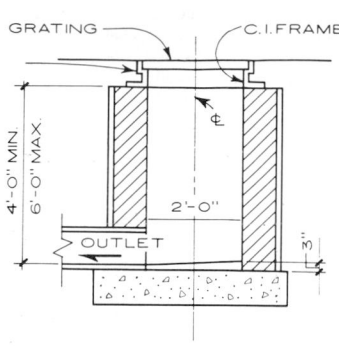

SECTION

YARD DRAINAGE INLET

NOTE:

Wall can be 8'' brick (shown) or 6'' concrete or 6'' solid concrete manhole blocks or precast units.

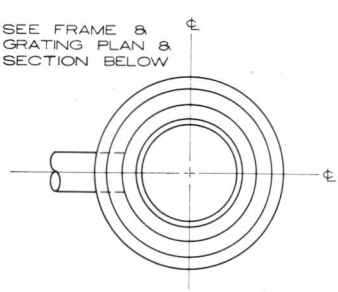

PLAN

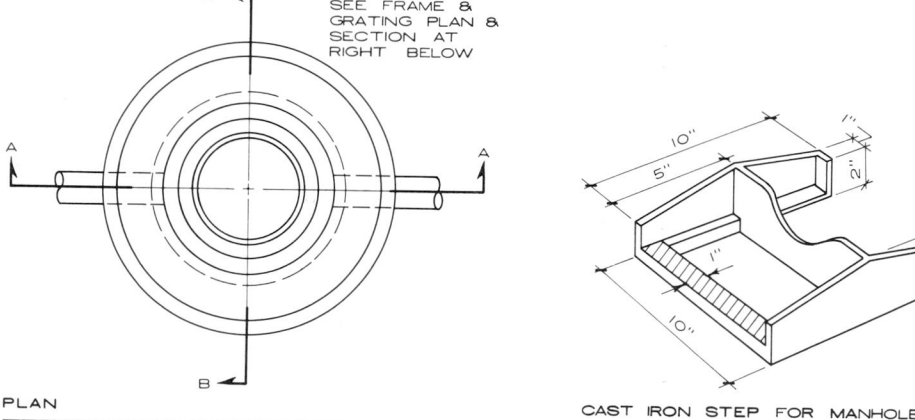

PLAN

YARD DRAINAGE BASIN
SCALE: 1/4''=1'-0''

CAST IRON STEP FOR MANHOLES

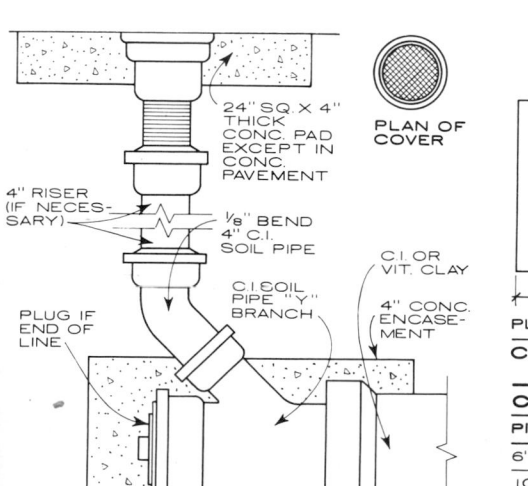

DETAIL OF INSPECTION BOX AND CLEAN-OUT (LAMP HOLE)
SCALE: 3/8''=1'-0''

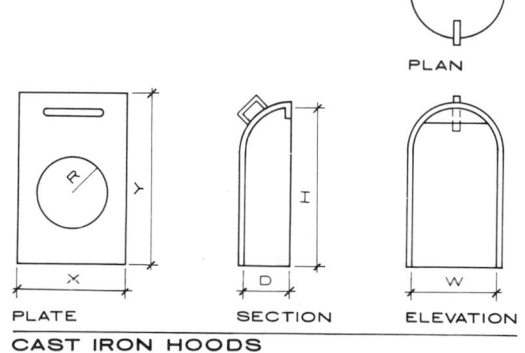

PLAN OF COVER

PLATE   SECTION   ELEVATION

CAST IRON HOODS

CAST IRON HOOD SIZES

PIPE SIZE	R	X	Y	H	W	D
6'' & 8'' OUTLET	5''	13 1/2''	23 1/2''	20 1/2''	11 1/2''	5 1/2''
10'' OUTLET	6''	15 1/4''	26 1/2''	23 1/2''	13 1/2''	6 1/2''
12'' OUTLET	7''	17 3/4''	29''	26''	15 3/4''	7 1/2''
15'' OUTLET	8 1/2''	20''	30''	27''	18''	9''
18'' OUTLET	10''	23''	33''	30''	21''	11''
20'' OUTLET	11''	25 1/2''	35''	32''	23 1/2''	11''

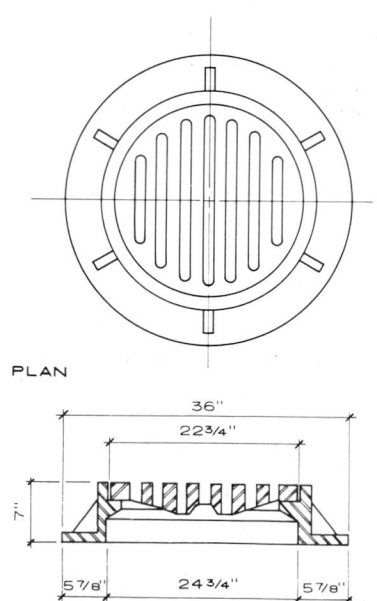

PLAN

SECTION

FRAME & GRATING FOR YARD DRAINAGE INLETS & BASINS
SCALE: 1/2''=1'-0''

B. J. Baldwin; Giffels & Rossetti, Inc.; Detroit, Michigan

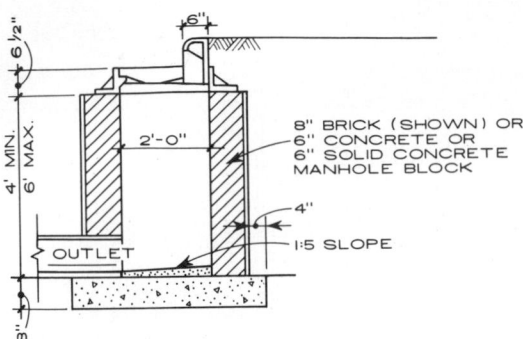

SECTION "A-A"

8" BRICK (SHOWN) OR
6" CONCRETE OR
6" SOLID CONCRETE
MANHOLE BLOCK

4"

1:5 SLOPE

OUTLET

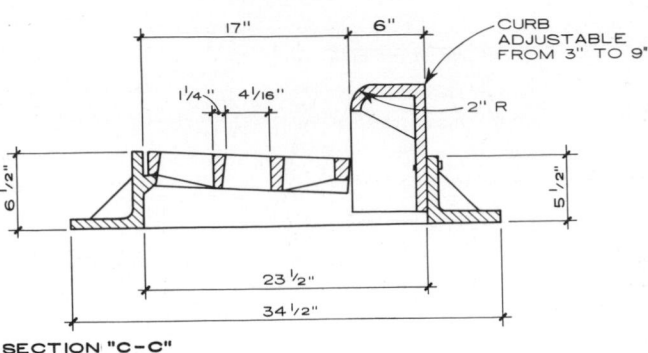

SECTION "C-C"

CURB
ADJUSTABLE
FROM 3" TO 9"

17"   6"
1¼" 4¹⁄₁₆"
2" R
6½"   5½"
23½"
34½"

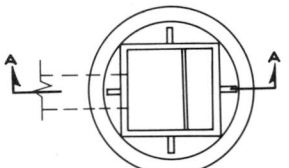

PLAN
ROAD TYPE INLET

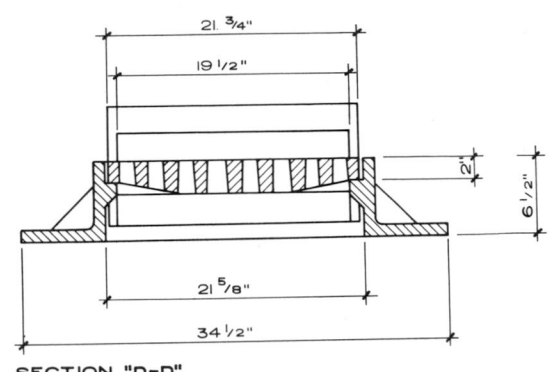

SECTION "D-D"

21.¾"
19½"
2"
6½"
21⁵⁄₈"
34½"

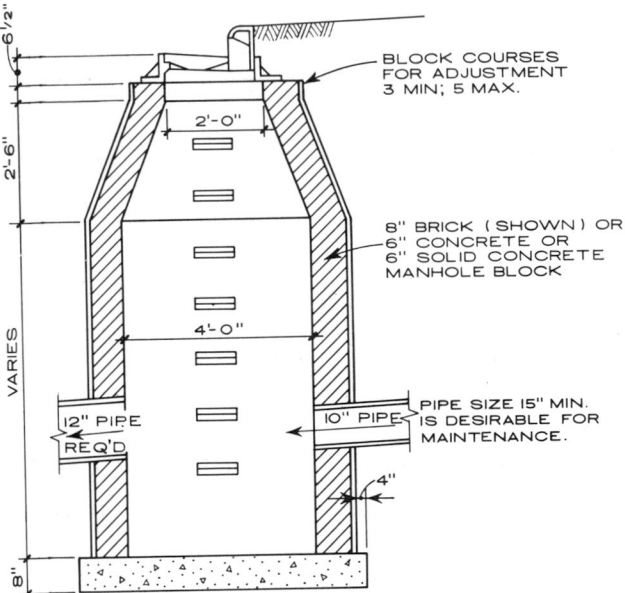

BLOCK COURSES
FOR ADJUSTMENT
3 MIN; 5 MAX.

8" BRICK (SHOWN) OR
6" CONCRETE OR
6" SOLID CONCRETE
MANHOLE BLOCK

PIPE SIZE 15" MIN.
IS DESIRABLE FOR
MAINTENANCE.

12" PIPE
REQ'D

10" PIPE

4"

SECTION "B-B"

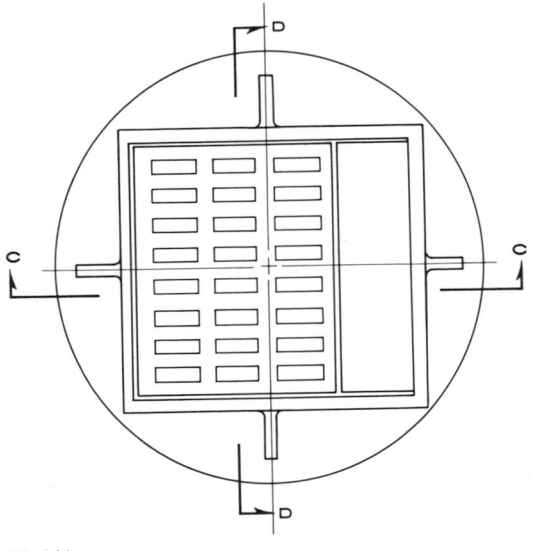

PLAN
**TYPICAL CASTING FOR
ROAD TYPE INLET OR
CATCH BASIN**

SCALE: ¾" = 1'-0"

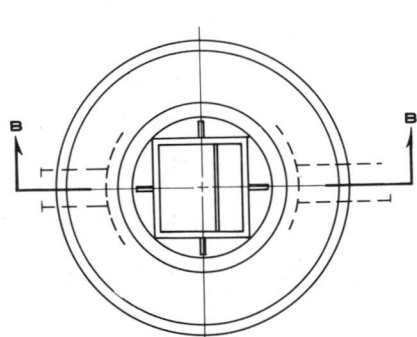

PLAN
ROAD TYPE CATCH BASIN

B. J. Baldwin; Giffels & Rossetti, Inc.; Detroit, Michigan

A
A

PLAN

2 SD + B
EARTH BEYOND
S
1'-0"
D
CHANNEL BANK
B

ELEVATION

12"
4"
SLOPE VARIES
18"
12" MIN
D
TO BE CARRIED DOWN AS REQUIRED FOR GOOD BEARING AND FROST PROTECTION
VARIES 24" MIN
3
12
CONCRETE

SECTION A-A

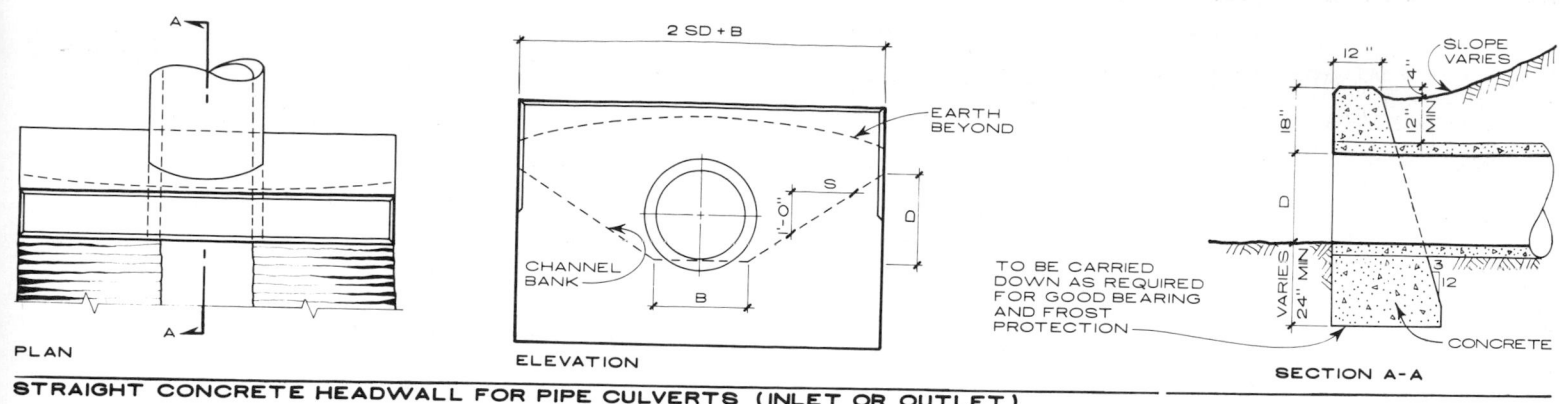

STRAIGHT CONCRETE HEADWALL FOR PIPE CULVERTS (INLET OR OUTLET)

F
E
A
G
H
J
I
D
C
B
30°
BATTER 3" PER FOOT
K
1/2"

PLAN

A
L
DIAM. PIPE
2'-0"

FRONT ELEVATION

1 1/2" TO 1
H
N
M
A
6"
18"
6"
D

SIDE ELEVATION

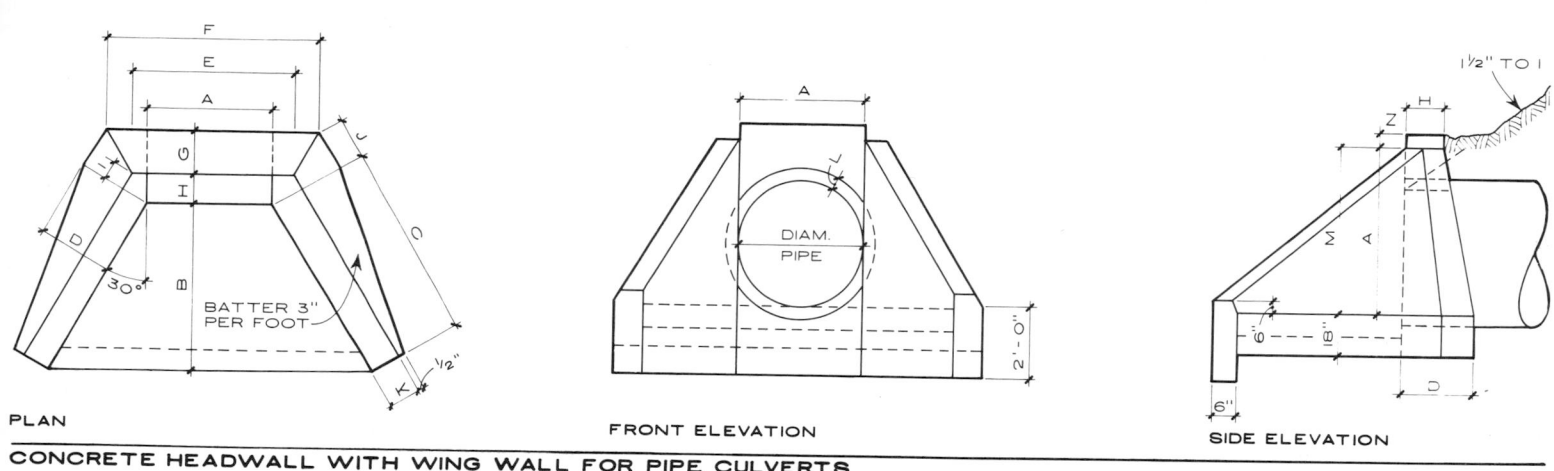

CONCRETE HEADWALL WITH WING WALL FOR PIPE CULVERTS

DIMENSIONS FOR HEADWALL WITH WING WALLS

DIAMETER OF PIPE	a	b	c	d	e	f	g	h	i	j	k	l	m	n
42"	42"	5'-0"	5'-9 1/4"	23 1/2"	4'-5 1/2"	5'-9"	13 1/2"	10"	5 3/4"	13 1/2"	10"	4 1/2"	4'-6"	3 1/2"
48"	48"	5'-6"	6'-4 1/4"	25"	4'-11 1/2"	6'-5"	15"	10"	5 3/4"	14 1/2"	10"	5"	5'-0"	4"
54"	54"	6'-0"	6'-11 1/8"	27 1/2"	5'-6 3/4"	7'-1 3/4"	16 1/2"	11"	6 3/8"	15 7/8"	11"	5 1/2"	5'-6"	4 1/2"
60"	60"	6'-6"	7'-6"	30"	6'-2"	7'-10 5/8"	18"	12"	7"	17 3/8"	12"	6"	6'-0"	5"

$D_1 > D$

WATER SURFACE FOR FULL CULVERT
EXIST. GR.
D
D1
RIP-RAP

SECTION

$D_1 < D$

WATER SURFACE FOR FULL CULVERT
EXIST. GR.
D
D1
CUTOFF WALL TO PREVENT UNDERMINING

SECTION

$D_1 < D$

WATER SURFACE FOR FULL CULVERT
D
D1

SECTION

$D_1 < D$

WATER SURFACE FOR FULL CULVERT
D
D1

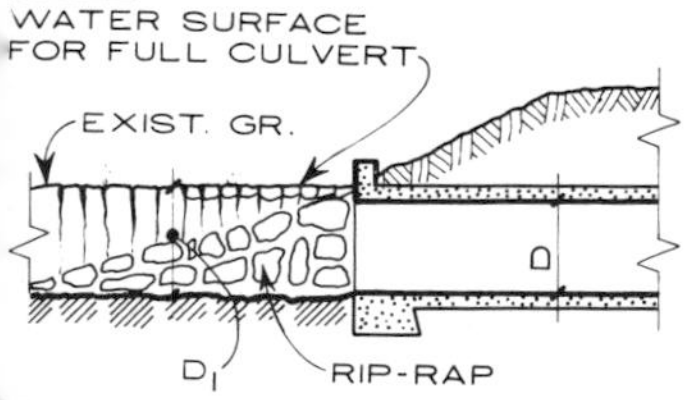

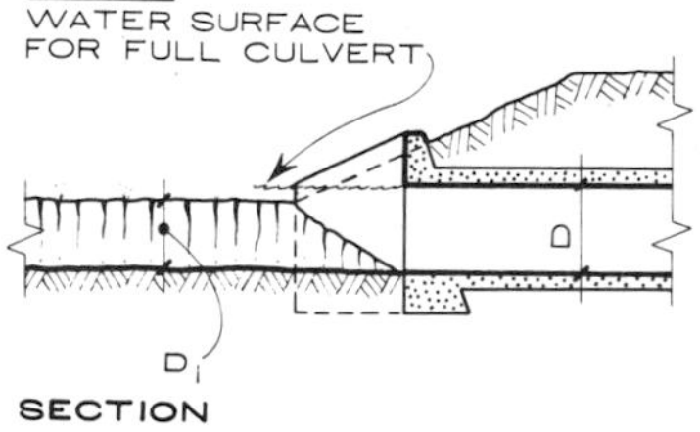

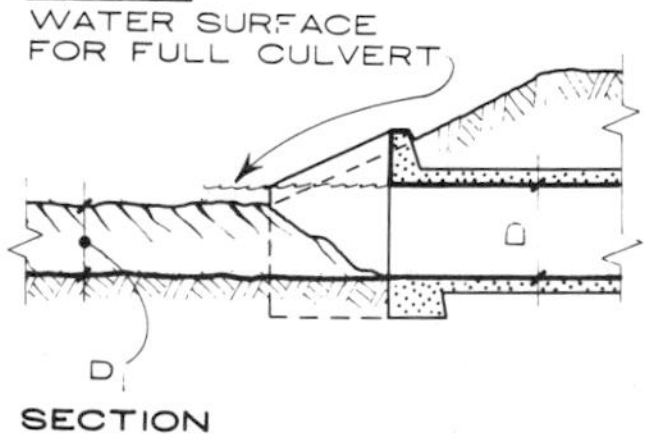

SECTION

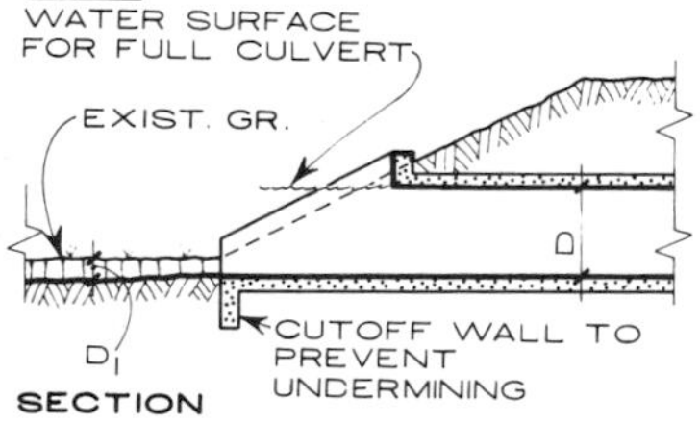

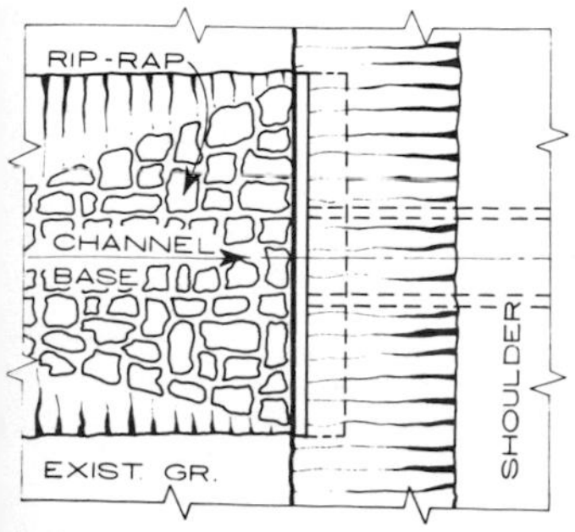

RIP-RAP
CHANNEL BASE
EXIST. GR.
SHOULDER

PLAN
STRAIGHT HEADWALL PARALLEL TO ROAD

FOR CASE WHERE TOP OF DITCH SIDE IS ABOVE TOP OF CULVERT OR PIPE

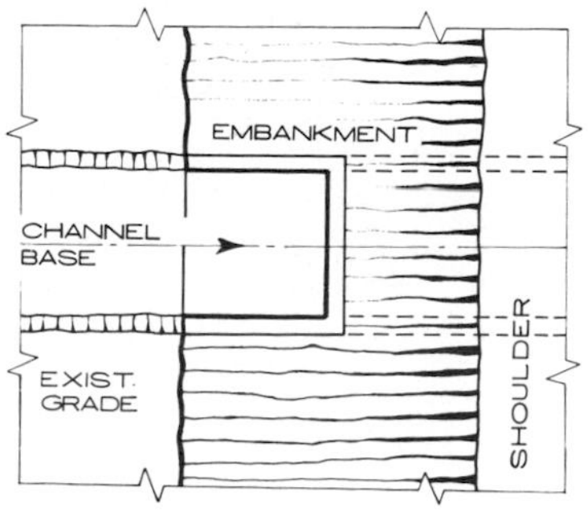

EMBANKMENT
CHANNEL BASE
EXIST. GRADE
SHOULDER

PLAN
WING WALLS NORMAL TO ROAD

SHALLOW DITCHES OR UNDERPASS

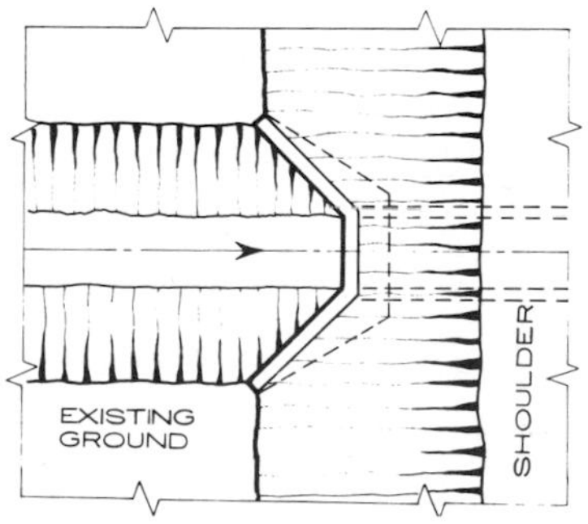

EXISTING GROUND
SHOULDER

PLAN
FLARED WING WALLS SYMMETRICAL

FOR CASES WHERE TOP OF PIPE IS ABOVE TOP OF DITCH SIDES

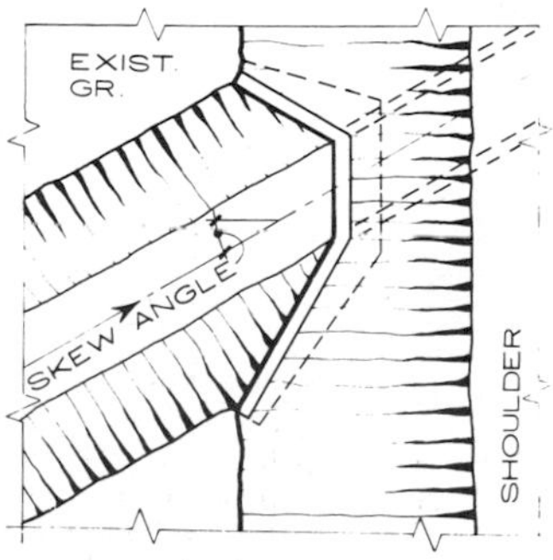

EXIST. GR.
SKEW ANGLE
SHOULDER

PLAN
FLARED WING WALLS SKEWED CULVERT

HEADWALL DESIGN AS CONTROLLED BY TOPOGRAPHY

PROTECTION AGAINST TERMITES & DECAY BY SOIL POISONING (For Termite Shields see Index)

CHEMICALS AND CONCENTRATIONS

CHEMICALS	CONCENTRATIONS	
Aldrin	0.5%	applied in water emulsion
Benzene Hexachloride (BHC)	0.8%	of gamma isomer applied in water emulsion
Chlordane	1.0%	applied in water emulsion
Dieldren	0.5%	applied in water emulsion
DDT	8.0%	in oil solution
Heptachlor	0.5%	in water emulsion

NOTES:

1. Other materials may be used provided they contain at least one of the above mentioned chemicals in the concentrations recommended.

2. Chemicals toxic to plants and animals. Should be applied by trained personnel.

3. Oil solutions shall not be used under concrete slabs or where the solution may come in contact with vapor barriers.

4. Where individual water supply systems are used well must be not less than 100 feet from treated area. Horizontal distance from treated area may be reduced to 50 feet where ground surface is effectively separated from water bearing formation by an extensive, continuous, impervious strata of clay, hardpan, rock etc.

APPLICATION-GENERAL.

Treatment shall not be made when the soil or fill is excessively wet or immediately after heavy rains, to avoid surface flow of the toxicant from application site. Surface flow of toxicants toward sources of individual water supply shall be avoided. Unless the treated areas are to be immediately covered, precautions shall be taken to prevent disturbance of the treatment by human or animal contact with the treated soil.

UNDER SLABS.

Under entire area of floor slab including porches and entrance platforms. Rate — 1 gal. per 10 sq. ft. In gravel fill of coarse material — 1 1/2 gal. per 10 sq. ft.

FOUNDATIONS.

1. Rate — 4 gal. per 10 lineal feet both sides of foundation, piers, interior foundation walls, around plumbing, etc.

   a. With concrete foundations or slab-on-grade apply to depth of one foot.

   b. With masonry foundations increase rate by multiplying by depth of foundation in feet.

2. Voids of unit masonry foundation walls and piers — 2 gal. per lineal foot to voids at bottom of foundation.

3. Application Methods:

   a. Chemical mixed with soil as it is replaced in trench — 1 ft. lifts.

   b. Chemical applied by rodding with soil injector rod inserted at 12 inch intervals — 6 inches from foundation wall. Penetration of rod to within 6 inches of top of footing. Disperse chemicals through rod under pressure according to soil type.

STANDARD SOIL CLASSIFICATION

SOIL TYPE	PRESSURE (PSI)
Granular — SW, SP, GW, GP	30 — 50
Intermediate — GM, GC, ML, SM, SC, OL, CL	50 — 150
Dense Impermeable Clays — MH, CH, OH	150 — 300

REGION 1 VERY HEAVY

REGION 2 MODERATE TO HEAVY

REGION 3 SLIGHT TO MODERATE

REGION 4 NONE TO SLIGHT

Lines defining areas approximate only. Local conditions may be more or less severe than indicated by the region classification.

Source:
Decay & Termites Study;
Bldg. Research Adv. Bd.

GEOGRAPHIC DISTRIBUTION OF TERMITE INFESTATION

Joseph A. Wilkes, AIA; Wilkes and Faulkner; Washington, D. C.

SLOPE SITE DEVELOPMENT RELATIONSHIP

AVERAGE % GRADE	DEVELOPMENT POTENTIAL	REMARKS
0–5%	Good for building sites, parking lots, play fields, roads.	Minimum necessity for grade changing devices. Minimum excavation for development.
5–10%	Good for building sites, roads, Fair for parking lots, play fields.	Minor necessity for grade changing devices. Minor excavation for development.
10–20%	Fair for building sites & roads. Difficult for parking lots, play fields.	Moderate use of grade changing devices. Moderate excavation for development.
20–40%	Difficult for building sites & roads. Very difficult for parking lots & play fields.	Considerable use of grade changing devices. Considerable excavation for development.
40%– OVER	Conservation area or buffer zone.	Extreme use of grade changing devices. Extreme excavation for development.

NOTE: Slope site development relationships may vary with local climate, topography and soil conditions.

SLOPE TERMINOLOGY :   % GRADE = 100 $\frac{V}{H}$

RATIO = H : V

EXAMPLE :

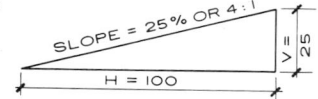

SLOPE = 25% OR 4:1

V = 25

H = 100

SLOPE - SURFACE TREATMENT RELATIONSHIPS

SURFACE TREATMENT	MAXIMUM SLOPE	DESIRABLE MAX. SLOPE	MINIMUM SLOPE	DESIRABLE MIN. SLOPE
CONCRETE SMOOTH FINISH	———	50% (1:1)	0.5%	1%
CONCRETE ROUGH FINISH	———	50% (1:1)	0.75%	1.5%
ASPHALT	———	50% (1:1)	1%	2%
BRICK	———	50% (1:1)	1%	2%
COBBLESTONES	———	50% (1:1)	1%	2%
LAWN	33.3% (3:1)	25% (4:1)	1%	2%
GROUND COVER PLANTS	50% (2:1)	33.3% (3:1)	2%	3%

GRADE CHANGE	V.C. LENGTH
3%	0
10%	4'
25%	6'
50%	10'

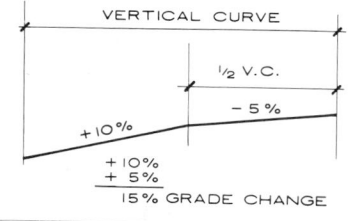

VERTICAL CURVE = V.C.

½ V.C.

+ 5 %

+10%

+10% − 5%

5% GRADE CHANGE

NOTE :

% grade change equals algebraic difference of grades of intersecting slopes.

uphill = + slope
downhill = − slope

VERTICAL CURVE

½ V.C.

− 5 %

+10%

+10% + 5%

15% GRADE CHANGE

DESIRABLE MINIMUM ROUNDING FOR CHANGES IN EARTH SLOPES

RELATIONSHIP OF SLOPE TO HORIZONTAL AND VERTICAL DISTANCES

GRADE	HORIZONTAL DISTANCES						
	100'	75'	50'	25'	10'	1'	0.1'
1%	1	0.75	0.5	0.25	0.1	0.01	0.001
2%	2	1.5	1.0	0.5	0.2	0.02	0.002
3%	3	2.25	1.5	0.75	0.3	0.03	0.003
4%	4	3.0	2.0	1.0	0.4	0.04	0.004
5%	5	3.75	2.5	1.25	0.5	0.05	0.005
6%	6	4.5	3.0	1.5	0.6	0.06	0.006
7%	7	5.25	3.5	1.75	0.7	0.07	0.007
8%	8	6.0	4.0	2.0	0.8	0.08	0.008
9%	9	6.75	4.5	2.25	0.9	0.09	0.009
10%	10	7.5	5.0	2.50	1.0	0.10	0.010
11%	11	8.25	5.5	2.75	1.1	0.11	0.011
12%	12	9.0	6.0	3.0	1.2	0.12	0.012
13%	13	9.75	6.5	3.25	1.3	0.13	0.013
14%	14	10.5	7.0	3.5	1.4	0.14	0.014
15%	15	11.25	7.5	3.75	1.5	0.15	0.015
20%	20	15.0	10.0	5.0	2.0	0.2	0.02
25%	25	18.75	12.5	6.25	2.5	0.25	0.025
50%	50	37.5	25.0	12.5	5.0	0.5	0.05

VERTICAL DISTANCES IN FEET

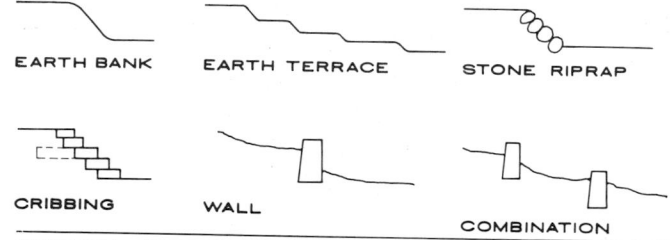

EARTH BANK   EARTH TERRACE   STONE RIPRAP

CRIBBING   WALL   COMBINATION

TYPICAL GRADE CHANGING DEVICES

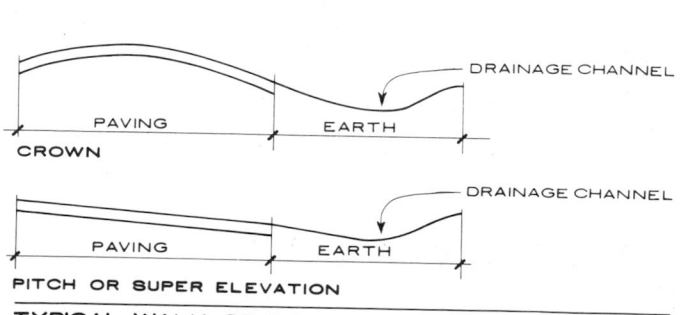

DRAINAGE CHANNEL

PAVING   EARTH

CROWN

DRAINAGE CHANNEL

PAVING   EARTH

PITCH OR SUPER ELEVATION

TYPICAL WALK OR ROAD CROSS SECTION

Floyd Zimmerman; Sasaki, Dawson, DeMay Associates, Inc.; Watertown, Massachusetts

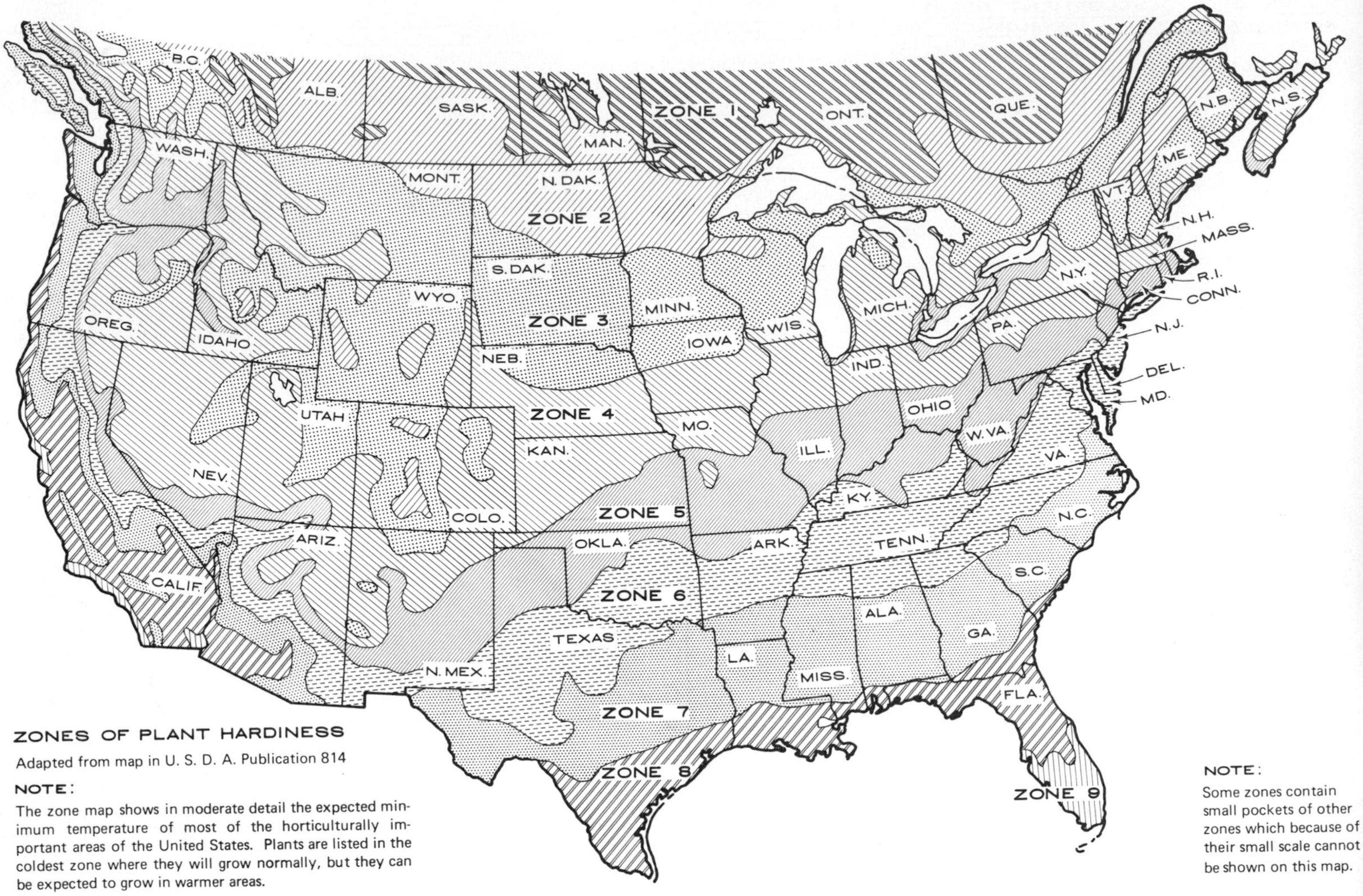

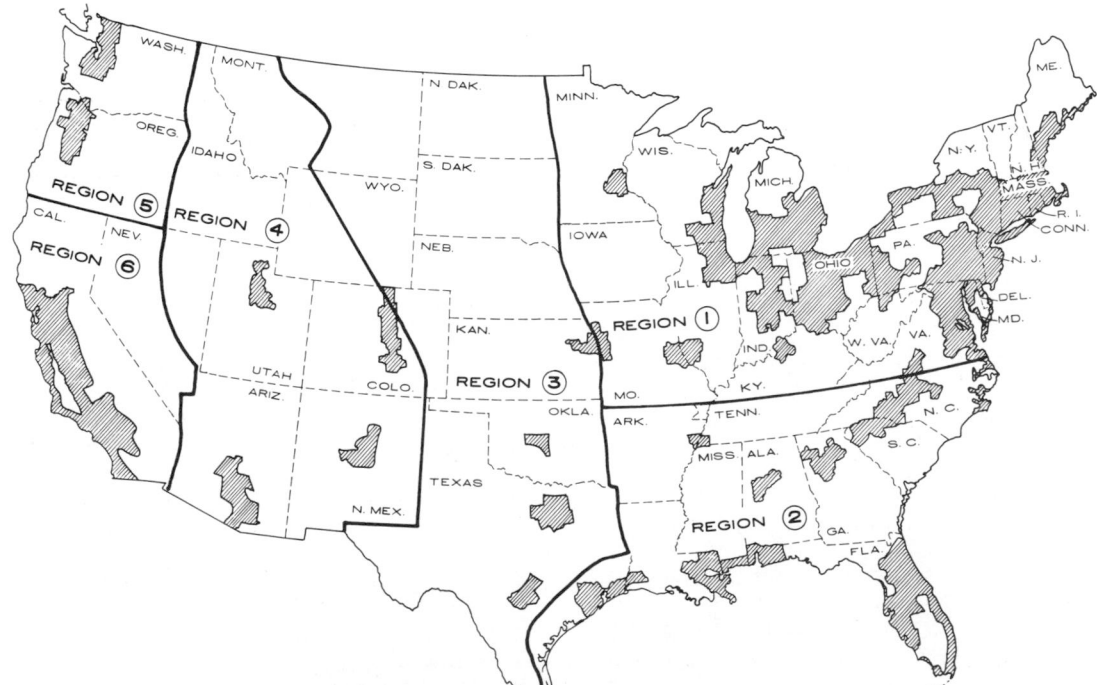

ZONES OF PLANT HARDINESS

Adapted from map in U. S. D. A. Publication 814

NOTE:

The zone map shows in moderate detail the expected minimum temperature of most of the horticulturally important areas of the United States. Plants are listed in the coldest zone where they will grow normally, but they can be expected to grow in warmer areas.

NOTE:

Some zones contain small pockets of other zones which because of their small scale cannot be shown on this map.

APPROXIMATE RANGE OF AVERAGE ANNUAL MINIMUM TEMPERATURES FOR EACH ZONE.

1.	−50° TO −40°	3.	−30° TO −20°	5.	−10° TO 0°	7.	10° TO 20°	9.	30° TO 40°
2.	−40° TO −30°	4.	−20° TO −10°	6.	0° TO 10°	8.	20° TO 30°		

PLANT REGIONS

REGION ①	THE NORTHEAST
REGION ②	THE SOUTHEAST
REGION ③	THE PLAINS
REGION ④	THE ROCKIES
REGION ⑤	THE PACIFIC NORTHWEST
REGION ⑥	THE PACIFIC SOUTHWEST
	AREA OF EMERGING URBANIZATION

NOTE:

Plant development is related to soil development and together are controlled by climate. The most commonly used ornamental trees and shrubs for a given area are related to the natural plant region and the hardiness zone of that area. No attempt is made here to show local conditions which would affect the selection of plant material.

RELATIONSHIP OF PLANT REGIONS TO URBAN AREAS

Laurence & Beatriz Coffin, Urban Planners & Landscape Architects; Washington, D. C.

PHYSICAL

CROWN: Trees increase each year in height and spread of branches by adding a new growth of twigs.

TRUNK: The tree trunk supports the crown and produces the bulk of the useful wood.

ANNUAL RINGS: Reveal age of tree by showing new growth added each year.

HEARTWOOD: This was once sapwood. It is now inactive wood giving strength and stiffness.

OUTER BARK: The outer bark protects tree from injuries.

ROOTS: The roots anchor the tree and help hold the soil against erosion.

PHYSIOLOGICAL

LEAVES: The leaves make food for the tree by combining carbon dioxide from the air and water from the soil in the presence of sunlight. Oxygen, a by-product, is released.

SAPWOOD: The sapwood, or xylem, carries the sap (water and nutrients) from roots to the leaves.

CAMBIUM: The cambium is a layer of cells between the bark and the wood. This is where growth in diameter occurs with the formation of annual rings of new wood inside and new bark outside.

INNER BARK: The inner bark, or phloem, carries food made in the leaves down to the branches, trunk, and roots.

ROOT HAIRS: The tiny root hairs absorb the minerals from soil moisture and send them up as nutrient salts in the sapwood to the leaves.

TREE FUNCTION

EFFECTS OF CITY GREEN-BELTS:

Observations quoted here are for temperate regions and are approximate. Greater discrepancies will occur in tropical regions. All observations will change with particular local conditions. They are only given as a working tool for the planning of urban green spaces.

AIR TEMPERATURE

A	B
90°F	75°–80°F
75°F	65°–70°F
60°F	58°–60°F
45°F	44°–48°F
30°F	29°–31°F
15°F	17°F

FLOOR TEMPERATURE

A	B
70°F	60°F
50°F	45°F
30°F	33°F
Frozen ground	Frozen depth reduced to half

LIGHT INTENSITY %

A	B
Cloudless 100%	5–50%
Cloudy 100%	15–75%

RELATIVE HUMIDITY

A	B
85%	77%
70%	75%
60%	60%

RELATIVE TEMPERATURE, HUMIDITY AND LIGHT INTENSITY OUTSIDE VS. INSIDE FOREST

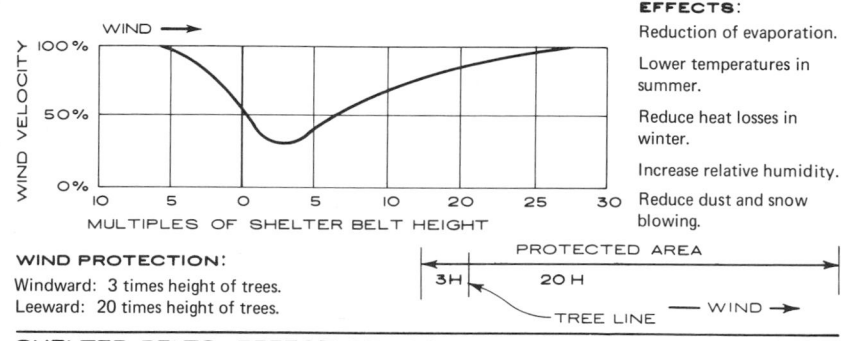

WIND RETARDATION EFFECTS:

Reduction of evaporation.

Lower temperatures in summer.

Reduce heat losses in winter.

Increase relative humidity.

Reduce dust and snow blowing.

WIND PROTECTION:

Windward: 3 times height of trees.
Leeward: 20 times height of trees.

SHELTER BELTS—EFFECT OF TREES ON WIND

TREE GROWTH AND CITY CONDITIONS

REQUIRED FACTORS FOR TREE GROWTH	AVERAGE CITY CONDITIONS IN COMPARISON WITH SURROUNDING RURAL AREA	NECESSARY CHANGES TO FOSTER TREE GROWTH IN CITIES	EFFECT OF TREES ON CITY CONDITIONS
LIGHT	Less illumination Decrease overall solar radiation		Decrease light intensity under tree canopies
AIR	More air pollution Air stagnation Formation of wind canyons	Physical control of air pollution	Purified air Dust reducing effect Wind protection
HEAT	Higher night time temperature Downtown heat islands Periodic temperature inversion		Cooling and regulatory effects
WATER	Less rainfall Lower relative humidity	Irrigation	Water conservation Relative humidity regulation
SOIL Must be capable of absorbing moisture There must be aereation There must be a supply of nutrients Must be free of harmful concentration of salts	Ground severely compacted with poor permeability to air and water Soil low in organic matter Soil affected by concentration of harmful chemicals	Preparation of soil Tree feeding	Increase ground permeability to air and water Soil stability

Laurence & Beatriz Coffin, Urban Planners & Landscape Architects; Washington, D. C.

Silhouettes indicate specimens of natural form, but varieties or forced forms possessing compact, spreading, columnar or pyramidal characteristics are available. The height at the ten year stage of development is given as an architectural design factor to be considered in the selection of tree sizes.

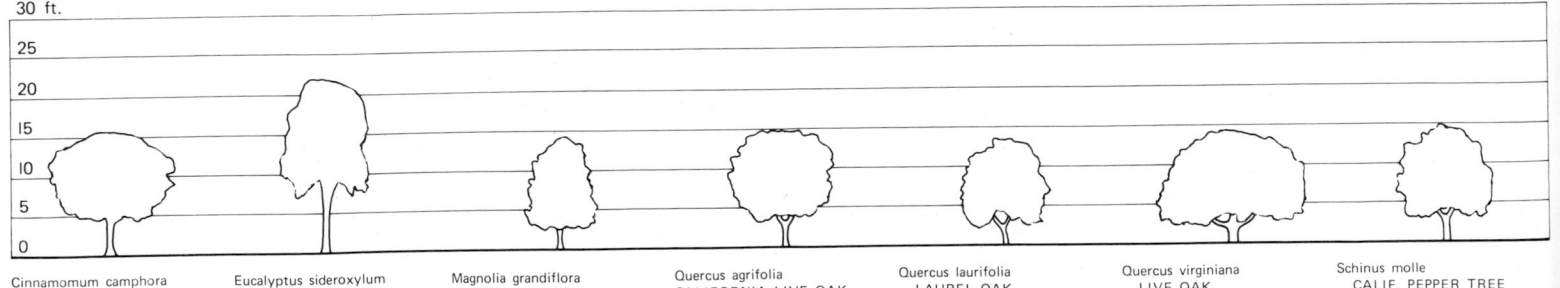

30 ft.

Acer platanoides
  NORWAY MAPLE
Zone 3
  Region 1, 2, 4, 5, 6
Mature: 50' H., 40' Spr.
Street planting
Spring: Yellow
Fall: Yellow

Acer rubrum
  RED MAPLE
Zone 3
  Region 1, 2
Mature: 60' H., 60' Spr.
Street planting
Spring: Red
Fall: Bright Red

Acer saccharum
  SUGAR MAPLE
Zone 3
  Region 1, 2
Mature: 80' H., 60' Spr.
Street planting
Spring: Yellow
Fall: Yellow, Red

Ginkgo biloba
  MAIDENHAIR TREE
Zone 4
  Region 1, 2, 3, 4, 5, 6
Mature: 60' H., 40' Spr.
Street planting
Fall: Yellow

Gleditsia triacanthos inermis
  THORNLESS HONEYLOCUST
Zone 4
  Region 1, 2, 3, 4
Mature: 60' H., 40' Spr.
Street planting

Platanus acerifolia
  LONDON PLANE TREE
Zone 5
  Region 1, 2, 3, 4, 6
Mature: 80' H., 60' Spr.
Street planting
Open habit

Platanus racemosa
  CALIFORNIA PLANE TREE
Zone 7
  Region 6
Mature: 60' H., 40' Spr.
Street planting
Picturesque form

30 ft.

Gymnocladus dioicus
  KENTUCKY COFFEE TREE
Zone 4
  Region 3
Mature: 75' H., 75' Spr.
Street planting
Spring: White
Winter: Structure

Populus nigra
  LOMBARDY POPLAR
Zone 2
  Region 1, 2, 3, 4, 6
Mature: 60' H., 15' Spr.
Screen
Fall: Yellow

Phellodendron amurense
  AMUR CORK TREE
Zone 3
  Region 1, 3, 5
Mature: 45' H., 30' Spr.
City conditions
Winter: Structure

Ulmus augustine americana
  AMERICAN AUGUSTINE ELM
Zone 2
  Region 1, 2, 3, 4, 5
Mature: 80' H., 80' Spr.
Street tree

Ulmus parvifolia
  CHINESE ELM
Zone 5
  Region 1, 2, 3, 6
Mature: 50' H., 40' Spr.
City conditions
Region 6: evergreen
Winter: Structure

Ulmus pumila
  SIBERIAN ELM
Zone 4
  Region: 3, 4, 5
Mature: 50' H., 40' Spr.
City conditions
Open habit

Cladrastis lutea
  AMERICAN YELLOWWOOD
Zone 3
  Region 1, 2, 3, (South)
Mature: 60' H., 40' Spr.
City conditions
Spring: White
Fall: Yellow

30 ft.

Fraxinus oregona
  OREGON ASH
Zone 6
  Region 5, 6
Mature: 80' H., 50' Spr.
Shade tree
Light green

Fraxinus pennsylvanica
  GREEN ASH
Zone 2
  Region 1, 2, 3, 4
Mature: 60' H., 40' Spr.
Street tree
Fall: Yellow

Quercus alba
  WHITE OAK
Zone 4
  Region 1, 2, 3
Mature: 90' H., 90' Spr.
Specimen planting
Fall: Violet-purple

Quercus borealis
  RED OAK
Zone 4
  Region 1, 2, 3, 4
Mature: 75' H., 75' Spr.
Street tree
Fall: Red

Quercus palustris
  PIN OAK
Zone 4
  Region 1, 2, 3, 4, 5, 6
Mature: 80' H., 40' Spr.
Street tree
Fall: Scarlet

Salix babylonica
  WEEPING WILLOW
Zone 6
  Region 2, 3, 4, 6
Mature: 50' H., 40' Spr.
Specimen planting
Spring: Yellow

Tilia cordata
  LITTLE-LEAF LINDEN
Zone 3
  Region 1, 2, 4
Mature 90' H., 50' Spr.
Street tree
Spring: Yellow

BROADLEAVED DECIDUOUS TREES Approximate ten year height for trees growing under favorable conditions.

30 ft.

Cinnamomum camphora
  CAMPHOR TREE
Zone 9
  Region 2, 6
Mature: 40' H., 60' Spr.
Street planting

Eucalyptus sideroxylum
  RED IRONBARK
Zone 9
  Region 6
Mature: 60' H., 40' Spr.
City conditions
Blue-gray

Magnolia grandiflora
  SOUTHERN MAGNOLIA
Zone 7
  Region 2, 6
Mature: 60' H., 70' Spr.
Specimen planting
Lustrous dark green

Quercus agrifolia
  CALIFORNIA LIVE OAK
Zone 9
  Region 6
Mature: 60' H., 70' Spr.
Street planting
Glossy dark green

Quercus laurifolia
  LAUREL OAK
Zone 7
  Region 2
Mature: 60' H., 60' Spr.
Specimen planting
Lustrous dark green

Quercus virginiana
  LIVE OAK
Zone 7
  Region 2
Mature: 60' H., 100' Spr.
Specimen planting
Fine texture

Schinus molle
  CALIF. PEPPER TREE
Zone 9
  Region 4, 6
Mature: 40' H., 30' Spr.
Street tree
Light green

BROADLEAVED EVERGREEN TREES Approximate ten year height for trees growing under favorable conditions.
Botanical name and Common name of trees given in this order. See Zones and Regions in given maps. H. = Height, Spr. = Spread

Laurence & Beatriz Coffin, Urban Planners & Landscape Architects; Washington, D. C.

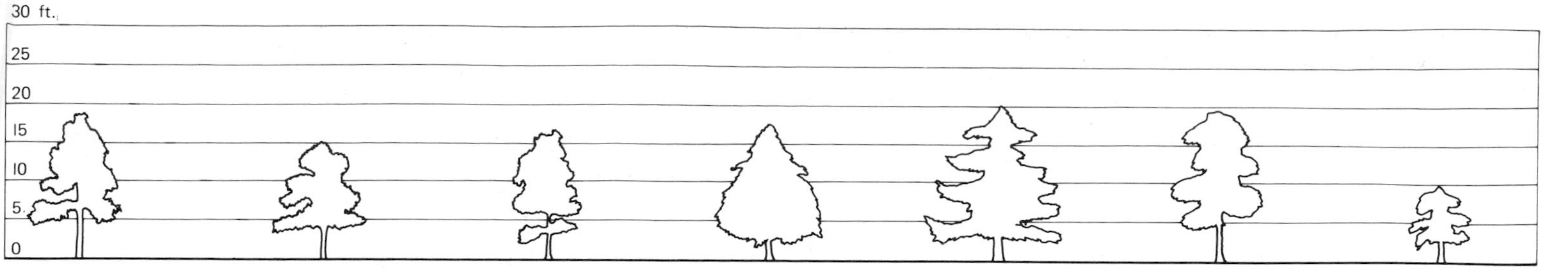

30 ft.
25
20
15
10
5
0

Pinus resinosa
RED PINE
Zone 2
Region 1
Mature: 75' H., 30' Spr.
Specimen planting
Dark green

Pinus nigra
AUSTRIAN PINE
Zone 4
Region 1, 4, 5, 6
Mature: 50' H., 40' Spr.
Specimen, hedge
Dense, Dark green

Pinus ponderosa
PONDEROSA PINE
Zone 3
Region 3, 4, 5, 6
Mature: 150' H.
Slow growth for 10 years,
after 1 foot per year

Pinus radiata
MONTEREY PINE
Zone 3
Region 5, 6
Mature: 50' H., 35' Spr.
Specimen planting
Open, Bright green

Pinus strobus
EASTERN WHITE PINE
Zone 2
Region 1, 2, 5
Mature: 100' H., 60' Spr.
Specimen, hedge
Open growth

Pinus sylvestris
SCOTCH PINE
Zone 2
Region 1, 2, 5
Mature: 75' H., 50' Spr.
Specimen planting
Bluish-green
Red trunk

Pinus thunbergi
JAPANESE BLACK PINE
Zone 4
Region 1, 2
Specimen planting
Asymmetrical
Dense, Dark green

30 ft.
25
20
15
10
5
0

Abies concolor
WHITE FIR
Zone 4
Region 1, 3, 4, 5, 6
Mature: 80' H., 50' Spr.
Specimen planting
Horizontal branching
Bluish-green

Cupresus macrocarpa
MONTEREY CYPRESS
Zone 7
Region 6
Mature: 75' H., 40' Spr.
Specimen planting
Dark yellow-green
Gray-green bark

Juniperus virginiana
EASTERN RED CEDAR
Zone 2
Region 1, 2, 3
Mature: 50' H., 30' Spr.
Specimen planting
Densely pyramidal

Cryptomeria japonica
CRYPTOMERIA
Zone 5
Region 1, 2, 5, 6
Mature: 100' H., 50' Spr.
Specimen, massing
Dark green

Larix decidua
EUROPEAN LARCH
Zone 2
Region 1
Mature: 100' H., 50' Spr.
Open
Yellow-green
Deciduous

Picea abies
NORWAY SPRUCE
Zone 2
Region 1, 2, 3
Mature: 150' H., 75' Spr.
Specimen planting
Dark yellow-green

Picea pungens
COLORADO BLUE SPRUCE
Zone 2
Region 1, 3, 4, 6
Mature: 80' H., 40' Spr.
Specimen planting
Blue

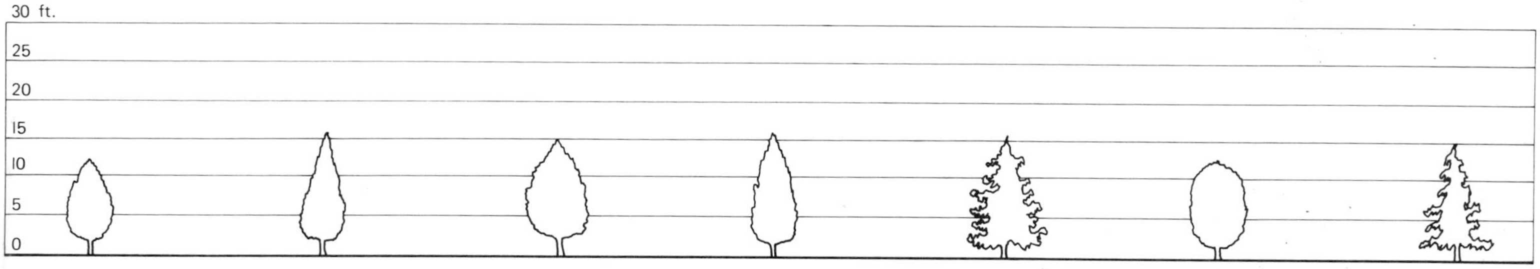

30 ft.
25
20
15
10
5
0

Chamaecyparis pisifera
SAWARA CYPRESS
Zone 3
Region 1, 3, 4, 6
Mature: 90' H., 40' Spr.
Open habit

Libocedrus decurrens
CALIF. INCENSE-CEDAR
Zone 5
Region 5, 6
Mature: 100' H., 35' Spr.
Dark yellow-green lustrous

Thuja orientalis
ORIENTAL ARBOR-VITAE
Zone 0
Region 2, 6
Mature: 40' H., 30' Spr.
Specimen
Lustrous

Thuja occidentalis
AMERICAN ARBOR-VITAE
Zone 2
Region 1, 2, 3, 4
Mature: 40' H., 20' Spr.
Specimen, hedge
Yellow-green

Taxodium distichum
COMMON BALD CYPRESS
Zone 4
Region 1, 2
Mature: 120'
Specimen planting
Deciduous

Taxus baccata
ENGLISH YEW
Zone 6
Region 1, 5, 6
Mature: 50' H., 70' Spr.
Specimen, hedge
Dark green

Tsuga canadensis
CANADA HEMLOCK
Zone 3
Region 1, 2, 6
Mature: 80' H., 50' Spr.
Specimen, hedge

CONIFER TREES (EVERGREEN UNLESS OTHERWISE INDICATED)

Exposure and atmospheric conditions will greatly affect this group of trees. They are not recommended for street planting or for locations with heavy air pollution. Approximate ten year height for trees growing under favorable conditions.

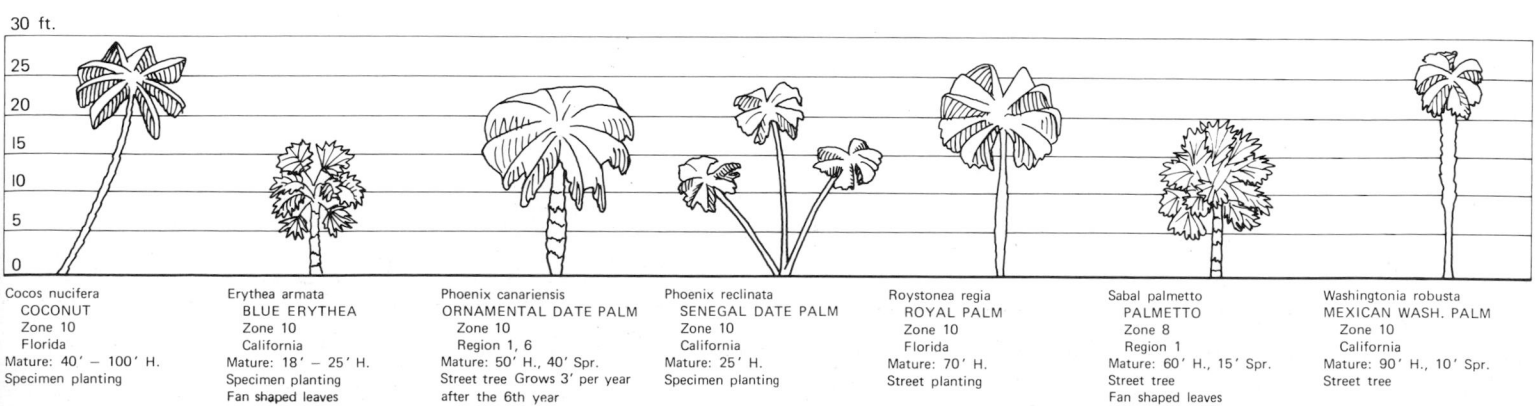

30 ft.
25
20
15
10
5
0

Cocos nucifera
COCONUT
Florida
Mature: 40' – 100' H.
Specimen planting

Erythea armata
BLUE ERYTHEA
Zone 10
California
Mature: 18' – 25' H.
Specimen planting
Fan shaped leaves

Phoenix canariensis
ORNAMENTAL DATE PALM
Zone 10
Region 1, 6
Mature: 50' H., 40' Spr.
Street tree Grows 3' per year
after the 6th year

Phoenix reclinata
SENEGAL DATE PALM
Zone 10
California
Mature: 25' H.
Specimen planting

Roystonea regia
ROYAL PALM
Zone 10
Florida
Mature: 70' H.
Street planting

Sabal palmetto
PALMETTO
Zone 8
Region 1
Mature: 60' H., 15' Spr.
Street tree
Fan shaped leaves

Washingtonia robusta
MEXICAN WASH. PALM
Zone 10
California
Mature: 90' H., 10' Spr.
Street tree

PALM TREES   APPROXIMATE TEN YEAR HEIGHT FOR TREES GROWING UNDER FAVORABLE CONDITIONS

Botanical name and Common name given in this order. See Zones and Regions in given maps. H. = Height Spr. = Spread.

Laurence & Beatriz Coffin, Urban Planners & Landscape Architects; Washington, D. C.

Betula populifolia
GREY BIRCH
Zone 2
  Region 1, 2, 3, 4, 5
Mature: 30' H., 20' Spr.
White bark
Fall: Yellow

Cornus florida
FLOWERING DOGWOOD
Zone 4
  Region 1, 2, 3(East)
Mature: 20' H., 25' Spr.
Spring: White or Pink
Fall: Red

Cornus nutalli
PACIFIC DOGWOOD
Zone 7
  Region 5, 6
Mature: 30' H., 30' Spr.
Spring: White
Fall: Scarlet and Yellow

Cercis canadensis
EASTERN REDBUD
Zone 4
  Region 1, 2, 4
Mature: 30' H., 30' Spr.
Spring: Purplish Pink
Fall: Yellow

Crataegus phaenopyrum
WASHINGTON HAWTHORN
Zone 4
  Region 1, 2
Mature: 30' H., 30' Spr.
Spring: White
Fall: Orange

Ilex opaca
AMERICAN HOLLY
Zone 5
  Region 1, 2
Mature: 40' H., 25' Spr.
Dark green, Red fruit
Evergreen

Lagerstroemia indica
CRAPE MYRTLE
Zone 7
  Region 2, 6
Mature: 20' H., 20' Spr.
Spring: Pink, Bluish
Dense

Acer palmatum
JAPANESE MAPLE
Zone 5
  Region 1, 2, 6
Mature: 20' H., 20' Spr.
Spring: Red
Fall: Red

Delonix regia
FLAME TREE
Zone 10
  Florida
Mature: 40' H., 40' Spr.
Summer: Red flowers
Fern-like folliage

Myrica californica
CALIFORNIA BAYBERRY
Zone 7
  Region 5, 6
Mature: 30' H., 15' Spr.
Bronze colored
Evergreen

Magnolia soulangeana
SAUCER MAGNOLIA
Zone 5
  Region 1, 2, 6
Mature: 25' H., 25' Spr.
Spring: White - Pink
Coarse texture

Malus (species)
FLOWERING CRAB
Zone 4
  Region 1, 2, 4
Mature: 25' H., 25' Spr.
Spring: White, Pink, Red
Dense

Prunus serrulata
ORIENTAL CHERRY
Zone 5, 6
  Region 1, 2, 5, 6
Mature: 25' H., 25' Spr.
Spring: White, Pink
Glossy bark

Photinia serrulata
CHINESE PHOTINIA
Zone 7
  Region 2, 6
Mature: 36' H., 25' Spr.
Spring: New growth Red
Lustrous evergreen

Botanical name and Common name of trees and shrubs given in this order. See Zones and Regions in given maps.

H. = Height   Spr. = Spread

MINOR TREES—ADAPTED TO CITY CONDITIONS, DECIDUOUS UNLESS OTHERWISE SPECIFIED.

SIZE	DECIDUOUS SHRUBS—WITHSTANDING CITY CONDITIONS				EVERGREEN SHRUBS—WITHSTANDING CITY CONDITIONS		
10' to 15' HIGH Scale 1" = 30'	Cornus racemosa GRAY DOGWOOD Zone 4 Region 1, 2 Red stalks Hedge	Hamamelis virginiana COMMON WITCH HAZEL Zone 4 Region 1, 2, 3 Fall: Yellow	Ligustrum amurense AMUR PRIVET Zone 3 Region 1, 2, 3, 5, 6 Nearly evergreen Hedge or specimen	Syringa vulgaris COMMON LILAC Zone 3 Region 1, 4, 5 Spring: Lilac Massing	Juniperus chinensus columnaris CHINESE JUNIPER Zone 4 Region 1, 2, 3 Hedge specimen	Taxus cupidata capitata JAPANESE YEW Zone 4 Region 1, 2, 3, 4, 5, 6 Specimen Dark green	Rhododendron maximum ROSEBAY RHODODENDRON Zone 3 Region 1, 2, 5 Spring: Pink Dark green, dense
6' to 10' HIGH Scale 1" = 20'	Aronia arbutifolia RED CHOKEBERRY Zone 5 Region 1, 2 Spring: White Fall: Red	Fremontia californica FLANNEL BUSH Zone 7 California Spring: Yellow Massing	Spirea prunifolia plena BRIDALWREATH SPIREA Zone 4 Region 1, 2, 3 Spring: White	Vibornum tomentosum DOUBLEFILE VIBURNUM Zone 2 Region 1, 2, 3, 4, 5, 6 Spring: White Massing	Taxus cuspidata JAPANESE YEW Zone 4 Region 1, 2, 3, 4, 5, 6 Hedge Dark green	Myrtus communis MYRTLE Zone 8–9 Region 2, 6 Hedge, Specimen Massing	Nerium oleander NERIUM Zone 7–8 Region 2, 3, 4, 6 Bamboo-like Light green—white flower
2' to 6' HIGH Scale 1" = 20'	Berberis thunbergi JAPANESE BARBERRY Zone 5 Region 1, 2, 3, 4, 5, 6 Fall: Scarlet Hedge	Forsythia intermediaspetabilis SHOWY BORDER FORSYTHIA Zone 5 Region 1, 2, 3, 4, 5, 6 Spring: Yellow Massing	Euonymus alata WINGED EUONYMUS Zone 3 Region 1, 2, 5, 6 Fall: Scarlet Hedge: Massing	Rosa rugosa RUGOSA ROSE Zone 2 Region 1, 2 Fall: Orange Hedge	Juniperus chinensis pfitzeriana PFITZER'S JUNIPER Zone 4 Region 1, 2 Feathery texture	Buxus suffruticosa DWARF BOX Zone 5 Region 2, 3, 6 Dark lustrous	Pinus mugo mughus MUGO PINE Zone 2 Region 1, 2, 4, 5, 6 Bright green Specimen, Massing
6" to 24" HIGH Used as ground cover	Cotoneaster horizontalis ROCK SPRAY Zone 4 Region 1, 2, 3, 4, 5, 6	Cytisus albus PORTUGUESE BROOM Zone 5 Region 1, 5 White flowers	Euonymus fortunei WINTER CREEPER Zone 2 Region 1, 2, 3, 4, 5, 6	Juniperus sabina tamariscifolia TAMARIX JUNIPER Zone 4 Region 3, 4, 5, 6	Juniperus chinensis sargenti SARGENT JUNIPER Zone 4 Region 1, 2	Hedera helix vars. ENGLISH IVY Zone 4 Region 1, 2	Pachistima cambyi CAMBYI PACHISTIMA Zone 5 Region 1, 2 Fall: Bronze

Silhouettes indicate specimens of natural form. Shrubs are adaptable to different height and forms by pruning. A wide range of varieties and exotic shrubs can be found throughout the plant regions. A few shrubs commonly used are listed here.

Laurence & Beatriz Coffin, Urban Planners & Landscape Architects; Washington, D. C.

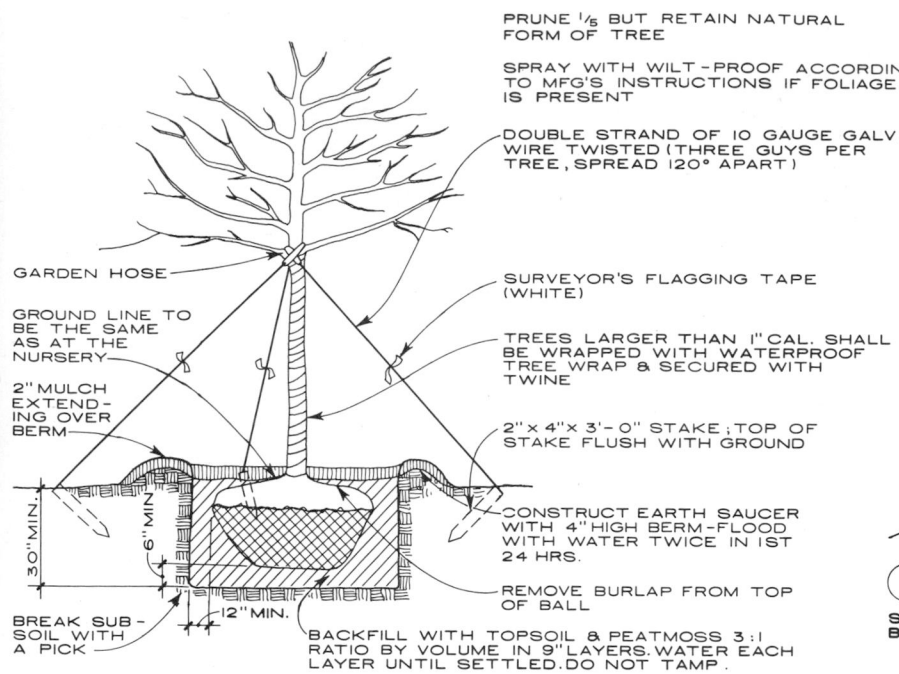

PRUNE ⅕ BUT RETAIN NATURAL FORM OF TREE

SPRAY WITH WILT-PROOF ACCORDING TO MFG'S INSTRUCTIONS IF FOLIAGE IS PRESENT

DOUBLE STRAND OF 10 GAUGE GALV. WIRE TWISTED (THREE GUYS PER TREE, SPREAD 120° APART)

GARDEN HOSE

GROUND LINE TO BE THE SAME AS AT THE NURSERY

SURVEYOR'S FLAGGING TAPE (WHITE)

2" MULCH EXTENDING OVER BERM

TREES LARGER THAN 1" CAL. SHALL BE WRAPPED WITH WATERPROOF TREE WRAP & SECURED WITH TWINE

2" x 4" x 3'-0" STAKE; TOP OF STAKE FLUSH WITH GROUND

CONSTRUCT EARTH SAUCER WITH 4" HIGH BERM - FLOOD WITH WATER TWICE IN 1ST 24 HRS.

30" MIN.   6" MIN.

BREAK SUB-SOIL WITH A PICK

12" MIN.

REMOVE BURLAP FROM TOP OF BALL

BACKFILL WITH TOPSOIL & PEATMOSS 3:1 RATIO BY VOLUME IN 9" LAYERS. WATER EACH LAYER UNTIL SETTLED. DO NOT TAMP.

PLANTING & GUYING DETAILS - FOR MINOR TREES 1½" CALIPER AND SMALLER, BALLED & BURLAPPED.

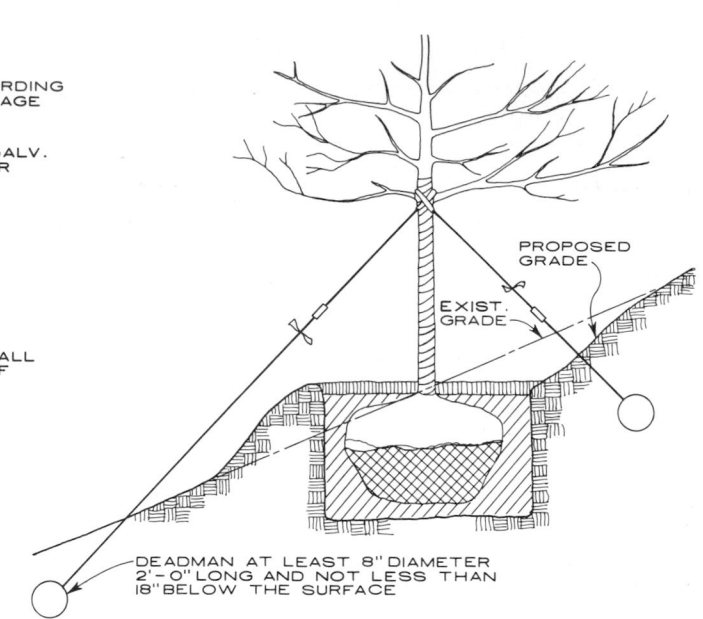

PROPOSED GRADE

EXIST. GRADE

DEADMAN AT LEAST 8" DIAMETER 2'-0" LONG AND NOT LESS THAN 18" BELOW THE SURFACE

SLOPE PLANTING DETAIL - FOR MAJOR & MINOR TREES, BALLED & BURLAPPED

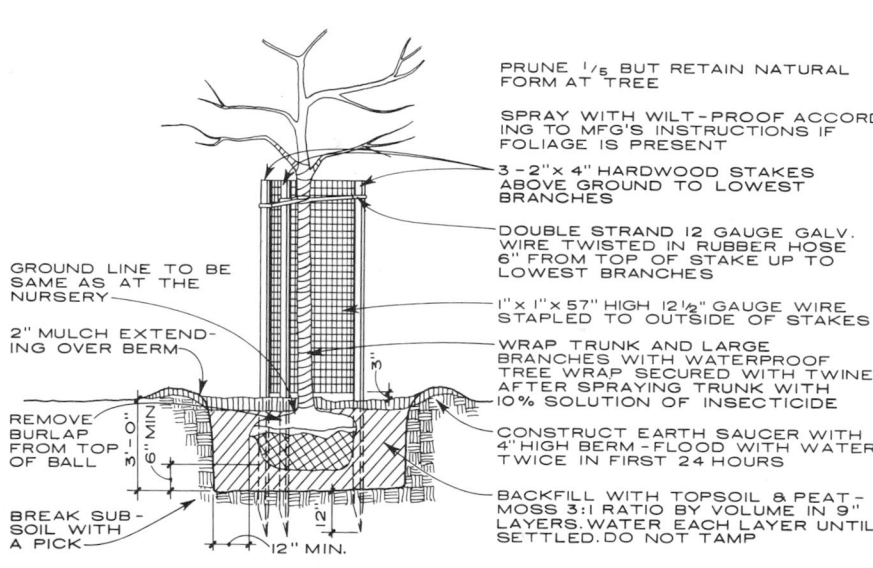

PRUNE ⅕ BUT RETAIN NATURAL FORM AT TREE

SPRAY WITH WILT-PROOF ACCORDING TO MFG'S INSTRUCTIONS IF FOLIAGE IS PRESENT

3 - 2" x 4" HARDWOOD STAKES ABOVE GROUND TO LOWEST BRANCHES

DOUBLE STRAND 12 GAUGE GALV. WIRE TWISTED IN RUBBER HOSE 6" FROM TOP OF STAKE UP TO LOWEST BRANCHES

GROUND LINE TO BE SAME AS AT THE NURSERY

1" x 1" x 57" HIGH 12½" GAUGE WIRE STAPLED TO OUTSIDE OF STAKES

2" MULCH EXTENDING OVER BERM

WRAP TRUNK AND LARGE BRANCHES WITH WATERPROOF TREE WRAP SECURED WITH TWINE AFTER SPRAYING TRUNK WITH 10% SOLUTION OF INSECTICIDE

REMOVE BURLAP FROM TOP OF BALL

CONSTRUCT EARTH SAUCER WITH 4" HIGH BERM - FLOOD WITH WATER TWICE IN FIRST 24 HOURS

BREAK SUB-SOIL WITH A PICK

12" MIN.

BACKFILL WITH TOPSOIL & PEAT-MOSS 3:1 RATIO BY VOLUME IN 9" LAYERS. WATER EACH LAYER UNTIL SETTLED. DO NOT TAMP

PLANTING & STAKING DETAIL - FOR MAJOR TREES 2" CALIPER AND LARGER, BALLED AND BURLAPPED.

STANDARD SHADE TREES—BALLED AND BURLAPPED

*CALIPER	HEIGHT RANGE	MAXIMUM HEIGHTS	MINIMUM BALL DIAM.	MINIMUM BALL DEPTH
1/2 to 3/4 in.	5 to 6 ft.	8 ft.	12 inches	9 inches
3/4 to 1 in.	6 to 8 ft.	10 ft.	14 inches	10 inches
1 to 1 1/4 in.	7 to 9 ft.	11 ft.	16 inches	12 inches
1 1/4 to 1 1/2 in.	8 to 10 ft.	12 ft.	18 inches	13 inches
1 1/2 to 1 3/4 in.	10 to 12 ft.	14 ft.	20 inches	14 inches
1 3/4 to 2 in.	10 to 12 ft.	14 ft.	22 inches	15 inches
2 to 2 1/2 in.	12 to 14 ft.	16 ft.	24 inches	16 inches
2 1/2 to 3 in.	12 to 14 ft.	16 ft.	28 inches	19 inches
3 to 3 1/2 in.	14 to 16 ft.	18 ft.	32 inches	20 inches
3 1/2 to 4 in.	14 to 16 ft.	18 ft.	36 inches	22 inches
4 to 5 in.	16 to 18 ft.	22 ft.	44 inches	26 inches
5 to 6 in.	18 and up.	26 ft.	48 inches	29 inches

*In the selection of trees from commercial nurseries, caliper indicates the diameter of the trunk taken 6 inches above the ground level up to and including 4 inch caliper size and 12" inches above the ground level for larger sizes.

SHRUBS & MINOR TREES BALLED AND BURLAPPED

HEIGHT RANGE	MINIMUM BALL DIAM.	MINIMUM BALL DEPTH
1 1/2 to 2 ft.	10 inches	8 inches
2 to 3 ft.	12 inches	9 inches
3 to 4 ft.	13 inches	10 inches
4 to 5 ft.	15 inches	11 inches
5 to 6 ft.	16 inches	12 inches
6 to 7 ft.	18 inches	13 inches
7 to 8 ft.	20 inches	14 inches
8 to 9 ft.	22 inches	15 inches
9 to 10 ft.	24 inches	16 inches
10 to 12 ft.	26 inches	17 inches

NOTE FOR STD. SHADE TREES AND SHRUBS AND MINOR TREES Ball sizes should always be of a diameter to encompass the fibrous and feeding root system necessary for the full recovery of the plant.

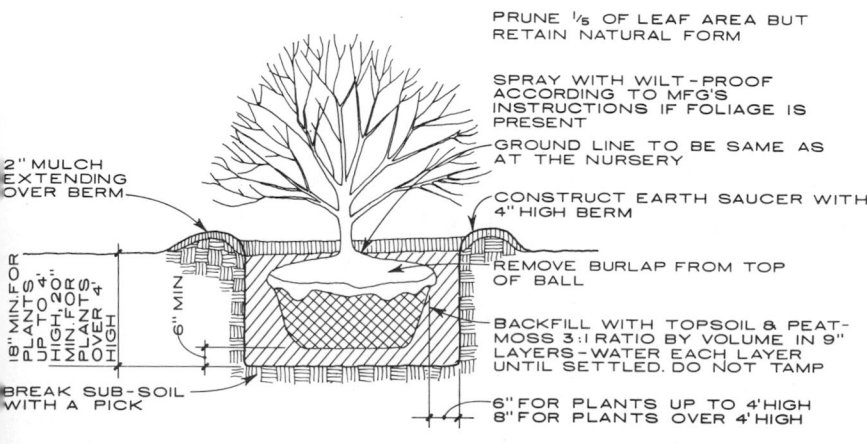

PRUNE ⅕ OF LEAF AREA BUT RETAIN NATURAL FORM

SPRAY WITH WILT-PROOF ACCORDING TO MFG'S INSTRUCTIONS IF FOLIAGE IS PRESENT

GROUND LINE TO BE SAME AS AT THE NURSERY

2" MULCH EXTENDING OVER BERM

CONSTRUCT EARTH SAUCER WITH 4" HIGH BERM

REMOVE BURLAP FROM TOP OF BALL

18" MIN. FOR PLANTS UP TO 4' HIGH, 20" MIN. FOR PLANTS OVER 4' HIGH   6" MIN.

BREAK SUB-SOIL WITH A PICK

BACKFILL WITH TOPSOIL & PEAT-MOSS 3:1 RATIO BY VOLUME IN 9" LAYERS - WATER EACH LAYER UNTIL SETTLED. DO NOT TAMP

6" FOR PLANTS UP TO 4' HIGH 8" FOR PLANTS OVER 4' HIGH

SHRUB PLANTING DETAIL - FOR ALL SHRUBS BALLED AND BURLAPPED

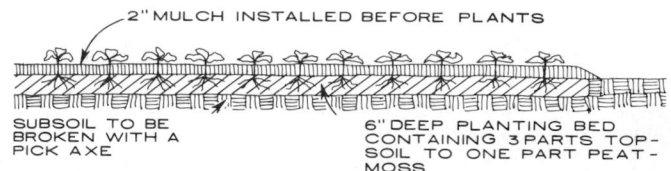

2" MULCH INSTALLED BEFORE PLANTS

SUBSOIL TO BE BROKEN WITH A PICK AXE

6" DEEP PLANTING BED CONTAINING 3 PARTS TOP-SOIL TO ONE PART PEAT-MOSS

GROUND COVER PLANTING DETAIL
NOTE: GROUND COVERS SHOULD BE POT OR CONTAINER GROWN

Laurence & Beatriz Coffin, Urban Planners & Landscape Architects; Washington, D. C.

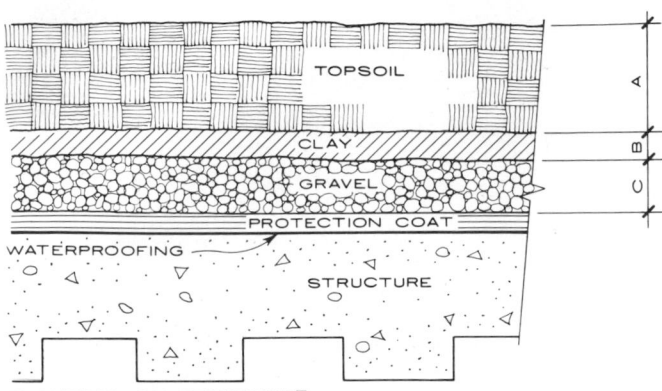

PLANTING ON STRUCTURE

NOTE: SAME DETAIL APPLIES TO LARGE PLANTERS.

PLANTING ITEM	DEPTHS		
	A	B	C
LAWNS	12"		4"
SHRUBS	24"	2"	4"
MINOR TREES	30"	2"	4"
* MAJOR TREES	36"	2"	4"

* Structural columns are usually placed directly under all major trees. Drainage to be provided within the gravel.

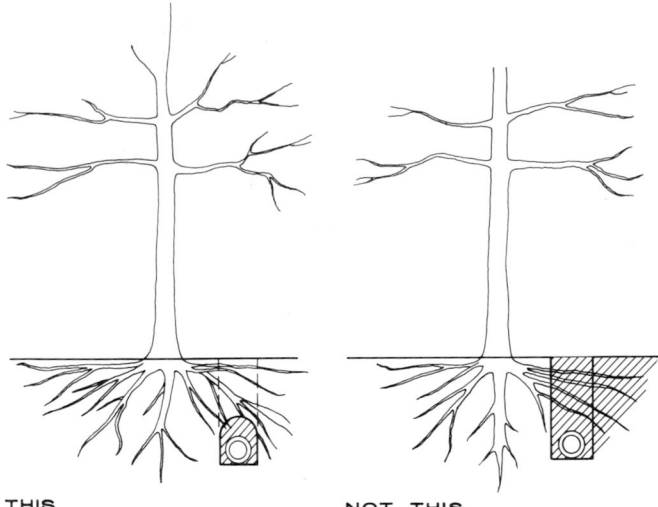

THIS   **NOT THIS**

Fewer roots are severed by tunneling under tree than by trenching.

UNDERGROUND UTILITIES NEAR EXISTING TREES

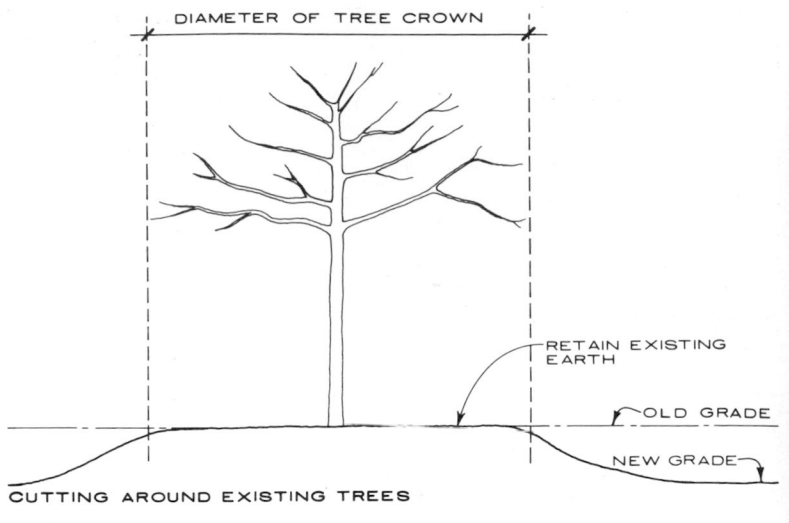

CUTTING AROUND EXISTING TREES

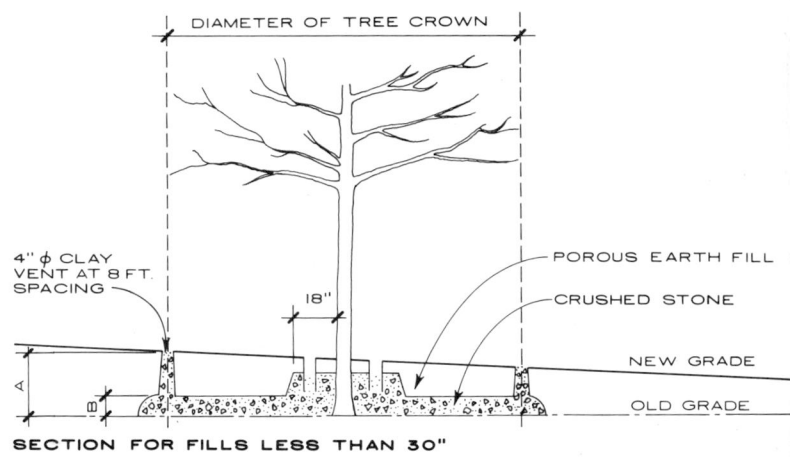

SECTION FOR FILLS LESS THAN 30"

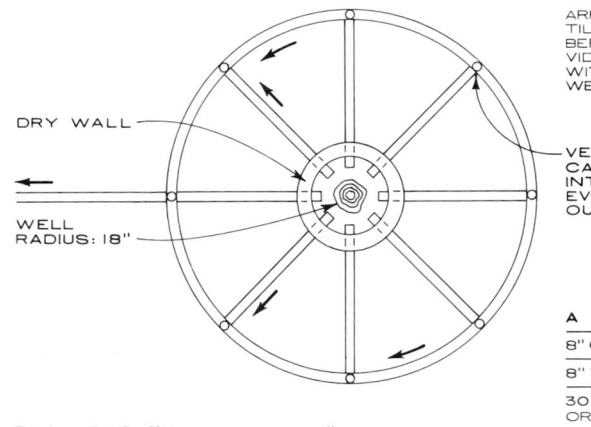

ARRANGEMENT OF CLAY TILE ON ORIGINAL GRADE BEFORE FILLING PROVIDES GOOD DRAINAGE WITH CENTRAL TREE WELL.

VENTS TO BE LOCATED AT THE TILE INTERSECTIONS AND EVERY 8 FT. IN THE OUTER RING.

A	B
8" OR LESS	
8" TO 30"	2" TO 6"
30" OR MORE	8" TO 12" OR MORE

PLAN: FOR FILLS OVER 30"
FILLING AROUND EXISTING TREES

NOTES:

1. Flood plants twice within 24 hours after planting.

2. Fertilize with 2 lbs. 5-10-10 while back-filling, but not around roots.

3. Ericaceous plants to receive a surface application of aluminum sulfate @ 1/2 lb/10 sq. ft.

4. Trees for special uses should be branched or pruned naturally according to type. Where a form of growth is desired which is not in accordance with a natural growth habit, this form should be specified, such as:

BUSH FORM — trees which start to branch close to the ground in the manner of a shrub.

CLUMPS — trees with three or more main stems starting from the ground.

CUT BACK OR SHEARED — trees that have been pruned back so as to multiply the branching structure and to develop a more formal effect.

TOPIARY — trees sheared or trimmed closely in a formal geometric pattern.

TOP-WORKED TREES — the height of stem and age of top should be specified.

5. Trees suitable for planting as street trees should be free of branches within the lower 60% of their height. Height of branching should bear a relation-ship to the size and kind of tree also, so that the crown of the tree will be in good balance with the trunk as the tree grows.

6. Container or pot grown plants should be grown in their containers sufficiently long for the new fibrous roots to have developed so that the root mat will retain its shape and hold together when removed from the container or pot.

(Notes and charts on sizes obtained from the American Association of Nurserymen, Inc.)

Laurence & Beatriz Coffin, Urban Planners & Landscape Architects; Washington, D. C.

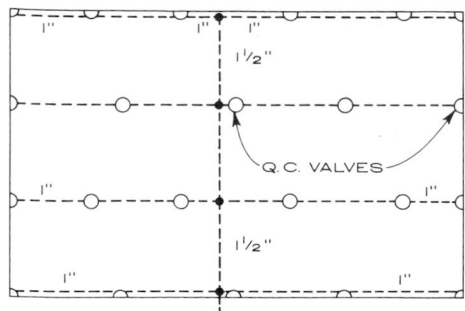

QUICK-COUPLING SYSTEM
UNIT COST 1.0

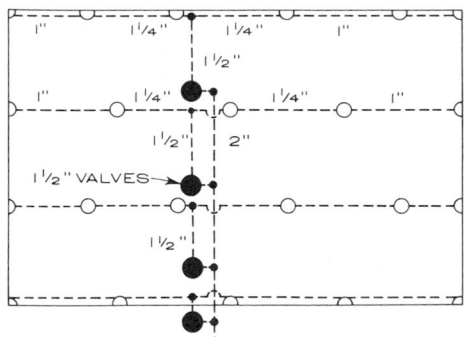

MANUAL ROTARY POP-UP SYSTEM
UNIT COST 1.45

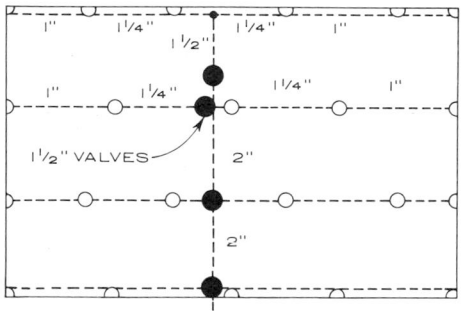

AUTOMATIC ROTARY POP-UP SYSTEM
UNIT COST 1.81

TYPICAL LAYOUTS - AREA 1.15 ACRES

GENERAL NOTES:

DESIGN FACTORS

a. Size of the supply line; b. length of supply line; c. available water pressure. These factors will govern the type of system, type of heads and pipe size to be used.

TYPES OF CONTROL

Quick coupler: this system is normally under pressure, and key is inserted where water is needed.

Manual: this system is turned on by use of a valve; all heads are in place.

Automatic: this system is operated from a central control unit. Each section is turned on for a period each day or on certain days of the week as pre-set. There are two basic types, Hydraulic or Electric, the latter being more common. The control valves are located at remote locations with control lines from the valves to the control unit. Control lines are buried with the pipe. This type of system not only cuts labor cost in operation but also pipe cost. The additional cost of this system will be paid for in about 3 to 5 years on the West Coast.

NOTE: Provide pipe sleeves under walks and thru walls for future controls and extension of system.

John Barclay; Seibert, Hunter, Shute & Plumley; Medford, Oregon

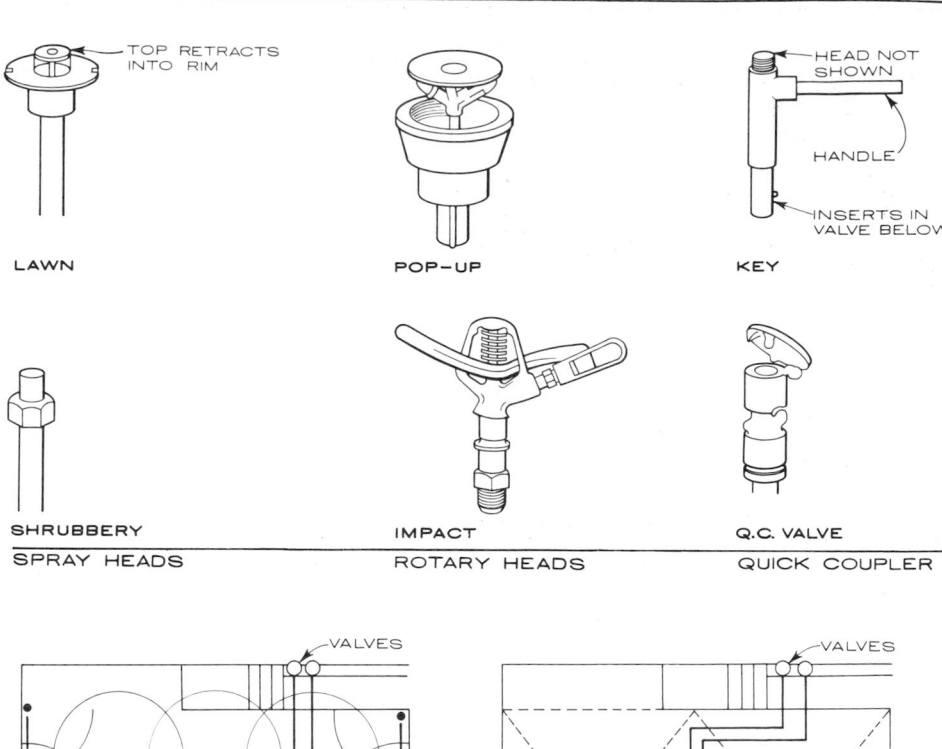

LAWN   POP-UP   KEY

SHRUBBERY   IMPACT   Q.C. VALVE
SPRAY HEADS   **ROTARY HEADS**   **QUICK COUPLER**

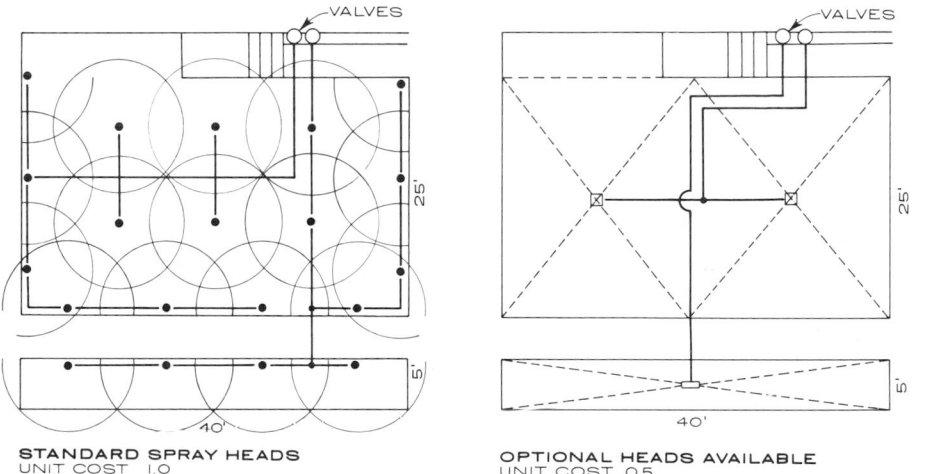

STANDARD SPRAY HEADS
UNIT COST 1.0

OPTIONAL HEADS AVAILABLE
UNIT COST 0.5

TYPICAL LAYOUT - RESIDENTIAL

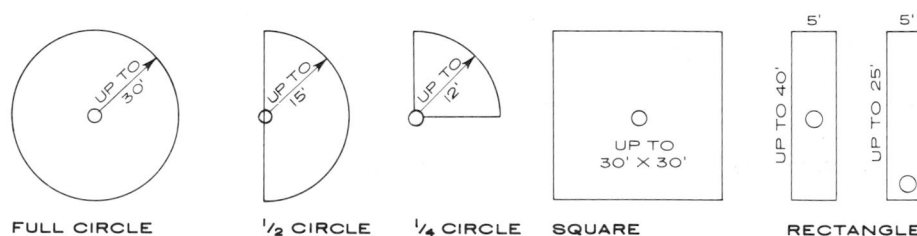

FULL CIRCLE   ½ CIRCLE   ¼ CIRCLE   SQUARE   RECTANGLE
COVERAGE SPRAY HEADS

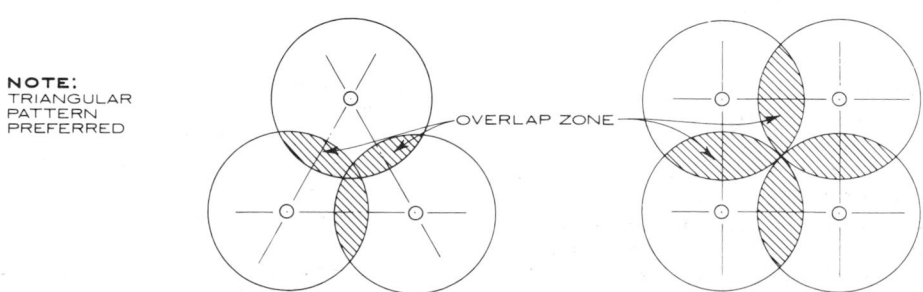

NOTE: TRIANGULAR PATTERN PREFERRED

OVERLAP ZONE

THIS TYPE OF HEAD WILL COVER UP TO APPROXIMATLY 350' DIAMETER WITH A 4" PIPE, 200 G.P.M. AND 100 # PRESSURE.

COVERAGE ROTARY HEADS

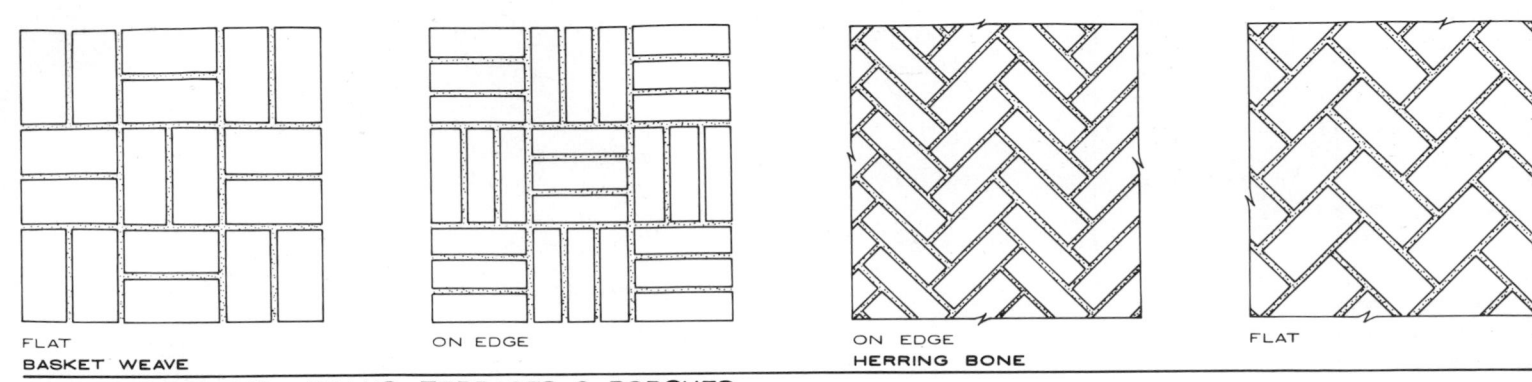

FLAT
BASKET WEAVE

ON EDGE

ON EDGE
HERRING BONE

FLAT

PAVING PATTERNS - WALKS, TERRACES & PORCHES

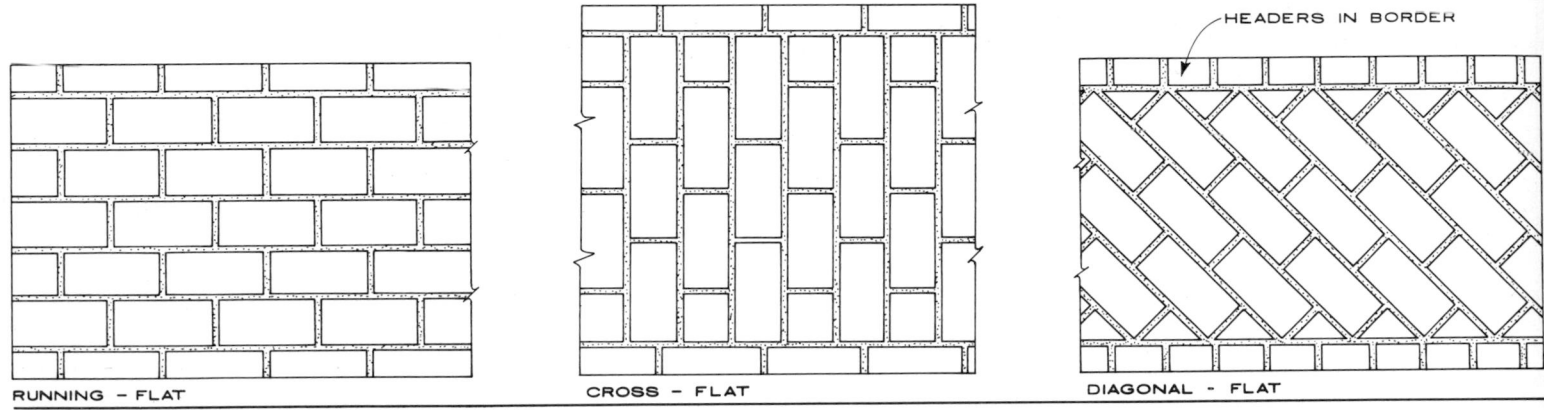

HEADERS IN BORDER

RUNNING - FLAT

CROSS - FLAT

DIAGONAL - FLAT

PATTERNS USUALLY USED FOR WALKS

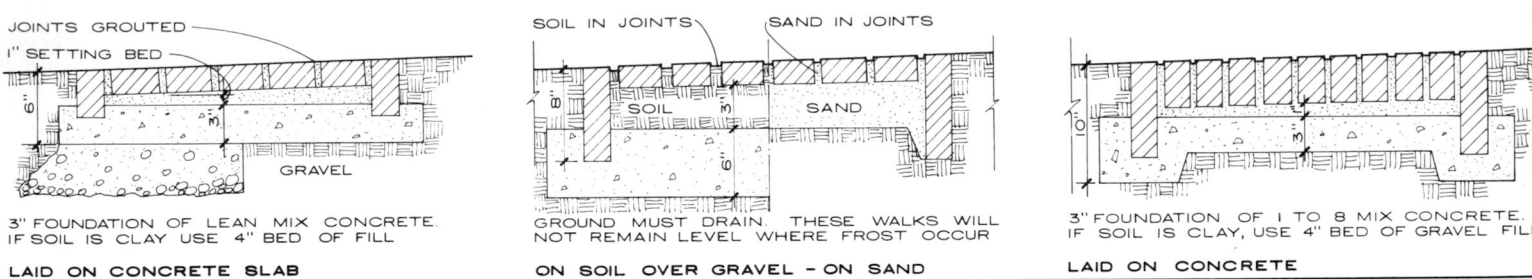

JOINTS GROUTED
1" SETTING BED
6"
GRAVEL

3" FOUNDATION OF LEAN MIX CONCRETE.
IF SOIL IS CLAY USE 4" BED OF FILL

LAID ON CONCRETE SLAB

SOIL IN JOINTS   SAND IN JOINTS
SOIL   SAND

GROUND MUST DRAIN. THESE WALKS WILL
NOT REMAIN LEVEL WHERE FROST OCCUR

ON SOIL OVER GRAVEL - ON SAND

3" FOUNDATION OF 1 TO 8 MIX CONCRETE.
IF SOIL IS CLAY, USE 4" BED OF GRAVEL FILL

LAID ON CONCRETE

SECTIONS OF TYPICAL WALKS OR TERRACES
SCALE : " = 1'-0"

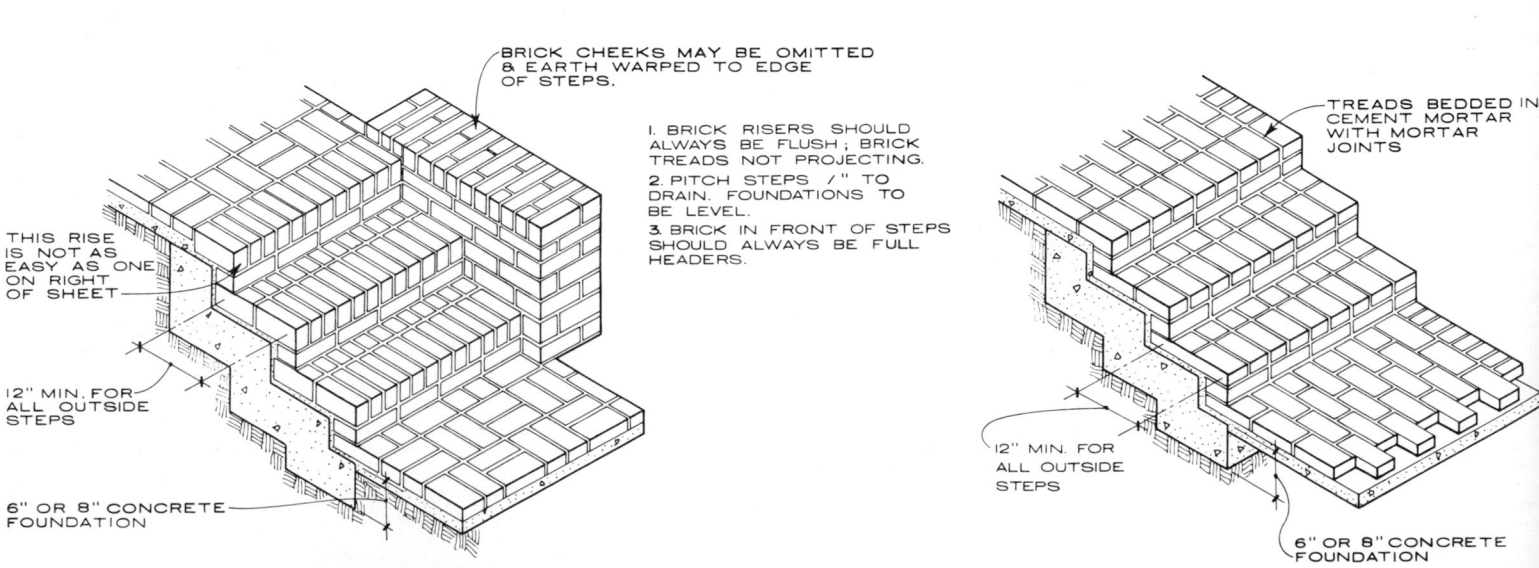

BRICK CHEEKS MAY BE OMITTED
& EARTH WARPED TO EDGE
OF STEPS.

1. BRICK RISERS SHOULD
ALWAYS BE FLUSH ; BRICK
TREADS NOT PROJECTING.
2. PITCH STEPS /" TO
DRAIN. FOUNDATIONS TO
BE LEVEL.
3. BRICK IN FRONT OF STEPS
SHOULD ALWAYS BE FULL
HEADERS.

THIS RISE
IS NOT AS
EASY AS ONE
ON RIGHT
OF SHEET

12" MIN. FOR
ALL OUTSIDE
STEPS

6" OR 8" CONCRETE
FOUNDATION

TREADS BEDDED IN
CEMENT MORTAR
WITH MORTAR
JOINTS

12" MIN. FOR
ALL OUTSIDE
STEPS

6" OR 8" CONCRETE
FOUNDATION

SEE SECTIONS ABOVE FOR FOUNDATIONS OF WALKS

WALKS - TERRACES - PORCHES - STEPS
SCALE : 3/8" = 1'- 0"

B. J. Baldwin; Giffels & Rossetti, Inc.; Detroit, Michigan

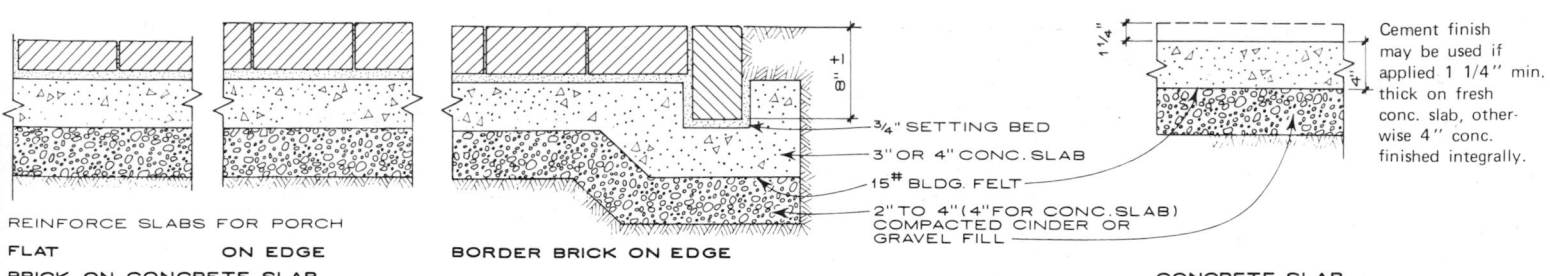

REINFORCE SLABS FOR PORCH

FLAT   ON EDGE

BRICK ON CONCRETE SLAB   BORDER BRICK ON EDGE

¾" SETTING BED
3" OR 4" CONC. SLAB
15# BLDG. FELT
2" TO 4" (4" FOR CONC. SLAB) COMPACTED CINDER OR GRAVEL FILL

CONCRETE SLAB

Cement finish may be used if applied 1 1/4" min. thick on fresh conc. slab, otherwise 4" conc. finished integrally.

SECTIONS THRU PAVING   SCALE ¾" = 1'-0"

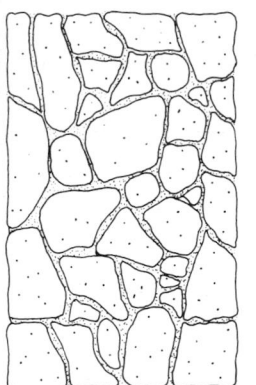 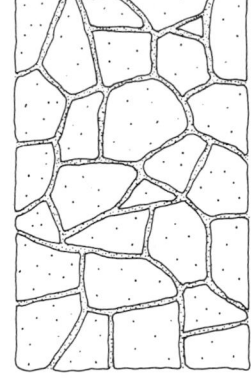 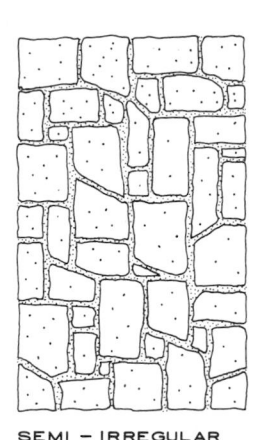 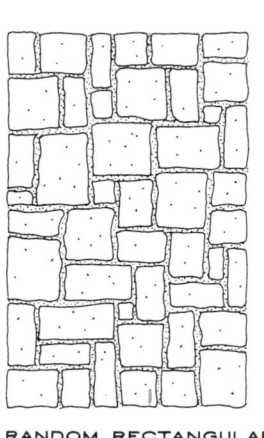 

IRREGULAR (NOT FITTED)   IRREGULAR (FITTED)   SEMI – IRREGULAR   RANDOM RECTANGULAR   RECTANGULAR (LIMITED SIZE)

NOTE: Stones are usually specified run of quarry but may be limited by specifying maximum and minimum sizes. Stones are shown as average size but may vary considerably according to the quarry.

FLAGSTONE PATTERNS   SCALE ⅛" = 1'-0"

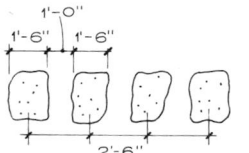 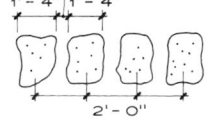 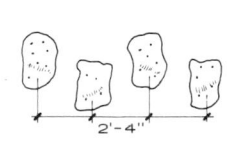 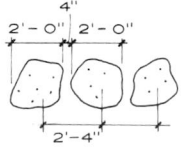

FOR LONG WALKS   FOR SHORT WALKS   MEDIUM SPACING

STEPPING STONES

NOTE: Walks may be from 1'-4" to 2'-4" wide. Spacing for short walks 2'-0"; spacing for longer walks 2'-4" to 2'-6". Stones are usually 1'-4" to 1'-6" average length.

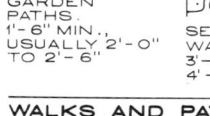 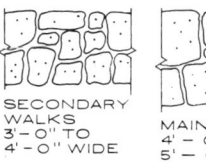 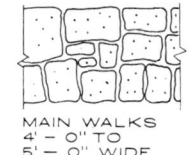

GARDEN PATHS. 1'-6" MIN., USUALLY 2'-0" TO 2'-6"   SECONDARY WALKS 3'-0" TO 4'-0" WIDE   MAIN WALKS 4'-0" TO 5'-0" WIDE

WALKS AND PATHS
SCALE : ⅛" = 1'-0"

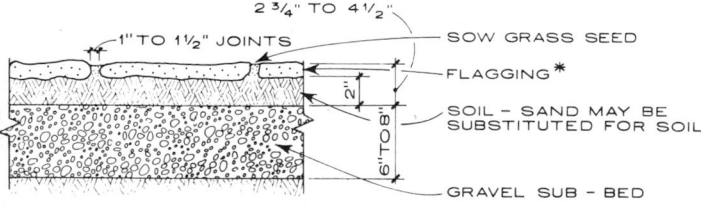

2 ¾" TO 4 ½"
1" TO 1½" JOINTS
SOW GRASS SEED
FLAGGING *
SOIL – SAND MAY BE SUBSTITUTED FOR SOIL
GRAVEL SUB - BED
2"
6" TO 8"

THIS TYPE WILL NOT STAY LEVEL WHERE FROST OCCURS

*SLATE ¾" TO 1"
QUARTZITE 1¼" TO 2½"
SANDSTONE 1½"

STONE DIRECTLY ON EARTH
SCALE: ¾" = 1'-0"

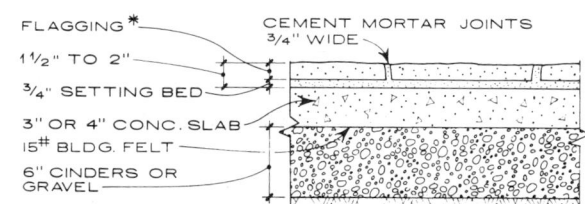

FLAGGING *
CEMENT MORTAR JOINTS ¾" WIDE
1½" TO 2"
¾" SETTING BED
3" OR 4" CONC. SLAB
15# BLDG. FELT
6" CINDERS OR GRAVEL

REINFORCE SLABS IF FOR PORCHES

*SLATE ¾" TO 1"
QUARTZITE ¾" TO 1"
SANDSTONE 1"

STONE ON CONCRETE SLAB

MATERIAL	SURFACE FINISH	EDGE FINISH
SLATE	Natural Split (quarry cleft)	Sawed or Hand Trimmed
QUARTZITE	Natural Split (quarry cleft)	Snapped Finish
SANDSTONE	Natural Split (quarry cleft) Rubbed, sawed, or planed	Flag Cut, Quarry Cut, Sawed or Rubbed

NOTE: Bluestone is a type of sandstone available in blue, gray, red, pink and greenish colors.

B. J. Baldwin; Giffels & Rossetti, Inc.; Detroit, Michigan

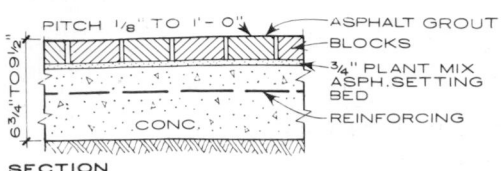

SECTION

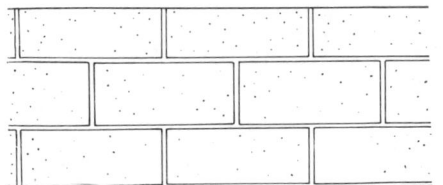

RECTANGULAR BLOCKS

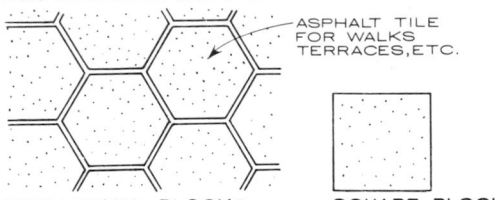

HEXAGONAL BLOCKS   SQUARE BLOCK

ASPHALT PAVING BLOCKS AND TILES
DIMENSIONS

PLANS

	RECTANGULAR		SQUARE	HEXAGONAL
DEPTHS	1 1/4", 1 1/2", 2", 2 1/2", 3"	1 1/4", 1 1/2",	1 1/2", 2"	1 1/4", 1 1/2", 2"
WIDTHS	8"		5"	8"	8 1/2"
LENGTHS	16"		12"	8"	8 1/2"

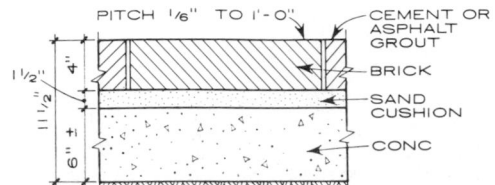

VITRIFIED PAVING BRICK
BRICK DIMENSIONS

DEPTHS	2 1/2", 3", 3 1/2", 4"
WIDTHS	3 1/2", 4"
LENGTHS	8 1/2"

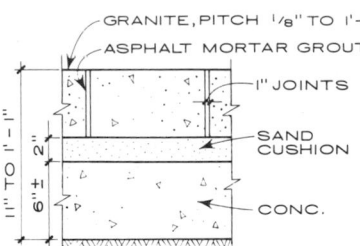

NOTE: If on earth use earth joints.

RUBBLE PAVEMENT STONE BLOCK

BLOCK DIMENSIONS

DEPTHS	3" TO 5"
WIDTHS	3" TO 5"
LENGTHS	4" TO 12"

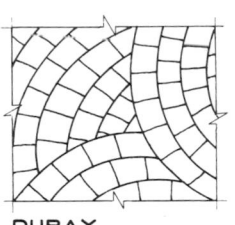

DURAX BLOCKS

Roughly cubed 2 3/4" to 3 1/2" granite blocks on edge. Usually laid in concentric circles with 1/2" joints.

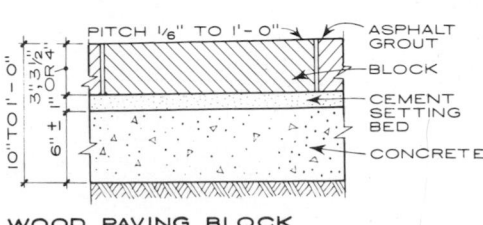

WOOD PAVING BLOCK
BLOCK DIMENSIONS

DEPTHS	3" Light Traffic
	3 1/2" Medium Traffic
	4" Heavy Traffic
WIDTHS	3 1/2" To 4"
LENGTHS	5" To 10", 8" Average

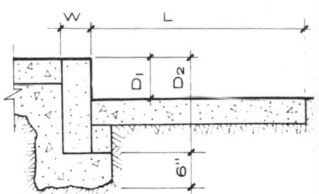

GRANITE CURBS

L	D	D	W
	4" To	16,	4",
3'- 0"	7"	18	5"
	4" To	18,	6",
6'- 0"	7"	20	7"

* Nominal, may vary 1" ±.
End joints usually set in mortar.

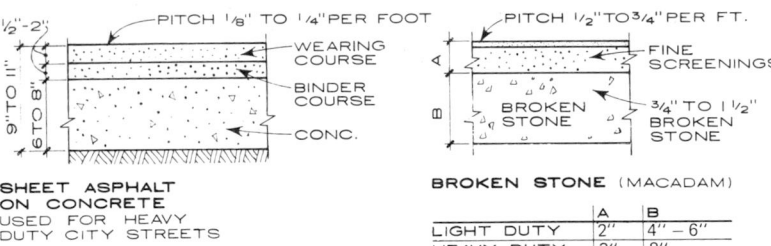

SHEET ASPHALT ON CONCRETE USED FOR HEAVY DUTY CITY STREETS

BROKEN STONE (MACADAM)

	A	B
LIGHT DUTY	2"	4" – 6"
HEAVY DUTY	3"	8"

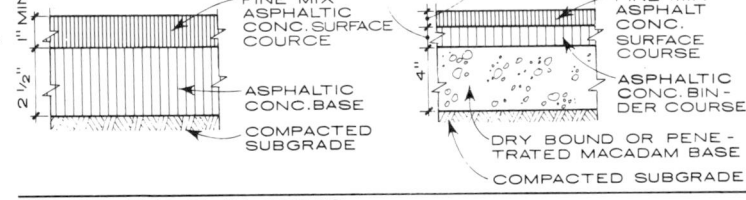

WALKS AND PLAY AREAS

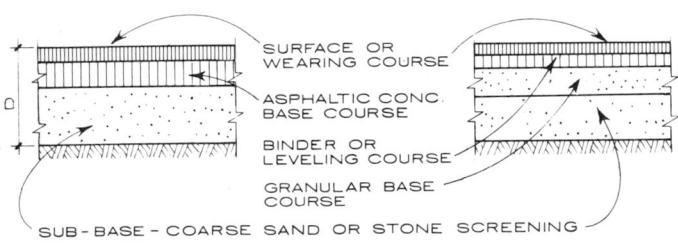

FULL DEPTH ASPHALTIC CONCRETE

COMBINATION – ASPHALTIC CONCRETE AND GRANULAR BASE COURSE

D = 1/2 TO 1/3 AVERAGE ANNUAL FROST PENETRATION

NOTE :

1. Excellent subgrade soils unaffected by moisture of frost include well-graded clean sharp sands and gravels. Good subgrade soils retain a substantial amount of load supporting capacity when wet. They include clean sands and sand gravels and soils free of detrimental amounts of plastic materials.

2. Medium subgrade soils (loams, silty sands and sand-gravels containing moderate amounts of clay and fine silts) retain a moderate degree of firmness under adverse moisture conditions.

3. Poor subgrade soils (those having appreciable amounts of clay and fine silt which becomes soft and plastic when wet and coarser silts and sandy loam) are frost susceptible.

B. J. Baldwin; Giffels & Rossetti, Inc.; Detroit, Michigan

PAVEMENT THICKNESS FOR LOCAL RESIDENTAL STREETS PARKING LOTS & DRIVEWAYS FOR PASSENGER CARS

SUBGRADE	FULL DEPTH ASPHALTIC CONCRETE		COMBINATION–ASPHALTIC CONC. & GRANULAR BASE		
	Surface Course (Min.)	Base Course	Asphaltic Concrete		Granular Base Course
GOOD TO EXCELLENT	1"	2 1/2"	Surface Course (min.)	Base Course	
MEDIUM	1"	3 1/2"	1"	2"	3"
POOR	1"	5"	1"	2"	6" (See Note //4)

PAVEMENT THICKNESS FOR FEEDER STREETS, PARKING LOTS & DRIVEWAYS FOR TRUCKS

SUBGRADE	FULL DEPTH ASPHALTIC CONCRETE		COMBINATION–ASPHALTIC CONC. & GRANULAR BASE		
	Surface Course (Min.)	Base Course	Asphaltic Concrete		Granular Base Course
GOOD TO EXCELLENT	1 1/2"	3 1/2"	Surface Course (min.)	Base Course	
MEDIUM	1 1/2"	5 1/2"	1 1/2"	3"	5"
POOR	1 1/2"	7 1/2"	1 1/2"	3"	9" (See Note //4)

4. On poor subgrade place 2 inches of coarse sand or stone screenings between subgrade and base to prevent intrusion of fine subgrade material into the base course.

5. Asphaltic pavements are particularly susceptible to failure if surface or subsurface drainage is inadequate. Slope surfaces at least 1/8" per foot toward properly sized inlets or ditches. Poor and medium subgrades often require underdrains properly spaced with carefully graded aggregrate filters.

6. Thicknesses and pavement designs other than those shown in the tables may be required in some areas. Good asphaltic pavement design considers material availability, stability of mix designs, quality of aggregates, weights and frequency of wheel loads, temperatures and other factors.

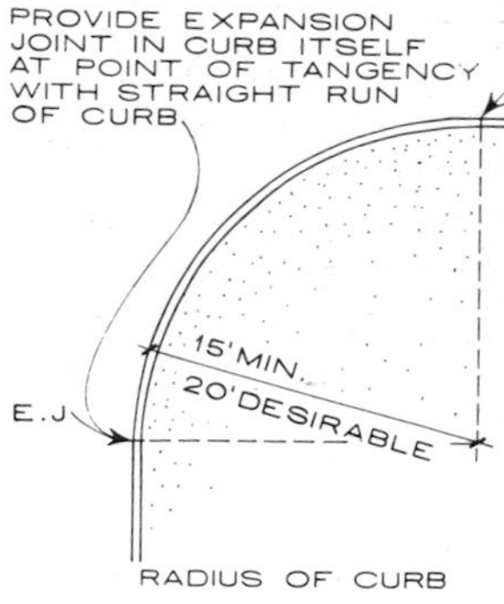

PROVIDE EXPANSION
JOINT IN CURB ITSELF
AT POINT OF TANGENCY
WITH STRAIGHT RUN
OF CURB

EXPANSION JOINT WHERE
SIDEWALK ABUTS CURB

6'-0" 6'-0" 6'-0" (MAXIMUM)

SCORED JOINTS
EXPANSION JOINT EVERY 30'-0"
JOINT IN CENTER OF WALK IF
OVER 15'-0" WIDE

15' MIN.
20' DESIRABLE

E.J.

RADIUS OF CURB

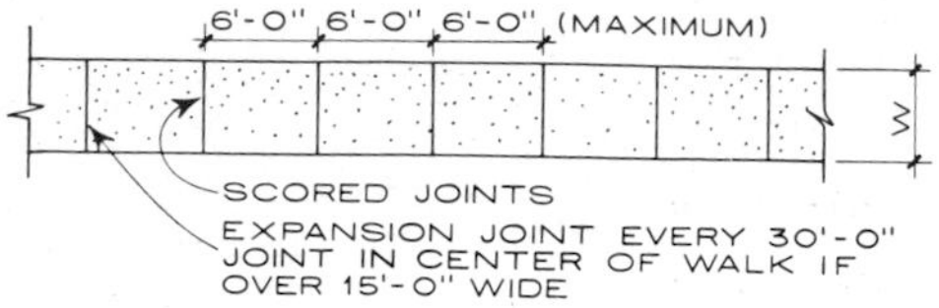

SIDEWALKS
SCALE : 1" = 20'-0"

SIDEWALK TYPE	W
MAIN SIDEWALK	5'-0" MIN.
SECONDARY SIDEWALK	4'-0" MIN.
ONE FAMILY HOUSE WALK	3'-0" MIN.
TWO FAMILY HOUSE WALK	4'-0" MIN.

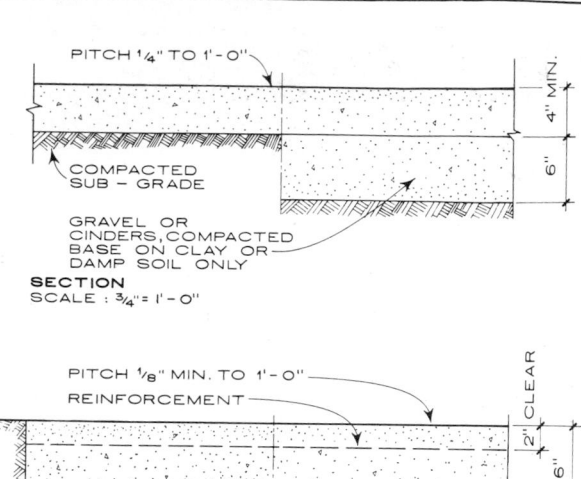

PITCH 1/4" TO 1'-0"
4" MIN.
6"
COMPACTED
SUB-GRADE
GRAVEL OR
CINDERS, COMPACTED
BASE ON CLAY OR
DAMP SOIL ONLY

SECTION
SCALE : 3/4" = 1'-0"

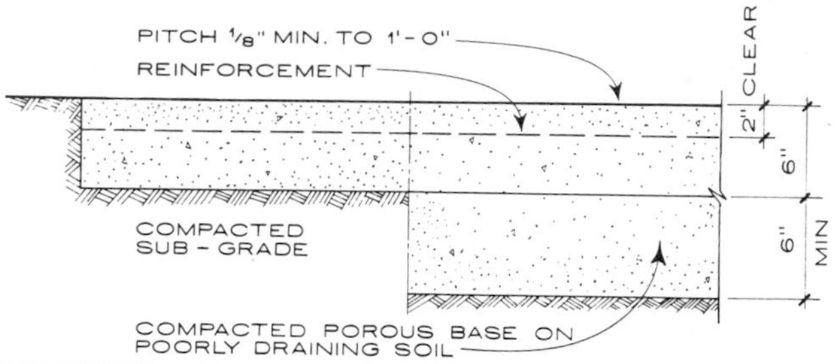

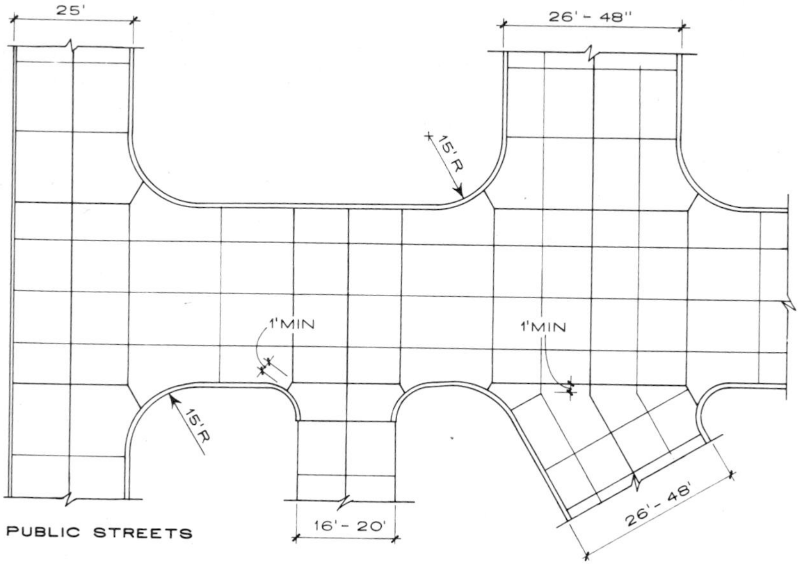

25'

26'-48'

15' R

1' MIN

1' MIN

15' R

16'-20'

26'-48'

PUBLIC STREETS

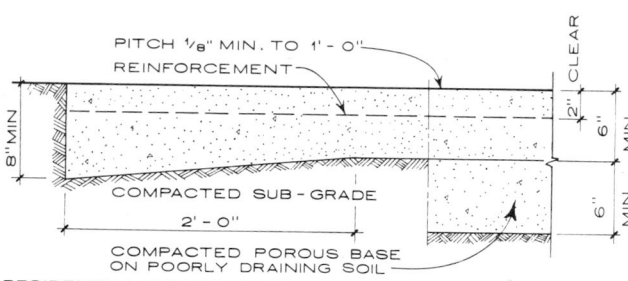

PITCH 1/8" MIN. TO 1'-0"
REINFORCEMENT
2" CLEAR
6"
COMPACTED
SUB-GRADE
6" MIN
COMPACTED POROUS BASE ON
POORLY DRAINING SOIL

RESIDENTIAL ROADS & DRIVEWAYS - TYPE A

PITCH 1/8" MIN. TO 1'-0"
REINFORCEMENT
2" CLEAR
6"
8" MIN
COMPACTED SUB-GRADE
2'-0"
6" MIN
COMPACTED POROUS BASE
ON POORLY DRAINING SOIL

RESIDENTIAL ROADS & DRIVEWAYS - TYPE B

ROAD SECTIONS SCALE 3/4" = 1'-0"

NOTE:
Design of roads depends on actual conditions of use.

25'

312' R

38' R

25'

38' R

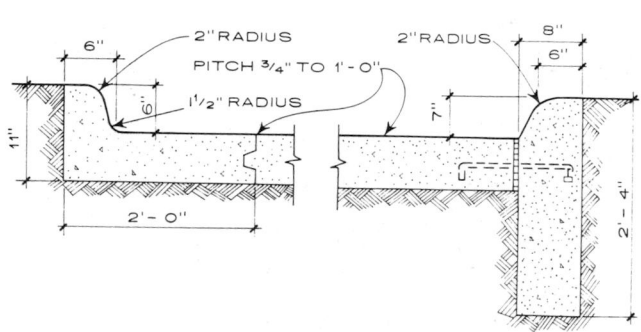

8" TO 11"   5" TO 8"
PITCH 1/8" MIN TO 1'-0"
REINFORCEMENT
R = 17 1/2"
17 1/2"
12"
5"
5" OR 6"

**FOR DRIVEWAYS AND MOUNTABLE SHOULDERS
INTEGRAL CURB**

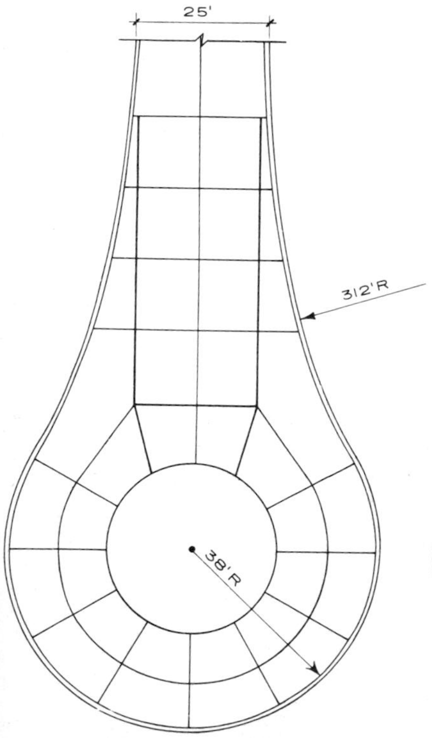

6"   2" RADIUS   2" RADIUS   8"
PITCH 3/4" TO 1'-0"   6"
1 1/2" RADIUS
11"   6"   7"
2'-0"   2'-4"

COMBINATION CURB & GUTTER

CURB SECTIONS SCALE 1/2" = 1'-0"

CUL DE SAC - OPEN CENTER 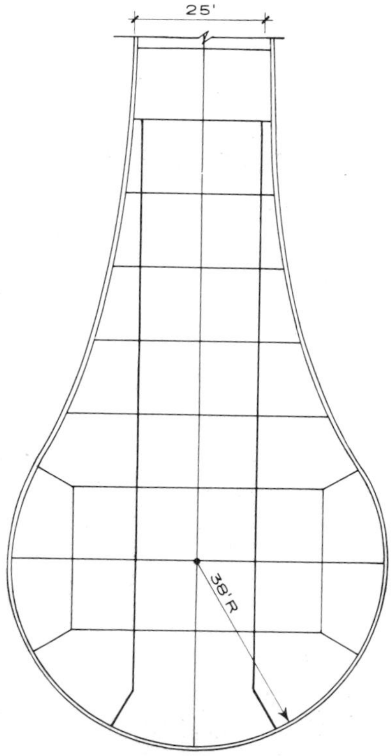   **FULLY PAVED**

PAVEMENT JOINT PLANS
NOTE:
Provide expansion joints where conc. pavement abuts other masonry structures.

NOTE:
Sidewalk perpendicular to (and terminating at) curb. Provide premoulded expansion joint.

B. J. Baldwin; Giffels & Rossetti, Inc.; Detroit, Michigan

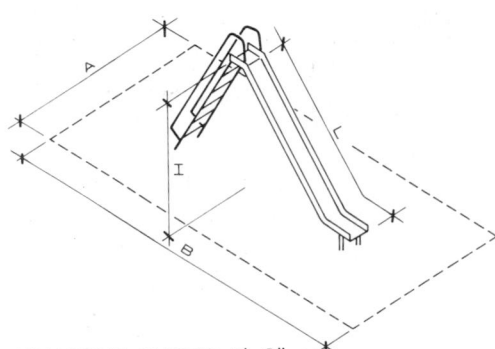

ADJACENT SLIDES: 7'-6"
(CHUTES C.TO C.) OTHERS 10' O.C.

SLIDES

H	L	NURSERY		STRAIGHT		RACER	
		A	B	A	B	A	B
5	10	8	20				
6	12	8	22				
7	14	8	24				
8	16			12	30	20	30
10	20			12	35	20	35
12	24			15	40	25	40
13½	30			15	45	25	45

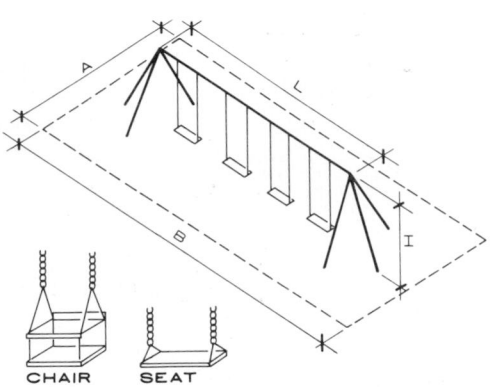

CHAIR   SEAT

SWINGS

NO SWINGS	CHAIR TYPE			SEAT TYPE						
	L	A	B	L	A	B	A	B	A	B
2	8	17	24	9	17	25	21	25	25	25
3	10	17	26	15	17	31	21	31	25	31
4	16	17	32	18	17	34	21	34	25	34
6	20,24	17	38	27,30	17	46	21	46	25	46
8				36	17	52	21	52	25	52
9				45	17	61	21	61	25	61
Height	8'			8',10',12'	8'		10'		12'	

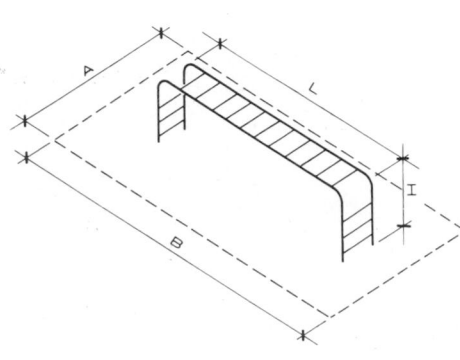

HORIZONTAL LADDER

HEIGHT	LENGTH	A	B
6	12	8	25
7½	16	8	30

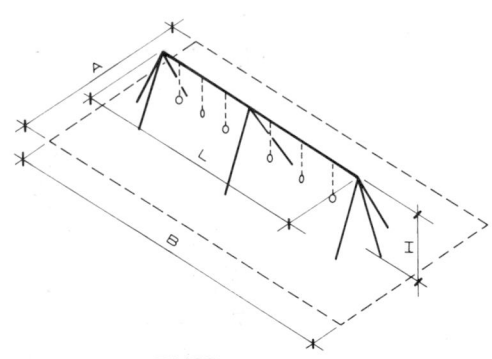

TRAVELING RINGS

HEIGHT	LENGTH	A	B
10	36	20	60
12	36	20	60
14	40	20	64

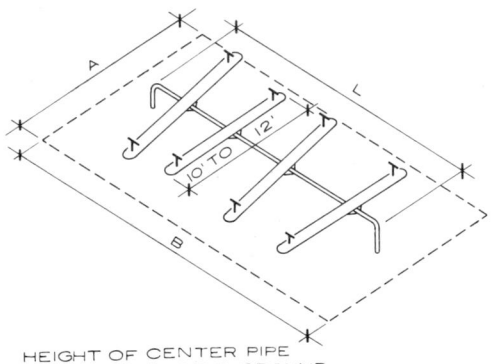

HEIGHT OF CENTER PIPE
1'-0" TO 3'-0" ABOVE GROUND

SEE - SAWS

BOARDS	1	2	3	4	6
L	3	6	9	12	18
A	20	20	20	20	20
B	5	10	15	20	25

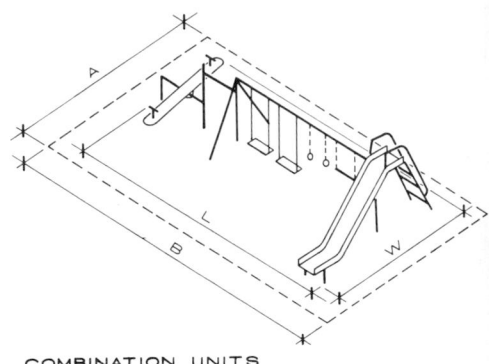

COMBINATION UNITS
ENCLOSURE LIMITS :
A = W + 12'-0"
B = L + 6'-0"
Types and no. of units is variable.

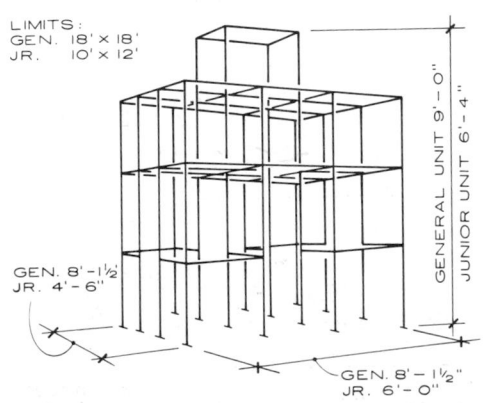

LIMITS :
GEN. 18' x 18'
JR. 10' x 12'

GENERAL UNIT 9'-0"
JUNIOR UNIT 6'-4"

GEN. 8'-1½
JR. 4'-6"

GEN. 8'-1½"
JR. 6'-0"

N.Y.C. HOUSING AUTH. STANDARD
CLIMBING APPARATUS

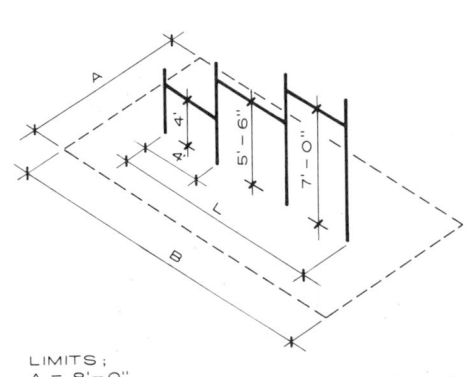

LIMITS :
A = 8'-0"
B = L +6'-0"

HORIZONTAL BARS

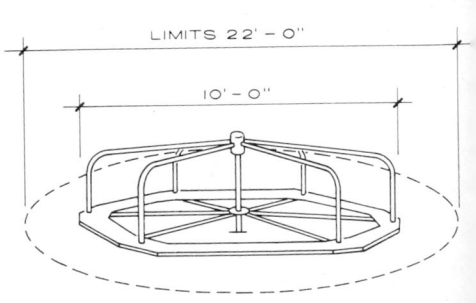

LIMITS 22'-0"
10'-0"

10 FT. DIAMETER IS CONSIDERED STAND-
ARD. OTHER DIAMETERS = 12',14'& 16'
LIMITS 24',26'& 28' DIA.

MERRY - GO - ROUND

Vincent F. Nauseda; Sasaki, Dawson, DeMay Associates, Inc.; Watertown, Massachusetts

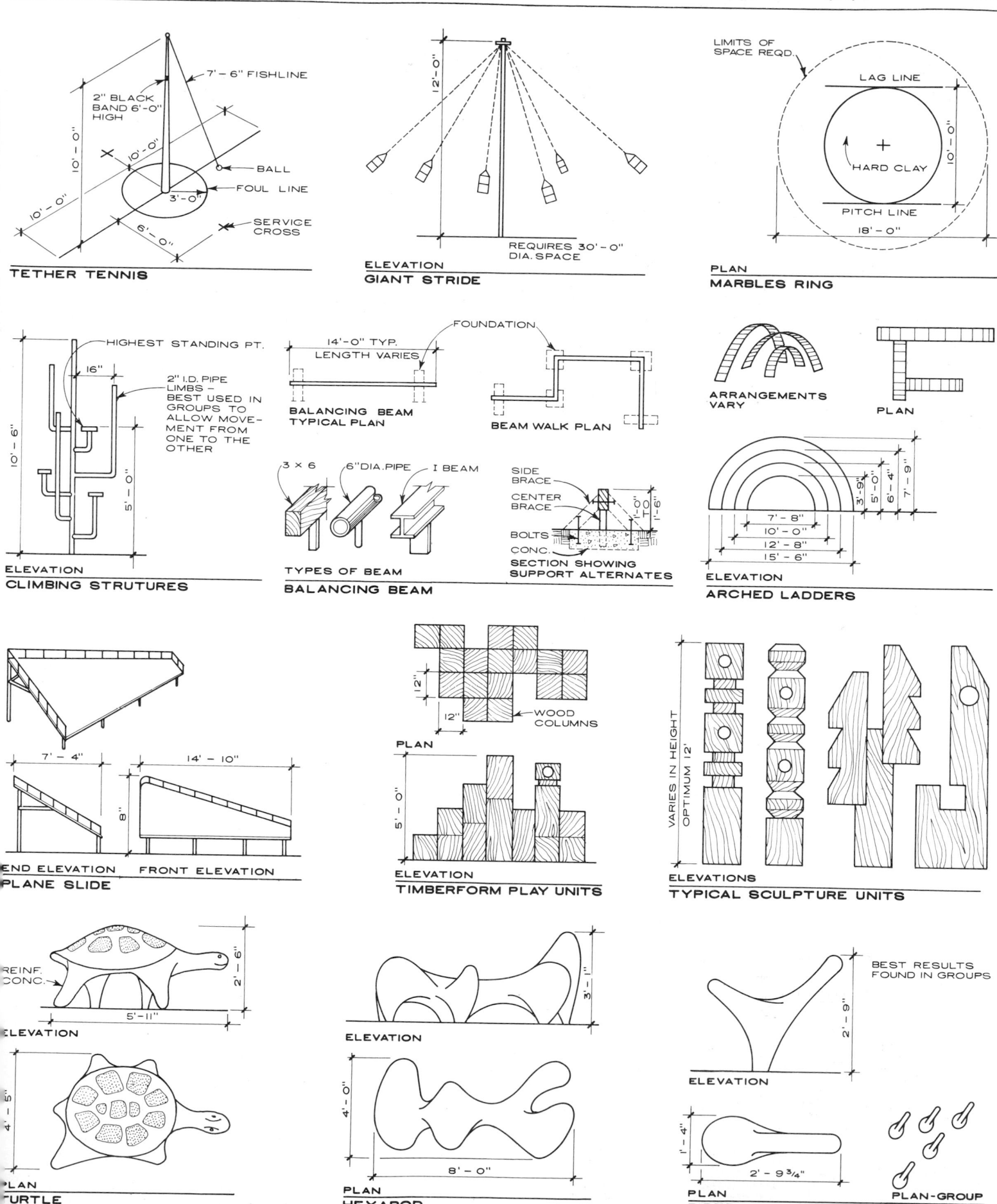

TETHER TENNIS
- 7'-6" FISHLINE
- 2" BLACK BAND 6'-0" HIGH
- 10'-0"
- 10'-0"
- BALL
- FOUL LINE
- 3'-0"
- 6'-0"
- SERVICE CROSS

ELEVATION
GIANT STRIDE
- 12'-0"
- REQUIRES 30'-0" DIA. SPACE

PLAN
MARBLES RING
- LIMITS OF SPACE REQD.
- LAG LINE
- 10'-0"
- HARD CLAY
- PITCH LINE
- 18'-0"

ELEVATION
CLIMBING STRUTURES
- HIGHEST STANDING PT.
- 16"
- 2" I.D. PIPE LIMBS – BEST USED IN GROUPS TO ALLOW MOVEMENT FROM ONE TO THE OTHER
- 10'-6"
- 5'-0"

BALANCING BEAM TYPICAL PLAN
- 14'-0" TYP. LENGTH VARIES
- FOUNDATION

BEAM WALK PLAN

TYPES OF BEAM
- 3 × 6
- 6" DIA. PIPE
- I BEAM

BALANCING BEAM
- SIDE BRACE
- CENTER BRACE
- BOLTS
- CONC.
- 1'-0"
- 1'-6"

SECTION SHOWING SUPPORT ALTERNATES

ARRANGEMENTS VARY
PLAN

ELEVATION
ARCHED LADDERS
- 3'-9"
- 5'-0"
- 6'-4"
- 7'-9"
- 7'-8"
- 10'-0"
- 12'-8"
- 15'-6"

END ELEVATION
FRONT ELEVATION
PLANE SLIDE
- 7'-4"
- 14'-10"
- 8"

PLAN
TIMBERFORM PLAY UNITS
- 12"
- 12"
- WOOD COLUMNS
- 5'-0"

ELEVATION

ELEVATIONS
TYPICAL SCULPTURE UNITS
- VARIES IN HEIGHT OPTIMUM 12'

TURTLE
PLAY ANIMALS
- REINF. CONC.
- 2'-6"
- 5'-11"
- 4'-5"
- ELEVATION
- PLAN

HEXAPOD
- 3'-1"
- 4'-0"
- 8'-0"
- ELEVATION
- PLAN

RIDER
- BEST RESULTS FOUND IN GROUPS
- 2'-9"
- 1'-4"
- 2'-9¾"
- ELEVATION
- PLAN
- PLAN-GROUP

Vincent F. Nauseda; Sasaki, Dawson, DeMay Associates, Inc.; Watertown, Massachusetts

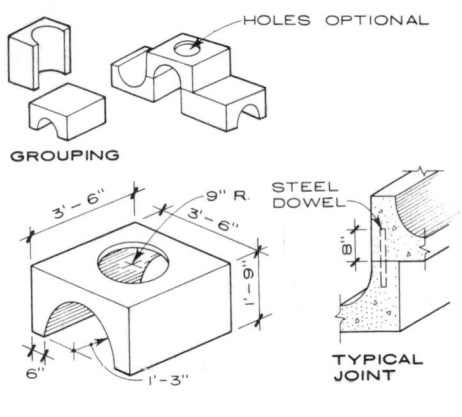

GROUPING

HOLES OPTIONAL

STEEL DOWEL

9" R.

3' - 6"

3' - 6"

6"

1' - 3"

TYPICAL JOINT

TYPICAL UNIT

CONCRETE CLIMBERS

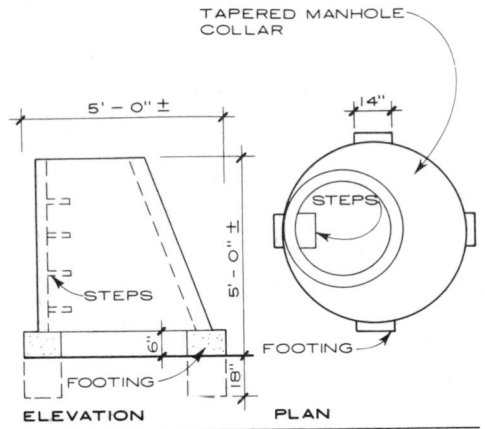

TAPERED MANHOLE COLLAR

5' - 0" ±

STEPS

FOOTING

14"

STEPS

FOOTING

ELEVATION   **PLAN**

FOX HOLE

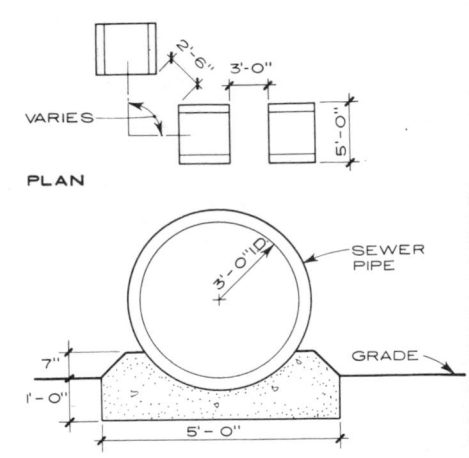

VARIES

2'-6"   3'-0"

5'-0"

PLAN

SEWER PIPE

3'-0"⌀

7"

1'-0"

GRADE

5' - 0"

SECTION

PIPE TUNNEL

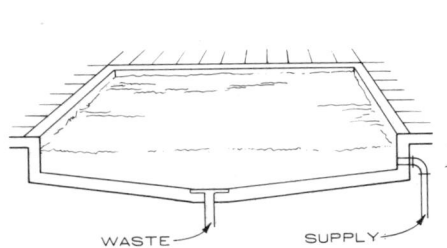

WASTE   SUPPLY

FILLED POOL

SCULPTURAL PLAY POOL

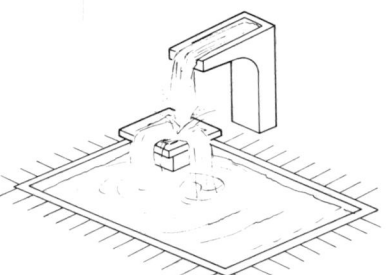

SCULPTURAL PLAY POOL

EDGE OF BOX (CONC., WOOD, BRICK)

SAND DEPTH VARIES-8" DESIRABLE MIN.

POROUS CONC. (OPTIONAL)

CRUSHED STONE OR GRAVEL

COMPACT EARTH

SECTION (SIZE & SHAPES VARY)

SANDBOX (GENERAL)

NOTES:

A. Filled & Play Pools requirements:
   1. maximum depth of 24"
   2. filtered and chlorinated water from recirculating system
   3. maximum turn-over cycle every 4 hrs. by use of recirculating system.
B. Spray Pool (general)
   No water is allowed to stand but is drained away without the use of a recirculating system.
Standards of sanitation in water treatment, circulation, etc., should be equal to those for swimming pools.

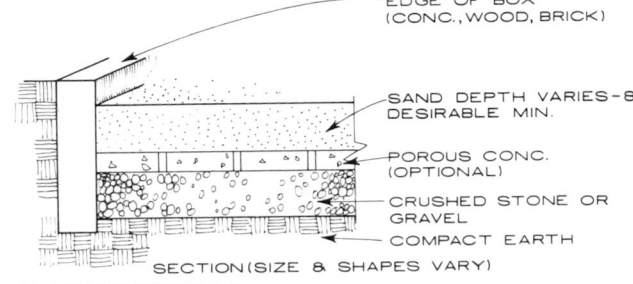

SCUPPER

WATER LEVEL

POROUS CONC.

SAND

DRAIN

CRUSHED STONE

CONTAINER

WATER SUPPLY & VALVE

BASE DRAIN & VALVE

DIAGRAMATIC SECTION

WATER WASHED SANDBOX

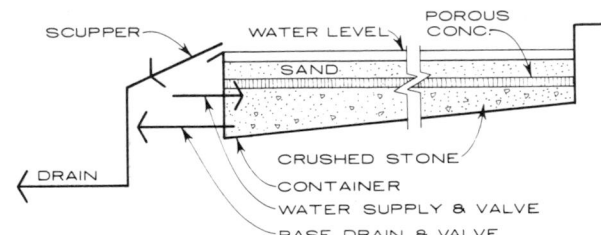

SPRAY HEAD

SUPPLY

WASTE

SPRAY POOL

WADING POOLS

SANDBOXES

Water is forced up through the sand, soaking it and causing impurities to be floated away along the top to the scupper and drain.

UNUSABLE ARTIFACTS

Many items unusual to the standard playground equipment line have a natural appeal to children. Items such as old cars, boats, carts, trees, logs, etc. When used discreetly and properly conditioned become a new source of playground equipment.

PEEL AWAY BARK AND SAND ROUGH EDGES

TRACTOR

1. remove all glass
2. weld all moving parts except crank and steering
3. strip all sharp objects
4. paint and secure to foundation

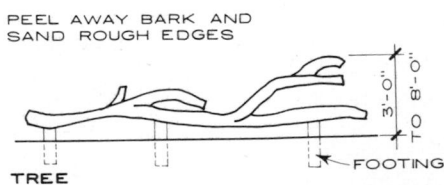

3'-0" TO 8'-0"

TREE

FOOTINGS

ANCHOR SECURELY, SAND AND PAINT.

WOOD ANCHOR

WOODEN BOAT

UNUSABLE ARTIFACTS AS STATIONARY EQUIPMENT

GENERAL PLANNING INFORMATION

EQUIPMENT	UNIT OF AREA IN SQ. FT	CAPACITY IN CHILDREN
SLIDE	450	4 — 6
HORIZONTAL LADDER	375	6 — 8
TRAVELING RINGS	625	4 — 6
GIANT STRIDE	1225	4 — 6
SMALL JUNGLE GYM	180	8 — 10
LOW SWING	150	1
HIGH SWING	250	1
SEE SAW	100	2
MEDIUM JUNGLE GYM	500	15 — 20
TETHER TENNIS	400	2
WADING POOL	3000	35 — 40
SAND BOY	300	12 — 15

Vincent F. Nauseda; Sasaki, Dawson, DeMay Associates, Inc.; Watertown, Massachusetts

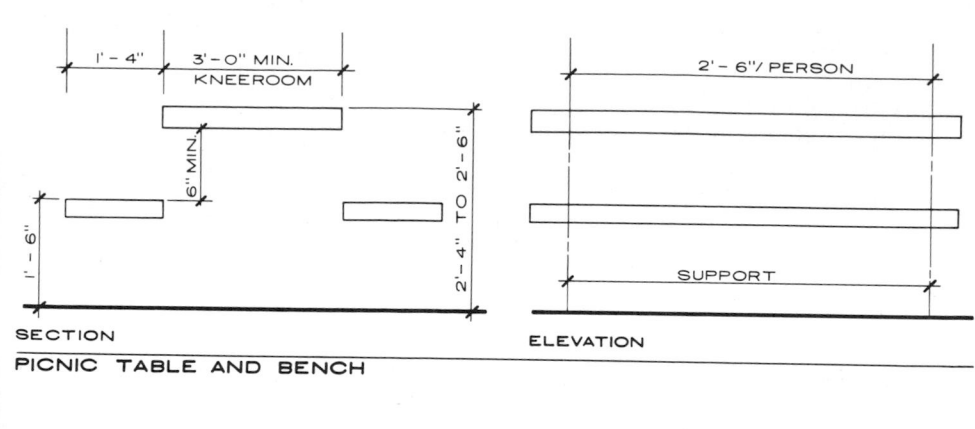

PICNIC TABLE AND BENCH

SECTION | ELEVATION

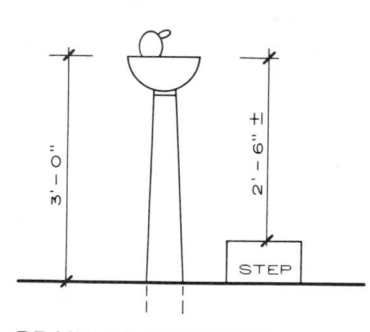

DRINKING FOUNTAIN

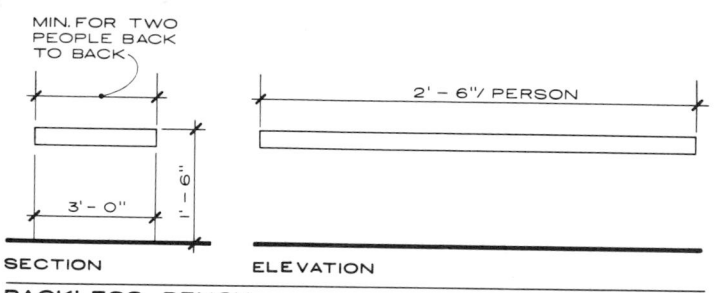

BACKLESS BENCH

SECTION | ELEVATION

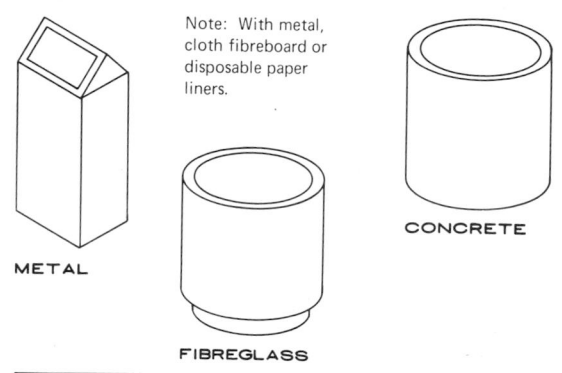

Note: With metal, cloth fibreboard or disposable paper liners.

METAL | FIBREGLASS | CONCRETE

TRASH CONTAINERS

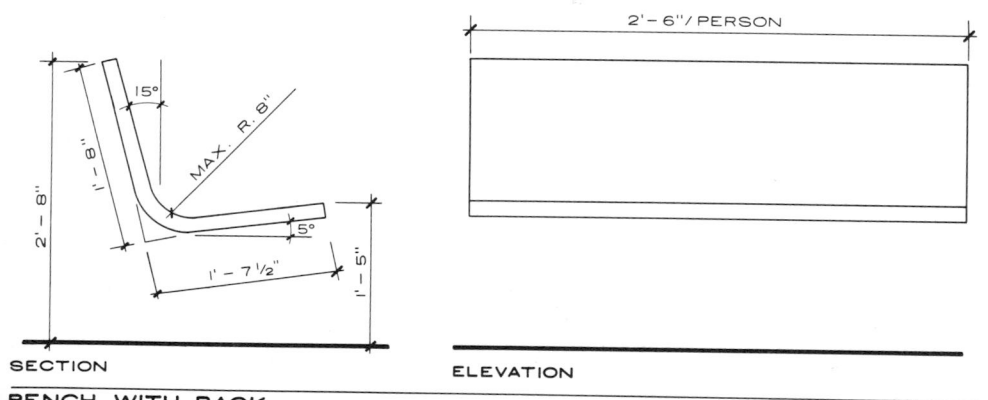

BENCH WITH BACK

SECTION | ELEVATION

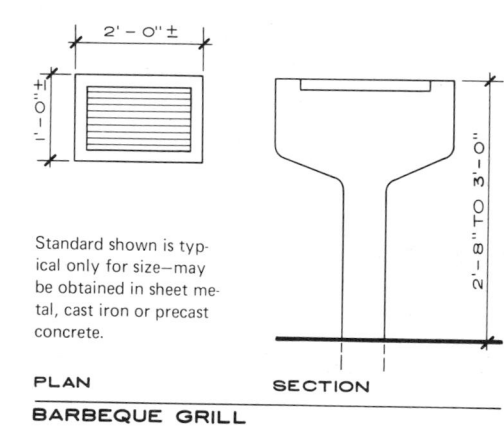

Standard shown is typical only for size—may be obtained in sheet metal, cast iron or precast concrete.

PLAN | SECTION

BARBEQUE GRILL

METAL | CUT STONE OR CONC. | SPLIT STONE | WOOD

BOLLARDS

REQUIREMENTS FOR A TYPICAL INTENSIVE USE AREA SERVING 60-80 PEOPLE IN ONE ACRE

ITEM	NO./ACRE
PICNIC TABLES	15 - 20
BARBEQUE GRILLS	5 - 7
TRASH CONTAINERS	5 - 7

NOTE: Drinking fountains serve 300' – 600' radius.

Richard H. Rogers; Sasaki, Dawson, DeMay Associates, Inc.; Watertown, Massachusetts

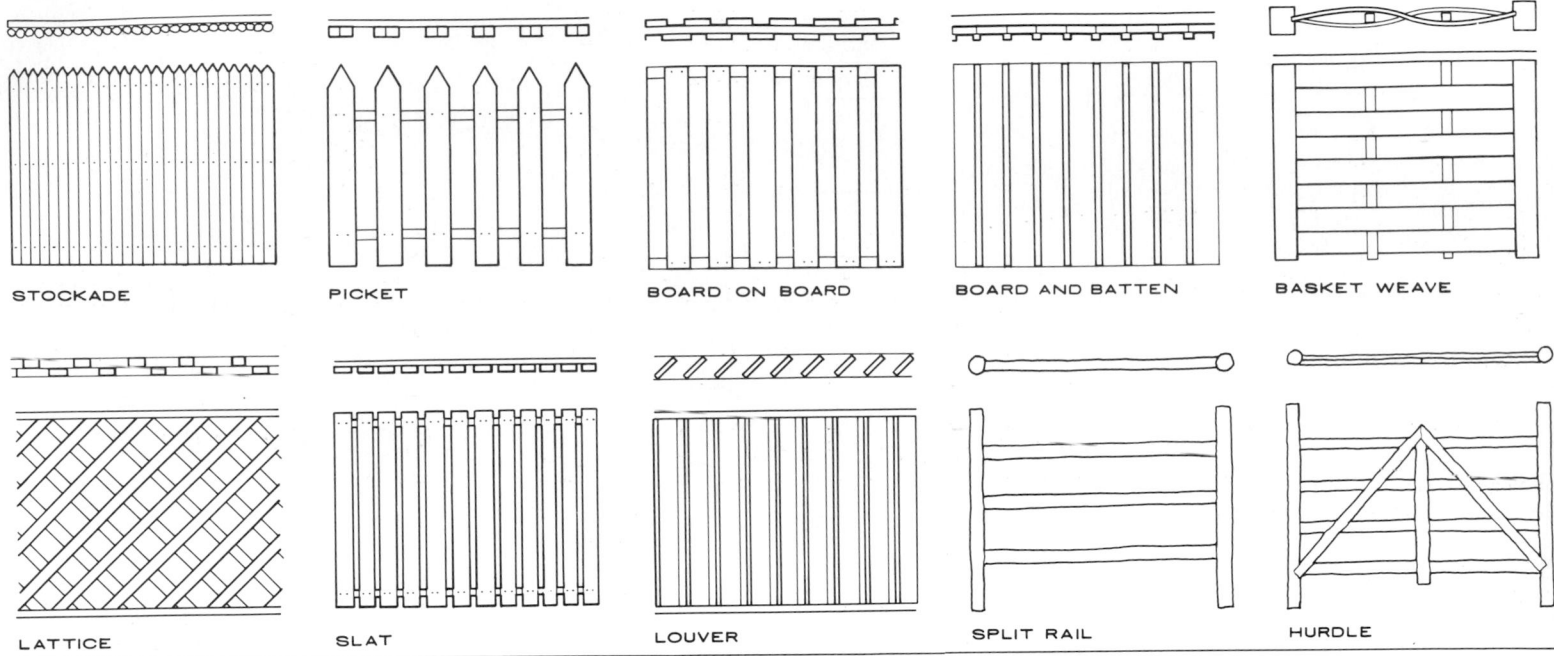

STOCKADE   PICKET   BOARD ON BOARD   BOARD AND BATTEN   BASKET WEAVE

LATTICE   SLAT   LOUVER   SPLIT RAIL   HURDLE

COMMON FENCE TYPES

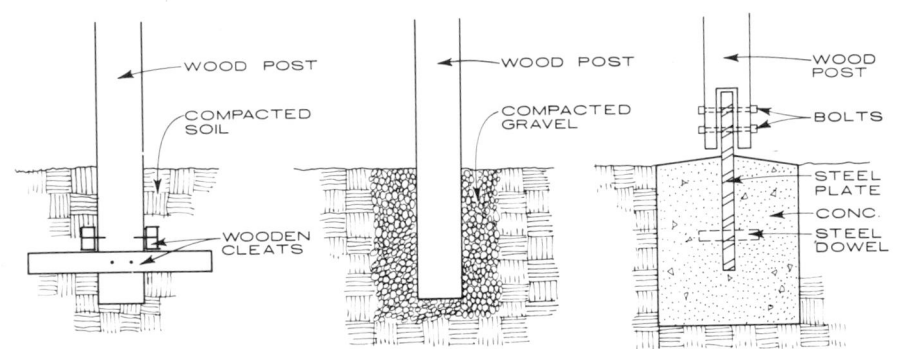

METHODS OF SETTING WOODEN POSTS

WOOD POST — COMPACTED SOIL — WOODEN CLEATS

WOOD POST — COMPACTED GRAVEL

WOOD POST — BOLTS — STEEL PLATE — CONC. — STEEL DOWEL

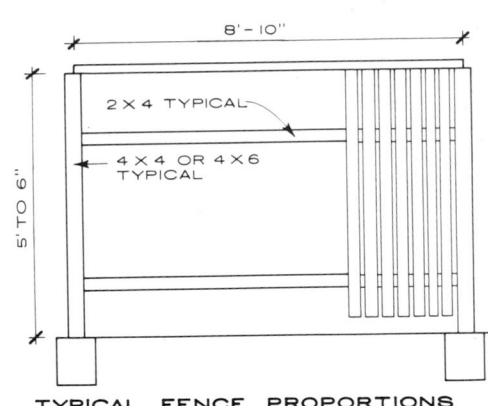

TYPICAL FENCE PROPORTIONS

8'–10"
2 X 4 TYPICAL
4 X 4 OR 4 X 6 TYPICAL
5' TO 6"

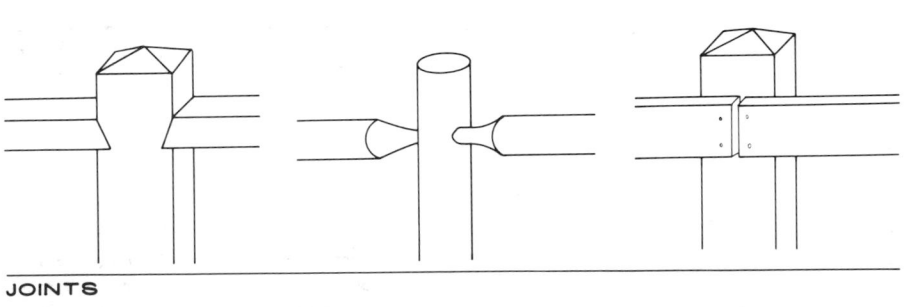

JOINTS

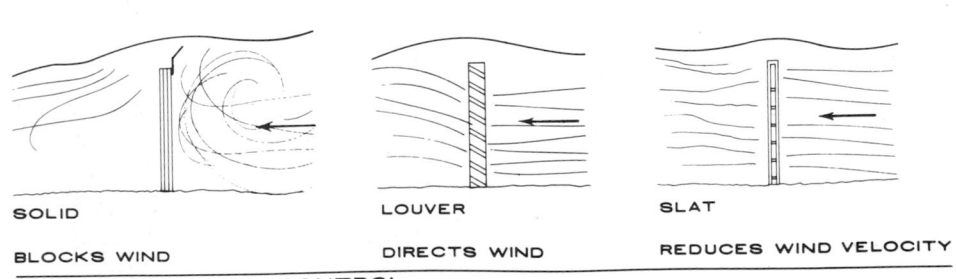

SOLID — BLOCKS WIND

LOUVER — DIRECTS WIND

SLAT — REDUCES WIND VELOCITY

FENCES FOR WIND CONTROL

POST ONE SIZE LARGER THAN FENCE

TENSION ALTERNATE

COMPRESSION ALTERNATE

TYPICAL GATE

Martina Mesmer; Sasaki, Dawson, DeMay Associates, Inc.; Watertown, Massachusetts

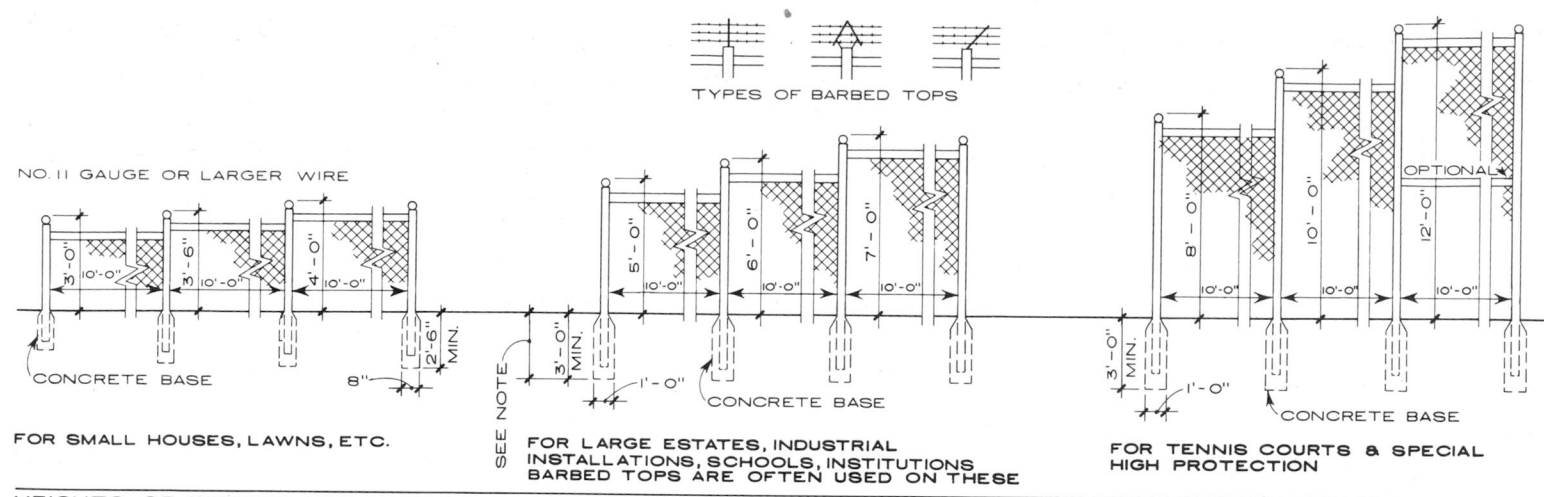

TYPES OF BARBED TOPS

NO. 11 GAUGE OR LARGER WIRE

CONCRETE BASE   8"

FOR SMALL HOUSES, LAWNS, ETC.

SEE NOTE

CONCRETE BASE

FOR LARGE ESTATES, INDUSTRIAL
INSTALLATIONS, SCHOOLS, INSTITUTIONS
BARBED TOPS ARE OFTEN USED ON THESE

OPTIONAL

CONCRETE BASE

FOR TENNIS COURTS & SPECIAL
HIGH PROTECTION

HEIGHTS OF FENCES FOR VARIOUS USES

See note at middle right for depth of concrete bases.

SCALE : 1/8" = 1'-0"

MATERIALS: (Sizes given are not standard but represent the average sizes used)

WIRE GUAGE:	Usually No. 11 or No. 9 W & M. For specially rugged use use No. 6. For tennis courts usually No. 11.
WIRE MESH:	Usually 2". For tennis courts usually 1 5/8" or 1 3/4" of chain link steel hot dip galvanized after weaving. Top and bottom salvage may be barbed or knuckled.
CORNER & END POSTS:	For lawn fences usually 2" O.D. For estate fences 2" for low and 2 1/2" for medium and 3" O.D. for heavy or high. For tennis courts 3" O.D.
LINE OR INTER- MEDIATE POSTS:	For lawn 1 3/8" or 2" O.D. round. For estate etc. 2", 2 1/4", 2 1/2" H or I sections. For tennis courts 2 1/2" round O.D. or 2 1/4" H or I sections.
GATE POSTS:	The same or next size larger than the corner posts. Footings for gate posts 3'—6" deep.
TOP RAILS:	1 5/8" O.D. except some lawn fence may be 1 3/8" O.D.
MIDDLE RAILS:	On 12'—0" fence same as top rail.
GATES:	Single or double any width desired.
POST SPACING:	Line posts 10'—0" O.C., 8'—0" O.C. may be used on heavy construction.

O.D. = Outside Diameter

NOTE:

Bottom of concrete base to be set
below frost line. (see local code).
Concrete base sizes shown are
recommended minimum and should
be redesigned for conditions where
soil is poor.

A.S.A. SCHEDULE 40 PIPE SIZES	SWING GATE OPENINGS	
	SINGLE GATE	DOUBLE GATE
2 1/2"	to 6'—0"	up to 12'—0"
3 1/2"	over 6' to 18'	over 12' to 26'
6"	over 13' to 18'	over 26' to 36'
8"	over 18' to 32'	over 36' to 64'

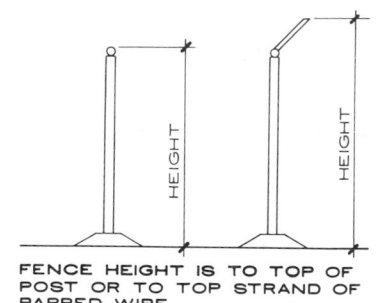

FENCE HEIGHT IS TO TOP OF
POST OR TO TOP STRAND OF
BARBED WIRE

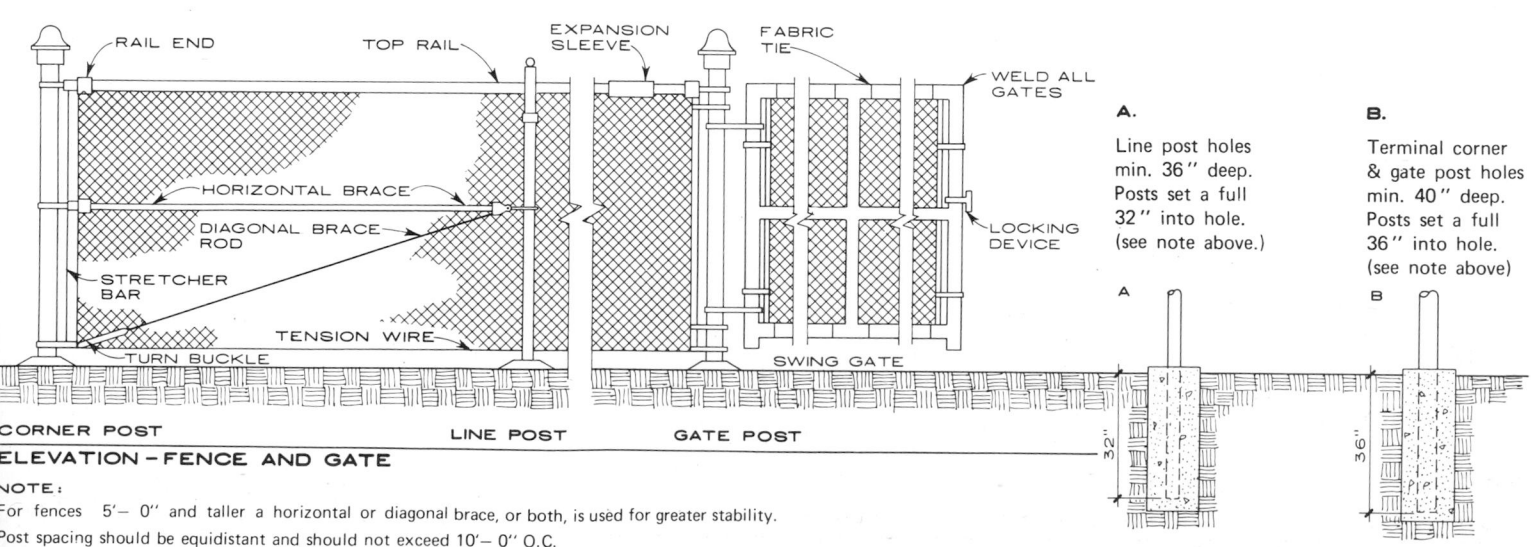

RAIL END   TOP RAIL   EXPANSION SLEEVE   FABRIC TIE

WELD ALL GATES

HORIZONTAL BRACE

DIAGONAL BRACE ROD

STRETCHER BAR

TENSION WIRE

TURN BUCKLE

LOCKING DEVICE

CORNER POST   LINE POST   GATE POST   SWING GATE

A.

Line post holes
min. 36" deep.
Posts set a full
32" into hole.
(see note above.)

B.

Terminal corner
& gate post holes
min. 40" deep.
Posts set a full
36" into hole.
(see note above)

A   B

32"   36"

ELEVATION — FENCE AND GATE

NOTE:

For fences 5'—0" and taller a horizontal or diagonal brace, or both, is used for greater stability.

Post spacing should be equidistant and should not exceed 10'—0" O.C.

Charles Driesen; Ewing Cole Erdman & Eubank; Philadelphia, Pennsylvania

CONCRETE CONSTRUCTION

TABLE OF ASTM STANDARD REINFORCING BAR SIZES

BAR SIZE DESIG-NATION	WEIGHT POUNDS PER FOOT	NOM. DIMENSIONS – ROUND SECT. DIAMETER (INCHES)	CROSS SECT. AREA SQ.IN.	PERIMETER (INCHES)
# 3	.376	.375	.11	1.178
# 4	.668	.500	.20	1.571
# 5	1.043	.625	.31	1.963
# 6	1.502	.750	.44	2.356
# 7	2.044	.875	.60	2.749
# 8	2.670	1.000	.79	3.142
# 9	3.400	1.128	1.00	3.544
#10	4,303	1.270	1.27	3.990
#11	5.313	1.410	1.56	4.430
#14	7.650	1.693	2.25	5.320
#18	3.600	2.257	4.00	7.090

NOTE:
Bar sizes #14 and #18 are generally not carried as local warehouse stock items.

CROSS OR DIAGONAL RIBS VARY IN HEIGHT FROM 4 TO 5% OF NOMINAL BAR DIAMETER

CONTINUOUS RIBS

NOMINAL DIAMETER

CROSS SECTION OF REINFORCING BAR

COMMON STYLES OF WELDED WIRE FABRIC – TWO WAY TYPE –

STYLE DESIGNATION	SECTIONAL AREA LONGI-TUDI-AL	TRANS-VERSE	WEIGHT LBS. PER 100 SQ.FT.
2 x 2 – 14/14	.030	.030	21
2 x 2 – 16/16	.018	.018	13
4 x 4 – 4/4	.120	.120	85
4 x 4 – 6/6	.087	.087	62
4 x 4 – 8/8	.062	.062	44
4 x 4 – 10/10	.043	.043	31
6 x 6 – 4/4	.080	.080	58
6 x 6 – 6/6	.058	.058	42
6 x 6 – 8/8	.041	.041	30
6 x 6 – 10/10	.029	.029	21

NOTE:
Style designation — First two numbers indicate longitudinal and tranverse wire spacing in inches and the later two, A.S. & W. wire gauge. The above commonly warehoused styles are furnished in (5) ft. wide by (150) ft. long smooth wire rolls; however 11 ga. fabric is furnished galvanized only.

Economic use of welded wire fabric in sheets or rolls in lieu of reinforcing varies from three tons for light weight fabric to fifteen tons for heavy weight fabric. On large jobs fabric can be made with deformed or galvanized wire, and with varying wire size and spacing.

NOTE
REBAR = REINFORCING BAR

STANDARD STEEL WIRE SIZES AND GAUGES

DIAMETER INCHES	A.S. & W. GAUGE	DIAMETER INCHES	AREA SQ. IN.	POUNDS PER FOOT
1/2	—	.5000	.19635	.6668
	7/0	.4900	.18857	.6404
	6/0	.4615	.16728	.5681
	5/0	.4305	.14556	.4943
	4/0	.3938	.12180	.4136
	3/0	.3625	.10321	.3505
	2/0	.3310	.086049	.2922
	0	.3065	.073782	.2506
	1	.2830	.062902	.2136
	2	.2625	.054119	.1838
1/4	—	.2500	.049087	.1667
	3	.2437	.046645	.1584
	4	.2253	.039867	.1354
	5	.2070	.033654	.1143
	6	.1920	.028953	.09832
	7	.1770	.024606	.08356
	8	.1620	.020612	.07000
	9	.1483	.017273	.05866
	10	.1350	.014314	.04861
	11	.1250	.011404	.03873
	12	.1055	.0087417	.02969
	13	.0915	.0065755	.02233
	14	.0800	.0050266	.01707
	15	.0720	.0040715	.01383
	16	.0625	.0030680	.01042

NOTE:
Wire sizes & gauges listed above are readily available in the production of welded wire fabric. #11 ga. wire or lighter is furnished galvanized only in the production of welded wire fabric. Intermediate sizes are available on large jobs.

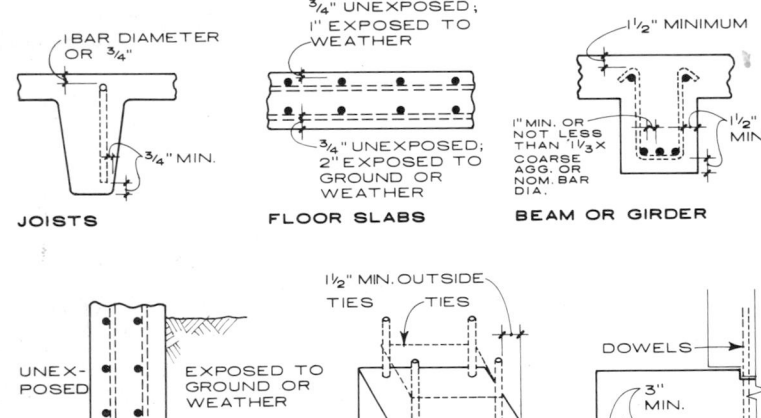

JOISTS

I BAR DIAMETER OR ³/₄"

³/₄" MIN.

FLOOR SLABS

³/₄" UNEXPOSED; 1" EXPOSED TO WEATHER

³/₄" UNEXPOSED; 2" EXPOSED TO GROUND OR WEATHER

BEAM OR GIRDER

1½" MINIMUM

1" MIN. OR NOT LESS THAN 1¹/₃× COARSE AGG. OR NOM. BAR DIA.

1½" MIN.

WALLS

UNEX-POSED

EXPOSED TO GROUND OR WEATHER

³/₄" MIN.

COLUMNS

1½" MIN. OUTSIDE TIES   TIES

1½" MIN. (#5 & SMALLER) 2" MIN. (#6 & LARGER)

FOOTINGS

DOWELS

3" MIN.

PROTECTION FOR REINFORCEMENT

MIN REBAR LAP SPLICING

Fy psi	TENSION LAP IN BAR diameters	COMPRESSION LAP IN BAR diameters
40,000	24	20
50,000	30	20
60,000	36	24
75,000	—	30

Minimum lap (12) inches
Maximum rebar size permitted in lap splice (No. 11)

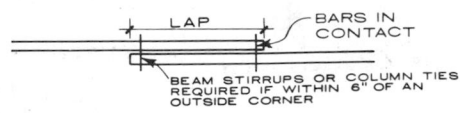

LAP   BARS IN CONTACT

BEAM STIRRUPS OR COLUMN TIES REQUIRED IF WITHIN 6" OF AN OUTSIDE CORNER

STANDARD REBAR HOOK DETAILS

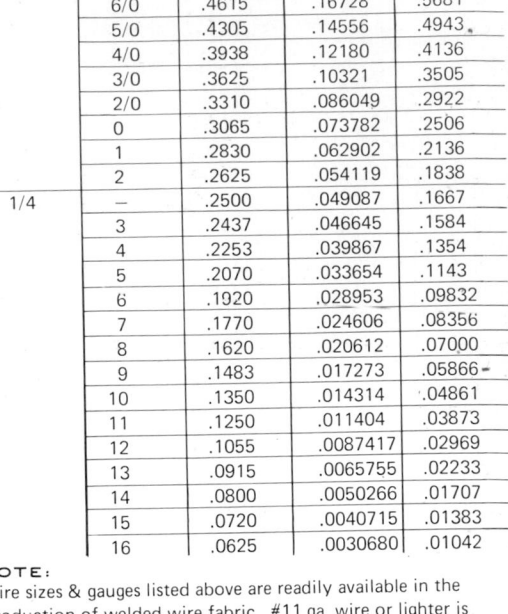

O – DETAILING DIM.
OVERALL BAR DIM.   HOOK

4D OR 2½" MINIMUM

180° HOOK

d = (1) Bar Diameter
D = 6d for No. 3 to No. 8 Bars
D = 8d for No. 9 to No. 11 Bars
J = D + 2d
H = 5d + D/2 (or) 2 1/2'' + d + D/2 minimum

O – DETAILING DIM.
OVERALL BAR DIM.   HOOK

12D

90° HOOK

d = (1) Bar Diameter
D = 6d for No. 3 to No. 8 bars
D = 8d for No. 9 to No. 11 bars
J = 13d + D/2

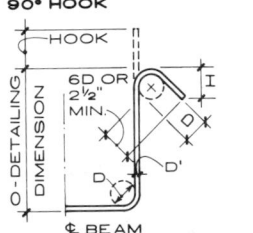

6D OR 2½" MIN.

Ȼ BEAM

135° HOOK STIRRUP – TIES SIMILAR

d = (1) Bar Diameter
D = 4d for No. 3 to No. 6 Bars
H = 1'' + d + D/2
When supporting bars are used, stirrup hooks may be bent to the diameter of the supporting bar.

TEMPERATURE REINFORCEMENT FOR STRUCTURAL FLOOR & ROOF SLAB
(IN PERCENTAGE OF CROSS – SECTIONAL AREA OF CONCRETE)

REINFORCEMENT	CONCRETE INTERIOR	EXTERIOR
Deformed Bars	.20%	.25%
Welded Wire Fabric	.18%	.22%

Slabs with embedded pressure piping (.20%) normal to it.

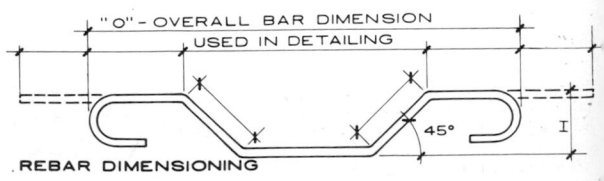

"O" – OVERALL BAR DIMENSION USED IN DETAILING

45°

REBAR DIMENSIONING

Irvin Bruce Schafer; Peoria, Illinois

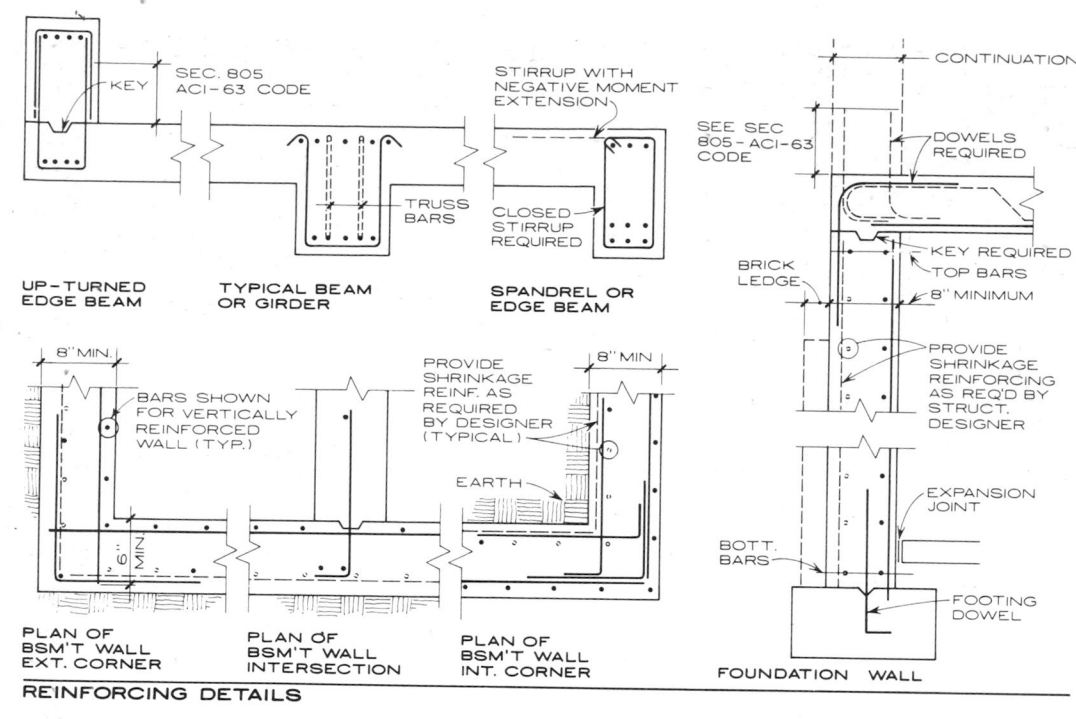

REINFORCING DETAILS

UP-TURNED EDGE BEAM

TYPICAL BEAM OR GIRDER

SPANDREL OR EDGE BEAM

PLAN OF BSM'T WALL EXT. CORNER

PLAN OF BSM'T WALL INTERSECTION

PLAN OF BSM'T WALL INT. CORNER

FOUNDATION WALL

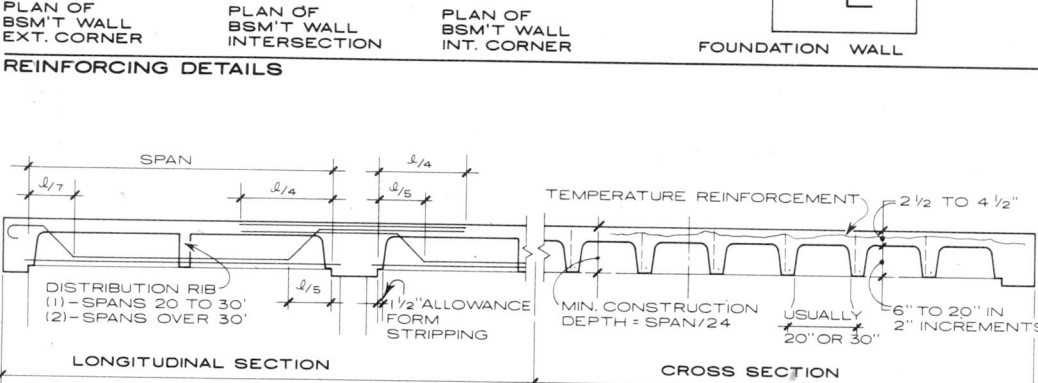

LONGITUDINAL SECTION

CROSS SECTION

ONE-WAY CONCRETE JOIST CONSTRUCTION

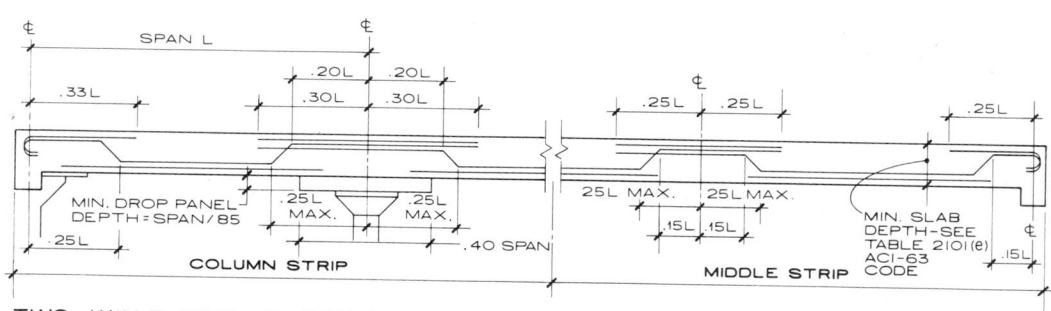

COLUMN STRIP

MIDDLE STRIP

TWO-WAY FLAT SLAB - SQUARE BAY CONSTRUCTION

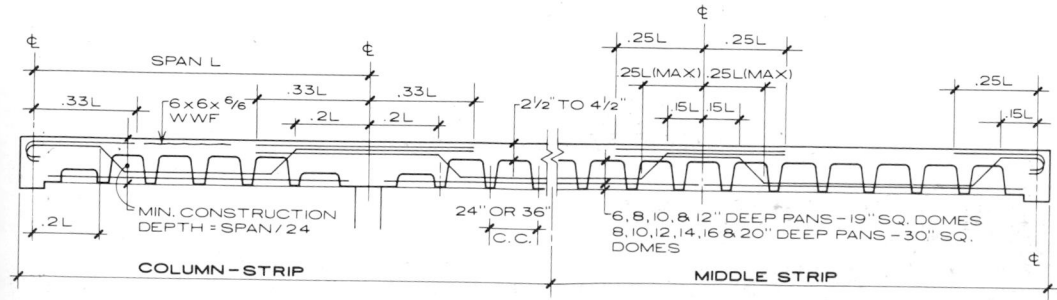

COLUMN-STRIP

MIDDLE STRIP

WAFFLE FLAT SLAB - SQUARE BAY CONSTRUCTION

CONCRETE FLOOR SYSTEMS

Irvin Bruce Schafer; Peoria, Illinois

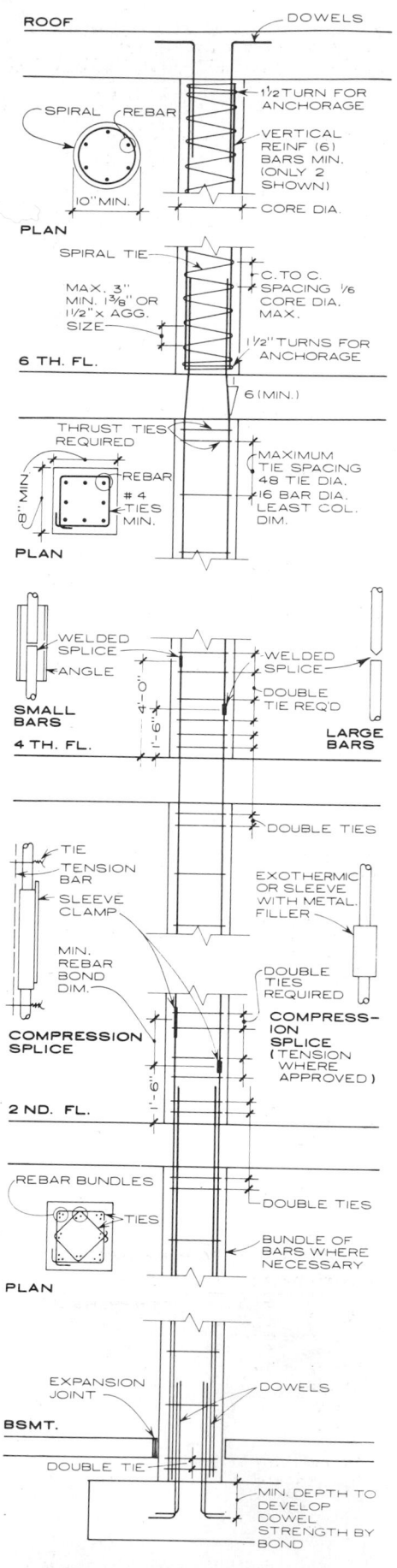

COMPOSITE OF MAJOR TYPES OF COLUMN REBAR

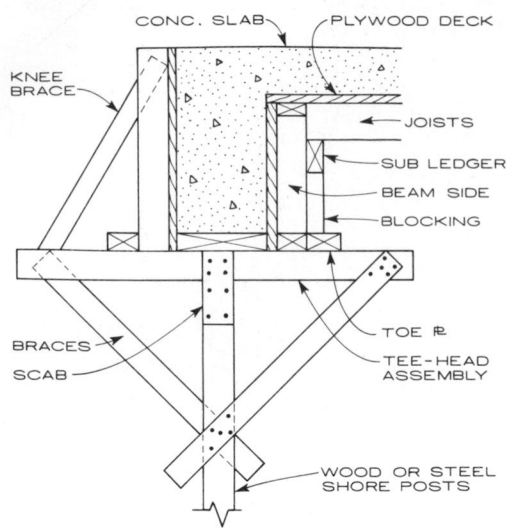

TYPICAL EXTERIOR SLAB AND BEAM
FORMING

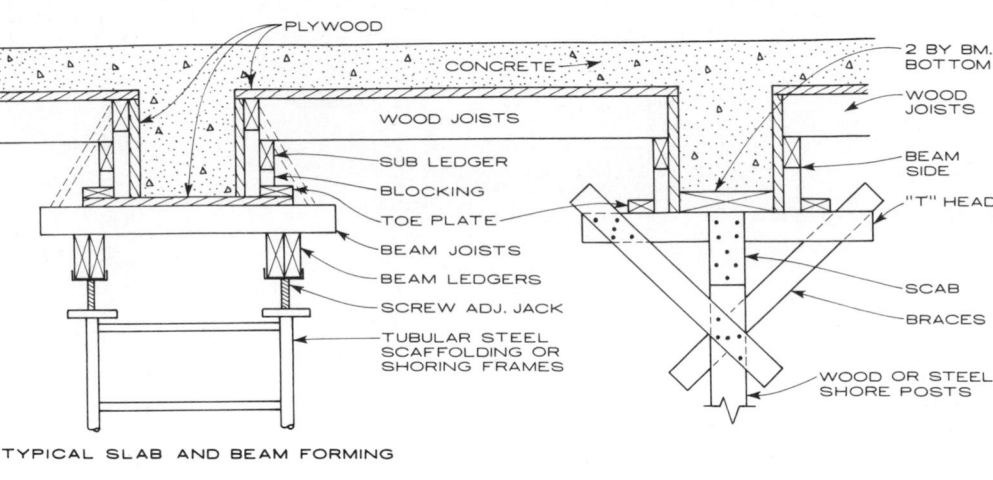

TYPICAL SLAB AND BEAM FORMING

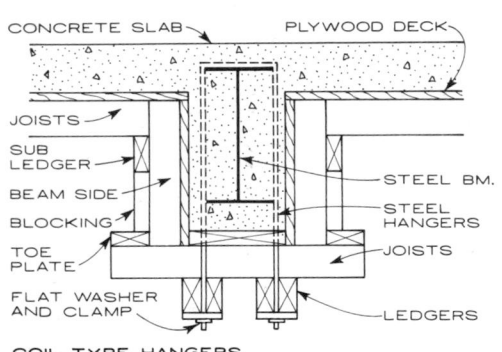

COIL TYPE HANGERS
TYPICAL SUSPENDED SLAB

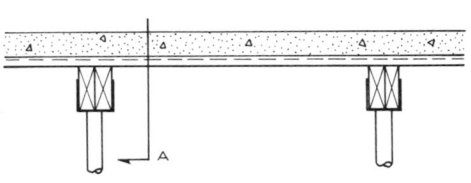

TYPICAL CORRUGATED STEEL FORMS

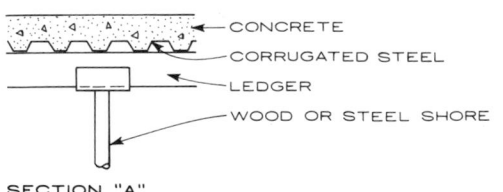

SECTION "A"
See manufacturer's catalogs for loads and spans.

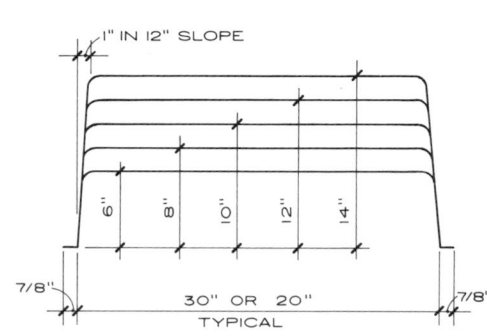

TYPICAL PATENTED STEEL FORMS
FOR CONC. JOIST FLOOR SYSTEMS

NOTE:

Smaller filler sizes are available for non typical conditions.

See manufacturer's catalogs.
Fiber forms also on market in similar size.
Plywood deck is required for forming.

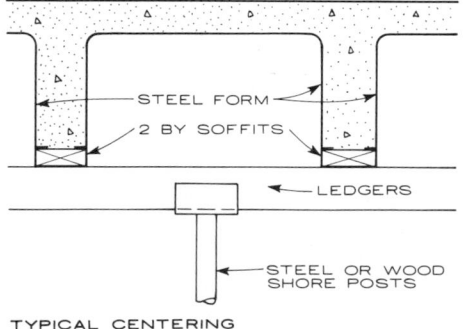

TYPICAL CENTERING

FORM DESIGN NOTE:

Sizes, grades, and spans of materials used in forming and shoring must be examined for structural strength prior to detailing.

Jack A. Clark; Baume and Polivnick; Denver, Colorado

COMPARATIVE COST OF FORMS * (BASED ON 4 USES)

Form type	Cost per sq. ft. one use	Number possible uses	Total cost per use	Lbs. per sq. ft.	Total cost per sq. ft.	Surface finish
Field built wood***	100	5	100**	9.5	100	Poor to good
Shop built wood	154	15	73	9.5	82	Fair to excellent
Composite Steel and wood	228	15	89	12	100	Good to excellent
Steel A242 plate	290	50	102	15	117	Good to excellent
Light gauge pre-formed steel	250	50	93	11	104	Good to excellent
Fiber glass reinforced plastic	423	30	133	7	140	Good to excellent

* Includes labor cost   ** Assume no re-use   *** Basic index = 100

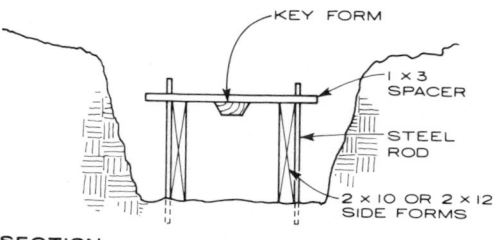

KEY FORM

1 x 3 SPACER

STEEL ROD

2 x 10 OR 2 x 12 SIDE FORMS

SECTION

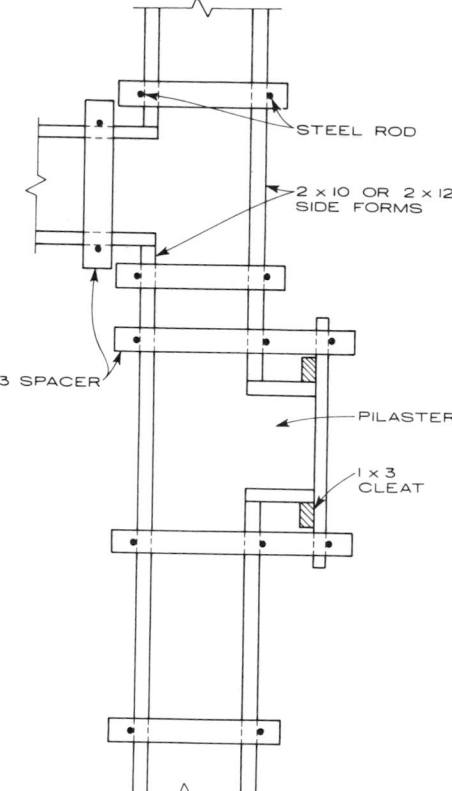

STEEL ROD

2 x 10 OR 2 x 12 SIDE FORMS

1 x 3 SPACER

PILASTER

1 x 3 CLEAT

PLAN
FOOTING FORMS

NOTE:

Steel rods driven at slight angle so predrilled spacer brings rods into vertical position. Spacers are at 3'– 0" to 4'– 0" o.c. and nailed into top of side forms with double-headed nails. If key form is required nail it to spacers.

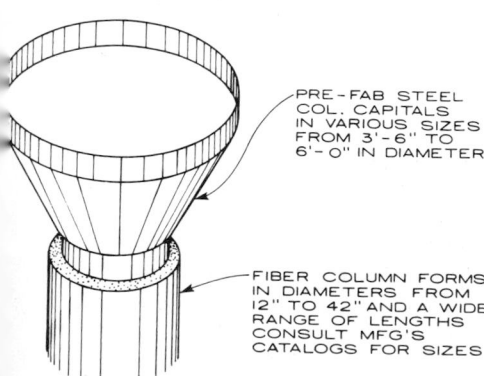

PRE-FAB STEEL COL. CAPITALS IN VARIOUS SIZES FROM 3'-6" TO 6'-0" IN DIAMETER

FIBER COLUMN FORMS IN DIAMETERS FROM 12" TO 42" AND A WIDE RANGE OF LENGTHS CONSULT MFG'S CATALOGS FOR SIZES

ROUND COLUMN FORMS

NOTE:

Steel round column forms also from 12" dia. to 48" dia. with or without steel column capitals.

Jack A. Clark; Baume and Polivnick; Denver, Colorado

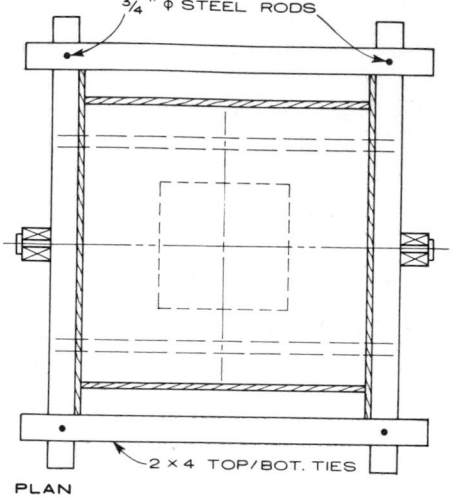

3/4" φ STEEL RODS

2 x 4 TOP/BOT. TIES

PLAN

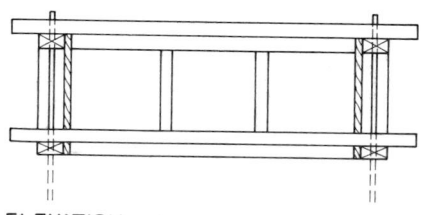

ELEVATION
PAD FOOTING FORM

NOTE:

3/4" φ steel rods used at each corner to lock and position form. If 2 x 4 stud side panels need additional strength add vertical stiffbacks with form ties thru center of footing.

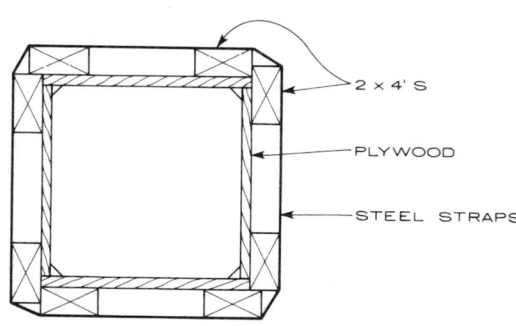

2 x 4'S

PLYWOOD

STEEL STRAPS

PLAN
COLUMNS TO 14" SQUARE

NOTE:

Height of column will change thickness and spaces of steel bands. Consult mfr.'s catalogs.

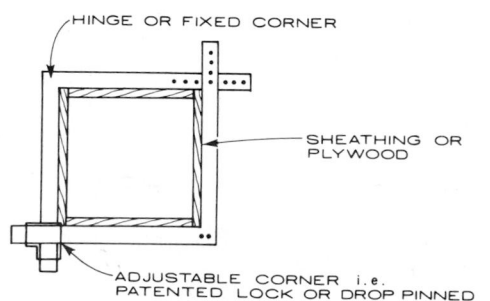

HINGE OR FIXED CORNER

SHEATHING OR PLYWOOD

ADJUSTABLE CORNER i.e. PATENTED LOCK OR DROP PINNED

PLAN
TYPICAL PATENTED COLUMN CLAMP

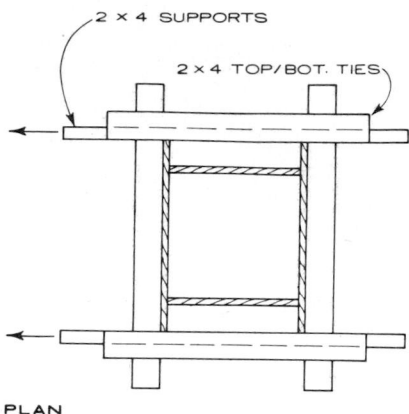

2 x 4 SUPPORTS

2 x 4 TOP/BOT. TIES

PLAN

ELEVATION
STEPPED FORM

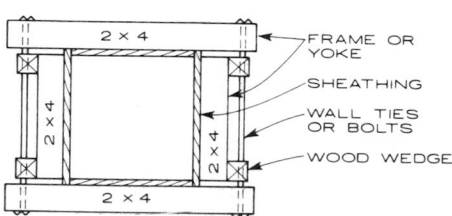

2 x 4

2 x 4

FRAME OR YOKE

SHEATHING

WALL TIES OR BOLTS

WOOD WEDGE

2 x 4

PLAN OF SQUARE & RECT. COLS.

NOTE:

Selection of sheathing (or plywood), type of column clamps (job built or patented metal types) and their spacing will depend on column height, rate of concrete pour, feet per hour and concrete temperature °F. also if concrete is to be vibrated during pour. Consult design guides for correct selection of materials to assure safe column forms.

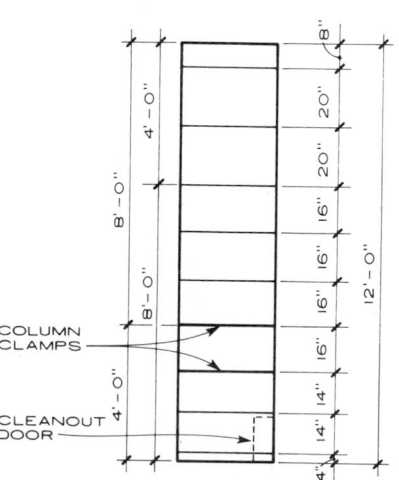

8"

20"

20"

16"

16"

16"

16"

14"

14"

4'-0"

8'-0"

8'-0"

4'-0"

12'-0"

COLUMN CLAMPS

CLEANOUT DOOR

TYPICAL COLUMN ELEVATION

NOTE:

Clamp spaces designed for 1" plywood. Note that clamps fall at plywood joints.

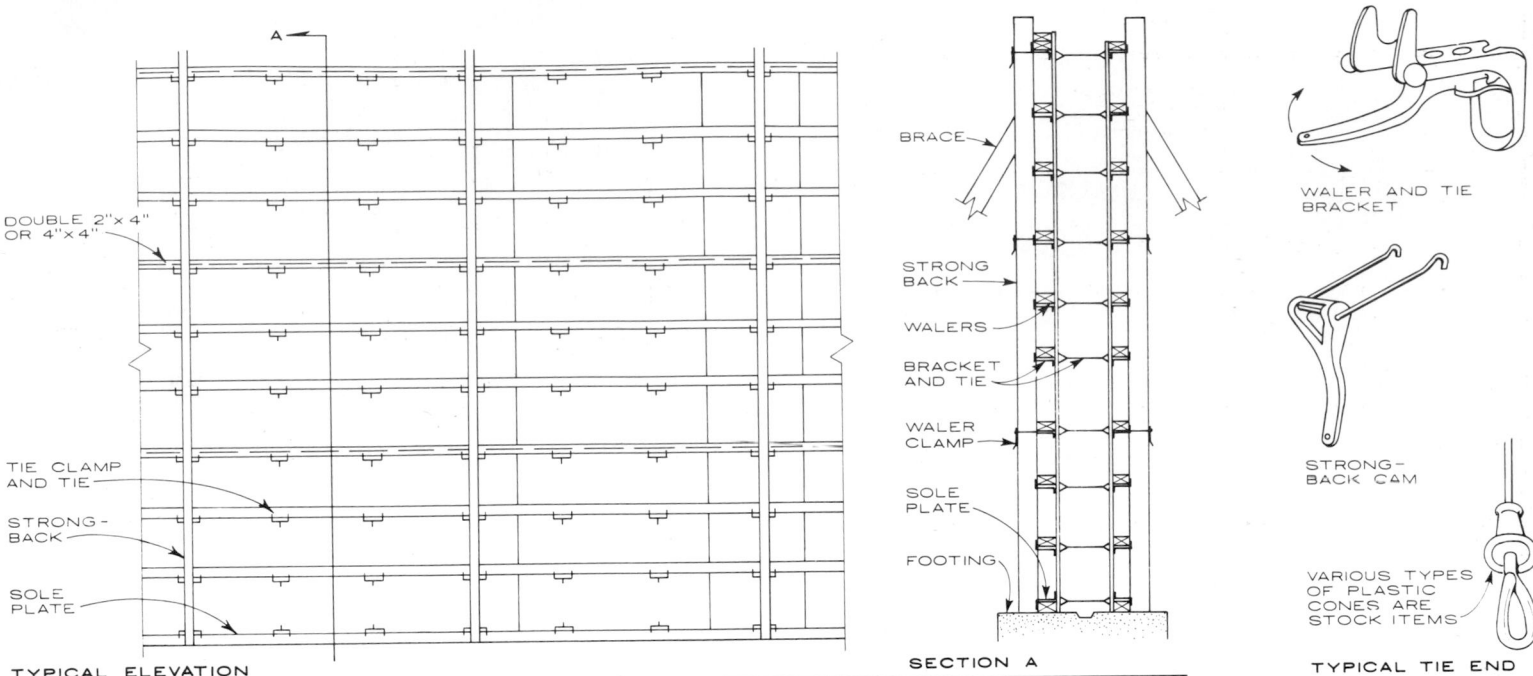

TYPICAL ELEVATION

SECTION A

TYPICAL TIE END

- BRACE
- STRONG BACK
- WALERS
- BRACKET AND TIE
- WALER CLAMP
- SOLE PLATE
- FOOTING

WALER AND TIE BRACKET

STRONG-BACK CAM

VARIOUS TYPES OF PLASTIC CONES ARE STOCK ITEMS

DOUBLE 2"x 4" OR 4"x 4"

TIE CLAMP AND TIE

STRONG-BACK

SOLE PLATE

WALL FORMS

NOTE:

Forms can be ganged by the use of 4 X 4's lag bolted to walers in place of 2 X 4 strongbacks. Metal lifting straps bolted to the tops of the strongbacks use special vertical angle to butt forms.

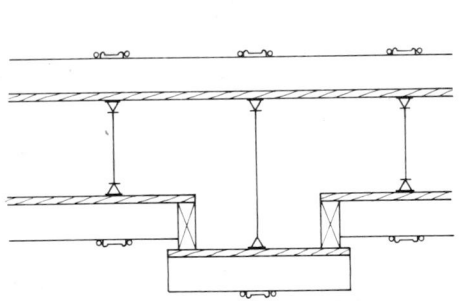

PLAN OF SMALL PILASTER

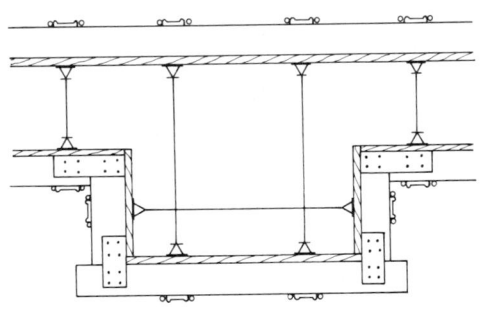

PLAN OF LARGE PILASTER

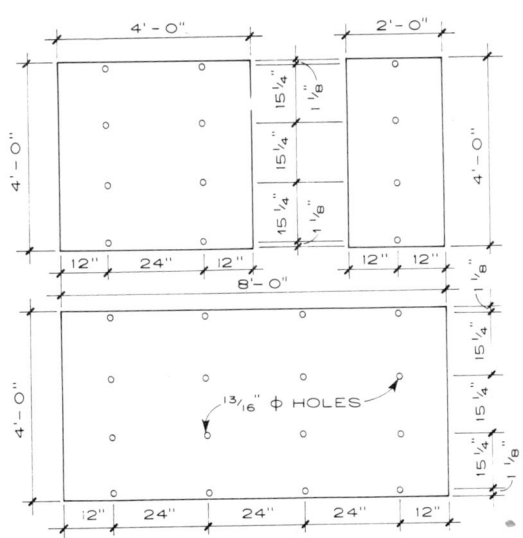

TYPICAL PANEL LAYOUT

$^{13}/_{16}$" ⌀ HOLES

NOTE:

Various types of steel edged with backing bar panels that interlock are also on the market with plywood faces from 3/4" to 1 1/2" thick attached to the metal frames.

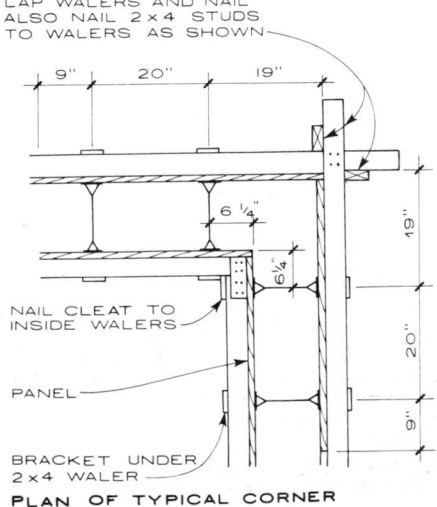

LAP WALERS AND NAIL ALSO NAIL 2 x 4 STUDS TO WALERS AS SHOWN

NAIL CLEAT TO INSIDE WALERS

PANEL

BRACKET UNDER 2 x 4 WALER

PLAN OF TYPICAL CORNER FOR 12" WALL

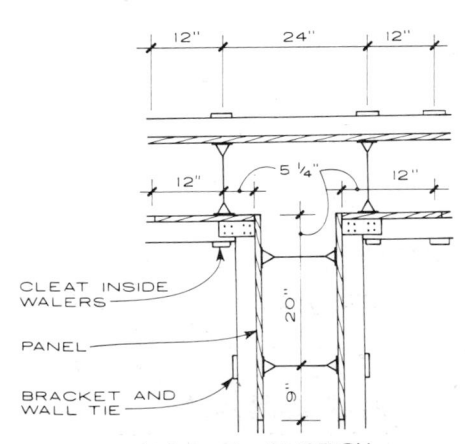

CLEAT INSIDE WALERS

PANEL

BRACKET AND WALL TIE

PLAN OF "T" WALL JUNCTION FOR 12" WALL

FORM DESIGN NOTES:

Pressure depends on rate of pour—feet per hour and concrete temperature °F. Vibration of concrete is also a factor in form pressure.

Provide clean-out doors at bottom of wall forms.

Various types of form ties are on the market. Some are not suitable for architectural concrete work, i.e. can not be withdrawn from the concrete.

Various plastic cones of 1 1/2" diameter and 1/2" deep can be used and the holes are left ungrouted to form a type of architectural feature.

Consult manufacturers catalogs for form design and tie strength information.

Jack A. Clark; Baume and Polivnick; Denver, Colorado

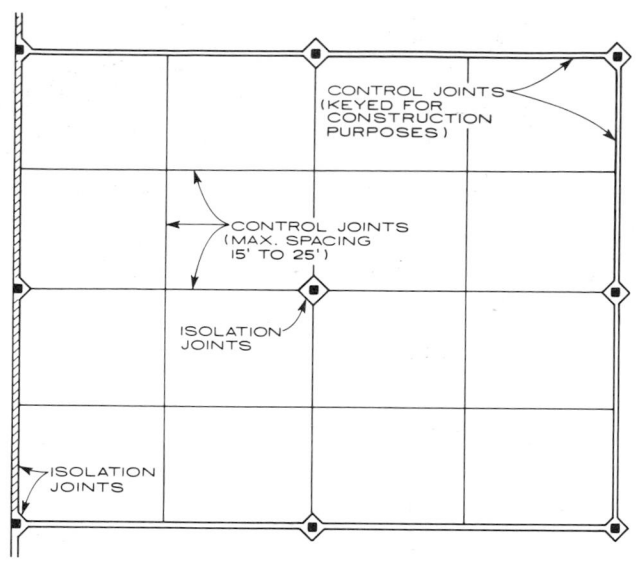

CONSTRUCTION PLAN FOR TYPICAL SLAB ON GRADE

CONTROL JOINTS FOR A FLOOR ON GRADE

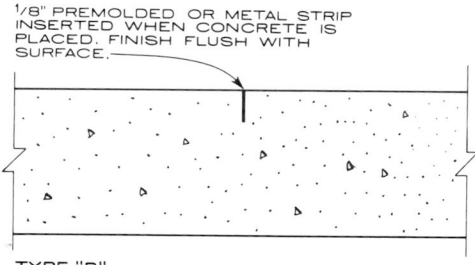

SAWED JOINT TO BE FILLED WITH LEAD OR JOINT FILLER

1/8"

1/5 T

T

TYPE "A"

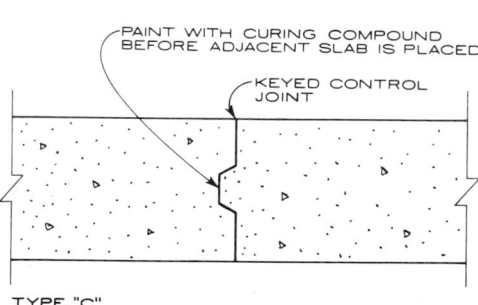

1/8" PREMOLDED OR METAL STRIP INSERTED WHEN CONCRETE IS PLACED. FINISH FLUSH WITH SURFACE.

TYPE "B"

PAINT WITH CURING COMPOUND BEFORE ADJACENT SLAB IS PLACED

KEYED CONTROL JOINT

TYPE "C"

CONTROL JOINT TYPES FOR FLOOR SLAB ON GRADE

NOTE:

In Types "A" or "B" lead or other metal strips should be installed in areas where small wheel trucks are used. In areas where trucks with pneumatic tires are used the joint filler in Type "A" or "B" or the keyed joint shown in Type "C" is satisfactory.

Jack A. Clark; Baume and Polivnick; Denver, Colorado
Heinzman and Clifton; Washington, D. C.

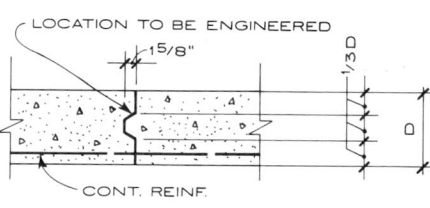

LOCATION TO BE ENGINEERED
1 5/8"
1/3 D
D
CONT. REINF.

TYPICAL SUSPENDED SLAB AND BEAM

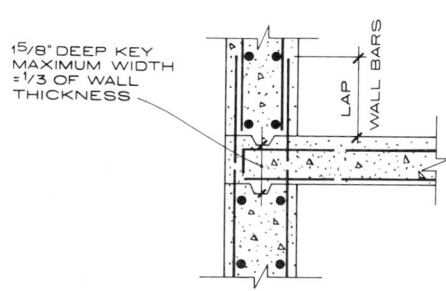

1 5/8" DEEP KEY MAXIMUM WIDTH = 1/3 OF WALL THICKNESS

LAP WALL BARS

TYPICAL SUSPENDED SLAB AT WALL

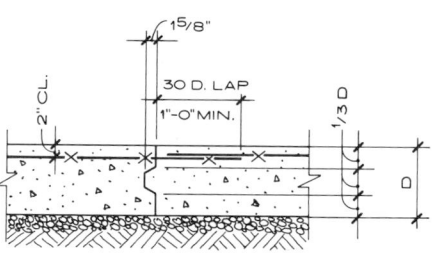

1 5/8"
2" CL.
30 D. LAP
1'-0" MIN.
1/3 D
D

TYPICAL SLAB ON GRADE

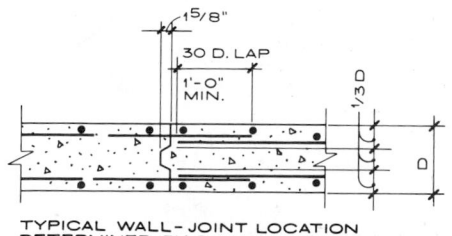

1 5/8"
30 D. LAP
1'-0" MIN.
1/3 D
D

TYPICAL WALL-JOINT LOCATION DETERMINED BY STRUCTURAL ENGINEER

CONSTRUCTION JOINT TYPES

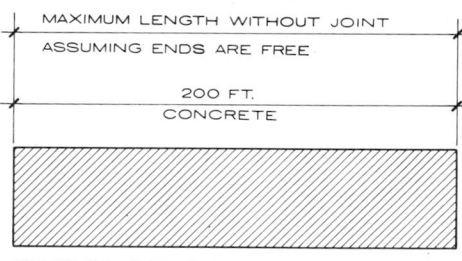

MAXIMUM LENGTH WITHOUT JOINT ASSUMING ENDS ARE FREE
200 FT.
CONCRETE

BUILDINGS WITHOUT JOINT

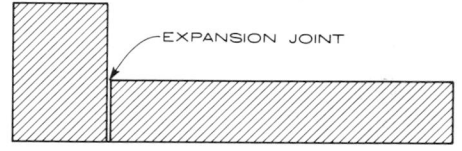

EXPANSION JOINT

TYPE "A" NEW BUILDING ADJOINING EXISTING BUILDING

TYPE "B" LONG LOW BUILDING ABUTTING HIGH BUILDING

TYPE "C" WINGS ADJOINING MAIN STRUCTURE

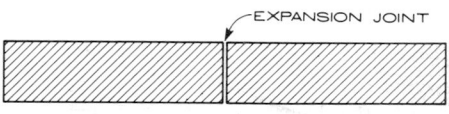

EXPANSION JOINT

LONG BUILDINGS

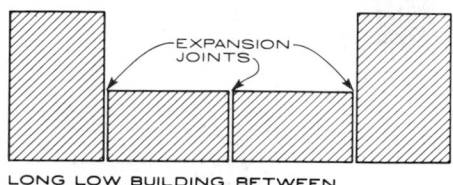

EXPANSION JOINTS

LONG LOW BUILDING BETWEEN HIGH WINGS

RECOMMENDED LOCATION OF EXPANSION JOINTS

GENERAL INFORMATION ON TYPES ON CONSTRUCTION:

1. A one way slab system is suitable for heavy loads on spans up to about 15 feet.

2. Pan-joist floors are economical for light loads on fairly long spans. In place of the metal or plastic pans. Paper tubes may also be used to reduce dead weight.

3. Two-way solid slabs are economical for medium to heavy loads on spans up to about 30 feet. They are justified when the ratio of long to short side of slab panel is 2 to 1 or less. Metal or plastic pans or "domes" may be used to reduce dead weight.

4. Flat slabs are girderless floor systems having drop panels and column capitals. They are well suited to carry either heavy or light loads as well as large concentrated loads, the drop panels providing the necessary increase in cross sectional area and depth to resist negative moments and shears.

5. Flat plates are girderless floor systems without drop panels or column capitals. Shear is an important consideration and in many cases special shearhead reinforcement has to be provided (two types are shown below). Domes may be used to reduce dead weight producing essentially a two-way joist system commonly referred to as a "waffle slab".

6. For the various floor systems shown the Architect can determine rather quickly which system of framing most economically suits a column spacing and superimposed loading. The graphs shown are based on designs for the dead weights of the floor systems plus the indicated superimposed loads.

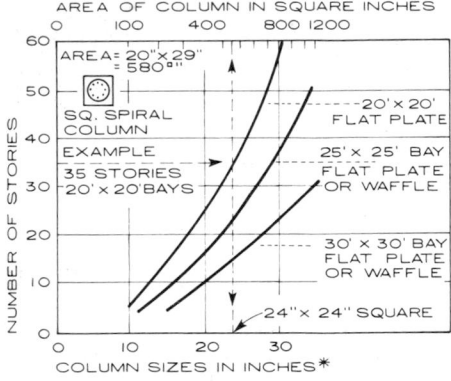

PRELIMINARY SIZES OF REINFORCED CONCRETE COLUMNS
FORMULA :

The area of any column in square inches for any story is:

$$A = \frac{N(W_D + 1/2\ W_L)B}{k}$$

A = column area in square inches
N = number of stories above
$W_D + W_L$ = dead and live loads (psf)
B = bay area (sq. ft.)
For 8% reinforcement + f'_c = 5,000 psi.
 k = 3,650 for f_y = 75,000 psi.
 k = 3,170 for f_y = 60,000 psi.

NOTE: The above equation and graph are based on Working Stress Design (ACI 318-63)

*Columns are square with 8% reinforcment f'_c = 5,000 psi, f_y = 75,000 psi and moment is negligible. In addition to the dead load of the structure, graph takes into account 35 psf for partitions, mechanical and ceiling. Assumed live load is 60 psf.

Jack A. Clark; Baume and Polivnick; Denver, Colorado
Frank Strasburger, C. E.; Strasburger & Soto; Washington, D. C.

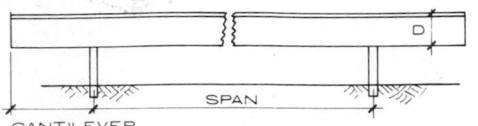

CANTILEVER
CROSS SECTION
FOLDED PLATED

Sufficient cantilever can help to counterbalance the span. The usual span to depth ratio varies from 1:10 to 1:15. Example: If span is 40' long, the usual minimum depth is about 40/10 or 4'.

FORMULA :
Volume of concrete in Cu.Yds/Sq.Ft = th/324a.
h = ft.   t = in.   a = ft.

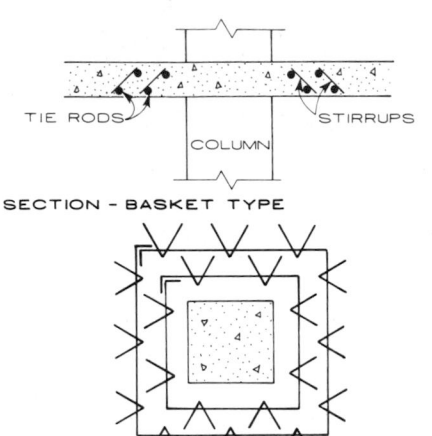

SECTION - BASKET TYPE

PLAN - BASKET TYPE

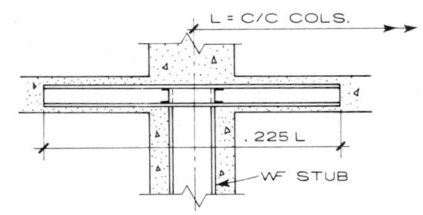

SECTION - STEEL GRILLAGE TYPE

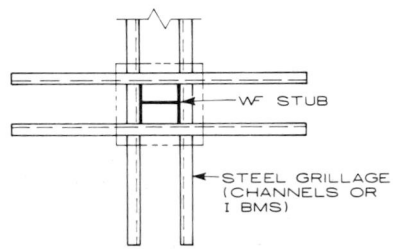

PLAN - STEEL GRILLAGE TYPE

TWO TYPES OF SHEARHEADS USED IN FLAT PLATE CONSTRUCTION

The steel grillage shearhead is usually made up of pairs of channels or I beams as shown. In the case of concrete columns this grillage is welded to a Wide Flange stub four to five feet long and embedded in the column. In the case of steel columns the grillage is welded to the column directly.

A distinct advantage of the steel grillage shearhead over the "basket" of stirrups shown is that it will allow openings in the slab adjacent to the columns. The width of these openings depends on the distance between grillage members i.e. the stub or column size. Intermediate exterior columns have three-quarter grillages and corner columns have half grillages.

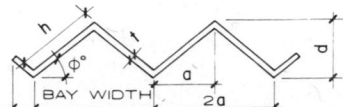

END SECT.— 2 SEGMENT FOLDED PL.
SCHEDULE - 2 SEGMENT FOLDED PLATE

SPAN	$\phi°$ MAX.	MIN.	d MAX.	MIN.	$2a^{(1)}$	$t^{(2)}$	REIN-FORCING[3]
40'	45°	25°	4'-0"	2'-9"	15'	4"	1.2 – 1.6
60'	45°	25°	6'-0"	4'-0"	20'	4",6"	1.9 – 2.7
75'	45°	25°	7'-6"	5'-0"	25'	4",6"	2.6 – 3.7
100'	45°	25°	10'-0"	6'-9"	30'	5",6"	4.0 – 5.2

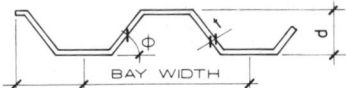

END SECTION - 4 SEGMENT FOLDED PL.
SCHEDULE - 4 SEGMENT FOLDED PLATE

SPAN	$\phi°$ MAX.	MIN.	d MAX.	MIN.	$2a^{(1)}$	$t^{(2)}$	REIN-FORCING[3]
40'	45°	30°	5'-0"	2'-6"	20'	3"	1.5 – 2.0
60'	45°	30°	6'-0"	4'-0"	25'	3",3 1/2"	2.0 – 3.0
75'	45°	30°	7'-6"	5'-0"	30'	3",4"	2.5 – 4.0
100'	45°	30°	10'-0"	6'-6"	40'	4",5"	4.0 – 6.0

Max. recommended slope is 45°.
1. values shown may vary w/arch. design.
2. average thickness in inches.
3. pounds/square foot of projected area.

GENERAL INFORMATION ON VARIOUS CONCRETE SHELL ELEMENTS

1. Domes are especially suitable for structures where spans are long and column-free space is required. Because strength is inherent in the shape, shell roofs are being designed with thicknesses as little as 2 1/2 inches.

2. The Hyperbolic Paraboloid shell roof is, in effect a three-dimensional "sheet" of concrete in which strength and rigidity are accomplished not by increasing the thickness of the sheet but by curving in space. Despite its double curvature, the shape can be formed entirely of straight pieces. Hyperbolic-Parabolids are exceptionally adaptable to churches, auditoriums and theatres.

3. Folded Plates (F/P's) are a form of shell roof with tremendous span and load-carrying abilities. They are being used more and more to provide great areas of column free space for industrial construction. Because of their ability to cantilever, they are also used in the design of schools, stores, and hangars.

4. Long Barrel Shells as opposed to short barrel shells have a small chord compared to span. To achieve full shell action support is required along the total periphery of each barrel. In practice this support along the straight edges are never fully restrained so that some bending moments in the shell have to be considered in the design. The support or stiffener along the curved edges usually consist of arch-type ribs spanning between the supporting columns. Since cantilevers are easily achieved the visible shell edge can be made as thin as the basic shell.

5. Inverted Umbrellas are hyperbolic paraboloid shells supported by single columns. Since walls are not load bearing they can be located where desired providing for great versatility of the interior space arrangement.

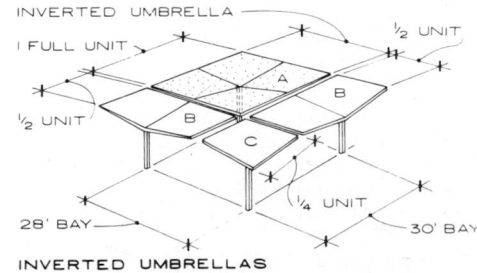

INVERTED UMBRELLAS

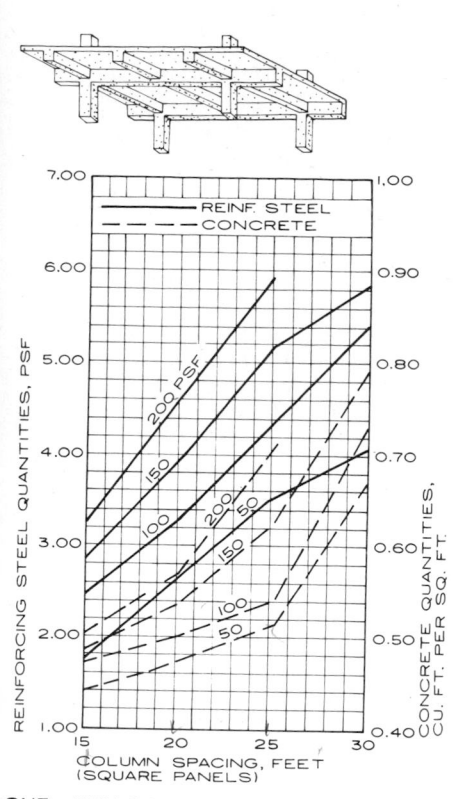

ONE – WAY SOLID SLAB
(SPAN = ½ THE COL. SPACING)

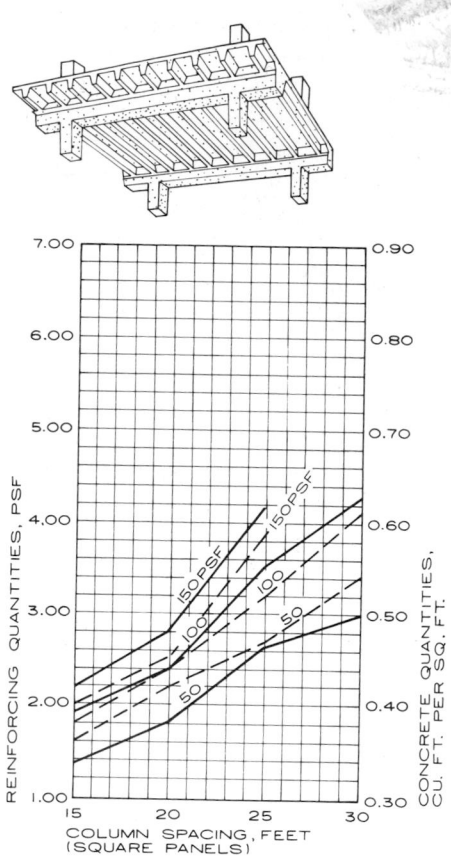

ONE WAY JOISTS
(20 IN. METAL PANS)

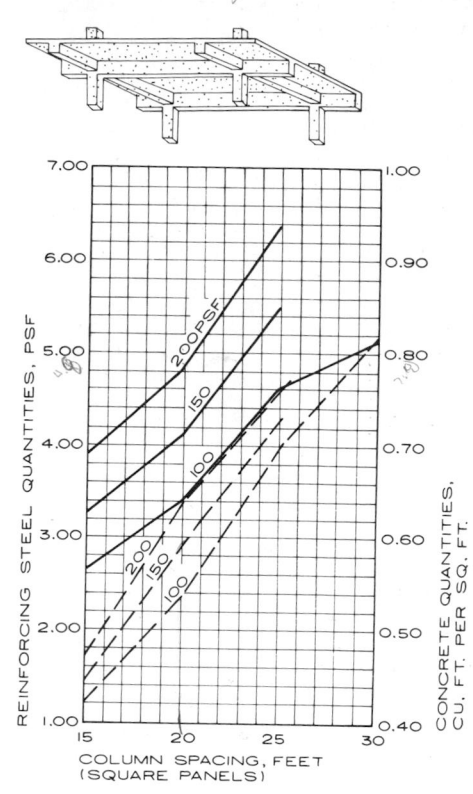

TWO - WAY SOLID SLAB

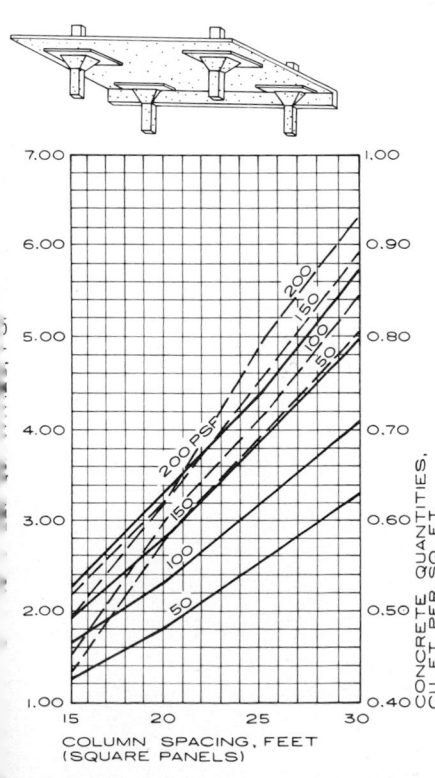

FLAT SLAB

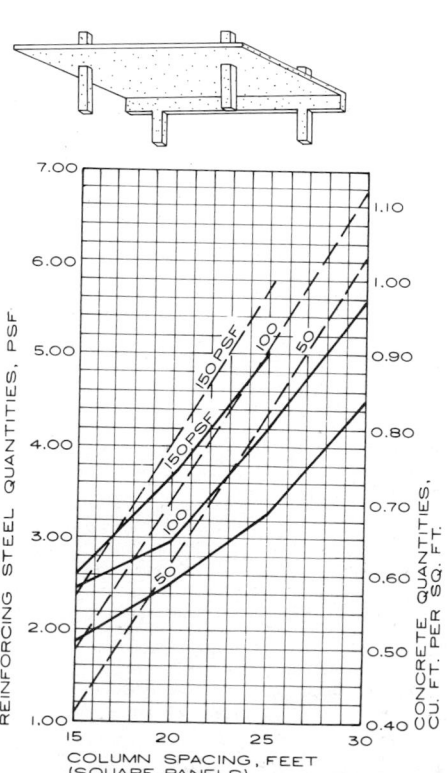

FLAT PLATE

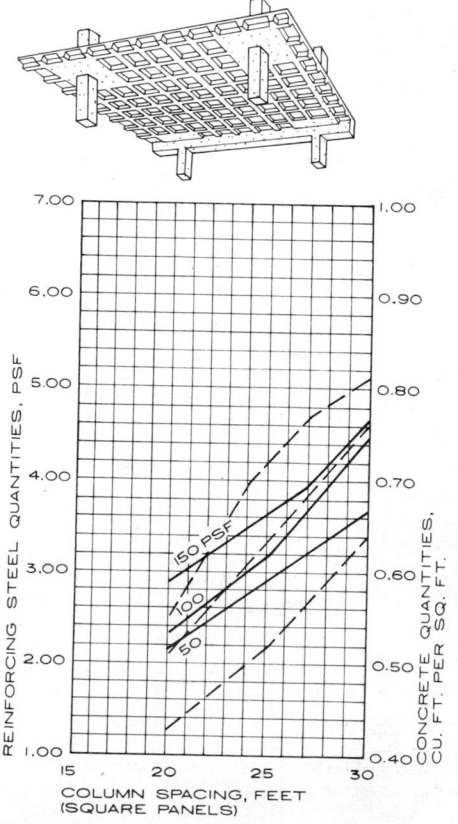

WAFFLE FLAT PLATE
(TWO - WAY JOIST WITHOUT BEAMS)

ck A. Clark; Baume and Polivnick; Denver, Colorado
ank Strasburger, C. E.; Strasburger & Soto; Washington, D. C.

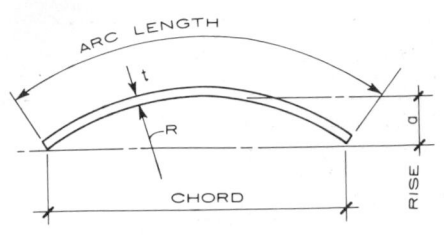

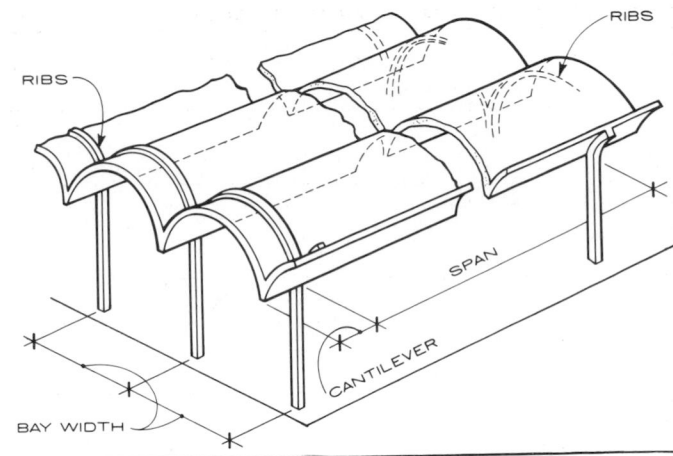

NOTES:

(1) For long-span multiple barrels, the usual span-to-depth ratio varies from 1:10 to 1:15.

(2) Pounds per square foot of projected area.

(3) Ribs, necessary to stiffen the shell at the supports, may be incorporated above or below the curved plane. Drawing at right shows both types.

BARREL SHELLS / SPAN DATA (I)

SPAN	BAY WIDTH	a	R	t	REINF.(2)
80'	30'	8'	25'	3"	3.5
100'	30'	10'	30'	3"	4.0
120'	35'	12'	30'	3"	4.5
140'	40'	14'	35'	3"	5.0
160'	45'	16'	35'	3 1/2"	6.5

LONG BARREL SHELLS

HYPERBOLIC PARABOLOID SPAN DATA

SPAN	PROJECTION MIN.- MAX.	X (I) MIN.-MAX.	a (2)	t (3)	REINF. (4)
50'	50' — 70'	3' — 5'	1'	2 3/4"	2 — 3 LB
60'	60' — 85'	4' — 6'	1'	2 3/4"	2 — 3 LB
75'	75' — 105'	6' — 9'	1 1/2'	3"	3 — 4 LB
100'	100' — 140'	9' — 13'	2'	3 1/4"	3 — 4 LB
125'	125' — 175'	13' — 20'	2 1/2'	3 1/2"	4 — 5 LB
150'	150' — 210'	17' — 25'	3'	4"	5 — 7 LB

(1) Figures given are recommended lower limits; maximum feasible limit = S/5.
(2) Average depth of edge beams.
(3) Average shell thickness in inches.
(4) Average reinforcing steel of hyperbolic paraboloids in pounds per square foot of surface.
(5) Width and location near edge may vary, in some h/p's edge beams taper towards the tip.

EDGE BEAM DETAIL

SEE NOTE (5)

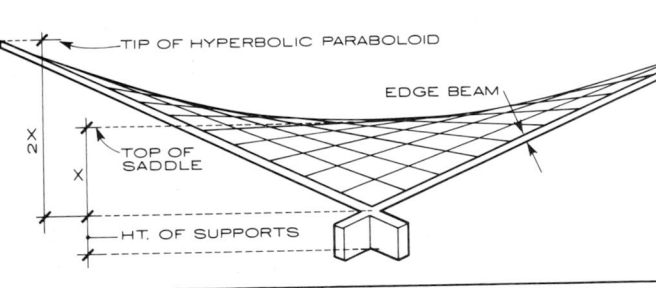

HYPERBOLIC PARABOLOID

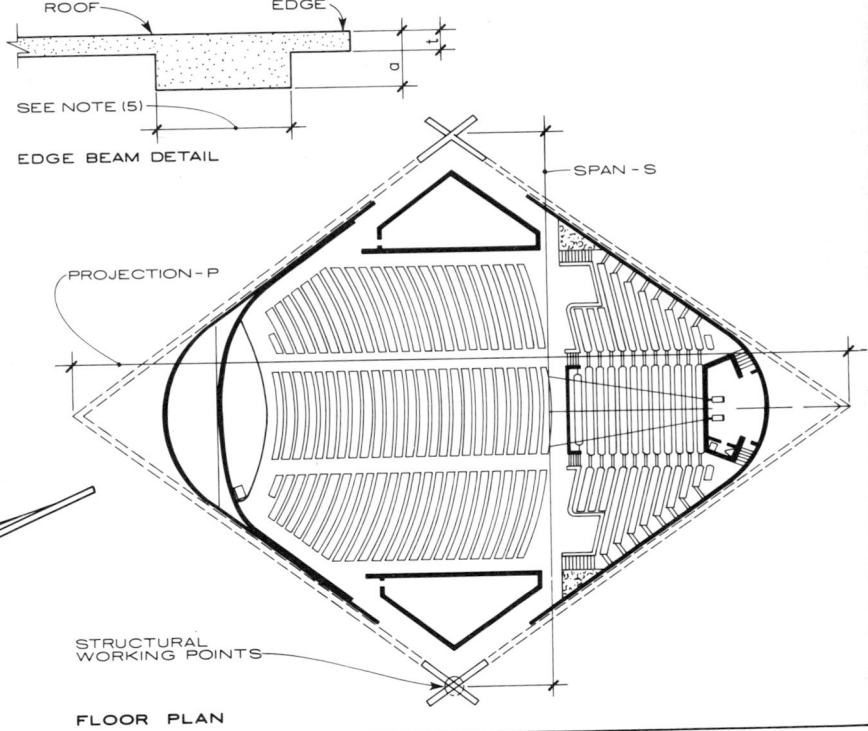

FLOOR PLAN

DOME / SPAN DATA

D	t	∅	a	R
100'	3"	30	13.4'	100'
		45	20.7'	70.7'
125'	3"	30	16.8'	125'
		45	25.9'	88.4'
150'	3 1/2" (3")	30	20.1'	150'
		45	31.0'	106.0'
175'	4" (3 1/2")	30	23.5'	175'
		45	36.2'	123.7'
200'	4 1/2" (4")	30	26.8'	200'
		45	41.4'	141.4'

NOTE:
Shell thickness "t" is usually increased by 50 to 75 per cent near the periphery.

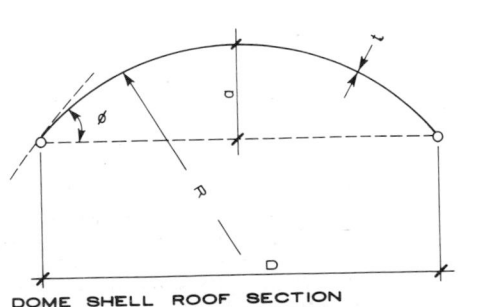

DOME SHELL ROOF SECTION

DONE SHELL ROOF

Jack A. Clark; Baume and Polivnick; Denver, Colorado

Frank Strasburger, C. E.; Strasburger & Soto; Washington, D. C.

TYPE REQUIRED FOR DIFFERENT CONDITIONS WITH SUPERIMPOSED LOADS SHOWN

SPAN IN FEET	RESIDENCE 40 P.S.F.	APT. BLDG. 60 P.S.F.	OFFICE BLDG. 80 P.S.F.	PUBLIC ASSEMBLY 100 P.S.F.	LIGHT INDUSTRIAL 125 P.S.F.	ROOF 30 P.S.F.
12						
14						
16					A	
18			A		P,W	
20		A			D,Q,AA	
22	A			D,Q	B,E	
24		FF	D,P,Q,AA	B,E,P	C,X,BB	A
26	P	D	B,E	C	F,M,GG	D
28		E	C	F	G,H,Y	
30	E	B,C,Q	F,GG	G,BB	J,HH	
32	B,C	F	G	H,M	N,Z	
34	F,Q	G,GG		K,J		F,O
36	AA,FF		S,BB	N,HH	R,CC,JJ	
38			H,M			
40	BB,GG	H,M,S,HH	J,N,U	L,Q,R,CC,JJ	T,DD,EE,KK,V	H,FF,O

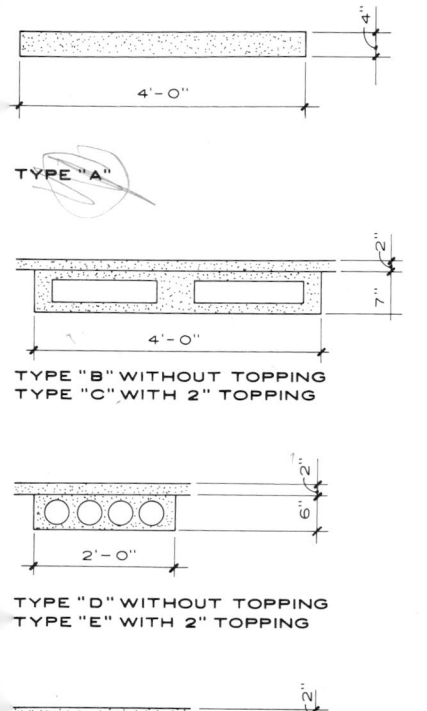

TYPE "A"

TYPE "B" WITHOUT TOPPING
TYPE "C" WITH 2" TOPPING

TYPE "D" WITHOUT TOPPING
TYPE "E" WITH 2" TOPPING

TYPE "F" — WITHOUT TOPPING
TYPE "G" — WITH 2" TOPPING

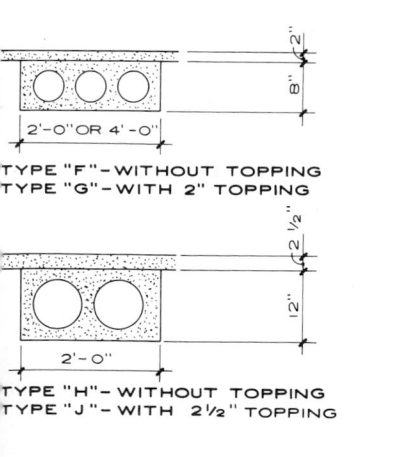

TYPE "H" — WITHOUT TOPPING
TYPE "J" — WITH 2½" TOPPING

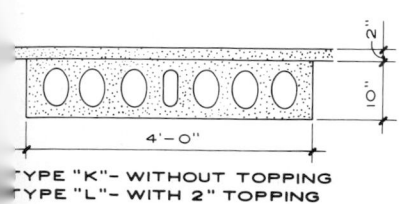

TYPE "K" — WITHOUT TOPPING
TYPE "L" — WITH 2" TOPPING

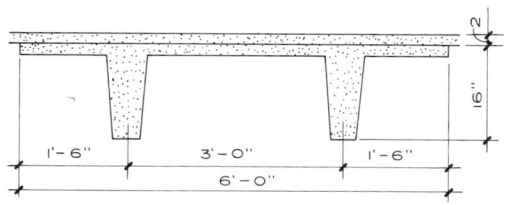

TYPE "M" – WITHOUT TOPPING
TYPE "N" – WITH 2" TOPPING

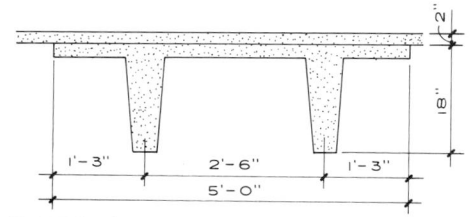

TYPE "Q" – WITHOUT TOPPING
TYPE "R" – WITH 2" TOPPING

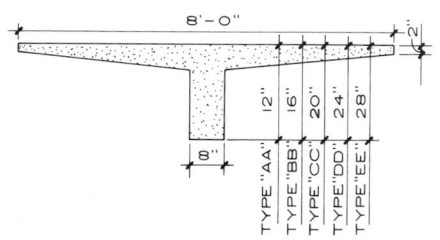

TYPE "S" – WITHOUT TOPPING
TYPE "T" – WITH 2" TOPPING

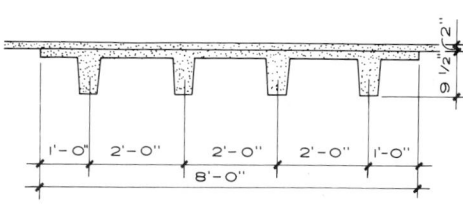

TYPE "O" – WITHOUT TOPPING
TYPE "P" – WITH 2" TOPPING

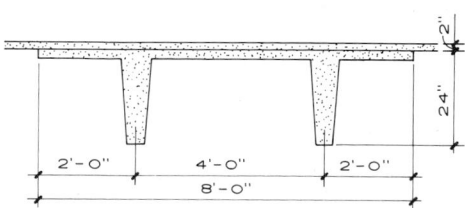

TYPE "U" – WITHOUT TOPPING
TYPE "V" – WITH 2" TOPPING

TYPE "W" TYPE "X" TYPE "Y" TYPE "Z"

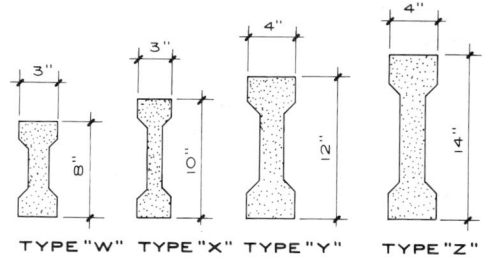

TYPE "AA" THRU "EE" – AS NOTED

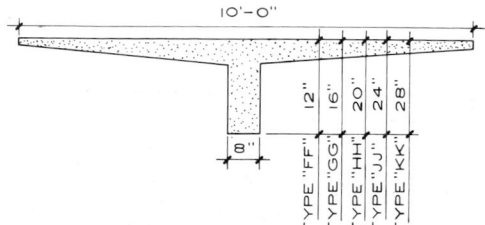

TYPE "FF" THRU "KK" – AS NOTED

NOTES:

With the exception of the four joists (Types W, X, Y, and Z) all the elements shown are prestressed and of hardrock concrete. Lightweight units are also available. To avoid needless repetition types have been indicated on table at the maximum span only for the superimposed load columns.

Since roof elements are usually used without the 3,000 p.s.i. structural topping slab the types having the topping have been omitted in the last column of the table.

When used for floor construction, topping is required to adjust for unevenness and camber in types shown.

Jack A. Clark; Baume and Polivnick; Denver, Colorado
Frank Strasburger, C. E.; Strasburger & Soto and Duncan Gray, C. E.; Washington, D. C.

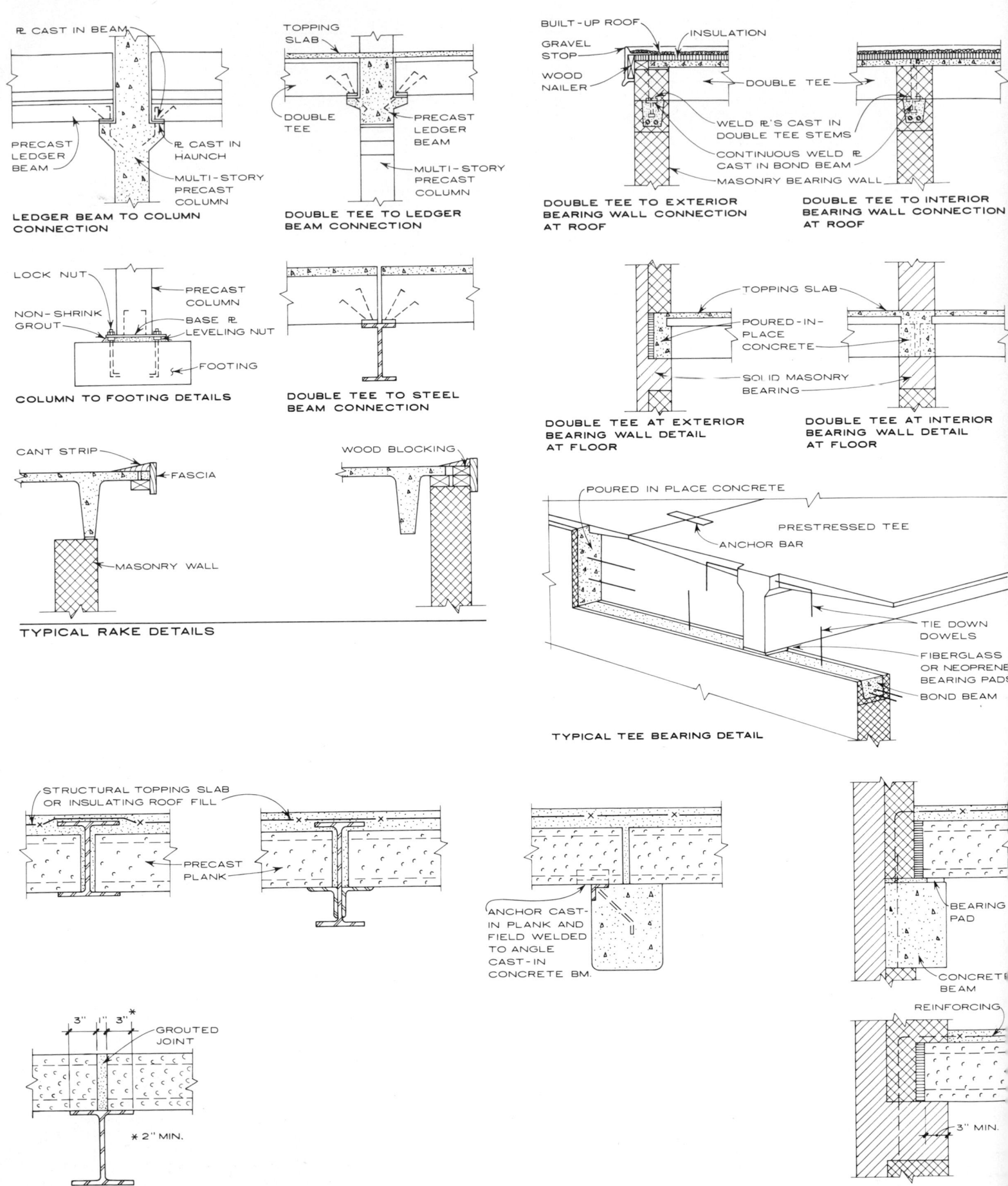

PL CAST IN BEAM

PRECAST LEDGER BEAM

PL CAST IN HAUNCH

MULTI-STORY PRECAST COLUMN

LEDGER BEAM TO COLUMN CONNECTION

TOPPING SLAB

DOUBLE TEE

PRECAST LEDGER BEAM

MULTI-STORY PRECAST COLUMN

DOUBLE TEE TO LEDGER BEAM CONNECTION

BUILT-UP ROOF
GRAVEL STOP
WOOD NAILER
INSULATION
DOUBLE TEE
WELD PL'S CAST IN DOUBLE TEE STEMS
CONTINUOUS WELD PL CAST IN BOND BEAM
MASONRY BEARING WALL

DOUBLE TEE TO EXTERIOR BEARING WALL CONNECTION AT ROOF

DOUBLE TEE TO INTERIOR BEARING WALL CONNECTION AT ROOF

LOCK NUT
NON-SHRINK GROUT
PRECAST COLUMN
BASE PL LEVELING NUT
FOOTING

COLUMN TO FOOTING DETAILS

DOUBLE TEE TO STEEL BEAM CONNECTION

TOPPING SLAB
POURED-IN-PLACE CONCRETE
SOLID MASONRY BEARING

DOUBLE TEE AT EXTERIOR BEARING WALL DETAIL AT FLOOR

DOUBLE TEE AT INTERIOR BEARING WALL DETAIL AT FLOOR

CANT STRIP
FASCIA
MASONRY WALL

WOOD BLOCKING

TYPICAL RAKE DETAILS

POURED IN PLACE CONCRETE
PRESTRESSED TEE
ANCHOR BAR
TIE DOWN DOWELS
FIBERGLASS OR NEOPRENE BEARING PADS
BOND BEAM

TYPICAL TEE BEARING DETAIL

STRUCTURAL TOPPING SLAB OR INSULATING ROOF FILL
PRECAST PLANK

ANCHOR CAST-IN PLANK AND FIELD WELDED TO ANGLE CAST-IN CONCRETE BM.

BEARING PAD
CONCRETE BEAM
REINFORCING

3" 3"
GROUTED JOINT
* 2" MIN.

3" MIN.

PRECAST PLANK FRAMING DETAILS

Jack A. Clark; Baume and Polivnick; Denver, Colorado

Frank Strasburger, C. E.; Strasburger & Soto and Duncan Gray, C. E.; Washington, D. C.

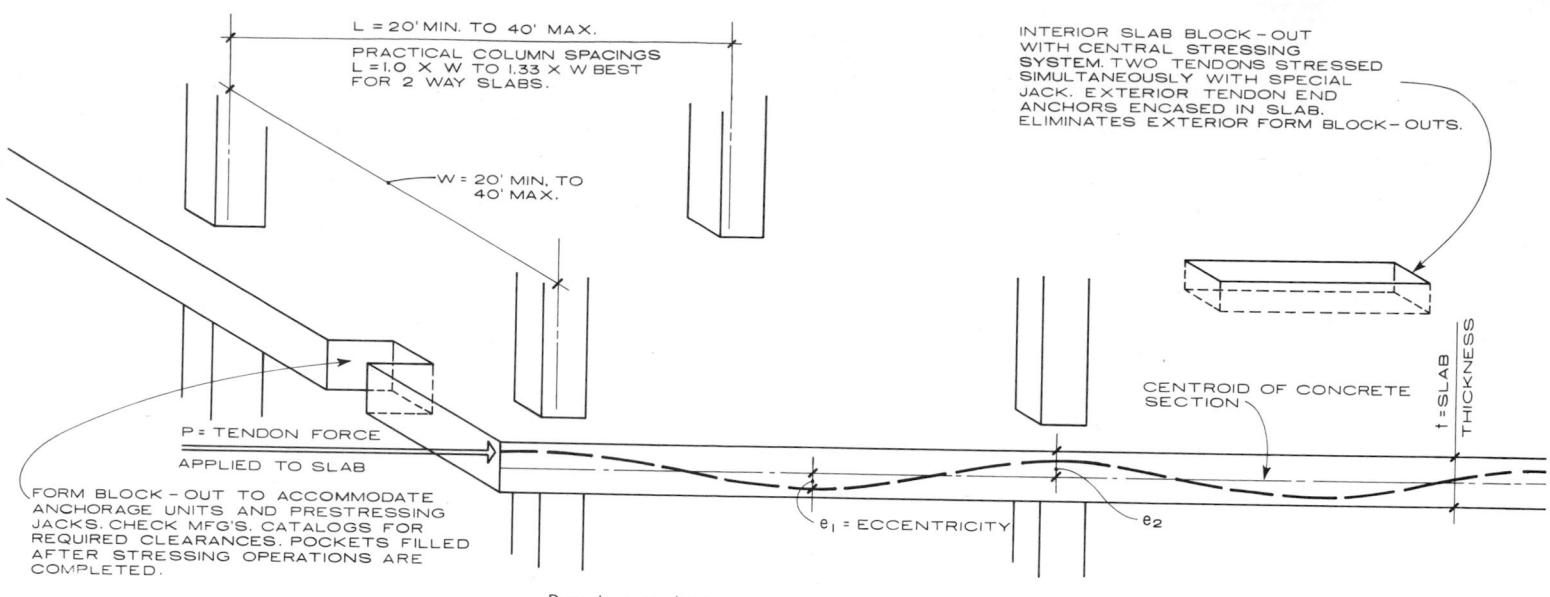

L = 20' MIN. TO 40' MAX.

PRACTICAL COLUMN SPACINGS L = 1.0 × W TO 1.33 × W BEST FOR 2 WAY SLABS.

W = 20' MIN. TO 40' MAX.

INTERIOR SLAB BLOCK-OUT WITH CENTRAL STRESSING SYSTEM. TWO TENDONS STRESSED SIMULTANEOUSLY WITH SPECIAL JACK. EXTERIOR TENDON END ANCHORS ENCASED IN SLAB. ELIMINATES EXTERIOR FORM BLOCK-OUTS.

CENTROID OF CONCRETE SECTION

t = SLAB THICKNESS

P = TENDON FORCE

APPLIED TO SLAB

e_1 = ECCENTRICITY

e_2

FORM BLOCK-OUT TO ACCOMMODATE ANCHORAGE UNITS AND PRESTRESSING JACKS. CHECK MFG'S. CATALOGS FOR REQUIRED CLEARANCES. POCKETS FILLED AFTER STRESSING OPERATIONS ARE COMPLETED.

Draped post-tension tendons pre-compress concrete to provide resistance to tensile stresses produced by flexual bending due to dead + live loads on floor. Maximum tendon spacing should not exceed 8 times slab thickness (t).

Practical solid slab thickness 6″ min. to about 10″ max. without drop panels. For long spans cast-in-place (not lift slabs) haunched slabs or drop panels may be used. Hollow slabs or waffle slabs can also be used to reduce dead load on long spans.

RECOMMENDED SPAN/DEPTH RATIO

FLOORS	42
ROOF	48

Check deflections, camber, and vibration.

GENERAL CONSIDERATIONS:

1. Concrete strength usually 4000 p.s.i. at 28 days and at least 3000 p.s.i. at time prestressing. Hardrock aggregate or lightweight concrete used. Low slump controlled mix is required to reduce shrinkage. Shrinkage after prestressing increases prestress losses.

2. Steel usually 240,000 p.s.i. to 270,000 p.s.i. minimum strength. Size should be small enough to permit proper curvature and accurate positioning in slab.

3. Tendons greased and wrapped or placed in smooth conduits to reduce frictional losses during stressing operations. Length of continuous tendons limited to about 100 feet if stressed from one end. Long tendons require simultaneous stressing from both ends to reduce friction losses. Tendons may be grouted after stressing or left un-bonded. Ultimate strength must be checked.

4. Minimum average prestress (Net prestress force/area of concrete) = 150 p.s.i. to 250 p.s.i. minimum average prestress required. Maximum average prestress usually 500 p.s.i. to avoid excessive creep losses.

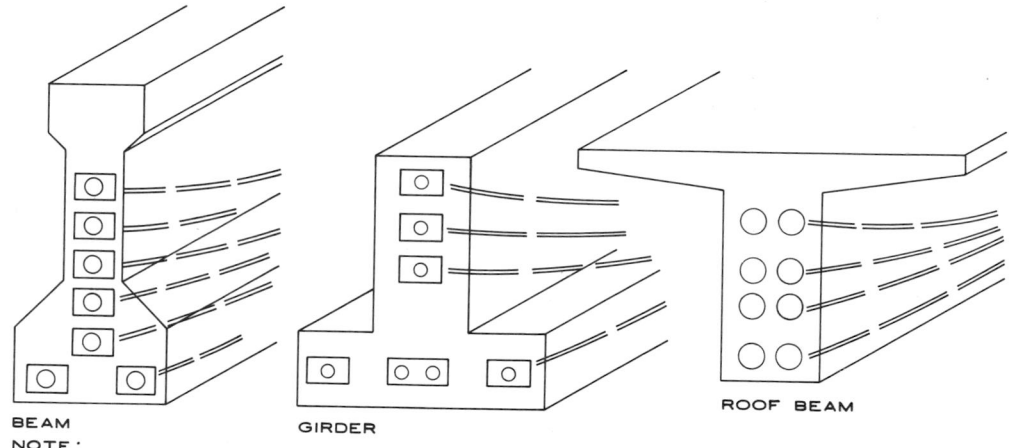

BEAM

GIRDER

ROOF BEAM

NOTE:

Post-tensioned beams and girders are prestressed by jacking tendons against the member itself. Permits casting at site for members too large or heavy for transporting from factory to site.

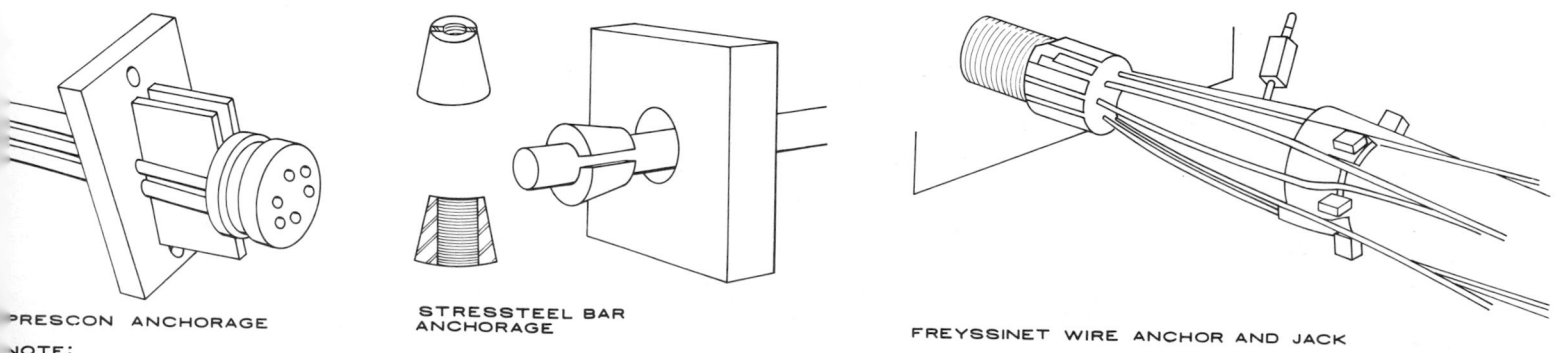

PRESCON ANCHORAGE

STRESSTEEL BAR ANCHORAGE

FREYSSINET WIRE ANCHOR AND JACK

NOTE:

Two-way post tensioned flat slabs average about 1 lb. of prestressing wire or strand per square foot for 24' to 28' bays. Additionally: at ordinary reinforcing steel runs about 0.5 lbs. per square foot.

Jack A. Clark; Baume and Polivnick; Denver, Colorado
Wright & Mok; Consulting Engineers; Silver Spring, Maryland

LIFT—SLAB CONSTRUCTION

GENERAL NOTES:

The lift slab method of construction basically consists of casting the reinforced concrete floor and roof slabs one on top of the other at or near ground level and, after curing, lifting to their final position by hydraulic jacks. By constructing in this manner, practically all of the structural work and a large portion of the electrical and mechanical work can be done within a few feet of the ground, thus facilitating the placement of materials and reducing the amount of labor required to perform these operations. The above applies to the following lift-shapes:

1. Space Frames (Steel or conc.)
2. Flat Slabs (Reinf. conc. postensioned, prestressed)
3. Vaults
4. Domes
5. Any structure for which in-place forming or erection is expensive or has disadvantages.

LIFT—SLAB RESTRICTIONS

1. Uniform slab thickness required.
2. Cantilevers required.
3. Columns should be located as uniformly as possible.
4. Openings must be located away from shear zone.

LIFT—SLAB ADVANTAGES

1. Forms: only slab edge and other minor forming required, most of it done at ground level.
2. Steel: reinforcing steel, postensioned, placed at ground level, no hoisting.
3. Concrete: placed at ground level, no hoisting.
4. Ceiling Treatment: no joint marks, grain markings or other blemishes to be removed by rubbing and cleaning.
5. Materials: use slabs as elevators to raise materials.
6. Electrical and Mechanical: sleeves for all floors can be set at one time.
7. Inclement Weather Protection: early erection of all slabs in any one section provides roof protection.

LIFTING METHOD (GENERAL)

Hydraulic jacks, especially designed for lift-slab construction, are placed on top of each column, ready to lift the slabs as soon as they attain required strength. Lifting rods are then connected to the steel lifting collars which are, by this time, a permanent part of the slab, occasionally two or more slabs are lifted at one time.

LIFTING COLLARS

One for each slab to be lifted, are stacked one atop another around each column at the time the columns are erected. They are made of steel and have fittings to which the lifting rods of each jack are connected.

LIFT SHAPE (GENERAL)

The concept involves the development of a structural steel skeleton in such a way that it can be fabricated on a flat plane, then lifted and "sprung" into final position for a spray coating of concrete or other material. The lift shape process is basically a technique of construction. While the lift shape technique involves a logical system of thrust and counterthrust, the structural analysis itself is not significantly different than for more conventional methods of designing thin shell concrete.

TILT—UP CONSTRUCTION

GENERAL NOTES:

Tilt up construction is a special form of precast concrete construction. Walls are cast on the site in a horizontal position, tilted to the vertical position, set in place and made an integral part of the completed structure. There are a great many different ways of designing and erecting such structures, particularly as to the details. Each designer and builder has his own methods and details which he is constantly trying to improve. It will be advantageous for the designer to consult with possible contractors before the design and construction details are definitely established. He should at least consider the personnel and equipment available in the area. Even small changes in design or construction procedure may result in appreciable saving in time and money as well as providing a better structure.

ADVANTAGES

Tilt up is adaptable to a wide range of uses and architectural effects. It has been used for many types of structures from private homes and garages to multi-story office buildings, although by far its greatest use has been for one story industrial and commercial buildings. Construction time is relatively short with this method.

DESIGN

Wall panels must be designed for the conditions to which they will be subjected in the completed structure and during erection. The general design of the building will determine whether the walls are load-bearing or non-load bearing with a continuous footing or supported on the column footings only. The design for these conditions after the walls of reinforced concrete built in the conventional manner, the only difference will be in details.

LIFTING STRESSES

Tilting a wall panel creates stresses not encountered in conventional cast-in place construction and with some pick-up arrangements an exact analysis may be rather involved. The method of attaching the lifting equipment must be known in order to determine the stresses. If the attachment is to a stiff channel or angle bolted to the top edge of the panel, the latter will be designed as a simply supported slab.

LOADS

The total load to be used in computing erection stresses must be assumed. In addition to the dead load of the slab, there is some resistance to the initial movement, the amount depending on the type of bond prevention material, surface condition of the floor, moisture condition lifting speed and possibly other factors. Experience indicates that where care is taken to prevent bond between the panel and floor, the initial resistance to movement is only slightly greater than that due to the weight of the slab.

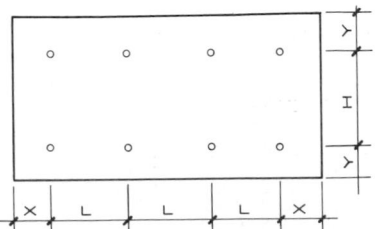

BEST RESULTS OCCUR WHEN CANTILEVERS ARE PROPORTIONED AS FOLLOWS:
Y = 25% H MIN; 40% H MAX.
X = 25% L MIN; 40% L MAX.

PLAN OF LIFT—SLAB

SCHEMATIC ISOMETRIC OF LIFT—SLAB METHOD

NOTE:

Schematic shows jacks at top of columns, lifting rods, shear bars under slabs. The slabs can be pre-stressed, post-tensioned, or reinforced concrete.

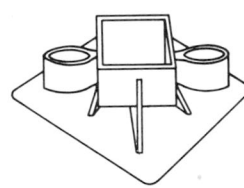

TYPICAL COLLAR USED IN LIFT—SLAB CONSTRUCTION

LIFT—SLAB CONSTRUCTION

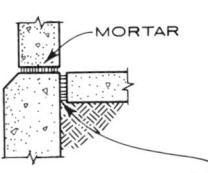

PREFERRED FOUNDATION DETAIL FOR TILT-UP CONSTRUCTION

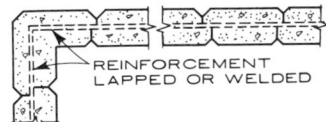

PANELS AS CURTAIN WALL
This detail to be used only as a closure and not where stiffness is required.

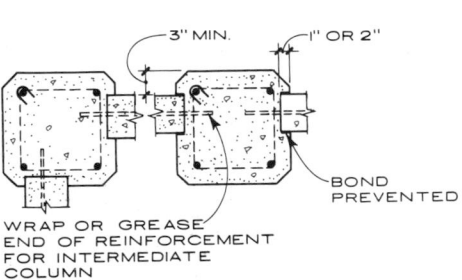

PANELS WITH STRUCTURE
Erect panels before pouring column.
Column wall joint typical where movement at joint is desired.

COLUMN—WALL JOINT DETAILS

TILT—UP CONSTRUCTION

James Morobitto; Baume and Polivnick; Denver, Colorado
Frank Strasburger, C. E.; Strasburger & Soto; Washington, D. C. and Heinzman and Clifton; Washington, D. C.

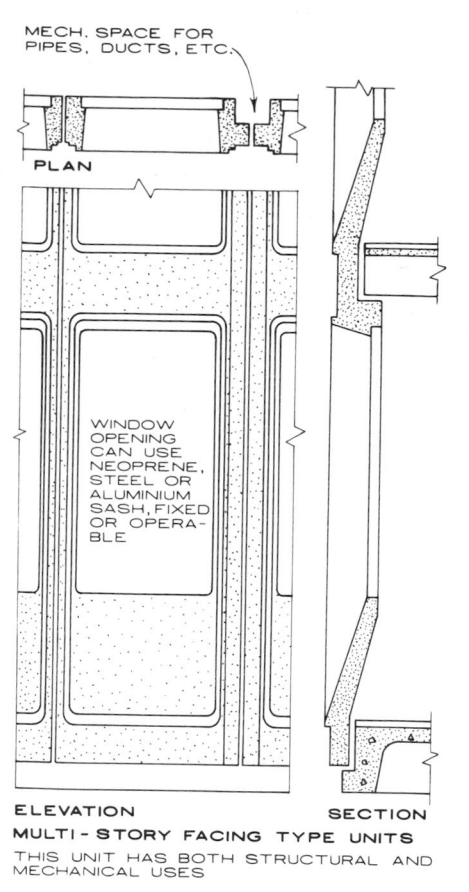

ELEVATION   **SECTION**

MULTI - STORY FACING TYPE UNITS

THIS UNIT HAS BOTH STRUCTURAL AND MECHANICAL USES

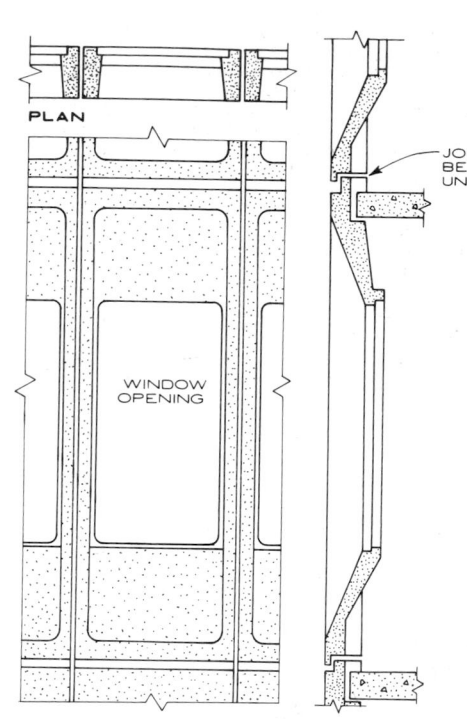

ELEVATION   **SECTION**

SINGLE STORY FACING TYPE UNITS

THIS UNIT HAS BOTH STRUCTURAL AND MECHANICAL USES

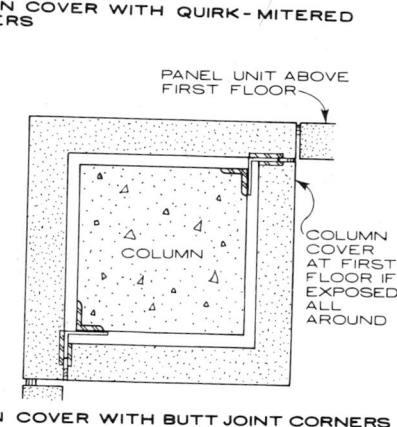

COLUMN COVER WITH QUIRK - MITERED CORNERS

COLUMN COVER WITH BUTT JOINT CORNERS

ADVANTAGE IS COLUMN COVER CAN BE COMBINED WITH FASCIA PANELS WITH OPEN FIRST FLOOR AREA.
ANCHORAGE SIMILAR TO QUIRK - MITERED CORNER

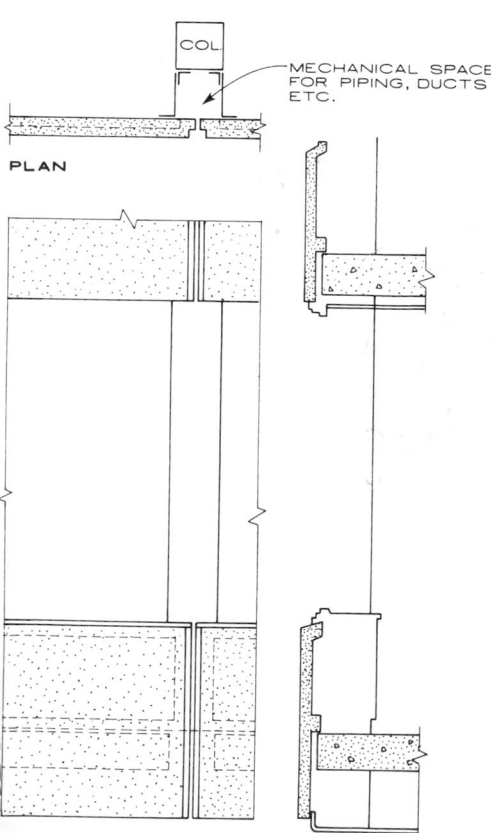

ELEVATION   **SECTION**

SPANDREL FACING TYPE UNITS

THESE ARE CANTILEVERED TO ALLOW MECHANICAL SPACE

BASIC TYPES

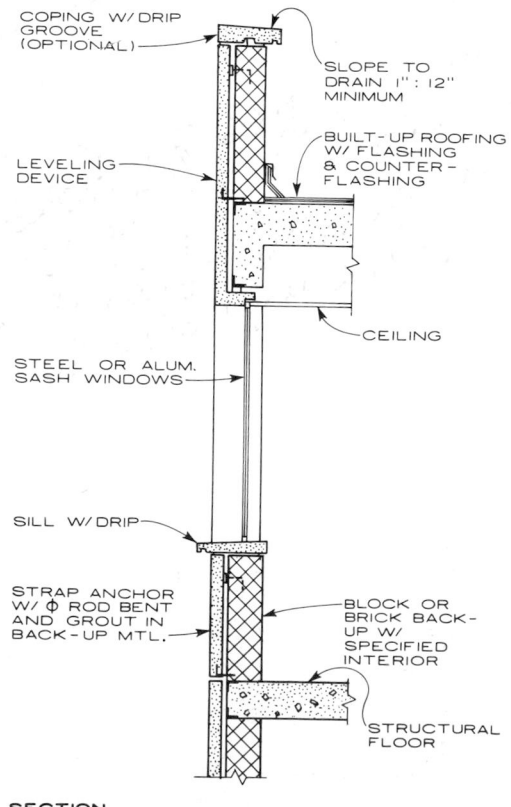

SECTION

FLAT FACING UNITS WITH COPING - RETURN AT WINDOW HEAD-WINDOW SILL

RECOMMENDED THICKNESSES:

Panels using up to 1 $\frac{1}{2}$" maximum size aggregate:

THICKNESS OF PANEL	MAXIMUM LENGTH
2"	6'- 0"
2 $\frac{1}{2}$"	8'- 0"
3"	10'- 0"
3 $\frac{1}{2}$"	13'- 0"
4"	15'- 0"
4 $\frac{1}{2}$"	18'- 0"
5"	23'- 0"
5 $\frac{1}{2}$"	25'- 0"
6"	27'- 0"
6 $\frac{1}{2}$"	30'- 0"
7"	35'- 0"
7 $\frac{1}{2}$"	38'- 0"
8"	40'- 0"

NOTE:

If maximum 1 $\frac{1}{2}$" aggregate is used minimum thickness should be 2 $\frac{1}{2}$", preferably 3".

POSSIBLE FINISHES

Panels can be made in an infinite variety of finishes and colors depending on the type and size of aggregate and matrix color chosen by the architect. Some of the most common are: Rough Exposed Aggregate; Honed; Polished; Smooth; Stippled; and Brushed. The designer may also choose to design a sculptered pattern or to have signs cast into panel.

ECONOMY

For a more economical job the designer should pick a width and height of unit that can be transported, handled and erected with a minimum of labor and maximum re-use of the unit form. Odd size units should, if at all possible, come from a portion of the typical unit so they may be cast from the typical units mold. Be sure to consult with your local manufacturer to ascertain his limitations, total economy, in your area and recommendations for your panel.

Jack A. Clark; Baume and Polivnick; Denver, Colorado

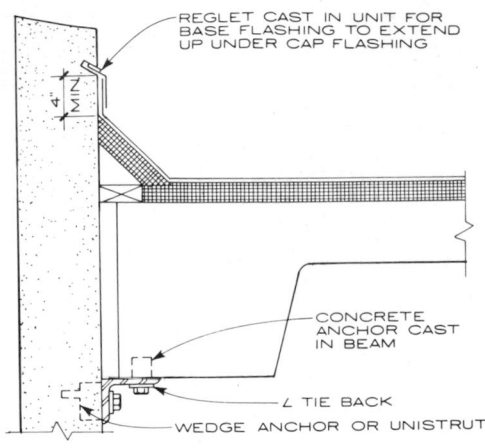

REGLET CAST IN UNIT FOR BASE FLASHING TO EXTEND UP UNDER CAP FLASHING

4" MIN

CONCRETE ANCHOR CAST IN BEAM

∠ TIE BACK

WEDGE ANCHOR OR UNISTRUT

SECTION AT ROOF LATERAL SUPPORT AT CONCRETE

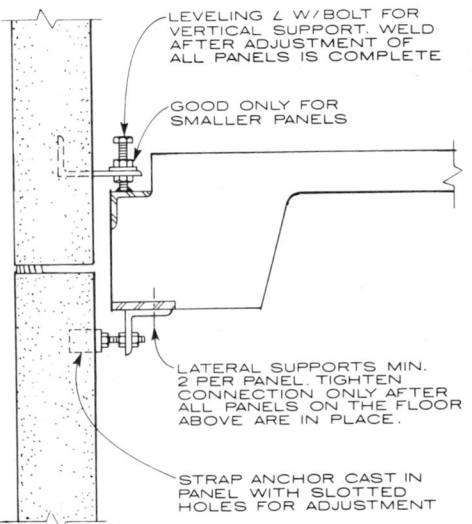

LEVELING ∠ W/BOLT FOR VERTICAL SUPPORT. WELD AFTER ADJUSTMENT OF ALL PANELS IS COMPLETE

GOOD ONLY FOR SMALLER PANELS

LATERAL SUPPORTS MIN. 2 PER PANEL. TIGHTEN CONNECTION ONLY AFTER ALL PANELS ON THE FLOOR ABOVE ARE IN PLACE.

STRAP ANCHOR CAST IN PANEL WITH SLOTTED HOLES FOR ADJUSTMENT

SECTION OF COMPRESSION SUPPORT AT INTERMEDIATE JOINTS

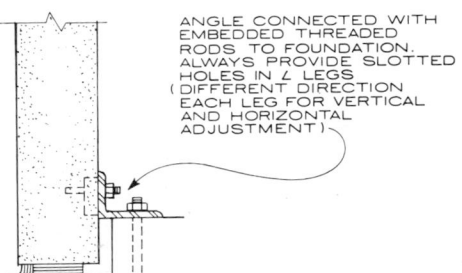

ANGLE CONNECTED WITH EMBEDDED THREADED RODS TO FOUNDATION. ALWAYS PROVIDE SLOTTED HOLES IN ∠ LEGS (DIFFERENT DIRECTION EACH LEG FOR VERTICAL AND HORIZONTAL ADJUSTMENT)

SECTION AT FOUNDATION

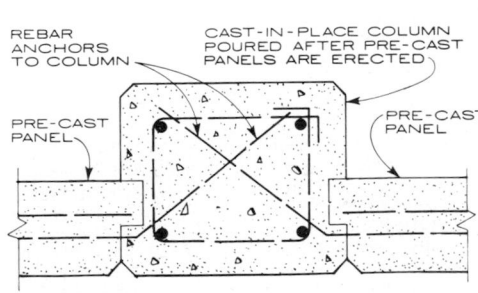

REBAR ANCHORS TO COLUMN

CAST-IN-PLACE COLUMN POURED AFTER PRE-CAST PANELS ARE ERECTED

PRE-CAST PANEL

PRE-CAST PANEL

PLAN DETAIL OF JOINT CONCRETE FRAME

Jack A. Clark; Baume and Polivnick; Denver, Colorado

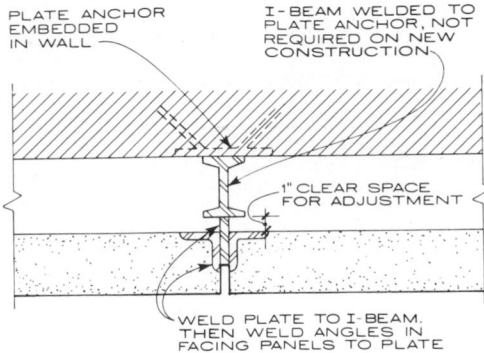

PLATE ANCHOR EMBEDDED IN WALL

I-BEAM WELDED TO PLATE ANCHOR, NOT REQUIRED ON NEW CONSTRUCTION.

1" CLEAR SPACE FOR ADJUSTMENT

WELD PLATE TO I-BEAM. THEN WELD ANGLES IN FACING PANELS TO PLATE

CONNECTION FOR ACCESS FROM FACE OF UNITS ONLY

NOTE:
The principal is the same for existing masonry, new masonry or structural steel.

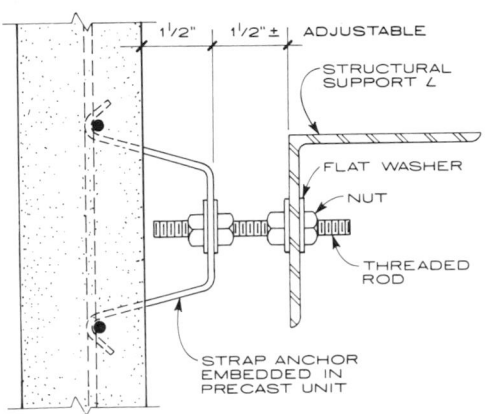

1½"   1½"±   ADJUSTABLE

STRUCTURAL SUPPORT ∠

FLAT WASHER

NUT

THREADED ROD

STRAP ANCHOR EMBEDDED IN PRECAST UNIT

TYPICAL PLAN SECTION OF STRAP ANCHOR CONNECTION AT STEEL

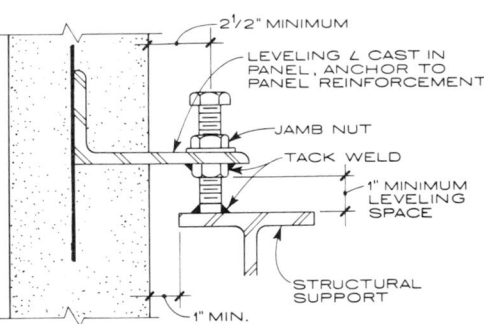

2½" MINIMUM

LEVELING ∠ CAST IN PANEL, ANCHOR TO PANEL REINFORCEMENT

JAMB NUT

TACK WELD

1" MINIMUM LEVELING SPACE

STRUCTURAL SUPPORT

1" MIN.

SECTION AT LEVELING DEVICE FOR STRUCTURAL STEEL BEAM

NOTE:
Adjustment minimums

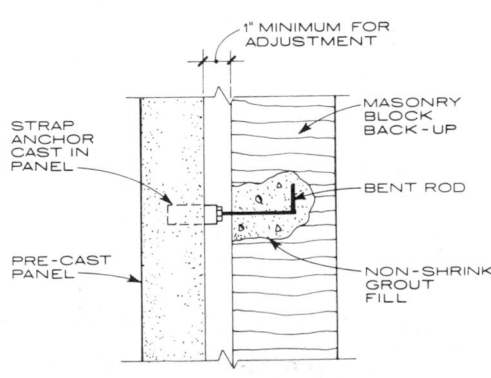

1" MINIMUM FOR ADJUSTMENT

STRAP ANCHOR CAST IN PANEL

MASONRY BLOCK BACK-UP

BENT ROD

PRE-CAST PANEL

NON-SHRINK GROUT FILL

SECTION AT CONNECTION OF FLAT PANELS TO MASONARY

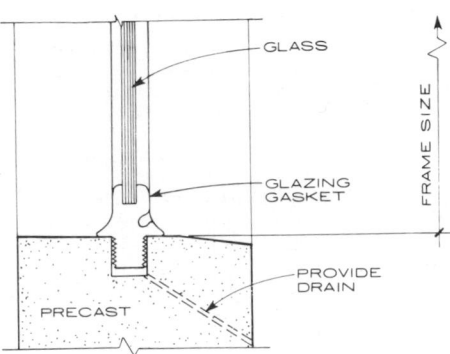

GLASS

GLAZING GASKET

FRAME SIZE

PROVIDE DRAIN

PRECAST

SILL DETAIL AT FIXED WINDOW JAMB SIMILAR

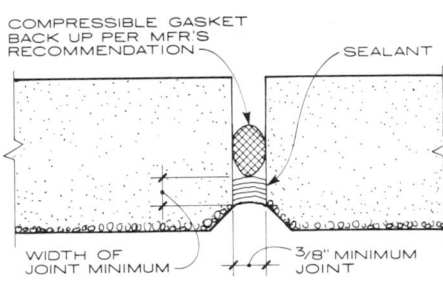

COMPRESSIBLE GASKET BACK UP PER MFR'S RECOMMENDATION

SEALANT

WIDTH OF JOINT MINIMUM

3/8" MINIMUM JOINT

SEALANT JOINT DETAIL

NOTE:
Joints can be used to great advantage by accenting them.

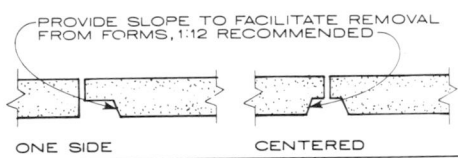

PROVIDE SLOPE TO FACILITATE REMOVAL FROM FORMS, 1:12 RECOMMENDED

ONE SIDE   CENTERED

REVEAL JOINTS

SOLID INSULATION BOARD

Solid insulation board surface applied to back of panel provides good values at reasonable cost.

CELLULAR CONCRETE

Cellular concrete has fair insulation values but requires greater thickness of the wall section.

FOAM PLASTIC CORE

Foam plastic core has fair insulation values. Used for double faced walls finished both sides. It is more expensive and requires greater handling control.

INSULATION METHODS

CONCRETE SURFACES – GENERAL

Architectural finishes are as varied and possible as the cost and effort expended to achieve them. There are three basic ways to improve or change the appearance of concrete:
1. By varying the materials, i.e. using a colored matrix and exposed aggregates.
2. Changing the mold or form by such means as a form liner.
3. By treating or tooling the concrete in the final stages of hardening by sandblasting or bush hammering.

The aim is to develop and secure maximum benefit from one of three features—color, texture and pattern—all of which are inter-related. Color is the easiest method of changing the appearance of concrete. It should not be used on a plain concrete surface with a series of panels since color matches are difficult to achieve. The exception is possible when white cement is used, usually as a base for the pigment to help reduce changes of color variation. Since white cement is expensive, many effects are tried with grey cement to avoid an entire plain surface. Colored concrete is most effective when it is used with an exposed aggregate finish.

VARYING MATERIALS AND EXPOSING SURFACES

1. Brushing surface about 18 hours after casting is least expensive method.
2. Washing and brushing surface sprayed with retarder 12 to 24 hours after casting.
3. Glue bed aggregate transfer method is used to face panels with expensive aggregates and varied textures by gluing the aggregate to a liner.
4. Sand bed aggregate transfer method is used to face panels with larger stones.
5. Hand-pressign aggregate after casting. Thismethod along with the sand aggregate method is used to double face panels.
5. Hand-pressing aggregate after casting. This method

FORM LINERS (PRESENTLY USED)

1. Sandblasted Douglas Fir or Long Leaf Yellow Pine dressed one side away from the concrete surface.
2. Flexible steel strip formwork adapted to curved surfaces (Schwellmer System).
3. Resin-coated, striated, or sandblasted plywood.
4. Rubber mats.
5. Thermoplastic sheets with high glass or texture laid over stone etc.
6. Formed plastics.
7. Plaster-of-paris molds for sculptured work.
8. Clay (sculpturing and staining concrete).
9. Masonite (Screen side).
10. Standard steel forms.
11. Wood boarding and reversed battens.
12. Square edged lumber dressed one side.

TOOLING SURFACES

1. Stamping with various tools or rollers.
2. Brooming.
3. Rubbing.
4. Scraping.
5. Grinding.
6. Bush-hammering.
7. Sandblasting.

KIND OF COMMON AGGREGATE

1. Quartz—clear, white, rose.
2. Marble—green, yellow, red, pink, blue, grey, white and black.
3. Granite—pink, grey, black and white.
4. "Gravels"—brown, reddish-brown.
5. Ceramic—full range.
6. Vitreous or glass—full range.

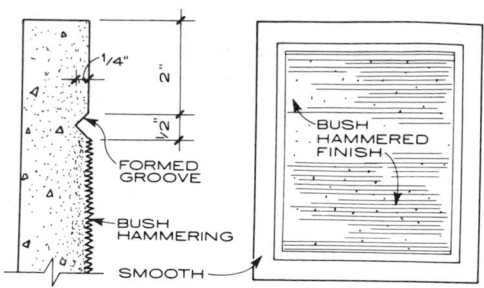

BUSH HAMMERING DETAILS

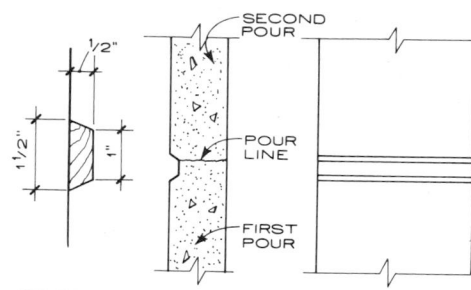

HORIZONTAL RUSTICATION AT CONSTRUCTION JOINT

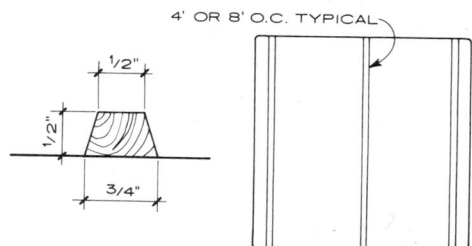
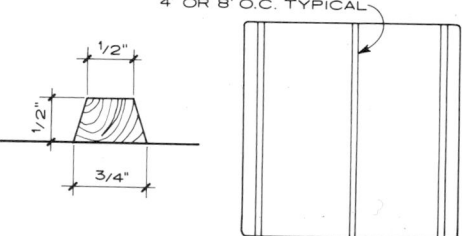
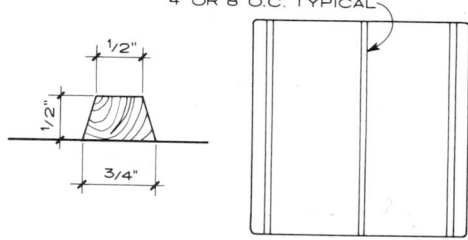
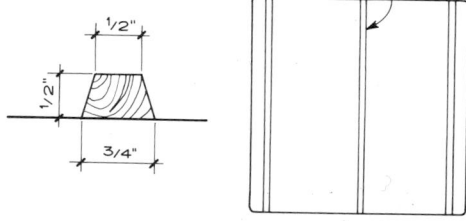

VERTICAL RUSTICATION – SMOOTH OR LIGHT SANDBLAST

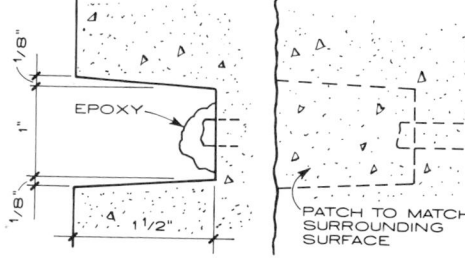

TIE-HOLE TREATMENT

PIECES OF FLAT STONE EMBEDDED IN SAND

LARGE EXPOSED AGGREGATE

AGGREGATES UNIFORM IN SIZE QUARTZ, MARBLE

EXPOSED GRAVEL AGGREGATE PANEL

EXPOSED AGGREGATE SURFACES

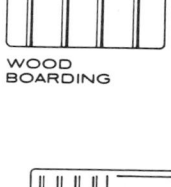

SANDBLASTED PLYWOOD

WOOD BOARDING

SQUARE EDGED LUMBER - DRESSED ONE SIDE

CORRUGATED VINYL PLASTIC

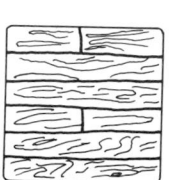

MOULDED PLASTIC FORM

RUBBER MATTING

CONCRETE PANEL
PLASTIC STONE

PLASTIC FILM OVER A STONE LAYER, DIMPLED CONCRETE

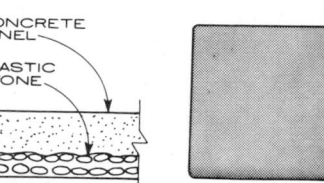

EXAMPLES OF TEXTURES OBTAINED BY USE OF FORM LINES

Jack A. Clark; Baume and Polivnick; Denver, Colorado

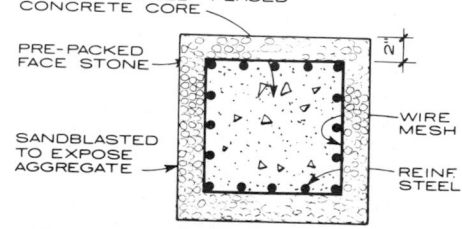

CONVENTIONALLY PLACED CONCRETE CORE
PRE-PACKED FACE STONE
SANDBLASTED TO EXPOSE AGGREGATE
WIRE MESH
REINF. STEEL

ARBETON EXPOSED AGGREGATE FINISH

CHAPTER 4

MASONRY CONSTRUCTION

BUILDING CODE REQUIREMENTS FOR MASONRY.   USAS A41.1—1953.0.

Scope: Minimum requirements for design and construction of non-reinforced masonry.   Does not cover veneer or fire protection requirements.

ALLOWABLE COMPRESSIVE STRESSES IN UNIT MASONRY

CONSTRUCTION AND GRADE OF UNIT	ALLOWABLE COMPRESSIVE STRESSES; GROSS CROSS-SECTIONAL AREA (EXCEPT AS NOTED) IN PSI				
	TYPE M MORTAR	TYPE S MORTAR	TYPE N MORTAR	TYPE O MORTAR	TYPE K MORTAR
SOLID BRICK MASONRY					
8,000 plus, psi	400	350	300	200	100
4,500 to 8,000, psi	250	225	200	150	100
2,500 to 4,500, psi	175	160	140	110	75
1,500 to 2,500, psi	125	115	100	75	50
GROUTED SOLID BRICK MASONRY					
4,500 plus, psi	350	275	200		
2,500 to 4,500, psi	275	215	155		
1,500 to 2,500, psi	225	175	125		
MASONRY OF HOLLOW UNITS	85	75	70		
HOLLOW WALLS (CAVITY OR MASONRY BONDED)* SOLID UNITS:					
2,500 plus, psi	140	130	110		
1,500 to 2,500, psi	100	90	80		
HOLLOW UNITS	70	60	55		

*On gross cross-sectional area of wall minus area of cavity between wythes.

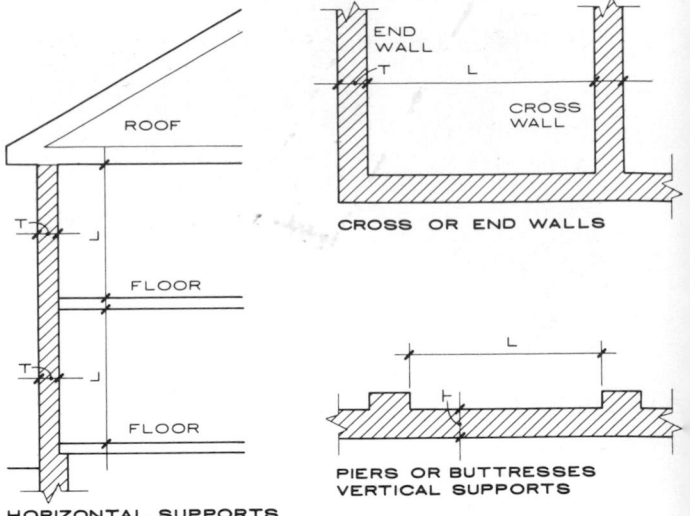

CROSS OR END WALLS

PIERS OR BUTTRESSES VERTICAL SUPPORTS

HORIZONTAL SUPPORTS

MAXIMUM RATIO OF UNSUPPORTED HEIGHT OR LENGTH TO NOMINAL THICKNESS

TYPE OF MASONRY	RATIO $\frac{L}{T}$
SOLID MASONRY BEARING WALLS	20
HOLLOW UNIT MASONRY BEARING WALLS	18
CAVITY WALLS	18*
NON-BEARING WALLS	36**

*Thickness equal to sum of the nominal thickness of the inner and outer widths.

**Based on actual thickness of partition including plaster.

LATERAL SUPPORT

BEARING WALLS—EXCEPTIONS (see adjacent sketch)

1.   Stiffened solid masonry bearing walls may be 12 inches thick for a height of 70'.
2.   The top story bearing wall of a building not exceeding 35 feet in height may be 8 inches in thickness.
3.   Walls of residential buildings not exceeding three stories or 35 feet in height may be eight inches in thickness.
4.   Walls above roof level, 12 feet or less in height, enclosing stairways, penthouses, etc. may be of 8 inch thickness.
5.   Hollow walls (metal tied or masonry bonded) shall not exceed 35 feet in height above their support, except that 10 inch cavity walls shall not exceed 25 feet in height.

EXTERIOR NONBEARING WALLS

Four inches less in thickness than required for bearing walls but not less than 8 inches except where 6 inch walls are permitted.

BEARING WALLS — MINIMUM THICKNESS

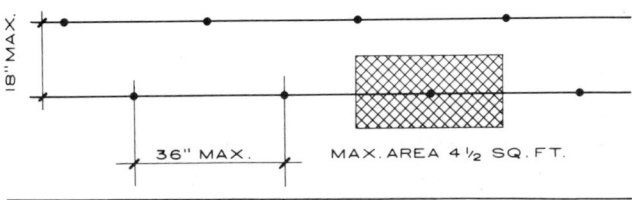

SPACING AND STAGGERING OF METAL TIES

BONDING OF SOLID UNITS

Headers—   4% of wall surface
maximum spacing, 24 in.

Metal ties—   3/16" diameter steel rod for
each 4 1/2 sq. ft.

NOTE:

Refer to Local Building Code for local code requirements for masonry.

Structural Clay Products Institute; McLean, Virginia

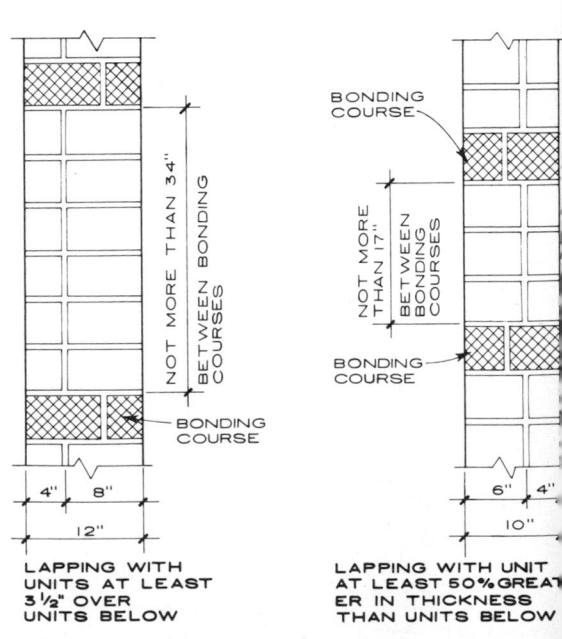

LAPPING WITH UNITS AT LEAST 3½" OVER UNITS BELOW

LAPPING WITH UNIT AT LEAST 50% GREATER IN THICKNESS THAN UNITS BELOW

BONDING OF HOLLOW UNITS

BUILDING CODE REQUIREMENTS FOR REINFORCED MASONRY, USAS A41.2-1960

Scope: Minimum requirements for design and construction of reinforced masonry built with solid or hollow masonry units.

COMPRESSIVE STRENGTH OF UNITS AND MASONRY

COMPRESSIVE STRENGTH OF UNITS	ASSUMED COMPRESSIVE STRENGTH OF MASONRY $f'm$*
1,000 to 1,500 psi	900 to 1,150 psi
Over 1,500 to 2,500 psi	1,151 to 1,550 psi
Over 2,500 to 4,000 psi	1,551 to 2,000 psi
Over 4,000 to 6,000 psi	2,001 to 2,400 psi
Over 6,000 to 8,000 psi	2,401 to 2,700 psi
Over 8,000 to 10,000 psi	2,701 to 2,900 psi
Over 10,000 to 12,000 psi	2,901 to 3,000 psi
Over 12,000 psi	3,000 psi

*Based on h/d of 2.0

NOTE:

Use gross area for masonry of solid units and net area for masonry of hollow units.

WALLS

Minimum thickness: 6 in.

Maximum unsupported height or length, 25 t

Allowable axial stress: 0.20 $f'm$ for h/t of 10 or less, and reduced proportionally to 0.15 $f'm$ for h/t of 25

Minimum reinforcement: 0.002 bt

MINIMUM REQUIRED STRESS VALUES

DESCRIPTION		ALLOWABLE STRESS
COMPRESSIVE:		
AXIAL	fm	See Walls & Columns
FLEXURAL	fm	0.33 f'm
SHEAR:		
BEAMS WITH NO WEB REINFORCEMENT	Vm	50 psi
BEAMS WITH WEB REINFORCEMENT	V	150 psi
BOND:		
PLAIN BARS	U	80 psi
DEFORMED BARS (ASTM A305)	U	160 psi
BEARING:	fm	0.25 f'm
MODULUS OF ELASTICITY:	Em	1.000 f'm
MODULUS OF RIGIDITY	Ev	400 f'm

COLUMNS

Minimum thickness, 12 in. (8 in. for minor columns)

Maximum unsupported height, 20 d

Allowable axial load (PV < 0.006)
$P = Ag [0.16 f'm + 0.52 pgf's]$ where $h/d \leq 10$
$P^1 = [1.3 - 0.03 h/d]$ where $h/d > 10$

RECOMMENDED BUILDING CODE REQUIREMENTS FOR ENGINEERED BRICK MASONRY, SCPI - MAY 1960

Scope: Minimum requirements for design and construction of brick masonry of solid units both non-reinforced and reinforced.

COMPRESSIVE STRENGTH OF UNITS AND MASONRY

COMPRESSIVE STRENGTH OF UNITS, psi	ASSUMED COMPRESSIVE STRENGTH, f'm, psi *		
	TYPE M MORTAR	TYPE S MORTAR	TYPE N MORTAR
14,000 PLUS	4600	3900	3200
12,000	4000	3400	2800
10,000	3400	2900	2400
8,000	2800	2400	2000
6,000	2200	1900	1600
4,000	1600	1400	1200
2,000	1000	900	800

* Based on h/d of 5.0
Mortar shall be mixture of portland cement (I, II, III) hydrated lime (5), and sand.

ALLOWABLE STRESSES FOR NON-REINFORCED BRICK MASONRY

DESCRIPTION	TYPE M OR S MORTAR	TYPE N MORTAR
TENSION IN FLEXURE		
NORMAL TO BED JOINTS	36	28
PARALLEL TO BED JOINTS	72	56
SHEAR	50	40

Allowable stresses:
Reinforced brick masonry similar to USAS A41.2 − 1960, except flexural compressive stress equal to 0.40 f'm.

WORKMANSHIP:

Allowable stresses shall be reduced by 1/3 when there is no engineering or architectural inspection.

ALLOWABLE VERTICAL LOADS

Non-reinforced Brick Masonry
Walls: $P = c(0.25 f'm) Ag$
Columns: $P = c(0.20 f'm) Ag$

Reinforced Brick Masonry
Walls: $P = (0.25 f'm) Ag$ for $h/t \leq 5$
Columns: $P = (0.20 f'm + 0.65 pgfs) Ag$ for $h/t \leq 5$
$P' = P [1 - (h/40 t)^3]$ for $h/t > 5$

STRESS REDUCTION FACTORS, C, FOR BRICK MASONRY *

h/t	e/t		
	0 to 1/20	1/6	1/3
5	1.00	0.66	0.32
10	0.92	0.63	0.27
15	0.79	0.56	0.22
20	0.64	0.42	0.16
25	0.49	0.36	0.12
30	0.38	0.27	0.08

* The slenderness ratio h/t of walls and columns shall be limited to 30 for walls and 25 for columns.

Structural Clay Products Institute; McLean, Virginia

NOTE:

Refer to Local Building Code for local code requirements for masonry.

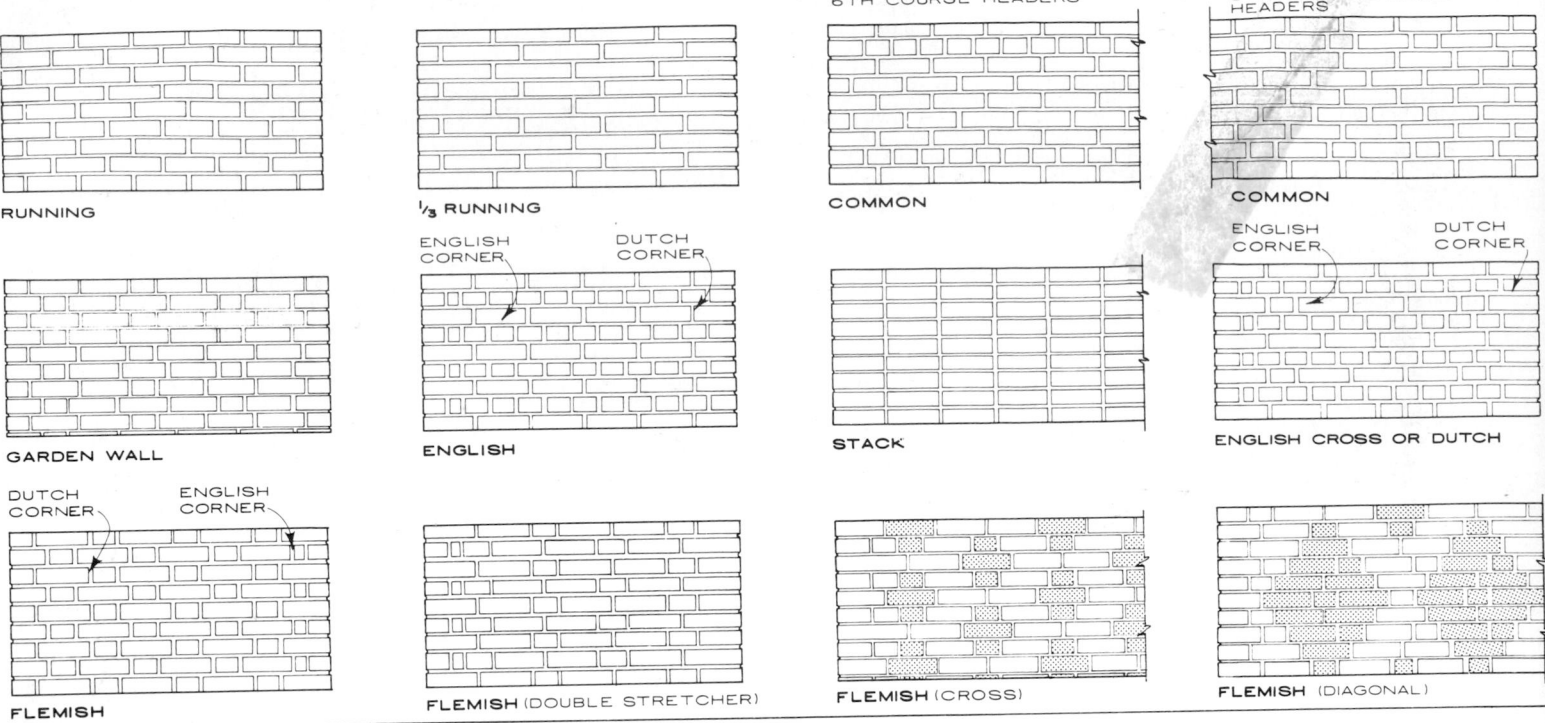

BRICK BONDS

Labels within the brick bonds figure: RUNNING, 1/3 RUNNING, 6TH COURSE HEADERS, COMMON, 6TH COURSE FLEMISH HEADERS, COMMON, GARDEN WALL, ENGLISH CORNER, DUTCH CORNER, ENGLISH, STACK, ENGLISH CORNER, DUTCH CORNER, ENGLISH CROSS OR DUTCH, DUTCH CORNER, ENGLISH CORNER, FLEMISH, FLEMISH (DOUBLE STRETCHER), FLEMISH (CROSS), FLEMISH (DIAGONAL)

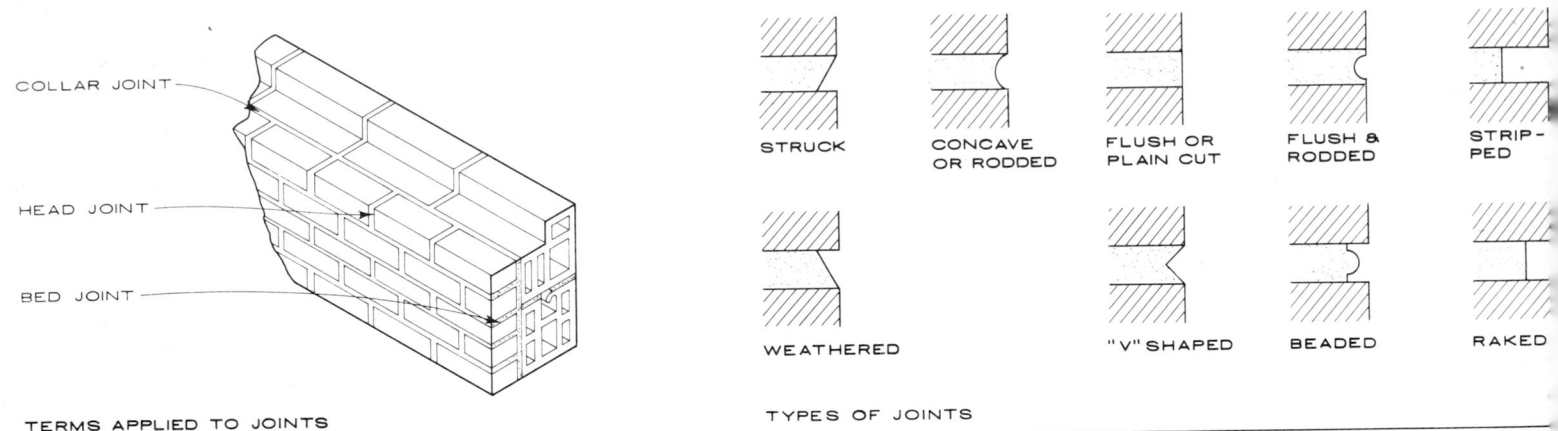

BRICK JOINTS

COLLAR JOINT, HEAD JOINT, BED JOINT

TERMS APPLIED TO JOINTS

STRUCK, CONCAVE OR RODDED, FLUSH OR PLAIN CUT, FLUSH & RODDED, STRIPPED, WEATHERED, "V" SHAPED, BEADED, RAKED

TYPES OF JOINTS

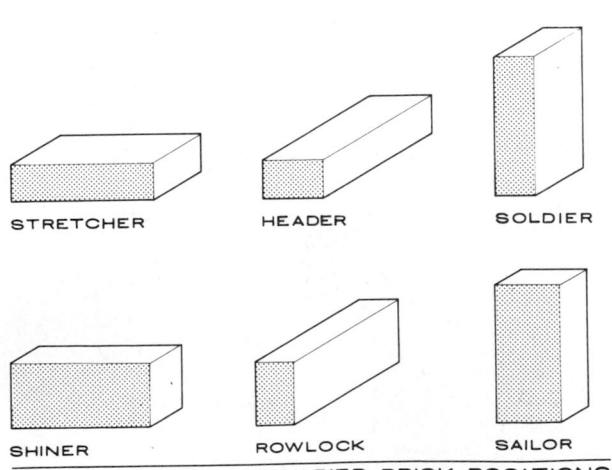

STRETCHER, HEADER, SOLDIER, SHINER, ROWLOCK, SAILOR

TERMS APPLIED TO VARIED BRICK POSITIONS

NOMINAL MODULAR SIZES OF BRICK

UNIT DESIGNATION	DIMENSIONS*			MODULAR COURSING
	THICKNESS	HEIGHT	LENGTH	
MODULAR	4"	2 2/3"	8"	3C = 8"
ENGINEER	4"	3 1/5"	8"	5C = 16"
ECONOMY	4"	4"	8"	1C = 4"
DOUBLE	4"	5 1/3"	8"	3C = 16"
ROMAN	4"	2"	12"	2C = 4"
NORMAN	4"	2 2/3"	12"	3C = 8"
NORWEGIAN	4"	3 1/5"	12"	5C = 16"
UTILITY[1]	4"	4"	12"	1C = 4"
TRIPLE	4"	5 1/3"	12"	3C = 16"
SCR BRICK	6"	2 2/3"	12"	3C = 8"
6" NORWEGIAN	6"	3 1/5"	12"	5C = 16"
6" JUMBO	6"	4"	12"	1C = 4"
8" JUMBO	8"	4"	12"	1C = 4"

[1] Also called Norman Economy, General and King Norman.

*For special shapes contact local brick manufacturers.

Structural Clay Products Institute; McLean, Virginia

4" x 2 2/3" x 8" NOMINAL

    BRICK SIZES:
       For 1/4" Joint   3 3/4" x 2 3/8" x 7 3/4"
      * For 3/8" Joint   3 5/8" x 2 1/4" x 7 5/8"
    ** For 1/2" Joint   3 1/2" x 2 3/16" x 7 1/2"

4" x 2 2/3" x 12" NOMINAL

    BRICK SIZES:
       For 1/4" Joint   3 3/4" x 2 3/8" x 11 3/4"
      * For 3/8" Joint   3 5/8" x 2 1/4" x 11 5/8"
    ** For 1/2" Joint   3 1/2" x 2 3/16" x 11 1/2"

SCR 6" x 2 2/3" x 12" NOMINAL
      For 1/2" Joint   5 1/2" x 2 1/8" x 11 1/2"

    Joint selected determines brick size
    3 courses = 2 modules (8")

NOMINAL HEIGHT OF 2 2/3" COURSES TO & OF JOINT.
READ FROM BOTTOM UP.

#	Height	#	Height
31	6'– 10 2/3"	61	13'– 6 2/3"
30	6'– 8"	60	13'– 4"
29	6'– 5 1/3"	59	13'– 1 1/3"
28	6'– 2 2/3"	58	12'– 10 2/3"
27	6'– 0"	57	12'– 8"
26	5'– 9 1/3"	56	12'– 5 1/3"
25	5'– 6 2/3"	55	12'– 2 2/3"
24	5'– 4"	54	12'– 0"
23	5'– 1 1/3"	53	11'– 9 1/3"
22	4'– 10 2/3"	52	11'– 6 2/3"
21	4'– 8"	51	11'– 4"
20	4'– 5 1/3"	50	11'– 1 1/3"
19	4'– 2 2/3"	49	10'– 10 2/3"
18	4'– 0"	48	10'– 8"
17	3'– 9 1/3"	47	10'– 5 1/3"
16	3'– 6 2/3"	46	10'– 2 2/3"
15	3'– 4"	45	10'– 0"
14	3'– 1 1/3"	44	9'– 9 1/3"
13	2'– 10 2/3"	43	9'– 6 2/3"
12	2'– 8"	42	9'– 4"
11	2'– 5 1/3"	41	9'– 1 1/3"
10	2'– 2 1/3"	40	8'– 10 2/3"
9	2'– 0"	39	8'– 8"
8	1'– 9 1/3"	38	8'– 5 1/3"
7	1'– 6 2/3"	37	8'– 2 2/3"
6	1'– 4"	36	8'– 0"
5	1'– 1 1/3"	35	7'– 9 1/3"
4	10 2/3"	34	7'– 6 2/3"
3	8"	33	7'– 4"
2	5 1/3"	32	7'– 1 1/3"
1	2 2/3"		

4" x 3 1/5" x 8" NOMINAL

    BRICK SIZES:
      * For 3/8" Joint   3 5/8" x 2 13/16" x 7 5/8"
      For 1/2" Joint   3 1/2" x 2 11/16" x 7 1/2"

    Joint selected determines brick size.
    5 courses = 4 modules (16").

NOMINAL HEIGHTS OF 3 1/5" COURSES TO & OF JOINT.
READ FROM BOTTOM UP.

#	Height	#	Height
29	7'– 8 4/5"	59	15'– 8 4/5"
28	7'– 5 3/5"	58	15'– 5 3/5"
27	7'– 2 2/5"	57	15'– 2 2/5"
26	6'– 11 1/5"	56	14'– 11 1/5"
25	6'– 8"	55	14'– 8"
24	6'– 4 4/5"	54	14'– 4 4/5"
23	6'– 1 3/5"	53	14'– 1 3/5"
22	5'– 10 2/5"	52	13'– 10 2/5"
21	5'– 7 1/3"	51	13'– 7 1/5"
20	5'– 4"	50	13'– 4"
19	5'– 0 4/5"	49	13'– 0 4/5"
18	4'– 9 3/5"	48	12'– 9 3/5"
17	4'– 6 2/5"	47	12'– 6 2/5"
16	4'– 3 1/5"	46	12'– 3 1/5"
15	4'– 0"	45	12'– 0"
14	3'– 8 4/5"	44	11'– 8 4/5"
13	3'– 5 3/5"	43	11'– 5 3/5"
12	3'– 2 2/5"	42	11'– 2 2/5"
11	2'– 11 1/5"	41	10'– 11 1/5"
10	2'– 8"	40	10'– 8"
9	2'– 4 4/5"	39	10'– 4 4/5"
8	2'– 1 3/5"	38	10'– 1 3/5"
7	1'– 10 2/5"	37	9'– 10 2/5"
6	1'– 7 1/5"	36	9'– 7 1/5"
5	1'– 4"	35	9'– 4"
4	1'– 0 4/5"	34	9'– 0 4/5"
3	9 3/5"	33	8'– 9 3/5"
2	6 2/5"	32	8'– 6 2/5"
1	3 1/5"	31	8'– 3 1/5"
		30	8'– 0"

4" x 4" x 8" NOMINAL

    BRICK SIZES:
       For 1/4" Joint   3 3/4" x 3 3/4" x 7 3/4"
      * For 3/8" Joint   3 5/8" x 3 5/8" x 7 5/8"
    ** For 1/2" Joint   3 1/2" x 3 1/2" x 7 1/2"

4" x 4" x 12" NOMINAL

    BRICK SIZES:
       For 1/4" Joint   3 3/4" x 3 3/4" x 11 3/4"
       For 3/8" Joint   3 5/8" x 3 5/8" x 11 5/8"
       For 1/2" Joint   3 1/2" x 3 1/2" x 11 1/2"

    Joint selected determines brick size.
    1 course = 1 module (4")

NOMINAL HEIGHTS OF 4" COURSES TO & OF JOINT.
READ FROM BOTTOM UP.

#	Height	#	Height
21	7'– 0"	43	14'– 4"
20	6'– 8"	42	14'– 0"
19	6'– 4"	41	13'– 8"
18	6'– 0"	40	13'– 4"
17	5'– 8"	39	13'– 0"
16	5'– 4"	38	12'– 8"
15	5'– 0"	37	12'– 4"
14	4'– 8"	36	12'– 0"
13	4'– 4"	35	11'– 8"
12	4'– 0"	34	11'– 4"
11	3'– 8"	33	11'– 0"
10	3'– 4"	32	10'– 8"
9	3'– 0"	31	10'– 4"
8	2'– 8"	30	10'– 0"
7	2'– 4"	29	9'– 8"
6	2'– 0"	28	9'– 4"
5	1'– 8"	27	9'– 0"
4	1'– 4"	26	8'– 8"
3	1'– 0"	25	8'– 4"
2	8"	24	8'– 0"
1	4"	23	7'– 8"
		22	7'– 4"

Not all sizes made in all sections of U. S.; check with local manufacturers for sizes available. Grid lines (— · — · —) are 4" modules.
* 3/8" Joint used for facing brick.
** 1/2" Joint used for glazed and structural units and building brick.

Structural Clay Products Institute; McLean, Virginia

VERTICAL BRICK COURSES

NUMBER OF BRICKS & JOINTS	HEIGHT		
	1/4" JOINTS	3/8" JOINTS	1/2" JOINTS
1 brk. & 1 jt.	2 1/2"	2 5/8"	2 3/4"
2 brks. & 2 jts.	5"	5 1/4"	5 1/2"
3 brks. & 3 jts.	7 1/2"	7 7/8"	8 1/4"
4 brks. & 4 jts.	10"	10 1/2"	11"
5 brks. & 5 jts.	1'- 0 1/2"	1'- 1 1/8"	1'- 1 3/4"
6 brks. & 6 jts.	1'- 3"	1'- 3 3/4"	1'- 4 1/2"
7 brks. & 7 jts.	1'- 5 1/2"	1'- 6 3/8"	1'- 7 1/4"
8 brks. & 8 jts.	1'- 8"	1'- 9"	1'-10"
9 brks. & 9 jts.	1'-10 1/2"	1'-11 5/8"	2'- 0 3/4"
10 brks. & 10 jts.	2'- 1"	2'- 2 1/4"	2'- 3 1/2"
11 brks. & 11 jts.	2'- 3 1/2"	2'- 4 7/8"	2'- 6 1/4"
12 brks. & 12 jts.	2'- 6"	2'- 7 1/2"	2'- 9"
13 brks. & 13 jts.	2'- 8 1/2"	2'-10 1/8"	2'-11 3/4"
14 brks. & 14 jts.	2'-11"	3'- 0 3/4"	3'- 2 1/2"
15 brks. & 15 jts.	3'- 1 1/2"	3'- 3 5/8"	3'- 5 1/4"
16 brks. & 16 jts.	3'- 4"	3'- 6"	3'- 8"
17 brks. & 17 jts.	3'- 6 1/2"	3'- 8 5/8"	3'-10 3/4"
18 brks. & 18 jts.	3'- 9"	3'-11 1/4"	4'- 1 1/2"
19 brks. & 19 jts.	3'-11 1/2"	4'- 1 7/8"	4'- 4 1/4"
20 brks. & 20 jts.	4'- 2"	4'- 4 1/2"	4'- 7"
21 brks. & 21 jts.	4'- 4 1/2"	4'- 7 1/8"	4'- 9 3/4"
22 brks. & 22 jts.	4'- 7"	4'- 9 3/4"	5'- 0 1/2"
23 brks. & 23 jts.	4'- 9 1/2"	5'- 0 3/8"	5'- 3 1/4"
24 brks. & 24 jts.	5'- 0"	5'- 3"	5'- 6"
25 brks. & 25 jts.	5'- 2 1/2"	5'- 5 5/8"	5'- 8 3/4"
26 brks. & 26 jts.	5'- 5"	5'- 8 1/4"	5'-11 1/2"
27 brks. & 27 jts.	5'- 7 1/2"	5'-10 7/8"	6'- 2 1/4"
28 brks. & 28 jts.	5'-10"	6'- 1 1/2"	6'- 5"
29 brks. & 29 jts.	6'- 0 1/2"	6'- 4 1/8"	6'- 7 3/4"
30 brks. & 30 jts.	6'- 3"	6'- 6 3/4"	6'-10 1/2"
31 brks. & 31 jts.	6'- 5 1/2"	6'- 9 3/8"	7'- 1 1/4"
32 brks. & 32 jts.	6'- 8"	7'- 0"	7'- 4"
33 brks. & 33 jts.	6'-10 1/2"	7'- 2 5/8"	7'- 6 3/4"
34 brks. & 34 jts.	7'- 1"	7'- 5 1/4"	7'- 9 1/2"
35 brks. & 35 jts.	7'- 3 1/2"	7'- 7 7/8"	8'- 0 1/4"
36 brks. & 36 jts.	7'- 6"	7'-10 1/2"	8'- 3"
37 brks. & 37 jts.	7'- 8 1/2"	8'- 1 1/8"	8'- 5 3/4"
38 brks. & 38 jts.	7'-11"	8'- 3 3/4"	8'- 8 1/2"
39 brks. & 39 jts.	8'- 1 1/2"	8'- 6 3/8"	8'-11 1/4"
40 brks. & 40 jts.	8'- 4"	8'- 9"	9'- 2"
41 brks. & 41 jts.	8'- 6 1/2"	8'-11 5/8"	9'- 4 3/4"
42 brks. & 42 jts.	8'- 9"	9'- 2 1/4"	9'- 7 1/2"
43 brks. & 43 jts.	8'-11 1/2"	9'- 4 7/8"	9'-10 1/4"
44 brks. & 44 jts.	9'- 2"	9'- 7 1/2"	10'- 1"
45 brks. & 45 jts.	9'- 4 1/2"	9'-10 1/8"	10'- 3 3/4"
46 brks. & 46 jts.	9'- 7"	10'- 0 3/4"	10'- 6 1/2"
47 brks. & 47 jts.	9'- 9 1/2"	10'- 3 3/8"	10'- 9 1/4"
48 brks. & 48 jts.	10'- 0"	10'- 6"	11'- 0"
49 brks. & 49 jts.	10'- 2 1/2"	10'- 8 5/8"	11'- 2 3/4"
50 brks. & 50 jts.	10'- 5"	10'-11 1/4"	11'- 5 1/2"
51 brks. & 51 jts.	10'- 7 1/2"	11'- 1 7/8"	11'- 8 1/4"
52 brks. & 52 jts.	10'-10"	11'- 4 1/2"	11'-11"
53 brks. & 53 jts.	11'- 0 1/2"	11'- 7 1/8"	12'- 1 3/4"
54 brks. & 54 jts.	11'- 3"	11'- 9 3/4"	12'- 4 1/2"
55 brks. & 55 jts.	11'- 5 1/2"	12'- 0 3/8"	12'- 7 1/4"
56 brks. & 56 jts.	11'- 8"	12'- 3"	12'-10"
57 brks. & 57 jts.	11'-10 1/2"	12'- 5 5/8"	13'- 0 3/4"
58 brks. & 58 jts.	12'- 1"	12'- 8 1/4"	13'- 3 1/2"
59 brks. & 59 jts.	12'- 3 1/2"	12'-10 7/8"	13'- 6 1/4"
60 brks. & 60 jts.	12'- 6"	13'- 1 1/2"	13'- 9"
61 brks. & 61 jts.	12'- 8 1/2"	13'- 4 1/8"	13'-11 3/4"
62 brks. & 62 jts.	12'-11"	13'- 6 3/4"	14'- 2 1/2"
63 brks. & 63 jts.	13'- 1 1/2"	13'- 9 3/8"	14'- 5 1/4"
64 brks. & 64 jts.	13'- 4"	14'- 0"	14'- 8"
65 brks. & 65 jts.	13'- 6 1/2"	14'- 2 5/8"	14'-10 3/4"
66 brks. & 66 jts.	13'- 9"	14'- 5 1/4"	15'- 1 1/2"
67 brks. & 67 jts.	13'-11 1/2"	14'- 7 7/8"	15'- 4 1/4"
68 brks. & 68 jts.	14'- 2"	14'-10 1/2"	15'- 7"
69 brks. & 69 jts.	14'- 4 1/2"	15'- 1 1/8"	15'- 9 3/4"
70 brks. & 70 jts.	14'- 7"	15'- 3 3/4"	16'- 0 1/2"
71 brks. & 71 jts.	14'- 9 1/2"	15'- 6 3/8"	16'- 3 1/4"
72 brks. & 72 jts.	15'- 0"	15'- 9"	16'- 6"
73 brks. & 73 jts.	15'- 2 1/2"	15'-11 5/8"	16'- 8 3/4"
74 brks. & 74 jts.	15'- 5"	16'- 2 1/4"	16'-11 1/2"
75 brks. & 75 jts.	15'- 7 1/2"	16'- 4 7/8"	17'- 2 1/4"
76 brks. & 76 jts.	15'- 9"	16'- 7 1/2"	17'- 5"

Structural Clay Products Institute; McLean, Virginia

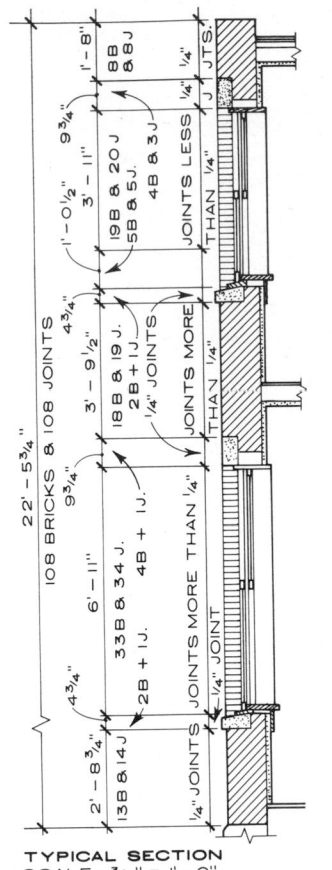

TYPICAL SECTION
SCALE: 3/16" = 1'- 0"

BRICK COURSES ADJUSTED TO DIMENSIONS

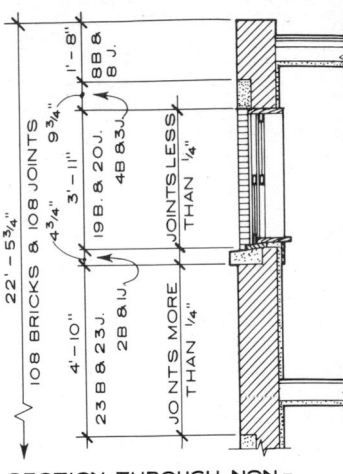

SECTION THROUGH NON-TYPICAL WINDOW
SCALE: 3/16" = 1'- 0"

NOTE:
Where window, door, vent, etc., dimensions and details are pre-determined, sizes of brick joints must be varied somewhat at different points of the building. In order to keep brick courses on the same line around the entire building, it is necessary to key all wall sections to each other.
* In the drawing shown, notice that the course of brick below the non-typical window sill must occur on the same line on every wall of the building — even though this window may occur on only one wall.

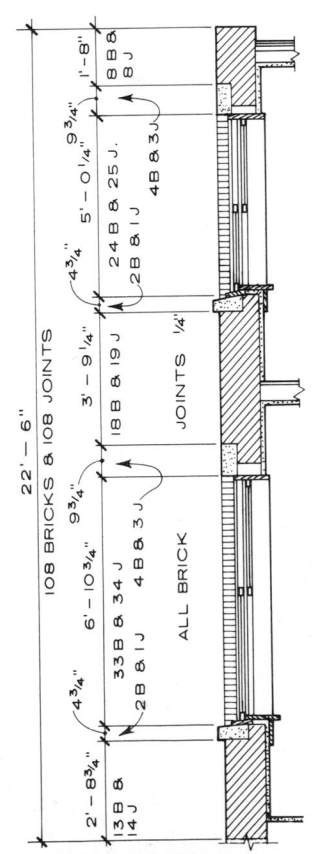

TYPICAL SECTION
SCALE: 3/16" = 1'- 0"

DIMENSIONS FIXED BY BRICK COURSES

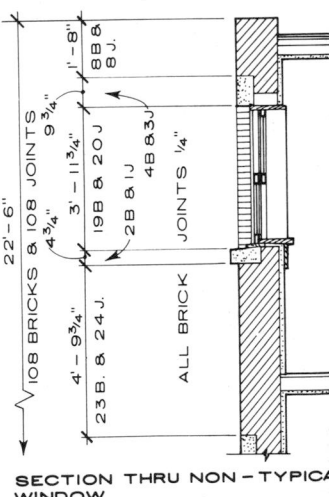

SECTION THRU NON-TYPICAL WINDOW
SCALE: 3/16" = 1'- 0"

NOTE:
Windows, doors, vents and other masonry opening details must be adjusted to achieve even brick coursing around entire bldg. Size of brick joint may be pre-determined or may depend on the height of windows used.

Other details — doors, vents, etc. — must be adjusted with reference to the brick coursing.

HORIZONTAL BRICK COURSES

NUMBER OF BRICKS & JOINTS	LENGTH OF COURSE		
	1/4" JOINTS	3/8" JOINTS	1/2" JOINTS
1 brks. & 0 jt.	0'- 8"	0'- 8"	0'- 8"
1 1/2 brks. & 1 jt.	1'- 0 1/4"	1'- 0 3/8"	1'- 0 1/2"
2 brks. & 1 jt.	1'- 4 1/4"	1'- 4 3/8"	1'- 4 1/2"
2 1/2 brks. & 2 jts.	1'- 8 1/2"	1'- 8 3/4"	1'- 9"
3 brks. & 2 jts.	2'- 0 1/2"	2'- 0 3/4"	2'- 1"
3 1/2 brks. & 3 jts.	2'- 4 3/4"	2'- 5 1/8"	2'- 5 1/2"
4 brks. & 3 jts.	2'- 8 3/4"	2'- 9 1/8"	2'- 9 1/2"
4 1/2 brks. & 4 jts.	3'- 1"	3'- 1 1/2"	3'- 2"
5 brks. & 4 jts.	3'- 5"	3'- 5 1/2"	3'- 6"
5 1/2 brks. & 5 jts.	3'- 9 1/4"	3'- 9 7/8"	3'- 10 1/2"
6 brks. & 5 jts.	4'- 1 1/4"	4'- 1 7/8"	4'- 2 1/2"
6 1/2 brks. & 6 jts.	4'- 5 1/2"	4'- 6 1/4"	4'- 7"
7 brks. & 6 jts.	4'- 9 1/2"	4'- 10 1/4"	4'- 11"
7 1/2 brks. & 7 jts.	5'- 1 3/4"	5'- 2 5/8"	5'- 3 1/2"
8 brks. & 7 jts.	5'- 5 3/4"	5'- 6 5/8"	5'- 7 1/2"
8 1/2 brks. & 8 jts.	5'- 10"	5'- 11"	6'- 0"
9 brks. & 8 jts.	6'- 2"	6'- 3"	6'- 4"
9 1/2 brks. & 9 jts.	6'- 6 1/4"	6'- 7 3/8"	6'- 8 1/2"
10 brks. & 9 jts.	6'- 10 1/4"	6'- 11 3/8"	7'- 0 1/2"
10 1/2 brks. & 10 jts.	7'- 2 1/2"	7'- 3 3/4"	7'- 5"
11 brks. & 10 jts.	7'- 6 1/2"	7'- 7 3/4"	7'- 9"
11 1/2 brks. & 11 jts.	7'- 10 3/4"	8'- 0 1/8"	8'- 1 1/2"
12 brks. & 11 jts.	8'- 2 3/4"	8'- 4 1/8"	8'- 5 1/2"
12 1/2 brks. & 12 jts.	8'- 7"	8'- 8 1/2"	8'- 10"
13 brks. & 12 jts.	8'- 11"	9'- 0"	9'- 2"
13 1/2 brks. & 13 jts.	9'- 3 1/4"	9'- 4 7/8"	9'- 6 1/2"
14 brks. & 13 jts.	9'- 7 1/4"	9'- 8 7/8"	9'- 10 1/2"
14 1/2 brks. & 14 jts.	9'- 11 1/2"	10'- 1 1/4"	10'- 3"
15 brks. & 14 jts.	10'- 3 1/2"	10'- 5 1/4"	10'- 7"
15 1/2 brks. & 15 jts.	10'- 7 3/4"	10'- 9 5/8"	10'- 11 1/2"
16 brks. & 15 jts.	10'- 11 3/4"	11'- 1 5/8"	11'- 3 1/2"
16 1/2 brks. & 16 jts.	11'- 4"	11'- 6"	11'- 8"
17 brks. & 16 jts.	11'- 8"	11'- 10"	12'- 0"
17 1/2 brks. & 17 jts.	12'- 0 1/4"	12'- 2 3/8"	12'- 4 1/2"
18 brks. & 17 jts.	12'- 4 1/4"	12'- 6 3/8"	12'- 8 1/2"
18 1/2 brks. & 18 jts.	12'- 8 1/2"	12'- 10 3/4"	13'- 1"
19 brks. & 18 jts.	13'- 0 1/2"	13'- 2 3/4"	13'- 5"
19 1/2 brks. & 19 jts.	13'- 4 3/4"	13'- 7 1/8"	13'- 9 1/2"
20 brks. & 19 jts.	13'- 8 3/4"	13'- 11 1/8"	14'- 1 1/2"
20 1/2 brks. & 20 jts.	14'- 1"	14'- 3 1/2"	14'- 6"
21 brks. & 20 jts.	14'- 5"	14'- 7 1/2"	14'- 10"
21 1/2 brks. & 21 jts.	14'- 9 1/4"	14'- 11 7/8"	15'- 2 1/2"
22 brks. & 21 jts.	15'- 1 1/4"	15'- 3 7/8"	15'- 6 1/2"
22 1/2 brks. & 22 jts.	15'- 5 1/2"	15'- 8 1/4"	15'- 11"
23 brks. & 22 jts.	15'- 9 1/2"	16'- 0 1/4"	16'- 3"
23 1/2 brks. & 23 jts.	16'- 1 3/4"	16'- 4 5/8"	16'- 7 1/2"
24 brks. & 23 jts.	16'- 5 3/4"	16'- 8 5/8"	16'- 11 1/2"
24 1/2 brks. & 24 jts.	16'- 10"	17'- 1"	17'- 4"
25 brks. & 24 jts.	17'- 2"	17'- 5"	17'- 8"
25 1/2 brks. & 25 jts.	17'- 6 1/4"	17'- 9 3/8"	18'- 0 1/2"
26 brks. & 25 jts.	17'- 10 1/4"	18'- 1 3/8"	18'- 4 1/2"
26 1/2 brks. & 26 jts.	18'- 2 1/2"	18'- 5 3/4"	18'- 9"
27 brks. & 26 jts.	18'- 6 1/2"	18'- 9 3/4"	19'- 1"
27 1/2 brks. & 27 jts.	18'- 10 3/4"	19'- 2 1/8"	19'- 5 1/2"
28 brks. & 27 jts.	19'- 2 3/4"	19'- 6 1/8"	19'- 9 1/2"
28 1/2 brks. & 28 jts.	19'- 7"	19'- 10 1/2"	20'- 2"
29 brks. & 28 jts.	19'- 11"	20'- 2 1/2"	20'- 6"
29 1/2 brks. & 29 jts.	20'- 3 1/4"	20'- 6 7/8"	20'- 10 1/2"
30 brks. & 29 jts.	20'- 7 1/4"	20'- 10 7/8"	21'- 2 1/2"
30 1/2 brks. & 30 jts.	20'- 11 1/2"	21'- 3 1/4"	21'- 7"
31 brks. & 30 jts.	21'- 3 1/2"	21'- 7 1/4"	21'- 11"
31 1/2 brks. & 31 jts.	21'- 7 3/4"	21'- 11 5/8"	22'- 3 1/2"
32 brks. & 31 jts.	21'- 11 3/4"	22'- 3 5/8"	22'- 7 1/2"
32 1/2 brks. & 32 jts.	22'- 4"	22'- 8"	23'- 0"
33 brks. & 32 jts.	22'- 8"	23'- 0"	23'- 4"
33 1/2 brks. & 33 jts.	23'- 0 1/4"	23'- 4 3/8"	23'- 8 1/2"
34 brks. & 33 jts.	23'- 4 1/4"	23'- 8 3/8"	24'- 0 1/2"
34 1/2 brks. & 34 jts.	23'- 8 1/2"	24'- 0 3/4"	24'- 5"
35 brks. & 34 jts.	24'- 0 1/2"	24'- 4 3/4"	24'- 9"
35 1/2 brks. & 35 jts.	24'- 4 3/4"	24'- 9 1/8"	25'- 1 1/2"
36 brks. & 35 jts.	24'- 8 3/4"	25'- 1 1/8"	25'- 5 1/2"
36 1/2 brks. & 36 jts.	25'- 1"	25'- 5 1/8"	25'- 10"
37 brks. & 36 jts.	25'- 5"	25'- 9 1/2"	26'- 2"
37 1/2 brks. & 37 jts.	25'- 9 1/4"	26'- 1 7/8"	26'- 6 1/2"
38 brks. & 37 jts.	26'- 1 1/4"	26'- 5 7/8"	26'- 10 1/2"
38 1/2 brks. & 38 jts.	26'- 5 1/2"	26'- 10 1/4"	27'- 3"

NUMBER OF BRICKS & JOINTS	LENGTH OF COURSE		
	1/4" JOINTS	3/8" JOINTS	1/2" JOINTS
39 brks. & 38 jts.	26'- 9 1/2"	27'- 2 1/4"	27'- 7"
39 1/2 brks. & 39 jts.	27'- 1 3/4"	27'- 6 5/8"	27'- 11 1/2"
40 brks. & 39 jts.	27'- 5 3/4"	27'- 10 5/8"	28'- 3 1/2"
40 1/2 brks. & 40 jts.	27'- 10"	28'- 3"	28'- 8"
41 brks. & 40 jts.	28'- 2"	28'- 7"	29'- 0"
41 1/2 brks. & 41 jts.	28'- 6 1/4"	28'- 11 3/8"	29'- 4 1/2"
42 brks. & 41 jts.	28'- 10 1/4"	29'- 3 3/8"	29'- 8 1/2"
42 1/2 brks. & 42 jts.	29'- 2 1/2"	29'- 7 3/4"	30'- 1"
43 brks. & 42 jts.	29'- 6 1/2"	29'- 11 3/4"	30'- 5"
43 1/2 brks. & 43 jts.	29'- 10 3/4"	30'- 4 1/8"	30'- 9 1/2"
44 brks. & 43 jts.	30'- 2 3/4"	30'- 8 1/8"	31'- 1 1/2"
44 1/2 brks. & 44 jts.	30'- 7"	31'- 0 1/2"	31'- 6"
45 brks. & 44 jts.	30'- 11"	31'- 4 1/2"	31'- 10"
45 1/2 brks. & 45 jts.	31'- 3 1/4"	31'- 8 7/8"	32'- 2 1/2"
46 brks. & 45 jts.	31'- 7 1/4"	32'- 0 7/8"	32'- 6 1/2"
46 1/2 brks. & 46 jts.	31'- 11 1/2"	32'- 5 1/4"	32'- 11"
47 brks. & 46 jts.	32'- 3 1/2"	32'- 9 1/4"	33'- 3"
47 1/2 brks. & 47 jts.	32'- 7 3/4"	33'- 1 5/8"	33'- 7 1/2"
48 brks. & 47 jts.	32'- 11 3/4"	33'- 5 5/8"	33'- 11 1/2"
48 1/2 brks. & 48 jts.	33'- 4"	33'- 10"	34'- 4"
49 brks. & 48 jts.	33'- 8"	34'- 2"	34'- 8"
49 1/2 brks. & 49 jts.	34'- 0 1/4"	34'- 6 3/8"	35'- 0 1/2"
50 brks. & 49 jts.	34'- 4 1/4"	34'- 10 3/8"	35'- 4 1/2"
50 1/2 brks. & 50 jts.	34'- 8 1/2"	35'- 2 3/4"	35'- 9"
51 brks. & 50 jts.	35'- 0 1/2"	35'- 6 3/4"	36'- 1"
51 1/2 brks. & 51 jts.	35'- 4 3/4"	35'- 11 1/8"	36'- 5 1/2"
52 brks. & 51 jts.	35'- 8 3/4"	36'- 3 1/8"	36'- 9 1/2"
52 1/2 brks. & 52 jts.	36'- 1"	36'- 7 1/2"	37'- 2"
53 brks. & 52 jts.	36'- 5"	36'- 11 1/2"	37'- 6"
53 1/2 brks. & 53 jts.	36'- 9 1/4"	37'- 3 7/8"	37'- 10 1/2"
54 brks. & 53 jts.	37'- 1 1/4"	37'- 7 7/8"	38'- 2 1/2"
54 1/2 brks. & 54 jts.	37'- 5 1/2"	38'- 0 1/4"	38'- 7"
55 brks. & 54 jts.	37'- 9 1/2"	38'- 4 1/4"	38'- 11"
55 1/2 brks. & 55 jts.	38'- 1 3/4"	38'- 8 5/8"	39'- 3 1/2"
56 brks. & 55 jts.	38'- 5 3/4"	39'- 0 5/8"	39'- 7 1/2"
56 1/2 brks. & 56 jts.	38'- 10"	39'- 5"	40'- 0"
57 brks. & 56 jts.	39'- 2"	39'- 9"	40'- 4"
57 1/2 brks. & 57 jts.	39'- 6 1/4"	40'- 1 3/8"	40'- 8 1/2"
58 brks. & 57 jts.	39'- 10 1/4"	40'- 5 3/8"	41'- 0 1/2"
58 1/2 brks. & 58 jts.	40'- 2 1/2"	40'- 9 3/4"	41'- 5"
59 brks. & 58 jts.	40'- 6 1/2"	41'- 1 3/4"	41'- 9"
59 1/2 brks. & 59 jts.	40'- 10 3/4"	41'- 6 1/8"	42'- 1 1/2"
60 brks. & 59 jts.	41'- 2 3/4"	41'- 10 1/8"	42'- 5 1/2"

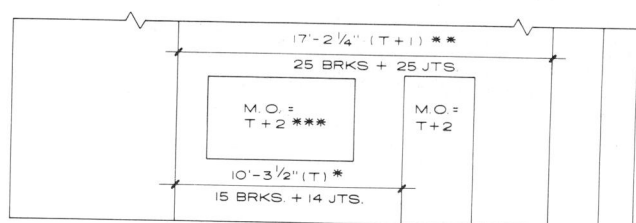

ELEVATION

17'-2 1/4" (T+1) ** — 25 BRKS + 25 JTS. — M.O. = T+2 *** — M.O. = T+2 — 10'-3 1/2" (T) * — 15 BRKS. + 14 JTS.

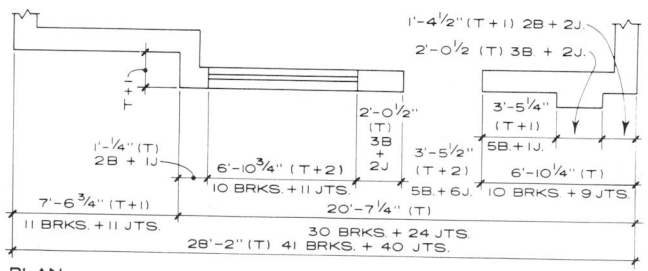

PLAN

1'-4 1/2" (T+1) 2B+2J — 2'-0 1/2" (T) 3B+2J — 3'-5 1/4" (T+1) 5B+1J — 2'-0 1/2" (T) 3B+2J — 3'-5 1/2" (T+2) — 1'-1/4" (T) 2B+1J — 6'-10 3/4" (T+2) 10 BRKS.+11 JTS. — 5B+6J — 6'-10 1/4" (T) 10 BRKS + 9 JTS. — 7'-6 3/4" (T+1) 11 BRKS.+11 JTS. — 20'-7 1/4" (T) — 28'-2" (T) 41 BRKS. + 40 JTS. — 30 BRKS + 24 JTS.

EXAMPLE SHOWING USE OF TABLE (WITH 1/4" JOINTS)

* T : Dimensions and no. of joints as given in above table, i.e. one joint less than the number of bricks.

** T+1: One brick joint added to figure given in table, i.e. number of bricks and joints equal.

*** T+2: Two brick joints added to figure given in table, i.e. one joint more than the number of bricks.

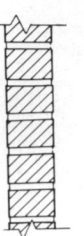
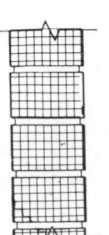
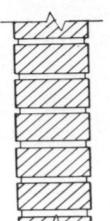

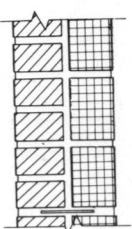
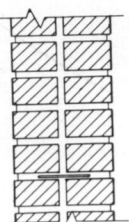
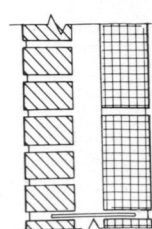

TYPE 1
4" BRICK PARTITION
MODULAR BRICK

TYPE 2
6" TILE WALL
6" X 4" X 12" TILE

TYPE 3
6" BRICK WALL
SCR BRICK

TYPE 4
8" TILE WALL
METAL – TIED; 4" X 5⅓" X 12" TILE

TYPE 5
8" BRICK AND TILE WALL
METAL – TIED; MODULAR BRICK; 4" X 5⅓" X 12" TILE

TYPE 6
8" BRICK WALL
METAL – TIED; MODULAR BRICK

TYPE 7
10" BRICK AND TILE CAVITY WALL
MODULAR BRICK, 4" X 8" X 16" TILE

PROPERTIES OF CLAY MASONRY WALLS

WALL TYPE NUMBER		1	2	3	4	5	6	7
ALLOWABLE COMPRESSIVE LOAD (LBS/LINEAR FT.)	TYPE M MORTAR	17,400 (a)	5,870	27,000 (a)	7,900 (b)	7,900 (b)	36,600 (a,b)	7,750 (c)
	TYPE S MORTAR	15,220 (a)	5,180	23,620 (a)	6,980 (b)	6,980 (b)	32,000 (a,b)	6,640 (c)
	TYPE N MORTAR	13,050 (a)	4,830	20,250 (a)	6,510 (b)	6,510 (b)	27,450 (a,b)	6,080 (c)
LATERAL SUPPORT SPACING (ft. – in.)	LOAD BEARING	6'–8" (f)	9'–0"	10'–0"	12'–0"	12'–0"	13'–4"	12'–0"
MATERIAL QUANTITY [g] (PER 100 SQ. FT.)	MORTAR CU. FT. (h)	5.50	3.30	7.90	5.70	10.40	14.10	6.70
	BRICK	675		450		675	1350	675
	TILE		300		450	225		113
	METAL TIES				23	23	23	23
"U" VALUE [k] (BTU/SQ.FT. – HR – F °)	UNINSULATED	0.76	0.42	0.68	0.33	0.41	0.54	0.30
WALL WEIGHT (LBS/SQ. FT.)	UNPLASTERED	37	41	58	60	67	78	64
AVG. SOUND RESISTANCE (DB)	UNPLASTERED	45	47	52	52	52	58	54
FIRE RESISTANCE (HRS.) [m]	UNPLASTERED	1	2 [n]	2	3	3	4	4

a – Brick compressive strength 8,000 psi plus.
b – Collar joints filled with mortar.
c – If loads bear on only one wythe, reduce allowable loads by 20%.
d – Brick compressive strength 2,500 psi plus.

e – Masonry compressive strength (f'm) = 3.000 psi; h/t = 25 (ASA A 41.2 – 1960)
f – Some buildings codes permit 8' – 0" (24t) for bearing partitions.
g – Waste is not included, as this will vary with the job. A waste factor of 2% is frequently applied for masonry units and 10% to 20% for mortar.

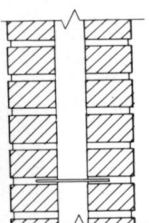
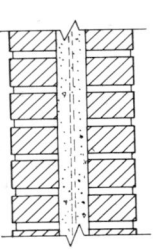
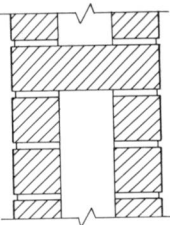
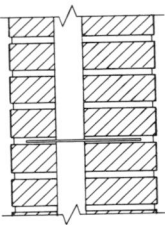

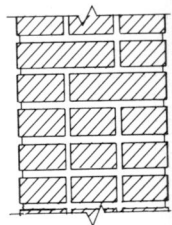

TYPE 8
10" BRICK AND BRICK CAVITY WALL
MODULAR BRICK

TYPE 9
10" REINFORCED BRICK WALL
MODULAR BRICK

TYPE 10
12" UTILITY WALL
UTILITY BRICK; HEADERS 2 FT. O.C. EACH WAY

TYPE 11
12" BRICK AND BRICK CAVITY WALL
NORMAN BRICK, SCR BRICK

TYPE 12
12" BRICK AND TILE WALL
METAL – TIED; MODULAR BRICK, 4" X 8" X 12" TILE, 4" X 5⅓" X 12" TILE

TYPE 13
12" BRICK WALL
MASONRY BOND; MODULAR BRICK

PROPERTIES OF CLAY MASONRY WALLS

WALL TYPE NUMBER		8	9	10	11	12	13
ALLOWABLE COMPRESSIVE LOAD (LBS/LINEAR FT.)	TYPE M MORTAR	15,200 (c,d)	52,000 (e)	14,700 (c,d)	19,400 (c,d)	12,000 (b)	56,000 (a)
	TYPE S MORTAR	14,100 (c,d)	52,000 (e)	13,650 (c,d)	18,100 (c,d)	10,580 (b)	49,000 (a)
	TYPE N MORTAR	11,950 (c,d)		11,500 (c,d)	15,300 (c,d)	9,860 (b)	42,000 (a)
LATERAL SUPPORT SPACING (FT.–IN.)	LOAD BEARING	12'–0"	20'–10"	18'–0"	15'–0"	18'–0"	20'–0"
MATERIAL QUANTITY [g] (PER 100 SQ. FT.)	MORTAR CU.FT. (h)	10.90	10.90	9.40	12.90	15.40	22.70
	BRICK	1350	1350	625	450 – 4" / 450 – 6"	675	2025
	TILE		GROUT 19.8 CU. FT.			150 – 4 x 8 x 12 / 225 – 4 x 5 1/3 x 12	
	METAL TIES (i)	23			23	23	
"U" VALUE [k] (BTU/SQ.FT. – HR – F °)	UNINSULATED	0.36	0.49	0.36	0.33	0.28	0.42
WALL WEIGHT (LBS/SQ. FT.)	UNPLASTERED	74	100	78	95	89	120
AVG. SOUND RESISTANCE (DB)	UNPLASTERED	58	58	57	58	57	60
FIRE RESISTANCE (HRS.) [m]	UNPLASTERED	4	4	4	4	4	4

h – Assumed mortar joint thicknesses, 3/8" for brick and 1/4" for tile (horiz. cell).
i – Based on one metal tie for each 4-1/2 sq. ft. for wall area. Increase quantity by 50% if building code requires one metal tie for each 3 sq. ft. of wall area.

k – Corrected for a 15-mph wind outside and still air inside.
m – Noncombustible or no members framed into wall.
n – One unit and 3 cells in wall thickness; units at least 71% solid.

Structural Clay Products Institute; McLean, Virginia

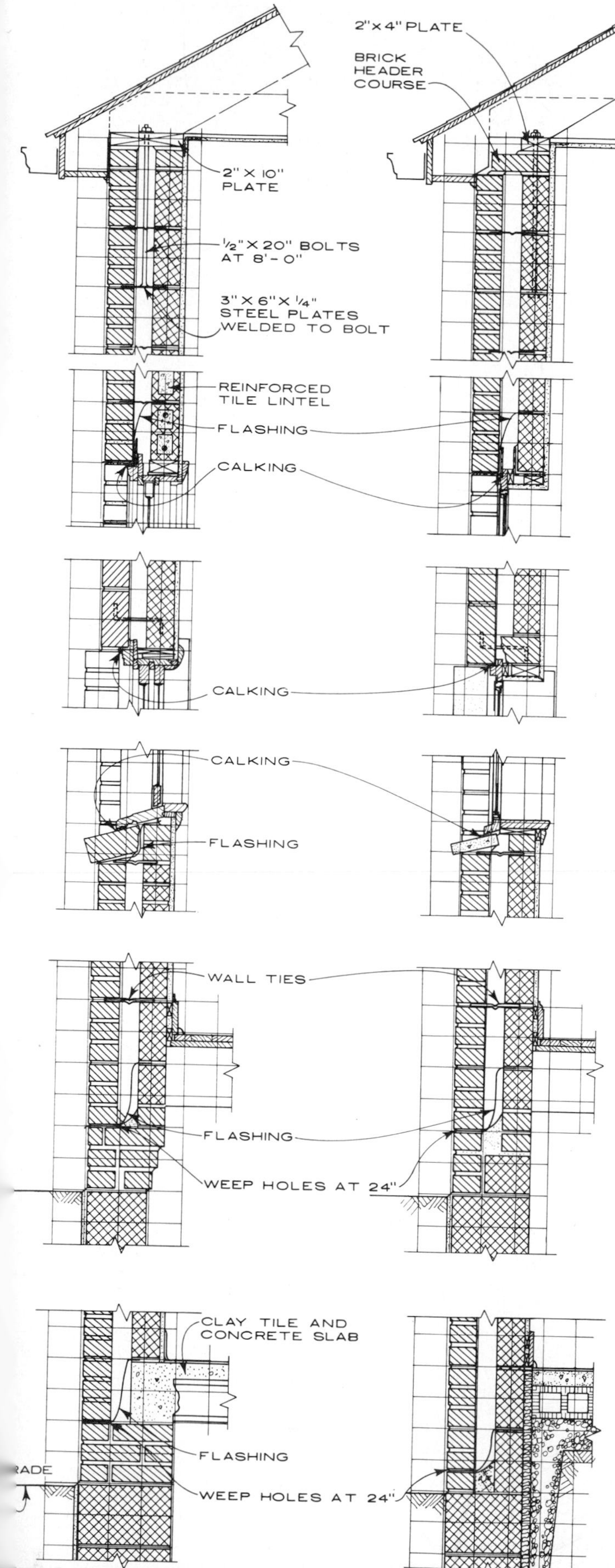

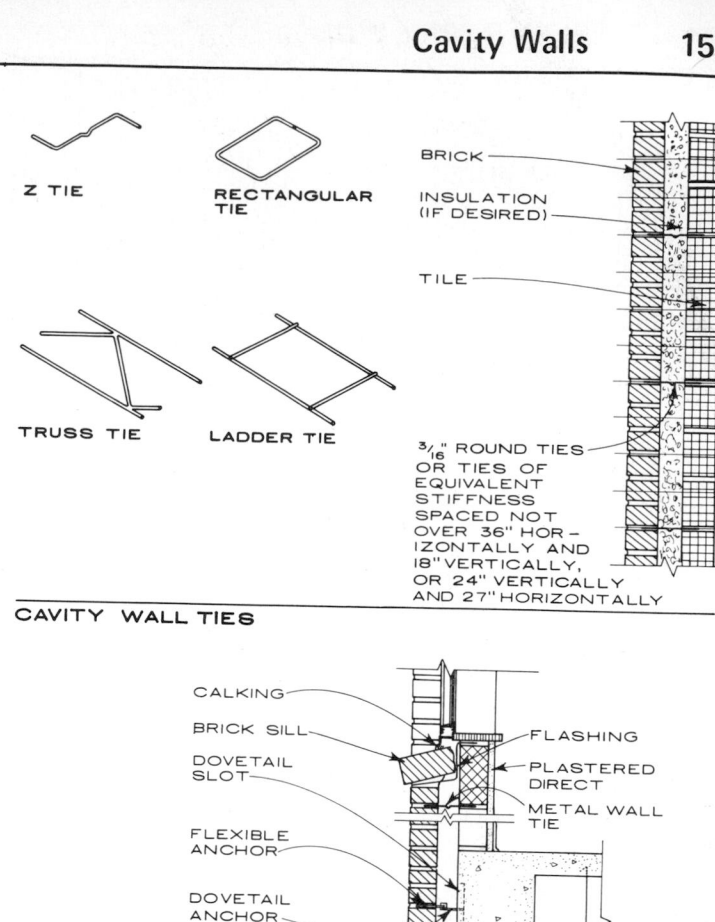

CAVITY WALL TIES

- Z TIE
- RECTANGULAR TIE
- TRUSS TIE
- LADDER TIE
- BRICK
- INSULATION (IF DESIRED)
- TILE
- 3/16" ROUND TIES OR TIES OF EQUIVALENT STIFFNESS SPACED NOT OVER 36" HORIZONTALLY AND 18" VERTICALLY, OR 24" VERTICALLY AND 27" HORIZONTALLY

Typical cavity wall sections (left):

- 2"x4" PLATE
- BRICK HEADER COURSE
- 2"X 10" PLATE
- 1/2"X 20" BOLTS AT 8'-0"
- 3"X 6"X 1/4" STEEL PLATES WELDED TO BOLT
- REINFORCED TILE LINTEL
- FLASHING
- CALKING
- CALKING
- CALKING
- CALKING
- FLASHING
- WALL TIES
- FLASHING
- WEEP HOLES AT 24"
- CLAY TILE AND CONCRETE SLAB
- FLASHING
- WEEP HOLES AT 24"
- GRADE

TYPICAL CAVITY WALL SECTIONS

ctural Clay Products Institute; McLean, Virginia

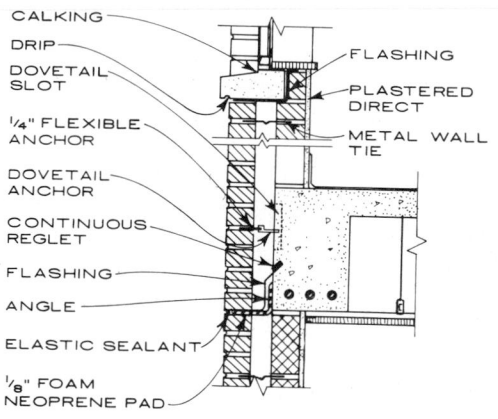

- CALKING
- BRICK SILL
- DOVETAIL SLOT
- FLEXIBLE ANCHOR
- DOVETAIL ANCHOR
- FLASHING
- PLASTERED DIRECT
- METAL WALL TIE

FLEXIBLE ANCHORAGE

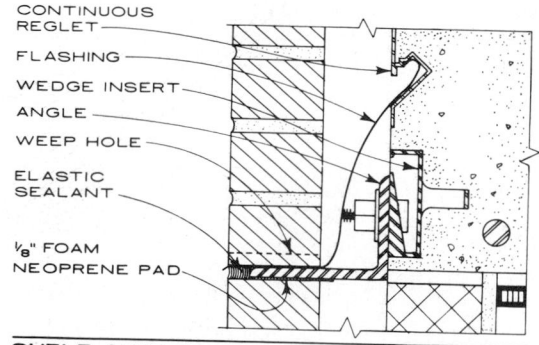

- CALKING
- DRIP
- DOVETAIL SLOT
- 1/4" FLEXIBLE ANCHOR
- DOVETAIL ANCHOR
- CONTINUOUS REGLET
- FLASHING
- ANGLE
- ELASTIC SEALANT
- 1/8" FOAM NEOPRENE PAD
- FLASHING
- PLASTERED DIRECT
- METAL WALL TIE

- CONTINUOUS REGLET
- FLASHING
- WEDGE INSERT
- ANGLE
- WEEP HOLE
- ELASTIC SEALANT
- 1/8" FOAM NEOPRENE PAD

SHELF ANGLES

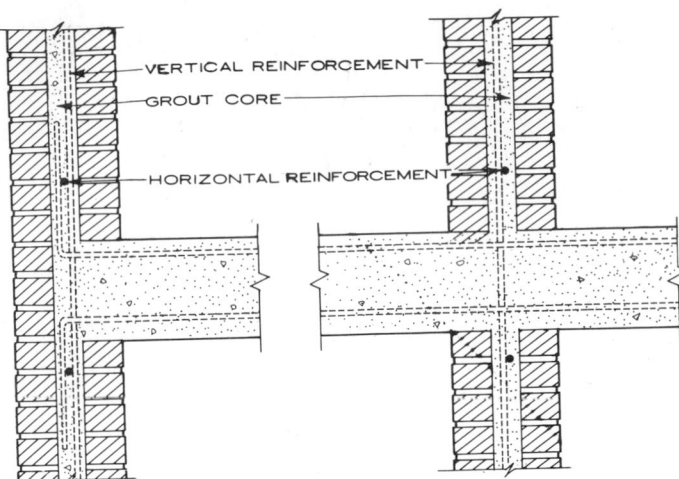

10"RBM BEARING WALLS – 8"REINFORCED CONCRETE FLOOR

Labels: VERTICAL REINFORCEMENT, GROUT CORE, HORIZONTAL REINFORCEMENT

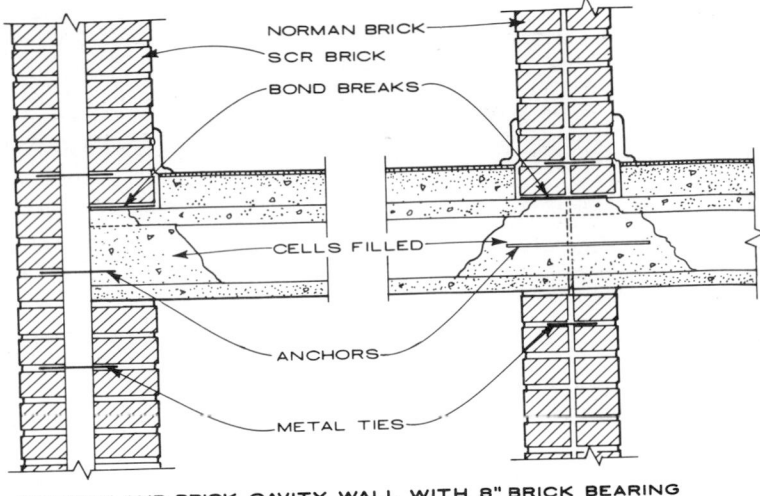

12" BRICK AND BRICK CAVITY WALL WITH 8" BRICK BEARING PARTITION – PRECAST CONCRETE FLOOR

Labels: NORMAN BRICK, SCR BRICK, BOND BREAKS, CELLS FILLED, ANCHORS, METAL TIES

NOTE:

1. Cavity may be insulated.

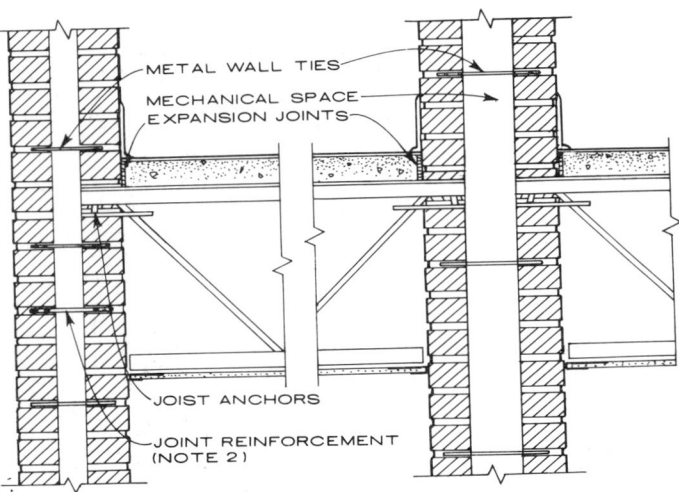

BRICK AND BRICK CAVITY BEARING WALLS – STEEL JOIST FLOOR

Labels: METAL WALL TIES, MECHANICAL SPACE EXPANSION JOINTS, JOIST ANCHORS, JOINT REINFORCEMENT (NOTE 2)

NOTES:

1. Cavity width may vary from 2″ to 4″ in nominal width.
2. Horizontal joint reinforcement may be desirable at joist bearing to act as a bond beam.
3. Insulation may be added if desired.

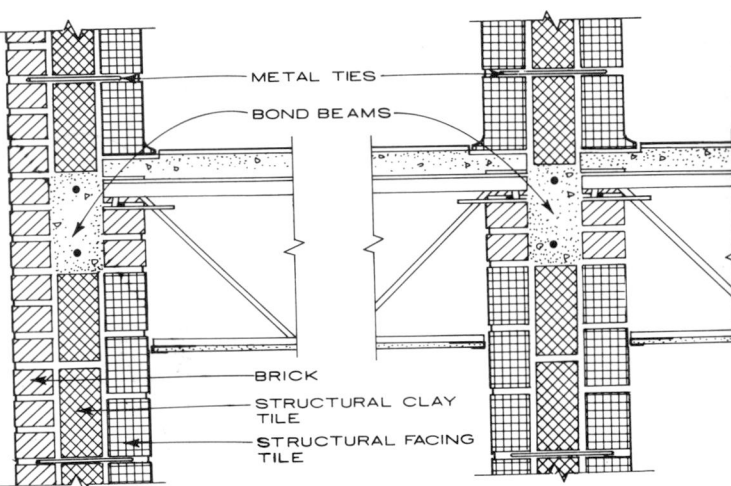

12" BRICK AND TILE BEARING WALLS – STEEL JOIST FLOOR

Labels: METAL TIES, BOND BEAMS, BRICK, STRUCTURAL CLAY TILE, STRUCTURAL FACING TILE

NOTE:

1. Bond beams are desirable at joists bearing to distribute stresses due to load and differential building movement.

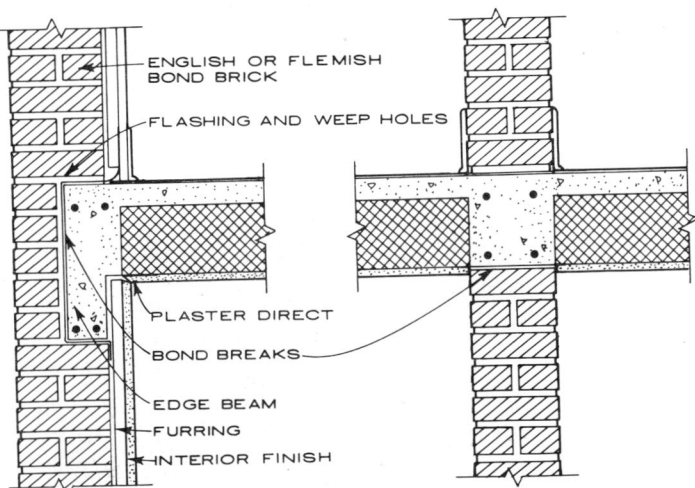

8"BRICK BEARING WALLS – 8" TILE AND CONCRETE FLOOR

Labels: ENGLISH OR FLEMISH BOND BRICK, FLASHING AND WEEP HOLES, PLASTER DIRECT, BOND BREAKS, EDGE BEAM, FURRING, INTERIOR FINISH

NOTES:

1. Metal ties may be used in lieu of masonry headers.
2. Edge beam helps control concrete curling.

Structural Clay Products Institute; McLean, Virginia

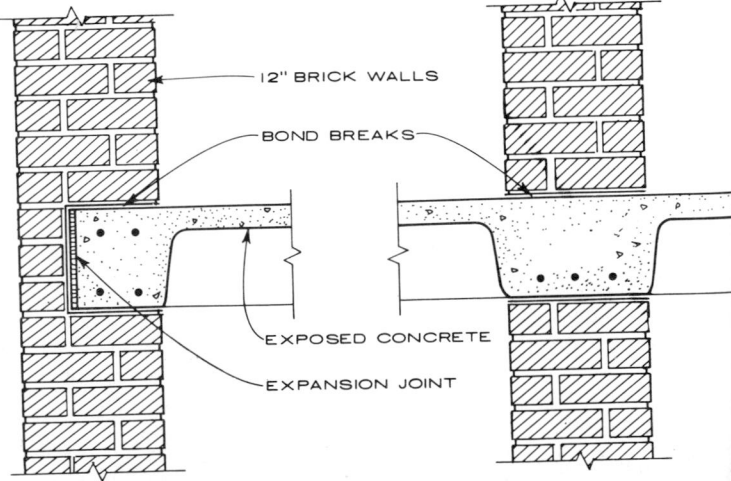

12"BRICK BEARING WALLS – 8" WAFFLE FLOOR

Labels: 12" BRICK WALLS, BOND BREAKS, EXPOSED CONCRETE, EXPANSION JOINT

NOTES:

1. Brick wall may be metal-tied in lieu of masonry headers.
2. Expansion joint may not be required between floor and exterior wall.

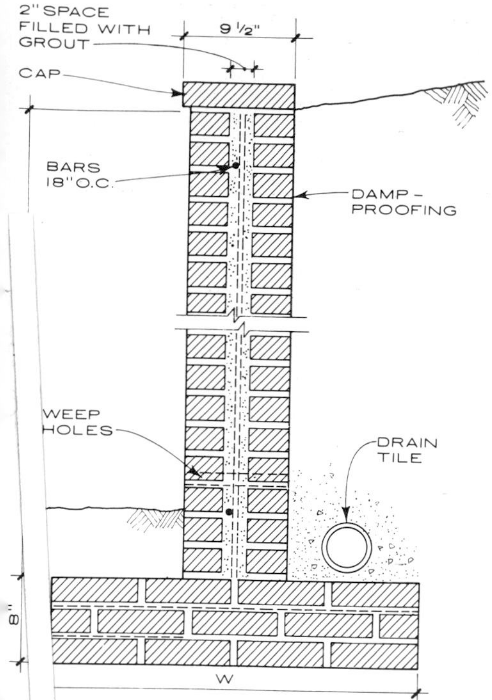

WALL SECTION

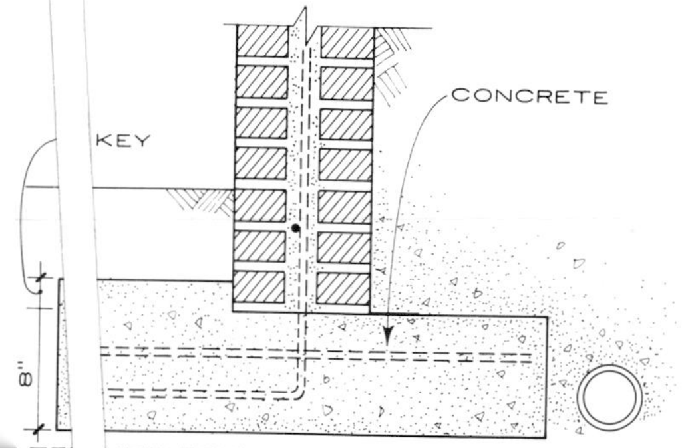

2" SPACE FILLED WITH GROUT

CAP

9 1/2"

BARS 18" O.C.

DAMP-PROOFING

WEEP HOLES

DRAIN TILE

8"

W

RETAINING WALLS

KEY

CONCRETE

ALTERNATE FOUNDATION

8"

REINFORCED PILASTERS

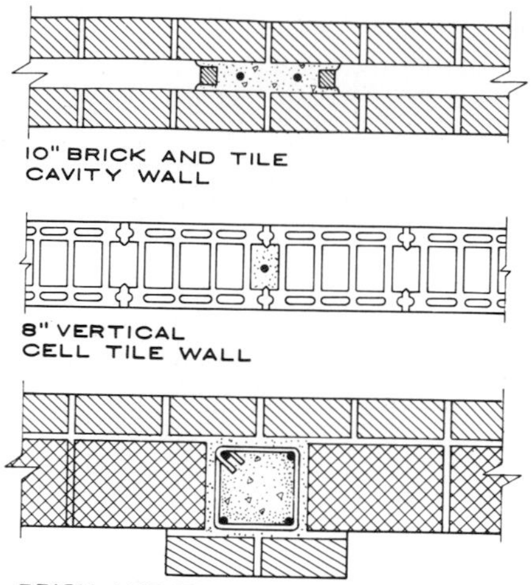

10" BRICK AND TILE CAVITY WALL

8" VERTICAL CELL TILE WALL

BRICK AND TILE COMPOSITE WALL

REINFORCED PIERS

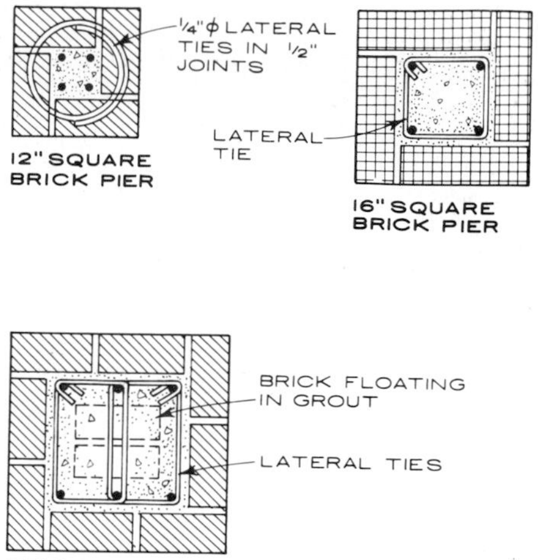

1/4"⌀ LATERAL TIES IN 1/2" JOINTS

12" SQUARE BRICK PIER

LATERAL TIE

16" SQUARE BRICK PIER

BRICK FLOATING IN GROUT

LATERAL TIES

20" SQUARE BRICK PIER

BOND BEAMS

HORIZONTAL STEEL

BEAM

BRICK FLOATING IN GROUT

TIE

VERTICAL STEEL

10"

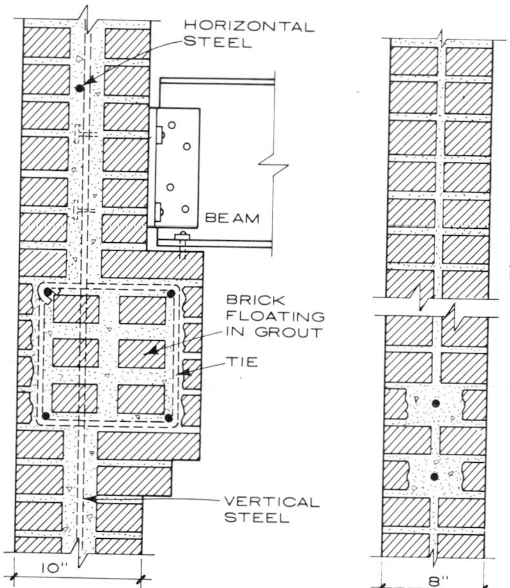

WALL SECTION & ALTERNATE

8"

5'-0'

SWIMMING POOLS

10"

3/16" METAL TIES @ 16" O.C. HORIZ. AND VERTICAL

@ 32" O.C.

#3 @ 16" O.C.

SEALANT

6.6.6 WIRE MESH

#3 @ 12" O.C.

4"

10"

5'-0"

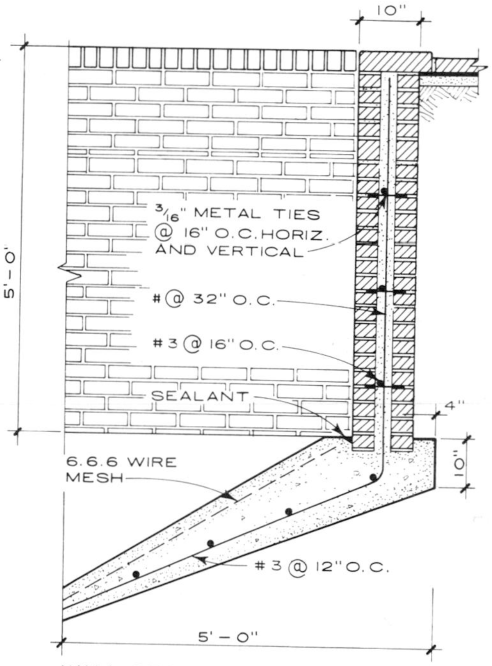

WALL SECTION - DIVING AREA

SLABS

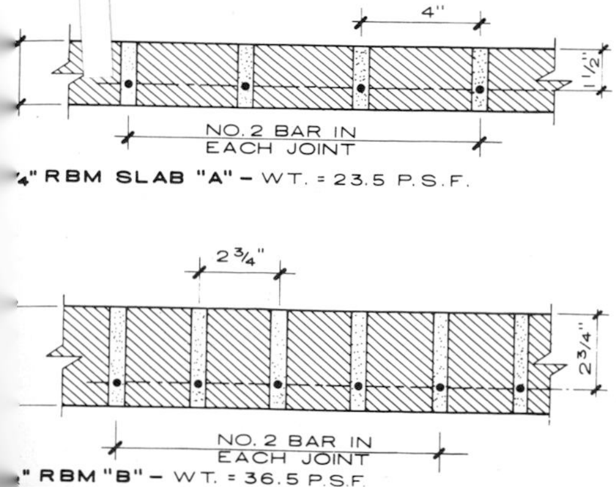

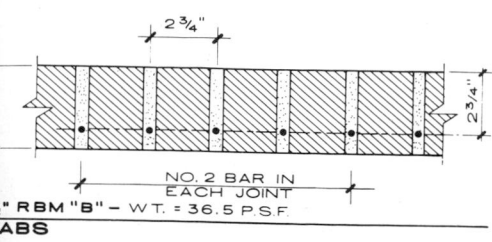

4"

1 1/2"

NO. 2 BAR IN EACH JOINT

4" RBM SLAB "A" - WT. = 23.5 P.S.F.

2 3/4"

2 3/4"

NO. 2 BAR IN EACH JOINT

RBM "B" - WT. = 36.5 P.S.F.

Architectural Clay Products Institute; McLean, Virginia

TABLE OF SAFE SUPERIMPOSED LOAD (LBS/FT^2) FOR RBM SLABS

SPAN LENGTH	SLAB A			SLAB B		
	BRICK UNIT COMPRESSIVE STRENGTH			BRICK UNIT COMPRESSIVE STRENGTH		
	4,000	6,600	12,000	4,000	6,600	12,000
2'-0''	204	206	210	588	597	603
3'-0''	128	130	132	379	385	389
4'-0''	87	91	93	276	280	283
5'-0''	47	58	68	196	217	221
6'-0''	25	33	40	125	151	155
7'-0''		18	23	82	101	104
8'-0''				55	69	71
9'-0''				36	47	48
10'-0''				22	31	32
11'-0''						20

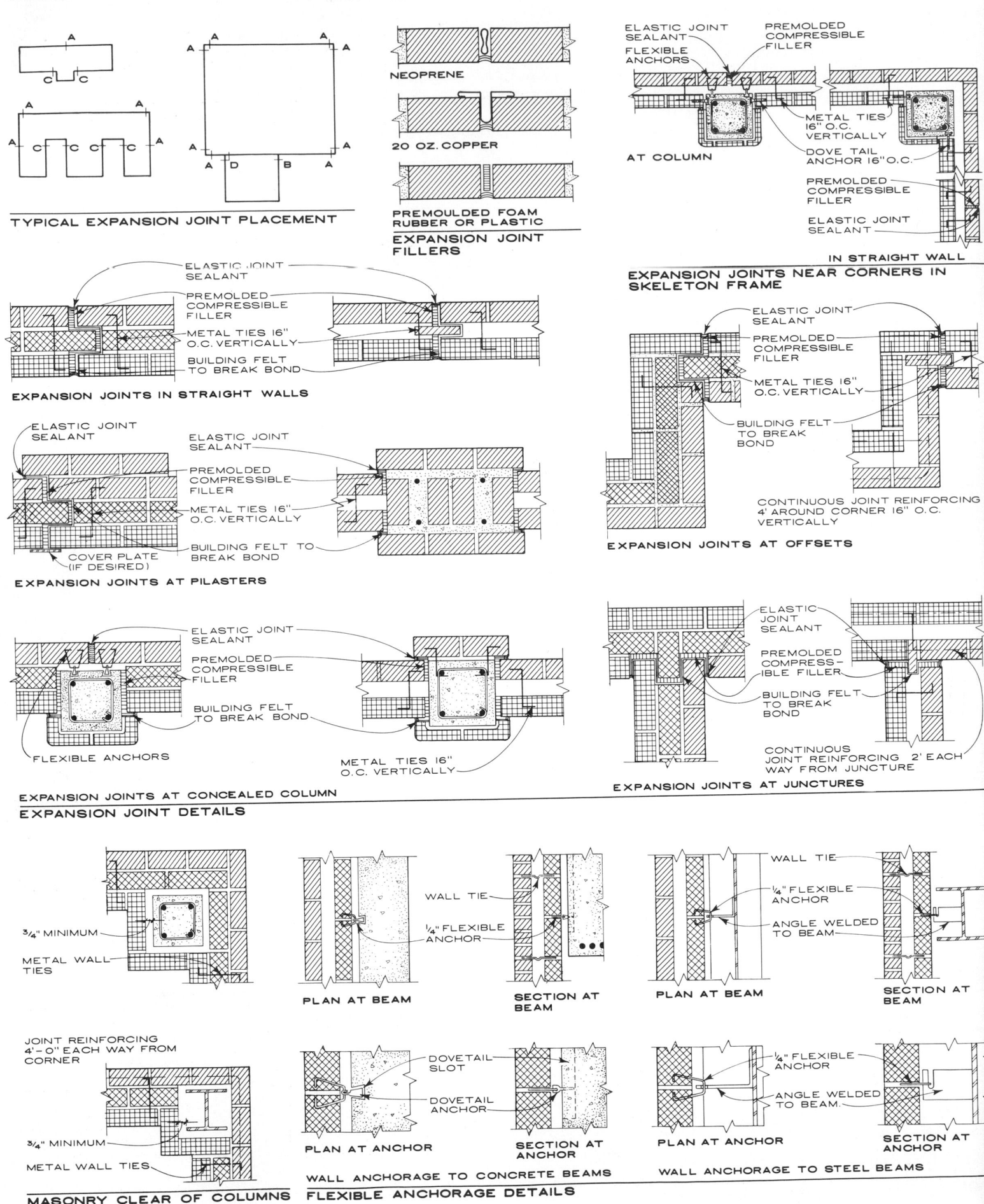

TYPICAL EXPANSION JOINT PLACEMENT

NEOPRENE

20 OZ. COPPER

PREMOULDED FOAM RUBBER OR PLASTIC

EXPANSION JOINT FILLERS

ELASTIC JOINT SEALANT

PREMOLDED COMPRESSIBLE FILLER

FLEXIBLE ANCHORS

METAL TIES 16" O.C. VERTICALLY

DOVE TAIL ANCHOR 16"O.C.

PREMOLDED COMPRESSIBLE FILLER

ELASTIC JOINT SEALANT

AT COLUMN

IN STRAIGHT WALL

EXPANSION JOINTS NEAR CORNERS IN SKELETON FRAME

ELASTIC JOINT SEALANT

PREMOLDED COMPRESSIBLE FILLER

METAL TIES 16" O.C. VERTICALLY

BUILDING FELT TO BREAK BOND

EXPANSION JOINTS IN STRAIGHT WALLS

ELASTIC JOINT SEALANT

ELASTIC JOINT SEALANT

PREMOLDED COMPRESSIBLE FILLER

METAL TIES 16" O.C. VERTICALLY

BUILDING FELT TO BREAK BOND

COVER PLATE (IF DESIRED)

EXPANSION JOINTS AT PILASTERS

ELASTIC JOINT SEALANT

PREMOLDED COMPRESSIBLE FILLER

BUILDING FELT TO BREAK BOND

METAL TIES 16" O.C. VERTICALLY

BUILDING FELT TO BREAK BOND

CONTINUOUS JOINT REINFORCING 4' AROUND CORNER 16" O.C. VERTICALLY

EXPANSION JOINTS AT OFFSETS

ELASTIC JOINT SEALANT

PREMOLDED COMPRESS- IBLE FILLER

BUILDING FELT TO BREAK BOND

CONTINUOUS JOINT REINFORCING 2' EACH WAY FROM JUNCTURE

ELASTIC JOINT SEALANT

PREMOLDED COMPRESSIBLE FILLER

BUILDING FELT TO BREAK BOND

METAL TIES 16" O.C. VERTICALLY

FLEXIBLE ANCHORS

EXPANSION JOINTS AT CONCEALED COLUMN

EXPANSION JOINTS AT JUNCTURES

EXPANSION JOINT DETAILS

3/4" MINIMUM

METAL WALL TIES

PLAN AT BEAM

WALL TIE

1/4" FLEXIBLE ANCHOR

SECTION AT BEAM

PLAN AT BEAM

WALL TIE

1/4" FLEXIBLE ANCHOR

ANGLE WELDED TO BEAM

SECTION AT BEAM

JOINT REINFORCING 4'-0" EACH WAY FROM CORNER

3/4" MINIMUM

METAL WALL TIES

PLAN AT ANCHOR

DOVETAIL SLOT

DOVETAIL ANCHOR

SECTION AT ANCHOR

PLAN AT ANCHOR

1/4" FLEXIBLE ANCHOR

ANGLE WELDED TO BEAM.

SECTION AT ANCHOR

MASONRY CLEAR OF COLUMNS

WALL ANCHORAGE TO CONCRETE BEAMS

WALL ANCHORAGE TO STEEL BEAMS

FLEXIBLE ANCHORAGE DETAILS

Structural Clay Products Institute; McLean, Virginia

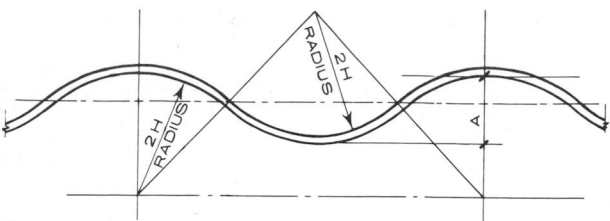

PLAN

Four inch thick Serpentine walls have been built with radii up to 20'-0'' in the South.

Radii under 7'-0'' are advisable in the North.

Use running bond.

No reinforcing is used in the wall.

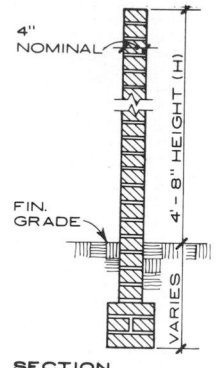

SECTION

SERPENTINE GARDEN WALLS

RELATIONSHIPS OF 4'' SERPENTINE WALLS

HEIGHT ABOVE FOUNDATION (H)	MAX. RADIUS NO MORE THAN 2H	MIN. DISTANCE A, NO LESS THAN H/2
2'-0''	4'-0''	1'-0''
2'-6''	5'-0''	1'-3''
3'-0''	6'-0''	1'-6''
3'-6''	7'-0''	1'-9''
4'-0''	8'-0''	2'-0''
4'-6''	9'-0''	2'-3''
5'-0''	10'-0''	2'-6''
5'-6''	11'-0''	2'-9''
6'-0''	12'-0''	3'-0''

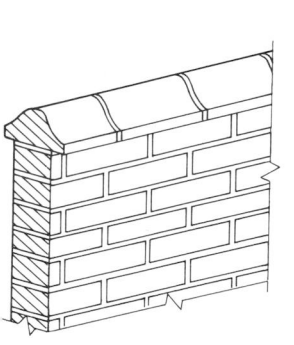

MOLDED BRICK

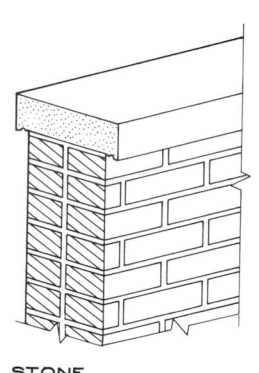

STONE

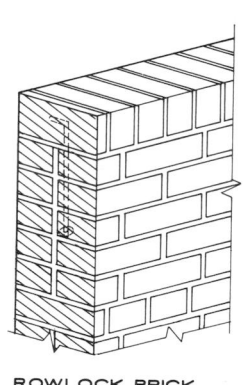

ROWLOCK BRICK

TYPICAL COPINGS

TABLE 1
PANEL WALL REINFORCING STEEL

WALL SPAN, ft.	MAXIMUM SPACING OF TWO NO. 2 BARS		
	WIND LOAD, P.S.F.		
	10	15	20
8	3'-8''	2'-4''	1'-10''
10	2'-4''	1'-7''	1'-2''
12	1'-8''	1'-1''	10''
14	1'-3''	10''	7''
16	11''	7''	6''

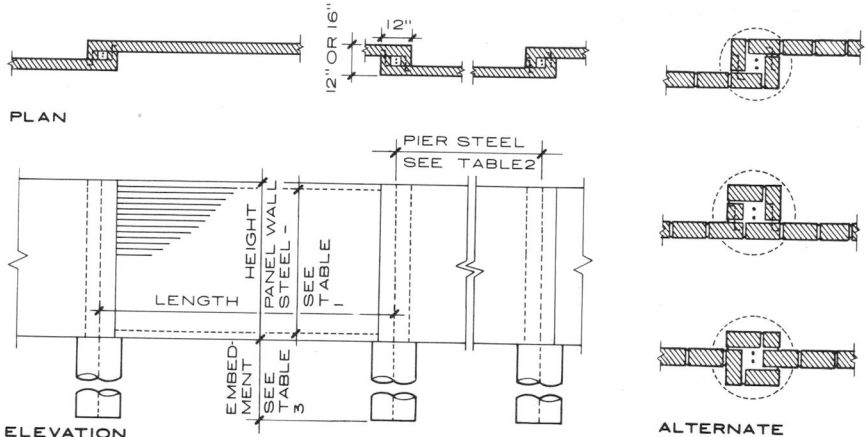

PLAN

ELEVATION

ALTERNATE PIERS

TABLE 2
PILASTER REINFORCING STEEL

WALL SPAN, FEET	WIND LOAD 10 P.S.F.			WIND LOAD 15 P.S.F.			WIND LOAD 20 P.S.F.		
	WALL HEIGHT, FEET			WALL HEIGHT, FEET			WALL HEIGHT, FEET		
	4	6	8	4	6	8	4	6	8
8	2#3	2#4	2#5	2#3	2#5	2#6	2#4	2#5	2#5*
10	2#3	2#4	2#5	2#4	2#5	2#7	2#4	2#6	2#6*
12	2#3	2#5	2#6	2#4	2#6	2#6*	2#4	2#6	2#7*
14	2#3	2#5	2#6	2#4	2#6	2#6*	2#5	2#6	2#7*
16	2#4	2#5	2#7	2#4	2#6	2#7*	2#5	2#6*	2#7*

*Requires 16-in. pilasters.

TABLE 3
REQUIRED EMBEDMENT OF 15-IN. PIER FOUNDATION

WALL SPAN, FEET	WIND LOAD 10 P.S.F.			WIND LOAD 15 P.S.F.			WIND LOAD 20 P.S.F.		
	WALL HEIGHT, FEET			WALL HEIGHT, FEET			WALL HEIGHT, FEET		
	4	6	8	4	6	8	4	6	8
8	2'-0''	2'-6''	2'-9''	2'-3''	2'-9''	3'-3''	2'-3''	3'-0''	3'-9''
10	2'-0''	2'-6''	3'-0''	2'-3''	3'-0''	3'-9''	2'-6''	3'-3''	4'-3''
12	2'-3''	2'-9''	3'-3''	2'-6''	3'-3''	4'-0''	2'-9''	3'-9''	4'-6''
14	2'-3''	3'-0''	3'-6''	2'-9''	3'-6''	4'-3''	3'-0''	4'-0''	4'-9''
16	2'-3''	3'-0''	3'-9''	2'-9''	3'-9''	4'-6''	3'-3''	4'-3''	5'-3''

PIER AND PANEL GARDEN WALLS

Structural Clay Products Institute; McLean, Virginia

TABLE OF RBM LINTELS

Superimposed Load (lbs. per lin. ft.)

Lintel L (ft.)	t (in.)	0 D	0 R	250 D	250 R	500 D	500 R	750 D	750 R	1000 D	1000 R	1250 D	1250 R	1500 D	1500 R
3	4	1.5	2 #2	4.1	2 #2	7.5	2 #2	10.8	2 #2	14.1	2 #2	17.5	2 #2	20.8	2 #2
	6		1 #3	2.9	1 #4	3.9	1 #5	5.0	1 #5	6.5	1 #5	8.0	1 #5	9.5	1 #5
	8		1 #3	2.6	1 #4	3.4	2 #3	4.0	2 #3	5.0	2 #3	6.0	2 #3	7.2	2 #3
	10		2 #3	2.4	2 #3	3.1	2 #3	3.7	3 #3	4.1	3 #3	4.9	3 #3	5.8	3 #3
	12		2 #3	2.3	2 #3	2.9	3 #3	3.4	3 #3	3.8	3 #3	4.2	4 #3	4.9	4 #3
4	4	2.3	2 #2	5.8	2 #2	10.3	2 #2	14.7	2 #2	19.2	2 #2	23.6	2 #2	28.1	2 #2
	6		1 #3	4.1	1 #4	5.3	1 #5	6.9	1 #5	8.9	1 #5	10.9	1 #5	12.9	1 #5
	8		1 #3	3.7	1 #4	4.7	2 #3	5.5	2 #3	6.8	2 #4	8.3	2 #4	9.8	2 #4
	10		2 #3	3.4	2 #3	4.3	2 #3	5.0	3 #3	5.6	3 #3	6.8	4 #3	7.9	4 #3
	12		2 #3	3.3	2 #3	4.0	3 #3	4.6	3 #3	5.2	3 #3	5.8	4 #3	6.7	4 #3
5	4	3.2	2 #2	7.7	2 #2	13.3	2 #2	18.8	2 #2	24.4	2 #2	30.0	2 #2	35.5	2 #2
	6		1 #3	5.3	1 #4	6.7	1 #5	8.7	1 #5	11.4	1 #5	13.9	1 #5	16.4	1 #5
	8		1 #4	4.8	2 #3	6.0	2 #4	7.0	2 #4	8.8	2 #4	10.7	2 #4	12.5	2 #4
	10		2 #3	4.5	3 #3	5.6	3 #3	6.4	3 #3	7.3	2 #4	8.7	2 #4	10.2	2 #4
	12		2 #3	4.3	3 #3	5.2	3 #3	6.0	2 #4	6.7	4 #3	7.5	4 #3	8.7	4 #3
6	4	4.2	2 #2	11.0	2 #2	18.6	2 #2	26.1	2 #2	33.7	2 #2				
	6		1 #4	6.6	1 #4	8.3	1 #5	11.1	1 #5	14.1	1 #5	17.1	1 #5	20.1	1 #5
	8		1 #4	6.0	1 #5	7.4	2 #4	8.7	2 #4	10.9	2 #4	13.1	2 #4	15.3	2 #4
	10		2 #3	5.7	3 #3	6.9	2 #4	7.9	2 #4	9.1	3 #4	10.8	3 #4	12.6	3 #4
	12		3 #3	5.5	2 #4	6.5	2 #4	7.4	3 #4	8.2	3 #4	9.3	3 #4	10.8	3 #4
7	4	5.5	2 #2	15.8	2 #2	26.1	2 #2	36.4	2 #2						
	6	5.3	1 #4	7.9	1 #5	9.8	1 #5	13.3	1 #5	16.8	1 #5	20.3	1 #5	23.8	1 #5
	8		2 #3	7.3	1 #5	8.9	2 #4	10.6	2 #4	13.2	2 #4	15.7	2 #4	18.3	2 #4
	10		3 #3	6.9	2 #4	8.3	3 #4	9.4	3 #4	11.0	3 #4	13.1	3 #4	15.1	3 #4
	12		3 #3	6.7	4 #3	7.8	3 #4	8.8	3 #4	9.7	3 #4	11.3	2 #5	13.0	2 #5
8	4	8.1	2 #2	21.6	2 #6	35.0	2 #2								
	6	6.5	1 #4	9.3	1 #5	11.7	1 #6	15.7	1 #6	19.7	1 #6	23.7	1 #6	27.7	1 #6
	8		1 #5	8.7	2 #4	10.4	1 #6	12.6	2 #5	15.5	2 #5	18.4	2 #5	21.4	2 #5
	10		3 #3	8.3	3 #4	9.7	3 #4	11.0	3 #4	13.1	3 #4	15.4	3 #4	17.7	3 #4
	12		2 #4	8.0	3 #4	9.2	3 #4	10.4	4 #4	11.5	4 #4	13.4	4 #4	15.3	4 #4
9	4	11.6	2 #2	28.6	2 #2										
	6	7.7	1 #5	10.8	1 #6	13.7	1 #6	18.2	1 #6	22.7	1 #6	27.2	1 #6	31.6	1 #6
	8		1 #5	10.1	1 #6	12.0	2 #5	14.7	2 #5	18.0	2 #5	21.3	2 #5	24.6	2 #5
	10		2 #4	9.6	3 #4	11.2	3 #4	12.6	3 #5	15.2	3 #5	17.8	3 #5	20.5	3 #5
	12		3 #4	9.3	3 #4	10.7	4 #4	11.9	4 #4	13.4	4 #4	15.6	4 #4	17.8	4 #4
10	4	15.9	2 #2	36.9	2 #2										
	6	9.1	1 #5	12.3	1 #6	15.8	1 #6	20.8	1 #6	25.8	1 #6	30.8	1 #6	35.7	1 #6
	8		2 #4	11.6	2 #5	13.6	2 #5	16.9	2 #5	20.5	2 #5	24.2	2 #5	27.9	2 #5
	10		3 #4	11.1	3 #4	12.8	3 #5	14.6	3 #5	17.5	3 #5	20.4	3 #5	23.3	3 #5
	12		3 #4	10.8	4 #4	12.2	4 #4	13.6	3 #5	15.5	3 #5	17.9	3 #5	20.3	3 #5

Notes:
1 It is recommended that a minimum of two courses of brick be provided above the reinforcements.
2 Table is calculated for brick units of 4,000 psi or greater in compressive strength and Type S mortar.
3 Table designed in accord with A 41.2 1960, A.S.A.

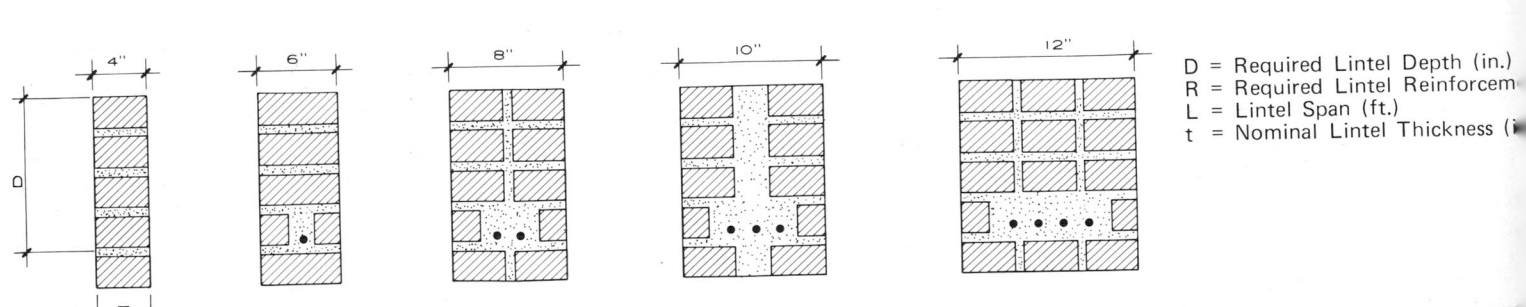

D = Required Lintel Depth (in.)
R = Required Lintel Reinforcem[ent]
L = Lintel Span (ft.)
t = Nominal Lintel Thickness (i[n.])

TYPICAL LINTEL DETAILS

Structural Clay Products Institute; McLean, Virginia

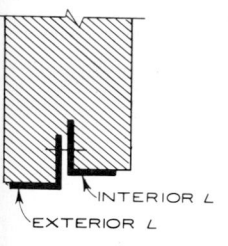
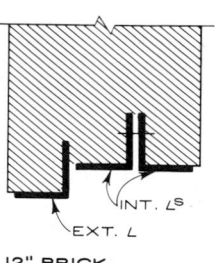
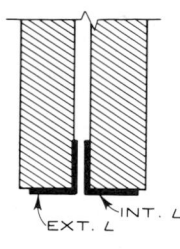
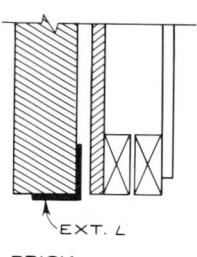
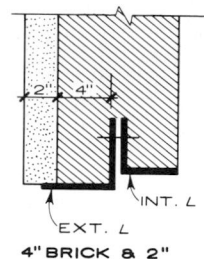
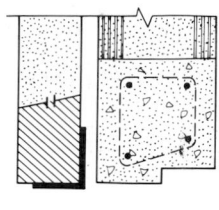

INTERIOR *L*
EXTERIOR *L*
8" BRICK

INT. *L*s
EXT. *L*
12" BRICK

EXT. *L*
INT. *L*
BRICK CAVITY WALL

EXT. *L*
BRICK VENEER

INT. *L*
EXT. *L*
4" BRICK & 2" STONE FACING

4" BRICK OR STONE WITH CONC. BLOCK OR CLAY TILE

LOOSE STEEL LINTELS FOR MASONRY — NO. & SIZE OF ANGLES REQUIRED

CLEAR SPAN	EXTERIOR ANGLES FOR BRICK OR STONE NO FLOOR LOAD 4"	4"+2" STONE	INTERIOR ANGLES WALL THI.	MAXIMUM FLOOR LOADS PER FOOT OF SPAN NONE	250	500	750	1000	1250	1500
4'-0" OR LESS	*L*-3 1/2 x 3 1/2 x 5/16	*L*-3 1/2 x 5 x 5/16	8	*L*-3 1/2 x 3 1/2 x 5/16	*L*-3 1/2 x 3 1/2 x 5/16	*L*-3 1/2 x 3 1/2 x 5/16	*L*-4 x 3 1/2 x 5/16	*L*-5 x 3 1/2 x 5/16	*L*-5 x 3 1/2 x 3/8	*L*-5 x 3 1/2 x 7/16
			12	2*L*s 3 1/2 x 3 1/2 x 5/16	2*L*s 3 1/2 x 3 1/2 x 5/16	2*L*s 3 1/2 x 3 1/2 x 5/16	2*L*s 3 1/2 x 3 1/2 x 5/16	2*L*s 3 1/2 x 3 1/2 x 5/16	*L*-5 x 3 1/2 x 3/8	*L*-5 x 3 1/2 x 7/16
5'-0"	*L*-3 1/2 x 3 1/2 x 5/16	*L*-3 1/2 x 5 x 5/16	8	*L*-3 1/2 x 3 1/2 x 5/16	*L*-3 1/2 x 3 1/2 x 5/16	*L*-5 x 3 1/2 x 5/16	*L*-5 x 3 1/2 x 3/8	*L*-5 x 3 1/2 x 7/16	*L*-6 x 3 1/2 x 3/8	*L*-7 x 4 x 3/8
			12	2*L*s 3 1/2 x 3 1/2 x 5/16	2*L*s 3 1/2 x 3 1/2 x 5/16	2*L*s 3 1/2 x 3 1/2 x 5/16	2*L*s 4 x 3 1/2 x 5/16	2*L*s 5 x 3 1/2 x 5/16	2*L*s 5 x 3 1/2 x 5/16	2*L*s 5 x 3 1/2 x 3/8
6'-0"	*L*-4 x 3 1/2 x 5/16	*L*-5 x 5 x 5/16	8	*L*-4 x 3 1/2 x 5/16	*L*-5 x 3 1/2 x 5/16	*L*-5 x 3 1/2 x 3/8	*L*-6 x 3 1/2 x 3/8	*L*-7 x 4 x 3/8	2*L*s 5 x 3 1/2 x 3/8	2*L*s 5 x 3 1/2 x 3/8
			12	2*L*s 4 x 3 1/2 x 5/16	2*L*s 4 x 3 1/2 x 5/16	2*L*s 5 x 3 1/2 x 5/16	2*L*s 5 x 3 1/2 x 5/16	2*L*s 5 x 3 1/2 x 3/8	2*L*s 6 x 3 1/2 x 3/8	2*L*s 6 x 3 1/2 x 3/8
7'-0"	*L*-4 x 3 1/2 x 5/16	*L*-5 x 5 x 5/16	8	*L*-4 x 3 1/2 x 5/16	*L*-5 x 3 1/2 x 3/8	*L*-6 x 4 x 3/8	*L*-7 x 4 x 3/8	*L*-8 x 4 x 7/16	2*L*s 7 x 4 x 3/8	2*L*s 7 x 4 x 3/8
			12	2*L*s 5 x 3 1/2 x 5/16	2*L*s 5 x 3 1/2 x 3/8	2*L*s 6 x 3 1/2 x 3/8	2*L*s 7 x 4 x 3/8	2*L*s 7 x 4 x 3/8	2*L*s 7 x 4 x 7/16	2*L*s 8 x 4 x 7/16
8'-0"	*L*-5 x 3 1/2 x 5/16	*L*-5 x 5 x 5/16	8	*L*-5 x 3 1/2 x 5/16	*L*-6 x 3 1/2 x 3/8	*L*-7 x 4 x 3/8	*L*-8 x 4 x 7/16	*L*-8 x 4 x 1/2	*L*-9 x 4 x 1/2	*L*-9 x 4 x 9/16
			12	2*L*s 5 x 3 1/2 x 5/16	2*L*s 5 x 3 1/2 x 7/16	2*L*s 6 x 3 1/2 x 3/8	2*L*s 7 x 4 x 3/8	2*L*s 7 x 4 x 3/8	2*L*s 7 x 4 x 7/16	2*L*s 8 x 4 x 7/16
9'-0"	*L*-5 x 3 1/2 x 3/8	*L*-5 x 5 x 3/8	8	*L*-5 x 3 1/2 x 3/8	*L*-7 x 4 x 3/8	*L*-8 x 4 x 7/16	*L*-8 x 4 x 1/2	*L*-9 x 4 x 1/2	2*L*s 7 x 4 x 7/16	2*L*s 8 x 4 x 7/16
			12	2*L*s 5 x 3 1/2 x 3/8	2*L*s 6 x 3 1/2 x 3/8	2*L*s 7 x 4 x 3/8	2*L*s 7 x 4 x 7/16	2*L*s 8 x 4 x 7/16	2*L*s 8 x 4 x 7/16	*L*-9 x 4 x 3/4
10'-0"	*L*-6 x 3 1/2 x 3/8	*L*-5 x 5 x 1/2	8	*L*-6 x 3 1/2 x 3/8	*L*-8 x 4 x 7/16	*L*-8 x 4 x 1/2	*L*-9 x 4 x 1/2	*L*-9 x 4 x 5/8	*L*-9 x 4 x 3/4	*L*-9 x 4 x 7/8
			12	2*L*s 6 x 3 1/2 x 3/8	2*L*s 7 x 4 x 3/8	2*L*s 8 x 4 x 7/16	2*L*s 8 x 4 x 1/2	2*L*s 8 x 4 x 1/2	2*L*s 9 x 4 x 1/2	2*L*s 9 x 4 x 1/2

NOTES:

For economy, a double channel ⊨ with pipe separators may be substituted for a pair of interior angles: 2-6" [ ] 8.2# for 2-7" x 4" x 3/8" and under; 2-7" [ ] 9.8# for 2-7" x 4" x 7/16" 2-8" [ ] 11.5# for 2-8" x 4" x 1/2" and under; 2-9" [ ] 13.4# for 2-9" x 4" x 1/2" and under.

When masonry lighter than brick is used over interior angles floor load may be increased by the difference in weight per sq. ft. times the width of the opening. Interior angles have been designed for floor load plus brick masonry of ht. = width of opening. fs = 20,000 #/□". Deflection max. 1/700 span.

6" min. bearing required for all lintels except single angles below heavy line require 8"; below dash line, 10". Omit floor load on lintel when distance to bottom of floor construction is greater than width of opening. Interior and exterior angles in 8" walls and interior angles in 12" walls are bolted together when clear span of opening is over 6'-0".

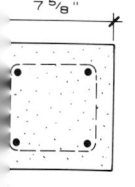
7 5/8"

ONE PIECE LINTELS

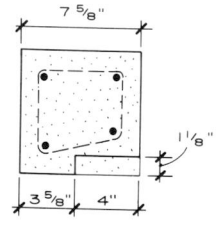
7 5/8"
1 1/8"
3 5/8" 4"

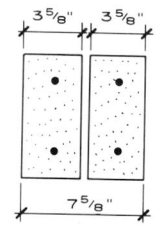
3 5/8" 3 5/8"
7 5/8"

TWO PIECE SPLIT LINTELS

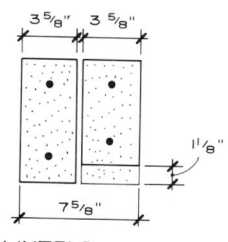
3 5/8" 3 5/8"
1 1/8"
7 5/8"

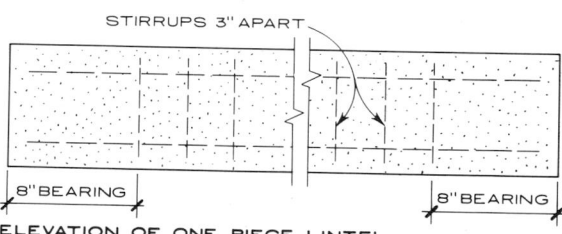
STIRRUPS 3" APART
8" BEARING
8" BEARING
ELEVATION OF ONE PIECE LINTEL

PRECAST CONCRETE LINTELS — NO. & SIZE OF REINFORCING BARS REQUIRED

LINTEL SIZE	CLEAR SPAN	LINTEL IN BRICK WALL 80 #/□' MAX. FLOOR LOAD IN LBS PER FOOT OF CLEAR SPAN. NONE	250	500	750	1000	LINTEL IN CONCRETE BLOCK WALL 50 MAX. FLOOR LOAD IN LBS PER FOOT OF CLEAR SPAN. NONE	250	500	750	1000
3 3/4" x 7 5/8"	4'-0"	Two # 3 φ	Two # 4 φ				Two # 3 φ	Two # 4 φ	Two # 4 φ		
	5'-0"	Two # 3 φ					Two # 3 φ				
	6'-0"	Two # 4 φ					Two # 3 φ				
	7'-0"						Two # 4 φ				
5 5/8" x 7 5/8"	4'-0"	Two # 3 φ	Two # 3 φ	Two # 4 φ	Two # 4 φ	Two # 5 φ [2]	Two # 3 φ	Two # 3 φ	Two # 4 φ	Two # 4 φ	Two # 4 φ [2]
	5'-0"	Two # 3 φ	Two # 4 φ	Two # 5 φ	Two # 5 φ [5]	Two # 6 φ [5]	Two # 3 φ	Two # 4 φ	Two # 4 φ	Two # 5 φ [4]	Two # 6 φ [4]
	6'-0"	Two # 4 φ	Two # 5 φ	Two # 6 φ [7]	Two # 7 φ [7]	Two # 8 φ [7]	Two # 3 φ	Two # 4 φ	Two # 5 φ [7]	Two # 6 φ [7]	Two # 7 φ [7]
	7'-0"	Two # 4 φ	Two # 6 φ [7]	Two # 8 φ [7]			Two # 3 φ	Two # 5 φ	Two # 6 φ [7]	Two # 7 φ [7]	
	8'-0"	Two # 5 φ	Two # 8 φ [7]				Two # 4 φ	Two # 6 φ [7]	Two # 7 φ [7]		
	9'-0"	Two # 6 φ					Two # 4 φ	Two # 8 φ [7]			
	10'-0"	Two # 7 φ					Two # 5 φ				

NOTES:

Lintels are modular sizes. fc = 3000 #/□"; fs = 20000 #/□". 4 in table = no. of stirrups at each end of lintel. Lintels above heavy line require bars at bottom only, location of which must be indicated on lintel.

by fabricator. Lintels below heavy line require top and bottom bars of the same size and stirrups as indicated. Two piece-split lintels can be used only if above heavy line and are not to carry floor loads unless

bottom of floor construction is at least 12" above top of lintel. To use one piece lintel in 12" walls, increase reinf. to 3 bars or equiv. area and increase allowable floor loads by 50%.

Philip R. Bates, AIA; Fresno, California

TABLE OF HOLLOW CLAY TILE LINTELS

LINTEL		SUPERIMPOSED LOAD (LBS. PER LIN. FT.)								
L (FT.)	t (IN.)	0		250		500		750		1000	
		D	R	D	R	D	R	D	R	D	R
4	4	5.8	1 #3	5.8	1 #3	9.8	1 #3				
	6	5.8	2 #3	5.8	2 #3	5.8	2 #3	9.8	2 #3	9.8	2 #3
	8	5.8	2 #3	5.8	2 #3	5.8	2 #3	5.8	2 #3	9.8	2 #3
5	4	5.8	1 #3	5.8	1 #3	9.8	1 #4				
	6	5.8	2 #3	5.8	2 #3	9.8	2 #3	9.8	2 #3		
	8	5.8	2 #3	5.8	2 #3	5.8	2 #3	9.8	2 #3	9.8	2 #4
6	4	5.8	1 #3	5.8	1 #5						
	6	5.8	2 #3	9.8	2 #3						
	8	5.8	2 #3	5.8	2 #3	5.8	2 #5	9.8	2 #4	9.8	2 #4

D = Effective Depth
R = Required Lintel Reinforcement
L = Lintel Span
t = Nominal Lintel Thickness

NOTES:

1. Table is calculated for tile masonry compressive strength (f'm) of 2000 psi.

2. Dead load of the lintel is included in the reinforcement requirements.

3. Table designed in accord with A 41.2–1960, A.S.A.

4. Lintel dead load assumed to be 135 pcf.

CONCRETE FILLED

D   5.8"

8" × 8"   6" × 8"   4" × 8"

D   9.8"

REINF. RODS

8" × 12"   6" × 12"   4" × 12"

TYPICAL HOLLOW CLAY TILE LINTEL DETAILS
STRUCTURAL CLAY PRODUCTS INSTITUTE

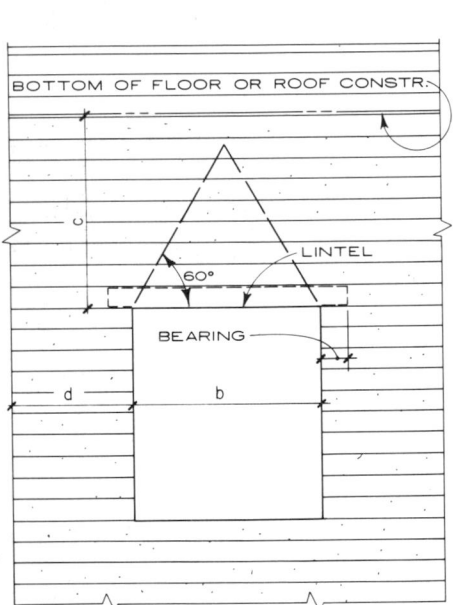

BOTTOM OF FLOOR OR ROOF CONSTR.

60°

LINTEL

BEARING

d   b

SIMPLE LINTEL WITH ARCH ACTION
c ≦ b ;   d ≦ b
CARRIES WALL LOAD ONLY IN TRIANGLE ABOVE OPENING

h_2

60°

b

h_1

60°

b

SIMPLE LINTEL WITHOUT ARCH ACTION
h_1 or h_2 < 0.6b
CARRIES LESS WALL LOAD THAN TRI‐ANGLE ABOVE OPENING

BOTTOM OF FLOOR OR ROOF CONSTR.

h

60°

b

LINTEL WITH FLOOR LOAD
c < b
CARRIES GREATER LOAD (AREA OF RECTANGLE) THAN △ ABOVE OPENING

TYPES OF LINTEL CONDITIONS — CONSULT STRUCTURAL HANDBOOKS FOR DESIGN FORMULAS

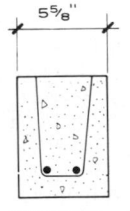

5 5/8"

6" LINTEL

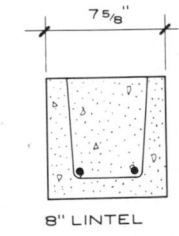

7 5/8"

8" LINTEL

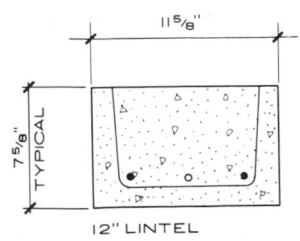

11 5/8"

7 5/8" TYPICAL

12" LINTEL

MAX. CLR. SPAN	WALL WIDTH	REBAR NO.–SIZE
6'-0"	6"	2-#3
8'-0"		2-#4
6'-0"	8"	2-#3
8'-0"		2-#4
6'-0"	12"	3-#3
8'-0"		3-#4

NOTES:

This type of lintel is used to carry concrete block or lighter wall construction only. It is not recommended to carry any floor loads.

PRECAST CONCRETE "U" LINTELS — NUMBER & SIZE OF REINFORCING BARS REQUIRED

Phillip R. Bates, AIA; Fresno, California

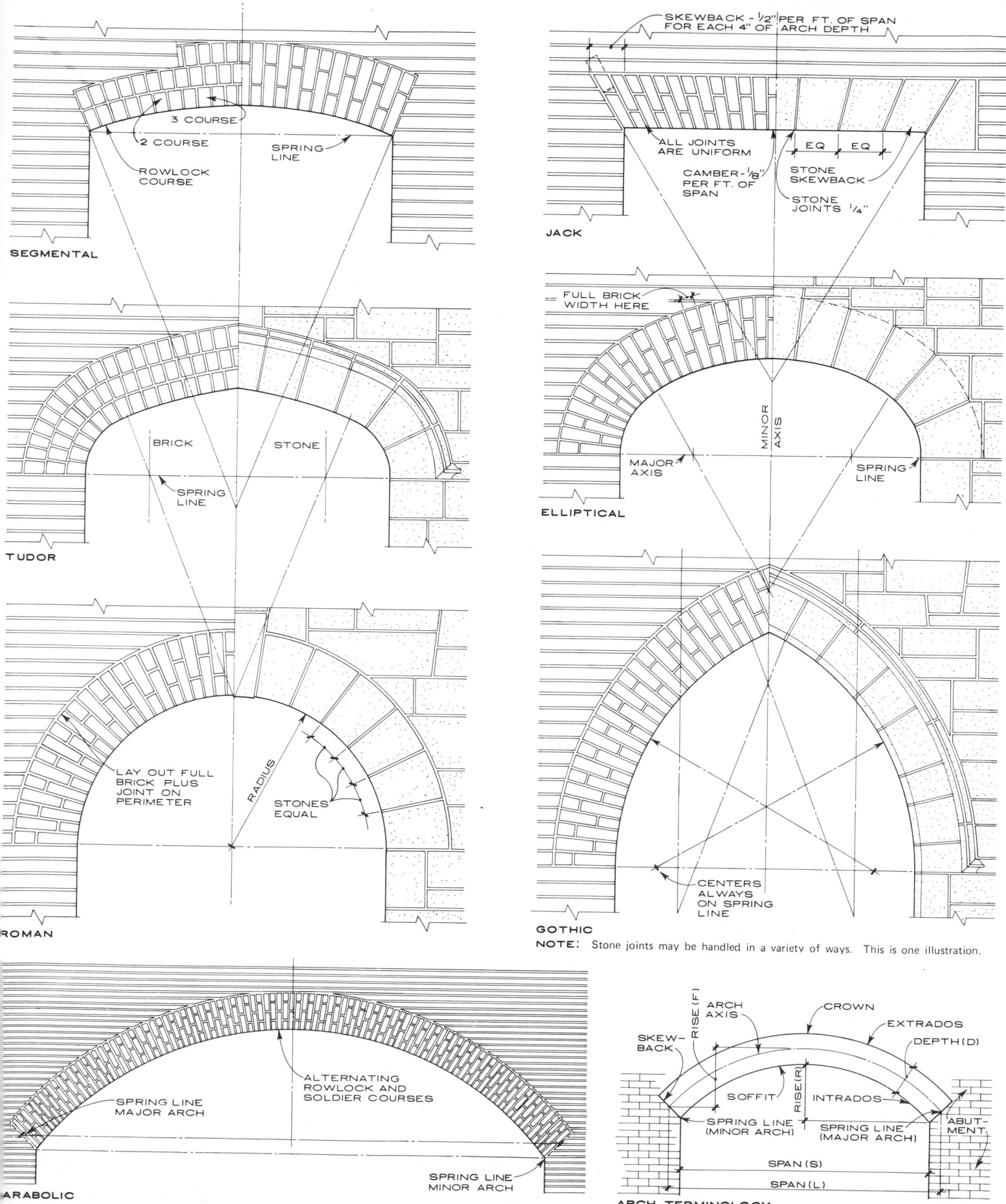

SEGMENTAL
- 3 COURSE
- 2 COURSE
- ROWLOCK COURSE
- SPRING LINE

JACK
- SKEWBACK - 1/2" PER FT. OF SPAN FOR EACH 4" OF ARCH DEPTH
- ALL JOINTS ARE UNIFORM
- CAMBER - 1/8" PER FT. OF SPAN
- EQ   EQ
- STONE SKEWBACK
- STONE JOINTS 1/4"

TUDOR
- BRICK   STONE
- SPRING LINE

ELLIPTICAL
- FULL BRICK WIDTH HERE
- MINOR AXIS
- MAJOR AXIS
- SPRING LINE

ROMAN
- LAY OUT FULL BRICK PLUS JOINT ON PERIMETER
- RADIUS
- STONES EQUAL

GOTHIC
- CENTERS ALWAYS ON SPRING LINE

NOTE: Stone joints may be handled in a variety of ways. This is one illustration.

PARABOLIC
- SPRING LINE MAJOR ARCH
- ALTERNATING ROWLOCK AND SOLDIER COURSES
- SPRING LINE MINOR ARCH

ARCH TERMINOLOGY
- ARCH AXIS
- RISE (F)
- CROWN
- EXTRADOS
- DEPTH (D)
- SKEWBACK
- SOFFIT
- RISE (R)
- INTRADOS
- SPRING LINE (MINOR ARCH)
- SPRING LINE (MAJOR ARCH)
- ABUTMENT
- SPAN (S)
- SPAN (L)

Structural Clay Products Institute; McLean, Virginia

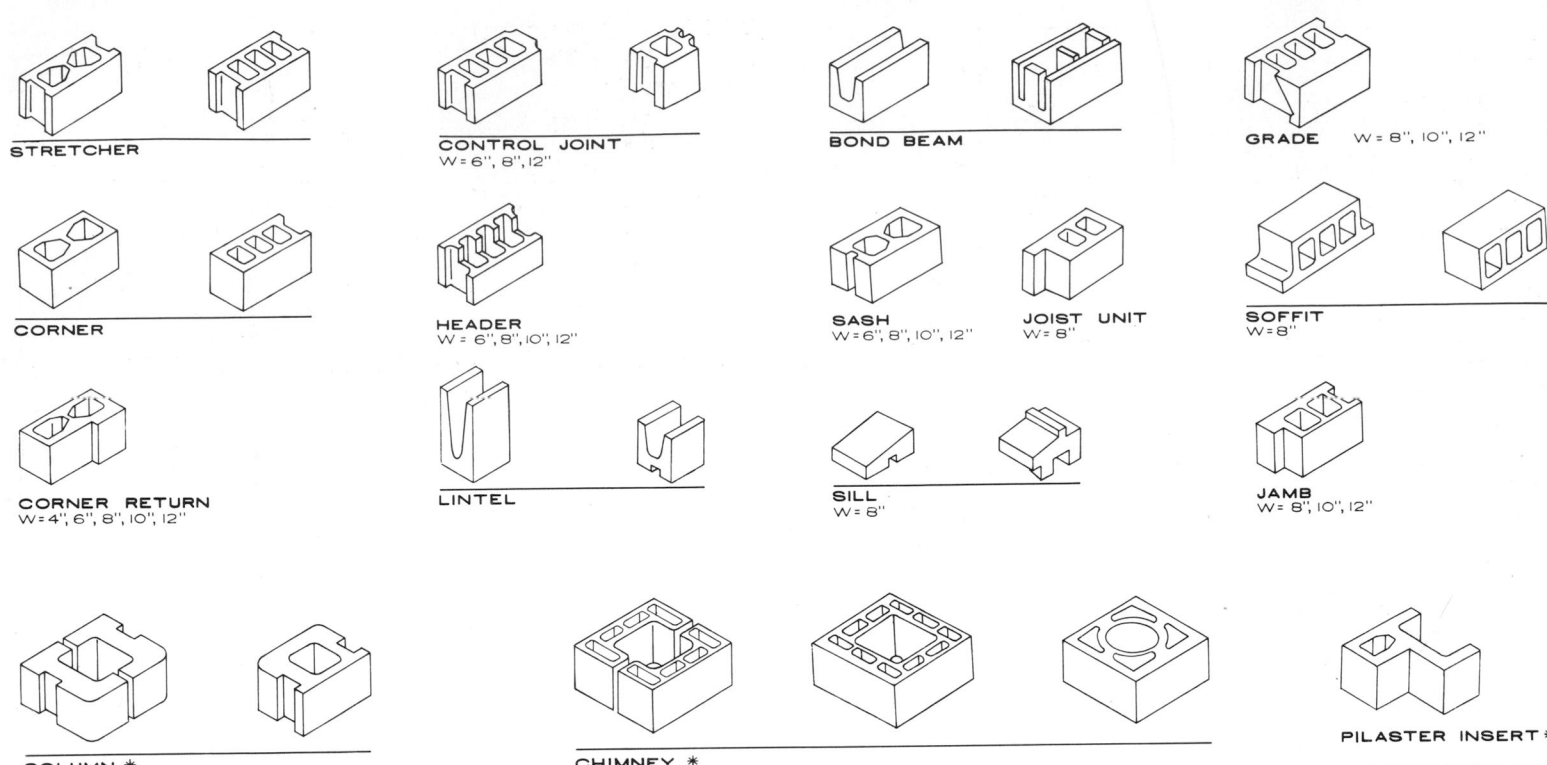

STRETCHER

CONTROL JOINT
W = 6", 8", 12"

BOND BEAM

GRADE   W = 8", 10", 12"

CORNER

HEADER
W = 6", 8", 10", 12"

SASH
W = 6", 8", 10", 12"

JOIST UNIT
W = 8"

SOFFIT
W = 8"

CORNER RETURN
W = 4", 6", 8", 10", 12"

LINTEL

SILL
W = 8"

JAMB
W = 8", 10", 12"

COLUMN *

CHIMNEY *

PILASTER INSERT *

TYPICAL CONCRETE BLOCK SHAPES

BLOCK SPECIFICATIONS AND FIRE RESISTANCE DATA

1. A solid (load bearing) concrete block is a unit whose cross-sectional area in every plane parallel to the bearing surface is not less than 75% of the gross cross-sectional area measured in the same plane. (ASTM C145—64T)

2. A hollow concrete block is a unit whose cross-sectional area in every plane parallel to the bearing surface is less than 75% of the gross cross-sectional area measured in the same plane. (ASTM C90—64T)

3. Actual dimension is $3/8''$ to $1/2''$ less than nominal shown.

4. All shapes shown are available in all dimensions given in chart except for width (W) which may be otherwise noted.
*. Available in special sizes (does not refer to table shown)

5. Because the number of shapes and sizes for concrete masonry screen units is virtually unlimited, it is advisable for the designer to check on availability of any specific shape during early planning.

6. Screen units should be of high quality, even though they seldom are employed in load-bearing construction. When tested with their hollow cells parallel to the direction of the load, screen units should have a compressive strength exceeding 1,000 psi of gross area; a quality of concrete unit comparable to "Specifications for Hollow Load-Bearing Concrete Masonry Units" ASTM C90—65T.

7. Building codes are quite specific in the degree of fire protection required in various areas of buildings. Local building regulations will govern the concrete masonry wall section best suited for specific applications. Fire-resistance ratings of concrete masonry walls are based on fire tests made at Underwriters' Laboratories, Inc., National Bureau of Standards, Portland Cement Association, and other recognized laboratories. Methods of test are described in ASTM E119 "Standard Method of Fire Tests of Building Construction and Materials".

8. The fire-resistance ratings of most concrete masonry walls are determined by heat transmission measured by temperature rise on the cold side. Fire endurance can be calculated as a function of the aggregate type used in the block unit, and the solid thickness of the wall, or the equivalent solid thickness of the wall when working with hollow units.

Robert S. Dame, R. A.; Kensington, Maryland

9. Equivalent thickness of hollow units is calculated from actual thickness and the percentage of solid materials. Both needed items of information are normally reported by the testing laboratory using standard ASTM procedures, such as ASTM C140 "Methods of Sampling and Testing Concrete Masonry Units". When walls are plastered or otherwise faced with fire-resistant materials, the thickness of these materials is included in calculating the equivalent thickness effective for fire-resistance. Estimated fire-resistance ratings shown in the table are for fully protected construction in which all structural members are of incombustible materials. Where combustible members are framed into walls, equivalent solid thickness protecting each such member should not be less than 93 percent of the thicknesses shown. Plaster is effective in increasing fire-resistance when combustible members are framed into masonry walls, as is filling core spaces with various fire-resistant materials.

10. The following are minimum equivalent thicknesses for rating of:

	1 hr.	2 hr.	3 hr.	4 hr.
Pumice	1.8	3.0	4.0	4.7
Expanded slag	2.2	3.3	4.2	5.0
Expanded shale or clay	2.5	3.7	4.7	5.5
Limestone, scoria, cinders unexpanded slag	2.7	4.0	5.0	5.9
Calcareous gravel	2.8	4.2	5.3	6.2
Siliceous gravel	3.0	4.5	5.7	6.7

Equivalent thickness is the solid thickness that would be obtained if the same amount of concrete contained in a hollow unit were recast without core holes. Calculate fire-resistance as follows: Equivalent thickness equals the percentage of block solidity (based on aggregate type) times actual block thickness (in.). Refer to table for hour rating of wall.

NOMINAL DIMENSIONS OF TYPICAL CONCRETE BLOCK SHAPES

HEIGHT (H)	LENGTH (L)	WIDTH (W)
4	8	2
8	12	3
	16	4
		6
		8
		10
		12

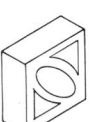

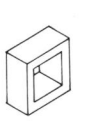

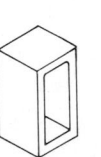

TYPICAL SCREEN BLOCK SHAPES

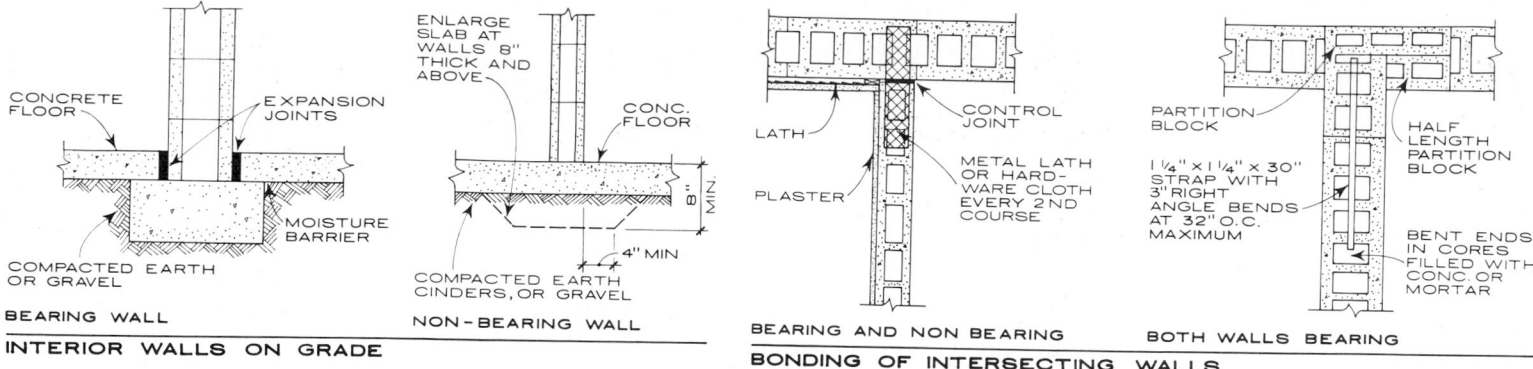

INTERIOR WALLS ON GRADE

BEARING WALL — CONCRETE FLOOR, EXPANSION JOINTS, MOISTURE BARRIER, COMPACTED EARTH OR GRAVEL

NON-BEARING WALL — ENLARGE SLAB AT WALLS 8" THICK AND ABOVE, CONC. FLOOR, 8" MIN, 4" MIN, COMPACTED EARTH CINDERS, OR GRAVEL

BONDING OF INTERSECTING WALLS

BEARING AND NON BEARING — LATH, PLASTER, CONTROL JOINT, METAL LATH OR HARD-WARE CLOTH EVERY 2ND COURSE

BOTH WALLS BEARING — PARTITION BLOCK, 1¼" × 1¼" × 30" STRAP WITH 3" RIGHT ANGLE BENDS AT 32" O.C. MAXIMUM, HALF LENGTH PARTITION BLOCK, BENT ENDS IN CORES FILLED WITH CONC. OR MORTAR

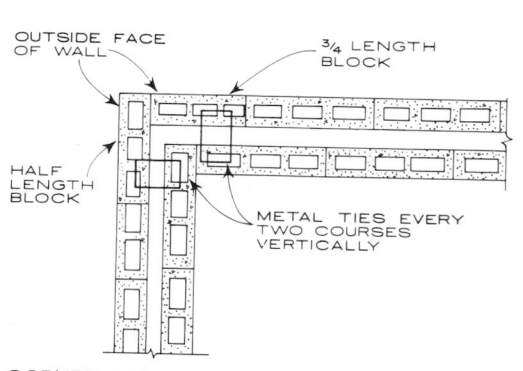

CORNER CONSTRUCTION-CAVITY WALL-PLAN VIEW

OUTSIDE FACE OF WALL, ¾ LENGTH BLOCK, HALF LENGTH BLOCK, METAL TIES EVERY TWO COURSES VERTICALLY

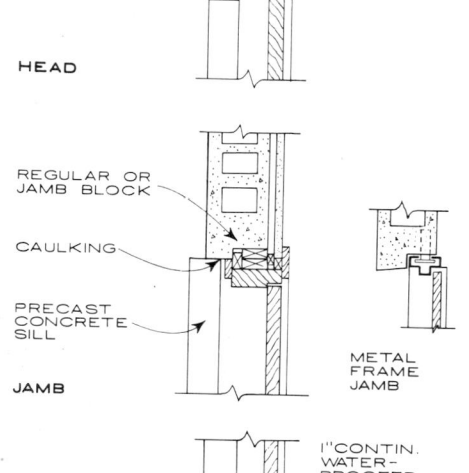

HEAD — PRECAST CONCRETE LINTEL, CAULKING

JAMB — REGULAR OR JAMB BLOCK, CAULKING, PRECAST CONCRETE SILL, METAL FRAME JAMB

FRAMING OF CAVITY WALL AND WOOD JOIST FLOOR

METAL TIES, FINISH FLOOR, JOIST ANCHOR, WOOD JOIST, MIN. BEARING OF 3" FOR WD. JOISTS (TYPICAL), SOLID CONCRETE BLOCK

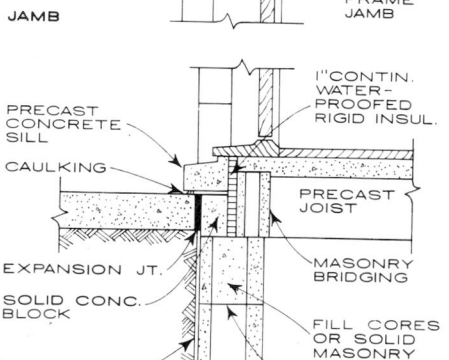

DOOR SILL AT FIRST FLOOR

PRECAST CONCRETE SILL, CAULKING, EXPANSION JT., SOLID CONC. BLOCK, WATER-PROOFING, 1" CONTIN. WATER-PROOFED RIGID INSUL., PRECAST JOIST, MASONRY BRIDGING, FILL CORES OR SOLID MASONRY, MET. LATH

CHIMNEY FOOTING ON INTERIOR WALL

2" (MIN. THICKNESS) CONCRETE-SLOPED, COMPACTED FILL, ASH-PIT, CLEAN-OUT DOOR, EXPAN. JOINT

NOTE:
Slope ashpit above cleanout door level for ease in sweeping out.

FRAMING OF WALL AND WOOD JOIST FLOOR

FINISH FLOOR, MASONRY BRIDGING, SOLID CONCRETE BLOCK, CONC. FILLED CORES OR SOLID CONCRETE MASONRY, METAL LATH, WOOD JOIST-MIN. BEARING OF 3" (TYPICAL), 1¼" × 1¼" TWISTED STEEL PLATE JOIST ANCHOR AT 6' INTERVALS OR EVERY 4TH JOIST

NOTE:
Joists parallel to and adjacent to walls anchored at 8 foot intervals. Anchors should engage three joists.

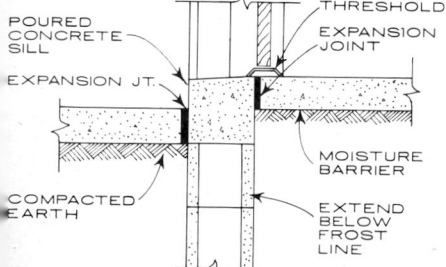

DOOR SILL AT BASEMENT

POURED CONCRETE SILL, EXPANSION JT., COMPACTED EARTH, METAL THRESHOLD, EXPANSION JOINT, MOISTURE BARRIER, EXTEND BELOW FROST LINE

CHIMNEY FOOTING ON EXTERIOR WALL

WATER PROOFING, GRAVEL OR STONE FILL, DRAIN TILE, ASH-PIT, CLEAN-OUT DOOR, CONC. FLOOR, EXPAN. JT.

NOTE:
Slope ashpit above floor level for ease in sweeping out.

FRAMING OF WALL AND SOFFIT BLOCK JOIST FLOOR (CONCRETE BLOCK JOIST FLOOR SIMILAR)

SOLID CONCRETE BLOCK, 1" CONTIN. WATER-PROOFED RIGID INSULATION, CONCRETE FLOOR, FILLED CORES OR SOLID MASONRY, METAL LATH

SCALE ALL DRAWINGS 1/2" = 1'-0"

Robert S. Dame, R. A.; Kensington, Maryland

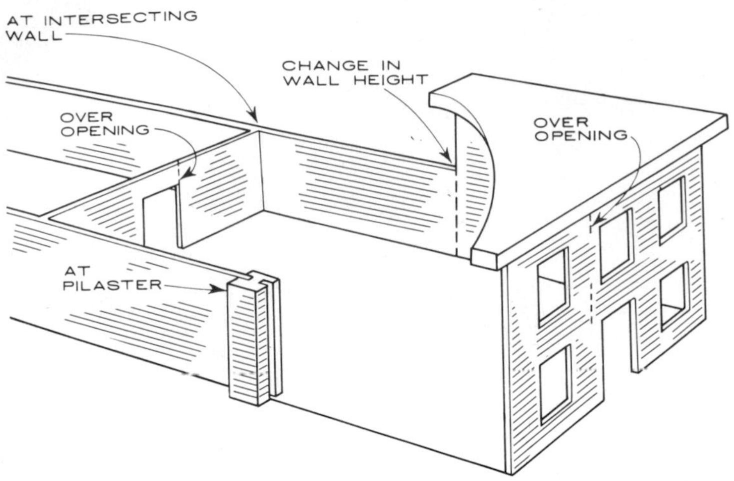
AT INTERSECTING WALL
CHANGE IN WALL HEIGHT
OVER OPENING
OVER OPENING
AT PILASTER

TYPICAL CONTROL JOINT LOCATIONS

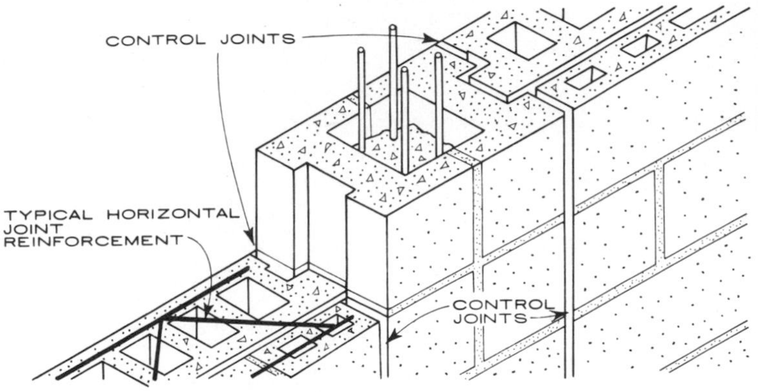
CONTROL JOINTS
TYPICAL HORIZONTAL JOINT REINFORCEMENT
CONTROL JOINTS

FLUSH WALL PILASTER AND CONTROL JOINTS

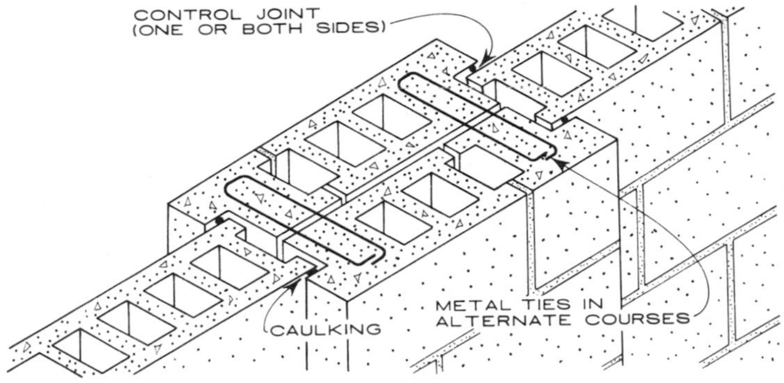
CONTROL JOINT (ONE OR BOTH SIDES)
CAULKING
METAL TIES IN ALTERNATE COURSES

CONTROL JOINT AT PIER

CONTROL JOINT SPACING FOR MOISTURE CONTROLLED, TYPE I, Q BLOCK UNITS

RECOMMENDED SPACING OF CONTROL JOINTS	VERTICAL SPACING OF JOINT REINFORCEMENT			
	NONE	24"	16"	8"
EXPRESSED AS RATIO OF PANEL LENGTH TO HEIGHT L/H	2	2½	3	4
PANEL LENGTH (L) NOT TO EXCEED [REGARDLESS OF HEIGHT (H)]	40'	45'	50'	60'

NOTE:

With horizontal bond beams at 4'– 0" o.c. vertically and control joints at 60'– 0" maximum o.c.

GENERAL CONSTRUCTION NOTES

There are three methods of controlling cracking in concrete unit masonry structures: product specifications which limit moisture movement (these limits are incorporated in "Q Block Specifications," the product standard of the industry's quality control program), steel reinforcement which increases crack resistance (bond beams or horizontal joint reinforcement), and control joints.

Control joints are employed in crack control to reduce restraint by accommodating movement of the masonry wall, or movement of structural elements adjacent to the wall. They are vertical separations built into the wall at locations where cracking is likely due to horizontal stress. Their spacing along the wall length will depend upon: (1) expected movement(s) of wall or other elements, (2) resistance of wall to horizontal tensile stress, and (3) the extent and location in the wall of windows, doors, recesses, chases, and other causes of stress concentration.

Generally, a control joint is placed at one side of an opening less than six feet in width and at both jambs of openings over six feet in width. Where concrete unit masonry is used as backup of other materials, extend control joints through facing if it is rigidly bonded (masonry bond). Control joint need not extend through facing when bond is flexible (metal ties).

Control joint should extend through plaster applied directly to masonry, but plaster on furring may not require vertical separation at control joint.

Provide horizontal slip plane where reinforced lintel beam terminates at a control joint. Provide horizontal slip plane at junction of roof and load-bearing masonry terminating at a control joint. Bond between roof and wall should be broken 12–15 feet back from corners, with slip plane.

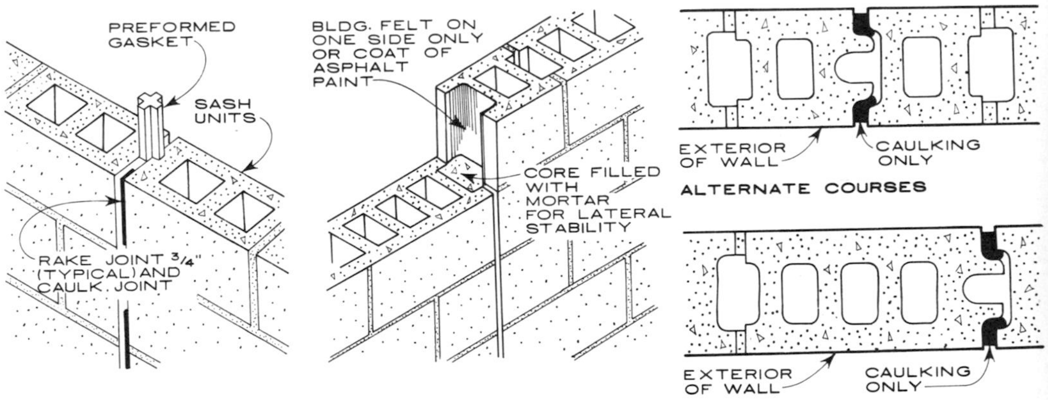
PREFORMED GASKET
SASH UNITS
RAKE JOINT ¾" (TYPICAL) AND CAULK. JOINT
BLDG. FELT ON ONE SIDE ONLY OR COAT OF ASPHALT PAINT
CORE FILLED WITH MORTAR FOR LATERAL STABILITY
EXTERIOR OF WALL
CAULKING ONLY
ALTERNATE COURSES
EXTERIOR OF WALL
CAULKING ONLY

SHEAR RESISTING FLUSH WALL CONTROL JOINTS

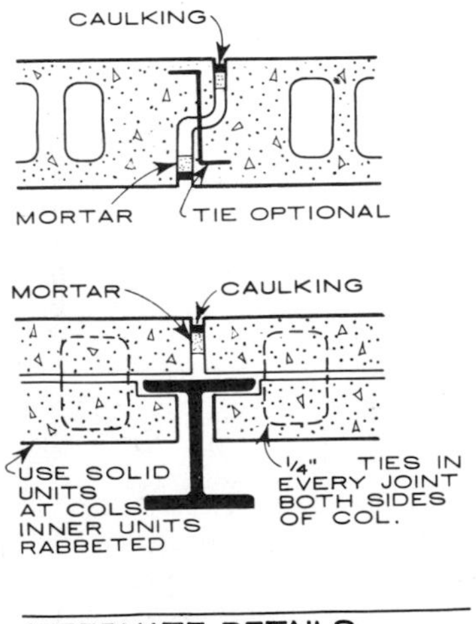
CAULKING
MORTAR
TIE OPTIONAL
MORTAR
CAULKING
USE SOLID UNITS AT COLS. INNER UNITS RABBETED
¼" TIES IN EVERY JOINT BOTH SIDES OF COL.

ALTERNATE DETAILS OF FLUSH CONTROL JOINTS

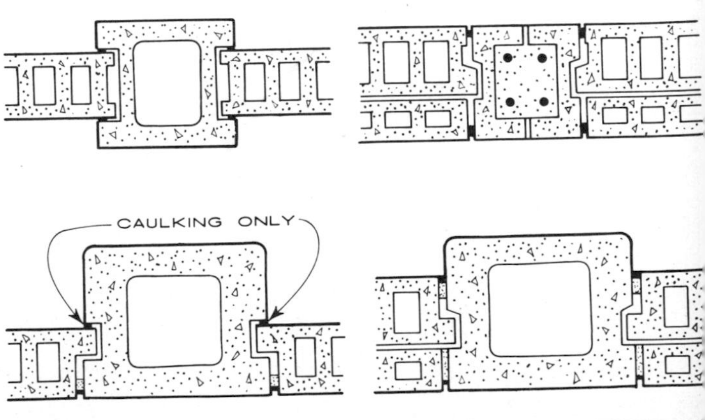
CAULKING ONLY

CONTROL JOINTS AT WALLS AND PILASTERS

Robert S. Dame, R. A.; Kensington, Maryland

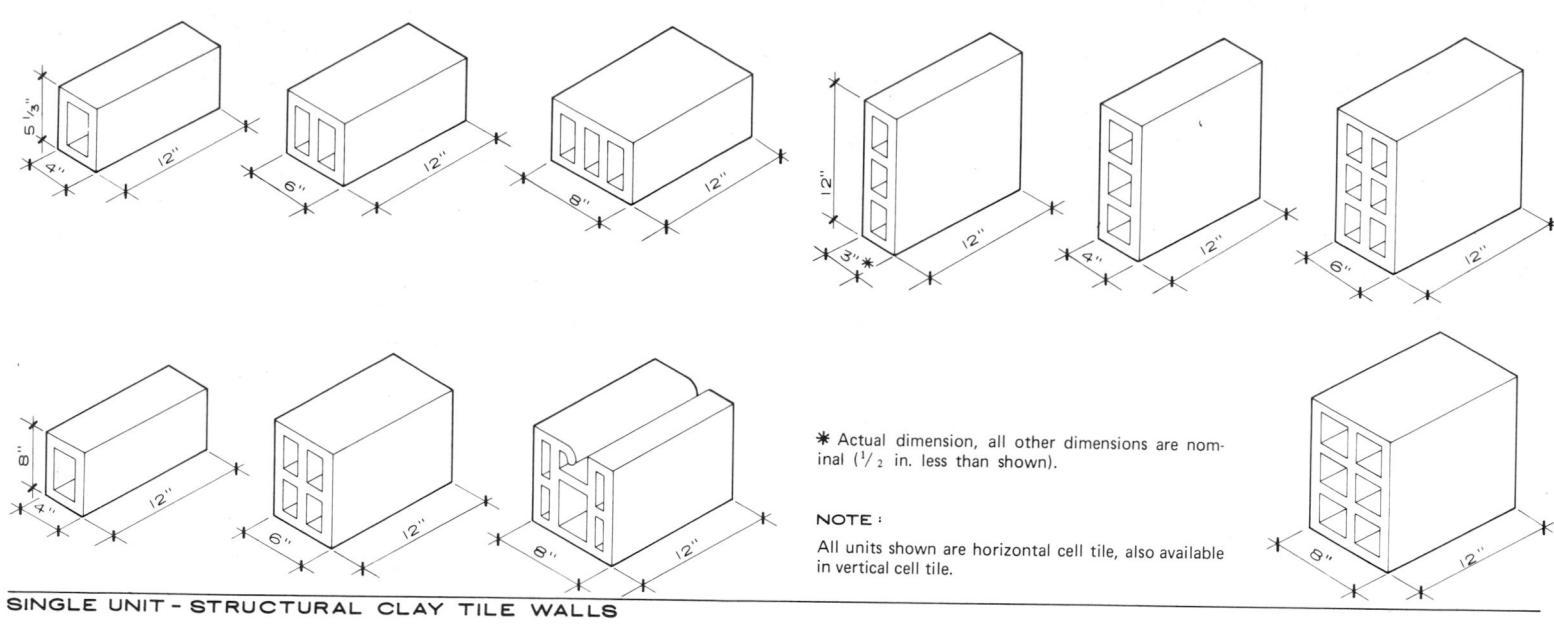

✱ Actual dimension, all other dimensions are nominal (1/2 in. less than shown).

NOTE :

All units shown are horizontal cell tile, also available in vertical cell tile.

SINGLE UNIT - STRUCTURAL CLAY TILE WALLS

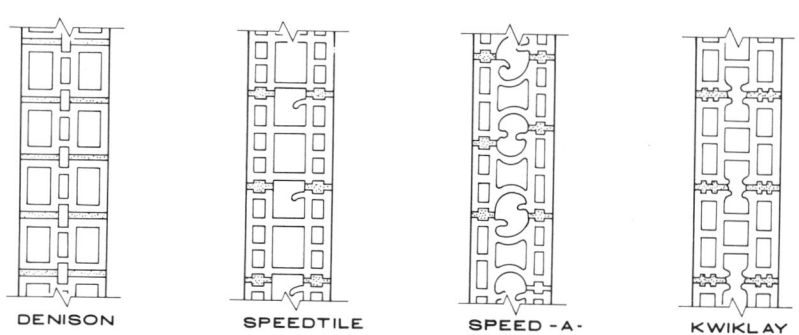

DENISON SPEEDTILE SPEED-A-BACKER KWIKLAY

SINGLE UNIT - STRUCTURAL CLAY TILE WALLS

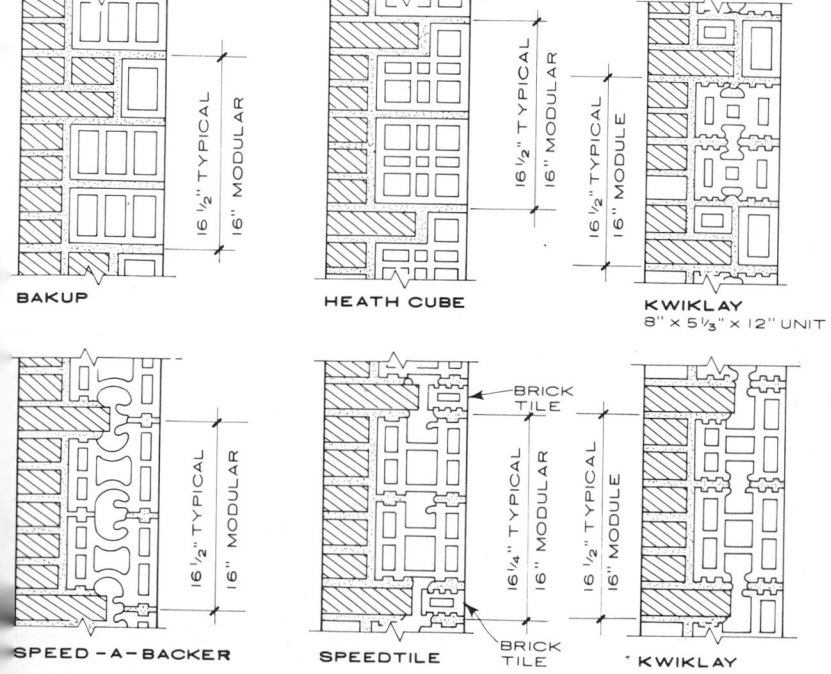

BAKUP HEATH CUBE KWIKLAY
8" × 5⅓" × 12" UNIT

SPEED-A-BACKER SPEEDTILE KWIKLAY

BRICK TILE
BRICK TILE

COMBINATION BRICK & CLAY TILE - 12" WALLS

Structural Clay Products Institute; McLean, Virginia

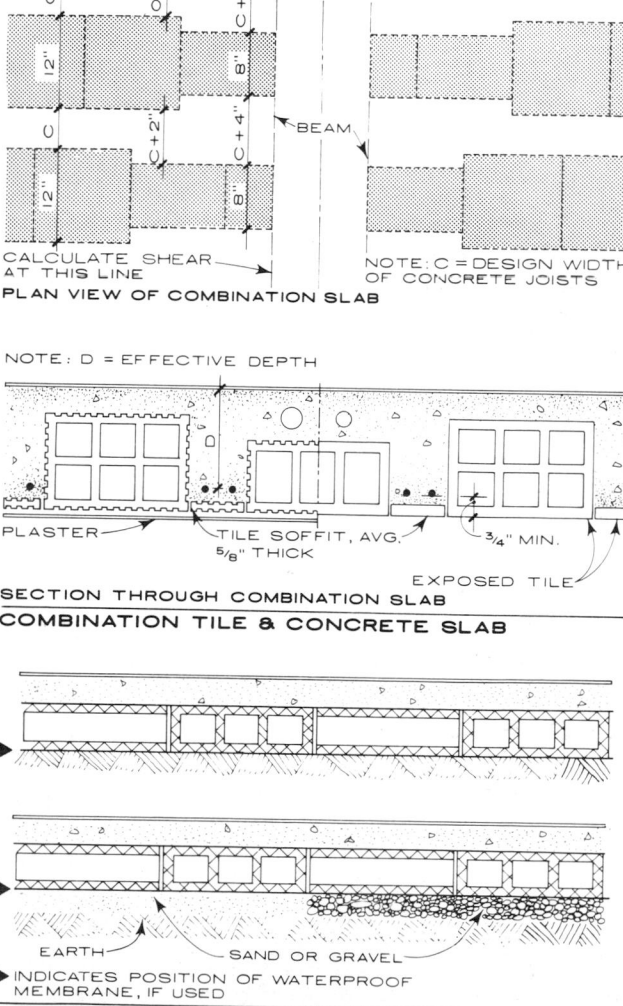

WIDTH OF BEAM

BEAM

CALCULATE SHEAR AT THIS LINE

NOTE: C = DESIGN WIDTH OF CONCRETE JOISTS

PLAN VIEW OF COMBINATION SLAB

NOTE: D = EFFECTIVE DEPTH

PLASTER

TILE SOFFIT, AVG. ⅝ THICK

¾" MIN.

EXPOSED TILE

SECTION THROUGH COMBINATION SLAB
COMBINATION TILE & CONCRETE SLAB

EARTH

SAND OR GRAVEL

▶ INDICATES POSITION OF WATERPROOF MEMBRANE, IF USED

SECTIONS THROUGH TYPICAL CLAY TILE SUBFLOORS

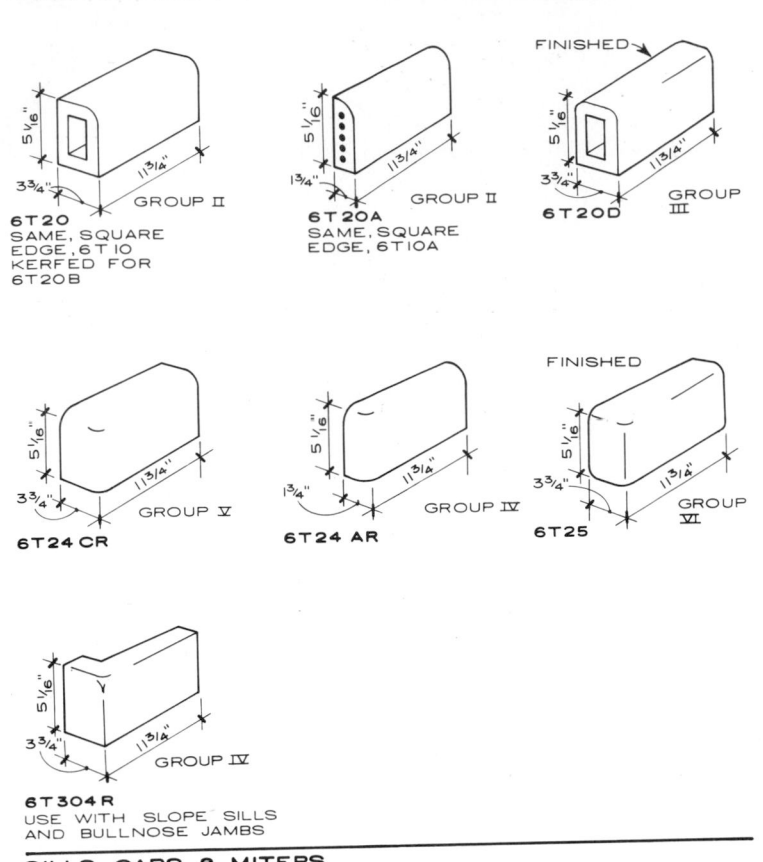

6T20 — GROUP II
SAME, SQUARE
EDGE, 6T10
KERFED FOR
6T20B

6T20A — GROUP II
SAME, SQUARE
EDGE, 6T10A

6T20D — GROUP III
FINISHED

6T24CR — GROUP V

6T24AR — GROUP IV

6T25 — GROUP VI
FINISHED

6T304R — GROUP IV
USE WITH SLOPE SILLS
AND BULLNOSE JAMBS

SILLS, CAPS & MITERS

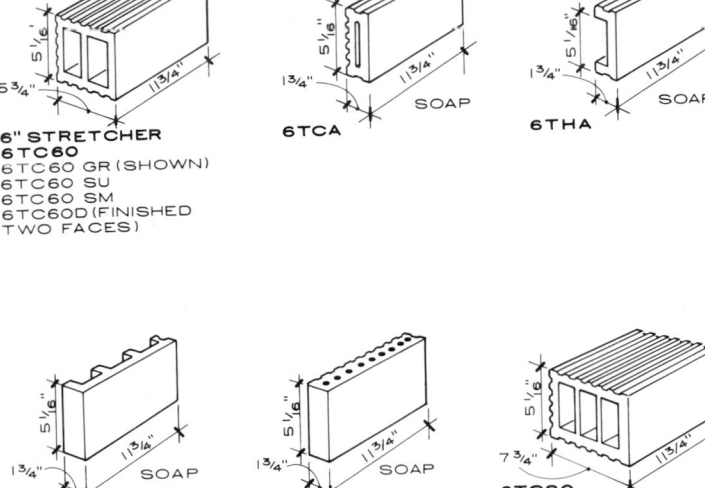

4″ STRETCHER 6TC
6TC GR
6TC SU (SHOWN)
6TC SM

4″ STRETCHER 6T
6T GR (SHOWN)
6TSU
6TSM

4″STRETCHER 6TCD (FINISHED 2 FACES)
FINISHED

6″ STRETCHER 6TC60
6TC60 GR (SHOWN)
6TC60 SU
6TC60 SM
6TC60D (FINISHED TWO FACES)

6TCA — SOAP

6THA — SOAP

6TVA — SOAP

6TA — SOAP

6TC80
6TC80 GR (SHOWN)
6TC80 SU

STRETCHER GROUP

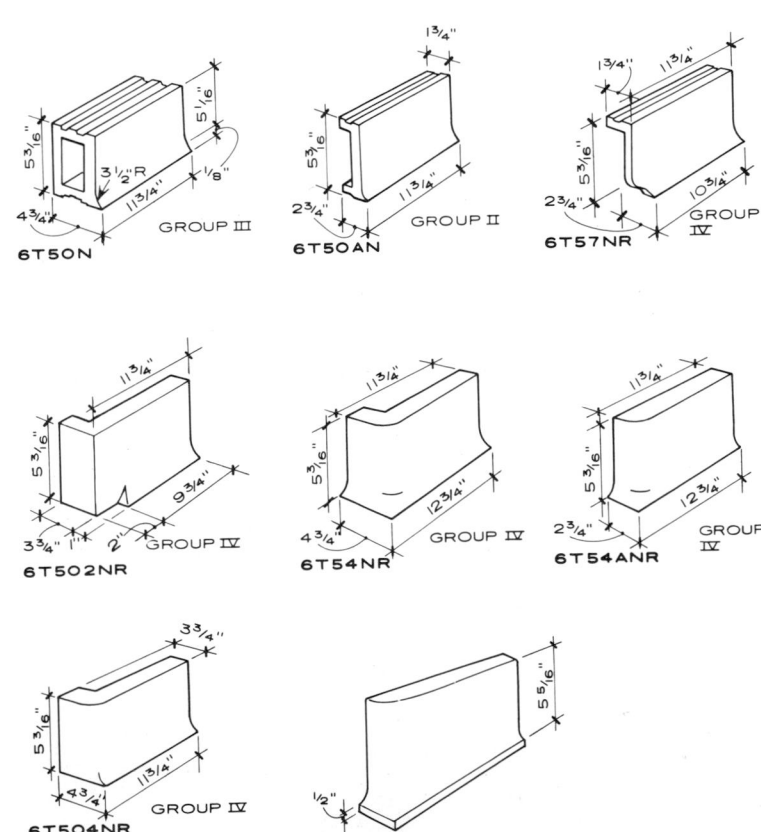

6T50N — GROUP III

6T50AN — GROUP II

6T57NR — GROUP IV

6T502NR — GROUP IV

6T54NR — GROUP IV

6T54ANR — GROUP IV

6T504NR — GROUP IV

COVE BASE (NON RECESSED EXCEPT AS NOTED)

RECESSED

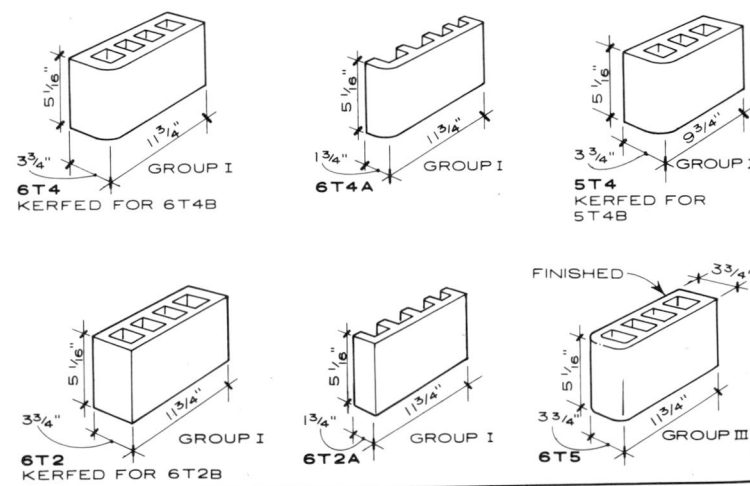

6T4 — GROUP I
KERFED FOR 6T4B

6T4A — GROUP I

5T4 — GROUP I
KERFED FOR 5T4B

6T2 — GROUP I
KERFED FOR 6T2B

6T2A — GROUP I

6T5 — GROUP III
FINISHED

CORNERS & JAMBS

GENERAL NOTES:

Number with suffix R denotes right hand shape; similar left hand shape takes suffix L.

Type and directions of scoring and coring are optional with the manufacturer. In general, the manufacturer standardizes on either the horizontal or vertical coring. This note also applies to 8w shapes shown on preceding page.

Structural Clay Products Institute; McLean, Virginia

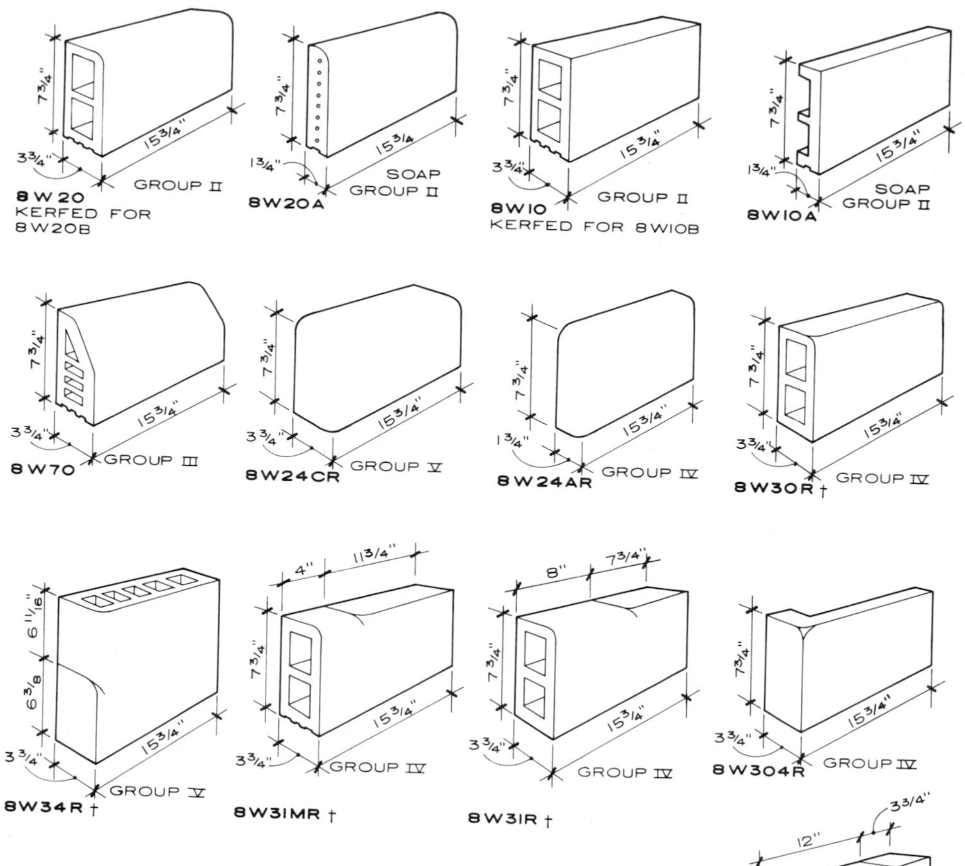

8W 20
KERFED FOR 8W20B
GROUP II
7 3/4" · 3 3/4" · 15 3/4"

8W20A
SOAP GROUP II
13/4" · 15 3/4"

8W10
KERFED FOR 8W10B
GROUP II
7 3/4" · 3 3/4" · 15 3/4"

8W10A
SOAP GROUP II
13/4" · 15 3/4"

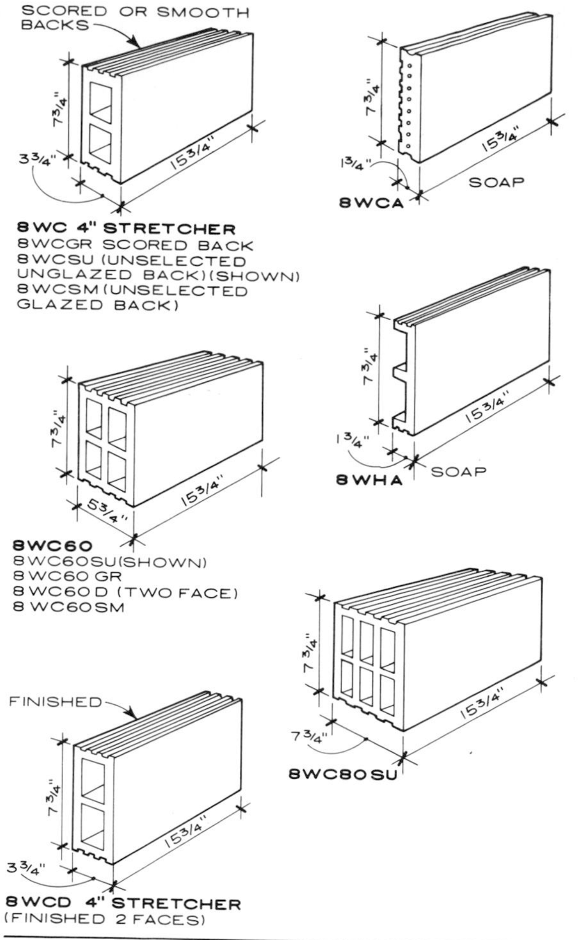

SCORED OR SMOOTH BACKS

8WC 4" STRETCHER
8WCGR SCORED BACK
8WCSU (UNSELECTED UNGLAZED BACK)(SHOWN)
8WCSM (UNSELECTED GLAZED BACK)
7 3/4" · 3 3/4" · 15 3/4"

8WCA SOAP
7 3/4" · 13/4" · 15 3/4"

8W70 GROUP III
7 3/4" · 3 3/4" · 15 3/4"

8W24CR GROUP V
7 3/4" · 3 3/4" · 15 3/4"

8W24AR GROUP IV
7 3/4" · 13/4" · 15 3/4"

8W30R † GROUP IV
7 3/4" · 3 3/4" · 15 3/4"

8WC60
8WC60SU(SHOWN)
8WC60 GR
8WC60 D (TWO FACE)
8WC60SM
7 3/4" · 15 3/4" · 5 3/4"

8WHA SOAP
7 3/4" · 13/4" · 15 3/4"

8W34R † GROUP V
6 1/16" · 6 3/8" · 3 3/4" · 15 3/4"

8W31MR † GROUP IV
4" · 113/4" · 7 3/4" · 3 3/4" · 15 3/4"

8W31R † GROUP IV
8" · 7 3/4" · 3 3/4" · 15 3/4"

8W304R GROUP IV
7 3/4" · 3 3/4" · 15 3/4"

FINISHED
8WCD 4" STRETCHER
(FINISHED 2 FACES)
7 3/4" · 3 3/4" · 15 3/4"

8WC80SU
7 3/4" · 7 3/4" · 15 3/4"

STRETCHER GROUP

GENERAL NOTE :
Suffix B denotes soap with 3 3/4" reveal or return.
Units designated † are kerfed for soap with 3 3/4" reveal.

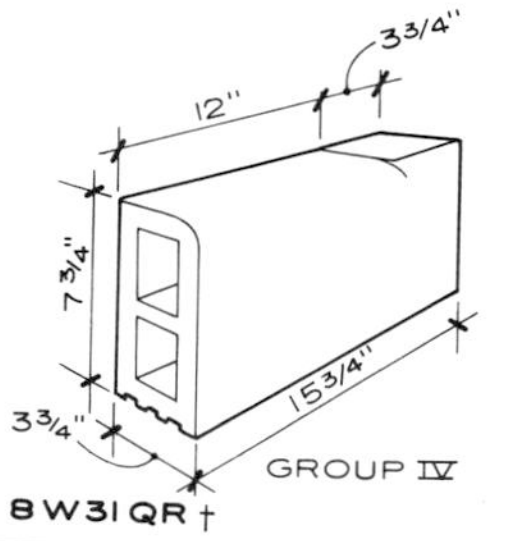

SILLS, CAPS & MITERS

8W31QR † GROUP IV
12" · 3 3/4" · 7 3/4" · 3 3/4" · 15 3/4"

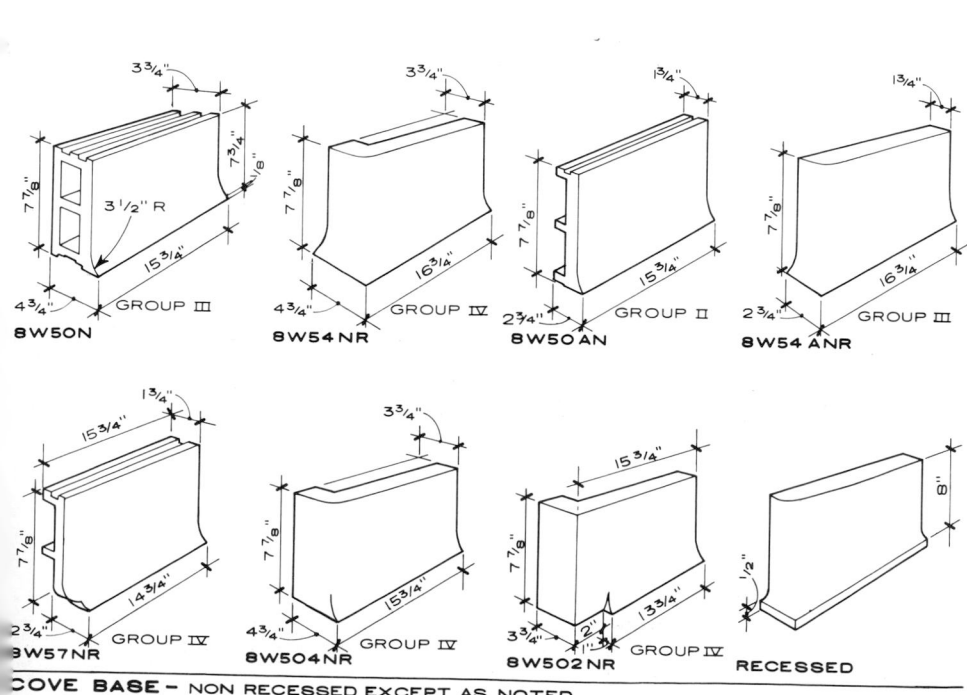

8W50N GROUP III
3 3/4" · 7 3/4" · 7 7/8" · 3 1/2" R · 15 3/4" · 4 3/4"

8W54NR GROUP IV
3 3/4" · 7 7/8" · 16 3/4" · 4 3/4"

8W50AN GROUP II
13/4" · 7 7/8" · 15 3/4" · 2 3/4"

8W54ANR GROUP III
13/4" · 7 7/8" · 16 3/4" · 2 3/4"

8W57NR GROUP IV
15 3/4" · 13/4" · 7 7/8" · 4 3/4" · 2 3/4"

8W504NR GROUP IV
3 3/4" · 15 3/4" · 7 7/8" · 4 3/4"

8W502NR GROUP IV
15 3/4" · 7 7/8" · 13/4" · 2" · 1" · 2 3/4"

RECESSED
8" · 1/2"

COVE BASE - NON RECESSED EXCEPT AS NOTED

Structural Clay Products Institute; McLean, Virginia

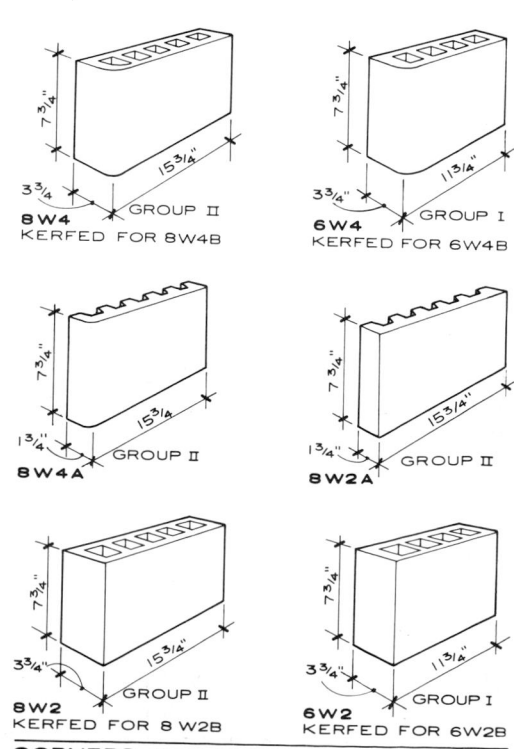

8W4 GROUP II
KERFED FOR 8W4B
7 3/4" · 3 3/4" · 15 3/4"

6W4 GROUP I
KERFED FOR 6W4B
7 3/4" · 13/4" · 15 3/4"

8W4A GROUP II
7 3/4" · 13/4" · 15 3/4"

8W2A GROUP II
7 3/4" · 13/4" · 15 3/4"

8W2 GROUP II
KERFED FOR 8W2B
7 3/4" · 3 3/4" · 15 3/4"

6W2 GROUP I
KERFED FOR 6W2B
7 3/4" · 3 3/4" · 13/4"

CORNERS & JAMBS

VERTICAL COURSING

NUMBER OF COURSES	5 1/3'' NOMINAL HEIGHT	8'' NOMINAL HEIGHT
1	5 5/16''	8''
2	10 5/8''	1' 4''
3	1' 4''	2' 0''
4	1' 9 5/16''	2' 8''
5	2' 2 5/8''	3' 4''
6	2' 8''	4' 0''
7	3' 1 5/16''	4' 8''
8	3' 6 5/8''	5' 4''
9	4' 0''	6' 0''
10	4' 5 5/16''	6' 8''
11	4' 10 5/8''	7' 4''
12	5' 4''	8' 0''
13	5' 9 5/16''	8' 8''
14	6' 2 5/8''	9' 4''
15	6' 8''	10' 0''
16	7' 1 5/16''	10' 8''
17	7' 6 5/8''	11' 4''
18	8' 0''	12' 0''
19	8' 5 5/16''	12' 8''
20	8' 10 5/8''	13' 4''
21	9' 4''	14' 0''
22	9' 9 5/16''	14' 8''
23	10' 2 5/8''	15' 4''
24	10' 8''	16' 0''
25	11' 1 5/16''	16' 8''
26	11' 6 5/8''	17' 4''
27	12' 0''	18' 0''
28	12' 5 5/16''	18' 8''
29	12' 10 5/8''	19' 4''
30	13' 4''	20' 0''
31	13' 9 5/16''	20' 8''
32	14' 2 5/8''	21' 4''
33	14' 8''	22' 0''
34	15' 1 5/16''	22' 8''
35	15' 6 5/8''	23' 4''
36	16' 0''	24' 0''
37	16' 5 5/16''	24' 8''
38	16' 10 5/8''	25' 4''
39	17' 4''	26' 0''
40	17' 9 5/16''	26' 8''
41	18' 2 5/8''	27' 4''
42	18' 8''	28' 0''
43	19' 1 5/16''	28' 8''
44	19' 6 5/8''	29' 4''
45	20' 0''	30' 0''
46	20' 5 5/16''	30' 8''
47	20' 10 5/8''	31' 4''
48	21' 4''	32' 0''
49	21' 9 5/16''	32' 8''
50	22' 2 5/8''	33' 4''

Note: For convenience in using scale, 1/3'' dimensions are changed to 5/16''

Bucks should be filled with mortar to provide sound attenuation

Panic-safe internal corners are possible using standard stretcher units in block bond with as few as 5 units, 3/8'' joints producing a quarter circle with radius of 1' 1 1/8'' or 9 units, 1/4'' joints with a radius of 1'-11''. See mfgrs data.

Structural Clay Products Institute; McLean, Virginia

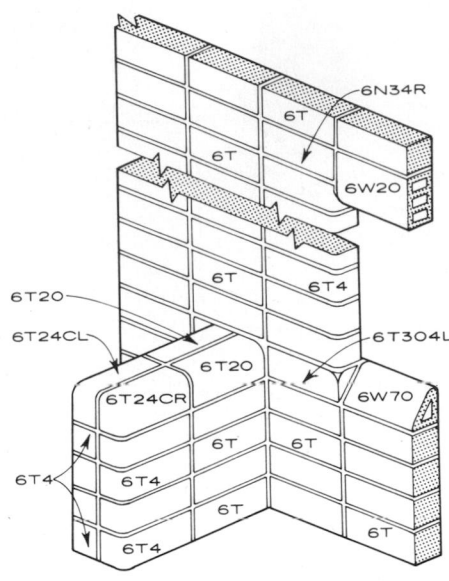

EIGHT INCH DOUBLE-FACED WING WALL BONDED TO MAIN WALL WITH TYPICAL BUTT JOINTS, STACK BOND

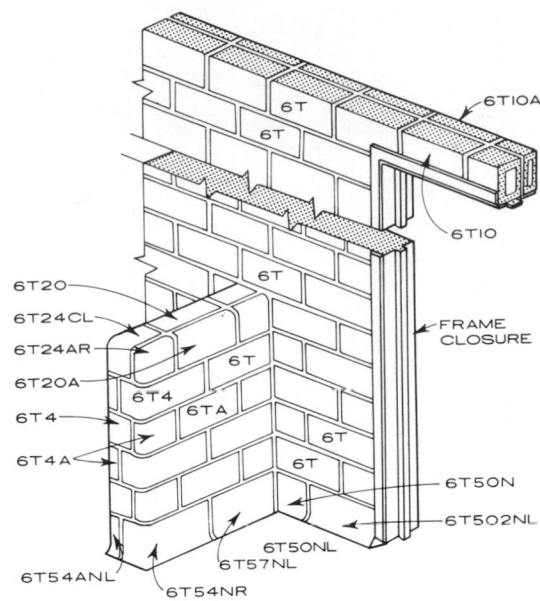

SIX INCH DOUBLE-FACED WING WALL BONDED TO MAIN WALL WITH TYPICAL BUTT JOINTS

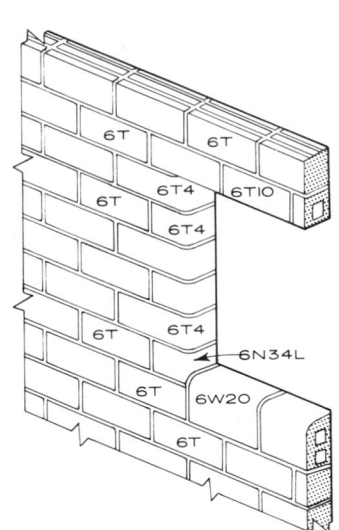

FOUR INCH SINGLE-FACED WALL WITH BULLNOSE SILL AND JAMB. SQUARE LINTEL RUNNING BOND

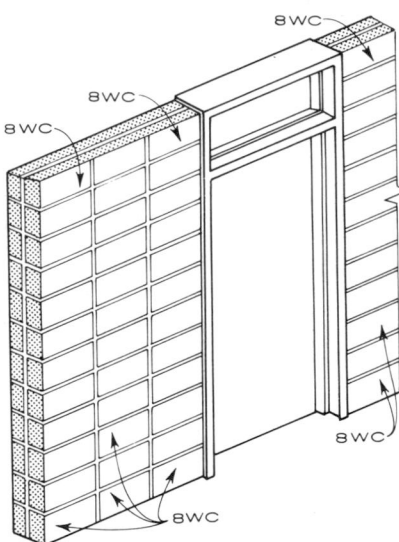

ECONOMY WALL CONSTRUCTION NO SHAPES REQUIRED FULL HEIGHT TRANSOM. 8W SERIES STACK BOND

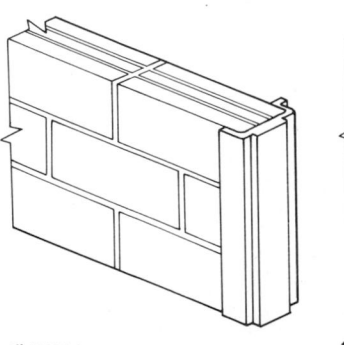

4'' WALL

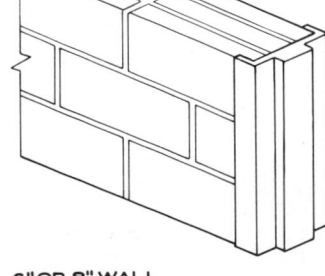

6''OR 8'' WALL

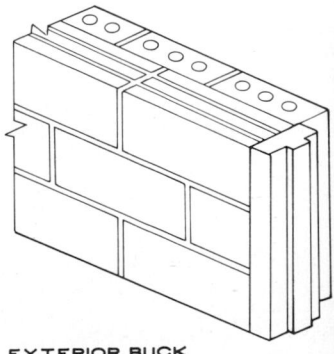

EXTERIOR BUCK

FRAME FITTINGS

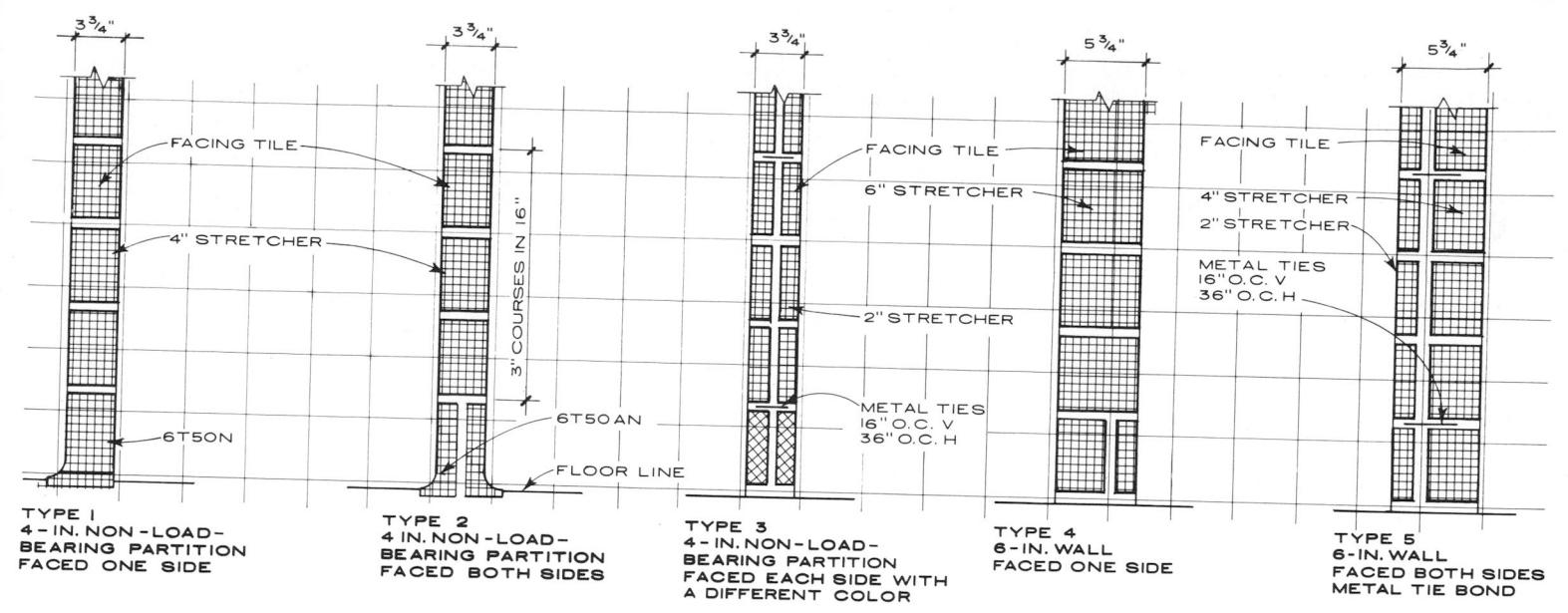

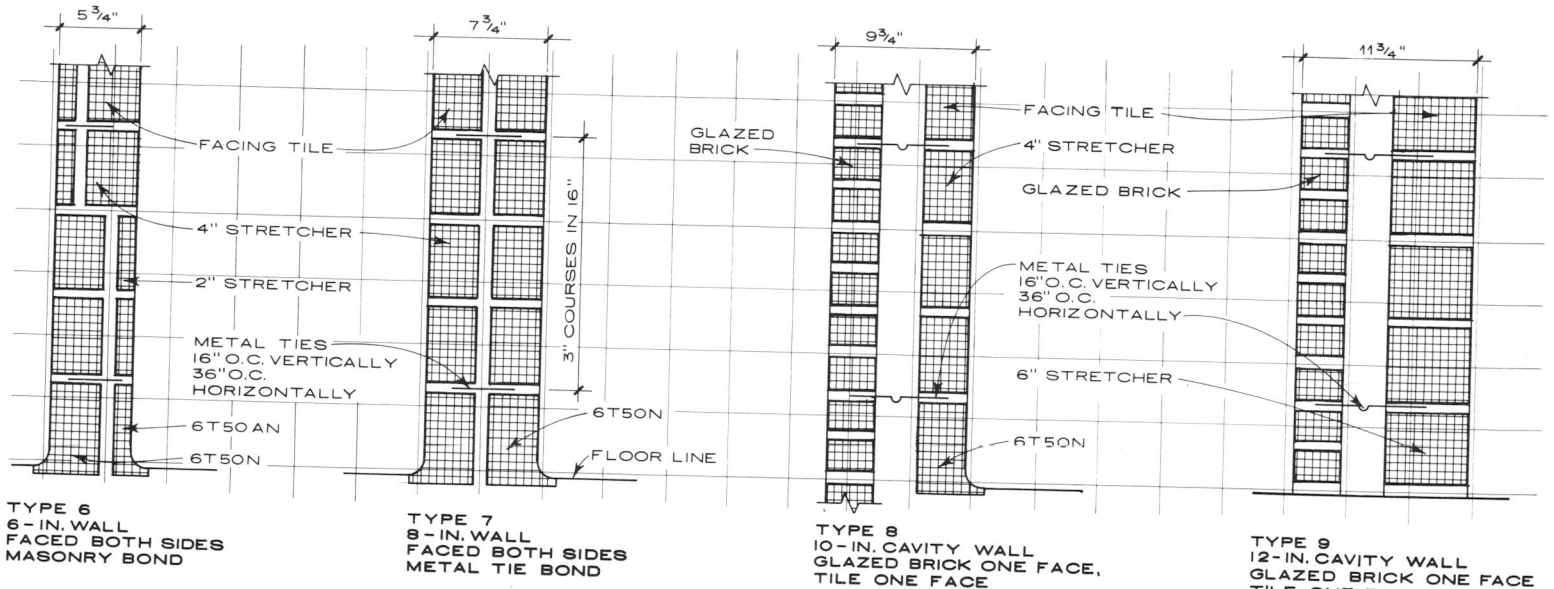

WALL SECTIONS AND PROPERTIES

	WALL TYPE NUMBER	1	2	3	4	5	6	7	8	9
ALLOWABLE LOAD (lb/linear ft)	TYPE M MORTAR (85 P.S.I.)				5870	5870	5870	7900	6300²	7970²
	TYPE S MORTAR (75 P.S.I.)				5180	5180	5180	6980	5400²	6840²
	TYPE N MORTAR (70 P.S.I.)				4830	4830	4830	6510	4950²	6270²
MATERIAL QUANTITY (per sq ft of wall)	MORTAR (CU. FT.) 25% WASTE ADDED	2.19	2.19	2.19¹	3.36	3.36¹	3.36¹	4.531¹	6.97	8.14
	FACING TILE 2% WASTE ADDED	230	230	460	230	230	230	460	230	230
	GLAZED BRICK 5% WASTE ADDED								230	230
	METAL TIES 2% WASTE ADDED			25.5		25.5		25.5	25.5	25.5
U VALUES (Btu/sq ft/hr/°F)	UNPLASTERED PARTITION	0.40	0.40	0.39						
	EXTERIOR WALL				0.35	0.34	0.34	0.30	0.30	0.23
	WITH 2-IN. INSULATION								0.10	0.03
LATERAL SUPPORT SPACING REQUIRED (ft)	NON-LOAD-BEARING	12	12	12	18	18	18	24	24	30
	LOAD-BEARING				9	9	9	12	12	15
WALL WEIGHT (psf)	UNPLASTERED	30	30	33	41	47	47	60	67	79
SOUND RESISTANCE (db)	UNPLASTERED	45	45	46	47	48	48	50	54	58

¹ If collar joint is filled, add 2.6 cu ft per 100 sq ft of wall.

² Eccentrically loaded. For concentric loading increase allowable load 25 per cent.

Structural Clay Products Institute; McLean, Virginia

GENERAL

Natural stone is employed in a wide variety of applications in building. Today it is used most extensively as a non-structural material and in combination with other materials as a facing, a veneer, or for decorative purposes. However, its use with precast, post-tensioned, and various sandwich and panel systems is increasing.

CAST STONE

Cast stone is used in much the same manner as cut stone. It is anchored in similar fashion except that much of the anchoring may be cast into the units during fabrication.

COMPOSITION

(see chart this page)

Stone is composed of mineral aggregates in varying mixture and formed over a long period of time by one or more of three basic processes. The variations in mineral content and process of formation dramatically affect the texture, color, and physical properties of the final stone. Vast differences in porosity, hardness, and structural characteristics may occur among samples of the same stone. This is particularly true of marbles, limestones, and sandstones.

The minerals are classified into the silica, silicate, and calcareous groups. The first two of these are quartz minerals or quartz with other metallic bases and are usually found in abundance in the harder, more durable stones depending on the nature of the binder or "cement". The calcareous group is made up largely of the lime minerals which are softer and often appear as the binder for the silicas.

PROCESS OF FORMATION

Stone is grouped into three classes according to the process of formation: 1) igneous — or volcanic, 2) sedimentary, and 3) metamorphic. These processes are often interdependent and many samples are the result of more than one process.

Igneous — or volcanic stone is formed from molten material heaved near the earth's surface and slowly cooled. It is usually crystalline and homogeneous in structure. Examples are granite and traprock.

Sedimentary stone is formed in layers of deposits of shell fragments, disintegrated stone, or sand which have been cemented under pressure below the surface of the earth. Sandstone, limestone, and some so-called marbles are in this class.

Metamorphic stone is formed through reconstitution due to great heat and additional pressure. Examples are marble, slate, and schist.

QUARRYING, CUTTING AND FINISHING

Rough stone is quarried by blasting from large deposits. It is then broken to size and dressed or shipped unfinished. Cut stone and veneer is quarried in blocks up to fifty tons by channeling, wire sawing, or drilling. The block is cut into slabs or pieces of desired size by gang sawing, diamond sawing, wire sawing, or machining. Final cutting and shaping may be done by splitting, shearing, machining, or hand tooling. Surface finishing, polishing, tooling, and special treatments such as heating, flaming, and chemical application are often employed for final texture and color. The final working processes are often performed by stone fabricators who are separate from the quarry. Sealing and final cleaning is usually performed at the job site.

PRINCIPAL BUILDING STONE

Igneous Group

> granite
> traprock
> lava stones

Sedimentary Group

> limestone: dolomitic, oolitic, crystalline, travertine marble.
>
> sandstone: bluestone, brownstone, silica sandstone, lime sandstone, and many conglomerate varieties.

Metamorphic Group

> marble*
> slate: clay slate, mica slate
> schist
> gneiss
> quartzite

*Note: many so-called marbles are actually dolomitic limestones and belong in the sedimentary group.

KINDS, CHARACTERISTICS & PROPERTIES OF STONE

GROUP BY MINERALS	MINERAL—ARCHITECTURAL CHARACTERISTIC	FOUND IN THESE STONES
SILICA MINERALS	QUARTZ—HARD, CRYSTALLINE, GLASSLIKE FRACTURE, COLORLESS IN PURE FORM, GRANULAR OR SANDY IN DISTRIBUTION, TAKES A GOOD POLISH	IMPORTANT COMPONENT OF: GRANITE MICA SCHIST GNEISS SANDSTONE
SILICATE MINERALS	FELDSPAR—HARD AND DENSE IN DURABLE ROCK, POROUS AND FLAWED IN LESS DURABLE STONE	USUALLY FOUND IN GRANITE, FOUND IN SOME SANDSTONES
	MICA—SOFT, CAUSES WEAKNESS UNLESS FINELY FLAKED AND EVENLY DISTRIBUTED, READILY SPLIT ALONG STRATA, USUALLY COLORLESS OR BLACK, HIGHLY REFLECTIVE ON SURFACE OF STONE	PREVALENT IN: SOME SLATES GRANITE MICA-SCHIST LIMESTONE SANDSTONE
	HORNBLENDE—HARD, DURABLE, CRYSTALLINE, BROWNISH-GREEN AND BLACK IN COLOR	IMPORTANT COMPONENT OF: GRANITE GNEISS
	SERPENTINE—SOFT, SOAPY IN STRUCTURE, GREEN OR YELLOW IN COLOR	IN SOME MARBLES, ESPECIALLY SERPENTINE MARBLE
CALCAREOUS MINERALS	CALCITE—SOFT, SOLUABLE, MAY CAUSE VOIDS OR PITTING, WHITE COLOR, (ALSO CEMENTING AGENT IN LIMESTONE AND SHALE)	LIMESTONE MARBLE TRAVERTINE DOLOMITE
NOTE: MANY SO-CALLED "MARBLES" AND "LIMESTONES" ARE ACTUALLY DOLOMITES DUE TO HIGH CONTENT OF DOLOMITE	DOLOMITE—HARDER THAN CALCITE, WHITE, USED IN MAKING LIME	LIMESTONE MARBLE DOLOMITE
	GYPSUM—SOFT, ACID RESISTANT, WHITE AND PALE COLORED	GYPSUM ALABASTER
	PYRITES—UNDESIRABLE IN BUILDING STONE, OXIDIZES AND STAINS, GRANULAR OR DEPOSITED IN POCKETS, YELLOW COLOR	NUMEROUS STONES IN VARIED AMOUNTS

IMPORTANT: Minerals found in building stone — the presence of these minerals and the degree to which they are found in any given sample greatly affects the properties and architectural characteristics of that particular sample of stone.

STRUCTURAL PROPERTIES OF REPRESENTATIVE STONES

STRUCTURAL PROPERTY		IGNEOUS ROCK		SEDIMENTARY ROCK		METAMORPHIC ROCK	
		GRANITE	TRAPROCK	LIMESTONE	SANDSTONE	MARBLE	SLATE
COMP.—ULTIMATE STRENGTH	(P.S.I.)	15,000–30,000	20,000	4,000–20,000	3,000–20,000	10,000–23,000	10,000–15,000
COMP.—ALLOWABLE WORKING STRESS	(P.S.I.)	800–1,500		500–1,000	400–700	500–900	1,000
SHEAR—ULTIMATE STRENGTH	(P.S.I.)	1,800–2,700		1,000–2,000	1,200–2,500	900–1,700	
SHEAR—ALLOWABLE WORKING STRESS	(P.S.I.)	200		200	150	150	
TENSION—ALLOWABLE WORKING STRESS	(P.S.I.)	150		125	75	125	
WEIGHT	(LBS. PER CU. FT.)	156–170	180–185	147–170	135–155	165–178	170–180
SPECIFIC GRAVITY		2.4–2.7	2.96	2.1–2.8	2.0–2.6	2.4–2.8	2.7–2.8
ABSORPTION OF WATER (PARTS BY WEIGHT)		1/750		1/38	1/24	1/300	1/430
MODULUS OF ELASTICITY	(P.S.I.)	6–10,000,000	12,000,000	4–14,000,000	1–7,500,000	4–13,500,000	12,000,000
COEFFICIENT OF EXPANSION	(P.S.F.)	0.0000040		0.0000045	0.0000055	0.0000045	0.0000058

NOTE: Individual samples vary greatly.

George M. Whiteside, III, AIA; Whiteside, Moeckel & Carbonell; Wilmington, Delaware

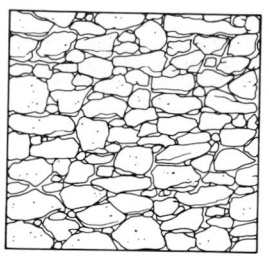
UNCOURSED FIELD STONE, ROUGH OR COMMON RUBBLE

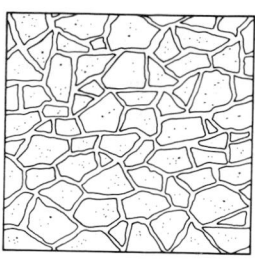
UNCOURSED COBWEB OR POLYGONAL RUBBLE

UNCOURSED AND ROUGHLY SQUARED

COURSED FIELDSTONE AND ROUGH OR COMMON RUBBLE

COURSED AND ROUGHLY SQUARED

RUBBLE AND ROUGHLY SQUARED STONE MASONRY – ELEVATIONS SHOWING FACE JOINTING

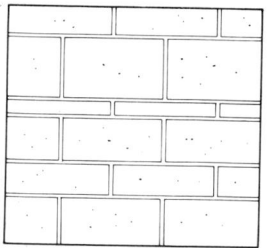
COURSED BROKEN BOND, RANGED

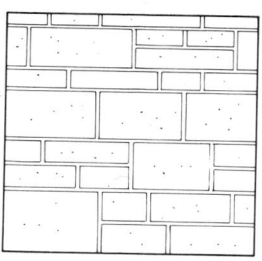
COURSED BROKEN BOND, BROKEN RANGE

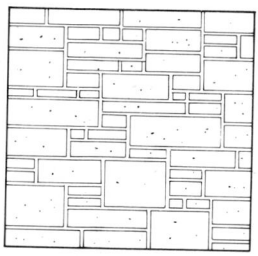
RANDOM, BROKEN COURSE AND RANGE

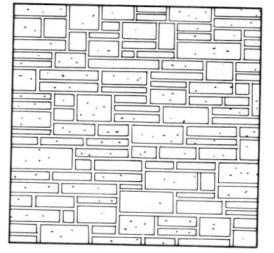
RANDOM, BROKEN COURSE AND RANGE, LONGSTONES

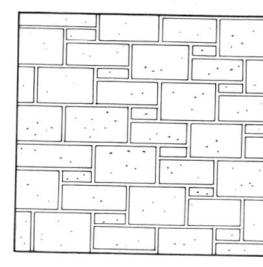
RANDOM COURSED PATTERN BOND

DIMENSIONED OR ASHLAR STONE MASONRY – ELEVATIONS SHOWING FACE JOINTING

GENERAL NOTES:

A course is a horizontal row of stone. Bond is the horizontal arrangement of vertical joints. A range is a course of uniform height or rise and running across the entire face of a wall.

A perch is nominally 16'– 6" long, 1'– 0" high, and 1'– 6" thick equalling 24 3/4 cubic feet. In some localities 16 1/2 cu. ft. and 22 cu. ft. are used.

Rubble work and roughly squared stone work is laid up with field stone or rough quarry stone. All hand dressing and rough squaring is done in the field by masons.

Ashlar masonry is cut to dimensions shown on shop drawings. It is cut, dressed, and finished to precise job requirements at the mill and then shipped to the site in its finished state.

ELEVATION — RISE "R" / LENGTH "L"

SECTION — RISE "R" / DEPTH "D"

DIMENSION RATIO

TYPE OF STONE	"R"	"L"	"D"
SOFT	1	3	2
HARD	1	5	3

RUBBLE STONE DIMENSION LIMITS

ROCK OR PITCH FACED
Rough, "rusticated", for all stones.

GANG SAWED
Smooth, visible saw marks, all stones.

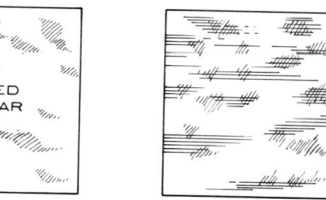
SHOT SAWED
Rough, more marked than gang, soft stones.

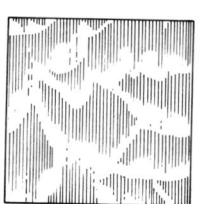
MACHINED (PLANER)
Smooth, some texture soft stones.

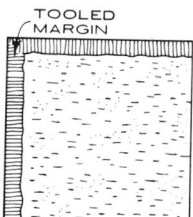
POINTED
Coarse, medium or fine, usually hard stones.

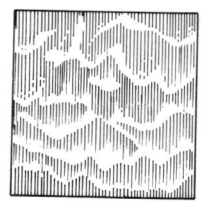
PEAN HAMMERED
Coarse, done after pointing, hard stones.

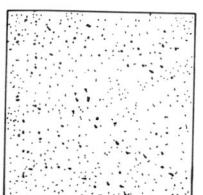
BUSH–HAMMERED
Medium texture for all stones.

PATENT BUSH–HAMMERED
4–8 cut in 7/8" –for all stones – esp. granite.

DROVE OR BOASTED
Soft stones.

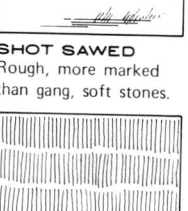
HAND TOOLED
Regular or random, for soft stones.

MACHINE TOOLED
Grooves 2–10 per inch, for all stones.

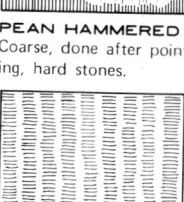
TOOTH CHISELED
Soft stones.

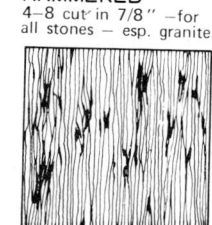
CRANDALLED
Regular & random – for soft stones.

PLUCKED
Machine textured for limestone.

VERY SMOOTH
CARBORUNDUM
Machine finish for limestone.

SMOOTH
WET RUBBED
Sand or carborundum grit for all stones.

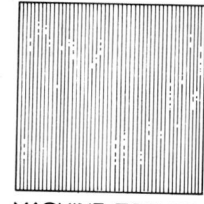
VERY SMOOTH
RUBBED & HONED
Usually for interior marble & granite.

VERY SMOOTH HIGH GLASS
HONED & POLISHED
Usually for marble & granite.

GRAPHIC SYMBOLS FOR TYPICAL STONE FINISHED

George M. Whiteside, III, AIA; Whiteside, Moeckel & Carbonell; Wilmington, Delaware

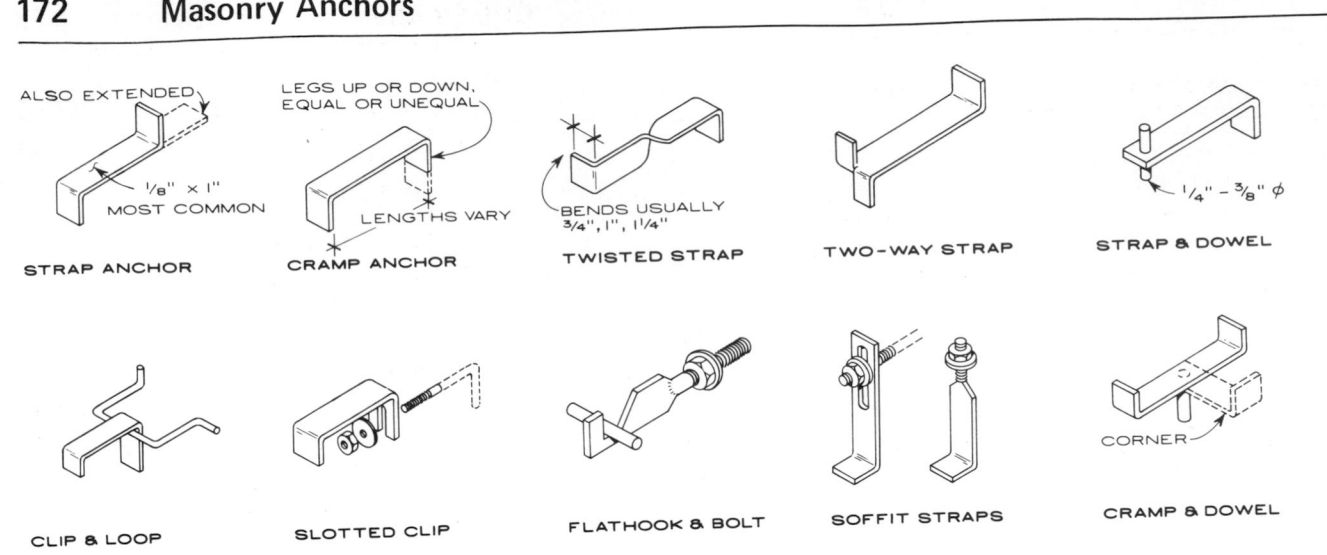

STRAP ANCHOR   CRAMP ANCHOR   TWISTED STRAP   TWO-WAY STRAP   STRAP & DOWEL   STRAP & ROD

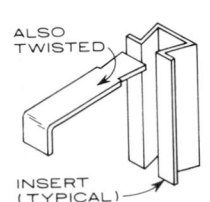 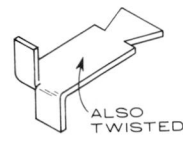 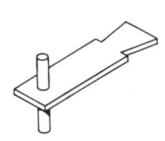 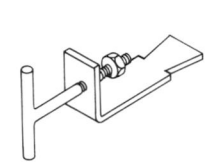 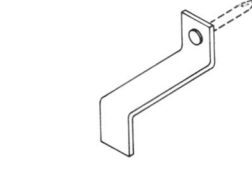 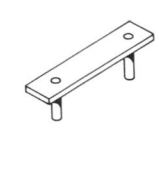

CLIP & LOOP   SLOTTED CLIP   FLATHOOK & BOLT   SOFFIT STRAPS   CRAMP & DOWEL   U-STRAP & RODS

DOVETAIL ANCHOR   TWO-WAY DOVETAIL   DOVETAIL & DOWEL   DOVETAIL CLIP & T-BOLT   CLIP & POWER STUD   STRAP & ROD CRAMP

FLAT STOCK ANCHORS FOR CUT STONE AND VENEER STONE

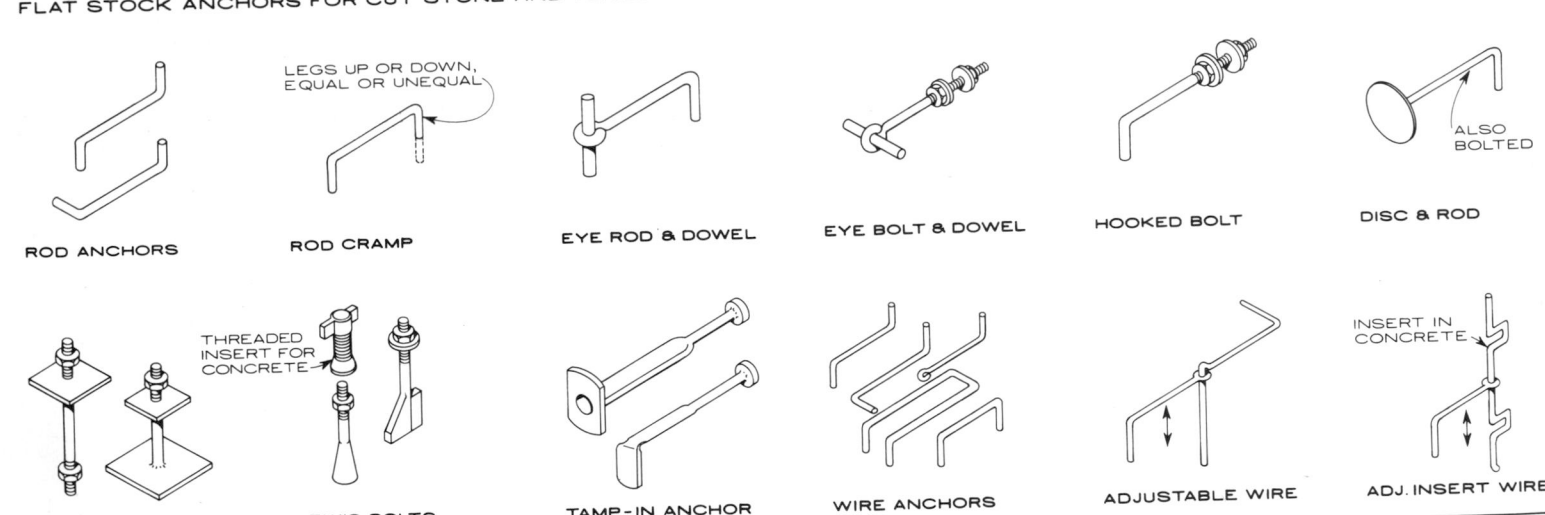

ROD ANCHORS   ROD CRAMP   EYE ROD & DOWEL   EYE BOLT & DOWEL   HOOKED BOLT   DISC & ROD

PLATE & BOLT   LEWIS BOLTS   TAMP-IN ANCHOR   WIRE ANCHORS   ADJUSTABLE WIRE   ADJ. INSERT WIRE

ROUND STOCK ANCHORS — ROD AND WIRE ANCHORS FOR CUT STONE AND VENEER STONE

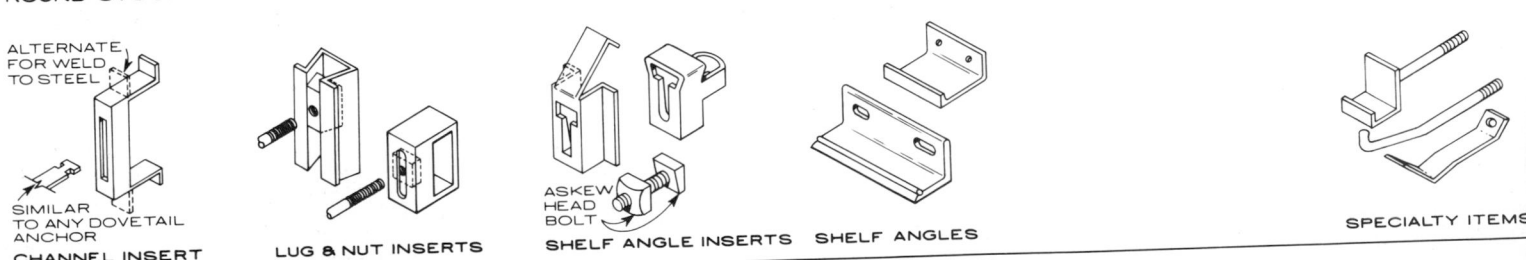

CHANNEL INSERT   LUG & NUT INSERTS   SHELF ANGLE INSERTS   SHELF ANGLES   SPECIALTY ITEMS

MISCELLANEOUS CONCRETE INSERTS, SUPPORT ANGLES, AND SPECIAL ANCHORS

ANCHOR DIMENSIONS AND MATERIALS
Standard flat stock anchors are made from strap 1"
and 1 1/4" wide by 1/8", 3/16" and 1/4" thick.
Lengths vary up to 6", 8", 10" and 12" standards
Dovetail anchors are usually 4 1/4" overall with 3 1/2"
projection from face of concrete. Bends are 3/4", 1"
and 1 1/4".

Round stock anchors are made from stock of any
diameter: 1/4" and 3/8" are most common for rods;
1/8" (#11 gauge) through 3/16" (#6 gauge) for wire
anchors; and 1/4" and 3/8" are most common for
dowels. Dowel lengths are usually 2" to 6".

Anchors should be corrosion resistant and usually non-
staining. Chromium-nickel stainless steel types 302
and 304 and eraydo alloy zinc are most corrosion and
stain resistant. Hot galvanized is poorest and prohibit
ed by some building codes. Copper, brass, and bronze
will stain under some conditions. Metals most commonly used are hot galvanized, eraydo alloy, brass,
bronze, monel, and stainless steel.

Local building codes often govern the types of metal
which may be used for stone anchors.

George M. Whiteside, III, AIA; Whiteside, Moeckel & Carbonell; Wilmington, Delaware

TABLE OF CUT STONE DIMENSIONS

THK.	A	B	C	D	E	F	G	H
2"	3/4"	1/2"	1/2"	1/2"	3/4"	1/2"	1 1/2"	2 1/4"
3"	1 3/4"	1"	1/2"	1/2"	3/4"	1/2"	2 1/2"	3 1/4"
4"	2 3/4"	1 1/2"	1/2"	1/2"	3/4"	1/2"	3 1/2"	4 1/4"
6"	3"	1 1/2"	1/2"	1/2"+	3/4"+	1/2"+	5 3/4"	6 1/4"
8"	4"	1 1/2"	1/2"	1/2"+	3/4"+	1/2"+	7 3/4"	8 1/2"

GENERAL NOTE:

1. Stone shall be of nominal thickness (1 1/8" ± 1/8", 2" ± 1/4", 3" ± 1/4", 4" ± 1/4", 6" ± 1/4", 8 1/4" ± 1/4").
2. A setting space of 1" larger than the nominal thickness is advisable. Back may be parged or slushed full.
3. 1/4" mortar joints usually used, but 3/16" or 1/8" may be used for close work.
4. Anchor material sometimes governed by local building codes.

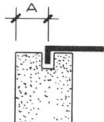
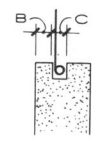
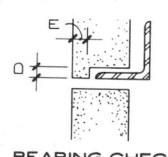

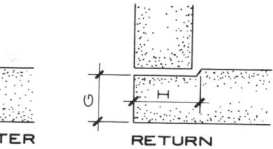

ANCHOR LOCATION   REGLET   BEARING CHECK   QUIRK MITER   RETURN

DETAILS OF TYPICAL STONE CUT-OUTS

On this page mortar, flashing and other ancillary materials necessary for sound, weatherproof construction have been omitted for the sake of clarity. See flashing pages.

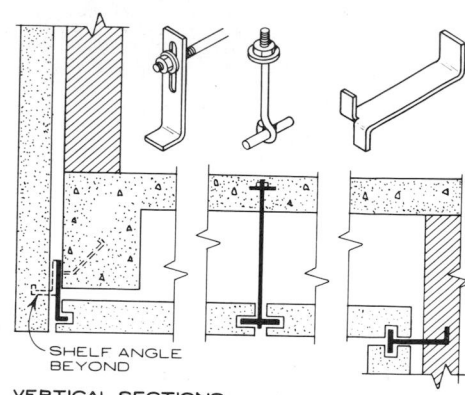

SHELF ANGLE BEYOND

VERTICAL SECTIONS

HUNG STONE TO CONCRETE SHOWING TYPICAL PROJECTED SOFFIT

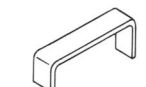

TYPICAL CRAMP   CRAMP AND DOWEL

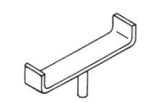
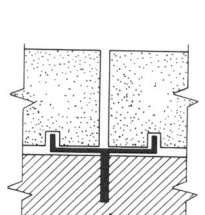

VERTICAL SECTION   VERTICAL PARALLEL SECTION

JOINT ANCHORING SHOWING CRAMP ANCHORS TO UNIT MASONRY BACK-UP

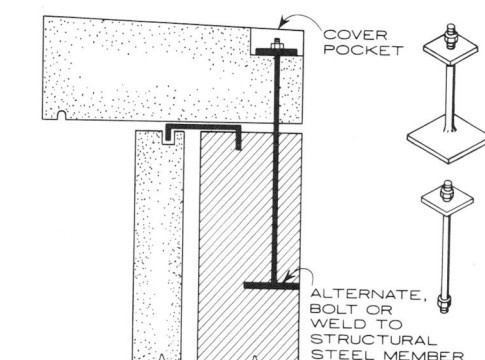

COVER POCKET

ALTERNATE, BOLT OR WELD TO STRUCTURAL STEEL MEMBER

VERTICAL SECTION

PROJECTING STONE TIE BACK USING PLATE AND BOLT ANCHOR

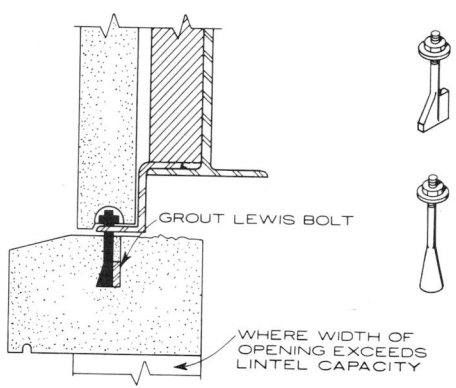

GROUT LEWIS BOLT

WHERE WIDTH OF OPENING EXCEEDS LINTEL CAPACITY

VERTICAL SECTION

RELIEF ANCHOR FOR STONE LINTEL SHOWING CLIP ANGLE AND LEWIS BOLT

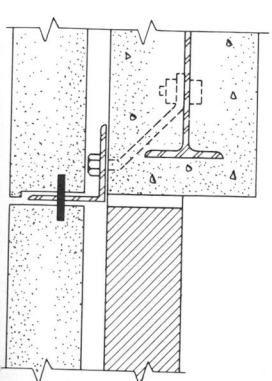

CONCRETE INSERT FOR DOVETAIL ANCHOR

PLAN SECTION

STONE FACING ANCHORED TO BACK-UP USING TWO-WAY ANCHORS

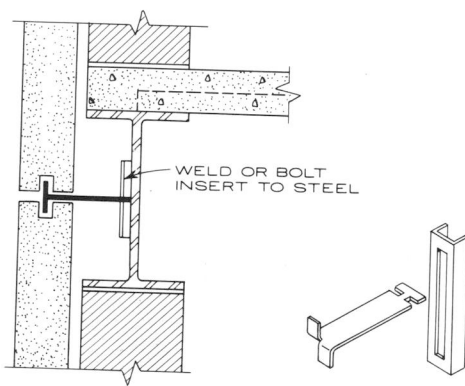

WELD OR BOLT INSERT TO STEEL

VERTICAL SECTION

STONE FACING ANCHORED TO SPANDREL BEAM USING CHANNEL INSERT AND TWO-WAY ANCHOR

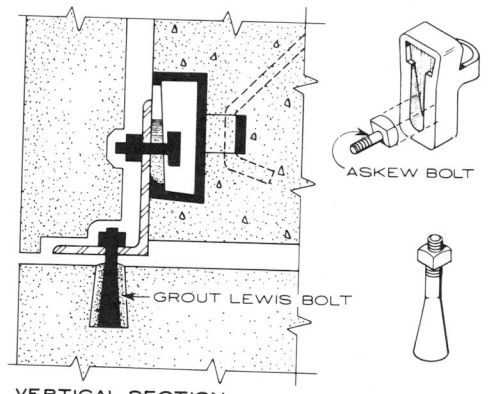

ASKEW BOLT

GROUT LEWIS BOLT

VERTICAL SECTION

CONCRETE INSERT, RELIEF ANGLE, AND LEWIS BOLT HUNG FROM CONCRETE BEAM

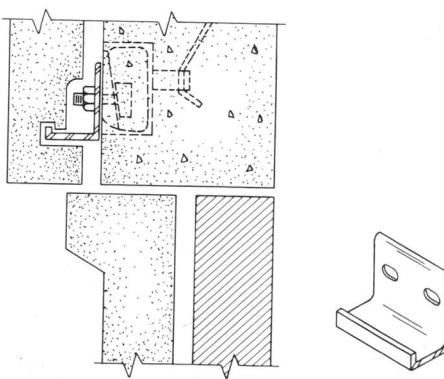

VERTICAL SECTION

ANGLE AND DOWEL AT SPANDREL USING BOLT BACK TO STEEL BEAM

VERTICAL SECTION

INSERT AND ANGLE ANCHOR SHOWING CONCEALED SUPPORT

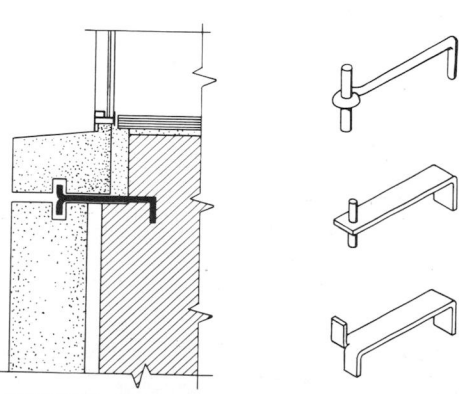

VERTICAL SECTION

SILL ANCHORING SHOWING TIE TO UNIT MASONRY BACK-UP

Harold Judefind and George M. Whiteside, III, AIA; Whiteside, Moeckel & Carbonell; Wilmington, Delaware

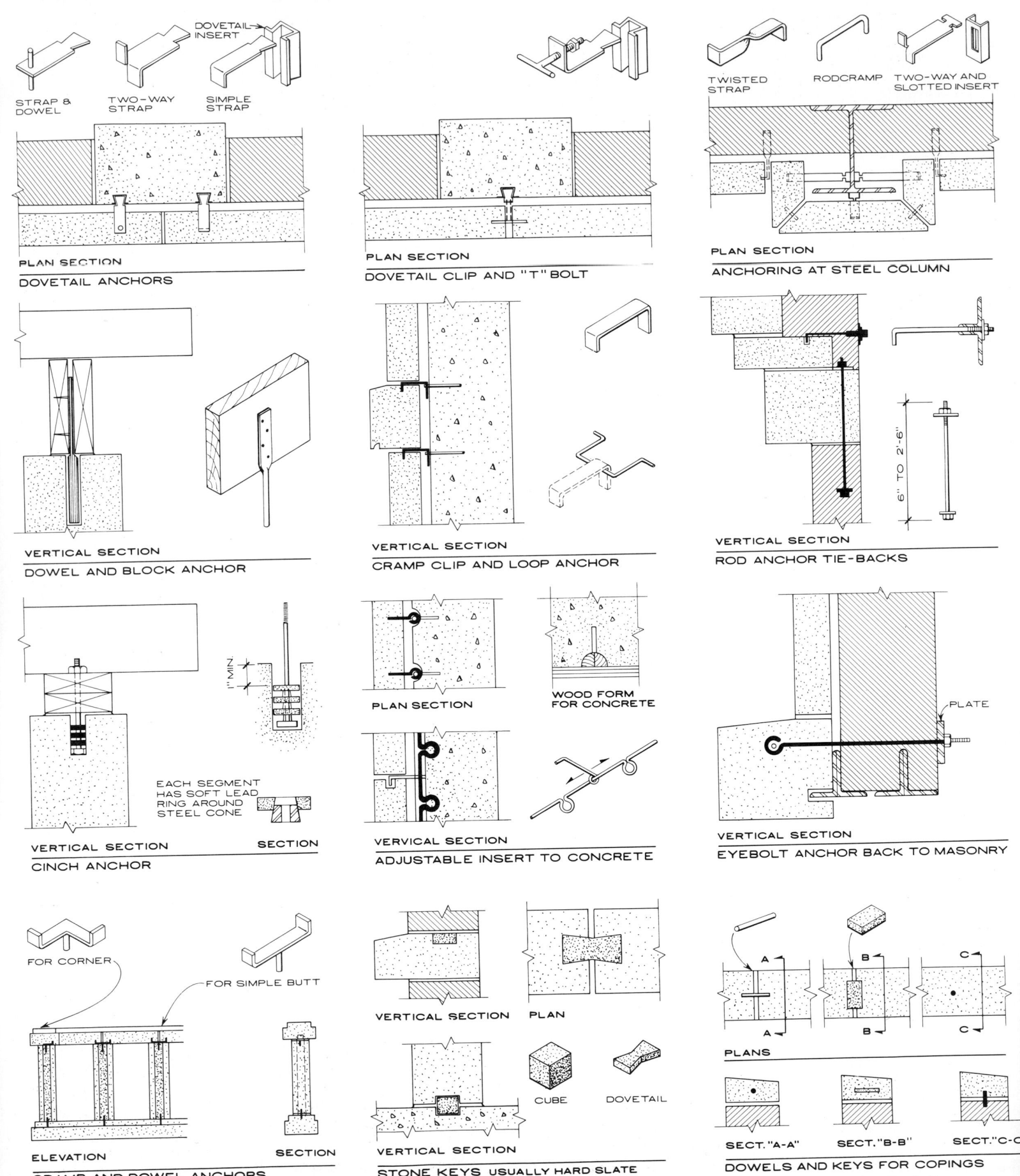

STRAP & DOWEL

TWO-WAY STRAP

SIMPLE STRAP

DOVETAIL INSERT

TWISTED STRAP

RODCRAMP

TWO-WAY AND SLOTTED INSERT

PLAN SECTION
DOVETAIL ANCHORS

PLAN SECTION
DOVETAIL CLIP AND "T" BOLT

PLAN SECTION
ANCHORING AT STEEL COLUMN

VERTICAL SECTION
DOWEL AND BLOCK ANCHOR

VERTICAL SECTION
CRAMP CLIP AND LOOP ANCHOR

VERTICAL SECTION
ROD ANCHOR TIE-BACKS

6" TO 2'-6"

VERTICAL SECTION   SECTION
CINCH ANCHOR

1" MIN.

EACH SEGMENT HAS SOFT LEAD RING AROUND STEEL CONE

PLAN SECTION

WOOD FORM FOR CONCRETE

VERVICAL SECTION
ADJUSTABLE INSERT TO CONCRETE

PLATE

VERTICAL SECTION
EYEBOLT ANCHOR BACK TO MASONRY

FOR CORNER

FOR SIMPLE BUTT

ELEVATION   SECTION
CRAMP AND DOWEL ANCHORS

VERTICAL SECTION   PLAN

CUBE   DOVETAIL

VERTICAL SECTION
STONE KEYS USUALLY HARD SLATE

A   B   C

A   B   C

PLANS

SECT. "A-A"   SECT. "B-B"   SECT. "C-C"
DOWELS AND KEYS FOR COPINGS

NOTE: On this page mortar, flashing and other ancillary materials necessary for sound, weatherproof construction have been omitted for the sake of clarity. See flashing pages.

Harold Judefind and George M. Whiteside, III, AIA; Whiteside, Moeckel & Carbonell; Wilmington, Delaware

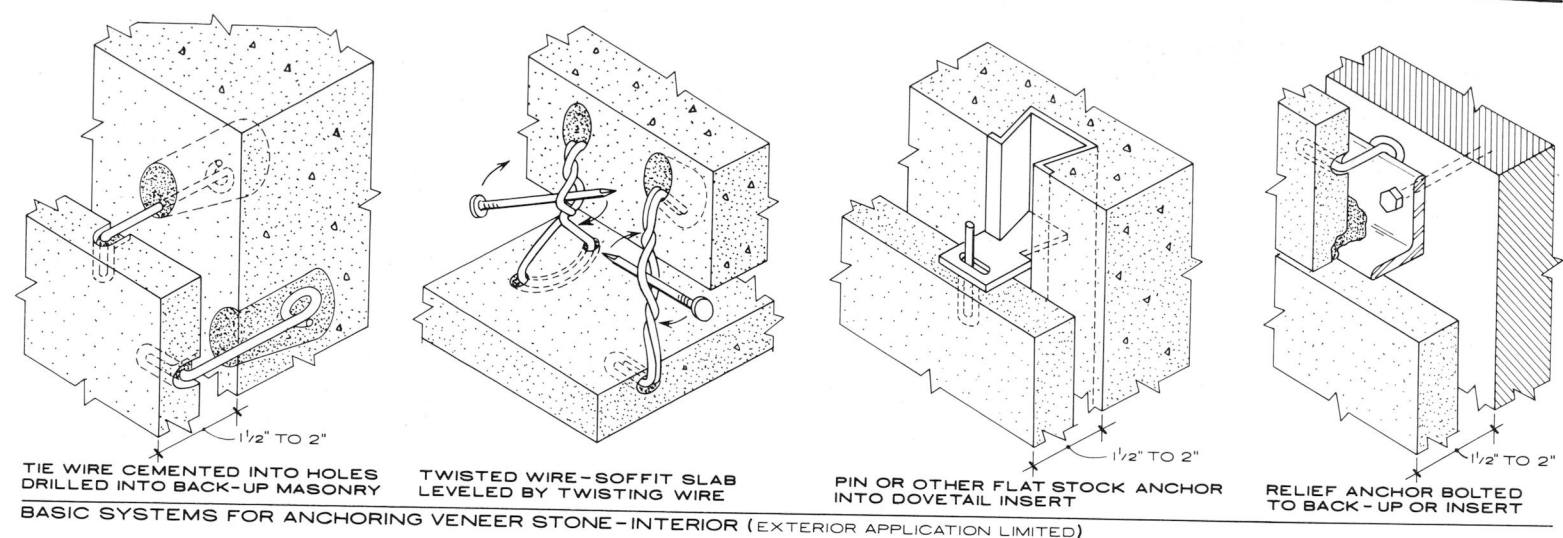

TIE WIRE CEMENTED INTO HOLES
DRILLED INTO BACK-UP MASONRY

TWISTED WIRE—SOFFIT SLAB
LEVELED BY TWISTING WIRE

PIN OR OTHER FLAT STOCK ANCHOR
INTO DOVETAIL INSERT

RELIEF ANCHOR BOLTED
TO BACK-UP OR INSERT

BASIC SYSTEMS FOR ANCHORING VENEER STONE—INTERIOR (EXTERIOR APPLICATION LIMITED)

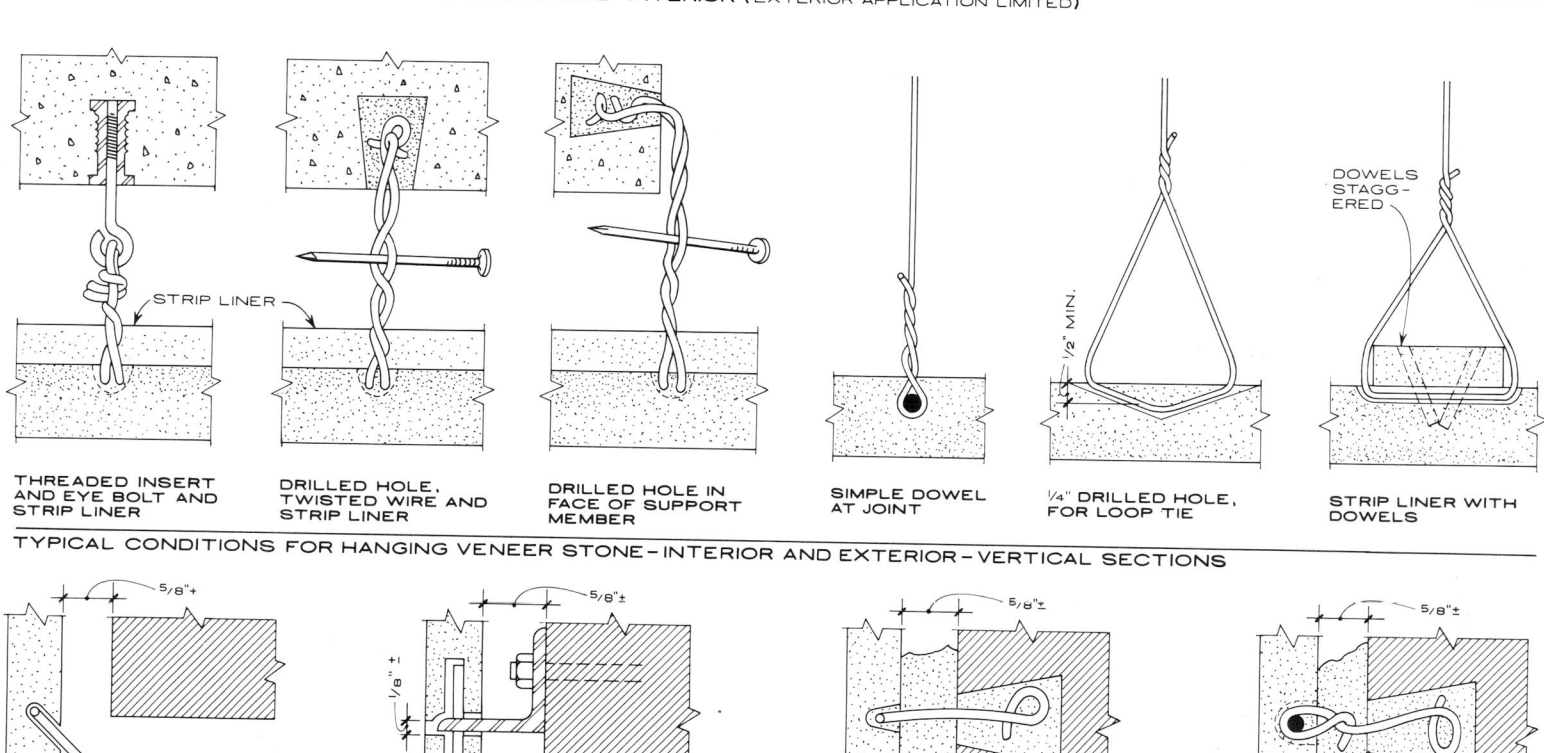

THREADED INSERT
AND EYE BOLT AND
STRIP LINER

DRILLED HOLE,
TWISTED WIRE AND
STRIP LINER

DRILLED HOLE IN
FACE OF SUPPORT
MEMBER

SIMPLE DOWEL
AT JOINT

1/4" DRILLED HOLE,
FOR LOOP TIE

STRIP LINER WITH
DOWELS

TYPICAL CONDITIONS FOR HANGING VENEER STONE—INTERIOR AND EXTERIOR—VERTICAL SECTIONS

PLAN—CRAMP JOINT
CORNER

SECTION—CLIP ANGLE
AND PIN (RELIEF SUPPORT)

PLAN—SIMPLE WIRE
ANCHOR

PLAN—WIRE ANCHOR
AND DOWEL

INTERIOR AND EXTERIOR PIN CONNECTIONS

INTERIOR WIRE ANCHORS TO DRILLED HOLES

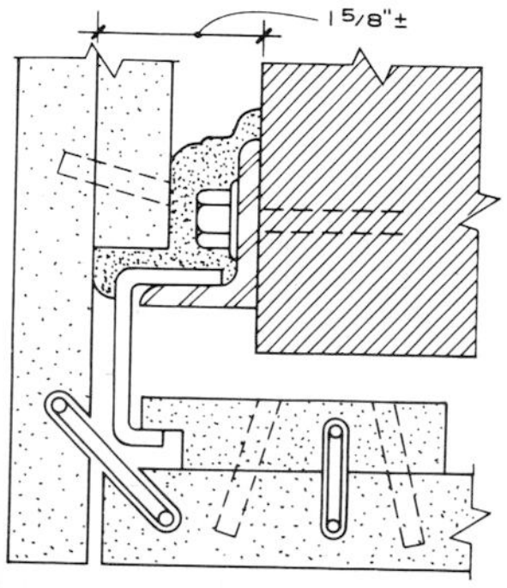

SOFFIT AND FASCIA

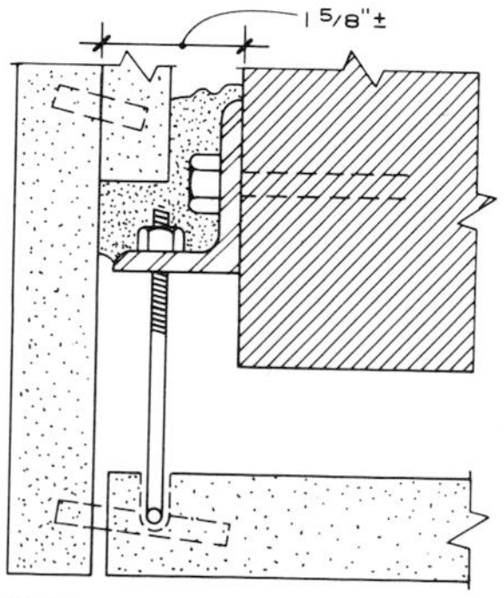

SOFFIT AND FASCIA

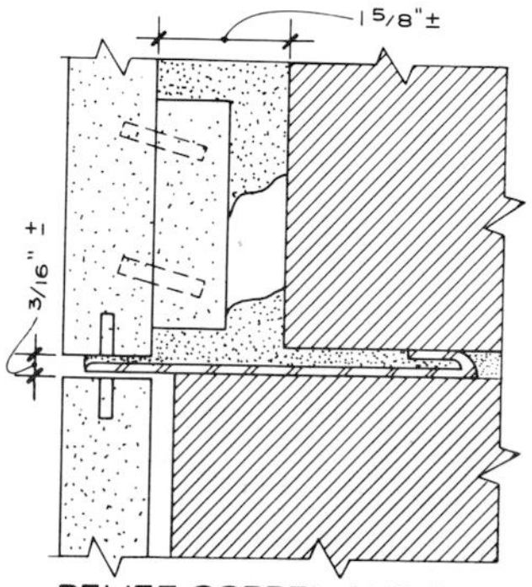

RELIEF CORBEL AND TIE-BACK

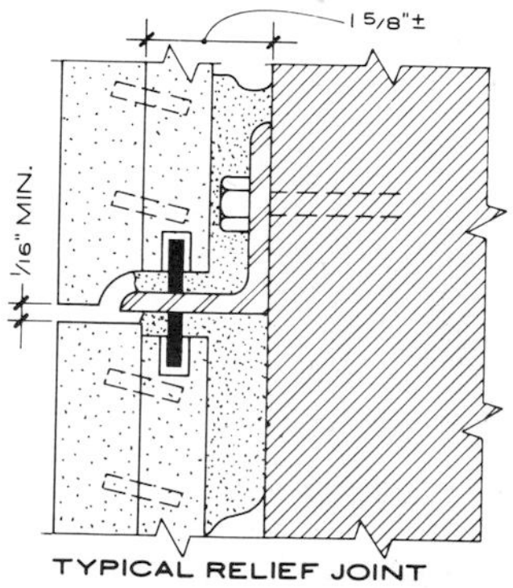

TYPICAL RELIEF JOINT

EXTERIOR VENEER (USUALLY MARBLE) USING STRIP LINERS AND DOWELS—VERTICAL SECTIONS

NOTE: Exterior use of thin veneer stone is not generally recommended for extensive application in all localities and under all exterior conditions.

J. Smith and George M. Whiteside, III, AIA; Whiteside, Moeckel & Carbonell; Wilmington, Delaware

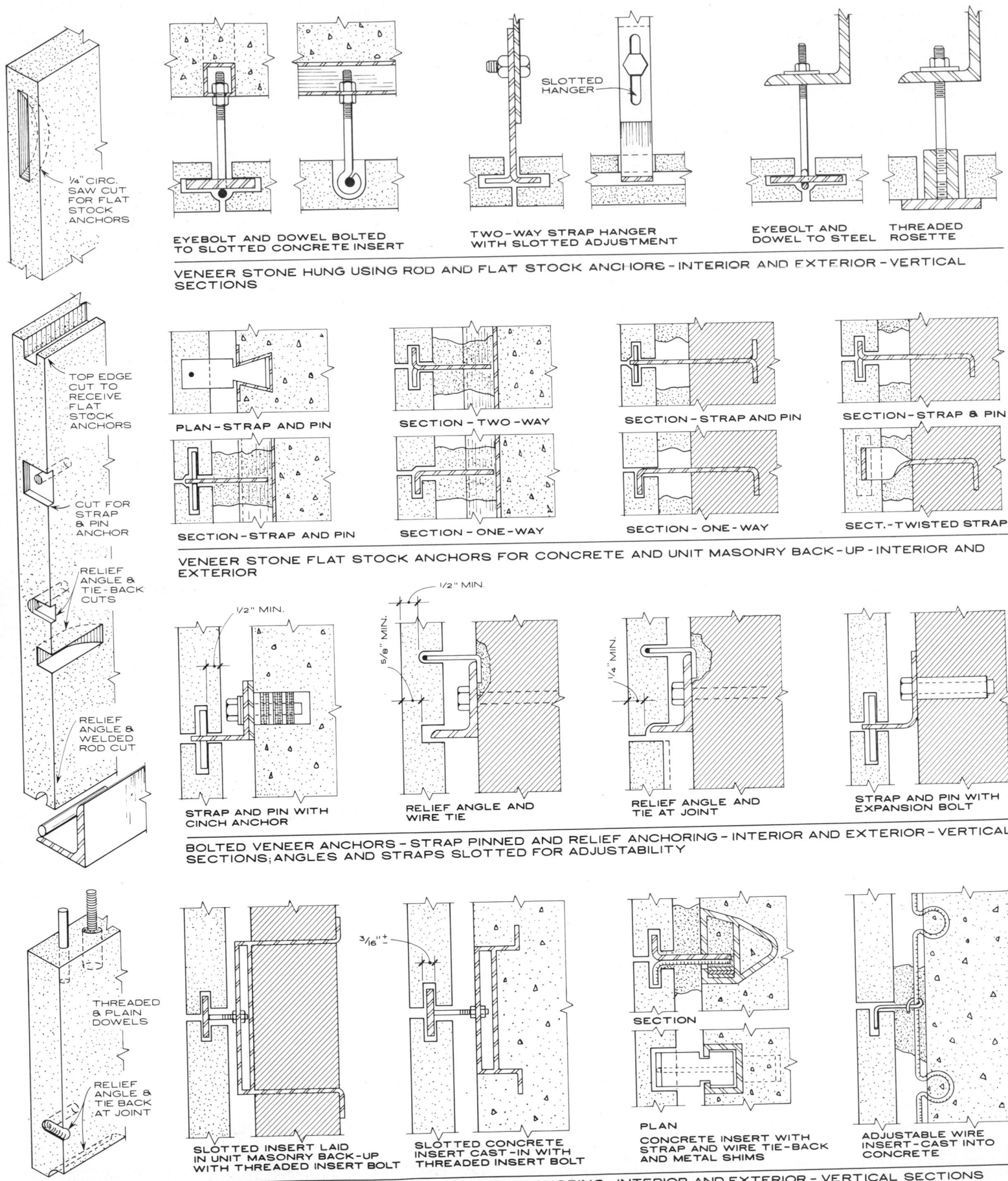

¼" CIRC. SAW CUT FOR FLAT STOCK ANCHORS

EYEBOLT AND DOWEL BOLTED TO SLOTTED CONCRETE INSERT

SLOTTED HANGER

TWO-WAY STRAP HANGER WITH SLOTTED ADJUSTMENT

EYEBOLT AND DOWEL TO STEEL

THREADED ROSETTE

VENEER STONE HUNG USING ROD AND FLAT STOCK ANCHORS – INTERIOR AND EXTERIOR – VERTICAL SECTIONS

TOP EDGE CUT TO RECEIVE FLAT STOCK ANCHORS

CUT FOR STRAP & PIN ANCHOR

RELIEF ANGLE & TIE-BACK CUTS

RELIEF ANGLE & WELDED ROD CUT

PLAN – STRAP AND PIN

SECTION – TWO-WAY

SECTION – STRAP AND PIN

SECTION – STRAP & PIN

SECTION – STRAP AND PIN

SECTION – ONE-WAY

SECTION – ONE-WAY

SECT. – TWISTED STRAP

VENEER STONE FLAT STOCK ANCHORS FOR CONCRETE AND UNIT MASONRY BACK-UP – INTERIOR AND EXTERIOR

½" MIN.

½" MIN.

⅝" MIN.

¼" MIN.

STRAP AND PIN WITH CINCH ANCHOR

RELIEF ANGLE AND WIRE TIE

RELIEF ANGLE AND TIE AT JOINT

STRAP AND PIN WITH EXPANSION BOLT

BOLTED VENEER ANCHORS – STRAP PINNED AND RELIEF ANCHORING – INTERIOR AND EXTERIOR – VERTICAL SECTIONS; ANGLES AND STRAPS SLOTTED FOR ADJUSTABILITY

THREADED & PLAIN DOWELS

RELIEF ANGLE & TIE BACK AT JOINT

TYPICAL CUTS

3/16"+

SLOTTED INSERT LAID IN UNIT MASONRY BACK-UP WITH THREADED INSERT BOLT

SLOTTED CONCRETE INSERT CAST-IN WITH THREADED INSERT BOLT

SECTION

PLAN

CONCRETE INSERT WITH STRAP AND WIRE TIE-BACK AND METAL SHIMS

ADJUSTABLE WIRE INSERT-CAST INTO CONCRETE

CONCRETE INSERT FOR VENEER STONE ANCHORING – INTERIOR AND EXTERIOR – VERTICAL SECTIONS

GENERAL NOTES: For exterior application 1 ¼" to 2" thick stone is recommended in most localities.

George M. Whiteside, III, AIA; Whiteside, Moeckel & Carbonell; Wilmington, Delaware

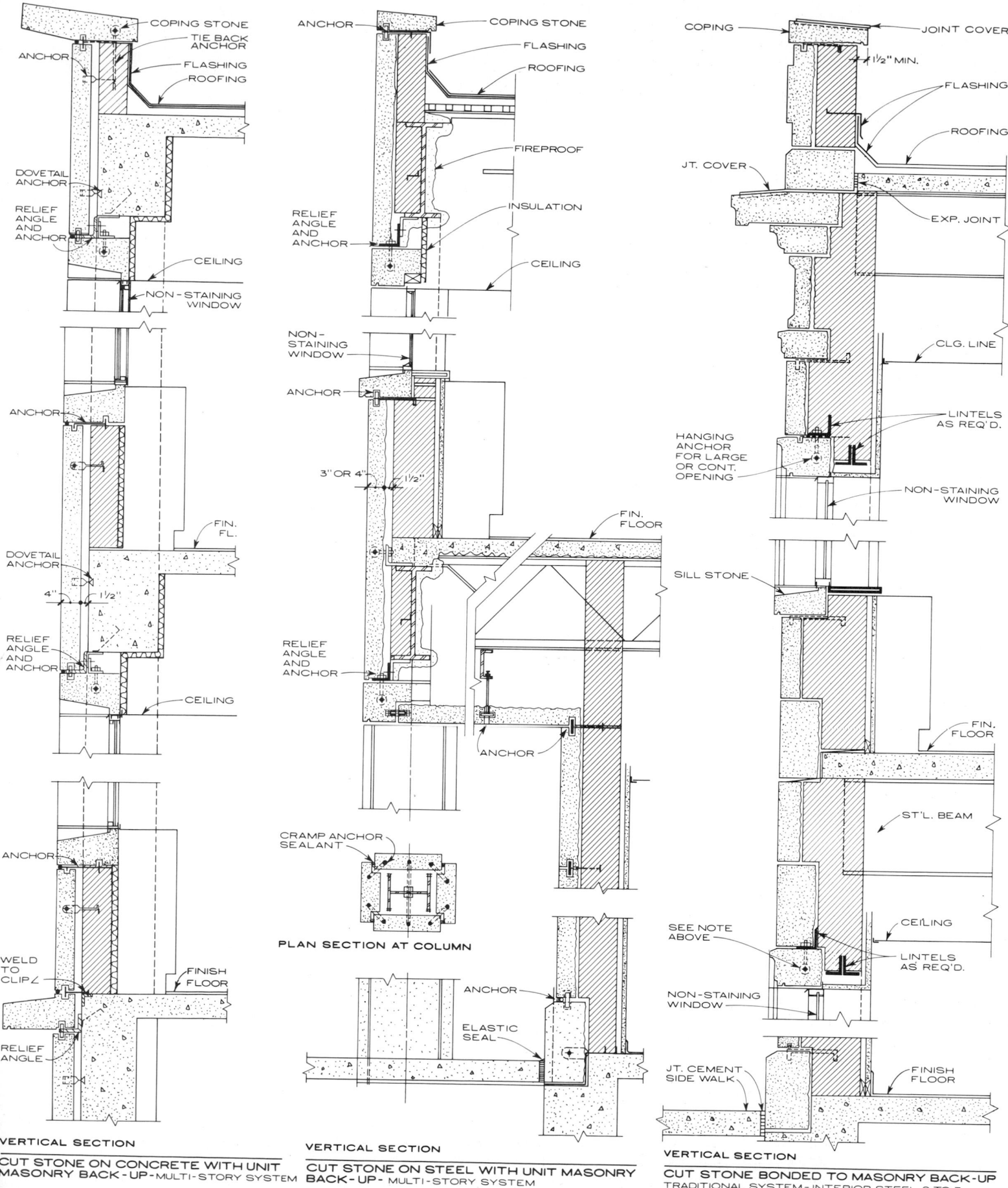

VERTICAL SECTION

CUT STONE ON CONCRETE WITH UNIT MASONRY BACK-UP-MULTI-STORY SYSTEM

VERTICAL SECTION

CUT STONE ON STEEL WITH UNIT MASONRY BACK-UP- MULTI-STORY SYSTEM

VERTICAL SECTION

CUT STONE BONDED TO MASONRY BACK-UP
TRADITIONAL SYSTEM-INTERIOR STEEL 2 TO 7 STORIES

Labels in diagrams: COPING STONE, TIE BACK ANCHOR, ANCHOR, FLASHING, ROOFING, DOVETAIL ANCHOR, RELIEF ANGLE AND ANCHOR, CEILING, NON-STAINING WINDOW, FIN. FL., DOVETAIL ANCHOR, 4", 1 1/2", RELIEF ANGLE AND ANCHOR, CEILING, ANCHOR, WELD TO CLIP ∠, FINISH FLOOR, RELIEF ANGLE

ANCHOR, COPING STONE, FLASHING, ROOFING, FIREPROOF, INSULATION, RELIEF ANGLE AND ANCHOR, CEILING, NON-STAINING WINDOW, ANCHOR, 3" OR 4", 1 1/2", FIN. FLOOR, RELIEF ANGLE AND ANCHOR, ANCHOR, CRAMP ANCHOR SEALANT, **PLAN SECTION AT COLUMN**, ANCHOR, ELASTIC SEAL

COPING, JOINT COVER, 1 1/2" MIN., FLASHING, ROOFING, JT. COVER, EXP. JOINT, CLG. LINE, HANGING ANCHOR FOR LARGE OR CONT. OPENING, LINTELS AS REQ'D., NON-STAINING WINDOW, SILL STONE, FIN. FLOOR, ST'L. BEAM, SEE NOTE ABOVE, CEILING, LINTELS AS REQ'D., NON-STAINING WINDOW, JT. CEMENT SIDE WALK, FINISH FLOOR

NOTE: On this page indications of flashing, caulking and mortar have been omitted at some points in order to retain clarity of details. See pages on flashing and caulking.

F. Hoover and George M. Whiteside, III, AIA; Whiteside, Moeckel & Carbonell; Wilmington, Delaware

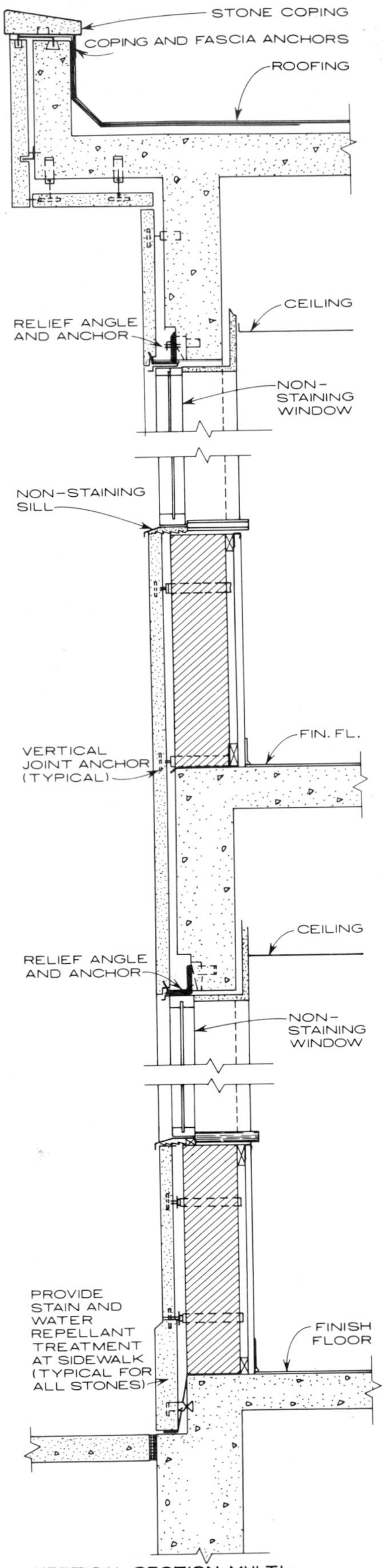

STONE COPING

COPING AND FASCIA ANCHORS

ROOFING

COPING

FLASHING

ROOFING

① (circle 1)

RELIEF ANGLE AND ANCHOR

CEILING

CEILING

NON-STAINING WINDOW

NON-STAINING WINDOW

MAXIMUM ANCHOR SPACING

NON-STAINING SILL

② (circle 2)

FINISH FLOOR

VERTICAL JOINT ANCHOR (TYPICAL)

FIN. FL.

③ (circle 3)

CEILING

CEILING LINE

RELIEF ANGLE AND ANCHOR

NON-STAINING WINDOW

STANDARD SYSTEM OF ANCHORING USED ON COLUMN & MASONRY UNITS

DOVETAIL ANCHOR

DOVETAIL ANCHOR

PROVIDE STAIN AND WATER REPELLANT TREATMENT AT SIDEWALK (TYPICAL FOR ALL STONES)

FINISH FLOOR

FINISH FLOOR

PLAN OF COLUMN

SIDEWALK

VERTICAL SECTION, MULTI-STORY SYSTEM

VENEER STONE ON CONCRETE WITH UNIT MASONRY BACK-UP

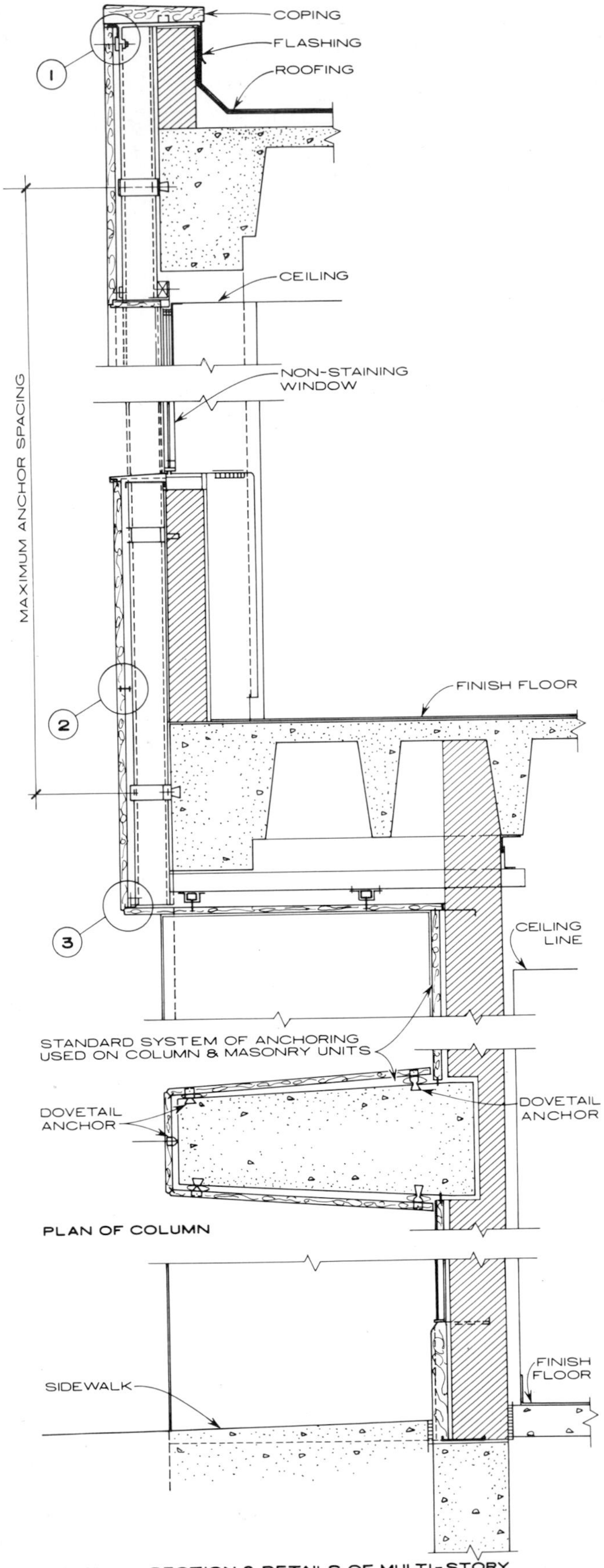

VERTICAL SECTION & DETAILS OF MULTI-STORY APPLICATION WITH OR WITHOUT MASONRY BACK-UP

THIN MARBLE VENEER ON GRID STRUT ANCHORING SYSTEM (ZIBELL ANCHORING SYSTEM)

GENERAL NOTE: 1 1/4" to 2" thickness recommended for most localities.

F. Hoover and George M. Whiteside, III, AIA; Whiteside, Moeckel & Carbonell; Wilmington, Delaware

DIM. STRUT "X" DEPTH

GRID STRUT

① **ANCHORING AT TOP OF MARBLE**

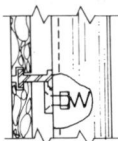 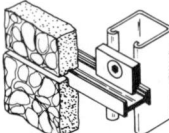

W

② **ANCHORING AT INTERMEDIATE JOINT**

 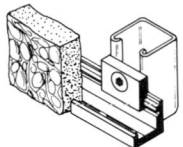

W

③ **ANCHORING AT BOTTOM OF MARBLE**

GRID STRUT SPACING RELATIVE TO SLAB HEIGHT – MARBLE

HEIGHT OF SLAB UP TO	GRID STRUT SPACING	
	7/8" TH'K.	1 1/4" TH'K.
2'–6"	4'–9"	4'–0"
3'–0"	4'–6"	3'–9"
3'–6"	4'–3"	3'–6"
4'–0"	4'–0"	3'–3"
4'–6"	3'–9"	3'–0"
5'–0"*	3'–6"	2'–9"
5'–6"*	3'–3"	2'–6"
6'–0"*	3'–3"	2'–3"

*FOR SLABS OVER 4'–6" HEIGHT USE INTERMEDIATE VERTICAL JOINT ANCHORING.

GRID ANCHOR SPACING & STRUT SIZE – MARBLE

MAXIMUM SPACING	ANCHOR	STRUT SIZE
7/8" TH.	1 1/4" TH.	WIDTH, DEPTH AND SHAPE
4'–0"	4'–0"	1 5/8" x 1 5/8"
7'–0"	6'–0"	1 5/8" x 2 7/16"
10'–0"	9'–0"	1 5/8" x 3 1/4"
15'–0"	13'–0"	1 5/8" x 4 7/8"

FOR DIM "X" SEE DETAIL 1 ABOVE
"X" = 1 5/8" FOR 7/8" MARBLE
"X" = 1 3/4" FOR 1 1/4" MARBLE

NOTE:

Flashing & Caulking required at certain points has been omitted in order to retain clarity of drawing at small scale. See pages on Flashing & Caulking.

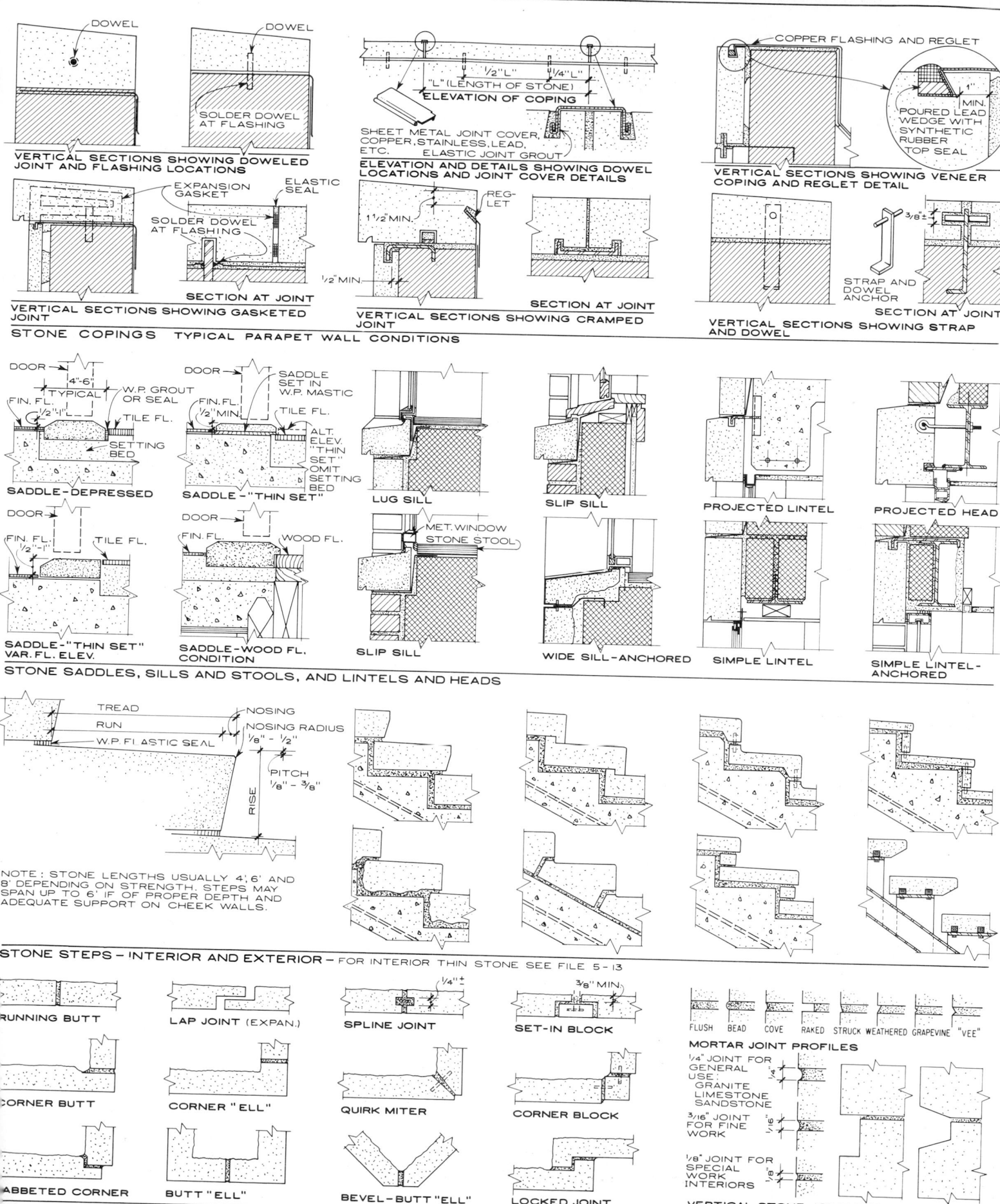

VERTICAL SECTIONS SHOWING DOWELED JOINT AND FLASHING LOCATIONS

DOWEL / DOWEL / SOLDER DOWEL AT FLASHING

VERTICAL SECTIONS SHOWING GASKETED JOINT

EXPANSION GASKET / ELASTIC SEAL / SOLDER DOWEL AT FLASHING

ELEVATION OF COPING

½"L / ¼"L / "L" (LENGTH OF STONE)

ELEVATION AND DETAILS SHOWING DOWEL LOCATIONS AND JOINT COVER DETAILS

SHEET METAL JOINT COVER, COPPER, STAINLESS, LEAD, ETC. / ELASTIC JOINT GROUT

VERTICAL SECTIONS SHOWING CRAMPED JOINT

1½" MIN. / REGLET / ½" MIN. / **SECTION AT JOINT**

VERTICAL SECTIONS SHOWING VENEER COPING AND REGLET DETAIL

COPPER FLASHING AND REGLET / 1" MIN. / POURED LEAD WEDGE WITH SYNTHETIC RUBBER TOP SEAL

VERTICAL SECTIONS SHOWING STRAP AND DOWEL

3/8"± / STRAP AND DOWEL ANCHOR / **SECTION AT JOINT**

STONE COPINGS   TYPICAL PARAPET WALL CONDITIONS

SADDLE - DEPRESSED

DOOR / 4"-6" TYPICAL / FIN. FL. / ½"-1" / W.P. GROUT OR SEAL / TILE FL. / SETTING BED

SADDLE - "THIN SET"

DOOR / FIN. FL. / ½" MIN. / SADDLE SET IN W.P. MASTIC / TILE FL. / ALT. ELEV. "THIN SET" OMIT SETTING BED

SADDLE - "THIN SET" VAR. FL. ELEV.

DOOR / FIN. FL. / ½"-1" / TILE FL.

SADDLE - WOOD FL. CONDITION

DOOR / FIN. FL. / WOOD FL.

LUG SILL

SLIP SILL

MET. WINDOW STONE STOOL

SLIP SILL

WIDE SILL - ANCHORED

PROJECTED LINTEL

SIMPLE LINTEL

PROJECTED HEAD

SIMPLE LINTEL - ANCHORED

STONE SADDLES, SILLS AND STOOLS, AND LINTELS AND HEADS

TREAD / RUN / NOSING / NOSING RADIUS 1/8" - 1/2" / W.P. PLASTIC SEAL / PITCH 1/8" - 3/8" / RISE

NOTE: STONE LENGTHS USUALLY 4', 6' AND 8' DEPENDING ON STRENGTH. STEPS MAY SPAN UP TO 6' IF OF PROPER DEPTH AND ADEQUATE SUPPORT ON CHEEK WALLS.

STONE STEPS - INTERIOR AND EXTERIOR - FOR INTERIOR THIN STONE SEE FILE 5-13

RUNNING BUTT

LAP JOINT (EXPAN.)

SPLINE JOINT / 1/4"±

SET-IN BLOCK / 3/8" MIN

MORTAR JOINT PROFILES

FLUSH / BEAD / COVE / RAKED / STRUCK / WEATHERED / GRAPEVINE / "VEE"

CORNER BUTT

CORNER "ELL"

QUIRK MITER

CORNER BLOCK

1/4" JOINT FOR GENERAL USE: GRANITE LIMESTONE SANDSTONE

3/16" JOINT FOR FINE WORK

1/8" JOINT FOR SPECIAL WORK INTERIORS

RABBETED CORNER

BUTT "ELL"

BEVEL - BUTT "ELL"

LOCKED JOINT

VERTICAL STONE JOINT PROFILES

STONE JOINTS - PLANS, PROFILES, AND MORTAR JOINT PROFILES

George M. Whiteside, III, AIA; Whiteside, Moeckel & Carbonell; Wilmington, Delaware

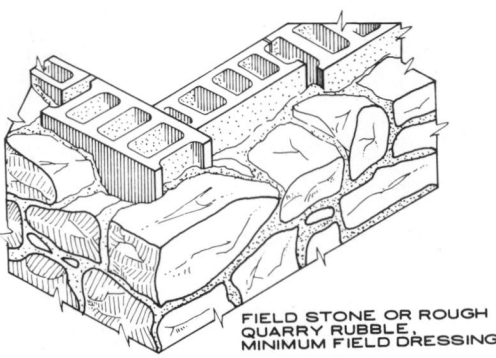

FIELD STONE OR ROUGH
QUARRY RUBBLE,
MINIMUM FIELD DRESSING

RUBBLE BONDED TO UNIT MASONRY

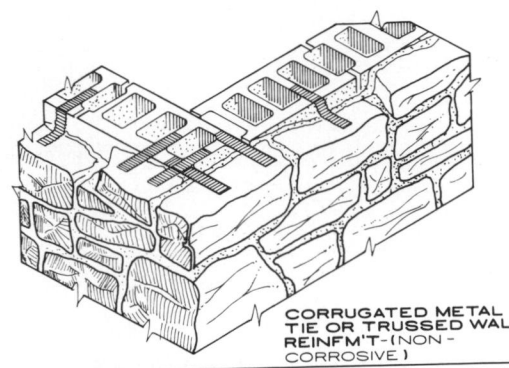

CORRUGATED METAL
TIE OR TRUSSED WALL
REINFM'T-(NON-
CORROSIVE)

ROUGHLY-SQUARED TIED TO UNIT MASONRY;
TRUSSED WALL REINFORCEMENT, BENT UP OR DOWN,
MAY BE USED AS TIE FOR STONE

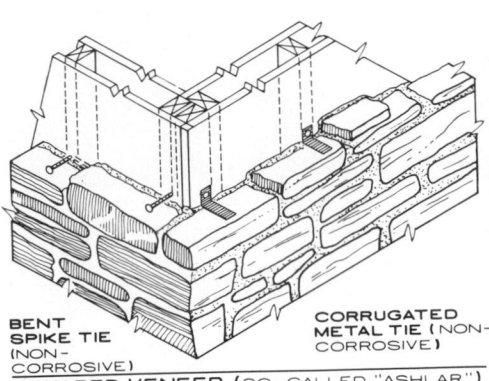

BENT
SPIKE TIE
(NON-
CORROSIVE)

CORRUGATED
METAL TIE (NON-
CORROSIVE)

SQUARED VENEER (SO-CALLED "ASHLAR")
TIED TO WOOD FRAME

1. All ties and anchors must be non-corrosive.

2. Dovetail anchors may be used for concrete back-up.

3. Stone joints are usually $1/2'' - 1''$ for rough work and $3/8'' - 3/4''$ for ashlar.

4. Non-staining cement mortar used on porous and light colored stones.

5. At all corners use extra ties and when possible large stones.

6. Stone thickness minimum 4'' — thinner stone sometimes used when permitted.

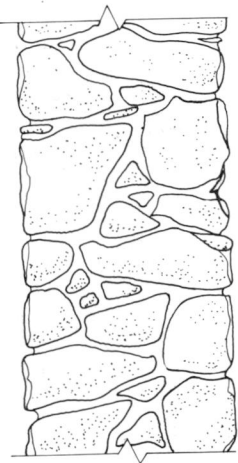

DOUBLE - FACED FIELD STONE
OR RUBBLE WALL; STONES
LAID IN THEIR NATURAL BED
AND PITCHED TO WEATHER;
WALL USUALLY 18" THICK
OR GREATER

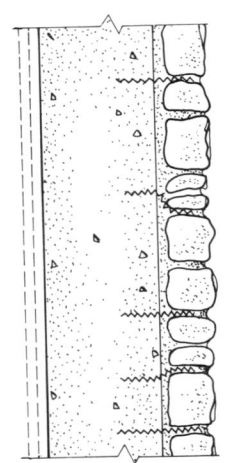

4"- 8" STONE CONCRETE
BACKED USING WALL TIES;
CONC. MAY BE FACED WITH
W.P. COMPOUND TO PREVENT
STAINING

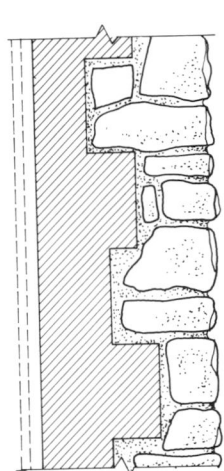

4"- 8" STONE BONDED
TO UNIT MASONRY BACK-
UP; VOIDS SLUSH FILLED;
HOLLOW CLAY TILE ALSO
USED; NO TIES REQUIRED

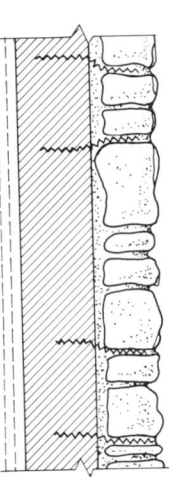

4"- 8" STONE TIED
TO UNIT MASONRY;
PROVIDE 1"- 2" AIR
SPACE OR SLUSH
FILL VOIDS AND
FURR INTERIOR
WALL SURFACE

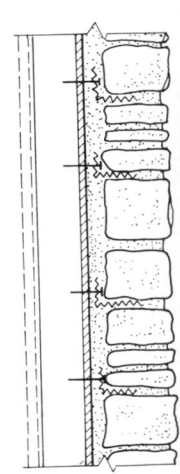

4"- 8" STONE TIED
TO WOOD FRAME;
USE WOOD
SHEATHING
AND W.P. FELT
OR W.P. SHEATHING
BOARD

RUBBLE, ROUGHLY - SQUARED, SQUARED, AND ASHLAR STONE WALLS SHOWING BACKING AND ANCHORING USUALLY LIMITED TO BUILDINGS
THREE STORIES HIGH OR LESS - VERTICAL SECTIONS

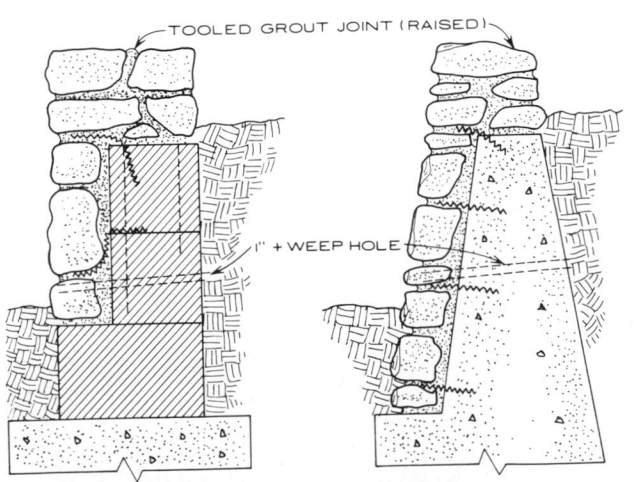

TOOLED GROUT JOINT (RAISED)

1" + WEEP HOLE

STONE FACED WALL WITH
UNIT MASONRY BACK-UP;
USE NON-CORROSIVE
TIES

STONE FACED WALL ON
CONCRETE; USE NON-
CORROSIVE TIES

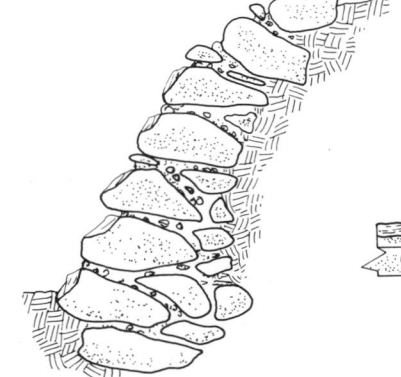

DRY LAID ROCK GARDEN WALL;
PITCH STONES TO CARRY RAIN
WATER INTO STONE POCKETS
AND RETAINED EARTH

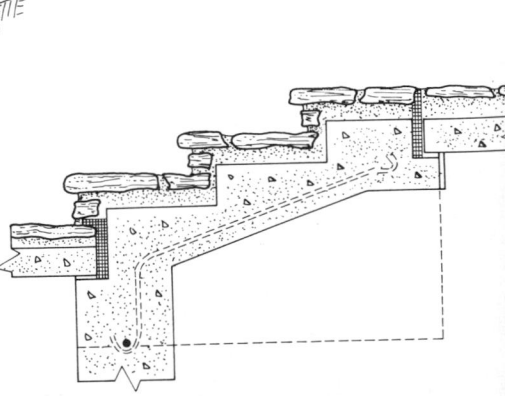

STONE STEPS AND GARDEN WALK;
CARRY CONC. WALK ONTO STEP FOOTING
AND ISOLATE WITH W.P. EXPANSION
MATERIAL AT JOINT

GARDEN WALLS AND STEPS OF ROUGH STONE - VERTICAL SECTIONS

George M. Whiteside, III, AIA; Whiteside, Moeckel & Carbonell; Wilmington, Delaware

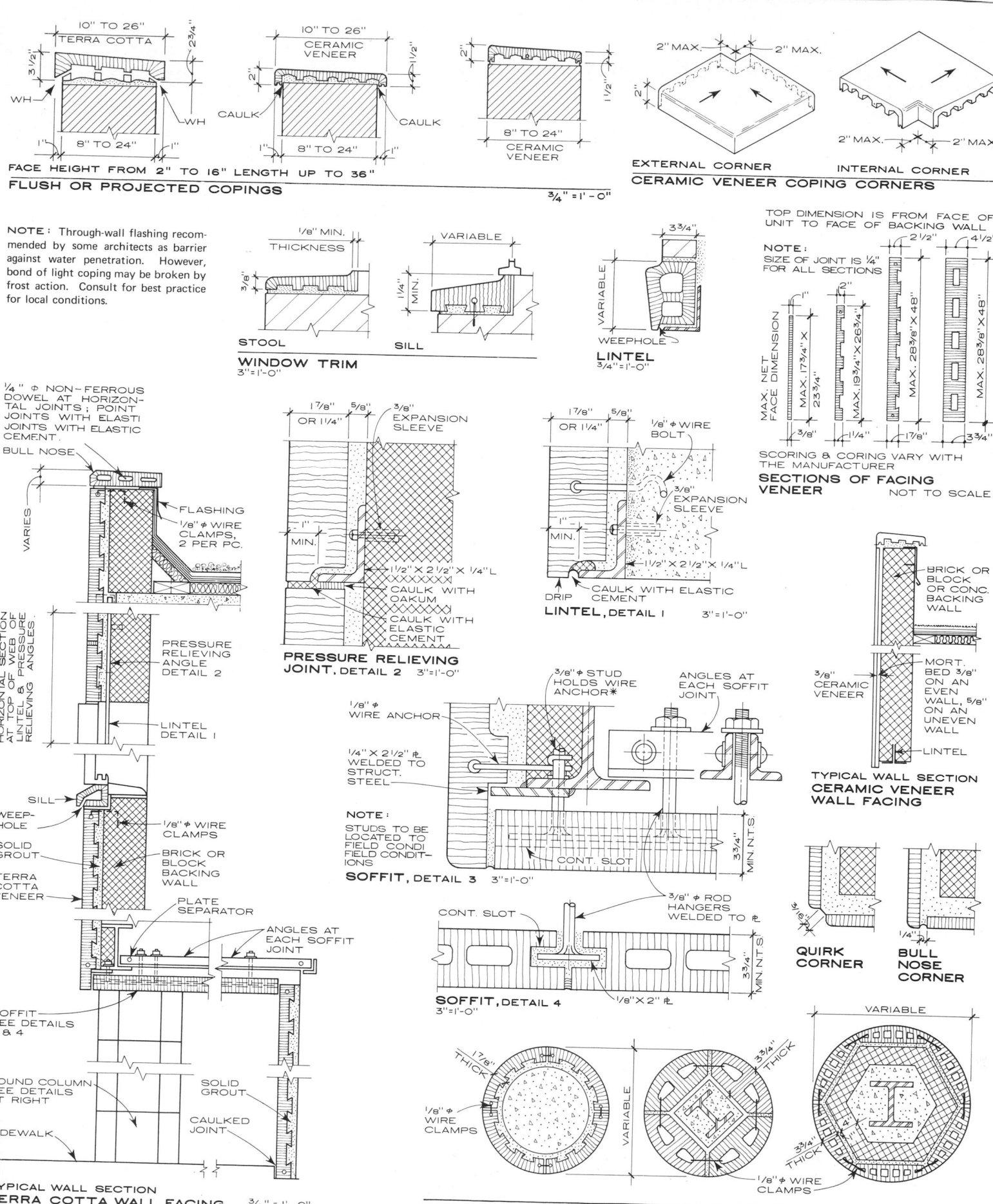

FACE HEIGHT FROM 2" TO 16" LENGTH UP TO 36"

FLUSH OR PROJECTED COPINGS

CERAMIC VENEER COPING CORNERS

EXTERNAL CORNER   INTERNAL CORNER

3/4" = 1'-0"

NOTE: Through-wall flashing recommended by some architects as barrier against water penetration. However, bond of light coping may be broken by frost action. Consult for best practice for local conditions.

WINDOW TRIM
3" = 1'-0"

STOOL   SILL

LINTEL
3/4" = 1'-0"

TOP DIMENSION IS FROM FACE OF UNIT TO FACE OF BACKING WALL

NOTE: SIZE OF JOINT IS 1/4" FOR ALL SECTIONS

SCORING & CORING VARY WITH THE MANUFACTURER

SECTIONS OF FACING VENEER   NOT TO SCALE

1/4" ∅ NON-FERROUS DOWEL AT HORIZONTAL JOINTS; POINT JOINTS WITH ELASTIC JOINTS WITH ELASTIC CEMENT.

PRESSURE RELIEVING JOINT, DETAIL 2   3" = 1'-0"

LINTEL, DETAIL 1   3" = 1'-0"

TYPICAL WALL SECTION CERAMIC VENEER WALL FACING

SOFFIT, DETAIL 3   3" = 1'-0"

NOTE: STUDS TO BE LOCATED TO FIELD CONDITIONS

SOFFIT, DETAIL 4
3" = 1'-0"

QUIRK CORNER   **BULL NOSE CORNER**

TYPICAL WALL SECTION TERRA COTTA WALL FACING   3/4" = 1'-0"

TERRA COTTA FACING ON ROUND COLUMNS   3/4" = 1'-0"

ax Martin Nathan, Rogers, Butler & Burgun; New York, New York

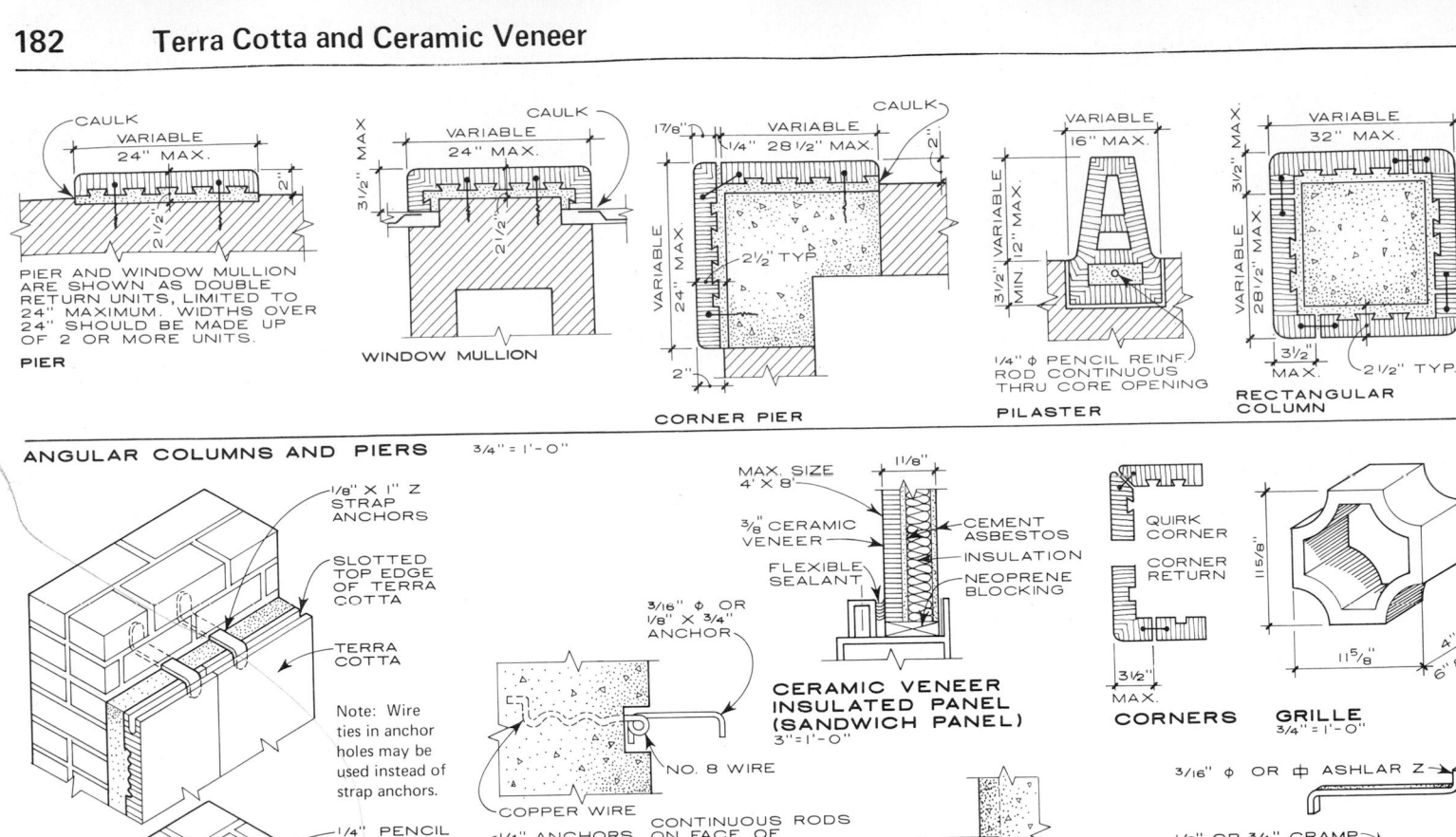

PIER

CAULK
VARIABLE 24" MAX.

PIER AND WINDOW MULLION ARE SHOWN AS DOUBLE RETURN UNITS, LIMITED TO 24" MAXIMUM. WIDTHS OVER 24" SHOULD BE MADE UP OF 2 OR MORE UNITS.

WINDOW MULLION

CAULK
VARIABLE 24" MAX.

CORNER PIER

CAULK
VARIABLE 28½" MAX.

PILASTER

VARIABLE 16" MAX.
¼" Φ PENCIL REINF. ROD CONTINUOUS THRU CORE OPENING

RECTANGULAR COLUMN

VARIABLE 32" MAX.

ANGULAR COLUMNS AND PIERS   ¾" = 1'-0"

1/8" × 1" Z STRAP ANCHORS
SLOTTED TOP EDGE OF TERRA COTTA
TERRA COTTA

Note: Wire ties in anchor holes may be used instead of strap anchors.

¼" PENCIL ROD
EYEBOLT OR LOOP ANCHOR
NO. 8 NON-FERROUS WIRE ANCHOR
TERRA COTTA

DOVETAIL ANCHOR SLOTS IN CONCRETE WALL
DOVETAIL ANCHORS
SLOTTED TOP EDGE OF TERRA COTTA
TERRA COTTA

ANCHORS FOR CONCRETE WALLS   1½" = 1'-0"

3/16" Φ OR 1/8" × 3/4" ANCHOR
COPPER WIRE
NO. 8 WIRE

¼" ANCHORS ABOUT 3'-0" O.C.
CONTINUOUS RODS ON FACE OF CONCRETE FOR ANCHORING TERRA COTTA
1/8" Φ OR 3/16" Φ ANCHORS ADJUSTABLE FOR POSITION

SLOT
DOVE-TAIL ANCHOR

CERAMIC VENEER INSULATED PANEL (SANDWICH PANEL)   3" = 1'-0"

MAX. SIZE 4' × 8'
3/8" CERAMIC VENEER
FLEXIBLE SEALANT
CEMENT ASBESTOS
INSULATION
NEOPRENE BLOCKING

CORNERS
QUIRK CORNER
CORNER RETURN

GRILLE   ¾" = 1'-0"
11 5/8"
6" 8"

STANDARD ANCHORS   1½" = 1'-0"
3/16" Φ OR Φ ASHLAR Z
1/8" OR 3/4" CRAMP
1/8" × 3/4" Z
½" ROUND
5/8" PINS AT JOINTS

GENERAL NOTES:

The architect selects texture, ceramic finish and color of exposed surface of terra cotta.

Texture: smooth, even plane, coarse-roughened; tooled, beveled, fluted; custom-designed.

Ceramic finish: Unglazed "natural earthy colors (body colors)"; red, gray, buff, brown, black; glazed, rough type, e.g., sanded glaze (slip-resisting); glazed, smooth, e.g., matte, satin or gloss.

Ceramic glaze colors (solid or mottled):
Unlimited range:
    monochrome (1 color, single-fired);
    polychrome (more than 1 color) e.g., murals;
    low-fired colors, e.g., gold, silver, vermilion.

Special applications of terra cotta (not covered):
    swimming pools
    ornamental terra cotta, e.g., cornices and column capitals;
    sculpture: bas-relief, e.g., sculptured patterns (standard or custom-designed) and cartouches. Free-standing sculpture.
    note: sculpture, ornamental and molded pieces can be made in larger dimensions than facing ashlar.
    bases and curbings, watertable and belt courses

SPECIAL NOTES:

Grilles: these can be open, or closed back, free standing screen walls, or perforated facades. Many grille designs are available.

Shelf angles: on multi-story buildings, roughly one shelf angle per story is needed.

Insulated ("sandwich") panels: also available 1 5/8" to 2 ¼" thick, with different insulation.

No. 8 nonferrous wire loose anchors are let into terra cotta anchor holes and then tied around exposed truss chord.

Concrete block backing wall with truss design masonry wall reinforcement. Gage of truss rods to be determined by structural engineer.

TERRA COTTA

CHOICE OF TYPE OF INSTALLATION
Anchored Type Units: 1" thick or more, exclusive of ribs;
Adhesive Type Units: 1 ¼" thick or less, including ribs.

ANCHORAGE OF TERRA COTTA

Max Martin Nathan, Rogers, Butler & Burgun; New York, New York

SCALE: 3/4" = 1'-0

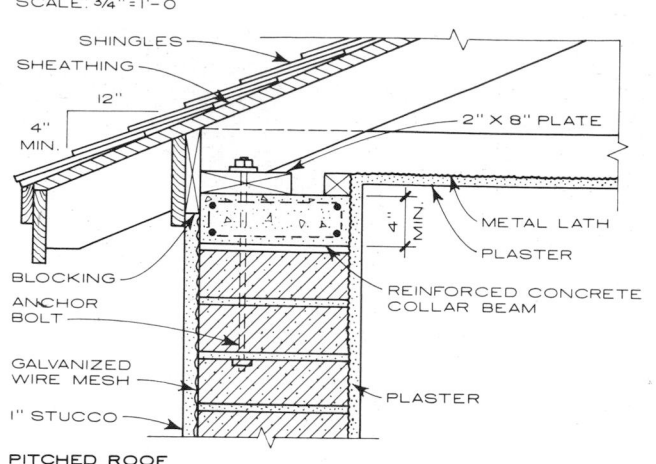

PITCHED ROOF

SHINGLES
SHEATHING
12"
4" MIN.
2" X 8" PLATE
METAL LATH
PLASTER
BLOCKING
ANCHOR BOLT
REINFORCED CONCRETE COLLAR BEAM
GALVANIZED WIRE MESH
1" STUCCO
PLASTER

WALL SECTION AT ROOF LINE

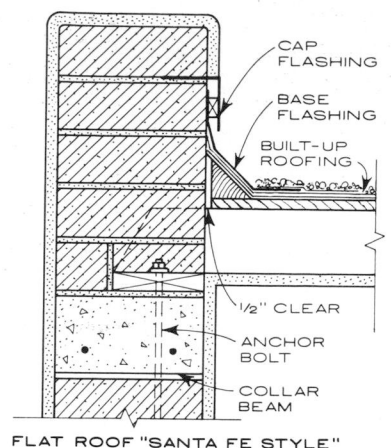

CAP FLASHING
BASE FLASHING
BUILT-UP ROOFING
1/2" CLEAR
ANCHOR BOLT
COLLAR BEAM

FLAT ROOF "SANTA FE STYLE"

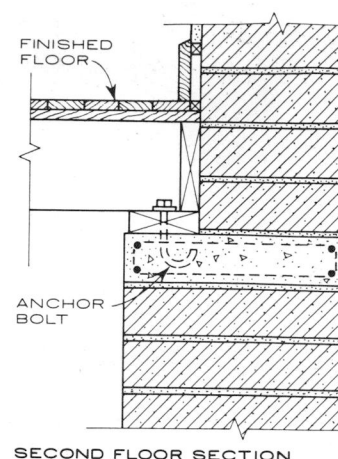

FINISHED FLOOR
ANCHOR BOLT

SECOND FLOOR SECTION

USUAL SIZES OF ADOBE BRICKS

H	L	W	H	L	W
4"	8"	16"	5"	12"	16"
4"	10"	16"	5"	10"	20"
4"	9"	18"	5"	12"	18"
4"	12"	18"	6"	12"	24"

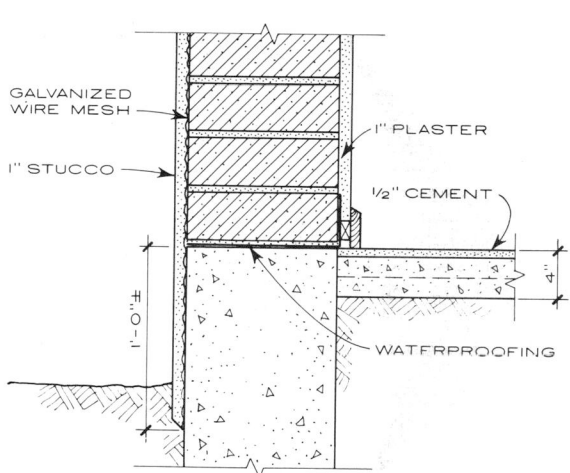

GALVANIZED WIRE MESH
1" STUCCO
1" PLASTER
1/2" CEMENT
WATERPROOFING
1'-0"

CONCRETE FLOOR

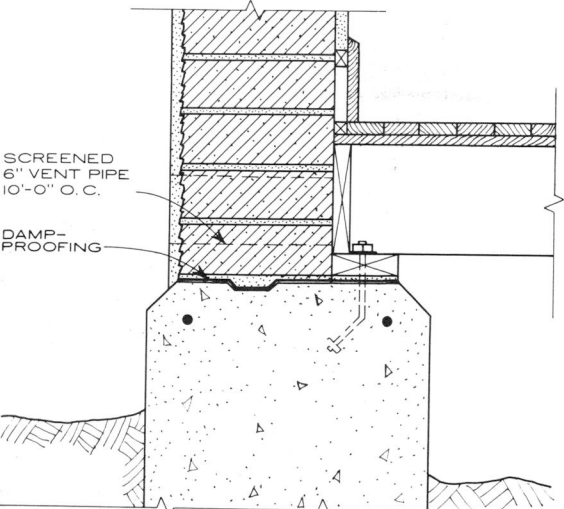

SCREENED 6" VENT PIPE 10'-0" O.C.
DAMP-PROOFING

WOOD FLOOR

WALL SECTIONS AT FLOOR LINE

David E. Miller; Troy, New York
Richard A. Morse, AIA; Tucson, Arizona

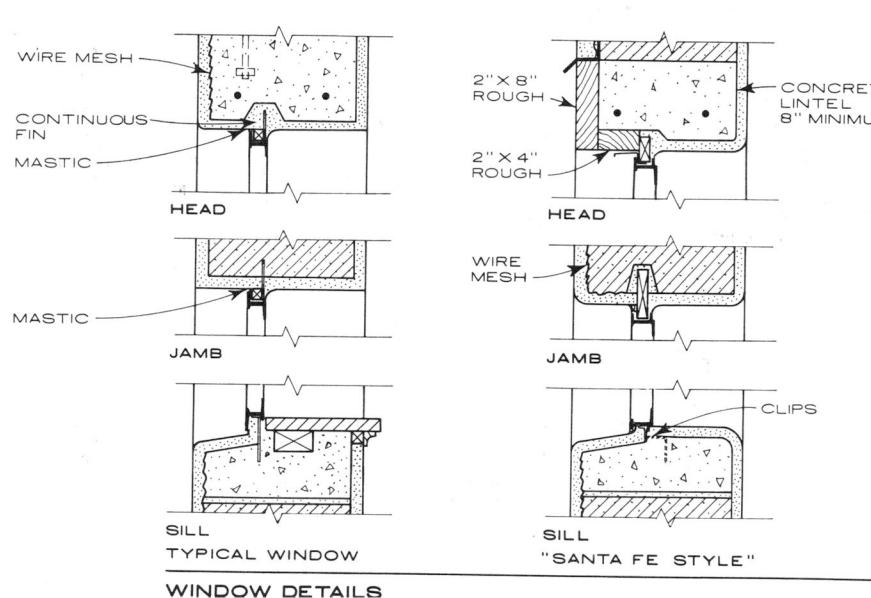

WIRE MESH
CONTINUOUS FIN
MASTIC

HEAD

2" X 8" ROUGH
2" X 4" ROUGH
CONCRETE LINTEL 8" MINIMUM

HEAD

MASTIC

JAMB

WIRE MESH

JAMB

CLIPS

SILL
TYPICAL WINDOW

SILL
"SANTA FE STYLE"

WINDOW DETAILS

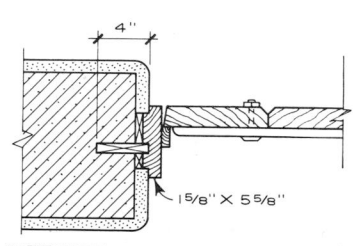

4"
1 5/8" X 5 5/8"

INTERIOR

USE PRESSED STEEL ANGLES AT HEAD

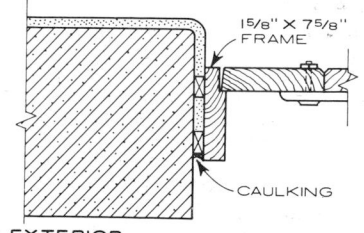

1 5/8" X 7 5/8" FRAME
CAULKING

EXTERIOR
DOOR JAMBS

NOTES:

1. These notes and details are for preliminary design only and presume masonry openings not over 3'– 4" wide. Verify by local FHA recommendations.

2. Bricks are either sun or kiln dried. Mortar is similar in composition to the brick. In laying up, allow time for equalizing of settlement and drying of mortar, and lay in uniform stages throughout the structure.

3. Sun baked adobe requires stucco on the exterior whereas burned adobe does not.

4. A continuous reinforced collar beam is recommended at roof plate not less than 4" thick reinforced with rods whose cross sectional area is at least 1/4 of 1% of cross sectional area of the course. When used as a lintel they should be at least 8" deep and reinforced same as collar beam. 4" deep concrete beams are recommended under window sills.

5. One story walls should be 12" thick in Arizona, 10" in New Mexico, and not exceed 12'– 0" in height; two story, 18" thick at first floor and 12" at second, not over 22'– 0" in height.

6. Fireplaces and chimneys of adobe are built similar to common brick construction. The inside of the fireplace should be lined with fire brick and the flues with flue lining. Tops of chimneys should be capped with concrete.

7. Arches can be built of adobe brick cut to the required shape or formed in special molds.

LAYOUT TABLE

NO. OF BLOCKS	6" $5\frac{3}{4} \times 5\frac{3}{4} \times 3\frac{7}{8}$	8" $7\frac{3}{4} \times 7\frac{3}{4} \times 3\frac{7}{8}$	12" $11\frac{3}{4} \times 11\frac{3}{4} \times 3\frac{7}{8}$
1	0'-6"	0'-8"	1'-0"
2	1'-0"	1'-4"	2'-0"
3	1'-6"	2'-0"	3'-0"
4	2'-0"	2'-8"	4'-0"
5	2'-6"	3'-4"	5'-0"
6	3'-0"	4'-0"	6'-0"
7	3'-6"	4'-8"	7'-0"
8	4'-0"	5'-4"	8'-0"
9	4'-6"	6'-0"	9'-0"
10	5'-0"	6'-8"	10'-0"
11	5'-6"	7'-4"	11'-0"
12	6'-0"	8'-0"	12'-0"
13	6'-6"	8'-8"	13'-0"
14	7'-0"	9'-4"	14'-0"
15	7'-6"	10'-0"	15'-0"
16	8'-0"	10'-8"	16'-0"
17	8'-6"	11'-4"	17'-0"
18	9'-0"	12'-0"	18'-0"
19	9'-6"	12'-8"	19'-0"
20	10'-0"	13'-4"	20'-0"
21	10'-6"	14'-0"	21'-0"
22	11'-0"	14'-8"	22'-0"
23	11'-6"	15'-4"	23'-0"
24	12'-0"	16'-0"	24'-0"
25	12'-6"	16'-8"	25'-0"

This table is based on Modular Coordination assuming $\frac{1}{4}$" mortar joints between glass blocks.

For minimum required opening height, find table dimension and add $\frac{3}{8}$".

For minimum required opening width, find table dimension and add $\frac{1}{2}$".

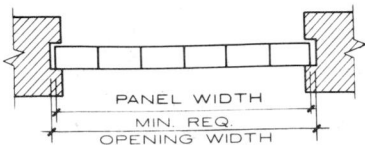

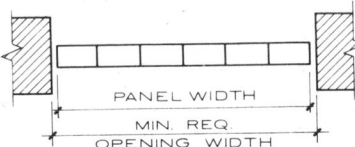

CHASE CONSTRUCTION

MAXIMUM PANEL AREA – 144 SQ. FT.
MAXIMUM HEIGHT – 20 FEET
MAXIMUM WIDTH – 25 FEET
MORTAR JOINTS = $\frac{1}{4}$ INCH

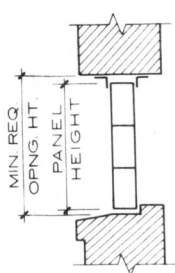

WALL ANCHOR CONSTRUCTION

MAXIMUM PANEL AREA – 100 SQ. FT.
MAXIMUM HEIGHT – 10 FEET
MAXIMUM WIDTH – 10 FEET
MORTAR JOINTS = $\frac{1}{4}$ INCH

ESTIMATING DATA
FOR 100 SQ. FT. OF PANEL $\frac{1}{4}$" MORTAR JOINTS

NOMINAL BLOCK SIZE	6"	8"	12"
NUMBER OF BLOCKS	400	225	100
PANEL WEIGHT, LBS.	2000	1800	1900
MORTAR VOLUME, CU. FT.	4.3	3.2	2.2

For design purposes, glass block panels weigh approximately 20 lbs. per sq. ft. installed. This applies to all sizes of blocks.

INSTALLATION

1. Sill area to be covered by mortar shall first have a heavy coat of asphalt emulsion and allowed to dry.

2. Adhere expansion strips to jambs and head with asphalt emulsion. Expansion strip must extend to sill.

3. When emulsion on sill is dry, place full mortar bed joint—do not furrow.

4. Set lower course of block. All mortar joints must be full and not furrowed. Steel tools must not be used to tap blocks in position. Mortar shall not bridge expansion joints. Visible width mortar joint shall be ¼" or as specified.

5. Install panel reinforcing in horizontal joints where required as follows:

(a) Place lower half of mortar bed joint. Do not furrow.

(b) Press panel reinforcing into place.

(c) Cover panel reinforcing with upper half of mortar bed and trowel smooth. Do not furrow.

(d) Panel reinforcing must run from end to end of panels and where used continuously must lap 6 inches. Reinforcing must not bridge expansion joints.

6. Place full mortar bed for joints not requiring panel reinforcing. Do not furrow.

7. Follow above instructions for succeeding courses. The number of blocks in successive lifts shall be limited to prevent squeezing out of mortar or movement of blocks.

8. Strike joints smoothly while mortar is still plastic and before final set. At this time rake out all spaces requiring caulking to a depth equal to the width of the spaces. Remove surplus mortar from faces of glass blocks and wipe dry. Tool joints smooth and concave, before mortar sets, so that exposed edges of blocks have sharp clean lines.

9. After final mortar set, pack oakum tightly between glass block panel and jamb and head construction. Leave space for caulking.

10. Caulk panels as indicated on details.

11. Final cleaning of glass block faces shall not be done until after final mortar set.

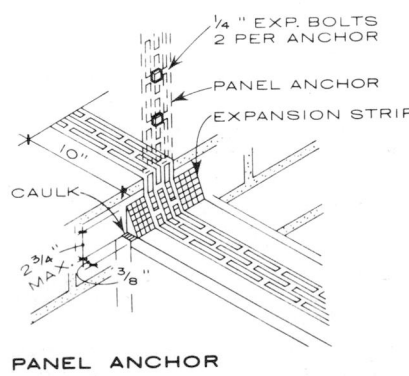

PANEL ANCHOR

Dotted lines show use on existing structure.

Robert D. Livingstone; Holden, Yang, Raemsch & Corser; New York, New York

GLASS BLOCK IN EXISTING WINDOW OPENING

Glass blocks and modules will fit nearly any existing window opening.

The drawings show typical head, sill and jamb section details for conventional window and glass block replacement. Notice how simple it is to work glass block into existing construction. It makes no difference if the opening is oddly shaped. Arches and irregular openings can be easily rebuilt to accommodate the glass blocks or modules by employing standard masonry construction techniques.

Many standard ribbon windows and ventilator attachments are available. These can be easily combined with glass blocks and modules.

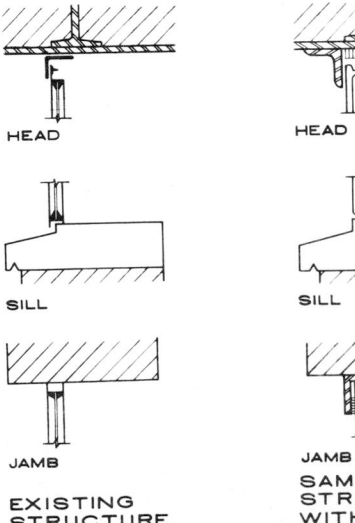

HEAD

HEAD

SILL

SILL

JAMB

JAMB

EXISTING STRUCTURE WITH SASH

SAME STRUCTURE WITH GLASS BLOCKS

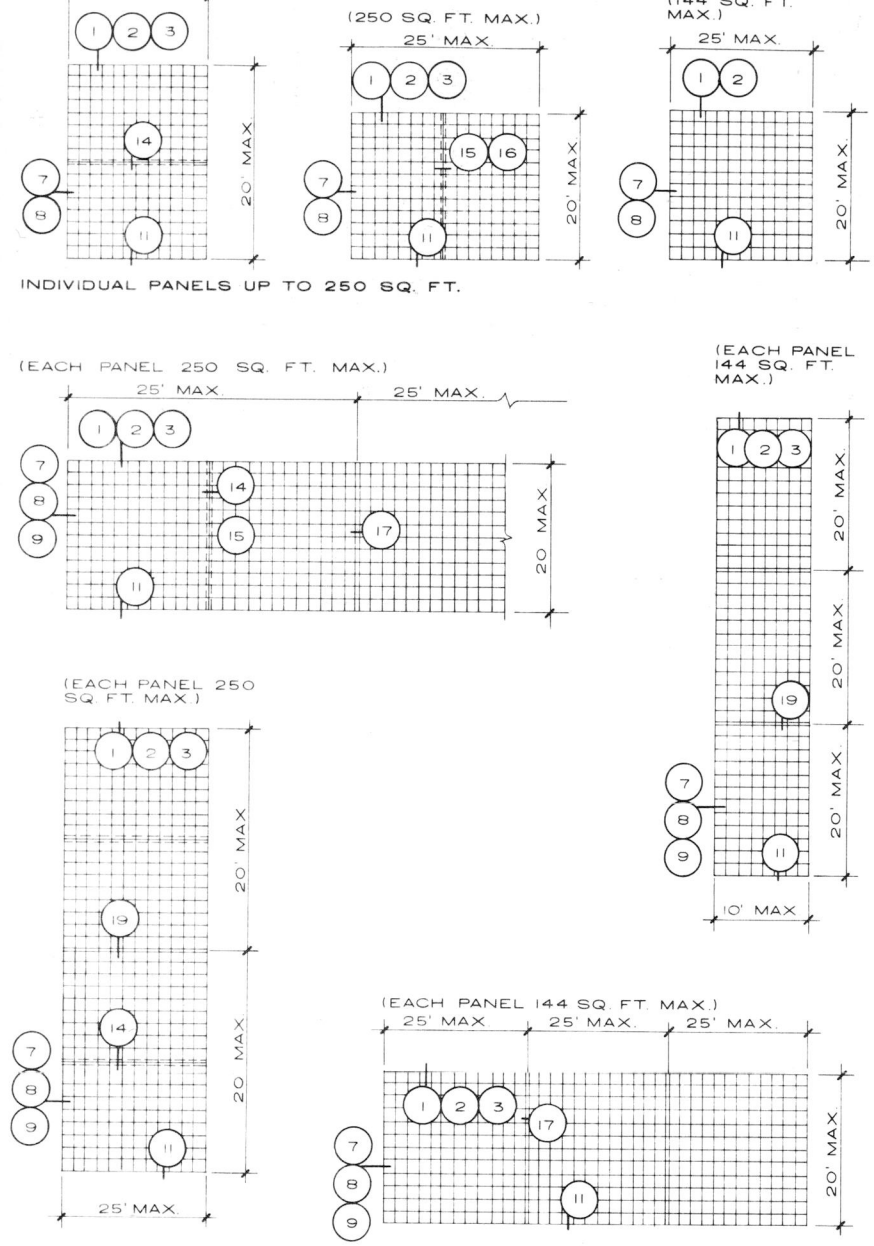

INDIVIDUAL PANELS UP TO 250 SQ. FT.

(EACH PANEL 250 SQ. FT. MAX.)

(EACH PANEL 250 SQ. FT. MAX.)

(EACH PANEL 144 SQ. FT. MAX.)

(EACH PANEL 144 SQ. FT. MAX.)

CONTINUOUS PANELS UP TO 250 SQ. FT.

EXTERIOR PANELS UP TO 250 SQ. FT.

INDIVIDUAL PANELS

CONTINUOUS PANELS

CONTINUOUS PANELS

EXTERIOR PANELS UP TO 100 SQ. FT.

INDIVIDUAL PANELS 250 SQ. FT. MAXIMUM AREA

INTERIOR PANELS

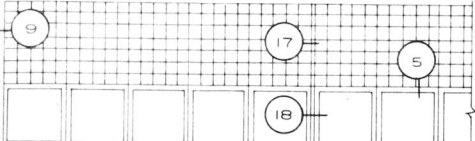

RIBBON WINDOWS

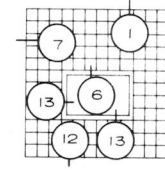

VENTILATORS

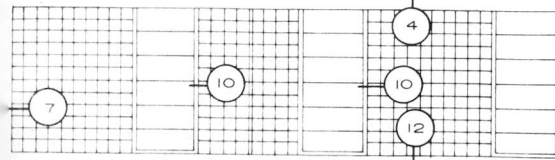

VERTICAL WINDOWS

GLASS BUILDING UNITS

1. These pages show elevations and sections of typical glass block panels. The large scale sections are typical head, jamb and sill details to show principles of construction only.

2. Any structural members must be calculated for safe loading, and local building codes checked for any possible restrictions on panel sizes or detail.

3. While single panels of glass block are limited to a maximum of 144 square feet, panel and curtain wall sections up to a maximum area of 250 square feet may be erected if properly braced to limit movement and settlement.

4. If chase construction cannot be used, substitute the panel anchor construction. Panel anchors are used to give lateral support for glass block panels.

5. Any glass block installation that is made in a frame construction shall have the wood adjacent to the mortar properly primed with asphalt emulsion.

6. Underwriters' Listing: glass block panels may be used for window openings subject to light fire exposure (class F openings).

7. Other types available are ornamental, sculptured and colored blocks of various sizes. Solid glass blocks (glass bricks) $2\frac{5}{16}$" thick x $5\frac{7}{8}$" x $8\frac{7}{8}$" for installation in detention windows.

Robert D. Livingstone; Holden, Yang, Raemsch & Corser; New York, New York

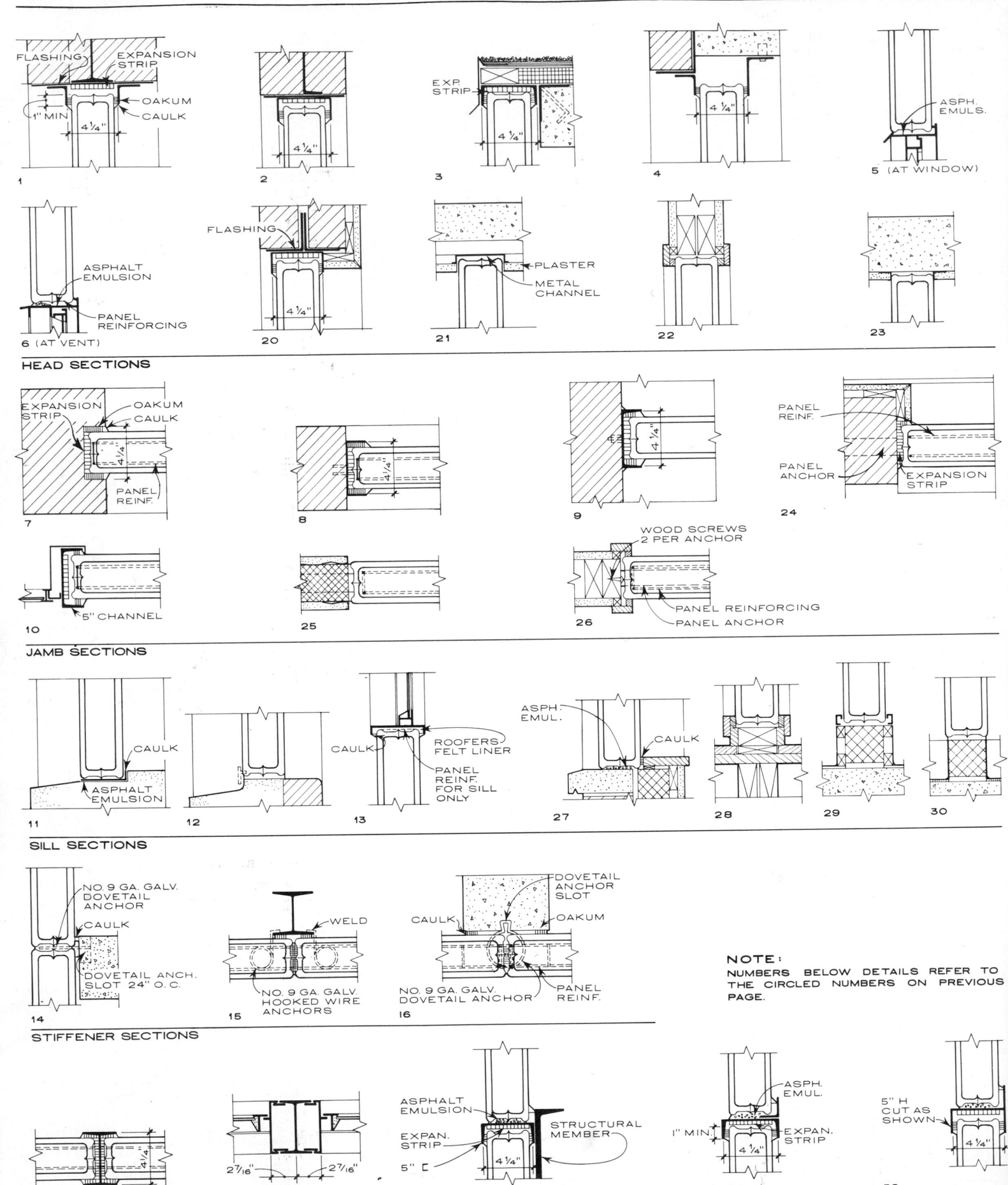

HEAD SECTIONS

JAMB SECTIONS

SILL SECTIONS

STIFFENER SECTIONS

NOTE:
NUMBERS BELOW DETAILS REFER TO THE CIRCLED NUMBERS ON PREVIOUS PAGE.

MULLIONS AND SHELF SECTIONS

Robert D. Livingstone; Holden, Yang, Raemsch & Corser; New York, New York

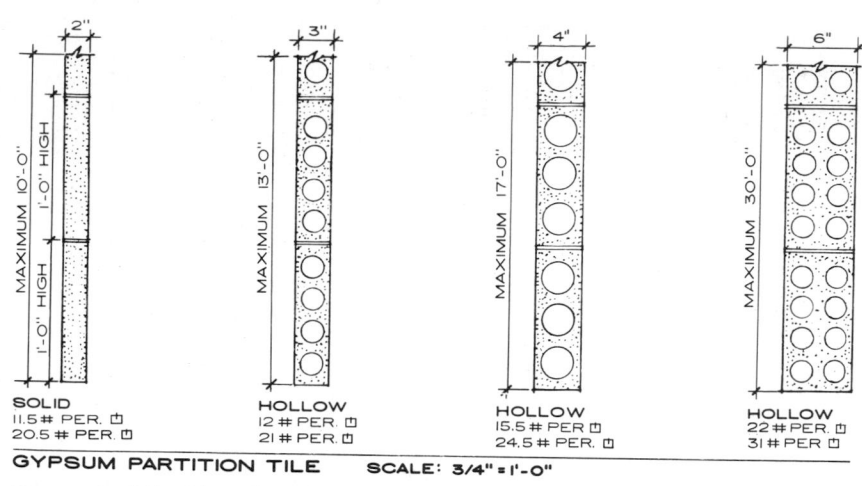

GYPSUM PARTITION TILE   SCALE: 3/4" = 1'-0"

SOLID
11.5# PER. ☐
20.5# PER. ☐

HOLLOW
12 # PER. ☐
21 # PER. ☐

HOLLOW
15.5# PER ☐
24.5# PER. ☐

HOLLOW
22 # PER. ☐
31 # PER ☐

Top row of weights without plaster, bottom row with two sides plastered; weight of plaster may be reduced by using light weight aggregate in place of sand aggregate. The limits of heights are the Underwriter's Laboratories recommendation, section through partitions.

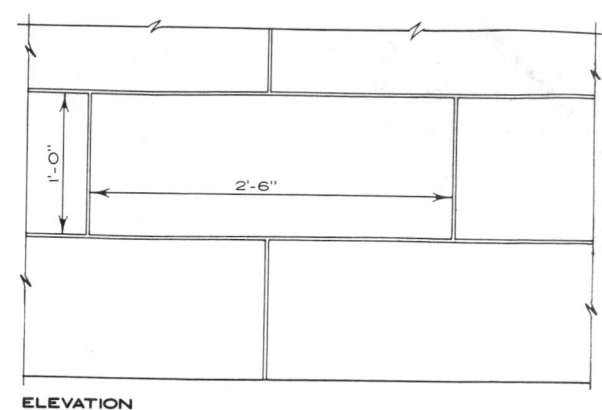

ELEVATION

This material not recommended where water or dampness are likely to exist such as baths, pools, showers etc. Partitions are set on base courses of concrete block in basements or where cement terrazzo or tile floors occur.

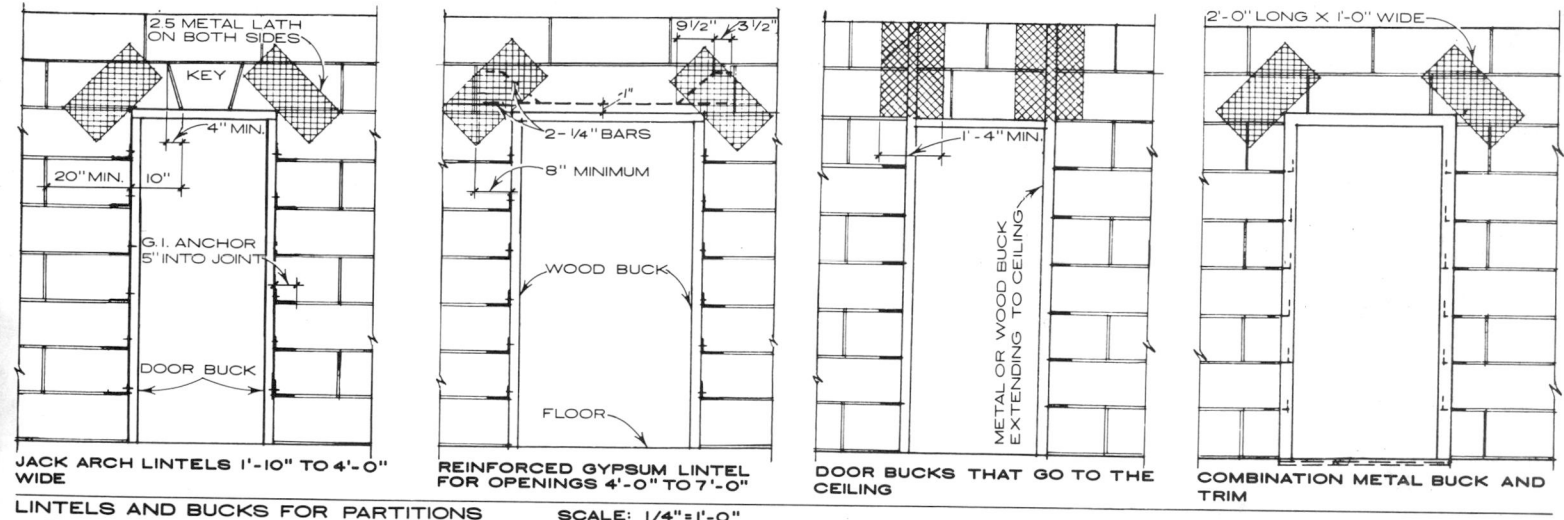

JACK ARCH LINTELS 1'-10" TO 4'-0" WIDE

REINFORCED GYPSUM LINTEL FOR OPENINGS 4'-0" TO 7'-0"

DOOR BUCKS THAT GO TO THE CEILING

COMBINATION METAL BUCK AND TRIM

LINTELS AND BUCKS FOR PARTITIONS   SCALE: 1/4"=1'-0"
LINTELS UP TO 1'-10" CAN BE SPANNED WITH TILE WITH 4" MINIMUM BEARING.

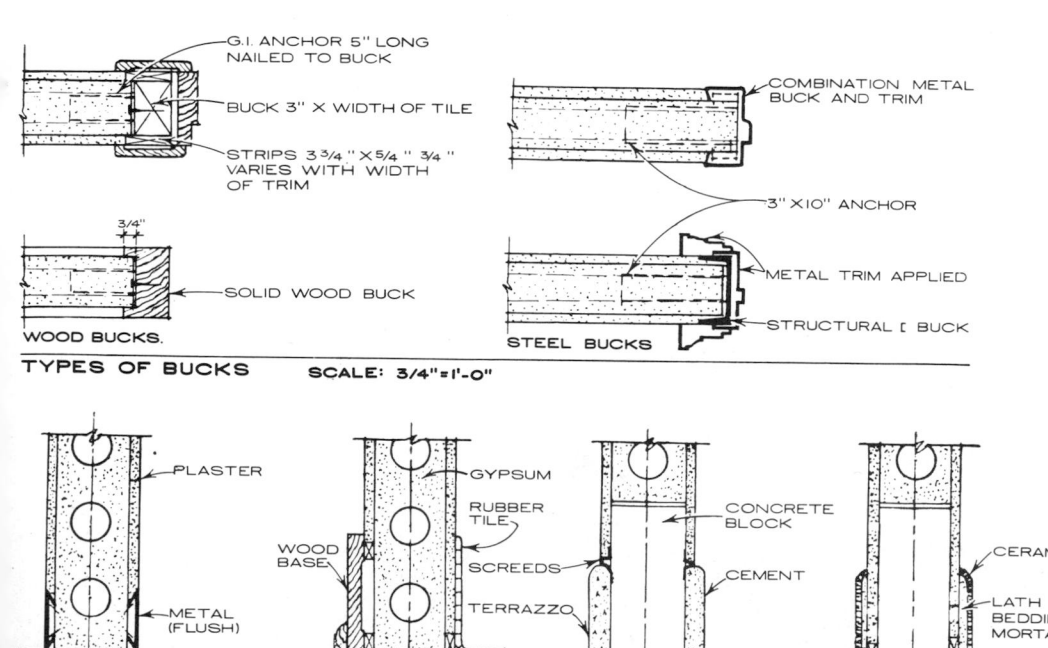

WOOD BUCKS.

STEEL BUCKS

TYPES OF BUCKS   SCALE: 3/4"=1'-0"

TYPES OF BASES   SCALE: 11/2"=1'-0"
WHERE EXCESSIVE MOISTURE IS EXPECTED, 12" CONCRETE BLOCK 1ST COURSE.

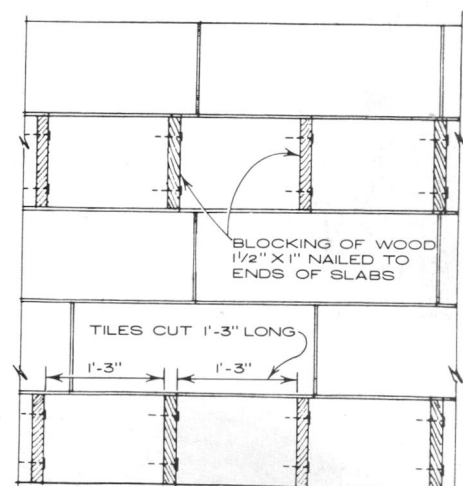

ELEVATION
SUCH AS FOR BLACKBOARDS ETC.
METHOD OF PROVIDING NAILING FOR HEAVY FIXTURES   SCALE: 1/2"=1'-0"

CHAPTER **5**

METALS

NOTE: ALL WOOD SIZES ARE NORMAL.

ROUGH CARPENTRY

	PENNY	INCHES	TYPE OF NAIL
1″ thick stock	8	$2\,^1/_2$	Common nails.
2″ thick stock	16 to 20	$3\,^1/_2$ or 4	Common nails.
3″ thick stock	40 to 60	5 or 6	Common nails or spikes.
Concrete Forms	variable		Common or double headed nails.
Framing for general use and for large members	10, 16, 20, 60	3, $3\,^1/_2$, 4, 6	Common nails or spikes depending on size of members.
Toe nailing studs, joists, etc.	10	3	Common nails.
Spiking usual plates and sills	16	$3\,^1/_2$	Common nails.
Toe nailing rafters and plates	10	3	Common nails.
Sheathing — roof and wall	8	$2\,^1/_2$	Common nails, may be zinc coated.
Finished rough flooring	8	$2\,^1/_2$	Common nails, may be zinc coated.

FINISH CARPENTRY

	PENNY	INCHES	TYPE OF NAIL
Moldings —— Sizes as required		$^7/_8$ to $1\,^1/_4$	Molding nails (brads).
Carpet strips, shoes	8	$2\,^1/_2$	Finishing or casing nails.
Door and window stops and members $^1/_4$″ to $^1/_2$″ thick	4	$1\,^1/_2$	Finishing or casing nails.
Ceiling, trim, casing, picture mold, base balusters and members $^1/_2$″ to $^3/_4$″ thick	6	2	Finishing or casing nails.
Ceiling, trim, casing, base, jambs, trim and members $^3/_4$″ to 1″ thick	8	$2\,^1/_2$	Finishing or casing nails.
Doors and window trim, boards and other members 1″ to $1\,^1/_4$″ thick	10	3	Finishing or casing nails.
Drop siding, 1″ thick	7 or 9	$2\,^1/_4$ or $2\,^3/_4$	Siding nails (7d), Casing nails (9d).
Bevel siding, $^1/_2$″ thick	6 or 8	2 or $2\,^1/_2$	Finishing nails (6d), Siding nails (8d).

WOOD FLOORING

	PENNY	INCHES	TYPE OF NAIL
See wood flooring page for nail sizes and types recommended.			Cut steel, wire, finishing, wire casing, flooring brads, parquet and flooring nails.

LATHING

	PENNY	INCHES	TYPE OF NAIL
Wood lath	3	$1\,^1/_4$	Blued lath nail.
Gypsum lath	3	$1\,^1/_4$	Blued common.
Fiber lath			
Metal lath, interior		1	Blued lath nails, staples or offset head nails.
Metal lath, exterior	3	$1\,^1/_4$	Self furring nails (double heads). Staples or cement coated.

SHEATHING OR SIDING

	PENNY	INCHES	TYPE OF NAIL
Asbestos $^3/_8$″ thick		$1\,^1/_4$	Galvanized roofing nail with $^7/_{16}$″ diameter head.
Fiber board $^1/_2$″ and $2\,^5/_{32}$″		$1\,^1/_2$ to 2	Galvanized roofing nail with $^7/_{16}$″ diameter head.
Gypsum board $^1/_2$″		$1\,^3/_4$	Galvanized roofing nail with $^7/_{16}$″ diameter head.
Plywood $^5/_{16}$″ and $^3/_8$″ thick	6	2	Common nails.
Plywood $^1/_2$″ and $^5/_8$″ thick	8	$2\,^1/_2$	Common nails.

ROOFING & SHEET METAL

	PENNY	INCHES	TYPE OF NAIL
Aluminum roofing	1	$1\,^3/_4$ to $2\,^1/_2$	Aluminum nail, neoprene washer optional.
Asbestos, corrugated or sheets	Depends on thickness		Leakproof roofing nails.
Asbestos shingles		1 to 2	See "Asbestos Cement Roofing and Siding."
Asphalt shingles			Galvanized large head roofing.
Copper cleats and flashing to wood			Copper wire or cut slating nails.
Copper cleats and flashing to prevent joints			Barbed copper nails.
Clay tile	4 to 6	$1\,^1/_2$ to 2	Copper nails.
Prepared felt roofing		1 to $1\,^1/_4$	Zinc roofing nails or large head roofing nails (barbed preferred). Heads may be reinforced.
Shingles, wood — usual size	3 to 4	$1\,^1/_4$ to $1\,^1/_2$	Zinc coated, copper wire shingle, copper clad shingle, cut iron
Shingles, wood — for heavy butts	4 to 8	$1\,^1/_2$ to $2\,^1/_2$	or cut steel.
Slate	Use nails 1″ larger than thickness of slate		Copper wire slating nail (large head). In dry climates zinc coated or copper clad nails may be used.
Tin, zinc roofing			Zinc coated nails (roofing or slating).
Monel roofing			Monel nail.
Nailing to sheet metal			Self tapping screws, helical drive scres.

TO CONCRETE OR CEMENT MORTAR

	PENNY	INCHES	TYPE OF NAIL
See following pages of fastening devices.			Concrete or cement nails (hardened), helical drive nails or drive bolts.

GENERAL NOTES:

1. Nail diameter, length, shape and surface affect holding power (withdrawal resistance and lateral resistance). See NFPA publications.

2. Materials: Zinc, brass, monel, copper, aluminum, iron or steel, stainless steel, copper bearing steel, muntz metal.

3. Coatings: Tin, copper, cement, brass plated, zinc, nickel, chrome, cadmium, etched acid, parkerized.

4. Forms: Smooth, barbed, helical, annular-ring.

5. Colors: Blue, bright, coppered, black (annealed).

6. Gauges shown are for steel wire (Washburn and Moen).

7. Abbreviations (for the following pages of fasteners only):

B = blunt	F = flat	O = oval
CS = countersunk	L = long	PC = pointing cone
D = diamond	N = narrow	R = round

 FLAT COMMON
 LARGE FLAT
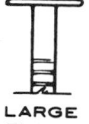 LARGE FLAT REINFORCED
 WIRE SPIKE
 CHECKERED ROOFING

 SINKERS CORKER
 TWINHEAD FLAT-CS
 L N ALSO BRAD
 DEEP OR P C
 CUPPED CS

 OVAL
 ROUND
 OVAL CS
 ROUND CS
 OFFSET

 HOOK
 NON-LEAK
 CONE
 HEADLESS DOWELS
 D BARGE SPIKES

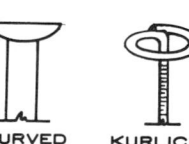 CURVED
 KURLICUE
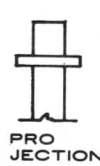 PROJECTION
 NUMERAL & LETTERED
 CUT NAIL
 BRAD HEAD

TYPES OF NAIL HEADS

 ROUND
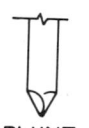 BLUNT
 DIAMOND
 LONG DIAMOND
 NEEDLE
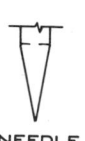

 CHISEL POINT
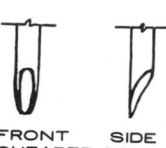 FRONT SHEARED / SIDE BEVEL
 FRONT CUT NAIL
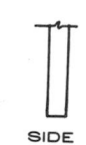 SIDE

TYPES OF NAIL POINTS

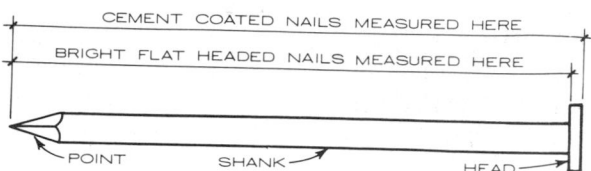

CEMENT COATED NAILS MEASURED HERE

BRIGHT FLAT HEADED NAILS MEASURED HERE

POINT   SHANK   HEAD

COMMON NAIL

LENGTH (IN INS.)	PENNY	GAUGE	DIAM. OF HEAD (IN INS.)	NO. OF NAILS PER LB.	SAFE WORKING RESISTANCE TO LATERAL SHEAR-LB.
1	2	15	$1\frac{1}{64}$	847	
$1\frac{1}{4}$	3	14	$1\frac{3}{64}$	543	
$1\frac{1}{2}$	4	$12\frac{1}{2}$	$\frac{1}{4}$	296	
$1\frac{3}{4}$	5	$12\frac{1}{2}$	$\frac{1}{4}$	254	
2	6	$11\frac{1}{2}$	$\frac{17}{64}$	167	48
$2\frac{1}{4}$	7	$11\frac{1}{2}$	$\frac{17}{64}$	150	
$2\frac{1}{2}$	8	$10\frac{1}{4}$	$\frac{9}{32}$	101	64
$2\frac{3}{4}$	9	$10\frac{1}{4}$	$\frac{9}{32}$	92.1	
3	10	9	$\frac{5}{16}$	66	80
$3\frac{1}{4}$	12	9	$\frac{5}{16}$	66.1	96
$3\frac{1}{2}$	16	8	$\frac{11}{32}$	47.4	128
4	20	6	$\frac{13}{32}$	29.7	160
$4\frac{1}{2}$	30	5	$\frac{7}{16}$	22.7	
5	40	4	$\frac{15}{32}$	17.3	
$5\frac{1}{2}$	50	3	$\frac{1}{2}$	13.5	
6	60	2	$\frac{17}{32}$	10.7	

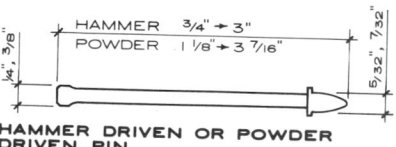

HAMMER 3/4" → 3"
POWDER 1 1/8" → 3 7/16"

HAMMER DRIVEN OR POWDER DRIVEN PIN

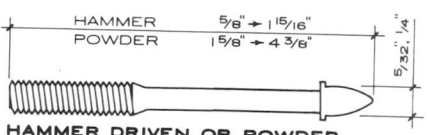

HAMMER 5/8" → 1 15/16"
POWDER 1 5/8" → 4 3/8"

HAMMER DRIVEN OR POWDER DRIVEN HEADLESS THREADED STUD

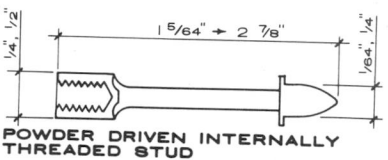

1 5/64" → 2 7/8"

POWDER DRIVEN INTERNALLY THREADED STUD

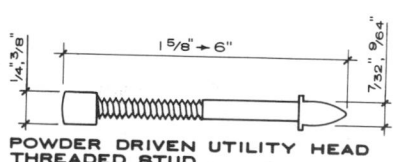

1 5/8" → 6"

POWDER DRIVEN UTILITY HEAD THREADED STUD

NOTE:

1. Thread sizes and lengths vary.

2. Hammer and power driven studs are intended for insertion into materials such as concrete, steel, etc.

3. Different stud heads and various attaching devices are available.

NAIL TYPE **		SIZE		MATERIAL
F ⸺⸺⸺⸺ D #14 GAUGE	BARBED NAILS	1/4" TO 1 1/2"		CEMENT COATED, BRASS, STEEL
LCSN ⸺⸺⸺⸺ D #14 GAUGE	CASING NAILS	2d TO 40d 6d TO 10d		BRIGHT, CEMENT COATED * CUPPED HEADS AVAILABLE IN ALUMINUM
O ALSO FLAT HEAD CS D #5 TO #10 GAUGE	CEMENT NAILS ALSO CALLED CONCRETE NAILS & HARDENED NAILS	1/2" TO 3"		SMOOTH, BRIGHT *OIL QUENCHED
LNF CUP HEAD AVAILABLE #15 TO #2 GAUGE	COMMON BRAD	2d TO 60d		BRIGHT—MAY BE SECURED WITH CUPPED HEAD, CEMENT COATED—USUALLY MADE IN HEAVY GAUGES
F	CUT COMMON NAILS OR CUT COMMON SPIKE	2d TO 60d 20d TO 100d		STEEL OR IRON * PLAIN OR ZINC COATED
LNF ⸺⸺⸺⸺ D GAUGE	COMMON NAILS (SHINGLE NAILS)	2d TO 60d		COPPER—CLAD
F ⸺⸺⸺⸺ D LIGHT GAUGE .095" HEAVY GAUGE .120"	COMMON BRASS WIRE NAILS	LIGHT GAUGE	1/2" 1" TO 3 1/2"	BRASS, ALUMINUM
		HEAVY GAUGE	3/4" – 6"	
F ⸺⸺⸺⸺ D .109 (ABOUT 12 GAUGE)	COMMON NAILS; (SHINGLE NAILS)	* 5/8" TO 6"		COPPER WIRE, ALUMINUM
F	STANDARD CUT NAILS (NON-FERROUS)	5/8" TO 6"		COPPER, MUNTZ METAL OR ZINC
F 2" LONG D #11 1/2 GAUGE	DOUBLE HEADED	*1 3/4", 2", *2 1/4", 2 1/2", *2 3/4", 3", 3 1/2", *4", *4 1/2"		BRIGHT, CEMENT COATED, MADE IN SEVERAL DESIGNS
CUPPED HEAD AVAILABLE D MADE IN 5 DIAMETERS	DOWEL PINS	5/8" TO 2"		BARBED – *CUPPED HEAD AVAILABLE
O D MADE IN 3 GAUGES	ESCUTCHEON PINS	1/4" TO 2"		BRIGHT STEEL, BRASS PLATED, BRASS, ALSO *NICKEL, SILVER, COPPER, ALUMINUM
F 6d – 2" D #10 GAUGE	FENCE NAILS	5d TO 20d		SMOOTH; BRIGHT, CEMENT COATED (GAUGE HEAVIER THAN COMMON)
LNF D #15 GAUGE	FINISHING NAIL, WIRE	2d TO 20d		SMOOTH; * CUPPED HEADS AVAILABLE (SMALLER GAUGE THAN USUAL COMMON BRAD)
	FINISHING NAILS	STANDARD FINE	3d TO 20d 6d TO 10d	CUT IRON AND STEEL
3d – 1 1/8" #15 & #16 GAUGE	FINE NAILS	*2d & 2d EX. FINE *3d & 3d EX. FINE		*BRIGHT – SMALLER GAUGE & HEADS THAN COMMON NAILS
PC B (ALSO WITH D. POINT) #14 GAUGE	FLOORING NAILS	*3d TO *20d 6d TO 20d		*BRIGHT & CEMENT COATED (DIFFERENT GAUGE) *CUPPED HEADS AVAILABLE
LNCS 6d – 2" D OR BLUNT D #11 GAUGE	FLOORING BRAD	6d TO 20d		SMOOTH; BRIGHT & CEMENT COATED CUPPED HEADS AVAILABLE

* NOT COVERED IN FEDERAL SPECIFICATIONS

** FOR LETTER CODE SEE FIRST PAGE OF THIS SERIE

NAIL TYPE **	SIZE		MATERIAL
NCSF 1⅛" NEEDLE #15 GAUGE — PARQUET FLOORING NAIL OR BRAD	1", 1⅛", 1¼"		SMOOTH OR BARBED
FLOORING NAILS	4d TO 10d		IRON OR STEEL (CUT)
OVAL, - ALSO CS HEAD 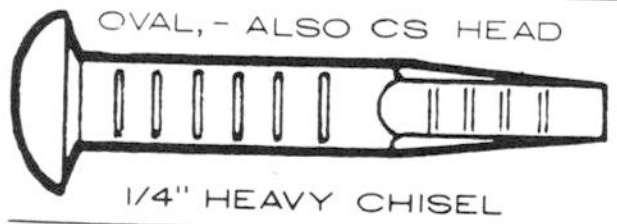 1/4" HEAVY CHISEL — HINGE NAILS	HEAVY: 1/4" TO 3/8" DIA. LIGHT-3/16" TO 1/4" DIA	1½" TO 4" LONG	SMOOTH, BRIGHT OR ANNEALED
OVAL LONG D 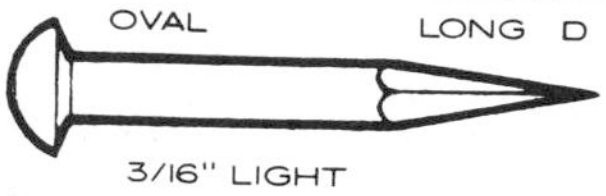 3/16" LIGHT — HINGE NAILS	HEAVY-1/4" DIA. LIGHT- 3/16" DIA.	1½" TO 3" ALSO TO *4"	SMOOTH, BRIGHT OR ANNEALED
F 3d-1⅛" D #15 GAUGE — LATH NAILS (WOOD)	2d, 2d LIGHT 3d 3d, LIGHT,3d HEAVY 4d.		BRIGHT (NOT RECOMMENDED) BLUED OR CEMENT COATED
F CHECKERED, OVAL CHISEL OR D 3/16"-1¼" GAUGE — GUTTER SPIKES	6" TO 10"		STEEL, ZINC COATED
O R #6½" GAUGE — HINGE NAILS	1½" TO 3"		STEEL, ZINC COATED
HOOK 1⅛" #12 GAUGE — LATH NAILS (METAL)	1⅛"		BRIGHT, BLUED, ZINC COATED, ANNEALED
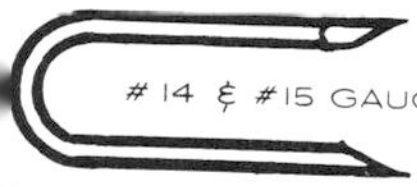 #14 & #15 GAUGE — LATH STAPLES	1" TO 1½"		BRIGHT, BLUED, ZINC COATED, ANNEALED
OFFSET F D #10 GAUGE 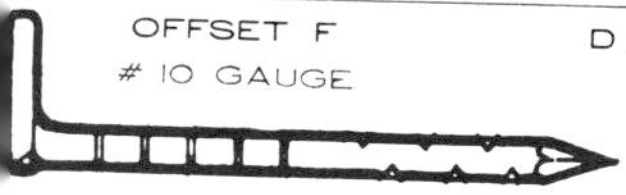 — * LATH OFFSET HEAD NAILS FOR SELF FURRING METAL LATH	1¼" TO 1¾" *		BRIGHT, ZINC COATED
F  #7-#9 GAUGE — MASONRY NAILS USED FOR FURRING STRIPS CLEATS, PLATES	1/2" TO 4"		HIGH CARBON STEEL, HEATED & TEMPERED
NCSF NEEDLE  #14 GAUGE — MOLDING NAILS (BRADS)	7/8" TO 1¼"		SMOOTH, BRIGHT OR CEMENT COATED
1/2" D 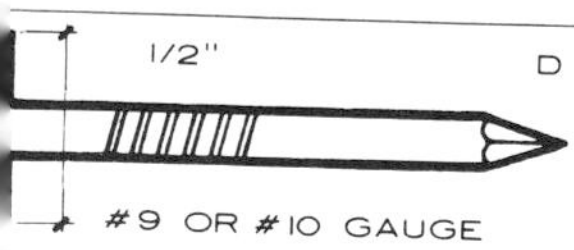 #9 OR #10 GAUGE — PLASTER-BOARD NAILS USED ALSO FOR WALL-BOARD ROCK LATH (5/16" HEAD)	1" TO 1¾" 1⅛" TO 1½"		* SMOOTH, BRIGHT OR CEMENT COATED, BLUED ALUMINUM
F D  #10 GAUGE — ROOFING NAILS (STANDARD)	3/4" TO 2"		BRIGHT, CEMENT COATED, ZINC COATED BARBED
F 1" SQ. CUP REINFORCED D  #12 GAUGE — ROOFING NAILS FOR BUILT-UP ROOFING	3/8" TO 2"		STEEL, ZINC COATED
UMBRELLA HEAD, FLAT HEAD AVAILABLE D  #9 TO #10 GAUGE — NEOPRENE WASHER ROOFING NAILS	1½" TO 2½"		STEEL, ZINC COATED
F 3/8" TO 1/2" D 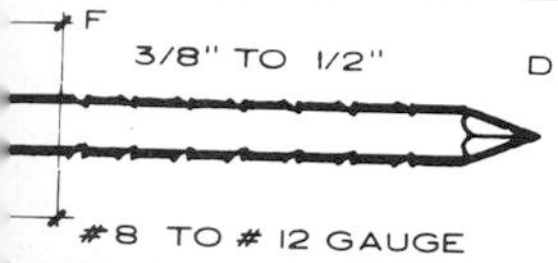 #8 TO #12 GAUGE — ROOFING NAILS LARGE HEAD	3/4" TO 1¾" ALSO *2" 3/4" TO 2½"		BARBED, BRIGHT OR ZINC COATED CHECKERED HEAD AVAILABLE ALUMINUM (ETCHED) NEOPRENE WASHER OPTIONAL

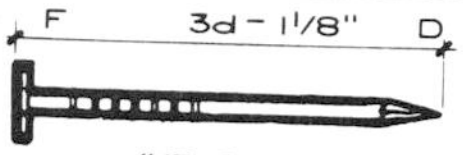

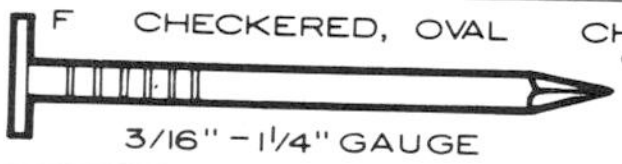

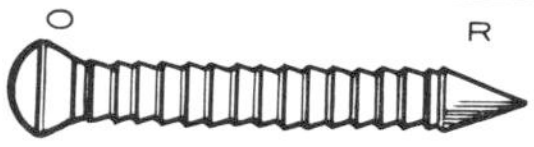

NOT COVERED IN FEDERAL SPECIFICATIONS

** FOR LETTER CODE, SEE THE PRECEDING PAGE

NAIL TYPE**	SIZE	MATERIAL
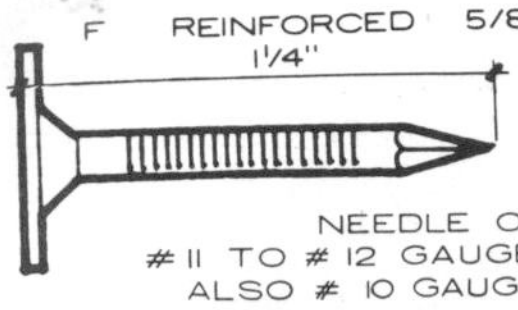 **F** REINFORCED 5/8" DIA. 1¼" **ROOFING NAILS LARGE HEAD** NEEDLE OR D # 11 TO # 12 GAUGE ALSO # 10 GAUGE	3/4" TO 1¼"	BRIGHT OR ZINC COATED
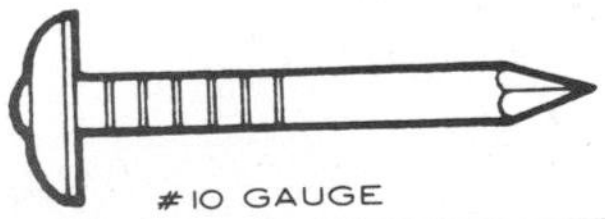 ***NON-LEAKING ROOFING NAIL** # 10 GAUGE	*1¾" TO 2"	*ZINC COATED, ALSO WITH LEAD HEADS
 **CUT SHEATHING NAILS**	3/4" TO 3"	COPPER OR MUNTZ METAL
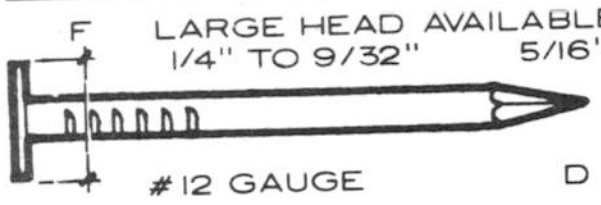 **F** LARGE HEAD AVAILABLE 1/4" TO 9/32" 5/16" DIA. **SHINGLE NAILS** # 12 GAUGE D	3d TO 6d 2d TO 6d	SMOOTH, BRIGHT, ZINC, CEMENT COATED, LIGHT AND HEAVY ALUMINUM
 **CUT SHINGLE NAILS**	2d TO 6d	IRON OR STEEL (CUT) PLAIN OR ZINC COATED
F D **SIDING NAILS** # 14 GAUGE	2d TO 40d 6d TO 10d	SMOOTH, BRIGHT OR CEMENT COATED SMALLER DIAMETER THAN COMMON NAILS * ALUMINUM
F D **SIDING NAILS USED FOR FENCES, TANKS, GATES, ETC.** # 11 GAUGE	2½" TO 3"	STEEL ZINC COATED
F 5/16" TO 3/8" **SLATING NAILS** SEVERAL GAUGES	3/8" HEAD — 1"TO 2" SMALL HEADS — 1"TO 2" COPPER WIRE — 7/8"-1½"	ZINC COATED, BRIGHT, CEMENT COATED, COPPER CLAD, COPPER
 **CUT SLATING NAILS, NON-FERROUS**	1¼" TO 2"	COPPER, ZINC OR MUNTZ METAL
 OVAL, SQUARE OR *ROUND HEAD CHISEL POINT 1/4" TO 5/8" SQ. **BARGE SPIKE, SQUARE**	3" TO 12" * ALSO 16"	PLAIN AND ZINC COATED USED FOR HARDWOOD
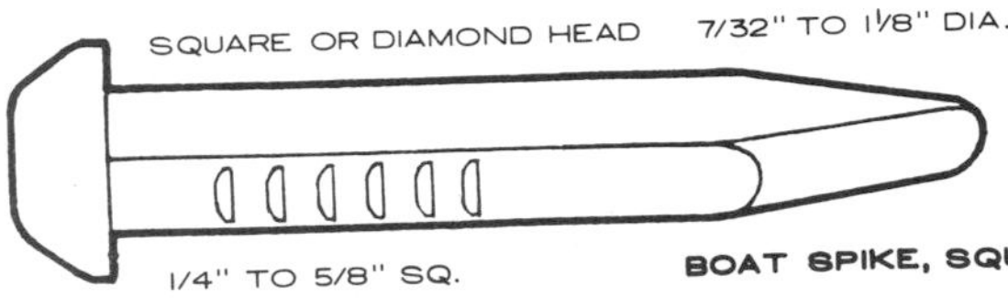 SQUARE OR DIAMOND HEAD 7/32" TO 1⅛" DIA. CHISEL POINT 1/4" TO 5/8" SQ. **BOAT SPIKE, SQUARE**	3" TO 12"	PLAIN AND ZINC COATED USED FOR HARD WOOD
 1" HEAD **ROOF DECK NAILS**	1" AND 1¾"	GALVANIZED - NAILS STEEL TUBE
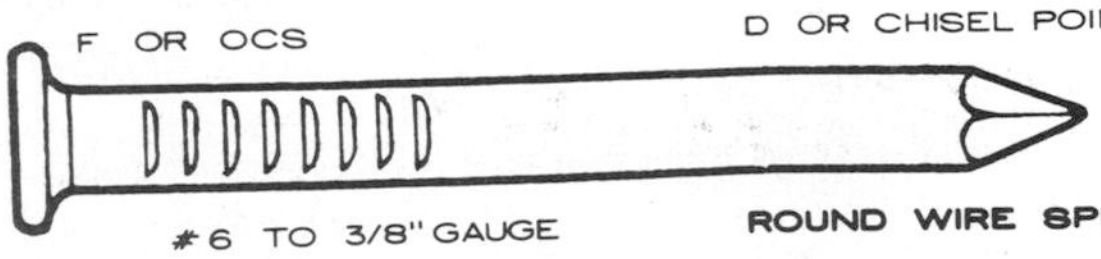 F OR OCS D OR CHISEL POINT # 6 TO 3/8" GAUGE **ROUND WIRE SPIKES**	10d TO 60d & 7" TO 12" *ALSO 16"	SMOOTH, BRIGHT OR ZINC COATED

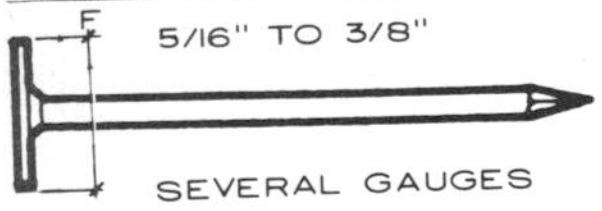

* NOT COVERED IN FEDERAL SPECIFICATIONS

** FOR LETTER CODE, SEE A PRECEDING PAGE IN THIS SERI

SCREW & BOLT LENGTHS (IN INCHES)

DIAMETER (IN INCHES)	CAP SCREWS — BUTTON HEAD	FLAT HEAD	HEXAGON HEAD	FILLISTER HEAD	BOLTS — MACHINE BOLT	CARRIAGE BOLT
1/4	1/2 – 2 1/4		1/2 – 3 1/2	3/4 – 3		
5/16	1/2 – 2 3/4		1/2 – 3 1/2	3/4 – 3 3/4	1/2 – 8	3/4 – 8
3/8		5/8 – 3	1/2 – 4	3/4 – 3 1/2	1/2 – 8	3/4 – 8
7/16		3/4 – 3	3/4 – 4	3/4 – 3 3/4	3/4 – 12	3/4 – 12
1/2		3/4 – 4	3/4 – 4 1/2	3/4 – 4	3/4 – 12	3/4 – 12
9/16		1 – 4	1 – 4 1/2	1 – 4	3/4 – 24	1 – 12
5/8		1 – 4	1 – 5	1 – 4	1 – 30	1 – 20
3/4		1 – 4	1 1/4 – 5	1 1/2 – 4 1/2	1 – 30	1 – 20
7/8			2 – 6	1 1/2 – 4 1/2	1 – 30	1 – 20
1			2 – 6	1 3/4 – 5	1 1/2 – 30	1 1/2 – 30

Length intervals = 1/8" increments up to 1", 1/4" increments from 1 1/4" to 4", 1/2" increments from 4 1/2" to 6".

Length intervals = 1/4" increments up to 6", 1/2" increments from 6 1/2" to 12", 1" increments over 12".

SHEET METAL & THREADING SCREWS

SHEET METAL GIMLET POINT. Hardened, self-tapping. Used in 28 to 6 gauge sheet metal; aluminum, plastic, slate, etc. Usual head types.

SHEET METAL BLUNT POINT. Hardened, self-tapping. Used in 28 to 18 gauge sheet metal. Made in 4 to 14 sizes and usual heads.

THREAD CUTTING-CUTTING SLOT. Hardened. Used in metals up to 1/4" thick. Sizes: 4 to 5/16", in usual head types. (Flat, oval, round, etc.).

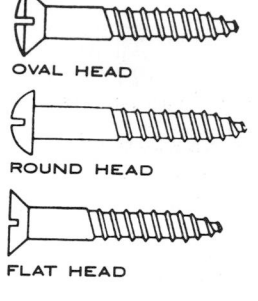

OVAL HEAD
ROUND HEAD
FLAT HEAD

WOOD SCREWS (IN INS.)

DIAM.	DECI. EQUIV.	LENGTH
0	.060	1/4 – 3/8
1	.073	1/4 – 1/2
2	.086	1/4 – 3/4
3	.099	1/4 – 1
4	.112	1/4 – 1 1/2
5	.125	3/8 – 1 1/2
6	.138	3/8 – 2 1/2
7	.151	3/8 – 2 1/2
8	.164	3/8 – 3
9	.177	1/2 – 3
10	.190	1/2 – 3 1/2
11	.203	5/8 – 3 1/2
12	.216	5/8 – 4
14	.242	3/4 – 5
16	.268	1 – 5
18	.294	1 1/4 – 5
20	.320	1 1/2 – 5
24	.372	3 – 5

Length intervals = 1/8" increments up to 1", 1/4" increments from 1 1/4" to 3", 1/2" increments from 3 1/2" to 5".

MACHINE SCREW & STOVE BOLT (IN INCHES)

STOVE BOLT DIAMETER (IN INS)	MACHINE SCREW DIAMETER	ROUND HEAD	FLAT HEAD	FILLISTER HEAD	OVAL HEAD	OVEN HEAD
	2	1/8 – 7/8		1/8 – 7/8		
	3	1/8 – 7/8		1/8 – 7/8		
	4	1/8 – 1 1/2	40 N.C.	1/8 – 1 1/2		
	4	1/8 – 1 1/2	36 N.C.	1/8 – 1 1/2		1/8 – 3/4
1/8	5	1/8 – 2		1/8 – 2		3/8 – 2
	6	1/8 – 2		1/8 – 2		1/8 – 1
5/32	8	3/16 – 3		3/16 – 3		3/16 – 2
3/16	10	3/16 – 6		3/16 – 3		1/4 – 6
	12	1/4 – 3		1/4 – 3		
1/4	1/4	5/16 – 6		5/16 – 3		3/8 – 6
5/16	5/16	3/8 – 6		3/8 – 3		3/4 – 6
3/8	3/8	1/2 – 5		1/2 – 3		3/4 – 5
1/2	1/2	1 – 4				

Length intervals = 1/16" increments up to 1/2", 1/8" increments from 5/8" to 1 1/4", 1/4" increments from 1 1/2" to 3", 1/2" increments from 3 1/2" to 6".

LAG BOLT (IN INCHES)

DIAM. (IN INS)	DECI. EQUIV.	LENGTH
1/4	.250	1 – 6
5/16	.313	1 – 10
3/8	.375	1 – 12
7/16	.438	1 – 12
1/2	.500	1 – 12
5/8	.625	1 1/2 – 16
3/4	.750	1 1/2 – 16
7/8	.875	2 – 16
1	1.00	2 – 16

Length intervals = 1/2" increments up to 8", 1" increments over 8".

NUTS

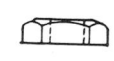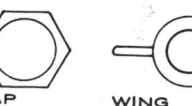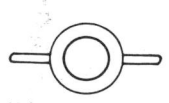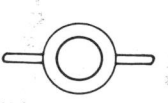

SQUARE HEXAGON CAP WING

HEADS

PHILLIPS

SLOTTED

NUT SIZES

Square and hexagon head nuts are available for ...screws and bolts listed; Cap nuts for all except nos. 2, 3, 4 (40 N.C. only), 5, and 9/16". ...ng nuts for all except nos. 2, 3, 4 (40 N.C.), 9/16", 5/8", 3/4", 7/8" and 1".

American Standard sizes by the American Institute of Bolt, Nut and Rivet Manufacturers. Many of listed items also stocked in aluminum, brass, copper, stainless steel, monel and bronze. Stove bolts have wider tolerances than machine screws.

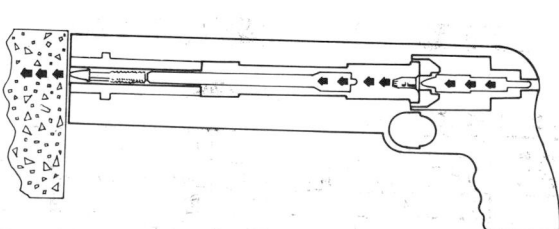

POWER ACTUATED SETTING DEVICE
LOW VELOCITY PRINCIPLE

The energy from a special industrial powder charge actuates a piston inside the tool barrel. The actuated piston sets drive pins instantly at low velocity. Drilling is eliminated.

SQUARE HEAD **HEADLESS**

SET SCREWS

Headless type with socket or slotted top made in sizes 4 to $1/2''$; in $1/2''$ to 5'' lengths.

Square head sizes $1/4''$ to 1''; $1/2''$ to 5'' lengths.

SOCKET TOP

SLOTTED TOP

CUT
Of steel and non-ferrous metals.

WASHERS

All types for bolts and screws of all sizes.

O.G. CAST
Made of cast metal.

SPRING LOCK
Of steel, monel metal, bronze and stainless steel.

EXTERNAL TOOTH ROCK
Of steel, monel metal, bronze, beryllium copper and stainless steel.

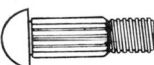

DARDELET "SELF-LOCKING" RIVET BOLT (IN INCHES)

DIAM.	LENGTH	DIAM.	LENGTH
$3/8$	$1\,1/8 \rightarrow 2\,1/4$	$3/4$	$1\,1/2 \rightarrow 4\,1/8$
$1/2$	$1\,1/4 \rightarrow 2\,3/4$	$7/8$	$1\,11/16 \rightarrow 5\,1/4$
$5/8$	$1\,3/8 \rightarrow 3\,5/8$	1	$2\,3/16 \rightarrow 5\,3/8$

Length intervals: $1/2''$ increments to 4'', 1'' increments over 4''.

ROUND **TRUSS** **FLAT** **COUNTER SUNK** **PAN**

RIVETS

Standard Rivets available with solid, tubular and split shanks of steel, brass, copper, aluminum, monel metal and stainless-steel; in diameters of $1/8''$ up to $7/16''$ and lengths of $3/16''$ up to 4 inches.

SPLIT RING (IN INCHES)

INSIDE DIAMETER	$2\,1/2$	4
DEPTH	$3/4$	1
BOLT DIAMETER	$1/2$	$3/4$
LUMBER MIN. DIMS.	RING-1 FACE	$1 \times 3\,5/8$	$1 \times 5\,1/2$
	RING-2 FACE	$1\,5/8 \times 3\,5/8$	$1\,5/8 \times 5\,1/2$

Made from SAE 1010 carbon steel.

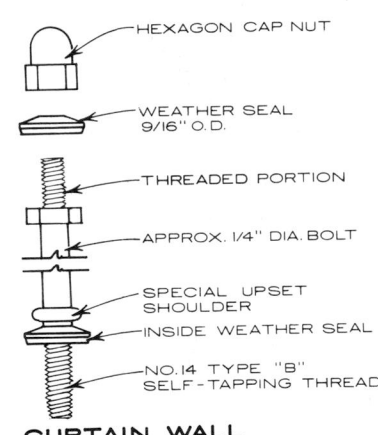

— HEXAGON CAP NUT
— WEATHER SEAL 9/16" O.D.
— THREADED PORTION
— APPROX. 1/4" DIA. BOLT
— SPECIAL UPSET SHOULDER
— INSIDE WEATHER SEAL
— NO.14 TYPE "B" SELF-TAPPING THREAD

CURTAIN WALL TOPSEAL FASTENER

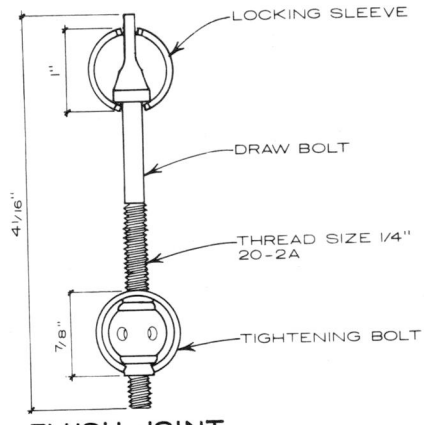

— LOCKING SLEEVE
— DRAW BOLT
— THREAD SIZE 1/4" 20-2A
— TIGHTENING BOLT
1"
4 1/16"
7/8"

FLUSH JOINT WOOD FASTENER

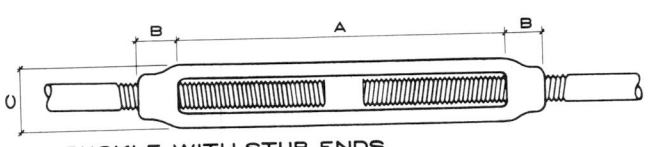

B A B

TURNBUCKLE WITH STUB ENDS

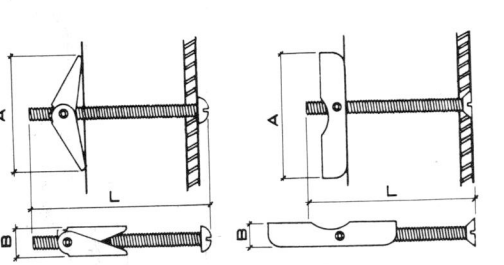

A L B

SPRING WING **TUMBLE** **RIVETED TUMBLE**

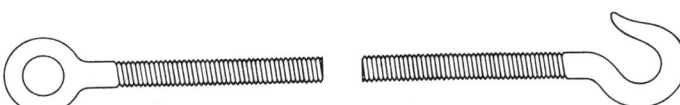

EYE **HOOK**

TURNBUCKLES (IN INCHES)

DIAMETER	$1/4$	$5/16$	$3/8$	$1/2$	$5/8$	$3/4$	$7/8$	1
DECI. EQUIV.	.250	.313	.375	.500	.625	.750	.875	1.00
A	4	$4\,1/2$	6''	6''	6''	6''	6''	6''
				9''	9''	9''		
				12''	12''	12''	12''	12''
B	$7/16$	$1/2$	$9/16$	$3/4$	$29/32$	$1\,1/16$	$1\,7/32$	$1\,3/8$
C	$3/4$	$7/8$	$31/32$	$1\,7/32$	$1\,1/2$	$1\,23/32$	$1\,7/8$	$2\,1/32$

DIAMETERS OVER 1'' AVAILABLE, NOT ALWAYS STOCKED.

TOGGLE BOLTS (IN INCHES)

DIAMETER		$1/8$	$5/32$	$3/16$	$1/4$	$5/16$	$3/8$	$1/2$
DECIMAL EQUIV.		.138	.164	.190	.250	.313	.375	.500
SPRING WING	A	1.438	1.875	1.875	2.063	2.750	2.875	4.625
	B	.375	.500	.500	.688	.875	1.000	1.250
	L	2-4	$2\,1/2$-4	2-6	$2\,1/2$-6	3-6	3-6	4-6
TUMBLE	A	1.250	2.000	2.000	2.250	2.750	2.750	
	B	.375	.500	.500	.688	.875	.875	
	L	2-4	$2\,1/2$-4	3-6	3-6	3-6	3-6	
RIVETED TUMBLE	A		2.000	2.000	2.250	2.750	2.750	3.375
	B		.375	.375	.500	.625	.688	.875
	L		$2\,1/2$-4	3-6	3-6	3-6	3-6	3-6

MACHINE BOLT ANCHORS & SHIELDS (IN INCHES)

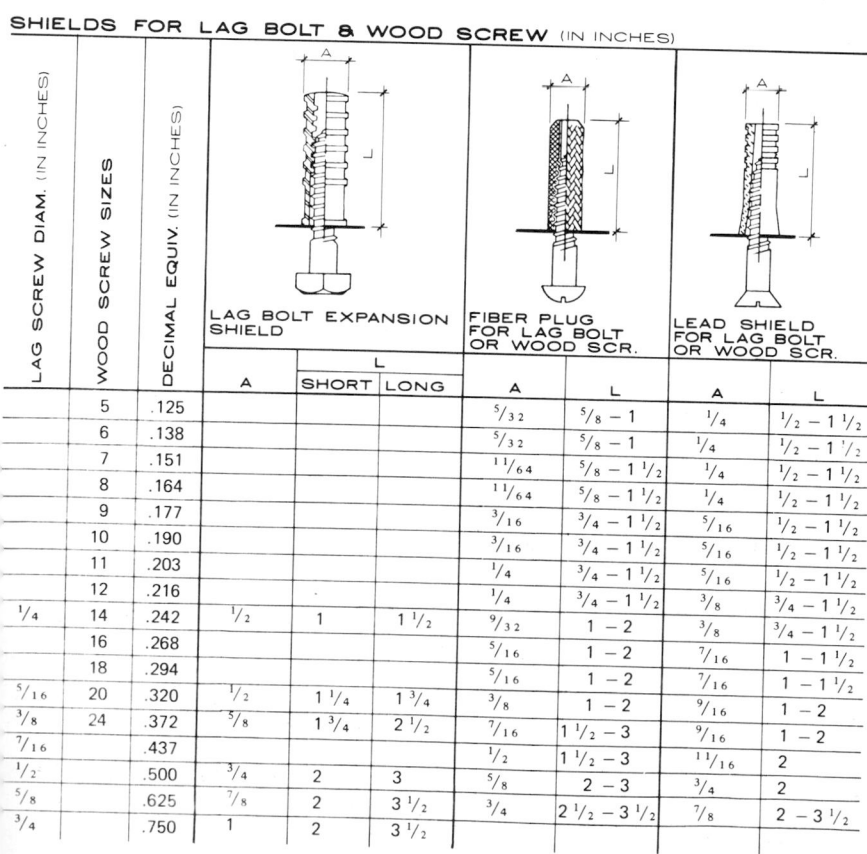

BOLT DIAM	THDS PER INCH	DECIMAL EQUIV. (IN INCHES)	SINGLE EXPANDING ANCHOR A	SINGLE EXPANDING ANCHOR L	MULTIPLE EXPANDING ANCHOR A	MULTIPLE EXPANDING ANCHOR L UNITS 1	MULTIPLE EXPANDING ANCHOR L UNITS 2	MULTIPLE EXPANDING ANCHOR L UNITS 3	SINGLE EXPANDING ANCHOR A	SINGLE EXPANDING ANCHOR L	DOUBLE ACTING SHIELD A	DOUBLE ACTING SHIELD L	MULTIPLE EXPANDING ANCHOR A	MULTIPLE EXPANDING ANCHOR L UNITS 1	MULTIPLE EXPANDING ANCHOR L UNITS 2
6	32	.138	1/4	3/8											
8	32	.164	5/16	1/2											
10	24	.190	3/8	5/8									1/2	7/8	1 1/8
12	24	.216	1/2	7/8											
1/4	20	.250	1/2	7/8					3/8	3/8	1/2	1 5/8	5/8	1 1/16	1 5/8
5/16	18	.312	5/8	1					1/2	1	5/8	1 7/8	5/8	1 1/16	1 5/8
3/8	16	.375	3/4	1 1/4	3/4	1 5/8	2 7/8	4 1/8	9/16	1 1/8	3/4	2 1/8	13/16	1 1/2	2 1/4
7/16	14	.437	7/8	1 1/2	1	1 3/4	3	4 1/4			7/8	2 3/8			
1/2	13	.500	7/8	1 1/2	1	1 3/4	3	4 1/4	3/4	1 1/2	7/8	2 3/8	1	1 3/4	2 5/8
5/8	11	.625	1 1/8	2	1 1/4	2 1/2	4 1/2	6 1/2	1	1 3/4	1	2 7/8	1 1/8	1 7/8	2 7/8
3/4	10	.750	1 1/4	2 1/4	1 1/2	2 3/4	4 3/4	6 7/8	1 1/8	2 1/4	1 1/4	4	1 3/8	2 1/2	3 3/4
7/8	9	.875	1 1/2	2 3/4	1 3/4	4	7	10			1 1/2	4 1/2	1 1/2	2 3/4	3 3/4
1	8	1.00	1 3/4	3 1/2	1 3/4	4	7	10	1 5/8	3	1 3/4	4 7/8	1 5/8	3 1/4	4 7/8

NOTE:

1. * Extension sleeve for deep setting.
2. Expansion shields and anchors shown are representative of many types, some of which may be used in single or multiple units.

Many are threaded for use with the head of the screw outside, some with the head inside and some types require setting tools to install.

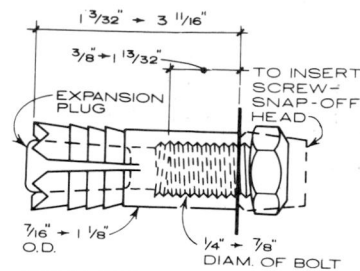

SELF DRILLING EXPANSION ANCHOR
(SNAP-OFF TYPE)

NOTE:

1. Refer to manufacturers for size variations within the limits shown, and for different types of bolts.
2. The anchor is made of case hardened steel and drawn carburizing steel.

SHIELDS FOR LAG BOLT & WOOD SCREW (IN INCHES)

LAG SCREW DIAM. (IN INCHES)	WOOD SCREW SIZES	DECIMAL EQUIV. (IN INCHES)	LAG BOLT EXPANSION SHIELD A	LAG BOLT EXPANSION SHIELD L SHORT	LAG BOLT EXPANSION SHIELD L LONG	FIBER PLUG FOR LAG BOLT OR WOOD SCR. A	FIBER PLUG FOR LAG BOLT OR WOOD SCR. L	LEAD SHIELD FOR LAG BOLT OR WOOD SCR. A	LEAD SHIELD FOR LAG BOLT OR WOOD SCR. L
	5	.125				5/32	5/8 - 1	1/4	1/2 - 1 1/2
	6	.138				5/32	5/8 - 1	1/4	1/2 - 1 1/2
	7	.151				11/64	5/8 - 1 1/2	1/4	1/2 - 1 1/2
	8	.164				11/64	5/8 - 1 1/2	1/4	1/2 - 1 1/2
	9	.177				3/16	3/4 - 1 1/2	5/16	1/2 - 1 1/2
	10	.190				3/16	3/4 - 1 1/2	5/16	1/2 - 1 1/2
	11	.203				1/4	3/4 - 1 1/2	5/16	1/2 - 1 1/2
	12	.216				1/4	3/4 - 1 1/2	3/8	3/4 - 1 1/2
1/4	14	.242	1/2	1	1 1/2	9/32	1 - 2	3/8	3/4 - 1 1/2
	16	.268				5/16	1 - 2	7/16	1 - 1 1/2
	18	.294				5/16	1 - 2	7/16	1 - 1 1/2
5/16	20	.320	1/2	1 1/4	1 3/4	3/8	1 - 2	9/16	1 - 2
3/8	24	.372	5/8	1 3/4	2 1/2	7/16	1 1/2 - 3	9/16	1 - 2
7/16		.437				1/2	1 1/2 - 3	11/16	2
1/2		.500	3/4	2	3	5/8	2 - 3	3/4	2
5/8		.625	7/8	2	3 1/2	3/4	2 1/2 - 3 1/2	7/8	2 - 3 1/2
3/4		.750	1	2	3 1/2				

NOTE:
For revised standard nomenclature for structural shapes see AISC Manual of Steel Construction 7th edition.

DIMENSIONS OF WF, B, JR, M, I STEEL SHAPES

D	WT.	d	b	b/2 + 2	b/2 + 5
	300	36 3/4	16 5/8		
	280	36 1/2	16 5/8	10 3/8	13 3/8
	260	36 1/4	16 1/2		
	245	36	16 1/2	10 1/4	13 1/4
36	230	35 7/8	16 1/2		
WF	194	36 1/2	12 1/8		
	182	36 3/8	12 1/8	8 1/8	11 1/8
	170	36 1/8	12		
	160	36	12		
	150	35 7/8	12	8	11
	135	35 1/2	12		
	240	33 1/2	15 7/8	10	13
	220	33 1/4	15 3/4		
33	200	33	15 3/4	9 7/8	12 7/8
WF	152	33 1/2	11 5/8	7 7/8	10 7/8
	141	33 3/4	11 1/2		
	130	33 1/8	11 1/2	7 3/4	10 3/4
	118	32 7/8	11 1/2		
	210	30 3/8	15 1/8	9 5/8	12 5/8
	190	30 1/8	15		
	172	29 7/8	15	9 1/2	12 1/2
30	132	30 1/4	10 1/2		
WF	124	30 1/8	10 1/2		
	116	30	10 1/2	7 1/4	10 1/4
	108	29 7/8	10 1/2		
	99	29 5/8	10 1/2		
	177	27 1/4	14 1/8	9 1/8	12 1/8
	160	27 1/8	14		
27	145	26 7/8	14	9	12
WF	114	27 1/4	10 1/8	7 1/8	10 1/8
	102	27 1/8	10		
	94	26 7/8	10	7	10
	84	26 3/4	10		
	160	24 3/4	14 1/8	9 1/8	12 1/8
	145	24 1/2	14		
	130	24 1/4	14	9	12
	120	24 1/4	12 1/8	8 1/8	11 1/8
24	110	24 1/8	12		
WF	100	24	12	8	11
	94	24 1/4	9		
	84	24 1/8	9		
	76	23 7/8	9	6 1/2	9 1/2
	68	23 3/4	9		
24	61	23 3/4	7		
B	55	23 1/2	7	5 1/2	8 1/2
	142	21 1/2	13 1/8	8 5/8	11 5/8
	127	21 1/4	13		
	112	21	13	8 1/2	11 1/2
21	96	21 1/8	9		
WF	82	20 7/8	9	6 1/2	9 1/2
	73	21 1/4	8 1/4		
	68	21 1/8	8 1/4		
	62	21	8 1/4	6 1/8	9 1/8
	55	20 3/4	8 1/4		
21	49	20 7/8	6 1/2		
B	44	20 5/8	6 1/2	5 1/4	8 1/4
	114	18 1/2	11 7/8	8	11
	105	18 3/8	11 3/4		
18	96	18 1/8	11 3/4	7 7/8	10 7/8
WF	85	18 3/8	8 7/8	6 1/2	9 1/2
	77	18 1/8	8 3/4		
	70	18	8 3/4	6 3/8	9 3/8
	64	17 7/8	8 3/4		

D	WT.	d	b	b/2 + 2	b/2 + 5
	60	18 1/4	7 1/2		
18	55	18 1/8	7 1/2		
WF	50	18	7 1/2	5	8
	45	17 7/8	7 1/2		
18	40	17 7/8	6		
B	35	17 3/4	6	5	8
	96	16 3/8	11 1/2		
	88	16 1/8	11 1/2	7 3/4	10 3/4
	78	16 3/8	8 5/8	6 3/8	9 3/8
16	71	16 1/8	8 1/2		
WF	64	16	8 1/2	6 1/4	9 1/4
	58	15 7/8	8 1/2		
	50	16 1/4	7 1/8	5 5/8	8 5/8
	45	16 1/8	7		
	40	16	7	5 1/2	8 1/2
	36	15 7/8	7		
16	31	15 7/8	5 1/2		
B	26	15 5/8	5 1/2	4 3/4	7 3/4
	730	22 1/2	17 7/8	11	14
	665	21 5/8	17 5/8	10 7/8	13 7/8
	605	21	17 3/8	10 3/4	13 3/4
	550	20 1/4	17 1/4	10 5/8	13 5/8
	500	19 5/8	17		
	455	19	16 7/8	10 1/2	13 1/2
	426	18 3/4	16 3/4		
	398	18 1/4	16 5/8	10 3/8	13 3/8
	370	18	16 1/2		
	342	17 1/2	16 3/8	10 1/4	13 1/4
	320	16 3/4	16 3/4	10 3/8	13 3/8
	314	17 1/4	16 1/4		
	287	16 3/4	16 1/8	10 1/8	13 1/8
	264	16 1/2	16		
	246	16 1/4	16		
	237	16 1/8	15 7/8	10	13
	228	16	15 7/8		
	219	15 7/8	15 7/8		
	211	15 3/4	15 3/4		
14	202	15 5/8	15 3/4		
WF	193	15 1/2	15 3/4		
	184	15 3/8	15 5/8	9	12
	176	15 1/4	15 5/8		
	167	15 1/8	15 5/8		
	158	15	15 1/2		
	150	14 7/8	15 1/2	9	12
	142	14 3/4	15 1/2		
	136	14 3/4	14 3/4		
	127	14 5/8	14 3/4		
	119	14 1/2	14 5/8	9 3/8	12 3/8
	111	14 3/8	14 5/8		
	103	14 1/4	14 5/8		
	95	14 1/8	14 1/2		
	87	14	14 1/2	9 1/4	12 1/4
	84	14 1/8	12		
	78	14	12	8	11
	74	14 1/4	10 1/8	7 1/8	10 1/8
	68	14	10		
	61	13 7/8	10	7	10
	53	14	8		
	48	13 3/4	8	6	9
	43	13 5/8	8		
	38	14 1/8	6 3/4		
	34	14	6 3/4	5 3/8	8 3/8
	30	13 7/8	6 3/4		

D	WT.	d	b	b/2 + 2	b/2 + 5
14	26	13 7/8	5		
B	22	13 3/4	5	4 1/2	7 1/2
	17.2	14	4	4	7
	190	14 3/8	12 5/8	8 3/8	11 3/8
	161	13 7/8	12 1/2		
	133	13 3/8	12 3/8	8 1/4	11 1/4
	120	13 1/8	12 3/8		
	106	12 7/8	12 1/4		
	99	12 3/4	12 1/4		
	92	12 5/8	12 1/8	8 1/8	11 1/8
	85	12 1/2	12 1/8		
	79	12 3/8	12 1/8		
	72	12 1/4	12		
	65	12 1/8	12	8	11
	58	12 1/4	10		
	53	12	10	7	10
	50	12 1/4	8 1/8	6 1/8	9 1/8
	45	12	8		
	40	12	8	6	9
	36	12 1/4	6 5/8	5 3/8	8 3/8
	31	12 1/8	6 1/2		
	27	12	6 1/2	5 1/4	8 1/4
	22	12 1/4	4		
12	19	12 1/8	4		
B	16.5	12	4	4	7
	14	11 7/8	4		
12 JR	11.8	12	3	3 1/2	6 1/2
	112	11 3/8	10 3/8		
	100	11 1/8	10 3/8	7 1/4	10 1/4
	89	10 7/8	10 1/4		
	77	10 5/8	10 1/4		
	72	10 1/2	10 1/8	7 1/8	10 1/8
	66	10 3/8	10 1/8		
10	60	10 1/4	10 1/8		
WF	54	10 1/8	10		
	49	10	10	7	10
	45	10 1/8	8		
	39	10	8	6	9
	33	9 3/4	8		
	29	10 1/4	5 3/4		
	25	10 1/8	5 3/4	4 7/8	7 7/8
	21	9 7/8	5 3/4		
10	29.1	9 7/8	5 15/16	5	8
M	22.9	9 7/8	5 3/4		
	21	9 7/8	5 3/4	4 7/8	7 7/8
	19	10 1/4	4		
10	17	10 1/8	4		
B	15	10	4	4	7
	11.5	9 7/8	4		
10 JR	9.0	10	2 3/4	3 3/8	6 3/8
	67	9	8 1/4		
	58	8 3/4	8 1/4		
	48	8 1/2	8 1/8	6 1/8	9 1/8
8	40	8 1/4	8 1/8		
WF	35	8 1/8	8		
	31	8	8	6	9
	28	8	6 1/2		
	24	7 7/8	6 1/2	5 1/4	8 1/4
	20	8 1/8	5 1/4		
	17	8	5 1/4	4 5/8	7 5/8
8	15	8 1/8	4		
B	13	8	4	4	7
	10	7 7/8	4		

D	WT.	d	b	b/2 + 2	b/2 + 5
	34.3	8	8		
	32.6	8	8	6	9
	28	8	6 5/8	5 3/8	8 3/8
	24	8	6 1/2	5 1/4	8 1/4
	22.5	8	5 3/8		
	20	8	5 3/8	4 3/4	7 3/4
	18.5	8	5 1/4		
	17	8	5 1/4	4 5/8	7 5/8
8 JR	6.5	8	2 1/4	3 1/8	6 1/8
7 JR	5.5	7	2 1/8	3 1/8	6 1/8
6	25	6 3/8	6		
WF	20	6 1/4	6	5	8
	15.5	6	6		
6	25	6	6	5	8
M	22.5	6	6 1/8	5 1/8	8 1/8
	20	6	6	5	8
6	16	6 1/4	4		
B	12	6	4	4	7
	8.5	5 7/8	4		
6 JR	4.4	6	1 7/8	3	6
5 M	18.9	5	5	4 1/2	7 1/2
5	18.5	5 1/8	5		
WF	16	5	5	4 1/2	7
4 WF	13	4 1/8	4	4	7
4 M	13	4	4	4	7
	120	24	8		
24	105.9	24	7 7/8	6	9
I	100	24	7 1/4		
	90	24	7 1/8	5 5/8	8 5/8
	79.9	24	7	5 1/2	8 1/2
	95	20	7 1/4	5 5/8	8 5/8
20	85	20	7	5 1/2	8 1/2
I	75	20	6 3/8	5 1/4	8 1/4
	65.4	20	6 1/4	5 1/8	8 1/8
18	70	18	6 1/4	5 1/8	8 1/8
I	54.7	18	6	5	8
15	50	15	5 5/8	4 7/8	7 7/8
I	42.9	15	5 1/2	4 3/4	7 3/4
	50	12	5 1/2	4 3/4	7 3/4
12	40.8	12	5 1/2		
I	35	12	5 1/8	4 5/8	7 5/8
	31.8	12	5	4 1/2	7 1/2
10	35	10	5	4 1/2	7 1/2
I	25.4	10	4 5/8	4 3/8	7 3/8
8	23	8	4 1/8	4 1/8	7 1/8
I	18.4	8	4	4	7
7	20	7	3 7/8	4	7
I	15.3	7	3 5/8	3 7/8	6 7/8
6	17.25	6	3 5/8	3 7/8	6 7/8
I	12.5	6	3 3/8	3 3/4	6 3/4
5	14.75	5	3 1/4	3 5/8	6 5/8
I	10	5	3	3 1/2	6 1/2
4	9.5	4	2 3/4		
I	7.7	4	2 5/8	3 3/8	6 3/8
3	7.5	3	2 1/2		
I	5.7	3	2 3/8	3 1/4	6 1/4

D = NOMINAL DEPTH IN INCHES
WT = WEIGHT IN LBS. PER FOOT
d = ACTUAL DEPTH IN INCHES
b = FLANGE WIDTH IN INCHES

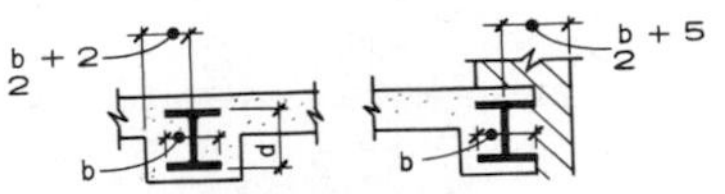

WF, B, JR, M, I SHAPES

H. Thompson, P. E.; Thompson & Czark; East Meadow, Long Island, New York

AMERICAN STANDARD STEEL CHANNEL SHAPES [

D	WT	d	b	D	WT	d	b
15 [	50	15	$3\frac{3}{4}$	8 [	18.75	8	$2\frac{1}{2}$
	40	15	$3\frac{1}{2}$		13.75	8	$2\frac{3}{8}$
	33.9	15	$3\frac{3}{8}$		11.5	8	$2\frac{1}{4}$
12 [	30	12	$3\frac{1}{8}$		8.5	8	$1\frac{7}{8}$
	25	12	3	7 [	14.75	7	$2\frac{1}{4}$
	20.7	12	3		12.25	7	$2\frac{1}{4}$
12 JR [	10.6	12	$1\frac{1}{2}$		9.8	7	$2\frac{1}{8}$
10 [	30	10	3	6 [	13	6	$2\frac{1}{8}$
	25	10	$2\frac{7}{8}$		10.5	6	2
	20	10	$2\frac{3}{4}$		8.2	6	$1\frac{7}{8}$
	15.3	10	$2\frac{5}{8}$	5 [	9	5	$1\frac{7}{8}$
10 JR [	8.4	10	$1\frac{1}{2}$		6.7	5	$1\frac{3}{4}$
	6.5	10	$1\frac{1}{8}$	4 [	7.25	4	$1\frac{3}{4}$
9 [	20	9	$2\frac{5}{8}$		5.4	4	$1\frac{5}{8}$
	15	9	$2\frac{1}{2}$	3 [	6	3	$1\frac{5}{8}$
	13.4	9	$2\frac{3}{8}$		5	3	$1\frac{1}{2}$
					4.1	3	$1\frac{3}{8}$

CAR AND SHIPBUILDING STEEL CHANNEL SHAPES [

D	WT	d	b	D	WT	d	b
18 [	58	18	$4\frac{1}{4}$	10 [	25.3	10	$3\frac{1}{2}$
	51.9	18	$4\frac{1}{8}$		21.9	10	$3\frac{1}{2}$
	45.8	18	4	9 [	25.4	9	$3\frac{1}{2}$
	42.7	18	4		23.9	9	$3\frac{1}{2}$
13 [	50	13	$4\frac{3}{8}$	8 [	22.8	8	$3\frac{1}{2}$
	40	13	$4\frac{1}{8}$		21.4	8	3
	35	13	$4\frac{1}{8}$		20	8	7
	31.8	13	4		18.7	8	3
12 [	50	12	$4\frac{1}{8}$	7 [	22.7	7	$3\frac{5}{8}$
	45	12	4		19.1	7	$3\frac{1}{2}$
	40	12	$3\frac{7}{8}$		17.6	7	3
	35	12	$3\frac{3}{4}$	6 [	18	6	$3\frac{1}{2}$
	37	12	$3\frac{5}{8}$		15.3	6	$3\frac{1}{2}$
	32.9	12	$3\frac{1}{2}$		16.3	6	3
	30.9	12	$3\frac{1}{2}$		15.1	6	3
10 [	41.1	10	$4\frac{5}{16}$		12	6	$2\frac{1}{2}$
	33.6	10	$4\frac{1}{8}$	4 [	13.8	4	$2\frac{1}{2}$
	28.5	10	4	3 [	7.6	3	$2\frac{1}{2}$
	28.3	10	$3\frac{1}{2}$		9.0	3	$2\frac{5}{16}$
	24.9	10	$3\frac{3}{8}$		7.1	3	2

EQUAL LEG STEEL ANGLE SECTIONS ∟

ANGLE LEG	AVAILABLE THICKNESS EXCEPT AS NOTED THUS												
	$1\frac{1}{8}$	1	$\frac{7}{8}$	$\frac{3}{4}$	$\frac{5}{8}$	$\frac{9}{16}$	$\frac{1}{2}$	$\frac{7}{16}$	$\frac{3}{8}$	$\frac{5}{16}$	$\frac{1}{4}$	$\frac{3}{16}$	$\frac{1}{8}$
8 × 8													
6 × 6													
5 × 5													
4 × 4													
$3\frac{1}{2}$ × $3\frac{1}{2}$													
3 × 3													
$2\frac{1}{2}$ × $2\frac{1}{2}$													
2 × 2													
$1\frac{3}{4}$ × $1\frac{3}{4}$													
$1\frac{1}{2}$ × $1\frac{1}{2}$													
$1\frac{1}{4}$ × $1\frac{1}{4}$													
1 × 1													

UNEQUAL LEG STEEL ANGLE SECTIONS ∟

ANGLE LEG	AVAILABLE THICKNESS EXCEPT AS NOTED THUS												
	$1\frac{1}{8}$	1	$\frac{7}{8}$	$\frac{3}{4}$	$\frac{5}{8}$	$\frac{9}{16}$	$\frac{1}{2}$	$\frac{7}{16}$	$\frac{3}{8}$	$\frac{5}{16}$	$\frac{1}{4}$	$\frac{3}{16}$	$\frac{1}{8}$
9 × 4													
8 × 6													
8 × 4													
7 × 4													
6 × 4													
6 × $3\frac{1}{2}$													
5 × $3\frac{1}{2}$													
5 × 3													
4 × $3\frac{1}{2}$													
4 × 3													
$3\frac{1}{2}$ × 3													
$3\frac{1}{2}$ × $2\frac{1}{2}$													
3 × $2\frac{1}{2}$													
3 × $2\frac{1}{2}$													
$2\frac{1}{2}$ × 2													
$2\frac{1}{2}$ × $1\frac{1}{2}$													
2 × $1\frac{1}{2}$													
2 × $1\frac{1}{4}$													
$1\frac{3}{4}$ × $1\frac{1}{4}$													

NOMENCLATURE

D = Nominal depth in inches
WT = Weight in lbs. per foot
d = Actual depth in inches
b = Flange width in inches

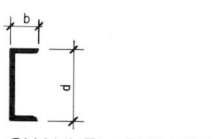 = Not available in this thickness

NOTE :

For revised standard nomenclature for structural shapes see AISC Manual of Steel Construction 7th edition.

ALUMINUM CHANNEL SHAPES [

D	WT	d	b
12 [	11.822	12	5
	8.274	12	4
10 [	8.36	10	$4\frac{1}{4}$
	6.138	10	$3\frac{1}{2}$
9 [	6.97	9	4
	4.983	9	$3\frac{3}{4}$
8 [	5.789	8	$3\frac{3}{4}$
	4.147	8	3
7 [	4.715	7	$3\frac{1}{2}$
	3.205	7	$2\frac{3}{4}$
6 [	4.03	6	$3\frac{1}{4}$
	2.834	6	$2\frac{1}{2}$
5 [	3.089	5	$2\frac{3}{4}$
	2.213	5	$2\frac{1}{4}$
4 [	2.331	4	$2\frac{1}{4}$
	1.738	4	2
3 [	1.597	3	$1\frac{3}{4}$
	1.135	3	$1\frac{1}{2}$
2 [	1.071	2	$1\frac{1}{4}$
	0.577	2	1

ALUMINUM I BEAM SHAPES

D	WT	d	b
12 I	14.292	12	7
	11.671	12	7
10 I	10.286	10	6
	8.646	10	6
9 I	8.36	9	$5\frac{1}{2}$
8 I	7.023	8	5
	6.181	8	5
7 I	5.80	7	$4\frac{1}{2}$
6 I	4.693	6	4
	4.03	6	4
5 I	3.699	5	$3\frac{1}{2}$
4 I	2.675	4	3
	2.31	4	3
3 I	2.03	3	$2\frac{1}{2}$
	1.637	3	$2\frac{1}{2}$

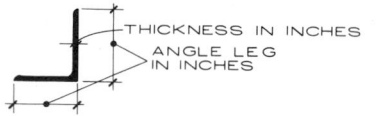

CHANNEL SHAPES

THICKNESS IN INCHES
ANGLE LEG IN INCHES

EQUAL AND UNEQUAL LEG ANGLES

I BEAM SHAPES

H. Thompson, P. E.; Thompson & Czark; East Meadow, Long Island, New York

MAXIMUM ALLOWABLE UNIFORM LOAD IN KIPS FOR BEAMS LATERALLY SUPPORTED * ASTM A‑36 STEEL

Length	6B 8.5	6B 12	6B 16	8B 10	8B 13	8B 15	8WF 17	8WF 20	8WF 24	8WF 28	8WF 31	10B 11.5	10B 15	10B 17	10B 19	10WF 21	10WF 25	10WF 29	10WF 33	12B 14	12B 16.5	12B 19	12B 22	12WF 27	12WF 31	12WF 36	12WF 40	14B 17.2	14B 22	14B 26
6	12	19	27	19	26	31	38	45	55	65	67	26	37	43	50	57	70	82	83	36	47	57	67	83	93	108		56	77	93
7	11	16	23	16	23	27	32	39	47	55	57	22	31	37	43	49	60	70	73	31	40	49	58	78	90	105		48	66	80
8	9	14	20	14	20	24	28	34	42	49	50	19	28	32	38	43	53	62	64	27	35	43	51	68	79	92	102	42	58	70
9	8	13	18	13	18	21	25	30	37	43	45	15	22	26	30	38	47	55	57	24	31	38	45	61	70	82	92	37	51	62
10	7	12	16	11	16	19	23	27	33	39	40	14	20	24	27	34	42	49	51	20	25	31	37	55	63	73	83	34	46	56
11	7	10	15	10	14	17	20	25	30	35	36	13	18	22	25	31	38	45	47	18	23	28	34	50	57	67	75	30	42	51
12	6	10	13	9	13	16	19	23	28	32	33	12	17	20	23	29	35	41	43	17	21	26	31	45	53	61	69	28	38	46
13	6	9	12	9	12	14	17	21	26	30	31	11	16	18	21	26	32	38	39	15	20	24	28	42	48	56	64	26	35	43
14				8	11	13	16	19	24	28	29	10	15	17	20	25	30	35	37	14	19	23	27	39	45	52	59	24	33	40
15				8	10	13	15	18	22	26	27	10	14	16	19	23	28	33	34	14	17	21	25	36	42	49	55	22	31	37
16				7	10	12	14	17	21	24	25	9	13	15	18	22	26	31	32	13	16	20	24	34	39	46	52	21	29	35
17				7	9	11	13	16	20	23	24	9	12	14	16	20	25	29	30	12	16	19	22	32	37	43	49	20	27	33
18												8	12	14	16	19	23	27	29	11	15	18	21	30	35	41	46	19	26	31
19												8	11	13	15	18	22	26	27	11	14	17	20	27	32	37	42	18	24	29
20												7	10	12	14	17	21	25	26	10	13	16	19	26	30	35	40	17	23	28
21																16	20	23	24	10	13	16	18	25	29	33	38	16	22	27
22																				9	12	15	18	24	27	32	36	15	21	25
23																				9	12	14	17	23	26	31	35	15	20	24
24																														

KIPS = 1000 POUNDS
D = TYPE OF BEAM
B = LIGHT BEAM
WF = WIDE FLANGE
WT = WEIGHT IN LBS PER FOOT
NOTE: VERIFY LATERAL SUPPORT WITH STRUCTURAL ENGINEERING CONSULTANT

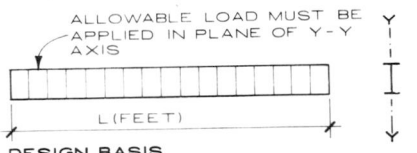

ALLOWABLE LOAD MUST BE APPLIED IN PLANE OF Y‑Y AXIS

L (FEET)

DESIGN BASIS

*NOTE:
For capacity of beams that are not shown see "AISC Manual of Steel Construction", 6th edition.

For revised standard nomenclature for structural shapes see AISC Manual of Steel Construction 7th edition.

MAXIMUM ALLOWABLE CONCENTRIC LOAD IN KIPS FOR COLUMNS OF ASTM A‑36 STEEL

EFFECTIVE LENGTH IN FEET "KH" WITH RESPECT TO LEAST RADIUS OF GYRATION

Depth	Weight	6	7	8	9	10	11	12	13	14	15	16	17	18	19	20	21	22	23
4 WF	13	62	57	51	45	39	32	27	23	20	17	15							
5 WF	16	83	79	74	69	64	58	52	46	39	34	30	27	24	21	19	18		
	18.5	97	92	87	81	75	69	62	55	47	41	36	32	29	26	23	21		19
6 WF	15.5	85	81	78	74	70	65	60	55	50	45	39	35	31	28	25	23	21	19
	20	109	105	101	96	91	85	80	74	67	61	54	48	42	38	34	31	28	26
	25	137	132	126	120	114	107	100	93	85	77	69	61	55	49	47	43	39	36
8 WF	24	133	128	123	118	113	107	101	94	88	81	73	66	59	53	47	43	39	36
	28	155	150	144	138	132	125	118	111	103	95	86	78	69	62	56	51	46	42
	31	178	174	169	164	159	154	148	142	136	130	123	117	110	102	95	87	79	72
3 φ	7.58	38	36	34	31	28	25	22	18	16	14	12	11	10	9				
	10.25	52	48	45	41	37	33	28	24	21	18	16	14	12					
	18.58	91	84	77	69	60	51	43	37	32	28	24	21	17	15	14	12	11	10
3½ φ	9.11	48	46	44	41	38	35	32	29	25	22	19	18	16	15				
	12.51	66	63	59	55	51	47	43	38	33	29	26	23	21	19	17	15	14	
4 φ	10.79	59	57	54	52	49	46	43	40	36	33	29	26	23	21	19			
	14.98	81	78	75	71	67	63	59	54	49	44	39	34	31	28	25	23	21	19
	27.54	147	140	133	126	118	109	100	91	81	70	62	55	49	44	39	36	32	30
5 φ	14.62	83	81	78	76	73	71	68	65	61	58	55	51	47	43	40	37	34	31
	20.78	118	114	111	107	103	99	95	91	86	81	76	71	65	59	53	48	44	40
	38.55	216	209	202	195	187	178	170	160	151	141	130	119	108	96	87	79	71	66
6 φ	18.97	110	108	106	103	101	98	95	92	89	86	82	79	75	71	67	63	59	55
	28.57	166	162	159	155	151	146	142	137	132	127	122	116	111	105	99	93	86	79
	53.16	306	299	292	284	275	266	257	247	237	227	216	205	193	181	168	155	142	130
3 X 3	8.8	44	41	38	34	31	27	23	19	17	14	13	11	10					
3½ X 3½	10.5	55	53	50	47	43	40	36	32	28	24	21	19	17	15	14	12		
4 X 4	12.02	66	63	60	57	54	51	48	44	40	36	32	29	26	23	21	19	17	16
5 X 5	15.42	88	86	83	81	78	75	72	69	66	62	59	55	51	47	43	39	35	32
6 X 6	18.82	110	108	106	103	101	98	95	93	90	87	83	80	77	73	69	66	62	58
3 X 2	7.10	28	23	18	15	12													
4 X 2	8.80	36	30	25	20	16													
4 X 3	10.5	53	50	46	42	38													
5 X 3	12.02	61	58	54	50	45													
6 X 3	13.72	70	66	62	58	53													
6 X 4	15.42	85	82	79	76	72													
8 X 4	18.82	105	101	97	93	89													

KIP = 1000 POUNDS
D = TYPE OF COLUMN
WT = WEIGHT IN LBS PER FOOT
WF = WIDE FLANGE
φ = PIPE
X = SQUARE OR RECTANGULAR TUBING
K = EFFECTIVE LENGTH FACTOR
(VERIFY WITH STRUCTURAL ENGINEERING CONSULTANT)

CONCENTRIC LOAD
COLUMN
FOR K SEE AISC MANUAL
DESIGN BASIS

NOTE:
For additional columns and actual dimensions of pipe see "AISC Manual of Steel Construction," 6th edition.

H. Thompson, P. E.; Thompson & Czark; East Meadow, Long Island, New York

PRELIMINARY SELECTION OF LIGHTWEIGHT STEELBEAMS AND LIGHTGAGE STEEL JOISTS

The tables used on this page on depths of joists and beams are not to be used for final design but are intended to serve as an aide to the architect in speeding selection of members for preliminary design and planning. The engineering design should of course be a separate and thorough process process involving a complete investigation of the pertinent conditions.

EXAMPLE: Assume a particular clear span. By selecting a spacing and estimating the total load, a member can immediately be selected from the table. NOTE: "Total Load." = Live Load plus Dead Load. Dead Load used in tables includes weight of joist or beam. For recommended Live Loads, see page on "Weights of Materials". Local code governs.

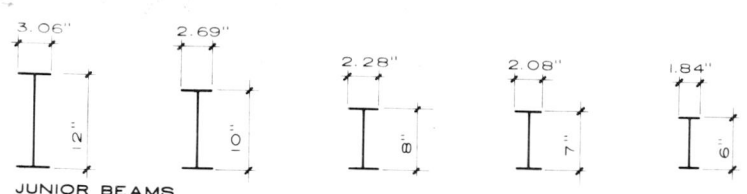

JUNIOR BEAMS

BRIDGING FOR J&L JUNIOR BEAMS

BEAM SPAN	BRIDGING SPACING
TO 14'–0"	1 row near center of span
14'–0" to 21'–0"	2 rows approx. at 1/3 points of span
21'–0" & over	3 rows approx. at 1/4 points of span

For wider spacing see manufacturer's literature

LOAD TABLE FOR J&L JUNIOR BEAMS

TOTAL LOAD PSI	SPACING INCHES	SPAN IN FEET						
		10	12	14	16	18	20	22
80	12	6	6	6	6	7	7	8
	16	6	6	6	7	8	8	10
	20	6	6	6	7	8	10	10
	24	6	6	7	7	8	10	10
100	12	6	6	6	6	7	8	10
	16	6	6	6	7	8	10	10
	20	6	6	7	7	8	10	10
	24	6	6	7	8	10	10	12
120	12	6	6	6	7	8	8	10
	16	6	6	7	7	8	10	10
	20	6	6	7	8	10	10	12
	24	6	7	7	8	10	10	12
140	12	6	6	6	7	8	10	10
	16	6	6	7	8	8	10	10
	20	6	7	7	8	10	10	12
	24	6	7	8	10	10	12	12
160	12	6	6	6	7	8	10	10
	16	6	6	7	8	10	10	12
	20	6	7	8	10	10	12	12
	24	6	7	8	10	10	12	12
180	12	6	6	7	8	10	10	10
	16	6	7	8	8	10	10	12
	20	6	7	8	10	10	12	12
	24	7	8	10	10	12	12	

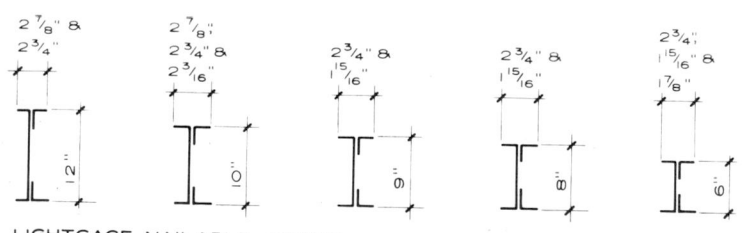

LIGHTGAGE NAILABLE JOISTS

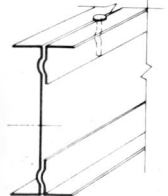

SECTION OBLIQUE

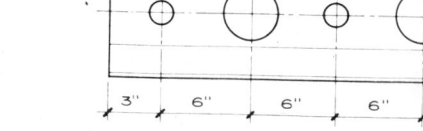

SIDE ELEVATION

LOAD TABLE FOR LIGHTGAGE STEEL JOISTS

TOTAL LOAD PSI	SPACING INCHES	SPAN IN FEET						
		10	12	14	16	18	20	22
80	12	6	6	6	8	8	8	10
	16	6	6	8	8	8	9	12
	20	6	8	8	8	9	10	12
	24	6	8	9	9	10	12	12
100	12	6	6	8	8	8	9	10
	16	6	8	8	8	9	10	12
	20	6	8	9	9	10	12	12
	24	6	8	9	10	12	12	—
120	12	6	6	8	8	9	9	10
	16	6	8	8	9	10	10	12
	20	6	8	9	10	12	12	—
140	12	6	8	8	9	10	10	12
160	12	6	8	9	9	10	12	12
180	12	6	8	9	10	10	12	—

BRIDGING FOR LIGHTGAGE STEEL JOISTS

JOIST SPAN	BRIDGING SPACING
TO 14'–0"	1 row at center of span
14'–0" to 20'–0"	2 rows 1/4 span apart, symmetrical about midspan
20'–0" & over	3 rows, 1/4 span apart.

Consult manufacturer's literature to determine economical members.

Jean Lesire, AIA; Arlington, Virginia

PRELIMINARY SELECTION OF OPEN WEB STEEL JOISTS

The table below on depths of Open Web Steel Joists is not to be used for final joist design but is intended to serve as an aid in speeding selection of steel joists for preliminary design and planning.

The final design must be a separate and thorough process, involving a complete investigation of the pertinent conditions. This page is not for that purpose.

EXAMPLE: Assume a particular clear span. By assuming a joist spacing and estimating the total load, a joist can immediately be selected from the table. Then proceed with preliminary design studies.

NOTE: "Total Safe Load" = Live Load plus Dead Load. Dead Load used in table below includes weight of joist. For recommended live loads, see pages on Weights of Materials. Local codes will govern.

Joint designation in table is that generally used on structural plans.

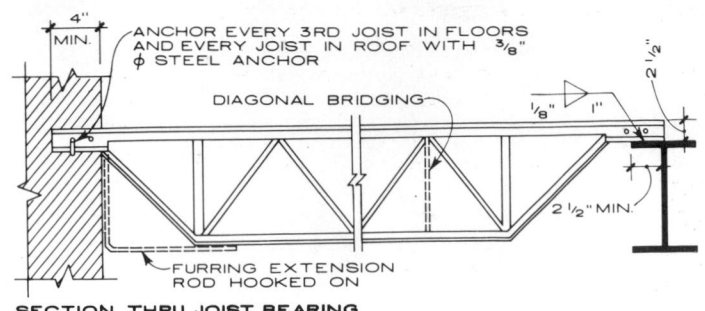

SECTION THRU JOIST BEARING

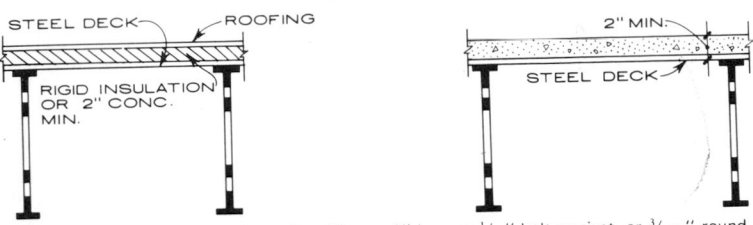

MINIMUM ATTACHMENTS: 2 welds, ea. 1" long or $1/2$" bolt or rivet, or $3/16$" round steel anchor fastened over beam flange.

BRIDGING SPACING

JOINT SPAN	MAXIMUM SPACING
To 14'-0"	1 row near center
14'-0" to 21'-0"	2 rows at $1/3$ points of span
21'-0" to 32'-0"	3 rows at $1/4$ points of span
32'-0" to 40'-0"	4 rows at $1/5$ points of span
40'-0" to 48'-0"	5 rows at $1/6$ points of span

NOTE: No span to exceed 24 times joist depth. Except for floors, the clear span of an H—series joist shall not exceed 20 times joist depth.

FIRE RESISTANCE RATINGS

HRS	TOP SLAB	CEILINGS
$3/4$	1" T & G on 2" x 2" wood strips attached to joist.	$3/4$" sanded gypsum plaster on expanded metal lath.
1 or $1 1/2$	2" reinf. conc., or 2" precast reinf. gypsum tile.	$3/4$" portland cement or sanded gypsum plaster on expanded metal lath.
	2" reinf. conc.	$5/8$" UL listed gypsum board
2	$2 1/2$" reinf. conc., or 2" reinf. gypsum tile with $1/4$" mortar finish.	$3/4$" sanded gypsum plaster on expanded metal lath.
	2" reinf. conc.	$5/8$" UL listed acoustical tile
	1" non-combustible insulation board over 18–22 gage steel roof deck.	$7/8$" vermiculite plaster on expanded metal lath.
3	$2 1/2$" reinf. conc., 2" reinf. gypsum tile with $1/2$" mortar finish.	1" gypsum plaster, or $3/4$" gypsum—vermiculite plaster on expanded metal lath.
4	$2 1/2$" reinf. conc., or 2" reinf. gypsum tile with $1/2$" mortar finish.	1" gypsum—vermiculite plaster on expanded metal lath.

Ratings are the result of tests made in accordance with ASTM standard E119.

LOAD TABLE—J SERIES (f_s = 22,000 psi)

TOTAL SAFE UNIFORMLY DISTRIBUTED LOAD LBS./FT.
NUMBER PRECEDING LETTER IS JOIST DEPTH; 14 J 5 IS 14" DEEP

JOIST DESIGNATION	8 J 2	10 J 3	12 J 4	14 J 5	16 J 6	18 J 7	20 J 7	22 J 7	24 J 7
8	475								
12	259	367	417						
16	146	232	313	388	450				
20		148	225	310	360	420	430		
24			156	220	299	350	358	375	
30					191	261	283	300	237
36								216	174
42								159	

CLEAR SPAN IN FEET

LOAD TABLE—H SERIES (f_s = 30,000 psi)

TOTAL SAFE UNIFORMLY DISTRIBUTED LOAD LBS./FT.
NUMBER PRECEDING LETTER IS JOIST DEPTH; 14 J 5 IS 14" DEEP

JOIST DESIGNATION	8 H 2	10 H 3	12 H 4	14 H 5	16 H 6	18 H 7	20 H 7	22 H 7	24 H 7
8	500								
12	333	417	533						
16	190	302	400	475	575				
20		193	300	380	460	520	540		
24			208	300	383	433	450	467	483
30					255	345	360	373	387
36						240	257	271	296
42								199	218

CLEAR SPAN IN FEET

Smith, Hinchman & Grylls Associates, Inc.; Detroit, Michigan

PRELIMINARY SELECTION OF LONG SPAN STEEL JOISTS

The table below on depths of Long Span Steel Joists is not to be used for final joist design but is intended to serve as an aid in speeding selection of steel joists for preliminary design and planning.

The final design must be a separate and thorough process, involving a complete investigation of the pertinent conditions. This page is not for that purpose.

EXAMPLE: assume a particular clear span. By assuming a joist spacing and estimating the total load, a joist can immediately be selected from the table. Then proceed with preliminary design studies.

NOTE: "Total Safe Load" = Live Load plus Dead Load. Dead Load used in table below includes weight of joist. For recommended live loads, see pages on Weights of Materials. Local codes will govern.

Joists will span to 96'—0" of clear opening, but from approximately 70'—0" to 96'—0" are primarily for roof construction.

Joist designation in table is that generally used on structural plans.

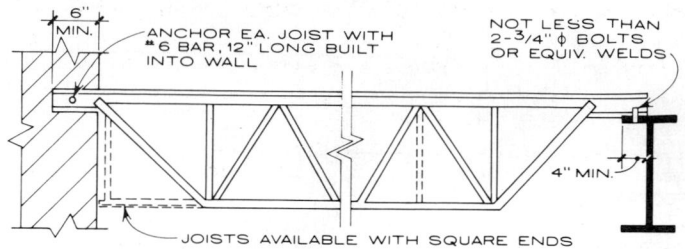

SECTION THRU JOIST BEARINGS

NOTE: FOR FIRE RESISTANT CONSTRUCTION SEE PAGE ON "OPEN WEB STEEL JOISTS"

BRIDGING SPACING

CHORD SIZE *	MAXIMUM SPACING
No. 02 to No. 08, incl.	10' — 0"
No. 09 to No. 14, incl.	16' — 0"
No. 15 to No. 19, incl.	21' — 0"

Joist span not to exceed 24 x depth for roofs, 20 x depth for floors.

* Last two digits of joist designation shown in load table.

LOAD TABLE

TOTAL SAFE UNIFORMLY DISTRIBUTED LOAD LBS/FT.

JOIST DESIGNATION	CLEAR SPAN IN FEET	25	30	35	40	45	50	55	60	65	70	75	80	85	90	96
LJ SERIES	18LJ07	616	465	344												
Based on allowable stress of 22,000 p.s.i.	20LJ08	699	585	447	344											
	24LJ09			575	464	368										
	28LJ10				465	387	323									
	32LJ11					451	374	315								
	36LJ12						397	339	292							
	40LJ13							441	385	338	300					
	44LJ14								403	357	319					
	48LJ15											383	342	300		
LH SERIES	18LH05	684	508	375												
Based on allowable stress of 33,000 p.s.i.	20LH06	822	635	469	361											
	24LH07			613	491	389										
	28LH08				456	371	308									
	32LH09					498	418	356								
	36LH10						413	357	311							
	40LH11							399	349	308	273					
	44LH12								383	339	300					
	48LH13										368	332	294			

NOTE: For deflection due to live load especially for LH-series of steel joists consult with structural engineer.

Smith, Hinchman & Grylls Associates, Inc.; Detroit, Michigan

ANGLES
HEAVY SHAPES

EQUAL LEG

SIZE	3/32	1/8	3/16	1/4	5/16	3/8	9/16	1/2
1/2 × 1/2		S						
5/8 × 5/8		S						
3/4 × 3/4		SA						
7/8 × 7/8		S						
1 × 1	A	SS SA	SS SA	SA				
1 1/8 × 1 1/8		S						
1 1/4 × 1 1/4		SS SA	SS SA	SS SA				
1 1/2 × 1 1/2		SS SA	SS SA	SS SA				
1 3/4 × 1 3/4		SA	SS SA	SS SA				
2 × 2		SS SA	SS SA	SS SA	SS SA	SA	SS SA	
2 1/2 × 2 1/2	A	SS SA	SS SA	SS SA	SA	SS SA		
3 × 3			SA	SS SA	SS SA	SA	SA	
3 1/2 × 3 1/2			SA	SA	SA	S	SA	
4 × 4			SS SA	SA	SA	S	SA	

UNEQUAL LEG

SIZE	1/8	3/16	1/4	5/16	3/8	1/2
1 × 5/8	S					
1 × 3/4	S					
1 3/8 × 7/8	S	S				
1 1/2 × 3/4	A					
1 1/2 × 1 1/4	A	SA	A			
1 3/4 × 1 1/4	SA	A	A			
2 × 1 1/4	S	S				
2 × 1 1/2	SA	SA	SA		A	
2 1/4 × 1 1/2	S					
2 1/2 × 1 1/2	A	SA	SA		SA	
2 1/2 × 2	A	SA	SA	SA	SA	S
3 × 2 1/2		SA	SA	SA	SA	S
3 × 2 1/2			SA	SA	SA	S
3 1/2 × 2 1/2			SA	SA	SA	S
3 1/2 × 3			SA	SA	SA	S
4 × 3			SA	SA	SA	SA

LIGHT SHAPES

EQUAL LEG

SIZE	1/16	1/8	3/16	1/4
1/2 × 1/2	A	A		
5/8 × 5/8		A		
3/4 × 3/4	A	A		
1 × 1	A	A	A	
1 1/4 × 1 1/4		A	A	
1 1/2 × 1 1/2		A	A	
1 3/4 × 1 3/4		A		
2 × 2	A	A	A	

UNEQUAL LEG

SIZE	3/32	1/8
3/8 × 3/4		A
1 × 1/2	A	A
1 × 3/4		A
1 1/4 × 1/2		A
1 1/2 × 3/4		A
1 1/2 × 1		A
2 × 1		A
2 × 1 1/2		A
3 1/2 × 1 1/4		A

LEGEND
S = STEEL
SS = STAINLESS STEEL
A = ALUMINUM

NOTE:
Weights of steel channels & angles shown on pages for structural steel and aluminum shapes.

ZEES
STEEL & ALUM ZEES

MAT'L	A	B	THICK
SA	2 11/16	3	1/4
S	2 11/16	3	3/8 1/2
S	3 1/16	4 1/16	1/4
S	3 1/8	4 1/16	5/16
S	3 3/16	4 1/8	3/8
S	3 1/4	5	5/16 1/2
S	3 5/16	5 1/16	3/8
S	3 1/2	6	3/8
A*	3 1/2	2 1/2	1/8

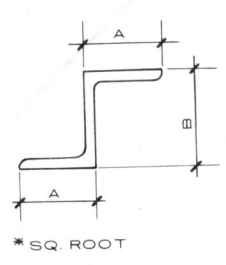

* SQ. ROOT

TEES

MAT'L	F	D	S	A	B	T₁	T₂

STEEL & ALUM. TEES BAR SIZE & STRUCTURAL / LIGHTWEIGHT ALUMINUM TEES

MAT'L	F	D	S	A	B	T₁	T₂
S	3/4	3/4	1/8	3/4	3/4	1/8	1/8
S	7/8	7/8	1/8	3/4	1 1/4	1/8	1/8
S	1	1	1/8 3/16	7/8	1 1/4	5/32	1/8
S	1 1/4	1 1/4	1/8 3/16 1/4	1	1/2	1/8	3/8
A	1 1/2	1 1/4	1/4	1	3/4	1/8	1/8
S	1 1/2	1 1/2	3/16	1	1	1/8	1/8
SA	1 1/2	1 1/2	1/4	1 1/4	7/8	1/8	1/8
A	2	2	1/4	2	3/4	1/8	1/8
S	2	2	5/16				
SA	2 1/4	2 1/4	1/4				
S	2 1/2	2 1/2	1/4 5/16 3/8				
A	3	3	3/8				
A	4	4	3/8				

LIGHT SHAPES
ALUMINUM

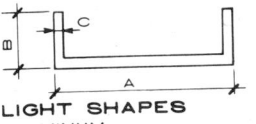

A	B	C	A	B	C	A	B	C
3/8	5/8	.109	1/4	1/4	1/8	5	2	3/16
1/2	3/8	1/8	1 1/2	1/2	1/8			
1/2	1/2	3/32	1 3/4	1/2	1/8			
1/2	3/4	1/8	1 3/4	3/4	1/8			
5/8	5/8	1/8	1 3/4	1	1/8			
3/4	3/8	1/8	2	1/2	1/8			
3/4	3/4	1/8	2	1	1/8			
1	1/2	1/8	2.1	.55	.100			
1	1	1/8	2 1/4	7/8	1/8			
1 1/4	1/2	1/8	2 1/2	1 1/2	1/8			
1 1/4	1/2	1/8	3	1/2	1/8			
1 1/4	3/4	1/8	3	1	1/8			

HEAVY SHAPES
STEEL & ALUMINUM

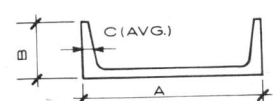

MAT'L	A	B	C
SA	3	1.410	.170
SA	3	1.498	.258
SA	3	1.596	.356
SA	4	1.580	.180
A	4	1.650	.247
SA	4	1.72	.320
SA	5	1.75	.190
SA	6	1.92	.200
A	6	1.95	.225
SA	6	2.03	.314
S	6	2.157	.437

STEEL BAR SIZE CHANNELS

3/4 × 5/16 × 1/8	1 1/8 × 9/16 × 3/16	2 × 1/2 × 1/8
3/4 × 3/8 × 1/8	1 1/4 × 1/2 × 1/8	2 × 9/16 × 3/16
7/8 × 3/8 × 1/8	1 1/2 × 9/16 × 3/16	2 × 5/8 × 1/4
7/8 × 7/16 × 1/8	1 1/2 × 3/4 × 1/8	2 × 1 × 3/16
1 × 3/8 × 1/8	1 1/2 × 1 1/2 × 3/16	2 × 1 × 3/16
1 × 1/2 × 1/8	1 3/4 × 1 1/2 × 3/16	2 1/2 × 5/8 × 3/16

Michael Newman; William A. Hall, AIA; New York, New York

STEEL ROUND

SIZE-NOMINAL INSIDE DIA.	OUTSIDE DIAM.	INSIDE DIAMETER STANDARD	EXTRA STRONG	DOUBLE EXTRA STRONG
1/8"	.405"	.269"	.215	
1/4"	.540"	.364"	.302	
3/8"	.675"	.493"	.423	
1/2"	.840	.622"	.546	.252
3/4"	1.050"	.824"	.742	.434
1"	1.315"	1.049"	.957	.599
1 1/4"	1.660"	1.380"	1.278	.896
1 1/2"	1.900"	1.610"	1.500	1.100
2"	2.375"	2.067"	1.939	1.503
2 1/2"	2.875"	2.469"	2.323	1.771
3"	3.500"	3.068"	2.900	2.300
3 1/2"	4.000"	3.548"	3.364	
4"	4.500"	4.026"	3.826	3.152
5"	5.563"	5.047"	4.813	4.063
6"	6.625"	6.065"	5.761	4.897
8"	8.625"	7.981"	7.625	6.875
10"	10.750"	10.020"	9.750	8.750
12"	12.750"	12.000	11.750	10.750

NOTES:

Round steel pipe is specified by nominal inside diameter followed by the terms "standard," "extra strong" and "double extra strong").

Rectangular & square & other shaped tubing is measured by outside dimension.

STEEL SQUARE

OUTSIDE DIM.	WALL THICKNESS									
1/2" X 1/2"	18	16								
5/8" X 5/8"	18	16								
3/4" X 3/4"	20	18	16	11						
7/8" X 7/8"	20	18	16	13						
1" X 1"	20	18	16	.073"	14	13	12	.102"	11	
1 1/4" X 1 1/4"	18	16	14	11	10	3/16"				
1 1/2" X 1 1/2"	18	16	14	11	.140	7	3/16"			
1 3/4" X 1 3/4"	16	14	11							
2" X 2"	16	14	13	7/64	11	1/8"	3/16"	.145	1/4"	
2 1/2" X 2 1/2"	14	11	.191"	3/16	1/4					
3" X 3"	14	11	5/32"	3/16	1/4					
3 1/2" X 3 1/2"	11	5/32"	3/16"	5	1/4"	5/16				
4" X 4"	11	3/16"	1/4"	5/16"	3/8"	1/2"				

ALL DIMENSIONS ARE BW GUAGE EXCEPT AS NOTED IN INCHES.

Tubing and pipe are available in various shapes and thicknesses for aluminum and bronze. Individual manufacturer's catalogs should be consulted for these metals. Some rectangular and square tubing has round corners. Extruded tubing has sharp, square corners.

STEEL RECTANGULAR

SIZE	WALL THICKNESS			
1 1/2 X 1	14	11	.083	.120
2 X 1	14		.083	
2 X 1 1/4	14		.083	
2 X 1 1/2	11		.120	
2 1/2 X 1	14		.083	
2 1/4 X 1 1/4	14		.083	
2 1/2 X 1/2	14	7	.083	.190
3 X 1	14		.083	
3 X 1 1/2	14	11	.083	.120
3 X 2	14	11	.083	.120
4 X 2	14	11	.083	.120
4 X 2 1/2	11		.120	
4 X 3	11	5/32"	.120	.156
5 X 2	3/16"	1/4	.188	.250
5 X 2 1/2	11	7	.120	.180
5 X 3	3/16"	1/4"	.188	.250
6 X 2	3/16"	1/4"	.188	.250
6 X 3	3/16"	1/4"	.188	.250
6 X 4	3/16"	1/4"	.188	.250
7 X 5	3/16"	1/4"	.188	.250
8 X 2	3/16"		.188	
8 X 3	3/16"	1/4"	.188	.250
8 X 4	3/16"	1/4"	.188	.250
8 X 6	3/16"	1/4"	.188	.250
10 X 2	3/16"		.188	
10 X 4	3/16"	1/4"	.188	.250
10 X 5	1/4"		.250	
10 X 6	1/4"	3/8"	.250	.313
10 X 8	1/4"	3/8"	.250	.375
12 X 2	3/16"		.188	
12 X 4	1/4"	3/8"	.250	.375
12 X 6	1/4"	3/8"	.250	.375

BW GUAGE OR INCHES AS NOTED

LEGEND:
S = STEEL
SS = STAINLESS STEEL
A = ALUMINUM

STEEL & STAINLESS STEEL FLATS & OTHER SHAPES

WIDTH INCHES / BW GAUGE	16	14	12	10	1/8	3/16	1/4	5/16	3/8	7/16	1/2	9/16	5/8	11/16	3/4	7/8	15/16	1	1 1/8	1 1/4	1 3/8	1 1/2	1 5/8	1 3/4	1 7/8	2
3/8	S	S	S	S	S	S	S			SS					SS			SS		SS		SS		SS		SS
1/2	S	S	S	S	S	S	S								SS			SS		SS		SS		SS		SS
5/8	S	S	S	S	S	S	S	S	S		S							SS								SS
3/4	S	S	S	S	S	S	S	S	S	S	S							SS		SS		SS		SS		SS
7/8	S	S	S	S	S	S	S	S	S		S		S		S											
1	S				S / SS	S / SS	S / SS	SS	S / SS	SS	S / SS	SS	S / SS	SS	S / SS	S		S / SS	S			SS		SS		SS
1 1/8	S				S	S	S		S		S				S			S								
1 1/4	S				S	S	S		S		S		S		S	S		S								
1 3/8		S			S	S	S		S		S		S		S			C								
1 1/2		S			S / SS	S / SS	S / SS	S	S / SS	S	S / SS		S / SS		S / SS	S		S		S						
1 5/8		S			S	S	S		S		S		S		S	S		S		S						
1 3/4		S			S	S	S		S		S		S		S		S		S		S					
2	S	S	S	S	S / SS	S / SS	S / SS	S	S / SS	S	S / SS		S / SS		SS	S		S		S		S	S			
2 1/4	S	S	S	S	S	S	S		S		S		S		S			S		S				S		
2 1/2	S		S	SS	S	S	SS		SS		S		SS	S	SS	S		S		S		S				S
2 3/4					S	S	S		S		S		S		S			S		S		S	S			
3		S		S	SS	SS	SS		SS		SS		SS		SS	S		S		S		S		S		SS
3 1/4				S	S	S		S		S		S		S		S		S		S						
3 1/2	S		S		S	S		S		S		S		S		S		S		S		S		S		S
3 3/4					S		S													S		S				
4	S	S	S	S	S	S	S		S		S		S		S			S		S		S		S		S
4 1/4					S																					
4 1/2		S	S	S	S	S	S		S		S		S		S			S		S		S		S		S
5		S	S	S	S	S	S		S		S		S		S			S		S		S		S		S
5 1/2		S	S	S	S	S	S		S		S		S		S			S		S		S		S		S
6		S	S	S	S	S	S		S		S		S		S			S		S		S		S		S
● ROUNDS	S / SS	S / SS	S / SS	SA / SS	S / SS	SA / SS	SA / SS	SA / SS	SA / SS	SA / SS	SA / SS	S / SS	SA / SS	SA / SS	S	SA / SS		SA / SS	SA / SS	SA / SS	SA / SS	SA / SS	A / SS	SA / SS		SA / SS
▲ HALF-ROUNDS					S		S		S		S				S											S
○ HEXAGONS	SS / A	SS / A	SS / A	SS / A	SS / A	SS / A	SS / A	SA / A	SA / A	SA	SA / SS	SA / SS	SA / SS	SS	SA / SS	SA / SS		SA / SS	SA / SS	A / SS	SA / SS	A / SS		S / SS		S / SS
□ SQUARES	SA / SS	SA / SS	SS		S	S / SS	S / SS	S / SS	SA / SS		S / SS	SA / SS	SA / SS		SA / SS	SA / SS		SA / SS	SA / SS	S / SS	SA / SS	S / SS		S / SS		S / SS
✚ PLATES	S	SA / SS	SA / SS	A / SS	AS / SS	SA	SA / SS		S / SS		SA / SS	SS	S		SA / SS	S		SA / SS		S		A / SS		S		SA / SS

Michael Newman; William A. Hall, AIA; New York, New York

GAUGE NO.	GRAPHIC SIZES	US STD. REVISED		UNITED STATES STANDARD (USS)		AMERICAN STEEL WIRE OR WASHBURN & MOEN (W & M)		BROWN AND SHARP (B & S) OR AMERICAN WIRE (AW) — For aluminum, copper, brass, bronze & nickel silver strip & wire and small sizes copper & brass tubing.		BIRMINGHAM WIRE (BWG) OR STUBS IRON WIRE — For hot and cold rolled steel strip. Flat steel wire. Steel, aluminum, bronze, monel stainless steel tubing & larger size copper and brass tubing.		MACHINE AND WOOD SCREWS		GRAPHIC SIZES	GAUGE NO.
		DECIMAL	FRACTION	DECIMAL	FRACTION	DECIMAL	FRACTION	DECIMAL	FRACTION	DECIMAL		DECIMAL	FRACTION		
000		.3750"	3/8"	.3750"	3/8"	.3625"	23/64"	.4096"	13/32"+	.425"	27/64"+	GRAPHIC SIZES DO NOT APPLY TO THIS COLUMN			000
00		.3437"	11/32"	.3437"	11/32"	.3310"	21/64"+	.3648"	23/64"+	.380"	3/8"+				00
0		.3125"	5/16"	.3125"	5/16"	.3065"	5/16"-	.3249"	21/64"-	.340"	11/32"-	.060"	1/16"		0
1		.2812"	9/32"	.2812"	9/32"	.2830"	9/32"	.2893"	19/64"-	.300"	19/64"+	.073"	5/64"-		1
2		.2656"	17/64"	.2656"	17/64"	.2625"	17/64"-	.2576"	1/4"+	.284"	9/32"+	.086"	3/32"-		2
3		.2391"	15/64"+	.2500"	1/4"	.2437"	1/4"-	.2294"	15/64"-	.259"	17/64"-	.099"	3/32"+		3
4		.2242"	7/32"+	.2344"	15/64"	.2253"	7/32"+	.2043"	13/64"+	.238"	15/64"+	.112"	7/64"+		4
5		.2092"	13/64"+	.2187"	7/32"	.2070"	13/64"+	.1819"	3/16"-	.220"	7/32"+	.125"	1/8"		5
6		.1943"	3/16"+	.2031"	13/64"	.1920"	3/16"+	.1620"	5/32"+	.203"	13/64"	.138"	9/64"-		6
7		.1793"	11/64"+	.1875"	3/16"	.1770"	11/64"+	.1443"	9/64"+	.180"	3/16"-	.151"	5/32"-		7
8		.1644"	11/64"-	.1719"	11/64"	.1620"	5/32"+	.1285"	1/8"+	.165"	11/64"-	.164"	11/64"-		8
9		.1495"	5/32"-	.1562"	5/32"	.1483"	9/64"+	.1144"	7/64"+	.148"	9/64"+	.177"	11/64"+		9
10		.1345"	9/64"-	.1406"	9/64"	.1350"	9/64"-	.1019"	7/64"-	.134"	9/64"-	.190"	3/16"+		10
11		.1196"	1/8"-	.1250"	1/8"	.1205"	1/8"-	.0907"	3/32"+	.120"	1/8"-	.203"	13/64"		11
12		.1046"	7/64"-	.1094"	7/64"	.1055"	7/64"-	.0808"	5/64"+	.109"	7/64"	.216"	7/32"-		12
13		.0897"	3/32"	.0938"	3/32"	.0915"	3/32"-	.0719"	5/64"-	.095"	3/32"+	—	—		13
14		.0747"	5/64"-	.0781"	5/64"	.0800"	5/64"+	.064"	1/16"+	.083"	5/64"+	.242"	1/4"-		14
15		.0673"	1/16"+	.0703"	5/64"-	.0720"	5/64"-	.0571"	1/16"-	.072"	5/64"-	—	—		15
16		.0598"	1/16"-	.0625"	1/16"	.0625"	1/16"	.0508"	3/64"+	.065"	1/16"+	.268"	17/64"+		16
17		.0538"	3/64"+	.0562"	1/16"-	.0540"	3/64"+	.0453"	3/64"-	.058"	1/16"-	—	—		17
18		.0478"	3/64"+	.0500"	3/64"+	.0475"	3/64"+	.0403"	3/64"-	.049"	3/64"+	.294"	19/64"		18
19		.0418"	3/64"-	.0437"	3/64"-	.0410"	3/64"-	.0359"	1/32"+	.042"	3/64"-	—	—		19
20		.0359"	1/32"+	.0375"	1/32"+	.0348"	1/32"+	.0320"	1/32"+	.035"	1/32"+	.320"	5/16"+		20
21		.0329"	1/32"+	.0344"	1/32"+	.0318"	1/32"+	.0285"	1/32"	.032"	1/32"+	—	—		21
22		.0299"	1/32"-	.0312"	1/32"	.0286"	1/32"-	.0253"	1/32"-	.028"	1/32"-	—	—		22
23		.0269"	1/32"-	.0281"	1/32"-	.0258"	1/32"-	.0226"	1/64"+	.025"	1/32"-	—	—		23
24		.0239"	1/32"-	.0250"	1/32"-	.0230"	1/64"+	.0201"	1/64"+	.022"	1/64"+	.372"	3/8"-		24
25		.0209"	1/64"+	.0219"	1/64"+	.0204"	1/64"+	.0179"	1/64"+	.020"	1/64"+	—	—		25
26		.0179"	1/64"+	.0187"	1/64"+	.0181"	1/64"+	.0159"	1/64"+	.018"	1/64"+	—	—		26
27		.0164"	1/64"+	.0172"	1/64"+	.0173"	1/64"+	.0142"	1/64"-	.016"	1/64"+	—	—		27
28		.0149"	1/64"+	.0156"	1/64"	.0162"	1/64"+	.0126"	1/64"-	.014"	1/64"-	—	—		28
29		.0135"	1/64"+	.0141"	1/64"-	.0150"	1/64"-	.0113"	1/64"-	.013"	1/64"-	—	—		29
30		.0120"	1/64"	.0125"	1/64"-	.0140"	1/64"-	.0100"	1/64"-	.012"	1/64"-	.450"	29/64"		30

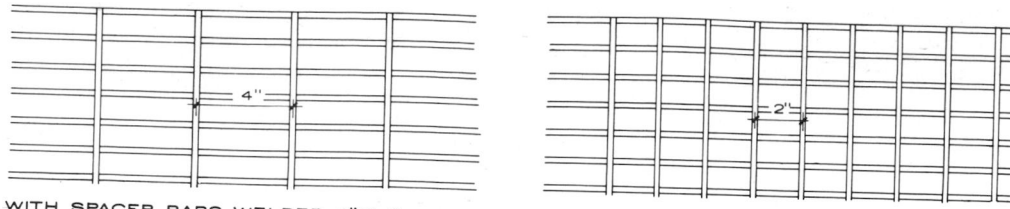

WITH SPACER BARS WELDED 4" O.C.　　　WITH SPACER BARS WELDED 2" O.C.

RECTANGULAR (WELDED OR PRESSURE LOCKED) 1½" = 1'-0"

NOTES :

Constructed of flat bearing bars with spacer bars at right angles. Spacer bars may be square, rectangular or other shape. Spacer bars connected to bearing bars by pressing into prepared slots, or by welding. Usually with open ends, or may have ends banded with flat bars of similar size as bearing bars welded. Standard bar spacing $^{15}/_{16}$" and 1 $^{3}/_{16}$". For usual bar sizes see "Table of Safe Loads for Gratings."

NOSING OF ANGLE AND ABRASIVE STRIP AND BAR ENDS

HEAVY FRONT AND BACK BEARING BARS AND BAR END PLATES

FLOOR PLATE NOSING, BAR END PLATES

TREADS

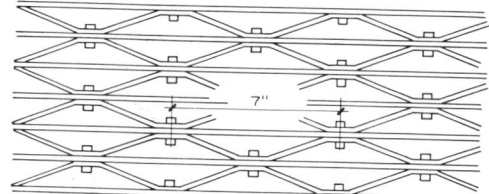

WITH SPACER BARS RIVETED APPROX. 7" O.C. USED FOR AVERAGE INSTALLATION

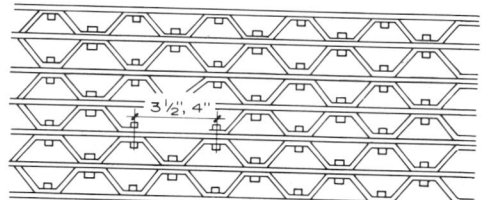

WITH SPACER BARS RIVETED 3½" OR 4" USED FOR HEAVY TRAFFIC AND WHERE WHEELED EQUIPMENT IS USED

RETICULATED (RIVETED) 1½" = 1'-0"

NOTES :

Construction of flat bearing bars and continuous bent spacer or reticuline bars riveted to the bearing bars. Usually with open ends or may have ends banded with flat bars of similar size as bearing bars, welded across ends. Normal spacing of bars: $^{7}/_{8}$", 1 $^{1}/_{8}$", 1 $^{3}/_{16}$", or 1 $^{1}/_{4}$". For usual bar sizes see "Table of Safe Loads for Gratings."

PLAIN NOSING BAR END PLATES

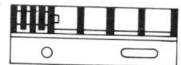

NOSING OF CLOSELY SPACED BARS, ANGLE ENDS

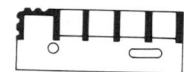

CHECKER PLATE NOSING, BAR END PLATES

TREADS

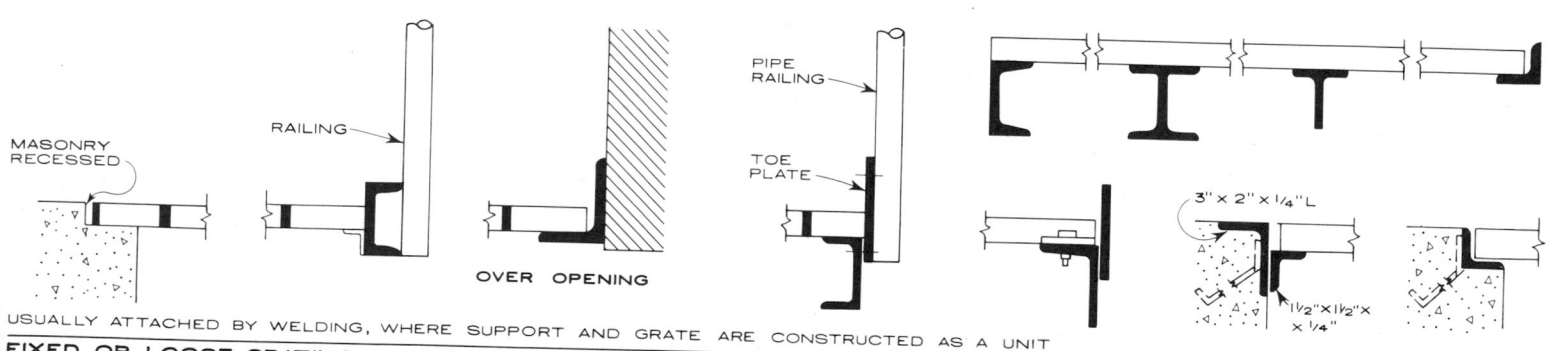

USUALLY ATTACHED BY WELDING, WHERE SUPPORT AND GRATE ARE CONSTRUCTED AS A UNIT

FIXED OR LOOSE GRATINGS 1½" = 1'-0"

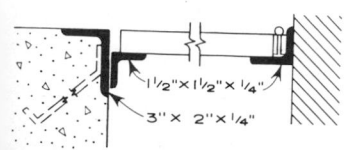
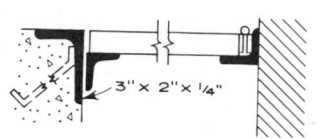
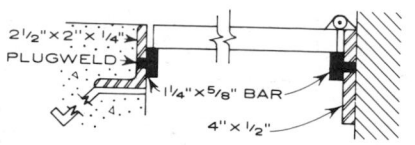
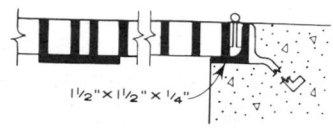

SIZES OF ANGLES SUPPORTING GRATING DEPEND ON DEPTH OF GRATING BARS

HINGED AREA GRATINGS 1½" = 1'-0"

Vicente Cordero, AIA; Arlington, Virginia

WIRE & WOVEN WIRE MESH

DIAMETER (INCHES)		GAUGE NO.	ACTUAL SIZE	MESH
DECIMAL	FRACTION			
.2437	1/4"	3		—
.2253	7/32"	4		—
.2070	13/64"	5		—
.1920	3/16"	6		2 1/2"
.1770	11/64"	7		2 1/4"
.1620	5/32"+	8		2"
.1483	5/32"−	9		1 3/4"
.1350	9/64"	10		1 1/2"
.1205	1/8"	11		1 1/4"
.1055	7/64"	12		1"
.0915	3/32"	13		—
.0800	5/64"	14		3/4"
.0625	1/16"	16		3/8" or 1/2"

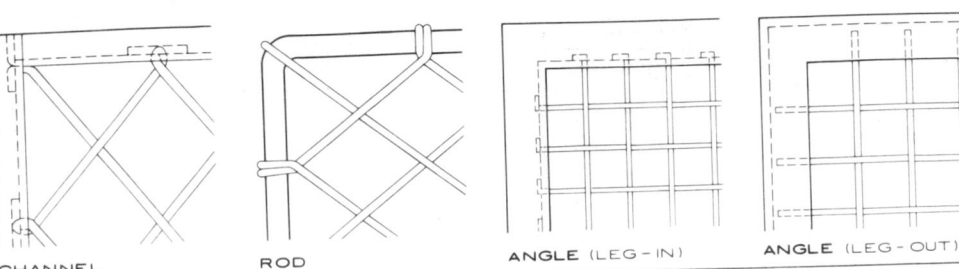

TYPES OF FRAME AND WOVEN WIRE MESH

CHANNEL   ROD   ANGLE (LEG-IN)   ANGLE (LEG-OUT)

RECOMMENDED USES FOR VARIOUS MESHES AND FRAMES

1/2" mesh #16 wire square or diamond	3/8" round or 1" channel	air intake screen, bird screen, window screen	galvanize after fabrication or use bronze
1" mesh #12 wire square or diamond	3/8" round or 1" channel	basement window guard, shelving, pipe railing screens	diamond mesh for strength
1 1/4" mesh #11 wire square or diamond	3/8" round or 1" channel	same as above, also animal cages	galvanize after fabrication
1 1/4" mesh #10 wire diamond	1 1/4" channel or 1" x 1/2" x 1/8"	heavy duty partitions as for tool cribs, elevator shafts, and stock rooms	ideal for factory use where trucking is done
1 1/2" mesh #10 wire diamond	1" or 1 1/4" x 1/2" x 1/8" channel	stockrooms, toolrooms, transformers, fire escape railings, stair enclosures, locker rooms, animal runways, lockers, etc.	standard multi-purpose construction (2" mesh can be used for economy)
1 1/2" mesh #10 wire	1" channel or 1/2" round	door and window guards	usual specification for insurance protection
2" mesh #6 wire	1 1/2" x 3/4" channel	same as for 1 1/2" mesh //10 wire	for heavy duty use

Woven wire available in stainless steel, aluminum, brass, bronze, copper, monel, etc. Can be round, square, flat, pressed, or crimped.

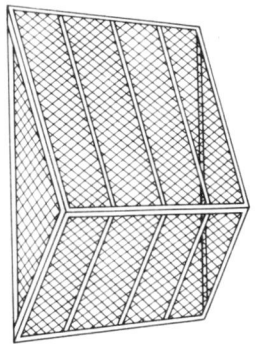

GUARD FOR VENTILATING SASH

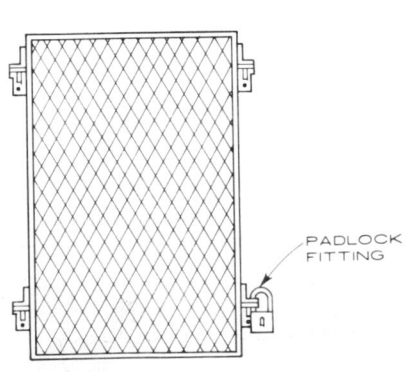

PADLOCK FITTING

REMOVABLE GUARD

WOVEN WIRE MESH WINDOW GUARDS

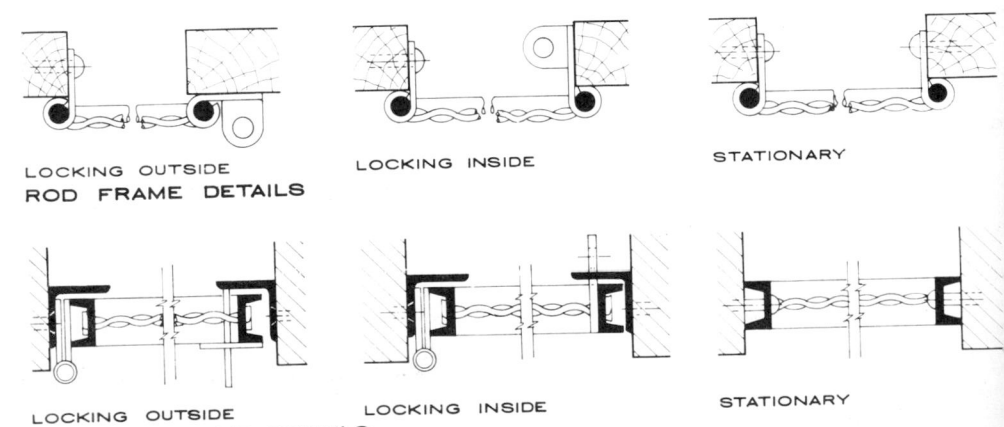

LOCKING OUTSIDE   LOCKING INSIDE   STATIONARY
ROD FRAME DETAILS

LOCKING OUTSIDE   LOCKING INSIDE   STATIONARY
CHANNEL FRAME DETAILS

J. Dean Morris; Morris and Redden; Eugene, Oregon

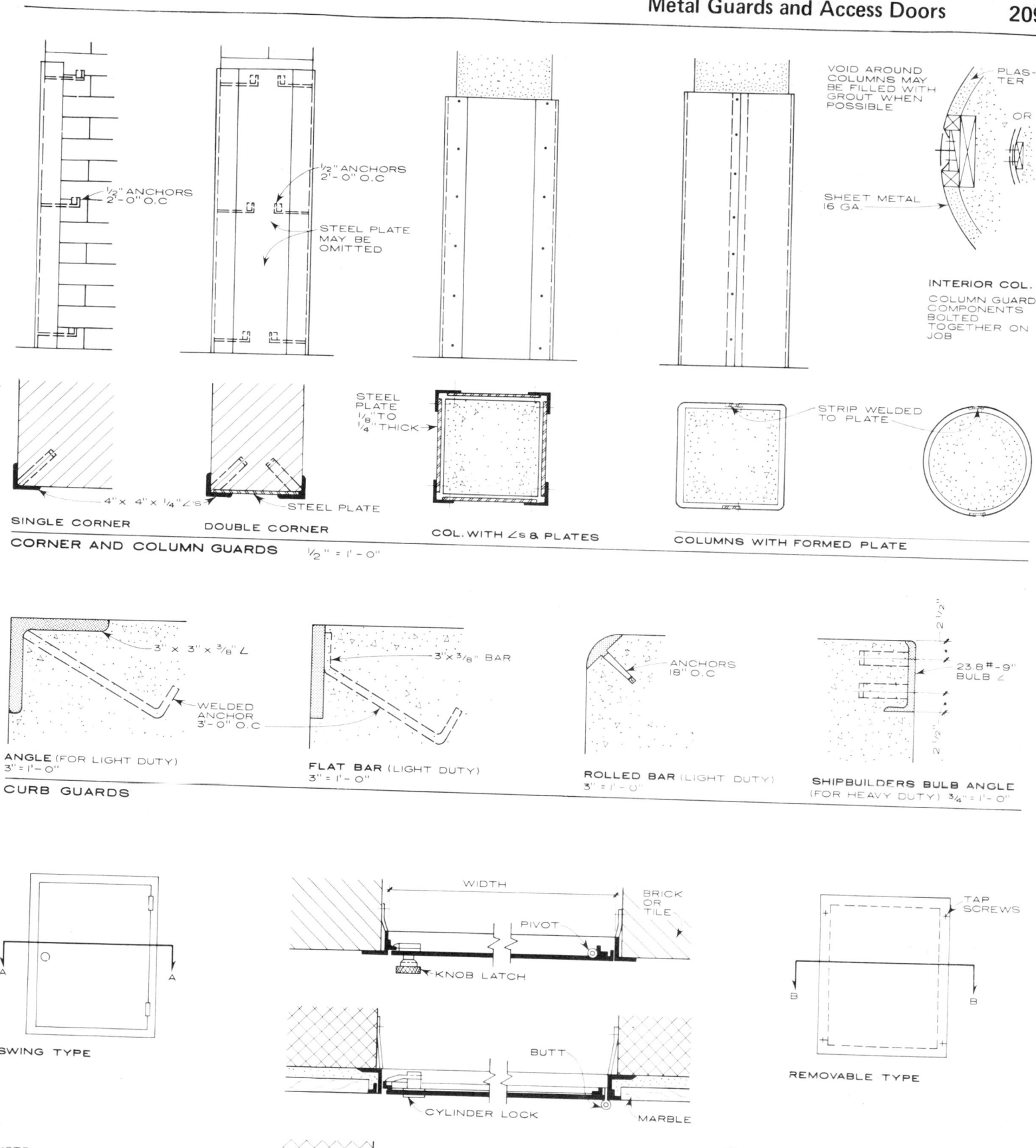

½" ANCHORS 2'-0" O.C

½" ANCHORS 2'-0" O.C

STEEL PLATE MAY BE OMITTED

VOID AROUND COLUMNS MAY BE FILLED WITH GROUT WHEN POSSIBLE

PLASTER

OR

SHEET METAL 16 GA.

INTERIOR COL.

COLUMN GUARD COMPONENTS BOLTED TOGETHER ON JOB

STEEL PLATE ⅛" TO ¼" THICK

STRIP WELDED TO PLATE

4" x 4" x ¼" ∠'s

STEEL PLATE

SINGLE CORNER   **DOUBLE CORNER**   **COL. WITH ∠s & PLATES**   **COLUMNS WITH FORMED PLATE**

CORNER AND COLUMN GUARDS ½" = 1'-0"

3" x 3" x ⅜" ∠

3" x ⅜" BAR

ANCHORS 18" O.C

2 ½"

23.8#-9 BULB ∠

2 ½"

WELDED ANCHOR 3'-0" O.C

ANGLE (FOR LIGHT DUTY) 3" = 1'-0"

FLAT BAR (LIGHT DUTY) 3" = 1'-0"

ROLLED BAR (LIGHT DUTY) 3" = 1'-0"

SHIPBUILDERS BULB ANGLE (FOR HEAVY DUTY) ¾" = 1'-0"

CURB GUARDS

WIDTH

BRICK OR TILE

PIVOT

TAP SCREWS

A   A

KNOB LATCH

B   B

SWING TYPE

CYLINDER LOCK   MARBLE

BUTT

REMOVABLE TYPE

BUTT

CAM LOCK   PLASTER

NOTE:
Frames usually set into building construction and door constructed to fit later. Doors may be hinged, set in with clips or fastened with screws. Hinges may be butt, pivot or surface. Assorted stock sizes from 8" x 8" to 24" x 36".

ACCESS DOORS   SECTIONS 1½" = 1'-0"

SECTIONS A-A

SECTION B-B

Vicente Cordero, AIA; Arlington, Virginia

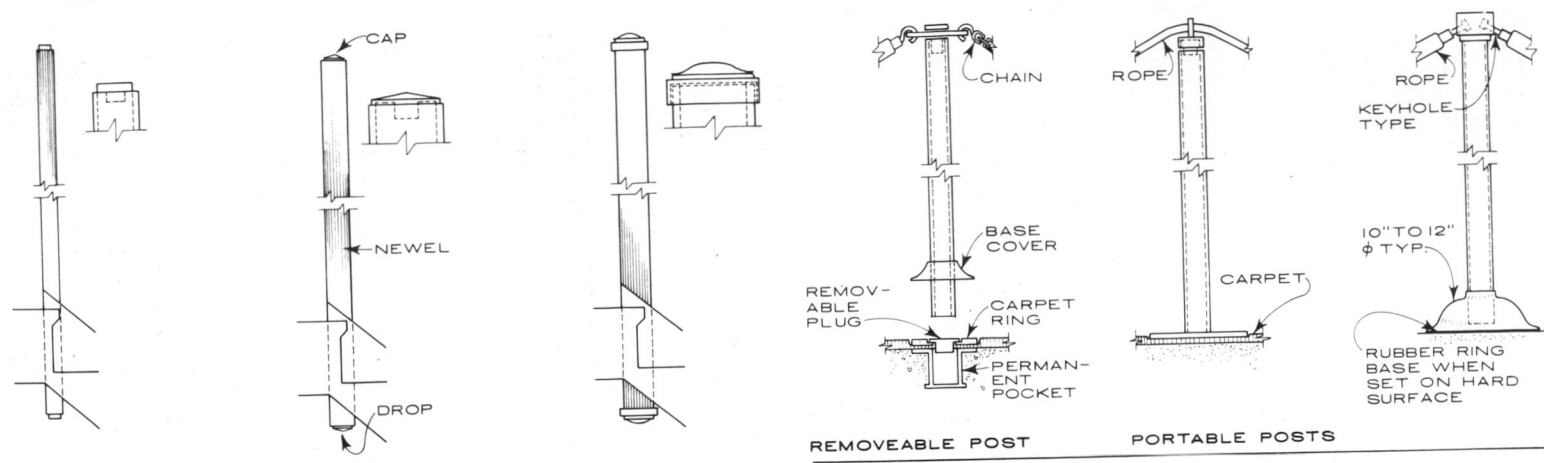

NEWELS OF STEEL PIPE AND TUBING WITH CAST OR PRESSED CAPS AND DROPS

REMOVEABLE POST   PORTABLE POSTS
CONTROL POSTS

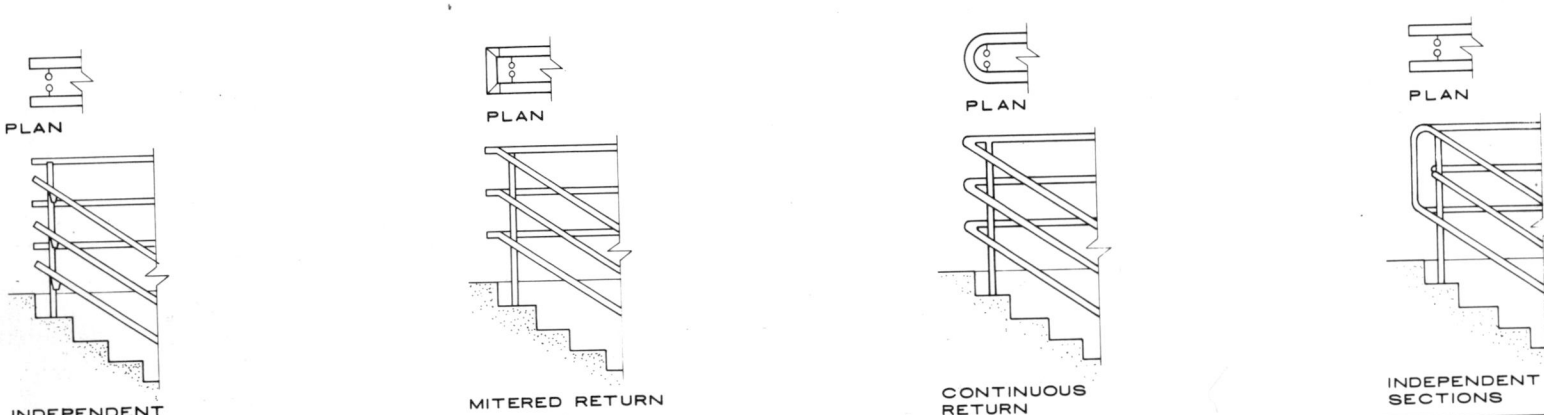

INDEPENDENT SECTIONS

MITERED RETURN

CONTINUOUS RETURN

INDEPENDENT SECTIONS

HANDRAIL RETURNS WITHOUT NEWELS

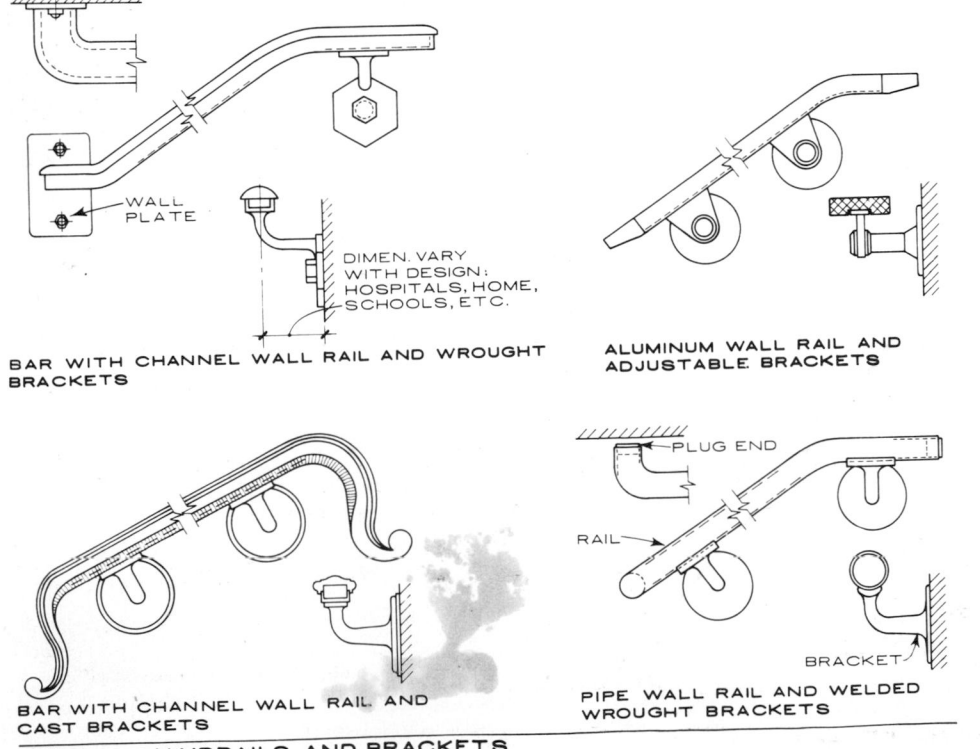

BAR WITH CHANNEL WALL RAIL AND WROUGHT BRACKETS

ALUMINUM WALL RAIL AND ADJUSTABLE BRACKETS

BAR WITH CHANNEL WALL RAIL AND CAST BRACKETS

PIPE WALL RAIL AND WELDED WROUGHT BRACKETS

TYPICAL HANDRAILS AND BRACKETS

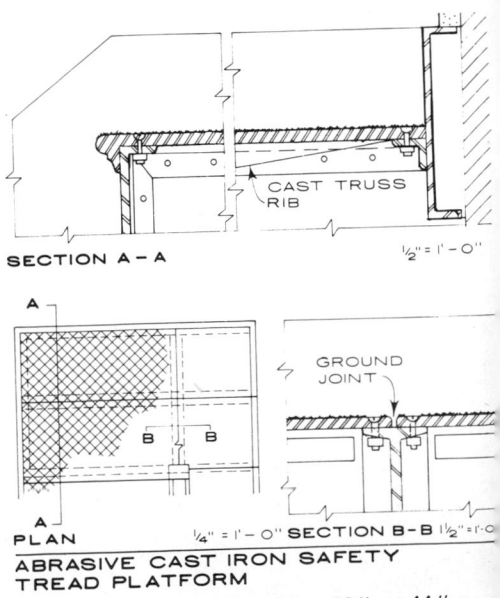

SECTION A - A   1/2" = 1'-0"

ABRASIVE CAST IRON SAFETY TREAD PLATFORM

Plate sizes are limited to 44" x 80" or 44" x 90". Plate thicknesses increase with size from 1/2" to 3/4". Material: Cast abrasive iron.

Paul R. Schieve, Sr. and Joseph Hornyak; Tippetts, Abbett, McCarthy, Stratton; New York, New York

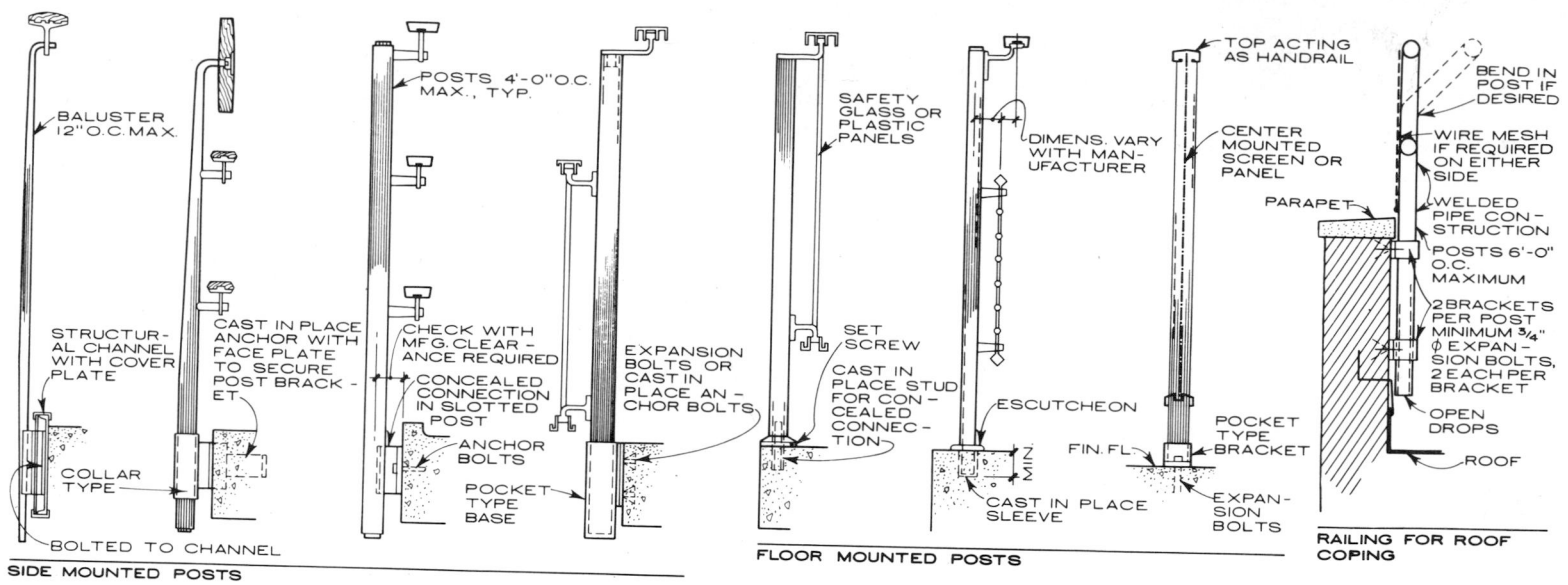

SIDE MOUNTED POSTS

FLOOR MOUNTED POSTS

RAILING FOR ROOF COPING

NOTE:

Three rail units usually 3'–6" high. Two rail units usually 3'–0" high. Rails and brackets may be secured to vertical members of glass wall construction, when properly reinforced.

TYPICAL POST AND RAIL DETAILS

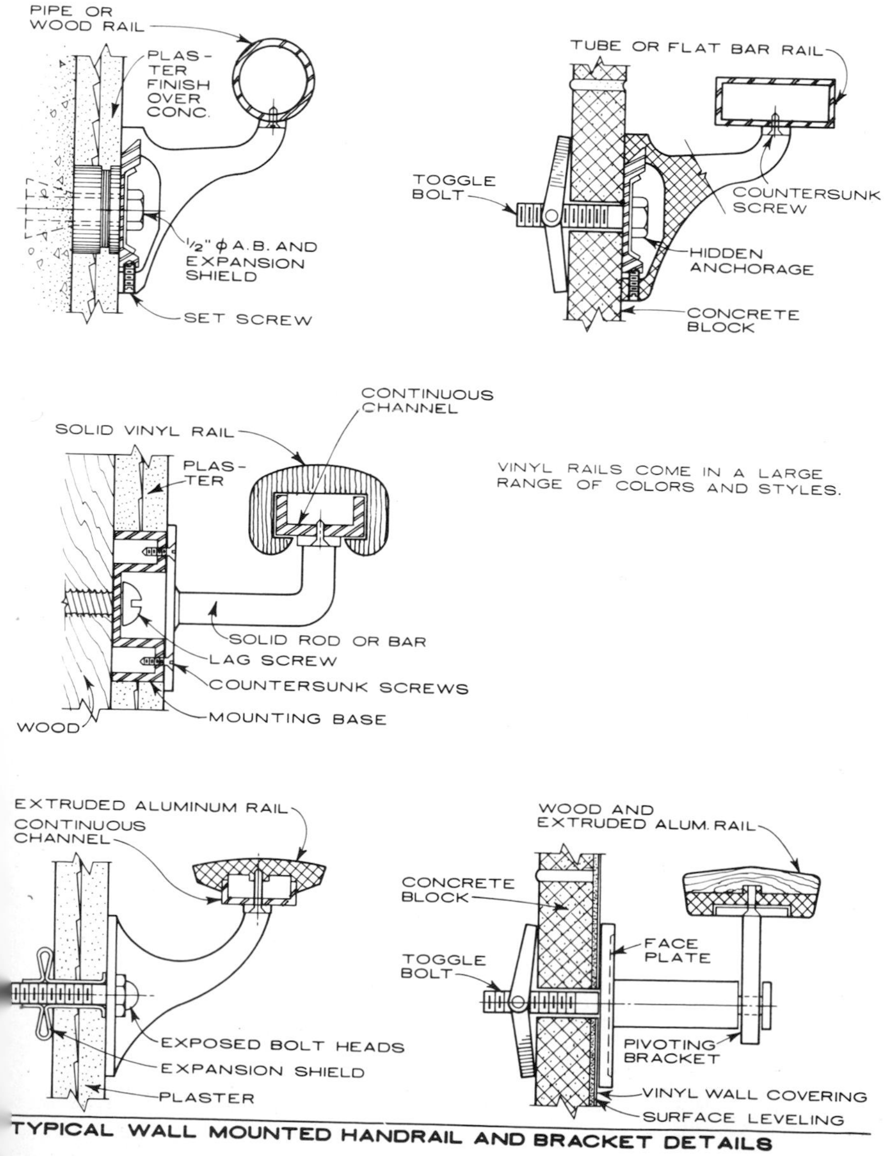

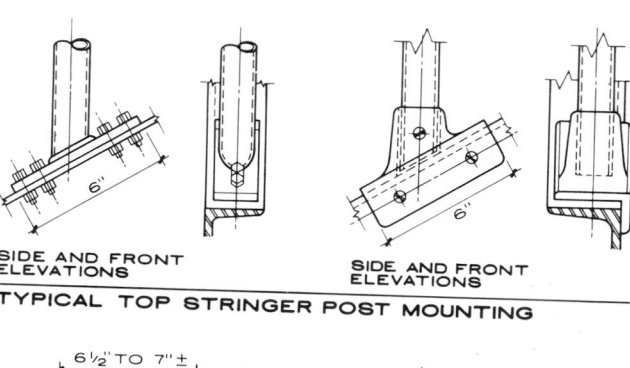

SIDE AND FRONT ELEVATIONS

SIDE AND FRONT ELEVATIONS

TYPICAL TOP STRINGER POST MOUNTING

VINYL RAILS COME IN A LARGE RANGE OF COLORS AND STYLES.

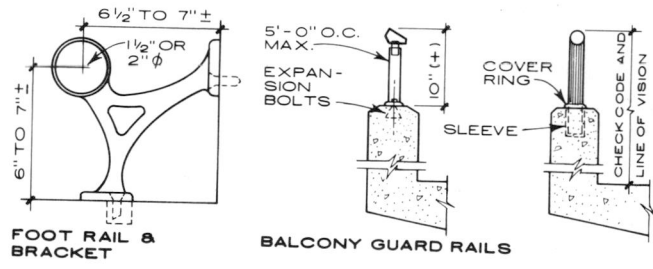

FOOT RAIL & BRACKET

BALCONY GUARD RAILS

ABRASIVE CAST IRON TRENCH COVER AND FRAME
SCALE : 1½" = 1'–0"
Made in abrasive cast iron over thickness ½" for 24" span to ¾" for 44" span.

MAT SINKAGE : NON-FERROUS METAL FRAME
1½" = 1'–0"

MAT THICKNESSES:

Rubber (solid or perforated): ¼", ⅜", ½" thick: Max. Size, 8'–6" x 15'–0".
Cocoa (sheared or unsheared): 1¼", 1½", 1¾" thick (Depress ¼" less than mat thick.)
Link Mats: Suggested Max. Width 6'–0" any shape or length. Frame to be of a non-ferrous metal.
Rubber ⅝", ½", Fibreboard ⅜".
Hardwood ⅝", Leather ⅝", Asphalt Felt ⅜".

TYPICAL WALL MOUNTED HANDRAIL AND BRACKET DETAILS

Paul R. Schieve, Sr. and Joseph Hornyak; Tippetts, Abbett, McCarthy, Stratton; New York, New York

CHAPTER **6**

CARPENTRY

ALLOWABLE UNIT STRESSES FOR STRESS GRADE LUMBER

Species & Commercial Grade	Light Framing	Joists & Planks	Beams & Stringers	Posts & Timbers	Decking	Extreme Fiber in Bending f	Horizontal Shear H	Compression Perpendicular to Grain $c_\perp$	Compression Parallel to Grain c	Modulus of Elasticity E
CEDAR, WESTERN RED					X	900		240		1,100,000
Select Dex					X	700		240		"
Commercial Dex										
DOUGLAS FIR, COAST REG'N			X			2050	120	455	1500	1,760,000
Dense Select Structural	X		X			1900	120	415	1400	"
Select Structural	X					1750	120	415	1400	"
1750f Industrial	X					1500	120	390	1200	"
1500f Industrial	X					1200	95	390	1000	"
1200f Industrial	X					1750	120	455	1400	"
Dense Construction		X	X			1500	120	390	1200	"
Construction		X	X			1200	95	390	1000	"
Standard		X				2050	120	455	1650	"
Dense Select Structural		X				1900	120	415	1500	"
Select Structural		X				1500	120	455	1400	"
Dense Construction				X		1200	120	390	1200	"
Construction				X		1500		390		"
Select Dex					X	1200		390		
Commercial Dex					X					
DOUGLAS FIR			X			2050	120	455	1500	1,760,000
Dense Select Structural	X					2300	125	455	1700	"
Dense Select Structural MC 15	X		X			1900	120	415	1400	"
Select Structural	X					2100	125	415	1550	"
Select Structural MC 15	X					1500	120	390	1200	"
1500f Industrial	X					1750	125	390	1400	"
1500f Industrial MC 15	X					1200	95	390	1000	"
1200f Industrial	X					1500	110	390	1200	"
1200f Industrial MC 15	X					2050	120	455	1650	"
Dense Select Structural		X				2300	125	455	1850	"
Dense Select Structural MC 15		X				1900	120	415	1500	"
Select Structural		X				2100	125	415	1650	"
Select Structural MC 15		X				1750	120	455	1400	"
Dense Construction		X				2050	125	455	1600	"
Dense Construction MC 15		X				1500	120	390	1200	"
Construction		X				1750	125	390	1400	"
Construction MC 15		X				1200	95	390	1000	"
Standard		X				1500	110	390	1200	"
Standard MC 15		X				1750	120	455	1200	"
Dense Construction			X			1500	120	390	1000	"
Construction–Decking			X			1900	120	455	1650	"
Dense Select Structural				X		1750	120	415	1500	"
Select Structural				X		1500	120	455	1400	"
Dense Construction				X		1200	120	390	1200	"
Construction–Decking				X						
HEMLOCK, EASTERN			X			1300	85	360	850	1,210,000
Select Structural	X		X			1200	60	360	775	"
Prime Structural		X				1100	60	360	650	"
Common Structural		X				950	60	360	600	"
Utility Structural		X						360	850	"
Select Structural					X			360		
FIR, WHITE					X	1100		365		1,210,000
Selected Decking					X	850		365		"
Commercial Decking										
HEMLOCK, WEST COAST			X			1600	100	365	1100	1,540,000
Select Structural	X					1500	100	365	1000	"
1500f Industrial	X					1200	80	365	900	"
1200f Industrial	X					1600	100	365	1200	"
Select Structural		X				1500	100	365	1100	"
Construction		X				1200	80	365	1000	"
Standard		X				1500	100	365	1000	"
Construction			X			1200	100	365	1100	"
Construction				X		1300		365		"
Select Dex					X	1000		365		
Commercial Dex					X					
HEMLOCK, WESTERN						1600	100	365	1100	1,540,000
Select Structural	X					1800	105	365	1200	"
Select Structural MC 15	X					1500	100	365	1000	"
1500f Industrial	X					1650	105	365	1150	"
1500f Industrial MC 15	X					1200	80	365	900	"
1200f Industrial	X									

Joseph A. Wilkes, AIA; Wilkes and Faulkner; Washington, D. C.

ALLOWABLE UNIT STRESSES FOR STRESS GRADE LUMBER

SPECIES & COMMERCIAL GRADE	AVAILABLE FOR FOLLOWING USES					ALLOWABLE UNIT STRESSES IN PSI				
	LIGHT FRAMING	JOISTS & PLANKS	BEAMS & STRINGERS	POSTS & TIMBERS	DECKING	EXTREME FIBER IN BENDING f	HORIZONTAL SHEAR H	COMPRESSION PERPENDICULAR TO GRAIN $C\perp$	COMPRESSION PARALLEL TO GRAIN C	MODULUS OF ELASTICITY E
HEMLOCK, WESTERN (CONT.)										
1200 f Industrial MC 15	X					1450	90	365	1050	1,540,000
Select Structural		X				1600	100	365	1200	"
Select Structural MC 15		X				1800	105	365	1300	"
Construction		X				1500	100	365	1100	"
Construction MC 15		X				1650	105	365	1250	"
Standard		X				1200	80	365	1000	"
Standard MC 15		X				1450	90	365	1150	"
Construction			X			1500	100	365	1000	"
Construction				X		1200	100	365	1100	"
Selected Decking					X	1300		365		"
Commercial Decking					X	1000		365		"
LARCH										
Dense Select Structural	X		X			2050	120	455	1500	1,760,000
Dense Select Structural MC 15	X					2300	125	455	1700	"
Select Structural	X		X			1900	120	415	1400	"
Select Structural MC 15	X					2100	125	415	1550	"
1500 f Industrial	X					1500	120	390	1200	"
1500 f Industrial MC 15	X					1750	120	390	1400	"
1200 f Industrial	X					1200	95	390	1000	"
1200 f Industrial MC 15	X					1500	110	390	1200	"
Dense Select Structural		X				2050	120	455	1650	"
Dense Select Structural MC 15		X				2300	125	455	1850	"
Select Structural		X				1900	120	415	1500	"
Select Structural MC 15		X				2100	125	415	1650	"
Dense Construction		X				1750	120	455	1400	"
Dense Construction MC 15		X				2050	125	455	1600	"
Construction		X				1500	120	390	1200	"
Construction MC 15		X				1750	125	390	1400	"
Standard		X				1200	95	390	1000	"
Standard MC 15		X				1500	110	390	1200	"
Dense Construction			X			1750	120	455	1200	"
Construction			X			1500	120	390	1000	"
Dense Select Structural				X		1900	120	455	1650	"
Select Structural				X		1750	120	415	1500	"
Dense Construction				X		1500	120	455	1400	"
Construction				X		1200	120	390	1200	"
Selected Decking					X	1500		390		"
Commercial Decking					X	1200		390		"
PINE, SOUTHERN										
Dense Structural 86 KD	2" Thick only					3000	165	455	2250	1,760,000
Dense Structural 58 KD	2" Thick only					2050	120	455	1650	"
No. 1 Dense KD	2" Thick only					2050	135	455	1760	"
No. 1 KD	2" Thick only					1750	135	390	1500	"
No. 2 KD	2" Thick only					1750	120	455	1300	"
No. 2 Dense KD	2" Thick only					1500	120	390	1100	"
Dense Structural 86	2", 3" & 4" Thick					2900	150	455	2200	"
Dense Structural 58	2", 3" & 4" Thick					1750	105	455	1450	"
No. 1 Dense	2" Thick only					1750	120	455	1550	"
No. 1	1" Thick only					1500	120	390	1350	"
No. 2 Dense	2", 3" & 4" Thick					1400	105	455	1050	"
No. 2	2", 3" & 4" Thick					1200	105	390	900	"
No. 1 Dense SR	3" & 4" Thick					1750	120	455	1750	"
No. 1 SR	3" & 4" Thick					1500	120	390	1500	"
Dense Structural 86	5" Thick & up					2400	150	455	1800	"
Dense Structural 58	5" Thick & up					1600	105	455	1300	"
No. 1 Dense SR	5" Thick & up					1600	120	455	1500	"
No. 1 SR	5" Thick & up					1400	120	390	1300	"
No. 2 Dense SR	5" Thick & up					1400	105	455	1050	"
No. 2 SR	5" Thick & up					1200	105	390	900	"
Industrial 86 KD	1", 1¼" & 1½" Thick					2600	165	390	1950	"
Industrial 58 KD	1", 1¼" & 1½" Thick					1750	120	390	1400	"
Industrial 50 KD	1", 1¼" & 1½" Thick					1500	120	390	1100	"
Industrial 86	1", 1¼" & 1½" Thick					2500	150	390	1900	"
Industrial 58	1", 1¼" & 1½" Thick					1500	105	390	1250	"
Industrial 50	1", 1¼" & 1½" Thick					1200	105	390	900	"
Select	1", 1¼" & 1½" Thick					1750	120	390	1350	"
Select No. 1					X	1200	105	390	900	"
Select No. 2					X	1200	105	390	900	"

Joseph A. Wilkes, AIA; Wilkes and Faulkner; Washington, D. C.

ALLOWABLE UNIT STRESSES FOR STRESS GRADE LUMBER

SPECIES & COMMERCIAL GRADE	AVAILABLE FOR FOLLOWING USES					ALLOWABLE UNIT STRESSES IN PSI				
	LIGHT FRAM-ING	JOISTS & PLANKS	BEAMS & STRING-ERS	POSTS & TIMBERS	DECK-ING	EXTREME FIBER IN BENDING	HORIZ-ONTAL SHEAR	COMPRES-SION PER-PENDICULAR TO GRAIN	COMPRES-SION PAR-ALLEL TO GRAIN	MODULUS OF ELAS-TICITY
						f	H	C⊥	c	E
PINE, NORWAY										
Prime Structural	X					1200	75	360	900	1,320,000
Common Structural	X					1100	75	360	775	"
Utility Structural	X					950	75	360	650	"
PINE (IDAHO WHITE, LODGEPOLE PONDEROSA & SUGAR)										1,100,000
Selected Decking					X	900		305		
Commercial Decking					X	700		305		
REDWOOD										1,320,000
Dense Structural		X	X	X		1700	110	320	1450	
Heart Structural		X	X	X		1300	95	320	1100	"
SPRUCE, EASTERN										1,320,000
1450f Structural Grade		X				1450	110	300	1050	
1300f Structural Grade		X				1300	95	300	975	"
1200f Structural Grade		X				1200	95	300	900	"
SPRUCE, ENGELMANN										1,100,000
Selected Decking					X	750		215		
Commercial Decking					X	600		215		"
SPRUCE, SITKA										1,320,000
Select Dex					X	1100		305		
Commercial Dex					X	850		305		"

Abbreviations: KD = Kiln Dried in accordance with Standard Grading Rules; SR = Stress Rated

WOOD COLUMNS ALLOWABLE SAFE LOADS FOR SIMPLE SOLID COLUMNS USING SIMPLIFIED DESIGN FORMULA AND TABLE.

FORMULA DERIVATION: From Euler Column Formula

$P/A = u \dfrac{\pi^2 E}{(L/r)^2}$ where P = Safe Load in Pounds
      A = Cross Section Area in in. sq.
      L/r = Slenderness Ratio
      E = Modulus of Elasticity
      u = Factor for end condition
      Pin end = 1

Applying reduction factor and adjustment for normal loading during formula becomes:

$P/A = \dfrac{.361 \, E}{(L/r)^2}$ Provided that P/A shall not exceed value for C, allowable unit compressive stress parallel to grain (See Table Allowable Stresses)

For wood columns Slenderness Ratio is expressed as
L/d where L is height in inches, d is least column dimension in inches

Formula then becomes: $P/A = \dfrac{.30 \, E}{(L/d)^2}$ or $P = \dfrac{A \cdot 30E}{(L/d)^2}$

Formula is further simplified by letting $Y = \dfrac{A \cdot 30}{(L/d)^2}$

For square columns of heights between 6 feet and 14 feet values of Y are given in table below.

EXAMPLE: Square Wood Column Height 10 feet
Nominal 6 x 6 Douglas Fir   E = 1,760,000 psi (see table)

d = 5.5 inches
A = 30.25 inches square
$L/d = 120/5.5 = 21.82$
$(L/d)^2 = 475$

$Y = \dfrac{A \cdot 3}{(L/d)^2} = \dfrac{30.25 \times .3}{475} = .019$

$P = YE = .019 \times 1,760,000 = 33,440$ pounds

NOTE: Values for Y not listed in table below may be derived from formula above.

TABLE OF VALUES FOR Y FOR SQUARE WOOD COLUMNS 4 X 4, 6, 8 X 8, 10 X 10 AND 12 X 12 FOR HEIGHTS FROM 6 FEET THROUGH 14 FEET. FOR P (ALLOW. LOAD) MULTIPLY Y X E MODULUS OF ELASTICITY   (See Table)

NOMINAL SIZE	ACTUAL SIZE	AREA		HEIGHT OF COLUMN IN FEET								
				6	7	8	9	10	11	12	13	14
4 x 4	3 9/16 x 3 9/16	12.67	Y	.0089	.0068	.0052	.00414	.00337	.00277	.00233		
6 x 6	5 1/2 x 5 1/2	30.25	Y	.0528	.0388	.0298	.0256	.0192	.0158	.0133	.0389	.0277
8 x 8	7 1/2 x 7 1/2	56.25	Y	.183	.135	.103	.0815	.0659	.0545	.0457	.101	.0865
10 x 10	9 1/2 x 9 1/2	90.25	Y	.475	.347	.265	.208	.170	.140	.117		.186
12 x 12	11 1/2 x 11 1/2	132.25	Y	1.017	.748	.567	.451	.367	.305	.254	.214	

Joseph A. Wilkes, AIA; Wilkes and Faulkner; Washington, D. C.

NOMINAL AND MINIMUM DRESSED SIZES OF SOFTWOOD LUMBER PRODUCTS

LUMBER PRODUCT	THICKNESS NOMINAL	MIN. DRESSED DRY	GREEN	FACE WIDTHS NOMINAL	MIN. DRESSED DRY	GREEN
BOARDS				2	$1\,^1/_2$	$1\,^9/_{16}$
				3	$2\,^9/_{16}$	$2\,^5/_8$
				4	$3\,^9/_{16}$	$3\,^5/_8$
				5	$4\,^1/_2$	$4\,^5/_8$
				6	$5\,^1/_2$	$5\,^5/_8$
	1	$^3/_4$	$^{25}/_{32}$	7	$6\,^1/_2$	$6\,^5/_8$
	$1\,^1/_4$	1	$1\,^1/_{32}$	8	$7\,^1/_2$	$7\,^5/_8$
	$1\,^1/_2$	$1\,^1/_4$	$1\,^9/_{32}$	9	$8\,^1/_2$	$8\,^3/_4$
				10	$9\,^1/_2$	$9\,^3/_4$
				11	$10\,^1/_2$	$10\,^3/_4$
				12	$11\,^1/_2$	$11\,^3/_4$
				14	$13\,^1/_2$	$13\,^3/_4$
				16	$15\,^1/_2$	$15\,^3/_4$
2 INCH DIMENSION				2	$1\,^1/_2$	$1\,^9/_{16}$
				3	$2\,^9/_{16}$	$2\,^5/_8$
				4	$3\,^9/_{16}$	$3\,^5/_8$
				6	$5\,^1/_2$	$5\,^5/_8$
	2	$1\,^1/_2$	$1\,^9/_{16}$	8	$7\,^1/_2$	$7\,^5/_8$
				10	$9\,^1/_2$	$9\,^3/_4$
				12	$11\,^1/_2$	$11\,^3/_4$
				14	$13\,^1/_2$	$13\,^3/_4$
				16	$15\,^1/_2$	$15\,^3/_4$
SHIPLAP $^3/_8$ INCH LAP				4	$3\,^1/_8$	$3\,^3/_{16}$
				6	$5\,^1/_{16}$	$5\,^3/_{16}$
				8	7	$7\,^1/_8$
	1	$^3/_4$	$^{25}/_{32}$	10	9	$9\,^1/_4$
				12	11	$11\,^1/_4$
				14	13	$13\,^1/_4$
				16	15	$15\,^1/_4$
SHIPLAP $^1/_2$ INCH LAP				4	3	$3\,^1/_{16}$
				6	$4\,^{15}/_{16}$	$5\,^1/_{16}$
				8	$6\,^7/_8$	7
	1	$^3/_4$	$^{25}/_{32}$	10	$8\,^7/_8$	$9\,^1/_8$
				12	$10\,^7/_8$	$11\,^1/_8$
				14	$12\,^7/_8$	$13\,^1/_8$
				16	$14\,^7/_8$	$15\,^1/_8$
CENTERMATCH $^1/_4$ INCH TONGUE				4	$3\,^1/_4$	$3\,^5/_{16}$
				5	$4\,^3/_{16}$	$4\,^5/_{16}$
	1	$^3/_4$	$^{25}/_{32}$	6	$5\,^3/_{16}$	$5\,^5/_{16}$
	$1\,^1/_4$	1	$1\,^1/_{32}$	8	$7\,^1/_8$	$7\,^1/_4$
	$1\,^1/_2$	$1\,^1/_4$	$1\,^9/_{32}$	10	$9\,^1/_8$	$9\,^3/_8$
				12	$11\,^1/_8$	$11\,^3/_8$
2 INCH DRESSED & MATCHED $^3/_8$ INCH TONGUE				4	$3\,^1/_8$	$3\,^3/_{16}$
				6	$5\,^1/_{16}$	$5\,^3/_{16}$
	2	$1\,^1/_2$	$1\,^9/_{16}$	8	7	$7\,^1/_8$
				10	9	$9\,^1/_4$
				12	11	$11\,^1/_4$
2 INCH SHIPLAP				4	3	$3\,^1/_{16}$
				6	$4\,^{15}/_{16}$	$5\,^1/_{16}$
	2	$1\,^1/_2$	$1\,^9/_{16}$	8	$6\,^7/_8$	7
				10	$8\,^7/_8$	$9\,^1/_8$
				12	$10\,^7/_8$	$11\,^1/_8$
DIMENSION OVER 2 INCH THICK DRY OR GREEN				3		$2\,^5/_8$
				4		$3\,^5/_8$
	$2\,^1/_2$	$2\,^1/_8$		6		$5\,^1/_2$
	3	$2\,^5/_8$		8		$7\,^1/_2$
	$3\,^1/_2$	3				
	$3\,^1/_2$	$3\,^1/_8$		10		$9\,^1/_2$
	4	$3\,^5/_8$		12		$11\,^1/_2$
				14		$13\,^1/_2$
				16		$15\,^1/_2$
TIMBERS DRY OR GREEN	5 and thicker	$^1/_2$ off		5 and thicker	$^1/_2$ off	

LUMBER PRODUCT	THICKNESS NOMINAL	MAX. M.C. 19%	FACE WIDTHS NOMINAL	MAX. M.C. 19%
FINISH	$^3/_8$	$^5/_{16}$	2	$1\,^1/_2$
	$^1/_2$	$^7/_{16}$	3	$2\,^9/_{16}$
	$^5/_8$	$^9/_{16}$	4	$3\,^9/_{16}$
	$^3/_4$	$^5/_8$	5	$4\,^1/_2$
	1	$^3/_4$	6	$5\,^1/_2$
	$1\,^1/_4$	1	7	$6\,^1/_2$
	$1\,^1/_2$	$1\,^1/_4$	8	$7\,^1/_4$
	$1\,^3/_4$	$1\,^3/_8$	9	$8\,^1/_4$
	2	$1\,^1/_2$	10	$9\,^1/_4$
	$2\,^1/_2$	2	11	$10\,^1/_4$
	3	$2\,^9/_{16}$	12	$11\,^1/_4$
	$3\,^1/_2$	$3\,^1/_{16}$	14	$13\,^1/_4$
	4	$3\,^9/_{16}$	16	$15\,^1/_4$
FLOORING DIMENSION GIVEN IS FACE DIMEN. EXCLUDING TONGUE	$^3/_8$	$^5/_{16}$	2	$1\,^3/_{16}$
	$^1/_2$	$^7/_{16}$	3	$2\,^1/_4$
	$^5/_8$	$^9/_{16}$	4	$3\,^1/_4$
	1	$^3/_4$	5	$4\,^3/_{16}$
	$1\,^1/_4$	1	6	$5\,^3/_{16}$
	$1\,^1/_2$	$1\,^1/_4$		
CEILING	$^3/_8$	$^5/_{16}$	3	$2\,^1/_4$
	$^1/_2$	$^7/_{16}$	4	$3\,^1/_4$
	$^5/_8$	$^9/_{16}$	5	$4\,^3/_{16}$
	$^3/_4$	$^{11}/_{16}$	6	$5\,^3/_{16}$
PARTITION			3	$2\,^1/_4$
	1	$^{23}/_{32}$	4	$3\,^1/_4$
			5	$4\,^3/_{16}$
			6	$5\,^3/_{16}$
STEPPING	1	$^3/_4$	8	$7\,^1/_4$
	$1\,^1/_4$	1	10	$9\,^1/_4$
	$1\,^1/_2$	$1\,^1/_4$	12	$11\,^1/_4$
	2	$1\,^1/_2$		
BEVEL SIDING	$^1/_2$	$^7/_{16}$ butt, $^3/_{16}$ tip	4	$3\,^9/_{16}$
	$^9/_{16}$	$^{15}/_{32}$ butt, $^3/_{16}$ tip	5	$4\,^1/_2$
	$^5/_8$	$^9/_{16}$ butt, $^3/_{16}$ tip	6	$5\,^1/_2$
	$^3/_4$	$^{11}/_{16}$ butt, $^3/_{16}$ tip	8	$7\,^1/_4$
	1	$^3/_4$ butt, $^3/_{16}$ tip	10	$9\,^1/_4$
			12	$11\,^1/_4$
BUNGALOW SIDING	$^3/_4$	$^{11}/_{16}$ butt, $^3/_{16}$ tip	8	$7\,^1/_4$
			10	$9\,^1/_4$
			12	$11\,^1/_4$
RUSTIC & DROP SIDING SHIPLAPPED $^3/_8$ INCH	$^5/_8$	$^9/_{16}$	4	$3\,^1/_8$
	1	$^{23}/_{32}$	5	$4\,^1/_{16}$
			6	$5\,^1/_{16}$
RUSTIC & DROP SIDING SHIPLAPPED $^1/_2$ INCH			4	3
			5	$3\,^{15}/_{16}$
	$^5/_8$	$^9/_{16}$	6	$4\,^{15}/_{16}$
	1	$^{23}/_{32}$	8	$6\,^5/_8$
			10	$8\,^5/_8$
			12	$10\,^5/_8$
RUSTIC & DROP SIDING DRESSED & MATCHED			4	$3\,^1/_4$
	$^5/_8$	$^9/_{16}$	5	$4\,^3/_{16}$
	1	$^{23}/_{32}$	6	$5\,^3/_{16}$
			8	$6\,^7/_8$
			10	$8\,^7/_8$

NOTE: Max. M.C. 19% = maximum moisture content 19%

Joseph A. Wilkes, AIA; Wilkes and Faulkner; Washington, D. C.

CEILING JOISTS

MAXIMUM ALLOWABLE LENGTHS "L" BETWEEN SUPPORTS

SIZE (NOMINAL) IN INCHES	SPACING (C TO C) IN INCHES	E=	1,000,000 Ft. In.	1,200,000 Ft. In.	1,400,000 Ft. In.	1,600,000 Ft. In.
2 × 4	12	L=	9— 4	10— 0	10— 6	11— 0
	16	L=	8— 7	9— 2	9— 8	10— 1
	24	L=	7— 7	8— 1	8— 6	8—11
2 × 6	12	L=	14— 2	15— 1	15—10	16— 7
	16	L=	13— 1	13—11	14— 8	15— 4
	24	L=	11— 8	12— 5	13— 1	13— 8
2 × 8	12	L=	18— 6	19— 8	20— 8	21— 7
	16	L=	17— 2	18— 3	19— 3	20— 1
	24	L=	15— 4	16— 4	17— 2	17—11
2 × 10	12	L=	22—11	24— 4	25— 7	26— 9
	16	L=	21— 5	22— 9	23—11	25— 0
	24	L=	19— 2	20— 5	21— 6	22— 5
2 × 12	12	L=	27— 2	28—11	30— 5	
	16	L=	25— 5	27— 1	28— 6	29— 9
	24	L=	23— 0	24— 5	25— 8	26—10

NOTES:

(The ceiling joist span lengths are based on the following):

1. Maximum allowable deflection = $^1/_{360}$ of the span length.

2. Dead load:
   A. Weight of joist (40 lbs. per cu. ft.).
   B. Lath and plaster ceiling (10 lbs. per cu. ft.).

3. Live load: none.

ATTIC FLOOR JOISTS

MAXIMUM ALLOWABLE LENGTHS "L" BETWEEN SUPPORTS

SIZE (NOMINAL) IN INCHES	SPACING (C TO C) IN INCHES	E=	1,000,000 Ft. In.	1,200,000 Ft. In.	1,400,000 Ft. In.	1,600,000 Ft. In.
2 × 4	12	L=	6— 6	6—11	7— 4	7— 8
	16	L=	6— 0	6— 4	6— 8	7— 0
	24	L=	5— 3	5— 7	5—10	6— 1
2 × 6	12	L=	10— 1	10— 8	11— 3	11— 9
	16	L=	9— 2	(— 9	10— 4	10— 9
	24	L=	8— 1	8— 7	9— 1	9— 6
2 × 8	12	L=	13— 4	14— 2	14—11	15— 7
	16	L=	12— 2	13— 0	13— 8	14— 3
	24	L=	10— 9	11— 5	12— 0	12— 7
2 × 10	12	L=	16— 9	17— 9	18— 8	19— 7
	16	L=	15— 4	16— 4	17— 2	17—11
	24	L=	13— 6	14— 5	15— 2	15—10
2 × 12	12	L=	20— 1	21— 4	22— 5	23— 6
	16	L=	18— 6	19— 7	20— 8	21— 7
	24	L=	16— 4	17— 4	18— 3	19— 1

NOTES:

(The attic floor joist span lengths are based on the following):

1. Maximum allowable deflection = $^1/_{360}$ of the span length.

2. Dead load:
   A. Weight of joist (40 lbs. per cu. ft.).
   B. Lath and plaster ceiling (10 lbs. per cu. ft.).
   C. Single thickness of flooring (2.5 to 3.0 lbs. per sq. ft.).

3. Live load: 20 lbs. per sq. ft. of floor area.

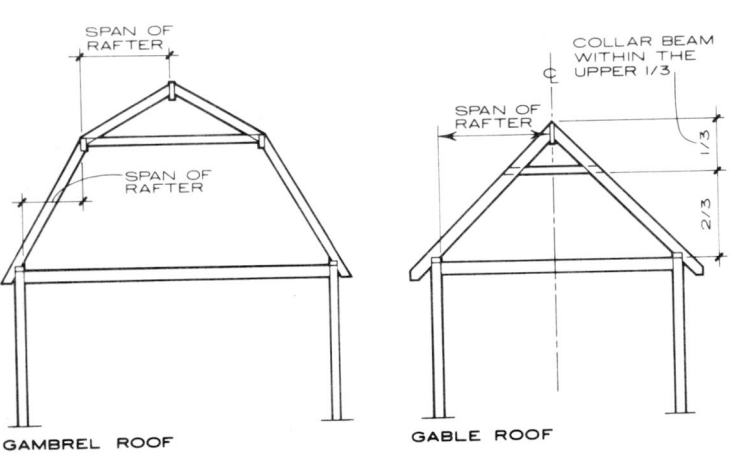

GAMBREL ROOF

GABLE ROOF

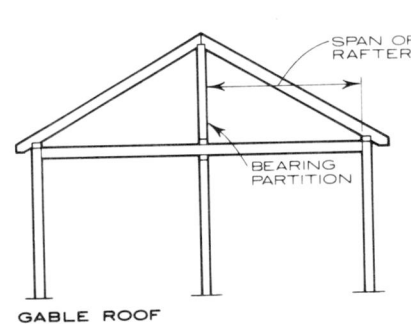

GABLE ROOF

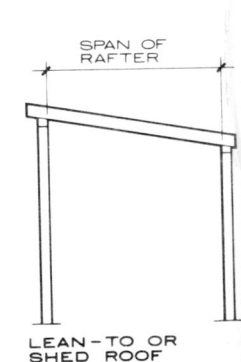

LEAN-TO OR SHED ROOF

NOTE:

(Applicable to this and the following pages on joist and rafter sizes).

SPANS LIMITED BY DEFLECTION were computed for the assumed loads to cause a deflection not exceeding $^1/_{360}$ of the span. The weight of plaster itself was ignored in the assumed loads for the deflection computations, because the initial deflection from the dead load occurs before plaster sets. The influence of live loads, rather than dead loads, when the ratio of live to dead loads is relatively high, is the principal factor to be considered. Also with joisted floors, flooring and bridging serve to distribute moving or concentrated loads to adjoining members. The omission of the plaster weight in load assumption applies to deflection computations only; the full dead and live load is considered when computing for strength.

SPANS LIMITED BY BENDING STRENGTH OF PIECE: may be used where ceilings are not plastered and deflection is not objectionable.

SPANS LIMITED BY HORIZONTAL SHEAR: For the heavier loads where horizontal shear may be a factor, the tables give the horizontal shear "H" induced by the load for each beam for the spans shown. If the horizontal shear "H" shown is greater than permitted for the material used, then select another joist size or a different spacing within the proper shear limit. The following symbols appear in tables:

E = modulus of elasticity.
f = extreme fiber stress in bending.
H = horizontal shear.
L = span length between supports.

DEAD LOAD ASSUMPTIONS: The following average weights of various materials were used as the basis for dead loads in computing the span lengths. All in lbs. per sq. ft.

Finished floor	2.5
Rough floor	2.5
Roof sheathing	2.5
Plaster and lath	10.9

Roof coverings:
  Group 1 Assumed as 2.5 lbs. per sq. ft. including:

Shingles	2.5
Copper sheets	1.5
Copper tile	1.75
Three-ply ready roofing	1.00

Group 2 Assumed as 8 lbs. per sq. ft. including

Five-ply felt and gravel	7
Slate, $^3/_{16}$"	7 $^1/_4$"
Roman tile	8
Spanish tile	8
Ludowici tile	8

Joists based on average weight of wood of 40 lbs. per cu. ft.

LIVE LOAD ASSUMPTIONS: Uniformly distributed.

PARTITIONS: Spans shown are computed for the given live load plus the dead load and do not provide for additional loads such as partitions. Where concentrated loads are imposed the spans should be re-computed to provide for them.

MEMBER SIZE (NOM)	S IN INCHES³
2 x 4	3.56
2 x 6	8.57
2 x 8	15.32
2 x 10	24.44
2 x 12	35.82
2 x 14	49.36
3 x 6	13.84
3 x 8	24.60
3 x 10	39.48
3 x 12	57.86
3 x 14	79.73

SECTION MODULUS

$$S = \frac{bd^2}{6}$$
(IN INCHES³)

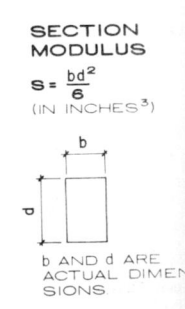

b AND d ARE ACTUAL DIMENSIONS

RAFTERS AND ROOF JOISTS   20 POUND LIVE LOAD   GROUP 1 ROOF COVERING

MAXIMUM ALLOWABLE LENGTHS "L" BETWEEN SUPPORTS.

From building code or other authority determine the allowable modulus of elasticity "E" (if span is to be limited by deflection) or the allowable extreme fiber stress in bending "f" (if span is to be determined by bending) for the species and grade of lumber used. Refer to the column below with corresponding value to determine the safe span for size and spacing of rafter and roof joist desired. Check span selected for deflection with spans for bending to see it does not exceed length permitted for bending stress "f" of material used.

SIZE (NOMINAL) IN INCHES	SPACING (C TO C) IN INCHES	SPAN "L" LIMITED BY DEFLECTION				SPAN "L" DETERMINED BY BENDING										
		E= 1,000,000	1,200,000	1,400,000	1,600,000	f= 900	1,000	1,100	1,200	1,300	1,400	1,500	1,600	1,700	1,800
		Ft In	Ft In	Ft In	Ft In	Ft In	Ft In	Ft In	Ft In	Ft In	Ft In	Ft In	Ft In	Ft In	Ft In
2 × 4	12	7-1	7-7	7-11	8-4	9-0	9-5	9-11	10-4	10-9	11-2	11-7	11-11	12-4	12-8
	16	6-6	6-11	7-3	7-7	7-10	8-3	8-8	9-0	9-5	9-9	10-1	10-5	10-9	11-1
2 × 6	12	10-11	11-7	12-2	12-9	13-8	14-5	15-1	15-9	16-5	17-1	17-8	18-3	18-9	19-4
	16	10-0	10-7	11-2	11-8	12-0	12-8	13-3	13-10	14-5	14-11	15-6	16-0	16-6	16-11
2 × 8	12	14-5	15-3	16-1	16-10	17-11	18-11	19-10	20-9	21-7	22-4	23-2	23-11	24-8	25-4
	16	13-3	14-0	14-9	15-5	15-9	16-8	17-5	18-3	19-0	19-8	20-4	21-0	21-8	22-4
2 × 10	12	18-0	19-2	20-2	21-1	22-4	23-7	24-9	25-10	26-11	27-11	28-11	29-10	30-9	
	16	16-7	17-8	18-7	19-5	19-9	20-10	21-10	22-10	23-9	24-8	25-6	26-4	27-2	27-11
2 × 12	12	21-7	23-0	24-2	25-3	26-8	28-1	29-6	30-10						
	16	19-11	21-2	22-3	23-4	23-8	24-11	26-1	27-3	28-5	29-6	30-6			
2 × 14	12	25-2	26-8	28-1	29-5	30-10									
	16	23-3	24-8	26-0	27-2	27-5	28-11	30-4							
3 × 6	12	12-7	13-4	14-1	14-8	16-11	17-10	18-8	19-6	20-4	21-1	21-10	22-6	23-3	23-11
	16	11-7	12-3	12-11	13-6	14-11	15-9	16-6	17-3	17-11	18-7	19-3	19-10	20-6	21-1
3 × 8	12	16-6	17-6	18-5	19-3	22-0	23-2	24-4	25-5	26-5	27-5	28-5	29-4	30-3	
	16	15-3	16-2	17-0	17-10	19-6	20-7	21-7	22-6	23-5	24-4	25-2	26-0	26-10	27-7
3 × 10	12	20-7	21-10	23-0	24-1	27-3	28-9	30-2							
	16	19-1	20-3	21-4	22-3	24-3	25-7	26-10	28-0	29-2	30-3				

NOTES:

1. Live load = 20 lbs. per sq. ft. of roof surface acting normal to surface.

2. See notes (first page of these tables) for data on which spans are based.

RAFTERS AND ROOF JOISTS   20 POUND LIVE LOAD   GROUP 2 ROOF COVERING

MAXIMUM ALLOWABLE LENGTHS "L" BETWEEN SUPPORTS

From building code or other authority determine the allowable modulus of elasticity "E" (if span is to be limited by deflection) or the allowable extreme fiber stress in bending "f" (if span is to be determined by bending) for the species and grade of lumber used. Refer to the column below with corresponding value to determine the safe span for size and spacing of rafter and roof joist desired. Check span selected for deflection with spans for bending to see it does not exceed length permitted for bending stress "f" of material used.

SIZE (NOMINAL) IN INCHES	SPACING (C TO C) IN INCHES	SPAN "L" LIMITED BY DEFLECTION				SPAN "L" DETERMINED BY BENDING										
		E= 1,000,000	1,200,000	1,400,000	1,600,000	f= 900	1,000	1,100	1,200	1,300	1,400	1,500	1,600	1,700	1,800
		Ft In	Ft In	Ft In	Ft In	Ft In	Ft In	Ft In	Ft In	Ft In	Ft In	Ft In	Ft In	Ft In	Ft In
2 × 4	12	6-8	7-1	7-6	7-10	8-2	8-7	9-0	9-5	9-10	10-2	10-6	10-11	11-3	11-6
	16	6-1	6-6	6-10	7-1	7-1	7-6	7-10	8-3	8-6	8-10	9-2	9-6	9-9	10-1
2 × 6	12	10-3	10-11	11-6	12-0	12-6	13-2	13-10	14-5	15-0	15-7	16-1	16-8	17-2	17-8
	16	9-5	10-0	10-6	11-0	10-11	11-6	12-1	12-7	13-1	13-7	14-1	14-6	15-0	15-5
2 × 8	12	13-7	14-5	15-2	15-10	16-5	17-4	18-2	19-0	19-9	20-6	21-2	21-11	22-7	23-3
	16	12-5	13-3	13-11	14-6	14-5	15-2	15-11	16-7	17-4	17-11	18-7	19-2	19-9	20-4
2 × 10	12	17-0	18-1	19-1	19-11	20-6	21-8	22-8	23-8	24-8	25-7	26-6	27-4	28-3	29-0
	16	15-8	16-7	17-6	18-3	18-1	19-0	20-0	20-10	21-8	22-6	23-4	24-1	24-10	25-6
2 × 12	12	20-5	21-9	22-10	23-11	24-8	25-10	27-2	28-4	29-6	30-7				
	16	18-10	20-0	21-0	22-0	21-8	22-10	23-11	25-0	26-1	27-2	28-1	29-1	30-0	
2 × 14	12	23-10	25-3	26-7	27-10	28-5	30-0								
	16	21-11	23-4	24-6	25-8	25-2	26-6	27-10	29-1	30-3					
3 × 6	12	11-10	12-7	13-3	13-10	15-6	16-4	17-2	17-11	18-7	19-4	20-0	20-8	21-3	21-11
	16	10-11	11-7	12-2	12-9	13-7	14-4	15-1	15-9	16-4	17-0	17-7	18-2	18-9	19-3
3 × 8	12	15-7	16-7	17-5	18-3	20-3	21-4	22-5	23-5	24-4	25-3	26-2	27-0	27-10	28-8
	16	14-4	15-3	16-1	16-9	17-11	18-10	19-9	20-8	21-6	22-4	23-1	23-10	24-7	25-3
3 × 10	12	19-6	20-9	21-10	22-10	25-2	26-6	27-10	29-1	30-3					
	16	18-0	19-2	20-2	21-1	22-4	23-6	24-8	25-9	26-10	27-10	28-10	29-9	30-8	
3 × 12	12	23-4	24-7	26-1	27-3	29-10	31-6								
	16	21-7	22-11	24-2	25-3	26-7	28-0	29-5	30-8						

NOTES:

Live load = 20 lbs. per sq. ft. of roof surface acting normal to surface.

See notes (first page of these tables) for data on which spans are based.

RAFTERS AND ROOF JOISTS   30 POUND LIVE LOAD   GROUP 1 ROOF COVERING

MAXIMUM ALLOWABLE LENGTHS "L" BETWEEN SUPPORTS

From building code or other authority determine the allowable modulus of elasticity "E" (if span is to be limited by deflection) or the allowable extreme fiber stress in bending "f" (if span is to be determined by bending) for the species and grade of lumber used. Refer to the column below with corresponding value to determine the safe span for size and spacing of rafter and roof joist desired. Check span selected for deflection with spans for bending to see it does not exceed length permitted for bending stress "f" of material used.

SIZE (NOMINAL) IN INCHES	SPACING (C TO C) IN INCHES	SPAN "L" LIMITED BY DEFLECTION				SPAN "L" DETERMINED BY BENDING									
		E = 1,000,000	1,200,000	1,400,000	1,600,000	f = 900	1,000	1,100	1,200	1,300	1,400	1,500	1,600	1,700	1,800
		Ft In	Ft In	Ft In	Ft In	Ft In	Ft In	Ft In	Ft In	Ft In	Ft In	Ft In	Ft In	Ft In	Ft In
2 X 4	12	6- 5	6- 9	7- 2	7- 6	7- 8	8- 1	8- 5	8- 10	9- 2	9- 6	9- 10	10- 2	10- 6	10- 10
	16	5- 10	6- 2	6- 6	6- 10	6- 8	7- 0	7- 4	7- 8	8- 0	8- 3	8- 7	8- 10	9- 2	9- 5
2 X 6	12	9- 10	10- 5	11- 0	11- 6	11- 9	12- 4	12- 11	13- 6	14- 1	14- 7	15- 1	15- 7	16- 1	16- 7
	16	9- 0	9- 7	10- 1	10- 6	10- 3	10- 9	11- 4	11- 10	12- 3	12- 9	13- 2	13- 8	14- 1	14- 6
2 X 8	12	13- 0	13- 10	14- 7	15- 3	15- 5	16- 3	17- 1	17- 10	18- 6	19- 3	19- 11	20- 7	21- 2	21- 10
	16	11- 11	12- 8	13- 4	13- 11	13- 6	14- 3	14- 11	15- 7	16- 3	16- 10	17- 5	18- 0	18- 7	19- 1
2 X 10	12	16- 4	17- 5	18- 4	19- 2	19- 4	20- 4	21- 4	22- 4	23- 3	24- 1	24- 11	25- 9	26- 7	27- 4
	16	15- 0	15- 11	16- 9	17- 6	17- 0	17- 10	18- 9	19- 7	20- 5	21- 2	21- 11	22- 7	23- 4	24- 0
2 X 12	12	19- 8	20- 11	22- 0	23- 0	23- 1	24- 4	25- 7	26- 8	27- 9	28- 10	29- 10	30- 10		
	16	18- 1	19- 2	20- 2	21- 1	20- 4	21- 5	22- 6	23- 6	24- 6	25- 5	26- 3	27- 2	28- 0	28- 9
2 X 14	12	22- 11	24- 4	25- 7	26- 9	26- 10	28- 4	29- 8	31- 0						
	16	21- 1	22- 5	23- 7	24- 8	23- 8	25- 0	26- 2	27- 4	28- 6	29- 6	30- 7			
3 X 6	12	11- 5	12- 1	12- 9	13- 4	14- 7	15- 4	16- 1	16- 10	17- 7	18- 2	18- 10	19- 5	20- 0	20- 7
	16	10- 5	11- 1	11- 8	12- 2	12- 9	13- 6	14- 2	14- 9	15- 4	15- 11	16- 6	17- 1	17- 7	18- 1
3 X 8	12	15- 0	15- 11	16- 9	17- 7	19- 1	20- 2	21- 1	22- 1	22- 11	23- 10	24- 8	25- 6	26- 3	27- 0
	16	13- 9	14- 8	15- 5	16- 1	16- 10	17- 9	18- 7	19- 5	20- 3	21- 0	21- 9	22- 5	23- 1	23- 9
3 X 10	12	18- 9	20- 0	21- 0	22- 0	23- 9	25- 1	26- 3	27- 6	28- 7	29- 8	30- 8			
	16	17- 4	18- 5	19- 4	20- 3	21- 0	22- 2	23- 3	24- 3	25- 3	26- 3	27- 2	28- 0	28- 11	29- 9

NOTES:

1. Live load = 30 lbs. per sq. ft. of roof surface acting normal to surface.

2. See notes (first page of these tables) for data on which spans are based.

RAFTERS AND ROOF JOISTS   30 POUND LIVE LOAD   GROUP 2 ROOF COVERING

MAXIMUM ALLOWABLE LENGTHS "L" BETWEEN SUPPORTS

From building code or other authority determine the allowable modulus of elasticity "E" (if span is to be limited by deflection) or the allowable extreme fiber stress in bending "f" (if span is to be determined by bending) for the species and grade of lumber used. Refer to the column below with corresponding value to determine the safe span for size and spacing of rafter and roof joist desired. Check span selected for deflection with spans for bending to see it does not exceed length permitted for bending stress "f" of material used.

SIZE (NOMINAL) IN INCHES	SPACING (C TO C) IN INCHES	SPAN "L" LIMITED BY DEFLECTION				SPAN "L" DETERMINED BY BENDING									
		E = 1,000,000	1,200,000	1,400,000	1,600,000	f = 900	1,000	1,100	1,200	1,300	1,400	1,500	1,600	1,700	1,800
		Ft In	Ft In	Ft In	Ft In	Ft In	Ft In	Ft In	Ft In	Ft In	Ft In	Ft In	Ft In	Ft In	Ft In
2 X 4	12	6- 1	6- 6	6- 10	7- 2	7- 1	7- 6	7- 10	8- 3	8- 7	8- 11	9- 2	9- 6	9- 9	10- 1
	16	5- 7	5- 11	6- 3	6- 6	6- 2	6- 6	6- 10	7- 2	7- 5	7- 9	8- 0	8- 3	8- 6	8- 9
2 X 6	12	9- 5	10- 0	10- 6	11- 0	10- 11	11- 6	12- 1	12- 8	13- 2	13- 8	14- 1	14- 7	15- 0	15- 6
	16	8- 7	9- 1	9- 7	10- 0	9- 6	10- 1	10- 7	11- 0	11- 6	11- 11	12- 4	12- 9	13- 1	13- 6
2 X 8	12	12- 5	13- 3	13- 11	14- 7	14- 5	15- 3	15- 11	16- 8	17- 4	18- 0	18- 8	19- 3	19- 10	20- 5
	16	11- 5	12- 1	12- 9	13- 4	12- 7	13- 4	13- 11	14- 7	15- 2	15- 9	16- 3	16- 10	17- 4	17- 10
2 X 10	12	15- 8	16- 8	17- 6	18- 4	18- 1	19- 1	20- 0	20- 11	21- 9	22- 7	23- 4	24- 1	24- 10	25- 7
	16	14- 4	15- 3	16- 0	16- 9	15- 10	16- 9	17- 6	18- 4	19- 1	19- 9	20- 6	21- 2	21- 10	22- 5
2 X 12	12	18- 10	20- 0	21- 1	22- 0	21- 8	22- 10	24- 0	25- 0	26- 1	27- 1	28- 0	28- 11	29- 10	30- 8
	16	17- 3	18- 4	19- 4	20- 2	19- 1	20- 1	21- 1	22- 0	22- 11	23- 9	24- 7	25- 5	26- 2	26- 11
2 X 14	12	22- 0	23- 4	24- 7	25- 8	25- 2	26- 7	27- 10	29- 1	30- 4					
	16	20- 2	21- 5	22- 7	23- 7	22- 2	23- 5	24- 6	25- 8	26- 8	27- 8	28- 8	29- 7	30- 6	
3 X 6	12	10- 11	11- 7	12- 2	12- 9	13- 8	14- 5	15- 1	15- 9	16- 5	17- 0	17- 7	18- 2	18- 9	
	16	10- 0	10- 7	11- 2	11- 8	12- 0	12- 7	13- 3	13- 10	14- 4	14- 11	15- 5	15- 11	16- 5	16- 11
3 X 8	12	14- 5	15- 3	16- 1	16- 10	17- 11	18- 11	19- 10	20- 8	21- 6	22- 4	23- 2	23- 11	24- 8	25- 4
	16	13- 2	14- 0	14- 9	15- 5	15- 9	16- 7	17- 5	18- 2	18- 11	19- 8	20- 4	21- 0	21- 8	22- 3
3 X 10	12	18- 0	19- 2	20- 2	21- 1	22- 4	23- 7	24- 9	25- 10	26- 10	27- 11	28- 10	29- 10	30- 9	
	16	16- 7	17- 7	18- 6	19- 5	19- 9	20- 9	21- 10	22- 9	23- 8	24- 7	25- 6	26- 3	27- 1	27- 11
3 X 12	12	21- 7	22- 11	24- 2	25- 3	26- 8	28- 1	29- 6	30- 9						
	16	19- 11	21- 2	22- 3	23- 3	23- 7	24- 10	26- 1	27- 3	28- 4	29- 5	30- 5			
3 X 14	12	25- 1	26- 8	28- 1	29- 4	30- 10									
	16	23- 2	24- 8	26- 0	27- 2	27- 5	28- 10	30- 3							

NOTES:

1. Live load = 30 lbs. per sq. ft. of roof surface acting normal to surface.

2. See notes (first page of these tables) for data on which spans are based.

RAFTERS AND ROOF JOISTS   40 POUND LIVE LOAD   GROUP 1 ROOF COVERING

MAXIMUM ALLOWABLE LENGTHS "L" BETWEEN SUPPORTS

From building code or other authority determine the allowable modulus of elasticity "E" (if span is to be limited by deflection) or the allowable extreme fiber stress in bending "f" (if span is to be determined by bending) for the species and grade of lumber used. Refer to the column below with corresponding value to determine the safe span for size and spacing of rafter and roof joist desired. Check span selected for deflection with spans for bending to see it does not exceed length permitted for bending stress "f" of material used.

Columns 3–6: **SPAN "L" LIMITED BY DEFLECTION** (E =). Columns 7–16: **SPAN "L" DETERMINED BY BENDING** (f =). All values in Ft–In.

SIZE (NOMINAL) IN INCHES	SPACING (C TO C) IN INCHES	E = 1,000,000	1,200,000	1,400,000	1,600,000	f = 900	1,000	1,100	1,200	1,300	1,400	1,500	1,600	1,700	1,800
2 × 4	12	5-11	6-3	6-7	6-11	6-9	7-2	7-6	7-10	8-2	8-5	8-9	9-0	9-4	9-7
2 × 4	16	5-4	5-9	6-0	6-3	5-11	6-3	6-6	6-10	7-1	7-4	7-7	7-10	8-1	8-4
2 × 6	12	9-1	9-8	10-2	10-8	10-5	11-0	11-6	12-0	12-6	13-0	13-5	13-10	14-4	14-9
2 × 6	16	8-4	8-10	9-3	9-8	9-1	9-7	10-0	10-6	10-11	11-4	11-9	12-1	12-6	12-10
2 × 8	12	12-1	12-10	13-6	14-1	13-9	14-6	15-2	15-10	16-6	17-2	17-9	18-4	18-11	19-5
2 × 8	16	11-0	11-8	12-4	12-11	12-0	12-8	13-3	13-10	14-4	14-11	15-5	15-11	16-5	17-0
2 × 10	12	15-2	16-1	17-0	17-9	17-3	18-2	19-1	19-11	20-9	21-6	22-3	23-0	23-8	24-6
2 × 10	16	13-11	14-9	15-6	16-3	15-1	15-11	16-8	17-5	18-2	18-10	19-6	20-2	20-9	21-4
2 × 12	12	18-4	19-5	20-5	21-4	20-8	21-10	22-11	23-11	24-10	25-10	26-9	27-7	28-5	29-3
2 × 12	16	16-9	17-9	18-9	19-7	18-2	19-2	20-1	21-0	21-10	22-8	23-5	24-3	24-11	25-8
2 × 14	12	21-4	22-7	23-10	24-11	24-1	25-5	26-7	27-10	28-11	30-0				
2 × 14	16	19-7	20-9	21-10	22-10	21-2	22-4	23-5	24-5	25-5	26-5	27-4	28-3	29-1	29-11
3 × 6	12	10-7	11-3	11-10	12-4	13-0	13-9	14-5	15-0	15-8	16-3	16-9	17-4	17-10	18-5
3 × 6	16	9-8	10-3	10-10	11-3	11-5	12-0	12-7	13-2	13-8	14-2	14-8	15-2	15-8	16-1
3 × 8	12	13-11	14-10	15-7	16-4	17-1	18-0	18-11	19-9	20-7	21-4	22-1	22-10	23-6	24-2
3 × 8	16	12-9	13-7	14-4	14-11	15-0	15-10	16-7	17-4	18-0	18-9	19-5	20-0	20-8	21-3
3 × 10	12	17-5	18-7	19-7	20-6	21-4	22-6	23-7	24-8	25-8	26-8	27-7	28-6	29-4	30-3
3 × 10	16	16-1	17-1	18-0	18-10	18-10	19-10	20-10	21-9	22-7	23-6	24-3	25-1	25-10	26-7
3 × 12	12	21-0	22-3	23-6	24-6	25-6	26-11	28-2	29-5	30-8					
3 × 12	16	19-4	20-6	21-7	22-7	22-6	23-9	24-11	26-0	27-1	28-1	29-1	30-3		
3 × 14	12	24-5	25-11	27-4	28-7	29-7	31-2								
3 × 14	16	22-6	23-11	25-2	26-4	26-2	27-7	28-11	30-3						

NOTES:

1. Live load = 40 lbs. per sq. ft. of roof surface acting normal to surface.

2. See notes (first page of these tables) for data on which spans are based.

RAFTERS AND ROOF JOISTS   40 POUND LIVE LOAD   GROUP 2 ROOF COVERING

MAXIMUM ALLOWABLE LENGTHS "L" BETWEEN SUPPORTS

From building code or other authority determine the allowable modulus of elasticity "E" (if span is to be limited by deflection) or the allowable extreme fiber stress in bending "f" (if span is to be determined by bending) for the species and grade of lumber used. Refer to the column below with corresponding value to determine the safe span for size and spacing of rafter and roof joist desired. Check span selected for deflection with spans for bending to see it does not exceed length permitted for bending stress "f" of material used.

Columns 3–6: **SPAN "L" LIMITED BY DEFLECTION** (E =). Columns 7–16: **SPAN "L" DETERMINED BY BENDING** (f =). All values in Ft–In.

SIZE (NOMINAL) IN INCHES	SPACING (C TO C) IN INCHES	E = 1,000,000	1,200,000	1,400,000	1,600,000	f = 900	1,000	1,100	1,200	1,300	1,400	1,500	1,600	1,700	1,800
2 × 6	12	8-9	9-4	9-10	10-3	9-10	10-5	10-11	11-4	11-10	12-3	12-9	13-2	13-6	13-11
2 × 6	16	8-0	8-6	8-11	9-4	8-7	9-1	9-6	9-11	10-4	10-8	11-1	11-5	11-9	12-2
2 × 8	12	11-7	12-4	13-0	13-7	13-0	13-9	14-5	15-0	15-8	16-3	16-10	17-4	17-11	18-5
2 × 8	16	10-7	11-3	11-11	12-5	11-4	12-0	12-7	13-2	13-8	14-2	14-8	15-2	15-7	16-1
2 × 10	12	14-8	15-7	16-5	17-1	16-4	17-3	18-1	18-11	19-8	20-5	21-1	21-10	22-6	23-2
2 × 10	16	13-5	14-3	15-0	15-8	14-4	15-1	15-10	16-6	17-2	17-10	18-5	19-0	19-7	20-2
2 × 12	12	17-8	18-9	19-9	20-7	19-8	20-9	21-9	22-8	23-7	24-6	25-4	26-2	27-0	27-9
2 × 12	16	16-2	17-2	18-1	18-11	17-0	18-2	19-0	19-11	20-8	21-6	22-3	23-1	23-10	24-7
2 × 14	12	20-7	21-10	23-0	24-1	22-10	24-1	25-3	26-5	27-6	28-6	29-6	30-6		
2 × 14	16	18-10	20-1	21-1	22-1	20-1	21-2	22-3	23-2	24-2	25-1	25-11	26-9	27-7	28-5
3 × 6	12	10-2	10-10	11-5	11-11	12-4	13-0	13-8	14-3	14-10	15-5	15-11	16-5	16-11	17-5
3 × 6	16	9-4	9-11	10-5	10-11	10-9	11-4	11-11	12-5	13-0	13-6	13-11	14-5	14-11	15-5
3 × 8	12	13-6	14-4	15-1	15-9	16-3	17-1	17-11	18-9	19-6	20-3	21-0	21-8	22-4	23-0
3 × 8	16	12-4	13-1	13-10	14-5	14-3	15-0	15-9	16-5	17-1	17-9	18-5	19-0	19-7	20-2
3 × 10	12	16-11	18-0	18-11	19-9	20-4	21-6	22-6	23-6	24-5	25-4	26-3	27-1	27-11	28-9
3 × 10	16	15-6	16-6	17-4	18-2	17-10	18-10	19-9	20-8	21-6	22-3	23-1	23-10	24-7	25-5
3 × 12	12	20-4	21-7	22-8	23-9	24-3	25-7	26-10	28-0	29-2	30-3				
3 × 12	16	18-8	19-10	20-11	21-10	21-5	22-7	23-8	24-9	25-9	26-9	27-8	28-7	29-5	30-3
3 × 14	12	23-8	25-1	26-5	27-8	28-2	29-8	31-2							
3 × 14	16	21-9	23-2	24-4	25-6	24-11	26-3	27-6	28-9	29-11	31-1				

NOTES:

Live load = 40 lbs. per sq. ft. of roof surface acting normal to surface.

See notes (first page of these tables) for data on which spans are based.

FLOOR JOISTS   LIVE LOAD = 40 POUNDS PER SQUARE FOOT

MAXIMUM ALLOWABLE LENGTHS "L" BETWEEN SUPPORTS

From building code or other authority determine the allowable modulus of elasticity "E" (if span is to be limited by deflection) or the allowable extreme fiber stress in bending "f" (if span is to be determined by bending) for the species and grade of lumber used. Refer to the column below with corresponding value to determine the safe span for size and spacing of rafter and roof joist desired. Check span selected for deflection with spans for bending to see it does not exceed length permitted for bending stress "f" of material used.

SIZE (NOMINAL) IN INCHES	SPACING (C TO C) IN INCHES	SPAN "L" LIMITED BY DEFLECTION				SPAN "L" DETERMINED BY BENDING									
		E = 1,000,000	1,200,000	1,400,000	1,600,000	"f" = 900	1000	1100	1200	1300	1400	1500	1600	1700	1800
		Ft In	Ft In	Ft In	Ft In	Ft In	Ft In	Ft In	Ft In	Ft In	Ft In	Ft In	Ft In	Ft In	Ft In
2 X 6	12	9- 1	9- 8	10- 2	10- 8	9- 6	10- 0	10- 5	10- 11	11- 4	11- 9	12- 3	12- 7	13- 0	13- 4
	16	8- 4	8- 10	9- 3	9- 8	8- 3	8- 8	9- 1	9- 6	9- 11	10- 3	10- 8	11- 0	11- 4	11- 8
2 X 8	12	12- 1	12- 10	13- 6	14- 1	12- 6	13- 2	13- 10	14- 5	15- 0	15- 7	16- 2	16- 8	17- 2	17- 8
	16	11- 0	11- 8	12- 4	12- 11	10- 11	11- 6	12- 1	12- 7	13- 1	13- 7	14- 1	14- 7	15- 0	15- 5
2 X 10	12	15- 2	16- 1	17- 0	17- 9	15- 9	16- 7	17- 5	18- 2	18- 11	19- 7	20- 4	21- 0	21- 7	22- 3
	16	13- 11	14- 9	15- 6	16- 3	13- 9	14- 6	15- 2	15- 10	16- 6	17- 2	17- 9	18- 4	18- 11	19- 5
2 X 12	12	18- 4	19- 5	20- 5	21- 4	18- 11	19- 11	20- 11	21- 10	22- 9	23- 7	24- 5	25- 2	26- 0	26- 9
	16	16- 9	17- 9	18- 9	19- 7	16- 7	17- 5	18- 3	19- 1	19- 11	20- 8	21- 4	22- 1	22- 9	23- 5
2 X 14	12	21- 4	22- 7	23- 10	24- 11	22- 0	23- 3	24- 4	25- 5	26- 6	27- 6	28- 5	29- 4	30- 3	
	16	19- 7	20- 7	21- 10	22- 10	19- 4	20- 4	21- 4	22- 4	23- 3	24- 1	24- 11	25- 9	26- 6	27- 4
3 X 6	12	10- 7	11- 3	11- 10	12- 4	11- 10	12- 6	13- 1	13- 8	14- 3	14- 9	15- 4	15- 10	16- 3	16- 9
	16	9- 8	10- 3	10- 10	11- 3	10- 4	10- 11	11- 5	12- 0	12- 5	12- 11	13- 4	13- 10	14- 3	14- 8
3 X 8	12	13- 11	14- 10	15- 7	16- 4	15- 7	16- 6	17- 3	18- 0	18- 9	19- 6	20- 2	20- 10	21- 6	22- 1
	16	12- 9	13- 7	14- 4	14- 11	13- 8	14- 5	15- 2	15- 10	16- 5	17- 1	17- 8	18- 3	18- 10	19- 4
3 X 10	12	17- 5	18- 7	19- 7	20- 6	19- 7	20- 7	21- 8	22- 7	23- 6	24- 5	25- 3	26- 1	26- 11	27- 8
	16	16- 1	17- 1	18- 0	18- 10	17- 2	18- 1	19- 0	19- 10	20- 8	21- 5	22- 2	22- 11	23- 7	24- 4
3 X 12	12	21- 0	22- 3	23- 6	24- 6	23- 5	24- 8	25- 10	27- 0	28- 1	29- 2	30- 2			
	16	19- 4	20- 6	21- 7	22- 7	20- 7	21- 9	22- 9	23- 10	24- 9	25- 9	26- 7	27- 6	28- 4	29- 2
3 X 14	12	24- 5	25- 11	27- 4	28- 7	27- 2	28- 8	30- 0							
	16	22- 6	23- 11	25- 2	26- 4	24- 0	25- 3	26- 6	27- 8	28- 10	29- 11	31- 0			

NOTE

Live load = 40 lbs. per sq. ft. with plastered ceiling.

NOTES:

1. Live load = 40 lbs. per sq. ft. with plastered ceiling, and
2. Live load = 50 lbs. per sq. ft. with unplastered ceiling.

FLOOR JOISTS   LIVE LOAD = 50 POUNDS PER SQUARE FOOT

MAXIMUM ALLOWABLE LENGTHS "L" BETWEEN SUPPORTS

From building code or other authority determine the allowable modulus of elasticity "E" (if span is to be limited by deflection) or the allowable extreme fiber stress in bending "f" (if span is to be determined by bending) for the species and grade of lumber used. Refer to the column below with corresponding value to determine the safe span for size and spacing of rafter and roof joist desired. Check span selected for deflection with spans for bending to see it does not exceed length permitted for bending stress "f" of material used.

SIZE (NOMINAL) IN INCHES	SPACING (C TO C) IN INCHES	SPAN "L" LIMITED BY DEFLECTION				SPAN "L" DETERMINED BY BENDING									
		E = 1,000,000	1,200,000	1,400,000	1,600,000	f = 900	1000	1100	1200	1300	1400	1500	1600	1700	1800
		Ft In	Ft In	Ft In	Ft In	Ft In	Ft In	Ft In	Ft In	Ft In	Ft In	Ft In	Ft In	Ft In	Ft In
2 X 6	12	8- 6	9- 1	9- 6	10- 0	8- 9	9- 2	9- 8	10- 1	10- 6	10- 11	11- 3	11- 8	12- 0	12- 4
	16	7- 9	8- 3	8- 8	9- 1	7- 7	8- 0	8- 5	8- 9	9- 2	9- 6	9- 10	10- 1	10- 5	10- 9
2 X 8	12	11- 4	12- 0	12- 8	13- 3	11- 7	12- 2	12- 9	13- 4	13- 11	14- 5	14- 11	15- 5	15- 11	16- 4
	16	10- 4	11- 0	11- 7	12- 1	10- 1	10- 7	11- 2	11- 8	12- 1	12- 7	13- 0	13- 5	13- 10	14- 3
2 X 10	12	14- 3	15- 2	15- 11	16- 8	14- 7	15- 4	16- 1	16- 10	17- 6	18- 2	18- 9	19- 5	20- 0	20- 7
	16	13- 0	13- 10	14- 7	15- 3	12- 8	13- 5	14- 0	14- 8	15- 3	15- 10	16- 5	16- 11	17- 5	17- 11
2 X 12	12	17- 2	18- 3	19- 3	20- 1	17- 6	18- 5	19- 4	20- 2	21- 0	21- 10	22- 7	23- 4	24- 1	24- 9
	16	15- 9	16- 9	17- 7	18- 5	15- 3	16- 1	16- 11	17- 8	18- 5	19- 1	19- 9	20- 5	21- 0	21- 8
2 X 14	12	20- 1	21- 4	22- 5	23- 6	20- 5	21- 6	22- 7	23- 7	24- 6	25- 5	26- 4	27- 3	28- 1	28- 10
	16	18- 5	19- 6	20- 7	21- 6	17- 10	18- 10	19- 9	20- 8	21- 6	22- 3	23- 1	23- 10	24- 7	25- 3
3 X 6	12	9- 11	10- 6	11- 1	11- 7	11- 0	11- 7	12- 1	12- 8	13- 2	13- 8	14- 2	14- 7	15- 1	15- 6
	16	9- 1	9- 8	10- 2	10- 7	9- 7	10- 1	10- 7	11- 0	11- 6	11- 11	12- 4	12- 9	13- 2	13- 6
3 X 8	12	13- 1	13- 11	14- 8	15- 4	14- 6	15- 3	16- 0	16- 9	17- 5	18- 1	18- 9	19- 4	19- 11	20- 6
	16	12- 0	12- 9	13- 5	14- 1	12- 8	13- 4	14- 0	14- 7	15- 3	15- 9	16- 4	16- 10	17- 5	17- 11
3 X 10	12	16- 6	17- 6	18- 5	19- 3	18- 2	19- 2	20- 1	21- 0	21- 10	22- 8	23- 5	24- 2	24- 11	25- 8
	16	15- 1	16- 1	16- 11	17- 8	15- 11	16- 9	17- 7	18- 4	19- 1	19- 10	20- 6	21- 3	21- 10	22- 6
3 X 12	12	19- 10	21- 1	22- 2	23- 2	21- 9	22- 11	24- 0	25- 1	26- 2	27- 1	28- 1	29- 0	29- 11	30- 9
	16	18- 2	19- 4	20- 4	21- 3	19- 1	20- 2	21- 1	22- 1	23- 0	23- 10	24- 8	25- 6	26- 3	27- 0
3 X 14	12	23- 1	24- 6	25- 10	27- 0	25- 3	26- 8	28- 0	29- 2	30- 5					
	16	21- 3	22- 7	23- 9	24- 10	22- 3	23- 6	24- 7	25- 9	26- 9	27- 9	28- 9	29- 8	30- 7	

NOTES: (For span length limited by deflection):

1. Maximum allowable deflection = $\frac{1}{360}$ of the span length.

2. Modulus of elasticity as noted for "E".

3. Dead load:
   A. Weight of joist.
   B. Double thickness of flooring (5 lbs.)
   C. Weight of plaster ceiling ignored.

4. Live load = 50 lbs. per sq. ft. with plastered ceiling.

NOTES: (For span length determined by bending):

1. Allowable stress in extreme fiber in bending as noted for "f".

2. Dead load:
   A. Weight of joist.
   B. Double thickness of flooring (5 lbs.)
   C. Plastered ceiling (10 lbs.).

3. Live load = 50 lbs. per sq. ft. with plastered ceiling.

   Live load = 60 lbs. per sq. ft. with unplastered ceiling.

FLOOR JOISTS   LIVE LOAD = 60 POUNDS PER SQUARE FOOT

MAXIMUM ALLOWABLE LENGTHS "L" BETWEEN SUPPORTS

From building code or other authority determine the allowable modulus of elasticity "E" (if span is to be limited by deflection) or the allowable extreme fiber stress in bending "f" (if span is to be determined by bending) for the species and grade of lumber used. Refer to the column below with corresponding value to determine the safe span for size and spacing of rafter and roof joist desired. Check span selected for deflection with spans for bending to see it does not exceed length permitted for bending stress "f" of material used.

SIZE (NOMINAL) IN INCHES	SPACING (C TO C) IN INCHES		SPAN "L" LIMITED BY DEFLECTION				SPAN "L" DETERMINED BY BENDING									
		E =	1,000,000	1,200,000	1,400,000	1,600,000	f = 900	1,000	1,100	1,200	1,300	1,400	1,500	1,600	1,700	1,800
			Ft In	Ft In	Ft In	Ft In	Ft In	Ft In	Ft In	Ft In	Ft In	Ft In	Ft In	Ft In	Ft In	Ft In
2 × 6	12	L =	8—1	8—7	9—1	9—6	8—2	8—7	9—0	9—5	9—9	10—2	10—6	10—10	11—2	11—6
		H =	45	49	52	54	46	49	51	54	56	59	61	63	65	67
	16	L =	7—4	7—10	8—3	8—7	7—1	7—6	7—10	8—2	8—6	8—10	9—2	9—5	9—9	10—0
		H =	54	58	61	64	52	55	58	61	64	66	69	71	74	76
2 × 8	12	L =	10—9	11—5	12—0	12—7	10—10	11—5	11—11	12—6	13—0	13—6	13—11	14—5	14—10	15—3
		H =	46	49	52	55	46	49	52	54	57	59	61	63	66	68
	16	L =	9—9	10—5	11—0	11—5	9—5	9—11	10—5	10—10	11—4	11—9	12—2	12—6	12—11	13—3
		H =	54	58	62	65	52	55	58	61	64	67	69	72	74	77
2 × 10	12	L =	13—6	14—5	15—2	15—10	13—7	14—4	15—0	15—8	16—4	17—0	17—7	18—2	18—8	19—3
		H =	46	49	52	55	46	49	52	54	57	59	62	64	66	68
	16	L =	12—4	13—2	13—10	14—6	11—10	12—6	13—1	13—8	14—3	14—9	15—4	15—10	16—4	16—9
		H =	55	59	62	65	52	55	58	61	64	67	70	72	75	77
2 × 12	12	L =	16—4	17—4	18—3	19—1	16—4	17—3	18—1	18—11	19—8	20—5	21—2	21—10	22—6	23—2
		H =	47	50	53	55	47	50	52	55	57	60	62	64	66	69
	16	L =	14—11	15—10	16—8	17—5	14—3	15—1	15—10	16—6	17—2	17—10	18—5	19—1	19—8	20—3
		H =	55	59	62	66	52	56	59	62	65	67	70	72	75	77
2 × 14	12	L =	19—1	20—3	21—4	22—4	19—1	20—2	21—2	22—1	23—0	23—10	24—8	25—6	26—3	27—0
		H =	47	50	53	56	47	50	53	55	58	60	62	65	67	69
	16	L =	17—6	18—7	19—6	20—5	16—9	17—7	18—6	19—3	20—1	20—10	21—7	22—3	23—0	23—8
		H =	55	59	63	66	53	56	59	62	65	68	70	73	75	78
3 × 6	12	L =	9—5	10—0	10—6	11—0	10—3	10—10	11—4	11—10	12—4	12—9	13—3	13—8	14—1	14—6
		H =	34	36	38	40	37	39	42	44	45	47	49	51	53	54
	16	L =	8—7	9—2	9—7	10—1	8—11	9—5	9—10	10—4	10—9	11—2	11—6	11—11	12—3	12—8
		H =	40	43	46	48	42	45	47	50	52	54	56	58	60	62
3 × 8	12	L =	12—6	13—3	13—11	14—7	13—6	14—3	15—0	15—8	16—3	16—11	17—6	18—1	18—7	19—2
		H =	34	37	39	41	38	40	42	44	46	48	50	51	53	55
	16	L =	11—5	12—1	12—9	13—4	11—10	12—6	13—1	13—8	14—3	14—9	15—3	15—9	16—3	16—9
		H =	41	44	46	49	43	45	48	50	52	54	56	58	60	62
3 × 10	12	L =	15—8	16—8	17—7	18—4	17—0	17—11	18—10	19—8	20—5	21—3	22—0	22—8	23—4	24—1
		H =	35	37	39	41	38	40	42	44	46	48	50	52	54	55
	16	L =	14—4	15—3	16—1	16—10	14—11	15—8	16—6	17—2	17—11	18—7	19—3	19—10	20—6	21—1
		H =	41	44	47	49	43	45	48	50	53	55	57	59	61	63
3 × 12	12	L =	18—10	20—1	21—1	22—1	20—5	21—6	22—7	23—7	24—6	25—5	26—4	27—2	28—0	28—10
		H =	35	38	40	42	38	41	43	45	47	49	51	52	54	56
	16	L =	17—4	18—5	19—4	20—3	17—11	18—10	19—9	20—8	21—6	22—4	23—1	23—10	24—7	25—4
		H =	42	45	47	50	43	46	48	51	53	55	57	59	61	63
3 × 14	12	L =	22—0	23—3	24—7	25—9	23—9	25—0	26—3	27—5	28—7	29—7	30—8			
		H =	36	38	40	42	39	41	44	47	49	51				
	16	L =	20—3	21—6	22—7	23—8	20—10	22—0	23—1	24—1	25—1	26—0	26—11	27—10	28—8	29—6
		H =	42	45	48	50	43	46	49	51	53	55	58	60	62	64
4 × 8	12	L =	13—9	14—7	15—5	16—1	15—9	16—7	17—4	18—2	18—11	19—7	20—3	20—11	21—7	22—3
		H =	28	30	32	34	33	35	37	38	40	42	43	45	46	48
	16	L =	12—7	13—5	14—1	14—9	13—9	14—6	15—3	15—11	16—6	17—2	17—9	18—4	18—11	19—6
		H =	33	36	38	40	37	39	41	43	45	47	49	50	52	54
4 × 10	12	L =	17—3	18—4	19—4	20—2	19—8	20—9	21—9	22—9	23—8	24—5	25—5	26—3	27—0	27—10
		H =	29	31	33	34	33	35	37	39	41	42	44	45	47	48
	16	L =	15—10	16—10	17—9	18—6	17—3	18—3	19—1	19—11	20—9	21—7	22—4	23—0	23—9	24—5
		H =	34	36	38	40	37	39	42	44	46	47	49	51	53	54

NOTES: (For span length limited by deflection):

1. Maximum allowable deflection = $1/360$ of the span length.

2. Modulus of elasticity as noted for "E".

3. Dead load:
   A. Weight of joist.
   B. Double thickness of flooring (5 lbs.).
   C. Weight of plaster ceiling ignored.

4. Weight of plaster ceiling was included in computing horizontal shear "H" induced by load.

NOTES: (For span length determined by bending):

1. Allowable stress in extreme fiber in bending as noted for "F".

2. Dead load:
   A. Weight of joist.
   B. Double thickness of flooring (5 lbs.).
   C. Plastered ceiling (10 lbs.).

3. Live load = 60 lbs. per sq. ft. with plastered ceiling.
   = 70 lbs. per sq. ft. with unplastered ceiling.

4. Total load was considered in computing horizontal shear "H" induced by load.

MONOPLANER WOOD TRUSSES, STEEL PLATE CONNECTED

Monoplaner trusses usually of 2'' nominal lumber, spaced 2'– 0'' o.c. Camber as required. Dry wall ceiling may be attached directly to trusses. Plywood sheathing staggered joints.

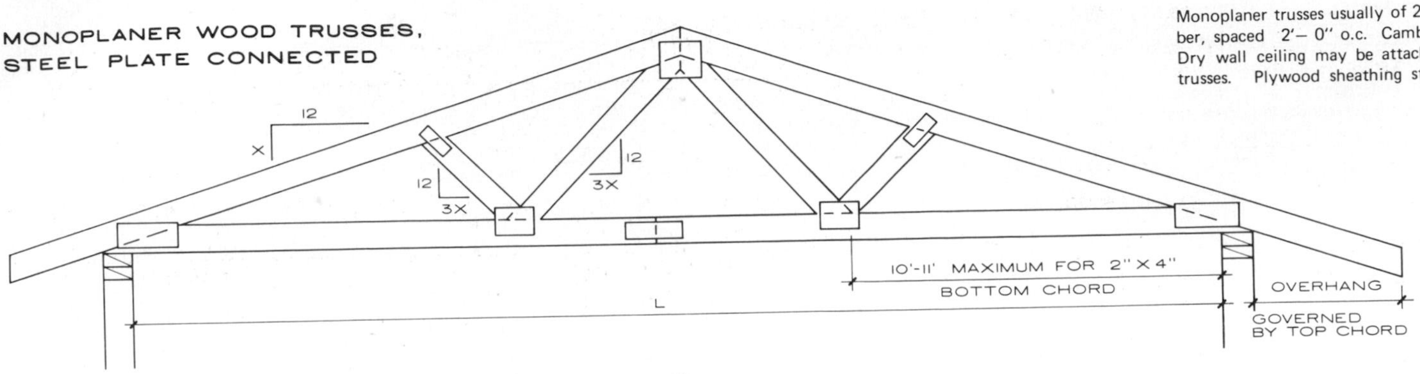

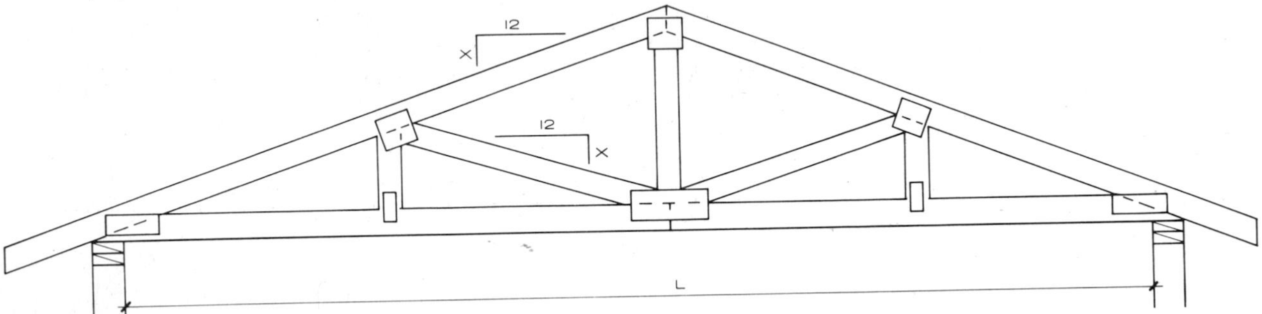

12

×

12

12

3×

3×

10'-11' MAXIMUM FOR 2"X 4"
BOTTOM CHORD

OVERHANG

L

GOVERNED
BY TOP CHORD

12

×

12

×

T

L

Approximate maximum spans for 2 x 4 and 2 x 6 top chords for trusses above (4 panel) using f = 1500 psi lumber with total loading of 55 psf including wind or 47.5 psf including snow.

APPROXIMATE MAXIMUM SPANS (see note, right)

×	L FOR 2 X 4	L FOR 2 X 6
1½	22'	30'
2	25'	32'
2½	26'	33'
3	27'	37'
4, 5, 6	28'	40'

All web members 2 x 4.

FOUR PANEL TRUSSES

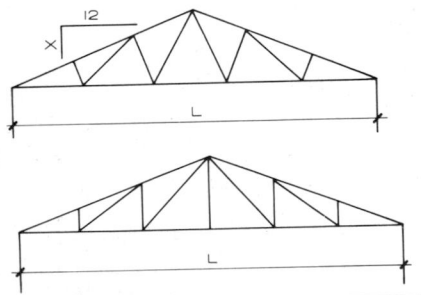

12

×

L

L

APPROXIMATE MAXIMUM SPANS (with 2 x 6 top and bottom chords ; f = 1500 psi.)

×	L FOR PINE	L FOR FIR
2½	49'	46'
3	52'	50'
3½	60'	59'
4, 5, 6	60'	60'

All web members 2 x 4.

SIX PANEL TRUSSES

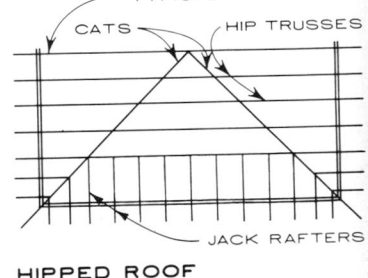

TYPICAL TRUSS

CATS

HIP TRUSSES

JACK RAFTERS

HIPPED ROOF

Plates manufactured from zinc-coated (hot dip process) sheet steel conforming to current ASTM A–93. Plates applied to both sides of joint offset ¼ inch with respect to each other. Where nails are required through connector plates they shall be 1½ inches long with $^9/_{32}$ inch head and a 0.12 inch (8d) deformed or annular ringed shank.

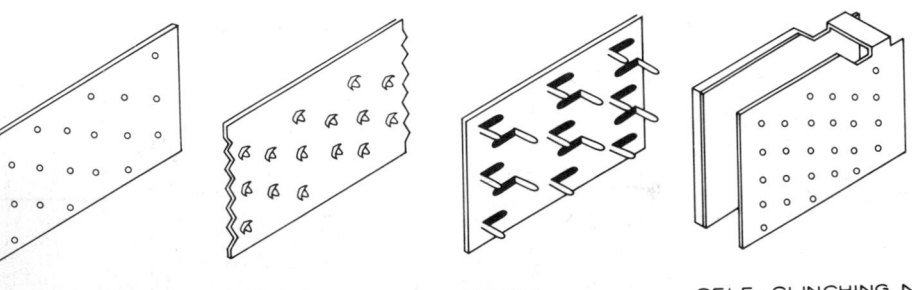

NAIL-ON
20 GAUGE

PRONGS
20 GAUGE

TEETH
14-20 GAUGE

SELF-CLINCHING NAILS
20 GAUGE

PLATE TYPES

GENERAL NOTES

1) Trusses designed in accordance with Truss Plate Institute Design Specifications for plate evaluation and National Design Specifications for nail values.

2) Plates sized for axial loads, eccentricity and net sec-

tion of metal.

3) Truss members shall be clamped in a mechanical or hydraulic jig with sufficient pressure to bring members into reasonable contact at all joints during application of

connector plates.

4) Provide adequate anchorage and erection bracing

Based on National Design Specifications for stress grade lumber and its fastenings.

Joseph A. Wilkes, AIA; Wilkes and Faulkner; Washington, D. C.

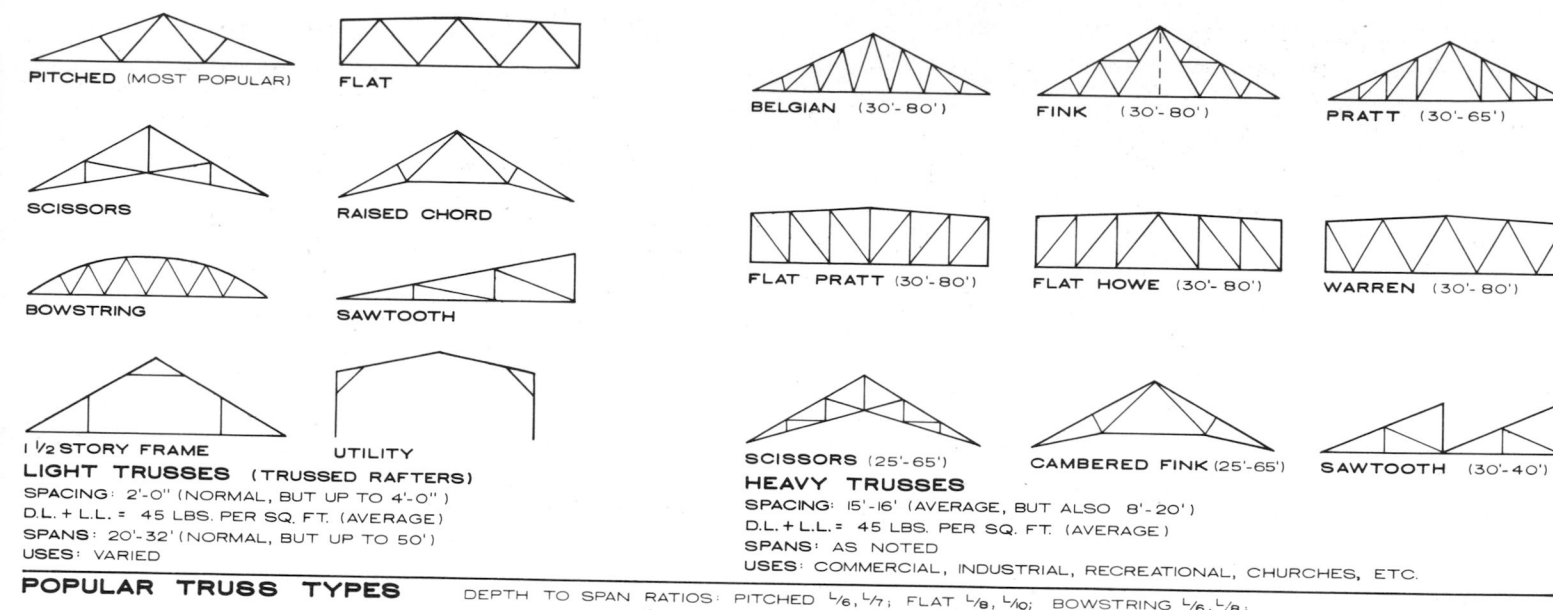

PITCHED (MOST POPULAR)   **FLAT**

SCISSORS   **RAISED CHORD**

BOWSTRING   **SAWTOOTH**

1 1/2 STORY FRAME   **UTILITY**

LIGHT TRUSSES (TRUSSED RAFTERS)
SPACING: 2'-0" (NORMAL, BUT UP TO 4'-0")
D.L. + L.L. = 45 LBS. PER SQ. FT. (AVERAGE)
SPANS: 20'-32' (NORMAL, BUT UP TO 50')
USES: VARIED

BELGIAN (30'-80')   **FINK** (30'-80')   **PRATT** (30'-65')

FLAT PRATT (30'-80')   **FLAT HOWE** (30'-80')   **WARREN** (30'-80')

SCISSORS (25'-65')   **CAMBERED FINK** (25'-65')   **SAWTOOTH** (30'-40')

HEAVY TRUSSES
SPACING: 15'-16' (AVERAGE, BUT ALSO 8'-20')
D.L. + L.L. = 45 LBS. PER SQ. FT. (AVERAGE)
SPANS: AS NOTED
USES: COMMERCIAL, INDUSTRIAL, RECREATIONAL, CHURCHES, ETC.

POPULAR TRUSS TYPES

DEPTH TO SPAN RATIOS: PITCHED $L/6$, $L/7$; FLAT $L/8$, $L/10$; BOWSTRING $L/6$, $L/8$;

LUMBER:
COMPRESSION PARALLEL TO GRAIN.......... 900 PSI
EXTREME FIBER IN BENDING...................1,200 PSI
MODULUS OF ELASTICITY................1,760,000 PSI

BASED ON NATIONAL DESIGN SPECIFICATIONS FOR STRESS GRADE LUMBER AND ITS FASTENINGS

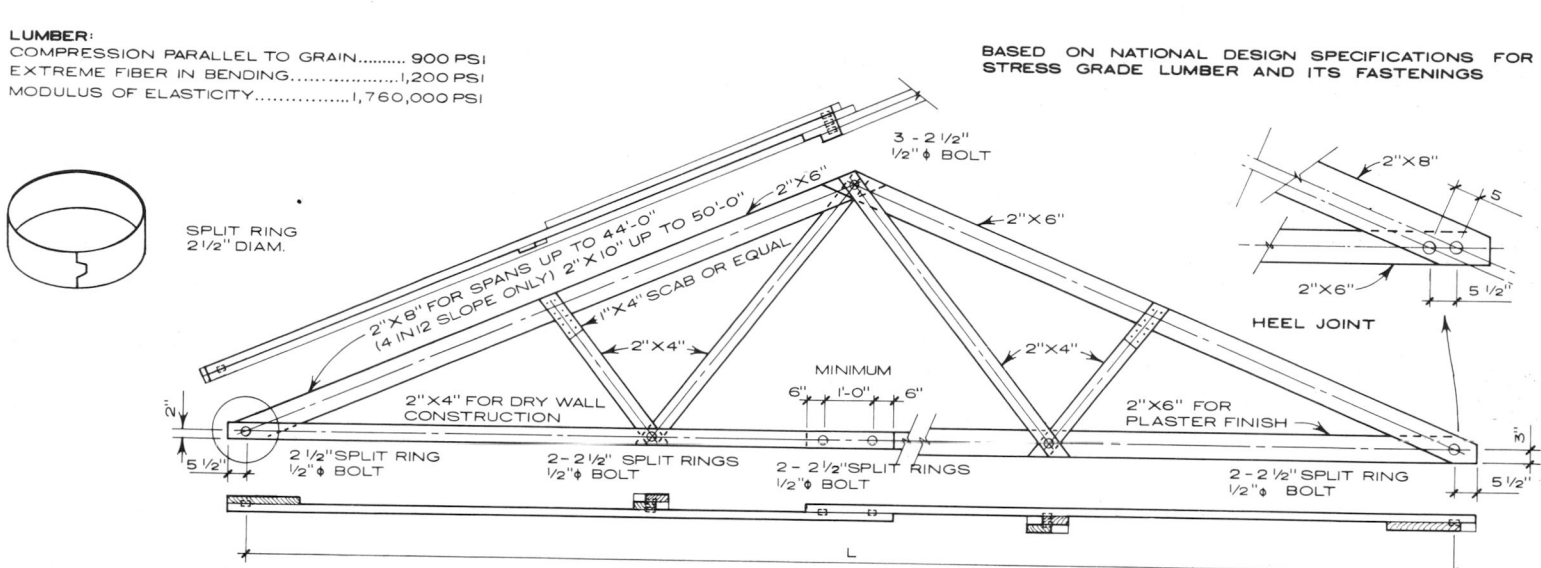

SPLIT RING 2 1/2" DIAM.

3 - 2 1/2"
1/2" φ BOLT

2"X8" FOR SPANS UP TO 44'-0" (4 IN 12 SLOPE ONLY) 2"X10" UP TO 50'-0"

2"X6"

2"X6"

1"X4" SCAB OR EQUAL

2"X4"

2"X4"

2"X8"

2"X6"

S

5 1/2"

HEEL JOINT

2"X4" FOR DRY WALL CONSTRUCTION

MINIMUM
6" 1'-0" 6"

2"X6" FOR PLASTER FINISH

2 1/2"SPLIT RING
1/2" φ BOLT

2 - 2 1/2" SPLIT RINGS
1/2" φ BOLT

2 - 2 1/2"SPLIT RINGS
1/2" φ BOLT

2 - 2 1/2"SPLIT RING
1/2" φ BOLT

2"

5 1/2"

5 1/2"

L

DETAIL OF RAFTER

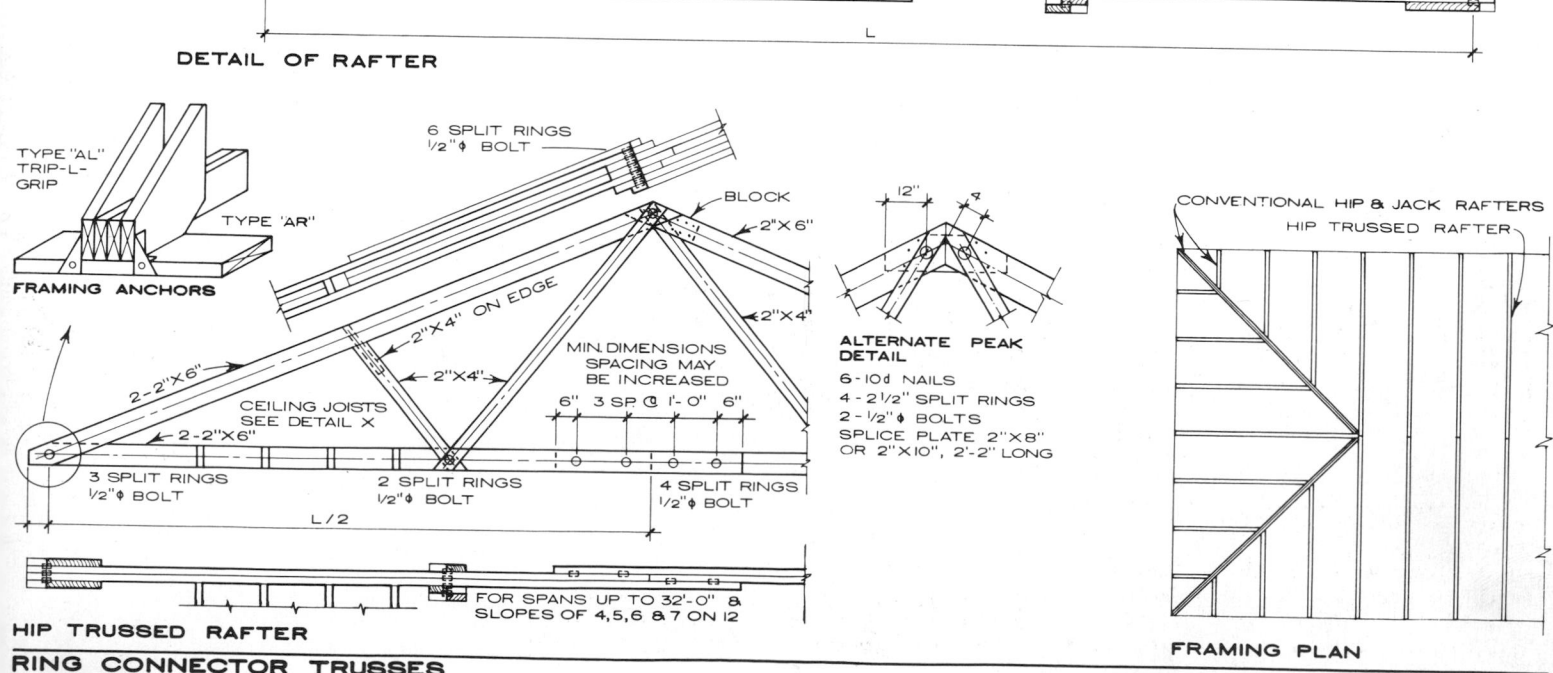

TYPE "AL"
TRIP-L-GRIP

TYPE 'AR'

FRAMING ANCHORS

6 SPLIT RINGS
1/2" φ BOLT

BLOCK

2"X6"

2"X4"

2"X4" ON EDGE

2-2"X6"

2"X4"

CEILING JOISTS
SEE DETAIL X

2-2"X6"

MIN. DIMENSIONS
SPACING MAY
BE INCREASED

6" 3 SP @ 1'-0" 6"

3 SPLIT RINGS
1/2" φ BOLT

2 SPLIT RINGS
1/2" φ BOLT

4 SPLIT RINGS
1/2" φ BOLT

L/2

FOR SPANS UP TO 32'-0" &
SLOPES OF 4,5,6 & 7 ON 12

12"

ALTERNATE PEAK DETAIL
6-10d NAILS
4 - 2 1/2" SPLIT RINGS
2 - 1/2" φ BOLTS
SPLICE PLATE 2"X8"
OR 2"X10", 2'-2" LONG

CONVENTIONAL HIP & JACK RAFTERS
HIP TRUSSED RAFTER

HIP TRUSSED RAFTER

FRAMING PLAN

RING CONNECTOR TRUSSES

Joseph A. Wilkes, AIA; Wilkes and Faulkner; Washington, D. C.

STRUCTURAL GLUED LAMINATED TIMBER

This is an engineered, stress-rated product of a timber laminating plant, comprising assemblies of specially selected and prepared wood laminations, securely bonded together with adhesives. The grain of all laminations is approximately parallel longitudinally. The laminations shall not exceed 2 inches net thickness. They may be comprised of end joined pieces to form any length, of pieces placed or glued edge-to-edge to make wider ones, or of pieces bent to curved form during gluing.

STANDARD WIDTHS OF MEMBERS

Nominal width	3"	4"	6"	8"	10"	12"	14"	16"
Net finished width	2 ¼"	3 ¼"	5" or 5 ¼"	7"	9"	11"	12 ½"	14 ½"

STANDARD DEPTHS OF MEMBERS

Industry recommended practice use nominal two inch thick lumber to produce straight members and curved members having radii of curvature within the bending radii limits for the species.

Nominal one inch thick lumber is normally used when the bending radius is too sharp to permit use of nominal two inch thick laminations.

Members of constant depth normally have a depth which is a multiple of the thickness of the laminating stock used.

ALLOWABLE UNIT STRESS RANGES FOR STRUCTURAL GLUED LAMINATED TIMBER – NORMAL DURATION OF LOADING

SPECIES	EXTREME FIBER IN BENDING, F_b (PSI)	TENSION PARALLEL TO GRAIN, F_t (PSI)	COMPRESSION PARALLEL TO GRAIN, F_c (PSI)	HORIZONTAL SHEAR, F_v (PSI)	COMPRESSION PERPENDICULAR TO GRAIN, $F_{c\perp}$ (PSI)	MODULUS OF ELASTICITY, E (PSI)
DRY CONDITIONS OF USE = MOISTURE CONTENT IN SERVICE LESS THAN 16%						
DOUGLAS FIR (COAST REGION)	1200 to 2600	1200 to 2600	1500 to 2200	165	385 and 450	1,800,000
DOUGLAS FIR AND LARCH	2000 to 2600	1600 to 2600	1500 to 2100	165	385 and 450	1,800,000
WEST COAST HEMLOCK	1600 to 2200	1800 to 2200	1500 to 1700	140	365	1,540,000
SOUTHERN PINE	1800 to 2600	2200 to 2600	1800 to 2000	200	385 and 450	1,800,000
CALIFORNIA REDWOOD	1400 to 2200	1800 to 2200	1800 to 2200	125	325	1,300,000
WET CONDITIONS OF USE = MOISTURE CONTENT IN SERVICE 16% OR MORE						
DOUGLAS FIR (COAST REGION)	950 to 2000	950 to 2000	1100 to 1600	145	260 and 305	1,600,000
DOUGLAS FIR AND LARCH	1600 to 2100	1300 to 2100	1100 to 1500	145	260 and 305	1,600,000
WEST COAST HEMLOCK	1200 to 1800	1400 to 1800	1100 to 1300	120	240	1,400,000
SOUTHERN PINE	1400 to 2100	1800 to 2000	1300 to 1500	175	260 and 300	1,600,000
CALIFORNIA REDWOOD	1100 to 1800	1500 to 1800	1300 to 1600	110	215	1,200,000

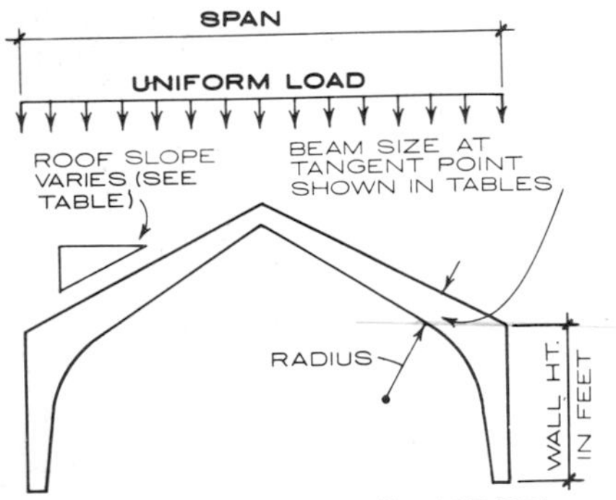

TYPICAL "TUDOR" THREE HINGED ARCH (ON WHICH TABLES BELOW ARE BASED)

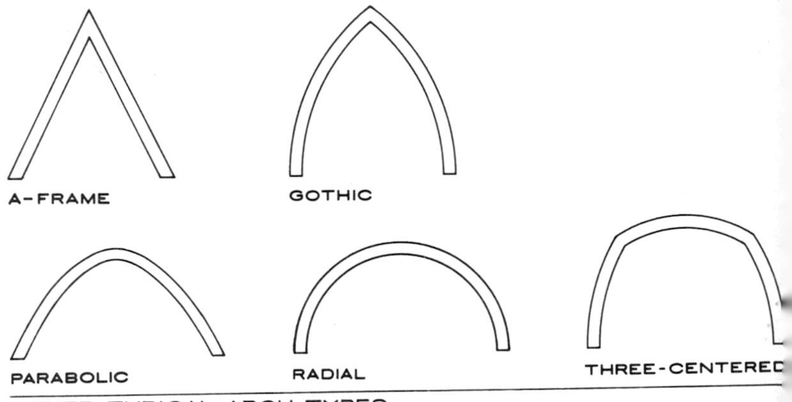

OTHER TYPICAL ARCH TYPES

Typical tangent point sections in inches based on a radius of 9'– 4" and on the following stresses: F_b = 2600psi, F_c = 1900psi, F_v = 165psi

SPAN		40'-0"					50'-0"				
WALL HT.		12	14	16	18	20	12	14	16	18	20
ROOF SLOPE	LOAD PLF										
3/12	600	5x16½	5x17¼	5x18¾	5x18¾	5x19½	5x20¼	7x18¾	7x19½	7x20¼	7x20¼
	800	5x19½	5x21	7x18	7x18¾	7x19½	7x19½	7x21	7x22½	7x23¼	7x24
	1,000	5x21¾	7x19½	7x20¾	7x21	7x21¾	7x21¾	7x24	7x24¾	7x25½	7x26¼
4/12	600	5x16½	5x17¼	5x18	5x18¾	5x19½	5x20¼	5x21	7x18¾	7x19½	7x20¼
	800	5x18¾	5x20¼	5x21	7x18	7x18¾	7x19½	7x21	7x21¾	7x22½	7x23¼
	1,000	5x21	7x18¾	7x19½	7x20¼	7x21	7x21¾	7x23¼	7x24	7x24¾	7x25½
6/12	600	5x15¾	5x16½	5x17¼	5x18	5x18¾	5x18¾	5x20¼	7x18	7x18¾	7x19½
	800	5x18	5x19½	5x20¼	5x21	7x18	7x18¾	7x19½	7x21	7x21¾	7x22½
	1,000	5x20¼	7x18	7x18¾	7x19½	7x20¼	7x20¼	7x21¾	7x23¼	7x24	7x24¾

SPAN		60'-0"					80'-0'				
WALL HT.		12	14	16	18	20	12	14	16	18	20
3/12	600	7x20¼	7x21¾	7x22½	7x24	7x24¾	7x27	9x25½	9x26¼	9x27¾	9x28½
	800	7x23¼	7x24¾	7x26¼	7x27¾	7x28½	9x27	9x29¼	9x30¾	9x32¼	9x33
	1,000	7x25½	7x27¾	9x26¼	9x27	9x27¾		9x33	9x33¾	9x35¼	9x36¾
4/12	600	7x19½	7x21	7x22½	7x23¼	7x24	7x25½	7x27¾	9x29¼	9x27	9x27¾
	800	7x22½	7x24¾	7x25½	7x27	7x27¾	9x25½	9x27¾	9x29¼	9x30¾	9x31½
	1,000	7x25½	7x27	7x29¼	9x27	9x27¾		9x31½	9x33	9x34½	9x35¼
6/12	600	5x21	7x19½	7x20¼	7x21	7x21¾	7x23¼	7x24¾	7x26¼	7x27¾	7x29¼
	800	7x20¼	7x21¾	7x23¼	7x24	7x24¾	7x26¼	7x28½	9x27	9x28½	9x29¼
	1,000	7x22½	7x24¾	7x25½	7x27	7x27¾	9x26¼	9x27¾	9x30	9x31½	9x33

SPAN		100'-0"				
WALL HT.		12	14	16	18	20
3/12	600	9x27¾	9x30	9x32¼	9x33¾	9x34[illegible]
	800		9x35¼	9x36¾	11x35¼	11x36
	1,000		9x35¼	11x37½	11x39	11x40[illegible]
4/12	600	9x26¼	9x28½	9x30	9x31½	9x33
	800		9x30	9x33	9x36¾	11x34[illegible]
	1,000		9x38¼	11x36¾	11x38¼	11x38[illegible]
6/12	600	7x27¾	9x26¼	9x27¾	9x29¼	9x30[illegible]
	800	9x29¼	9x30	9x32¼	9x33¾	9x35[illegible]
	1,000	9x31½	9x33¾	9x36	11x34½	11x36

TYPICAL "TUDOR" THREE HINGED ARCH SECTIONS (CONT.)

Typical tangent point sections in inches based on a radius of 7'– 0" and on the following stresses: Fb = 2400 psi, Fc = 2000 psi, Fv = 200 psi.

SPAN		40'-0"					50'-0"					60'-0"					80'-0"					100'-0"				
WALL HT.		12	14	16	18	20	12	14	16	18	20	12	14	16	18	20	12	14	16	18	20	12	14	16	18	20
ROOF SLOPE	LOAD PLF																									
3/12	500	5¼x16½	5¼x17¼	5¼x19½	5¼x19½	5¼x20¼	5¼x20¼	5¼x21¾	5¼x22½	5¼x24	5¼x25½	5¼x21¾	7 x21¾	7 x23¼	7x24	7x24¾	7x24	7x26¼	7x28½	7x30	7x30¾	7x28½	7x31½	7x33¾	9x31½	9x33
	700	5¼x19½	5¼x20¼	5¼x22¾	5¼x23¼	5¼x24¾	5¼x23¼	5¼x25½	7 x24	7 x24	7 x25½	7 x21¾	7 x24	7 x26¼	7x27	7x29¼	7x28½	7x31½	7x33¾	7x35¼	9x32¼	9x30	9x33	9x35¼	9x37½	9x39
	900	5¼x21	5¼x24¾	5¼x26¼	7 x23¼	7 x24	7 x23¼	7 x25½	7 x27	7 x28½	7 x29¼	7 x26¼	7 x28½	7 x30	7x31½	7x33	9x28½	9x31½	9x33¾	9x35¼	9x36¾	11x31½	11x33¾	9x39¾	9x42	9x44¼
5/12	500	5¼x16½	5¼x17¼	5¼x18¾	5¼x19½	5¼x20¼	5¼x18¾	5¼x21	5¼x22½	5¼x23¼	5 x24	5¼x21¾	5¼x24	7 x22½	7x22½	7x24	7x22½	7x24¾	7x26¼	7x27¾	7x29¼	7x26¼	7x29¼	7x30¾	7x33	7x34½
	700	5¼x19½	5¼x21	5¼x22½	5¼x22½	5¼x24	5¼x23¼	5¼x24¾	5¼x26¼	7 x22½	7 x24¾	7 x21¾	7 x24¾	7 x26¼	7x27	7x27¾	7x27	7x29¼	7x31½	7x33	7x34½	7x31½	7x34½	9x32¼	9x34½	9x36
	900	5¼x21¾	5¼x22¾	5¼x24¾	5¼x25½	7 x23¼	7 x22½	7 x24	7 x23½	7 x27	7 x27¾	7 x25½	7 x27	7 x29¼	7x32¼	7x32¼	7x30	7x33	7x35¼	9x33	9x34½	9x32¼	9x34½	9x36¾	9x38¼	9x40½
7/12	500	5¼x15	5¼x16½	5¼x18	5¼x18¾	5¼x19½	5¼x19½	5¼x20¼	5¼x21	5¼x21¾	5¼x23¼	5¼x21	5¼x22½	5¼x24	7x21¾	7x22½	7x21	7x23¼	7x24¾	7x26¼	7x27	7x24¾	7x27	7x28½	7x30	7x31½
	700	5¼x17¼	5¼x20¼	5¼x21	5¼x21¾	5¼x23¼	5¼x22½	5¼x24	5¼x25½	5¼x26¼	7 x24	7 x21	7 x23¼	7 x24	7x25½	7x26¼	7x25½	7x27¾	7x29¼	7x30¾	7x32¼	7x29¼	7x31½	7x33¾	9x31½	9x33
	900	5¼x20¼	5¼x23¼	5¼x24¾	5¼x24¾	5¼x25½	5¼x24¾	7 x23¼	7 x24¾	7 x25½	7 x27	7 x24¾	7 x26¼	7 x27¾	7x29¼	7x30¾	7x28½	7x30¾	7x33	7x34½	9x32¼	9x29¼	9x31½	9x33¾	9x36	9x37½

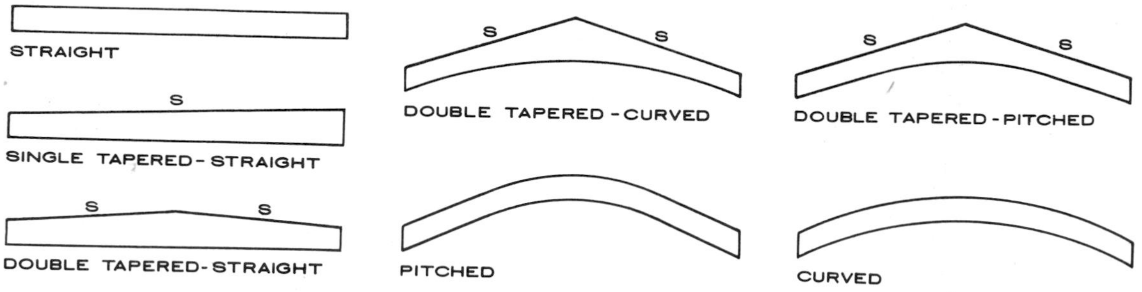
STRAIGHT
S
SINGLE TAPERED-STRAIGHT
S S
DOUBLE TAPERED-STRAIGHT
S S
DOUBLE TAPERED-CURVED
PITCHED
S S
DOUBLE TAPERED-PITCHED
CURVED

NOTES:

1. Beam names describe the top and bottom surfaces of the beam. The words before the hyphen describe the top surface; the word following the hyphen describes the bottom surface.
2. "S" designates a sawn surface. In general "tapered" refers to a sawn surface, and "pitched" to an unsawn sloped surface. Sawn surfaces on the tension side of a beam should be avoided.
3. Chart below applies to straight beams.

LAMINATED ROOF BEAM & PURLIN DESIGN CHART:

TYPICAL SINGLE SPAN SIMPLY SUPPORTED GLUED LAMINATED BEAMS (MEMBER SIZES IN INCHES)

SPAN (FT.)	SPACING (FT.)	TOTAL LOAD CARRYING CAPACITY IN POUNDS PER SQ. FT. 30 PSF	35 PSF	40 PSF	45 PSF	50 PSF	55 PSF
12	6	3 1/4 x 6 1/2	3 1/4 x 6 1/2	3 1/4 x 8 1/8	3 1/4 x 8 1/8	3 1/4 x 8 1/8	3 1/4 x 8 1/8
	8	3 1/4 x 6 1/2	3 1/4 x 8 1/8	3 1/4 x 8 1/8	3 1/4 x 8 1/8	3 1/4 x 8 1/8	3 1/4 x 8 1/8
	12	3 1/4 x 8 1/8	3 1/4 x 8 1/8	3 1/4 x 9 3/4	3 1/4 x 9 3/4	3 1/4 x 9 3/4	3 1/4 x 9 3/4
	16	3 1/4 x 9 3/4	3 1/4 x 9 3/4	3 1/4 x 9 3/4	3 1/4 x 11 3/8	3 1/4 x 11 3/8	3 1/4 x 11 3/8
16	6	3 1/4 x 8 1/8	3 1/4 x 9 3/4	3 1/4 x 9 3/4	3 1/4 x 9 3/4	3 1/4 x 9 3/4	3 1/4 x 9 3/4
	8	3 1/4 x 9 3/4	3 1/4 x 9 3/4	3 1/4 x 9 3/4	3 1/4 x 11 3/8	3 1/4 x 11 3/8	3 1/4 x 11 3/8
	12	3 1/4 x 11 3/8	3 1/4 x 11 3/8	3 1/4 x 11 3/8	3 1/4 x 13	3 1/4 x 13	3 1/4 x 14 5/8
	16	3 1/4 x 11 3/8	3 1/4 x 13	3 1/4 x 13	3 1/4 x 14 5/8	3 1/4 x 14 5/8	3 1/4 x 16 1/4
20	8	3 1/4 x 11 3/8	3 1/4 x 13	3 1/4 x 13	3 1/4 x 13	3 1/4 x 13	3 1/4 x 14 5/8
	12	3 1/4 x 13	3 1/4 x 14 5/8	3 1/4 x 14 5/8	3 1/4 x 16 1/4	3 1/4 x 16 1/4	5 1/4 x 14 5/8
	16	3 1/4 x 14 5/8	3 1/4 x 16 1/4	5 1/4 x 13	5 1/4 x 14 5/8	5 1/4 x 14 5/8	5 1/4 x 16 1/4
	18	3 1/4 x 16 1/4	5 1/4 x 13	5 1/4 x 14 5/8	5 1/4 x 14 5/8	5 1/4 x 16 1/4	5 1/4 x 16 1/4
24	8	3 1/4 x 14 5/8	3 1/4 x 14 5/8	3 1/4 x 14 5/8	3 1/4 x 16 1/4	3 1/4 x 16 1/4	5 1/4 x 14 5/8
	12	3 1/4 x 16 1/4	3 1/4 x 16 1/4	5 1/4 x 14 5/8	5 1/4 x16 1/4	5 1/4 x 16 1/4	5 1/4 x 16 1/4
	16	5 1/4 x 14 5/8	5 1/4 x 16 1/4	5 1/4 x 16 1/4	5 1/4 x 17 7/8	5 1/4 x 17 7/8	5 1/4 x 19 1/2
	18	5 1/4 x 16 1/4	5 1/4 x 16 1/4	5 1/4 x 17 7/8	5 1/4 x 17 7/8	5 1/4 x 19 1/2	5 1/4 x 21 1/8
28	8	3 1/4 x 16 1/4	3 1/4 x 16 1/4	5 1/4 x 14 5/8	5 1/4 x 16 1/4	5 1/4 x 16 1/4	5 1/4 x 16 1/4
	12	5 1/4 x 16 1/4	5 1/4 x 16 1/4	5 1/4 x 17 7/8	5 1/4 x 17 7/8	5 1/4 x 17 7/8	5 1/4 x 19 1/2
	16	5 1/4 x 17 7/8	5 1/4 x 17 7/8	5 1/4 x 19 1/2	5 1/4 x 21 1/8	5 1/4 x 21 1/8	5 1/4 x 22 3/4
	18	5 1/4 x 17 7/8	5 1/4 x 19 1/2	5 1/4 x 21 1/8	5 1/4 x 21 1/8	5 1/4 x 22 3/4	5 1/4 x 24 3/8
32	8	5 1/4 x 16 1/4	5 1/4 x 16 1/4	5 1/4 x 17 7/8	5 1/4 x 17 7/8	5 1/4 x 17 7/8	5 1/4 x 19 1/2
	12	5 1/4 x 17 7/8	5 1/4 x 19 1/2	5 1/4 x 19 1/2	5 1/4 x 21 1/8	5 1/4 x 21 1/8	5 1/4 x 22 3/4
	16	5 1/4 x 19 1/2	5 1/4 x 21 1/8	5 1/4 x 22 3/4	5 1/4 x 22 3/4	5 1/4 x 24 3/8	5 1/4 x 24 3/8
	18	5 1/4 x 21 1/8	5 1/4 x 21 1/8	5 1/4 x 22 3/4	5 1/4 x 24 3/8	5 1/4 x 26	5 1/4 x 26
40	12	5 1/4 x 22 3/4	5 1/4 x 22 3/4	5 1/4 x 24 3/8	5 1/4 x 24 3/8	5 1/4 x 26	7 x 24 3/8
	16	5 1/4 x 24 3/8	5 1/4 x 26	5 1/4 x 26	7 x 26	7 x 26	7 x 27 5/8
	18	5 1/4 x 26	5 1/4 x 26	7 x 26	7 x 26	7 x 27 5/8	7 x 29 1/4
	20	5 1/4 x 26	7 x 24 3/8	7 x 26	7 x 27 5/8	7 x 29 1/4	7 x 30 7/8
50	12	7 x 24 3/8	7 x 27 5/8	7 x 27 5/8	7 x 29 1/4	7 x 29 1/4	7 x 30 7/8
	16	7 x 27 5/8	7 x 29 1/4	7 x 30 7/8	7 x 30 7/8	7 x 32 1/2	7 x 34 1/8
	18	7 x 29 1/4	7 x 30 7/8	7 x 30 7/8	7 x 32 1/2	7 x 34 1/8	9 x 32 1/2
	20	7 x 29 1/4	7 x 30 7/8	7 x 32 1/2	7 x 34 1/8	9 x 32 1/2	9 x 34 1/8
60	12	7 x 29 1/4	7 x 30 7/8	7 x 32 1/2	7 x 34 1/8	9 x 32 1/2	9 x 34 1/8
	16	7 x 32 1/2	7 x 34 1/8	9 x 32 1/2	9 x 34 1/8	9 x 35 3/4	9 x 37 3/8
	18	7 x 34 1/8	9 x 32 1/2	9 x 34 1/8	9 x 35 3/4	9 x 37 3/8	9 x 39
	20	9 x 32 1/2	9 x 34 1/8	9 x 35 3/4	9 x 37 3/8	9 x 39	9 x 40 5/8

NOTES:

Sizes subject to increase if live load exceeds 75% of total load. Allowable deflection is 1/180 of the span for total load.
Basic allowable bending stress is 2400 psi for sections above dividing line (– – – –) and 2600 psi for sections below.
15% increase for short time loading and depth effect factor applied to each section.
Beam weight must be subtracted from total load carrying capacity.

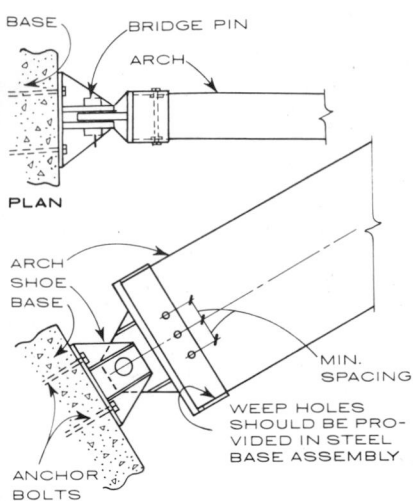

SIDE ELEVATION
TRUE HINGE ANCHORAGE
FOR ARCHES

Recommended for arches where true hinge action is desired

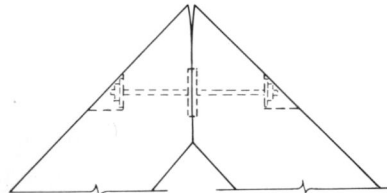

ARCH PEAK CONNECTIONS

This connection is intended for arches with a slope of 4:12 and greater, and will transfer both vertical forces (shear) and horizontal forces (tension and compression). It consists of two shear plates back to back and a through bolt or threaded rod with washers counterbored into the arch. To avoid local crushing of the peak tips of the arch due to dead load deflection, the tips are often beveled off as shown.

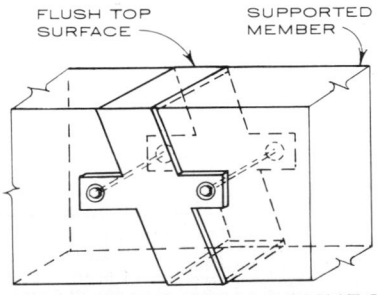

CANTILEVER BEAM CONNECT-
ION-SADDLE TYPE WITH
TENSION TIE·ASSEMBLY

It is necessary to let the plate into the top face of the supporting member and also into the bottom face of the supported member only when both beams are of the same depth. If the supported member is of lesser depth, then it is not necessary to let the bottom of the saddle plate into the bottom face of the supported member in order to obtain end grain bearing.

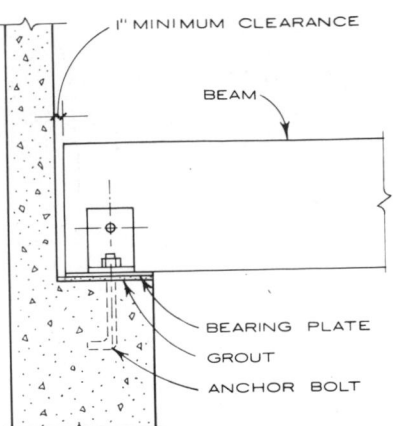

BEAM ANCHORAGE

This detail is intended for anchorages which are required to resist both uplift and horizontal forces. It may have one or more anchor bolts in masonry and one or more bolts with or without shear plates through the beam.

Provide minimum of one inch clearance or impervious moisture barrier on all wall contact surfaces, ends, sides and tops (if masonry exists above beam end).

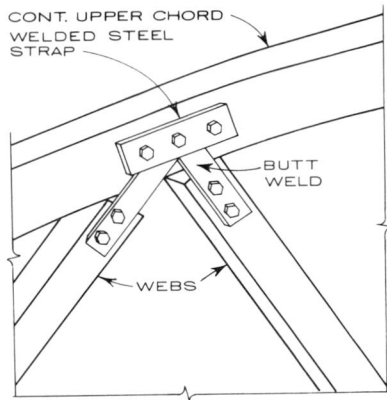

TRUSS CONNECTION
MONOCHORD STEEL STRAP
ASSEMBLY

Provide minimum of $1/4$ inch clearance between web ends and chords.

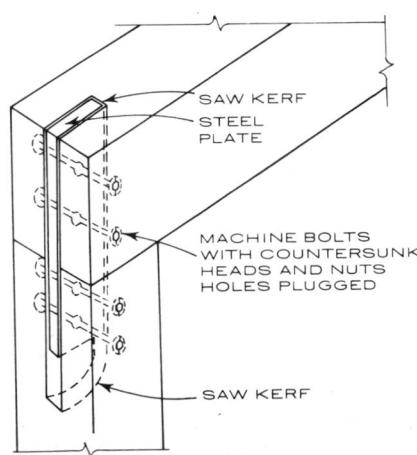

GIRDER TO COLUMN
CONNECTION (CONCEALED)

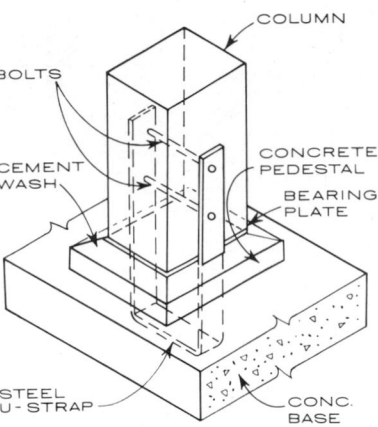

U-STRAP COLUMN
ANCHORAGE TO
CONCRETE BASE

This detail is recommended for industrial buildings and warehouses to resist both horizontal forces and uplift. Moisture barrier is recommended. It may be used with shear plates.

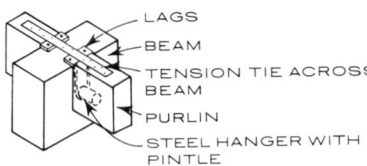

PURLIN HANGER-
CONCEALED TYPE

This connection is used for light and moderate loads. Hardware is completely concealed. It is recommended for laminated and well seasoned purlins but not for unseasoned wood.

BEAM HANGER

When supported members are seasoned material, the top of the supported member may be set flush with the top of the hanger strap.

When supported members are of unseasoned material, the hangers should be so dimensioned that the top edge of the supported member is raised above the top of the supporting member, or top of hanger strap to allow for shrinkage as the members season in place. For supported members with moisture content at or above fiber saturation when installed, the distance raised should be about 5% of the members depth above its bearing point.

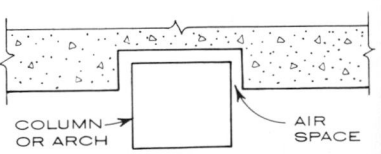

WOOD MEMBER SET IN
MASONRY WALL POCKET

Provide minimum of one inch air space between member and wall pocket or provide adequate moisture barrier.

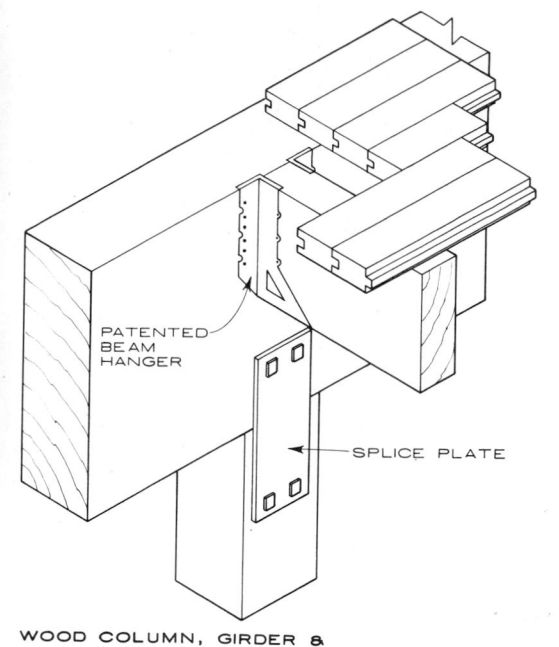

PATENTED
BEAM
HANGER

SPLICE PLATE

**WOOD COLUMN, GIRDER &
BEAM OR PURLIN**

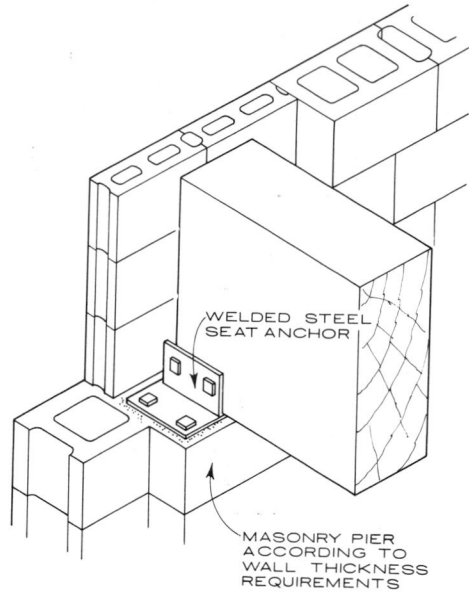

WELDED STEEL
SEAT ANCHOR

MASONRY PIER
ACCORDING TO
WALL THICKNESS
REQUIREMENTS

**WOOD GIRDER SUPPORTED BY
MASONRY WALL**

STEEL
ANGLE
CONNECTOR

WOOD BEAM
SUPPORTS
GLUE LAMINAT-
ED TO WOOD
COLUMN

**WOOD COLUMN WITH
LAMINATED BEAM SEATS**

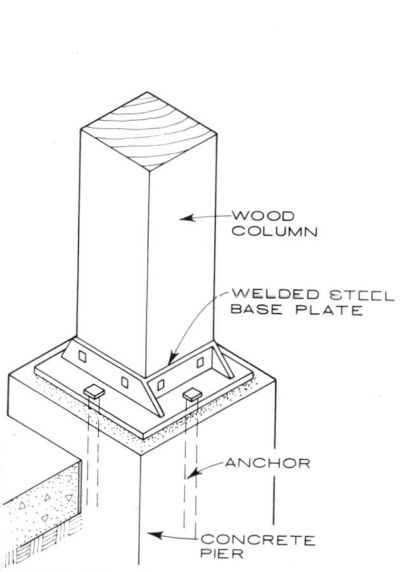

WOOD
COLUMN

WELDED STEEL
BASE PLATE

ANCHOR

CONCRETE
PIER

**WOOD COLUMN ANCHORED
TO CONCRETE PIER**

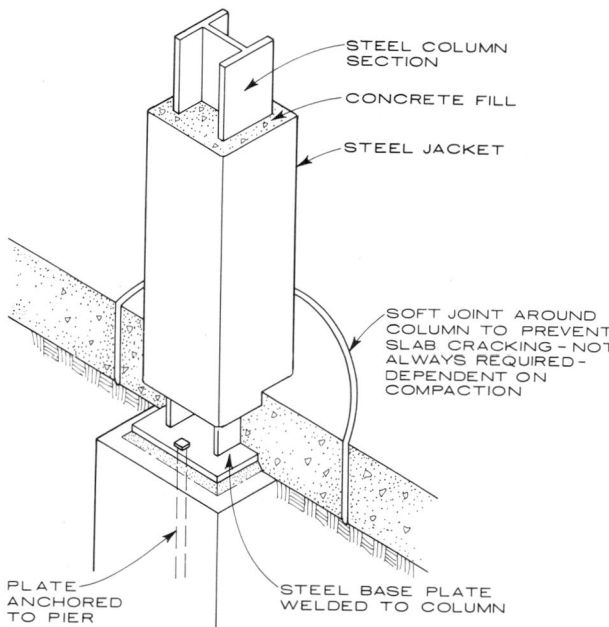

STEEL COLUMN
SECTION

CONCRETE FILL

STEEL JACKET

SOFT JOINT AROUND
COLUMN TO PREVENT
SLAB CRACKING - NOT
ALWAYS REQUIRED -
DEPENDENT ON
COMPACTION

PLATE
ANCHORED
TO PIER

STEEL BASE PLATE
WELDED TO COLUMN

COMPOSITE STEEL CONCRETE COLUMN
USED IN TIMBER CONSTRUCTION WHERE LOADS
OR CODES REQUIRE

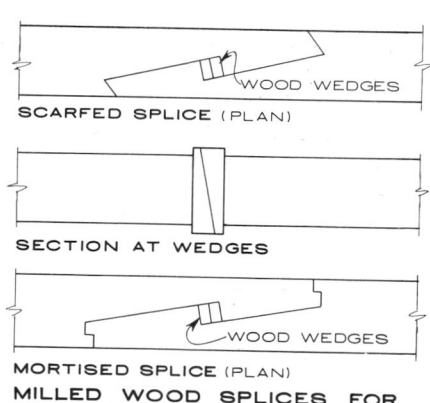

WOOD WEDGES

SCARFED SPLICE (PLAN)

SECTION AT WEDGES

WOOD WEDGES

MORTISED SPLICE (PLAN)
**MILLED WOOD SPLICES FOR
GIRDERS**

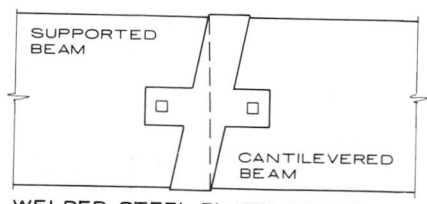

SUPPORTED
BEAM

CANTILEVERED
BEAM

WELDED STEEL PLATE SPLICE
SEE LAMINATED BEAM DETAILS

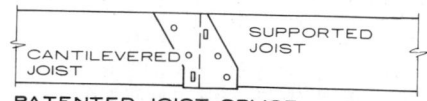

SUPPORTED
JOIST

CANTILEVERED
JOIST

PATENTED JOIST SPLICE
FOR USE WITH CANTILEVERED FLOOR
JOISTS - 16 GA. STEEL

**METAL CONNECTOR SPLICES
FOR CANTILEVERED BEAMS**

**GIRDER, BEAM & JOIST
SPLICING**

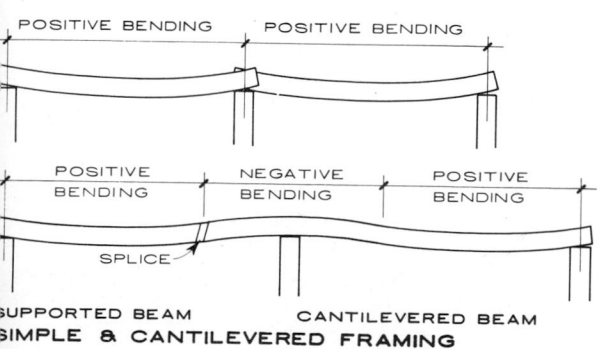

POSITIVE BENDING   POSITIVE BENDING

POSITIVE
BENDING   NEGATIVE
BENDING   POSITIVE
BENDING

SPLICE

SUPPORTED BEAM   CANTILEVERED BEAM
SIMPLE & CANTILEVERED FRAMING

This illustration shows the "positive" or downward
bending that occurs in conventional framing with simple spans.

This illustration shows the combination of "positive"
(downward) and "negative" (upward) bending that occurs with beams spliced at quarterpoint producing supported beam and cantilevered beam. The two types of
bending counterbalance each other, which produces
more uniform stresses and uses material more efficiently. In-line joists simplify plywood subflooring.

Joseph A. Wilkes, AIA; Wilkes and Faulkner; Washington, D. C.

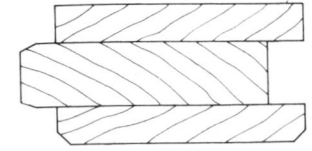

TONGUE & GROOVE

SIZES

NOMINAL	ACTUAL
2 × 6	1 5/8 × 5 FACE
2 × 8	1 5/8 × 7 FACE

V GROOVE

SIZES

NOMINAL	ACTUAL
3 × 6	2 5/8 × 5 1/4 FACE
4 × 6	3 1/2 × 5 1/4 FACE

STRIATED

LAMINATED

SIZES

NOMINAL	ACTUAL
3 × 6,8,10	2 1/4 × 5 1/2, 7 1/2, 9 1/2
3(SUPER THICK) × 6,8	2 5/8 × 5 1/2, 7 1/2
4 × 6,8	3 1/16 × 5 1/2, 7 1/2
5 × 6,8	3 13/16 × 5 1/2, 7 1/2

TYPES OF WOOD DECKING

INSULATION FACTORS (U) BTU/HR., SQ. FT., DEGREE F.

SPECIES	DECK THICKNESS NOM.	ACT.	INSULATION THICKNESS 0	1/2"	1"	1 1/2"	2"
INLAND RED CEDAR	3"	2 1/4"	.24	.18	.14	.12	.10
	3" (super)	2 5/8"	.22	.16	.13	.12	.10
	4"	3 1/16"	.19	.15	.12	.11	.09
	5"	3 13/16"	.15	.13	.11	.09	.08
SOUTHERN YELLOW PINE DOUGLAS FIR/LARCH	3"	2 1/4"	.30	.21	.16	.13	.11
	3" (super)	2 5/8"	.27	.20	.15	.12	.10
	4"	3 1/16"	.24	.18	.14	.12	.10
	5"	3 13/16"	.20	.15	.13	.11	.10
WHITE FIR IDAHO WHITE PINE	3"	2 1/4"	.27	.19	.15	.12	.11
	3" (super)	2 5/8"	.24	.18	.14	.12	.11
	4"	3 1/16"	.21	.16	.13	.11	.10
	5"	3 13/16"	.17	.14	.12	.10	.09

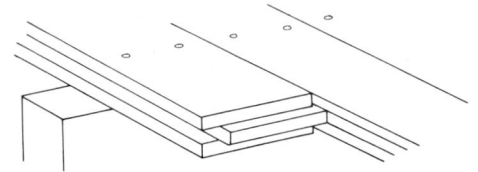

2 SPIKES PER PLANK AT BEAM

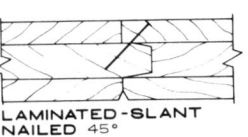

LAMINATED-SLANT NAILED 45° 30" O.C.

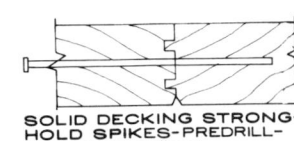

SOLID DECKING STRONG-HOLD SPIKES-PREDRILL-ED HOLES 30" O.C.

NAILING DECKING

WOOD DECKING DESIGN CHART—ALLOWABLE UNIFORMLY DISTRIBUTED TOTAL ROOF LOADS-PSF

THICKNESS	SPAN IN FEET	INLAND RED CEDAR E=1,200,000PSI F=950 BENDING SIMPLE	CONTIN.	DEFLECTION SIMPLE 1/240	CONTIN. 1/240	IDAHO WHITE FIR INLAND WHITE FIR E=1,500,000PSI F=950 BENDING SIMPLE	CONTIN.	DEFLECTION SIMPLE 1/240	CONTIN. 1/240	DOUGLAS FIR/LARCH SOUTHERN YELLOW PINE E=1,800,000PSI F=1635 BENDING SIMPLE	CONTIN.	DEFLECTION SIMPLE 1/240	CONTIN. 1/240
3"	10	62	52	30	45	62	52	37	52	106	88	44	67
	11	51	42	22	34	51	42	28	42	88	73	33	50
	12	43	36	17	26	43	36	22	33	74	61	26	39
	13	37	30	13	20	37	30	17	25	63	52	20	30
	14	31	26	11	16	31	26	13	20	54	45	16	24
	15	27	23	9	13	27	23	11	17	47	39	13	20
3" (superthick)	10	85	71	47	71	85	71	59	71	147	122	71	107
	11	70	59	36	54	70	59	44	59	121	101	53	80
	12	59	50	27	41	59	50	34	50	102	85	41	62
	13	51	42	22	33	51	42	27	40	87	72	32	49
	14	44	36	17	26	44	36	22	33	75	62	26	39
	15	38	31	14	21	38	31	18	27	65	54	21	32
	16	33	28	12	17	33	28	14	23	57	48	17	26
4"	10	114	96	74	96	114	96	93	96	197	164	111	164
	11	95	78	56	78	95	78	70	78	163	136	84	126
	12	80	67	43	65	80	67	53	67	137	114	64	97
	13	68	56	34	51	68	56	43	56	116	97	51	77
	14	58	48	27	41	58	48	34	48	100	84	41	61
	15	51	42	22	33	51	42	28	42	87	73	33	50
	16	44	38	18	27	44	38	23	34	77	64	23	41
	17	40	33	15	23	40	33	19	28	68	57	23	34
	18	35	29	13	19	35	29	16	24	61	51	19	29
	19	31	27	11	16	31	27	13	21	55	45	16	25
5"	10	178	150	144	150	178	150	178	150	307	256	215	256
	11	148	123	108	123	148	123	135	123	254	212	162	212
	12	124	104	83	104	124	104	104	104	213	178	125	178
	13	106	88	65	88	106	88	82	88	182	152	98	148
	14	91	76	52	76	91	76	66	76	157	131	79	119
	15	79	66	43	64	79	66	53	66	137	114	64	96
	16	69	59	35	53	69	59	44	59	120	100	53	79
	17	62	52	29	44	62	52	37	52	106	89	37	56
	18	56	45	25	37	56	45	31	45	95	79	31	47
	19	49	42	21	32	49	42	26	39	85	71	31	47
	20	44	37	18	27	44	37	23	34	77	64	27	41

Joseph A. Wilkes, AIA; Wilkes and Faulkner; Washington, D. C.

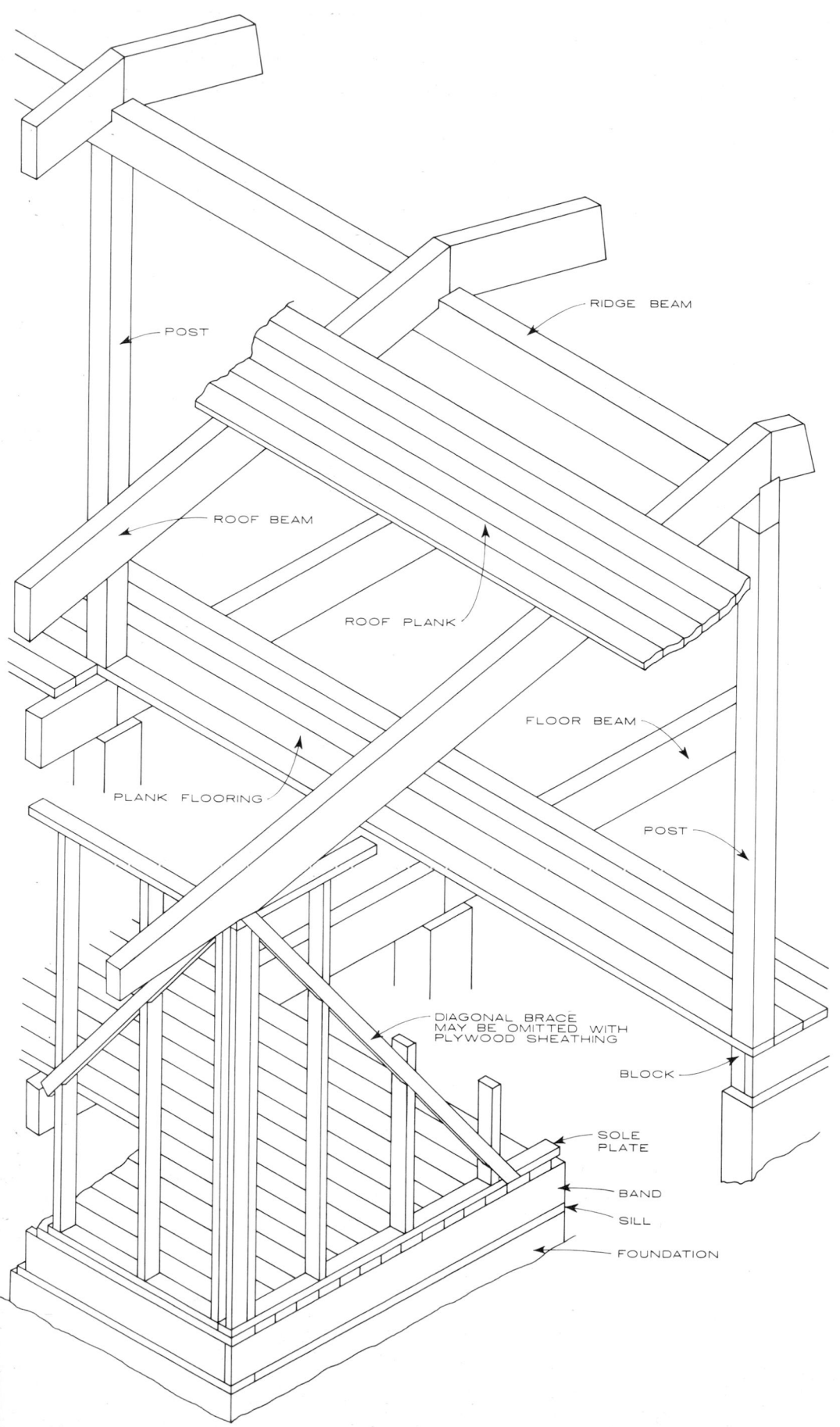

TYPICAL PLANK AND BEAM FRAMING FOR ONE STORY HOUSE

Joseph A. Wilkes, AIA; Wilkes and Faulkner; Washington, D. C.

DESCRIPTION

Use of two inch nominal thickness plank for subfloors or roofs supported on beams spaced 6 to 8 feet apart.

PRINCIPLES OF DESIGN

Two inch plank used more efficiently when continuous over more than one span.

Uses standard lumber lengths such as 12, 14 and 16 feet with beams 6, 7 or 8 feet apart.

Design permitting, end joints between supports allows use of random lengths.

ADVANTAGES OF SYSTEM

Architectural effect provided by exposed plank and beam ceiling. Added effective height of ceiling at no increase in wall height.

Fewer members permits savings in labor.

Cross-bridging not required.

LIMITATIONS OF SYSTEM

Bearing partitions and heavy loads such as bathtubs, refrigerators etc., may require additional framing. Concealment must be provided for wiring, piping and duct work.

Insulation value of two inch deck may be adequate, but where additional insulation is required it may be attached below deck or as rigid insulation above deck under roofing.

CONSTRUCTION DETAILS AND FASTENING

Members of built-up beams should be securely spiked together from both outside faces. Spaced beams should be blocked at frequent intervals, and each member should be securely nailed to blocking. Where planks butt over a single member, a nominal beam width of three or more inches is necessary to provide a suitable bearing and nailing surface for the planks. Planks should be both blind and face-nailed to the beam. In this construction posts (rather than studs) carry the loads, which are concentrated and must be designed for conditions, but not smaller than 4 x 4 inches. Built-up posts should be spiked together.

When solid beams butt at a column, a nominal column dimension of 6 or more inches parallel to direction of beam is recommended to provide suitable bearing. Spike bearing blocks to column where necessary to increase bearing surface.

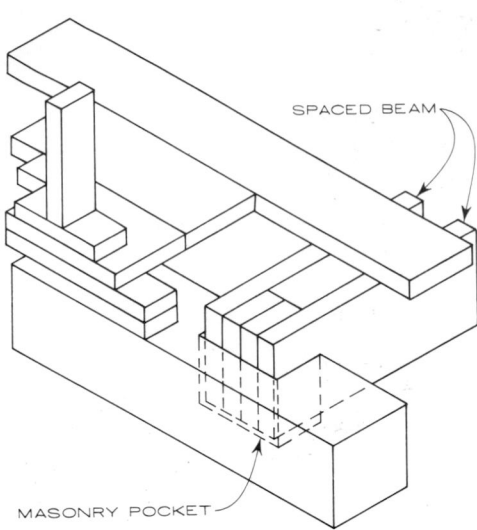

FIRST FLOOR FRAMING AT EXTERIOR WALL BEAM SET IN FOUNDATION

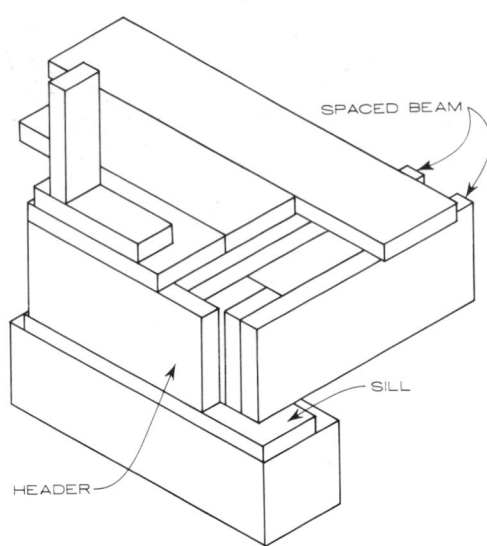

FIRST FLOOR FRAMING AT EXTERIOR WALL BEAM BEARING ON SILL

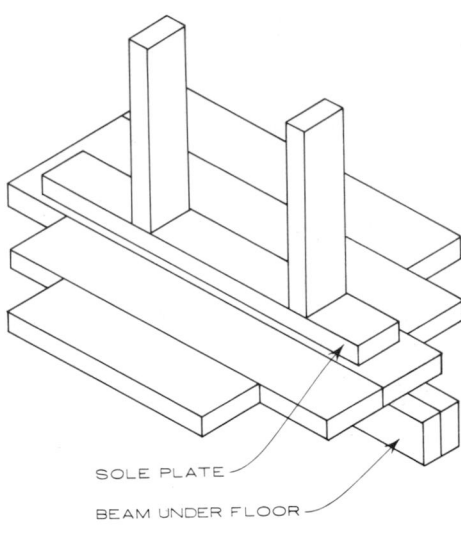

NON-BEARING PARTITION PARALLEL TO PLANK SUPPORTED BY BEAM UNDER FLOOR

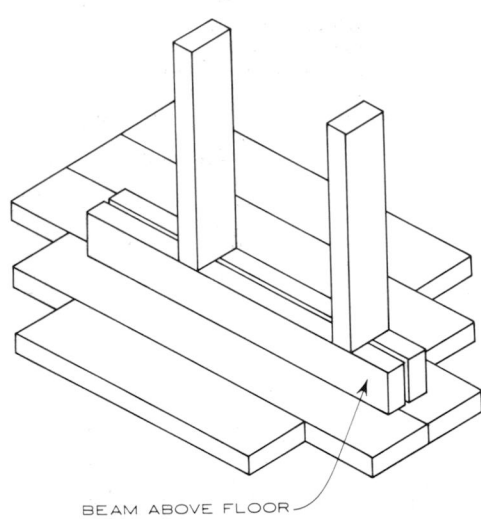

NON-BEARING PARTITION PARALLEL TO PLANK SUPPORTED BY BEAM ABOVE FLOOR

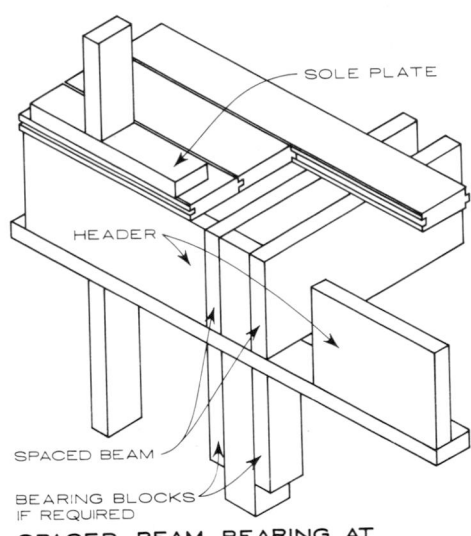

SPACED BEAM BEARING AT EXTERIOR WALL

The details in this column are preferable from the standpoint of equalizing shrinkage of horizontal lumber partition supports.

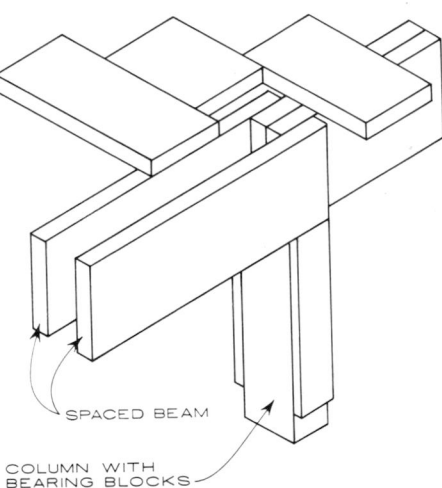

SPACED BEAM BEARING OVER BASEMENT SUPPORT

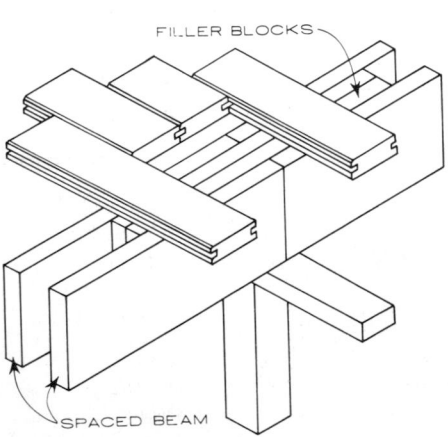

SPACED BEAM BEARING OVER I INTERIOR POST

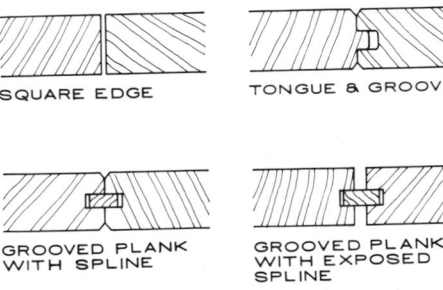

JOINT TYPES IN EXPOSED PLANK CEILINGS

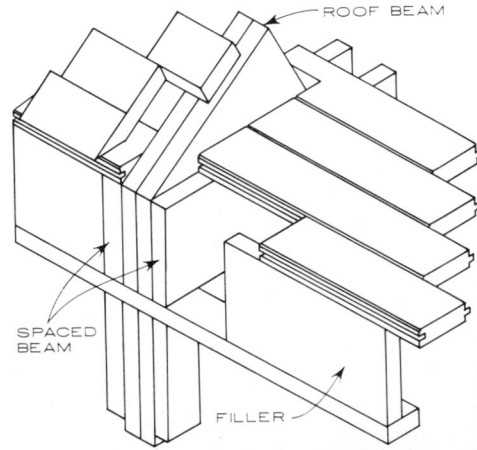

SOLID ROOF BEAM AND SPACED FLOOR BEAM BEARING ON EXTERIOR WALL

Joseph A. Wilkes, AIA; Wilkes and Faulkner; Washington, D. C.

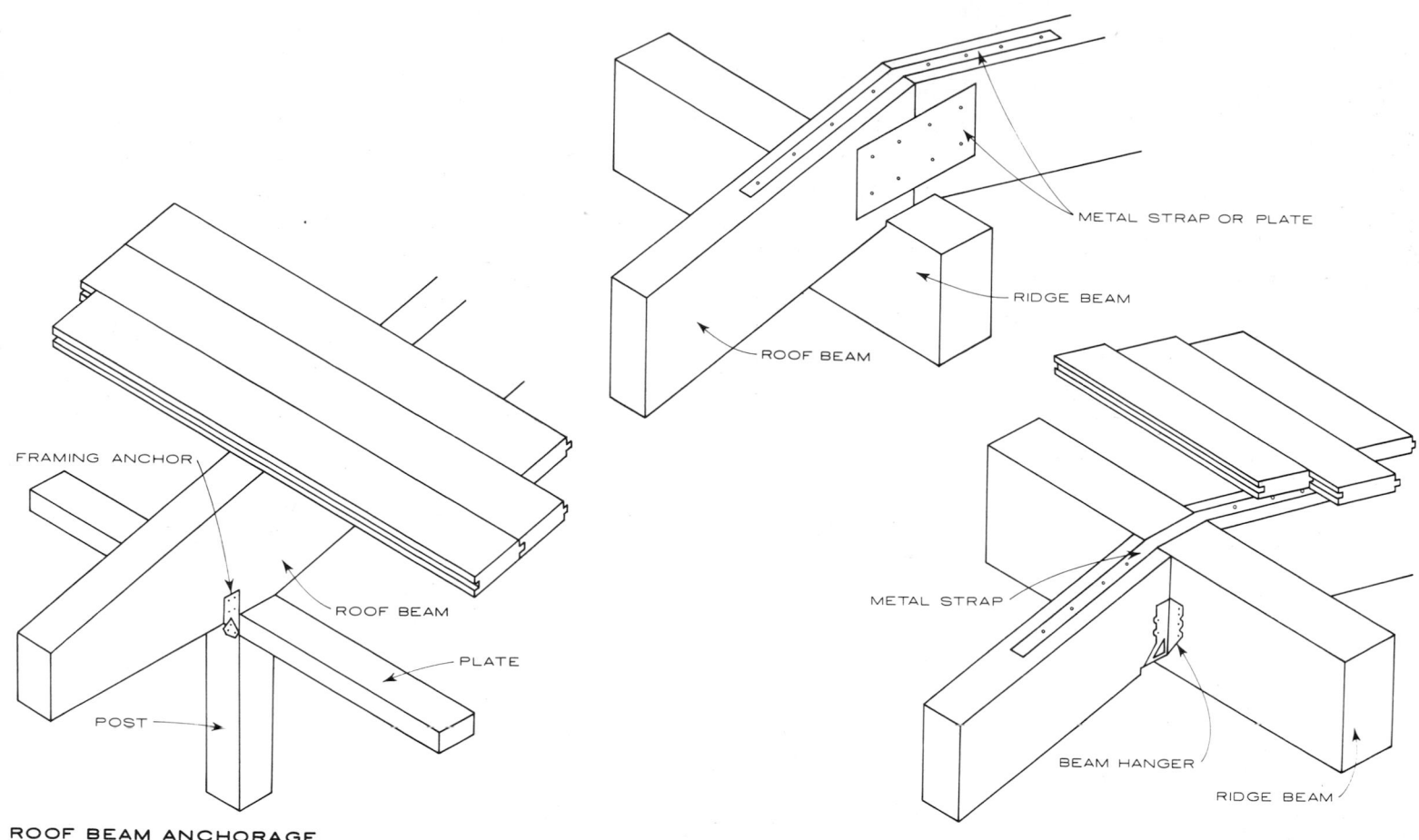

FRAMING ANCHOR

ROOF BEAM

PLATE

POST

ROOF BEAM ANCHORAGE

METAL STRAP OR PLATE

RIDGE BEAM

ROOF BEAM

METAL STRAP

BEAM HANGER

RIDGE BEAM

DESIGN TABLE FOR NOMINAL TWO-INCH PLANK

Required values for fiber stress in bending (f) and modulus of elasticity (E) to support safely a live load of 20, 30, or 40 pounds per square foot within a deflection limitation of $1/_{300}$. See tables on pages for "Lumber Grades and Allowable Stresses".

SPAN IN FEET	LIVE LOAD psf	TYPE A		TYPE B		TYPE C		TYPE D	
		f (psi)	E (psi)	f (psi)	E (psi)	f (psi)	E (psi)	f (psi)	E (psi)
6	20	310	570,000	310	230,000	250	30,000	310	40,000
	30	410	850,000	410	350,000	330	450,000	410	600,000
	40	510	1,130,000	510	470,000	410	600,000	510	800,000
7	20	420	900,000	420	370,000	330	480,000	420	640,000
	30	560	1,350,000	560	560,000	450	710,000	560	950,000
	40	700	1,800,000	700	750,000	560	950,000	700	1,270,000
8	20	543	1,340,000	543	557,000	434	707,000	543	948,000
	30	724	2,010,000	724	835,000	580	1,060,000	724	1,422,000
	40	906	2,670,000	906	1,110,000	720	1,410,000	906	1,890,000

Joseph A. Wilkes, AIA; Wilkes and Faulkner; Washington, D. C.

FLOOR AND ROOF BEAMS – DESIGN TABLES 20 POUNDS PSF

Required values for fiber stress in bending (f) and modulus of elasticity (E) for the sizes shown to support safely a live load of 20 pounds per square foot with a deflection limitation of $1/300$
1 = span in inches.

SPAN OF BEAM	NOMINAL SIZE OF BEAM	6'-0" f	6'-0" E	7'-0" f	7'-0" E	8'-0" f	8'-0" E
10'	2-3x6	1020	925000	1190	1080000	1360	1240000
	1-3x8	1100	730000	1280	855000	1460	970000
	2-2x8	890	590000	1030	690000	1180	790000
	1-4x8	790	530000	920	620000	1050	705000
	3-2x8	590	395000	690	460000	790	525000
	2-3x8	550	365000	640	425000	730	485000
	2-2x10	550	290000	640	340000	730	390000
11'	2-3x6	1230	1130000	1440	1440000	1640	1650000
	1-3x8	1320	970000	1540	1140000	1760	1300000
	2-2x8	1070	785000	1250	920000	1430	1050000
	1-4x8	960	705000	1120	825000	1270	940000
	3-2x8	710	525000	830	615000	950	700000
	2-3x8	660	485000	780	565000	880	650000
	2-2x10	660	390000	780	455000	880	520000
12'	2-3x6	1470	1600000				
	1-3x8	1580	1260000	1840	1470000		
	2-2x8	1270	1020000	1490	1190000	1700	1360000
	1-4x8	1140	915000	1330	1070000	1510	1220000
	3-2x8	850	680000	990	795000	1130	910000
	2-3x8	790	630000	920	735000	1050	840000
	1-6x8	750	605000	880	705000	1000	805000
	2-2x10	790	505000	920	590000	1050	670000
13'	1-3x8	1850	1600000				
	2-2x8	1500	1300000	1740	1440000	1990	1730000
	1-4x8	1340	1160000	1550	1280000	1780	1550000
	3-2x8	990	865000	1160	960000	1330	1160000
	2-3x8	920	800000	1080	885000	1230	1070000
	1-6x8	880	770000	1030	850000	1180	1020000
	2-2x10	920	640000	1080	705000	1230	850000
	1-3x10	1150	790000	1350	875000	1540	1050000
	1-4x10	830	570000	970	630000	1110	760000
14'	3-2x8	1150	1080000	1350	1260000	1540	1440000
	2-3x8	1070	1000000	1250	1170000	1430	1340000
	1-6x8	1030	960000	1200	1120000	1370	1280000
	1-3x10	1340	990000	1570	1150000	1780	1320000
	2-2x10	1070	810000	1260	935000	1430	1070000
	1-4x10	970	715000	1130	835000	1290	955000
	3-2x10	720	525000	840	625000	960	710000
	2-3x10	670	495000	780	575000	890	660000
	1-6x10	640	470000	750	550000	850	630000
	4-2x10	540	405000	630	417000	720	535000
	2-2x12	740	450000	870	525000	990	600000
15'	3-2x8	1320	1330000	1550	1540000	1770	1770000
	2-3x8	1230	1230000	1440	1430000	1640	1640000
	1-6x8	1180	1170000	1370	1370000	1570	1570000
	1-3x10	1540	1210000	1800	1410000	2050	1610000
	2-2x10	1230	1020000	1440	1140000	1640	1310000
	1-4x10	1110	875000	1300	1020000	1480	1170000
	3-2x10	820	655000	960	761000	700	872000
	2-3x10	770	605000	900	705000	1030	805000
	1-6x10	740	580000	860	675000	980	770000
	4-2x10	620	510000	725	570000	830	655000
	2-2x12	850	553000	990	645000	1140	737000
	1-4x12	760	495000	890	576000	1020	660000
16'	2-3x8	1410	1490000	1650	1740000		
	2-2x10	1410	1190000	1650	1390000	1880	1590000
	1-4x10	1260	1070000	1470	1240000	1680	1420000
	3-2x10	940	795000	1100	930000	1250	1060000
	2-3x10	880	740000	1020	860000	1170	985000
	1-6x10	840	705000	970	820000	1110	935000
	4-2x10	700	595000	820	695000	940	795000
	1-8x10	610	515000	710	600000	810	690000
	1-3x12	1200	830000	1400	970000	1600	1110000
	2-2x12	970	670000	1130	785000	1290	895000
	1-4x12	870	600000	1010	705000	1150	805000
	3-2x12	650	448000	750	522000	860	597000

SPAN OF BEAM	NOMINAL SIZE OF BEAM	6'-0" f	6'-0" E	7'-0" f	7'-0" E	8'-0" f	8'-0" E
17'	2-2x10	1590	1430000	1860	1670000		
	1-4x10	1430	1280000	1670	1490000	1900	1710000
	3-2x10	1060	955000	1240	1110000	1410	1270000
	2-3x10	990	885000	1150	1030000	1310	1180000
	1-6x10	940	845000	1100	980000	1250	1120000
	4-2x10	790	715000	930	835000	1060	955000
	1-8x10	690	620000	810	720000	920	825000
	1-3x12	1350	1000000	1580	1160000	1800	1330000
	2-2x12	1090	805000	1280	940000	1450	1080000
	1-4x12	980	720000	1140	840000	1300	960000
	3-2x12	730	535000	850	625000	970	715000
	2-3x12	680	500000	790	580000	900	665000
18'	1-4x10	1600	1520000	1870	1780000		
	3-2x10	1190	1130000	1370	1320000	1570	1510000
	2-3x10	1110	1050000	1300	1230000	1480	1400000
	1-6x10	1060	1000000	1230	1170000	1410	1340000
	4-2x10	890	850000	1040	995000	1190	1130000
	1-8x10	780	735000	910	860000	1030	980000
	1-3x12	1520	1190000	1780	1380000	2020	1580000
	2-2x12	1230	960000	1430	1120000	1630	1280000
	1-4x12	1100	855000	1280	1000000	1460	1140000
	3-2x12	820	640000	960	745000	1090	850000
	2-3x12	760	595000	890	690000	1010	790000
	1-6x12	720	570000	840	660000	960	750000
19'	3-2x10	1320	1340000	1550	1560000	1760	1780000
	2-3x10	1230	1240000	1440	1440000	1650	1650000
	1-6x10	1170	1180000	1370	1370000	1570	1570000
	4-2x10	990	1000000	1160	1170000	1320	1340000
	2-4x10	890	900000	1040	1040000	1190	1190000
	1-8x10	860	870000	1010	1010000	1150	1160000
	1-3x12	1680	1400000	1970	1630000		
	2-2x12	1360	1130000	1590	1320000	1820	1510000
	1-4x12	1220	1010000	1430	1180000	1630	1350000
	3-2x12	910	755000	1060	825000	1210	1000000
	2-3x12	840	700000	980	815000	1130	1860000
	1-6x12	800	670000	940	780000	1070	890000
20'	3-2x10	1470	1550000				
	2-3x10	1370	1440000	1600	1680000		
	1-6x10	1300	1370000	1520	1600000		
	4-2x10	1100	1160000	1280	1360000	1470	1550000
	2-4x10	990	1040000	1150	1220000	1320	1390000
	1-8x10	960	1010000	1120	1180000	1280	1340000
	2-2x12	1510	1310000	1770	1530000	2020	1750000
	1-4x12	1350	1170000	1580	1370000	1800	1570000
	3-2x12	1010	873000	1180	1020000	1350	1160000
	2-3x12	940	810000	1090	950000	1250	1080000
	1-6x12	890	775000	1040	905000	1190	1030000
	4-2x12		655000		765000		875000
21'	2-3x10	1500	1670000				
	1-6x10	1430	1590000	1680	1850000		
	4-2x10	1210	1350000	1420	1570000		
	2-4x10	1090	1210000	1270	1410000	1450	1610000
	1-8x10	1050	1170000	1230	1360000	1400	1550000
	2-2x12	1660	1520000	1950	1770000		
	1-4x12	1490	1360000	1740	1580000	1990	1810000
	3-2x12	1110	1010000	1300	1180000	1480	1350000
	2-3x12	1030	940000	1200	1100000	1380	1250000
	1-6x12	970	895000	1130	1050000	1310	1200000
	4-2x12	830	740000	970	885000	1110	1010000
	2-4x12	750	680000	870	795000	990	907000
22'	4-2x10	1330	1550000				
	2-4x10	1200	1380000	1400	1620000		
	1-8x10	1160	1350000	1350	1570000	1550	1790000
	1-4x12	1640	1560000				
	3-2x12	1220	1160000	1420	1360000	1630	1550000
	2-3x12	1130	1080000	1320	1260000	1520	1440000
	1-6x12	1080	1030000	1260	1210000	1450	1370000
	4-2x12	920	870000	1070	1020000	1230	1160000
	2-4x12	820	785000	960	915000	1100	1040000
	5-2x12	730	700000	860	815000	980	930000
	3-3x12	750	720000	880	840000	1010	960000

Joseph A. Wilkes, AIA; Wilkes and Faulkner; Washington, D. C.

FLOOR AND ROOF BEAMS – DESIGN TABLES 30 POUNDS PSF

Required values for fiber stress in bending (f) and modulus of elasticity (E) for the sizes shown to support safely a live load of 30 pounds per square foot with a deflection limitation of $^1/_{300}$
1 = span in inches.

Span of Beam	Nominal Size of Beam	6'-0" f	6'-0" E	7'-0" f	7'-0" E	8'-0" f	8'-0" E
10'	2-3x6	1360	1390000	1590	1620000		
	1-3x8	1460	1090000	1700	1280000	1950	1460000
	1-4x8	1050	795000	1220	925000	1400	1060000
	3-2x8	790	590000	920	690000	1050	790000
	2-3x8	730	545000	850	640000	970	730000
	2-4x8	530	400000	610	465000	700	530000
	2-2x10	740	435000	860	515000	980	585000
11'	1-3x8	1770	1460000	2060	1690000		
	1-4x8	1270	1060000	1490	1240000	1700	1410000
	3-2x8	950	790000	1110	920000	1270	1050000
	2-3x8	880	730000	1030	850000	1180	970000
	2-4x8	640	530000	750	620000	850	710000
	2-2x10	890	585000	1040	680000	1180	780000
	1-3x10	1100	720000	1290	840000	1480	960000
12'	1-4x8	1510	1370000	1770	1600000		
	2-2x8	1130	1020000	1320	1190000	1510	1360000
	2-3x8	1050	945000	1230	1100000	1400	1260000
	2-4x8	760	685000	880	800000	1010	915000
	1-6x8	1000	905000	1170	1050000	1340	1210000
	2-2x10	1060	755000	1230	880000	1410	1010000
	3-2x10	750	505000	820	590000	940	675000
	2-3x10	660	465000	760	545000	880	620000
13'	1-4x8	1780	1750000				
	3-2x8	1330	1300000	1550	1520000	1770	1740000
	2-3x8	1230	1210000	1440	1400000	1650	1600000
	2-4x8	890	875000	1040	1020000	1190	1170000
	1-6x8	1180	1050000	1370	1350000	1570	1540000
	2-2x10	1240	965000	1450	1120000	1650	1280000
	3-2x10	830	640000	970	750000	1100	855000
	2-3x10	770	595000	900	695000	1030	790000
	1-4x10	1110	860000	1300	1000000	1480	1150000
14'	3-2x8	1540	1620000				
	2-3x8	1430	1500000	1670	1750000		
	2-4x8	1030	1090000	1210	1280000	1380	1450000
	1-6x8	1370	1440000	1600	1680000		
	2-2x10	1490	1200000	1680	1400000	1930	1600000
	3-2x10	960	800000	1120	935000	1280	1070000
	2-3x10	890	740000	1050	865000	1200	980000
	1-4x10	1290	1070000	1510	1250000	1720	1430000
	1-6x10	850	710000	1000	825000	1140	940000
	2-4x10	650	535000	750	625000	860	715000
15'	2-4x8	1190	1340000	1380	1560000	1580	1780000
	1-6x8	1570	1770000				
	2-2x10	1650	1480000	1930	1720000		
	3-2x10	1100	985000	1280	1150000	1470	1310000
	2-3x10	1030	910000	1200	1060000	1370	1220000
	1-4x10	1480	1320000	1730	1540000	1970	1760000
	1-6x10	980	870000	1140	1020000	1300	1060000
	2-4x10	740	660000	865	770000	990	880000
	4-2x10	830	740000	960	860000	1100	980000
	1-8x10	720	640000	840	745000	960	850000
	2-2x12	1040	830000	1330	970000	1510	1110000
	1-4x12	1020	745000	1190	870000	1350	990000
16'	2-2x10	1880	1780000				
	3-2x10	1250	1190000	1460	1390000	1670	1590000
	2-3x10	1170	1100000	1360	1290000	1550	1470000
	1-4x10	1690	1600000				
	1-6x10	1110	1050000	1300	1230000	1480	1410000
	2-4x10	840	810000	980	950000	1120	1070000
	4-2x10	940	895000	1100	1040000	1250	1190000
	1-8x10	830	720000	950	905000	1090	1030000
	2-2x12	1290	1010000	1510	1180000	1720	1340000
	1-4x12	1160	900000	1350	1050000	1540	1200000
	3-2x12	860	670000	1000	785000	1150	895000
	2-3x12	800	620000	930	730000	1070	830000

Span of Beam	Nominal Size of Beam	6'-0" f	6'-0" E	7'-0" f	7'-0" E	8'-0" f	8'-0" E
17'	3-2x10	1420	1430000	1650	1670000		
	2-3x10	1320	1330000	1540	1550000	1760	1770000
	1-6x10	1260	1260000	1470	1480000	1680	1690000
	2-4x10	950	960000	1110	1120000	1270	1280000
	4-2x10	1060	1070000	1240	1250000	1420	1430000
	1-8x10	920	930000	1080	1080000	1230	1240000
	2-2x12	1460	1210000	1700	1410000	1950	1610000
	1-4x12	1310	1080000	1520	1260000	1750	1440000
	3-2x12	970	805000	1140	1080000	1300	1070000
	2-3x12	900	750000	1060	870000	1210	1000000
	4-2x12	730	605000	850	705000	970	805000
	2-4x12	650	545000	760	635000	870	725000
18'	2-3x10	1480	1580000				
	1-6x10	1410	1510000	1650	1760000		
	2-4x10	1070	1140000	1250	1330000	1430	1520000
	4-2x10	1190	1280000	1390	1490000	1590	1700000
	1-8x10	1040	1100000	1210	1290000	1380	1470000
	2-2x12	1640	1440000	1910	1680000		
	1-4x12	1470	1290000	1710	1500000	1950	1710000
	3-2x12	1090	960000	1270	1120000	1460	1280000
	2-3x12	1010	890000	1180	1040000	1350	1190000
	4-2x12	820	720000	960	840000	1090	960000
	2-4x12	730	650000	860	755000	980	860000
	5-2x12	660	575000	770	670000	870	765000
19'	1-6x10	1570	1770000				
	2-4x10	1190	1340000	1390	1560000	1590	1780000
	4-2x10	1330	1500000	1550	1750000		
	1-8x10	1150	1300000	1340	1510000	1540	1720000
	1-4x12	1630	1510000	1900	1760000		
	3-2x12	1220	1120000	1420	1310000	1620	1500000
	2-3x12	1140	1040000	1320	1220000	1500	1390000
	4-2x12	910	845000	1060	980000	1210	1120000
	2-4x12	820	760000	950	885000	1090	1010000
	5-2x12	730	675000	850	785000	970	900000
	1-6x12	1070	995000	1250	1160000	1430	1330000
	3-3x12	750	695000	880	810000	1000	925000
20'	1-8x10	1150	1510000	1340	1760000		
	3-2x12	1210	1310000	1410	1530000	1620	1750000
	2-3x12	1120	1220000	1310	1420000	1500	1630000
	4-2x12	910	1090000	1060	1150000	1210	1310000
	2-4x12	810	885000	950	1030000	1090	1180000
	5-2x12	730	790000	850	920000	970	1050000
	1-6x12	1070	1160000	1250	1360000	1430	1550000
	3-3x12	750	810000	880	945000	1000	1080000
	1-8x12	790	850000	920	995000	1050	1140000
	1-10x12	620	670000	720	780000	830	895000
	4-3x12	560	610000	660	710000	750	815000
	2-3x14	810	755000	950	880000	1090	1010000
21'	3-2x12	1490	1640000				
	2-3x12	1380	1470000	1600	1700000		
	4-2x12	1110	1180000	1300	1370000	1480	1570000
	2-4x12	1000	1060000	1160	1240000	1330	1410000
	5-2x12	890	945000	1040	1100000	1190	1260000
	1-6x12	1310	1400000	1530	1620000		
	3-3x12	920	975000	1070	1130000	1220	1290000
	1-8x12	970	1030000	1020	1190000	990	1360000
	1-10x12	760	805000	880	940000	1010	1450000
	4-3x12	690	730000	800	850000	920	970000
	2-3x14	1000	905000	1160	1050000	1330	1200000
	1-6x14	950	865000	1110	1010000	1270	1150000
22'	4-2x12	1220	1310000	1420	1530000	1630	1740000
	2-4x12	1090	1180000	1280	1370000	1460	1570000
	5-2x12	980	1050000	1140	1225000	1300	1400000
	1-6x12	1430	1550000	1680	1800000		
	3-3x12	1010	1080000	1180	1260000	1340	1440000
	1-8x12	1050	1040000	1230	1330000	1410	1510000
	1-10x12	830	890000	970	1040000	1110	1190000
	4-3x12	750	810000	880	945000	1010	1080000
	2-3x14	1090	1000000	1280	1170000	1460	1340000
	1-6x14	1040	960000	1220	1120000	1390	1280000
	3-3x14	730	670000	850	780000	970	890000
	2-4x14	790	725000	920	845000	1060	965000

Joseph A. Wilkes, AIA; Wilkes and Faulkner; Washington, D. C.

FLOOR AND ROOF BEAMS - DESIGN TABLES 40 POUNDS PSF

Required values for fiber stress in bending (f) and modulus of elasticity (E) for the sizes shown to support safely a live load of 40 pounds per square foot within a deflection limitation of $^1/_{300}$

1 = span in inches.

SPAN OF BEAM	NOMINAL SIZE OF BEAM	6'-0" f	6'-0" E	7'-0" f	7'-0" E	8'-0" f	8'-0" E
10'	1-3x8	1820	1460000	2130	1690000		
	2-2x8	1480	1180000	1720	1380000	1970	1580000
	1-4x8	1320	1060000	1540	1230000	1750	1410000
	1-6x8	870	700000	1020	815000	1160	930000
	2-2x10	920	585000	1070	680000	1220	775000
	1-3x10	1140	885000	1330	840000	1520	960000
	1-4x10	820	520000	960	610000	1090	695000
11'	2-2x8	1780	1570000				
	1-4x8	1600	1410000	1860	1650000		
	1-6x8	1060	930000	1230	1090000	1410	1240000
	2-2x10	1110	775000	1300	905000	1490	1035000
	1-3x10	1380	960000	1610	1120000	1840	1280000
	1-4x10	1000	695000	1160	810000	1330	925000
	3-2x10	740	515000	860	605000	990	690000
12'	1-6x8	1250	1210000	1460	1410000	1670	1610000
	3-2x8	1410	1360000	1650	1590000	1890	1820000
	2-2x10	1360	1010000	1560	1180000	1760	1340000
	1-3x10	1630	1250000	1910	1450000	2190	1660000
	1-4x10	1180	900000	1380	1050000	1580	1200000
	3-2x10	880	670000	1030	785000	1170	895000
	2-3x10	810	620000	950	730000	1090	830000
	1-6x10	780	595000	910	695000	1040	790000
	2-4x10	590	450000	690	535000	790	600000
13'	1-6x8	1470	1530000				
	2-3x8	1540	1600000				
	2-4x8	1110	1170000	1300	1360000	1490	1550000
	3-2x10	1010	855000	1180	1000000	1380	1140000
	2-2x10	1550	1280000	1810	1500000	2070	1710000
	1-3x10	1920	1580000				
	2-3x10	960	790000	1120	925000	1280	1150000
	1-4x10	1390	1150000	1620	1340000	1850	1530000
	2-4x10	690	575000	810	670000	920	765000
14'	2-4x8	1290	1450000	1510	1690000		
	3-2x10	1200	1070000	1400	1240000	1600	1420000
	2-3x10	1110	990000	1300	1150000	1490	1320000
	1-4x10	1610	1430000	1890	1660000		
	2-4x10	800	715000	940	830000	1070	950000
	3-3x10	740	660000	870	765000	990	880000
	1-6x10	1060	940000	1240	1100000	1420	1260000
	1-8x10	780	690000	910	805000	1040	920000
	4-2x10	900	800000	1050	930000	1200	1060000
	2-2x12	1250	900000	1440	1050000	1650	1200000
15'	3-2x10	1380	1310000	1610	1530000	1840	1750000
	2-3x10	1290	1220000	1500	1420000	1710	1620000
	2-4x10	930	880000	1080	1020000	1240	1170000
	3-3x10	860	810000	1000	945000	1140	1080000
	1-6x10	1220	1160000	1430	1350000	1630	1540000
	1-8x10	900	850000	1050	990000	1200	1130000
	4-2x10	1030	985000	1210	1150000	1380	1310000
	2-2x12	1420	1110000	1660	1290000	1900	1480000
	3-2x12	950	735000	1110	860000	1260	985000
	1-3x12	1760	1370000	2050	1600000		
	4-2x12	710	555000	830	645000	950	740000
	2-3x12	880	685000	1030	800000	1170	915000
16'	3-2x10	1570	1590000				
	2-3x10	1460	1480000	1700	1720000		
	2-4x10	1050	1070000	1230	1250000	1410	1430000
	3-3x10	970	985000	1130	1150000	1290	1310000
	1-6x10	1390	1410000	1630	1640000		
	1-8x10	1020	1030000	1190	1200000	1360	1380000
	4-2x10	1170	1190000	1370	1390000	1570	1590000
	2-2x12	1610	1340000	1880	1570000		
	3-2x12	1080	895000	1260	1050000	1440	1200000
	4-2x12	810	670000	940	785000	1080	895000
	5-2x12	640	550000	750	630000	860	720000
	2-3x12	1000	830000	1170	970000	1330	1110000

SPAN OF BEAM	NOMINAL SIZE OF BEAM	6'-0" f	6'-0" E	7'-0" f	7'-0" E	8'-0" f	8'-0" E
17'	2-3x10	1640	1760000				
	2-4x10	1190	1280000	1390	1490000	1580	1700000
	3-3x10	1100	1180000	1280	1370000	1460	1570000
	1-8x10	1150	1240000	1340	1440000	1530	1650000
	3-2x12	1220	1070000	1420	1250000	1620	1430000
	4-2x12	910	805000	1060	940000	1210	1070000
	5-2x12	730	645000	850	750000	970	860000
	2-3x12	1130	995000	1310	1160000	1500	1330000
	3-3x12	750	665000	880	770000	1000	885000
	2-4x12	820	725000	950	840000	1090	965000
	1-6x12	1070	950000	1250	1110000	1430	1270000
	1-8x12	790	700000	920	810000	1050	930000
18'	2-4x10	1330	1510000	1550	1770000		
	3-3x10	1230	1390000	1430	1630000		
	1-8x10	1290	1460000	1510	1720000		
	3-2x12	1360	1270000	1590	1490000	1810	1700000
	4-2x12	1020	950000	1190	1120000	1360	1270000
	5-2x12	820	760000	950	890000	1090	1020000
	2-3x12	1270	1180000	1480	1380000	1680	1580000
	3-3x12	840	785000	980	920000	1120	1050000
	2-4x12	920	855000	1070	1000000	1220	1145000
	1-6x12	1200	1120000	1400	1320000	1600	1520000
	1-8x12	880	825000	1030	970000	1180	1100000
	3-4x12	610	570000	710	665000	810	760000
19'	3-3x10	1370	1640000				
	3-2x12	1520	1500000	1770	1750000		
	4-2x12	1140	1130000	1330	1310000	1520	1500000
	5-2x12	910	900000	1060	1050000	1210	1200000
	2-3x12	1410	1390000	1650	1620000		
	3-3x12	940	925000	1100	1080000	1250	1230000
	2-4x12	1020	1010000	1190	1180000	1360	1350000
	1-6x12	1340	1330000	1560	1550000	1790	885000
	1-8x12	990	975000	1150	1140000	1310	1300000
	3-4x12	680	675000	790	785000	910	895000
	4-3x12	700	695000	820	810000	940	925000
	2-6x12	670	665000	780	770000	890	885000
20'	3-2x12	1680	1750000				
	4-2x12	1260	1310000	1470	1530000	1680	1750000
	5-2x12	1010	1050000	1180	1230000	1350	1400000
	3-3x12	1040	1080000	1210	1260000	1390	1440000
	2-4x12	1130	1180000	1320	1370000	1510	1570000
	1-6x12	1460	1550000				
	1-8x12	1090	1140000	1270	1330000	1450	1520000
	3-4x12	750	785000	880	920000	1000	1050000
	4-3x12	780	810000	910	950000	1040	1080000
	2-6x12	740	775000	870	905000	990	1030000
	1-10x12	850	890000	1000	1040000	1140	1190000
	2-3x14	1130	1000000	1320	1170000	1510	1340000
21'	4-2x12	1390	1520000	1620	1770000		
	5-2x12	1110	1210000	1300	1420000	1490	1620000
	3-3x12	1150	1250000	1340	1460000	1530	1670000
	2-4x12	1240	1360000	1450	1590000		
	1-8x12	1200	1320000	1400	1540000	1600	1750000
	3-4x12	830	910000	970	1060000	1110	1210000
	4-3x12	860	940000	1000	1100000	1150	1260000
	2-6x12	820	895000	960	1040000	1090	1190000
	1-10x12	940	1030000	1100	1210000	1260	1380000
	2-3x14	1240	1160000	1450	1360000	1660	1550000
	1-6x14	1190	1110000	1390	1300000	1590	1480000
	2-4x14	900	840000	1050	980000	1200	1120000
22'	4-2x12	1530	1750000				
	5-2x12	1220	1400000	1430	1620000		
	3-3x12	1260	1440000	1470	1680000		
	3-4x12	910	1050000	1060	1220000	1210	1390000
	4-3x12	940	1080000	1100	1260000	1260	1440000
	2-6x12	900	1030000	1050	1190000	1200	1370000
	1-10x12	1040	1190000	1210	1390000	1380	1590000
	2-3x14	1360	1340000	1590	1560000	1820	1780000
	1-6x14	1310	1280000	1530	1490000	1740	1700000
	2-4x14	990	970000	1160	1130000	1320	1280000
	3-3x14	910	895000	1060	1040000	1210	1190000
	3-4x14	660	645000	770	750000	880	865000

Joseph A. Wilkes, AIA; Wilkes and Faulkner; Washington, D. C.

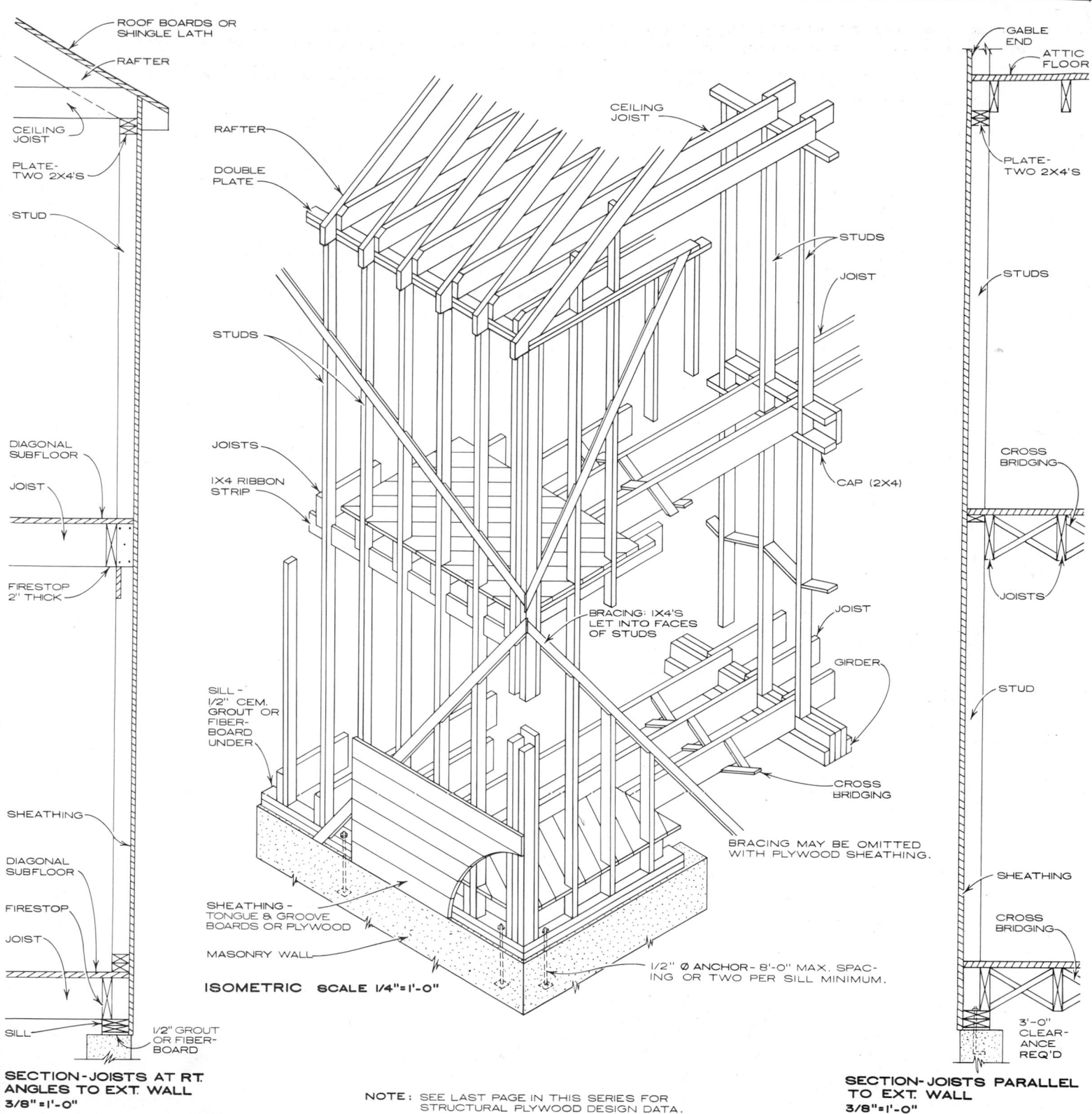

ROOF BOARDS OR SHINGLE LATH

RAFTER

CEILING JOIST

PLATE- TWO 2X4'S

STUD

DIAGONAL SUBFLOOR

JOIST

FIRESTOP 2" THICK

SHEATHING

DIAGONAL SUBFLOOR

FIRESTOP

JOIST

SILL

1/2" GROUT OR FIBER- BOARD

SECTION-JOISTS AT RT. ANGLES TO EXT. WALL
3/8"=1'-0"

RAFTER

DOUBLE PLATE

STUDS

JOISTS

1X4 RIBBON STRIP

SILL- 1/2" CEM. GROUT OR FIBER- BOARD UNDER

SHEATHING- TONGUE & GROOVE BOARDS OR PLYWOOD

MASONRY WALL

ISOMETRIC SCALE 1/4"=1'-0"

CEILING JOIST

STUDS

JOIST

CAP (2X4)

BRACING: 1X4'S LET INTO FACES OF STUDS

JOIST

GIRDER

CROSS BRIDGING

BRACING MAY BE OMITTED WITH PLYWOOD SHEATHING.

1/2" Ø ANCHOR- 8'-0" MAX. SPAC- ING OR TWO PER SILL MINIMUM.

NOTE : SEE LAST PAGE IN THIS SERIES FOR STRUCTURAL PLYWOOD DESIGN DATA.

GABLE END

ATTIC FLOOR

PLATE- TWO 2X4'S

STUDS

CROSS BRIDGING

JOISTS

STUD

SHEATHING

CROSS BRIDGING

3'-0" CLEAR- ANCE REQ'D

SECTION-JOISTS PARALLEL TO EXT. WALL
3/8"=1'-0"

NOTES:

BALLOON FRAME

Studs continuous to roof, supporting second floor joists. System produces minimum vertical movement and is often selected for two story stone or brick veneer or stucco.

FIRESTOPPING

All concealed spaces in the framing should be firestopped with 2 inch thick blocking, accurately fitted to fill openings and arranged to prevent drafts from one space to another.

Joseph A. Wilkes, AIA; Wilkes and Faulkner; Washington, D. C.

EXTERIOR WALL FRAMING

One Story Buildings: 2x4's, 16 or 24'' o.c.
Two Story Buildings: 2x4's, 16'' o.c.
Three Story Buildings: 2x4's, 16'' o.c.

BRACING EXTERIOR WALLS

Suitable sheathing acts as bracing for exterior walls. Additional strength and stiffness, if required, may be provided by 1x4 members let into the outside face of the studs at a 45º angle and properly secured top and bottom and into the studs.

BRIDGING FOR FLOOR JOISTS

May be omitted when flooring is properly nailed to joists. However, where nominal depth-to-thickness ratio of joists exceeds 6, bridging should be installed at 8' − 0'' intervals. (FHA also allows omission of bridging under certain conditions — see FHA publication No. 300, 1963, revised 1965.)

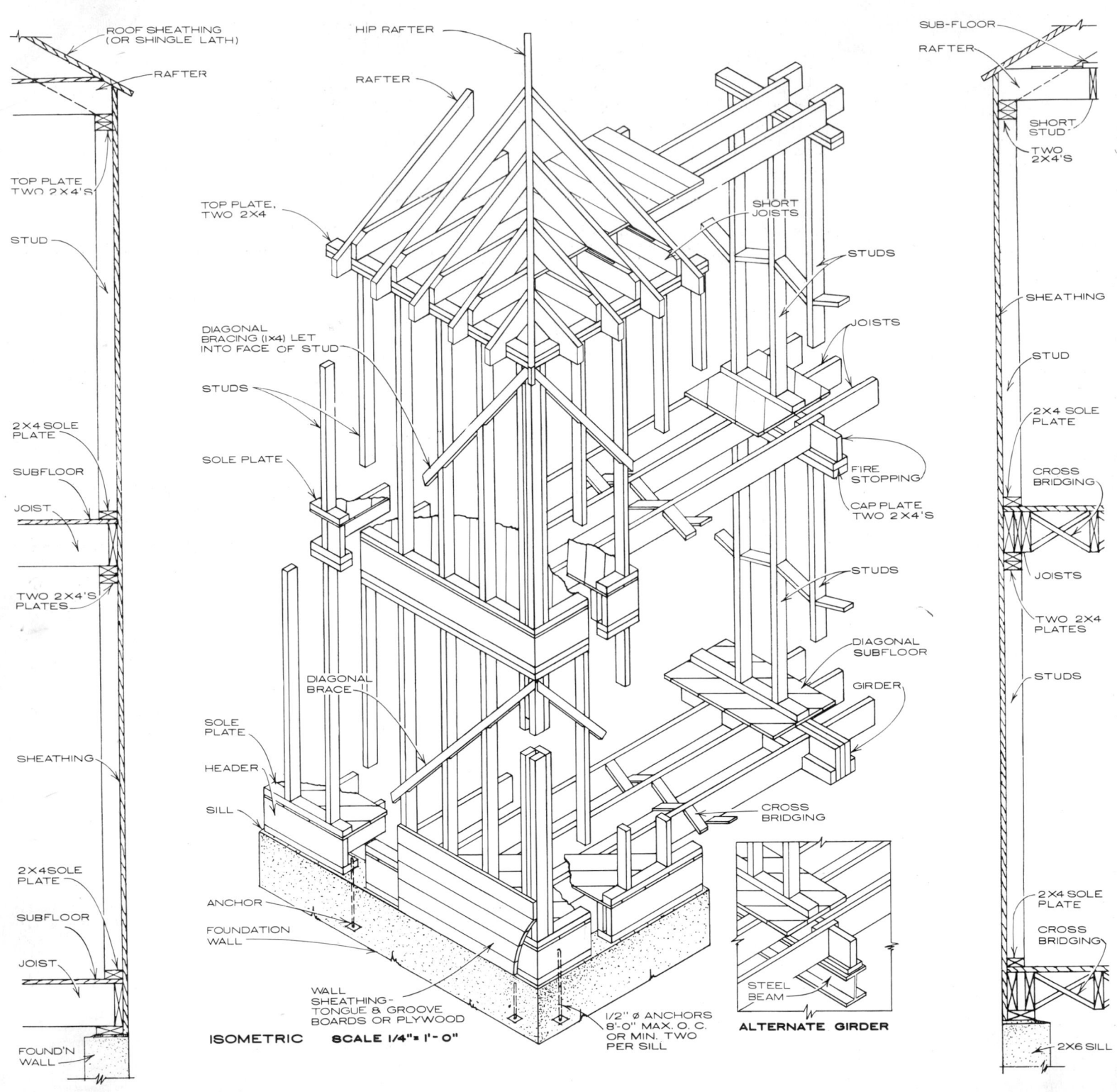

ROOF SHEATHING (OR SHINGLE LATH)

RAFTER

TOP PLATE TWO 2×4'S

STUD

2×4 SOLE PLATE

SUBFLOOR

JOIST

TWO 2×4'S PLATES

SHEATHING

2×4 SOLE PLATE

SUBFLOOR

JOIST

FOUND'N WALL

HIP RAFTER

RAFTER

TOP PLATE, TWO 2×4

DIAGONAL BRACING (1×4) LET INTO FACE OF STUD

STUDS

SOLE PLATE

DIAGONAL BRACE

SOLE PLATE

HEADER

SILL

ANCHOR

FOUNDATION WALL

WALL SHEATHING-TONGUE & GROOVE BOARDS OR PLYWOOD

ISOMETRIC   SCALE 1/4"= 1'-0"

1/2" Ø ANCHORS 8'-0" MAX. O. C. OR MIN. TWO PER SILL

SHORT JOISTS

STUDS

JOISTS

FIRE STOPPING

CAP PLATE TWO 2×4'S

STUDS

DIAGONAL SUBFLOOR

GIRDER

CROSS BRIDGING

STEEL BEAM

ALTERNATE GIRDER

SUB-FLOOR

RAFTER

SHORT STUD

TWO 2×4'S

SHEATHING

STUD

2×4 SOLE PLATE

CROSS BRIDGING

JOISTS

TWO 2×4 PLATES

STUDS

2×4 SOLE PLATE

CROSS BRIDGING

2×6 SILL

SECTION- CEILING JOISTS PARALLEL TO RAFTERS: FLOOR JOISTS PERPENDICULAR TO EXTERIOR WALLS   SCALE 3/8"=1'-0"

SECTION- CEILING JOISTS PERPENDICULAR TO RAFTERS: FLOOR JOISTS PARALLEL TO EXTERIOR WALLS.   SCALE: 3/8"=1'-0"

NOTES:

WESTERN OR PLATFORM FRAMING

Subfloor extends to outer edge of the frame and provides a flat, work surface at each floor. Common practice is to assemble walls on subfloor and tilt them into place. Arrangement of members in platform framing equilizes vertical shrinkage within the structure.

FIRESTOPPING

All concealed spaces in framing with 2" blocking, fitted to openings and arranged to prevent drafts between spaces.

Joseph A. Wilkes, AIA; Wilkes and Faulkner; Washington, D. C.

EXTERIOR WALL FRAMING

One Story Buildings: 2x4's, 16" or 24" o.c.
Two & Three Stories: 2x4's, 16" o.c.

BRACING EXTERIOR WALLS

Suitable sheathing acts as bracing. Where required for additional stiffness or bracing, 1x4's may be let into outer face of studs at 45° angle secured top, bottom and to studs.

BRIDGING FOR FLOOR JOISTS

May be omitted when flooring is properly nailed to joists. However, where nominal depth-to-thickness ratio of joists exceeds 6 bridging should be installed at 8' − 0" intervals. (F.H.A. also allows omission of bridging under certain conditions--see F.H.A. publication No. 300, 1963, revised 1965.)

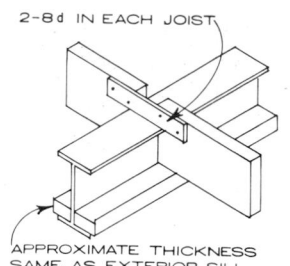

2-8d IN EACH JOIST

APPROXIMATE THICKNESS
SAME AS EXTERIOR SILL
TO EQUALIZE SHRINKAGE
ON WOOD BLOCKING

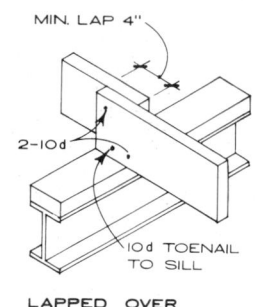

MIN. LAP 4"

2-10d

10d TOENAIL
TO SILL

**LAPPED OVER
WOOD SILL**

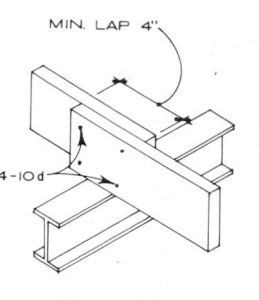

MIN. LAP 4"

4-10d

**LAPPED OVER
GIRDER**

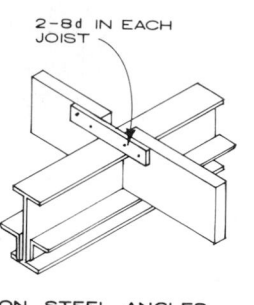

2-8d IN EACH
JOIST

ON STEEL ANGLES

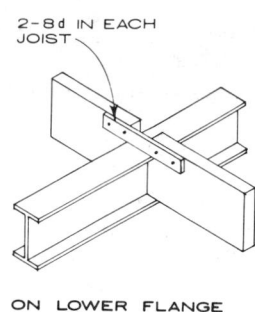

2-8d IN EACH
JOIST

ON LOWER FLANGE

WOOD JOISTS SUPPORTED ON STEEL GIRDERS

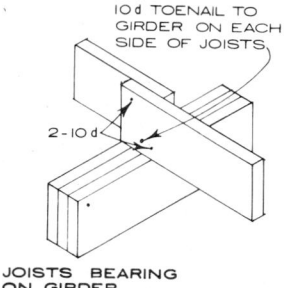

10d TOENAIL TO
GIRDER ON EACH
SIDE OF JOISTS

2-10d

**JOISTS BEARING
ON GIRDER**
MIN. LAP 4"

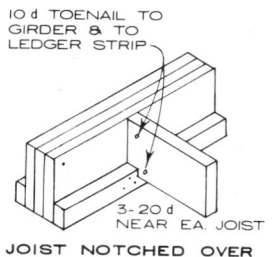

10d TOENAIL TO
GIRDER & TO
LEDGER STRIP

3-20d
NEAR EA. JOIST

**JOIST NOTCHED OVER
LEDGER STRIP**
NOTCHING OVER BEARING
NOT RECOMMENDED

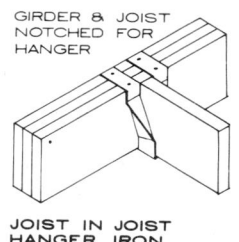

GIRDER & JOIST
NOTCHED FOR
HANGER

**JOIST IN JOIST
HANGER IRON**
ALSO CALLED STIRRUP
OR BRIDLE IRON

10d TOENAIL
TO GIRDER

TWO
10d

.3-20d
NEAR
EA. JOIST

**OVERLAPPING JOISTS
NOTCHED OVER GIRDER**
BEARING ONLY ON LEDGER,
NOT ON TOP OF GIRDER

TWO 8d IN
EACH JOIST

2-10d
TOENAIL
TO GIRDER

3-20d
NEAR
EA. JOIST

**JOISTS NOTCHED
OVER GIRDER**
BEARING ONLY ON
LEDGER, NOT ON TOP
OF GIRDER

WOOD JOISTS SUPPORTED ON WOOD GIRDERS

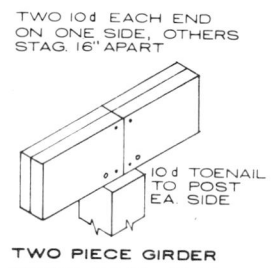

TWO 10d EACH END
ON ONE SIDE, OTHERS
STAG. 16" APART

10d TOENAIL
TO POST EA. SIDE

TWO PIECE GIRDER
GIRDER JOINTS ONLY
AT SUPPORTS

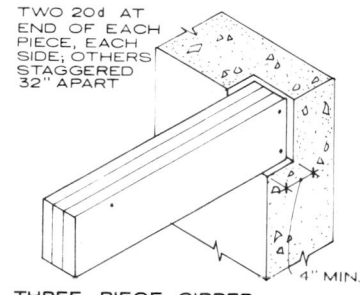

TWO 20d AT
END OF EACH
PIECE, EACH
SIDE; OTHERS
STAGGERED
32" APART

4" MIN.

THREE PIECE GIRDER
FOR FOUR PIECE GIRDER: ADD
NAILED WITH 20d TO THREE PC.

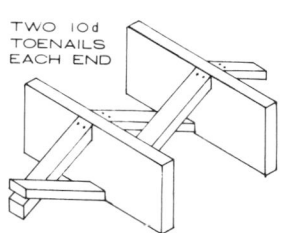

TWO 10d
TOENAILS
EACH END

1" X 3" CROSS BRIDGING
LOWER ENDS NOT NAILED,
UNTIL FLOORING IS LAYED

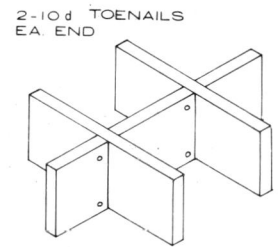

2-10d TOENAILS
EA. END

SOLID BRIDGING
USED UNDER PARTITIONS
FOR HEAVY LOADING

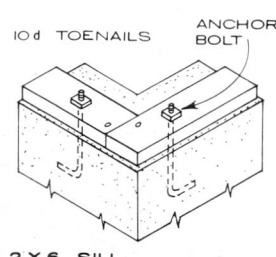

10d TOENAILS

ANCHOR
BOLT

2 X 6 SILL

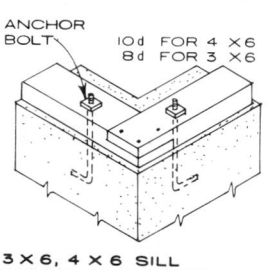

ANCHOR
BOLT

10d FOR 4 X 6
8d FOR 3 X 6

3 X 6, 4 X 6 SILL
HALVED AT CORNERS

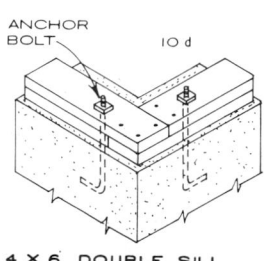

ANCHOR
BOLT

10d

4 X 6 DOUBLE SILL
NAILS STAGGERED ALONG
SILL 24" ON CENTER

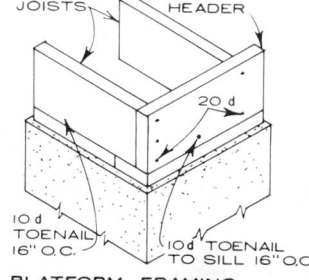

JOISTS

HEADER

20d

10d
TOENAIL
16" O.C.

10d TOENAIL
TO SILL 16" O.C.

PLATFORM FRAMING
TOENAIL TO SILL NOT
REQUIRED IF DIAGONAL
SHEATHING USED

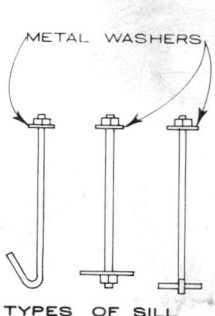

METAL WASHERS

**TYPES OF SILL
ANCHOR BOLTS**

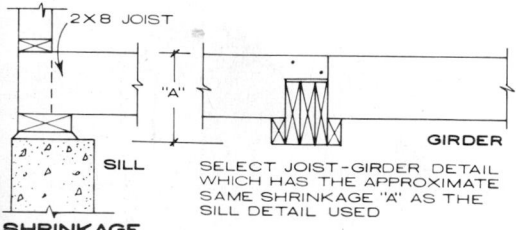

2 X 8 JOIST

"A"

GIRDER

SILL

SELECT JOIST-GIRDER DETAIL
WHICH HAS THE APPROXIMATE
SAME SHRINKAGE "A" AS THE
SILL DETAIL USED

SHRINKAGE

1/2" = 1'-0"

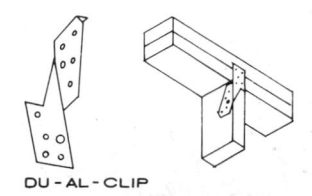

DU-AL-CLIP

METAL FRAMING DEVICES

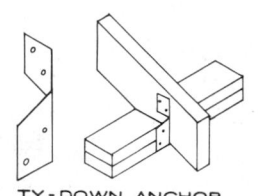

TY-DOWN ANCHOR

16 - 18 GAUGE ZINC COATED STEEL

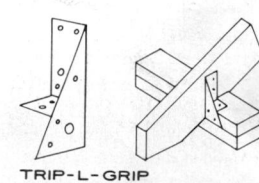

TRIP-L-GRIP

Joseph A. Wilkes, AIA; Wilkes and Faulkner; Washington, D. C.

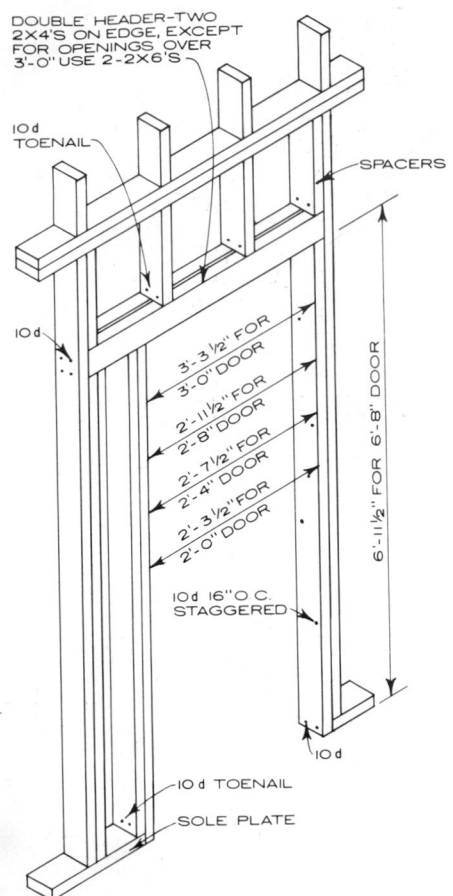

DOUBLE HEADER-TWO 2×4'S ON EDGE, EXCEPT FOR OPENINGS OVER 3'-0" USE 2-2×6'S

10d TOENAIL

SPACERS

10d

3'-3½" FOR 3'-0" DOOR
2'-11½" FOR 2'-8" DOOR
2'-7½" FOR 2'-4" DOOR
2'-3½" FOR 2'-0" DOOR

6'-11½" FOR 6'-8" DOOR

10d 16" O.C. STAGGERED

10d

10d TOENAIL

SOLE PLATE

DOOR OPENING
FOR ROUGH OPENINGS UP TO 3'-1½" WIDE

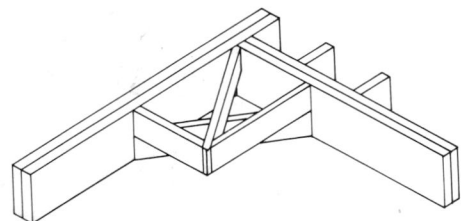

SMALL CANTILEVER PLATFORM
(SUCH AS HEARTHS)

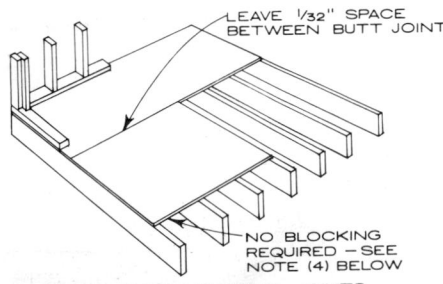

LEAVE 1/32" SPACE BETWEEN BUTT JOINTS

NO BLOCKING REQUIRED - SEE NOTE (4) BELOW

STAGGER SHEET BEARING JOINTS
PLYWOOD SUBFLOORING

NOTES:

1. These values apply for Structural I and II, Standard sheathing and C-C Exterior grades only.

2. Identification Index appears on all panels except 1 1/8" and 1 1/4" panels.

3. In some nonresidential buildings, special conditions may impose heavy concentrated loads and heavy traffic requiring subfloor constructions in excess of these minimums.

Joseph A. Wilkes, AIA; Wilkes and Faulkner; Washington, D. C.

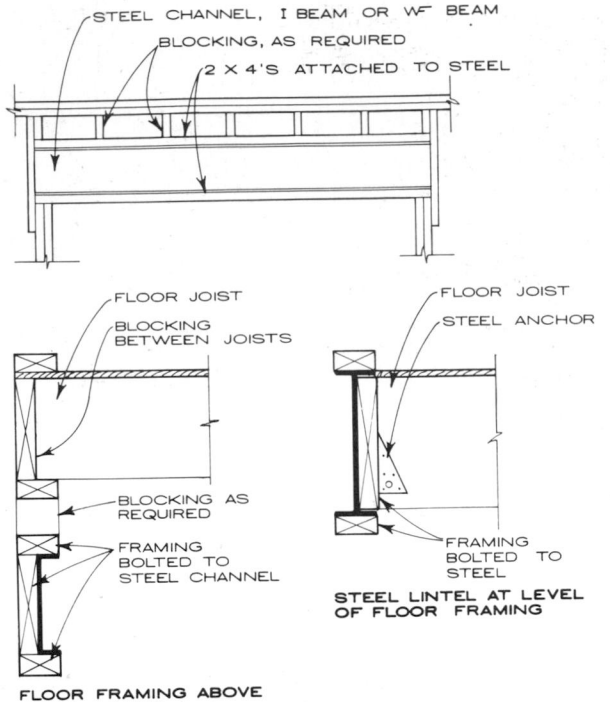

STEEL CHANNEL, I BEAM OR W BEAM
BLOCKING, AS REQUIRED
2 × 4'S ATTACHED TO STEEL

FLOOR JOIST
BLOCKING BETWEEN JOISTS

FLOOR JOIST
STEEL ANCHOR

BLOCKING AS REQUIRED

FRAMING BOLTED TO STEEL CHANNEL

FRAMING BOLTED TO STEEL

STEEL LINTEL AT LEVEL OF FLOOR FRAMING

FLOOR FRAMING ABOVE STEEL LINTEL

STEEL LINTELS FOR WIDE OPENINGS

NOTE:

STEEL LINTELS SELECTED FROM STEEL BEAM DESIGN TABLES ON BASIS OF FLOOR, WALL, & ROOF LOADS CARRIED OVER OPENING.

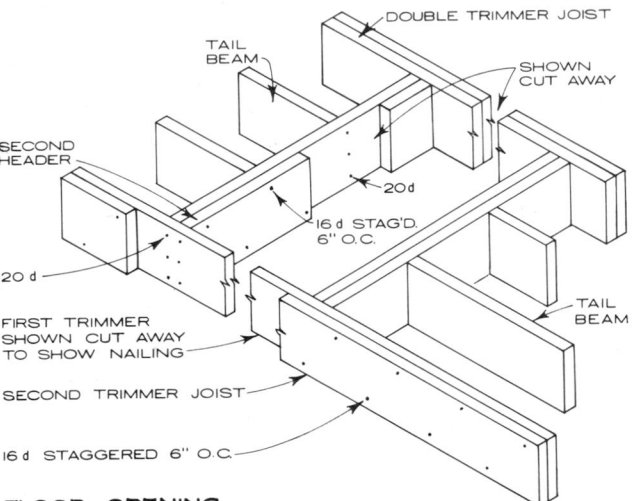

DOUBLE TRIMMER JOIST
TAIL BEAM
SHOWN CUT AWAY
SECOND HEADER
20d
16d STAG'D. 6" O.C.
20d
TAIL BEAM
FIRST TRIMMER SHOWN CUT AWAY TO SHOW NAILING
SECOND TRIMMER JOIST
16d STAGGERED 6" O.C.

FLOOR OPENING

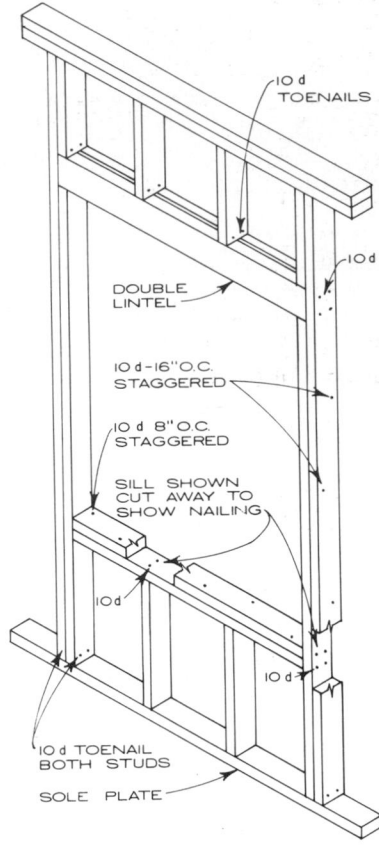

10d TOENAILS

DOUBLE LINTEL

10d-16" O.C. STAGGERED

10d 8" O.C. STAGGERED

SILL SHOWN CUT AWAY TO SHOW NAILING

10d

10d

10d TOENAIL BOTH STUDS

SOLE PLATE

WINDOW OPENING

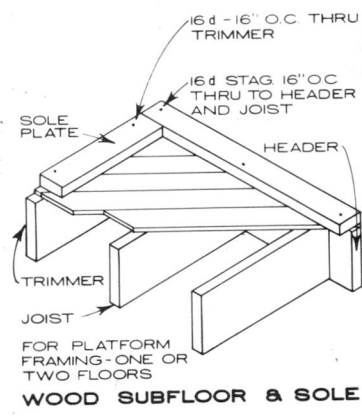

16d - 16" O.C. THRU TRIMMER

16d STAG. 16" O.C. THRU TO HEADER AND JOIST

SOLE PLATE

HEADER

TRIMMER

JOIST

FOR PLATFORM FRAMING- ONE OR TWO FLOORS

WOOD SUBFLOOR & SOLE

PLYWOOD SUBFLOORING - THICKNESS, SPAN, NAIL SPACING   NOTES: 1, 3, & 4
FOR DIRECT APPLICATION OF T&G WOODSTRIP AND BLOCK FLOORING & LIGHTWEIGHT CONCRETE

PANEL IDENTIFICATION INDEX	PLYWOOD THICKNESS (INCHES)	MAXIMUM SPAN (INCHES)	NAIL SIZE & TYPE	NAIL SPACING	
				PANEL EDGES	INTERMEDIATE
30/12	5/8	12(6)	8d common	6	10
32/16	1/2, 5/8	16(7)	8d common(8)	6	10
36/16	3/4	16(7)	8d common	6	10
42/20	5/8, 3/4, 7/8	20(7)	8d common	6	10
48/24	3/4, 7/8	24	8d common	6	10
1 1/8" Groups 1 & 2	1 1/8	48	10d common	6	6
1 1/4" Groups 3 & 4	1 1/4	48	10d common	6	6

4. Edges shall be tongue and grooved or supported with blocking for square edge wood flooring, unless separate underlayment layer (1/4" minimum thickness) is installed.

5. Spans limited to values shown because of possible effect of concentrated loads. At indicated maximum spans, floor panels carrying Identification Index numbers will support uniform loads of more than 100 psf.

6. May be 16" if 25/32" wood strip flooring is installed at right angles to joists.

7. May be 24" if 25/32" wood strip flooring is installed at right angles to joists.

8. 6d common nail permitted if plywood is 1/2".

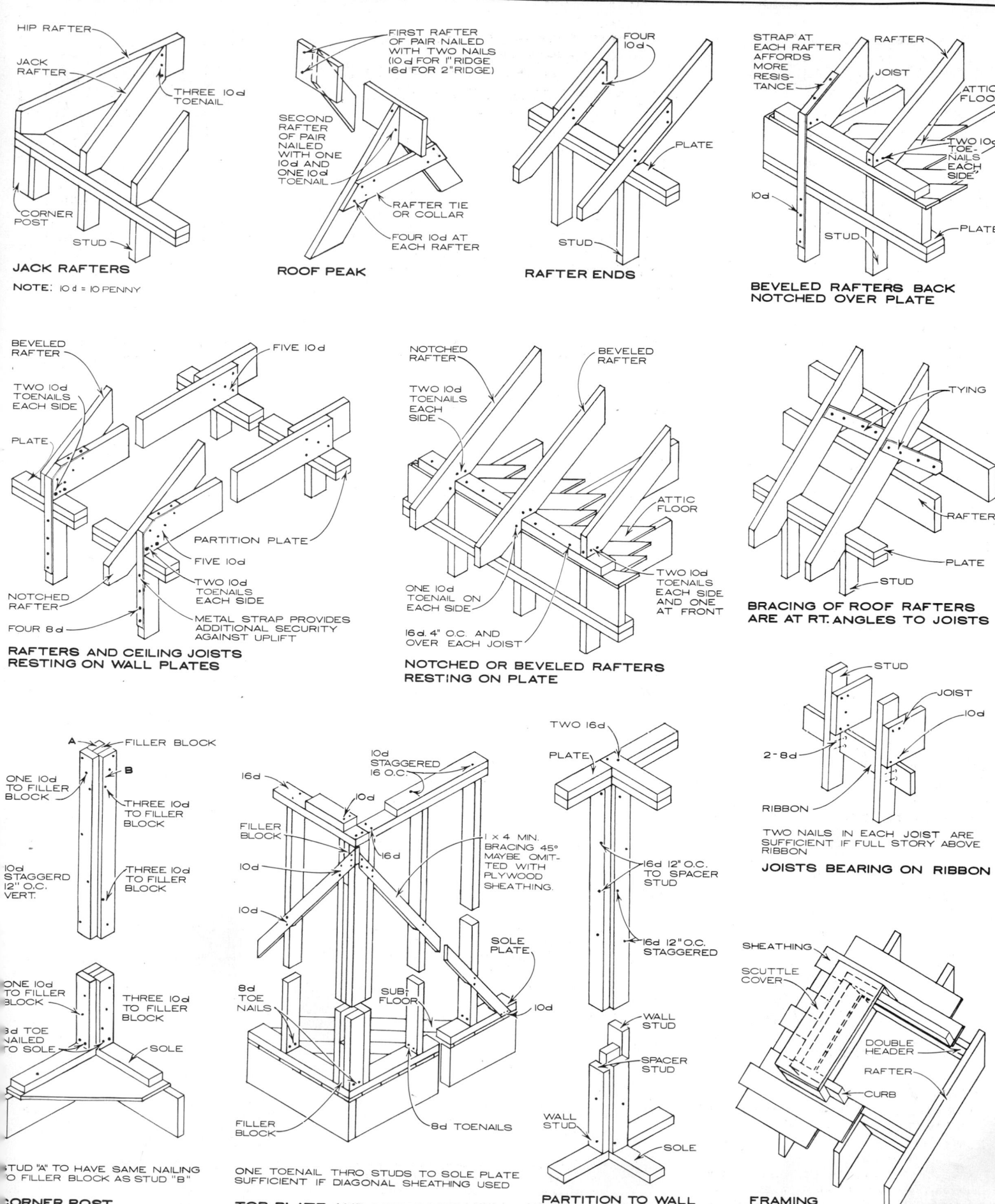

JACK RAFTERS

NOTE: 10d = 10 PENNY

ROOF PEAK

RAFTER ENDS

BEVELED RAFTERS BACK NOTCHED OVER PLATE

RAFTERS AND CEILING JOISTS RESTING ON WALL PLATES

NOTCHED OR BEVELED RAFTERS RESTING ON PLATE

BRACING OF ROOF RAFTERS ARE AT RT. ANGLES TO JOISTS

JOISTS BEARING ON RIBBON

TWO NAILS IN EACH JOIST ARE SUFFICIENT IF FULL STORY ABOVE RIBBON

CORNER POST

STUD "A" TO HAVE SAME NAILING TO FILLER BLOCK AS STUD "B"

TOP PLATE AND LET-IN BRACING

ONE TOENAIL THRO STUDS TO SOLE PLATE SUFFICIENT IF DIAGONAL SHEATHING USED

PARTITION TO WALL CONNECTION

FRAMING AT SCUTTLE

Joseph A. Wilkes, AIA; Wilkes and Faulkner; Washington, D. C.

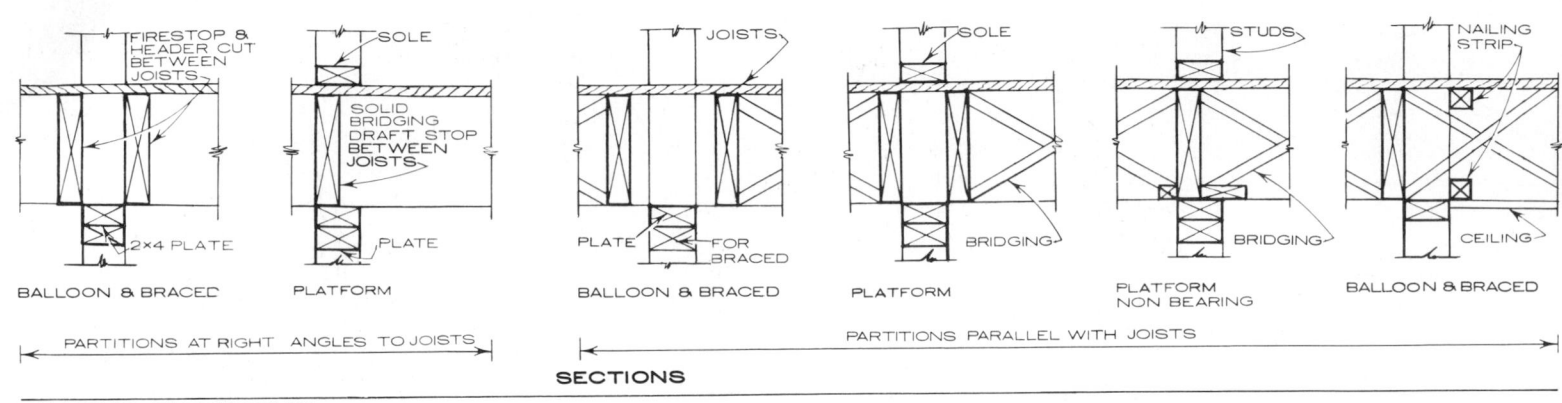

BEARING PARTITIONS

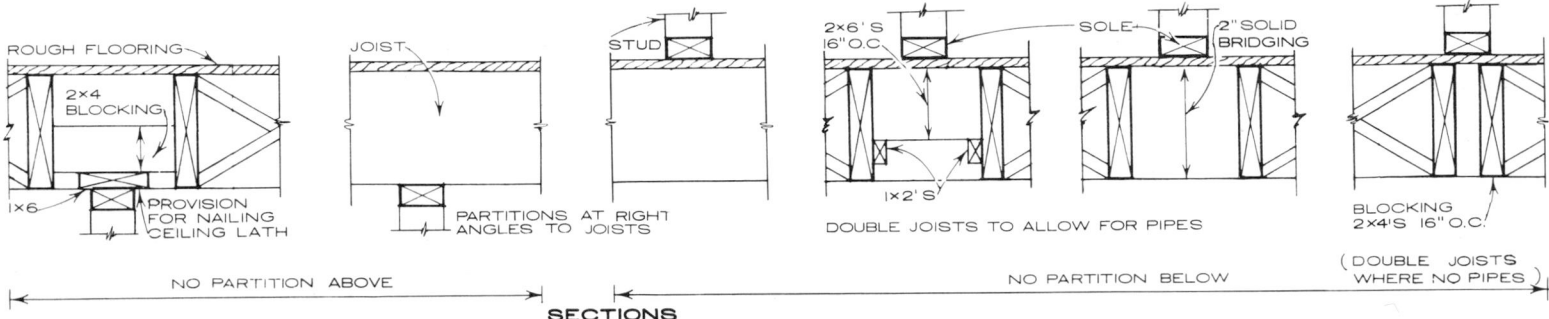

NON-BEARING PARTITIONS

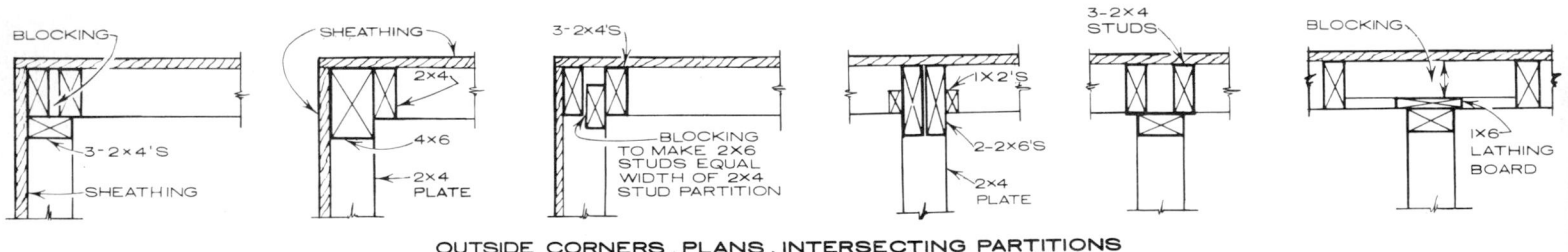

OUTSIDE CORNERS, PLANS, INTERSECTING PARTITIONS

WALL FRAMING
SCALE: 3/4"=1'-0"

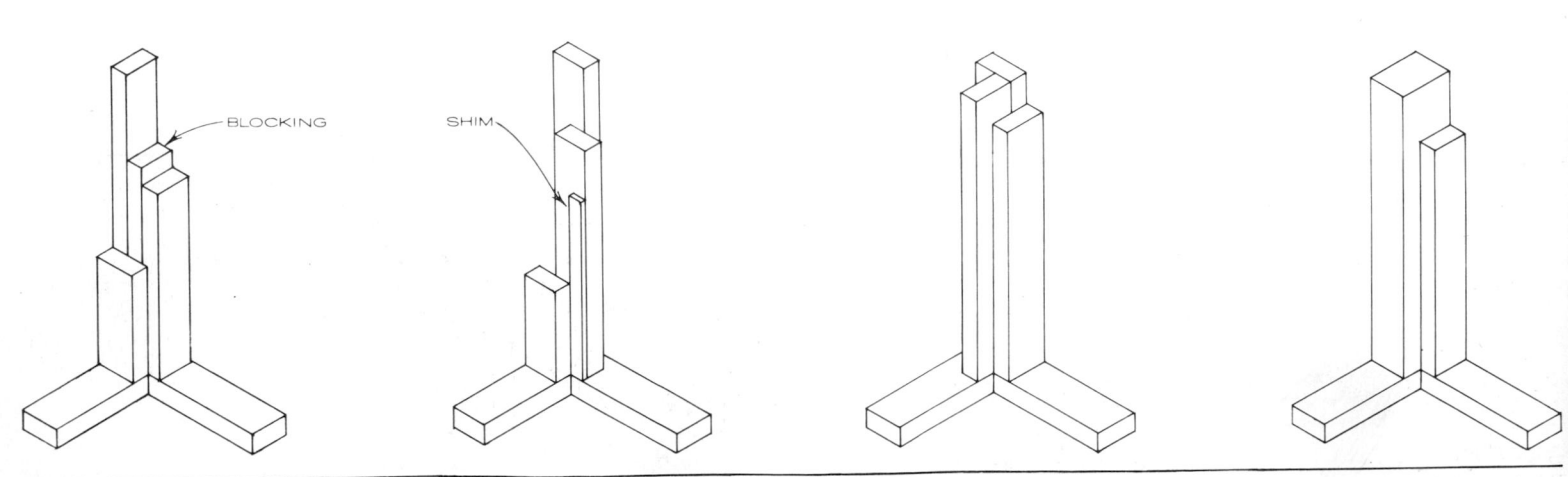

ASSEMBLY OF STUDS AT OUTSIDE CORNER

Joseph A. Wilkes, AIA; Wilkes and Faulkner; Washington, D. C.

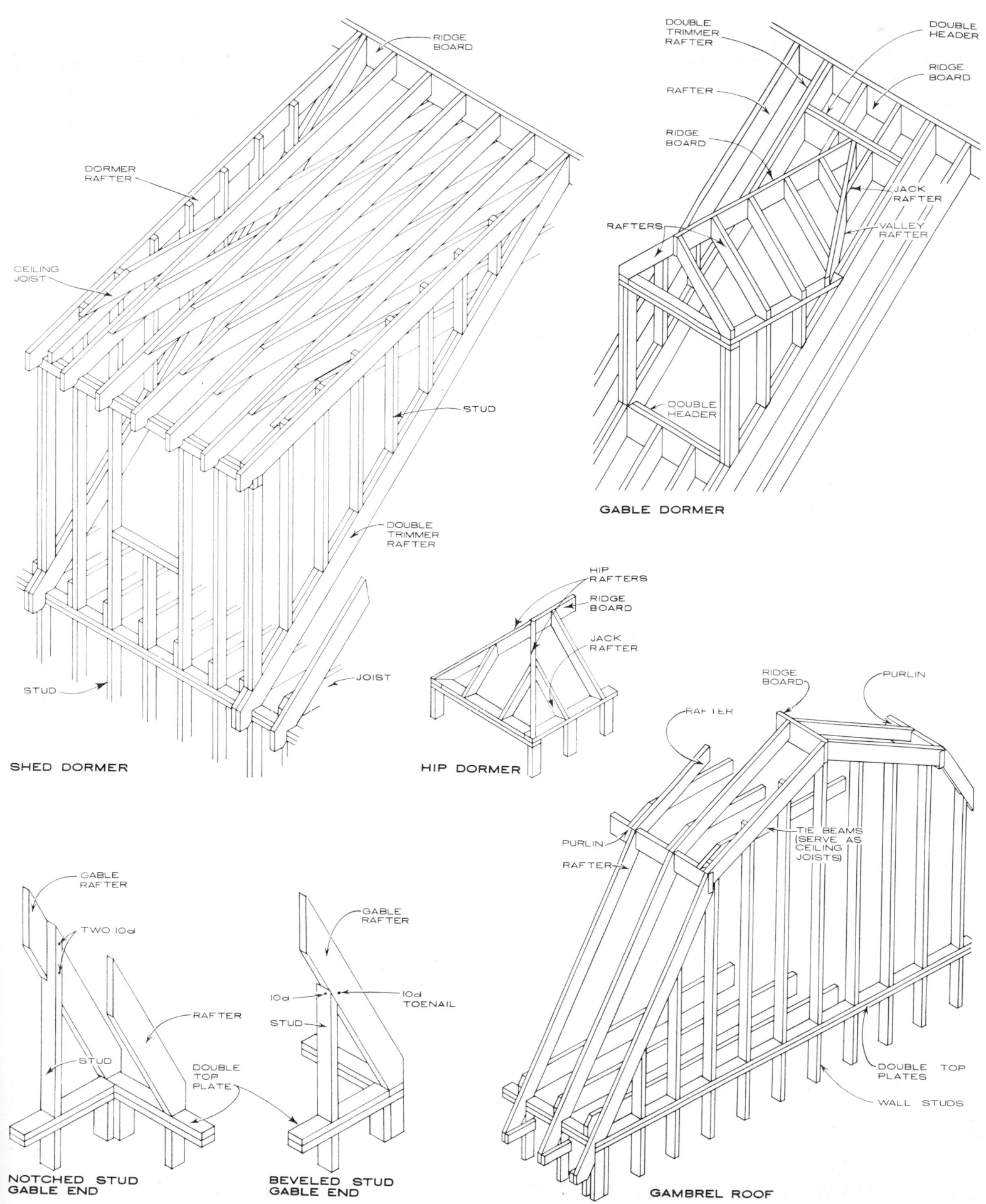

RIDGE BOARD

DORMER RAFTER

CEILING JOIST

STUD

DOUBLE TRIMMER RAFTER

STUD

JOIST

SHED DORMER

DOUBLE TRIMMER RAFTER

DOUBLE HEADER

RAFTER

RIDGE BOARD

RAFTERS

DOUBLE HEADER

JACK RAFTER

VALLEY RAFTER

GABLE DORMER

HIP RAFTERS

RIDGE BOARD

JACK RAFTER

HIP DORMER

RIDGE BOARD

PURLIN

RAFTER

PURLIN

RAFTER

TIE BEAMS (SERVE AS CEILING JOISTS)

DOUBLE TOP PLATES

WALL STUDS

GAMBREL ROOF

GABLE RAFTER

TWO 10d

RAFTER

STUD

DOUBLE TOP PLATE

NOTCHED STUD GABLE END

GABLE RAFTER

10d

10d TOENAIL

STUD

BEVELED STUD GABLE END

Joseph A. Wilkes, AIA; Wilkes and Faulkner; Washington, D. C.

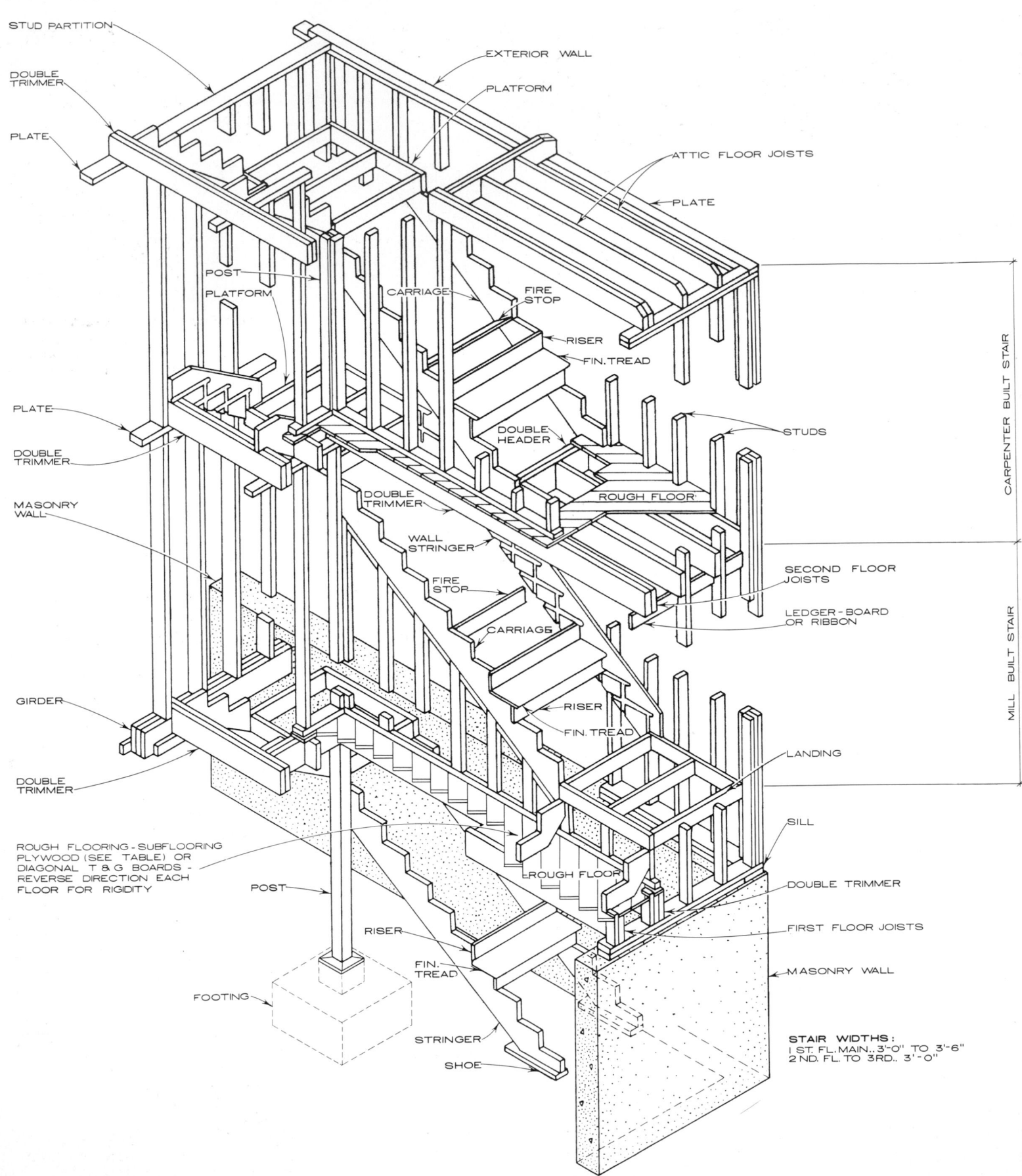

STUD PARTITION

DOUBLE TRIMMER

PLATE

EXTERIOR WALL

PLATFORM

ATTIC FLOOR JOISTS

PLATE

POST

PLATFORM

CARRIAGE

FIRE STOP

RISER

FIN. TREAD

DOUBLE HEADER

STUDS

PLATE

DOUBLE TRIMMER

DOUBLE TRIMMER

ROUGH FLOOR

MASONRY WALL

WALL STRINGER

SECOND FLOOR JOISTS

FIRE STOP

LEDGER-BOARD OR RIBBON

CARRIAGE

GIRDER

RISER

FIN. TREAD

DOUBLE TRIMMER

LANDING

ROUGH FLOORING-SUBFLOORING PLYWOOD (SEE TABLE) OR DIAGONAL T & G BOARDS - REVERSE DIRECTION EACH FLOOR FOR RIGIDITY

POST

ROUGH FLOOR

SILL

DOUBLE TRIMMER

FIRST FLOOR JOISTS

MASONRY WALL

FOOTING

RISER

FIN. TREAD

STRINGER

SHOE

CARPENTER BUILT STAIR

MILL BUILT STAIR

STAIR WIDTHS :
1 ST. FL. MAIN.. 3'-0" TO 3'-6"
2 ND. FL. TO 3RD.. 3'-0"

ISOMETRIC VIEW OF STAIRS
SCALE: 1/4" = 1'-0"

Joseph A. Wilkes, AIA; Wilkes and Faulkner; Washington, D. C.

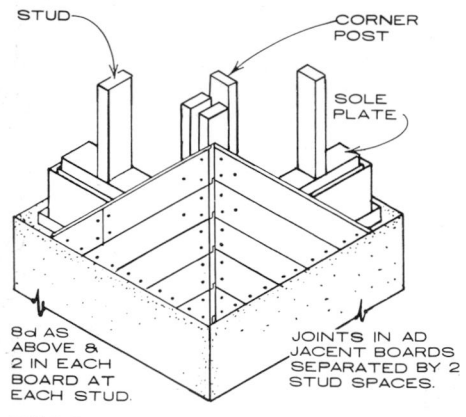

STUD

CORNER POST

SOLE PLATE

8d AS ABOVE & 2 IN EACH BOARD AT EACH STUD.

JOINTS IN ADJACENT BOARDS SEPARATED BY 2 STUD SPACES.

DIAGONAL WOOD WALL SHEATHING

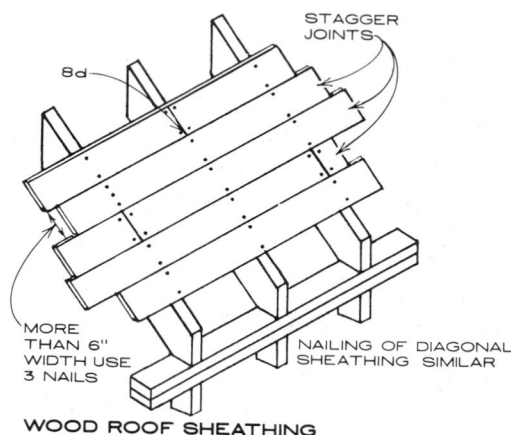

STAGGER JOINTS

8d

MORE THAN 6" WIDTH USE 3 NAILS

NAILING OF DIAGONAL SHEATHING SIMILAR

WOOD ROOF SHEATHING

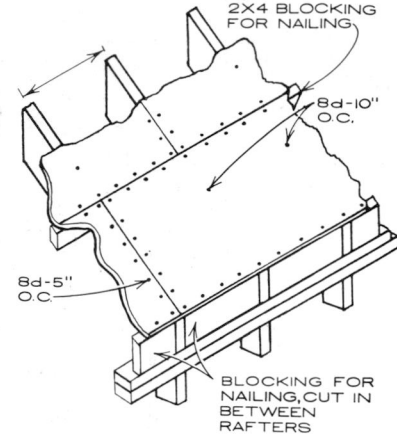

2X4 BLOCKING FOR NAILING

8d–10" O.C.

8d–5" O.C.

BLOCKING FOR NAILING, CUT IN BETWEEN RAFTERS

PLYWOOD ROOF- SHEATHING

Nailing and blocking required. See page on Structural Plywood Data for Plywood Roof Decking Table which gives thickness-span information.

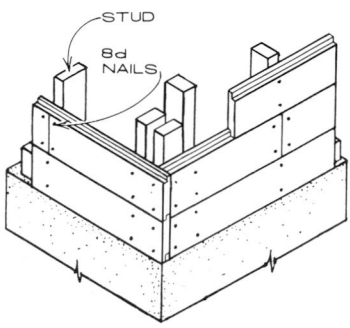

STUD

8d NAILS

HORIZONTAL

FOR BOARDS WIDER THAN 8" USE THREE NAILS IN PLACE OF TWO.

WOOD WALL SHEATHING

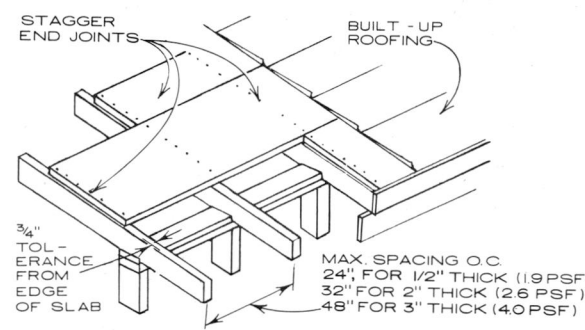

STAGGER END JOINTS

BUILT - UP ROOFING

3/4" TOLERANCE FROM EDGE OF SLAB

MAX. SPACING O.C.
24" FOR 1/2" THICK (1.9 PSF)
32" FOR 2" THICK (2.6 PSF)
48" FOR 3" THICK (4.0 PSF)

INSULATING ROOF DECK
SCALE: 1/4" = 1'-0"

ROOF SHEATHING AND DECKING

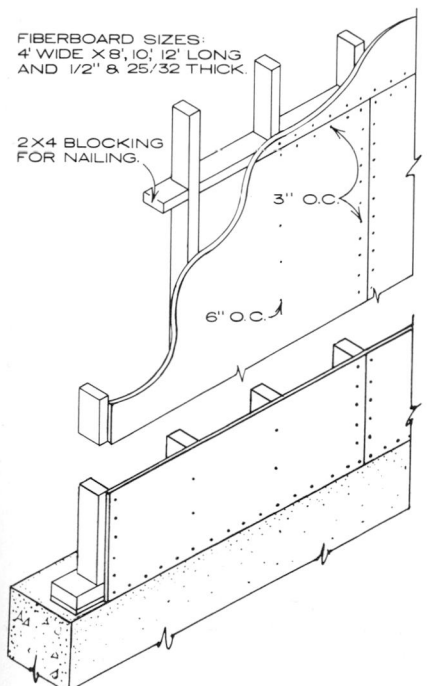

FIBERBOARD SIZES: 4' WIDE X 8', 10', 12' LONG AND 1/2" & 25/32" THICK.

2X4 BLOCKING FOR NAILING.

3" O.C.

6" O.C.

VERTICAL

FIBERBOARD WALL SHEATHING

NAILS - 7/16" HEAD, GALV. RFG. 1 1/2" THICK SHEATHING & 1 3/4" TO 2" FOR 25/32" THICK. ALL BOARDS NAILED 3/8" IN FROM EDGES NAIL SIZES & SPACINGS VARY SLIGHTLY WITH SOME MFRS. "ASPHALT COATED" & "ASPHALT IMPREGNATED" BDS. MADE.

NOTE:
More comprehensive data on plywood sheathing may be found on page on softwood plywood.

Joseph A. Wilkes, AIA; Wilkes and Faulkner; Washington, D. C.

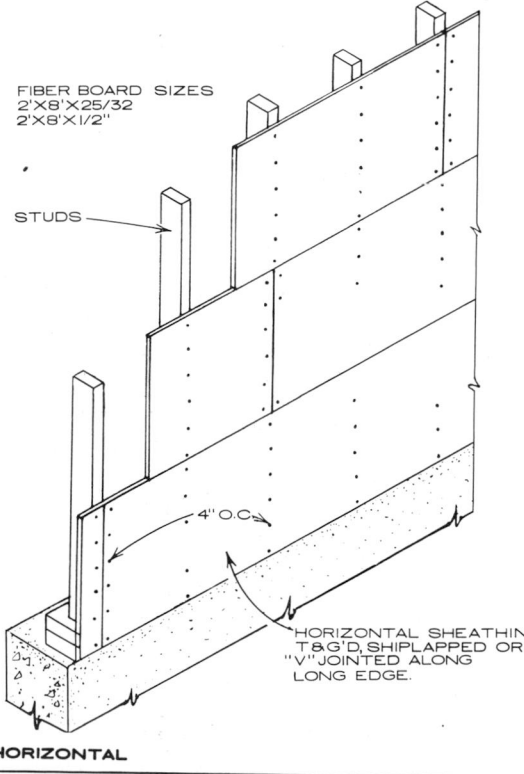

FIBER BOARD SIZES
2'X8'X25/32
2'X8'X1/2"

STUDS

4" O.C.

HORIZONTAL SHEATHING T&G'D, SHIPLAPPED OR "V" JOINTED ALONG LONG EDGE.

HORIZONTAL

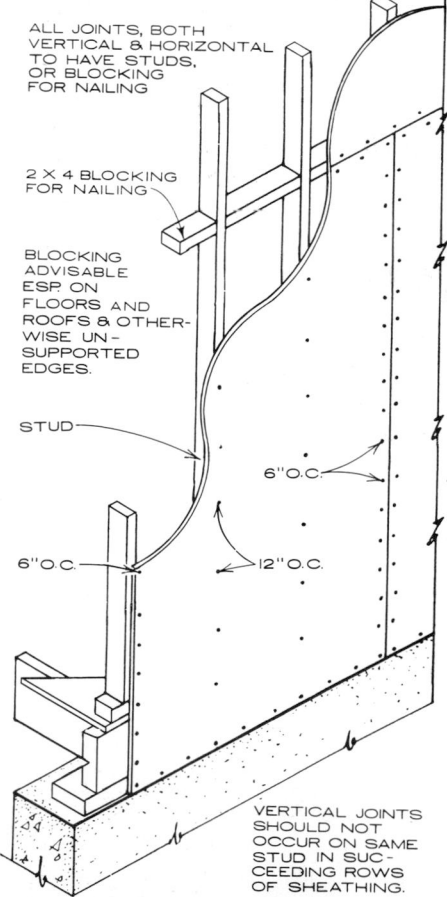

ALL JOINTS, BOTH VERTICAL & HORIZONTAL TO HAVE STUDS, OR BLOCKING FOR NAILING

2 X 4 BLOCKING FOR NAILING

BLOCKING ADVISABLE ESP. ON FLOORS AND ROOFS & OTHERWISE UNSUPPORTED EDGES.

STUD

6" O.C.

6" O.C.

12" O.C.

VERTICAL JOINTS SHOULD NOT OCCUR ON SAME STUD IN SUCCEEDING ROWS OF SHEATHING.

PANELS 4'-0" WIDE X 8'-0" HIGH

PLYWOOD WALL-SHEATHING

CLASSIFICATION OF SPECIES

GROUP I	GROUP 2	GROUP 3	GROUP 4
Douglas fir 1 *	Cedar, Port Orford	Alder, red	Cedar
Larch, Western	Douglas fir 2 **	Cedar, Alaska yellow	Incense
			Western red
Pine, Southern	Fir	Pine	Fir, subalpine
Loblolly	California red	Lodgepole	
Longleaf	Grand	Ponderosa	Pine, sugar
Shortleaf	Noble	Redwood	Poplar, Western
Slash	Pacific silver		
Tanoak	White		Spruce, Engelmann
	Hemlock, Western		
	Lauan	* Douglas fir 1—Washington, Oregon, Calif-	
	Red	ornia, Idaho, Montana,	
	White	Wyoming, British Columbia,	
	Pine, Western White	Alberta.	
	Spruce, Sitka	** Douglas fir 2—Nevada, Utah, Colorado,	
		Arizona, New Mexico.	

VENEERS GRADES USED IN PLYWOOD

N — Special order "natural finish" veneer. Select all heartwood or all sapwood. Free of open defects. Allows some repairs.

A — Smooth and paintable. Neatly made repairs permissible. Also used for natural finish in less demanding applications.

B — Solid surface veneer. Circular repair plugs and tight knots permitted.

C — Knotholes to 1". Occasional knotholes $1/2$" larger permitted providing total width of all knots and knotholes with a specified section does not exceed certain limits. Limited splits permitted. Minimum veneer permitted in Exterior-type plywood.

C PLUGGED — Improved C veneer with splits limited to $1/8$" in width and knotholes and borer holes limited to $1/4$" by $1/2$".

D — Permits knots and knotholes to $2 1/2$" in width and $1/2$" larger under certain specified limits. Limited splits permitted.

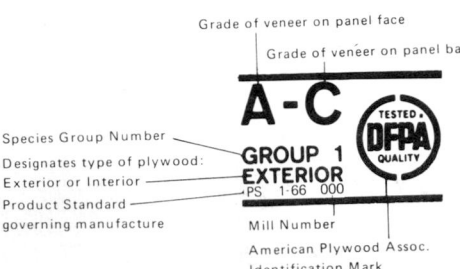

TYPICAL BACK STAMP   TYPICAL EDGE STAMP

TYPICAL DFPA GRADE TRADEMARKS

NOTE:

All the Interior grades shown are also available with Exterior glue. However these grades permit D veneer and are not an adequate substitute for Exterior type plywood which is limited to C or better veneer throughout. Also all grades shown, except Plyform, are available tongue and grooved in panels $1/2$", $5/8$", $3/4$" and $1 1/8$".

PLYWOOD ROOF DECKING TABLE. SEE INDEX FOR PAGE FOR SUBFLOORING TABLE, AND FOR WALL SHEATHING.

PANEL IDENT. INDEX	PLYWOOD THICKNESS (INCH)	MAX. SPAN (INCHES) (NOTE 4)	UNSUPPORTED EDGE—MAX. LENGTH (INCHES) (NOTE 5)	ALLOWABLE ROOF LOADS (PSF) (NOTES 6 & 7) (SPACING OF SUPPORTS (INCHES) CENTER TO CENTER)										
				12	16	20	24	30	32	36	42	48	60	72
12/0	$5/16$	12	12	100 (130)										
16/0	$5/16, 3/8$	16	16	130 (170)	55 (75)									
20/0	$5/16, 3/8$	20	20		85 (110)	45 (55)								
24/0	$3/8, 1/2$	24	24		150 (160)	75 (100)	45 (60)							
30/12	$5/8$	30	26			145 (165)	85 (110)	40 (55)						
32/16	$1/2, 5/8$	32	28				90 (105)	45 (60)	40 (50)					
36/16	$3/4$	36	30				125 (145)	65 (85)	55 (70)	35 (50)				
42/20	$5/8, 3/4, 7/8$	42	32					80 (105)	65 (90)	45 (60)	35 (40)			
48/24	$3/4, 7/8$	48	36						105 (115)	75 (90)	55 (55)	40 (40)		
2 4 1	$1 1/8$	72	48							160 (160)	95 (95)	70 (70)	45 (45)	25 (30)
$1 1/8''$ G 1&2	$1 1/8$	72	48							145 (145)	85 (85)	65 (65)	40 (40)	30 (30)
$1 1/4''$ G 3&4	$1 1/4$	72	48							160 (165)	95 (95)	75 (75)	45 (45)	25 (35)

NOTE:

1. Applies to Standard, Structural I and II and C-C grades only.

2. For applications where the roofing is to be guaranteed by a performance bond, recommendations may differ somewhat from these values. Contact American Plywood Association for bonded roof recommendations.

3. Use 6d common smooth, ring-shank or spiral thread nails for $1/2$" thick or less, and 8d common smooth, ring-shank or spiral thread for plywood 1" thick or less (if ring-shank or spiral thread nails same diameter as common). Use 8d ring-shank or spiral thread or 10d

common smooth shank nails for 2-4-1, $1 1/8$" and $1 1/4$" panels. Space nails 6" at panel edges and 12" at intermediate supports. Except that where spans are 48" or more, nails shall be 6" at all supports.

4. These spans shall not be exceeded for any load conditions.

5. Provide adequate blocking, tongue and grooved edges or other suitable edge support such as Plyclips when spans exceed indicated value. Use two Plyclips for 48" or greater spans and one for lesser spans.

6. Uniform load deflection limitation: $1/180$th of the span under live load plus dead load, $1/240$th under live load only. First number shown is allowable live load, and allowable total load is shown with parentheses.

7. Allowable roof loads were established by laboratory test and calculations assuming uniformly distributed loads.

Joseph A. Wilkes, AIA; Wilkes and Faulkner; Washington, D.C.

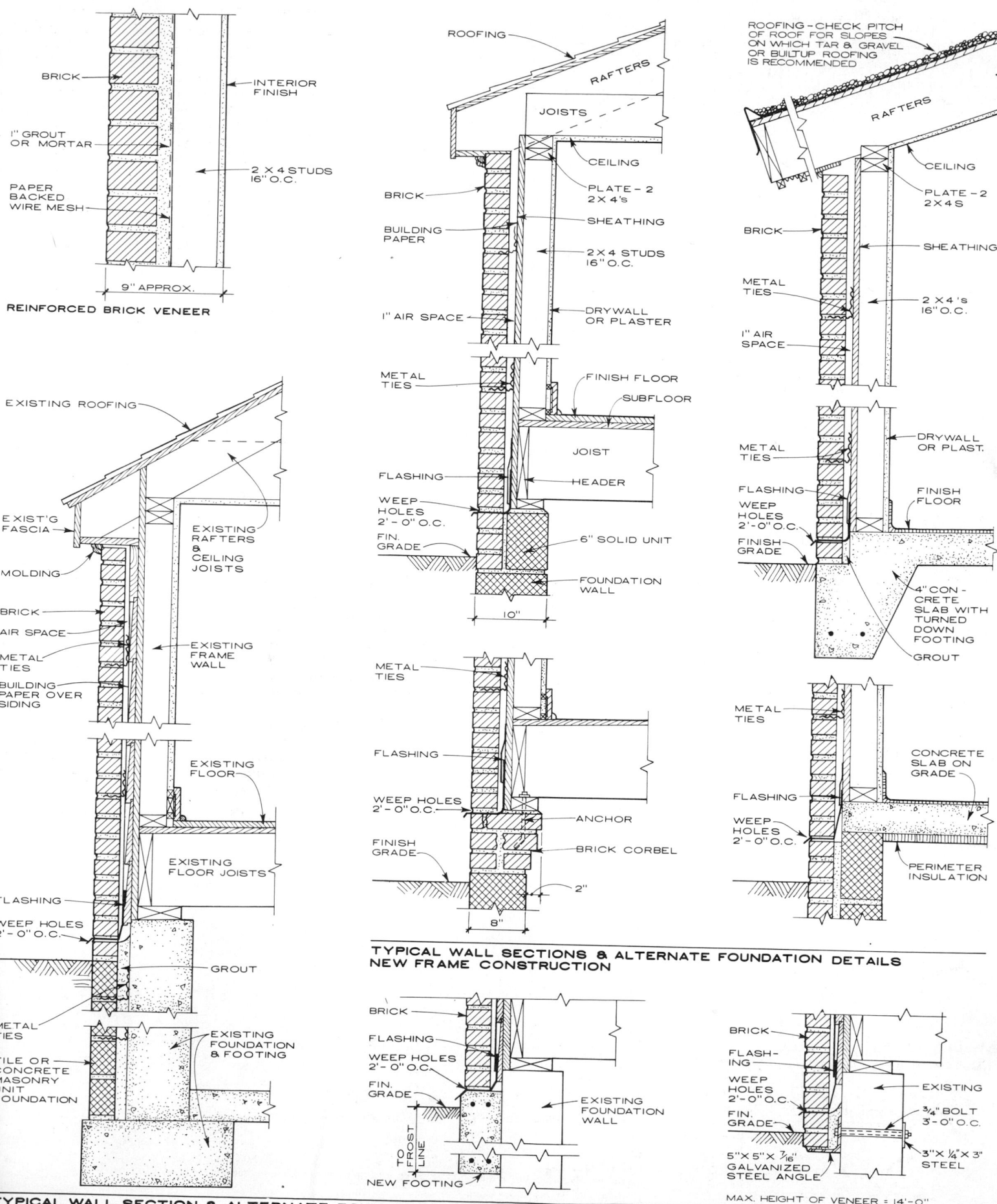

BRICK

INTERIOR FINISH

1" GROUT OR MORTAR

PAPER BACKED WIRE MESH

2 X 4 STUDS 16" O.C.

9" APPROX.

REINFORCED BRICK VENEER

EXISTING ROOFING

EXIST'G FASCIA

MOLDING

BRICK

AIR SPACE

METAL TIES

BUILDING PAPER OVER SIDING

EXISTING RAFTERS & CEILING JOISTS

EXISTING FRAME WALL

EXISTING FLOOR

EXISTING FLOOR JOISTS

FLASHING

WEEP HOLES 2'-0" O.C.

GROUT

METAL TIES

TILE OR CONCRETE MASONRY UNIT FOUNDATION

EXISTING FOUNDATION & FOOTING

TYPICAL WALL SECTION & ALTERNATE FOUNDATION DETAILS/EXISTING FRAME CONSTRUCTION

ROOFING

RAFTERS

JOISTS

CEILING

PLATE - 2 2 X 4's

BRICK

BUILDING PAPER

SHEATHING

2 X 4 STUDS 16" O.C.

1" AIR SPACE

DRYWALL OR PLASTER

METAL TIES

FINISH FLOOR

SUBFLOOR

JOIST

HEADER

FLASHING

WEEP HOLES 2'- 0" O.C.

FIN. GRADE

6" SOLID UNIT

FOUNDATION WALL

10"

METAL TIES

FLASHING

WEEP HOLES 2'- 0" O.C.

FINISH GRADE

ANCHOR

BRICK CORBEL

2"

8"

TYPICAL WALL SECTIONS & ALTERNATE FOUNDATION DETAILS NEW FRAME CONSTRUCTION

BRICK

FLASHING

WEEP HOLES 2'- 0" O.C.

FIN. GRADE

TO FROST LINE

NEW FOOTING

EXISTING FOUNDATION WALL

ROOFING - CHECK PITCH OF ROOF FOR SLOPES ON WHICH TAR & GRAVEL OR BUILTUP ROOFING IS RECOMMENDED

RAFTERS

CEILING

PLATE - 2 2 X 4S

BRICK

METAL TIES

1" AIR SPACE

SHEATHING

2 X 4's 16" O.C.

DRYWALL OR PLAST.

METAL TIES

FLASHING

WEEP HOLES 2'- 0" O.C.

FINISH GRADE

FINISH FLOOR

4" CON-CRETE SLAB WITH TURNED DOWN FOOTING

GROUT

METAL TIES

FLASHING

WEEP HOLES 2'- 0" O.C.

CONCRETE SLAB ON GRADE

PERIMETER INSULATION

BRICK

FLASH-ING

WEEP HOLES 2'- 0" O.C.

FIN. GRADE

5" X 5" X 7/16" GALVANIZED STEEL ANGLE

3/4" BOLT 3'- 0" O.C.

EXISTING

3" X 1/4" X 3" STEEL

MAX. HEIGHT OF VENEER = 14'-0"

Structural Clay Products Institute; McLean, Virginia

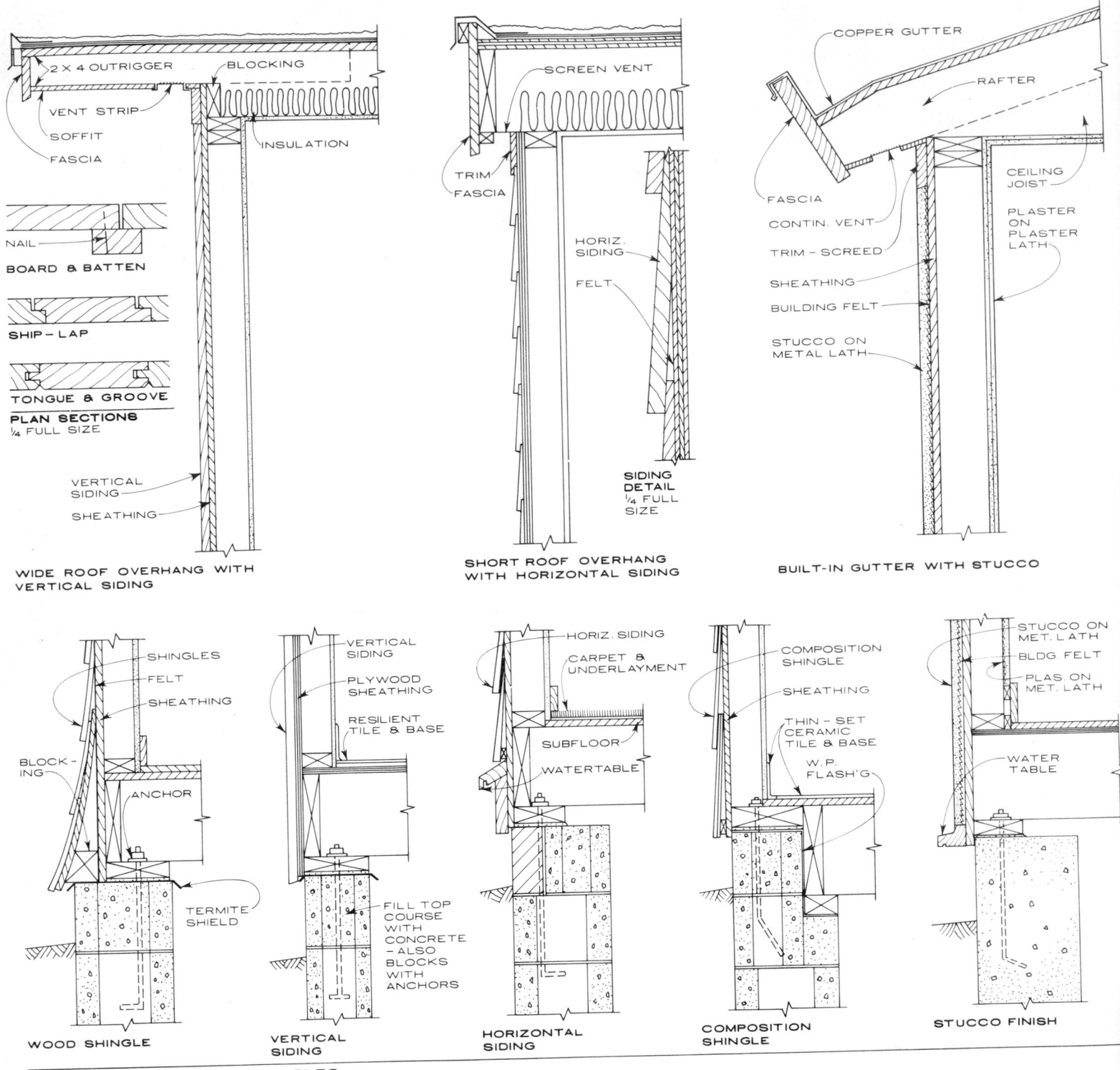

PLAN SECTIONS
¼ FULL SIZE

2 × 4 OUTRIGGER — BLOCKING
VENT STRIP
SOFFIT
FASCIA
INSULATION

NAIL
BOARD & BATTEN

SHIP – LAP

TONGUE & GROOVE

VERTICAL SIDING
SHEATHING

WIDE ROOF OVERHANG WITH VERTICAL SIDING

SCREEN VENT
TRIM
FASCIA
HORIZ. SIDING
FELT

SIDING DETAIL
¼ FULL SIZE

SHORT ROOF OVERHANG WITH HORIZONTAL SIDING

COPPER GUTTER
RAFTER
FASCIA
CONTIN. VENT
TRIM – SCREED
SHEATHING
BUILDING FELT
STUCCO ON METAL LATH
CEILING JOIST
PLASTER ON PLASTER LATH

BUILT-IN GUTTER WITH STUCCO

SHINGLES
FELT
SHEATHING
BLOCKING
ANCHOR
TERMITE SHIELD

WOOD SHINGLE

VERTICAL SIDING
PLYWOOD SHEATHING
RESILIENT TILE & BASE
FILL TOP COURSE WITH CONCRETE – ALSO BLOCKS WITH ANCHORS

VERTICAL SIDING

HORIZ. SIDING
CARPET & UNDERLAYMENT
SUBFLOOR
WATERTABLE

HORIZONTAL SIDING

COMPOSITION SHINGLE
SHEATHING
THIN – SET CERAMIC TILE & BASE
W.P. FLASH'G

COMPOSITION SHINGLE

STUCCO ON MET. LATH
BLDG. FELT
PLAS. ON MET. LATH
WATER TABLE

STUCCO FINISH

SIDING, SILLS AND WATERTABLES

NOTE : Components of details of watertable types are interchangeable.

EAVES SOFFIT MATERIALS

MATERIAL	THICKNESS	FINISH	REMARKS
ALUMINUM SHEET	.019 Gauge	Prefinished	Flat formed sheets or rolled; plain or perforated for venting. Use only aluminum nails or staples.
CEMENT – ASBESTOS	¼ Inch	Unfinished or Prefinished	Plain or perforated.
GYPSUM BOARD	¼ Inch	Painted	Protect from weather; water resistant available.
HARDBOARD	½ Inch	Painted	Perforated – plain and prefinished.
INSULATING BOARDS	¼ Inch	Painted	See manufacturers data.
PLYWOOD	¼ – ½ Inch	Painted, Stained or Prefinished	Plain or rough sawn textured; prefinished and medium density overlaid.
WOOD BOARDS	¼ – ³/₈ – ½ Inch	Painted, Stained or Prefinished	Square edged; tongue and grooved, ship-lapped; cedar, cypress, fir, pine and redwood most commonly used, plain or rough sawn.
	½ – ¾ Inch	Painted or Stained	

Joseph A. Wilkes, AIA; Wilkes and Faulkner; Washington, D. C.

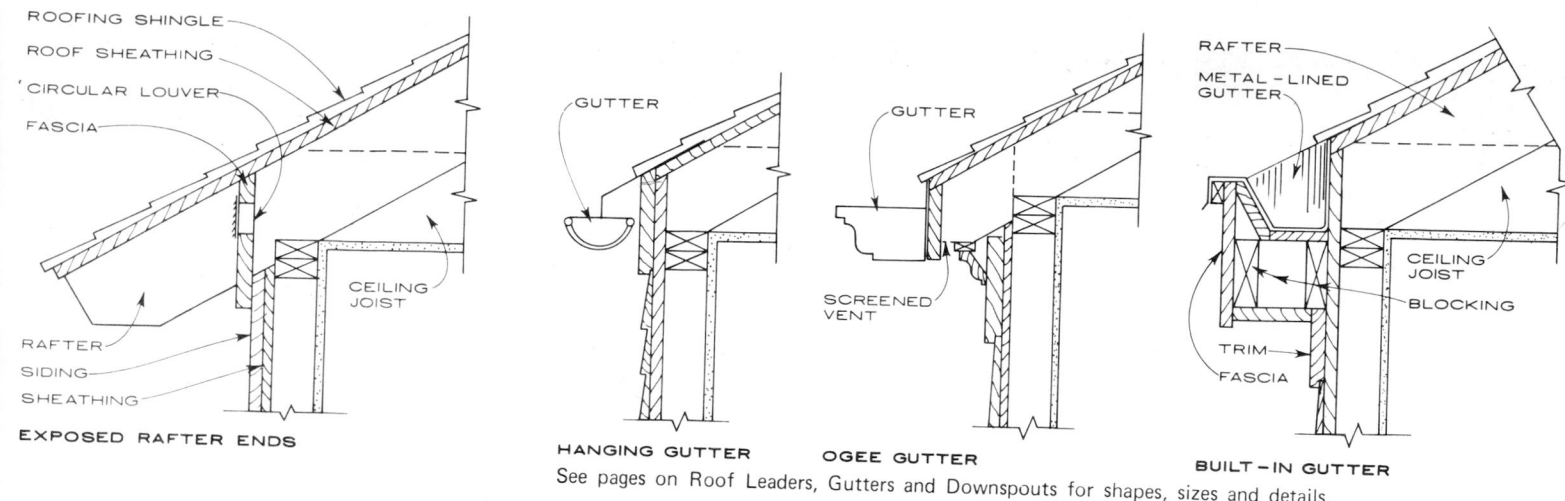

ROOFING SHINGLE
ROOF SHEATHING
CIRCULAR LOUVER
FASCIA

CEILING JOIST

RAFTER
SIDING
SHEATHING

EXPOSED RAFTER ENDS

GUTTER

SCREENED VENT

HANGING GUTTER

GUTTER

OGEE GUTTER

RAFTER
METAL-LINED GUTTER

CEILING JOIST

BLOCKING

TRIM
FASCIA

BUILT-IN GUTTER

See pages on Roof Leaders, Gutters and Downspouts for shapes, sizes and details.

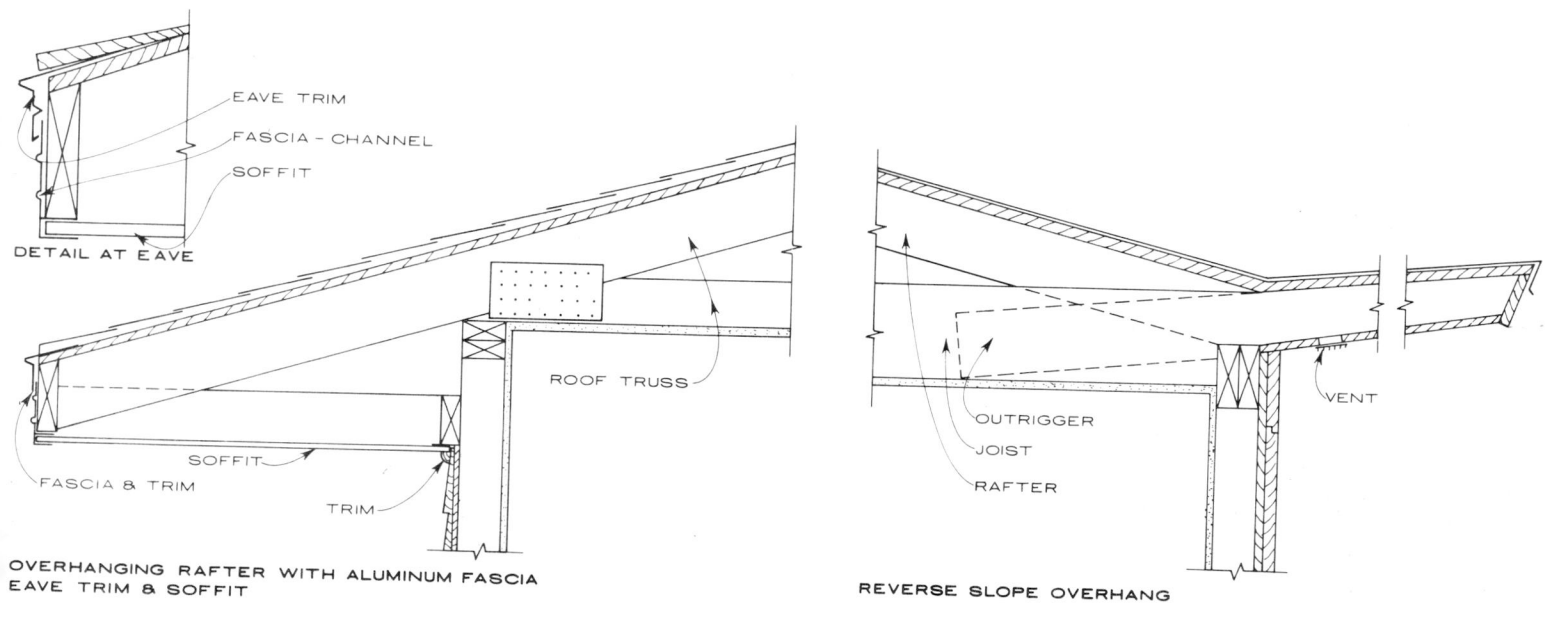

EAVE TRIM
FASCIA – CHANNEL
SOFFIT

DETAIL AT EAVE

ROOF TRUSS

SOFFIT

FASCIA & TRIM

TRIM

**OVERHANGING RAFTER WITH ALUMINUM FASCIA
EAVE TRIM & SOFFIT**

OUTRIGGER
JOIST
RAFTER

VENT

REVERSE SLOPE OVERHANG

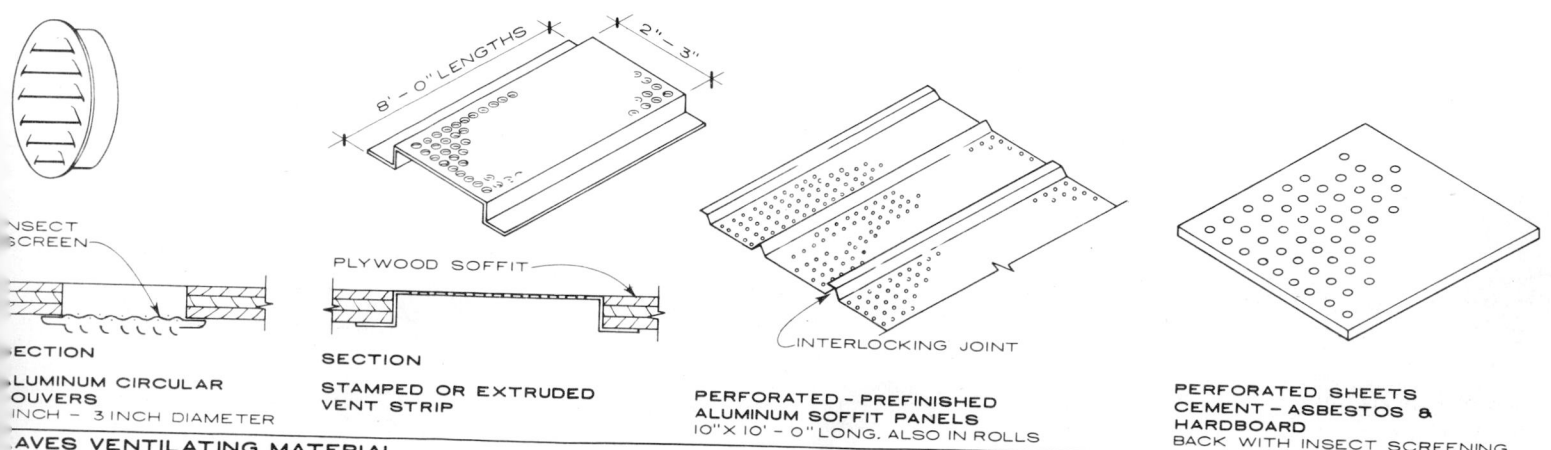

8' - 0" LENGTHS

2" – 3"

INSECT SCREEN

PLYWOOD SOFFIT

INTERLOCKING JOINT

**SECTION
ALUMINUM CIRCULAR
LOUVERS
INCH – 3 INCH DIAMETER**

**SECTION
STAMPED OR EXTRUDED
VENT STRIP**

**PERFORATED – PREFINISHED
ALUMINUM SOFFIT PANELS
10"X 10' – 0" LONG. ALSO IN ROLLS**

**PERFORATED SHEETS
CEMENT – ASBESTOS &
HARDBOARD
BACK WITH INSECT SCREENING**

EAVES VENTILATING MATERIAL

Ventilation of all rafter spaces required to prevent condensation and rot.

All vents should be protected from insect infestation by metallic or fiber glass screen cloth where perforations in material are greater than 1/10 inch.

Joseph A. Wilkes, AIA; Wilkes and Faulkner; Washington, D. C.

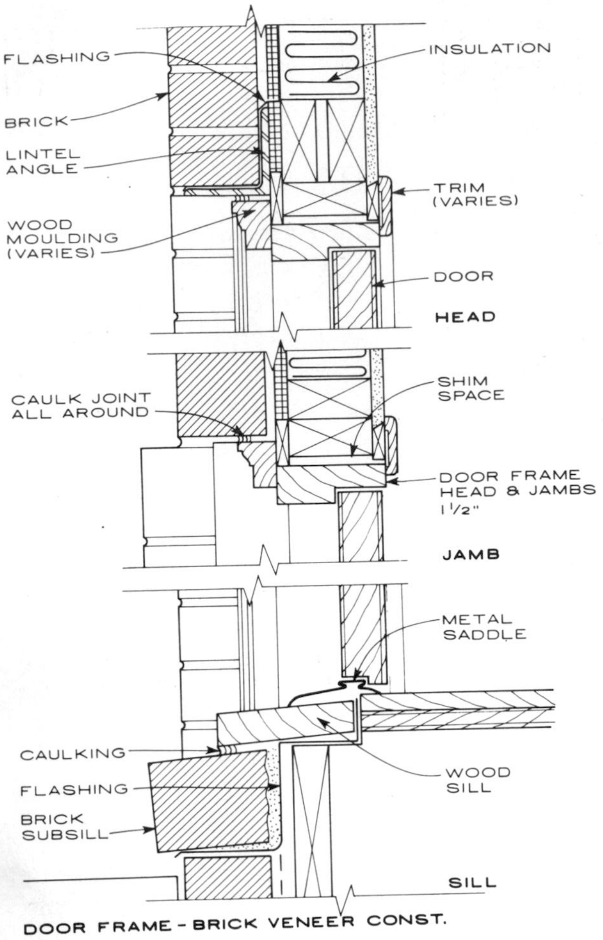

FLASHING

BRICK

LINTEL ANGLE

WOOD MOULDING (VARIES)

INSULATION

TRIM (VARIES)

DOOR

HEAD

CAULK JOINT ALL AROUND

SHIM SPACE

DOOR FRAME HEAD & JAMBS 1 1/2"

JAMB

METAL SADDLE

CAULKING

FLASHING

BRICK SUBSILL

WOOD SILL

SILL

DOOR FRAME - BRICK VENEER CONST.

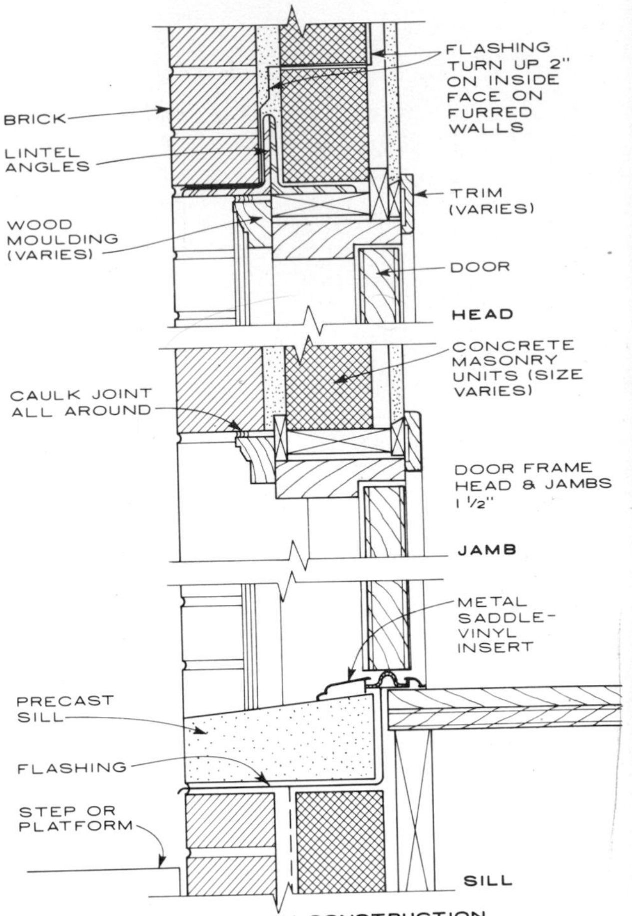

BRICK

LINTEL ANGLES

WOOD MOULDING (VARIES)

FLASHING TURN UP 2" ON INSIDE FACE ON FURRED WALLS

TRIM (VARIES)

DOOR

HEAD

CONCRETE MASONRY UNITS (SIZE VARIES)

CAULK JOINT ALL AROUND

DOOR FRAME HEAD & JAMBS 1 1/2"

JAMB

METAL SADDLE - VINYL INSERT

PRECAST SILL

FLASHING

STEP OR PLATFORM

SILL

DOOR FRAME - MASONRY CONSTRUCTION

NOTE: Flashing at masonry sills should make bond with waterproofing of Basement wall (dash lines above). See page on "Spandrel and Damp Course Flashing."

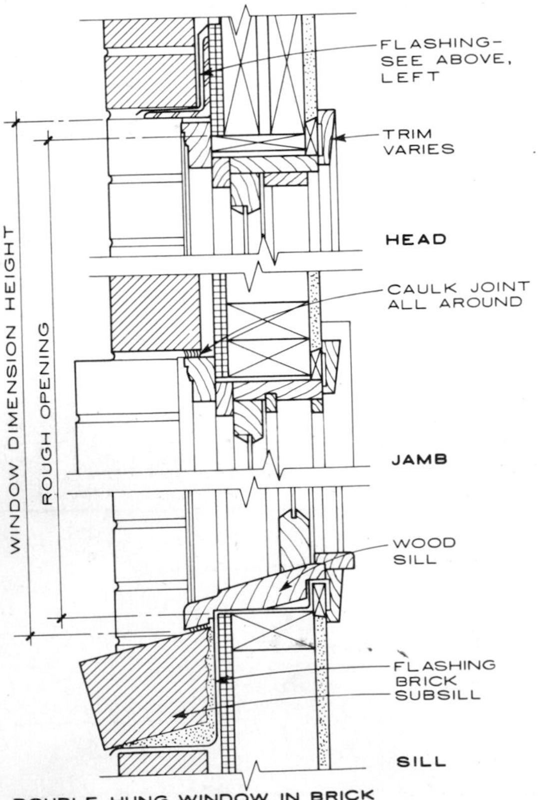

FLASHING - SEE ABOVE, LEFT

TRIM VARIES

HEAD

CAULK JOINT ALL AROUND

JAMB

WINDOW DIMENSION HEIGHT

ROUGH OPENING

WOOD SILL

FLASHING BRICK SUBSILL

SILL

DOUBLE HUNG WINDOW IN BRICK VENEER CONSTRUCTION

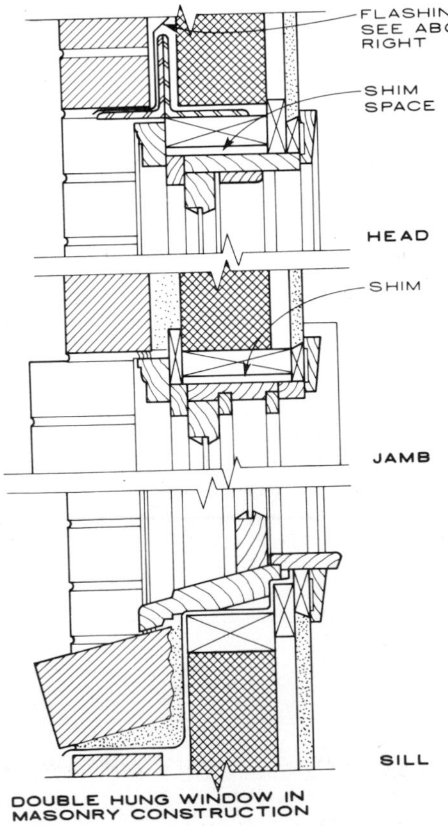

FLASHING - SEE ABOVE, RIGHT

SHIM SPACE

HEAD

SHIM

JAMB

SILL

DOUBLE HUNG WINDOW IN MASONRY CONSTRUCTION

HEAD

JAMB

SILL

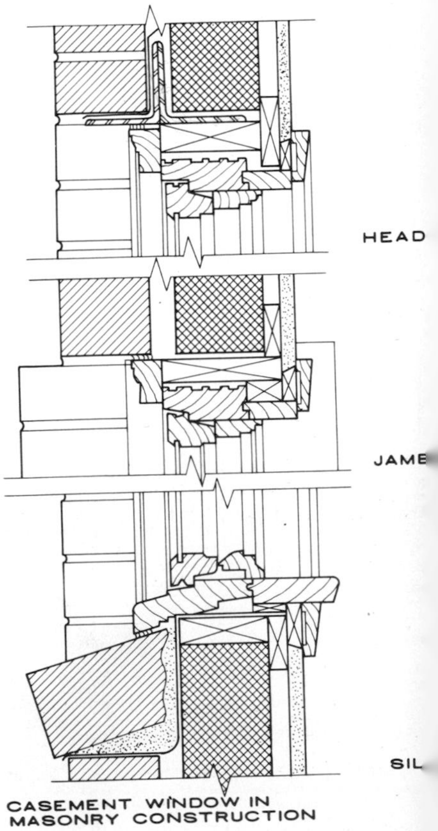

CASEMENT WINDOW IN MASONRY CONSTRUCTION

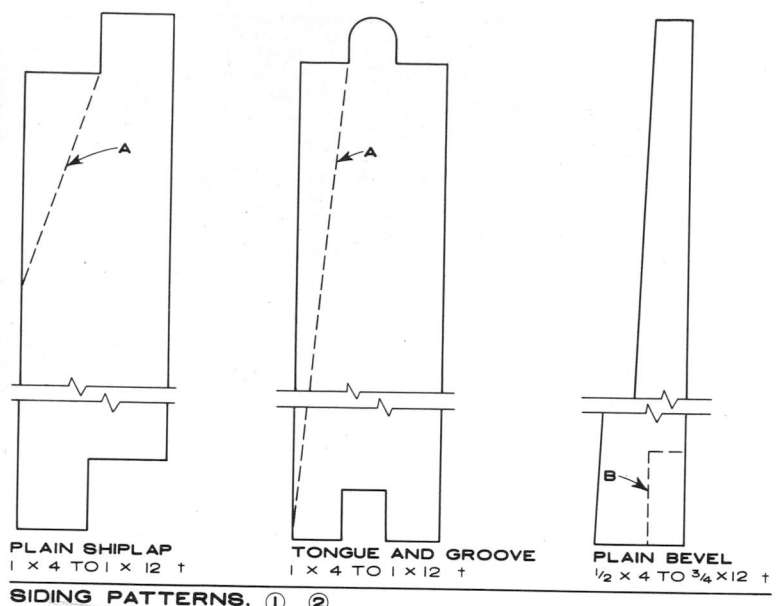

PLAIN SHIPLAP
1 X 4 TO 1 X 12 †

TONGUE AND GROOVE
1 X 4 TO 1 X 12 †

PLAIN BEVEL
½ X 4 TO ¾ X 12 †

SPLINE
½ X 1⅜ †

DOUBLE GROOVE
1 X 3 TO 1 X 12 †

TONGUE AND GROOVE
1 X 3 TO 1 X 12 †

SIDING PATTERNS, ① ②
DIAGRAMATIC DETAILS OF STANDARD SIDING PATTERNS

A = Numerous standard patterns available in fir, hemlock, spruce, cedar, redwood and others.

B = Rabbeted, bevel, and other variations available.

Strips and boards available in a variety of woods and sizes

can be used in combination to provide many board and batten effects.

For specific wood characteristics, grades, sizes, physical properties, definition of terms, application, storage and

handling, and specification requirements, contact lumber associations and or representatives active in area of use.

† Nominal sizes generally available.

PANEL PATTERNS, ① ②
DIAGRAMATIC DETAILS OF STANDARD PANEL PATTERNS

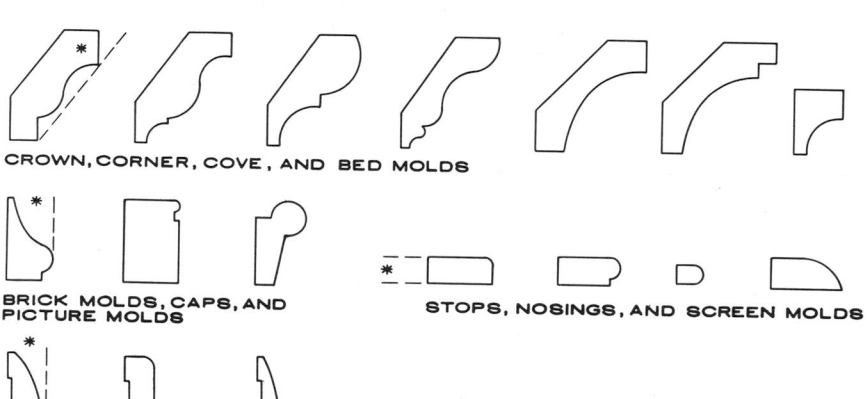

CROWN, CORNER, COVE, AND BED MOLDS

BRICK MOLDS, CAPS, AND PICTURE MOLDS

STOPS, NOSINGS, AND SCREEN MOLDS

CASING BASES, AND CHAIR RAILS

ROUNDS, HALF ROUNDS, QUARTER ROUNDS

TYPICAL TRIM PATTERNS AVAILABLE

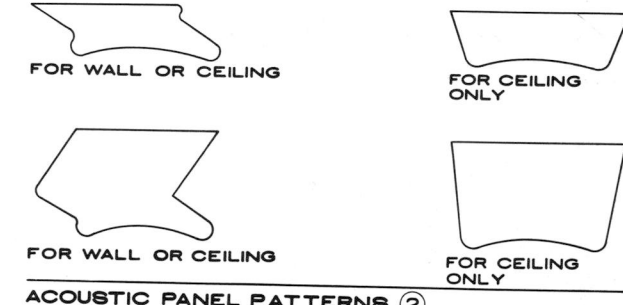

FOR WALL OR CEILING

FOR CEILING ONLY

FOR WALL OR CEILING

FOR CEILING ONLY

ACOUSTIC PANEL PATTERNS ②

Examples of special application units available as standard patterns.

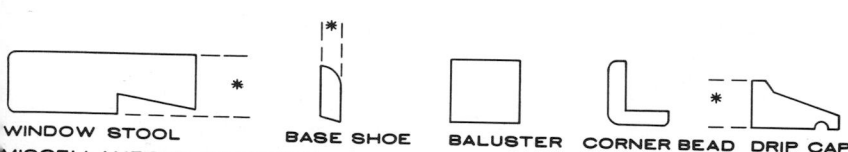

WINDOW STOOL

BASE SHOE

BALUSTER

CORNER BEAD

DRIP CAP

MISCELLANEOUS PATTERNS

STANDING AND RUNNING TRIM PATTERNS ③ ⑤ ⑥

Numerous patterns and dimensions of trim are produced in a variety of hard and soft woods for interior and exterior use. For a complete line of patterns, sizes, and wood species available, contact lumber associations and or representatives active in area of use.

Material thickness and configuration of member are major cost factors. Size and shape variations are so numerous that indication of dimensions is not feasible.

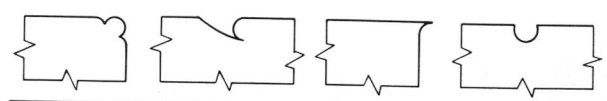

CUSTOM DESIGN PATTERNS ④ ⑥

Custom designs can be economically manufactured if designed with thought to minimum handling, simple cutting, head adjustment, and use of standard finish sizes.

Custom design cut limitations illustrated above should be avoided, since they require a special knife or several runs through the machine.

The organizations listed below were sources for information per numbered references and are provided for obtaining information not available in area of use.

① West Coast Lumber Inspection Bureau

② California Redwood Association

③ Western Pine Association

④ Southern Pine Association

⑤ United States Department of Commerce (Office of Technical Services)

⑥ Architectural Woodwork Institute

. E. Heidtmann and R. Paccone; Sargent, Webster, Crenshaw & Folley; Syracuse, New York

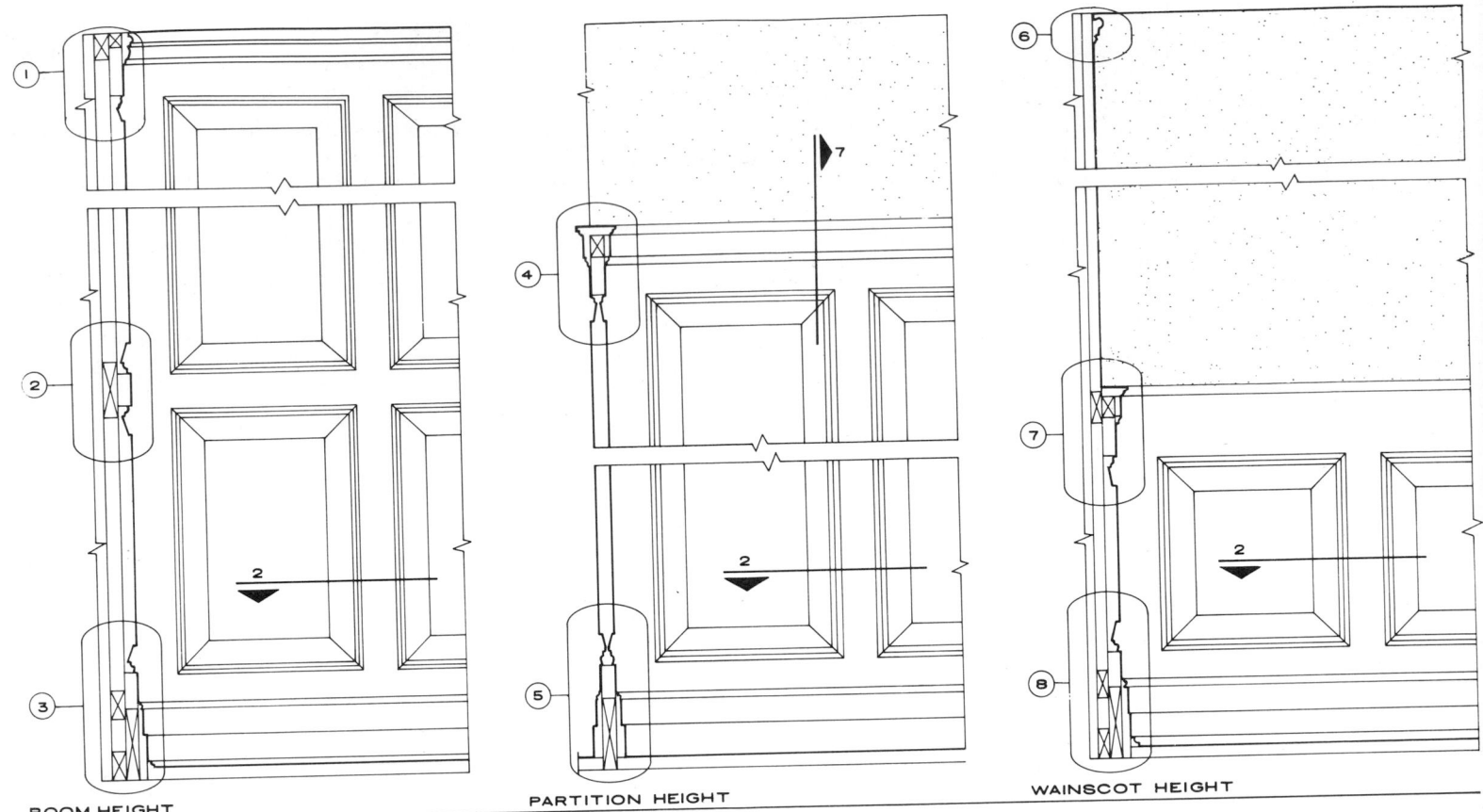

ROOM HEIGHT

PARTITION HEIGHT

WAINSCOT HEIGHT

STILE AND RAIL PANELING

VERTICAL BOARDS

VERTICAL BOARDS

HORIZONTAL BOARDS

RECESSED JOINT

BATTEN JOINT

INTEGRAL JOINT

ROOM HEIGHT

PARTITION HEIGHT

WAINSCOT HEIGHT

VERTICAL AND HORIZONTAL BOARD PANELING

NOTES :

1. For details indicated refer to next page.

2. For information on plywood paneling, refer to interior plywood pages.

3. Basic types of stile and rail, and board paneling and their characteristics, and limitations are illustrated. Dimensions for moulds, rails, and boards will vary with conditions and design.

4. Wood paneling characteristically has poor sound qualities, check methods necessary to achieve decibel reduction required.

5. Investigate codes in force for fire rated back-up requirements of wood paneling on studs.

H. E. Heidtmann and R. Paccone; Sargent, Webster, Crenshaw & Folley; Syracuse, New York

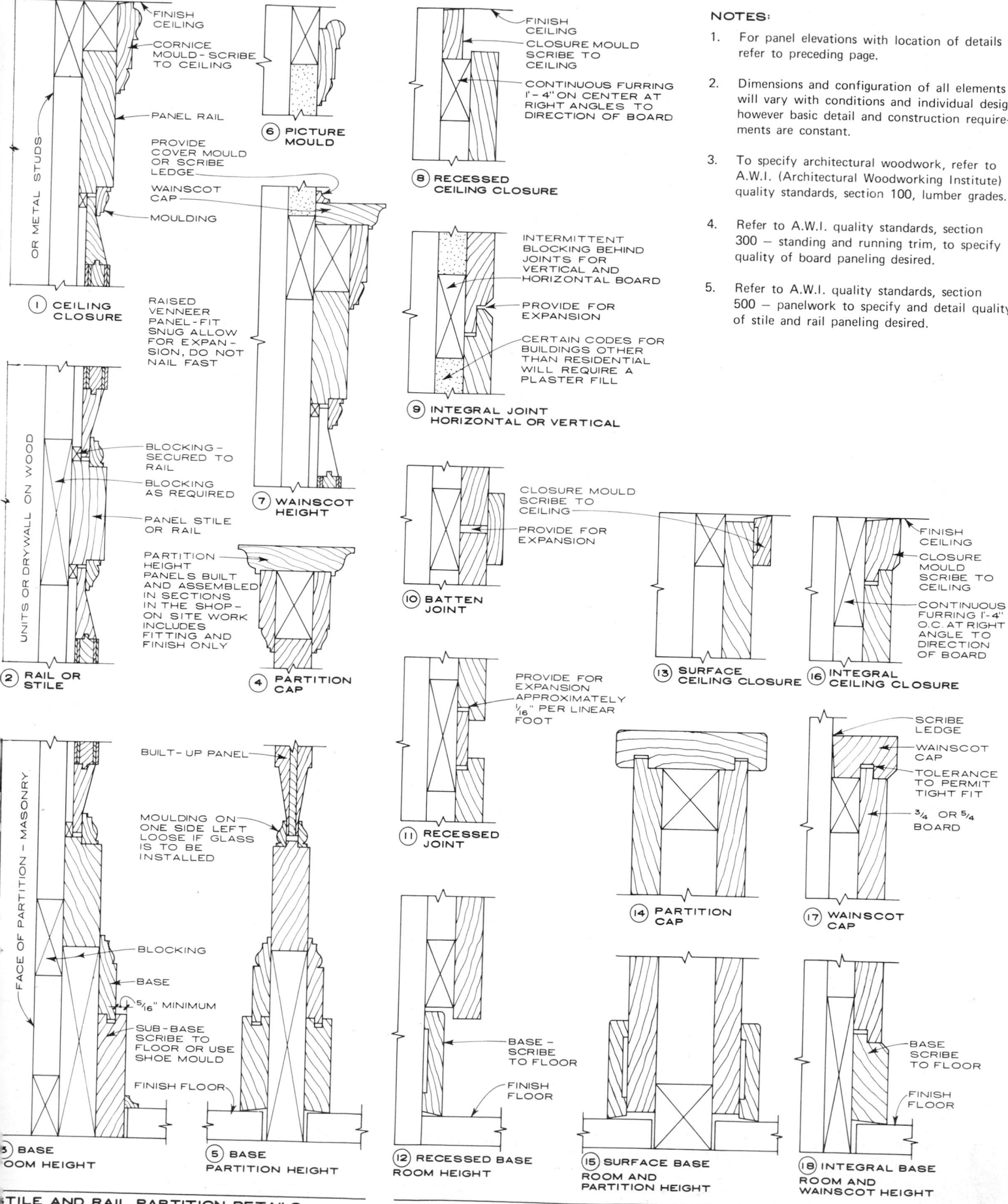

NOTES:

1. For panel elevations with location of details refer to preceding page.

2. Dimensions and configuration of all elements will vary with conditions and individual design, however basic detail and construction requirements are constant.

3. To specify architectural woodwork, refer to A.W.I. (Architectural Woodworking Institute) quality standards, section 100, lumber grades.

4. Refer to A.W.I. quality standards, section 300 — standing and running trim, to specify quality of board paneling desired.

5. Refer to A.W.I. quality standards, section 500 — panelwork to specify and detail quality of stile and rail paneling desired.

① CEILING CLOSURE

② RAIL OR STILE

③ BASE ROOM HEIGHT

④ PARTITION CAP

⑤ BASE PARTITION HEIGHT

⑥ PICTURE MOULD

⑦ WAINSCOT HEIGHT

⑧ RECESSED CEILING CLOSURE

⑨ INTEGRAL JOINT HORIZONTAL OR VERTICAL

⑩ BATTEN JOINT

⑪ RECESSED JOINT

⑫ RECESSED BASE ROOM HEIGHT

⑬ SURFACE CEILING CLOSURE

⑭ PARTITION CAP

⑮ SURFACE BASE ROOM AND PARTITION HEIGHT

⑯ INTEGRAL CEILING CLOSURE

⑰ WAINSCOT CAP

⑱ INTEGRAL BASE ROOM AND WAINSCOT HEIGHT

STILE AND RAIL PARTITION DETAILS

VERTICAL AND HORIZONTAL BOARD DETAILS

E. Heidtmann and R. Paccone; Sargent, Webster, Crenshaw & Folley; Syracuse, New York

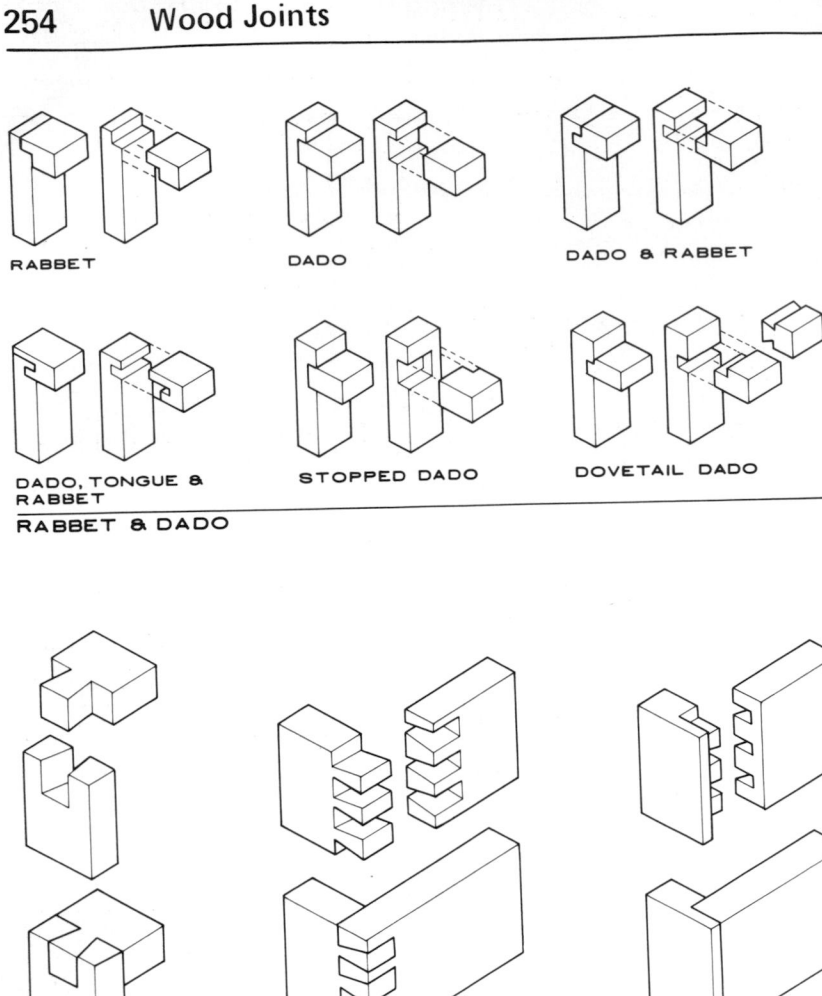

RABBET   DADO   DADO & RABBET

DADO, TONGUE & RABBET   STOPPED DADO   DOVETAIL DADO

RABBET & DADO

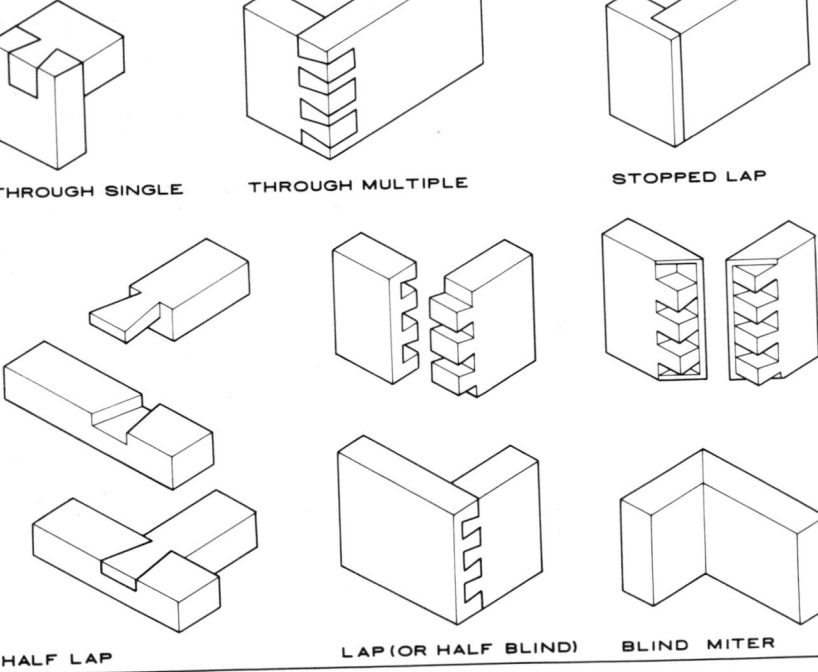

THROUGH SINGLE   THROUGH MULTIPLE   STOPPED LAP

HALF LAP   LAP (OR HALF BLIND)   BLIND MITER

DOVETAIL

NOTES:

1. Wood joints may be grouped into three classes: (1) right angle joints, (2) end joints, and (3) edge joints.

2. End joints are used to increase the length of a wood member. By proper utilization of end joints short lengths can be used which might otherwise have been wasted.

3. Edge joints are used to increase the width of a wood member. By giving narrow widths greater use of narrow stock may result.

4. A rabbet (rebate) is a right angle cut made along a corner edge of a wood member. A dado is a rectangular groove cut across the grain of a wood member. If this groove extends along the edge or face of a wood member (being cut parallel to the grain) it is known as a plough (plow).

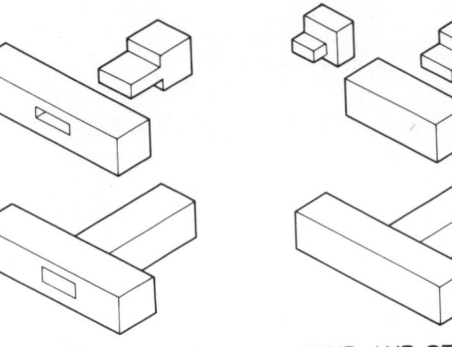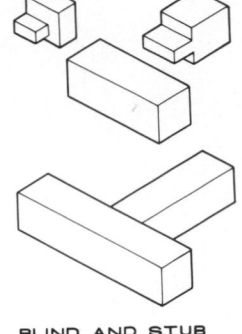

FULL (OR THROUGH)   BLIND AND STUB

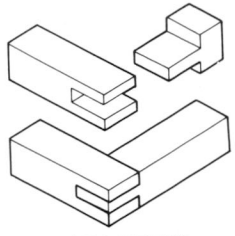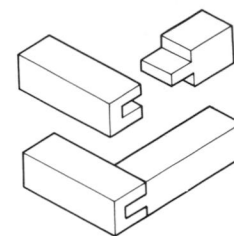

SHIP (OR OPEN)   HALF BLIND

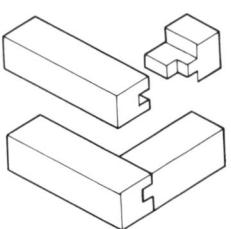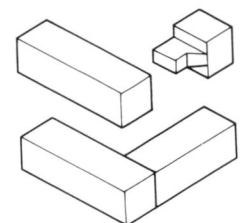

HAUNCH   HAUNCH — BLIND

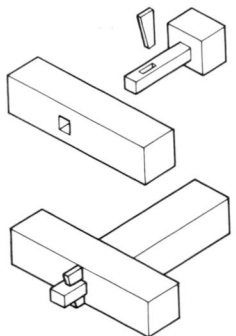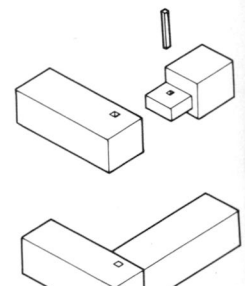

KEYED   PINNED BLIND

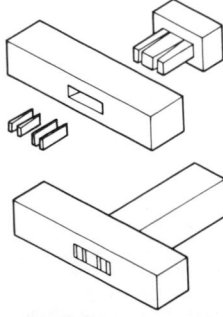

WEDGED

MORTISE & TENON

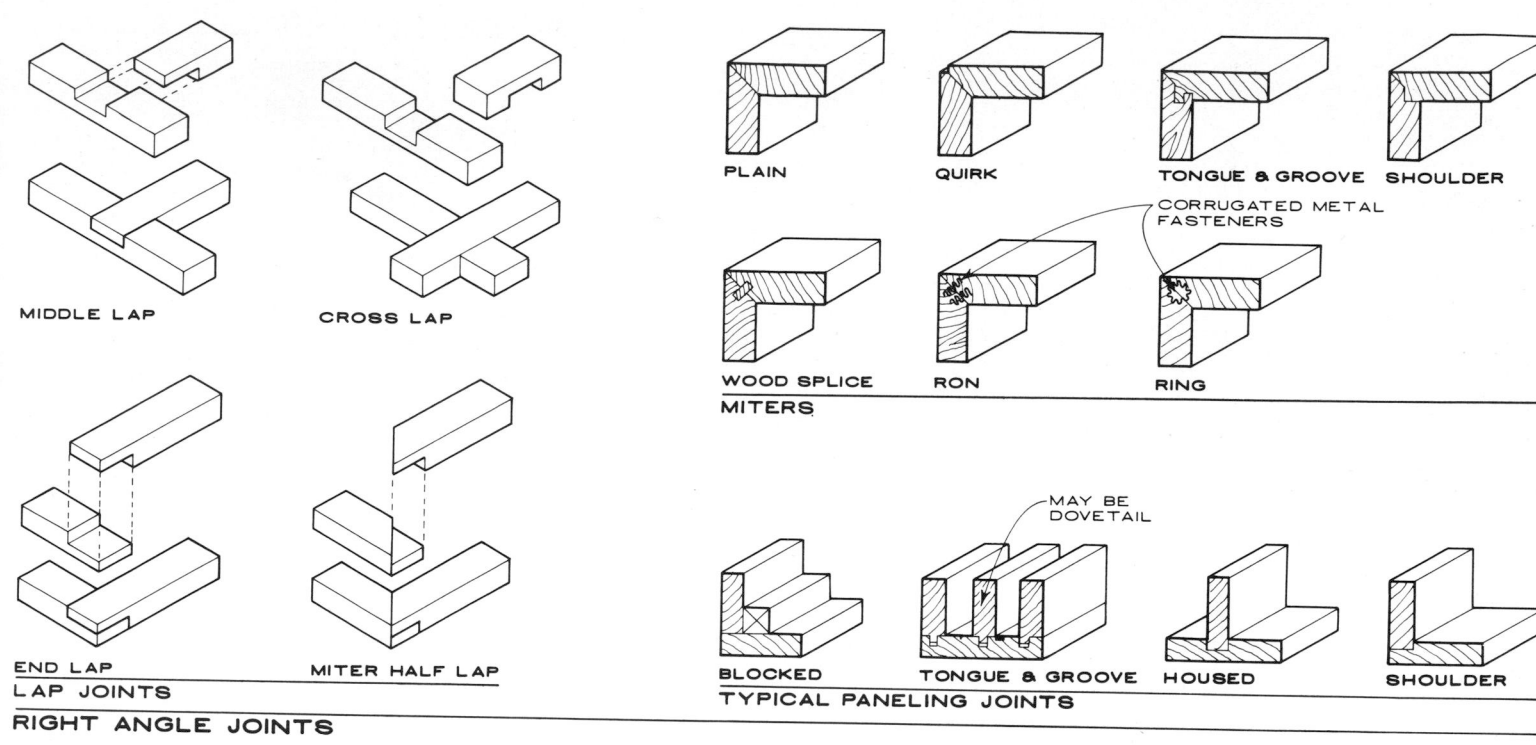

RIGHT ANGLE JOINTS

MIDDLE LAP

CROSS LAP

END LAP

MITER HALF LAP

LAP JOINTS

PLAIN   **QUIRK**   **TONGUE & GROOVE**   **SHOULDER**

CORRUGATED METAL FASTENERS

WOOD SPLICE   **RON**   **RING**

MITERS

MAY BE DOVETAIL

BLOCKED   **TONGUE & GROOVE**   **HOUSED**   **SHOULDER**

TYPICAL PANELING JOINTS

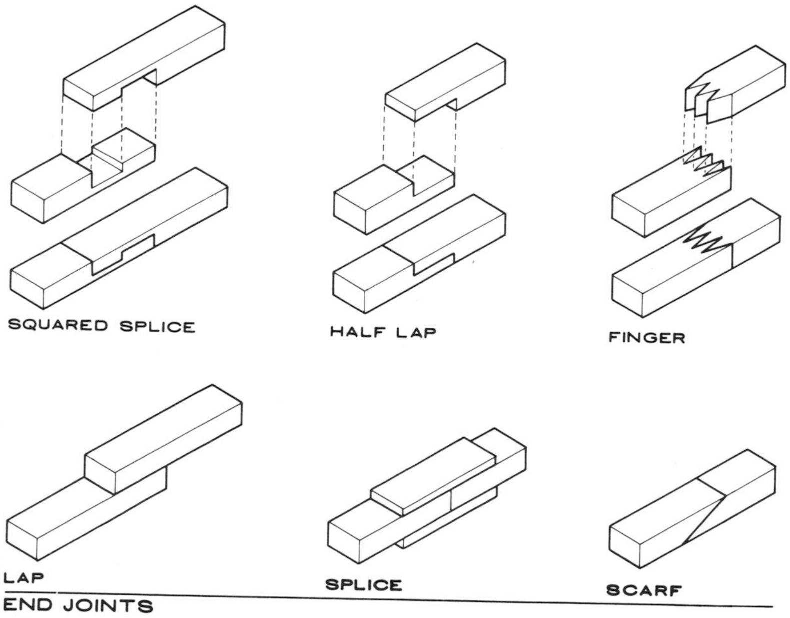

END JOINTS

SQUARED SPLICE

HALF LAP

FINGER

LAP

SPLICE

SCARF

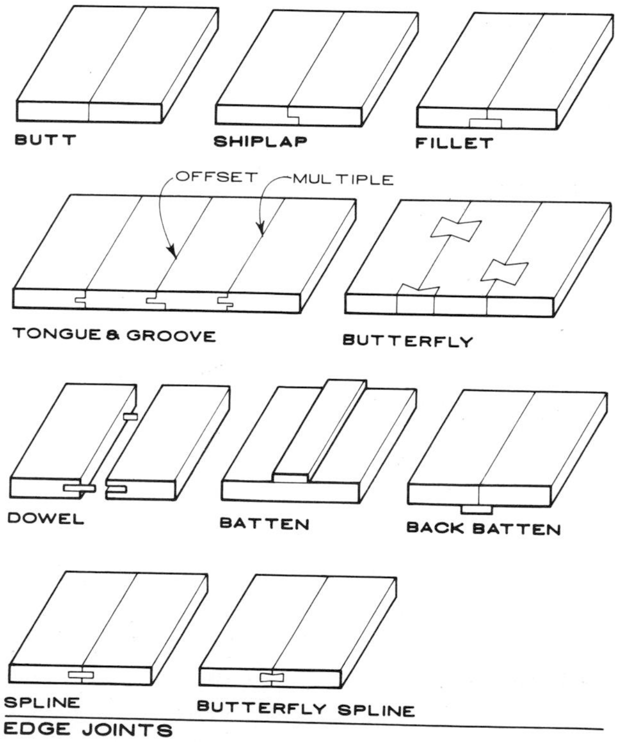

BUTT   **SHIPLAP**   **FILLET**

OFFSET   MULTIPLE

TONGUE & GROOVE

BUTTERFLY

DOWEL   **BATTEN**   **BACK BATTEN**

SPLINE   **BUTTERFLY SPLINE**

EDGE JOINTS

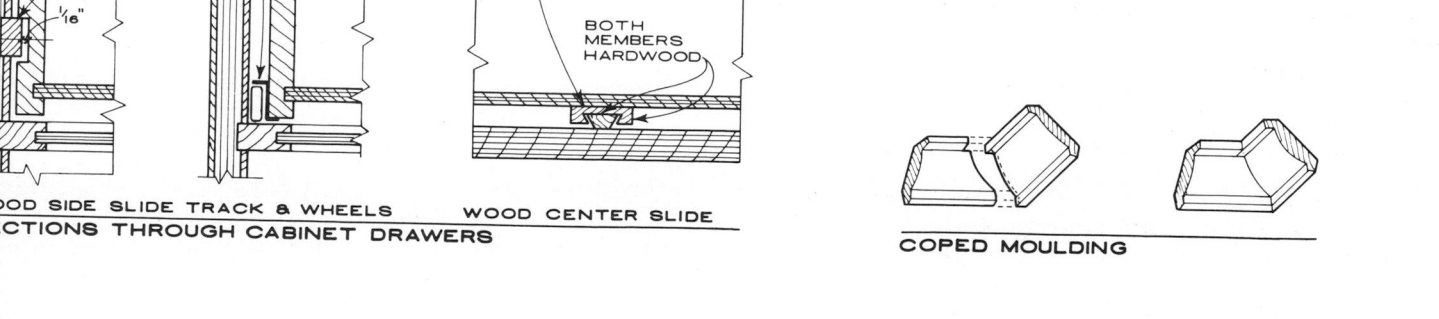

HARDWOOD

1/16"

EXTENSION GUIDES ALSO AVAILABLE

PATENTED METAL GUIDES ARE AVAILABLE

BOTH MEMBERS HARDWOOD

WOOD SIDE SLIDE TRACK & WHEELS   **WOOD CENTER SLIDE**

SECTIONS THROUGH CABINET DRAWERS

COPED MOULDING

VENEER GRADES

N	Special order "natural finish" veneer. Select all heartwood or all sapwood. No open defects. Some repairs allowed.
A	Smooth & paintable. Neat repairs permissible. Also used for natural finish in less demanding applications.
B	Solid surface veneer. Circular repair plugs & tight knots permitted.
C	Knotholes to 1". Occasional knotholes 1/2" larger within certain limits in specified section. Limited splits permitted. Mini-m veneer for Exterior-type plywood.
C	Improved C veneer with splits limited to 1/8" wide & knotholes & borer holes limited to 1/4" by 1/2".
D	Permits knots & knotholes to 2 1/2" wide & 1/2" larger under certain specified limits. Limited splits permitted.

KEY DEFINITIONS

GROUP
Refers to species used in manufacturing plywood. Species are classified into groups based on stiffness. Group number in grade-trademarks refers to species of face and back veneers.

STANDARD SHEATHING
Interior sheathing grade replacing former C-D grade. Subflooring, wall sheathing, roof decks, pallets, crates, some engineered applications.

STRUCTURAL I, STRUCTURAL II
Unsanded grades for use where strength is most important. Examples: box beams, gusset plates, stressed skin panels, shipping containers, bins. Both grades made only with exterior glue. Structural I is limited to Group I species and available in all exterior grades. Structural II permits Groups 1, 2, or 3 species.

IDENTIFICATION INDEX NUMBER
2 numbers separated by a slash appearing in grade-trademarks of all sheathing grades. Numbers indicate spacing in inches for supports, no. on left for roof decking with 35 p.s.f. minimum loading. No. on right for subflooring with 100 p.s.f. loading.

CLASS I, CLASS II
Applies only to Plyform grades. Indicates species mix permitted under Product Standard PS-166. Class I is stronger than Class II.

CLASSIFICATION OF SPECIES

GROUP 1	GROUP 2	GROUP 3
Douglas fir 1	Cedar, Port	Alder, red
Larch, Western	Orford	Cedar, Alaska
Pine, Southern	Douglas fir 2	yellow
Loblolly	Fir	Pine
Longleaf	California red	Lodgepole
Shortleaf	Grand	Ponderosa
Slash	Noble	Redwood
Tanoak	Pacific silver	
	White	GROUP 4
	Hemlock,	Cedar
	Western	Incense
	Lauan	Western red
	Red	Fir, subalpine
	White	Pine, sugar
	Pine, Western	Poplar, Western
	white	Spruce,
	Spruce, Sitka	Engelman

NOTES FOR SPECIALTY GRADES OF PLYWOOD (See Table)

(1) Sanded both sides except for decorative or other surfaces.
(2) Available in group 1, 2, 3, or 4 unless otherwise noted.
(3) Standard 4' x 8' panel size. Others available.
(4) Also available in Structural I.
(5) Panel sizes 4' x 7', 8', 9', 10'.
(6) Also horiz. lap siding 3/8 x 12, 16 to 16' long.

Foster C. Parriott; James M. Hunter & Associates; Boulder, Colorado

GUIDE TO APPEARANCE GRADES OF PLYWOOD (1)

	GRADE SYMBOLS (2)	DESCRIPTION AND MOST COMMON USES	FACE	BACK	INNER PLIES	1/4"	3/8"	1/2"	5/8"	3/4"	1"
INTERIOR TYPE	N-N, N-A N-B INT-DFPA	Natural fin. cab. quality. lor both sides select all heartw'd or all sapw'd veneer. For furniture of natural fin., cab. doors, built-ins, special items.	N	N A B	C					•	
	N-D INT-DFPA	Natural finish paneling. Special order.	N	D	D	•					
	A-A INT-DFPA	Interior applications where both sides will be on view. Built-ins, cabinets, furniture, partitions. Face smooth and suitable for painting.	A	A	D		•	•	•	•	•
	A-B INT-DFPA	Uses similar to Int. A-A but appearance of 1 side is less important and 2 smooth solid surfaces are required.	A	B	D		•	•	•	•	•
	A-D INT-DFPA	Interior use where appearance of 1 side only is important. Paneling, built-ins, shelves, partitions.	A	D	D		•	•	•	•	•
	B-B INT-DFPA	Int. utility panel for 2 smooth sides. Permits circular plugs. Paintable.	B	B	D		•	•	•	•	•
	B-D INT-DFPA	Int. utility panel for 1 smooth side. For backing, sides of built-ins, shelving (industry).	B	D	D		•	•	•	•	•
EXTERIOR TYPE	A-A EXT-DFPA (4)	Use where appearance of both sides is important. Fences, built-ins, signs, boats, cabinets, commercial refrigerators, tote boxes, ducts.	A	A	C		•	•	•	•	•
	A-B EXT-DFPA (4)	Use similar to A-A EXT panels, but where appearance of 1 side is less important.	A	B	C		•	•	•	•	•
	A-C EXT-DFPA (4)	Exterior use where appearance of only 1 side is important. Sidings, soffits, fences, structural uses, farm bldgs., commercial refrigerators.	A	C	C		•	•	•	•	•
	B-C EXT-DFPA (4)	Outdoor utility pan. for farm serv. & work bldgs.	B	C	C		•	•	•	•	•
	B-B EXT-DFPA	Outdoor utility pan. with solid paintable faces.	B	B	C		•	•	•	•	•

NOTES: (1) Sanded both sides.
(2) Available in Group 1, 2, 3, or 4.
(3) Standard 4 x 8 panel sizes. Others available.
(4) Also available in Structural 1.

GUIDE TO CONSTRUCTION GRADES OF PLYWOOD

	GRADE SYMBOLS (1) (2)	DESCRIPTION AND MOST COMMON USES	FRONT	BACK	INNER PLIES	1/4	5/16	3/8	1/2	5/8	3/4	7/8	1 1/8
INTERIOR TYPE	STANDARD INT-DFPA (4)	Unsanded interior sheathing grade for floors, walls, and roofs.	C	D	D		•	•	•	•	•	•	•
	STRUCTURAL I and STRUCTURAL II INT-DFPA	Unsanded structural grades where strength is most important. Made only with exterior glue. Structural I limited to Group I species for all plies. Structural II permits Group 1, 2, or 3 species.	C	D	D			•	•	•	•	•	
	UNDERLAYMENT INT-DFPA (4)	Underlayment or combination subfloor-underlayment for resilient floor coverings, carpeting. Ply beneath face is C or better. Sanded or touch-sanded as specified.	C plgd/plygd	D	C & D	•			•	•	•		
	C-D PLUGGED INT-DFPA (4)	Utility built-ins, backing for wall & ceiling tile. Not under layment substitute. Unsanded or touch-sanded.	C plg	D	D			•	•	•	•		
	Z-4-1 INT-DFPA (5)	Comb. subfloor-under layment. For resil. Floor cov., carpet, wd. strip flooring. Exterior glue for moist areas. Unsanded or touch-sanded.	C plg	D	C & D								•
EXTERIOR TYPE	C-C EXT-DFPA (4)	Waterproof bond for subflooring & roof deck, siding for service bldgs. Unsanded.	C	C	C		•	•	•	•	•		
	C-C PLUGGED EXT-DFPA (4)	Base for resilient floors & tile backing in moist areas. Refrig. or controlled atmosphere rooms. Sanded or touch-sanded.	C plg	C	C	•		•	•	•	•		
	STRUCTURAL I C-C EXT-DFPA	Engineered applications requiring full exterior — type panels of all group 1 woods: Unsanded.	C	C	C			•	•	•	•		
	PLYFORM CLASS I & II, B-B EXT-DFPA	Concr. forms, high re-use factor. Sanded 2 sides. Edge-sealed, mill-oiled. Special restr. on species. Also in HDO.	B	B	C					•	•		

NOTES: (1) Interior grades available with exterior glue.
(2) Avail. + & g 1/2, 5/8, 3/4, 1 1/8, except Plyform.
(3) Standard 4 x 8 panel size. Others available.
(4) Available in Group 1, 2, 3, or 4.
(5) Available in Group 1, 2, 3 only.

GUIDE TO SPECIALTY GRADES OF PLYWOOD (1)(2) — SEE NOTES AT BOTTOM LEFT.

	GRADES SYMBOLS	DESCRIPTION AND MOST COMMON USES	FRONT	BACK	INNER PLIES	5/16	3/8	1/2	5/8	3/4	1
INTERIOR	DECORATIVE PANELS	Rough textured faces. Accent walls, etc.	B+	D	D	•	•	•			
	PLYRON INT-DFPA	Hardboard faces standard; standard, tempered, screened, smooth. Counter tops, shelves, cab. doors, floors.			C D			•	•	•	
EXTERIOR TYPE	HDO (6) EXT-DFPA (4)	High density overlay, hard resin fiber. Paint not req. Conc. forms, signs, acid tanks, cabs., ctr. tops.	A B	A B	C pl.		•	•	•	•	•
	MDO (4) EXT-DFPA (6)	Medium density overlay, smooth opaque resin fibe; heat fused. Paint base. Siding etc.		B	B C Cpl.	•	•	•	•	•	
	303 SPEC-SID'G EXT-DFPA (5)(6)	Special surface treatm't. See following pages.	B+	C	C				•	•	•
	T 1-II EXT-DFPA (5)	1/4 x 3/8 parallel grooves. Sid'g.	C+	C	C				•	•	

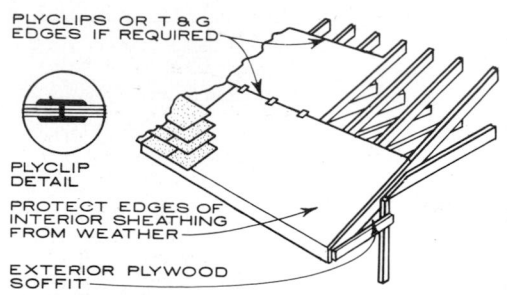

PLYCLIPS OR T & G EDGES IF REQUIRED

PLYCLIP DETAIL

PROTECT EDGES OF INTERIOR SHEATHING FROM WEATHER

EXTERIOR PLYWOOD SOFFIT

GABLE ROOF

BUILT-UP ROOFING

EXTERIOR PLYWOOD AT OPEN SOFFIT

INTERIOR SHEATHING

FLAT-LOW SLOPE ROOF

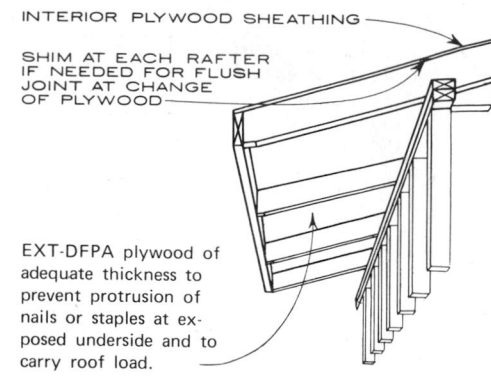

INTERIOR PLYWOOD SHEATHING

SHIM AT EACH RAFTER IF NEEDED FOR FLUSH JOINT AT CHANGE OF PLYWOOD

EXT-DFPA plywood of adequate thickness to prevent protrusion of nails or staples at exposed underside and to carry roof load.

OPEN SOFFIT

PLYWOOD ROOF SHEATHING (4)

ALLOWABLE GRADES	PANEL IDENT. INDEX	PLYWOOD THK. (IN.)	MAX SPAN (5) (IN.)	UNSUP-PORTED EDGE MAX. (IN.) (1)	ALLOWABLE ROOF LOADS (P.F.S.) (2)(3) SPACING OF SUPPORTS (IN. C TO C)									
					16	20	24	30	32	36	42	48	60	72
	16/0	5/16, 3/8	16	16	55									
DFPA STR I	20/0	5/16, 3/8	20	20	85	45								
	24/0	3/8, 1/2	24	24	150	75	45							
DFPA STR II	30/12	5/8	30	26		145	85	40						
	32/16	1/2, 5/8	32	28			90	45	40					
DFPA C-C EXT.	36/16	3/4 ~	36	30			125	65	55	35				
	42/20	5/8, 3/4, 7/8	42	32				80	65	45	35			
DFPA STD	48/24	3/4, 7/8	48	36					105	75	55	40		
W/EXT. GLUE	2-4-1	1 1/8	72	48						175	105	80	50	30
DFPA STD	Gps. 1&2	1 1/8	72	48						145	85	65	40	30
	Gps. 3&4	1 1/4	72	48						160	95	75	45	25

(1) **Provide adequate blocking, T & G edges or other suitable edge support such as Plyclips when unsupported edge exceeds these lengths.**

(2) Uniform load deflection limitation: 1/180 th of the span under live load plus dead load. 1/240 th under live load only.

(3) Allowable loads were established by laboratory tests and calculations assuming uniformly distributed loads.

(4) Plywood continuous over 2 or more spans; grain of face plys across supports.

(5) These spans shall not be exceeded for any load conditions.

NAIL SCHEDULE: (common)
6d nail for 1/2" thick or less; 8d nail for 1" thick or less: 10d or 8d ring-shank for 2-4-1 1 1/8" & 1 1/4". Space 6" at edges & 12" in field, spans 48" or more nail 6" at all supports.

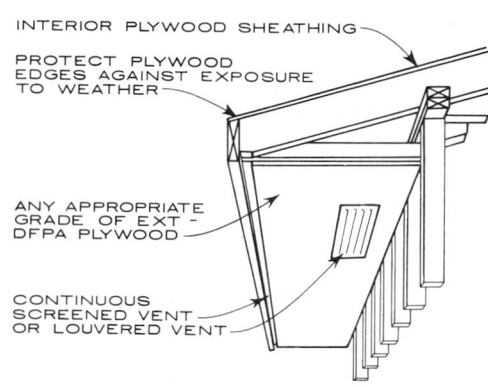

INTERIOR PLYWOOD SHEATHING

PROTECT PLYWOOD EDGES AGAINST EXPOSURE TO WEATHER

ANY APPROPRIATE GRADE OF EXT - DFPA PLYWOOD

CONTINUOUS SCREENED VENT OR LOUVERED VENT

SOFFIT NAILING SCHEDULE

PLYWOOD THICK-NESS	MAX. SUPPORT SPACING	NAIL SIZE	NAIL SPACING	
			EDGE	FIELD
3/8"	24"	6d	6	12
5/8"	48"	8d	6	12

CLOSED SOFFIT

PLYWOOD SUBFLOORING (1)

ALLOWABLE GRADES	PANEL IDENT. INDEX (2)(3)	PLYWOOD THK. (IN.)	MAX. SPAN (4) (IN.)	NAIL SIZE AND TYPE (COMMON)	NAIL SPACING (IN.)	
					PANEL EDGES	INTERMEDIATE
	30/12	5/8	12 (5)	8d	6	10
DFPA STRUCT. I	32/16	1/2, 5/8	16 (6)	8d (7)	6	10
DFPA STRUCT. II	36/16	3/4	16 (6)	8d	6	10
DFPA C-C EXT.	42/20	5/8, 3/4, 7/8	20 (6)	8d	6	10
DFPA STANDARD W/EXT. GLUE	48/24	3/4, 7/8	24	8d	6	10
DFPA STANDARD	2-4-1&Gps. 1&2	1 1/8	48	10d	6	6
	1 1/4" Gps. 3&4	1 1/4	48	10d	6	6

(1) Plywood continuous over 2 or more spans; grain of face plys across supports.

(2) Identification Index appears on all panels except 1 1/8" and 1 1/4".

(3) Special conditions may impose heavy concentrated loads requiring subfloor constructions in excess of these minimums.

(4) Spans limited to values shown because of possible effect of concentrated loads.

(5) May be 16" with 25/32" wood strip flooring at right angles to joists.

(6) May be 24" with 25/32" wood strip flooring at right angles to joists.

(7) 6d common nails permitted if plywood is 1/2".

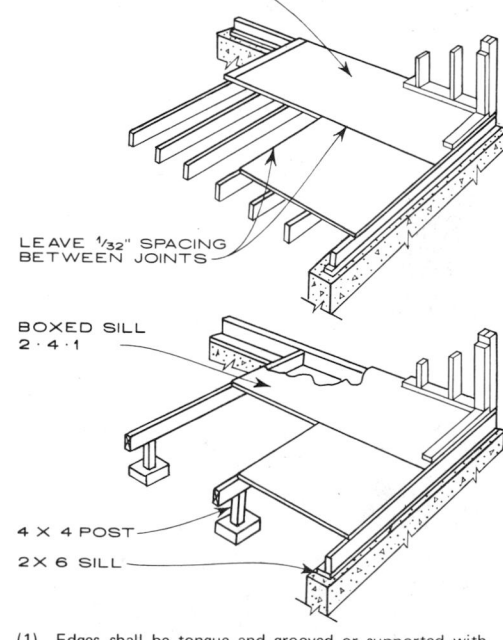

CONVENTIONAL PLYWOOD SUBFLOORING (1) OR COMBINED SUBFLOOR - UNDERLAYMENT (2)

LEAVE 1/32" SPACING BETWEEN JOINTS

BOXED SILL 2-4-1

4 X 4 POST

2 X 6 SILL

COMBINED SUBFLOOR-UNDERLAYMENT (1)

PLYWOOD GRADE	PLYWOOD SPECIES GROUP	MAXIMUM SUPPORT SPACING (2)(3)						NAIL SPACING (INCHES) (4)	
		16" O.C.		24" O.C.		48" O.C.			
		PANEL THICK-NESS	DEFORMED SHANK NAIL SIZE d	PANEL THICK-NESS	DEFORMED SHANK NAIL SIZE d	PANEL THICK-NESS	DEFORMED SHANK NAIL SIZE d	PANEL EDGES	INTER-MEDIATE
UNDERLAYMENT	1	1/2"	6d	3/4"	6d			6	10
UNDERLAYMENT W/EXT. GLUE	2&3	5/8"	6d	7/8"	8d			6	10
C-C PLUGGED	4	3/4"	6d	1"	8d			6	10
2-4-1 (5)	1, 2, &3					1 1/8"	8d	6	6

(1) For direct application of tile; carpeting, linoleum, or other non-structural flooring. Plywood continuous over two or more spans; grain of face plys across supports. Seasoned framing lumber is recommended.

(2) Edges shall be tongue and grooved, or supported with framing.

(3) In some buildings, special conditions may impose loads requiring heavier construction.

(4) Set nails 1/16" (1/8" for 2-4-1) and lightly sand subfloor at joints if resilient flooring is to be applied.

(5) May use 10d common smooth shank if supports well-seasoned.

(1) Edges shall be tongue and grooved or supported with blocking for square edge wood flooring, unless separate underlayment (1/4" min. thickness) is installed.

(2) T & G edges or support with edge blocking.

PLYWOOD FLOOR SYSTEMS

Foster C. Parriott; James M. Hunter & Associates; Boulder, Colorado

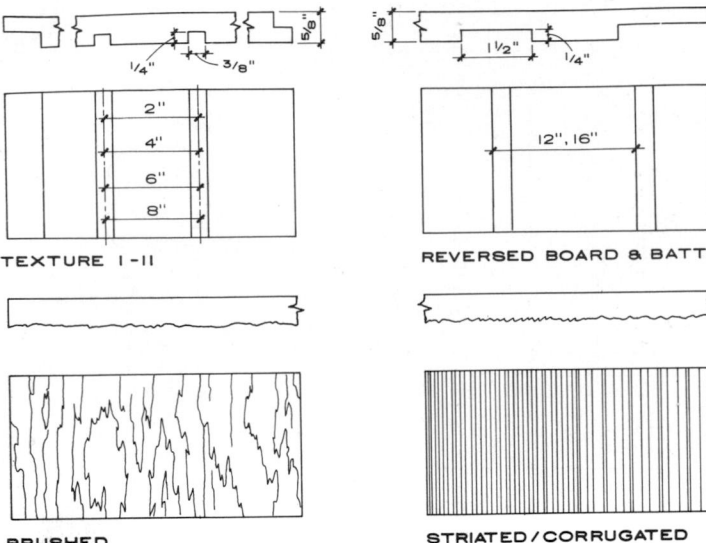

TEXTURE 1-11

REVERSED BOARD & BATTEN

CIRCULAR SAWN

ROUGH SAWN & KERFED

BRUSHED

STRIATED / CORRUGATED

GROOVES 1/32" W., .08" D.

FINELINE

HORIZONTAL - LAPPED MDO & ROUGH SAWN

PLYWOOD SIDING T 1-11 & 303 SPECIAL. SEE GUIDE TO SPECIALTY GRADES OF PLYWOOD.

Most patterns and textures available in medium density overlay (MDO) for painting and weathering qualities. Standard width: 4'-0"

No sheathing required except for horizontal lap siding when no let-in corner bracing is used. Standard lengths: 7', 8', 9', 10'. Standard thickness: 5/8", others available.

Sizes: 3/8" x 12", 16", to 16' long. 5/16" available to use w/ sheath. Other widths available.

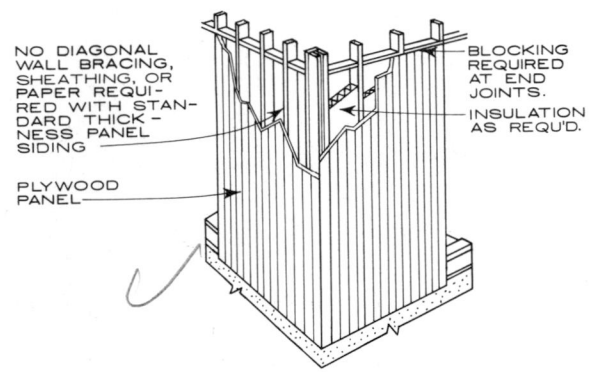

NO DIAGONAL WALL BRACING, SHEATHING, OR PAPER REQUIRED WITH STANDARD THICKNESS PANEL SIDING

PLYWOOD PANEL

BLOCKING REQUIRED AT END JOINTS.

INSULATION AS REQU'D.

PANEL SIDING VERTICAL "APPLICAT'N"

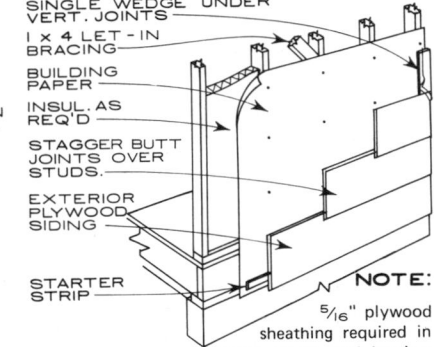

SINGLE WEDGE UNDER VERT. JOINTS
1 x 4 LET-IN BRACING
BUILDING PAPER
INSUL. AS REQ'D
STAGGER BUTT JOINTS OVER STUDS.
EXTERIOR PLYWOOD SIDING
STARTER STRIP

NOTE:
5/16" plywood sheathing required in absence of diagonal bracing.

PLYWOOD LAP SIDING "APPLICAT'N"

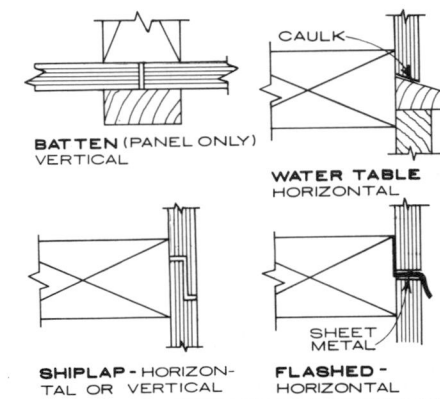

BATTEN (PANEL ONLY) VERTICAL

CAULK

WATER TABLE HORIZONTAL

SHIPLAP - HORIZONTAL OR VERTICAL

SHEET METAL

FLASHED - HORIZONTAL

JOINT SUGGESTIONS

CURVED STRESSED SKIN PANELS

FOLDED PLATE ROOFS

RADIAL FOLDED PLATE ROOFS

DELTA STRUCTURES

SOME SIMPLE RESIDENTIAL ELEMENTS: PLYWOOD GUSSET TRUSSES

NAILED PLYWOOD BOX BEAMS

FIR PLYWOOD COMPONENTS

Glued structural assemblies of plywood and lumber. Fabrication licensed by Plywood Fabricator Service, Inc., affiliate of American Plywood Assoc.
Some basic shapes: box beams, flat stressed skin panels.

NAILING CHART FOR PLYWOOD SIDING

APPLICATION	PLYWOOD THICKNESS (IN.)		MAX. SPACING OF SUPPORTS (C.-C.)	NAIL SIZE & TYPE (a)	NAIL SPACING (INCHES)	
					Panel Edges	Intermediate
Panel Siding (b)	3/8"	(c)	16"	6d Casing or Siding	6"	12"
	1/2"		24"	6d Casing or Siding	6"	12"
	5/8" or thicker		24"	8d Casing or Siding	6"	12"
Lap Siding or Bevel Siding	3/8"	(d)	16"	6d Casing or Siding	One nail per stud along bottom edge	4" at vert. joint
	1/2"		20"	8d Casing or Siding		8" at studs
	5/8"		24"	8d Casing or Siding		(siding wider than 12")

NOTES:

(a) Use galvanized, aluminum, or other non-corrosive nails. Use same schedule for panel siding and siding over sheathing.

(b) Battens applied with 8d non-corrosive casing nails spaced 12" o.c. staggered.

(c) Over separate sheathing 3/8" panel siding may be used over supports 24" o.c.

(d) Over separate sheathing 5/16" MDO plywood lap siding may be used over supports spaced 16" o.c.

FIR PLYWOOD BENDING

PANEL THK.	MINIMUM BENDING RADIUS (FT.)	
	ACROSS GRAIN	PARALLEL TO GRAIN
1/4"	2'	5'
5/16"	2'	6'
3/8"	3'	8'
1/2"	6'	12'
5/8"	8'	16'
3/4"	12'	20'

Shorter radii can be developed by selection for bending of areas that are free of knots and short grains, and/or by wetting or steaming, at the risk of possible fractures. Exterior glue is recommended.

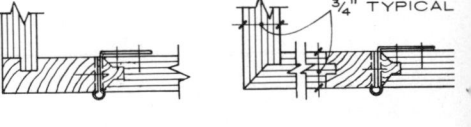

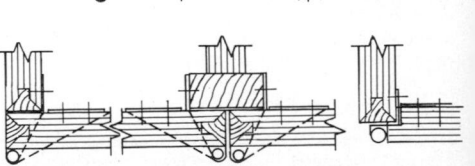

3/4" TYPICAL

PLYWOOD CABINET DOORS

For plywood doors or cabinets, use hardware that will screw into face of plywood, as edge has poor screw-holding properties.

Foster C. Parriott; James M. Hunter & Associates; Boulder, Colorado

TYPES OF HARDWOOD PLYWOOD

TECHNICAL	Fully waterproof bond—approx. equal strength in 2 directions.
TYPE 1 (EXT.)	Fully waterproof bond—full weather exposure, resist organisms.
TYPE 11 (INT.)	Water resistant bond.
TYPE 111 (INT.)	Moisture—resistant bond.

GRADES OF HARDWOOD PLYWOOD

PREMIUM GRADE (1)	Slight imperfections.
GOOD GRADE (1)	For natural finishes, no sharp contrasts.
SOUND GRADE (2)	For smooth painted surfaces.
UTILITY GRADE (3)	Open defects permitted but limited in size, species not selected, no matching.
BACKING GRADE (4)	Many flaws permitted, species not selected. No matching.
SPECIALTY GRADE	Non-conforming for special uses, matching, etc. Grade and type by agreement.

NUMBER OF PLIES

Odd number in pairs on opposite sides of core. For Technical Type, plies parallel to finish plies provide 40%–60% of total thickness.

SOME POPULAR SPECIES OF HARDWOOD VENEERS

Dense: white ash, yellow birch, black maple, red oak, rosewood, teak.

Medium Dense: black ash, gum, Afr. mahogany, red maple, prima vera, American walnut.

Low Density: aspen, American basswood, American chestnut, yellow poplar.

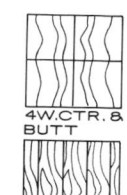

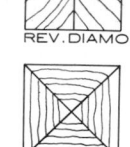
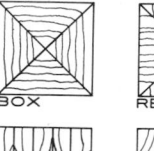
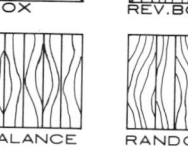
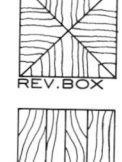

BOOK   SLIP   DIAMOND   REV.DIAMOND "V"

CHECKER BD.   4W.CTR.& BUTT   HERRINGBONE   BOX   REV.BOX

VERT.BUTT HORIZ.BOOK   LOT   CENTER   BALANCE   RANDOM

VENEER MATCHING

STANDARD SIZES & THICKNESSES OF HARDWOOD PLYWOOD

WIDTHS: 18", 24", 32", 36", 48"	Tolerance $\pm$ $^1/_{32}$"
LENGTHS: 48", 60", 72", 84", 96", 120"	Tolerance $\pm$ $^1/_{32}$"

THICKNESSES: $^1/_8$", $^3/_{16}$", $^1/_4$", $^5/_{16}$", $^3/_8$", $^1/_2$", $^5/_8$", $^3/_4$", $^{13}/_{16}$", $^7/_8$", 1"

Tolerances: Unsanded panels: $\pm$ $^1/_{32}$"
Sanded panels: + 0" − $^1/_{32}$"
$^1/_4$" wall panels + 0" − $^3/_{64}$"

Data supplied by Hardwood Plywood Manufacturers Association and by U.S. Plywood, Division of U.S. Plywood—Champion Papers, Inc.

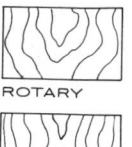

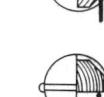

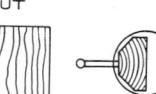

ROTARY

FLAT SLICING

QUARTER SLICING

HALF ROUND

RIFT.CUT

BACK CUT

VENEER CUTTING

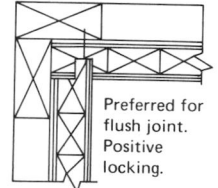

Preferred for flush joint. Positive locking.

INSIDE CORNER

Usually used. Joint is glued.

OUTSIDE CORNER

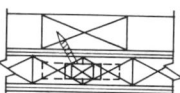

Spline usually $^1/_4$" x $^5/_8$". Dowels 6" to 12" o.c.

DOWEL & SPLINE

Tongue usually $^1/_4$" wide, $^5/_{16}$" deep. Dowels sometimes added.

TONGUE & GROOVE

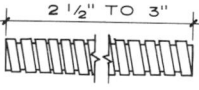

2 $^1/_2$" TO 3"

Glue spirals No. 8–10 dowels approx. $^3/_8$".

DOWEL

VENEER

EXPOSED PLYWOOD SPLINE

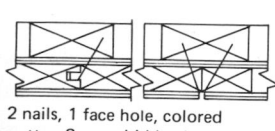

2 nails, 1 face hole, colored putty. Screws hidden by joint preferred for possible removal of panels. #10 or #12 size usual.

NAILS AND SCREWS RECOMMENDED

3" x 2" clips 16" o.c. Allow 1" at ceil. to drop panel into place.

METAL CLIPS

MATCHING HARDWOOD END   CONCEALED CROSSBAND   VENEER EDGEBAND

PANEL EDGES

DETAILS FOR QUALITY INTERIOR HARDWOOD PLYWOOD PANELING
LUMBER CORE PLYWOOD SHOWN

Foster C. Parriott; James M. Hunter & Associates; Boulder, Colorado

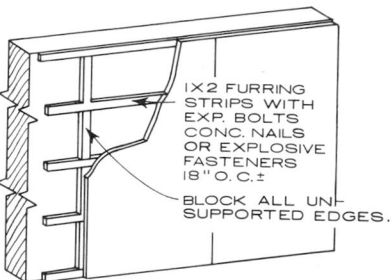

1X2 FURRING STRIPS WITH EXP. BOLTS CONC. NAILS OR EXPLOSIVE FASTENERS 18" O.C.±

BLOCK ALL UNSUPPORTED EDGES.

Many city bldg. codes require spaces between furring be filled (rough plaster trowelled in) to prevent flue action. On old plaster walls furring strips required to be set in the old plaster.

OVER MASONRY WALLS

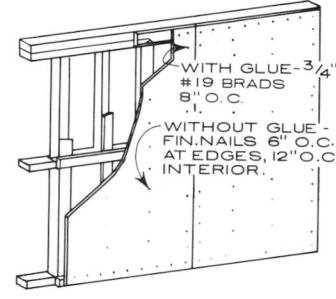

WITH GLUE-$^3/_4$" #19 BRADS 8" O.C.

WITHOUT GLUE - FIN.NAILS 6" O.C. AT EDGES, 12"O.C. INTERIOR.

$^1/_4$" x 2" tir plywood strips used when in doubt about dryness of framing. Glue recommended for quality work. Furring often nailed thru old plaster to framing, but nailing direct to framing is recommended.

ON FRAME WALLS

CASING OR FINISH NAILS USED

PANEL THICKNESS	NAIL SIZE
$^1/_4$"	4d
$^3/_8$"	6d
$^1/_2$"	6d
$^3/_4$"	8d

INTERIOR WALL AND FURRING APPLICATION

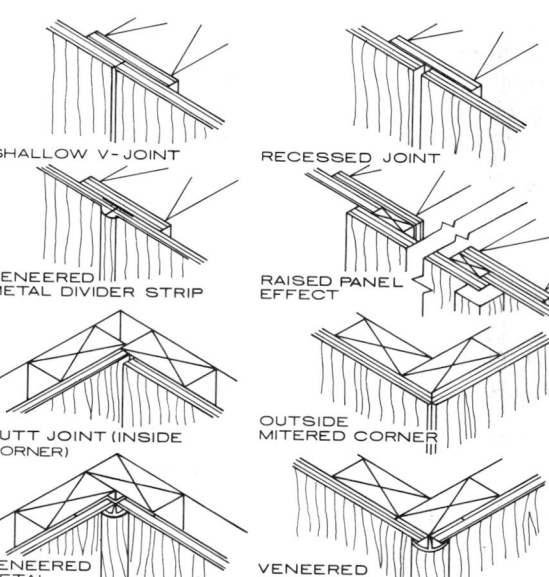

SHALLOW V-JOINT

RECESSED JOINT

VENEERED METAL DIVIDER STRIP

RAISED PANEL EFFECT

BUTT JOINT (INSIDE CORNER)

OUTSIDE MITERED CORNER

VENEERED METAL MOLDING

VENEERED METAL MOLDING

SOME INTERIOR JOINT DETAILS

LAMINATED HARDWOOD BLOCK FLOORING

STANDARD SIZE	9" x 9" x $^1/_2$"	
GRADES	Grade A (Prime) finished or unfinished	
	Grade B (Standard) finished or unfinished	
SPECIES	HIGH DENSITY	MEDIUM DENSITY
	Beech, American	Cherry, black
	Birch, yellow, sweet	Sapele
	Hickory	Walnut, American
	Maple, sugar (hard)	
	Maple, black (hard)	LOW DENSITY
	Oak, commercial, red	Poplar, yellow
	Oak, commercial, white	
	Pecan, commercial	
	Teak	
PLIES	3 at right angles, offset to provide tongues and grooves.	
APPLICATION	Laid in mastic over concrete or other suitable sub-floor.	

Data supplied by Hardwood Plywood Manufacturers Association (HPMA). Samples tested under U.S. Commercial Standard CS–233–63.

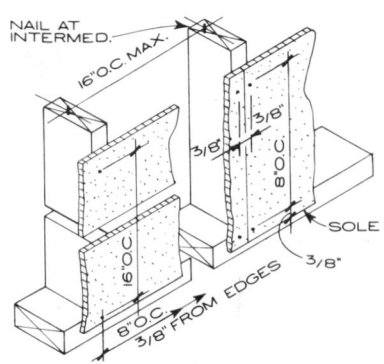

NAILS AND SPACING

Nails: Flat, casing or button head. Drive screw nails to penetrate into solid wood. Drilling for nails and fasteners is unneccessary on type "U" or "F" boards on any thickness up to and including 1/4".

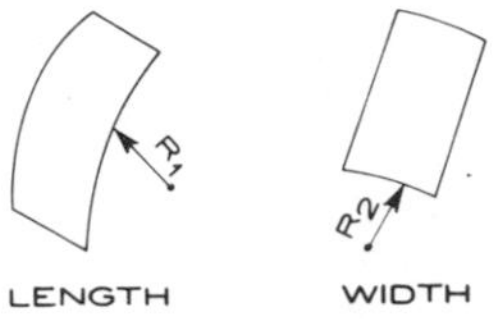

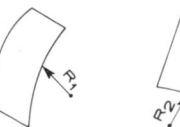

LENGTH   WIDTH

MIN. BENDING RADII

THICK.	R₁	R₂
1/8"	30"	36"
3/16"	36"	54"

(Unscored boards only.)

SIZES
Boards—4' X 4', 8', 9', 10', 12' usually 1/8" & 3/16" thick. For interior finishes—1/8" X 4' X 4' tile-like scored boards also available.

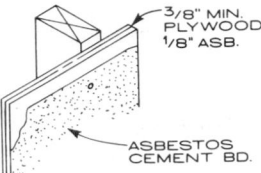

ON WOOD STUDS OVER BACKING

Asbestos cement board has an Underwriters Laboratory fire resistance rating of zero combustibility, zero flame spread and zero toxic smoke production. Backing with gyp. board increases its fire resistance and is recommended. 1/8" board should have a 3/8" min. gyp. backing. 3/8" asb. cement board may be used without backing if cats are placed behind all joints.

ON FURRING OVER MASONRY OR PLASTER

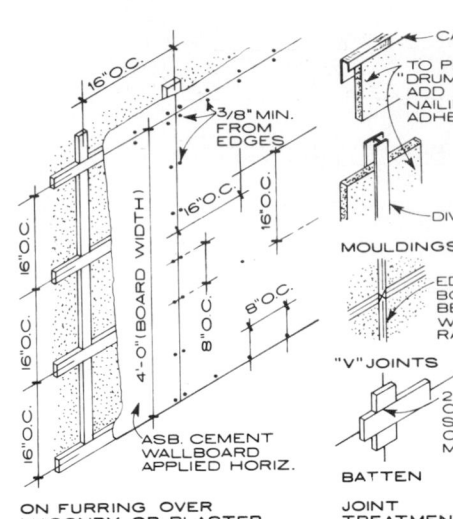

MOULDINGS

"V" JOINTS

BATTEN

JOINT TREATMENTS

ASBESTOS CEMENT WALLBOARDS

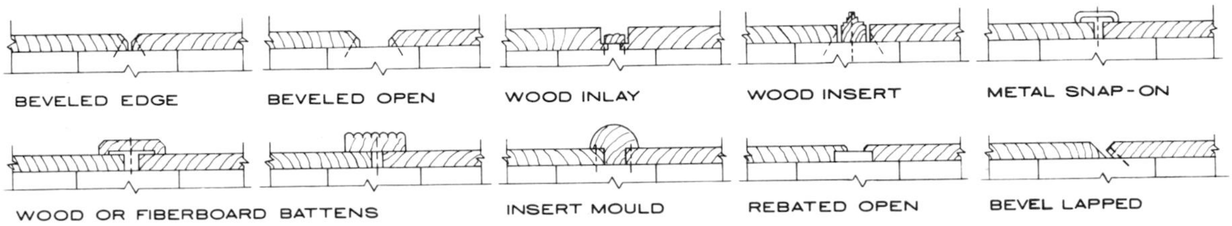

BEVELED EDGE   BEVELED OPEN   WOOD INLAY   WOOD INSERT   METAL SNAP-ON

WOOD OR FIBERBOARD BATTENS   INSERT MOULD   REBATED OPEN   BEVEL LAPPED

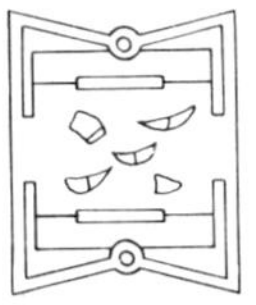

NAILED TO FACE OF STUD, FASTENER ALLOWS FOR EXPANSION. WALLBOARD IS CLINCHED BY STRIKING WITH BLOCK.

JOINTS APPLICABLE TO WALLBOARD PANELS

UPSON FLOATING FASTENER (FOR WALLBOARD)

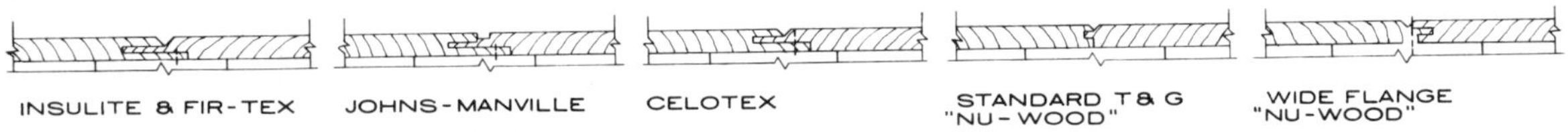

INSULITE & FIR-TEX   JOHNS-MANVILLE   CELOTEX   STANDARD T & G "NU-WOOD"   WIDE FLANGE "NU-WOOD"

JOINTS APPLICABLE TO WALLBOARD PLANKS

CLIPS FOR T & G JOINTS IN "NU-WOOD"

CONCEALED FASTENERS

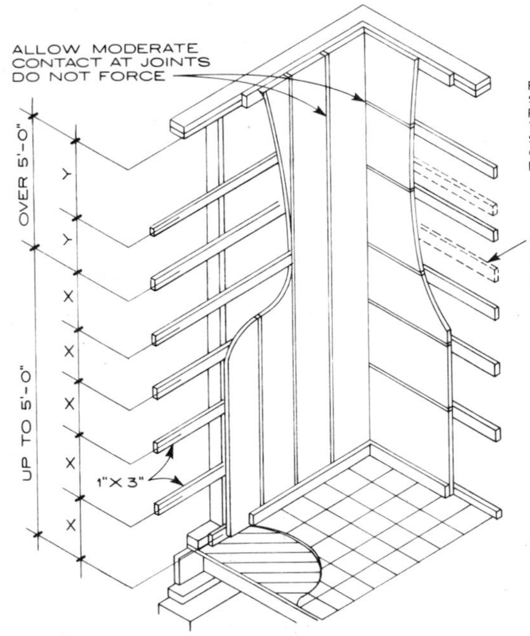

ALLOW MODERATE CONTACT AT JOINTS DO NOT FORCE

OVER 5'-0"

UP TO 5'-0"

1" X 3"

FIBERBOARD TILE: SIZES 12" & 16" SQ., 12" X 24" & 16" X 32", 1/2" THICK, PLAIN OR PERFORATED, EDGES T & G OR WIDE FLANGE. APPLIED SAME AS FIBERBOARD PLANK. GENERALLY USED ON CEILINGS BUT MAY BE USED ON WALLS.

FOR HORIZONTAL PLANK, LATH MUST BE PROVIDED BEHIND EACH JOINT. ADDITIONAL FURRING REQUIRED WHEN 16" PLANK IS USED.

NAILS SPACED IN ACCORDANCE WITH FURRING OR 12" O.C. FOR CONTINUOUS BACKING. PLANKS MAY ALSO BE SECURED BY ADHESIVE (SEE MFR.).

FOR NAIL SIZES & TYPES, SEE MFR.'S RECOMMENDATIONS.

SPACING OF FURRING VARIES WITH PLANK THICKNESS. FOR 1/2" PLANK "X" SHOULD BE 9", "Y"=12". FOR 3/4" PLANK "X" SHOULD BE 12", "Y"=16".

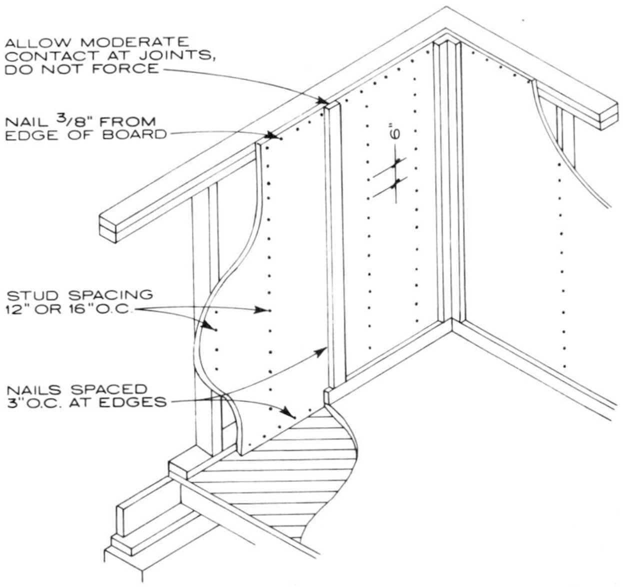

ALLOW MODERATE CONTACT AT JOINTS, DO NOT FORCE

NAIL 3/8" FROM EDGE OF BOARD

STUD SPACING 12" OR 16" O.C.

NAILS SPACED 3" O.C. AT EDGES

6"

PLANK   **PANELS**

VEGETABLE FIBER WALLBOARDS FOR INTERIORS – METHODS OF APPLYING INTERIOR FIBERBOARD

WALLBOARD AND FIBERBOARD SIZES

DESIGNATION		SIZES	THICKNESS
WALLBOARD, BUILDING: BOARD, STRUCTURAL: FIBERBOARD, INSULATING BOARD OR STRUCTURAL INSULATING BOARD.	PANEL	Generally available in widths of 4'—0" and lengths from 4'—0" to 12'—0" in increments of 1'—0" (no 11'—0" lengths made). Several boards are manufactured in sizes 8'—0" X 14'—0" & 16'—0" (Homasote & Upson). A 4'—0" X 14'—0" & 16'—0" is made (Upson). Largest board made is 8'—0" X 18'—0" (Upson).	3/8", 15/32 (Homasote) 1/2", & 3/4"
	PLANKS	Generally available in widths of 8", 10", 12", 16", and in lengths of 8'—0", 10'—0", 12'—0". A few planks are made in 6'—0" lengths.	1/2" & 3/4"

Ferd Scheeler; Skidmore, Owings and Merrill; Chicago, Illinois

TYPES OF GYPSUM BOARDS

THICK-NESS	WIDTH & EDGE	STOCK LENGTHS	GYPSUM BOARDS
1″ or 1 5/8″	Square 6′ or 8′	Clg. ht. up to 10′	Gypsum board studs are laminated strips of gypsum board cut to specified lengths and widths for use with semi-solid partition system.
1/2″ or 5/8″	4′ square	8′, 9′	Sound type of boards are wood fiber products for use with gypsum wall board systems to reduce sound transmission. There is one type for use where combustible materials are permitted. A second type is fire-retardant treated for use in noncombustible constructions.
3/8″ or 1/2″ or 5/8″	4′ beveled 4′ square (grain patterns only)	8′, 9′, & 10′ sp. & custom to sp. length	Gypsum board colored and textured with vinyl-surfaced material are available in many standard, special and custom colors. 5/8″ thickness boards are also available in fire rated gypsum board.
3/8″ or 1/2″ special order	4′ square	8′, 9′ & 10′	Paper covered gypsum board panels. See manufacturers literature for types wood grain patterns, textures, and colors that they have available.
regular 3/8″ or 1/2″ Fire-rated 5/8″	2′ & 4′ sq. 3′ t. & g. & square	Up to 12′ 8′	Backing board in all thicknesses is recommended for the base layer for 2-layer wallboard application. 1/2″ backing board and 5/8″ fire-rated board are for acoustical tile application.
1/2″ 5/8″ spec. order	4′ tapered	8′, 12′	Moisture resistant gypsum board is a wallboard specially processed for use as a base for ceramic tile and other non-absorbent wall tiles in bath and shower areas. The board is tapered on the edges so joints above the area to be tiled can be treated in the usual manner.
1/2″ or 5/8″	4′ square	11′ (std.)	Vinyl-surfaced backing gypsum board is a waterproofed gypsum wallboard base for the application of ceramic and other non-absorbent type wall tiles in bath and shower areas. Cut-outs and joints are sealed with vinyl tape. Fittings are caulked, and tile is set, both with waterproof tile adhesive. 5/8″ thickness boards are also available in fire rated gypsum board.

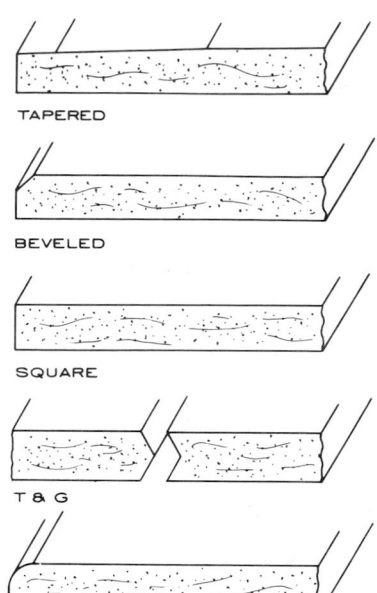

TAPERED

BEVELED

SQUARE

T & G

ROUNDED

TYPES OF EDGES

APPLICATION METHODS FOR VARIOUS DRYWALL THICKNESS

THICK-NESS	APPROX. WEIGHT LB/SQ.FT.	SIZE	LOCATION	APPLICATION METHOD	MAX SPACING OF FRAMING
1/4″	1.1	4′ X 8′ X 12′	OVER EXIST. FRAM'G.	HORIZONTAL OR VERTICAL	
3/8″	1.5	4′ X 8′ X 14′	CEILINGS	HORIZONTAL	16″
3/8″	1.5	4′ X 8′ X 14′	SIDEWALLS	HORIZONTAL OR VERTICAL	16″
1/2″	2.0	4′ X 8′ X 14′	CEILINGS	HORIZONTAL, VERTICAL	24″ H., 16″ V.
1/2″	2.0	4′ X 8′ X 14′	SIDEWALLS	HORIZONTAL OR VERTICAL	24″
5/8″	2.5	4′ X 8′ X 14′	CEILINGS	HORIZONTAL, VERTICAL	24″ H., 16″ V.
5/8″	2.5	4′ X 8′ X 14′	SIDEWALLS	HORIZONTAL OR VERTICAL	24″
1″	4.0	4′ X 8′ X 12′		FOR LAMINATED PARTITIONS	

NAIL TYPES AND USES

NAILS	WALLBOARD THICKNESS	NAIL	SPACING WALL	SPACING CEILING
GWB-54 ANN-ULAR RING NAILS 1/4″ HEAD, 1 1/4″ LONG 1 3/8″ LONG	3/8″	1 1/8″ GWB-54	8″	7″
	1/2″	1 1/4″ GWB-54	8″	7″
	5/8″	1 3/8″ GWB-54	8″	7″
	3/8″ BACKING	1 1/4″ GWB-54	8″	7″
	1/2″ BACKING	1 3/8″ GWB-54	8″	7″
COOLER TYPE 4d, 1 3/8″ LONG 7/32″ HEAD, 14 GA. 5d 1 5/8″ LONG 15/64″ HEAD, 13 1/2 GA. 6d 1 7/8″ LONG 1/4″ HEAD, 13 GA.	1/4″	1″ PENETRATION	8″	7″
	3/8″	4d COOLER	8″	7″
	1/2″ TYPE "X"	5d COOLER	7″	6″
	5/8″ TYPE "X"	6d COOLER	7″	6″

METAL STUD SIZE AND SPACING

STUD SIZE	STUD SPACING	SPAN 6′-0″	SPAN 8′-0″	SPAN 10′-0″
2 1/2″	16″	21.5	8.6	4.8
	24″	14.3	5.7	3.2
3 1/4″	16″	33.3	13.3	7.3
	24″	22.2	8.9	4.9
3 5/8″	16″	33.3	13.3	7.3
	24″	22.2	8.9	4.9
4″	16″	33.3	13.3	7.3
	24″	22.2	8.9	4.9

MAX. BENDING FOR DRYWALL

BENDING RADII

THICKNESS	LENGTHWISE	WIDTH
1/4″	5′-0″	15′-0″
3/8″	7′-6″	25′-0″
1/2″	20′-0″	—

Shorter radii may be obtained by moistening face and back so that water will soak well into core of board.

FURRING FOR 1/2″ & 5/8″ SINGLE LAYER WALLBOARD

FURRING MEMBER	FURRING MEMBER SPACING 24″ O.C.	16″ O.C.	12″ O.C.
RESIL. FURR. CHAN.	2′-0″	2′-0″	2′-0″
FURRING CHANNEL	4′-0″	4′-6″	5′-0″
1 5/8″ SCREW STUDS	5′-0″	5′-6″	6′-0″
2 1/2″ SCREW STUDS	6′-0″	6′-6″	7′-0″
3 5/8″ SCREW STUDS	8′-0″	8′-6″	9′-0″

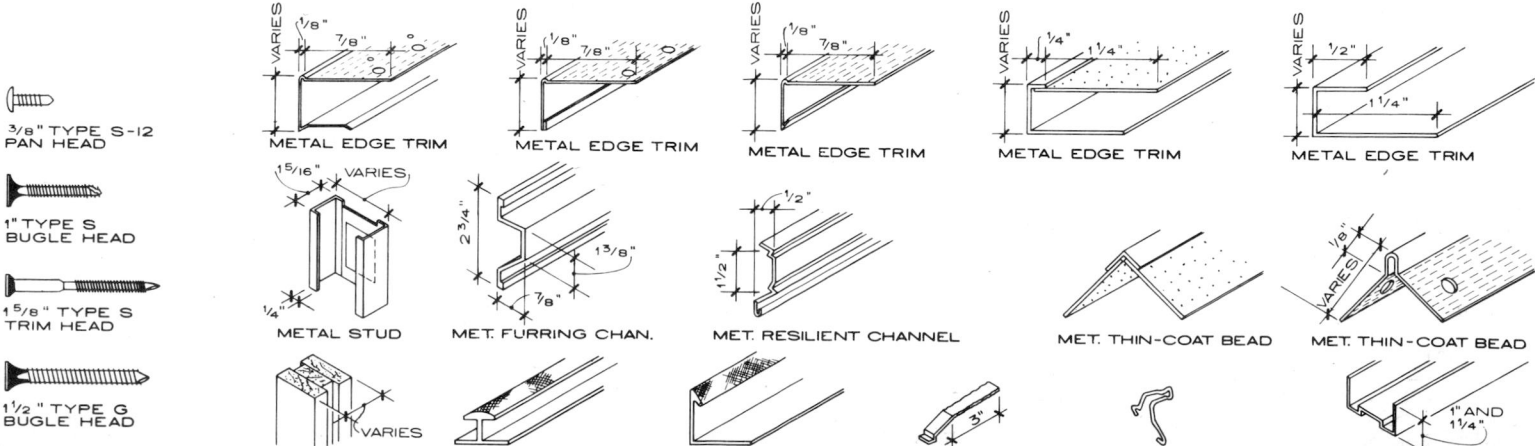

3/8″ TYPE S-12 PAN HEAD

1″ TYPE S BUGLE HEAD

1 5/8″ TYPE S TRIM HEAD

1 1/2″ TYPE G BUGLE HEAD

TYPES OF DRYWALL SCREWS

METAL EDGE TRIM

METAL EDGE TRIM

METAL EDGE TRIM

METAL EDGE TRIM

METAL EDGE TRIM

METAL STUD

MET. FURRING CHAN.

MET. RESILIENT CHANNEL

MET. THIN-COAT BEAD

MET. THIN-COAT BEAD

GYPSUM STUD

PRE-FINISHED DIVIDER

PRE-FINISHED CORNER

ADJUSTABLE WALL FURRING BRACKET

METAL FURRING CHANNEL CUP

METAL RUNNER

GYPSUM DRYWALL ACCESSORIES AND COMPONENTS

Ferd Scheeler; Skidmore, Owings and Merrill; Chicago, Illinois

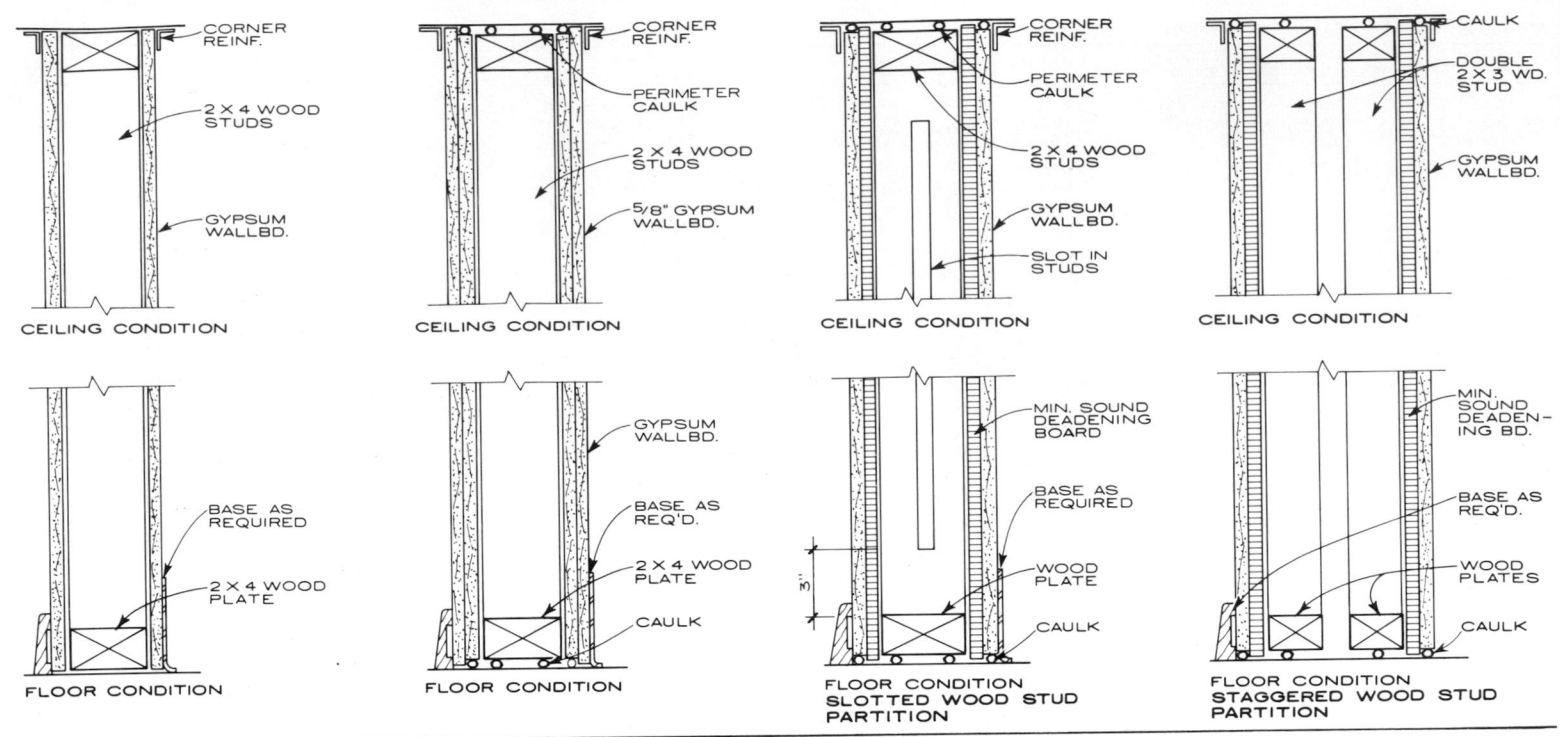

GYPSUM WOOD FRAMED TYPE PARTITIONS

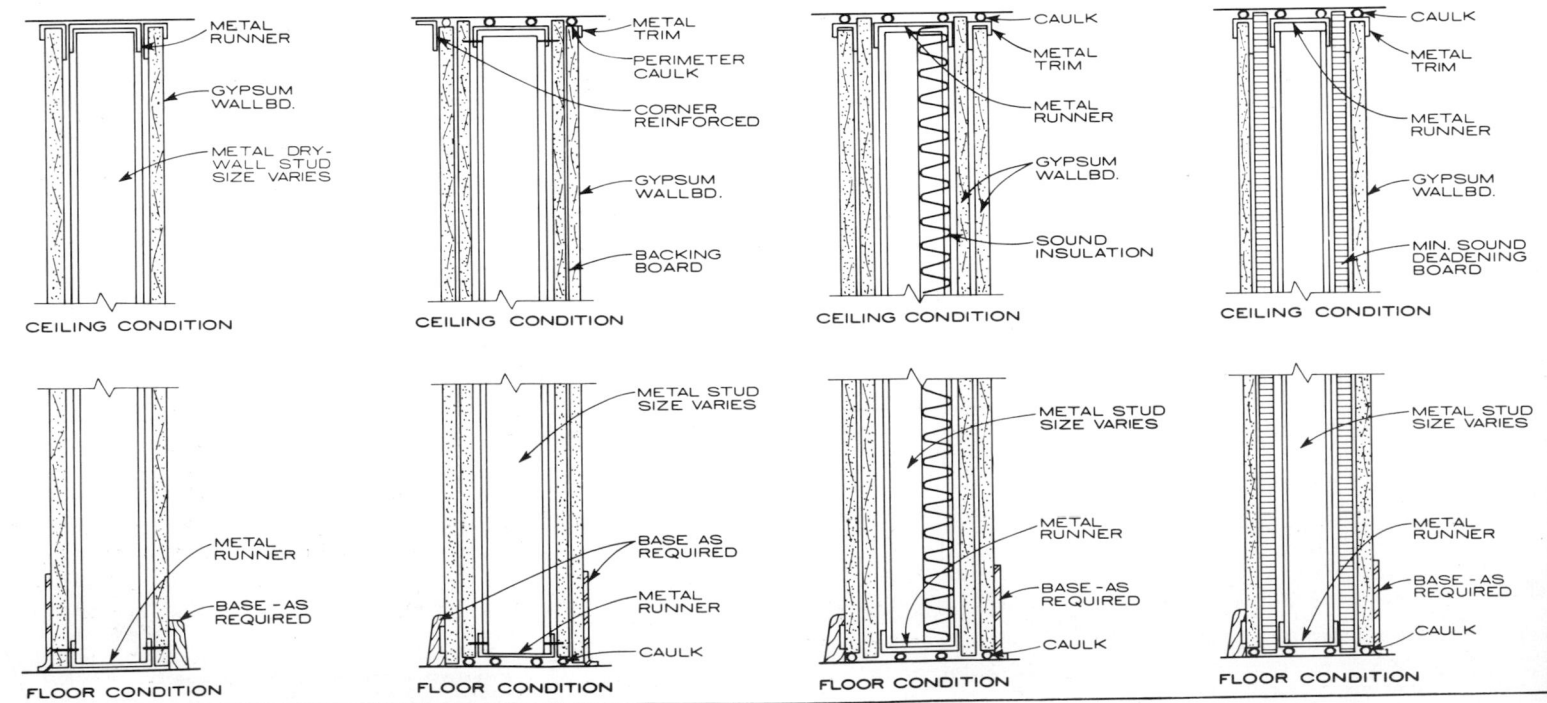

GYPSUM METAL FRAMED TYPE PARTITIONS

Ferd Scheeler; Skidmore, Owings and Merrill; Chicago, Illinois

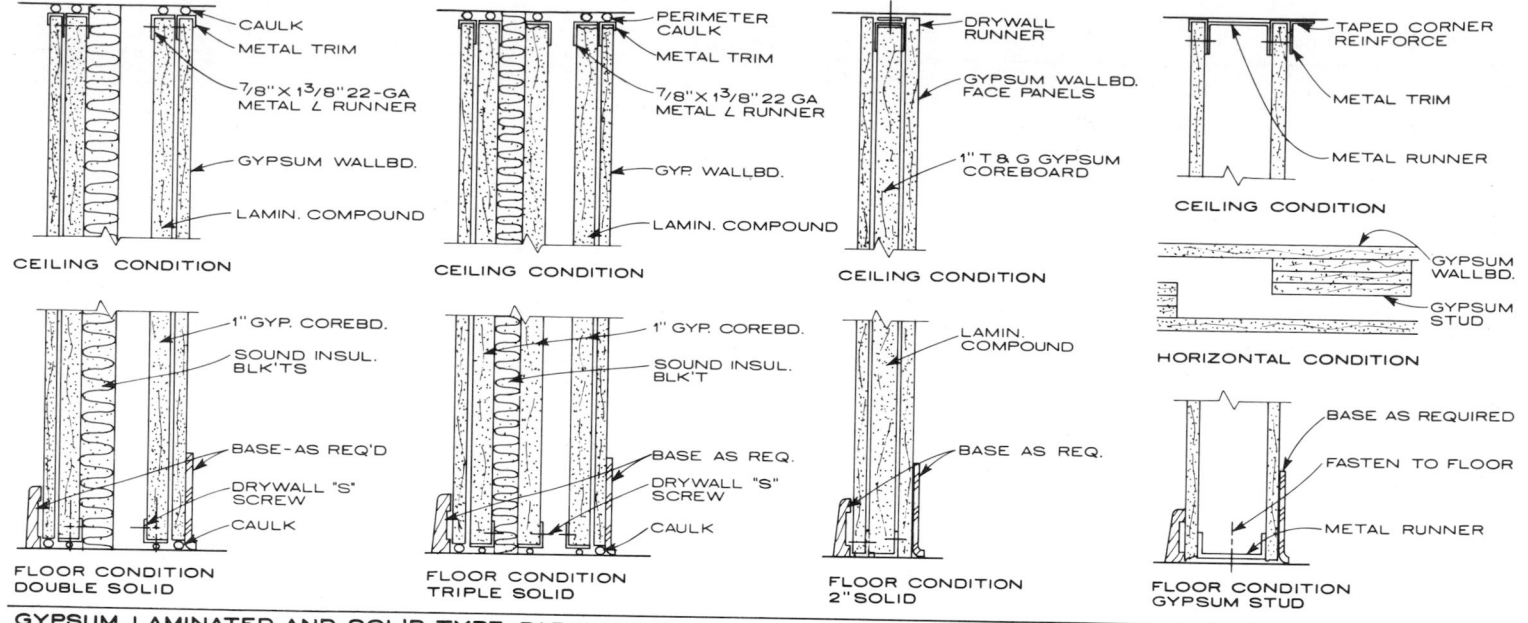

GYPSUM LAMINATED AND SOLID TYPE PARTITIONS

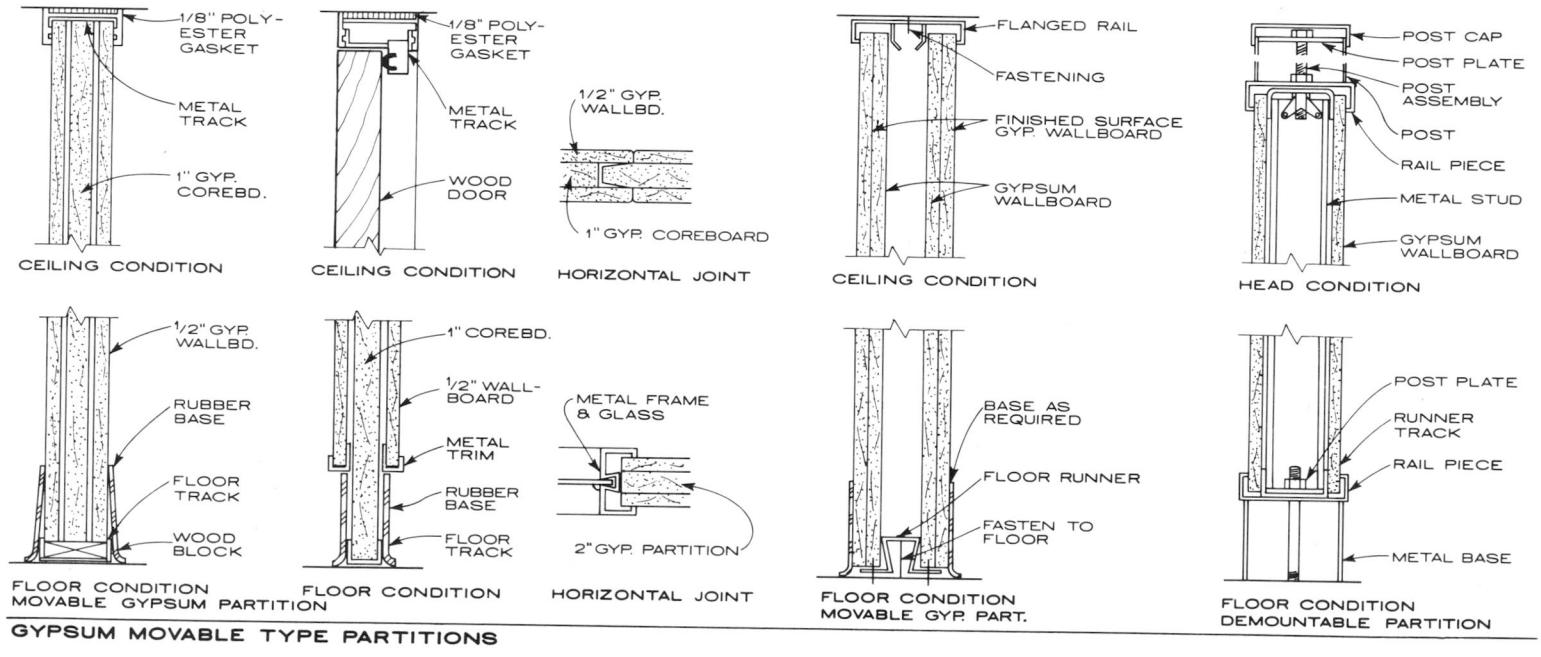

GYPSUM MOVABLE TYPE PARTITIONS

GYPSUM DRYWALL CEILING TYPES

Ferd Scheeler; Skidmore, Owings and Merrill; Chicago, Illinois

DESCRIPTION OF PARTITIONS	FIRE RATING	SOUND RATING	RELATIVE COST INDEX	COMMENTS
WOOD FRAMED TYPE				
WOOD STUD 2 LAYERS 5/8" LABEL GYPSUM WALLBOARD, 2 X 4 AT 16" O.C., BASE LAYER 6D NAILS AT 6" O.C., FACE LAYER LAMIN. TO BASE, JOINTS FINISHED	2 HRS.	38 STC	161	WIDTH 6 1/8", SEE SECTION ON CONSTRUCTION DETAIL PAGE
STAGGERED WOOD STUD 5/8" LABEL GYP. WALLBOARD, 2 ROWS 2 X 3 STAGGERED & SEPARATE PLATES 1" APART, BASE LAYER OF 1/2" WOOD FIBER SOUND DEAD BOARD ATT. WITH 6D CTD. NAILS, FACE LAYER 7D CTD. NAILS 7" O.C., JOINTS FIN.	1 HR.	53 STC	175	WIDTH 8 1/2, SEE SECTION ON CONSTRUCTION DETAIL PAGE
WOOD STUD RESIL. 5/8" LABEL GYP. BD. 2 X 4 AT 16" O.C., 3" INSUL. BLANKETS, RESILIENT CHANNEL ONE SIDE SPACED 24" O.C., BD. ATT. WITH 1" TYPE S SCREWS, OPP. SIDE DIRECT ATT. WITH 1 1/4" TYPE W SCREWS, JOINTS FINISHED	1 HR.	52 STC	134	WIDTH 5 1/2"
SLOT WOOD STUD 5/8" LABEL GYP. WALLBD., 2 X 4 SLOTTED STUDS 16" O.C., BASE LAYER OF 1/2" WOOD FIBER SOUND DEAD BOARD, 2 SIDES ATT. WITH 5D CTD. NAILS 12" O.C., FACE LAYER 6D CTD NAILS 8" O.C., JOINTS FINISHED	1 HR.	49 STC	155	WIDTH 5 7/8", SEE SECTION ON CONSTRUCTION DETAIL PAGE
SLOT WOOD STUD 5/8" LABEL GYP. BD., 2 X 4 SLOT. STUDS 16" O.C., SINGLE LAYER SCREW APPL. ONE SIDE, 2 LAYERS OPP. SIDE BASE LAYER SCREW APPL. & FACE LAYER LAMIN., PERIM. CAULK.	1 HR.	48 STC	143	WIDTH 5 1/2", SEE SECTION ON CONSTRUCTION DETAIL PAGE
WOOD STUD RESIL. LABEL GYP. BD. 2 LAYERS ONE SIDE & 1 LAYER OPP. SIDE 2 X 4 X 16" O.C., RESIL. CHAN. BOTH SIDES SPA. HORIZ. 24" O.C., 1 LAYER 5/8" BD. SCREW ATT. ONE SIDE, OPP. SIDE BASE LAYER OF 5/8" WALLBD. SCREW ATT. & FACE LAYER OF 1/2" WALLBD. LAMIN., JOINTS FIN., PERIMETER CAULKED	1 HR.	48 STC	146	WIDTH 6 1/2"
WOOD STUD 1/2" GYP. WALLBD., 2 X 4 AT 16" O.C., BASE LAYER 1/2" SOUND DEADENING BOARD ATTACHED WITH 1 5/8" CTD. NAILS 12" O.C., WALLBOARD FACE LAYER STRIP LAMIN. & 2 1/4" CTD. NAILS 24" O.C. INTO WOOD STUDS	45 MIN.	42 STC	162	WIDTH 5 5/8", SEE SECTION ON CONSTRUCTION DETAIL PAGE
METAL FRAMED TYPE				
METAL STUD 2 LAYERS 5/8" LABEL GYP. WALLBD. EA. SIDE, 3 5/8" MTL. STUDS 24" O.C., BASE LAYER SCREW ATT., FACE LAYER LAMIN., 1 1/2" INSUL. BLK'TS, PERIMETER CAULKED	2 HRS.	55 STC	176	WIDTH 6 1/8", SEE SECTION ON CONSTRUCTION DETAIL PAGE
METAL STUD 2 LAYERS 1/2" LABEL GYP. WALLBD. EA. SIDE, 2 1/2" MTL. STUDS 24" O.C., 1 1/2" INSUL. BLK'TS. STAPLED, WALLBD. APPL. VERT. & JOINTS STAG., BASE LAYER SCREW ATT., FACE LAYER STRIP LAMIN. & SCREWS CENTER BET'N. STUDS, PERIM. CAULK.	2 HRS.	54 STC	173	WIDTH 4 1/2", SEE SECTION ON CONSTRUCTION DETAIL PAGE
METAL STUD 5/8" LABEL GYP. WALLBD., 3 5/8" MT'L. STUDS 24" O.C., 2 LAYER, BASE LAYER 1/2" MIN. FIBER SOUND DEAD BD. EA. SIDE SCREW ATT., WALLBD. FACE LAYER LAMIN. & SCREW ATT., JOINTS STAG. & FIN., PERIMETER CAULKED	2 HRS.	52 STC	186	WIDTH 5 7/8", SEE SECTION ON CONSTRUCTION DETAIL PAGE
METAL STUD 2 LAYERS 5/8" LABEL GYP. WALLBD., 3 5/8" MTL. STUDS 24" O.C., 3" INSUL. BLKTS., 2 LAYERS WALLBD., LAMIN. ONE SIDE, OPP. SIDE 2 LAYERS WALLBD. SEPAR. BY RESIL. CHAN. SPACED HORIZ. 24" O.C. SCREW ATT., FACE JOINTS FIN.	2 HRS.	51 STC	187	WIDTH 6 1/2", SEE SECTION ON CONSTRUCTION DETAIL PAGE
METAL STUD 2 LAYERS 5/8" LABEL GYP. WALLBD., 3 5/8" MTL. STUDS 24" O.C., 2 LAYERS WALLBD. SCREW ATT. ONE SIDE, OPP. SIDE 2 LAYERS WALLBD. SEPAR. BY RESIL. CHAN. SPACED HORIZ. 24" O.C. SCREW ATT., FACE JOINTS FIN.	2 HRS.	50 STC	173	WIDTH 6 5/8"
METAL STUD 2 LAYERS 5/8" LABEL GYP. BD. PLAIN OR VINYL FACED, 3 5/8" STUDS 24" O.C., BASE LAYER SCREW ATT., FACE LAYER LAMIN. OR SCREW ATT., JTS. FIN. OR UNFIN.	2 HRS.	46 STC	157	WIDTH 6 1/8", SEE SECTION ON CONSTRUCTION DETAIL PAGE
METAL STUD 2 LAYERS 1/2" LABEL GYP. BD., 1 5/8" MTL. STUDS 24" O.C., 2 LAYERS EA. SIDE VERT. APPL. & SCREW ATT. JOINTS STAG. & FIN.	2 HRS.		156	WIDTH 3 5/8", SEE SECTION ON CONSTRUCTION DETAIL PAGE
METAL STUD 1/2" LABEL GYP. BD., 3 5/8" MTL. STUDS 24" O.C., SINGLE LAYER WALLBD. ONE SIDE APPL. VERT. & SCREW ATT., 1" INSUL. BLK'TS ONE SIDE 2 LAYER WALLBD. OPP. SIDE APPL. VERT. & SCREW ATT., JTS. STAG. & FIN., PERIMETER CAULKED	1 1/2 HRS.	51 STC	156	WIDTH 5 1/8"
METAL STUD 1/2" LABEL GYP. WALLBD., 1 5/8" MTL. STUDS 24" O.C., 2 LAYER, BASE LAYER 1/2" MIN. FIBER SOUND DEAD BD. SCREW ATT., WALLBD. FACE LAYER STRIP LAMIN. & SCREW ATT., JOINTS STAG. & FIN.	1 HR.	48 STC	167	WIDTH 3 5/8", SEE SECTION ON CONSTRUCTION DETAIL PAGE
METAL STUD 1/2" LABEL GYP. BD., 3 5/8" STUDS 24" O.C., SINGLE LAYER BD. EA. SIDE APPL. VERT. & SCREW ATT., 1" INSUL. BLK'TS ONE SIDE, JTS. FIN., PERIMETER CAULK.	1 HR.	47 STC	138	WIDTH 4 5/8"
METAL STUD 5/8" LABEL GYP. BD., 3 5/8" MTL. STUDS, 24" O.C., WALLBD. SINGLE LAYER SCREW ATT. 12" O.C., JOINTS FIN., PERIMETER PARTITION CAULKED	1 HR.	42 STC	106	WIDTH 4 7/8", SEE SECTION ON CONSTRUCTION DETAIL PAGE
METAL STUD 5/8" LABEL GYP. BD., 1 5/8" MTL. STUDS 24" O.C., WALLBD. SINGLE LAYER, SCREW ATT. 12" O.C., JOINTS FIN., PERIMETER CAULKED	1 HR.	38 STC	105	WIDTH 2 7/8"

Ferd Scheeler; Skidmore, Owings and Merrill; Chicago, Illinois

DESCRIPTION OF PARTITIONS	FIRE RATING	SOUND RATING	RELATIVE COST INDEX	COMMENTS
LAMINATED AND SOLID TYPES				
DOUBLE SOLID DRYWALL 1/2" GYPSUM WALLBOARD, TWO ROWS OF 1" COREBOARD SPACED 1 1/8" APART, ST'L. RUNNERS, LAMIN. & SCREW ATTACH. EA. FACE	2 HRS.	46 STC	150	WIDTH 4 1/8", SEE SECTION ON CONSTRUCTION DETAIL PAGE
SOLID DRYWALL VENT SHAFT 5/8" LABEL GYPSUM WALLBOARD FACES EACH SIDE OVER 1" GYPSUM COREBOARD, FACE LAYERS LAMIN. & SCREW ATT., JOINTS STAG. & UNFIN. 3/8" X 1 3/8" L RUNNERS HORIZ. AT FLR., CLG., & QUARTER POINTS	2 HRS.		124	WIDTH 2 1/4"
SOLID DRYWALL 5/8" LABEL GYP. WALLBD. FACES EA. SIDE OVER 1" GYPSUM COREBOARD, FACE LAYERS LAMIN., JOINTS STAGGERED AND FINISHED	2 HRS.	34 STC	124	WIDTH 2 1/4", SEE SECTION ON CONSTRUCTION DETAIL PAGE
SOLID DRYWALL 1/2" LABEL GYP. WALLBD. FACES EA. SIDE OVER 1" GYP. COREBOARD, FACE LAYERS LAMIN., JOINTS STG. & FIN., MT'L. TRACK AT FLR., 1/2" MT'L. TRIM AT WALL & CLG.	2 HRS.		120	WIDTH 2", DIFFICULT TO INSTALL OUTLET BOXES
TRIPLE SOLID DRYWALL 1/2" GYP. WALLBD., 3 ROWS OF 1" GYP. COREBD. EA. SPACED MIN. 1 1/8" & 1/2" APART, 1 1/2" INSUL. AFT. TO BACK OF ONE OUTER ROW, WALLBD. LAMIN. & SCREW ATTACHED TO OUTER ROWS, JOINTS FINISHED	2 HRS.	59 STC	210	WIDTH 6 1/4", DIFFICULT INSTALLATION AT PIPE CHASES, SEE SECTION ON CONSTRUCTION DETAIL PAGE
SOLID DRYWALL 1/2" GYP. WALLBD. FACES EA. SIDE OVER 1" GYP. COREBD. FACE LAYERS LAMIN., JOINTS STAG. & FIN., 1" SQ. WOOD RUNNER EACH SIDE	1 1/2 HRS.		105	WIDTH 2", DIFFICULT TO INSTALL OUTLET BOXES
GYPSUM STUD WALL 5/8" LABEL GYP. WALLBD., 1 5/8" X 6" LAMIN. GYP. STUDS 24" O.C., WALLBD. SCREW ATT. BOTH SIDES 18" O.C.	1 HR.		113	WIDTH 2 7/8", SEE SECTION ON CONSTRUCTION DETAIL PAGE
MOVABLE TYPE				
MOV. PART.—DOUBLE DRYWALL SOUND WALL SPEC. 5/8" GYP. BD. FACE PANELS LAMIN. TO 5/8" GYP. CORE STRIPS PLACED TO FORM PANEL JTS., 2 ROWS SPA. 2 1/8" APART, 2" INSUL. BLANKETS IN CHASE, V-JOINTS UNFINISHED	2 HRS.	50 STC	266	WIDTH 6"
MOV. PART.—DOUBLE DRYWALL SOUND WALL SPEC. 5/8" GYP. BD. FACE PANELS LAMIN. TO 5/8" GYP. CORE STRIPS TO FORM PANEL JTS., 2 ROWS SPA. 1 3/8" APART, V-JOINTS UNFINISHED	1 HR.	45 STC	234	WIDTH 5 1/8", SEE SECTION ON CONSTRUCTION DETAIL
MOV. DEMOUNTABLE PART. 1/2" VINYL FACED LABEL GYP. WALLBD. & BATTENS SCREW ATT., 2 1/2" MT'L. STUDS 24" O.C., 2" INSUL. SOUND BLANKETS	1 HR.	49 STC	187	WIDTH 3 1/2"
MOV. PART.—STANDARD SOLID DRYWALL PARTITION SPEC. 5/8" GYP. WALLBD. FACE PANELS LAMIN. TO SPEC. 1" GYP. CORE UNITS 24" WIDE, V-JOINTS UNFINISHED	1 HR.	36 STC	188	WIDTH 2 1/4", SEE SECTION ON CONSTRUCTION DETAIL PAGE
MOV. WALL PART. CONCEALED "H" STUDS 24" O.C., 2" INSUL. SOUND BLK'TS 3/4" X 24" BEVEL EDGE PANELS MILL LAMIN., JOINTS UNFINISHED		45 STC	180	WIDTH 3 5/8", SEE SECTION ON CONSTRUCTION DETAIL PAGE
MOV. WALL PART. CONCEALED "H" STUDS 24" O.C. BRIDGED, 2" INSUL. SOUND ATTEN. BLK'TS, 3/4" X 24" BEVEL EDGE PANELS MILL LAMIN., JTS. UNFINISHED	45 MIN.	45 STC	186	WIDTH 3 5/8"
MOV. DEMOUNTABLE PART. 1/2" VINYL OR PAPER FACED LABEL GYP. WALLBD. & BATTENS SCREW ATT., 2 1/2" MT'L. STUDS 24" A.C.		42 STC	172	WIDTH 3 1/2", SEE SECTION ON CONSTRUCTION DETAIL PAGE
DRYWALL CEILING TYPING				
RESIL. 5/8" LABEL GYP. BD. CEILING 1" NOM. SUB & FIN. FLR., 2 X 10 JOIST 16" O.C., RESIL. CHAN. SPAC. 24" O.C., WALLBD. ATT. WITH 1" & 1 5/8" TYPE S SCREWS, JOINTS FIN.	1 HR.	45 STC	CLG. MAT. 36	CLG. WGT. 3 LB./SQ. FT., SEE SECTION ON CONSTRUCTION DETAIL PAGE
RESIL. 1/2" LABEL GYP. BD. CEILING 1 1/4" NOM. WD. SUB. & FIN. FLR., 2 X 10 WD. JOIST 16" O.C., RESIL. CHAN. SPAC. 24" O.C., WALLBD. ATT. WITH 1" TYPE S SCREWS, JOINTS FIN.	1 HR.		CLG. MAT. 33	CLG. WGT. 3 LB/SQ. FT.
RESIL. GYP. BD. CEILING 1 1/4" NOM. WD. SUB & FIN. FLR., 2 X 10 WD. JOIST 16" O.C., RESIL. CHAN. SCREW ATT. TO JOIST, WALLBD. ATT. WITH 1" TYPE S SCREWS, JOINTS FIN.	1 HR.	47 STC	CLG. MAT. 34	CLG. WGT. 3 LB/SQ. FT.
RESIL. GYP. BD. CEILING 1 1/4" NOM. WD. SUB & FIN. FLR., 4402 CARPET & 4002 PAD, 2 X 10 WD. JOIST 16" A.C., RESIL. CHAN. SCREW ATT. TO JOIST, WALLBD. ATT. WITH 1" TYPE S SCREWS, JOINTS FIN.	1 HR.	47 STC	CLG. MAT. 34	CLG. WGT. 3 LB/SQ. FT. SEE SECTION ON CONSTRUCTION DETAIL PAGE
RESIL. GYP. BD. CEILING 1 1/4" NOM. WD. SUB & FIN. FLR., 3" INSUL. WOOL BLK'TS. BET'W. JTS., 2 X 10 WOOD JOISTS 16" O.C., RESIL. CHAN. SCREW ATT., BD. ATT. WITH 1" TYPE S SCREWS, JOINTS FIN.	1 HR.	59 STC	CLG. MAT. 46	CLG. WGT. 3 LB/SQ. FT., SEE SECTION ON CONSTRUCTION DETAIL PAGE
5/8" BACKING LABEL GYP. BD. CEILING 24 GA. NAIL. CHAN., WALLBD. ATT. WITH ANN. NAILS 6" O.C., JOINTS UNFIN., 2" CONC. ON METAL LATH FUR. OVER BAR JOIST	1 HR.		CLG. MAT. 45	CLG. WGT. 3 LB/SQ. FT.
1/2" LABEL GYP. BD. CEILING 1" NOM. WD. SUB & FIN. FLR., 2 X 10 WOOD JOIST 16" O.C., WALLBD. ATT. WITH 5D CEM. CTD. NAILS 6" O.C., JOINTS FINISHED	1 HR.		CLG. MAT. 23	CLG. WGT. 3 LB/SQ. FT.
5/8" LABEL GYP. BD. CEILING 1" NOM. WD. SUB & FIN. FLR., 2 X 10 WOOD JOIST 16" O.C., 3" INSUL. WOOL BLK'TS. BETW. JOISTS, WALLBD. ATT. WITH 6D NAILS 6" O.C., JOINTS FIN.	1 HR.	40 STC	CLG. MAT. 35	CLG. WGT. 3 LB/SQ. FT.
5/8" LABEL GYP. BD. CEILING AMER. PLYWOOD ASSOC. 2-4-1 FIR., 4 X 10 WD. JOIST 48" O.C., MT'L. FUR. CHAN. SPA. 24" O.C., WALLBD. ATT. WITH 1" TYPE S SCREWS, JOISTS FINISHED	1 HR.		CLG. MAT. 36	CLG. WGT. 3 LB/SQ. FT.
5/8" LABEL GYPSUM WALLBOARD CEILING 1/2" CR. CHAN. 4" O.C., MT'L. FUR. CHAN. 24" O.C., WALLBD. SCREW ATTACHED 12" O.C., JOINTS FINISHED			CLG. MAT. 60	CLG. WGT. 3 LB/SQ. FT.

Ferd Scheeler; Skidmore, Owings and Merrill; Chicago, Illinois

PARTICLE BOARD - TYPES, PROPERTIES, SIZES

TYPE	DENSITY (GRADE)	CLASS	MODULUS OF RUPTURE PSI	MODULUS OF ELASTICITY	SCREW HOLDING FACE (LBS.)	THICK. (INCHES)	LENGTH & WIDTH
1.	A. HIGH DENSITY 50+ P.C.F.	1	2400	350,000	450	$3/8''$	4' x 16' or multiples
		2	3400	350,000		$1/2, 5/8, 1 1/16''$	4' x 16', 6' x 12' or mult.
	B. MEDIUM DENSITY 37 – 50 P.C.F.	1	1600	250,000	225	$3/4''$	up to 4' x 16', 6' x 12'
		2	2400	400,000	225	1'' to 2''	4' x 16', 6' x 12' or mult.
	C. LOW DEN. 37 P.C.F. & UNDER	1	800	150,000	125		
		2	1400	250,000	175		
2.	A. HIGH DEN. 50 P.C.F. & OVER	1	2400	350,000	450		
		2	3400	500,000	500		
	B. MEDIUM DENSITY 50(-) P.C.F.	1	1800	250,000	225		
		2	2500	450,000	250		

Particle Board is made of wood flakes and chips pressed in a resin binder.

Edge finishing and joint details are generally similar to those of plywood paneling.

Type 1 made with urea-formaldehyde resin binders suitable for interior applications.
Type 2 made with phenolic resin binders suitable for certain exterior applications.

TYPES AND USES OF PARTICLE BOARD:

Corestock — bonded flakes or particles—for furniture, casework, panels, doors, etc.
Wood Veneered — for furniture, panels, dividers, cabinets, etc.
Overlaid — faced w/impreg. fiber, hardb'd, plstc. sh's, for sink tops, panels, doors, etc.
Embossed — heavily textured in patterns by heated roller—for int. panels, etc.
Filled — surface filled and sanded, ready for paint—for firm flat, true surfaces.
Exterior — made w/phenol. resins for weather resist.—for exterior covering.
Toxic-Treated — chemical-treated to resist insects, mold, decay-producing fungi.
Primed or Undercoated — factory-applied basecoat for regular or filled board.
Floor Underlayment — engineered specifically for use under carpet or resilient covering.
Fire-Retardant — particles treated w/chemicals to reduce flame-spread characteristics.

HARDBOARD - TYPES & SIZES

TYPE	USE OR DESCRIPTION	SURFACES	$1/12$	$1/10$	$1/8$	$3/16$	$7/32$	$1/4$	$5/16$	$3/8$
STANDARD	Normal interior, protected exterior applications (int. fin., cabinets, display, etc.)	S1S	●	●	●	●		●	●	
		S2S		●	●	●		●	●	●
TEMPERED	Where strength and wear count, for exterior use. Wainscots, work surfaces, siding, signs, etc.	S1S			●	●		●	●	
		S2S							●	
SERVICE	Moderate strength hardboard for non severe conditions (interior finish, porch ceilings, eaves, etc.)	S1S						●	●	●
		S2S			●	●	●	●		●
TEMPERED SERVICE	Improved hardness, stiffness, water resistance for Servicegrade	S1S						●		
		S2S							●	
TREATED	Processed with special additives during manufacture and with surface treatments (oils, resins)	S1S			●	●		●		
		S2S								
UNDERLAYMENT	Servicegrade underlay for resilient floor coverings.	S1S						●	●	
CONCRETE FORM BOARDS	Tempered and further processed for max. performance as conc. form liner.	S1S								
SIDING	Treated lap or panel (see drawing)	S1S					●		●	
PERFORATED	Standard or tempered, unfinished or prefinished, holes 1'' o.c. each way.	S1S			●			●	●	
TEXTURED	Patterns pressed or grooved on tempered hardboard: Tile — 4'' squares; embossed leather, wd. grain, basket weave; striated; grooved.	S1S / S2S				●		●		
FACTORY FINISHED	Primed or coated. Factory sealed or filled.	S1S / S2S		●	●					
LAMINATED	Decorative printed — wd. gr. etc. Special purpose with adhesives.									

Standard Sizes: standard width 4', 5' also available. Standard commercial lengths 4', 6', 8', 12', 16'. 4' x 18' available.

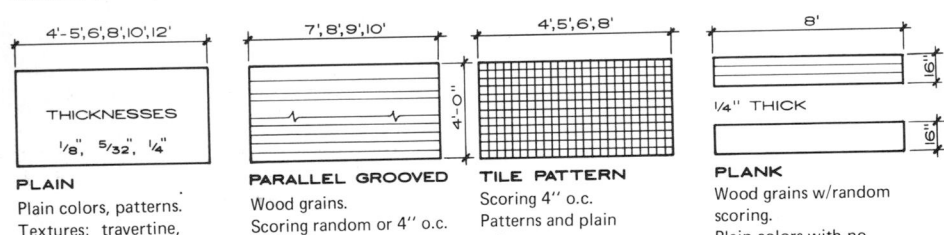

PLAIN — 4'-5',6',8',10',12'; THICKNESSES $1/8''$, $5/32''$, $1/4''$
Plain colors, patterns. Textures: travertine, leather, tapestry. Wood grains.

PARALLEL GROOVED — 7',8',9',10'
Wood grains. Scoring random or 4" o.c. $1/4''$ thick.

TILE PATTERN — 4',5',6',8'; 4'-0"
Scoring 4" o.c. Patterns and plain colors. Thicknesses $5/32''$, $1/8''$

PLANK — 8'; $1/4''$ THICK
Wood grains w/random scoring. Plain colors with no scoring.

Finish is baked-on melamine silicone plastic. Some finishes not recommended for wet areas.

Other Products:
Ceiling tile t&g $1/4''$ x 12 x 12 (Barclay) $1/4$ x 16 x 16 (Marlite) Plain white and pattern on white
Pegboard $5/32$, $1/4$ x 4' x 8'. Holes 1" o.c. both ways. Colors and patterns.
Hollow Core Panels: $5/8$ x 2' x 4', 8'. Plain colors and wood grain finishes.
Trim and aluminum moldings available in matched colors, woodgrains, and patterns.

PREFINISHED PLASTIC COATED HARDBOARD PANELS

HARDBOARD NAILING REQUIREMENTS

	SIZES & TYPES OF HARDBOARD	WHERE USED	SIZE OF NAIL	TYPE	SPACING AROUND EDGE	IN PANEL
INTERIOR	$3/16''$ std. & tempered	walls & ceilings	$1 1/4''$	C & F	4''	6''
	$1/4''$ & $5/16''$ std. & tempered		$1 1/2''$	C, F	4''	6''
	.215 underlayment	floor	$1 1/4''$	RG, DS BB & CS	6''	6''
	$3/16''$ & $1/4''$ finished floor	floor	$1 1/4''$	CC	3''	6''
EXT.	$3/16''$, $1/4''$ & $5/16''$ over sheathing	vertical	$2 1/4''$	S & GB	3''	12''
	$3/16''$, $1/4''$ & $5/16''$ no sheathing	panel siding	2''	S & GB	3''	6''
	$1/4''$ & $5/16''$ plain lap	horizontal	$2 1/2''$	S & GB	3''	16''
	$1/4''$ & $5/16''$ with shadow strip	lap siding	3''	S & GB	3''	16''

C—casing nail; F—finishing; RG—ring grooved; DS—drive screw; BB—barbed box; CS—coated sinker; CC—coated casing; S—galvan. siding; GB—gal. box.

WALL TILE - METAL, ENAMELED METAL, PLASTIC, CORK, LEATHER

Aluminum — Synthetic resin enamel
Aluminum — Porcelain enamel
Steel — Porcelain enamel
Stainless Steel — Polished
Copper — Polished
Polystyrene plastic.

$4 1/4$ x $4 1/4$
$8 1/2$ x $8 1/2$
Some:
$2 1/4$ x $8 1/2$
halves, doubles, 5 x 5, 10, 10 x 10, 20 (met.)

Vinyl plastic — $1/8$ x 9 x 9, 12 x 12 stand. 9, 18 x 18, 24 x 24, 12 x 36, 18 x 36, 36 x 36 custom.
Cork tile — 3 x 8–9 x 9–2, 6, 12 x 12–12 x 24. $1/8$ to $1/2$ th.
Cork brick — $3/8$ x 2 x 12 – $3/4$ x 2 s.f. panel
Cork Ins. for Dec. Walls — 12 x 36 x $1/4$, $1/2$, 1" th.
Leather lam. to alum. $4 1/4$ x $4 1/4$ etc.
Adhesive to smooth, firm backing. Trim shapes.

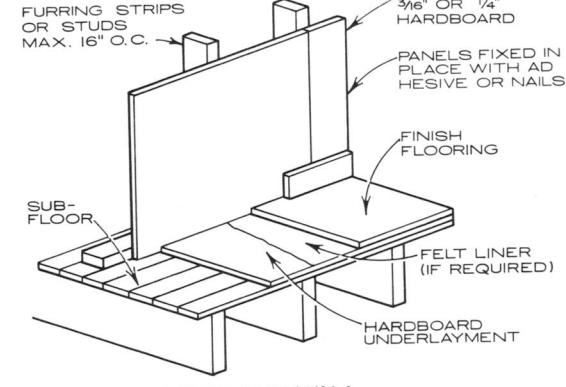

INTERIOR FLOOR AND WALL

EXTERIOR APPLICATION OF HARDBOARD

Foster C. Parriott; James M. Hunter & Associates; Boulder, Colorado

STOCK SIZES - PLASTIC LAMINATES

PRODUCT	THICK-NESS	WIDTH (INCHES)					LENGTH (INCHES)					
		24	30	36	48	60	60	72	84	96	120	144
FORMICA	1/32" *				●					●	●	
MICARTA		●	●	●	●	●		●	●			
FORMICA	1/20"	●	●	●	●	●	●	●		●		●
MICARTA		●	●	●	●			●		●	●	●
FORMICA	1/16"	●	●	●	●	●		●		●		●
MICARTA			●	●	●	●		●		●	●	●

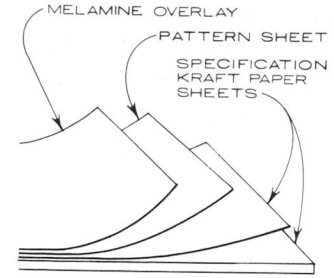

LAMINATED PLASTIC VENEER

(labels: MELAMINE OVERLAY, PATTERN SHEET, SPECIFICATION KRAFT PAPER SHEETS)

INSTALLATION NOTES:

Where panels are to be secured to wall with concealed clips, allow sufficient installation space at top.

Where woodgrains are to be used, indicate direction of grain on drawings.

Show backer sheets on drawings.

Avoid joints within panels, use stock width panel sizes. General purpose $1/16"$ plastic laminate can be bent cold to a 4" radius, providing epoxy thermosetting adhesives are used. Field bending using contact adhesives is not recommended for $1/16"$ plastic laminate; use $1/20"$ postforming plastic laminate instead which can be bent to a radii as small as $3/4"$. Edge banding grade can be bent to a 3" radius using contact adhesives at room temperatures and to a $3/4"$ radius at temperatures between 325° and 360°F.

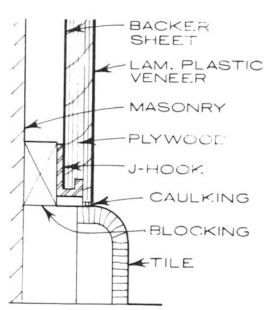
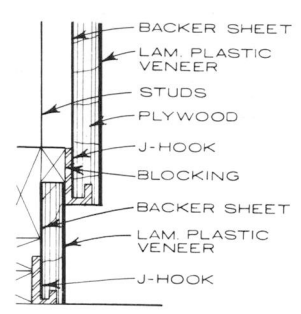
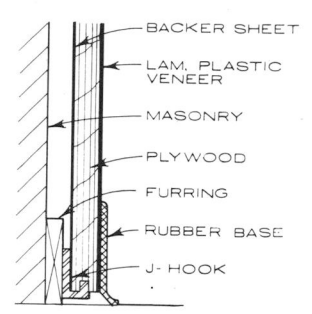

BASEBOARDS

(left labels: BACKER SHEET, LAM. PLASTIC VENEER, MASONRY, PLYWOOD, J-HOOK, CAULKING, BLOCKING, TILE)

(center labels: BACKER SHEET, LAM. PLASTIC VENEER, STUDS, PLYWOOD, J-HOOK, BLOCKING, BACKER SHEET, LAM. PLASTIC VENEER, J-HOOK)

(right labels: BACKER SHEET, LAM. PLASTIC VENEER, MASONRY, PLYWOOD, FURRING, RUBBER BASE, J-HOOK)

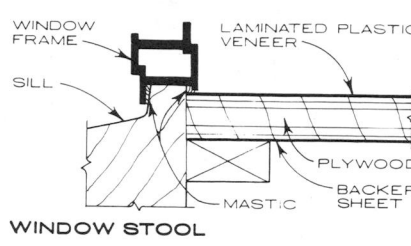

WINDOW STOOL

(labels: WINDOW FRAME, LAMINATED PLASTIC VENEER, SILL, PLYWOOD, MASTIC, BACKER SHEET)

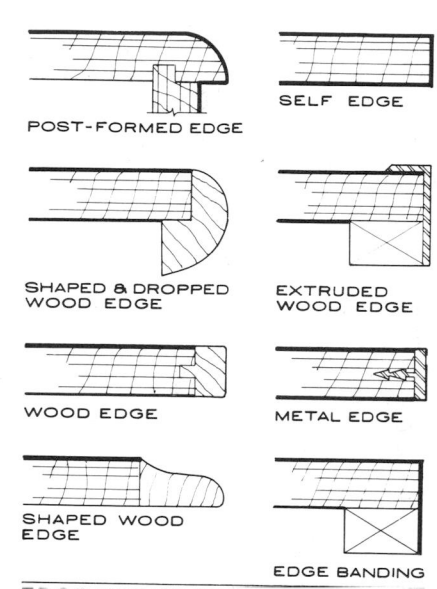

EDGE TREATMENTS

POST-FORMED EDGE | SELF EDGE
SHAPED & DROPPED WOOD EDGE | EXTRUDED WOOD EDGE
WOOD EDGE | METAL EDGE
SHAPED WOOD EDGE | EDGE BANDING

COUNTERS

GENERAL PURPOSE
(labels: 3/4" PLYWOOD, 1/16" LAMINATED PLASTIC VENEER, BACKER SHEET, METAL EDGE MOLDING, METAL COVE MOLDING)

BAR TOP
(labels: FINISHED BLOCK, BACKER SHEET, 3/4" PLYWOOD, SHAPED WOOD BLOCKING, 1/20" POSTFORMED LAM. PLASTIC VENEER)

POSTFORMING
(labels: BACKER SHEET, SHAPED WOOD BLOCKING, 3/4" PLYWOOD, 1/20" POSTFORMED LAM. PLASTIC VENEER)

EDGE BANDING
(labels: BACKER SHEET, 3/4" PLYWOOD, EDGE BLOCK, 1/16" LAM. PLASTIC VENEER)

NOTES:

Plywood with heavily grained or rotary cut top ply should not be used as figure will show thru.

BACKING MATERIALS

Gum, Birch, Poplar, Mahogany, vertical grain fir, finished plywood; hardboard and wood particle board: hollow metal and aluminum.

ADHESIVES

Contact adhesive for field application to plywood, wood particle board, or hard board. Thermosetting adhesives under pressure for shop application.

BACKER SHEETS

$1/16"$ or $1/32"$ unfinished plastic laminate should be used on opposite surface to prevent warpage.

FINISHES

Gloss, satin, furniture finish, velvet surface, low glare, oil rub and textured. Laminated plastic panels with a variety of backing materials are available.

BRAND NAMES

Consoweld, Formica, Melamite, Micarta, Nevamar, Panelyte, Pionite, Textolite and others.

Thorsen & Thorshov Associates, Inc., AIA; Minneapolis, Minnesota

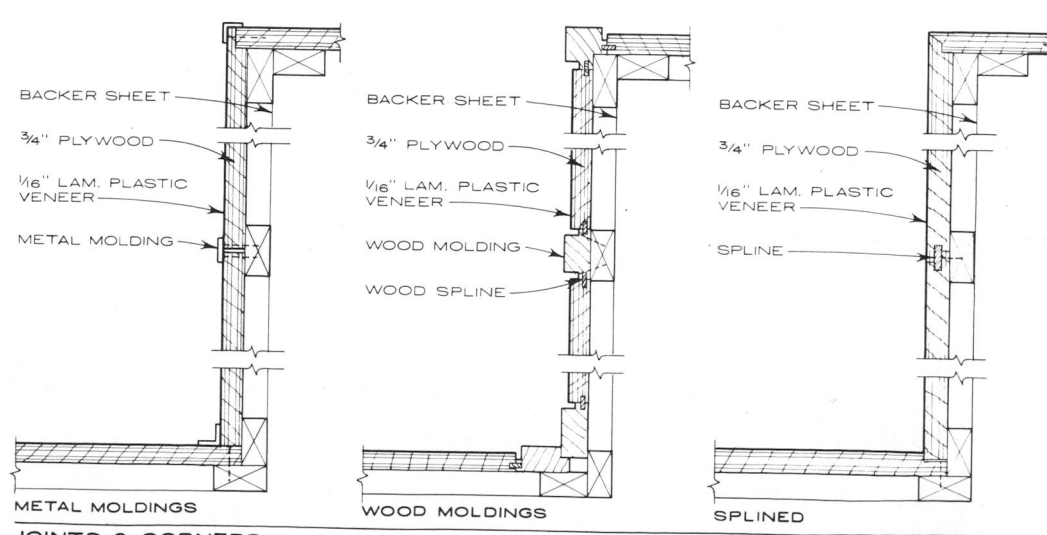

JOINTS & CORNERS

METAL MOLDINGS
(labels: BACKER SHEET, 3/4" PLYWOOD, 1/16" LAM. PLASTIC VENEER, METAL MOLDING)

WOOD MOLDINGS
(labels: BACKER SHEET, 3/4" PLYWOOD, 1/16" LAM. PLASTIC VENEER, WOOD MOLDING, WOOD SPLINE)

SPLINED
(labels: BACKER SHEET, 3/4" PLYWOOD, 1/16" LAM. PLASTIC VENEER, SPLINE)

THERMAL AND MOISTURE PROTECTION

BUILT-UP ROOFING

DECK OR SUBSTRATE	SURFACING	SLOPE IN./FT(1)	BASE SHEET(2)	PLYFELTS	PLYCEMENT LBS./SQ./PLY	SURFACE BITUMEN	U/L(4) RATING
WOOD OR OTHER NAILABLE TYPE DECK (Consult deck or roof manufacturers for recommendations on type of Fasteners)	Gravel—400 lbs./sq.	Up to 1″	Over wood—2 plies tar saturated felt nailed over sheathing paper. Over others—43 lb. asphalt coated organic felt nailed	3—15 lb. tar saturated organic	Coal tar pitch 25 lbs.	Coal tar pitch 75 lbs.	A
	Slag—300 lbs./sq.	Up to 3″	45 lb. asphalt coated asbestos nailed	2—15 lb. asphalt saturated asbestos	Hot asphalt 20—25 lbs (3)	Hot asphalt 60—70 lbs. (3)	A
	Marble chips 400-500 lbs./sq.		43 lb. asphalt coated organic nailed	3—15 lb. asphalt saturated organic			
	Smooth surface (Black)	Up to 6″	45 lb. asphalt coated asbestos	3—15 lb asphalt saturated asbestos	Hot asphalt 25 lbs (3)	Hot asphalt 20 lbs. Roof coating 1—gallon Emulsion 3 gallons (3)	A available on some constructions. Consult U/L or roofing mfr.
			43 lb asphalt coated organic nailed				
	Mineral surface (Various colors)	½″ to 6″	Sheathing paper over wood deck	2—15 lb. felts nailed to deck and mopped to each other.	Hot asphalt 25 lbs.	80 lb. asbestos cap sheet in hot asphalt	A
		3″ to 9″	Sheathing paper over wood deck. (Limited to 15 yr. bond)			55 lb. duplex organic cap sheet in hot asphalt	None
NON-NAILABLE DECK OR INSULATION	Gravel—400 lbs./sq. Slag—300 lbs./sq.	Up to 1″	43 lb. asphalt coated organic in hot asphalt	3—15 lb. tar saturated organic felt	Coal tar pitch 25 lb.	Coal tar pitch 75 lb.	A
	Marble chips 400—500 lbs./sq.	Up to 3″	45 lb. asphalt coated asbestos in hot asphalt	2—15 lb. asphalt saturated asbestos	Hot asphalt 20—25 lbs. (3)	Hot asphalt 60—70 lbs. (3)	A
			43 lb. asphalt coated organic in hot asphalt	3—15 lb. asphalt saturated organic			
	Smooth surface (Black)	Up to 6″	45 lb. asphalt coated asbestos in hot asphalt	3—15 lb. asphalt saturated asbestos	Hot asphalt 20—25 lbs. (3)	Hot asphalt 20 lbs. or Roof coating 1—gallon or Emulsion 3 gallons (3)	A available on some constructions. Consult U/L or roofing mfr.
	Mineral surface (various colors)	½″ to 6″	None	2—15 lb. felts mopped solidly to deck with asphalt	Hot asphalt 20-25 lbs.	80 lb. asbestos cap sheet in hot asphalt	A
		3″ to 9″	None (Limited to 15 yr. bond)			55 lb. duplex organic cap sheet in hot asphalt	None

NOTES:

(1) On notes over 1″ per foot back-nailing of all felts is usually required for all constructions.

(2) Except in nailed construction the coated base sheet is always applied in hot steep grade asphalt. Use 35 lbs. per square over most insulations.

(3) Type of asphalt to be used varies according to slope. Consult a manufacturers specification.

(4) Underwriters Laboratories Rated systems must be applied with materials bearing the Underwriters Laboratories label showing it as "Listed for Built-Up Roof Coverings," and must be applied strictly in accordance with Underwriters Laboratories application procedure. Not all standard specifications as shown here will meet the requirements. If Underwriters Laboratories Rating is required consult Underwriters Laboratories or roofing manufacturer before writing specifications.

SCHEDULE OF FELT OVERLAP (INCHES)

ORGANIC BASE SHEET	4
ASBESTOS BASE SHEET	2
2-PLY FELTS	19
3-PLY FELTS	24⅔
4-PLY FELTS	27½
ASBESTOS MINERAL SURFACE CAP SHEET	2
ORGANIC DUPLEX MINERAL SURFACE CAP SHEET	19

Developed by: Marvin H. Saline, AIA, Architect; Charlotte, North Carolina; from data furnished by: Robert M. Stafford, P. E., Consulting Engineer; Charlotte, North Carolina

ROOFING SHINGLES AND ROOFING TILE

TYPE	DESCRIPTION	SLOPE Minimum in/ft.	WEIGHT lbs/sq.	SIZE	BUTT THICK-NESS	UNDERLAY	FASTENERS	EXPOSURE	COLOR & TEXTURE	U/L RATING
MINERAL FIBER	Individual American Method	3"	540	16" long Widths- 6", 8", 9", 10" or random	1/4"	1 or 2 plies of 15 lb or 30 lb felt	Corrosion Resistant Nails	7"	6 slate-like colors	A (3)
	American Method Strip	3"	325	14" x 30"	5/32"			6"	Various Colors Textured	A (3)
	Dutch Lap	5"	265	16" x 16"	5/32"		Corrosion resistant nails and storm anchors	12" x 13"	Various	B (3)
	French or Hexagonal	5"	245	16" x 16"	5/32"			13" x 13"	Various	B (3)
	Ranch Design	3"	255	12" x 24"	5/32"			20 x 9"	Various	B (3)
ALUMINUM	Shake-Style Porcelain Enamelled	4"	39 to 58	10" x 48" 12" x 36"	3/4" 1"	2 plies 30 lb felt	aluminum screw shank nails	10" 12"	Various colors shake textured or striated	None
	4-Way Interlocking	4"	40	8" x 7 1/4" 8" x 14 1/2"	3/8"	15 lb or 30 lb felt	Aluminum Nails	Inter-locking	Various colors smooth and embossed	None
SLATE	Commercial Grade—Smooth	4"	700 to 800	Random width 6" to 14" lengths from 10" to 26" in 2" increments	3/16" to 1/4"	1-ply 30 lb felt	Large head copper or galv. slaters' nails and slaters' cement	3 1/2" to 11 1/2" (2)	Various colors or variegated shades	None
	Quarry Run Rough (1)		825 to 3600 (2)		3/16" to 1"					
PORCELAIN Enamel on Iron	Individual American Method	3"	225	10" x 10"	About 1"	1 ply 30 lb felt plus 18" felt strips between tile	Special sealing nails supplied with tile	10"	Many colors and various glosses	None
WOOD Red Cedar Most types and sizes available in Cypress, Redwood, White Cedar	No. 1 Handsplit and Resawn	4"	200 to 450	Lengths 18" to 32" widths random	1/2" to 1 1/4"	Spaced sheathing 30 lb felt interlayment with shakes	Corrosion resistant nails	Maximums 7 1/2" for 18" 10" for 24" 13" for 32"	Natural or various stains various textures	None (5)
	No. 1 Tapersplit		260	Length 24" widths random	1/2" to 5/8"					
	No. 1 Straight-split (Barn)		200 to 260	Lengths 18" to 24" widths random	3/8"					
CLAY TILE (4)	Shingle — Flat	6"	800 to 1600	Lengths 12",15", 24" Widths 5",7",8"	3/8" to 1"	30 lb or 45 lb felt	Copper Nails	5" to 11"	Blues, Greys, Greens, and Reds Smooth or Scored	None
	Interlocking— Flat English	4"	800	8" x 13 1/4"				10"		
	Interlocking Closed		800	8 3/4" x 11"	3/4" and 7/8"			8"		
	French Corrugated	4 1/2"	1000 to 1600	9" x 16"	3/8"			13"		
	Spanish Rounded		850	9 1/4" x 13 1/4"	1/2"			10 1/4"		
	Barrel—Mission Curved		1350	Lengths 14", 16", 18" Widths 6" to 8"	1/2"			11", 13", 15"		
	Roman		1400	Length 13"	1"			10"		
	Greek		1450	Length 13"	1"			10"		
CEMENT TILE	Bermuda	2 1/2"	1050	15 3/4" x 8 3/4"	2"	30 lb felt and 90 lb mineral surfaced roll roofing	Set in bed of cement mortar	13 1/2" x 9"	Natural, White and many pastel colors	None
	Flat Shingle		900	15" x 8 1/4"	1"			13 1/2" x 8 1/2"		
	Spanish			15" x 8 3/4"	—			13" x 8"		

NOTES:

(1) Special quarry selection of sizes, thicknesses, and colors for random application is available.

(2) Exposures and weights are calculated for tile laid with 3" double headlap. Variation from this will increase or decrease total weight. To determine exposure for 3" double headlap deduct 3" from shingle length and divide result by 2.

(3) Underwriters Laboratories Rating applies only for slopes 4" per foot and over. Asbestos felt or coated felt must be used as underlayment.

(4) Many other size and shapes available in certain geographic areas. Consult local manufacturers or agents.

(5) Underwriters Laboratories Rating Class C is available.

Developed by: Marvin H. Saline, AIA, Architect; Charlotte, North Carolina; from data furnished by: Robert M. Stafford, P. E., Consulting Engineer; Charlotte, North Carolina

ASPHALT SHINGLES AND ROLL ROOFING

TYPE	DESCRIPTION	SLOPE in/ft Min. Max.	WEIGHT lb./Square	SIZE	UNDERLAY	FASTENERS	EXPOSURE	COLOR & TEXTURE	U/L RATING
ASPHALT ORGANIC FELT	2 - Tab Strip Self-Sealing	3" 12" (1)	300	12" x 36"	15 lb. Asphalt Saturated felt	Nails or Staples (Exposed corner of Dutch Lap fastened with copper clip or staple)	5"	Smooth - Various Colors and Blends	C - Wind Resistant
	3 - Tab Standard Strip	4" 12" (1)	235				(2)		C
	3 - Tab Strip Self-Sealing	3" — (1)	235				10"		C - Wind Resistant
	Individual Dutch Lap	4" 12"	165	12" x 36"				Smooth - or textured various colors and blends	C
	Individual American		330				5"		C
	2 and 3 Tab Hexagonal		195	11 1/3" x 36"					
ASPHALT - ASBESTOS FELT	2 - Tab Strip Self-Sealing	3" 12" (1)	325	12" x 36"	15 lb. Asphalt saturated felt	Nails or Staples	5" (2)	Smooth Various Colors	A
ASPHALT - GLASS and ORGANIC FELT	2 - Tab Strip Self-Sealing	3" 12" (1)	325	12" x 36"	15 lb. Asphalt saturated felt	Nails or Staples	5" (2)	Smooth - extra large granules various colors	A - Wind Resistant
ASPHALT ROLL ROOFING	Smooth with Mica, Sand, or Talc Surfacing Both Sides	1" —	45 55 65	36" wide 1" sq. roll		Nails and Cold Application Cement	33" maximum for single ply application	Black	C
	Mineral Surfaced Single Coverage		90					various colors and blends	
	Double Coverage		110	36" wide 1/2 sq. roll			17"		
	Pattern Edge	4" —	105	36" wide 1 sq. roll			16"		

NOTES :

1. These shingles may be used on slopes down to 2" per foot when over 2-ply underlayment applied according to industry recommendations.

2. Strip shingles may be applied with 4" exposure. Increase weight and quantities by 25%.

3. Underwriters Laboratories Ratings shown are limited to specific application procedures. Consult Underwriters Laboratories or manufacturer for details. All materials used in Underwriters Laboratories Rated constructions must carry the appropriate Underwriters Laboratories Label.

STANDING SEAM, FLAT SEAM AND BATTEN SEAM ROOFING

TYPE	DESCRIPTION	SLOPE min. in/ft	SIZE	THICKNESS	WEIGHT lbs./Square	UNDERLAY	FASTENER
COPPER	Standing Seam, Pan or Roll Method	2 1/2"	20" x 48" 20" x 96" 24" x 96"	16 oz. 20 oz.	125 155	15 lb. roofing felt and rosin paper	Copper cleats and nails, Sheets are locked at seams or battens. Flat seams soldered
	Batten Seam Pan Method	3"	30" x 120"				
	Flat Seam	1/4"	14" x 20"				
COPPER BEARING STEEL	Standing Seam Roll Method	2"	26 1/2" x 50'	24 ga.	130	None	Cleats and nails
	Pressed Standing Seam	1/4"	25" x 12'	24 ga.	150		
LEAD with 4% to 6% Antimony	Batten and Standing Seam Flat Seam	1/4"	not over 24" x 96"	.0391 (2.5 lb) .0468 (3 lb)	300 360	30 lb. roofing felt and rosin paper	Copper cleats and nails.
TIN (1) (2) (Terne Plate)	Batten Seam	2 1/2"	14", 20", 24" or 28" x 50" (3)	.012 .015	62 76	Rosin paper	Terne cleats and roofing nails with double lock seams
	Standing Seam	2 1/2"					
	Flat Seam	1/4"	14" x 20" 20" x 28"				
TITANIUM - COPPER ZINC ALLOY (4)	Batten or Standing Seam Pan Method	3"	20" x 120"	.027	125	15 lb. roofing felt and rosin paper	T-C-Z cleats and roofing nails with double lock seams
			24" x 120"	.032	150		
STAINLESS STEEL	Continuous weld Standing Seam	1/4"	20" wide up to 60' long	28 ga. 30 ga.	72 58	None	Stainless steel sliding cleats spot-welded to one flange

NOTES:

1. Terne Plate is copper-bearing steel coated both sides with lead-tin alloy (80% lead-20% tin).

2. Terne must be shop-coated or painted one coat underside, and primed and painted two coats on exposed side. Long oil base paint is recommended.

3. Expansion seams must be provided on runs exceeding 30 feet where both ends are free to move or exceeding 15' where ends are securely fastened.

4. T-C-Z alloy will weather to dull grey. It may be painted for color on exposed side.

Developed by: Marvin H. Saline, AIA, Architect; Charlotte, North Carolina; from data furnished by: Robert M. Stafford, P. E., Consulting Engineer; Charlotte, North Carolina

CORRUGATED AND CRIMPED ROOFING

TYPE	DESCRIPTION	SLOPE min. in/ft	WEIGHT lbs./square	SIZE	THICKNESS	EXPOSURE OR LAP	COLOR AND TEXTURE	FASTENER
IRON AND STEEL OR GALVANIZED IRON	2 2/3" Corrugations with 1/2" or 7/8" depth	3"	Uncoated from 548 to 69. Coated from 568 to 90. Add approx. 10% for 3" corrugations	Widths 27 1/2" and 32 3/4" Lengths from 2' to 45'	Gauges from 12 to 29	24" or 32 3/4" wide End lap 6" minimum.	Uncoated galvanized or several colors of coatings	Corrosion-resistant self-tapping screws, bolts, welded studs, power-driven fasteners or nails in wood. All use neoprene washers.
	3" Corrugations with 3/4" depth			Widths 27 1/2" and 33 1/2". Lengths from 2' to 45'		24" or 30" wide. End lap 6" min.		
PROTECTED METAL (steel) (1)	Corrugated Sheet 2.7" corrugations 9/16" deep	(2)	From 244 to 147	Width 33" Lengths to 12'	Gauges from 18 to 24	29 3/4" wide. End lap 6" minimum	Smooth black or several colors	Same as for Corrugated Steel
	Mansard Sheet 6 beads per sheet			Width 30" Lengths to 12'		27" wide. End lap 6" min.		
	V-Beam Sheet 5.4" pitch and 1 5/8" deep 5 vees per sheet		From 278 to 167	Width 30" Lengths to 12'				
ALUMINUM	Corrugated Sheet 2.67" corrugations 7/8" deep	3	41.4	Widths 35" or 48 1/3" Length 3' to 30'	.024"	1 1/2 corrugation side lap. 6" min. end lap.	Plain mill or stucco in natural and various colors of acrylic enamel	Same as for corrugated steel, except use aluminum nails and sheet metal screws
	Curved corrugated sheet same corrugations (5)		55.2	Widths 33 3/4" Length 3' to 16'	.032"			
	V-Beam Sheet 4 7/8" pitch and 1 3/4" deep top and bottom flats 3/4"	2	58.4 72.2 90.3	Width 41 5/8" Length 3' to 30'	.032" .040" .050"	1 Vee Side lap (4)		
	Concealed Clip Panels (Reynolds Metals Co.)	(5)	68.9 86.1 107.7	Width 13.35" Length 3' to 39'	.032" .040" .050"	Width 12" End lap 6" minimum	Stucco only same colors as above	Clips with sheets locked at side laps
CORRUGATED ASBESTOS CEMENT	4.2" Corrugations 1 1/2" deep	3	410	Width 42" Length to 12"	3/8"	1 corrugation side lap 6" min end lap	Smooth natural or various colors of acrylic enamel	Bolts and clips, self-tapping screws, power driven studs, or drive screws over wood
	Curved Sheet Min. radius (length) 5' Min. radius (width) 4'			Width 42" Length 6' to 12'				
CORRUGATED STRUCTURAL GLASS	2 1/2" Corrugations 1" deep	3	6.3 lbs per square foot	Width 47 1/2" Lengths to 12'	3/8"	2 corrugations side lap 6" min end lap	Smooth or pebble finish. Obscure natural (6)	Same as for corrugated asbestos cement except with neoprene washers.
CORRUGATED FIBER GLASS Reinforced Plastic (7) (8)	1 1/4" Corrugations 1/4" Deep	1	Approx. 40	Width 26" Lengths 8', 10', 12'	6 and 8 oz.	1 and 2 Corrugation side lap. 8" min. end lap.	Many colors, translucent, opaque, or transparent smooth or pebble finish also in "diffuser" white	Self-tapping screws, drive screws, nails. All with neoprene washers.
	2 1/2" Corrugations 1/2" deep			Widths 26", 34" 40" Lengths 8', 10" 12'	5, 6, 8, 11 oz.			
	4.2" Corrugations 1 1/16" deep			Width 42" Lengths 8', 9', 10' 11', 12'	8 oz.			
	2.67" Corrugations 7/8" deep			Width 35' Length 8', 10', 12'	6 and 8 oz.			
	5-V Crimp 1/2" deep			Width 26" Lengths 8', 10', 12'	6 and 8 oz.			
	5.3 V Crimp 1" deep			Width 29" Lengths 7'—6", 9', 10' 6"	8 oz.			
CORRUGATED PLASTIC Non-Reinforced Plastic	2.67" Corrugations 9/16" deep	1	Approx. 40	Width 50 1/2" Lengths 8', 10', 12', 16', 20'	5 and 8 oz.	1 Corrugation side lap 8" min end lap	Same as for reinforced Plastic	Same as for reinforced plastic

NOTES:

1. Panels are made of a steel core covered both sides by an asbestos felt applied in hot zinc dipping then asphalt-impregnated. A colored weatherproof coating is then applied.

2. Corrugated and mansard sheets may be used on 4" min. slope with laps unsealed and on 3" min. slope with laps sealed. V-Beam sheets may be used on 3" min. slope with laps unsealed and on 1 1/2" min. slope with laps sealed.

3. Minimum curvature radius 18".

4. Use 9" min. side lap on slopes from 2" to 3". Use 6" min. side lap on slopes above 3".

5. May be used on min. 1/2" slope when only one (1) course used on slope. When more than one course the min. slope is 4".

6. Available in limited tints from some manufactures.

7. Available in General Purpose, Type I, and Five Retardant, Type II, except 5 oz. weight only in Type I.

8. For detail product information and physical properties consult a manufacturer or:

The Fiberglass Reinforced Panel Council
Council of the Plastics Industry, Inc.
250 Park Ave., New York, N.Y. 10017

Developed by: Marvin H. Saline, AIA, Architect; Charlotte, North Carolina; from data furnished by: Robert M. Stafford, P. E., Consulting Engineer; Charlotte, North Carolina

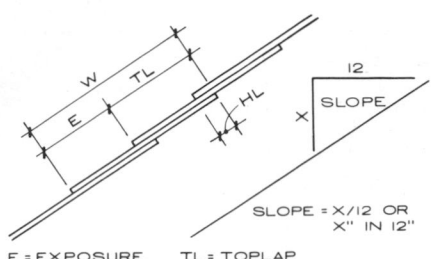

E = EXPOSURE   TL = TOPLAP
HL = HEADLAP   SL = SIDELAP
W = WIDTH FOR STRIP SHINGLES OR
    LENGTH FOR INDIVIDUAL SHINGLES

SLOPE = X/12 OR X" IN 12"

SCHEDULE OF SHINGLE TYPES

DESCRIPTION	DESIGN	WEIGHT	L	W	E	TL	HL	SL
Three tab square butt strip		235 lb.	36"	12"	5"	7"	2"	
Two tab square butt strip		235 lb.* 300 lb.*	36"	12"	5"	7"	2"	
Three tab hexagonal strip		195 lb.	36"	12"	5"	7"	2"	
Two tab hexagonal strip		195 lb.	36"	12"	5"	7"	2"	
American giant individual		330 lb.	12"	16"	5"	11"	6"	
Dutchlap giant individual		165 lb.	16"	12"	10"	2"		3"

*Available in self-sealing type shingle.

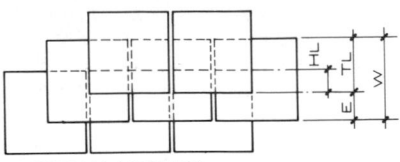

AMERICAN METHOD

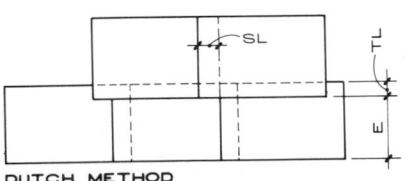

DUTCH METHOD

NOMENCLATURE: ASPHALT & COMPOSITION SHINGLES

SCHEDULE OF UNDERLAYMENT

SLOPE	TYPE OF UNDERLAYMENT
Normal slope: 4 in 12 and up	Single layer of 15 lb. asphalt saturated felt over entire roof
Low slope: 2 in 12 to 4 in 12*	Two layers of 15 lb. asphalt saturated felt over entire roof

*Square butt strip shingles only; requires "Wind-resistant" shingles or cemented tabs.

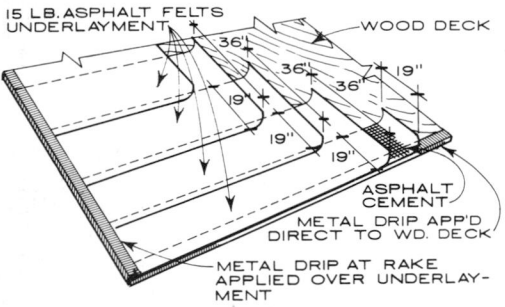

APPLICATION OF UNDERLAYMENT ON LOW SLOPE ROOFS

Use only enough nails to hold underlayment in place until shingles are laid.

NAILING OF SHINGLES RECOMMENDATION

DECK TYPE	NAIL LENGTH
1" Wood sheathing	1 1/4"
3/8" Plywood	7/8"
1/2" Plywood	1"
Reroofing over asphalt shingles	1 3/4"

NAIL TYPES
SMOOTH
ANNULAR THREADED
SCREW THREADED

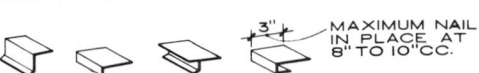

MAXIMUM NAIL IN PLACE AT 8" TO 10" CC.

DRIP EDGE SHAPES
PREFORMED CORROSION-RESISTANT METAL

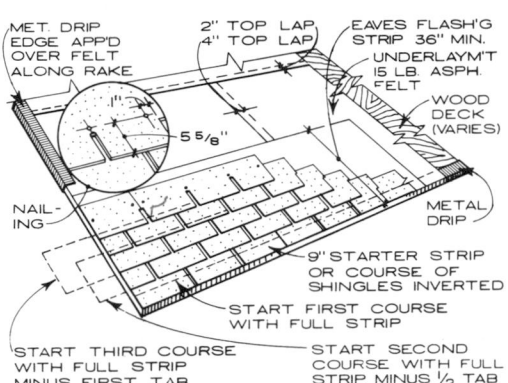

HIP & RIDGE

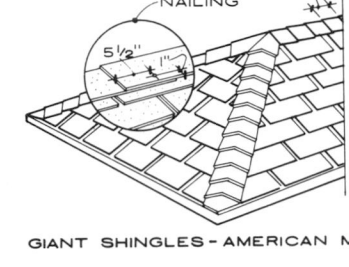

GIANT SHINGLES - AMERICAN METHOD

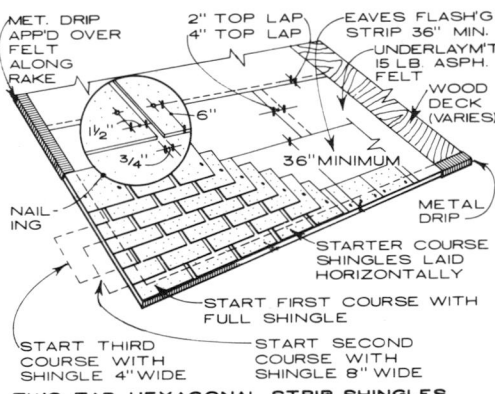

TWO TAB HEXAGONAL STRIP SHINGLES

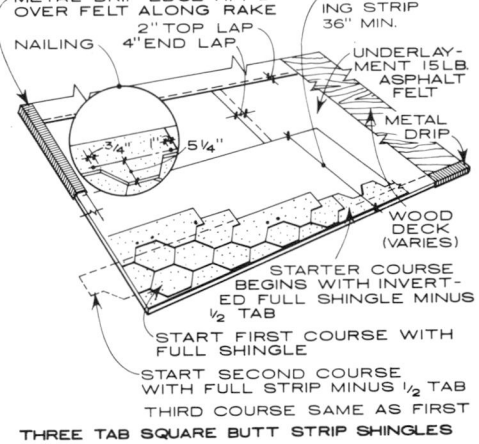

THREE TAB SQUARE BUTT STRIP SHINGLES

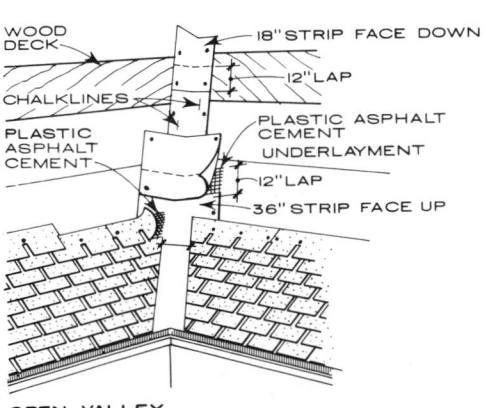

OPEN VALLEY
*Valley width should be 6" wide at ridge and spread wider at the rate of 1/8"/foot downward to eave. Establish valley width using chalkline from ridge to cove.

APPLICATION DIAGRAMS

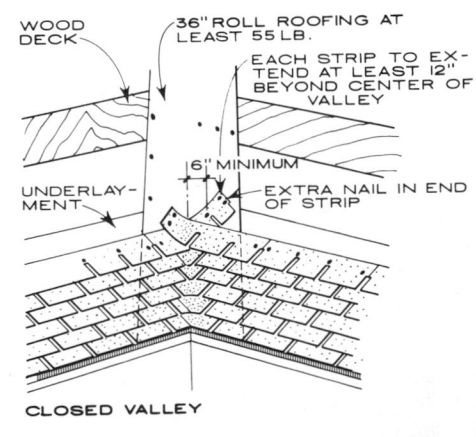

CLOSED VALLEY

Developed by: Holroyd and Gray, Architects; Charlotte, North Carolina; from data furnished by: Robert M. Stafford, P. E.; Consulting Engineer; Charlotte, North Carolina

NOMENCLATURE

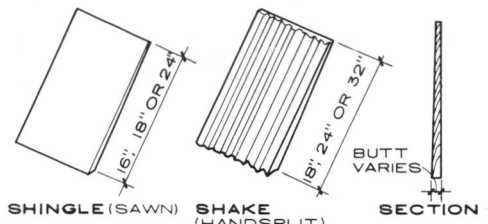

SHINGLE (SAWN)   SHAKE (HANDSPLIT)   SECTION

Species: Shingles and shakes are available in Red cedar, Redwood and Tidewater red cypress.

SCHEDULE OF SHINGLE TYPES

GRADE*	SIZE	EXPOSURE (AT LISTED SLOPES)		
		5 IN 12 AND UP	4 IN 12	3 IN 12
1, 2 & 3	24"	7½"	6¾"	5¾"
1, 2 & 3	18"	5½"	5"	4¼"
1, 2 & 3	16"	5"	4½"	3¾"

* Grade description:

No. 1 = Premium grade: 100% heartwood, 100% clear and 100% edge grain.

No. 2 = Intermediate grade: not less than 10" clear on 16" shingles, 11" clear on 18" shingles and 16" clear on 24" shingles. Flat grain and limited sap wood permitted.

No. 3 = Utility grade: 6" clear on 16" and 18" shingles, 10" clear on 24" shingles. (For economy applications and secondary buildings.)

SCHEDULE OF SHAKE TYPES

TYPE	SIZE LENGTH & THICKNESS	EXPOSURE* 4 IN 12 SLOPE
HANDSPLIT AND RESAWN	18" x ½" to ¾"	7½"
	18" x ¾" to 1¼"	7½"
	24" x ¾" to 1¼"	10"
	24" x ½" to ¾"	10"
	32" x ¾" to 1¼"	13"
TAPERSPLIT	24" x ½" to ⅝"	10"
STRAIGHT-SPLIT (BARN)	18" x ⅜"	7½"
	24" x ⅜"	10"

* Roof slopes less than 4 in 12 not recommended for shakes without special construction. See table of "Underlayment and sheathing."

SHINGLES & SHAKES USED FOR ROOFING

EXPOSURE FOR SHINGLES & SHAKES USED FOR SIDING

SHINGLE LENGTH	EXPOSURE OF SHINGLES	
	SGL. COURSE	DBL. COURSE
16"	6" TO 7½"	8" TO 12"
18"	6" TO 8½"	9" TO 14"
24"	8" TO 11½"	12" TO 16"

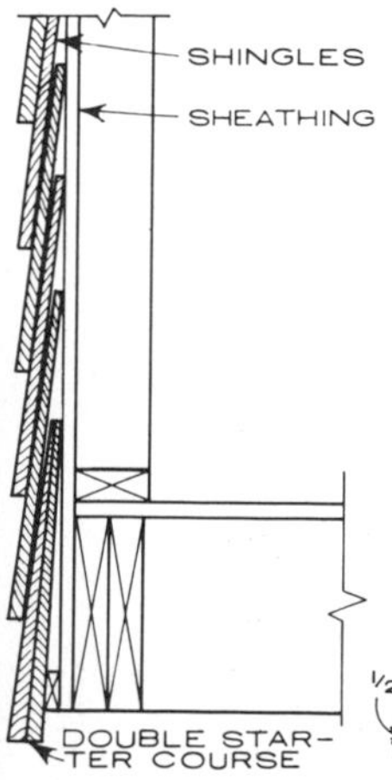

SHINGLES
SHEATHING
SHINGLE BACKER OR ASPHALT IMPREGNATED BACKER BOARD
½"
DOUBLE STARTER COURSE
TRIPLE STARTER COURSE

SINGLE COURSING APPLICATION   DOUBLE COURSING APPLICATION

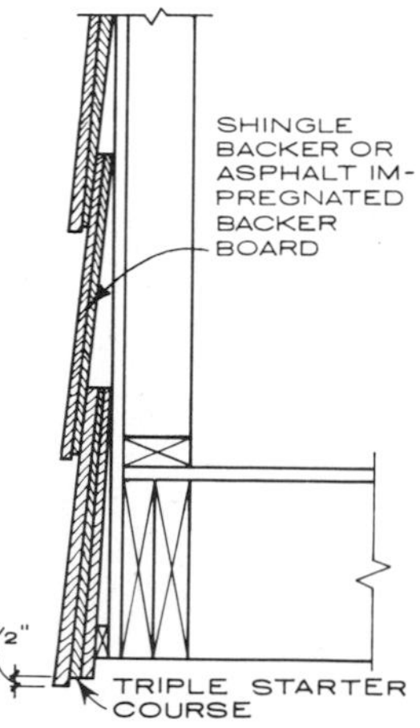

WOOD SHINGLES & SHAKES FOR SIDING

UNDERLAYMENT AND SHEATHING

ROOFING TYPE	SHEATHING	UNDERLAYMENT	NORMAL SLOPE		LOW SLOPE	
WOOD SHINGLES	Spaced	No underlayment required	5 in 12 and up	No underlayment required	3 in 12 to 5 in 12(2)	No underlayment required
	Solid (1)	No. 15 asphalt saturated felt.	5 in 12 and up	No underlayment required	3 in 12 to 5 in 12(2)	No underlayment required (3).
WOOD SHAKES	Spaced	No. 30 asphalt saturated felt (interlayment).	4 in 12 and up	Underlayment starter course; interlayment over entire roof.		Shakes not recommended on slopes less than 4 in 12 with spaced sheathing.
	Solid (1) (4)	No. 30 asphalt saturated felt (interlayment).	4 in 12 and up	Underlayment starter course; interlayment over entire roof.	3 in 12 to 4 in 12 (2) (5)	Single layer underlayment over entire roof; interlayment over entire roof.

(1) May be desirable for added insulation and to minimize air infiltration.

(2) Requires reduced weather exposure.

(3) May be desirable for protection of sheathing.

(4) Recommended for areas subject to winddriven snow.

(5) Shake exposure as follows: 10" for 32" shake, 7½" for 24" shake and 5½" for 18" shake.

Eaves flashing: Recommended in severe climates or where design temperature is 0 degrees or colder.

A. Normal slope: Apply an additional course of underlayment. Extend from eave up to a point 12" inside interior wall line.

B. Low slope: Apply an additional course of underlayment cemented down. Extend to a point 24" inside interior wall line.

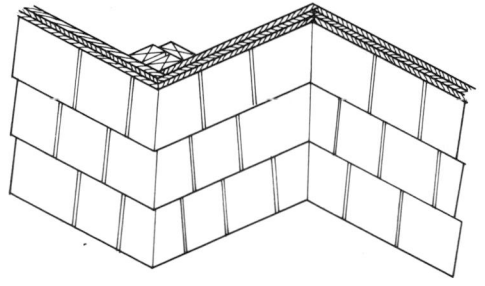

18" WIDE, 30 LB. INTERLAYMENT OVER TOP PORTION OF EACH COURSE OF SHAKES
1½" MINIMUM OFFSET
RAFTERS
EXPOSURE
EXPOSURE X 2
¼" MIN.
1 TO 1½"
DOUBLE STARTER COURSE
36" WIDE 30 LB FELT STARTER STRIP
SPACED SHEATHING, 1" x 4" OR 1" x 6", SPACING EQUAL TO SHAKE EXPOSURE

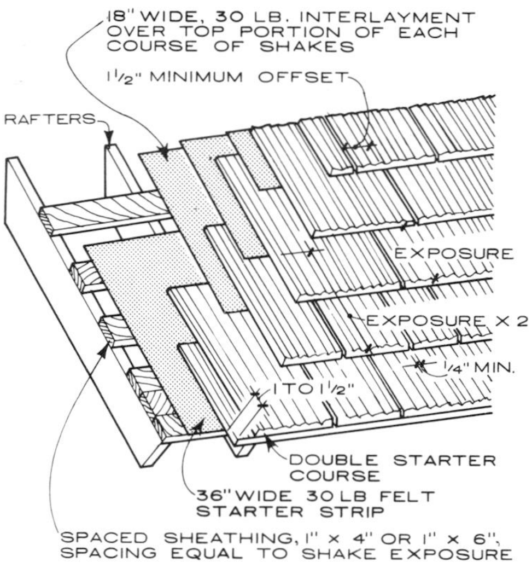

INSTALLATION OF SHAKES OVER SPACED SHEATHING (4 IN 12 MIN.)

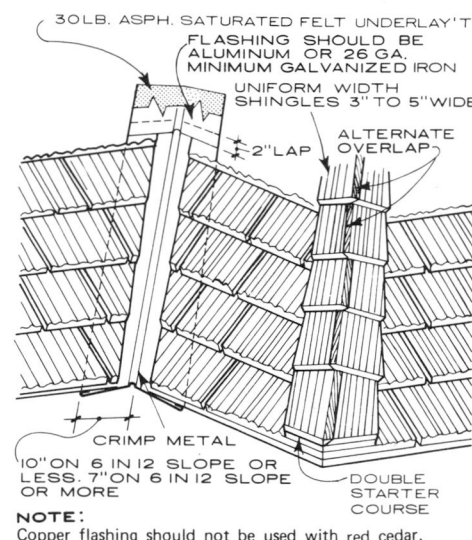

30 LB. ASPH. SATURATED FELT UNDERLAY'T
FLASHING SHOULD BE ALUMINUM OR 26 GA. MINIMUM GALVANIZED IRON
UNIFORM WIDTH SHINGLES 3" TO 5" WIDE
ALTERNATE OVERLAP
2" LAP
CRIMP METAL
10" ON 6 IN 12 SLOPE OR LESS. 7" ON 6 IN 12 SLOPE OR MORE
DOUBLE STARTER COURSE

NOTE: Copper flashing should not be used with red cedar.

VALLEY HIP & RIDGE APPLICATION OF SHAKES & SHINGLES

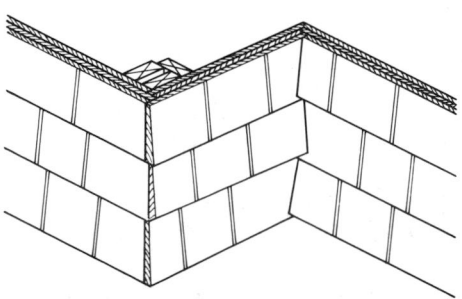

MITERED OUTSIDE & INSIDE CORNERS (RECOMMENDED)

WOVEN OUTSIDE & INSIDE CORNERS (MORE ECONOMICAL)

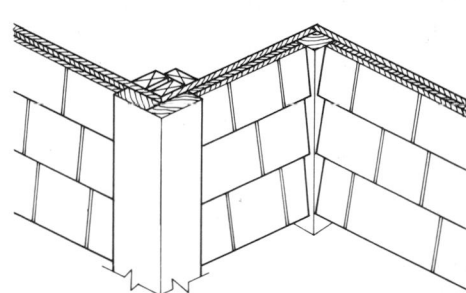

CORNER BOARDS OUTSIDE & INSIDE CORNERS

NAILING
THICKNESS AND NAILS

16" long	5 butts = 2"	3d
18" long	5 butts = 2¼"	3d
24" long	4 butts = 2"	4d
25" to 27"	1 butt = ½"	5 or 6d
25" to 27"	1 butt = ⅝" to 1¼"	7 or 8d

SHEATHING NOTES

Sheathing may be strip-type, solid 1" x 6" diagonal type, plywood, fibreboard or gypsum. Horizontal wood nailing strips, 1" x 2", should be used over fibreboard and gypsum sheathing. Space strips equal to shingle exposure.

Developed by: Holroyd and Gray, Architects; Charlotte, North Carolina; from data furnished by: Robert M. Stafford, P. E.; Consulting Engineer; Charlotte, North Carolina

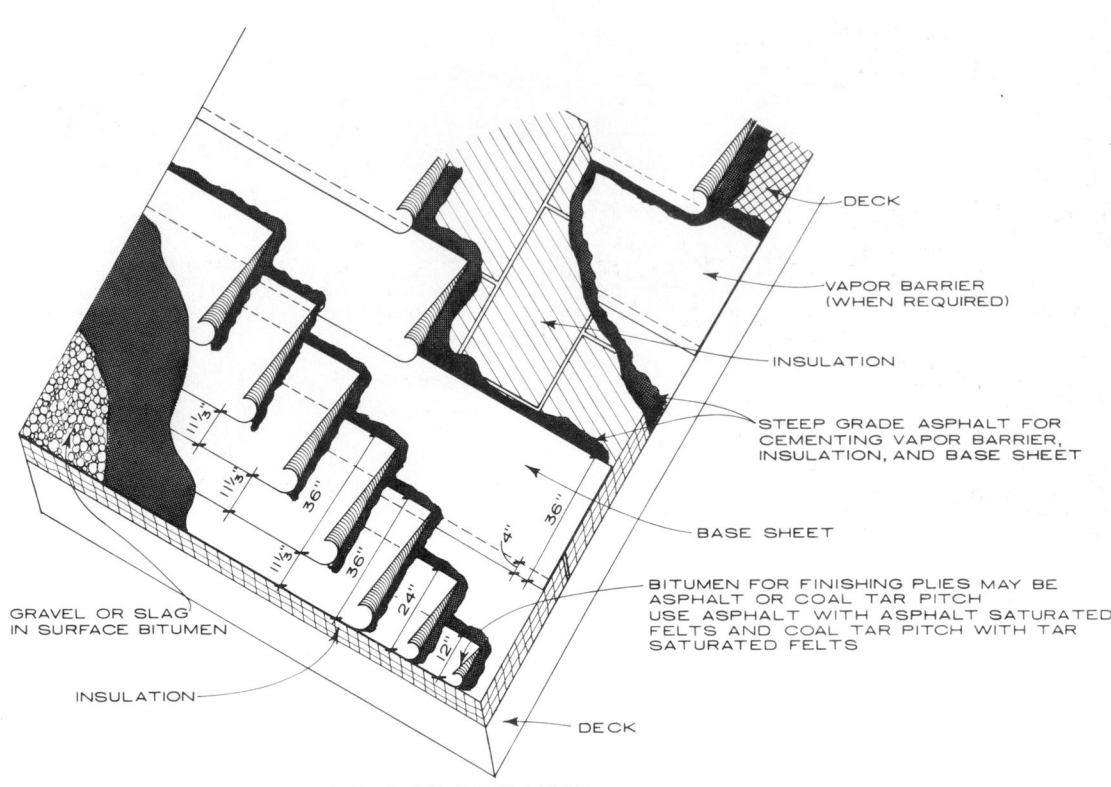

DECK

VAPOR BARRIER
(WHEN REQUIRED)

INSULATION

STEEP GRADE ASPHALT FOR
CEMENTING VAPOR BARRIER,
INSULATION, AND BASE SHEET

BASE SHEET

BITUMEN FOR FINISHING PLIES MAY BE
ASPHALT OR COAL TAR PITCH
USE ASPHALT WITH ASPHALT SATURATED
FELTS AND COAL TAR PITCH WITH TAR
SATURATED FELTS

GRAVEL OR SLAG
IN SURFACE BITUMEN

INSULATION

DECK

PATTERN FOR NAILING BASE
SHEET OR VAPOR BARRIER OVER
NAILABLE DECK

20 YEAR TYPE BUILT-UP ROOF OVER INSULATION

NOTES:

For smooth surface roofs omit gravel or slag. On slopes over 1″ per
foot back-nailing of all felts along top edge is usually required.

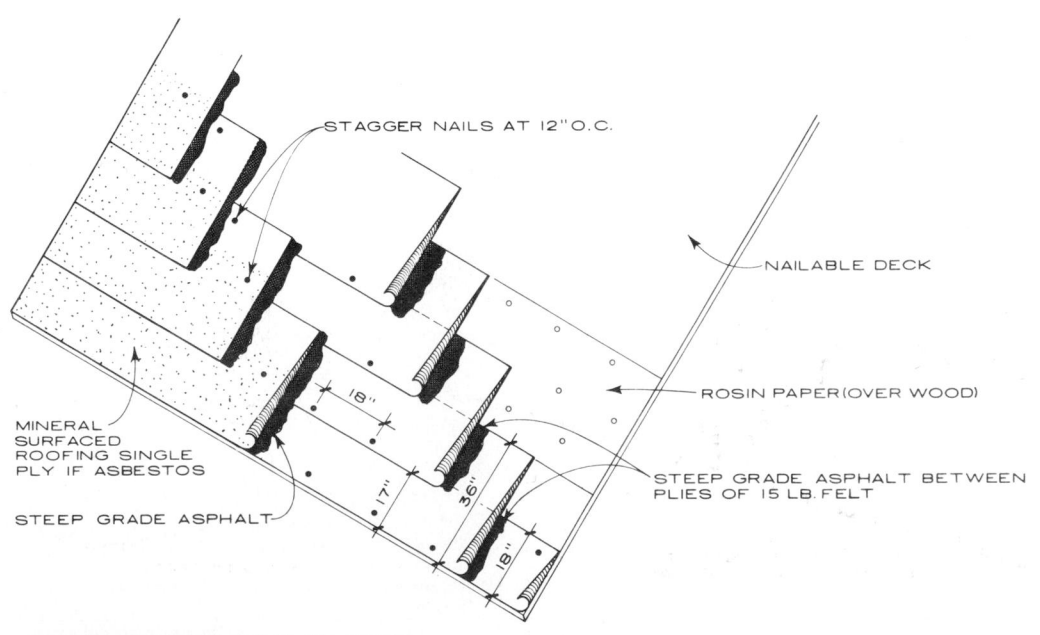

STAGGER NAILS AT 12″ O.C.

NAILABLE DECK

ROSIN PAPER (OVER WOOD)

MINERAL
SURFACED
ROOFING SINGLE
PLY IF ASBESTOS

STEEP GRADE ASPHALT

STEEP GRADE ASPHALT BETWEEN
PLIES OF 15 LB. FELT

NOTES:

Over non-nailable deck or insulation omit rosin paper
and cement solidly with asphalt.
Nailing strips must be provided.

Minimum slope for organic felt = 3″ per ft.

Minimum slope for asbestos felt = 1/2″ per ft.

MINERAL SURFACE BUILT-UP ROOF

Developed by: Angelo J. Forlidas, AIA; Charlotte, North Carolina; from data furnished by: Robert M. Stafford, P. E.; Consulting Engineer; Charlotte, North Carolina

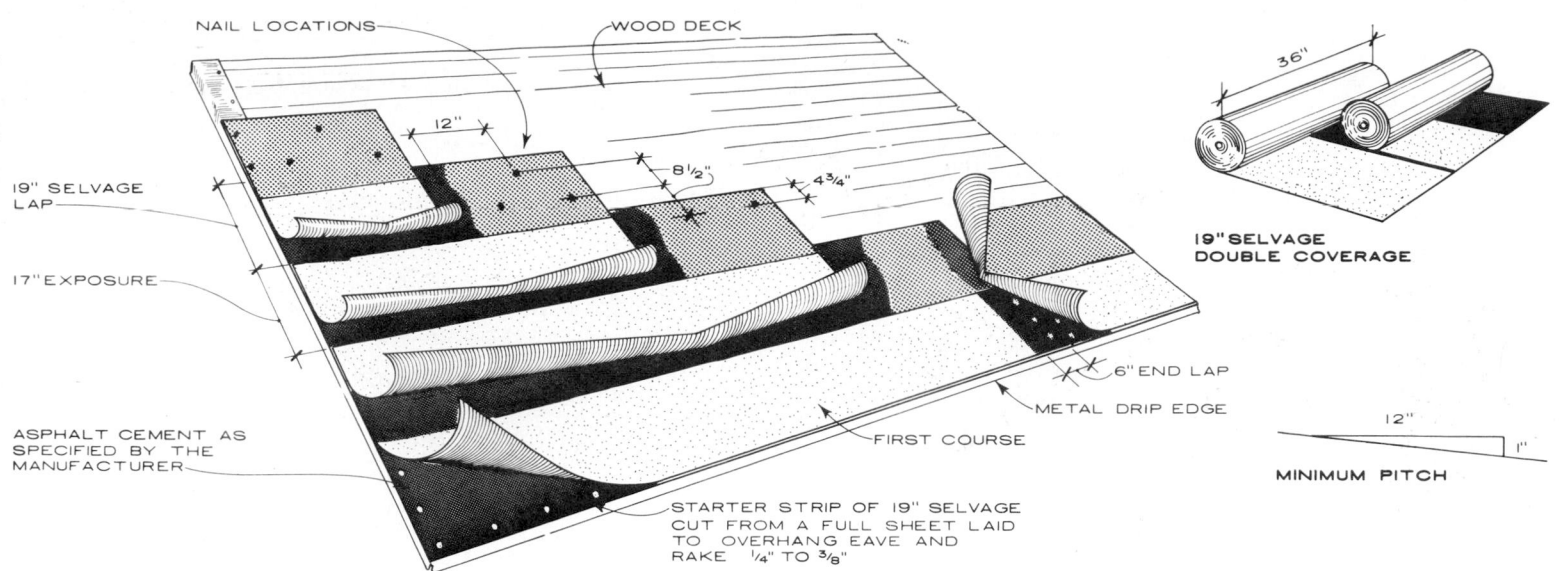

NAIL LOCATIONS

WOOD DECK

12"

8½"

4¾"

19" SELVAGE
LAP

17" EXPOSURE

ASPHALT CEMENT AS
SPECIFIED BY THE
MANUFACTURER

6" END LAP

METAL DRIP EDGE

FIRST COURSE

STARTER STRIP OF 19" SELVAGE
CUT FROM A FULL SHEET LAID
TO OVERHANG EAVE AND
RAKE ¼" TO ⅜"

36"

19" SELVAGE
DOUBLE COVERAGE

12"
1"

MINIMUM PITCH

ROLL ROOFING – DOUBLE COVERAGE – CEMENTED PARALLEL TO THE EAVES

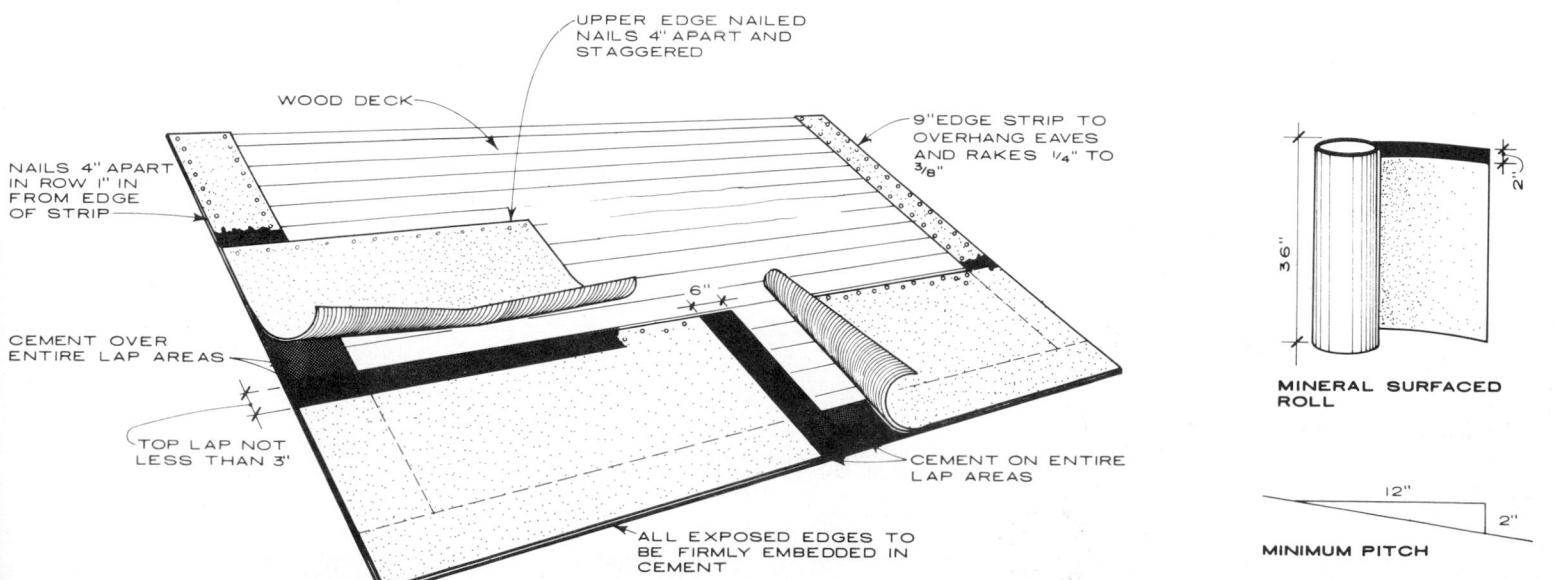

UPPER EDGE NAILED
NAILS 4" APART AND
STAGGERED

WOOD DECK

9" EDGE STRIP TO
OVERHANG EAVES
AND RAKES ¼" TO
⅜"

NAILS 4" APART
IN ROW 1" IN
FROM EDGE
OF STRIP

6"

CEMENT OVER
ENTIRE LAP AREAS

TOP LAP NOT
LESS THAN 3"

CEMENT ON ENTIRE
LAP AREAS

ALL EXPOSED EDGES TO
BE FIRMLY EMBEDDED IN
CEMENT

36"

2"

MINERAL SURFACED
ROLL

12"
2"

MINIMUM PITCH

ROLL ROOFING – CONCEALED NAILING

Developed by: Angelo J. Forlidas, AIA; Charlotte, North Carolina; from data furnished by: Robert M. Stafford, P. E.; Consulting Engineer; Charlotte, North Carolina

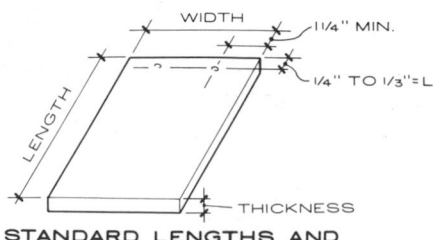

STANDARD LENGTHS AND WIDTHS OF SLATES

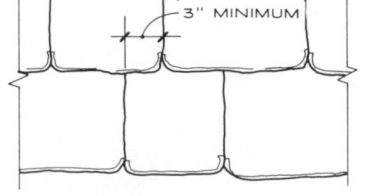

PROPER JOINTING

PITCHED ROOF

LENGTH	WIDTH
10″ *	6″, 7″, 8″
12″ *	6″, 7″, 8″, 9″, 10″
14″ *	7″, 8″, 9″, 10″, 12″
16″	8″, 9″, 10″, 12″
18″	9″, 10″, 11″, 12″
20″	10″, 11″, 12″, 14″
22″	11″, 12″, 14″
24″	12″, 14″

The above slates are split in these thicknesses: $3/16$″, $1/4$″, $3/8$″, $1/2$″, $3/4$″, 1″, $1 1/4$″, $1 1/2$″, $1 3/4$″, and 2″.

* $1/2$″ and over not often used in these sizes.

Random widths are usually used.

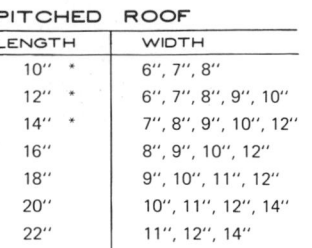

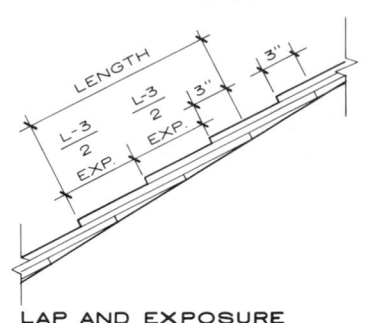

LAP AND EXPOSURE

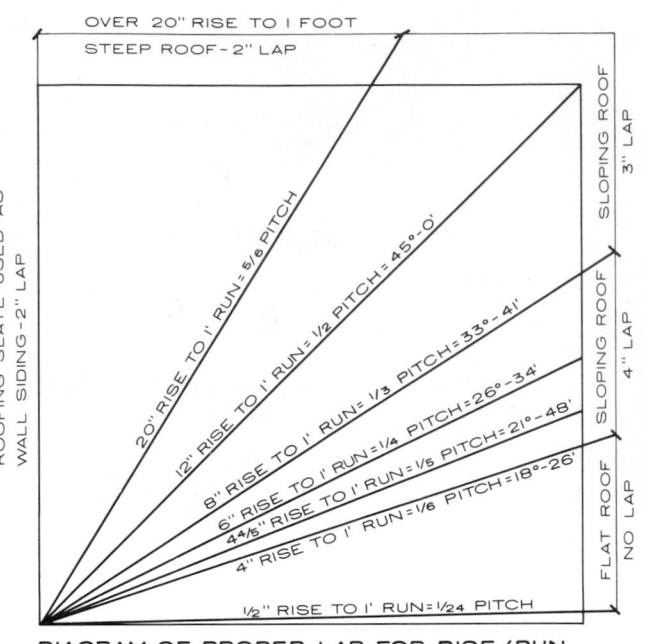

DIAGRAM OF PROPER LAP FOR RISE / RUN

FLAT ROOF

LENGTH	WIDTH
6″	6″, 8″, 9″
10″	6″, 7″, 8″
12″	6″, 7″, 8″

$1/4$″ to $3/8$″—Promenade or heavy service.

$3/16$″—Ordinary and light service.
$3/4$″ to $1 1/4$″—Special terraces, walks, etc.
May be used and set in cement.

GENERAL NOTES:

Commercial Standard is the Quarry run of $3/16$″ thickness and includes tolerable variations above and below $3/16$″.

"Full $3/16$ slate" or "$3/16$" or "not less than $3/16$" indicates hand picked selection with minimum variation. On other sizes reasonable plus tolerances only are permissible, thus a $1/2$″ slate must be full $1/2$″ or slightly thicker.

"Textural" is a rough textured slate roof with uneven butts and a variation in thickness and size; generally not applied to slate over $3/8$″ thick.

"Graduated" is a textural roof of large size slates, and more variation in thickness, size and color.

A square of Roofing Slate means a sufficient number of slates of any size to cover 100 sq. ft. with 3″ lap.

For flat roofs a square would cover more than 100 sq. ft.

Standard Nomenclature for slate color: black, blue black, mottled gray, purple, green, mottled purple and green, purple variegated, red. The above should be preceded by the word "Unfading" or "Weathering."

Other colors and combinations are termed specials.

Proper Jointing: pitched roofs.
3″ minimum vertical overlap.
Horizontal overlap varies with pitch; see diagram.

Felt:
With Commercial Standard Slate use 15# saturated felt.
With textural roofs use 30# felt.
With Graduated roofs use 30# for $3/4$″ slate and 45#, 55#, or 65# prepared roll roofing for heavier slate.

Nail Fastening:
Refer to Section 5:01 for Slating nails.
Each slate punched with 2 nail holes.
Use nails 1″ longer than thickness of slate.

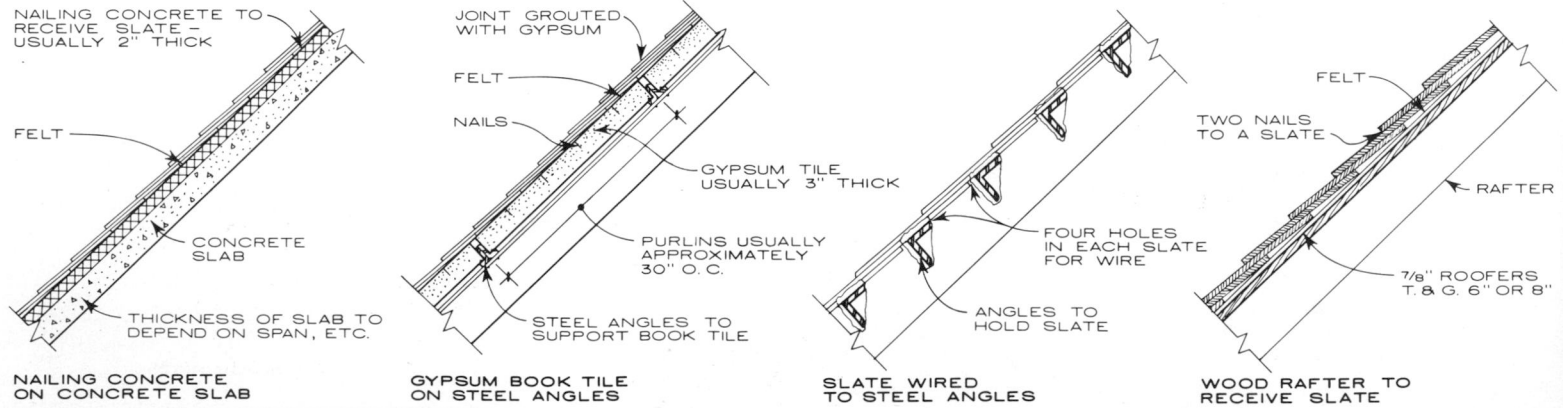

TYPES OF ROOFS TO RECEIVE SLATE
SCALE: $3/4$″ = 1′-0″

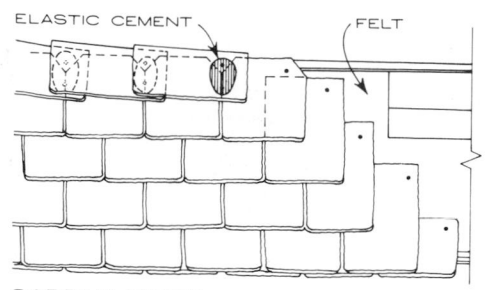

SADDLE RIDGE

ELASTIC CEMENT
FELT

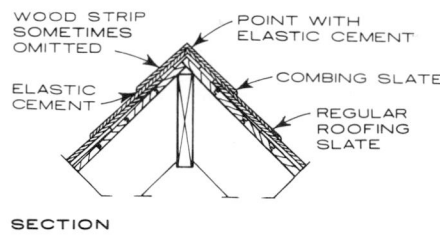

WOOD STRIP SOMETIMES OMITTED
POINT WITH ELASTIC CEMENT
ELASTIC CEMENT
COMBING SLATE
REGULAR ROOFING SLATE

SECTION

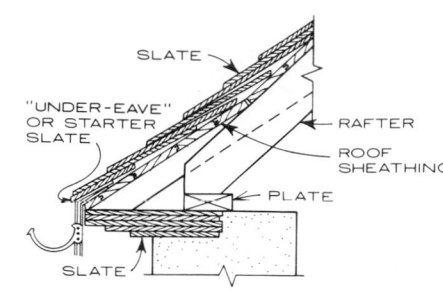

SLATE
"UNDER-EAVE" OR STARTER SLATE
RAFTER
ROOF SHEATHING
PLATE
SLATE

EAVE

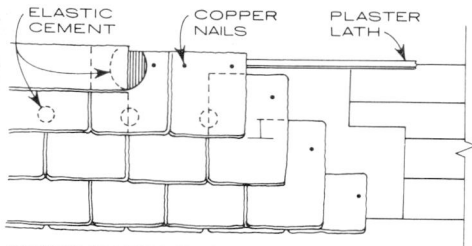

ELASTIC CEMENT
COPPER NAILS
PLASTER LATH

STRIP SADDLE RIDGE

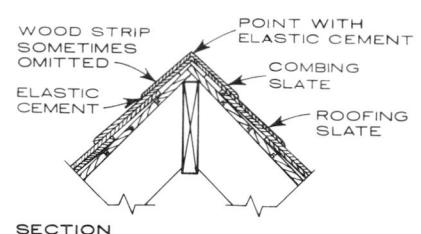

WOOD STRIP SOMETIMES OMITTED
POINT WITH ELASTIC CEMENT
COMBING SLATE
ELASTIC CEMENT
ROOFING SLATE

SECTION

SLATE
SLATE
1/2"

GABLE RAKE

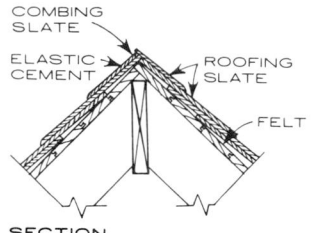

COMBING SLATE
ELASTIC CEMENT
ROOFING SLATE
FELT

SECTION

COMB RIDGE

COMB RIDGE

Combing slate—1 side only.

Project over side of ridge away from prevailing wind.

Coxcomb ridge—when combing slate is laid alternately projecting on either side of ridge.

Combing slate can be laid with grain running horizontally or vertically.

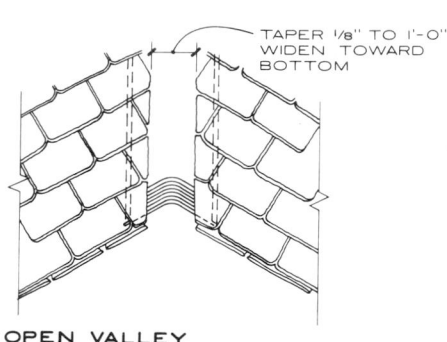

TAPER 1/8" TO 1'-0" WIDEN TOWARD BOTTOM

OPEN VALLEY

FELT
PLASTER LATH
ELASTIC CEMENT
POINT WITH CEMENT
A
A

SADDLE HIP

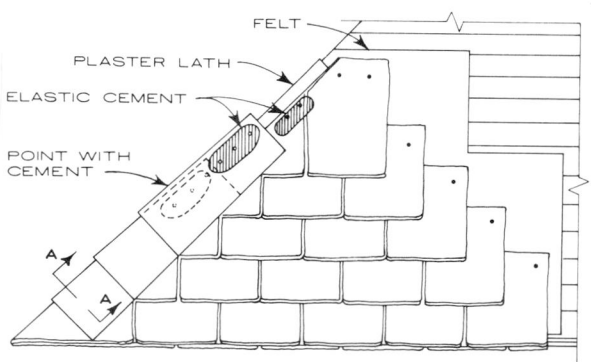

SECTION A-A

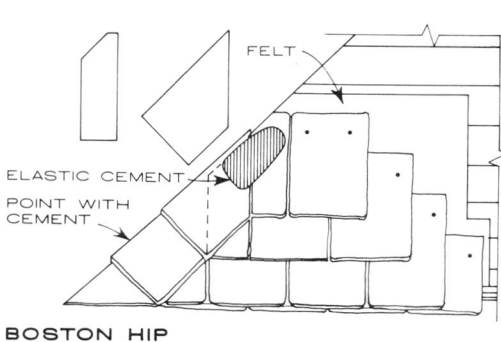

FELT
ELASTIC CEMENT
POINT WITH CEMENT

BOSTON HIP

Plaster lath sometimes omitted. Hip slates are sometimes smaller slates. On less expensive work strip saddle hips are laid with butt joints which do not always join with roof courses.

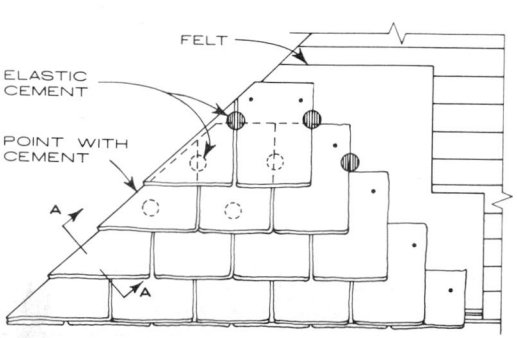

FELT
ELASTIC CEMENT
POINT WITH CEMENT
A
A

MITERED HIP

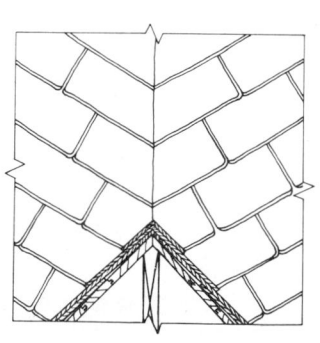

SECTION A-A

FELT
ELASTIC CEMENT
POINT WITH CEMENT

FANTAIL HIP

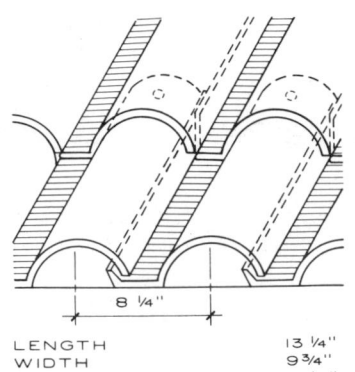

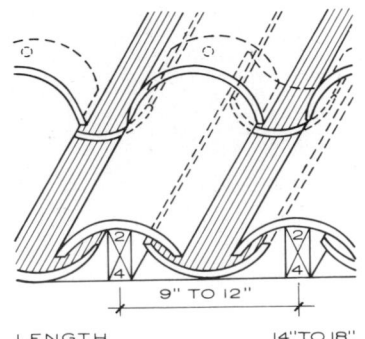

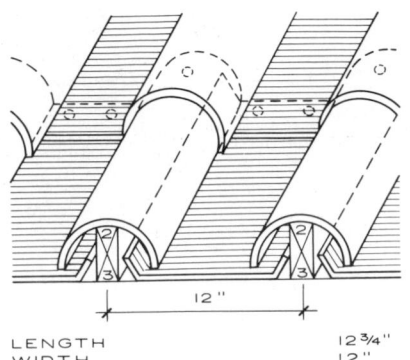

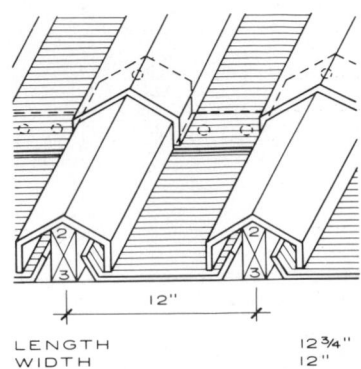

	SPANISH
LENGTH	13 1/4"
WIDTH	9 3/4"
AVERAGE EXPOSURE	10 1/4"
MINIMUM LAP	3"
AVERAGE WEIGHT PER SQ	900 #

SPANISH

	STRAIGHT BARREL MISSION
LENGTH	14" TO 18"
WIDTH	8"
AVERAGE EXPOSURE	11" TO 15"
MINIMUM LAP	3"
AVERAGE WEIGHT PER SQ	1250 #

STRAIGHT BARREL MISSION

	ROMAN
LENGTH	12 3/4"
WIDTH	12"
AVERAGE EXPOSURE	10"
MINIMUM LAP	3"
AVERAGE WEIGHT PER SQ	1100 #

ROMAN

	GREEK
LENGTH	12 3/4"
WIDTH	12"
AVERAGE EXPOSURE	10"
MINIMUM LAP	3"
AVERAGE WEIGHT PER SQ	1250 #

GREEK

NOTES:

1. Minimum slope for above roof tile is 4 1/2" in 12".

2. Sizes vary according to manufacturer.

3. Specials such as ridge, rake, closures, vary with manufacturer.

4. Minimum of 30// felt on all decking.

5. All details shown on this page are of Spanish tile. Details for Mission, Roman, and Greek are similar.

6. Use non-corrosive nails.

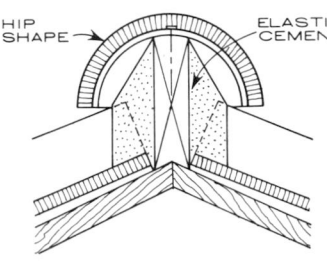

HIP SECTION

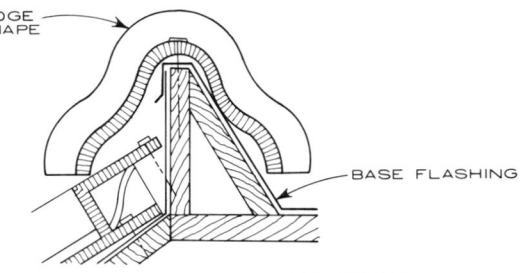

RIDGE AND DECK SECTION

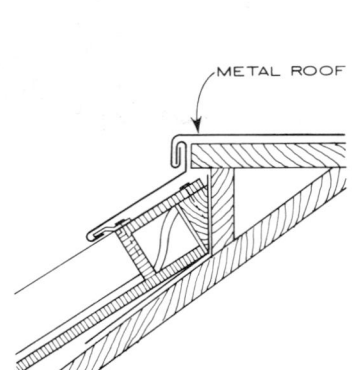

DECK WITH FLASHING OVER TOP OF TILE

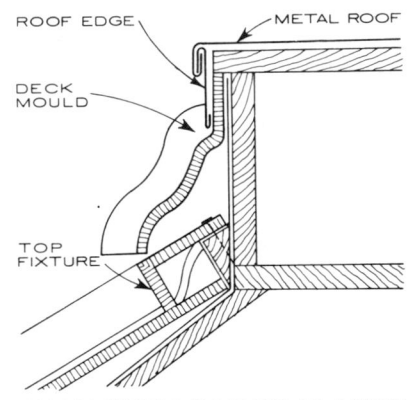

DECK WITH RAISED FLANGE

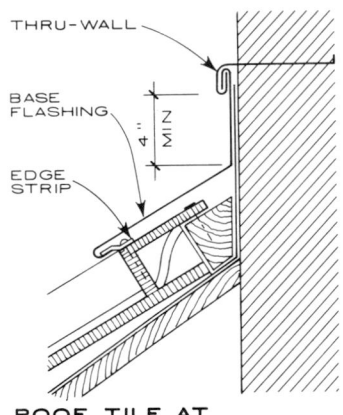

ROOF TILE AT MASONRY WALL

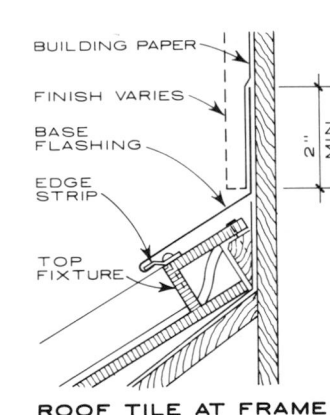

ROOF TILE AT FRAME WALL

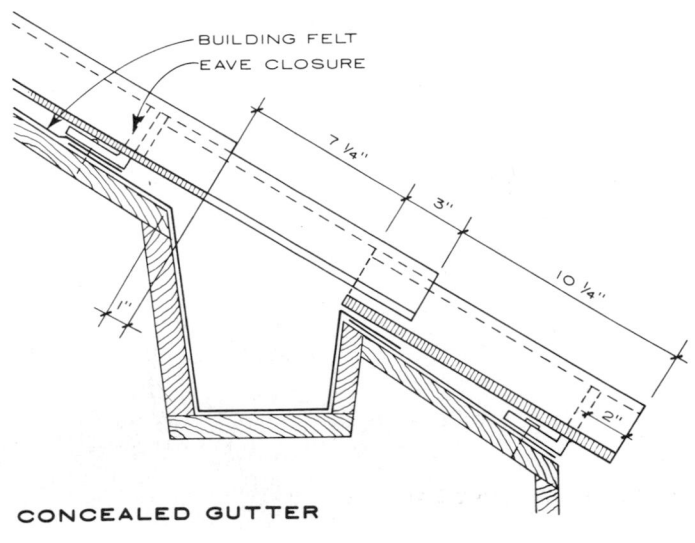

CONCEALED GUTTER

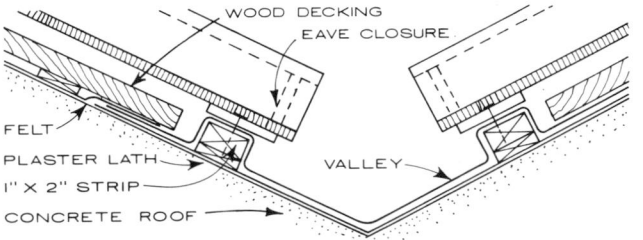

VALLEY ON CONCRETE ROOF

SECTION AT RAKE

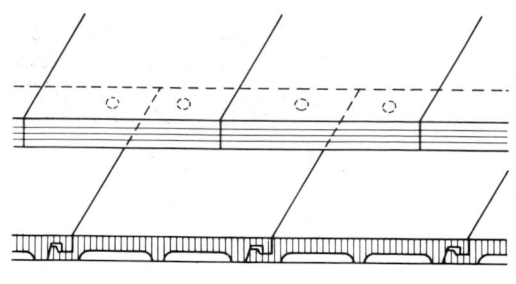

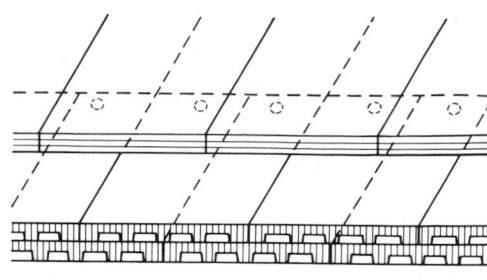

	CLOSED	ENGLISH
LENGTH	11"	13 1/4"
WIDTH	8 3/4"	8 3/4"
AVERAGE EXPOSURE	8"	10 1/8"
MINIMUM LAP	3"	3"
AVERAGE WEIGHT PER SQ	900#	900#

ENGLISH AND CLOSED INTERLOCKING TILE

NOTES:

1. Minimum slope 4 1/2 " in 12".

2. Sizes vary according to manufacturer.

3. Specials such as ridge, rake, closures, vary with manufacturer.

4. Minimum of 30// felt on all decking.

5. Unless otherwise noted all details are of English—Closed Tile; French Tile is similar.

6. Use non-corrosive nails.

LENGTH	16 1/4"
WIDTH	9"
AVERAGE EXPOSURE	13"
MINIMUM LAP	3"
AVERAGE WEIGHT PER SQ	1000#

FRENCH TILE

LENGTH	12" AND 15"
WIDTH	6", 7", AND 9"
AVERAGE EXPOSURE	LENGTH − 2 1/2"
MINIMUM LAP	SEE DETAIL BELOW
AVERAGE WEIGHT PER SQ	1100#

SHINGLE TILE

NOTES:

1. Minimum slope for above roof tile is 6" in 12".

2. Sizes vary according to manufacturer.

3. Specials such as ridge, rake, closures, vary with manufacturer.

4. Minimum of 30// felt on all decking.

5. Use non-corrosive nails.

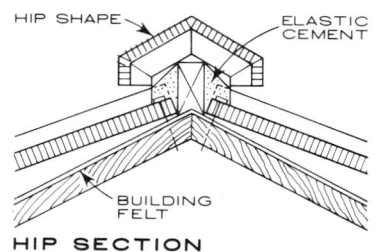

HIP SECTION

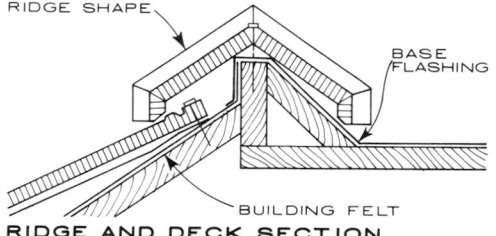

RIDGE AND DECK SECTION

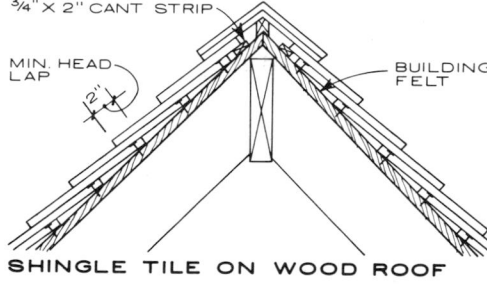

SHINGLE TILE ON WOOD ROOF

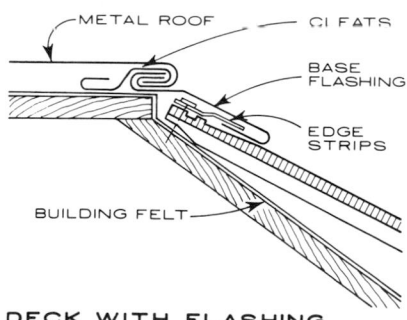

DECK WITH FLASHING OVER TOP OF TILE

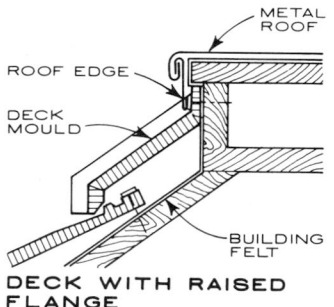

DECK WITH RAISED FLANGE

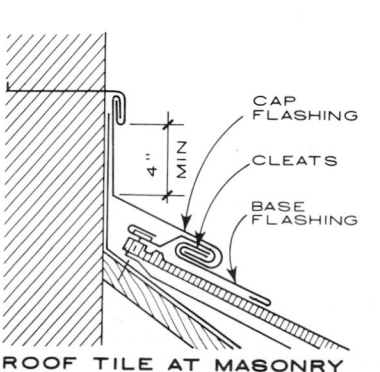

ROOF TILE AT MASONRY WALL

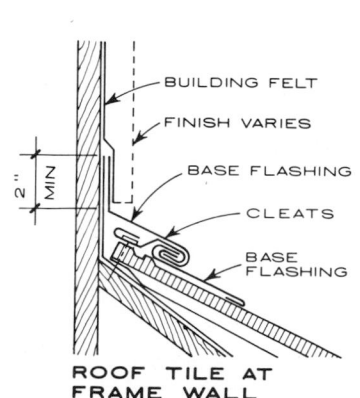

ROOF TILE AT FRAME WALL

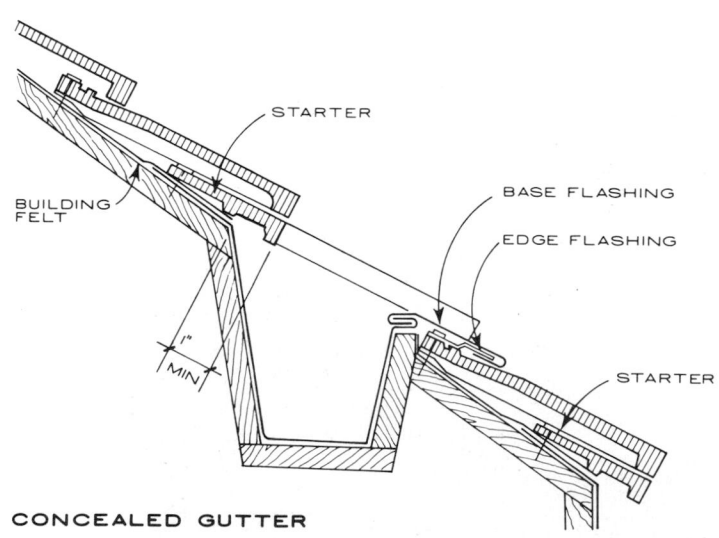

CONCEALED GUTTER

GENERAL NOTES

1. Detail drawings for metal roof types are diagrammatic only. Roofing underlayments have been omitted for clarity. The indication of adjoining construction is included merely to establish its relation to the sheet metal work and is not intended as a recommendation of architectural design. Any details which may suggest an architectural period do not limit the application of sheet metal to that or any other architectural style.

2. Weights of metals and roof slopes indicated on detail drawings are minimum as recommended by the Sheet Metal and Air Conditioning Contractors' National Association and may vary from recommendations of some manufacturers.

3. Metals used must be of a thickness or gauge heavy enough and in correct proportion to the breadth and scale of the work. Provide expansion joints for freedom of movement.

4. Prevent direct contact of metal roofing with dissimilar metals which cause electrolysis.

5. The chart at right indicates comparative weights of sheet metals in relation to their common gauge number or thickness identification. The usual method of designating thicknesses of these metals is as follows:

Aluminum	thousandths of an inch
Copper	ounces per sq. foot
Monel	B & S gauge no.
Stainless Steel	U.S. Standard gauge no.
Galvanized Sheet	U.S. Standard gauge no.

To avoid any misunderstanding when specifying the gauge number of any metal, always indicate the decimal thickness of the gauge required.

COMPARATIVE WEIGHTS PER SQUARE FOOT OF SHEET METALS

B & S GAUGE		ALUM.	COPPER	COPPER	MONEL	U.S. STANDARD GAUGE	STAINLESS STEEL	STAINLESS STEEL	GALVANIZED SHEET	GALVANIZED SHEET
GAUGE NO.	THICK-NESS (IN.)	LBS./FT.2	OZ./FT.2	LBS./FT.2	LBS./FT.2	GAUGE NO.	THICK-NESS (IN.)	LBS./FT.2	THICK-NESS (IN.)	LBS./FT.2
—	1/8 .1250	1.762								
9	.1144	1.605								
—	7/64 .1094	1.542								
10	.1019	1.436								
—	3/32 .0938	1.322								
11	.0907	1.282								
12	.0808	1.141								
—	5/64 .0781	1.101								
13	.0720	1.014								
—	.0645		48	3.00						
14	.0641	0.901		2.97	2.94	14	.0781	3.28	.080	3.28
—	1/16 .0625	0.881		2.90	2.87					
15	.0571	0.803		2.65	2.62	15	.0703	2.95	.071	2.97
—	.0533		40	2.50						
16	.0508	0.718		2.36	2.33	16	.0625	2.63	.064	2.66
—	.0483		36	2.25						
—	3/64 .0469	0.661		2.17	2.15					
17	.0453	0.634		2.10	2.08	17	.0563	2.36	.058	2.41
—	.0431		32	2.00						
18	.0403	0.563		1.87	1.84	18	.0500	2.10	.052	2.16
19	.0359	0.507		1.66	1.64	19	.0438	1.84	.046	1.91
—	.0323		24	1.50						
20	.0320	0.451		1.48	1.47	20	.0375	1.58	.040	1.66
—	1/32 .0313	0.441		1.45	1.44					
21	.0285	0.394		1.32	1.31	21	.0344	1.44	.037	1.53
—	.0270		20	1.25						
22	.0253	0.352		1.17	1.16	22	.0313	1.31	.034	1.41
23	.0226	0.324		1.05	1.04	23	.0281	1.18	.031	1.28
—	.0216		16	1.00						
24	.0201	0.282		0.932	0.923	24	.0250	1.05	.028	1.16
25	.0179	0.253		0.830	0.822	25	.0219	0.919	.025	1.03
26	.0159	0.224		0.737	0.730	26	.0188	0.788	.022	0.906
—	1/64 .0156	0.220		0.725	0.717					
27	.0142	0.200		0.658	0.652	27	.0172	0.722	.020	0.844
—	.0135		10	0.625						
28	.0126	0.177		0.584	0.579	28	.0156	0.656	.019	0.781
29	.0113	0.159		0.524	0.519	29	.0141	0.593	.017	0.719
—	.0108		8	0.500						
30	.0100	0.141		0.464	0.159	30	.0125	0.526	.016	0.656

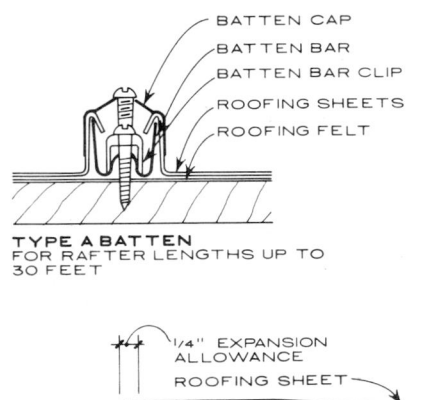

TYPE A BATTEN
FOR RAFTER LENGTHS UP TO 30 FEET

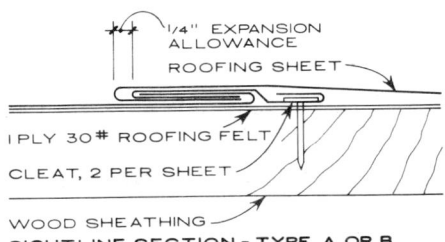

SIGHTLINE SECTION - TYPE A OR B BATTEN

Do not nail through roofing sheets. Use clips, cleats and nails for attachment. All bends and seams should be with a radius at least equal to twice the thickness of the sheet. Cleats should be spaced 10 to 12 inches o.c. The strongest joints are obtained by lock seaming or spot welding. Joints must allow for expansion of metal.

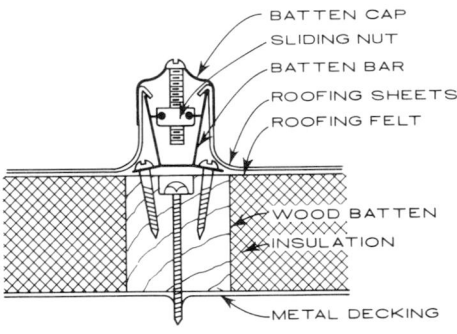

TYPE B BATTEN
FOR RAFTER LENGTHS OVER 30 FEET

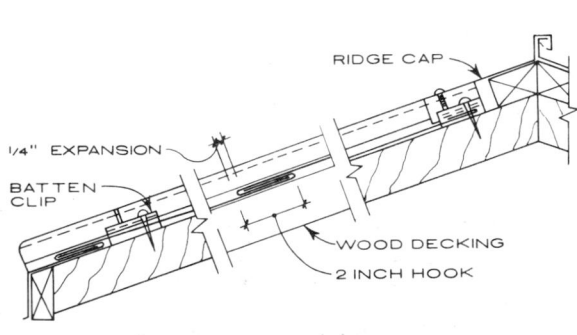

SECTION THRU TYPE A BATTEN

NOTES:

Batten roof system fabricated in Aluminum, Copper, Monel Metal or Stainless Steel is adaptable for pitched roofs (minimum pitch 1 1/2 in. per ft.), barrel roof and spires. Design flexibility of batten permits use on domes and parabolic structures.

Roofing Materials:
  Aluminum:
    Roof sheets; .032 in. thick, .040 in. thick minimum for domes and parabolic shaped roofs.
    Batten bars and caps; .051 in. thick.
    Standard batten spacing:
      34 1/2" for batten system A
      33 3/4" for batten system B
    Horizontal sight lines: Vary from 114 1/2 in. to 156 1/2 in. on centers to suit job conditions.
    Finishes: Variety. Consult manufacturer.

  Stainless Steel or Monel Metal:
    Roof sheets; 24 gauge.
    Battens and caps; 20 gauge, all material type 302
    Standard batten spacing and sheet sizes:
      Same as aluminum.
    Finishes: Variety. Consult manufacturer.

  Copper:
    Roof sheets; 16 ounce.
    Battens and caps; 20 ounce.
    Standard batten spacing:
      28 1/2" for batten system A
      27 3/4" for batten system B
    Standard horizontal sight line on 114 1/2 in. centers.

Sheet sizes and batten centers listed above are standards, but are variable, especially on unusually shaped roofs. Do not exceed 48 in. batten centers.

PREFABRICATED METAL BATTEN DETAILS

Emory E. Hinkel, Jr.; A. G. Odell, Jr. and Associates; Charlotte, North Carolina

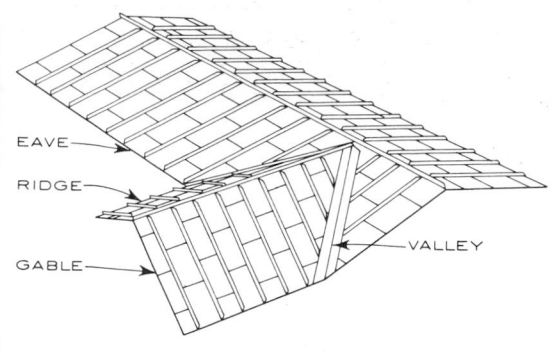

STANDING SEAM METAL ROOF

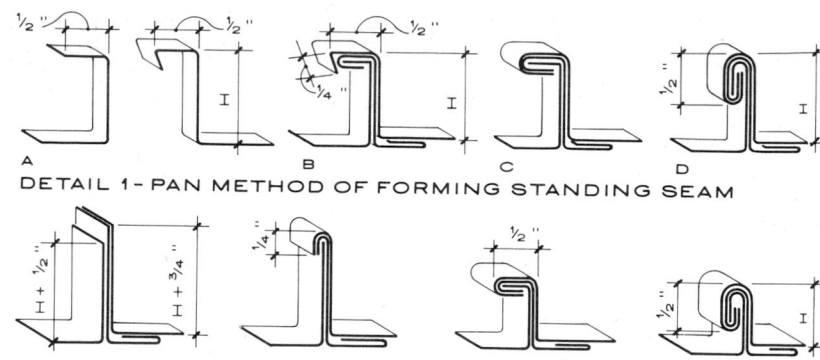

DETAIL 1- PAN METHOD OF FORMING STANDING SEAM

DETAIL 2- FIELD METHOD OF FORMING STANDING SEAM

GAGE AND PAN WIDTHS FOR STANDING SEAM ROOFS

WIDTH OF SHEET (INCHES)	WIDTH OF PAN (INCHES)			RECOMMENDED GAGES		
	SEAM HEIGHT 7/8 IN.	SEAM HEIGHT 1 IN.	SEAM HEIGHT 1 1/4 IN.	GALV. STEEL (GAGE)	COPPER (OUNCES)	PAINTED TERNE (POUNDS)
20	17 1/4	16 3/4	16 1/4	26	16	40
22	19 1/4	18 3/4	18 1/4	26	16	40
24	21 1/4	20 3/4	20 1/4	26	16	40
26	23 1/4	22 3/4	22 1/4	24	20	40
28	25 1/4	24 3/4	24 1/4	24	20	40

RIDGE

ALTERNATE RIDGE

RIDGE

A   B

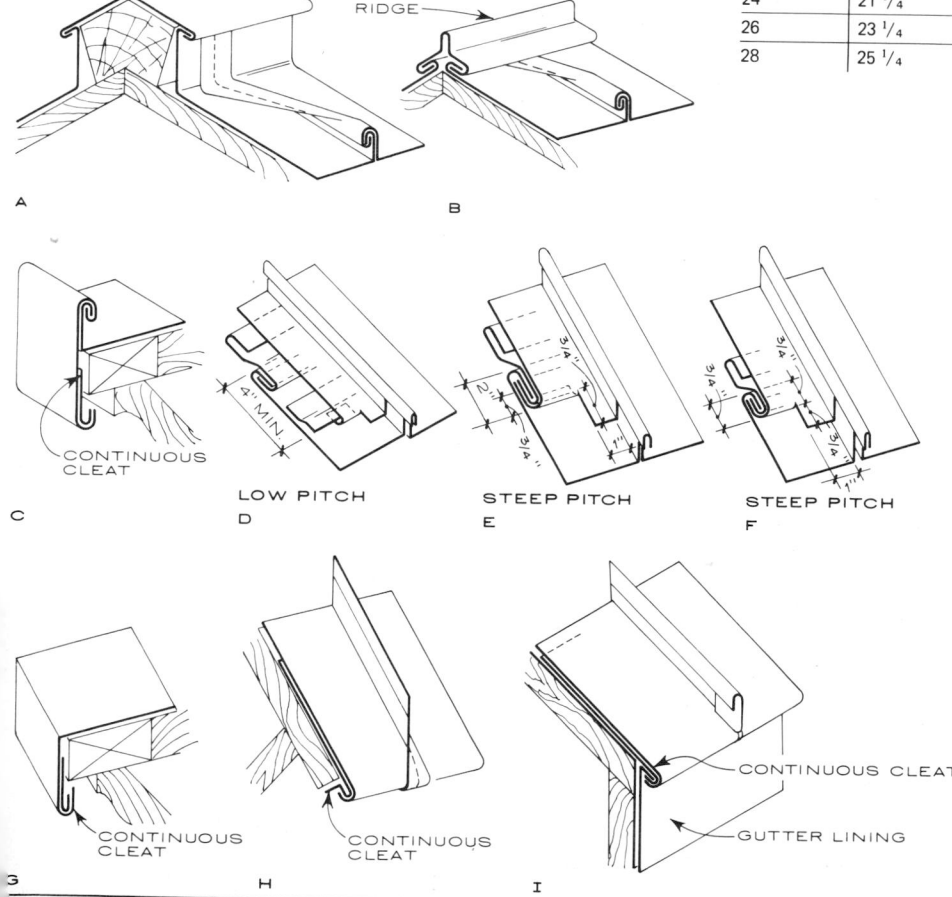

CONTINUOUS CLEAT

LOW PITCH

STEEP PITCH

STEEP PITCH

C   D   E   F

CONTINUOUS CLEAT

CONTINUOUS CLEAT

CONTINUOUS CLEAT

GUTTER LINING

G   H   I

DETAIL 3- STANDING SEAM CONSTRUCTION

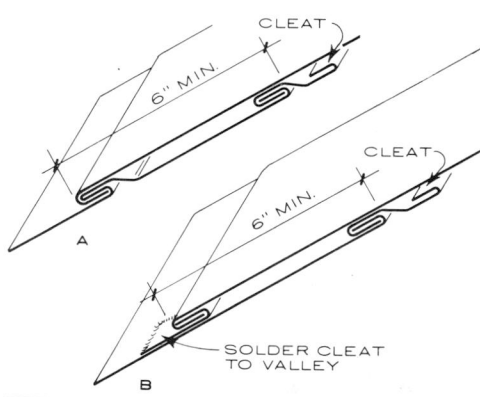

CLEAT

6" MIN.

CLEAT

6" MIN.

A

SOLDER CLEAT TO VALLEY

B

DETAIL 4- ROOFING AT VALLEY

A- BATTEN SEAM AND STANDING SEAM

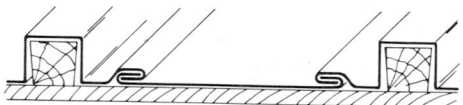

B- BATTEN SEAM AND FLAT SEAM

DETAIL 5- COMBINATION OF ROOF TYPES

NOTES:

Standing seam roofing may be applied on slopes of 3 in. per foot or greater, and when the distance between ridge and eaves does not exceed 30'— 0". If the surface to receive the roofing is other than wood, nailing strips must be provided to receive the cleats. The surface should be thoroughly dry, smooth, and covered with the underlayment as recommended.

The spacing of seams may vary between reasonable limits to suit the architectural style of a given building. The two methods of installing standing seam roofing are the pan and the roll method. In the pan method, the sides of the sheets are formed as shown in A of detail 1. Top and bottom edges of pans are formed as shown in D, E or F of detail 3. Pans are installed with cleats spaced not more than 12 in. on center. Each pan is locked to the one below as shown in D, E or F of detail 3. The adjacent row of pans is next installed and the standing seams completed as in C and D of detail 1.

The roll method consists of a series of long sheets joined together at their ends with double flat lock seams and sent to the job in rolls. The standing seam is field formed as shown in A of detail 2. The roofing is installed in lengths reaching from the eave to the ridge and attached with cleats spaced not more than 12 in. on center. After second length is installed and cleated in place, the standing seam is formed as shown in detail 2.

H of detail 3 shows method of terminating metal roofing at the eave where roofing is locked over a continuous cleat. I of detail 3 shows method of terminating metal roofing at a built-in gutter. Roofing is loose locked to a continuous cleat and the flange on back edge of gutter. Seam terminations must be soldered. A and B of detail 3 show methods of terminating metal roofing at the ridge. C and G of detail 3 illustrate methods of terminating metal roofing at the gable. Methods of joining metal roofing to a valley are shown in A and B of detail 4.

Emory E. Hinkel, Jr.; A. G. Odell, Jr. and Associates; Charlotte, North Carolina

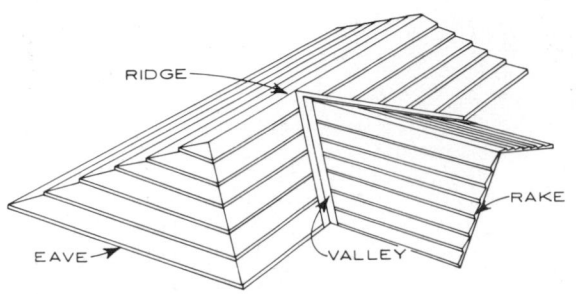

BERMUDA TYPE METAL ROOF

RIDGE • RAKE • EAVE • VALLEY

RECOMMENDED GAGES OR WEIGHTS FOR PAN WIDTHS

WIDTH OF SHEET (INCHES)	WIDTH OF PAN "D" (INCHES)	COPPER (OUNCES)	GALVANIZED STEEL (GAGE)	STAINLESS STEEL (GAGE)	TERNE (POUNDS)
20	16½	16	26	28	40
22	18½	16	26	28	40
24	20½	16	26	26	40
26	22½	20	24	26	40
28	24½	20	24	26	40

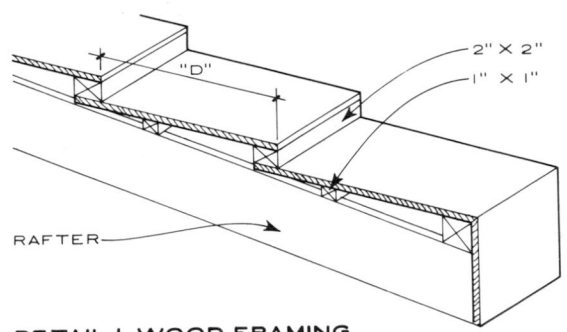

DETAIL 1–WOOD FRAMING

2" X 2" — 1" X 1" — "D" — RAFTER

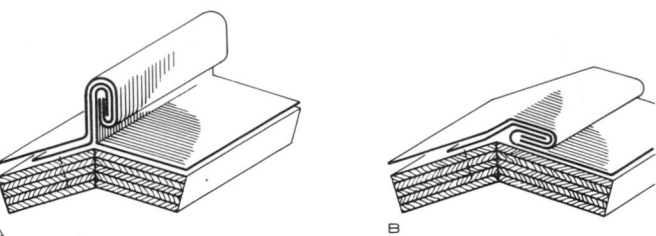

DETAIL 5–SEAM TYPES AT HIP OR RIDGE

A   B

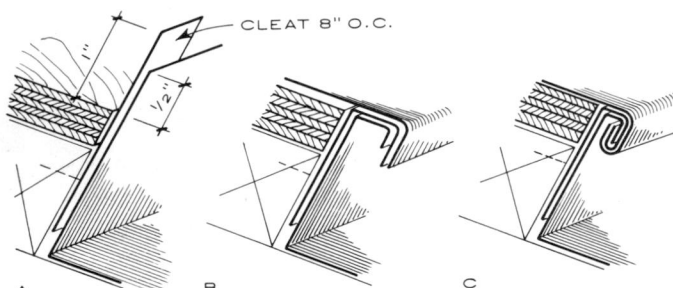

DETAIL 2–CONSTRUCTION AT BATTEN

CLEAT 8" O.C.   A   B   C

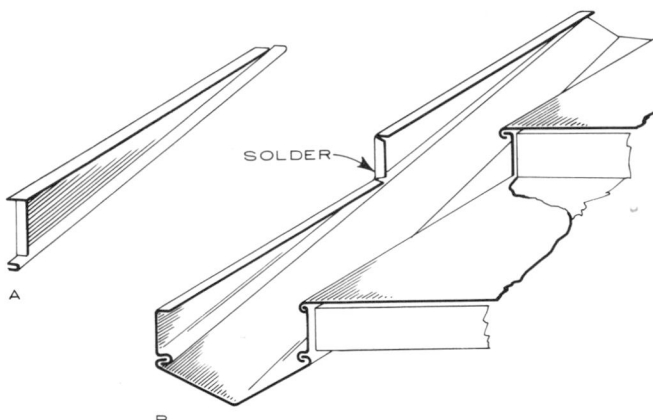

DETAIL 6–CONSTRUCTION AT CLOSURE AND VALLEY

SOLDER   A   B

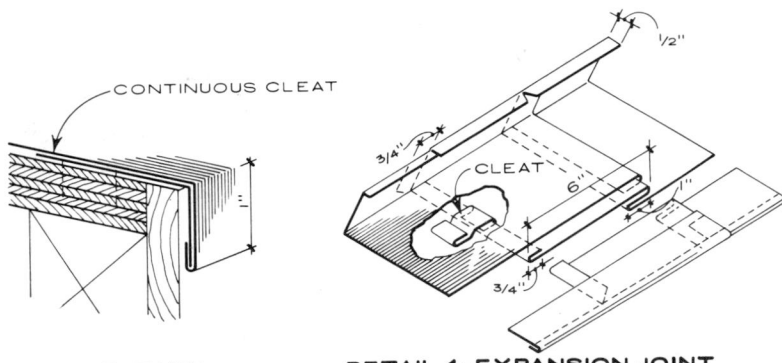

DETAIL 3–EAVE

CONTINUOUS CLEAT

DETAIL 4–EXPANSION JOINT

½"   ¾"   CLEAT   6"   ¾"

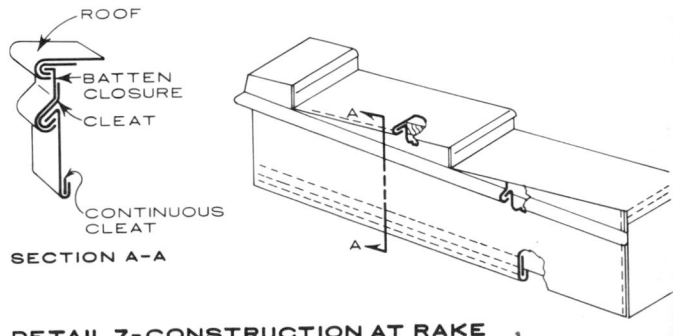

DETAIL 7–CONSTRUCTION AT RAKE

ROOF   BATTEN CLOSURE   CLEAT   CONTINUOUS CLEAT   SECTION A–A

NOTES:

The Bermuda roof may be used for roofs having a slope greater than 2½ in. per foot. Wood framing must be provided as shown in detail 1. Dimension "D" and gage of metal will depend upon the size of sheet used. See chart.

The surface to receive the metal roofing should be thoroughly dry and covered by a saturated roofing felt. A rosin paper should be applied over the felt to avoid bonding between felt and metal.

Bermuda roof is applied beginning at the eave. The first pan is hooked over a continuous cleat as shown in detail

3. The upper portion of the first and each succeeding pan is attached as shown in detail 2. Cleats spaced on 8 in. centers are nailed to batten as in A of detail 2. Joint is developed as shown in B of detail 2 and malleted against batten as shown in C of detail 2. All cross seams are single locked and soldered except at expansion joints. Cross seams should be staggered. Expansion joints should be used at least every 25 ft. and formed as shown in detail 4. Roofing is joined at hip or ridge by use of a standing seam as shown in A of detail 5. Seam may be malleted down as shown in B of detail 5.

Detail 6 shows the method of forming valleys. Valley sections are lapped 8 in. in direction of flow. Individual closures for sides of valley are formed as shown in A of detail 6 and must be soldered as indicated in B of detail 6. A method of terminating the roof at rake is shown in detail 7. The face plate (optional) is held in place by continuous cleats at both top and bottom. The batten closure is formed as a cleat to hold edge of roof pan as shown in section A–A of detail 7.

Emory E. Hinkel, Jr.; A. G. Odell, Jr. and Associates; Charlotte, North Carolina

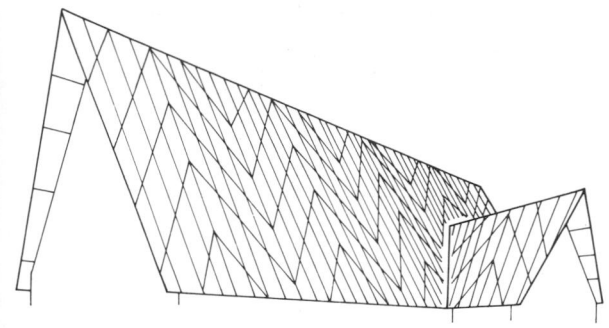

CHEVRON DESIGN METAL ROOF

DETAIL 1- SUGGESTED PATTERNS FOR CHEVRON
ROOFING

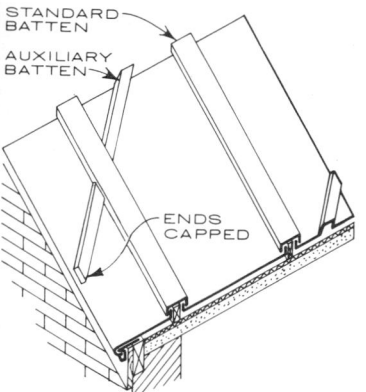

DETAIL 2- GABLE END

DETAIL 3- BATTEN
INTERSECTION

DETAIL 4- VALLEY

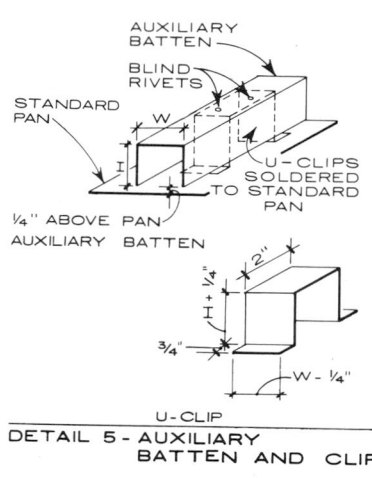

DETAIL 5- AUXILIARY
BATTEN AND CLIP

NOTES:

A chevron design roof or vertical wall is made by using auxiliary battens in conjunction with standard batten seam construction. Auxiliary battens are ornamental and are not a functional part of the roof. The size and shape of the auxiliary batten can vary to suit architectural appearance. The auxiliary battens are formed as channels and are held in place by metal U clips as shown in detail 5.

The U clips should be spaced not more than 2 ft. apart and not less than two clips should be used on any auxiliary batten. The clips are soldered to the metal pans and the auxiliary batten is attached to the clips with metal rivets.

To prevent the entrapment of water in back of the auxiliary battens, the lower edge of the batten should be at least 1/4 in. above the top surface of the standard pan.

Where the end of the auxiliary batten butts the standard batten, a 1/4 in. space between the members should be provided, as shown in detail 3.

At the gable, the ends of the auxiliary battens can be left open or they can be closed by folding over a tab provided on the end of the batten.

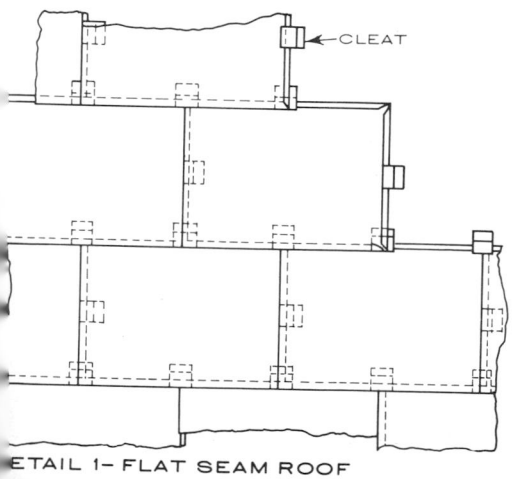

DETAIL 1- FLAT SEAM ROOF

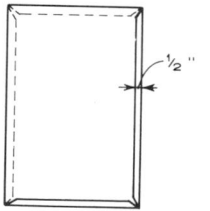

DETAIL 2- ROOFING SHEET

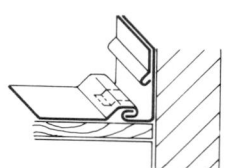

DETAIL 4- JUNCTION AT
PARAPET WALL

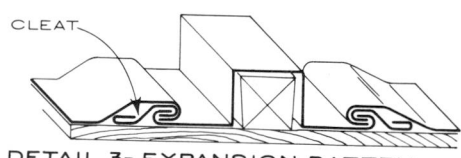

DETAIL 3- EXPANSION BATTEN

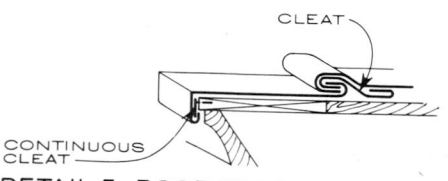

DETAIL 5- ROOF EDGE

NOTES:

The flat seam method of roofing as illustrated is most commonly used on roofs of slight pitch or for the covering of curved surfaces such as towers or domes.

The joints connecting the sheets of roofs having a pitch greater than 1/2 in. per ft. may be sealed with caulking compound or white lead. The joints of roofs having a pitch of less than 1/2 in. per ft. must be malleted and thoroughly sweated full with solder.

Roofs of slight pitch should be divided by expansion battens as shown in detail 3, into sections not exceeding ft. square.

The surface upon which the roof is installed should be thoroughly dry, smooth, and covered with the underlayment as recommended on another page in this series.

The roof is composed of pans formed from metal sheets of a size found on another page in this series.

The metal sheets may be pre-tinned if required, 1 1/2 in. back from all edges and on both sides of the sheet. Pans are formed by notching and folding the sheets as shown in detail 2.

The pans are held in place by cleating as shown. After

pans are in place, all seams are malleted and soldered or sealed.

Detail 4 shows the junction of a roof and a parapet wall. Metal base flashing is cleated to deck on 2 ft. centers and extended up wall. 8 in. pans are locked and soldered to base flashing. Metal counter flashing covers 4 in. of the base flashing. Detail 5 illustrates the installation of flashing at edge of roof. Flashing is formed as shown and attached to the face by a continuous cleat nailed on 1 ft. centers and cleated to the roof deck. Pans are locked and soldered or sealed to the flashing.

Gory E. Hinkel, Jr.; A. G. Odell, Jr. and Associates; Charlotte, North Carolina

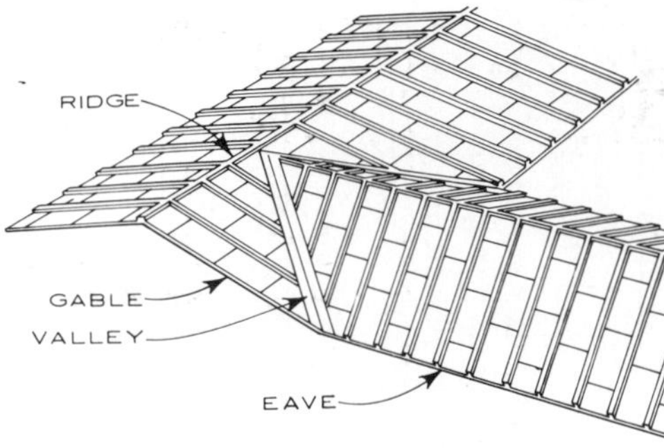

RIDGE

GABLE

VALLEY

EAVE

BATTEN SEAM METAL ROOF

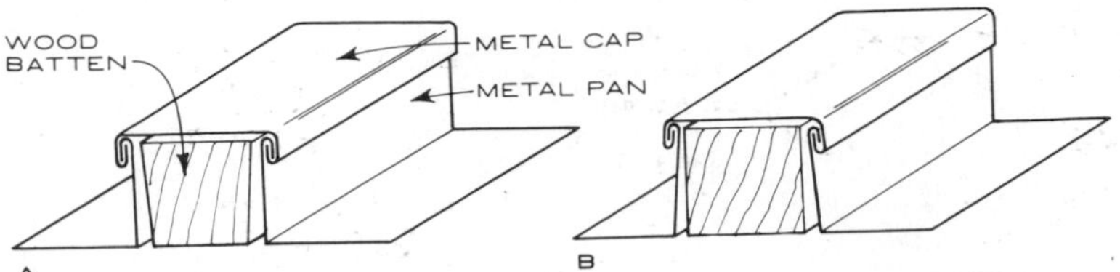

WOOD BATTEN — METAL CAP — METAL PAN

A — B

DETAIL 1-BATTEN ALTERNATES FOR METAL ROOFING

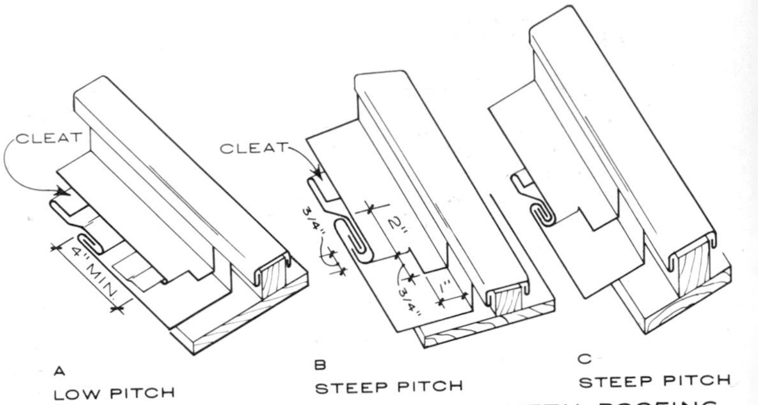

CLEAT — CLEAT

3/4" — 2" — 4" MIN — 3/4"

A — LOW PITCH

B — STEEP PITCH

C — STEEP PITCH

DETAIL 3- TRANSVERSE SEAM IN METAL ROOFING

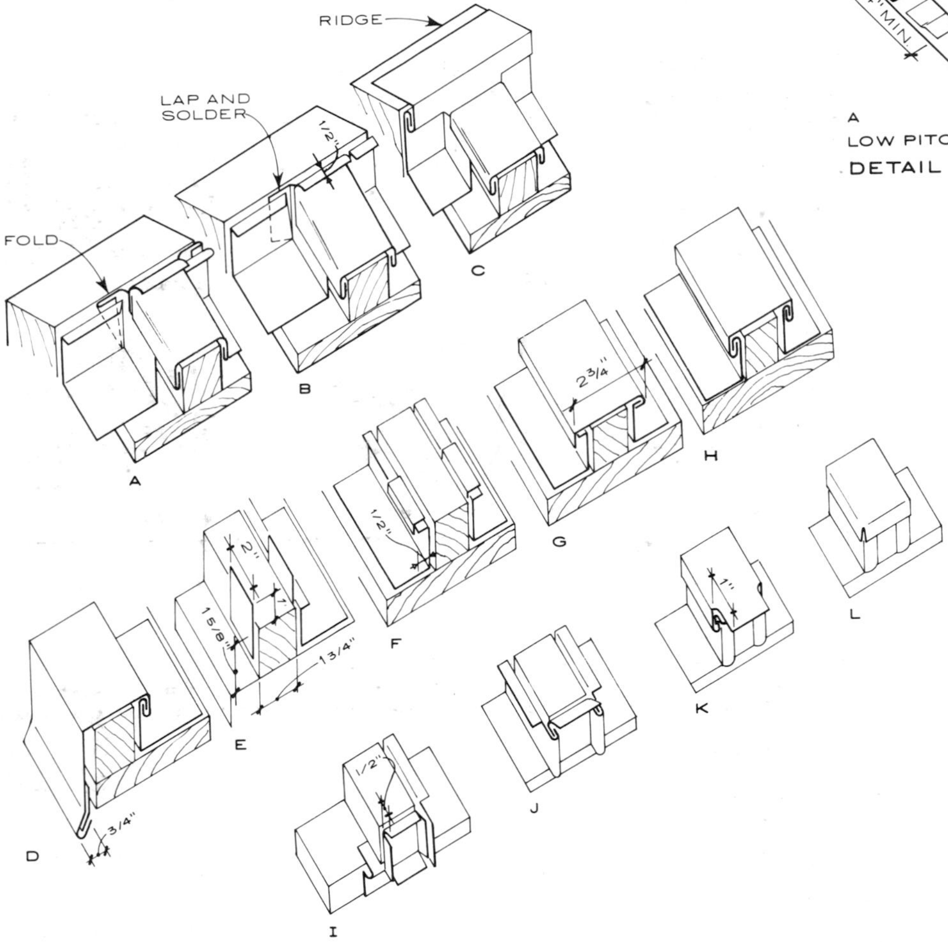

RIDGE

LAP AND SOLDER

1/2"

FOLD

A — B — C — 2 3/4" — H

2" — 1/2" — G

1 5/8" — 1" — F — L

E — 1 3/4" — K

D — 3/4" — J — 1"

1/2" — I

DETAIL 2- BATTEN CONSTRUCTION FOR METAL ROOFING

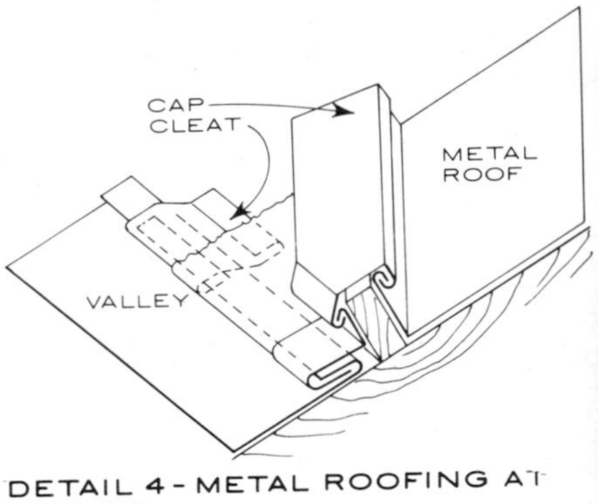

CAP CLEAT — METAL ROOF

VALLEY

DETAIL 4- METAL ROOFING AT VALLEY

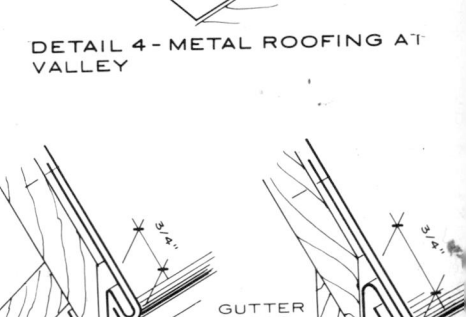

3/4" — 3/4"

GUTTER LINING

A — B

DETAIL 5- METAL EDGE STRIP AT EAVES

NOTES:

Copper (minimum 16 oz.), terne (minimum 40 lb.), or aluminum (minimum 0.032 in.) is recommended for batten seam roofing.

Batten seam roofing may be applied on slopes of 3 in. per ft. or greater. If the surface to receive the roofing is other than wood, the battens should be bolted in place. The surface to receive the roofing should be thoroughly dry, smooth, and covered with the underlayment as recommended by the manufacturer.

The spacing of the wood battens may vary within reasonable limits to suit the architectural style and scale of the building, but the recommended maximum distance is 20 in. between battens. Care should be taken to space the battens in such a manner that waste of metal is held to a minimum.

Battens may be shaped as shown in A or B of detail 1. A is preferred as it automatically makes allowance for expansion. When battens shown in B are used, care must be taken to provide for expansion by bending the metal where it meets the batten at greater than 90 degrees.

Sheets are formed into pans with each side turned up 2 1/8 in. A 1/2 in. flange is turned toward the center of the pan as shown in F, G, and H of detail 2. At lower end of the pan, the sheet is notched and a hook edge is formed as in A, B or C of detail 3. For low pitched roofs the upper end of the sheet is formed as in A of detail 3. On steeper roofs the upper end is formed as shown in B or C of detail 3.

Pans are installed, starting at the eave, and held in place

with cleats spaced not over 12 in. on center as shown in of detail 2. Each pan is hooked to the one below it a cleated into place. After pans are in place, a cap is stalled over the batten as shown in G and H of detail

A, B and C of detail 2 show methods of terminating me roofing at the ridge.

D of detail 2 shows method of joining metal roofing at gable.

Detail 4 shows method of joining metal roofing at a vall

I, J, K and L of detail 2 show method of closing the bat ends.

A and B of detail 5 show alternate edge strips at eav

Emory E. Hinkel, Jr.; A. G. Odell, Jr. and Associates; Charlotte, North Carolina

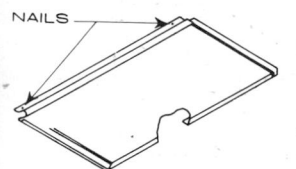

NAILS

Use alum. or hot-dipped zinc coated nails. For exposed nails use washers.

Sizes: 8" x 7 1/4", 1'- 2 1/2"
Finishes: Wood grain stipple embossed.

INTERLOCKING SHINGLE

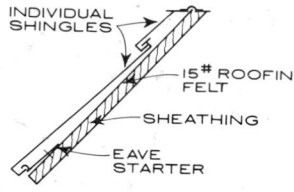

INDIVIDUAL SHINGLES
15# ROOFING FELT
SHEATHING
EAVE STARTER

SECTION THRU ROOF

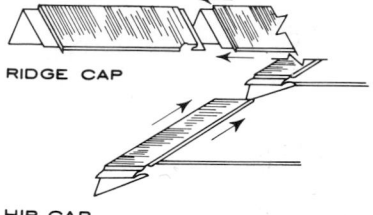

RIDGE CAP

HIP CAP

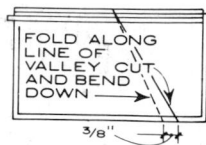

FOLD ALONG LINE OF VALLEY CUT AND BEND DOWN
3/8"

Use aluminum flashing only with aluminum shingles and siding. Never use copper in contact with aluminum.

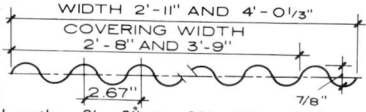

WIDTH 2'-11" AND 4'-0 1/3"
COVERING WIDTH 2'-8" AND 3'-9"
2.67"   7/8"

Length: 3'- 0" to 30'- 0" by 6" increments; Thickness: .024" for 2'- 11" width and .032" for 4'- 0 1/3" width; Finishes: Plain mill, stucco texture.

CORRUGATED ROOFING DIMENSIONS & DATA

LOADING TABLE FOR CORRUGATED ROOFING

DESIGN LOAD LBS. PER SQ. FT.	MAX. RECOMM. SPAN LENGTH IN INCHES			
	1 OR 2 SPANS		3 OR MORE SPANS	
	.024" T	.032" T	.024" T	.032" T
20	80	91	89	102
25	71	84	79	94
30	65	77	73	86
35	60	71	67	79
40	56	67	63	75
45	53	63	59	70
50	50	60	56	67

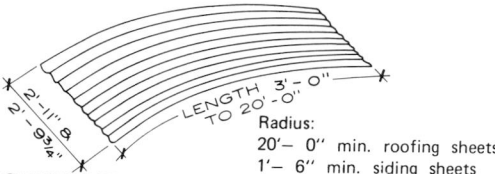

LENGTH 3'- 0" TO 20'- 0"
2'-11" & 2'-9 3/4"
Radius:
20'- 0" min. roofing sheets
1'- 6" min. siding sheets

CORRUGATED ROOFING & SIDING

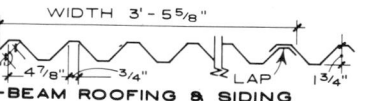

WIDTH 3'- 5 5/8"
4 7/8"   3/4"   LAP   1 3/4"

V-BEAM ROOFING & SIDING

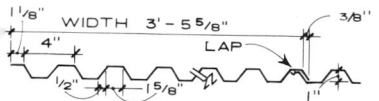

WIDTH 3'- 5 5/8"
1 1/8"   3/8"
4"   LAP
1/2"   1 5/8"   1"

Length: 3'- 0" to 30'- 0" by 6" increments; Thickness: .032" and .040"; Finish: No. E-5 pattern, stucco texture.

RIBBED INDUSTRIAL SIDING

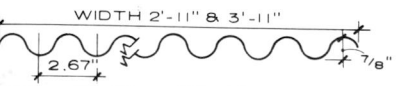

WIDTH 2'-11" & 3'-11"
2.67"   7/8"

Length: 3'- 0" to 30'- 0" by 6" increments; Thickness: .024" and .032"; Finish: Plain mill, No. E-5 pattern, stucco texture.

CORRUGATED SIDING

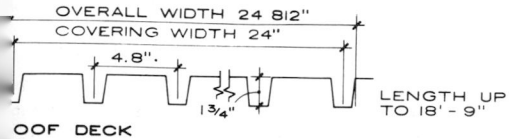

OVERALL WIDTH 24 & 12"
COVERING WIDTH 24"
4.8"
1 3/4"
LENGTH UP TO 18'- 9"

ROOF DECK

CORRUGATED AND OTHER FORMED ALUMINUM ROOFING AND SIDING

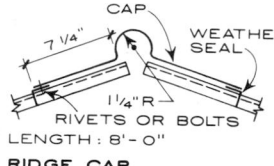

CAP   WEATHER SEAL
7 1/4"
1 1/4" R
RIVETS OR BOLTS
LENGTH: 8'- 0"

RIDGE CAP

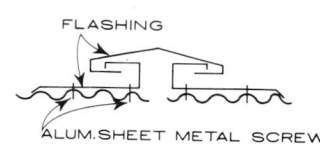

FLASHING
ALUM. SHEET METAL SCREWS

EXPANSION JOINT

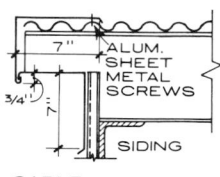

7"   ALUM. SHEET METAL SCREWS
3/4"   7"
SIDING

CABLE

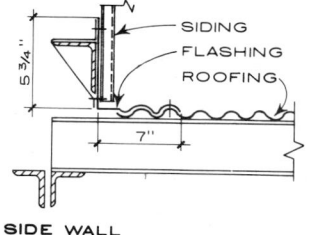

ALUM. WEATHER SEAL
2"
SHEET METAL SCREW
6"
SHEET METAL SCREW
FLASHING
2"

EAVE

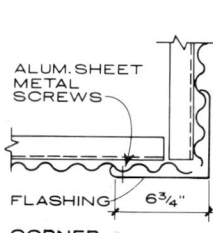

SIDING
FLASHING
ROOFING
5 3/4"
7"

SIDE WALL

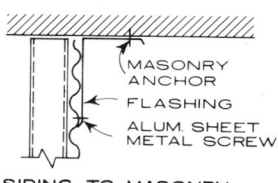

ALUM. SHEET METAL SCREWS
FLASHING   6 3/4"

CORNER

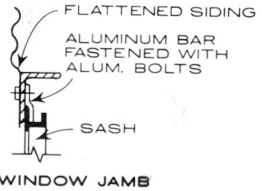

MASONRY ANCHOR
FLASHING
ALUM. SHEET METAL SCREW

SIDING TO MASONRY

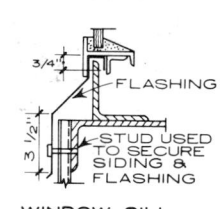

FLATTENED SIDING
ALUMINUM BAR FASTENED WITH ALUM. BOLTS
SASH

WINDOW JAMB

FLASHING
3/4"
STUD USED TO SECURE SIDING & FLASHING
3 1/2"

WINDOW SILL

FLASHING DETAILS

NOTE:

CORRUGATED ROOFING (MINIMUM ROOF PITCH 3" IN 12")

End lap should be 6" min.; side lap, 1 1/2" corrugation. Fasten only through crown of corrugation. Space fasteners every fourth corrugation; for extreme wind conditions, space at every third corrugation. For side lap fasteners space 12" o.c. max.

V-BEAM ROOFING (MINIMUM ROOF PITCH 3" IN 12")

End laps should be 6" min.; side lap, one rib. Fasten only through valley of rib. Space fasteners every rib at end of supports. For side lap fasteners, space 12" o.c. max.

V-BEAM SIDING

End lap should be 4"; side lap one rib. Fasten only through valley of corrugation. Space fasteners every rib at ends of sheet and every other rib at intermediate supports. For side lap fasteners, space 12" o.c. max.

CORRUGATED SIDING

End lap should be 4" min.; side lap, one corrugation. Fastening may be through high or low corrugation. Space fasteners every fourth corrugation; for extreme wind, every third corrugation. For side lap fasteners space 12" o.c. max.

RIBBED INDUSTRIAL SIDING

Space sheet fasteners every other rib valley (8"). Space side lap fasteners 12" max. thru rib-valley only. End laps min. 4". Side lap should be one rib and laid away from prevailing wind.

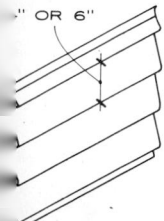

4" OR 6"

Covering width 2'- 0"
Height 8', 10', 12'
Thickness: .024"
Finish: smooth mill wood grain, stipple embossed.
Side lap 2" min. should be laid away from prevailing wind.

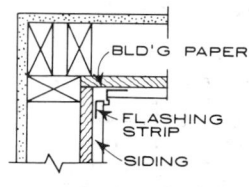

BLD'G PAPER
FLASHING STRIP
SIDING

INTERNAL CORNER

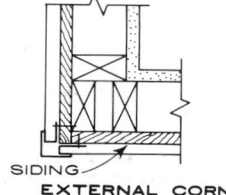

SIDING

EXTERNAL CORNER

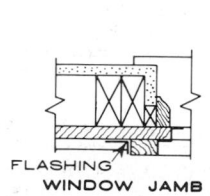

FLASHING
WINDOW JAMB

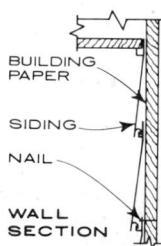

BUILDING PAPER
SIDING
NAIL

WALL SECTION

LAPBOARD SIDING AND INSTALLATION DETAILS

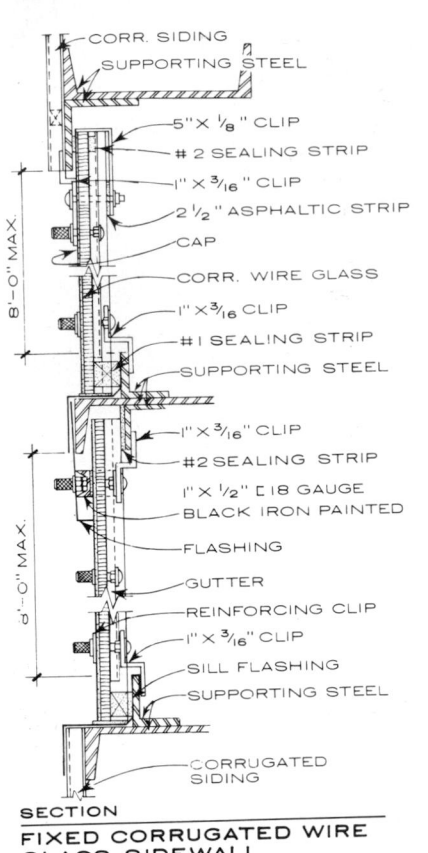

SECTION

FIXED CORRUGATED WIRE GLASS SIDEWALL

Labels: CORR. SIDING / SUPPORTING STEEL / 5" X 1/8" CLIP / #2 SEALING STRIP / I" X 3/16" CLIP / 2 1/2" ASPHALTIC STRIP / CAP / CORR. WIRE GLASS / I" X 3/16" CLIP / #I SEALING STRIP / SUPPORTING STEEL / I" X 3/16" CLIP / #2 SEALING STRIP / I" X 1/2" L 18 GAUGE BLACK IRON PAINTED / FLASHING / GUTTER / REINFORCING CLIP / I" X 3/16" CLIP / SILL FLASHING / SUPPORTING STEEL / CORRUGATED SIDING / 8'-0" MAX. / 8'-0" MAX.

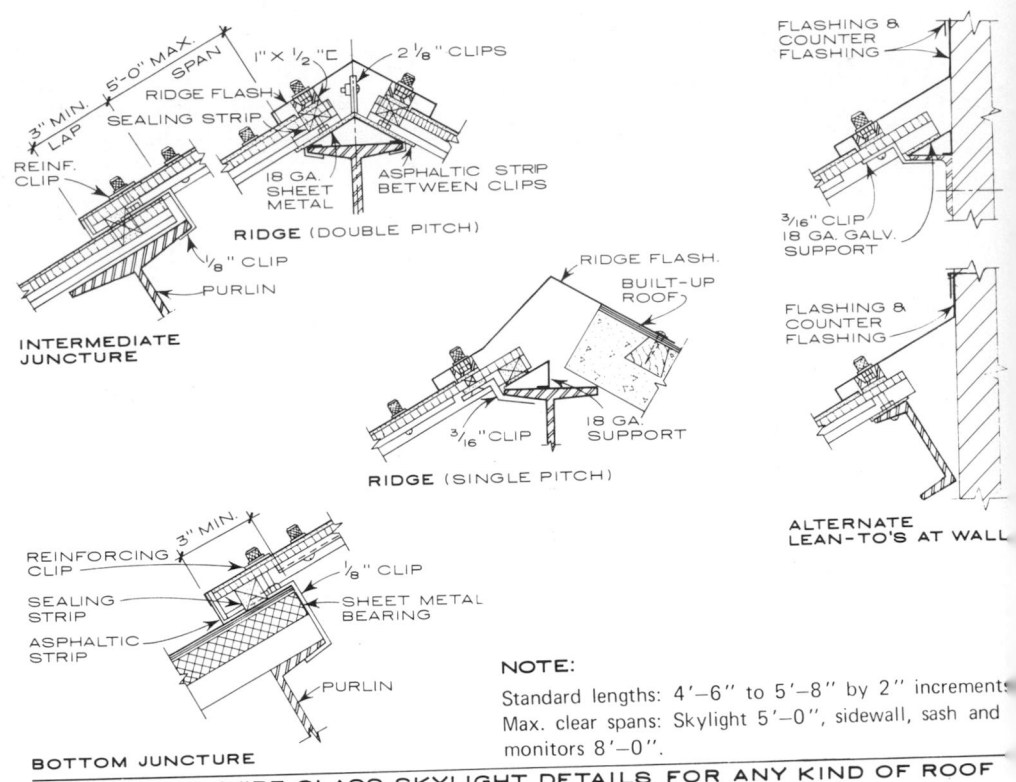

INTERMEDIATE JUNCTURE

RIDGE (DOUBLE PITCH)

RIDGE (SINGLE PITCH)

BOTTOM JUNCTURE

ALTERNATE LEAN-TO'S AT WALL

CORRUGATED WIRE GLASS SKYLIGHT DETAILS FOR ANY KIND OF ROOF

Corrugated wire glass has only limited availability.
Check source before specifying.

NOTE:

Standard lengths: 4'–6" to 5'–8" by 2" increments
Max. clear spans: Skylight 5'–0", sidewall, sash and
monitors 8'–0".

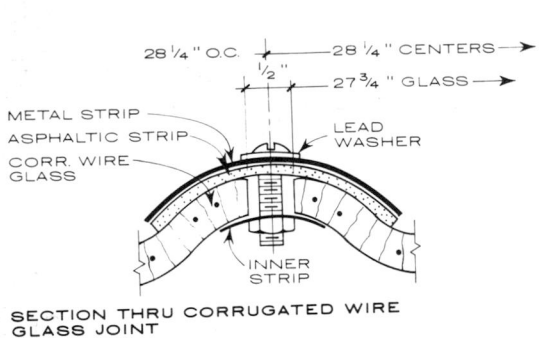

SECTION THRU CORRUGATED WIRE GLASS JOINT

Labels: 28 1/4" O.C. / 28 1/4" CENTERS / 27 3/4" GLASS / 1/2" / METAL STRIP / ASPHALTIC STRIP / CORR. WIRE GLASS / LEAD WASHER / INNER STRIP

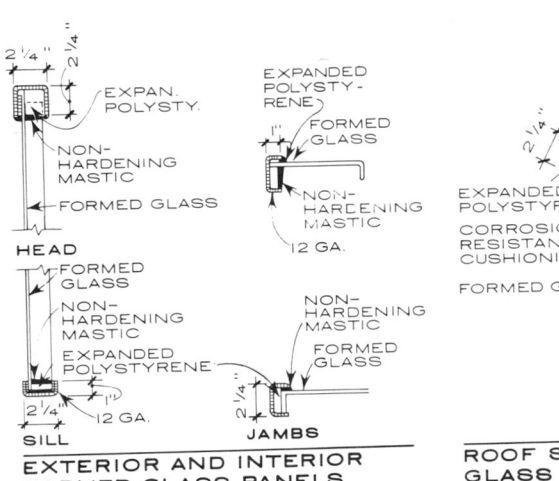

HEAD

SILL

JAMBS

EXTERIOR AND INTERIOR FORMED GLASS PANELS

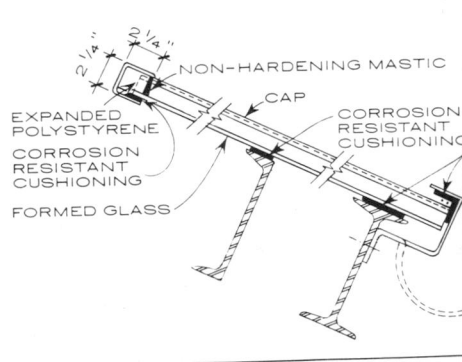

ROOF SYSTEM—WIRED FORMED GLASS

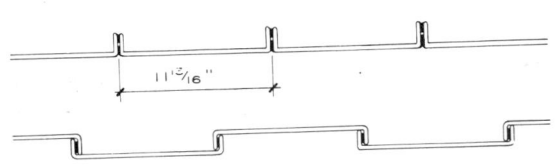

SINGLE GLAZING

11 13/16"

SEALANT, NON-HARDENING MASTIC

SPLIT DOUBLE

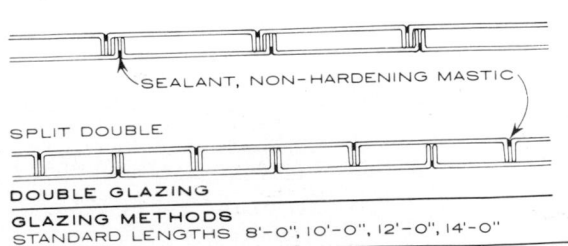

DOUBLE GLAZING

GLAZING METHODS
STANDARD LENGTHS 8'-0", 10'-0", 12'-0", 14'-0"

FORMED GLASS INSTALLATION DETAILS

LOAD DATA (VALUES IN LBS/SF)

	UNWIRED			WIRED		
SPAN	6'–0"	9'–0"	12'–0"	6'–0"	9'–0"	12'–
FLANGE OPP. LOAD	42	15	*	30	13	*
DOUBLE GLAZED	90	30	17	65	26	13
FLANGE TOWARD LOAD	117	54	29	97	49	22

*   NOT RECOMMENDED

J. F. Hayes and J. W. Meade; Hayes and Hough; Philadelphia, Pennsylvania

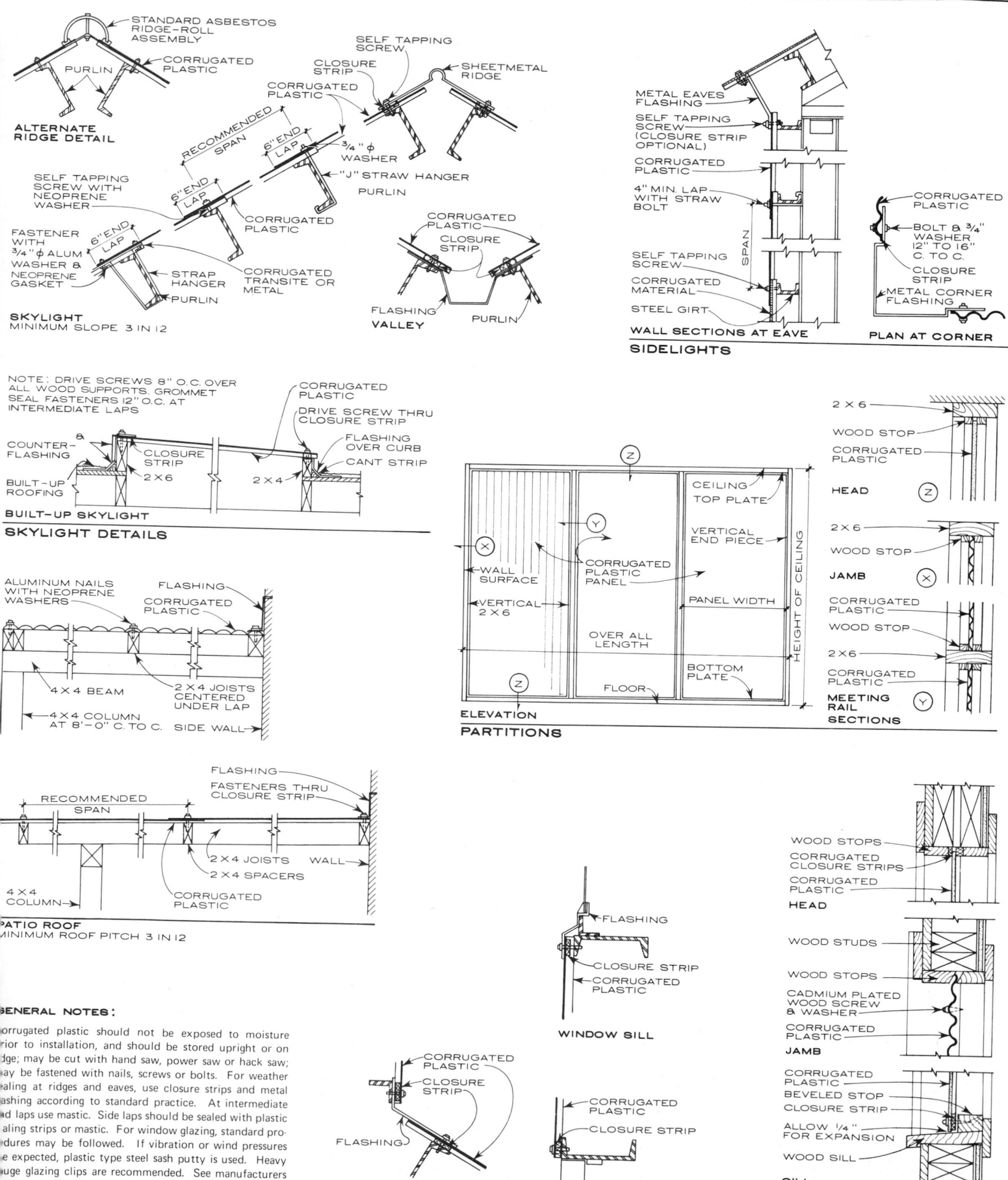

STANDARD ASBESTOS RIDGE-ROLL ASSEMBLY
PURLIN
CORRUGATED PLASTIC

ALTERNATE RIDGE DETAIL

SELF TAPPING SCREW WITH NEOPRENE WASHER
FASTENER WITH ¾" φ ALUM WASHER & NEOPRENE GASKET
6" END LAP
STRAP HANGER
PURLIN
CORRUGATED PLASTIC
CORRUGATED TRANSITE OR METAL

RECOMMENDED SPAN
6" END LAP
6" END LAP
¾" φ WASHER
"J" STRAW HANGER
PURLIN

SKYLIGHT MINIMUM SLOPE 3 IN 12

SELF TAPPING SCREW
CLOSURE STRIP
CORRUGATED PLASTIC
SHEETMETAL RIDGE

CORRUGATED PLASTIC
CLOSURE STRIP
FLASHING
PURLIN

VALLEY

METAL EAVES FLASHING
SELF TAPPING SCREW (CLOSURE STRIP OPTIONAL)
CORRUGATED PLASTIC
4" MIN. LAP WITH STRAW BOLT
SELF TAPPING SCREW
CORRUGATED MATERIAL
STEEL GIRT
SPAN

WALL SECTIONS AT EAVE

CORRUGATED PLASTIC
BOLT & ¾" WASHER 12" TO 16" C. TO C.
CLOSURE STRIP
METAL CORNER FLASHING

PLAN AT CORNER

SIDELIGHTS

NOTE: DRIVE SCREWS 8" O.C. OVER ALL WOOD SUPPORTS. GROMMET SEAL FASTENERS 12" O.C. AT INTERMEDIATE LAPS.
COUNTER-FLASHING
BUILT-UP ROOFING
CLOSURE STRIP
2 X 6
CORRUGATED PLASTIC
DRIVE SCREW THRU CLOSURE STRIP
FLASHING OVER CURB
CANT STRIP
2 X 4

BUILT-UP SKYLIGHT

SKYLIGHT DETAILS

ALUMINUM NAILS WITH NEOPRENE WASHERS
FLASHING
CORRUGATED PLASTIC
4 X 4 BEAM
2 X 4 JOISTS CENTERED UNDER LAP
4 X 4 COLUMN AT 8'-0" C. TO C.   SIDE WALL

Z
Y
X
WALL SURFACE
VERTICAL 2 X 6
CEILING TOP PLATE
VERTICAL END PIECE
CORRUGATED PLASTIC PANEL
PANEL WIDTH
OVER ALL LENGTH
BOTTOM PLATE
FLOOR
Z
HEIGHT OF CEILING

ELEVATION

PARTITIONS

2 X 6
WOOD STOP
CORRUGATED PLASTIC

HEAD   Z

2 X 6
WOOD STOP

JAMB   X

CORRUGATED PLASTIC
WOOD STOP
2 X 6
CORRUGATED PLASTIC

MEETING RAIL   Y

SECTIONS

FLASHING
FASTENERS THRU CLOSURE STRIP
RECOMMENDED SPAN
2 X 4 JOISTS
2 X 4 SPACERS
WALL
CORRUGATED PLASTIC
4 X 4 COLUMN

PATIO ROOF MINIMUM ROOF PITCH 3 IN 12

FLASHING
CLOSURE STRIP
CORRUGATED PLASTIC

WINDOW SILL

CORRUGATED PLASTIC
CLOSURE STRIP

DOOR HEAD

CORRUGATED PLASTIC
CLOSURE STRIP
FLASHING

SIDEWALL-ROOF FLASHING

TYPICAL DETAILS

WOOD STOPS
CORRUGATED CLOSURE STRIPS
CORRUGATED PLASTIC

HEAD

WOOD STUDS
WOOD STOPS
CADMIUM PLATED WOOD SCREW & WASHER
CORRUGATED PLASTIC

JAMB

CORRUGATED PLASTIC
BEVELED STOP
CLOSURE STRIP
ALLOW ¼" FOR EXPANSION
WOOD SILL

SILL

SECTIONS

GENERAL NOTES:

Corrugated plastic should not be exposed to moisture prior to installation, and should be stored upright or on edge; may be cut with hand saw, power saw or hack saw; may be fastened with nails, screws or bolts. For weather sealing at ridges and eaves, use closure strips and metal flashing according to standard practice. At intermediate and laps use mastic. Side laps should be sealed with plastic sealing strips or mastic. For window glazing, standard procedures may be followed. If vibration or wind pressures are expected, plastic type steel sash putty is used. Heavy gauge glazing clips are recommended. See manufacturers literature for detailed methods of installation. Standard lengths 8'-0", 10'-0", 12'-0", 14'-0" depending on pattern.

F. Hayes and J. W. Meade; Hayes and Hough; Philadelphia, Pennsylvania

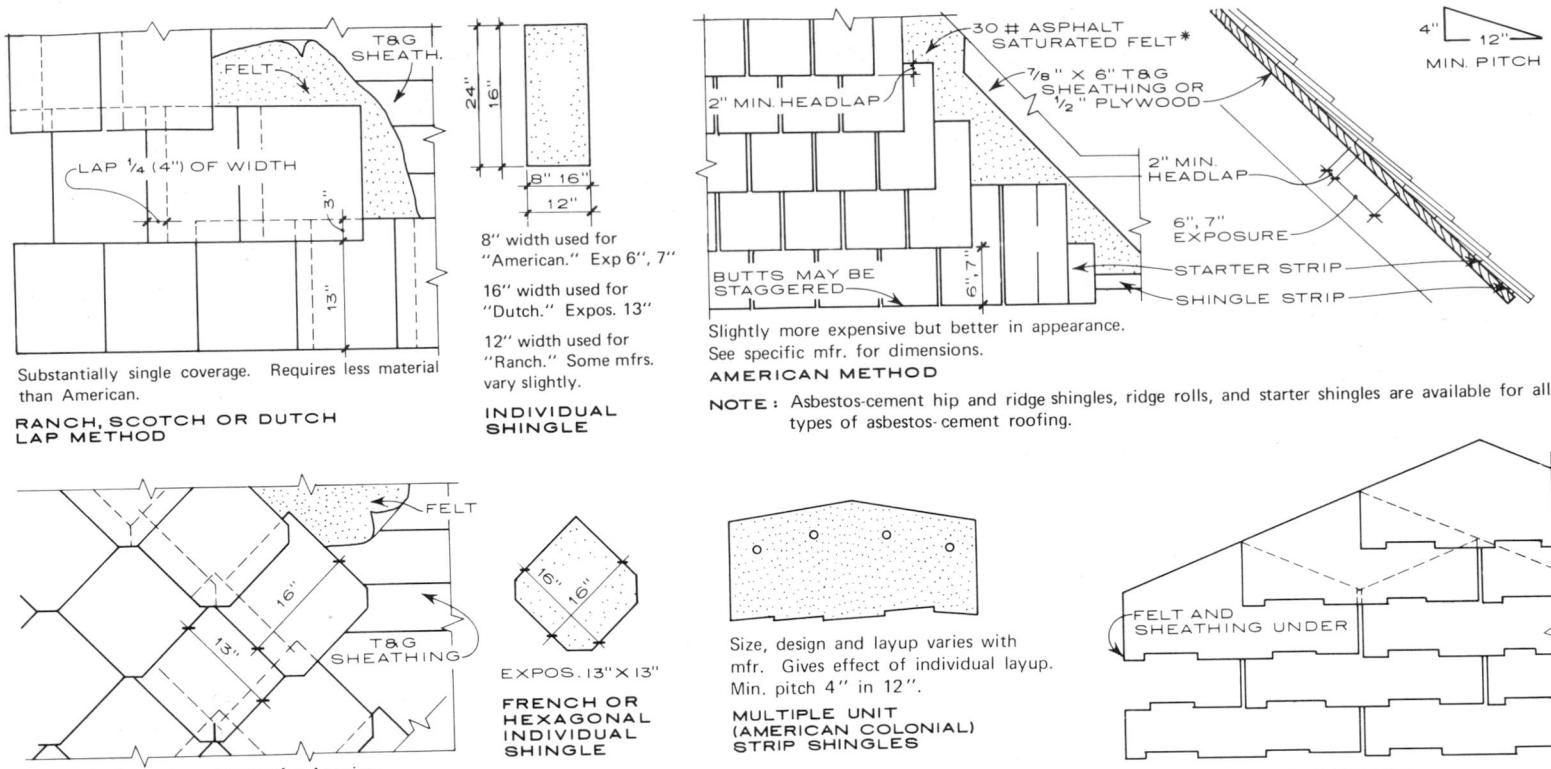

RANCH, SCOTCH OR DUTCH LAP METHOD

Substantially single coverage. Requires less material than American.

INDIVIDUAL SHINGLE

8" width used for "American." Exp 6", 7"

16" width used for "Dutch." Expos. 13"

12" width used for "Ranch." Some mfrs. vary slightly.

AMERICAN METHOD

Slightly more expensive but better in appearance. See specific mfr. for dimensions.

NOTE : Asbestos-cement hip and ridge shingles, ridge rolls, and starter shingles are available for all types of asbestos-cement roofing.

FRENCH OR HEXAGONAL METHOD

Inexpensive but not as waterproof as American.

FRENCH OR HEXAGONAL INDIVIDUAL SHINGLE

EXPOS. 13" X 13"

MULTIPLE UNIT (AMERICAN COLONIAL) STRIP SHINGLES

Size, design and layup varies with mfr. Gives effect of individual layup. Min. pitch 4" in 12".

MULTIPLE UNIT METHOD

ASBESTOS—CEMENT ROOFING SHINGLES

All shingles have uniform thickness of 5/32".
Use 1 1/4" galv. or aluminum needle point nails.

Min. slope: 4" in 12" for shingles, over single layer underlayment. 30# asphalt felt* recommended.

Consult manufacturer for slopes less than 4" in 12".

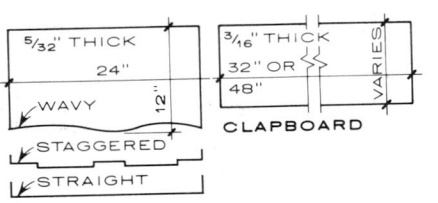

SIDING SHINGLES

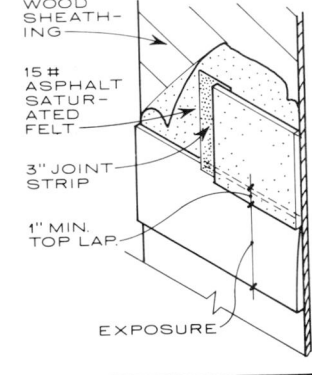

Asbestos-cement siding may be applied over non-lumber sheathing using wood under coursing strips or insulating backer board. Use 1 1/4" aluminum nails or self-clinching nails. Refer to mfrs' data for proper fasteners and dimensions.

ASBESTOS-CEMENT * SHEET SIZES *

TYPE	USE	SIZES			
		1/8"	3/16"	1/4"	3/8"
"F" (flexible)	Interiors & exteriors requiring high strength & density, smooth surface, low moisture absorption.	48"x48",96" 120"&144"	48"x48",96" 120"&144"	48"x48",96" 120"&144"	48"x48",96" 120"&144"
"U" (utility)	Interiors & exteriors general utility and construction.		48"x48",96" 120"&144"	48"x48",96" 120"&144"	48"x48",96" 120"&144"

* Both "F" and "U" width are specified in Federal Specification SS-B-775—Color: Stone grey, also available primed and prefinished in color. Sheets up to 1/4" thick do not have to be drilled for nailing. Nails: galv. or aluminum, min. length 1" plus sheet thickness. Nail 8"— 12" on all edges, 16" o.c. on intermediate studs.

ASBESTOS—CEMENT * SIDING

* The new term "Mineral Fiber" is synonymous with Asbestos-Cement.

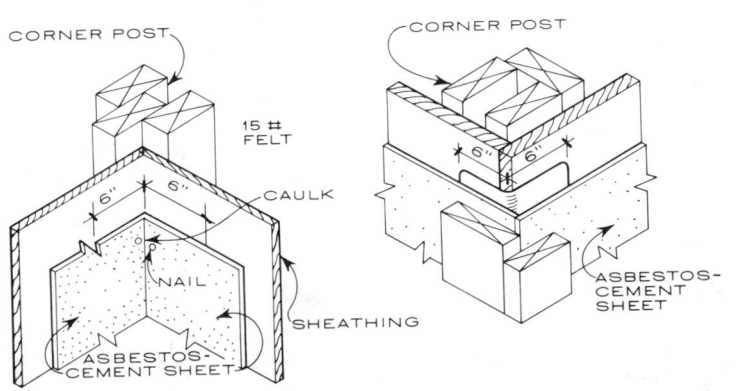

INSIDE CORNER   **OUTSIDE CORNER**   **VERTICAL BATTEN**

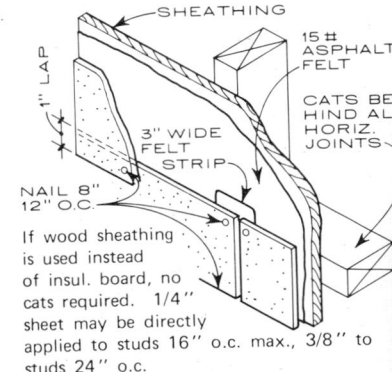

If wood sheathing is used instead of insul. board, no cats required. 1/4" sheet may be directly applied to studs 16" o.c. max., 3/8" to studs 24" o.c.

EXTERIOR WALLS

ASBESTOS—CEMENT BOARD-EXTERIOR WALLS

NOTE: All underlay material should be designated as breather typ

Anthony Forjohn; Cope & Lippincott, Architects; Philadelphia, Pennsylvania

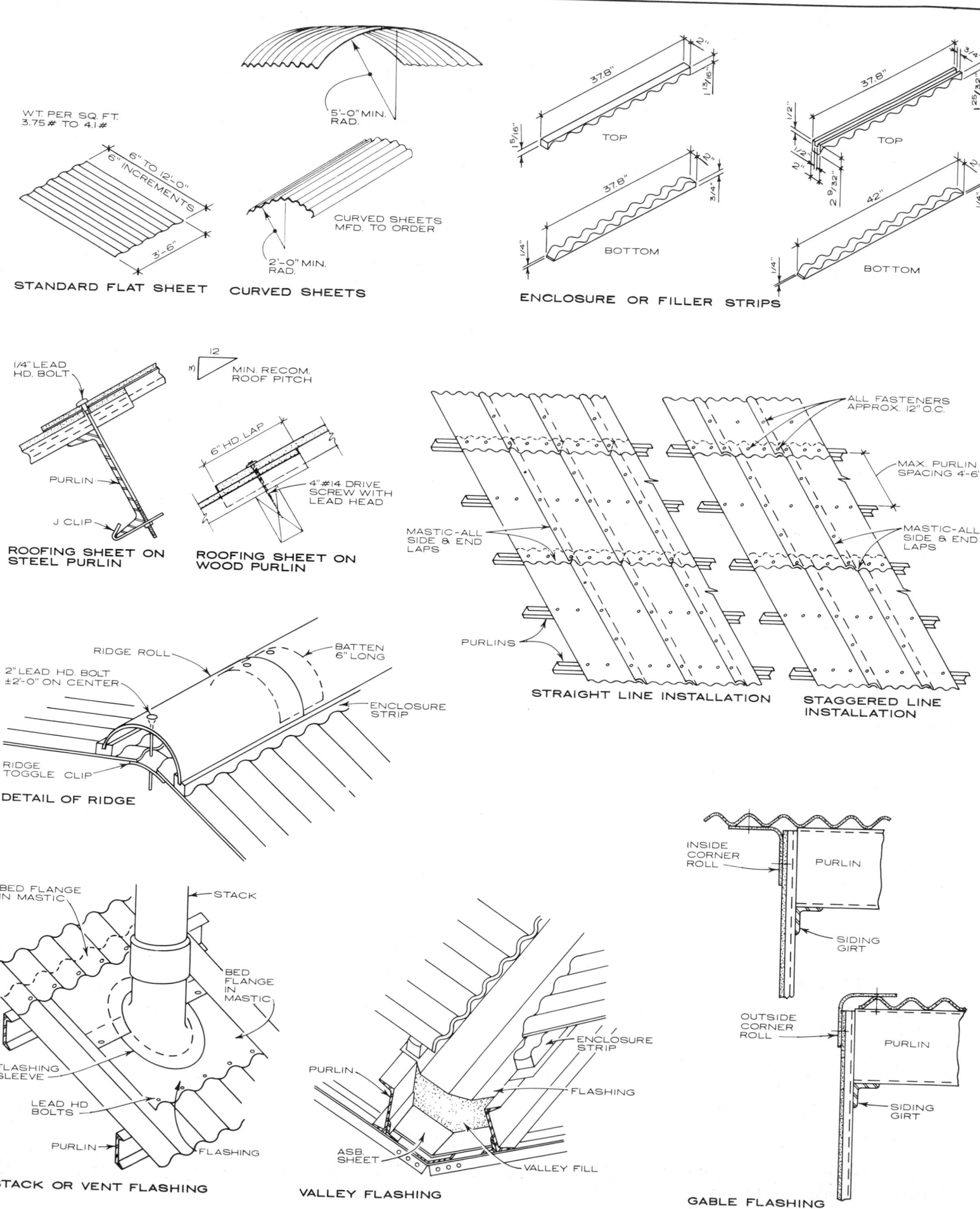

WT. PER SQ. FT.
3.75# TO 4.1#

6" TO 12'-0"
6" INCREMENTS

3'-6"

STANDARD FLAT SHEET

5'-0" MIN. RAD.

2'-0" MIN. RAD.

CURVED SHEETS MFD. TO ORDER

CURVED SHEETS

37.8"

TOP

BOTTOM

ENCLOSURE OR FILLER STRIPS

1/4" LEAD HD. BOLT

PURLIN

J CLIP

ROOFING SHEET ON STEEL PURLIN

12
3
MIN. RECOM. ROOF PITCH

6" HD. LAP

4" #14 DRIVE SCREW WITH LEAD HEAD

ROOFING SHEET ON WOOD PURLIN

ALL FASTENERS APPROX. 12" O.C.

MAX. PURLIN SPACING 4'-6"

MASTIC-ALL SIDE & END LAPS

PURLINS

STRAIGHT LINE INSTALLATION

STAGGERED LINE INSTALLATION

RIDGE ROLL

BATTEN 6" LONG

2" LEAD HD. BOLT ±2'-0" ON CENTER

ENCLOSURE STRIP

RIDGE TOGGLE CLIP

DETAIL OF RIDGE

BED FLANGE IN MASTIC

STACK

BED FLANGE IN MASTIC

FLASHING SLEEVE

LEAD HD BOLTS

PURLIN

FLASHING

STACK OR VENT FLASHING

ENCLOSURE STRIP

PURLIN

FLASHING

ASB. SHEET

VALLEY FILL

VALLEY FLASHING

INSIDE CORNER ROLL

PURLIN

SIDING GIRT

OUTSIDE CORNER ROLL

PURLIN

SIDING GIRT

GABLE FLASHING

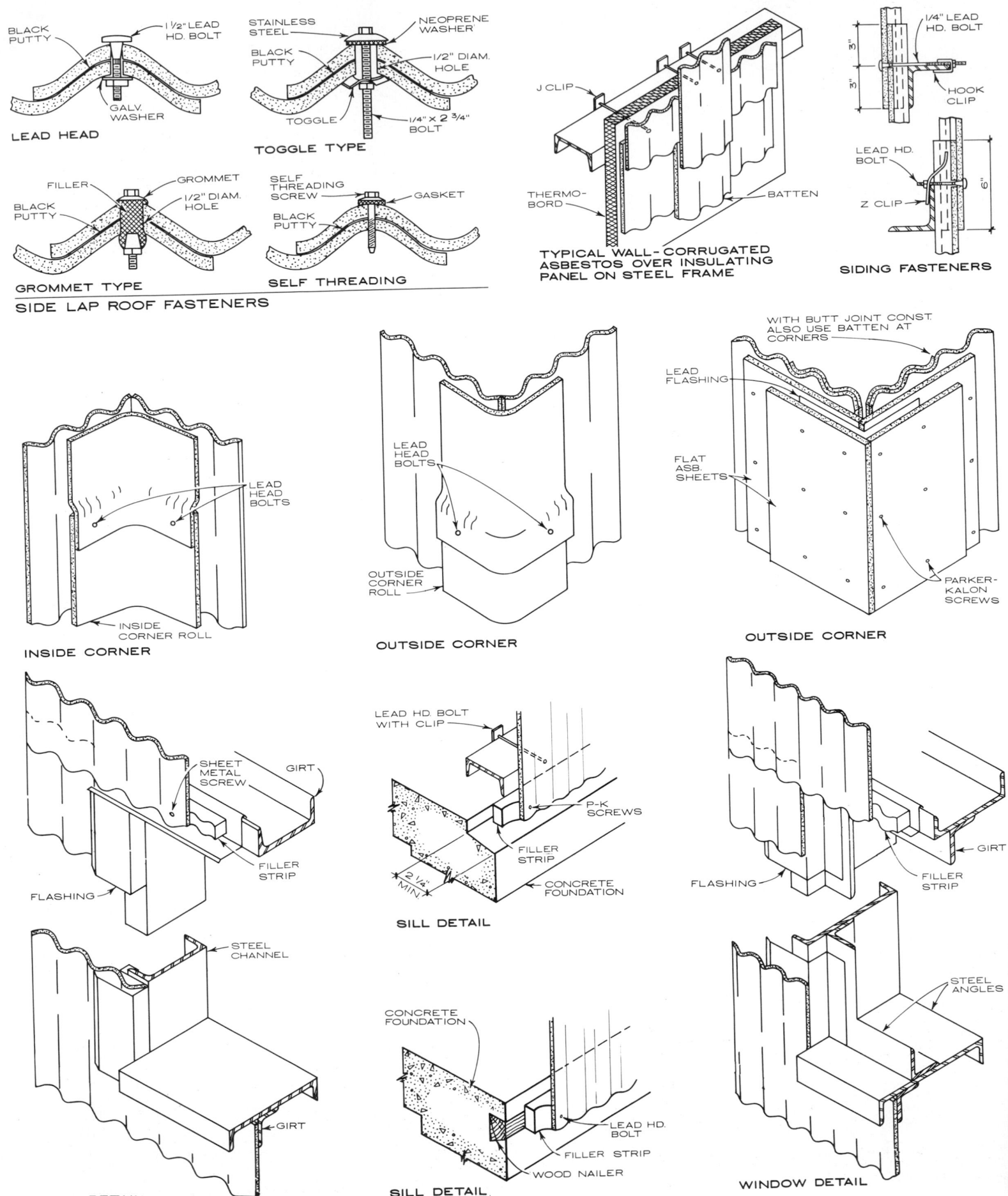

LEAD HEAD

TOGGLE TYPE

GROMMET TYPE

SELF THREADING

SIDE LAP ROOF FASTENERS

TYPICAL WALL - CORRUGATED ASBESTOS OVER INSULATING PANEL ON STEEL FRAME

SIDING FASTENERS

INSIDE CORNER

OUTSIDE CORNER

OUTSIDE CORNER

SILL DETAIL

DOOR DETAIL

SILL DETAIL.

WINDOW DETAIL

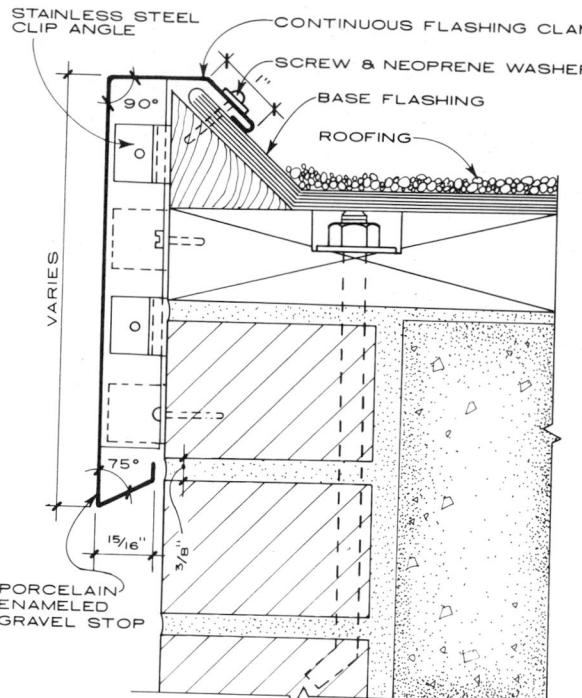

TYPICAL GRAVEL STOP DETAIL   NO SCALE

STAINLESS STEEL CLIP ANGLE
CONTINUOUS FLASHING CLAMP
SCREW & NEOPRENE WASHER
BASE FLASHING
ROOFING
90°
75°
VARIES
15/16"
3/8
PORCELAIN ENAMELED GRAVEL STOP

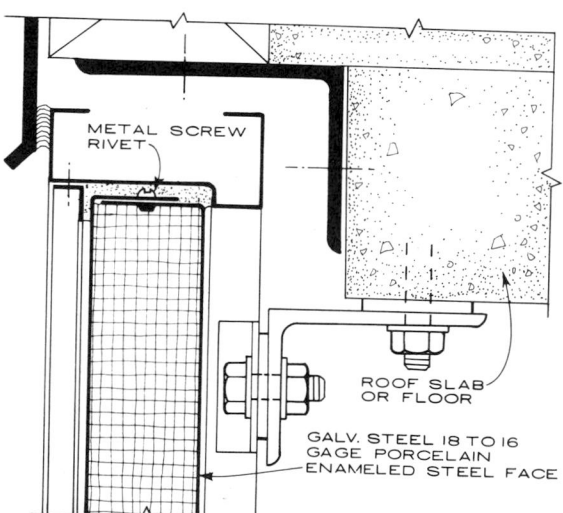

METAL SCREW RIVET
ROOF SLAB OR FLOOR
GALV. STEEL 18 TO 16 GAGE PORCELAIN ENAMELED STEEL FACE

TYPICAL INSULATED PANEL INSTALLATION AT ROOF SLAB (FLOOR SIMILAR)   NO SCALE

See Curtain Wall manufacturers' catalogs for other installation details.
See Panel manufacturers for other panel edge conditions.

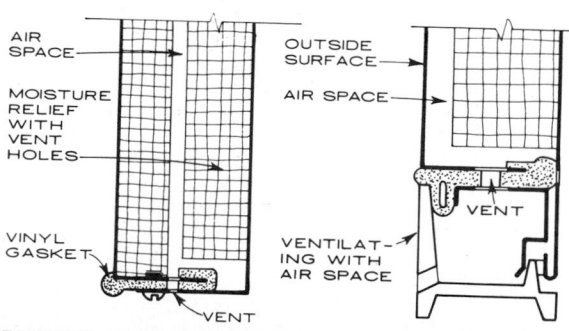

AIR SPACE
MOISTURE RELIEF WITH VENT HOLES
VINYL GASKET
VENT
OUTSIDE SURFACE
AIR SPACE
VENT
VENTILATING WITH AIR SPACE

DETAILS FOR CONTROLLING MOISTURE AND CONDENSATION IN INSULATED PANELS
WHERE NEEDED IN HIGH THERMAL CONTRAST AREAS

Porcelain Enamel Institute, Inc.; Washington, D. C.

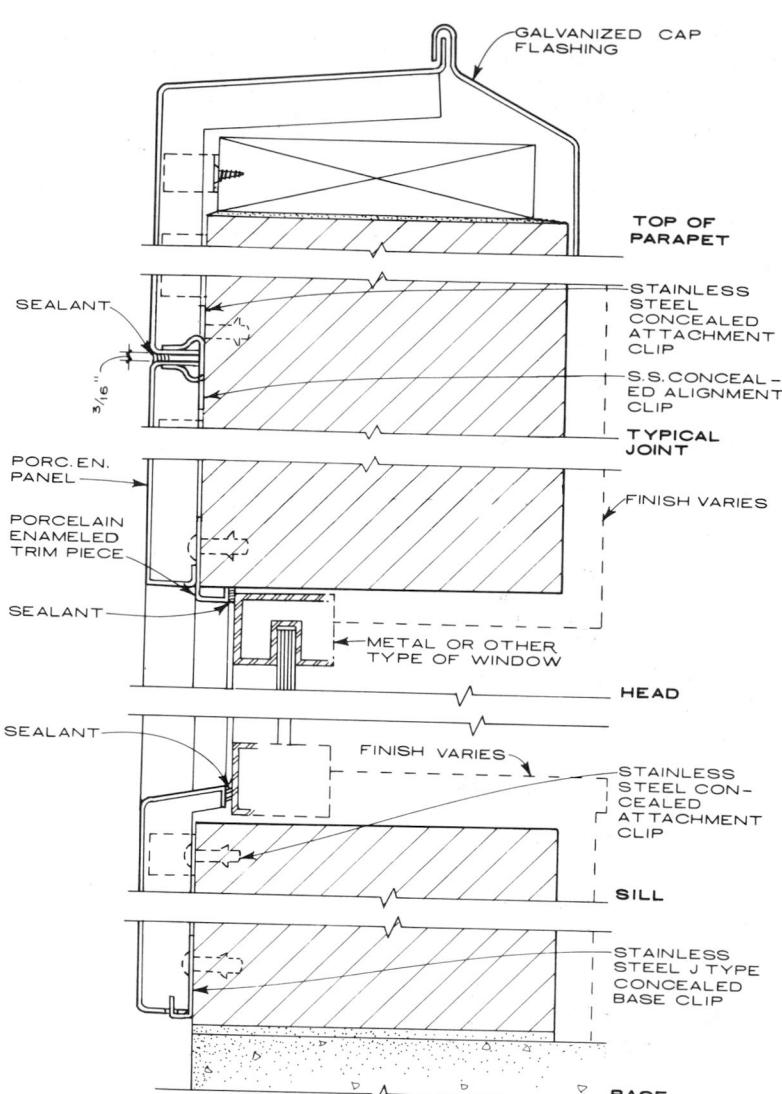

GALVANIZED CAP FLASHING
TOP OF PARAPET
SEALANT
STAINLESS STEEL CONCEALED ATTACHMENT CLIP
S.S. CONCEALED ALIGNMENT CLIP
TYPICAL JOINT
3/16"
PORC. EN. PANEL
PORCELAIN ENAMELED TRIM PIECE
SEALANT
FINISH VARIES
METAL OR OTHER TYPE OF WINDOW
HEAD
SEALANT
FINISH VARIES
STAINLESS STEEL CONCEALED ATTACHMENT CLIP
SILL
STAINLESS STEEL J TYPE CONCEALED BASE CLIP
BASE

TYPICAL SECTIONS THRU MASONRY WALL WITH PORCELAIN ENAMELED VENEER FACE   NO SCALE

NOTE:
For larger panels stiffeners may be necessary. Stiffener spacing is usually 12" to 18" O.C. Stiffeners are shaped with open side facing front of panel. Size approx. 3" long x a fraction less than panel depth.

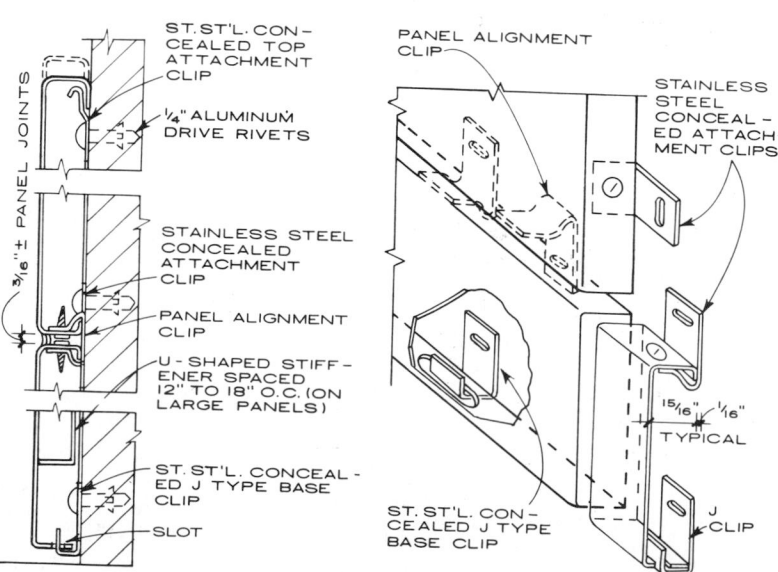

ST. ST'L. CONCEALED TOP ATTACHMENT CLIP
1/4" ALUMINUM DRIVE RIVETS
PANEL ALIGNMENT CLIP
STAINLESS STEEL CONCEALED ATTACHMENT CLIP
PANEL ALIGNMENT CLIP
STAINLESS STEEL CONCEALED ATTACHMENT CLIPS
STAINLESS STEEL CONCEALED ATTACHMENT CLIP
PANEL ALIGNMENT CLIP
U-SHAPED STIFFENER SPACED 12" TO 18" O.C. (ON LARGE PANELS)
3/16" ± PANEL JOINTS
ST. ST'L. CONCEALED J TYPE BASE CLIP
SLOT
15/16" 1/16"
TYPICAL
ST. ST'L. CONCEALED J TYPE BASE CLIP
J CLIP

TYPICAL VENEER TYPE PANEL ATTACHMENT DETAILS

CUSTOM SHAPES:

"Framed Dome": Triangular pieces and members super-imposed on structural frame of triangular units. Glazing may be of: Glass, clear or tinted, plain or reinforced; Plastics, clear or translucent.

Multiple pyramids: Special gutter member required between pyramids (see detail). May be superimposed over building structure or space frame.

Architectural designs: vaults, domes, flat, to conform to building designs.

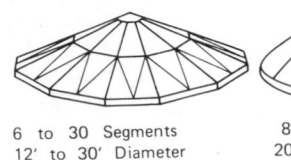

6 to 30 Segments
12' to 30' Diameter

8 to 36 Segments
20' to 100' Diameter

A wide variety of standard arrangements and sizes, also custom variations, are available.

DOMES
NOTES:

Common maximum spacing of rafters is 2'— 0". This varies with span and size and/or weight of members.

Condensation must be conducted down and out.

Screws, nuts, etc., exposed on exterior must be protected with lead washers or neoprene grommets.

GLAZING

Glass — Clear, tinted, translucent; plain, tempered or reinforced.

Plastic — Clear, tinted, translucent, single sheet or sandwich panel.

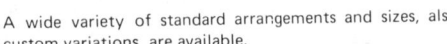

SINGLE PITCH

TURRET - DOUBLE PITCH

CONTINUOUS RIDGE VENTILATOR

ROLL - AWAY

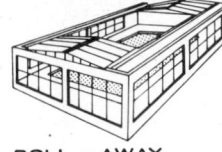

TOP HINGED VENTILATING

SOME BASIC STANDARD SHAPES

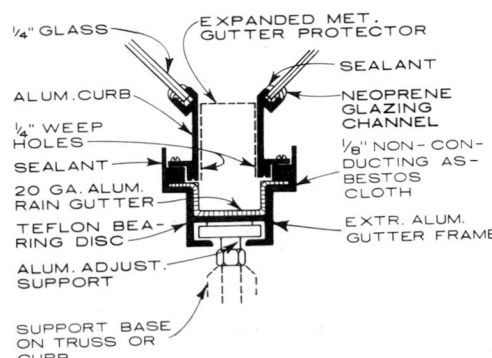

- ¼" GLASS
- EXPANDED MET. GUTTER PROTECTOR
- ALUM. CURB
- SEALANT
- NEOPRENE GLAZING CHANNEL
- ¼" WEEP HOLES
- SEALANT
- ⅛" NON - CONDUCTING ASBESTOS CLOTH
- 20 GA. ALUM. RAIN GUTTER
- TEFLON BEARING DISC
- EXTR. ALUM. GUTTER FRAME
- ALUM. ADJUST. SUPPORT
- SUPPORT BASE ON TRUSS OR CURB

A GUTTER & SUPPORT ASSEMBLY

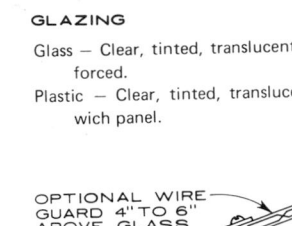

- OPTIONAL WIRE GUARD 4"TO 6" ABOVE GLASS
- RIDGE CAP
- LAP BAR
- NEOPRENE GASKET
- CONDENSATE GUTTERS
- RIDGE
- OPTIONAL INNER GLAZING
- GLASS
- WEEP HOLES
- RAFTER BAR
- HORIZONTAL LAP JOINT
- CURB

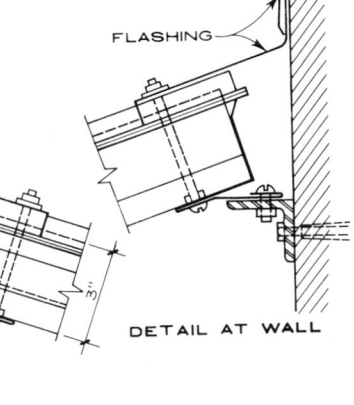

- FLASHING

DETAIL AT WALL

VARIOUS MATERIALS USED IN FORMED METAL - DRY GLAZED SKYLIGHTS	
Aluminum	Monel metal
Galvanized steel	Stainless steel
Copper	Lead—coated steel
Lead—coated copper	

Choice of material influenced by special fumes, appearance, etc.

FORMED METAL - DRY GLAZED SKYLIGHT

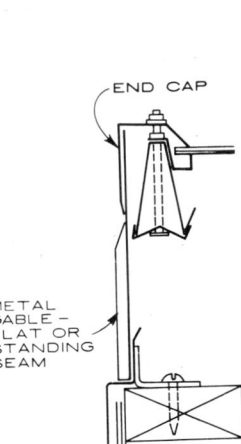

- END CAP
- METAL GABLE — FLAT OR STANDING SEAM

GABLE SECTION

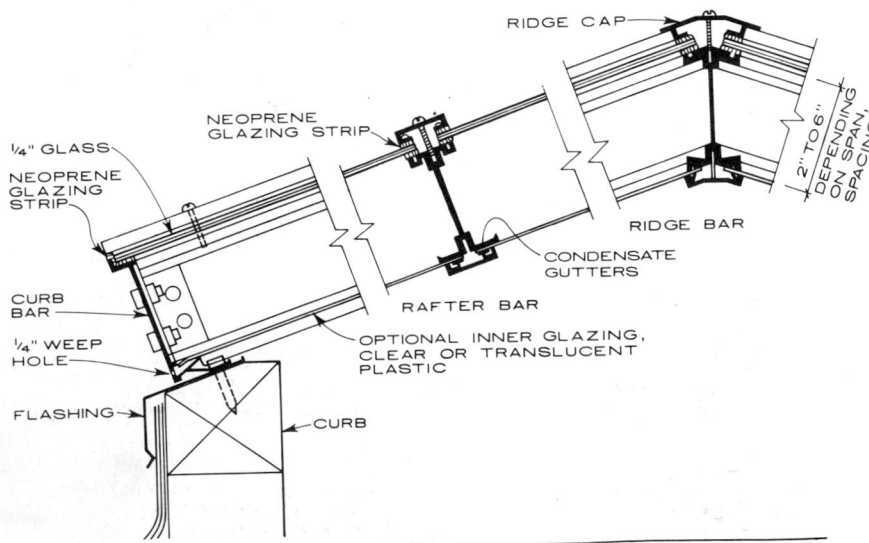

- RIDGE CAP
- NEOPRENE GLAZING STRIP
- ¼" GLASS
- NEOPRENE GLAZING STRIP
- 2"TO 6" DEPENDING ON SPAN, SPACING
- RIDGE BAR
- CONDENSATE GUTTERS
- CURB BAR
- RAFTER BAR
- ¼" WEEP HOLE
- OPTIONAL INNER GLAZING, CLEAR OR TRANSLUCENT PLASTIC
- FLASHING
- CURB

EXTRUDED ALUMINUM SKYLIGHT

Foster C. Parriott; James M. Hunter & Associates; Boulder, Colorado

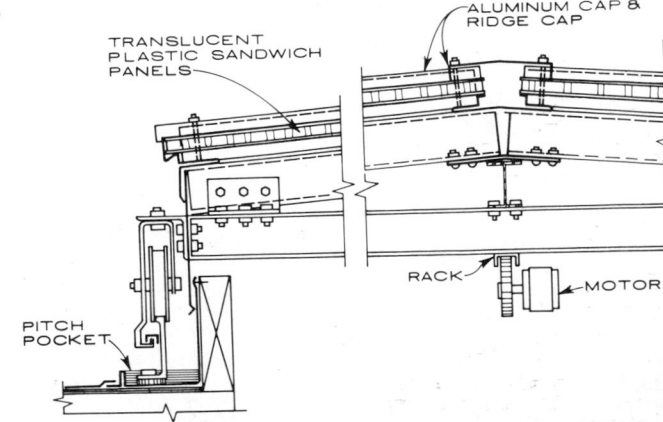

- ALUMINUM CAP & RIDGE CAP
- TRANSLUCENT PLASTIC SANDWICH PANELS
- RACK
- MOTOR
- PITCH POCKET

ROLL - AWAY SKYLIGHT -ONE OF SEVERAL DESIGNS

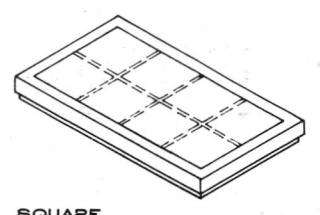

SQUARE
MIN. 3'-0" X 3'-0"
MAX. 4'-0" X 4'-0"
RECTANGULAR
MIN. 2'-0" X 4'-0"
MAX. 3'-0" X 6'-0"
FLAT PANEL Ⓐ Ⓑ

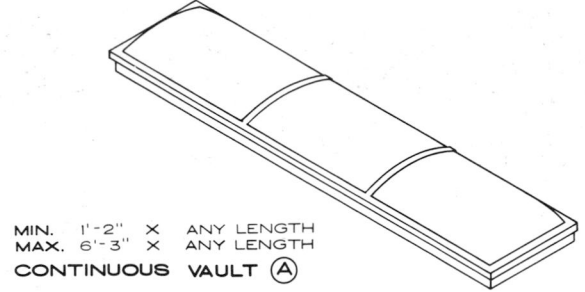

MIN. 1'-2" X ANY LENGTH
MAX. 6'-3" X ANY LENGTH
CONTINUOUS VAULT Ⓐ

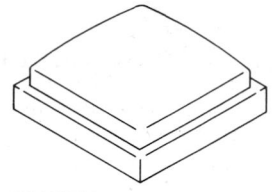

SQUARE
MIN. 1'-2¼" X 1'-2¼"
MAX. 6'-3" X 6'-3"
RECTANGULAR
MIN. 1'-2¼" X 1'-10¼"
MAX. 3'-11" X 5'-6"
ONE PIECE DOME Ⓒ

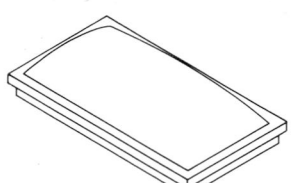

MIN. 1'-2¼" X 1'-10¼"
MAX. 7'-9¼" X 9'-5¼"
RECTANGULAR DOME Ⓐ Ⓑ

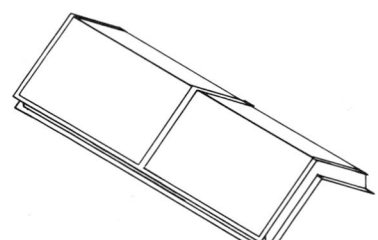

MIN. 1'-6" X ANY LENGTH
MAX. 4'-0" X ANY LENGTH
RIDGE TYPE Ⓐ Ⓑ

NOTES:

1. The stock skylights shown are available in the following frames:
   Ⓐ With curb frame (installed on job built curb).
   Ⓑ With integral curb and flashing (installed directly on roof).
   Ⓒ As a single plastic unit without integral curb or frame (installed either on job built curb or directly on roof).

2. Dimensions noted are interior opening sizes and are minimum-maximum only. Cn

2. Dimensions noted are interior opening sizes and are minimum-maximum only. Consult manufacturers for special sizes and for variations in style and shape.

3. Domes are available in various light controlling types and colors, in single, double or triple dome arrangements.

4. Accessories are interior ceiling domes, darkening shades, ceiling grid diffusers, and light controlled ceiling shutters.

5. Interior well liners are not usually furnished with standard skylight unit.

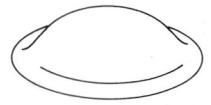

CIRCULAR
MIN. 1'-6"
MAX. 4'-0"
SQUARE
MIN. 1'-2¼" X 1'-2¼"
MAX. 6'-3" X 6'-3"
RECTANGULAR
MIN. 1'-2¼" X 1'-10¼"
MAX. 3'-11" X 5'-6"
ONE PIECE DOME Ⓒ

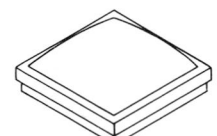

MIN. 1'-5½" X 1'-5½"
MAX. 6'-6¼" X 6'-6¼"
PYRAMID TYPE Ⓐ Ⓑ

MIN. 1'-2¼" X 1'-2¼"
MAX. 7'-11¾" X 7'-11¾"
SQUARE DOME Ⓐ Ⓑ

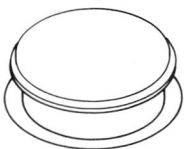

MIN. 2'-0"
MAX. 7'-7¼"
CIRCULAR DOME Ⓑ

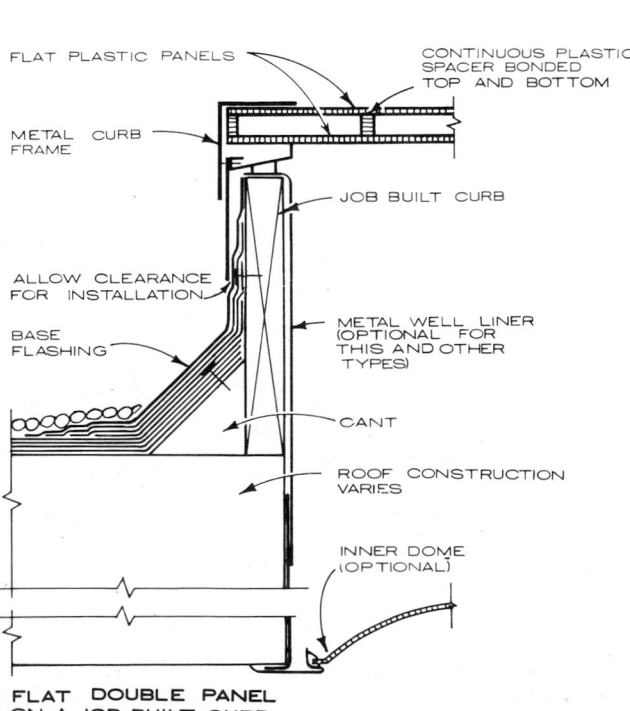

FLAT PLASTIC PANELS
CONTINUOUS PLASTIC SPACER BONDED TOP AND BOTTOM
METAL CURB FRAME
JOB BUILT CURB
ALLOW CLEARANCE FOR INSTALLATION
METAL WELL LINER (OPTIONAL FOR THIS AND OTHER TYPES)
BASE FLASHING
CANT
ROOF CONSTRUCTION VARIES
INNER DOME (OPTIONAL)

FLAT DOUBLE PANEL ON A JOB BUILT CURB
SCALE 1½" = 1'-0"

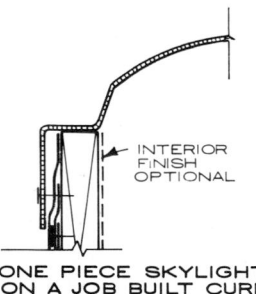

INTERIOR FINISH OPTIONAL

ONE PIECE SKYLIGHT ON A JOB BUILT CURB
SCALE 1½" = 1'-0"

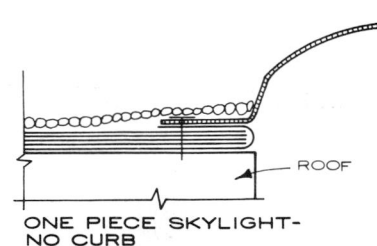

ROOF

ONE PIECE SKYLIGHT- NO CURB
SCALE 1½" = 1'-0"

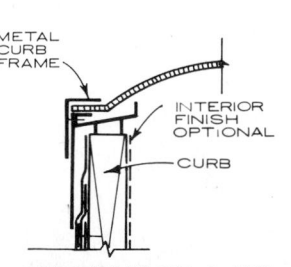

METAL CURB FRAME
INTERIOR FINISH OPTIONAL
CURB

SKYLIGHT ON A JOB BUILT CURB
SCALE 1½" = 1'-0"

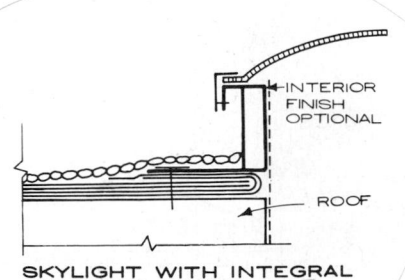

INTERIOR FINISH OPTIONAL
ROOF

SKYLIGHT WITH INTEGRAL CURB & FLASHING
SCALE 1½" = 1'-0"

WIDTH OF RECTANGULAR GUTTERS FOR GIVEN ROOF AREAS AND RAINFALL INTENSITIES

NOTE:

The terms "leader," "conductor," and "downspout" all mean the same thing.

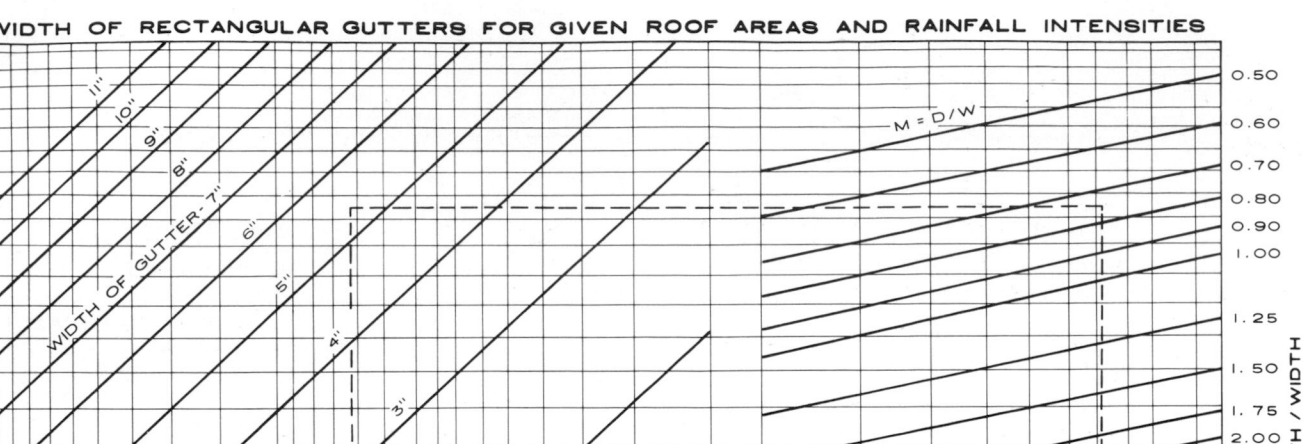

IA = RAINFALL INTENSITY × AREA

L = LENGTH OF GUTTER IN FEET

SAMPLE PROBLEM:

To size rectangular gutter for a building 120 x 30 ft. located in New York City. This building has a flat roof with a raised roof edge on three sides. A gutter is to be located on one of the 120 ft. sides. So that each section of gutter will not exceed 50 ft., three downspouts will be used with 2 gutter expansion joints. The area to be drained by each section of gutter will be 1200 sq. ft., the rainfall intensity from map below is 6 in., the length of each gutter section is 40 ft., and the ratio of gutter depth to width is 0.75. On chart above find the vertical line representing L = 40. Proceed vertically along this line to its intersection with the oblique line representing M = 0.75. Pass horizontally to the left to intersect the vertical line representing IA = 7200. The point of intersection occurs between the oblique line representing gutter widths of 5 and 6 in. The required width of gutter is, therefore, 6 in. and its depth need be only 4 1/2 in.

DESIGN AREAS FOR PITCHED ROOFS

PITCH	FACTOR
LEVEL TO 3 IN./FT.	1.00
4 TO 5 IN./FT.	1.05
6 TO 8 IN./FT.	1.10
9 TO 11 IN./FT.	1.20
12 IN./FT.	1.30

NOTE: When a roof is sloped neither the plan nor actual area should be used in sizing drainage. Multiply the plan area by the factor shown above to obtain design area.

INFLUENCE OF GUTTER SHAPE ON DESIGN

1. RECTANGULAR GUTTERS:

Use graph at top of page.

2. IRREGULAR SHAPES:

Determine equivalent rectangular size and use same method.

3. SEMICIRCULAR GUTTERS:

First size downspout from tables below. Then use gutter 1 inch larger in diameter.

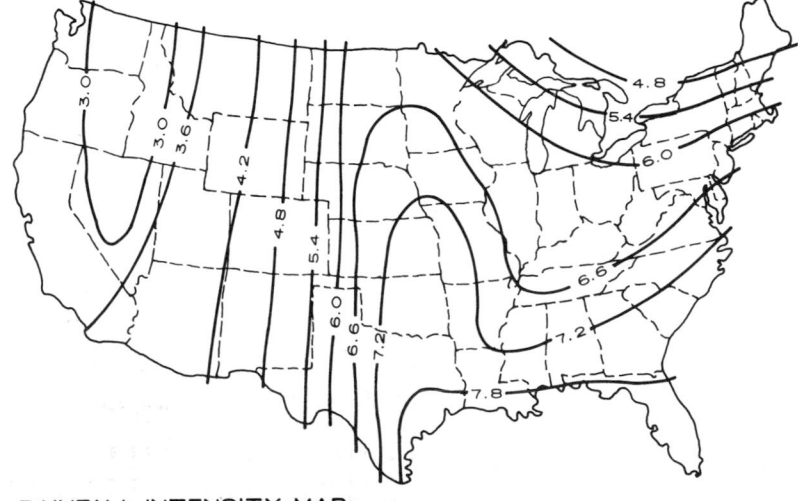

RAINFALL INTENSITY MAP

NOTE:

Map shows hourly rainfall in inches for 5 minute periods to be expected once in 10 yrs. This is normally adequate for design but record storms have gone twice as high in some areas. For important work see local records.

Lawrence W. Cobb, AIA; Columbia, South Carolina

DOWNSPOUT CAPACITY

INTENSITY IN IN./HR. LASTING 5 MIN.	SQ. FT. ROOF/ SQ. IN. DOWN-SPOUT
2	600
3	400
4	300
5	240
6	200
7	175
8	150
9	130
10	120
11	110

GENERAL NOTES:

Most gutters are run level for appearance. However, a slope of 1/16 in. per foot is desirable for drainage.

For residential work allow 100 sq. ft. of roof area per 1 sq. in. of downspout.

DOWNSPOUT SIZES

TYPE	AREA SQ. IN.	NOM. SIZE IN.	ACT. SIZE IN.
PLAIN ROUND	7.07	3	3
	12.57	4	4
	19.63	5	5
	28.27	6	6
CORR. ROUND	5.94	3	3
	11.04	4	4
	17.72	5	5
	25.97	6	6
CORR. RECT.	3.80	2	1 3/4 x 2 1/4
	7.73	3	2 3/8 x 3 1/4
	11.70	4	2 3/4 x 4 1/4
	18.75	5	3 3/4 x 5
PLAIN RECT.	3.94	2	1 3/4 x 2 1/4
	6.00	3	2 x 3
	12.00	4	3 x 4
	20.00	5	3 3/4 x 4 3/4
	24.00	6	4 x 6

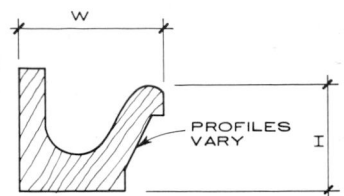

WOOD GUTTERS

REDWOOD	FIR
3″ H x 4″ W	3″ H x 4″ W
4″ H x 4″ W	4″ H x 5″ W
4″ H x 6″ W	4″ H x 6″ W
	5″ H x 7″ W

NOTE:
Wood gutters are still in use in New York State and the New England States.

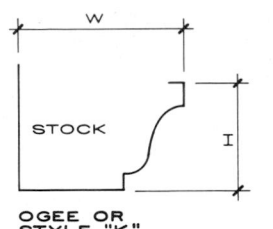

RECTANGULAR   **BEVELED**

METAL GUTTER NOTES:

Various sizes and other shapes available.

Always keep front 1/2 inch lower than back of gutter.

Do not use width less than 4 inches except for canopies and small porches. Min. ratio of depth to width should be 3 to 4.

METAL GUTTER SHAPES AND SIZES

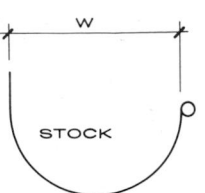

OGEE OR STYLE "K"

2 1/2″ H x 3″ W	
2 3/4″ H x 4″ W	G A
3 3/4″ H x 5″ W	G A
4 3/4″ H x 6″ W	G
5 1/4″ H x 7″ W	
6″ H x 8″ W	

SEMICIRCULAR OR HALF-ROUND

4″ W	G
5″ W	G A
6″ W	G A
7″ W	G
8″ W	G

Stock sizes marked "G" for galv., "A" for aluminum.

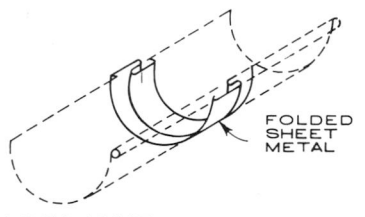

SECTION A-A   **ELEVATION**

BRASS JOINT FITTINGS AVAILABLE

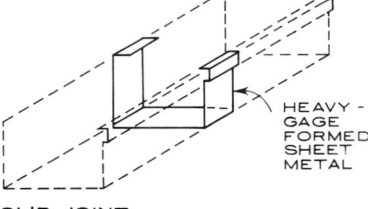

SECTION   **PLAN**   SCALE: 1½″=1′-0″

SPLICED JOINT IN WOOD GUTTER

RECOMMENED MINIMUM GAUGES FOR METAL GUTTER

GIRTH-INCHES	GALV. STEEL GAUGE	COPPER OZ.	ALUMINUM INCHES	STAINLESS STEEL GAUGE
UP TO 15	26	16	0.025	26
16 TO 20	24	16	0.032	26
21 TO 25	22	20	0.051	24
26 TO 30	20	24	0.064	22
31 TO 35	18	24	—	20
OVER 35	16	—	—	18

NOTES:

Girth is width of sheet metal from which gutter is fabricated.

Sizes listed in table at top of page but not marked as stock are available on special order. Other metals available on special order.

EXPANSION JOINTS

Wherever straight runs exceed 60 ft. in length, provide expansion joints similar to that shown for built-in gutters.

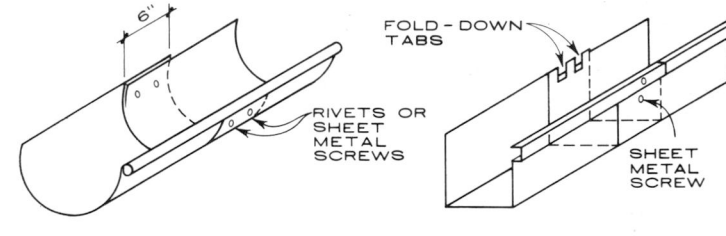

LOCK JOINT   **SLIP JOINT**   **LAP JOINT**   **LAP JOINT**

NOTES: All jointing methods are applicable to most gutter shapes. Lap joint is most common.

Seal all joints with mastic or by soldering. These joints do not provide expansion.

SPLICED JOINTS IN METAL GUTTERS

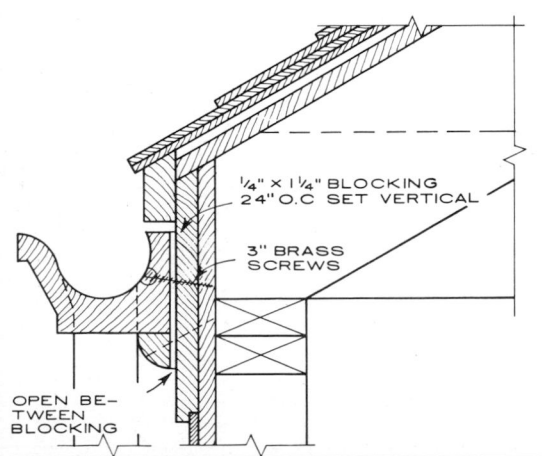

TYPICAL WOOD GUTTER DETAIL-1½″=1′-0″

Lawrence W. Cobb, AIA; Columbia, South Carolina

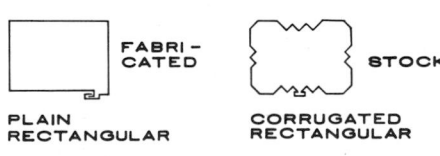

PLAIN RECTANGULAR   **CORRUGATED RECTANGULAR**

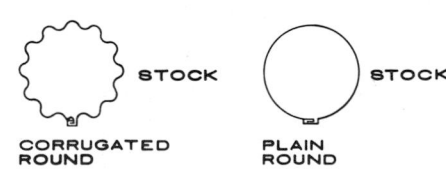

CORRUGATED ROUND   **PLAIN ROUND**

NOTES:

Space downspouts 20 ft. min., 50 ft. max., generally. Extreme max. 60 ft.

Do not use size smaller than 7.00 in area except for canopies.

Corrugated shapes resist freezing better than plain shapes.

Elbows available: 45°, 60°, 75°, 90°.

MINIMUM METAL GAUGES

GALVANIZED IRON	26 GA.
STAINLESS STEEL	28 GA.
ALUMINUM	0.025 IN.
COPPER	16 OZ.

STANDARD DOWNSPOUT SHAPES

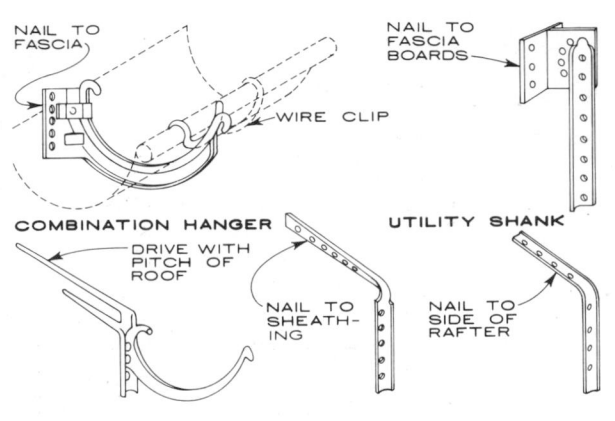

NAIL TO FASCIA

WIRE CLIP

COMBINATION HANGER

DRIVE WITH PITCH OF ROOF

NAIL TO SHEATHING

UTILITY SHANK

NAIL TO FASCIA BOARDS

NAIL TO SIDE OF RAFTER

DRIVE HANGER   **VARIOUS SHANKS**

SHANK AND CIRCLE HANGERS
Available in malleable and wrought copper, bronze, stainless steel and aluminum. Only a sampling of the wide variety of shapes available is shown. See mfrs. literature.

GUTTER HANGERS

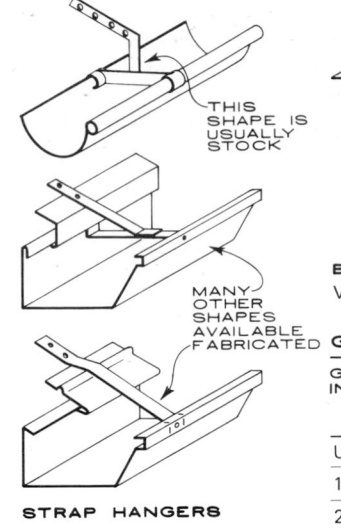

THIS SHAPE IS USUALLY STOCK

MANY OTHER SHAPES AVAILABLE FABRICATED

STRAP HANGERS

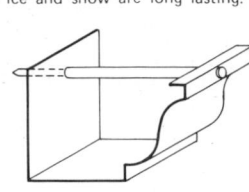

NOTE: Gutter hangers are normally spaced 3'-0" O.C. Reduce to 1'-6" O.C. where ice and snow are long lasting.

BRACKET HANGER
Various shapes are available.

SPIKE AND FERRULE
Not recommended if girth is over 15 in.

GUTTER BRACKET OR STRAP SIZES

GIRTH INCHES	GALV. STEEL INCHES	COPPER INCHES	ALUM. INCHES	STAINLESS INCHES
UP TO 15	1/8 x 1	1/8 x 1	3/16 x 1	1/8 x 1
15 TO 20	3/16 x 1	1/4 x 1	1/4 x 1	1/8 x 1 1/2
20 TO 24	1/4 x 1 1/2	1/4 x 1 1/2	1/4 x 2	1/8 x 2

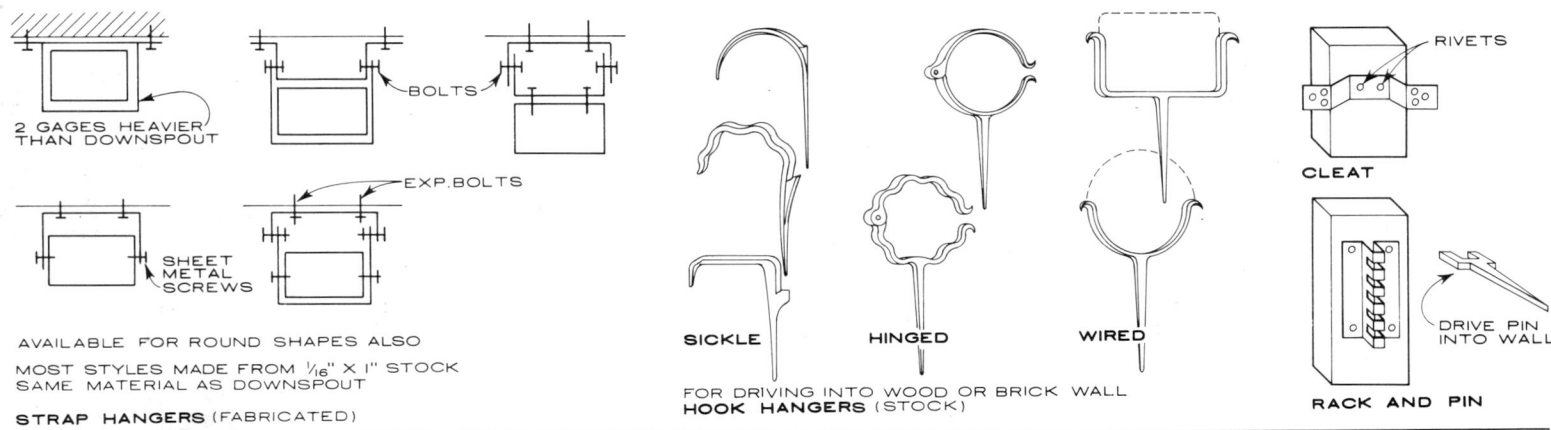

2 GAGES HEAVIER THAN DOWNSPOUT

BOLTS

EXP. BOLTS

SHEET METAL SCREWS

AVAILABLE FOR ROUND SHAPES ALSO

MOST STYLES MADE FROM 1/16" X 1" STOCK SAME MATERIAL AS DOWNSPOUT

STRAP HANGERS (FABRICATED)

SICKLE   **HINGED**   **WIRED**

FOR DRIVING INTO WOOD OR BRICK WALL

HOOK HANGERS (STOCK)

RIVETS

CLEAT

DRIVE PIN INTO WALL

RACK AND PIN

DOWNSPOUT HANGERS

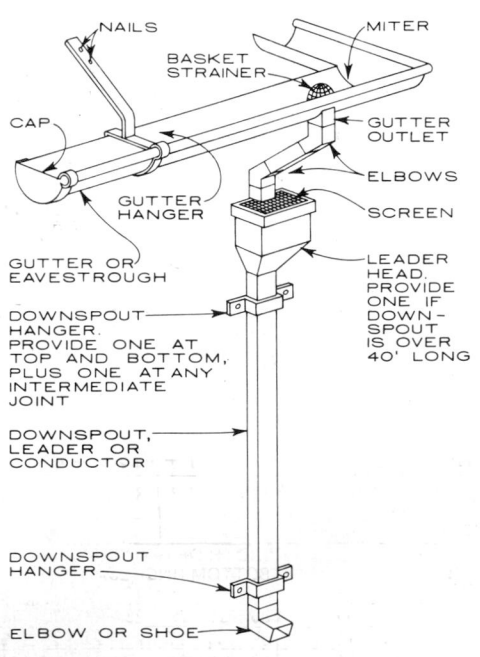

NAILS

BASKET STRAINER

MITER

CAP

GUTTER HANGER

GUTTER OUTLET

ELBOWS

SCREEN

GUTTER OR EAVESTROUGH

DOWNSPOUT HANGER. PROVIDE ONE AT TOP AND BOTTOM, PLUS ONE AT ANY INTERMEDIATE JOINT

LEADER HEAD. PROVIDE ONE IF DOWNSPOUT IS OVER 40' LONG

DOWNSPOUT, LEADER OR CONDUCTOR

DOWNSPOUT HANGER

ELBOW OR SHOE

PARTS OF A GUTTER

Lawrence W. Cobb, AIA; Columbia, South Carolina

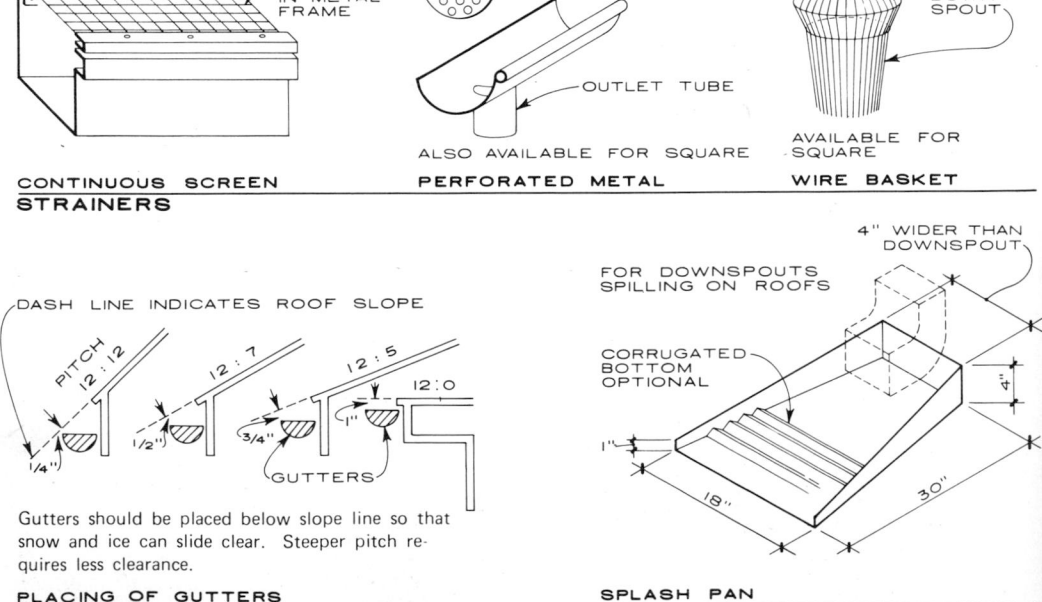

1/4" MESH SCREEN IN METAL FRAME

CONTINUOUS SCREEN

INSTALL AT EACH DOWNSPOUT

OUTLET TUBE

ALSO AVAILABLE FOR SQUARE

PERFORATED METAL

INSTALL AT EACH DOWNSPOUT

AVAILABLE FOR SQUARE

WIRE BASKET

STRAINERS

DASH LINE INDICATES ROOF SLOPE

PITCH 12:12   12:7   12:5   12:0

1/4"   1/2"   3/4"   1"

GUTTERS

Gutters should be placed below slope line so that snow and ice can slide clear. Steeper pitch requires less clearance.

PLACING OF GUTTERS

STRAINERS

4" WIDER THAN DOWNSPOUT

FOR DOWNSPOUTS SPILLING ON ROOFS

CORRUGATED BOTTOM OPTIONAL

1"   4"   18"   30"

SPLASH PAN

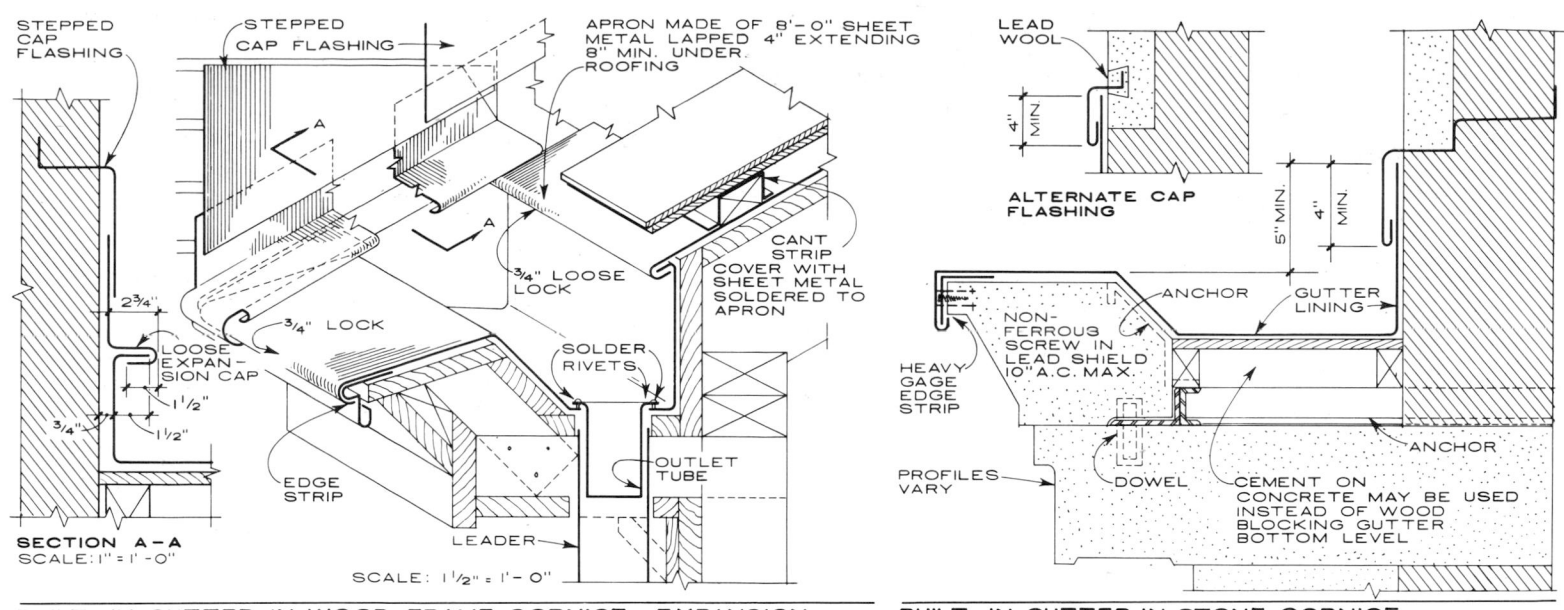

SECTION A-A
SCALE: 1" = 1'-0"

BUILT-IN GUTTER IN WOOD FRAME CORNICE - EXPANSION JOINT AT BRICK WALL

SCALE: 1 1/2" = 1'-0"

BUILT-IN GUTTER IN STONE CORNICE
SCALE: 3/4" = 1'-0"

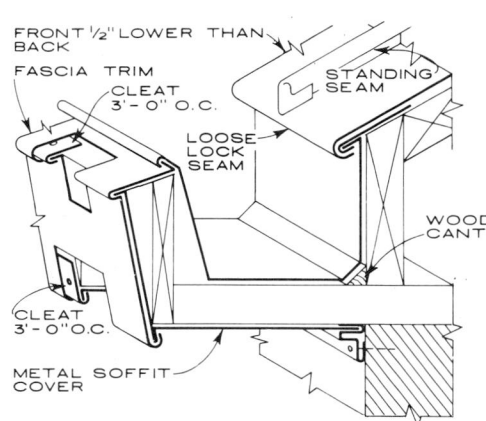

WITH METAL SOFFIT COVER
SCALE: 1 1/2" = 1'-0"

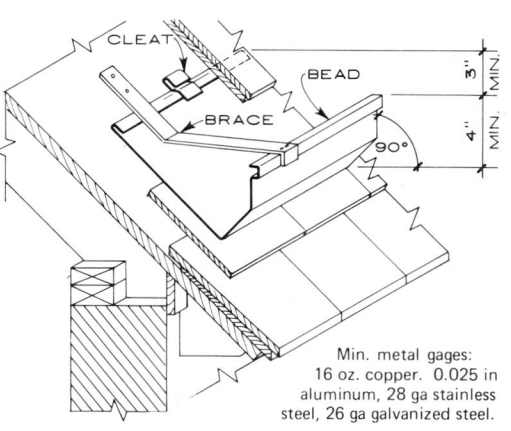

Min. metal gages: 16 oz. copper. 0.025 in aluminum, 28 ga stainless steel, 26 ga galvanized steel.

WATER DIVERTER - FOR ENTRANCES & SLOPING CANOPIES - SCALE: 3/4" = 1'-0"

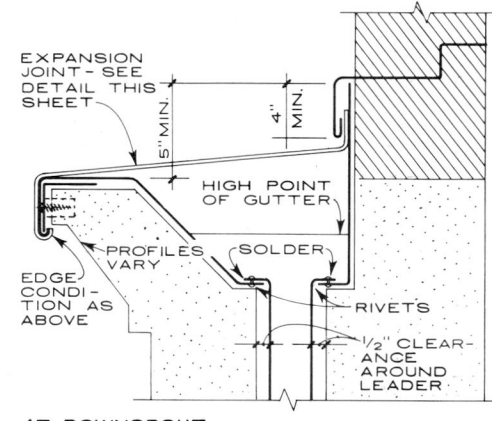

AT DOWNSPOUT
SCALE: 3/4" = 1'-0"

ALLOWANCES FOR GUTTER EXPANSION

COPPER OR ST. STL.			GALVANIZED STL.		
TEMP F	30'	60'	TEMP F	30'	60'
E @ 170	1/4"	1/4"	E @ 170	1/4"	1/4"
120	7/16"	5/8"	120	3/8"	1/2"
100	1/2"	3/4"	100	7/16"	5/8"
75	9/16"	7/8"	75	1/2"	3/4"
35	11/16"	1 1/8"	35	9/16"	7/8"
0	13/16"	1 3/8"	0	5/8"	1"
B	2"	3 1/4"	B	1-3/4"	2 1/2"
C	1/2"	13/16"	C	7/16"	5/8"
D	1/2"	13/16"	D	7/16"	5/8"

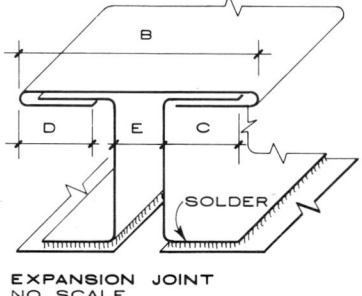

EXPANSION JOINT
NO SCALE

DIAGRAM OF GUTTER LINING
NO SCALE

Gutter lining fixed at downspout moving to and from expansion joint.

3'-0" IF GIRTH OF GUTTER EXCEEDS 36" MAX. 8'-0" MAX.

ALUMINUM			ZINC		
TEMP F	30'	60'	TEMP F	30'	60'
E @ 170	1/4"	1/4"	E @ 170	1/4"	1/4"
120	1/2"	3/4"	120	9/16"	7/8"
100	5/8"	1"	100	11/16"	1 1/16"
75	3/4"	1 1/4"	75	7/8"	1 1/2"
35	15/16"	1 5/8"	35	1 1/8"	2"
0	1 1/8"	2"	0	1 3/8"	2 1/2"
B	2 3/4"	4 1/2"	B	3"	5 1/2"
C	11/16"	1 1/8"	C	3/4"	1 3/8"
D	11/16"	1 1/8"	D	3/4"	1 3/8"

MAXIMUM DISTANCE BETWEEN EXPAN. JOINT & DOWNSPOUT (FT) BUILT IN GUTTER

SIDE ANGLES OF GUTTER	16 OZ. COPPER / 26 GA. STAINLESS / 40 LB. TERNE — WIDTH GUTTER BOTTOM (IN)			20 OZ. COPPER / 24 GA. STAINLESS / 40 LB. TERNE — WIDTH GUTTER BOTTOM (IN)					24 OZ. COPPER / 22 GA. STAINLESS STL. / 40 LB. TERNE — WIDTH GUTTER BOTTOM (INCHES)						
	4	6	8	4	6	8	10	12	4	6	8	10	12	14	16
45°–90°	22	18	16	28	24	21	18	17	36	31	26	23	21	20	18
60°–90°	23	19	17	31	26	22	20	18	39	33	28	25	23	21	19
90°–90°	26	21	19	34	29	25	22	20	42	36	31	27	25	23	21
45°–60°	18	16	14	25	22	18	16	14	32	27	24	21	19	17	16

Lawrence W. Cobb, AIA; Columbia, South Carolina

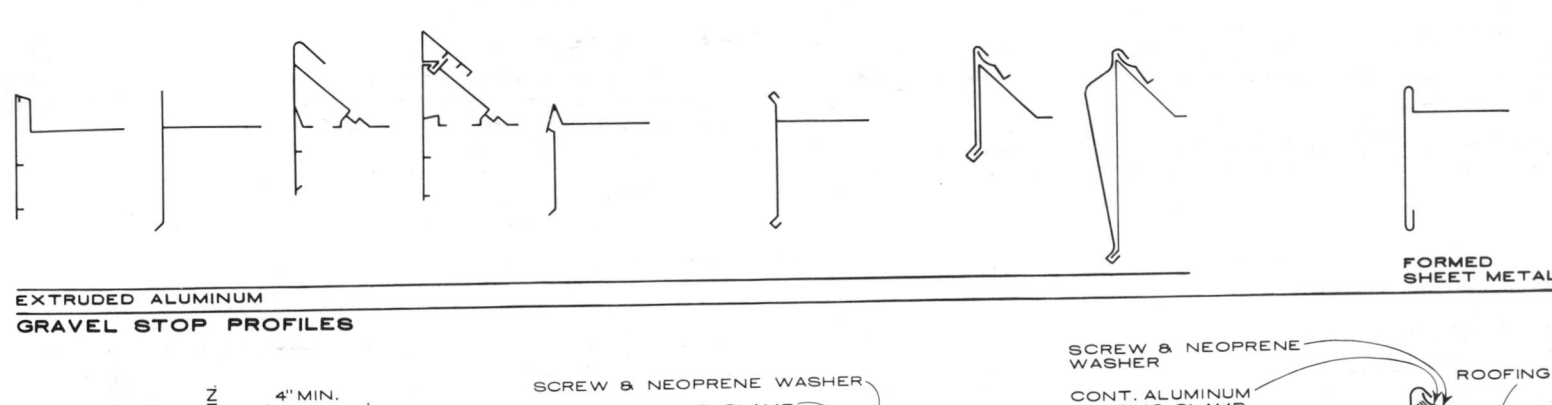

FORMED
SHEET METAL

EXTRUDED ALUMINUM

GRAVEL STOP PROFILES

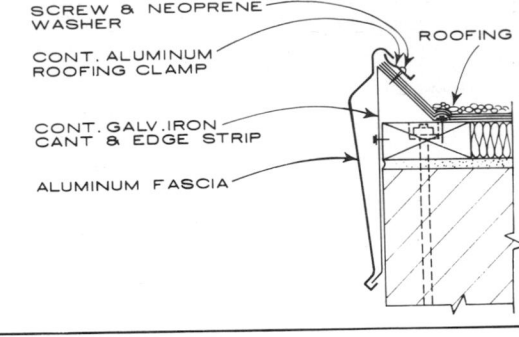

CONT. METAL
PITCH DAM

GRAVEL STOP

CONT. METAL
EDGE STRIP

1" MIN.

4" MIN.

ROOFING

3/4" LOCK

1" MIN.

FORMED SHEET METAL

SCREW & NEOPRENE WASHER

CONT. FLASHING CLAMP

GRAVEL STOP CLAMP

GRAVEL STOP

CONT. METAL
PITCH DAM

BASE
FLASHING

ROOFING

EXTRUDED ALUMINUM

SCREW & NEOPRENE
WASHER

CONT. ALUMINUM
ROOFING CLAMP

CONT. GALV. IRON
CANT & EDGE STRIP

ALUMINUM FASCIA

ROOFING

GRAVEL STOP DETAILS
NOTE: USE NEOPRENE WASHERS @ ALL FASTENERS

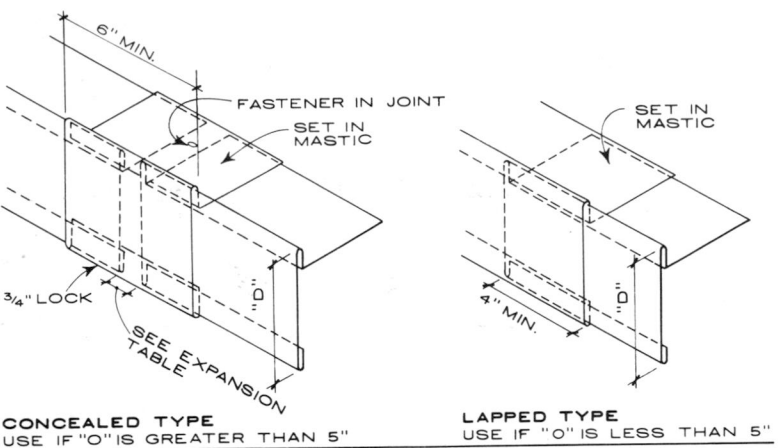

6" MIN.

FASTENER IN JOINT

SET IN
MASTIC

3/4" LOCK

SEE EXPANSION
TABLE

"D"

CONCEALED TYPE
USE IF "O" IS GREATER THAN 5"

SET IN
MASTIC

4" MIN.

"D"

LAPPED TYPE
USE IF "O" IS LESS THAN 5"

GRAVEL STOP EXPANSION JOINTS

FORMED ALUMINUM
JOINT COVER

ALUMINUM ANCHOR-GUTTER
BAR BELOW

EXTRUDED ALUMINUM
COPING COVER

1 1/4"

4"

EXTRUDED ALUMINUM

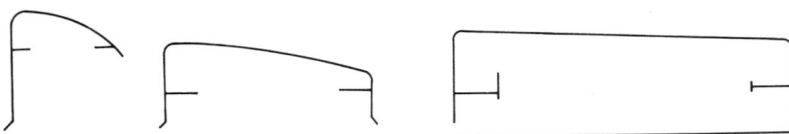
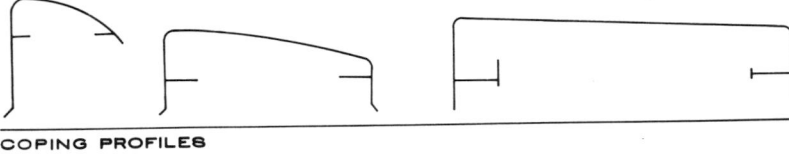

COPING PROFILES

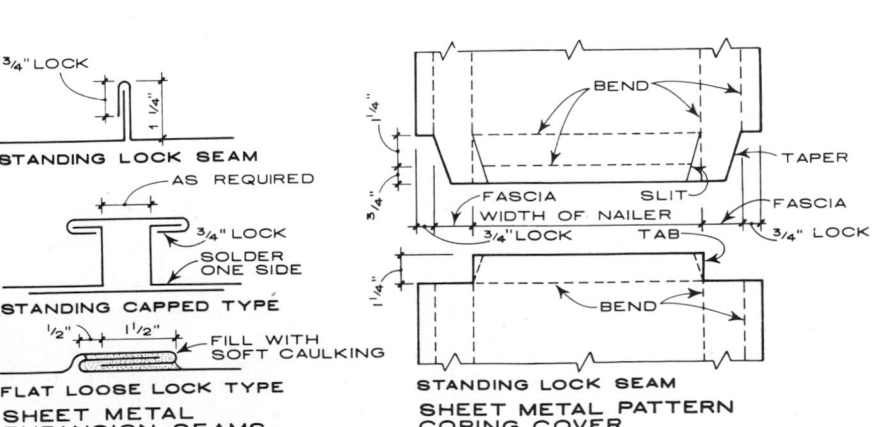

3/4" LOCK

1 1/4"

STANDING LOCK SEAM

AS REQUIRED

3/4" LOCK

SOLDER
ONE SIDE

STANDING CAPPED TYPE

1/2"   1 1/2"

FILL WITH
SOFT CAULKING

FLAT LOOSE LOCK TYPE

**SHEET METAL
EXPANSION SEAMS**

BEND

1/4"

3/4"

FASCIA   SLIT
WIDTH OF NAILER
3/4" LOCK   TAB

TAPER

FASCIA

3/4" LOCK

1/4"

BEND

STANDING LOCK SEAM

**SHEET METAL PATTERN
COPING COVER**

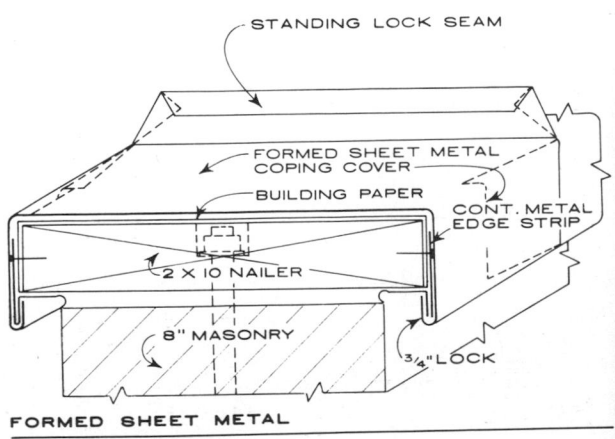

STANDING LOCK SEAM

FORMED SHEET METAL
COPING COVER

BUILDING PAPER

CONT. METAL
EDGE STRIP

2 X 10 NAILER

8" MASONRY

3/4" LOCK

FORMED SHEET METAL

COPING DETAILS

Ferebee, Walters and Associates; Charlotte, North Carolina

DEFINITIONS:

Waterproofing is a system intended to prevent the passage of water through walls and floors.

Dampproofing is to prevent the passage of moisture or collection of water vapors. A system that is not capable of withstanding hydrostatic pressures.

GENERAL NOTES:

1. Membrane, hydrolithic and chemical admixtures in concrete are typical types of waterproofing and dampproofing systems. Choice of the appropriate system depends upon the prevailing hydrostatic conditions. Consult manufacturers for system properties and uses.
2. Specify installation to conform strictly to the recommendations of the manufacturer of the system selected.
3. The details on the fellowing pages are typical conditions only.

TYPICAL SYSTEMS

TYPE	DESCRIPTION	GENERAL USES
MEMBRANES	Tar or asphalt bitumens on and between layer(s) of felt made of rag, asbestos and wood fiber or of fabric made of cotton and glass. Butyl rubber and polyvinyl chloride sheets with laps sealed with adhesives and cements.	Exterior, below grade on walls and under floors. Under walking surfaces of roofs.
HYDROLITHIC COATINGS	Sprayed, troweled or brushed on coatings of asphaltic bitumens and plastics. Coatings of plaster or cement mixed with ferrous particles.	Exterior, below grade on walls. Interior, below grade on walls and floors.
CONCRETE ADMIXTURES	Liquid, paste or powder admixtures used integrally to render concrete impermeable.	Walls and floors above and below grade, concrete canopies and covered walks.
METAL WATERPROOFING	Plain metal sheets, and metal sheets coated with fabric and/or plastic sheets sealed by soldering, adhesives and cements. Generally the metal is lead or copper.	Shower stalls and pans, pools, around floor and roof drains. Under walking surfaces on roofs.

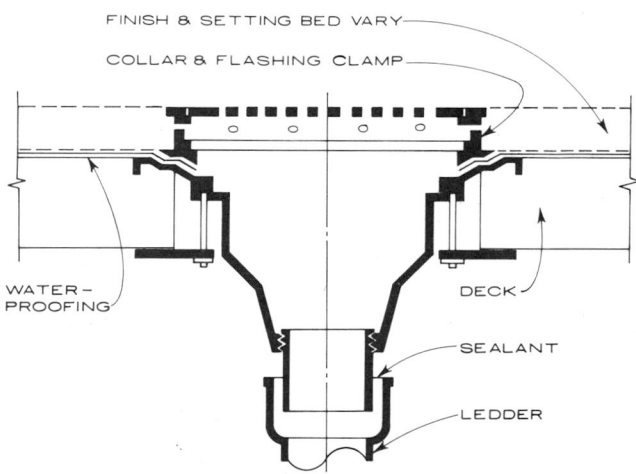

DRAIN IN WATERPROOFED WALKING SURFACE

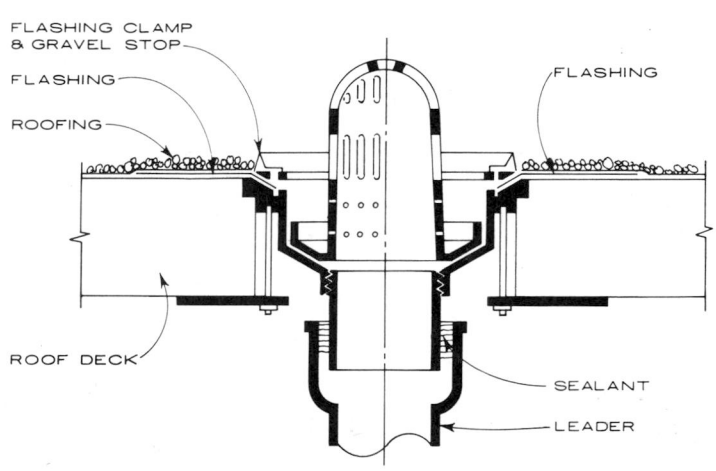

ROOF DRAIN

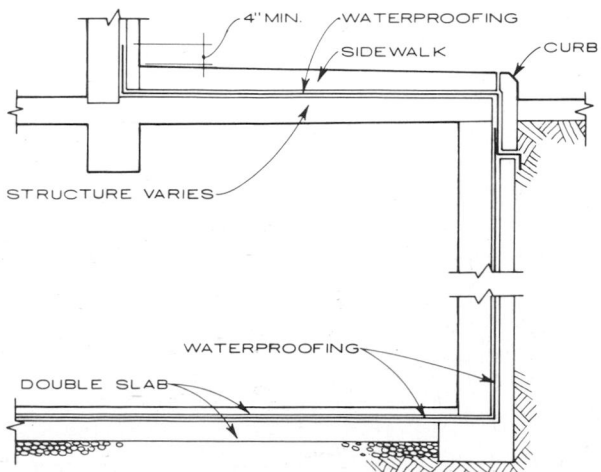

SIDEWALK VAULT – MEMBRANE AND METAL WATERPROOFING

William C. Nichols, AIA; Atlanta, Georgia

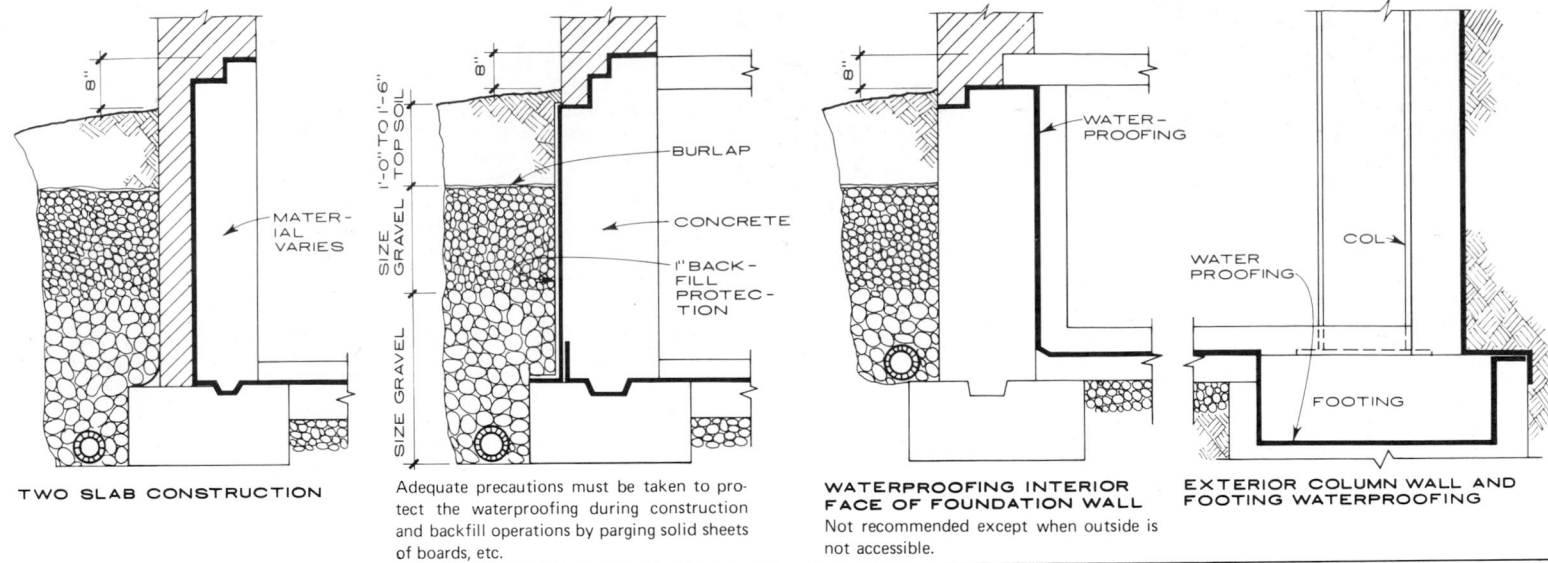

TWO SLAB CONSTRUCTION

Adequate precautions must be taken to protect the waterproofing during construction and backfill operations by parging solid sheets of boards, etc.

WATERPROOFING INTERIOR FACE OF FOUNDATION WALL
Not recommended except when outside is not accessible.

EXTERIOR COLUMN WALL AND FOOTING WATERPROOFING

EXTERIOR WALLS – TWO SLAB CONSTRUCTION – MEMBRANE AND METAL TYPES

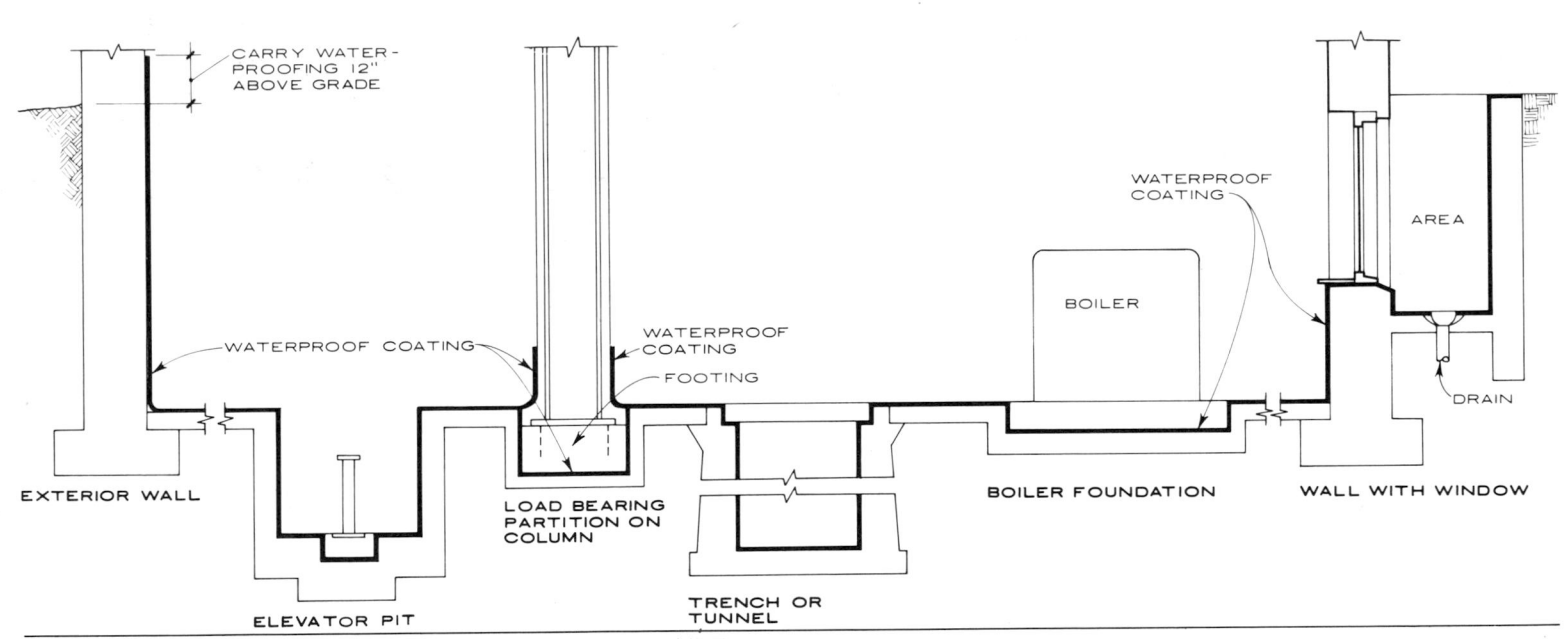

EXTERIOR WALL

ELEVATOR PIT

LOAD BEARING PARTITION ON COLUMN

TRENCH OR TUNNEL

BOILER FOUNDATION

WALL WITH WINDOW

WATERPROOF COATING METHOD – HYDROLITHIC TYPE
RECOMMENDED ONLY WHEN OUTSIDE IS NOT ACCESSIBLE

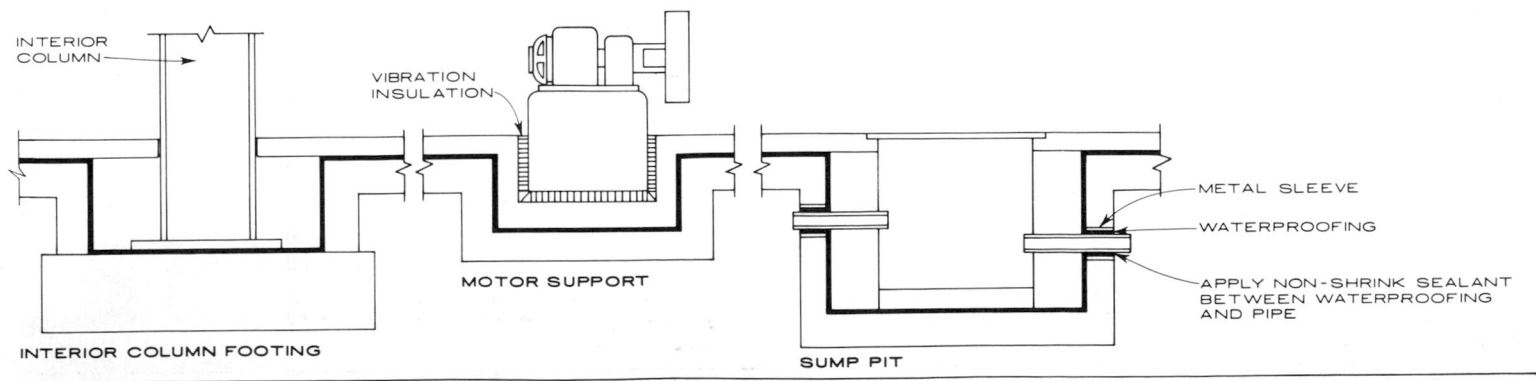

INTERIOR COLUMN FOOTING

MOTOR SUPPORT

SUMP PIT

WATERPROOFING WITH PROTECTIVE SLAB – MEMBRANE TYPE

William C. Nichols, AIA; Atlanta, Georgia

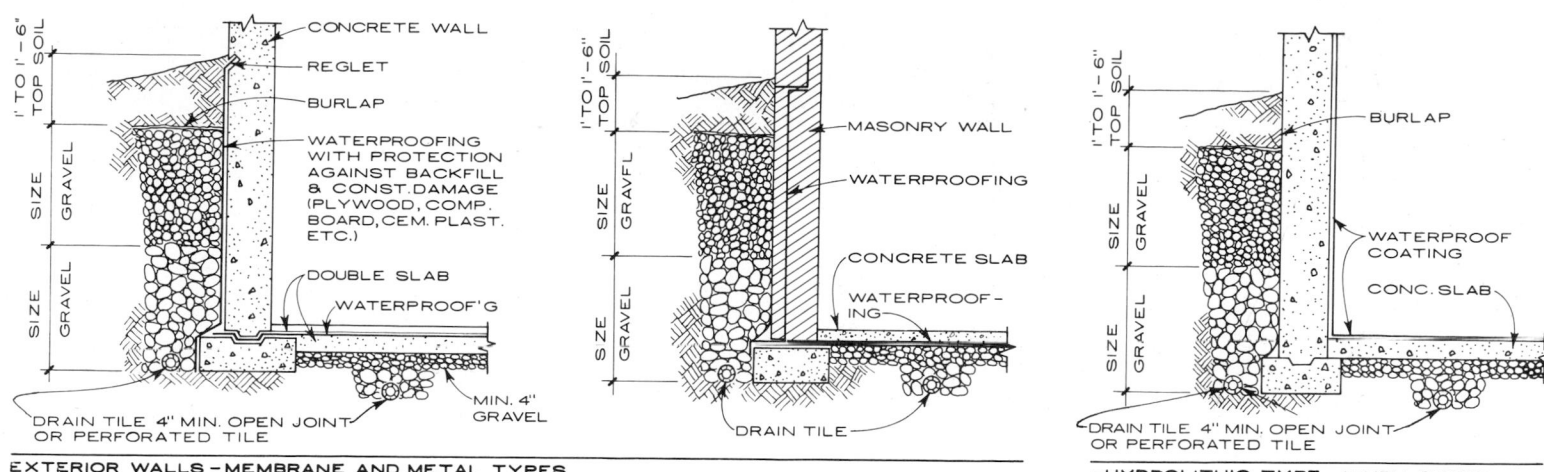

EXTERIOR WALLS – MEMBRANE AND METAL TYPES

– HYDROLITHIC TYPE – WHEN OUTER SIDE IS NOT ACCESSIBLE

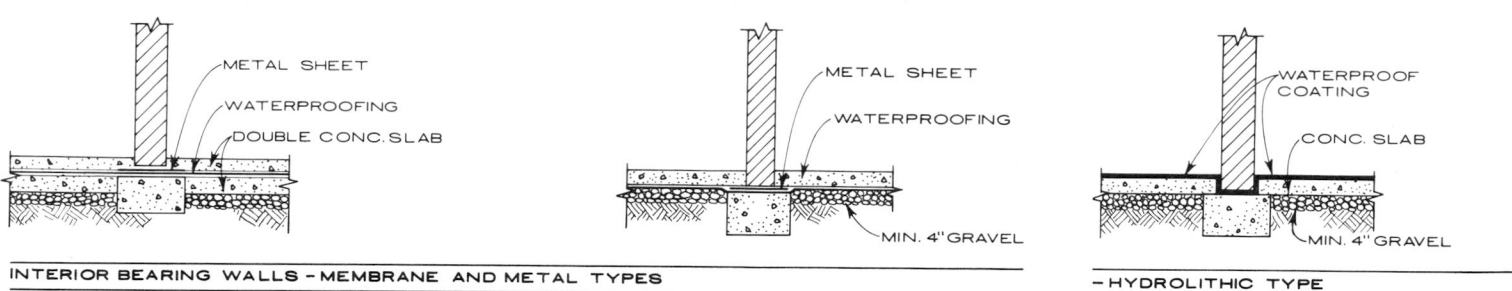

INTERIOR BEARING WALLS – MEMBRANE AND METAL TYPES

– HYDROLITHIC TYPE

RESIDENTIAL WATERPROOFING – BASEMENTS BELOW GRADE

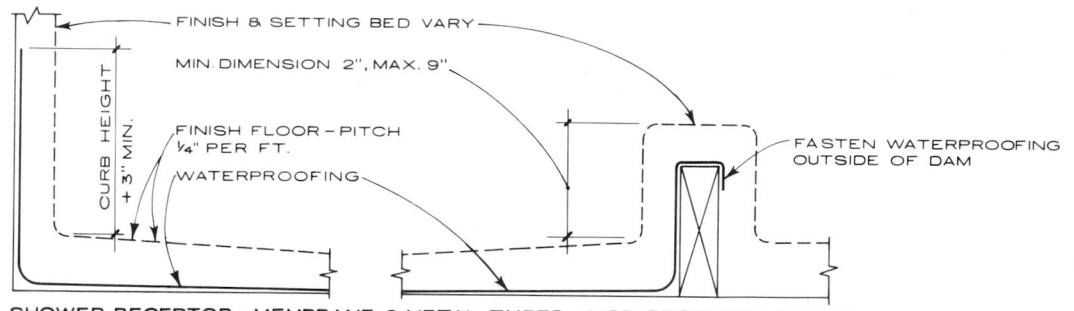

SHOWER RECEPTOR – MEMBRANE & METAL TYPES – MOP RECEPTOR SIMILAR

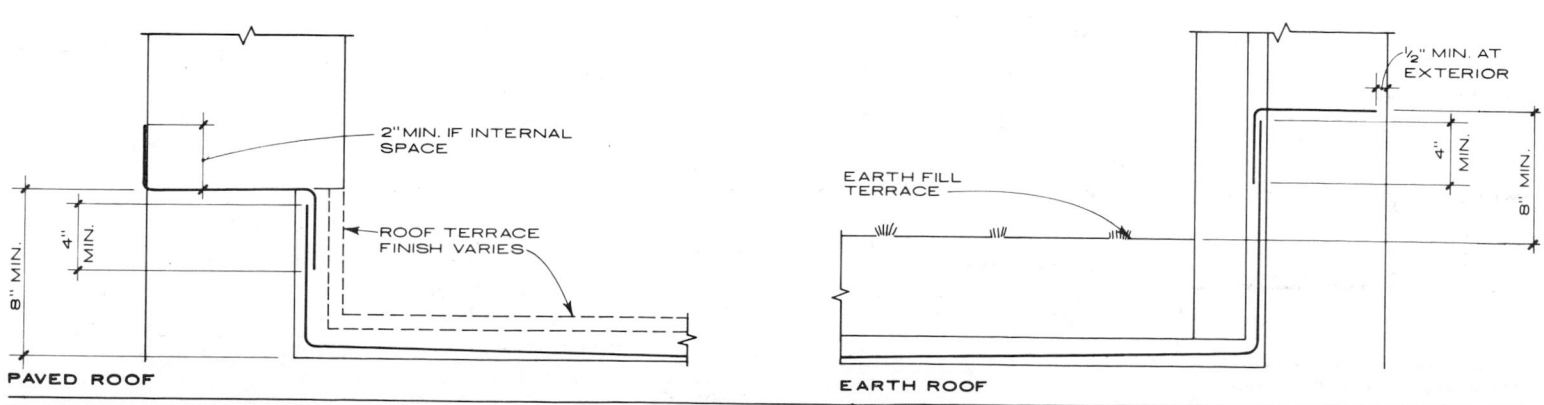

PAVED ROOF

EARTH ROOF

FLASHING BETWEEN WALL AND SPECIAL ROOF COVERING – MEMBRANE AND METAL TYPES

William C. Nichols, AIA; Atlanta, Georgia

FLASHING DEFINITION: Pieces of sheet metal to prevent the leakage or driving-in of rain water at the joints around the openings, the joints or angles between a roof or floor and any vertical surface against which it abuts.

MINIMUM THICKNESSES (GAUGES OR WEIGHT) FOR COMMON FLASHING CONDITIONS

MATERIAL / CONDITIONS	A BASE COURSE	B WALL OPENINGS HEAD AND SILL	C THRU-WALL	D SPANDREL	E CAP FLASHING	F BASE FLASHING	G VERTICAL SURFACE	H HORIZONTAL SURFACE	J ROOF EDGE	K VALLEY OR GUTTER	L RIDGES – HIPS	M CRICKETS	N CHIMNEY PAN	O LEDGE FLASHING	P ROOF PENETRATIONS	R COPING WIDTH	S EDGE STRIPS	T CLEATS	NOTE REFERENCE
COPPER	10 OZ	10 OZ	10 OZ	10 OZ	16 OZ	16 OZ	16 OZ	20 OZ	16 OZ	16 OZ	16 OZ	16 OZ	16 OZ	16 OZ	16 OZ	16 OZ	20 OZ	20 OZ	NOTE #6
ALUMINUM	.019"	.019"	.019"	.019"	.019"	.019"	.019"	.019"	.019"	.019"	.019"	.019	.019"	.019"	.019"	.040"	.032"	.024"	NOTE #5
STAINLESS STEEL	30 GA	30 GA	30 GA	30 GA	26 GA	26 GA	30 GA	30 GA	26 GA	26 GA	26 GA	26 GA	30 GA	26 GA	26 GA	26 GA	24 GA	24 GA	NOTE #2
GALVANIZED STEEL	26 GA	26 GA	26 GA	26 GA	26 GA	26 GA	26 GA	24 GA	24 GA	24 GA	24 GA	24 GA	26 GA	24 GA	24 GA	24 GA	22 GA	26 GA	NOTE #4
ZINC ALLOY	.027"	.027"	.027"	.027"	.027"	.027"	.020"	.027"	.027"	.027"	.027"	.027"	.027"	.027"	.027"	.027"	.032"	.040"	NOTE #3
LEAD	3 #	2½ #	2½ #	2½ #	2½ #	2½ #	3 #	3 #	3 #	3 #	2½ #	3 #	3 #	3 #	3 #	3 #	20 #	40 #	NOTE #8
PAINTED TERNE	40 #	40 #	40 #	40 #	20 #	20 #	40 #	40 #	20 #	40 #	20 #	40 #	20 #	40 #	40 #	⊠	20 #	40 #	NOTE #7
ELASTIC	SEE NOTE 7																		

GENERAL NOTES:

1. All sizes and weights of material given in chart are minimum. Actual conditions may require greater strength.

2. All galvanized steel must be painted.

3. With lead flashing use 16 oz. copper cleats. If any part is exposed, use 3 # lead cleats.

4. Coat zinc with asphaltum paint when in contact with redwood or cedar. High acid content (in these woods only) develops stains.

5. Type 302 stainless steel is an all purpose flashing type. Cleats not needed.

6. Use only aluminum manufactured for the purpose of flashing. Cleats not needed.

7. See manufacturers literature for use and types of elastic flashing.

8. In general cleats will be same material as flashing, but heavier weight or thicker gauge.

9. In selecting metal flashing precaution must be taken not to place flashing in direct contact with dissimilar metals that cause electrolysis.

10. Spaces marked ⊠ in chart are uses not recommended for that material.

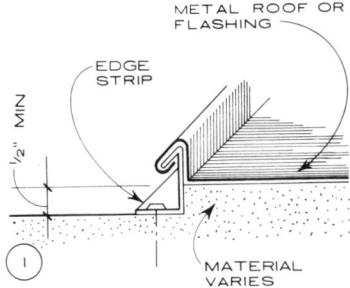

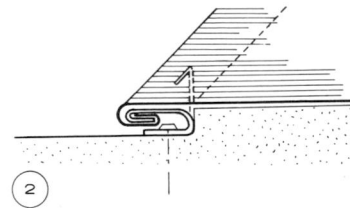

DEVELOPMENT OF EDGE
(HOLD DOWN) **STRIPS**

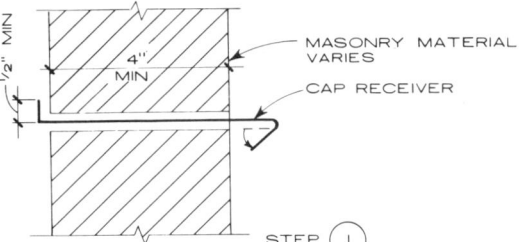

STEP 1

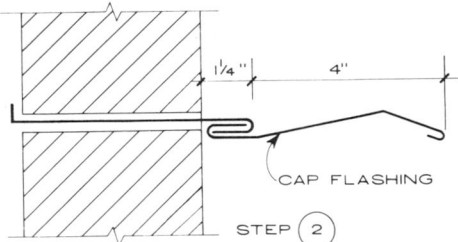

STEP 2

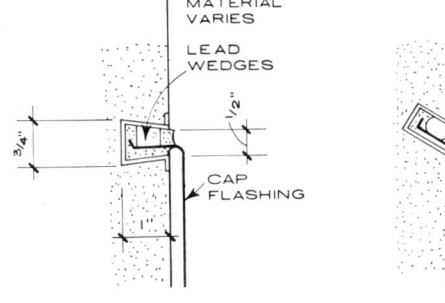

METAL REGLETS CAST IN PLACE

TYPICAL REGLETS

NOTE:
Various types of metal reglets are available for cast in place & masonry work; see manufacturer's literature. Where material permits, reglets may be sawn. Flashing is secured in reglets with lead wedges at max. 12" cc, fill reglet with non-hardening waterproof compound.

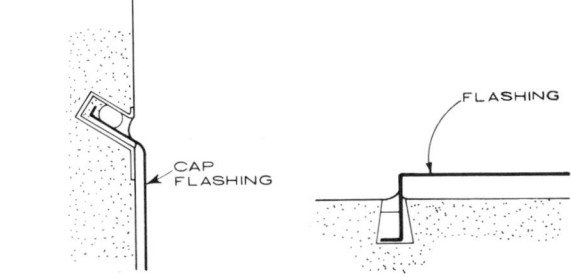

REGLET SAWED IN MATERIAL

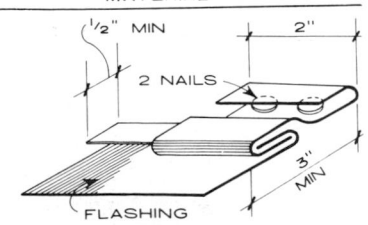

TYPICAL CLEAT

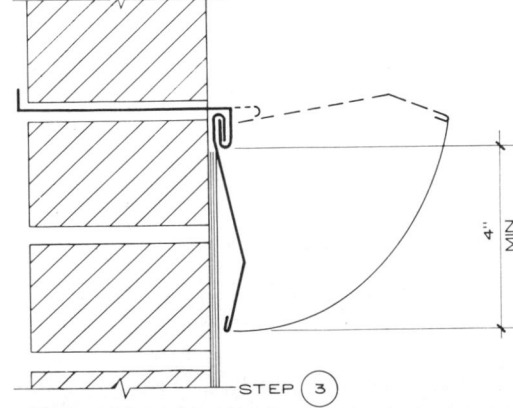

STEP 3

DEVELOPMENT OF CAP FLASHING
NOTE:
Hem in cap flashing recommended for stiffness; but may be omitted if heavier gauge material used.

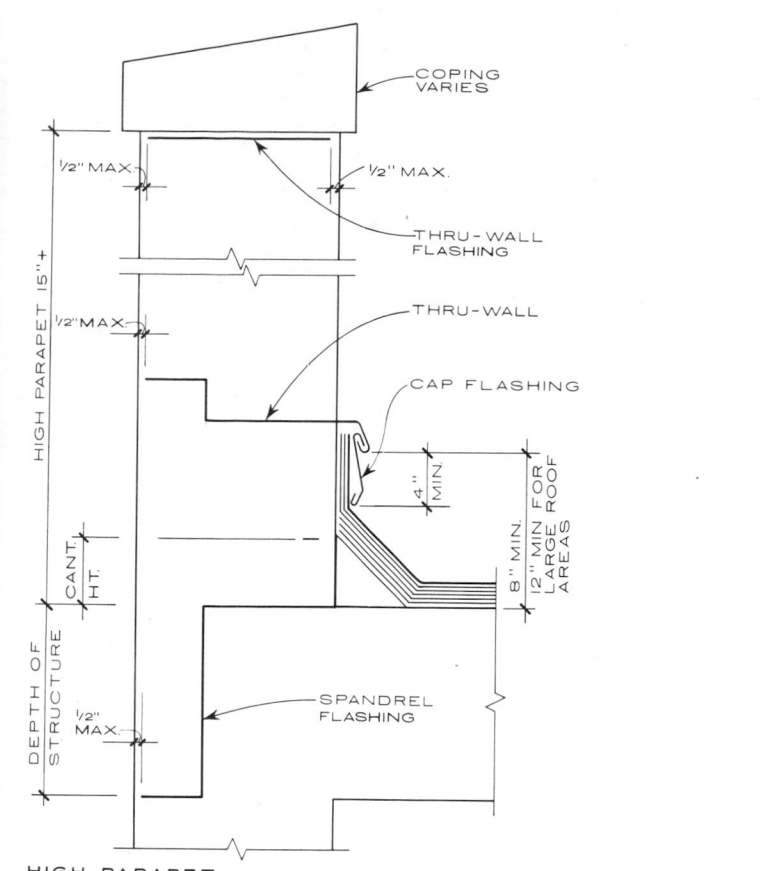

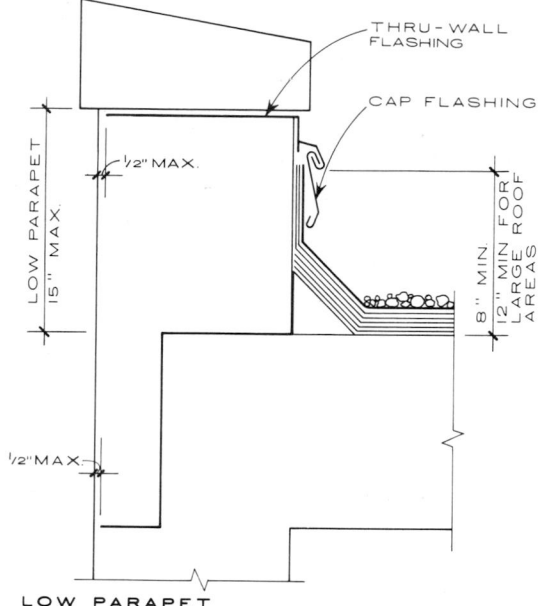

NOTE: WALL MATERIAL VARIES

HIGH PARAPET

LOW PARAPET

PARAPET FLASHING

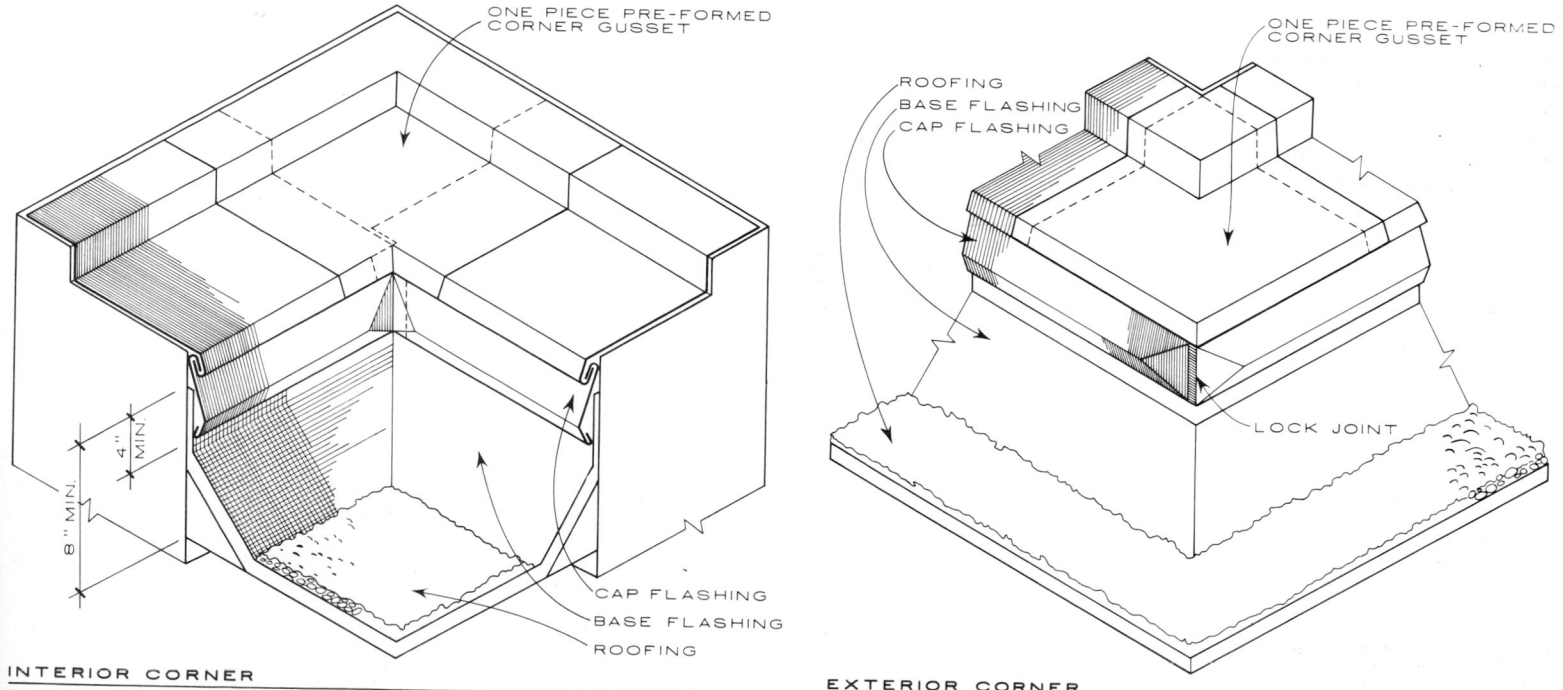

INTERIOR CORNER

EXTERIOR CORNER

PARAPET FLASHING AT CORNERS

NOTES:

1. Use loose lock joints set in non-hardening compound for adjacent pieces of flashing.

2. Where flashing turns corner insert gusset and solder at corners only.

3. Lap all vertical joints min. 4″. Cap flashing must lap base flashing min. 4″.

4. Thru-wall flashing not recommended for earthquake areas.

5. A deformed surface pattern is recommended for all thru-wall flashing.

6. The above details presume no expansion joints needed.

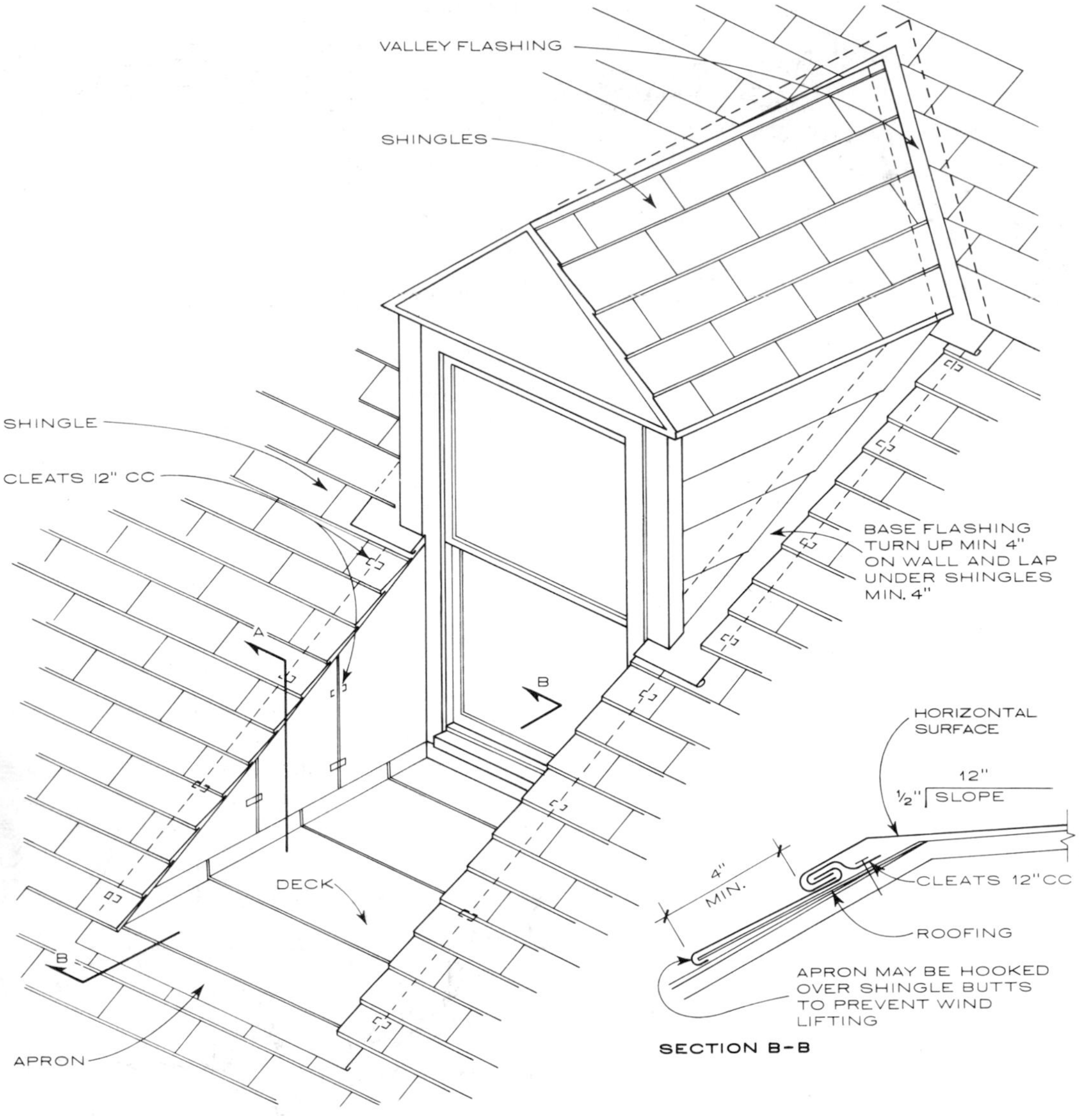

VALLEY FLASHING

SHINGLES

SHINGLE

CLEATS 12" CC

A

B

DECK

B

APRON

DORMER FLASHING

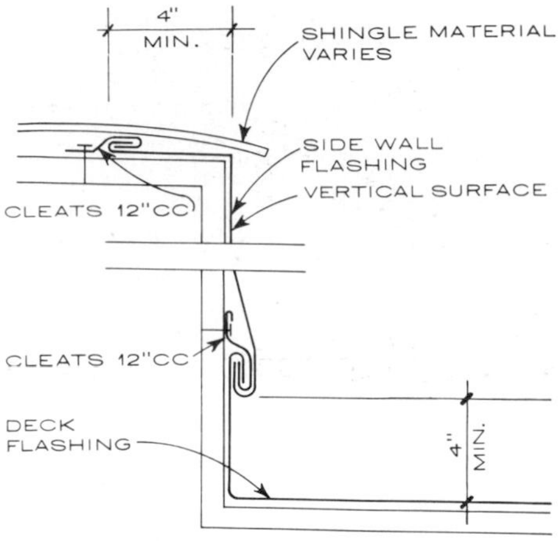

BASE FLASHING
TURN UP MIN 4"
ON WALL AND LAP
UNDER SHINGLES
MIN. 4"

4"
MIN.

SHINGLE MATERIAL
VARIES

SIDE WALL
FLASHING

VERTICAL SURFACE

CLEATS 12"CC

CLEATS 12"CC

DECK
FLASHING

4"
MIN.

SECTION A-A

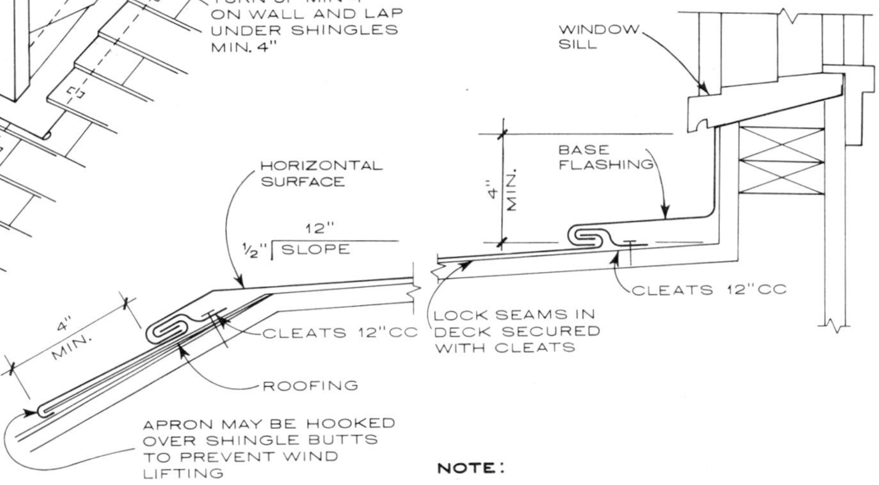

HORIZONTAL
SURFACE

$\frac{1}{2}$" | 12" | SLOPE

4"
MIN.

CLEATS 12"CC

ROOFING

APRON MAY BE HOOKED
OVER SHINGLE BUTTS
TO PREVENT WIND
LIFTING

SECTION B-B

WINDOW
SILL

BASE
FLASHING

4"
MIN.

CLEATS 12"CC

LOCK SEAMS IN
DECK SECURED
WITH CLEATS

NOTE:

Separate pieces of base flashing are installed as each
course of shingles is applied. The upper edge of each
piece should extend 2'' above each course of shingles.
The lower edge should be 1/2'' above the butts of the
shingles forming the next course.

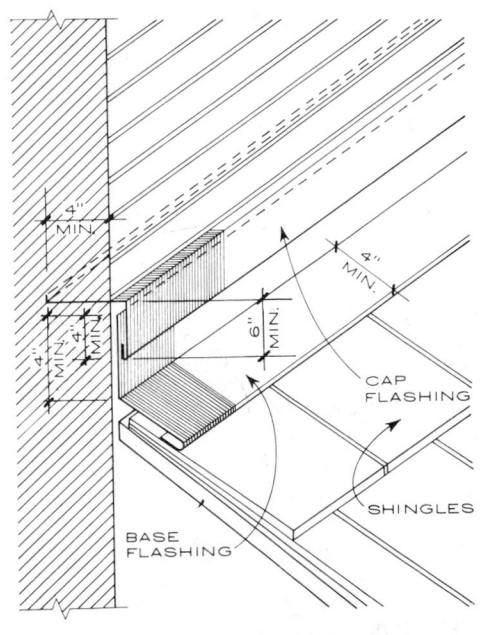

4"
MIN.

4"
MIN.

4"
MIN.

6"
MIN.

CAP
FLASHING

SHINGLES

BASE
FLASHING

**APRON FLASHING WHERE ROOF SLOPES
FROM WALL**

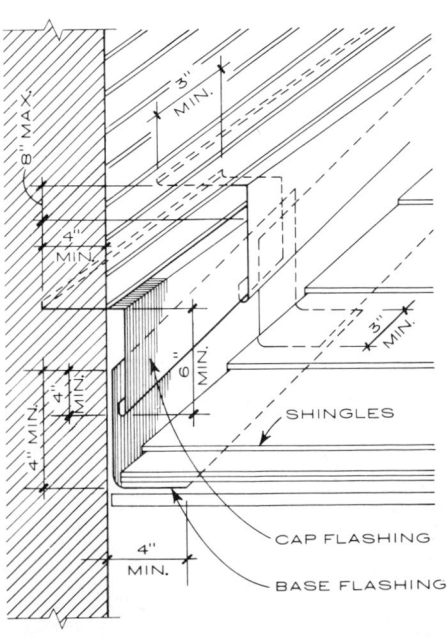

3"
MIN.

8" MAX.

4"
MIN.

6"
MIN.

4"
MIN.

3"
MIN.

SHINGLES

CAP FLASHING

BASE FLASHING

4"
MIN.

**SEPARATE PIECES OF BASE
FLASHING**

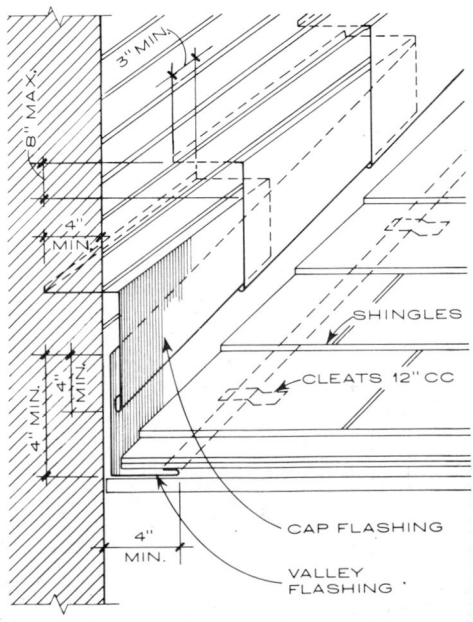

3" MIN.

8" MAX.

4"
MIN.

4"
MIN.

SHINGLES

CLEATS 12" CC

CAP FLASHING

VALLEY
FLASHING

4"
MIN.

RUNNER BASE FLASHING

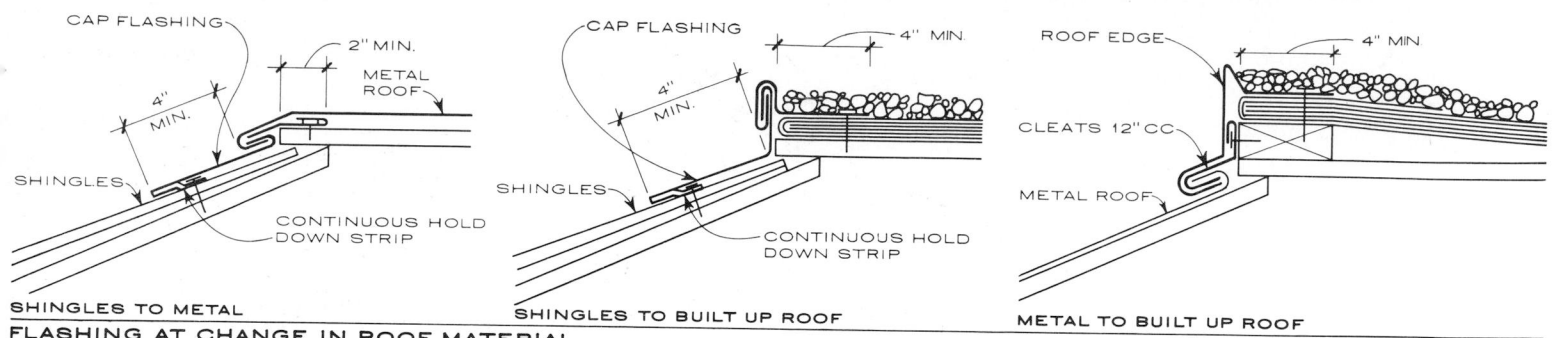

CAP FLASHING | 2" MIN. | METAL ROOF
4" MIN.
SHINGLES
CONTINUOUS HOLD DOWN STRIP

SHINGLES TO METAL

CAP FLASHING | 4" MIN.
4" MIN.
SHINGLES
CONTINUOUS HOLD DOWN STRIP

SHINGLES TO BUILT UP ROOF

ROOF EDGE | 4" MIN
CLEATS 12" CC
METAL ROOF

METAL TO BUILT UP ROOF

FLASHING AT CHANGE IN ROOF MATERIAL

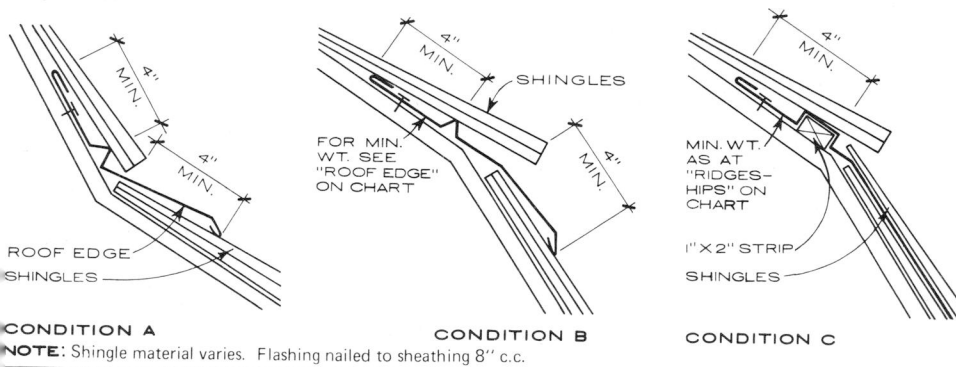

4" MIN.
4" MIN.
ROOF EDGE
SHINGLES

CONDITION A

4" MIN.
SHINGLES
FOR MIN. WT. SEE "ROOF EDGE" ON CHART
4" MIN.

CONDITION B

4" MIN.
MIN. WT. AS AT "RIDGES-HIPS" ON CHART
1" X 2" STRIP
SHINGLES

CONDITION C

NOTE: Shingle material varies. Flashing nailed to sheathing 8" c.c.

FLASHING OF BREAK IN SLOPE OF SHINGLE ROOFS

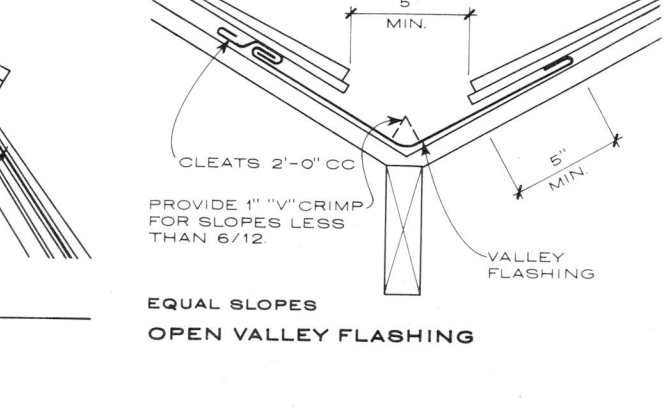

SHINGLE MATERIAL VARIES
5" MIN.
CLEATS 2'-0" CC
PROVIDE 1" "V" CRIMP FOR SLOPES LESS THAN 6/12
5" MIN.
VALLEY FLASHING

EQUAL SLOPES
OPEN VALLEY FLASHING

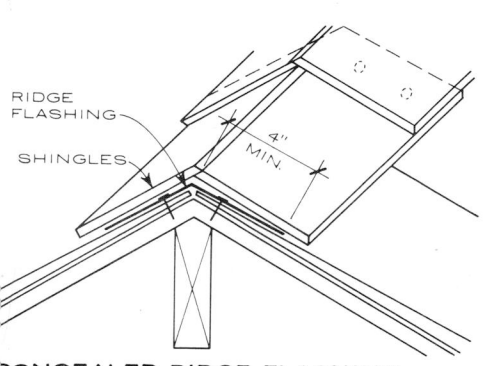

RIDGE FLASHING
SHINGLES
4" MIN.

CONCEALED RIDGE FLASHING
NOTE:

idge flashing formed in 10' lengths and lapped
". Flashing is nailed to sheathing after shingles
re installed, then flashing is covered with ridge
hingles.

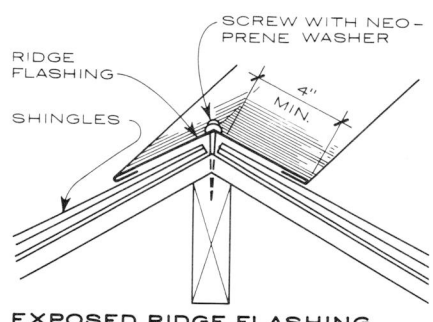

SCREW WITH NEO-PRENE WASHER
RIDGE FLASHING
SHINGLES
4" MIN.

EXPOSED RIDGE FLASHING
NOTE:

Ridge flashing formed in 10' lengths and lapped 4".

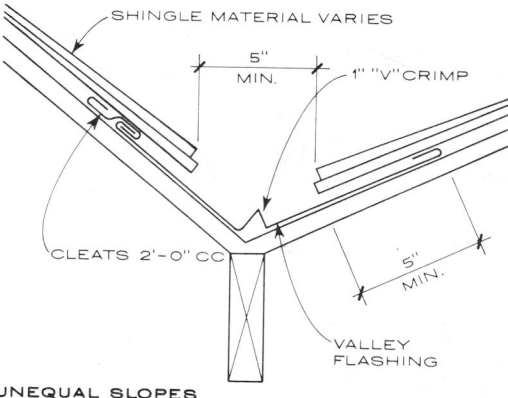

SHINGLE MATERIAL VARIES
5" MIN.
1" "V" CRIMP
CLEATS 2'-0" CC
5" MIN.
VALLEY FLASHING

UNEQUAL SLOPES
OPEN VALLEY FLASHING

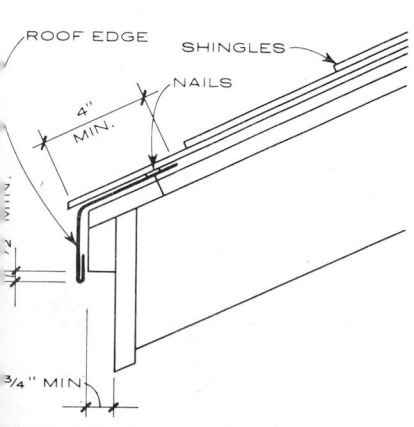

ROOF EDGE | SHINGLES
NAILS
4" MIN.
3/4" MIN.

OOF EDGE FLASHING

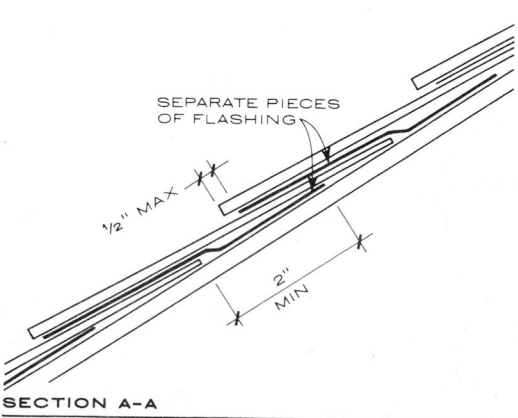

SEPARATE PIECES OF FLASHING
1/2" MAX
2" MIN

SECTION A-A
CONCEALED VALLEY FLASHING

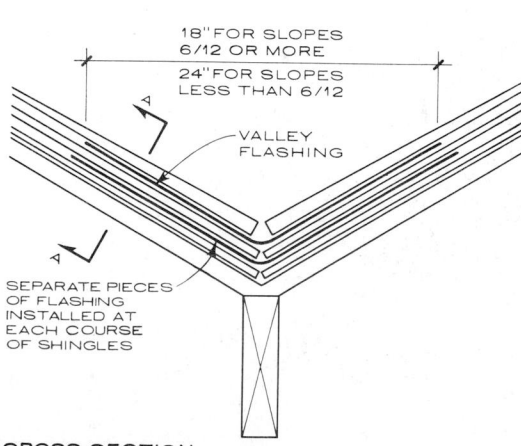

18" FOR SLOPES 6/12 OR MORE
24" FOR SLOPES LESS THAN 6/12
VALLEY FLASHING
SEPARATE PIECES OF FLASHING INSTALLED AT EACH COURSE OF SHINGLES

CROSS SECTION

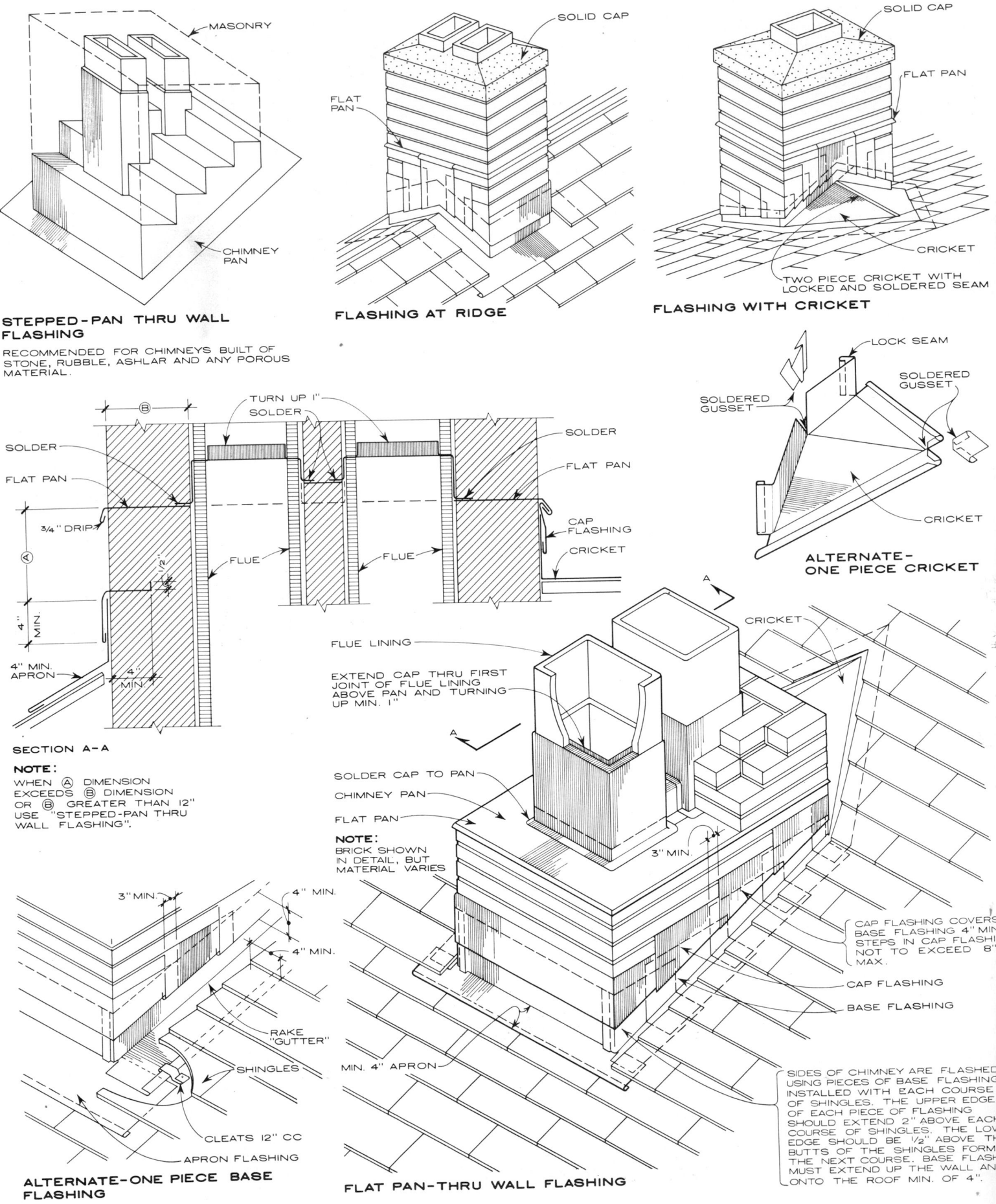

STEPPED-PAN THRU WALL FLASHING

RECOMMENDED FOR CHIMNEYS BUILT OF STONE, RUBBLE, ASHLAR AND ANY POROUS MATERIAL.

FLASHING AT RIDGE

FLASHING WITH CRICKET

TWO PIECE CRICKET WITH LOCKED AND SOLDERED SEAM

MASONRY

CHIMNEY PAN

SOLID CAP

FLAT PAN

SOLID CAP

FLAT PAN

CRICKET

ALTERNATE-ONE PIECE CRICKET

LOCK SEAM

SOLDERED GUSSET

SOLDERED GUSSET

CRICKET

SOLDER

TURN UP 1"

SOLDER

SOLDER

FLAT PAN

FLAT PAN

CAP FLASHING

CRICKET

3/4" DRIP

FLUE

FLUE

4" MIN.

4" MIN. APRON

4" MIN.

SECTION A-A

NOTE:
WHEN Ⓐ DIMENSION EXCEEDS Ⓑ DIMENSION OR Ⓑ GREATER THAN 12" USE "STEPPED-PAN THRU WALL FLASHING".

FLUE LINING

EXTEND CAP THRU FIRST JOINT OF FLUE LINING ABOVE PAN AND TURNING UP MIN. 1"

SOLDER CAP TO PAN

CHIMNEY PAN

FLAT PAN

NOTE:
BRICK SHOWN IN DETAIL, BUT MATERIAL VARIES

A

A

CRICKET

3" MIN.

CAP FLASHING COVERS BASE FLASHING 4" MIN STEPS IN CAP FLASHI NOT TO EXCEED 8" MAX.

CAP FLASHING

BASE FLASHING

3" MIN.

4" MIN.

4" MIN.

RAKE "GUTTER"

SHINGLES

CLEATS 12" CC

APRON FLASHING

ALTERNATE-ONE PIECE BASE FLASHING

MIN. 4" APRON

FLAT PAN-THRU WALL FLASHING

SIDES OF CHIMNEY ARE FLASHED USING PIECES OF BASE FLASHING INSTALLED WITH EACH COURSE OF SHINGLES. THE UPPER EDGE OF EACH PIECE OF FLASHING SHOULD EXTEND 2" ABOVE EACH COURSE OF SHINGLES. THE LOW EDGE SHOULD BE 1/2" ABOVE TH BUTTS OF THE SHINGLES FORM THE NEXT COURSE. BASE FLASH MUST EXTEND UP THE WALL AN ONTO THE ROOF MIN. OF 4".

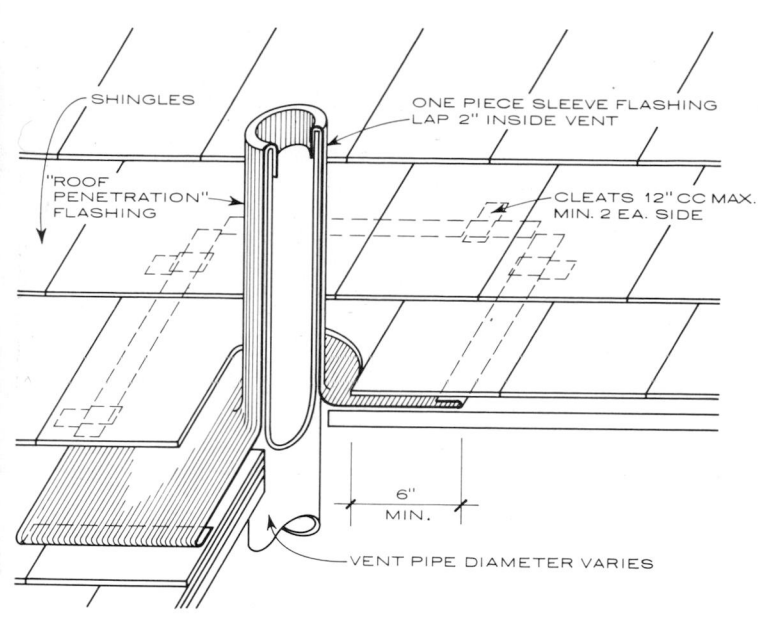

SHINGLES

ONE PIECE SLEEVE FLASHING LAP 2" INSIDE VENT

"ROOF PENETRATION" FLASHING

CLEATS 12" CC MAX. MIN. 2 EA. SIDE

6" MIN.

VENT PIPE DIAMETER VARIES

VENT IN PITCHED ROOF

LAP MIN. 2" INSIDE VENT

WEIGHT OF MATERIAL SAME AS FOR ROOF PENETRATIONS

3" MIN.

SOLDERED LAP SEAM

BUILT UP ROOF

8" MINIMUM

6" MIN.

VENT PIPE DIAMETER VARIES

VENT IN FLAT ROOF

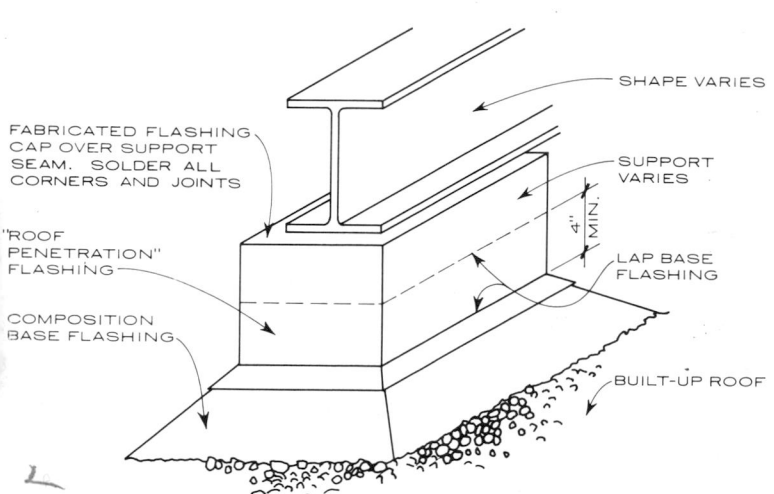

SHAPE VARIES

FABRICATED FLASHING CAP OVER SUPPORT SEAM. SOLDER ALL CORNERS AND JOINTS

SUPPORT VARIES

4" MIN.

LAP BASE FLASHING

"ROOF PENETRATION" FLASHING

COMPOSITION BASE FLASHING

BUILT-UP ROOF

FLASHING OF BEAM SUPPORT AT ROOF

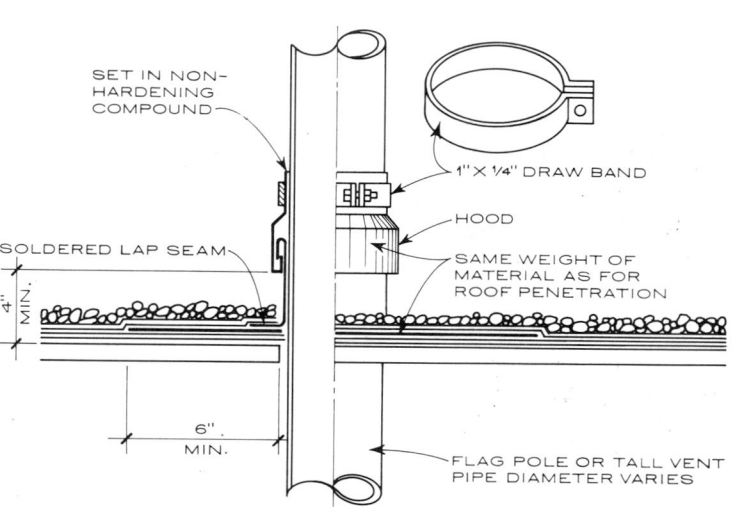

SET IN NON-HARDENING COMPOUND

1" X 1/4" DRAW BAND

HOOD

SOLDERED LAP SEAM

SAME WEIGHT OF MATERIAL AS FOR ROOF PENETRATION

4" MIN.

6" MIN.

FLAG POLE OR TALL VENT PIPE DIAMETER VARIES

TALL PIPE THRU ROOF

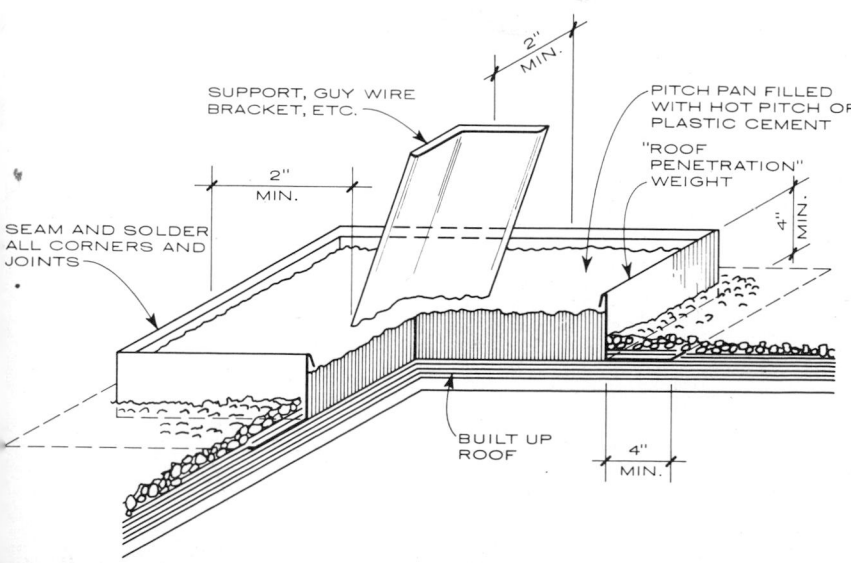

2" MIN.

SUPPORT, GUY WIRE BRACKET, ETC.

PITCH PAN FILLED WITH HOT PITCH OR PLASTIC CEMENT

"ROOF PENETRATION" WEIGHT

2" MIN.

4" MIN.

SEAM AND SOLDER ALL CORNERS AND JOINTS

BUILT UP ROOF

4" MIN.

PITCH PAN FLASHING OF SMALL PENETRATION THRU ROOF

NOTE:

Precaution must be taken to prevent pitch from running down support during hot weather.
Methods vary according to condition, i.e., vibrating machinery, water tank.
Consult roofing expert for such conditions.

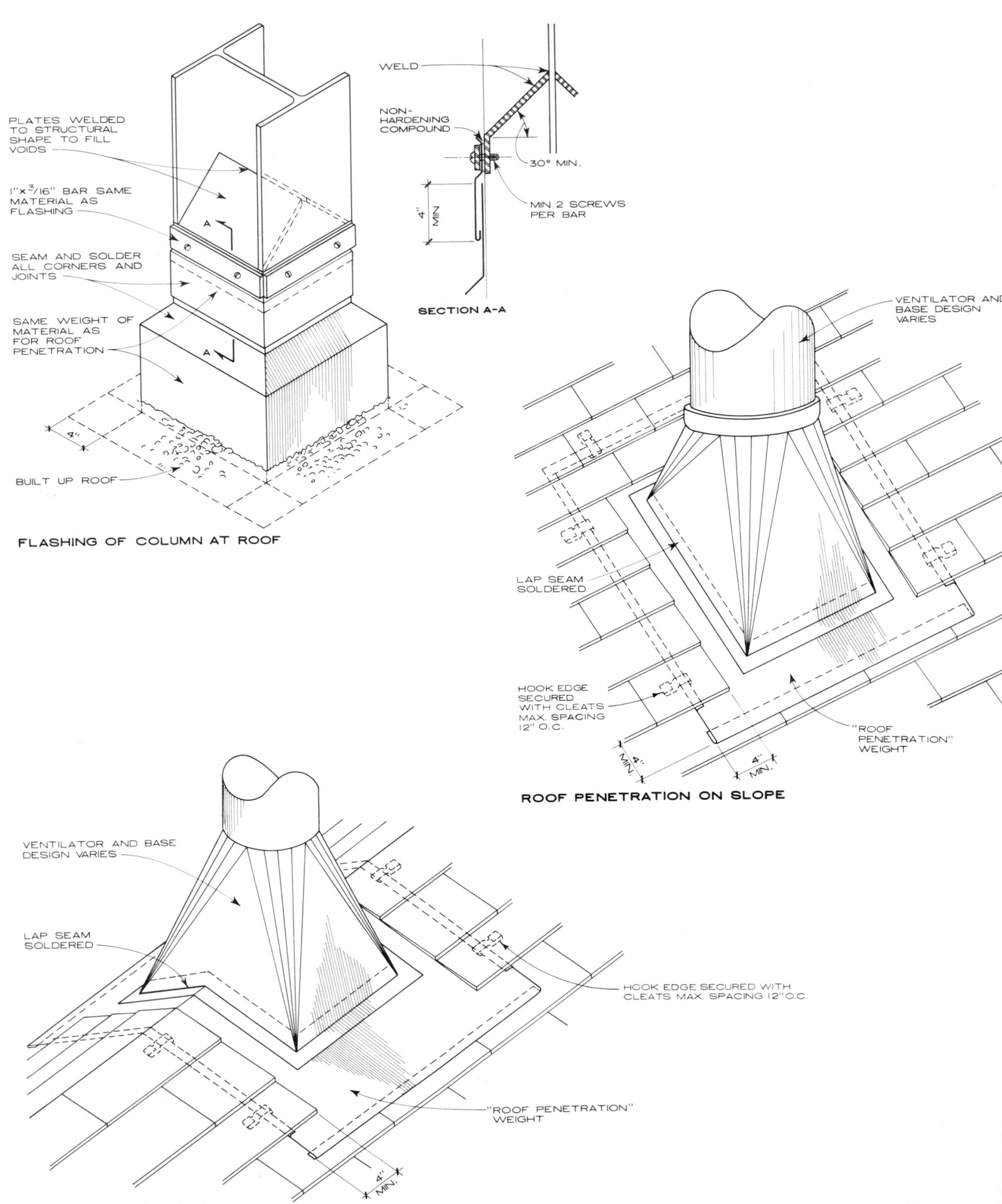

PLATES WELDED TO STRUCTURAL SHAPE TO FILL VOIDS

1"x³/16" BAR SAME MATERIAL AS FLASHING

SEAM AND SOLDER ALL CORNERS AND JOINTS

SAME WEIGHT OF MATERIAL AS FOR ROOF PENETRATION

A

A

BUILT UP ROOF

4"

FLASHING OF COLUMN AT ROOF

WELD

NON-HARDENING COMPOUND

30° MIN.

MIN. 2 SCREWS PER BAR

4" MIN

SECTION A-A

VENTILATOR AND BASE DESIGN VARIES

LAP SEAM SOLDERED

HOOK EDGE SECURED WITH CLEATS MAX. SPACING 12" O.C.

4" MIN.   4" MIN.

"ROOF PENETRATION" WEIGHT

ROOF PENETRATION ON SLOPE

VENTILATOR AND BASE DESIGN VARIES

LAP SEAM SOLDERED

HOOK EDGE SECURED WITH CLEATS MAX. SPACING 12"O.C.

"ROOF PENETRATION" WEIGHT

4" MIN.

ROOF PENETRATION AT RIDGE

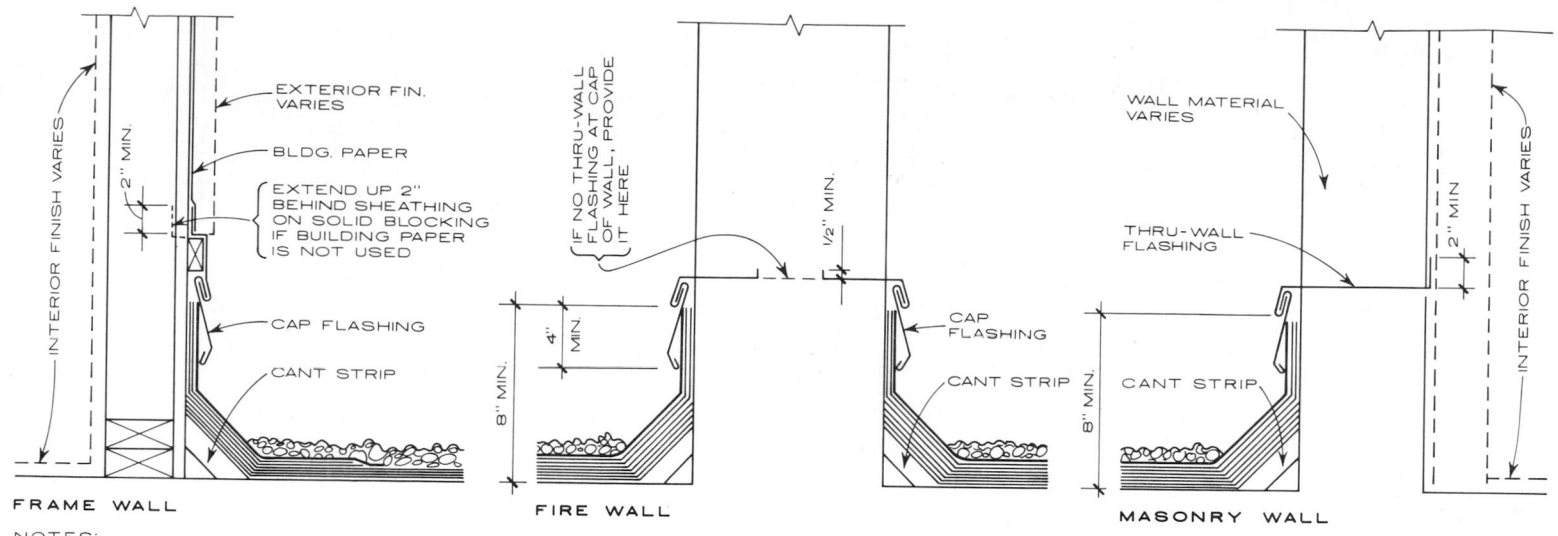

NOTES:
1. CAP FLASHING MUST LAP BASE FLASHING 4"
2. THROUGH WALL FLASHING NOT RECOMMENDED IN EARTHQUAKE AREAS.

FLASHING BETWEEN WALL AND BUILT-UP ROOFING

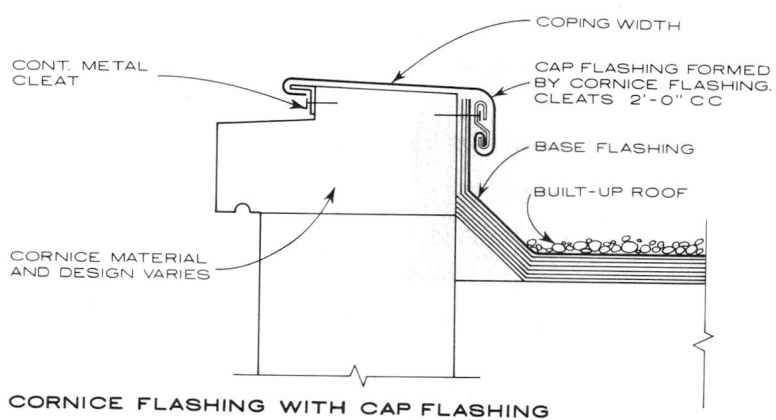

CORNICE FLASHING WITH CAP FLASHING

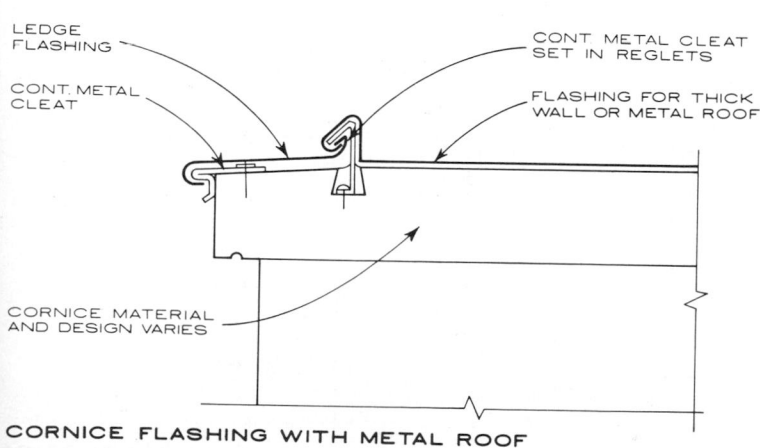

CORNICE FLASHING WITH METAL ROOF

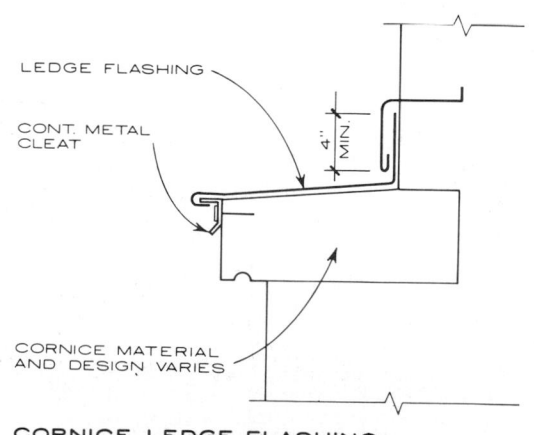

CORNICE LEDGE FLASHING

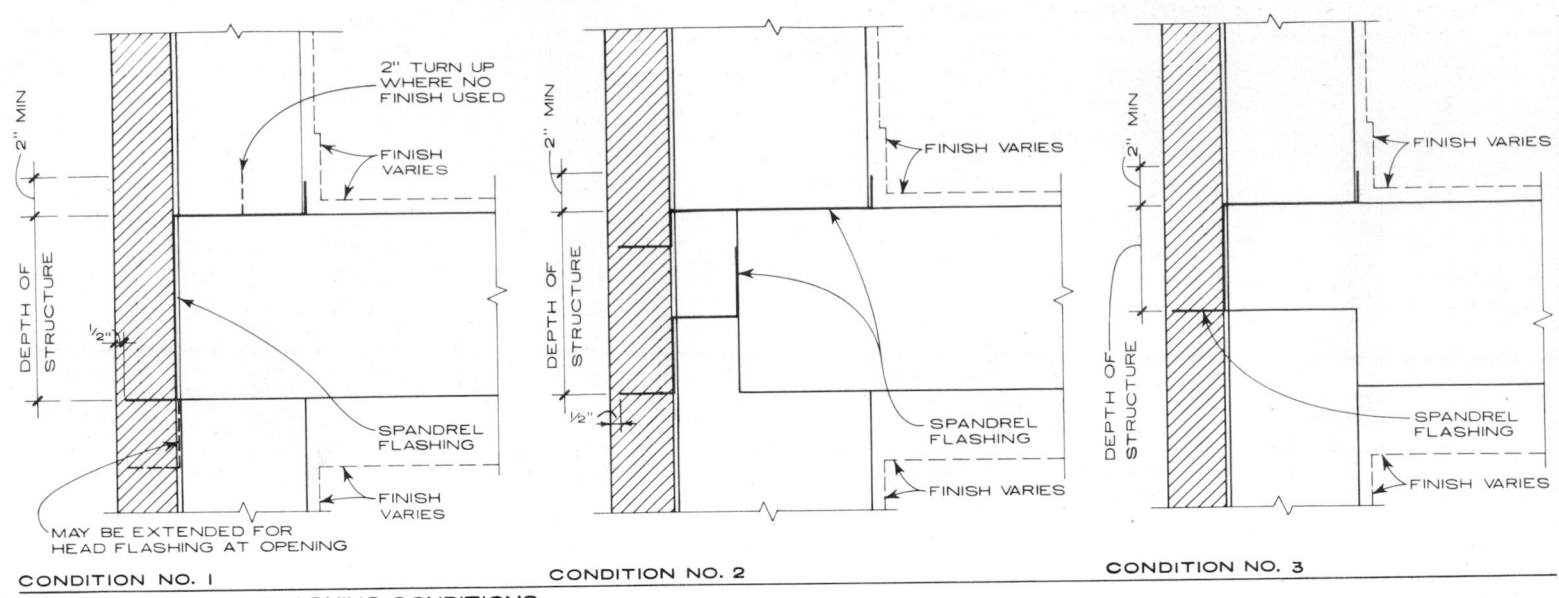

CONDITION NO. 1   CONDITION NO. 2   CONDITION NO. 3

TYPICAL SPANDREL FLASHING CONDITIONS

NOTE:

Material and shape of floor structure varies. Flashing recommended for full depth of structure in wall.

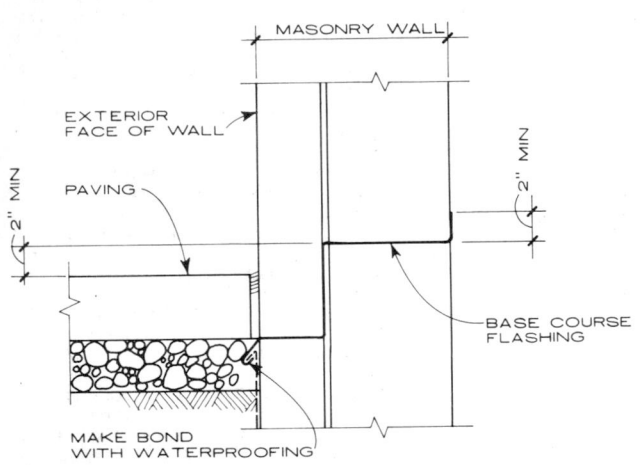

DAMP COURSE AT PAVING AND WALL

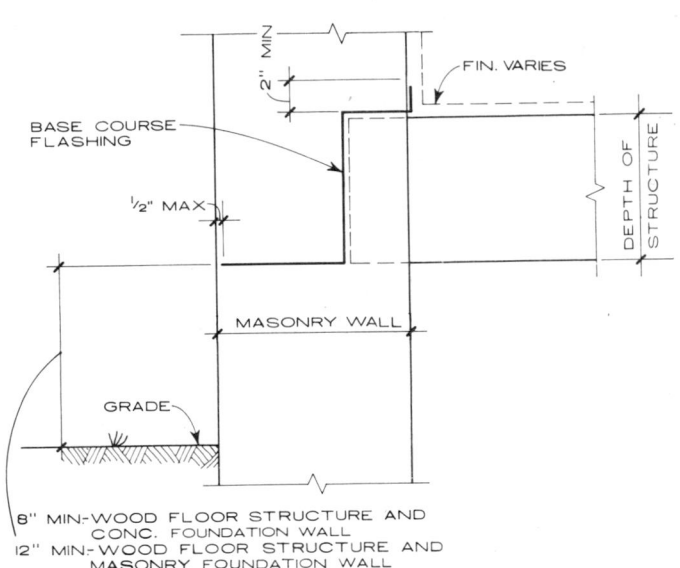

DAMP COURSE AT FLOOR CONSTRUCTION

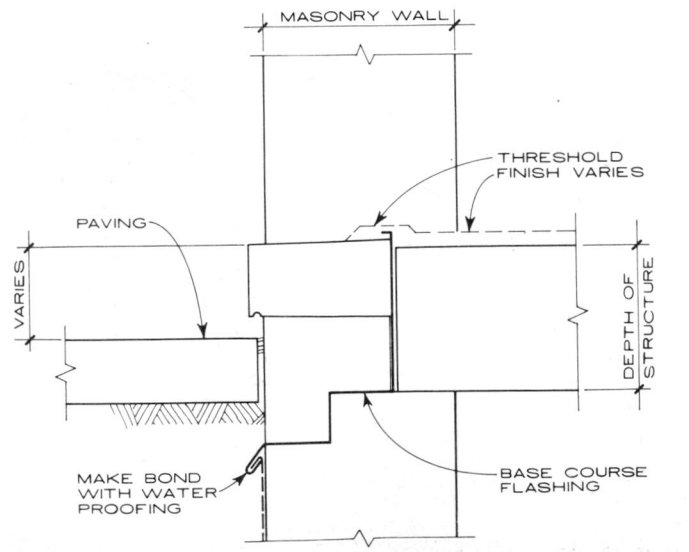

DAMP COURSE AT SILL OF MASONRY CONSTRUCTION

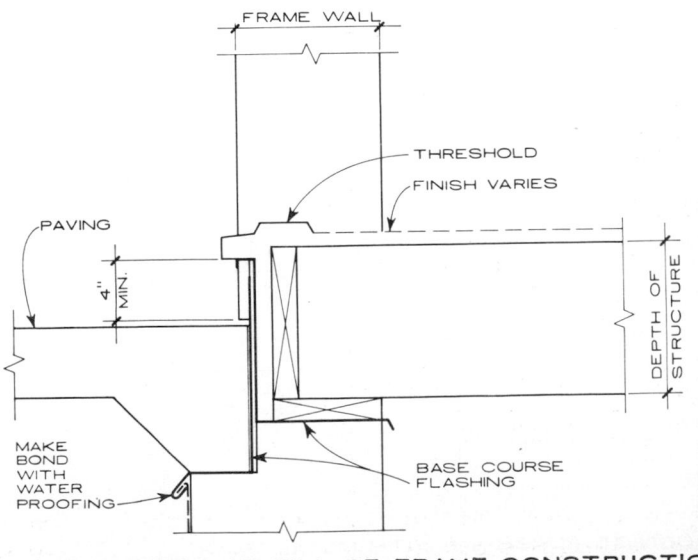

DAMP COURSE AT SILL OF FRAME CONSTRUCTION

THERMAL EXPANSION COEFFICIENTS OF MATERIALS
(INCHES PER DEGREE FAHRENHEIT)

METALS AND ALLOYS		STONE AND MASONRY	
Aluminum (wrought)	.0000128	Ashlar masonry	.0000035
Bronze	.0000101	Brick masonry	.0000034
Copper	.0000098	Cement (portland)	.0000070
Iron (wrought)	.0000067	Clay tile (structural)	.0000033
Lead	.0000159	Concrete	.0000065
Monel metal	.0000078	Granite	.0000040
Steel (medium)	.0000067	Limestone	.0000038
Steel (stainless)	.0000099	Marble	.0000056
Zinc (rolled)	.0000178	Plaster	.0000092
Timber (parallel to fiber)		Rubble masonry	.0000035
Fir	.0000021	Sandstone	.0000044
Maple	.0000036	Glass	
Oak	.0000027	Glass (common)	.0000047
Pine	.0000030		

FORMULA FOR MATERIAL EXPANSION
Multiply span (in inches) of material X 100 degrees (average difference in Fahrenheit temperature between summer and winter) X the coefficient of thermal expansion of the material Span X 100° F. X coefficient of thermal expansion.

JOINT SPACING
No single recommendation on positioning and spacing of expansion joints can be applicable to all structures. Guide lines set forth here should be used with caution and each building design analyzed before placement of joints. refer to STRUCTURAL CLAY PRODUCTS INSTITUTE publications for additional information.

EXPANSION JOINT WIDTH
The width of an expansion joint is generally assumed as 1" (one inch). The actual amount of expansion to be expected from a given material and situation should be calculated. Where additional "skin joints" are provided in cavity wall construction (general note number 3), joint width may be reduced to 1/2" (one-half inch) to facilitate calking and a neat appearance.

GENERAL NOTES:
Most architectural building materials are affected by temperature changes to the extent that movement in the form of expansion and contraction occur in response to normal temperature changes. Expansion joints are provided to allow for such movement to prevent cracks, breakage, distortion, malfunctioning or other unforseen developments which could be caused by such movement. Normally these expansion joints must occur where indicated by isometric "LOCATION OF EXPANSION JOINTS" of this page, and must provide complete separation of materials, and cut through entire building from top of footing or foundation wall to the roof and through parapet. This is accomplished by the use of double columns and girders, or by slip planes. Additional expansion joints may be required in certain other situations and building elements as follows:

1. Joints in roof may be required at more frequent intervals because of severe exposure. Where additional roof joints are provided and do not provide complete building separation, the roof slab should not be rigidly connected to the supporting structure in order for the joints to function.
2. Provide additional expansion joints thru parapet walls located between joints required by other criteria. If parapet wall is doweled to the structural frame and reinforced, these additional joints may be omitted. Joints should be placed near corners to avoid displacement of the parapet.
3. In masonry cavity wall construction, provide additional expansion joints in the exterior wythe of masonry for full height of wall including parapets, and located between joints required by other criteria. The exterior wythe of masonry in cavity wall construction shall be tied to the interior wythe or back-up material with flexible anchors in order for the joints to function.
4. Provide horizontal expansion joints at all shelf angles provided for the support of masonry walls or panels by a structural frame. Shelf angles should be interrupted at frequent intervals ot allow for thermal movement.
5. Provide expansion joints (soft joints, slip channels, etc.) at interior partitions which abutt underside of floor or roof structure above in buildings which have exterior bearing or shear walls of exposed concrete. Joints should also be provided where deflection of floor and roof slabs is anticipated to the extent that abutting partition could be crushed.
6. Expansion joints or slip planes may be required in many minor exterior elements of a building where a material occurs in such volume of length that thermal movement may create a problem; for example, metal railing, metal wall panels, curtain wall, gravel stops, glass blocks, plate glass, concrete paving, sidewalks, etc.

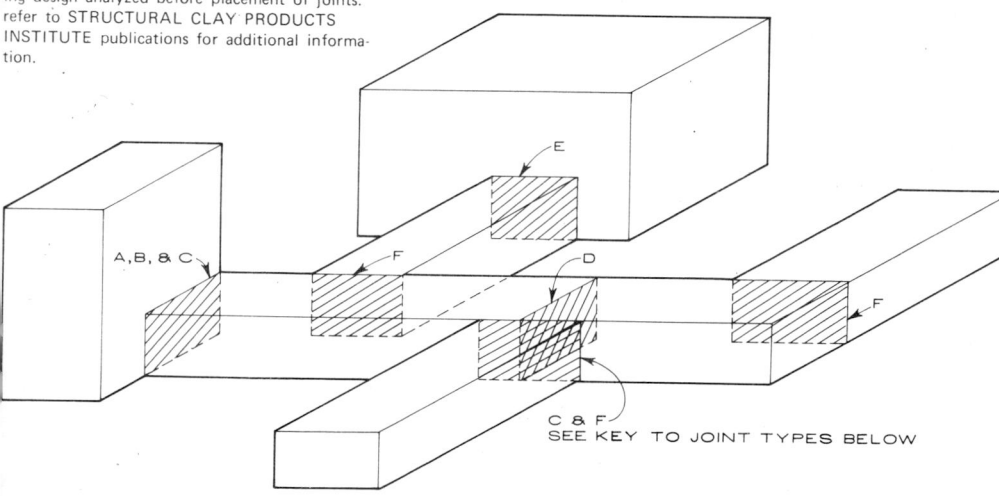

SEE KEY TO JOINT TYPES BELOW

LOCATIONS OF EXPANSION JOINTS
SEE "JOINT SPACING" NOTE ABOVE

EXPANSION JOINT TYPES
A. New building adjoining existing building.
B. Long low building abutting higher building.
C. Wings adjoining main structure.
D. Long building (exceeding maximums indicated below).
E. Long low connecting wings between buildings.
F. Intersections at wings of "L", "T", or "U" shaped buildings.

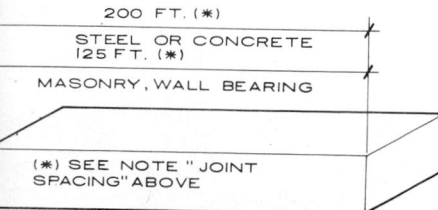

200 FT. (*)

STEEL OR CONCRETE 125 FT. (*)

MASONRY, WALL BEARING

(*) SEE NOTE "JOINT SPACING" ABOVE

MAXIMUM ALLOWANCE WITHOUT JOINTS
(ASSUMING ENDS OF STRUCTURE ARE FREE)

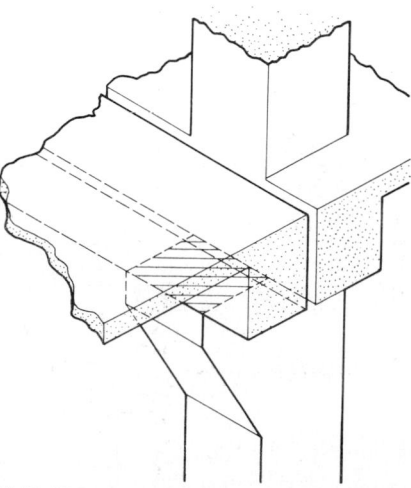

DOUBLE COLUMNS   SLIP PLANE

JOINTS IN CONCRETE STRUCTURE

Robert D. Abernathy; J. N. Pease Associates; Charlotte, North Carolina

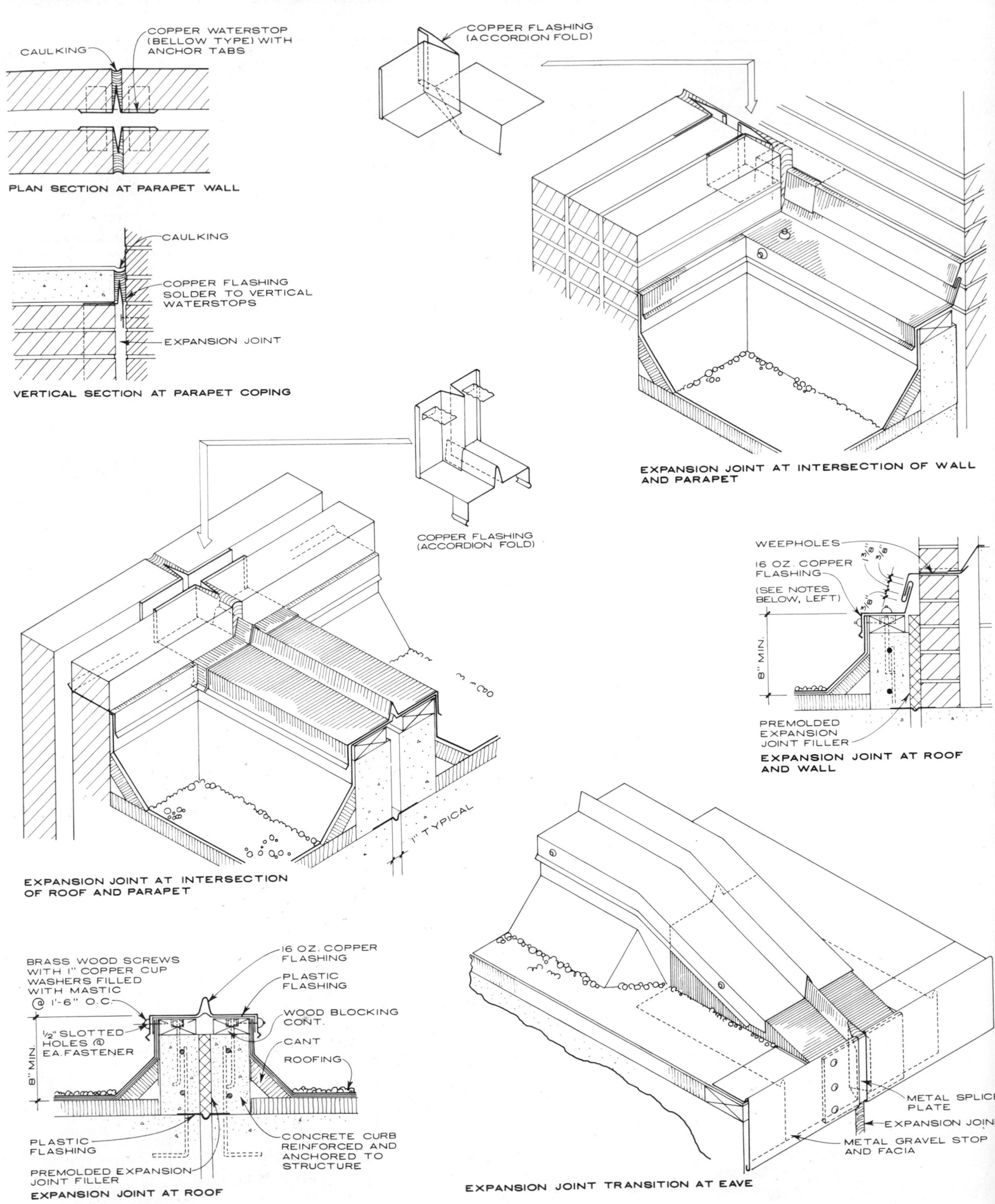

CAULKING

COPPER WATERSTOP (BELLOW TYPE) WITH ANCHOR TABS

PLAN SECTION AT PARAPET WALL

CAULKING

COPPER FLASHING SOLDER TO VERTICAL WATERSTOPS

EXPANSION JOINT

VERTICAL SECTION AT PARAPET COPING

COPPER FLASHING (ACCORDION FOLD)

COPPER FLASHING (ACCORDION FOLD)

EXPANSION JOINT AT INTERSECTION OF WALL AND PARAPET

1" TYPICAL

EXPANSION JOINT AT INTERSECTION OF ROOF AND PARAPET

WEEPHOLES

16 OZ. COPPER FLASHING (SEE NOTES BELOW, LEFT)

3/8", 3/8", 3/8"

8" MIN.

PREMOLDED EXPANSION JOINT FILLER

EXPANSION JOINT AT ROOF AND WALL

BRASS WOOD SCREWS WITH 1" COPPER CUP WASHERS FILLED WITH MASTIC @ 1'-6" O.C.

1/2" SLOTTED HOLES @ EA. FASTENER

8" MIN.

16 OZ. COPPER FLASHING

PLASTIC FLASHING

WOOD BLOCKING CONT.

CANT

ROOFING

PLASTIC FLASHING

PREMOLDED EXPANSION JOINT FILLER

CONCRETE CURB REINFORCED AND ANCHORED TO STRUCTURE

EXPANSION JOINT AT ROOF

METAL SPLICE PLATE

EXPANSION JOINT

METAL GRAVEL STOP AND FACIA

EXPANSION JOINT TRANSITION AT EAVE

Robert D. Abernathy; J. N. Pease Associates; Charlotte, North Carolina

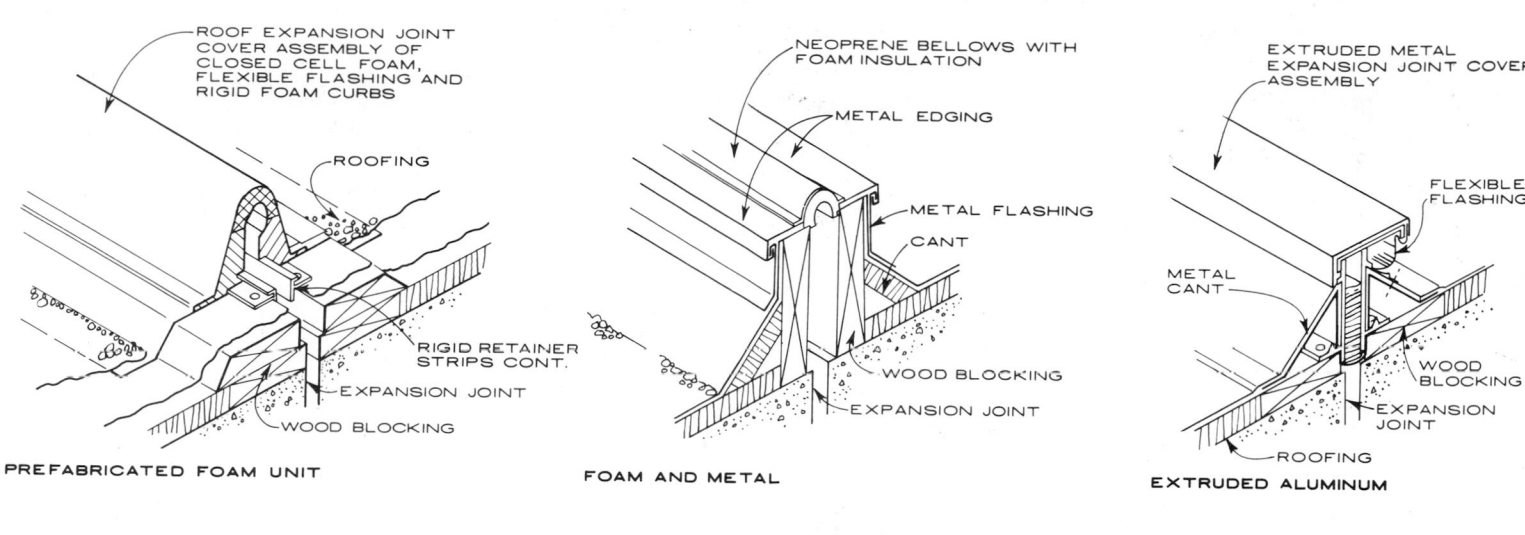

PREFABRICATED FOAM UNIT

ROOF EXPANSION JOINT COVER ASSEMBLY OF CLOSED CELL FOAM, FLEXIBLE FLASHING AND RIGID FOAM CURBS

ROOFING

RIGID RETAINER STRIPS CONT.

EXPANSION JOINT

WOOD BLOCKING

FOAM AND METAL

NEOPRENE BELLOWS WITH FOAM INSULATION

METAL EDGING

METAL FLASHING

CANT

WOOD BLOCKING

EXPANSION JOINT

EXTRUDED ALUMINUM

EXTRUDED METAL EXPANSION JOINT COVER ASSEMBLY

FLEXIBLE FLASHING

METAL CANT

WOOD BLOCKING

EXPANSION JOINT

ROOFING

A large selection of prefabricated assemblies to cover roof expansion joints are available from various manufacturers, with component parts such as "T" intersections and eave transition assemblies to satisfy most situations encountered.

Roof expansion joint covers may be fashioned from common building and roofing materials such as sheet metal, sheet vinyl, and synthetic rubber, with satisfactory results.

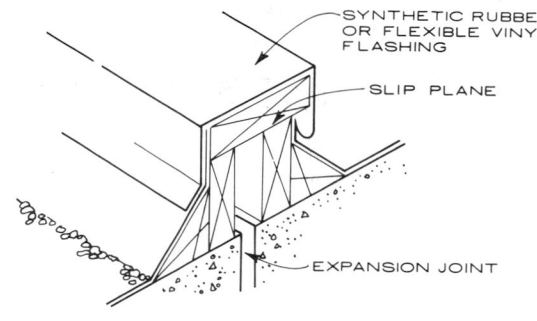

WOOD AND FLEXIBLE FLASHING

SYNTHETIC RUBBER OR FLEXIBLE VINYL FLASHING

SLIP PLANE

EXPANSION JOINT

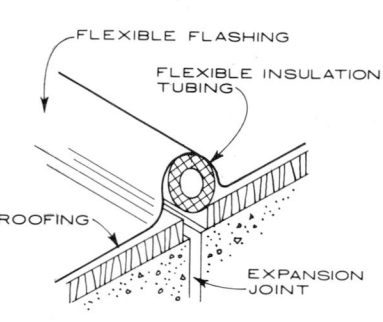

FOAM AND FLEXIBLE FLASHING

FLEXIBLE FLASHING

FLEXIBLE INSULATION TUBING

ROOFING

EXPANSION JOINT

EXPANSION JOINT COVERS AT ROOF WITH PREFABRICATED COMPONENTS

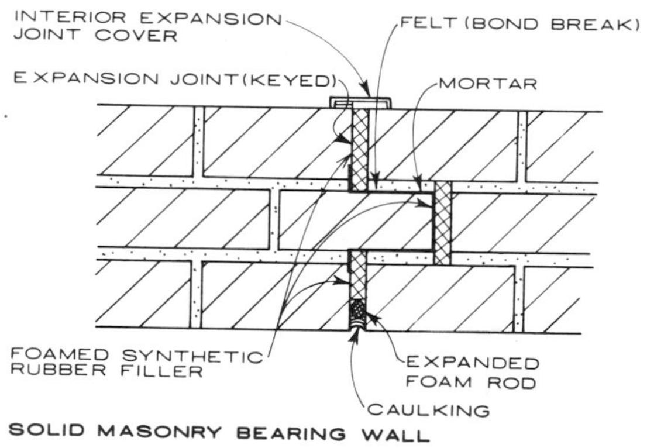

SOLID MASONRY BEARING WALL

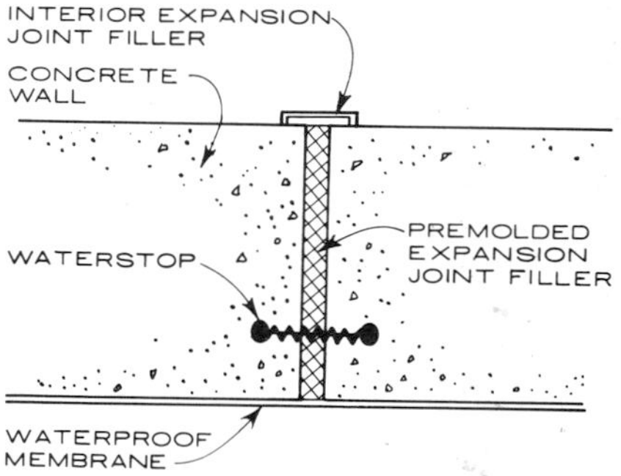

INTERIOR EXPANSION JOINT COVER

EXPANSION JOINT (KEYED)

FELT (BOND BREAK)

MORTAR

FOAMED SYNTHETIC RUBBER FILLER

EXPANDED FOAM ROD

CAULKING

CONCRETE FOUNDATION WALL

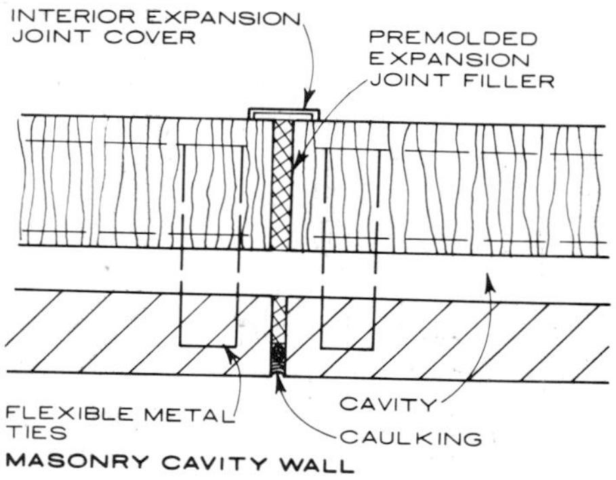

INTERIOR EXPANSION JOINT FILLER

CONCRETE WALL

WATERSTOP

PREMOLDED EXPANSION JOINT FILLER

WATERPROOF MEMBRANE

MASONRY CAVITY WALL

INTERIOR EXPANSION JOINT COVER

PREMOLDED EXPANSION JOINT FILLER

FLEXIBLE METAL TIES

CAVITY

CAULKING

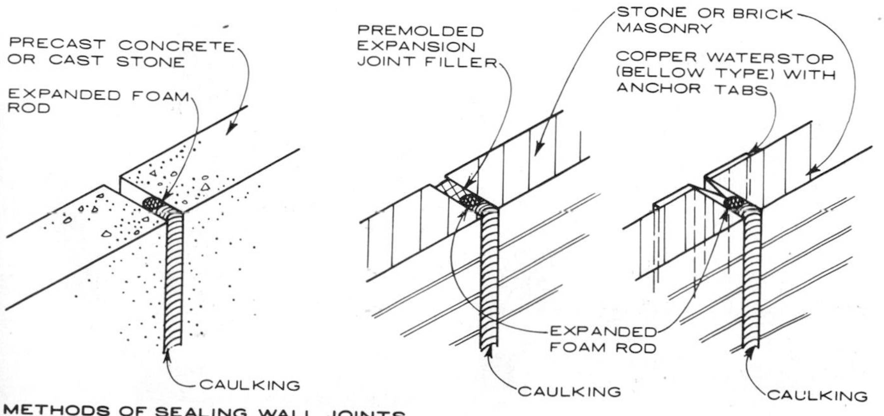

METHODS OF SEALING WALL JOINTS

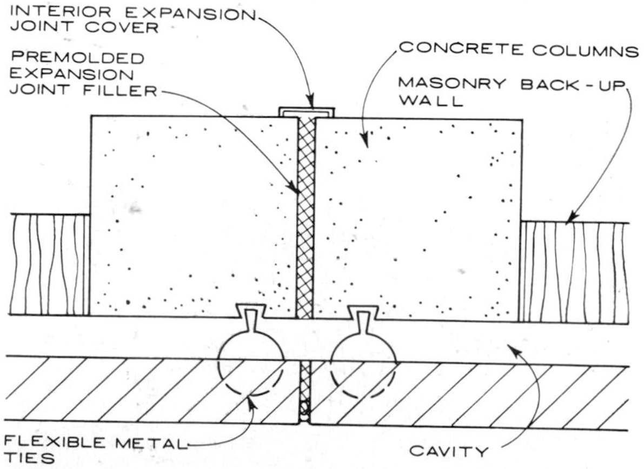

PRECAST CONCRETE OR CAST STONE

EXPANDED FOAM ROD

CAULKING

PREMOLDED EXPANSION JOINT FILLER

STONE OR BRICK MASONRY

COPPER WATERSTOP (BELLOW TYPE) WITH ANCHOR TABS

EXPANDED FOAM ROD

CAULKING

CAULKING

CAVITY WALL AT COLUMNS

INTERIOR EXPANSION JOINT COVER

PREMOLDED EXPANSION JOINT FILLER

CONCRETE COLUMNS

MASONRY BACK-UP WALL

FLEXIBLE METAL TIES

CAVITY

EXPANSION JOINTS AT WALLS

Robert D. Abernathy; J. N. Pease Associates; Charlotte, North Carolina

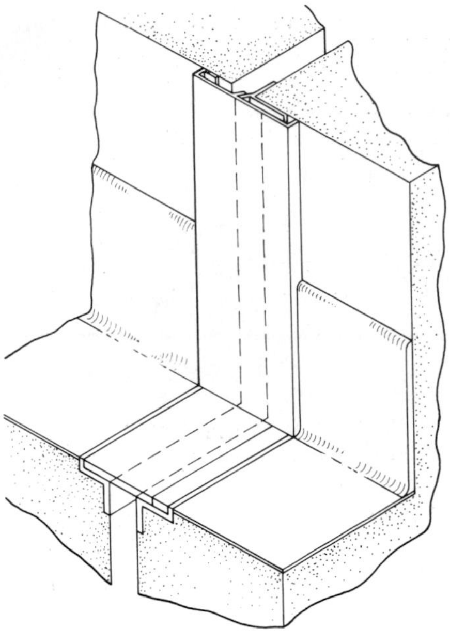

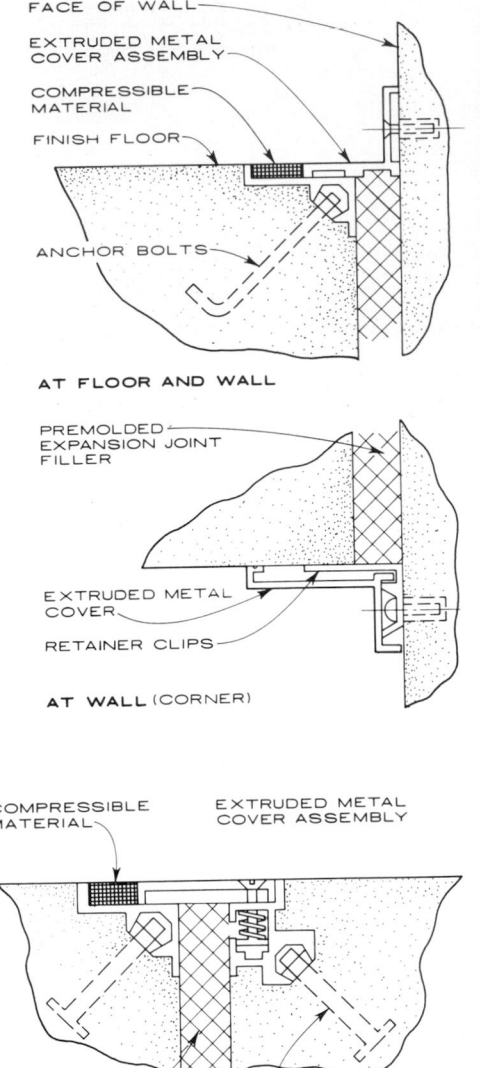

AT FLAT BASE

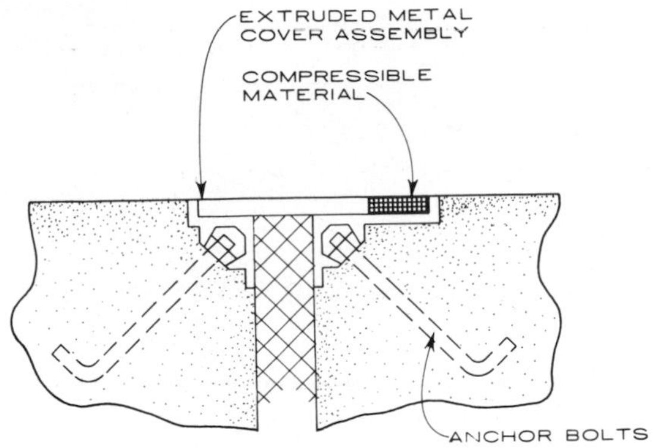

AT PROJECTING BASE

EXTRUDED METAL COVER ASSEMBLY

COMPRESSIBLE MATERIAL

ANCHOR BOLTS

AT FLOOR

PREMOLDED EXPANSION JOINT FILLER

RETAINER CLIPS

EXTRUDED METAL COVER

AT WALL

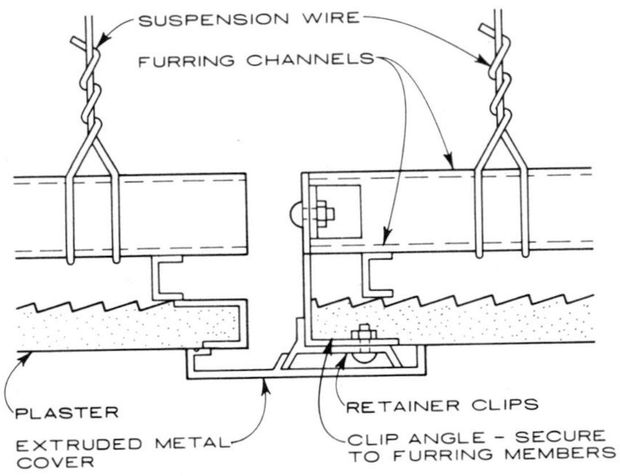

SUSPENSION WIRE

FURRING CHANNELS

PLASTER

EXTRUDED METAL COVER

RETAINER CLIPS

CLIP ANGLE – SECURE TO FURRING MEMBERS

AT SUSPENDED CEILING

FACE OF WALL

EXTRUDED METAL COVER ASSEMBLY

COMPRESSIBLE MATERIAL

FINISH FLOOR

ANCHOR BOLTS

AT FLOOR AND WALL

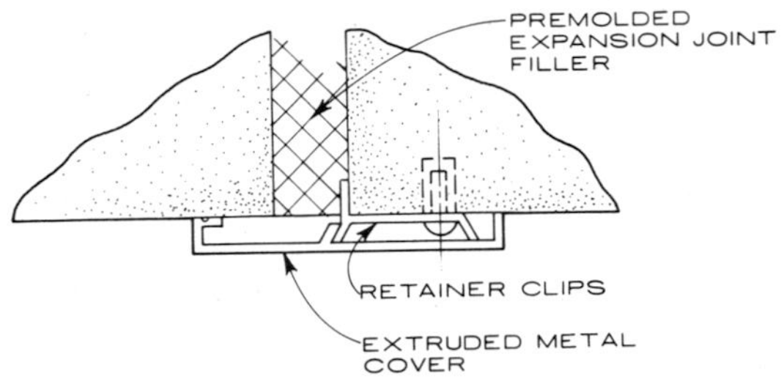

PREMOLDED EXPANSION JOINT FILLER

EXTRUDED METAL COVER

RETAINER CLIPS

AT WALL (CORNER)

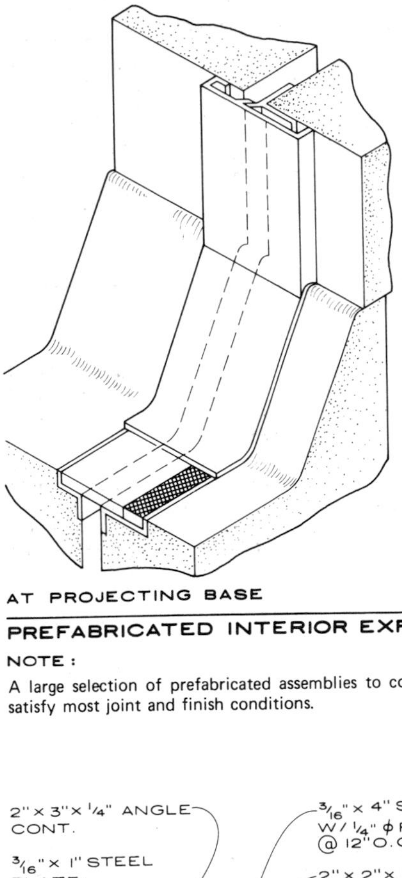

COMPRESSIBLE MATERIAL

EXTRUDED METAL COVER ASSEMBLY

PREMOLDED EXPANSION JOINT FILLER

ANCHOR BOLTS

SEISMIC FLOOR JOINT COVER

NOTE :

Expansion joint covers which will respond to differential movement, both laterally and horizontally, should be provided at joints in structures located where seismic action (earth tremors and quakes) may be expected or where differential settlement is anticipated.

PREFABRICATED INTERIOR EXPANSION JOINT COVERS

NOTE :

A large selection of prefabricated assemblies to cover interior expansion joints are available from various manufacturers to satisfy most joint and finish conditions.

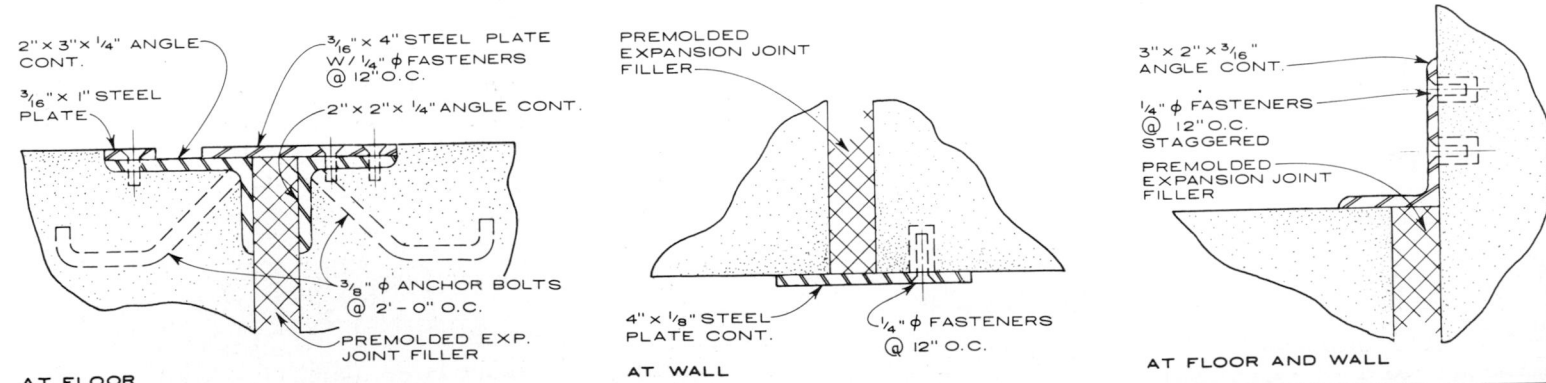

2" x 3" x 1/4" ANGLE CONT.

3/16" x 1" STEEL PLATE

3/16" x 4" STEEL PLATE W/ 1/4" φ FASTENERS @ 12" O.C.

2" x 2" x 1/4" ANGLE CONT.

3/8" φ ANCHOR BOLTS @ 2'-0" O.C.

PREMOLDED EXP. JOINT FILLER

AT FLOOR

PREMOLDED EXPANSION JOINT FILLER

4" x 1/8" STEEL PLATE CONT.

1/4" φ FASTENERS @ 12" O.C.

AT WALL

3" x 2" x 3/16" ANGLE CONT.

1/4" φ FASTENERS @ 12" O.C. STAGGERED

PREMOLDED EXPANSION JOINT FILLER

AT FLOOR AND WALL

PLATE AND ANGLE TYPE INTERIOR EXPANSION JOINT COVERS

Robert D. Abernathy; J. N. Pease Associates; Charlotte, North Carolina

APPLICATION OF VENTILATORS

	SCHOOLS	COMMERCIAL	INDUSTRIAL	APARTMENTS	MOTELS	RESIDENTIAL
Fresh Air Intake	◢	◢				
Pressure Relief	◢	◢				
Combustion Air	◢	◢				
Attic Vent Or Fan	◢	◢	◢	◢		
Gravity Vent	◢	◢				
Sky Light / Vent Or Fan	◢	◢	◢	◢	◢	◢
Power Exhaust	◢	◢	◢			
Corrosive Fume Exhaust	◢	◢	◢			
Toilet Exhaust	◢	◢	◢	◢	◢	◢

AREA USES

	NO. OF MINUTES SUGGESTED FOR ONE AIR CHANGE		
Assembly Halls	5	To	10
Bakeries	2	To	5
Boiler Rooms	2	To	4
Cafeterias	3	To	5
Dormitories	5	To	10
Dry Cleaning Plants	1	To	5
Engine Rooms	1	To	3
Factory Buildings	5	To	10
Garages	3	To	5
Generator Rooms	3	To	5
Gymnasiums	3	To	10
Kitchens	2	To	3
Laboratories	3	To	10
Laundries	3	To	5
Machine Shops	3	To	5
Mills	5	To	10
Offices	5	To	10
Pump Rooms	5	To	10
Restaurants	5	To	10
Shops	2	To	10
Stores	5	To	10
Toilets	3	To	5
Transformer Rooms	1	To	5
Warehouses	10	To	30

TYPICAL ACCESSORIES:

Bird screen, galvanized or aluminum; self acting dampers, horizontal or vertical mount for lowest static and complete weatherproof assurance when closed, thermal acoustic curb bases.

ROOF VENTILATORS

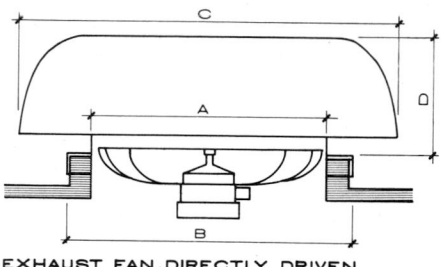

AIR INTAKE, RELIEF & GRAVITY VENTILATION

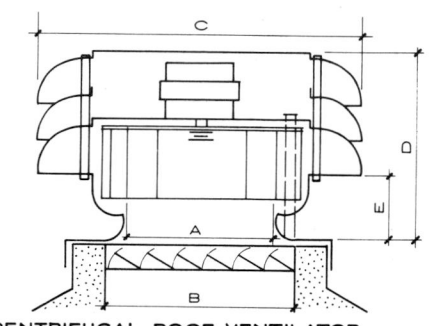

EXHAUST FAN, DIRECTLY DRIVEN

CENTRIFUGAL ROOF VENTILATOR

TYPES & SHAPES OF UNITS

NOTE:

To determine the amount of air required in CFM, divide the area volume in cubic feet by the minute air change derived from the table below.

Example: In an area 50' x 40' x 20', the calculated volume is 40,000 cu. ft. If a four-minute air change is required, the volume to be exhausted is 10,000 cubic feet per minute.

To insure quiet air intake, divide CFM requirement by desired throat velocity to obtain square foot throat area. Intake face velocities are more satisfactory when kept at 600 fpm. or below.

CFM ratings vary with manufacturer according to H.P. of motor, pulley sizes and design. Diameter of blades are considered standard up to 48 inches. Not all sizes are made by all manufacturers.

When discharging a fan into an attic space, it should be centrally located over the area to be ventilated. When the attic is unfinished, install a vertical discharge fan in the attic floor. When the attic is finished, install a horizontal fan in an outside wall of the attic so it will discharge with the prevailing winds.

ENGINEERING DATA & CAPACITY

SIZE (IN INCHES)				GRAVITY CFM *	FRESH AIR INTAKE	
A	B	C	D		CFM	THROAT FPM
6	10	14	6	75	270	1080
12	16	20	9	305	750	750
18	26	29	11	720	1686	750
24	32	36	16	1260	2700	675
30	38	51	19	1980	6240	998
36	44	61	20	2880	9600	1067

* CFM BASED ON 20 FT. STACK HT., 20°F TEMP. DIFF. & 4 MPH WIND VEL.

ENGINEERING DATA & CAPACITY

SIZE (INCHES)				BLADE SIZE	H.P.	R.P.M	CFM vs/S.P.	
A	B	C	D				F.A.	1/8 "S.P.
10	14	20	10	8	1/60	1550	250	200
12	16	20	10	8	1/60	1550	515	300
19	23	29	6	12	1/20	1140	1025	560
23	27	36	10	16	1/15	1050	2000	1200
25	29	36	10	18	1/12	1050	2400	1500

ENGINEERING DATA & CAPACITY

SIZE (IN INCHES)					H.P.	R.P.M.	CFM vs/S.P.	
A	B	C	D	E			F.A.	1/8 "S.P.
6	6 1/2	13	10 1/2	2 1/2	1/35	1050	218	99
8	8 1/2	18 1/8	13	3 1/8	1/20	1050	611	495
10 5/8	12 1/2	25 3/4	16 1/2	4 7/8	1/12	860	1037	885
12 1/2	17 1/2	30 3/4	18	4 13/16	1/6	860	2008	1800
14 3/4	19 1/2	34 1/4	22	6 11/16	1/6	565	2457	2100
19 5/16	24 1/2	44 1/16	26	7 1/2	1/2	565	4965	4430
23 3/4	30 1/2	52 3/4	31	8 7/8	1	565	7898	7380
30 3/4	35 1/2	66 7/8	37	9 9/16	5	565	18270	17550

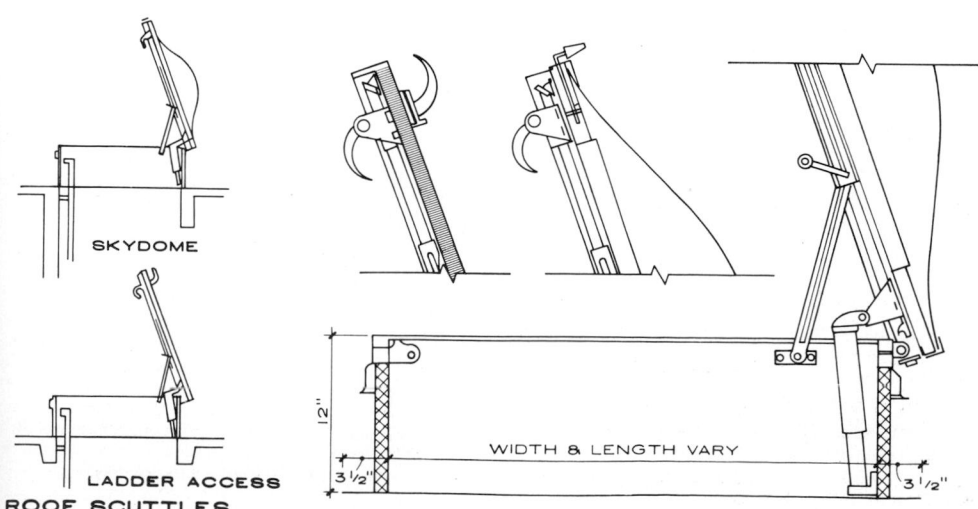

SKYDOME

LADDER ACCESS

ROOF SCUTTLES

12"

WIDTH & LENGTH VARY

3 1/2"

3 1/2"

HATCH TYPES:

SINGLE LEAF, DOUBLE LEAF, SMOKE & FIRE RELIEF, SKYDOMES

HATCH SIZES:

2'-6" x 2'-6", x 3'-0", x 4'-0", x 4'-6", x 8'-0"
3'-6" x 3'-6", x 4'-0", x 5'-0", x 6'-0", x 8'-0"

MATERIALS AVAILABLE & WEIGHTS:

SHEET STEEL	2'-6" x 3'-0"	160 lbs.
	2'-6" x 8'-0"	350 lbs.
GALVANIZED STL.	2'-6" x 3'-0"	165 lbs
	2'-6" x 8'-0"	360 lbs.
ALUMINUM	2'-6" x 3'-0"	85 lbs.
	2'-6" x 8'-0"	170 lbs.
COPPER	2'-6" x 3'-0"	150 lbs.
	2'-6" x 8'-0"	335 lbs.

NOTE: Designs of units vary with manufacturer but are similar.

Chester L. Helt, AIA; Jean G. Surratt and Associates; Charlotte, North Carolina

DEFINITIONS & SYMBOLS

BRITISH THERMAL UNIT (Btu): a common unit of heat defined generally as the quantity of heat required to raise the temperature of one pound of water one degree Fahrenheit.

DEGREE DAYS (DD): a measure based on climatic conditions of the severity of a heating period, usually an entire season. From weather records for each day the difference between 65° F. and the mean temperature is determined. The sum of these differences for all the days in the heating season is the Degree Days for that locality.

DEWPOINT: the temperature at which a cooling air-water vapor mixture becomes completely saturated (100% relative humidity) and is on the verge of some moisture condensing into water. It varies with barometric pressure.

EMITTANCE (e): a rating of the ability of a material to give off heat as radiant energy. It is equal to the amount of heat absorbed (that not reflected), so the sum of emittance and reflectance, expressed as percent, is 100%. It is also defined as the ratio of heat radiated by a material to that of a "black body" under similar conditions. It is applicable only when the surface faces an air space. See Reflectance. The same ratio applied to opaque and optically flat surfaces is called emissivity; for ordinary materials, emittance is preferred.

HUMIDITY, ABSOLUTE: the weight of water vapor in pounds per cubic foot.

HUMIDITY, PERCENTAGE: indicates the weight of moisture that air at a given temperature is holding in vapor form to what it could hold at that same temperature when fully saturated, as percent.

HUMIDITY, RELATIVE (RH): the ratio of the actual vapor pressure at a given temperature to the saturation vapor pressure at the same temperature.

ISOTHERM: designates a line on a graph joining points of equal temperature.

OVERALL HEAT TRANSMISSION COEFFICIENT (U or $1/R_T$): the reciprocal (divided into 1) of the Total Thermal Resistance. "U" has been the unit used to express heat flow through a building section including air spaces $3/4$ inch or greater and air films. Technically, it is heat transmission in Btu's per hour per square foot per degree F difference from air to air. While it has been used to calculate heat loss or gain, it is recommended that it be

abandoned in favor of the more easily used Total Thermal Resistance (R_T).

PERM: unit of vapor transmission rate of 1 grain per square foot per hour per inch of mercury pressure difference. (from permeance)

REFLECTANCE: a rating of the ability of a material to reflect heat by radiation. It is the ratio of the radiant heat reflected by a surface to that of a "black body" (a theoretical body that absorbs all radiation falling on it) under similar conditions. No symbol is used because ratings are based on emittance. For opaque and optically flat surfaces the optimum value of reflectance is reflectivity: for ordinary materials, reflectance is preferred.

REP: a reciprocal (1/perm) which indicates resistance to water vapor transfer.

SURFACE AIR FILM COEFFICIENT (f): the heat flow in Btu per hour per square foot between an exposed surface and the adjacent air. f_i is inside surface coefficient, f_0 is outside surface coefficient. It indicates the conductance of heat through the air film that clings to all surfaces. Film resistance is preferably expressed as 1/f.

THERM: a unit of 100,000 Btu of heat.

THERMAL CONDUCTIVITY (k or 1/r): the reciprocal of Thermal Resistivity. "k factor" has been the unit expressing heat flow in Btu's per hour, through one square foot of material which is exactly one inch thick for one degree F difference between its surfaces. While it has been used for comparing insulating efficiencies of homogeneous materials (uncoated solid insulation, wood, building board) it is recommended that Thermal Resistivity (r) be used to simplify calculations. Thermal conductivities of a series of materials must not be added.

THERMAL CONDUCTANCE (C or 1/R): the reciprocal of Thermal Resistance. "C" has been the unit expressing heat flow in Btu's per hour per square foot of a given thickness for one degree F temperature difference between its surfaces. While it has been used for comparing insulating efficiencies of materials and constructions of several materials of stated thicknesses, it is recommended that it be replaced by Thermal Resistance, R, to simplify calculations. Conductances of a series of materials must not be added.

THERMAL RESISTANCE (R): a unit for the rate of heat flow through a given thickness of a homogeneous or com-

posite material, or construction assembly with or without cavities or reflective surfaces. It is measured by the temperature difference in degrees F between the two exposed faces required to cause one Btu to flow through one square foot per hour. Resistances may be added. (R = temp. diff. F/Btu for one sq. ft., hr).

THERMAL RESISTIVITY (r): a unit for the rate of heat flow through a homogeneous material exactly one inch thick. It is measured by the temperature difference in degrees F between the smooth parallel faces required to cause one Btu to flow through one square foot per hour. Resistivities may be added. (r = temp. diff. F/Btu inch for one sq. ft., hr).

TOTAL THERMAL RESISTANCE (R_T): an expression of the total resistance to heat flow through a complete building section or construction assembly, including internal air spaces with or without emittances or reflectances, and external air films. Total thermal resistance is usually expressed as R_T of typical section per sq. ft. hr. and the value for one construction may be compared directly with another on the basis of more or less heat flow for the same temperatures.

VAPOR BARRIER: a material which does not readily permit passage of water vapor. Normally, an acceptable material is rated at one perm or preferably less in many building applications.

VAPOR PERMEABILITY: a property of a material measured by the amount of water vapor (grains per square foot per hour for one inch of mercury pressure difference) which passes through an inch-thickness. Unit: perm-inch.

VAPOR PERMEANCE: similar to vapor permeability except that permeance, like conductance, is a performance of the material as tested or used regardless of thickness. Unit: Perm, is usually the unit of concern to designers.

VAPOR PRESSURE: the pressure created by water vapor in a space, whether air is present or not. Saturated vapor pressure is determined only by temperature.

VAPOR RESISTANCE: the reciprocal (1/perm) of vapor permeance. A rating of the resistance of a material or an assembly to the passage of water vapor. Unit: Rep. In a series, reps may be added.

VAPOR RESISTIVITY: similar to vapor resistance except that it is a rating of a material exactly one inch thick. Unit: Rep/inch.

THERMAL TRANSMISSION

Problems in performance of building construction (materials and their assembly are usually associated with uncontrolled or undesirable temperature or moisture or both. Combined heat and moisture flows are complex, and because of their interaction, neither should be considered independently of the other.

Most materials used in building construction have been tested to establish how much heat they will transmit under

standard conditions. While those evaluations are subject to manufacturing and testing tolerances and require judgment in their final application, published test values are normally accepted for calculation purposes.

Heat transmission coefficients are usually given as conductivities (k) or conductances (C) which have their counter parts: resistivity (r) or resistance (R). Each is the reciprocal of its counterpart as given in the definitions above.

The k or C value of a material has been the basis for comparing thermal properties, but these values cannot be added to find the conductance of a building section made up of different materials. Resistivity (r) and resistance (R) values can be added and their use greatly simplifies heat flow calculations. In such calculations the symbol R is used for resistance because resistivity values are the resistance for exactly one inch of thickness only.

(CONTINUED

Owen L. Delevante, AIA; Glen Rock, New Jersey
E. C. Shuman, P. E.; Consulting Engineer; State College, Pennsylvania

THERMAL TRANSMISSION (CONT.)

Traditionally, the total resistance (R_t) of a building section has been selected or computed and then converted to its reciprocal, the Overall Heat Transmission Coefficient (U) to establish a unit expressing heat passage through the section. However, that conversion is basically redundant and it introduces unnecessary chances for arithmetic errors. Design or analysis of a building section should preferably be in terms of a total resistance value (R_t) required or available. The general procedure for calculating the total resistance value (R_t) of a building section is:

1. Select the design outdoor weather and other conditions of temperature, wind direction and wind speed, sun angle, sun heat if applicable and the indoor air temperature that is to be maintained in each room during the coldest or hottest weather.

2. List all component elements of the section (including air spaces $3/4$" or greater except where such a space is necessary to the effectiveness of reflective material) beginning with the surface air film resistance of one face and ending with the surface resistance of the other face.

3. Against each component (except surface air films) show the thickness involved (actual, not nominal) unless test values are given as conductances.

4. Against each component, list the resistance for the thickness shown. See following tables. Resistivities can be multiplied or divided to adjust for thickness. For example, if the resistivity (for 1") is 3.70, then the resistance of $1/2$ inch would be 1.85 and of 2 inches, 7.40.

5. Add the resistances and divide the temperature differential (F) from inside to outside by the total resistance (R_t) of the section to determine the heat transmission rate in Btu per hour per square foot of the section.

Note: The foregoing does not include consideration of heat losses due to air infiltration through cracks and openings and ventilation air. Such losses should be computed in accordance with procedures set forth in references and used to determine design of heating plant. Nor does it consider sun loads during heating seasons.

The solution to the basic problem of acceptable heat flow rate is the selection of the most appropriate materials for the building section and design of the heating plant with a capacity at maximum output just equal to the heating loss which develops under the most severe weather conditions. Economics usually interferes with the attainment of this ideal because weather records show that most severe weather conditions do not repeat themselves every year. If heating systems were designed with adequate capacity for the maximum weather conditions on record, there would be considerable excess capacity during most of the operating life of the system.

In many cases, occasional failure of a heating plant to maintain a preselected indoor design temperature during brief periods of severe weather is not critical. Of critical importance is the nature of the occupancy and the performance of the building (sections) and heating plant expected by the owner. A basic consideration in cold weather for most healthy persons is the temperature of the indoor surface of the outer wall of the room, including windows. With indoor air temperature of 72°–75°F at 5 feet above the floor, most people will be significantly less comfortable when the wall surface temperature is 60°F than when it is 68°F. Similar considerations should be made for ceiling and floor temperatures in accordance with the tables below:

RECOMMENDED MINIMUM THERMAL RESISTANCES (R)

OUTDOOR AIR TEMP. F.	INDOOR SURFACE TEMPERATURES °F				
	60	FAIR 64	MED. 66	GOOD 68	FLOOR * MIN.
+30	2.3	3.4	5.1	10.0	1.7
+20	2.8	4.2	6.4	12.5	2.2
+10	3.4	5.1	7.8	14.5	2.6
0	3.9	6.0	9.2	17.0	3.0
−10	4.4	6.8	10.1	20.0	3.4
−20	5.1	7.8	11.3	23.0	3.9
−30	5.7	8.4	12.8	25.0	4.4
−40	6.4	10.2	14.5	28.0	4.8

* not desirable for children

THERMAL PERFORMANCE REFERENCE VALUES

	EFFECTIVE THERMAL RESISTANCE (R) CONDUCIVE TO COMFORT			
	EXCELLENT	GOOD	MODERATE	MINIMAL
CEILING	24	19	13	9
WALLS	13	11	8	7
FLOOR OVER VENTED CRAWL SPACE	19	13	9	7

In selecting materials for a building section, use of an insulating material with the recommended effective thermal resistance value can eliminate consideration of the resistance of the other materials in meeting resistance requirements of the section. However, this does not eliminate the need for analysing the moisture vapor control provided by the section.

Compilation of summer cooling loads involves the same principles as in determining heating loads but adds new factors such as moisture heat load (latent heat), solar gain, heat from occupants, lights and equipment and time lag due to the heat capacity of the structure. It is wise to consult an expert in this field even before the orientation and fenestration of a proposed new air-conditioned building is fixed. For general design purposes it is sufficient to note that air cooling costs several times as much as air heating on a unit basis of volume and time, and that the thermal insulation installed to conserve heat in winter works equally well to reduce heat gain and cooling costs in the summer.

MOISTURE VAPOR MIGRATION

Moisture is present as vapor in ordinary air and as absorbed moisture in most building materials. It may be present in the free liquid state or as ice in the solid state within the range of temperatures encountered in many buildings. Problems involving moisture may arise from changes in moisture content, from the presence of excessive moisture, or from effects associated with its changes in state.

Design and construction of buildings must consider the behavior of moisture, particularly the change from the vapor to the liquid or solid state, known as condensation. Moisture problems involving condensation are most likely to occur in buildings in any climate where there is a source of moisture vapor at temperatures above normal, or in cooled structures, and in buildings in cold climates.

Most moisture problems in residences occur in winter and

become increasingly critical as homes are built smaller and tighter. The residences must permit escape or migration of moisture vapor originating from cooking, laundering, bathing, breathing and perspiration of people as well as from humidifiers, automatic washers and dryers, and the bare earth in a crawl space or basement, or walls.

This migration must be limited to acceptable rates because moisture in air is a gas which occupies all the space along with the air.

Moisture vapor can act independently of the air since its properties do not depend on the presence of air. It exerts its own pressure, and can move about through air in a space, or move through materials under differences in vapor pressure independently of the air. Moisture vapor flows only from high toward low pressure.

Moisture in building materials usually has a marked effect upon the transmission of heat through them. Particularly, in porous materials saturated with water there is likely to be a migration of moisture to the cold side under the influence of the temperature gradient. This can occur by a process of evaporation, vapor flow, and condensation within the material, a substantial amount of heat being transferred as latent heat of vapor, particularly in the case of open fibrous material.

Moisture should not be allowed to migrate and accumulate in building construction unless place of accumulation is designed specifically to handle moisture in any of its three forms: vapor, liquid or solid.

Owen L. Delevante, AIA; Glen Rock, New Jersey
E. C. Shuman, P. E.; Consulting Engineer; State College, Pennsylvania

MATERIAL & DESCRIPTION		DENSITY (lb per cu ft)	RESISTANCE (R)[a] Per inch thickness (1/k)	For thickness listed (1/C)
BUILDING BOARDS, PANELS, FLOORING, ETC.				
Asbestos-cement board		120	0.25	—
Asbestos-cement board	1/8 in.	120	—	0.033
Gypsum or plaster board	3/8 in.	50	—	0.32
Gypsum or plaster board	1/2 in.	50	—	0.45
Plywood		34	1/25	—
Sheathing, wood fiber (impreg. or coated) 25/32"		20		2.06
		22	2.44	—
		25	2.27	—
Wood fiber board, lam. or homogeneous		26	2.38	—
		33	1.82	—
Wood fiber, hardboard type		65	0.72	—
Wood fiber, hardboard type	1/4 in.	65	—	0.18
Wood subfloor	25/32 in.	—	—	0.98
Wood, hardwood finish	3/4 in.	—	—	0.68
BUILDING PAPER				
Vapor-permeable felt		—	—	0.06
Vapor-seal, 2 layers of mopped 15 lb felt		—	—	0.12
Vapor-seal, plastic film		—	—	Negl.
FINISH FLOORING MATERIALS				
Carpet and fibrous pad		—	—	2.08
Carpet and rubber pad		—	—	1.23
Cork tile	1/8 in.	—	—	0.28
Terrazzo	1 in.	—	—	0.08
Tile-asphalt, linoleum, vinyl, rubber		—	—	0.05
INSULATING MATERIALS				
Blanket and Batt[b]				
Mineral wool, fibrous form processed		0.5	3.12	—
from rock, slag, or glass		1.5–4.0	3.70	—
Wood fiber		3.2–3.6	4.00	—
Boards and Slabs				
Cellular glass	90°F	9	2.44	—
	60°F		2.56	—
	30°F		2.70	—
	0°F		2.86	—
	−30°F		3.00	—
Corkboard	90°F	6.5–8.0	3.57	—
	60°F		3.70	—
	30°F		3.85	—
	0°F		4.00	—
	90°F	12	3.22	—
	60°F		3.33	—
	30°F		3.45	—
	0°F		3.57	—
Glass fiber	90°F	4–9	3.85	—
	60°F		4.17	—
	30°F		4.55	—
	0°F		4.76	—
	−30°F		5.26	—
Expanded rubber (rigid)	75°F	4.5	4.55	—
Expanded polyurethane (R-11 blown)	100°F	1.5–2.5	5.56	—
(Thickness 1 in. & greater)	75°F		5.88	—
	50°F		6.25	—
	25°F		5.88	—
	0°F		5.88	—
Expanded polystyrene, extruded	75°F	1.9	3.85	—
	60°F		4.00	—
	30°F		4.17	—
	0°F		4.55	—
	−60°F		5.26	—
Expanded polystyrene,	75°F	1.0	3.57	—
molded beads	30°F		3.85	—
	0°F		4.17	—
Mineral wool with resin binder	90°F	15	3.45	—
	60°F		3.57	—
	30°F		3.70	—
	0°F		4.00	—
Mineral fiberboard, wet felted				
Core or roof insulation		16–17	2.94	—
Acoustical tile		18	2.86	—
Acoustical tile		21	2.73	—
Mineral fiberboard, wet molded				
Acoustical tile[c]		23	2.38	—
Wood or can fiberboard				
Acoustical tile[c]	1/2 in.	—	—	1.19
Acoustical tile[c]	3/4 in.	—	—	1.78
Interior finish (plank, tile)		15	2.86	

MATERIAL & DESCRIPTION		DENSITY (lb per cu ft)	RESISTANCE (R)[a] Per inch thickness (1/k)	For thickness listed (1/C)
INSULATING MATERIALS				
Boards and Slabs (continued)				
Insulating roof deck				
Approximately	1-1/2 in.	—	—	4.17
Approximately	2 in.	—	—	5.56
Approximately	3 in.	—	—	8.33
Wood shredded (cemented, preformed slabs)		22	1.67	
Loose Fill				
Mineral wool	90°F	2.0–5.0	3.33	—
(glass, slag, or rock)	60°F		3.70	—
	30°F		4.00	—
	0°F		4.35	—
Perlite (expanded)	90°F	5.0–8.0	2.63	—
	60°F		2.78	—
	30°F		2.94	—
	0°F		3.12	—
Vermiculite (expanded)	90°F	7.0–8.2	2.08	—
	60°F		2.18	—
	30°F		2.27	—
	0°F		2.38	—
	90°F	4.0–6.0	2.22	—
	60°F		2.33	—
	30°F		2.50	—
	0°F		2.63	—
Roof Insulation[d]				
Preformed, for use above deck				
Approximately	1/2 in.	—	—	1.39
Approximately	1 in.	—	—	2.78
Approximately	1-1/2 in.	—	—	4.17
Approximately	2 in.	—	—	5.26
Approximately	2-1/2 in.	—	—	6.67
Approximately	3 in.	—	—	8.33
Cellular glass		—	2.56	—
MASONRY MATERIALS - CONCRETES				
Cement mortar		116	0.20	—
Gypsum-fiber concrete,				
87-1/2% gypsum, 12-1/2% wood chips		51	0.60	—
Lightweight aggregates including		120	0.19	—
expanded shale, clay or slate;		100	0.28	—
expanded slags; cinders; pumice;		80	0.40	—
perlite; vermiculite; also		60	0.59	—
cellular concretes		40	0.86	—
		30	1.11	—
		20	1.43	—
Sand & gravel or stone aggregate		140	0.11	—
(oven dried)				
Sand & gravel or stone aggregate		140	0.08	—
(not dried)				
Stucco		116	0.20	—
MASONRY UNITS				
Brick, common[d]		120	0.20	—
Brick, face[e]		130	0.11	—
Clay tile, hollow: 1 cell deep	3 in.	—	—	0.80
1 cell deep	4 in.	—	—	1.11
2 cells deep	6 in.	—	—	1.52
2 cells deep	8 in.	—	—	1.85

Owen L. Delevante, AIA; Glen Rock, New Jersey

E. C. Shuman, P. E.; Consulting Engineer; State College, Pennsylvania

MATERIAL & DESCRIPTION		DENSITY (lb per cu ft)	RESISTANCE (R)[a] Per inch thickness (1/k)	RESISTANCE (R)[a] For thickness listed (1/C)
MASONRY UNITS				
Concrete blocks, three oval core:				
Sand & gravel aggregate	4 in.	—	—	0.71
	8 in.	—	—	1.11
	12 in.	—	—	1.28
Cinder aggregate	3 in.	—	—	0.86
	4 in.	—	—	1.11
	8 in.	—	—	1.72
	12 in.	—	—	1.89
Lightweight aggregate	3 in.	—	—	1.27
(expanded shale, clay, slate	4 in.	—	—	1.50
or slag; pumice)	8 in.	—	—	2.00
	12 in.	—	—	2.27
Concrete blocks, rectangular core: f				
Sand & gravel aggregate				
2 core, 8 in. 36 lb. g		—	—	1.04
Lightweight aggregate (expanded shale, clay, slate or slag; pumice)				
3 core, 6 in. 19 lb. g	45 F	—	—	1.65
2 core, 8 in. 24 lb. g	45 F	—	—	2.18
3 core, 12 in. 38 lb. g	45 F	—	—	2.48
Granite, marble		150—175	0.05	
Stone, lime or sand		—	0.08	
Gypsum partition tile:				
3 × 12 × 30 in. solid		—	—	1.26
3 × 12 × 30 in. 4-cell		—	—	1.35
4 × 12 × 30 in. 3-cell		—	—	1.67
METALS				
Aluminum		159—175	0.0007	
Brass, red		524—542	0.0014	
Brass, yellow		524—542	0.0014	
Copper, cast rolled		550—555	0.0004	
Iron, gray cast		438—445	0.0030	—
Iron, pure		474—493	0.0023	—
Lead		704	0.0040	—
Steel, cold drawn		490	0.0032	
Steel, stainless, type 304			0.0055	
Zinc, cast			0.0013	
PLASTERING MATERIALS				
Cement plaster, sand aggregate		116	0.20	—
Sand aggregate	1/2 in.	—	—	0.10
Sand aggregate	3/4 in.	—	—	0.15
Gypsum plaster:				
Lightweight aggregate	1/2 in.	45	—	0.32
Lightweight aggregate	5/8 in.	45	—	0.39
Lightweight aggregate, on metal lath	3/4 in.	—	—	0.47
Perlite aggregate		45	0.67	—
Sand aggregate		105	0.18	—
Sand aggregate	1/2 in.	105	—	0.09
Sand aggregate	5/8 in.	105	—	0.11
Sand aggregate, on metal lath	3/4 in.	—	—	0.1
Vermiculite aggregate		45	0.59	—
ROOFING				
Asbestos-cement shingles		120	—	0.21
Asphalt roll roofing		70	—	0.15
Asphalt shingles		70	—	0.44
Built-up roofing	3/8 in.	70	—	0.33
Slate	1/2 in.	—	—	0.05
SIDING MATERIALS				
(On Flat Surface)				
Shingles:				
Asbestos-cement		120	—	0.21
Wood, 16 in., 7-1/2 in. exposure		—	—	0.87
Wood, double, 16 in., 12 in. exposure		—	—	1.19
Wood, plus insul. backer board, 5/16 in.		—	—	1.40
Siding:				
Asbestos-cement, 1/4 in., lapped		—	—	0.21
Asphalt insulating siding (1/2 in. bd.)		—	—	1.46
Wood, drop, 1 × 8 in.		—	—	0.79
Wood, bevel, 1/2 × 8 in., lapped		—	—	0.81
Wood, bevel, 3/4 × 10 in., lapped		—	—	1.05
Architectural glass		—	—	0.10

MATERIAL & DESCRIPTION		DENSITY (lb per cu ft)	RESISTANCE (R)[a] Per inch thickness (1/k)	RESISTANCE (R)[a] For thickness listed (1/C)
WOODS				
Maple, oak, and similar hardwoods		45	0.91	—
Fir, pine, and similar softwoods		32	1.25	—
Fir, pine, and similar softwoods				
	25/32 in.	32	—	0.98
	1-5/8 in.	32	—	2.03
	2-5/8 in.	32	—	3.28
	3-5/8 in.	32	—	4.55
Door, 1-3/4 in. thick solid wood core				1.96

AIR SURFACES

Position of Surface	Direction of Heat Flow	Type of Surface Non-Reflective Materials Resistance (R)	Type of Surface Reflective Aluminum Coated Paper Resistance (R)	Type of Surface Highly Reflective Foil Resistance (R)
STILL AIR				
Horizontal	Upward	0.61	1.10	1.32
45° slope	Upward	0.62	1.14	1.37
Vertical	Horizontal	0.68	1.35	1.70
45° slope	Down	0.76	1.67	2.22
Horizontal	Down	0.92	2.70	4.55
MOVING AIR (any position)				
15 mph wind	Any	0.17 W	—	—
7-1/2 mph wind	Any	0.25 S	—	—

AIR SPACES

Position of Air Space and Thickness (inches)		Heat Flow Dir.	Sea-son	Types of Surfaces on Opposite Sides Both Surfaces Non-Reflective Materials Resistance (R)	Types of Surfaces on Opposite Sides Aluminum Coated Paper/ Non-Reflective Materials Resistance (R)	Types of Surfaces on Opposite Sides Foil/ Non-Reflective Materials Resistance (R)
Horizontal	3/4	Up	W	0.87	1.71	2.23
	3/4		S	0.76	1.63	2.26
	4		W	0.94	1.99	2.73
	4		S	0.80	1.87	2.75
45° slope	3/4	Up	W	0.94	2.02	2.78
	3/4		S	0.81	1.90	2.81
	4		W	0.96	2.13	3.00
	4		S	0.82	1.98	3.00
Vertical	3/4	Down	W	1.01	2.36	3.48
	3/4		S	0.84	2.10	3.28
	4		W	1.01	2.34	3.45
	4		S	0.91	2.16	3.44
45° slope	3/4	Down	W	1.02	2.40	3.57
	3/4		S	0.84	2.09	3.24
	4		W	1.08	2.75	4.41
	4		S	0.90	2.50	4.36
Horizontal	3/4	Down	W	1.02	2.39	3.55
	1-1/2		W	1.14	3.21	5.74
	4		W	1.23	4.02	8.94
	3/4		S	0.84	2.08	3.25
	1-1/2		S	0.93	2.76	5.24
	4		S	0.99	3.38	8.08

Owen L. Delevante, AIA; Glen Rock, New Jersey

E. C. Shuman, P. E.; Consulting Engineer; State College, Pennsylvania

GLASS, GLASS BLOCK & PLASTIC SHEET[i]

MATERIAL & DESCRIPTION	OVERALL HEAT TRANSMISSION COEFFICIENT (U)	SEASONS	RESISTANCE (R)
VERTICAL PANELS—EXTERIOR			
Flat Glass			
Single glass	1.13	Winter	0.89
	1.06	Summer	0.94
Insulating glass, two lights of glass			
3/16 in. air space	0.69	Winter	1.44
	0.64	Summer	1.56
1/4 in. air space	0.65	Winter	1.55
	0.61	Summer	1.65
1/2 in. air space	0.58	Winter	1.72
	0.56	Summer	1.79
Insulating glass, three lights of glass			
1/4 in. air spaces	0.47	Winter	2.13
	0.45	Summer	2.22
1/2 in. air spaces	0.36	Winter	2.78
	0.35	Summer	2.86
Storm windows			
1 in. — 4 in. air space	0.56	Winter	1.79
	0.54	Summer	1.85
Glass Block			
6 × 6 × 4 in. thick (nom.)	0.60	Winter	1.67
	0.57	Summer	1.76
8 × 8 × 4 in. thick (nom.)	0.56	Winter	1.79
	0.54	Summer	1.85
—with cavity divider	0.48	Winter	2.08
	0.46	Summer	2.17
12 × 12 × 4 in. thick (nom.)	0.52	Winter	1.92
	0.50	Summer	2.00
—with cavity divider	0.44	Winter	2.27
	0.42	Summer	2.38
12 × 12 × 2 in. thick (nom.)	0.60	Winter	1.67
	0.57	Summer	1.76
Single Plastic Sheet	1.09	Winter	.92
	1.00	Summer	1.00
HORIZONTAL PANELS—EXTERIOR			
Flat Glass			
Single glass	1.22	Winter	0.82
	0.83	Summer	1.20
Insulating glass, two lights of glass			
3/16 in. air space	0.75	Winter	1.34
	0.49	Summer	2.04
1/4 in. air space	0.70	Winter	1.43
	0.46	Summer	2.17
1/2 in. air space	0.66	Winter	1.52
	0.44	Summer	2.27
Glass Block			
11 × 11 × 3 in. thick with cavity divider	0.53	Winter	1.89
	0.35	Summer	2.86
12 × 12 × 4 in. thick with cavity divider	0.51	Winter	1.96
	0.34	Summer	2.94
Plastic Bubbles[k]			
Single walled	1.15	Winter	.87
	0.80	Summer	1.25
Double walled	0.70	Winter	1.43
	0.46	Summer	2.17

Owen L. Delevante, AIA; Glen Rock, New Jersey
E. C. Shuman, P. E.; Consulting Engineer; State College, Pennsylvania

NOTES:

a. Resistances are representative values for dry materials and are intended as design (not specification) values for materials in normal use. Unless shown otherwise in descriptions of materials, all values are for 75 F mean temperature.

b. Includes paper backing and facing if any. In cases where insulation forms a boundary (highly reflective of otherwise) of an air space, refer to appropriate table for the insulating value of the air space. Some manufacturers of batt and blanket insulation mark their products with R value, but they can assure only the quality of the material as shipped.

c. Average values only are given since variations depend upon density of the board and on the type, size and depth of perforations.

d. Thicknesses supplied by different manufacturers may vary depending upon the particular material.

e. Values will vary if density varies from that listed.

f. Data on rectangular core concrete blocks differs from the data for oval core blocks due to core configuration, different mean temperature and different unit weight. Weight data on oval core blocks not available.

g. Weight of units approx. 7-5/8 high by 15-5/8 long are given to describe blocks tested. Values are for one square foot area.

h. Thermal resistance of metals is so low that in building constructions it is usually ignored. Values shown emphasize relatively easy flow of heat along or through metals so that they are usually heat leaks, inward or out.

i. Spaces of uniform thickness bounded by moderately smooth surfaces.

j. Values shown not applicable to interior installations of materials listed.

k. Winter is heat flow up; summer is heat flow down.

l. Based on area of opening, not on total surface area.

Based on data from ASHRAE HANDBOOK OF FUNDAMENTALS, 1967, Chapters 23 and 26

U	R_T
2.00	0.50
1.80	0.56
1.60	0.63
1.50	0.67
1.40	0.72
1.30	0.77
1.20	0.83
1.10	0.91
1.00	1.00
.90	1.11
.80	1.25
.70	1.43
.60	1.67
.58	1.72
.56	1.79
.54	1.85
.52	1.92
.50	2.00
.48	2.08
.46	2.17
.44	2.27
.42	2.38
.40	2.50
.38	2.63
.36	2.78
.34	2.94
.32	3.13
.30	3.33
.28	3.57
.26	3.85
.24	4.17
.22	4.55
.20	5.00
.19	5.26
.18	5.55
.17	5.88
.16	6.25
.15	6.67
.14	7.15
.13	7.69
.12	8.35
.11	9.09
.10	10.00
.09	11.11
.08	12.50
.07	14.29
.06	16.67
.05	20.00
.04	25.00

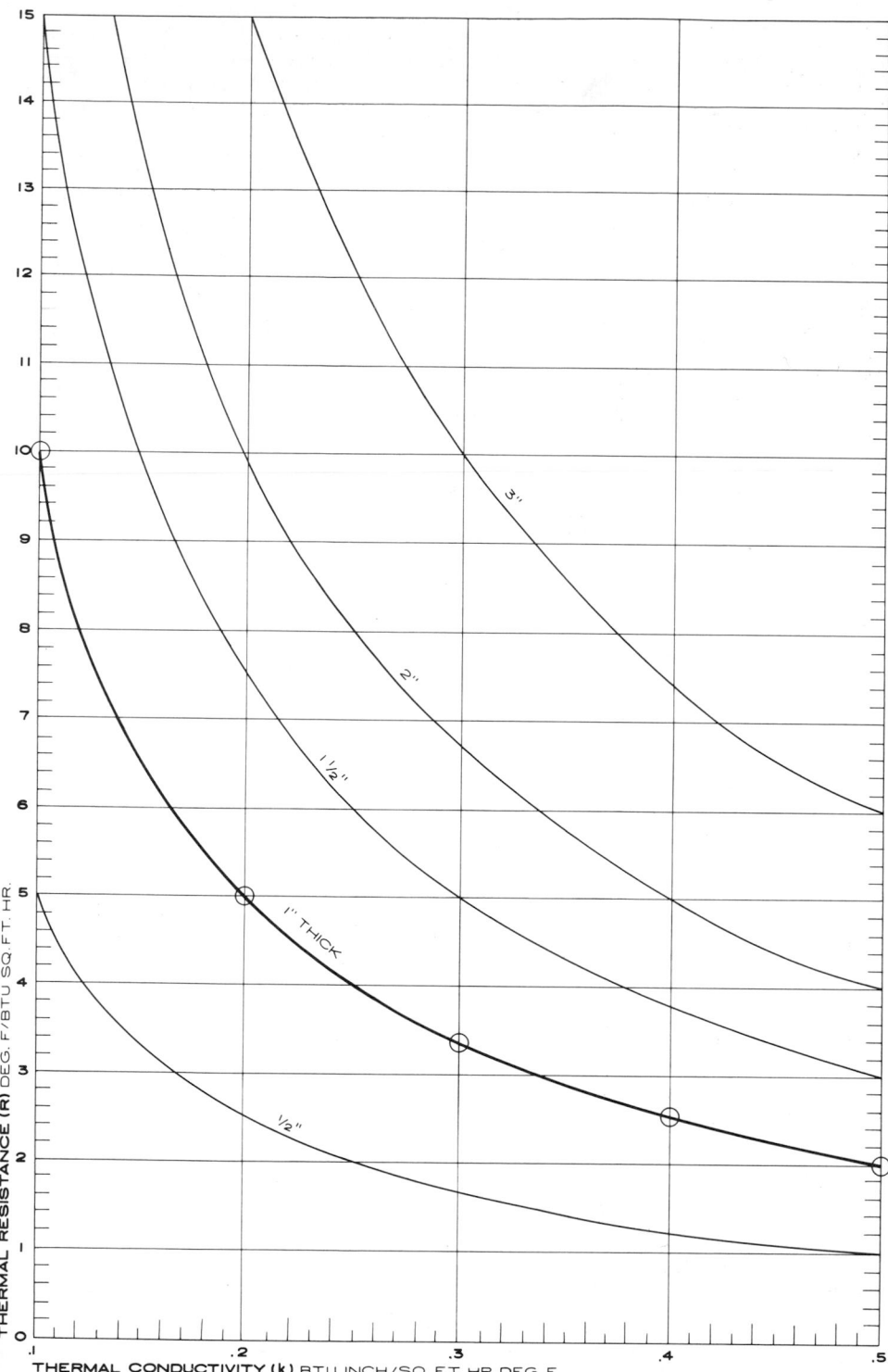

THERMAL RESISTANCE (R) DEG. F/BTU SQ.FT.HR.

THERMAL CONDUCTIVITY (k) BTU INCH/SQ.FT. HR DEG.F

Thermal resistances for combinations of materials, spaces with or without emittances or reflectances, and air films are additive while conductances (C factor) and conductivities (k factor) are not. Convert all C, k, and U factors to R values. Heat flow values are identical for both procedures, but calculations are simpler if only R values are used.

$$\text{Btu per hour, sq. ft.} = \frac{\text{Temp. diff. F}}{R}$$

TOTAL THERMAL RESISTANCE (R_T). An expression of the total resistance to heat flow through a complete building section or construction assembly, including internal air spaces with or without emittances or reflectances, and external air films. Total thermal resistance is usually expressed as R_T of typical section per sq. ft. hr. and the value for

one construction may be compared directly with another on the basis of more or less heat flow for the same temperatures.

OVERALL HEAT TRANSMISSION COEFFICIENT (U or $1/R_T$): the reciprocal (divided into 1) of the Total Thermal Resistance. "U" has been the unit used to express heat flow through a building section including air spaces 3/4 inch or greater and air films. Technically, it is heat transmission in Btu's per hour per square foot per degree F difference from air to air. While it has been used to calculate heat loss or gain, it is recommended that it be abandoned in favor of the more easily used Total Thermal Resistance (R_T).

THERMAL RESISTANCE (R). A unit for the rate ·

of heat flow through a given thickness of a homogeneous or composite material, or construction assembly with or without cavities or reflective surfaces. It is measured by the temperature difference in degrees F between the two exposed faces required to cause one Btu to flow through one square foot per hour. Resistances may be added. (R = temp. diff. F/Btu for one sq. ft., hr.)

THERMAL RESISTIVITY(r). A unit for the rate of heat flow through a homogeneous material exactly one inch thick. It is measured by the temperature difference in degrees F between the smooth parallel faces required to cause one Btu to flow through one square foot per hour. Resistivities may be added. (r = temp. diff. F/Btu inch for one sq. ft., hr.)

Lawrence Conde; Frost Associates, Architects; New York, New York
E. C. Shuman, P. E.; Consulting Engineer; State College, Pennsylvania

WOOD FRAME CONSTRUCTION

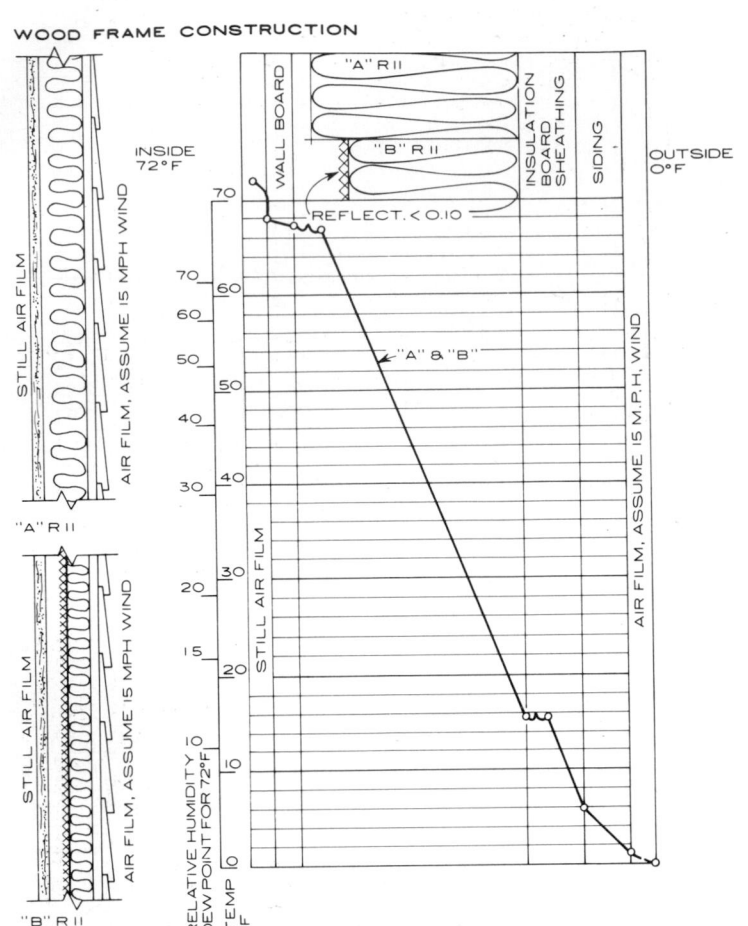

	WALL "A"			WALL "B"		
	R F/Btu*	°F Diff. Due to R*	Temp °F*	R F/Btu*	°F Diff Due to R*	Temp °F*
Indoor room air			72.0			72.0
Still air film (indoor)	0.68	3.2		0.68	3.2	
Indoor face of wall board			68.8			68.8
Gypsum or plaster board (1/2 in.)	0.45	2.1		0.45	2.1	
Back face of wall board			66.7			66.7
Stud air space remaining	negl.	—				
Inner face of insulation			66.7			66.7
Thermal insulation, R11-wo/refl.	11.00	51.37				
-w/refl.				11.00	51.37	
Outer face of insulation			15.3			15.3
Inner face of sheathing			15.3			15.3
Sheathing, 25/32 in., 20 lb.	2.06	9.6		2.06	9.6	
Outer face of sheathing			5.7			5.7
Inner face of siding			5.7			5.7
Siding, wood, 3/4 x 10, lapped	1.05	4.9		1.05	4.95	
Outer face of siding			0.8			0.8
Outdoor air film (15 mph wind)	0.17	0.80		0.17	0.80	
Outdoor air			0			0
TOTALS	15.41	72.0		15.41	72.0	

Heat Loss/sf = $\dfrac{\text{Temp. Diff., Room to Outdoors}}{\text{Total Resistance, R}} = \dfrac{72-0}{15.41} = 4.7$ Btu/hr. applies to insulated areas only; studs and other materials are heat paths which increase heat loss.

Wall "A"—Full thick fibrous insulation R11, non-reflective faces, air spaces insufficient to provide any significant resistance.

Wall "B"—Reflective faced fibrous insulation, R11 with the facing; air space 3/4 in. or more in width required with the facing to provide R11; that space must not be counted a second time.

Insulation thicknesses are not specified but only the R value of the material as manufactured; proper installation is implied.

*
Decimals are used to check calculations only — fractional Btu's are usually of no consequence.

MASONRY CAVITY WALL CONSTRUCTION

	WALL "A"			WALL "B"		
	R F/Btu*	°F Diff. Due to R*	Temp °F*	R F/Btu*	°F Diff Due to R*	Temp °F*
Indoor room air			72.0			72.0
Still air film (indoor)	0.68	10.55		0.68	4.16	
Indoor face of wall board			61.45			67.84
Gypsum or plaster board (1/2 in.)	0.45	6.98		0.45	2.76	
Back face of wall board			54.47			65.08
Furring air space (3/4 in.)	0.90	13.95		0.90	5.52	
Inner face of concrete block			40.52			59.56
Concrete block, 8 in., 3 oval core sand & gravel	1.11	17.10		1.11	6.80	
Outer face of concrete block			23.42			52.76
"A" cavity, 2 in. air space	0.90	13.95		—	—	
"B" cavity, filled w/insulation R8	—	—		8.0	49.04	
Inner face of face brick			9.47			3.72
Face brick, nom. 4 in.	0.44	6.83		0.44	2.70	
Outer face of face brick			2.64			1.02
Outdoor air film (15 mph wind)	0.17	2.63		0.17	1.04	
Outdoor air			0			0
TOTALS	4.65	72.01		11.75	72.02	

Heat Loss/sf = $\dfrac{\text{Temp. Diff., Room to Outdoors}}{\text{Total Resistance, R}} = \dfrac{72-0}{4.65} = 15.5$ Btu/hr. $\dfrac{72-0}{11.75} = 6.13$ Btu/hr.

Wall "A"—2 in. open cavity

Wall "B"—2 in. cavity filled with insulation R8. (Verify if water-repellent type is required) R value is for material as manufactured; proper installation is implied.

*Decimals are used to check calculations only—fractional Btu's are usually of no consequence.

NOTE: In tabulation the considerable difference between the temperatures of inside surfaces of the two walls. Occupants of conventional rooms with Wall "A" will be less comfortable than with Wall "B" because of colder inside surface temperature; 61°F vs. 68°F.

Owen L. Delevante, AIA; Glen Rock, New Jersey
E. C. Shuman, P. E.; Consulting Engineer; State College, Pennsylvania

MATERIAL[a]	PERMEANCE (PERM)	PERMEABILITY (PERM-INCH)
Materials Used in Construction		
Concrete (1:2:4 mix)	—	3.2
Brick-masonry (4 in. thick)	0.8–1.1	—
Concrete block (8 in. cored, limestone agg.)	2.4	—
Asbestos-cement board (0.2 in. thick)	0.54	—
Plaster on metal lath 3/4 in.)	15	—
Plaster on plain gypsum lath (with studs)	20	—
Gypsum wallboard (3/8 in. plain)	50	—
Struct. insulating bd. (sheathing qual.)	—	20–50
Struct. insulating bd. (int., uncoated, 1/2 in.)	50–90	—
Hardboard (1/8 in. standard)	11	—
Hardboard (1/8 in. tempered)	5	—
Built-up roofing (hot-mopped)	0.0	—
Wood, fir sheathing, 3/4 in.	2.9	—
Plywood (douglas-fir, exterior glue, 1/4 in.)	0.7	—
Plywood (douglas-fir, interior glue, 1/4 in.)	1.9	—
Acrylic, glass fiber reinforced sheet, 56 mil	0.12	—
Polyester, glass fiber reinforced sheet, 48 mil	0.05	—
Thermal Insulations		
Cellular glass	—	0.0
Mineral wool, unprotected	29.0	—
Expanded polyurethane (R-11 blown)	—	0.4–1.6
Expanded polystyrene-extruded	—	1.2
Expanded polystyrene-bead	—	2.0–5.8
Plastic and Metal Foils and Films[b]		
Aluminum foil (1 mil)	0.0	—
Polyethylene (4 mil)	0.08	—
Polyethylene (6 mil)	0.06	—
Polyethylene (8 mil)	0.04	—
Polyester (1 mil)	0.7	—
Polyvinylchloride, unplasticized (2 mil)	0.68	—
Polyvinylchloride, plasticized (4 mil)	0.8–1.4	—
Building Papers, Felts, Roofing Papers[c]		
Duplex sheet, asp. lam., alum. foil one side (43)[d]	0.176	—
Saturated and coated roll roofing (326)[d]	0.24	—
Kraft paper and asp. lam., reinf. 30-120-30 (34)[d]	1.8	—
Asp.-saturated, coated vapor-barrier paper (43)[d]	0.6	—
Asp.-saturated, not coated sheathing paper (22)[d]	20.2	—
15-lb asphalt felt (70)[d]	5.6	—
15-lb tar felt (70)[d]	18.2	—
Single-kraft, double infused (16)[d]	42	—
Liquid-Applied Coating Materials		
Paint-2 coats		
Aluminum varnish on wood	0.3–0.5	—
Enamels on smooth plaster	0.5–1.5	—
Primers and sealers on interior insulation board	0.9–2.1	—
Misc. primers plus 1 coat flat oil paint on plas.	1.6–3.0	—
Flat paint on interior insulation bd.	4	—
Water emulsion on interior insulation bd.	30–85	—
Paint-3 coats		
Ext. paint, white lead and oil on wood siding	0.3–1.0	—
Ext. paint, white lead-zinc oxide and oil on wood	0.9	—
Styrene-butadiene latex coating, 2 oz./sq. ft.	11	—
Polyvinyl acetate latex coating, 4 oz./sq. ft.	5.5	—
Asphalt cut-back bastic, 1/16 in. dry	0.14	—
3/16 in. dry	0.0	—
Hot melt asphalt, 2 oz./sq. ft.	0.5	—
3.5 oz./sq. ft.	0.1	—

a. Vapor transmission rates listed will permit comparisons of materials but selection of vapor barrier materials should be based on rates obtained from the manufacturer or from laboratory tests. A range of values shown indicates variation among mean values for materials that are similar but of different density. Values are intended for design guidance only.

b. Usually installed as vapor barriers. If used as exterior finish and elsewhere near cold side, special considerations are required.

c. Low permeance sheets used as vapor barriers. High permeance used elsewhere in construction.

d. Basis weight in lb. per 500 sq. ft.

Based on data from ASHRAE HANDBOOK OF FUNDAMENTALS, 1967, Chapter 19.

Owen L. Delevante, AIA; Glen Rock, New Jersey
E. C. Shuman, P. E.; Consulting Engineer; State College, Pennsylvania

BUILDING SECTION ANALYSIS FOR POTENTIAL CONDENSATION

Any building section may be analyzed by simple calculations to determine if and where condensation might occur and what might be done in selection of materials or their assembly to eliminate that possibility. The section may or may not contain a vapor barrier or it may contain a relatively imperfect barrier; the building section may include cold-side materials of comparatively high resistance to the passage of vapor (and this is highly undesirable). It is to be avoided. With few exceptions, the vapor resistance at or near the warm surface should be five times that of any component.

The table at left gives permeances and permeability of building and vapor barrier materials and those values can be used in analysis of building sections by the following simple method:

1. List the materials, without surface films or air spaces, in the order of their appearance in the building section, beginning with the inside surface material and working to the outside.

2. Against each material list the permeance (or permeability) value from the table or a more accurate value if available from tests or manufacturers data. Where a range is given, select an average value or use judgment in assigning a value based on the character and potential installation method of the material proposed for use.

3. Start at the top of the list and note any material that has less permeance than the materials above it on the list. At that point the possibility exists that vapor leaking through the first material may condense on the second, provided the dew-point (condensation point) is reached and the movement is considerable. In that case, provide ventilation through the cold-side material or modify the design to eliminate or change the material to one of greater permeance.

4. If the leakage is slight (or the difference in permeance small), judgment should be used to estimate, by the severity of the climate and the duration of cold periods, whether condensation during these transient conditions is likely to be sufficiently troublesome to warrant either ventilation or a change in design of the building section.

EXAMPLE Nº 1

	Estimated Permeance
Plaster, painted 2 coats	3.0
Vapor Barrier	1.0 (lowest)
Insulation	29.0
Wood sheathing	2.9
4" Brick veneer	1.1 (next)

In this example the vapor barrier transmits 1 grain of moisture per square foot per hour for each unit of vapor pressure difference and nothing else transmits less. However, the cold brick veneer is nearly as low in permeance so it is advisable to make certain that the vapor barrier is expertly installed, with all openings at pipes, outlet boxes or joints carefully fitted or sealed. Alternatively, the brick veneer may have open mortar joints near the top and bottom to serve both as weep holes and as vapor release openings. They will also ventilate the wall and help reduce heat gain in summer.

EXAMPLE Nº 2

	Estimated Permeance
Flat oil paint on plaster	3.0
Furred space	—
8" concrete block	2.4
4" Brick veneer	1.1 (lowest)

Vapor (under pressure) would easily pass through the interior finish, be slowed up by the concrete block and nearly stopped by the cold brick veneer. Unless this design is radically improved, the masonry will become saturated and may cause serious water stains or apparent "leaks" in cold weather. In addition, alternating freezing and thawing of condensation within the masonry wall can cause physical damage to the construction.

EXAMPLE Nº 3

AIR SPACE (PLENUM)

	Estimated Permeance
Mineral wool ac. tile	29.0
Gypsum wallboard (susp.)	50.0
Concrete slab	2.0
Roof Insulation	29.0
Roofing, built-up	.24 (lowest)

First resistance to vapor flow occurs at the concrete roof slab which would be fairly cool because of the protection provided in the insulating value of the acoustical tile and the air space formed by the suspended ceiling. Moisture would probably condense on the underside of the slab in high humidity conditions but it is certain that some fo the vapor would continue to move through the slab, the insulation above and then condense on the underside of the cold roofing. It would flow back as water, saturating the insulation (and reducing its effectiveness), then the deck and would eventually drip to the ceiling below. This hazardous condition might not be observed for a long time because the gypsum lath and the acoustical tile would first soak up the water dripping from above.

First recommended correction is a vapor barrier on the top of the concrete roof slab with sufficient insulation above to keep the vapor barrier above the dew-point temperature of the interior air. An alternative would be a vapor barrier on the back of the gypsum lath with insulation resting on the lath and adequate venting of the air space (plenum) to the outside air.

EXAMPLES OF USE OF THIS CHART

1.

	Dry Bulb	Wet Bulb	RH	Dew Point
a.	75°F	75°F	100%	75°F
b.	75	73	90	72
c.	75	71	80	69
d.	75	63	50	55

2. Assume RH is designed for a specific room temperature. At intersection of 35% RH & 68°F Dry Bulb read horizontally to find Dew Point or cold surface temperature at which condensation will occur—40°F. At same intersection read 53°F Wet Bulb room temperature.

3.

Known	Obtain
a. Wet & Dry Bulb Temperatures	RH, Dew Point & Vapor Pressure
b. RH & Wet Bulb Temperature	Dry Bulb Temp., Dew Point & Vapor Pressure
c. RH & Dry Bulb Temperature	Wet Bulb Temp., Dew Point & Vapor Pressure

4. Vapor Pressure Scale. Assume that a black roof had been installed at a temperature of 72°F with moisture vapor in or under the roofing exerting a pressure of .4 P.S.I.A. Temperature of a black roof in service can be as high as 160°F. The 88°F gain in temperature would induce a 4.3 P.S.I.A. or 619 P.S.F. gain in vapor pressure. This is the reason for rapid and easy growth of blisters in roofing once they have started.

NOTE: Outdoor air temperature will not ordinarily be the indoor surface temperature of doors and windows and their frames. Their indoor surface temperatures may be warmer by an amount sufficient to avoid condensation.

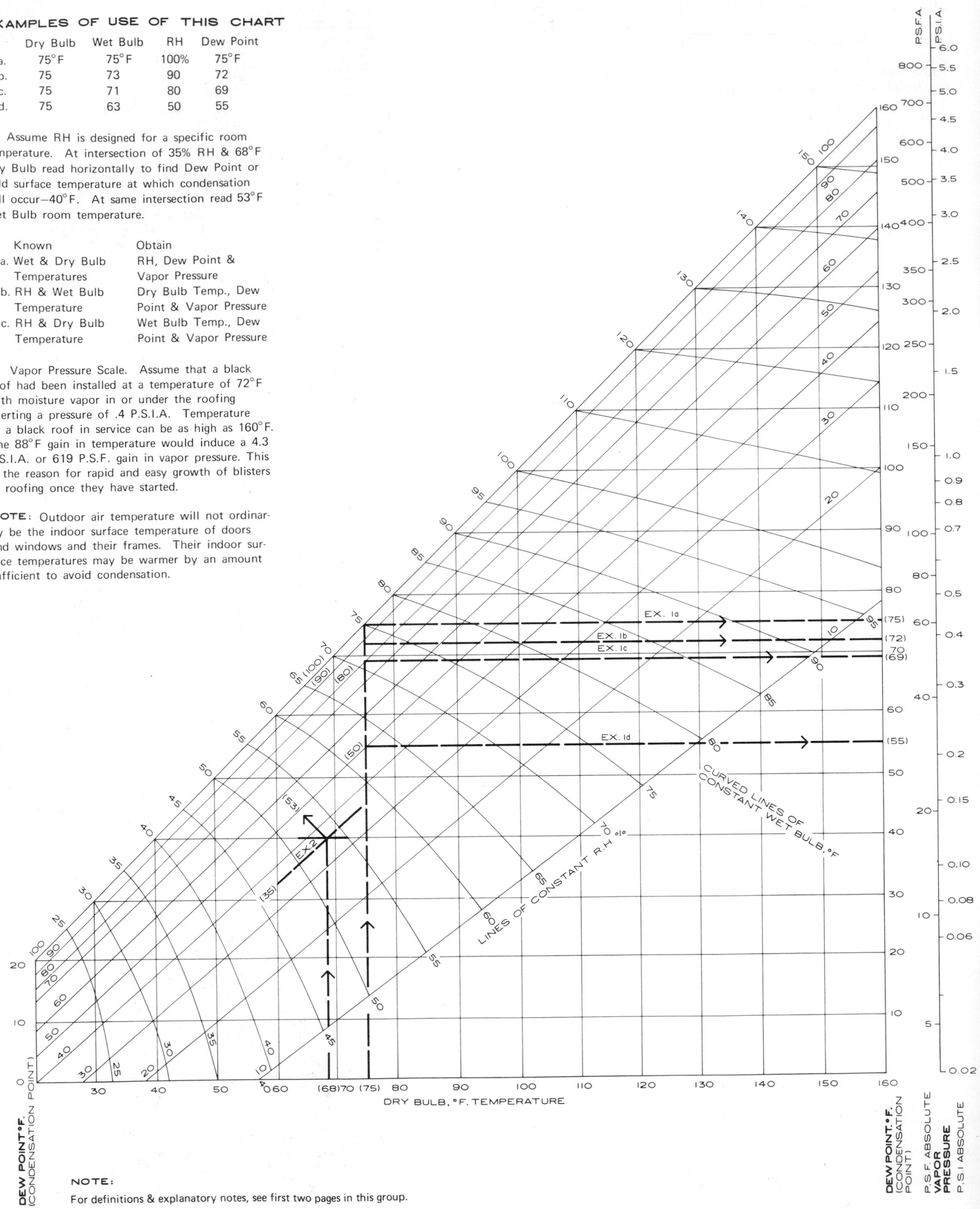

CURVED LINES OF CONSTANT WET BULB, °F.

LINES OF CONSTANT R.H.

DEW POINT °F. (CONDENSATION POINT)

DRY BULB, °F. TEMPERATURE

DEW POINT °F. (CONDENSATION POINT)

P.S.F. ABSOLUTE VAPOR PRESSURE

P.S.I. ABSOLUTE

P.S.F.A.   P.S.I.A.

NOTE:
For definitions & explanatory notes, see first two pages in this group.

Lawrence Conde; Frost Associates, Architects; New York, New York
E. C. Shuman, P. E.; Consulting Engineer; State College, Pennsylvania

CHAPTER 8

CURTAIN WALLS, DOORS, WINDOWS, GLASS

CLASSIFICATION BY NATURE OF COMPONENTS

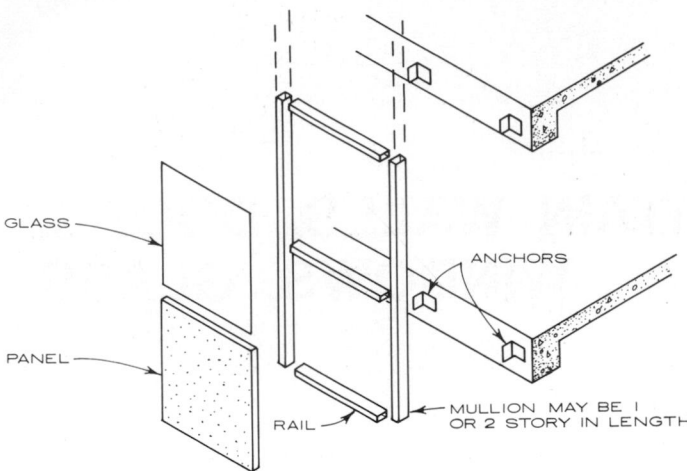

GLASS

PANEL

ANCHORS

RAIL

MULLION MAY BE 1
OR 2 STORY IN LENGTH

I.   GRID SYSTEM (STICK)
FRAMING MEMBERS VISUALLY PROMINENT
COMPONENTS INSTALLED PIECE BY PIECE

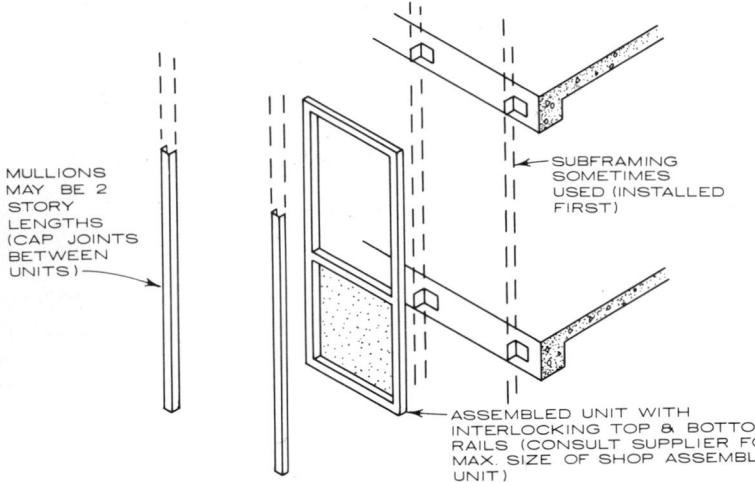

MULLIONS
MAY BE 2
STORY
LENGTHS
(CAP JOINTS
BETWEEN
UNITS)

SUBFRAMING
SOMETIMES
USED (INSTALLED
FIRST)

ASSEMBLED UNIT WITH
INTERLOCKING TOP & BOTTOM
RAILS (CONSULT SUPPLIER FOR
MAX. SIZE OF SHOP ASSEMBLED
UNIT)

2.   GRID SYSTEM (PANEL AND MULLION)
FRAMING MEMBERS VISUALLY PROMINENT
PANEL PREASSEMBLED & INSTALLED AS SHOWN

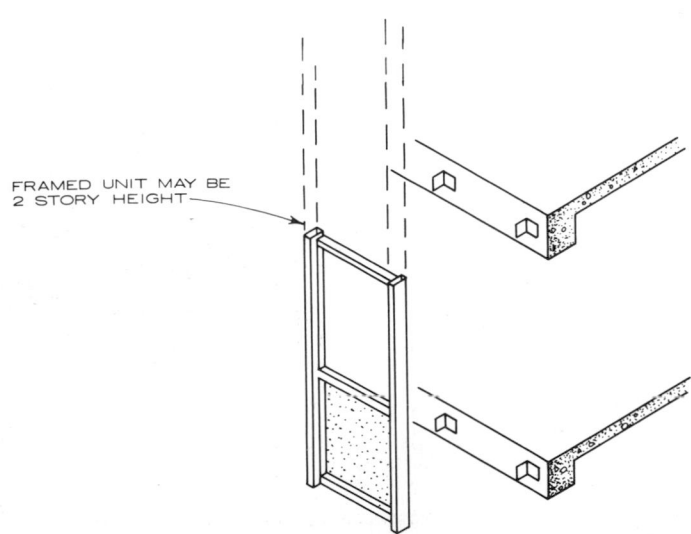

FRAMED UNIT MAY BE
2 STORY HEIGHT

3.   PANEL SYSTEM
COMPLETELY PREASSEMBLED UNITS; MAY OR MAY NOT INCLUDE INTERIOR FINISH

CLASSIFICATION BY USAGE

A CUSTOM TYPE

Walls designed specifically for one project, using specially designed parts and details. Such walls may be used on buildings of any height, but are more typical of multistoried structures. Included in this category are the highly publicized (and often more expensive) walls which serve as design pacesetters.

B COMMERCIAL TYPE

Walls made up principally of parts and details standardized by the manufacturer and assembled either in the manufacturer's stock patterns or in accord with the architect's design. This type is offered by many manufacturers and is typically used on one and two story buildings, but may be used on taller structures. Commercial walls offer lower cost because of quantity production, and also offer the advantages of proven performance.

C INDUSTRIAL TYPE

Walls in which ribbed, fluted, or otherwise preformed metal sheets in stock sizes are used, along with standard metal sash, as the principal components. This type of metal curtain wall has a long history of satisfactory performance, and, in its insulated form, finds wide use in many important buildings outside the industrial field.

GENERAL NOTES:

1. Mullions which extend through the wall and are exposed on both exterior and interior of the building, should include a thermal break (especially if they are aluminum).

2. When mullions serve as guide rails for roof mounted window washing platforms or "rigs," mullions should be designed as a track and reinforced against thrust, using information on loads from cleaning equipment manufacturer.

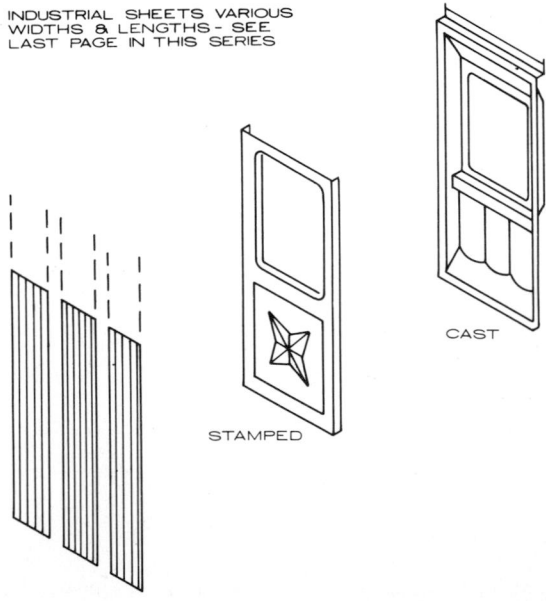

INDUSTRIAL SHEETS VARIOUS
WIDTHS & LENGTHS - SEE
LAST PAGE IN THIS SERIES

CAST

STAMPED

ALTERNATE PANEL TYPES

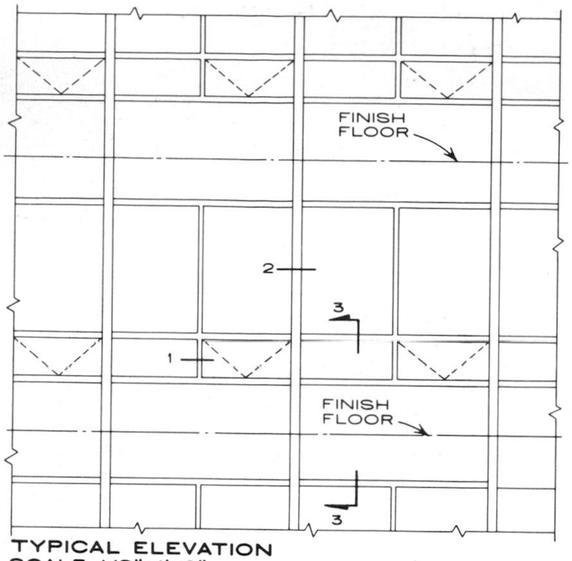

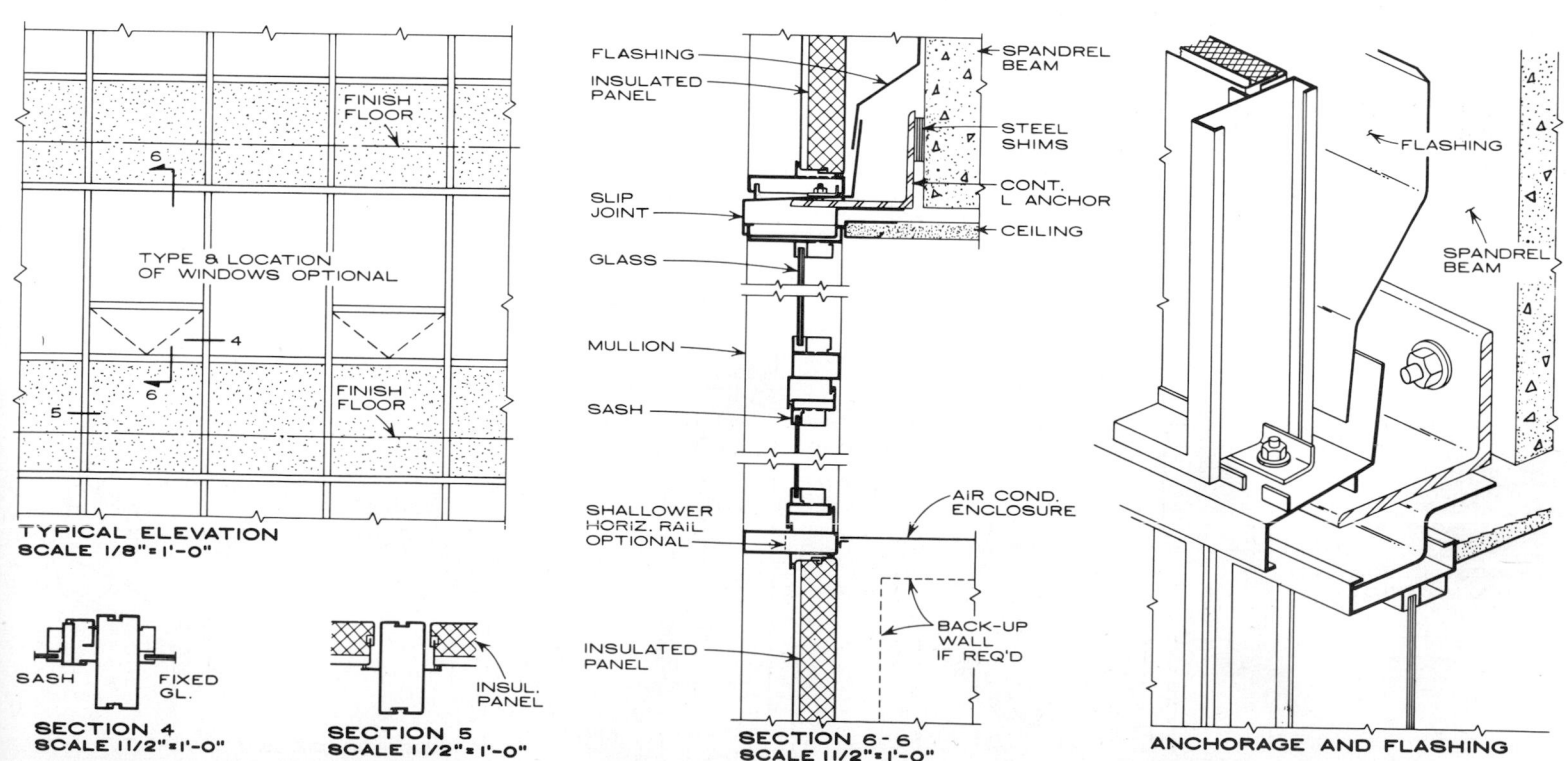

TYPICAL ELEVATION
SCALE 1/8"=1'-0"

FINISH FLOOR

FINISH FLOOR

SECTION 1
SCALE 1 1/2"=1'-0"

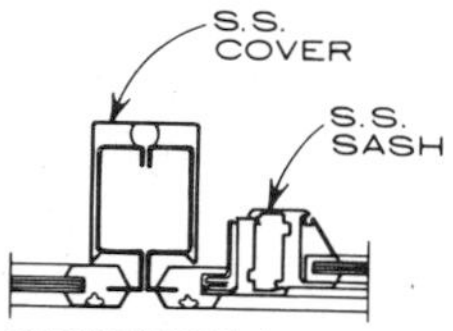

S.S. COVER
S.S. SASH

SECTION 2
SCALE 1 1/2"=1'-0"

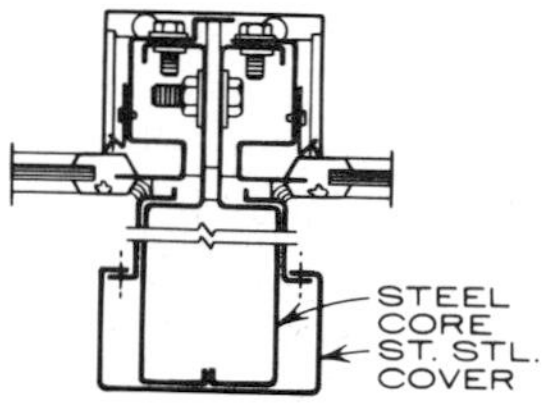

STEEL CORE ST. STL. COVER

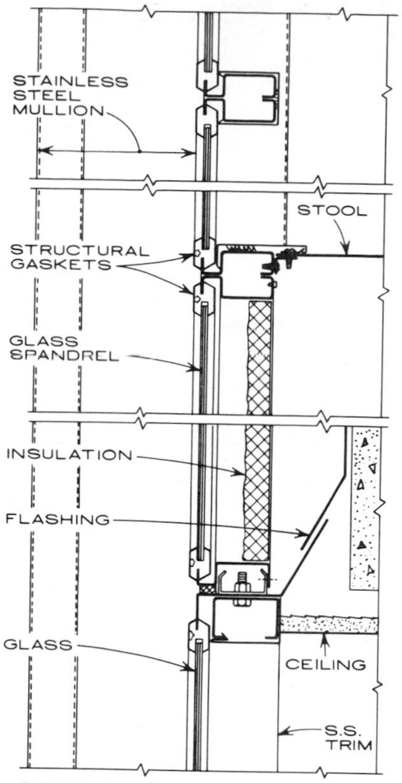

STAINLESS STEEL MULLION

STOOL

STRUCTURAL GASKETS

GLASS SPANDREL

INSULATION

FLASHING

GLASS

CEILING

S.S. TRIM

SECTION 3-3
SCALE 1 1/2"=1'-0"

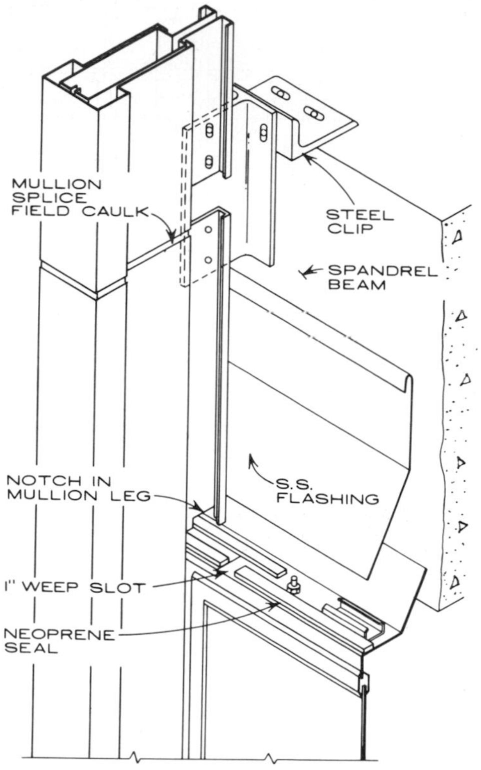

MULLION SPLICE FIELD CAULK

STEEL CLIP

SPANDREL BEAM

NOTCH IN MULLION LEG

S.S. FLASHING

1" WEEP SLOT

NEOPRENE SEAL

ANCHORAGE AND FLASHING

CUSTOM TYPE-GRID DESIGN-STAINLESS STEEL-MULTI-STORY PANEL & MULLION SYSTEM USING STRUCTURAL GASKETS

TYPICAL ELEVATION
SCALE 1/8"=1'-0"

FINISH FLOOR

TYPE & LOCATION OF WINDOWS OPTIONAL

FINISH FLOOR

SECTION 4
SCALE 1 1/2"=1'-0"

SASH   FIXED GL.

SECTION 5
SCALE 1 1/2"=1'-0"

INSUL. PANEL

FLASHING

INSULATED PANEL

SLIP JOINT

GLASS

MULLION

SASH

SHALLOWER HORIZ. RAIL OPTIONAL

INSULATED PANEL

SPANDREL BEAM

STEEL SHIMS

CONT. L ANCHOR

CEILING

AIR COND. ENCLOSURE

BACK-UP WALL IF REQ'D

SECTION 6-6
SCALE 1 1/2"=1'-0"

FLASHING

SPANDREL BEAM

ANCHORAGE AND FLASHING

COMMERCIAL TYPE-GRID DESIGN-ALUMINUM-TYPICAL MULTI-STORY PANEL (OR UNIT) SYSTEM-SPLIT MULLIONS (WALL ERECTED IN PRE-ASSEMBLED UNITS, SUPPORTED BY SHELF ANGLES AT EACH FLOOR)

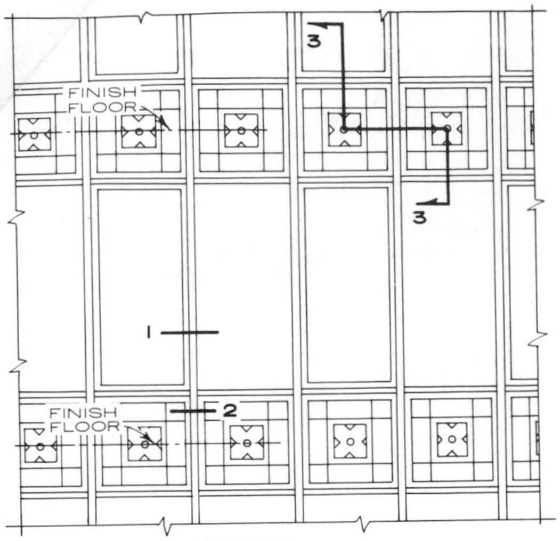

TYPICAL ELEVATION
SCALE 1/8"=1'-0"
WINDOW & PANEL TYPES OPTIONAL

FINISH FLOOR

FINISH FLOOR

MULLION SIZES & SHAPES OPTIONAL

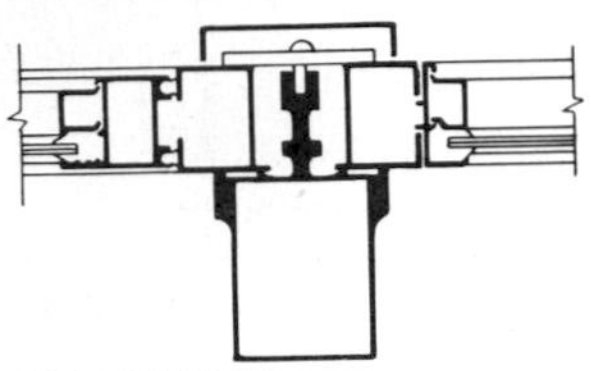

SECTION 1
SCALE 1 1/2"=1'-0"

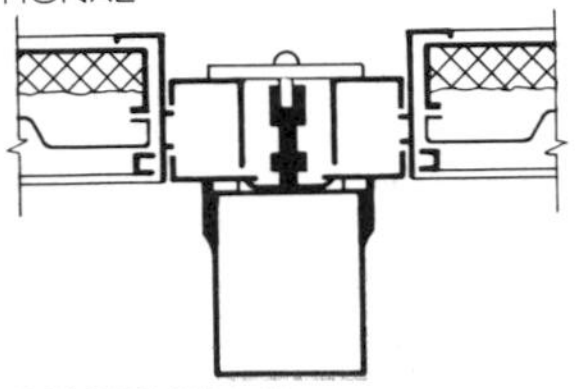

SECTION 2
SCALE 1 1/2"=1'-0"

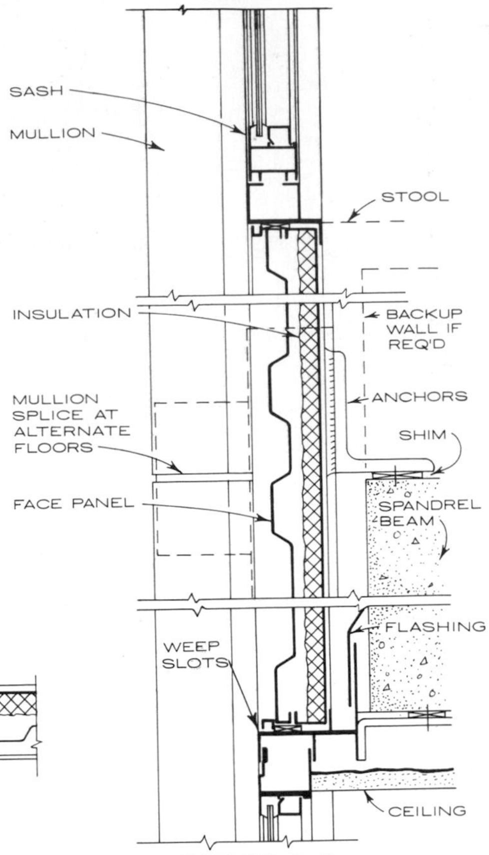

SASH
MULLION
STOOL
INSULATION
BACKUP WALL IF REQ'D
MULLION SPLICE AT ALTERNATE FLOORS
ANCHORS
SHIM
FACE PANEL
SPANDREL BEAM
WEEP SLOTS
FLASHING
CEILING

SECTION 3-3
SCALE 1 1/2"=1'-0"

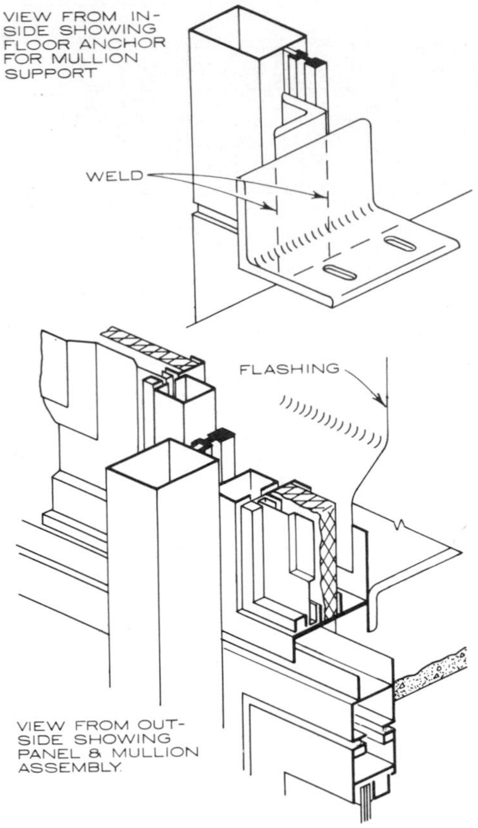

VIEW FROM IN-SIDE SHOWING FLOOR ANCHOR FOR MULLION SUPPORT

WELD

FLASHING

VIEW FROM OUT-SIDE SHOWING PANEL & MULLION ASSEMBLY.

ANCHORAGE & FLASHING
MULLIONS INSTALLED FIRST; PANELS INSTALLED FROM BUILDING FLOORS

COMMERCIAL TYPE GRID DESIGN ALUMINUM —TYPICAL MULTI-STORY PANEL-AND-MULLION DESIGN

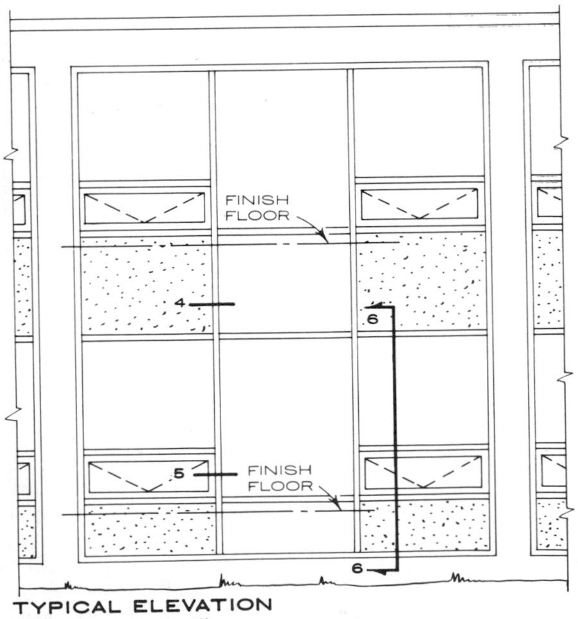

TYPICAL ELEVATION
SCALE 1/8"=1'-0"
WINDOW & PANEL TYPES OPTIONAL

FINISH FLOOR

FINISH FLOOR

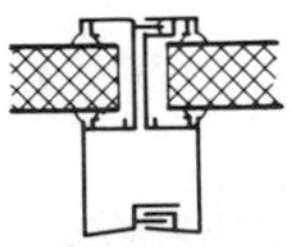

SECTION 4
SCALE 1 1/2"=1'-0"

SECTION 5
SCALE 1 1/2"=1'-0"

INSULATED PANEL
SPLIT MULLION
DRAPERY POCKET
FIXED GLASS
SASH
STOOL
INSULATED PANEL
ADJUSTABLE SILL
ANCHOR
FLOOR

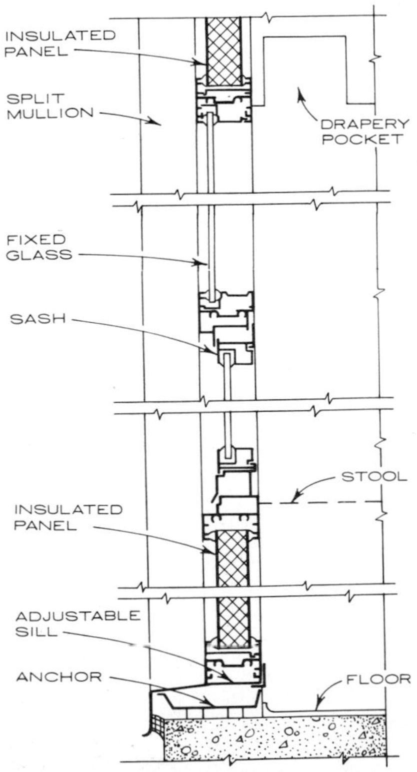

SECTION 6-6
SCALE 1 1/2"=1'-0"

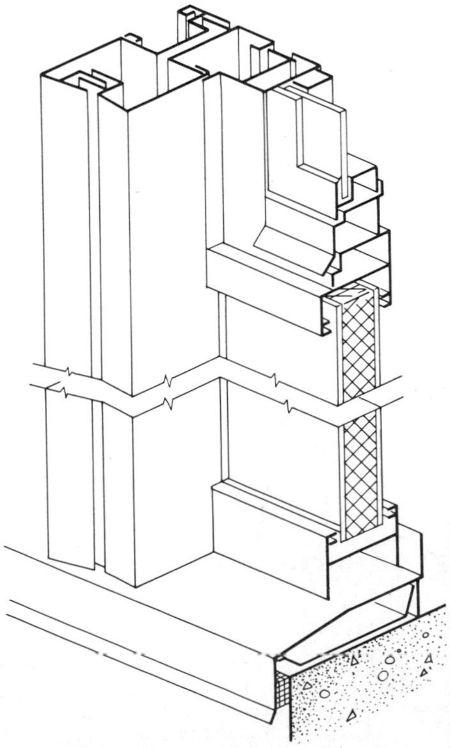

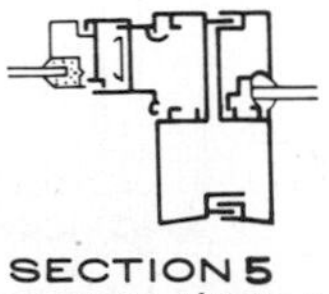

ANCHORAGE & FLASHING
COMPLETELY PRE-ASSEMBLED UNITS INSTALLED IN INTERLOCKING FASHION

COMMERCIAL TYPE, GRID DESIGN, ALUMINUM. SPLIT-MULLION PANEL SYSTEM FOR ONE OR TWO STORY USE

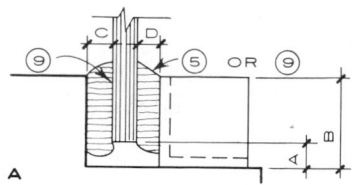

A TAPE GLAZING

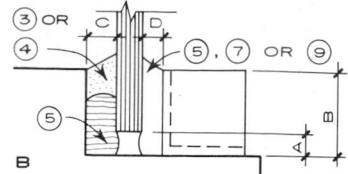

B ELASTOMERIC COMPOUND WITH TAPE

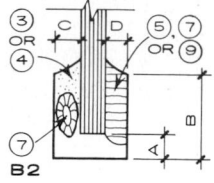

B1 OIL–BASE GLAZING COMPOUND & TAPE OR PREFORMED SEALANT

B2 TAPE AND PREFORMED SEALANT

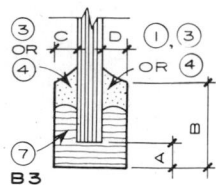

B3 OIL–BASE GLAZING COMPOUND WITH PREFORMED SEALANT

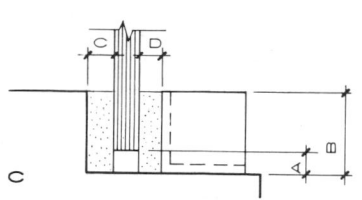

C IMPREGNATED URETHENE FOAM

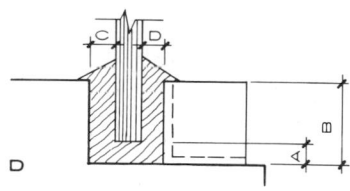

D GASKET GLAZING

CURTAIN WALL GLAZING DETAILS

NOTES:

1. Curtain wall glazing is for
   A. larger glass surfaces
   B. locations of greater movement and vibration

2. Details shown apply also to thick glass, including insulating glass and panels.

3. Except in details B3 and D, setting blocks at bottom edge and resilient spacer shims at all other edges should be used. Not shown in above details.

SEALANT MATERIALS

1. Oil base glazing compound	wet
2. Non-skinning compound—polybutene	wet
3. Two part rubber base compound—polysulfide	wet
4. One part elastic compound—polysulfide, silicone	wet
5. Polybutene ribbon or tape	wet
6. Impregnated wool felt	dry
7. Neoprene or butyl—cured	dry
8. Polyvinyl chloride	dry
9. Butyl ribbon or tape—partially cured	wet
10. Impregnated urethene	wet

PREFORMED SQUARE AND RECTANGULAR SHAPES FOR SETTING BLOCKS AND SHIMS

HEIGHT	LENGTH (INCHES)					
INCHES	50	50-55	55	60-65	70	90 DUROMETERS
$1/16$		$1/8$				
$3/32$		$1/2$	$3/8$		$7/8$	
$1/8$		$5/16, 1/8, 3/8$				$1/8, 7/32, 5/16, 3/8, 7/16, 1/2, 11/16, 15/16$
$3/16$	$1/2$	$5/32$				$3/16, 5/16$
$7/32$		$1/8$	$1/8, 3/8$	$5/8$		$3/16$
$1/4$						$3/8, 1/2, 5/8, 13/16, 1$
$3/8$						$3/8, 1/2, 5/8, 3/4$
$7/16$					$7/16$	$7/16, 9/16$
$1/2$						$1/2, 3/4$

Channels available:
of 55—75 durometers @ $1/8$″, $3/16$″, $1/4$″, and $5/16$″ glass openings
of 45—75 durometers @ $3/8$″, $1/2$″, $5/8$″, and $3/4$″ glass openings
thickness varies from $1/16$″ to $1/2$″

Tubing and Cord available:
full range of durometers, I.D. and O.D. and wall thicknesses.

Wedges and special shapes available.

ACRYLIC PLASTIC GLAZING

Glazing details essentially apply; however, greater expansion clearance and rabbet engagement depth need to be allowed for larger panes.
Sealants need to be elastic and with greater cross section; and may be used on only one side.

CURTAIN WALL DETAILS: A, B, C & D EDGE CLEARANCES

CLEARANCE	SIZE SQ. FT.	THICKNESS					C & D DIM.
		$3/16$	$7/32$	$1/4$	$5/16$	$3/8 - 1/2$	
A EDGE	up to 25	$1/4$	$1/4$	$1/4$	$1/4$	$1/4$	$1/8$
	over 25 to 70	$1/4$	$1/4$	$1/4$	$1/4$	$1/4$	$1/8$
	over 70 to 84			$1/4$	$1/4$	$1/4$	$1/8$
	over 84			$1/4$	$1/4$	$9/32$	$1/8$
RABBET DEPTH B	up to 25	$5/8$	$5/8$	$5/8$	$5/8$	$5/8$	$1/8$
	over 25 to 70	$3/4$	$3/4$	$3/4$	$3/4$	$3/4$	$1/8$
	over 70 to 84			$3/4$	$3/4$	$7/8$	$1/8$
	over 84			$3/4$	$3/4$	$7/8$	$1/8$

Note: for glass larger or thicker, consult mfr.

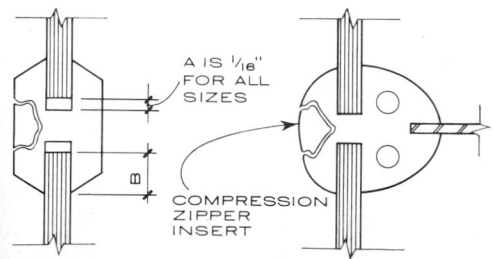

A IS $1/16$″ FOR ALL SIZES

COMPRESSION ZIPPER INSERT

MUNTIN TYPES

NOTE: Details shown apply to thick glass including insulating glass and panels.

"B" DIMENSION FOR MUNTIN TYPE STRUCTURAL GASKETS

GLASS THICKNESS	$3/16$ OR $7/32$	$1/4$	$5/16$	$3/8, 1/2,$ OR $3/4$
Up to 25 sq. ft.	$1/2$	$1/2$	$1/2$	$5/8$
Over 25 to 75 sq. ft.	$1/2$	$1/2$	$5/8$	$5/8$
Over 75 to 100 sq. ft.		$5/8$	$5/8$	$3/4$

STRUCTURAL GASKETS

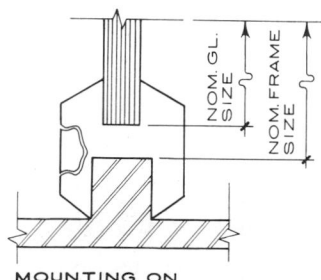

MOUNTING ON METAL FRAME

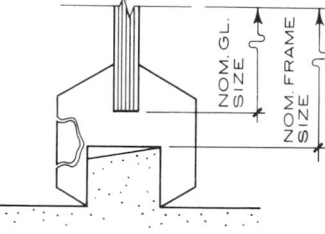
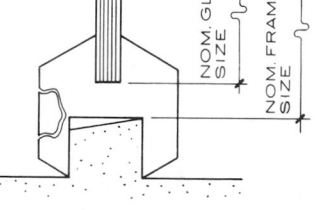

MOUNTING ON PRECAST BASE

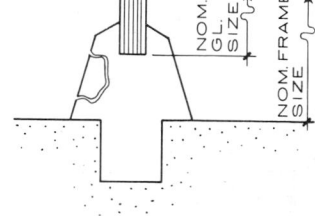

RECESSED IN GROOVE

PERIMETER TYPES

NOTE: Some authorities recommend coating lug or groove with a non-hardening sealant to prevent water being forced or blown under or around gasket.

Suspended glazing is used for large openings where visibility, unhampered by metal framing members, is desired.
Glass is hung from metal clamps and is in tension.
Max. height is limited by availability from manufacturer.
Max. widths & thicknesses are determined by wind loads.

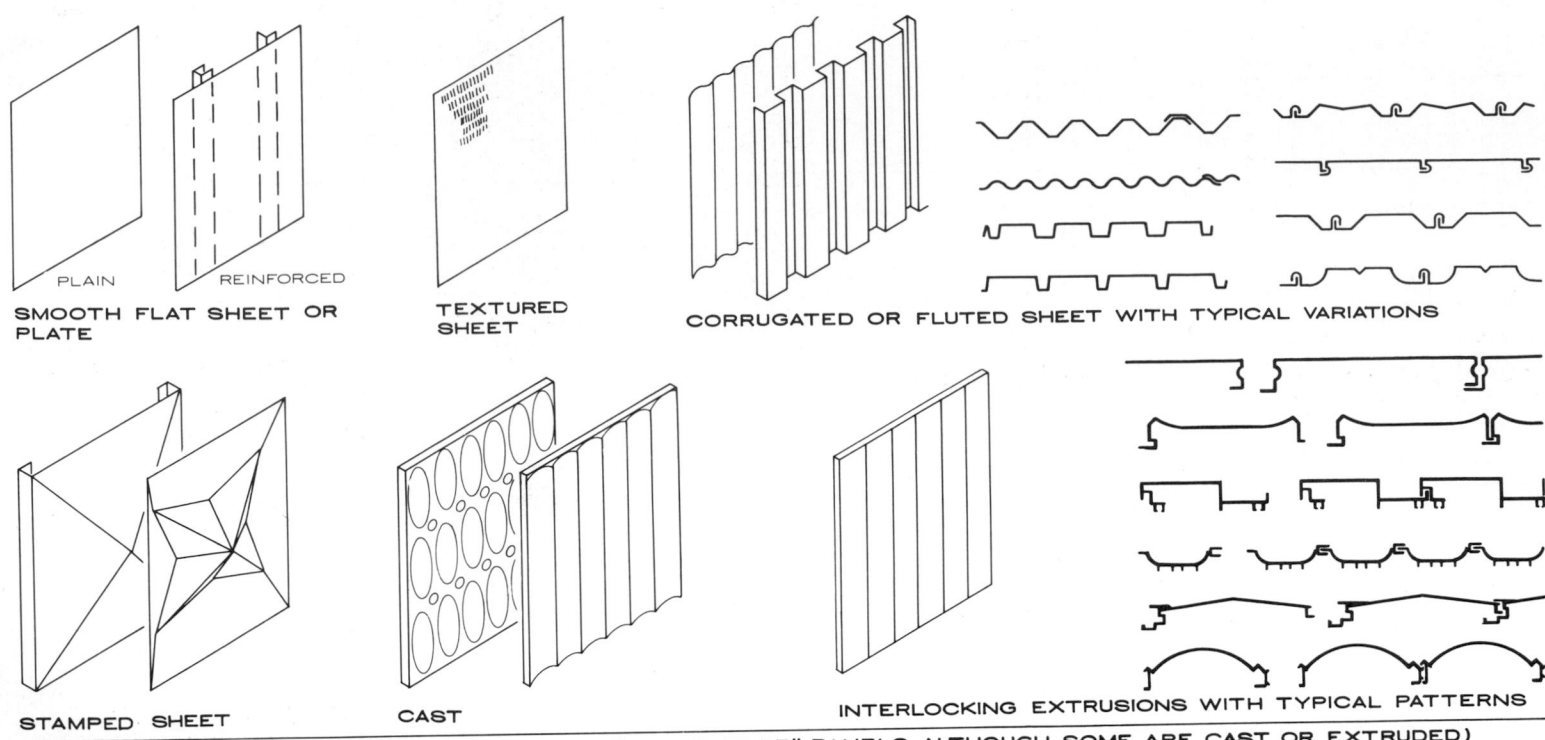

PLAIN   REINFORCED

SMOOTH FLAT SHEET OR PLATE

TEXTURED SHEET

CORRUGATED OR FLUTED SHEET WITH TYPICAL VARIATIONS

STAMPED SHEET

CAST

INTERLOCKING EXTRUSIONS WITH TYPICAL PATTERNS

SKIN OR FACING PANELS (ALSO KNOWN AS "SHEET TYPE" PANELS ALTHOUGH SOME ARE CAST OR EXTRUDED)
INSULATION, IF ANY, IS INSTALLED SEPARATELY

1. Anchorage devices, should permit 3-dimensional adjustment.

2. Anchors must be designed to withstand wind loads acting outward as well as inward.

3. Anchors must be firmly secured in position after final assembly and adjustment of wall components.

4. All anchorage members must be protected against corrosion.

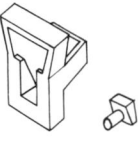
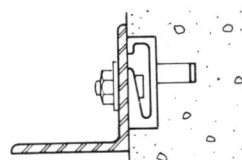

Malleable c.i. insert provides adjustable support.

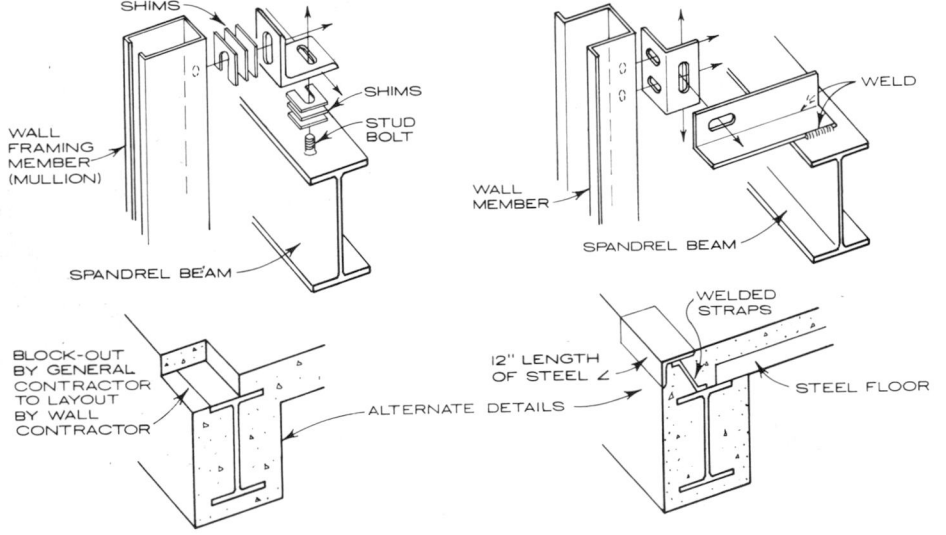

SHIMS

SHIMS

WALL FRAMING MEMBER (MULLION)

STUD BOLT

WALL MEMBER

WELD

SPANDREL BEAM

SPANDREL BEAM

BLOCK-OUT BY GENERAL CONTRACTOR TO LAYOUT BY WALL CONTRACTOR

WELDED STRAPS

12" LENGTH OF STEEL ∠

STEEL FLOOR

ALTERNATE DETAILS

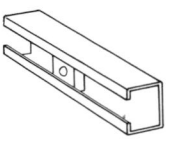
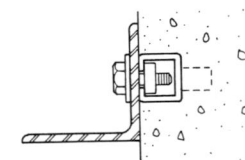

Continuous galv. steel channel insert in lengths to 20' providing attachment at any point, anchorage at 4" intervals.

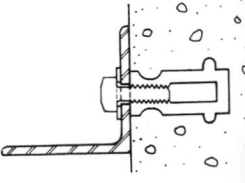

Threaded malleable iron insert, with bolts $1/4$" to $3/4$" diameter.

STEEL STRUCTURE

CONCRETE STRUCTURE

BASIC PRINCIPLES OF METAL CURTAIN WALL ATTACHMENT & ANCHORAGE

2 $1/8$"

2 HR. FIRE RATED

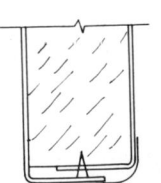
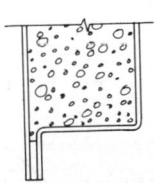
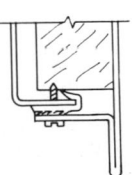

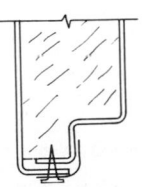

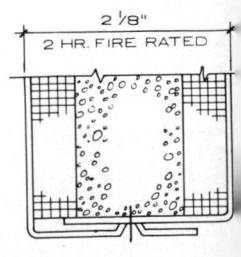

MECHANICALLY ASSEMBLED "ARCHITECTURAL" PANELS (I.E. NOT INDUSTRIAL)-
EDGE DETAILS - OUTSIDE FACE IS TO LEFT OF ALL PANELS

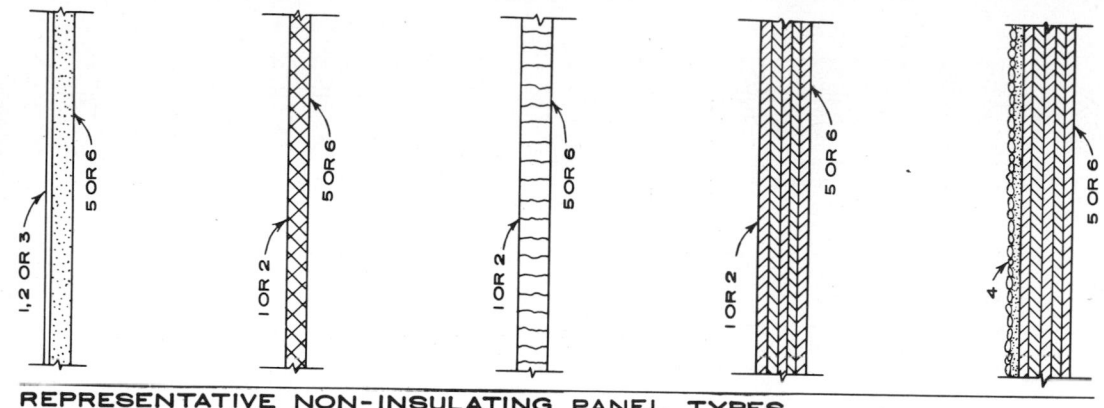

REPRESENTATIVE NON-INSULATING PANEL TYPES
(EXTERIOR FACE ON LEFT)

TYPICAL FACING MATERIALS

1. Aluminum or stainless steel sheet, smooth or textured.
2. Porcelain enameled metal.
3. Glass-reinforced plastic sheet.
4. Stone chips in plastic matrix.
5. Galvanized bonderized steel sheet.
6. Aluminum sheet.
7. Cement-asbestos board.
8. Tempered hardboard.
9. Ceramic tile in plastic matrix.
10. Opaque colored glass.

TYPICAL CORE MATERIALS

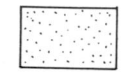 CEMENT ASBESTOS

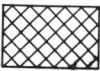 TEMPERED HARDWOOD

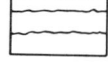 ALUMINUM HONEYCOMB

 MARINE PLYWOOD

 PAPER HONEYCOMB

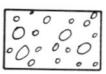 FOAMED PLASTIC

 CELLULAR GLASS

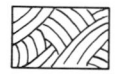 IMPREGNATED WOOD FIBER BOARD

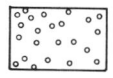 PERLITE BEADS IN MINERAL BINDER

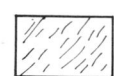 FIBROUS GLASS — ALUMINUM FOIL

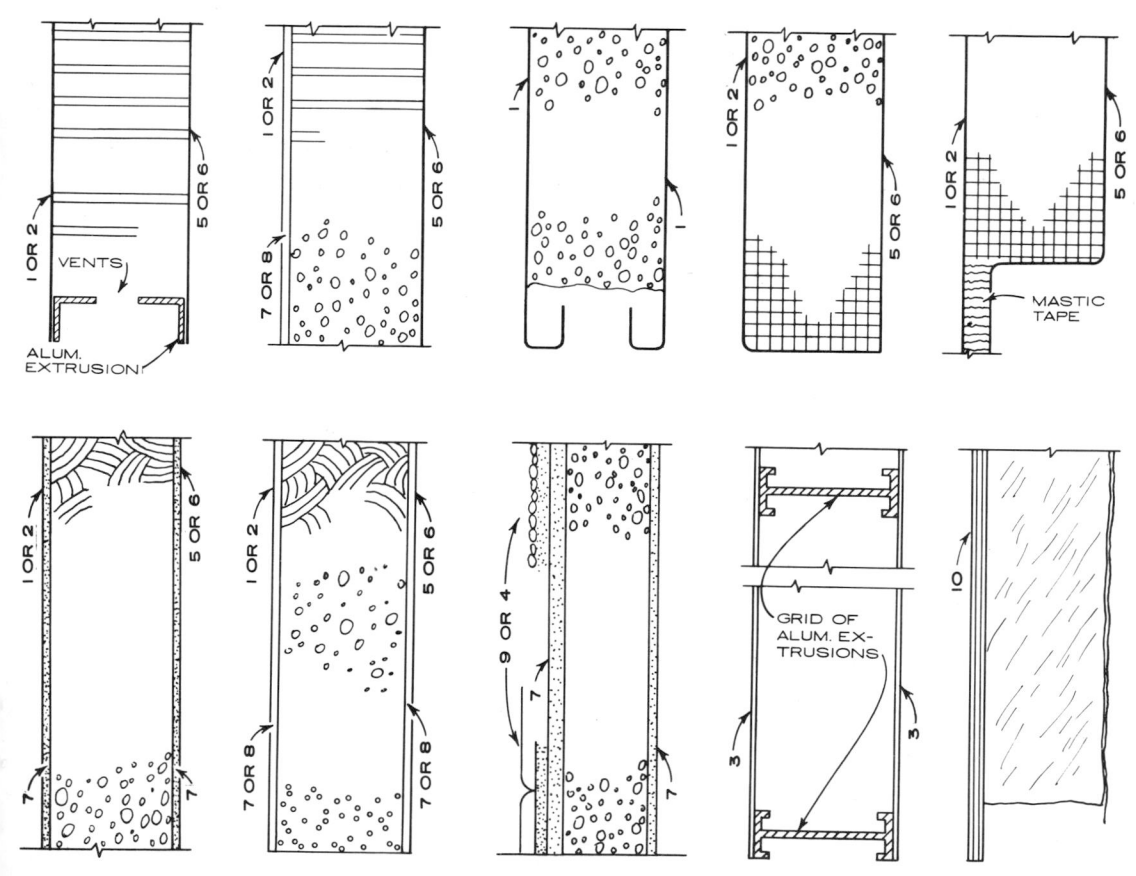

REPRESENTATIVE INSULATING PANEL TYPES   (EXTERIOR FACE ON LEFT)

PROPERTIES OF COMMON CORE MATERIALS

MATERIAL	DENSITY LB/CU.FT.	APPROX. K-VALUE	SENSITIVITY TO MOISTURE	FIRE RESISTANCE
PAPER HONEYCOMB	2.5 to 7.0	.45 to .55	slight, if impregnated	poor
PAPER HONEYCOMB, WITH FOAMED PLASTIC FILL	4.5 to 10.0	.20 to .35	slight	poor
PAPER HONEYCOMB, WITH VERMICULITE FILL	5 to 14	.35 to .40	high	fair, if faced with steel or cement asbestos
POLYSTYRENE FOAM	1.7 to 2.3	.23 to .27	none	poor
POLYURETHANE FOAM	1.5 to 2.0	.12 to .15	none	poor
IMPREGNATED WOOD FIBERBOARD	20	.36 to .38	slight	UL rating-incombustible
CELLULAR GLASS	9	.39	none	excellent
PERLITE BEADS IN MINERAL BINDER	11	.33	none	good

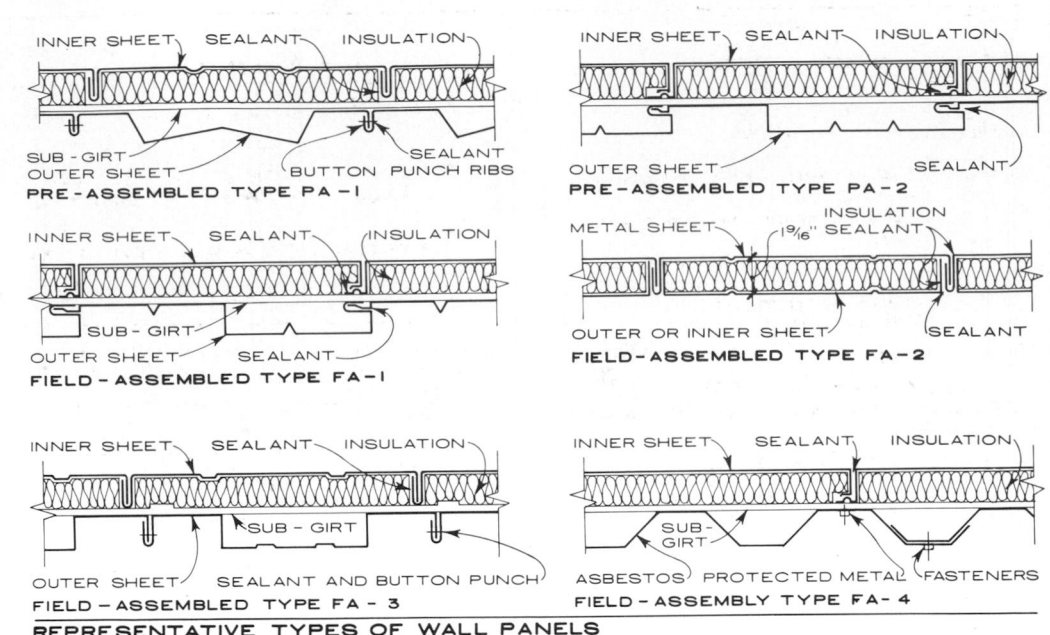

RECESSED FEATURE STRIP

PROJECTING FEATURE STRIP

SUB-GIRT CLOSURES

ACCESSORIES
MATERIAL : .062 EXTRUDED ALUMINUM
SCALE : 1½" = 1'-0"

PRE-ASSEMBLED TYPE PA-1

FIELD-ASSEMBLED TYPE FA-1

FIELD-ASSEMBLED TYPE FA-3

PRE-ASSEMBLED TYPE PA-2

FIELD-ASSEMBLED TYPE FA-2

FIELD-ASSEMBLY TYPE FA-4

REPRESENTATIVE TYPES OF WALL PANELS
SCALE : 1½" = 1'-0"

NOTE:

Types of panels shown are representative of the many assemblies of components available. Typical applied finishes available for outer sheets are acrylics, vinyls, alkyds, fluoropolymers, porcelain enamel and on aluminum only, various anodized finishes. Typical available length of sheets is 40 feet. Span and wind load must be considered in the selection of panel components and spacing of girts.

Spans given in the table are based on panel components shown, with 12 inch wide liner sheets and 20 psf wind load deflection L/180 except FA4 based on 20 psf wind load deflection L/126. Consult manufacturers for verification of data given herein and for thermal and acoustical ratings of panels designed for these purposes.

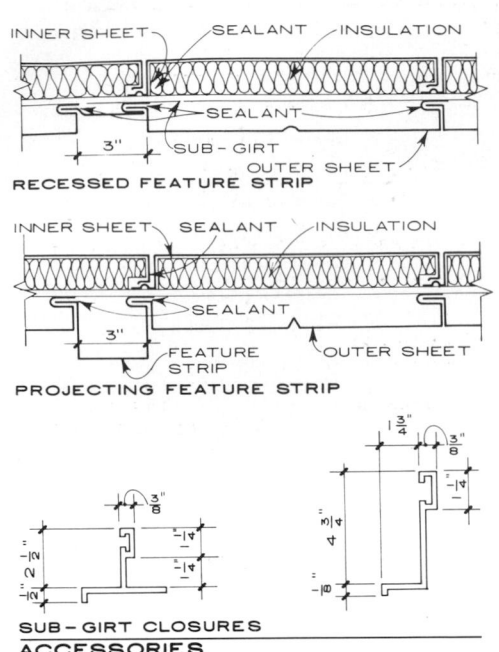

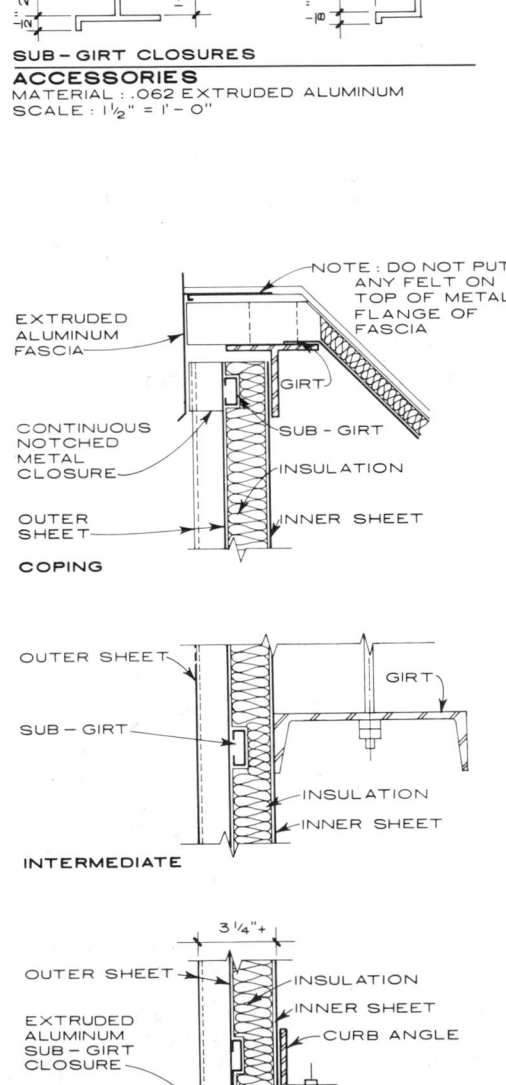

EXTRUDED ALUMINUM FASCIA

NOTE : DO NOT PUT ANY FELT ON TOP OF METAL FLANGE OF FASCIA

CONTINUOUS NOTCHED METAL CLOSURE

OUTER SHEET

COPING

OUTER SHEET

SUB-GIRT

INTERMEDIATE

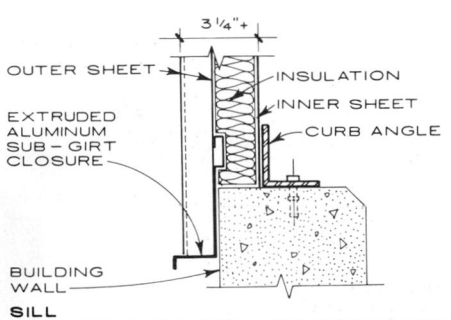

OUTER SHEET

EXTRUDED ALUMINUM SUB-GIRT CLOSURE

BUILDING WALL

SILL

CONSTRUCTION DETAILS OF FIELD-ASSEMBLED INSULATED METAL WALLS
SCALE = 1½" = 1'-0"

TABLE OF SPANS FOR TYPES OF WALL PANELS SHOWN ABOVE

TYPE	OUTER SHEET	INNER SHEET	SINGLE SPAN	MULTI SPAN	TYPE	OUTER SHEET	INNER SHEET	SINGLE SPAN	MULTI SPAN
	PANEL SHEETS		SPAN IN FEET			PANEL SHEETS		SPAN IN FEET	
FA1	16 GA. AL.	18 GA. ST.	9.6	11.8	FA4	18 GA. ST.	18 GA. ST.	13.4	18.0
	16 GA. AL	20 GA. ST.	9.08	11.08		20 GA. ST.	20 GA. ST.	12.08	16.16
	18 GA. ST.	20 GA. ST.	10.9	13.8		22 GA. ST.	22 GA. ST.	11.16	15.0
FA2	16 GA. AL.	18 GA. ST.	10.3	12.7	PA1	16 GA. AL.	18 GA. ST.	11.2	13.9
	16 GA. AL.	20 GA. ST.	9.7	12.0		16 GA. AL.	20 GA. ST.	10.7	13.2
	18 GA. ST.	20 GA. ST.	11.6	14.4		18 GA. ST.	20 GA. ST.	12.3	15.2
FA3	16 GA. AL.	18 GA. ST.	10.0	12.4	PA2	16 GA. AL.	18 GA. ST.	10.8	10.8
	16 GA. AL.	20 GA. ST.	9.6	11.8		16 GA. AL.	20 GA. ST.	9.7	9.7
	18 GA. ST.	20 GA. ST.	11.9	14.6		18 GA. ST.	20 GA. ST.	11.9	11.9

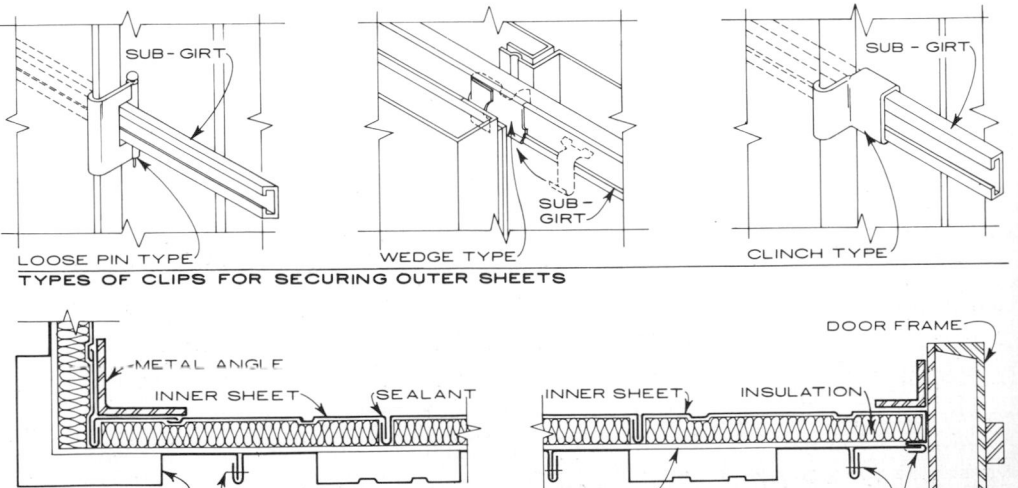

LOOSE PIN TYPE

WEDGE TYPE

CLINCH TYPE

TYPES OF CLIPS FOR SECURING OUTER SHEETS

METAL ANGLE

METAL CORNER

SEALANT AND BUTTON PUNCH

OUTSIDE CORNER

DOOR FRAME

INNER SHEET

INSULATION

SUB-GIRT

SEALANT AND BUTTON PUNCH

SEALANT

JAMB AT DOOR

ESSENTIALS OF A GOOD JOINT SEAL

1. THE SEALANT:

Must be appropriate for the application;

Must have: properly balanced adhesive and cohesive strength, elasticity
the ability to recover from compression and extension,
the ability to retain its essential properties under prolonged exposure to weather,
a reasonable curing time, and
a shelf life of at least six months;

Must be non-staining.

2. THE JOINT CONFIGURATION:

Must be sized in proportion to the amount of movement that is anticipated;

Must provide ample depth of sealant contact;

Must be designed to prevent any local overstressing of the sealant.

3. THE APPLICATION:

As a general rule, all contact surfaces must be thoroughly clean and dry;

A primer must be used whenever so recommended by the manufacturer;

In butt joints, the sealant must be well compacted by tooling.

JOINT PROPORTIONS

BUTT JOINTS

COMPRESSED   NORMAL   EXTENDED

w	t
Minimum—at least 2 x maximum amount of movement expected	Minimum—$1/4''$ or under certain conditions, in metal $1/8''$
$1/4''$ to $1/2''$	Masonry = W / Metal $1/4''$
$1/2''$ to $1''$	Masonry $1/2''$ / Metal = W/2
over $1''$	Masonry—$1/2''$

LAP JOINTS

COMPRESS   NORMAL   EXTENDED

w	t
Minimum—2t or $3/8''$ —whatever is less	Minimums: Masonry—$1/8''$ Metal—$1/16''$ if placed before parts are joined; otherwise $1/8''$
Otherwise width is immaterial	

Above dimensions should be increased if installation is made at temperatures above 90°F or below 40°F.

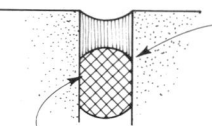

Top surface of back-up should be rounded. Sealant should not bond to back-up material.

Back-up material should be compressible and compatible, e.g. polyethylene foam, neoprene or butyl rope. Do not use oakum, bituminous or impregnated metals.

BACK-UP OF DEEP BUTT JOINTS

INSUFFICIENT CONTACT DEPTH

TOOLING INSURES FULL CONTACT DEPTH

WRONG — NOT TOOLED   RIGHT — TOOLED

TOOLING OF BUTT JOINTS

CHARACTERISTICS OF COMMON ELASTOMERIC SEALANTS

	ACRYLIC (SOLVENT-RELEASES) (ONE-PART)	POLYSULFIDE		POLYURETHANE (TWO-PART)	SILICONE (ONE-PART)
		TWO-PART	ONE-PART		
CHIEF INGREDIENTS	Acrylic terpolymer, inert pigments, stabilizer and selected fillers	Polysulfide polymers, activators, pigments, plasticizers, inert fillers, gelling and curing agents		Polyurethane prepolymer, inert fillers, pigment, plasticizers, accelerators, activators and extenders	Siloxane polymer, pigment and selected fillers
PERCENT SOLIDS	85 – 95	95 – 100	95 – 100	95 – 100	95 – 100
CURING PROCESS	Solvent release and very slow chemical cure	Chemical reaction with curing agent	Chemical reaction with moisture in the air	Chemical reaction with curing agent	Chemical reaction with moisture in the air
CURING CHARACTERISTICS	Skins on exposed surface; interior remains soft and tacky	Cures uniformly thru out; rate affected by temperature and humidity	Skins over, cures progressively inward; final cure uniform thruout	Cures uniformly thru out; rate affected by temperature and humidity	Cures progressively inward; final cure uniform thru out
PRIMER	Generally not required	Manufacturer's approved primer required for porous surfaces, sometimes for other surfaces		Mfr's. approved primer required for most surfaces	Mfr's. approved primer required for most surfaces
APPLICATION TEMPERATURE, °F	40 – 120 must be heated	40 – 100	60 – 100	40 – 120	0 – 120
TACK-FREE TIME	1 to 7 days	6 to 24 hours	6 to 72 hours	1 to 24 hours	1 hour or less
HARDNESS, SHORE A CURED 1 TO 6 MONTHS AGED 5 YEARS	0 – 25 / 45 – 55	15 – 45 / 30 – 60	25 – 35 / 40 – 50	20 – 40 / 35 – 55	20 – 40 / 35 – 55
TOXICITY	Non-toxic	Curing agent is toxic	Contains toxic ingredients	Toxic; gloves recommended for handling	Non-toxic
USE CHARACTERISTICS	Excellent adhesion; poor low-temperature flexibility; not usable in traffic areas; unpleasant odor for 5 – 12 days	Wide range of appropriate applications; curing time depends on temperature and humidity	Unpleasant odor; broad range of cured hardnesses available	Sets very fast; broad range of cured hardnesses; excellent for concrete joints and traffic areas.	Requires contact with air for curing; low abrasion resistance; not tough enough for use in traffic areas

Wayne F. Koppes, AIA; Basking Ridge, New Jersey

INTRODUCTION:

The following is a selection of hollow metal details from various manufacturers. They are in no way intended to favor a manufacturer or a product. Details vary. Consult manufacturers literature.

Hollow metal is divided into a frame section and a door section. The frame section can be used with wood doors. Both sections are complete in themselves.

NOMENCLATURE

Active Leaf	The door leaf of a pair in which the lock is normally installed.
Astragal (overlapping)	A vertical molding attached to the meeting edge of one leaf of a pair of doors for protection against weather conditions and to retard passage of smoke, flame and gasses.
Astragal (split)	A vertical molding attached to both leaves at a pair of doors at the meeting edge for protection against weather conditions.
Barrier Screen	See Smoke Screen.
Beveled Edge	The edge at a door that is not at a 90° angle to the face of the door (std. bevel is 1/8″ in 2″).
Blank Jamb	Vertical member of frame without hardware preparation. Used when doors are furnished with push and pull hardware or surface mounted strikes and single active floor hinges.
Borrowed Light	Four-sided frame prepared for glass installation in field.
Bullnose Trim	The face & jamb width joined by a radius rather than a 90° break.
Cabinet Jamb	Frame in three or more pieces applied as the finished frame over rough buck.
Cap	See Soffit.
Cased Opening	Frame section which does not have any stops.
Covemold Frame	Frame having contour faces (exposed) simulating contour of wood frame.
Cut-Out	A preparation for hardware and/or accessories.
Double Acting Door	Type of door prepared for pivot or spring type hinge permitting the door to swing 90° in either direction.
Double Egress Frame	Double rabbeted double frame prepared to receive two single-acting doors swinging in opposite directions.
Dutch Door	Door having two separate leaves, one hung above the other. Shelf on lower leaf, optional.

Face	Exposed part of frame parallel to face of wall.
Filler Plate	A blank plate used to fill mortised cutouts.
Flat Frame	Frame having flat faces exposed.
Floor Clearance	Distance between bottom of door and finished floor.
Glass Stop	Fixed trim on a glass tight door against which glass is set.
Glazing Bead	A removable trim at glazing opening to hold glass securely in place.
Hand	Term used to designate direction in which door swings.
Handing	The swinging of the door e.g., right hand or left hand. To determine the hand of a door, view the door from the outside. The side that the hinges are on is the hand of the door. If the door swings away from the viewer, the hand is a regular hand, i.e. right or left hand. If the door swings to the viewer, the door is reverse swing, i.e. right hand reverse swing or left hand reverse swing.
Head	Horizontal frame member at top of door opening or top member of transom frames.
Header	See Head.
Hinge Backset	Distance from edge to hinge to stop on frame.
Hinge Filler Plate	Plate installed for a hinge cut-out when no hinge is required.
Inactive Leaf	The door leaf in a pair of doors which is normally held closed by top and bottom bolts.
Jamb	Vertical frame member; between door and glass or wall; between glass and door or wall. See also Mullion.
Jamb Depth	Over-all width of frame section.
Knock Down (KD) Frame	Door frame furnished by manufacturer in three or more basic parts for assembly in field.
Lock Backset	Distance from edge of door to centerline of cylinder or knob.
Masonry Box	See Plaster Guard.
Mortise Preparation	Reinforcing drilling and tapping for hardware which is to be mortised into door or frame.
Mullion	Vertical or horizontal frame member; between glass and glass, or door and door.
Muntin	Non-structural member used to subdivide an open area in frame or door.

Opening Size	Size of frame opening measured between rabbets and finished floor.
Plaster Guard	Metal shield attached behind hinge and strike reinforcement to prevent mortar or plaster from entering mounting holes.
Return	See Backband.
Reveal	That part of the backband which extends beyond finished wall.
Reveal	Distance from face of frame to surface of finished wall.
Reversing Channel	See End Channel.
Reverse Bevel	Refers to hand of door or lock when doors swing to outside.
Rough Opening	Size of wall opening into which frame is installed.
Rubber Silencer	A part attached to the stop of a frame to cushion the closing of door.
Section Width	See Jamb Depth.
Single Acting Door	Type of door prepared for a pivot type or spring-type single-acting hinge permitting the door to swing 90° in one direction only.
Smoke Screen	A door frame combined with sidelights on either or both sides of door openings, including transom opening when and if required.
Soffit	Underside of stop on frame.
Split Jambs	Frames with jamb width in two pieces.
Stilts	See Floor Struts.
Stop	Part of frame against which door closes or glass rests.
Strike Stile	Vertical member of an inactive door leaf which receives the strike.
Strut Guide	Metal piece attached inside throat of frame which guides and holds ceiling strut to frame (usually incorporated in clip).
Sub Buck	See Rough Buck.
Surface Hardware Preparation	Reinforcing or machining or both, for hardware which is applied to surface of door or frame in field.
Top & Bottom Cap	Horizontal channel used in doors which do not have a flush top or bottom.
Transom Bar	The part of a transom frame which separates the top of the door from the transom.
Trim	(1) See face. (2) An applied face.
Trimmed Opening	See Cased Opening.

James W. G. Watson, AIA; Ronald A. Spahn and Associates; Cleveland Heights, Ohio

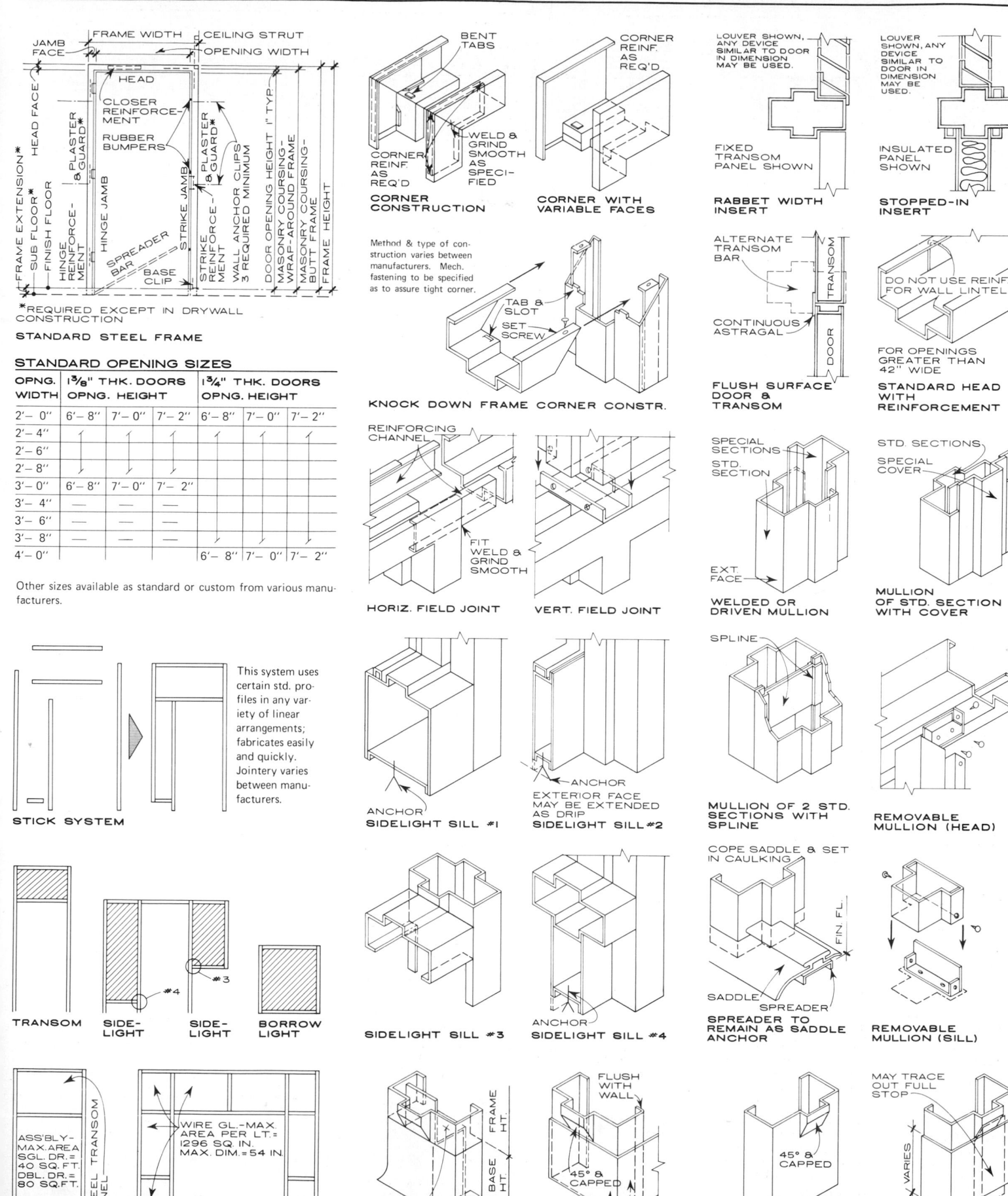

STANDARD STEEL FRAME

*REQUIRED EXCEPT IN DRYWALL CONSTRUCTION

STANDARD OPENING SIZES

OPNG. WIDTH	1⅜" THK. DOORS OPNG. HEIGHT			1¾" THK. DOORS OPNG. HEIGHT		
2'- 0"	6'- 8"	7'- 0"	7'- 2"	6'- 8"	7'- 0"	7'- 2"
2'- 4"	✓	✓	✓	✓	✓	✓
2'- 6"						
2'- 8"						
3'- 0"	6'- 8"	7'- 0"	7'- 2"			
3'- 4"	—	—	—			
3'- 6"						
3'- 8"						
4'- 0"				6'- 8"	7'- 0"	7'- 2"

Other sizes available as standard or custom from various manufacturers.

This system uses certain std. profiles in any variety of linear arrangements; fabricates easily and quickly. Jointery varies between manufacturers.

STICK SYSTEM

TRANSOM   SIDE-LIGHT   SIDE-LIGHT   BORROW LIGHT

ASS'BLY-MAX. AREA SGL. DR.= 40 SQ. FT. DBL. DR. = 80 SQ. FT.

STEEL TRANSOM PANEL

WIRE GL.-MAX. AREA PER LT. = 1296 SQ. IN. MAX. DIM. = 54 IN.

SMOKE SCREENS   1½ HR. WITH STEEL ¾ HR. WITH WIRE GL.

CORNER CONSTRUCTION
BENT TABS
CORNER REINF. AS REQ'D
WELD & GRIND SMOOTH AS SPECIFIED

CORNER WITH VARIABLE FACES
CORNER REINF. AS REQ'D

Method & type of construction varies between manufacturers. Mech. fastening to be specified as to assure tight corner.

TAB & SLOT
SET SCREW

KNOCK DOWN FRAME CORNER CONSTR.

REINFORCING CHANNEL
FIT WELD & GRIND SMOOTH

HORIZ. FIELD JOINT   **VERT. FIELD JOINT**

ANCHOR
SIDELIGHT SILL #1

ANCHOR
EXTERIOR FACE MAY BE EXTENDED AS DRIP
SIDELIGHT SILL #2

SIDELIGHT SILL #3

ANCHOR
SIDELIGHT SILL #4

FASTEN CLIP TO STRUCT. SLAB
FRAME HT.
BASE HT.
CUT-OFF FRAME

FLUSH WITH WALL
45° & CAPPED
ROOM BASE CONT.
CUT-OFF STOP

RABBET WIDTH INSERT
LOUVER SHOWN, ANY DEVICE SIMILAR TO DOOR IN DIMENSION MAY BE USED.
FIXED TRANSOM PANEL SHOWN

STOPPED-IN INSERT
LOUVER SHOWN, ANY DEVICE SIMILAR TO DOOR IN DIMENSION MAY BE USED.
INSULATED PANEL SHOWN

FLUSH SURFACE DOOR & TRANSOM
ALTERNATE TRANSOM BAR
CONTINUOUS ASTRAGAL
TRANSOM
DOOR

STANDARD HEAD WITH REINFORCEMENT
DO NOT USE REINF. FOR WALL LINTEL.
FOR OPENINGS GREATER THAN 42" WIDE

WELDED OR DRIVEN MULLION
SPECIAL SECTIONS
STD. SECTION
EXT. FACE

MULLION OF STD. SECTION WITH COVER
STD. SECTIONS
SPECIAL COVER

MULLION OF 2 STD. SECTIONS WITH SPLINE
SPLINE

REMOVABLE MULLION (HEAD)

COPE SADDLE & SET IN CAULKING
FIN. FL.
SADDLE
SPREADER
SPREADER TO REMAIN AS SADDLE ANCHOR

REMOVABLE MULLION (SILL)

45° & CAPPED
HOSPITAL STOP

MAY TRACE OUT FULL STOP
VARIES
SPAT

James W. G. Watson, AIA; Ronald A. Spahn and Associates; Cleveland Heights, Ohio

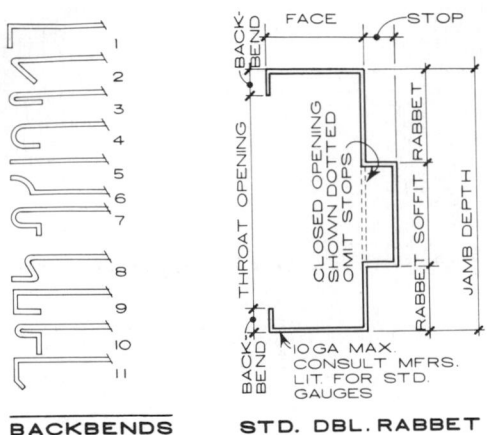

BACKBENDS   **STD. DBL. RABBET**

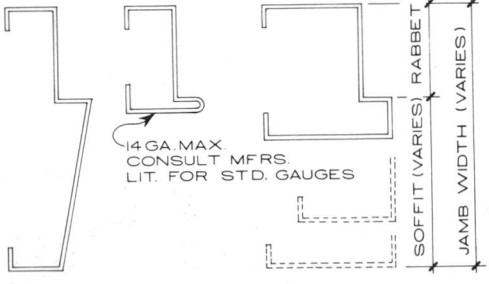

VARIOUS SINGLE RABBETS

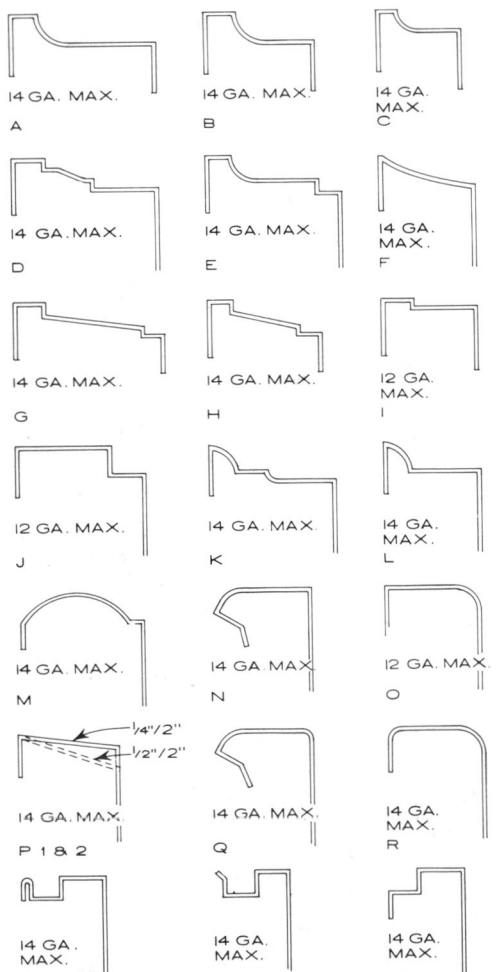

VARIOUS FACES

VARIOUS STANDARD PROFILES [1]

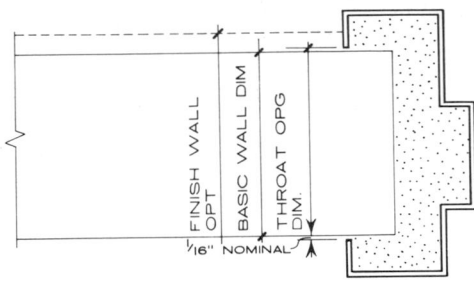

JAMB DEPTH	2¾	3	3¾	4¾	5½	5¾	6¾	7¾	8¾	12¾
RABBET [3]	SINGLE		1⁵⁄₁₆ STD. FOR 1¾" DOOR							
SOFFIT [3]	RABBET									
RABBET [3]	ONLY		1⁹⁄₁₆ STD. FOR 1⅜" DOOR							
BACKBEND	½	⁷⁄₁₆	½	½	¾	½	½	½	½	½
THROAT	1¾	2⅛	2	3¾	4	4¾	5¾	6¾	7¾	11¾

NOTES:
1. Many others available. Consult mfrs. list for dimensions and options.
2. Depths vary in ⅛" increments to 12¾" max.
3. Omit stops for cased opening frames.
4. Std. stop ⅝", ½" min. + std. face 2", 1" min.

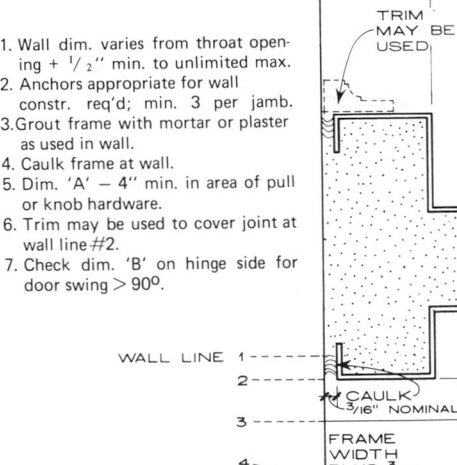

1. Basic wall dim. < throat opening dim. Fin wall mat'l (dotted may encroach on backbend).
2. Anchors appropriate for wall constr. Req'd. min. 3 per jamb.
3. Fill frame w/mortar or plaster as used in wall.
4. Grout frame, backbend at masonry wall.
5. Backbend may vary as selected.

WRAP-AROUND FRAMES

1. Wall dim. varies from throat opening + ½" min. to unlimited max.
2. Anchors appropriate for wall constr. req'd; min. 3 per jamb.
3. Grout frame with mortar or plaster as used in wall.
4. Caulk frame at wall.
5. Dim. 'A' — 4" min. in area of pull or knob hardware.
6. Trim may be used to cover joint at wall line #2.
7. Check dim. 'B' on hinge side for door swing > 90°.

BUTT FRAME

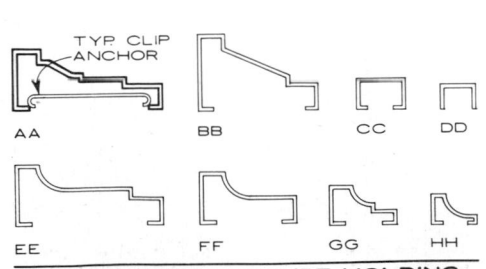

VARIOUS TRIM & SCRIBE MOLDING

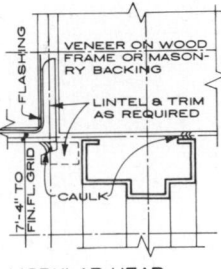

MODULAR HEAD WOOD CONSTRUCTION

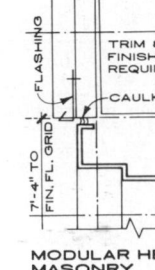

MODULAR HEAD MASONRY CONSTRUCTION

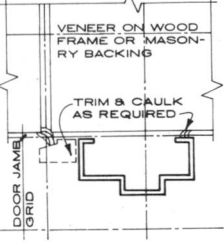

MODULAR JAMB WOOD CONSTRUCTION

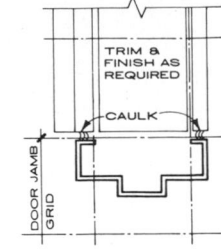

MODULAR JAMB MASONRY CONSTRUCTION

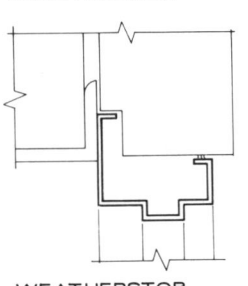

WEATHERSTOP HEAD #1

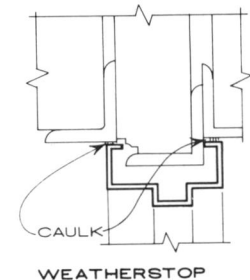

WEATHERSTOP HEAD #2

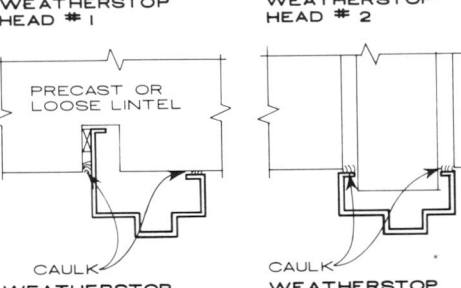

WEATHERSTOP JAMB #1   **WEATHERSTOP JAMB #2**

VARIOUS INSTALLATIONS

NOTES:
1. Some details vary between manufacturers.
2. Stock frames stocked in warehouse prior to receipt of order. Certain profiles are warehoused locally.
3. Standard frames manufactured from existing jigs and tooling upon receipt of order. Certain profiles are readily available.
4. Custom frames manufactured in response to specific dimensional requirements of a particular customer. Custom profiles are available with relative delay.
5. Selection should reflect anticipated requirements of construction schedule.
6. Certain detail features will constitute a custom frame, verify with manufacturer.

James W. G. Watson, AIA; Ronald A. Spahn and Associates; Cleveland Heights, Ohio

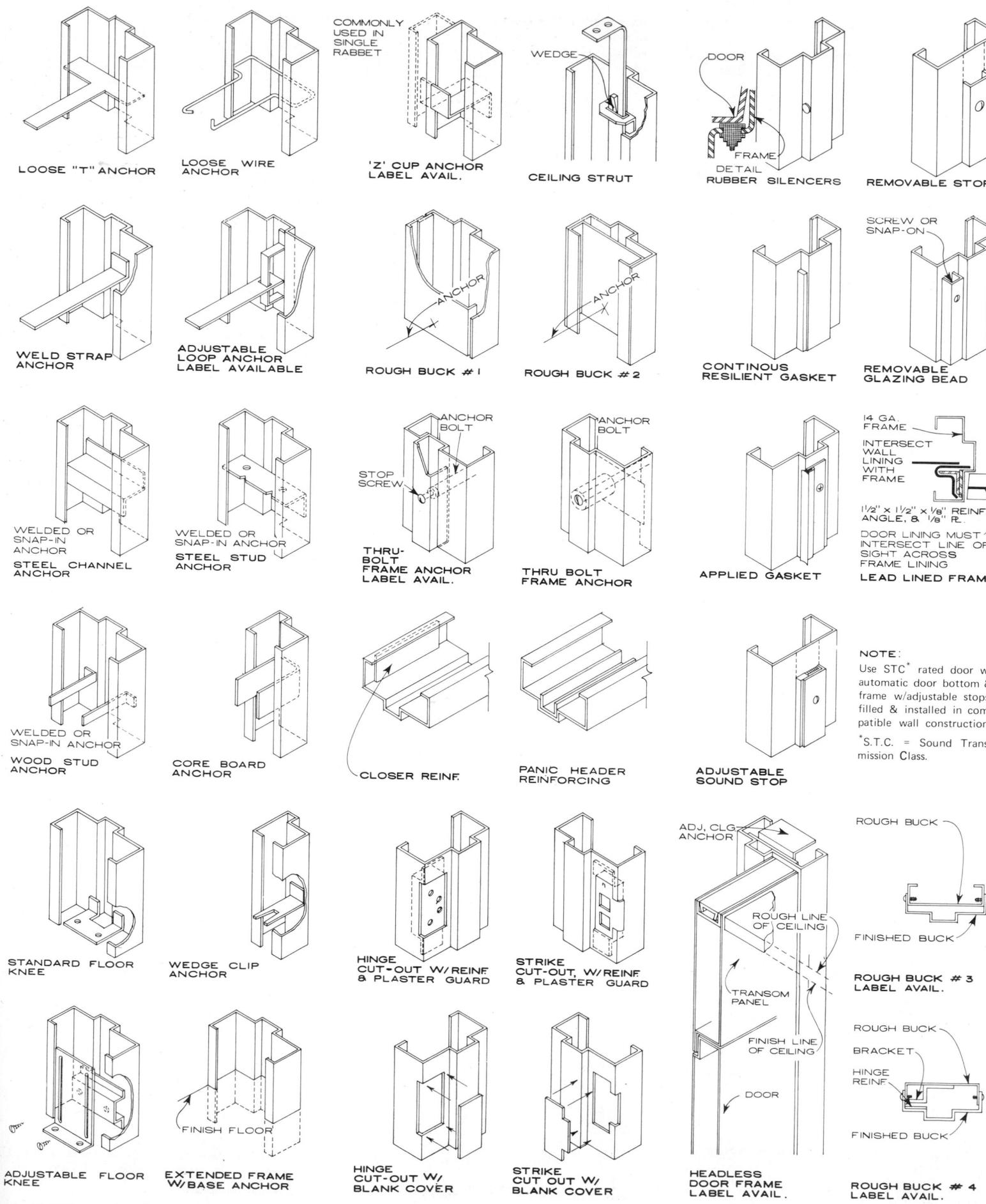

LOOSE "T" ANCHOR

LOOSE WIRE ANCHOR

COMMONLY USED IN SINGLE RABBET

'Z' CUP ANCHOR LABEL AVAIL.

WEDGE

CEILING STRUT

DOOR

FRAME DETAIL RUBBER SILENCERS

REMOVABLE STOP

WELD STRAP ANCHOR

ADJUSTABLE LOOP ANCHOR LABEL AVAILABLE

ANCHOR

ROUGH BUCK #1

ANCHOR

ROUGH BUCK #2

CONTINOUS RESILIENT GASKET

SCREW OR SNAP-ON

REMOVABLE GLAZING BEAD

WELDED OR SNAP-IN ANCHOR

STEEL CHANNEL ANCHOR

WELDED OR SNAP-IN ANCHOR

STEEL STUD ANCHOR

ANCHOR BOLT

STOP SCREW

THRU-BOLT FRAME ANCHOR LABEL AVAIL.

ANCHOR BOLT

THRU BOLT FRAME ANCHOR

APPLIED GASKET

14 GA. FRAME

INTERSECT WALL LINING WITH FRAME

1½" x 1½" x ⅛" REINF. ANGLE, & ⅛" R.

DOOR LINING MUST INTERSECT LINE OF SIGHT ACROSS FRAME LINING

LEAD LINED FRAME

WELDED OR SNAP-IN ANCHOR

WOOD STUD ANCHOR

CORE BOARD ANCHOR

CLOSER REINF.

PANIC HEADER REINFORCING

ADJUSTABLE SOUND STOP

NOTE:
Use STC* rated door w/ automatic door bottom & frame w/adjustable stops; filled & installed in compatible wall construction.

*S.T.C. = Sound Transmission Class.

STANDARD FLOOR KNEE

WEDGE CLIP ANCHOR

HINGE CUT-OUT W/REINF & PLASTER GUARD

STRIKE CUT-OUT, W/REINF & PLASTER GUARD

ADJ. CLG. ANCHOR

ROUGH LINE OF CEILING

TRANSOM PANEL

FINISH LINE OF CEILING

DOOR

ROUGH BUCK

FINISHED BUCK

ROUGH BUCK #3 LABEL AVAIL.

ADJUSTABLE FLOOR KNEE

EXTENDED FRAME W/BASE ANCHOR

FINISH FLOOR

HINGE CUT-OUT W/ BLANK COVER

STRIKE CUT OUT W/ BLANK COVER

HEADLESS DOOR FRAME LABEL AVAIL.

ROUGH BUCK

BRACKET

HINGE REINF.

FINISHED BUCK

ROUGH BUCK #4 LABEL AVAIL.

James W. G. Watson, AIA; Ronald A. Spahn and Associates; Cleveland Heights, Ohio

LOAD BEARING FRAMES

STRUCT-URAL HEADER TUBE AS REQ'D.

LOAD BEARING WALL HEAD #1

BEARING PLATE

LOAD BEARING WALL HEAD #2

ANCHOR

SPACER

LOAD BEARING WALL JAMB #1

WALL CONTINUOUS AND ANCHORAGE VARIES

LOAD BEARING WALL JAMB #2

LOAD BEARING WALL MULLION #1

LOAD BEARING WALL MULLION #2

LOAD BEARING WALL CORNER #1

LOAD BEARING WALL CORNER #2

MULLION MAY BE CONTINUOUS TO FL.

LOAD BEARING WALL SILL #1

FLASHING

SETTING BED

BEARING PLATE

LOAD BEARING WALL SILL #2

NOTES:

1. Hollow metal frames may be designed (and rein-forced) to be loadbearing.

2. Two proprietary systems shown; others possible at de-signers option.

James W. G. Watson, AIA; Ronald A. Spahn and Associates; Cleveland Heights, Ohio

SECURITY FRAME

DOUBLE FRAME WITH FIXED MULLION OPTIONAL

SPECIAL POCKET & REINF. FOR ELEC-TRIC LOCK OPTIONAL

SHIPPING SPREADER

FULL MITRE & CONTIN. WELD

BORROW LIGHT

INSERT AVAILABLE

HEAVY FLOOR CLIP

ELEVATIONS

PROFILE VARIES DOUBLE STOP REQUIRED

TOOL RESISTING BAR OPTIONAL

WINDOW JAMB   **MUNTIN**

BUTT OR WRAP-AROUND FRAME, BACKBENDS VARY

CORRUGATED MASONRY ANCHORS

DOOR JAMB   **GLASS INSERT #1**

EXTRUDED ALUMINUM MOLDING

BULLET RESISTING GLASS

GLASS INSERT #2   **GLASS INSERT #3**

9-11 GAGE FLATTENED EXPANDED METAL

1/8" LOUVER BLADES ARCWELDED TO DOOR

EXPANDED WIRE   **LOUVER**

9-11 GAGE FLATTENED EXPANDED METAL

CONTINUOUS STAINLESS STEEL HINGE

SPEAKING DEVICE   **FOOD PASS INSERT**

LABELED OPENINGS

The letters A, B, C, D, and E, used by labeling agencies and codes, refer to location of opening.

A. Walls between separate buildings; fire walls; curtain and division wall to high hazard contents (transformer vaults, film storage vaults, etc.)

B. Openings for vertical shafts (stairwells, elevators, fire partitions, refuse vaults, incinerator rooms, incinerator chutes, walls and partitions within stage enclosures, separating garage from other occupancies.)

C. Openings in corridors and room partitions.

D. Openings in exterior walls subject to severe fire exposure.

E. Openings in exterior walls subject to moderate fire exposure.

NOTE:
Labeled frames (except w/sidelights and/or transoms) are neither classified A, B, C, D, or E, nor are hour rated.

Labeled frames may be shipped prior to labeled doors.

LABELED FRAMES

A fire door frame shall be of a design and construction that when in combination with a suitable fire door and hardware, the assembly will protect the opening in which it is installed against the passage of flame and in certain wall constructions against the passage of heat.

Design, construction and installation must be tested in accordance with ASTM Designation E—152.

Consult local codes and/or governing authorities for requirements concerning fire resistivity; design size conformance to test prodecures and identification of such.

Labeling is a service which may be satisfactory to governing authorities as identification of compliance with their regulations.

Where permitted, certain proprietary devices and systems exceeding stated limits may be available.

Consult manufacturer's literature.

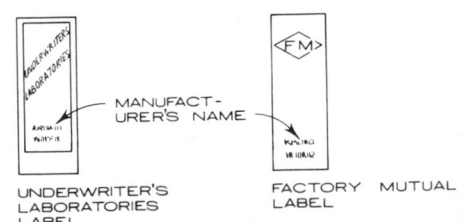

MANUFACT-URER'S NAME

UNDERWRITER'S LABORATORIES LABEL   **FACTORY MUTUAL LABEL**

FRAME REQUIREMENTS

1. Maximum size: S/sw is 4'—0" x 10'—0", Pr/sw is 8'—0" x 10'—0".

2. Jamb depth: $2\frac{5}{8}$" minimum.

3. Stop: $\frac{5}{8}$" minimum.

4. Face: $1\frac{1}{4}$" minimum.

5. Anchors: approved masonry, steel stud, wood stud, plaster partition, expansion bolts, 3 min./jamb < 90".

6. Gauge: 16 gauge minimum.

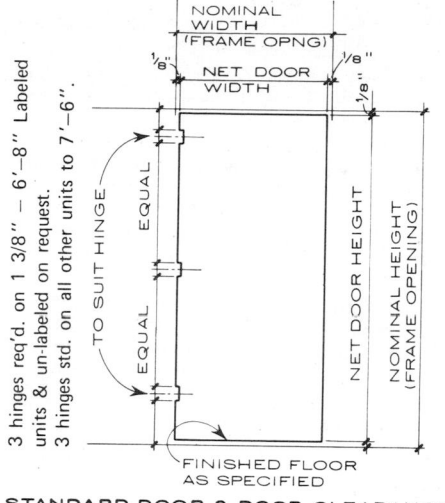

STANDARD DOOR & DOOR CLEARANCE

3 hinges req'd. on 1 3/8" — 6'-8" Labeled units & un-labeled on request. 3 hinges std. on all other units to 7'-6".

Tubular stiles & rails compose structural elements.

Stiles and rails hold in place a flush or recessed panel.

A recessed panel door is generally considered an industrial type door. May be used for decorative purposes.

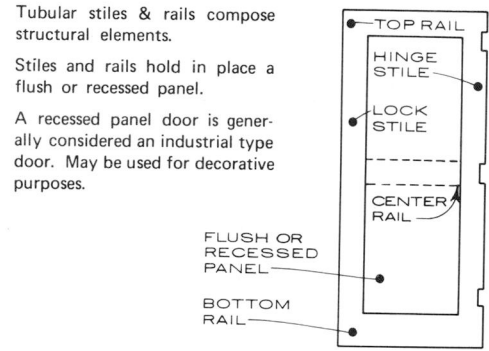

STILE & RAIL CONSTRUCTION

Relatively wide center panel connected to hinge & lock stile by interlocking and/or welding—forming 2 exposed vertical seams on door face.

Inverted channel closes top & bottom.

Exterior door is furnished with cap.

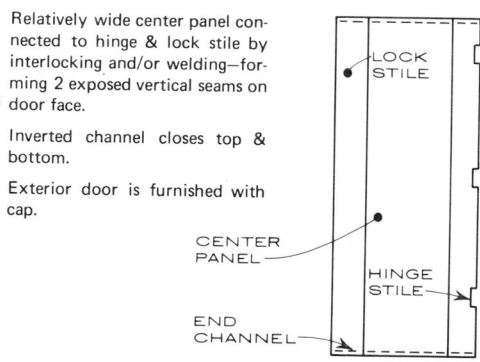

STILE & PANEL CONSTRUCTION

Pan type or enclosed grid construction.

No seams visible on face.

Exposed seams may be on vertical edges where two pans join.

Top &/or bottom of door may be flush or recessed.

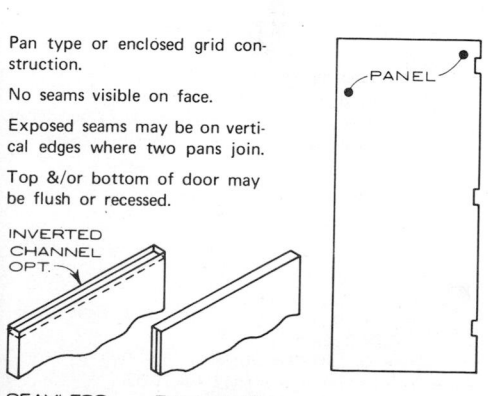

FLUSH CONSTRUCTION

James W. G. Watson, AIA; Ronald A. Spahn and Associates; Cleveland Heights, Ohio

DOOR TYPES

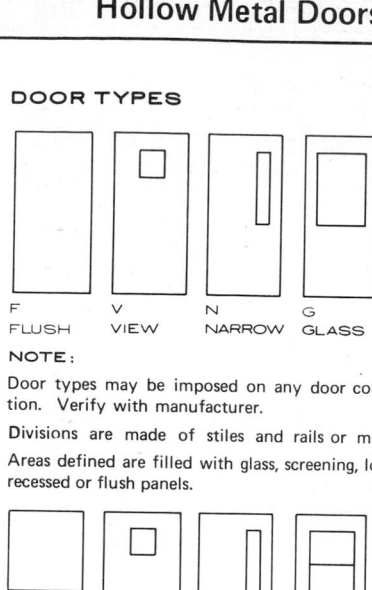

F FLUSH   V VIEW   N NARROW   G GLASS   FG FULL GLASS

NOTE:

Door types may be imposed on any door construction. Verify with manufacturer.

Divisions are made of stiles and rails or muntins.

Areas defined are filled with glass, screening, louvers, recessed or flush panels.

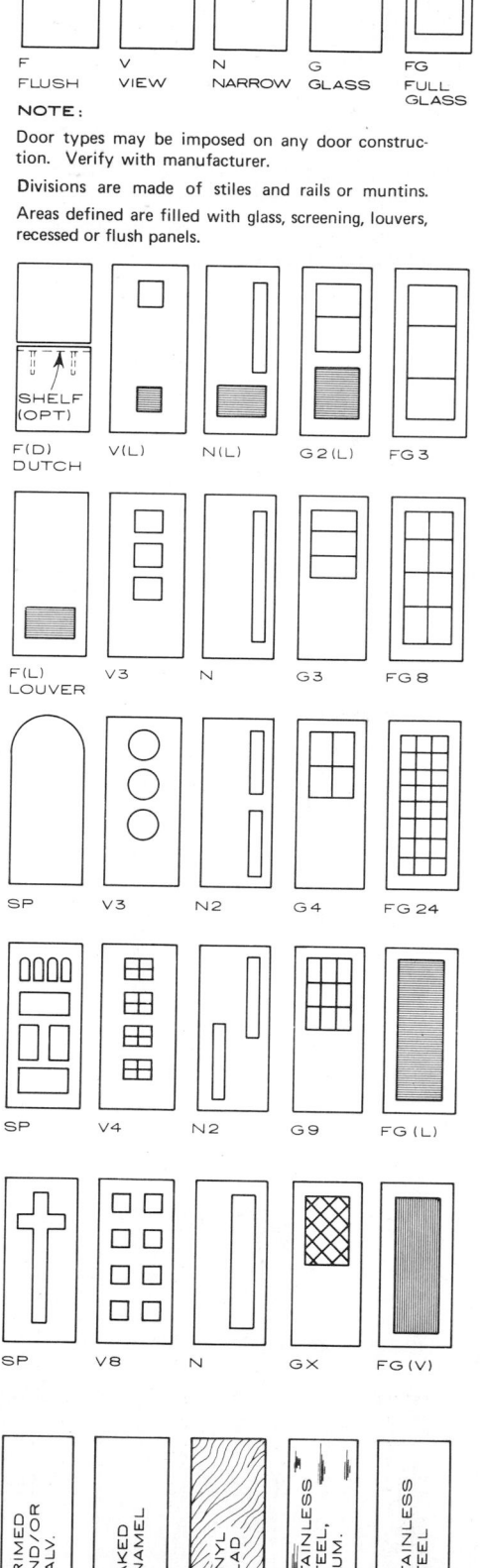

F(D) DUTCH   V(L)   N(L)   G2(L)   FG3

F(L) LOUVER   V3   N   G3   FG8

SP   V3   N2   G4   FG 24

SP   V4   N2   G9   FG (L)

SP   V8   N   GX   FG (V)

STANDARD   FINISH PAINT   APPLIED   TEXTURED, EMBOSSED   POLISHED

PRIMED AND/OR GALV. — BAKED ENAMEL — VINYL CLAD — STAINLESS STEEL, ALUM. — STAINLESS STEEL

FINISHES

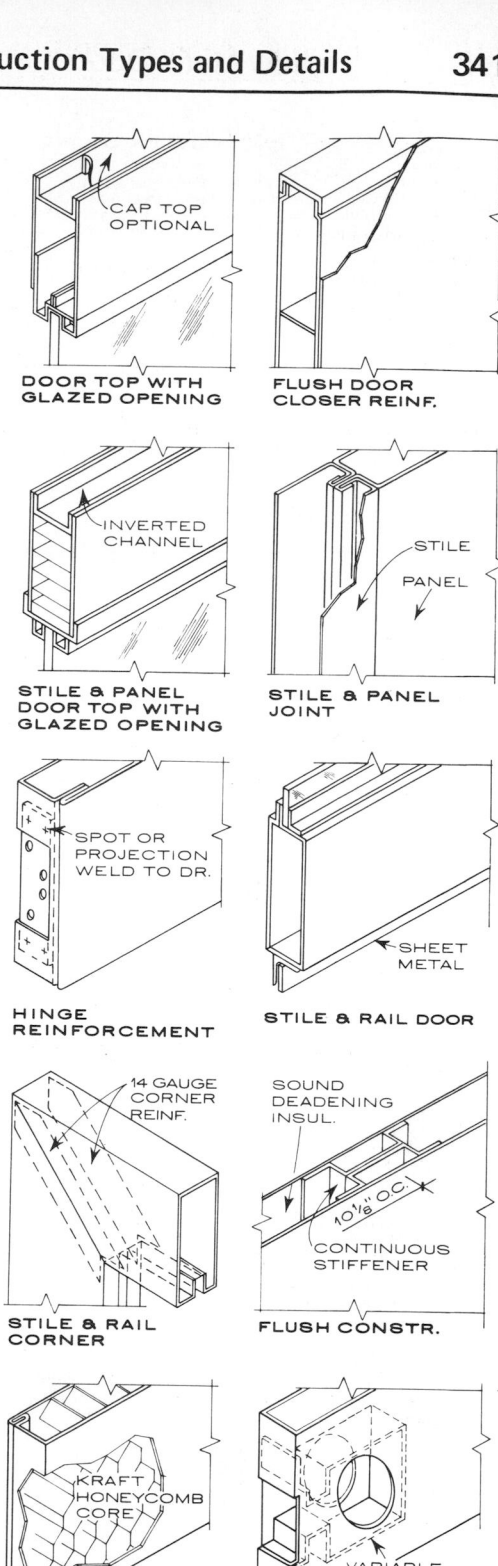

DOOR TOP WITH GLAZED OPENING   CAP TOP OPTIONAL

FLUSH DOOR CLOSER REINF.

STILE & PANEL DOOR TOP WITH GLAZED OPENING   INVERTED CHANNEL

STILE & PANEL JOINT   STILE PANEL

HINGE REINFORCEMENT   SPOT OR PROJECTION WELD TO DR.

STILE & RAIL DOOR   SHEET METAL

STILE & RAIL CORNER   14 GAUGE CORNER REINF.

FLUSH CONSTR.   SOUND DEADENING INSUL.   CONTINUOUS STIFFENER   10 1/8" O.C.

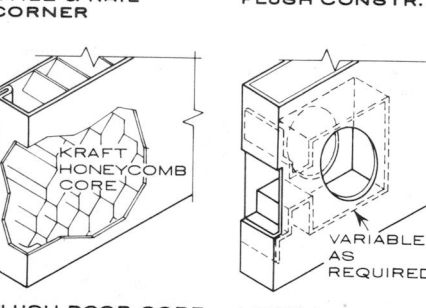
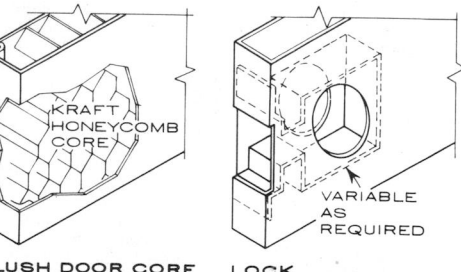

FLUSH DOOR CORE   KRAFT HONEYCOMB CORE

LOCK REINFORCEMENT   VARIABLE AS REQUIRED

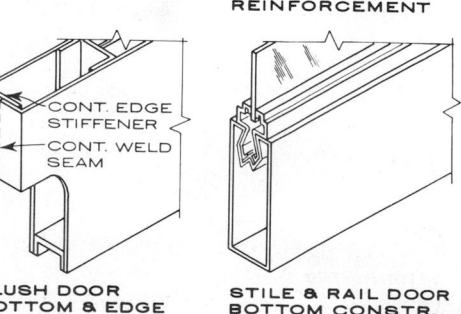

FLUSH DOOR BOTTOM & EDGE CONSTR.   CONT. EDGE STIFFENER   CONT. WELD SEAM

STILE & RAIL DOOR BOTTOM CONSTR.

MINIMUM STEEL GA. 16 & 18 GA. DOORS

item	min. ga.	equivalent min. thickness (in.)
rails, stiles & panels	18	0.0449
composite		
perimeter channel	18	0.0499
face	22	0.0284
reinforcement		
lock	14	0.0710
hinge	10	0.1271
closer	12	0.0972
surface app. hdw.	14	0.0710
glass moldings	20	0.0344
glass muntins	22	0.0284

MINIMUM STEEL GA. 20 GA. DOORS

item	min. ga.	equivalent min. thickness (in.)
rails, stiles & panels	20	0.0344
composite		
perimeter channel	16	0.0568
face	20	0.0344
reinforcement		
lock	14	0.0710
hinge	12	0.0972
closer	12	0.0972
surface app. hdw.	14	0.0710

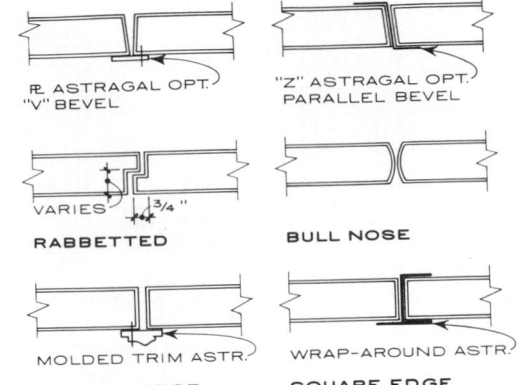

RL. ASTRAGAL OPT. "V" BEVEL

"Z" ASTRAGAL OPT. PARALLEL BEVEL

RABBETTED   VARIES   3/4"

BULL NOSE

MOLDED TRIM ASTR.   SQUARE EDGE

WRAP-AROUND ASTR.   SQUARE EDGE

MEETING STILES

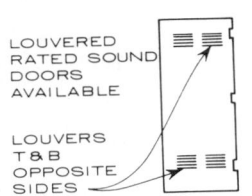

LOUVERED RATED SOUND DOORS AVAILABLE

LOUVERS T & B OPPOSITE SIDES

DOUBLE GLAZED USED WITH ADJUSTABLE STOP

AUTOMATIC BOTTOM

SOUND TRANSMISSION CLASS (STC) IS DETERMINED BY AN ASTM TEST

SOUND DOOR

STRUCTURAL MINERAL, FOAM, OR FIBER CORE

METAL SHEETS BONDED TO CORE BY WATERPROOF ADHESIVE

PERIMETER CHANNEL

ANHYDROUS CORE

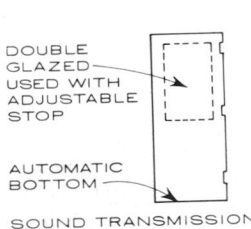

A FIBROUS MATERIAL BONDED TO BOTH FACE SHEETS

HONEYCOMB CORE

"Z" MEMBER, CHANNELS, OR FORMED TRUSS

NORMALLY SOUND DEADENED OR INSULATED

GRID STIFFENERS

 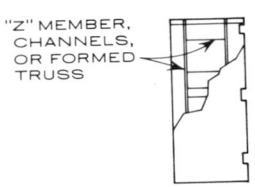

"Z" MEMBER, CHANNELS, OR FORMED TRUSS

NORMALLY SOUND DEADENED OR INSULATED

HORIZONTAL STIFFENERS

"Z" MEMBER, CHANNELS, OR FORMED TRUSS

NORMALLY SOUND DEADENED OR INSULATED

VERTICAL STIFFENERS

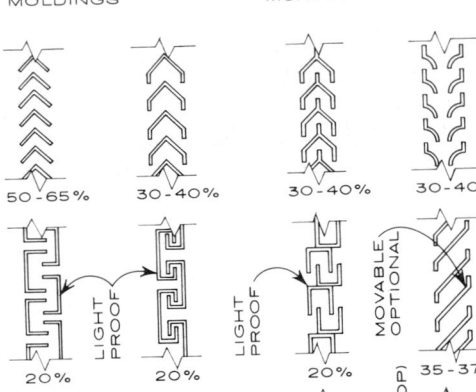
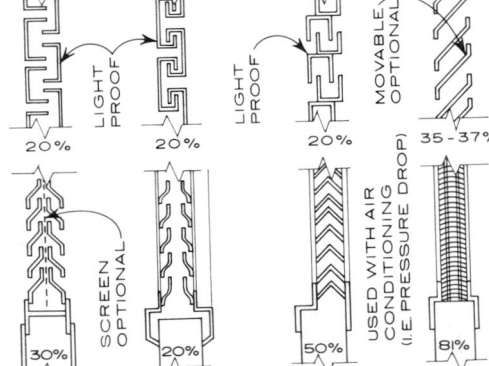

MOLDINGS   MUNTIN

50-65%   30-40%   30-40%   30-40%

20%   20%   20%   35-37%

LIGHT PROOF   LIGHT PROOF   MOVABLE OPTIONAL

30%   20%   50%   81%

SCREEN OPTIONAL   USED WITH AIR CONDITIONING (I.E. PRESSURE DROP)

DOOR LOUVERS (% FREE AREA INDICATED)

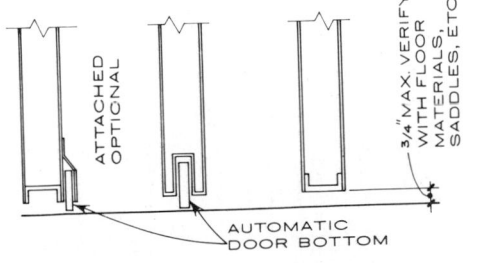

ATTACHED OPTIONAL

3/4" MAX. VERIFY WITH FLOOR MATERIALS, SADDLES, ETC.

AUTOMATIC DOOR BOTTOM

DOOR BOTTOMS

James W. G. Watson, AIA; Ronald A. Spahn and Associates; Cleveland Heights, Ohio

LABELED DOORS

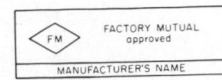

UNDERWRITER'S LABORATORY
FIRE DOOR No. ☐
RATING: 3 HR. (A) TEMP. RISE 250°
MANUFACTURER'S NAME

FM   FACTORY MUTUAL approved
MANUFACTURER'S NAME

A firedoor shall be of a design and a construction that when in combination with a suitable firedoor frame & hardware the assembly will protect the opening in which it is installed against the passage of flame & in certain wall constructions against the passage of heat.

Design, construction & installation must be tested in accordance with ASTM Designation E—152. Consult local codes &/or governing authorities for requirements concerning fire resistivity; design size, conformance to test procedures & identification of such.

Labeling is a service which may be satisfactory to governing authorities as identification of compliance with their regulations.

Where permitted, certain proprietary devices & systems exceeding stated limits may be used. Consult manufacturer's literature.

RATING—GLAZING REQUIREMENTS

A*   3 hr. rating; no glazing permitted.

B*   1 1/2 hr. rating; 100 sq. in. of glazing per door leaf.

C   3/4 hr. rating; max. 1296 sq. in. of glazing per light. Max. dim. per light — 54". Min. dim. per light — 3".

D   1 1/2 hr. rating; no glazing permitted.

E   3/4 hr. rating; Max. 720 sq. in. of glazing per light. Max. dim. per light — 54".

NOTE:

All hardware used on U.L. labeled doors must be approved & listed by U.L. Laboratories & be as classified by NFPA.

All labeled doors must be used with labeled frames. Max. door sizes correspond to max. frame opening sizes.

U.L. Oversize Certificate available for oversize openings.

See table of U.L. size requirements on following page.

A fire label on a door indicates that that door has been considered from the fire protection viewpoint without reference to electrical or accidental hazard features (which are covered by separate listings).

*A, B & D doors are available with Heat Transmission Ratings of: 250°F
           650°F
           NOT RATED

*Available on Composite Doors only.

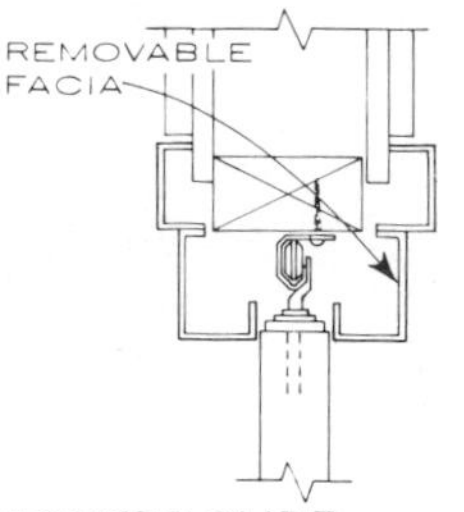

POCKET SLIDE DOOR HEAD

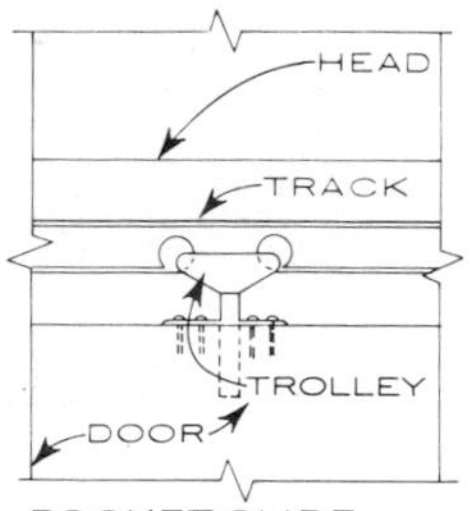

POCKET SLIDE DOOR TRACK

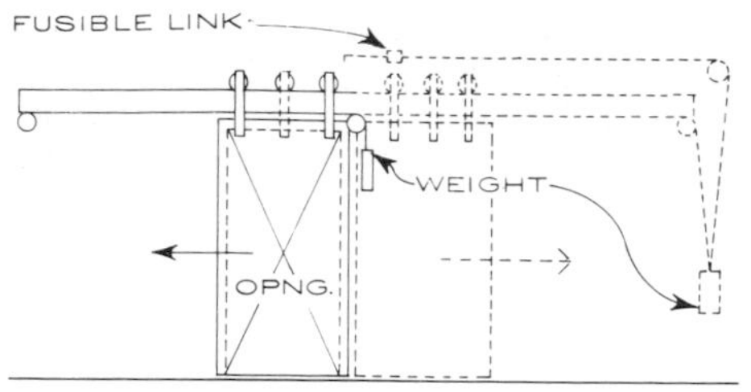

INDUSTRIAL DOOR--HORIZONTAL TRACK

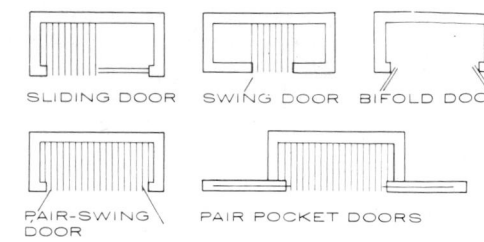

CLOSET DOOR ACCESS COMPARISON

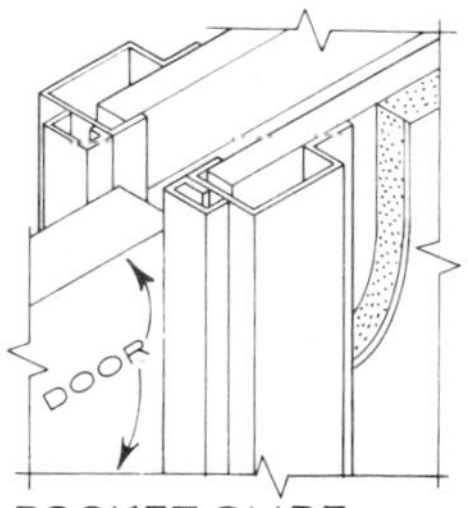

SLIDING DOOR   SWING DOOR   BIFOLD DOOR

PAIR-SWING DOOR   PAIR POCKET DOORS

POCKET SLIDE DOOR JAMB

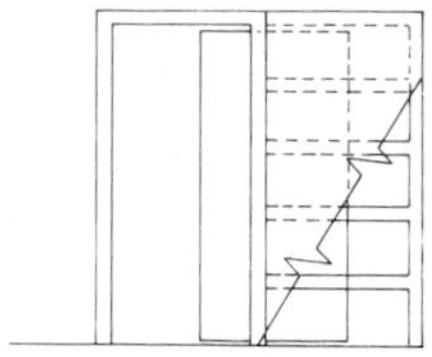

POCKET SLIDE DOOR ELEVATION

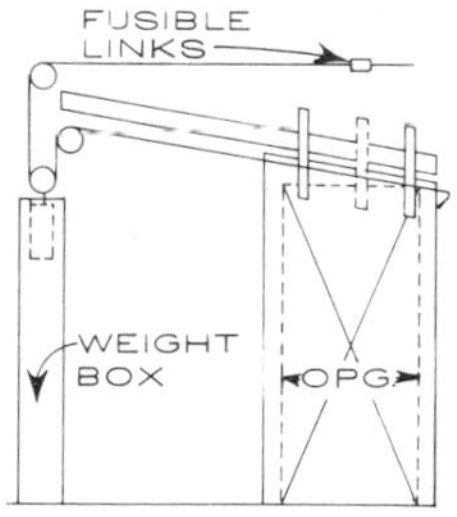

SLOPED TRACK

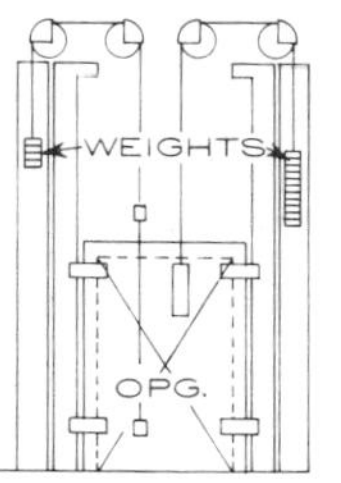

VERTICAL TRACK

BIFOLD JAMB

BIFOLD JAMB

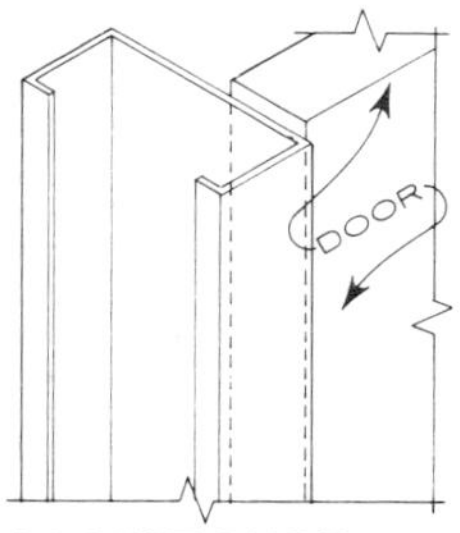

POCKET SLIDE DOOR JAMB

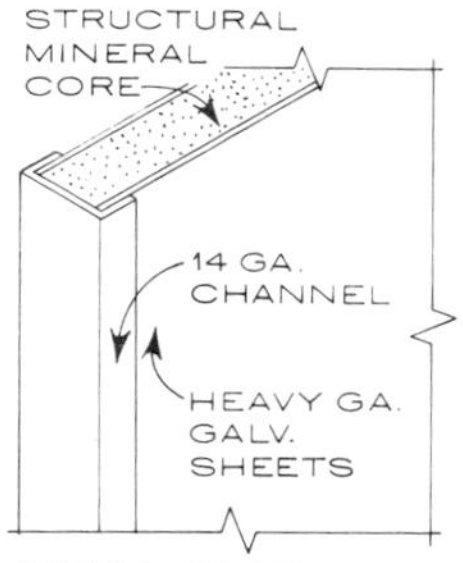

METAL CLAD CONSTRUCTION

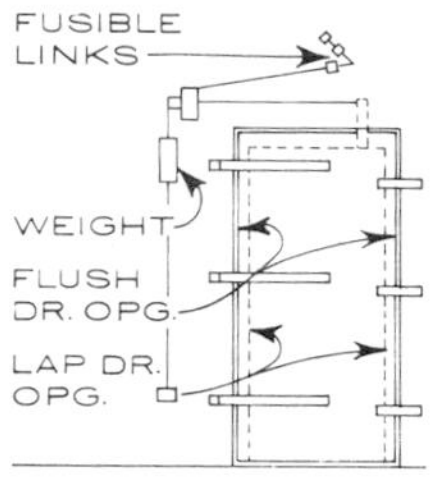

FLUSH OR LAP SWING DOOR

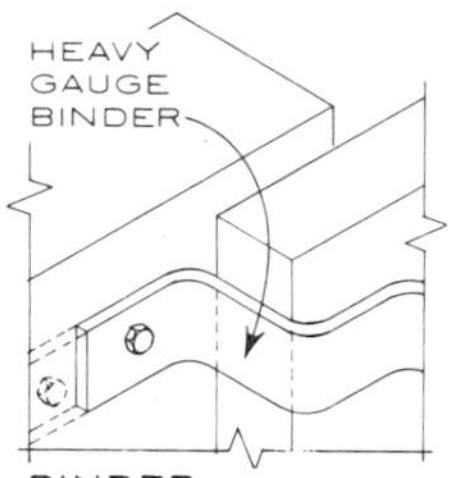

BINDER

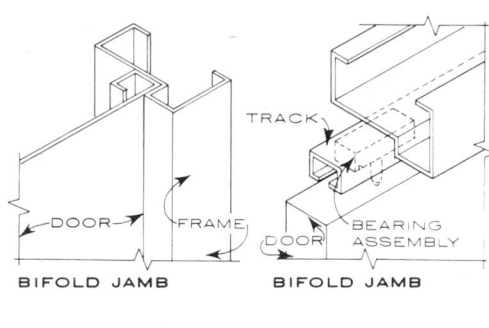

BIFOLD DOOR TYPES (MIX OR MATCH)

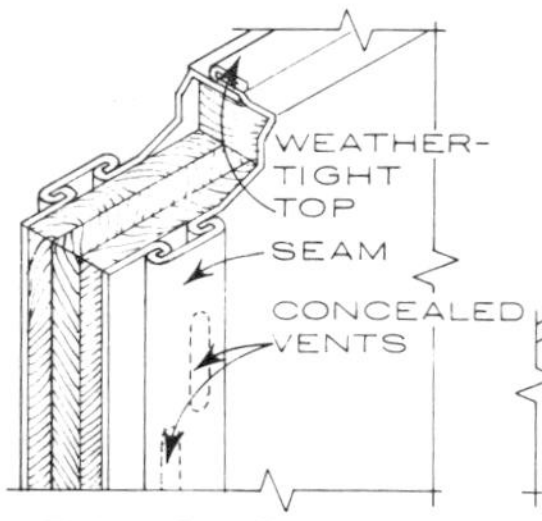

METAL CLAD CONSTRUCTION

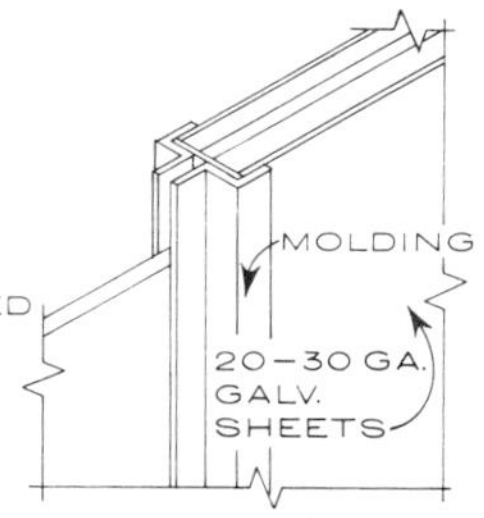

VISION PANEL

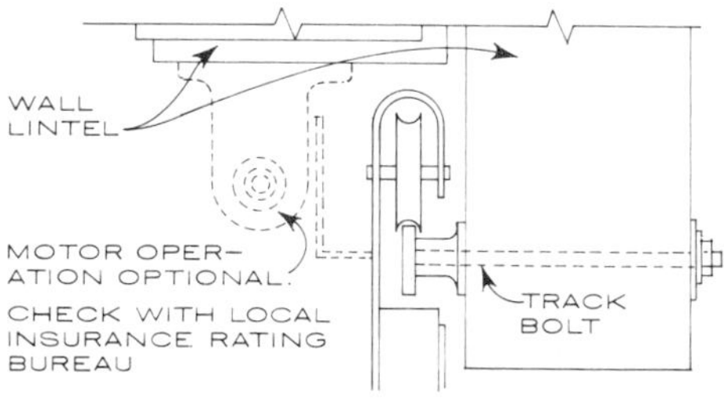

INDUSTRIAL SLIDING DOOR--HEAD

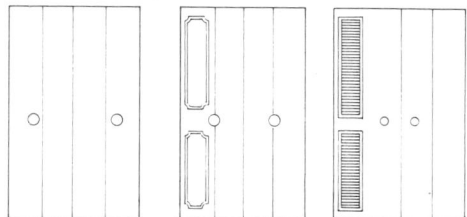

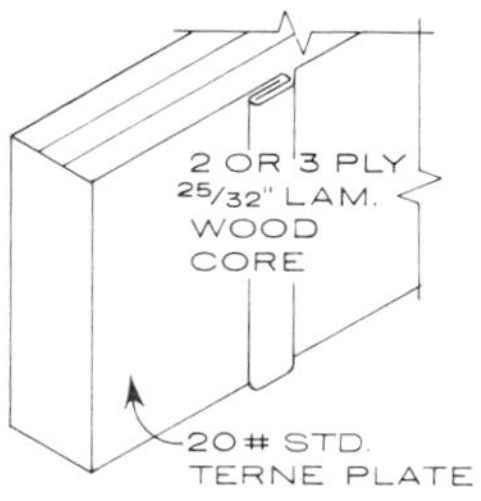

BIFOLD DOOR SIZES
TWO PANEL UNITS

NOM. DOOR SIZE	WIDTH	OPNG. WIDTH	FINISHED HEIGHTS 6'–8" UNITS	7'–6" UNITS	8'–0" UNITS
1'–6"	17 1/2"	18 1/2"	6'–8 3/4"	7'–5 1/4"	7'–11 1/4"
2'–0"	23 1/2"	24 1/2"	6'–8 3/4"	7'–5 1/4"	7'–11 1/4"
2'–6"	29 1/2"	30 1/2"	6'–8 3/4"	7'–5 1/4"	7'–11 1/4"
3'–0"	35 1/2"	36 1/2"	6'–8 3/4"	7'–5 1/4"	7'–11 1/4"

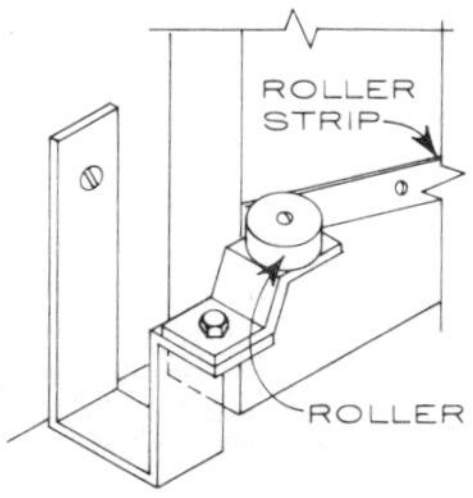

FOUR PANEL UNITS

NOM. DOOR SIZE	WIDTH	OPNG. WIDTH	6'–8" UNITS	7'–6" UNITS	8'–0" UNITS
3'–0"	35"	36"	6'–8 3/4"	7'–5 1/4"	7'–11 1/4"
4'–0"	47"	48"	6'–8 3/4"	7'–5 1/4"	7'–11 1/4"
5'–0"	59"	60"	6'–8 3/4"	7'–5 1/4"	7'–11 1/4"
6'–0"	71"	72"	6'–8 3/4"	7'–5 1/4"	7'–11 1/4"

TIN CLAD CONSTRUCTION

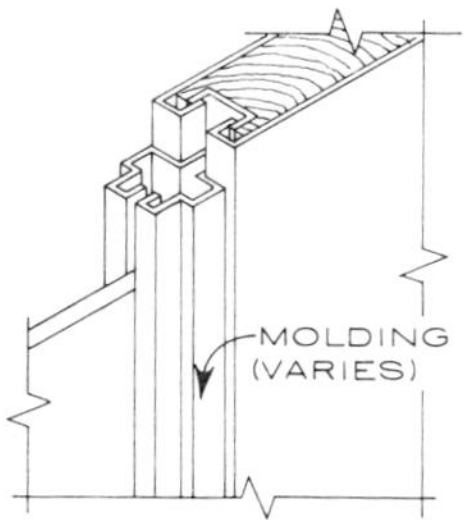

KALAMEIN GLAZING

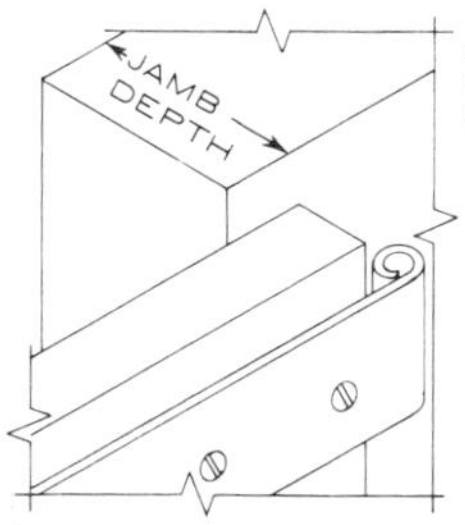

SWING LAP JAMB

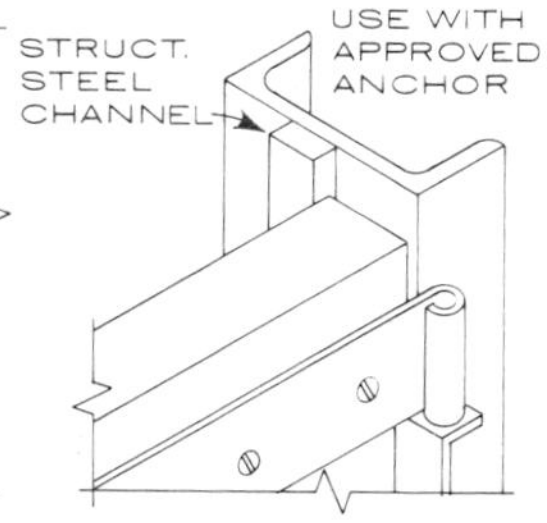

U.L. APPROVED JAMB

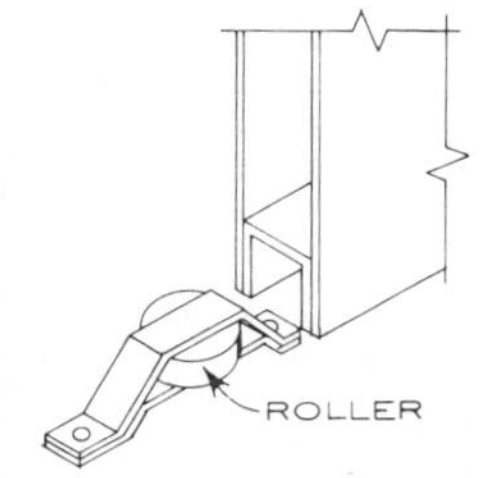

UNDERWRITERS SPECIFICATIONS–FIRE DOOR

class	hourly rating	operation	maximum size width	height	area
A	3	S/SW	6'–0"	12'–0"	72 sq.
		PR/SW	10'–0"	12'–0"	120
		S/SW	12'–0"	12'–0"	120
		PR/SW	12'–0"	12'–0"	120
B	1 1/2	S/SL	10'–0"	10'–0"	80
C	3/4	S/SW	10'–0"	10'–0"	60
D	1 1/2	PR/SW	10'–0"	10'–0"	80
E	3/4	S/SL	10'–0"	10'–0"	80
		S/SW	16'–0"	10'–0"	60
		PR/SL	10'–0"	10'–0"	80

Note: for glass requirements see another page in this series.

COMBINATIONS

NOM. OPNG. WIDTH	STD. 1/2 UNIT & FULL UNIT COMB.	FINISHED OPNG. WIDTH
7'–0"	1'–6" + 4'–0" + 1'–6"	83"
7'–6"	2'–6" + 5'–0"	89 1/2"
8'–0"	4'–0" + 4'–0"	95"
8'–0"	3'–0" + 6'–0"	107 1/2"
10'–0"	5'–0" + 5'–0"	119"
11'–0"	2'–6" + 6'–0" + 2'–6"	131"
12'–0"	6'–0" + 6'–0"	143"

Note: To combine doors for oversized opening: use full units (4-fold) in multiples or in combination with half units (2-fold); many variations of width and panel effects may be obtained. Consult manufacturers' literature.

FLOOR GUIDE # 1

FLOOR GUIDE # 2

James W. G. Watson, AIA; Ronald A. Spahn and Associates; Cleveland Heights, Ohio

GENERAL NOTES FOR ALL WOOD DOORS:

Kiln dried wood, moisture content @ 6 — 12%.

Type 1 doors: Fully waterproof bond ext. and int.
Type 11 doors: Water resistant bond. Int. only.

Tolerances: Height, width, thickness, squareness and warp per NWMA STANDARDS and vary with solid vs. built-up construction.

Prefit: Doors @ $3/16$" less in width and $1/8$" less in height than nominal size, $\pm 1/32$" tolerance, with vertical edges eased.

Premachining: Doors mortised for locks and cut out for hinges when so specified.
Grading:

Premium: For transparent finish. Good/custom: For paint or transparent finish. Sound: For paint, with 2 coats completely covering defects.

FLUSH WOOD DOORS:

CORE MATERIAL
SOLID CORES:

Wood block, single specie, @ $2 1/2$" max. width, surfaced two sides, without spaces or defects impairing strength or visible thru hdwd. veneer facing.

HOLLOW CORES:

Wood, wood derivative, or class A insul. board.

FINISHED EDGES:

Hdwd. edge strips on stiles to match face. Hdwd. or soft end strips on top and bottom st
Hdwd. edge strips on stiles to match face. Hdwd. or soft end strips on top and bottom rails.

TYPES OF WOOD FACES:

Standard thickness face veneers @ $1/20$" — $1/36$", bonded to hardwood, crossband @ $1/10$" — $1/16$". Most economical and widely used, inhibits checking, difficult to refinish or repair face damage, for use on all cores.

$1/8$" Sawn veneers, bonded to crossband, easily refinished and repaired.

For use on staved block and stile and rail solid cores. $1/4$" Sawn veneers: same as $1/8$" but without crossband on stile and rail solid cores with horizontal blocks. Decorative grooves can be cut into faces.

LIGHT & LOUVER OPENINGS:

Custom made to specifications. Wood beads and slats to match face veneer. 5" min. between opening and edge of door.

Hollow core: Cut-out area max. $1/2$ height of door. Door not guaranteed with openings greater than 40%.
Exterior doors: Weatherproofing required to prevent moisture from leaking into core.

FACTORY FINISHING:

Partial: Sealing coats applied, final job finish.
Complete: Requires prefit and premachining.

SPECIAL FACING:

High or medium-low density overlay faces of phenolic resins and cellulose fibers fused to inner faces of hardwood in lieu of final veneers as base for final opaque finish only.

$1/16$" min. laminated plastic bonded to $1/16$" min. wood back of two or more piles.

$1/8$" hardboard, smooth one or two sides.

SPECIAL CORES:
SOUND INSULATING DOORS:

Transmission loss rating @ 35 — 42 decibels. Thicknesses @ $1 3/4$", $2 1/4$", $2 1/2$", and 3". Barrier faces separated by a void or damping compound to keep faces from vibrating in unison. Special stops, gaskets, and threshold devices required. Mfrs. requirements as to wd. frames and wall specs.

FIRE RATED DOORS:

"B" label @ $1 1/2$ and 1 hr., "C" label @ $3/4$ hr.

LEAD LINED DOORS:

See U/L requirements. Optional location within door construction of $1/32$" to $1/2$" continuous lead sheet from edge to edge which may be reinforced with lead bolts.

GROUNDED DOORS:

Wire mesh located at center of core, grounded with copper wire through hinges to frame.

TYPES OF FLUSH DOORS

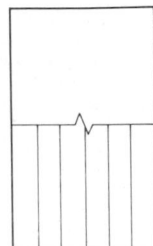

PLAIN: SOLID/HOLLOW
"V" GROOVE: SOLID

TYPES OF HOLLOW CORES:

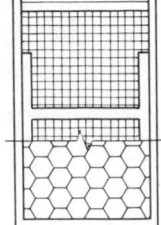

LADDER:
Horizontal strips, equally spaced, flat or arched, notched into stiles.

IMPLANTED BLANKS:
Spirals or other forms separated or joined, implanted between & supporting outer faces of door.

MESH:
Interlocked, horizontal & vertical strips, equally spaced, notched into stiles, or expandable cellular or honey-comb core.

TYPES OF SOLID CORES:

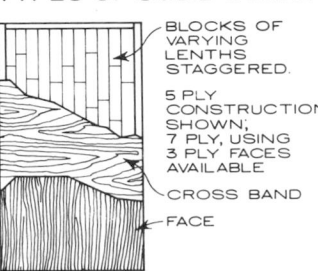

BLOCKS OF VARYING LENTHS STAGGERED.
5 PLY CONSTRUCTION SHOWN; 7 PLY, USING 3 PLY FACES AVAILABLE
CROSS BAND
FACE

CONTINUOUS BLOCK STAVED CORE:
Bonded staggered blocks bonded to face panels. Most widely used & economical solid core.

FRAMED BLOCK STAVED CORE:
Non-bonded staggered blocks laid up within stile rail frame, bonded to face panels.

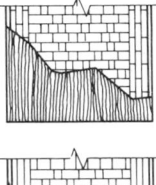

STILE AND RAIL:
Horizontal blocks when cross banding is not used. Vertical panel blocks when cross banding is used.

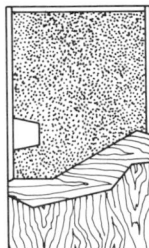

PARTICLE BOARD:
Extremely heavy, more soundproof, not yet covered by (1964) commercial standards.

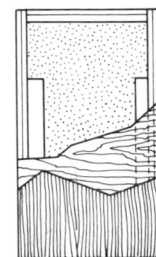

MINERAL COMPOSITION:
Lightest weight of all cores. Details, as cut-outs, difficult. Low screw holding strength.

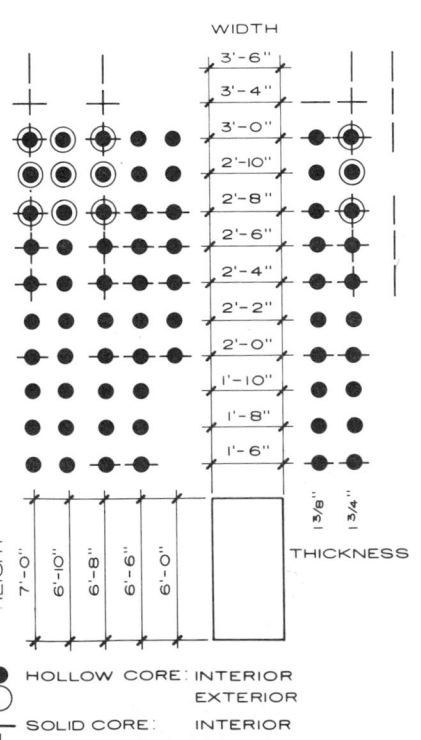

WIDTH

HOLLOW CORE: INTERIOR / EXTERIOR
SOLID CORE: INTERIOR / EXTERIOR

STANDARD SIZES

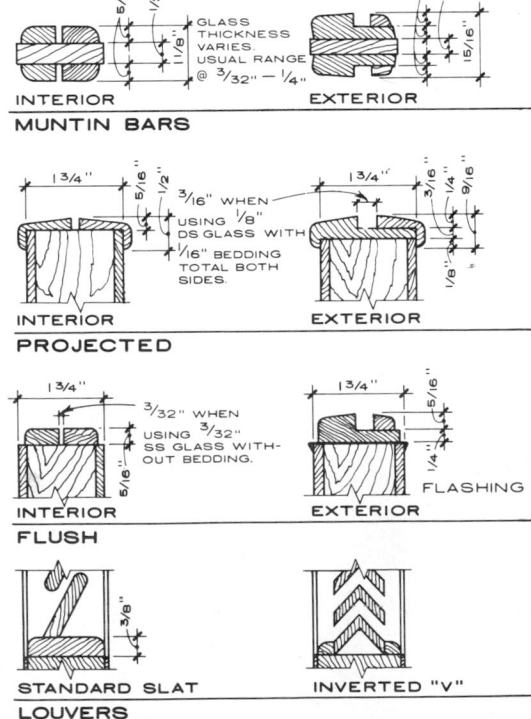

GLASS THICKNESS VARIES, USUAL RANGE @ $3/32$" — $1/4$"
INTERIOR   EXTERIOR
MUNTIN BARS

$3/16$" WHEN USING $1/8$" DS GLASS WITH $1/16$" BEDDING TOTAL BOTH SIDES.
INTERIOR   EXTERIOR
PROJECTED

$3/32$" WHEN USING $3/32$" SS GLASS WITH-OUT BEDDING.
INTERIOR   EXTERIOR
FLASHING
FLUSH

STANDARD SLAT   INVERTED "V"
LOUVERS
STOCK OPENING & LOUVER DETAIL
SCALE: 3"=1'-0"

GLASS & WOOD PANEL DOORS

CONSTRUCTION

Solid pine or built-up stiles, rails and vertical members or mullions, doweled as in NWMA std.

BUILT-UP MEMBERS

Core as in solid core of flush doors.
Edge and end strips as in flush doors.
Face veneers: Hdwd. @ $1/8''$ min.

PANELS

Flat: 3 ply hdwd. or soft.
Raised—2 sides: Solid hdwd. or soft or built-up of 2 or more plies.

STICKING, GLASS STOPS & MUNTINS

Cove or bead or ovolo, solid, matching face.

KEY TO SELECTED STD. TYPES BELOW

Ponderosa pine: Numbered series.
Hardwood veneer: Lettered series.
Entrance doors of stock designs also available in addition to exterior doors shown.

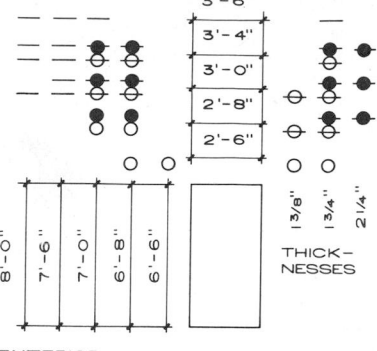

KEY TO SYMBOLS

● Hardwood veneer.
○ Ponderosa pine.
— 1 light & divided light.
Divided lights @
8: Lights @ 2 wide 4 high.
10: Lights @ 2 wide 5 high.
12: Lights @ 3 wide 4 high.
15: Lights @ 3 wide 5 high.
5 horizontal lights.
Interior:
Hdwd. veneer: Available in all sizes.
Pond. pine: 12 & 15 lights.
Not available @ $2'-0''$ wide.
Exterior:
Hdwd. veneer only.
Available in all sizes.

STANDARD SIZES   INTERIOR   EXTERIOR

SELECTED STANDARD DOOR TYPES:

100/A   101/S   102/B   103/D   104/—   106/I   107/F   108/L   109/M   113/—

INTERIOR

Stiles and top rail: $4^{3}/4''$; except 101/S: $4^{1}/4''$. Bottom rail: $9^{5}/8''$; except 101/S: $9^{1}/4''$ or $9^{1}/2''$; 104: $8''$.

Cross rail: 104: $4^{11}/16''$; 103/D and 107/F; $6^{5}/8''$; 108/L and M: $3^{7}/8''$; 109: $3^{1}/4''$; 113: $2^{1}/8''$.

Lock rail: 102/B, 106/1 and 108/L: $8''$; 104: $7^{7}/8''$. Mullions: 106/1 and 109: $4^{5}/8''$; 108/L and M: $3^{7}/8''$; 113: $2^{1}/8''$.

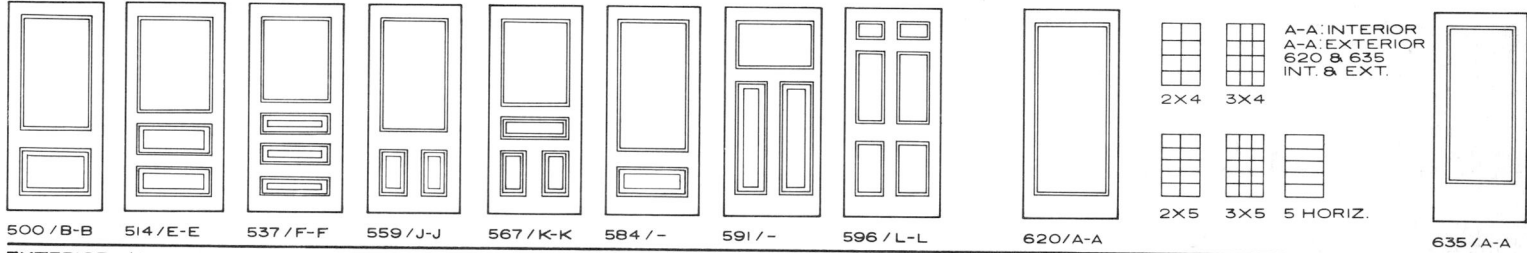

A-A: INTERIOR
A-A: EXTERIOR
620 & 635
INT. & EXT.

2×4   3×4
2×5   3×5   5 HORIZ.

500/B-B   514/E-E   537/F-F   559/J-J   567/K-K   584/—   591/—   596/L-L   620/A-A   635/A-A

EXTERIOR (AVAILABLE IN SINGLE & DIVIDED LIGHTS)

Stiles and top rail: $4^{3}/4''$; except 500, 584, 591 and 596: $5^{1}/2''$; 635: 635: $6^{1}/2''$, 635: $3'-0''$ and under: Top rail @ $5^{1}/2''$.

Bottom rail: $9^{5}/8''$; except B-B: $9^{3}/4''$; 635: $18^{1}/2''$. Lock rail: 500: $9^{5}/8''$; B-B, 559/J-J, 596/L-L: $8''$; 514/E-E: $4^{5}/8''$.

Cross rail and mullions: 591 and 596: $5^{3}/8''$; 559/J-J and 567/K-K: $4^{5}/8''$; L-L: $3^{7}/8''$. Cross rail only: 584: $5^{1}/2''$; 514/E-E and 537/F-F: $4^{5}/8''$.

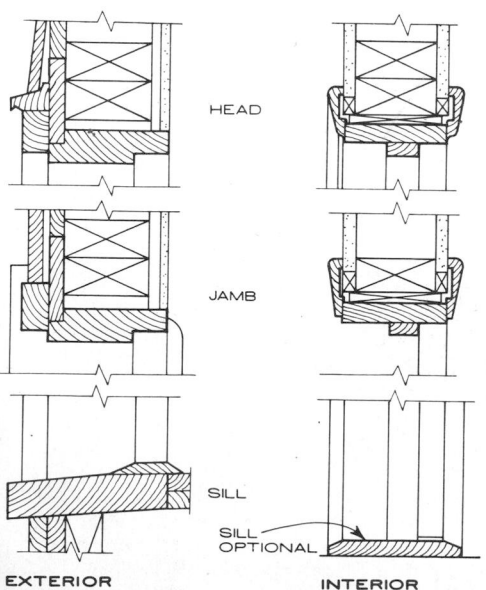

HEAD
JAMB
SILL
SILL OPTIONAL

EXTERIOR   INTERIOR

DOOR FRAMES
SCALE: $1^{1}/2'' = 1'-0''$

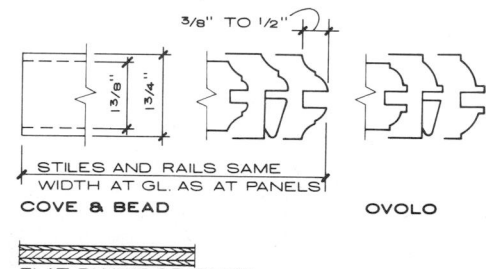

STILES AND RAILS SAME
WIDTH AT GL. AS AT PANELS

COVE & BEAD   OVOLO

FLAT PLYWOOD PANEL

SOLID OR LAMINATED

BEVEL RAISED PANEL   HIP RAISED PANEL

STICKING AND PANEL DETAILS
SCALE: $3'' = 1'-0''$

DOOR HUNG HERE

ADJUSTABLE DOOR FRAME
SCALE: $1^{1}/2'' = 1'-0''$

JALOUSIES

$1^{3}/4''$ rim type door as in panel door construction with square sticking and fitted with full or half alum. framed inserts housing $4''$ high clear or obscure glass louvers.
Usual widths @ $2'-6''$, $2'-8''$, and $3'-0''$.
Heights standard.

Simultaneous louver activation outward (similar to venetian blind) by roto operator.

Full frame with 17 louvers with double operators for top 9 and lower 8.

Half frame with 8 louvers—single operators.

Left or right side operation with jambs punched for both and metal plate to cover side not used.

Storm sash/screens on interior.

DUTCH DOORS

Divided door with top half independent of lower. Horiz. meeting rail w/ or w/o interior shelf. Provide WS, separate locking devices and joining hardware for both leaves to act in unison.

SCREEN/STORM DOORS

$1^{1}/8''$ screen, storm or combination doors. $1''$ greater height than nom. due to sill bevel. Combination: Interchange screen/glass inserts.

See index for garage doors and for hardware for doors.

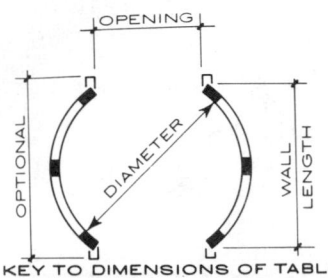

KEY TO DIMENSIONS OF TABLE

SIZES OF STANDARD DOORS

Diameter	Opening		Wall Length	
	Mfr. #1	Mfr. #2	Mfr. #1	Mfr. #2
5'- 6"	3'- 8 3/4"		4'- 3 1/4"	
5'-10"	3'-11 1/2"	3'-11 5/8"	4'- 6 1/4"	4'- 6 1/4"
6'- 0"	4'- 1"	4'- 1"	4'- 7 3/8"	4'- 7 5/8"
6'- 2"	4'- 2 1/2"	4'- 2 1/2"	4'- 8 13/16"	4'- 9 1/8"
6'- 4"	4'- 4"	4'- 3 7/8"	4'-10 1/4"	4'-10 1/2"
6'- 6"	4'- 5 1/4"	4'- 5 1/4"	4'-11 5/8"	4'-11 7/8"
6'- 8"	4'- 6 3/4"	4'- 6 5/8"	5'- 1"	5'- 1 1/4"
6'-10"	4'- 8"	4'- 8 1/8"	5'- 2 5/8"	5'- 2 3/4"
7'- 0"	4'- 9 1/2"	4'- 9 1/2"	5'- 3 7/8"	5'- 4 1/8"
7'- 2"	4'-11"	4'-10 7/8"	5'- 5 1/4"	5'- 5 1/2"
7'- 4"	5'- 0 3/8"	5'- 0 3/8"	5'- 6 11/16"	5'- 7"
7'- 6"	5'- 1 3/4"		5'- 8 3/16"	

LOCKED 45°
(COMMON)

LOCKED 90°
(RARE)

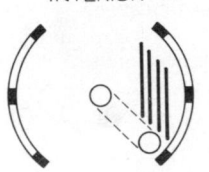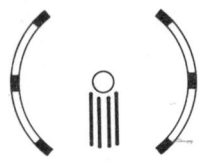

BOOK FOLDED (RARE) **SIDE OPEN**
TWO ABOVE POSITIONS REQUIRE
OVERHEAD SPEED CONTROL

NOTE :
Preset emergency device allows doors to collapse under 60# — 180# pressure.

Curved sliding night doors available for security.

Enclosure walls and wings may be designed to roll aside.

CENTRAL OPEN

ONE WING COLLAPSED FOR NIGHT SWING DOOR
(RARE)

FULL PANIC COLLAPSED POSITION
(ALL DOORS)

PLANS SHOWING LOCKED & FOLDED WING POSITIONS

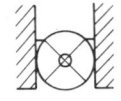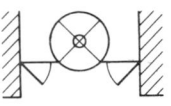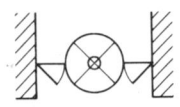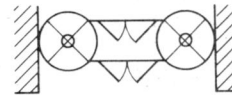

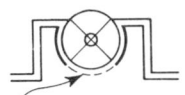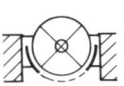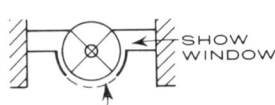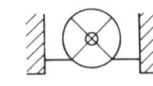

CURVED SLIDING NIGHT DOORS — IF CODE PERMITS

SHOW WINDOW

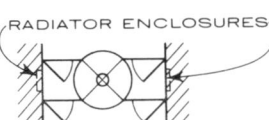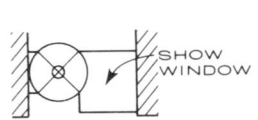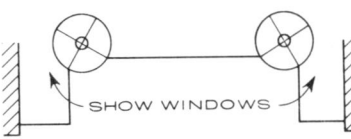

RADIATOR ENCLOSURES

SHOW WINDOW

SHOW WINDOWS

LAYOUT TYPES

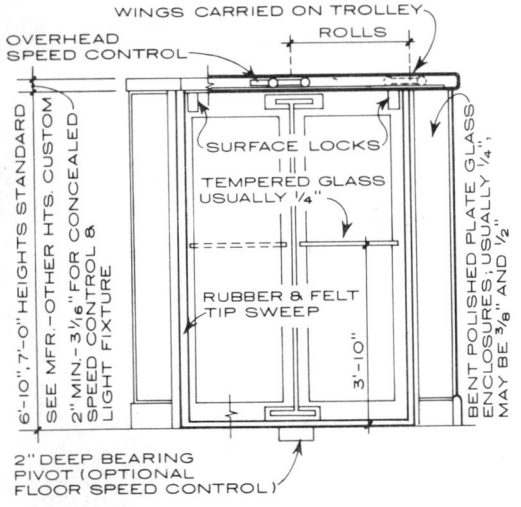

ELEVATION & SECTION 1/4" = 1'-0"

OVERHEAD SPEED CONTROL
WINGS CARRIED ON TROLLEY ROLLS
SURFACE LOCKS
TEMPERED GLASS USUALLY 1/4"
RUBBER & FELT TIP SWEEP
BENT POLISHED PLATE GLASS ENCLOSURES; USUALLY 1/4", MAY BE 3/8" AND 1/2"
6'-10", 7'-0" HEIGHTS STANDARD — SEE MFR.-OTHER HTS. CUSTOM
2" MIN.-3 1/16" FOR CONCEALED SPEED CONTROL & LIGHT FIXTURE
2" DEEP BEARING PIVOT (OPTIONAL FLOOR SPEED CONTROL)
3'-1 0"

DESIGN CONSIDERATIONS

Theoretical capacity each way = 2880 per hr.

Practical capacity = 2000 per hr. For general use, allow 6'- 6" diameters. Use 7'- 0" dia. for hotels and department stores. Motor drive optional with constant low speed or 1/4 point mechanism. Stainless steel, aluminum or bronze finish available. Wall enclosure may be all metal, all glass, partial glass or housed in construction. Provide heating and cooling source integral with or immediately adjacent to enclosure.

Codes may credit 50% of legal exiting requirements by means of revolving doors. Some do not credit any and require hinged door adjacent. Integral exit fixture required if freestanding legal exit.

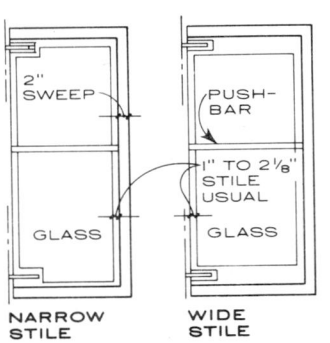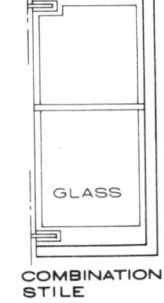

NARROW STILE **WIDE STILE** **COMBINATION STILE**

2" SWEEP
GLASS
PUSH-BAR
1" TO 2 1/8" STILE USUAL
GLASS
GLASS

WING TYPES 3/16" = 1'-0"

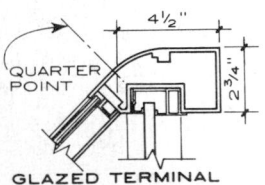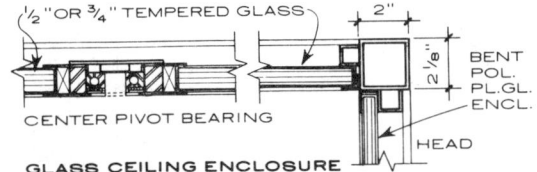

GLAZED TERMINAL

QUARTER POINT
4 1/2"
2 3/4"

GLASS CEILING ENCLOSURE

1/2" OR 3/4" TEMPERED GLASS
2"
2 1/8"
BENT POL. PL. GL. ENCL.
CENTER PIVOT BEARING
HEAD

METAL FACING
TO SUIT 2" MIN.
SEE ELEV.
1/4"
BENT POL. PL. GLASS ENCLOS.
19/16" TO 2"

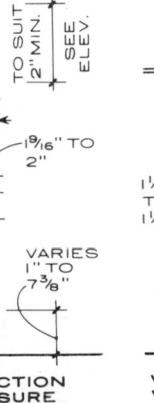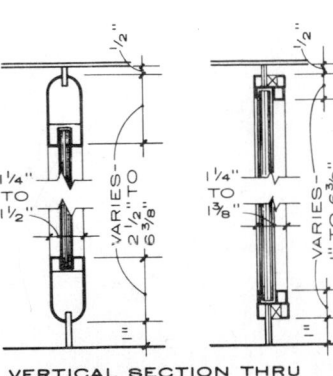

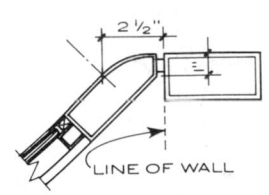

INTEGRAL DUCT & GRILLE TERMINAL
4 3/4" TO VARY TO SUIT

WALL OR SIDELIGHT TERMINAL
2 1/2"
LINE OF WALL

SELF-FRAMED SIDELIGHT
2 3/4"
3/4"
STANDARD TUBULAR MULLION

VERTICAL SECTION THRU ENCLOSURE
VARIES 1" TO 7 3/8"

VERTICAL SECTION THRU WINGS
1/2"
1 1/4" TO 1 1/2"
VARIES 2 1/2" TO 6 3/8"
1 1/4" TO 1 3/8"
VARIES 1" TO 6 3/8"

SPECIAL ENCLOSURE POST DETAILS

DETAILS SCALE: 1/2" = 1'-0"

Warren Anderson; The Perkins and Will Partnership; Chicago, Illinois

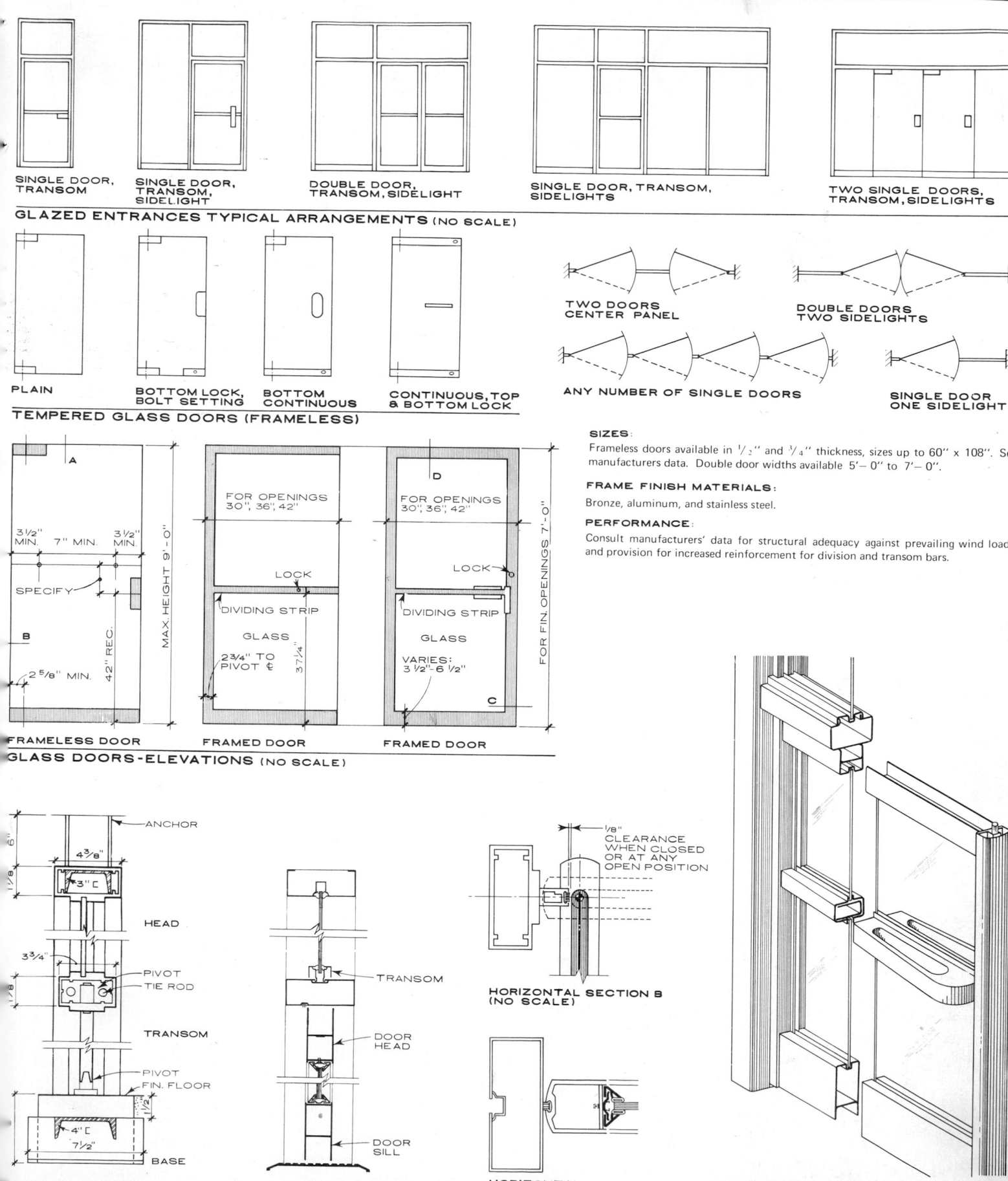

SINGLE DOOR, TRANSOM

SINGLE DOOR, TRANSOM, SIDELIGHT

DOUBLE DOOR, TRANSOM, SIDELIGHT

SINGLE DOOR, TRANSOM, SIDELIGHTS

TWO SINGLE DOORS, TRANSOM, SIDELIGHTS

GLAZED ENTRANCES TYPICAL ARRANGEMENTS (NO SCALE)

PLAIN

BOTTOM LOCK, BOLT SETTING

BOTTOM CONTINUOUS

CONTINUOUS, TOP & BOTTOM LOCK

TEMPERED GLASS DOORS (FRAMELESS)

TWO DOORS CENTER PANEL

DOUBLE DOORS TWO SIDELIGHTS

ANY NUMBER OF SINGLE DOORS

SINGLE DOOR ONE SIDELIGHT

SIZES:

Frameless doors available in $1/2''$ and $3/4''$ thickness, sizes up to 60'' x 108''. See manufacturers data. Double door widths available 5'—0'' to 7'—0''.

FRAME FINISH MATERIALS:

Bronze, aluminum, and stainless steel.

PERFORMANCE:

Consult manufacturers' data for structural adequacy against prevailing wind loads and provision for increased reinforcement for division and transom bars.

FRAMELESS DOOR

FRAMED DOOR

FRAMED DOOR

GLASS DOORS—ELEVATIONS (NO SCALE)

VERTICAL SECTION A
SCALE: 1 1/2" = 1'-0"

VERTICAL SECTION D
SCALE: 1 1/2" = 1'-0"

HORIZONTAL SECTION C
SCALE: 3" = 1'-0"

HORIZONTAL SECTION B
(NO SCALE)

ISOMETRIC OF DOOR FRAME, SIDELIGHT & TRANSOM

DOOR DETAILS

Daniel Schwartzman, FAIA & Associates, Francis Gunther, Graphics Coordinator; New York, New York

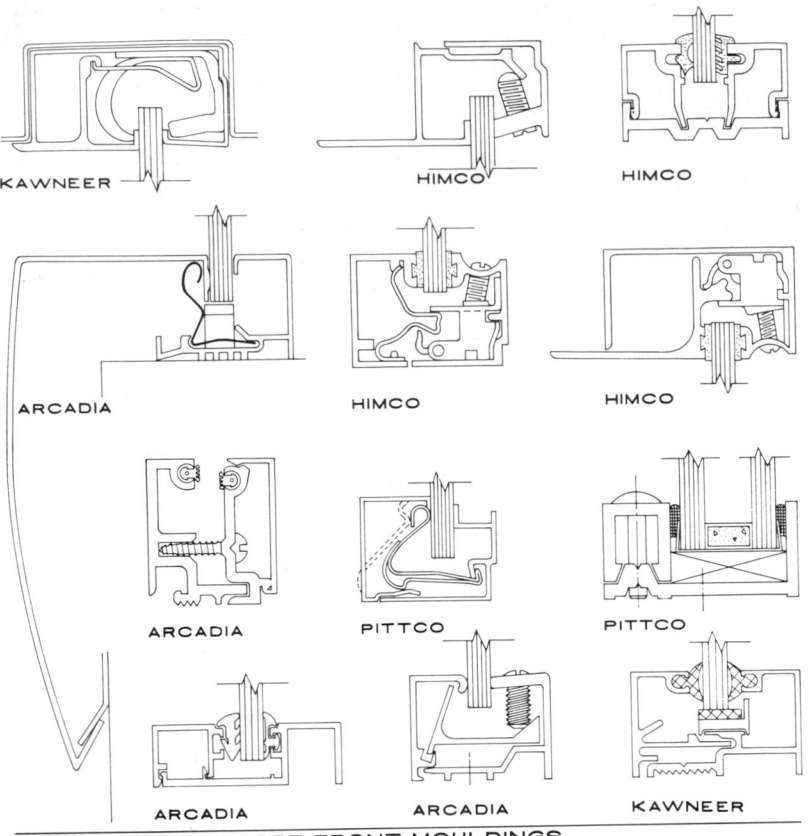

KAWNEER   HIMCO   HIMCO

ARCADIA   HIMCO   HIMCO

ARCADIA   PITTCO   PITTCO

ARCADIA   ARCADIA   KAWNEER

SELECTION OF STORE FRONT MOULDINGS
FROM LEADING MANUFACTURERS
SCALE: ONE-HALF SIZE

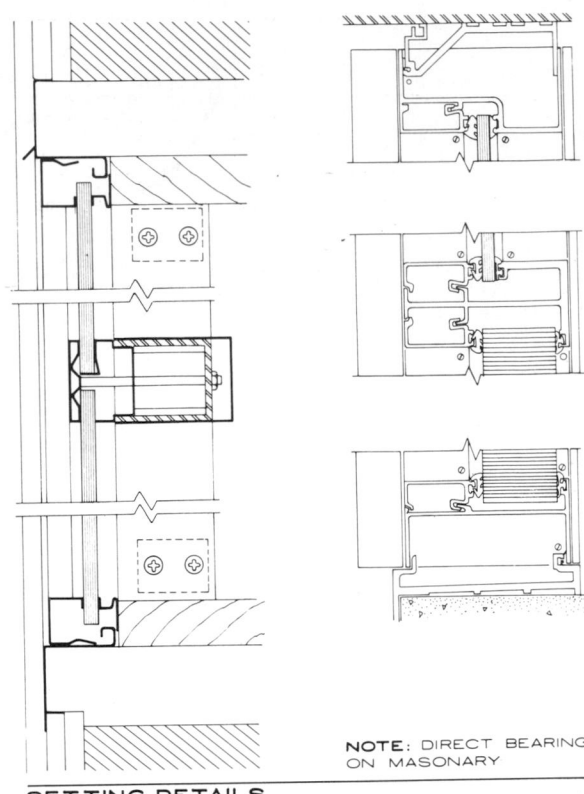

NOTE: DIRECT BEARING ON MASONARY

SETTING DETAILS
SCALE: QUARTER SIZE

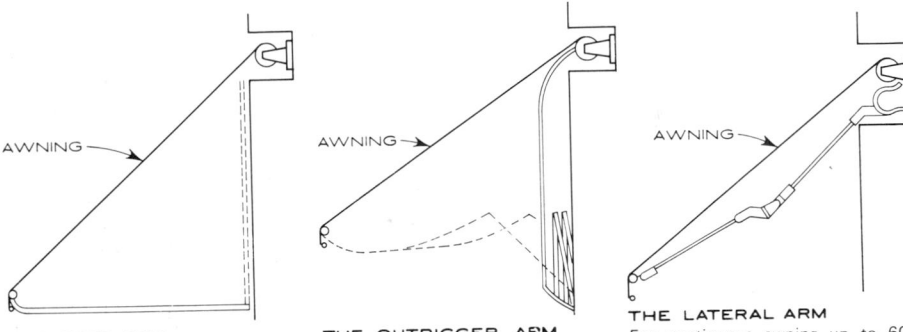

AWNING   AWNING   AWNING

THE PIPE ARM

The roller L is at least 12'–0"
above sidewalk. The pipe arm
hinged 7'–0" above sidewalk.

THE OUTRIGGER ARM

The roller L at least 9'–6" a-
bove sidewalk. Concealed arms
in jamb recess.

THE LATERAL ARM

For continuous awning up to 60'
long. Awning box only support.
Concealed arms in recessed awning
box.

TYPES OF ARM OPERATORS

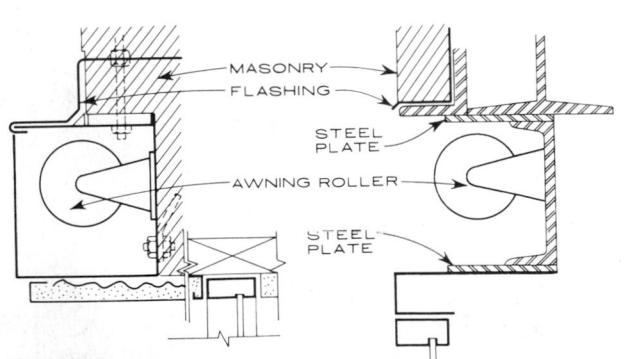

MASONRY
FLASHING
STEEL PLATE
AWNING ROLLER
STEEL PLATE

AWNING MATERIALS:

1. Canvas
2. Interlocking metal slats
   a. aluminum
   b. bronze
   c. stainless steel
3. Fiberglass

AWNING OPERATORS:

1. Detachable handle control
2. Gear box & shaft
   (concealed or exposed)
   with removable handle
   inside or outside of
   building
3. Electric control

TYPICAL CONSTRUCTION DETAILS
SCALE: 1½" = 1'–0"

AWNING DETAILS

Daniel Schwartzman, FAIA & Associates, Francis Gunther, Graphics Coordinator; New York, New York

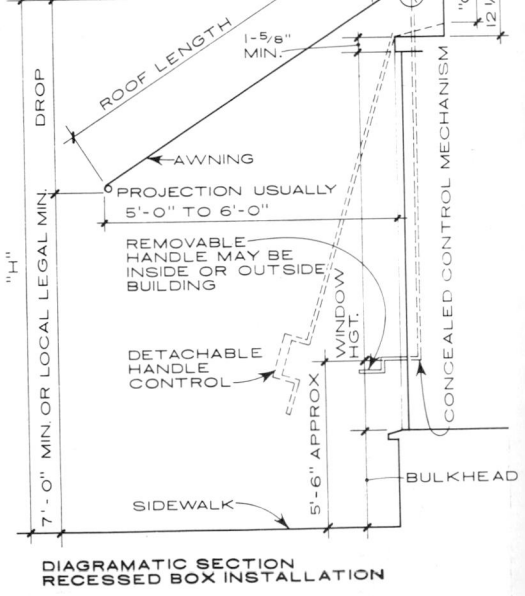

Ȼ AWNING ROLLER
DROP
ROOF LENGTH
AWNING
1-5/8" MIN.
PROJECTION USUALLY 5'–0" TO 6'–0"
REMOVABLE HANDLE MAY BE INSIDE OR OUTSIDE BUILDING
DETACHABLE HANDLE CONTROL
"H" 7'–0" MIN. OR LOCAL LEGAL MIN.
SIDEWALK
WINDOW HGT.
5'–6" APPROX.
CONCEALED CONTROL MECHANISM
BULKHEAD
"A"
"C"
12 ½"

DIAGRAMATIC SECTION
RECESSED BOX INSTALLATION

AWNING BOX CLEARANCES:

Recessed box sizes		"H"	"A"	"B"	"C"
A. lateral arm type	9'–6" to 11'–0"	10"	10 ½"	10"	
	9'–6" to 12'–0"	10 ½"	12"	10"	
	9'–6" to 14'–0"	11"	13 ½"	10"	
B. outrigger arm type	varies	6'–2"	6'–2"	6'–2"	

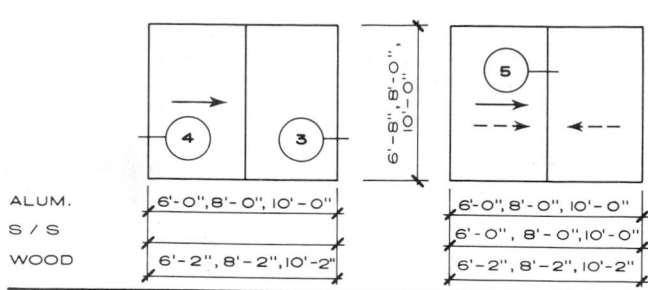
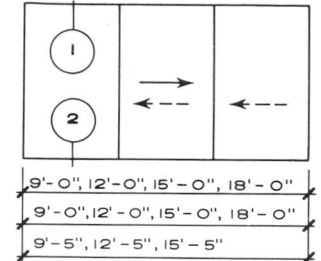
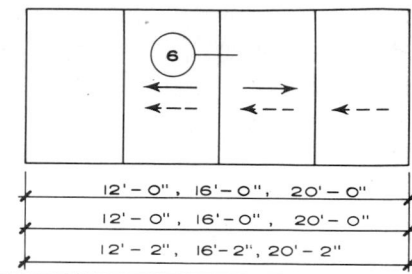

ALUM.	6'-0", 8'-0", 10'-0"	6'-0", 8'-0", 10'-0"	9'-0", 12'-0", 15'-0", 18'-0"	12'-0", 16'-0", 20'-0"
S/S		6'-0", 8'-0", 10'-0"	9'-0", 12'-0", 15'-0", 18'-0"	12'-0", 16'-0", 20'-0"
WOOD	6'-2", 8'-2", 10'-2"	6'-2", 8'-2", 10'-2"	9'-5", 12'-5", 15'-5"	12'-2", 16'-2", 20'-2"

RESIDENTIAL SLIDING DOOR DIMENSIONS
DIMENSIONS SHOWN ARE NOMINAL STOCK SIZES

S/S = STAINLESS STEEL

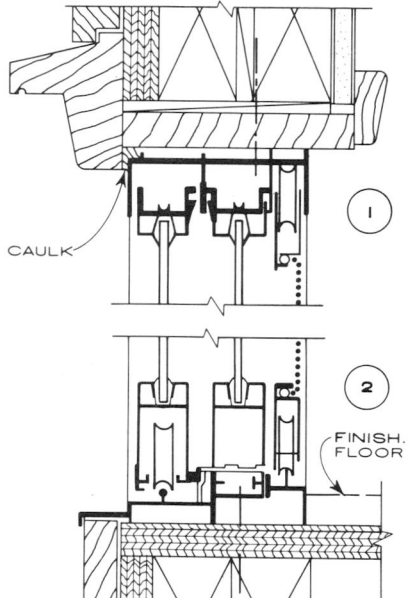

CAULK

FINISH. FLOOR

NOTE:

Details shown are for wood frame construction. Interior and exterior finishes and trim are optional. See manufacturer's data for typical installation details.

Screens are available for all doors. Details show screens on interior; consult specific manufacturers literature to determine if screens are furnished interior only, exterior only or are available either way.

Glazing may be polished plate, tempered, or thermal insulating glass or a combination thereof.

See manufacturer's data for special sizes, locking devices, and finishes.

In wood sliding door details, the parts furnished by the door manufacturer are shown in a heavy outline. The other parts of framing and trim shown hatched would be furnished by others.

In metal sliding doors, only the metal parts are furnished by the manufacturer.

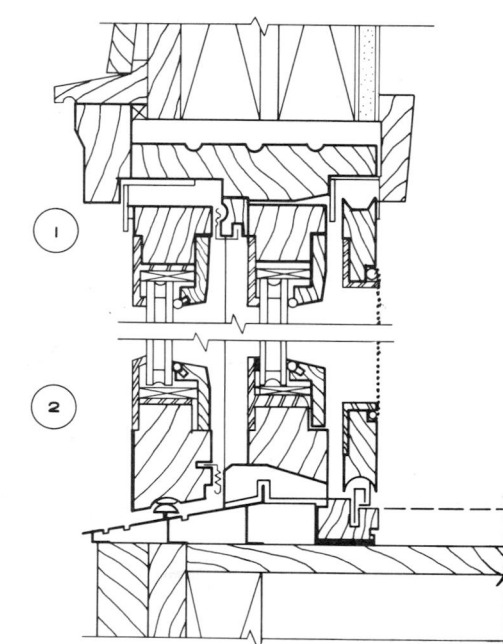

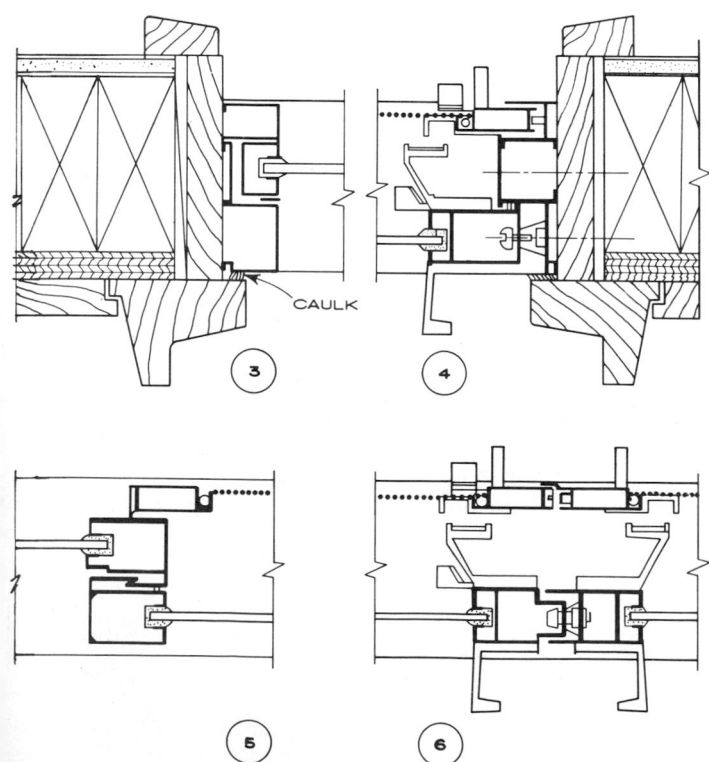

CAULK

METAL SLIDING DOOR DETAILS

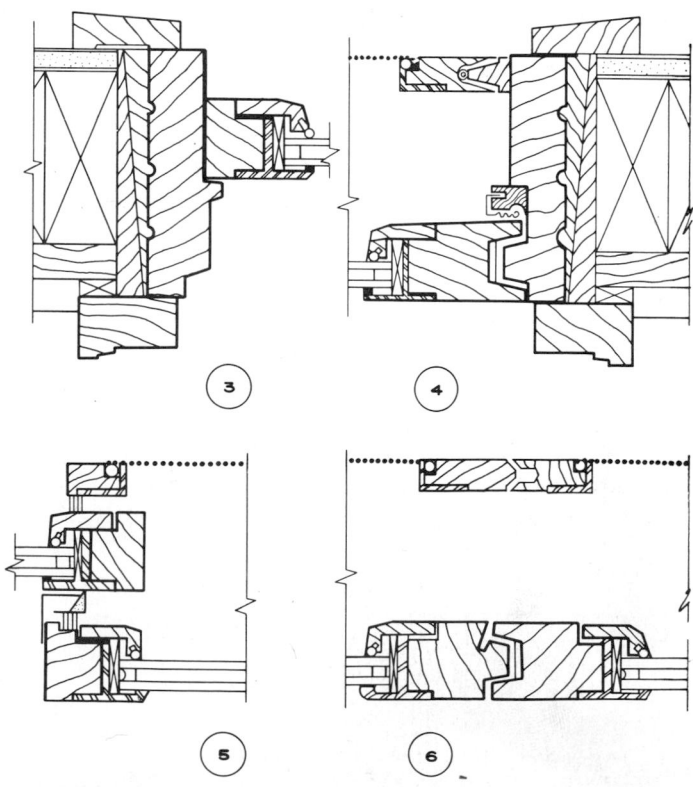

WOOD SLIDING DOOR DETAILS

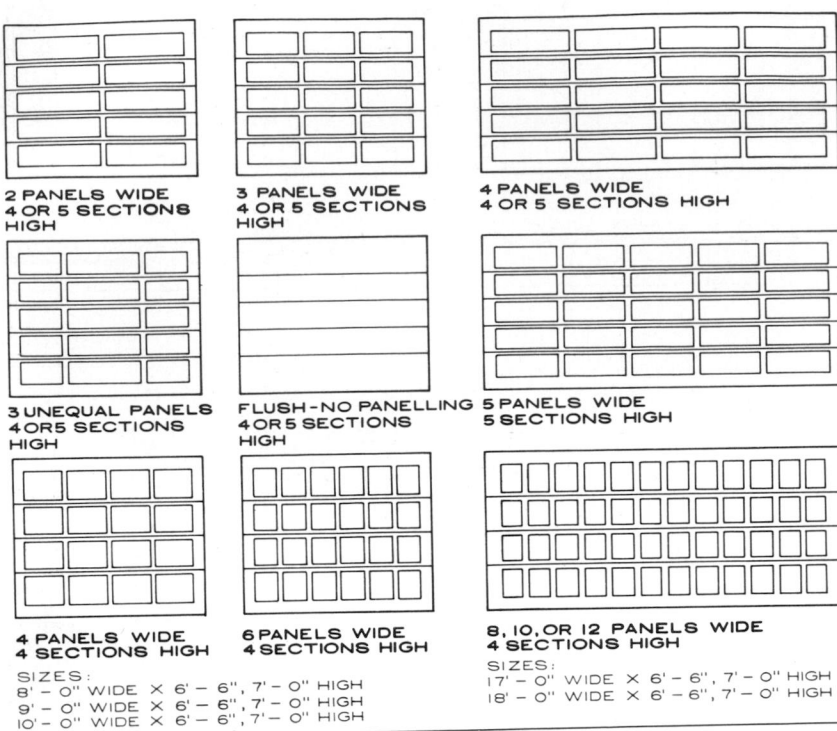

2 PANELS WIDE 4 OR 5 SECTIONS HIGH

3 PANELS WIDE 4 OR 5 SECTIONS HIGH

4 PANELS WIDE 4 OR 5 SECTIONS HIGH

3 UNEQUAL PANELS 4 OR 5 SECTIONS HIGH

FLUSH-NO PANELLING 4 OR 5 SECTIONS HIGH

5 PANELS WIDE 5 SECTIONS HIGH

4 PANELS WIDE 4 SECTIONS HIGH

6 PANELS WIDE 4 SECTIONS HIGH

8, 10, OR 12 PANELS WIDE 4 SECTIONS HIGH

SIZES :
8' – 0" WIDE X 6' – 6", 7' – 0" HIGH
9' – 0" WIDE X 6' – 6", 7' – 0" HIGH
10' – 0" WIDE X 6' – 6", 7' – 0" HIGH

SIZES :
17' – 0" WIDE X 6' – 6", 7' – 0" HIGH
18' – 0" WIDE X 6' – 6", 7' – 0" HIGH

WOOD DOORS STANDARD STOCK DESIGNS AND SIZES

NOTE :

Glazed panels may be located as desired. 3 section doors also available. Other stock designs and sizes available varying with manufacturers. Also available 8' – 0" wide x 7' – 6", 8' – 0" high.

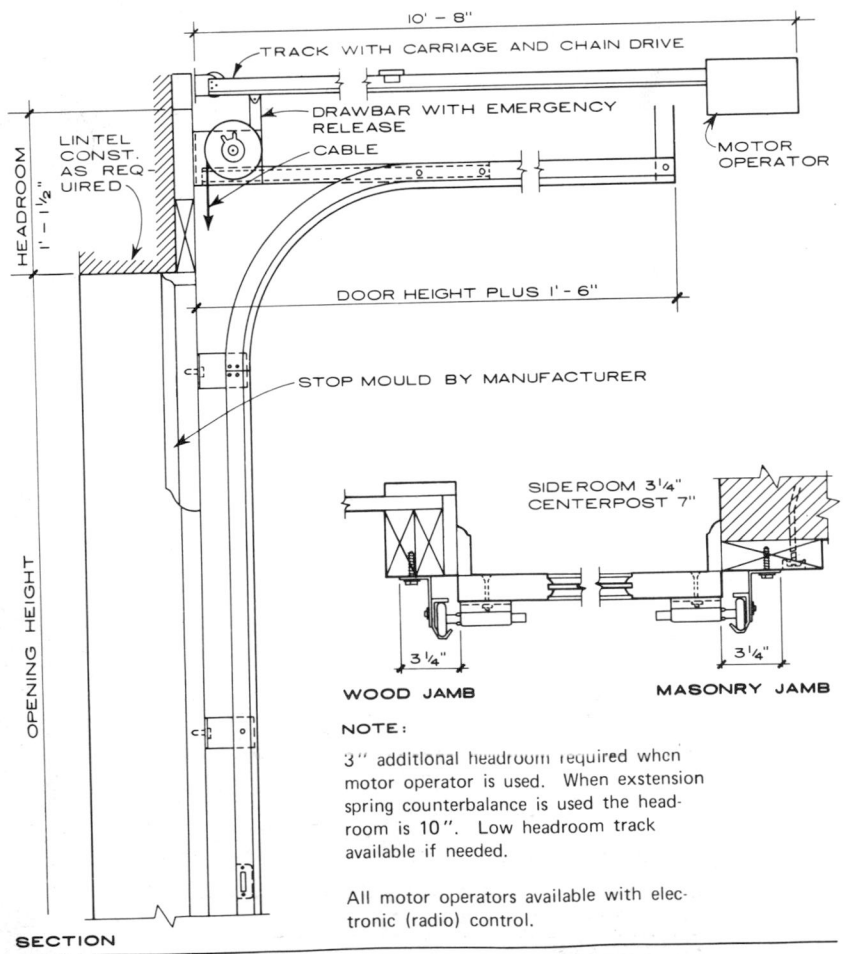

SECTION

INSTALLATION DETAILS

10' – 8"

TRACK WITH CARRIAGE AND CHAIN DRIVE

DRAWBAR WITH EMERGENCY RELEASE

CABLE

MOTOR OPERATOR

LINTEL CONST. AS REQUIRED

HEADROOM 1'-1½"

DOOR HEIGHT PLUS 1'-6"

STOP MOULD BY MANUFACTURER

OPENING HEIGHT

SIDEROOM 3¼"
CENTERPOST 7"

3¼"   3¼"

WOOD JAMB   **MASONRY JAMB**

NOTE :

3" additional headroom required when motor operator is used. When exstension spring counterbalance is used the headroom is 10". Low headroom track available if needed.

All motor operators available with electronic (radio) control.

Eugene Patrick Holden; Dale E. Selzer, AIA, Architect; Dallas, Texas

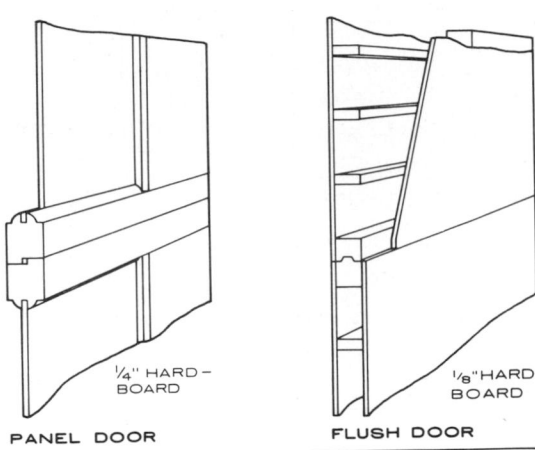

¼" HARD-BOARD

⅛" HARD-BOARD

PANEL DOOR   **FLUSH DOOR**

TYPICAL DETAILS OF WOOD DOORS

All doors available with torsion or extension spring counterbalance.

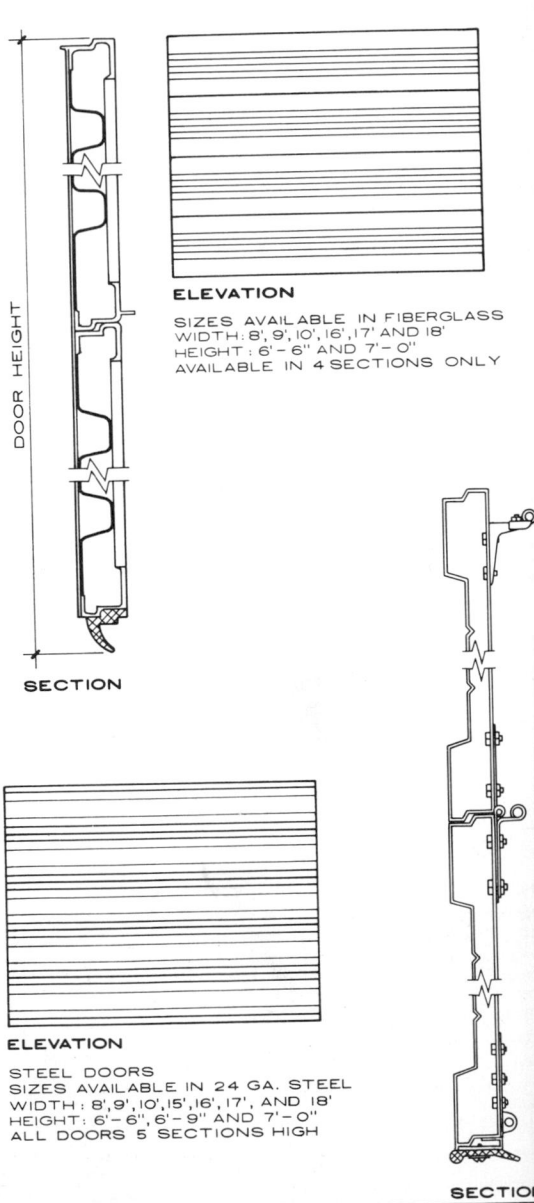

ELEVATION

SIZES AVAILABLE IN FIBERGLASS
WIDTH: 8', 9', 10', 16', 17' AND 18'
HEIGHT : 6'-6" AND 7'-0"
AVAILABLE IN 4 SECTIONS ONLY

DOOR HEIGHT

SECTION

ELEVATION

STEEL DOORS
SIZES AVAILABLE IN 24 GA. STEEL
WIDTH : 8', 9', 10', 15', 16', 17', AND 18'
HEIGHT : 6'-6", 6'-9" AND 7'-0"
ALL DOORS 5 SECTIONS HIGH

SECTION

FIBERGLASS AND STEEL DOORS

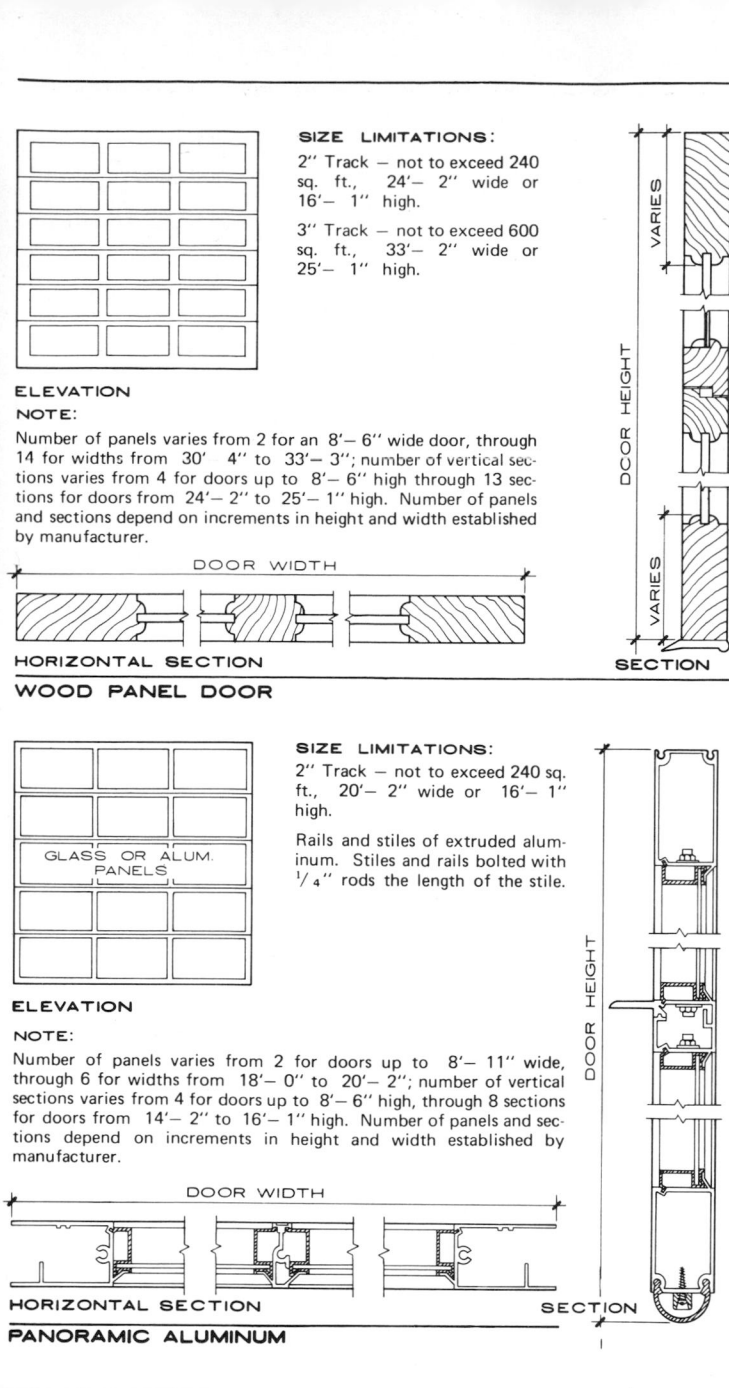

SIZE LIMITATIONS:

2" Track — not to exceed 240 sq. ft., 24'— 2" wide or 16'— 1" high.

3" Track — not to exceed 600 sq. ft., 33'— 2" wide or 25'— 1" high.

ELEVATION

NOTE:

Number of panels varies from 2 for an 8'— 6" wide door, through 14 for widths from 30'— 4" to 33'— 3"; number of vertical sections varies from 4 for doors up to 8'— 6" high through 13 sections for doors from 24'— 2" to 25'— 1" high. Number of panels and sections depend on increments in height and width established by manufacturer.

DOOR WIDTH

HORIZONTAL SECTION

WOOD PANEL DOOR

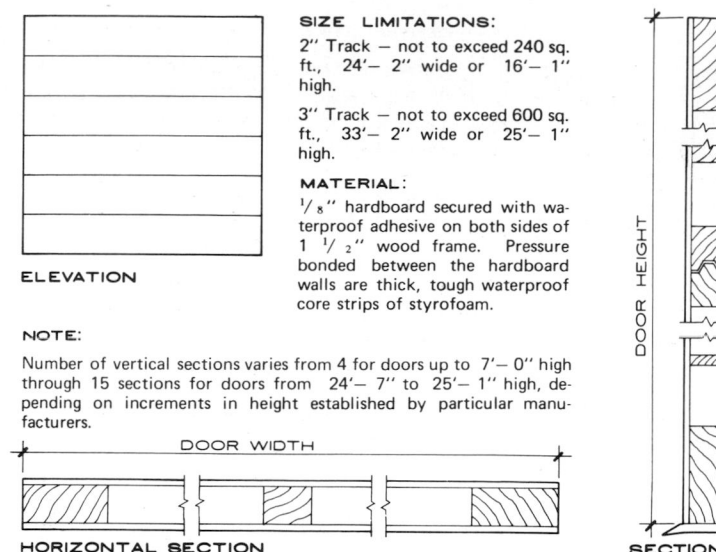

SIZE LIMITATIONS:

2" Track — not to exceed 240 sq. ft., 24'— 2" wide or 16'— 1" high.

3" Track — not to exceed 600 sq. ft., 33'— 2" wide or 25'— 1" high.

MATERIAL:

1/8" hardboard secured with waterproof adhesive on both sides of 1 1/2" wood frame. Pressure bonded between the hardboard walls are thick, tough waterproof core strips of styrofoam.

ELEVATION

NOTE:

Number of vertical sections varies from 4 for doors up to 7'— 0" high through 15 sections for doors from 24'— 7" to 25'— 1" high, depending on increments in height established by particular manufacturers.

DOOR WIDTH

HORIZONTAL SECTION

FLUSH WOOD DOOR

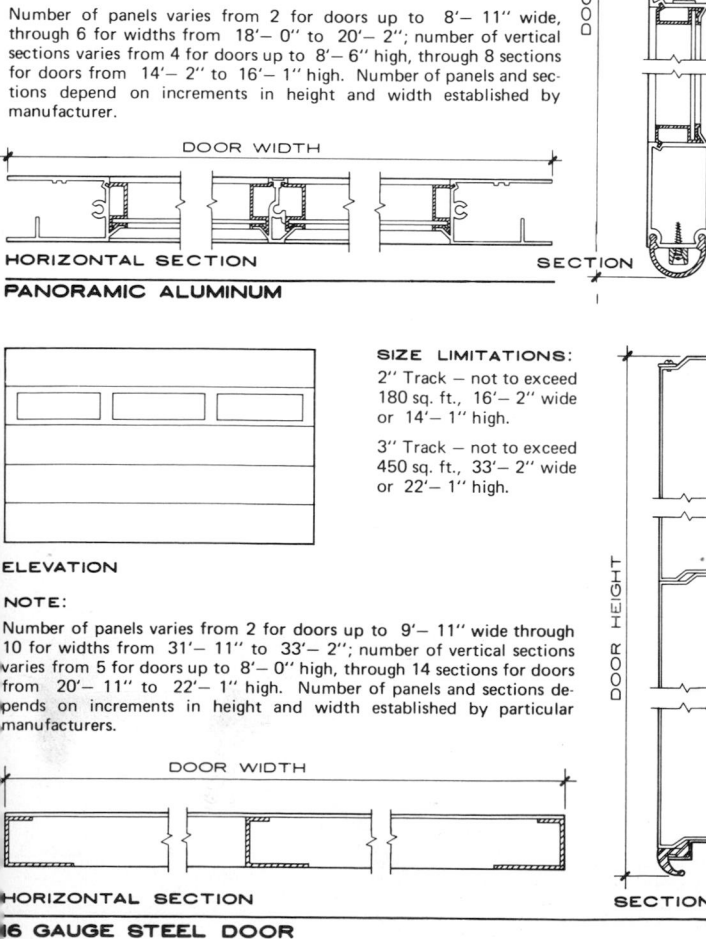

SIZE LIMITATIONS:

2" Track — not to exceed 240 sq. ft., 20'— 2" wide or 16'— 1" high.

Rails and stiles of extruded aluminum. Stiles and rails bolted with 1/4" rods the length of the stile.

GLASS OR ALUM. PANELS

ELEVATION

NOTE:

Number of panels varies from 2 for doors up to 8'— 11" wide, through 6 for widths from 18'— 0" to 20'— 2"; number of vertical sections varies from 4 for doors up to 8'— 6" high, through 8 sections for doors from 14'— 2" to 16'— 1" high. Number of panels and sections depend on increments in height and width established by manufacturer.

DOOR WIDTH

HORIZONTAL SECTION

PANORAMIC ALUMINUM

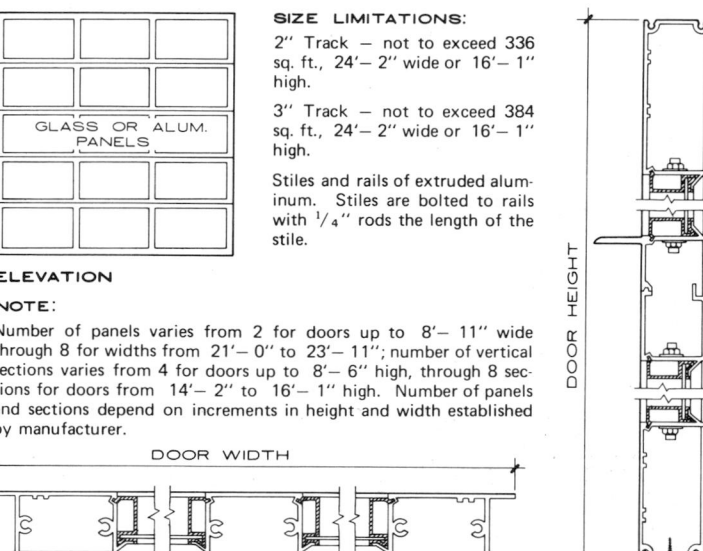

SIZE LIMITATIONS:

2" Track — not to exceed 336 sq. ft., 24'— 2" wide or 16'— 1" high.

3" Track — not to exceed 384 sq. ft., 24'— 2" wide or 16'— 1" high.

Stiles and rails of extruded aluminum. Stiles are bolted to rails with 1/4" rods the length of the stile.

GLASS OR ALUM. PANELS

ELEVATION

NOTE:

Number of panels varies from 2 for doors up to 8'— 11" wide through 8 for widths from 21'— 0" to 23'— 11"; number of vertical sections varies from 4 for doors up to 8'— 6" high, through 8 sections for doors from 14'— 2" to 16'— 1" high. Number of panels and sections depend on increments in height and width established by manufacturer.

DOOR WIDTH

HORIZONTAL SECTION

HEAVY DUTY ALUMINUM

SIZE LIMITATIONS:

2" Track — not to exceed 180 sq. ft., 16'— 2" wide or 14'— 1" high.

3" Track — not to exceed 450 sq. ft., 33'— 2" wide or 22'— 1" high.

ELEVATION

NOTE:

Number of panels varies from 2 for doors up to 9'— 11" wide through 10 for widths from 31'— 11" to 33'— 2"; number of vertical sections varies from 5 for doors up to 8'— 0" high, through 14 sections for doors from 20'— 11" to 22'— 1" high. Number of panels and sections depends on increments in height and width established by particular manufacturers.

DOOR WIDTH

HORIZONTAL SECTION

16 GAUGE STEEL DOOR

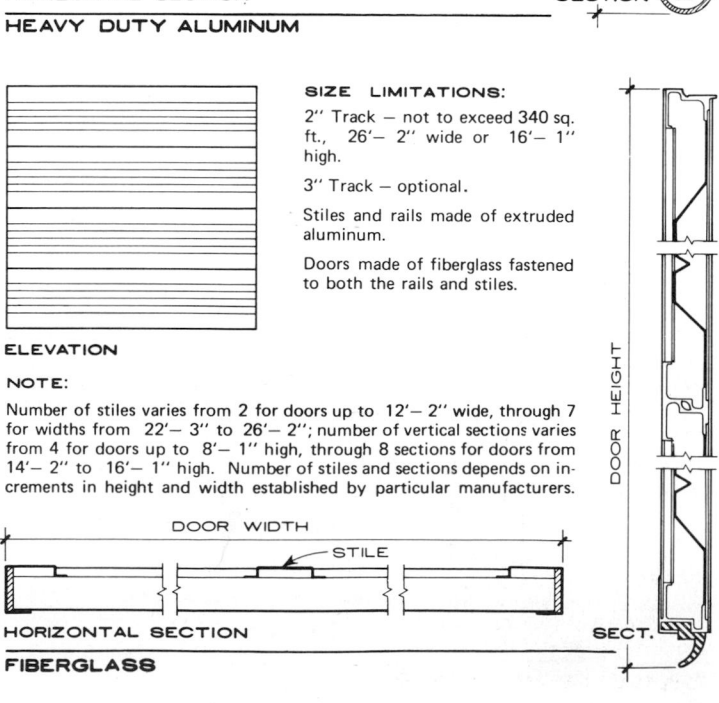

SIZE LIMITATIONS:

2" Track — not to exceed 340 sq. ft., 26'— 2" wide or 16'— 1" high.

3" Track — optional.

Stiles and rails made of extruded aluminum.

Doors made of fiberglass fastened to both the rails and stiles.

ELEVATION

NOTE:

Number of stiles varies from 2 for doors up to 12'— 2" wide, through 7 for widths from 22'— 3" to 26'— 2"; number of vertical sections varies from 4 for doors up to 8'— 1" high, through 8 sections for doors from 14'— 2" to 16'— 1" high. Number of stiles and sections depends on increments in height and width established by particular manufacturers.

DOOR WIDTH

— STILE

HORIZONTAL SECTION

FIBERGLASS

Eugene Patrick Holden; Dale E. Selzer, AIA, Architect; Dallas, Texas

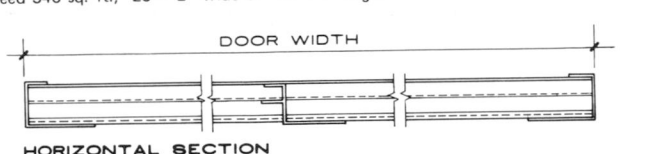

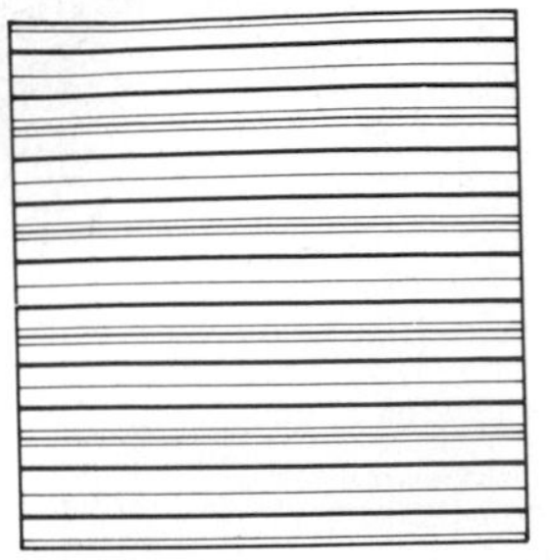

ELEVATION

CENTER STILE		SECTION	
DOOR WIDTH	NO. OF STILES	DOOR HEIGHT	NO. OF SECTIONS
to 12'-2"	2	to 8'-1"	4
12'-3" to 16'-2"	3	8'-2" to 10'-1"	5
16'-3" to 19'-2"	4	10'-2" to 12'-1"	6
19'-3" to 22'-2"	5	12'-2" to 14'-1"	7
22'-3" to 26'-2"	7	14'-2" to 16'-1"	8
26'-3" to 33'-2"	9	16'-2" to 18'-1"	9
		18'-2" to 20'-1"	10
		20'-2" to 22'-1"	11
		22'-2" to 24'-1"	12
		24'-2" to 25'-1"	13

GENERAL INFORMATION:

1. Standard commercial doors are designed to 20 #/ft.^{2} wind load.

2. All doors are available with sash sections or sash openings in standard section.

3. Doors are available using 20 or 24 gauge steel sections on the top and bottom and intermediate fiberglass sections.

4. Larger openings can be enclosed by using 2 or more doors with removable or swing up center posts. When the center posts are removed or raised, the entire opening is clear.

5. Doors of larger sizes can be manufactured with special engineering.

SIZE LIMITATIONS FOR STANDARD SIZES ON STANDARD TRACK:

20 ga., 2" track—not to exceed 240 sq. ft., 24'-2" wide or 16'-1" high.
        3" track—not to exceed 600 sq. ft., 33'-2" wide or 25'-1" high.
24 ga., 2" track—not to exceed 340 sq. ft., 26'-2" wide or 16'-1" high.

HORIZONTAL SECTION

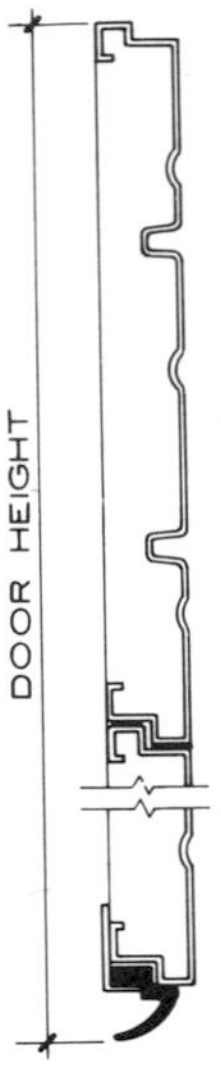

SECTION

COMBINED DOOR - 20 AND 24 GAUGE STEEL AND FIBERGLASS

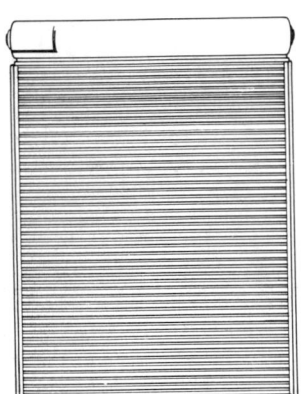

CURTAIN
Available in sizes listed below.

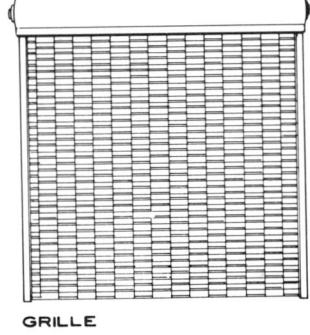

GRILLE
Available in sizes listed below: galvanized or stainless steel or aluminum.

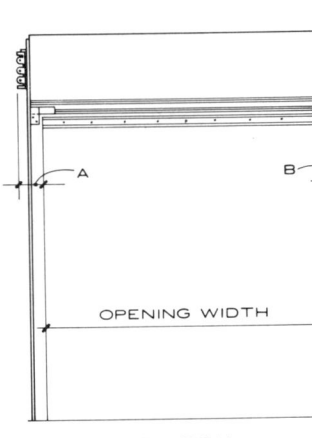

FRAME ELEVATION

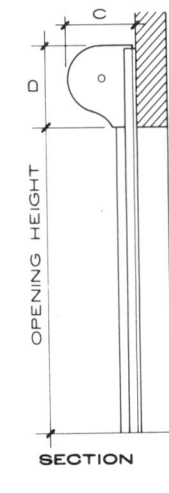

SECTION

DIMENSION TABLE

HEIGHT	0' TO 5'-11"				6'-0" TO 8'-0"				6'-0" TO 8'-0"			
WIDTH	A	B	C	D	A	B	C	D	A	B	C	D
TO 10'-0"	5	5	13	15	5	5	13	15	5	5	15	17

HEIGHT	0' TO 5'-9"				5'-10" TO 10'-1"				10'-2" TO 14'-1"			
WIDTH	A	B	C	D	A	B	C	D	A	B	C	D
TO 12'-0"	6	8½	13	15	6	8½	15	17	6	8½	19	21
12'-1" TO 15'-6"	6	8½	17	19	6	8½	17	19	6	8½	19	21
15'-7" TO 24'-4"	7	9	17	19	7	9	19	21	7	9	19	21
24'-5" TO 32'-10"	7	9½	17	19	7	9½	19	21	7	9½	19	21

HEIGHT	14'-1" TO 17'-9"				17'-10" TO 23'-9"				23'-10" TO 28'-10"			
WIDTH	A	B	C	D	A	B	C	D	A	B	C	D
TO 15'-6"	6	8½	19	21	6	8½	21	23	6	8½	23	25
15'-7" TO 24'-4"	7	9	21	23	7	9	23	25	7	9	25	27
24'-5" TO 32'-10"	7	9½	21	23	7	9½	23	25	7	9½	25	27

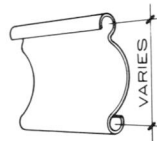

ROLLED SLAT
Available in galvanized, stainless steel and aluminum.

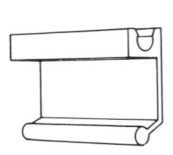

EXTRUDED ALUMINUM SLAT
For use with rolling counter doors.

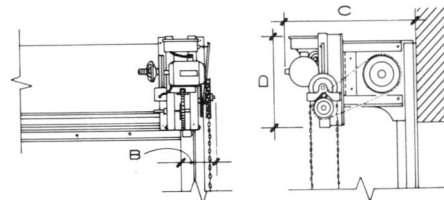

HOOD MOUNTED OPERATOR
Dimension "D" will be 23" minimum.
Dimension "C" will increase 15".

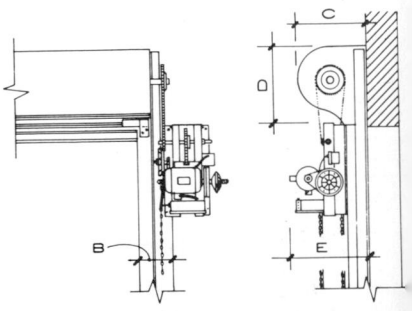

WALL MOUNTED OPERATOR
Dimension "B" will increase by 12".
Dimension "E" will be 20" for all doors.

NOTE:
Doors can be manufactured to be installed under the lintel and between the jambs when side or headroom are less than the above dimensions. Also doors can be manufactured to be installed on outside of building. This type door approved for V.L. Class A fire rating.

ROLLING METAL DOORS & GRILLES

Eugene Patrick Holden; Dale E. Selzer, AIA, Architect; Dallas, Texas

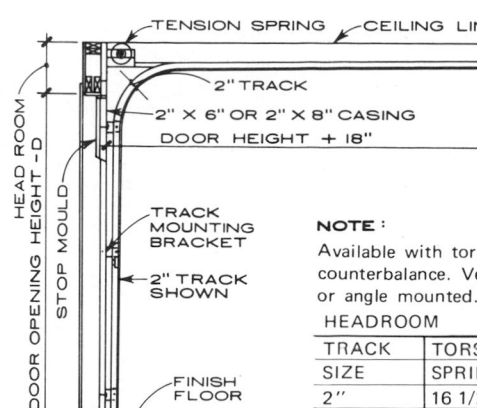

TENSION SPRING — CEILING LINE
2" TRACK
2" X 6" OR 2" X 8" CASING
DOOR HEIGHT + 18"
HEAD ROOM
DOOR OPENING HEIGHT-D
STOP MOULD
TRACK MOUNTING BRACKET
2" TRACK SHOWN
FINISH FLOOR

NOTE:

Available with torsion or extension spring counterbalance. Vertical tracks can be bracket or angle mounted.

HEADROOM

TRACK SIZE	TORSION SPRINGS	EXTENSION SPRINGS
2"	16 1/2"	18"
3"	18 1/2"	22"

STANDARD HEADROOM TRACK – 2" OR 3"

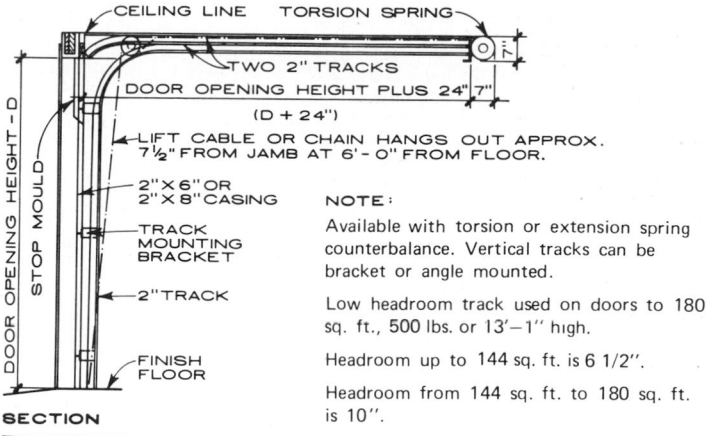

CEILING LINE   TORSION SPRING
TWO 2" TRACKS
DOOR OPENING HEIGHT PLUS 24" 7"
(D + 24")
LIFT CABLE OR CHAIN HANGS OUT APPROX. 7 1/2" FROM JAMB AT 6'-0" FROM FLOOR.
DOOR OPENING HEIGHT-D
STOP MOULD
2" X 6" OR 2" X 8" CASING
TRACK MOUNTING BRACKET
2" TRACK
FINISH FLOOR

NOTE:

Available with torsion or extension spring counterbalance. Vertical tracks can be bracket or angle mounted.

Low headroom track used on doors to 180 sq. ft., 500 lbs. or 13'-1" high.

Headroom up to 144 sq. ft. is 6 1/2".

Headroom from 144 sq. ft. to 180 sq. ft. is 10".

SECTION

LOW HEADROOM TRACK – 2"

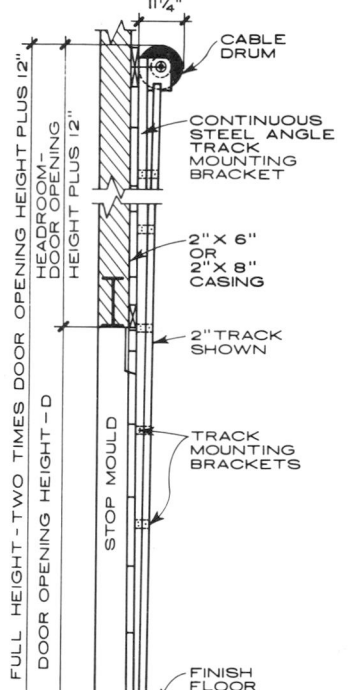

11 1/4"
CABLE DRUM
CONTINUOUS STEEL ANGLE TRACK MOUNTING BRACKET
FULL HEIGHT-TWO TIMES DOOR OPENING HEIGHT
HEADROOM-DOOR OPENING HEIGHT PLUS 12"
DOOR OPENING HEIGHT PLUS 12"
2" X 6" OR 2" X 8" CASING
2" TRACK SHOWN
DOOR OPENING HEIGHT-D
STOP MOULD
TRACK MOUNTING BRACKETS
FINISH FLOOR

NOTE:

Torsion spring or weight counterbalance.

Tracks can be bracket or angle mounted.

FULL VERTICAL TRACK – 2" OR 3"

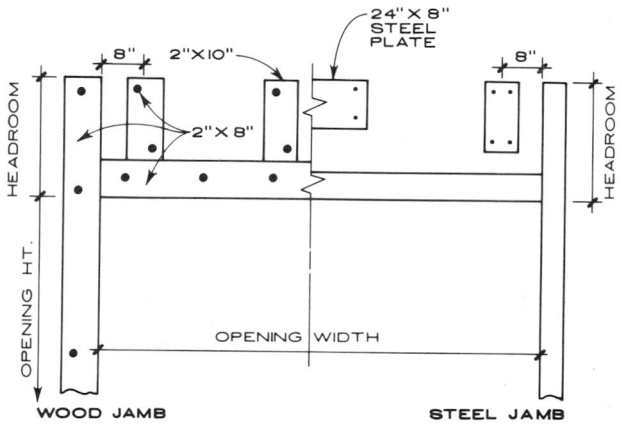

24" X 8" STEEL PLATE
8"   2" X 10"
2" X 8"
8"
HEADROOM
HEADROOM
OPENING HT.
OPENING WIDTH

WOOD JAMB   STEEL JAMB

All pads and plates to be flush with wood or steel jambs.

Wide or heavy doors which require more than two springs will require pads additional to those shown in the above detail.

INTERIOR ELEVATION OF DOOR OPENING

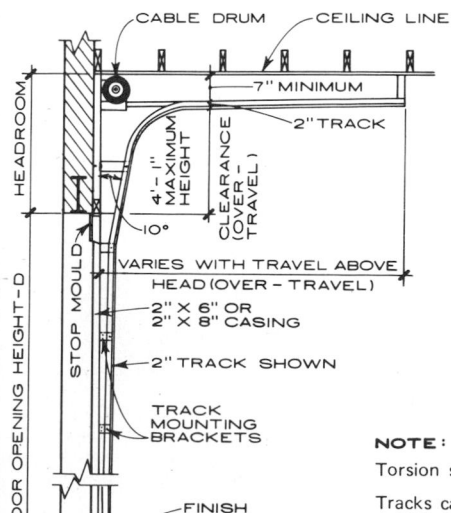

CABLE DRUM   CEILING LINE
7" MINIMUM
2" TRACK
4'-1" MAXIMUM HEIGHT
CLEARANCE (OVER-TRAVEL)
10°
VARIES WITH TRAVEL ABOVE HEAD (OVER-TRAVEL)
2" X 6" OR 2" X 8" CASING
2" TRACK SHOWN
HEADROOM
DOOR OPENING HEIGHT-D
STOP MOULD
TRACK MOUNTING BRACKETS
FINISH FLOOR

NOTE:

Torsion spring counterbalance only.

Tracks can be bracket or angle mounted.

Maximum usable headroom is 11'-6".

LIFT CLEARANCE TRACK – 2" OR 3"

Eugene Patrick Holden; Dale E. Selzer, AIA, Architect; Dallas, Texas

NOTE:

For weight counterbalance doors, additional sideroom is required.

See note for asterisk at Table for Steel Jamb sideroom below.

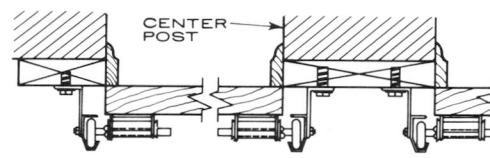

CENTER POST

WOOD JAMBS

SIDEROOM

TRACK SIZE	SIDEROOM	FOR DOORS		CENTER POST
2"	3"	to 12'-1" high		6"
2"	3 1/2"	12'-2" to 14'-1"	*	7"
2"	4 1/2"	14'-2" to 16'-1"	*	9"
3"	5"	to 320 sq. ft.	*	10"
3"	5 1/2"	over 320 sq. ft.	*	11"

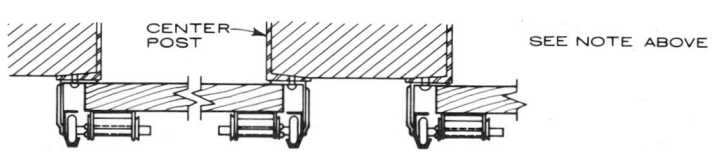

CENTER POST   SEE NOTE ABOVE

STEEL JAMBS

SIDEROOM

TRACK SIZE	SIDEROOM	FOR DOORS		CENTER POST
2"	4"	to 12'-1" high		8"
2"	4 1/2"	12'-2" to 14'-1"	*	9"
2"	5 1/2"	14'-2" to 16'-1"	*	11"
3"	6"	to 320 sq. ft.	*	12"
3"	7"	over 320 sq. ft.	*	14"

* 16 ga. steel doors over 168 sq. ft. Use 3" angle mounted track with 7" sideroom, 14" center post.

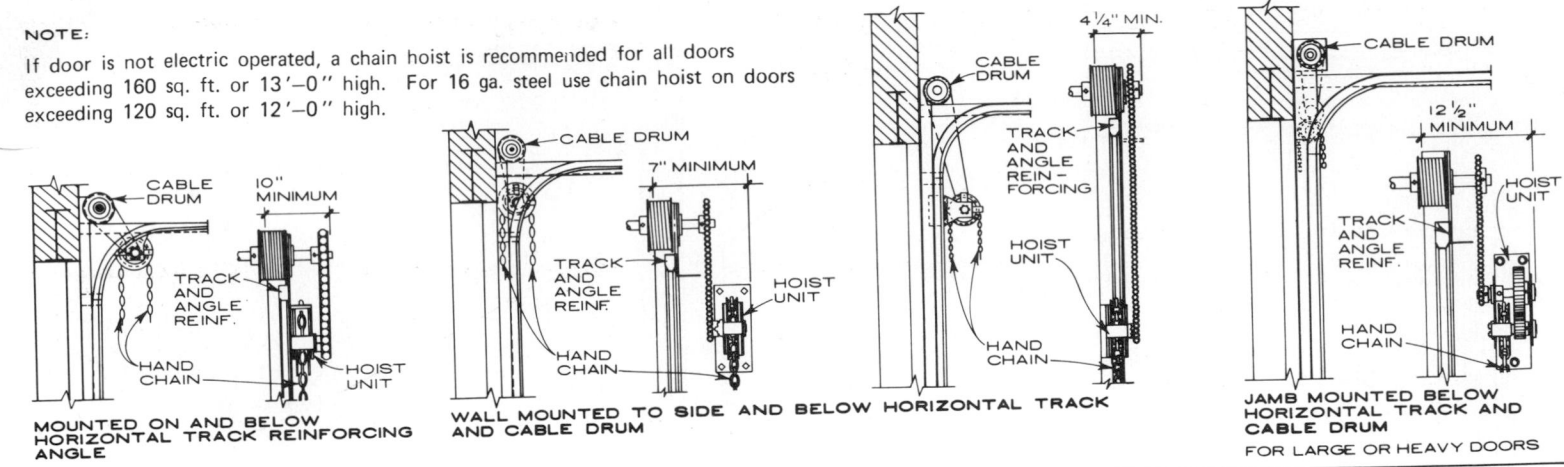

NOTE:

If door is not electric operated, a chain hoist is recommended for all doors exceeding 160 sq. ft. or 13'-0" high. For 16 ga. steel use chain hoist on doors exceeding 120 sq. ft. or 12'-0" high.

MOUNTED ON AND BELOW HORIZONTAL TRACK REINFORCING ANGLE

WALL MOUNTED TO SIDE AND BELOW HORIZONTAL TRACK AND CABLE DRUM

WALL MOUNTED TO SIDE AND BELOW HORIZONTAL TRACK

JAMB MOUNTED BELOW HORIZONTAL TRACK AND CABLE DRUM
FOR LARGE OR HEAVY DOORS

CHAIN HOIST OPERATORS – MINIMUM SIDE ROOM CLEARANCE

NOTE: All chain hoist operators require additional sideroom clearance. Operator may be mounted on left or right side as shown; on the left greater sideroom is required. Dimensions shown are from door jamb to projection of operator.

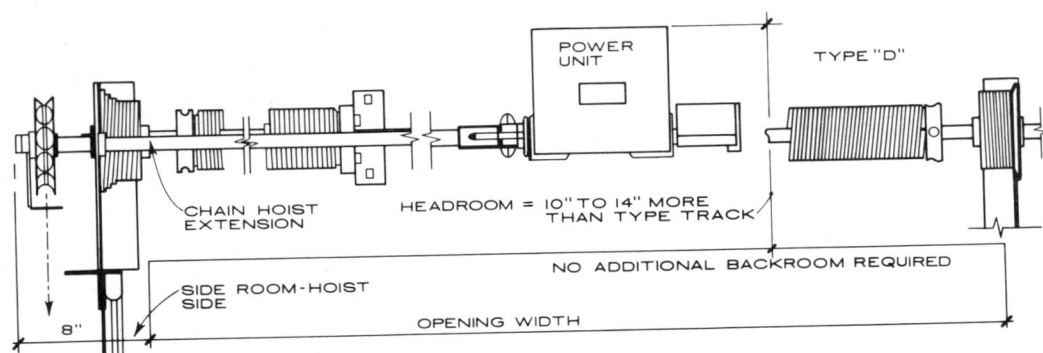

CENTER MOUNTED OPERATOR

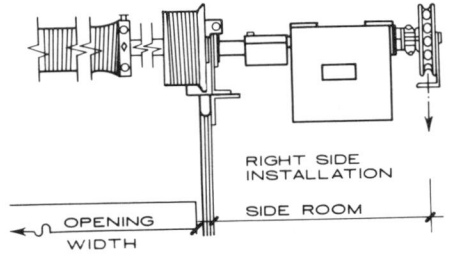

SIDE MOUNTED OPERATOR

SIDEROOM WIDTHS FOR HEAVY COMMER-CIAL USE – 20" FOR 2" TRACK AND 21" FOR 3" TRACK. FOR INDUSTRIAL USE, WIDTHS ARE 23" FOR 2" TRACK AND 24" FOR 3" TRACK.

NOTES:
CENTER MOUNTED
Same principle as side mounted operator except power unit is located on front wall above door opening. No additional sideroom is needed. Needs from 10" to 14" additional headroom; 3" additional sideroom on chain hoist side.

NOTES:
SIDE MOUNTED
Power unit is mounted on inside front wall to the right or left of the door and is connected to the crosshead shaft with a drive chain and sprockets or an adjustable coupling. Power is applied to the shaft to raise the door. The door closes by its own weight with the speed controlled by the operator.

No extra headroom required. Needs 20" to 24" of sideroom on mounting side.
Side mounted operators are available with direct coupled or chain drive, depending on installation condition.

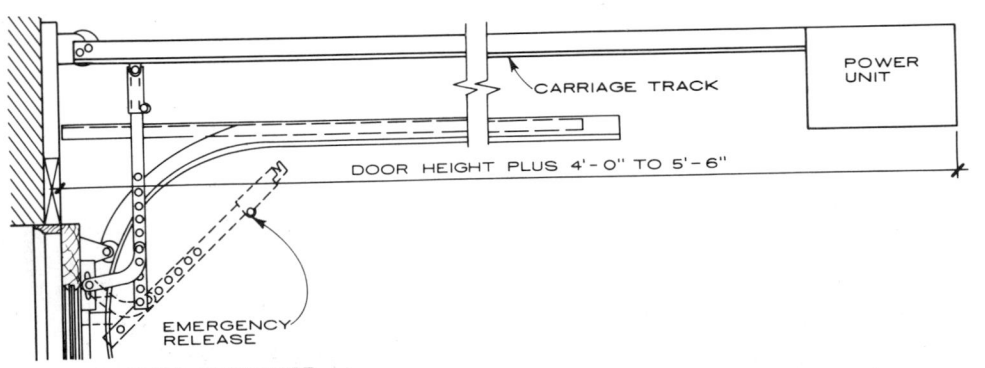

DRAWBAR TYPE OPERATOR
NOTE:
Power unit is mounted between, above and to the rear of horizontal tracks of door. A chain-driven carriage slides forward and back in its own tracks, which run from power unit to front wall above door. An arm linking the carriage and

the door applies force to open and close the door as the carriage moves backward and forward.
Door requires a minimum of 2" additional head room above tracks plus 1" to 3 1/2" more at power unit. No additional sideroom is required.

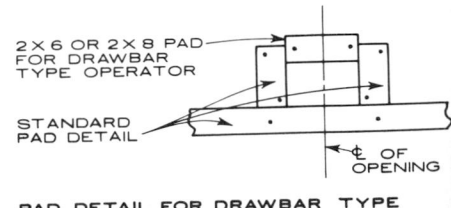

PAD DETAIL FOR DRAWBAR TYPE OPERATORS

Drawbar type is not recommended for use on extra large doors nor with lift clearance track installations. Emergency chain hoists are not normally used on drawbar type operators.

ELECTRIC MOTOR OPERATORS NO SCALE

Available in all standard voltages, frequency and phase. Control can be by 2 or 3 button push button station, pull switches, photoelectric, radio control (single c multiple), time delay closing and/or reversing or stop only safety switch. For Operator Selector chart see manufacturers data.

Eugene Patrick Holden; Dale E. Selzer, AIA, Architect; Dallas, Texas

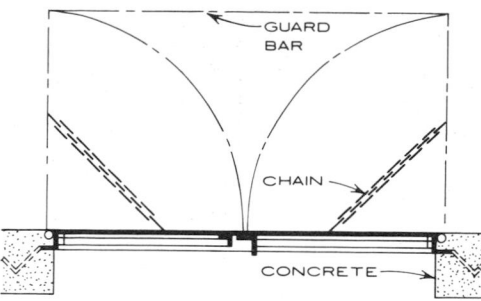

ELEVATION OF SIDEWALK DOOR
SCALE 1/2"= 1'-0"

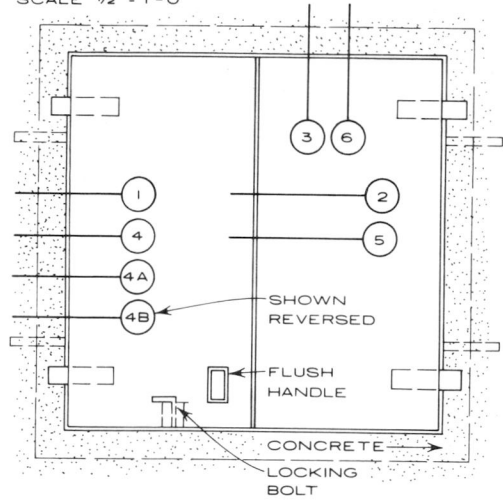

PLAN OF SIDEWALK DOOR

NOTE: SIDEWALK DOORS

Doors are usually of steel reinforced with angles, tees, or bars; and may also be of aluminum floor plate for weight reduction, and of safety type metal. Frames are usually of structural slopes with anchors into masonry or floor construction. Hinges can be set flush or on the surface and may be of cast iron, or steel, fitted with brass or bronze pins. Lifting handles are usually set flush and are essential where doors are to be operated from above. Locking is usually by a heavy barrel bolt on the underside. Guard bars and chains are required to hold doors in open position and to protect the opening. Door leaves of floor plate for ordinary construction may be 3/16" or 1/4" thickness with stiffeners to support the load. Plates of greater thickness may be used in order to handle greater live loads and possible deflections.

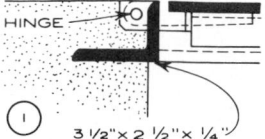
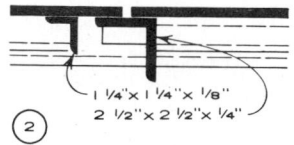
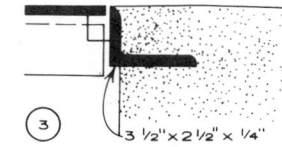

DETAILS - STANDARD FRAME
SCALE 1 1/2"= 1'-0"

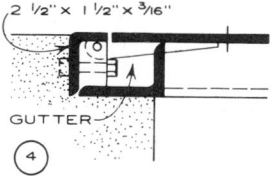
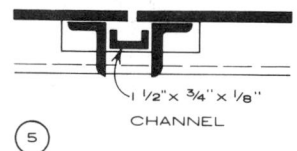
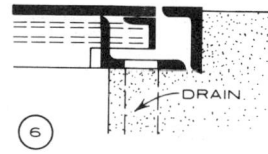

DETAILS - DRAIN AND GUTTER
SCALE 1 1/2"= 1'-0"

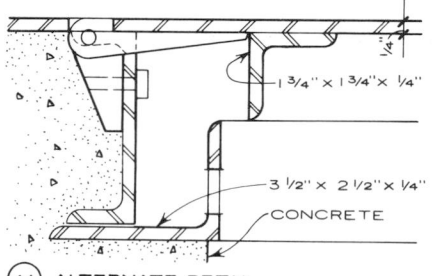

4A ALTERNATE DETAIL
FOR HEAVY DUTY AND LARGE DOORS
I BEAM MAY BE USED IN PLACE
OF CHANNEL

4B ALTERNATE DETAIL

DETAILS - ALTERNATE DRAIN AND GUTTER   SCALE 3"=1'-0"

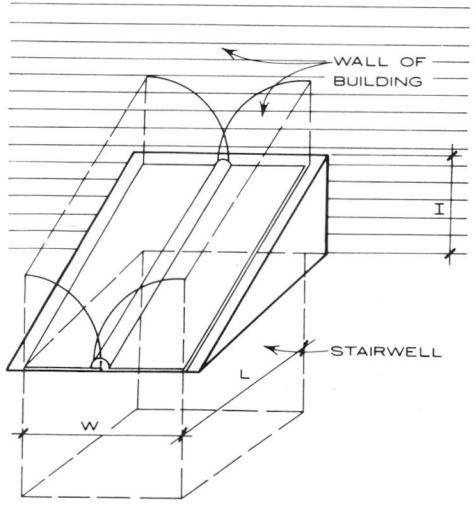

CELLAR DOOR OPENINGS

TYPE	LENGTH	WIDTH	HEIGHT
A	4'-6"	3'-4"	2'-6"
B	5'-0"	3'-8"	1'-10"
C	5'-8"	4'-0"	1'-7 1/2"

DOORS ARE MADE TO FIT THE ABOVE OPENINGS. THEY ARE MANUFACTURED TO ORDER.

CELLAR DOORS

Richard Malesardi and Associates, Architects; Washington, D. C.

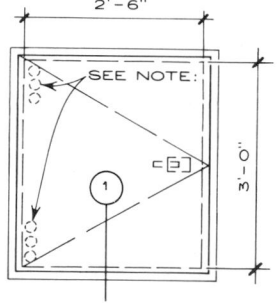

NOTE:

Compression spring operators open smoke hatch instantly when heat breaks 160° fusible link.

Hatches are available in single leaf or double leaf for larger openings.

PLAN OF SMOKE HATCH

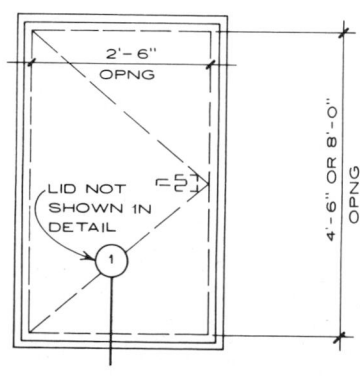

PLAN OF ROOF HATCH

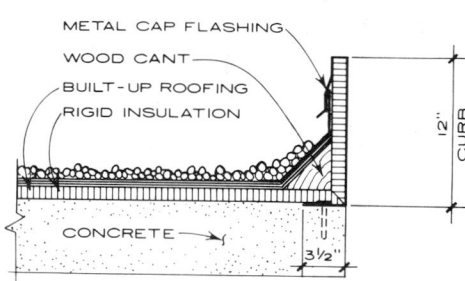

1B DETAIL @ CONCRETE ROOF

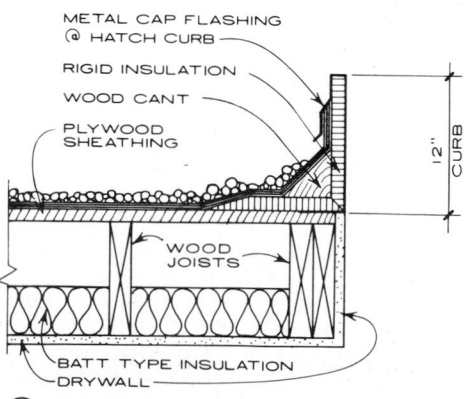

1A DETAIL @ WOOD ROOF

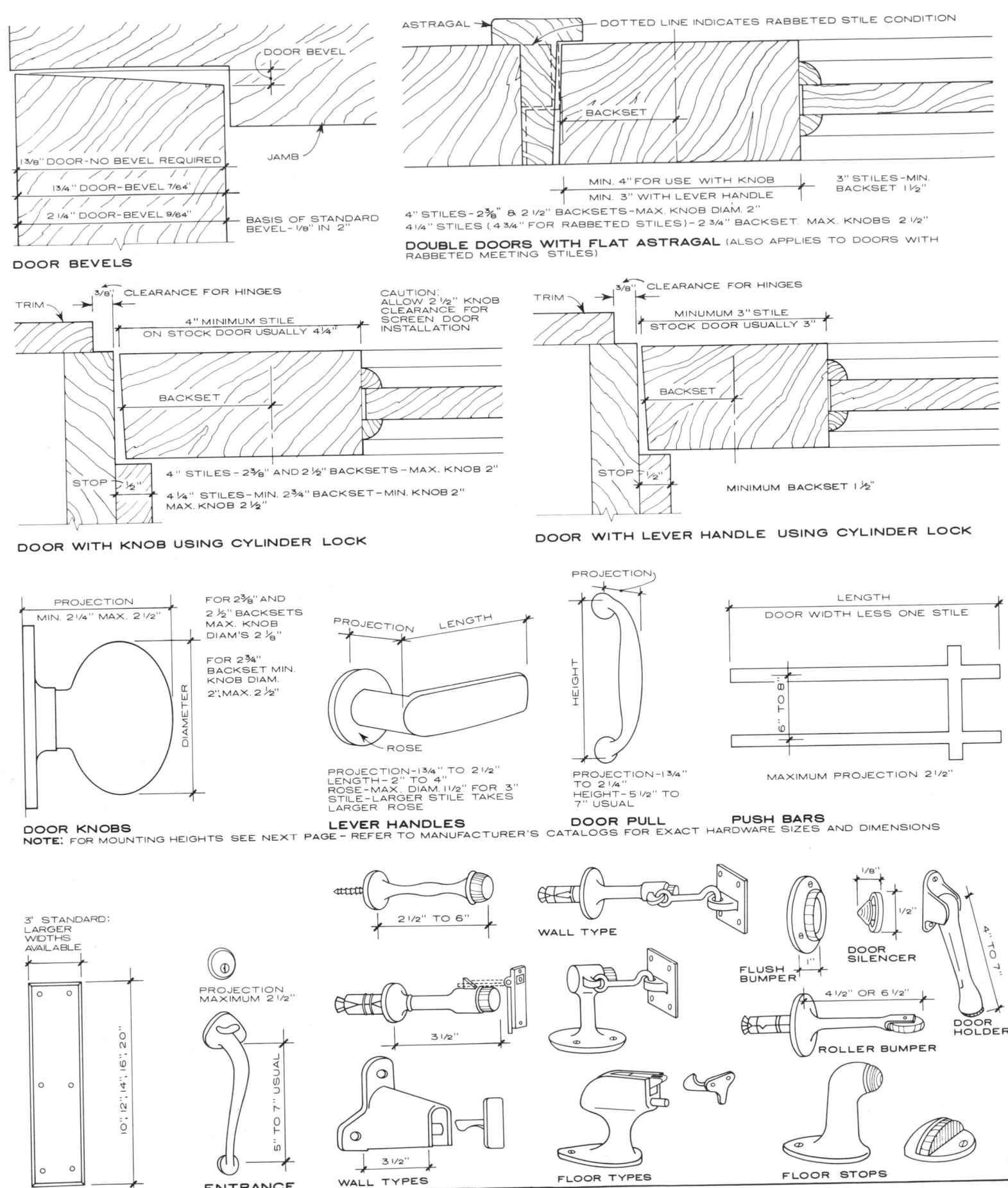

DOOR BEVELS

DOOR BEVEL

DOOR BEVEL

JAMB

1 3/8" DOOR-NO BEVEL REQUIRED

1 3/4" DOOR-BEVEL 7/64"

2 1/4" DOOR-BEVEL 9/64"

BASIS OF STANDARD BEVEL- 1/8" IN 2"

ASTRAGAL

DOTTED LINE INDICATES RABBETED STILE CONDITION

BACKSET

MIN. 4" FOR USE WITH KNOB

MIN. 3" WITH LEVER HANDLE

3" STILES-MIN. BACKSET 1 1/2"

4" STILES-2 3/8" & 2 1/2" BACKSETS-MAX. KNOB DIAM. 2"

4 1/4" STILES (4 3/4" FOR RABBETED STILES)-2 3/4" BACKSET. MAX. KNOBS 2 1/2"

DOUBLE DOORS WITH FLAT ASTRAGAL (ALSO APPLIES TO DOORS WITH RABBETED MEETING STILES)

TRIM

3/8" CLEARANCE FOR HINGES

4" MINIMUM STILE ON STOCK DOOR USUALLY 4 1/4"

CAUTION: ALLOW 2 1/2" KNOB CLEARANCE FOR SCREEN DOOR INSTALLATION

BACKSET

STOP 1 1/2"

4" STILES - 2 3/8" AND 2 1/2" BACKSETS - MAX. KNOB 2"

4 1/4" STILES - MIN. 2 3/4" BACKSET - MIN. KNOB 2" MAX. KNOB 2 1/2"

DOOR WITH KNOB USING CYLINDER LOCK

TRIM

3/8" CLEARANCE FOR HINGES

MINUMUM 3" STILE STOCK DOOR USUALLY 3"

BACKSET

STOP 1 1/2"

MINIMUM BACKSET 1 1/2"

DOOR WITH LEVER HANDLE USING CYLINDER LOCK

PROJECTION MIN. 2 1/4" MAX. 2 1/2"

FOR 2 3/8" AND 2 1/2" BACKSETS MAX. KNOB DIAM'S 2 1/8"

FOR 2 3/4" BACKSET MIN. KNOB DIAM. 2", MAX. 2 1/2"

DIAMETER

DOOR KNOBS

PROJECTION   LENGTH

ROSE

PROJECTION-1 3/4" TO 2 1/2"
LENGTH-2" TO 4"
ROSE-MAX. DIAM. 1 1/2" FOR 3" STILE-LARGER STILE TAKES LARGER ROSE

LEVER HANDLES

PROJECTION

HEIGHT

PROJECTION-1 3/4" TO 2 1/4"
HEIGHT-5 1/2" TO 7" USUAL

DOOR PULL

LENGTH

DOOR WIDTH LESS ONE STILE

6" TO 8"

MAXIMUM PROJECTION 2 1/2"

PUSH BARS

NOTE: FOR MOUNTING HEIGHTS SEE NEXT PAGE – REFER TO MANUFACTURER'S CATALOGS FOR EXACT HARDWARE SIZES AND DIMENSIONS

3" STANDARD: LARGER WIDTHS AVAILABLE

10", 12", 14", 16", 20"

PUSH PLATE

PROJECTION MAXIMUM 2 1/2"

5" TO 7" USUAL

ENTRANCE HANDLE

2 1/2" TO 6"

WALL TYPE

3 1/2"

3 1/2"

WALL TYPES

FLOOR TYPES

FLUSH BUMPER

1"

1/8"

1/2"

DOOR SILENCER

4 1/2" OR 6 1/2"

ROLLER BUMPER

4" TO 7"

DOOR HOLDER

FLOOR STOPS

STOPS AND HOLDERS

F. J. Trost; SMS Partnership, Architects; Stamford, Connecticut

American Society of Architectural Hardware Consultants; Mill Valley, California

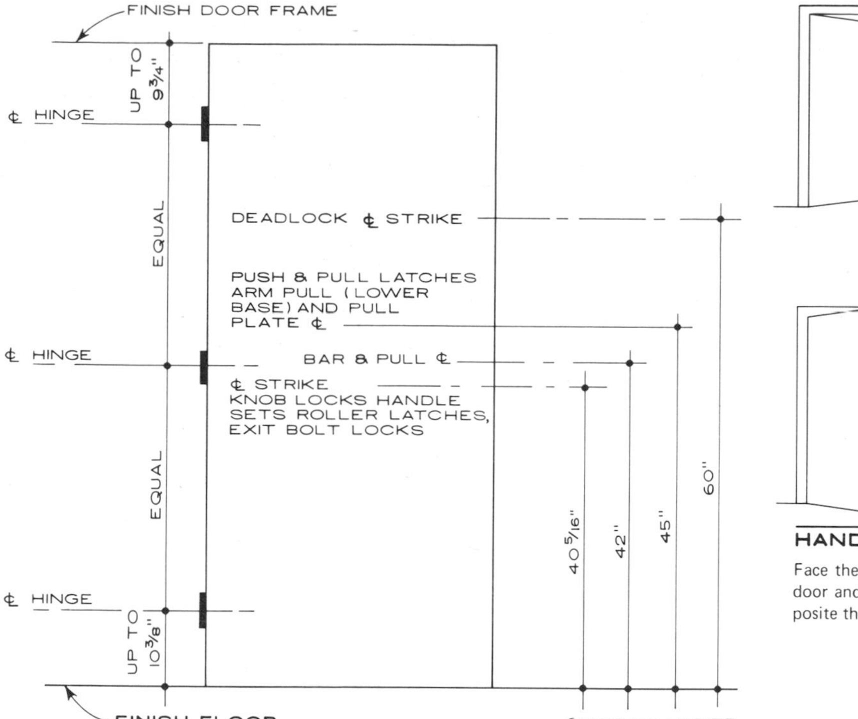
FINISH DOOR FRAME
UP TO 9¾"
℄ HINGE
EQUAL
DEADLOCK ℄ STRIKE
PUSH & PULL LATCHES ARM PULL (LOWER BASE) AND PULL PLATE ℄
℄ HINGE
BAR & PULL ℄
℄ STRIKE KNOB LOCKS HANDLE SETS ROLLER LATCHES, EXIT BOLT LOCKS
EQUAL
60"
45"
42"
40 5/16"
℄ HINGE
UP TO 10⅜"
FINISH FLOOR
MAY BE VARIED TO SUIT NEED OF SPECIFIC INSTALLATIONS

RECOMMENDED DOOR HARDWARE LOCATIONS

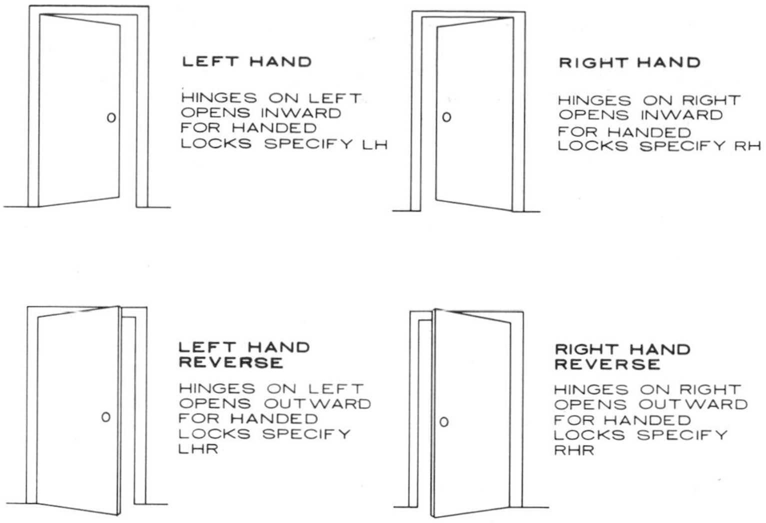
LEFT HAND
HINGES ON LEFT OPENS INWARD FOR HANDED LOCKS SPECIFY LH
RIGHT HAND
HINGES ON RIGHT OPENS INWARD FOR HANDED LOCKS SPECIFY RH
LEFT HAND REVERSE
HINGES ON LEFT OPENS OUTWARD FOR HANDED LOCKS SPECIFY LHR
RIGHT HAND REVERSE
HINGES ON RIGHT OPENS OUTWARD FOR HANDED LOCKS SPECIFY RHR

HANDS OF DOORS

Face the outside of the door to determine its hand. The outside is the street side of an entrance door and the corridor side of a room door. The outside of a communicating door is the side opposite the hinges.

American Standards Association Lock Strikes A–115V–1959 for metal door frames. To determine proper length of lip measure from ℄ of strike to edge of jamb and add 1/4". Outside strike dimensions standard for all lock types shown.

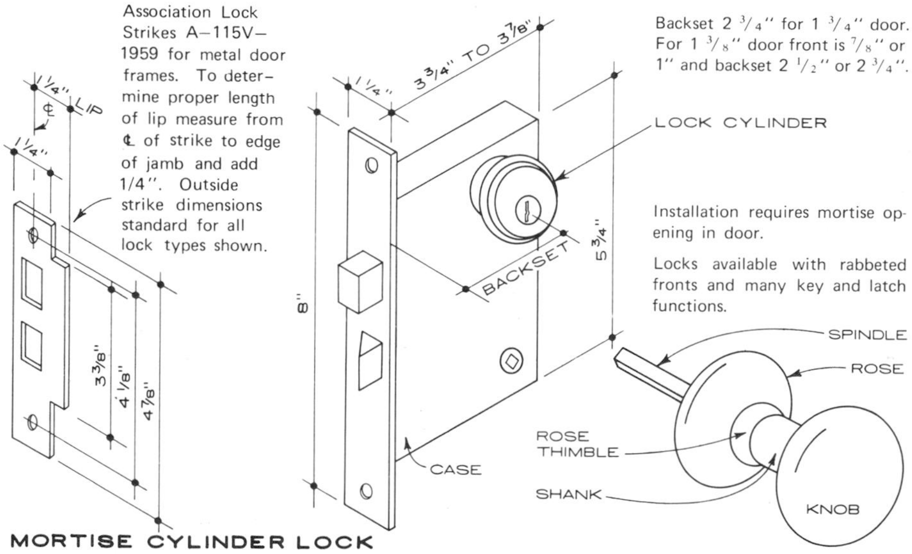
1/4"
LIP
1¼"
3⅜"
4 1/8"
4⅞"
1 1/4"
3¾" TO 3⅞"
8"
BACKSET
5¾"
LOCK CYLINDER
CASE
SPINDLE
ROSE
ROSE THIMBLE
SHANK
KNOB

Backset 2 3/4" for 1 3/4" door. For 1 3/8" door front is 7/8" or 1" and backset 2 1/2" or 2 3/4".

Installation requires mortise opening in door.

Locks available with rabbeted fronts and many key and latch functions.

MORTISE CYLINDER LOCK

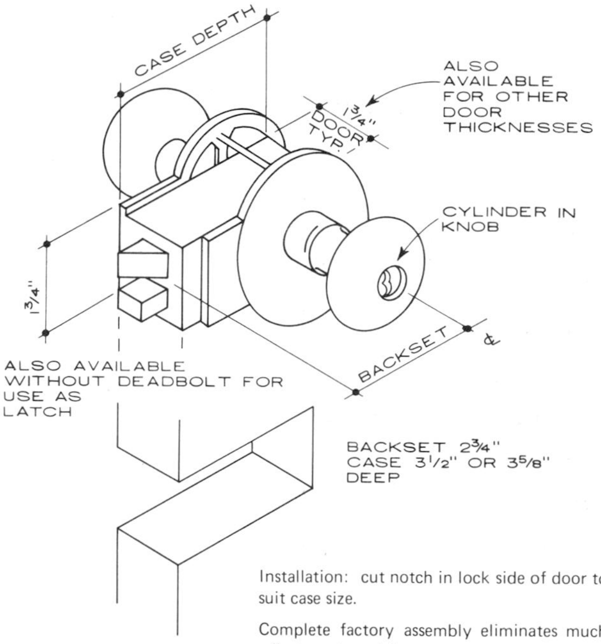
CASE DEPTH
1¾" DOOR TYP.
ALSO AVAILABLE FOR OTHER DOOR THICKNESSES
CYLINDER IN KNOB
1¾"
BACKSET
℄
ALSO AVAILABLE WITHOUT DEADBOLT FOR USE AS LATCH
BACKSET 2¾" CASE 3 1/2" OR 3⅝" DEEP

Installation: cut notch in lock side of door to suit case size.

Complete factory assembly eliminates much adjustment on job.

UNIT LOCK

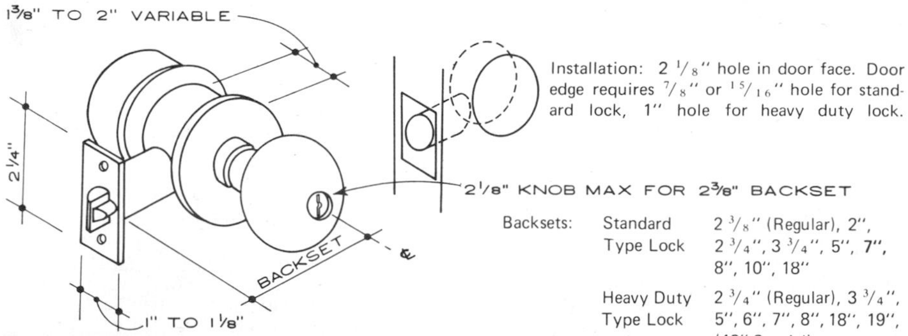
1⅜" TO 2" VARIABLE
2¼"
BACKSET
℄
1" TO 1⅛"
2 1/8" KNOB MAX FOR 2⅜" BACKSET

Installation: 2 1/8" hole in door face. Door edge requires 7/8" or 15/16" hole for standard lock, 1" hole for heavy duty lock.

Backsets:	Standard Type Lock	2 3/8" (Regular), 2", 2 3/4", 3 3/4", 5", 7", 8", 10", 18"
	Heavy Duty Type Lock	2 3/4" (Regular), 3 3/4", 5", 6", 7", 8", 18", 19", (42" Special)

CYLINDRICAL LOCK

Available in standard type (residential & light commercial) & heavy duty-type (institutional commercial)

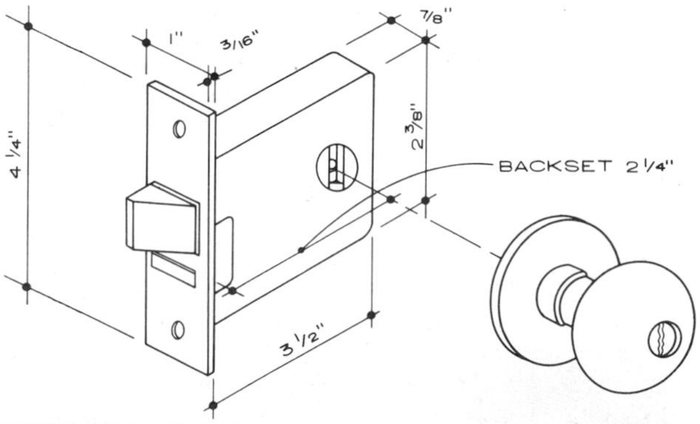
1"
3/16"
7/8"
4 1/4"
2⅜"
BACKSET 2¼"
3 1/2"

INTEGRALOCK

Mortise type installation. Combines features of mortise and cylinder locks.

F. J. Trost; SMS Partnership, Architects; Stamford, Connecticut
American Society of Architectural Hardware Consultants; Mill Valley, California

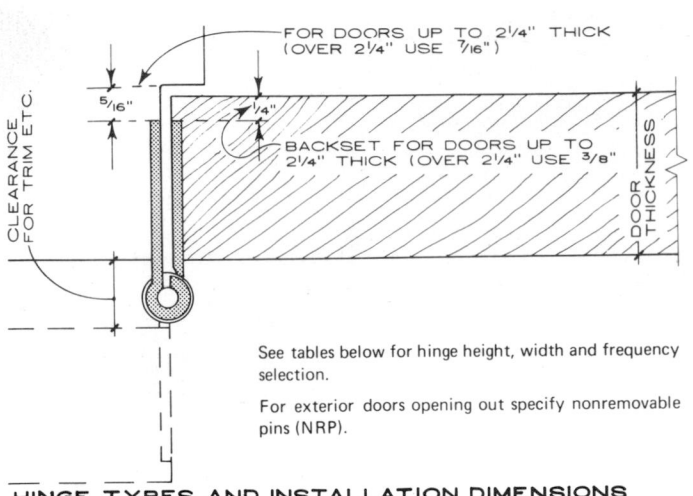

FOR DOORS UP TO 2¼" THICK (OVER 2¼" USE ⁷⁄₁₆")

5/16"

1/4"

BACKSET FOR DOORS UP TO 2¼" THICK (OVER 2¼" USE ³⁄₈")

CLEARANCE FOR TRIM ETC.

DOOR THICKNESS

See tables below for hinge height, width and frequency selection.

For exterior doors opening out specify nonremovable pins (NRP).

HINGE TYPES AND INSTALLATION DIMENSIONS

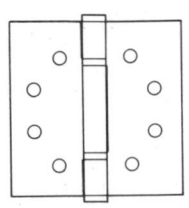

TEMPLATE

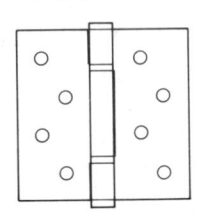

NON-TEMPLATE (FOR WOOD DOORS)

STANDARD FOR ALL HINGES

ROUNDED TO AVOID ATTACHING WEARING APPAREL ETC.

BUTTON TIP   HOSPITAL TIP
CONSULT MANUFACTURERS FOR OTHER AVAILABLE TIPS

NOTE:

1. Use 2 hinges on doors less than 5'—0" high. Add 1 hinge for each additional 2'—6" of door height. Always specify 3 hinges per door.

2. Use ball bearing hinges on doors equipped with closers.

3. Use high frequency hinges on high frequency openings, average frequency hinges on average frequency openings, low frequency hinges on low frequency openings.

4. 2 or 4 ball or oilite bearings available on most hinge types (4 for extra heavy).

HINGE SELECTION TABLES

HINGE HEIGHT—DETERMINED BY DOOR WIDTH AND THICKNESS

DOOR THICKNESS	DOOR WTH.	HINGE HGT.
3/4" to 1 1/8" CABINET	to 24	2 1/2
7/8" & 1 1/8" SCREEN OR COMB.	to 36	3
1 3/8"	to 36	3 1/2
1 3/4"	to 36	4
	over 36-41	4 1/2
	42 to 48	4 1/2*
2", 2 1/4", 2 1/2"	to 42	5
	over 42	6
TRANSOMS		
1 1/4" & 1 3/8"		3
1 3/4"		3 1/2
2", 2 1/4", 2 1/2"		4

NOTE: Height of a hinge is always first dimension not including tips.
* Extra heavy hinges should be specified for heavy doors and doors where high frequency service is expected. Extra heavy hinges should be 4 1/2", 5", & 6" sizes.

HINGE WIDTH—DETERMINED BY DOOR THICKNESS AND CLEARANCE REQUIRED

DOOR THICKNESS	CLEARANCE REQUIRED *	HINGE WIDTH
1 3/8	1 1/4	3 1/2
	1 3/4	4
1 3/4	1	4
	1 1/2	4 1/2
	2	5
	3	6
2	1	4 1/2
	1 1/2	5
	2 1/2	6
2 1/4	1	5
	2	6
2 1/2	3/4	5
	1 3/4	6
3	3/4	6
	2 3/4	8
	4 3/4	10

* NOTE: Clearance is computed for door flush with casing.

FREQUENCY OF DOOR OPERATION

TYPE OF BUILDING AND DOOR	ESTIMATED FREQUENCY		
	DAILY	YEARLY	
LARGE DEPT. STORE ENTRANCE	5,000	1,500,000	HIGH FREQUENCY
LARGE OFFICE BUILDING ENTRANCE	4,000	1,200,000	
THEATER ENTRANCE PERFORMANCE	1,000	450,000	
SCHOOL ENTRANCE	1,250	225,000	
SCHOOL TOILET DOOR	1,250	225,000	
STORE OR BANK ENTRANCE	500	150,000	
OFFICE BUILDING TOILET DOOR	400	118,000	
SCHOOL CORRIDOR DOOR	80	15,000	AVERAGE FREQUENCY
OFFICE BUILDING CORRIDOR DOOR	75	22,000	
STORE TOILET DOOR	60	18,000	
DWELLING ENTRANCE	40	15,000	
DWELLING TOILET DOOR	25	9,000	LOW FREQ.
DWELLING CORRIDOR DOOR	10	3,600	
DWELLING CLOSET DOOR	6	2,200	

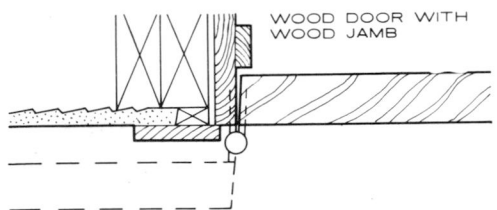

WOOD DOOR WITH WOOD JAMB

FULL MORTISE NON TEMPLATE

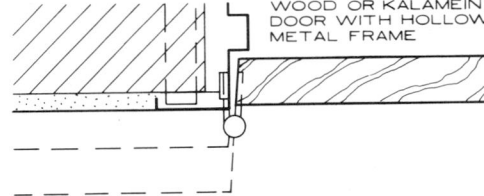

WOOD OR KALAMEIN DOOR WITH HOLLOW METAL FRAME

FULL MORTISE TEMPLATE

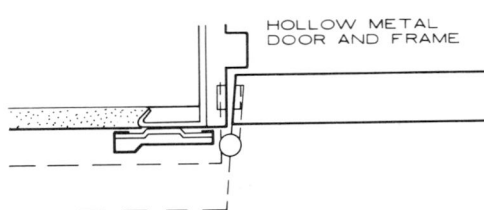

HOLLOW METAL DOOR AND FRAME

FULL MORTISE TEMPLATE

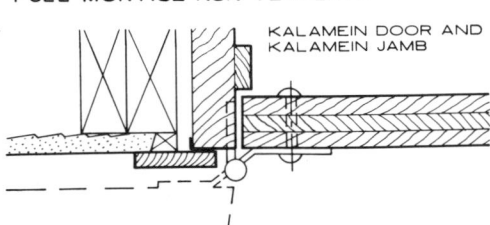

KALAMEIN DOOR AND KALAMEIN JAMB

HALF SURFACE TEMPLATE

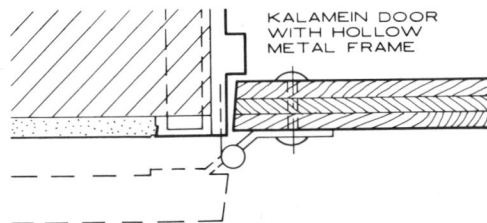

KALAMEIN DOOR WITH HOLLOW METAL FRAME

HALF SURFACE TEMPLATE

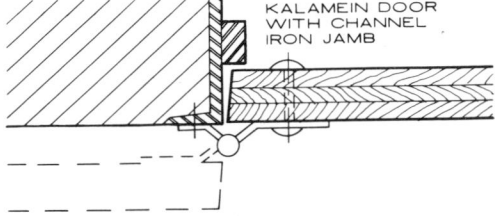

KALAMEIN DOOR WITH CHANNEL IRON JAMB

FULL SURFACE TEMPLATE

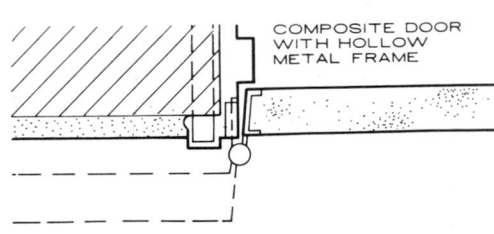

COMPOSITE DOOR WITH HOLLOW METAL FRAME

FULL MORTISE TEMPLATE

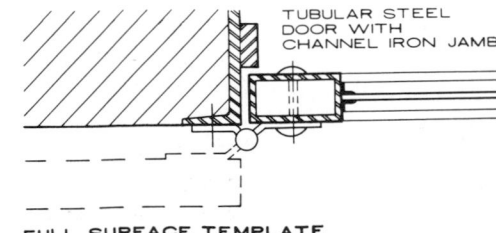

TUBULAR STEEL DOOR WITH CHANNEL IRON JAMB

FULL SURFACE TEMPLATE

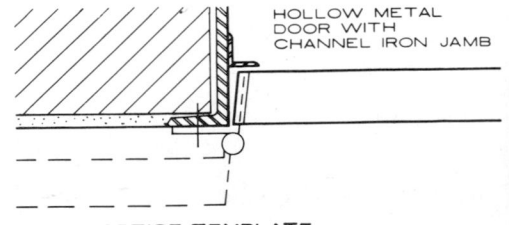

HOLLOW METAL DOOR WITH CHANNEL IRON JAMB

HALF MORTISE TEMPLATE

F. J. Trost; SMS Partnership, Architects; Stamford, Connecticut
American Society of Architectural Hardware Consultants; Mill Valley, California

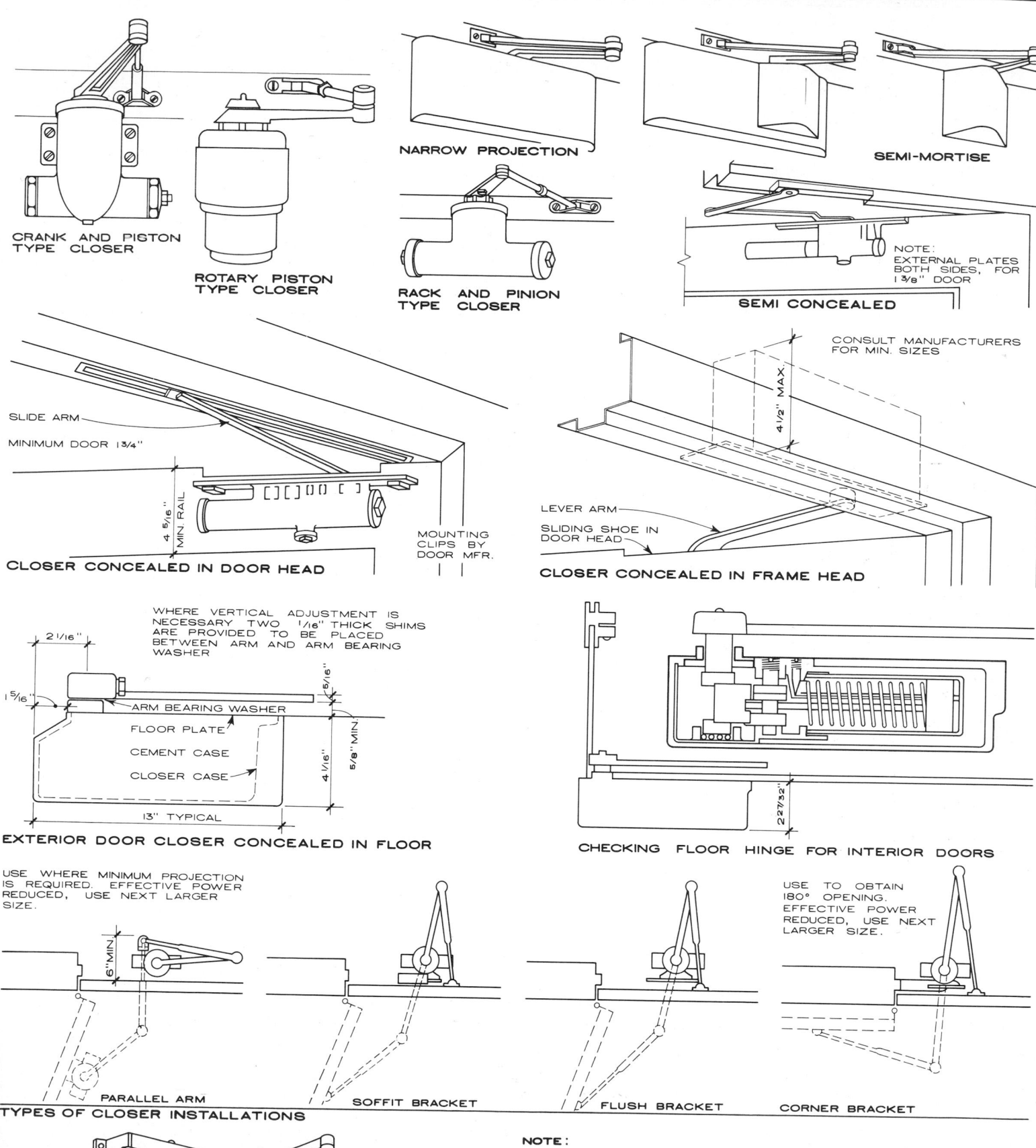

CRANK AND PISTON TYPE CLOSER

ROTARY PISTON TYPE CLOSER

NARROW PROJECTION

RACK AND PINION TYPE CLOSER

SEMI-MORTISE

NOTE: EXTERNAL PLATES BOTH SIDES, FOR 1 3/8" DOOR

SEMI CONCEALED

SLIDE ARM

MINIMUM DOOR 1 3/4"

4 5/16" MIN. RAIL

MOUNTING CLIPS BY DOOR MFR.

CLOSER CONCEALED IN DOOR HEAD

CONSULT MANUFACTURERS FOR MIN. SIZES

4 1/2" MAX.

LEVER ARM

SLIDING SHOE IN DOOR HEAD

CLOSER CONCEALED IN FRAME HEAD

WHERE VERTICAL ADJUSTMENT IS NECESSARY TWO 1/16" THICK SHIMS ARE PROVIDED TO BE PLACED BETWEEN ARM AND ARM BEARING WASHER

2 1/16"

1 5/16"

5/16"

ARM BEARING WASHER

FLOOR PLATE

CEMENT CASE

CLOSER CASE

4 1/16"

5/8" MIN.

13" TYPICAL

EXTERIOR DOOR CLOSER CONCEALED IN FLOOR

22 7/32"

CHECKING FLOOR HINGE FOR INTERIOR DOORS

USE WHERE MINIMUM PROJECTION IS REQUIRED. EFFECTIVE POWER REDUCED, USE NEXT LARGER SIZE.

6" MIN.

PARALLEL ARM

SOFFIT BRACKET

FLUSH BRACKET

USE TO OBTAIN 180° OPENING. EFFECTIVE POWER REDUCED, USE NEXT LARGER SIZE.

CORNER BRACKET

TYPES OF CLOSER INSTALLATIONS

PROVIDES MAXIMUM HEADROOM

TOP JAMB INSTALLATION

NOTE:

For functions, size tables, dimensions and application of all types of closing devices, refer to manufacturers catalogs.

CAUTION

Check headroom on brackets for low projection.

F. J. Trost; SMS Partnership, Architects; Stamford, Connecticut
American Society of Architectural Hardware Consultants; Mill Valley, California

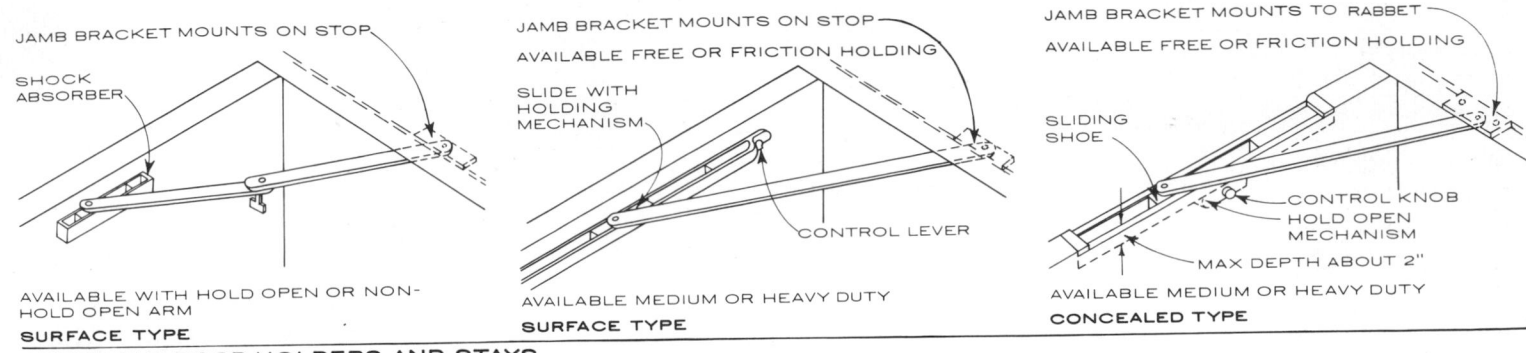

JAMB BRACKET MOUNTS ON STOP

SHOCK ABSORBER

AVAILABLE WITH HOLD OPEN OR NON-HOLD OPEN ARM

SURFACE TYPE

JAMB BRACKET MOUNTS ON STOP

AVAILABLE FREE OR FRICTION HOLDING

SLIDE WITH HOLDING MECHANISM

CONTROL LEVER

AVAILABLE MEDIUM OR HEAVY DUTY

SURFACE TYPE

JAMB BRACKET MOUNTS TO RABBET

AVAILABLE FREE OR FRICTION HOLDING

SLIDING SHOE

CONTROL KNOB
HOLD OPEN MECHANISM

MAX DEPTH ABOUT 2"

AVAILABLE MEDIUM OR HEAVY DUTY

CONCEALED TYPE

OVERHEAD DOOR HOLDERS AND STAYS

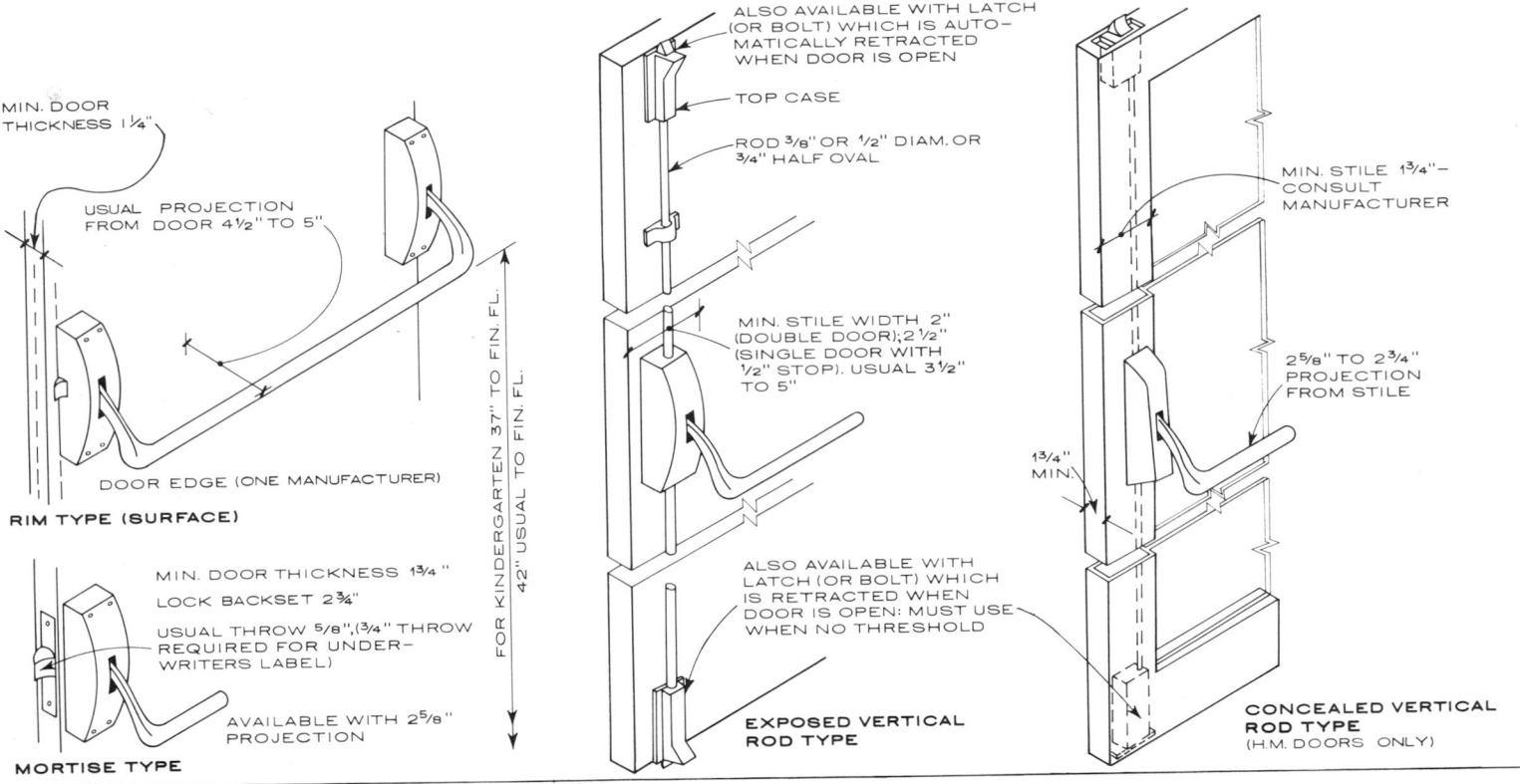

MIN. DOOR THICKNESS 1¼"

USUAL PROJECTION FROM DOOR 4½" TO 5"

DOOR EDGE (ONE MANUFACTURER)

RIM TYPE (SURFACE)

MIN. DOOR THICKNESS 1¾"

LOCK BACKSET 2¾"

USUAL THROW ⅝",(¾" THROW REQUIRED FOR UNDER-WRITERS LABEL)

AVAILABLE WITH 2⅝" PROJECTION

MORTISE TYPE

FOR KINDERGARTEN 37" TO FIN. FL.
42" USUAL TO FIN. FL.

ALSO AVAILABLE WITH LATCH (OR BOLT) WHICH IS AUTO-MATICALLY RETRACTED WHEN DOOR IS OPEN

TOP CASE

ROD ⅜" OR ½" DIAM. OR ¾" HALF OVAL

MIN. STILE WIDTH 2" (DOUBLE DOOR);2½" (SINGLE DOOR WITH ½" STOP). USUAL 3½" TO 5"

ALSO AVAILABLE WITH LATCH (OR BOLT) WHICH IS RETRACTED WHEN DOOR IS OPEN: MUST USE WHEN NO THRESHOLD

EXPOSED VERTICAL ROD TYPE

MIN. STILE 1¾"-CONSULT MANUFACTURER

2⅝" TO 2¾" PROJECTION FROM STILE

1¾" MIN.

CONCEALED VERTICAL ROD TYPE
(H.M. DOORS ONLY)

PANIC EXIT MECHANISMS

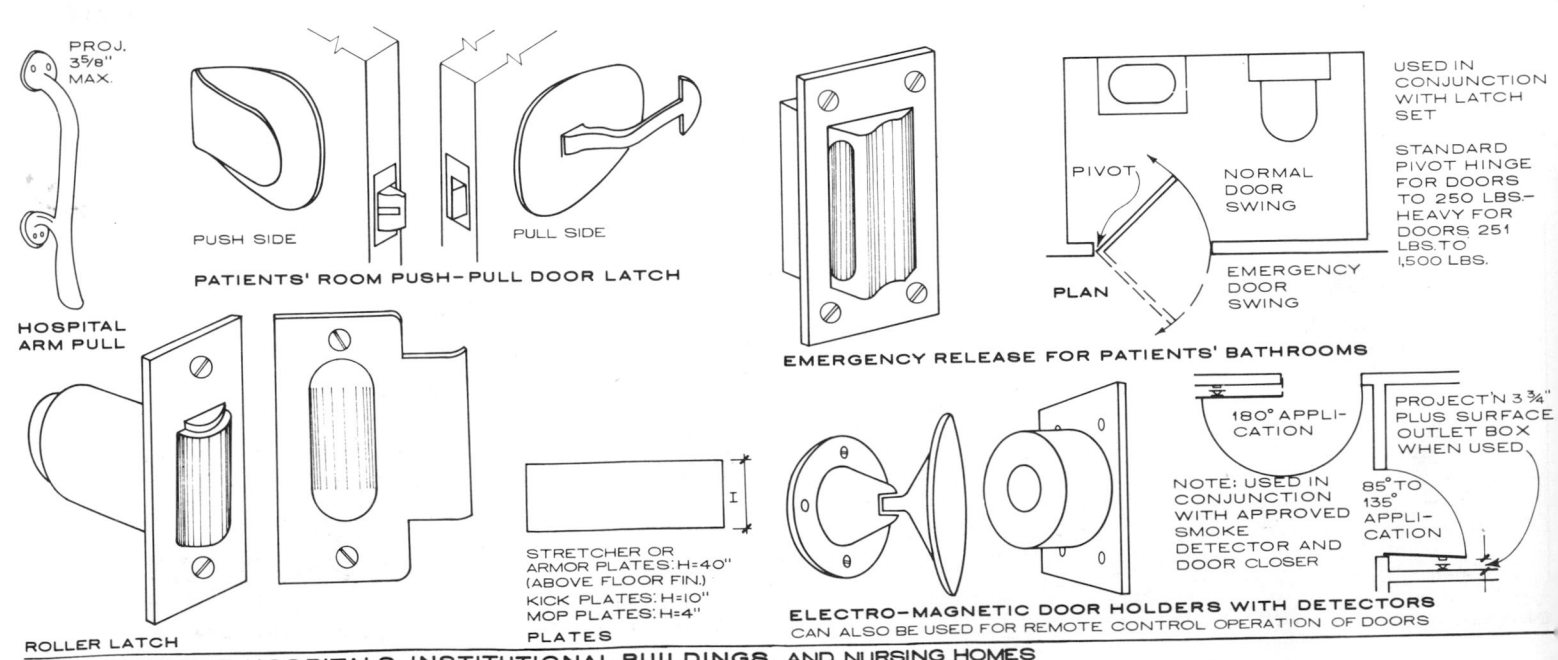

PROJ. 3⅝" MAX.

HOSPITAL ARM PULL

PUSH SIDE

PULL SIDE

PATIENTS' ROOM PUSH-PULL DOOR LATCH

EMERGENCY RELEASE FOR PATIENTS' BATHROOMS

PIVOT

NORMAL DOOR SWING

PLAN

EMERGENCY DOOR SWING

USED IN CONJUNCTION WITH LATCH SET

STANDARD PIVOT HINGE FOR DOORS TO 250 LBS-HEAVY FOR DOORS 251 LBS.TO 1,500 LBS.

STRETCHER OR ARMOR PLATES: H=40" (ABOVE FLOOR FIN.)
KICK PLATES: H=10"
MOP PLATES: H=4"

PLATES

ROLLER LATCH

ELECTRO-MAGNETIC DOOR HOLDERS WITH DETECTORS
CAN ALSO BE USED FOR REMOTE CONTROL OPERATION OF DOORS

NOTE: USED IN CONJUNCTION WITH APPROVED SMOKE DETECTOR AND DOOR CLOSER

180° APPLI-CATION

85° TO 135° APPLI-CATION

PROJECT'N 3¾" PLUS SURFACE OUTLET BOX WHEN USED

HARDWARE FOR HOSPITALS, INSTITUTIONAL BUILDINGS, AND NURSING HOMES

F. J. Trost; SMS Partnership, Architects; Stamford, Connecticut
American Society of Architectural Hardware Consultants; Mill Valley, California

HARDWARE SYMBOLS & FINISHES

SYMBOL	FINISH
USP	Primed For Painting
US 3	Bright Brass
US 4	Dull Brass
US 10	Dull Bronze
US 10B	Dull Bronze, Oxidized And Oil Rubbed
US 14	Nickel Plated, Bright
US 26	Chromium Plated, Bright
US 26D	Chromium Plated, Dull
US 27	Satin Aluminum, Lacquered
US 28	Satin Aluminum, Anodized
US 32	Stainless Steel, Polished
US 32D	Stainless Steel, Dull

NOTE:

Finishes noted are federal approved with samples on file (except US 10 B — no sample). For other finishes consult manufacturers.

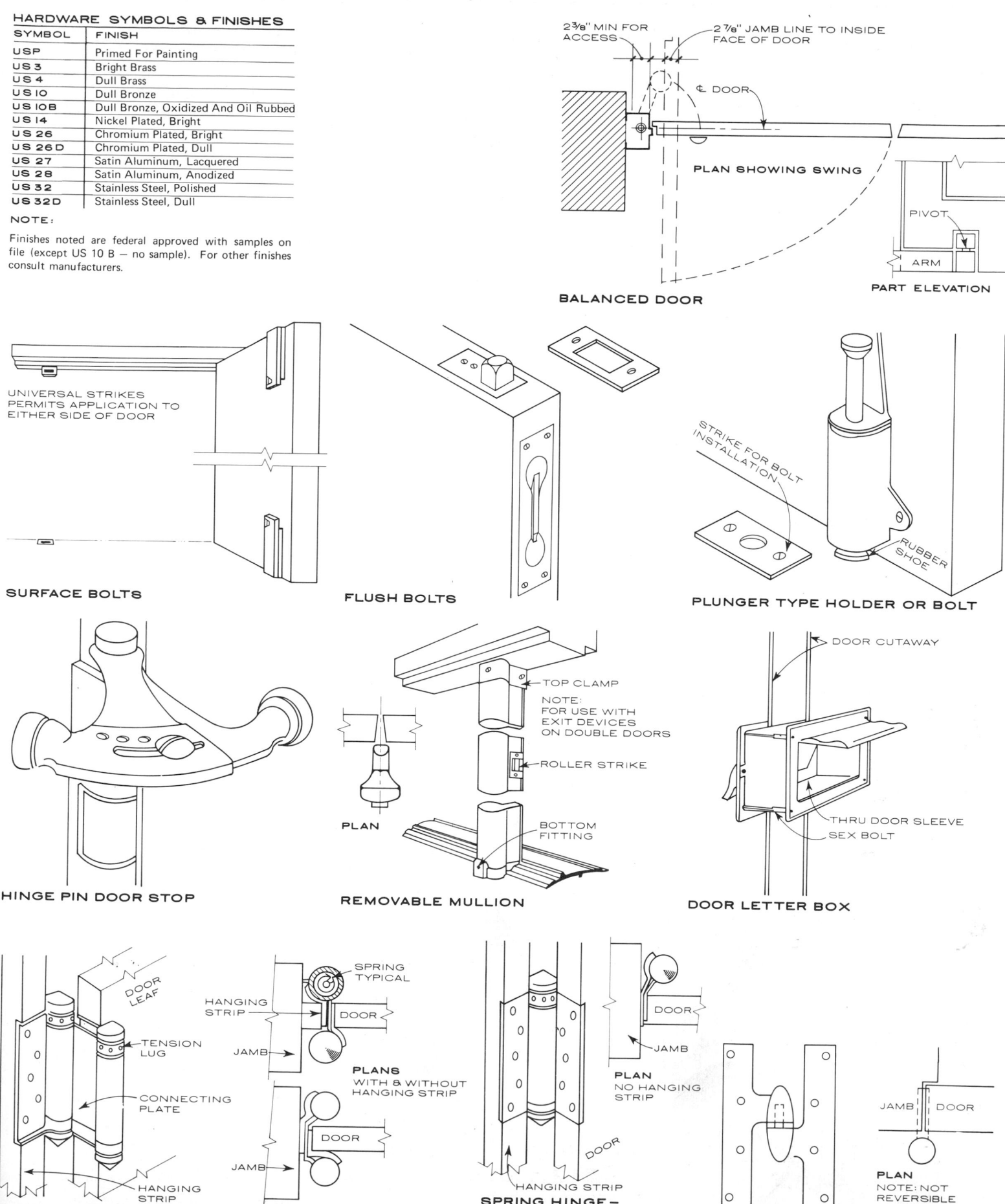

BALANCED DOOR

PART ELEVATION

SURFACE BOLTS

FLUSH BOLTS

PLUNGER TYPE HOLDER OR BOLT

HINGE PIN DOOR STOP

REMOVABLE MULLION

DOOR LETTER BOX

SPRING HINGE—DOUBLE ACTING

SPRING HINGE— SINGLE ACTING

OLIVE KNUCKLE HINGE

F. J. Trost; SMS Partnership, Architects; Stamford, Connecticut

American Society of Architectural Hardware Consultants; Mill Valley, California

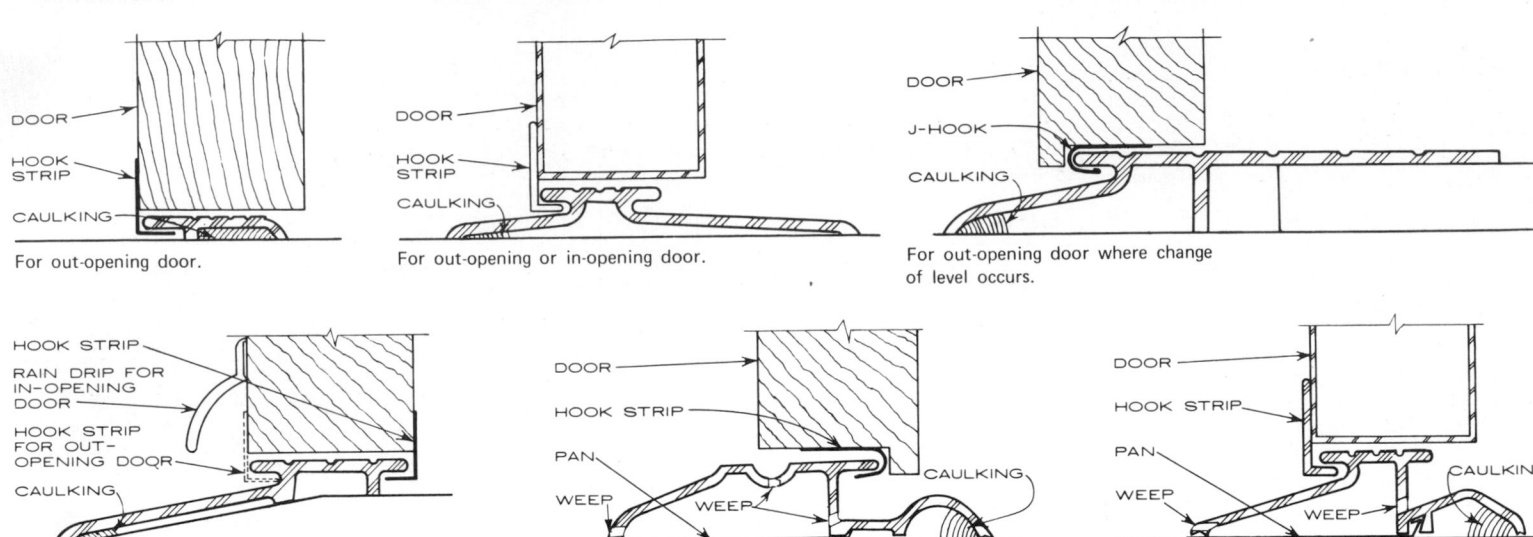

DOOR
HOOK STRIP
CAULKING

For out-opening door.

DOOR
HOOK STRIP
CAULKING

For out-opening or in-opening door.

DOOR
J-HOOK
CAULKING

For out-opening door where change of level occurs.

HOOK STRIP
RAIN DRIP FOR IN-OPENING DOOR
HOOK STRIP FOR OUT-OPENING DOOR
CAULKING

For in-opening door (as shown) and out-opening door where change of level occurs.

DOOR
HOOK STRIP
PAN
WEEP
WEEP
CAULKING

For in-opening door.

DOOR
HOOK STRIP
PAN
WEEP
WEEP
CAULKING

For out-opening door.

INTERLOCKING THRESHOLDS

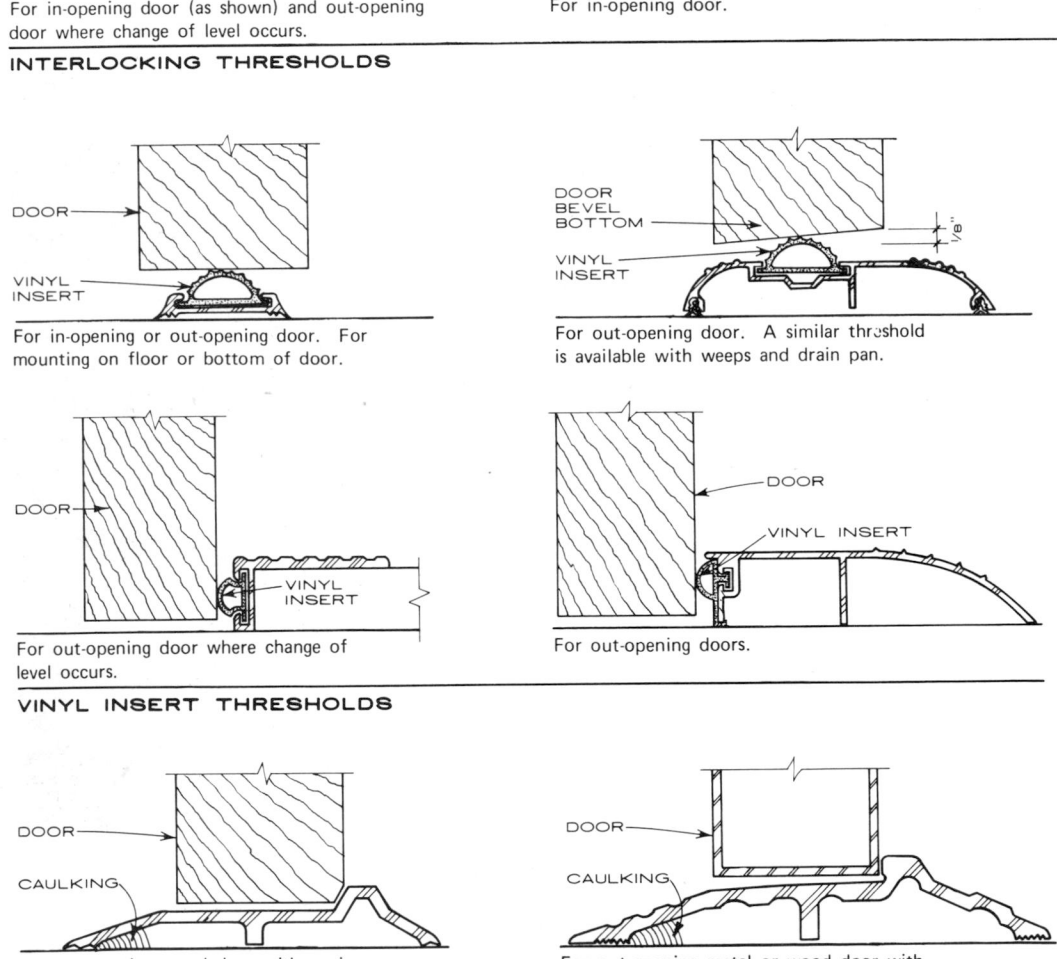

DOOR
VINYL INSERT

For in-opening or out-opening door. For mounting on floor or bottom of door.

DOOR BEVEL BOTTOM
VINYL INSERT

For out-opening door. A similar threshold is available with weeps and drain pan.

DOOR
VINYL INSERT

For out-opening door where change of level occurs.

DOOR
VINYL INSERT

For out-opening doors.

VINYL INSERT THRESHOLDS

DOOR
CAULKING

For out-opening wood door with panic exit hardware.

DOOR
CAULKING

For out-opening metal or wood door with panic hardware.

LATCH TRACK THRESHOLDS

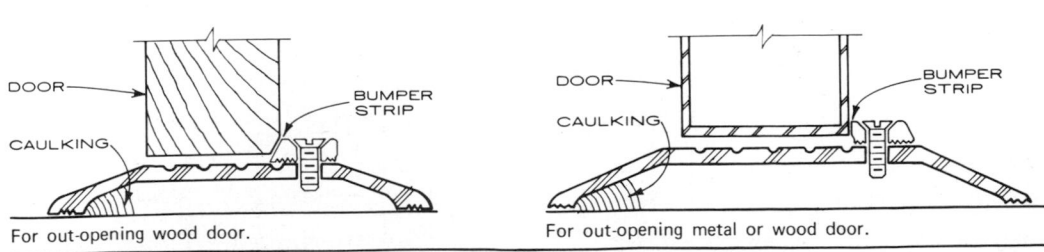

DOOR
BUMPER STRIP
CAULKING

For out-opening wood door.

DOOR
BUMPER STRIP
CAULKING

For out-opening metal or wood door.

FLAT SADDLE THRESHOLDS

Dan Cowling and Associates, Inc.; Little Rock, Arkansas

EXTRUDED METAL   ROLLED METAL

SURFACE HOOKS

EXTRUDED METAL

ROLLED METAL

CONCEALED HOOKS

INTERLOCKING HOOK STRIPS

SCALE: FULL SIZE

NOTE:

Hook strips are available in aluminum, brass, bronze, and zinc, and vary in thickness and dimensions. Consult manufacturers catalogs.

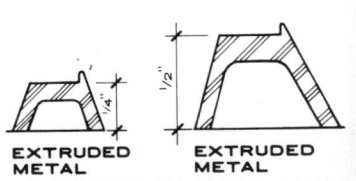

EXTRUDED METAL   EXTRUDED METAL

THRESHOLD ELEVATORS

SCALE: FULL SIZE

NOTE:

Available in alum. and bronze. Consult manufacturers' catalogs.

GENERAL NOTE:

Thresholds are available in bronze and aluminum with a wide selection of shapes and dimensions.

All scales $1/2$ full size, except as noted.

NOTE:

Threshold profiles vary from mfr. to mfr. Consult mfr. catalog for additional sizes. Std. length is 18' to 20' or saddles may be cut to size. Anchors to wood floors are screws; to terrazzo or cement floors, screws in fiber plugs or expansive metal anchors; to concrete, screws tapped to clips set in concrete.

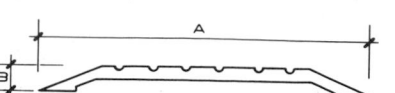

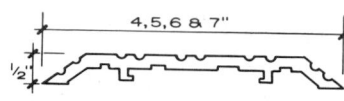

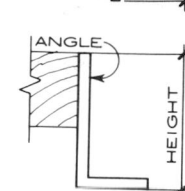

FLOOR TILE / HEIGHT

ANGLE / HEIGHT

JOINT STRIP

Used for division of floors of different materials

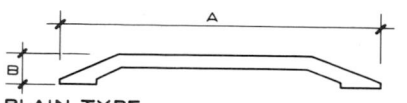

PLAIN TYPE

BRASS		ALUMINUM				BRONZE	
A	B	A	B	A	B	A	B
3"	1/4"	4 5/64"	3/32"	4"		2 1/2 & 3	1/4"
2 1/4"	3/16"	2 1/4"	3/16"	4 5/64"	1/2"	4, 5	
4, 5 & 6	1/2"	2 1/2, 3"	1/4"	5 & 6		& 6	1/2"
		2 1/4"	3/16"	4"	7/16"		

FLUTED TYPES

BRASS		ALUM.		BRONZE		STEEL	
A	B	A	B	A	B	A	B
3, 3 1/2		3, 4		3	5/16"	3 & 4	1/2"
4, 5	1/2"	5, 6		3	3/8"	5 1/2	9/16"
& 6		6 1/4"	1/2"	4, 4 1/2		5 1/2	
		7		5, 6	1/2"	& 7	5/8"
		7 1/2		& 7			
		3, 4	5/8"	6 & 7	5/8"		
		5 & 6					

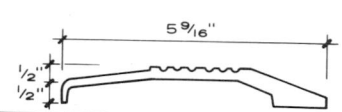

PLAIN AND FLUTED SADDLES AND JOINT STRIPS FOR INTERIORS

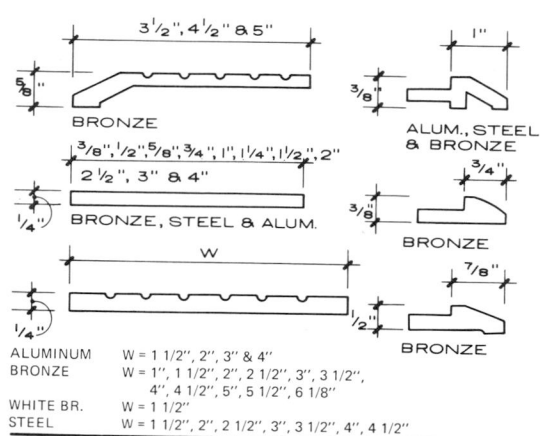

BRONZE — 3 1/2", 4 1/2" & 5"

ALUM., STEEL & BRONZE

BRONZE, STEEL & ALUM. — 3/8", 1/2", 5/8", 3/4", 1", 1 1/4", 1 1/2", 2", 2 1/2", 3" & 4"

BRONZE

BRONZE

ALUMINUM	W = 1 1/2", 2", 3" & 4"
BRONZE	W = 1", 1 1/2", 2", 2 1/2", 3", 3 1/2", 4", 4 1/2", 5", 5 1/2", 6 1/8"
WHITE BR.	W = 1 1/2"
STEEL	W = 1 1/2", 2", 2 1/2", 3", 3 1/2", 4", 4 1/2"

ASSEMBLED SADDLED COMPONENTS

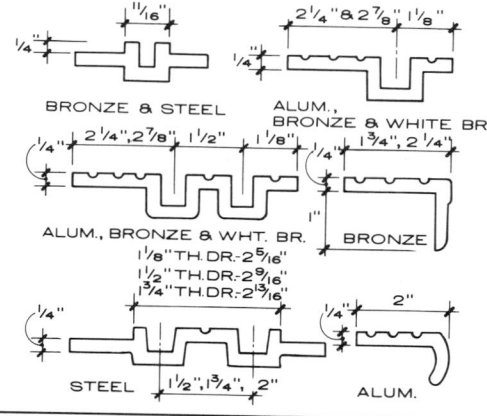

BRONZE & STEEL

ALUM., BRONZE & WHITE BR.

ALUM., BRONZE & WHT. BR.
1 1/8" TH. DR.-2 5/16"
1 1/2" TH. DR.-2 9/16"
1 3/4" TH. DR.-2 13/16"

BRONZE — 1 3/4", 2 1/4"

STEEL — 1/2", 1 3/4", 2"

ALUM. — 2"

SLIDING DOOR SADDLE COMPONENTS

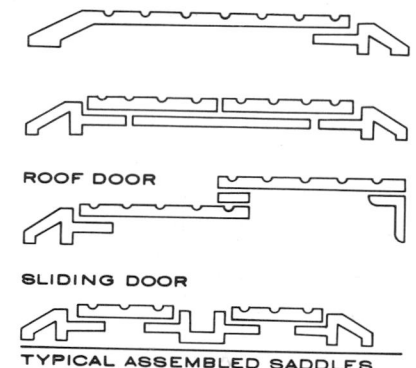

ROOF DOOR

SLIDING DOOR

TYPICAL ASSEMBLED SADDLES

By combining component saddles may be made to any width, joints will not show as flutes, pattern is identical

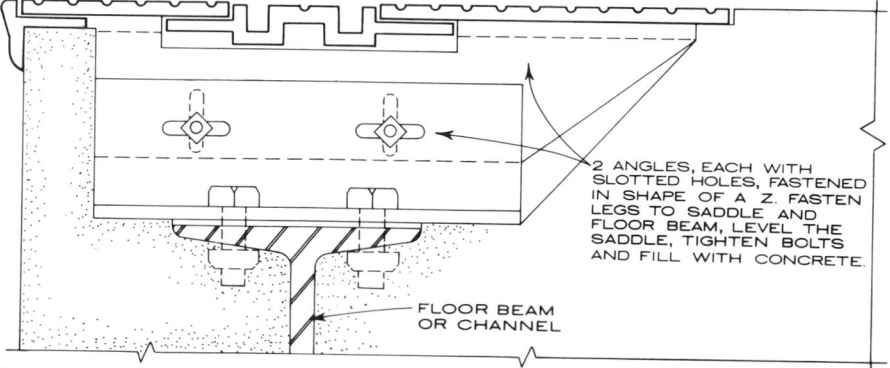

2 ANGLES, EACH WITH SLOTTED HOLES, FASTENED IN SHAPE OF A Z. FASTEN LEGS TO SADDLE AND FLOOR BEAM, LEVEL THE SADDLE, TIGHTEN BOLTS AND FILL WITH CONCRETE.

FLOOR BEAM OR CHANNEL

ELEVATOR SADDLE CONSTRUCTION
SCALE: 3" = 1'-0"

THRESHOLD — CUTOUT — WALL

WALL — THRESHOLD

CUTOUT

CUTOUT FOR FLOOR HINGES
SCALE: 3/4" = 1'-0"

Threshold assemblies may also be cut or notched to fit mullions or columns.

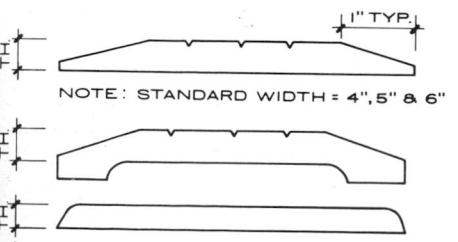

1" TYP.

NOTE: STANDARD WIDTH = 4", 5" & 6"

RECOMMENDED PRACTICE

TH.	IRON	BRONZE	ALUMINUM	NICKEL
1/4		to 6" wide	to 10" wide	to 6" wide
5/16	to 6" wide	to 10" wide	to 18" wide	to 10" wide
3/8	to 12" wide	to 18" wide	to 24" wide	to 14" wide
7/16	to 24" wide	to 24" wide	to 36" wide	to 18" wide
1/2	to 30" wide	to 30" wide	to 42" wide	to 24" wide
5/8	to 42" wide	to 42" wide	to 42" wide	to 30" wide
3/4	to 42" wide	to 42" wide	to 42" wide	to 30" wide

length to 9'-6". When width exceeds 32" length should not exceed 7'-6".

CAST METAL ABRASIVE SURFACE SADDLES

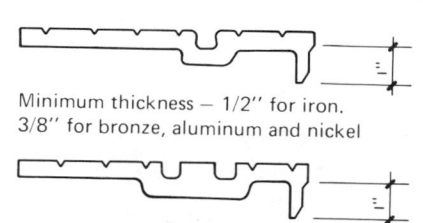

Minimum thickness — 1/2" for iron. 3/8" for bronze, aluminum and nickel

ELEVATOR DOOR SADDLE

Saddles with floor hinge cut-outs, as shown above also available.

Dan Cowling and Associates, Inc.; Little Rock, Arkansas

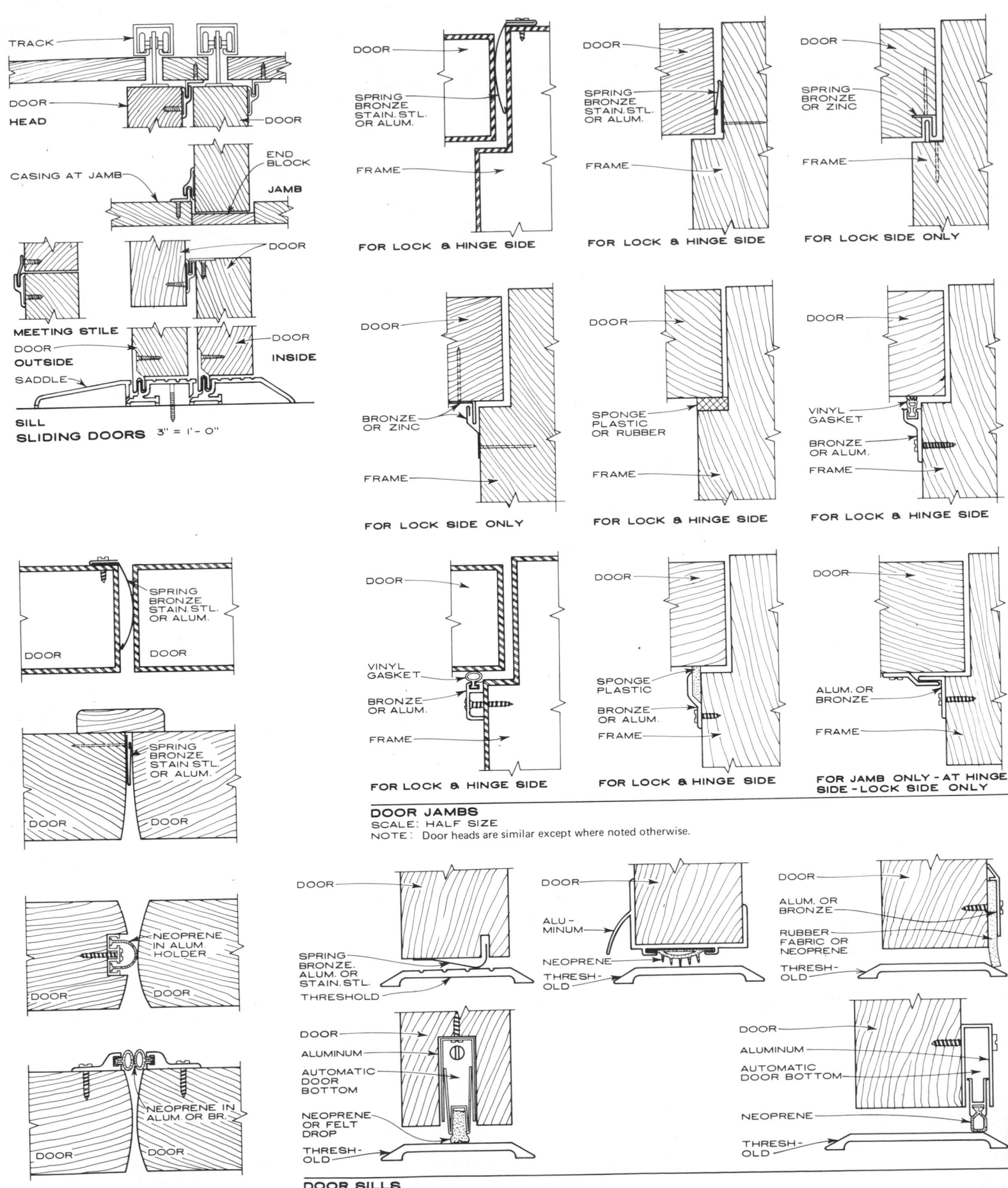

TRACK

DOOR

HEAD

CASING AT JAMB

END BLOCK

JAMB

DOOR

MEETING STILE

DOOR

OUTSIDE

INSIDE

DOOR

SADDLE

SILL

SLIDING DOORS 3" = 1'-0"

DOOR

SPRING BRONZE STAIN. STL. OR ALUM.

FRAME

FOR LOCK & HINGE SIDE

DOOR

SPRING BRONZE STAIN. STL. OR ALUM.

FRAME

FOR LOCK & HINGE SIDE

DOOR

SPRING BRONZE OR ZINC

FRAME

FOR LOCK SIDE ONLY

DOOR

BRONZE OR ZINC

FRAME

FOR LOCK SIDE ONLY

DOOR

SPONGE PLASTIC OR RUBBER

FRAME

FOR LOCK & HINGE SIDE

DOOR

VINYL GASKET

BRONZE OR ALUM.

FRAME

FOR LOCK & HINGE SIDE

DOOR

VINYL GASKET

BRONZE OR ALUM.

FRAME

FOR LOCK & HINGE SIDE

DOOR

SPONGE PLASTIC

BRONZE OR ALUM.

FRAME

FOR LOCK & HINGE SIDE

DOOR

ALUM. OR BRONZE

FRAME

FOR JAMB ONLY - AT HINGE SIDE - LOCK SIDE ONLY

DOOR JAMBS
SCALE: HALF SIZE
NOTE: Door heads are similar except where noted otherwise.

SPRING BRONZE STAIN. STL. OR ALUM.

DOOR

DOOR

SPRING BRONZE STAIN STL. OR ALUM.

DOOR

DOOR

NEOPRENE IN ALUM. HOLDER

DOOR

DOOR

NEOPRENE IN ALUM. OR BR.

DOOR

DOOR

MEETING STILES

DOOR

SPRING BRONZE. ALUM. OR STAIN. STL.

THRESHOLD

DOOR

ALUMINUM

NEOPRENE

THRESHOLD

DOOR

ALUM. OR BRONZE

RUBBER FABRIC OR NEOPRENE

THRESHOLD

DOOR

ALUMINUM

AUTOMATIC DOOR BOTTOM

NEOPRENE OR FELT DROP

THRESHOLD

DOOR

ALUMINUM

AUTOMATIC DOOR BOTTOM

NEOPRENE

THRESHOLD

DOOR SILLS
SCALE: HALF SIZE

Dan Cowling and Associates, Inc.; Little Rock, Arkansas

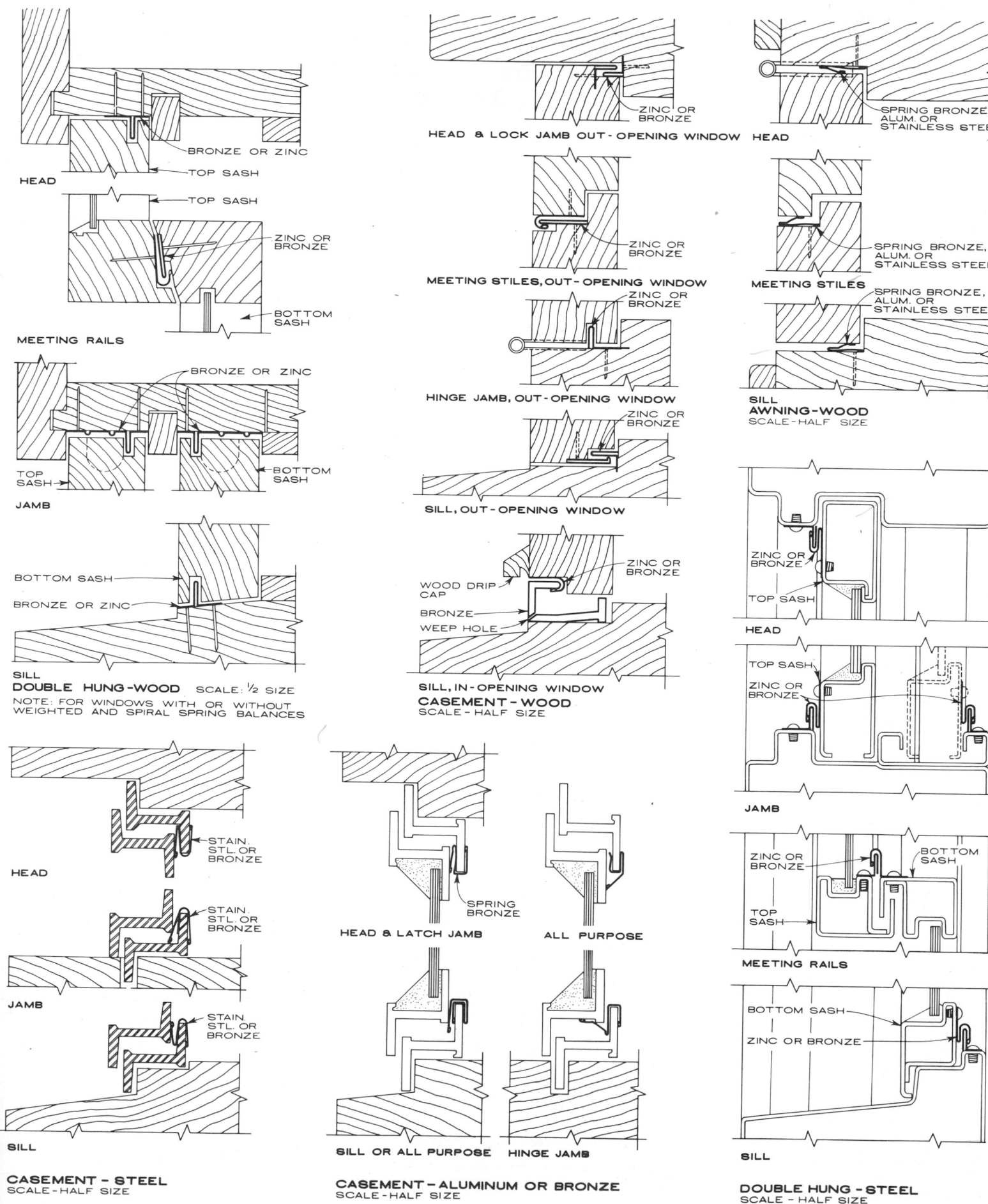

HEAD

BRONZE OR ZINC
TOP SASH

TOP SASH

MEETING RAILS

ZINC OR BRONZE

BOTTOM SASH

BRONZE OR ZINC

TOP SASH

JAMB

BOTTOM SASH

BOTTOM SASH

BRONZE OR ZINC

SILL
DOUBLE HUNG-WOOD SCALE: 1/2 SIZE
NOTE: FOR WINDOWS WITH OR WITHOUT WEIGHTED AND SPIRAL SPRING BALANCES

ZINC OR BRONZE
HEAD & LOCK JAMB OUT-OPENING WINDOW

ZINC OR BRONZE
MEETING STILES, OUT-OPENING WINDOW

ZINC OR BRONZE
HINGE JAMB, OUT-OPENING WINDOW

ZINC OR BRONZE
SILL, OUT-OPENING WINDOW

ZINC OR BRONZE
WOOD DRIP CAP
BRONZE
WEEP HOLE
SILL, IN-OPENING WINDOW
CASEMENT-WOOD
SCALE-HALF SIZE

SPRING BRONZE, ALUM. OR STAINLESS STEEL
WINDOW HEAD

SPRING BRONZE, ALUM. OR STAINLESS STEEL
MEETING STILES

SPRING BRONZE, ALUM. OR STAINLESS STEEL

SILL
AWNING-WOOD
SCALE-HALF SIZE

ZINC OR BRONZE
TOP SASH
HEAD

TOP SASH
ZINC OR BRONZE
JAMB

ZINC OR BRONZE
BOTTOM SASH
TOP SASH
MEETING RAILS

BOTTOM SASH
ZINC OR BRONZE
SILL
DOUBLE HUNG -STEEL
SCALE - HALF SIZE

HEAD
STAIN. STL. OR BRONZE

STAIN. STL. OR BRONZE
JAMB

STAIN. STL. OR BRONZE

SILL
CASEMENT - STEEL
SCALE-HALF SIZE

SPRING BRONZE
HEAD & LATCH JAMB
ALL PURPOSE

SILL OR ALL PURPOSE
HINGE JAMB
CASEMENT-ALUMINUM OR BRONZE
SCALE-HALF SIZE

Dan Cowling and Associates, Inc.; Little Rock, Arkansas

GENERAL NOTES:

1. The word "window," as used in the following pages, includes the frame as well as fixed and movable units within the frame.

2. All dimensions are window dimensions (W.D.) unless otherwise noted.

3. A ventilator is a movable unit of a window, vertical or horizontal, hinged or pivoted.

4. Size of any single glass area is determined by:
A. the location of window
B. the strength of glass
C. the manufacturer's standards.

5. Windows may be obtained which vary from the standard sizes shown; in this case consult manufacturer for possible changes in details and price.

6. "Western" refers to the states of California, Oregon, Utah, Washington, Idaho, Nevada, and Arizona.

7. "Eastern" refers to states other than the "Western" states.

8. Number of muntins shown is not standard, but may vary in number and size.

9. Aluminum window classification:
A. The Architectural Aluminum Manufacturer's Association (AAMA) designates all windows as either Architectural or Residential. Architectural refers to windows suitable for either commercial or monumental type buildings; Residential refers to windows suitable for residential type buildings only.
B. Alloy, thickness, weight and shape vary among manufacturers, but all windows must meet minimum AAMA

test specifications in order to be certified in either of the two categories. No simple chart (as shown below for steel) is available for aluminum.

STEEL WINDOW CLASSIFICATION BY THE STEEL WINDOW INSTITUTE:

	MINIMUM DEPTH OF ANY FRAMING MEMBER (INCHES)	MINIMUM WEIGHT OF WINDOW (LBS./LINEAL/FOOT) OR MINIMUM THICKNESS OF ANY SECTION THROUGH WINDOW (INCHES)
STANDARD INTERMEDIATE	$1\frac{1}{4}$	3.0
HEAVY INTERMEDIATE	$1\frac{5}{16}$	3.5
HEAVY CUSTOM	$1\frac{1}{2}$	4.2
RESIDENTIAL	1	2
ARCHITECTURAL PROJECTED	$1\frac{3}{8}$	$\frac{1}{8}$

10. All elevations are shown from the outside. In vertical sections, the outside of the building is shown to the left; in horizontal sections, the outside is below the detail.

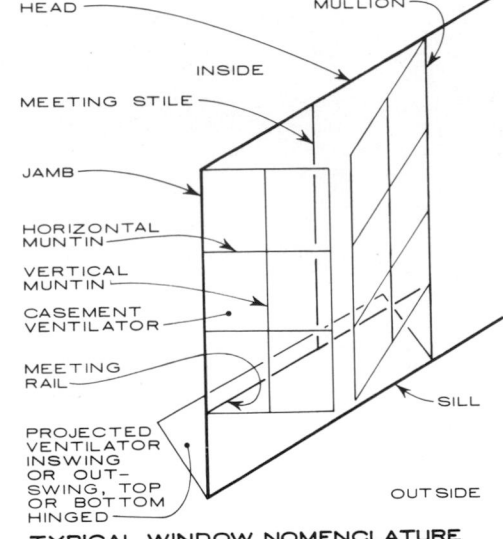

TYPICAL WINDOW NOMENCLATURE
COMBINATION CASEMENT AND PROJECTED WINDOW IS SHOWN IN THIS EXAMPLE

SYMBOLS & CONVENTIONS
(AS USED ON ARCHITECTURAL DRAWINGS)

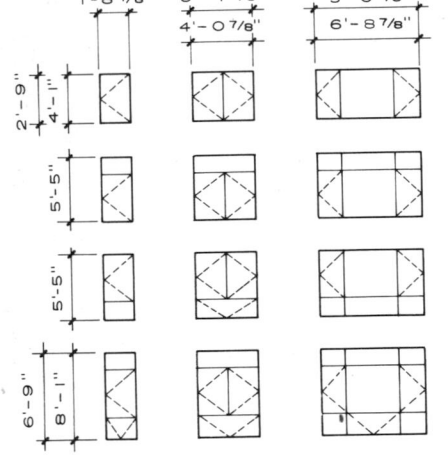

COMBINATION (CASEMENT, PROJECTED, FIXED)
Alum: Architectural
Steel: Standard Intermediate
Heavy Intermediate

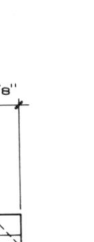

COMBINATION (CASEMENT, FIXED)
Alum: No standard by AAMA
Steel: Standard Intermediate
Heavy Intermediate

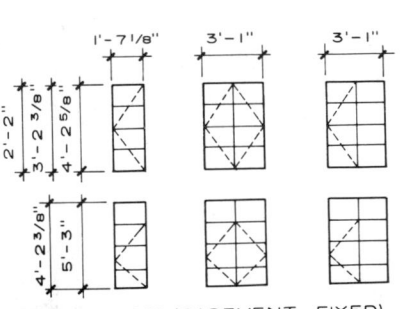

COMBINATION (CASEMENT, FIXED)
Alum: Residential
Steel: Residential (Eastern)

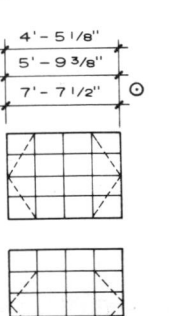

* Aluminum only
⊙ Steel only

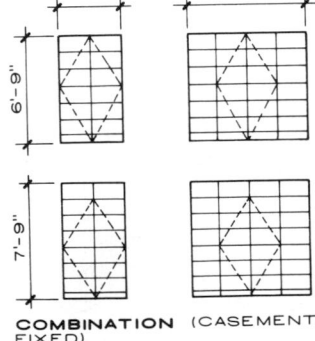

COMBINATION (CASEMENT, FIXED)
Alum: No standard by AAMA
Steel: Special units shown designed for use as doors for porches, patios, etc.

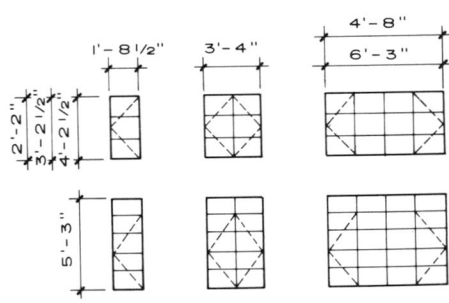

COMBINATION (CASEMENT, FIXED)
Alum: Residential (Western—Type X)
Steel: No standard by Steel Window Institute

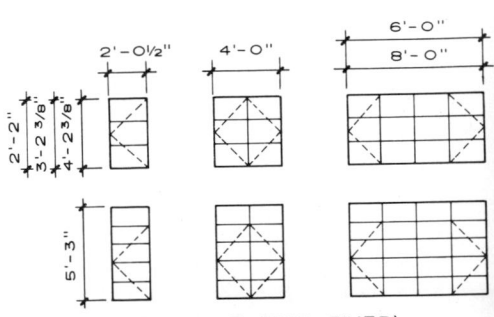

COMBINATION (CASEMENT, FIXED)
Alum: Residential (Western—Type XW)
Steel: No standard by Steel Window Institute

CASEMENT WINDOWS

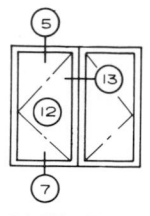
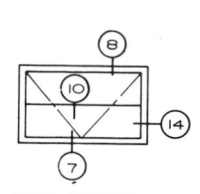
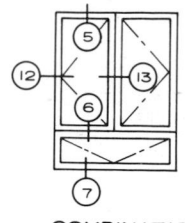
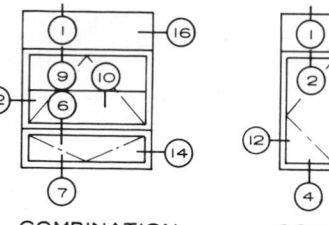
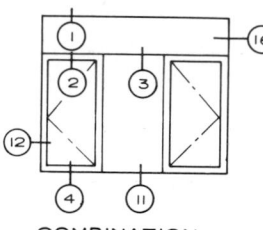
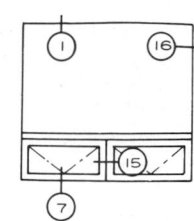

CASEMENT **PROJECTED** **COMBINATION (CASEMENT – PROJECTED)** **COMBINATION (PROJECTED – FIXED)** **COMBINATION (CASEMENT – FIXED)** **COMBINATION (PROJECTED – FIXED) ALSO KNOWN AS "CLASSROOM"**

A CASEMENT, PROJECTED, OR COMBINATION WINDOW

(casement, projected, fixed) is used where maximum light and ventilation are important factors.

High-up projected-out sash needs chain or motor operators to open and close. Hand operated sash hardware, whether inward or outward opening, must be within arm reach of average person standing on floor, or else have some mechanical or nonmechanical device (a pole) to extend arm reach.

See Index for pages on "Dimensions of the Human Figure."

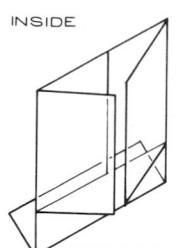
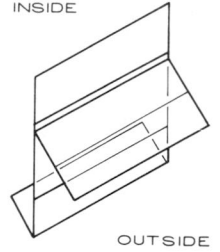
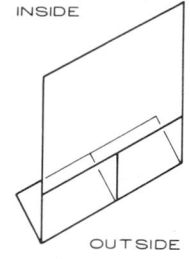

INSIDE ... OUTSIDE

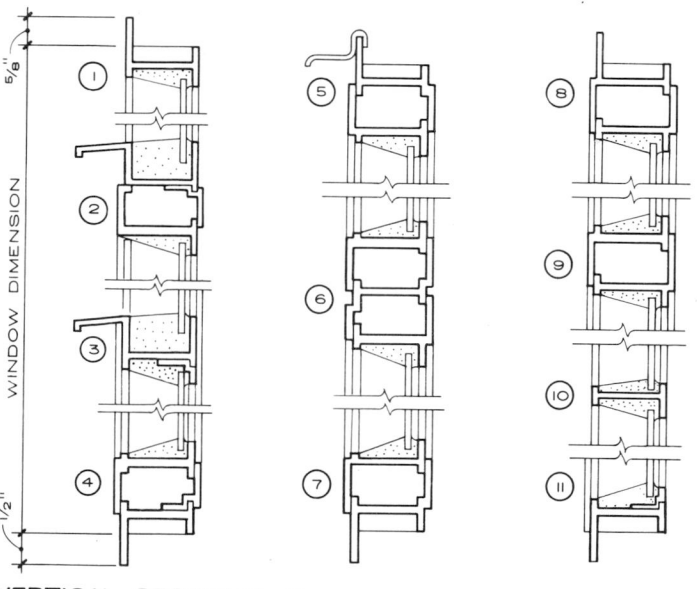

VERTICAL SECTIONS (ALUMINUM)
SCALE: 3" = 1'-0"

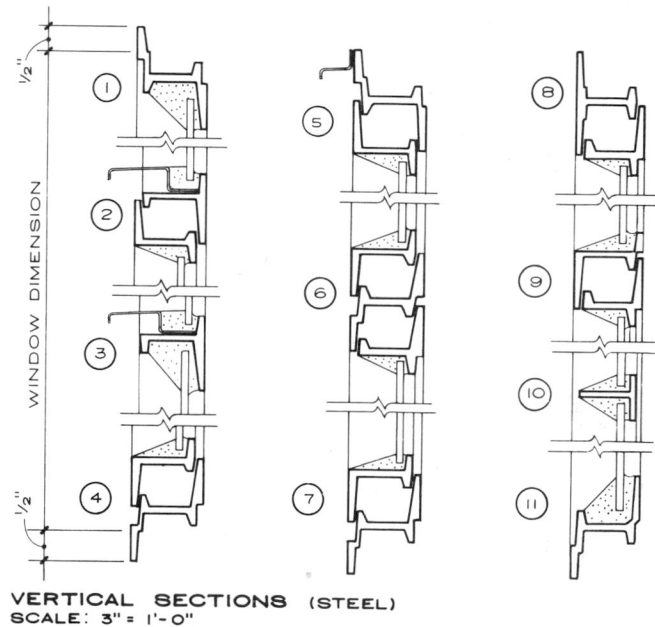

VERTICAL SECTIONS (STEEL)
SCALE: 3" = 1'-0"

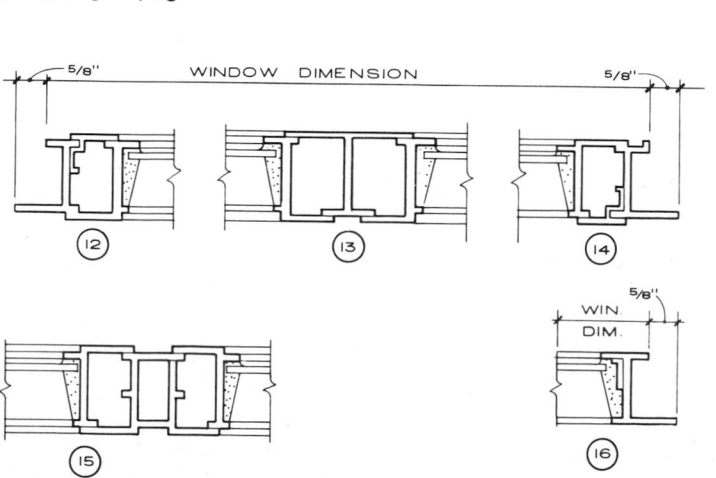

HORIZONTAL SECTIONS (ALUMINUM)
SCALE: 3" = 1'-0"

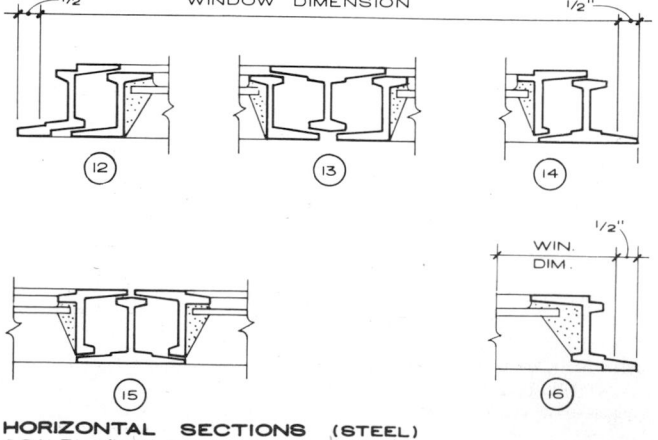

HORIZONTAL SECTIONS (STEEL)
SCALE: 3" = 1'-0"

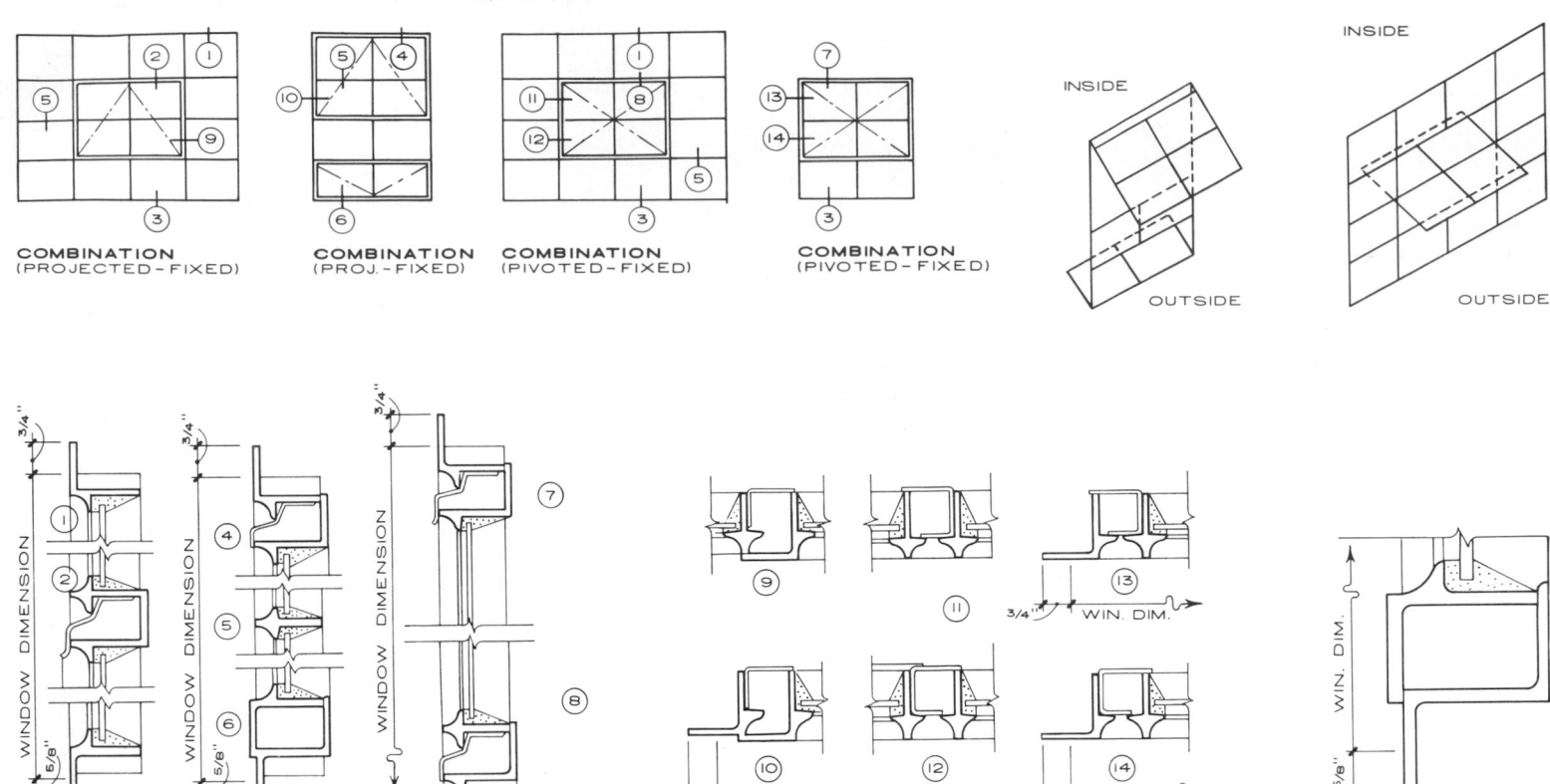

INDUSTRIAL STEEL WINDOWS

Industrial steel windows (projected, pivoted, fixed) consist of either "commercial projected" or "horizontal pivoted" windows and are used in industrial buildings, warehouses, etc., because their cost is usually less than similar windows. They may be hand operated or mechanically operated in groups.

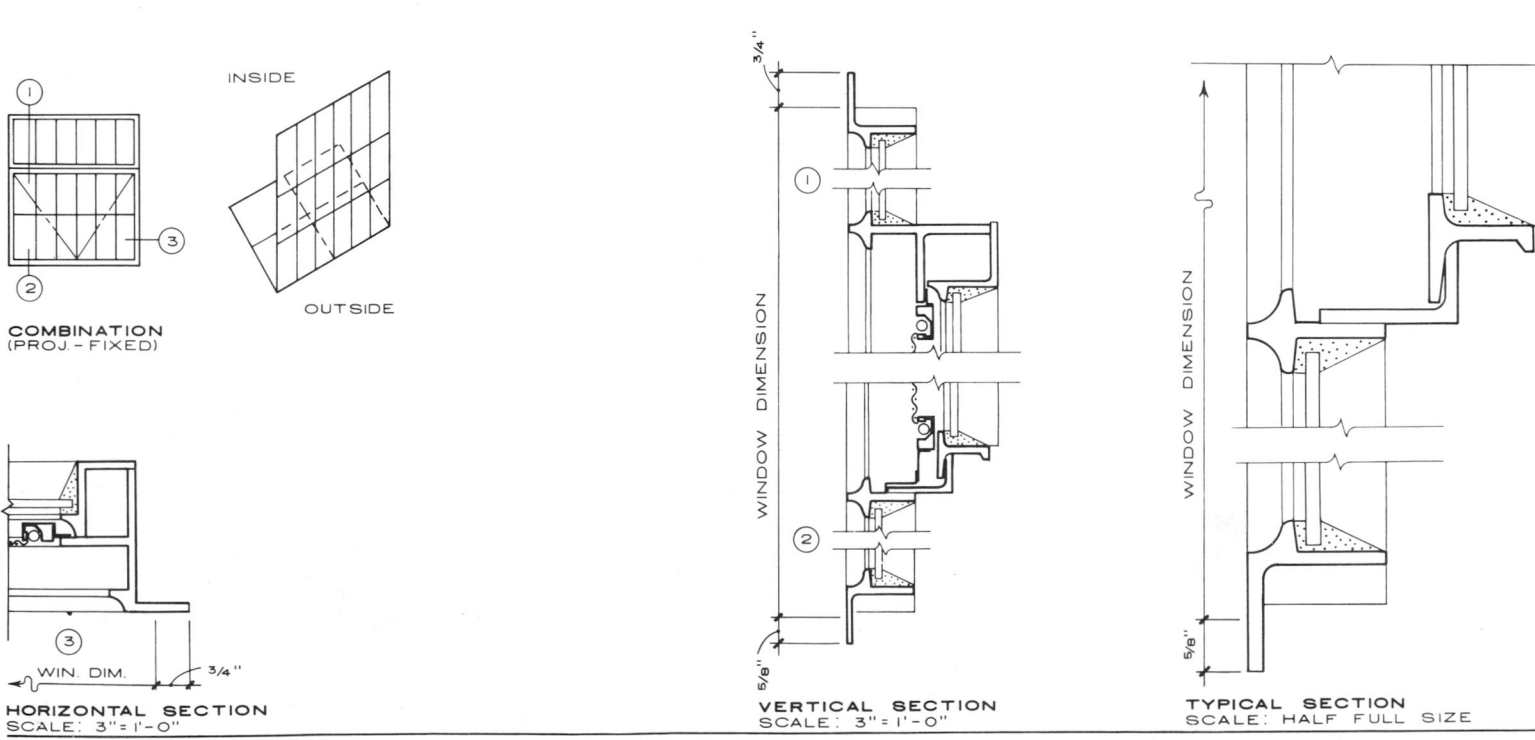

STEEL SECURITY WINDOWS

A steel security window (projected, fixed) is a hopper type window used where protection is required. It is similar to an industrial window except that the narrowly spaced security bars (which are in a common frame with the window) remain fixed while the ventilator moves. Screens available if required.

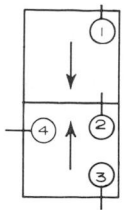

DOUBLE HUNG

A Dougle Hung Window (or single hung window) is used where maximum light and flush interior and exterior bldg. appearance are important factors.

A Single Hung Window (not shown) is generally the same as a double hung window except that the frame for the upper fixed light is an integral part of the head and jamb members.

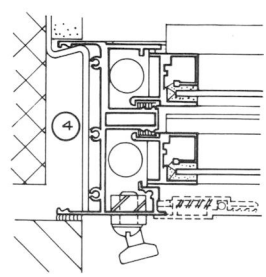

HORIZONTAL SECTION (ALUMINUM)
SCALE: 3"=1'-0"

DOUBLE HUNG WINDOWS

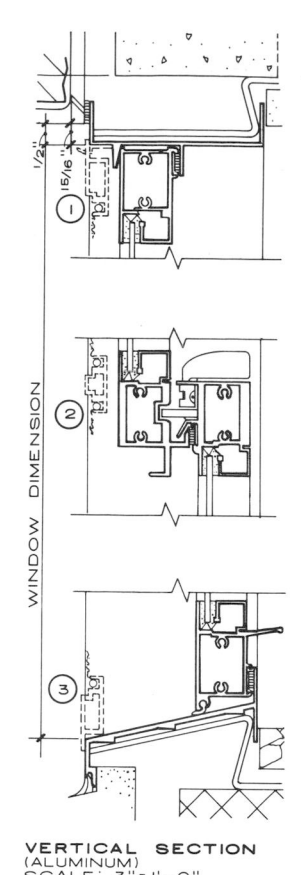

VERTICAL SECTION
(ALUMINUM)
SCALE: 3"=1'-0"

NOTE:

Steel frame and ventilators are of box tubular construction.

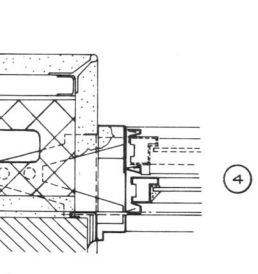

HORIZONTAL SECTION (STEEL)
NO SCALE

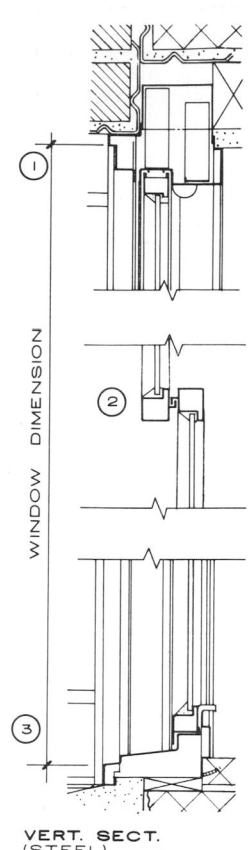

VERT. SECT.
(STEEL)
NO SCALE

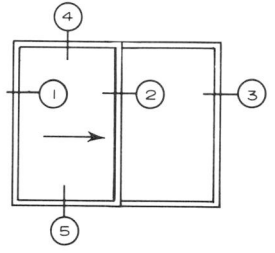

HORIZONTAL SLIDING

A Horizontal Sliding Glass Window (single or double) is used where maximum light, flush interior and exterior bldg. appearance, simple manual operation, and accessibility are important factors.

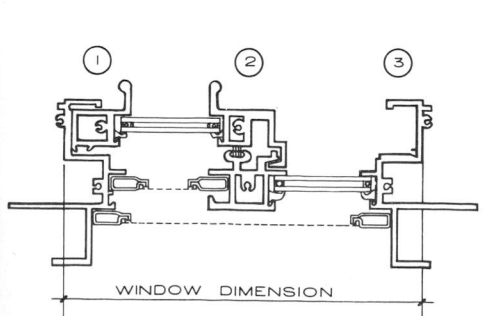

HORIZONTAL SECTION (ALUMINUM)
SCALE: 3"=1'-0"

SLIDING WINDOWS

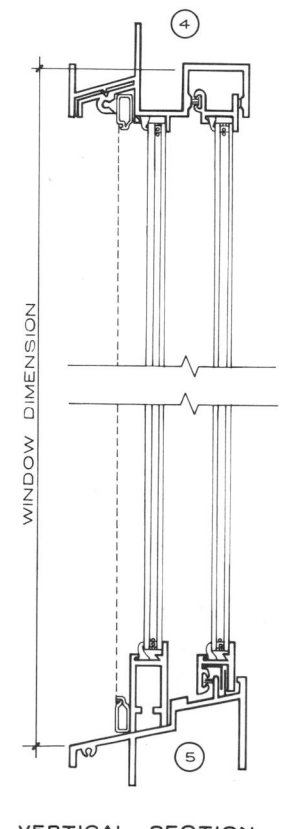

VERTICAL SECTION
(ALUMINUM)
SCALE: 3"=1'-0"

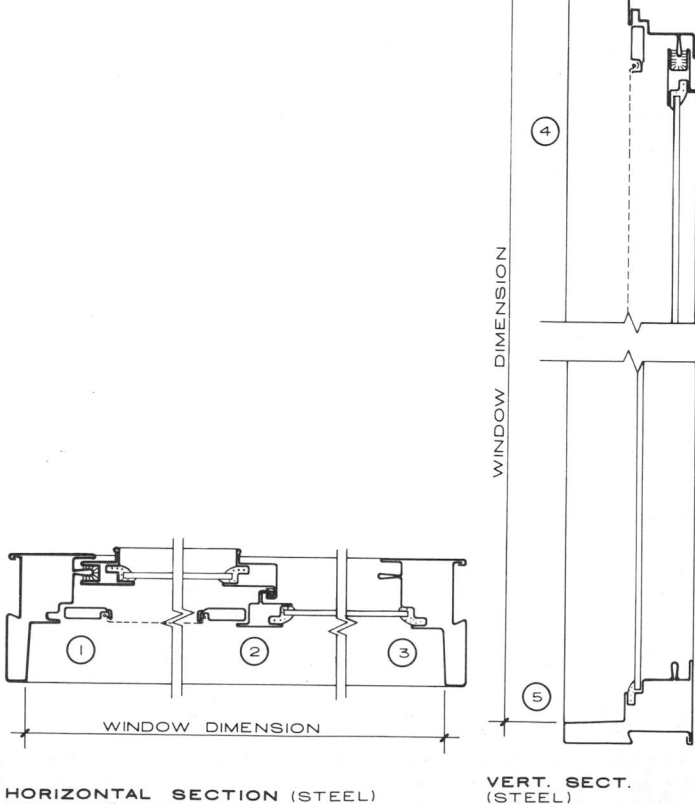

HORIZONTAL SECTION (STEEL)
SCALE: 3"=1'-0"

VERT. SECT.
(STEEL)
SCALE: 3"=1'-0"

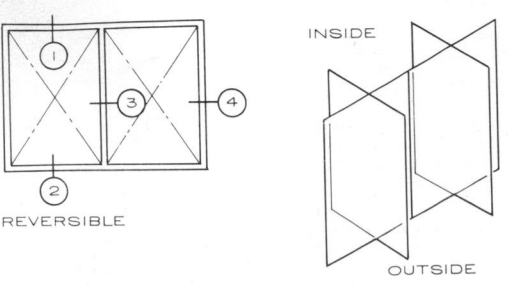

REVERSIBLE

A Reversible window is used mostly in multistory, air conditioned buildings where window washing from the interior is desired. It is normally opened for cleaning only; however, it may be combined with a hopper if ventilation is required.

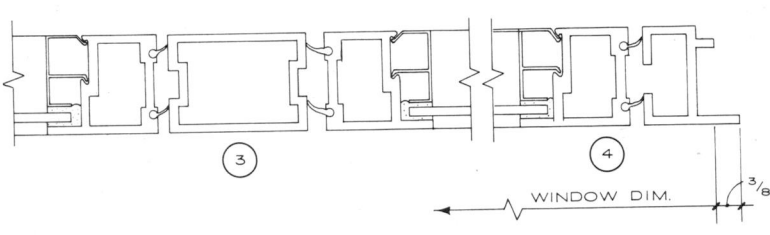

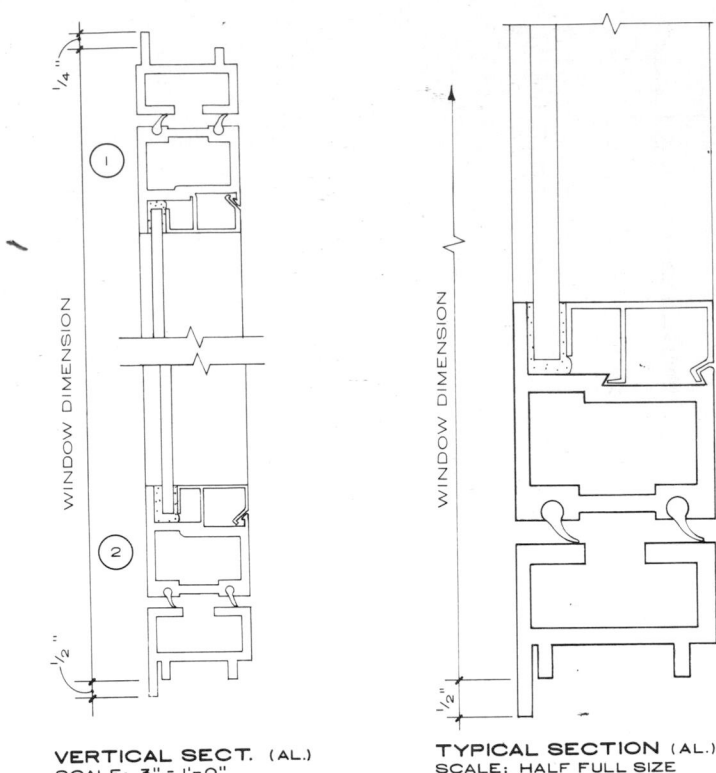

HORIZONTAL SECTION (ALUMINUM)
SCALE: 3" = 1'-0"

REVERSIBLE WINDOW

VERTICAL SECT. (AL.)
SCALE: 3" = 1'-0"

TYPICAL SECTION (AL.)
SCALE: HALF FULL SIZE

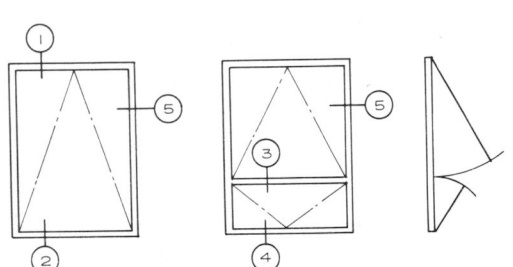

PROJECTED (SPECIAL)

A Projected (special) window is used mostly in multistory, air conditioned buildings where window washing from the interior is desired. It is normally opened for cleaning only; however, it may be combined with a hopper if ventilation is required.

For such use see alternate below.

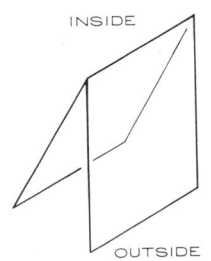

FULL SASH PRO-
JECTED WITH
HOPPER VENT
FOR VENTILATION

ALTERNATE—KEY OPERATED

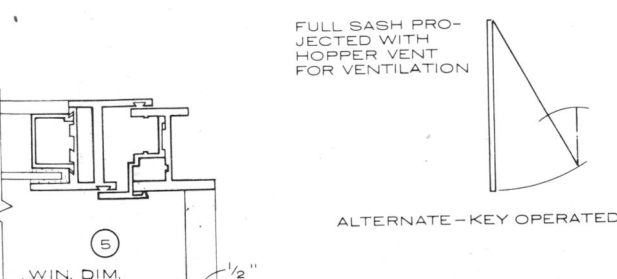

HORIZONTAL SECTION (AL.)
SCALE: 3" = 1'-0"

PROJECTED WINDOW

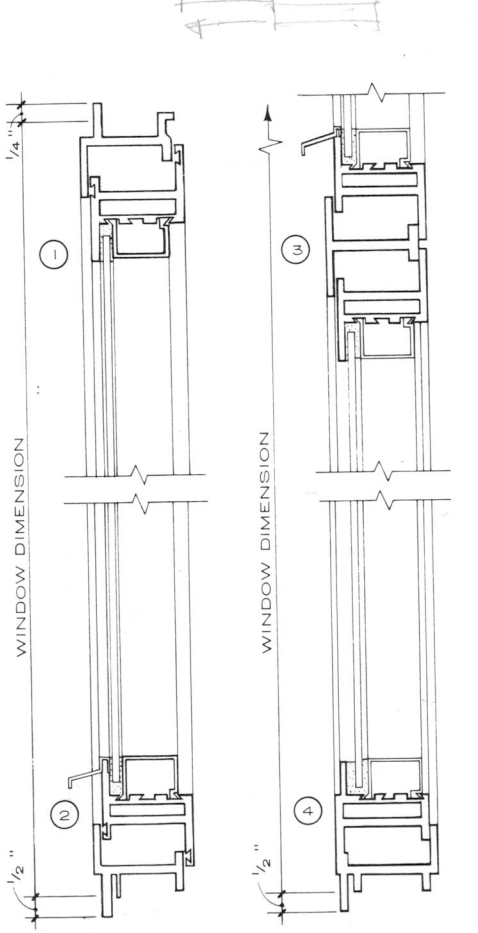

VERTICAL SECTION (ALUMINUM)
SCALE: 3" = 1'-0"

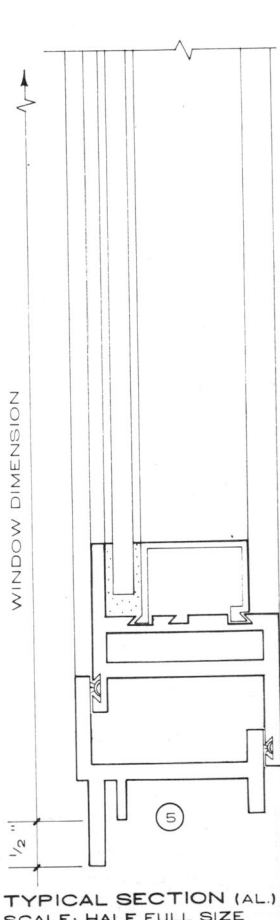

TYPICAL SECTION (AL.)
SCALE: HALF FULL SIZE

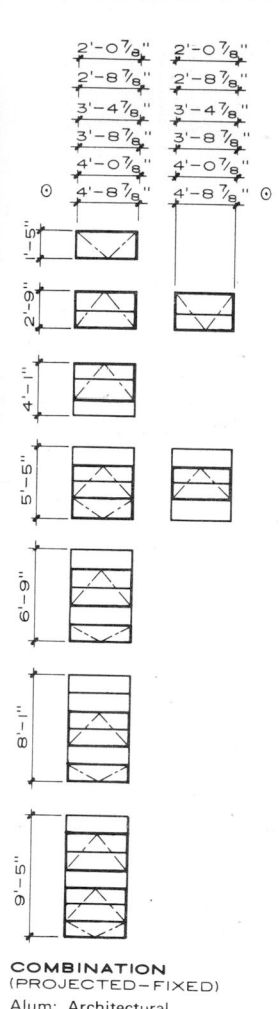

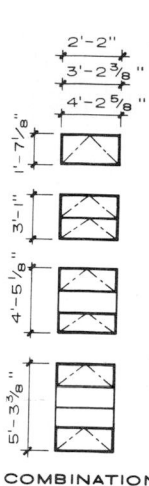

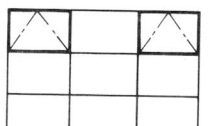

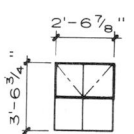

COMBINATION
(PROJECTED–FIXED)
Alum: Architectural
Steel: Std. Intermediate
Heavy Intermediate
Arch. Projected
⊙ Steel only

COMBINATION
(PROJECTED–FIXED)
Alum: Residential
Steel: No std. by SWI

COMBINATION
(PROJECTED–FIXED)
Alum: No std. by AAMA
Steel: Residential
No std. sizes by SWI

COMBINATION
(PROJECTED–FIXED)
This type known as
"utility"
Alum: No std. by AAMA
Steel: Special utility
classification

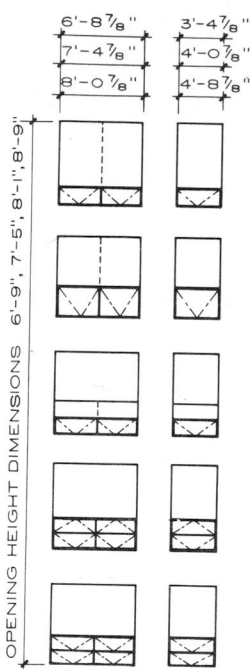

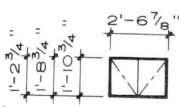

COMBINATION
(PROJECTED–FIXED)
This type known as "classroom window"
Alum: No special "classroom" category by AAMA
Steel: Std. Intermediate
Heavy Intermediate

PROJECTED
This type known as "basement"
Alum: Residential
Steel: Residential

OPENING HEIGHT DIMENSIONS 6'-9", 7'-5", 8'-1", 8'-9"

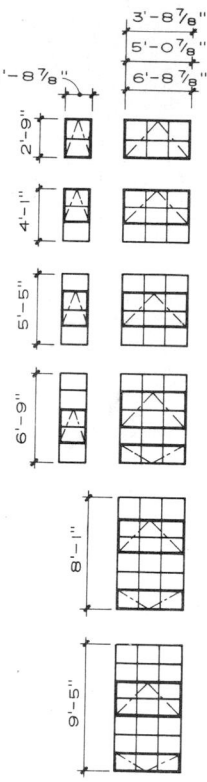

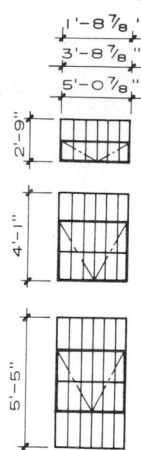

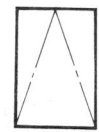

COMBINATION
(PROJECTED–FIXED)
This type known as "commercial proj."
Alum: No std. by AAMA
Steel: Arch. Projected

COMBINATION
(PROJECTED–FIXED)
This type known as "security window"
Alum: No std. by AAMA
Steel: Min. detention
Moderate detention
Max. detention

PROJECTED
(SPECIAL)
Alum: Architectural
No std. sizes by AAMA
Steel: No std. by SWI

NOTE:

Electric motor or mechanical chain control should be provided for high outward-opening projecting sash.

PROJECTED WINDOW

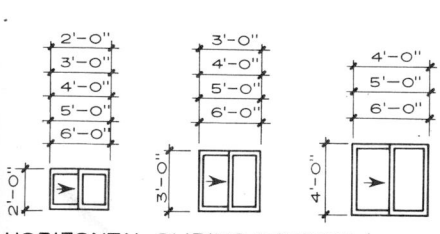

HORIZONTAL SLIDING WINDOW
Alum: Residential
Steel: No std. sizes by SWI

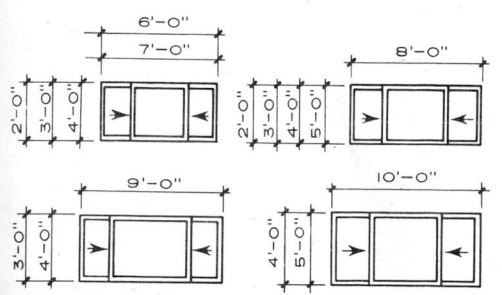

COMBINATION WINDOW (HOR. SLIDING–FIXED)
Alum: Residential
Steel: No std. sizes by SWI

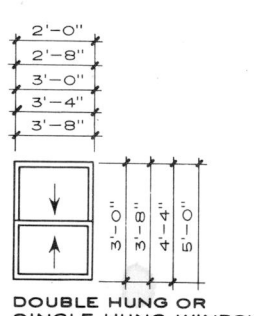

DOUBLE HUNG OR SINGLE HUNG WINDOW
Alum: Residential
Steel: No std. by SWI

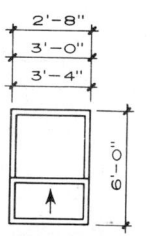

SINGLE HUNG WINDOW
Alum: Residential
Steel: No std. by SWI

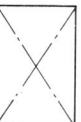

REVERSIBLE WINDOW
(SPECIAL)
Alum: Architectural
No std. sizes by AAMA
Steel: No std. by SWI

JALOUSIE WINDOW
Alum: Architectural
No std. sizes by SJAC, Inc.
Steel: No std. by SWI

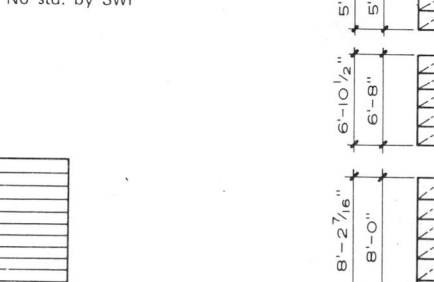

STD. SIZES
MODULAR SIZES

AWNING WINDOW
Alum: Architectural
Residential
Steel: Heavy Intermediate
No std. sizes by SWI

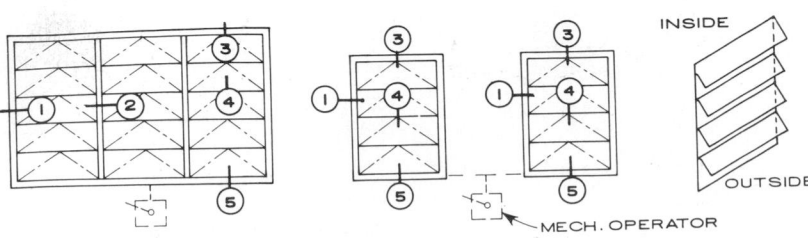

AWNING

AN AWNING WINDOW is one whose movable units consist of a group of hand operated or gear operated outward projecting ventilators, all of which move in unison. It is used where maximum height and ventilation is required in inaccessible areas such as upper parts of gymnasiums or auditoriums. Hand operation is limited to one window only, while a single gear operator may be connected to two or more awning windows.

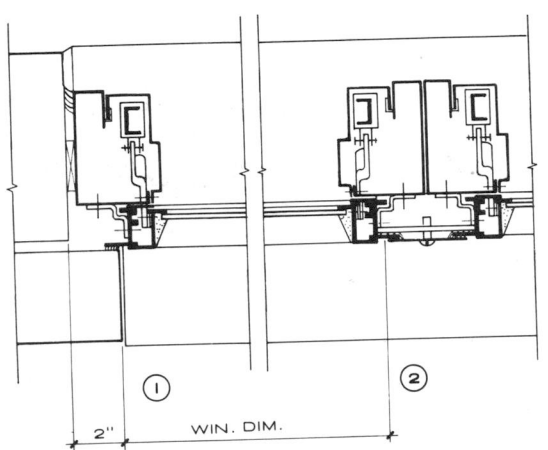

HORIZONTAL SECTION (ALUMINUM)
SCALE: 1½" = 1'-0"

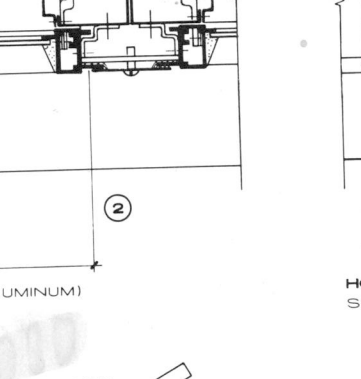

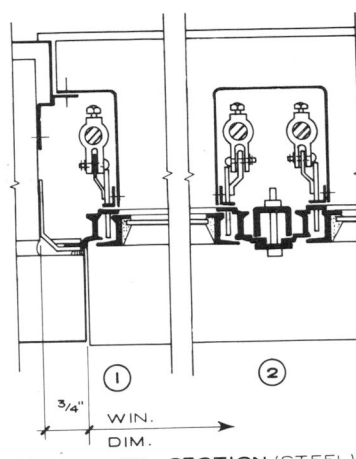

HORIZONTAL SECTION (STEEL)
SCALE: 1½" = 1'-0"

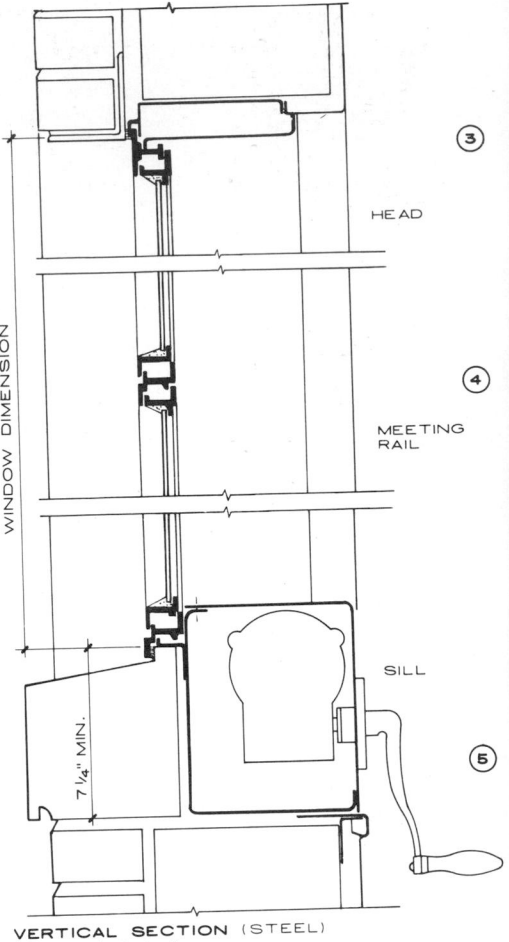

VERTICAL SECTION (STEEL)
SCALE: 1½" = 1'-0"

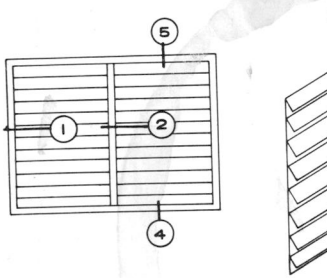

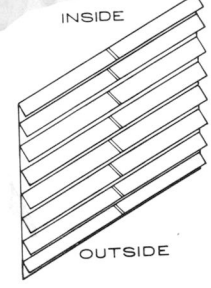

JALOUSIE

A JALOUSIE WINDOW (ALUMINUM) consists of a series of operable overlapping glass louvers which pivot in unison. It may be combined in the same frame with a series of operable opaque louvers for climate control. It is used mostly in residential type constructions in southern climates, where maximum ventilation and flush exterior and interior appearance is desired.

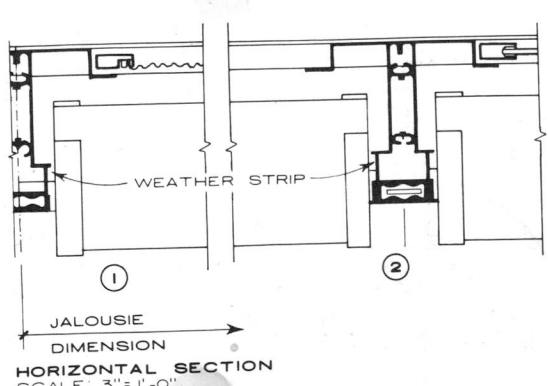

HORIZONTAL SECTION
SCALE: 3" = 1'-0"

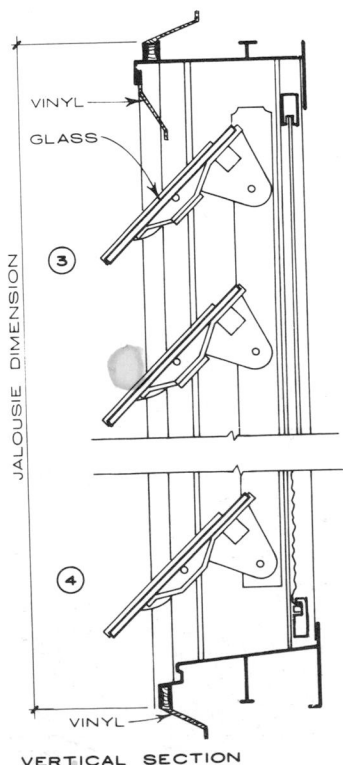

VERTICAL SECTION
SCALE: 3" = 1'-0"

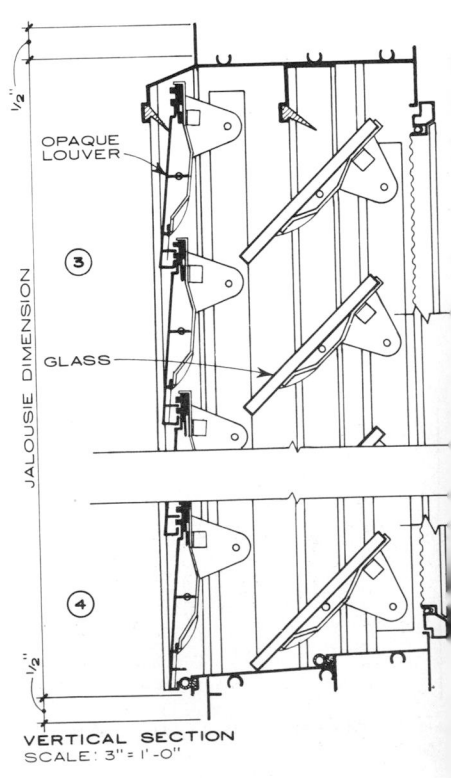

VERTICAL SECTION
SCALE: 3" = 1'-0"

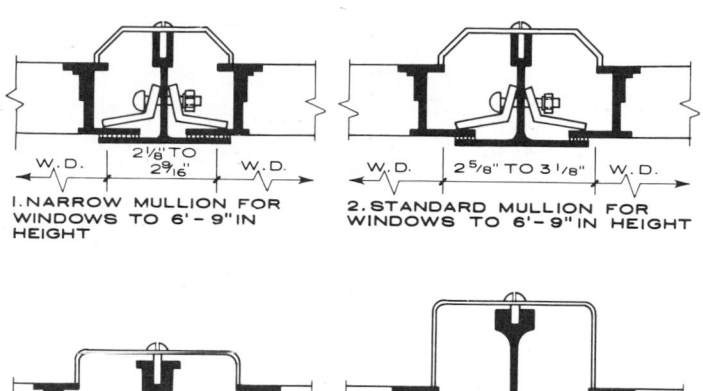

1. NARROW MULLION FOR WINDOWS TO 6'- 9" IN HEIGHT

2. STANDARD MULLION FOR WINDOWS TO 6'- 9" IN HEIGHT

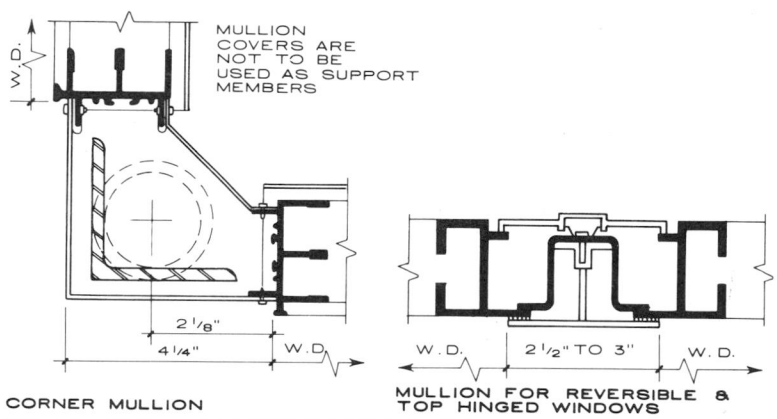

3. STANDARD MULLION FOR WINDOWS 6'- 9" TO 8'- 1" IN HT.

4. STANDARD MULLION FOR WINDOWS HIGHER THAN 8'- 1"

NOTE:

MULLIONS 1 THROUGH 4 ARE USED WITH CASEMENT AND PROJECTED WINDOWS.
W. D. = WINDOW DIMENSION

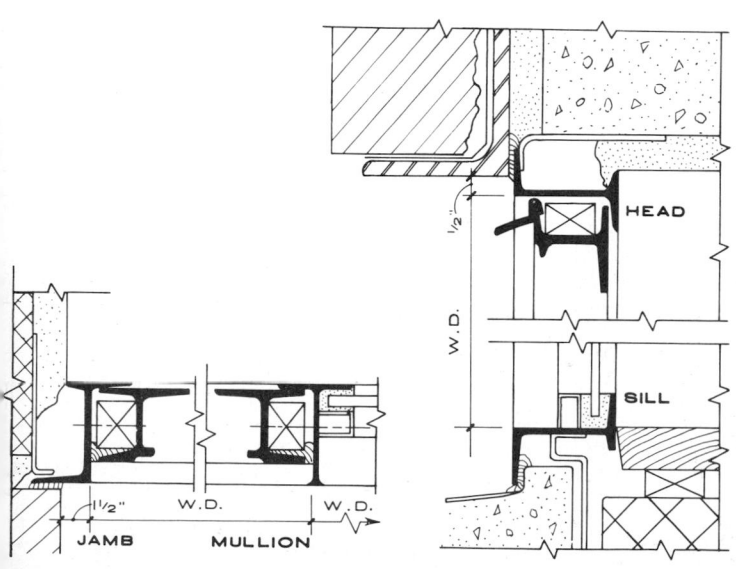

MULLION COVERS ARE NOT TO BE USED AS SUPPORT MEMBERS

CORNER MULLION

MULLION FOR REVERSIBLE & TOP HINGED WINDOWS

ALUMINUM MULLIONS
SCALE : 3" = 1'- 0"

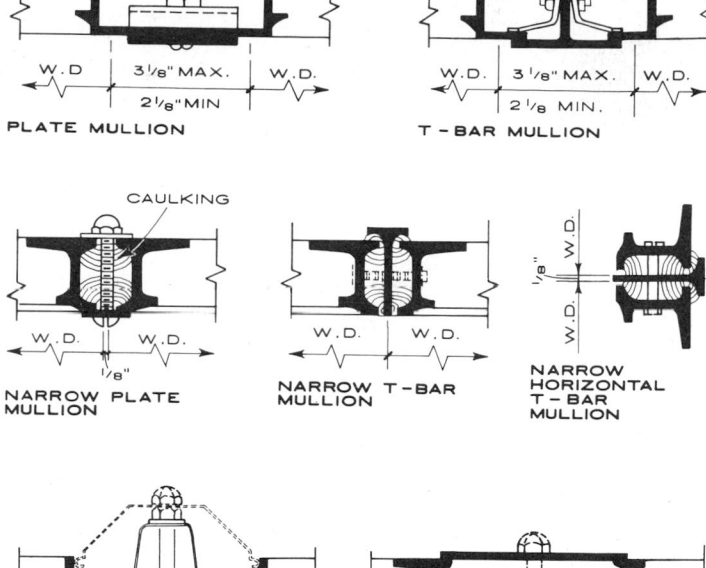

PLATE MULLION

T - BAR MULLION

CAULKING

NARROW PLATE MULLION

NARROW T-BAR MULLION

NARROW HORIZONTAL T - BAR MULLION

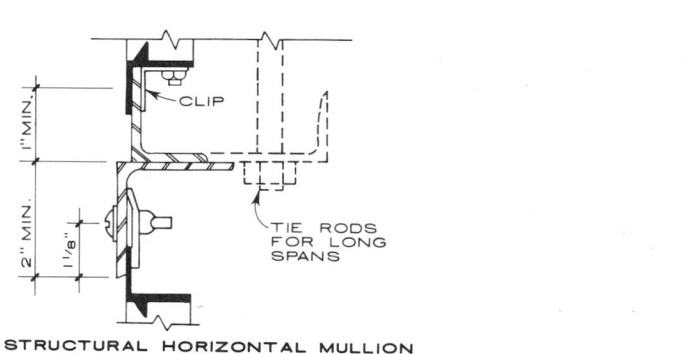

MULLIONS WITH COVERS FOR LARGE OPENINGS

CLIP

TIE RODS FOR LONG SPANS

STRUCTURAL HORIZONTAL MULLION

STEEL MULLIONS
SCALE : 3" = 1'- 0"

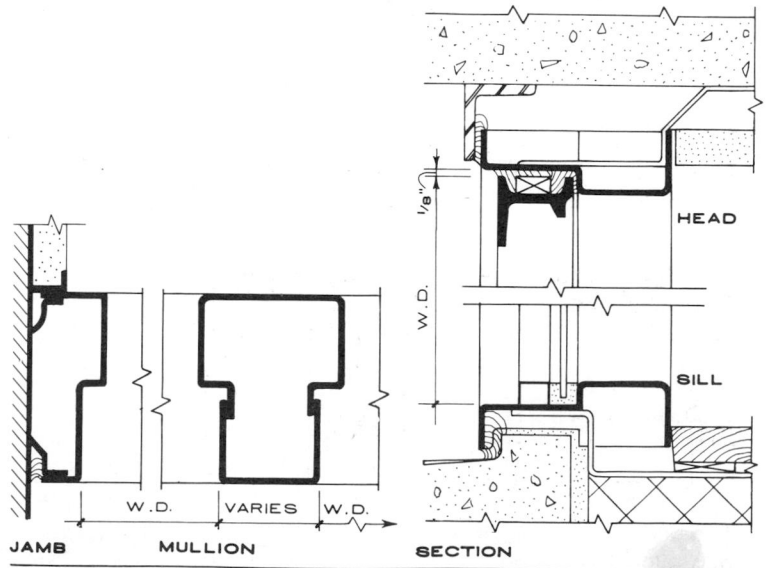

HEAD

SILL

JAMB   MULLION

HOT - ROLLED STEEL SUB - FRAME
SCALE : 3" = 1'- 0"

JAMB   MULLION   SECTION

HEAD

SILL

FORMED STEEL SUB FRAME (#12, #14 GA. STEEL)
SCALE : 3" = 1'- 0"

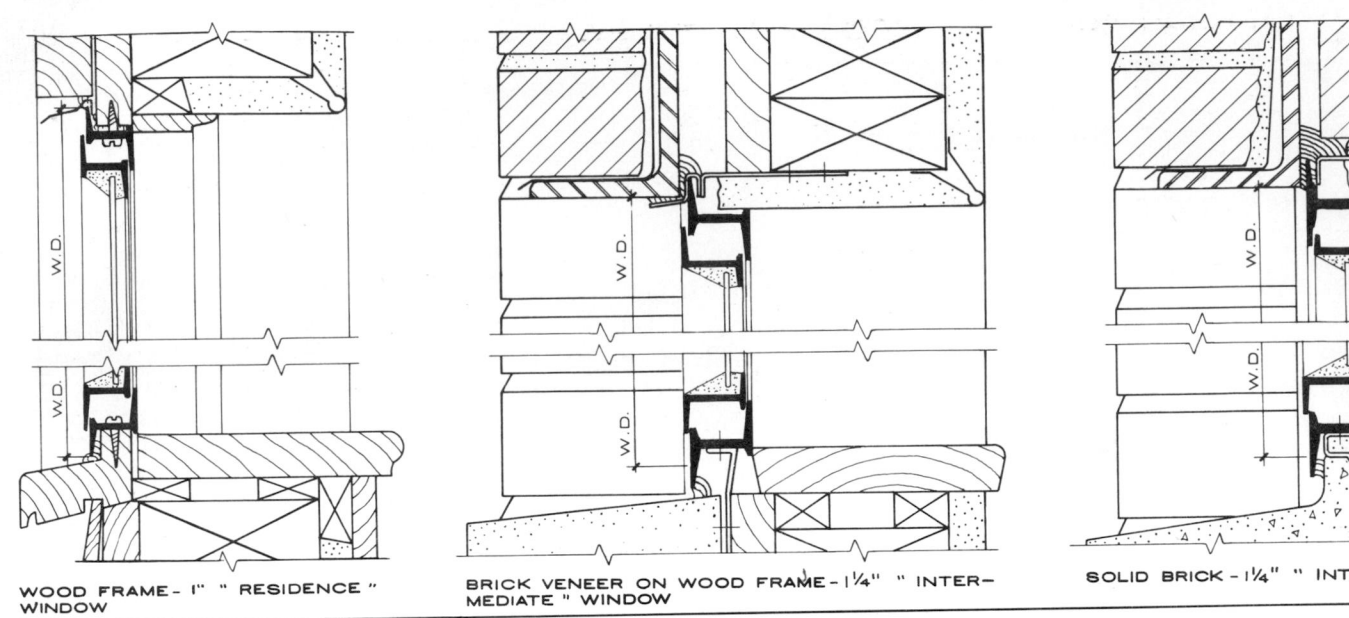

WOOD FRAME - 1" " RESIDENCE "
WINDOW

BRICK VENEER ON WOOD FRAME - 1¼" " INTER-
MEDIATE " WINDOW

SOLID BRICK - 1¼" " INTERMEDIATE "

SCALE : 3" = 1'-0"

STEEL CASEMENTS

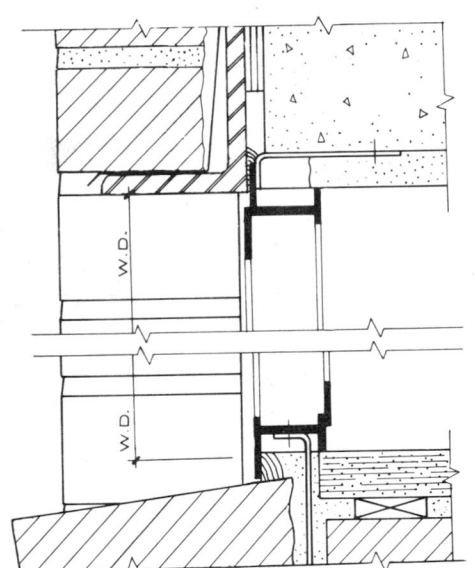

BRICK WITH CONC. SPANDREL (ALUM.)
PROJECTED
SCALE : 3" = 1'-0"

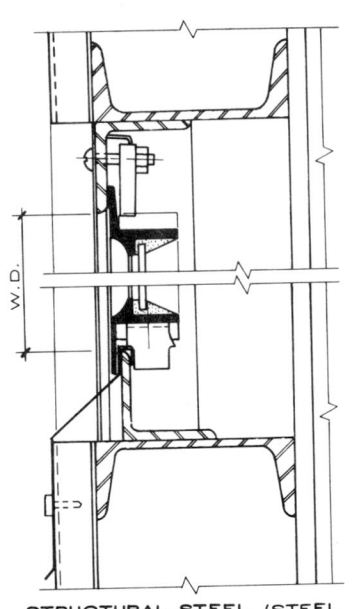

STRUCTURAL STEEL (STEEL
"INDUSTRIAL" WINDOW) FIXED
SCALE : 3" = 1'-0"

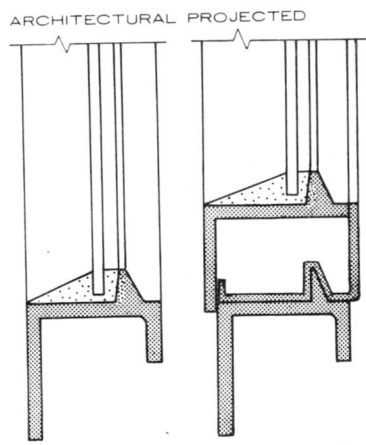

ARCHITECTURAL PROJECTED

TYPICAL SECTIONS GLAZING
TYPES (STEEL)
SCALE : HALF FULL SIZE

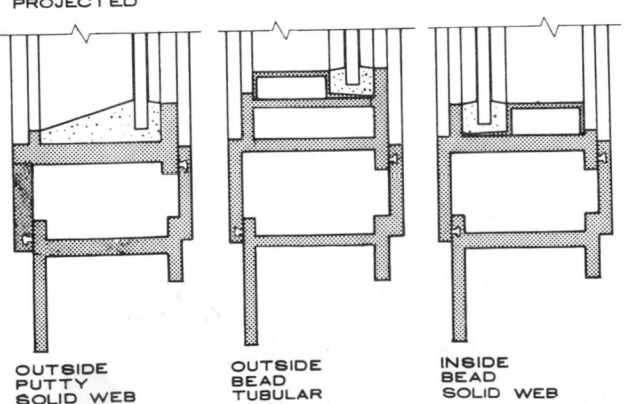

PROJECTED

OUTSIDE
PUTTY
SOLID WEB

OUTSIDE
BEAD
TUBULAR

INSIDE
BEAD
SOLID WEB

TYPICAL SECTIONS - GLAZING TYPES (ALUMINUM)
SCALE HALF FULL SIZE

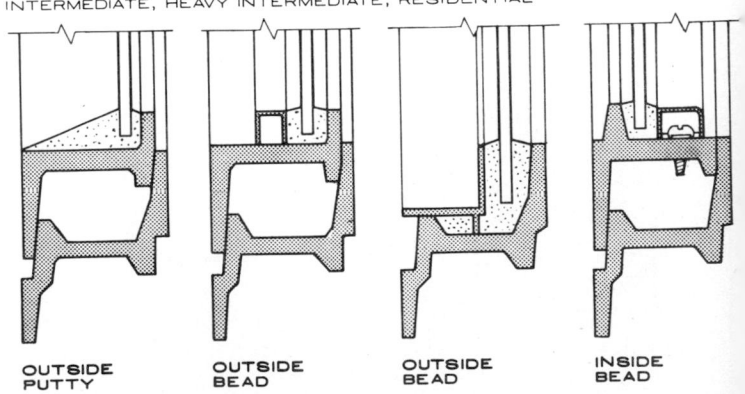

INTERMEDIATE, HEAVY INTERMEDIATE, RESIDENTIAL

OUTSIDE
PUTTY

OUTSIDE
BEAD

OUTSIDE
BEAD

INSIDE
BEAD

TYPICAL SECTIONS - GLAZING TYPES (STEEL)
SCALE HALF FULL SIZE

TYPICAL OPERATING HARDWARE FOR METAL WINDOWS NO SCALE

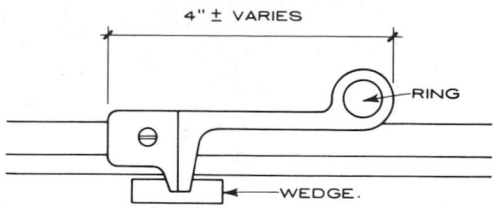

TYPICAL (CAM) LOCKING HANDLE

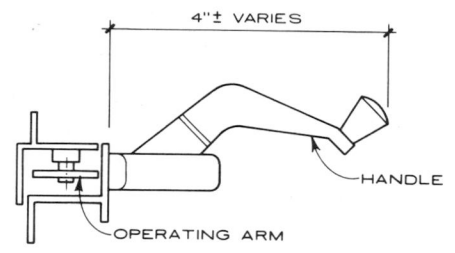

TYPICAL CRANK (ROTO) OPERATOR

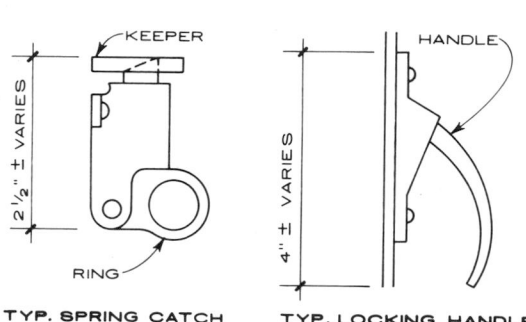

TYP. SPRING CATCH   **TYP. LOCKING HANDLE**

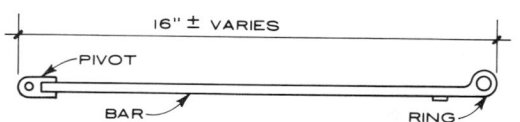

TYPICAL STAY BAR (PUSH BAR)

OTHER TYPES OF HARDWARE:

1. Concealed cam hardware.
2. Hardware with removable handles for A.C. buildings. Also key locks.
3. Sliding window hardware.
4. D. H. window hardware (sweeplock).
5. Telescoping adjuster.
6. Chain, pole & cord operated hardware.
7. Hardware for security windows.
8. Heavy duty, electrical powered hardware for group window control.

FINISHES INCLUDE:

1. Steel: diecast, lacquered & painted.
2. Aluminum: wide range of finishes and colors. Generally match window finish.
3. Bronze
4. White bronze & nickel bronze

Charles F. D. Egbert, AIA; Architect; Washington, D. C.

EXTRUDED ALUMINUM SILLS

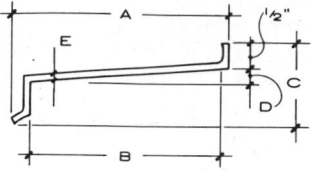

For Lug Sills
Extend into brick joints at window jambs and allow 1/4" space for expansion at ends.

For Continuous Sills
At joints allow 1/4" to 3/8" expansion and flash joints.

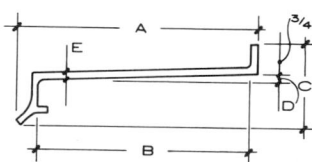

Used for continuous line of windows. Provide 1/4" to 3/8" expansion space at jamb or butt joints of continuous sills.

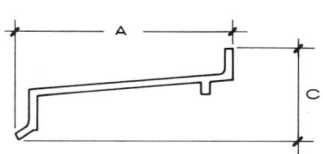

Sills may be made to fit posts or mullions, and may be mitered at corners. Sills over eight feet in length should have central anchorage to keep them in proper position.

* Non-warehouse items

Refer to aluminum manufacturers catalogs.

A	B	C	D	E	Std. No.*
3 7/16"	3"	1 9/16"	3/16"	3/32"	37734
3 29/32"		1 1/2"			P-3684
3 15/16"	3 1/2"	1 19/32"	7/32"	3/32"	37735
4 13/32"		1 17/32"			P-3683
4 7/16"	4"	1 5/8"	1/4"	3/32"	37736
4 7/8"		1 9/16"			3686
4 15/16"	4 1/2"	1 21/32"	9/32"	3/32"	37737
5 3/8"		1 9/16"			3687
5 7/16"	5"	1 11/16"	5/16"	3/32"	37738
5 7/8"		1 5/8"			3685
5 15/16"	5 1/2"	1 23/32"	11/32"	3/32"	37739
9 1/16"	8 1/2"	1 31/32"	7/32"	5/32"	37745
3 1/2"	2 3/4"	1 13/16"	3/16"	1/8"	54684
4"	3 1/4"	1 27/32"	7/32"	1/8"	54685
4 1/2"	3 3/4"	1 7/8"	1/4"	1/8"	54686
					9558
5"	4 1/4"	1 29/32"	9/32"	1/8"	54687
					13008
5 1/2"	4 3/4"	1 15/16"	5/16"	1/8"	54688
					13009
6"	5 1/4"	1 31/32"	11/32"	1/8"	54689
6 9/16"	5 3/4"	2"	3/8"	5/32"	54690
7 9/16"	6 3/4	2 1/16"	7/16"	5/32"	54691
8 1/8"	7 1/4"	2 5/32"	15/32"	3/16"	54692
9 1/8"	8 1/4"	2 7/32"	17/32"	3/16"	54693
3 1/2"		1 9/16"			P-3692
4"		1 19/32"			P-3691
4 1/2"		1 5/8"			P-3690
5"		1 21/32"			P-3126
5 1/2"		1 11/16"			P-3127
6"		1 23/32"			P-3128
9 1/16"		1 29/32"			P-3230

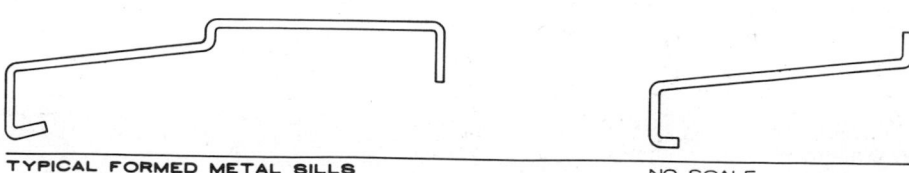

TYPICAL FORMED METAL SILLS
SHAPES MADE TO ORDER   NO SCALE

GENERAL NOTES :

NOMENCLATURE : STD. WINDOW TYPES

DH: Double Hung
SH: Single Hung
HS: Horizontal Sliding
C: Casement
A: Awning
H: Hopper
B: Basement
P: Picture

Above units used singly and, except P, in groups of 2 or 3—mullion or triple units, or more.

A/H may be vertically stacked w/ 1 sash/frame and w/ 2 or more sash/frame.

P units used in combination w/ DH/SH/HS/C/A/H/B and conform in construction to same.

WOOD SPECIE :

For frames, window and storm sash, and screens. Frames: not more than 2 species. Sash or screen: 1 specie only.

Ponderosa Pine	Doug. Wh. Fir	W. Larch
So. Y. Pine	Sitka Spruce	Incense Cedar
Idaho Wh. Pine	Englemann Spruce	Cypress
Sugar Pine	No. Wh. Pine	W. Red Cedar
Lodgepole Pine	Redwood	W.Coast Hemlock

MOISTURE CONTENT :

6-12% at time of fabrication.

PRESERVATIVE TREATMENT :

Protection against moisture, decay and termites. Latest edition of Commercial Standard CS262: water-repellent preservative non-pressure treatment for all wood parts after cutting.

MINIMUM GRADING REQUIREMENTS :

All exposed parts to be free from defects except for minor deviations. Lt. Brown stain and lt. to moderate streaks allowed. Unexposed parts w/o structurally unsound defects.

CONSTRUCTION

WINDOW FRAME :

$3/4''$ min. side and head jambs. C: $3/4''$ and $1 5/16''$. A/H: $1 1/16''$ min. side jambs w/ 2 or more sash/frame. Side jambs dadoed to receive head jamb and sill.

$5 1/4''$ jamb width incl. blind stop when reqd., for std. brick veneer or wood faced frame wall with $3/4''$ sheathing and $7/8''$ lath and pl. Add extenders to thinner jambs or for thicker walls.

Blind stop @ jamb thk. + $1/2''$ projection: DH/SH/S/C/spec. $1/2'' × 3/4''$ parting stop let into jambs: DH/SH.

$1 5/16'' × 7 1/8''$ 1-piece sill w/ 14° bevel (3'':12''). A/H: $1 1/16''$ min. thickness with 1 sash/frame.

2-piece sill: $2 3/32'' × 5 5/16''$ main and $1 5/16'' × 3 1/2''$ undersill. A/H: undersill a bearing sill for stacked sash. Alt. 2-piece sill: $1 5/16''$ main sill and nosing. A/H: $1 1/16''$ min. thk. main sill and nosing w/ 1 sash/frame.

$3/4'' × 1 3/4''$ min. mitered side and head ext. casings. Alternate: brick molding, narrower than casing. $3/4''$ min. thk. drip cap w/ $3/8''$ min. projection.

Int. head casing mitered to side casings. Int. head and side stops line opening above stool. $3/4''$ thk. stool @ 1'' projection beyond casing. Apron: trim below stool, align with head casing.

"Picture Frame" or "Full Bound" interior trim: mitered casing of equal width on four sides of opening, eliminating stool and apron.

Mullion casing, int. and ext., for mullion/triple units.

WINDOW & STORM SASH AND SCREENS :

Mortised and tenoned w/ slotted construction. Screens: as above, or dowelled construction.

Std. thicknesses of wood sash varies w/ mfgrs.
$1 3/8''$ nominal regular sash: $1 11/32''$ actual.
$1 5/8''$ nom. regular sash: A/H w/ 2 or more sash/frame.
$1 3/4''$ nom. picture and hotbed sash: $1 11/16''$ actual.
$2 1/4''$ nominal picture sash: $2 7/32''$ actual.
$2 5/8''$ nominal picture sash: $2 19/32''$ actual.
Institutional sash at least $1 3/4''$ thick.
$1 1/8''$ nominal pl. rail wdw. and storm sash and screens:
$1 3/32''$ actual $3/4''$ screens: $21/32''$ actual.

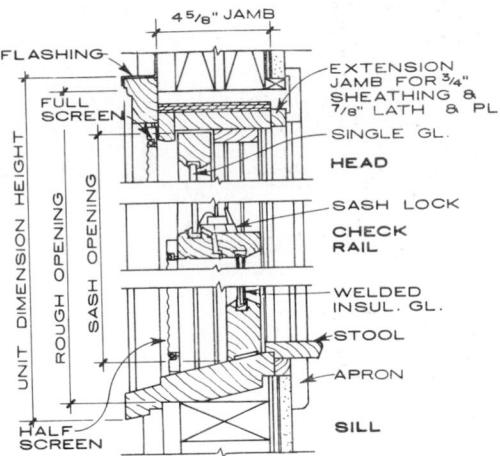

VERTICAL SECTIONS (10012)
SCALE : $1 1/2'' = 1' - 0''$

OPERATING SASH (10012)

FLASHING
FULL SCREEN
UNIT DIMENSION HEIGHT
ROUGH OPENING
SASH OPENING
HALF SCREEN

$4 5/8''$ JAMB
EXTENSION JAMB FOR $3/4''$ & $7/8''$ SHEATHING LATH & PL.
SINGLE GL.
HEAD
SASH LOCK
CHECK RAIL
WELDED INSUL. GL.
STOOL
APRON
SILL

ANDERSEN DOUBLE HUNG

Parting stop integral w/ jamb liner.
Rigid vinyl jamb liners as both track for sash and WS.
Additional woven pile WS inserts in stiles of sash.
Spring tension metal WS at top rail of top sash.
Meeting rail and bottom rail of bottom.

EXTERIOR CASING
BLIND STOP
INTERIOR TRIM
WELDED INSUL. GL.
HEAD
1" INSUL. GL.
SILL

PICTURE SASH

ROUGH OPENING WIDTH
SASH OPNG. LINE OF STOOL
SINGLE GL.
WELDED INSUL. GL.
OPERATING SASH
SELF-STORING STORM & SCREEN COMBINATION
FULL SCREEN
LINE OF SILL
HALF SCREEN
PICTURE SASH
UNIT DIMENSION WIDTH

JAMB   SUPPORT MULLION   TYP. MULLION   MULLION POST   MULLION POST

PLAN SECTIONS
SCALE : $1 1/2'' = 1' - 0''$

$4 5/8''$ jamb w/ $1/2''$ shthg. and $1/2''$ interior. Finish shown, no jamb extenders required.

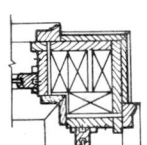

CORNER AND BOW WINDOWS :

Similar adaptation for casement and other applicable window types.

TYPICAL CORNER DETAIL
SCALE : $3/4'' = 1' - 0''$

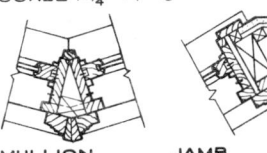

MULLION   JAMB

TYPICAL BOW WINDOW DETAILS
SCALE : $3/4'' = 1' - 0''$

30° or 45° or any angle as required for assembly of 3 or more standard window units.

STOCK SNAP-IN BARS AND GRIDS

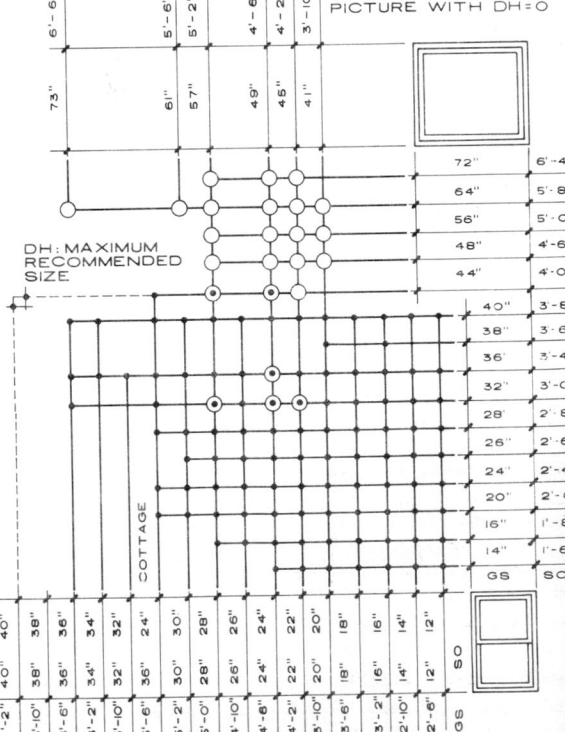

PICTURE WITH DH=0

DH: MAXIMUM RECOMMENDED SIZE

COTTAGE

SO = SASH OPENING   DOUBLE HUNG = •
GS = GLASS SIZE   PICTURE WITH DH = ○

TYPICAL STANDARD SIZES (5 MANUFACTURERS)

CONSTRUCTION

Bars & muntins separate gl. opngs. w/i single sash. Bars: hor. or vert., full wth. or hgt. of gl. opng. Muntins: H or V, from stile or rail to bar, bar to bar. Bars & muntins also diagonal. Acrylic plastic or wd. snap-in bars & grids avail., in reg. or diamond patterns for 1-light sash.

1-light sash: single pane of glass w/o bars & muntins. Divided light or "cut-up" sash: glass panes separated by bars & muntins.

Sticking: solid, of any design allowing reqd. rabbet for type of glass & thickness of sash.

Storm sash (double glazing) may be applied to outside or inside of sash or outside of frame.

Screen sash applied to outside or inside of frame, depending on window type.

Storm & screen sash in outside of frame @ 1" greater than SO height w/ 14° bevelled bot. edge. 3/4" screen may have oval bottom edge. Height further increased with 2-piece sill.

DH: half-sliding or full screens available.
DH/S: combination self-storing storm-screen sash available w/ 1 half-screen & w storm panels.
Alum. frames for storm & screen sash available.

NAILING-EXTERIOR FASTENING

Hot dip galvanized or non-staining metal.

WEATHERSTRIPPING

Mfrs. option, of rigid durable material suitable for normal continuous operation; installed in frame, sash, or both which meets allowable air infiltration stds. @ 25 mph wind pressure.

Usual materials are S.S., anodized alum., vinyl plastic or molded fiber lined with felt or neoprene rolled into retention grooves.

GLAZING & GLAZING METHODS

ss & ds wdw. gl. w/ 1 1/8", 1 3/8", & 1 3/4" sash.
ssB, unless otherwise specified, 76 U.I. max.
dsB: 100 U.I. maximum.
Face puttying, adhesive bedding, or wood stop glazing.
3/8" & 7/16" ins. gl. w/ 1 3/8" & 1 3/4" sash. 1/16" clearance each side. 1" insulating glass w/ 2 1/4" & thicker sash. 1/4" clearance each side. Wood stop or flexible vinyl glazing w/ ins. gl. Storm sash deleted w/ use of insulating glass.

SCREENING

Alum., galv. stl. or brz.: grooved w/ spline or tacked. Vinyl coated fiber cloth: grooved w/ spline only. Each with flush or applied mitered stops. 18x14 or 18x16 mesh.

HARDWARE

All hardware, including operating devices, fasteners, etc. to be non-rusting metal or steel with rust-resistant finish.

DOUBLE HUNG & SINGLE HUNG

Pulleys with cords and sash weights obsolete.

Spring counterbalance: clock spring w/i revolving drum wrapped w/ tape or cord attached to stiles of sash. 2 per sash, overhead or jamb installation. Flat space-saving overhead type also available.

Tension spring balance or pretensioned spiral balance with inner torque rod: tube enclosure, with attaching arms to sash. 1 or 2 per sash, vertically housed in stile rout or incorporated in jamb liner weatherstripping.

Adj. pressure WS of flexible vinyl or metal w/spring compression action, or rigid w/ compress. spring backing.

Sash activated by application of pressure, with hold at any position by release of pressure. Sash may be removable with all types.

Provide sash lock and sash lift.

HORIZONTAL SLIDING

Top of sill & head jamb with track or guide of molded plastic or metal which requires no paint or finish and permits easy operation of sash. Also provides weatherstrip.

Meeting stile lock w/ handle & recessed finger grips.
Continued.

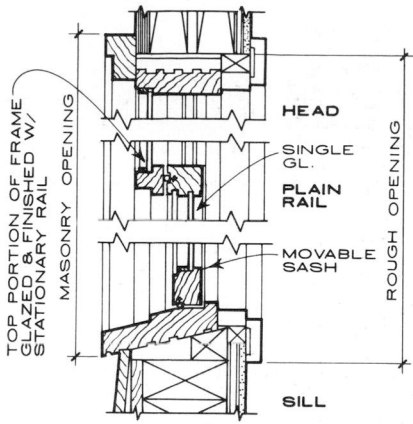

VERTICAL SECTION

HEAD — SINGLE GL. — PLAIN RAIL — MOVABLE SASH — SILL

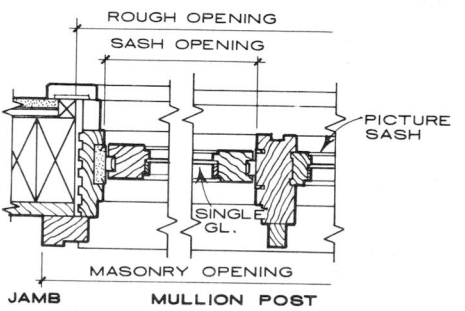

PLAN SECTION
CARADCO SINGLE HUNG

Tubular vinyl WS at meeting rail & bottom rail of movable sash. Alum. jamb liners as track for sash, with urethane foam strip backing on 1 side for floating WS & sash removal.

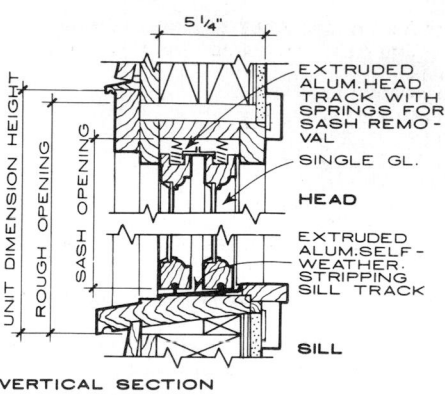

5 1/4"

EXTRUDED ALUM. HEAD TRACK WITH SPRINGS FOR SASH REMOVAL — SINGLE GL. — HEAD — EXTRUDED ALUM. SELF-WEATHER. STRIPPING SILL TRACK — SILL

VERTICAL SECTION

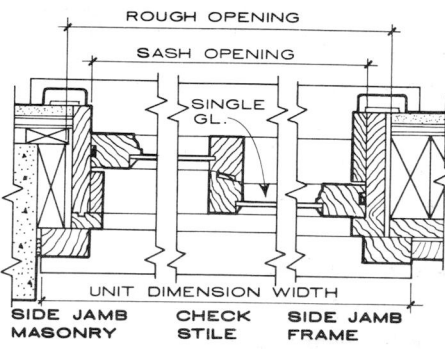

PLAN SECTION
WOODCO HORIZONTAL SLIDING

Polyvinyl WS insert in sash stile. Spring tension metal WS at meeting rail. Sash lock pressure seals meeting stile.

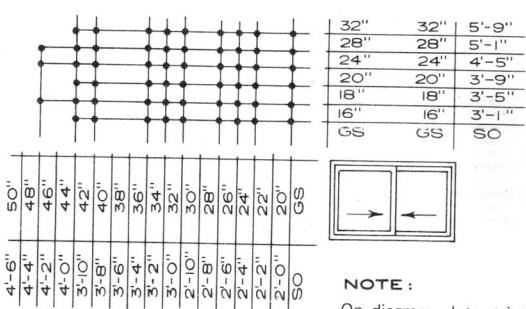

32"	32"	5'-9"
28"	28"	5'-1"
24"	24"	4'-5"
20"	20"	3'-9"
18"	18"	3'-5"
16"	16"	3'-1"
GS	GS	SO

NOTE: SO = SASH OPENING GS = GLASS SIZE

NOTE: On diagram, dots at intersections of lines indicate that size of window is manufactured.

HORIZONTAL SLIDING WINDOWS
TYPICAL STANDARD SIZES (3 MFRS.)

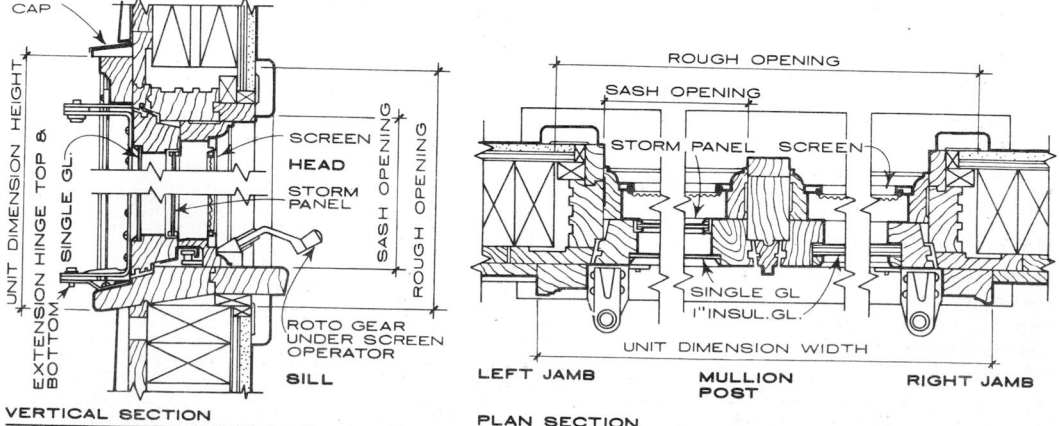

VERTICAL SECTION
MALTA CASEMENT

Spring tension alum. Ws makes contact with sash and frame at all points.

PLAN SECTION

LEFT JAMB — MULLION POST — RIGHT JAMB

SCALE ALL DRAWINGS 1 1/2" = 1'-0"

HDWE. & OPERATING MECHANISMS

CASEMENT

Outswinging or inswinging:
Hinged always as viewed from the outside. Usual fastening to side jamb by extension; double acting or concealed supporting arm hinges. Supporting arms provide friction for manual operation.

Outswinging: for mechanical operation provide holding or friction device to hold sash open at any predetermined position. More sophisticated devices are roto worm gear or folding push bar with locking device.

Side jamb lock, 2/sash @ 2'– 8'' or higher. Plunger type sash lock for inswinging sash.

AWNING & HOPPER

Sash usually hinged on sliding tracks on side jambs, allowing in or out operation of sash and provides friction for manual operation.

A: push bar operator w/ locking device for sash activation and holding, or roto or lever operator. 2 or more sash/frame: roto operators w/ torque bar activates all sash in unison.

Manual operation: provide sash lock, plunger type for H.

NAILING - EXTERIOR FASTENING

Hot dip galvanized or non-staining metal.

STANDARD LAYOUTS & OPENING SIZES

Dimensions always given as width x height.

GS = glass size (in.): clear dimensions between stiles and rails inclusive of muntins and bars.

SO = sash opng. (ft. and in.): OA dims. of sash.

RO = rough opng. (ft. and in.): frame opening in wall required to receive window unit.

Sash stiles @ 2'' nominal width.
Sash meeting stile @ 1'' nominal width: S only.
Sash top rail @ 2'' nominal width.
Sash meeting rail @ 1'' nominal width: DH/SH.
Sash bottom rail @ 3'' nominal width.
Window frame sill bevel @ 2''.

RO fitting allow: at side and head jambs @ $3/4$''.

SO width = gl. width(s) + stiles involved.
SO height = gl. width(s) + rails involved.

RO width = SO + side jambs + fitting allowance
RO height = SO + head jamb + fitting allow. + sill bevel.

The above dimensions serve as a rough rule of thumb, only, for all window types. Act. stile and rail face dims. vary due to cut-ups of sash. Size variations due to mfrs., WS installations, and with DH/SH with type of balance used.

MODULAR SIZES

CS 163–64 list opng. sizes for all sash except pl. rail & barn sash as conforming to modular coordination.

Mfrs. sizes subscribe only w/ DH and by-passing S. Glass widths @ 4'' intervals and glass heights @ 2''.

SO widths: GS + 4'': DH and total GS + 5'': by-pass S.

SO heights: total GS + 4'' + 2'': DH and GS + 4'': by-pass S. Mfrs. additions and omissions as dictated by demand.

C/A/H: wide variance of available sizes and not applicable to modular coordination.

B: modular width @ 2 bldg. blocks of 16'' long ea.
B: modular hgt. @ 1 $1/2$, 2, 2 $1/2$, and 3 bks. @ 8'' high.

DOUBLE HUNG WINDOWS

Frame with operative top and bottom sash which may be removable or pivoted.

Standard DH unit with upper and lower sash @ same GS and meeting rail at center of opening.

Front or cottage type: top sash smaller than bottom sash and meeting rail above center of opng.

Meeting rail: bot. rail of top sash and top rail of bot.

Check rail: usual meeting rail for DH windows. 1 $3/8$'' thks. of meeting rail increased to compensate for $1/2$'' parting stop separating sash. Bevelled and dadoed projections of ea. rail w/ WS. GS @ 12'' x 12'' – 44'' x 40'' for 1–light sash. Widths greater than 40'' seldom used and sizes greater than 44'' x 40'' cannot be properly balanced.

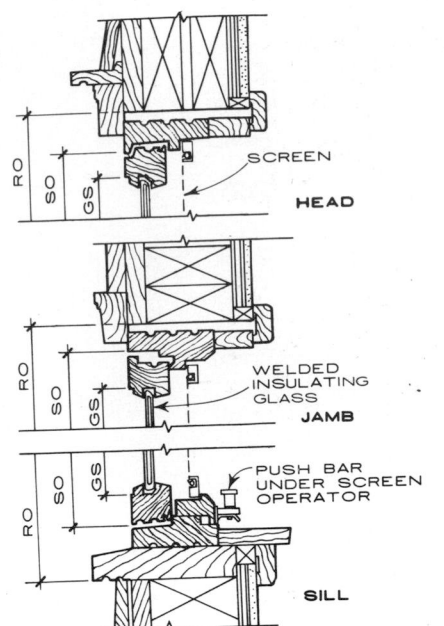

HEAD
SCREEN

JAMB
WELDED INSULATING GLASS

SILL
PUSH BAR UNDER SCREEN OPERATOR

USED AS AWNING - FRAME WALL

HEAD
STORM PANEL

JAMB
SCREEN

SILL
SINGLE GL.

USED AS CASEMENT - BRICK VENEER

CONVERTIBLE WINDOWS: AWNING - HOPPER - CASEMENT; MULTI-PURPOSE

Spring tension S.S. Window stripping at all sides of sash.

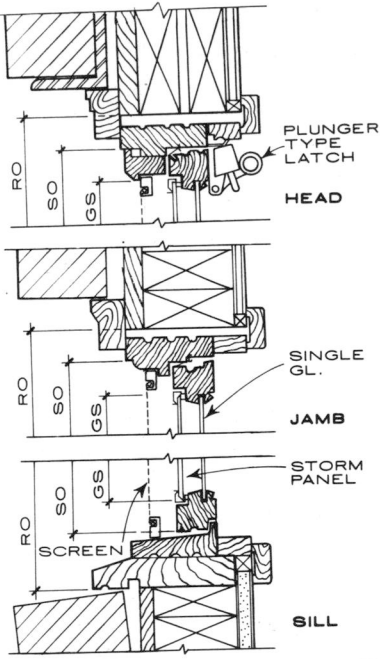

HEAD
PLUNGER TYPE LATCH

JAMB
SINGLE GL.

SILL
STORM PANEL
SCREEN

USED AS HOPPER - BRICK VENEER

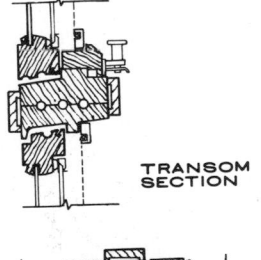

TRANSOM SECTION

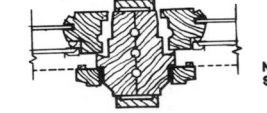

MULLION SECTION

SCALE : 1 $1/2$'' = 1'– 0''

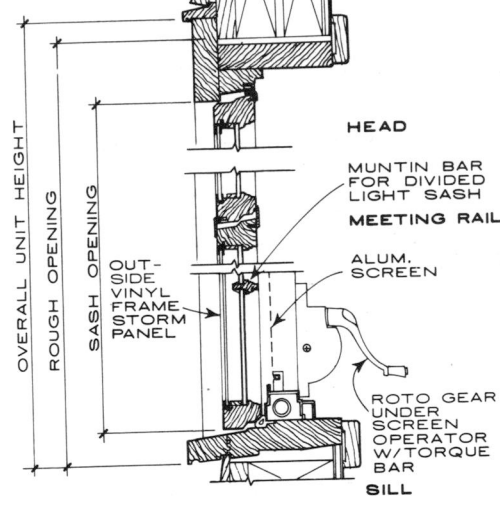

HEAD
MUNTIN BAR FOR DIVIDED LIGHT SASH
MEETING RAIL
ALUM. SCREEN
OUTSIDE VINYL FRAME STORM PANEL
ROTO GEAR UNDER SCREEN OPERATOR W/ TORQUE BAR
SILL

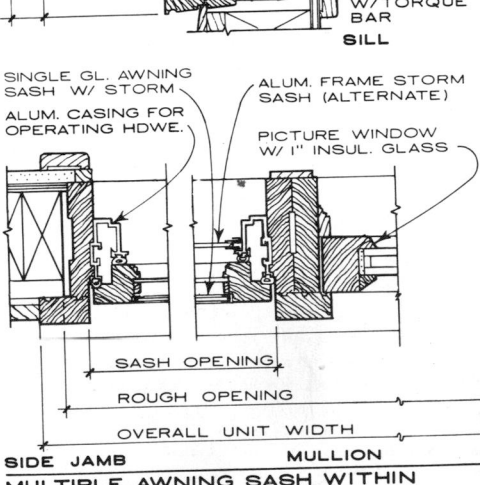

SINGLE GL. AWNING SASH W/ STORM
ALUM. CASING FOR OPERATING HDWE.
ALUM. FRAME STORM SASH (ALTERNATE)
PICTURE WINDOW W/ 1'' INSUL. GLASS

SASH OPENING
ROUGH OPENING
OVERALL UNIT WIDTH

SIDE JAMB   **MULLION**

MULTIPLE AWNING SASH WITHIN SINGLE FRAME

Vinyl tubular window stripping at head, jambs and sill. Solid overlap vinyl W.S. at meeting rails.

Operating hdwe. enclosed in alum. casing. All sash react in unison, 70° opening. Lower sash first to open, last to close for partial ventilation.

All sash locked in unison with pressure seal to weather stripping

PLAIN RAIL DH WINDOW

1−1/8″ sash, either one fixed, other operative. Meeting rail thks. same as stiles and jamb w/o parting stop, so no separation between sash. Movable sash slides against fixed sash. Movable sash w/ bolts that engage holes in side jambs for holding sash open at any one of a number of predetermined positions.

SINGLE HUNG WINDOWS

Frame w/ stationary top sash or top section of frame glazed w/ bottom check rail and operative bottom sash which may be removable. GS: 1−light sash @ 20″x16″ − 44″x26″.

HORIZONTAL SLIDING WINDOWS

Frame with all sash operative or one or more operative sash with stationary sash. Operative sash may be removable. L, R, or center portion of frame may be glazed & w/ meeting stile(s) in lieu of stationary sash. Stiles, rails & meeting stiles: 1−3/8″ min. face dim. SO for 2 sash/frame @ approx. 3′x2′ − 5′−6:x6′. Commercial Standard limits glass height to 50″.

CASEMENT WINDOWS

Frame with one or more outswinging, inswinging, or stationary sash. French casement extends to floor. Stiles & top rail @ 1″−2″, bottom rail @ 3″ nom. Alternate: "Full Bound" sash. Outswinging: screen inside, regular or self-storing flexible type with operation similar to a window shade. SO range for 1 sash/frame @ 1′−4″x2′−2″ − 2′x6′.

AWNING/HOPPER WINDOWS

Frame with 1 or more operating sash. Awning: bottom of sash swings outward. Hopper: top of sash swings inward. Stiles and rails @ 1−1/2″ − 2″. Awning/hopper sash may be used as casement. Glass size: 1−light sash @ 27″x14″ − 48″x32″.

BASEMENT WINDOWS

Inswinging sash: awning or hopper type. 1, 2, or 3 light sash: modular & non-modular. Non-modular SO @ 1′−8″x1′−4″ − 3′,4:x2′−4″.

MISCELLANEOUS WINDOW TYPES

BARN OR UTILITY SASH:
Single sash window unit @ 1−1/8″ or 1−3/8″ thk. Raised through split head jamb with ploughed runways in side jambs. Spring bolts hold sash open in predetermined positions.

HOTBED SASH:
Used in plant cold frames & other greenhouse activities. 3−light @ 1−3/8″ or 1−3/4″ thick.

TRANSOM SASH:
1−light @ 1−3/8″ thick.

WINDOW JALOUSIES:
Wood sash frame with alum. insert frame housing 4″ high clear or obscure glass louvers. SO: 1′−7″x2′−0−1/4″ − 3′−1″x6′−11−3/4″, used singly, or as mullion, triple units or greater.

VINYL CLAD WINDOW UNITS:
DH/SH/HS/C/A/H & P windows. Sash & ext. portions of frame encased in vinyl.

FIRE WINDOWS:
Sash glazed with wired glass @ 1/4″ min. thk.

BOW WINDOWS:
DH/C/A/H/P & combinations of adjoining stock units from 3 to 8 wide, usually 5, installed on 12′−15′ radius, joined by special mullions. Head soffit and window seat may be included.

STANDARD WINDOW HEIGHT:
6′−8″ above fin. fl. DH not recommended for use over counter or sink.

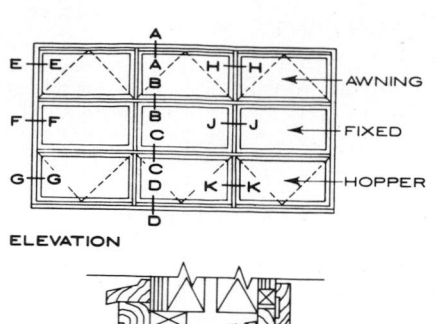

ELEVATION

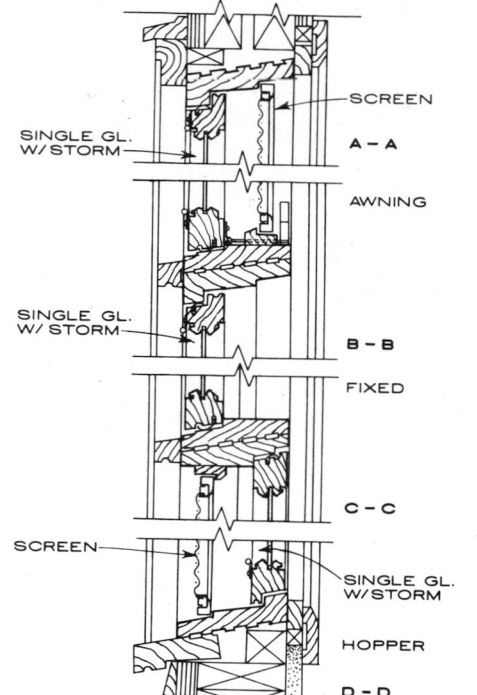

SINGLE GL. W/ STORM — A − A

AWNING

SINGLE GL. W/ STORM — B − B

FIXED

C − C

SCREEN

SINGLE GL. W/ STORM

HOPPER

D − D

VERTICAL SECTIONS

CARADCO COMBINED UNITS

Spring tension alum. WS at all sides of sash. Hopper version of these units can be used as casements—singly, in series, & combined with picture units.

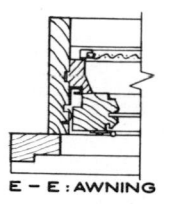
E − E : AWNING

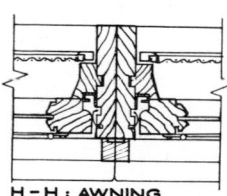
H−H : AWNING

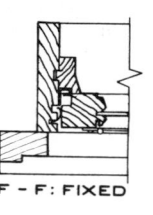
F − F : FIXED

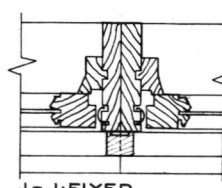
J − J : FIXED

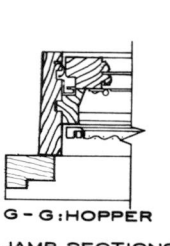
G − G : HOPPER

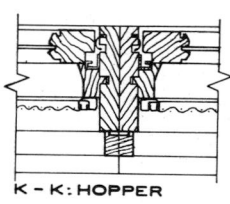
K − K : HOPPER

JAMB SECTIONS   MULLION SECTIONS

CARADCO COMBINED UNITS : AWNING − HOPPER − FIXED. PICTURE WITH AWNING/HOPPER

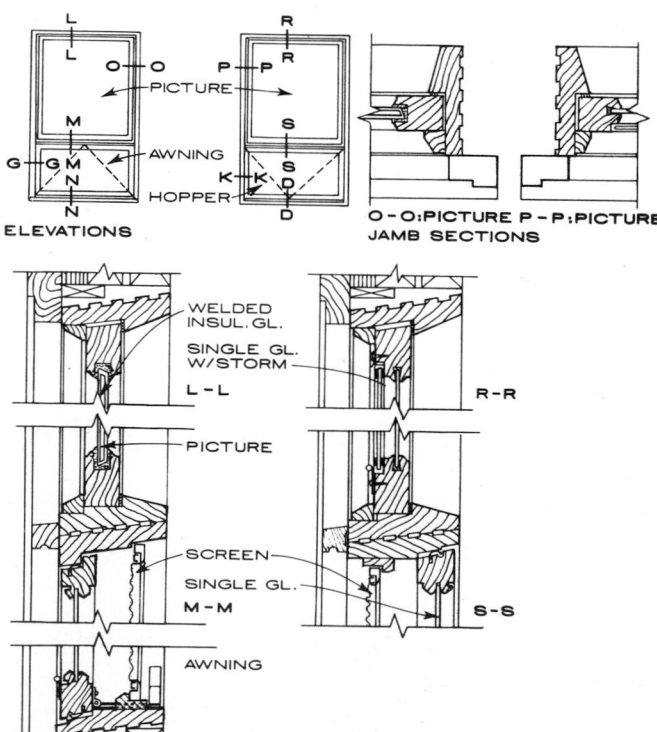

ELEVATIONS

PICTURE
AWNING
HOPPER

WELDED INSUL. GL.
SINGLE GL. W/ STORM
L − L
R − R

PICTURE
M − M
S − S

SCREEN
SINGLE GL.

AWNING
N − N

VERTICAL SECTIONS

O − O : PICTURE   P − P : PICTURE
JAMB SECTIONS

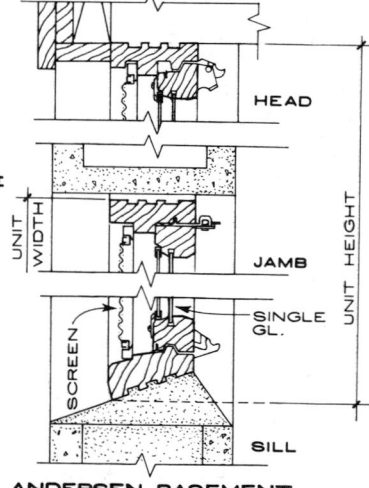

HEAD
JAMB
SINGLE GL.
SCREEN
SINGLE GL.
SILL
UNIT WIDTH
UNIT HEIGHT

ANDERSEN BASEMENT

Modular sizes:
2 blks. wide x 2, 2 1/2, or 3 high.

1 light glazing only.
Removable sash & dual purpose hinges for opening from top or bottom.

MAIN SILL & UNDERSILL

MAIN SILL & NOSING

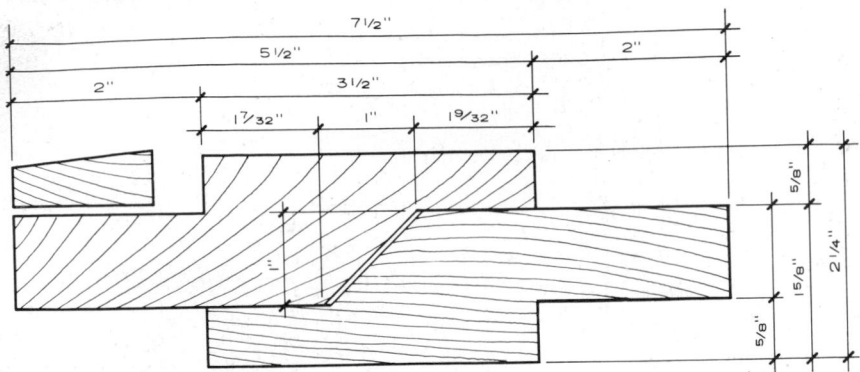

WOOD FRAME MEMBER
SCALE: HALF FULL SIZE

NOTE:

The following details illustrate how a 2" x 6" member (nominal dimension) may be milled in a single shape which can then be used to form most parts of the frames for windows, doors, and glass, including their heads, jambs, sills, mullions and posts. Members may be cut to a shape other than this and used equally well; the profile shown is an example only of this method of a multiuse wood frame member.

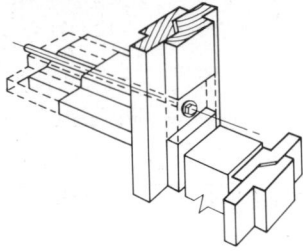

TENSION ROD DETAIL

Tension rods may be placed thru transom pieces to decrease deflection of transom under excessive glass or panel loads.

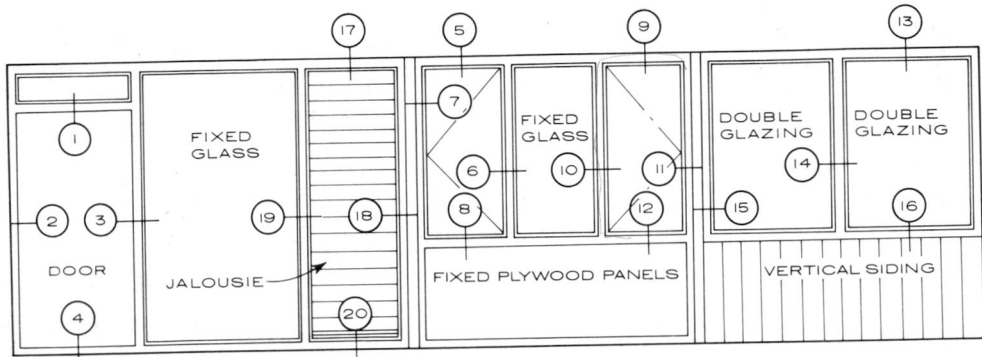

KEY ELEVATION

FIXED GLASS

DOOR

JALOUSIE

FIXED GLASS

FIXED PLYWOOD PANELS

DOUBLE GLAZING

DOUBLE GLAZING

VERTICAL SIDING

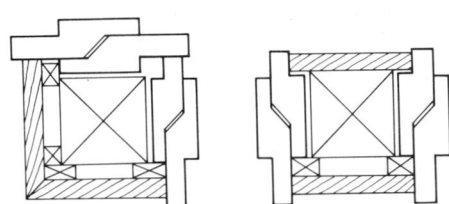

GENERAL APPLICATION OF POST
SCALE: 1 1/2" = 1'-0"

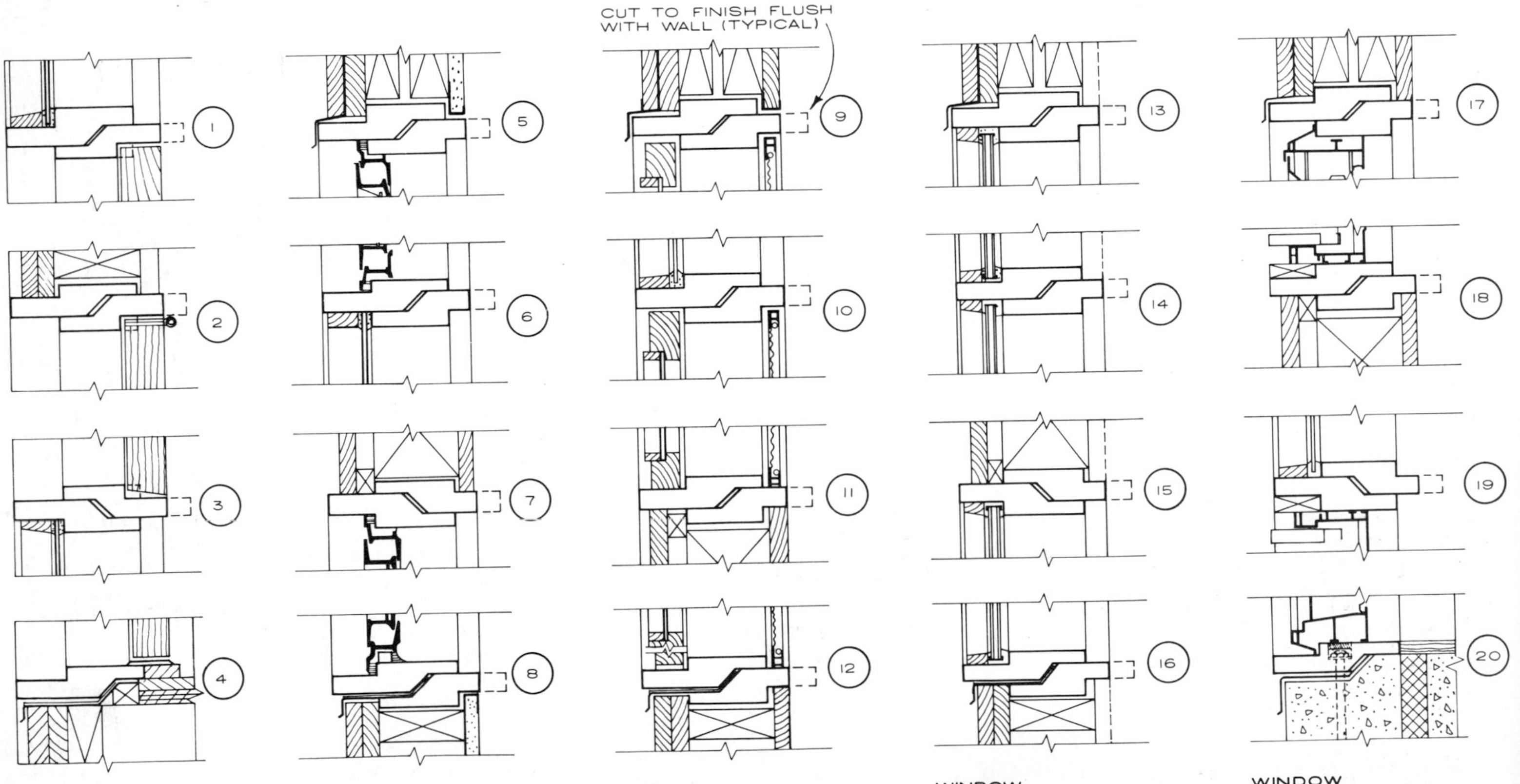

CUT TO FINISH FLUSH
WITH WALL (TYPICAL)

DOOR

WINDOW (STEEL)

WINDOW (WOOD)

WINDOW (DOUBLE GLAZING)

WINDOW (JALOUSIE)

DETAILS (OUTSIDE OF BUILDING IS SHOWN TO THE LEFT)
SCALE: 1 1/2" = 1'-0"

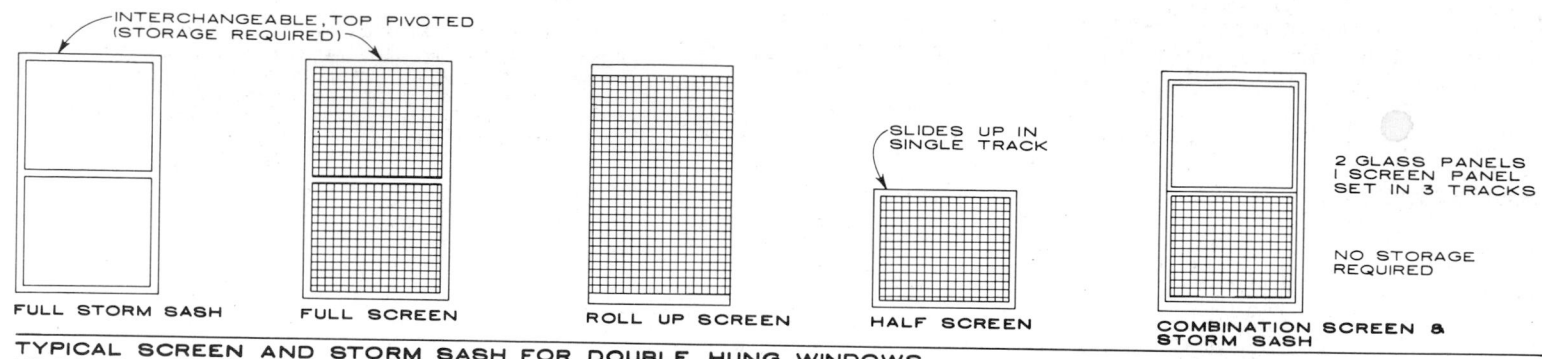

INTERCHANGEABLE, TOP PIVOTED
(STORAGE REQUIRED)

SLIDES UP IN
SINGLE TRACK

2 GLASS PANELS
1 SCREEN PANEL
SET IN 3 TRACKS

NO STORAGE
REQUIRED

FULL STORM SASH   FULL SCREEN   ROLL UP SCREEN   HALF SCREEN   COMBINATION SCREEN &
STORM SASH

TYPICAL SCREEN AND STORM SASH FOR DOUBLE HUNG WINDOWS
NO SCALE

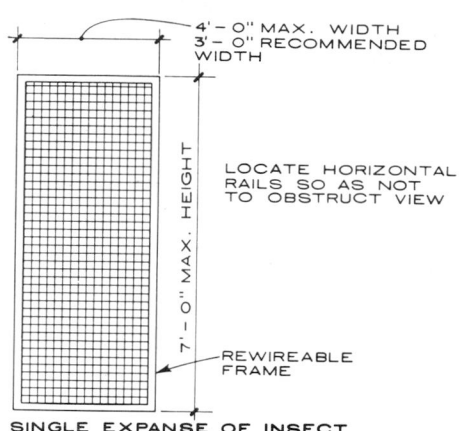

4' – 0" MAX. WIDTH
3' – 0" RECOMMENDED
WIDTH

7' – 0" MAX. HEIGHT

LOCATE HORIZONTAL
RAILS SO AS NOT
TO OBSTRUCT VIEW

REWIREABLE
FRAME

**SINGLE EXPANSE OF INSECT
SCREEN FOR PORCHES**
NO SCALE

STORM WINDOW FASTENED
TO CASEMENT (PIGGY BACK)

SCREEN ON INSIDE

**TYPICAL CASEMENT WINDOW
STORM SASH AND SCREEN**
NO SCALE

FULL STORM SASH
AND SCREEN,
INTERCHANGEABLE

**TYPICAL SLIDING WINDOW
STORM SASH AND SCREEN**
NO SCALE

TYPES OF SCREENING
TYPICAL 18 x 14 OR 18 x 16
WIRES PER INCH MESH

ALUMINUM - MILL FINISH
ALUMINUM - ANODIZED (GREEN OR
BLACK)
FIBERGLASS - HARD TO KEEP CLEAN
EXPANDS AND CONTRACTS
STAINLESS STEEL - EXPENSIVE
BRONZE - VERY EXPENSIVE

OTHER TYPES OF SCREENS
SEE MFR. INFORMATION

DETENTION
PROTECTION
SAFETY

Charles F. D. Egbert, AIA; Architect; Washington, D. C.

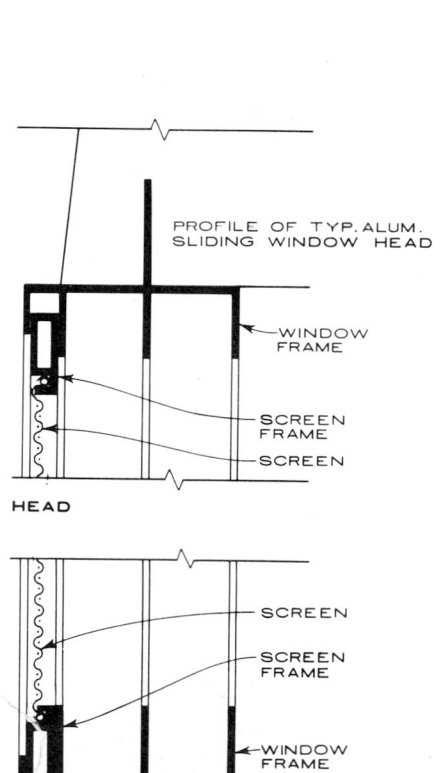

PROFILE OF TYP. ALUM.
SLIDING WINDOW HEAD

WINDOW
FRAME

SCREEN
FRAME

SCREEN

HEAD

SCREEN

SCREEN
FRAME

WINDOW
FRAME

PROFILE OF TYP. ALUM.
SLIDING WINDOW SILL

SILL

**TYPICAL SCREEN INSTALLATION
ON SLIDING ALUM. WINDOW**
SCALE: HALF FULL SIZE

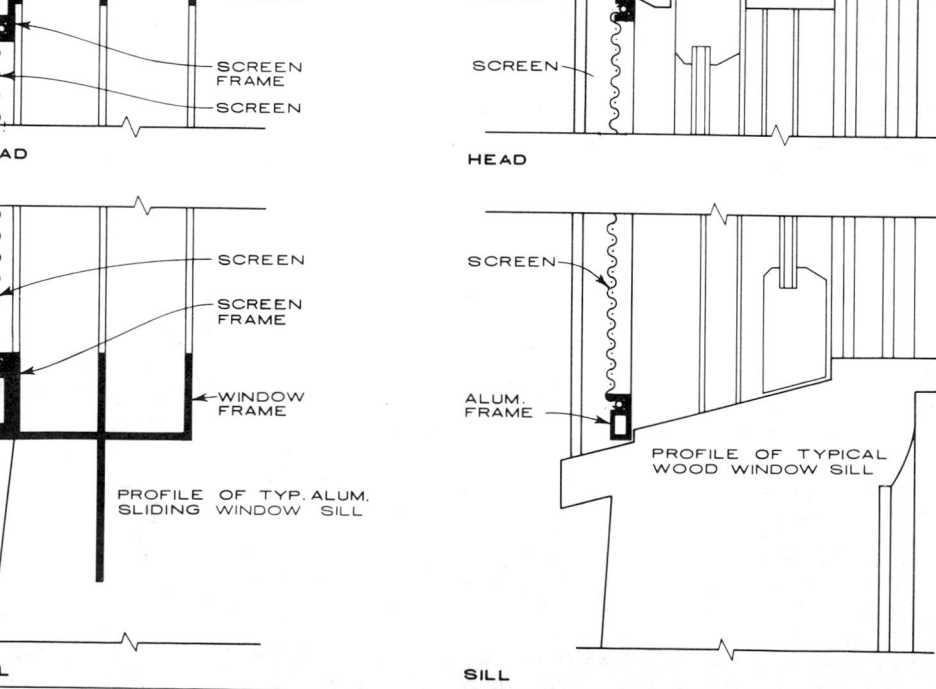

PROFILE OF TYPICAL
WOOD WINDOW HEAD

ALUM.
FRAME

SCREEN

HEAD

SCREEN

ALUM.
FRAME

PROFILE OF TYPICAL
WOOD WINDOW SILL

SILL

**TYPICAL SCREEN INSTALLATION
ON D.H. WOOD WINDOW**
SCALE: 3" = 1' – 0"

BASIC TYPES OF GLASS

Type of glass	Thick. in.	Wt./ s. f.	Quality	Max. stock size in.	Remarks

SHEET GLASS

Made by a flat or vertical draw process which produces transparent, natural flat-fired polished surfaces. Inherent surface wave is negligible in sizes less than 50 u.i. For larger sizes install with wave running horizontal for minimum distortion.

STANDARD

		oz.			
Picture		1/16	16	AA,A,B	90 u.i.
Window ss		3/32	19	AA,A,B	90 u.i.
ds		1/8	26	AA,A,B,G	140 u.i. G @ 20 x 24, T @ 36 x 66 comm.
hs		3/16	40	AA,A,B	120 x 84 T @ 50 x 92
hs		7/32	45	AA,A,B	120 x 84 HS @ 72 x 120, T @ 72 x 108
hs		1/4	52	AA,A,B	120 x 84 HS @ 72 x 168, T @ 72 x 108
hs		3/8	84	AA,A,B	60 x 84
hs		7/16	86	A,B	60 x 84

SOLAR HEAT & GLARE CONTROL

Window hs		1/8	26	glaz.	60 x 84 VLT @ 31%
hs		3/16	40	glaz.	120 x 84 VLT @ 61%, T @ 50 x 92
hs		7/32	46	glaz.	120 x 84 VLT @ 56%, HS @ 72 x 120, T @ 72 x 108
hs		7/32	46	glaz.	60 x 84 VLT @ 14%
hs		1/4	52	glaz.	120 x 84 HS @ 72 x 168

FLOAT GLASS

Formed by floating on surface of molten tin, with annealing process producing transparent flat flass. Grinding and polishing not required.

STANDARD	1/4	3.24	glaz.	122 x 200	HS @ 72 x 168, T @ 72 x 108

PLATE GLASS

Transparent flat glass ground and polished after rolling.

STANDARD

		lbs.			
Regular	1/8	1.64	glaz.,mir. glaz.,silv.	130 x 80	
	1/4	3.28	glaz.,mir. glaz.,silv.	130 x 240	twin ground for mirrors HS @ 72 x 168, T @ 72 x 120
Heavy duty	5/16	4.10	comm.	130 x 240	
	3/8	4.92	comm.	125 x 281	T @ 85 x 110
	1/2	6.56	comm.	125 x 281	T @ 96 x 120

also available in 5/8, 3/4, 7/8, and 1 — standard thicknesses

SOLAR HEAT & GLARE CONTROL

Regular	13/64	2.67	comm., glaz.	84 x 120	bronze, gray
	1/4	3.29	comm., glaz.	124 x 214	bronze gray, blue green HS @ 72 x 168, T @ 72 x 120
Heavy duty	3/8	4.93	comm.	120 x 280	bronze, gray, blue green T @ 72 x 120
	1/2	6.57	comm.	120 x 278	bronze, gray. T @ 96 x 120

HEAVY ROUGH PLATE: one or both sides not polished after rolling.

	17/64	3.47	comm.	76 x 138	clear, bronze, gray, glue green— polished 1 side, T @ 72 x 120
	9/32	3.70	comm.	130 x 240	clear
				124 x 214	bronze, gray, blue green HS @ 72 x 168, T @ 72 x 120
	7/16	5.75	comm.	130 x 240	clear
				120 x 280	bronze, gray, blue green T @ 85 x 110

also available in 9/16 — clear, bronze, gray; 13/16 — clear and 1-1/8 — clear standard thicknesses.

VARIATIONS OF BASIC TYPES OF GLASS

TEMPERED GLASS   Standard types and max. sizes given in above table. Process of reheating and sudden cooling of base glass which greatly increases mechanical strength and resistance to thermal stresses.
3-5 times as strong as base glass.
Cannot be altered after tempering.
Special limitations as to placement size and configuration of cutout areas. Pulverizes when broken.

HEAT STRENGTHENED GLASS — Std types and max. sizes given in above table.
As per tempered glass above, except:
Twice as strong as base glass.
Does not pulverize when broken.

BENT GLASS
Cylindrical and conic shapes bent to desired curvature. Within limits.
Shapes must be supported during tempering process.
Twice as strong as base glass.

PATTERNED GLASS
Semitransparent rolled glass varying from almost clear to almost obscure. Greater obscurity achieved by special patterns and finishes. Diffusion types with permanent glare reducing finish applied to pattern size or both sides of glass not recommended for partitions.
Decorative types as per table below.

	1/8	1.75	comm.	48 x 120	Special finishes available: 1 or
	1/8	2.0	comm.	96 x 132	2 sides — satin, frosted, and glare
	7/32	3.6	comm.	96 x 132	reducing. Max. sizes may vary in
	3/8	5.0	comm.	60 x 144	some instances. Also available in SHGC, tempered and white trans- lucent glass.
	3/8	6.3		50 x 144	Structural corrugated @ 1" o.a.

Approved by National Board of Fire Underwriters as a fire retardant glass.

	1/4	3.5	comm.	72 x 130	Max. sizes vary with mfgrs. Square or diamond pattern, hexagonal (vert. or hor. chicken wire.) polished or various types of patterned glass.

Type of glass	Thick. in.	Wt./ s. f.	Quality	Max. stock size	Remarks

MIRRORS

Regular	AS, SG, FG, and			PG	clear and SHGC glass PG: avail. with copper back max. size @ 84" x 120"
One-way	1/8	as PG	as PG	30 x 80	clear and SHGC plate, safety
	1/4	as PG	as PG	30 x 80	plate, tempered plate; for greater thicknesses consult mfr. for stock sizes

SPANDREL GLASS

Clear sheet, float, plate or wire glass.
Opaque with vitreous color fire-fused to back.
Glass is heat strengthened in the process.
2-5 times as strong as base glass.
Fire-fused surface always faces back-up wall
Unless with integral insulation and vapor barrier 1/2" air space is required between spandrel glass and back-up.
Variety of standard colors available.
Special finishes available.
Pinholes and nonuniformity of color apparent if used without back-up.

Thick. in.	Wt./ s. f. lbs.	Max. stock size	Remarks
1/4	3.3	72 x 168	FG, FG
9/32	3.62	72 x 168	HRP
5/16	4.25	60 x 120	patterned glass
3/8	4.95	72 x 168	PG
1-1/4	3.6	72 x 168	PG 1" fiber glass insulation with aluminum foil
1-1/4	3.9	72 x 168	HRP vapor barrier applied to 1/4" spandrel glass
1/4	3.3	72 x 168	PG,FG both spandrel and vision areas
9/32	3.62	72 x 168	HRP in one panel

LAMINATED GLASS

SAFETY GLASS
Tough transparent plastic sandwiched under heat and pressure between 2 layers of sheet or plate glass.
When fractured particles tend to adhere to plastic
Plastic tinted to control glare, light and heat.
Thicker plastic for sound absorption.

Thick. in.	Wt./ s. f. lbs.	Max. stock size	Type of glass	Remarks
3/16	2.42	15 s. f.	ss + ss	clear
7/32	2.49	15 s. f.	ss + ss	clear or tinted
15/64	2.91	15 s. f.	ss + ds	clear or tinted
1/4	3.32	15 s. f.	ds + ds	clear, also sound control @ 46 x 120, clear or tinted.
1/4	3.25	72 x 138	1/8" PG + 1/8" PG	clear or tinted
5/16	3.5	66 x 120	1/8" PG + 1/8" PG	clear, also sound control @ 46 x 144, clear or tinted.

also available in thicknesses of 3/8", 1/2", 5/8", 3/4", 7/8" and 1" with maximum size @ 72 x 138 clear or tinted PG.

BULLET RESISTING GLASS
Safety glass with laminations of 3-5 layers of plate glass.
Thickness range @ 3/4" — 3".
Max. stock size @ 72" x 138" at thicknesses thru 1-3/16".
Beyond 1-3/16" thickness max. size determined by weight.

CATHEDRAL (ART) GLASS
1/8" thickness, max. size @ 32 x 84, many colors and patterns.

INSULATING GLASS
Two pieces of glass, separated by hermetically sealed air space.
Glass edge: 3/16" air space with sheet glass.
Metal edge: 1/4 or 1/2' air space with sheet, float, plate, or patterned glass.
Tempered, laminated and wired glass available in limited size range.
Triple glazing insulating glass available for special applications.

Edge type	Thick. gl. in.	Type of glass	o. a. thick. in. 3/16" air space	Wt./ s. f. lbs.	Max. s. f.	Remarks
Glass	3/32	ssA + ssA	3/8	2.4	10	max. dim. @ 70"
	1/8	dsA + dsA	7/16	3.2	24	max. dim. @ 70"
			1/4" 1/2" air space			
Metal	1/8	dsA + dsA	9/16 13/16	3.25	16	
	1/8	SHGC hs + dsA	9/16 13/16	3.25	12	
	1/8	reg PG + reg PG	9/16 13/16	3.25	12	
	1/8	SHGC PG + reg PG	19/32 27/32	3.25	16	
	1/8	patt. + patt.	1/2 3/4	3.25	16	
	3/16	hs + hs	23/32 31/32	5.25	27	
	3/16	SHGC hs + hs	11/16 15/16	5.25	27	
	1/4	PG or FG + PG or FG	27/32 1-3/32	6.5	70	
	1/4	SHGC PG + PG or FG	27/32 1-3/32	6.5	50	HS @ 70 s. f.
	7/32	patt. + patt.	25/32 1-1/32	6.25	33.3	

SPECIAL PROPRIETARY GLASS   by Corning Glass Works
Flexible Glass—"Chemcor"; chemically tempered. 3-5 times strength of heat tempered glass can be bent, returns to original shape on release of pressure.
Ceramic Glass—"Pyroceram": opaque, produced in sheets, white or colored.

ABBREVIATIONS

comm.	— commercial	patt.	— patterned
ds.	— double strength	PG.	— Plate Glass
FG.	— Float Glass	silv.	— silvering
G	— greenhouse	SG.	— Sheet Glass
glaz.	— glazing	SHGC.	— Solar Heat and Glare Control
HRP.	— Heavy Rough Plate	ss.	— single strength
hs.	— heavy sheet	T.	— Tempered
HS.	— Heat Strengthened	u.i.	— united inches = Length + Width
mir.	— mirror	VLT.	— Visual Light Transmittance

Data shown represents one or more manufacturers in each instance.

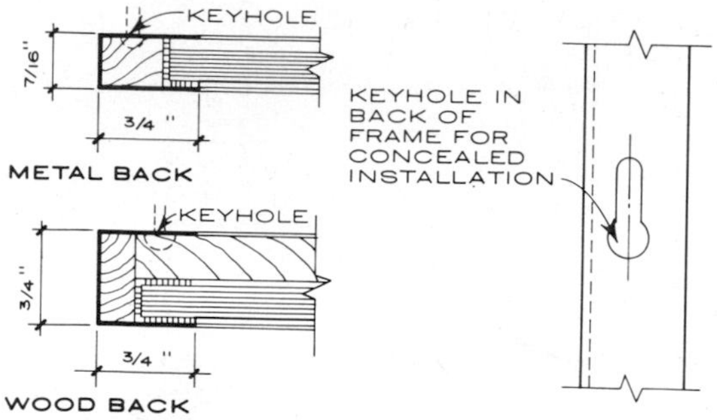
KEYHOLE
7/16"
3/4"
METAL BACK
KEYHOLE
3/4"
3/4"
WOOD BACK
KEYHOLE IN BACK OF FRAME FOR CONCEALED INSTALLATION

MIRROR WITH METAL FRAME

Available in brass, bronze and nickel silver with any polished or plated finish.

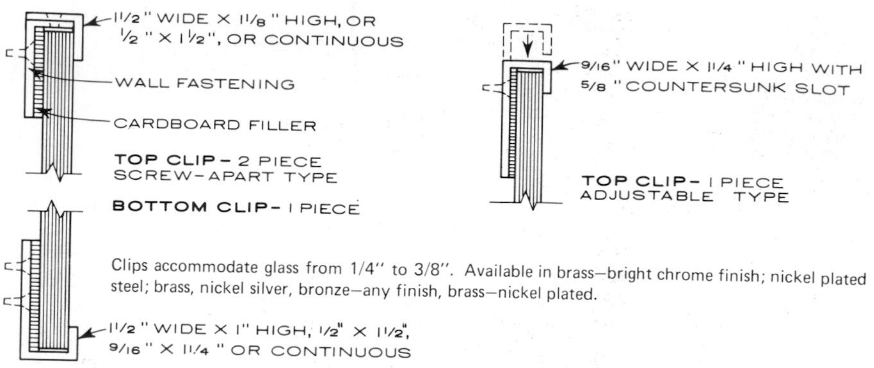
1 1/2" WIDE X 1 1/8" HIGH, OR 1/2" X 1 1/2", OR CONTINUOUS
WALL FASTENING
CARDBOARD FILLER
TOP CLIP – 2 PIECE SCREW-APART TYPE
BOTTOM CLIP – 1 PIECE
1 1/2" WIDE X 1" HIGH, 1/2" X 1 1/2", 9/16" X 1 1/4" OR CONTINUOUS
9/16" WIDE X 1 1/4" HIGH WITH 5/8" COUNTERSUNK SLOT
TOP CLIP – 1 PIECE ADJUSTABLE TYPE

Clips accommodate glass from 1/4" to 3/8". Available in brass—bright chrome finish; nickel plated steel; brass, nickel silver, bronze—any finish, brass—nickel plated.

MIRROR CLIPS

MIRROR GLAZING DETAILS
SCALE: HALF FULL SIZE

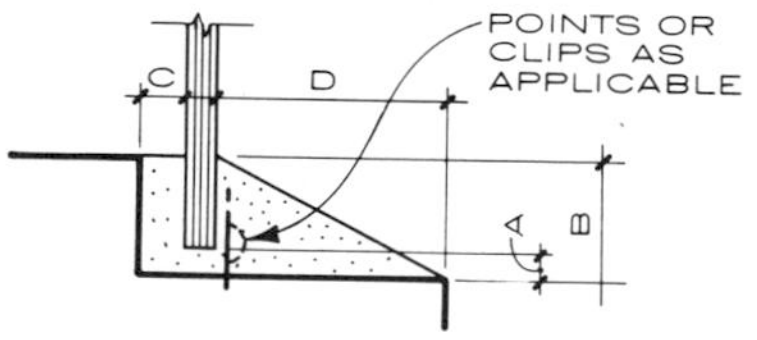
POINTS OR CLIPS AS APPLICABLE
C
D
A
B

FACE GLAZING
(WOOD OR METAL)

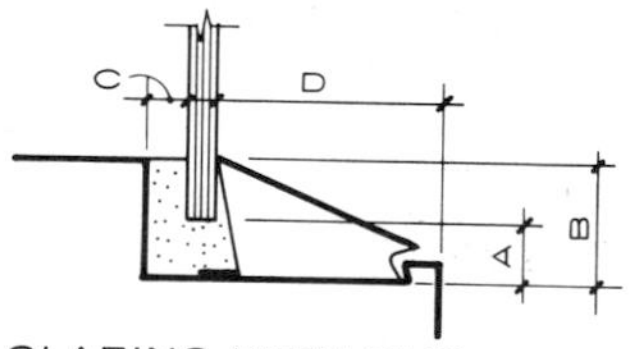
C
D
A
B

GLAZING WITH CLIP
(METAL)

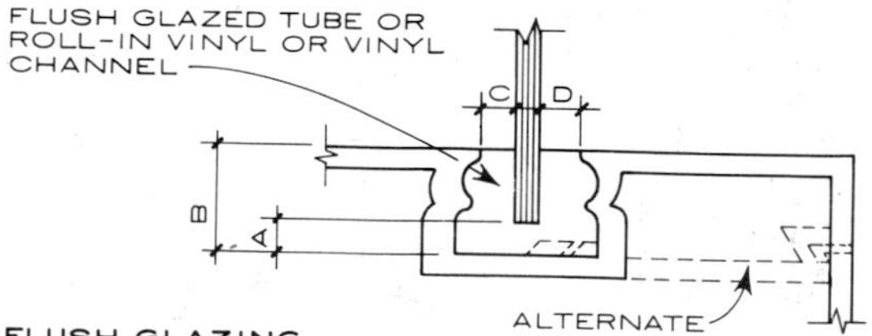
FLUSH GLAZED TUBE OR ROLL-IN VINYL OR VINYL CHANNEL
C
D
A
B
ALTERNATE WITH SNAP-ON CLIP

FLUSH GLAZING
(METAL)

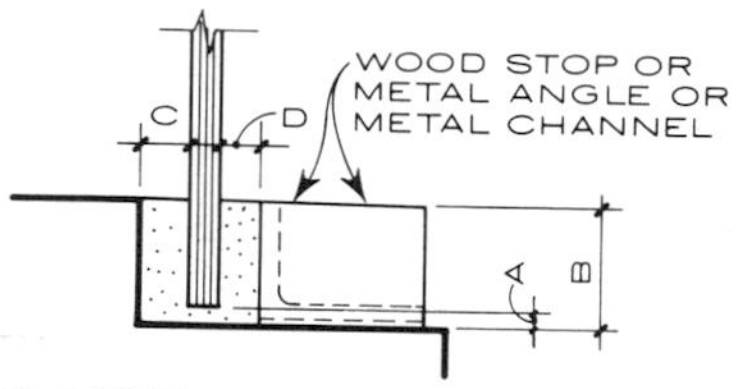
WOOD STOP OR METAL ANGLE OR METAL CHANNEL
C
D
A
B

GLAZING WITH STOP
(WOOD OR METAL)

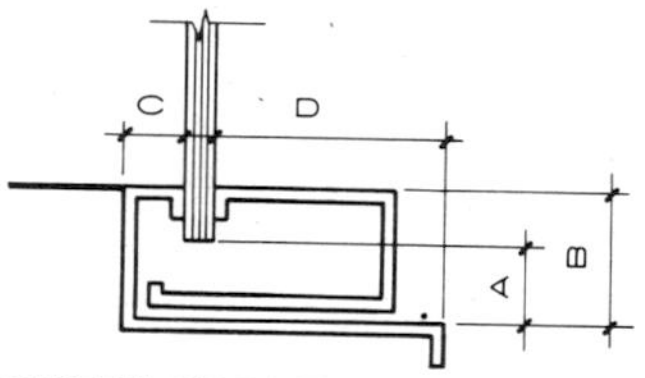
C
D
A
B

STORE FRONT SASH GLAZING
(METAL)

NOTE:

1. "A" & "B" dimensions are shown on chart.
2. "C" dimension is 1/16" for glass up to 5 sq. ft. 1/8" min. on all over 5 sq. ft. except for store front sash which is 0".
3. "D" dimension for face glazing is 3/8" min. For clip glazing and store front sash glazing, dimension is 0"; For flush glazing, the dimension is 1/8".

EDGE CLEARANCES A & B FOR SINGLE GLAZING DETAILS

GLASS TYPE	THICKNESS (INCHES)	GLASS AREA (SQ.FT.)	SIZE WIDTH OR HEIGHT (IN.)	A DIM. (IN.) ALLOW CLEARANCE HEAD, SILL, JAMB	B DIM. (IN.) RABBET DEPTH (MIN.)
SHEET	ss 3/32	5	40	1/16	3/8
	ss 3/32	14	50	1/6	7/16
	ds 1/8	5	40	1/16	3/6
	ds 1/8	25	80	1/8	7/16
	hs 3/16	25	120	11/62	1/2
	hs 3/16	70	120	15/62	5/8
	hs 7/32	25	120	11/64	1/2
	hs 7/32	70	120	15/64	5/8
SPANDREL & HEAT-STRENGTHENED	1/4	25	80	5/32	1/2
	1/4	84	168	1/4	5/8
	3/8	25	80	5/32	1/2
	3/8	84	168	1/4	5/8

GLASS TYPE (CON'T)	THICKNESS (INCHES)	GLASS AREA (SQ.FT.)	SIZE WIDTH OR HEIGHT (IN.)	A DIM. (IN.) ALLOW CLEARANCE HEAD, SILL, JAMB	B DIM. (IN.) RABBET DEPTH (MIN.)
POLISHED PLATE CLEAR & TINTED	1/8	25	128	11/64	1/2
	1/8	67	128	15/64	5/8
	1/4	100	120	11/64	1/2
	1/4	140	156	1/4	5/8
	1/4	207	229	11/32	3/4
	5/16	207	229	11/32	3/4
	3/8	258	286	3/8	3/4
	3/8	258	286	7/16	7/8
	1/2	258	286	7/16	7/8

NOTE: FOR GLASS LARGER OR THICKER THAN SHOWN, CONSULT MANUFACTURER.

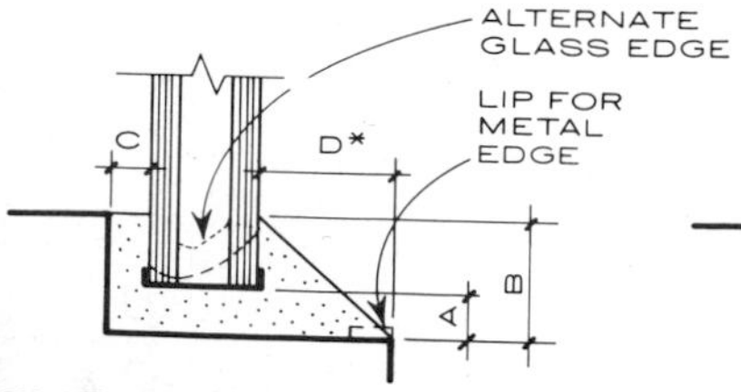
ALTERNATE GLASS EDGE
LIP FOR METAL EDGE
C
D*
A
B

FACE GLAZING
(WOOD OR METAL)

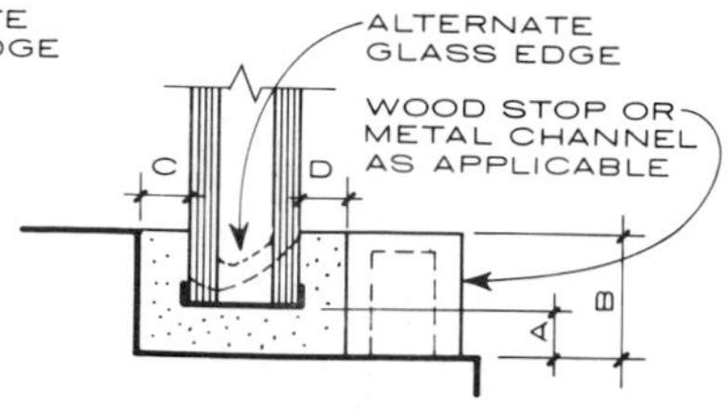
ALTERNATE GLASS EDGE
WOOD STOP OR METAL CHANNEL AS APPLICABLE
C
D
A
B

GLAZING WITH STOP
(WOOD OR METAL)

EDGE CLEARANCES A B C D

TYPE	THICK. (INCHES)	MAX. SQ.FT.	MIN. DIM. (INCHES) A	B	C	D*	D
GLASS EDGE S.S	3/8	TO 10	1/8	5/8	1/8	1/2	1/8
GLASS EDGE D.S	7/16	TO 24	1/8	5/8	1/8	1/2	1/8
METAL EDGE	9/16 13/16	12	1/8	5/8	1/8	1/2	1/8
METAL EDGE	11/16 15/16	27	1/4	3/4	1/8	5/8	1/8
METAL EDGE	13/16 1 1/16	70	1/4	3/4	1/8	5/8	1/8

DOUBLE GLAZING DETAILS
SCALE: HALF FULL SIZE

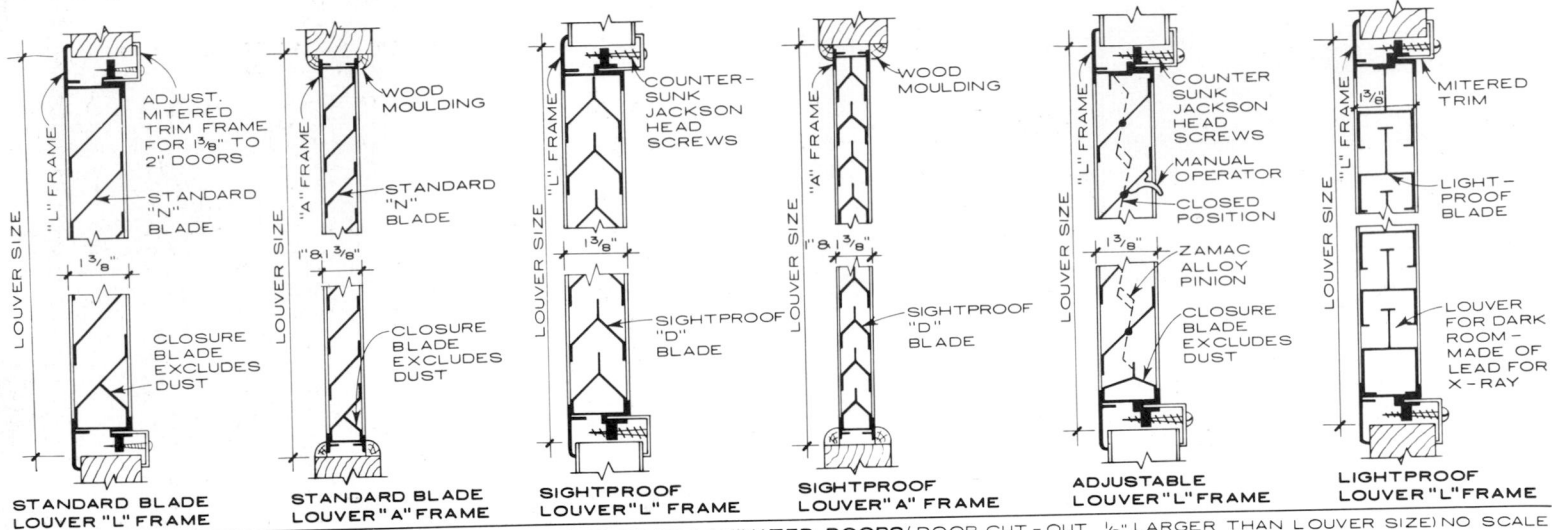

STANDARD BLADE LOUVER "L" FRAME — ADJUST. MITERED TRIM FRAME FOR 1⅜" TO 2" DOORS · STANDARD "N" BLADE · CLOSURE BLADE EXCLUDES DUST · "L" FRAME · LOUVER SIZE · 1⅜"

STANDARD BLADE LOUVER "A" FRAME — WOOD MOULDING · STANDARD "N" BLADE · CLOSURE BLADE EXCLUDES DUST · "A" FRAME · LOUVER SIZE · 1" & 1⅜"

SIGHTPROOF LOUVER "L" FRAME — COUNTER-SUNK JACKSON HEAD SCREWS · SIGHTPROOF "D" BLADE · "L" FRAME · LOUVER SIZE · 1⅜"

SIGHTPROOF LOUVER "A" FRAME — WOOD MOULDING · SIGHTPROOF "D" BLADE · "A" FRAME · LOUVER SIZE · 1" & 1⅜"

ADJUSTABLE LOUVER "L" FRAME — COUNTER SUNK JACKSON HEAD SCREWS · MANUAL OPERATOR · CLOSED POSITION · ZAMAC ALLOY PINION · CLOSURE BLADE EXCLUDES DUST · "L" FRAME · LOUVER SIZE · 1⅜"

LIGHTPROOF LOUVER "L" FRAME — MITERED TRIM · LIGHTPROOF BLADE · LOUVER FOR DARK ROOM — MADE OF LEAD FOR X-RAY · "L" FRAME · LOUVER SIZE · 1⅜"

DOOR LOUVERS — FOR WOOD, HOLLOW METAL, & PLASTIC LAMINATED DOORS (DOOR CUT-OUT ⅛" LARGER THAN LOUVER SIZE) NO SCALE

NOTE: See pages on wood and metal doors for other door louver designs.

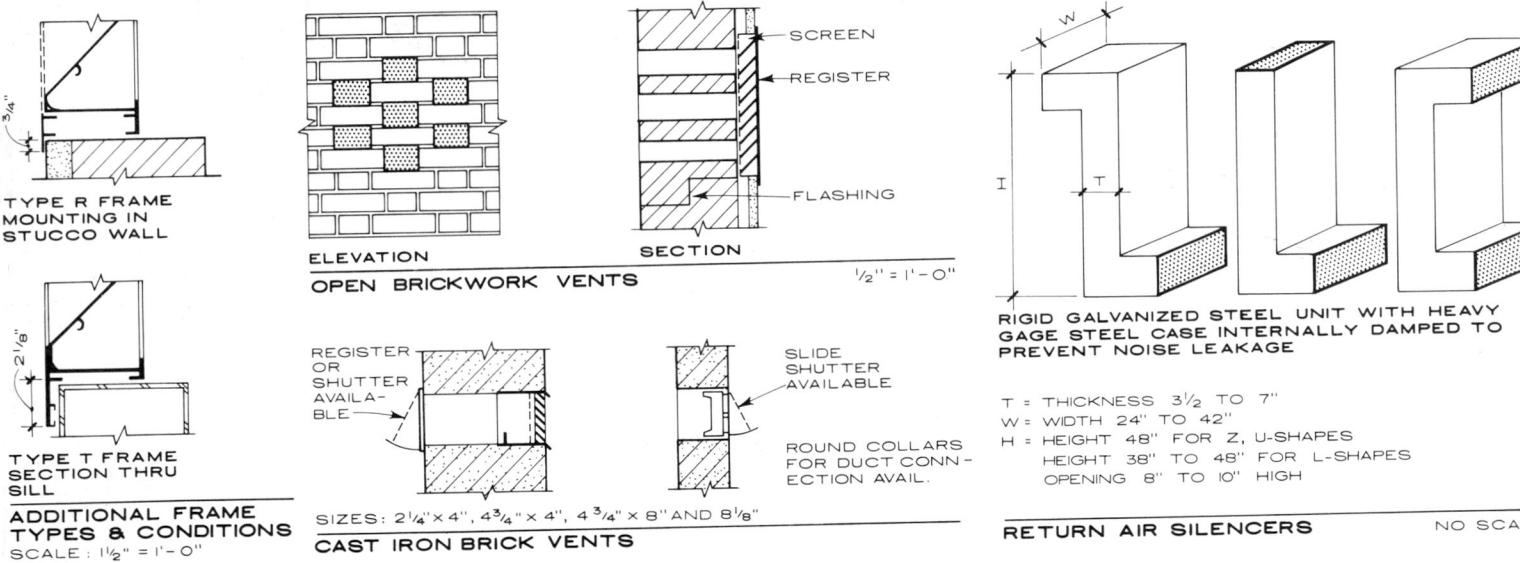

TYPE R FRAME MOUNTING IN STUCCO WALL — ¾"

TYPE T FRAME SECTION THRU SILL — 2⅛"

ADDITIONAL FRAME TYPES & CONDITIONS
SCALE : 1½" = 1'-0"

OPEN BRICKWORK VENTS — ELEVATION · SECTION · SCREEN · REGISTER · FLASHING · ½" = 1'-0"

CAST IRON BRICK VENTS — REGISTER OR SHUTTER AVAILABLE · SLIDE SHUTTER AVAILABLE · ROUND COLLARS FOR DUCT CONNECTION AVAIL. · SIZES: 2¼" × 4", 4¾" × 4", 4¾" × 8" AND 8⅛"

RETURN AIR SILENCERS — RIGID GALVANIZED STEEL UNIT WITH HEAVY GAGE STEEL CASE INTERNALLY DAMPED TO PREVENT NOISE LEAKAGE

T = THICKNESS 3½ TO 7"
W = WIDTH 24" TO 42"
H = HEIGHT 48" FOR Z, U-SHAPES
    HEIGHT 38" TO 48" FOR L-SHAPES
    OPENING 8" TO 10" HIGH

NO SCALE

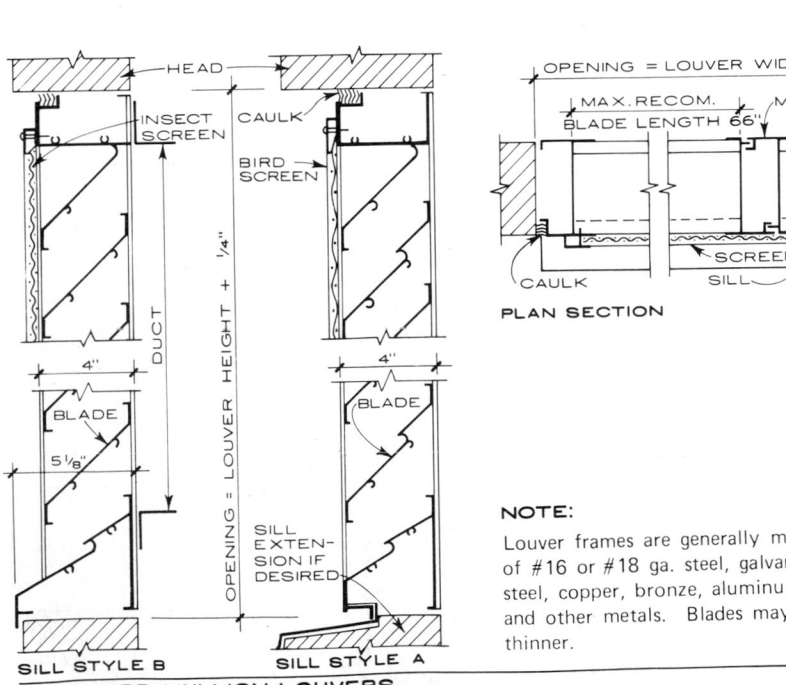

STANDARD MULLION LOUVERS — HEAD · INSECT SCREEN · CAULK · BIRD SCREEN · DUCT · OPENING = LOUVER HEIGHT + ¼" · BLADE · 5⅛" · 4" · SILL EXTENSION IF DESIRED · SILL STYLE B · SILL STYLE A

OPENING = LOUVER WIDTH + ¼" · MAX. RECOM. BLADE LENGTH 66" · MULLION · CAULK · SCREEN · SILL · **PLAN SECTION**

NOTE: Louver frames are generally made of #16 or #18 ga. steel, galvanized steel, copper, bronze, aluminum, and other metals. Blades may be thinner.

1½" = 1'-0"

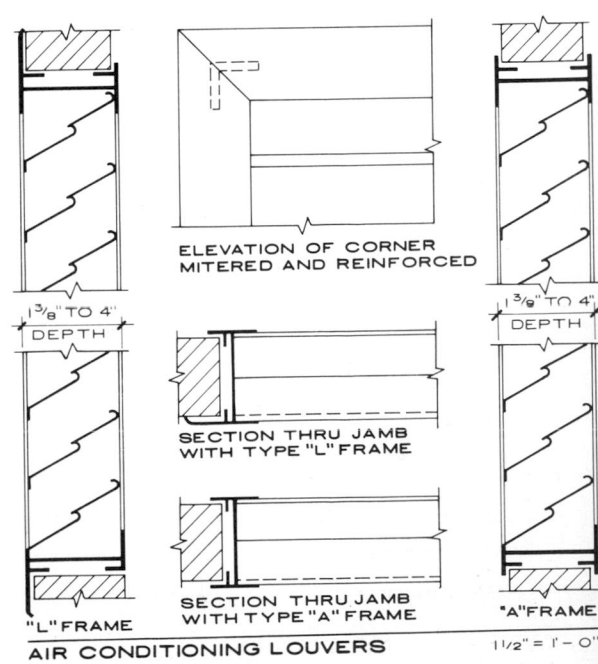

AIR CONDITIONING LOUVERS — ELEVATION OF CORNER MITERED AND REINFORCED · "L" FRAME · 1⅜" TO 4" DEPTH · SECTION THRU JAMB WITH TYPE "L" FRAME · SECTION THRU JAMB WITH TYPE "A" FRAME · "A" FRAME · 1⅜" TO 4" DEPTH · 1½" = 1'-0"

Charles Driesen; Ewing Cole Erdman & Eubank; Philadelphia, Pennsylvania

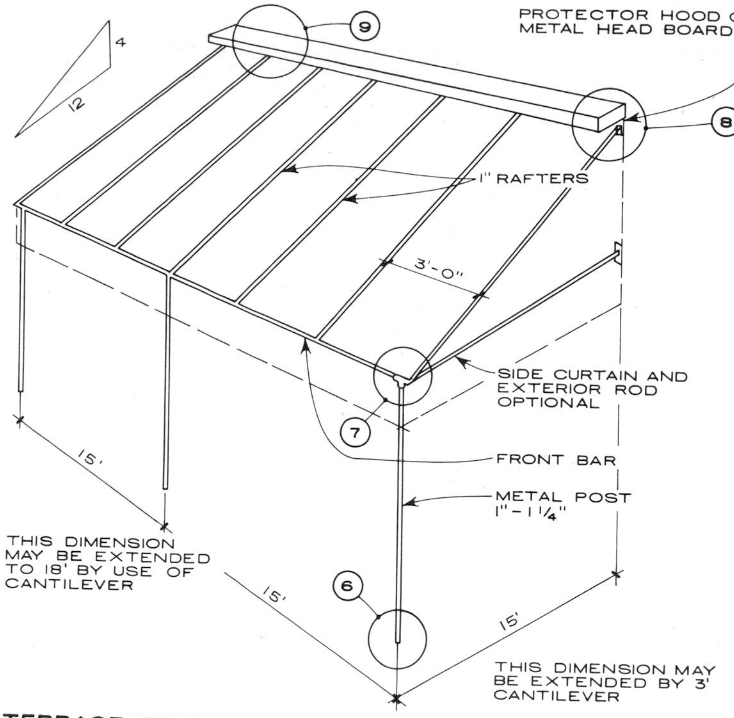

TERRACE OR ROOF AWNINGS

PROTECTOR HOOD GALV. METAL HEAD BOARD

9

8

1" RAFTERS

3'-0"

SIDE CURTAIN AND EXTERIOR ROD OPTIONAL

7

FRONT BAR

METAL POST 1"—1¼"

6

15'

THIS DIMENSION MAY BE EXTENDED TO 18' BY USE OF CANTILEVER

15'

15'

THIS DIMENSION MAY BE EXTENDED BY 3' CANTILEVER

4

12

NOTES: TERRACE OR ROOF AWNINGS

To provide complete sun protection and shade, the overall length of the awning bar should extend 3 inches past the glass line on both sides. For proper sun shade protection, awnings should project at least as far forward from the face of the window as the bottom of the window is below the front bar of the awning.

The wall measurement of an awning is the distance down the face of the building from the point where the awning attaches to the face of the building (or from the center of the roller in the case of the roller type awning).

The projection of an awning is the distance from the face of the building to the front bar of the awning in its correct projected position.

Right and left of an awning are your right and left as you are facing the awning looking into the building.

Framework consists of galvanized steel pipe, with non-rattling fittings. Awning is lace-on type canvas with rope reinforced eave. Protector hood is galvanized sheet metal or either bronze, copper, or aluminum.

Roller type awnings are also available as well as pre-enameled aluminum and concealed recess awnings. Pre-enameled aluminum is corrugated and is available in a wide range of colors.

Concealed recess awnings require a recess box (size depending on measurements of awning) with hinged type fascia cover in the front construction of the building. Sizes of members should be checked by calculation for conditions not similar to those shown on this page.

NOTES: CANOPIES

Nylon adjusted to frame with leather straps or rope reinforced lashing eave.

Spans:

Frames up to 6'—0" width require 5 rafters.
Frames 6'—0" to 8'—0" width require 7 rafters.
Frames 8'—0" to 11'—0" width require 9 rafters.
Frames 11'—0" to 15'—0" width require 11 rafters.

Canopy frame specifications:

Uprights: 1¼" galvanized pipes.
Rafters: 1" galvanized pipe to 15'—0" length.
Bows: 1" body bows; ¾" head bows.
Side braces: ⅝" steel or brass.

9

8

7

6

5

4

3

RAFTER ENDS DROP FORGED STEEL GALV. TYPICAL

2

1

CAP PLUG

BRONZE WATERPROOF SOCKETS SET FLUSH IN CONCRETE

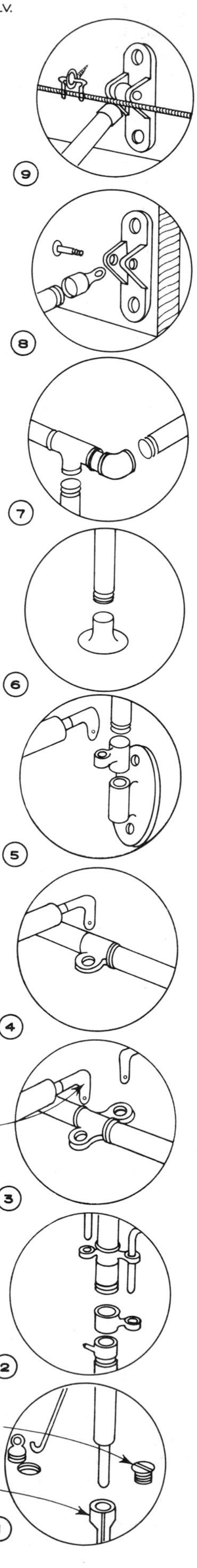

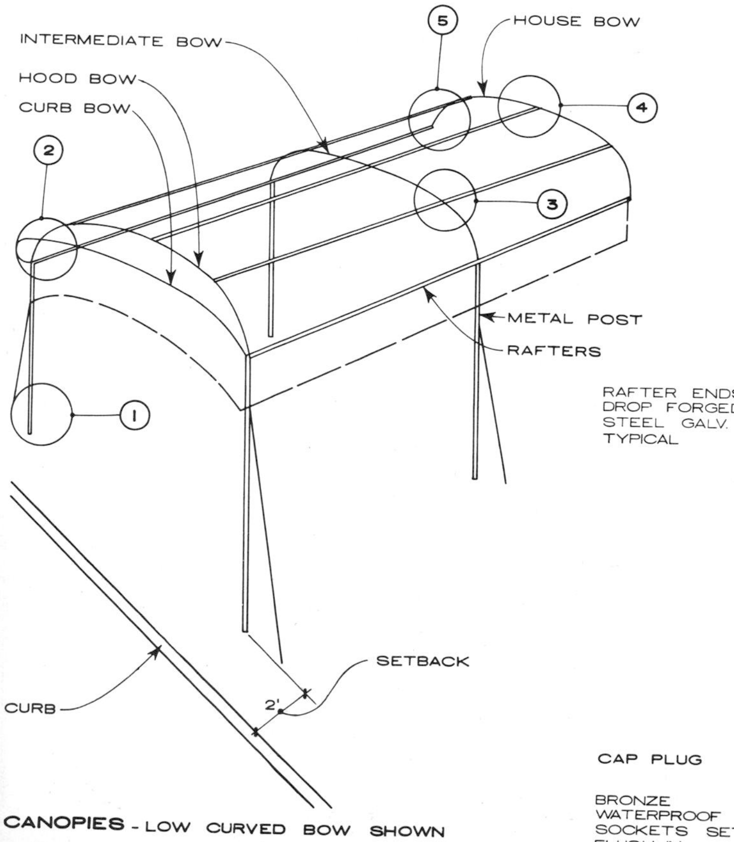

CANOPIES - LOW CURVED BOW SHOWN

INTERMEDIATE BOW
HOOD BOW
CURB BOW

2

5   HOUSE BOW

4

3

1

METAL POST

RAFTERS

SETBACK

CURB   2'

NOTE:

CONSULT LOCAL BUILDING CODE FOR LIMITATIONS ON HEIGHT AND SETBACK.

Richard Malesardi and Associates, Architects; Washington, D. C.

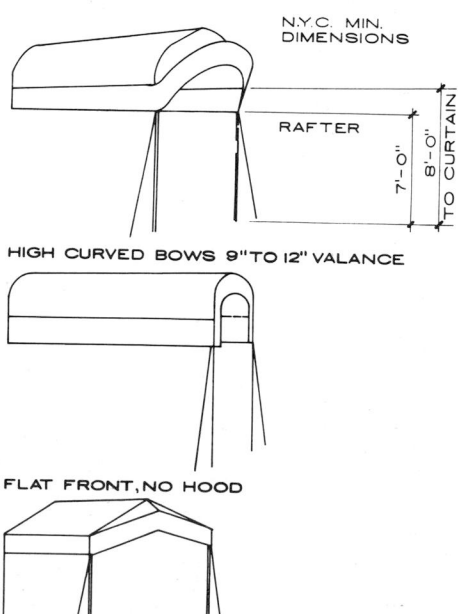

N.Y.C. MIN. DIMENSIONS

RAFTER

7'-0"   8'-0" TO CURTAIN

HIGH CURVED BOWS 9" TO 12" VALANCE

FLAT FRONT, NO HOOD

GABLE BOW, STRAIGHT CURTAIN

CANOPY TYPES

CHAPTER **9**

FINISH MATERIALS

2.5 AND 3.4 LBS. PER SQ. YD.; 24" & 27"
WIDE × 8'-0" LONG

DIAMOND MESH EXPANDED METAL LATH

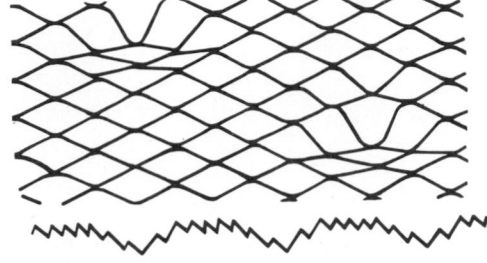

¼" DEEP "DIMPLES" 1½" OR 1¾" O.C.;
24" & 27" WIDE × 8'-0" LONG

SELF-FURRING DIAMOND MESH LATH

3/8" OR 3/4"   11/32 OR 11/16"

3/8" AND 3/4" DEEP RIBS; 4½" AND 6" O.C.; 27" AND 24" WIDE; 8' AND 8', 10' AND 12' LONG RESPECTIVELY

RIB EXPANDED METAL LATH

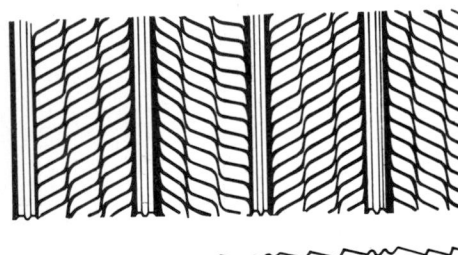

2.75 AND 2.4 LBS. PER SQ. YD., 24" W. × 8' L.

FLAT RIB EXPANDED METAL LATH

GYPSUM LATH:

Gypsum lath is composed of an air-entrained gypsum core sandwiched between two sheets of fibrous absorbent paper and used as a basecoat for gypsum plaster. See page on SPECIAL SYSTEMS.
PLAIN GYPSUM LATH is 3/8" and 1/2" thick, 48" lg. and 16" wide (16 1/5" in the Western U.S.).
PERFORATED GYPSUM LATH is plain gypsum lath with 3/4" diameter holes punched 4" o.c. in both directions to provide mechanical key to plaster.
INSULATING GYPSUM LATH is plain gypsum lath with aluminum foil laminated to the backside.
LONG LENGTH GYPSUM LATH 16" and 24" wide, in lengths up to 12' is available insulated or plain with square or vee-jointed T & G edges.

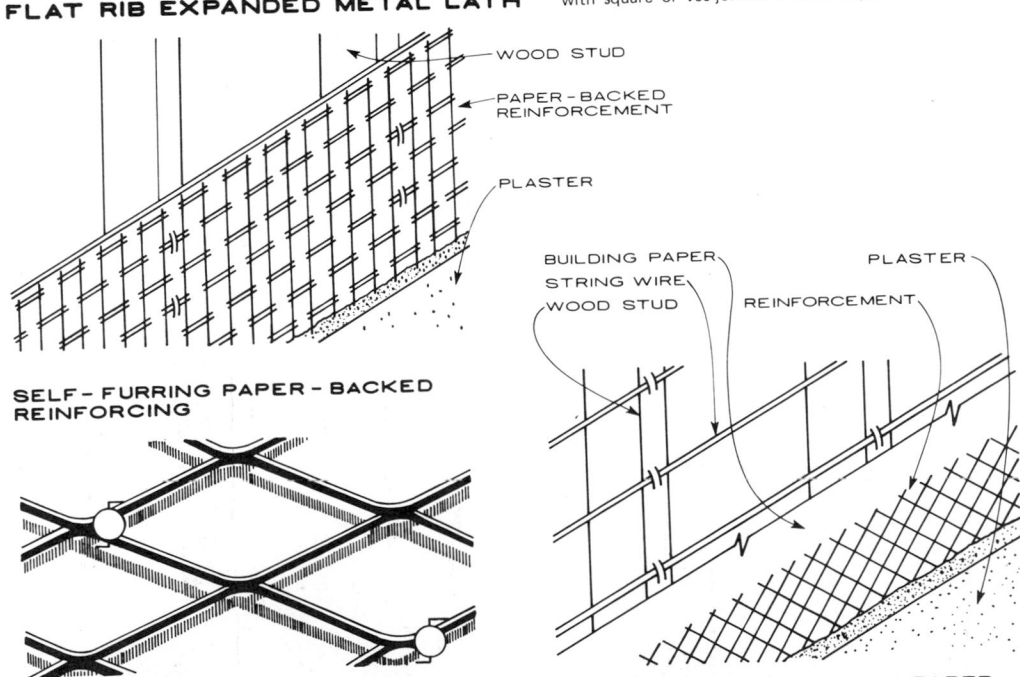

WOOD STUD
PAPER-BACKED REINFORCEMENT
PLASTER

SELF-FURRING PAPER-BACKED REINFORCING

BUILDING PAPER
STRING WIRE
WOOD STUD
PLASTER
REINFORCEMENT

STUCCO MESH
1 3/8" × 3/8" DIAMOND MESH; 48" W. × 8'-2" L.

STRING WIRES & BUILDING PAPER

MISCELLANEOUS LATHING SYSTEMS FOR OPEN WOOD FRAME CONST.

Douglas S. Stenhouse, AIA; Washington, D. C.

DEFINITIONS

AGGREGATE—Inert material used as filler with a cementitious material and water to produce plaster or concrete. Usually implies sand, perlite or vermiculite.

BASECOAT—Any plaster coat applied prior to the application of finish coat.

BEAD—A strip of galvanized sheet metal with a formed projected nosing and one or two perforated and (in some cases) expanded flanges. The nosing serves as a ground to establish plaster thicknesses while the flange(s) provide a means for attachment to the plaster base.

CALCINED—Having had water driven off chemically or by heat, altering chemical and physical characteristics of a material.

CLIP—A device made of wire or sheet metal for attaching various types of lath to the substructure and lath sheets to one another.

FIBERED—Pertaining to basecoat plaster containing animal, vegetable or glass fibers of sufficient length to increase cohesiveness of mix.

FURRING—Elements used to maintain space between finished and unfinished surfaces.

GAUGING—Cementitious material, usually calcined gypsum, Keene's cement or portland cement combined with lime putty to provide and control set.

GROUND—A formed metal shape or wood strip that acts as a combined edge and gauge for various thicknesses of plaster to be applied to a plaster base. Wood grounds are also used as a nailing base for various types of trim.

GYPSUM—Hydrous calcium sulphate, a natural mineral in crystalline form.

GYPSUM READY-MIXED PLASTERS—Basecoat or finish coat plasters with ingredients combined at mill and requiring only addition of water at job. Basecoat plaster mixes contain calcined gypsum and an aggregate. Finish plasters contain finely ground calcined gypsum and various proprietary products to influence color and texture.

HYDRATED LIME—Dry, relatively stable lime, produced by heating quicklime with just enough water to satisfy its chemical affinity for water under conditions of its hydration.

KEENE'S CEMENT—Any hydrous calcined sulphate, finish plaster composed of calcined gypsum and an accelerator used as gauging for lime putty.

LIME—Obtained by burning various types of limestone, consisting of oxides or hydroxides of calcium and magnesium.

LIME PLASTER—Basecoat plaster of hydrated lime and an aggregate.

LIME PUTTY—Material resulting from mixing hydrated lime with water to form a thick paste.

NEAT PLASTER—Basecoat plaster, fibered or unfibered, used for job mixing with aggregates.

PERLITE—Siliceous volcanic glass containing silica and alumina expanded by heat for use as a lightweight plaster aggregate.

PLASTER—Cementitious material or combination of cementitious materials and aggregate that when mixed with suitable amount of water forms a plastic mass that sets and hardens when applied to a surface. May denote exterior or interior use.

PORTLAND CEMENT—Manufactured combination of limestone and an argillaceous substance.

SCREED—A device secured to a surface which serves as a guide for subsequent applications of plaster. Thicknesses and widths vary with the thicknesses desired for each operation.

STUCCO—Plaster used in exterior applications. The term does not connote any specific combination of materials.

VERMICULITE—Micaceous mineral of silica, magnesium and alumina oxides made up in a series of parallel plates or laminae and expanded by heat for use as a lightweight plaster aggregate.

GENERAL NOTES:

No attempt is being made in these pages to recommend thicknesses, proportions or mixes of various plastering materials and finishes. Systems and methods of application vary widely depending upon local traditions and innovations promoted by the industry. The list of definitions above is provided to familiarize one with the basic terms used in the trade. Consult your local plastering sub-contractor and industry representatives for specific data.

See page on Gypsum Block Partitions.

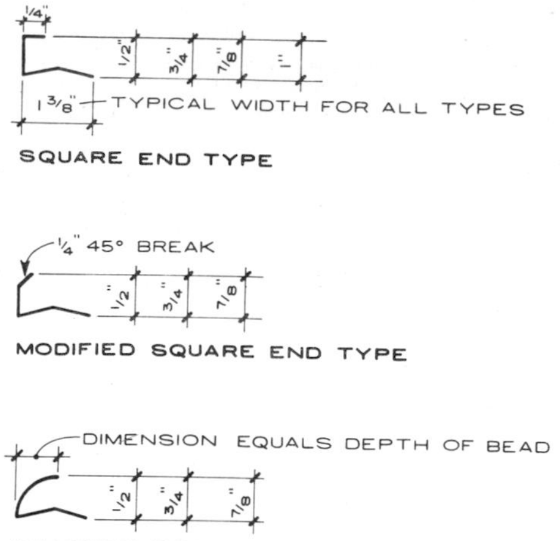

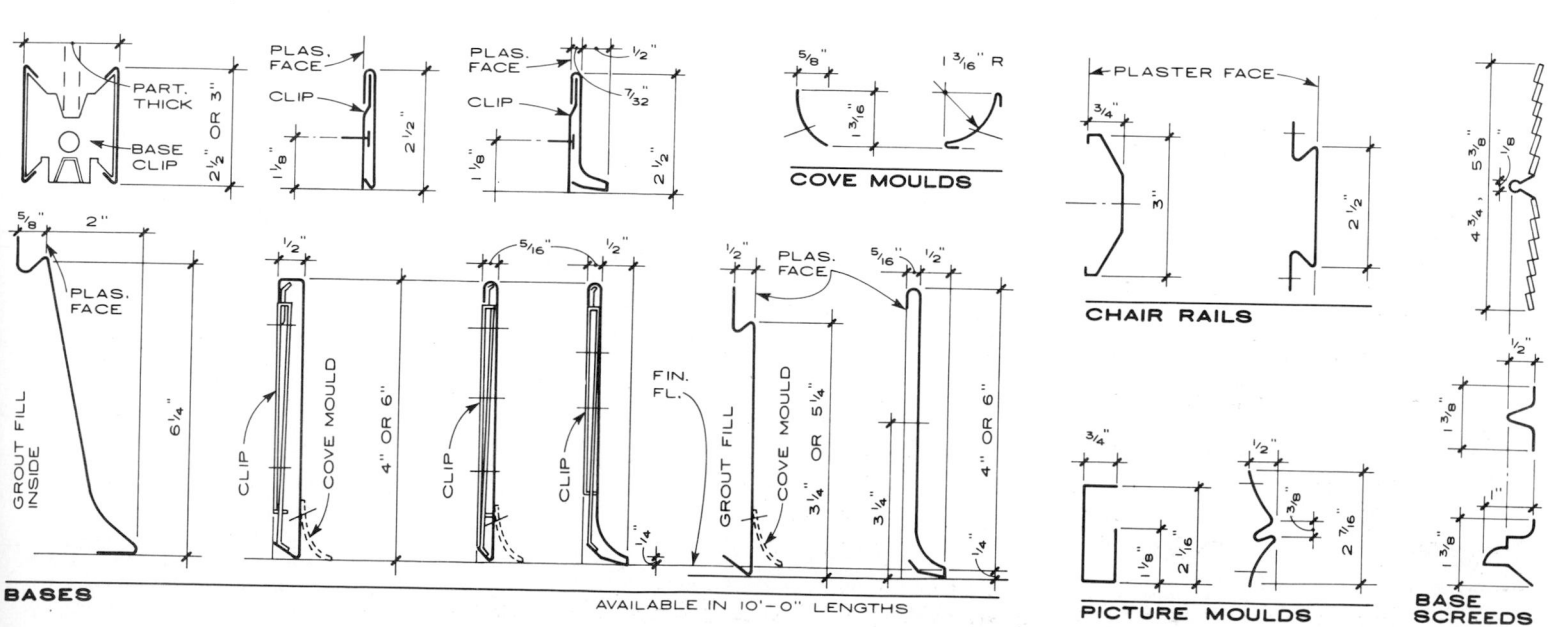

1/4"
1/2" 3/4" 7/8" 1"
1 3/8" TYPICAL WIDTH FOR ALL TYPES
SQUARE END TYPE
1/4" 45° BREAK
1/2" 3/4" 7/8"
MODIFIED SQUARE END TYPE
DIMENSION EQUALS DEPTH OF BEAD
1/2" 3/4" 7/8"
QUARTER ROUND END TYPE

SOLID WING CASING BEADS

SHAPES INDICATED ARE AVAILABE IN 24 GAUGE GALVANIZED STEEL

1/4"
1/2" 5/8" 3/4" 7/8" 1" 1 1/8" 1 1/4"
3 1/8" TYPICAL FOR ALL TYPES
SQUARE END TYPE
1/4" 45° BREAK
1/2" 3/4"
MODIFIED SQUARE END TYPE
DIMENSION EQUALS DEPTH OF BEAD
1/2" 3/4"
QUARTER ROUND END TYPE

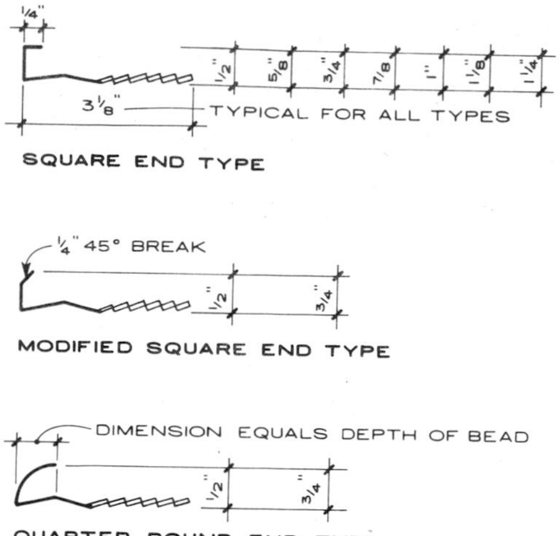

EXPANDED WING CASING BEADS

SHAPES INDICATED ARE AVAILABE IN 24 GAUGE GALVANIZED STEEL

1/4"
CONSTANT
1" 2" 2 1/4" 2 1/2"
VARIES
3 1/4"
FLAT TYPE
2"
1/4"
3"
R = 1 1/2"
ROUNDED TYPE

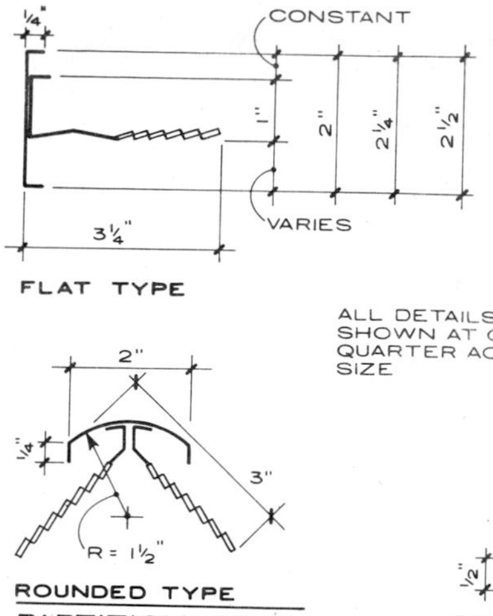

ALL DETAILS ARE SHOWN AT ONE QUARTER ACTUAL SIZE

PARTITION CAPS

1 3/8"
3/8"
1/2"

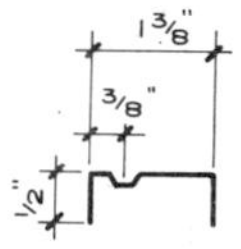

STOP MOULD

CONSULT MANUFACTURERS' CATALOGS FOR LENGTHS, GAUGES AND METAL COMPOSITION WHERE NOT NOTED

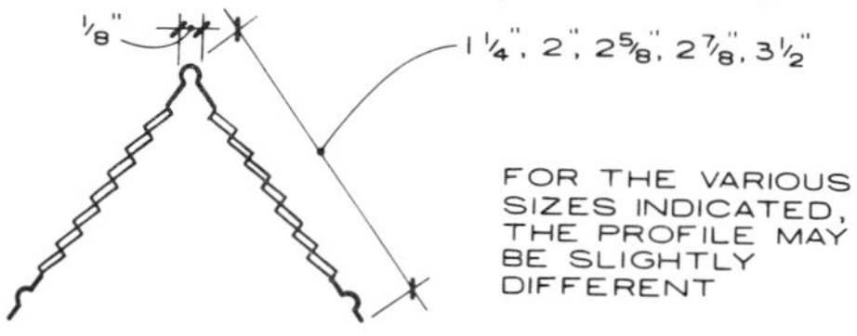

1/8"
1 1/4", 2", 2 5/8", 2 7/8", 3 1/2"

FOR THE VARIOUS SIZES INDICATED, THE PROFILE MAY BE SLIGHTLY DIFFERENT

EXPANDED WING CORNER BEAD

1/8"
1 1/2"

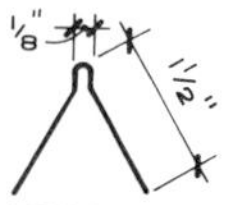

ARCH OR FLEXIBLE CORNER BEAD

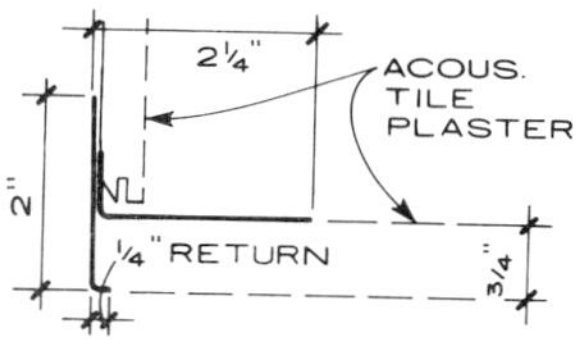

2 1/4"
ACOUS. TILE PLASTER
2"
1/4" RETURN
3/4"

PLASTER AND ACOUSTICAL TILE TERMINAL

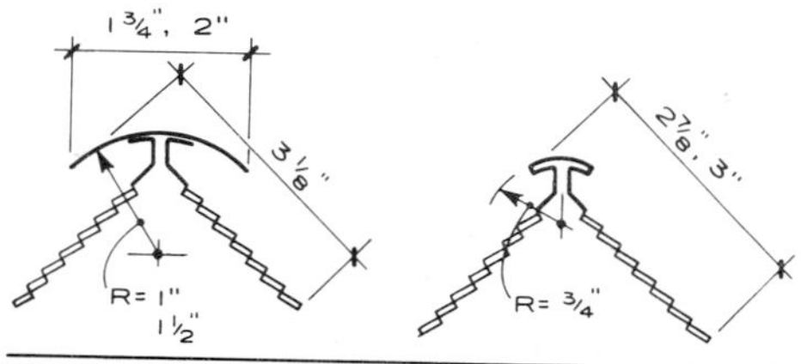

1 3/4", 2"
3 1/8"
R = 1 1/2"
2 7/8", 3"
R = 3/4"

BULL NOSE CORNER BEADS

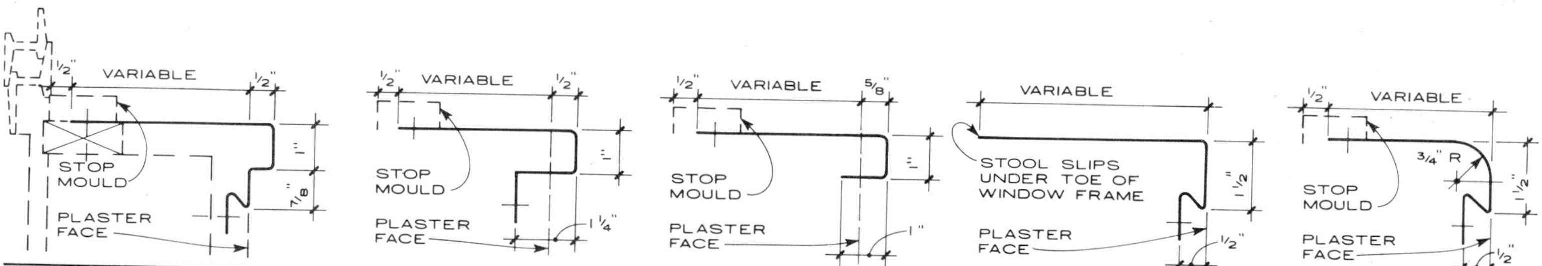

1/2" VARIABLE 1/2"
STOP MOULD
PLASTER FACE
1"
7/8"
1/2" VARIABLE 1/2"
STOP MOULD
PLASTER FACE
1"
1 1/4"
1/2" VARIABLE 5/8"
STOP MOULD
PLASTER FACE
1"
1"
VARIABLE
STOOL SLIPS UNDER TOE OF WINDOW FRAME
PLASTER FACE
1 1/2"
1/2"
1/2" VARIABLE
3/4" R
STOP MOULD
PLASTER FACE
1 1/2"
1/2"

WINDOW STOOLS

AVAILABLE IN 14 AND 16 GAUGE GALV. STEEL

PART. THICK
BASE CLIP
2 1/2" OR 3"
PLAS. FACE
CLIP
1 1/8"
2 1/2"
PLAS. FACE
CLIP
1/2"
7/32"
1 1/8"
2 1/2"
5/8" 2"
PLAS. FACE
GROUT FILL INSIDE
6 1/4"
1/2"
CLIP
COVE MOULD
4" OR 6"
5/16" 1/2"
CLIP
CLIP
1/4"
FIN. FL.
1/2"
PLAS. FACE
5/16" 1/2"
GROUT FILL
COVE MOULD
3 1/4" OR 5 1/4"
3 1/4"
4" OR 6"
1/4"

BASES

AVAILABLE IN 10'-0" LENGTHS

5/8"
1 3/16"
1 3/16" R

COVE MOULDS

PLASTER FACE
3/4"
3"
2 1/2"

CHAIR RAILS

3/4"
1 1/8"
2 1/16"
1/2"
3/8"
2 7/16"

PICTURE MOULDS

4 3/4", 5 3/8"
1/8"
1/2"
1 3/8"
1"
1 3/8"

BASE SCREEDS

Douglas S. Stenhouse, AIA; Washington, D. C.

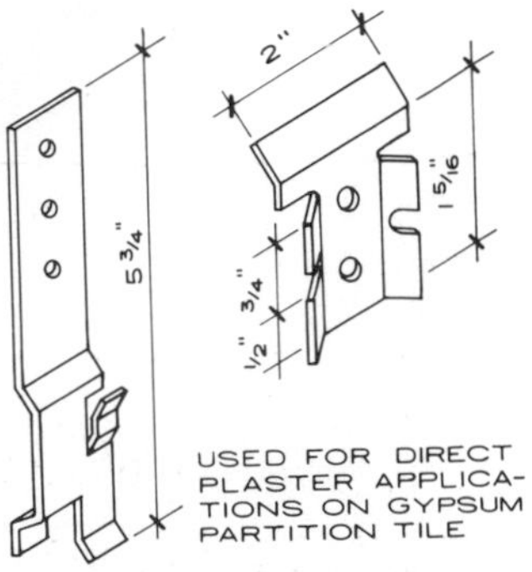

MASONRY BASE CLIPS

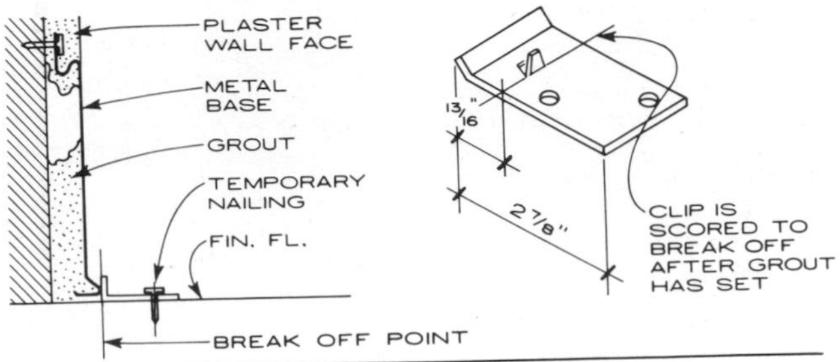

USED FOR DIRECT PLASTER APPLICATIONS ON GYPSUM PARTITION TILE

2"
5 3/4"
3/4"
1/2"
1 5/16"

METAL BASE RETAINING CLIP

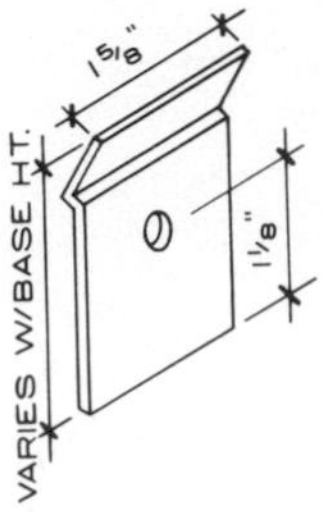

- PLASTER WALL FACE
- METAL BASE
- GROUT
- TEMPORARY NAILING
- FIN. FL.
- BREAK OFF POINT

13/16"
2 7/8"

CLIP IS SCORED TO BREAK OFF AFTER GROUT HAS SET

METAL BASE SPLICE PLATE

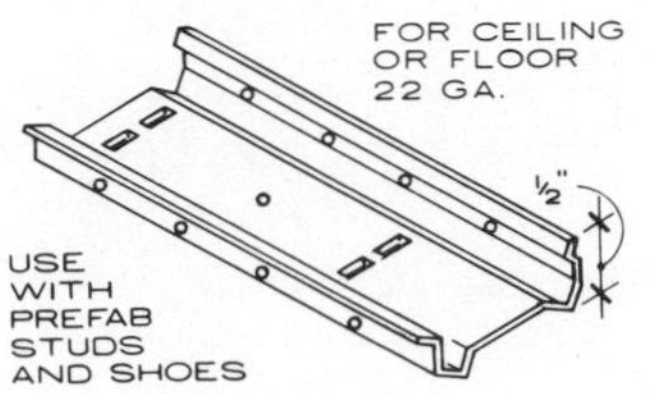

1 5/8"
1 1/8"
VARIES W/BASE HT.

STANDARD RUNNER

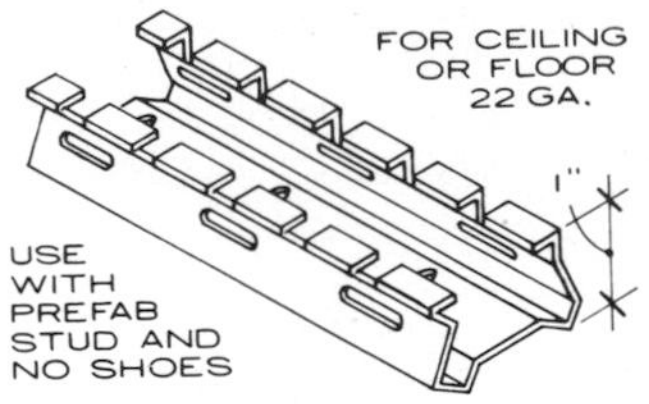

FOR CEILING OR FLOOR 22 GA.
1/2"
USE WITH PREFAB STUDS AND SHOES

SNAP-IN RUNNER

FOR CEILING OR FLOOR 22 GA.
1"
USE WITH PREFAB STUD AND NO SHOES

ROLL FORMED RUNNER

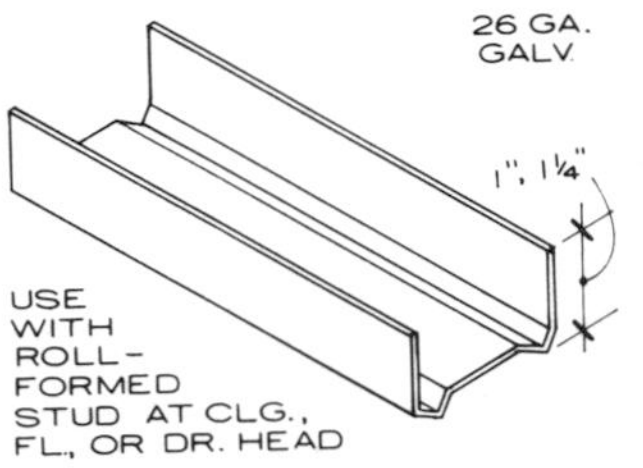

26 GA. GALV
1", 1 1/4"
USE WITH ROLL-FORMED STUD AT CLG., FL, OR DR. HEAD

TYPICAL STUD TRACKS

NOTE:

For 6'' wide prefabricated studs, snap-in runner must have shoes. Roll formed runner may be used for framing all wall openings. Available in 10 foot lengths.

STUD SIZE	DIMENSION "A"
1 5/8"	1 7/16"
2 1/2"	2 5/16"
3 1/4"	3 1/16"
4"	3 13/16"
6"	5 13/16"

AVAILABLE IN 16 GAUGE STL.

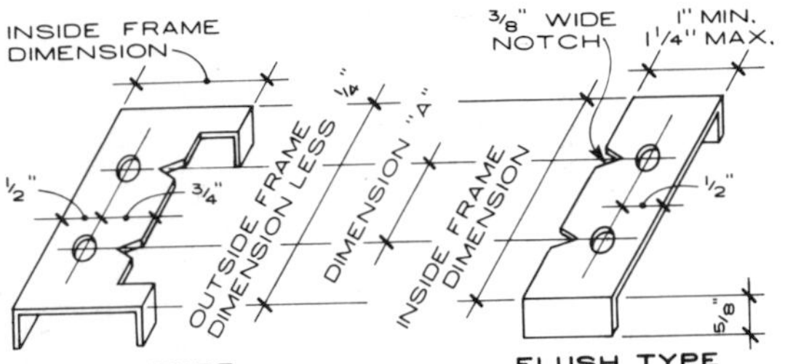

REVEAL TYPE

INSIDE FRAME DIMENSION
OUTSIDE FRAME DIMENSION LESS DIMENSION "A"
1/2"
3/4"

FLUSH TYPE

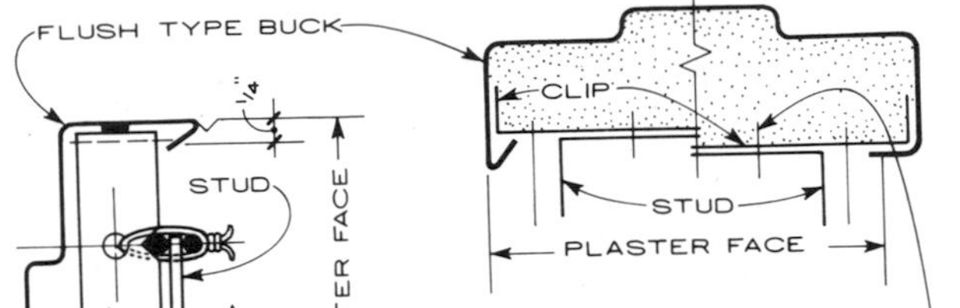

3/8" WIDE NOTCH
1" MIN. 1 1/4" MAX.
INSIDE FRAME DIMENSION
1/2"
5/8"

PREFABRICATED OR PUNCHED STUD SYSTEM

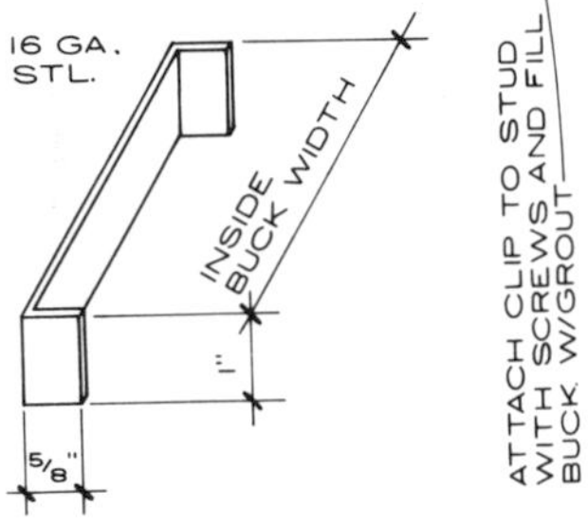

BUCK DETAIL

FLUSH TYPE BUCK
STUD
18 GA. TIE WIRE
REVEAL DEPTH
REVEAL TYPE BUCK
PLASTER FACE

CLIP
STUD
PLASTER FACE
ATTACH CLIP TO STUD WITH SCREWS AND FILL BUCK W/GROUT

ROLL-FORMED STUD SYS.

16 GA. STL.
INSIDE BUCK WIDTH
1"
5/8"

METAL DOOR BUCK ANCHOR CLIPS AND APPLICATIONS

PUNCHED CHANNEL

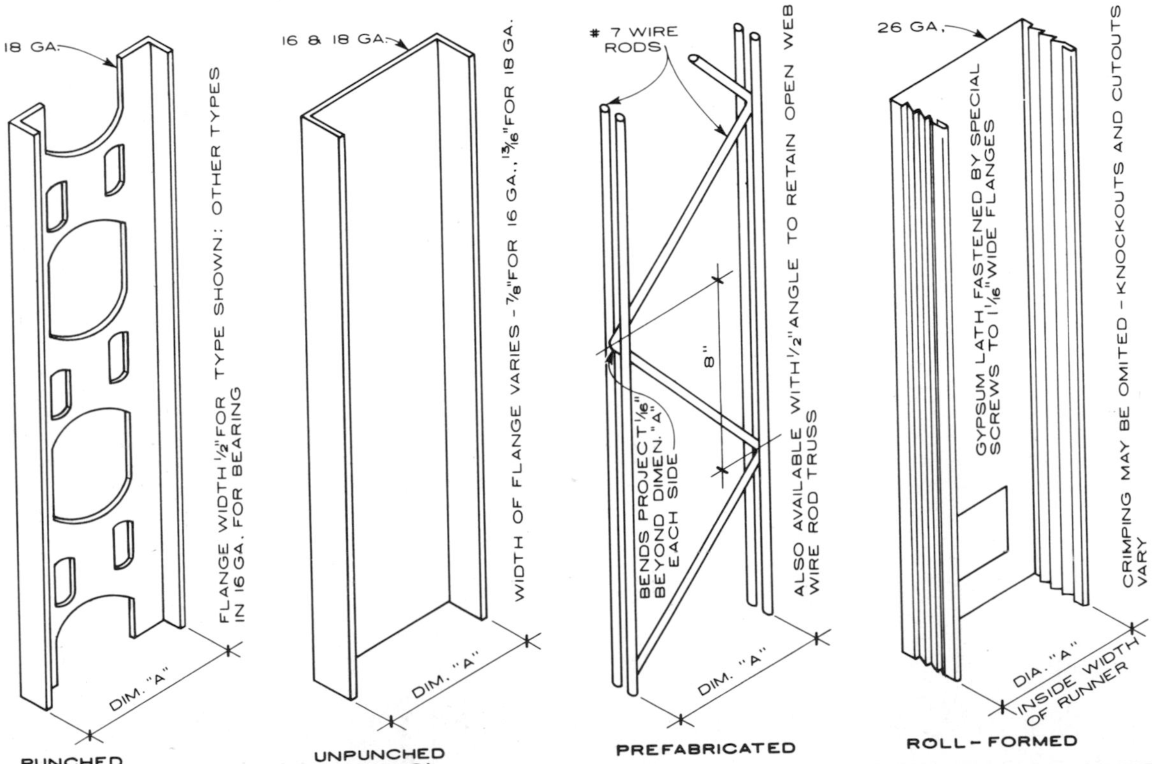

18 GA.
FLANGE WIDTH 1/2" FOR TYPE SHOWN; OTHER TYPES IN 16 GA. FOR BEARING
DIM. "A"

UNPUNCHED (BEARING)

16 & 18 GA.
WIDTH OF FLANGE VARIES - 7/8" FOR 16 GA., 13/16" FOR 18 GA.
DIM. "A"

PREFABRICATED

7 WIRE RODS
8"
BENDS PROJECT 1/16" BEYOND DIMEN. "A" EACH SIDE
ALSO AVAILABLE WITH 1/2" ANGLE TO RETAIN OPEN WEB WIRE ROD TRUSS
DIM. "A"

ROLL-FORMED

26 GA.
GYPSUM LATH FASTENED BY SPECIAL SCREWS TO 1 1/16" WIDE FLANGES
CRIMPING MAY BE OMITED - KNOCKOUTS AND CUTOUTS VARY
DIA. "A"
INSIDE WIDTH OF RUNNER

SHOE

22 GA.
7", 8 1/2"

COLUMN CLIPS

20 GA. GALV.
FOR LOCKING TOGETHER PR. OF PUNCHED STUDS
20 GA. GALV.
FOR LOCKING TOGETHER PR. OF ANGLE-TYPE PREFAB STUDS

STUD TYPE	DIM. "A" (INCHES)
PUNCHED	1 5/8, 1 7/8, 2, 2 1/2, 3 1/4, 4, 6
UNPUNCHED	2 1/2, 3 1/4, 3 5/8, 4, 6
PREFAB	1 5/8, 2 1/2, 3 1/4, 4, 6
ROLL-FORMED	1 5/8, 2 1/2, 3 5/8
NAILABLE	2 1/2, 3 1/4, 4

Nailable studs have two point clinching action similar to nailable suspension system illust. on next page. Refer to manufacturers' catalogs for lengths, finishes, recomm. design loads and heights.

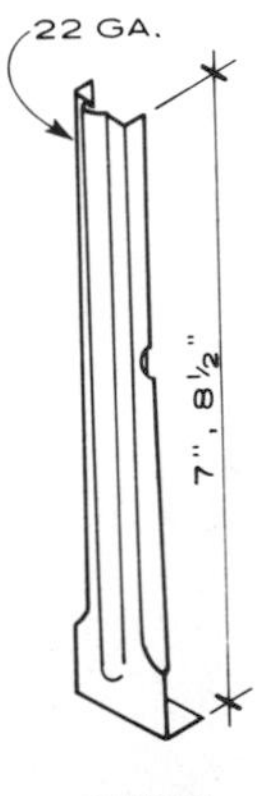

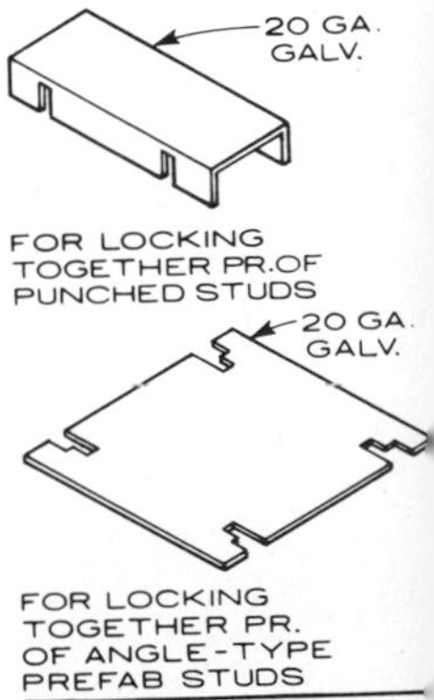

TYPICAL METAL STUD TYPES AND ACCESSORIES (NON-BEARING UNLESS OTHERWISE NOTED)

Douglas S. Stenhouse, AIA; Washington, D. C.

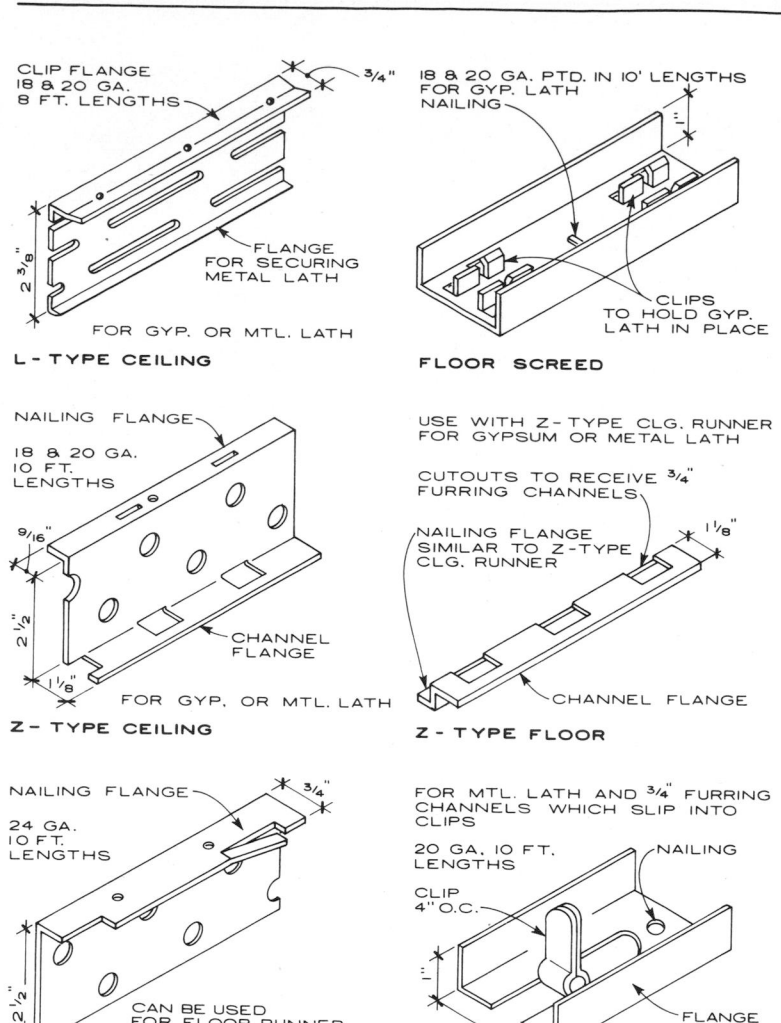

CLIP FLANGE 18 & 20 GA. 8 FT. LENGTHS

3/4"

FLANGE FOR SECURING METAL LATH

2 3/8"

FOR GYP. OR MTL. LATH

L - TYPE CEILING

18 & 20 GA. PTD. IN 10' LENGTHS FOR GYP. LATH NAILING

CLIPS TO HOLD GYP. LATH IN PLACE

FLOOR SCREED

NAILING FLANGE

18 & 20 GA. 10 FT. LENGTHS

9/16"

2 1/2"

1 1/8"

CHANNEL FLANGE

FOR GYP. OR MTL. LATH

Z - TYPE CEILING

USE WITH Z-TYPE CLG. RUNNER FOR GYPSUM OR METAL LATH

CUTOUTS TO RECEIVE 3/4" FURRING CHANNELS

NAILING FLANGE SIMILAR TO Z-TYPE CLG. RUNNER

1 1/8"

CHANNEL FLANGE

Z - TYPE FLOOR

NAILING FLANGE

3/4"

24 GA. 10 FT. LENGTHS

2 1/2"

CAN BE USED FOR FLOOR RUNNER WHERE METAL BASE IS NOT SPECIFIED

PRONG TYPE FLOOR & CLG.

FOR MTL. LATH AND 3/4" FURRING CHANNELS WHICH SLIP INTO CLIPS

20 GA. 10 FT. LENGTHS

CLIP 4" O.C.

NAILING

1"

2" OR 2 1/4"

FLANGE MAY SERVE AS SCREED AND MTL. BASE

CLIP-TYPE FLOOR & CLG.

STUDLESS FLOOR AND CEILING TRACKS AND RUNNERS

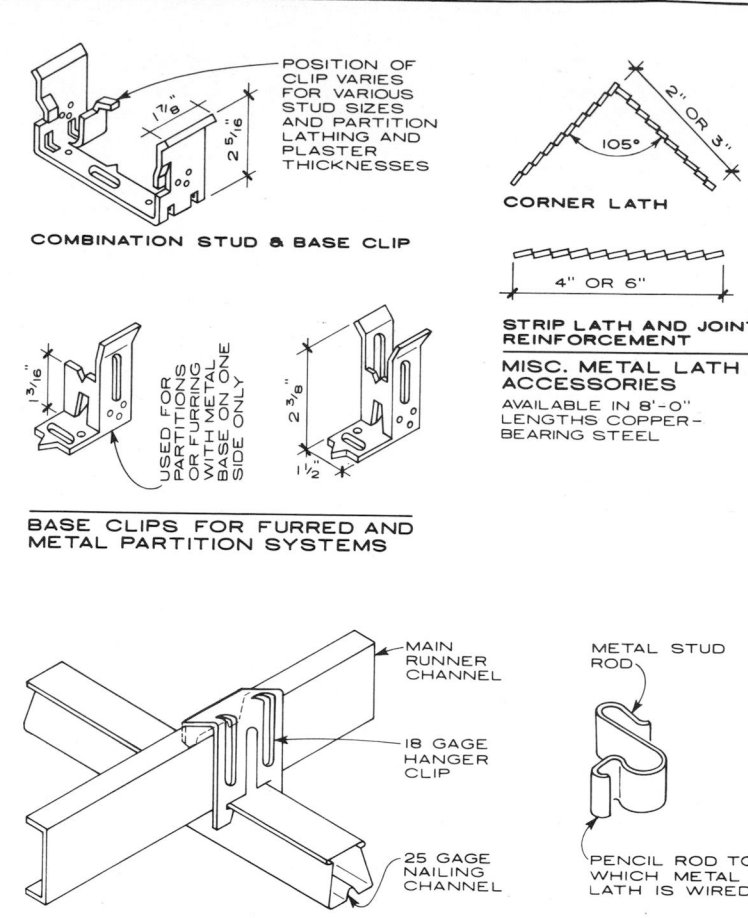

POSITION OF CLIP VARIES FOR VARIOUS STUD SIZES AND PARTITION LATHING AND PLASTER THICKNESSES

7/8"

2 5/16"

COMBINATION STUD & BASE CLIP

1 3/16"

USED FOR PARTITIONS OR FURRING WITH METAL BASE ON ONE SIDE ONLY

2 3/8"

1 1/2"

BASE CLIPS FOR FURRED AND METAL PARTITION SYSTEMS

2" OR 3"

105°

CORNER LATH

4" OR 6"

STRIP LATH AND JOINT REINFORCEMENT

MISC. METAL LATH ACCESSORIES

AVAILABLE IN 8'-0" LENGTHS COPPER-BEARING STEEL

MAIN RUNNER CHANNEL

18 GAGE HANGER CLIP

25 GAGE NAILING CHANNEL

NAILABLE GYPSUM LATH SUSPENSION SYSTEM

METAL STUD ROD

PENCIL ROD TO WHICH METAL LATH IS WIRED

RESILIENT PREFABRICA- TED STUD CLIP

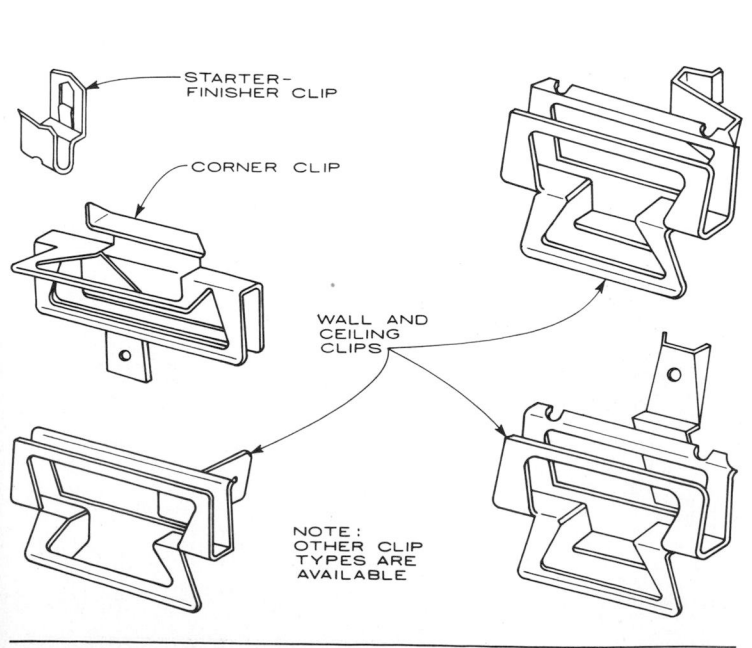

STARTER- FINISHER CLIP

CORNER CLIP

WALL AND CEILING CLIPS

NOTE: OTHER CLIP TYPES ARE AVAILABLE

CLIPS FOR RESILIENT GYPSUM LATH SUSP. SYSTEM

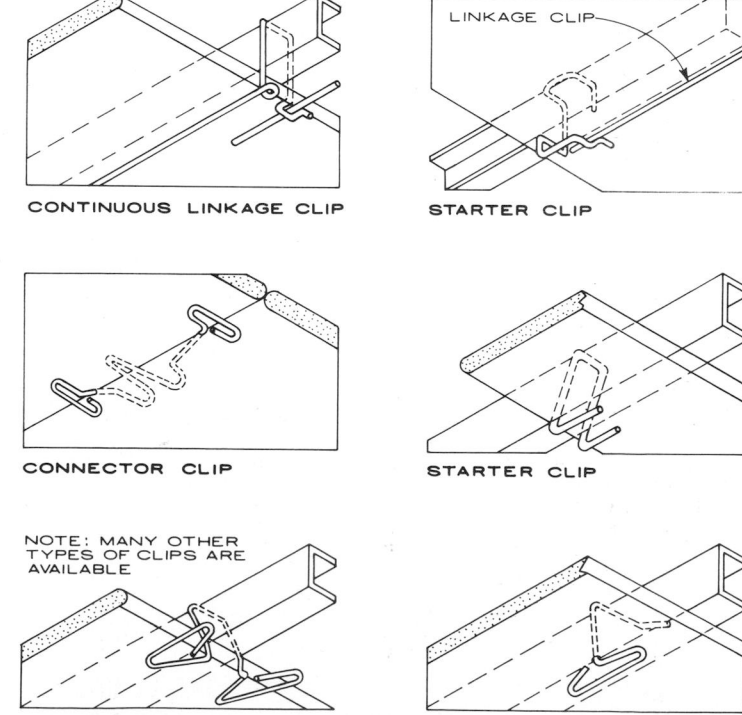

CONTINUOUS LINKAGE CLIP

LINKAGE CLIP

STARTER CLIP

CONNECTOR CLIP

STARTER CLIP

NOTE: MANY OTHER TYPES OF CLIPS ARE AVAILABLE

CHANNEL CLIP

CENTER CLIP

CLIPS FOR NON-RESILIENT GYPSUM LATH SUSP. SYST.

Douglas S. Stenhouse, AIA; Washington, D. C.

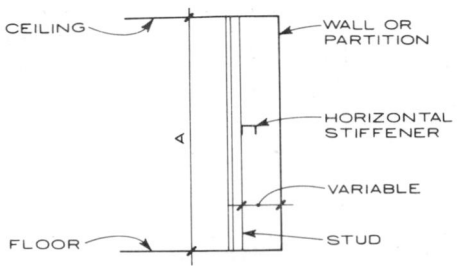

UNBRACED FURRING

RECOMMENDED MAXIMUM UNSUPPORTED HEIGHT "A" FOR STUD SPACING

STUD TYPE	12"O.C.	16"O.C.	19"O.C.	24"O.C.
¾" CHANNEL	9'-0"	8'-0"	7'-0"	6'-0"
1½" CHANNEL	12'-0"	10'-0"	9'-0"	8'-0"
2" CHANNEL	13'-0"	11'-0"	10'-0"	9'-0"
2" PREFAB	11'-0"	10'-0"	9'-0"	8'-0"
2½" PREFAB	14'-0"	12'-0"	11'-0"	10'-0"
3¼" PREFAB	20'-0"	17'-0"	16'-0"	14'-0"

NOTES:

1—When overall height of furring exceeds dimension "B" recommended for specific stud heights, install horizontal bracing as recommended in braced framing table.

2—Horizontal stiffeners (not less than 3/4" cold-rolled channels) spaced the same distance vertically as attachments to the wall are recommended for all unbraced (free-standing) furring. For stud spacing less than 16" O.C. use maximum spacing for stiffeners of 4'–6" O.C. vertically, 3'–6" O.C. for stud spacing greater than 16".

3—Wall furring using long length gypsum lath should not exceed 12'–0" in height and horizontal bracing should be located at intervals not greater than 3'–0" vertically.

4—Where regular-sized sheets of insulating gypsum lath are used, horizontal bracing should be placed at intervals not greater than 4'–6" vertically.

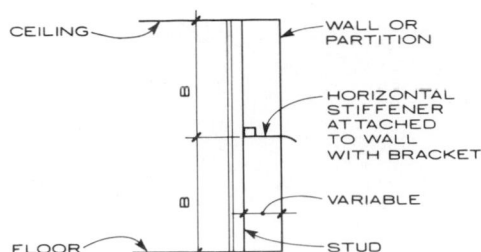

BRACED FURRING

RECOMMENDED MAX. SPACING "B" BETWEEN HORIZ. BRACING FOR STUD SPACING

STUD TYPE	12"O.C.	16"O.C.	19"O.C.	24"O.C.
¾" CHANNEL	7'-0"	6'-0"	5'-0"	5'-0"
1½" CHANNEL	9'-0"	9'-0"	7'-0"	6'-0"
2" CHANNEL	10'-0"	9'-0"	8'-0"	7'-0"
2" PREFAB	9'-0"	8'-0"	7'-0"	6'-0"
2½" PREFAB	11'-0"	10'-0"	9'-0"	8'-0"
3¼" PREFAB	16'-0"	14'-0"	13'-0"	11'-0"

RECOMMENDED HEIGHTS OF WALL FURRING – METAL CHANNEL AND PREFABRICATED STUD

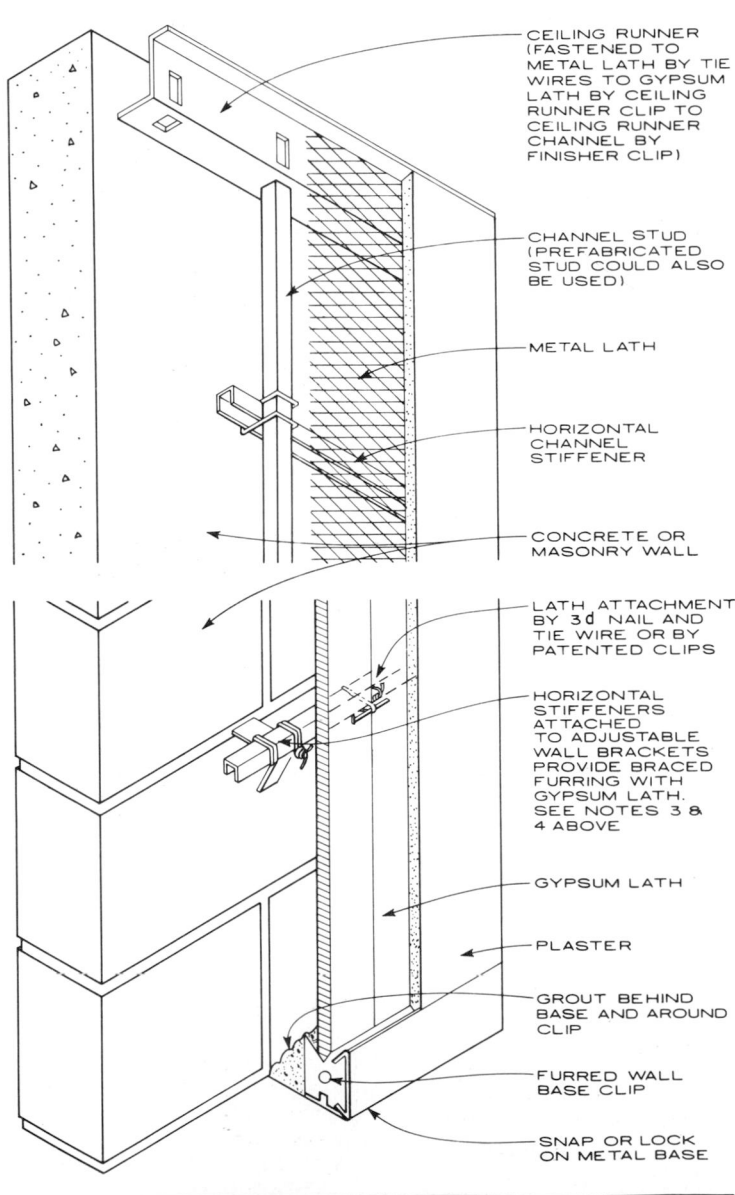

INSIDE FURRING OF EXTERIOR MASONRY WALLS

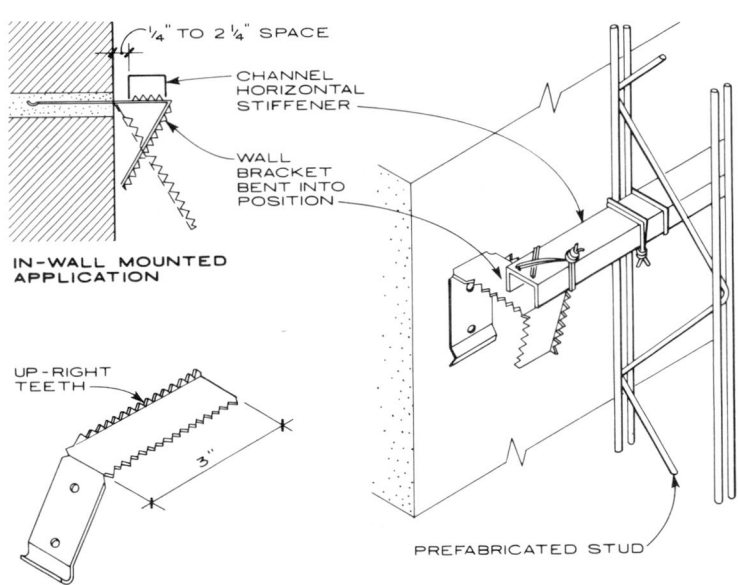

IN-WALL MOUNTED APPLICATION

BRACKET

SURFACE-MOUNTED APPLICATION

ADJUSTABLE WALL FURRING BRACKET DETAILS

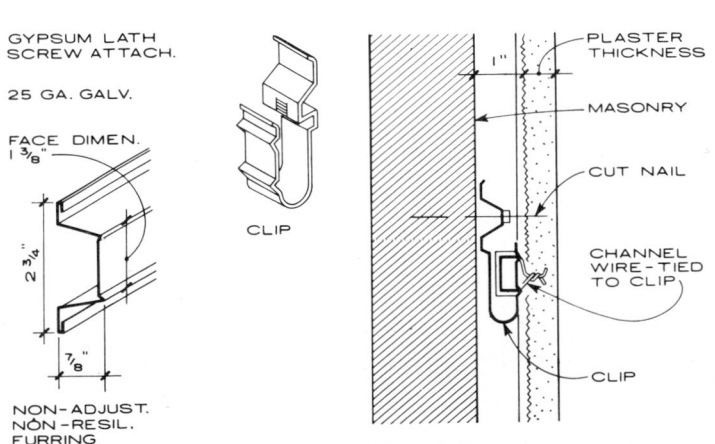

NON-ADJUST. NON-RESIL. FURRING CHANNEL

RESILIENT WALL FURRING CLIP DETAILS

Douglas S. Stenhouse, AIA; Washington, D. C.

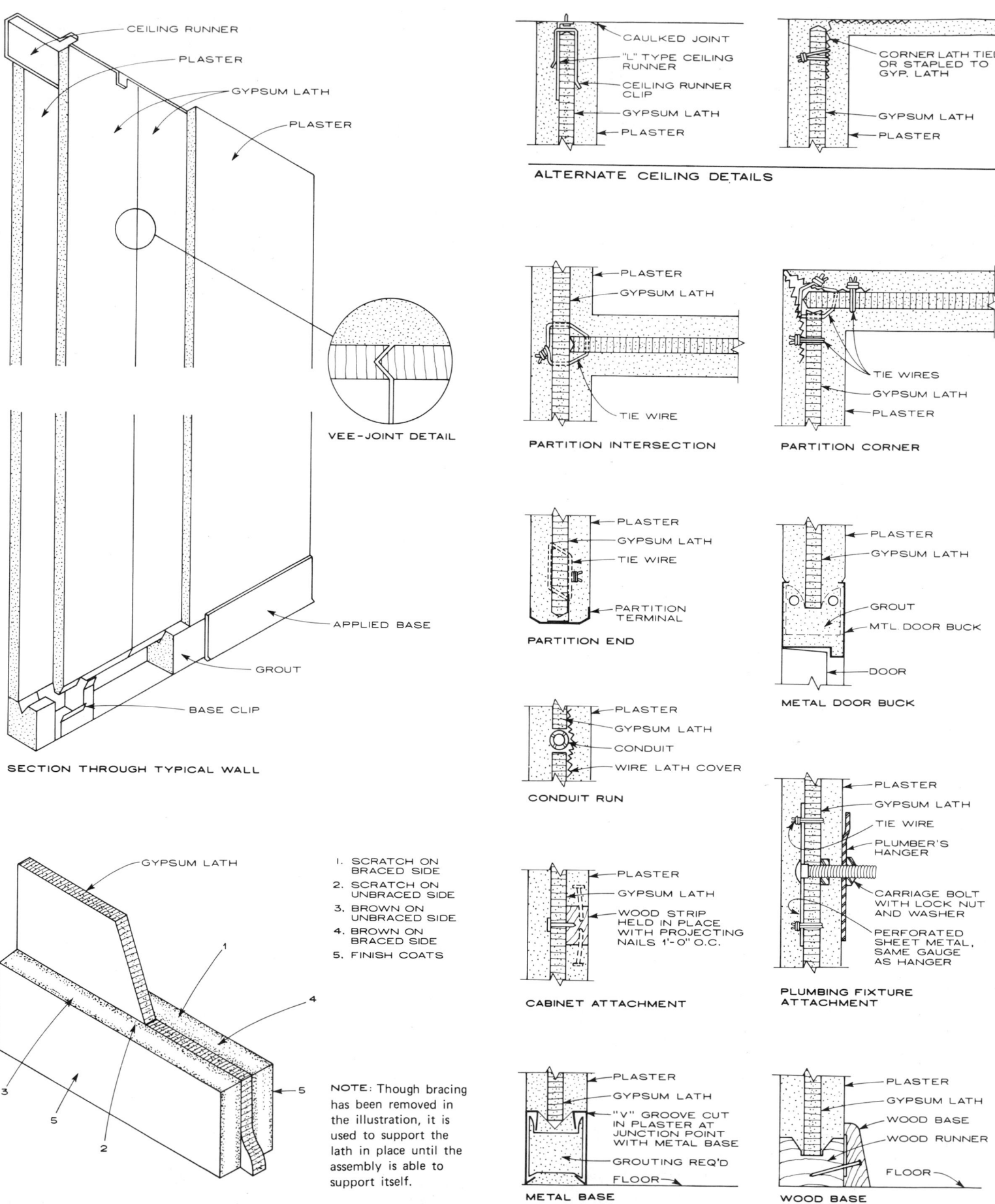

CEILING RUNNER

PLASTER

GYPSUM LATH

PLASTER

VEE-JOINT DETAIL

SECTION THROUGH TYPICAL WALL

APPLIED BASE

GROUT

BASE CLIP

GYPSUM LATH

1. SCRATCH ON BRACED SIDE
2. SCRATCH ON UNBRACED SIDE
3. BROWN ON UNBRACED SIDE
4. BROWN ON BRACED SIDE
5. FINISH COATS

NOTE: Though bracing has been removed in the illustration, it is used to support the lath in place until the assembly is able to support itself.

SEQUENCE OF PLASTER APPLICATION

Douglas S. Stenhouse, AIA; Washington, D. C.

CAULKED JOINT
"L" TYPE CEILING RUNNER
CEILING RUNNER CLIP
GYPSUM LATH
PLASTER

CORNER LATH TIED OR STAPLED TO GYP. LATH
GYPSUM LATH
PLASTER

ALTERNATE CEILING DETAILS

PLASTER
GYPSUM LATH
TIE WIRE

PARTITION INTERSECTION

TIE WIRES
GYPSUM LATH
PLASTER

PARTITION CORNER

PLASTER
GYPSUM LATH
TIE WIRE
PARTITION TERMINAL

PARTITION END

PLASTER
GYPSUM LATH
GROUT
MTL. DOOR BUCK
DOOR

METAL DOOR BUCK

PLASTER
GYPSUM LATH
CONDUIT
WIRE LATH COVER

CONDUIT RUN

PLASTER
GYPSUM LATH
WOOD STRIP HELD IN PLACE WITH PROJECTING NAILS 1'-0" O.C.

CABINET ATTACHMENT

PLASTER
GYPSUM LATH
TIE WIRE
PLUMBER'S HANGER
CARRIAGE BOLT WITH LOCK NUT AND WASHER
PERFORATED SHEET METAL, SAME GAUGE AS HANGER

PLUMBING FIXTURE ATTACHMENT

PLASTER
GYPSUM LATH
"V" GROOVE CUT IN PLASTER AT JUNCTION POINT WITH METAL BASE
GROUTING REQ'D
FLOOR

METAL BASE

PLASTER
GYPSUM LATH
WOOD BASE
WOOD RUNNER
FLOOR

WOOD BASE

MISCELLANEOUS DETAILS

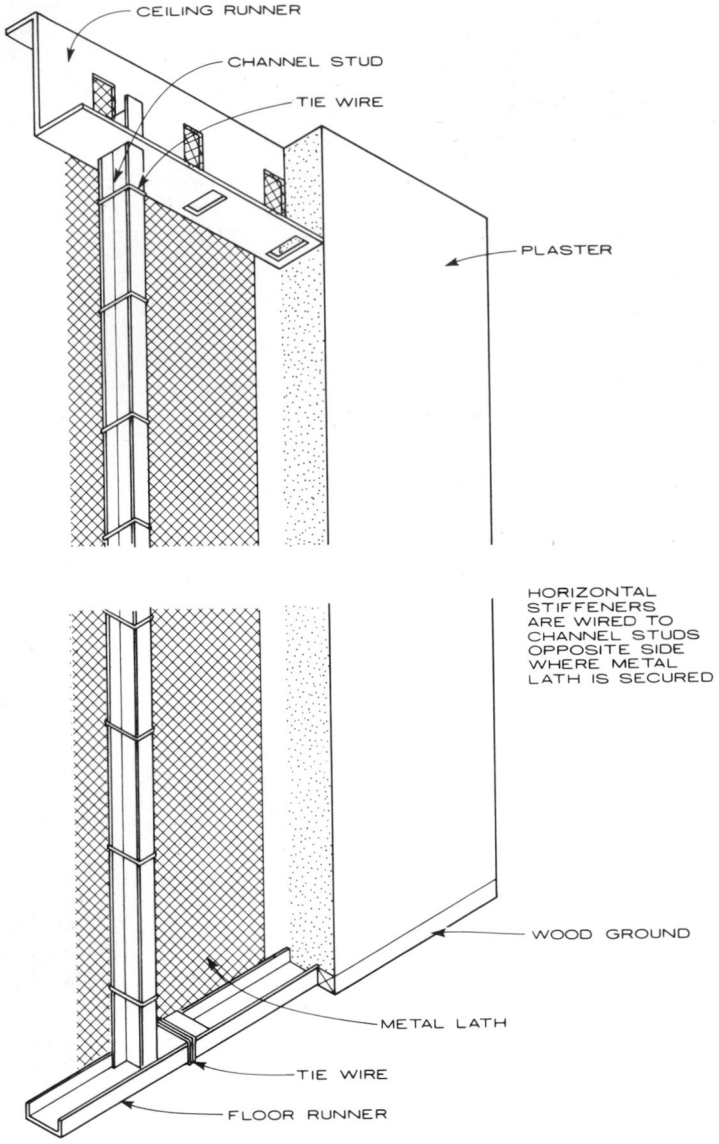

SECTION THROUGH TYPICAL WALL

- CEILING RUNNER
- CHANNEL STUD
- TIE WIRE
- PLASTER
- HORIZONTAL STIFFENERS ARE WIRED TO CHANNEL STUDS OPPOSITE SIDE WHERE METAL LATH IS SECURED
- WOOD GROUND
- METAL LATH
- TIE WIRE
- FLOOR RUNNER

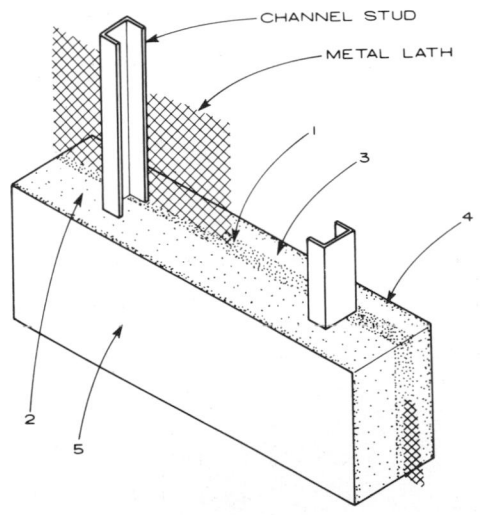

SEQUENCE OF PLASTER APPLICATION

- CHANNEL STUD
- METAL LATH

1. SCRATCH ON LATH SIDE
2. BACK - UP ON CHANNEL SIDE
3. BROWN COAT ON LATH SIDE
4. FINISH COAT
5. FINISH COAT

NOTE - Though bracing has been removed in the illustration, it is required to support lath until the partition is able to support itself.

Douglas S. Stenhouse, AIA; Washington, D. C.

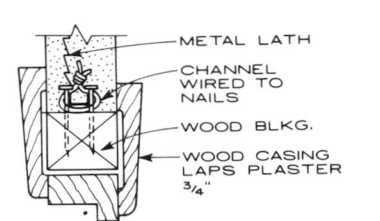

ALTERNATE CEILING DETAILS

- CEILING LINE
- CHANNEL STUD WIRED TO METAL LATH
- CEILING LINE
- 2 ∠ OR CLIP TYPE CEILING RUNNER (SEE PAGE ON JOINTS)
- CHANNEL STUD
- CHANNEL STUD PUNCHED THRU CEILING LATH AND TIED TO FURRING CHANNELS
- MAIN RUNNER CHANNEL AND HANGER WIRE
- USE OF CHANNEL OR PENCIL TO ALIGN STUDS IS OPTIONAL
- METAL LATH
- CHANNEL STUD

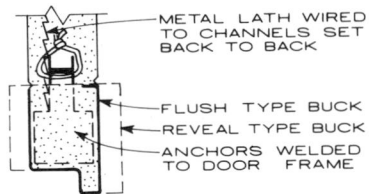

WOOD BUCK DETAIL

- METAL LATH
- CHANNEL WIRED TO NAILS
- WOOD BLKG.
- WOOD CASING LAPS PLASTER 3/4"

LIGHTSWITCH OR OUTLET DTL.

- CONDUIT
- CHANNEL STUD
- METAL LATH
- SHALLOW TYPE BOX
- COVER PLATE
- SWITCH
- 2" PARTITION

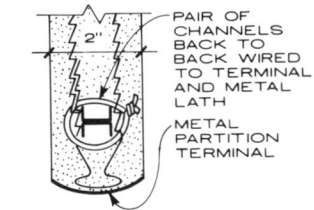

METAL DOOR BUCK DETAIL (STUDLESS SYSTEM SIMILAR)

- METAL LATH WIRED TO CHANNELS SET BACK TO BACK
- FLUSH TYPE BUCK
- REVEAL TYPE BUCK
- ANCHORS WELDED TO DOOR FRAME

PARTITION END DETAIL (STUDLESS SYSTEM SIM.)

- 2"
- PAIR OF CHANNELS BACK TO BACK WIRED TO TERMINAL AND METAL LATH
- METAL PARTITION TERMINAL

RESILIENT/WOOD BASE DETAIL

- METAL LATH WIRED TO CHANNEL
- WD. NAILING STRIPS WIRED TO STUDS
- 2 ∠ OR CLIP TYPE FLOOR RUNNER MAY BE USED
- FLOOR LINE

METAL BASE DETAIL

- METAL LATH WIRED TO CHANNEL
- BASE CLIP SECURED TO EACH STUD BY TONGUE AND NAILED TO FLOOR

TABLE FOR CHANNEL STUD SIZE PARTITION THICKNESS AND HEIGHT

HEIGHT	THICK	CHANNEL
12 FT	2"	3/4" 300 LBS
14 FT	2 1/4"	PER 1000 FT
16 FT	2 1/2"	
18 FT	2 3/4"	1 1/2" 475 LBS
20 FT	3"	PER 1000 FT
24 FT*	3 1/4"	

*For heights over 20' furnish channels spaced 6' vertically.
**Spacing for partitions 16' high or less. For greater heights see note above or reduce stud spacings 25%.

CHANNEL STUD SPACING

TYPE OF MTL LATH	WEIGHT #/SQ YD	SPACING IN INCHES
DIAMOND	2.5	12
FLAT EXP.	3.4	16
FLAT RIB	2.75	16
FLAT RIB	3.4	24**

Weights include lath only.

PARTITION LENGTH	LIMITS
< 10 FEET HIGH	NONE
> 10 FEET HIGH	2 x HT
> 14 FEET HIGH	1 1/2 x HT
> 20 FEET HIGH	1 x HT

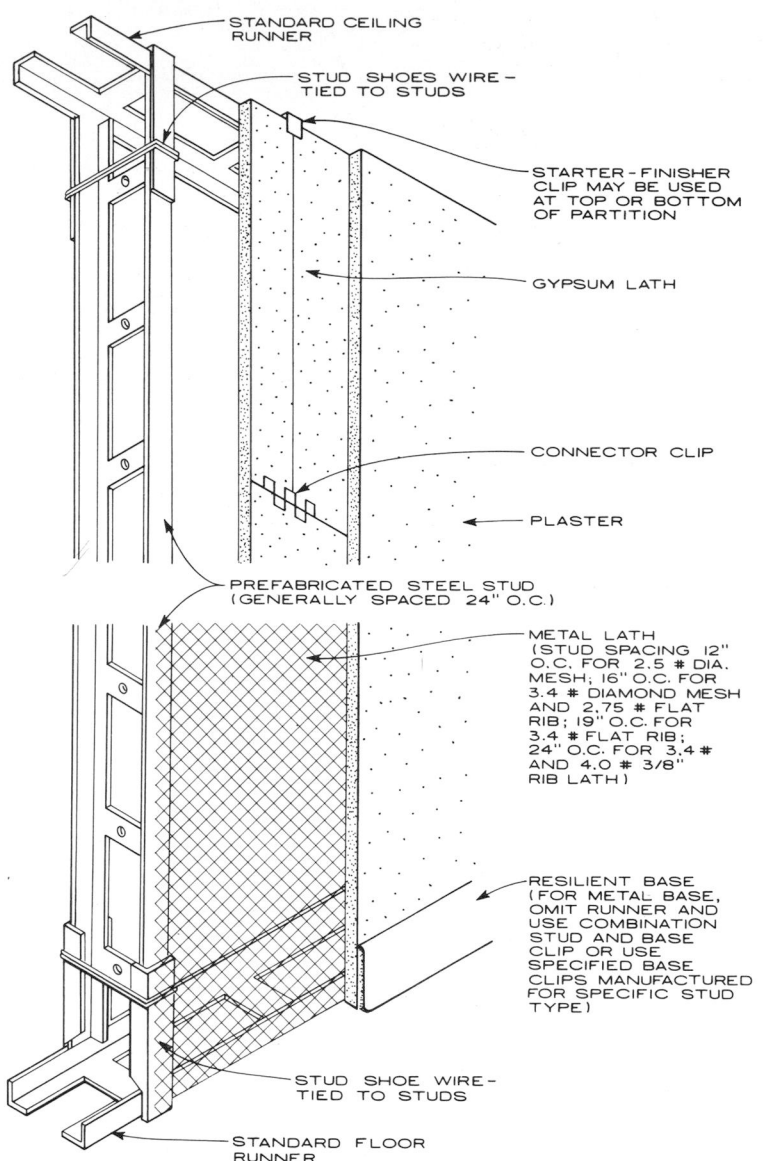

SECTION THROUGH TYPICAL WALL

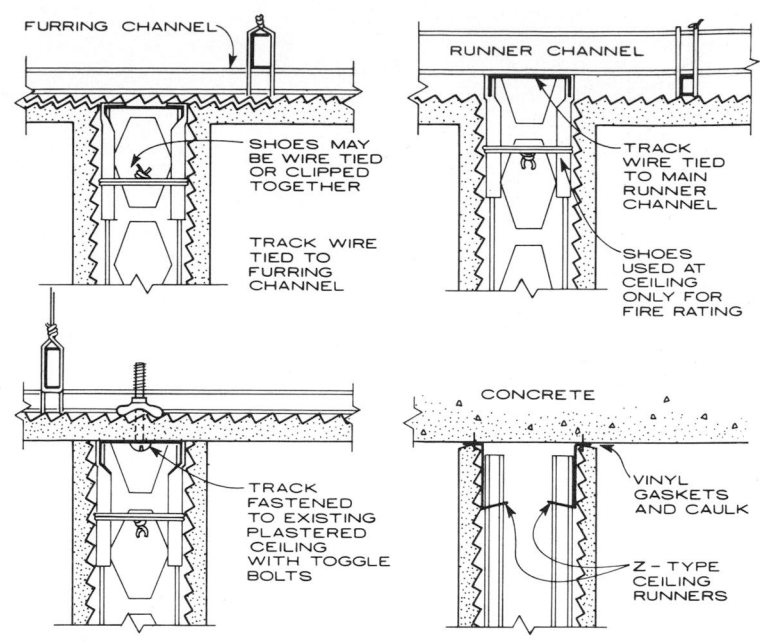

ALTERNATE CEILING DETAIL

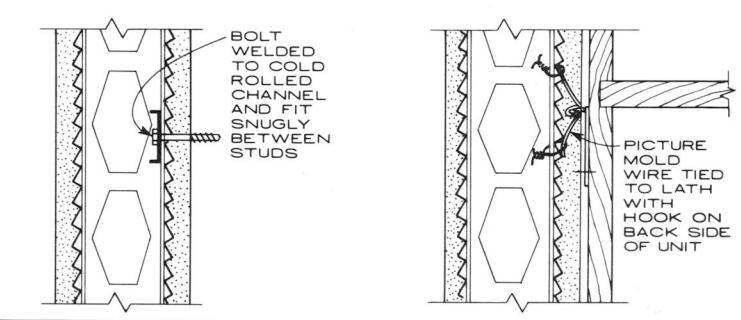

WALL - SUPPORTED ATTACHMENT DETAILS

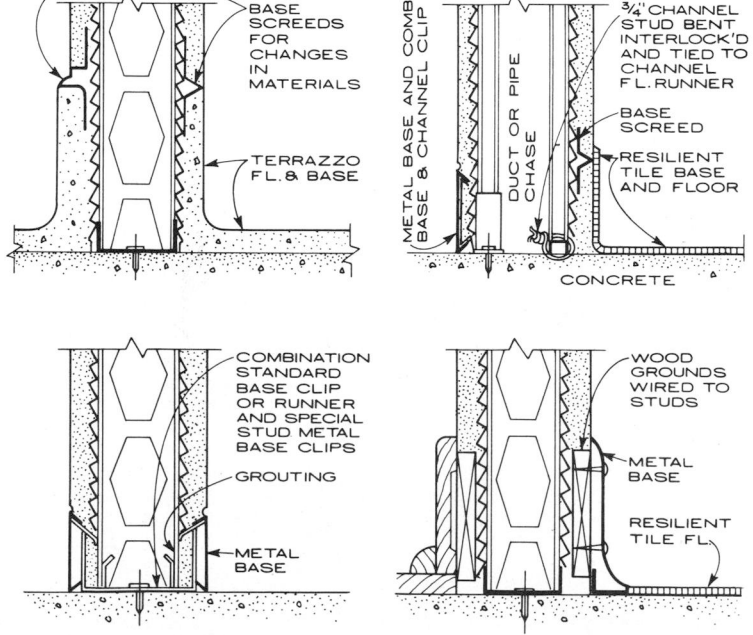

ALTERNATE BASE DETAILS

STUD SPACING AND PARTITION HEIGHT LIMITATIONS

STUD TYPE		PARTITION THICKNESS	MAXIMUM HEIGHT FOR STUD SPACING		
			24" o.c.	19" o.c.	16" o.c.
PREFAB	1 5/8"	3 1/8"			9'
	2"	3 1/2"		9'	10'
	2 1/2"	4"	9'	14'	15'
	3 1/4"	4 3/4"	13'	18'	21'
	4"	5 1/2"	16'	20'	22'
	6"	7 1/2"	20'	24'	26'
DOUBLE ROW OF 3/4" CHANNELS HORIZ. BRACED	3"				14'
	4"				16'
	5"				20'

Plaster thickness is computed thus:
1. 3/4" from stud face or 5/8" from face of metal lath.
2. For 3/8" rib expanded metal lath laid up with ribs against studs, add 1/2".
3. For 3/8" gypsum lath with 1/2" plaster, add 1/4".

NOTES for use of table:
1. 24" spacing of studs not recommended for rib expanded metal lath less than nominal 3/8" or for gypsum lath less than 1/2"
2. Maximum heights are indicated for partition lengths < 1 1/2 x height. For greater lengths reduce height 20%.
3. Horizontal bracing for double row channel studs shall be spaced vertically no greater than 4'-0" o.c.

Douglas S. Stenhouse, AIA; Washington, D. C.

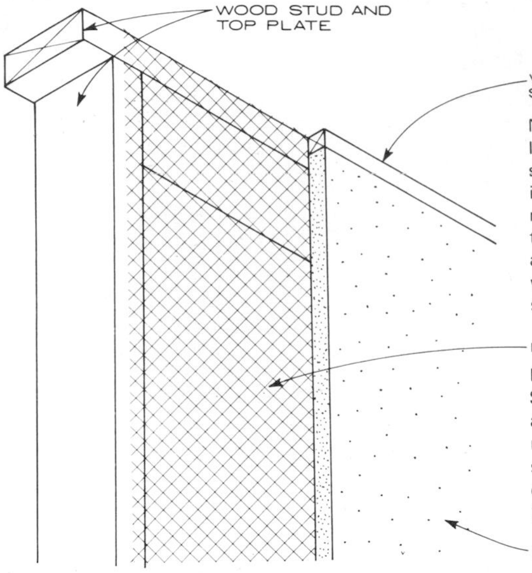

WOOD STUD AND TOP PLATE

WOOD GROUND FOR SECURING WOOD TRIM

NOTE: Install corner lath where plaster intersects ceiling and trim is omitted. Casing bead may also be used to terminate wall surface and act as screed when when wall surface stops short of ceiling.

METAL LATH

NOTE: Stud spacing for 2.5# and 3.4# diamond mesh. 2.75# flat rib shall be 16″ o.c. 19″ o.c. for 3.4# flat rib, 24″ o.c. for 3/4″ rib.

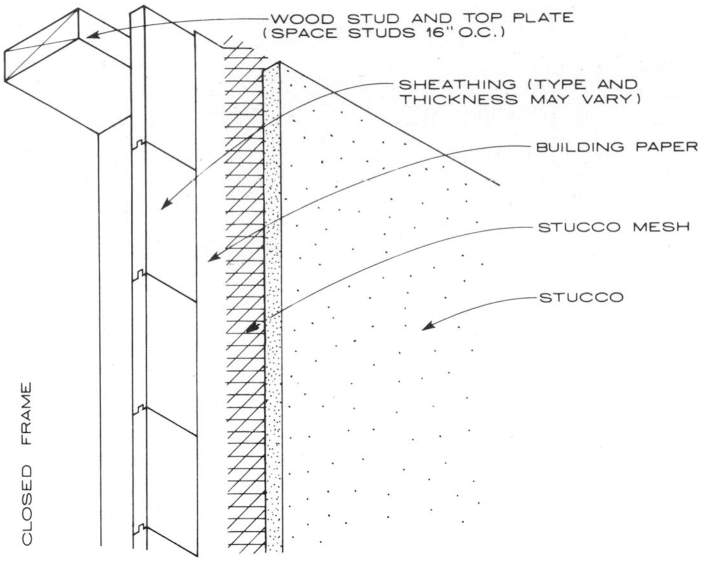

PLASTER

WOOD STUD AND TOP PLATE (SPACE STUDS 16″ O.C.)

SHEATHING (TYPE AND THICKNESS MAY VARY)

BUILDING PAPER

STUCCO MESH

STUCCO

CLOSED FRAME

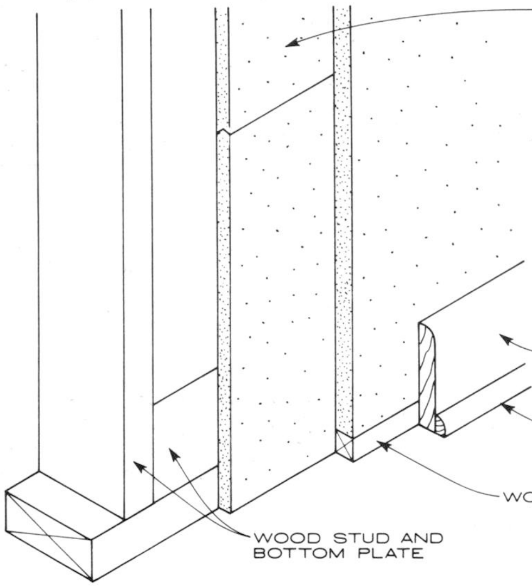

OPEN FRAME

GYPSUM LATH

NOTE: Resilient and non-resilient clip systems are often used for attaching gypsum lath to wood frame.

Spacing of studs shall not exceed 16″ o.c. for 3/8″ gypsum lath or 24″ o.c. for 1/2″ lath.

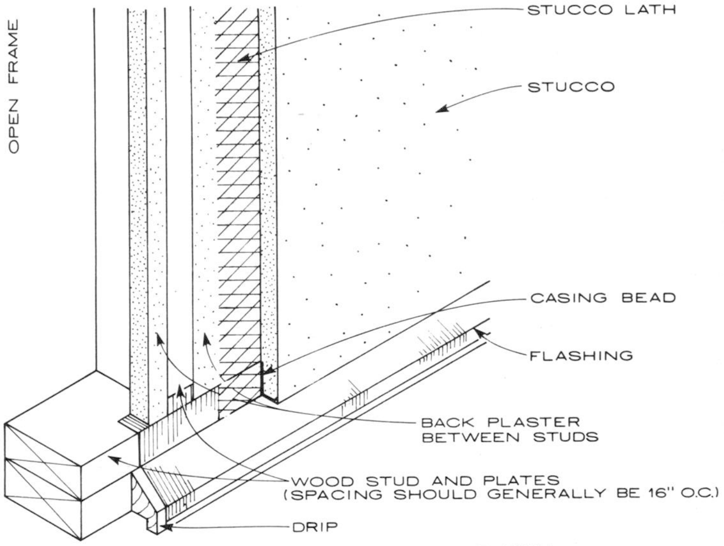

WOOD BASE

SHOE MOULD

WOOD GROUND

WOOD STUD AND BOTTOM PLATE

STUCCO LATH

STUCCO

CASING BEAD

FLASHING

BACK PLASTER BETWEEN STUDS

WOOD STUD AND PLATES (SPACING SHOULD GENERALLY BE 16″ O.C.)

DRIP

SECTIONS THROUGH TYPICAL PARTITION

SECTIONS THROUGH TYPICAL EXTERIOR WALL

WOOD STUD PARTITION AND WALL SYSTEMS

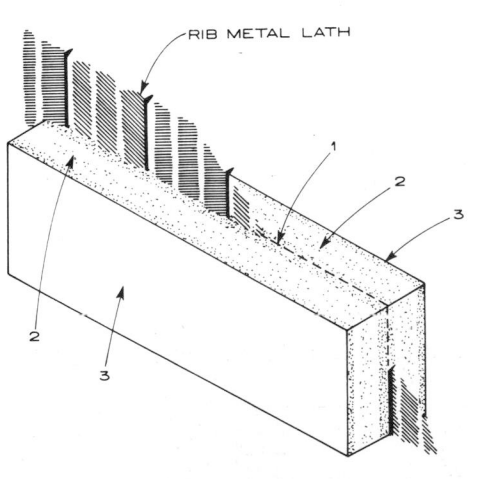

RIB METAL LATH

1. SCRATCH COAT
2. BROWN COAT
3. FINISH COAT

NOTE - Hollow studless partitions are similar to solid type. They are used where a furred space is required. They are formed simply by introducing a second layer of rib lath and pulling the two apart to create a space in between. Details are similar.

NOTE - Though bracing has been removed in the illustration it is required to support lath until the partition is able to support itself.

SEQUENCE OF PLASTER APPLICATION

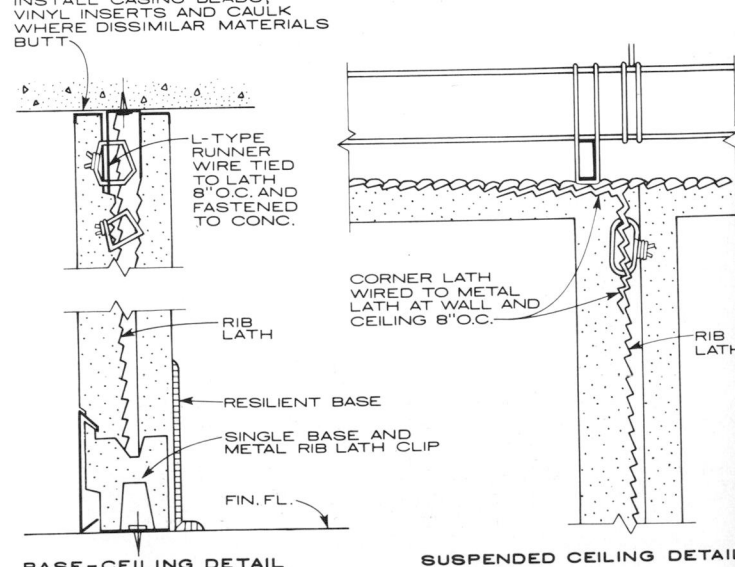

INSTALL CASING BEADS, VINYL INSERTS AND CAULK WHERE DISSIMILAR MATERIALS BUTT

L-TYPE RUNNER WIRE TIED TO LATH 8″ O.C. AND FASTENED TO CONC.

CORNER LATH WIRED TO METAL LATH AT WALL AND CEILING 8″ O.C.

RIB LATH

RESILIENT BASE

SINGLE BASE AND METAL RIB LATH CLIP

FIN. FL.

RIB LATH

BASE-CEILING DETAIL

SUSPENDED CEILING DETAIL

METAL LATH (STUDLESS, SOLID) PARTITION SYSTEM AND DETAILS (Channel stud solid and hollow partition details are similar)

Douglas S. Stenhouse, AIA; Washington, D. C.

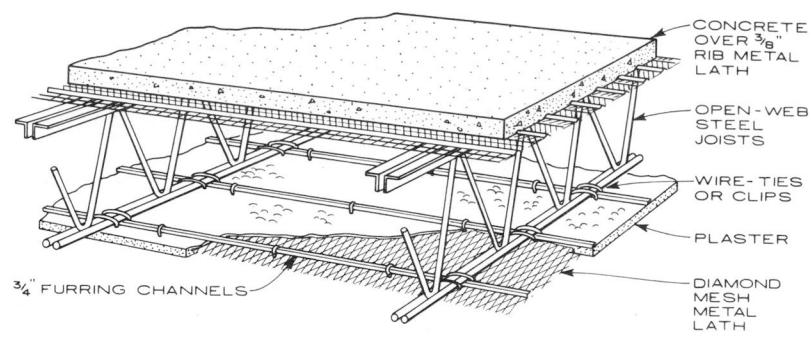

FURRED METAL LATH ON OPEN WEB STEEL JOISTS
(Rib metal lath may be substituted for Diamond Mesh Lath and furring channels)

Labels: CONCRETE OVER 3/8" RIB METAL LATH; OPEN-WEB STEEL JOISTS; WIRE-TIES OR CLIPS; PLASTER; DIAMOND MESH METAL LATH; 3/4" FURRING CHANNELS

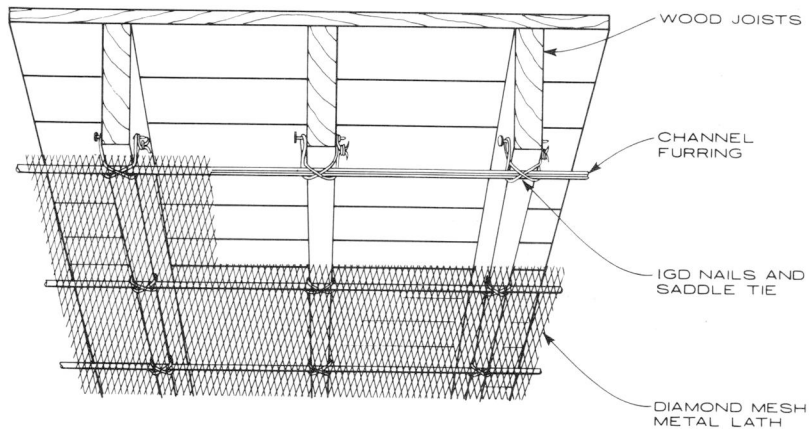

FURRED METAL LATH ON WOOD JOISTS
(Lath may be nailed directly to joists with 1 1/2" barbed roofing nail 7/16" head, 6" O.C., though this "contact" system is more subject to cracking due to wood shrinkage)

Labels: WOOD JOISTS; CHANNEL FURRING; IGD NAILS AND SADDLE TIE; DIAMOND MESH METAL LATH

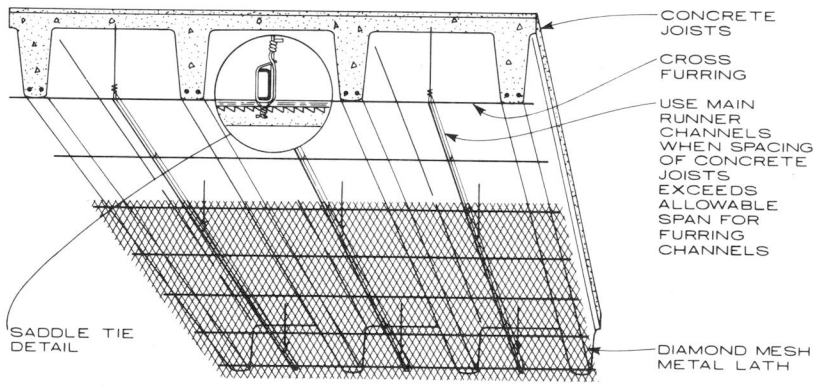

FURRED METAL LATH CEILING ON CONCRETE JOISTS

Labels: CONCRETE JOISTS; CROSS FURRING; USE MAIN RUNNER CHANNELS WHEN SPACING OF CONCRETE JOISTS EXCEEDS ALLOWABLE SPAN FOR FURRING CHANNELS; DIAMOND MESH METAL LATH; SADDLE TIE DETAIL

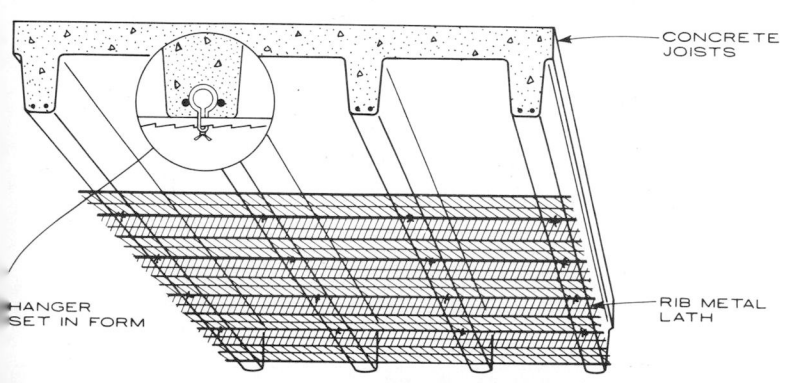

(CONTACT) RIB METAL LATH ON CONCRETE JOISTS

Labels: CONCRETE JOISTS; HANGER SET IN FORM; RIB METAL LATH

Douglas S. Stenhouse, AIA; Washington, D. C.

SPACING AND SELECTION OF FURRING AND SUSPENSION SYSTEM COMPONENTS

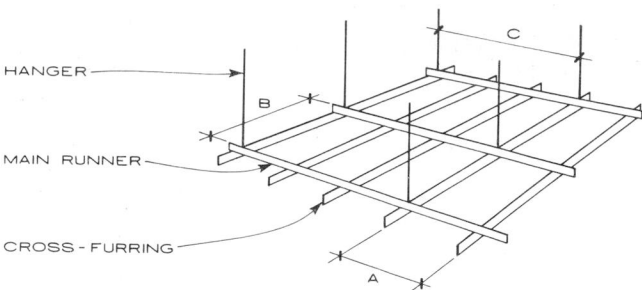

Labels: HANGER; MAIN RUNNER; CROSS-FURRING; A; B; C

HOW TO USE TABLES

1. Select lath and plaster system.
2. Determine spacing of cross-furring channels ("A").
3. Determine spacing of main runner channels ("B").
4. Determine hanger support spacing for main runner ("C").
5. Calculate area of ceiling supported by hanger.
6. Select hanger type from table.

MAXIMUM SPACING "A" OF SUPPORTS FOR LATHING SYSTEMS

TYPE OF LATH		LBS PER SQ.		WOOD	STEEL
		YARD	FOOT	CONC.	
GYPSUM	3/8" PLAIN	13.5	1.5	16"	16"
	1/2" PLAIN	18.0	2.0	16"	16"
	1/2" VENEER BASE	16.2	1.8	16"	16"
	5/8" VENEER BASE	20.3	2.25	16"	16"
METAL	DIAMOND MESH	3.4	.38	13 1/2"	16"
	FLAT RIB	2.75	.31	16"	12"
	FLAT RIB	3.4	.38	19"	19"
	3/8" RIB	3.4	.38	24"	24"
	3/8" RIB	4.0	.44	24"	24"
	3/4" RIB	5.4	.60	36"	36"
	WELDED WIRE	1.4	.15	16"	16"
	PAPER BACKED WIRE	1.95	.21	24"	24"

MAXIMUM SPACING "B" BETWEEN MAIN RUNNERS

CROSS FURRING TYPE	CROSS FURRING SPACING "A"			
	12"	16"	19"	24"
1/4" DIAM. PENCIL ROD	2'-0"	—	—	—
3/8" DIAM. PENCIL ROD	2'-6"	—	2'-0"	—
3/4" CRC, HRC (.3 LB/FT)	—	4'-0"	3'-6"	3'-0"
1" HRC (.41 LB/FT)	5'-0"	—	4'-6"	4'-0"

MAXIMUM SPACING "C" BETWEEN HANGERS

MAIN RUNNER TYPE	MAIN RUNNER SPACING "B"				
	3'-0"	3'-6"	4'-0"	4'-6"	5'-0"
3/4" CRC (.3 LB/FT)	2'-0"	—	—	—	—
1 1/2" CRC (.875 LB/FT)	4'-0"	3'-6"	3'-0"	—	—
1 1/2 HRC (1.12 LB/FT)	—	—	—	4'-0"	—
2" CRC (.59 LB/FT)	—	—	5'-0"	—	—
2" HRC (1.26 LB/FT)	—	—	—	—	5'-0"
1/2" × 1/2" × 3/16" STL ∠	—	5'-0"	—	—	—

HANGER TYPE SELECTION TABLE

MAXIMUM CLG AREA	MINIMUM SIZE OF HANGER	
12.5 SQ. FT.	9 GAGE	9 gage wire
16 SQ. FT.		8 gage wire
18 SQ. FT.		3/16" diam. mild steel rod
25 SQ. FT.		1" × 3/16" mild steel flat

TIE WIRE SELECTION TABLE

	SUPPORT	MAX. CLG. AREA	MINIMUM SIZE HANGER
CROSS FURR'G	CONG	8 sq. ft.	14 gage wire
	SIZ, WD	8	16 gage wire (2 loops)
MAIN RUNNERS	SINGLE HANGERS BETWEEN BEAMS	8 sq. ft.	12 gage wire
		12	10 gage wire
		16	8 gage wire
	DOUBLE WIRE LOOPS AT SUPPORTS	8 sq. ft.	14 gage wire
		12	12 gage wire
		16	11 gage wire

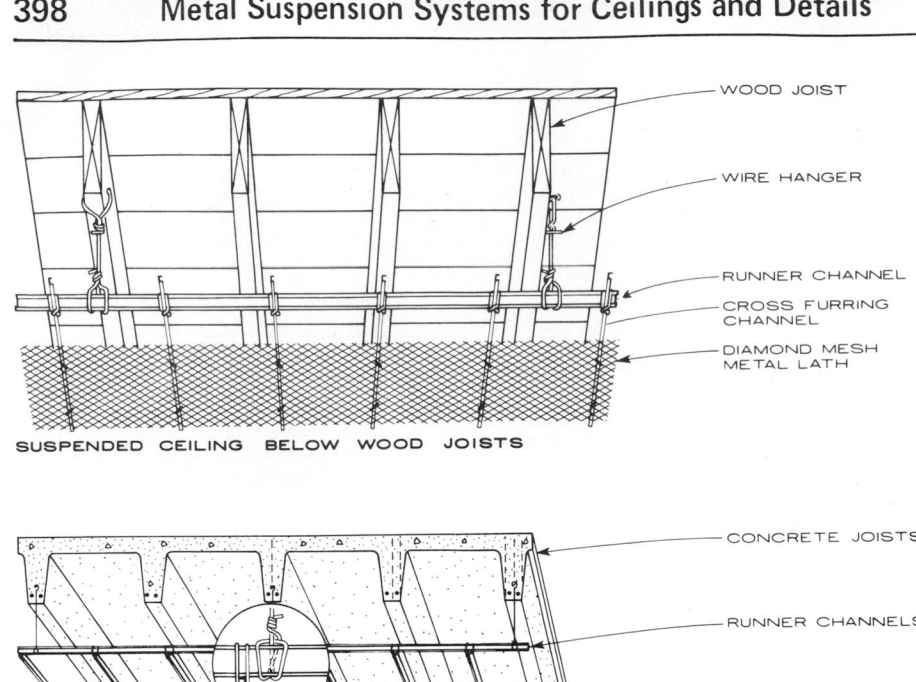

WOOD JOIST

WIRE HANGER

RUNNER CHANNEL

CROSS FURRING CHANNEL

DIAMOND MESH METAL LATH

SUSPENDED CEILING BELOW WOOD JOISTS

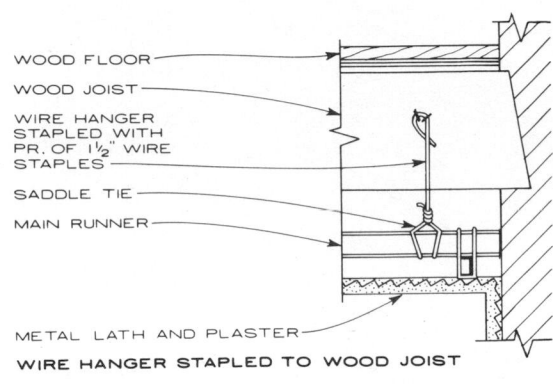

WOOD FLOOR

WOOD JOIST

WIRE HANGER STAPLED WITH PR. OF 1½" WIRE STAPLES

SADDLE TIE

MAIN RUNNER

METAL LATH AND PLASTER

WIRE HANGER STAPLED TO WOOD JOIST

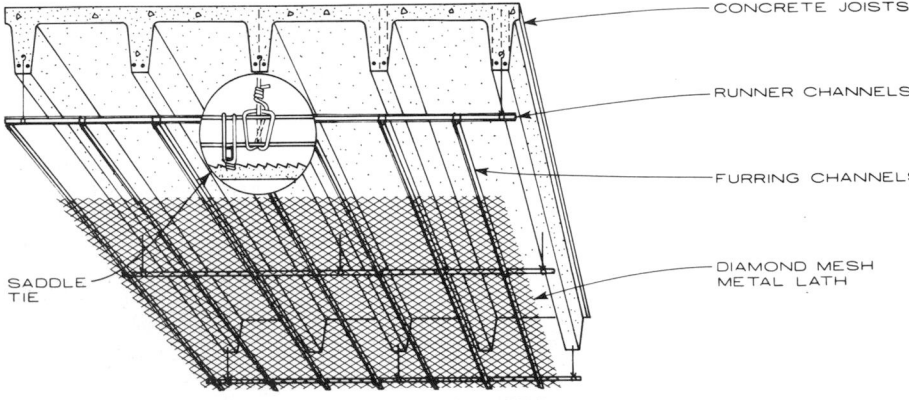

CONCRETE JOISTS

RUNNER CHANNELS

FURRING CHANNELS

DIAMOND MESH METAL LATH

SADDLE TIE

SUSPENDED CEILING BELOW CONCRETE JOISTS

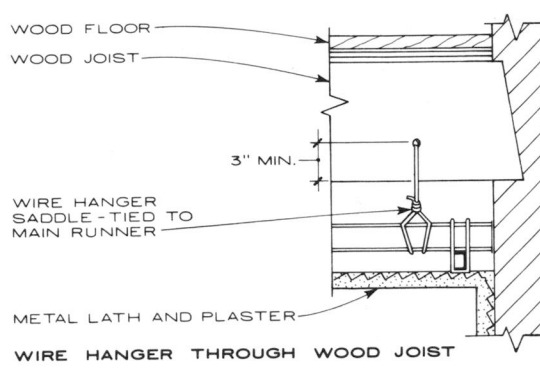

WOOD FLOOR

WOOD JOIST

3" MIN.

WIRE HANGER SADDLE-TIED TO MAIN RUNNER

METAL LATH AND PLASTER

WIRE HANGER THROUGH WOOD JOIST

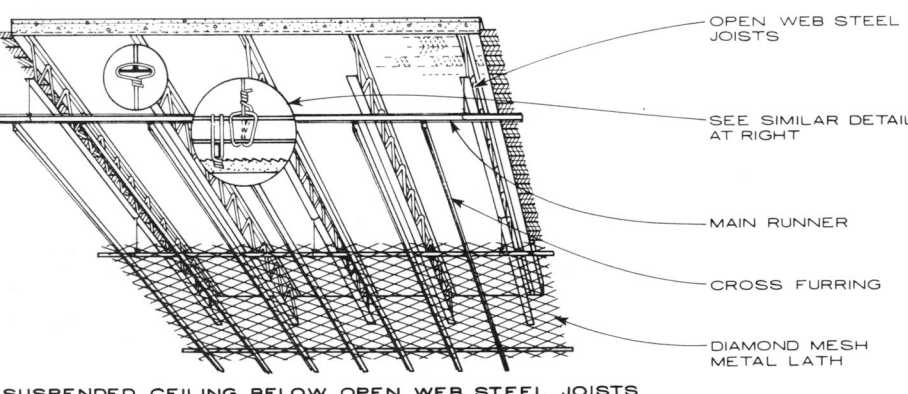

OPEN WEB STEEL JOISTS

SEE SIMILAR DETAIL AT RIGHT

MAIN RUNNER

CROSS FURRING

DIAMOND MESH METAL LATH

SUSPENDED CEILING BELOW OPEN WEB STEEL JOISTS

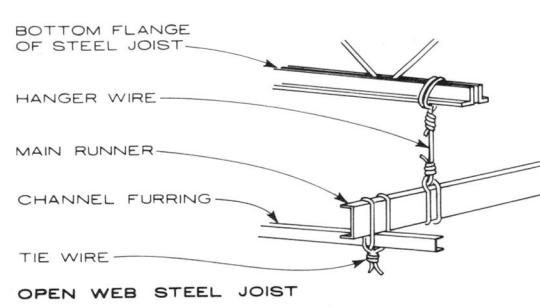

BOTTOM FLANGE OF STEEL JOIST

HANGER WIRE

MAIN RUNNER

CHANNEL FURRING

TIE WIRE

OPEN WEB STEEL JOIST

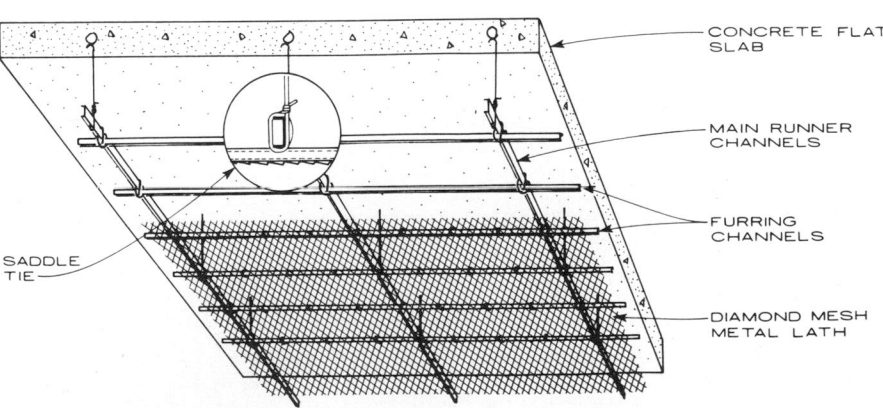

CONCRETE FLAT SLAB

MAIN RUNNER CHANNELS

FURRING CHANNELS

SADDLE TIE

DIAMOND MESH METAL LATH

SUSPENDED CEILING BELOW CONCRETE FLAT SLAB

Douglas S. Stenhouse, AIA; Washington, D. C.

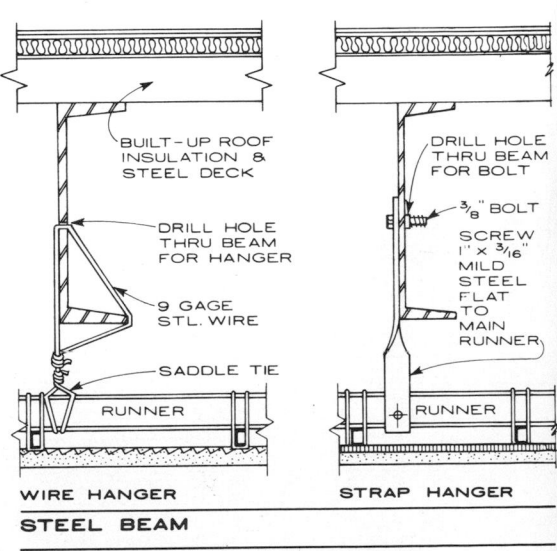

BUILT-UP ROOF INSULATION & STEEL DECK

DRILL HOLE THRU BEAM FOR HANGER

9 GAGE STL. WIRE

SADDLE TIE

RUNNER

DRILL HOLE THRU BEAM FOR BOLT

⅜" BOLT

SCREW 1" × 3/16" MILD STEEL FLAT TO MAIN RUNNER

RUNNER

WIRE HANGER

STRAP HANGER

STEEL BEAM

MISCELLANEOUS SUSPENSION DETAILS

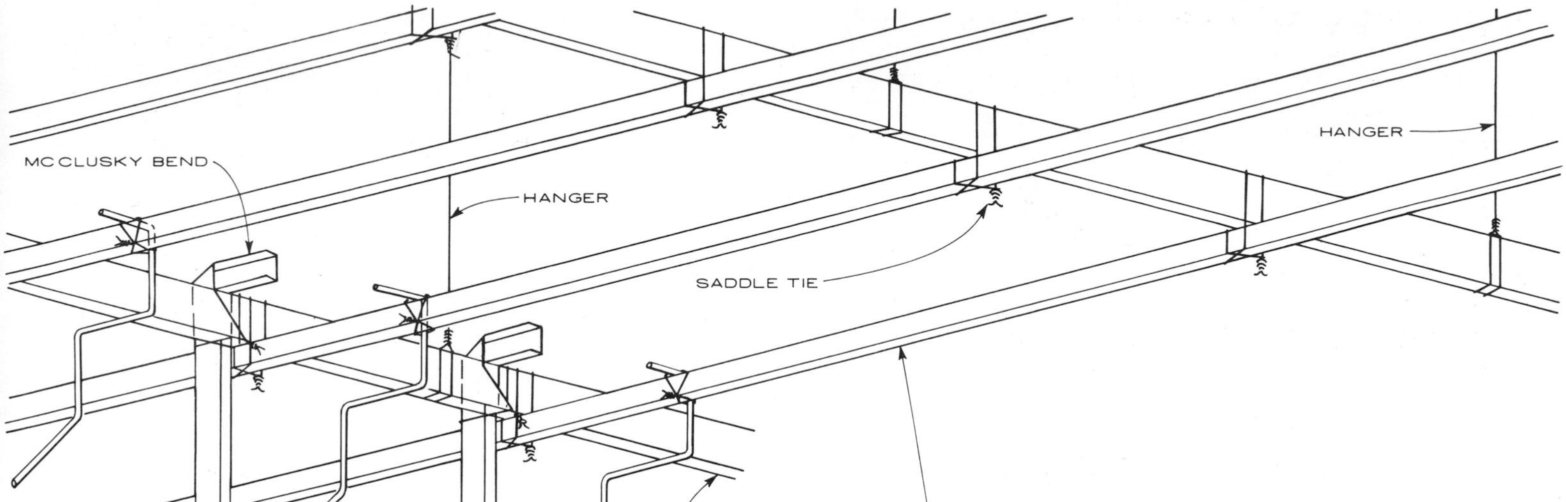

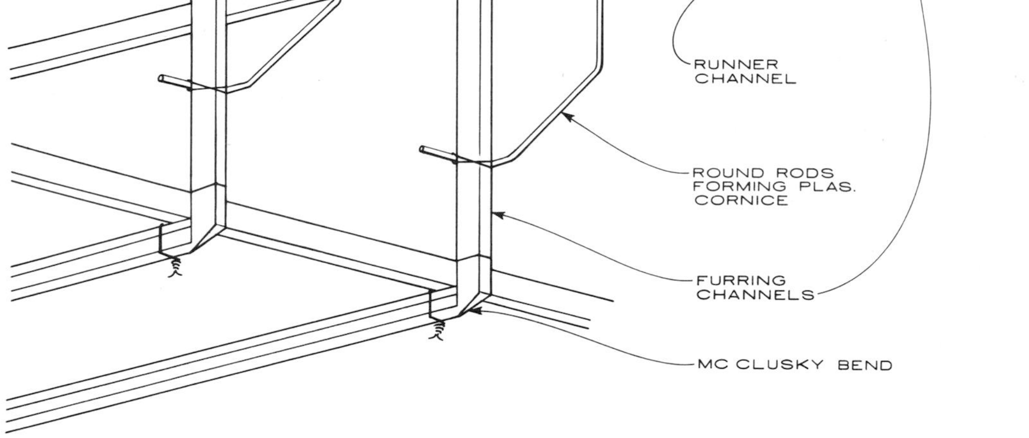

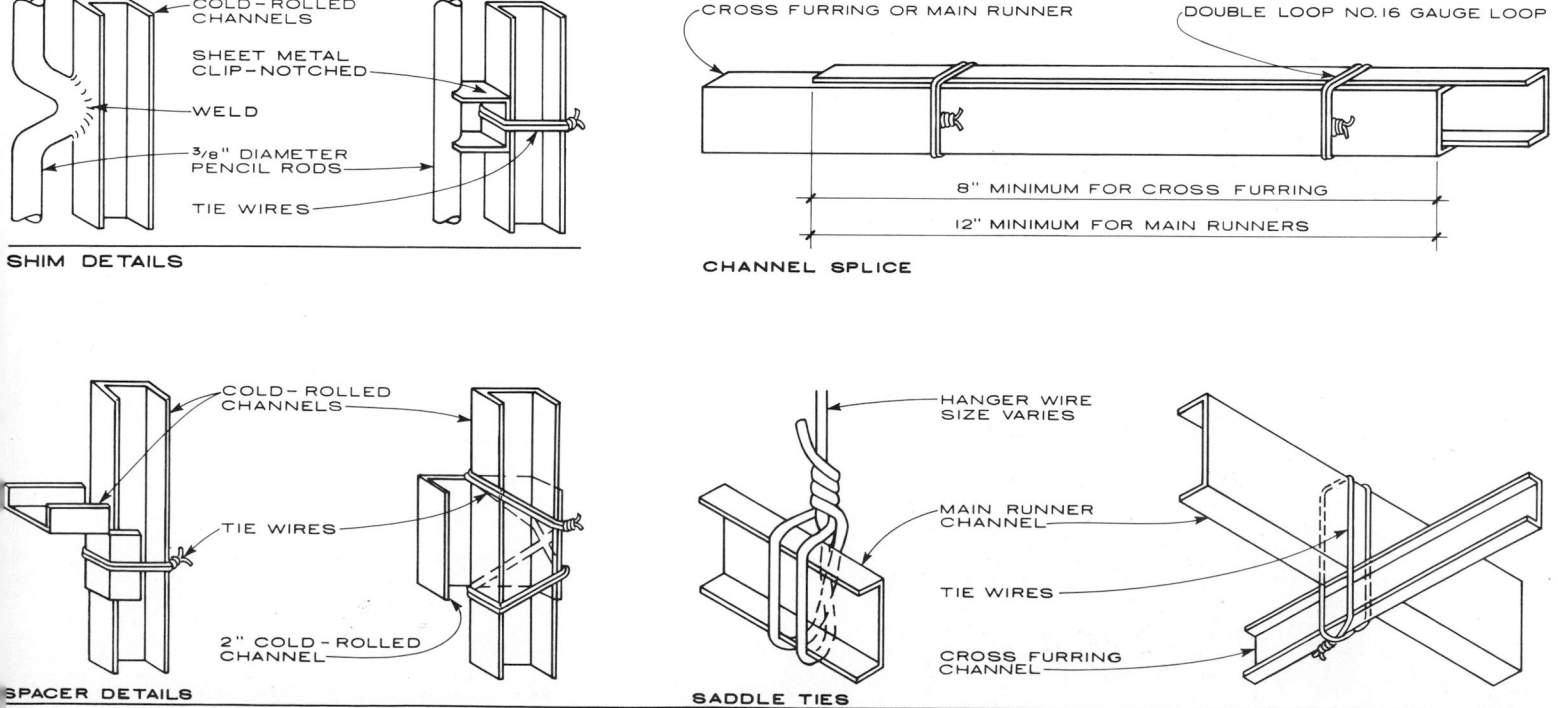

MCCLUSKY BEND

HANGER

HANGER

SADDLE TIE

RUNNER CHANNEL

ROUND RODS FORMING PLAS. CORNICE

FURRING CHANNELS

MC CLUSKY BEND

TYPICAL METAL COMPONENTS OF A LATH SUPPORTING STRUCTURE

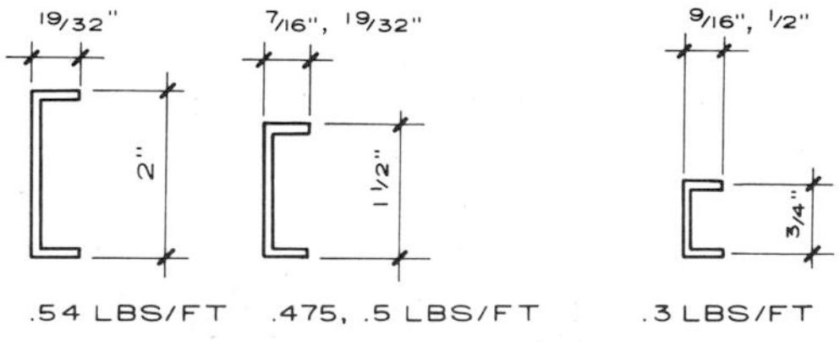

19/32"	7/16", 19/32"	9/16", 1/2"
2"	1 1/2"	3/4"
.54 LBS/FT	.475, .5 LBS/FT	.3 LBS/FT
RUNNERS		FURRING

TYPICAL COLD-ROLLED CHANNEL SHAPES

Heat-rolled channels (HRC) generally run heavier than cold-rolled channels (CRC). Shapes illustrated are available in 16 ga., 16 and 20 ft. standard lengths.

Galvanizing of all components is recommended where moisture is a factor, extra heavy galvanizing for swimming pools.

See page on Suspended Ceiling Systems for instructions for selection of components.

COLD-ROLLED CHANNELS

SHEET METAL CLIP-NOTCHED

WELD

3/8" DIAMETER PENCIL RODS

TIE WIRES

SHIM DETAILS

CROSS FURRING OR MAIN RUNNER

DOUBLE LOOP NO.16 GAUGE LOOP

8" MINIMUM FOR CROSS FURRING

12" MINIMUM FOR MAIN RUNNERS

CHANNEL SPLICE

COLD-ROLLED CHANNELS

TIE WIRES

2" COLD-ROLLED CHANNEL

SPACER DETAILS

HANGER WIRE SIZE VARIES

MAIN RUNNER CHANNEL

TIE WIRES

CROSS FURRING CHANNEL

SADDLE TIES

TYPICAL METAL CHANNEL SUSPENSION AND FURRING DETAILS

Douglas S. Stenhouse, AIA; Washington, D. C.

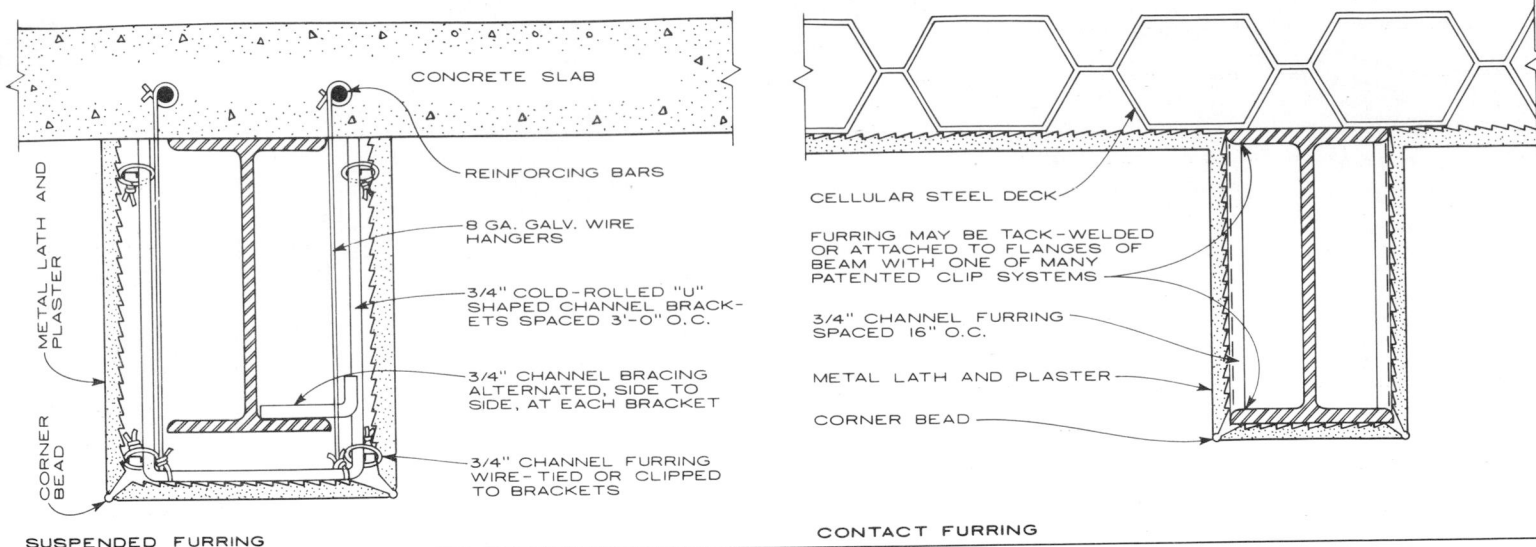

CONCRETE SLAB

REINFORCING BARS

8 GA. GALV. WIRE HANGERS

3/4" COLD-ROLLED "U" SHAPED CHANNEL BRACK-ETS SPACED 3'-0" O.C.

3/4" CHANNEL BRACING ALTERNATED, SIDE TO SIDE, AT EACH BRACKET

3/4" CHANNEL FURRING WIRE-TIED OR CLIPPED TO BRACKETS

METAL LATH AND PLASTER

CORNER BEAD

CELLULAR STEEL DECK

FURRING MAY BE TACK-WELDED OR ATTACHED TO FLANGES OF BEAM WITH ONE OF MANY PATENTED CLIP SYSTEMS

3/4" CHANNEL FURRING SPACED 16" O.C.

METAL LATH AND PLASTER

CORNER BEAD

SUSPENDED FURRING

CONTACT FURRING

BASIC SYSTEMS OF BEAM AND GIRDER PLASTER FIREPROOFING

GYPSUM LATH MAY BE USED IN LIEU OF METAL LATH. VARIOUS SPRAYED-ON NON-PLASTER TYPE SYSTEMS ARE ALSO COMMONLY USED

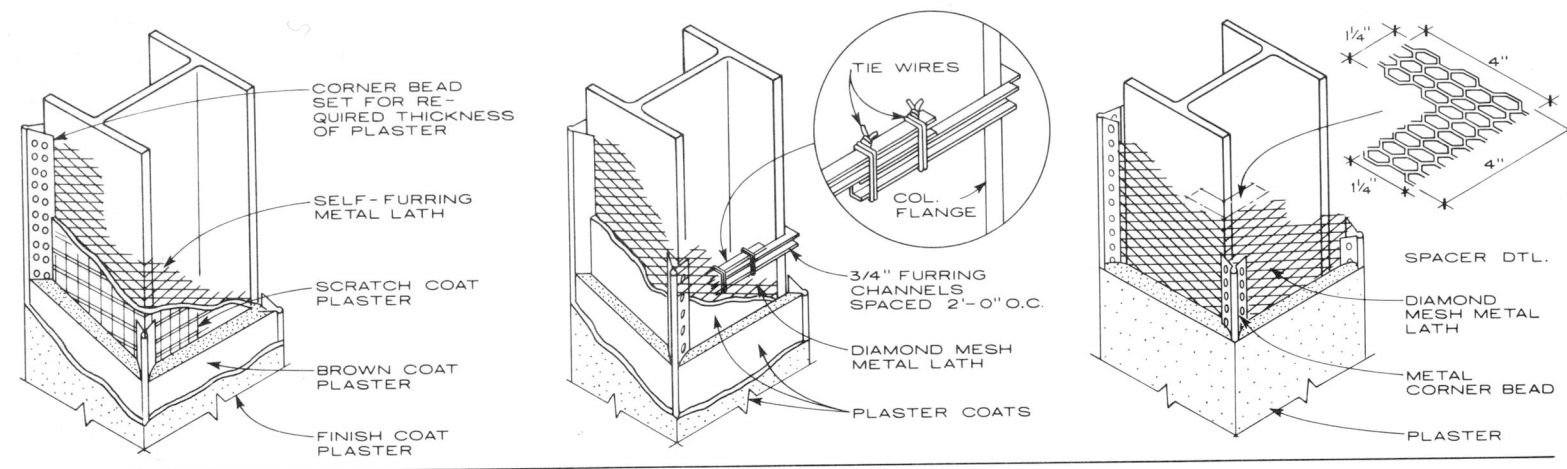

CORNER BEAD SET FOR RE-QUIRED THICKNESS OF PLASTER

SELF-FURRING METAL LATH

SCRATCH COAT PLASTER

BROWN COAT PLASTER

FINISH COAT PLASTER

TIE WIRES

COL. FLANGE

3/4" FURRING CHANNELS SPACED 2'-0" O.C.

DIAMOND MESH METAL LATH

PLASTER COATS

SPACER DTL.

DIAMOND MESH METAL LATH

METAL CORNER BEAD

PLASTER

BASIC SYSTEMS FOR COLUMN FIREPROOFING

GYPSUM LATH MAY BE USED IN LIEU OF METAL LATH

CONSULT LOCAL BUILDING CODE AND UNDERWRITERS' LABORATORIES INC. FOR VARIOUS COMBINATIONS OF APPROVED MATERIALS, THICK-NESSES AND CORRESPONDING FIRE RATINGS

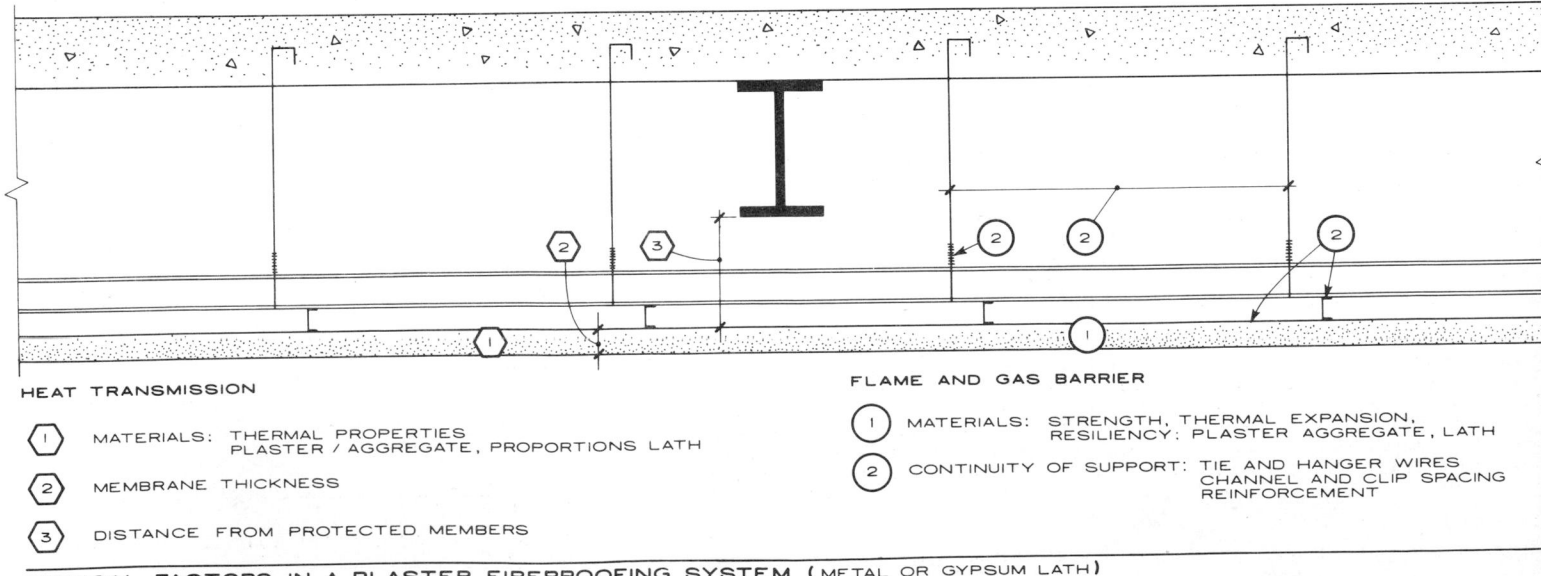

HEAT TRANSMISSION

(1) MATERIALS: THERMAL PROPERTIES PLASTER / AGGREGATE, PROPORTIONS LATH

(2) MEMBRANE THICKNESS

(3) DISTANCE FROM PROTECTED MEMBERS

FLAME AND GAS BARRIER

(1) MATERIALS: STRENGTH, THERMAL EXPANSION, RESILIENCY: PLASTER AGGREGATE, LATH

(2) CONTINUITY OF SUPPORT: TIE AND HANGER WIRES CHANNEL AND CLIP SPACING REINFORCEMENT

CRITICAL FACTORS IN A PLASTER FIREPROOFING SYSTEM (METAL OR GYPSUM LATH)

Douglas S. Stenhouse, AIA; Washington, D. C.

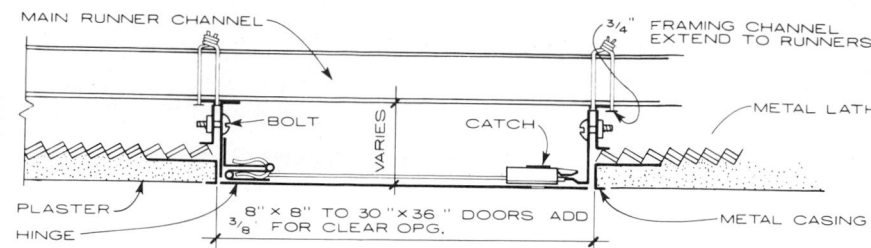

MAIN RUNNER CHANNEL
3/4" FRAMING CHANNEL EXTEND TO RUNNERS
BOLT
VARIES
CATCH
METAL LATH
PLASTER
HINGE
8" x 8" TO 30"x36" DOORS ADD 3/8" FOR CLEAR OPG.
METAL CASING

FLUSH METAL FACE

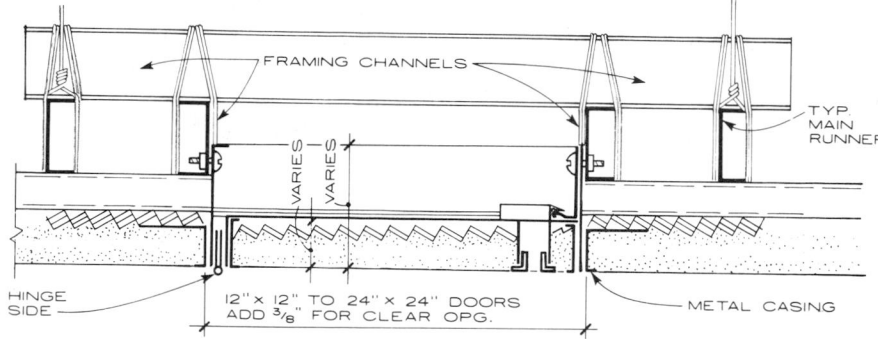

FRAMING CHANNELS
TYP. MAIN RUNNER
VARIES — VARIES
HINGE SIDE
12"x 12" TO 24"x 24" DOORS ADD 3/8" FOR CLEAR OPG.
METAL CASING

FLUSH PLASTER FACE

METAL ACCESS DOORS AND FRAMES

NOTE:
GAGE OF METAL, NO. OF LOCKS, HINGES VARY. FIRE-RATED DOORS AVAILABLE

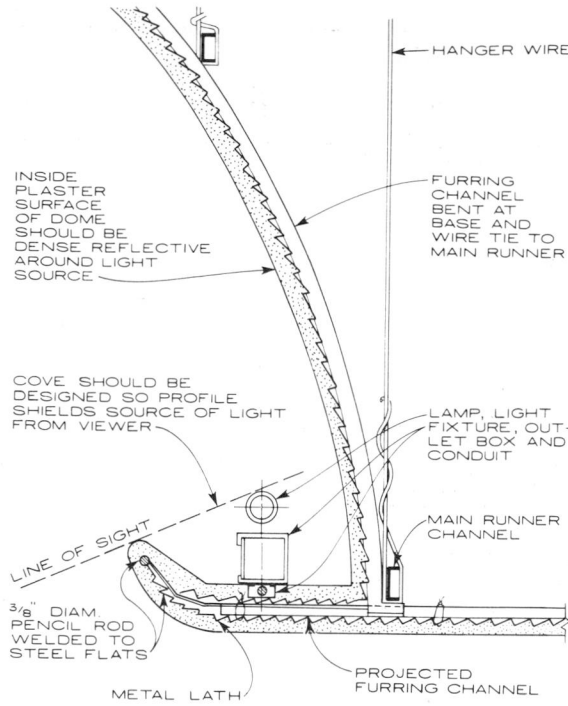

HANGER WIRE

INSIDE PLASTER SURFACE OF DOME SHOULD BE DENSE REFLECTIVE AROUND LIGHT SOURCE

FURRING CHANNEL BENT AT BASE AND WIRE TIE TO MAIN RUNNER

COVE SHOULD BE DESIGNED SO PROFILE SHIELDS SOURCE OF LIGHT FROM VIEWER

LINE OF SIGHT

LAMP, LIGHT FIXTURE, OUT-LET BOX AND CONDUIT

MAIN RUNNER CHANNEL

3/8" DIAM. PENCIL ROD WELDED TO STEEL FLATS

METAL LATH

PROJECTED FURRING CHANNEL

DETAIL OF DOME SHOWING LIGHT COVE

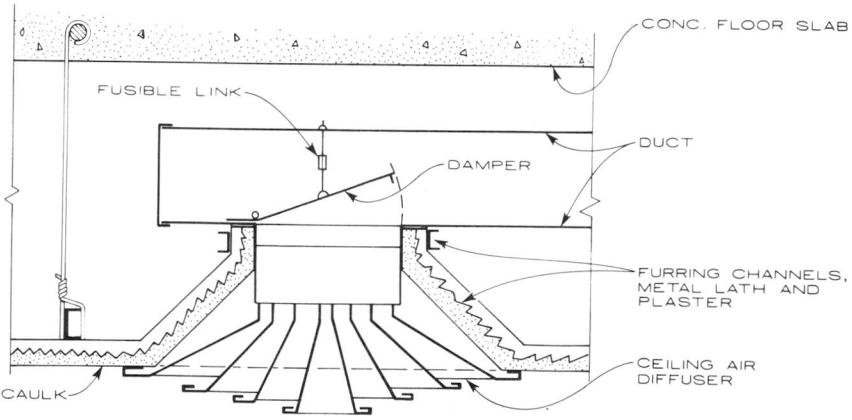

CONC. FLOOR SLAB
FUSIBLE LINK
DUCT
DAMPER
FURRING CHANNELS, METAL LATH AND PLASTER
CEILING AIR DIFFUSER
CAULK

DUCT OPENING IN FIRE-RATED CEILING

NOTES ON ORNAMENTAL PLASTER

Historically, Moorish, Bavarian, Italian, French and English craftsmen have left us a heritage of ornamental plaster work, for which there is increasing interest and demand. The entire subject is discussed in great detail in a rare but informative book entitled, Plastering by William Millar, published in 1897 by B. T. Batsford, London, England. Very briefly, the following are basic types of ornamental plasterwork still being employed by the trade.

RUNNING A CORNICE:

This type of field work is accomplished over basecoats formed to approximate the desired profile. Metal lath is wire-tied or welded to steel flats, pencil rods and bent furring channels. The final white coat finish is laid down by dragging a 22 gage sheet metal, wood-backed form across on guides, working from a scaffold. This form is precisely shaped to produce the final profile, allowing 1/8" tolerances for bedding any precast ornament that may be set in place by coating surfaces with a latex compound and thin coat of lime putty.

PRECAST ORNAMENT:

Castings of complete cornices, pediments, arches, columns, rosettes, ceiling and wall panels can be made in the shop with glue, gelatin, silicone rubber and plaster moulds, depending on whether they are intended for reuse or are designed so that they can be separated and refitted together again. Waste moulds are generally made of plaster with inside surfaces greased to reduce bond and absorption. Rubber and gelatin moulds are used for repetive castings. Where detailed, in-depth castings must be made, small individual moulds are bound together by a mother mould. Hemp fiber, burlap or mosquito netting, depending upon the thickness of the casting, are used for reinforcement.

SCAGLIOLA AND GRAFFITO:

These are, respectively, imitation marble and two-dimensional fresco-type work requiring considerable artistry.

Douglas S. Stenhouse, AIA; Washington, D. C.

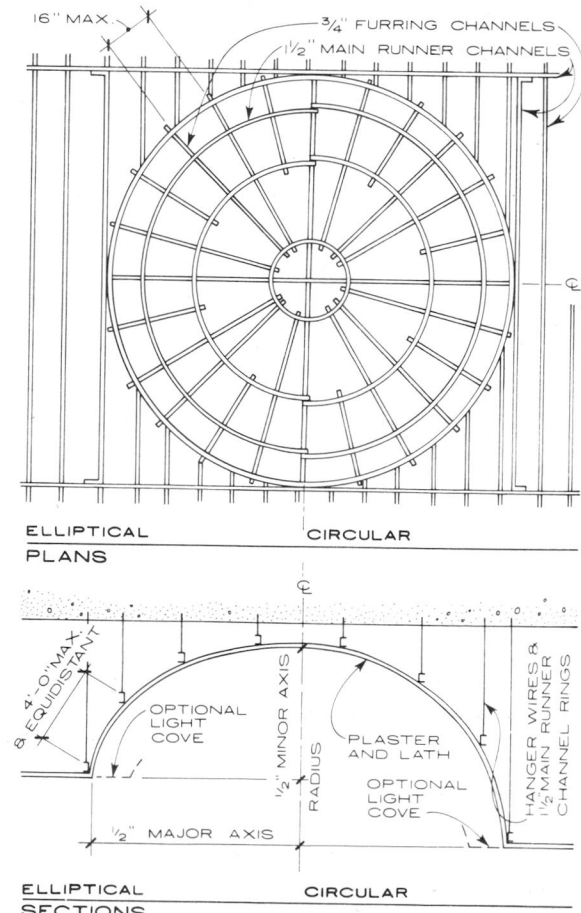

16" MAX.
3/4" FURRING CHANNELS
1 1/2" MAIN RUNNER CHANNELS

ELLIPTICAL   CIRCULAR
PLANS

8 4'-0" MAX. EQUIDISTANT
OPTIONAL LIGHT COVE
1/2 MINOR AXIS
1/2 RADIUS
PLASTER AND LATH
OPTIONAL LIGHT COVE
HANGER WIRES & 1 1/2" MAIN RUNNER CHANNEL RINGS
1/2" MAJOR AXIS

ELLIPTICAL   CIRCULAR
SECTIONS

FURRING, SUSPENSION SYSTEM FOR DOMED CEILING

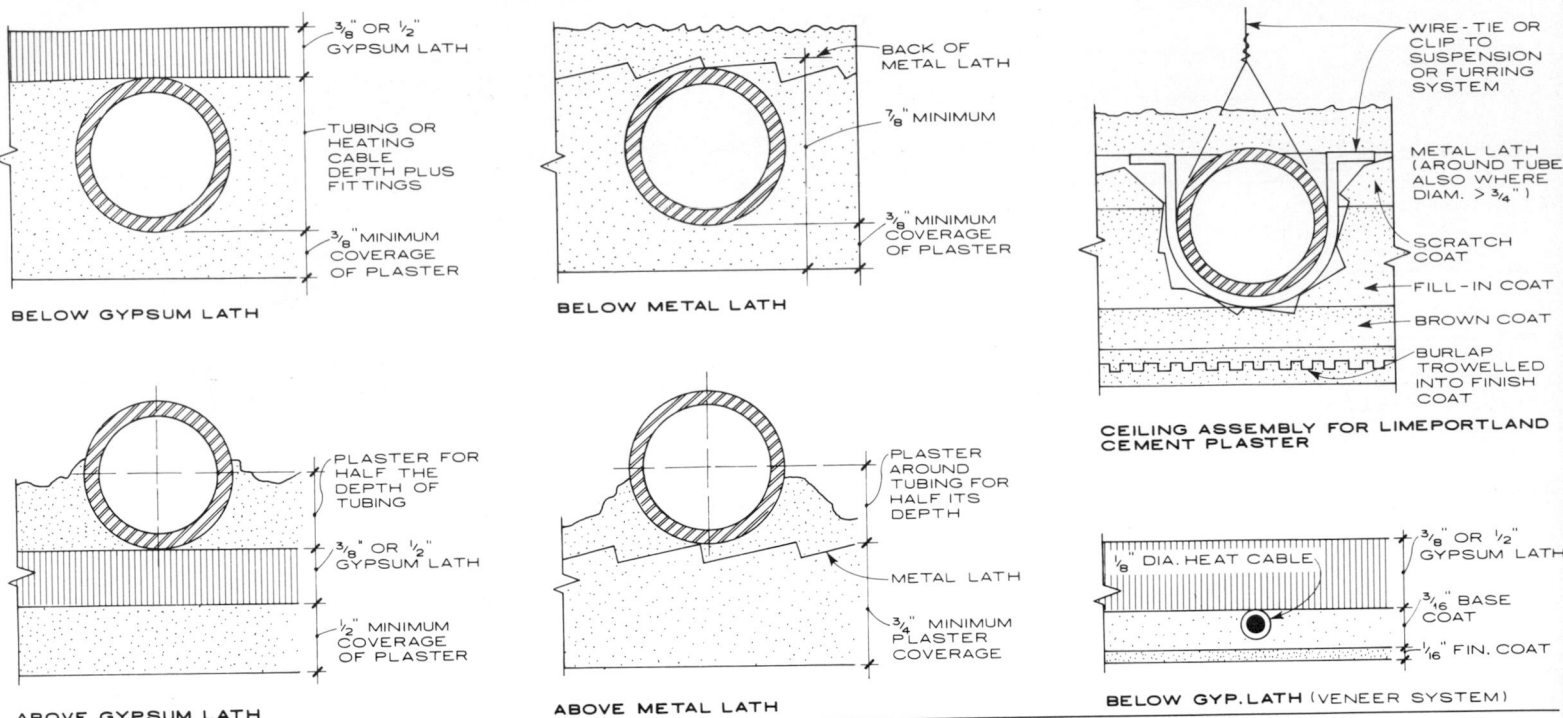

BELOW GYPSUM LATH
- 3/8" OR 1/2" GYPSUM LATH
- TUBING OR HEATING CABLE DEPTH PLUS FITTINGS
- 3/8" MINIMUM COVERAGE OF PLASTER

BELOW METAL LATH
- BACK OF METAL LATH
- 7/8" MINIMUM
- 3/8" MINIMUM COVERAGE OF PLASTER

CEILING ASSEMBLY FOR LIMEPORTLAND CEMENT PLASTER
- WIRE - TIE OR CLIP TO SUSPENSION OR FURRING SYSTEM
- METAL LATH (AROUND TUBE ALSO WHERE DIAM. > 3/4")
- SCRATCH COAT
- FILL-IN COAT
- BROWN COAT
- BURLAP TROWELLED INTO FINISH COAT

ABOVE GYPSUM LATH
- PLASTER FOR HALF THE DEPTH OF TUBING
- 3/8" OR 1/2" GYPSUM LATH
- 1/2" MINIMUM COVERAGE OF PLASTER

ABOVE METAL LATH
- PLASTER AROUND TUBING FOR HALF ITS DEPTH
- METAL LATH
- 3/4" MINIMUM PLASTER COVERAGE

BELOW GYP. LATH (VENEER SYSTEM)
- 1/8" DIA. HEAT CABLE
- 3/8" OR 1/2" GYPSUM LATH
- 3/16" BASE COAT
- 1/16" FIN. COAT

PLASTER SYSTEMS FOR RADIANT HEATING IN CEILING

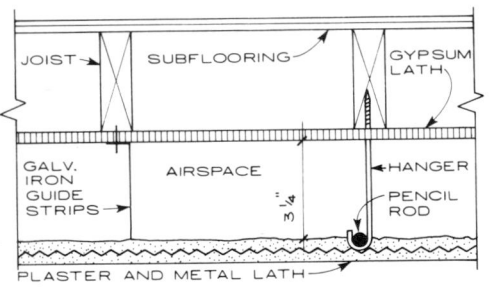

- JOIST
- SUBFLOORING
- GYPSUM LATH
- GALV. IRON GUIDE STRIPS
- AIRSPACE
- HANGER
- PENCIL ROD
- PLASTER AND METAL LATH

GUIDE STRIP AND SUSPENSION DETAILS

NEW SYSTEMS OF PLASTERING

Technological advances have provided the plaster trade several new systems highly competitive with traditional drywall. None, like drywall, are recommended for excessively moist areas, but they are claimed to be neater, cleaner operations that are installed quickly, the finish coat directly over the base coat after the latter has had a chance to set. Installations can be made on masonry by using special furring channels with foam insulation in between channels at exterior walls. The systems involve spraying an aluminum sulphate catalyst over a lath base which must be damp before the base coat is applied. Finish coats may be trowelled smooth, floated or textured, and their appearance is identical to conventional plastering systems. One system employs a two-coat $1/16$" base and finish on standard gypsum lath with conventional beads and corner lath. Other veneer systems use special lath boards 4' wide, 8, 9, 10 and 12 feet long, covered with an absorptive paper. Either $3/8$", $1/2$" and $5/8$" thick lath board may be used with the two-coat veneer system, but $1/2$" and $5/8$" thicknesses only on one-coat jobs. Two-coat systems have $1/16$" base and finish coats. One-coat systems are a minimum $3/32$" thick. Both require special glass-coated fiber "tape" and beads.

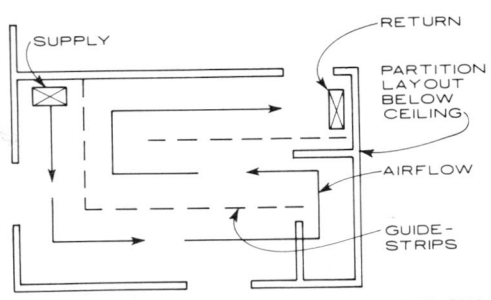

- SUPPLY
- RETURN
- PARTITION LAYOUT BELOW CEILING
- AIRFLOW
- GUIDE-STRIPS

PLAN SHOWING GUIDE STRIPS & AIR FLOW

PLASTER CEILING PLENUMS FOR WARM AIR RADIANT HEATING IN CLG.

Warm air circulated through wall and ceiling plenums is another method of providing the benefits of radiant heat. It may be used to great advantage in buildings that require a great deal of ventilation, and it is relatively simple in comparison with other types of radiant heating systems. Dampers are installed in supply ducts to provide individually regulated room temperatures. Various systems of attachment are employed for suspending the lower ceiling from supports above. The gage of the wire hangers will vary depending upon the support system and spacing.

Douglas S. Stenhouse, AIA; Washington, D. C.

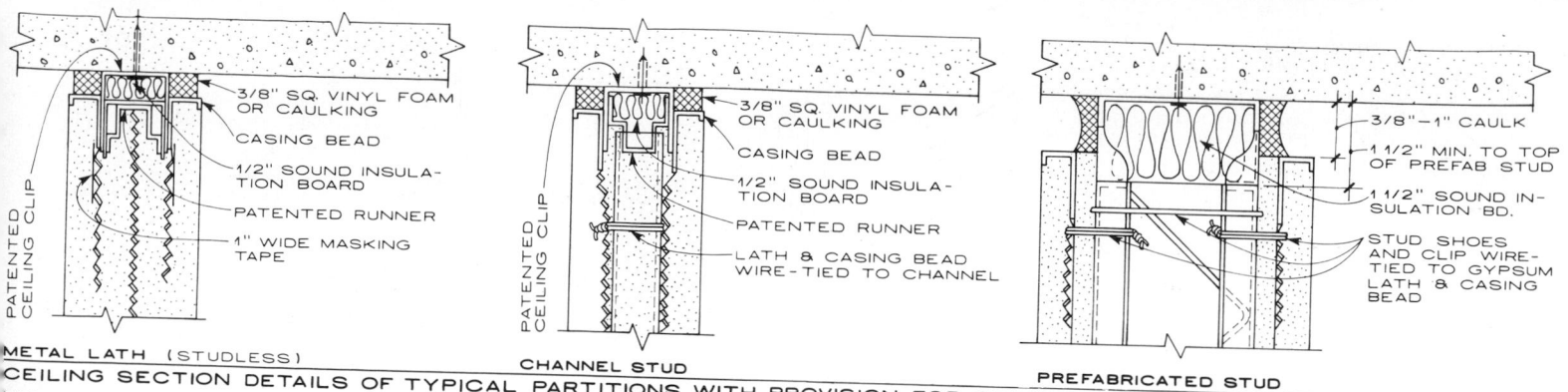

3/8" SQ. VINYL FOAM OR CAULKING
CASING BEAD
1/2" SOUND INSULA-TION BOARD
PATENTED RUNNER
1" WIDE MASKING TAPE
PATENTED CEILING CLIP
METAL LATH (STUDLESS)

3/8" SQ. VINYL FOAM OR CAULKING
CASING BEAD
1/2" SOUND INSULA-TION BOARD
PATENTED RUNNER
LATH & CASING BEAD WIRE-TIED TO CHANNEL
PATENTED CEILING CLIP
CHANNEL STUD

3/8"–1" CAULK
1 1/2" MIN. TO TOP OF PREFAB STUD
1 1/2" SOUND IN-SULATION BD.
STUD SHOES AND CLIP WIRE-TIED TO GYPSUM LATH & CASING BEAD
PREFABRICATED STUD

CEILING SECTION DETAILS OF TYPICAL PARTITIONS WITH PROVISION FOR CEILING DEFLECTION
(WALL SECTIONS SIMILAR)

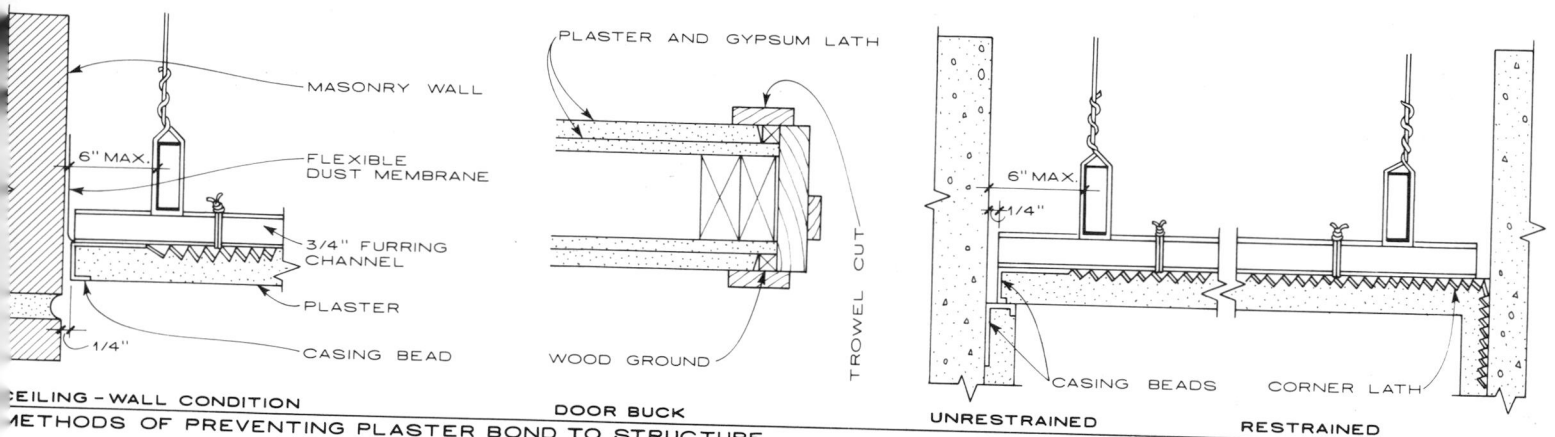

MASONRY WALL
6" MAX.
FLEXIBLE DUST MEMBRANE
3/4" FURRING CHANNEL
PLASTER
CASING BEAD
1/4"
CEILING–WALL CONDITION

PLASTER AND GYPSUM LATH
WOOD GROUND
TROWEL CUT
DOOR BUCK

6" MAX.
1 1/4"
CASING BEADS   CORNER LATH
UNRESTRAINED   RESTRAINED

METHODS OF PREVENTING PLASTER BOND TO STRUCTURE

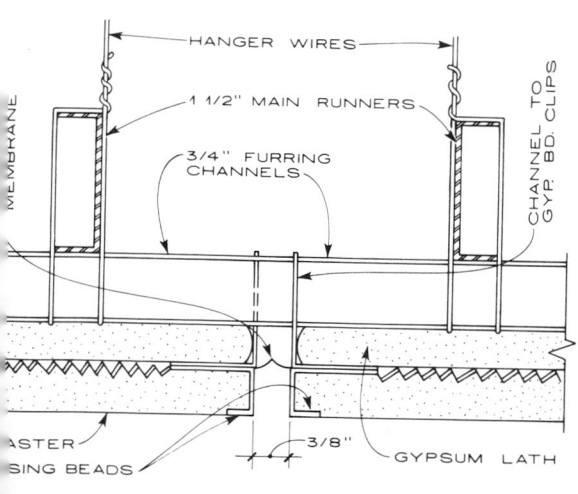

HANGER WIRES
1 1/2" MAIN RUNNERS
3/4" FURRING CHANNELS
CHANNEL TO GYP. BD. CLIPS
MEMBRANE
PLASTER
CASING BEADS
3/8"
GYPSUM LATH

CEILING CONTROL JOINT FOR GYPSUM LATH
(METAL LATH CONDITION SIMILAR)

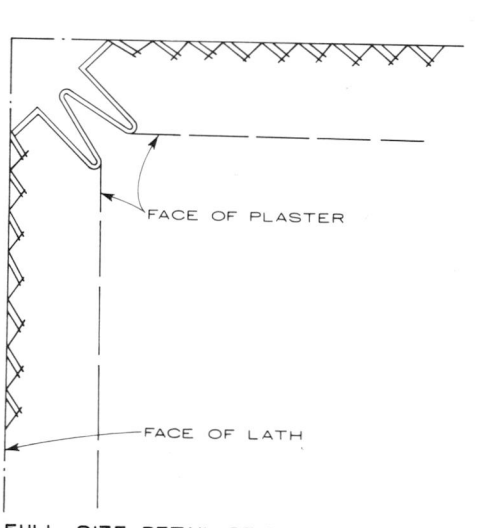

FACE OF PLASTER
FACE OF LATH

FULL-SIZE DETAIL OF PATENTED CORNER EXPANSION JOINT

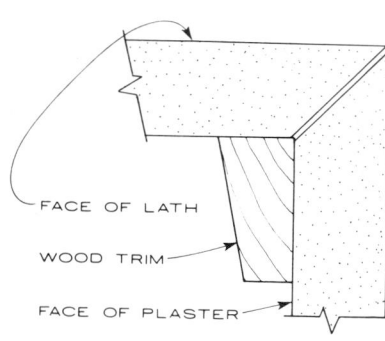

FACE OF LATH
WOOD TRIM
FACE OF PLASTER

TROWEL CUT CONCEALED BY WOOD TRIM

NOTE:
As for this detail and the detail above for wood door buck the pur-pose for most wood trim is to cover places where plaster is preordained to crack.

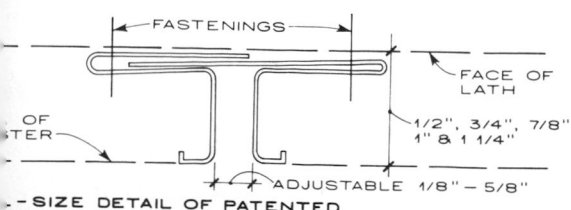

FASTENINGS
FACE OF LATH
1/2", 3/4", 7/8" 1" & 1 1/4"
FACE OF PLASTER
ADJUSTABLE 1/8" – 5/8"

FULL-SIZE DETAIL OF PATENTED CEILING OR WALL CONTROL JOINT

S. Stenhouse, AIA; Washington, D. C.

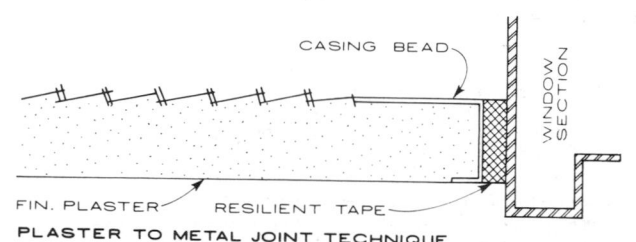

CASING BEAD
WINDOW SECTION
FIN. PLASTER   RESILIENT TAPE

PLASTER TO METAL JOINT TECHNIQUE

GLAZED WALL TILE
Nominal thickness = ⁵/₁₆'', Actual = ³/₃₂'' to ³/₈''.

Normally used on interior walls or where freezing temperature will not be encountered. For exposure to freezing use frost proof glazed tile. For light or moderate traffic on floors use an extra duty crystalline glaze.

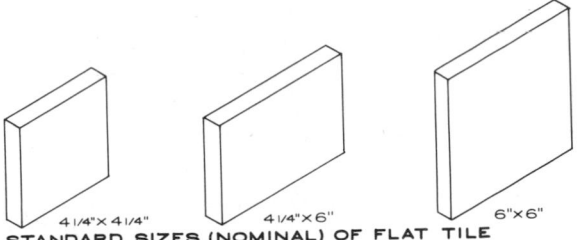

STANDARD SIZES (NOMINAL) OF FLAT TILE

Actual tile size is ¹/₁₆'' less (joint size);

Special sizes available from some manufacturers: 4 ¹/₄'' x 8 ¹/₄'', 6'' x 9'', 6'' x 12'', 3'' x 3'', 3'' x 6'', 4'' octagon, 1 ³/₈'' x 1 ³/₈''.

Shapes shown to the right are standard trimmers. Special trimmer shapes are available from some manufacturers.

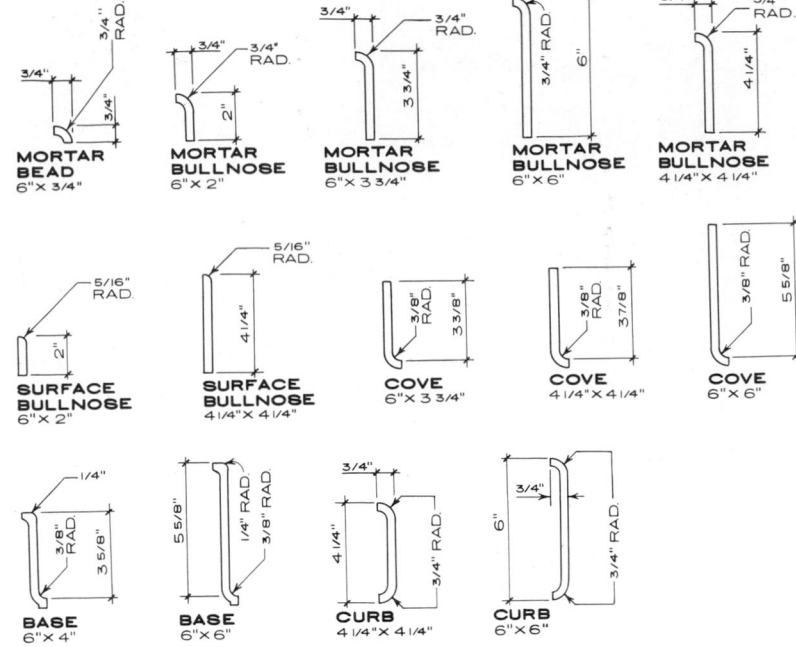

CERAMIC MOSAIC TILE
Nominal thickness = ¹/₄'', Actual = ³/₁₆'' to ⁵/₁₆''.

Available in porcelain and natural clay type. Porcelain mosaics have clear bright colors and have low absorption (.05% or less). Natural clay mosaics have muted earthy colors and have water absorption of .05% to 3.0%.

STANDARD SIZES (NOMINAL) OF FLAT TILE

Actual tile size is ¹/₁₆'' less (joint size).

Special shapes available from some manufacturers.

Shapes shown to the right are standard trimmers. Special trimmer shapes are available from some manufacturers.

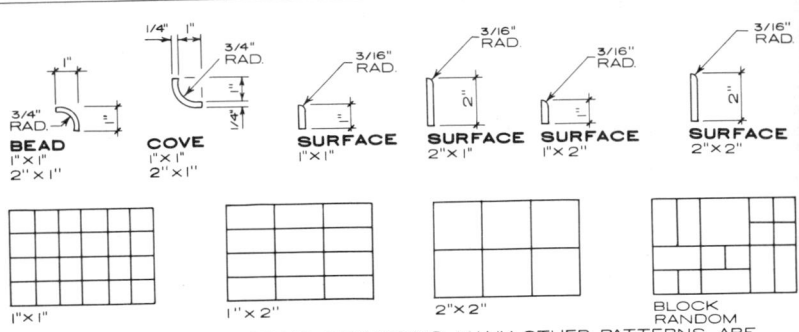

TYPICAL CERAMIC MOSAIC PATTERNS. MANY OTHER PATTERNS ARE AVAILABLE.

QUARRY TILE AND PAVERS
Quarry tile is produced from natural clays and shales by the extrusion process. A paver is similar in size to a quarry tile but is produced by the dust pressed method with materials similar to those used for ceramic mosaic tile.

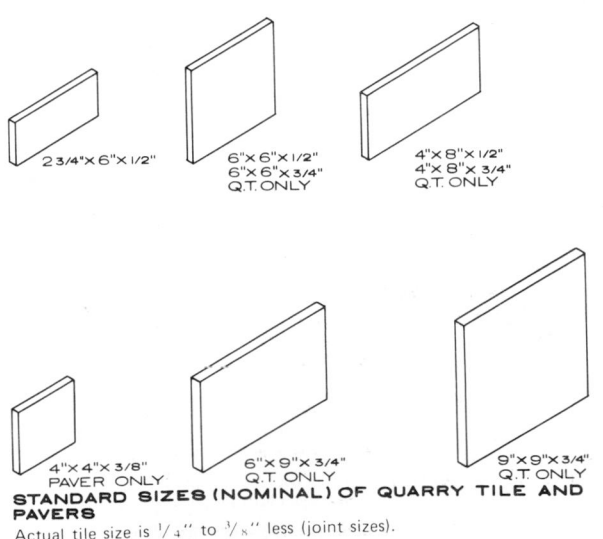

STANDARD SIZES (NOMINAL) OF QUARRY TILE AND PAVERS

Actual tile size is ¹/₄'' to ³/₈'' less (joint sizes).

Special shapes available from some manufacturers.

Shapes shown to the right are standard trimmers. Special trimmer shapes are available from some manufacturers.

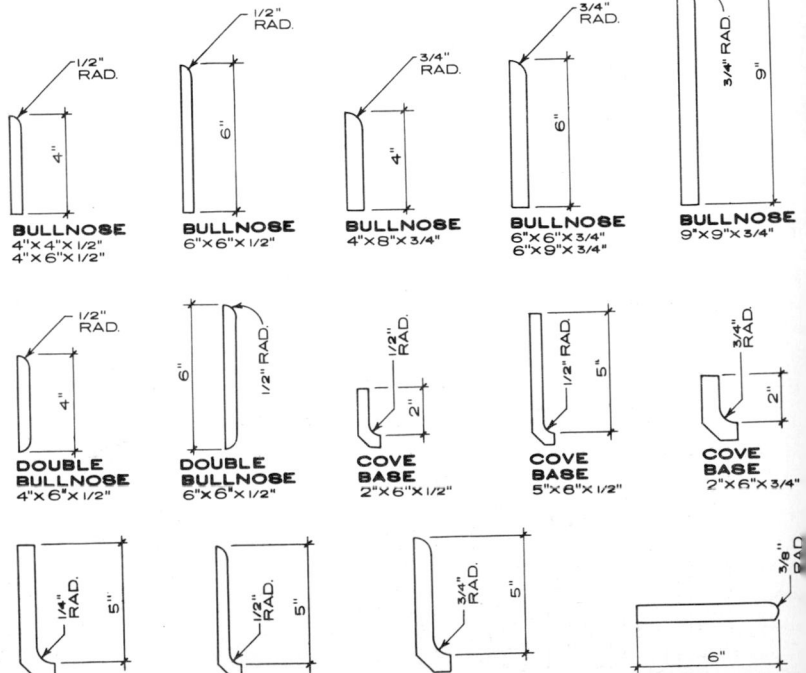

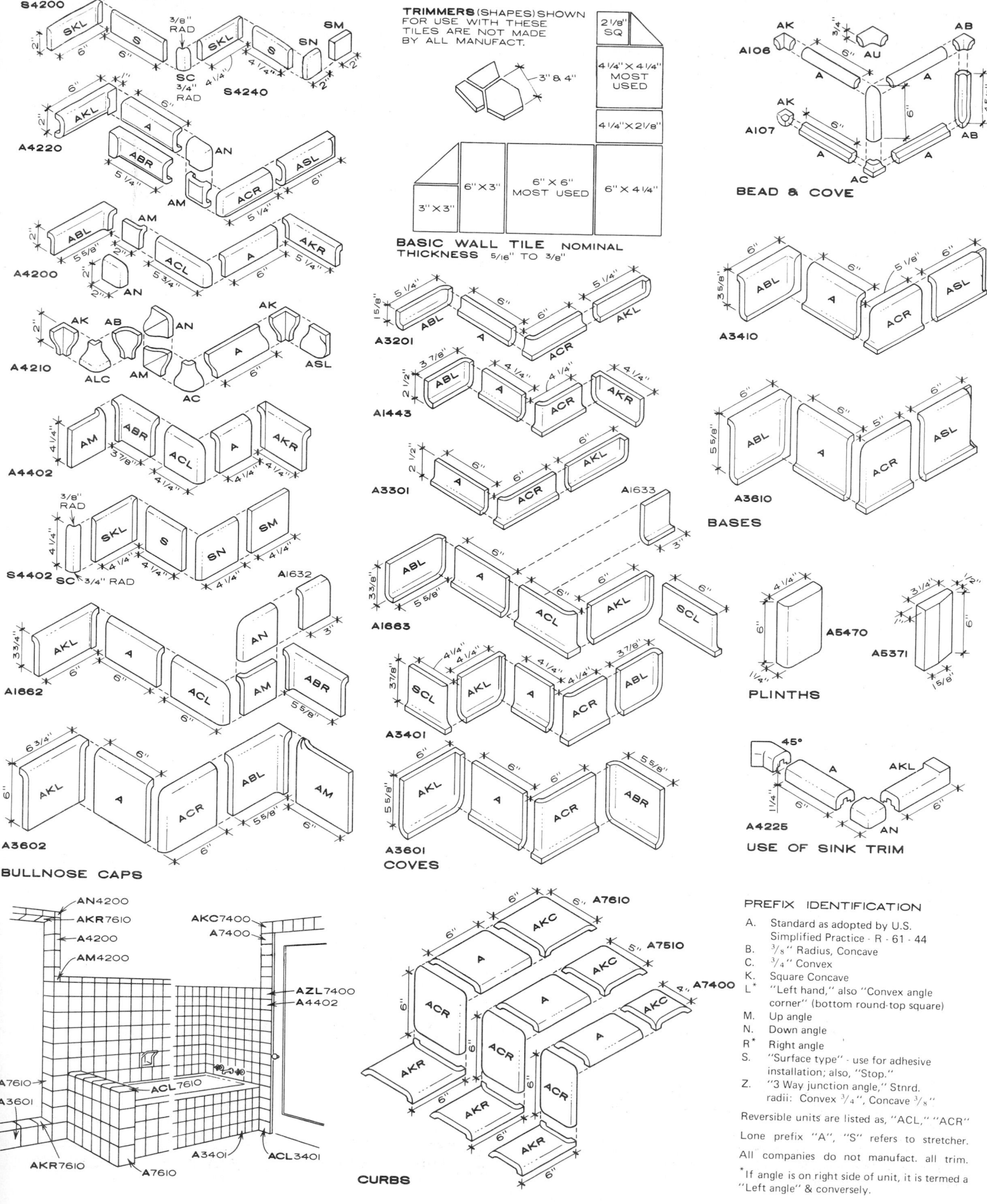

S4200

S4240

A4220

A4200

A4210

A4402

S4402

A1662

A3602

BULLNOSE CAPS

TRIMMERS (SHAPES) SHOWN FOR USE WITH THESE TILES ARE NOT MADE BY ALL MANUFACT.

3" & 4"

2 1/8" SQ

4 1/4" X 4 1/4" MOST USED

4 1/4" X 2 1/8"

6" X 3"

6" X 6" MOST USED

6" X 4 1/4"

3" X 3"

BASIC WALL TILE NOMINAL THICKNESS 5/16" TO 3/8"

A3201

A1443

A3301

A1633

A1663

A3401

A3601

COVES

BEAD & COVE

A106

A107

A3410

A3610

BASES

A5470

A5371

PLINTHS

A4225

USE OF SINK TRIM

A7610

A7510

A7400

CURBS

PREFIX IDENTIFICATION

A. Standard as adopted by U.S. Simplified Practice · R · 61 · 44
B. 3/8" Radius, Concave
C. 3/4" Convex
K. Square Concave
L* "Left hand," also "Convex angle corner" (bottom round-top square)
M. Up angle
N. Down angle
R* Right angle
S. "Surface type" - use for adhesive installation; also, "Stop."
Z. "3 Way junction angle," Stnrd. radii: Convex 3/4", Concave 3/8"

Reversible units are listed as, "ACL," "ACR"

Lone prefix "A", "S" refers to stretcher.

All companies do not manufact. all trim.

*If angle is on right side of unit, it is termed a "Left angle" & conversely.

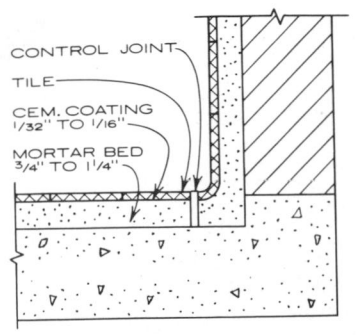

MORTAR METHOD
Used on slab-on-grade construction where no bending stresses occur and on structural slabs of limited area.

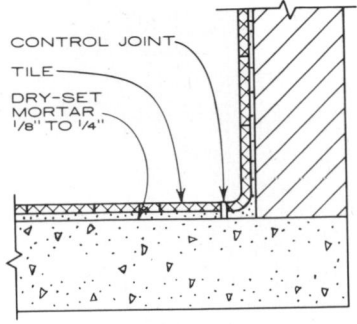

THIN-SET METHOD
Used on smooth clean concrete or cement mortar that is well cured.

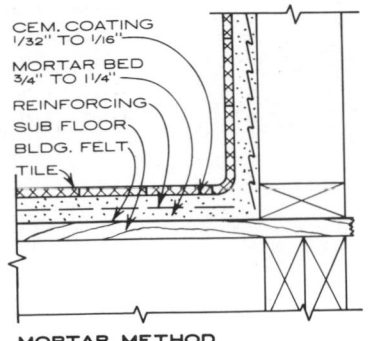

MORTAR METHOD
Used over all wood floors that are structurally sound.

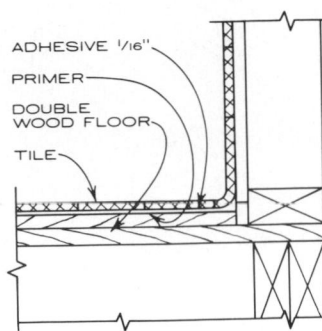

THIN-SET METHOD
Used over wood floors exposed to light or moderate traffic.

TILE INSTALLATION DETAILS FOR INTERIOR FLOORS

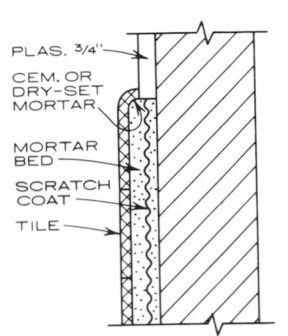

MORTAR METHOD
Used over clean, sound, dimensionally stable masonry or concrete.

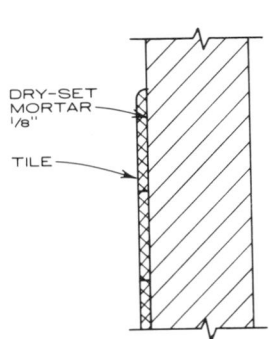

THIN-SET METHOD
Used over clean, sound, dimensionally stable masonry or concrete.

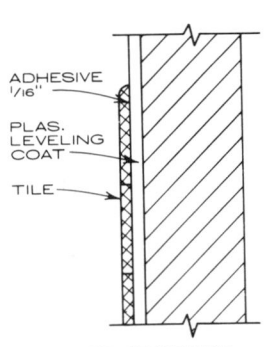

ORGANIC ADHESIVE METHOD
Used over sound dimensionally stable masonry or concrete with leveling coat.

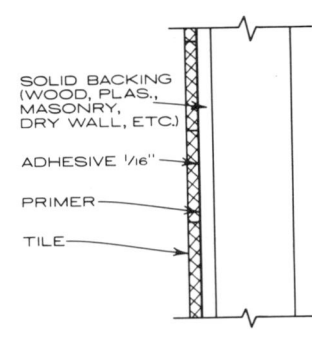

ORGANIC ADHESIVE METHOD
Used in interiors over gypsum wallboard, plaster, plywood or other smooth surfaces.

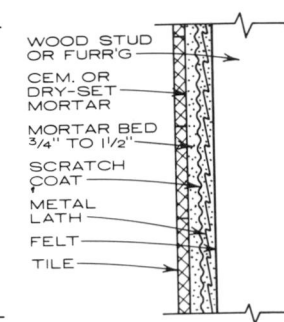

MORTAR METHOD
Used over dry, well braced wood studs or furring.

TILE INSTALLATION DETAILS FOR INTERIOR WALLS

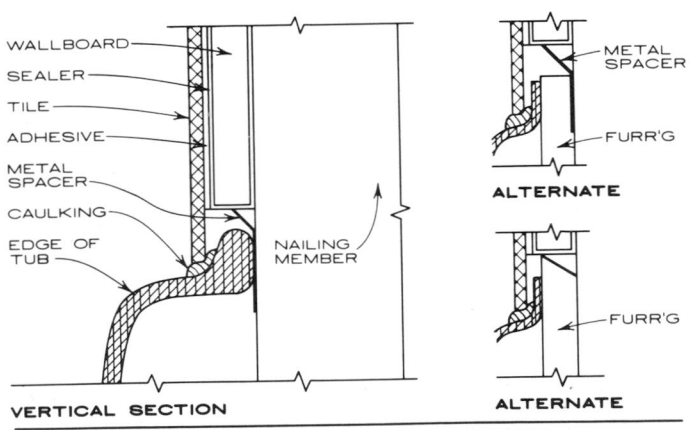

VERTICAL SECTION   **ALTERNATE**

TILE TUB ENCLOSURES WITH WALLBOARD

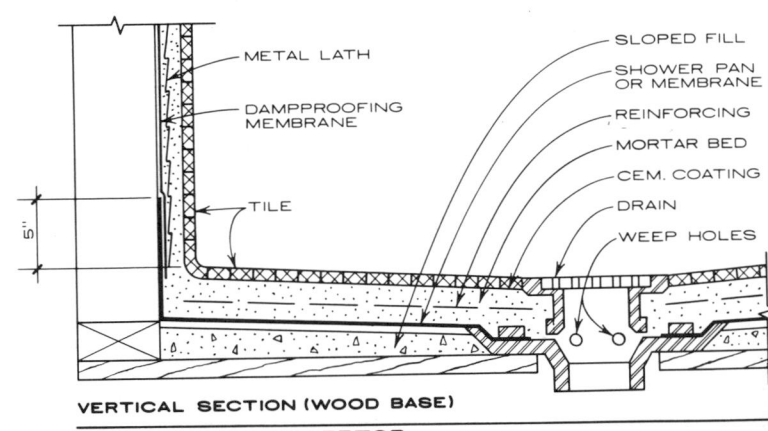

VERTICAL SECTION (WOOD BASE)

TILE SHOWER RECEPTOR

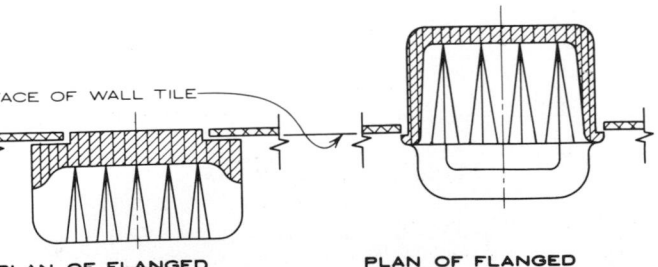

PLAN OF FLANGED SURFACE TYPE   **PLAN OF FLANGED TYPE**   **PLAN OF FLUSH TYPE**

TYPES OF CERAMIC WALL ACCESSORIES

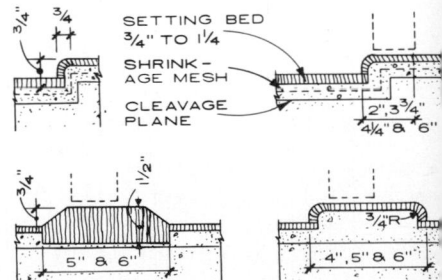

CERAMIC TILE SADDLES

TYPICAL COVERINGS AND AVAILABLE SIZES

DESCRIPTION	WIDTH	TRIMMED WIDTH	LENGTH PER SINGLE ROLL	MINIMUM QUANTITY SOLD
Burlap Paper backed, may be vinyl coated.	36″		4 Yards	Single roll
Canvas May be pre-finished or prepared for painting.	24″ 27″ 48″		5 Yards	Single roll
Cork Crushed cork laminated to cloth backing	50″	48″	35 Yards	Lineal yard
Cork Paper Thin cork veneer laminated to paper backing	28″ 30″	26″	5 Yards	Single roll
Fabric Paper backed	36″ 40″		4 Yards 3 Yards	Single roll Lineal yard
Felt May be paper backed	54″	53″		Lineal yard
Grass Cloth Woven natural fibers, paper backed. Color varies considerably from one lot to another.	30″ 36″	34–35″	5 Yards 4 Yards	Single roll Single roll
Paper: American	20″ 27″ 30″ 36″ 41″ 48″	18″ 25″ 28″ 34″ 39″ 46″	7 Yards 5 Yards 3 Yards	Single roll
English	22″	21″	11 Yards	Single roll
Flocked Widths vary according to pattern.	29″	27″	5 Yards	Double roll Silk: Triple roll
Foil	30″	Pre-trimmed	5 Yards	Single roll
French	19–21″	17–19″	7 Yards	Single roll
Handprinted Sheets	24″ 35″ 30″ 26″ 40″ 40″		40″ 45″ 48″ 40″ 53″ 75″	By the sheet
Murals Variable	32″ 40″ 48″ 48″ 126″		68″ 108″ 108″ 75″ 108″	By the panel or by the square foot.
Scenic Variable	28″	26″	5 Yards	Single roll
Silk	30″	Pre-trimmed	5 Yards	Single roll
Paper backed	36″	Pre-trimmed	4 Yards	
Textures Texture (such as sand) added to canvas ground. Usually plastic coated.	3′ 4′		12 Feet 36 Feet	Single roll By the square foot
Vinyl See notes on vinyl-coated wall coverings at right.				
Wood Veneer Cloth or paper backed. Sometimes requires finishing.	12″ 18″ 21″ 24″		8, 10, 12 ft.	By the square foot

NOTE: This list represents typical coverings and typical sizes available.

ISD Incorporated, Chicago and New York

TABLE OF COVERAGE

Room Size	Maximum Number of Single Rolls Required Using 30 Sq. Ft. per Roll					Yards of Border	Single Rolls for Ceiling
	8 Foot Ceiling	9 Foot Ceiling	10 Foot Ceiling	11 Foot Ceiling	12 Foot Ceiling		
8 x 10	10	11	12	13	14	12	3
9 x 12	11	13	14	15	17	14	4
10 x 10	11	12	13	15	16	14	4
10 x 12	12	13	15	16	18	15	4
10 x 14	13	14	16	18	19	16	5
12 x 14	14	16	17	19	21	18	6
12 x 16	15	17	19	21	22	19	7
12 x 18	16	18	20	22	24	20	8
12 x 20	17	19	21	23	26	22	8
14 x 16	16	18	20	22	24	20	8
14 x 18	17	19	21	23	26	22	8
14 x 20	18	20	22	25	27	23	10
14 x 22	19	22	24	26	29	24	11
16 x 18	18	20	22	25	27	23	10
16 x 20	19	22	24	26	29	24	11
16 x 22	21	23	25	28	30	26	12
16 x 24	21	24	27	29	32	27	13
18 x 20	21	23	25	28	30	26	12

To find number of rolls needed, calculate square footage and divide by 30 (sq. ft. per roll). Subtract $2/3$ roll for each door and window opening.

VINYL WALL COVERING

Federal Specification CCC-W-408, issued May 8, 1963, provides for vinyl coated wall covering standard requirements. The following notes are taken from that specification.

There are three types and two classes of vinyl wall covering:

Type I	Light Duty	7 ounces per sq.yd.	For use as a maintenance-free covering for areas not subjected to abrasion or wear traffic, and for ceilings.
Type II	Medium Duty	13 ounces per sq.yd.	For general use in areas where there is average traffic and scuffing.
Type III	Heavy Duty	22 ounces per sq.yd.	For use only as wainscot or lower wall protection for areas exposed to damage by moveable equipment or to abusive conditions such as exist in hospitals.

Class I   Regular Finish
Class II   Mildew-Resistant Finish

Composition may be of three layers, the first being a supporting material of cotton cloth, nonwoven fiberglass, asbestos, or other suitable material. Supporting material for Class 2 must be mildew-resistant treated. The second layer is a coating compound of plasticized polymerized or copolymerized vinyl-chloride resin which is applied to the outside of the supporting material in a continuous film. This layer is integrally pigmented. A clear coating may be added as a third layer if it is necessary in order to meet the physical requirements noted in the specification.

TYPE	Pieces per Roll	Yardage per Roll
Type I	Single piece	Not less than 72 square feet plus 1 foot tolerance.
Type II	2 pieces	Not less than 15 yards or more than 45 yards.
Type III	4 pieces 6 pieces	15 to 30 yards Over 30 yards

NOTE: All pieces to be in 3-yard lengths or multiples thereof.

The specification also includes requirements and test procedures as to breaking strength, tear strength, hydrostatic resistance, abrasion resistance, flame resistance, char length, colorfastness to light, shrinkage, cold crack, blocking, heat aging, and crocking. Manufacturers should be able to supply all information concerning specification requirements and test data upon request.

STRIP FLOORING OAK —NATIONAL OAK MANUFACTURERS ASSOCIATION

SIZES				NAILING				QUANTITIES FOR ESTIMATING	
THICKNESS		FACE WIDTHS	NAILING	NOM. SIZE	O.C.	NAIL SIZE		% FLOOR AREA INCREASE	COUNT-ED
NOM.	ACT.								
25/32"	25/32"	1 1/2" 2" 2 1/4"	Blind	25/32" x 2 1/4"	10"	8d cut steel		33 1/3%	1" x 3"
* 1/2"	15/32"	1 1/2" 2"	Blind	25/32" x 2"	10"	8d cut steel		37 1/2%	1" x 2 3/4"
* 3/8"	11/32"	1 1/2" 2"	Blind	25/32" x 1 1/2"	12"	8d cut steel		50%	1" x 2 1/4"
* 5/16"	10/32"	1 1/2" 2"	Surface	1/2" x 2"	10"	6d wire fin.		25%	1" x 2 1/2"
				1/2" x 1 1/2"	10"	6d wire fin.		33 1/2%	1" x 2"
				3/8" x 2"	8"	4d wire casing		25%	1" x 2 1/2"
				3/8" x 1 1/2"	8"	4d wire casing		33 1/3%	1" x 2"
				5/16" x 2"	5"	1" barbed wire		—	1" x 2"
				5/16" x 1 1/2"	2/7"	Floor brad #15		—	1" x 1 1/2"

*These should always be used over sub-flooring.
Narrow widths cost more laid.

For irregularities add 5% more for waste.

HOLLOW BACK
25/32" x 2 1/4" T&G

GROOVES
1/2" x 2" T&G

GROOVES
3/8" x 2" T&G

FLAT BACK
5/16" x 2" SQ. EDGE

TONGUE AND GROOVE SIDES AND ENDS
DETAILS OF TYPES

STANDARD GRADES

GRADE	ALLOWABLE DEFECTS	BUNDLE LENGTHS	USES
CLEAR: Quartered or Plain Sawed	Face practically free from defects except 3/8" bright sap.	2'-0" & up Aver. 4'-3"	Fine domestic work, clubs, hotels, also churches, schools.
SELECT: Quartered or Plain Sawed	Sap, pin worm holes streaks, slight working imperfections, small, tight knots—1 to every 3'-0".	2'-0" and up. Average	Medium domestic work, schools, offices, stores & institutions.
No. 1 COMMON Plain Sawed	Shall be of such nature as will make and lay a sound floor without cutting.	3'-9" 2'-0" and up. Aver. 3'-0"	Low priced homes, lofts, factories.
No. 2 COMMON Plain Sawed	May contain defects of all types. Will lay a serviceable floor.	1'-3" and up. Aver. 2'-6"	Low priced homes, lofts, factories.

1 1/4" Shorts: plain or quartered sawed, No. 1 Common or better, No. 2 Common, defects as per No. 1 and No. 2 Common above, pieces @ 9" to 18", uses as No. 2 Common above.

Grades do not consider the question of color.

STRIP FLOORING: BEECH, BIRCH, NORTHERN HARD MAPLE —MAPLE FLOORING MANUFACTURING ASSOCIATION

SIZES									NAILING			QUANTITIES FOR ESTIMATING		
TYPE	THICKNESS CUT FROM	ACT.	FW = FACE WIDTHS			(2)	(2)		ACT. THK.	O.C.	NAIL SIZE	% FLOOR AREA INCREASE		
												FW 1 1/2"	25/32"	3/8"tk
STD.	1"	25/32"	1 1/2" 2" 2 1/4" 3 1/4" 2 1/2" 3 1/2"						25/32"	12" to 16"	2 1/4" #5 Spiral Fl. Screw Nail	53%	36 1/3%	
STD.	1 1/4"	33/32"	1 1/2" 2" 2 1/4" 3 1/4" 2 1/2" 3 1/2"						33/32"	Do	Do	2"	40 1/2%	28%
STD.	1 1/2"	41/32"	— — 2 1/4" 3 1/4"			—	—		41/32"	Do	Reg. Spec. Nails	2 1/4"	36 1/3%	25 1/2%
STD.	2"	53/32"	— — 2 1/4" 3 1/4"			—	—		53/32"	Do	Do	3 1/4"	27%	—
SPEC.(1)	1"	3/8"	1 1/2" 2" 2 1/4"			—	—		3/8"	9"	1/2" #1 Spiral Fl. Screw Nail	2 1/2"	23%	—
SPEC.(1)	1"	1/2"	1 1/2" 2" 2 1/4"			—	—		1/2"	Do	Do	3 1/2"	24 3/7%	—
SPEC.(1)	1"	5/8"	1 1/2" 2" 2 1/4"			—	—		5/8"	Do	Do	See note (3)		

1. Not currently produced, special orders only.
2. 2 1/2" & 3 1/2": jointed (square edged) only, also 3 1/4", 1 1/2", 2", 2 1/4", 3 1/4": T & G sides and ends.
3. For 1/2" & 5/8" thicknesses: same as 25/32". For 33/32" as per 25/32" + 25%. For 41/32" as per 25/32" + 50%. For 53/32" as per 25/32" + 100%.

Standard measurement: 1/2" & thicker: all widths are measured 3/4" of length as waste for matching. 3/8"—all widths @ 1/2". Jointed flooring—all widths @ 3/4" except for 2 1/2" face @ 1/2".

STANDARD GRADES

GRADE	USES
1st: 2' thru 8' bundles. 33% max. under 4' 17% max. @ 2'	Highest standard made: Fine houses, apartments, churches, public buildings, clubs, gyms, dance floors, hotels, offices, skating rinks, schools.
2nd: 2' thru 8' bundles. 45% max. under 4' 25% max. @ 2'	Slight imperfections permitted: same uses as above, but where imperfections are not objectionable or when color finish is desired.
3rd: 1 1/4" thru 8' bundles 65% max. under 4' 27% max. @ 1 1/4'	Serviceable for factories, warehouses, workshops, farms, industrial buildings, stores, low cost housing and homes.
Special Color Grades (Marked color variations not a defect except in Special Grades.)	Finest grades produced, available only in limited quantities. Selected 1st Grade Light—selected for light color. Selected 1st Grade Amber—selected for amber color.
Combination Grades	2nd and Better Grade: combination of 1st & 2nd grades in all thicknesses and widths. Third and Better Grade: combination of 1st, 2nd and 3rd grades, thickness and widths.

STANDARD T & G: scratch back (V grooves)
Thicknesses: 25/32", 33/32", 41/32", 53/32"
Widths: 1 1/2", 2", 2 1/4", 3 1/4"

SPECIAL T & G
Thicknesses, 3/8", 1/2", 5/8"
Widths: 1 1/2", 2", 2 1/4"

JOINTED (SQUARE EDGED)
Thickness: 25/32", 33/32"
Widths: 2 1/2", 3 1/4", 3 1/2"

STRIP FLOORING: SOFTWOOD —WESTERN WOOD PRODUCTS ASSOCIATION AND SOUTHERN PINE ASSOCIATION

SIZES

FIN. THK.	FACE WIDTHS					QUANTITIES FOR ESTIMATING		
5/16"	1 1/2"	2 3/8"	3 1/4"	4 1/4"	5 3/16"	Size: add to floor area as follows:		
7/16"	1 1/2"	2 3/8"	3 1/4"	4 1/4"	5 3/16"	25/32" x 2 3/8" @ 27%	1 1/16" x 2 3/8" @ 58%	1 5/16" x 2 3/8" @ 90%
9/16"	1 1/2"	2 3/8"	3 1/4"	4 1/4"	5 3/16"	x 3 1/4" @ 23%	x 3 1/4" @ 54%	x 3 1/4" @ 85%
25/32"	1 1/2"	2 3/8"	3 1/4"	4 1/4"	5 3/16"	x 5 3/16" @ 15%	x 5 3/16" @ 43%	x 5 3/16" @ 72%
1 1/16"	1 1/2"	2 3/8"	3 1/4"	4 1/4"	5 3/16"	Also add 3% to 5% to above for waste.		
1 5/16"	1 1/2"	2 3/8"	3 1/4"	4 1/4"	5 3/16"			

	SHIPLAP	T & G	SPLINE		SHIPLAP	T & G	SPLINE
25/32"	3/8" lap: 3 1/8", 5 1/8", 7 1/8", 9 1/8", 11 1/8", 13 1/8", 15 1/8"	1/4" tongue: 3 1/4", 5 3/16", 7", 9", 11"	1 5/16"			1/4" tongue: 3 1/4", 5 3/16", 7", 9", 11"	3 1/2", 5 1/2", 7 1/2", 9 1/2", 11 1/2"
	1/2" lap: 3", 5", 7", 9", 11", 13", 15"		1 5/8"	1/2" lap: 3", 5", 7", 9", 11"	3/8" tongue: 3 1/8", 5 1/8", 7", 9", 11"		
1 1/16"		1/4" tongue: 3 1/4", 5 3/16", 7", 9", 11"	2 5/8" 3 5/8" 4 5/8"			" " "	" " "

AVAILABLE SPECIES AND GRADES

SPECIES	FLAT GRAIN	EDGE GRAIN	MIXED GRAIN
Douglas Fir	C & Btr., D-Flg. Select Merchantable Construction, Standard Boards	B & Btr., C, D- Flooring	C & Btr., D, E—Flooring
Douglas Fir, Western Larch Eastern Hemlock	B & Btr., C Select, D Select, No.'s 1, 2 Common D & Btr., No.'s 1, 2, 3 Common	B & Btr., C Select, D Select	
Hemlock	C & Btr., D-Flooring, Select Merchantable, Construction. Standard Boards	B & Btr., C, D	C & Btr., D, E—Flooring
Southern Pine	B & B, C, C & Btr., D, No. 2	B & B, C, C & Btr., D, No. 2	

BLOCKS, SQUARES & PLANKS —MAPLE FLOORING MANUFACTURING ASSOCIATION

FABRICATED BLOCKS & SQUARES

MAPLE, BEECH, BIRCH	1 1/2" STRIPS	2" STRIPS	2 1/4" STRIPS
25/32" & 33/32" Thick	7 1/2" x 7 1/2" & 9" x 9"	8" x 8" & 10" x 10"	6 3/4" x 6 3/4" & 9" x 9"

Note: Maple also made into single slats. Thickness @ 25/32" & 33/32" for end to end pattern; @ 33/32" to 2 1/2" for edge grain pattern. Face widths @ 1 1/2", 2" 2 1/4", & 3 1/4" for end to end pattern; @ 1 1/8", 1 5/16", 1 3/8" & 1 3/4" for edge grain pattern. Face lengths @ 8" to 16", usually 12", for end to end pattern; usually 12" for edge grain pattern.

Flooring Blocks: T & G on wd. or conc., for patterns, squares, or herringbone.
Single Piece Blocks: for square & herringbone patterns, side & end T & G. Thicknesses @ 25/32" & 33/32", face widths @ 1 1/2", 2", 2 1/4", face lengths as desired from 6 3/4" to 13 1/2".

Planks: Solid oak, teak, walnut, mahogany & pine. Sizes not std. but usually available: 33/32" & 25/32" tk., 4" to 8" wide, 4" to 12" long in plain oak & teak. Planks screwed, nailed, plugged or butterflied.
These materials available for parquetry, in blocks. (See maple sizes.)

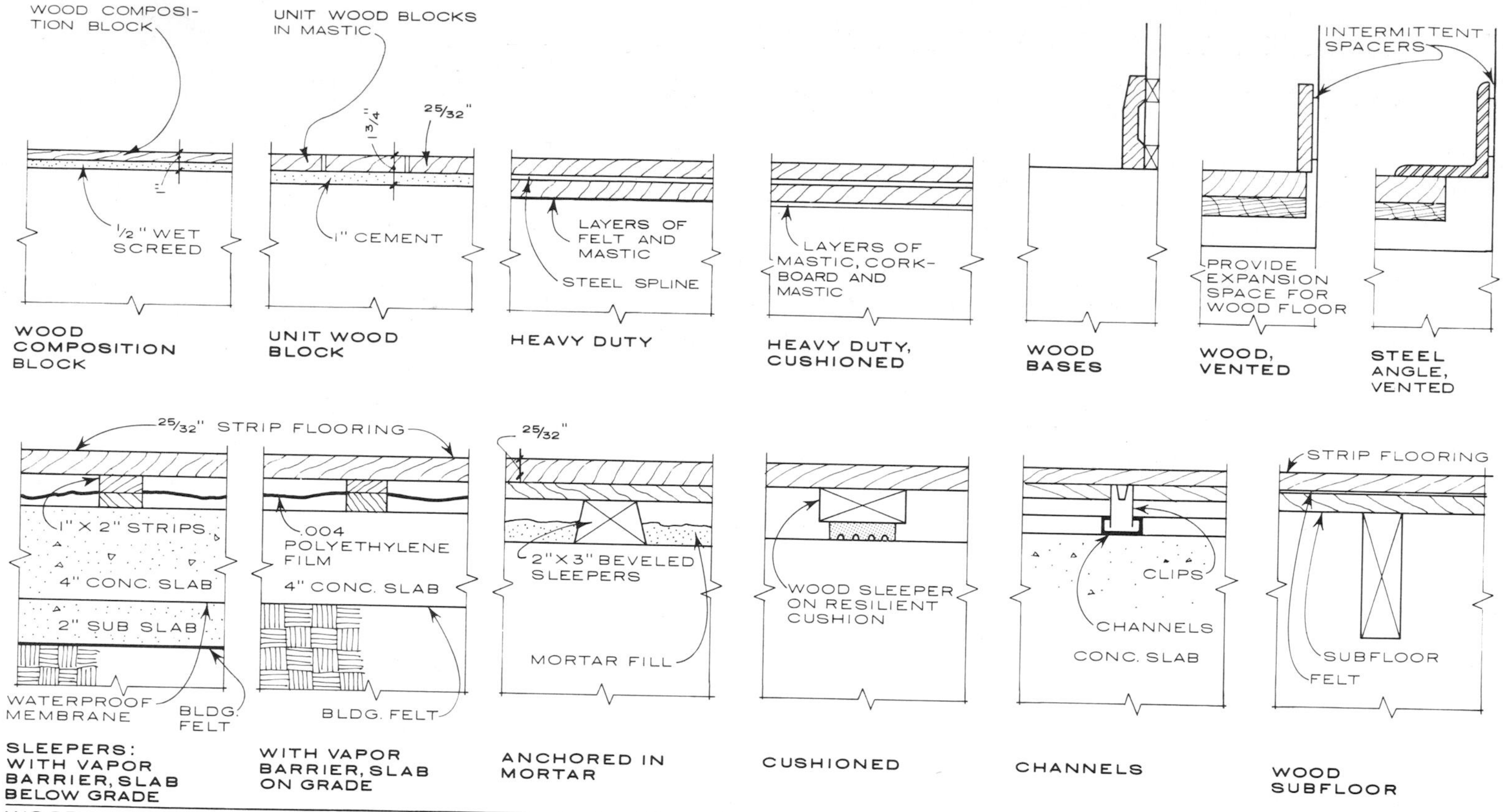

WOOD COMPOSITION BLOCK | UNIT WOOD BLOCKS IN MASTIC | 3/4" | 25/32" | INTERMITTENT SPACERS

1/2" WET SCREED | 1" CEMENT | LAYERS OF FELT AND MASTIC | STEEL SPLINE | LAYERS OF MASTIC, CORK-BOARD AND MASTIC | PROVIDE EXPANSION SPACE FOR WOOD FLOOR

WOOD COMPOSITION BLOCK | UNIT WOOD BLOCK | HEAVY DUTY | HEAVY DUTY, CUSHIONED | WOOD BASES | WOOD, VENTED | STEEL ANGLE, VENTED

25/32" STRIP FLOORING | 25/32" | STRIP FLOORING

1" X 2" STRIPS | .004 POLYETHYLENE FILM | 2" X 3" BEVELED SLEEPERS | WOOD SLEEPER ON RESILIENT CUSHION | CLIPS |
4" CONC. SLAB | 4" CONC. SLAB | MORTAR FILL | | CHANNELS | SUBFLOOR
2" SUB SLAB | | | | CONC. SLAB | FELT
WATERPROOF MEMBRANE | BLDG. FELT | | | |
BLDG. FELT

SLEEPERS: WITH VAPOR BARRIER, SLAB BELOW GRADE | WITH VAPOR BARRIER, SLAB ON GRADE | ANCHORED IN MORTAR | CUSHIONED | CHANNELS | WOOD SUBFLOOR

WOOD FLOORING

CEMENT TOPPING | CEMENT TOPPING | CEMENT TOPPING | FELT | WOOD SUBFLOOR | 5/8" PLYWOOD ON JOISTS
4" CONC. SLAB | 4" CONC. SLAB | | WOOD SUBFLOOR | 1/4" HARD-BOARD OR 3/8" PLYWOOD |
2" SUB SLAB | | | | |
BLDG. FELT | BLDG. FELT | | | |
WATERPROOF MEMBRANE

SLAB BELOW GRADE | SLAB ON GRADE | SLAB ABOVE GRADE | WOOD SUBFLOOR | WOOD SUBFLOOR | WOOD SUBFLOOR | VINYL BASE

RESILIENT FLOORING

TABLE OF RESILIENT FLOORING CHARACTERISTICS

TYPE OF RESILIENT FLOORING	BASIC COMPONENTS	(A) SUBFLOOR APPLICATION	RECOMMENDED LOAD LIMIT	DURABILITY (B)	RESIS. TO HEEL DAMAGE	EASE OF MAINT.	GREASE RESIS.	SURFACE ALKALAI RESIS.	RESIS. TO STAINING	CIGARETTE BURN RESISTANCE	RESILIENCE	QUIETNESS
VINYL SHEET	Vinyl Resins With Fiber Back	B-O-S	75-100	2-3	2-5	1-2	1	1-3	3-4	4	4	4
HOMOGENEOUS VINYL TILE	Vinyl Resins	B-O-S	150-200	1-3	1-4	2-4	1	1-2	1-5	2-5	2-5	2-5
VINYL ASBESTOS TILE	Vinyl Resins & Asbestos Fibers	B-O-S	25	2	4-5	2-3	2	4	2	6	6	6
CORK TILE W/ VINYL COATING	Raw Cork & Vinyl Resins	S	150	4	3	2	1	1	5	3	3	3
CORK TILE	Raw Cork & Resins	S	75	5	4	4	4	5	4	1	1	1
RUBBER TILE	Rubber Compound	B-O-S	200	2	4	4	3	2	1	2	2	2
LINOLEUM	Cork, Wood, Floor & Oleoresins	S	75	3	4-5	4-5	1	4	2	4	4	4
ASPHALT TILE	Resins, Asphalt Compounds—Asbestos	B-O-S	25	3-4	4	4	5	5	4	7	7	6

(A) B: BELOW GRADE ; O: ON GRADE ; S: SUSPENDED
(B) NUMERALS INDICATE SUBJECTIVE RATINGS (RELATIVE RANK OF EACH FLOOR TO OTHERS LISTED ABOVE) "I" INDICATING HIGHEST.

Bruce A. Kenan, AIA; Pederson, Hueber, Hares & Glavin; Syracuse, New York

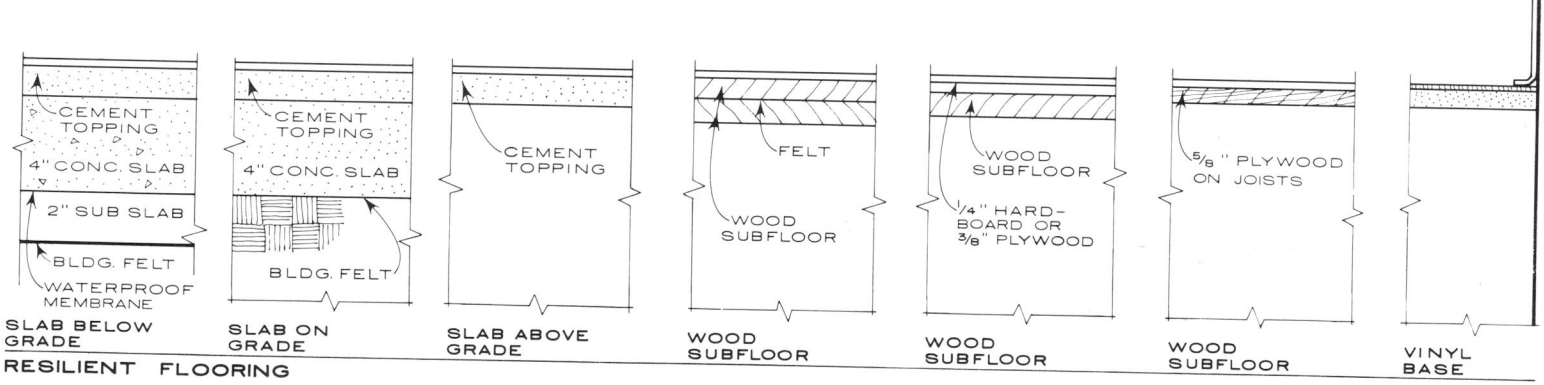

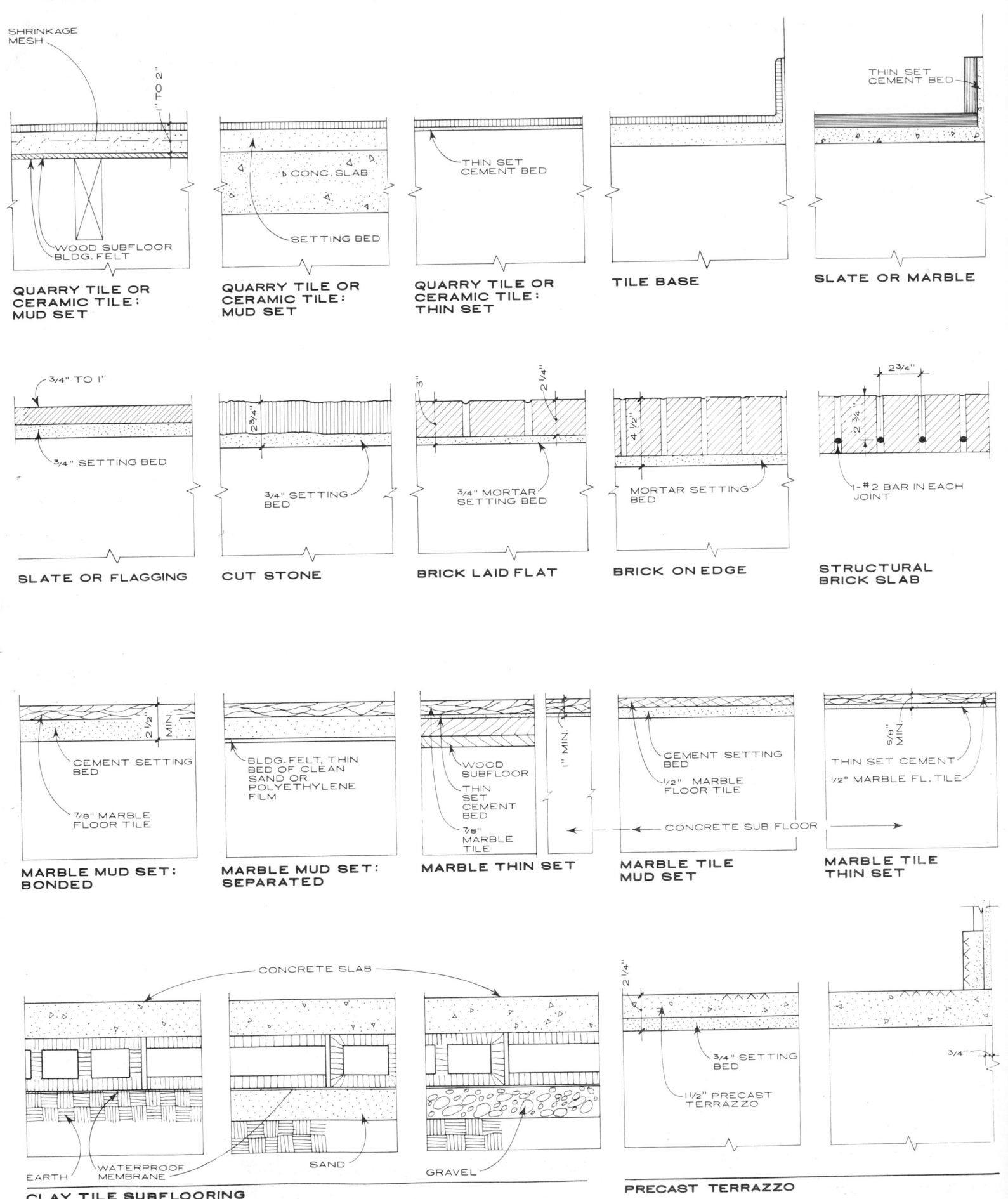

SHRINKAGE MESH

1" TO 2"

WOOD SUBFLOOR
BLDG. FELT

**QUARRY TILE OR
CERAMIC TILE:
MUD SET**

CONC. SLAB

SETTING BED

**QUARRY TILE OR
CERAMIC TILE:
MUD SET**

THIN SET
CEMENT BED

**QUARRY TILE OR
CERAMIC TILE:
THIN SET**

TILE BASE

THIN SET
CEMENT BED

SLATE OR MARBLE

3/4" TO 1"

3/4" SETTING BED

SLATE OR FLAGGING

2 3/4"

3/4" SETTING
BED

CUT STONE

3"   2 1/4"

3/4" MORTAR
SETTING BED

BRICK LAID FLAT

4 1/2"

MORTAR SETTING
BED

BRICK ON EDGE

2 3/4"

2 3/4"

1-#2 BAR IN EACH
JOINT

**STRUCTURAL
BRICK SLAB**

2 1/2" MIN.

CEMENT SETTING
BED

7/8" MARBLE
FLOOR TILE

**MARBLE MUD SET:
BONDED**

BLDG. FELT, THIN
BED OF CLEAN
SAND OR
POLYETHYLENE
FILM

**MARBLE MUD SET:
SEPARATED**

1" MIN.

WOOD
SUBFLOOR

THIN
SET
CEMENT
BED

7/8"
MARBLE
TILE

MARBLE THIN SET

CEMENT SETTING
BED

1/2" MARBLE
FLOOR TILE

CONCRETE SUB FLOOR

**MARBLE TILE
MUD SET**

5/8" MIN.

THIN SET CEMENT

1/2" MARBLE FL. TILE

**MARBLE TILE
THIN SET**

CONCRETE SLAB

EARTH   WATERPROOF
MEMBRANE   SAND   GRAVEL

CLAY TILE SUBFLOORING

2 1/4"

3/4" SETTING
BED

1 1/2" PRECAST
TERRAZZO

3/4"

PRECAST TERRAZZO

Bruce A. Kenan, AIA; Pederson, Hueber, Hares & Glavin; Syracuse, New York

SCALE: 1½" = 1'-0" EXCEPT AS NOTED

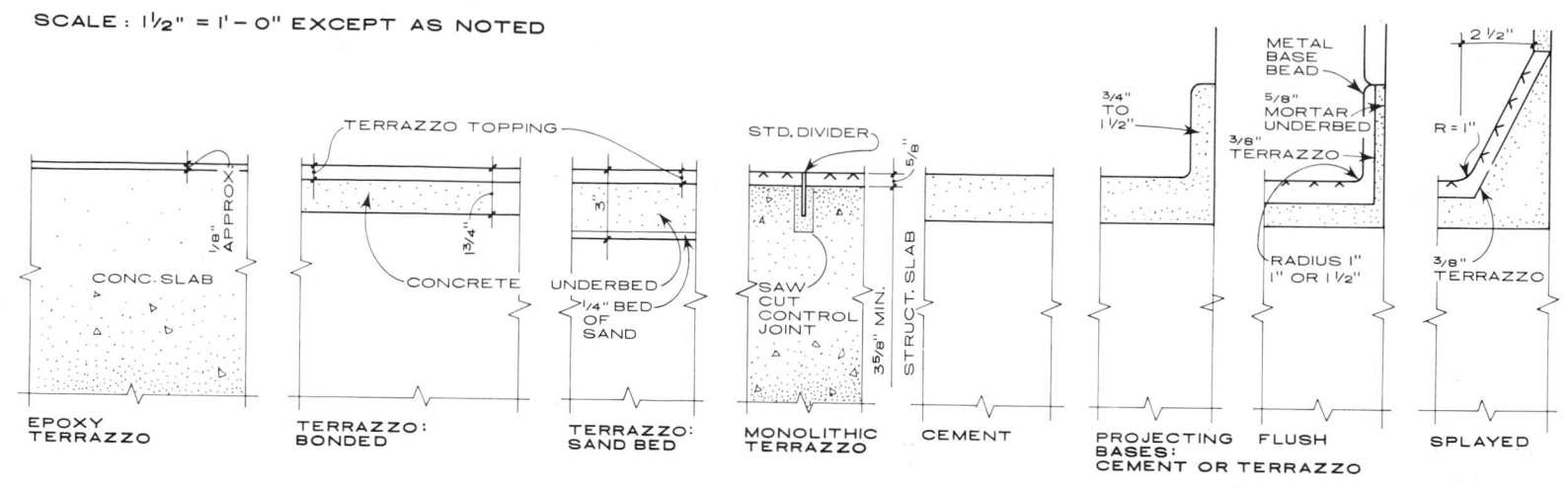

EPOXY TERRAZZO

TERRAZZO: BONDED

TERRAZZO: SAND BED

MONOLITHIC TERRAZZO

CEMENT

PROJECTING BASES: CEMENT OR TERRAZZO

FLUSH

SPLAYED

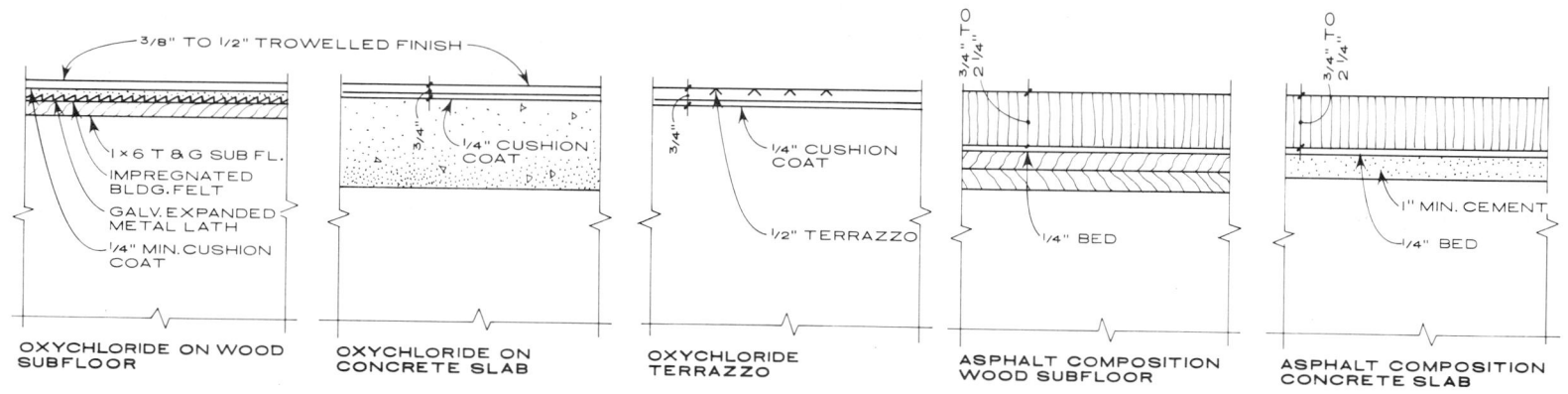

OXYCHLORIDE ON WOOD SUBFLOOR

OXYCHLORIDE ON CONCRETE SLAB

OXYCHLORIDE TERRAZZO

ASPHALT COMPOSITION WOOD SUBFLOOR

ASPHALT COMPOSITION CONCRETE SLAB

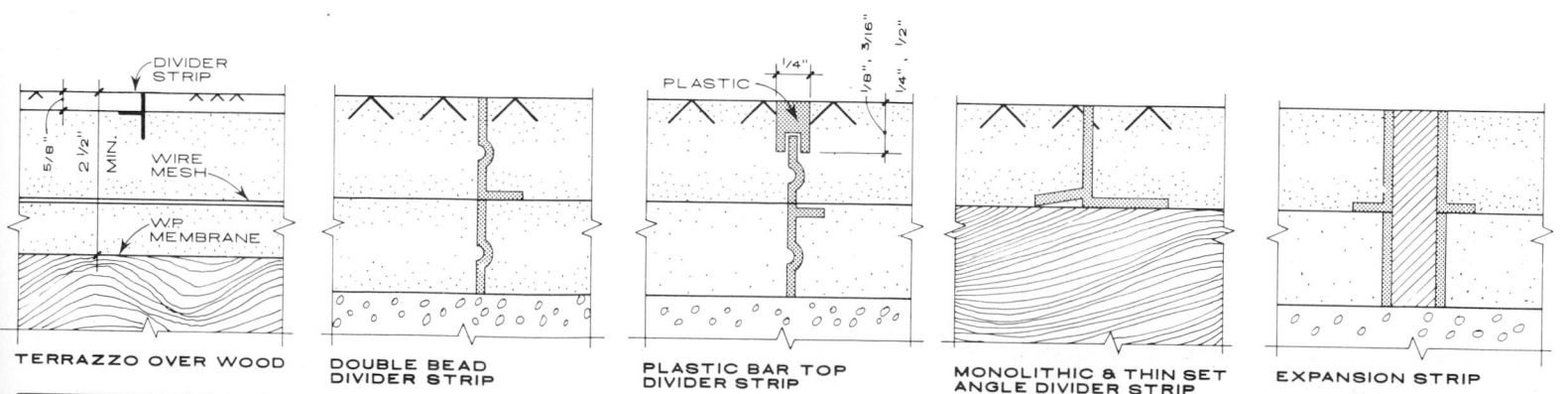

TERRAZZO OVER WOOD

DOUBLE BEAD DIVIDER STRIP

PLASTIC BAR TOP DIVIDER STRIP

MONOLITHIC & THIN SET ANGLE DIVIDER STRIP

EXPANSION STRIP

TYPES OF FLOORING (NO SCALE BUT STRIPS SHOWN LARGER THAN OTHER DETAILS FOR CLARITY)

Bruce A. Kenan, AIA; Pederson, Hueber, Hares & Glavin; Syracuse, New York

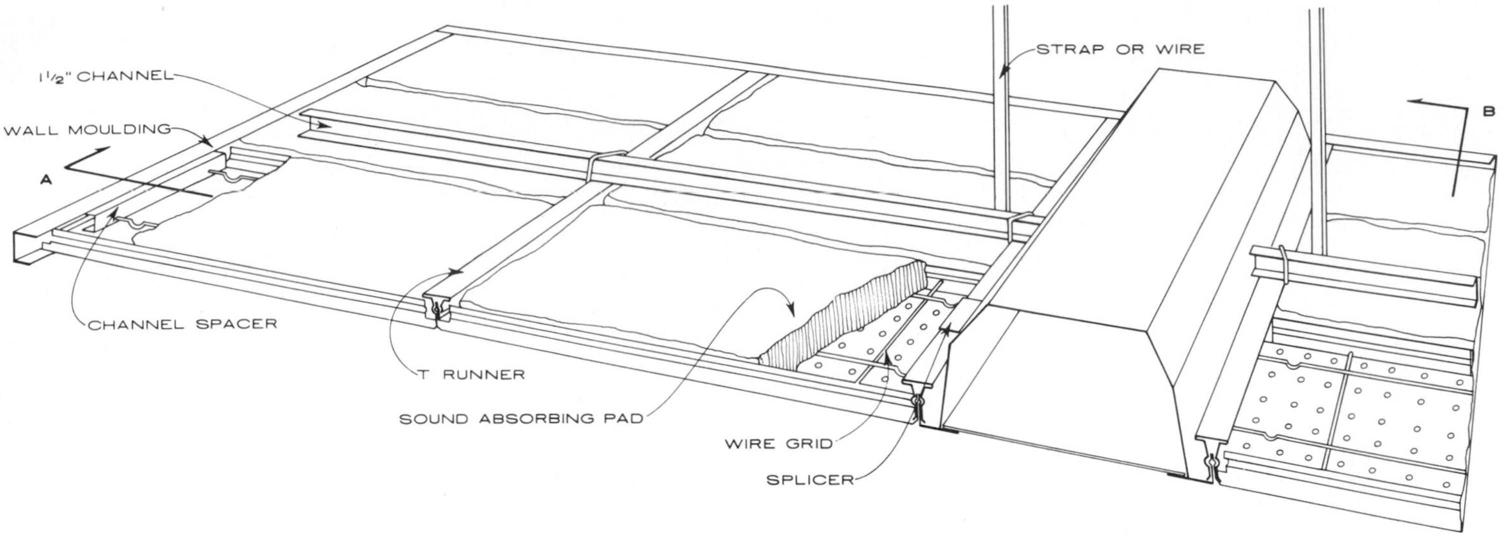

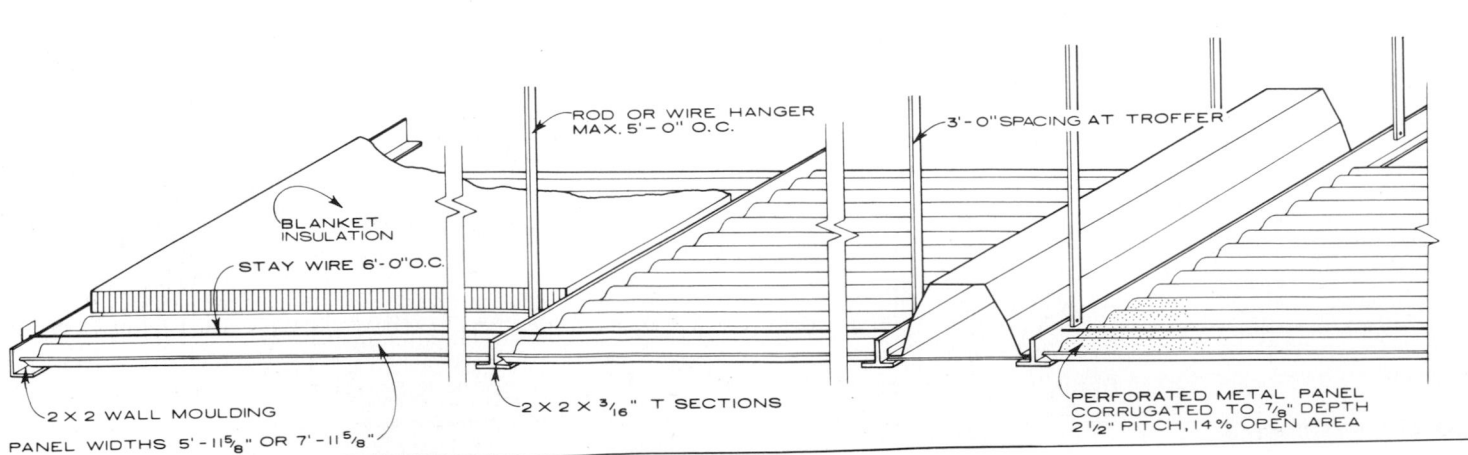

1½" CHANNEL

WALL MOULDING

A

CHANNEL SPACER

T RUNNER

SOUND ABSORBING PAD

WIRE GRID

SPLICER

STRAP OR WIRE

B

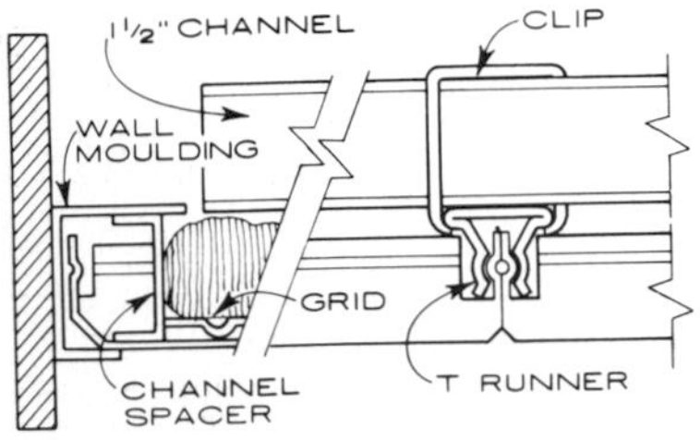

DETAIL A

1½" CHANNEL

CLIP

WALL MOULDING

GRID

CHANNEL SPACER

T RUNNER

DETAIL B

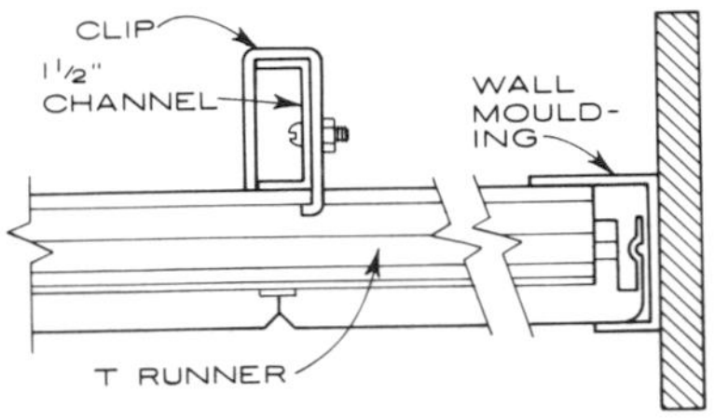

CLIP

1½" CHANNEL

WALL MOULD-ING

T RUNNER

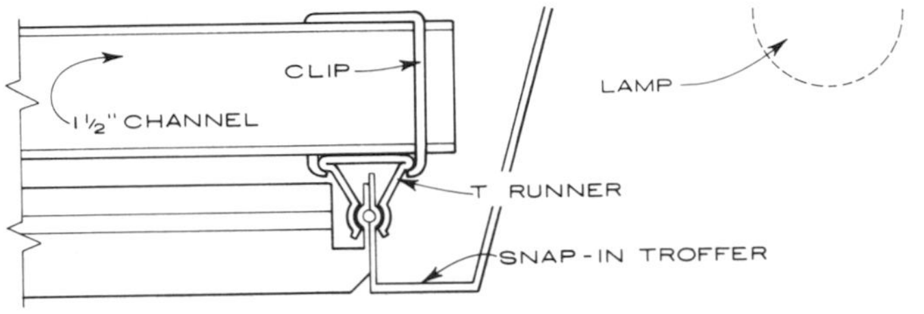

LIGHTING TROFFER DETAIL

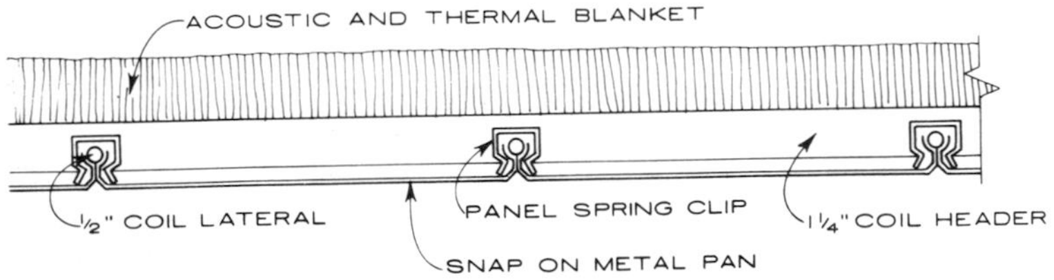

1½" CHANNEL

CLIP

LAMP

T RUNNER

SNAP-IN TROFFER

ACOUSTIC AND THERMAL BLANKET

½" COIL LATERAL

PANEL SPRING CLIP

1¼" COIL HEADER

SNAP ON METAL PAN

METAL PAN W/HEATING & COOLING COILS

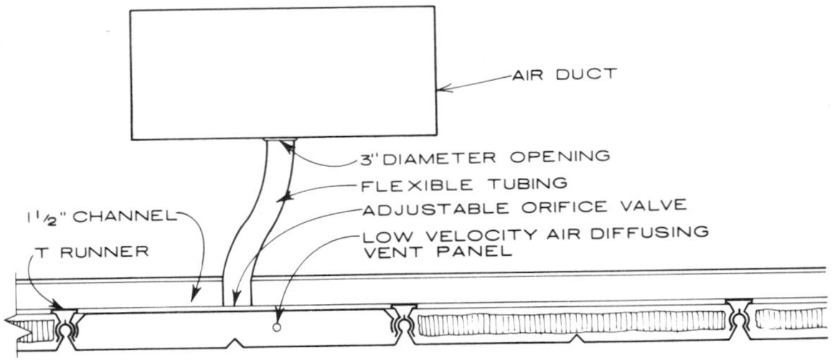

METAL PAN SUSPENDED CEILING SYSTEMS

AIR DUCT

3" DIAMETER OPENING

FLEXIBLE TUBING

ADJUSTABLE ORIFICE VALVE

LOW VELOCITY AIR DIFFUSING VENT PANEL

1½" CHANNEL

T RUNNER

METAL PAN W/AIR DIFFUSING PANELS

ROD OR WIRE HANGER MAX. 5'-0" O.C.

3'-0" SPACING AT TROFFER

BLANKET INSULATION

STAY WIRE 6'-0" O.C.

2 X 2 WALL MOULDING

PANEL WIDTHS 5'-11⅝" OR 7'-11⅝"

2 X 2 X ³⁄₁₆" T SECTIONS

PERFORATED METAL PANEL CORRUGATED TO ⅞" DEPTH 2½" PITCH, 14% OPEN AREA

PERFORATED METAL ACOUSTICAL CEILING SYSTEM

Stephen M. Albert; Boulder, Colorado

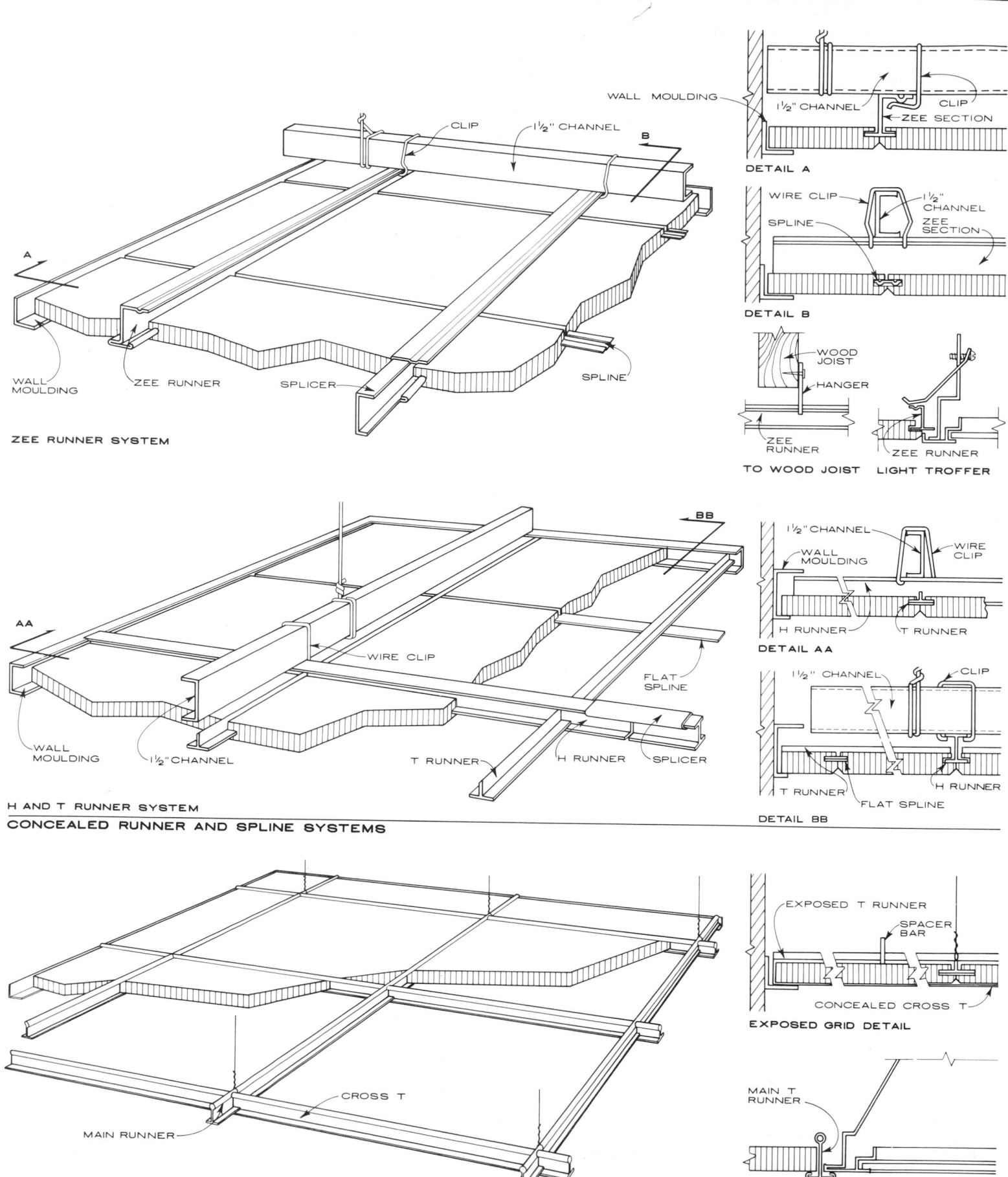

WALL MOULDING

1½" CHANNEL

CLIP

ZEE SECTION

DETAIL A

WIRE CLIP

SPLINE

1½" CHANNEL

ZEE SECTION

DETAIL B

WOOD JOIST

HANGER

ZEE RUNNER

TO WOOD JOIST

ZEE RUNNER

LIGHT TROFFER

CLIP

1½" CHANNEL

B

A

WALL MOULDING

ZEE RUNNER

SPLICER

SPLINE

ZEE RUNNER SYSTEM

BB

1½"CHANNEL

WALL MOULDING

WIRE CLIP

H RUNNER

T RUNNER

DETAIL AA

1½" CHANNEL

CLIP

T RUNNER

FLAT SPLINE

H RUNNER

DETAIL BB

AA

WIRE CLIP

FLAT SPLINE

WALL MOULDING

1½"CHANNEL

T RUNNER

H RUNNER

SPLICER

H AND T RUNNER SYSTEM

CONCEALED RUNNER AND SPLINE SYSTEMS

EXPOSED T RUNNER

SPACER BAR

CONCEALED CROSS T

EXPOSED GRID DETAIL

MAIN T RUNNER

LIGHT TROFFER

CROSS T

MAIN RUNNER

EXPOSED GRID SYSTEM

Stephen M. Albert; Boulder, Colorado

ACOUSTICAL TILE AND SUSPENDED CEILING — SUMMARY

	DETAILS FOLLOW	HANGER SPACING	SIZE – PRINCIPAL STRUCT. MEMB.	SHAPE – PRINCIP. STRUCT. MEMB.	SPACING PRINCIPAL STRUCT. MEMB.	SIZE – SECONDARY MEMBER	SHAPE	SPACING SECONDARY STRUCT. MEMB.	SPLINE SPACING	WALL TO PRIM. STRUCT. MEMB. (MAXIMUM)	TROFFER SIZES	NOTES
APPLIED, NAIL OR ADHESIVE	X										12 X 12 REC.	ADHESIVE 4 CORNERS
SUSP. NAILING CHANNEL	X	4'-0"	1 1/2"	⊏	4'-0"		⋈	16"		2"		
CONCEALED SPLINE	X		1 1/2"	⊏	4'-0" o.c.	1 1/2"	⊥	12" o.c.	12" or 24"	12"	12 X 12 or 24	
SEMI-EXPOSED GRID	X	2'-0"		⊥	2'-0" o.c.		⊥	12" o.c.		12"	12 X 24	spacer bar 5'-0" o.c.
EXPOSED GRID	X	3'-0"		⊥	2'-0" o.c.		⊥	2–4' o.c.		48"	24 X 24 or 48	
LUMINAIR CEILING	X	30" o.c.	17 1/2"	truss	4'-0" o.c.					12"	48 X 48 or 50 X 50	details, see mfr.
METAL PAN	X		1 1/2"	⊏	4'-0" o.c.			24" o.c.		12"		
METAL LOUVERED	X	36" o.c.		⊥	36" o.c.		⋈				3" X 3" X 3" cells	lamp to grid — 80% A
SUSP. CORRUG. PLASTIC	X	3'-4'0" o.c.	1 1/2"	⊥	2'-6" – 5'-0"	1"	∿					

Do not cement acoustical tile to underside of an uninsulated concrete, steel, or gypsum roof deck where temperature differentials are likely to cause condensation or where deck is exposed to extreme heat.

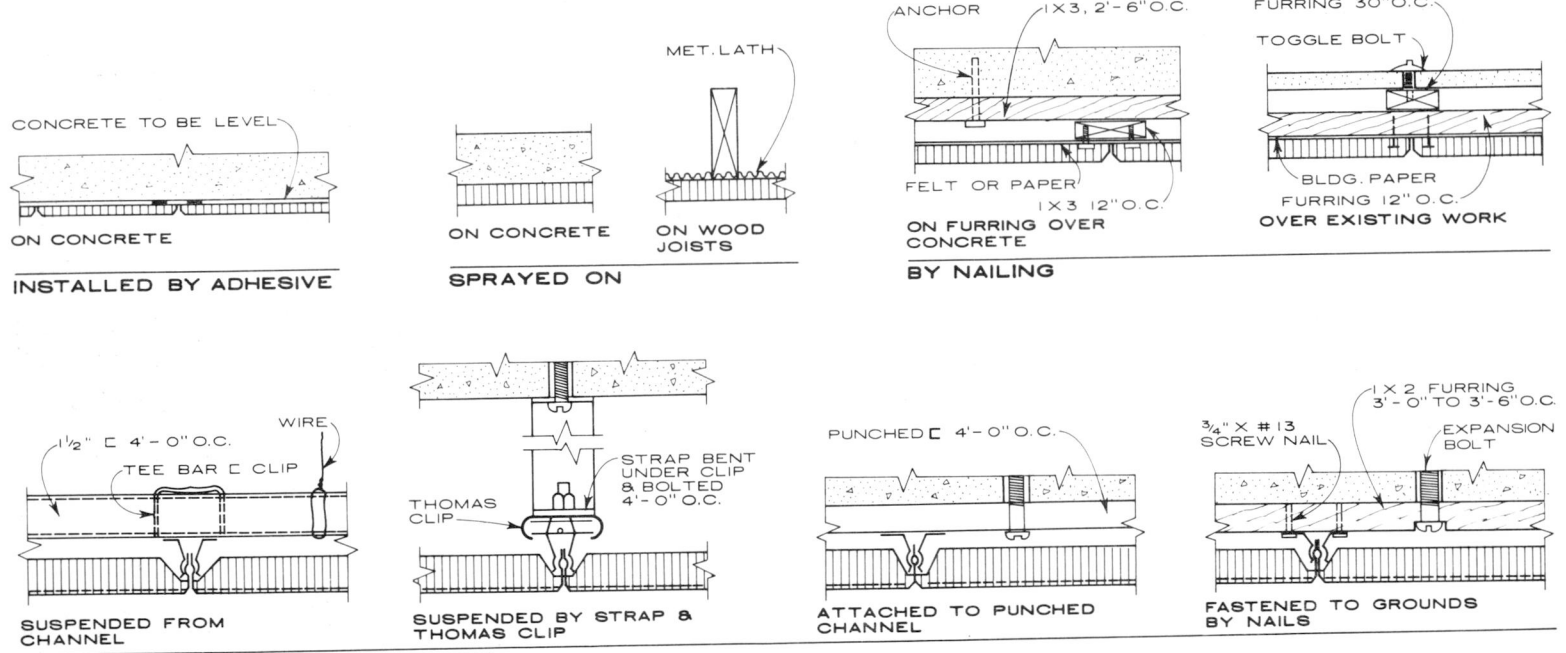

INSTALLED BY ADHESIVE   SPRAYED ON   BY NAILING

ON CONCRETE — CONCRETE TO BE LEVEL

ON CONCRETE   ON WOOD JOISTS — MET. LATH

ON FURRING OVER CONCRETE — ANCHOR, 1X3, 2'-6" O.C., FELT OR PAPER, 1X3 12" O.C.

OVER EXISTING WORK — FURRING 30" O.C., TOGGLE BOLT, BLDG. PAPER, FURRING 12" O.C.

TEE BAR SYSTEMS FOR METAL PAN

SUSPENDED FROM CHANNEL — 1 1/2" ⊏ 4'-0" O.C., WIRE, TEE BAR ⊏ CLIP

SUSPENDED BY STRAP & THOMAS CLIP — THOMAS CLIP, STRAP BENT UNDER CLIP & BOLTED 4'-0" O.C.

ATTACHED TO PUNCHED CHANNEL — PUNCHED ⊏ 4'-0" O.C.

FASTENED TO GROUNDS BY NAILS — 3/4" X #13 SCREW NAIL, 1 X 2 FURRING 3'-0" TO 3'-6" O.C., EXPANSION BOLT

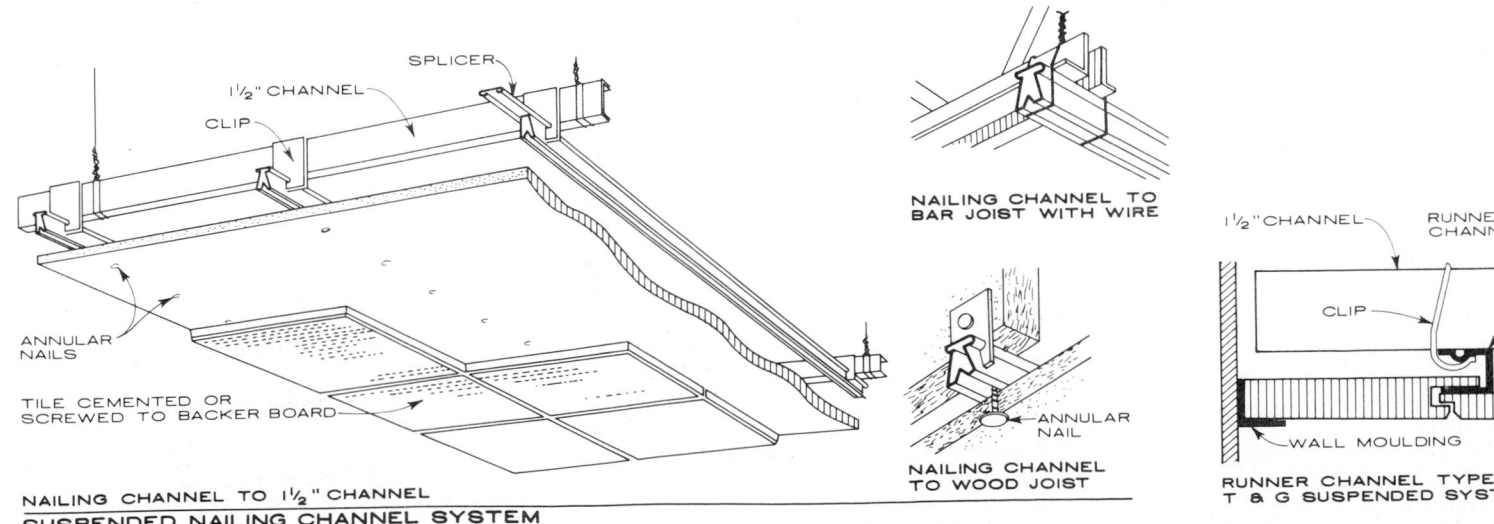

SUSPENDED NAILING CHANNEL SYSTEM

NAILING CHANNEL TO 1 1/2" CHANNEL — SPLICER, 1 1/2" CHANNEL, CLIP, ANNULAR NAILS, TILE CEMENTED OR SCREWED TO BACKER BOARD

NAILING CHANNEL TO BAR JOIST WITH WIRE

NAILING CHANNEL TO WOOD JOIST — ANNULAR NAIL

RUNNER CHANNEL TYPE T & G SUSPENDED SYSTEM — 1 1/2" CHANNEL, RUNNER CHANNEL, CLIP, WALL MOULDING

Stephen M. Albert; Boulder, Colorado

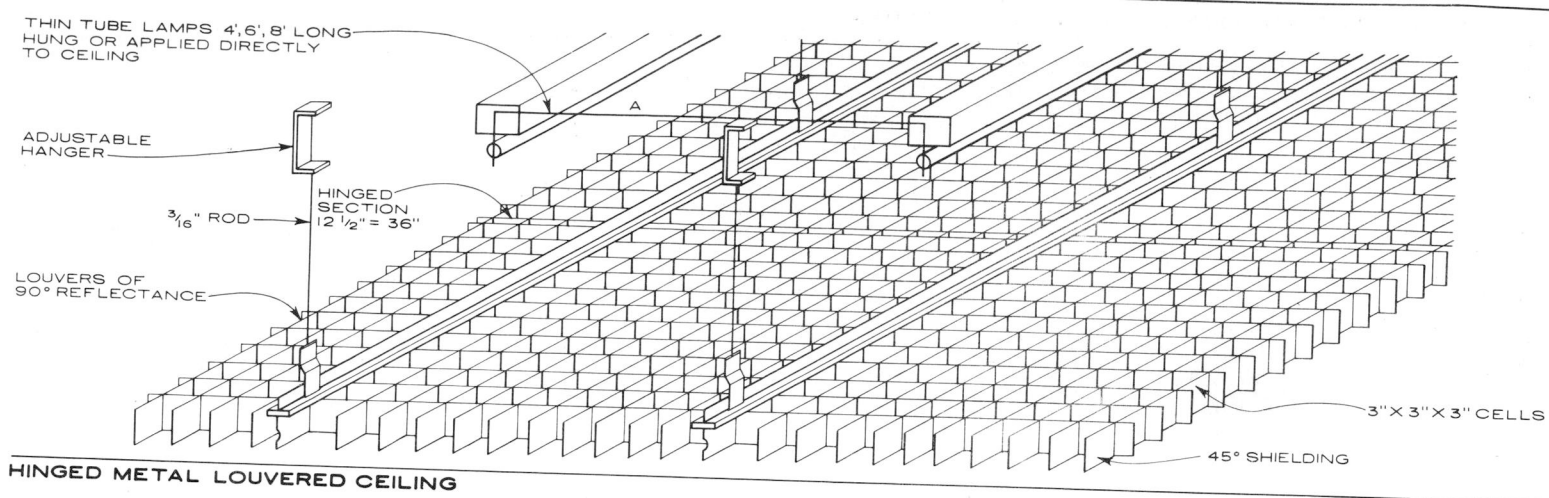

THIN TUBE LAMPS 4', 6', 8' LONG
HUNG OR APPLIED DIRECTLY
TO CEILING

ADJUSTABLE
HANGER

³/₁₆" ROD

HINGED
SECTION
12 ½" = 36"

LOUVERS OF
90° REFLECTANCE

A

3"X 3"X 3" CELLS

45° SHIELDING

HINGED METAL LOUVERED CEILING

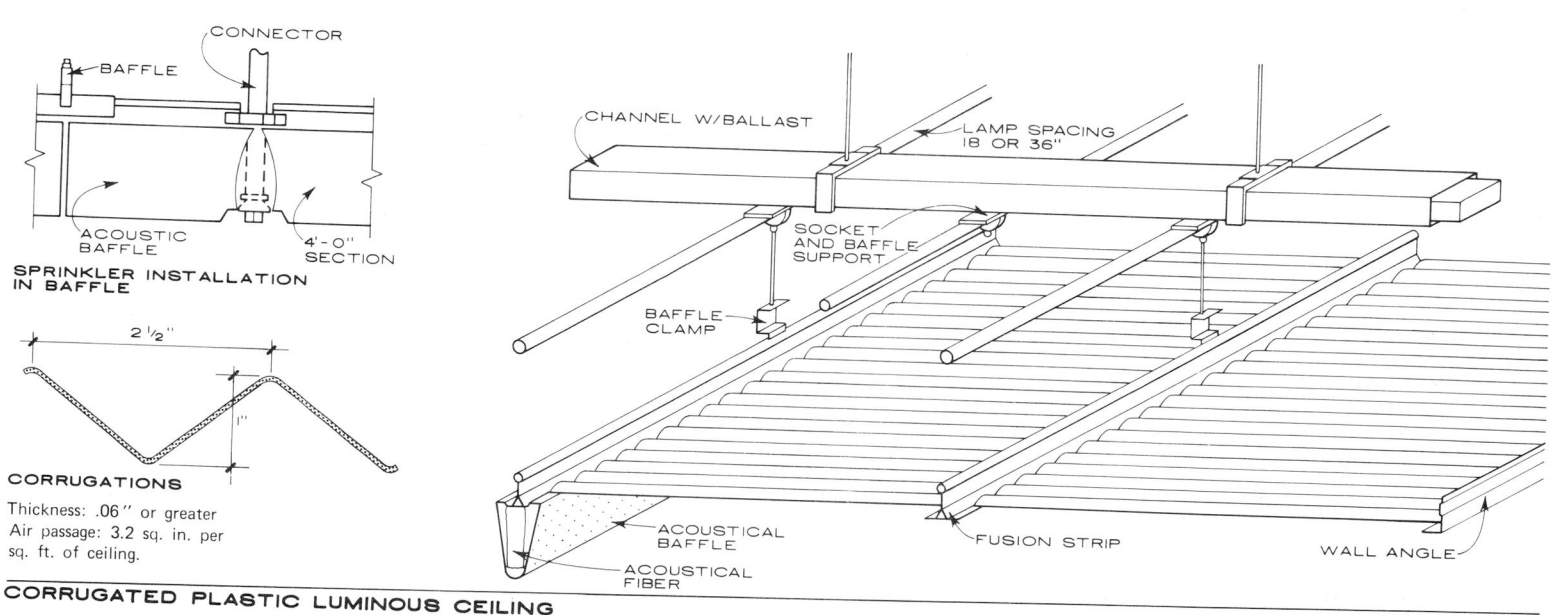

BAFFLE

CONNECTOR

ACOUSTIC
BAFFLE

4'-0"
SECTION

**SPRINKLER INSTALLATION
IN BAFFLE**

2 ½"

1"

CORRUGATIONS

Thickness: .06" or greater
Air passage: 3.2 sq. in. per
sq. ft. of ceiling.

CHANNEL W/BALLAST

LAMP SPACING
18 OR 36"

SOCKET
AND BAFFLE
SUPPORT

BAFFLE
CLAMP

ACOUSTICAL
BAFFLE

ACOUSTICAL
FIBER

FUSION STRIP

WALL ANGLE

CORRUGATED PLASTIC LUMINOUS CEILING

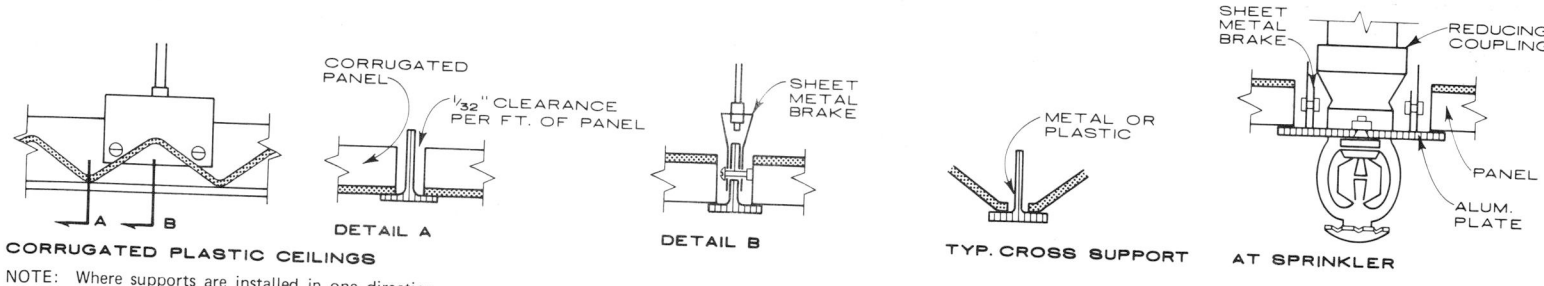

CORRUGATED
PANEL

¹/₃₂" CLEARANCE
PER FT. OF PANEL

SHEET
METAL
BRAKE

METAL OR
PLASTIC

SHEET
METAL
BRAKE

REDUCING
COUPLING

PANEL

ALUM.
PLATE

CORRUGATED PLASTIC CEILINGS

DETAIL A

DETAIL B

TYP. CROSS SUPPORT

AT SPRINKLER

NOTE: Where supports are installed in one direction
only, hangers should be braced above plastic to prevent
side play.

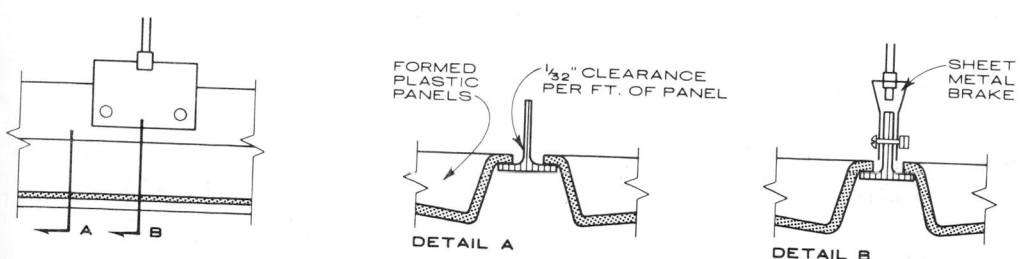

FORMED
PLASTIC
PANELS

¹/₃₂" CLEARANCE
PER FT. OF PANEL

SHEET
METAL
BRAKE

FORMED PLASTIC CEILINGS

DETAIL A

DETAIL B

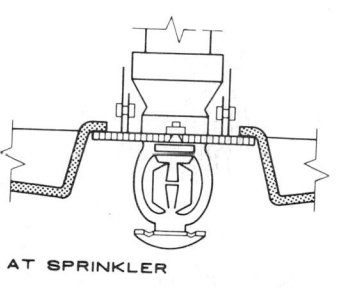

AT SPRINKLER

STANDARD SUPPORTS FOR FORMED AND CORRUGATED PLASTIC CEILINGS

Stephen M. Albert; Boulder, Colorado

GENERAL NOTES:

Many variations of the typical types shown are available such as slanted, rounded, or tapered tops and ends; grooved, ribbed, fluted and shaped faces; as well as other decorative treatment.

Refer to the following sections for:

a) Standard Metal Shapes

b) Metal Stair Nosings

MATERIALS AND FINISHES:

Aluminum
Regular polish: bright or satin texture.
Clear or color anodized: smooth, spun, or hammered texture.
Stainless Steel: satin finish.
Screws: nickel plated where exposed.
Insert strips: bronze or plastic—standard colors.

D.O.F. = DEPTH OF FACE

LEGEND

 INDICATES BACK-UP MATERIAL (PLYWOOD, PLASTER OR OTHER DENSE SURFACE)

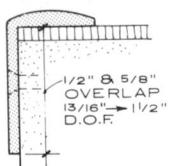

13/32" & 11/16" OVERLAP
7/8" → 1 3/8" D.O.F.

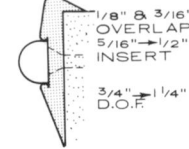

1/4" OVERLAP
3/4" → 1 1/4" D.O.F.

1/16" → 1/8" MATERIAL
5/8" → 1 1/2" D.O.F.

5/64" → 1/8" MATERIAL
13/16" → 1 3/32" D.O.F.

1/16" → 1/8" MATERIAL
3/4" → 1 1/16" D.O.F.

1/2" & 5/8" OVERLAP
13/16" → 1 1/2" D.O.F.

3/16" & 1/4" OVERLAP
5/16" → 2" D.O.F.

1/8" & 3/16" OVERLAP
5/16" → 1/2" INSERT
3/4" → 1 1/4" D.O.F.

5/16" → 1 25/32" FACE

BUTT TYPE
CONCEALED FLANGES: TAPERED OR STRAIGHT

OVERLAP TYPE

ROLL DOWN TYPE

APPLIED AFTER TYPES

TEE TYPE

NOSINGS

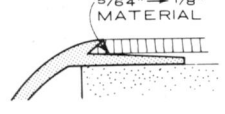

5/64" → 1/8" MATERIAL

1/8" & 1/4" UNDER FLANGE

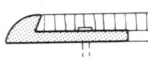

1/16" → 3/16" MATERIAL

1/16" → 1/8" MATERIAL

1/8" & 3/16" MATERIAL

1/8" & 3/16" MATERIAL

SINK (FLAT RIM) OR DOORWAY: BUTT & ROLL DOWN TYPES
CONCEALED FLANGES: TAPERED OR STRAIGHT

BUTT TYPES

EDGINGS

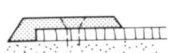

3/32" → 5/32" MATERIAL
3/8" → 1 3/16" WIDTHS

3/4" → 1 9/32" WIDTHS

1" → 2 1/2" WIDTHS

1 3/64" → 2 1/8" WIDTHS

EDGE BINDER
OVERLAP TYPES

SEAM BINDER

OVERLAP TYPE
CARPET EDGE BINDERS

TAP DOWN TYPE

EDGINGS

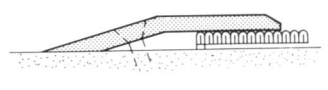

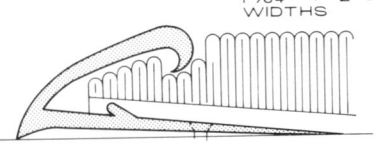

1/16" → 9/32" MATERIAL

1/32" → 1/4" MATERIAL

1/16" → 1/8" MATERIAL

1/16" → 3/8" MATERIAL

21/64" OVERLAP

SLOTTED HOLES

1/32" → 1/2" MATERIAL

OUTSIDE TYPES
CONCEALED FLANGES: TAPERED

INSIDE TYPE

OUTSIDE
APPLIED AFTER TYPE

CONCEALED FLANGE

CORNERS

CAP MOULDING

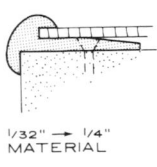

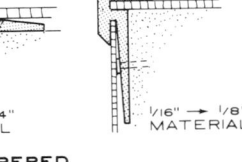

1/32" → 3/8" MATERIAL

1/16" → 5/32" MATERIAL

7/16" → 2" FACE

CONCEALED FLANGE - TAPERED

APPLIED AFTER

COVE AND BATHTUB EDGING

COVE

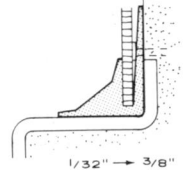

1/16" → 1/2" MATERIAL

CONCEALED FLANGE

DIVISION BAR

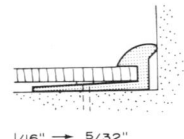

TAG PLACED HERE

7/8" → 3 11/16" WIDTHS
3/4" → 3 1/2" TAGS

1/2" → 1" BACK FASTENING
1 1/16" → 2 3/16" FACE
7/8" → 2" TAGS

STRAIGHT

CURVED

TAG MOULDINGS

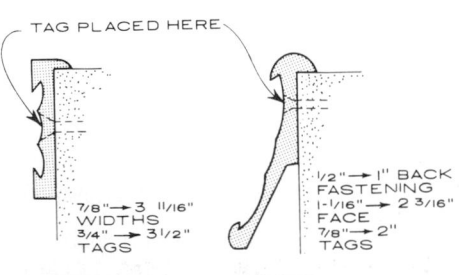

INSIDE

OUTSIDE

RIGHT/LEFT
END STOPS

CORNERS
UP TO 5/32" MATERIAL

COVE BASE

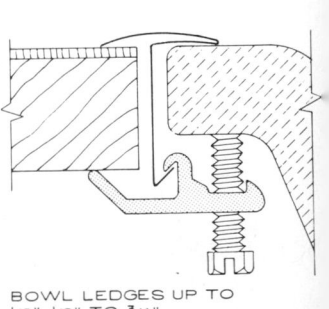

BOWL LEDGES UP TO 1/2", 1/2" TO 3/4", 3/4" TO 1 1/8"

SINK AND LAVATORY FRAME

ARCHITECTURAL GRAPHIC STANDARDS AND THE UNIFORM SYSTEM

Within the limits of Architectural Graphic Standards' fundamental emphasis on graphic presentation of design and construction information, the contents of this edition are arranged in Chapters substantially paralleling the sixteen Divisions of the Uniform System for Construction Specifications, Data Filing & Cost Accounting.

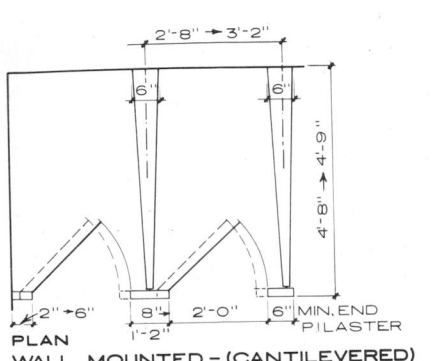

PLAN
WALL MOUNTED – (CANTILEVERED)
RECOMMENDED ONLY WITH FIRM WALL
ANCHORAGE (OVERHEAD BRACING ALSO
AVAILABLE)

NOTE:
STD. = STANDARD ADULT DIMENSIONS
JR. = JUNIOR, CHILDRENS DIMENSIONS

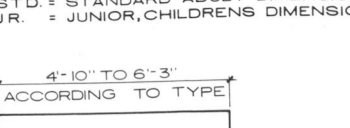

ALCOVE (RECESSED)
OVERHEAD BRACED IS
MOST FREQUENTLY USED

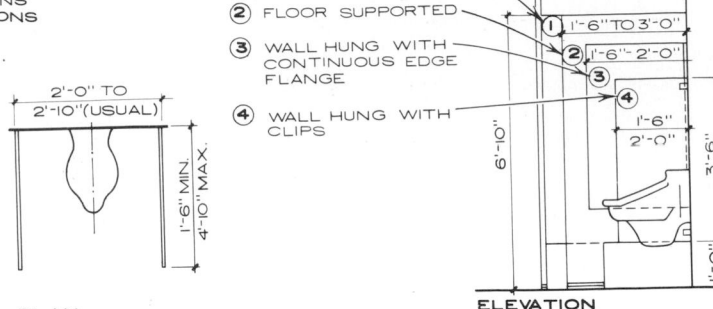

① PILASTER BRACED
② FLOOR SUPPORTED
③ WALL HUNG WITH CONTINUOUS EDGE FLANGE
④ WALL HUNG WITH CLIPS

PLAN
URINAL SCREENS

ELEVATION

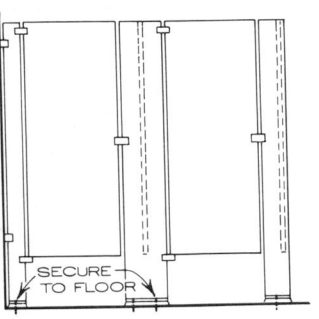

FRONT ELEVATION
FLOOR SUPPORTED
METAL GAUGES: DOORS- 22, PILASTERS-16, PANELS- 20
JUNIOR STALLS MOST COMMONLY AVAILABLE IN FLOOR SUPPORTED

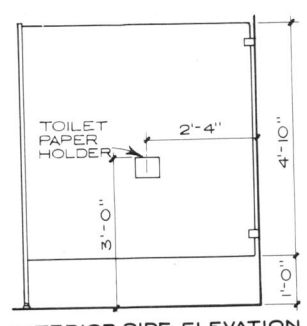

INTERIOR SIDE ELEVATION

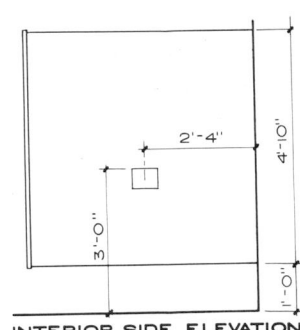

FRONT ELEVATION
WALL MOUNTED
METAL GAUGES: DOORS- 22, PILASTERS-16, PANELS-20

INTERIOR SIDE ELEVATION

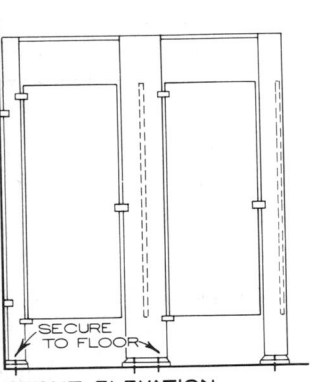

FRONT ELEVATION
OVERHEAD BRACED
METAL GAUGES: DOORS-22, PILASTERS-16, PANELS-20

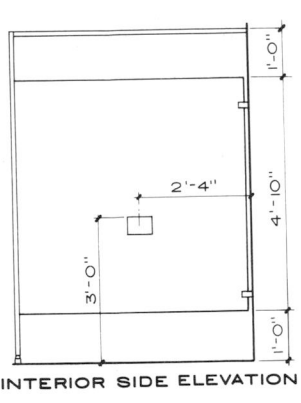

INTERIOR SIDE ELEVATION

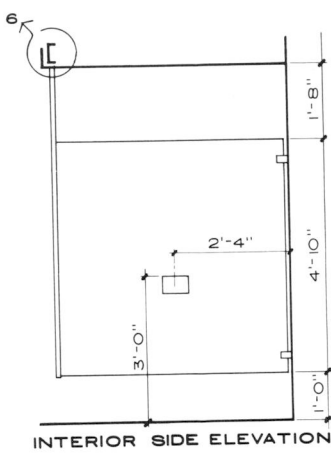

FRONT ELEVATION
CEILING HUNG
METAL GAUGES: DOORS-22, PILASTERS-16, PANELS-20

INTERIOR SIDE ELEVATION

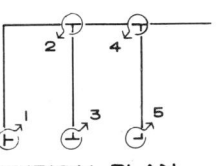

TYPICAL PLAN

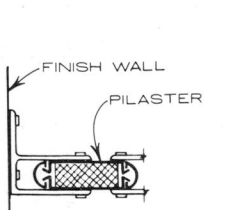

DETAIL 1.

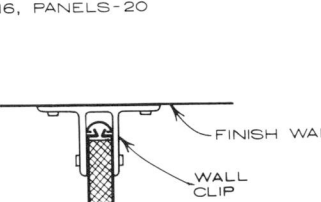

DETAIL 2.

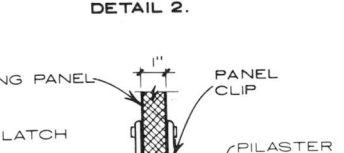

DETAIL 3.

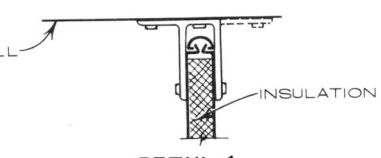

DETAIL 4.

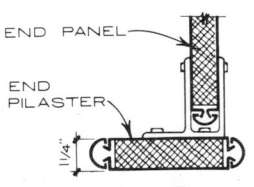

DETAIL 5.

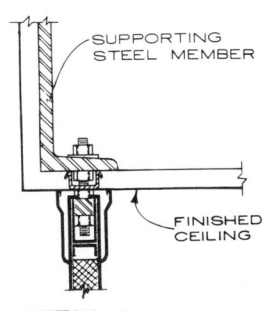

DETAIL 6.

SEE MANUFACTURERS
LITERATURE FOR ADDI-
TIONAL CEILING HUNG
ENCLOSURE DETAILS

DETAILS
SCALE: 1½" = 1'-0"

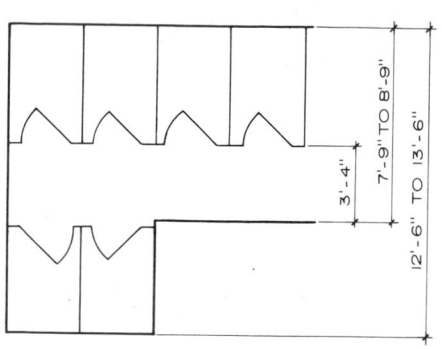

SPACE REQUIREMENTS

**PLAN OF STANDARD W.C. COMPARTMENT
(TYPICAL FOR METAL OR MARBLE)**

GENERAL NOTES:

1. Compartment types: ceiling hung (marble or metal), overhead braced, wall hung (metal only).

2. Metal finishes: baked-on enamel, porcelain enamel, stainless steel.

3. A = Standard compartment widths: 2'-6", 2'-8", 2'-10", 3'-0" (2'-10" is most frequently used).

4. B = Standard door widths: 1'-8", 1'-10", 2'-0", 2'-2", 2'-4", 2'-6". (2'-0" metal doors are standard with marble compartments). Non-standard sizes which are sometimes used: 1'-11", 2'-3", 2'-5".

5. C = Standard pilaster widths: 3", 4", 5", 6", 8", 10", 1'-0". Non-standard sizes which are sometimes used: 2", 7", 1'-2".

GENERAL PLANNING DATA

GENERAL NOTE FOR HARDWARE

Door hardware for tollet stalls may be adjusted to hold door open when stall is not in use. A 30° angle is frequently used.

MARBLE ENCLOSURES

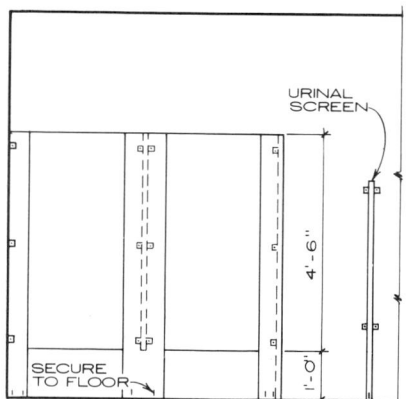

**FRONT ELEVATION
FLOOR SUPPORTED
SCALE: 1/4"=1'-0"**

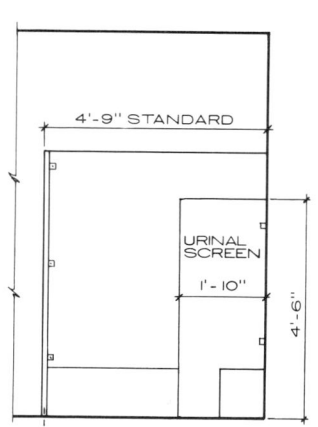

SIDE ELEVATION

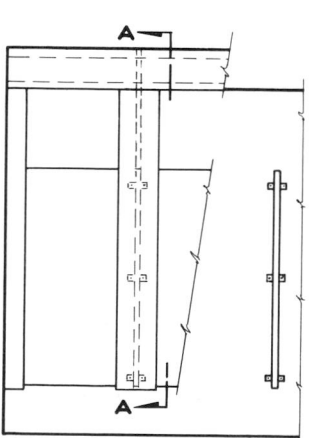

**FRONT ELEVATION
CEILING HUNG
SCALE: 1/4"=1'-0"**

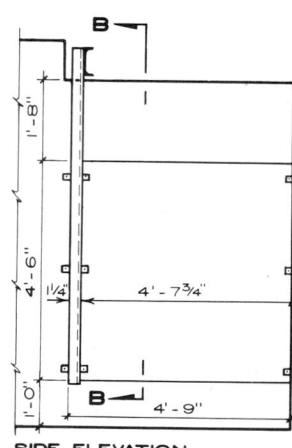

SIDE ELEVATION

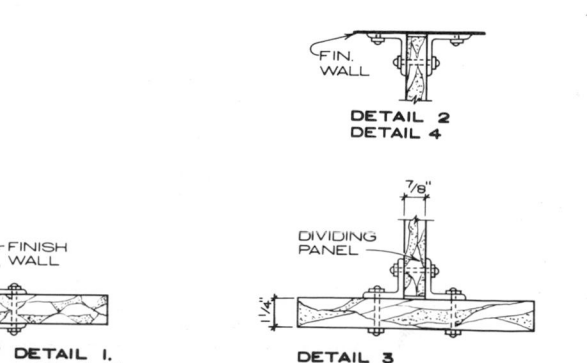

**DETAIL 2
DETAIL 4**

**DETAIL 1.
1 1/2"=1'-0"**

**DETAIL 3
1 1/2"=1'-0"**

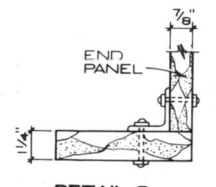

**DETAIL 5
1 1/2"=1'-0"**

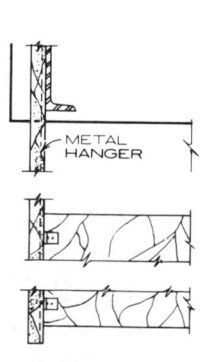

**SECTION A-A
3/4"=1'-0"**

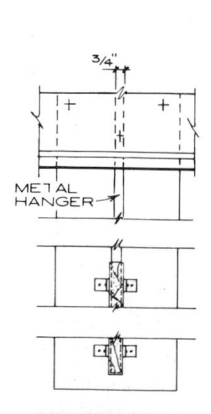

**SECTION B-B
3/4"=1'-0"**

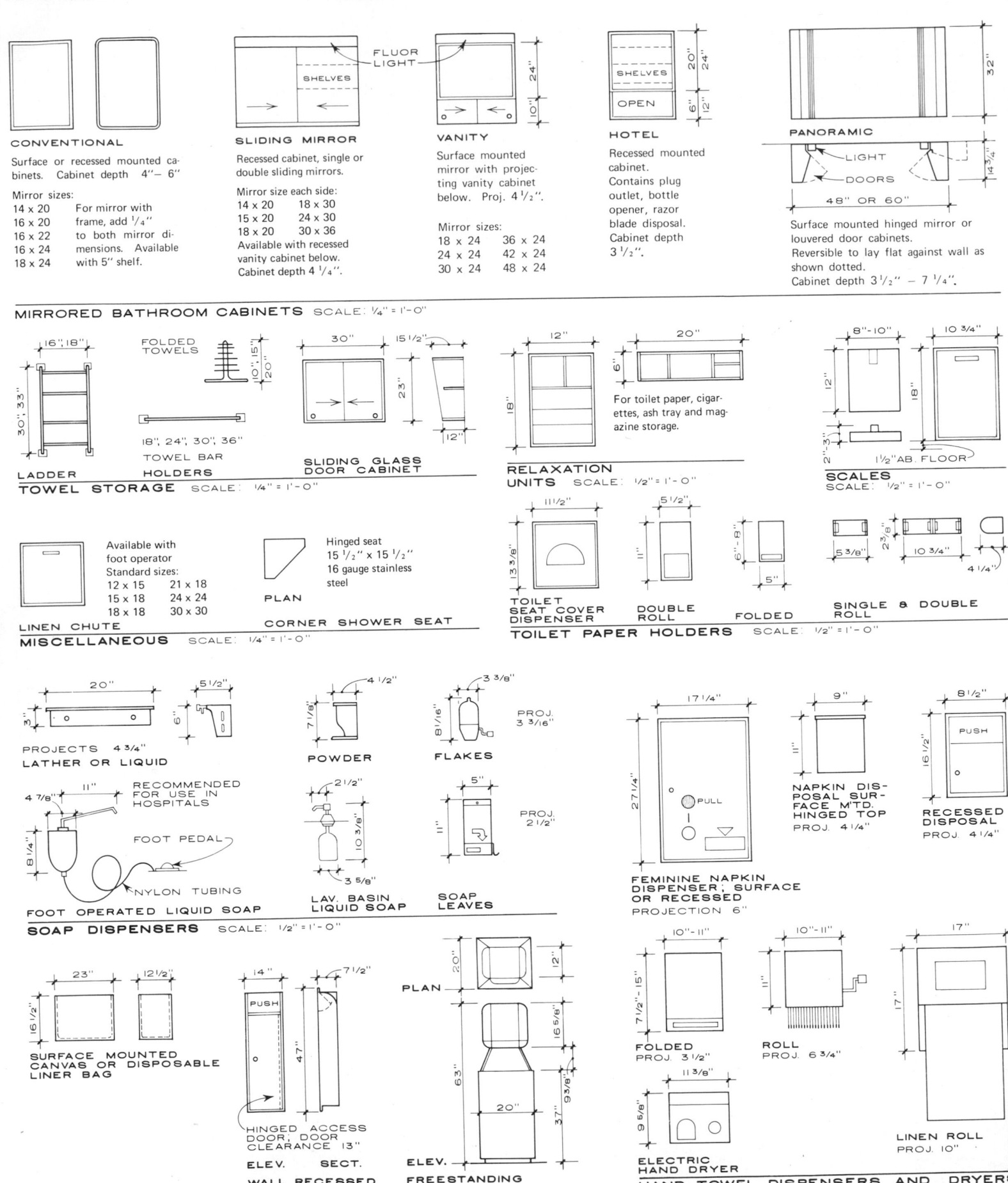

CONVENTIONAL

Surface or recessed mounted cabinets. Cabinet depth 4"– 6"

Mirror sizes:
14 x 20   For mirror with
16 x 20   frame, add ¼"
16 x 22   to both mirror dimensions. Available
16 x 24   with 5" shelf.
18 x 24

SLIDING MIRROR

Recessed cabinet, single or double sliding mirrors.

Mirror size each side:
14 x 20   18 x 30
15 x 20   24 x 30
18 x 20   30 x 36
Available with recessed vanity cabinet below. Cabinet depth 4 ¼".

VANITY

Surface mounted mirror with projecting vanity cabinet below. Proj. 4 ½".

Mirror sizes:
18 x 24   36 x 24
24 x 24   42 x 24
30 x 24   48 x 24

HOTEL

Recessed mounted cabinet. Contains plug outlet, bottle opener, razor blade disposal. Cabinet depth 3 ½".

PANORAMIC

Surface mounted hinged mirror or louvered door cabinets. Reversible to lay flat against wall as shown dotted. Cabinet depth 3 ½" – 7 ¼".

MIRRORED BATHROOM CABINETS SCALE: ¼" = 1'-0"

FOLDED TOWELS

18", 24", 30", 36"
TOWEL BAR

LADDER   HOLDERS

SLIDING GLASS DOOR CABINET

TOWEL STORAGE SCALE: ¼" = 1'-0"

For toilet paper, cigarettes, ash tray and magazine storage.

RELAXATION UNITS SCALE: ½" = 1'-0"

SCALES SCALE: ½" = 1'-0"

Available with foot operator
Standard sizes:
12 x 15   21 x 18
15 x 18   24 x 24
18 x 18   30 x 30

LINEN CHUTE

Hinged seat
15 ½" x 15 ½"
16 gauge stainless steel

PLAN

CORNER SHOWER SEAT

MISCELLANEOUS SCALE: ¼" = 1'-0"

TOILET SEAT COVER DISPENSER

DOUBLE ROLL   FOLDED

SINGLE & DOUBLE ROLL

TOILET PAPER HOLDERS SCALE: ½" = 1'-0"

PROJECTS 4¾"
LATHER OR LIQUID

POWDER   FLAKES

PROJ. 3 3/16"

PROJ. 2 ½"

RECOMMENDED FOR USE IN HOSPITALS

FOOT PEDAL

NYLON TUBING

FOOT OPERATED LIQUID SOAP

LAV. BASIN LIQUID SOAP

SOAP LEAVES

SOAP DISPENSERS SCALE: ½" = 1'-0"

FEMININE NAPKIN DISPENSER; SURFACE OR RECESSED
PROJECTION 6"

NAPKIN DISPOSAL SURFACE M'TD. HINGED TOP
PROJ. 4 ¼"

RECESSED DISPOSAL
PROJ. 4 ¼"

SURFACE MOUNTED CANVAS OR DISPOSABLE LINER BAG

PUSH

HINGED ACCESS DOOR; DOOR CLEARANCE 13"

ELEV.   SECT.
WALL RECESSED

PLAN

ELEV.
FREESTANDING

WASTE RECEPTACLES   SCALE: ¼" = 1'-0"

FOLDED
PROJ. 3 ½"

ROLL
PROJ. 6 ¾"

ELECTRIC HAND DRYER

LINEN ROLL
PROJ. 10"

HAND TOWEL DISPENSERS AND DRYERS
SCALE: ½" = 1'-0"

H. E. Hallenbeck, AIA; J. Anthony Cappuccilli, Architects, AIA; Syracuse, New York

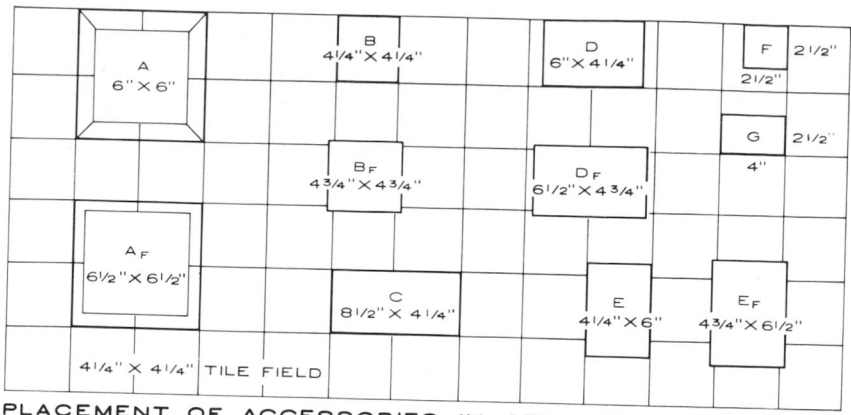

PLACEMENT OF ACCESSORIES IN CERAMIC TILE

CERAMIC ACCESSORIES

FLUSH TYPE: Face of accessory in same plane as surface of adjacent tile.

FLANGE TYPE: Accessory overlaps adjacent tile $1/4$" on all sides for conventional set, and $3/16$" on all sides for thin-set.

INSTALLATION METHOD:
A. Conventional mortar set.
B. Adhesive or thin-set, maximum depth of accessory $5/16$".

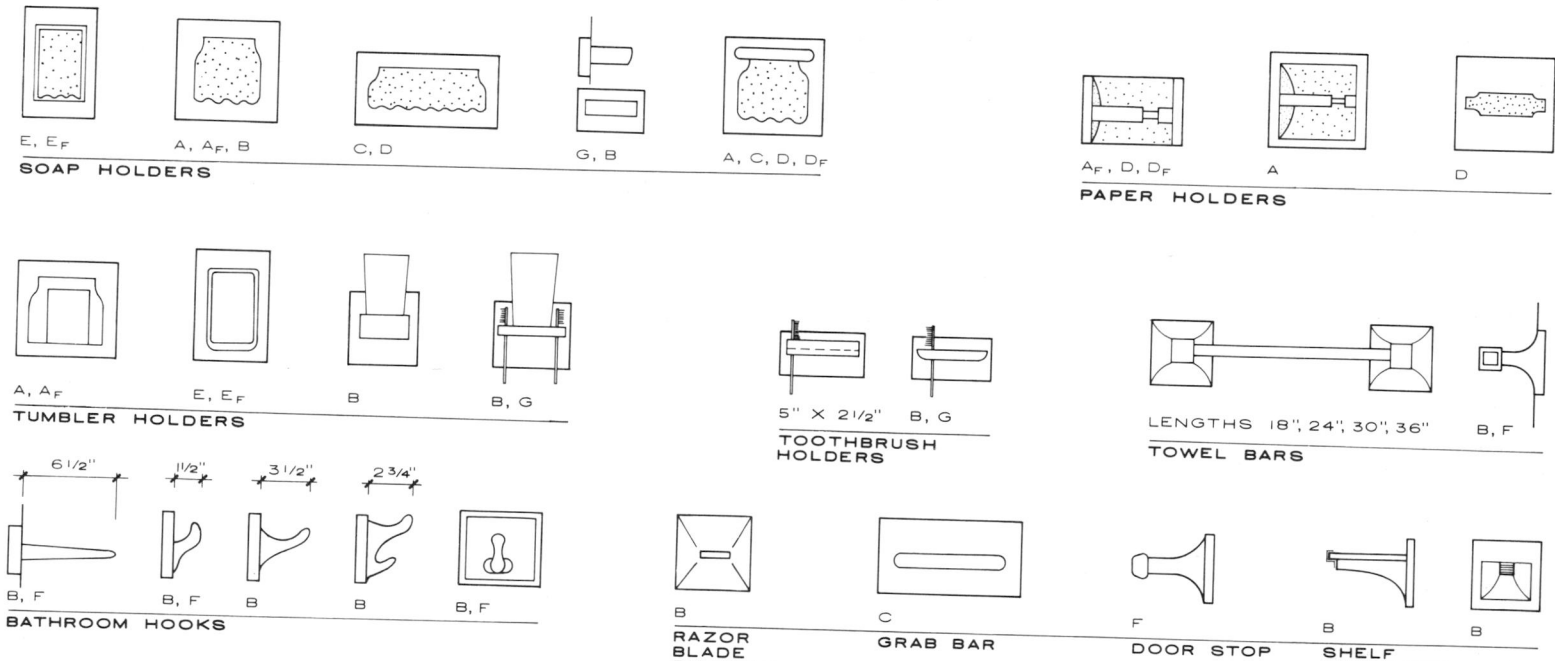

SOAP HOLDERS

PAPER HOLDERS

TUMBLER HOLDERS

TOOTHBRUSH HOLDERS

TOWEL BARS

BATHROOM HOOKS

RAZOR BLADE DISPOSAL

GRAB BAR

DOOR STOP

SHELF SUPPORTS

ACCESSORIES

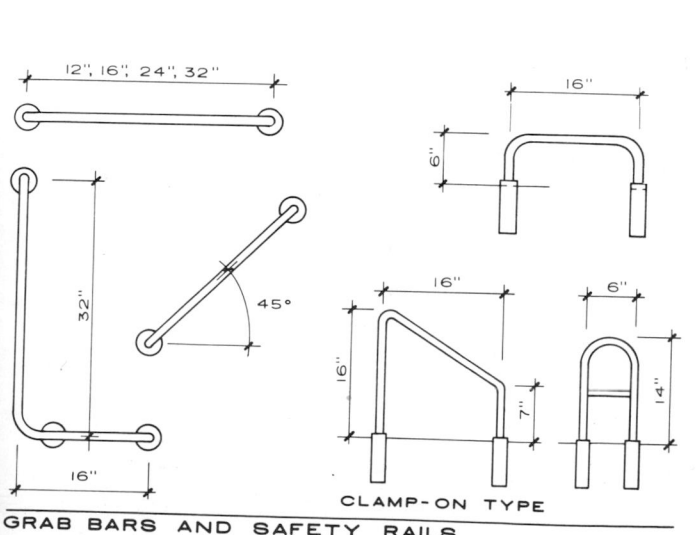

GRAB BARS AND SAFETY RAILS

CLAMP-ON TYPE

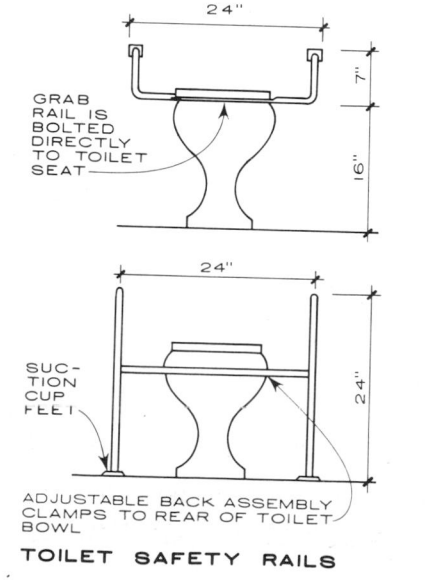

GRAB RAIL IS BOLTED DIRECTLY TO TOILET SEAT

SUCTION CUP FEET

ADJUSTABLE BACK ASSEMBLY CLAMPS TO REAR OF TOILET BOWL

TOILET SAFETY RAILS

GRAB RAILS:

LIGHT DUTY 1" O.D.
HEAVY DUTY 1¼" O.D.
AVAILABLE IN STAINLESS STEEL OR CHOME PLATED.

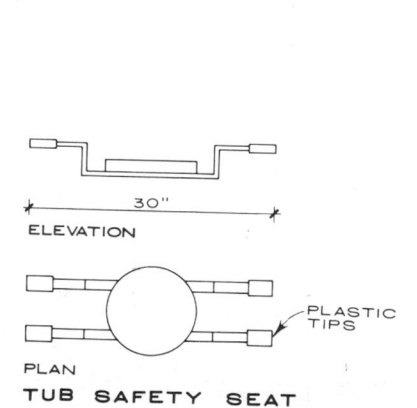

ELEVATION

PLASTIC TIPS

PLAN

TUB SAFETY SEAT

H. E. Hallenbeck, AIA; J. Anthony Cappuccilli, Architects, AIA; Syracuse, New York

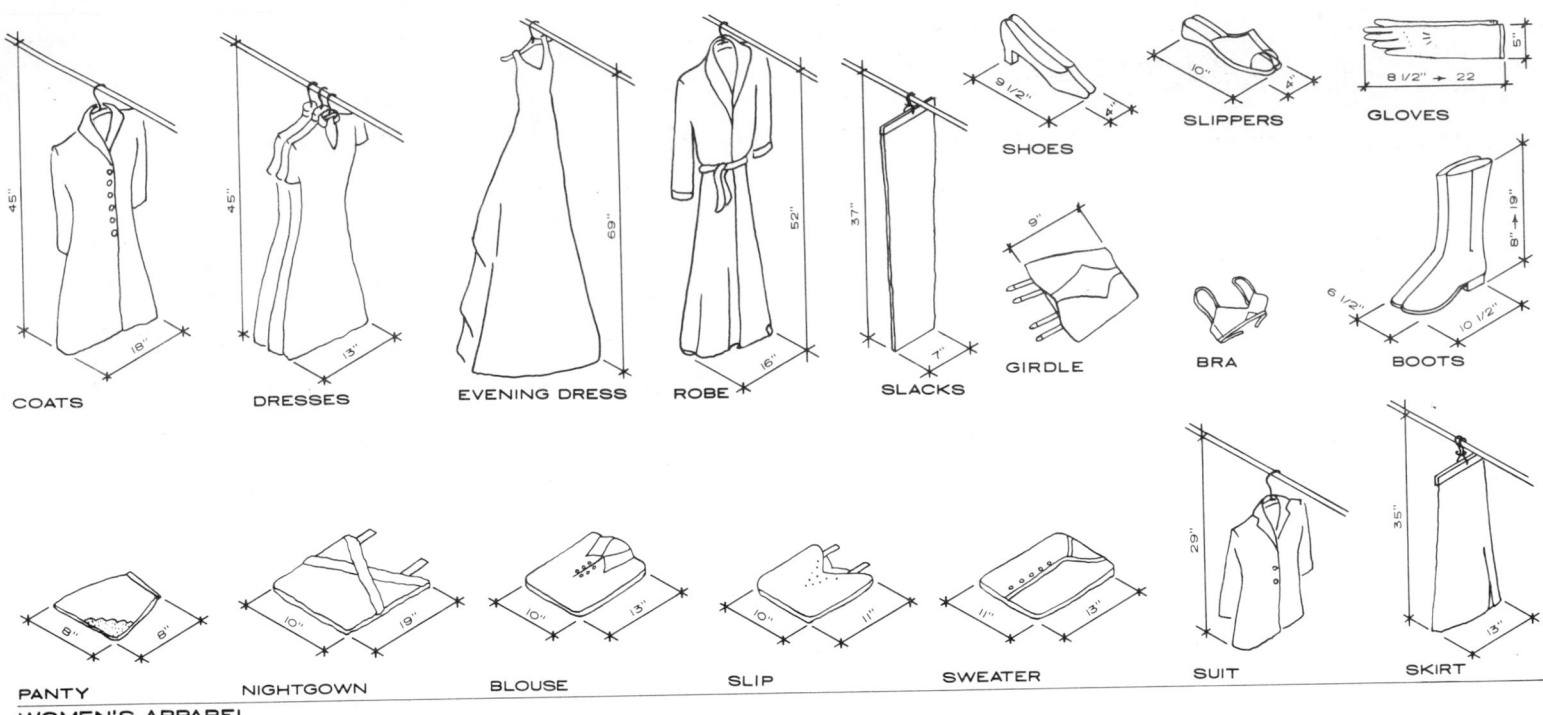

SHOES   SLIPPERS   GLOVES

COATS   DRESSES   EVENING DRESS   ROBE   SLACKS   GIRDLE   BRA   BOOTS

PANTY   NIGHTGOWN   BLOUSE   SLIP   SWEATER   SUIT   SKIRT

WOMEN'S APPAREL

HANDKERCHIEFS

COATS   SUITS   TROUSERS   SLACKS   BOW TIE   TIE   CANE   UMBRELLA

SHIRT   SWEATER   PAJAMAS   HAT   MUFFLER   SHORTS

SLIPPERS   RUBBERS   GLOVES   SHOES   SOCKS   BOOTS

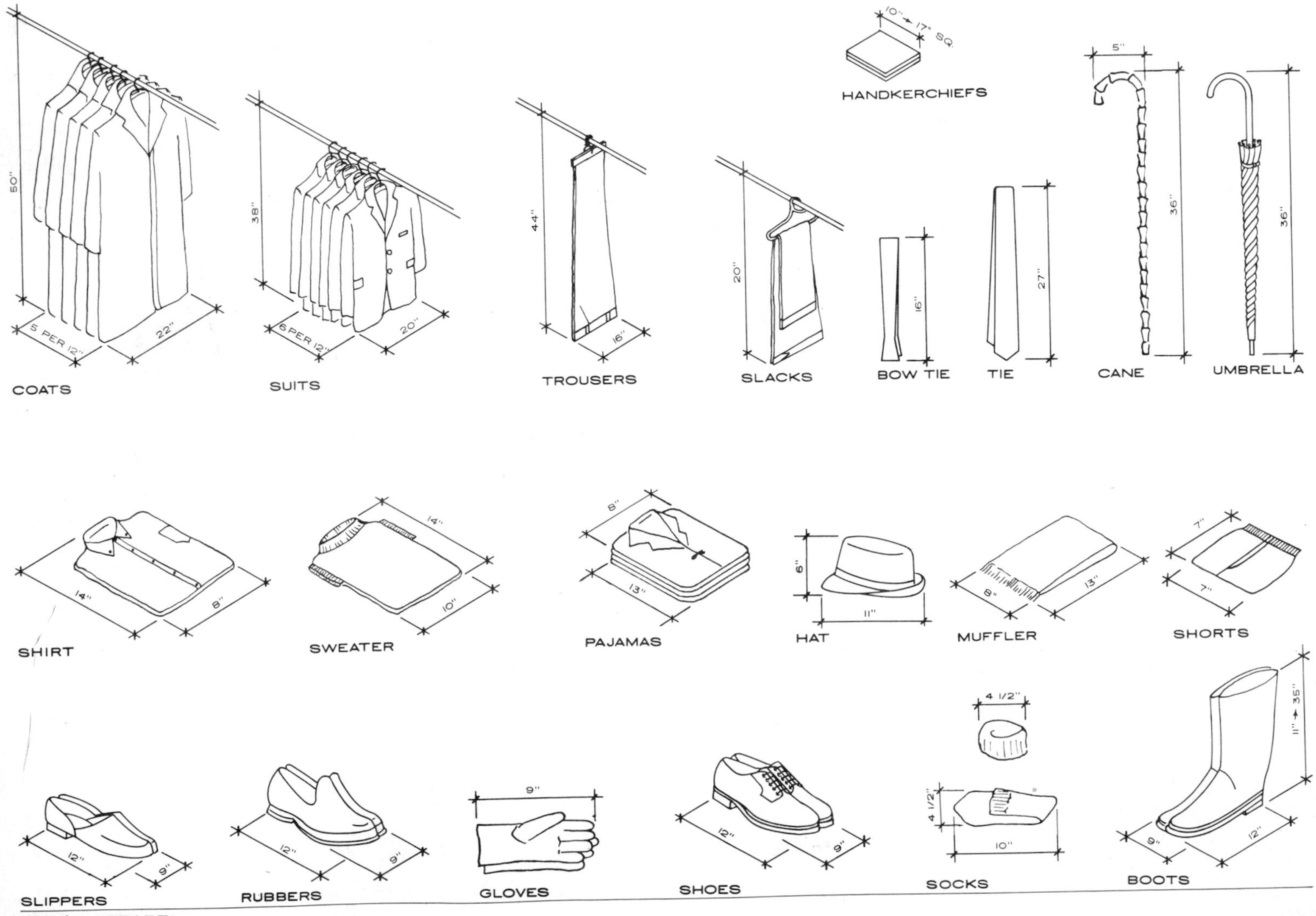

MEN'S APPAREL

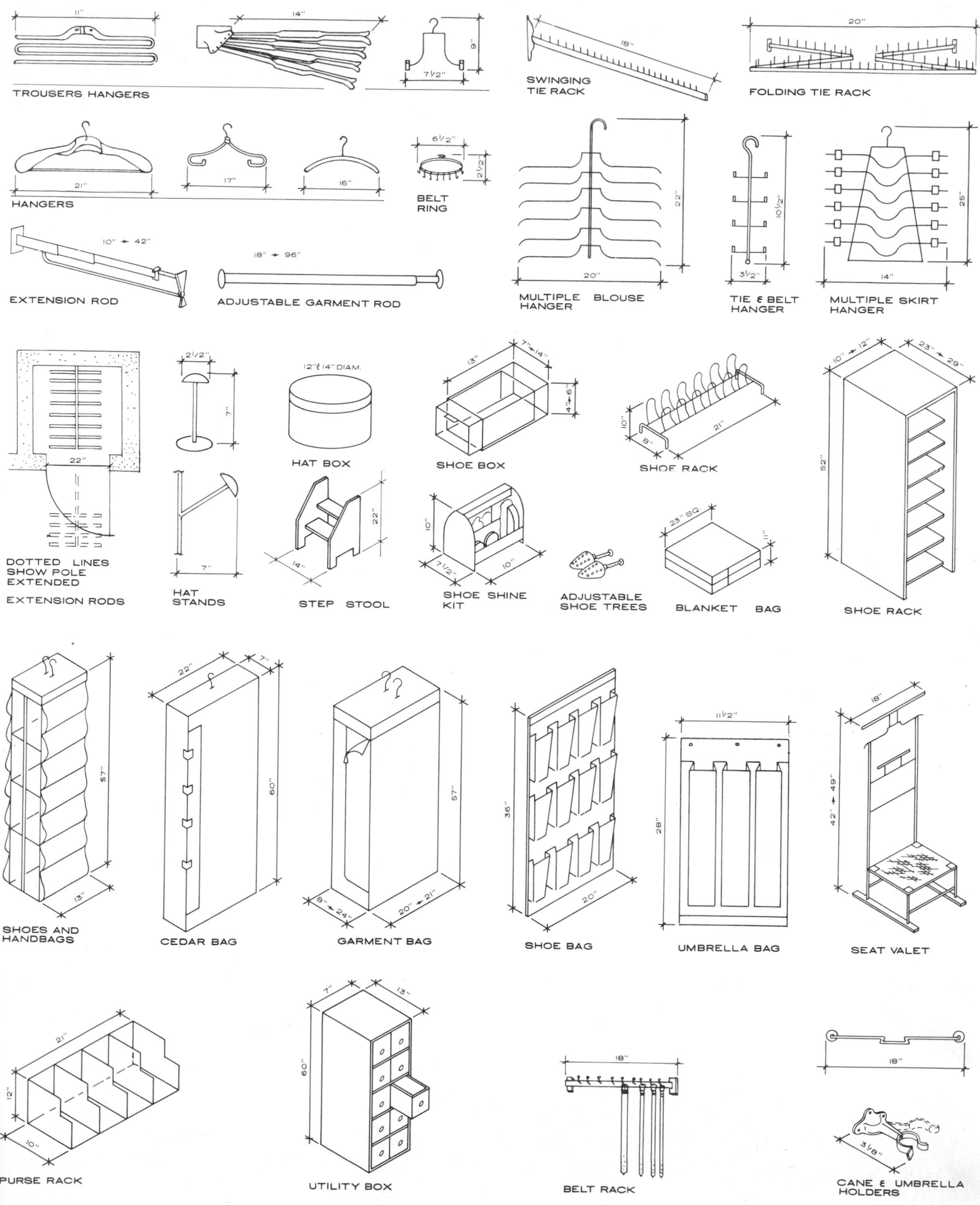

TROUSERS HANGERS

SWINGING TIE RACK

FOLDING TIE RACK

HANGERS

BELT RING

MULTIPLE BLOUSE HANGER

TIE & BELT HANGER

MULTIPLE SKIRT HANGER

EXTENSION ROD

ADJUSTABLE GARMENT ROD

DOTTED LINES SHOW POLE EXTENDED

EXTENSION RODS

HAT STANDS

HAT BOX

STEP STOOL

SHOE BOX

SHOE SHINE KIT

SHOE RACK

ADJUSTABLE SHOE TREES

BLANKET BAG

SHOE RACK

SHOES AND HANDBAGS

CEDAR BAG

GARMENT BAG

SHOE BAG

UMBRELLA BAG

SEAT VALET

PURSE RACK

UTILITY BOX

BELT RACK

CANE & UMBRELLA HOLDERS

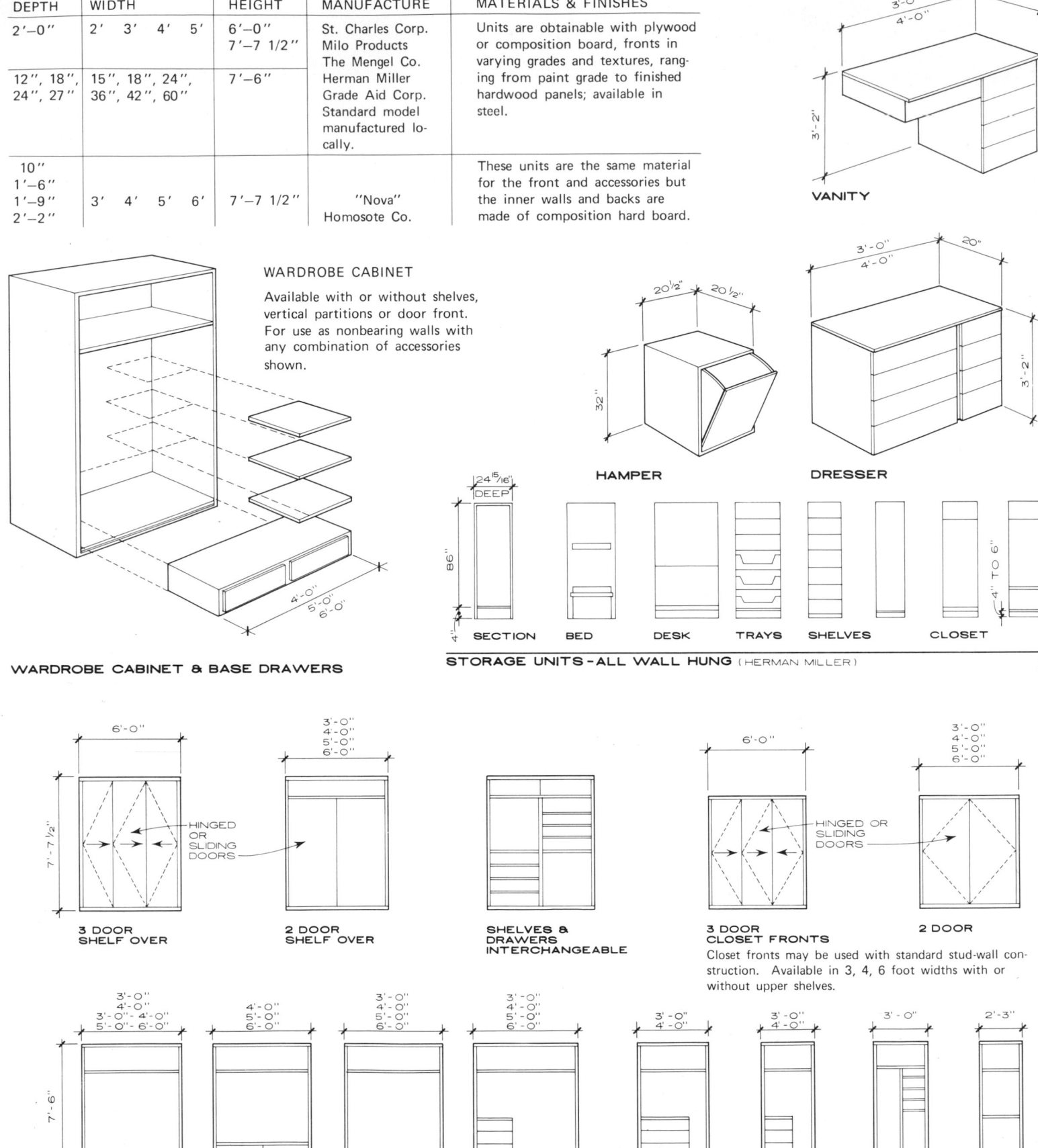

DEPTH	WIDTH	HEIGHT	MANUFACTURE	MATERIALS & FINISHES
2'-0"	2' 3' 4' 5'	6'-0" 7'-7 1/2"	St. Charles Corp. Milo Products The Mengel Co. Herman Miller Grade Aid Corp. Standard model manufactured lo- cally.	Units are obtainable with plywood or composition board, fronts in varying grades and textures, rang- ing from paint grade to finished hardwood panels; available in steel.
12", 18", 24", 27"	15", 18", 24", 36", 42", 60"	7'-6"		
10" 1'-6" 1'-9" 2'-2"	3' 4' 5' 6'	7'-7 1/2"	"Nova" Homosote Co.	These units are the same material for the front and accessories but the inner walls and backs are made of composition hard board.

VANITY

WARDROBE CABINET

Available with or without shelves,
vertical partitions or door front.
For use as nonbearing walls with
any combination of accessories
shown.

HAMPER   DRESSER

24 15/16" DEEP

86"

4"

SECTION   BED   DESK   TRAYS   SHELVES   CLOSET

STORAGE UNITS – ALL WALL HUNG (HERMAN MILLER)

WARDROBE CABINET & BASE DRAWERS

3 DOOR
SHELF OVER

HINGED
OR
SLIDING
DOORS

2 DOOR
SHELF OVER

SHELVES &
DRAWERS
INTERCHANGEABLE

3 DOOR
CLOSET FRONTS

HINGED OR
SLIDING
DOORS

2 DOOR

Closet fronts may be used with standard stud-wall construction. Available in 3, 4, 6 foot widths with or
without upper shelves.

WARDROBE

WARDROBE
LOWER
DRAWERS

STORAGE
CABINET

WARDROBE
TRAY CHEST

DRESSER

VANITY-DESK

LINEN &
STORAGE
CLOSETS

STORAGE UNIT & CLOSET FRONTS

Hugh Newell Jacobsen, AIA; Washington, D. C.

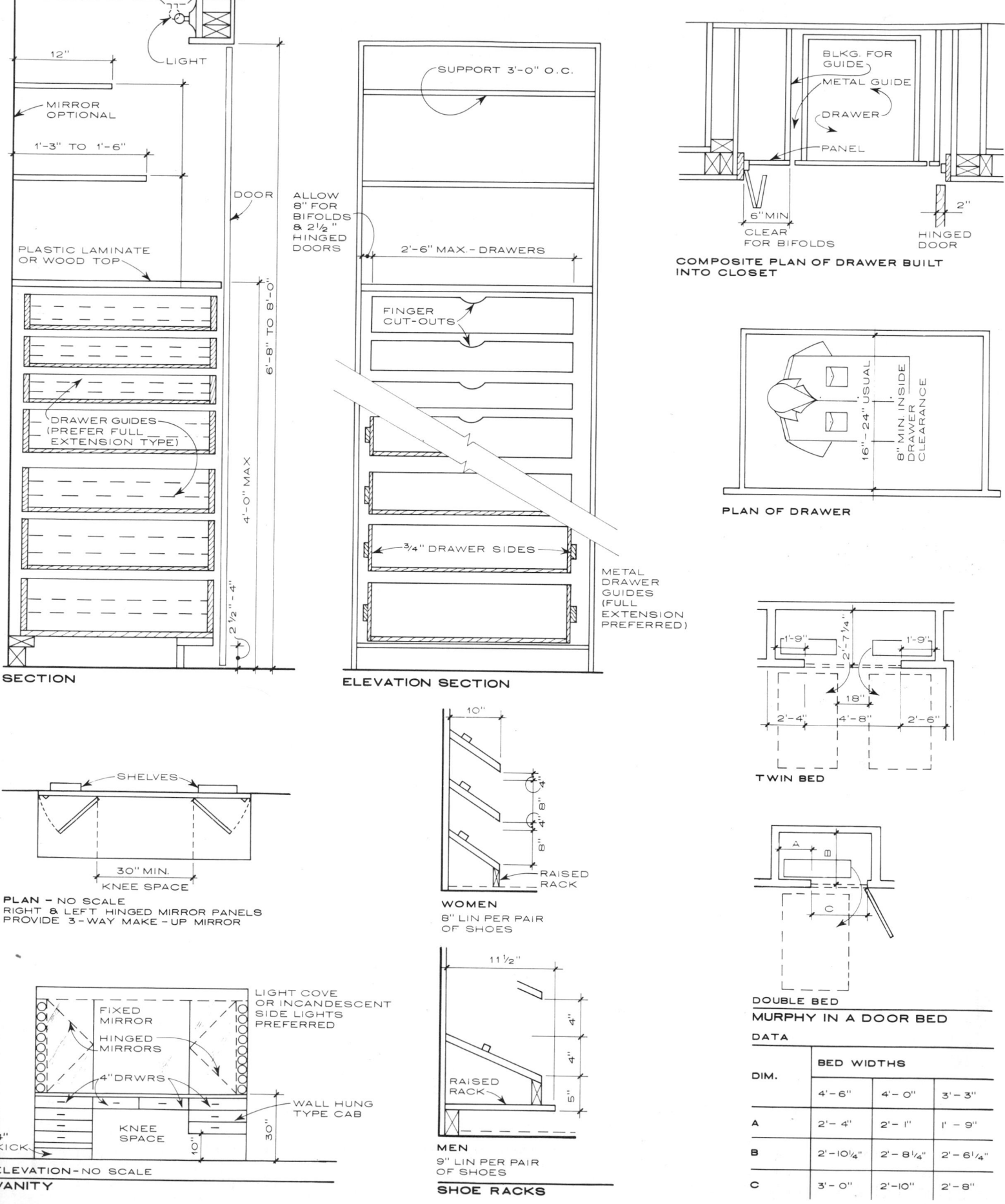

SECTION

12"

LIGHT

MIRROR OPTIONAL

1'-3" TO 1'-6"

DOOR

PLASTIC LAMINATE OR WOOD TOP

ALLOW 8" FOR BIFOLDS & 2½" HINGED DOORS

6'-8" TO 8'-0"

DRAWER GUIDES (PREFER FULL EXTENSION TYPE)

4'-0" MAX

2½"-4"

ELEVATION SECTION

SUPPORT 3'-0" O.C.

2'-6" MAX. - DRAWERS

FINGER CUT-OUTS

¾" DRAWER SIDES

METAL DRAWER GUIDES (FULL EXTENSION PREFERRED)

COMPOSITE PLAN OF DRAWER BUILT INTO CLOSET

BLKG. FOR GUIDE
METAL GUIDE
DRAWER
PANEL

6" MIN CLEAR FOR BIFOLDS

2"

HINGED DOOR

PLAN OF DRAWER

16" MIN. INSIDE DRAWER CLEARANCE

8" MIN.
16"-24" USUAL

PLAN - NO SCALE
RIGHT & LEFT HINGED MIRROR PANELS PROVIDE 3 - WAY MAKE - UP MIRROR

SHELVES

30" MIN. KNEE SPACE

VANITY

ELEVATION-NO SCALE

FIXED MIRROR

HINGED MIRRORS

4" DRWRS

4" KICK

KNEE SPACE

LIGHT COVE OR INCANDESCENT SIDE LIGHTS PREFERRED

WALL HUNG TYPE CAB

30"

WOMEN
8" LIN PER PAIR OF SHOES

10"

4"

8"

4"

8"

RAISED RACK

MEN
9" LIN PER PAIR OF SHOES

11½"

4"

4"

4"

5"

RAISED RACK

SHOE RACKS

TWIN BED

1'-9"   1'-9"

2'-7¼"

18"

2'-4"   4'-8"   2'-6"

DOUBLE BED

A

C

MURPHY IN A DOOR BED

DATA

DIM.	BED WIDTHS		
	4'-6"	4'-0"	3'-3"
A	2'-4"	2'-1"	1'-9"
B	2'-10¼"	2'-8¼"	2'-6¼"
C	3'-0"	2'-10"	2'-8"

R. E. Powe, Jr.; Hugh N. Jacobsen, AIA; Washington, D. C.

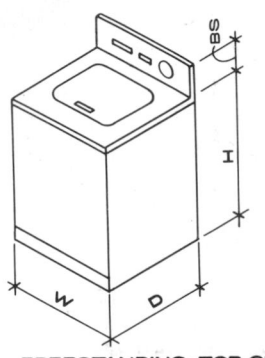

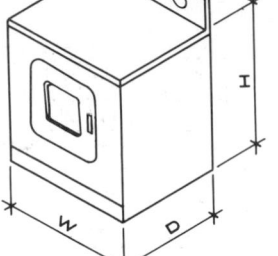

FREESTANDING-TOP OR FRONT LOADING

UNDER COUNTER

AUTOMATIC WASHERS (SOME HAVE KICK SPACES, SOME NOT)

FREESTANDING

UNDER COUNTER

AUTOMATIC WASHER-DRYER COMBINATIONS
(SOME HAVE KICK SPACES, SOME NOT)

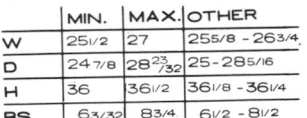

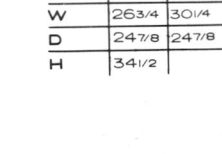

	MIN.	MAX.	OTHER
W	25 1/2	27	25 5/8 - 26 3/4
D	24 7/8	28 23/32	25 - 28 5/16
H	36	36 1/2	36 1/8 - 36 1/4
BS	6 3/32	8 3/4	6 1/2 - 8 1/2

	MIN.	MAX.
W	26 3/4	30 1/4
D	24 7/8	24 7/8
H	34 1/2	

	MIN.	MAX.	OTHER
W	30	34 1/16	25 5/8
D	24 1/2	25 9/16	28
H	35 3/4	36	
BS	7	7 5/8	9 7/8

	MIN.	MAX.
W	30	34 1/16
D	24 3/4	25 9/16
H	34 1/2	35 3/4

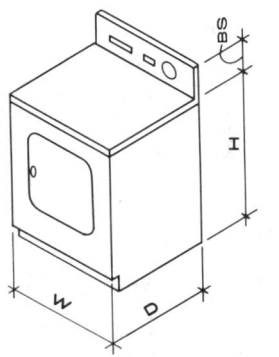

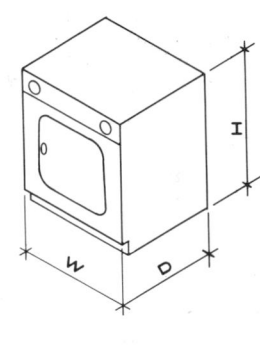

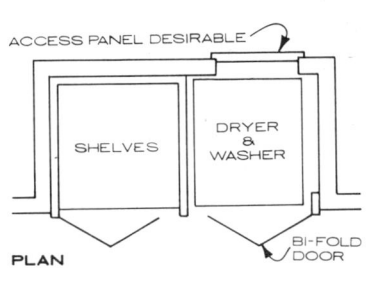

ACCESS PANEL DESIRABLE

SHELVES

DRYER & WASHER

PLAN

BI-FOLD DOOR

WRINGER CLEARANCE 3'-10"- 4'-1"

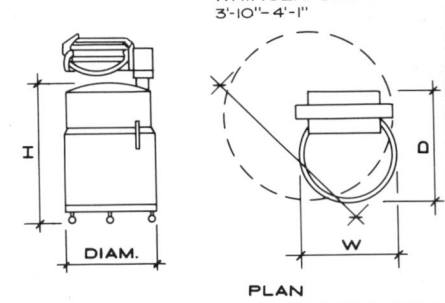

DIAM.

PLAN

WRINGER WASHERS

FREESTANDING FRONT LOADING

UNDER COUNTER

AUTOMATIC DRYERS

	MIN.	MAX.	OTHER
W	26 3/4	31 1/2	27 - 31
D	24 7/8	28 23/32	25 - 28 5/16
H	36	36 1/2	36 1/8 - 36 1/4
BS	6 3/32	8 3/4	6 1/2 - 8 1/2

	MIN.	MAX.
W	26 3/4	
D	24 7/8	
H	34 1/2	

	MIN.	MAX.	OTHER
W	23 1/4	27 1/4	24 - 27
D	24	29 3/4	26 - 28
H	33	46	35 1/2 - 38 1/4
DIAM.	23	29	23 1/8 - 23 1/2

GENERAL NOTES:

See kitchen & laundry layout pages for locations of washers & dryers and wall chases for pipes & vents and for dishwasher locations.

Where clearances of doors of machines (when open) may be a problem, check manufacturers catalog for "open-door" dimension.

All dimensions given are actual ones but certain variations in body design may affect actual depths of models. Check all units for exact voltage. Some units available with gas.

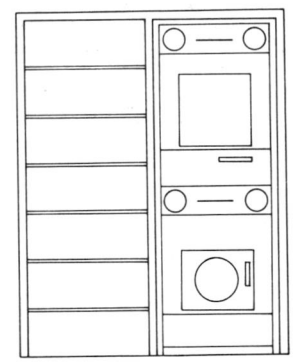

ELEVATION

STACKED WASHER & DRYER WITH CLOSETS OR SHELVES

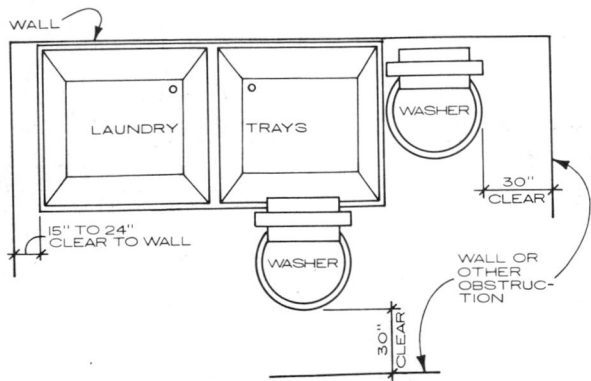

WALL

LAUNDRY

TRAYS

WASHER

WASHER

15" TO 24" CLEAR TO WALL

30" CLEAR

WALL OR OTHER OBSTRUCTION

30" CLEAR

PLAN OF TUB AND WRINGER WASHER WITH CLEARANCES

R. E. Powe, Jr.; Hugh N. Jacobsen, AIA; Washington, D. C.

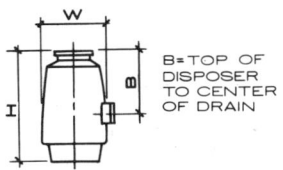

B = TOP OF DISPOSER TO CENTER OF DRAIN

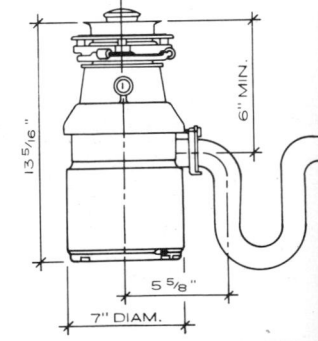

6" MIN.

5 5/8"

7" DIAM.

	MIN.	MAX.	OTHER
W	7 1/8	10 3/4	7 3/8 → 9 1/2
B	5 1/2	9 1/8	6 5/8 → 8 3/4
H	12	16 1/8	12 5/8 → 16

GARBAGE DISPOSER UNITS

NOTE:

Do not place on joint Dining-Kitchen wall because of noise.
Check manufacturers details for different models.

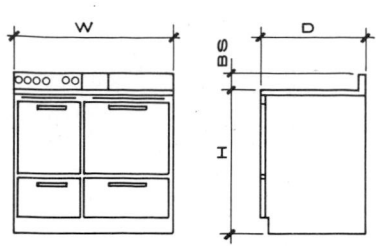

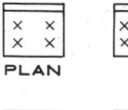

PLAN

ELEV. (POSSIBLE VARIATIONS)

STANDARD RANGE (FREE STANDING)

ONE OVEN-FOUR UNITS

	MIN.	MAX.	OTHER
W	19 1/2	40	21-30
D	24 1/4	27 1/2	25 - 26 1/4
H	35 1/8	36 1/8	35 1/4 - 36
BS	4 11/16	12 1/2	8 1/4 - 11 1/2

TWO OVENS FOUR UNITS

	MIN.	MAX.	OTHER
W	40		
D	25	27 1/2	25 1/2 - 26 1/4
H	35 1/8	36	35 1/4
BS	8 1/4	11 1/8	8 1/8 - 10 3/8

SYMBOLS
O - OVEN
B - BROILER
G - REVOLVING GRILL
X - BURNER, GAS OR ELECTRIC
W - WARMING OVEN
S - STORAGE
R - ROTISSERIE

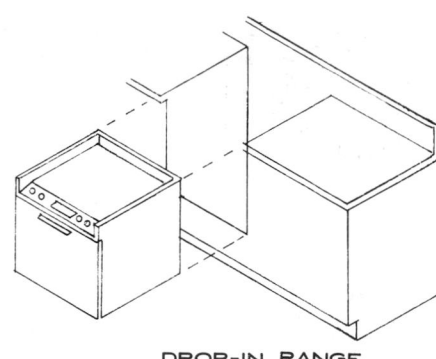

DROP-IN RANGE

	MIN.	MAX.	OTHER
W	22 7/8	30	23 7/8
D	22 7/8	25	22 1/2 24
H	23	24 1/16	23 1/2

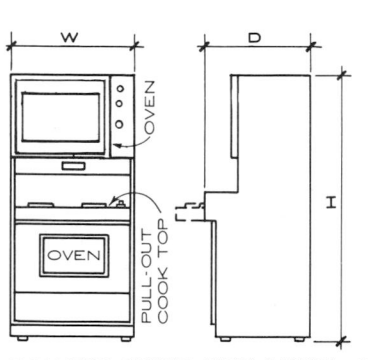
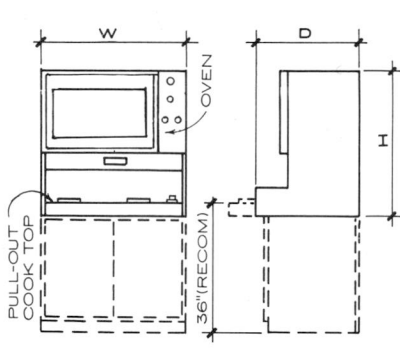

RANGES WITH EYE LEVEL OVENS

DOUBLE OVEN-4 UNITS

	MIN.	MAX.	OTHER
W	29 7/8	30	
D	25 1/2	27 5/8	25 5/8 - 27 1/2
H	61 1/2	71 1/4	63 3/4 - 67 7/16

SINGLE OVEN TOP ONLY-4 UNITS

	MIN.	MAX.	OTHER
W	29 13/16	38 7/8	29 7/8
D	25 1/2	27 5/8	27 1/4
H	33 1/2	41 1/6	36 3/4

DOUBLE OVEN TOP ONLY-4 UNITS

	MIN.	MAX.	OTHER
W	39	40 1/4	40
D	25 1/2	27 5/8	26 3/4
H	34 7/8	36 3/4	

NOTE:
SELF CLEANING OVENS MUST VENT TO OUTSIDE

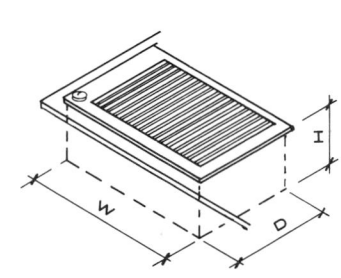

BUILT-IN BROILER

	MIN.	MAX.	OTHER
W	19	28 5/8	19 5/8 - 28
D	19 3/4	20 3/4	
H	11	13 1/2	

WARMING DRAWER

		CABINET OPEN
W	23 3/4	22 1/2
H	10 1/4	9

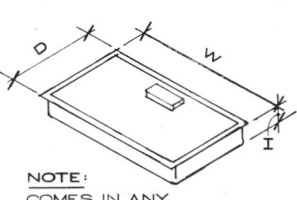

NOTE:
COMES IN ANY ARRANGEMENT

BUILT-IN COOK TOP ELECTRIC OR GAS

	MIN.	MAX.
W	12	48
D	18	22
H	2	3

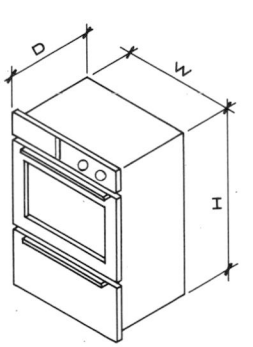

OVEN & BROILER

	MIN.	MAX.	OTHER
W	21	24 1/4	22 1/2 - 24
D	21 1/8	24	22 1/2 - 22 11/16
H	38	40 7/16	40 3/16

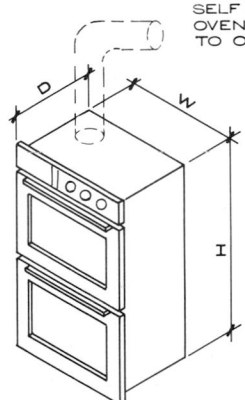

DOUBLE OVEN

	MIN.	MAX.	OTHER
W	21	24 1/4	22 1/2 - 24
D	21 1/8	24	22 1/2 - 22 11/16
H	39 1/4	50 3/8	42 - 46 13/16

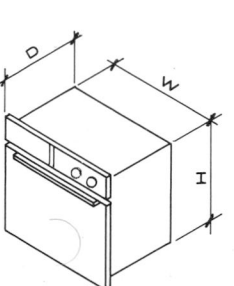

SINGLE OVEN

	MIN.	MAX.	OTHER
W	21	24 1/4	22 1/2 - 24
D	21 1/8	24	22 1/2 - 22 11/16
H	23 1/2	26 7/8	25

BUILT-IN WALL OVENS (GAS OR ELECTRIC)

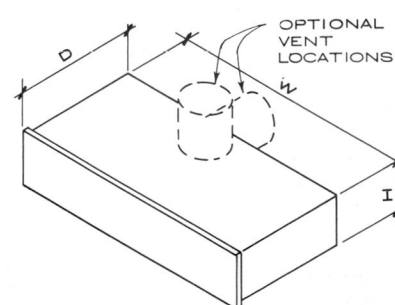

OPTIONAL VENT LOCATIONS

RANGE HOOD

	MIN.	MAX.	OTHER
W	24	72	30-66
D	12	27 1/2	17-26
H	5 1/2	8 5/8	5 5/8 - 7 1/2

Range hoods are available with vents as shown or with no vent. The following accessories are available with hoods: fans, filters, lights, etc. (see manufacturers).

NOTES:

1. Check manufacturers requirements for rough clearances.

2. Dimensions shown are in inches.

3. Optional equipment available for ranges or wall ovens are broilers and rotisseries.

R. E. Powe, Jr.; Hugh N. Jacobsen, AIA; Washington, D. C.

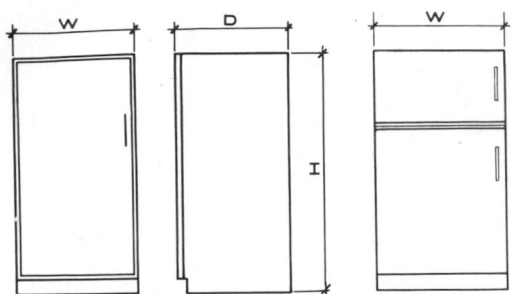

REFRIGERATORS CONVENTIONAL TYPE WITH FREEZERS—ONE & TWO DOORS

TO 13.0 CU. FT.

	MIN.	MAX.	OTHER
W	24	31	28–30
D	$28^3/_8$	$29^3/_4$	$28^3/_4$–$29^1/_4$
H	$55^3/_8$	68	$56^1/_2$–$64^1/_4$
LBS	33	119	55–98
CU.FT.	9.0	12.5	9.5–12.13

TO 19.0 CU. FT.

	MIN.	MAX.	OTHER
W	$30^1/_2$	$33^3/_4$	31–33
D	$23^1/_8$	$29^1/_8$	$25^3/_4$ – $28^3/_4$
H	63	$69^1/_2$	64–68
LBS	103	205	105–183
CU.FT.	13.5	18.8	13.7–17.0

TO 26.0 CU.FT. (DOUBLE DOORS-S/S)

	MIN.	MAX.	OTHER
W	41	48	$35^3/_4$
D	$23^1/_8$	$28^1/_8$	$29^1/_2$
H	63	$65^1/_2$	66
LBS	183	444	
CU.FT.	16.81	26.0	21.3

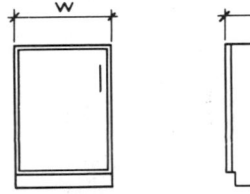

REFRIGERATOR-UNDER COUNTER

TO 7.0 CU.FT.

	MIN.	MAX.	OTHER
W	$23^3/_4$	36	$23^7/_8$–24
D	$27^7/_{16}$	26	$24^5/_8$–$25^3/_8$
H	$34^1/_4$	$34^1/_2$	
LBS	19	30	25–26
CU.FT.	5.0	6.62	6.08–6.4

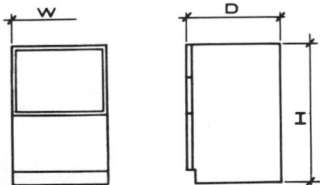

ICE CUBE MAKER

	MIN.	MAX.	OTHER
W	$14^1/_4$	36	16–$18^1/_8$
D	25	$34^1/_2$	$34^{13}/_{32}$
H	17	24	23–$23^{23}/_{32}$

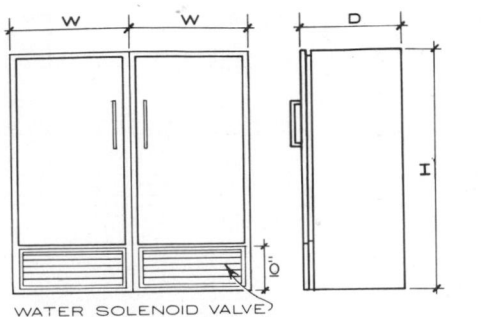

WATER SOLENOID VALVE LOCATED BEHIND GRILLE

REFRIGERATOR-FREEZER COMBINATION BUILT-IN WALL TYPE

	MIN.	MAX.	OTHER
W	33	36	
D	$23^{13}/_{16}$	24	$23^7/_8$
H	$41^3/_{32}$	$58^1/_4$	$42^7/_8$

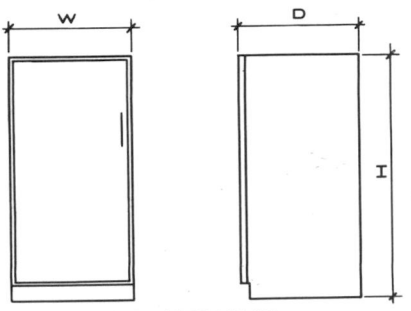

FREEZERS—UPRIGHT

4.0-12.0 CU. FT.

	MIN.	MAX.	OTHER
W	24	32	28–30
D	$28^1/_2$	$30^7/_8$	$29^1/_4$–$29^5/_8$
H	$56^1/_2$	64	$57^1/_2$–$59^3/_4$
LBS	336	416	352–406
CU.FT.	9.6	11.9	10.1–11.6

12.1-20.0 CU. FT.

	MIN.	MAX.	OTHER
W	$30^1/_2$	32	
D	$24^{11}/_{16}$	$33^1/_8$	$28^1/_8$–$30^7/_8$
H	$63^1/_4$	71	64–$69^3/_4$
LBS	441	710	473–648
CU.FT.	12.6	20.2	13.5–18.5

NOTE:

1. Door swings opposite to those shown are available.

2. Location, type and size of freezer varies within combination units.

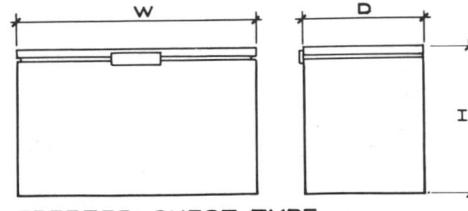

FREEZER-CHEST TYPE

	MIN.	MAX.	OTHER
W	40	$70^3/_8$	$46^1/_4$–60
D	28	$31^1/_2$	$30^5/_{16}$
H	$35^3/_4$	$36^5/_8$	$36^5/_{16}$
LBS	420	798	525–682
CU.FT.	12.0	22.8	15.0–19.5

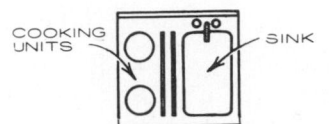

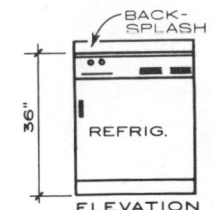
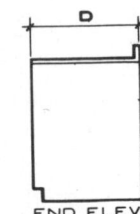

KITCHEN UNITS (KITCHENETTES)

COUNTER TOP DIMENSIONS 2 UNITS (GAS OR ELEC.)

	MIN.	MAX.	OTHER
W	24	48	29–40
D	$21^7/_8$	28	24–$26^1/_8$
BS	4	6	

3 UNITS (GAS OR ELEC.)

	MIN.	MAX.
W	28	29
D	28	28
BS	4	6

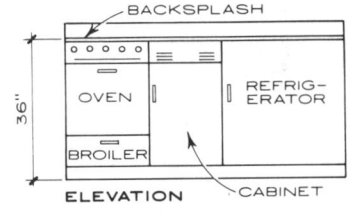

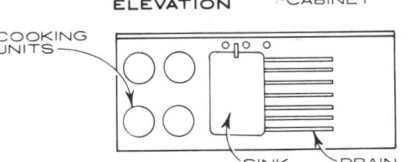

COUNTER TOP DIMENSIONS 2 UNITS (GAS OR ELEC.)

	MIN.	MAX.	OTHER
W	42	78	48–72
D	$25^{13}/_{16}$	$26^3/_4$	$26^1/_2$
BS	4	6	

3 UNITS (GAS OR ELEC.)

	MIN.	MAX.	OTHER
W	42	72	48–69
D	$24^1/_2$	28	25–$26^1/_2$
BS	4	6	

4 UNITS (GAS OR ELEC.)

	MIN.	MAX.	OTHER
W	48	87	50–84
D	24	25	$24^1/_2$
BS	4	6	$4^3/_4$

NOTE:

1. Matching upper storage cabinets available from manufacturers of kitchenettes.

2. When standard refrigerators & freezers are built into cabinet work, consult manufacturers literature for ventilation requirements, back clearance and door swing clearance.

R. E. Powe, Jr.; Hugh N. Jacobsen, AIA; Washington, D. C.

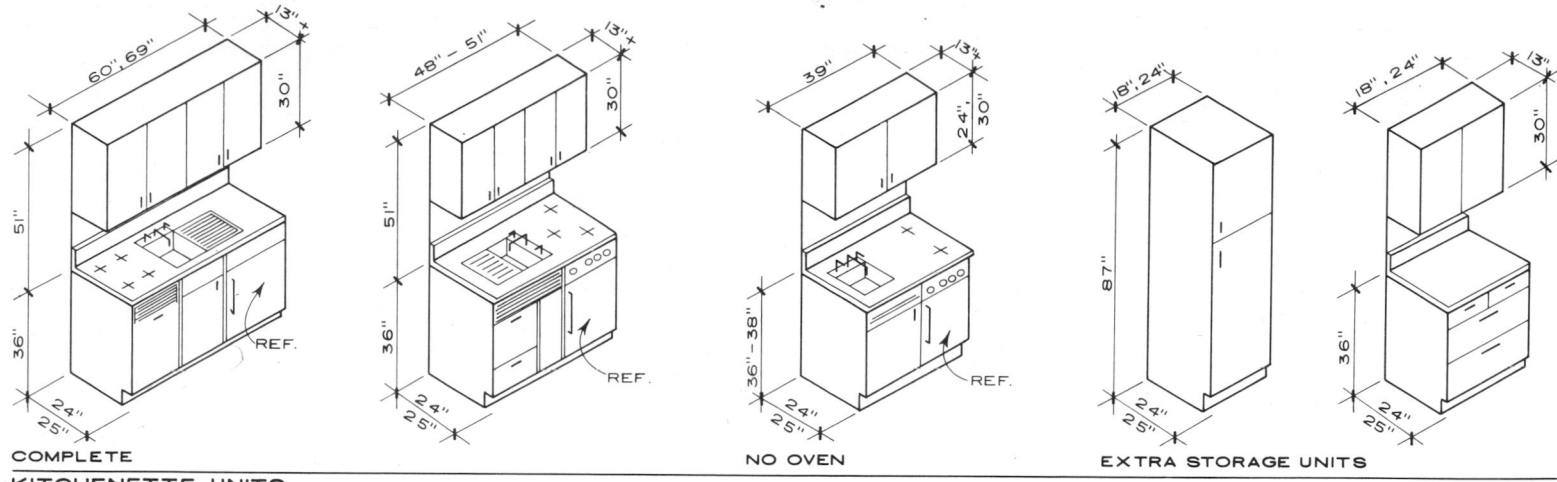

COMPLETE   **NO OVEN**   **EXTRA STORAGE UNITS**

KITCHENETTE UNITS

Lights and outlets optional, all units 84″ to 87″ high.

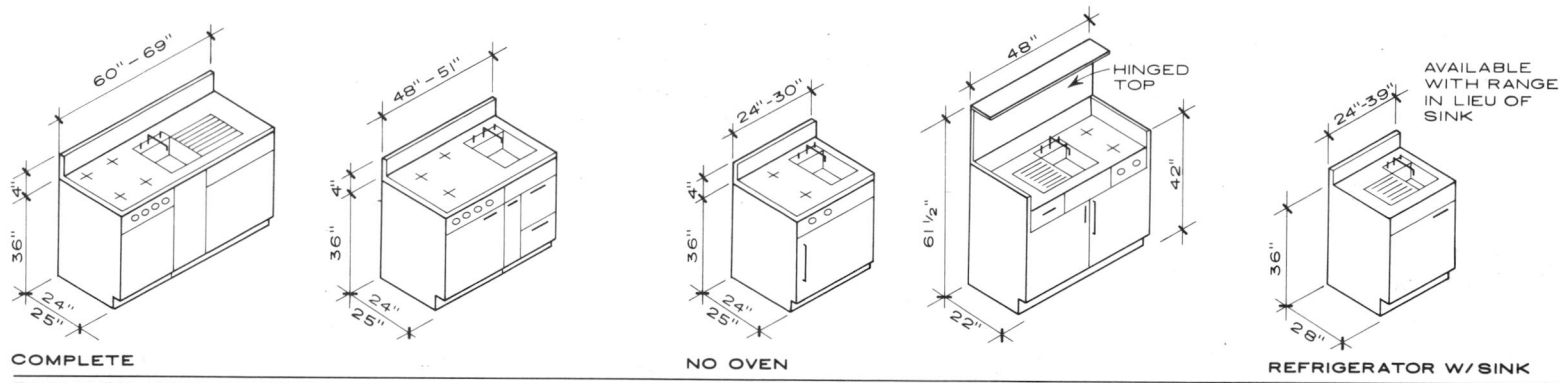

COMPLETE   **NO OVEN**   **REFRIGERATOR W/SINK**

PACKAGE KITCHENETTES

See manufacturer's data for actual dimensions.

NOTE:

Check clearance of refrigerator door and hardware against adjoining doors, jambs, roll-up door tracks etc.
Check clearance of lighting fixtures by upper cabinet doors, particularly when ceiling is furred down.

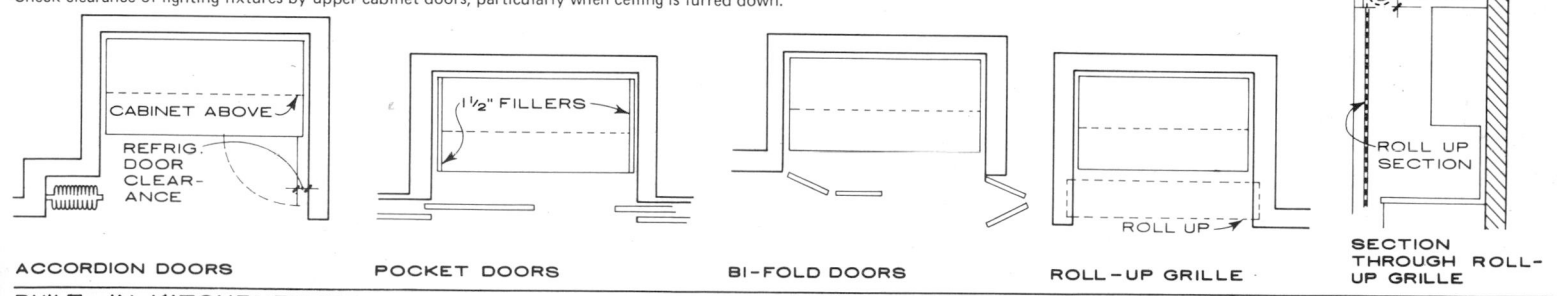

ACCORDION DOORS   **POCKET DOORS**   **BI-FOLD DOORS**   **ROLL-UP GRILLE**   **SECTION THROUGH ROLL-UP GRILLE**

BUILT-IN KITCHENETTES

Consult Local Building codes for kitchenette and built-in kitchenette requirements.
Recess widths: allow 3″ longer than sizes shown above. Provide for air circulation so warm air from refrigerator is not trapped in kitchen recess.

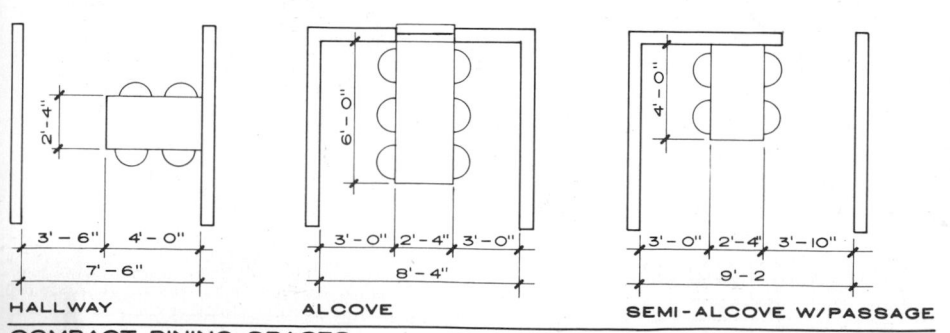

HALLWAY   **ALCOVE**   **SEMI-ALCOVE W/PASSAGE**

COMPACT DINING SPACES

NOTE:

See pages on Commercial Food Facilities for Dining Booths and Counters.

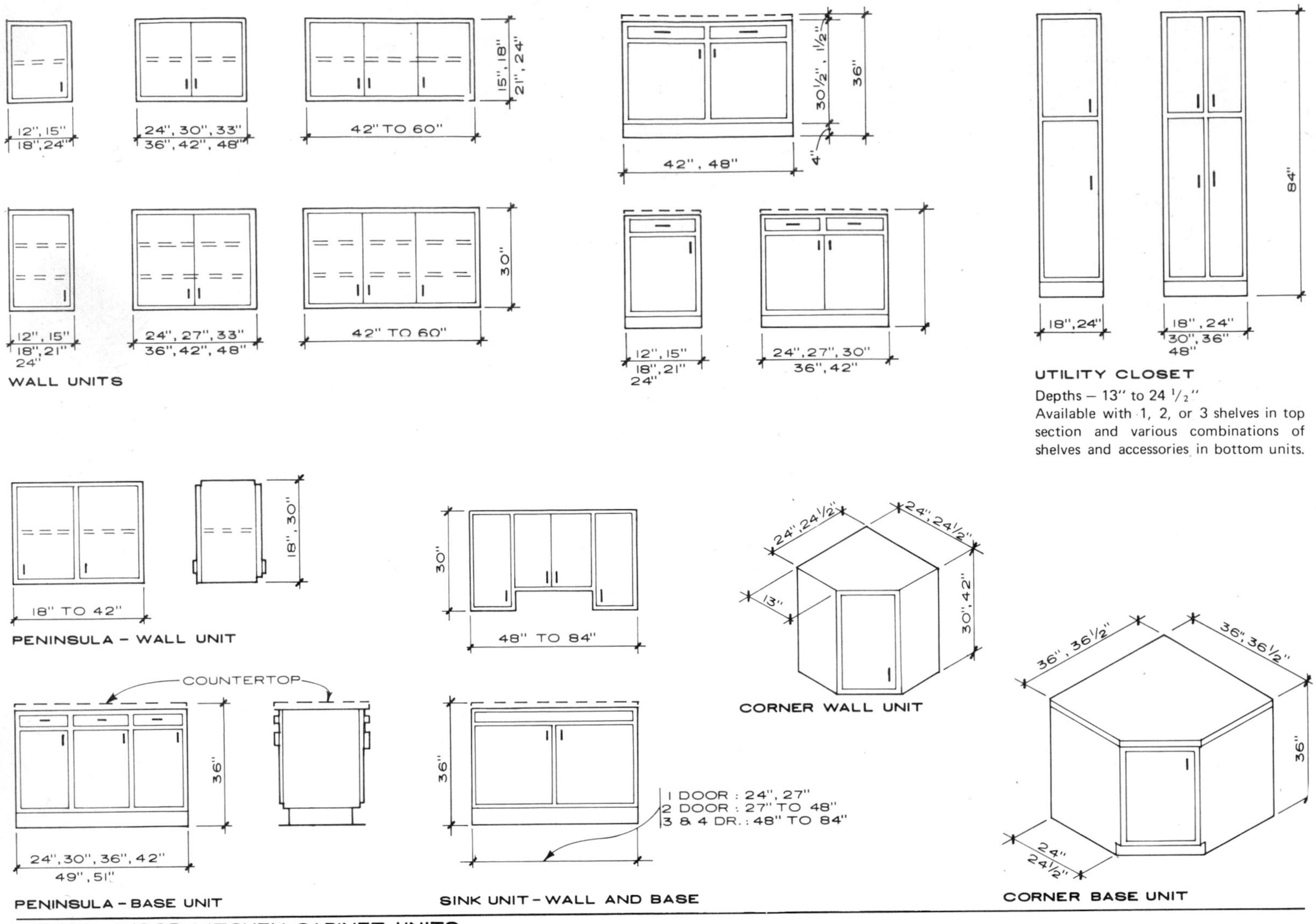

WALL UNITS

12", 15"
18", 24"

24", 30", 33"
36", 42", 48"

42" TO 60"

15", 18"
21", 24"

12", 15"
18", 21"
24"

24", 27", 33"
36", 42", 48"

42" TO 60"

30"

42", 48"

30½", 1½"

36"

4"

12", 15"
18", 21"
24"

24", 27", 30"
36", 42"

UTILITY CLOSET

18", 24"

18", 24"
30", 36"
48"

84"

Depths — 13" to 24 ½"
Available with 1, 2, or 3 shelves in top section and various combinations of shelves and accessories in bottom units.

PENINSULA – WALL UNIT

18" TO 42"

18", 30"

PENINSULA – BASE UNIT

COUNTERTOP

36"

24", 30", 36", 42"
49", 51"

SINK UNIT – WALL AND BASE

30"

48" TO 84"

36"

1 DOOR : 24", 27"
2 DOOR : 27" TO 48"
3 & 4 DR.: 48" TO 84"

CORNER WALL UNIT

24", 24½"

24", 24½"

13"

30", 42"

CORNER BASE UNIT

36", 36½"

36", 36½"

36"

24"
24½"

TYPICAL WOOD KITCHEN CABINET UNITS

Depth of wall units: 13" and 16". Depth of base units: 24" and 24 ½". Base units available with or without top drawer.

See "Metal Kitchen Cabinets" page for other combinations of drawers, cupboards, and accessories available for wood cabinets. Wood bases are integral with cabinet.

Filler pieces are available separate or integral. Consu manufacturers' data for additional information.

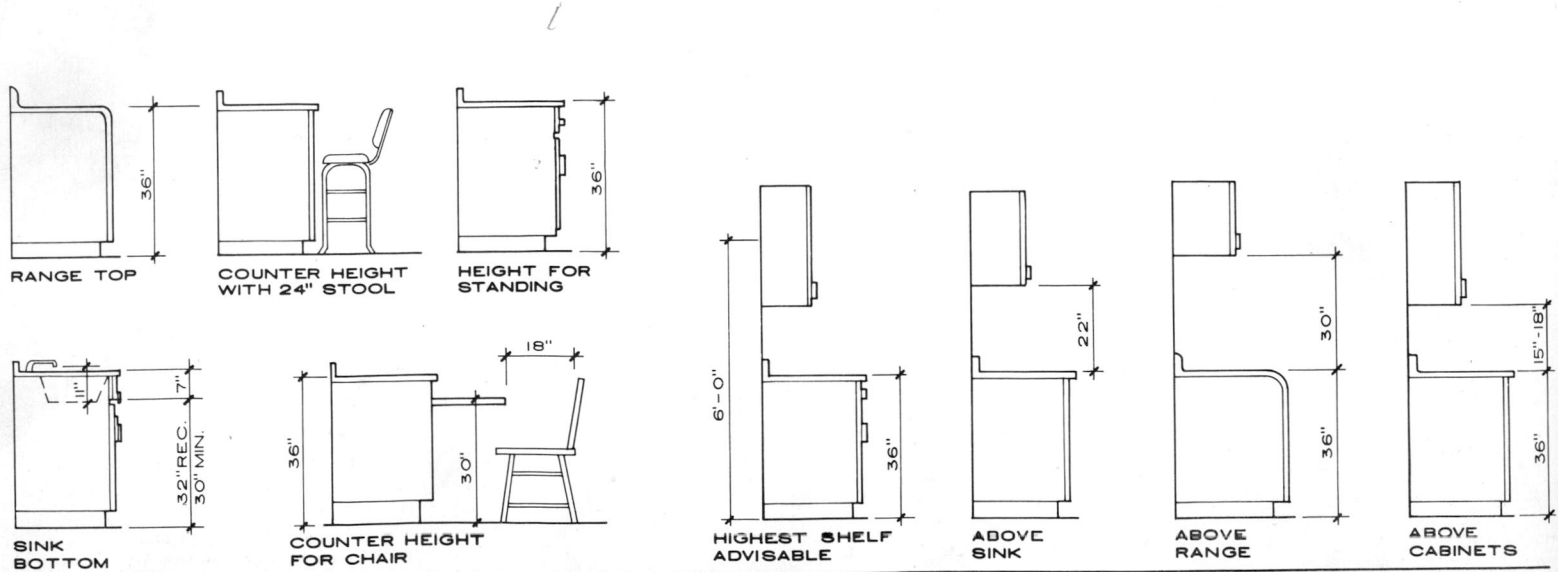

RANGE TOP — 36"

COUNTER HEIGHT WITH 24" STOOL

HEIGHT FOR STANDING — 36"

SINK BOTTOM — 7" — 32" REC. 30" MIN.

COUNTER HEIGHT FOR CHAIR — 18" — 36" — 30"

HIGHEST SHELF ADVISABLE — 6'-0" — 36"

ABOVE SINK — 22" — 36"

ABOVE RANGE — 30" — 36"

ABOVE CABINETS — 15"-18" — 36"

IDEAL WORK HEIGHTS AND CLEARANCES ABOVE COUNTERS

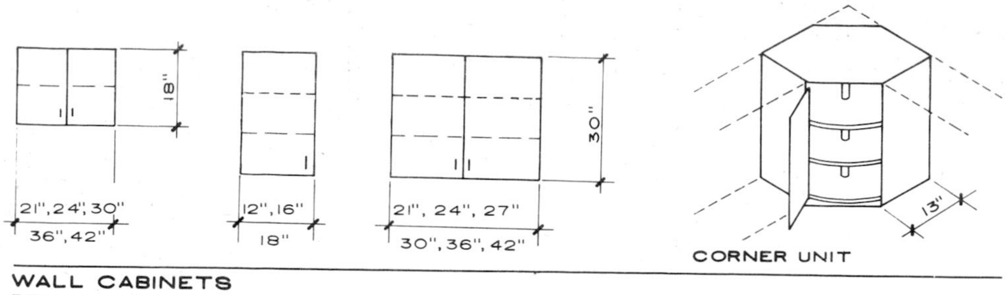

18"

21", 24", 30"
36", 42"

12", 16"
18"

21", 24", 27"
30", 36", 42"

30"

13"

CORNER UNIT

WALL CABINETS
DEPTH = 13"

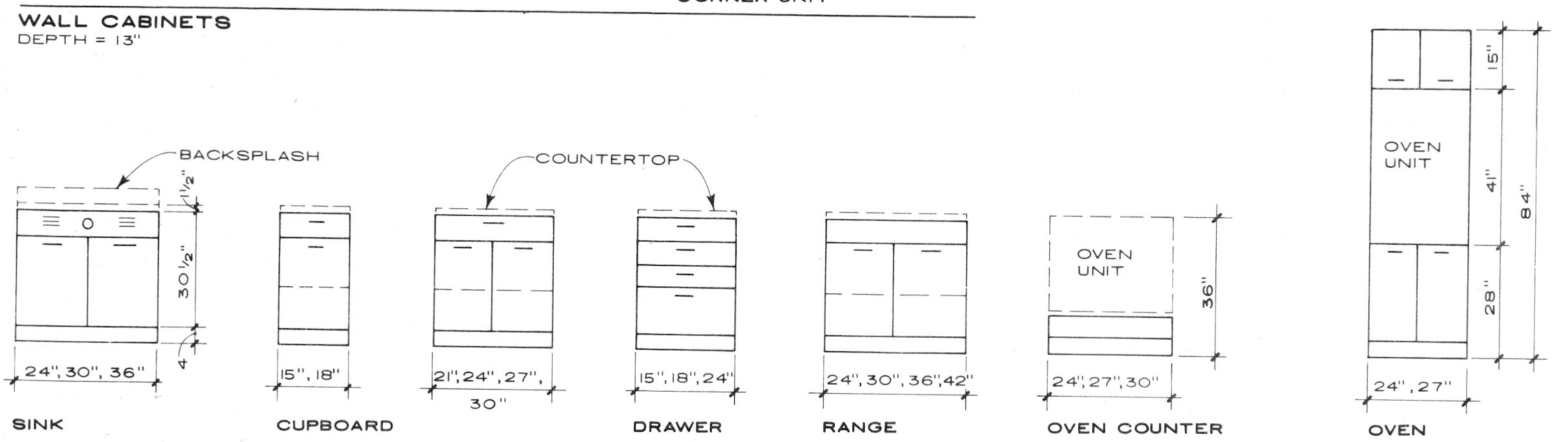

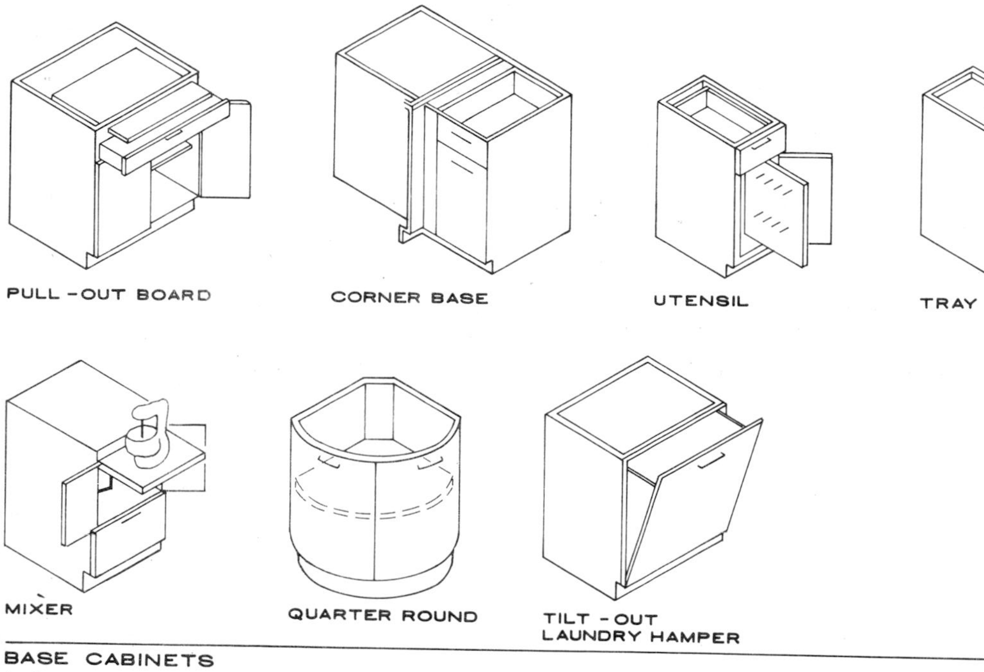

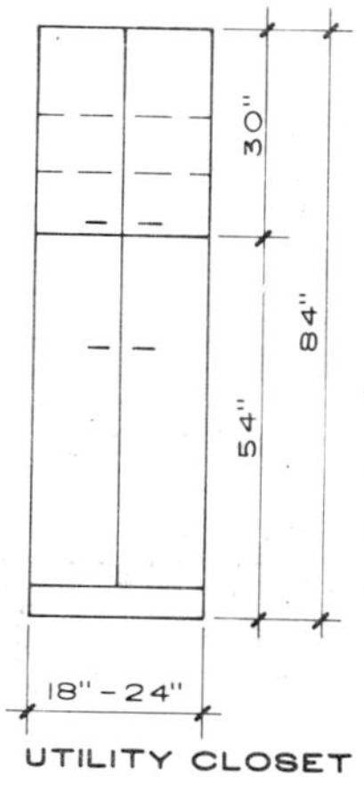

BACKSPLASH

COUNTERTOP

1 1/2"

30 1/2"

4"

24", 30", 36"

15", 18"

21", 24", 27",
30"

15", 18", 24"

24", 30", 36", 42"

OVEN
UNIT

36"

24", 27", 30"

SINK　　**CUPBOARD**　　**DRAWER**　　**RANGE**　　**OVEN COUNTER**

OVEN
UNIT

15"

41"

28"

84"

24", 27"

OVEN

PULL-OUT BOARD　　**CORNER BASE**　　**UTENSIL**　　**TRAY**

30"

84"

54"

18" – 24"

UTILITY CLOSET

Furnished with either
6 wire shelves or with
2 each of the following:
wire shelves, broom
holders and coat hooks.
Depth of unit 13" or
24 1/2".

MIXER　　**QUARTER ROUND**　　**TILT-OUT
LAUNDRY HAMPER**

BASE CABINETS

Depth = 24 1/2"
Bases are integral with cabinets.

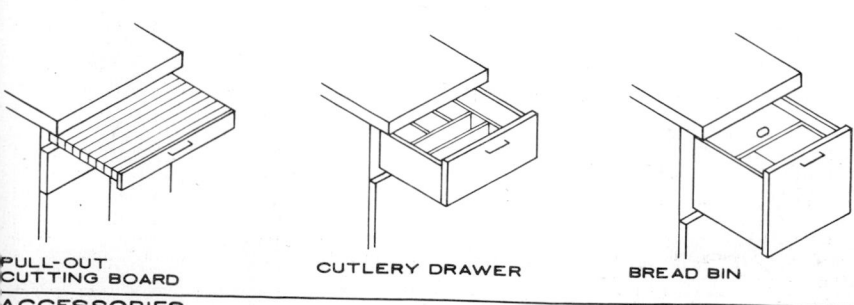

**PULL-OUT
CUTTING BOARD**　　**CUTLERY DRAWER**　　**BREAD BIN**

ACCESSORIES

NOTE :

Sizes and units shown are most common.

Basic units are available with or without top drawer.

Counter tops may be of stainless steel, plastic laminate on
wood, laminated wood or linoleum on wood.

Filler pieces are available for most stack sizes to fit ends or
inside corners of wall, base and full height units.

See manufacturer's data for filler pieces, special sizes, units,
accessories and finishes.

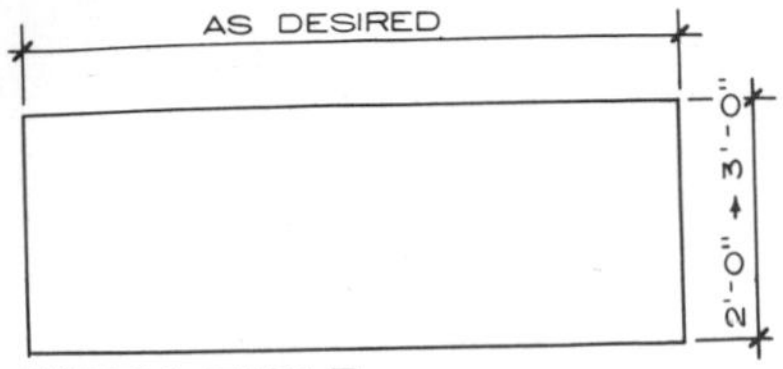

AS DESIRED

3'-0" / **2'-0"**

WORK TABLE
WOOD & METAL TOPS, METAL LEGS, DRAWERS & UNDERSHELVES
HT. 34" TO 36".

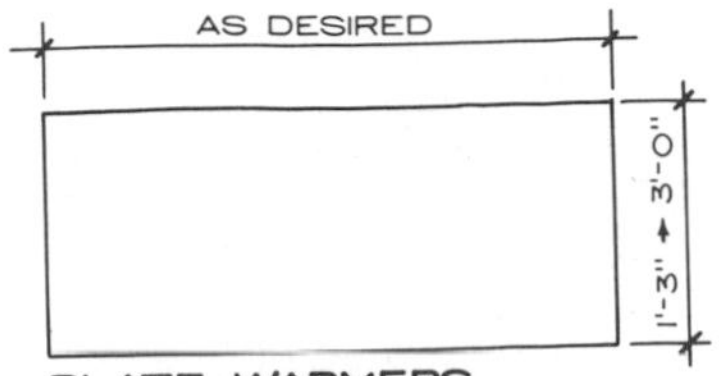

AS DESIRED

3'-0" / **1'-3"**

PLATE WARMERS
METAL TOPS, BODY DOORS & SHELVES HEATED BY GAS, ELECTRICITY OR STEAM. MAY BE FREE-STANDING OR BUILT-IN OTHER FIXTURES
HT. 2'-6" TO 6'-0"

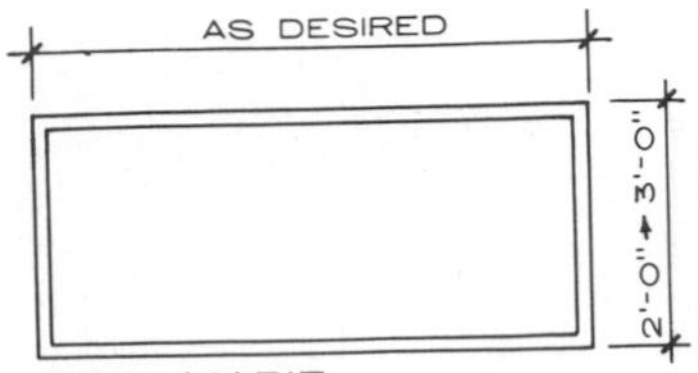

AS DESIRED

3'-0" / **2'-0"**

BAIN MARIE
METAL HEATED BY GAS, ELECTRICITY OR STEAM. MAY BE FREE STANDING OR SET INTO COOK'S TABLE
HT. 34" TO 36"

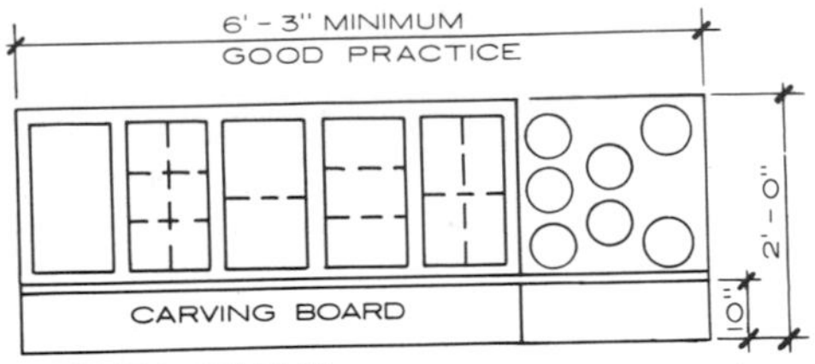

6'-3" MINIMUM
GOOD PRACTICE

2'-0"

CARVING BOARD

STEAM TABLE

1. Top openings are 12" x 20" or 12" x 18". Pans are full, half, third, quarter or sixth sizes, ϕ's = 6 ½", 8 ½" & 10 ½".

2. Table may be dry heated (gas or electric) or wet steam heated (gas, electric or steam).

3. Table may be freestanding or fitted into cook's tables or counters, may have a serving shelf above, a lower area fitted with a warming unit, etc.

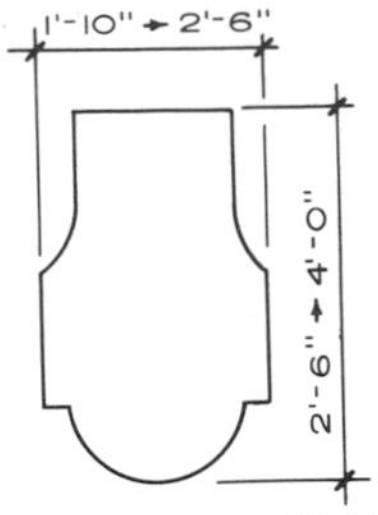

1'-10" ← 2'-6"   **2'-6" ← 4'-0"**

MIXING MACHINE
MANY TYPES & SIZES
HT. 26" TO 65"

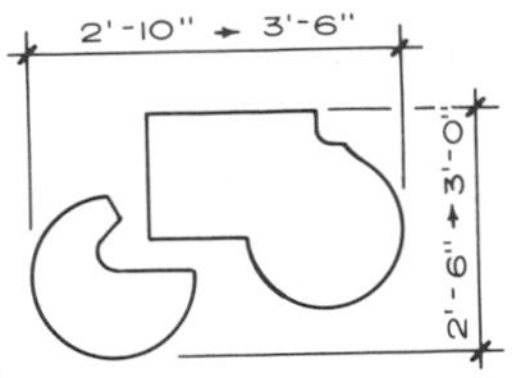

2'-10" ← 3'-6"   **2'-6" ← 3'-0"**

FOOD CUTTER
MANY TYPES & SIZES
HT. 17" TO 22". ON LEGS OR TABLE

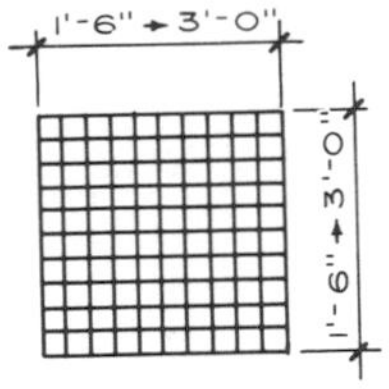

1'-6" ← 3'-0"   **1'-6" ← 3'-0"**

BUTCHER BLOCK
WOOD ON LEGS
HT. 34" TO 36"

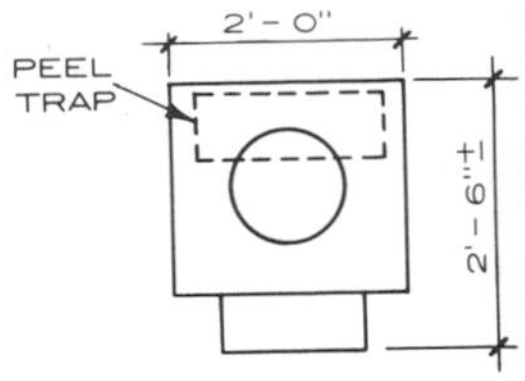

2'-0"   PEEL TRAP   **2'-6" ± 1'**

PARER
MANY TYPES & SIZES
HT. 48" TO 62"

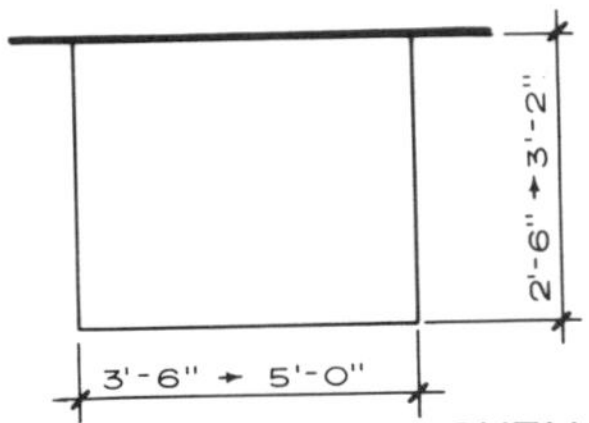

2'-6" ← 3'-2"

3'-6" ← 5'-0"

BAKE & ROAST OVEN
GAS OR ELECTRIC. MANY TYPES & SIZES
HT. 46" TO 66"

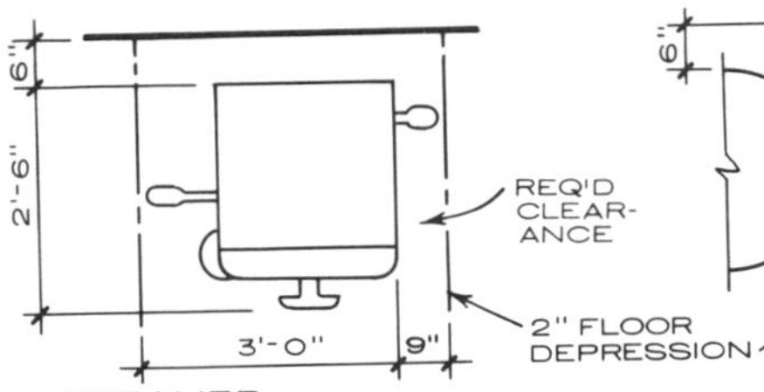

6"   **2'-6"**   REQ'D CLEARANCE   2" FLOOR DEPRESSION

3'-0"   **9"**

STEAMER
STEAM, GAS OR ELECTRIC
APPROX. HT. 60"

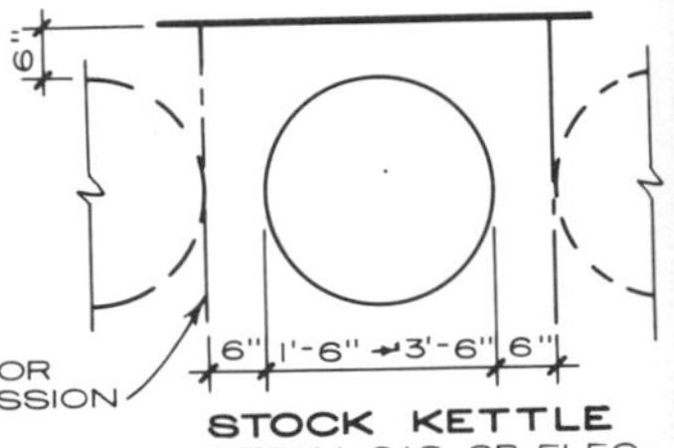

6"   **6"**

6" ← 1'-6" ← 3'-6" ← 6"

STOCK KETTLE
STEAM, GAS OR ELECTRIC. MANY TYPES & SIZES
HT. 32" TO 34"

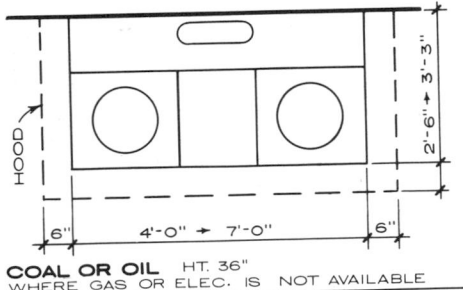

2'-6" ← 3'-3"

HOOD

6"   4'-0" ← 7'-0"   6"

COAL OR OIL   HT. 36"
WHERE GAS OR ELEC. IS NOT AVAILABLE

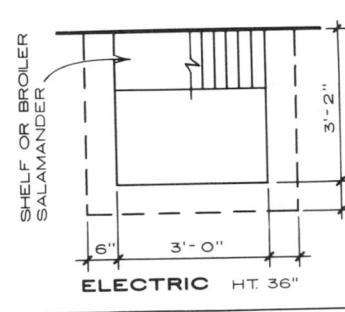

SHELF OR BROILER SALAMANDER

3'-2"

6"   3'-0"

ELECTRIC   HT. 36"

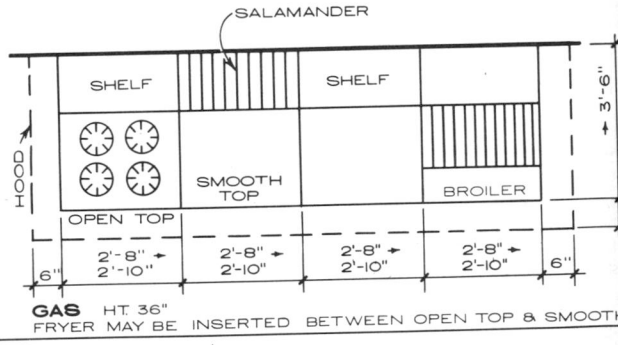

SALAMANDER

3'-6"

SHELF   SHELF

OPEN TOP   SMOOTH TOP   BROILER

HOOD

6"   2'-8" ← 2'-10"   2'-8" ← 2'-10"   2'-8" ← 2'-10"   2'-8" ← 2'-10"   6"

GAS   HT. 36"
FRYER MAY BE INSERTED BETWEEN OPEN TOP & SMOOTH

RANGES

MISC. KITCHEN MACHINES

Meat saws
Meat grinders
Meat slicers
Bread slicers
Silver washers
Silver burnishers
Dish washers
Glass washers
Toasters
Griddles
Hot plates
Ice makers
Ice cream cabinets

NOTES

1. Provide hoods connected to mechanically ventilated ductwork, or other approved type of ventilation for bake and roast ovens, steamers, stock kettles, fryers and ranges.

2. Ranges, fryers and ovens should have legs or be set on masonry platforms.

3. Steamers, parers and kettles should be placed in depressed floor areas with drains, or provide properly sloped troughs with drains in floor at front of equipment. Acid resistant grout recommended for tile in these areas.

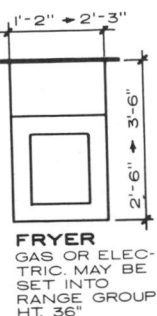

1'-2" ← 2'-3"

2'-6" ← 3'-6"

FRYER
GAS OR ELECTRIC. MAY BE SET INTO RANGE GROUP
HT. 36"

Anthony J. Amendola, AIA; Forest Hills, New York

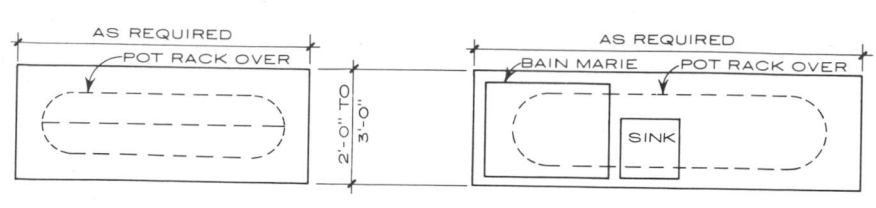

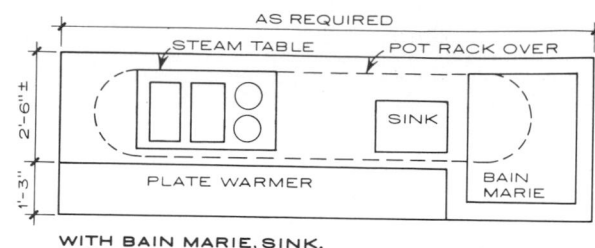

PLAIN
COOK'S TABLES

WITH BAIN MARIE & SINK

WITH BAIN MARIE, SINK, STEAM TABLE & PLATE WARMER

These tables are available in many sizes, types, and designs. Design is based on intended use. Pot racks located over tables can be hung from ceiling or supported on standards. Space between tables and ranges is usually 3'–6''.

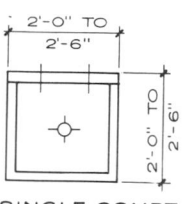

SINGLE COMPT.
UTILITY

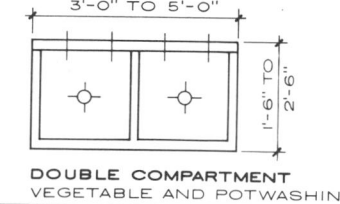

DOUBLE COMPARTMENT
VEGETABLE AND POTWASHING

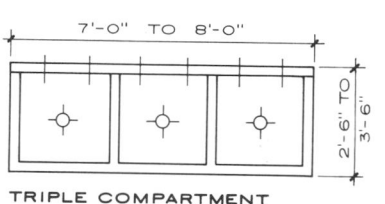

TRIPLE COMPARTMENT
POT WASHING

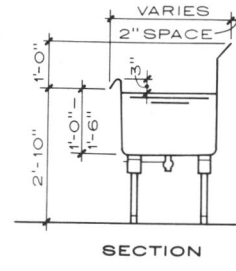

SECTION

SINKS

Can be fabricated in any size required. Corners, horizontally or vertically, can be of square or round design. Usually furnished with drainboards at one or both ends. Drainboards can be any length, widths same as sink. Can be designed to set into top of cook's table, counter, work or dish table. Sinks can be supported on chair carriers imbedded in wall instead of on legs.

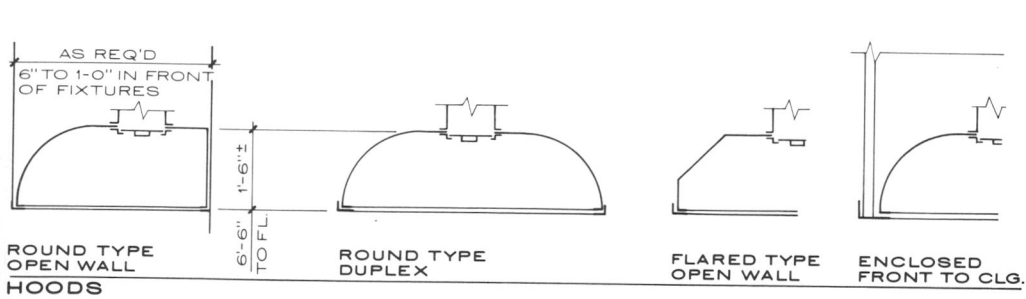

ROUND TYPE OPEN WALL

ROUND TYPE DUPLEX

FLARED TYPE OPEN WALL

ENCLOSED FRONT TO CLG.

HOODS

Many types and designs of hoods are possible. All can be made of galvanized iron or stainless steel. Enclosed fronts can be metal furring and plaster, tile, or metal sheets. Place hood over ranges, kettles, steamers, ovens, dishwashers, glasswashers, urns, etc. Connect to vent system and exhaust to outside air. Install grease filters over all range, fryer and oven areas or as required by local codes.

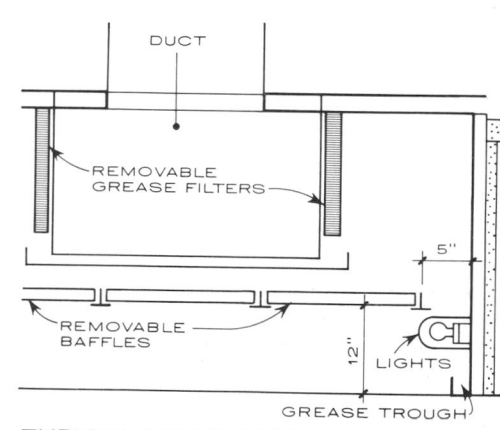

TYPICAL HOOD DETAIL WITH GREASE FILTERS

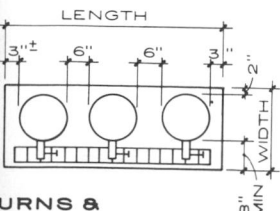

URNS & URN STANDS

2 PIECE SET				3 PIECE SET						URN SIZES		
CAPACITY (GALS.)		STAND SIZE		CAPACITY (GALS.)			STAND SIZE			CAPACITY (GALS.)		DIA.
COFFEE	WATER	LENGTH	WIDTH	COFFEE	WATER	COFFEE	LENGTH	WIDTH	COFFEE	WATER	(IN.)
3	6	2'-10"	1'-9"	3	6	3	4'-3	1'-9"	3	6	11
4	8	3'-0"	1'-10"	4	8	4	4'-6"	1'-10"	4	8	12
5	10	3'-0"	1'-11"	5	10	5	4'-10"	1'-11"	5	10	13
6	12	3'-4"	2'-0"	6	12	6	5'-0"	2'-0"	6	12	14
8	16	3'-6"	2'-1"	8	16	8	5'-4"	2'-1"	8	15	15
10	20	3'-8"	2'-2"	10	20	10	5'-6"	2'-2"	10	20	16

Urn stands are made to accommodate the number and sizes of urns set upon them. Urns are made in many designs and sizes for coffee, tea, chocolate, water, fruit juices, etc.

They may be heated by gas, steam, or electricity. "Combination" type urns are available for holding both coffee and water in one unit.

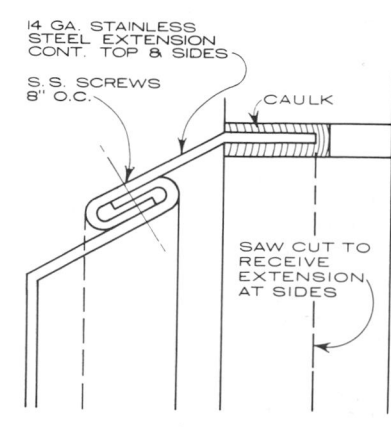

WALL SPLASH DETAIL
(WHEN CLOSURE IS REQUIRED)

Anthony J. Amendola, AIA; Forest Hills, New York

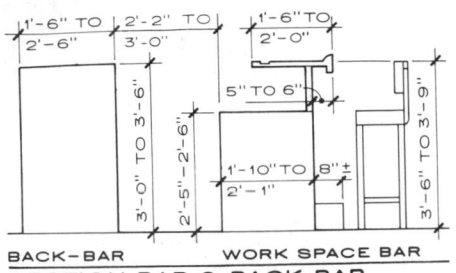

BACK-BAR   WORK SPACE BAR

SECTION-BAR & BACK-BAR

NOTE:

All stock units shown fit under bars in various sizes and combinations, as may be required by design.

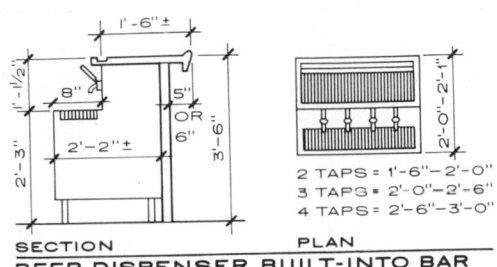

SECTION   PLAN

2 TAPS = 1'-6"-2'-0"
3 TAPS = 2'-0"-2'-6"
4 TAPS = 2'-6"-3'-0"

BEER DISPENSER BUILT-INTO BAR

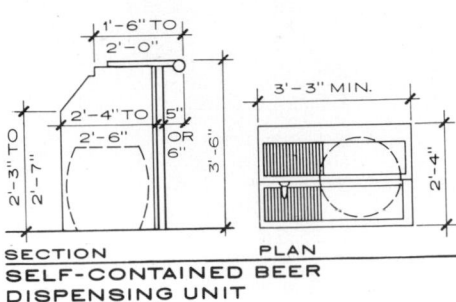

SECTION   PLAN

SELF-CONTAINED BEER DISPENSING UNIT

SLIDE COVER

ICE STORAGE CABINET

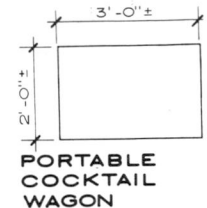

PORTABLE COCKTAIL WAGON

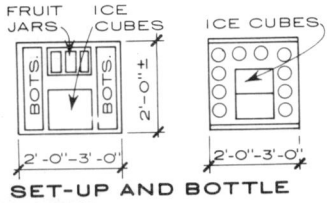

FRUIT JARS   ICE CUBES   ICE CUBES

BOTS.   BOTS.

SET-UP AND BOTTLE RACKS

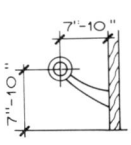

SANDWICH BOARD

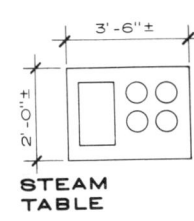

STEAM TABLE

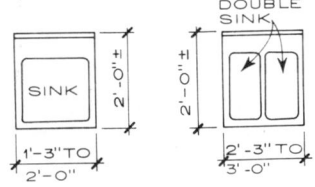

SINK   DOUBLE SINK

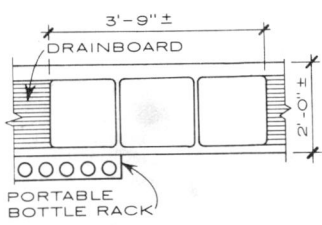

DRAINBOARD

PORTABLE BOTTLE RACK

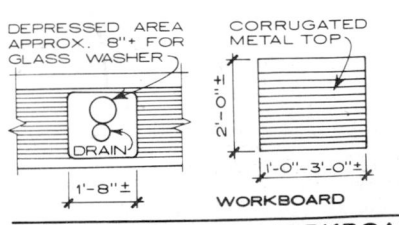

DEPRESSED AREA APPROX. 8"± FOR GLASS WASHER

DRAIN

CORRUGATED METAL TOP

WORKBOARD

UNITS OF SINK & WORKBOARDS

Anthony J. Amendola, AIA; Forest Hills, New York

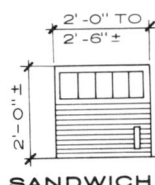

GENERALLY 1¾" DIA.

METAL RAILS

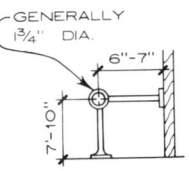

TERRAZZO ETC.

MASONRY STEP

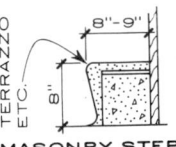

METAL CORNER

WOOD STEP

FOOT RAILS AND STEPS

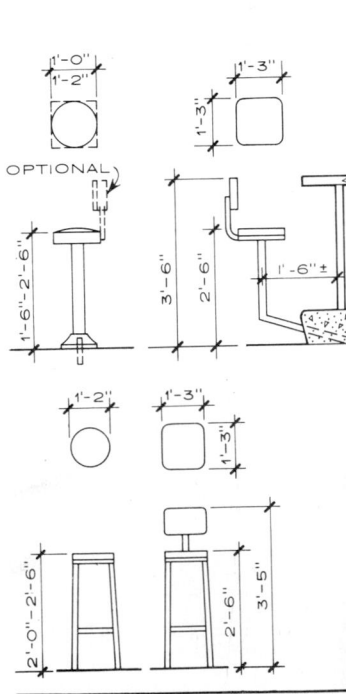

OPTIONAL

STOOLS
THERE ARE MANY STYLES AND SHAPES AVAILABLE

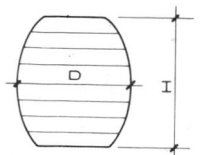
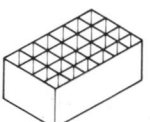

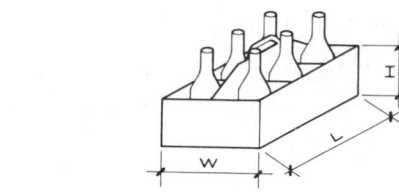

Cardboard or Wood
Cases; 16" to 19" x 11"
to 13" x 8" to 10" h.

CHAMPAGNE BUCKET

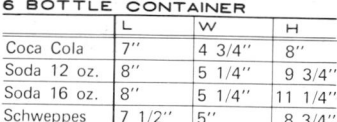

KEGS

	D	H
Full	23"	25"
1/2	17 1/8"	25"
1/4	14 1/2"	16 1/2"

Kegs, usually aluminum.
Full keg holds 496 8 oz.
glasses.

BEER

BOTTLES

	D	H
Small	2 3/4"	6"
Av'g.	2 3/4"	9"
Quart	3 1/2"	9 3/4"

Can Sizes: 2 5/8"
diameter. 4 3/4"
or 6 1/4" high.
Packed also in 6-Packs.

BOTTLES

	D	H
Wine	3"	14 1/2"
Whiskey	3 1/2"	11 1/2"
Gin	3 1/4"	11 1/2"
Champagne 1/5	3 1/2"	12 3/4"
Brandy	3"	12"
(fine champagne)	3 1/2"	10 1/2"
Vermouth — 30 oz.	3 1/4"	12 1/2"
— 25 3/5 oz.	3"	12 1/4"

Sizes given are for std. round bottles.
Wine sizes vary with type.
Size given is usual max.

LIQUOR

BOTTLES

	D	H
Quart	3 3/8"	11 3/4"
Pint—Max.	2 1/2"	11"
Split	2 1/4"	8"
12 oz. Soda	2 1/2"	9 1/2"

Can Sizes: 2 5/8" diameter
4 3/4" high, packed in six-
packs of 5 1/4" Wide, 8 1/4"
long, 5" high

6 BOTTLE CONTAINER

	L	W	H
Coca Cola	7"	4 3/4"	8"
Soda 12 oz.	8"	5 1/4"	9 3/4"
Soda 16 oz.	8"	5 1/4"	11 1/4"
Schweppes	7 1/2"	5"	8 3/4"

MIXES AND SOFT DRINKS

CONTAINER SIZES

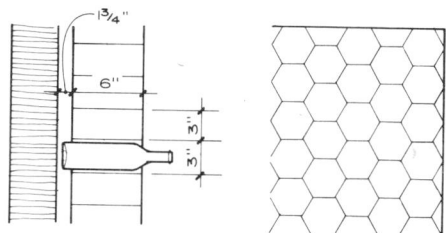

SMALL SIZE FOR PINTS
CAPACITY 14 BOTTLES PER SQ. FT.

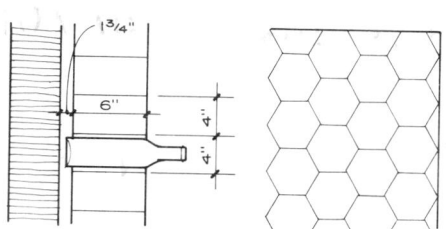

MEDIUM SIZE FOR QUARTS
CAPACITY 9 1/2 BOTTLES PER SQ. FT.

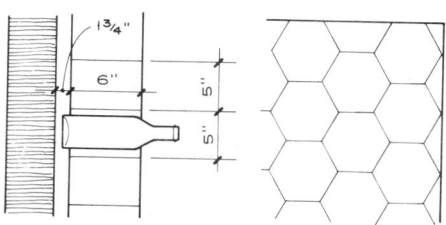

LARGE SIZE FOR CORDIALS
CAPACITY 6 1/2 BOTTLES PER SQ. FT.

METAL HONEYCOMB BOTTLE STORAGE RACKS

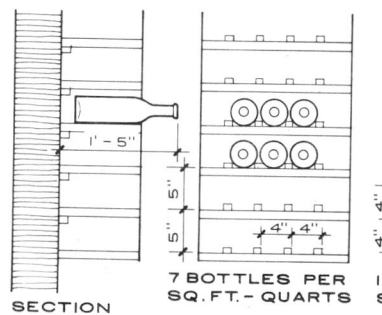

SECTION

WOOD BOARD SHELVES

7 BOTTLES PER
SQ. FT. - QUARTS

12 BOTTLES PER
SQ. FT. - QUARTS

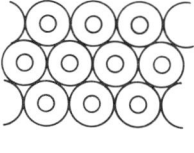

Bottle Size	Number per sq. ft.
2 1/2" d.	20
2 3/4" d.	18
3" d.	14
3 1/2" d.	9

These figures also for
standing bottles.

STACKED BOTTLES

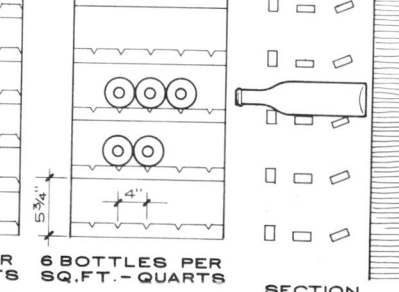

11 BOTTLES PER
SQ. FT. - QUARTS

6 BOTTLES PER
SQ. FT. - QUARTS

SECTION

WOOD SLAT SHELVES

BOTTLE STORAGE

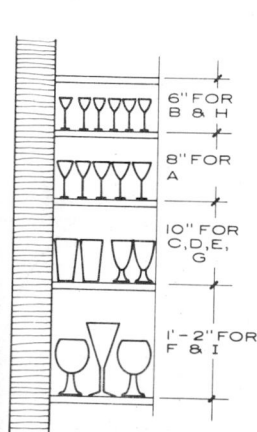

6" FOR B & H	
8" FOR A	
10" FOR C, D, E, G	
1'-2" FOR F & I	

Lineal feet for 1 doz. glasses on 1'-0" shelf

Type		Glass d.	Glass h.	Lin. ft. of shelf
A	Cordial	1/2"–2"	3 1/2"–4"	4"–5"
B	Cocktail	2 1/2"–3"	2"–4"	8"–10"
C	Wine	2"–2 1/2"	5"	5"–8"
D	Champag.	3 1/2"–4"	5"–6"	16"–19"
E	Beer	3 1/2"	5"	16"
F	Pilsener	3"	8 1/2"	12"
G	Highball	2 3/4"	5 1/2"	9"
H	Old. Fash.	3"	3 1/4"	12"
I	Brandy	4"–5"	6"–8"	19"–36"

The above are average sizes and allowances. No standards
exist.

SECTION

GLASS STORAGE

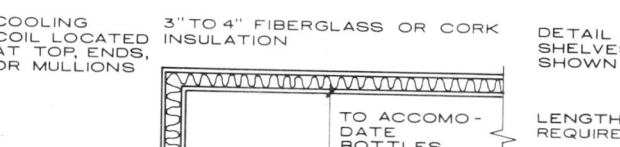

COOLING COIL located AT TOP, ENDS, OR MULLIONS

3" TO 4" FIBERGLASS OR CORK INSULATION

DETAIL OF SHELVES AS SHOWN ABOVE

TO ACCOMO-DATE BOTTLES

LENGTH AS REQUIRED

PLAN

WINE BOTTLE STORAGE REFRIGERATOR

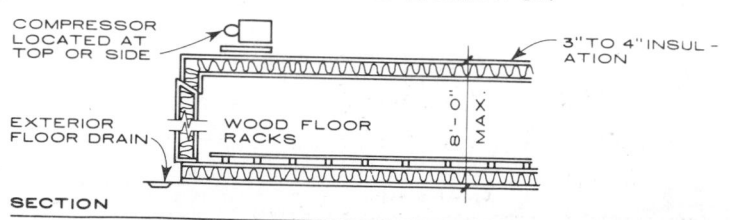

COMPRESSOR LOCATED AT TOP OR SIDE

3" TO 4" INSUL-ATION

EXTERIOR FLOOR DRAIN

WOOD FLOOR RACKS

8'-0" MAX.

SECTION

WALK-IN BEER COOLER

J. C. Mayer; William B. Tabler, FAIA; New York, New York

CENTER TRACK

Center track—supported at either the floor or ceiling. Panels are connected to each other and are either manually or power operated.

NOTE : SOME SETS OF DOORS START WITH A HALF PANEL.

€ OF TRACK

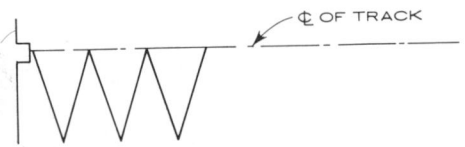

EDGE TRACK

Edge track—supported at either the floor or ceiling. Panels are connected to each other and are either manually or power operated.

€ OF TRACK

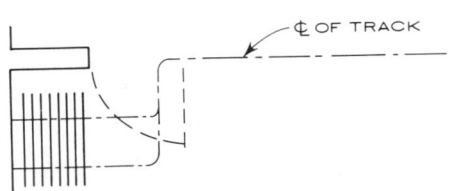

STACKING POCKET

Ceiling suspended, unconnected panels, manually operated only.

€ OF TRACK

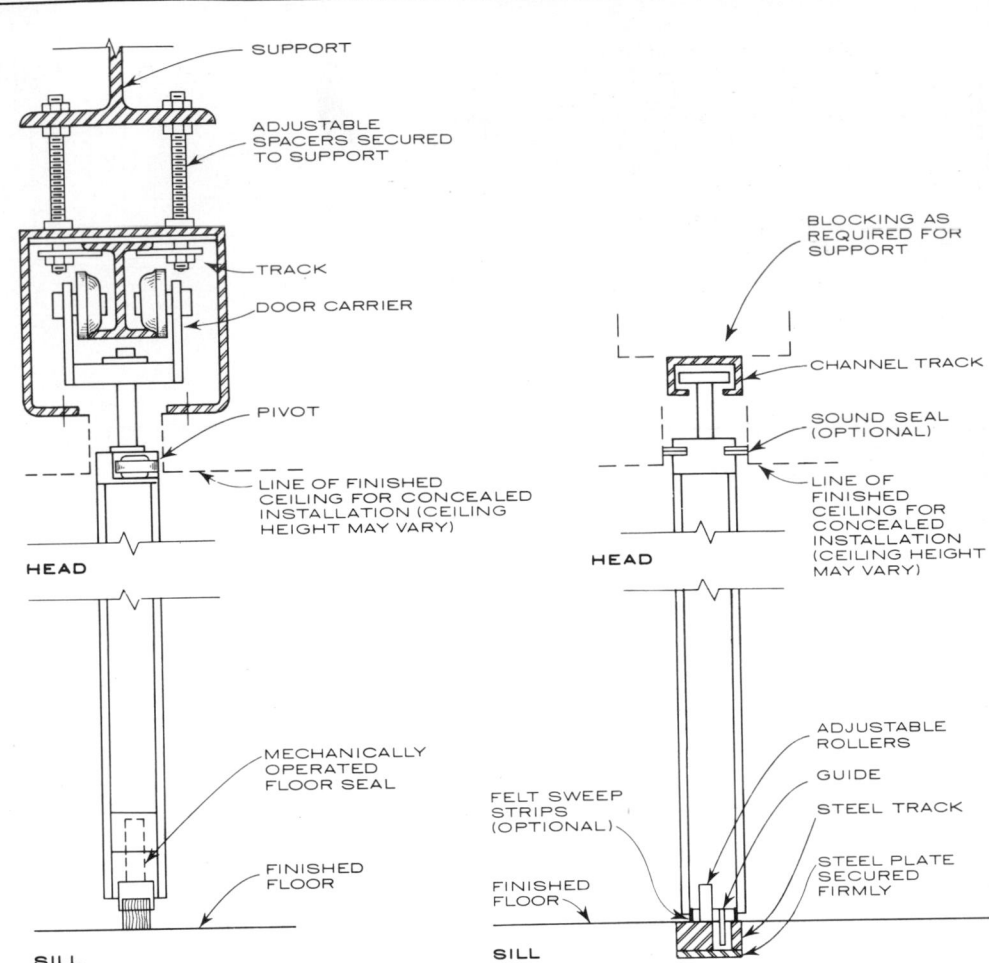

SUPPORT

ADJUSTABLE SPACERS SECURED TO SUPPORT

TRACK

DOOR CARRIER

PIVOT

LINE OF FINISHED CEILING FOR CONCEALED INSTALLATION (CEILING HEIGHT MAY VARY)

HEAD

MECHANICALLY OPERATED FLOOR SEAL

FINISHED FLOOR

SILL

BLOCKING AS REQUIRED FOR SUPPORT

CHANNEL TRACK

SOUND SEAL (OPTIONAL)

LINE OF FINISHED CEILING FOR CONCEALED INSTALLATION (CEILING HEIGHT MAY VARY)

HEAD

ADJUSTABLE ROLLERS

GUIDE

STEEL TRACK

FELT SWEEP STRIPS (OPTIONAL)

STEEL PLATE SECURED FIRMLY

FINISHED FLOOR

SILL

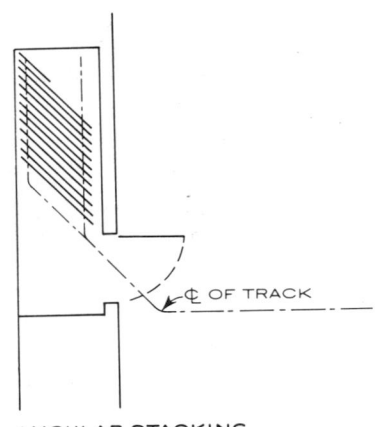

ANGULAR STACKING

€ OF TRACK

€ OF TRACK

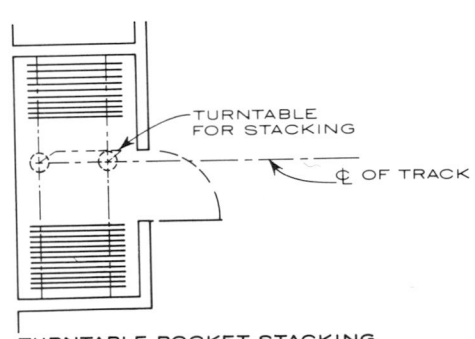

TURNTABLE FOR STACKING

€ OF TRACK

TURNTABLE POCKET STACKING

Door panels are stacked on a pair of overhead tracks.

Manually operated track switches are provided to transfer panels to parallel stacking tracks as indicated.

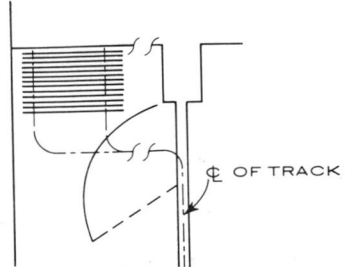

€ OF TRACK

REMOTE STACK LOCATION WITH RIDE PANEL PASSAGE DOOR

VARIATIONS OF TYPE STACKING

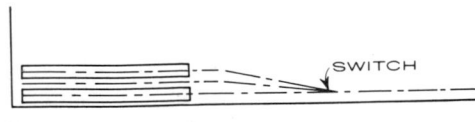

SWITCH

STACKING WITH SWITCHES

JAMB-DETAIL "1"
SCALE: 1½" = 1'-0"

JAMB-DETAIL "2"
SCALE: 1½" = 1'-0"

NOTES:

1. Panel thickness, width, height, finish and acoustic quality vary dependent upon size of opening, usage and manufacturer.

2. Enclosures for movable partitions vary. See manufacturers literature for required clearances in pockets.

3. Overhead structure must be sufficient to support movable partition and must be properly anchored and braced.

4. Leaf type partitions are recommended where rigidity and flat plane storage are important factors.

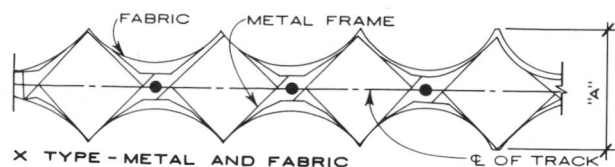

X TYPE - METAL AND FABRIC

"X" Type door is built of a metal frame with a vinyl fabric covering. Various insulation materials produce a wide range of acoustic properties. Dimensions given vary according to manufacturer. "A" Dimension varies from 3 $\frac{1}{4}$" – 8 $\frac{1}{2}$".

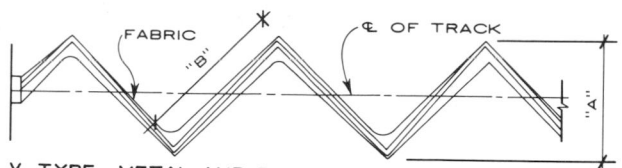

V TYPE - METAL AND FABRIC

"A" Dimension varies from 3 $\frac{1}{2}$" – 10 $\frac{3}{8}$" in extended position:

"B" Dimension varies from 2" – 4 $\frac{5}{8}$".

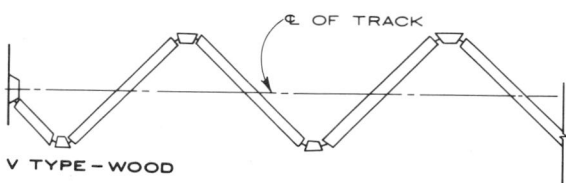

V TYPE - WOOD

"V" Type door is available in metal with fabric covering or in solid wood panels.

TYPICAL ACCORDION PARTITIONS

"X" and "V" Types may be installed on a curved track with a minimum radius of 3 – 6".

All "X" and "V" partitions are ceiling supported and may be manually or power operated.

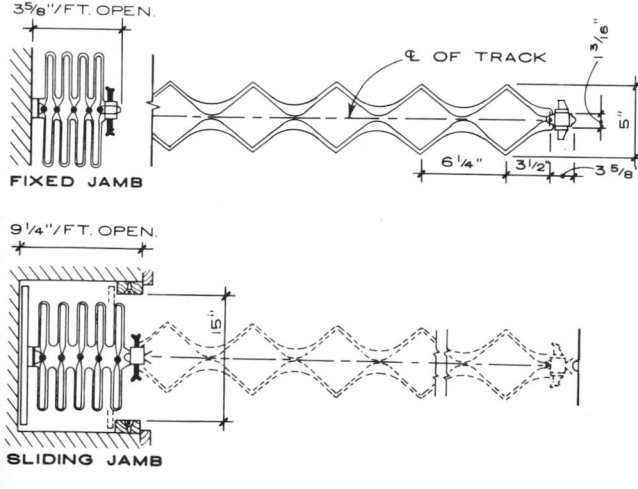

FIXED JAMB

SLIDING JAMB

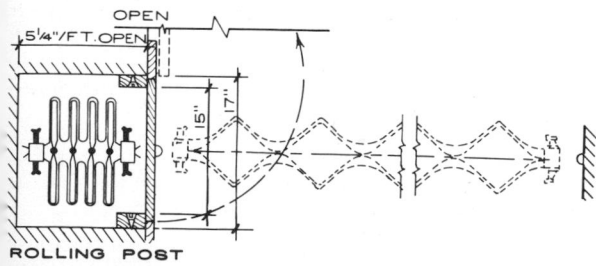

ROLLING POST

STACKING ARRANGEMENTS

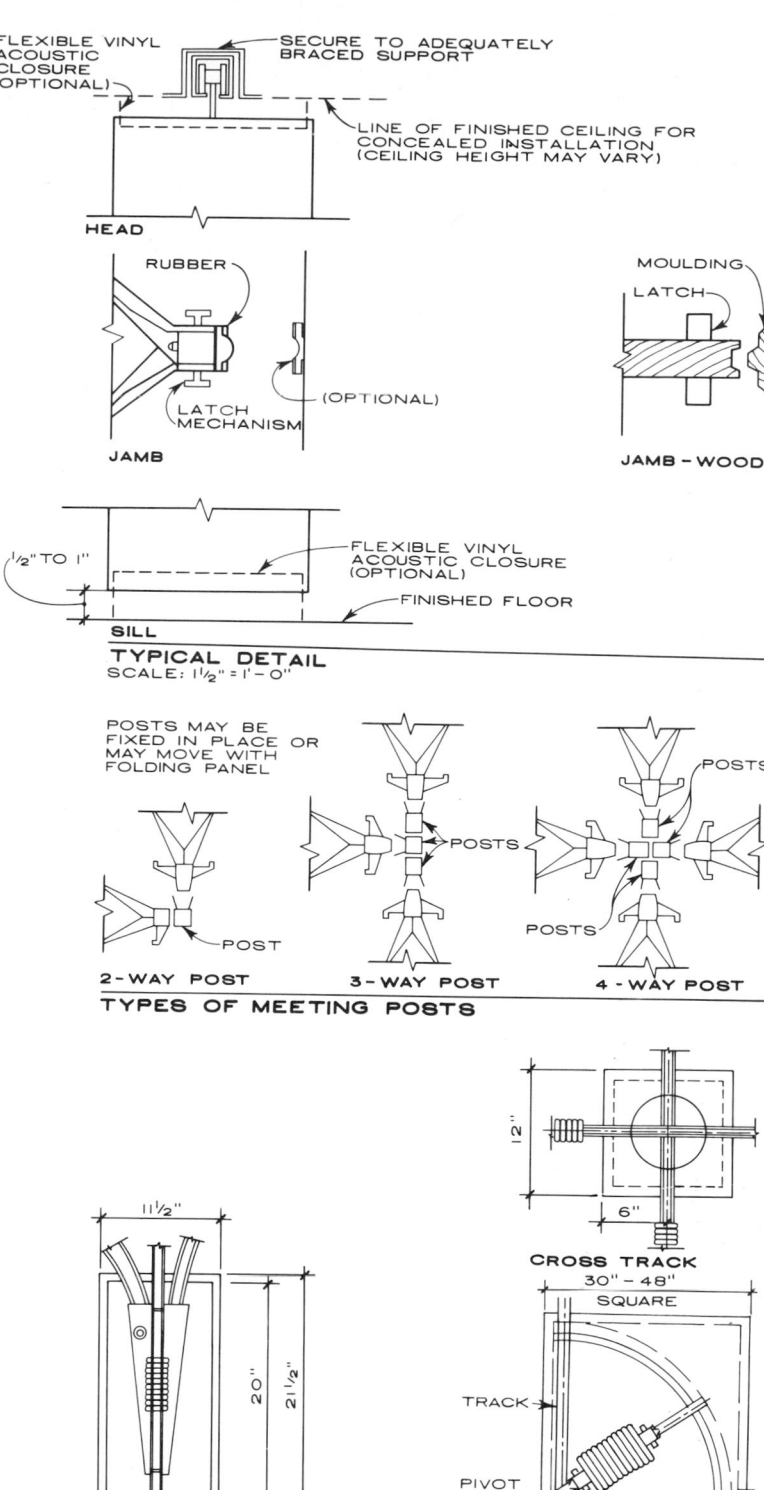

HEAD

JAMB

JAMB - WOOD

SILL

TYPICAL DETAIL
SCALE: 1 $\frac{1}{2}$" = 1' – 0"

TYPES OF MEETING POSTS

2 - WAY POST   3 - WAY POST   4 - WAY POST

POSTS MAY BE FIXED IN PLACE OR MAY MOVE WITH FOLDING PANEL

CROSS TRACK

3 - WAY SWITCH   PIVOT SWITCH

TRACK - SWITCHES

GENERAL NOTES

1. Panel thickness, width, height, finish and acoustic quality vary, dependent upon size of opening, usage and manufacturer. Dimensions given vary according to manufacturer.

2. Enclosures for operable partitions vary. See manufacturer's literature for required clearances in pockets.

3. Overhead structure must be sufficient to support operable partition and must be properly anchored and braced.

4. The accordion type partition is recommended for small openings, which does not however, preclude its use for large openings.

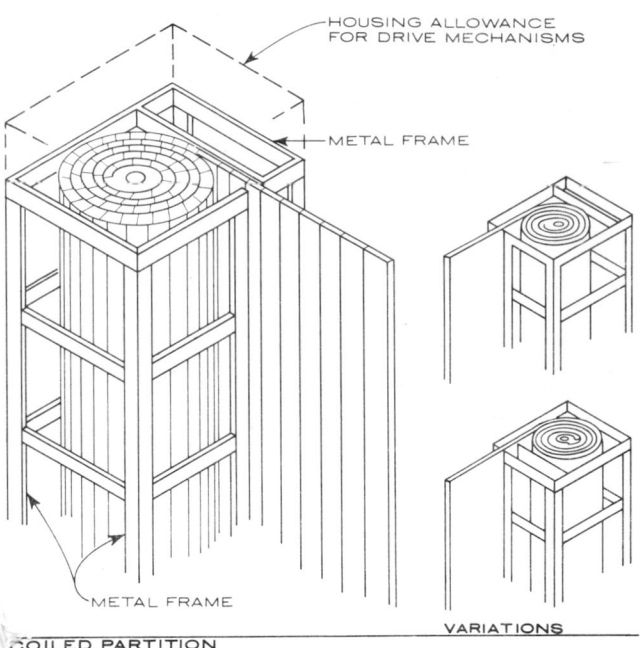

HOUSING ALLOWANCE FOR DRIVE MECHANISMS

METAL FRAME

METAL FRAME

METAL FRAME

COILED PARTITION
METAL FRAME IS STANDARD MANU-
FACTURER'S EQUIPMENT WITH ALL
COILED PARTITIONS

VARIATIONS

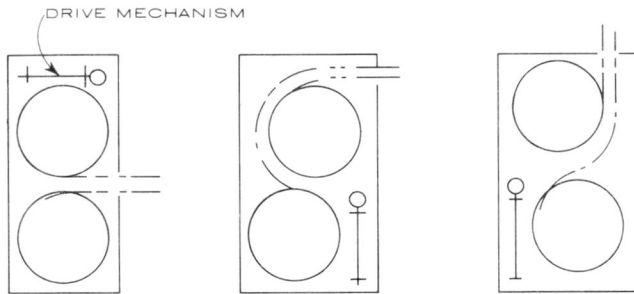

DRIVE MECHANISM

DOUBLE PARTITION COIL BOXES
(USED MOSTLY FOR ACOUSTIC PURPOSES)

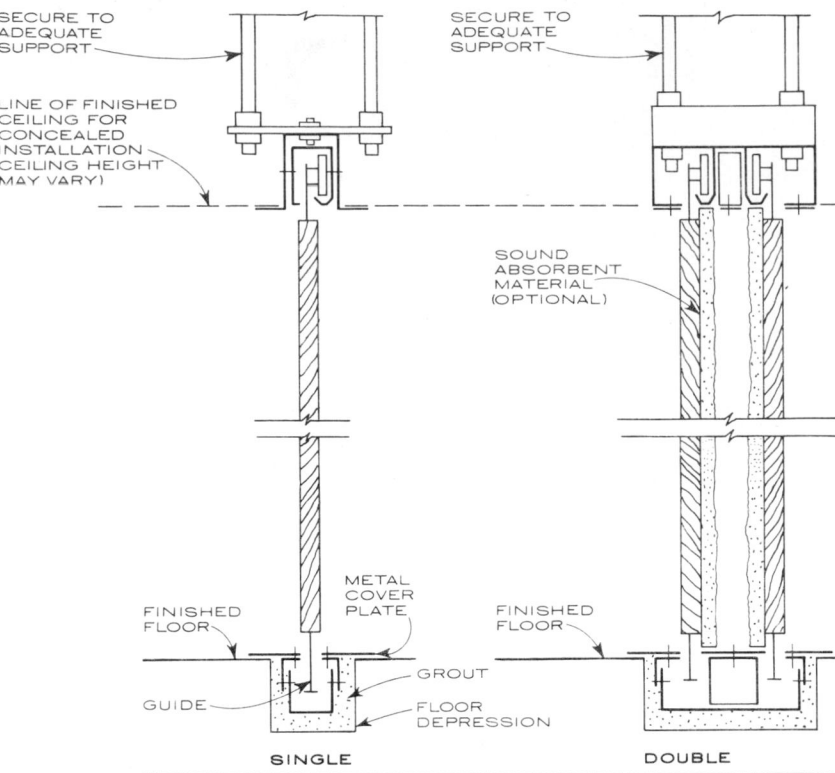

SECURE TO ADEQUATE SUPPORT

SECURE TO ADEQUATE SUPPORT

LINE OF FINISHED CEILING FOR CONCEALED INSTALLATION (CEILING HEIGHT MAY VARY)

SOUND ABSORBENT MATERIAL (OPTIONAL)

FINISHED FLOOR

METAL COVER PLATE

FINISHED FLOOR

GUIDE

GROUT

FLOOR DEPRESSION

SINGLE

DOUBLE

SECTIONS

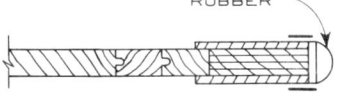

RUBBER

LEAD STILE

NOTES:

1. All coiled partitions are ceiling supported and may be operated by one of the four following methods:
   A. Full manual: Manually extended and manually retracted.
   B. Manual-mechanical: Manually extended and retracted by hand crank.
   C. Full mechanical: Extended and retracted by hand crank.
   D. Electrical: Electric motor extends and retracts.

2. Required floor depression = $2\frac{3}{4}''$ below finished floor (if operating mechanism is overhead). Floor depression = 5'' to 6'' (if operating mechanism is below floor).

3. Minimum radius for coiled partition tract = 2'– 0''.

4. Standard material is wood strips, but other materials may be substituted or used in conjunction with wood, such as metal strips, metal grilles, etc.

5. This is the most flexible partition for curved installations.

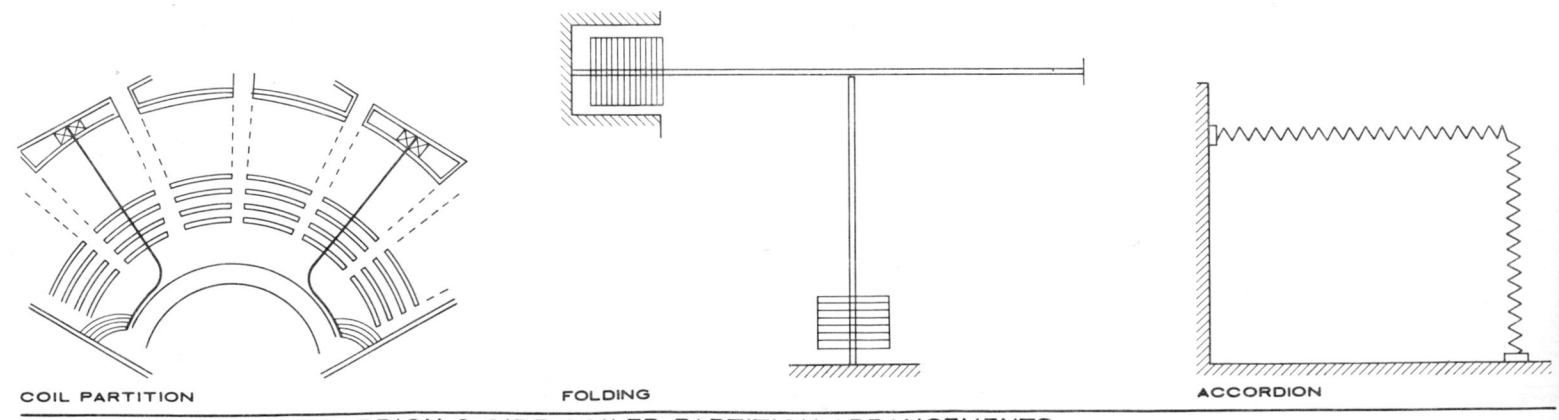

COIL PARTITION

FOLDING

ACCORDION

TYPICAL FOLDING ACCORDION & SIDE COILED PARTITION ARRANGEMENTS

RECOMMENDED USE HEIGHT OF CHALKRAIL ABOVE FLOOR

Sight line requirements not incorporated.

	RECOMMENDATION BY:			
	REX WHITAKER ALLEN AND ASSOCIATES	SAN FRANCISCO UNIFIED SCHOOL DISTRICT	ODELL MACCONNELL ASSOCIATES EDUCATIONAL PLANNING CONSULTANT	
			PUPIL USE	TEACHER USE
KINDERGARTEN	20''	24''	22''	30''
1ST–3RD GRADE	30''	27''	24''	30''
4TH–6TH GRADE	30''	34''	26''	30''
7TH–8TH GRADE	34''		28''	30''
JUNIOR HIGH SCHOOL	36''	36''	30''	30''
SENIOR HIGH SCHOOL	36''	36''	30''	30''

TACKBOARD SIZES

	THICKNESS	MAXIMUM SIZE	COLORS AVAILABLE
1/4'' CORK MOUNTED ON 1/4'' PLYWOOD OR ON HARDBOARD	$1/2''$	4' x 12'	tan, gray, green, blue
1/8'' CORK MOUNTED ON 3/8'' FIBERBOARD	$1/2''$	4' x 12'	tan, gray, green
UNMOUNTED CORK	$1/4''$	4' x 80' 6' x 90'	tan, gray, green, blue
1/4'' VINYL COVERED CORK ON 1/4'' PLYWOOD OR ON HARDBOARD	$1/2''$	4' x 12'	12 standard colors special colors available
UNMOUNTED 1/4'' VINYL COVERED CORK	$1/4''$	4' x 50'	12 standard colors special colors available
VINYL COVERED 1/2'' FIBERBOARD	$1/2''$	4' x 12'	8 standard colors special colors available

CHALKBOARD SIZES

	THICKNESS	HEIGHTS	LENGHTS	STANDARD COLORS
PORCELAIN GLASS	varies	3' – 4'	to 20'	11 standard
NUCITE GLASS	$1/4''$	3' – 4'	to 12'	6
SLATE	$1/4''$ to $3/8''$	3' – 4'	to 6'	black
INTEGRAL COLORS CEMENT ASBESTOS	$3/16''$ and $1/4''$	3' and 4'	6' and 8'	brown, green, gray
A COMPOSITION PAINTED ON CEM. ASB. OR HARDBOARD	$3/16''$ and $1/4''$	3' – 4'	to 12' to 16'	6 to 8 plus custom

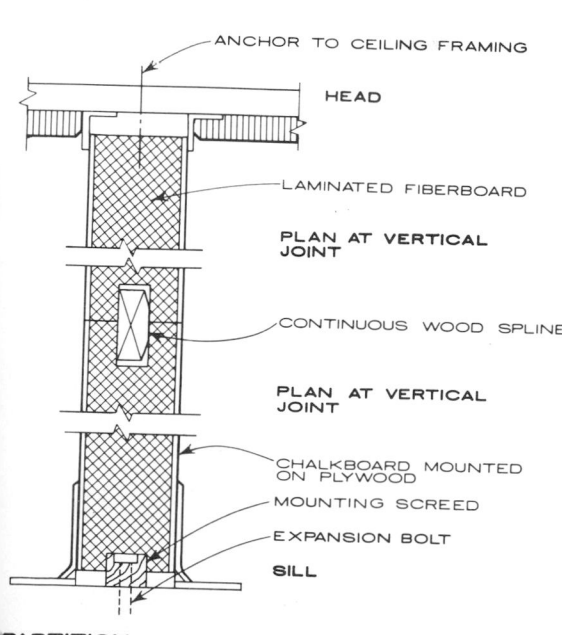

PARTITION

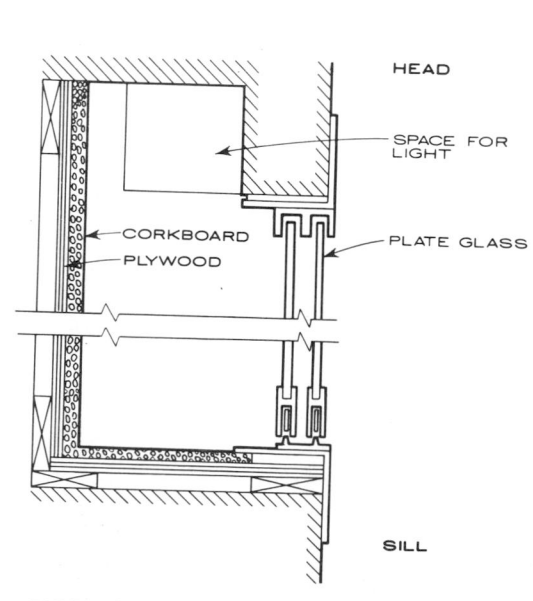

DISPLAY CASE

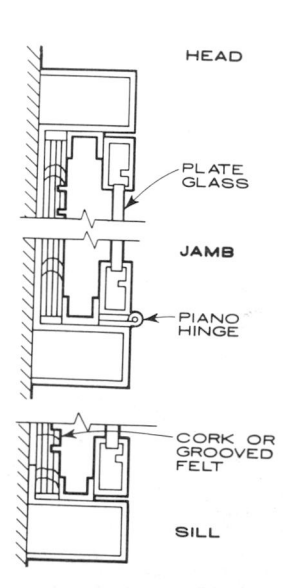

BULLETIN BOARD

Rex Whitaker Allen and Associates; San Francisco, California

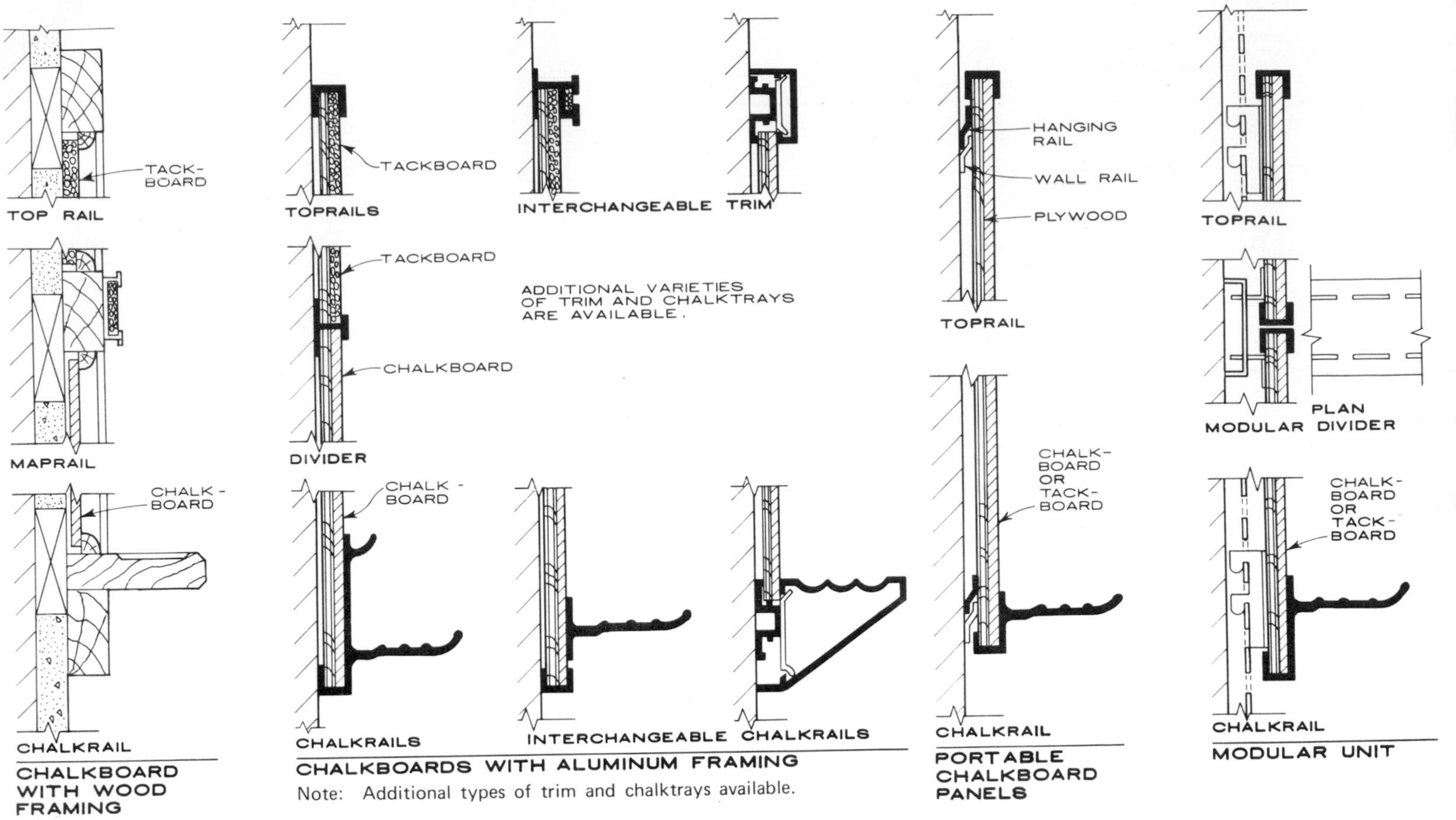

TACK-BOARD

TOP RAIL

TACKBOARD

TOPRAILS

INTERCHANGEABLE TRIM

HANGING RAIL

WALL RAIL

PLYWOOD

TOPRAIL

TOPRAIL

MAPRAIL

TACKBOARD

CHALKBOARD

DIVIDER

ADDITIONAL VARIETIES OF TRIM AND CHALKTRAYS ARE AVAILABLE.

TOPRAIL

PLAN MODULAR DIVIDER

CHALK-BOARD

CHALKRAIL

CHALKBOARD WITH WOOD FRAMING

CHALK-BOARD

CHALKRAILS

INTERCHANGEABLE CHALKRAILS

CHALKBOARDS WITH ALUMINUM FRAMING

Note: Additional types of trim and chalktrays available.

CHALK-BOARD OR TACK-BOARD

CHALKRAIL

PORTABLE CHALKBOARD PANELS

CHALK-BOARD OR TACK-BOARD

CHALKRAIL

MODULAR UNIT

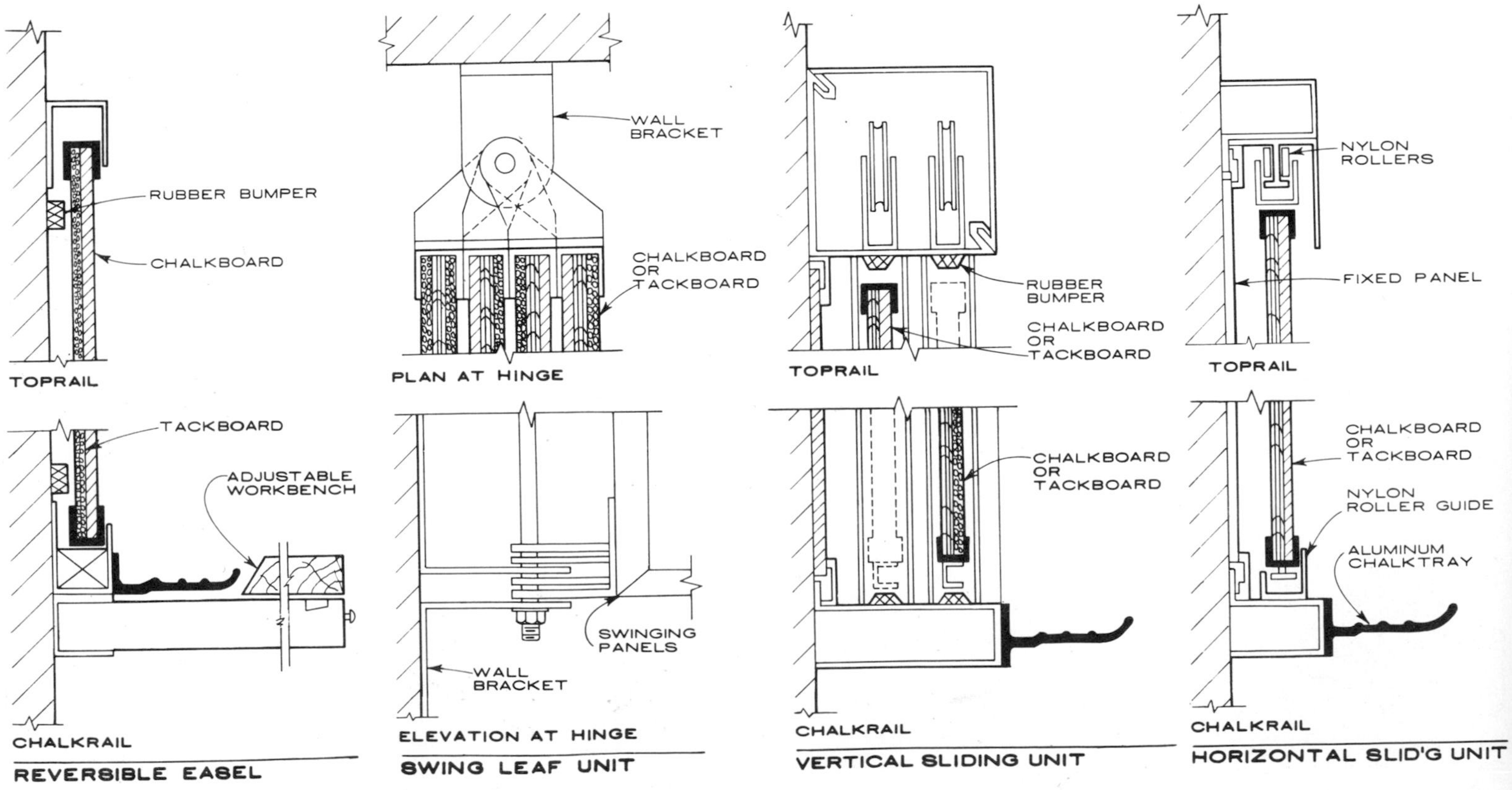

RUBBER BUMPER

CHALKBOARD

TOPRAIL

TACKBOARD

ADJUSTABLE WORKBENCH

CHALKRAIL

REVERSIBLE EASEL

WALL BRACKET

CHALKBOARD OR TACKBOARD

PLAN AT HINGE

SWINGING PANELS

WALL BRACKET

ELEVATION AT HINGE

SWING LEAF UNIT

RUBBER BUMPER

CHALKBOARD OR TACKBOARD

TOPRAIL

CHALKBOARD OR TACKBOARD

CHALKRAIL

VERTICAL SLIDING UNIT

NYLON ROLLERS

FIXED PANEL

TOPRAIL

CHALKBOARD OR TACKBOARD

NYLON ROLLER GUIDE

ALUMINUM CHALKTRAY

CHALKRAIL

HORIZONTAL SLID'G UNIT

Rex Whitaker Allen and Associates; San Francisco, California

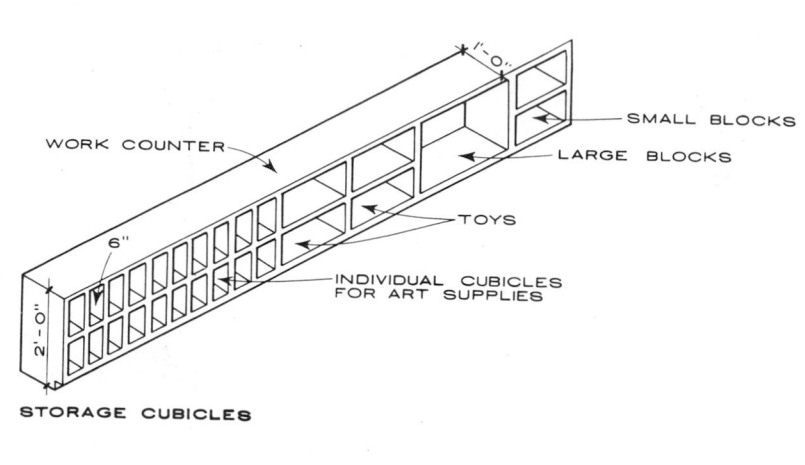

STORAGE CUBICLES

WORK COUNTER
SMALL BLOCKS
LARGE BLOCKS
TOYS
INDIVIDUAL CUBICLES FOR ART SUPPLIES
1"-0"
6"
2'-0"

COTS

4'-8"
2'-0"

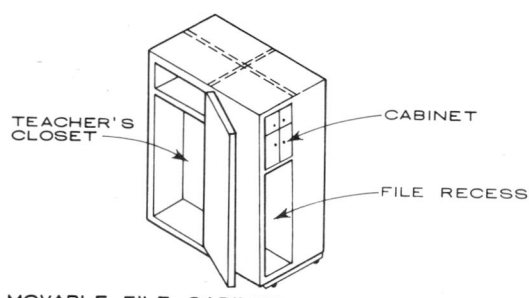
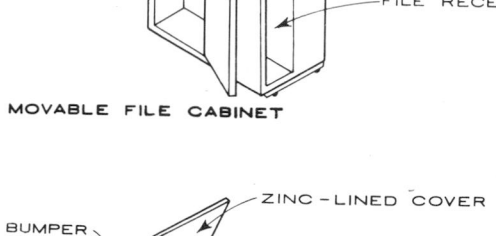

MOVABLE FILE CABINET

TEACHER'S CLOSET
CABINET
FILE RECESS

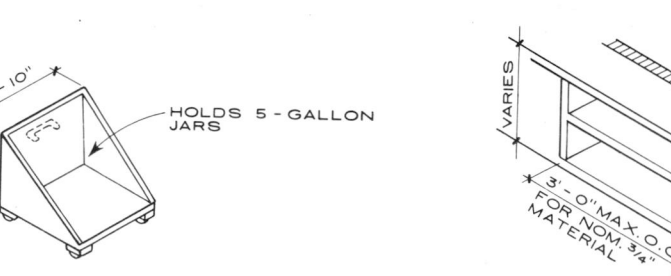

SEAT & STORAGE CUBICLES

1'-8"
1'-0"
1'-8"
2'-0"
1'-0"

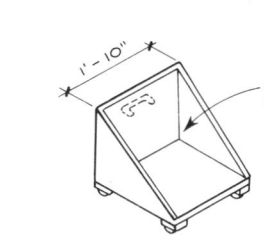

CLAY TRUCK

ZINC-LINED COVER
BUMPER
LINOLEUM LINED
RUBBER TIRES
1'-6"
4"

ALTERNATE CLAY TRUCK

1'-10"
HOLDS 5-GALLON JARS

WORK COUNTER & OPEN SHELVING

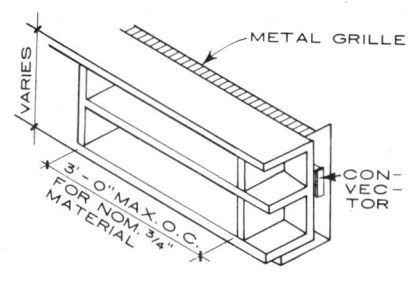

METAL GRILLE
VARIES
CON-VEC-TOR
3'-0" MAX. O.C. FOR NOM. 3/4" MATERIAL

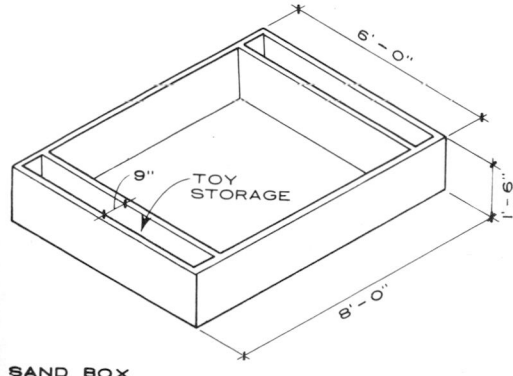

SAND BOX

6'-0"
9"
TOY STORAGE
1'-6"
8'-0"

RECORD PLAYER UNIT

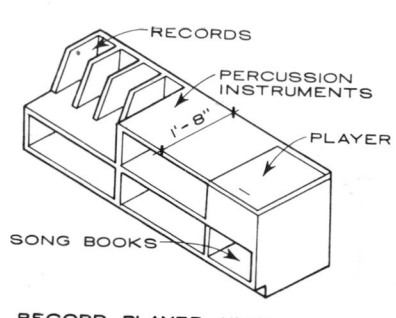

RECORDS
PERCUSSION INSTRUMENTS
PLAYER
1'-8"
SONG BOOKS

PAPER STORAGE UNIT

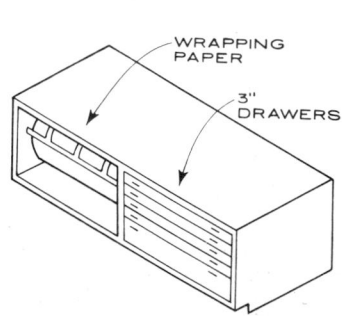

WRAPPING PAPER
3" DRAWERS

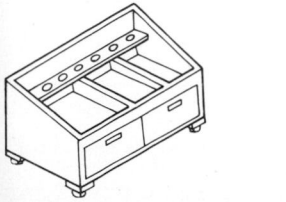

CARPENTRY TOOL CART

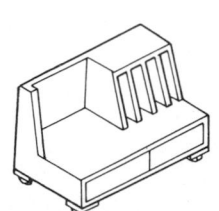

MUSIC CART

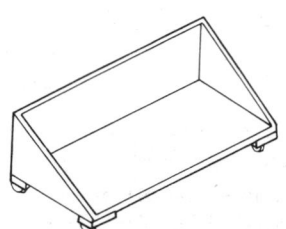

REST MAT CART

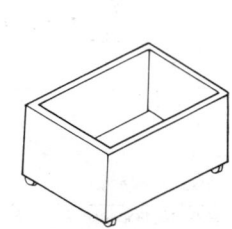

BLOCK CART

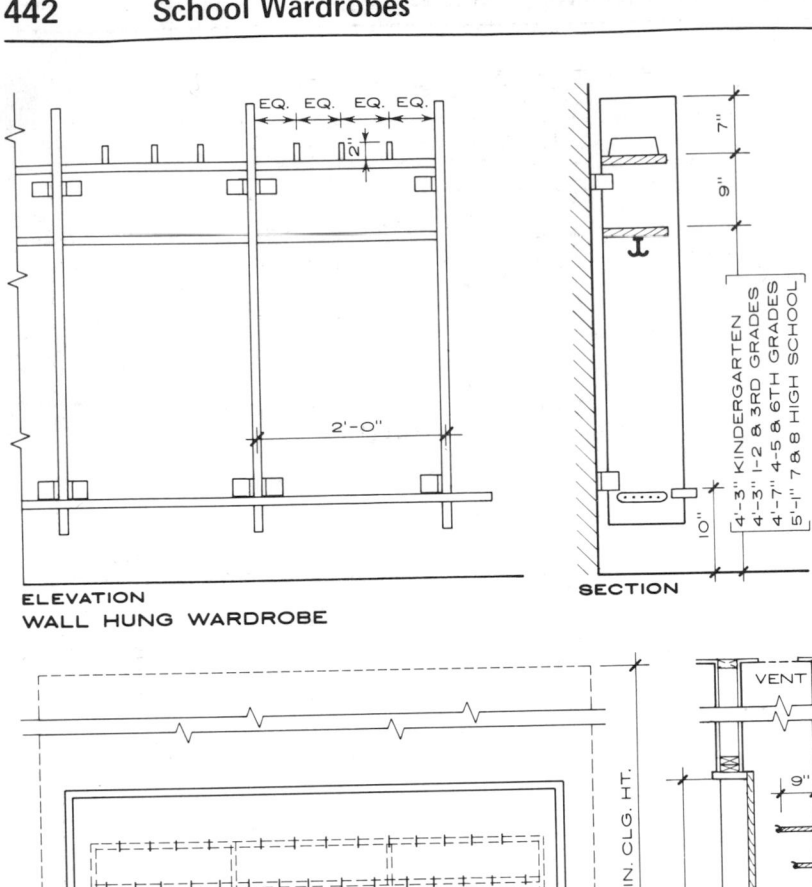

EQ. EQ. EQ. EQ.

2"

2'-0"

ELEVATION
WALL HUNG WARDROBE

7"

9"

10"

4'-3" KINDERGARTEN
4'-3" 1-2 & 3RD GRADES
4'-7" 4-5 & 6TH GRADES
5'-1" 7 & 8 HIGH SCHOOL

SECTION

SHELF FOR LUNCH BOX
HAT, GLOVES

9" PER PUPIL

6"

SEE TABLE OF FIXTURE HTS.

ELEVATION
OPEN CUBICLE WARDROBE

SLOPED FLOOR OR DRIP PAN FOR CARRYING OFF WATER

SECTION
SCALE: 1/2" = 1'-0"

VENT

9'-6" MIN. CLG. HT.

6'-0"

9"

SHELVES WITH HOOK STRIPS

UNDERCUT DOOR FOR VENT SPACE

ELEVATION   **SECTION**

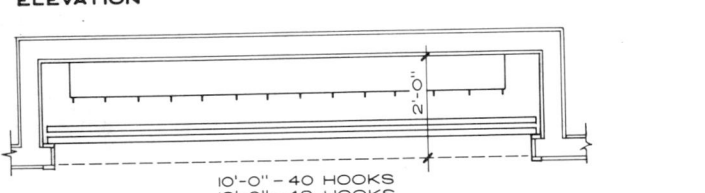

2'-0"

10'-0" – 40 HOOKS
12'-0" – 48 HOOKS

PLAN
VERTICAL-SLIDING DOOR WARDROBE
SCALE: 1/4" = 1'-0"

SCREENED EXHAUST VENT

1'-9" MIN.

12" MIN.

1'-4"

6'-0" – 6'-4"

HANGING SPACE ON PIVOTING DOOR

SCREENED EXHAUST VENT

2'-0" – 2'-4"

10"

9"

7"

9"

4"

RAISED DOOR FOR VENTILATION

SEE CHART SHOWING FIXTURE HTS.

SHELF FOR OVERSHOES, MAY INCLUDE DRIP PAN BELOW

6'-0" – 6'-4"

HANGING SPACE ON REAR WALL

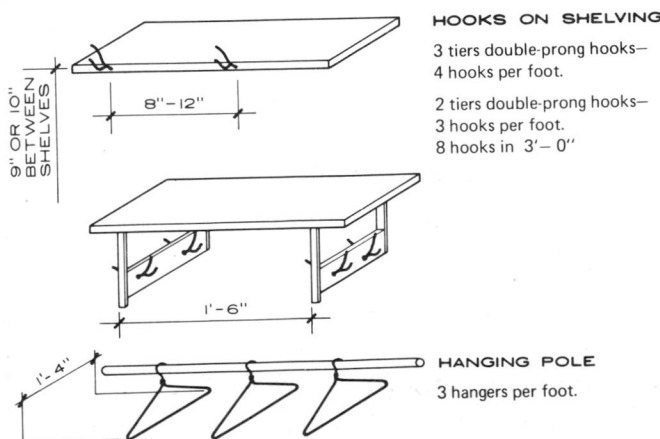

HOOKS ON SHELVING

3 tiers double-prong hooks—
4 hooks per foot.

2 tiers double-prong hooks—
3 hooks per foot.
8 hooks in 3'-0"

9" OR 10" BETWEEN SHELVES

8"-12"

1'-6"

1'-4"

HANGING POLE
3 hangers per foot.

HANGING DEVICES

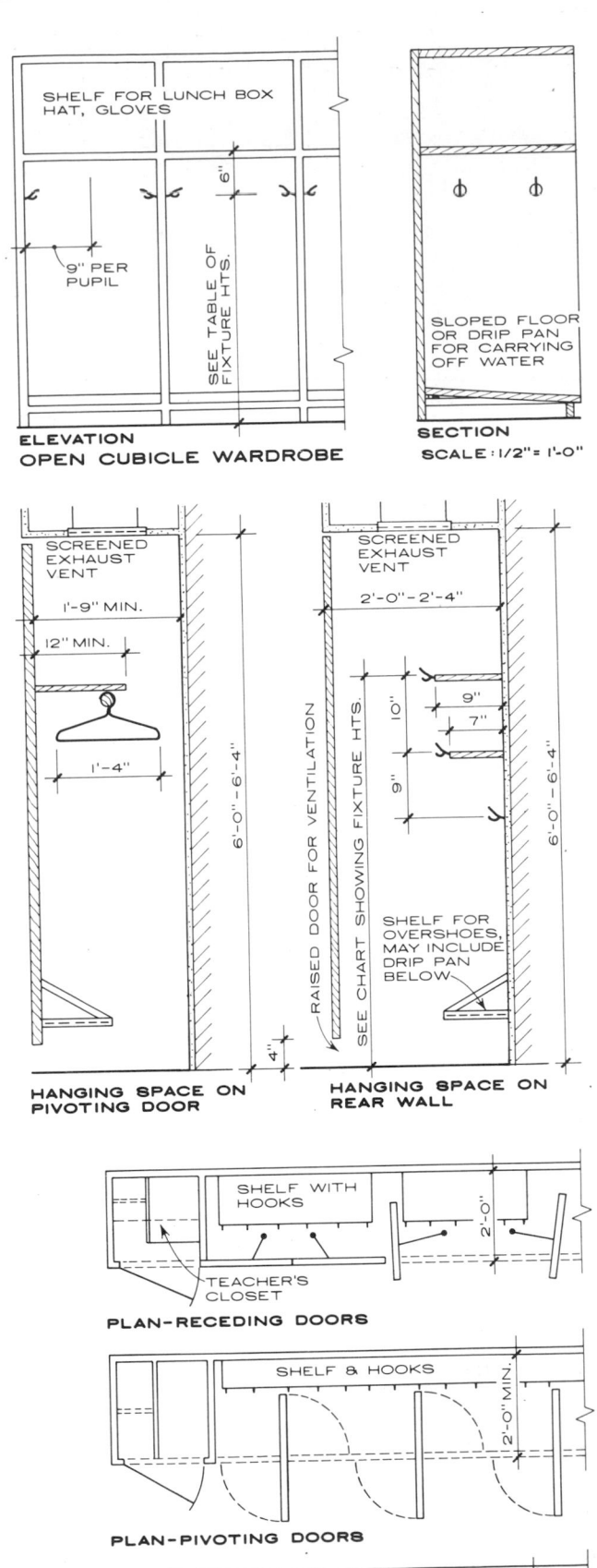

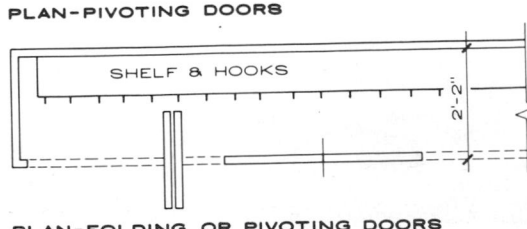

SHELF WITH HOOKS

2'-0"

TEACHER'S CLOSET

PLAN–RECEDING DOORS

SHELF & HOOKS

2'-0" MIN.

PLAN–PIVOTING DOORS

SHELF & HOOKS

2'-2"

PLAN–FOLDING OR PIVOTING DOORS

Reed B. Fuller; Stetson–Spina Associates; Palm Beach, Florida

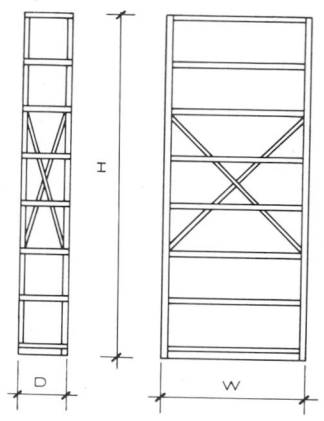

TYPICAL BASIC UNIT

SIZES TYPICAL WITH MOST MANUFACTURERS

W	D	H
24"	9"	3' – 3"
30"	12"	6' – 3"
36"	15"	7' – 3"
42"	18"	8' – 3"
48"	24"	10' – 3"
	30"	
	36"	

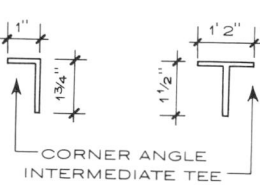

CORNER ANGLE
INTERMEDIATE TEE

TYPICAL UPRIGHTS

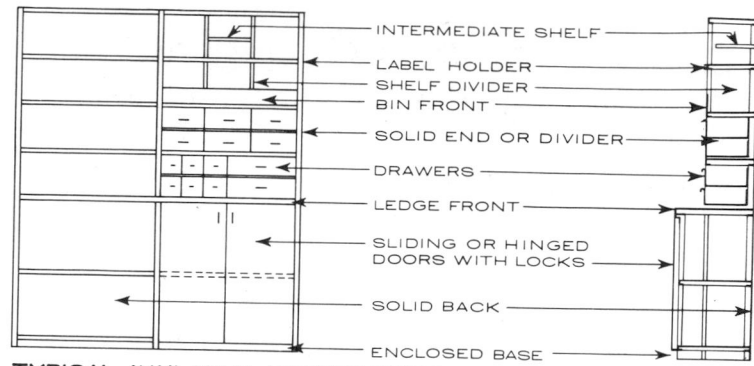

INTERMEDIATE SHELF
LABEL HOLDER
SHELF DIVIDER
BIN FRONT
SOLID END OR DIVIDER
DRAWERS
LEDGE FRONT
SLIDING OR HINGED DOORS WITH LOCKS
SOLID BACK
ENCLOSED BASE

TYPICAL AVAILABLE ACCESSORIES

NOTES:

1. Shelving is available as bolted type, which forms separate movable units more permanent in nature or as clipped type, which forms continuous shelving but is more easily set up and dismantled.

2. Shelving is available in grey, green or tan from most manufacturers or in many custom colors at an additional charge.

3. Shelves are adjustable on 1" centers.

4. Diagonal bracing may be eliminated when solid backs or ends are used.

SOLID SHELF UNITS

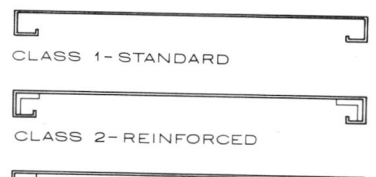

CLASS 1 – STANDARD

CLASS 2 – REINFORCED

CLASS 3 – HEAVY DUTY

LOAD CAPACITY CLASSES
(SEE CHART AT RIGHT)

TABLE OF SHELF CAPACITIES BY SHELF CLASS - APPROXIMATE WEIGHTS COMMON TO MOST MANUFACTURERS

SHELF WIDTH	UNIFORM LOAD IN POUNDS		
	CLASS 1	CLASS 2	CLASS 3
24"	900	1500	2000
30"	800	1300	1800
36"	700	1200	1500
42"	350	800	1200
48"	300	700	1000

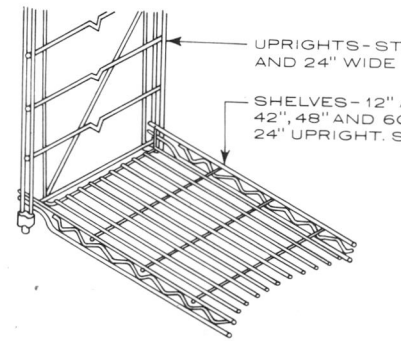

UPRIGHTS – STANDARD OR REINFORCED – 12", 18", AND 24" WIDE AND 53", 63", 73", AND 88" HIGH.

SHELVES – 12" AND 18" DEEP AND 24", 30", 36", 42", 48" AND 60" LONG. USE TWO 12" SHELVES WITH 24" UPRIGHT. SHELVES ADJUST ON 5" CENTERS.

NOTES:

1. Chrome finish at base price, stainless steel available at $3 \frac{1}{2}$ times base price.

2. Approved by National Sanitation Foundation for food storage.

3. Available accessories include corner braces, dividers, bottle shelves, back and side ledges.

ERECTA SHELF WIRE SHELVING

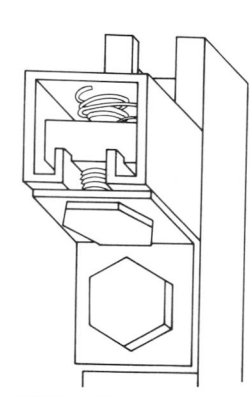

1. Channels available in a wide variety of sizes and combination of sizes, in 12, 14, and 16 gauges and lengths of 10 and 20 feet.

2. Attachment by bolts with spring-loaded nuts and a variety of fittings.

3. System provides unlimited flexibility of spacing and loading for heavy-duty storage on owners choice of shelving material.

UNISTRUT METAL FRAMING

CLOSED DIMENSIONS

ROWS	22"	24"	30"
3	2' – 11 3/4"	3' – 1 3/4"	3' – 11 3/4"
4-20	Add 1/4" per row		
21	5' – 1 7/8"	5' – 3 7/8"	6' – 1 7/8"
22-30	Add 1/2" per row		

OPEN DIMENSIONS

ROWS	22"	24"	30"
3	4' – 9 3/8"	5' – 1 3/8"	6' – 5 1/4"
4-30	Add per row		
	22"	24"	30"

NOTES:

Units are available either fixed or portable, hand or motor operated, closed or semi-closed.

Accessories include end rails, end closure panels, aisle steps, scorers table, integral or portable power units.

Vinyl coated steel seats instead of wood are available depending on manufacturer.

1. Figure capacity at 16" to 18" per person.

2. H = $9 \frac{5}{8}$" or $11 \frac{5}{8}$".
   Total height = $7 \frac{3}{8}$" + H x number of rows.

3. Maximum length per unit: 20' – 0".
   Minimum length per unit: 8' – 0" to 10 rows, 6" more per row to 20 rows, 13' – 0" to 30 rows.

CLOSED DIMENSION
AUTOMATIC CLOSURE PANEL
2 x 8 BUCK
30"
CLOSED TYPE WITH BACKREST
CLOSED TYPE
SEMI-CLOSED TYPE
WOOD SEATS, FOOTBOARDS, RISERS, ETC.
22" X 24"
9 1/4"
11 1/4"
STEEL FRAME
6"
1'-5"
AUTOMATIC FLOOR LOCK

COMPOSITE SECTION

TELESCOPING GYM SEATING

Richard H. Newton; Chappelle and Crothers Associates, Architects; Philadelphia, Pennsylvania

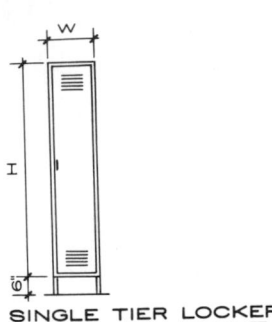

SINGLE TIER LOCKER

SINGLE TIER

W	D	H
9"	1'-0"	
	1'-3"	
	1'-6"	
1'-0"	1'-0"	
	1'-3"	
	1'-6"	
	1'-9"	
1'-3"	1'-3"	5'-0"
	1'-6"	6'-0"
	1'-9"	
1'-6"	1'-6"	
	1'-9"	
	2'-0"	
2'-0"	1'-6"	
	1'-9"	
	2'-0"	

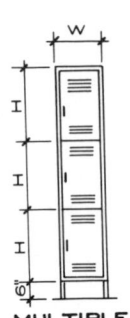

MULTIPLE TIER LOCKERS:

DOUBLE TIER

W	D	H
9"	1'-0"	2'-6"
	1'-3"	3'-0"
	1'-6"	
1'-0"	1'-0"	2'-6"
	1'-3"	3'-0"
	1'-6"	3'-6"
1'-3"	1'-3"	
	1'-6"	

3 TIER

W	D	H
9"	1'-0"	1'-8"
	1'-3"	2'-0"
1'-0"	1'-6"	

4 TIER

W	D	H
1'-0"	1'-0"	
	1'-3"	
	1'-6"	
1'-3"	1'-3"	1'-3"
	1'-6"	
1'-6"	1'-6"	

5 AND 6 TIER

W	D	H
1'-0"	1'-0"	
	1'-3"	
	1'-6"	1'-0"
1'-3"	1'-3"	
	1'-6"	1'-0"
	1'-9"	1'-2 2/5"
1'-6"	1'-6"	1'-0"

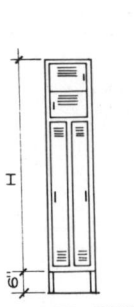

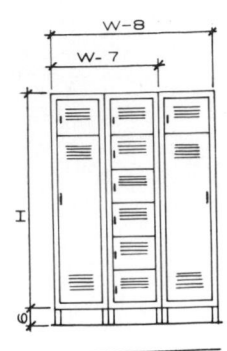

MULTI-PERSON LOCKERS:

2 PERSON

W	D	H
1'-3"	1'-3"	5'-0"
	1'-6"	6'-0"
1'-6"	1'-9"	6'-0"
	1'-9"	

7 PERSON

W	D	H
3'-0"	1'-6"	6'-0"
	1'-9"	

8 TIER

W	D	H
4'-6"	1'-9"	6'-0"

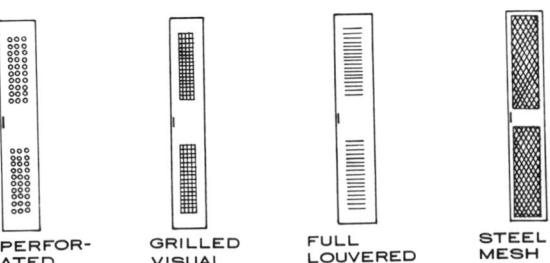

PERFORATED	GRILLED VISUAL	FULL LOUVERED	STEEL MESH

DOOR VARIATIONS

GENERAL NOTES:

1. Locker frame and door is usually of no. 16 gauge steel; sides, back, top and bottom of no. 20 to no. 24 gauge steel. Finishes vary.

2. The standard locker types may be varied as follows:

A. Door types as shown.

B. Sides of perforated sheet steel or expanded mesh to meet specific ventilation requirements.

C. Optional equipment includes sloped top, closed base, 6" legs and a variety of interior fittings such as hooks, shelves, partitions, etc.

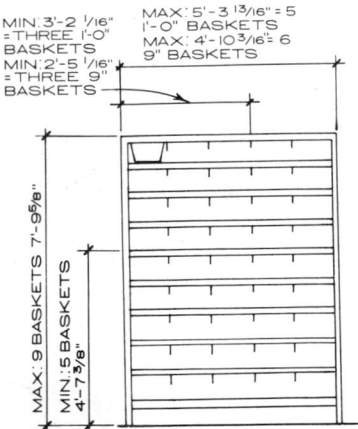

MIN: 3'-2 1/16" = THREE 1'-0" BASKETS
MIN: 2'-5 1/16" = THREE 9" BASKETS
MAX: 5'-3 13/16" = 5 1'-0" BASKETS
MAX: 4'-10 3/16" = 6 9" BASKETS
MAX: 9 BASKETS 7'-9 5/8"
MIN: 5 BASKETS 4'-7 5/8"

BASKET RACK

NOTE:

Basket racks are arranged in single row or double (back to back) row. Single row depth is 1'-1 1/4".

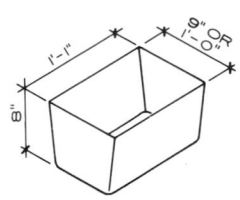

LOCKER BASKETS

MATERIALS:

1. Sides and bottom of perforated steel with louvered ends.

2. All surfaces of wire mesh with perforated steel ends.

3. All surfaces of wire mesh.

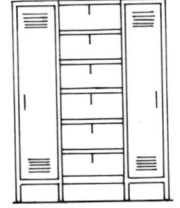

COMBINATION

NOTE:

Standard combination shown has a capacity of twelve 9" baskets and two single tier lockers. However, a variety of combinations for different capacities are available.

NOTES:

Checking lockers are available in enameled carbon steel, or stainless steel for heavy duty use, as in transportation terminals. Locks are provided with built-in multiple coin selector, owner adjustable for coins, tokens, or "free" operations.

Lockers are available without legs for recessed installation. Overall height is 6'-0", some models, 5'-0". A variety of bases are available for free-standing or movable installation.

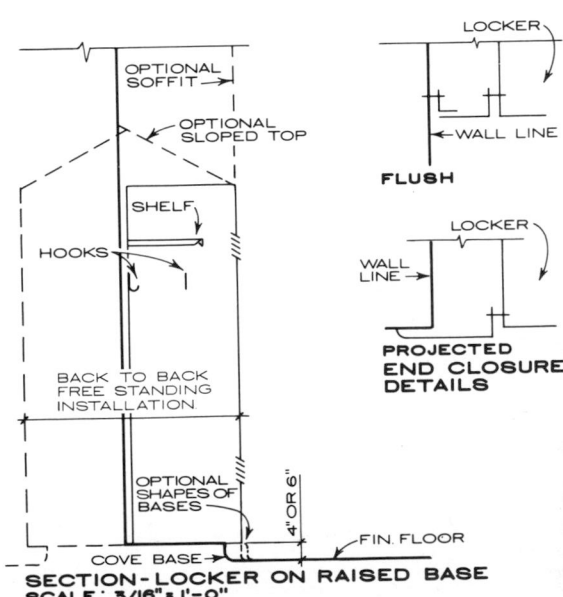

SECTION-LOCKER ON RAISED BASE
SCALE: 3/16" = 1'-0"

The shelf and 2 hooks shown are considered standard equipment.

TYPES	W	D	H
1 SINGLE TIER	9"	1'-6"	6'-0"
	1'-0"		
2 DOUBLE TIER	9"	1'-6"	3'-0"
	1'-0"		
4 FOUR TIER	1'-3"	1'-6"	4 1'-3"
		2'-0"	3 1'-1"
		2'-7"	1 1'-10"
5 FIVE TIER	1'-0"	1'-3"	1'-0"
		1'-6"	1'-2 5/8"
		1'-9"	
6 SIX TIER	1'-0"	1'-3"	1'-0"
		1'-6"	
		1'-9"	

CHECKING LOCKERS

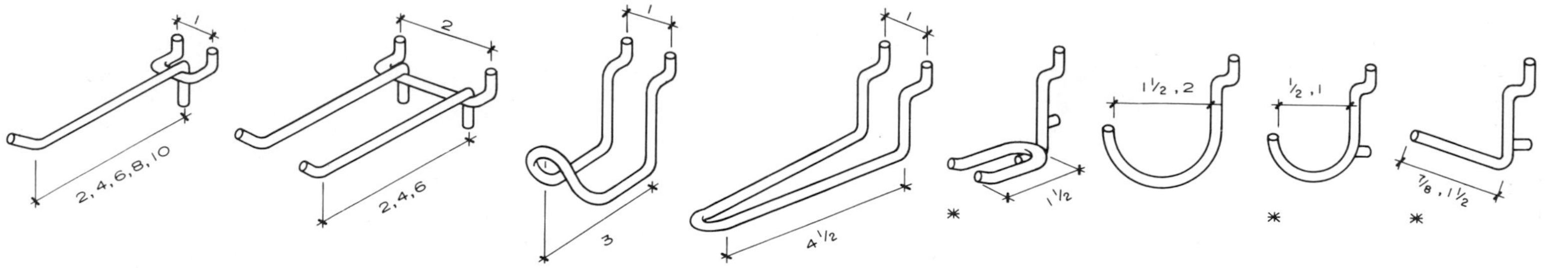

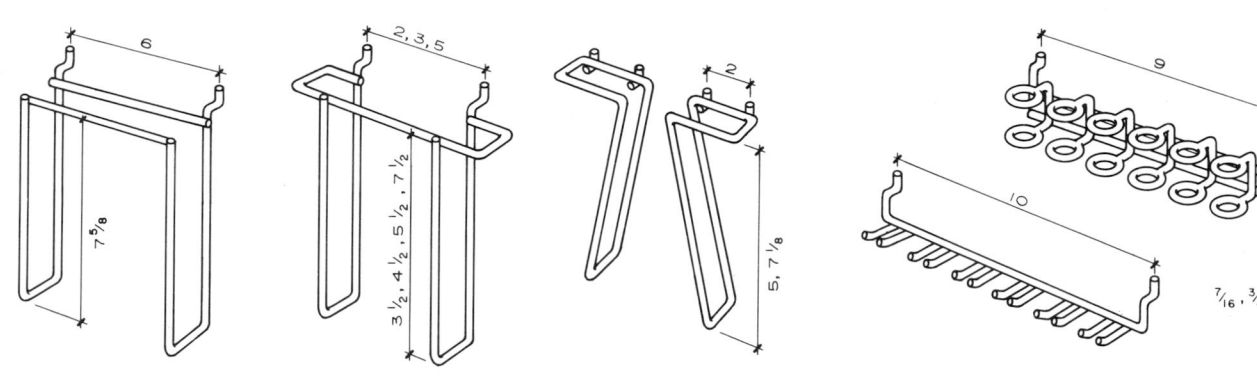

SINGLE AND DOUBLE HOOKS

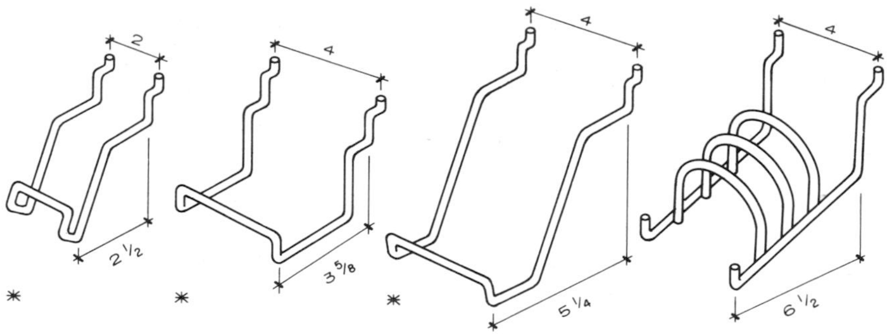

EASELS

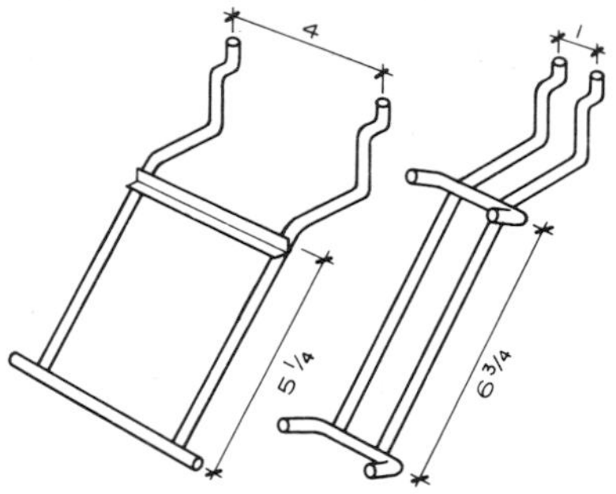

SHOE BRACKETS

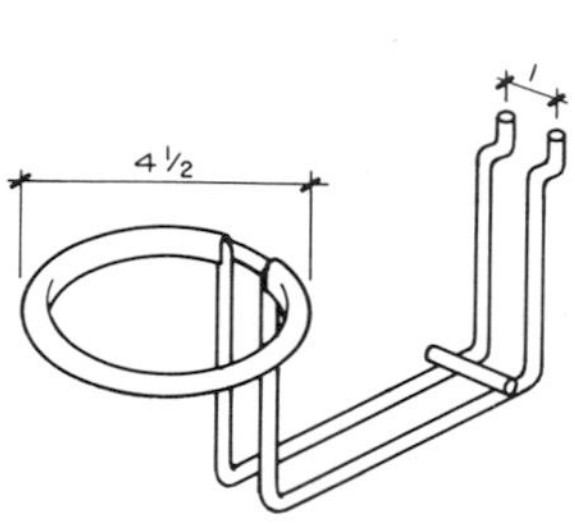

HAT BRACKET

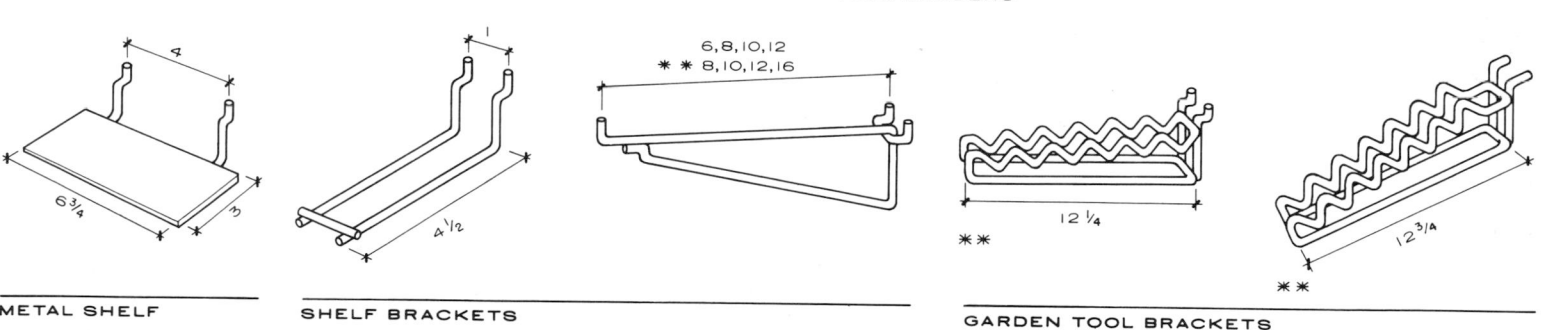

LITERATURE RACKS

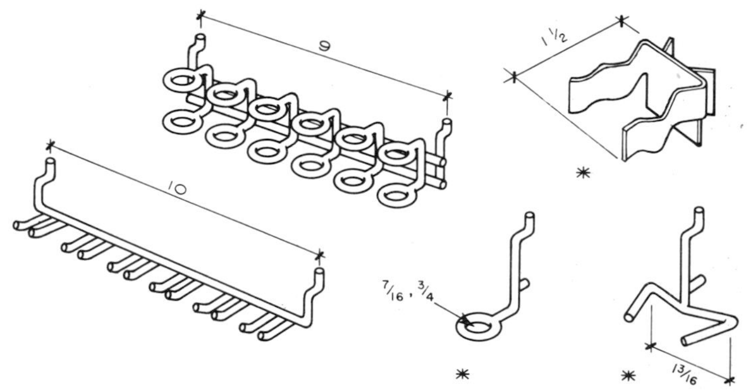

TOOL HOLDERS

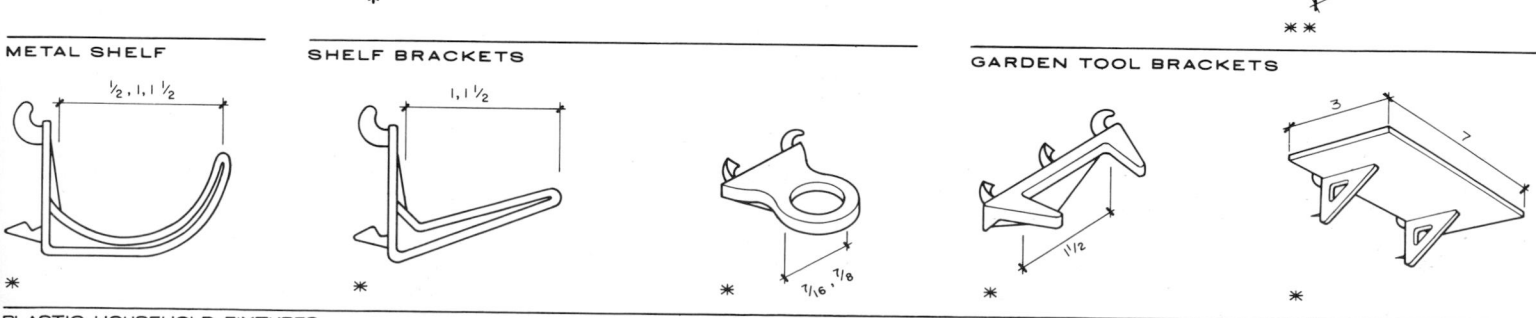

METAL SHELF   **SHELF BRACKETS**

GARDEN TOOL BRACKETS

PLASTIC HOUSEHOLD FIXTURES

NOTE:

Perforated board fixtures are generally for use with $1/8$" or $1/4$" hardboard.

✳ To be used with $1/8$" board only.

✳✳ To be used with $1/4$" board only.

Above data is incomplete. Consult manufacturers catalogs for a complete listing of fixtures and dimensions.

Geddes, Brecher, Qualls, Cunningham, Architects; Philadelphia, Pennsylvania

BOOK CAPACITY

No definite formula can be given for finding the number of books per gross stack room areas. Many variables must be considered: size and kind of books (folios, bound periodicals, etc.); number and width of aisles; stairways, lifts, carrels, etc.; whether calculations are based on ultimate capacity. Variance has been found to run from 13½ — 19 books/sq. ft., according to local conditions. For rough rule of thumb, allow 16 books/sq. ft. of gross area.

SHELF CAPACITY & WIDTH

TYPE OF BOOK	VOLS. PER. LIN. FT.	SHELF WIDTH
CIRCULATING	7	8"
FICTION & ECONOMICS	7	8"
HISTORY & GEN. LIT.	7	8"
REFERENCE	7	10"
TECHNICAL - SCIENTIFIC	6	10"
MEDICAL	5	8"
LAW & PUBLIC DOCUM'TS	4 - 5	8"
BOUND PERIODICALS	5	10"-12"
U.S. PATENT SPEC.	2	8"

cu. ft. of book range weighs 25#

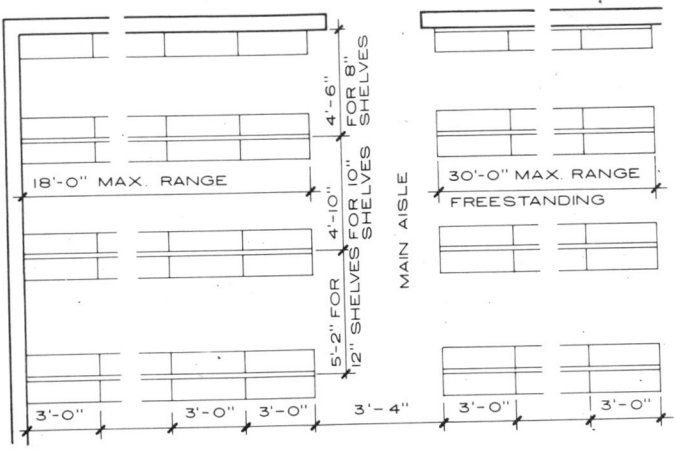

STACK RANGES SCALE- ⅛"=1'-0"

TIE CHANNEL

CELLULAR STEEL (2") OR REINFORCED CONC. (3½" MIN.) STACK DECK

ADJUSTABLE BRACKET

ADJUSTABLE SHELF

MULTI-TIER BOOKSTACKS

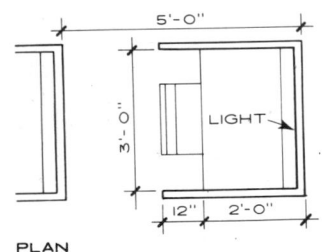

PLAN

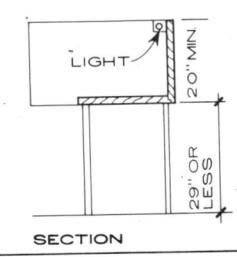

LIGHT

SECTION

STUDY CARRELS SCALE- ¼"=1'-0"

Dimensions for study carrels indicated here have been found to give students enough enclosure so that they are not easily disturbed by other activities. Less enclosure than this will result in student distractions. The principal light source should be from the ceiling. However, a supplementary individual light will usually be needed to reduce shadows on the working surface caused by side panels & bookshelves.

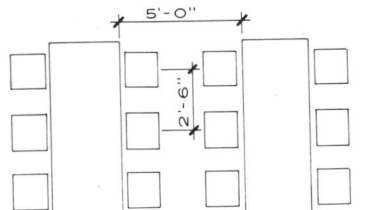

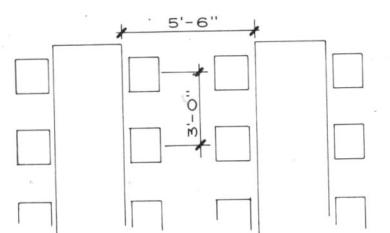

Standard tables:
- 3'- 0" x 5'- 0"
- 3'- 0" x 7'- 6"
- 3'- 4" x 10'- 0"

Small reading tables: 4'- 0" diameter.
Tables used in colleges, libraries, etc., made to order — 3'- 6" wide and desired length.

SEATING & SPACING OF TABLES

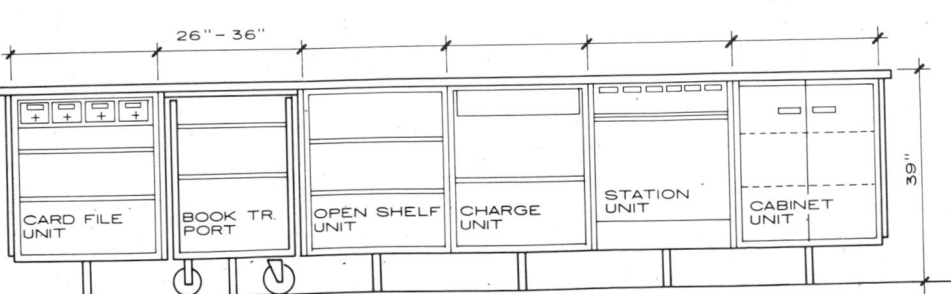

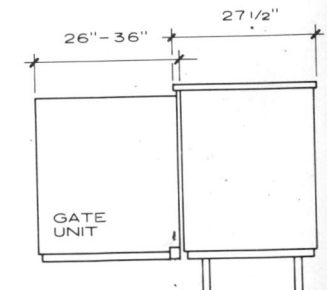

GATE UNIT

CARD FILE UNIT   BOOK TR. PORT   OPEN SHELF UNIT   CHARGE UNIT   STATION UNIT   CABINET UNIT

SECTIONAL CHARGING DESKS SCALE- ¼"=1'-0"

Circulation desks are available in modular units varying in widths between 26" & 36" and include station units, charge machine units, card file units, book return units, book truck ports, shelving & cabinet units, gate units, and end & corner units.

Roland A. Gallimore, AIA; Geddes, Brecher, Qualls, Cunningham, Architects; Philadelphia, Pennsylvania

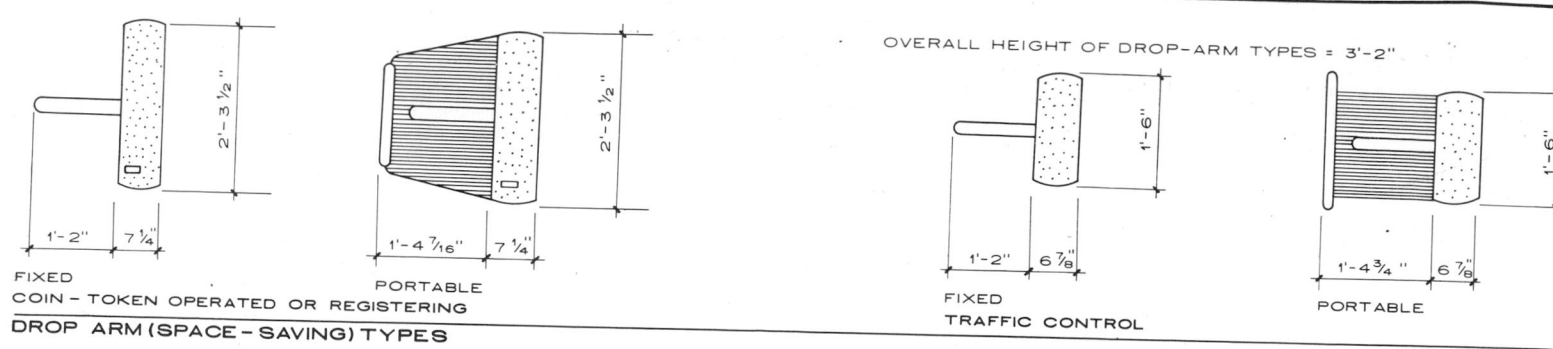

OVERALL HEIGHT OF DROP-ARM TYPES = 3'-2"

2'-3½" 2'-3½" 1'-6" 1'-6"

FIXED
COIN – TOKEN OPERATED OR REGISTERING
1'-2" 7¼"

PORTABLE
1'-4 7/16" 7¼"

FIXED
TRAFFIC CONTROL
1'-2" 6 7/8"

PORTABLE
1'-4¾" 6 7/8"

DROP ARM (SPACE – SAVING) TYPES

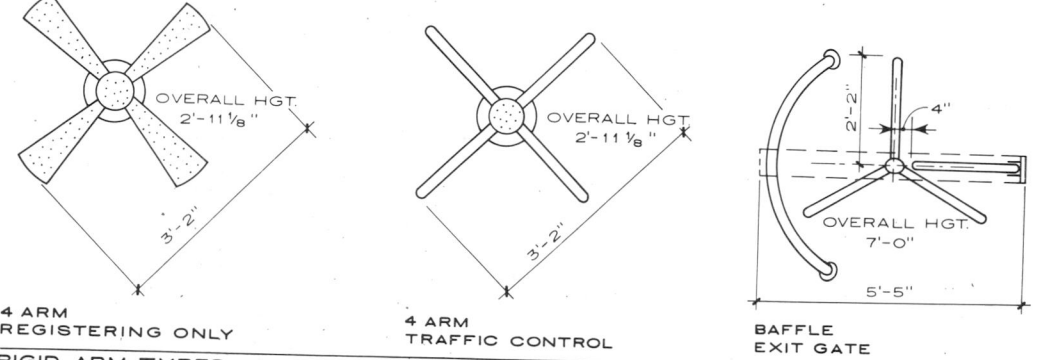

OVERALL HGT. 2'-11 1/8"
3'-2"

4 ARM
REGISTERING ONLY

OVERALL HGT. 2'-11 1/8"
3'-2"

4 ARM
TRAFFIC CONTROL

2'-2" 4"
OVERALL HGT. 7'-0"
5'-5"

BAFFLE
EXIT GATE

RIGID ARM TYPES

SYMBOLS

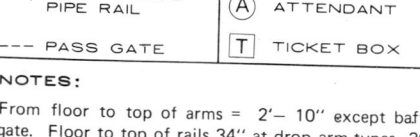

1½ STANDARD PIPE RAIL

(A) ATTENDANT

--- PASS GATE

[T] TICKET BOX

NOTES:

From floor to top of arms = 2'– 10" except baffle gate. Floor to top of rails 34" at drop arm types—36" min., 39" max. at rigid arm types.

All types available in clockwise or counterclockwise rotation.

Automatic bell counter optional.

Codes often require 22" min. clear width at legal turnstile exits. Codes usually credit 0 to 50% of total exiting requirements via turnstiles. Usually require legal exit adjacent. Verify with local code.

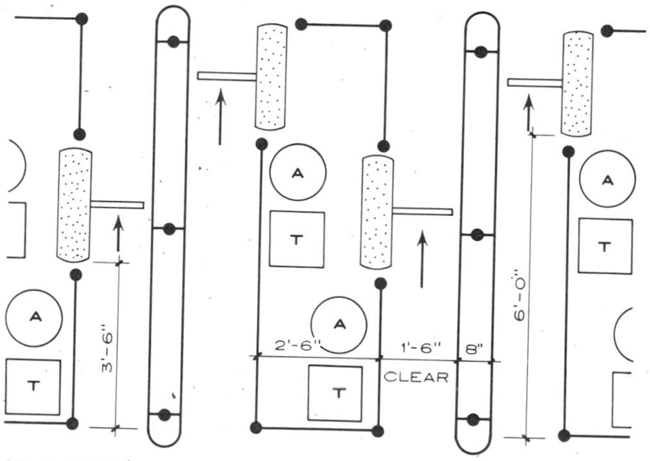

STAGGERED

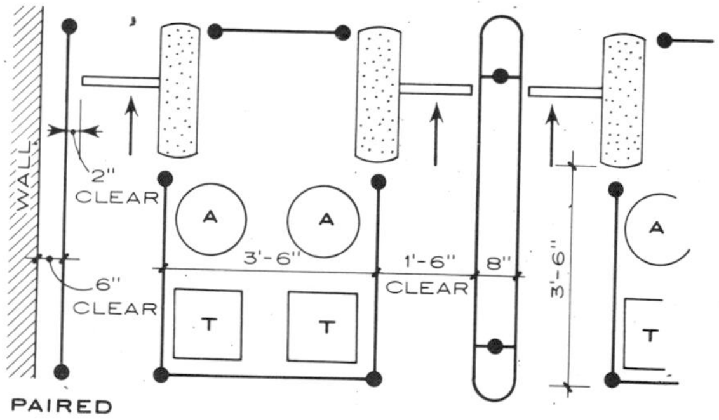

(A) (A) T T
3'-6" 2'-6" 1'-6" 8" 6'-0" CLEAR

PAIRED

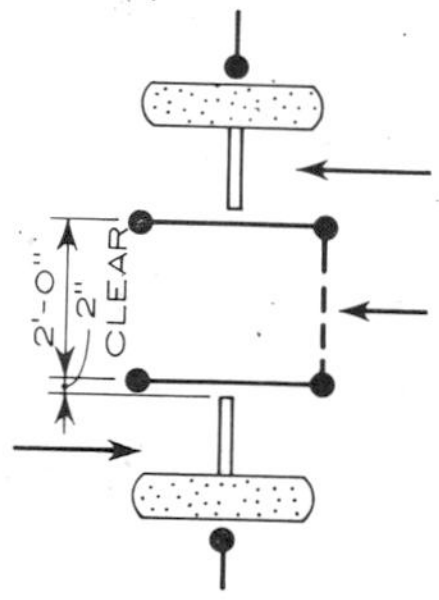

WALL
2" CLEAR
6" CLEAR
(A) (A)
3'-6" 1'-6" 8"
T T
3'-6"

PAY ENTER-FREE EXIT

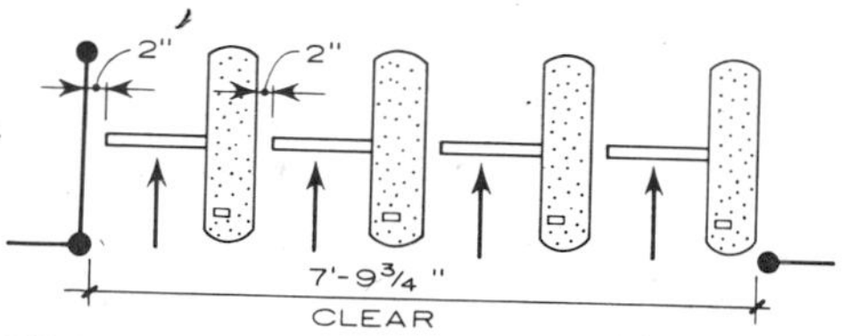

2'-0" 2" CLEAR

TYPICAL INSTALLATION

WALL
2" CLEAR
6" CLEAR
(A) (A) (A)
1'-6" 2'-0" 3'-6"
T T T

GROUPED

2" 2"
7'-9¾"
CLEAR

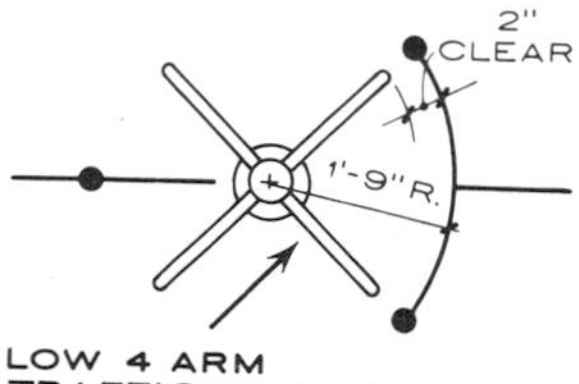

LOW 4 ARM TRAFFIC CONTROL

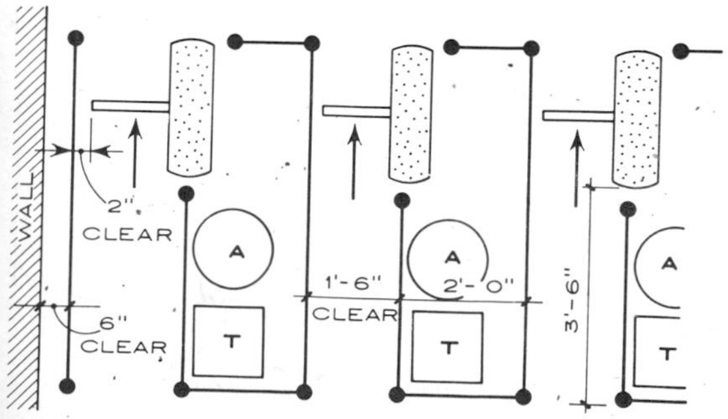

2" CLEAR
1'-9" R.

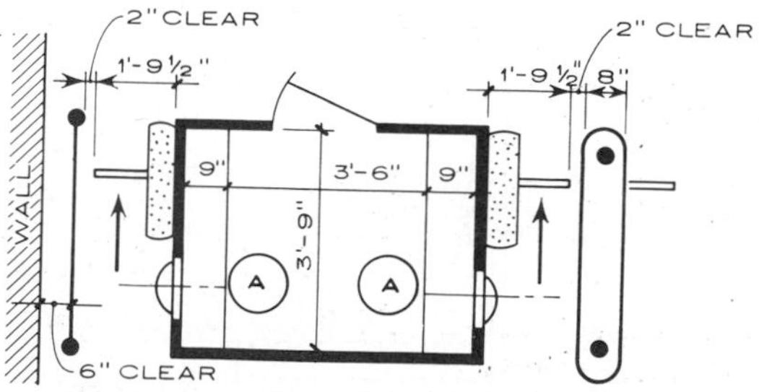

CASHIER ATTENDED

WALL
2" CLEAR
1'-9½"
9" 3'-6" 9"
3'-9"
2" CLEAR
1'-9½" 8"
(A) (A)
6" CLEAR

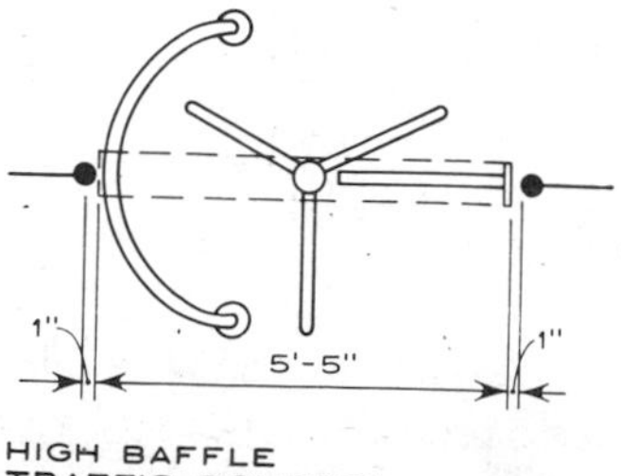

HIGH BAFFLE TRAFFIC CONTROL

1" 5'-5" 1"

UNIT

Warren Anderson; The Perkins and Will Partnership; Chicago, Illinois

GENERAL PLANNING NOTES

While planning is in the early stage, consult with the Post Office Department, Washington, D.C. for suggestions and guidance regarding facilities to provide the best possible service.

For methods of providing the security required for mail rooms, the architect is referred to the local postmaster.

It is suggested that off-the-street loading and unloading be provided.

Mail Room — General — A security type room is necessary to protect the mail until delivered. The mail room should be located at the platform level and if possible have its own access door to the platform for off-hour service and building security, except where there is call window or lock box service, in which case the mail room should be located at the principal building entrance level. A thirty-inch (30″) security type door to the platform should be provided. Standard interior environmental conditions should be provided in this space. Mail room door locks may be conventional Builder's Hardware. The Post Office Department will change tumblers of the locks and retain all keys.

The size of mail room and services provided by the Post Office from a mail room will vary depending upon the size and occupancy of the building. The Post Office Department has established criteria and definitions of building sizes according to delivery manpower requirements: Small — 100,000 sq. ft. or less of leasable office space, Medium — 100,000 to 200,000 sq. ft. of leasable office space, and Large — over 200,000 sq. ft. and six floors (levels).

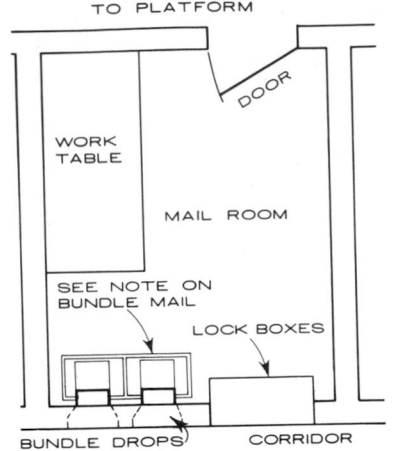

PLAN – SMALL OFFICE BUILDING

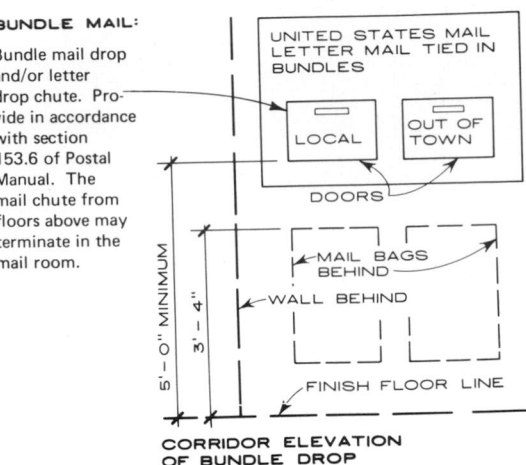

BUNDLE MAIL:

Bundle mail drop and/or letter drop chute. Provide in accordance with section 153.6 of Postal Manual. The mail chute from floors above may terminate in the mail room.

CORRIDOR ELEVATION OF BUNDLE DROP

PLAN – MEDIUM SIZE AND LARGE OFFICE BUILDINGS

For small office buildings a planning factor of $\frac{1}{2}$ sq. ft. of mail room for each 1,000 sq. ft. of leasable office space is generally adequate with a minimum size of 36 sq. ft. A lock box section should be considered when there are more than 10 tenants.

In a medium sized office building the planning factor for the mail room size is 1.5 sq. ft. for each 1,000 sq. ft. of leasable space. Planning should include provision for lock boxes and also for a Dutch door to serve as a service window for providing other services to tenants. The backs of all lockboxes in the mail room shall have secure doors with a suitable fastening device. These doors can be hinged or sliding type. The best location for the mail room is near the elevators and adjacent to the truck platform. Where 100 or more tenant firms are expected, the lockboxes may be omitted.

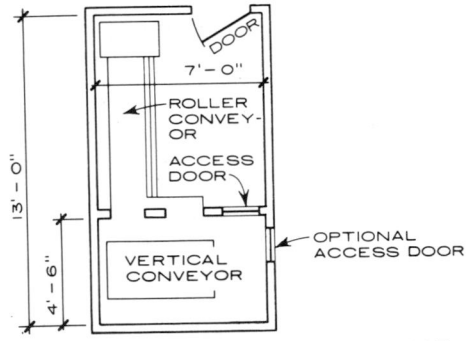

PLAN – AT EACH MULTI-TENANT FLOOR

Additional small areas will be required on each multi-tenant floor for servicing by vertical conveyor. The central mail room at the platform level would house the terminal of the vertical conveyor.

See also, page on Mail Chutes and page on Miscellaneous Conveyors, for additional information.

PLAN – VERY LARGE OFFICE BUILDINGS

Main Mail Room — 150 tenant firms — the plan is the same however, the dimensions would be 26 feet by 27 feet (20′ Min.) or a minimum of 670 sq. ft. and so on, see table below.

In a large office building the main mail room will provide additional services and the planning factor should be approximately 3 sq. ft. per 1,000 square feet of leasable space. This may be reduced substantially where there are several single tenant floors or multi-floor tenants. Use planning factor or data from Space Requirements Table, whichever is smaller.

SPACE REQUIREMENTS TABLE FOR MAIN MAIL ROOM WITH VERTICAL CONVEYOR.

NUMBER OF TENANT FIRMS IN BUILDING	SPACE REQUIRED IN SQUARE FEET
50	400
51 – 100	535
101 – 150	670
151 – 200	805
201 – 250	940
251 – 300	1075
301 – 350	1210
351 – 400	1345
401 – 450	1480
451 – 500	1615

NOTE:

For Vertical Conveyors and Tray Storage for handling of mail in large office buildings see catalogs of manufacturers of conveying equipment.

Robert S. Dame, R. A.; Kensington, Maryland

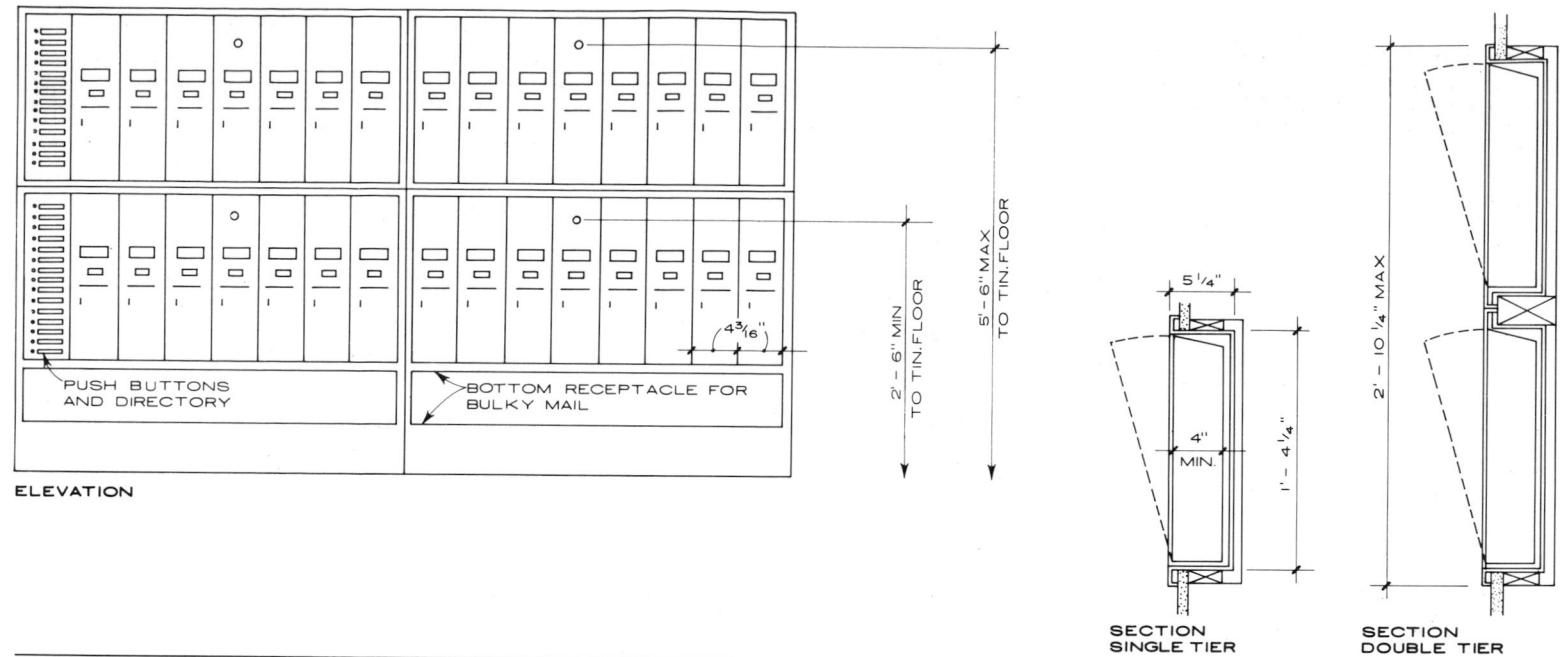

PUSH BUTTONS AND DIRECTORY

BOTTOM RECEPTACLE FOR BULKY MAIL

4³/₁₆"

2'-6" MIN. TO TIN.FLOOR

5'-6" MAX. TO TIN.FLOOR

ELEVATION

VERTICAL TYPE INSTALLATION

5¼"

4" MIN.

1'-4¼"

SECTION SINGLE TIER

2'-10¼" MAX.

SECTION DOUBLE TIER

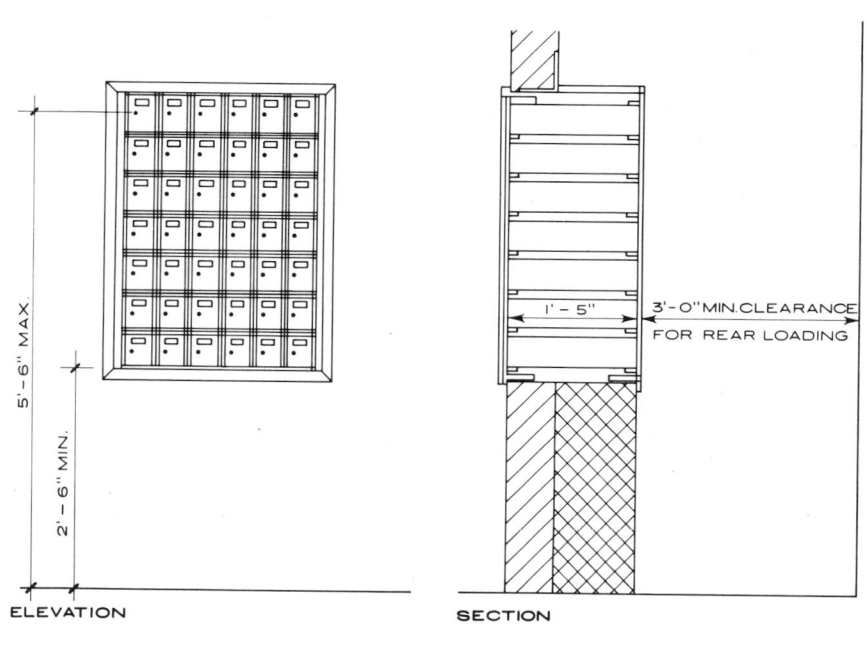

5'-6" MAX.

2'-6" MIN.

ELEVATION

1'-5"

3'-0" MIN. CLEARANCE FOR REAR LOADING

SECTION

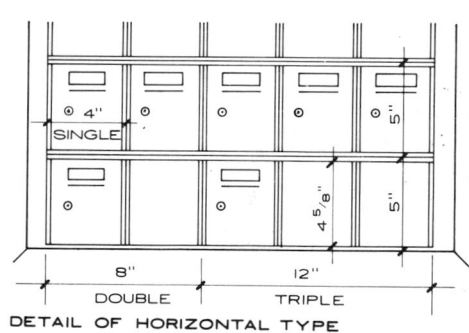

4" SINGLE

5"

4⅝"

5"

8"
DOUBLE

12"
TRIPLE

DETAIL OF HORIZONTAL TYPE

505

COMPARTMENT DOOR WITH KEY LOCK

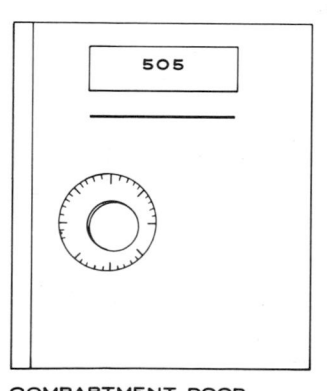

505

COMPARTMENT DOOR WITH COMBINATION LOCK

HORIZONTAL TYPE INSTALLATION

Franz W. Krebs, AIA; Silver Spring, Maryland

GENERAL NOTE:

Supply alphabetical directory of all persons receiving mail in installations of 15 receptacles or more. Government approved mailboxes are made in 3 — 12 units to a gang. Each gang supply with mounting for a master lock. Push buttons for telephones can be installed in frame with mailboxes, but must be accessible for maintenance without access to mailboxes.

Mailboxes must be constructed to receive long letter mail 4 1/2" wide and bulky magazines 14 1/2" long, and 3 1/2" in diameter. Post Office recommends rear loading type boxes with a mail room 3'—0" wide to permit undisturbed loading. For detailed Post Office regulations see P.O.D. publication 17.

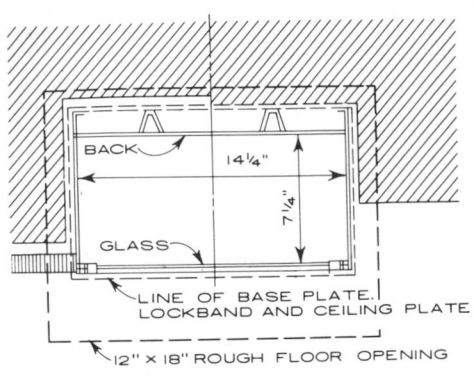

PACKAGE CHUTE – PLAN

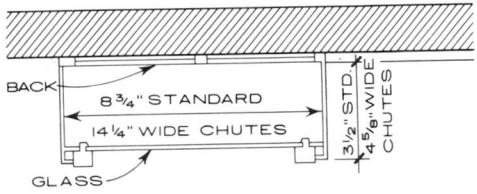

MAIL CHUTE – PLAN

1. May be recessed.
2. Use wide chutes for 8″ x 10″ envelopes.

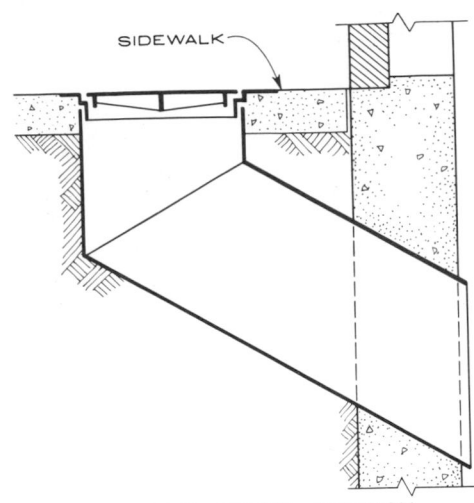

SIDEWALK COAL CHUTE – SECTION
Coal chute of cast iron ring and cover placed outside of building and connected to coal storage by steel hopper of 12 or 14 guage.

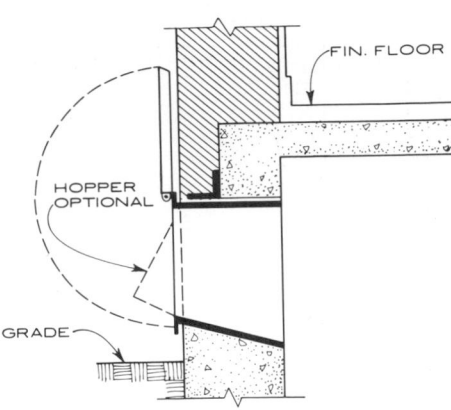

FOUNDATION COAL CHUTE – SECTION
Used where the coal room ceiling is high enough above grade to allow space for the chute.

TYPE OF DOOR	NOMINAL DOOR SIZE	
	WIDTH	HEIGHT
SOLID STEEL OR GLAZED 3 LIGHTS	24″	18″
	33″	24″

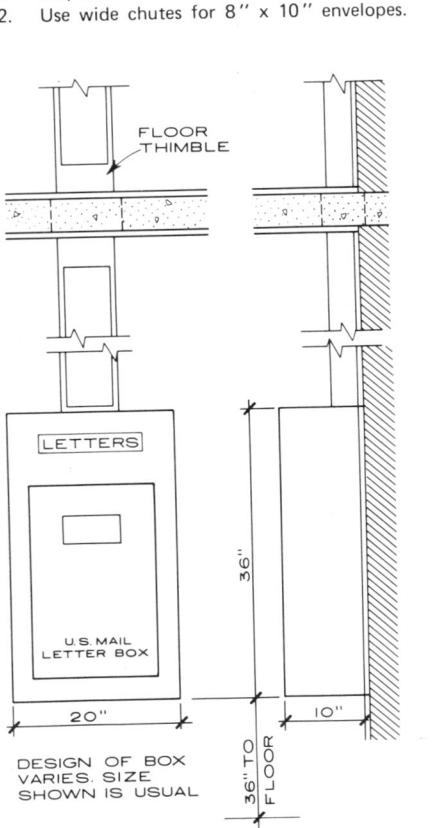

ELEVATIONS

MAIL CHUTES AND BOXES

NOTES:
Rough floor opening 8″ x 12″ for single chute, and 8″ x 24″ for double chute. Box must be withing 100′ of main entrance. Chute of aluminum, bronze or stainless steel. Glazed front may be used in public buildings hotels, railroad stations, business and office buildings four stories and over, apartment houses of forty families or over with permission of Post Office Department. Main entrance must be unlocked during business hours.

Franz W. Krebs, AIA; Silver Spring, Maryland

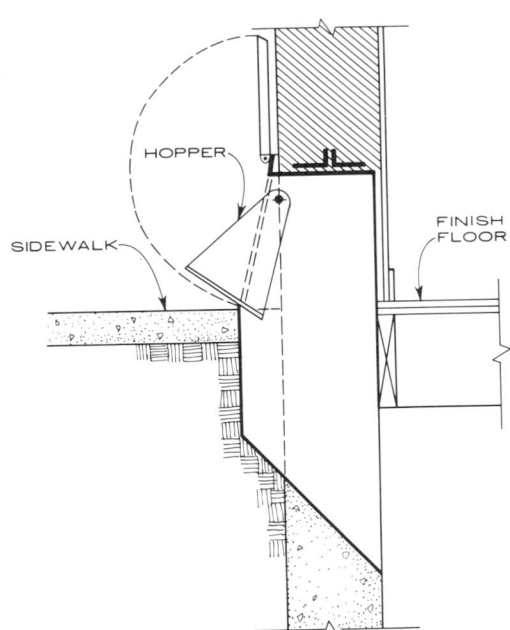

FOUNDATION COAL CHUTE – SECTION
Used where the first floor is on or near grade level. Body of the chute extending down into the foundation.

TYPE OF DOOR	NOMINAL DOOR SIZE	
	WIDTH	HEIGHT
SOLID STEEL	25″	18″
	33″	22″

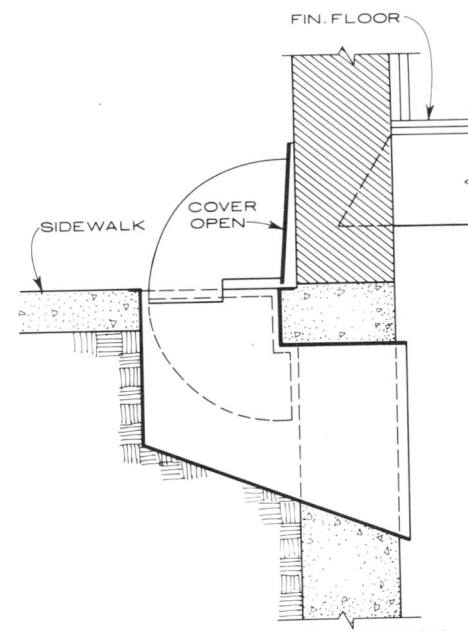

GRADE LINE COAL CHUTE – SECTION
Used where the first floor is on or near grade level.

TYPE OF DOOR	NOMINAL DOOR SIZE	
	WIDTH	LENGTH
CAST, MALLEABLE IRON	26″	19″
	32″	21″
	24″	16″
STEEL FLOOR PLATE	19″	19″
	21″	26″
	27″	32″

COAL CHUTES

NOTES:
Coal chutes are not made as catalog items. Above details are construction guidelines. Coal chutes are usually constructed of steel or malleable iron, and are set into building walls during construction. The sizes given are nominal.

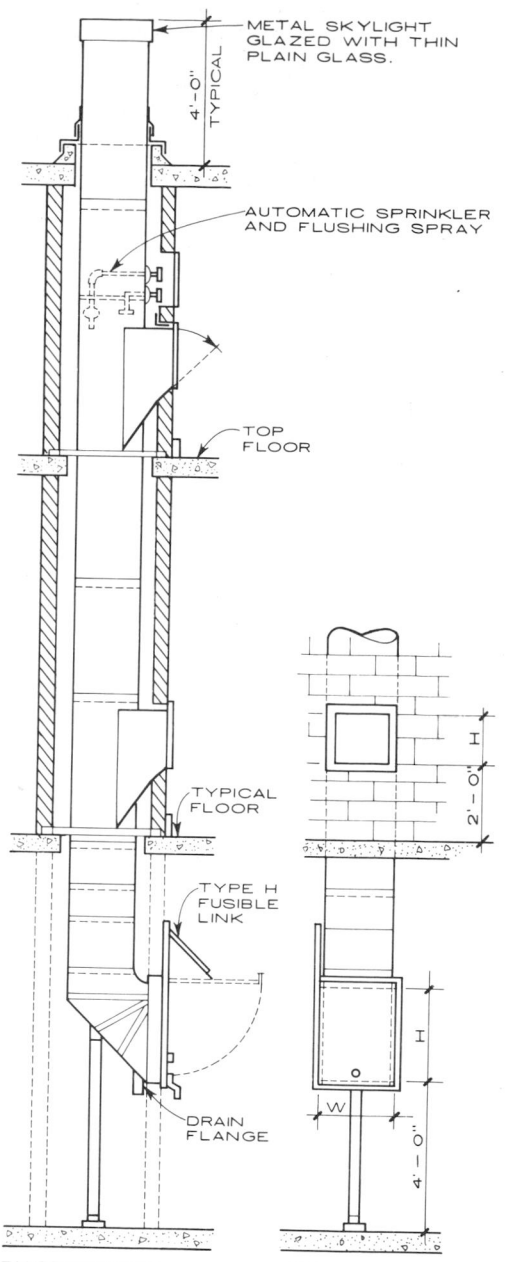

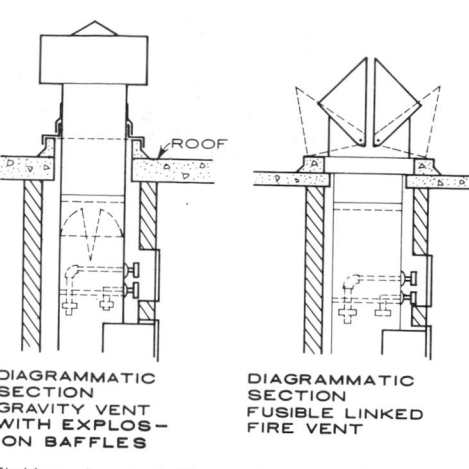

DIAGRAMMATIC SECTION GRAVITY VENT WITH EXPLOSION BAFFLES

DIAGRAMMATIC SECTION FUSIBLE LINKED FIRE VENT

Flashing and counterflashing at roof penetrations is necessary to provide watertight connection with roofing material, but cannot be shown in any detail at this scale. See pages on flashing.

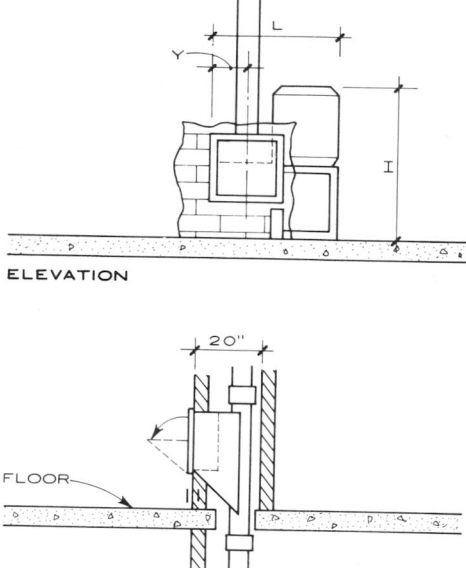

ELEVATION

DIAGRAMMATIC SECTION

ELEVATION

RUBBISH OR LINEN CHUTE

DIAGRAMMATIC SECTION

RUBBISH CHUTE

PLAN

RUBBISH AND LINEN CHUTES

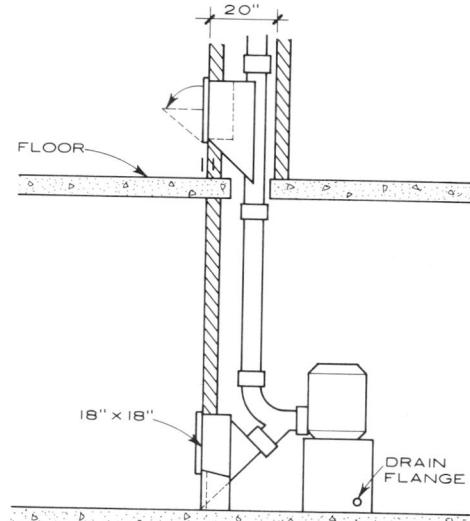

SECTION WET COLLECTOR SYSTEM

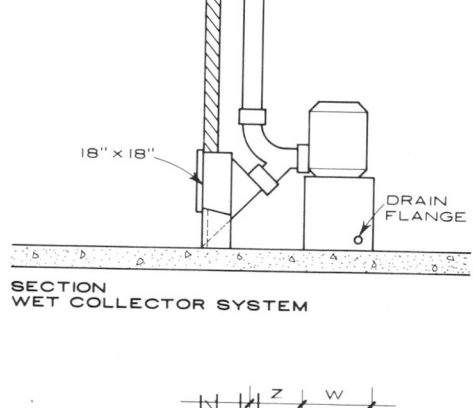

SECTION DRY COLLECTOR SYSTEM

RECOMMENDED DOOR SIZES (IN INCHES)

Chute dia.	LINEN OR PAPER		RUBBISH OR GARBAGE		DISCHARGE	
	Bottom Hinge w x h	Side Hinge w x h	Bottom Hinge w x h	Side Hinge w x h	Type H	Type A
36	30 x 30	30 x 30	24 x 24	24 x 24	36 x 48	36
28	24 x 24	24 x 24	21 x 18	21 x 21	28 x 36	28
24	21 x 18	21 x 21	18 x 18	18 x 18	24 x 30	24
20	18 x 18	18 x 18	15 x 18	15 x 15	20 x 30	20
18	15 x 18	15 x 15	15 x 18	15 x 15	18 x 30	18
15	12 x 15	12 x 12	12 x 12	12 x 12	15 x 24	15
12	12 x 15	12 x 12	12 x 15		12 x 24	12

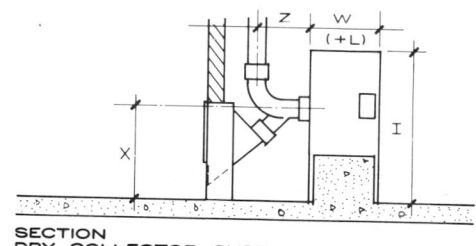

DUST CHUTES

No. Intakes	Size Riser	Motor h.p.	Type Collector	L	W	H	X	Y	Z
1–6	8"	1 1/2	wet	34	18	41	24 1/2	8 1/2	10
			dry	36	20	42	24 1/2	10 1/2	10
7–12	10"	3	wet	40 3/8	22	57 1/4	37	10 1/4	10
			dry	40	24	81	45 1/2	12	12

NOTES ON CHUTES:

Fire underwriters recommend:

1. Linen chutes should extend full diameter thru the roof as specified on the rubbish chute, and be capped with a metal skylight glazed with thin plain glass.

2. Intermediate automatic sprinklers are recommended at alternate floors.

Franz W. Krebs, AIA; Silver Spring, Maryland

Chutes are fabricated from #18 Ga. aluminized steel, or aluminum. One expansion joint per story; intake doors stainless steel, side or bottom hinged with or without underwriters Class B label.

Discharge Type A aluminized steel (no underwriters label), or type H hopper with or without underwriters Class B

label.

Chutes are usually secured to floor with clamp type supports 3/16" x 1 1/4" steel.

Riser of dust chutes 8" or 10" diameters. Aluminum dry parts, stainless steel wet.

FIRE CLASSIFICATION

CLASS A
Incipient fires on which quenching and the cooling effect of water is of prime importance. Fires of wood, paper, textile and rubbish.

CLASS B
Incipient fires on which blanketing or smothering effect of extinguishing is of prime importance. Fire of gasoline, oil, grease and fat.

CLASS C
Incipient fires in electrical equipment where the use of non-conducting extinguishing agent is needed.

OCCUPANCY CLASSIFICATION

CLASS I
Light hazard occupancies (schools, offices, and public buildings) require one unit of extinguishing capacity for every 2,500 square feet of floor area for use on Class A fires and one unit for every 625 square feet for use on Class B fires.

CLASS II
Ordinary hazard occupancies (dry goods and warehouses) require one unit of extinguishing capacity for every 1,250 square feet of floor space for use on Class A fires and one unit for every 625 square feet of floor area for use on Class B fires.

CLASS III
Extra hazard occupancies (paint shops, etc.) require additional units of extinguishing capacity beyond the requirements specified for ordinary hazard occupancies at the discretion of local authorities.

NOTES:
1. Classifications from the National Board of Fire Underwriters.
2. In all cases check the requirements of local codes.

WATER BASE EXTINGUISHERS

	PRESSURIZED CLASS A ONLY	CARTRIDGE CLASS A ONLY	PUMP TANK CLASS A ONLY		LOADED STREAM CLASS A & B	SODA–ACID CLASS A ONLY	FOAM CLASS A & B
CAPACITY IN GALLONS	2 1/2	2 1/2	2 1/2	5	2 1/2	2 1/2	2 1/2
HEIGHT	25"	25"	26"	28"	27"	24"	24"
DIAMETER	8"	8"	8"	11"	8"	8"	8"
WEIGHT (LBS)	28	26	36	55	42	34	34
CLASS	2A	2A	2A	4A	2A, 1/2 B	2A	2A,4B
RECHARGE	Weigh cylinder and check annually. In all cases, follow instructions on extinguisher label.					Recharge after use, discharge and recharge annually.	
EFFECTIVE RANGE	45–55 ft.		30–40 ft.		35–40 ft.	30–40 ft.	35–40 ft.
PRESSURE SOURCE	compressed air	gas cartridge	hand pump		pressure	chemical reaction	
TEMPERATURE EFFECT	will freeze	will freeze	will freeze		will operate at −40°F.	will freeze	will freeze
METHOD OF EXTINGUISHING	quenches, cools	quenches, cools	quenches, cools		alka-metal salt quenches, cools and fireproofs	quenches, cools	smothers, cools

NOTE: All water base extinguishing agents are electric conductors.

CARBON DIOXIDE
CLASS B & C FIRES

CAP. IN LBS.	2 1/2	5	10	15	20
HEIGHT	18"	17"	22"	26"	26"
DIAMETER	4"	6"	7"	7"	8"
WEIGHT (LBS.)	10	18	35	44	55
CLASS	1B,C	1B,C	4B,C	4B,C	4B,C
HEIGHT	16"	15"	26"	30"	37"
DIAMETER	7"	10"	13"	12"	11"
WEIGHT (LBS.)	12	17	34	44	55
CLASS	1B,C	1B,C	4B,C	4B,C	4B,C
HEIGHT	18"	17"	26"	33"	33"
DIAMETER	9"	9"	11"	11"	12"
WEIGHT (LBS.)	9	17	34	42	55
CLASS	1B,C	1B,C	4B,C	4B,C	4B,C

EFFECTIVE RANGE
3 to 8 feet
DISCHARGE TIME
2 1/2 lbs., 12 sec.; 5 lbs., 22 sec.; 10 lbs., 23 sec.; 15 lbs., 26 sec.; 20 lbs., 25 sec.
RECHARGE
after use.
PRESSURE SOURCE
compressed gas.
TEMPERATURE EFFECT
will operate at minus 40°F.
ELECTRICAL CONDUCTIVITY
will not conduct.

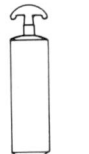

HAND PUMP   PRESSURIZED

VAPORIZING LIQUID
CLASS B & C FIRES—HAND PUMP

CAP. IN QTS.	1	1 1/2
HEIGHT	14"	18"
DIAMETER	3"	3"
WEIGHT (LBS.)	7	10
CLASS	1 1/2 B,C	1/2 B,C

Discharge time about one minute.

CLASS B & C FIRES
PRESSURIZED

CAP. IN QTS.	1	1 1/2
HEIGHT	14"	15"
DIAMETER	3"	3 1/2"
WEIGHT (LBS.)	7 1/2	9 1/2
CLASS	1/2 B,C	1/2 B,C

EFFECTIVE RANGE:
1 and 1 1/2 qt. pump — 20–30 ft.
pressurized — 1 qt. 25–30 ft.
RECHARGE:
after use.
PRESSURE SOURCE:
pump or pressurized.
TEMPERATURE EFFECT:
will operate at minus 40°F.
ELECTRICAL CONDUCTIVITY:
will not conduct.

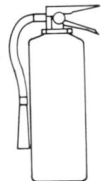

Dimensions below are for 2 makes of extinguisher to show relative sizes.

DRY CHEMICAL
CLASS B & C ONLY

CAP. IN LBS.	5	10	20	30
HEIGHT	19"	21"	22"	30"
DIAMETER	5"	6"	8"	8"
WEIGHT (LBS.)	15	33	48	70
CLASS	4B,C	8B,C	16B,C	20B,C
HEIGHT	13"	22"	21"	25"
DIAMETER	5"	7"	9"	9"
WEIGHT (LBS.)	12	21	35	50
CLASS	4B,C	8B,C	16B,C	20B,C

EFFECTIVE RANGE
10 to 20 feet.
DISCHARGE TIME
5 lbs., 10 sec.; 10 lbs., 11 sec.; 20 lbs., 15 sec.; 30 lbs., 24 sec.
RECHARGE
after use.
PRESSURE SOURCE
compressed gas.
TEMPERATURE EFFECT
will operate at minus 40°F.
ELECTRICAL CONDUCTIVITY
will not conduct.

Dimensions below are for 3 makes of extinguisher to show relative sizes.

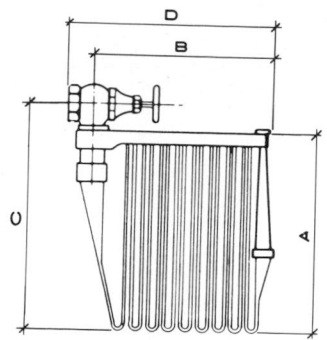

SWING RACK SEMI-AUTOMATIC
1½" LINEN HOSE

HOSE CAPACITY	25	50	75	100
A	10"	20"	24"	27"
B	15"	16"	19"	20"
C	14"	23"	27"	32"
D	17"	18"	20"	22"
WIDTH	4"	4"	4"	4"

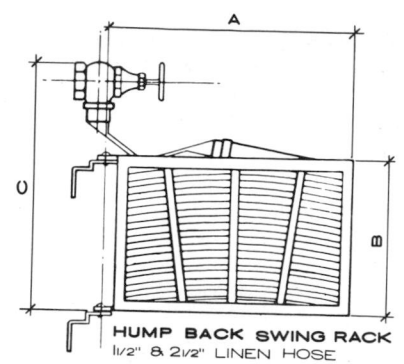

HUMP BACK SWING RACK
1½" & 2½" LINEN HOSE

HOSE CAPACITY	50	100	150	200
A	30"	30"	34"	40"
B	17"	21"	28"	39"
C	30"	33"	40"	50"
WIDTH 1½" HOSE	4"	4"	4"	4"
WIDTH 2½" HOSE	6"	6"	6"	6"

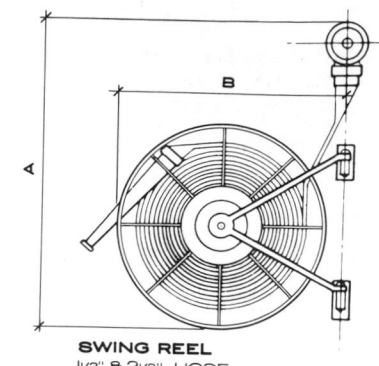

SWING REEL
1½" & 2½" HOSE

HOSE CAPACITY	50	100	150
A	38"	38"	36"
B	21"	27"	31"
WIDTH 1½" HOSE	4"	4"	4"
WIDTH 2½" HOSE	6"	6"	6"

FIRE HOSE RACK & REELS

NOTE:

Recommended hose size for use with building standpipes should not exceed 1½" in diameter and 75 feet in length. A larger hose used by amateurs is likely to tangle and cause excessive water damage.

A connection for 2½" hose should be available to each station for the use of firemen. Many codes require 2½" outlets at all standpipes.

By using a reducing coupling 1½" hose can be attached. When a 2½" stream is required the coupling may be removed. Industrial installations use 2½" hoses and train personnel in the use of the heavier equipment. Valves may be located 5'– 6" above floor (check local code).

Unlined woven linen hose is recommended for use on standpipe installations. Cotton rubber lined hose is standard for fire department and heavy equipment hose.

Tables show rack & reels for 1½" & 2½" linen hose only. Consult manufacturer's literature for rack & reel dimensions when other types & sizes of hose are used.

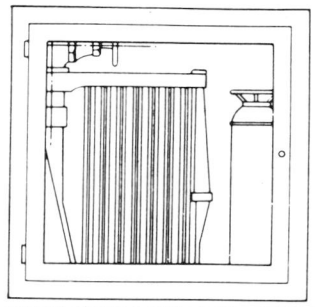

75 FT. 1½" LINEN HOSE, RACK & ANGLE VALVE   2½ GAL. EXTINGUISHER
2'-9"X2'-9"X8½" TO 2'-11"X2'-11"X9"

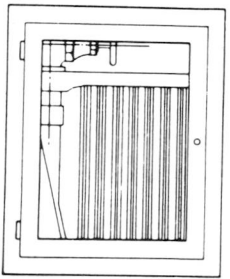

75 FT. 1½" LINEN HOSE, RACK & ANGLE VALVE.
1'-9"X2'-5"X8" TO 1'-4"X2'-7"X8½"

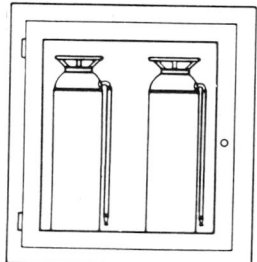

TWO 2½ GAL. EXTINGUISHERS
1'-11"X2'-9"X7" TO 2'-2"X2'-11"X8"

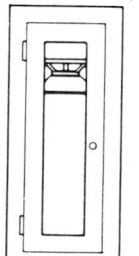

ONE 2½ GAL. EXTINGUISHER
1'-0"X2'-6"X8" TO 1'-4"X2'-7"X8½"
NOTE: RESIDENTIAL EXTINGUISHER CABINET 1'-5"X7"X2"

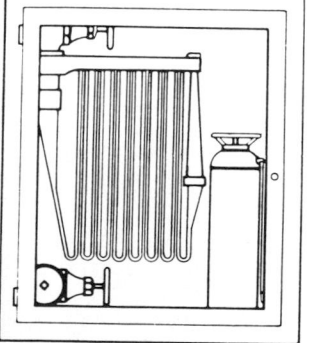

75 FT. 1½" LINEN HOSE & RACK 1½" & 2½" ANGLE VALVE 2½ GAL. EXTINGUISHER
2'-9"X3'-4"X8½ TO 2'-10"X3'-7"X9"

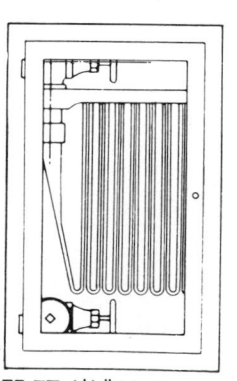

75 FT. 1½" LINEN HOSE & RACK 1½" & 2½" ANGLE VALVE
1'-11"X3'-3"X8½" TO 2'-4"X3'-4"X9"

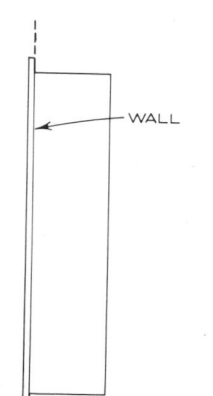

WALL

RECESSED

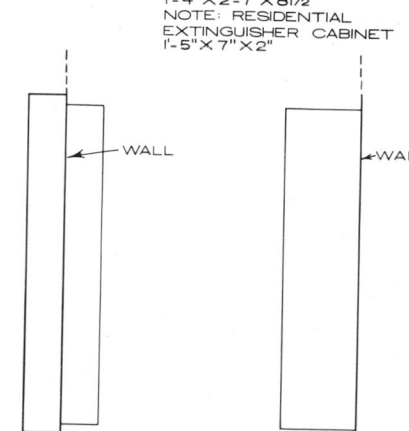

WALL

WALL

SEMI-RECESSED

SURFACE MOUNTED

FIRE HOSE & EXTINGUISHER CABINETS

NOTE:

Cabinets are #18 gauge steel with glass doors as shown or with doors of metal, wood, mirror, etc.

Consult manufacturer's literature for cabinets with special features such as: Revolving door, twin doors, pivoting door with attached extinguisher, curved door, etc.

Cabinets are obtainable for 25, 50, 75, & 100 foot hose racks. Rough dimensions are shown.

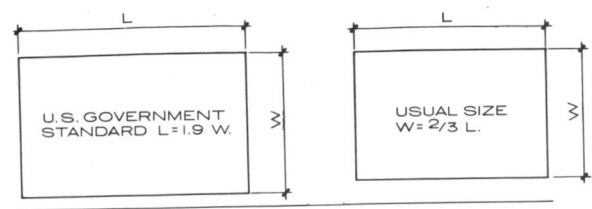

PROPORTIONS OF U.S. FLAG

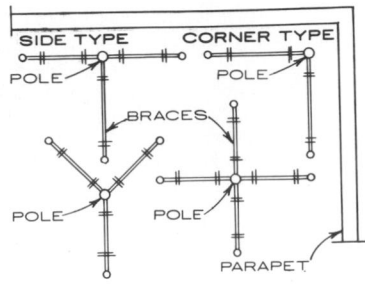

BRACING PLAN FOR POLE ON ROOF

U.S. FLAG SIZES AS MANUFACTURED AND USED

WIDTH	LENGTH	WIDTH	LENGTH
3'-0"	5'-0"	10'-0"	18'-0"
4'-0"	6'-0"	10'-0"	19'-0"
4'-4"	5'-6"	12'-0"	20'-0"
5'-0"	8'-0"	15'-0"	25'-0"
5'-0"	9'-6"	20'-0"	30'-0"
6'-0"	10'-0"	20'-0"	38'-0"
8'-0"	12'-0"	26'-0"	45'-0"
10'-0"	15'-0"		

BALL — FROM 5" DIAM. ON 20'-0" POLE TO 14" DIAM. ON 125'-0" POLE.

TILTING POLE UNIT — PIVOT FOR MAINTENANCE, COUNTER WEIGHT

FOUNDATION FOR GROUND SET POLE — METAL COLLAR, POLE, CAULKING, WEDGES, DRY SAND, CONCRETE, METAL TUBE, WEDGES, LIGHTNING PROTECTION, 10% OF POLE HGT. 3'-0" MIN.

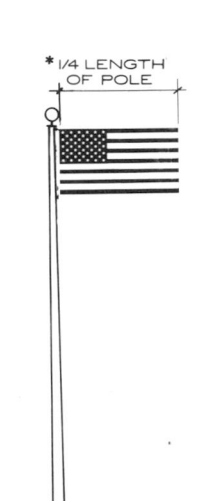

POLE ON GROUND — *1/4 LENGTH OF POLE

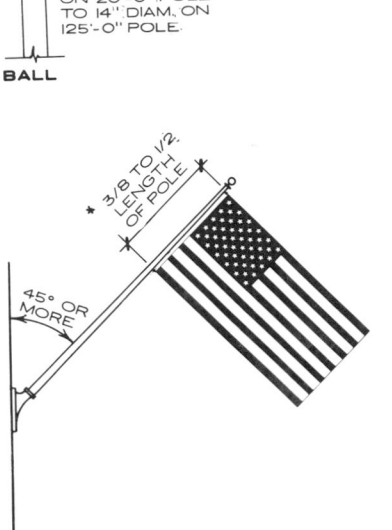

OUTRIGGER POLES FOR FLAGS ON BUILDING FRONTS — 3/8 TO 1/2 LENGTH OF POLE, 45° OR MORE

FOR FLAGS ON ROOFS — *1/3 LENGTH OF POLE

SIZE OF FLAG IN RELATION TO POLE HEIGHT

RECOMMENDED FLAG SIZES

POLE	FLAG SIZE	POLE	FLAG SIZE
15'-0"	3'-0" x 5'-0"	50'-0"	8'-0" x 12'-0"
20'-0"	4'-0" x 6'-0"	60'-0"	8'-0" x 12'-0"
25'-0"	4'-0" x 6'-0"	65'-0"	9'-0" x 15'-0"
30'-0"	5'-0" x 8'-0"	70'-0"	9'-0" x 15'-0"
35'-0"	5'-0" x 8'-0"	80'-0"	10'-0" x 15'-0"
40'-0"	6'-0" x 10'-0"	90'-0"	10'-0" x 15'-0"
45'-0"	6'-0" x 10'-0"	100'-0"	12'-0" x 18'-0"

NOTE:

Outrigger poles require bracing for lengths over 13'-0", and are available in entasis tapered shapes of bronze, aluminum and stainless steel.

*For windy weather, smaller flags than the above are generally used.

RELATION OF HEIGHT OF POLE TO HEIGHT OF BLDG.

HEIGHT OF POLE	HEIGHT OF BLDG.
20'-0"	1 to 2 stories
25'-0"	3 to 5 stories
33'-0" to 35'-0"	6 to 10 stories
40'-0" to 50'-0"	11 to 15 stories
60'-0" to 75'-0"	over 15 stories

NOTE:

This rule serves for preliminary assumptions

POLE SIZES AS GENERALLY MANUFACTURED (STEEL)

LIGHTWEIGHT SWAGED JOINED SECTIONS

HT.	BASE DIAM.	TOP DIAM.
20'-0"	3 1/2"	2 3/8"
25'-0"	4"	2 3/8"
30'-0"	4 1/2"	2 3/8"
35'-0"	4 1/2"	2 3/8"
40'-0"	5"	2 3/8"
45'-0"	5"	2 3/8"
50'-0"	5 9/16"	2 3/8"
60'-0"	6 5/8"	2 3/8"
70'-0"	7 5/8"	2 3/8"
75'-0"	8 5/8"	2 3/8"
80'-0"	9 5/8"	2 3/8"
90'-0"	10 3/4"	2 3/8"
100'-0"	11 3/4"	2 3/8"

SWAGED

HEAVYWEIGHT SWAGED JOINED SECTIONS

HT.	BASE DIAM.	TOP DIAM.
20'-0"	4"	2 7/8"
25'-0"	4 1/2"	2 7/8"
30'-0"	5"	2 7/8"
40'-0"	5 9/16"	2 7/8"
50'-0"	6 5/8"	2 7/8"
60'-0"	7 5/8"	2 7/8"
70'-0"	8 5/8"	2 7/8"
75'-0"	9 5/8"	2 7/8"
80'-0"	10 3/4"	2 7/8"
90'-0"	11 3/4"	2 7/8"
100'-0"	12 3/4"	2 7/8"
125'-0"	14"	2 7/8"

SWAGED

EXTRA HEAVYWEIGHT SWAGED JOINED SECTIONS

HT.	BASE DIAM.	TOP DIAM.
25'-0"	5"	3 1/2"
30'-0"	5 9/16"	3 1/2"
35'-0"	6 5/8"	3 1/2"
40'-0"	7 5/8"	3 1/2"
45'-0"	8 5/8"	3 1/2"
50'-0"	8 5/8"	3 1/2"
55'-0"	9 5/8"	3 1/2"
60'-0"	10 3/4"	3 1/2"
70'-0"	11 3/4"	4"
75'-0"	12 3/4"	4"
80'-0"	12 3/4"	4"
90'-0"	14"	4"
100'-0"	16"	4"

SWAGED

CONE TAPERED OR ENTASIS TAPERED

HT.	BASE DIAM.	TOP DIAM.
20'-0"	5"	3 1/4"
25'-0"	5 9/16"	3 1/4"
30'-0"	6"	3 1/4"
35'-0"	6 5/8"	3 1/4"
40'-0"	7 5/8"	3 1/4"
50'-0"	8 5/8"	3 1/4"
60'-0"	10 3/4"	3 1/4"
70'-0"	11 3/4"	3 1/4"
75'-0"	12 3/4"	4"
80'-0"	14"	4"
90'-0"	15"	4"
100'-0"	16"	4"

CONE   ENTASIS

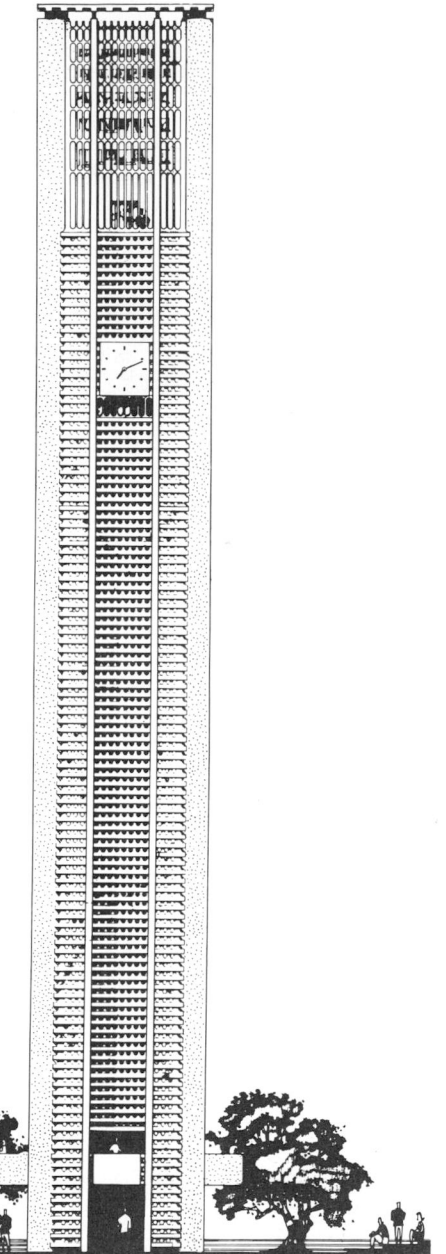

UNIVERSITY OF CALIFORNIA, RIVERSIDE   22' SQUARE x 161'

BELL SYSTEMS DESCRIPTIONS

CLASSIFICATION:
PEAL . . . . . .2–8 BELLS
CHIME . . . . .9–22 BELLS
CARILLON . .23+ BELLS

PLAYING METHOD
1. MANUAL
       Keyboard levers "batons"
       Electric console
2. AUTOMATIC
       Roll Player
       Programed hour strike
       Swinging bell ringer

BELL STRIKE MECHANISMS:
1. Wire cables connecting
bell clapper to clavier keyboard.
2. Electric operated hammer
fastened adjacent to bell. The
above playing methods and
bell strike mechanisms can be
interchanged to provide an
automatic as well as a manually operated system.

CLOCK SYSTEMS DESCRIPTIONS

SYSTEM 1
One electric master clock programmed to control secondary
clocks. Secondary clocks with
self-correcting reset devices to
keep all clocks coordinated.

Master clock programmed to
control bell strike mechanisms
on the quarter, half, and full
hour.

SYSTEM 2
One synchronous electric
motor driven clock with
mechanically operated
shafts direct to indicators
on clock face.

Movement size correlated
to size and quantity of
clocks.

Clock dial design and size
is unrestricted. A minimum
clock dial radius is equal
to 1/15 of its height above
the ground.

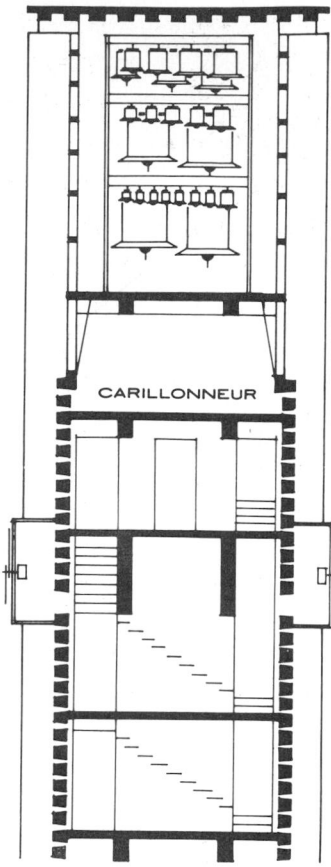

CARILLONNEUR

SECTION

GENERAL INFORMATION

Provide maximum wall openings at belfry area.

Provide separate areas for
both bell and clock move-
ments.

Provide vibration isolators
at each bell support to
prevent vibration to structure.

Cast bronze bells of:
    80% pure copper
    20% pure tin

The minimum space below
the largest bell to the belfry
floor should equal the large
bell diameter.

BELL DATA — FOUR OCTAVES

A' = 435 VIBRATIONS

NOTE	POUNDS	DIAMETER	HEIGHT	NOTE	POUNDS	DIAMETER	HEIGHT	NOTE	POUNDS	DIAMETER	HEIGHT	NOTE	POUNDS	DIAMETER	HEIGHT
B	5665	60"	52"	C_2	583	30"	25"	C_3	119	17"	14"	C_4	40	11"	9"
C_1	4730	60"	50"	$C^\#_2$	484	38"	24"	$C^\#_3$	108	16"	14"	$C^\#_4$	37	10"	9"
D_1	3300	53"	44"	D_2	407	27"	22"	D_3	99	15"	13"	D_4	35	10"	9"
$D^\#_1$	2750	50"	42"	$D^\#_2$	341	25"	21"	$D^\#_3$	90	15"	13"	$D^\#_4$	34	10"	8"
E_1	2332	47"	40"	E_2	290	24"	20"	E_3	81	14"	12"	E_4	33	9"	8"
F_1	1910	44"	37"	F_2	253	22"	18"	F_3	75	14"	12"	F_4	32	9"	8"
$F^\#_1$	1683	42"	35"	$F^\#_2$	220	21"	18"	$F^\#_3$	68	13"	11"	$F^\#_4$	31	9"	7"
G_1	1408	40"	33"	G_2	198	20"	18"	G_3	62	13"	11"	G_4	30	9"	7"
$G^\#_1$	1188	38"	32"	$G^\#_2$	176	20"	16"	$G^\#_3$	57	12"	11"	$G^\#_4$	29	8"	7"
A_1	1000	36"	30"	A_2	154	18"	16"	A_3	53	12"	10"	A_4	28	8"	7"
$A^\#_1$	836	33"	28"	$A^\#_2$	141	18"	15"	$A^\#_3$	48	11"	10"	$A^\#_4$	26	8"	7"
B_1	704	31"	25"	B_2	130	17"	15"	B_3	44	11"	9"	B_4	25	8"	7"

A. Quincy Jones, FAIA, and Associates, Architects; Los Angeles, California

NOTES:

Data processing equipment on this page is shown to assist the architect with sizes in planning and to indicate the degree of variation in size and design of equipment. Many other variaties of equipment by other manufacturers are available.

Each installation is unique and equipment is constantly changing. Flexibility in planning and accessibility to supporting mechanical systems are requirements. Pedestal floors provide support for uniform or concentrated loads. Space below floor serves as plenum, duct space, electrical cables for computers, etc. Equipment supplier must be contacted at initial planning.

GENERAL DESIGN REQUIREMENT:

1. Heating and electrical system: separate from building to minimize shut downs. Temperature 60°–90°, humidity 20%–80% with filtered, dust-free air.
2. Walls: non-combustible and sound treated.
3. Floors: accessible and non-combustible and to retard sound vibration.
4. Ceiling: acoustic type and non-combustible.
5. Lighting: 60 to 80 foot candles desirable, 40 ft. candles minimum. Avoid direct sunlight.
6. Doors: large enough to accomodate equipment.
7. Fire detection system.

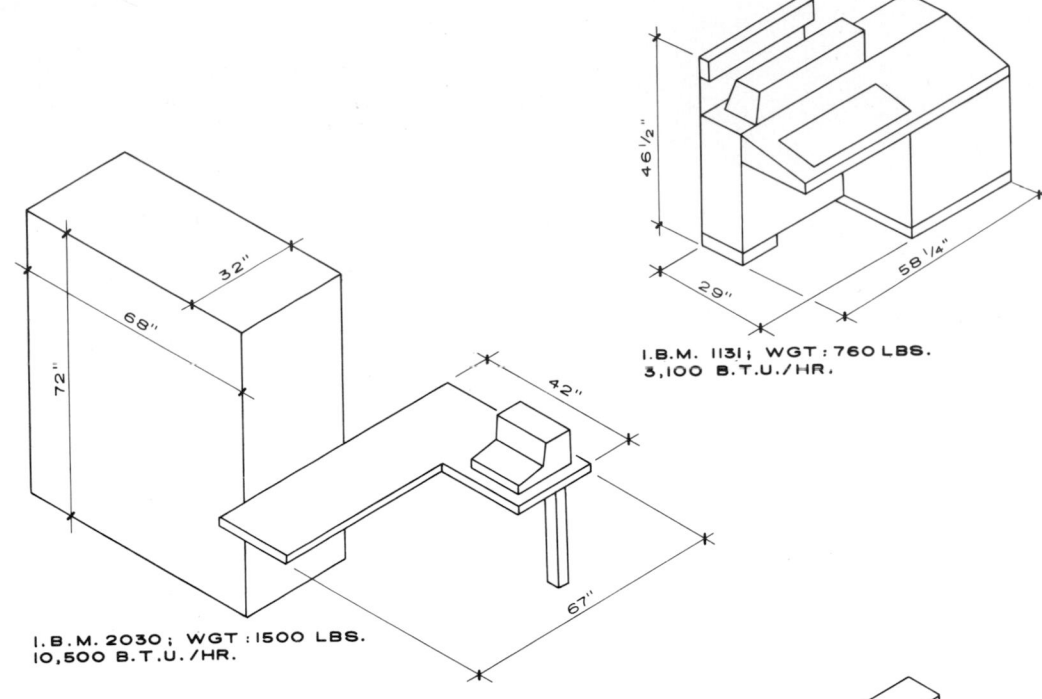

I.B.M. 1131; WGT: 760 LBS.
3,100 B.T.U./HR.

I.B.M. 2030; WGT: 1500 LBS.
10,500 B.T.U./HR.

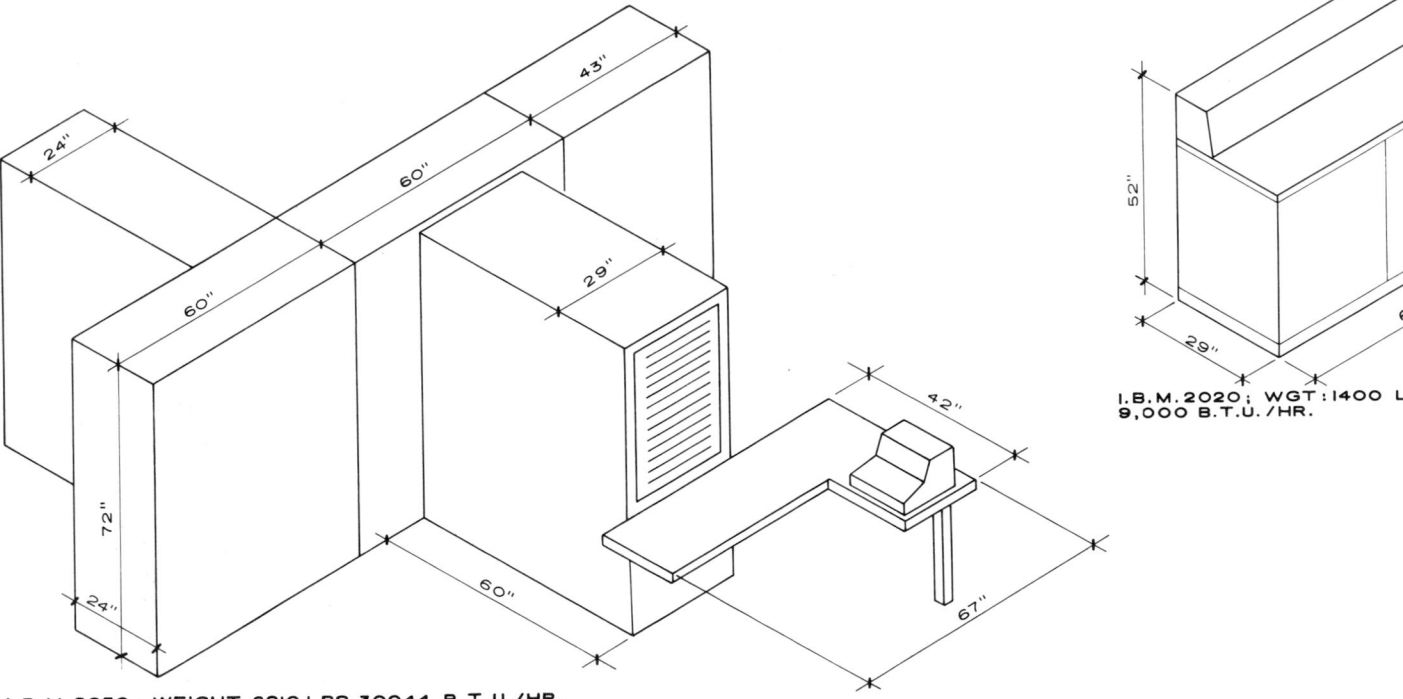

I.B.M. 2050; WEIGHT 6910 LBS. 30044 B.T.U./HR.

I.B.M. 2020; WGT: 1400 LBS.
9,000 B.T.U./HR.

CENTRAL PROCESSING UNITS

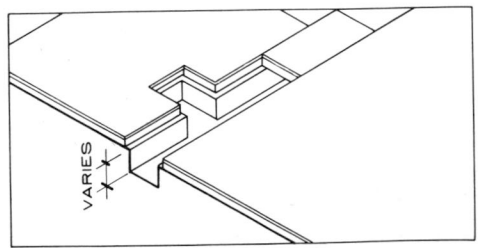

RACEWAY FLOORS
COVERS REMOVABLE/CUTOUTS IN COVERS

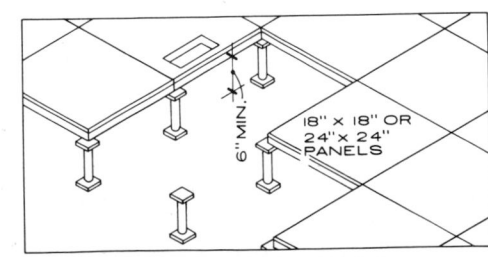

18" x 18" OR 24" x 24" PANELS

PEDESTAL SUPPORTED PANELS
PANELS REMOVABLE/CUTOUTS IN PANELS

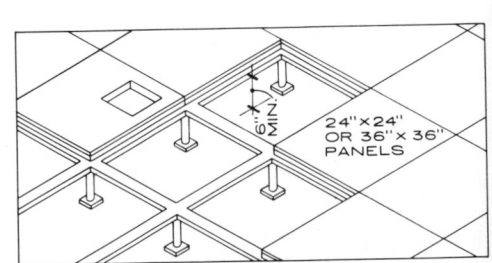

24" x 24" OR 36" x 36" PANELS

SUBFRAMING SUPPORTED PANELS
PANELS REMOVABLE/CUTOUTS IN PANELS

ACCESSIBLE COMPUTER FLOOR SYSTEMS

Robert L. Plumley, AIA; Seibert, Hunter, Shute & Plumley; Medford, Oregon

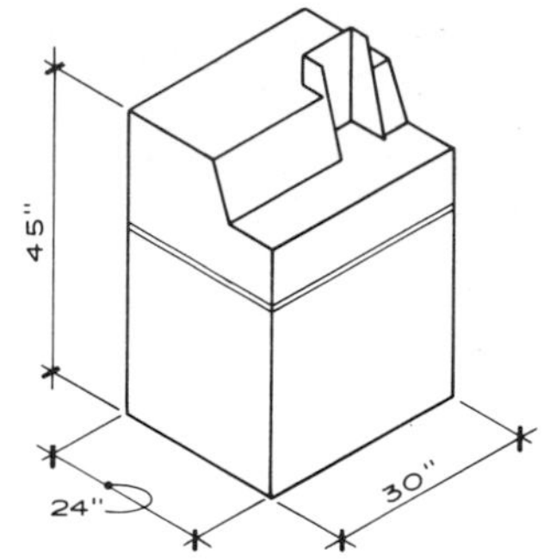

CARD READER
WGT: 440 LBS.
1,200 B.T.U./HR.

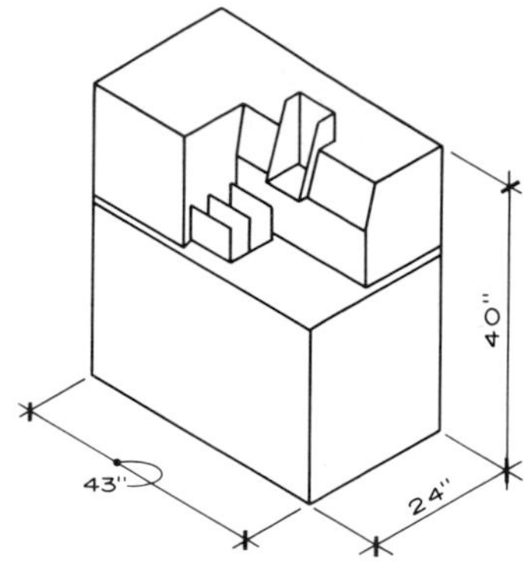

45"
24"
30"

CARD READ PUNCH
WGT: 575 LBS.
2,200 B.T.U./HR.

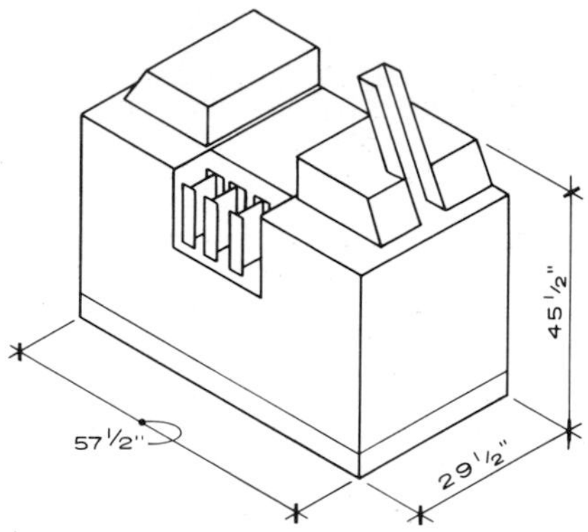

40"
43"
24"

CARD READ PUNCH
WGT: 1050 LBS.
3,000 B.T.U./HR.

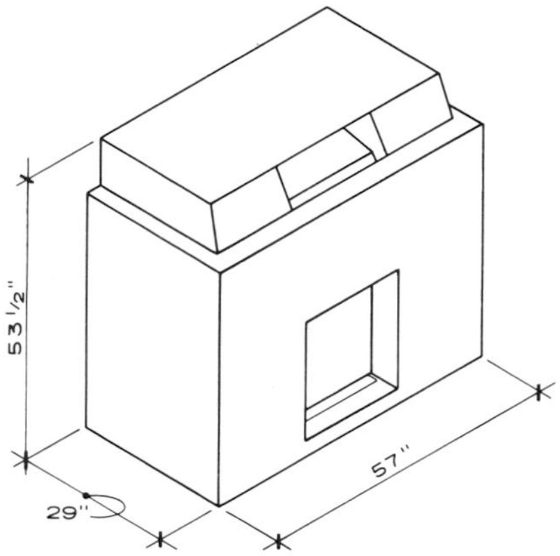

45½"
57½"
29½"

PRINTER
WGT: 825 LBS.
4,500 B.T.U./HR.

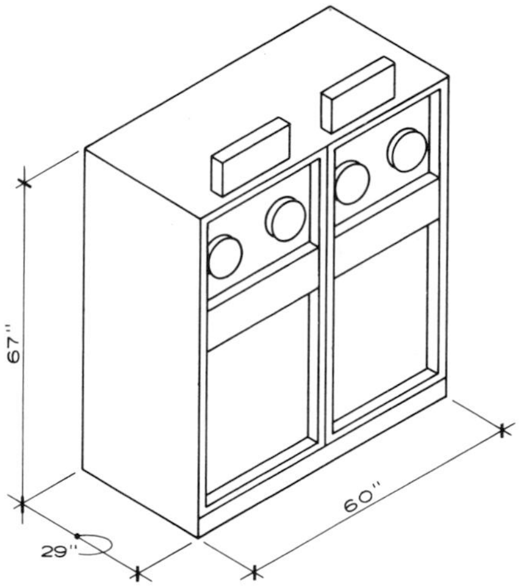

53½"
29"
57"

MAGNETIC TAPE UNIT (DBE.)
WGT: 1600 LBS.
7,000 B.T.U./HR.

67"
29"
60"

CONTROL UNIT
WGT: 1000 LBS.
7,000 B.T.U./HR.

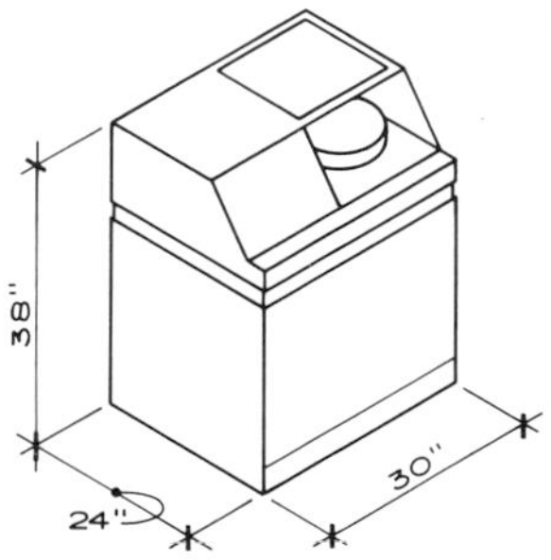

60"
32"
46"

DISK STORAGE DRIVE
WGT: 390 LBS.
2,000 B.T.U./HR.

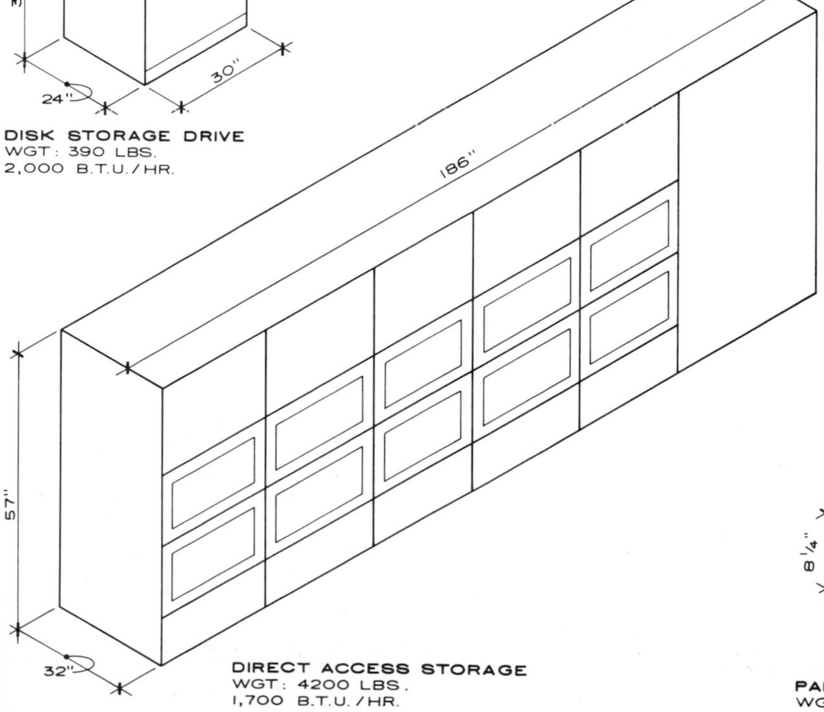

38"
24"
30"

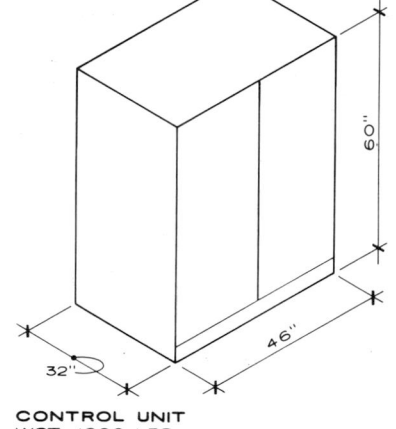

DISPLAY STATION
WGT: 45 LBS.
477 B.T.U./HR.

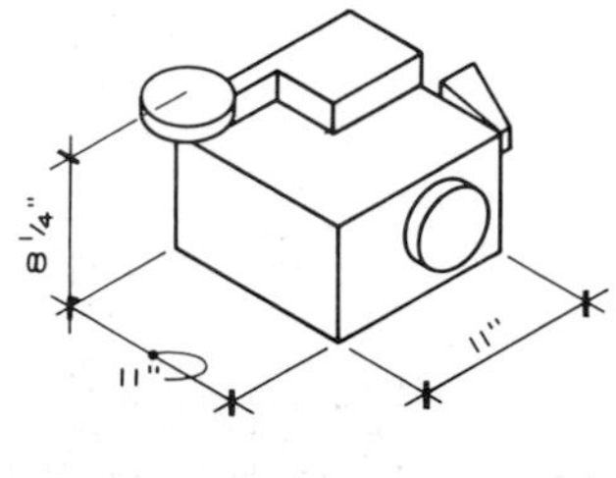

17½"
13¾"
19½"

DIRECT ACCESS STORAGE
WGT: 4200 LBS.
1,700 B.T.U./HR.

186"
57"
32"

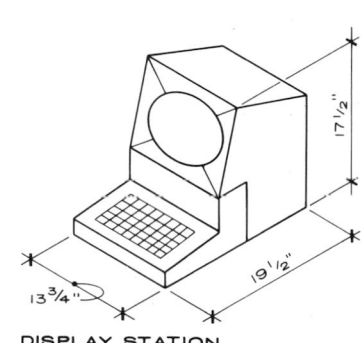

PAPER TAPE PUNCH
WGT: 26 LBS

8¼"
11"
11"

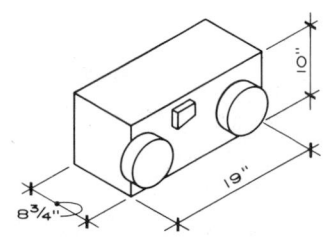

PAPER TAPE RECORDER
WGT: 15 LBS.

10"
8¾"
19"

Robert L. Plumley, AIA; Seibert, Hunter, Shute & Plumley; Medford, Oregon

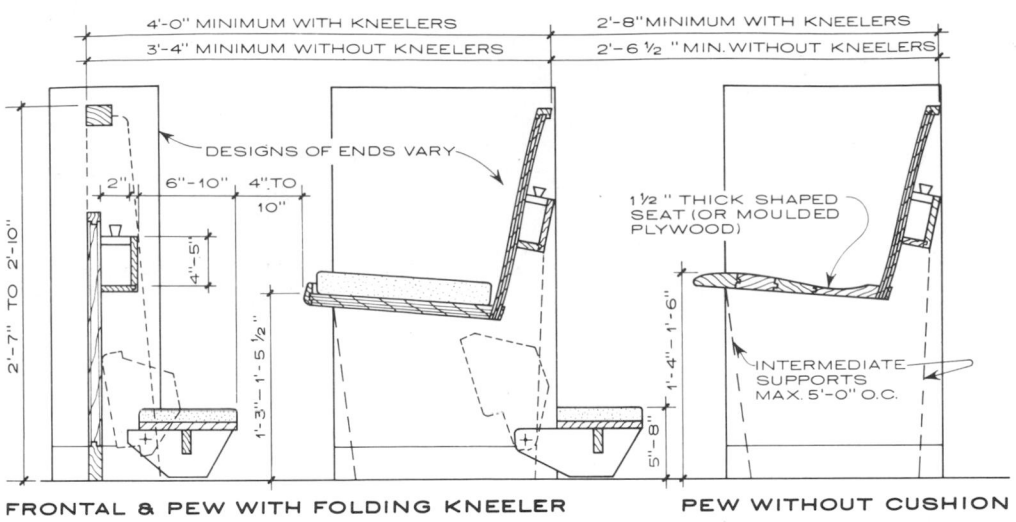

4'-0" MINIMUM WITH KNEELERS
3'-4" MINIMUM WITHOUT KNEELERS
2'-8" MINIMUM WITH KNEELERS
2'-6 ½" MIN. WITHOUT KNEELERS

DESIGNS OF ENDS VARY

1 ½" THICK SHAPED SEAT (OR MOULDED PLYWOOD)

INTERMEDIATE SUPPORTS MAX. 5'-0" O.C.

FRONTAL & PEW WITH FOLDING KNEELER

PEW WITHOUT CUSHION

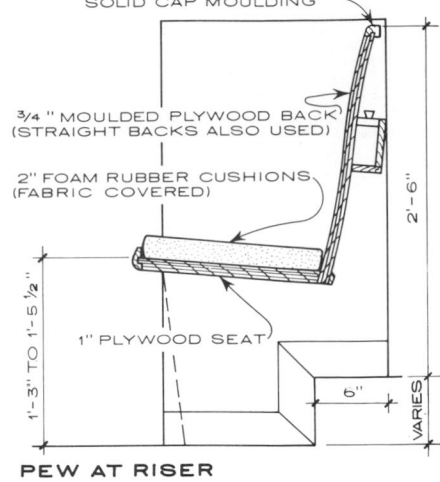

SOLID CAP MOULDING

¾" MOULDED PLYWOOD BACK (STRAIGHT BACKS ALSO USED)

2" FOAM RUBBER CUSHIONS (FABRIC COVERED)

1" PLYWOOD SEAT

PEW AT RISER

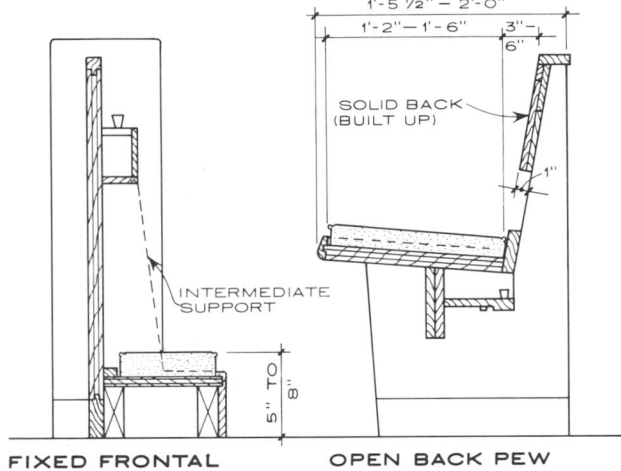

SOLID BACK (BUILT UP)

INTERMEDIATE SUPPORT

FIXED FRONTAL   **OPEN BACK PEW**

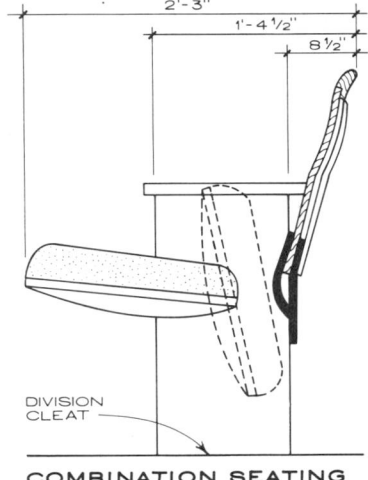

2'-3"
1'-4 ½"
8 ½"

DIVISION CLEAT

COMBINATION SEATING

PEW SPACING BACK TO BACK			PEW SPACING SEAT WIDTH *		
NO. OF SPACES	2'-10" SPACING	2'-8" SPACING	NO. OF PERSONS	1'-8" SEAT WIDTH	1'-6" SEAT WIDTH
1	2'-10"	2'-8"	1	1'-8"	1'-6"
2	5'-8"	5'-4"	2	3'-4"	3'-0"
3	8'-6"	8'-0"	3	5'-0"	4'-6"
4	11'-4"	10'-8"	4	6'-8"	6'-0"
5	14'-2"	13'-4"	5	8'-4"	7'-6"
6	17'-0"	16'-0"	6	10'-0"	9'-0"
7	19'-10"	18'-8"	7	11'-8"	10'-6"
8	22'-8"	21'-4"	8	13'-4"	12'-0"
9	25'-6"	24'-0"	9	15'-0"	13'-6"
10	28'-4"	26'-8"	10	16'-8"	15'-0"
20	56'-8"	53'-4"	11	18'-4"	16'-6"
30	85'-0"	80'-0"	12	20'-0"	18'-0"
40	113'-4"	106'-8"	13	21'-8"	19'-6"
50	141'-8"	133'-4"	14	23'-4"	21'-0"
			15	not recommended	

*When pews have ends, thickness of ends must be added to dimensions.

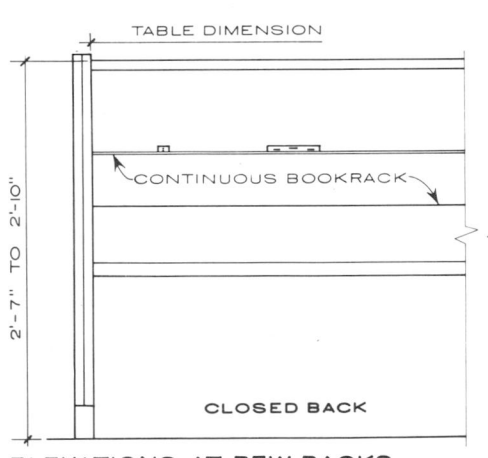

TABLE DIMENSION

CONTINUOUS BOOKRACK

CLOSED BACK

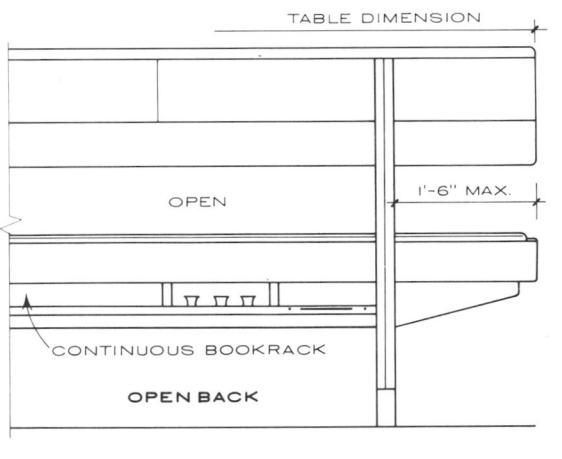

TABLE DIMENSION

OPEN

1'-6" MAX.

CONTINUOUS BOOKRACK

OPEN BACK

ELEVATIONS AT PEW BACKS

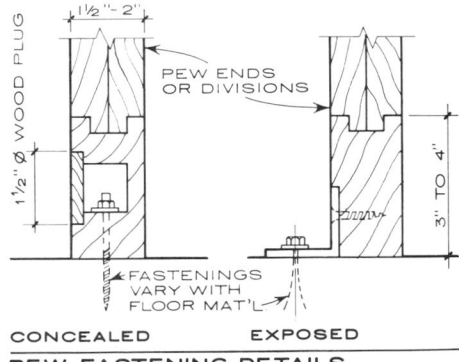

1 ½" Ø WOOD PLUG

PEW ENDS OR DIVISIONS

FASTENINGS VARY WITH FLOOR MAT'L

CONCEALED   EXPOSED

PEW FASTENING DETAILS

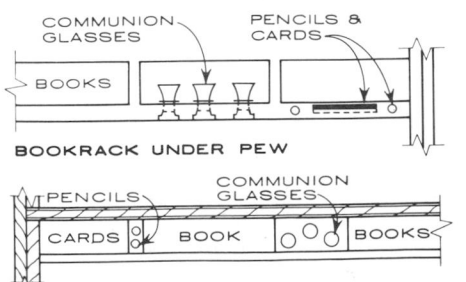

COMMUNION GLASSES

PENCILS & CARDS

BOOKS

BOOKRACK UNDER PEW

PENCILS
COMMUNION GLASSES
CARDS   BOOK   BOOKS

BOOKRACK ON PEW BACK

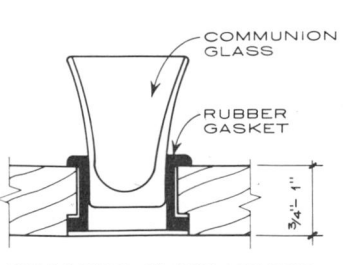

COMMUNION GLASS

RUBBER GASKET

COMMUNION GLASS HOLDER

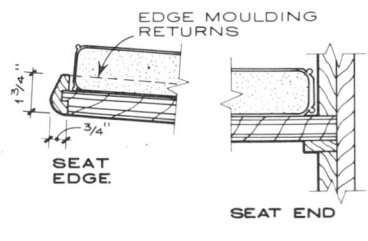

EDGE MOULDING RETURNS

SEAT EDGE.

SEAT END

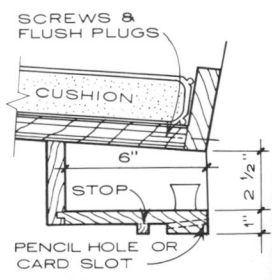

SCREWS & FLUSH PLUGS

CUSHION

STOP

PENCIL HOLE OR CARD SLOT

BOOKRACK

TYPICAL DETAILS

Harold E. Wagoner, FAIA and Associates; Philadelphia, Pennsylvania

STANDARD CARPET AND RUG SIZES

CARPET	AVAILABLE WIDTHS
SYNTHETIC FIBERS	4'–6'', 6', 7'–6'', 9', 12', 15'
WOOL FIBERS	9', 12', 15'
Stair Width	2'–3''
SPONGE BONDED or RUBBER BACKED	4'–6'', 12'
CARPET PAD	
ALL HAIR, HAIR AND FIBER, RUBBERIZED HAIR AND FIBER	2'–3'', 3', 4'–6'', 6', 9', 12'
FOAM RUBBER	3', 6'
SPONGE RUBBER	3', 4'–6'', 9'

CROSS SECTION OF READILY AVAILABLE SIZES

	WIDTH	LENGTH
AREA RUGS		
RECTANGULAR	3'	5'
	4'	6', 7', 10'
	5'	8'
	6'	8', 9'
	8'	10', 12'
	9'	12'
	10'	13', 14'
	12'	14', 15', 18'
SQUARE & ROUND	4'	4'
	5'	5'
	6'	6'
	9'	9'
	12'	12'
HEMP RUGS	6'	9'
	8'	10'
	9'	12', 36' ROLLS
	12'	15'
HANDWOVEN RUGS	2'	2'–4'', 3'–2'', 4', 4'–8''
(such as RYA or	3'–4''	4', 4'–4'', 5'–10''
FLAT WOVEN)	4'	4'–5', 5', 5'–10'', 6'–8''
	5'	5'–6'', 6'–8'', 7'–4'', 8'–4''
	6'–8''	8'–4'', 10'
	9'–10''	13'
MACHINE WASHABLE		
RECTANGULAR	1'–5''	2'
	2'	3', 3'–6'', 6'
	3'	5'
	4'	6'
	6'	9'
	8'	10'
	9'	12'
ROUND	2', 3', 5', 6' Diam.	
ORIENTAL		
MOROCCAN	4'	6'
	6'	9'
	8'	10''
	9'	12''
	12'	15', 18' (sometimes)
*PERSIAN		
DOZAR	4'–3''	6'–11''
KELLEGI	5'–11''	16'–4''
KENAREH (Runner)	3'	8' to 20'
PUSHTI	2'	3'
QALI	5'–11''	10'
YASTIK	10'' to 1'–3''	1'–8'' to 2'–7''
ZARCHEREK	2'–4''	4'–7''
ZARONIM	3'–5''	5'
OUTDOOR/INDOOR	3'	Sold by the yard and in
	9'	12'' squares.
	12'	

ISD Incorporated, Chicago and New York

STANDARD LINEN SIZES

	SIZE	SUGGESTED FOLDED SIZE
FLAT SHEET		
TWIN	72 x 108	9 x 13 1/2
DOUBLE	81 x 108	10 1/8 x 13 1/2
QUEEN SIZE	90 x 115	11 1/4 x 14 3/8
KING SIZE	108 x 120	13 1/2 x 15
FITTED SHEET		
TWIN	39 x 76	9 3/4 x 9 1/2
DOUBLE	54 x 76	13 1/2 x 9 1/2
QUEEN SIZE	60 x 80	15 x 10
KING SIZE	72 x 84	18 x 10 1/2
PILLOW CASE		
STANDARD	21 x 33	7 x 11
KING	21 x 45	7 x 15
BLANKET		
TWIN	66 x 90	16 1/2 x 22 1/2
	72 x 90	18 x 22 1/2
DOUBLE	80 x 90	20 x 22 1/2
QUEEN/KING	108 x 90	27 x 22 1/2
HAND TOWEL	11 x 18	5 1/2 x 9
	12 x 20	6 x 10
FACE TOWEL	15 x 26	7 1/2 x 13
	16 x 32	8 x 16
	18 x 36	9 x 18
BATH TOWEL	22 x 44	11 x 11
	24 x 48	12 x 12
	26 x 50	13 x 12 1/2
	28 x 52	14 x 13
BATH SHEET	36 x 68	12 x 17
	44 x 72	14 3/4 x 18
WASH CLOTH	9 x 9	4 1/2 x 9
	12 x 12	6 x 12
	14 x 14	7 x 14
BATH MAT	20 x 30	10 x 7 1/2
	20 x 34	10 x 8 1/2
	22 x 36	10 x 9
TABLE CLOTH		
RECTANGULAR	52 x 52	
	52 x 70	
	62 x 85	
	62 x 104	
	70 x 90	
	70 x 126	
ROUND	72'' DIAM.	
	90'' DIAM.	
OVAL	52 x 70	
	64 x 84	
	72 x 90	
NAPKIN	14 x 14	4 3/4 x 7
	18 x 18	6 x 9
	22 x 22	7 1/2 x 11
DISH TOWEL	16 x 30	8 x 15
	18 x 36	9 x 18
	20 x 32	10 x 16

NOTE: There is no standard method of folding linens.

*NOTE ON PERSIAN RUGS:

Sizes are examples. Names do not refer to types, but to size.

TYPE OF SLAT	SIZE		PULLEY OPERATED	OSCILLATING LIFT
2" ALUMINUM	Blind	Maximum width	16'– 0"	20'– 0"
		Maximum length	20'– 0"	16'– 0"
		Maximum area	120 Sq. Ft.	245 Sq. Ft.
		Head box	2" H x 2 3/8" W	5 5/8" x 4 7/8"
	Pocket	Width "W"	4 1/2"	7 1/4"
		Height "H"	2 1/2" + 3/4" per linear foot of blind height.	7 3/4" + 3/4" per linear foot of blind height.
1" ALUMINUM	Blind	Maximum width	12'– 0"	
		Maximum length	10'– 0"	
		Maximum area	120 Sq. Ft.	
		Head box	1 1/2" sq. to 2 1/4"	
	Pocket	Width "W"	2 1/2"	
		Height "H"	1 1/2" to 2 1/4" + 1/2" per linear foot of blind height.	Not available
2" STEEL		Usually limited to small blinds—maximum area = 80 Sq. Ft.; other data as for aluminum.		
WOOD		Rarely used—maximum area 80 Sq. Ft.		

NOTE:

Pulley operated blinds up to 69 7/8"—single pull. Larger blinds—compound pull.

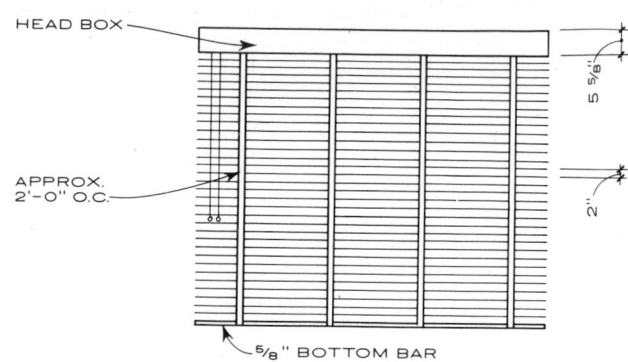

HORIZONTAL VENETIAN BLINDS

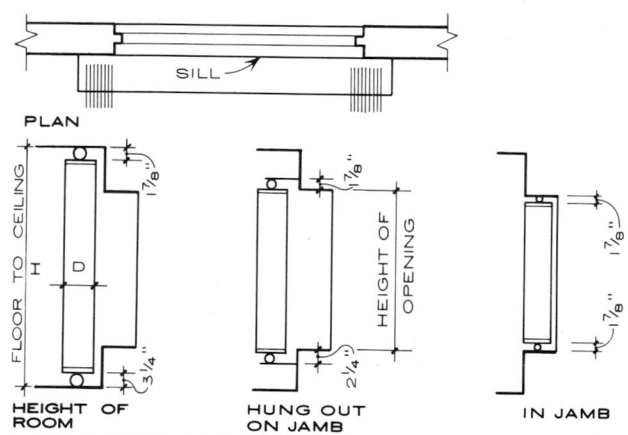

VERTICAL VENETIAN BLINDS

	THRU VU	SIMON VENTI-LIGHTER	VERTICAL LOUVERED BLIND
SINGLE SPAN WIDTH LIMIT	12'–0"	10'–0"	16'–0"
HEIGHT	UP TO 25'–0"	10'–0"	UP TO 24'–0"
DEPTH OF VANE	3 1/2", 5", 7 1/2"	5" TO 7"	METAL 4"–7" FABRIC 3"–10"

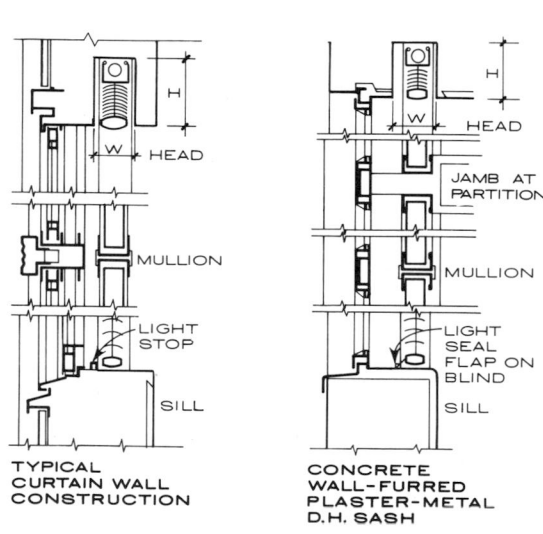

TYPICAL CURTAIN WALL CONSTRUCTION

CONCRETE WALL–FURRED PLASTER–METAL D.H. SASH

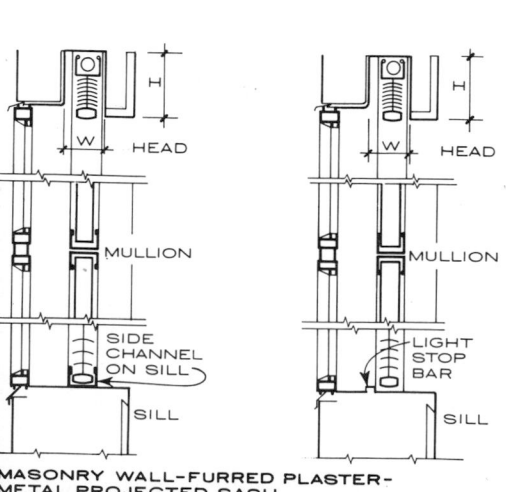

MASONRY WALL–FURRED PLASTER–METAL PROJECTED SASH

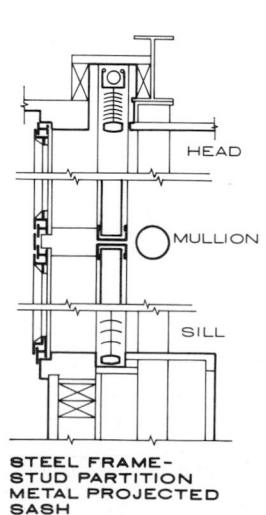

STEEL FRAME–STUD PARTITION METAL PROJECTED SASH

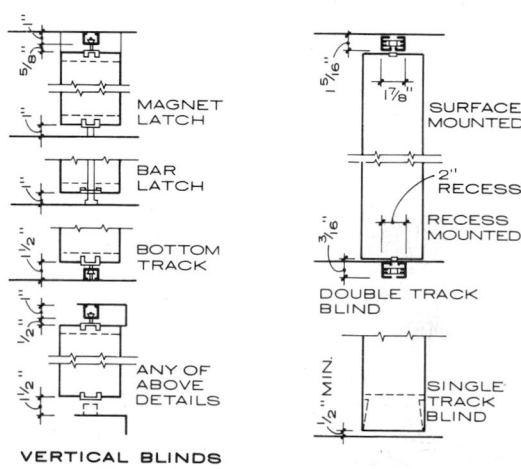

VERTICAL BLINDS

VARIOUS SUGGESTED INSTALLATION METHODS

Stewart R. James; Kilham Beder & Chu; New York, New York

TWO CHANNEL EXTRUDED ALUMINUM TRACK — CORD PULL FLUSH, RECESSED OR BRACKET MOUNTED

		GRABER	KIRSCH
MAXIMUM LENGTH — TWO WAY DRAW		42'—0"	32'—0"
MAXIMUM LENGTH — ONE WAY DRAW		30'—0"	16'—0"
MAXIMUM LENGTH — MULTIPLE DRAW		60'—0"	64'—0"
MAXIMUM FABRIC WEIGHT — TWO WAY		110 lbs.	80 lbs.
	ONE WAY	75 lbs.	80 lbs.
	MULTIPLE	150 lbs.	160 lbs.
PROJECTION & BRACKETS REQUIRED		48" apart at ends 24" projection 3/4" to 5"	No brackets space screws 16" on centers
CURVE		12" radius	Cannot be curved
PLEAT SPACING		4" to 6"	4" to 6"
CEILING POCKET FOR DRAPERY ONLY		5" front to back minimum	

HAND PULL — RARELY USED EXCEPT FOR HOSPITAL CUBICLES

NOTES:

Fullness of fabric lining and pleating determine exact width at gathering space (bunching). For 100% fullness (double width): Basic allowance = 1/3 of window width. For bunching this includes overlap and pulleys.

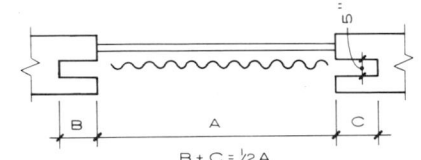

TWO — WAY DRAW

B + C = 1/2 A

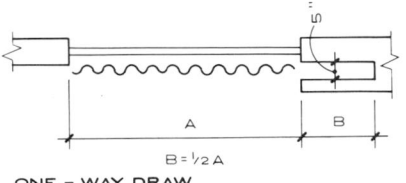

ONE — WAY DRAW

B = 1/2 A

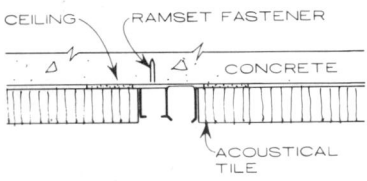

TO CONCRETE

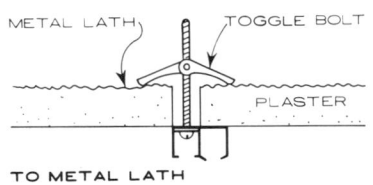

TO METAL LATH

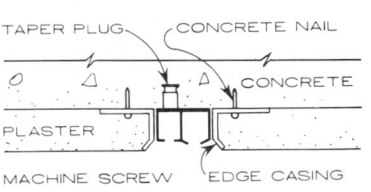

TO CONCRETE

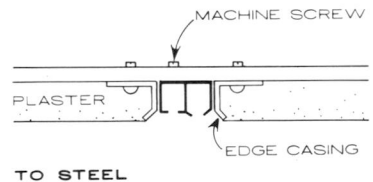

TO STEEL

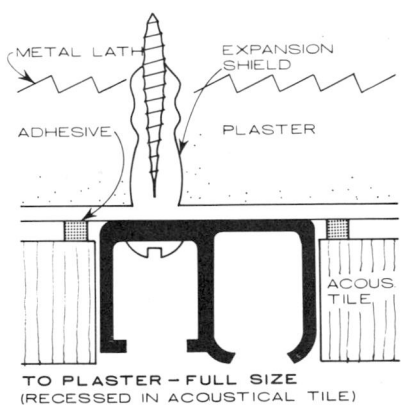

TO PLASTER — FULL SIZE (RECESSED IN ACOUSTICAL TILE)

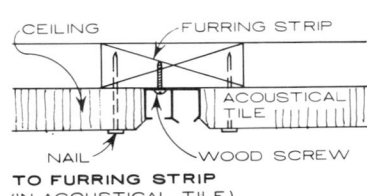

TO METAL LATH (RECESSED)

TO FURRING STRIP (IN ACOUSTICAL TILE)

VARIOUS INSTALLATION DETAILS

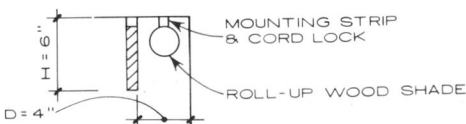

DEPTH OF POCKET REQUIRED = DIAMETER + 1/2"
HEIGHT OF POCKET REQUIRED = DIAMETER + 2 1/2"

ROLL - UP WOOD SHADES — HOLLAND (TEMLITE)

SHADE HEIGHT	DIAM. ROLLED	SHADE HEIGHT	DIAM. ROLLED	SHADE HEIGHT	DIAM. ROLLED	SHADE HEIGHT	DIAM. ROLLED
3'—0"	3 1/2"	5'—0"	4"	7'—0"	4 3/4"	9'—0"	5 1/8"
4'—0"	3 3/4"	6'—0"	4 3/8"	8'—0"	5"	10'—0"	5 1/2"

Stewart R. James; Kilham Beder & Chu; New York, New York

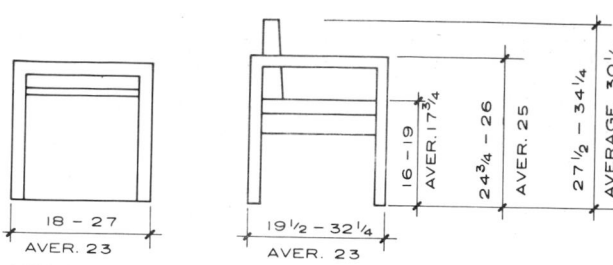

ARM CHAIR DIMENSIONS

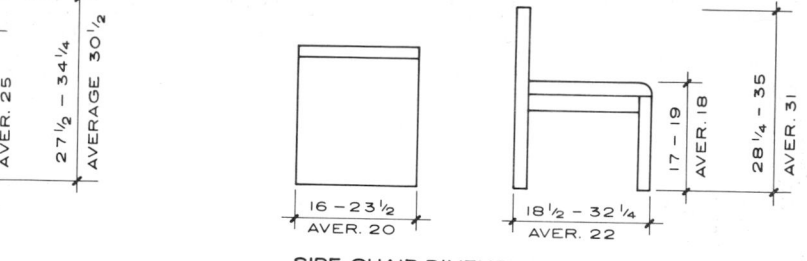

SIDE CHAIR DIMENSIONS

W 16
D 20
H 35

VIENNA CHAIR
THONET INDUSTRIES

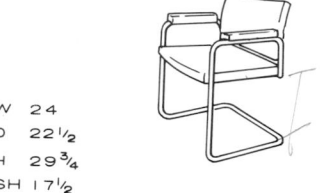

W 24
D 22½
H 29¾
SH 17½

POLARIS ARM CHAIR
STENDIG, INC.

W 22¾
D 22½
H 30
SH 18

RIEMERSCHMID CHAIR
DUNBAR FURN. CORP.

W 22
D 21¼
H 33
SH 18½

EAMES ARM CHAIR
HERMAN MILLER INC.

W 26
D 23½
H 32
SH 18½

SAARINEN CHAIR
KNOLL ASSOCIATES, INC.

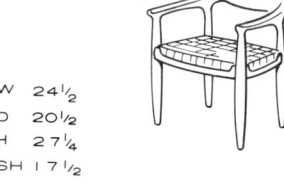

W 24½
D 20½
H 27¼
SH 17½

HANS WEGNER CHAIR
GEORG JENSEN, INC.

W 21½
D 20
H 31¾
SH 17¾

SIDE CHAIR
KNOLL ASSOCIATES, INC.

W 19½
D 20½
H 32
SH 18

PRAGUE ARM CHAIR
STENDIG, INC.

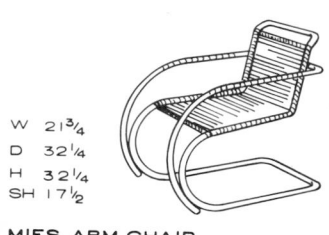

W 21¾
D 32¼
H 32¼
SH 17½

MIES ARM CHAIR
STENDIG, INC.

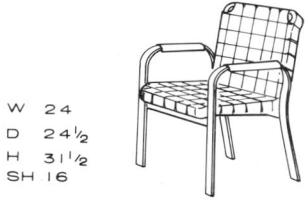

W 24
D 24½
H 31½
SH 16

AALTO ARM CHAIR
ICF, INC.

W 19½
D 21½
H 29¼
SH 18

MOLDED PLYWOOD CHAIR
HERMAN MILLER INC.

W 22½
D 19¾
H 29½
SH 18

MAGISTRETTI CHAIR
STENDIG, INC.

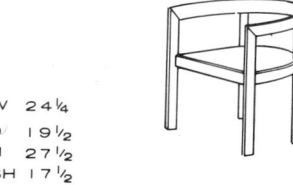

W 24¼
D 19½
H 27½
SH 17½

PARIS ARM CHAIR
STENDIG, INC.

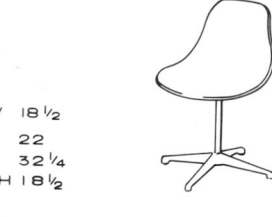

W 18½
D 22
H 32¼
SH 18½

SWIVEL CHAIR
HERMAN MILLER INC.

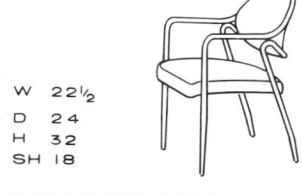

W 22½
D 24
H 32
SH 18

PETITT ARM CHAIR
KNOLL ASSOCIATES, INC.

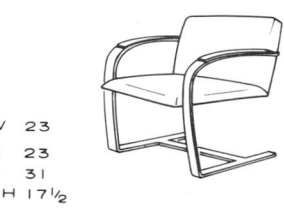

W 23
D 23
H 31
SH 17½

BRNO CHAIR
KNOLL ASSOCIATES, INC.

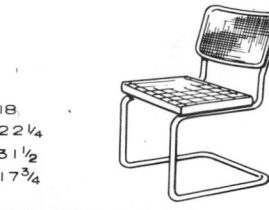

W 18
D 22¼
H 31½
SH 17¾

BREUER SIDE CHAIR
STENDIG, INC.

W 25
D 22
H 29½
SH 18½

UPHOLSTERED ARM CHAIR
HERMAN MILLER INC.

W 21¼
D 22
H 30½
SH 18

CORBUSIER ARM CHAIR
STENDIG, INC.

W 21
D 22½
H 30
SH 18

BERTOIA SIDE CHAIR
KNOLL ASSOCIATES, INC.

D Incorporated, Chicago and New York

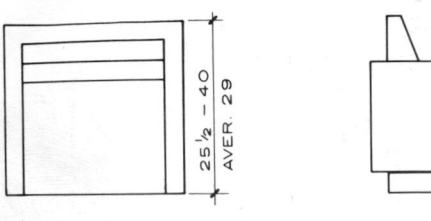
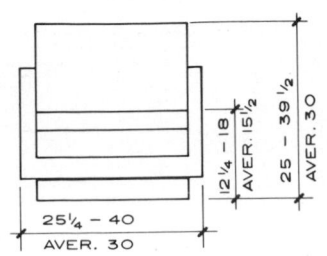

25½ – 40
AVER. 29

20½ – 25
AVER. 22½

12¼ – 18
AVER. 15½

25 – 39½
AVER. 30

25¼ – 40
AVER. 30

TYPICAL LOUNGE CHAIR DIMENSIONS

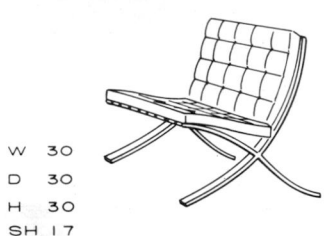

W 30
D 30
H 30
SH 17

BARCELONA CHAIR
KNOLL ASSOCIATES, INC.

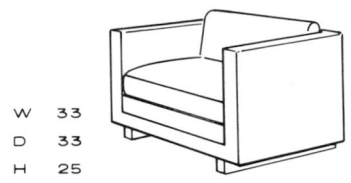

W 33
D 33
H 25
SH 15½

LOUNGE CHAIR
WARD BENNETT DESIGNS
BRICKEL ASSOCIATES, INC.

W 28
D 26½
H 31

BUBBLE LOUNGE CHAIR
STOW/DAVIS FURN. CORP.

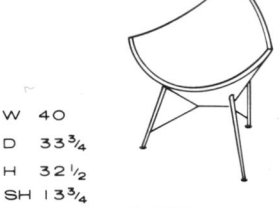

W 40
D 33¾
H 32½
SH 13¾

COCONUT CHAIR
HERMAN MILLER INC.

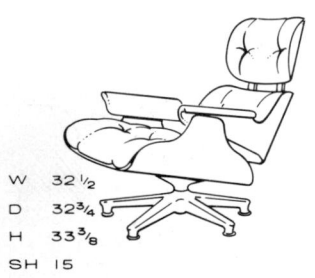

W 32½
D 32¾
H 33⅜
SH 15

LOUNGE CHAIR
HERMAN MILLER INC.

W 27
D 27
H 28
SH 16½

TAMPERE SWIVEL CHAIR
STENDIG INC.

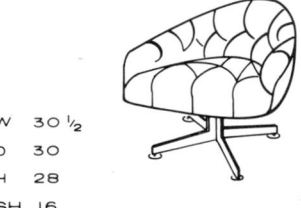

W 30½
D 30
H 28
SH 16

TUFTED LOUNGE CHAIR
LEHIGH FURN. CORP.

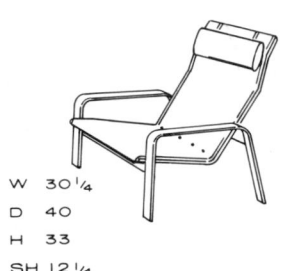

W 30¼
D 40
H 33
SH 12¼

ADJUSTABLE CHAIR
STENDIG INC.

W 35
D 30
H 26½
SH 16

SUISSE BARREL CHAIR
STENDIG INC.

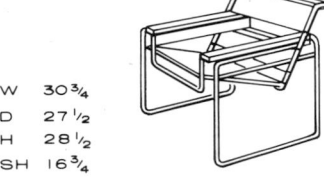

W 30¾
D 27½
H 28½
SH 16¾

WASSILY CHAIR
STENDIG INC.

W 34
D 31
H 42
SH 15

SWAN CHAIR
FRITZ HANSEN INC.

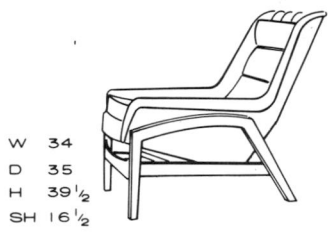

W 34
D 35
H 39½
SH 16½

ADJUSTABLE CHAIR
DUX. INC.

W 27
D 34
H 29

OTTOMAN:
W 27
D 24
H 15½

LOUNGE CHAIR
DUNBAR FURN. CORP.

W 40
D 34
H 35½

OTTOMAN:
W 25½
D 20
H 16

SAARINEN CHAIR
KNOLL ASSOCIATES

W 36
D 36½
H 34¼

FOOT STOOL:
W 24
D 21
H 15¾

SWIVEL LOUNGE CHAIR
STENDIG INC.

ISD Incorporated, Chicago and New York

RECTANGULAR

WIDTH	LENGTH	APPROX. SEAT
5'–0''	20'–0''	20–22
4'–6''	18'–0''	18–20
4'–6''	16'–0''	16–18
4'–6''	14'–0''	14–16
4'–0''	12'–0''	12–14
4'–0''	11'–0''	10–12
4'–0''	10'–0''	10–12
4'–0''	9'–0''	8–10
4'–0''	8'–0''	8–10
3'–6''	9'–0''	8–10
3'–6''	8'–0''	8–10
3'–6''	7'–6''	6–8
3'–6''	7'–0''	6–8
3'–0''	7'–0''	6–8
3'–0''	6'–6''	6–8
2'–6''	5'–6''	4–6
2'–6''	5'–0''	4–6

BOAT SHAPED

WIDTH CENTER	END	LENGTH	APPROX. SEAT.
6'–0''	4'–0''	20'–0''	20–24
5'–6''	4'–0''	18'–0''	18–20
5'–6''	4'–0''	16'–0''	16–18
5'–0''	3'–6''	14'–0''	14–16
4'–6''	3'–6''	12'–0''	12–14
4'–0''	3'–2''	11'–0''	10–12
4'–0''	3'–2''	10'–0''	10–12
3'–6''	3'–0''	9'–0''	8–10
3'–6''	3'–0''	8'–0''	8–10
3'–0''	2'–10''	7'–0''	6–8
3'–0''	2'–10''	6'–0''	6–8

SQUARE

WIDTH	LENGTH	APPROX. SEAT.
5'–0''	5'–0''	8–12
4'–6''	4'–6''	4–8
4'–0''	4'–0''	4–8
3'–6''	3'–6''	4
3'–0''	3'–0''	4

ROUND

DIAMETER	CIRCUM.	APPROX. SEAT.
8'–0''	25'–1''	10–12
7'–0''	21'–8''	8–10
6'–0''	18'–9''	7–8
5'–0''	15'–7''	6–7
4'–6''	14'–1''	5–6
4'–0''	12'–6''	5–6
3'–6''	11'–0''	4–5

SOURCE: LEHIGH FURN. CORP.

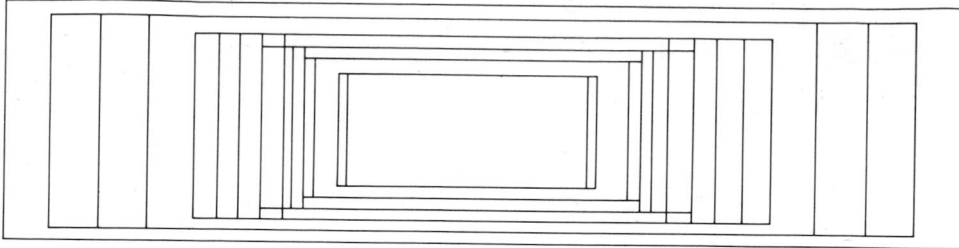

TABLE PLANS

L 60
W 20 OPENS TO 40
H 29

FLIP-TOP TABLE
DUNBAR FURNITURE CORP.

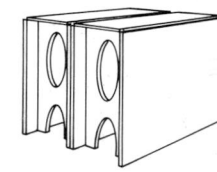

L 16 EXTENDS TO 116
W 35 1/2
H 29

DOUBLE DROP LEAF TABLE
GEORG JENSEN INC.

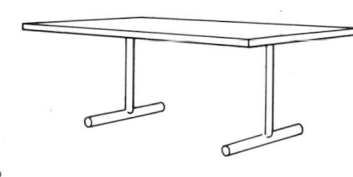

L 60
W 30
H 28 1/2

CONFERENCE / DINING TABLE
STENDIG INCORPORATED

L 84
W 36
H 28 1/2

CONFERENCE TABLE
ROFFMAN ASSOCIATES, INC.

48'' DIAM.
H 28 (OR 25 1/2)

CONFERENCE / DINING TABLE
ZOGRAPHOS DESIGNS LTD.

L 96
W 36/42
H 29

CONFERENCE / DINING TABLE
LEHIGH FURNITURE CORP.

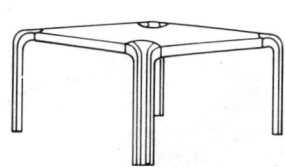

L 36
W 36
H 28

AALTO DINING TABLE
ICF, INCORPORATED

ISD Incorporated, Chicago and New York

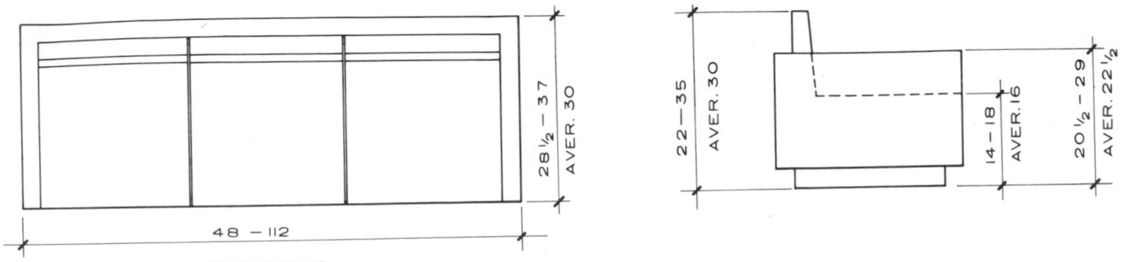

TYPICAL SOFA DIMENSIONS

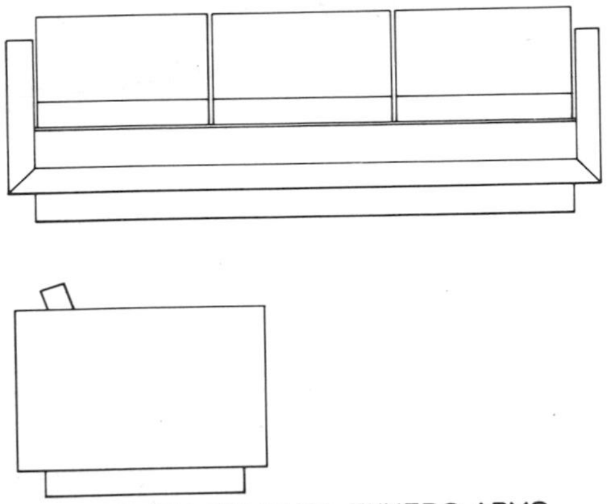

28½ – 37   AVER. 30

48 – 112

22 – 35   AVER. 30

14 – 18   AVER. 16

20½ – 29   AVER. 22½

A. LOOSE PILLOW BACK, TUXEDO ARMS, PLATFORM BASE

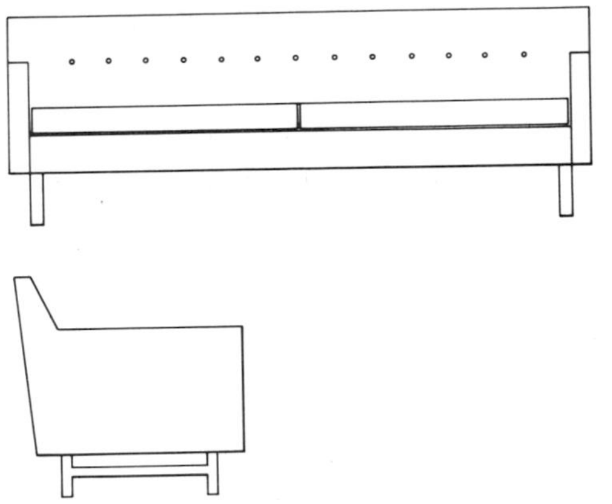

B. LAWSON ARM AND BACK, RUNNER LEGS

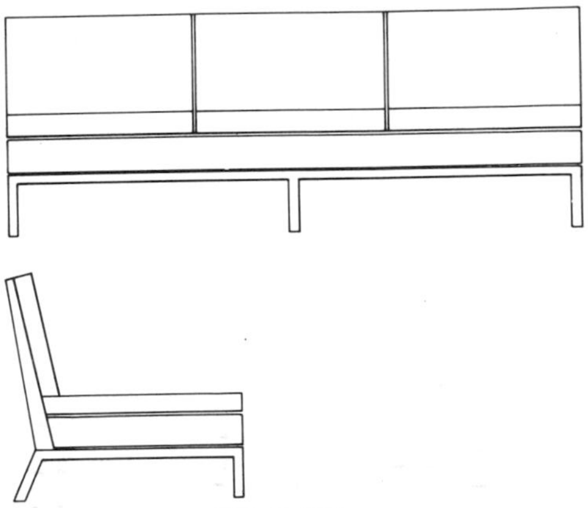

C. ARMLESS, STEEL BASE

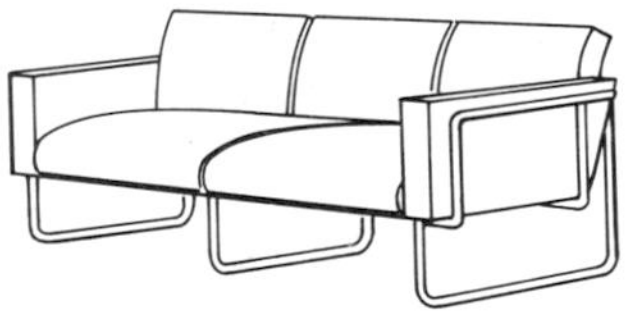

W   55
D   31½
H   28½
SH   16½

TWO – SEAT SOFA
STENDIG INCORPORATED

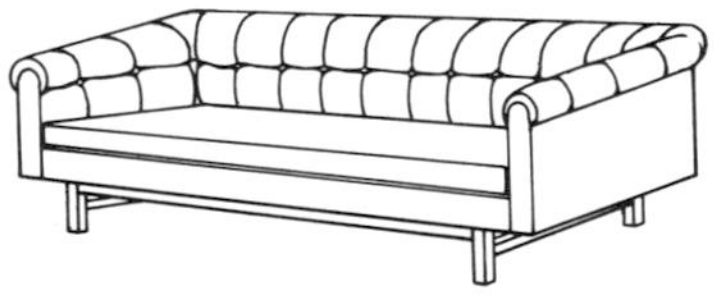

W   72
D   29½
H   28

ROLL ARM SOFA
DIRECTIONAL CONTRACT FURN.

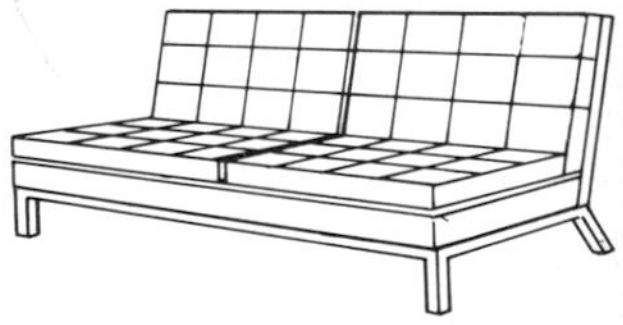

W   56
D   30
H   31½
SH   15½

ARMLESS SETTEE
KNOLL ASSOCIATES, INC.

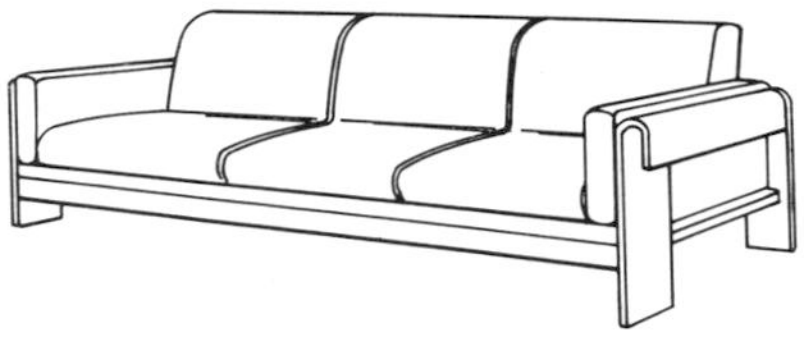

W   83¼
D   30
H   27
SH   14

BASTIANO SOFA
STENDIG INCORPORATED

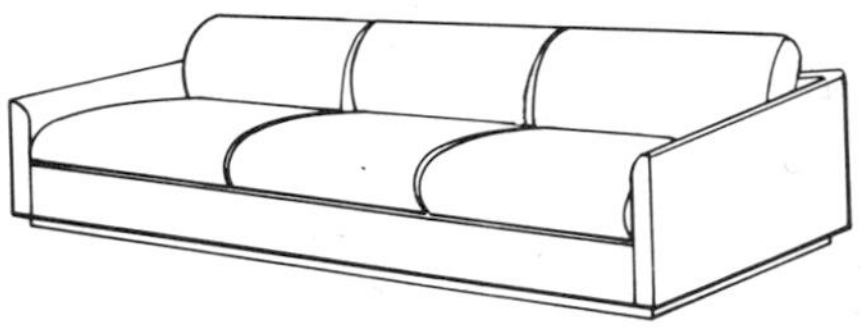

W   86
D   33½
H   22
SH   16

SOFA
LEHIGH FURNITURE CORPORATION

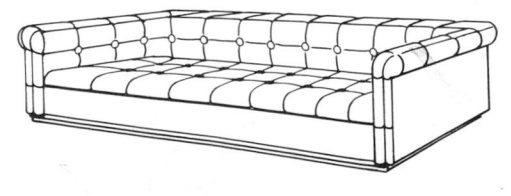

W   101½
D   36
H   24
SH   14

BISCUIT – TUFTED SOFA
DUNBAR FURNITURE CORPORATION

W   108
D   35½
H   29
SH   17

NINE – FOOT SOFA
DUNBAR FURNITURE CORPORATION

ISD Incorporated, Chicago and New York

STANDARD MATTRESS SIZES

CRIB	$22\frac{1}{4} \times 38\frac{3}{4}$		
	$25\frac{1}{4} \times 50\frac{3}{4}$		
	$31\frac{1}{4} \times 56\frac{3}{4}$		
BUNK	30 x 75		
	33 x 75		
DORMITORY & HOSPITAL	36 x 75	36 x 80	
TWIN	39 x 75	39 x 80	39 x 84
THREE-QUARTER	48 x 75		
DOUBLE	54 x 75	54 x 80	54 x 84
QUEEN-SIZE		60 x 80	60 x 84
KING-SIZE		72 x 80	72 x 84
		76 x 80	76 x 84

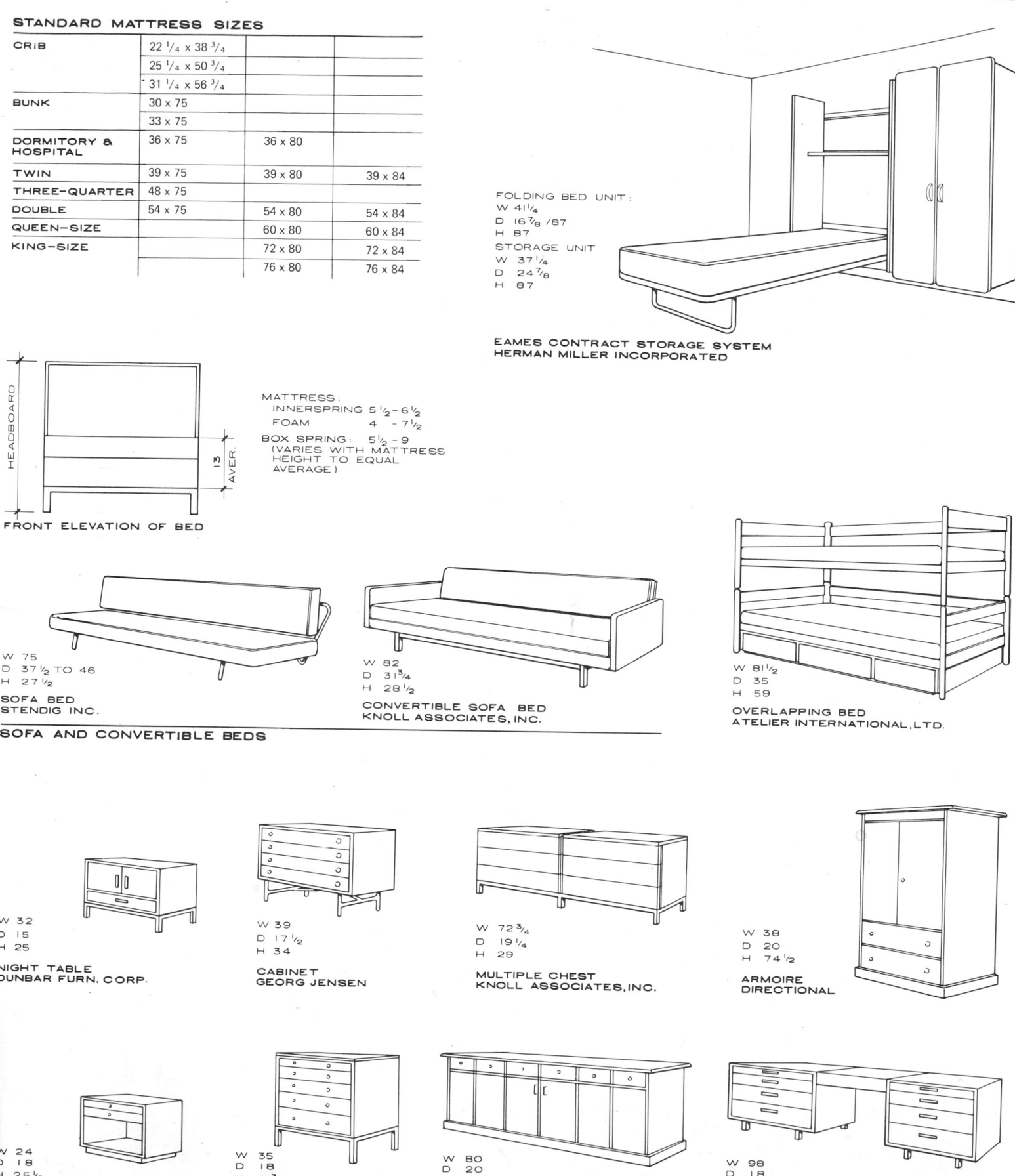

FOLDING BED UNIT:
W 41 1/4
D 16 7/8 /87
H 87

STORAGE UNIT
W 37 1/4
D 24 7/8
H 87

EAMES CONTRACT STORAGE SYSTEM
HERMAN MILLER INCORPORATED

MATTRESS:
INNERSPRING 5 1/2 - 6 1/2
FOAM 4 - 7 1/2

BOX SPRING: 5 1/2 - 9
(VARIES WITH MATTRESS HEIGHT TO EQUAL AVERAGE)

HEADBOARD / 13 AVER.

FRONT ELEVATION OF BED

W 75
D 37 1/2 TO 46
H 27 1/2

SOFA BED
STENDIG INC.

W 82
D 31 3/4
H 28 1/2

CONVERTIBLE SOFA BED
KNOLL ASSOCIATES, INC.

W 81 1/2
D 35
H 59

OVERLAPPING BED
ATELIER INTERNATIONAL, LTD.

SOFA AND CONVERTIBLE BEDS

W 32
D 15
H 25

NIGHT TABLE
DUNBAR FURN. CORP.

W 39
D 17 1/2
H 34

CABINET
GEORG JENSEN

W 72 3/4
D 19 1/4
H 29

MULTIPLE CHEST
KNOLL ASSOCIATES, INC.

W 38
D 20
H 74 1/2

ARMOIRE
DIRECTIONAL

W 24
D 18
H 25 1/2

NITE TABLE
HARVEY PROBBER

W 35
D 18
H 41 3/4

HIGH CHEST
DUNBAR FURN.

W 80
D 20
H 34 1/2

DRESSER
DIRECTIONAL

W 98
D 18
H 29 1/2

CABINETS W/SUSPEND. VANITY
HARVEY PROBBER INC.

BEDROOM FURNITURE

SD Incorporated, Chicago and New York

TYPICAL END OR SIDE TABLE DIMENSIONS

DESCRIPTION	DEPTH		WIDTH		HEIGHT	
	MIN.	MAX.	MIN.	MAX.	MIN.	MAX.
RECTANGULAR	19	28	21	48	17	28
SQUARE	15	32	15	32	17	28
ROUND	16	30	16	30	18	22½

TYPICAL LOW TABLE DIMENSIONS

DESCRIPTION	DEPTH		WIDTH		HEIGHT	
	MIN.	MAX.	MIN.	MAX.	MIN.	MAX.
RECTANGULAR	15½	24	24	86	12	18
SQUARE	36	42	36	42	15	17
ROUND	30	42	30	42	15	16½

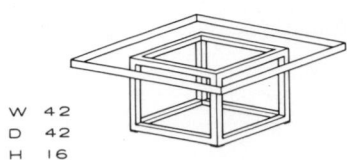

W 42
D 42
H 16

TABLE
HARVEY PROBBER INC.

W 27
D 19
H 25

TABLE
DUNBAR FURN. CORP.

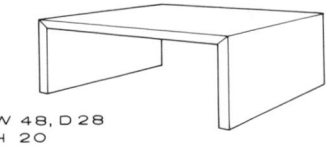

W 48, D 28
H 20

PANEL TABLE
INTREX INC.

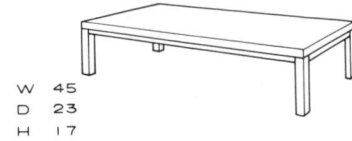

W 45
D 23
H 17

COFFEE TABLE
KNOLL ASSOCIATES, INC.

DIAM. 16
H 20½

SIDE TABLE
KNOLL ASSOCIATES

W 21½
D 19
H 17½

BREUER TABLE
STENDIG INC.

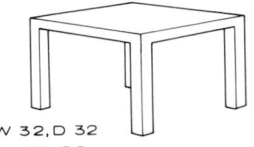

W 32, D 32
H 17-28

PARSONS TABLE
DIRECTIONAL

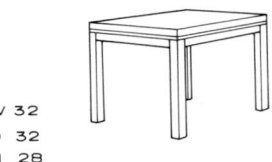

W 32
D 32
H 28

SQUARE TABLE
JENS RISOM

W 40
D 40
H 17

BARCELONA TABLE
KNOLL ASSOCIATES, INC.

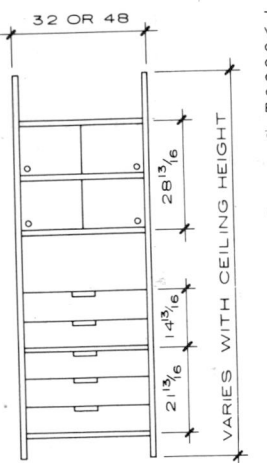

32 OR 48

28 13/16

14 3/16

21 13/16

VARIES WITH CEILING HEIGHT

THE CSS IS A SYSTEM IN
WHICH INTERCHANGEABLE
COMPONENTS ARE HUNG
ON EITHER WALL MOUNTED
OR FREE STANDING POLES.
COMPONENTS MAY BE REMOV-
ED OR ADDED AT ANY TIME.

COMPONENTS INCLUDE:
    SHELVES
    LIGHTING
    CHALKBOARDS
    CASE WITH FLIPPER
  OR SLIDING DOORS
    DRAWERS, ETC.

W 23
D 17
H 39

SILVER CHEST
DUNBAR FURN.

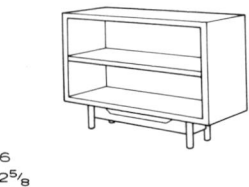

W 36
D 12⅝
H 31½

LOW BOOKCASE
JENS RISOM DESIGN

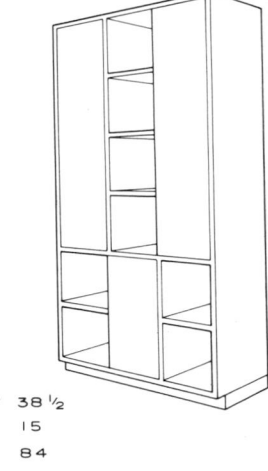

W 38½
D 15
H 84

CABINET
HARVEY PROBBER

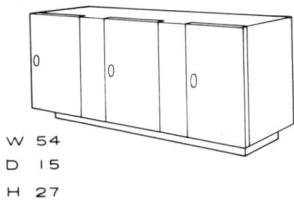

W 20
D 10
H 22

TELEPHONE TABLE
CUMBERLAND

W 54
D 15
H 27

CABINET
DUNBAR FURN.

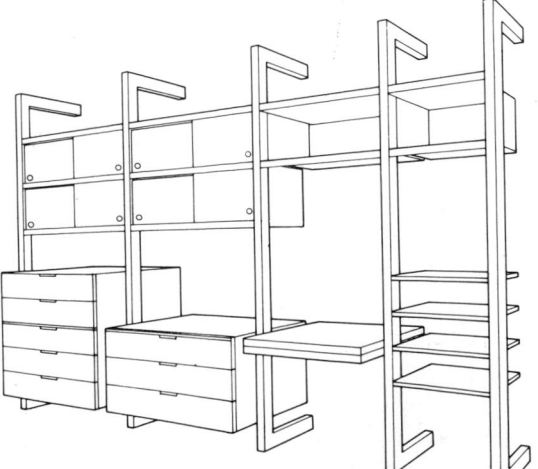

COMPREHENSIVE STORAGE SYSTEM
HERMAN MILLER INC.

ISD Incorporated, Chicago and New York

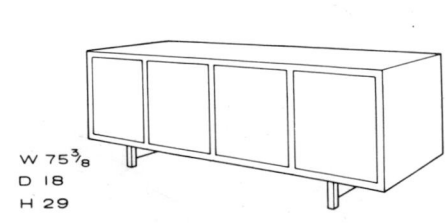

W 75⅜
D 18
H 29

SIDEBOARD
KNOLL ASSOCIATES, INC.

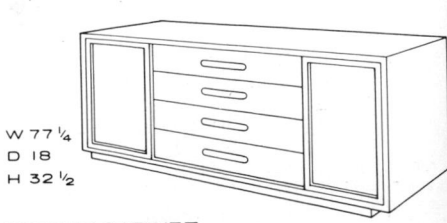

W 77¼
D 18
H 32½

BUFFET CABINET
HARVEY PROBBER INC.

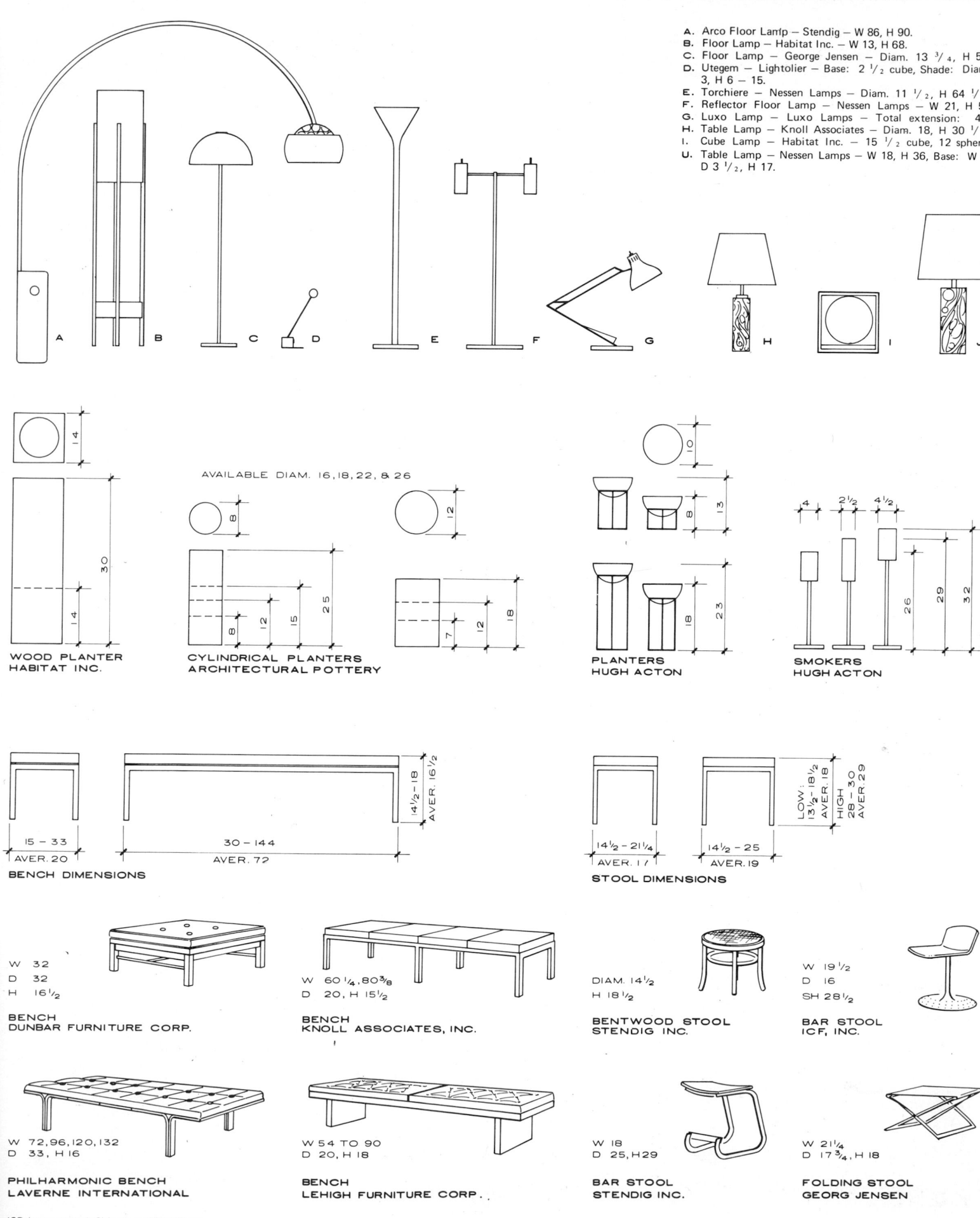

A. Arco Floor Lamp — Stendig — W 86, H 90.
B. Floor Lamp — Habitat Inc. — W 13, H 68.
C. Floor Lamp — George Jensen — Diam. 13 3/4, H 56.
D. Utegem — Lightolier — Base: 2 1/2 cube, Shade: Diam. 3, H 6 — 15.
E. Torchiere — Nessen Lamps — Diam. 11 1/2, H 64 1/2.
F. Reflector Floor Lamp — Nessen Lamps — W 21, H 50
G. Luxo Lamp — Luxo Lamps — Total extension: 45.
H. Table Lamp — Knoll Associates — Diam. 18, H 30 1/2.
I. Cube Lamp — Habitat Inc. — 15 1/2 cube, 12 sphere.
J. Table Lamp — Nessen Lamps — W 18, H 36, Base: W 7, D 3 1/2, H 17.

WOOD PLANTER
HABITAT INC.

AVAILABLE DIAM. 16, 18, 22, & 26

CYLINDRICAL PLANTERS
ARCHITECTURAL POTTERY

PLANTERS
HUGH ACTON

SMOKERS
HUGH ACTON

BENCH DIMENSIONS

15 – 33   AVER. 20
30 – 144   AVER. 72
14 1/2 – 18   AVER. 16 1/2

STOOL DIMENSIONS

14 1/2 – 21 1/4   AVER. 17
14 1/2 – 25   AVER. 19
LOW: 13 1/2 – 18 1/2   AVER. 18
HIGH: 28 – 30   AVER. 29

W 32
D 32
H 16 1/2

BENCH
DUNBAR FURNITURE CORP.

W 60 1/4, 80 3/8
D 20, H 15 1/2

BENCH
KNOLL ASSOCIATES, INC.

DIAM. 14 1/2
H 18 1/2

BENTWOOD STOOL
STENDIG INC.

W 19 1/2
D 16
SH 28 1/2

BAR STOOL
ICF, INC.

W 72, 96, 120, 132
D 33, H 16

PHILHARMONIC BENCH
LAVERNE INTERNATIONAL

W 54 TO 90
D 20, H 18

BENCH
LEHIGH FURNITURE CORP.

W 18
D 25, H 29

BAR STOOL
STENDIG INC.

W 21 1/4
D 17 3/4, H 18

FOLDING STOOL
GEORG JENSEN

ISD Incorporated, Chicago and New York

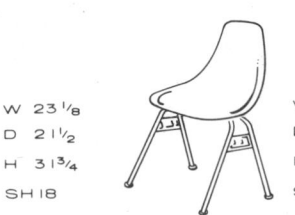

W	23 1/8
D	21 1/2
H	31 3/4
SH	18

**PLASTIC STACK CHAIR
HERMAN MILLER, INC.**

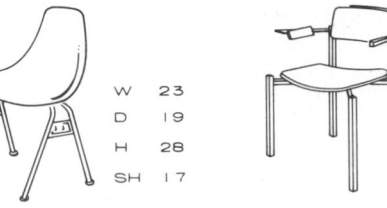

W	23
D	19
H	28
SH	17

**KIKI STACK ARM CHAIR
STENDIG INC.**

W	18
D	18
H	30
SH	17

**40/4 ROWLAND CHAIR
GENERAL FIREPROOF**

W	21
D	21 1/2
H	32
SH	17 3/4

**ALBINSON CHAIR
KNOLL ASSOCIATES**

W	19 1/2
D	20
H	33 1/2
SH	17 3/4

**STACKING CHAIR
HANSEATIC FURN.**

RECTANGULAR

L	W
60, 72 84, 96	18
60, 72 84, 96	24
60, 72 84, 96	30
60, 72 84, 96	36

SQUARE

36	36
42	42
48	48
60	60

ROUND

48 DIAM.
54 DIAM.
60 DIAM.

4 15/16"

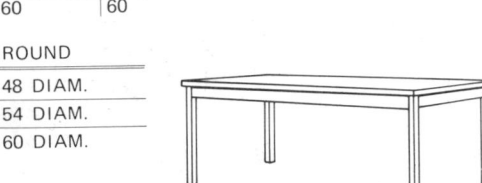

**FOLDING TABLE
HOWE FOLDING FURNITURE**

RECTANGULAR

L	W
60, 66 72	33
42, 48, 54, 60, 66, 72, 78, 84, 90, 96	36

SQUARE

24	24
30	30
36	36
42	42
48	48

ROUND

24 DIAM.
30 DIAM.
36 DIAM.

Increase by 6" to 72"

2 1/2"

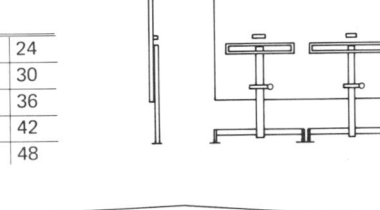
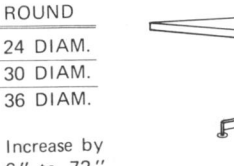

**TILT TOP TABLE
HUGH ACTION**

RECTANGULAR

L	W
53	33

SQUARE

33	33

**STACK TABLE
HANSEATIC FURNITURE CO.**

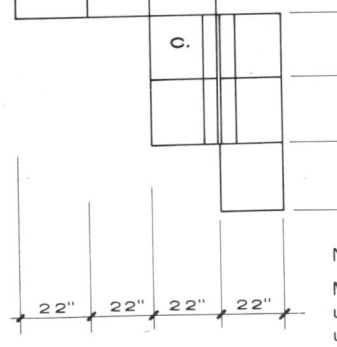

AVAILABLE UNITS:

A. BENCH UNIT
B. TABLE UNIT
C. MODULAR BACK UNIT

SEAT HT. — 17 1/4"

NOTE:

Maximum length for one bench is five units. Almost any layout possible with use of straight and right angle connector plates.

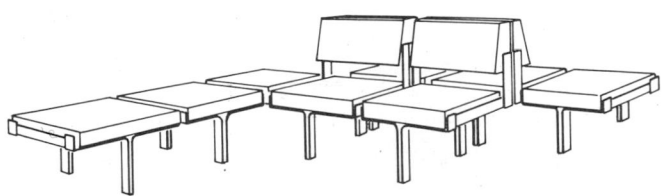

**LINK BENCH MODULAR SEATING SYSTEM
UG FURNITURE COMPANY INC.**

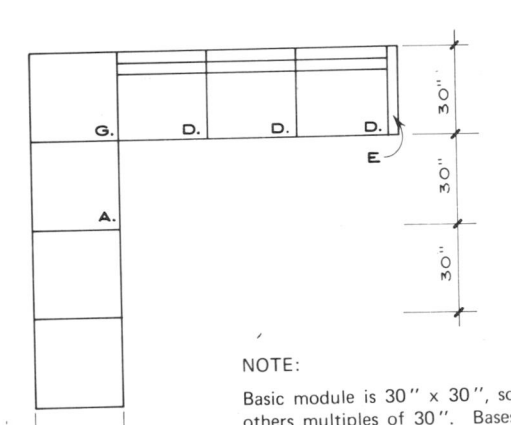

AVAILABLE UNITS:

A. CUSHION UNIT
B. SEAT UNIT
C. 2-SEAT UNIT
D. 3-SEAT UNIT
E. ARM UNIT
F. 15" TABLE TOP
G. 30" TABLE TOP

SEAT HT. — 15"
BACK HT. — 28"

NOTE:

Basic module is 30" x 30", some unit lengths are half, others multiples of 30". Bases available to accomodate two to four units.

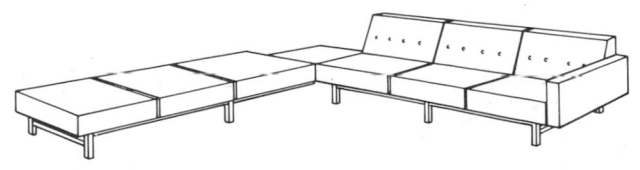

**MODULAR SEATING SYSTEM
HERMAN MILLER INCORPORATED**

ISD Incorporated, Chicago and New York

A. PORTABLE T.V. W 9, D 8 3/4, H 10
B. PORTABLE RADIO W 12 1/2, D 5 3/8, H 10 1/4
C. TABLE RADIO W 14 3/4, D 7, H 5 1/2
D. PORTABLE T.V. W 12 1/2, D 9 5/8, H 8 1/8

E. MODULAR SOUND SYSTEM; MAIN UNIT: W 23, D 14 1/4, H 8 1/2
SPEAKER: W 11 1/2, D 9 7/8, H 19 1/2
F. PORTABLE STEREO W 51 3/8, D 15 13/16, H 18 7/16
G. TABLE RADIO W 13 9/16, D 5 11/16, H 7 1/8
H. CLOCK RADIO W 15 1/4, D 6 1/8, H 7 3/4

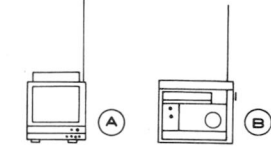

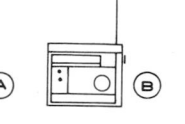

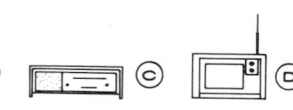

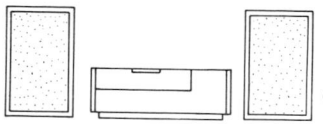

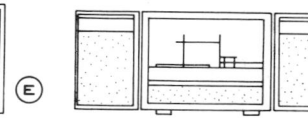

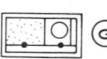

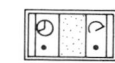

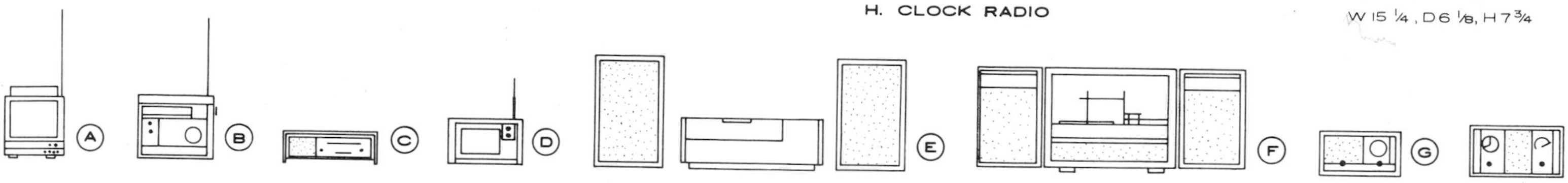

RADIOS AND STEREO CONSOLES

	SIZE VARIATIONS		
	WIDTH	DEPTH	HEIGHT
RADIOS			
PORTABLE	7 – 12 1/2	2 – 5	5 – 10
TABLE MODEL	10 1/2 – 16	3 – 8 1/2	5 – 10
CLOCK RADIO	11 – 15	4 – 8	4 1/2 – 9
STEREO CONSOLES	40	17	26 – 28
	52 – 58	17 – 20	25 – 30
	60 – 68	16 1/2 – 21	25 – 31
	71 – 74	16 1/2 – 21	23 – 28
TV/STEREO COMBINATION	62 – 71	18 1/2 – 21	28 – 32

W 27 1/2
D 16 7/8
H 18 1/2
TABLE MODEL TV

W 32
D 17 3/4
H 29 5/8
CONSOLE TV

TELEVISION

SCREEN SIZE		SIZE VARIATIONS		
		WIDTH	DEPTH	HEIGHT
23" (295 sq. ")	CONSOLE	40 1/2 – 68	19 – 22	28 – 32
	TABLE MODEL	29	16	21
22" (282 sq. ")	CONSOLE	28 – 40	15 – 17 1/2	29 – 34
	TABLE MODEL	26	16 – 17	18 – 19
20" (212 to 227 sq. ")	TABLE MODEL	26	16	20
	PORTABLE	23 – 24	13 – 14	17
19" (184 sq. ")	TABLE MODEL	23	13	17
	PORTABLE	23 – 24	13	17
18" (172 to 180 sq. ")	CONSOLE	29	18	30 1/2
	TABLE MODEL	25	17	17 1/2
	PORTABLE	18 – 22	13	17 – 19
16" (141 sq. ")	PORTABLE	19	12	14
15" (125 sq. ")	PORTABLE	19 1/2	11 1/2	13
12" (74 to 79 sq. ")	PORTABLE	16 – 17	10 – 11	11 – 12
9" (40 sq. ")	PORTABLE	12 1/2	10	8

W 60
D 17
H 25 5/8
STEREO CONSOLE

W 72
D 16 1/2
H 26
STEREO CONSOLE

W 68 1/4
D 20 1/2
H 30 5/8
TV/STEREO COMBINATION

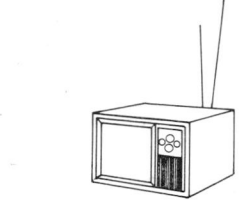

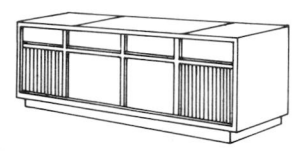

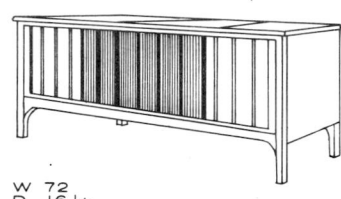

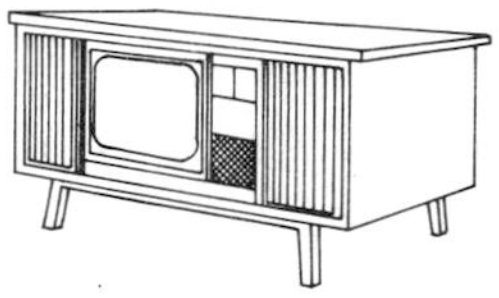

W 48 11/16
D 19 3/8
H 30 5/16
CONSOLE TV

RADIOS, STEREOS AND TELEVISION SETS

ALL DIMENSIONS IN INCHES

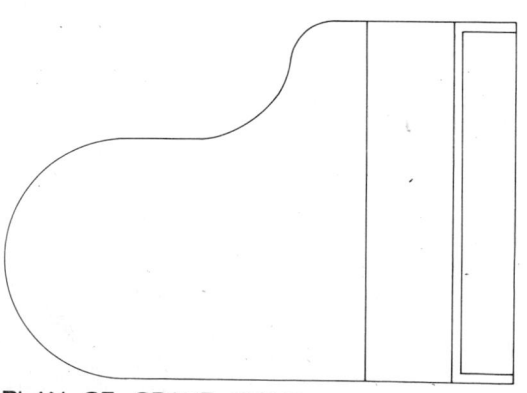

PLAN OF GRAND PIANO

GRAND PIANOS

	LENGTH	WIDTH	HEIGHT
CONCERT GRAND	9'	5'	3' – 4"
MUSIC ROOM GRAND	7'	5'	3' – 4"
PARLOR GRAND	6' – 3"	4' – 10"	3' – 4"
BABY GRAND	5' – 2"	4' – 10"	3' – 2"
UPRIGHT PIANOS			
SPINET	4' – 10"	2' – 0 1/2"	3'
	4' – 10"	2' – 0 1/2"	3' – 4"
STUDIO	4' – 10"	2' – 0 3/4"	3' – 9"

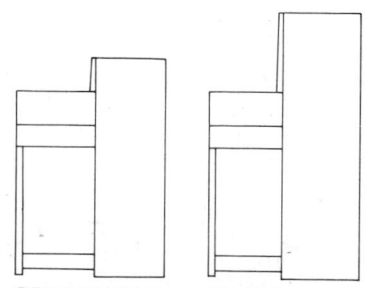

SPINET PIANO STUDIO PIANO
ELEVATIONS
UPRIGHT PIANOS

PIANOS

ISD Incorporated, Chicago and New York

STANDARD JUVENILE MATTRESS SIZES

TYPE	LENGTH	WIDTH	TYPE	LENGTH	WIDTH
BASSINET	36 38¾	18 22¼	6—YEAR CRIB	51 56¾	27 31¼
JUNIOR CRIB	46 50¾	23 25¼	YOUTH BED	66 76	33 36

W 25½
L 51
H 31½

JUNIOR CRIB
THE CHILDREN'S WORKBENCH

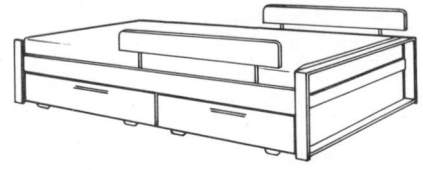

W 37½
L 79
H 12 + 5" GUARD RAILS

YOUTH BED WITH STORAGE
THE CHILDREN'S WORKBENCH

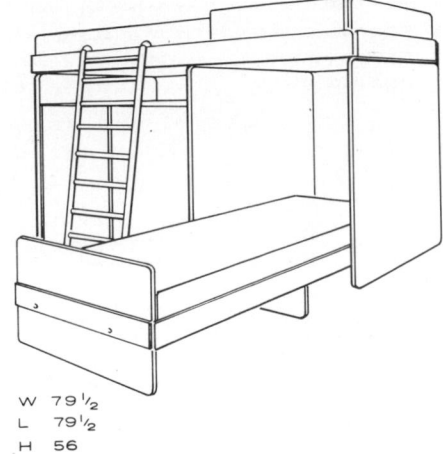

W 79½
L 79½
H 56

MAGISTRETTI BED SYSTEM
ATELIER INTERNATIONAL, LTD.

STANDARD HEIGHTS

SEAT HEIGHT	AGE GROUP	TABLE HEIGHT
TO 12"	1 TO 4	TO 22"
12" — 14"	5, 6, 7	22" — 25"
13" — 17"	8, 9, 10	24" — 29"
15" — 18"	11, 12, 13	26" — 30"

DIAM. 17
H 22½

ROUND TABLE
BURKE

W 31½
D 23½
H 23½

AALTO TABLE
ICF, INC.

W 15¾
D 16¼
H 24
SH 14½ OR
W 13⅛
D 13⅜
H 20
SH 12¼

CHILD'S CHAIR
KNOLL ASSOCIATES, INC.

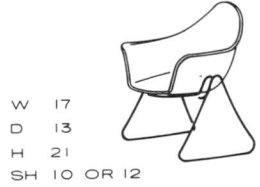

W 17
D 13
H 21
SH 10 OR 12

STACKING CHAIR
HANSEATIC FURN. CO.

W 15
D 16
H 24
SH 15

CHILDREN'S CHAIR
ICF, INC.

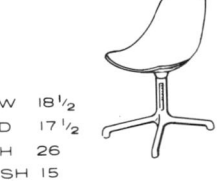

W 18½
D 17½
H 26
SH 15

CHAIR
BURKE

UNIT CONTAINS:
OPEN STORAGE,
DRAWERS, TOY BOX,
WARDROBE.

W 35
D 12
H 46

WARDROBE
THE CHILDREN'S WORKBENCH

W 36
D 17¾
H 29¼

CHEST
CHILDREN'S WORKB.

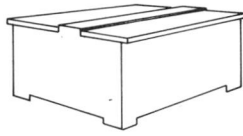

W 29
D 30
H 21

DESK W/HINGED TOP
DESIGN GROUP

W 41½
D 14
H 29½

BOOKCASE/BENCH
CHILDREN'S WORKB.

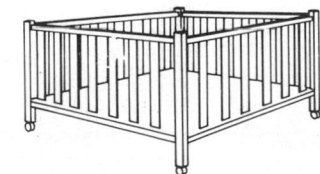

W 40
D 40
H 28
FOLDS TO: 5 x 40

PLAY YARD

W 23⅜
D 23¾
H 20½ - 28½

FEEDING TABLE
WELSH CO.

H 28
SH 21

HIGH CHAIR
CHILDREN'S WORKB.

TYPICAL UNIT
HAS HINGED
SEAT LID;
REMOVABLE
TRAY

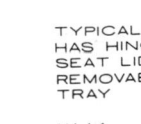

W 14
D 12
H 16

POTTY CHAIR

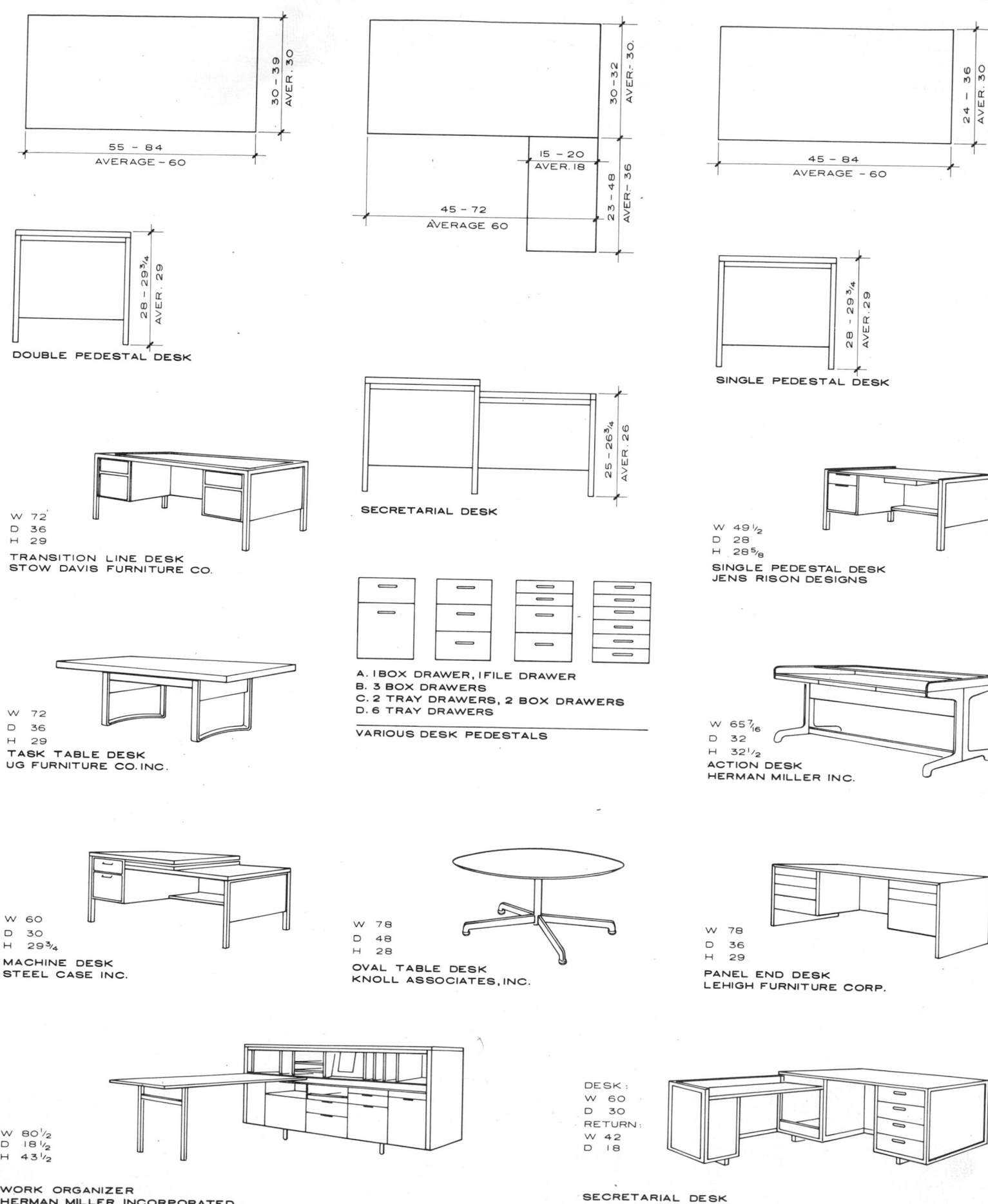

30 – 39
AVER. 30

55 – 84
AVERAGE – 60

28 – 29¾
AVER. 29

DOUBLE PEDESTAL DESK

W 72
D 36
H 29

TRANSITION LINE DESK
STOW DAVIS FURNITURE CO.

W 72
D 36
H 29

TASK TABLE DESK
UG FURNITURE CO. INC.

W 60
D 30
H 29¾

MACHINE DESK
STEEL CASE INC.

30 – 32
AVER. 30

15 – 20
AVER. 18

45 – 72
AVERAGE 60

23 – 48
AVER. 36

25 – 26¾
AVER. 26

SECRETARIAL DESK

A. 1 BOX DRAWER, 1 FILE DRAWER
B. 3 BOX DRAWERS
C. 2 TRAY DRAWERS, 2 BOX DRAWERS
D. 6 TRAY DRAWERS

VARIOUS DESK PEDESTALS

W 78
D 48
H 28

OVAL TABLE DESK
KNOLL ASSOCIATES, INC.

24 – 36
AVER. 30

45 – 84
AVERAGE – 60

28 – 29¾
AVER. 29

SINGLE PEDESTAL DESK

W 49½
D 28
H 28⅝

SINGLE PEDESTAL DESK
JENS RISON DESIGNS

W 65⁷⁄₁₆
D 32
H 32½

ACTION DESK
HERMAN MILLER INC.

W 78
D 36
H 29

PANEL END DESK
LEHIGH FURNITURE CORP.

W 80½
D 18½
H 43½

WORK ORGANIZER
HERMAN MILLER INCORPORATED

DESK:
W 60
D 30
RETURN:
W 42
D 18

SECRETARIAL DESK
CORRY JAMESTOWN CORPORATION

ISD Incorporated, Chicago and New York

TYPICAL CREDENZA DIMENSIONS

	WIDTH	DEPTH	HEIGHT
ONE COMPONENT	27 to 30	17 3/4 to 21	25 1/2 to 29 3/4
TWO COMPONENT	37 1/4 to 41 1/2	17 3/4 to 21	25 1/2 to 29 3/4
THREE COMPONENT	44 3/4 to 60 1/2	17 3/4 to 21	25 1/2 to 29 3/4
FOUR COMPONENT	62 1/4 to 79 3/4	17 3/4 to 21	25 1/2 to 29 3/4
FIVE COMPONENT	95 3/4 to 98 1/2	17 3/4 to 21	25 1/2 to 29 3/4

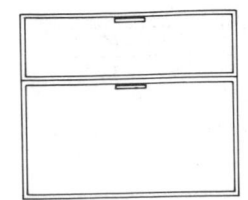
A. BOX DRAWER
B. FILE DRAWER

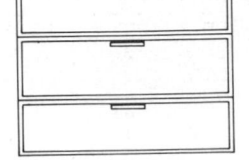
A. BOX DRAWER
B. BOX DRAWER
C. BOX DRAWER

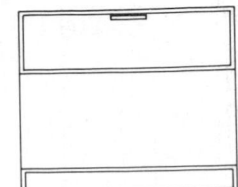
A. BOX DRAWER
B. PULL – OUT
   DICTATION SLIDE

TYPICAL CREDENZA COMPONENTS

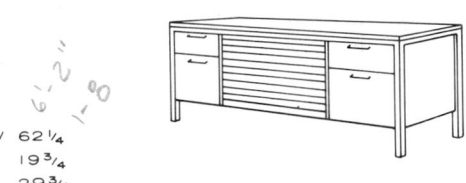
W 62 1/4
D 19 3/4
H 29 3/4
CREDENZA WITH TAMBOUR UNIT
STEELCASE INC.

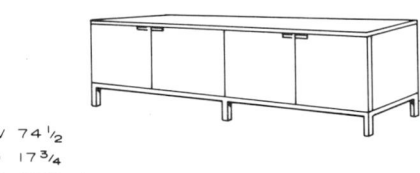
W 74 1/2
D 17 3/4
H 25 1/2
CABINET
KNOLL ASSOCIATES, INC.

W 84
D 20
H 29
CREDENZA WITH KNEEHOLE
STOW DAVIS FURNITURE CO.

W 15
D 20 1/2
H 25 1/2
AALTO STORAGE UNIT
GF, INC.

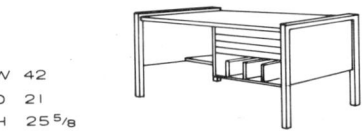
W 42
D 21
H 25 5/8
TYPING TABLE
JENS RISOM DESIGN

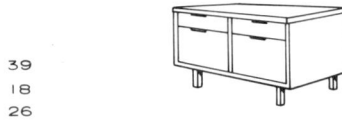
W 39
D 18
H 26
CABINET
HARVEY PROBBER, INC.

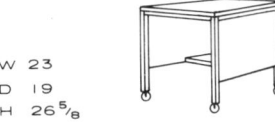
W 23
D 19
H 26 5/8
TYPING TABLE
STEELCASE, INC.

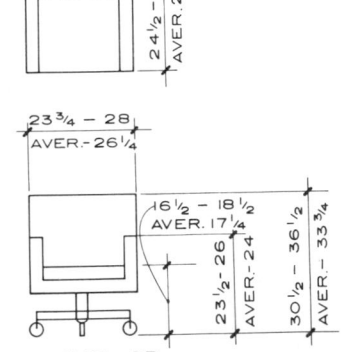
SWIVEL OR
SWIVEL POSTURE CHAIR

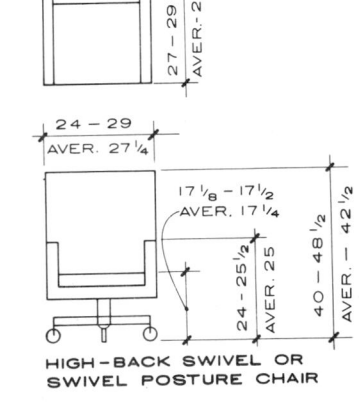
HIGH-BACK SWIVEL OR
SWIVEL POSTURE CHAIR

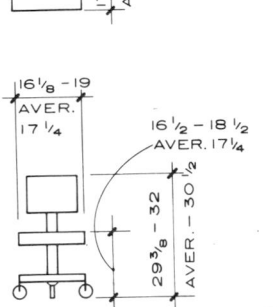
SECRETARIAL POSTURE
CHAIR

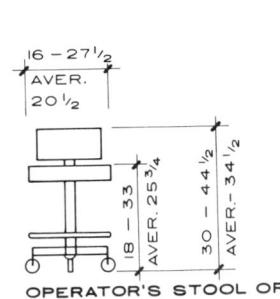
OPERATOR'S STOOL OR
DRAFTING STOOL

W 27 1/4
D 27 3/4
H 36 1/2 - 38 1/2
SWIVEL ARM CHAIR
KNOLL ASSOCIATES, INC.

W 24
D 29 1/2
H 48 1/2 (ADJ)
HIGH BACK SWIVEL
STOW DAVIS FURN. CO.

W 17 1/4
D 27
H 30 - 34 1/2
SECRETARIAL CHAIR
STEELCASE INC.

W 18
D 20
H 35 - 42
SWIVEL - BASE STOOL
KNOLL ASSOCIATES, INC.

ISD Incorporated, Chicago and New York

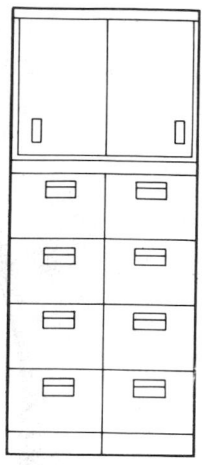

TYPICAL OVERFILE STORAGE

DESCRIPTION	WIDTH	HEIGHT	DEPTH
OVER 2 LETTER	29 3/4	25 5/8	28 9/16
OVER 2 LEGAL	35 3/4	OR	
OVER 3 LETTER	44 5/8	36 3/4	
OVER 3 LEGAL	53 5/8		

TYPICAL VERTICAL FILES

DESCRIPTION	WIDTH	HEIGHT	DEPTH
5-DR. LETTER	14 7/8	59 1/4	28 9/16
LEGAL	17 7/8	59 1/4	
4-DR. LETTER	14 7/8	50 1/2	
LEGAL	17 7/8	50 1/2	
3-DR. LETTER	14 7/8	41 1/4	
LEGAL	17 7/8	41 1/4	
2-DR. LETTER	14 7/8	29 3/4	
LEGAL	17 7/8	29 3/4	

INSIDE DRAWER DIMENSIONS

DESCRIPTION	WIDTH	HEIGHT	DEPTH
LETTER	12 1/4	10 1/2	26 3/4
LEGAL	15 1/4	10 1/2	26 3/4

TYPICAL VERTICAL FILES

TYPICAL OVERFILE STORAGE

DESCRIPTION	WIDTH	HEIGHT	DEPTH
LETTER SIZE	36	26	15
LEGAL SIZE	36	26	18

TYPICAL LATERAL FILES

DESCRIPTION	WIDTH	HEIGHT	DEPTH
7-DR. LETTER	36	88 3/8	15
LEGAL	36	88 3/8	18
6-DR. LETTER	36	76 3/8	15
LEGAL	36	76 3/8	18
5-DR. LETTER	36	63 3/4	15
LEGAL	36	63 3/4	18
4-DR. LETTER	36	51 3/4	15
LEGAL	36	51. 3/4	18
3-DR. LETTER	36	41	15
LEGAL	36	41	18
2-DR. LETTER	36	29	15
LEGAL	36	29	18

TYPICAL LATERAL FILES

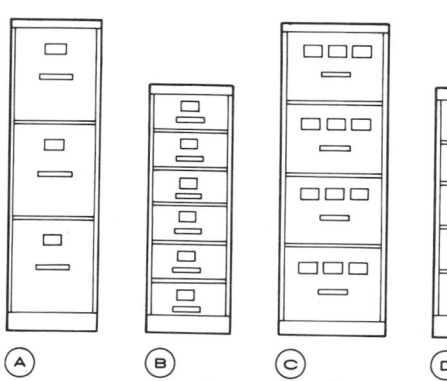
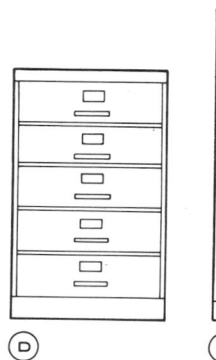

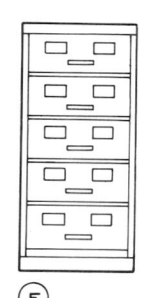

SPECIAL FILING CASES

VARIOUS SPECIAL FILES

	DESCRIPTION	WIDTH	HEIGHT	DEPTH
A.	LEDGER SHEET FILE	14 7/8	52 3/8	28 9/16
B.	CHECK FILE	12 7/8	41 1/4	
C.	DOCUMENT FILE	17 7/8	52 3/8	
D.	CARD RECORD FILE SIX-DRAWER (3x5, 4x6 CARDS)	25 1/8	41 1/4	
	FIVE-DRAWER (3x5, 4x6, 5x8 CARDS)	25 1/8	41 1/4	
E.	TABULATING CARD FILE	20 9/16	52 3/8	
F.	5x8 CARD FILE	19	41 1/4	

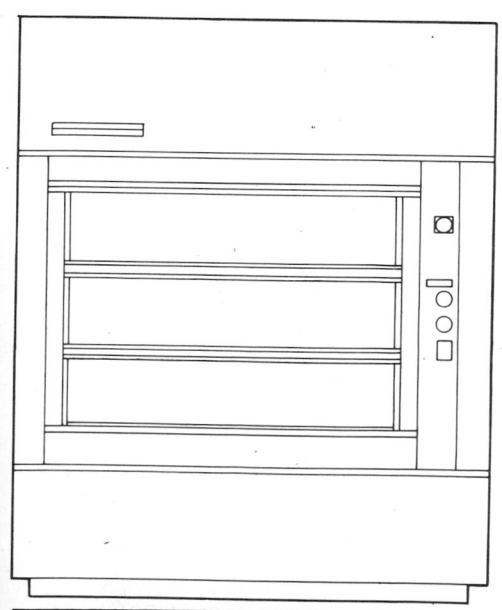

RECORDS RETRIEVAL

AUTOMATED RETRIEVAL SYSTEM

An automated system which allows for the retrieval of records in a matter of seconds. Records are stored in the unit on carriers. Each carrier is individually suspended and equally spaced on a conveyor system. The operator sits or stands at a posting board and at the touch of a button the proper carrier moves into position so that a record may be pulled or filed. In the event of card trays, where there may be 2—6 trays per carrier, the correct tray slides forward.

Records which may be stored in these units include file folders, binders, reference books, ledgers, tape reels, microfilm, and cards.

VARIOUS OVERALL UNIT SIZES

WIDTH	HEIGHT	DEPTH
91 1/4	95 1/2	42 OR 70 7/16
91 1/4	107 1/2	42 OR 70 7/16
91 1/4	119 1/2	42 OR 70 7/16
77 7/8	95 1/2	36 1/4
77 7/8	107 1/2	36 1/4
77 7/8	119 1/2	36 1/4

FIRE INSULATED FILES

DESCRIPTION	WIDTH	HEIGHT	DEPTH
4-DR. LETTER	17	52	29 13/16
LEGAL	20 1/4	52	
3-DR. LETTER	17	40 11/16	
LEGAL	20 1/4	40 11/16	
2-DR. LETTER	17	27 5/8	
LEGAL	20 1/4		

ISD Incorporated, Chicago and New York

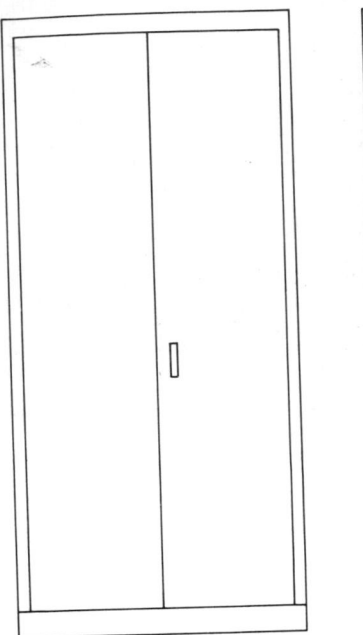
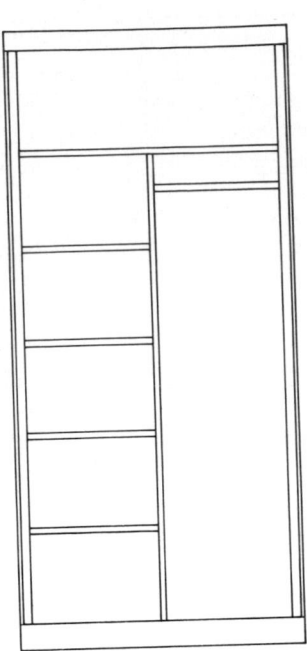

CLOSED STEEL WARDROBE CABINETS

DESCRIPTION	WIDTH	DEPTH	HEIGHT
Cabinet with one stationary shelf and coat rod	20, 36	19 ⁵/₈	78
Cabinet with four adjustable shelves, one stationary shelf and coat rod	36	19 ⁵/₈	78

CLOSED STEEL STORAGE CABINETS

	WIDTH	DEPTH	HEIGHT
Cabinet with four adjustable shelves	20, 36	19 ⁵/₈	78

STEEL STORAGE SHELVING UNITS

DESCRIPTION	HEIGHT	WIDTH	DEPTH
Basic structure consists of posts and adjustable shelves. To these may be added backs, sides, sloped shelves, bin dividers, doors, etc., as required.	min. 3′–3″ with 12″ increases to 12′–3″	36	9
		36, 42	12, 15, 18, 24
		48	12, 18, 24
		36	30, 36

STEEL BOOK AND LIBRARY SHELVING UNITS

2 Adj. shelves	42	36	single: 10 ¹/₈
6 Adj. shelves	84, 90		double: 20 ¹/₄

TYPICAL STEEL COUNTER HEIGHT UNITS

DESCRIPTION	WIDTH	DEPTH	HEIGHT
A. File unit	varies as required	28 ⁷/₁₆	41 ⁷/₈
B. Single cupboard	21 ¹⁵/₁₆ 23 ¹³/₁₆		
Double cupboard	38 ¹/₄ 43 ³/₄		
C. Knee space w/box drawer and foot rail	21 ¹³/₁₆ 32 ⁷/₈		
D. Open storage for plain or roller shelves	18 ¹/₄ 21 ¹⁵/₁₆ 34 ³/₄		
E. Cabinet with cash drawer	23 ¹³/₁₆		

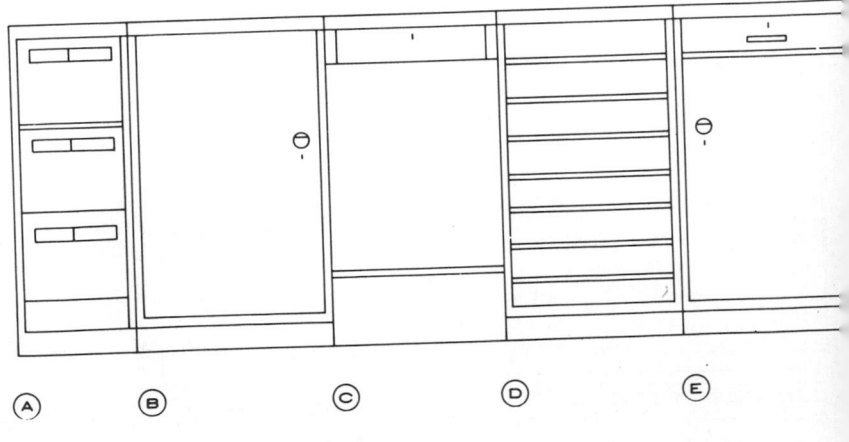

ISD Incorporated, Chicago and New York

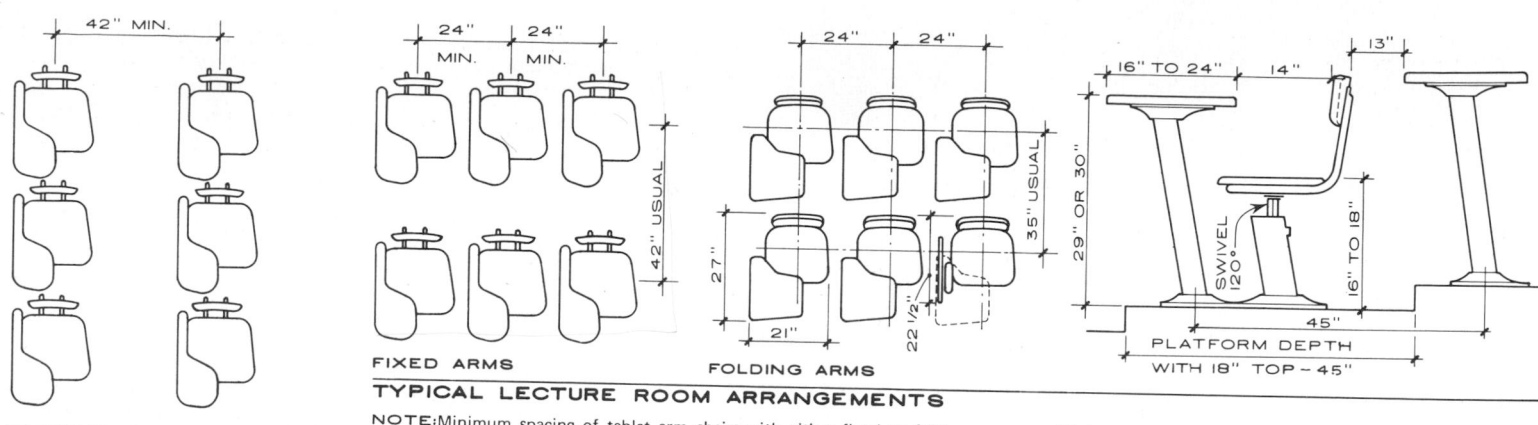

TYPICAL CLASSROOM ARRANGEMENT

FIXED ARMS

FOLDING ARMS

TYPICAL LECTURE ROOM ARRANGEMENTS

NOTE: Minimum spacing of tablet arm chairs with either fixed or folding arms is governed by manufacturers who make various sizes of tablet arms.

Minimum spacing for fixed pedestal seating alone (no tablet arms) is 32".

SWIVEL 120°

PLATFORM DEPTH WITH 18" TOP — 45"

FIXED PEDESTAL CHAIRS WITH FOLDING OR FIXED TABLET ARMS

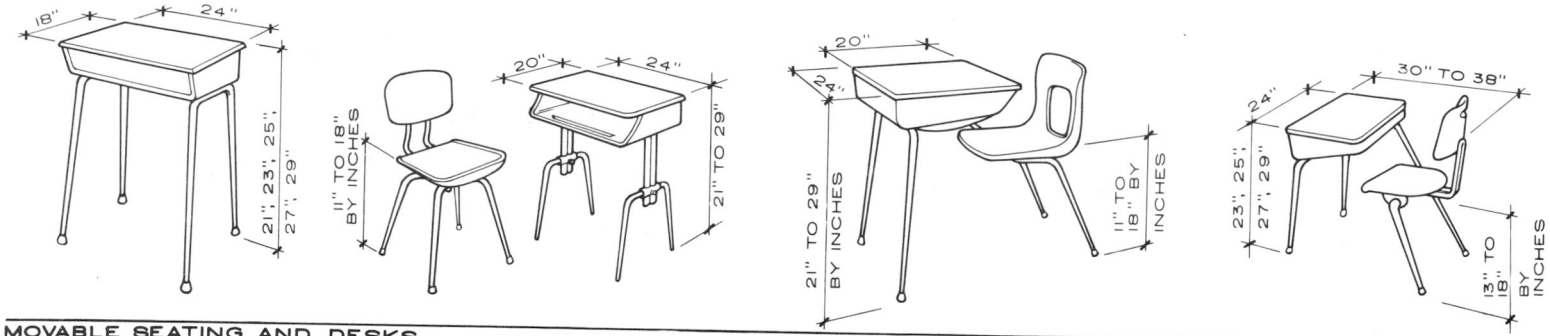

MOVABLE SEATING AND DESKS

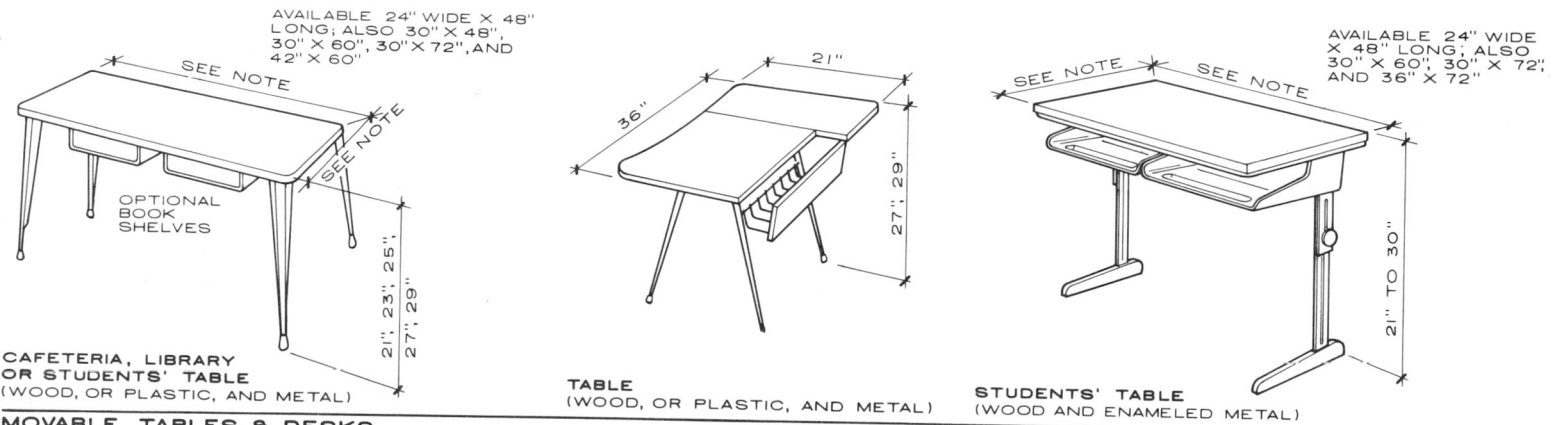

AVAILABLE 24" WIDE X 48" LONG; ALSO 30" X 48", 30" X 60", 30" X 72", AND 42" X 60"

OPTIONAL BOOK SHELVES

CAFETERIA, LIBRARY OR STUDENTS' TABLE (WOOD, OR PLASTIC, AND METAL)

TABLE (WOOD, OR PLASTIC, AND METAL)

AVAILABLE 24" WIDE X 48" LONG; ALSO 30" X 60", 30" X 72", AND 36" X 72"

STUDENTS' TABLE (WOOD AND ENAMELED METAL)

MOVABLE TABLES & DESKS

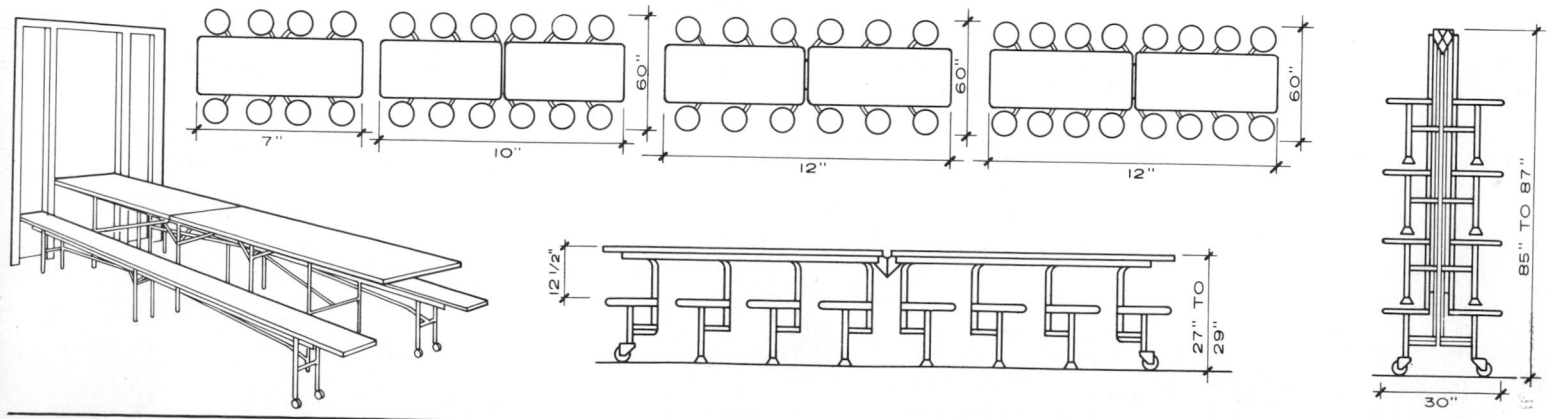

MOBILE OR STATIONARY ONE-FOLD TABLES WITH ATTACHABLE STOOLS, CHAIRS OR BENCHES

Reed B. Fuller; Stetson–Spina Associates; Palm Beach, Florida

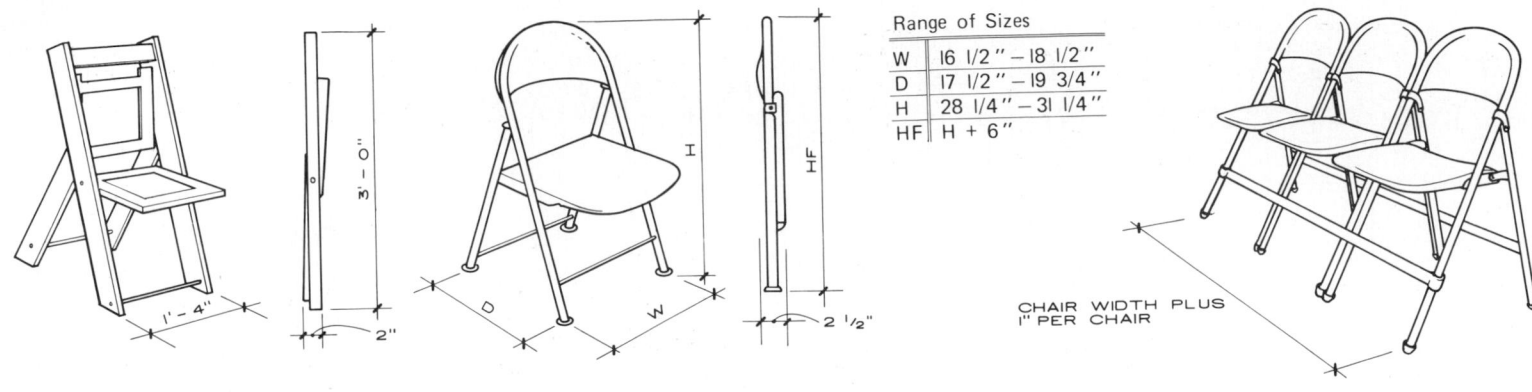

Range of Sizes	
W	16 1/2″ – 18 1/2″
D	17 1/2″ – 19 3/4″
H	28 1/4″ – 31 1/4″
HF	H + 6″

CHAIR WIDTH PLUS
1″ PER CHAIR

WOOD FOLDING CHAIR   TUBULAR STEEL FOLDING CHAIR   CHAIRS IN CLAMPED POSITION

SIZES OF FOLDING CHAIRS

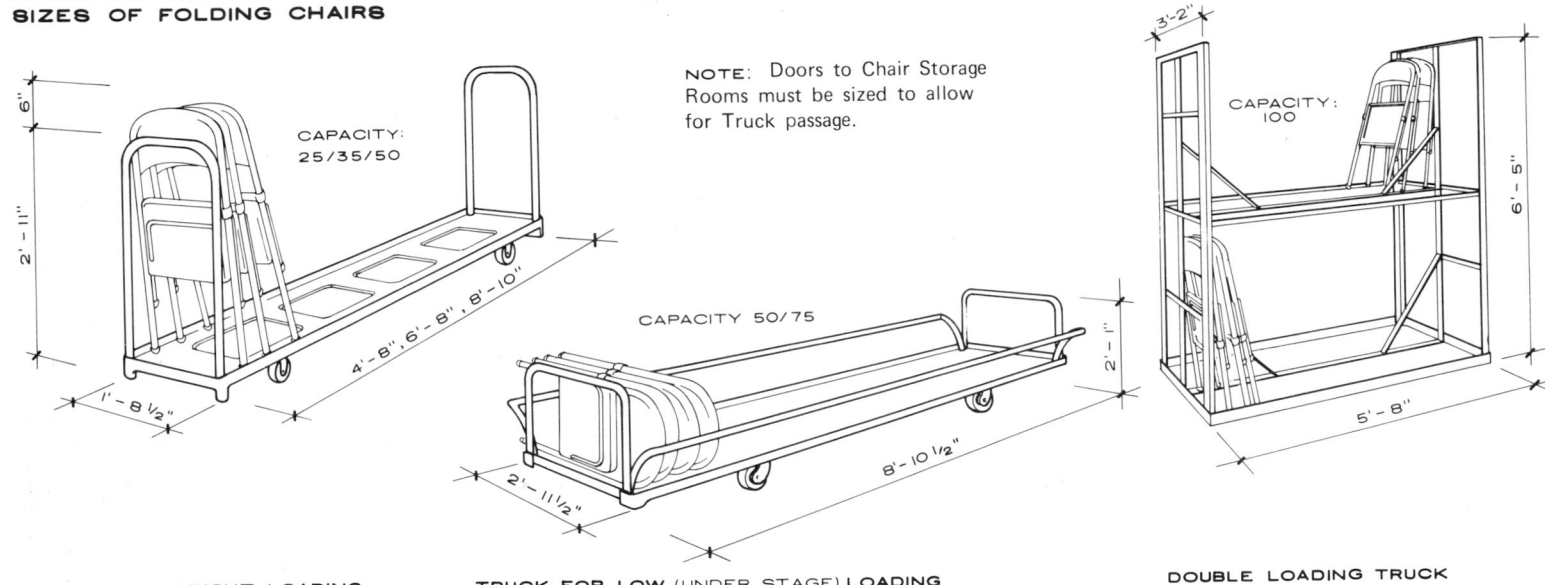

CAPACITY:
25/35/50

NOTE: Doors to Chair Storage
Rooms must be sized to allow
for Truck passage.

CAPACITY:
100

CAPACITY 50/75

TRUCK FOR UPRIGHT LOADING   TRUCK FOR LOW (UNDER STAGE) LOADING   DOUBLE LOADING TRUCK

CHAIR TRUCK STORAGE

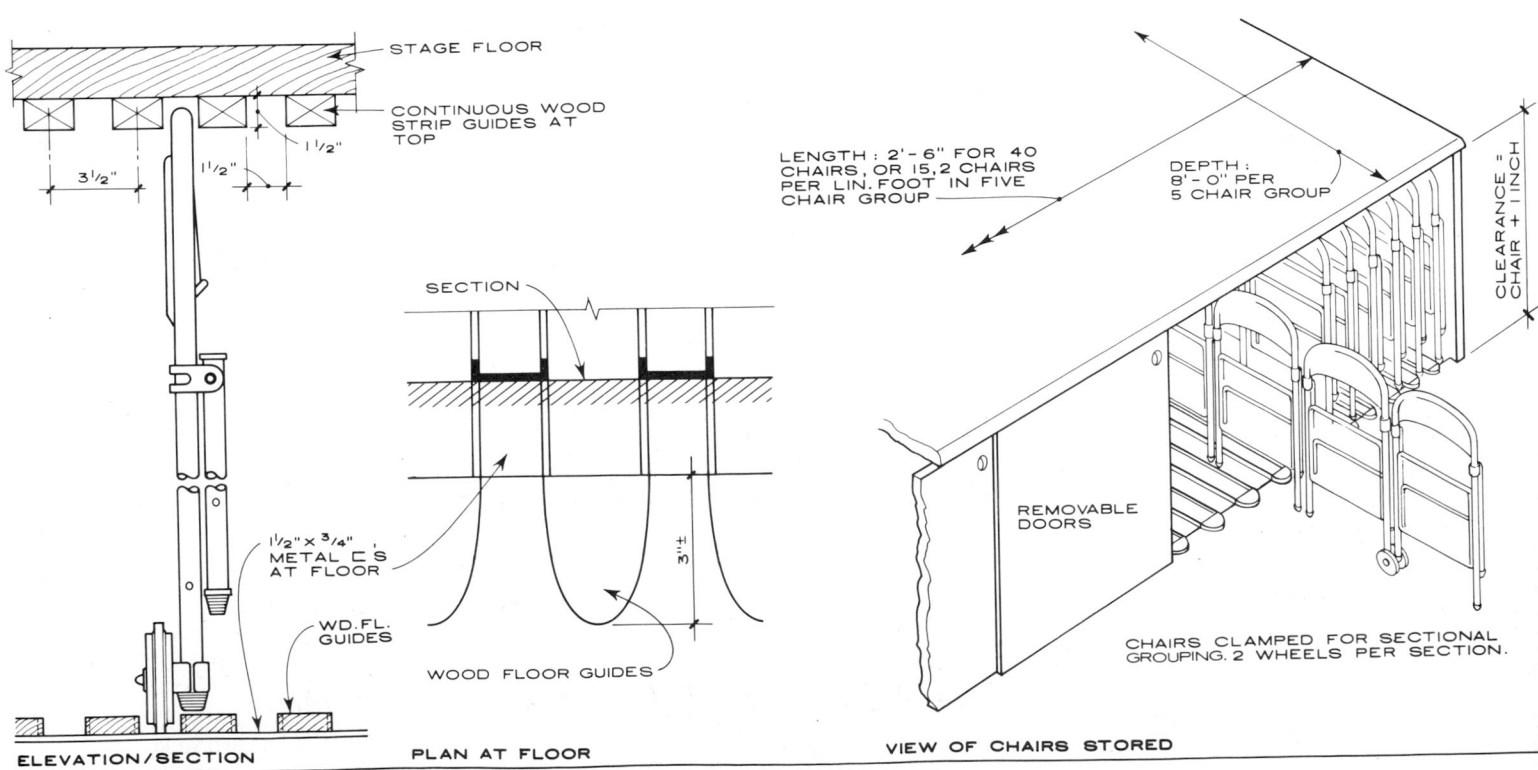

STAGE FLOOR

CONTINUOUS WOOD
STRIP GUIDES AT
TOP

LENGTH : 2'-6" FOR 40
CHAIRS, OR 15,2 CHAIRS
PER LIN. FOOT IN FIVE
CHAIR GROUP

DEPTH :
8'- 0" PER
5 CHAIR GROUP

CLEARANCE =
CHAIR + 1 INCH

SECTION

1 1/2" x 3/4"
METAL ⊏'s
AT FLOOR

WD. FL.
GUIDES

WOOD FLOOR GUIDES

REMOVABLE
DOORS

CHAIRS CLAMPED FOR SECTIONAL
GROUPING. 2 WHEELS PER SECTION.

ELEVATION/SECTION   PLAN AT FLOOR   VIEW OF CHAIRS STORED

TRACK DEVICE FOR STORAGE OF CHAIRS UNDER STAGE PLATFORM

J. C. Mayer; William B. Tabler, FAIA; New York, New York

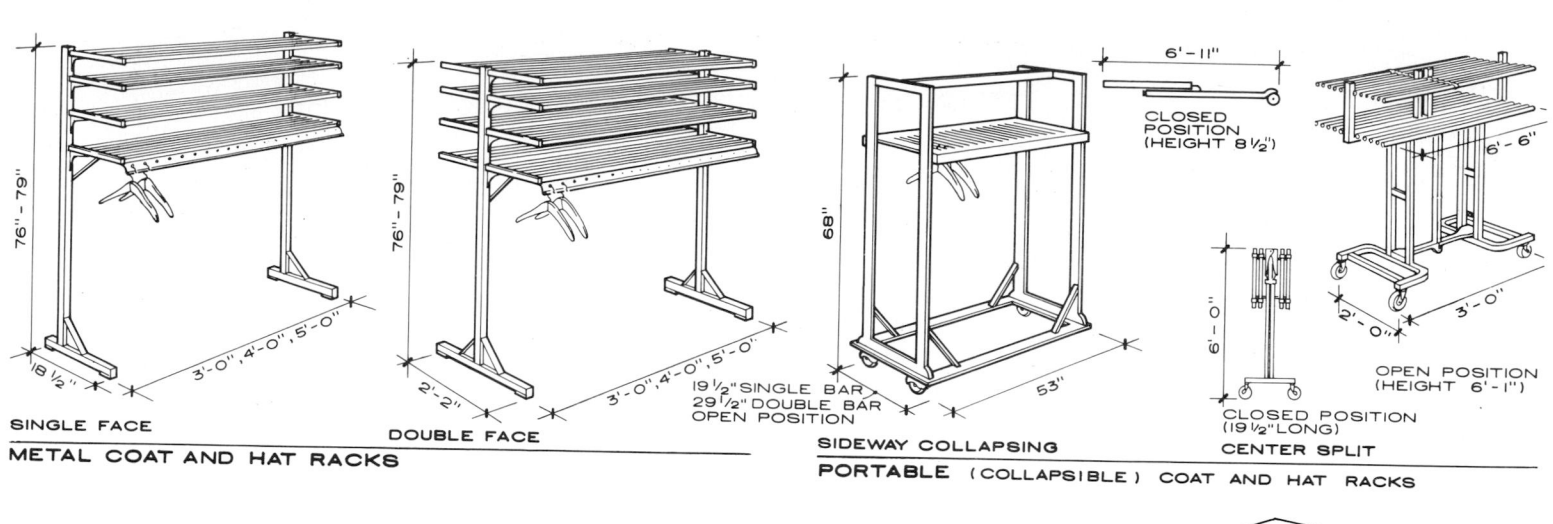

SINGLE FACE   DOUBLE FACE

METAL COAT AND HAT RACKS

19½"SINGLE BAR
29½"DOUBLE BAR
OPEN POSITION

SIDEWAY COLLAPSING

CLOSED POSITION
(HEIGHT 8½')

CLOSED POSITION
(19½"LONG)

OPEN POSITION
(HEIGHT 6'-1")

CENTER SPLIT

PORTABLE (COLLAPSIBLE) COAT AND HAT RACKS

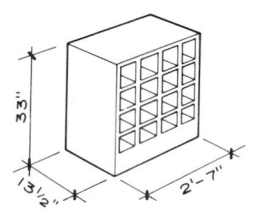

OVERSHOE RACK   UMBRELLA RACK

NOTE:

Allow ¾ sq. ft. per person which allows for coat on hanger, hat, umbrella and overshoes. Allow approximately 20% of hanger capacity for overshoe - umbrella racks. Standard hanger spacing is 3" o.c. (4 per lin. ft.). Capacity may be increased 25% by spacing 2½" o.c. (5 per lin. ft.). Use of hooks increases capacity to 8 per lin. ft.

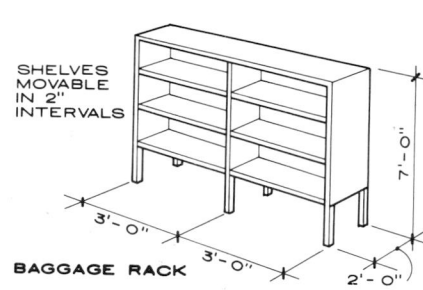

SHELVES
MOVABLE
IN 2"
INTERVALS

BAGGAGE RACK

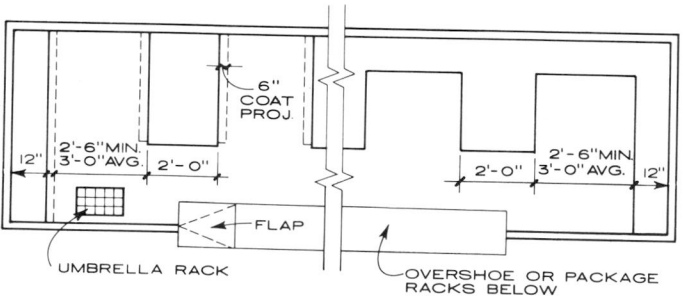
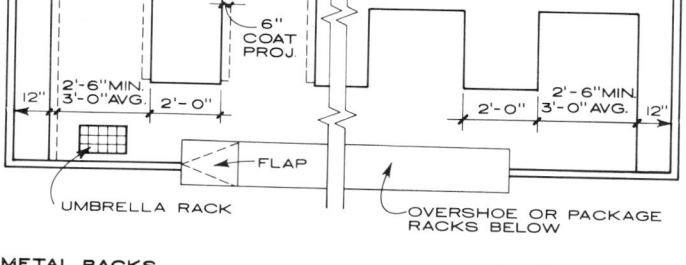

6"
COAT
PROJ.

2'-6"MIN.
3'-0"AVG.

2'-6"MIN.
3'-0"AVG.

FLAP

UMBRELLA RACK

OVERSHOE OR PACKAGE
RACKS BELOW

METAL RACKS   WOOD RACKS

TYPICAL CHECKROOM LAYOUT

VERTICAL
SUPPORT

DOUBLE FACE   SINGLE FACE

WOOD CHECKROOM SHELVING

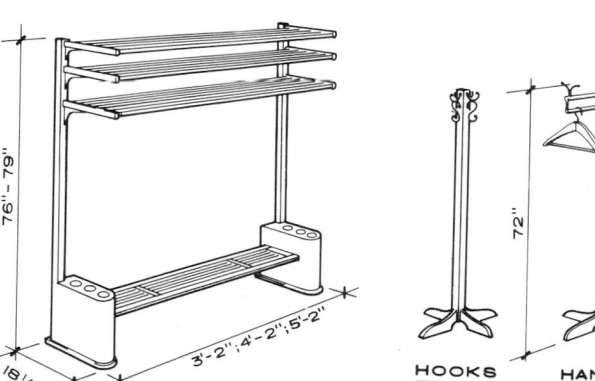

COMBINATION COAT, HAT, UMBRELLA, OVERSHOE RACK

Above model may be mounted back-to-back. Portable models are mounted on casters. Models available with or without umbrella and overshoe racks.

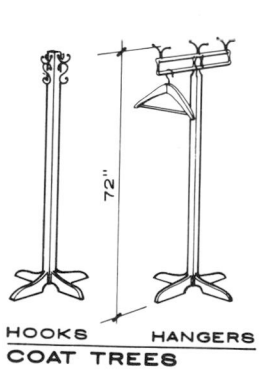

HOOKS   HANGERS

COAT TREES

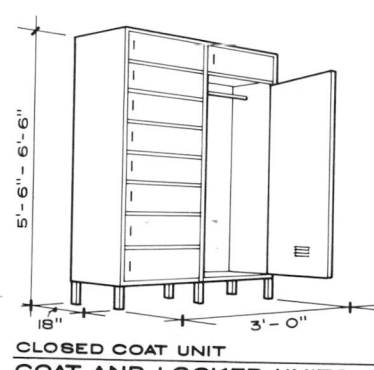

CLOSED COAT UNIT   OPEN COAT UNIT

COAT AND LOCKER UNITS

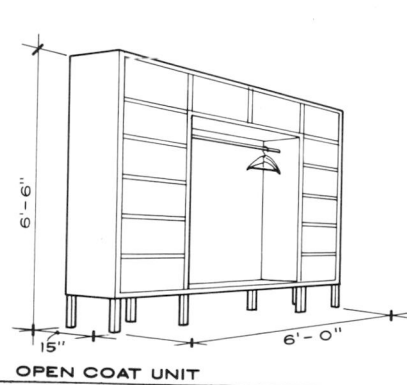

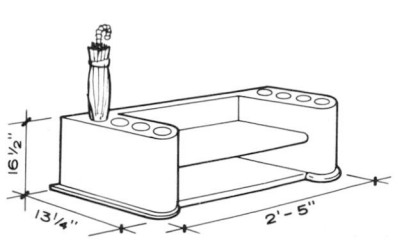

UMBRELLA & OVERSHOE RACK

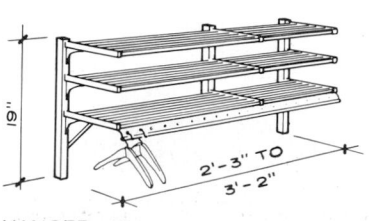

HOOK-WALL RACK   HANGER-WALL RACK

J. C. Mayer; William B. Tabler, FAIA; New York, New York

Adjustable metal or wood legs.

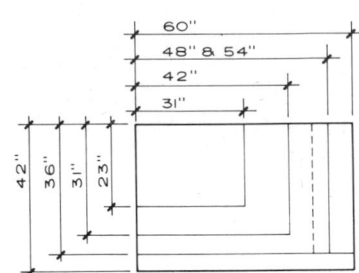

PLAN
BASIC TABLE

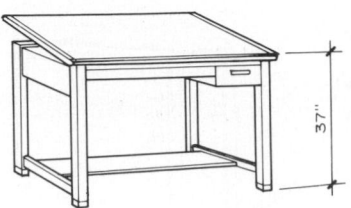

Drafting &/or engineering table available in wood, steel or in combination. Various drawer and pedestal arrangements available. See manufacturer's literature.

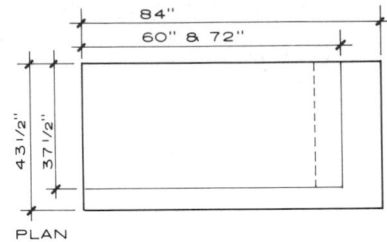

PLAN
TYPICAL DRAFTING TABLE

35 1/4" TO 44" ADJUSTMENT

Adjusts to desired height by foot pedal, takes any stop, vertical or horizontal.

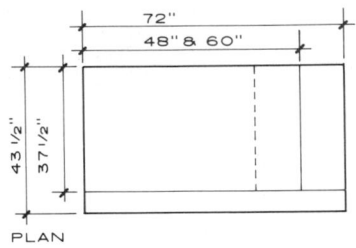

PLAN
"AUTO-SHIFT" DRAWING TABLE

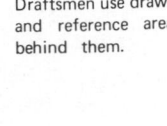

Draftsmen use drawers and reference area behind them.

"Auto-shift" provides drawing and reference in only 36 sq. ft. per man.

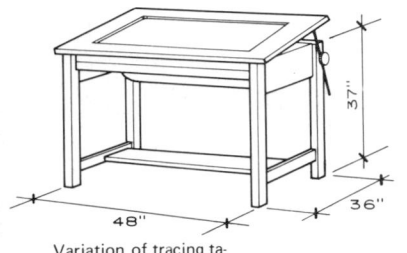

Variation of tracing table available on base similar to basic table.
TRACING TABLES

Tracing tables are obtainable with 22" x 24" or 24" x 36" glass tracing units.

Portable boards available with tracing areas up to 24" x 36 3/4".

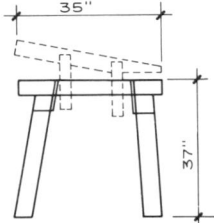

Adjustable trestles or horses available; adjust from 39" to 47" in height.
TRESTLES & BOARDS

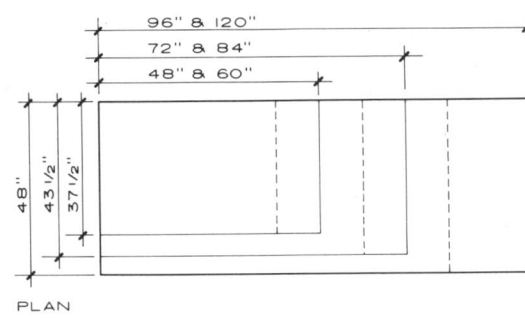

PLAN

DRAFTING & TRACING TABLES, TRESTLES & BOARDS

FIXED HT. 28" TO 30"

BACK ADJUSTS 10" TO 13½" ABOVE SEAT

VARIABLE SEAT HEIGHTS FROM 17½" TO 34"

STOOLS & CHAIRS

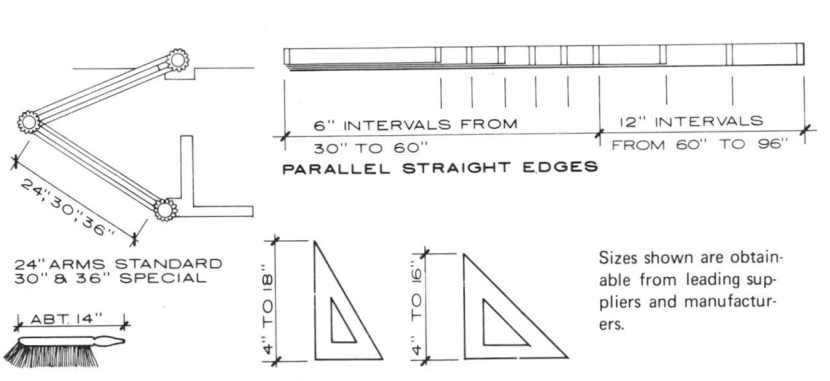

24" ARMS STANDARD 30" & 36" SPECIAL

ABT. 14"

6" INTERVALS FROM 30" TO 60"   12" INTERVALS FROM 60" TO 96"
PARALLEL STRAIGHT EDGES

4" TO 18"   4" TO 16"

Sizes shown are obtainable from leading suppliers and manufacturers.

18"

6" INTERVALS FROM 18" TO 60"

"T" SQUARES

DRAFTING EQUIPMENT

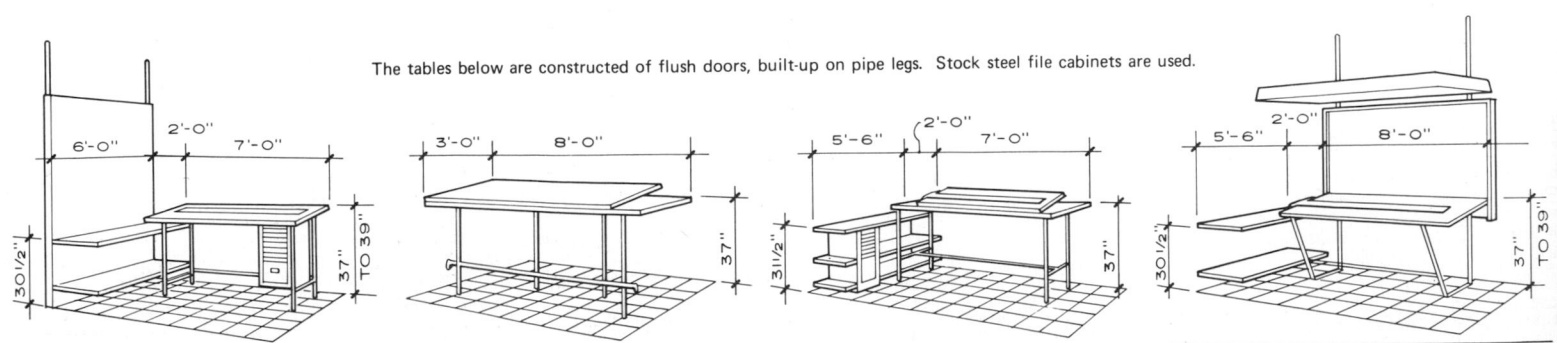

The tables below are constructed of flush doors, built-up on pipe legs. Stock steel file cabinets are used.

SPECIAL DRAFTING TABLE INSTALLATIONS

Richard Robinson; The Spitznagel Partners, Inc.; Sioux Falls, South Dakota

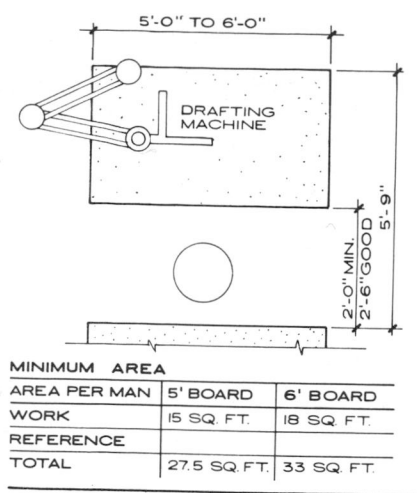

MINIMUM AREA

AREA PER MAN	5' BOARD	6' BOARD
WORK	15 SQ. FT.	18 SQ. FT.
REFERENCE		
TOTAL	27.5 SQ. FT.	33 SQ. FT.

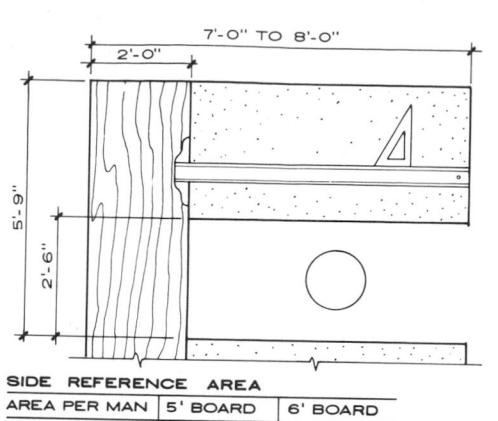

SIDE REFERENCE AREA

AREA PER MAN	5' BOARD	6' BOARD
WORK	15 SQ. FT.	18 SQ. FT.
REFERENCE	11 SQ. FT.	11 SQ. FT.
TOTAL	38.5 SQ. FT.	44 SQ. FT.

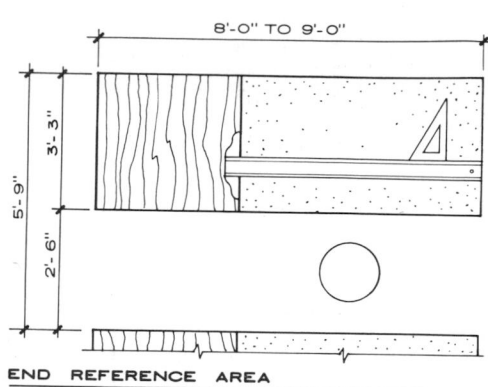

END REFERENCE AREA

AREA PER MAN	5' BOARD	6' BOARD
WORK	15 SQ. FT.	18 SQ. FT.
REFERENCE	9 SQ. FT.	9 SQ. FT.
TOTAL	44 SQ. FT.	49.5 SQ. FT.

PLANS OF DRAFTING UNITS
SCALE: 1/4" = 1'-0"

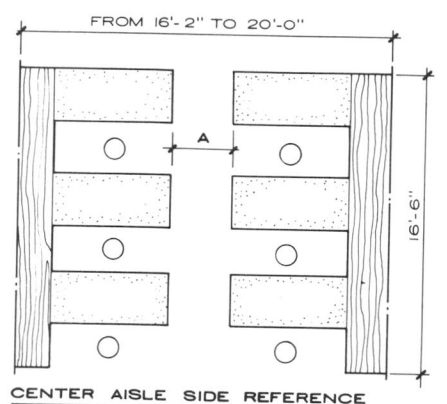

CENTER AISLE SIDE REFERENCE

AREA PER MAN	5' BOARD	6' BOARD
MINIMUM	44.25 SQ. FT.	49.75 SQ. FT.
GOOD	46.75 SQ. FT.	52.25 SQ. FT.
EXCELLENT	49.50 SQ. FT.	55 SQ. FT.

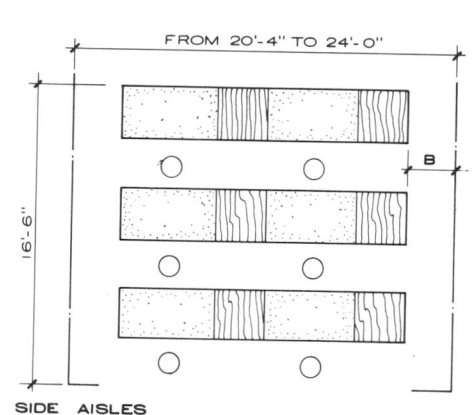

SIDE AISLES

AREA PER MAN	5' BOARD	6' BOARD
MINIMUM	56 SQ. FT.	61.50 SQ. FT.
GOOD	57.75 SQ. FT.	63.50 SQ. FT.
EXCELLENT	60.50 SQ. FT.	66 SQ. FT.

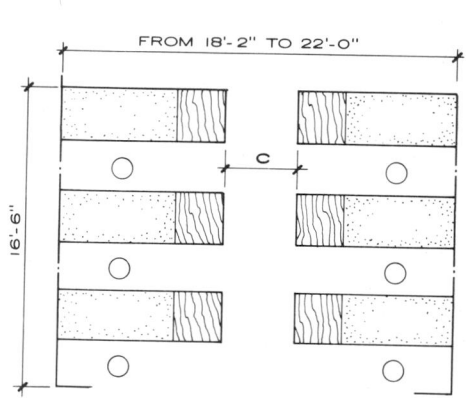

CENTER AISLE END REFERENCE

AREA PER MAN	5' BOARD	6' BOARD
MINIMUM	55 SQ. FT.	61 SQ. FT.
GOOD	57.50 SQ. FT.	63.25 SQ. FT.
EXCELLENT	60.50 SQ. FT.	66 SQ. FT.

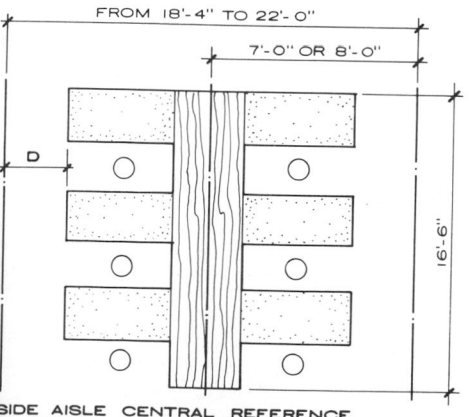

SIDE AISLE CENTRAL REFERENCE

AREA PER MAN	5' BOARD	6' BOARD
MINIMUM	50.25 SQ. FT.	55.75 SQ. FT.
GOOD	52.25 SQ. FT.	57.75 SQ. FT.
EXCELLENT	55 SQ. FT.	60.50 SQ. FT.

SIDE AISLE WITH STORAGE AREA

AREA PER MAN	5' BOARD	6' BOARD
MINIMUM	86.25 SQ. FT.	91.75 SQ. FT.
GOOD	88 SQ. FT.	93.50 SQ. FT.
EXCELLENT	90.75 SQ. FT.	96.75 SQ. FT.

PLANS OF COMPARATIVE DRAFTING AREAS
SCALE: 3/32" = 1'-0"

NOTES:

Dimensions shown are based on the use of 3' x 5' and 3' x 6' drafting tables. If larger tables are used they will replace reference areas and the total areas will not increase. Provide one large table for detailing, reference, and wrapping.

The draftsman requires 80 to 100 footcandles of light on his board or approximately 6 watts per square foot. Avoid sharp contrasts of light in drafting room. The board illumination should never be more than seven times as bright as the surroundings. Fluorescent trough fixtures are most practical when hung diagonally to tables.

For the medium-sized architectural drafting office 100 square feet per man is ideal. This includes areas for drafting, reference, plan storage, aisle and supply. Reception, office, conference, and wash rooms are not included.

AISLE WIDTHS

AISLE	A	B	C	D	E
MIN.	2'-2"	2'-2"	2'-2"	2'-2"	2'-2"
GOOD	3'-0"	2'-6"	3'-0"	2'-6"	2'-6"
EXCEL.	4'-0"	3'-0"	4'-0"	3'-0"	3'-0"

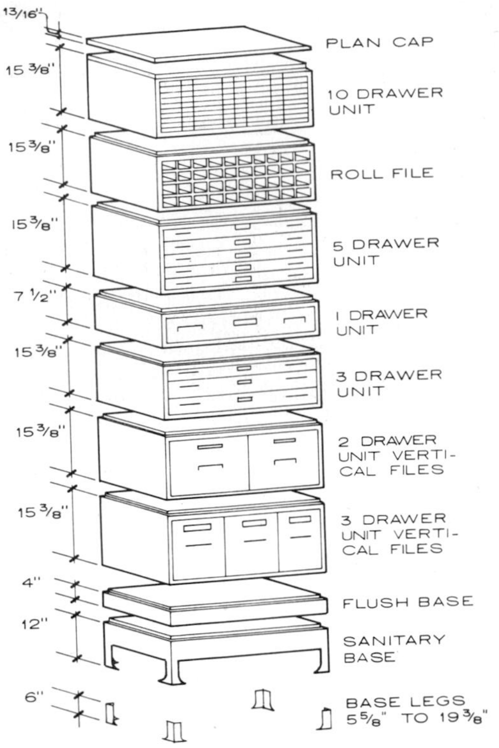

13/16"
15 3/8"
15 3/8"
15 3/8"
7 1/2"
15 3/8"
15 3/8"
15 3/8"
4"
12"
6"
PLAN CAP
10 DRAWER UNIT
ROLL FILE
5 DRAWER UNIT
1 DRAWER UNIT
3 DRAWER UNIT
2 DRAWER UNIT VERTICAL FILES
3 DRAWER UNIT VERTICAL FILES
FLUSH BASE
SANITARY BASE
BASE LEGS 5 5/8" TO 19 3/8"

PLAN FILE

Steel shown, wood similar; depth 28 1/2" to 50 1/2"; width 40 3/4" to 79 5/16"; drawer extends 26" to 42".

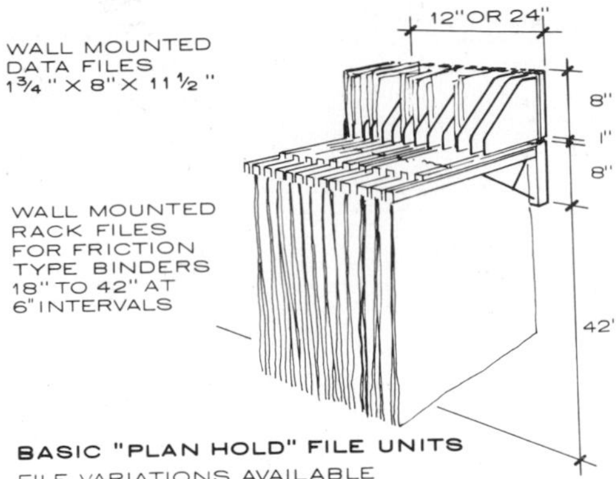

WALL MOUNTED DATA FILES 1 3/4" X 8" X 11 1/2"
WALL MOUNTED RACK FILES FOR FRICTION TYPE BINDERS 18" TO 42" AT 6" INTERVALS
12" OR 24"
8"
1"
8"
42"

BASIC "PLAN HOLD" FILE UNITS

FILE VARIATIONS AVAILABLE ON ROLLING STANDS AND CIRCULAR CAROUSEL STANDS.

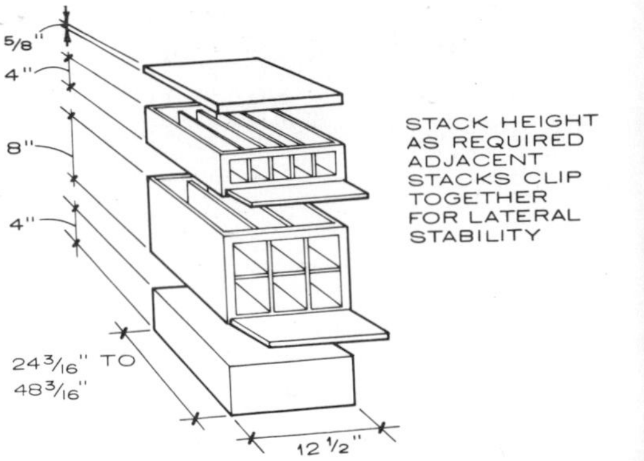

5/8"
4"
8"
4"
24 3/16" TO 48 3/16"
12 1/2"
STACK HEIGHT AS REQUIRED ADJACENT STACKS CLIP TOGETHER FOR LATERAL STABILITY

TYPICAL ROLL FILE UNITS

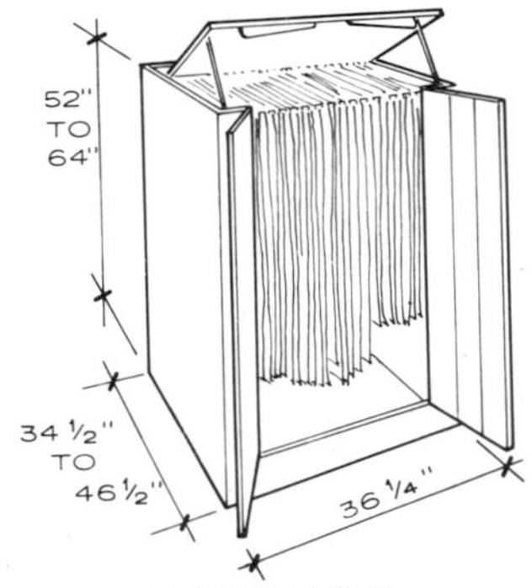

52" TO 64"
34 1/2" TO 46 1/2"
36 1/4"

CABINET CLIP FILE

52"
27" TO 39"
16"

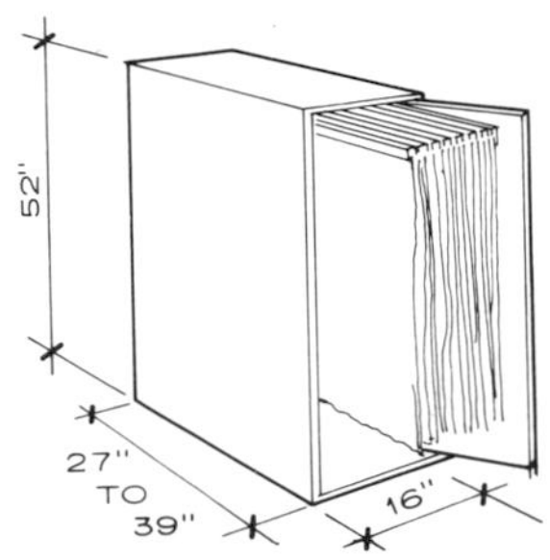

CABINET VERTICAL FILES

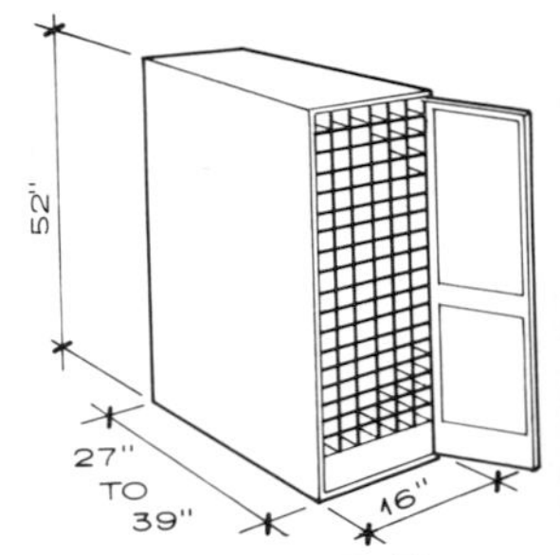

52"
27" TO 39"
16"

CABINET ROLL FILE

72"
18"
44 3/4" TO 56 3/4"

VERTICAL FILE

61 3/4"
28"
25"
22 3/16"

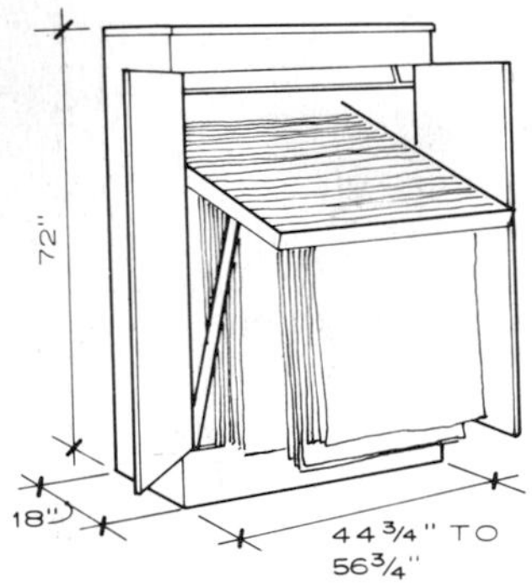

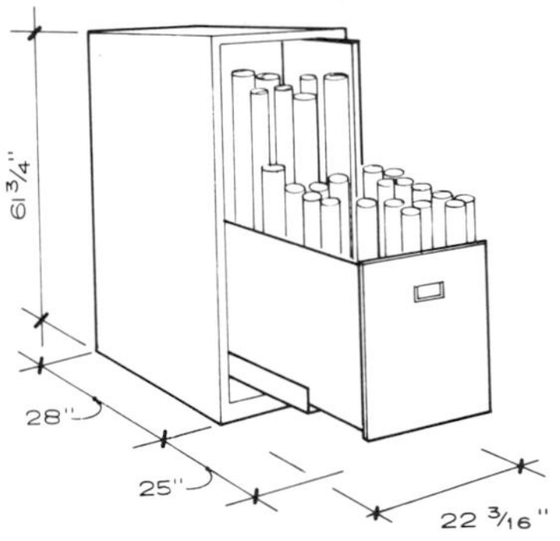

VERTICAL ROLL FILE

39 1/4" TO 42"
41 7/8" TO 54 3/8"
14 1/2" TO 26 1/4"

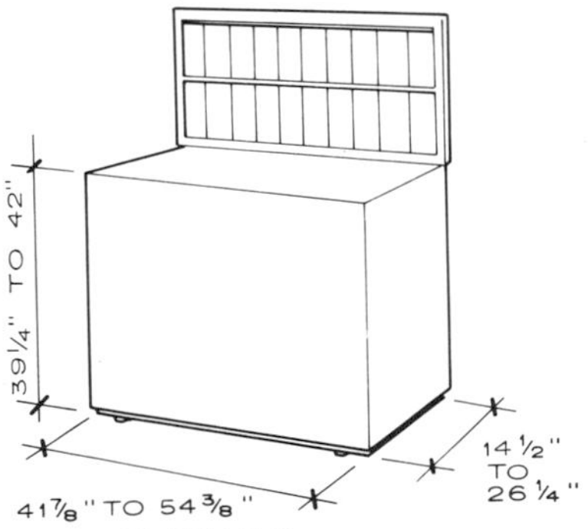

VERTICAL PLAN FILE

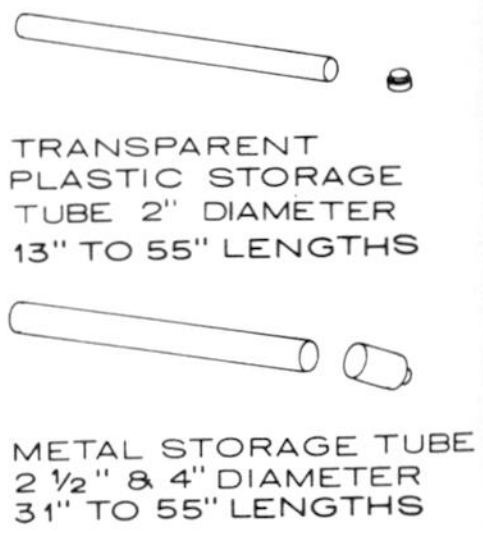

TRANSPARENT PLASTIC STORAGE TUBE 2" DIAMETER 13" TO 55" LENGTHS
METAL STORAGE TUBE 2 1/2" & 4" DIAMETER 31" TO 55" LENGTHS

STORAGE TUBES

FILING AND STORAGE EQUIPMENT

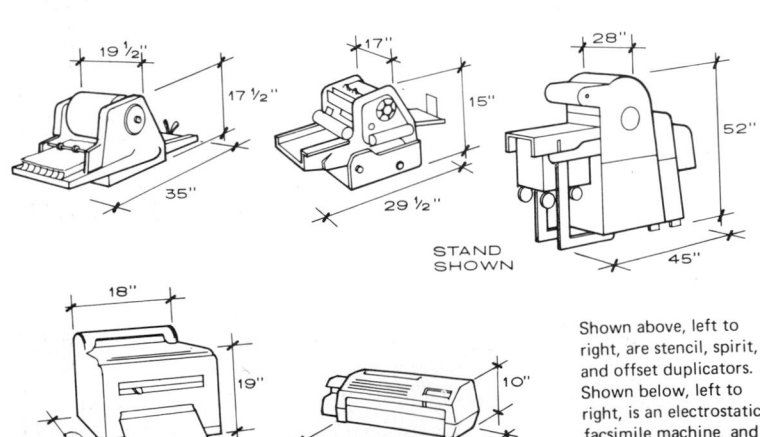

19 1/2"
17 1/2"
35"
17"
15"
29 1/2"
28"
52"
45"
STAND SHOWN

18"
19"
26 3/4"
10"
25 1/2"
10 1/2"

Shown above, left to right, are stencil, spirit, and offset duplicators. Shown below, left to right, is an electrostatic facsimile machine and a photocopy machine.

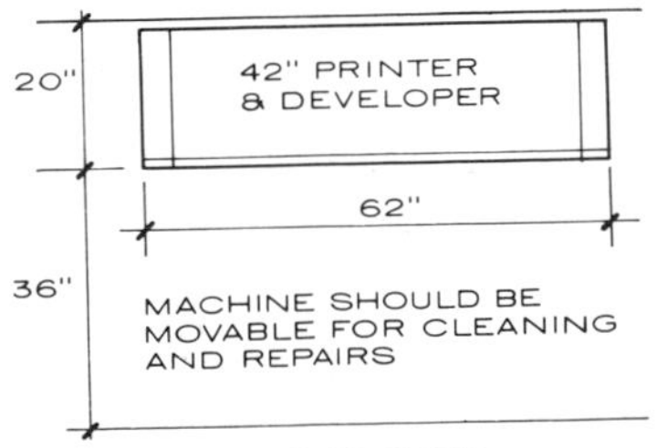

20"
42" PRINTER & DEVELOPER
62"
36"
MACHINE SHOULD BE MOVABLE FOR CLEANING AND REPAIRS

PRINTER & DEVELOPER

The process used determines the requirements of space, light, plumbing and ventilation.

For reproduction of tracings a printing and developing unit is necessary. The printer is above the developing unit. With the two units and the proper chemicals and paper, blueprints, black and white and bluelines, and other types of copy are possible.

When choosing equipment the size and type process is determined by the individual requirements of the office.

The machines should be ventilated for heat and chemical fumes. The 42" machine is the most commonly used in medium sized offices.

REPRODUCTION EQUIPMENT

Richard Robinson; The Spitznagel Partners, Inc.; Sioux Falls, South Dakota

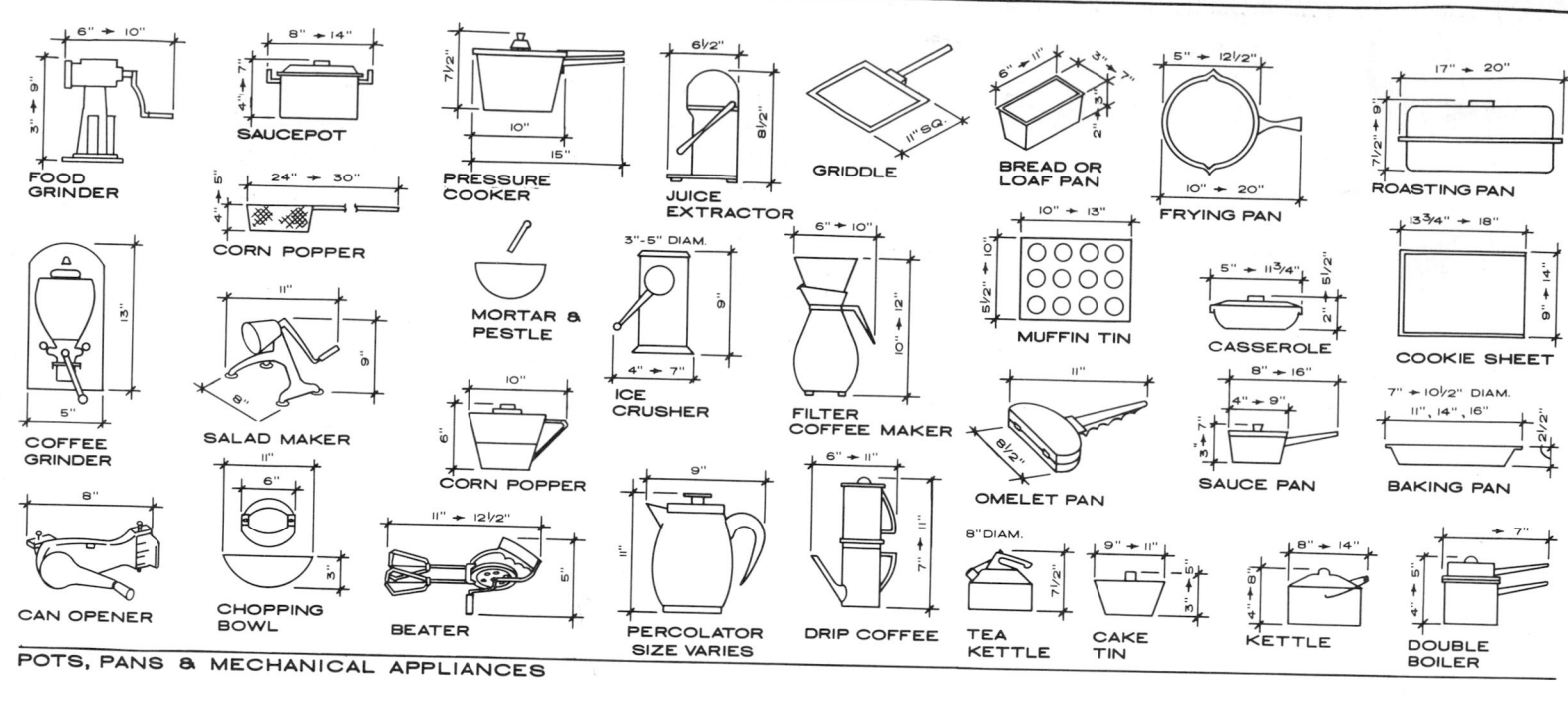

FOOD GRINDER · **SAUCEPOT** · **PRESSURE COOKER** · **JUICE EXTRACTOR** · **GRIDDLE** · **BREAD OR LOAF PAN** · **FRYING PAN** · **ROASTING PAN**

CORN POPPER · **MORTAR & PESTLE** · **ICE CRUSHER** · **FILTER COFFEE MAKER** · **MUFFIN TIN** · **CASSEROLE** · **COOKIE SHEET**

COFFEE GRINDER · **SALAD MAKER** · **CORN POPPER** · **OMELET PAN** · **SAUCE PAN** · **BAKING PAN**

CAN OPENER · **CHOPPING BOWL** · **BEATER** · **PERCOLATOR SIZE VARIES** · **DRIP COFFEE** · **TEA KETTLE** · **CAKE TIN** · **KETTLE** · **DOUBLE BOILER**

POTS, PANS & MECHANICAL APPLIANCES

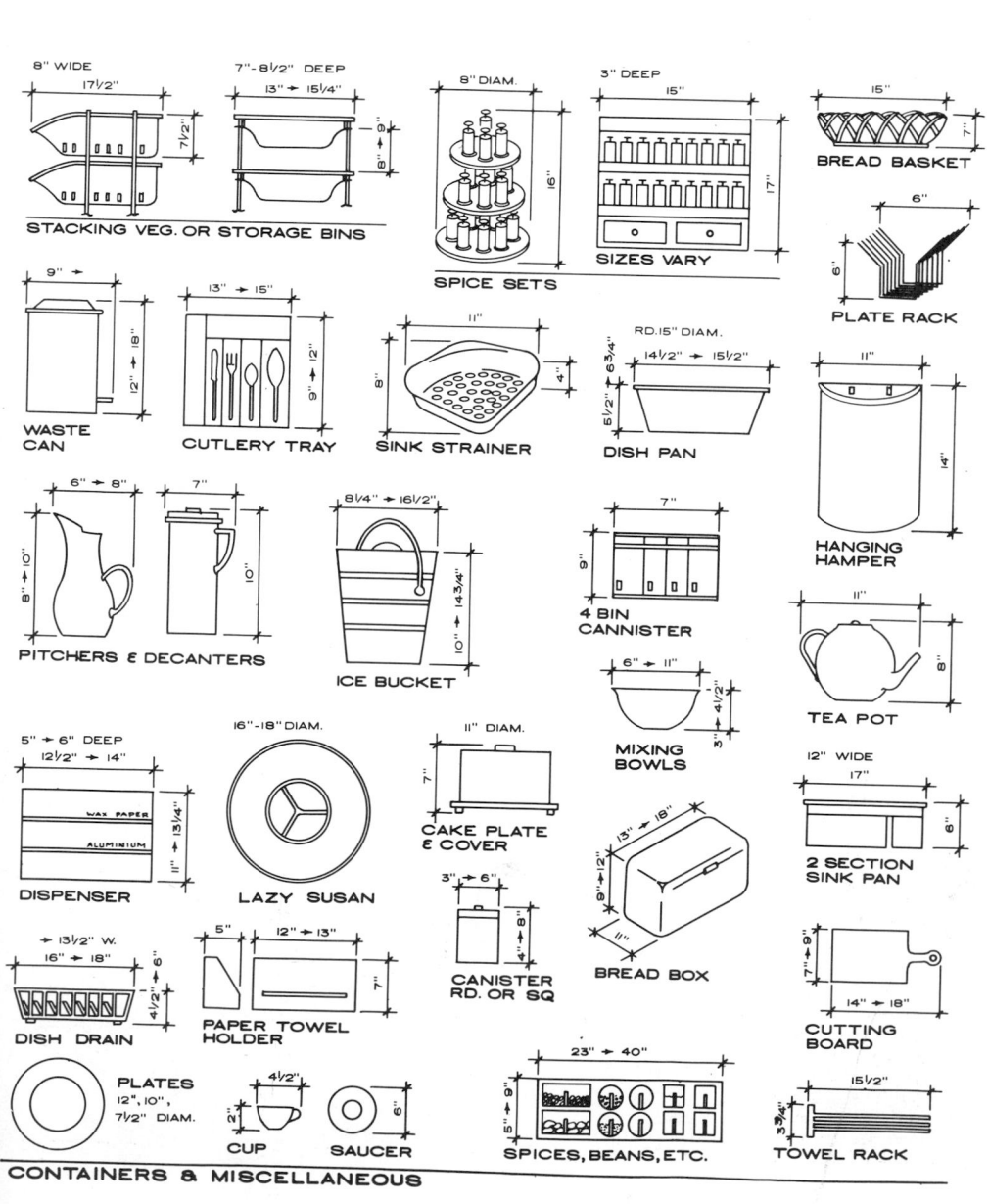

STACKING VEG. OR STORAGE BINS · **SPICE SETS** · **SIZES VARY** · **BREAD BASKET** · **PLATE RACK**

WASTE CAN · **CUTLERY TRAY** · **SINK STRAINER** · **DISH PAN** · **HANGING HAMPER**

PITCHERS & DECANTERS · **ICE BUCKET** · **4 BIN CANNISTER** · **TEA POT**

DISPENSER · **LAZY SUSAN** · **CAKE PLATE & COVER** · **MIXING BOWLS** · **BREAD BOX** · **2 SECTION SINK PAN**

DISH DRAIN · **PAPER TOWEL HOLDER** · **CANISTER RD. OR SQ** · **CUTTING BOARD**

PLATES 12", 10", 7½" DIAM. · **CUP** · **SAUCER** · **SPICES, BEANS, ETC.** · **TOWEL RACK**

CONTAINERS & MISCELLANEOUS

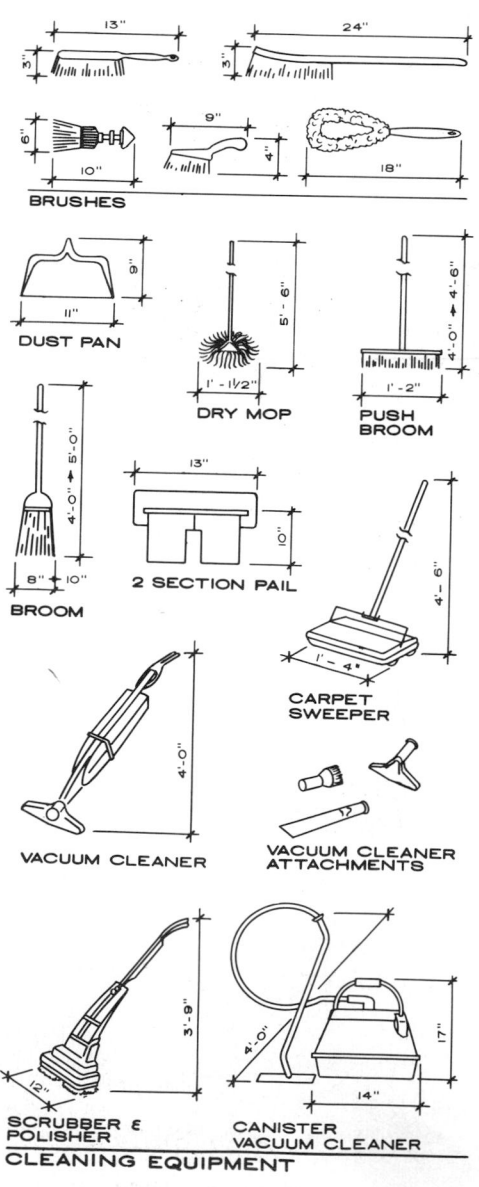

BRUSHES · **DUST PAN** · **DRY MOP** · **PUSH BROOM**

BROOM · **2 SECTION PAIL** · **CARPET SWEEPER**

VACUUM CLEANER · **VACUUM CLEANER ATTACHMENTS**

SCRUBBER & POLISHER · **CANISTER VACUUM CLEANER**

CLEANING EQUIPMENT

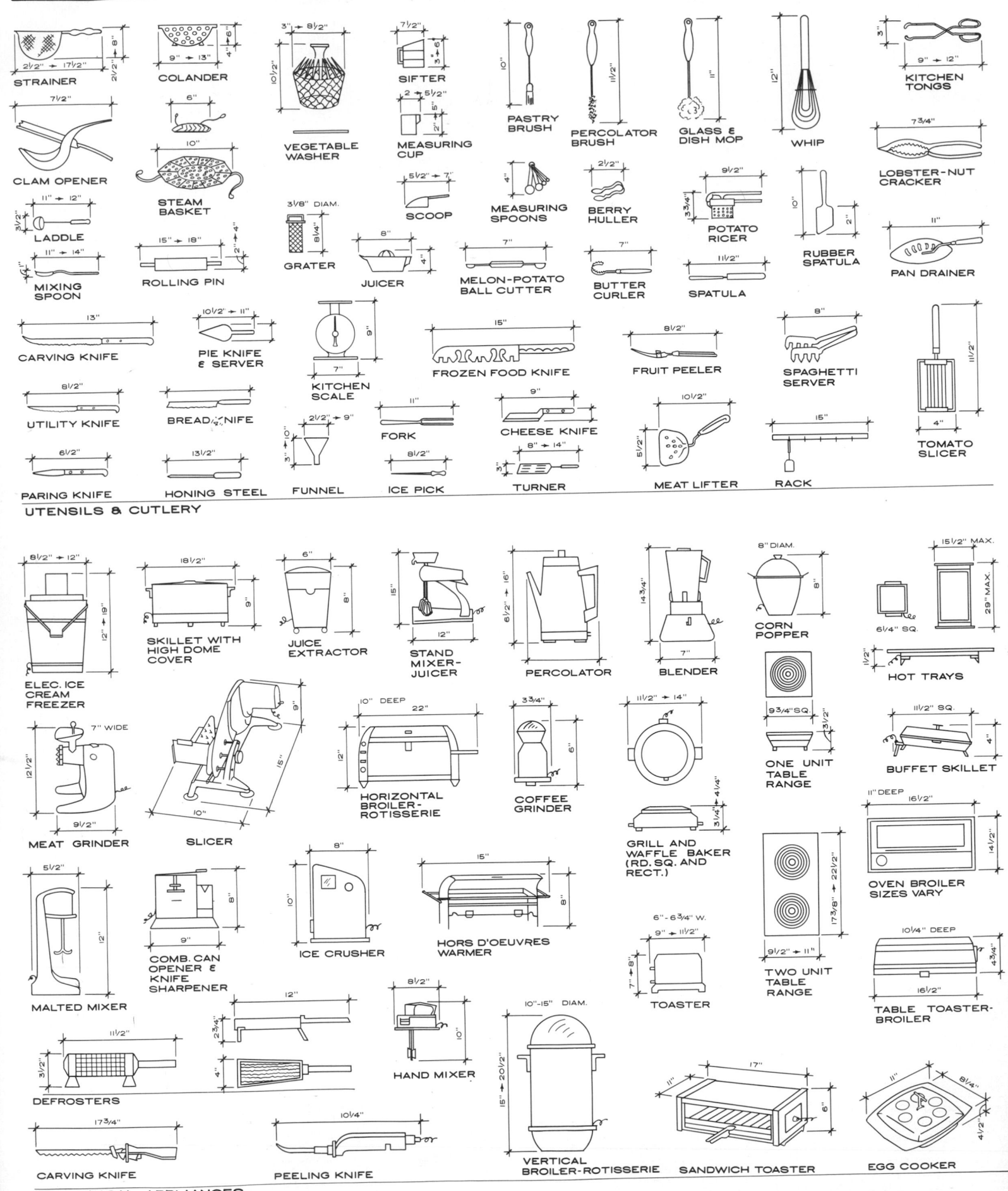

STRAINER

COLANDER

SIFTER

VEGETABLE WASHER

MEASURING CUP

PASTRY BRUSH

PERCOLATOR BRUSH

GLASS & DISH MOP

WHIP

KITCHEN TONGS

CLAM OPENER

STEAM BASKET

SCOOP

MEASURING SPOONS

BERRY HULLER

POTATO RICER

RUBBER SPATULA

LOBSTER-NUT CRACKER

LADDLE

GRATER

JUICER

MELON-POTATO BALL CUTTER

BUTTER CURLER

SPATULA

PAN DRAINER

MIXING SPOON

ROLLING PIN

CARVING KNIFE

PIE KNIFE & SERVER

KITCHEN SCALE

FROZEN FOOD KNIFE

FRUIT PEELER

SPAGHETTI SERVER

UTILITY KNIFE

BREAD KNIFE

FORK

CHEESE KNIFE

MEAT LIFTER

RACK

TOMATO SLICER

PARING KNIFE

HONING STEEL

FUNNEL

ICE PICK

TURNER

UTENSILS & CUTLERY

ELEC. ICE CREAM FREEZER

SKILLET WITH HIGH DOME COVER

JUICE EXTRACTOR

STAND MIXER-JUICER

PERCOLATOR

BLENDER

CORN POPPER

HOT TRAYS

MEAT GRINDER

SLICER

HORIZONTAL BROILER-ROTISSERIE

COFFEE GRINDER

GRILL AND WAFFLE BAKER (RD. SQ. AND RECT.)

ONE UNIT TABLE RANGE

BUFFET SKILLET

MALTED MIXER

COMB. CAN OPENER & KNIFE SHARPENER

ICE CRUSHER

HORS D'OEUVRES WARMER

TOASTER

TWO UNIT TABLE RANGE

OVEN BROILER SIZES VARY

TABLE TOASTER-BROILER

DEFROSTERS

HAND MIXER

VERTICAL BROILER-ROTISSERIE

SANDWICH TOASTER

EGG COOKER

CARVING KNIFE

PEELING KNIFE

ELECTRICAL APPLIANCES

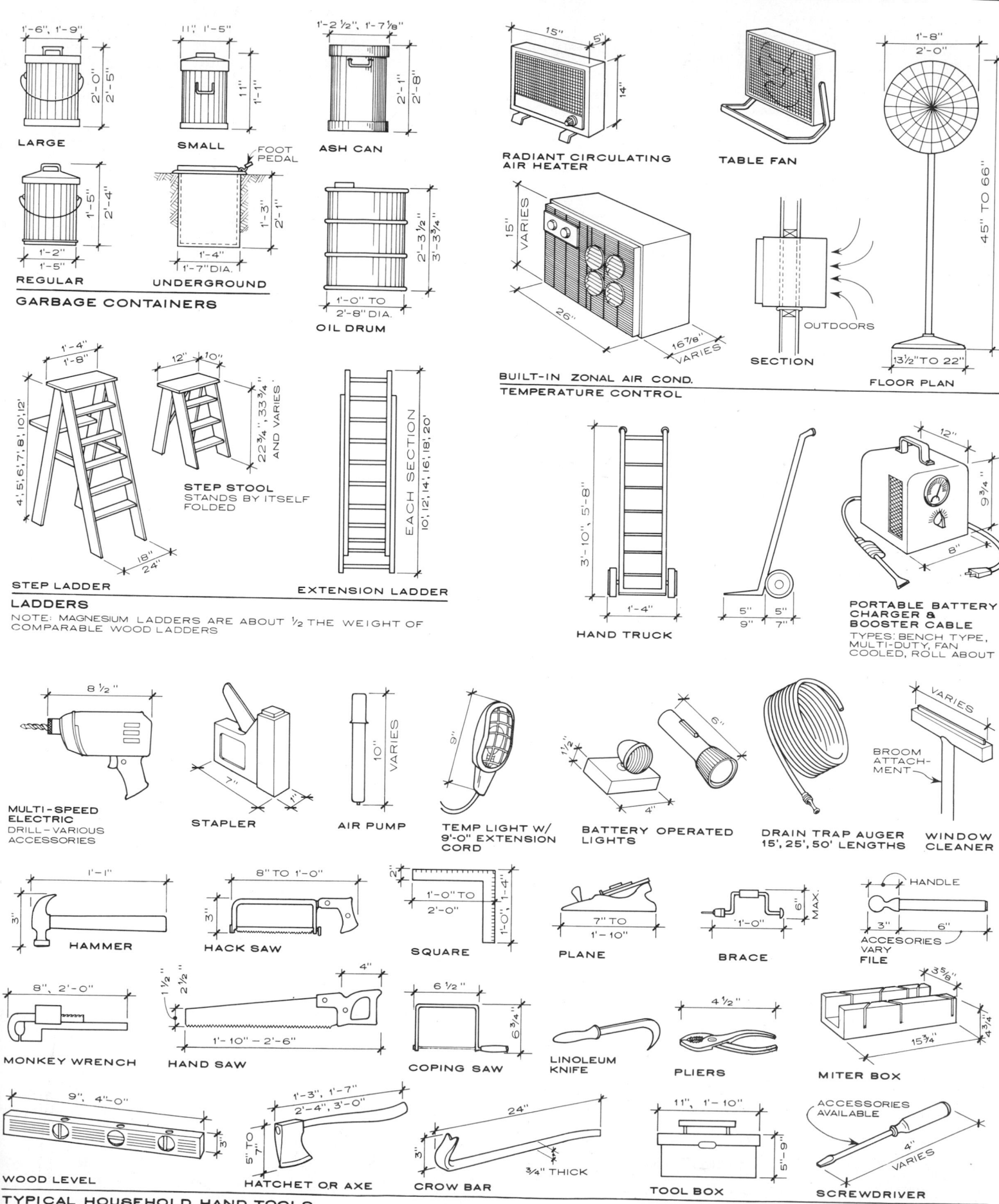

GARBAGE CONTAINERS

LARGE — 1'-6", 1'-9" / 2'-0", 2'-5"

SMALL — 11", 1'-5" / 11", 1'-1"

ASH CAN — 1'-2½", 1'-7⅛" / 2'-1", 2'-8"

REGULAR — 1'-2", 1'-5" / 1'-5", 2'-4"

UNDERGROUND — FOOT PEDAL / 1'-4", 1'-7" DIA. / 1'-3", 2'-1"

OIL DRUM — 2'-3½", 3'-3¾" / 1'-0" TO 2'-8" DIA.

LADDERS

STEP LADDER — 1'-4", 1'-8" / 18", 24" / 4', 5', 6', 7', 8', 10', 12'

STEP STOOL — STANDS BY ITSELF FOLDED — 12", 10" / 22¾", 33¾" AND VARIES

EXTENSION LADDER — EACH SECTION 10', 12', 14', 16', 18', 20'

NOTE: MAGNESIUM LADDERS ARE ABOUT ½ THE WEIGHT OF COMPARABLE WOOD LADDERS

TEMPERATURE CONTROL

RADIANT CIRCULATING AIR HEATER — 15", 5", 14"

TABLE FAN

FLOOR PLAN — 1'-8", 2'-0" / 45" TO 66" / 13½" TO 22"

BUILT-IN ZONAL AIR COND. — 15", 26", 16⅞" VARIES

SECTION — OUTDOORS

HAND TRUCK — 3'-10", 5'-8" / 1'-4" / 5", 9" / 5", 7"

PORTABLE BATTERY CHARGER & BOOSTER CABLE — 12", 9¾", 8"
TYPES: BENCH TYPE, MULTI-DUTY, FAN COOLED, ROLL ABOUT

MULTI-SPEED ELECTRIC DRILL – VARIOUS ACCESSORIES — 8½"

STAPLER — 7", 1"

AIR PUMP — 10" VARIES

TEMP LIGHT W/ 9'-0" EXTENSION CORD — 9"

BATTERY OPERATED LIGHTS — 1½", 6", 4"

DRAIN TRAP AUGER 15', 25', 50' LENGTHS

WINDOW CLEANER — VARIES — BROOM ATTACHMENT

TYPICAL HOUSEHOLD HAND TOOLS

HAMMER — 1'-1", 3"

HACK SAW — 8" TO 1'-0", 3"

SQUARE — 2", 1'-0" TO 2'-0", 1'-0" TO 1'-4"

PLANE — 7" TO 1'-10"

BRACE — 1'-0", 6" MAX.

FILE — HANDLE / ACCESSORIES VARY / 3", 6"

MONKEY WRENCH — 8", 2'-0"

HAND SAW — 1½", 2½", 4" / 1'-10" — 2'-6"

COPING SAW — 6½", 6¾"

LINOLEUM KNIFE

PLIERS — 4½"

MITER BOX — 3⅝", 4¾", 15¾"

WOOD LEVEL — 9", 4'-0", 3"

HATCHET OR AXE — 1'-3", 1'-7" / 2'-4", 3'-0" / 5" TO 7"

CROW BAR — 24", 3", ¾" THICK

TOOL BOX — 11", 1'-10" / 5", 9"

SCREWDRIVER — ACCESSORIES AVAILABLE / 4" VARIES

R. E. Powe, Jr.; Hugh N. Jacobsen, AIA; Washington, D. C.

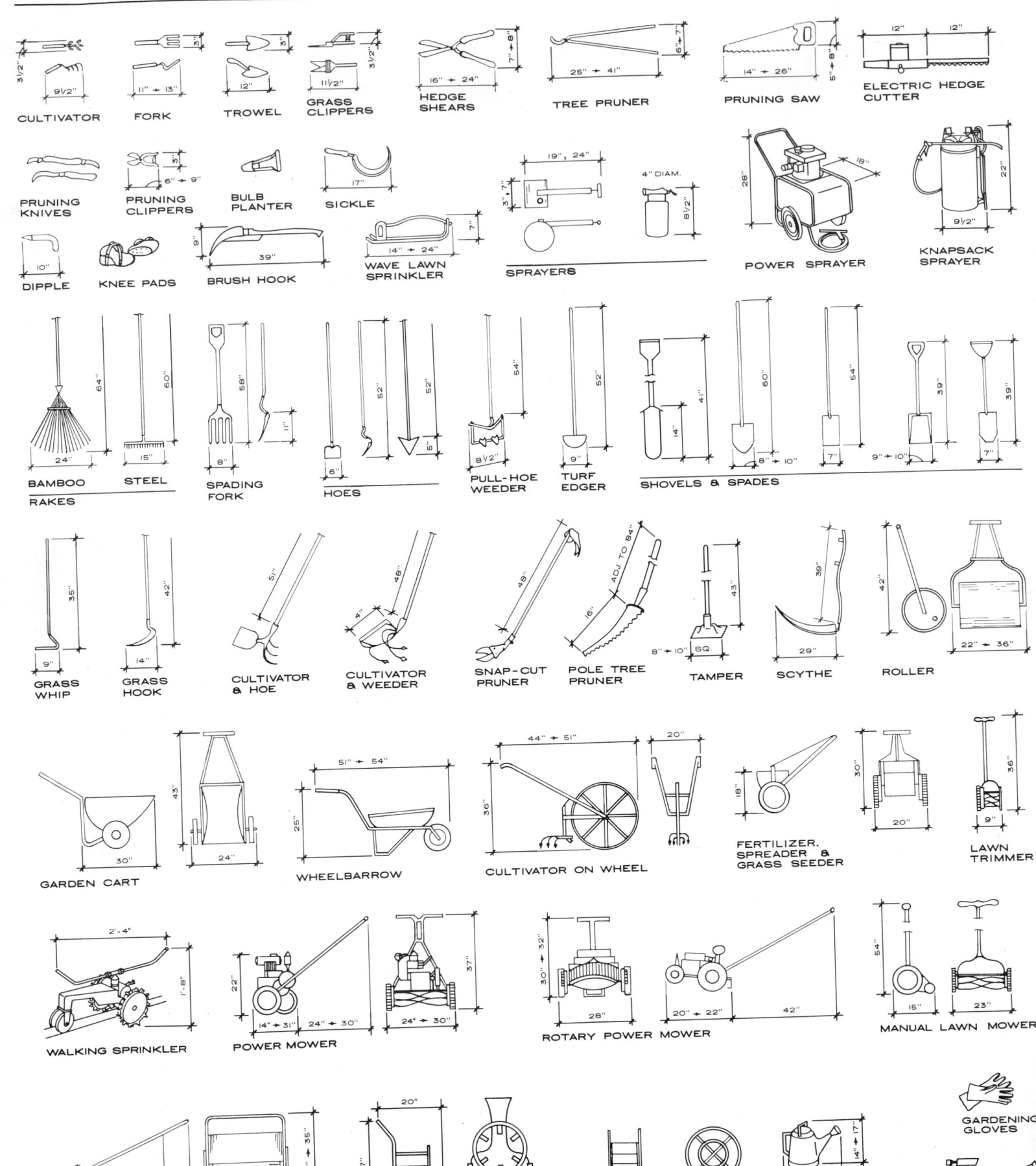

CULTIVATOR — FORK — TROWEL — GRASS CLIPPERS — HEDGE SHEARS — TREE PRUNER — PRUNING SAW — ELECTRIC HEDGE CUTTER

PRUNING KNIVES — PRUNING CLIPPERS — BULB PLANTER — SICKLE — SPRAYERS — POWER SPRAYER — KNAPSACK SPRAYER

DIPPLE — KNEE PADS — BRUSH HOOK — WAVE LAWN SPRINKLER

BAMBOO — STEEL — RAKES — SPADING FORK — HOES — PULL-HOE WEEDER — TURF EDGER — SHOVELS & SPADES

GRASS WHIP — GRASS HOOK — CULTIVATOR & HOE — CULTIVATOR & WEEDER — SNAP-CUT PRUNER — POLE TREE PRUNER — TAMPER — SCYTHE — ROLLER

GARDEN CART — WHEELBARROW — CULTIVATOR ON WHEEL — FERTILIZER, SPREADER & GRASS SEEDER — LAWN TRIMMER

WALKING SPRINKLER — POWER MOWER — ROTARY POWER MOWER — MANUAL LAWN MOWER

LAWN SWEEPER — HOSE REELS — WATERING CAN — GARDENING GLOVES — HOSE NOZZLES

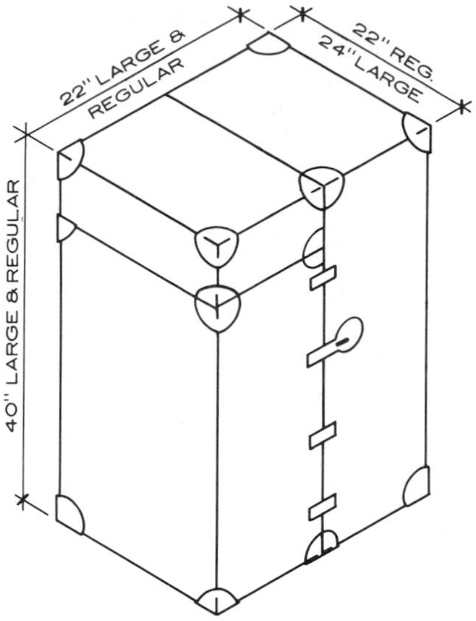

WARDROBE
HANGER SECTION:
REGULAR: 10"
LARGE: 12"

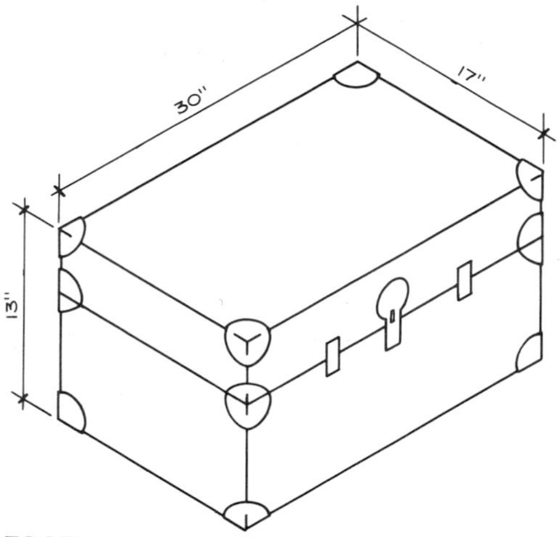

FOOT LOCKER OR CAMP TRUNK
DRESS TRUNK SIMILAR CONSTRUCTION
22"→24" H. 21"→22"D. 36"—39"W.

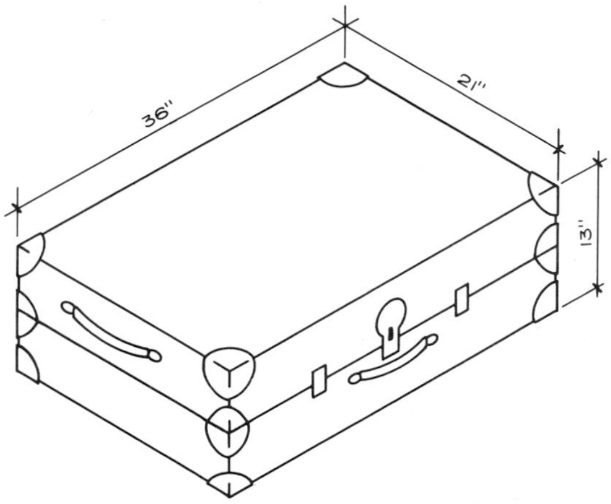

STEAMER

TRUNKS

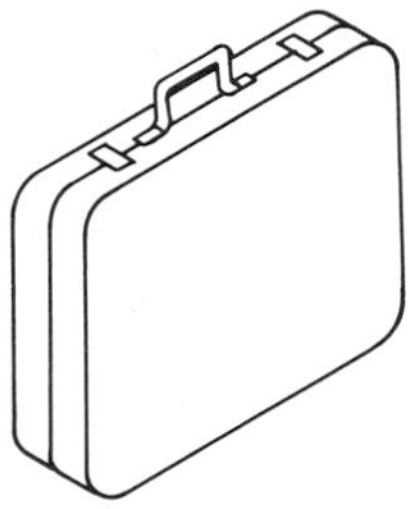

MEN'S LUGGAGE
AVAILABLE IN MATCHED SETS.

	H	W	D
3 SUITER	20	26	8 1/2
2 SUITER	20	26	6 3/4
WEEK-ENDER	15 1/2	20 1/2	7

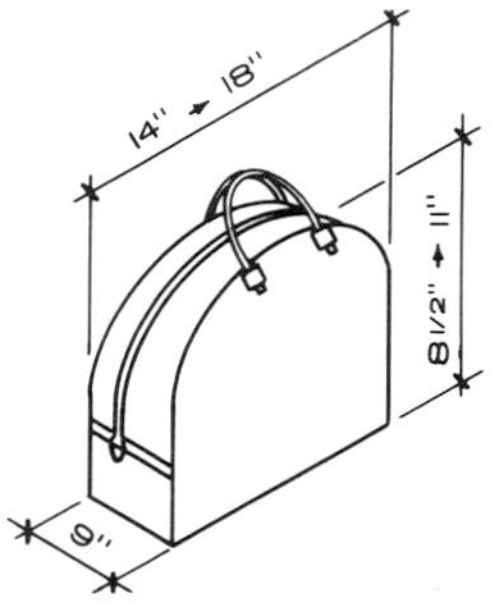

CLUB BAG

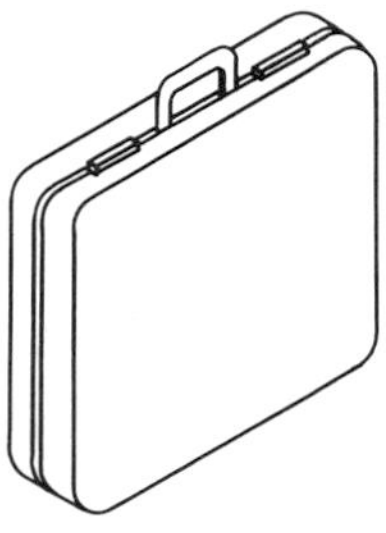

WOMEN'S LUGGAGE
AVAILABLE IN MATCHED SETS

	H	W	D
X LARGE	19 1/4	26 1/4	8
PULLMAN	18	24 1/2	7 3/4
WEEK-ENDER	16 1/4	22	6 3/4

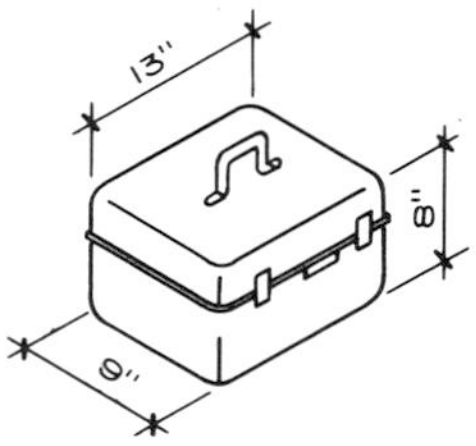

TRAIN CASE

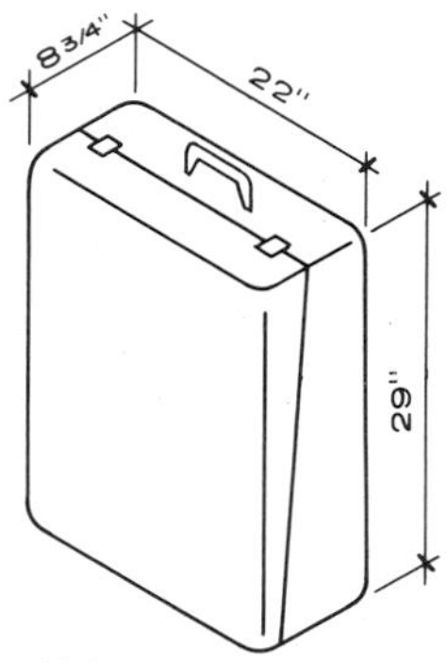

JACKNIFE

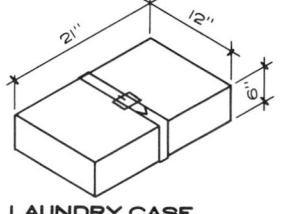

LAUNDRY CASE

HAT BOX

HAT & SHOE

GLADSTONE

TOTE BAG

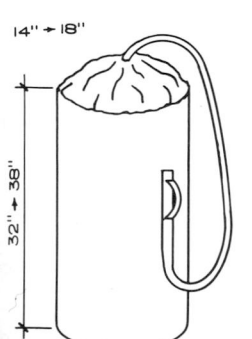

DUFFEL BAG

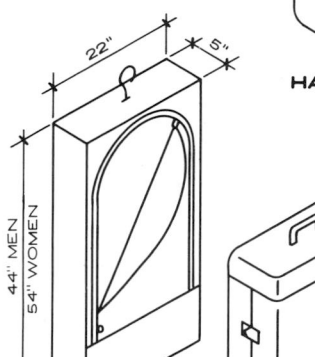

FOLDING GARMENT BAG

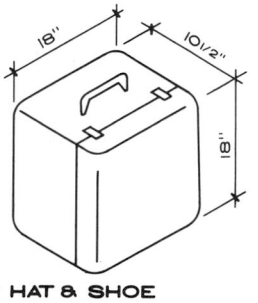
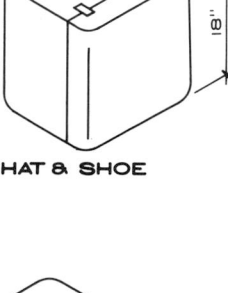

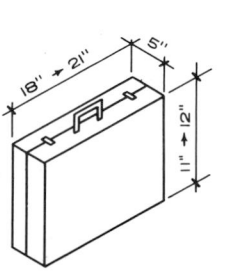
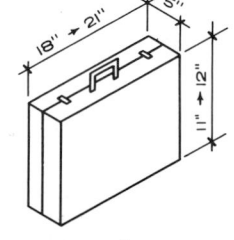

ATTACHÉ CASE

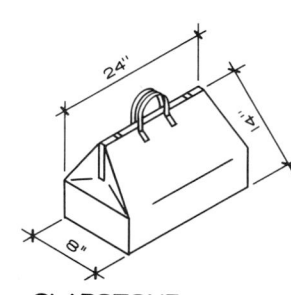

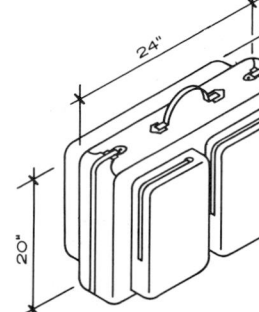

FLIGHT BAG

BAGS & CASES

Dimensions shown are maximum of several models. If several styles exist, the longest, widest, and highest dimension found in the group are given.

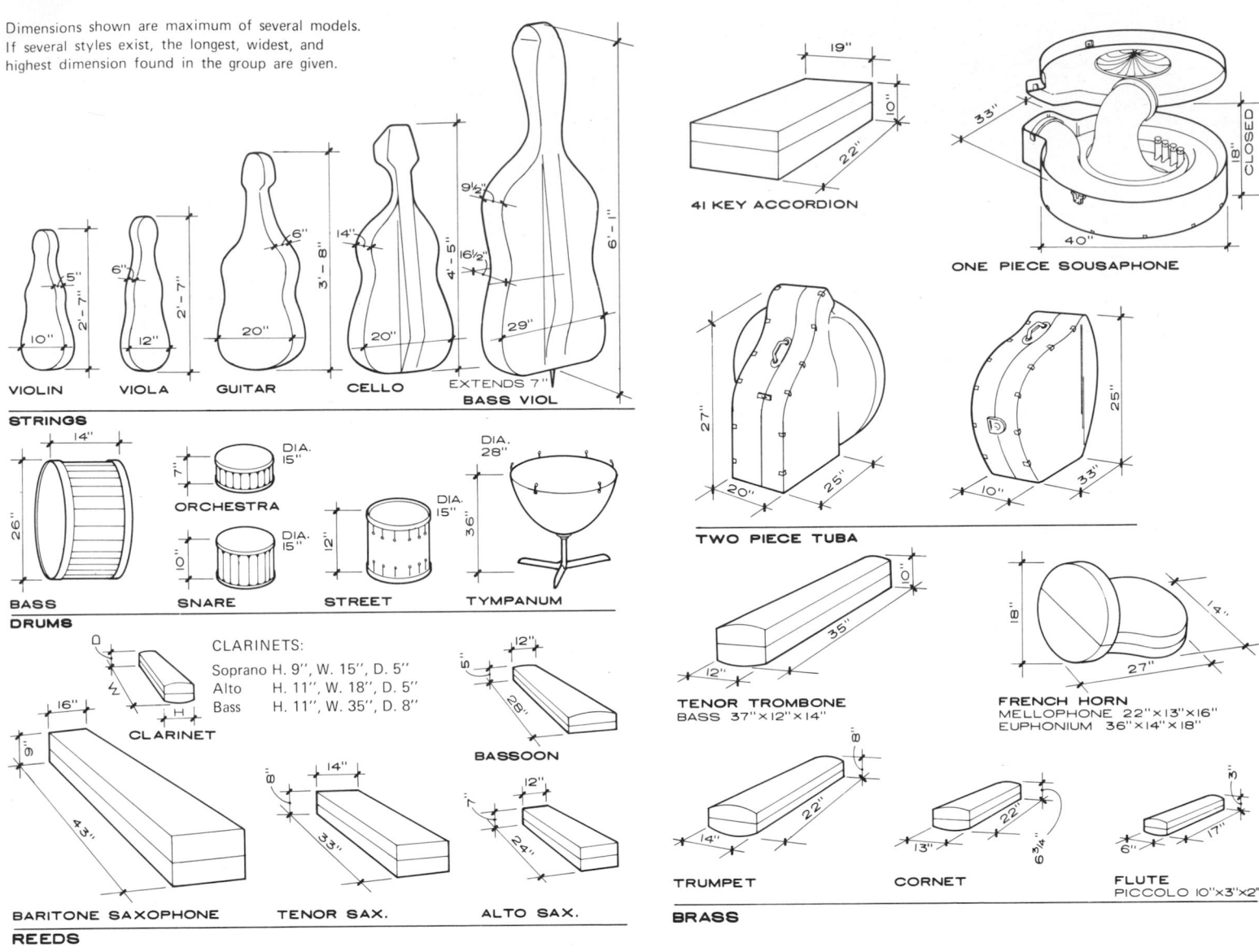

STRINGS

VIOLIN · VIOLA · GUITAR · CELLO · BASS VIOL (EXTENDS 7")

DRUMS

BASS · ORCHESTRA · SNARE · STREET · TYMPANUM

REEDS

CLARINETS:
Soprano H. 9", W. 15", D. 5"
Alto   H. 11", W. 18", D. 5"
Bass   H. 11", W. 35", D. 8"

CLARINET · BASSOON · BARITONE SAXOPHONE · TENOR SAX. · ALTO SAX.

41 KEY ACCORDION

ONE PIECE SOUSAPHONE

TWO PIECE TUBA

TENOR TROMBONE
BASS 37"×12"×14"

FRENCH HORN
MELLOPHONE 22"×13"×16"
EUPHONIUM 36"×14"×18"

TRUMPET · CORNET · FLUTE
PICCOLO 10"×3"×2"

BRASS

MUSIC RACK, WHEN OPEN INCREASES "H" 8" TO 10"

MAX. SIZE SHEET MUSIC ALL INSTRUMENTS.

TONE BOX · ORGAN

ORGANS AND TONE BOXES

MFR.	MODEL AND/OR TYPE	SIZES** (Inches)				APP. WT. (#)	TONE BOXES* MODEL	SIZES** (Inches)			APP. WT. (#)
		H	W	D1	D2			H	W	D	
CONN	541 Minuet	35	47	24	–	248	150	14	30	21	39
	626 Rhapsody	40	53	28	38	339	250	30	30	21	115
	630 Serenade	41	57	29	40	405					
	720 Artist	43	58	29	46	543					
	825 Classic	48	58	29	46	610					
HAMMOND	Spinet †	38	45	26	–	270	PR–40	38	32	18	130
	25 Pedal home †	39	49	29	49	445	Q & QR40	37	31	18	121
	25 Pedal Church	39	49	29	49	450	Series 10	42	33	18	125
	32 Pedal Church	40	57	29	48	545					
WURLITZER	4017 Spinet †	35	44	23	–	163	202	41	29	21	165
	4070 Spinet †	36	44	25	–	188	2025	41	29	21	171
	4140 Spinet †	38	47	25	–	221					
	4300 Deluxe Spinet †	38	47	25	–	250					
	4500 Console †	43	53	30	42	376					
	4502 Church †	43	52	22	42	376					
	4520 Theatre †	49	58	24	43	407					
	4700 Concert †	49	63	23	59	550					

* By each mfr. any tone box will suit any organ.
** Dimensions are to the nearest inch above fraction
† These organs have their own speakers built in.

NOTE:

Organs and tone box models listed are in current production. For best acoustical results consult mfr. on organ and tone box placement. 3/4" conduit is required for cable from organ to tone box if wiring is to be concealed.

ORGANS AND TONE BOXES

Jean Lesire, AIA; Arlington, Virginia

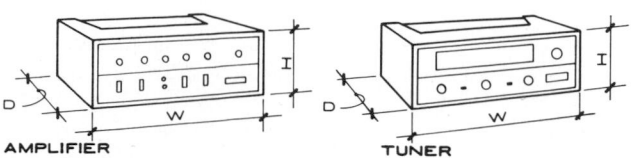

AMPLIFIERS AND TUNERS

	MUSIC POWER (Watts) or TYPE	SIZE (inches)		
		W	H	D
AMPLIFIER	65	15	5	12
	120	15	5	13
	150	15	8	12
TUNER	FM Stereo	15	5	12
	FM Stereo	17	5	13
	FM Stereo, AM, Short Wave	15	5	12

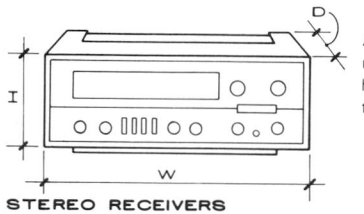

All dimensions are maximum, the depth measured from control knobs to rear heat sink, fuse spot or antenna in extended position whichever is greater.

STEREO RECEIVERS

TUNER SECTION	AMPLIFIER SECTION MUSIC POWER (Watts)	SIZE (Inches)		
		W	H	D
FM	70	15	5	12
AM-FM	55	15	5	13
FM	65	18	6	14
FM	75	18	6	15
AM-FM	75	18	6	19
FM	90	17	5	13
AM-FM	90	17	5	15
FM	120	17	5	13

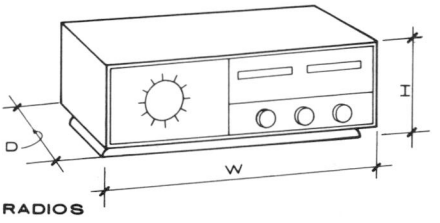

RADIOS

TYPE	SIZE (Inches)		
	W	H	D
AM TABLE RADIO	13	7	5
AM-FM TABLE RADIO	14	8	6
AM CLOCK RADIO	13	7	6
AM-FM CLOCK RADIO	13	4	7

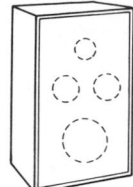

*Can be placed horizontally or vertically
**Read as follow = Bookshelf speaker 1/1.5—2/5—1/12 is equipped with one 1.5" φ treble speaker, two 5" φ midrange speakers and one 12" φ bass speaker.

SPEAKER SYSTEMS

TYPE	LOUDSPEAKER FEATURE**	SIZE (Inches)		
		W	H	D
COMPACT* SPEAKER	1/2.5—1/6	7	13	6
	1/2.5—1/8	10	20	9
BOOK-SHELF* SPEAKER	1/2.5—1/10	23	13	11
	1/1.5—2/5—1/12	25	14	12
	1/2.5—1/6—1/12	25	14	12
	1/1.5—1/5—1/6—1/12	25	14	12
CONSOLE SPEAKER	1/2—1/8—1/15	25	31	15
	1/1.5—2/5—2/6—2/12	27	27	14
	2/2—1/5—1/8—1/18	31	27	17

SPEAKER DIMENSIO DIMENSIONS
10½"W x 18"H x 7½"D

CONTROL CENTER DIMENSIONS: 18"W X 9"H X 14"D
(HEIGHT INCLUDES AUTOMATIC SPINDLE)

STEREO MUSIC SYSTEM

TELEVISION RECEIVERS

	TYPE	SCREEN DIAGONAL (Inches)	SIZE (Inches)		
			W	H	D
BLACK & WHITE TV	PORTABLE	8	10	8	10
		11	16	11	11
		15	19	17	11
		18	24	18	13
		19	23	16	13
		20	25	17	15
	TABLE	22	26	20	17
	CONSOLE	22	35	29	16
COLOR TV	PORTABLE	14	20	14	17
	TABLE	18	25	20	19
		20	27	21	21
		23	29	22	22
	CONSOLE	20	32	32	21
		23	51	31	24

GENERAL NOTE : Because products are subject to continuous changes, the data shown on this page should only be used for preliminary studies.

Jean Lesire, AIA; Arlington, Virginia

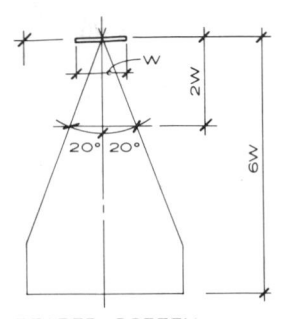

BEADED SCREEN

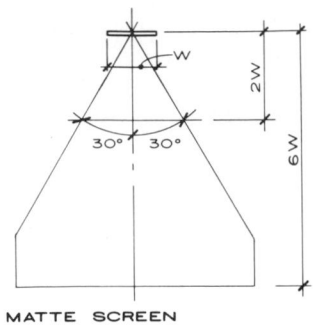

MATTE SCREEN

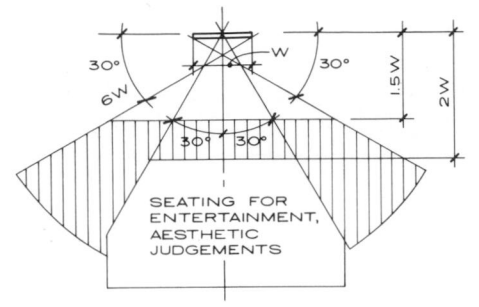

LENTICULAR SCREEN
(SHADED AREA—SATISFACTORY SEATING
FOR INFORMATIONAL MATERIAL ONLY)

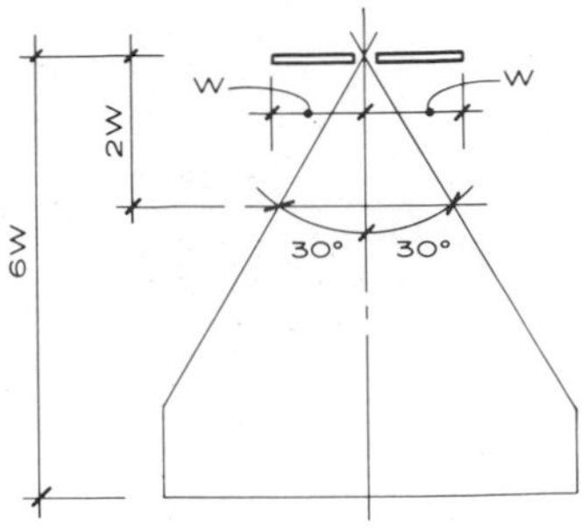

COMPARISON PROJECTION
(MATTE OR LENTICULAR
SCREEN)

RECOMMENDED SEATING LAYOUTS
NOTE: W = WIDTH OF SCREEN

AVERAGE SLIDE PROJECTOR DISTANCE (FT.) ACCORDING TO SCREEN WIDTH

PROJECTOR LENS FOCAL LENGTH	40" 2×2	40" SUPER SLIDES	50" 2×2	50" SUPER SLIDES	60" 2×2	60" SUPER SLIDES	70" 2×2	70" SUPER SLIDES	84" 2×2	84" SUPER SLIDES	8'-0" 2×2	8'-0" SUPER SLIDES	9'-0" 2×2	9'-0" SUPER SLIDES	10'-0" 2×2	10'-0" SUPER SLIDES	12'-0" 2×2	12'-0" SUPER SLIDES	14'-0" 2×2	14'-0" SUPER SLIDES	16'-0" 2×2	16'-0" SUPER SLIDES
3"	7'	7'	9'	8'	11'	10'	13'	12'	16'	14'	18'	16'	20'	18'	22'	20'	27'	24'	31'	28'	36'	32'
4"	10'	9'	12'	12'	15'	14'	17'	16'	21'	19'	24'	22'	27'	25'	30'	28'	36'	33'	42'	39'	48'	44'
5"	12'	11'	16'	14'	19'	17'	22'	19'	26'	23'	30'	27'	34'	30'	37'	33'	45'	40'	52'	47'	60'	53'
6"	15'	13'	19'	17'	22'	20'	26'	23'	31'	28'	36'	32'	40'	36'	45'	40'	54'	48'	63'	56'	72'	64'
7"	17'	15'	22'	18'	26'	22'	30'	27'	37'	31'	42'	37'	47'	43'	52'	48'	63'	53'	73'	64'	84'	75'
8"	20'	17'	25'	22'	30'	27'	35'	31'	42'	37'	48'	43'	54'	48'	60'	53'	72'	64'	84'	75'	95'	85'

THE 2 × 2 SLIDES ARE 23MM × 34MM MASKS—HORIZONTAL FORMAT
THE SUPERSLIDES ARE 38MM × 38MM

To find projector-to-screen distance required to fill screen with image for other slide types listed below, multiply the distance given for 2 x 2 slides of corresponding lens focal length by the factors given below:

30 x 30 mm mask
126 (26 1/2 x 26 1/2 mm)
Single frame filmstrip (17 1/2 x 23 mm)
3 1/4 x 4 in. slides (3 in. wide mask)
2 3/4 x 2 3/4 slides (2 1/4 in. square mask)

EXAMPLE 1:
given:
8' wide screen
6" lens focal length
2 x 2 slides
find:

distance required from projector to screen to fill screen width with image.
from table = 36'

EXAMPLE 2:
given:
8' wide screen
5" lens focal length
single frame filmstrip
find:

distance required from projector to screen to fill screen width with image. (from table for 2 x 2) — 30' x 1.48 = 44.4'

SCREEN TYPES AND SIZES:

Tripod screens: 30" x 40" to 72" x 96". Bottom of screen to floor usually 3' to 4' (adjustable).

Table or wall-hung screens: 18" x 24" to 36" x 36".

Ceiling or wall-hung: 30" x 40" to 72" x 96" and 6' x 8' to 15' x 20'.

Electrically operated: 6' x 8' to 12' x 12' and 11' x 14' to 18' x 18'.

Lace and grommet: custom made to any size. Economical in large size for stages having fly lofts, not recommended otherwise.

To determine screen size for cinemascope projection, first find the proper size for conventional projection, and double the width, minimum height — four feet.

Polarized transluscent screens are used for rear projection, of glass or plastics.

SEATING CAPACITY

SCREEN WIDTH	SEATING AREA (SQ. FT.)	CAPACITY AT 6 SQ. FT. PER PERSON
40"	135	23
50"	238	40
60"	340	57
70"	482	80
84"	654	110
8'	848	141
9'	1078	180
10'	1338	220
12'	2000	334
14'	2592	432
16'	3378	563

MOVIE PROJECTOR DISTANCE (FT.)

LENS FOCAL LENGTH 16MM	8MM	40"	50"	60"	70"	84"	8'	9'	10'	12'	14'	16'
1½"		13'	17'	20'	23'	28'	32'	36'	40'	48'	56'	64'
1⅝"	¾"	14'	18'	22'	25'	31'	35'	39'	44'	52'	61'	70'
2"	⅞"	18'	22'	26'	31'	37'	42'	47'	53'	63'	74'	84'
2.21"	1"	19'	24'	29'	34'	41'	46'	52'	58'	70'	81'	93'
2½"	—	22'	27'	33'	38'	46'	53'	59'	66'	79'	92'	105'
3"		26'	33'	40'	46'	55'	63'	71'	79'	95'	110'	126'
	1½"	29'	36'	44'	53'	61'	70'	78'	87'	104'	122'	139'
3½"		31'	38'	46'	54'	64'	74'	83'	92'	110'	128'	147'
4"		35'	44'	53'	61'	73'	84'	95'	105'	122'	147'	169'
22MM	SUP 8	14'	17'	21'	24'	29'	33'	37'	42'	50'	58'	66'
28MM	SUP 8	17'	22'	26'	30'	37'	42'	47'	53'	63'	74'	84'

OVERHEAD PROJECTOR DISTANCE (FT.)

LENS FOCAL LENGTH	40"	50"	60"	70"	84"	8'	9'	10'	12'	COPY SIZE
8.8"	3'	4'	5'	6'	7'	7'	8'			8 x 10
12.5"	5'	6'	7'	9'	10'	11'				10 x 10
14"	5'	7'	7'	8'	11'	12'	13'	15'		10 x 10
15½"		6'	8'	9'	11'	12'	14'	15'	18'	10 x 10
18"		8'	10'	12'	13'	14'	17'	20'		10 x 10
22"		10'	11'	13'	15'	19'	22'	26'		10 x 10
24"		12'	13'	14'	18'	21'	23'	26'	29'	10 x 10
26"		15'	16'	17'	20'	23'	25'	27'	31'	10 x 10
30"		15'	17'	20'	23'	26'	30'	33'	39'	10 x 10
36"		18'	21'	24'	28'	31'	35'	39'	43'	10 x 10
40"		22'		27'	32'	35'	40'	45'		10 x 10

Robert A. Brent; Hellmuth, Obata & Kassabaum, Inc.; St. Louis, Missouri

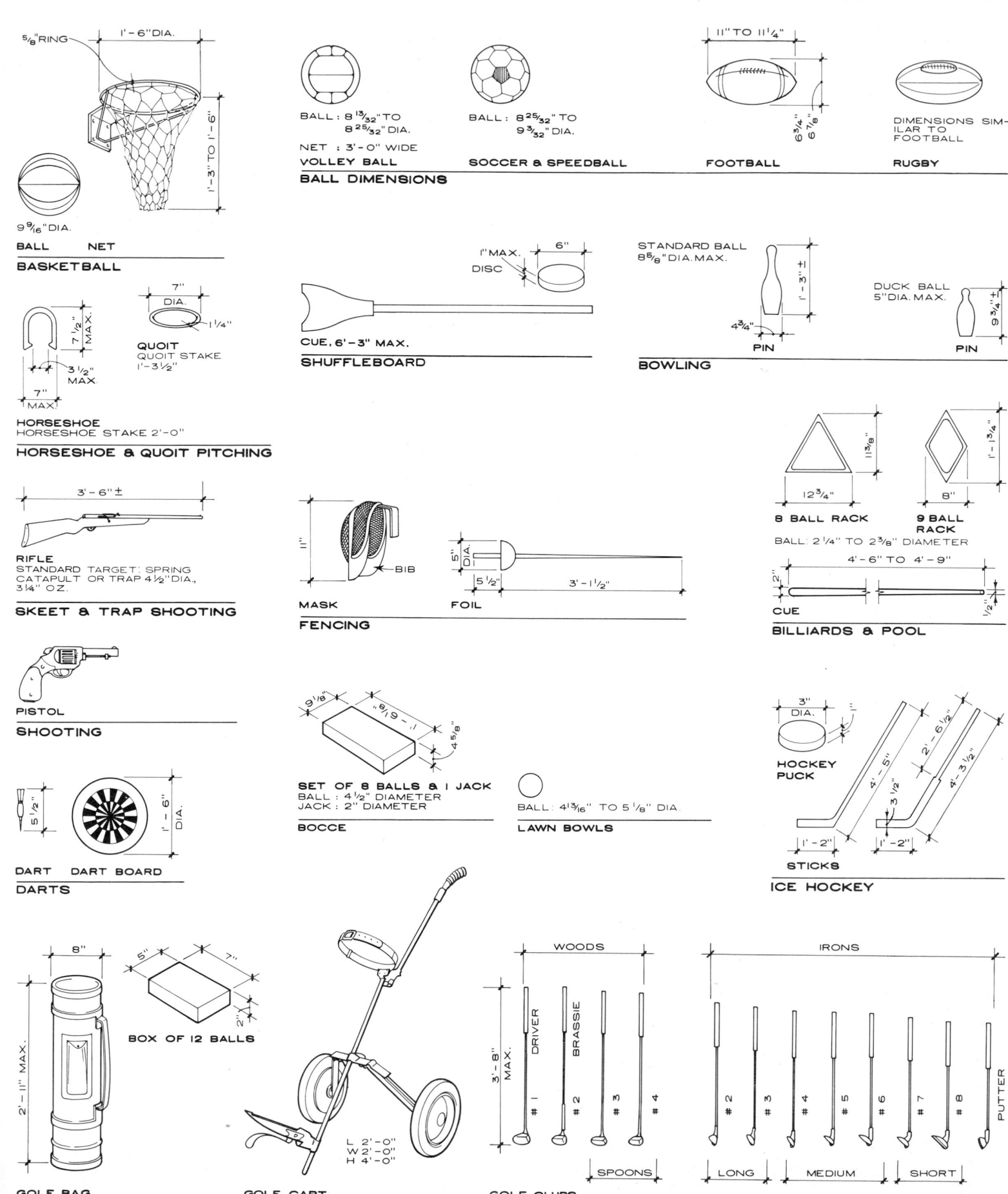

BASKETBALL

5/8" RING

1'-6" DIA.

1'-3" TO 1'-6"

9 9/16" DIA.

BALL NET

BALL DIMENSIONS

BALL: 8 13/32" TO 8 25/32" DIA.

NET: 3'-0" WIDE

VOLLEY BALL

BALL: 8 25/32" TO 9 3/32" DIA.

SOCCER & SPEEDBALL

11" TO 11 1/4"

6 3/4"
6 7/8"

FOOTBALL

DIMENSIONS SIMILAR TO FOOTBALL

RUGBY

HORSESHOE & QUOIT PITCHING

7 1/2" MAX.

3 1/2" MAX.

7" MAX.

HORSESHOE
HORSESHOE STAKE 2'-0"

7" DIA.

1 1/4"

QUOIT
QUOIT STAKE 1'-3 1/2"

SHUFFLEBOARD

1" MAX.

6"

DISC

CUE, 6'-3" MAX.

BOWLING

STANDARD BALL 8 5/8" DIA. MAX.

1'-3"±

4 3/4"

PIN

DUCK BALL 5" DIA. MAX.

9 3/4"±

PIN

SKEET & TRAP SHOOTING

3'-6"±

RIFLE
STANDARD TARGET: SPRING CATAPULT OR TRAP 4 1/2" DIA., 3 1/4" OZ.

FENCING

11"

MASK BIB

5" DIA.

5 1/2"

3'-1 1/2"

FOIL

BILLIARDS & POOL

11 3/8"

12 3/4"

8 BALL RACK

1'-3 3/4"

8"

9 BALL RACK

BALL: 2 1/4" TO 2 3/8" DIAMETER

4'-6" TO 4'-9"

2"

1/2"

CUE

SHOOTING

PISTOL

BOCCE

9 1/8"

1'-6 1/8"

4 5/8"

SET OF 8 BALLS & 1 JACK
BALL: 4 1/2" DIAMETER
JACK: 2" DIAMETER

LAWN BOWLS

BALL: 4 13/16" TO 5 1/8" DIA.

ICE HOCKEY

3" DIA.

HOCKEY PUCK

4'-5"

3 1/2"

1'-2"

2'-6 1/2"

4'-3 1/2"

1'-2"

STICKS

DARTS

5 1/2"

1'-6" DIA.

DART DART BOARD

GOLF (FOR MOTORIZED GOLF CARTS FOR PASSENGERS, SEE MISCELLANEOUS VEHICLES)

8"

2'-11" MAX.

GOLF BAG

5"

7"

2"

BOX OF 12 BALLS

L 2'-0"
W 2'-0"
H 4'-0"

GOLF CART

WOODS

3'-8" MAX.

#1 DRIVER #2 BRASSIE #3 #4

SPOONS

IRONS

#2 #3 #4 #5 #6 #7 #8 PUTTER

LONG MEDIUM SHORT

GOLF CLUBS

Jacques J. Amsellem, AIA; Silver Spring, Maryland

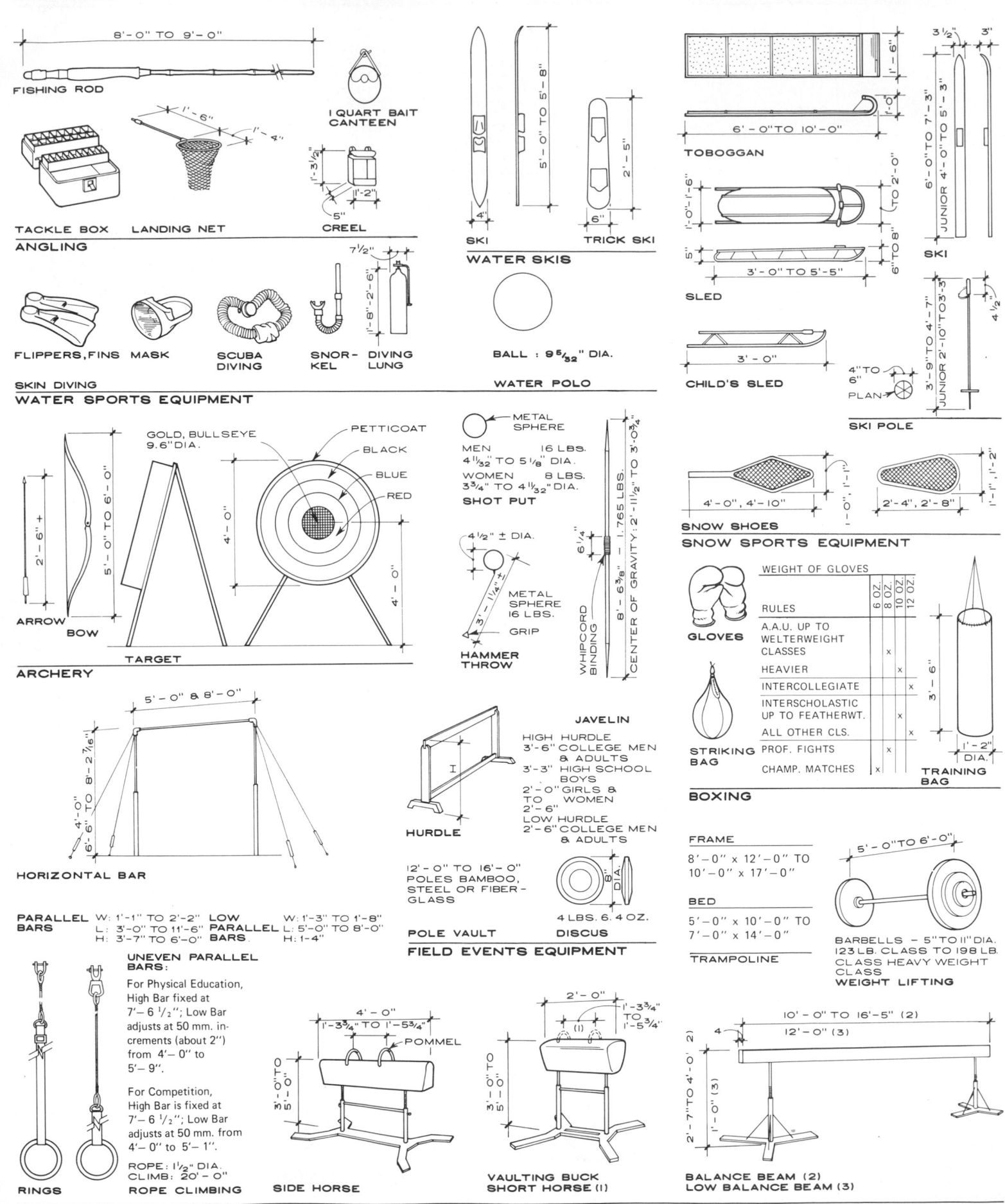

FISHING ROD 8'-0" TO 9'-0"

TACKLE BOX   **LANDING NET**   **CREEL**

I QUART BAIT CANTEEN

ANGLING

FLIPPERS, FINS   **MASK**   **SCUBA DIVING**   **SNOR-KEL**   **DIVING LUNG**

SKIN DIVING

WATER SPORTS EQUIPMENT

SKI   **TRICK SKI**

WATER SKIS

BALL : 9 5/32" DIA.

WATER POLO

TOBOGGAN 6'-0" TO 10'-0"

SLED

CHILD'S SLED 3'-0" TO 5'-5"

SKI

SKI POLE

GOLD, BULLSEYE 9.6" DIA.   **PETTICOAT**   **BLACK**   **BLUE**   **RED**

ARROW   **BOW**   **TARGET**

ARCHERY

SHOT PUT
METAL SPHERE
MEN   16 LBS.   4 11/32" TO 5 1/8" DIA.
WOMEN   8 LBS.   3 3/4" TO 4 11/32" DIA.

HAMMER THROW
4 1/2" ± DIA.
METAL SPHERE 16 LBS.
GRIP

JAVELIN
CENTER OF GRAVITY: 2'-11 1/2" TO 3'-0 3/4"
WHIPCORD BINDING

SNOW SHOES 4'-0", 4'-10"   2'-4", 2'-8"

SNOW SPORTS EQUIPMENT

GLOVES   **STRIKING BAG**

WEIGHT OF GLOVES				
RULES	6 OZ.	8 OZ.	10 OZ.	12 OZ.
A.A.U. UP TO WELTERWEIGHT CLASSES		X		
HEAVIER			X	
INTERCOLLEGIATE				X
INTERSCHOLASTIC UP TO FEATHERWT.			X	
ALL OTHER CLS.			X	
PROF. FIGHTS		X		
CHAMP. MATCHES	X			

TRAINING BAG

BOXING

HORIZONTAL BAR 5'-0" & 8'-0"

PARALLEL BARS
W: 1'-1" TO 2'-2"
L: 3'-0" TO 11'-6"
H: 3'-7" TO 6'-0"

LOW PARALLEL BARS.
W: 1'-3" TO 1'-8"
L: 5'-0" TO 8'-0"
H: 1-4"

UNEVEN PARALLEL BARS:

For Physical Education, High Bar fixed at 7'-6 1/2"; Low Bar adjusts at 50 mm. increments (about 2") from 4'-0" to 5'-9".

For Competition, High Bar is fixed at 7'-6 1/2"; Low Bar adjusts at 50 mm. from 4'-0" to 5'-1".

ROPE: 1 1/2" DIA. CLIMB: 20'-0"

RINGS   **ROPE CLIMBING**   **SIDE HORSE**   **POMMEL**

HURDLE
HIGH HURDLE
3'-6" COLLEGE MEN & ADULTS
3'-3" HIGH SCHOOL BOYS
2'-0" GIRLS & WOMEN
TO 2'-6"
LOW HURDLE
2'-6" COLLEGE MEN & ADULTS

POLE VAULT
12'-0" TO 16'-0"
POLES BAMBOO, STEEL OR FIBER-GLASS

DISCUS
4 LBS. 6.4 OZ.

FIELD EVENTS EQUIPMENT

FRAME
8'-0" x 12'-0" TO 10'-0" x 17'-0"

BED
5'-0" x 10'-0" TO 7'-0" x 14'-0"

TRAMPOLINE

BARBELLS — 5" TO 11" DIA. 123 LB. CLASS TO 198 LB. CLASS HEAVY WEIGHT CLASS

WEIGHT LIFTING

VAULTING BUCK SHORT HORSE (1)

BALANCE BEAM (2) 10'-0" TO 16'-5" (2)
LOW BALANCE BEAM (3) 12'-0" (3)

GYMNASIUM EQUIPMENT

Jacques J. Amsellem, AIA; Silver Spring, Maryland

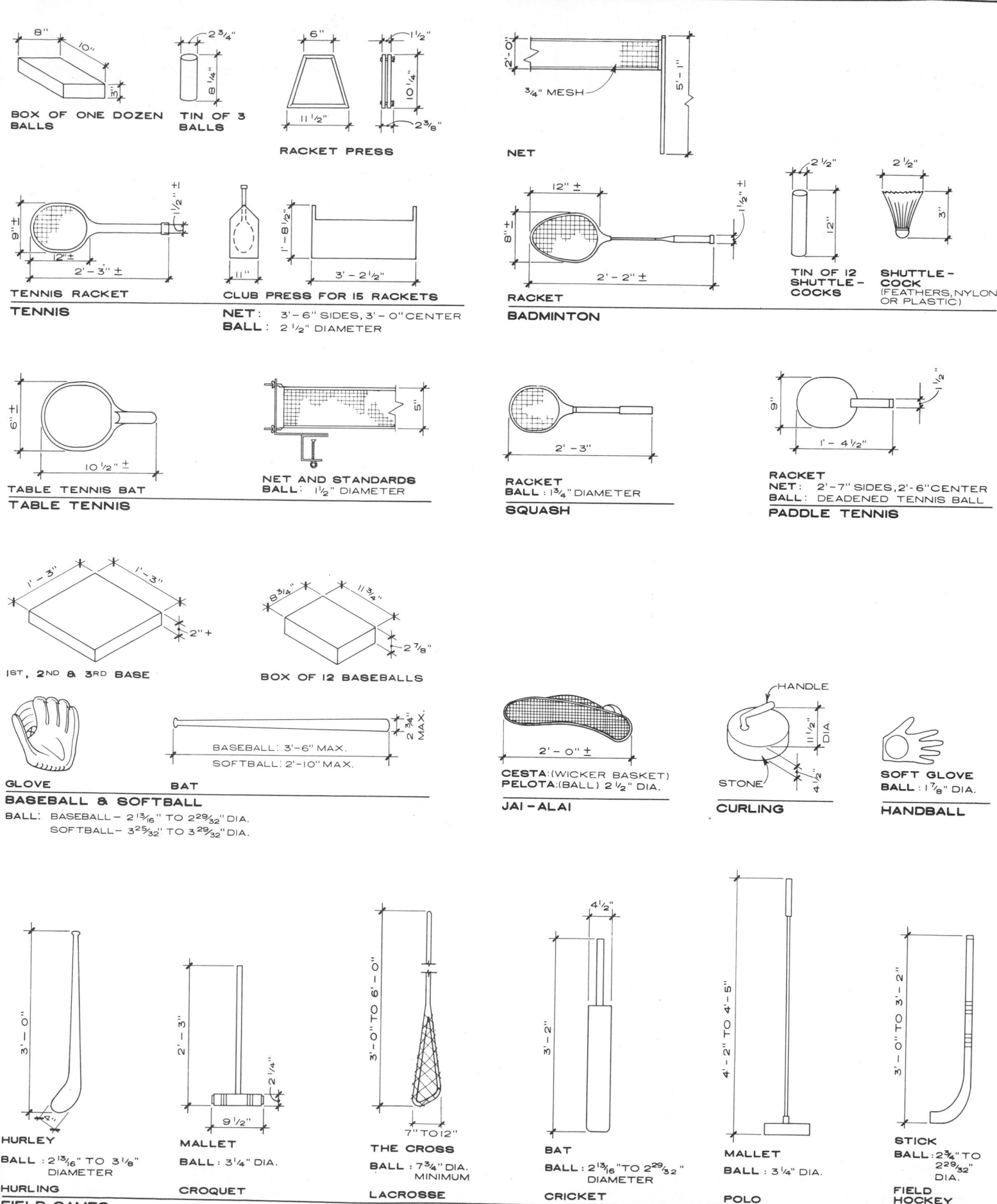

BOX OF ONE DOZEN BALLS

TIN OF 3 BALLS

RACKET PRESS

NET

3/4" MESH

TENNIS RACKET

CLUB PRESS FOR 15 RACKETS

TENNIS
NET: 3'-6" SIDES, 3'-0" CENTER
BALL: 2 1/2" DIAMETER

RACKET

BADMINTON

TIN OF 12 SHUTTLE-COCKS

SHUTTLE-COCK
(FEATHERS, NYLON OR PLASTIC)

TABLE TENNIS BAT
TABLE TENNIS

NET AND STANDARDS
BALL: 1 1/2" DIAMETER

RACKET
BALL: 1 3/4" DIAMETER
SQUASH

RACKET
PADDLE TENNIS
NET: 2'-7" SIDES, 2'-6" CENTER
BALL: DEADENED TENNIS BALL

1ST, 2ND & 3RD BASE

BOX OF 12 BASEBALLS

GLOVE   BAT
BASEBALL & SOFTBALL
BALL: BASEBALL — 2 13/16" TO 2 29/32" DIA.
SOFTBALL — 3 25/32" TO 3 29/32" DIA.

BASEBALL: 3'-6" MAX.
SOFTBALL: 2'-10" MAX.

CESTA: (WICKER BASKET)
PELOTA: (BALL) 2 1/2" DIA.
JAI-ALAI

HANDLE
STONE
CURLING

SOFT GLOVE
BALL: 1 7/8" DIA.
HANDBALL

HURLEY
BALL: 2 13/16" TO 3 1/8" DIAMETER
HURLING

MALLET
BALL: 3 1/4" DIA.
CROQUET

THE CROSS
BALL: 7 3/4" DIA. MINIMUM
LACROSSE

BAT
BALL: 2 13/16" TO 2 29/32" DIAMETER
CRICKET

MALLET
BALL: 3 1/4" DIA.
POLO

STICK
BALL: 2 3/4" TO 2 29/32" DIA.
FIELD HOCKEY

FIELD GAMES

Jacques J. Amsellem, AIA; Silver Spring, Maryland

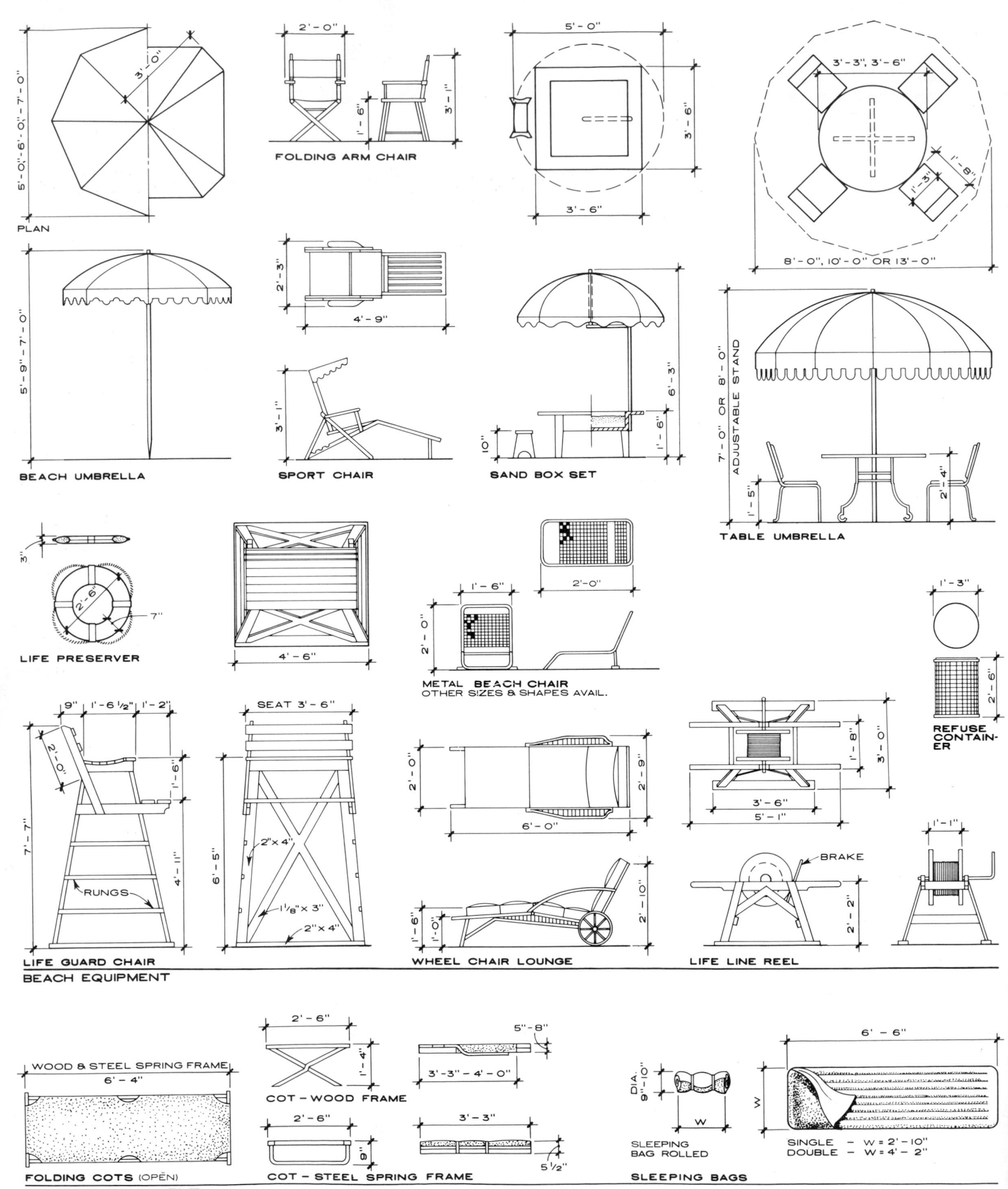

PLAN

BEACH UMBRELLA

FOLDING ARM CHAIR

SPORT CHAIR

SAND BOX SET

ADJUSTABLE STAND

TABLE UMBRELLA

LIFE PRESERVER

METAL BEACH CHAIR
OTHER SIZES & SHAPES AVAIL.

REFUSE CONTAINER

LIFE GUARD CHAIR

RUNGS

WHEEL CHAIR LOUNGE

BRAKE

LIFE LINE REEL

BEACH EQUIPMENT

WOOD & STEEL SPRING FRAME

FOLDING COTS (OPEN)

COT - WOOD FRAME

COT - STEEL SPRING FRAME

SLEEPING BAG ROLLED

SLEEPING BAGS

SINGLE - W = 2'-10"
DOUBLE - W = 4'-2"

CAMPING EQUIPMENT

Jacques J. Amsellem, AIA; Silver Spring, Maryland

ASSEMBLED CONSTRUCTION

TOP SURFACE SUITABLE TO RECIEVE FINISH FLOOR – (WITH MINIMAL USE OF MASTIC TYPE UNDERLAYMENT)

| FLOOR SYSTEM | NO. | PHYSICAL PROPERTIES | | | | | |
		STANDARD SIZE	WEIGHT P.S.F.	DEPTH OF SYSTEM	ELECTRICAL CONDUIT SPACE	BOTTOM OK FOR FINISH	SOUND TRANSM.*
WOOD JOIST	1	6", 8", 10", 12"	5 – 8	6 1/2" – 12 1/2"	Between Joists	No	Poor
WOOD BEAM & PLANK / PLYWOOD	2	2", 3", 4" Plank 1 1/8" Plywood	6 – 16	10" – 22"	None	Yes	Poor
STRESSED SKIN PLYWOOD	3	3 1/2" – 12 1/2"	4 – 7.5	3 1/2" – 12 1/2"	Between Joists	Yes	Poor
STEEL JOIST	4	8" – 24"	32 – 36	10 1/2" – 26 1/2"	Between Joists	No	Poor
COMPOSITE FLOOR SLAB	5		45 – 75	3 1/2" – 6 1/2"	In Slab	No	Fair
CELLULAR STEEL FLOOR	6	1 1/2" – 6"	40 – 50	4" – 9"	In Cells	Yes	Fair
UNIT MASONRY PLANK	7	4", 6", 8", 10"	40 – 80	6" – 12"	In Cells, Topping	Yes	Good
PRECAST CONCRETE PLANK	8	4", 6", 8", 10"	40 – 75	5 1/2" – 12"	In Cells, Topping	Yes	Good
CONCRETE SLAB (ONE WAY)	9		50 – 120	4" – 10"	In Slab	No	Good
CONCRETE SLAB (TWO WAY)	10		72 – 120	6" – 10"	In Slab	No	Very Good
CONCRETE PAN JOIST	11	6", 8", 10", 12", 14"	40 – 90	8" – 17"	In Slab	No	Good
CONCRETE WAFFLE SLAB	11A	6" – 20"	73 – 104	8" – 24"	In Slab	Yes	Good
CONCRETE FLAT PLATE	12		75 – 150	6" – 12"	In Slab	Yes	Very Good
CONCRETE FLAT SLAB	13		90 – 170	10" – 16"	In Slab	Yes	Very Good
PRECAST CONCRETE DOUBLE TEE	14	6" – 16"	50 – 70	8" – 18"	Topping	No	Good
PRESTRESSED CONCRETE SINGLE TEE	15	16" – 36"	70 – 90	18" – 38"	Topping	No	Good
COMPOSITE SLAB / BEAM	16		35 – 70	3 1/2" – 6"	In Slab	No	Good

*Refer to acoustical pages for specific data.

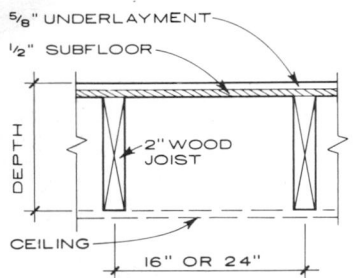

Fire rating possible with appropriate
1. ceiling.

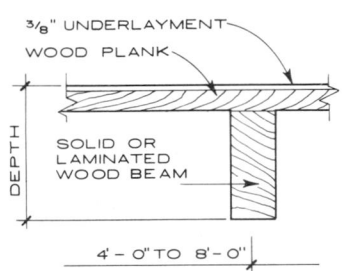

Substitute 1 1/8" plywood for plank
and underlayment if beams are 48"
2. o.c.

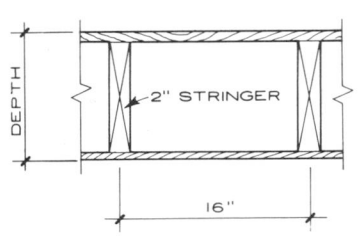

Top skin: 3/4" underlayment plywood
glued to stringers. Bottom skin: 3/8"
plywood or check U.L. list for mat'ls.
3. required for fire rating.

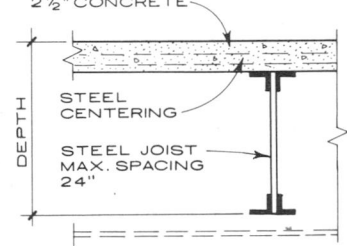

4. Ceiling required for fire rating.

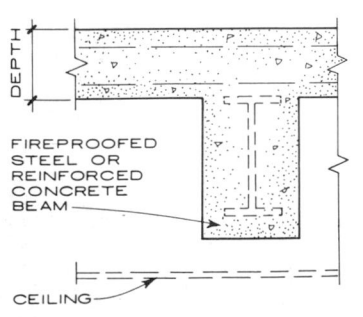

9.

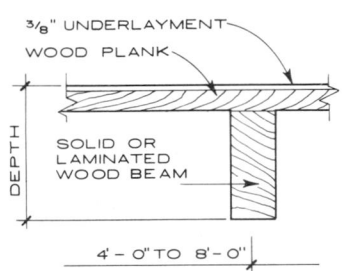

10.

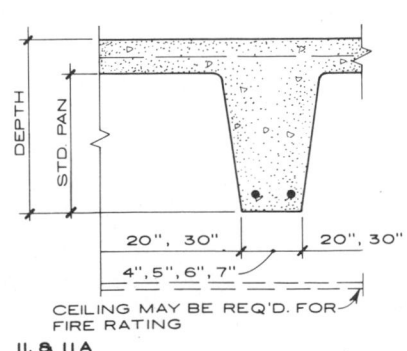

CEILING MAY BE REQ'D. FOR
FIRE RATING
11. & 11A

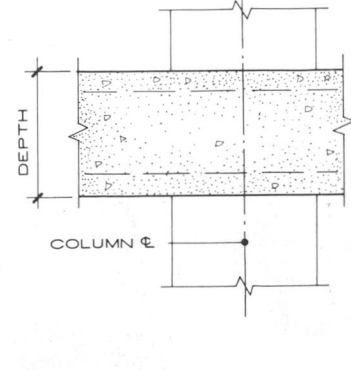

12.

John W. Robertson, AIA; Robertson–Richards, Architects; Syracuse, New York

CEILINGS ARE INDICATED WHERE USUALLY REQUIRED

STRUCTURAL PROPERTIES					FIRE RESISTANCE		NOTE	NO.	FOR LOCAL DATA	
LIVE LOAD P.S.F.	SPAN RANGE	STRUCTURAL FRAMES	BAY SIZE CHARACTER	CREEP** DEFLECTION	PROTECTED BY	HOURS			COST $ P.S.F.	SOURCE
Up to 50	Up to 18'	Wood Masonry	None	Yes	Ceiling	1 Combust.		1.		
Up to 50	10' – 22'	Wood Masonry	Equal Span	Yes	Check Local Acceptance of Fire Resisting Treatments			2.		
Up to 75	9' – 30'	Wood, Steel Masonry	None	Yes	Ceiling	1 Combust.		3.		
50 to 100	Up to 40'	Steel Masonry	None	No	Ceiling	2 – 3*		4.		
60 to 200	6' – 14'	Steel	None	No	Spray-On Ceiling	3 – 4		5.		
60 to 150	8' – 16'	Steel	None	No	Spray-On Ceiling	3 – 4		6.		
60 to 150	Up to 32'	Steel, Mas. Concrete	None	Yes	Self	3 – 4		7.		
60 to 150	Up to 36'	Steel, Mas. Concrete	None	Yes	Self	3 – 4		8.		
60 to 150	Up to 25'	Steel Concrete	None	Yes	Concrete	1 – 4	For specific construction requirements for fire rating, refer to testing agency reports.	9.		
60 to 250	10' – 30'	Steel Concrete	L≤1.33W* L≤1.5L'	Yes	Concrete	2 – 4		10.		
60 to 150	20' – 32'	Concrete	None	Yes	Ceiling	2 – 4		11.		
60 to 200	20' – 50'	Concrete	L ≤1.33W* L ≤1.2L'	Yes	Ceiling May Be Req'd.	2 – 4		11A.		
60 to 100	15' – 25'	Poured Conc. or Lift-Slab	L ≤1.33W* L ≤1.2L'	Yes	Concrete	2 – 4		12.		
60 to 250	15' – 35'	Concrete	L ≤1.33W* L ≤1.2L'	Yes	Concrete	2 – 4		13.		
60 to 150	15' – 35'	Concrete Masonry	None	Yes	Concrete	2		14.		
60 to 150	25' – 65'	Concrete Masonry	None	Yes	Concrete	2		15.		
60 to 200	Up to 35'	Steel	None	Yes	Concrete	1 – 4		16.		

* L = Length, W = Width and L' = Length of adjacent bay, ≤ = Equal to or not greater than

** Long term creep or deflection due to dead load or sustained live load.

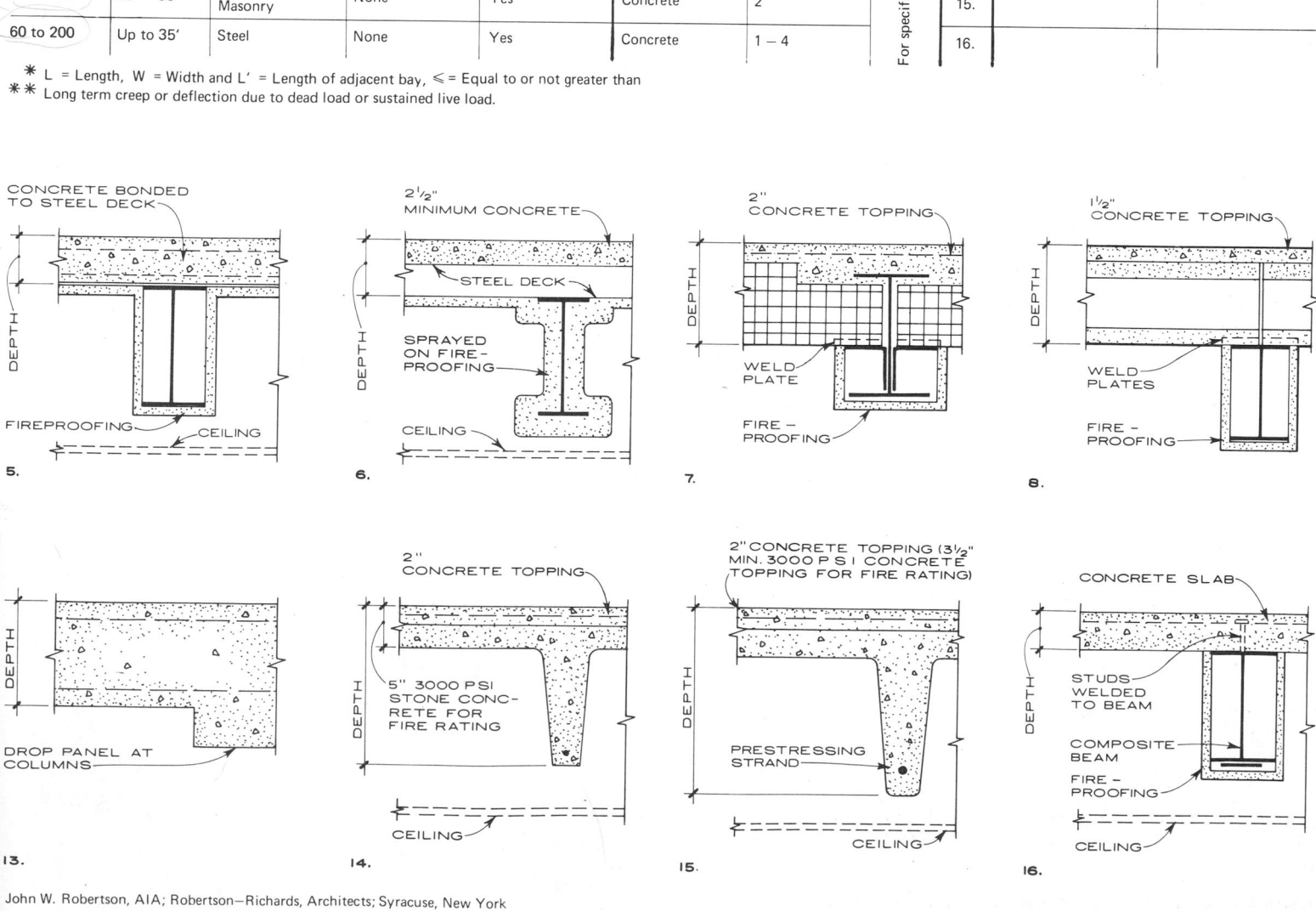

5. CONCRETE BONDED TO STEEL DECK — DEPTH — FIREPROOFING — CEILING

6. 2½" MINIMUM CONCRETE — STEEL DECK — SPRAYED ON FIRE-PROOFING — DEPTH — CEILING

7. 2" CONCRETE TOPPING — WELD PLATE — FIRE-PROOFING — DEPTH

8. 1½" CONCRETE TOPPING — WELD PLATES — FIRE-PROOFING — DEPTH

13. DROP PANEL AT COLUMNS — DEPTH

14. 2" CONCRETE TOPPING — 5" 3000 PSI STONE CONCRETE FOR FIRE RATING — CEILING — DEPTH

15. 2" CONCRETE TOPPING (3½" MIN. 3000 P S I CONCRETE TOPPING FOR FIRE RATING) — PRESTRESSING STRAND — CEILING — DEPTH

16. CONCRETE SLAB — STUDS WELDED TO BEAM — COMPOSITE BEAM — FIRE-PROOFING — CEILING — DEPTH

John W. Robertson, AIA; Robertson–Richards, Architects; Syracuse, New York

TOP SURFACE SUITABLE TO RECEIVE INSULATION

ROOF SYSTEMS	NO.	PHYSICAL PROPERTIES					INSUL. K=27			
		STD. THICKNESS	WEIGHT P.S.F.	DEPTH OF SYSTEM	CONDUIT PIPE SPACE	INSULATING "U" VALUE	U=.1	U=.15	SOUND TRANSM.	BOT. OK FOR FIN.
WOOD JOIST	1.	4", 6", 8", 10", 12"	5—8	4" To 12"	Thru Joist	.35	2"	1 1/4"	Poor	No
WOOD PLANK	2.	2", 3", 4", 5"	4—8	2" To 5"	None	.24—.15	1 1/2"	1"—0"	Poor	Yes
STRESSED SKIN PANEL	3.	3 1/4", 8 1/4"	3—6	3 1/4" To 8 1/4"	None	.35	2"	1 1/4"	Poor	Yes
STEEL JOIST / POURED GYP.	4.	8" To 48"	11—19	11" To 51"	Between Joists	.2	1 1/4"	1/2"	Fair	No
STEEL JOIST / INSUL. DECK	5.	2" To 3"	6—8	9 1/2" To 51"	Between Joists	.2—.15	1 1/4"	1/2"—0"	Fair	No
STEEL BEAM / PRECAST PLANK	6.	2" To 3"	14	8" To 15"	None	.45	2"	1 1/4"	Poor	Yes
STEEL DECK / INSUL. OR FILL	7.	3 5/8" To 7 1/4"	6—24	3 5/8" To 7 1/4"	In Clg.	.21—.1	1 1/2"—0"	1/2"—0"	Fair/Fill Poor/Insul	Yes
LONG SPAN STEEL DECK	8.	1 1/2" To 7 1/2"	2—10.8	1 1/2" To 7 1/2"	In Clg.	.67	2 1/2"	1 1/2"	Poor	Yes
UNIT MASONRY PLANKS	9.	4", 6", 8", 10"	20—55	4" To 10"	In Cells Exposed	.4—.27	2"	1"	Good	Yes
PRECAST CONC. PLANKS	10.	4", 6", 8", 10"	40—75	4" To 10"	In Cells Exposed	.48—.35	2"	1 1/4"	Good	Yes
CONC. SLAB (ONE WAY)	11.	3"—10"	50—125	3" To 10"	In Slab	.70	2 1/2"	1 1/2"	Good	No
CONC. SLAB (TWO WAY)	12.	6"—10"	75—125	6" To 10"	In Slab	.70	2 1/2"	1 1/2"	Very Good	No
CONC. PAN JOIST	13.	Std. Pans 6", 8", 10", 12", 14"	39—76	8" To 17"	In Slab	.70	2 1/2"	1 1/2"	Good	No
CONC. WAFFLE SLAB	14.	Std. Pans 8", 10", 12", 14"	73—104	11" To 17"	In Slab	.70	2 1/2"	1 1/2"	Good	No
CONC. FLAT SLAB	15.	6" To 12"	75—150	6" To 12"	In Slab	.56	2 1/2"	1 1/2"	Very Good	No
PRECAST CONC. DBL. TEE	16.	8" To 24"	35—54	8" To 24"	None	.70	2 1/2"	1 1/2"	Good	Yes
PRECAST CONC. SINGLE TEE	17.	12" To 48"	65—84	12" To 48"	None	.70	2 1/2"	1 1/2"	Good	Yes
COMPOSITE SLAB / BEAM	18.	3 1/2" To 6"	35—70	3 1/2" To 6"	In Slab	.70	2 1/2"	1 1/2"	Very Good	No
WOOD TRUSS	19.	1/2"	8—14	72" To 120"	Between Trusses	.57	2 1/4"	1 1/2"	Poor	No

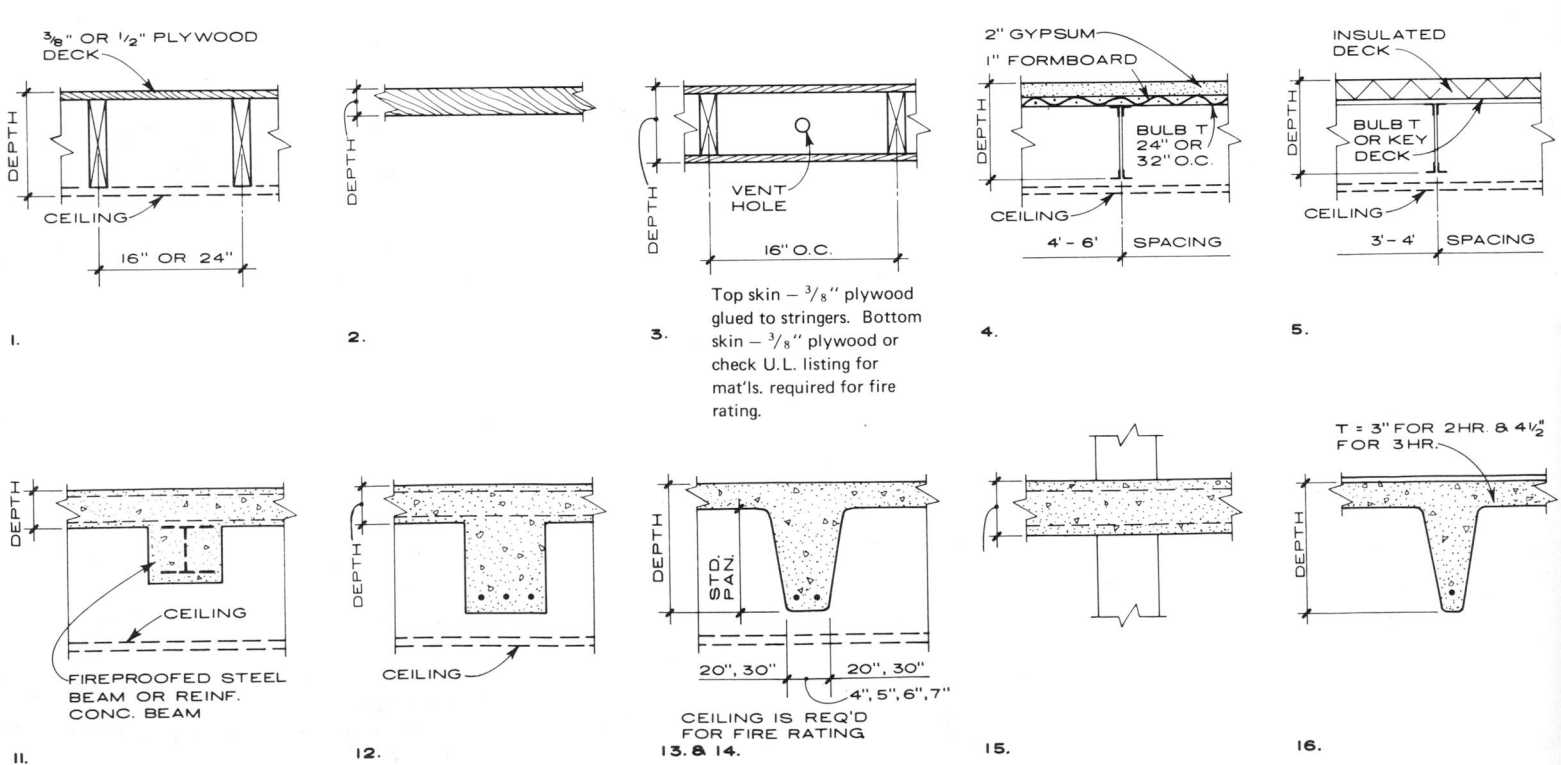

1. 3/8" OR 1/2" PLYWOOD DECK — DEPTH — CEILING — 16" OR 24"

2. DEPTH

3. VENT HOLE — 16" O.C. — DEPTH

Top skin — 3/8" plywood glued to stringers. Bottom skin — 3/8" plywood or check U.L. listing for mat'ls. required for fire rating.

4. 2" GYPSUM — 1" FORMBOARD — DEPTH — BULB T 24" OR 32" O.C. — CEILING — 4'-6' SPACING

5. INSULATED DECK — DEPTH — BULB T OR KEY DECK — CEILING — 3'-4' SPACING

11. DEPTH — CEILING — FIREPROOFED STEEL BEAM OR REINF. CONC. BEAM

12. DEPTH — CEILING

13. & 14. DEPTH — STD. PAN — 20", 30" — 20", 30" — 4", 5", 6", 7" — CEILING IS REQ'D FOR FIRE RATING

15. DEPTH

16. T = 3" FOR 2 HR. & 4 1/2" FOR 3 HR. — DEPTH

John W. Robertson, AIA; Robertson—Richards, Architects; Syracuse, New York

CEILINGS ARE INDICATED WHERE USUALLY REQUIRED

STRUCTURAL PROPERTIES					FIRE RESISTANCE				LOCAL DATA		
LIVE LOAD P.S.F.	SPAN RANGE	STRUCTURAL FRAME	BAY SIZE CHARACTER	CREEP *** DEFLECTION	PROTECTED BY	HOURS	NOTE	NO.			
Up To 40 #	Up To 20'	Wood Masonry	None	Yes	None	None		1.			
Up To 40 #	10' To 14'	Wood Masonry	Equal	Yes	Check local acceptance of fire resisting treatments.			2.			
Up To 40 #	11' To 25'	Wd., Stl., Masonry	4'—0'' Module	Yes	See detail 1 Combust.			3.			
Up To 40 #	Up To 96'	Steel Masonry	None	No	None	None		4.			
Up To 50 #	Up To 96'	Steel Masonry	None	No	Ceiling	2		5.			
Up To 40 #	15' To 25'	Steel	None	Yes	Ceiling	2		6.			
Up To 40 #	Up To 9'	Steel	None	No	Spray on Ceiling	2,3		7.			
Up To 40 #	Up To 33'	Masonry Steel	None	No	Spray on Ceiling	2		8.			
Up To 45 #	Up To 33'	Stl., Mas., Conc.	None	Yes	Self	2		9.			
Up To 40 #	15' To 50'	Conc., Mas., Steel	None	Yes	Self	2		10.			
Up To 60 #	Up To 25'	Steel Conc.	None	Yes	Conc.	$3/4$—4		11.			
Up To 60 #	10' To 30'	Conc.	L≤1.33W L≤1.5L' †	Yes	Conc.	2—4		12.			
Up To 60 #	20' To 34'	Conc.	None	Yes	Ceiling	2—4		13.			
Up To 60 #	20' To 50'	Conc.	L≤1.33W L≤1.2L' †	Yes	Ceiling	2—4		14.			
60 #	15' To 30'	Conc.	L≤1.33W L≤1.2L' †	Yes	Conc.	2—4		15.			
Up To 60 #	15' To 75'	Conc. Masonry	None	Yes	Conc.	2		16.			
Up To 60 #	25' To 110'	Conc. Masonry	None	Yes	Conc.	2		17.			
Up To 60 #	Up To 35'	Steel	None	Yes	Ceiling Conc.	1—4		18.			
Up To 40 #	30' To 50'	Wood Masonry	None	Yes	None	None		19.			

For specific construction requirements for fire rating, refer to testing agency reports.

† L = Length, W = Width and L' = Length of adjacent bay.

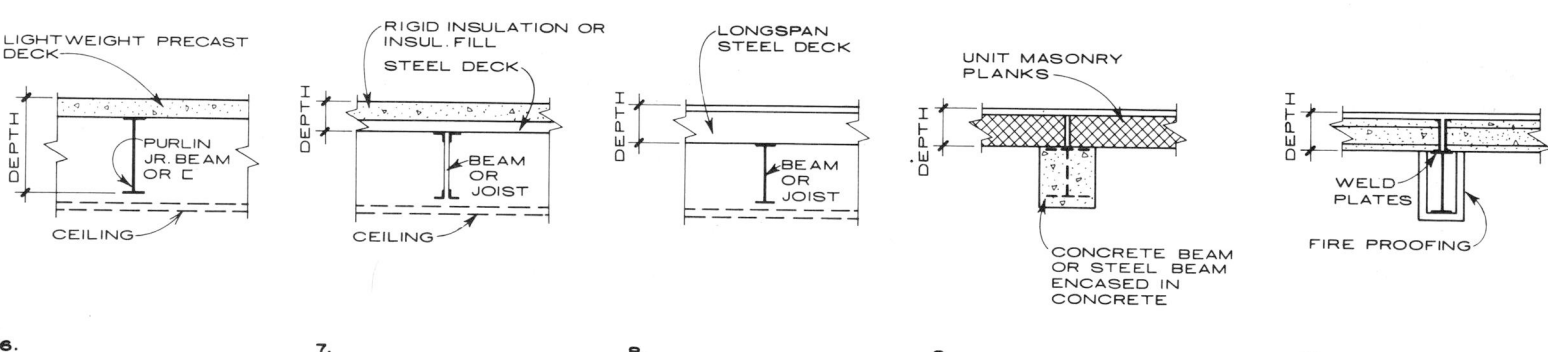

6. 7. 8. 9. 10.

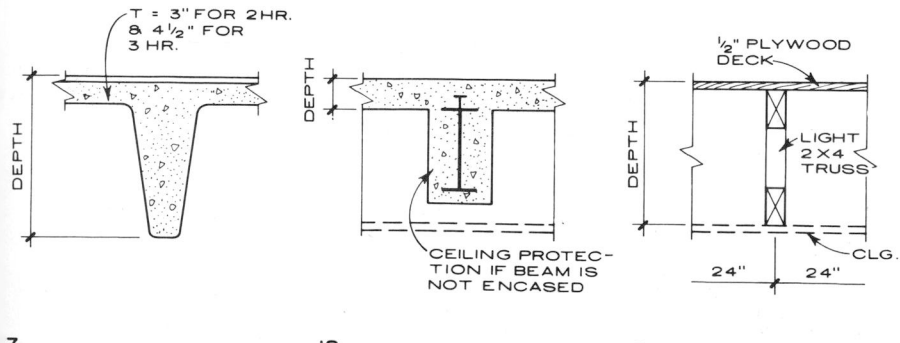

7. 18. 19.

* Thickness of insulation with a K value of .27 which must be added to obtain the given value of "U".

** Refer to acoustical pages for specific data.

*** Long term creep or deflection due to dead load or sustained live load.

T Topping desirable for smooth surface for adhering insulation & may be req'd. for fire rating.

John W. Robertson, AIA; Robertson—Richards, Architects; Syracuse, New York

ROOF DECKS

* Dimensions vary from manufacturer to manufacturer and are shown for preliminary space allowance.

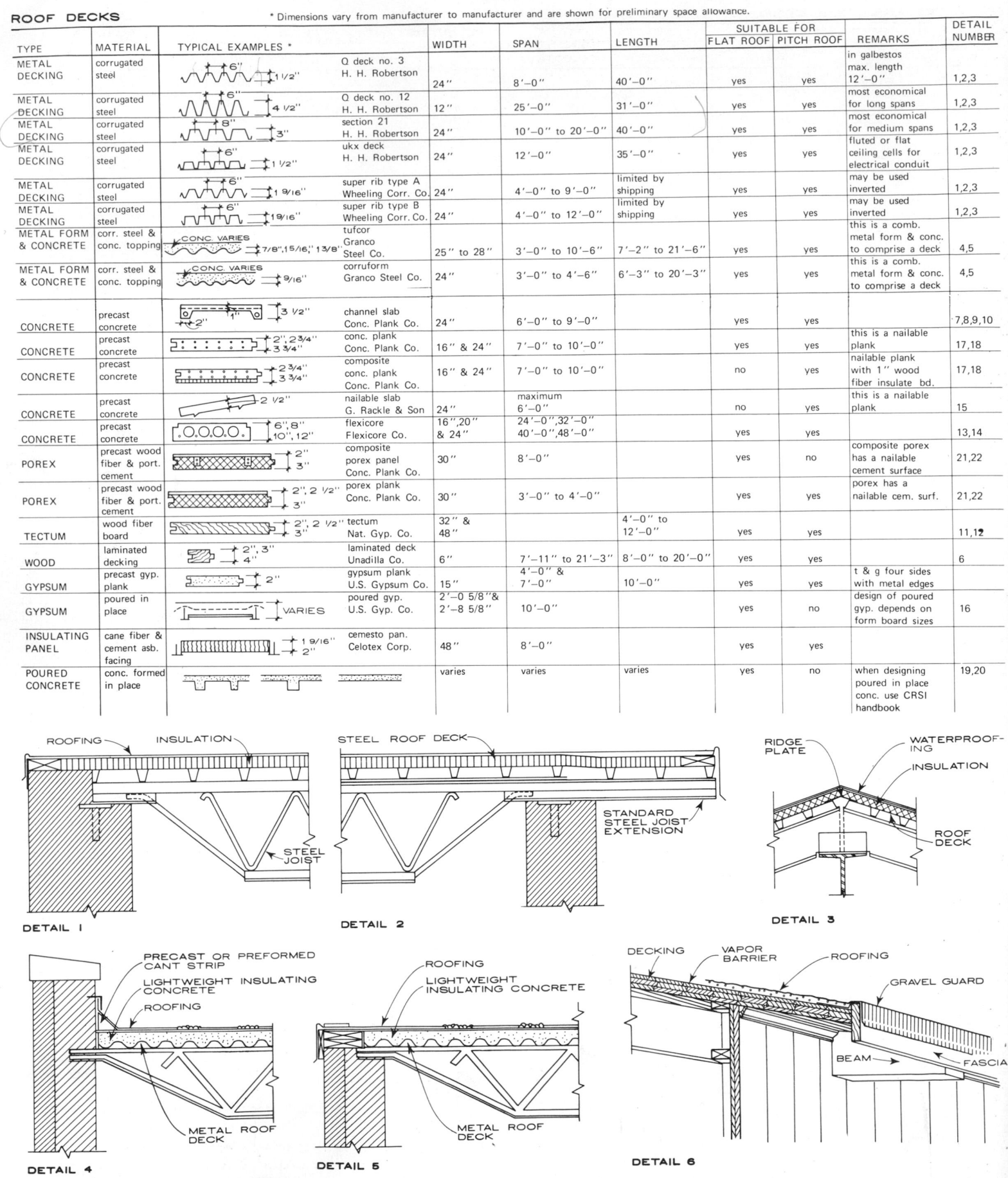

TYPE	MATERIAL	TYPICAL EXAMPLES *	WIDTH	SPAN	LENGTH	SUITABLE FOR FLAT ROOF	PITCH ROOF	REMARKS	DETAIL NUMBER
METAL DECKING	corrugated steel	Q deck no. 3 H. H. Robertson	24"	8'-0"	40'-0"	yes	yes	in galbestos max. length 12'-0"	1,2,3
METAL DECKING	corrugated steel	Q deck no. 12 H. H. Robertson	12"	25'-0"	31'-0"	yes	yes	most economical for long spans	1,2,3
METAL DECKING	corrugated steel	section 21 H. H. Robertson	24"	10'-0" to 20'-0"	40'-0"	yes	yes	most economical for medium spans	1,2,3
METAL DECKING	corrugated steel	ukx deck H. H. Robertson	24"	12'-0"	35'-0"	yes	yes	fluted or flat ceiling cells for electrical conduit	1,2,3
METAL DECKING	corrugated steel	super rib type A Wheeling Corr. Co.	24"	4'-0" to 9'-0"	limited by shipping	yes	yes	may be used inverted	1,2,3
METAL DECKING	corrugated steel	super rib type B Wheeling Corr. Co.	24"	4'-0" to 12'-0"	limited by shipping	yes	yes	may be used inverted	1,2,3
METAL FORM & CONCRETE	corr. steel & conc. topping	tufcor Granco Steel Co.	25" to 28"	3'-0" to 10'-6"	7'-2" to 21'-6"	yes	yes	this is a comb. metal form & conc. to comprise a deck	4,5
METAL FORM & CONCRETE	corr. steel & conc. topping	corruform Granco Steel Co.	24"	3'-0" to 4'-6"	6'-3" to 20'-3"	yes	yes	this is a comb. metal form & conc. to comprise a deck	4,5
CONCRETE	precast concrete	channel slab Conc. Plank Co.	24"	6'-0" to 9'-0"		yes	yes		7,8,9,10
CONCRETE	precast concrete	conc. plank Conc. Plank Co.	16" & 24"	7'-0" to 10'-0"		yes	yes	this is a nailable plank	17,18
CONCRETE	precast concrete	composite conc. plank Conc. Plank Co.	16" & 24"	7'-0" to 10'-0"		no	yes	nailable plank with 1" wood fiber insulate bd.	17,18
CONCRETE	precast concrete	nailable slab G. Rackle & Son	24"	maximum 6'-0"		no	yes	this is a nailable plank	15
CONCRETE	precast concrete	flexicore Flexicore Co.	16",20" & 24"	24'-0",32'-0" 40'-0",48'-0"		yes	yes		13,14
POREX	precast wood fiber & port. cement	composite porex panel Conc. Plank Co.	30"	8'-0"		yes	no	composite porex has a nailable cement surface	21,22
POREX	precast wood fiber & port. cement	porex plank Conc. Plank Co.	30"	3'-0" to 4'-0"		yes	yes	porex has a nailable cem. surf.	21,22
TECTUM	wood fiber board	tectum Nat. Gyp. Co.	32" & 48"		4'-0" to 12'-0"	yes	yes		11,12
WOOD	laminated decking	laminated deck Unadilla Co.	6"	7'-11" to 21'-3"	8'-0" to 20'-0"	yes	yes		6
GYPSUM	precast gyp. plank	gypsum plank U.S. Gypsum Co.	15"	4'-0" & 7'-0"	10'-0"	yes	yes	t & g four sides with metal edges	
GYPSUM	poured in place	poured gyp. U.S. Gyp. Co.	2'-0 5/8" & 2'-8 5/8"	10'-0"		yes	no	design of poured gyp. depends on form board sizes	16
INSULATING PANEL	cane fiber & cement asb. facing	cemesto pan. Celotex Corp.	48"	8'-0"		yes	yes		
POURED CONCRETE	conc. formed in place		varies	varies	varies	yes	no	when designing poured in place conc. use CRSI handbook	19,20

DETAIL 1

DETAIL 2

DETAIL 3

DETAIL 4

DETAIL 5

DETAIL 6

NOTE:

See pages on roofing and flashing for conditions at metal roof edges (gravel guards), for flashing, and at junctures of metal flanges of flashing materials with roofing.

Morris Winkler; Curtin, Kane, Gere and Ashley, AIA; Syracuse, New York

ROOF DECKS SEE NOTE AT BOTTOM OF PRECEDING PAGE

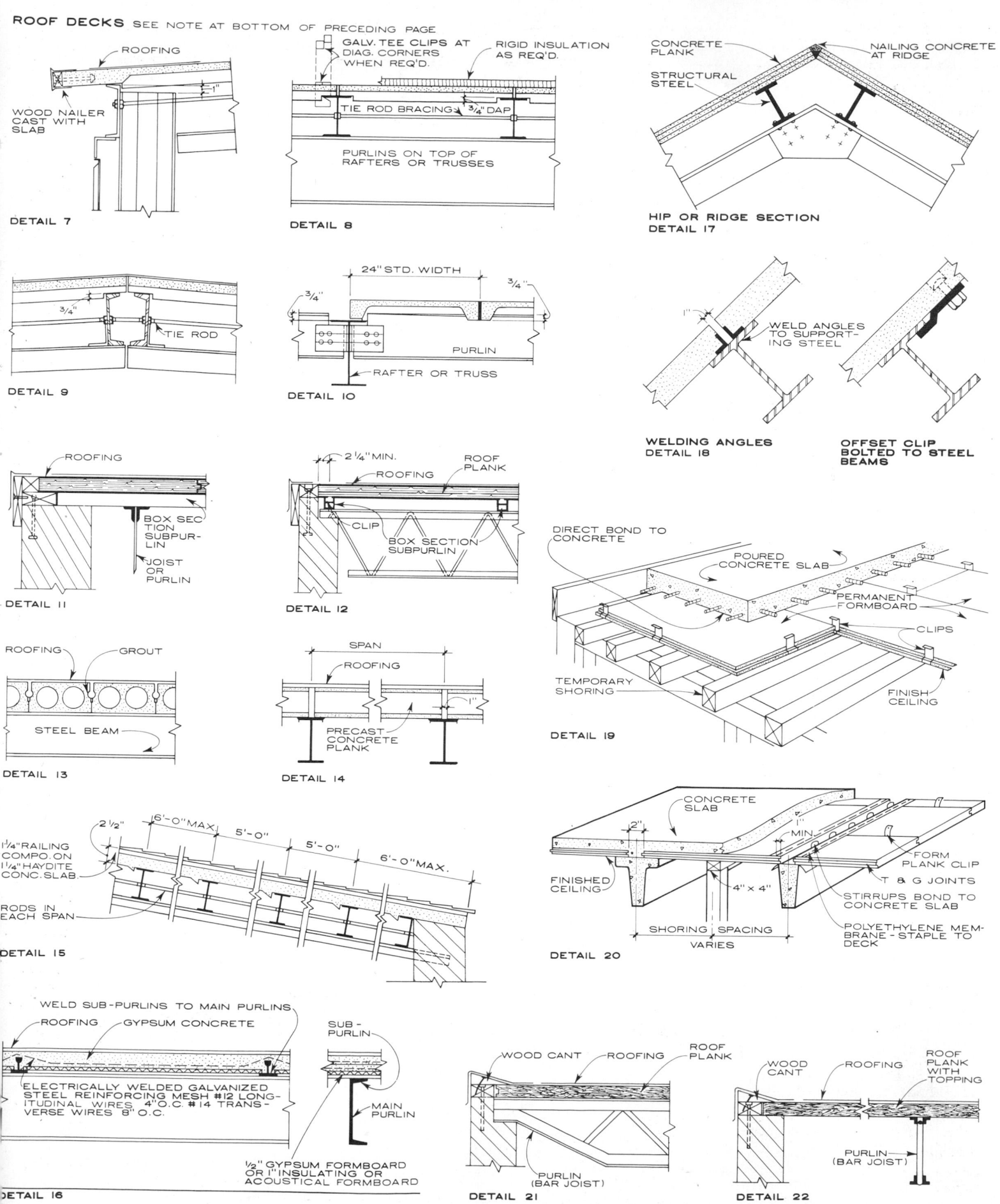

ROOFING

WOOD NAILER
CAST WITH
SLAB

1"

DETAIL 7

GALV. TEE CLIPS AT
DIAG. CORNERS
WHEN REQ'D.

RIGID INSULATION
AS REQ'D.

TIE ROD BRACING   ¾" DAP

PURLINS ON TOP OF
RAFTERS OR TRUSSES

DETAIL 8

CONCRETE
PLANK

STRUCTURAL
STEEL

NAILING CONCRETE
AT RIDGE

HIP OR RIDGE SECTION
DETAIL 17

¾"

TIE ROD

DETAIL 9

24" STD. WIDTH

¾"   ¾"

PURLIN

RAFTER OR TRUSS

DETAIL 10

1"

WELD ANGLES
TO SUPPORT-
ING STEEL

WELDING ANGLES
DETAIL 18

OFFSET CLIP
BOLTED TO STEEL
BEAMS

ROOFING

BOX SEC-
TION
SUBPURLIN

JOIST
OR
PURLIN

DETAIL 11

2¼" MIN.

ROOFING

ROOF PLANK

CLIP

BOX SECTION
SUBPURLIN

DETAIL 12

DIRECT BOND TO
CONCRETE

POURED
CONCRETE SLAB

PERMANENT
FORMBOARD

CLIPS

TEMPORARY
SHORING

FINISH
CEILING

DETAIL 19

ROOFING   GROUT

STEEL BEAM

DETAIL 13

SPAN

ROOFING

1"

PRECAST
CONCRETE
PLANK

DETAIL 14

CONCRETE
SLAB

2"   1"   MIN.

FINISHED
CEILING

4" X 4"

SHORING SPACING
VARIES

FORM
PLANK CLIP

T & G JOINTS

STIRRUPS BOND TO
CONCRETE SLAB

POLYETHYLENE MEM-
BRANE - STAPLE TO
DECK

DETAIL 20

1¼" RAILING
COMPO. ON
1¼" HAYDITE
CONC. SLAB.

2½"   6'-0" MAX.   5'-0"   5'-0"   6'-0" MAX.

RODS IN
EACH SPAN

DETAIL 15

WELD SUB-PURLINS TO MAIN PURLINS
ROOFING   GYPSUM CONCRETE

SUB-
PURLIN

ELECTRICALLY WELDED GALVANIZED
STEEL REINFORCING MESH #12 LONG-
ITUDINAL WIRES 4" O.C. #14 TRANS-
VERSE WIRES 8" O.C.

MAIN
PURLIN

½" GYPSUM FORMBOARD
OR 1" INSULATING OR
ACOUSTICAL FORMBOARD

DETAIL 16

WOOD CANT   ROOFING

ROOF
PLANK

PURLIN
(BAR JOIST)

DETAIL 21

WOOD
CANT   ROOFING

ROOF
PLANK
WITH
TOPPING

PURLIN
(BAR JOIST)

DETAIL 22

Morris Winkler; Curtin, Kane, Gere and Ashley, AIA; Syracuse, New York

GENERAL NOTES:

Choose quiet, protected site; orient building with doors and windows facing away from noise sources.

Arrange building spaces with noisy equipment and noisy activities together, away from quiet spaces.

Choose quiet mechanical equipment.

Consider acoustical properties of all materials, systems and constructions before choosing any.

THE NATURE OF SOUND

Sound is a vibration in an elastic medium; its production requires a source and a path; it travels to a receiver (the human ear, usually).

Air, fluids, and building materials are paths; materials possess mass, and therefore inertia; their oscillating motion when excited by acoustical energy is governed by laws of motion.

FREQUENCY OF COMMON SOUNDS

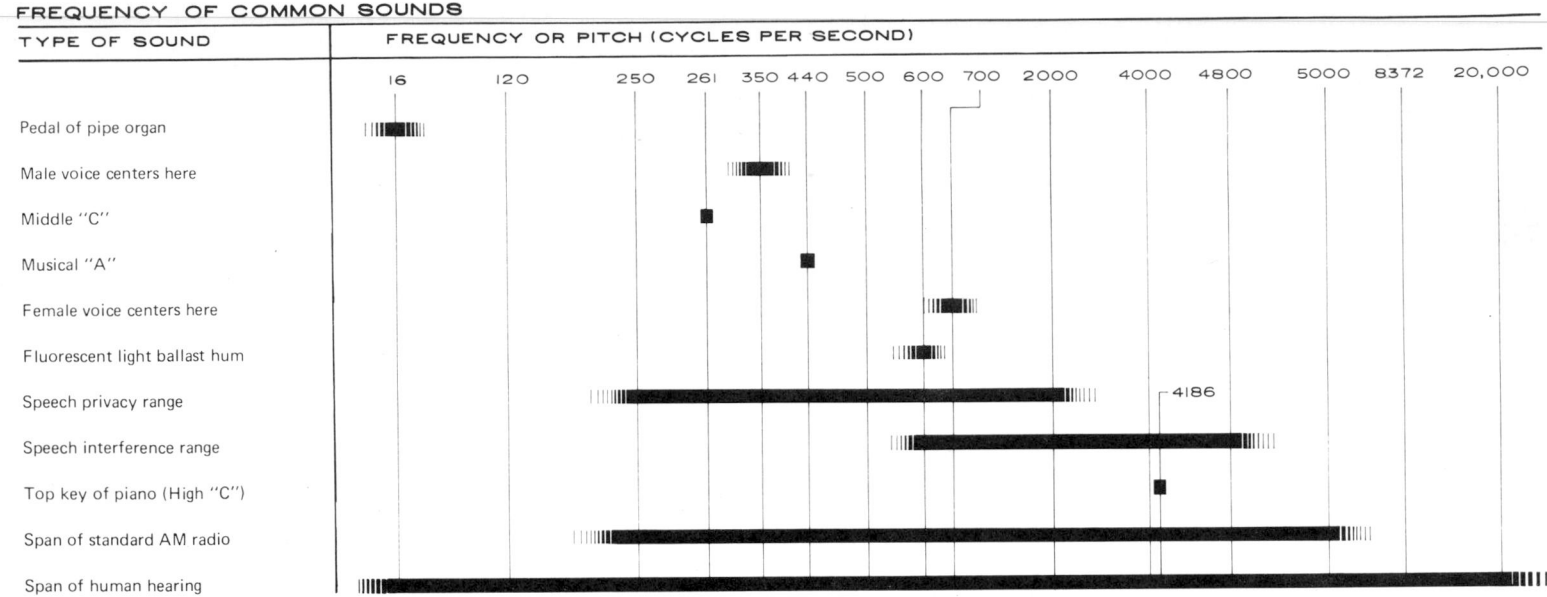

TYPE OF SOUND	FREQUENCY OR PITCH (CYCLES PER SECOND)

Pedal of pipe organ
Male voice centers here
Middle "C"
Musical "A"
Female voice centers here
Fluorescent light ballast hum
Speech privacy range
Speech interference range
Top key of piano (High "C")
Span of standard AM radio
Span of human hearing

RELATIONSHIP OF SOUND INTENSITY, LEVEL, AND LOUDNESS

INTENSITY (RELATIVE ENERGY – UNITS)	SOUND PRESSURE LEVEL (DECIBELS)	LOUDNESS
100,000,000,000,000	140	Jet aircraft and artillery fire
10,000,000,000,000	130	Threshold of pain
1,000,000,000,000	120	Near elevated train
100,000,000,000	110	Inside propeller plane
10,000,000,000	100	
1,000,000,000	90	Full symphony or band
100,000,000	80	Inside auto at high speed
10,000,000	70	Conversation, face to face
1,000,000	60	Inside general office
100,000	50	
10,000	40	Inside private office
1,000	30	Inside bedroom — Inside empty theater
100	20	
10	10	
1	0	Threshold of hearing

NOTE:

The decibel number represents a ratio (actually 10 x the logarithm) of the Intensity measured to a reference intensity roughly equivalent to the threshold of hearing.

SUBJECTIVE EFFECT OF CHANGE IN SOUND PRESSURE LEVEL

CHANGE IN SOUND PRESSURE LEVEL	CHANGE IN APPARENT LOUDNESS
3 dB	Just perceptible
5 dB	Clearly noticeable
10 dB	Twice as loud (or 1/2)
15 dB	Big change
20 dB	Much louder (or quieter)

Glenn A. Kahley; Vincent G. Kling and Associates; Philadelphia, Pennsylvania
Lyle F. Yerges, Consulting Engineer; Downers Grove, Illinois

1. USE OF THE STRUCTURE
SUBJECTIVE NEEDS—DETERMINES CRITERIA

TYPE OF SPACE	RECOMMENDED NOISE CRITERION CURVE
BROADCAST STUDIOS	NC15 – 20
CONCERT HALLS	NC20
LEGITIMATE THEATERS (500 SEATS, NO AMPLIFICATION)	NC20 – 25
MUSIC ROOMS	NC25
SCHOOL ROOMS (NO AMPLIFICATION)	NC25
CONFERENCE ROOMS FOR 50	NC25
APARTMENTS AND HOTELS	NC25 – 30
ASSEMBLY HALLS (AMPLIFICATION)	NC25 – 30
HOMES (SLEEPING AREAS)	NC25 – 35
CONFERENCE ROOMS FOR 20	NC30
MOTION PICTURE THEATERS	NC30
HOSPITALS	NC30
CHURCHES	NC30
COURTROOMS	NC30
LIBRARIES	NC30
SMALL PRIVATE OFFICES	NC30 – 35
RESTAURANTS	NC45
COLISEUMS FOR SPORTS ONLY (AMPLIFICATION)	NC40
STENOGRAPHIC OFFICES (TYPING AND BUSINESS MACHINES)	NC50
FACTORIES	NC40 – 65

NOTE: Each noise criteria curve is a code for specifying permissible sound pressure levels in eight octave bands. It is intended that in no one frequency band should the specfied level be exceeded.

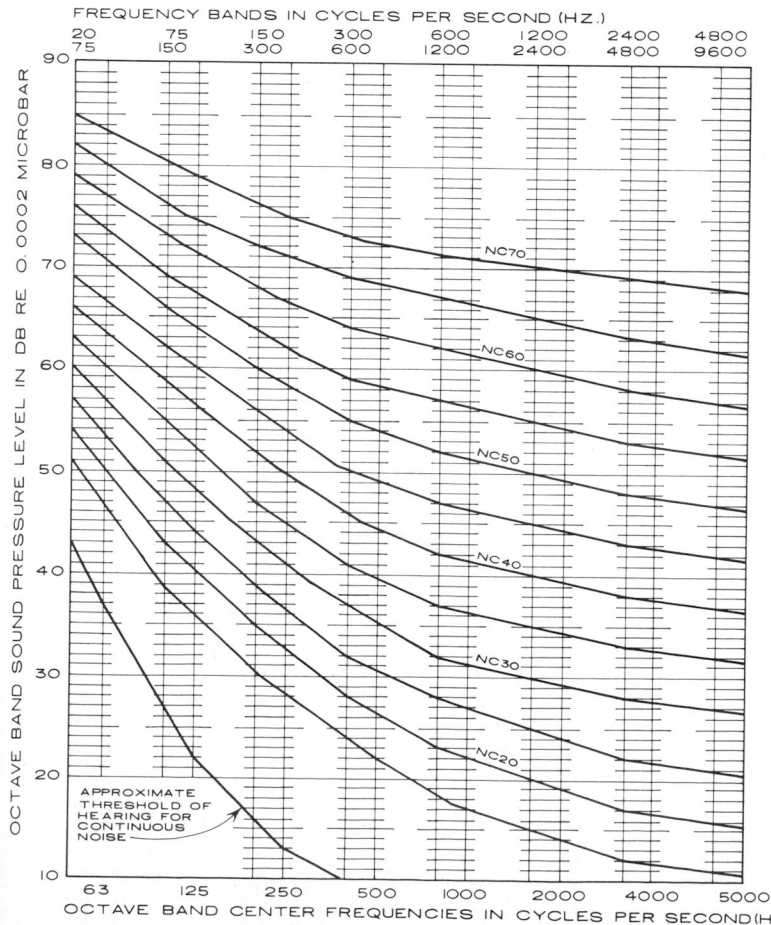

FREQUENCY BANDS IN CYCLES PER SECOND (HZ.)

THE NC – CURVES (NOISE CRITERIA) BASED UPON HUMAN RESPONSE TO SOUND PRESSURE LEVEL AND FREQUENCY*

* COURTESY T. J. SCHULTZ, JOURNAL OF THE ACOUSTICAL SOCIETY OF AMERICA 43.637

Hussein A. Saleh; Vincent G. Kling and Associates; Philadelphia, Pennsylvania
Lyle F. Yerges, Consulting Engineer; Downers Grove, Illinois

2. NOISE SOURCES—INTERIOR AND EXTERIOR— DETERMINE CONTROL PROVISIONS

(A)

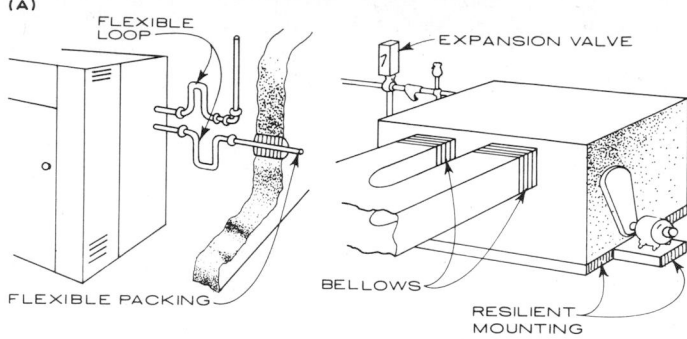

NOTE:

Avoid or minimize noise sources. Choose quiet equipment. Use vibration isolation, sound absorbent duct lining, resilient pipe connectors. Design for low flow velocities in pipes and ducts.

(B)

Orient spaces to minimize transmission problems. Space windows of adjoining apartments maximum distance apart. Place noisy areas back-to-back. Place closets between noisy and quiet areas.

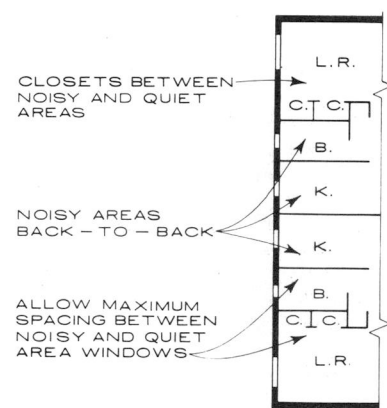

CLOSETS BETWEEN NOISY AND QUIET AREAS

NOISY AREAS BACK – TO – BACK

ALLOW MAXIMUM SPACING BETWEEN NOISY AND QUIET AREA WINDOWS

3. ACOUSTICAL DESIGN

(A)

Choose materials, systems, and constructions to control sound transmission.

(B)

Design shapes, areas, volumes and surfaces to accomplish desirable interior accoustical conditions.

(C)

Economic factors:

"Build in" good acoustics.
Choose simplest construction meeting criteria.
Law of diminishing returns quickly limits benefits of increasing any variable (such as weight, thickness, etc.)
It is much cheaper to avoid noise problems in original design or in choice of equipment than to correct them later.

STC-rating number (see another page in this series for explanation) in this chart indicates approximate center of a range; for example:

STC-37 means STC-35 to less than STC-40
STC-42 means STC-40 to less than STC-45 etc.

Test procedures and variables in construction require a tolerance of approximately ± 2 to 3dB. The ear recognizes 3 dB change as just noticeable.

All STC-numbers are based upon laboratory data. Actual field installations usually test approximately 3 to 5 dB lower.

Performance criteria assume normal background level in "Room Being Considered" and average construction cost range for building.

For low-cost construction or high background level, criteria may be reduced 3 to 5 points. For high-cost construction or low background level, criteria may be increased 3 to 5 points.

The following table is a fairly reliable, conservative guide for choosing partition constructions. It assumes no holes, "leaks" or significant "flanking paths"; a so-called normal spectrum of background sound in the room; no unusual or extreme extraneous noise conditions; and no "special" conditions or highly critical uses for the spaces. For auditori-

ums, theaters, recording studios, music schools, and similar areas; for large hotels, apartments, dormitories and similar buildings; and for any structure where the amount of wall construction is large enough to make the economic multiplier very large, professional advice is the only safe economical course.

BACKGROUND SOUND (often referred to as "masking"):

A. Low background level. . .Under NC-25. Quiet suburban or residential areas. No ventilating or mechanical equipment sounds. Little or no traffic noise.

B. Normal or average background level . . . NC-25
Continued on next page.

SOUND ISOLATION CRITERIA

TYPE OF OCCUPANCY	WALL, PARTITION, OR PANEL BETWEEN		SOUND ISOLATION REQUIREMENT
	ROOM CONSIDERED AND	ADJACENT AREA	
Executive areas, doctors' suites, confidential privacy requirements	Office	Adjacent offices	STC 47
		General office areas	STC 42
		Corridor or lobby	STC 47
		Washrooms and toilet areas	STC 47
		Exterior of building	STC 42
		Kitchen and dining areas	STC 47
		Manufacturing areas and mechanical equipment rooms	STC 52
Normal office areas, normal privacy requirements.	Office	Adjacent offices	STC 37
		General office areas	STC 37
		Corridor or lobby	STC 37
		Washrooms and toilet areas	STC 42
		Exterior of building	STC 37
		Kitchen and dining areas	STC 42
		Manufacturing areas and mechanical equipment rooms	STC 47
Any normal occupancy, using conference rooms for group meetings or discussions	Conference Rooms	Other conference rooms	STC 42
		Adjacent offices	STC 42
		General office areas	STC 42
		Corridor or lobby	STC 42
		Washrooms and toilet areas	STC 47
		Exterior of building	STC 37
		Kitchen and dining areas	STC 47
		Manufacturing or other noisy interior areas	STC 47
Normal business offices, drafting areas, banking floors, etc.	Large General Office Areas	Corridors or lobby	STC 32
		Exterior of building	STC 32
		Data processing areas	STC 37
		Manufacturing areas and mechanical equipment areas	STC 42
		Kitchen and dining areas	STC 37
Office in manufacturing, laboratory, or test areas	Shop and Laboratory Offices	Adjacent offices	STC 37
		Manufacturing, laboratory, or test areas	STC 42
		Washrooms and toilet areas	STC 37
		Corridor or lobby	STC 32
		Exterior of building	STC 32
Motels and urban hotels	Bedrooms	Adjacent bedrooms, separate occupancy	STC 47
		Bathrooms, separate occupancy	STC 47
		Living rooms, separate occupancy	STC 47
		Dining areas	STC 47
		Corridor, lobby, or public spaces	STC 47
		Mechanical equipment rooms	STC 52
		Exterior of building:	
		Normal street or highway noise	STC 42
		Heavy highway traffic	STC 47
		Airport noise	STC 47
Apartments, multiple dwelling building	Bedrooms	Adjacent bedrooms, separate occupancy	STC 47
		Bathrooms, separate occupancy	STC 47
		Bathrooms, same occupancy	STC 37
		Living rooms, separate occupancy	STC 47
		Living rooms, same occupancy	STC 42
		Kitchen areas, separate occupancy	STC 47
		Kitchen areas, same occupancy	STC 42
		Mechanical equipment rooms	STC 52
		Corridors, lobby, public spaces	STC 47
		Exterior of building	STC 42

Hussein A. Saleh; Vincent G. Kling and Associates; Philadelphia, Pennsylvania
Lyle F. Yerges, Consulting Engineer; Downers Grove, Illinois

to under NC-35. Some distant traffic noise or light street traffic. Some ventilating air sound and occasional low level mechanical equipment sounds.

C. High background level . . . over NC-35. Street noise and traffic sounds. Noisy central ventilating system or window air conditioner unit.

Note: All of these background levels assume no unusual sounds such as persistent pure tones, distinct and unusual signals, strongly perceptible vibration, or similar stimuli.

All exterior or other areas which are the source of "extraneous" noise are assumed to have a normal or usual noise level and type of noise for such areas.

If extraordinarily high noise levels exist, as in the near vicinity of engine test stands, airports with heavy jetplane traffic, or near heavily traveled highways with heavy truck traffic, or in similar circumstances, increase all isolation requirements by up to 5 points — or consult a qualified acoustical consultant.

FLOORS should provide isolation against:

AIR-BORNE SOUND at least equal to that of the partitions and preferably 3 to 5 points better.

STRUCTURE-BORNE (IMPACT) SOUND: at least equal to the FHA criterion of (see 9th Pg. in this series) (for floors immediately above the following spaces)

Multi-family dwelling rooms, hotels, motels etc.	INR = 0
Single family dwelling rooms	No requirement
School classrooms	INR = −5
Offices	INR = −5
Auditoriums, lecture rooms, and similar spaces	INR = +5
Radio studios, music areas, and similar spaces	Use professional consultants.

SOUND ISOLATION CRITERIA

TYPE OF OCCUPANCY	WALL, PARTITION, OR PANEL BETWEEN ROOM CONSIDERED AND ADJACENT AREA		SOUND ISOLATION REQUIREMENT
Apartments, multiple dwelling building	Living Rooms	Adjacent living rooms, separate occupancy	STC 47
		Bathrooms, separate occupancy	STC 47
		Bathrooms, same occupancy	STC 42
		Kitchen areas, separate occupancy	STC 47
		Kitchen areas, same occupancy	STC 42
		Mechanical equipment rooms	STC 52
		Exterior of building	STC 37
Private, single family residences	Bedrooms	Adjacent bedrooms	STC 37
		Living rooms	STC 42
		Bathrooms, not directly connected with bedroom	STC 42
		Kitchen areas	STC 42
		Exterior of building	STC 37
Private, single family residences	Living Rooms	Adjacent bathrooms	STC 42
		Kitchen areas	STC 42
		Exterior of building	STC 37
Normal school buildings without extraordinary or unusual activities or requirements.	Classrooms	Adjacent classrooms	STC 37
		Laboratories	STC 42
		Corridor or public areas	STC 37
		Kitchen and dining areas	STC 42
		Shops	STC 47
		Recreational areas	STC 47
		Music rooms	STC 47
		Mechanical equipment rooms	STC 52
		Toilet areas	STC 42
		Exterior of building	STC 37
Normal school buildings without extraordinary or unusual activities or requirements	Large Music or Drama Areas	Adjacent music or drama rooms	STC 52
		Corridor or public areas	STC 47
		Practice rooms	STC 47
		Shops	STC 47
		Recreational areas	STC 47
		Laboratories	STC 47
		Toilet areas	STC 47
		Mechanical equipment rooms	STC 52
		Exterior of building	STC 47
	Music Practice Rooms	Adjacent practice rooms	STC 47
		Corridors and public areas	STC 47
	Language Laboratories	Same as for theaters, concert halls, auditorium, etc.	
	Counseling Offices	Same as for executive offices	
Any occupancy where serious performances are given. Requirements may be relaxed for elementary schools or non-critical types of occupancy.	Theaters, Concert Halls, Lecture Halls	Adjacent similar areas	STC 52
		Corridors and public areas	STC 47
		Recreational areas	STC 52
		Mechanical equipment spaces	STC 52
		Classrooms	STC 47
		Laboratories	STC 47
		Shops	STC 52
		Toilet areas	STC 52
		Exterior of building	STC 52
Any occupancy where serious amateur or any professional work is done	Radio, TV, Recording Studios	Use professional consultants. This is an extremely critical type of area.	

Giovanni Petri, AIA; Vincent G. Kling and Associates; Philadelphia, Pennsylvania
Lyle F. Yerges, Consulting Engineer; Downers Grove, Illinois

FIGURE I

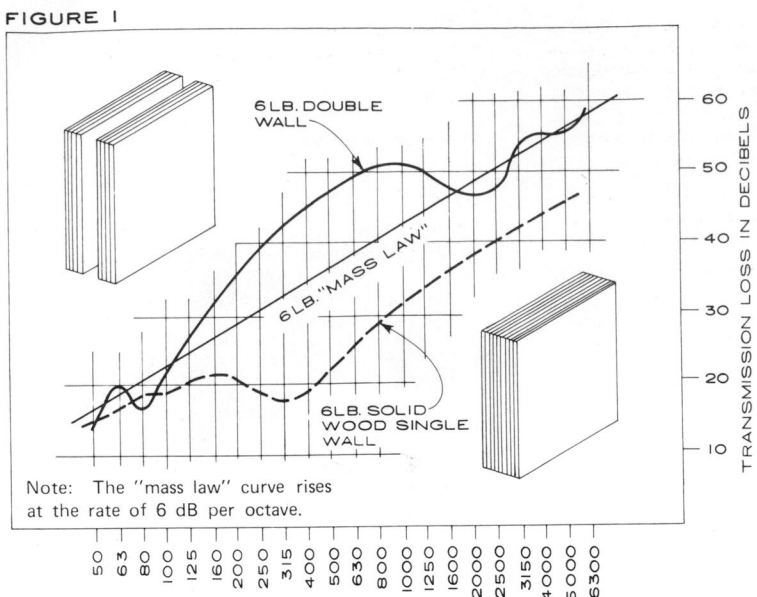

Note: The "mass law" curve rises at the rate of 6 dB per octave.

ONE - THIRD OCTAVE BAND CENTER FREQUENCY IN CYCLES/SECOND

EXPLANATORY NOTES:

TRANSMISSION LOSS (TL) refers to attenuation of sound passing through construction when tested according to ASTM E90—66T. The actual graph of the test provides the best rating method.

Sound Transmission through walls or floors and ceiling varies with the frequency of sound and the weight (or mass) and stiffness of the construction.

For all solid panels, a dip occurrs in the Transmission Loss curve; this is the "coincidence dip", related to the stiffness and mass of the wall.

Theoretically, the Transmission Loss varies at the rate of 6dB per doubling (or halving) of the weight of the construction. For example:

Weight—lb./sq. ft.:	5	10	20	40	80	160
TL@ 400 c.p.s. —dB:	33	39	45	51	57	63

A single solid panel behaves less well than the "mass law" would predict; a true double wall with separate, unconnected wythes performs better than the "mass law" predicts.

The Transmission Loss tends to increase about 5dB for each doubling of the air space between wythes (minimum effective space approximately 2"). For example:

Air Space (inches):	3	6	12	24	48
TL (decibels):	40	45	50	55	60

Resilient attachment of surface "skins" to studs or structural surfaces provides same effect as separates wythes.

Soft, resilient, absorptive materials in the cavity between wythes, particularly for light-weight staggered-stud construction, improves Transmission Loss.

"Visco-elastic" (somewhat resilient but not fully elastic) materials, such as certain insulation boards, etc. —"dampen" or restrict the vibration of panels. When used with rigid panels (such as gypsum boards), they increase Transmission Loss appreciably. Installation details recommended by manufacturers should be followed.

FIGURE 2

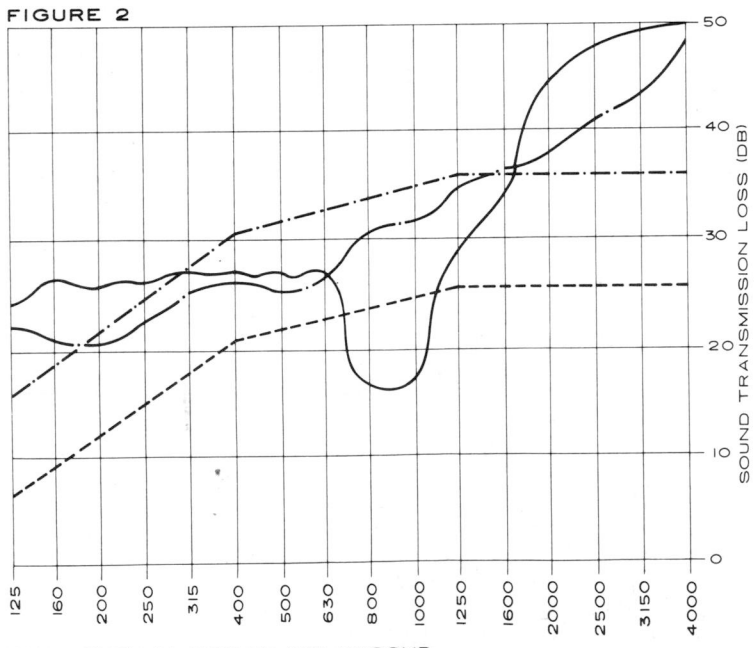

FREQUENCY IN CYCLES PER SECOND

——— Partition with 31 dB average, 22STC   · — · Partition with 31 dB average, 32STC

– – – – Sound transmission class contour   · — · — Sound transmission class contour

Allan R. Niemeyer; Vincent G. Kling and Associates; Philadelphia, Pennsylvania

Lyle F. Yerges, Consulting Engineer; Downers Grove, Illinois

DEFINITIONS

ATTENUATION: reduction or lessening (from root word meaning "to thin out as a string or fiber").

CENTER FREQUENCY OF AN OCTAVE BAND: the frequency in the center of the entire 2/1 range of the octave.

NOISE REDUCTION: This refers to the actual difference in Sound-Pressure Level between two spaces being considered. It is what the ear hears and what we are actually interested in. It is dependent not only on the Transmission Loss of the walls, floors and ceilings, but also the Sound Absorption present in the room being considered.

OCTAVE: a frequency ratio of 2/1. For example, from Middle "C" (261) to one octave higher (522) or one octave lower (130).

SOUND TRANSMISSION CLASS (STC): a rating system which compares the TL test curve for a construction with a "standard contour" which reflects known subjective response to the TL performance. The contour is fitted to the test curve of the constructions, and the relative vertical position of the contour determines the Sound Transmission Class and compares the rank-order constructions. See Figure 2 for example.

Figure 1 compares two constructions with identical numerical average TL but widely differing effectiveness. The relative position of the standard contours indicates a 10-point superiority for one construction.

SOUND TRANSMISSION CLASS CURVE: a three-segment "contour", shaped to match approximately the ear's evaluation of the importance of the sound pressure in the frequency ranges spanned by the segments of the curve. The contour is matched to the actual results of an actual test, and the rating of the construction is given according to the vertical position of the contour.

The SOUND TRANSMISSION LOSS at all frequencies, from 125 to 4000 cps, is important (in varying degrees), so a single number or an average is meaningless. The shape of the entire TL curve (from a test) as related to the standard contour is important. Deep dips (as in curve A) are deadly, but the numerical average misses this dip; the contour properly evaluates its effect. The STC rating is a numerical rank-ordering of the vertical position of the contour as the contour is fitted to the test curve.

The STC-RATING of ordinary "base constructions" is listed in the following tables. The tabulated results represent reasonable averages of many tests by several laboratories and testing agencies. While the values may differ slightly from published data from a specific laboratory or manufacturer, they are conservative and representative of the particular construction described. (See another page for further explanation and qualification.) For any construction with unique details or characteristics, refer if possible to actual laboratory test data and the qualifying descriptive details of the test specimen.

SOUND TRANSMISSION LOSS – STUD FRAMED WALLS AND PARTITIONS

BASE CONSTRUCTION		WEIGHT (lb/ft²)	STC RATING	PLANS (NO SCALE)
	1/4" PLYWOOD – NAILED TO STUDS	2 1/2	24	
	1/2" WOOD FIBERBOARD – NAILED TO STUDS	3 1/2	28	
2" x 4" WOOD STUDS 16" O.C. (UNLESS OTHERWISE NOTED)	1/2" GYPSUM BOARD – NAILED TO STUDS (JOINTS TAPED AND SEALED)	5 3/4	32	
	3/8" GYPSUM LATH-NAILED TO STUDS – 1/2" SANDED GYPSUM PLASTER (2 COATS)	15	35	
	METAL LATH-NAILED TO STUDS – 7/8" SANDED GYPSUM PLASTER (3 COATS)	20	37	
3 5/8" MET. STUDS 24" O.C.	5/8" GYPSUM BOARD-SCREW ATTACHMENT TO STUDS (JOINTS TAPED AND SEALED)	6	39	
3 1/4" METAL STUDS 16" O.C. (UNLESS OTHERWISE NOTED)	3/8" GYPSUM LATH-CLIPPED TO STUDS – 1/2" SANDED GYPSUM PLASTER (2 COATS)	15	40	
	METAL LATH-CLIPPED TO STUDS – 3/4" SANDED GYPSUM PLASTER (3 COATS)	19	37	

NOTE:

Combinations of channels or similar sections to produce a similar air space between opposite surfaces provide approximately the same STC ratings. Arrangements of channels or studs to produce completely independent (non-connected) wythes provide approximately the same improvement in STC rating (10 points) as staggered studs.

MODIFICATIONS TO BASE CONSTRUCTION

MODIFICATION	STC RATING IMPROVEMENT	PLANS (NO SCALE)
SURFACE SKIN WEIGHT	Doubling 1 Side = +3 points Doubling 2 Sides = +5 points	
RESILIENT ATTACHMENT OF SURFACE	To 1 Side = +6 points To 2 Sides = +10 points	
STAGGERED STUDS	+9 points	
SLOTTED STUDS	+8 points	
RESILIENT DAMPING BOARD LAYER UNDER SURFACE SKINS	Surface adhesively applied according to specific procedures recommended by the Gypsum Board Manufacturer +10 points.	
ABSORPTION IN CAVITY	+5 points	

Cumulative improvement of any combinations of these modifications is calculated thus: largest number + 1/2 next largest + 1/2 next largest etc.

EXAMPLE:

Given a "Base Construction," such as 1/2" Gypsum Board on wood studs = STC – 33.

Change to:

Staggered studs (+10 points)	=	10 points
Add:		
Absorption in cavity (+5 points) 1/2 x 5 points	=	2 1/2 points
Add:		
One additional 1/2" gypsum board to one side only (+3 points) 1/2 x 3 points	=	1 1/2 points
	Total	14 points

Therefore, "Base Construction" increases from STC 33 to STC 47.

Sterlin G. Daniel; Vincent G. Kling and Associates; Philadelphia, Pennsylvania
Lyle F. Yerges, Consulting Engineer; Downers Grove, Illinois

SOUND TRANSMISSION LOSS—WALLS AND PARTITIONS OF MASONRY AND CONCRETE

BASE CONSTRUCTION		WEIGHT (lb./ft.^{2})	STC RATING	PLANS (NO SCALE)
WALLS OF CONCRETE MASONRY UNITS	4" LIGHTWEIGHT *	20	36	
	4" DENSE	30	38	
	6" LIGHTWEIGHT *	28	41	
	6" DENSE	43	43	
	8" LIGHTWEIGHT *	34	46	
	8" DENSE	55	48	
	12" LIGHTWEIGHT *	50	51	
	12" DENSE	80	53	
SOLID BRICK WALLS	4" BRICK †	38	41	
	8" BRICK †	80	49	
	12" BRICK †	120	54	
SOLID CONCRETE WALLS	6" REINFORCED DENSE CONCRETE	75	46	
	8" REINFORCED DENSE CONCRETE	95	51	
	12" REINFORCED DENSE CONCRETE	145	56	

*Sealed against air leakage with 2 coats of sealer paint both sides or similarly sealed.

†Careful workmanship: Air-tight joints and surface sealed.

MODIFICATIONS TO THE BASE CONSTRUCTIONS PRODUCE CORRESPONDING IMPROVEMENTS IN STC-RATING

MODIFICATION	STC RATING IMPROVEMENT		PLANS (NO SCALE)
SAND FILLED CORES		+ 3 points	
1/2" SANDED PLASTER (OR SIMILAR SURFACE SKIN)	1 Side	+ 2 points	
	2 Sides	+ 4 points	
RIGIDLY FURRED SURFACE SKIN	1 Side	+ 7 points	
	2 Sides	+ 10 points	
RESILIENTLY ATTACHED SURFACE SKIN	1 Side	+ 12 points	
	2 Sides	+ 15 points	
ABSORPTION IN CAVITY	1 Side	+ 3 points	
	2 Sides	+ 5 points	
DIVIDING WALL INTO SEPARATE WYTHES WITH 4" AIR SPACE		+ 15 points	

FORMULA:

Cumulative improvement of any combination of these modifications is calculated thus:
Largest number + next largest number + next largest number, etc.

EXAMPLE:

Given a base construction such as 4" Lightweight Block = STC-36

Add:

Resilient plaster skin
one side   =   12 points

Add:

Sand in cores   =   3 points

Add:

Plaster on opposite
side   =   2 points
                      Total   17 points

Therefore "base construction" increases from STC-36 to STC-53.

Josue S. Gutierrez; Vincent G. Kling and Associates; Philadelphia, Pennsylvania

Lyle F. Yerges, Consulting Engineer; Downers Grove, Illinois

SOUND TRANSMISSION LOSS — STUDLESS AND SPECIAL DRYWALL CONSTRUCTION

BASE CONSTRUCTION		WEIGHT (lbs./ft.²)	STC RATING	PLANS (NO SCALE)
STUDLESS CONSTRUCTION	2″ PANEL, SANDED GYPSUM PLASTER ON METAL LATH ✳, WITH OR WITHOUT IMBEDDED CHANNELS	18	34	
	2 1/2″ PANEL, SANDED GYPSUM PLASTER ON SEPARATE LAYERS OF GYPSUM LATH	19	38	
SPECIAL DRYWALL CONSTRUCTION	2 1/4″ SOLID LAMINATED GYPSUM BOARD	10	30	
	5/8″ GYPSUM BOARD LAYERS LAMINATED TO 1 5/8″ x 6″ GYPSUM STRIPS	7	34	
	DOUBLE SOLID DRYWALL — 2 SEPARATE WYTHES OF 1/2″ GYPSUM BOARD LAMINATED TO 1″ GYPSUM BOARD WITH 1 1/8″ AIR SPACE	14	46	

✳ Gypsum lath instead of metal lath provides approximately the same STC rating.

NOTES: 1. To calculate the effect of variations in weight or air space, See "Control of air borne sound transmission."
2. For the effect of other construction variables, see a preceding page on "Sound Transmission."

WINDOWS AND GLAZING

CONSTRUCTION	THICKNESS	WEIGHT (lbs./ft.²)	STC RATING
D.S. GLASS	1/8″	1 1/2	21
PLATE GLASS	1/4″	3.2	26
INSULATING GLASS	1″	6 1/2	32
LAMINATED ACOUSTICAL GLASS*	9/32″	3 1/4	36
GLASS BLOCK	3 3/4″	20	40
SPACED GLASS (1/4″ – 2″ AIR SPACE- 1/4″)	2 1/2″	6 1/2	42

✳ "Acousta-Pane 36"

SOLID SINGLE SHEET MATERIALS

CONSTRUCTION	THICKNESS	WEIGHT (lb./ft.²)	STC RATING
ALUMINUM	0.025	.35	19
PLYWOOD	1/4″	.73	22
CELLULOSE FIBERBOARD	1/2″	.75	22
PLATE GLASS	1/4″	3.2	26
SHEET STEEL	18 GAGE	2.0	30
LEAD	1/16″	3.9	34

DOORS ✳

CONSTRUCTION	THICKNESS	WEIGHT (lb./ft.²)	STC RATING
HOLLOW CORE WOOD	1 3/4″	3 1/2	26
SOLID CORE WOOD	1 3/4″	5	29
HOLLOW METAL	1 3/4″	5	30
PACKED METAL	1 3/4″	7	32
SPECIAL ACOUSTICAL	1 3/4″	6	35
SOLID CORE WOOD	2 1/4″	7	32
SPECIAL ACOUSTICAL	2 1/2″	8	38

✳ Fully gasketed, all edges and bottom. "Leaky" gaskets or no gaskets can reduce STC RATINGS by 5 to 15 points.

William Lukens; Vincent G. Kling and Associates; Philadelphia, Pennsylvania
Lyle F. Yerges, Consulting Engineer; Downers Grove, Illinois

MOVABLE AND OPERABLE PARTITIONS

STC ratings range from STC-18 to STC-44 (up to STC-55 for special double wall assemblies) depending upon construction, weight, and tightness of seals and closures.

Generally, performance parallels comparable fixed wall construction if edges and perimeters are well sealed.

HOLES AND OPENINGS

Holes and openings, such as door undercuts and louvers, perimeters of pipes and ducts, and similar joints however small, seriously degrade transmission loss performance of constructions.
One square inch of opening transmits as much sound as about 100 sq. ft. of a 40 dB wall.
High frequencies escape through small holes, all frequencies through long cracks.

FORMULA:

Cumulative improvement of any combinations of these modifications is calculated thus: largest number + next largest + next largest, etc.

EXAMPLE:

Given a "Base Construction" such as Double Solid Drywall (STC = 46)

Change to:

TRIPLE SOLID DRYWALL

Add:
2 Air Spaces of 1 1/8″   =   5 points
Add:
1 Layer of 1″ Gypsum
Board in cavity   =   2 points
Add:
Absorption in one cavity   =   5 points

Total = 12 points

Therefore, "Base construction" increases from STC-46 to STC-58.

GENERAL NOTES:

In addition to "air-borne" sound transmission, floors are subject to impact or structureborne transmission of noises such as footfalls, dropped objects, scraping furniture.

Impact noise rating INR refers to a rating system which compares the effectiveness of floor constructions in isolating against transmission of impact sounds to spaces below the floor. It is based upon an international standards organization test method which employs a tapping machine of known performance characteristics.

A "standard contour" which reflects subjective response to noise is fitted to the curve of the noise level measured in the room below the floor. The relative vertical position of the contour determines the impact noise rating and compares and rank-orders constructions.

The tapping test method is based upon experience gained largely from tests of the heavy masonry floor constructions widely used in european apartment and multifamily buildings. It tends to over-rate the effectiveness of floor coverings such as carpet; it does not appear to evaluate properly the effect of heavy, slow impacts nor of low-frequency impact sound; and it does not reflect accurately the performance of lightweight floor constructions such as the more common U'
the more common U.S. woodjoist floors and similar systems.

While some government agencies include INR requirements in their specifications', the method has not been adopted in this country, and it has not been accepted as an ASTM standard.

Field measurements of sound pressure levels in the room underneath a floor construction on which a standard tapping machine is operating should not exceed this curve by more than the tolerances specified in section III—A—3 of the text of F.H.A. no. 750 guide, Impact Noise Control in Multifamily Dwellings.

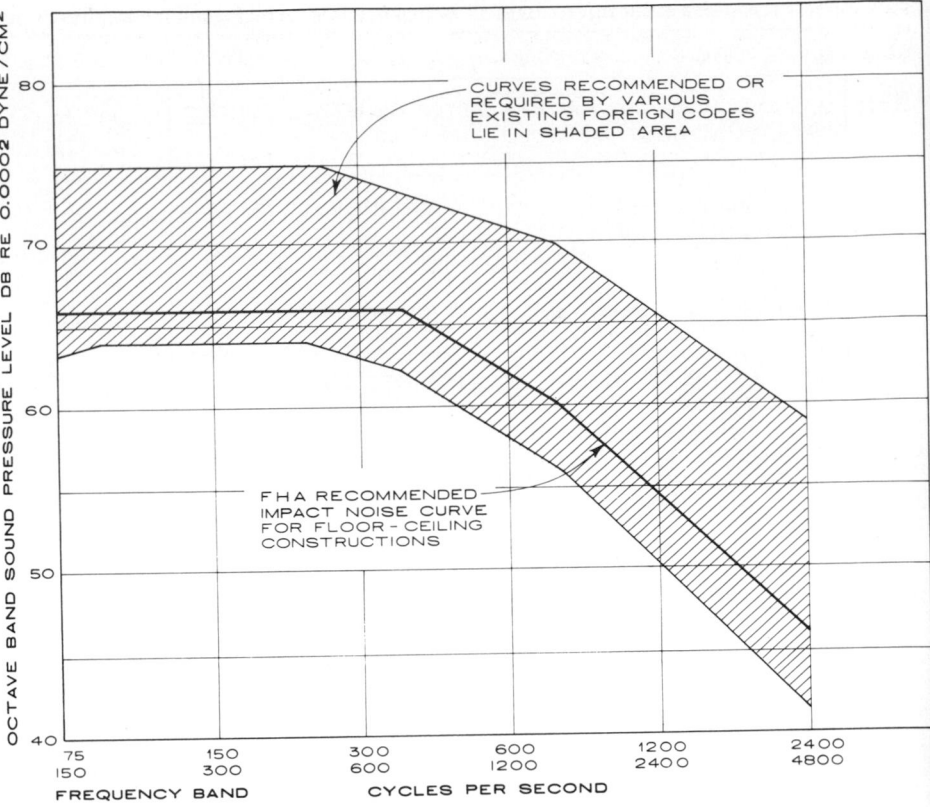

IMPACT NOISE CURVE

STRUCTURAL FLANKING

Edge attachment and junctions of walls, partitions, floors and ceiling can cause large differences in TL performance. The transverse waves set up in continuous, stiff, lightweight walls or floors can carry sound a long distance from the source to other parts of the structure. Curtainwalls and thin concrete floors on bar joists are particularly subject to this weakness.

Properly designed discontinuities, such as shown in adjacent sketches, are helpful in reducing structural flanking.

A resilient joint between wall and partition or partition and floor can often appreciably improve TL performance.

Flanking via inter-connected air volumes, as in balloon framing, can reduce TL as must as 10 dB.

Continuous pipes, conduits or ducts can act as transmission paths from room to room. Care must also be taken to isolate such services from the structure.

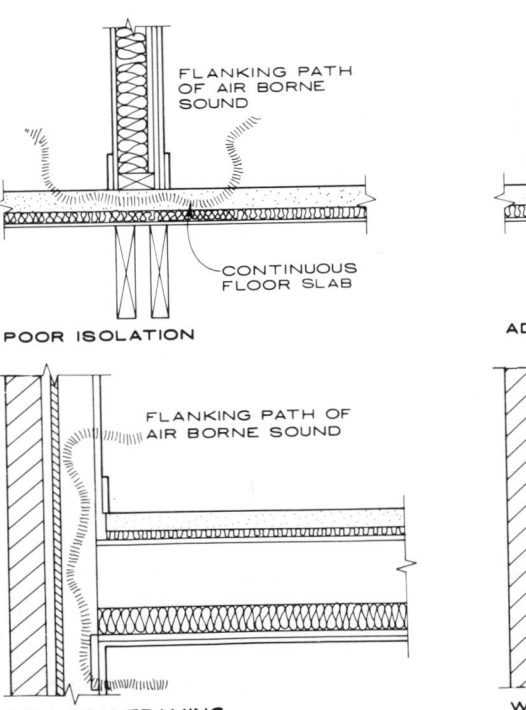

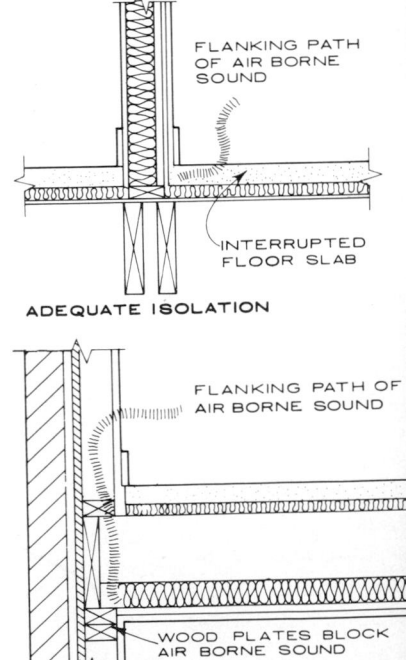

Herman DeJong; Vincent G. Kling and Associates; Philadelphia, Pennsylvania
Lyle F. Yerges, Consulting Engineer; Downers Grove, Illinois

For a discussion of STC-rating of floor constructions, see "Control of Air Borne Sound Transmission" and "Sound Transmission Loss" pages.

The INR (Impact Noise Rating) of constructions in the following tables follows the procedure of the FHA No. 750 guide, since this rating system now has considerable acceptance in the United States, and the system is reasonably comparable with European systems.

SOUND TRANSLATION LOSS AND IMPACT NOISE RATINGS – WOOD FRAMED FLOORS

2" x 10" WOOD JOISTS – 16" O.C. UNLESS OTHERWISE NOTED

BASE CONSTRUCTION	WEIGHT (lb./ft.^{2})	STC RATING	INR RATING	SECTIONS
1/2" PLYWOOD SUBFLOORS AND STANDARD OAK FLOORING – NAILED TO JOISTS	8	25	−28	
DITTO – PLUS 5/8" GYPSUM BOARD CEILING NAILED TO UNDERSIDE OF JOISTS	10	37	−17	
DITTO – EXCEPT 3/8" GYPSUM LATH AND 1/2" SANDED PLASTER	15	39	−15	
DITTO – EXCEPT METAL LATH AND 7/8" SANDED GYPSUM PLASTER (3 COATS)	17	39	−15	

MODIFICATIONS TO BASE CONSTRUCTION

MODIFICATION	STC RATING IMPROVEMENT	INR RATING IMPROVEMENT	SECTIONS
RESILIENT SUSPENSION OF CEILING	+10	+8	
"FLOATING RAFT" – ROUGH FLOORING AND FINISH FLOORING ON 1" x 3" SLEEPERS RESTING ON BUT NOT NAILED THROUGH RESILIENT FIBER BOARD	+10	+8	
STAGGERED JOISTS – CEILING INDEPENDENT OF FLOOR	+8	+7	
RESILIENT DAMPING BOARD LAYER BETWEEN SUBFLOOR AND FINISH FLOOR UNDERLAYMENT (UNDERLAYMENT ADHESIVELY APPLIED TO DAMPING BOARD)	+7	0 to +2	
ABSORPTION IN CAVITY: (**ONLY WHEN CEILING RESILIENTLY SUSPENDED OR ON STAGGERED JOISTS; LITTLE OR NO IMPROVEMENT IN RIGID CONSTRUCTION)	+3	+7*	
VINYL TILE	0	0	
3/32" LINOLEUM	0	+5	
1/4" CORK TILE	0	+10 to +15	
CARPET AND PAD	0	+20 to +25	

FORMULA

Cumulative improvement of any combination of these modifications is calculated thus: largest number + next largest number + next largest ... etc.

EXAMPLE:

A base construction such as 2" x 10" joists, with 1/2" plywood subfloors and standard oak flooring with 5/8" gypsum board ceiling nailed to joists (STC = 37, INR = −17)

	STC	INR
	37 points	−17 points
Add: Resilient suspension of ceiling =	10	+ 8
Add: Heavy carpet on thick pad =	0	+25
Total	47 points	+16 points

Therefore, "Base Construction" increases from STC = 37, INR = −17 to STC = 47, INR = +16.

Donald L. Downs; Vincent G. Kling and Associates; Philadelphia, Pennsylvania
Lyle F. Yerges, Consulting Engineer; Downers Grove, Illinois

SOLID REINFORCED CONCRETE FLOOR SLABS

BASE CONSTRUCTION	WEIGHT (lb./ft.²)	STC RATING	INR RATING	SECTION (NO SCALE)
4″ REINFORCED DENSE CONCRETE	50	41	−17	
6″ REINFORCED DENSE CONCRETE	75	46	−17	
8″ REINFORCED DENSE CONCRETE	95	51	−16	

RIBBED CONCRETE FLOORS

BASE CONSTRUCTION	WEIGHT (lb./ft.²)	STC RATING	INR RATING	SECTION (NO SCALE)
RIBBED CONCRETE—2″ SLAB ON 4″ HOLLOW FILLER BLOCKS	65	45	−22	
RIBBED CONCRETE—2″ SLAB ON 6″ HOLLOW FILLER BLOCKS	80	49	−21	
RIBBED CONCRETE—2 1/2″ SLAB ON 6″ RIBS 2′−0″ ON CENTERS	55	41	−17	
RIBBED CONCRETE—4″ SLAB ON 6″ RIBS 2′−0″ O.C.	75	46	−17	

CONCRETE ON CELLULAR METAL FLOORS *

BASE CONSTRUCTION	WEIGHT (lb./ft.²)	STC RATING	INR RATING	SECTION (NO SCALE)
2″ CONCRETE ON LIGHT CELLULAR METAL FLOOR	35	38	−22	

CONCRETE ON STEEL JOISTS *

BASE CONSTRUCTION	WEIGHT (lb./ft.²)	STC RATING	INR RATING	SECTION (NO SCALE)
2″ TO 2 1/2″ CONCRETE ON LATH OR LIGHT METAL FORMS	35	37	−24	

* These floors tend to particularly susceptible to horizontal "flanking" unless special precautions are taken at edges and supports. (See page on "Control of Structure-Borne Sound Transmission."

Bernard J. Cywinski; Vincent G. Kling and Associates; Philadelphia, Pennsylvania
Lyle F. Yerges, Consulting Engineer; Downers Grove, Illinois

MODIFICATIONS TO CONCRETE FLOOR "BASE" CONSTRUCTION

MODIFICATION	STC RATING IMPROVEMENT	INR RATING IMPROVEMENT	SECTION — NO SCALE
"FLOATING RAFT": ROUGH FLOORING AND FINISH FLOORING ON SLEEPERS RESTING ON RESILIENT FIBER BOARD OR BLANKET ON RUBBER OR SPRING CLIPS.	+12	+20	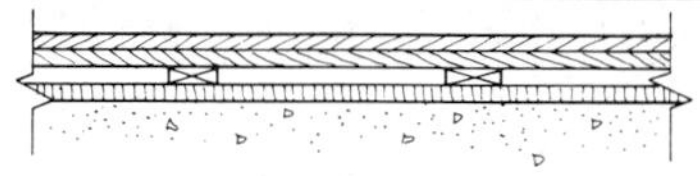
DITTO — BUT SLEEPERS DIRECTLY ON CONCRETE; NO RESILIENT MATERIAL.	+7	+15	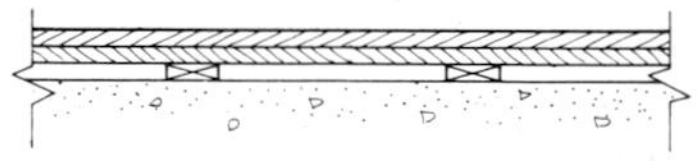
"FLOATING" CONCRETE TOPPING ON 1" THICK GLASS FIBER MAT OR EQUIVALENT.	+10	+15	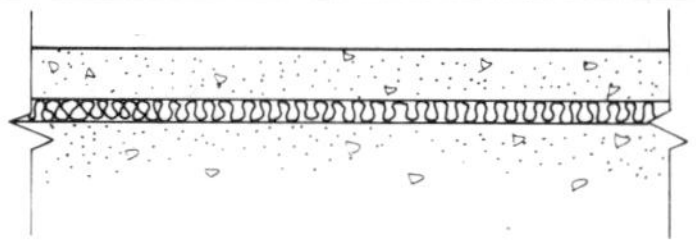
SUSPENDED CEILING ON RESILIENT RUNNERS. RESILIENT CLIPS, OR WIRE HANGERS, SUSTANTIAL AIR SPACE.	+12	+8	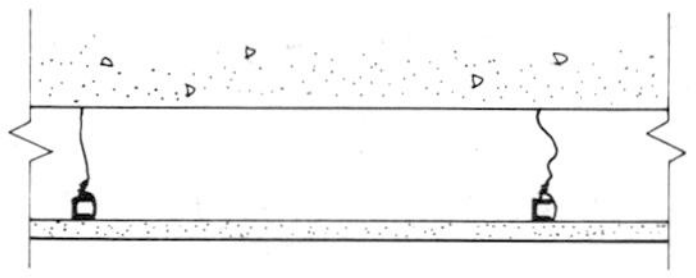
RIGIDLY FURRED CEILING SKIN; VERY SMALL AIR SPACE.	+7	0	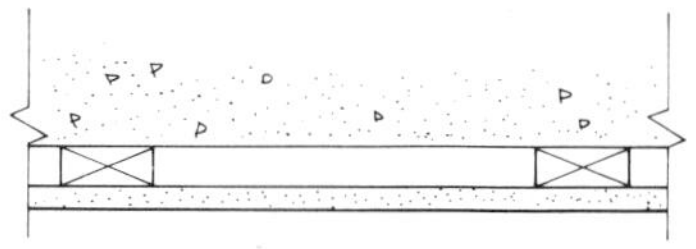
1/2" SANDED PLASTER OR SIMILAR SURFACE SKIN	+2	0	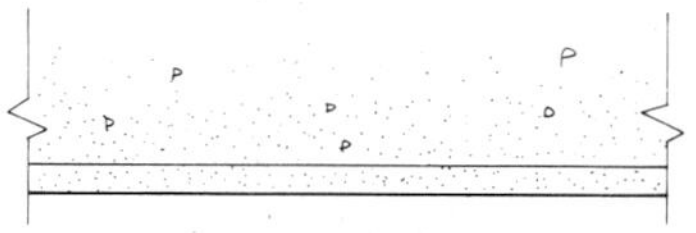
RESILIENT DAMPING BOARD UNDER FLOORING	0	+10	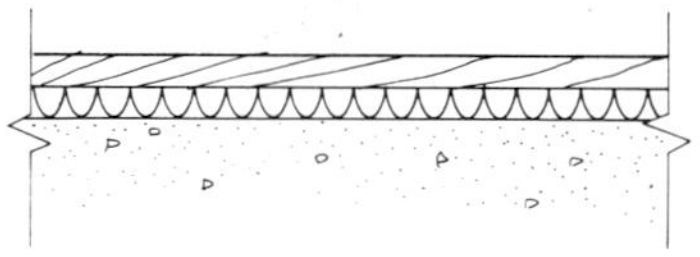
ABSORPTION IN CAVITY: † (ONLY WHEN CEILING RESILIENTLY SUSPENDED; LITTLE OR NO IMPROVEMENT IN RIGID CONSTRUCTION)	+3	+5†	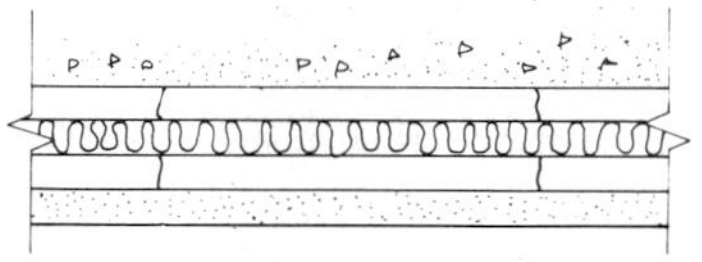
WOOD FINISH FLOORING AT LEAST 1/2" THICK, SET IN MASTIC	0	+7	
VINYL TILE *	0	0	
CARPET AND PAD *	0	+20 TO +30	
3/32" LINOLEUM	0	+3 TO +5	
1/4" CORK TILE	0	+10 TO +15	

* Except on concrete on steel joists or concrete on cellular metal floors, where values are: Vinyl tile — STC improvement = 0, INR improvement = +5, Carpet and Pad — STC improvement = 0, INR improvement = +25 to +40.

FORMULA:

Cumulative improvement of any combination of these modifications is calculated thus: largest number + next largest number + next largest number...etc.

EXAMPLE:

Given a "Base Construction" such as 6" Reinforced Dense Concrete, bare surface, (STC = 46, INR = −17).

		STC	INR
Add: "Floating Raft"	=	+ 12 points	+ 20 points
Add: 3/32" Linoleum	=	+ 0	+ 4
Total		12 points	24 points

Therefore, "Base Construction" increases from STC = 46, INR = −17 to STC = 58, INR = +7.

C. Perry Burdon; Vincent G. Kling and Associates; Philadelphia, Pennsylvania
Lyle F. Yerges, Consulting Engineer; Downers Grove, Illinois

NOTES ON SOUND ABSORBENTS

Sound absorbents convert acoustic energy into heat by internal friction of vibrating air within their porous structure. Their efficiency depends upon their thickness, density, (weight and amount of interconnected porosity) surface (% open), and their mounting method (particularly the air space behind them).

See graphs below.

All building materials and furnishings absorb some energy. Particularly effective are:

1. Carpets (especially on felt pads) unless carpet has heavily starched or latex back coating.

2. Heavy gathered draperies and fabrics.

3. Upholstered furniture.

4. Acoustical absorbents.

Thin paneling materials (glass, plywood $1/4''$ or less, sheet metal) with deep air space behind them are fairly effective absorbers in low frequencies (under 300 cps.)

Sound absorbents are used to:

1. Control noise (unwanted sound) within a space;

2. Control unwanted reflections (echoes and "flutters") from surfaces; and

3. Control reverberation (persistence of sound after source has ceased; high speed, multiple reflections within space) within a space.

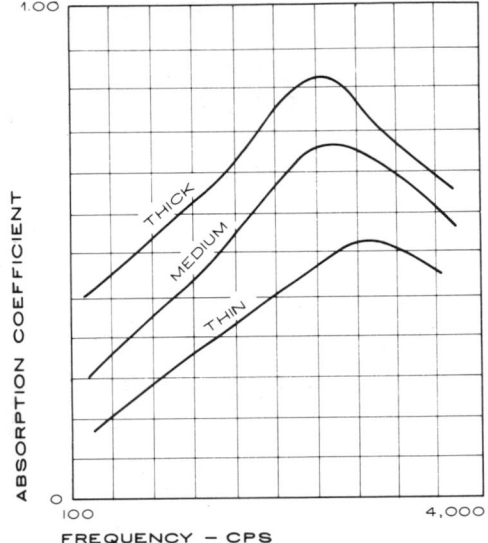

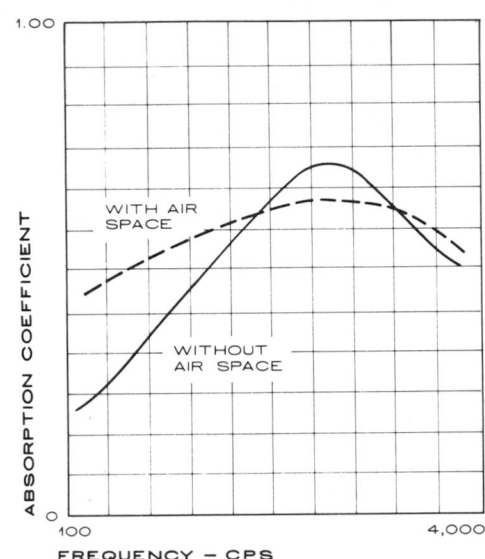

ROOM ACOUSTICS

Room acoustics (within a space) are influenced by:

1. Shape and configuration

2. Room cubic volume and

3. Amount of absorption present.

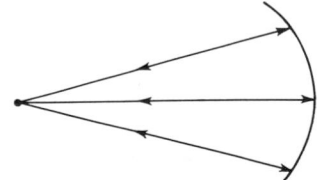

1. FOCUSED BY CONCAVE SURFACES

Avoid such configurations, if possible, or make the radial very short or long. Like an optical lens, such surfaces make "hot spots" which are very objectionable.

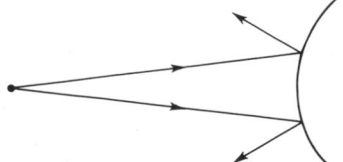

2. DIFFUSED BY CONVEX SURFACES

Where possible, use convex surfaces and deep texture on large surfaces to diffuse sound pleasantly, just as matte finish surfaces diffuse light into soft pleasant reflections. Texture, however, must be very deep—about 6" or so, to diffuse sound; fine sandpaper surfaces have almost no effect in sound diffusion.

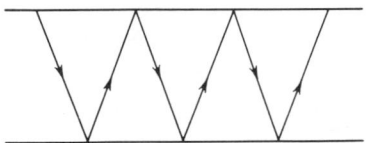

3. REFLECTED BETWEEN PARALLEL SURFACES

If surfaces are about 70' away or more, distinct echoes may be reflected from them. Avoid having direct sound and reflected sound following paths more than 50' different in length. Large parallel surfaces as little as 20' apart can produce rapid, repeated reflections called "flutter".

EFFECTS OF SURFACE FORM ON SOUND ENERGY

Paul Ti - Fu Wang; Vincent G. Kling and Associates; Philadelphia, Pennsylvania

Lyle F. Yerges, Consulting Engineer; Downers Grove, Illinois

ACOUSTICAL DESIGN

For a discussion of architectural acoustical design of spaces, refer to a publication of the Acoustical Materials Association, "The Use of Architectural Acoustical Materials—Theory and Practice", or to textbooks or reference books. Do not assume that adequate acoustical design involves covering the entire ceiling of a space with acoustical tile. In many cases this can be a mistake with serious consequences.

ACOUSTICAL MATERIALS

Acoustical materials are applied plasters, fibrous matrices, tiles, lay-in panels, blankets, boards, or hanging units which are specifically designed to absorb sound. Materials vary in type, appearance, composition, and performance.

For a detailed listing of available materials, their characteristics and performance, refer particularly to the current edition of the annually published Bulletin of the Acoustical Materials Association, "Performance Data of Architectural Acoustical Materials."

SOUND ABSORPTION COEFFICIENT

Sound Absorption Coefficient of a material is the ratio of sound absorbing effectiveness (at a specific frequency) of one square foot of the material to one square foot of a perfectly absorbtive material. It is expressed in a decimal value (such as .70) or in percent. Normally, acoustical absorbents are tested at 125, 250, 500, 1000, 2000 and 4000 cycles.

NOISE REDUCTION COEFFICIENT

An arithmetic average, to nearest .05, of the four middle frequencies (250–2000) is called the Noise Reduction Coefficient. The resulting number is a good means of comparing the performance characteristics of similar products and in calculating anticipated reductions in noise levels (if the noise is predominantly at those frequencies).

SOUND TRANSMISSION LOSS OF SOUND ABSORBENTS

Most sound abosrbents are lightweight and porous. As a result, they usually have low TL values. Like blotters, they absorb but they don't prevent transmission through them. Unless partitions go to the structural slab above, only the TL up through the ceiling, over the top of the partition and down through the ceiling on the other side can be considered.

SOUND ATTENUATION FACTORS

The Acoustical Materials Association, in the above Bulletin, publishes Sound Attenuation Factors (roughly, the TL via the path through the ceiling, over the top of the partition) for the more commonly used acoustical materials. The ceiling STC should equal the STC—contour for the partition between the spaces under consideration.

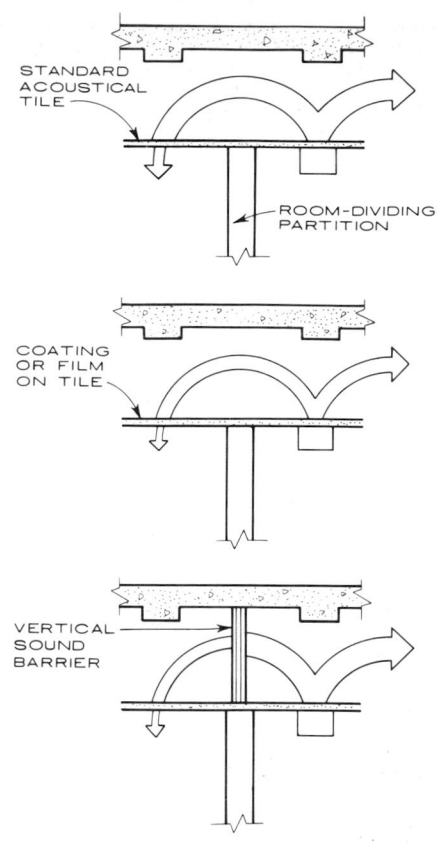

STANDARD ACOUSTICAL TILE

ROOM-DIVIDING PARTITION

COATING OR FILM ON TILE

VERTICAL SOUND BARRIER

SOUND TRANSMISSION THROUGH CEILINGS

CONSIDERATIONS FOR THE ACOUSTICAL DESIGN OF SPACES

1. Don't assume that acoustical design means covering the entire ceiling with acoustical tile.

2. Don't use "pure" geometric shapes. Concave, circular, or elliptical surfaces, cubical rooms, etc. require special consideration.

3. Don't surround the acoustical "source" with absorbent materials.

4. Don't penetrate or pierce walls, floors, or enclosing partitions unless absolutely necessary.

5. Don't ignore the mechanical and electrical systems; they not only generate noise, but they provide "leaks" and paths for sound transmission.

6. Don't assume that sound control is some form of applied "treatment" or hardware accessory.

7. Don't choose equipment based upon initial cost alone, assuming that problems which may arise can be cheaply corrected later with acoustical materials.

1. Do use absorptive materials on surfaces which might otherwise cause objectionable reflections.

2. Do use diffuse, convex surfaces designed to distribute sound to listening areas.

3. Do keep the "sending" or source end of a room hard and reflective.

4. Do maintain the integrity of walls and enclosing surfaces; seal all holes and openings.

5. Do consider the mechanical and electrical equipment as an integral part of the building's acoustical design.

6. Do use qualified professional advice on any space with acoustically critical requirements.

7. Do avoid noise problems by choosing quiet equipment, acoustically adequate constructions; choose all materials for their acoustical properties as well as for their other characteristics.

Daniel S. Briggs; Vincent G. Kling and Associates; Philadelphia, Pennsylvania
Lyle F. Yerges, Consulting Engineer; Downers Grove, Illinois

USE OF ABSORPTION IN COMMON OCCUPANCIES[1]

ROOM OCCUPANCY	CEILING[2] FULL	PARTIAL	NRC RANGE .45 — .65	.65 — .75	OVER .75	WALL TREATMENT[3]	SPECIAL[4]
PRIVATE OFFICES	X			X			
GENERAL OFFICE SPACES	X			X			
COMPUTER AND ACCOUNTING ROOMS	X				X	X	
CLASSROOMS, ELEMENTARY	X			X			
CLASSROOMS, SECONDARY AND COLLEGE		X		X		X	
LANGUAGE LABORATORIES	X			X		X	X
LIBRARIES	X			X			
LABORATORIES	X			X			
MEETING AND CONFERENCE ROOMS	X < 700 sq. ft.	X > 700 sq. ft.		X		X	
GYMNASIUMS, ARENAS, AND RECREATIONAL SPACES	X			X			X
SCHOOL AND INDUSTRIAL SHOPS, FACTORIES, ETC.	X				X	X	X
STORES AND COMMERCIAL SHOPS	X			X			
KITCHENS	X				X		
RESTAURANTS	X			X		X	
CORRIDORS	X			X		X	
LOBBIES	X			X			
RESIDENTIAL LIVING ROOMS	X	X					
RESIDENTIAL BEDROOMS	X	X					
HOSPITAL ROOMS	X			X			
CHURCHES							X
AUDITORIUMS							X
CONCERT HALLS							X
THEATERS							X
LECTURE ROOMS							X
MECHANICAL EQUIPMENT ROOMS							X
RADIO, RECORDING, AND T.V. STUDIOS							X

NOTES:

1. This table lists conservative "rule—of—thumb" recommendations for the use of absorption in common occupancies. For further information, refer to publications of the Acoustical Materials Association, various books and publications, or to a qualified acoustical consultant.

2. Or an equivalent amount of distributed absorption provided by carpets, draperies, furnishings, etc.

3. Sidewall treatment advisable in addition to ceiling treatment to reduce reflections, flutter, or echo, to further reduce noise, or to control reverberation.

4. Highly complex applications, usually requiring services of an acoustical consultant. May require special forms or types of absorption, or, in some instances, none at all.

Giovanni Petri, AIA; Vincent G. Kling and Associates; Philadelphia, Pennsylvania

Lyle F. Yerges, Consulting Engineer; Downers Grove, Illinois

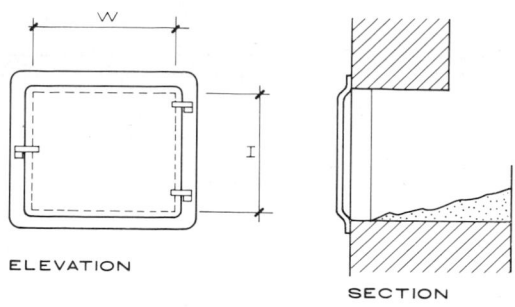

ELEVATION

SECTION

CLEANOUT OR ASHPIT DOORS

OPENING SIZES

W		H	W		H
4"	x	8"	12"	x	10"
5"	x	8"	12"	x	12"
8"	x	8"	12"	x	18"
8"	x	10"	18"	x	24"
10"	x	10"	24"	x	24"
12"	x	8"			

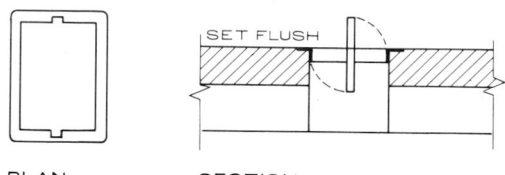

SET FLUSH

PLAN   **SECTION**

USUAL OPENING SIZES

4"	x	8"	5"	x	8"
4 1/2"	x	9"	7"	x	10"
5"	x	7"			

ASH DUMPS, TILTING TYPE

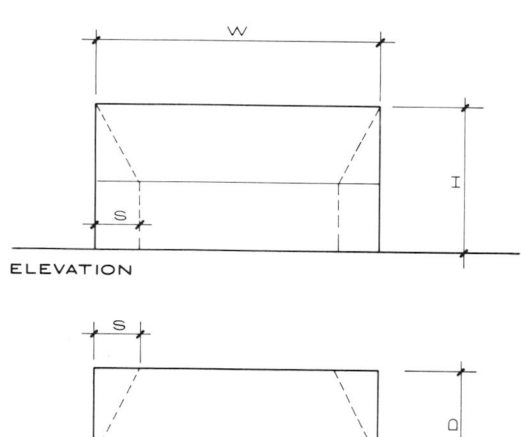

ELEVATION

PLAN

FIREPLACE OPENING SIZES

W	H	D	S
2'-0"	1'-6" to 1'-9"	1'-4" to 1'-6"	
2'-6"	1'-9" to 1'-10 1/2"	1'-6" to 1'-7"	
2'-8"	1'-9" to 2'-0"	1'-6" to 1'-8"	
2'-10"	2'-0"	1'-8"	
3'-0"	2'-0"	1'-8"	6 1/2"
3'-4"	2'-0"	1'-8"	6 1/2"
3'-6"	2'-0"	1'-8"	6"
4'-0"	2'-1 1/2"	1'-9"	6"
4'-6"	2'-3" to 2'-6"	1'-10" to 2'-0"	9"
5'-0"	2'-6" to 2'-9"	2'-0" to 2'-2"	9"
6'-0"	2'-9" to 3'-0"	2'-2" to 2'-4"	9"

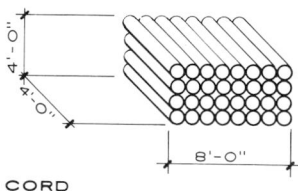

CORD
(ONE CORD = 128 CU FT)

USUAL LOG LENGTHS

1'-4", 2'-0", 2'-6" and 4'-0"

TO SELECT LOGS:

Allow 3" minimum clearance between log and each side of fireplace. Smaller logs thus used with splay.

LOGS

NOTE:

Larger openings than those shown may have hoods to lower openings or hobs to raise inner hearth.

Robert B. Martin, AIA; Lincoln City, Oregon

SCALE: 3/4" = 1'-0"

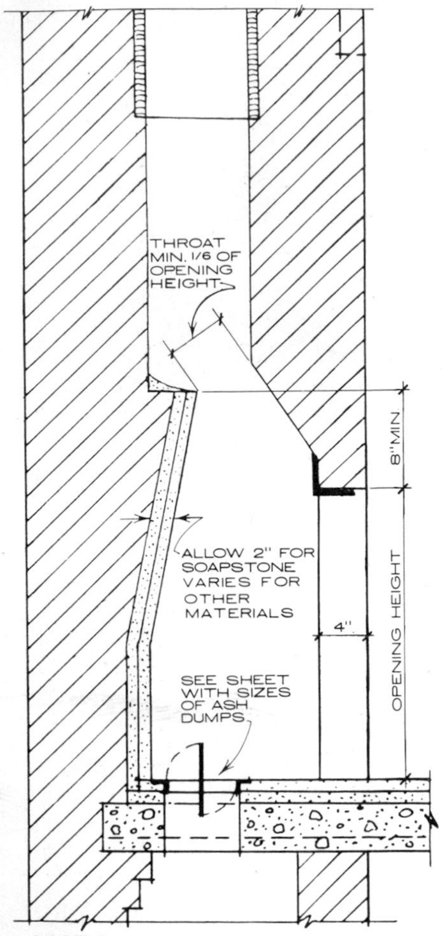

THROAT MIN. 1/6 OF OPENING HEIGHT

ALLOW 2" FOR SOAPSTONE VARIES FOR OTHER MATERIALS

SEE SHEET WITH SIZES OF ASH DUMPS

8" MIN

4"

OPENING HEIGHT

SECTION
FIREPLACE WITHOUT DAMPER

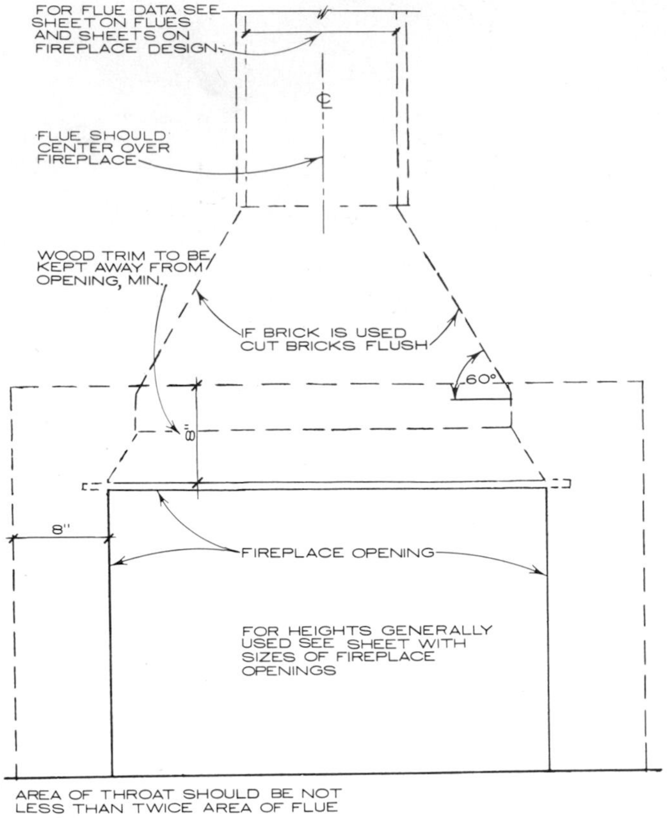

FOR FLUE DATA SEE SHEET ON FLUES AND SHEETS ON FIREPLACE DESIGN

FLUE SHOULD CENTER OVER FIREPLACE

WOOD TRIM TO BE KEPT AWAY FROM OPENING, MIN.

IF BRICK IS USED CUT BRICKS FLUSH

60°

8"

8"

FIREPLACE OPENING

FOR HEIGHTS GENERALLY USED SEE SHEET WITH SIZES OF FIREPLACE OPENINGS

AREA OF THROAT SHOULD BE NOT LESS THAN TWICE AREA OF FLUE

ELEVATION

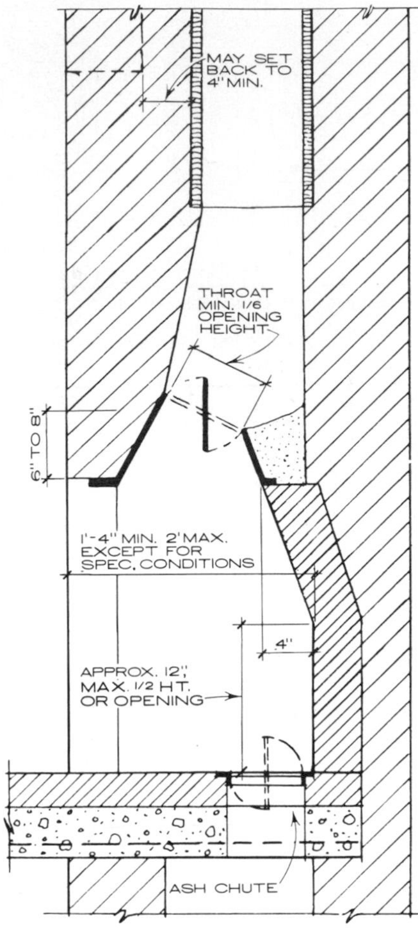

MAY SET BACK TO 4" MIN.

THROAT MIN. 1/6 OPENING HEIGHT

6" TO 8"

1'-4" MIN. 2' MAX. EXCEPT FOR SPEC. CONDITIONS

APPROX. 12" MAX. 1/2 HT. OR OPENING

4"

ASH CHUTE

SECTION
FIREPLACE WITH DAMPER

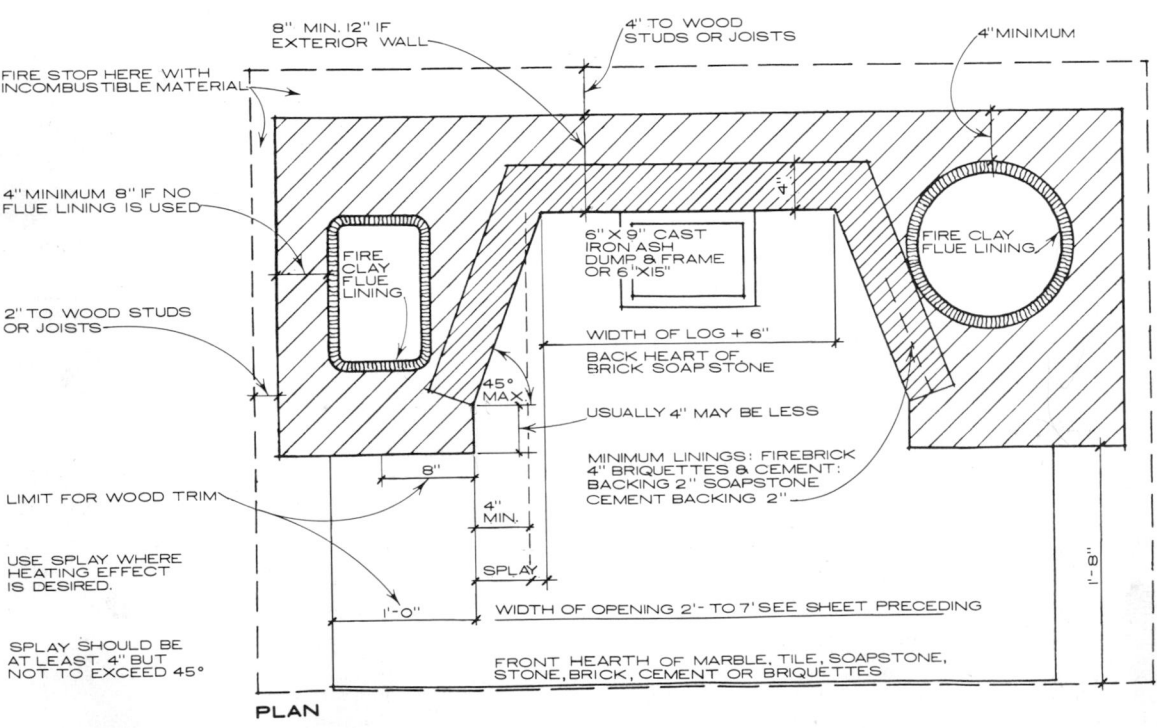

8" MIN. 12" IF EXTERIOR WALL

4" TO WOOD STUDS OR JOISTS

4" MINIMUM

FIRE STOP HERE WITH INCOMBUSTIBLE MATERIAL

4" MINIMUM 8" IF NO FLUE LINING IS USED

FIRE CLAY FLUE LINING

2" TO WOOD STUDS OR JOISTS

4"

6" X 9" CAST IRON ASH DUMP & FRAME OR 6" X 15"

FIRE CLAY FLUE LINING

45° MAX

WIDTH OF LOG + 6"

BACK HEART OF BRICK SOAP STONE

USUALLY 4" MAY BE LESS

MINIMUM LININGS: FIREBRICK 4" BRIQUETTES & CEMENT: BACKING 2" SOAPSTONE CEMENT BACKING 2"

LIMIT FOR WOOD TRIM

USE SPLAY WHERE HEATING EFFECT IS DESIRED.

SPLAY SHOULD BE AT LEAST 4" BUT NOT TO EXCEED 45°

8"

4" MIN.

SPLAY

1'-0"

WIDTH OF OPENING 2'- TO 7' SEE SHEET PRECEDING

1'-8"

FRONT HEARTH OF MARBLE. TILE, SOAPSTONE, STONE, BRICK, CEMENT OR BRIQUETTES

PLAN

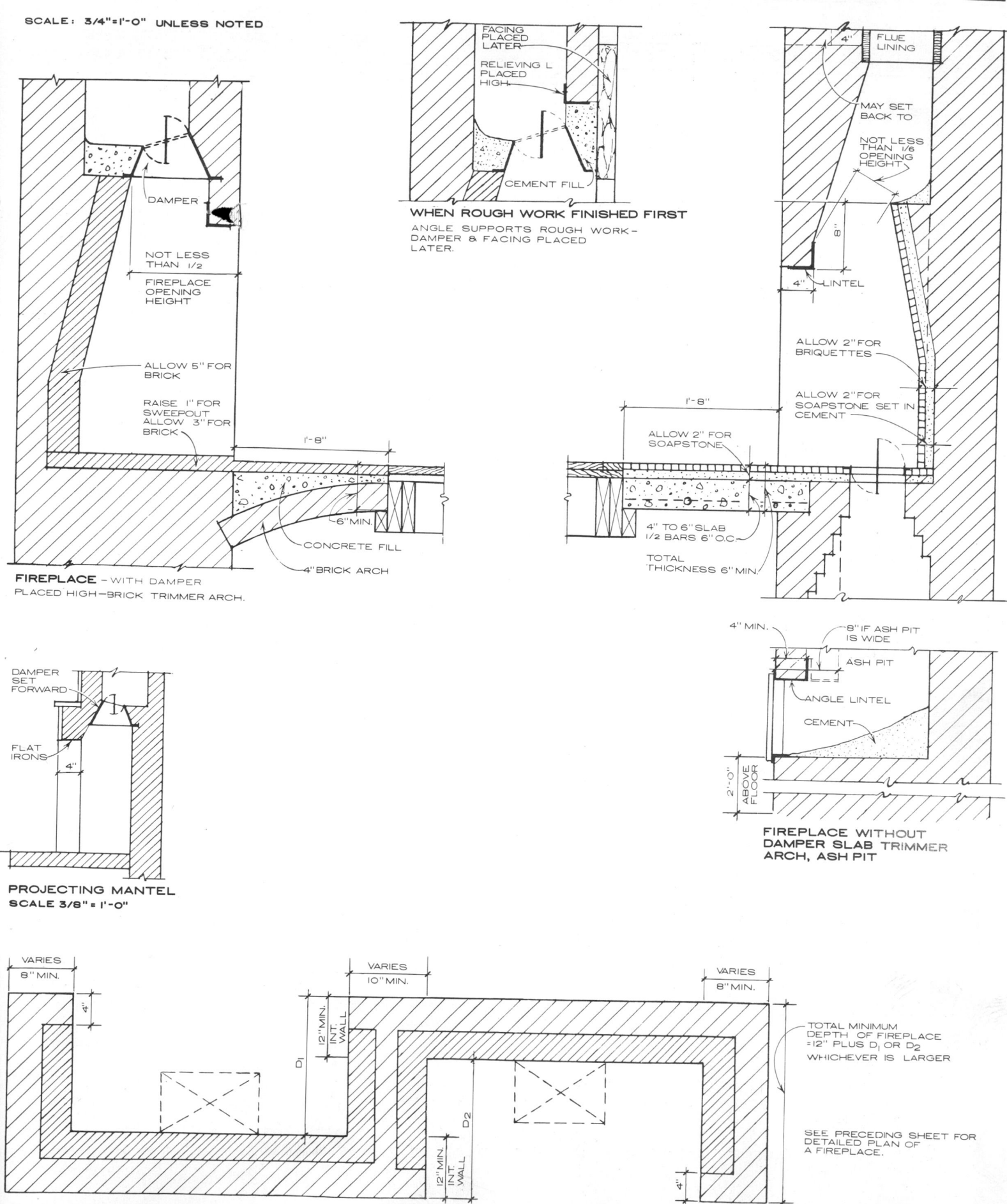

SCALE: 3/4"=1'-0" UNLESS NOTED

FACING PLACED LATER

RELIEVING L PLACED HIGH

4"

CEMENT FILL

WHEN ROUGH WORK FINISHED FIRST

ANGLE SUPPORTS ROUGH WORK —
DAMPER & FACING PLACED
LATER.

4"   FLUE LINING

MAY SET BACK TO

NOT LESS THAN 1/6 OPENING HEIGHT

8"

4"   LINTEL

ALLOW 2" FOR BRIQUETTES

ALLOW 2" FOR SOAPSTONE SET IN CEMENT

DAMPER

NOT LESS THAN 1/2

FIREPLACE OPENING HEIGHT

ALLOW 5" FOR BRICK

RAISE 1" FOR SWEEPOUT ALLOW 3" FOR BRICK

1'-8"

6" MIN.

CONCRETE FILL

4" BRICK ARCH

FIREPLACE – WITH DAMPER
PLACED HIGH—BRICK TRIMMER ARCH.

1'-8"

ALLOW 2" FOR SOAPSTONE

4" TO 6" SLAB 1/2 BARS 6" O.C.

TOTAL THICKNESS 6" MIN.

DAMPER SET FORWARD

FLAT IRONS

4"

PROJECTING MANTEL
SCALE 3/8" = 1'-0"

4" MIN.

8" IF ASH PIT IS WIDE

ASH PIT

ANGLE LINTEL

CEMENT

2'-0" ABOVE FLOOR

**FIREPLACE WITHOUT
DAMPER SLAB TRIMMER
ARCH, ASH PIT**

VARIES 8" MIN.

4"

VARIES 10" MIN.

12" MIN. INT. WALL

D_1

VARIES 8" MIN.

12" MIN. INT. WALL

D_2

TOTAL MINIMUM DEPTH OF FIREPLACE =12" PLUS D_1 OR D_2 WHICHEVER IS LARGER

SEE PRECEDING SHEET FOR DETAILED PLAN OF A FIREPLACE.

4"

SIDE-BY-SIDE FIREPLACES

DAMPER SIZES / FINISHED FIREPLACE OPENING / ROUGH MASONRY

| CONTROL | | THROAT | | | OVERALL | | | FINISHED FIREPLACE OPENING | | | | | | THROAT | WTH. | DEPTH | SMOKE CHAMB. | FLUE LINING SIZES | | | RND. | MODULAR |
| POKER NO. | ROTARY NO. | BOT | | | | | | WTH. | HGT. | DEPTH | BACK | VERT. BACK | SLOPE BACK | | | | | RECTANGULAR | | | | |
		T	A	O	L	B	W	A	B	C	D	E	F	G	H	I	J	K	L	M	K	L M
224	324	24	17 5/16	4 1/4	28 1/2	21	9 7/8	24	24	16	11	14	15	8 3/4	32	20	19	11 3/4	8 1/2 × 8 1/2	8	10	8 × 12
230	330	30	23 5/16	4 1/4	34 1/2	27	9 7/8	26	24	16	13	14	15	8 3/4	34	20	21	12 3/4	8 1/2 × 8 1/2	8	11	8 × 12
								28	24	16	15	14	15	8 3/4	36	20	21	11 1/2	8 1/2 × 13	10	12	8 × 12
								30	29	16	17	14	18	8 3/4	38	20	24	12 1/2	8 1/2 × 13	10	13	12 × 12
233	333	33"	26 5/16	4 1/4	37 1/2	30	9 7/8	32	29	16	19	14	21	8 3/4	40	20	24	13 1/2	8 1/2 × 13	10	14	12 × 12
								36	29	16	23	14	21	8 3/4	44	20	27	15 1/2	13 × 13	12	16	12 × 12
236	336	36	29 5/16	4 1/4	40 1/2	33	9 7/8	40	29	16	27	14	21	8 3/4	48	20	29	17 1/2	13 × 13	12	17	16 × 16
242	342	42	35 5/16	4 1/4	46 1/2	39	9 7/8	42	32	16	29	14	23	8 3/4	50	20	32	18 1/2	13 × 13	12	20	16 × 16
248	348	48	41 5/16	4 1/4	52 1/2	45	9 7/8	48	32	18	33	14	23	13	56	22	37	21 1/2	13 × 13	15	20	16 × 20
254	354	54	42 1/2	7	58 1/2	46	14 5/8	54	37	20	37	16	27	13	68	24	45	25	13 × 18	15	26	16 × 20
260	360	60	49 1/2	7	64 1/2	53	14 5/8	60	37	22	42	16	27	13	72	27	45	27	13 × 18	18	26	16 × 20
								60	40	22	42	16	29	13	72	27	45	27	18 × 18	18	26	20 × 20
272	372	72	60 1/2	7	76 1/2	64	14 5/8	72	40	22	54	16	29	13	84	27	56	33	18 × 18	18	32	20 × 20
*284	*384	84	73 1/2	7	88 1/2	77	14 5/8	84	40	24	64	20	26	13	96	29	67	36	20 × 20	20	36	20 × 20
*296	*396	96	85 3/4	7	100 1/2	89	14 5/8	96	40	24	76	20	26	13	108	29	75	42	24 × 24	22	42	20 × 20

* TWO VALVE PLATES

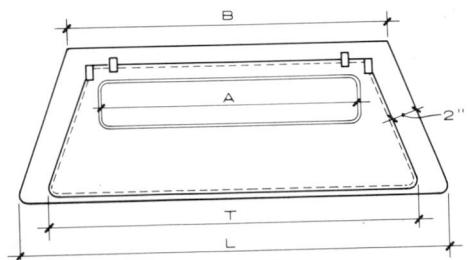

PLAN OF DAMPER

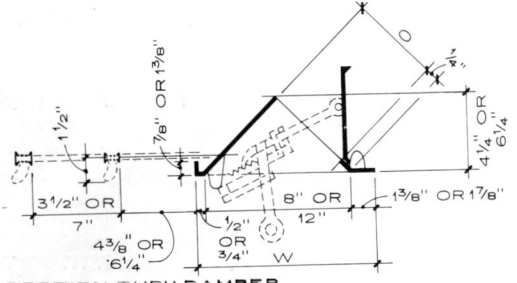

SECTION THRU DAMPER

Where two dimensions are shown the smaller applies to Dampers 248—348 and under, the larger to 254—354 and over. Both operating devices are shown.

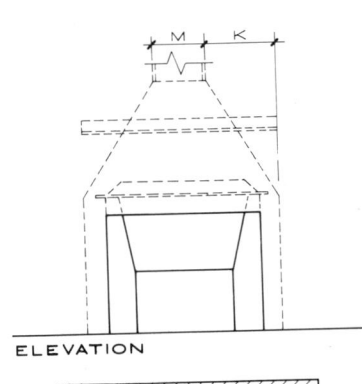

ELEVATION

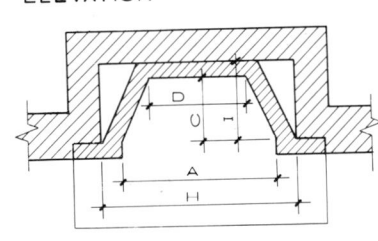

PLAN

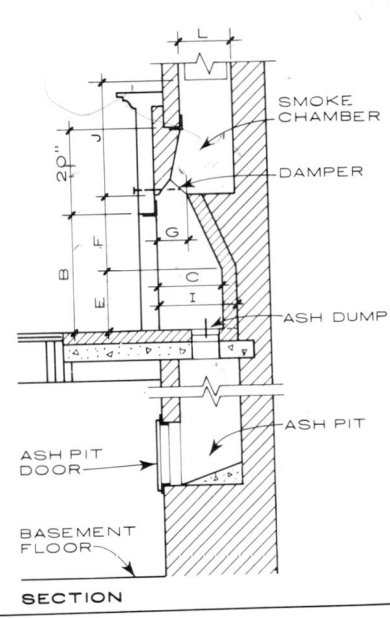

SECTION

DONLEY THROAT AND DAMPER

STEEL DAMPERS

DAMPER NO.	WIDTH OF FIREPLACE	A	B	C	D	E
24 A 26	24" TO 26"	28 1/4	26 3/4	13	24	9 1/2
28 A 30	27" TO 30"	32 1/4	30 3/4	13	28	9 1/2
32 A 34	31" TO 34"	36 1/4	34 3/4	13	32	9 1/2
36 A 38	35" TO 38"	40 1/4	38 3/4	13	36	9 1/2
40 A 42	39" TO 42"	44 1/4	42 3/4	13	40	9 1/2
44 A 46	43" TO 46"	48 1/4	46 3/4	13	44	9 1/2
48 A 50	47" TO 50"	52 1/4	50 3/4	13	48	9 1/2
52 A 54	51" TO 54"	56 1/4	54 3/4	13	52	9 1/2
58 A 60	57" TO 60"	62 1/2	60 3/4	13	58	9 1/2

CAST IRON DAMPERS

DAMPER NO.	WIDTH OF FIREPLACE	A	B	C	D	E
M 24	24" TO 26"	28	21	13 1/2	24	10
M 30	27" TO 30"	34	26 3/4	13 1/2	30	10
M 33	31" TO 34"	37	29 3/4	13 1/2	33	10
M 36	35" TO 38"	40	32 3/4	13 1/2	36	10
M 42	39" TO 42"	46	38 3/4	13 1/2	48	10
M 48	43" TO 46"	52	44 3/4	13 1/2	48	10
M 54	47" TO 50"	57 1/2	50 1/2	13 1/2	54	10
M 60	51" TO 54"	64	56 1/2	14 1/2	60	11 1/2
M 72	57" TO 60"	76	68	14 1/2	72	11 1/2

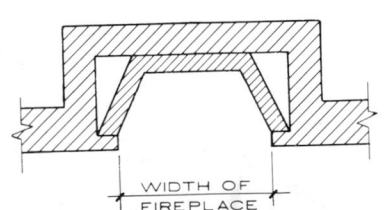

PLAN

All dampers are available with a break proof steel valve operated by poker-type or rotary-face control.

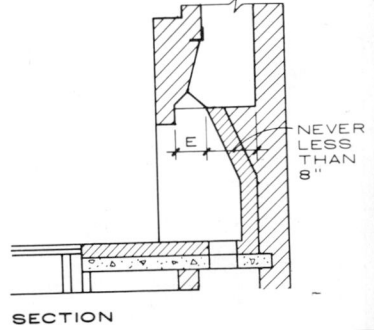

SECTION

NEVER LESS THAN 8"

MAJESTIC THROATS AND DAMPERS

Robert B. Martin, AIA; Lincoln City, Oregon

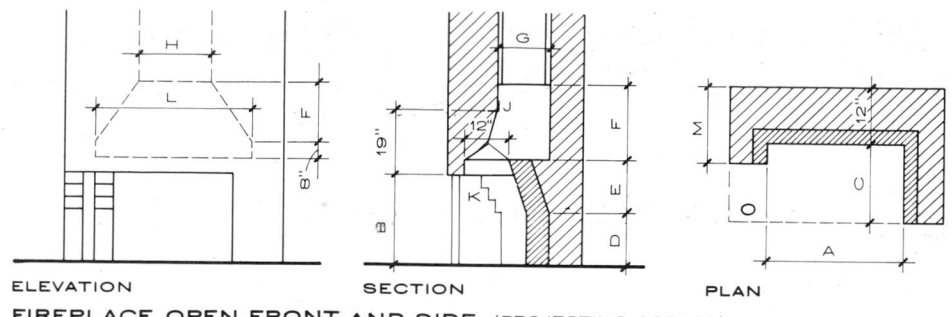

NOTE:

Back flange of damper must be fully supported on masonry to protect from heat.
Do not build in solidly at ends; allow for expansion.
Facing allowed for 4''; this will vary with material used.
All dampers on this page: Donley Bros. Co.

LINTEL ANGLE SIZE FOR COLUMN "J" BELOW:

A: 3'' x 3'' x ³/₁₆''
B: 3 ½'' x 3'' x ¼''

ELEVATION   SECTION   PLAN

FIREPLACE OPEN FRONT AND SIDE (PROJECTING CORNER)

DAMPER NO.	A	B	C	D	E	F	OLD FLUE SIZE		NEW FLUE SIZE		L	M	ANGLE J (2 REQD)	PLATE LINTEL K	CORNER POST HEIGHT
							G	H	G	H					
528	28	26½	16	14	20	29⅓	13	13	12	12	36	16	A-36	11 X 16	26½
532	32	26½	16	14	20	32	13	13	12	16	40	16	A-42	11 X 16	26½
536	36	26½	16	14	20	35	13	13	12	16	44	16	A-48	11 X 16	26½
540	40	29	16	14	20	35	13	18	16	16	48	16	B-54	11 X 16	29
548	48	29	20	14	24	43	13	18	16	16	56	20	B-60	11 X 16	29
554	54	29	20	14	23	45	13	18	16	16	62	20	B-72	11 X 16	29
560	60	29	20	14	23	51	13	18	16	20	68	20	B-78	11 X 16	29

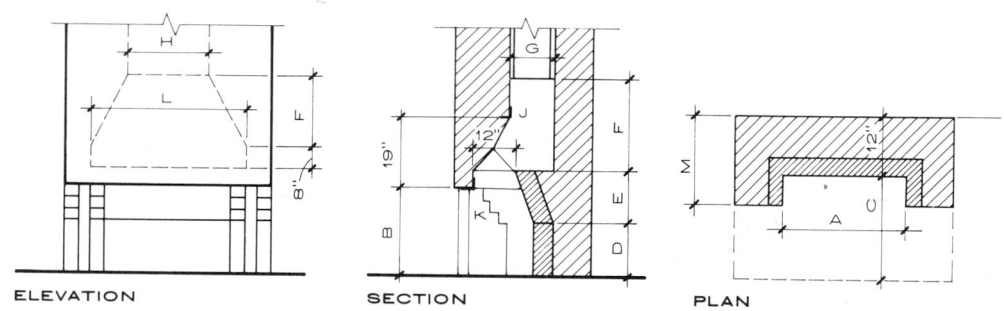

NOTE:

Support back flange of damper on masonry. Do not build solidly at ends

LINTEL ANGLE SIZE FOR COLUMN "J" BELOW:

A: 3'' x 3'' x ³/₁₆''
B: 3 ½'' x 3'' x ¼''

ELEVATION   SECTION   PLAN

FIREPLACE OPEN THREE SIDES: (TWO SHORT, ONE LONG)

DAMPER NO.	A	B	C	D	E	F	OLD FLUE SIZE		NEW FLUE SIZE		L	M	ANGLE J (2 REQD.)	PL. LINTEL K (2 REQD.)	CORNER POST HT. (2 REQD.)
							G	H	G	H					
528	28	26½	20	14	18	27	13	13	12	16	36	20	A-42	11 X 16	26½
532	32	26½	20	14	18	32	13	13	16	16	40	20	A-48	11 X 16	26½
536	36	26½	20	14	18	32	13	18	16	16	44	20	A-48	11 X 16	26½
540	40	29	20	14	21	35	13	18	16	16	48	20	B-54	11 X 16	29
548	48	29	20	14	21	40	13	18	16	20	56	20	B-60	11 X 16	29
554	54	29	20	14	23	45	18	18	16	20	62	20	B-72	11 X 16	29
560	60	29	20	14	23	51	18	18	16	20	68	20	B-78	11 X 16	29

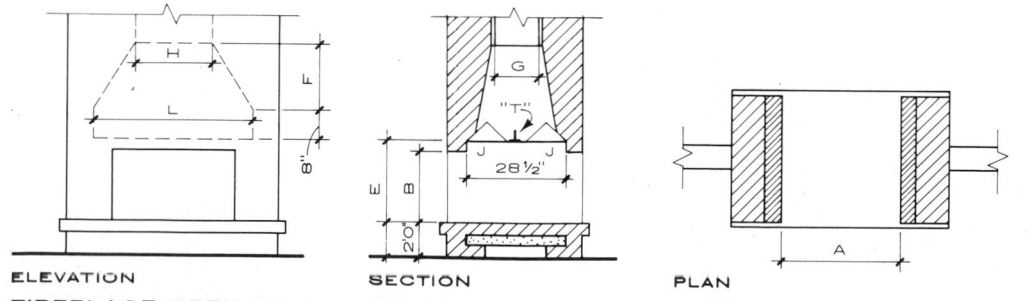

NOTE:

Tee and damper not to be built in solidly at ends.

LINTEL ANGLE SIZE FOR COLUMN "J" BELOW:

A: 3'' x 3'' x ³/₁₆''
B: 3 ½'' x 3'' x ¼''

ELEVATION   SECTION   PLAN

FIREPLACE OPEN FRONT AND BACK (FIREPLACE OPEN THREE SIDES—ONE SHORT, TWO LONG—SIMILAR TO THIS)

DAMPER NO. (2 REQUIRED)	A	B	E	F	OLD FLUE SIZE		NEW FLUE SIZE		ANGLE J (2 REQUIRED)	L	TEE LENGTH
					G	H	G	H			
528	28	24	35	19	13	13	12	16	A-36	36	35
532	32	29	35	21	13	18	16	16	A-40	40	39
536	36	29	35	21	13	18	16	20	A-42	44	43
540	40	29	35	35	18	18	16	20	A-48	48	47
548	48	32	37	37	18	18	20	20	B-54	56	55

Robert B. Martin, AIA; Lincoln City, Oregon

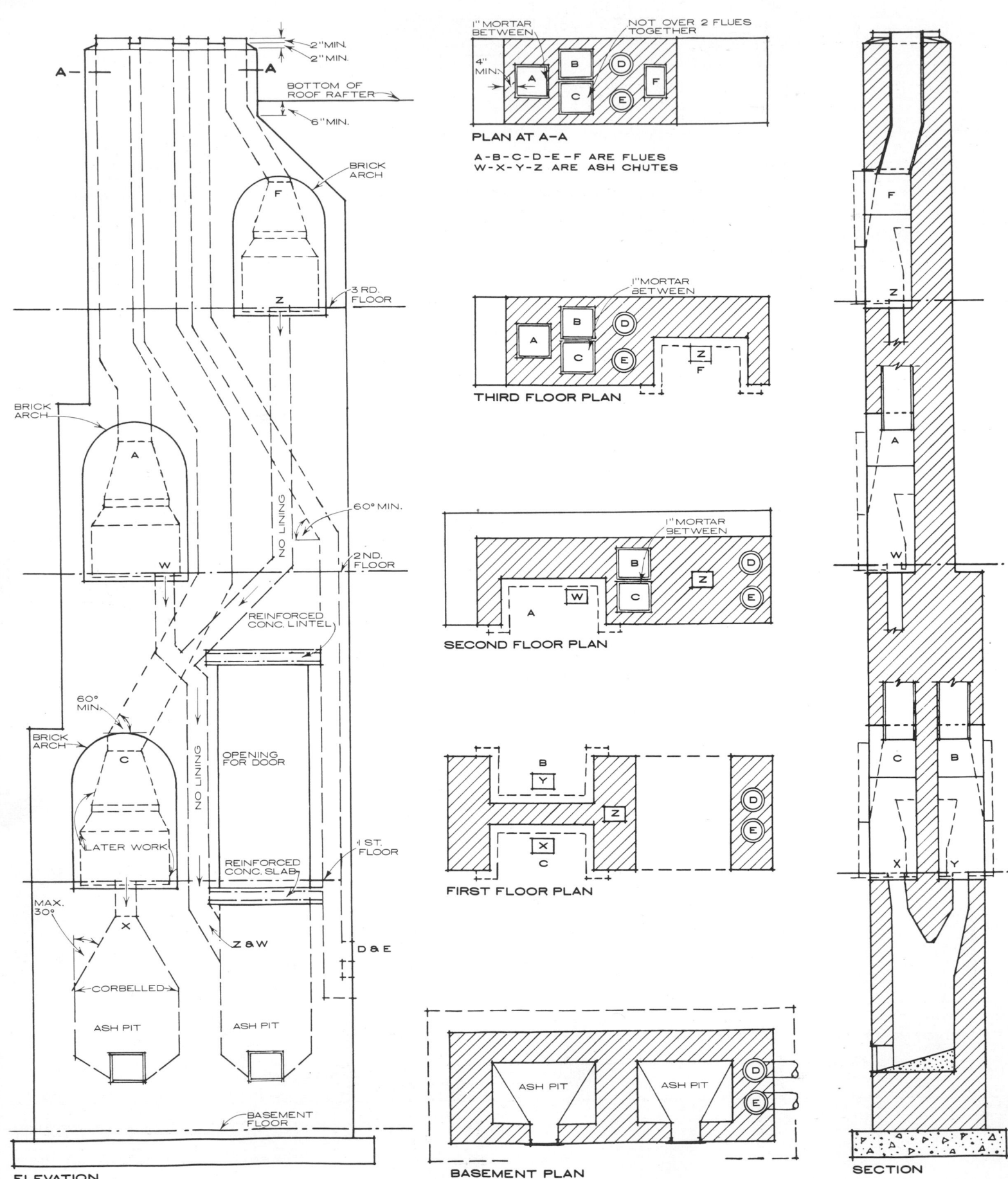

CHIMNEY CONSTRUCTION INDICATING FIREPLACES TO BE BUILT LATER
SCALE: ¼" = 1'-0"

2"MIN.
2"MIN.

BOTTOM OF
ROOF RAFTER

6"MIN.

BRICK
ARCH

F

3 RD.
FLOOR

Z

BRICK
ARCH

A

60° MIN.

W

2ND.
FLOOR

REINFORCED
CONC. LINTEL

NO LINING

60°
MIN.

BRICK
ARCH

C

OPENING
FOR DOOR

LATER WORK

1 ST.
FLOOR

NO LINING

REINFORCED
CONC. SLAB

MAX.
30°

X

Z & W

D & E

CORBELLED

ASH PIT

ASH PIT

BASEMENT
FLOOR

ELEVATION

1" MORTAR
BETWEEN

NOT OVER 2 FLUES
TOGETHER

4"
MIN.

A

B

D

F

C

E

PLAN AT A–A

A – B – C – D – E – F ARE FLUES
W – X – Y – Z ARE ASH CHUTES

1"MORTAR
BETWEEN

A

B

D

C

E

Z

F

THIRD FLOOR PLAN

1"MORTAR
BETWEEN

B

D

A

W

C

Z

E

SECOND FLOOR PLAN

B

Y

Z

D

X

E

C

FIRST FLOOR PLAN

ASH PIT

ASH PIT

D

E

BASEMENT PLAN

F

Z

A

W

C

B

X

Y

SECTION

SCALE : 1/4"=1'-0"

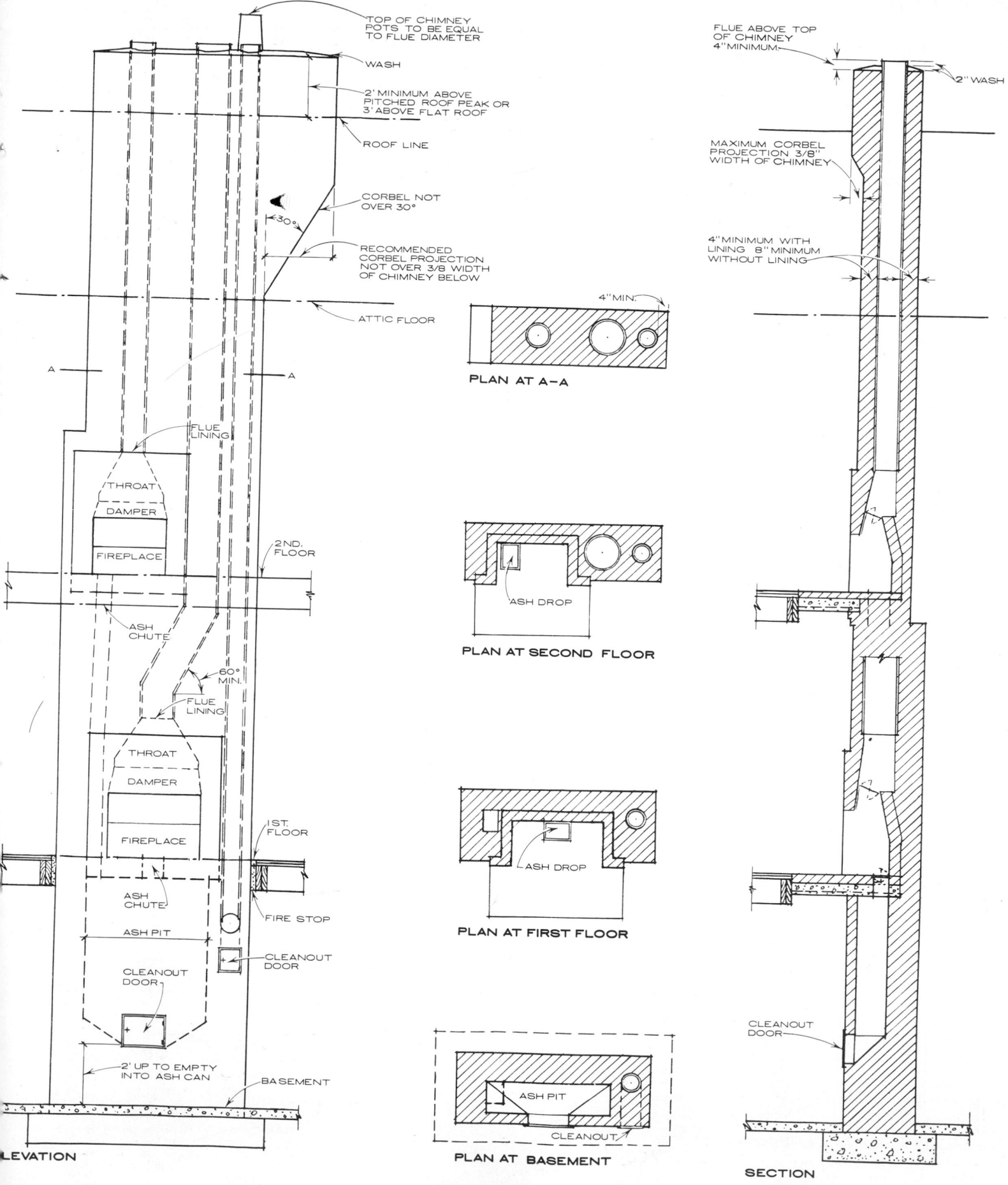

TOP OF CHIMNEY POTS TO BE EQUAL TO FLUE DIAMETER

WASH

2' MINIMUM ABOVE PITCHED ROOF PEAK OR 3' ABOVE FLAT ROOF

ROOF LINE

CORBEL NOT OVER 30°

30°

RECOMMENDED CORBEL PROJECTION NOT OVER 3/8 WIDTH OF CHIMNEY BELOW

ATTIC FLOOR

A

A

FLUE LINING

THROAT

DAMPER

FIREPLACE

2ND. FLOOR

ASH CHUTE

60° MIN.

FLUE LINING

THROAT

DAMPER

FIREPLACE

1ST. FLOOR

ASH CHUTE

FIRE STOP

ASH PIT

CLEANOUT DOOR

CLEANOUT DOOR

2' UP TO EMPTY INTO ASH CAN

BASEMENT

ELEVATION

4" MIN.

PLAN AT A-A

ASH DROP

PLAN AT SECOND FLOOR

ASH DROP

PLAN AT FIRST FLOOR

ASH PIT

CLEANOUT

PLAN AT BASEMENT

FLUE ABOVE TOP OF CHIMNEY 4" MINIMUM

2" WASH

MAXIMUM CORBEL PROJECTION 3/8" WIDTH OF CHIMNEY

4" MINIMUM WITH LINING 8" MINIMUM WITHOUT LINING

CLEANOUT DOOR

SECTION

CHIMNEYS & FIREPLACES SHOWING FRAMING & FIRESTOPPING IN WOOD CONSTRUCTION
SCALE 3/8"= 1'-0"

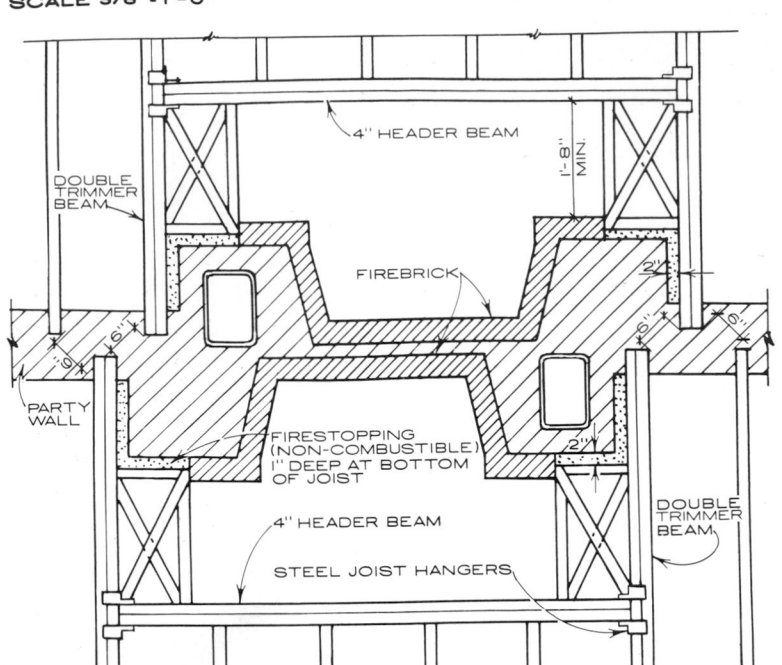

FIREPLACES BACK TO BACK IN PARTY WALL
SHOWING SPACING BETWEEN JOISTS

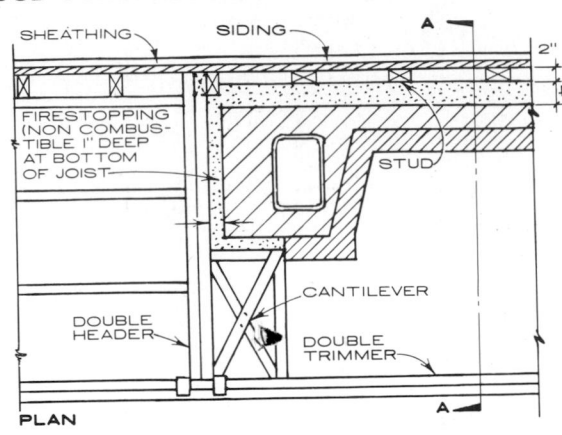

PLAN

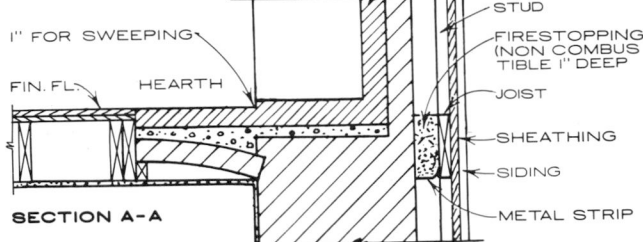

SECTION A-A

FIREPLACE IN EXTERIOR FRAME
WALL - BRICKWORK CONCEALED

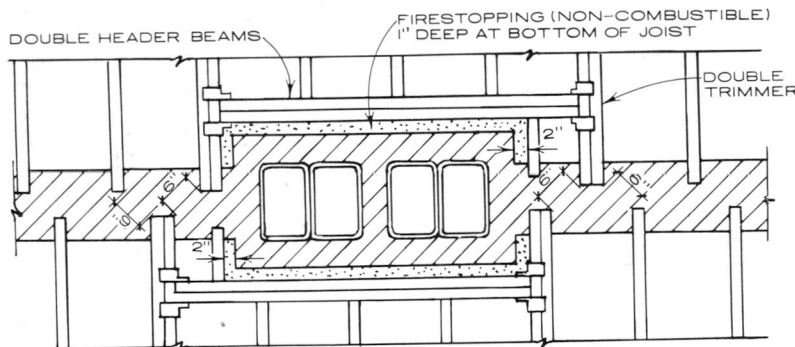

CHIMNEY IN PARTY WALL SHOWING SPACING
BETWEEN JOISTS AND FIRESTOPPING

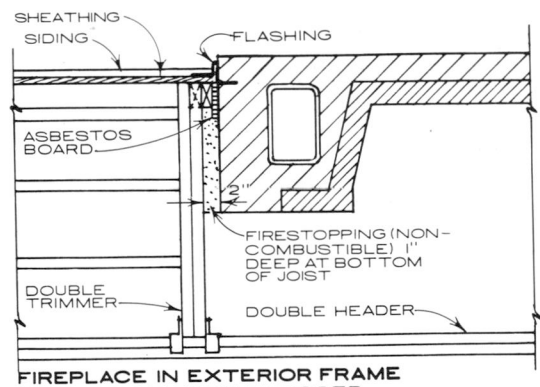

FIREPLACE IN EXTERIOR FRAME
WALL-BRICKWORK EXPOSED

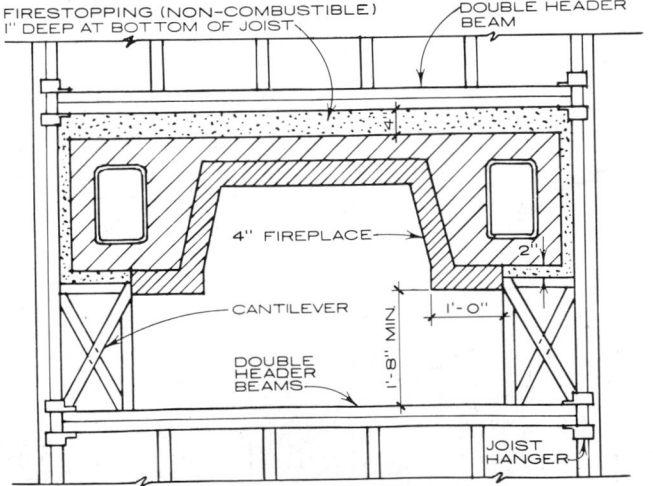

FIREPLACE FRAMING & FIRESTOPPING

NOTE: FIREPLACE SPLAY IS FOR
HEATING PURPOSES ONLY.

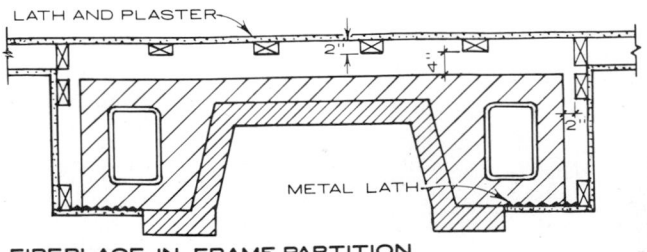

FIREPLACE IN FRAME PARTITION

SCALE: 1/2" = 1'-0"

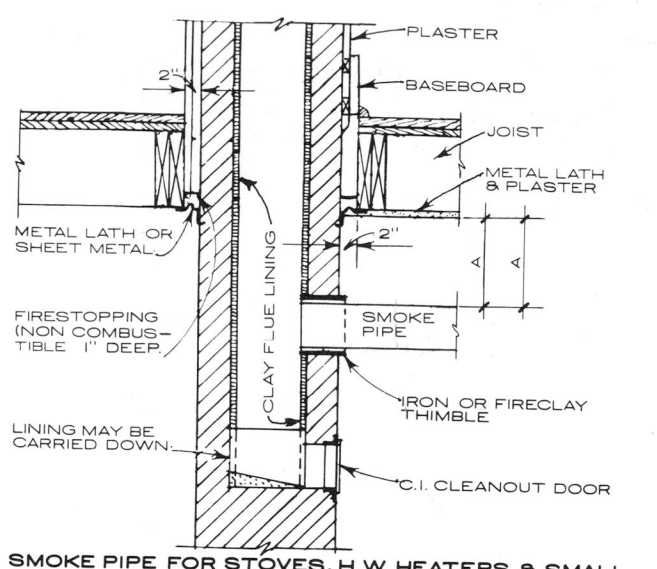

PLASTER

BASEBOARD

JOIST

METAL LATH & PLASTER

2"

METAL LATH OR SHEET METAL

FIRESTOPPING (NON COMBUSTIBLE) 1" DEEP.

CLAY FLUE LINING

2"

A A

SMOKE PIPE

LINING MAY BE CARRIED DOWN.

IRON OR FIRECLAY THIMBLE

C.I. CLEANOUT DOOR

SMOKE PIPE FOR STOVES, H.W. HEATERS & SMALL RANGES - CONNECTIONS & CLEARANCES.

SMOKE PIPE CONNECTIONS AND CLEARANCES

A = 9" WITH SHEET METAL SHIELD 1" FROM CEILING AND EXTENDING 1'-0" BOTH SIDES ENTIRE LENGTH SMOKE PIPE

A = 1'-6" WHEN USING NO METAL SHIELD BETWEEN CEILING AND SMOKE PIPE

A = 3'-0" WHEN USING NO METAL SHIELD WITH MEDIUM HEAT APPLIANCES

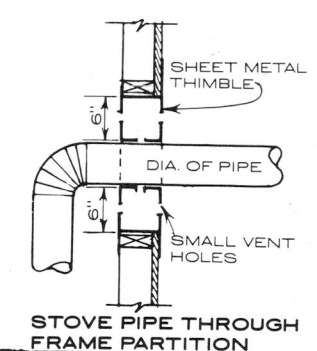

SHEET METAL THIMBLE

6"

DIA. OF PIPE

6"

SMALL VENT HOLES

STOVE PIPE THROUGH FRAME PARTITION

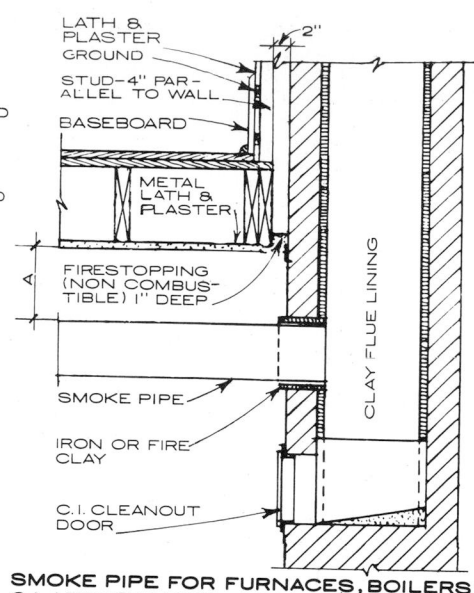

LATH & PLASTER GROUND

2"

STUD-4" PARALLEL TO WALL

BASEBOARD

METAL LATH & PLASTER

A

FIRESTOPPING (NON COMBUSTIBLE) 1" DEEP

CLAY FLUE LINING

SMOKE PIPE

IRON OR FIRE CLAY

C.I. CLEANOUT DOOR

SMOKE PIPE FOR FURNACES, BOILERS & LARGE RANGES - CONNECTIONS & CLEARANCES.

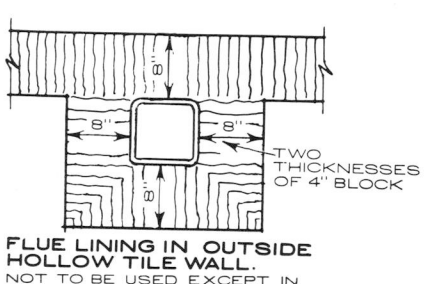

8"

8" 8"

8"

TWO THICKNESSES OF 4" BLOCK

FLUE LINING IN OUTSIDE HOLLOW TILE WALL.

NOT TO BE USED EXCEPT IN CONNECTION WITH HOLLOW TILE WALL.

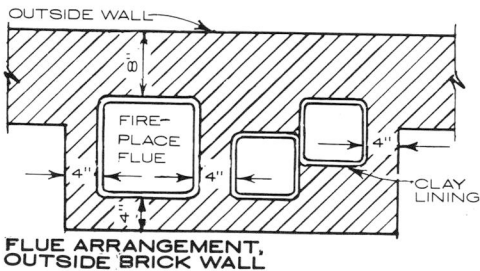

OUTSIDE WALL

8"

FIRE-PLACE FLUE

4" 4"

4"

4"

CLAY LINING

FLUE ARRANGEMENT, OUTSIDE BRICK WALL

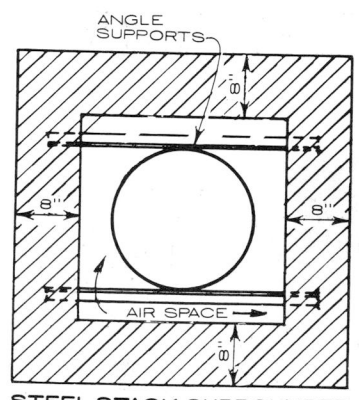

ANGLE SUPPORTS

8"

8"

8"

AIR SPACE

8"

STEEL STACK SURROUNDED WITH BRICK
USED FOR LARGE BOILERS

8"

4

DRESSED STONE

4" 8"

1" MIN.

OUTSIDE WALL - RUBBLE

FLUE ARRANGEMENTS IN STONE CHIMNEY

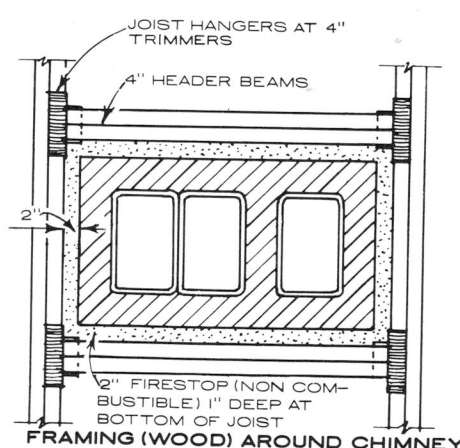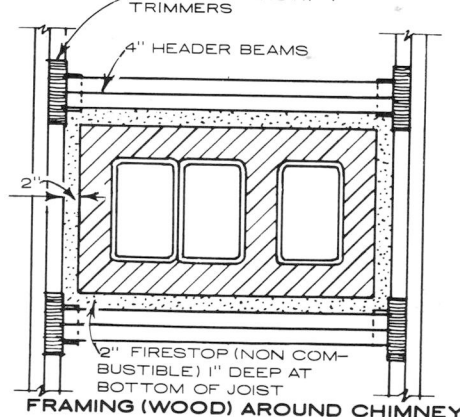

JOIST HANGERS AT 4" TRIMMERS

4" HEADER BEAMS

2"

2" FIRESTOP (NON COMBUSTIBLE) 1" DEEP AT BOTTOM OF JOIST

FRAMING (WOOD) AROUND CHIMNEY

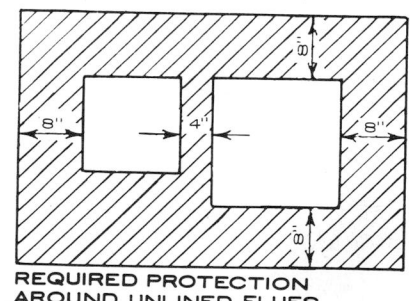

8"

8" 4" 8"

8"

REQUIRED PROTECTION AROUND UNLINED FLUES

TYPE B = NONCOMBUSTIBLE CORROSION RESISTANT MATERIAL FOR VENTING OF GAS APPL..

TYPE BW = NONCOMBUSTIBLE CORROSION RESISTANT MATERIAL FOR VENTING RECESSED GAS HEATERS

TYPE C = SHEET COPPER MATERIAL NOT LESS THAN 24 GUAGE GALVANIZED IRON MATERIAL NOT LESS THAN 20 GAUGE

1" CLEARANCE FROM COMBUSTIBLE MATERIAL

FLUE FROM GAS BURNING EQUIPMENT

CLAY CHIMNEY POT

CEMENT WASH

SETTING OF CHIMNEY POT

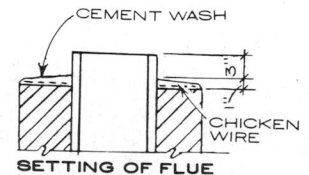

CEMENT WASH

3"

1"

CHICKEN WIRE

SETTING OF FLUE LINING WITHOUT POT

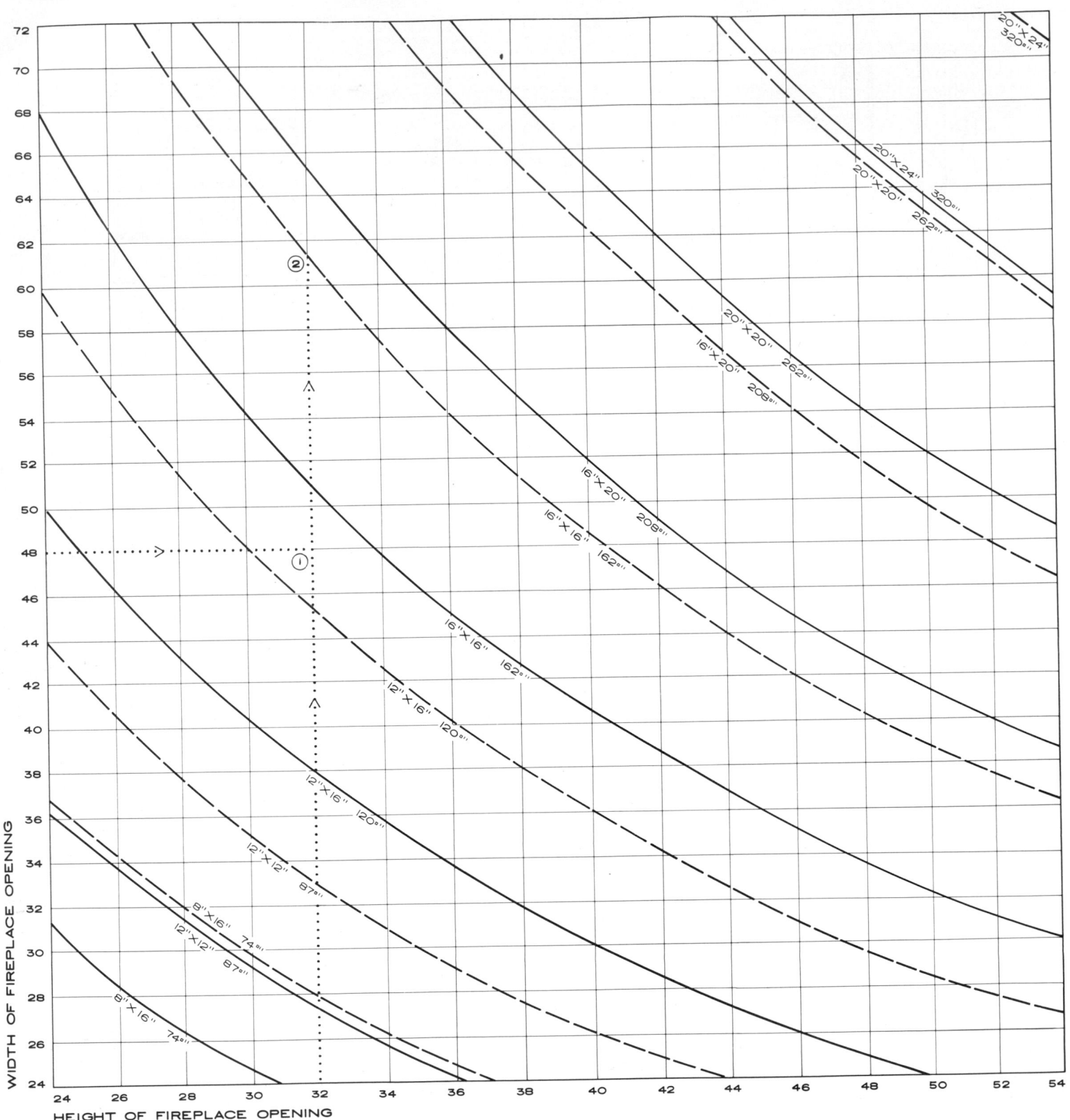

WIDTH OF FIREPLACE OPENING

HEIGHT OF FIREPLACE OPENING

─────── Recommended flue size — 1/10 of fireplace area.

─ ─ ─ ─ Recommended minimum flue size 1/12 of fireplace area.

NOTE:

Charts are based on net flue areas.

Modular flues only made in rectangular sizes. If round flue is desired for modular chimney, use non-modular round flue.

If flue is less than 20 feet high, it is advisable to use the next larger flue size unless intersection ① falls well below the fireplace area curve.

PROBLEM

Find proper modular flue size, at 1/12 fireplace area, for a fireplace 48" wide and 32" high.

SOLUTION

① Find intersection of 48" width with 32" height of fireplace.

② Proper flue size is nearest curve (for 1/12 area) above intersection, in this case, 16" x 16".

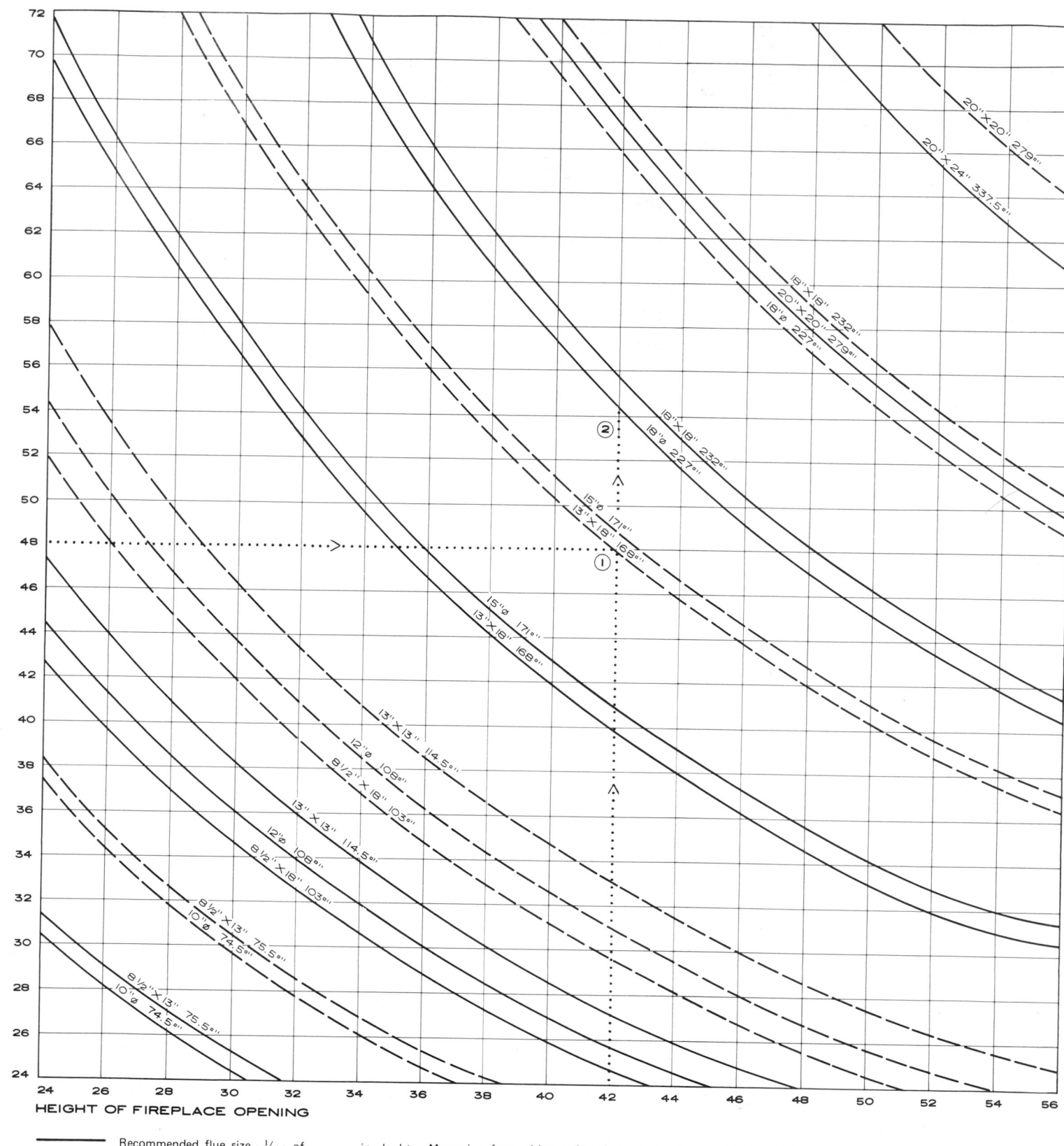

WIDTH OF FIREPLACE OPENING

HEIGHT OF FIREPLACE OPENING

—————— Recommended flue size - $1/10$ of fireplace area.

– – – – – Recommended minimum flue size $1/12$ area of fireplace.

EXPLANATION OF CHIMNEY HEIGHT:

The F.H.A. measures height of chimney from the throat and the Department of Agriculture measures it from the hearth; despite discrepancy, these charts have long been used measuring from either point, and their validity is not in doubt. Measuring from either point gives results of sufficient accuracy for good fireplace design.

NOTES:

Charts are based on minimum net inside flue areas.

For chimney less than 35' high, use $1/10$ ratio for flue, over 35', use $1/12$ ratio. If flue is less than 20' high, it is advisable to use next larger flue size, unless intersection ① falls well below the curve.

Smallest flue recommended for any fireplace is 10" diameter.

PROBLEM

Find proper flue size at $1/10$ fireplace area for fireplace 48" wide and 42" high.

SOLUTION

① Find intersection of 48" width with 42" height of fireplace.

② Proper flue size is nearest curve (for $1/10$ area) above intersection, in this case, 18" ⌀. For rectangular flue, continue to next curve for $1/10$ area: 18" x 18".

ROUND FLUE LININGS

AREA (sq. in.)	A	T	LENGTH
26	6″	$5/8$″	2′– 0″
47	8″	$3/4$″	2′– 0″
74.5	10″	$7/8$″	2′– 0″
108	12″	1″	2′– 0″
171	15″	$1\,1/8$″	2′– 0″
240	18″	$1\,1/4$″	2′– 0″
298	20″	$1\,3/8$″	2′– 0″
433	24″	$1\,5/8$″	2′– 0″
551	27″ *	2″	2′– 6″
683	30″ *	$2\,1/8$″	2′– 6″
829	33″ *	$2\,1/4$″	2′– 6″
989.5	36″ *	$2\,1/2$″	2′– 6″

* Not available in some localities

Areas shown are net inside areas.

Wall thicknesses shown are minimum required.

Nominal flue sizes for round flues is interior diameter, outside dimensions for non-modular rectangular flues. Nominal dimensions for modular flue linings are actual dimensions plus $1/2$″.

Verify with local manufacturers for available types and sizes of flue linings.

RECTANGULAR FLUE LININGS
STANDARD

AREA (sq. in.)	A	B	T
22	$4\,1/2$″	$8\,1/2$″	$5/8$″
36	$4\,1/2$″	13″	$5/8$″
51	$8\,1/2$″	$8\,1/2$″	$5/8$″
79	$8\,1/2$″	13″	$3/4$″
108	$8\,1/2$″	18″	$7/8$″
125	13″	13″	$7/8$″
168	13″	18″	$7/8$″
232	18″	18″	$1\,1/8$″
279	20″	20″	$1\,3/8$″
338	20″	24″	$1\,1/2$″
420	24″	24″	$1\,1/2$″

All flue linings listed above are 2′– 0″ long.

Fireplace flue sizes: $1/10$ area of fireplace opening recommended. $1/12$ area is minimum.

Flue area should never be less than 70 sq. in. for fireplace of 840 sq. in. opening or smaller.

Flues for stoves and ranges and room heaters: 39 sq. in. minimum using rectangular flue, or 6″ dia. (inside) using round flue.

RECTANGULAR FLUE LININGS
MODULAR

AREA (sq. in.)	A	B	T
15	4″	8″	$1/2$″
20	4″	12″	$5/8$″
27	4″	16″	$3/4$″
35	8″	8″	$5/8$″
57	8″	12″	$3/4$″
74	8″	16″	$7/8$″
87	12″	12″	$7/8$″
120	12″	16″	1″
162	16″	16″	$1\,1/8$″
208	16″	20″	$1\,1/4$″
262	20″	20″	$1\,3/8$″
320	20″	24″	$1\,1/2$″
385	24″	24″	$1\,5/8$″

All flue linings listed above are 2′– 0″ long, also available, on request, in 12″ lengths.

For proper flue sizes for fireplaces using modular flue linings see page titled: Modular Flue Sizes for Fireplaces.

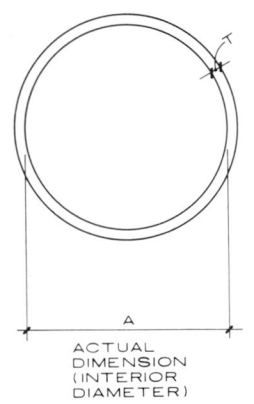

ROUND

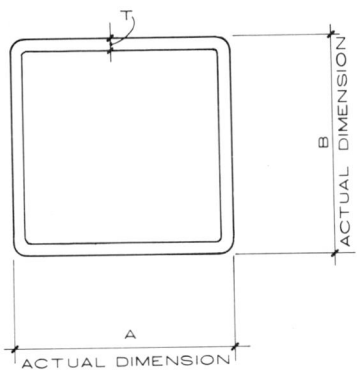

STANDARD

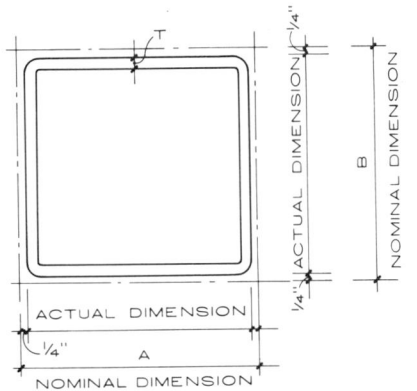

Cross section of flue lining shall fit within rectangle of dimension corresponding to nominal size.

MODULAR

CLAY FLUE LININGS

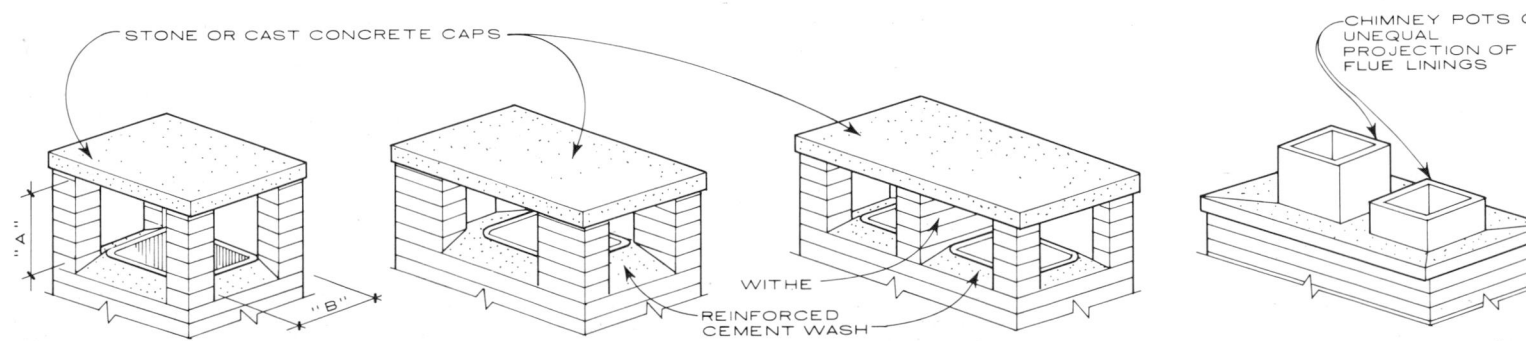

Chimney hoods to prevent downdraft due to adjoining hills, buildings, trees, etc.

"A" should be $1/4$ greater than "B" in all hooded chimneys.

Chimney hoods also serve as water protection for seldom used flues.

Withe between flues is the best method of preventing downdraft.

Unequal projection of flues above the stack is a safeguard against smoke pouring out of one flue and down the other.

CHIMNEY HOODS & POTS

Robert B. Martin, AIA; Lincoln City, Oregon

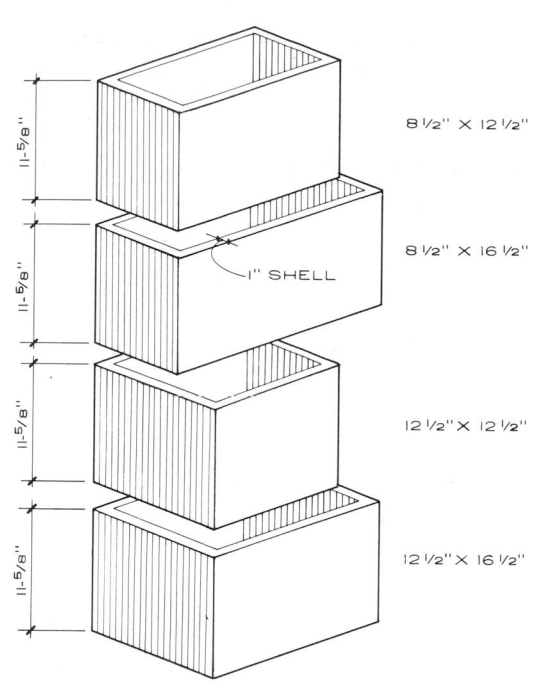

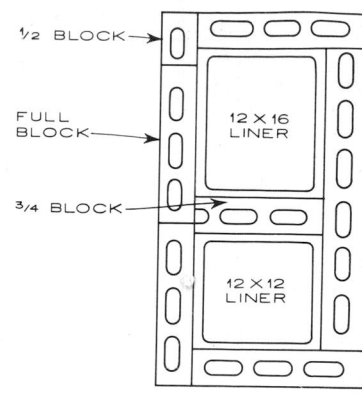

8 ½" X 12 ½"

8 ½" X 16 ½"

1" SHELL

12 ½" X 12 ½"

12 ½" X 16 ½"

Recommended by the International Conference of Building Officials as required by the Uniform Building Code.

Internally mixed brick red color.

½ BLOCK

FULL BLOCK

¾ BLOCK

12 X 16 LINER

12 X 12 LINER

EXPANDED SHALE FLUE LININGS

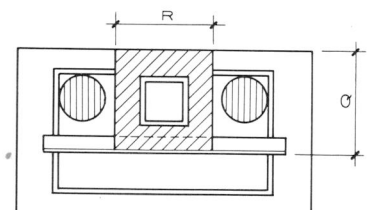

PLAN ABOVE HEATSAVER

R

Q

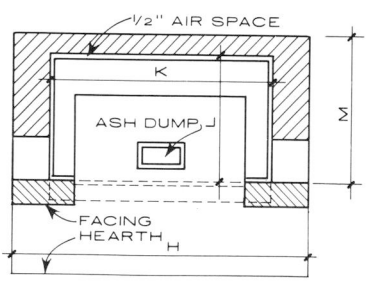

½" AIR SPACE

K

ASH DUMP J

M

FACING HEARTH H

PLAN ABOVE HEARTH

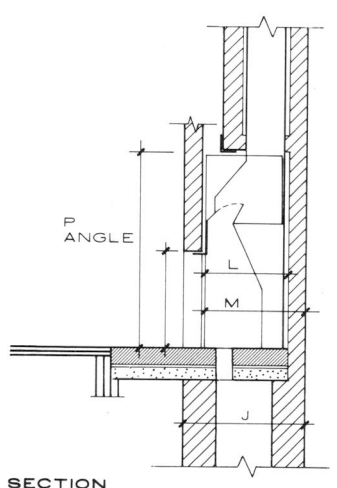

P ANGLE

L

M

J

SECTION

Hot air duct may terminate anywhere in same or adjacent room above top of circulator.

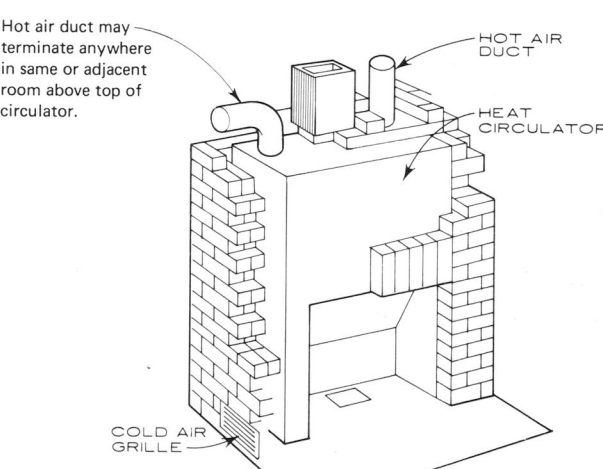

HOT AIR DUCT

HEAT CIRCULATOR

COLD AIR GRILLE

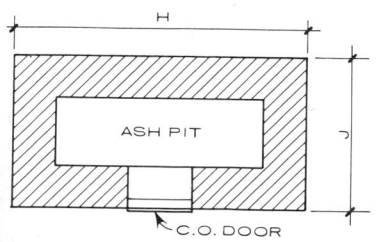

H

ASH PIT

J

C.O. DOOR

PLAN BELOW HEARTH

ROUGH MASONRY DIMENSIONS IN INCHES

NO.	H	J	K	L	M	N	P	STANDARD FLUE	MODULAR FLUE
28	52	32	36	24	28	26 $^2/_3$	56	13 x 13	12 x 12
32	56	32	40	24	28	26 $^2/_3$	56	13 x 13	12 x 12
36	60	32	44	24	28	26 $^2/_3$	56	13 x 13	12 x 12
40	72	32	56	24	28	29 $^1/_3$	66 $^2/_3$	13 x 13	12 x 16
48	80	32	64	24	28	29 $^1/_3$	66 $^2/_3$	13 x 13	12 x 16
60	92	36	76	28	32	32	80	13 x 18	16 x 20

NOTES: Figures given are nominal sizes to conform to modular dimensions. The thickness of facing will vary with material used. The wall back of the Heatsaver as shown is 4" thick. If this is an exterior wall it should be 8", and dimension M increased 4".

Q and R measurements can be determined by adding wall thickness to flue size dimensions. Since wall thickness can vary, Q and R are not given in the table. Minimum wall thickness is 4". On the 28" unit only, the R measurement cannot be more than 20", or the warm air opening through the casing, as shown on the drawing, will be distorted.

HEAT CIRCULATOR FIREPLACE

Robert B. Martin, AIA; Lincoln City, Oregon

Listed by Underwriters Laboratories, Inc., as acceptable for venting all listed gas appliances equipped with draft hoods.

Sized from 3 inches I.D. to 24 inches I.D.

Can be installed from 1 to 3 inches from combustible construction. (See current Underwriters Laboratories, Inc., Gas and Oil Equipment List for distances for each manufacturers product.)

ROUND PIPE

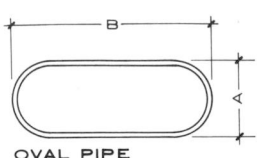

OVAL PIPE
TYPE B GAS VENTS

NOTE:

SEE ANOTHER PAGE IN THIS SERIES FOR FLUES FROM GAS BURNING EQUIPMENT

Oval pipe of 4 and 6 inch sizes listed as acceptable for use in 2 x 4 stud walls and 2 x 6 stud walls, studs on 16 inch centers.

Engineered capacity tables for properly sizing vent systems available from vent manufacturers. Parts available in straight lengths, adjustable lengths, fixed and adjustable elbows, tees, increasers, adaptors, round to oval and oval to round, flashings, storm collars and caps.

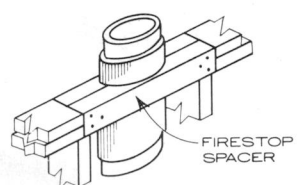

MULTI-STORY
UPPERFLOORS

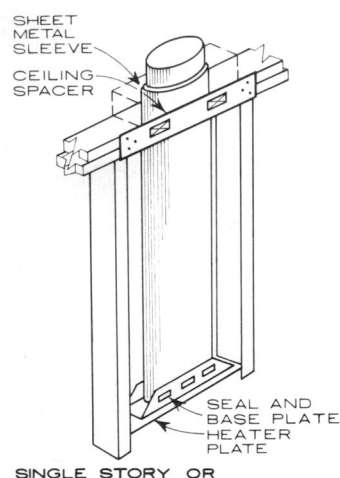

SINGLE STORY OR
FIRST FLOOR OF
MULTI-STORY

TYPE BW GAS VENTS CHIMNEYS

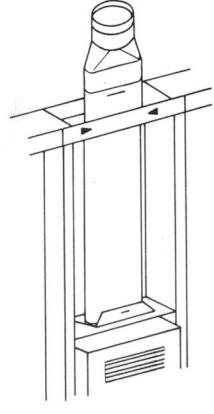

Similar to type B 4" oval except additional parts are supplied. The only vent acceptable for use in 2 x 4 walls for venting listed gas fired vented wall furnaces.

Consists of pipe-base plate, seal, ceiling spacer and fire stop spacer. Type BW gas vents shall have listed capacity not less than that of the listed vented wall furnaces to which they are connected.

Chimneys consisting entirely of factory made parts which are designed to be assembled with other parts of the same model without requiring field construction. Produced in sizes from 6" I.D. to 12" I.D. Listings for 1" or 2" distance from enclosure walls and roof structure.

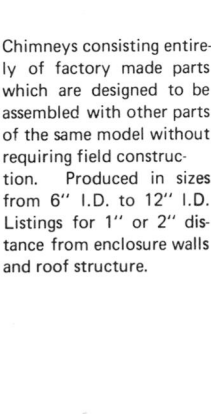

Approved for use with residential and industrial low heat appliances using solid, liquid or gaseous fuel including domestic type incinerators, fireplace stoves, and when so listed, may be used with masonry fireplaces.

Maximum allowable height determined by U.L. listing varies from 8' to 60'.

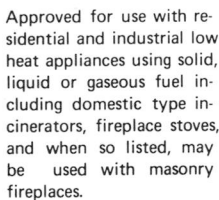

FACTORY BUILT CHIMNEY

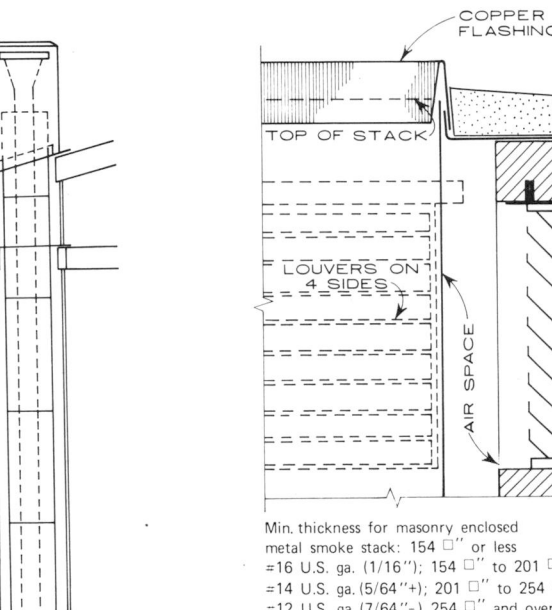

Min. thickness for masonry enclosed metal smoke stack: 154 □" or less =16 U.S. ga. (1/16"); 154 □" to 201 □" =14 U.S. ga. (5/64"+); 201 □" to 254 □" =12 U.S. ga. (7/64"-) 254 □" and over. =10 U.S. ga. (9/64"-)

TOP OF METAL SMOKESTACK WITH BRICK SURROUNDS

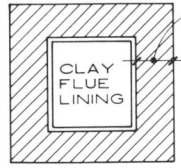

Chimneys for stoves, cooking ranges, warm air, hot water and low pressure steam heating furnaces, low heat industrial appliances, portable type incinerators, fireplaces.

LOW HEAT APPLIANCES

Chimneys for high pressure steam boilers, smoke houses, and other medium heat appliances other than incinerators. Continue firebrick up 25' min. N.Y.C. firebrick up 50' min.

MEDIUM HEAT APPLIANCES

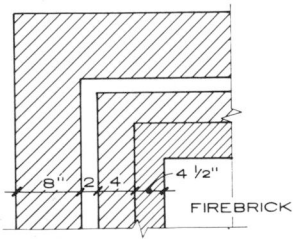

Chimneys for cupolas, brass furnaces, porcelain baking kilns, and other high heat appliances.

HIGH HEAT APPLIANCES

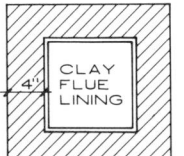

FOR RESIDENCE BLDGS., INSTITUTIONAL BLDGS., CHURCHES, SCHOOLS & RESTAURANTS.

For domestic type incinerators where firebox or charging compartment is not larger than 5 cu. ft.

CHIMNEYS FOR INCINERATORS

For apartment house type incinerators. Continue fire brick up 10' above roof of combustion chamber for grate area 7 □' or less; 40' above for grate area exceeding 7 □'.

MINIMUM CHIMNEY REQUIREMENTS

Robert B. Martin, AIA; Lincoln City, Oregon

GENERAL NOTE :

Based on advice of the late Frederick N. Whitley, fireplace and chimney specialist.

The open floor plan makes useful multi-opening and free standing fireplaces. Design requirements for such fireplaces vary from those of conventional fireplaces. The following rules of thumb are given to aid in achieving proper function of these newer fireplaces.

Trouble factors encountered in the design for most fireplaces are:
1. Flue too small
2. Damper throat too narrow
3. Omission of smoke shelf
4. Smoke chamber inadequate in volume

Proper functioning of fireplaces is dependent not only on fireplace and flue design, but also on the following:

1. Height of flue and its projection above various types of roof.
2. Neighboring and adjoining conditions, such as terrain, trees and buildings.
3. Wind directions and climate

Certain cross draft conditions within a room may cause the following types of fireplace to smoke without regard to the design of chimney or fireplace.

1. Fireplace open front and side
2. Fireplace open front and back
3. Fireplace open three sides (one long and two short sides)
4. Fireplace open three sides (two long and one short sides)
5. Fireplace open four sides.

Rules of thumb design data follow, below and to right:

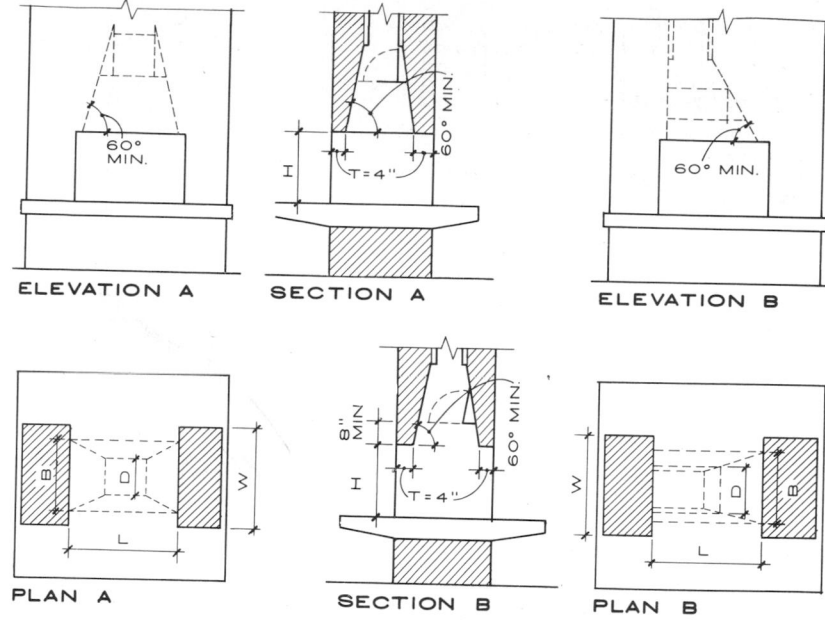

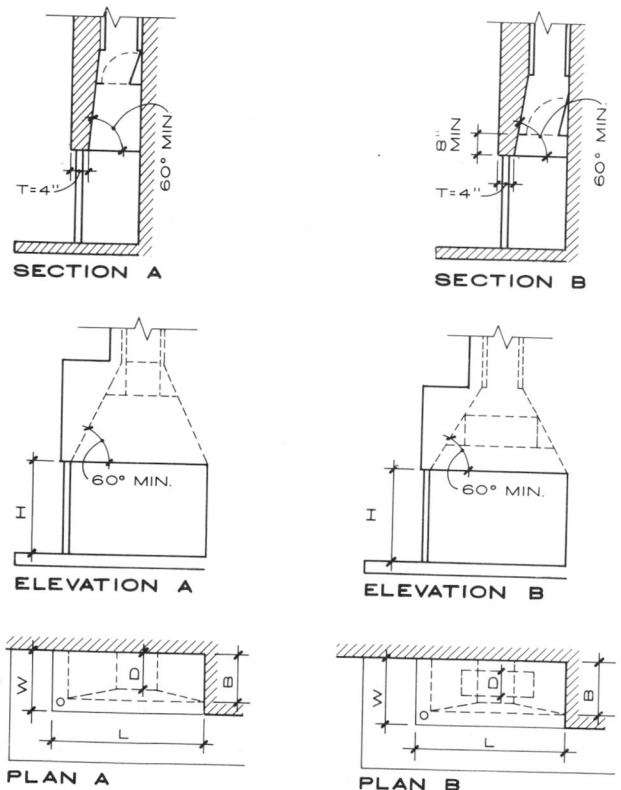

FIREPLACE OPEN FRONT AND SIDE

H   height from top of hearth to bottom of facing

B   (depth of burning area) $^2/_3$ H minus 4"

W   (width of fireplace) B plus T

D   (damper at bottom of flue, Section A) = free area of flue

D   (damper closer to fire, Section B) = twice the free area of the flue. Set damper a minimum 8" (preferably 12") from bottom of smoke chamber as shown.

FLUE : free flue area = $^1/_2$ of H x (L + W)

Robert B. Martin, AIA; Lincoln City, Oregon

FIREPLACE OPEN FRONT AND BACK

H   height from top of hearth to bottom of facing

B   (depth of burning area) $^5/_6$ H minus 8", but never less than 24"

W   (width of fireplace) = B plus T plus T

D   (damper at bottom of flue, Section A) = free area of flue

D   (damper closer to fire, Section B) = twice free area of flue. Set damper a minimum 8" (preferably 12") from bottom of smoke chamber. Operatable part of damper when open should extend entire length of smoke chamber as shown.

FLUE : free area (i.e., inside dimensions of flue) = $^1/_2$ of H x (L plus W)

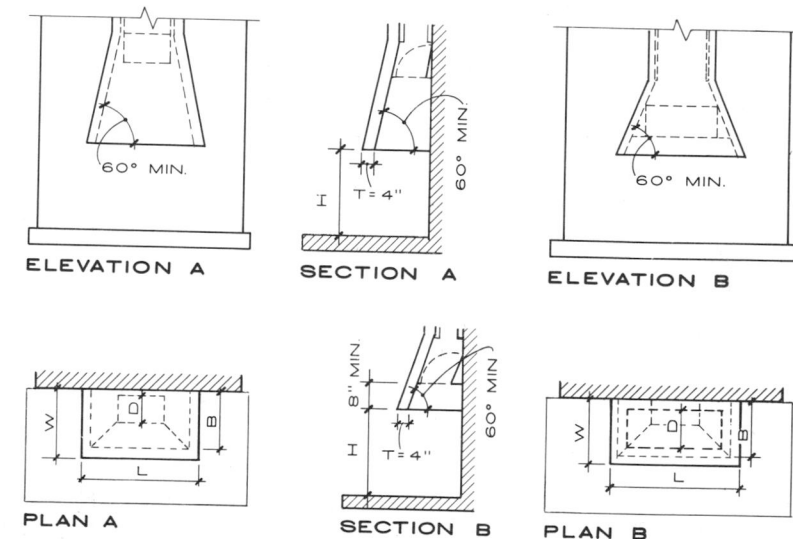

FIREPLACE OPEN THREE SIDES (ONE LONG AND TWO SHORT SIDES)

H   height from top of hearth to bottom of facing

B   (depth of burning area) = $^2/_3$ H minus 4"

W   (width of fireplace) = B plus T

D   (damper at bottom of flue, Section A) = free area of flue

D   (damper closer to fire, Section B) = twice free area of flue. Set damper a minimum 8" (preferably 12") from bottom of smoke chamber. Operatable part of damper when open should extend entire length of smoke chamber as shown.

FLUE : free area = $^1/_{12}$ of H x (L plus 2W)

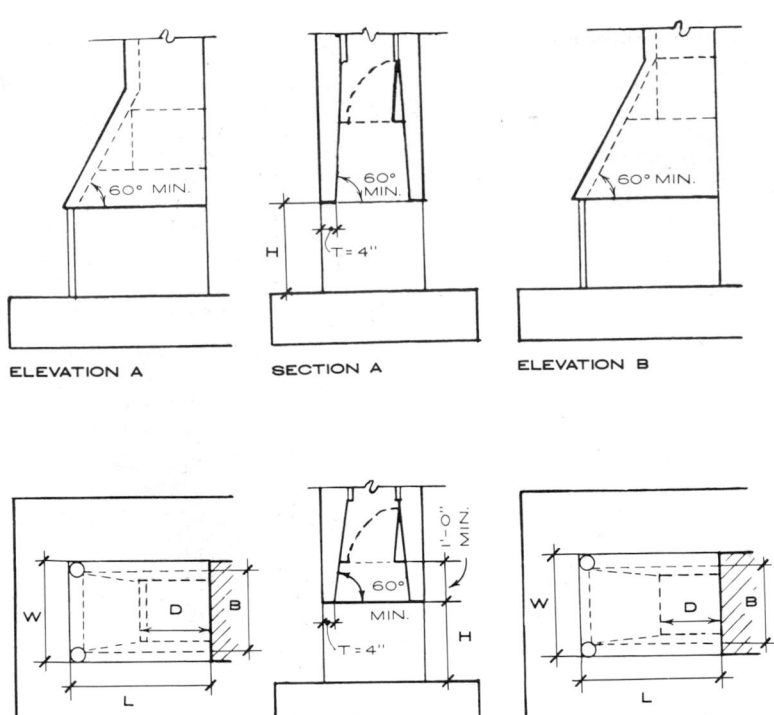

ELEVATION A   SECTION A   ELEVATION B

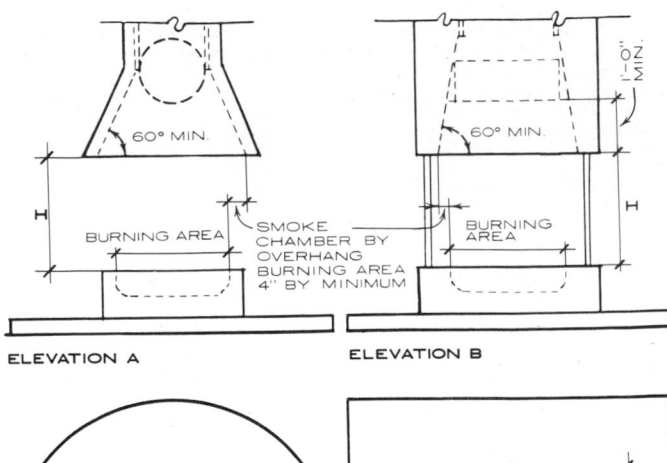

ELEVATION A   ELEVATION B

PLAN A   SECTION B   PLAN B

FIREPLACE OPEN THREE SIDES
(TWO LONG AND ONE SHORT SIDE)

1. H = height from top of hearth to bottom.

2. B (depth) of burning area) = $5/6$ H minus 8″, but never less than 24″.

3. W (width of fireplace) = B plus T plus T.

4. D (damper at bottom of flue, Sect. A) = free area of flue.

5. D (damper closer to fire, Sect. B) = twice free area of flue. Set damper a minimum of 12″ from bottom of smoke chamber. Operatable part of damper when open should extend entire length of smoke chamber, as shown.

6. Flue: free area = $1/12$ of H x (2L plus W).

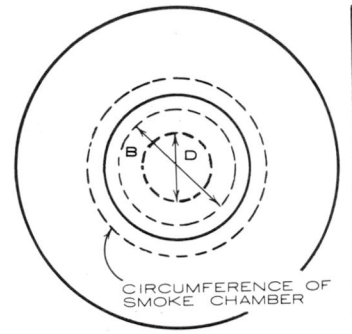

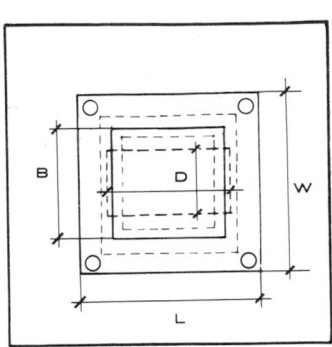

CIRCUMFERENCE OF SMOKE CHAMBER

PLAN A   PLAN B

FIREPLACE OPEN FOUR SIDES

1. H (height from top of hearth to bottom of facing) must never exceed the longest dimension of the burning area. It is recommended that H never exceed 28″.

2. B (burning area, circular fireplace, Elev. A) = 32″ minimum diameter.

3. B (burning area, square or rectangular fireplace) = 24″ minimum dimension.

4. D (damper at bottom of flue, Elev. A) = area of flue.

5. D (damper closer to fire, Elev. B) = twice flue area. Set damper a minimum of 12″ from bottom of smoke chamber. Operatable part of damper when open should extend entire length of smoke chamber, as shown.

6. Flue, circular fireplace: free area = $1/12$ of H x 3.14 x (B plus 8″).

7. Flue, square or rectangular fireplace: free area = $1/12$ of H x (2L plus 2W).

GENERAL NOTES:

In addition to proper damper and flue size, the flue height and fresh air necessary to support combustion are factors which should not be overlooked in fireplace design. The following rules of thumb make allowance for these factors:

1. In a one story flat roofed building the flue should extend 8′–0″ above the roof.

2. In a flat roofed building of two or more stories the flue should extend 6′–0″ above the roof.

3. In a one story pitched roof building the flue should extend 4′–0″ above the roof ridge.

4. In a pitched roof building of two stories or more the flue should extend 4′–0″ above the roof ridge.

5. Fresh air to support combustion and proper draft is often supplied by crack leakage around doors and windows. It can also be supplied by leaving a space between the floor and the bottoms of doors in the room where the fireplace is located. However, in air-conditioned buildings, where cracks and crevices are weather-stripped and insulated, it is more of a problem to supply the proper quantity of fresh air. The following formulas indicate the quantities of fresh air necessary for the various fireplaces. Letters shown in formulas are on the diagrams for each fireplace.

Fireplace open front and side: cubic feet per minute of fresh air = (L plus W) x H x 60. Fireplace open front and back: c.f.m. fresh air = 2L x H x 60.

Fireplace open three sides (one long and two short sides): c.f.m. fresh air = (L plus 2W) x H x 60.

Fireplace open three sides (two long and one short side): c.f.m. fresh air = (2L plus W) x H x 60.

Fireplace open four sides:
Circular: c.f.m. fresh air = 3.14 x (B plus 8″) x H x 60.

Square or rectangular: c.f.m. fresh air = (2L plus 2W) x H x 60.

NOTE:

Consult local building codes on all details of fireplace construction and chimney heights.

This and the following pages show examples of special fireplaces. Variations in design may be achieved by use of different dampers.
1. Low dampers with separate lintels and more elaborate masonry work. Two dampers often required.
2. High dampers with integral lintels and a minimum of masonry work.
Relative costs will vary with each condition.

USING HIGH DAMPER

USING TWO LOW DAMPERS

END ELEVATIONS OF ALTERNATE FIRE PLACE

USING SPECIAL DAMPER

PLAN AT ROOF

SECTION

FIREPLACE OPEN FOUR SIDES

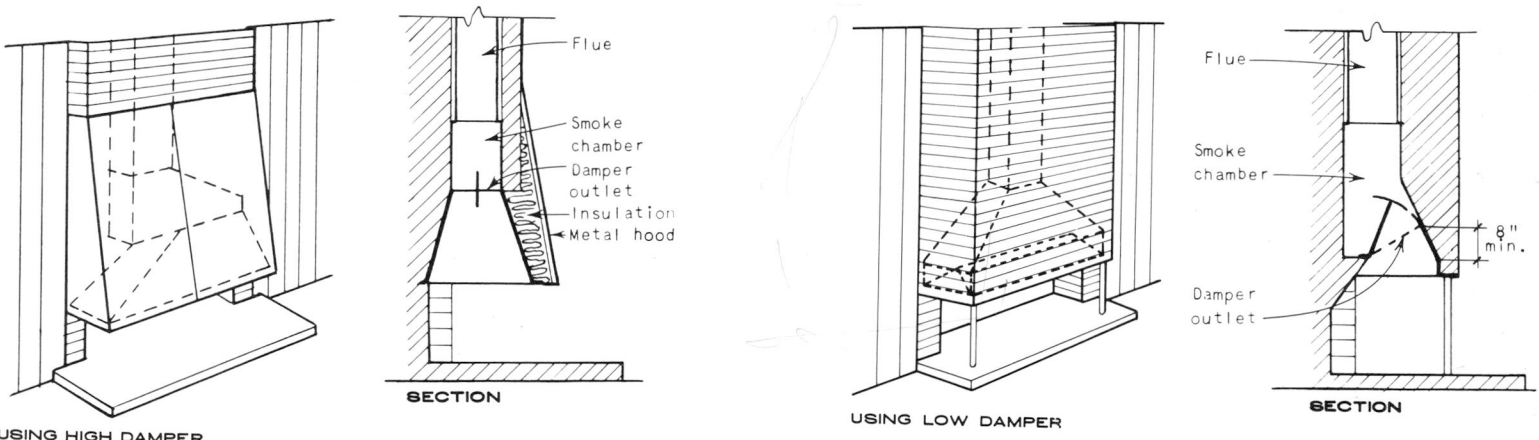

USING HIGH DAMPER

SECTION

USING LOW DAMPER

SECTION

FIREPLACE OPEN THREE SIDES
(ONE LONG AND TWO SHORT SIDES)

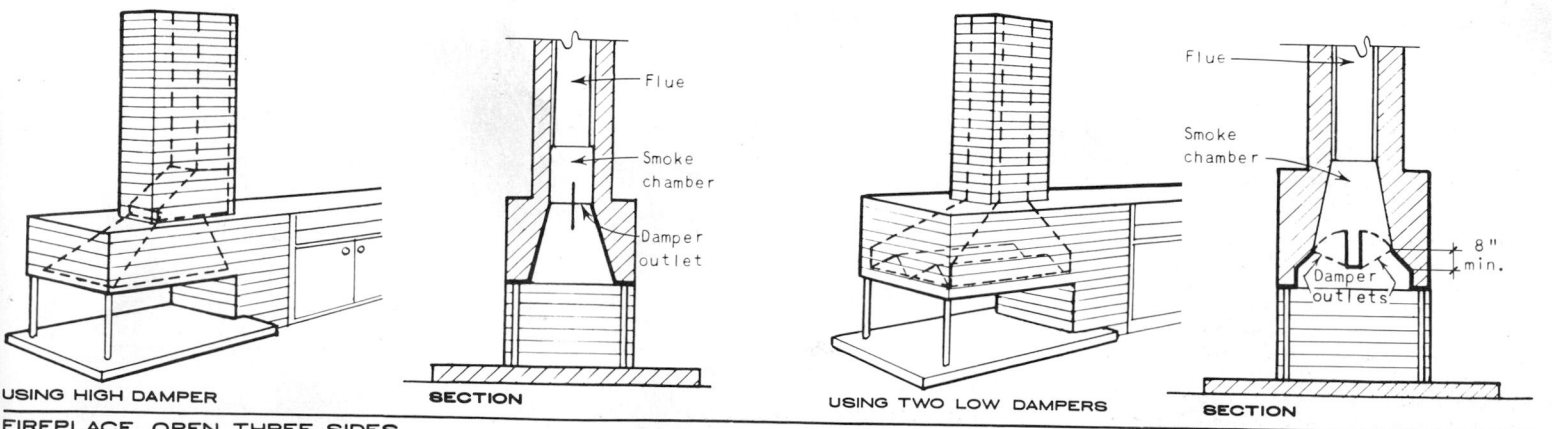

USING HIGH DAMPER

SECTION

USING TWO LOW DAMPERS

SECTION

FIREPLACE OPEN THREE SIDES
(TWO LONG AND ONE SHORT SIDE)

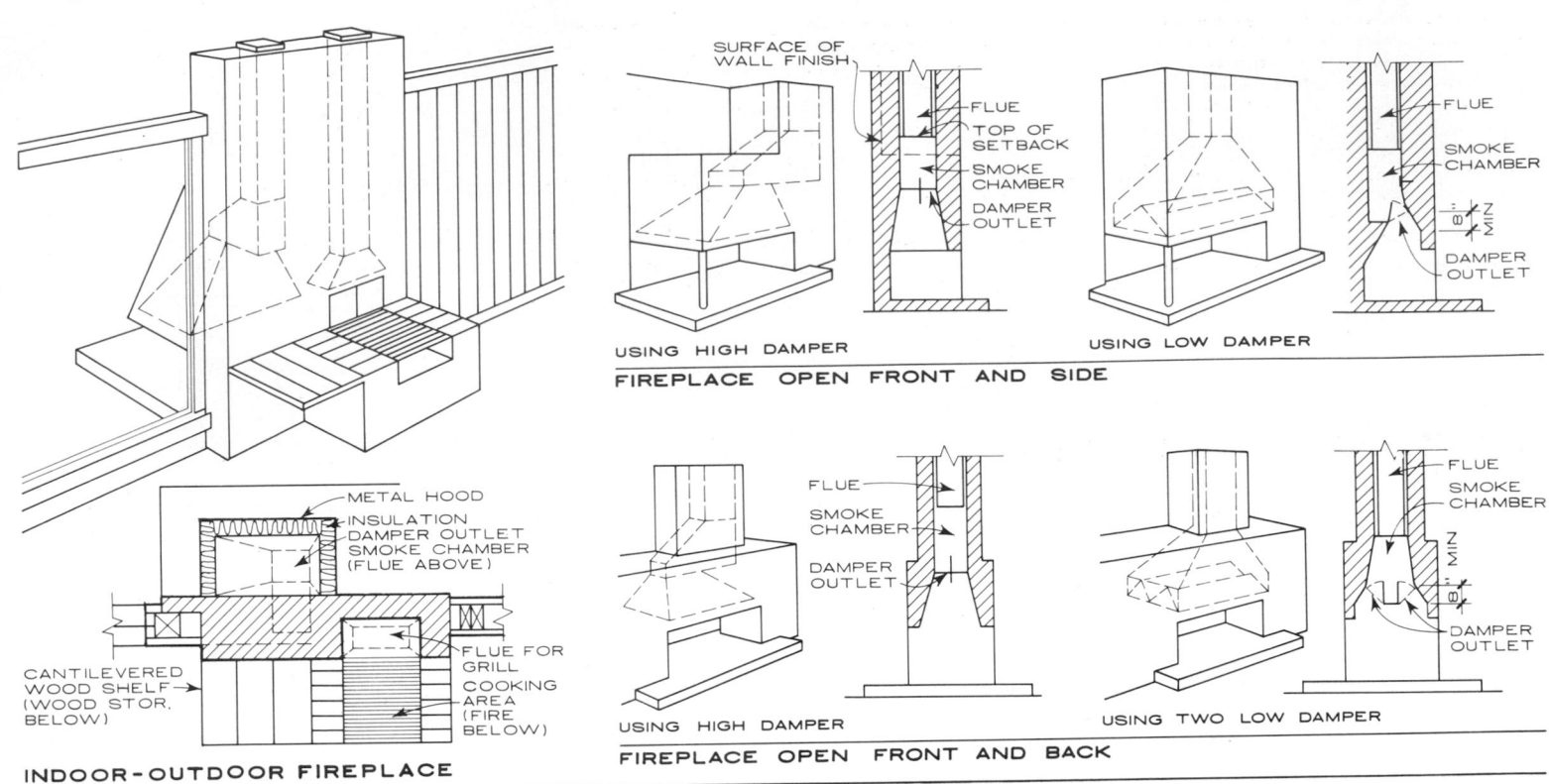

USING HIGH DAMPER

USING LOW DAMPER

FIREPLACE OPEN FRONT AND SIDE

INDOOR-OUTDOOR FIREPLACE

USING HIGH DAMPER

USING TWO LOW DAMPER

FIREPLACE OPEN FRONT AND BACK

EXAMPLES OF PREFABRICATED METAL FIREPLACES

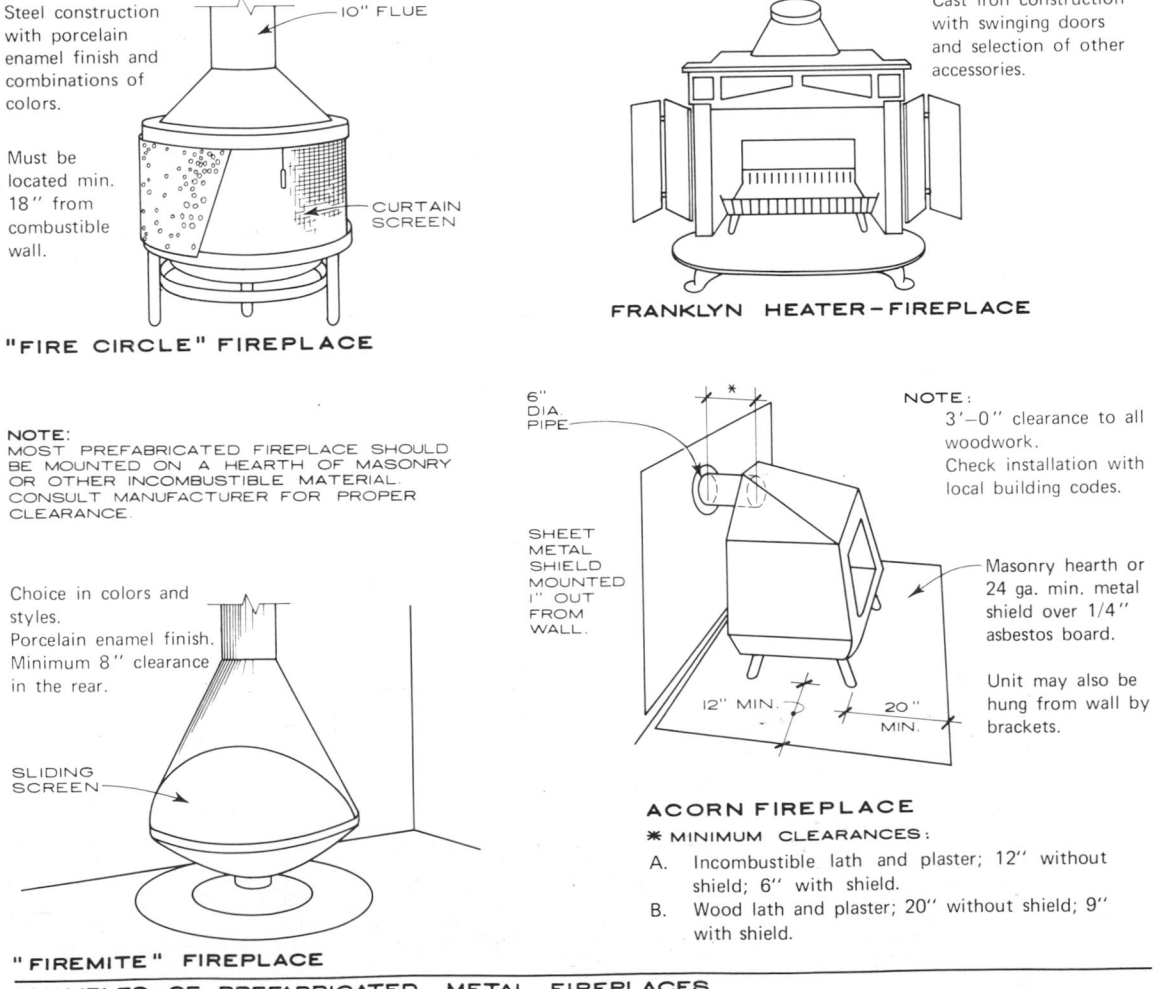

Steel construction with porcelain enamel finish and combinations of colors.

Must be located min. 18″ from combustible wall.

10″ FLUE

CURTAIN SCREEN

"FIRE CIRCLE" FIREPLACE

Cast iron construction with swinging doors and selection of other accessories.

FRANKLYN HEATER-FIREPLACE

NOTE:
MOST PREFABRICATED FIREPLACE SHOULD BE MOUNTED ON A HEARTH OF MASONRY OR OTHER INCOMBUSTIBLE MATERIAL. CONSULT MANUFACTURER FOR PROPER CLEARANCE.

Choice in colors and styles.
Porcelain enamel finish.
Minimum 8″ clearance in the rear.

SLIDING SCREEN

"FIREMITE" FIREPLACE

EXAMPLES OF PREFABRICATED METAL FIREPLACES

6″ DIA. PIPE

SHEET METAL SHIELD MOUNTED 1″ OUT FROM WALL.

12″ MIN.   20″ MIN.

NOTE:
3′-0″ clearance to all woodwork.
Check installation with local building codes.

Masonry hearth or 24 ga. min. metal shield over 1/4″ asbestos board.

Unit may also be hung from wall by brackets.

ACORN FIREPLACE

✳ MINIMUM CLEARANCES:
A. Incombustible lath and plaster; 12″ without shield; 6″ with shield.
B. Wood lath and plaster; 20″ without shield; 9″ with shield.

FLUE

SMOKE CHAMBER

DAMPER OUTLET

SECTION
PRECAST CONCRETE FIREPLACE

COURTESY OF DON SCHOLZ

Robert B. Martin, AIA; Lincoln City, Oregon

The automatic flue fed incinerator is designed for incineration of all types of waste including ordinary household rubbish, kitchen garbage, pathological waste and others. The system incorporates two flues, a charging flue and an exhaust flue. In some cases, existing boiler flues can be utilized as the exhaust flue.

The heart of the flue fed system is the gas washer. Its functions are to eliminate fly ash and to reduce temperatures of exhaust gases to 600°F maximum, so that the induced draft fan can handle them properly. Manufacturers should supply test reports by an independent organization.

A good incinerator will have automatic start up of entire system when the temperature rises in the combustion chamber. If matches or cigarettes are thrown down the chute igniting the rubbish prematurely; rather than allow emission of smoke out of the hopper doors, the entire system is reactivated and will operate as intended until such time as the temperature decreases and the system automatically shuts down.

Economy is a factor that should be considered in choosing incineration equipment. For example, a time cycle which allows the ignition burner to operate on predetermined settings. These settings can be from 30 seconds to 30 minutes (usually for 60 seconds every hour) and allow the burner to operate as it is intended—merely to ignite rubbish which has been charged into the incinerator. The incinerator design indicated below is recognized by leading air pollution authorities. One of the design features is use of a firebrick lined steel breeching to complete secondary combustion, rather than the use of the two pass system. This feature allows the utilization of the full output of the burner in completing combustion. This design completely eliminates any possibility of smoke emission from hopper doors.

Operation should be continuous and automatic, thereby eliminating set charging periods, thus increasing convenience to the tenants and avoiding storage of refuse inside apartments.

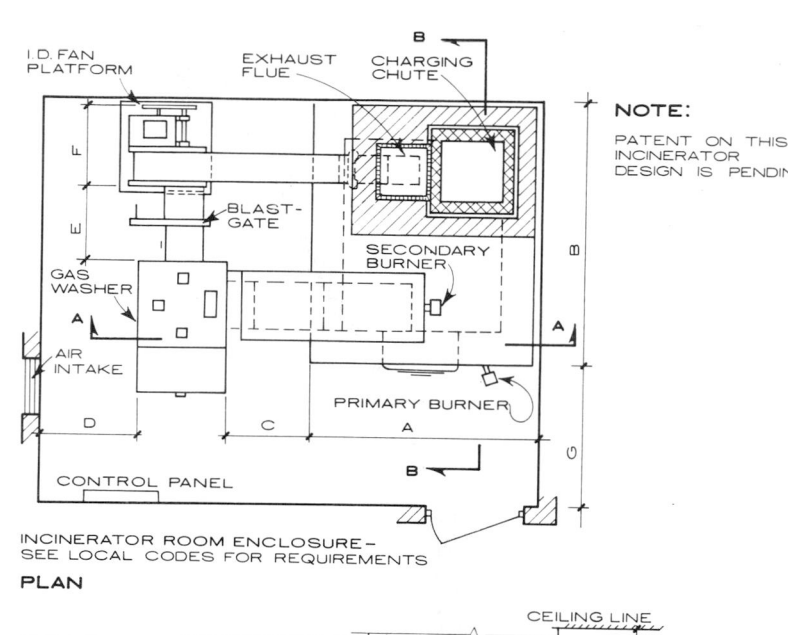

NOTE:

PATENT ON THIS INCINERATOR DESIGN IS PENDING

INCINERATOR ROOM ENCLOSURE—SEE LOCAL CODES FOR REQUIREMENTS

PLAN

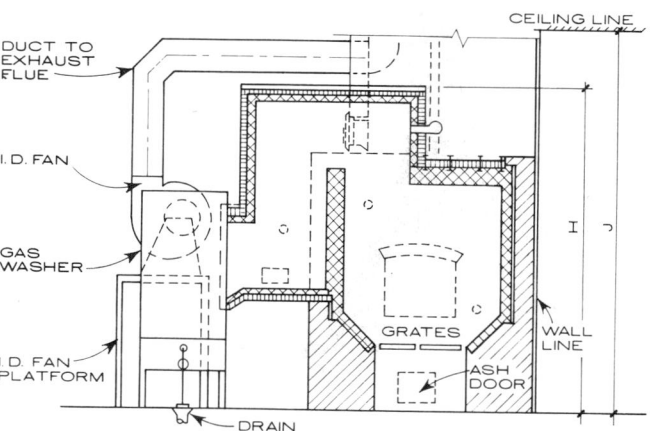

SECTION A-A

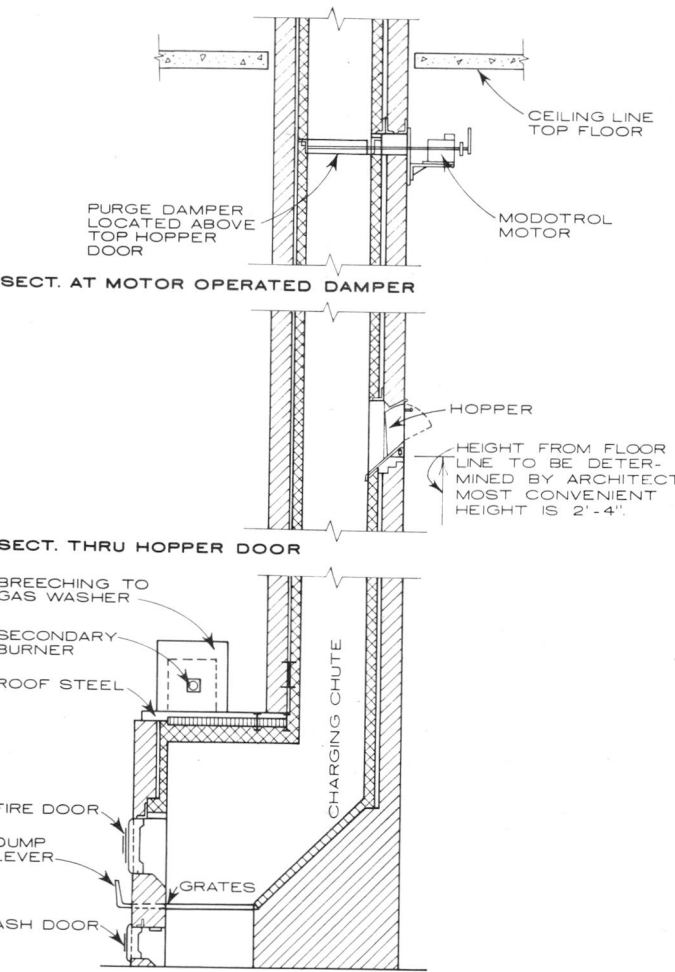

SECT. AT MOTOR OPERATED DAMPER

SECT. THRU HOPPER DOOR

SECTION B-B

DIMENSIONS OF FLUE FED INCINERATORS

A	B	C	D	E	F	G MIN.	H	J	CAPACITY (LB./HR.)	NO. OF ROOMS (APT. HSE.)	CHARGING CHUTE SIZE	VENTILATION AIR (CFM @ 70°F)	EXHAUST FLUE SIZE
4'–6''	7'–6''	1'–5 1/4''	2'–6''	1'–0''	2'–2''	6'–3''	8'–3 3/4''	10'–6''	50	100	22 1/2'' x 22 1/2''	90	8 1/2'' x 13''
4'–9''	7'–9''	1'–7 3/4''	2'–6''	1'–0''	2'–2''	6'–6''	9'–2 1/4''	10'–6''	100	200	22 1/2'' x 22 1/2''	125	13'' x 13''
5'–7''	8'–3''	1'–7 3/4''	2'–6''	1'–6''	2'–4''	7'–0''	9'–7 3/4''	12'–0''	150	300	27'' x 27''	190	13'' x 18''
5'–7''	8'–3''	2'–2 1/4''	2'–6''	1'–6''	2'–4''	7'–0''	9'–6 1/4''	12'–0''	200	400	27'' x 27''	250	13'' x 18''
6'–3''	8'–9''	2'–2 1/4''	2'–6''	1'–9''	2'–4''	7'–0''	9'–10 3/4''	12'–0''	250	500	27'' x 27''	310	18'' x 18''
6'–3''	8'–9''	2'–2 1/4''	2'–6''	2'–0''	2'–8''	7'–6''	10'–0 3/4''	12'–0''	300	600	27'' x 27''	375	20'' x 20''
7'–2''	8'–9''	2'–6 3/4''	3'–0''	2'–0''	2'–8''	7'–6''	10'–5 3/4''	12'–0''	350	700	27'' x 27''	440	20'' x 24''
7'–2''	8'–9''	3'–1 1/4''	3'–0''	2'–0''	2'–8''	7'–6''	10'–8 1/4''	12'–2''	400	800	27'' x 27''	500	24'' x 24''
7'–9''	8'–9''	3'–1 1/4''	3'–0''	2'–0''	3'–1''	7'–6''	11'–1 3/4''	12'–2''	450	900	27'' x 27''	565	24'' x 24''
7'–9''	9'–0''	3'–1 1/4''	3'–0''	2'–0''	3'–1''	7'–9''	11'–2 3/4''	12'–2''	500	1000	27'' x 27''	625	24'' x 24''
8'–3''	9'–3''	3'–1 1/4''	3'–0''	2'–0''	3'–6''	8'–0''	11'–1 3/4''	12'–3''	550	1100	27'' x 27''	720	24'' x 24''
8'–3''	9'–5''	3'–1 1/4''	3'–0''	2'–0''	3'–6''	8'–3''	11'–6 3/4''	12'–6''	600	1200	27'' x 27''	750	24'' x 24''

Milo Dvirka, P. E.; Consulting Engineer; Long Island City, New York

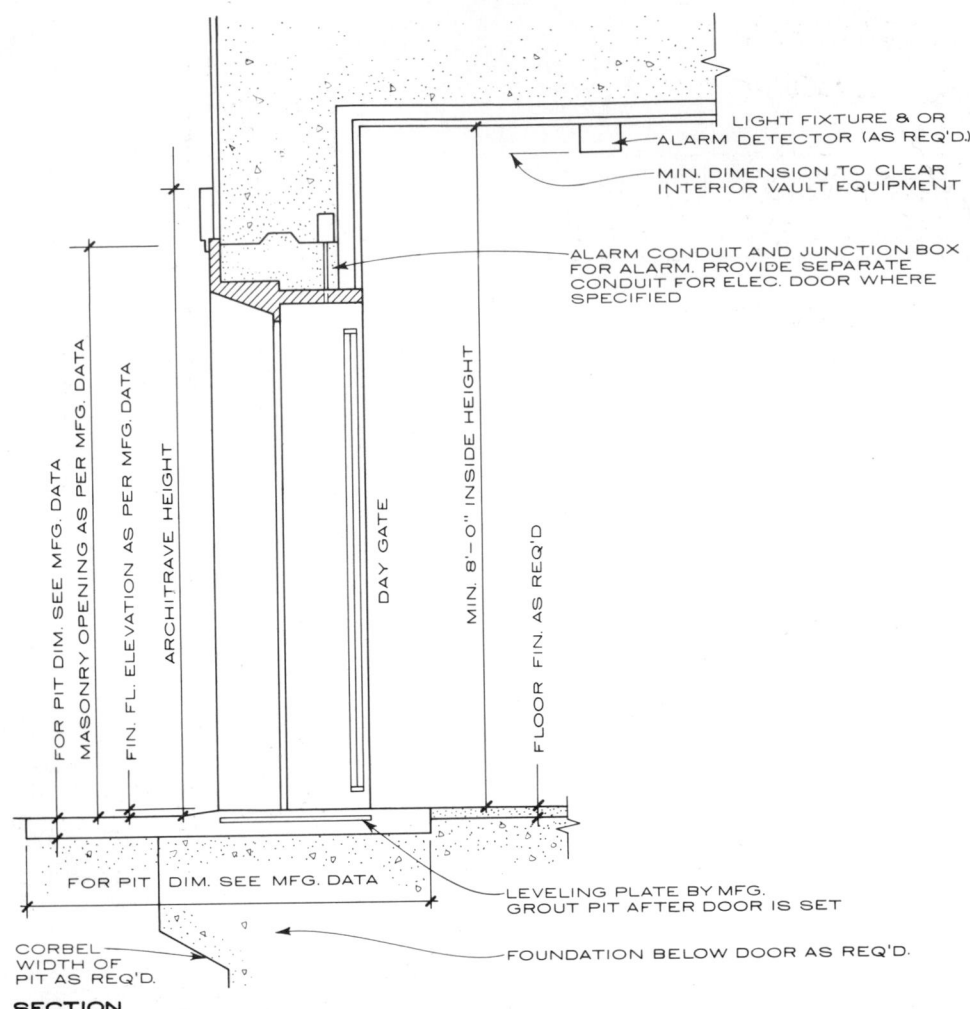

LIGHT FIXTURE & OR
ALARM DETECTOR (AS REQ'D.)

MIN. DIMENSION TO CLEAR
INTERIOR VAULT EQUIPMENT

ALARM CONDUIT AND JUNCTION BOX
FOR ALARM. PROVIDE SEPARATE
CONDUIT FOR ELEC. DOOR WHERE
SPECIFIED

FOR PIT DIM. SEE MFG. DATA

MASONRY OPENING AS PER MFG. DATA

FIN. FL. ELEVATION AS PER MFG. DATA

ARCHITRAVE HEIGHT

DAY GATE

MIN. 8'-0" INSIDE HEIGHT

FLOOR FIN. AS REQ'D

FOR PIT DIM. SEE MFG. DATA

LEVELING PLATE BY MFG.
GROUT PIT AFTER DOOR IS SET

FOUNDATION BELOW DOOR AS REQ'D.

CORBEL
WIDTH OF
PIT AS REQ'D.

SECTION

NOTE :

Vault doors, walls, floors and ceilings are always chosen to conform with insurance requirements. The maximum rating for a vault including the doors is a No. 10R classification. For further information see "Manual of Burglary Insurance" issued by the National Bureau of Casualty Underwriters, N.Y.C. and "Merchandise Vaults and Safes" issued by the National Board of Fire Underwriters, N.Y.C. Various types of wall, floor and ceiling construction and door thicknesses are possible. For the most commonly used types, see classification table. The average minimum vault size is 8'– 6" x 12'– 0".

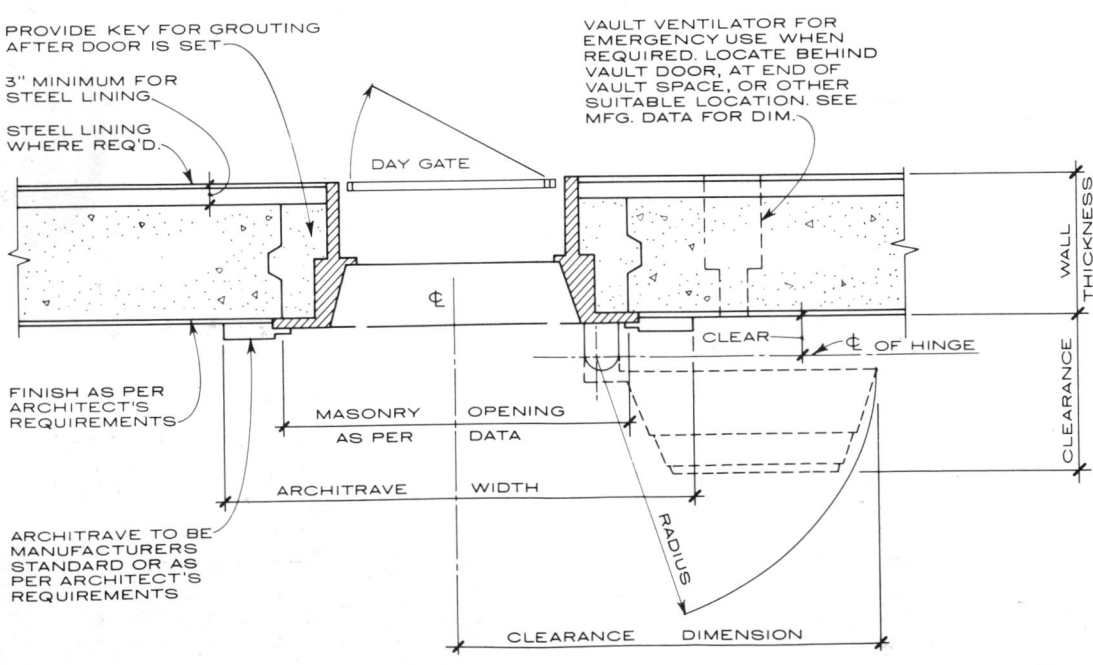

PROVIDE KEY FOR GROUTING
AFTER DOOR IS SET

3" MINIMUM FOR
STEEL LINING

STEEL LINING
WHERE REQ'D.

VAULT VENTILATOR FOR
EMERGENCY USE WHEN
REQUIRED. LOCATE BEHIND
VAULT DOOR, AT END OF
VAULT SPACE, OR OTHER
SUITABLE LOCATION. SEE
MFG. DATA FOR DIM.

DAY GATE

WALL THICKNESS

CLEAR

℄ OF HINGE

CLEARANCE

FINISH AS PER
ARCHITECT'S
REQUIREMENTS

MASONRY   OPENING
AS PER   DATA

ARCHITRAVE   WIDTH

RADIUS

ARCHITRAVE TO BE
MANUFACTURERS
STANDARD OR AS
PER ARCHITECT'S
REQUIREMENTS

CLEARANCE   DIMENSION

PLAN

Onofrio V. Bertolini; The Office of Alfred Easton Poor; New York, New York

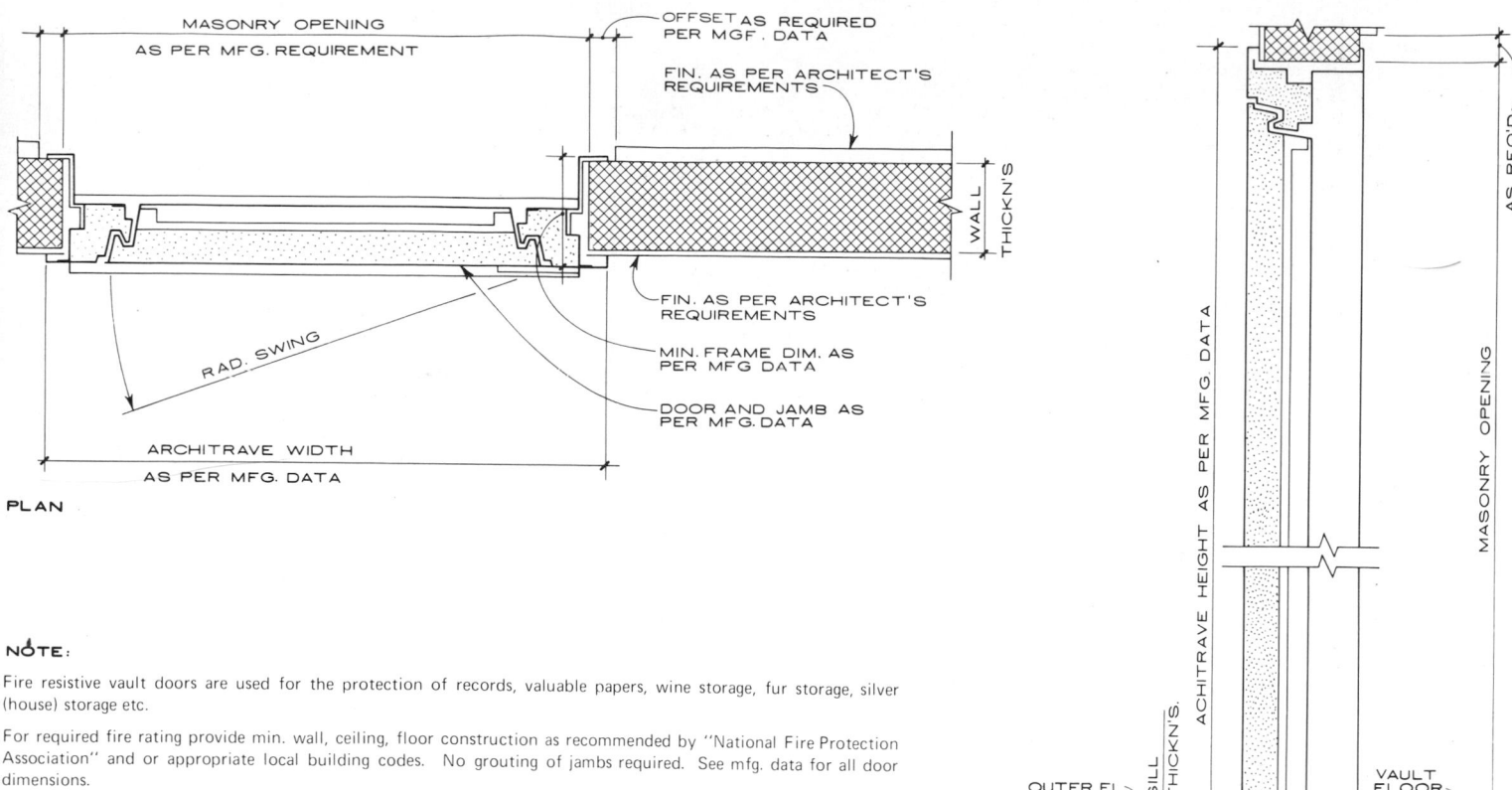

PLAN

SECTION

NOTE:

Fire resistive vault doors are used for the protection of records, valuable papers, wine storage, fur storage, silver (house) storage etc.

For required fire rating provide min. wall, ceiling, floor construction as recommended by "National Fire Protection Association" and or appropriate local building codes. No grouting of jambs required. See mfg. data for all door dimensions.

For minimum protection of office records, etc. in modern fireproof buildings conventional labeled fireproof hollow metal door and steel frame may meet requirements.

½, 1, 2, 4, & 6 HR. RATED FIRE RESISTIVE VAULT DOOR

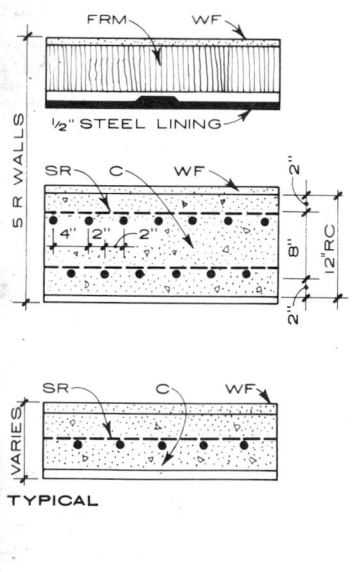

TYPICAL

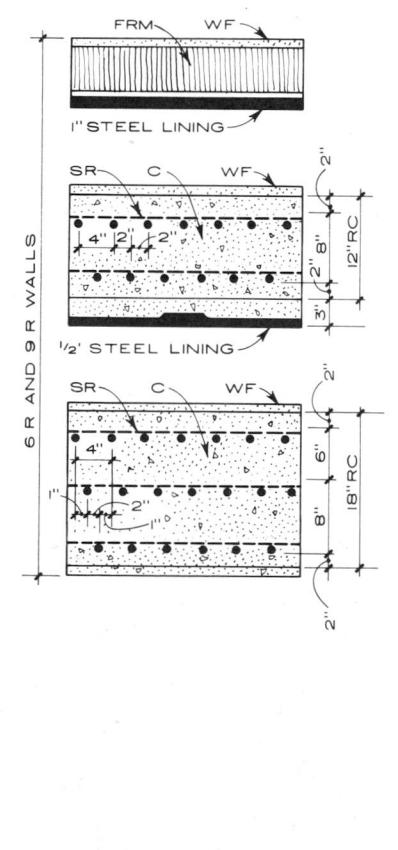

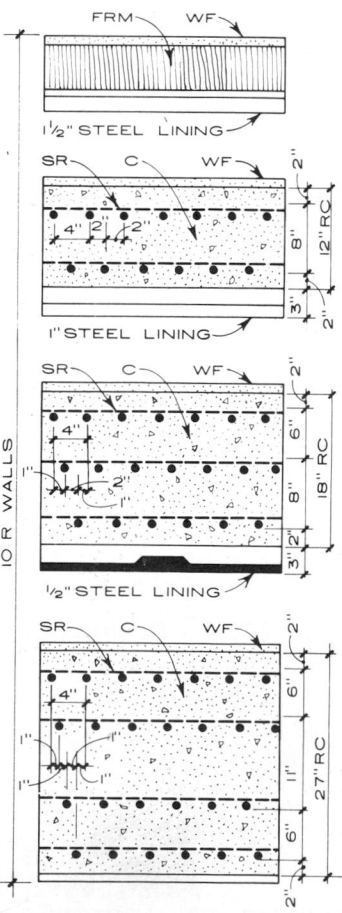

FRM = FIRE RESISTIVE MATERIAL
SR = STEEL REINFORCING
C = CONCRETE
RC = REINFORCED CONCRETE
WF = WALL FINISH

5R & 6R CLASSIFICATION	— 3 1/2"
9R CLASSIFICATION	— 7"
10R CLASSIFICATION	— 9 1/2"

VAULT CLASSIFICATION AND DOOR THICKNESS

Onofrio V. Bertolini; The Office of Alfred Easton Poor; New York, New York

NOTE:

The drawings below illustrate the use of a 9-point dimension grid which expresses the minimum desirable dimensions to be used when either specifying or designing a kidney or rectangular shaped pool for residential use.

Width, length, and depth dimensions may apply to any shape residential pool.

The minimum length with diving board and wading area is 30'. The average length of a residential pool is 40'.

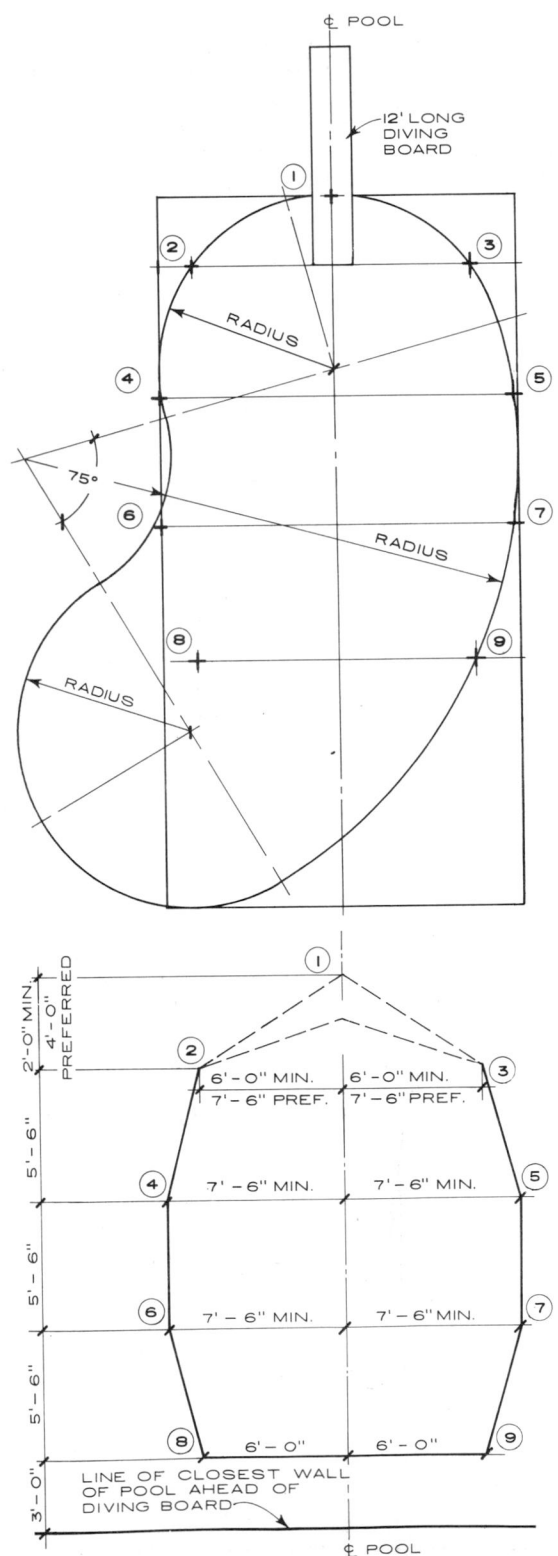

9 POINT GRID DIMENSION PLAN

Kenneth Jacobsen; R. Jackson Smith, AIA; Eggers & Higgins; New York, New York

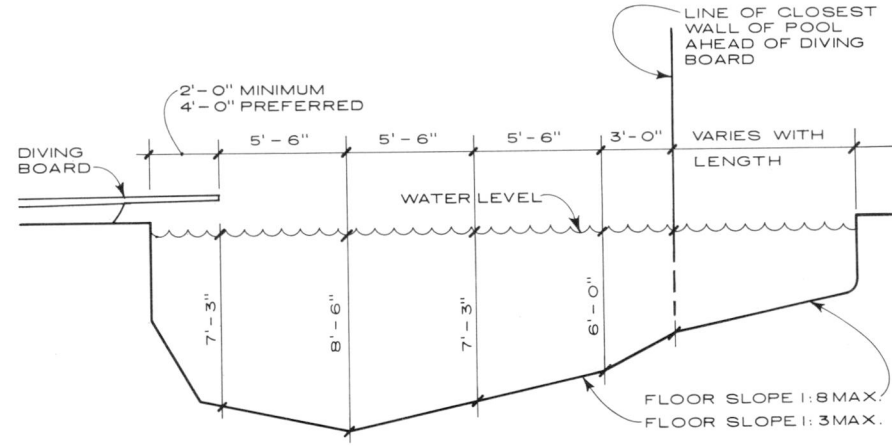

ISOMETRIC OVERLAY VIEW

LONGITUDINAL SECTION AT CENTERLINE

PERMITS AND RESTRICTIONS:

Required in most areas from building, health, plumbing, and electrical departments and zoning board. Check for setback restrictions and easements covering power and telephone lines, sewers and storm drains.

SITE CONSIDERATIONS:

Check the site for the following conditions, any of which will increase the cost considerably:

1. Fill more than 3' below pool deck.

2. Hard rock which will require drilling and blasting.

3. The presence of underground water or springs neccessitating pumping.

4. Accessibility of the site for mechanical equipment, minimum entry 8'— 0'' wide x 7'— 8'' high, with a grade easy enough for a truck to reach the site.

5. Locate the pool where it will get the most sun during swimming season. Place deep end if possible, so a diver dives away from, not into, the afternoon sun. Avoid overhanging tree branches near the pool.

6. The slope of the site should be as near level as possible; a steep slope requires retaining walls for the pool.

CONSTRUCTION AND SHAPES:

Pools may be made of reinforced concrete, either poured on the job, precast or gunite sprayed; concrete block, steel, aluminum, or plastic with or without block back-up. Concrete, aluminum, and steel pools are available in any shape: rectangular, square, kidney, oval, or free-form. Complete plastic installations and plastic pool liners with various back-ups are available only in manufacturers' standard shapes and sizes.

For practical purposes a rectangular pool is the most satisfactory giving the longest swimming distance.

POOL CAPACITY:

(Rule of Thumb): 36 sq. ft. for each swimmer, 100 sq. ft. for each diver. Pool 20' x 40' accomodates 14 persons at a time but since not everyone is in pool at once, pool and surrounds adequate for 30 — 40 people.

FILTER REQUIREMENTS:

Filter shall be sheltered, motor and electrical equipment shall be waterproofed.

GENERAL:

Public pools are generally considered as those belonging to municipalities, schools, country clubs, hotels, motels, apartments, and resorts. Permits for their construction are required in most areas from local and state Boards of Health as well as the departments of Building, Plumbing and Electricity.

Community pools should be integrated with existing and projected recreational facilities, such as picnic areas and parks, for maximum usage. Transportation access should be good, and there should be ample parking space. In a hot climate, enough shade should be provided, particularly in the lounging areas, and so located that it can be easily converted to spectator space by erection of bleachers.

Most local codes require that public pools have: (1) multiple unit filters, (2) mechanical chlorination, (3) a prescribed floor slope, (4) scum gutters in very large pools.

POOL DESIGN

Formerly most public pools were designed to meet competitive swimming requirements. The trend today is to provide for competitive dimensions and also design for all-around use. The following should be considered:

- Ratio of shallow water to deep water. Formerly 60% pool area 5' deep and less was considered adequate. Now 80% is considered more realistic.
- Ratio of loungers to bathers. Generally, no more than one-third of people attending a public pool are in the water at one time. Consequently the 6' to 8' walks formerly surrounding pools and used for lounging have been enlarged so that lounging area now approximates pool size. For Capacity Formula see "Public Swimming Pool Capacity" diagram on another page.

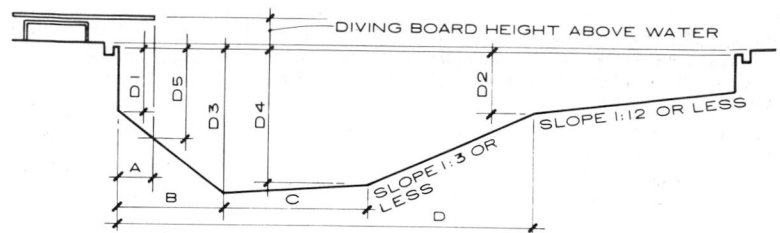

RECOMMENDED DIMENSIONS

BOARD HEIGHT ABOVE WATER		D1 (3)	D2	D3	D4	D5	A	B	C	D
24 inches	MIN	5'-0"	4'-6"	8'-0"	8'-0"		2'-6"	6'-0"	6'-0"	24'-0"
	MAX		5'-6"				4'-0"	10'-0"		
1 meter	MIN	5'-0"	4'-6"	8'-6"	8'-0"	7'-6"	5'-0"	6'-0"	9'-0"	30'-0"
	MAX		5'-6"				6'-0"	10'-0"		
3 meters	MIN	5'-0"	4'-6"	12'-0"	11'-6"	8'-6"	5'-0"	6'-0"	9'-0"	35'-0"
	MAX		5'-6"				6'-0"	10'-0"		

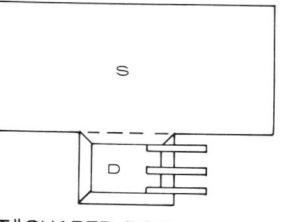

"T" SHAPED POOL

Provides large shallow area(s). Diving area off to one side. Water in large part of pool from 4'-6" to 5'-0" deep, adequate for regular competitive events.

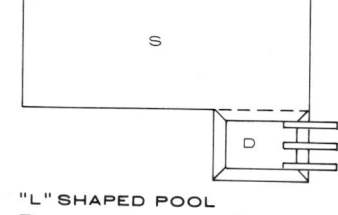

"L" SHAPED POOL

These two shapes generally desired for large 50 meter pools.

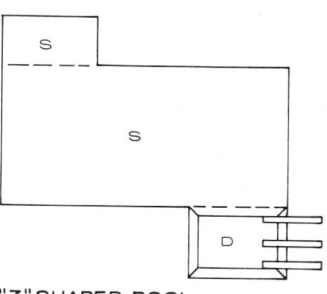

"Z" SHAPED POOL

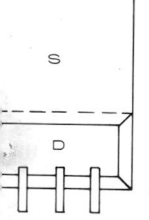

RECTANGULAR POOL

Standard design. Good for competitive swimming & indoor pool design. Shallow area often inadequate.

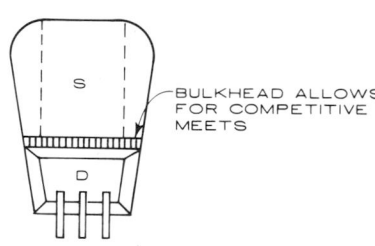

FAN - SHAPED POOL

Successful where there is a high percentage of children. Largest area for shallow depth. Deep area can be roped off or separated by bulkhead.

BULKHEAD ALLOWS FOR COMPETITIVE MEETS

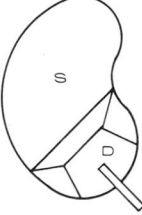

FREE - FORM POOL

Kidney & oval shapes are the most common free-forms. Use only where competitive meets are not a consideration.

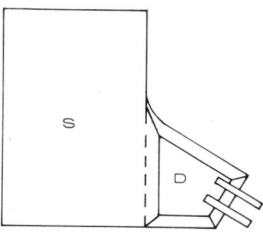

MODIFIED "L" POOL

Provides for separate diving area. Shallow area with 4'-0" min. depth may be roped off for competitive meets.

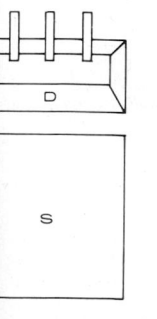

BULKHEAD

MULTIPLE POOLS

Separate pools for beginners, divers and swimmers. Ultimate in desirability especially if pool is intended for large numbers of people. Variation at left shows single pool and bulkhead over it with advantage that swimmers are kept out of area reserved for beginners. Both designs may use common filtration system.

WADING POOLS

Generally provided in connection with community and family club pools. Placed away from swimming area to avoid congestion. If near swimming pool, wading area should be fenced off for children's protection. To add play appeal provide spray fittings and small fountains in pool. Also provide seats and benches for adults who accompany children to pool.

PUBLIC POOL SHAPES

NOTE: S = Swimming Pool, D = Diving Pool, B = Beginners Pool

Kenneth Jacobsen; R. Jackson Smith, AIA; Eggers & Higgins; New York, New York

LENGTH OF POOLS:

25 yards is the minimum length for American records, and meets interscholastic and intercollegiate requirements. (Pool should be 75' – 1 1/2" long to allow for electronic timing panels at one end.)
50 meters (164' – 0 1/2") is minimum for world (F.I.N.A.) records. Add 3 1/2" for electronic timing devices.

WIDTH OF POOLS:

Drawing below shows 7' lanes. 6' lanes with pool width a multiple of 6' also meet general racing requirements. Strictly competitive pools should have 7' lanes.
Min. width of 25 yard pool is 36' (6' lanes) or 42' (7' lanes). With outside lanes, min. widths are 38' or 45'. 60' width (8 lanes) is desirable.

NOTE:

Gutters at sides of pool are desirable to reduce wave action in swimming meets or water polo. See lighting standards and diving board standards on other pages of this series for additional requirements for competitive pools.

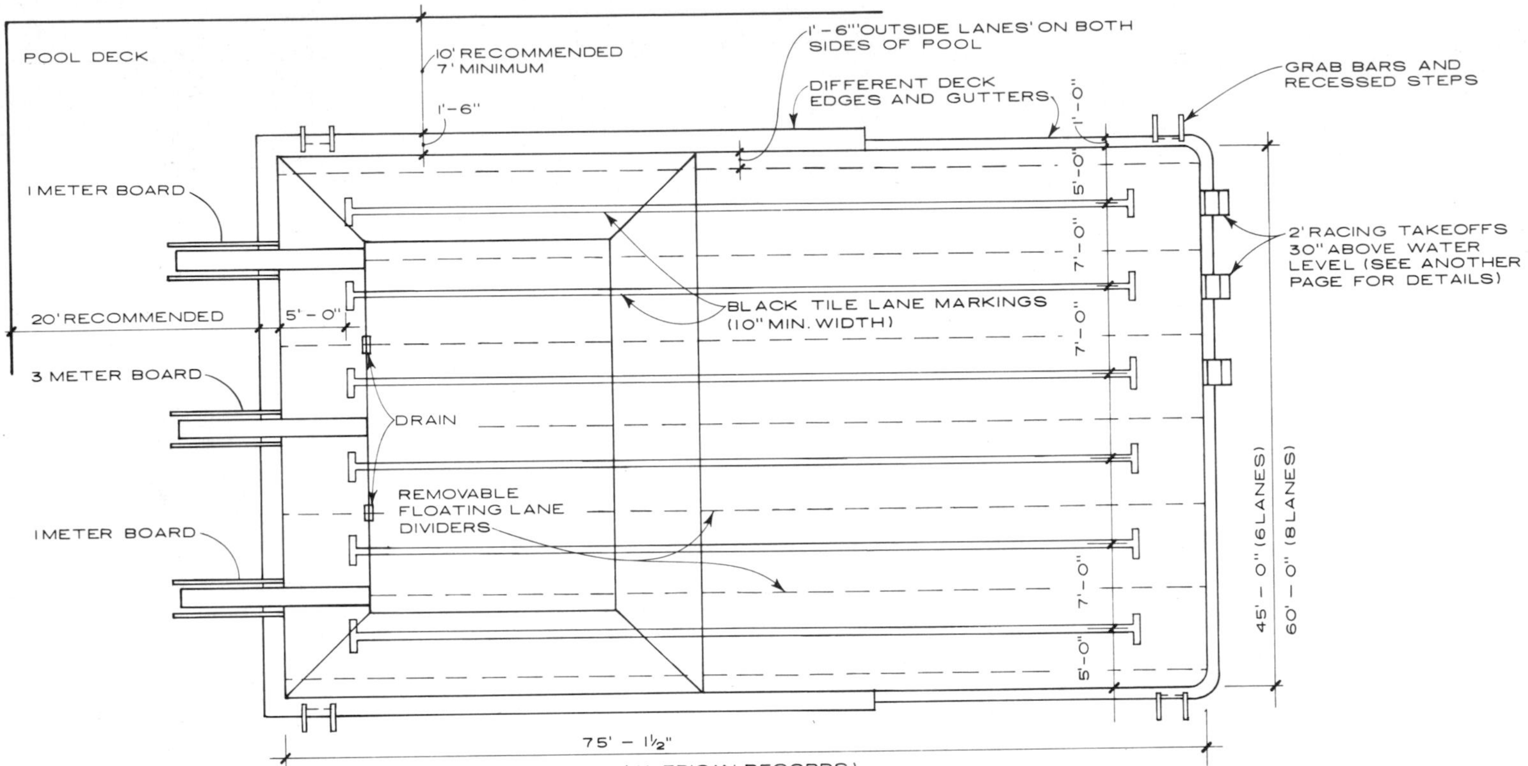

PLAN

LONGITUDINAL SECTION

25 YARD POOL

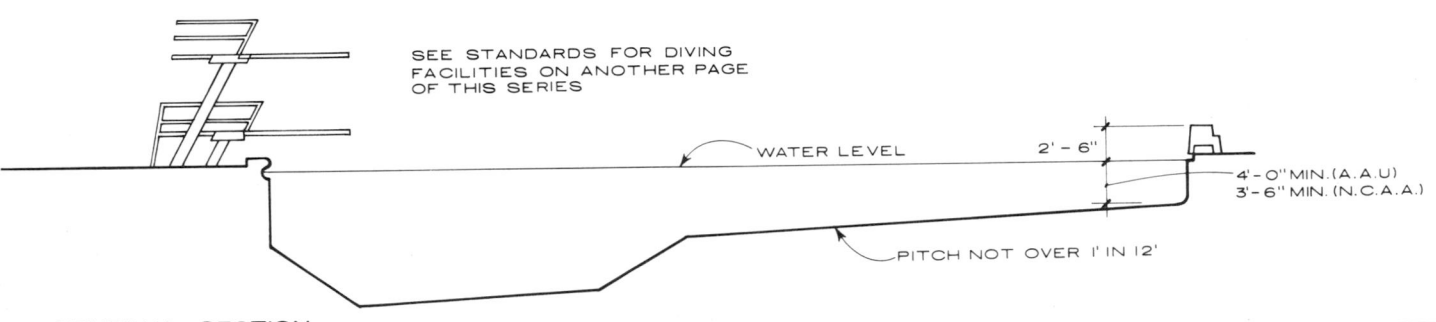

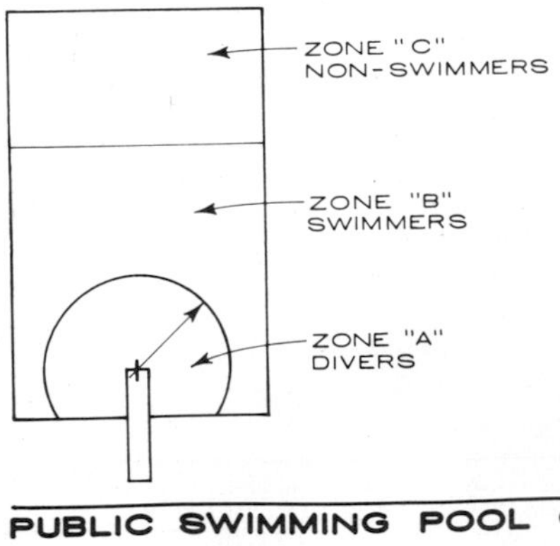

Swimming pool capacity requirements vary from one locality to another: check local regulations. The following is suggested by the American Public Health Association.

FORMULA DERIVATION:

ZONE "A" Diving area defined by 10' radius from diving board or platform.
12 divers per board; 2 – 3 in water, the rest on shore.
Or allow 300 sq. ft. of pool water surface per board.

ZONE "B" Swimming area; 24 sq. ft. per swimmer. Based on volume displaced by each swimmer (4/5 square of average ht.) and adjusted by the number of swimmers using pool at one time. (2/3 total swimmers).

ZONE "C" Non-swimmer area. 10 sq. ft. per person. Based on volume displaced by person (1/2 area allowed per swimmer) and adjusted by number not using water—50% (in some pools with large number of non-swimmers, figure may be as high as 75%).

FORMULA:

$$\text{Max. pool capacity} = 12 \times \text{No. diving boards or platforms} + \frac{\text{Area Zone "B"}}{24} + \frac{\text{Area Zone "C"}}{10}$$

PUBLIC SWIMMING POOL CAPACITY

Kenneth Jacobsen; R. Jackson Smith, AIA; Eggers & Higgins; New York, New York

GENERAL NOTES:

For judging competitive meets, A.A.U. officials recommend the springboard and diving platform arrangement indicated below in plan. Diving dimensions meet A.A.U. and F.I.N.A. standards. Fifty meters is minimum length for world records.

NOTE:

* Length should be 164' — 4" allowing an extra 3 — 1/2" to compensate for possible future tile facing, structural defects and electrical timing panels.

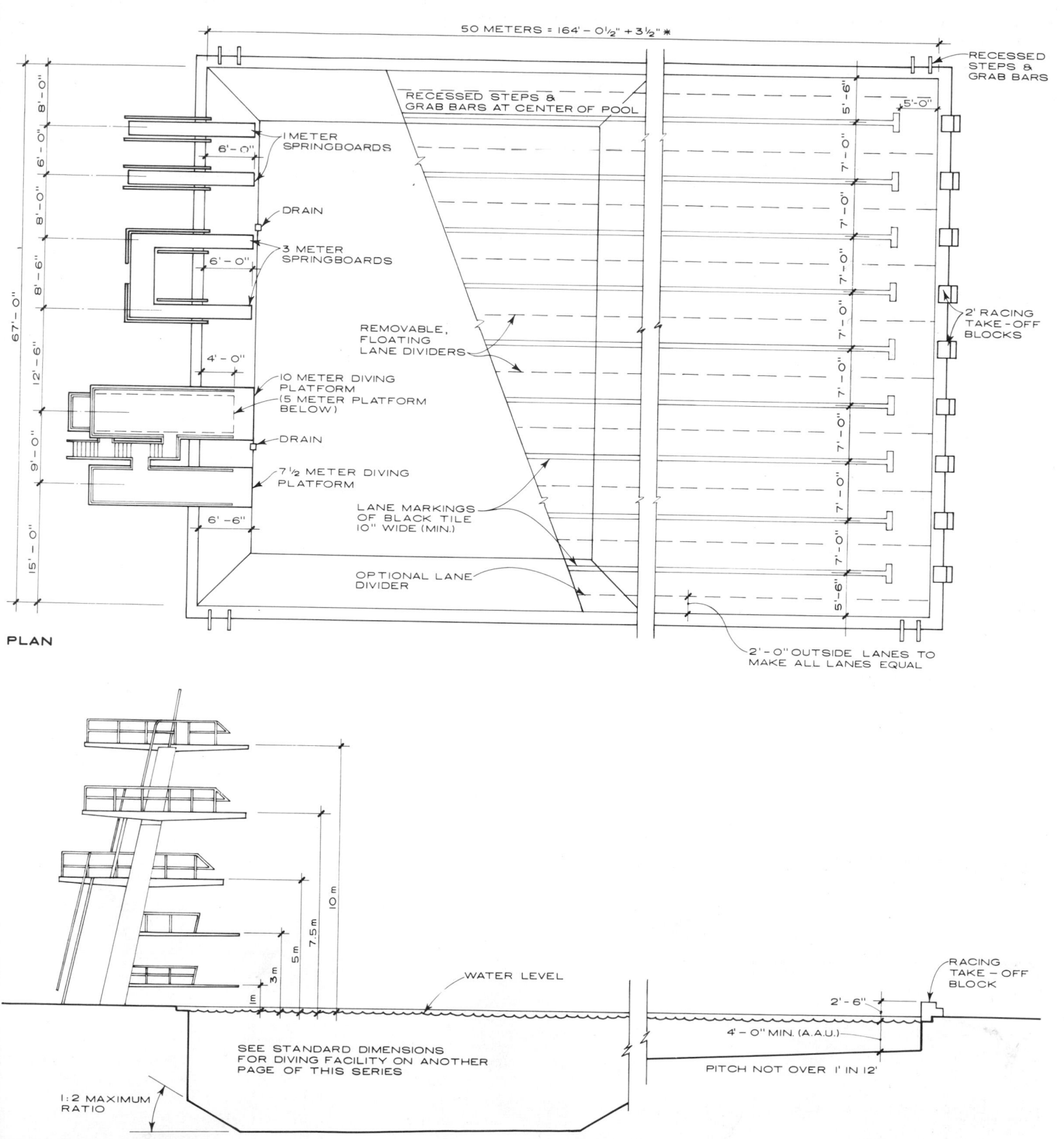

50 METERS = 164' — 0½" + 3½" *

RECESSED STEPS & GRAB BARS

RECESSED STEPS & GRAB BARS AT CENTER OF POOL

1 METER SPRINGBOARDS

6' — 0"

DRAIN

3 METER SPRINGBOARDS

6' — 0"

REMOVABLE, FLOATING LANE DIVIDERS

2' RACING TAKE-OFF BLOCKS

4' — 0"

10 METER DIVING PLATFORM (5 METER PLATFORM BELOW)

DRAIN

7½ METER DIVING PLATFORM

LANE MARKINGS OF BLACK TILE 10" WIDE (MIN.)

6' — 6"

OPTIONAL LANE DIVIDER

PLAN

2' — 0" OUTSIDE LANES TO MAKE ALL LANES EQUAL

67' — 0"   8' — 0"   8' — 0"   6' — 0"   8' — 0"   8' — 6"   12' — 6"   9' — 0"   15' — 0"

5' — 6"   5' — 0"   7' — 0"   7' — 0"   7' — 0"   7' — 0"   7' — 0"   7' — 0"   7' — 0"   5' — 6"

10 m   7.5 m   5 m   3 m

WATER LEVEL

RACING TAKE — OFF BLOCK

2' — 6"

4' — 0" MIN. (A.A.U.)

SEE STANDARD DIMENSIONS FOR DIVING FACILITY ON ANOTHER PAGE OF THIS SERIES

PITCH NOT OVER 1' IN 12'

1:2 MAXIMUM RATIO

LONGITUDINAL SECTION

Kenneth Jacobsen; R. Jackson Smith, AIA; Eggers & Higgins; New York, New York

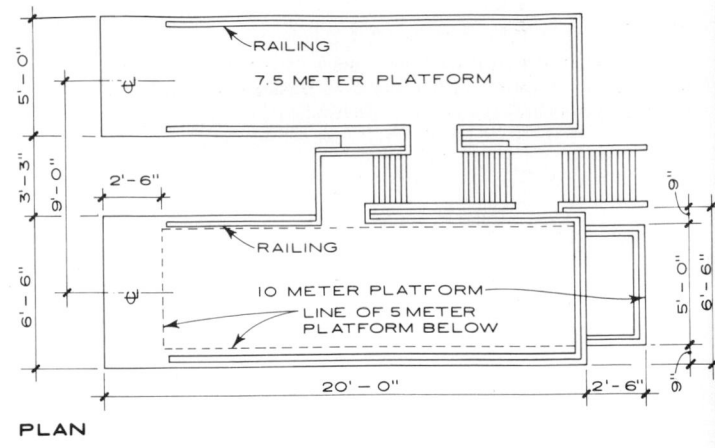

RAILING

7.5 METER PLATFORM

5'-0"

3'-3"

9'-0"

2'-6"

RAILING

6'-6"

IO METER PLATFORM

LINE OF 5 METER
PLATFORM BELOW

9"

5'-0"

6'-6"

9"

20'-0"

2'-6"

9"

PLAN

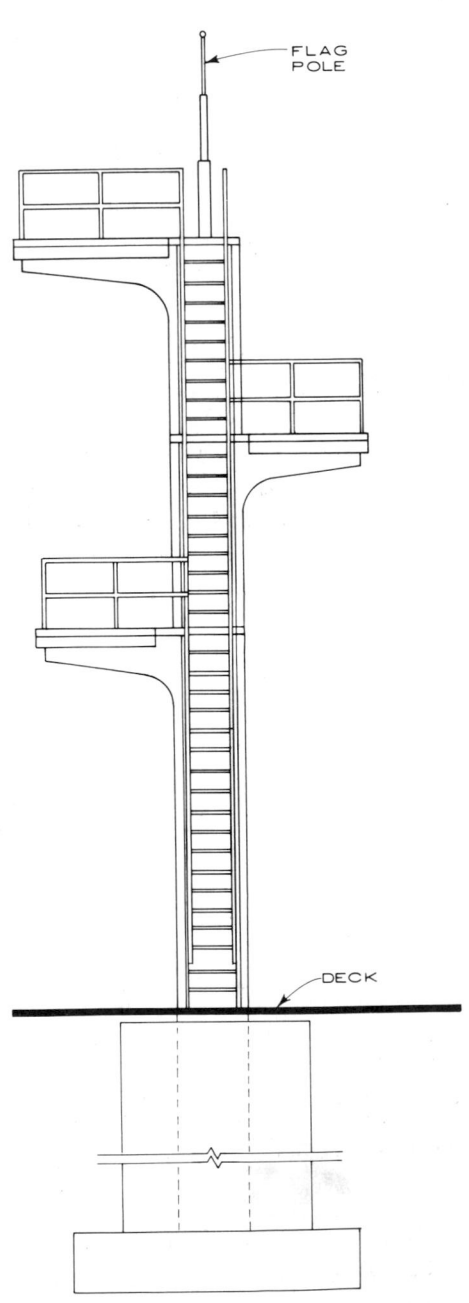

FLAG
POLE

DECK

REAR ELEVATION

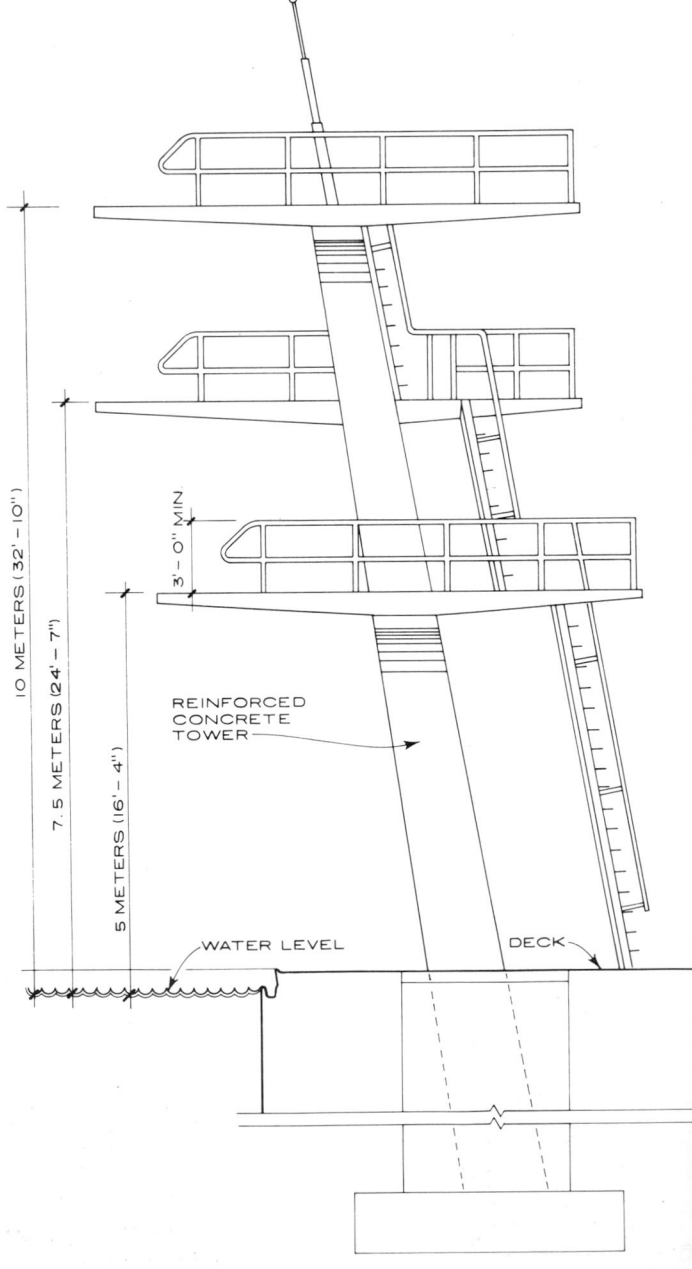

IO METERS (32'-10")

7.5 METERS (24'-7")

5 METERS (16'-4")

3'-0" MIN

REINFORCED
CONCRETE
TOWER

WATER LEVEL

DECK

SIDE ELEVATION

Kenneth Jacobsen; R. Jackson Smith, AIA; Eggers & Higgins; New York, New York

GENERAL NOTES:

Both 1 meter and 3 meter boards are required for amateur, collegiate and international meets. All boards shall have a non-slip surface.

Foundations are shown to approximate scale but dimensions should be determined by calculation.

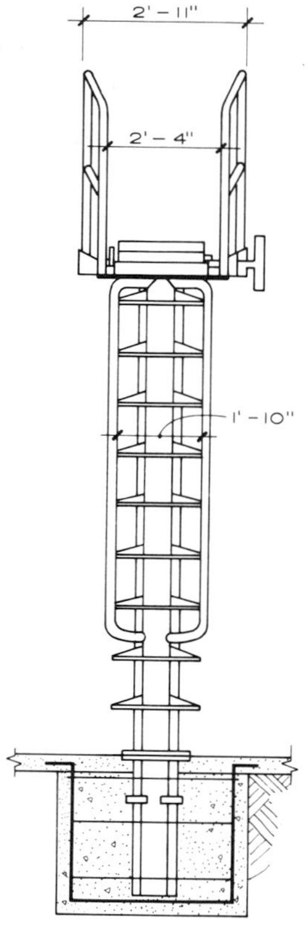

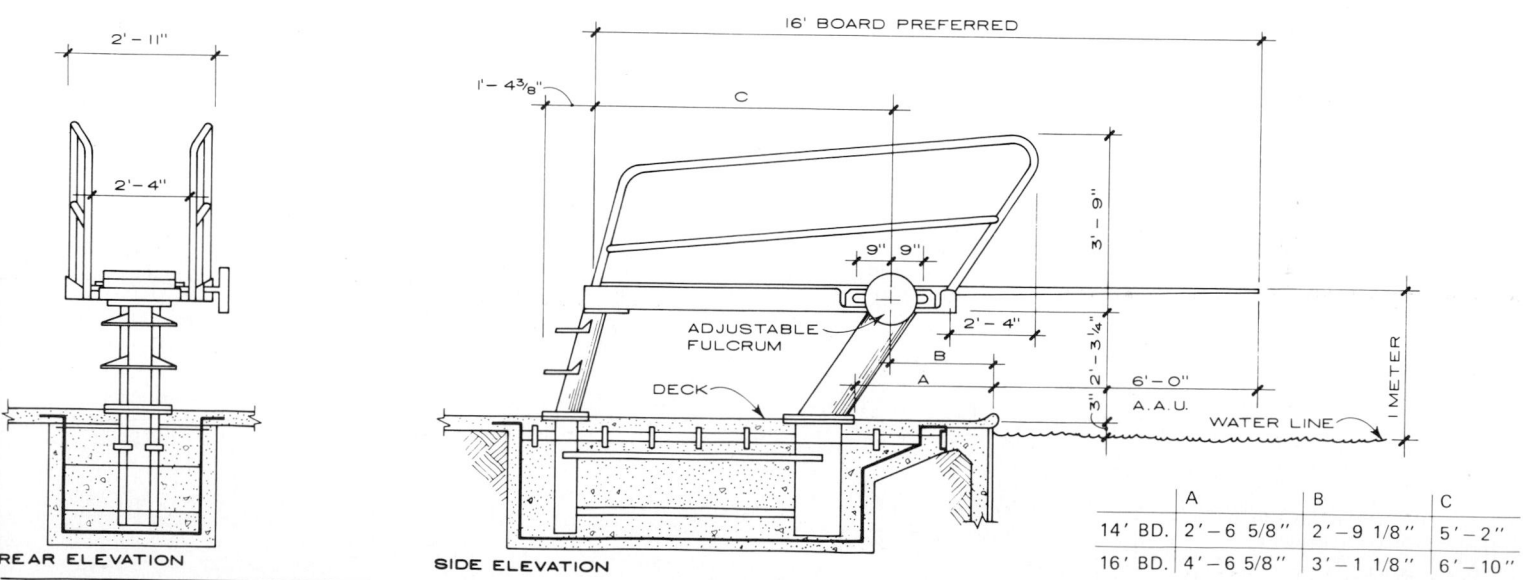

THREE METER DIVING BOARD — NO SCALE

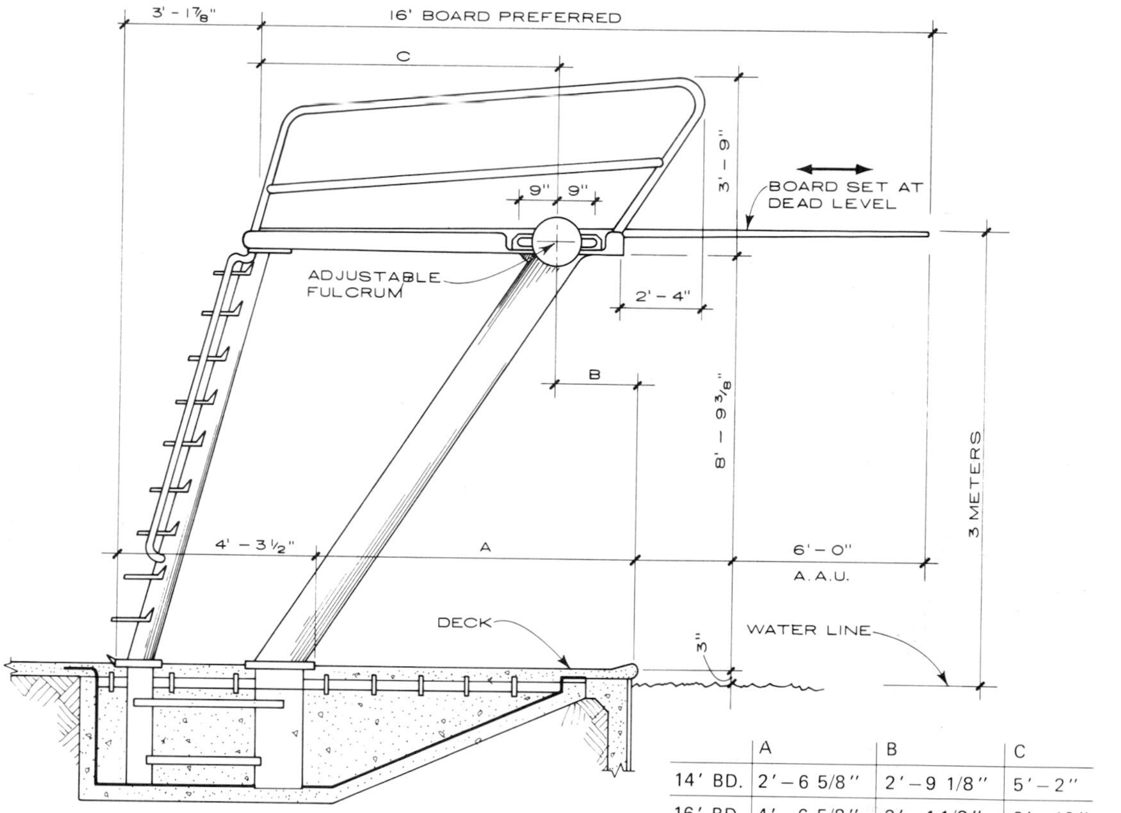

	A	B	C
14' BD.	2'–6 5/8"	2'–9 1/8"	5'–2"
16' BD.	4'–6 5/8"	3'–1 1/8"	6'–10"

REAR ELEVATION   SIDE ELEVATION

ONE METER DIVING BOARD — NO SCALE

	A	B	C
14' BD.	2'–6 5/8"	2'–9 1/8"	5'–2"
16' BD.	4'–6 5/8"	3'–1 1/8"	6'–10"

REAR ELEVATION   SIDE ELEVATION

Kenneth Jacobsen; R. Jackson Smith, AIA; Eggers & Higgins; New York, New York

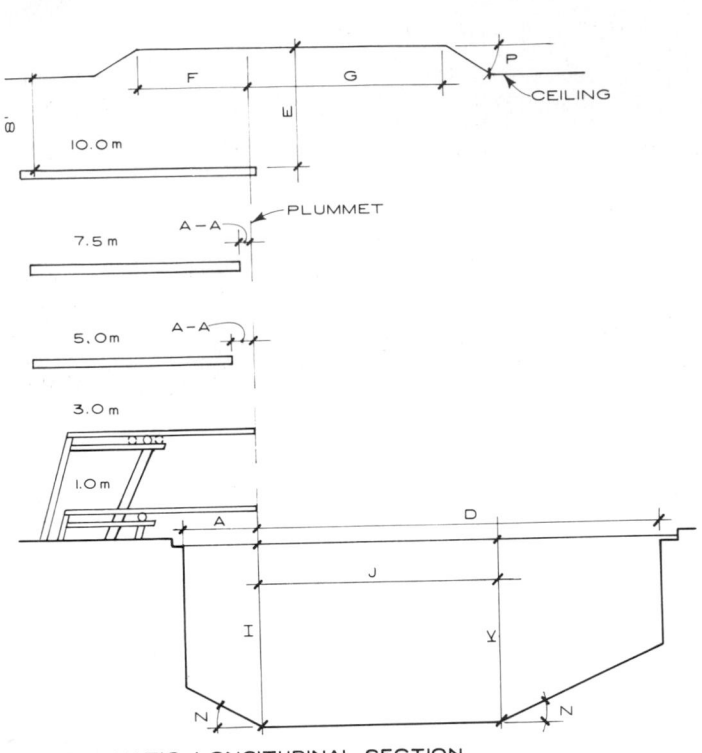

DIAGRAMMATIC LONGITUDINAL SECTION

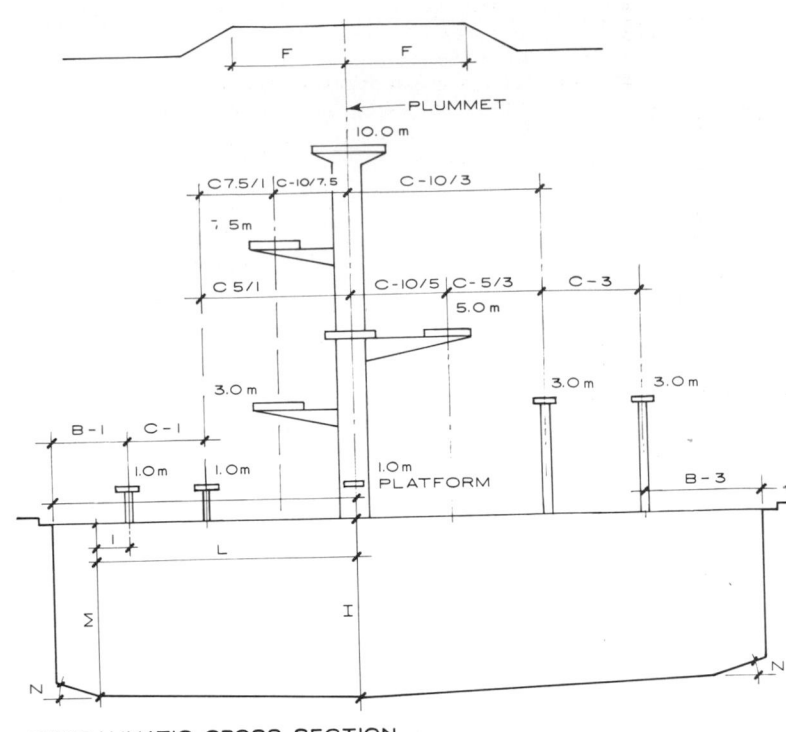

DIAGRAMMATIC CROSS SECTION

FINA INTERNATIONAL AMATEUR SWIMMING AND DIVING FEDERATION STANDARDS

DIMENSIONS FOR DIVING FACILITIES			SPRINGBOARDS 1 METER	SPRINGBOARDS 3 METER	PLATFORMS 1 METER	PLATFORMS 3 METER	5 METER	7.5 METER	10 METER
		LENGTH	16'-0"	16'-0"	15'-0"	16'-0"	20'-0"	20'-0"	20'-0"
		WIDTH	1'-8"	1'-8"	1'-8"	2'-6"	5'-0"	5'-0"	6'-6"
		HEIGHT	3'-3"	9'-10"	3'-3"	9'-10"	16'-4"	24'-7"	32'-10"
A	FROM PLUMMET: BACK TO POOL WALL	DESIG.	A-1	A-3	A-1 (pl)	A-3 (pl)	A-5	A-7.5	A-10
		MIN.	5'-0"	5'-0"	4'-0"	4'-0"	4'-0"	5'-0"	5'-0"
		PREF.	6'-0"	6'-0"			5'-0"		
A-A	FROM PLUMMET: BACK TO PLATFORM DIRECTLY BELOW	DESIG.					AA-5/1	A-7.5/3	AA-10/5
		MIN.					2'-6"	2'-6"	2'-6"
		PREF.					5'-0"	5'-0"	5'-0"
B	FROM PLUMMET: TO POOL WALL AT SIDE	DESIG.	B-1	B-3	B-1 (pl)	B-3 (pl)	B-5	B-7.5	B-10
		MIN.	8'-0"	12'-0"	7'-6"	9'-6"	14'-0"	15'-0"	17'-0"
		PREF.	10'-0"						
C	FROM PLUMMET TO ADJACENT PLUMMET	DESIG.	C-1	C-3 / C-3/1			C-5/3	C-5/1 / C-7.5/1	C-10/7.5 / C-10/5 / C-10/3
		MIN.	6'-0"	6'-0" / 6'-0"			7'-0"	7'-0" / 7'-0"	9'-0" / 9'-0" / 9'-0"
		PREF.	8'-0"	8'-0" / 8'-10"			10'-0"	10'-0" / 10'-0"	12'-0"
D	FROM PLUMMET TO POOL WALL AHEAD	DESIG.	D-1	D-3	D-1 (pl)	D-3 (pl)	D-5	D-7.5	D-10
		MIN.	29'-0"	34'-0"	26'-0"	31'-0"	34'-0"	36'-0"	45'-0"
		PREF.							
E	PLUMMET, FROM BOARD TO CEILING OVERHEAD	DESIG.	E-1	E-3	E-1 (pl)	E-3 (pl)	E-5	E-7.5	E-10
		MIN.	16'-0"	16'-0"	10'-0"	10'-0"	10'-0"	10'-6"	11'-0"
		PREF.					11'-0"	11'-0"	16'-0"
F	CLEAR OVERHEAD, BEHIND AND EACH SIDE OF PLUMMET	DESIG.	F-1 / E-3	F-3 / E-3	F-1 (pl)	F-3 (pl)	F-5 / E-5	F-7.5 / E-7.5	F-10
		MIN.	8'-0" / 16'-0"	8'-0" / 16'-0"	9'-0"	9'-0"	9'-0" / 10'-0"	9'-0" / 10'-6"	9'-0"
		PREF.					11'-0"	11'-0"	
G	CLEAR OVERHEAD, AHEAD OF PLUMMET	DESIG.	G-1 / E-3	G-3 / E-3	G-1 (pl)	G-3 (pl)	G-5 / E-5	G-7.5 / E-7.5	G-10
		MIN.	16'-0" / 16'-0"	16'-0" / 16'-0"	16'-0"	16'-0"	16'-0" / 10'-0"	16'-0" / 10'-6"	20'-0"
		PREF.					11'-0"	11'-0"	
H	DEPTH OF WATER AT PLUMMET	DESIG.	H-1	H-3	H-1 (pl)	H-3 (pl)	H-5	H-7.5	H-10
		MIN.	11'-0"	12'-0"	11'-0"	11'-0"	12'-0"	13'-6"	15'-0"
		PREF.	12'-0"	13'-0"			13'-0"	15'-0"	16'-0"
J-K	DISTANCE, DEPTH OF WATER, AHEAD OF PLUMMET	DESIG.	J-1 / K-1	J-3 / K-3	J/K-1 (pl)	J/K-3 (pl)	J-5 / K-5	J-7.5 / K-7.5	J-10 / K-10
		MIN.	20'-0" / 10'-9"	20'-0" / 11'-9"	16'/10'-9"	20'/10'-9"	20'-0" / 11'-9"	26'-0" / 13'-0"	40'-0" / 14'-0"
		PREF.	11'-9"	12'-9"			12'-9"		15'-0"
L-M	DISTANCE, DEPTH OF WATER, EACH SIDE OF PLUMMET	DESIG.	L-1 / M-1	L-3 / M-3	L/M-1 (pl)	L/M-3 (pl)	L-5 / M-5	L-7.5 / M-7.5	L-10 / M-10
		MIN.	8'-0" / 10'-9"	10'-6" / 11'-9"	7'/10'-9"	9'/10'-9"	14'-0" / 11'-9"	15'-0" / 13'-0"	17'-0" / 14'-0"
		PREF.	11'-9"	12'-9"			12'-9"		15'-0"
N P	MAXIMUM ANGLE OF SLOPE TO REDUCE DIMENSION BEYOND FULL REQUIREMENTS	POOL BOTTOM = 30 Degrees (Approximately 1 foot vertical to 2 feet horizontal)							
		CEILING HEIGHT = 30 Degrees							

Kenneth Jacobsen; R. Jackson Smith, AIA; Eggers & Higgins; New York, New York

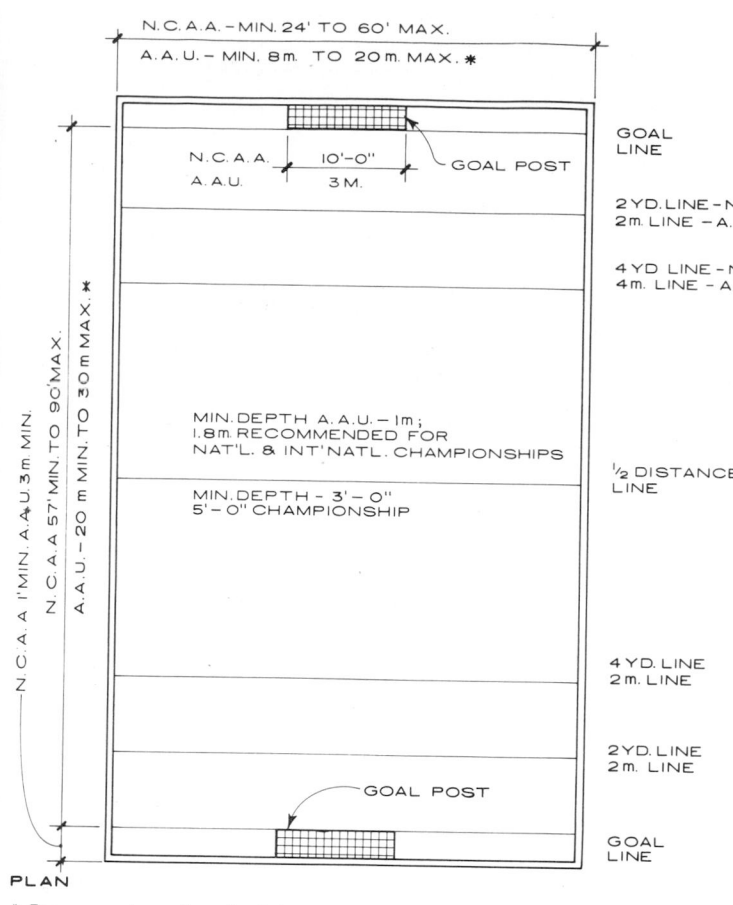

N.C.A.A. – MIN. 24' TO 60' MAX.
A.A.U. – MIN. 8 m. TO 20 m. MAX. *

N.C.A.A. I' MIN. A.A.U. 3 m. MIN.
N.C.A.A. 57' MIN. TO 90' MAX. *
A.A.U. – 20 m MIN. TO 30 m MAX. *

N.C.A.A.   10'-0"   — GOAL POST
A.A.U.   3 M.

GOAL LINE

2 YD. LINE – NCAA
2 m. LINE – A.A.U.

4 YD. LINE – NCAA
4 m. LINE – A.A.U

MIN. DEPTH A.A.U. – 1m;
1.8m. RECOMMENDED FOR
NAT'L. & INT'NATL. CHAMPIONSHIPS

MIN. DEPTH – 3'-0"
5'-0" CHAMPIONSHIP

½ DISTANCE LINE

4 YD. LINE
2 m. LINE

2 YD. LINE
2 m. LINE

GOAL POST

GOAL LINE

PLAN

* For womens' matches, the A.A.U. recommends measurements of 25 m. x 17 m.
One meter equals 3.28 ft. To obtain equivalent dimensions in feet, multiply by 3.28. A.A.U. figures are expressed in meters.

WATER POLO

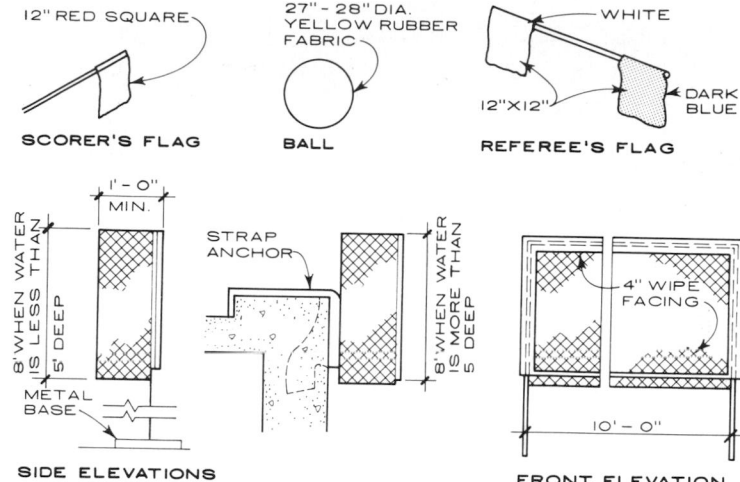

12" RED SQUARE

SCORER'S FLAG

27" - 28" DIA.
YELLOW RUBBER
FABRIC

BALL

WHITE

12" X 12"

DARK BLUE

REFEREE'S FLAG

1'-0" MIN.

8' WHEN WATER IS LESS THAN 5' DEEP

METAL BASE

STRAP ANCHOR

8' WHEN WATER IS MORE THAN 5' DEEP

4" WIPE FACING

10'-0"

SIDE ELEVATIONS

FRONT ELEVATION

N.C.A.A. GOALS

NOTES:

Distinctive marks must be provided on both sides of field of play indicating goal lines, 2 & 4 yd. (or meter) lines, and 1/2 distance between goal lines. These must be clearly visable from any position within the field of play. Allow sufficient space on walkways so referees may move freely from end to end of field of play. Provide space at goal lines for goal judges.

GOAL REQUIREMENTS

Posts and crossbar, rigid and perpendicular. A.A.U., wood or metal, 3 " sq., painted white; N.C.A.A., metal, 1 1/2 dia., painted yellow or orange. Nets to hang loosely on frame.

For A.A.U., the underside of the crossbar must be 0.90 meters above water surface when water is 1.50 meters or more in depth, and 2.40 meters from the bottom of the bath when the depth of the water is less than 1.50 meters.

Frames are custom made with bracing placed where necessary. It is recommended that they be collapsible for easy storage. Anchorage methods depend on pool design, with those above commonly used, or brass couplings may be placed in pool walls to which frame is attached. If pool is longer than required length, one of the goals may be floated & anchored with guy wires.

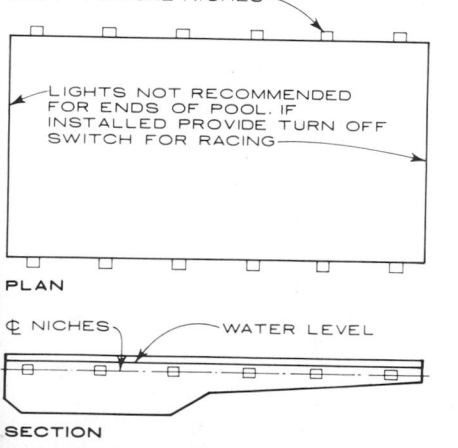

LIGHT FIXTURE NICHES

LIGHTS NOT RECOMMENDED FOR ENDS OF POOL. IF INSTALLED PROVIDE TURN OFF SWITCH FOR RACING

PLAN

₵ NICHES   WATER LEVEL

SECTION

UNDERWATER POOL LIGHTING

NOTES FOR WET AND DRY NICHE UNDERWATER LIGHTS

Underwater lighting type and distance "A" should be in accordance with NEC and NFPA regulations. Cite N.B.F.U. grounding requirements.

Underwater lights will require 0.5 to 2.0 watts per sq. ft. of water area and should be sized accordingly.

Box connections for dry or wet niches should be a minimum of 4'-0" away from the side wall of the pool and 8" above the deck. Low voltage wiring should be used for all dry or wet niche lighting fixtures. This requires a transformer located, by code, a specific distance away from pool wall and above deck.

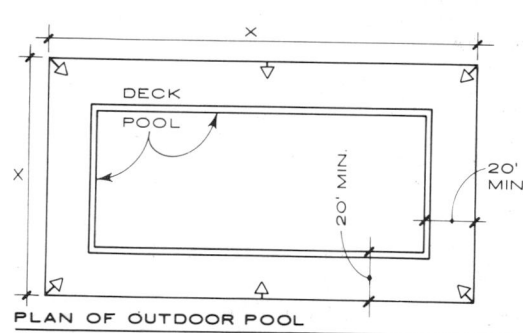

X

DECK

POOL

20' MIN.

20' MIN.

X

PLAN OF OUTDOOR POOL

OVERHEAD FLOOD LIGHTING

NOTE:

Distance "X" for spacing of lights not to exceed four times the actual mounting height of lamp in light fixture.

INTERIOR ABOVE WATER LIGHTING

The A.A.U. states that "sufficient over head lighting be installed with concentration directly over finish line. 40 foot-candles at a height of 3 ft. above the water surface is recommended. Buildings housing indoor pools should not have windows facing pool-ends, to prevent glare at finish and turns."

SWIMMING POOL LIGHTING

OUTDOOR ABOVE WATER LIGHTING

Flood lights should be mounted at least 20 ft. above the water. Select lamps to allow 1.0 watt per sq. ft. min. for floodlights. Consult A.A.U. or N.C.A.A. for specific requirements for championship meets. A.A.U. rules for championship meets require a minimum of 40 foot-candles 3 feet above the water surface.

Kenneth Jacobsen; R. Jackson Smith, AIA; Eggers & Higgins; New York, New York

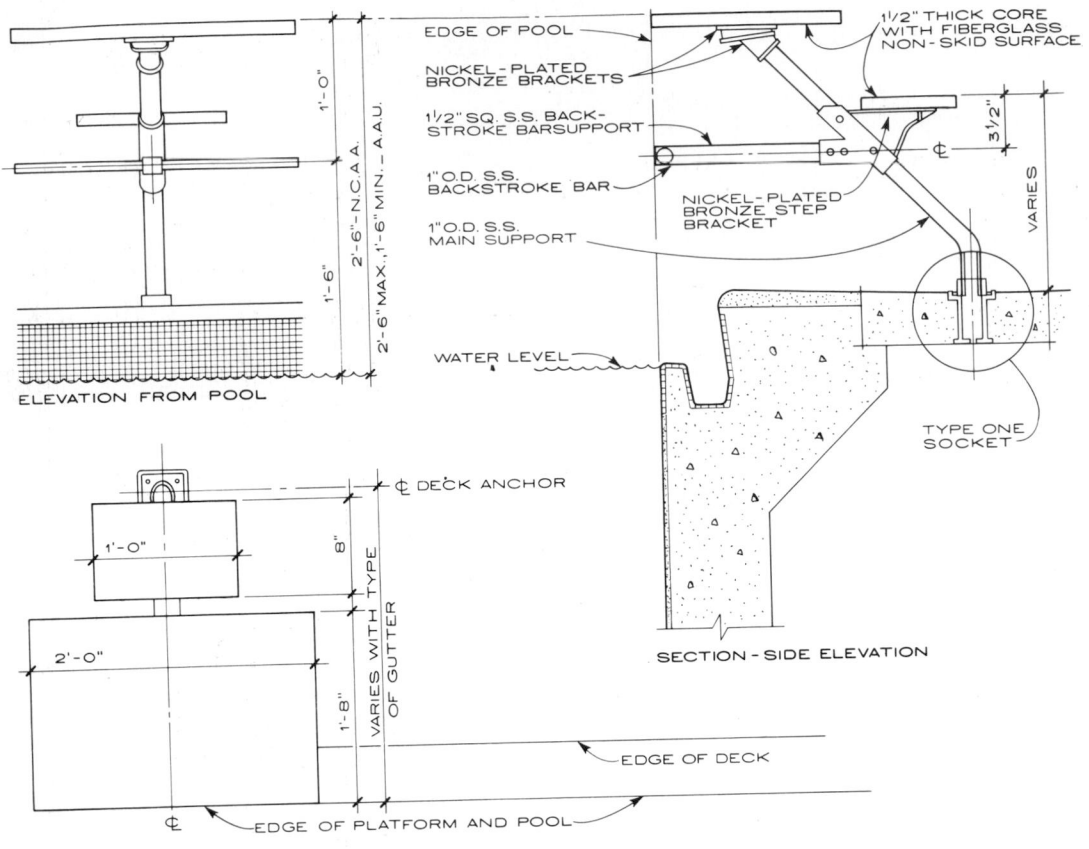

EDGE OF POOL

NICKEL-PLATED BRONZE BRACKETS

1½" SQ. S.S. BACK-STROKE BARSUPPORT

1" O.D. S.S. BACKSTROKE BAR

1" O.D. S.S. MAIN SUPPORT

1½" THICK CORE WITH FIBERGLASS NON-SKID SURFACE

NICKEL-PLATED BRONZE STEP BRACKET

WATER LEVEL

1'-0"

1'-6"

2'-6" N.C.A.A.

2'-6" MAX., 1'-6" MIN.-A.A.U.

3½"

VARIES

TYPE ONE SOCKET

ELEVATION FROM POOL

SECTION - SIDE ELEVATION

℄ DECK ANCHOR

1'-0"

2'-0"

8"

1'-8"

VARIES WITH TYPE OF GUTTER

EDGE OF DECK

EDGE OF PLATFORM AND POOL

STARTING PLATFORM

SCALE: 3/4" = 1'-0"

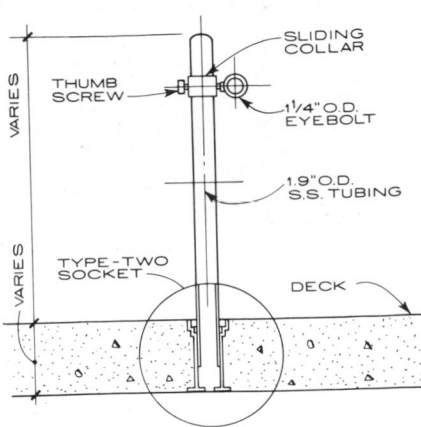

SLIDING COLLAR

THUMB SCREW

1¼" O.D. EYEBOLT

1.9" O.D. S.S. TUBING

TYPE-TWO SOCKET

DECK

VARIES

VARIES

DECK STANCHION

Used to hang splash curtains, backstroke warning and other types of finish line markers. Various types of eyebolt anchorages (top, side, fixed or adjustable) are available.

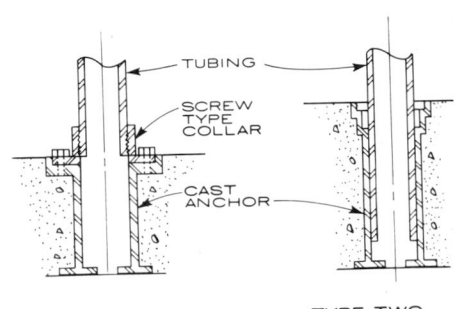

TUBING

SCREW TYPE COLLAR

CAST ANCHOR

TYPE ONE   TYPE TWO

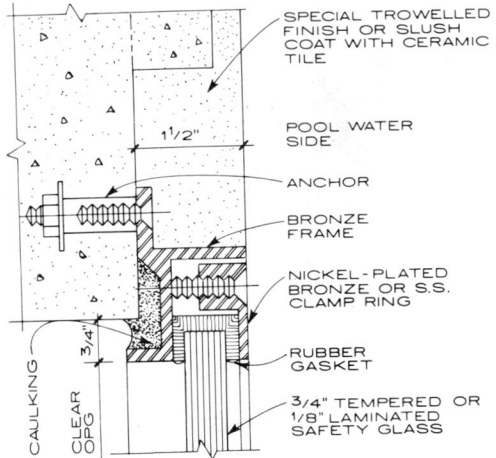

SPECIAL TROWELLED FINISH OR SLUSH COAT WITH CERAMIC TILE

POOL WATER SIDE

ANCHOR

BRONZE FRAME

NICKEL-PLATED BRONZE OR S.S. CLAMP RING

RUBBER GASKET

3/4" TEMPERED OR 1/8" LAMINATED SAFETY GLASS

1½"

3/4"

CAULKING

CLEAR OPG.

UNDERWATER OBSERVATION WINDOW

Standard rectangular type available for 2'-0" X 2'-0" up to 3'-0" X 5'-0" clear openings. 1'-6" diameter round type also standard.

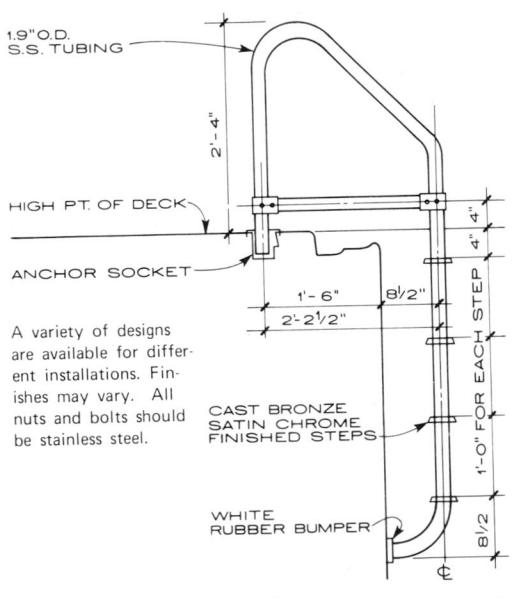

1.9" O.D. S.S. TUBING

HIGH PT. OF DECK

ANCHOR SOCKET

2'-4"

1'-6"

2'-2½"

4"

4"

1'-0" FOR EACH STEP

8½"

8½"

CAST BRONZE SATIN CHROME FINISHED STEPS

WHITE RUBBER BUMPER

A variety of designs are available for different installations. Finishes may vary. All nuts and bolts should be stainless steel.

LADDERS AND GRAB RAILS

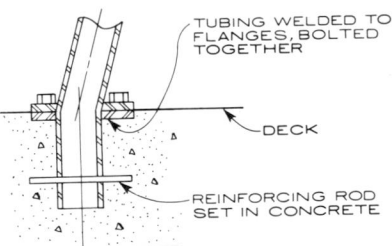

TUBING WELDED TO FLANGES, BOLTED TOGETHER

DECK

REINFORCING ROD SET IN CONCRETE

FLANGED BASE SOCKET
(For diving stands and lifeguard chairs)

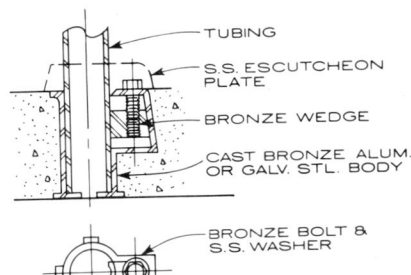

TUBING

S.S. ESCUTCHEON PLATE

BRONZE WEDGE

CAST BRONZE ALUM. OR GALV. STL. BODY

BRONZE BOLT & S.S. WASHER

LUG ON CAST BODY

ANCHOR SOCKET

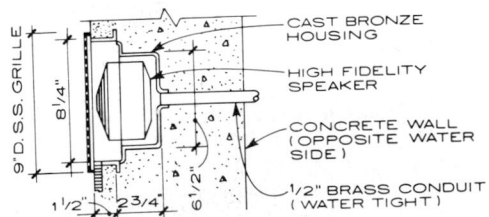

CAST BRONZE HOUSING

HIGH FIDELITY SPEAKER

CONCRETE WALL (OPPOSITE WATER SIDE)

½" BRASS CONDUIT (WATER TIGHT)

9" D. S.S. GRILLE

8¼"

6½"

½"

2¾"

UNDERWATER SPEAKER

(Underwater wet niche lights are similar)

Douglas S. Stenhouse, AIA; Washington, D. C.

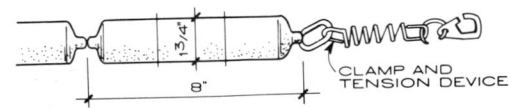

3/4"

8"

CLAMP AND TENSION DEVICE

PLASTIC FLOAT RACING LANE MARKERS

OTHER MISCELLANEOUS EQUIPMENT:
Wet and dry niche underwater lights, lifeguard chairs, slides, pennant marking lines, inlet fittings also available. Standard drain fittings may be used.

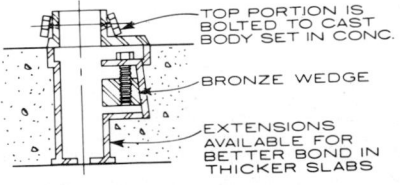

TOP PORTION IS BOLTED TO CAST BODY SET IN CONC.

BRONZE WEDGE

EXTENSIONS AVAILABLE FOR BETTER BOND IN THICKER SLABS

CLAMP FLANGE ANCHOR SOCKET
DECK SOCKET DETAILS

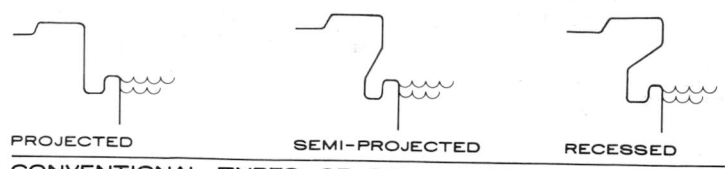

CONVENTIONAL TYPES OF SCUM GUTTERS

PROJECTED   SEMI-PROJECTED   RECESSED

Exit from pool more difficult as swimmers must raise themselves 12″ to 16″ rather than 2″ to 3″ for more contemporary types. Some Boards of Health disapprove of fully recessed types, claiming them to be difficult to clean and dangerous to those who may catch an arm or foot in same.

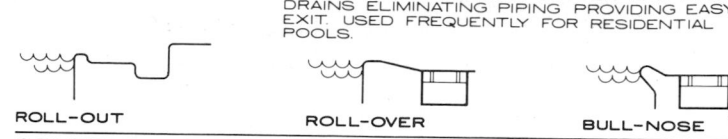

THESE TYPES COMBINE GUTTER AND DECK DRAINS ELIMINATING PIPING PROVIDING EASY EXIT. USED FREQUENTLY FOR RESIDENTIAL POOLS.

ROLL-OUT   ROLL-OVER   BULL-NOSE

CONTEMPORARY TYPES OF GUTTERS

Pools can be flooded easily to carry off floating foreign matter. If used for competitive swimming meets, platforms or take-off blocks are required to raise swimmer minimum 1′— 6″ above water level. Even in conventional type gutter pools, portable rather than permanent starting blocks are used.

TYPES OF SWIMMING POOL GUTTERS

Swimming pool gutters serve four basic purposes: (1) to drain off surface debris, (2) to dampen surface waves for racing, (3) to act as an overflow thereby keeping water level even, and (4) to provide an exit from the pool water to the deck. Different types may be combined around pool perimeter.

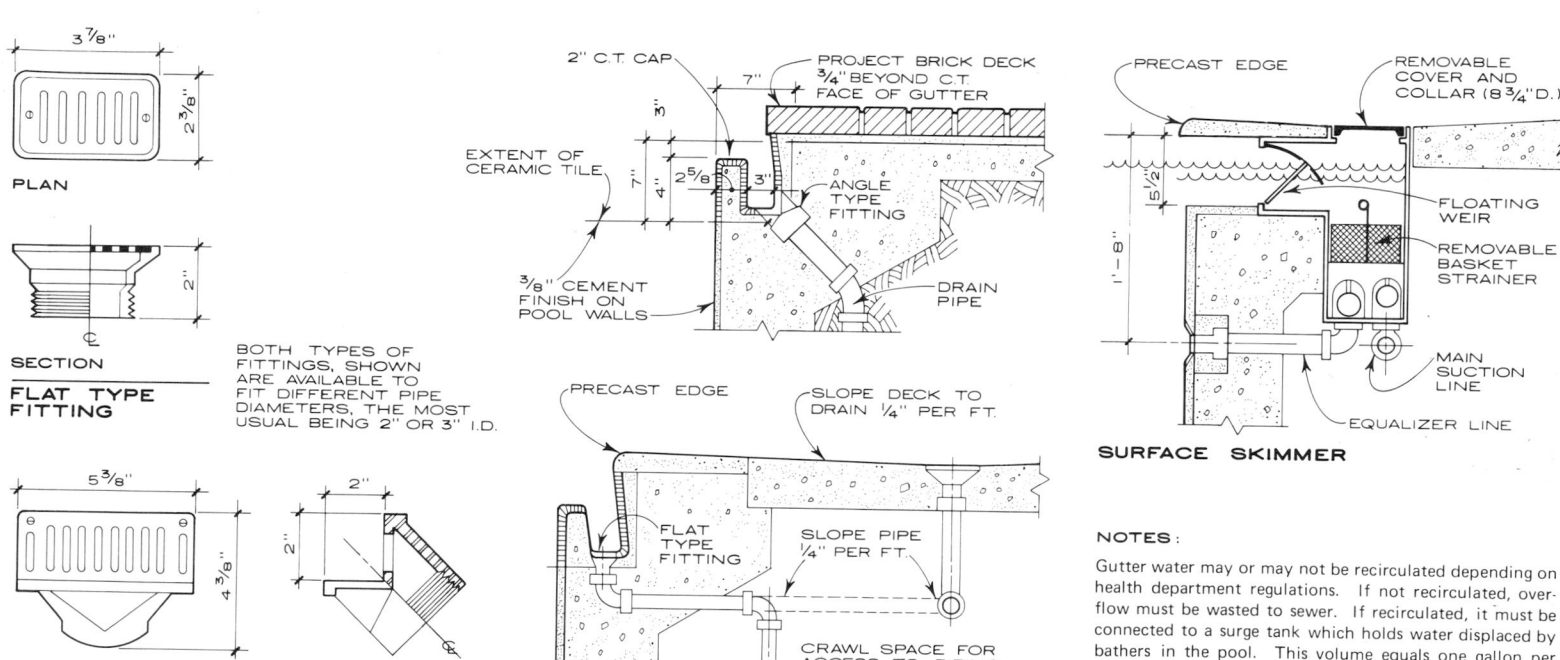

PLAN

SECTION

FLAT TYPE FITTING

BOTH TYPES OF FITTINGS, SHOWN ARE AVAILABLE TO FIT DIFFERENT PIPE DIAMETERS, THE MOST USUAL BEING 2″ OR 3″ I.D.

ELEVATION   SECTION

ANGLE TYPE FITTING

2″ C.T. CAP — PROJECT BRICK DECK ¾″ BEYOND C.T. FACE OF GUTTER

EXTENT OF CERAMIC TILE

ANGLE TYPE FITTING

⅜″ CEMENT FINISH ON POOL WALLS

DRAIN PIPE

PRECAST EDGE — SLOPE DECK TO DRAIN ¼″ PER FT.

FLAT TYPE FITTING

SLOPE PIPE ¼″ PER FT.

CRAWL SPACE FOR ACCESS TO PIPING

SCUM GUTTER DETAILS

PRECAST EDGE — REMOVABLE COVER AND COLLAR (8¾″ D.)

FLOATING WEIR

REMOVABLE BASKET STRAINER

MAIN SUCTION LINE

EQUALIZER LINE

SURFACE SKIMMER

NOTES:

Gutter water may or may not be recirculated depending on health department regulations. If not recirculated, overflow must be wasted to sewer. If recirculated, it must be connected to a surge tank which holds water displaced by bathers in the pool. This volume equals one gallon per square foot of pool surface. The surface skimmer operates by suction of filter pump. It is not approved by all Boards of Health. (See pages on Filter Systems).

CONVENTIONAL SCUM GUTTER AND SKIMMER DETAILS, COMPONENTS AND ASSEMBLIES   NO SCALE

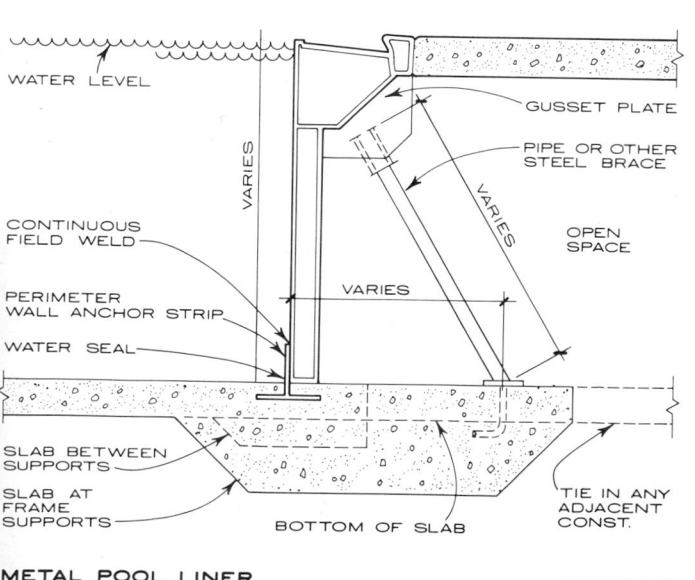

WATER LEVEL

GUSSET PLATE

PIPE OR OTHER STEEL BRACE

OPEN SPACE

VARIES

CONTINUOUS FIELD WELD

PERIMETER WALL ANCHOR STRIP

WATER SEAL

SLAB BETWEEN SUPPORTS

SLAB AT FRAME SUPPORTS

BOTTOM OF SLAB

TIE IN ANY ADJACENT CONST.

METAL POOL LINER   NO SCALE

Type often used in rooftop or other above grade installations where weight is a primary factor in design.

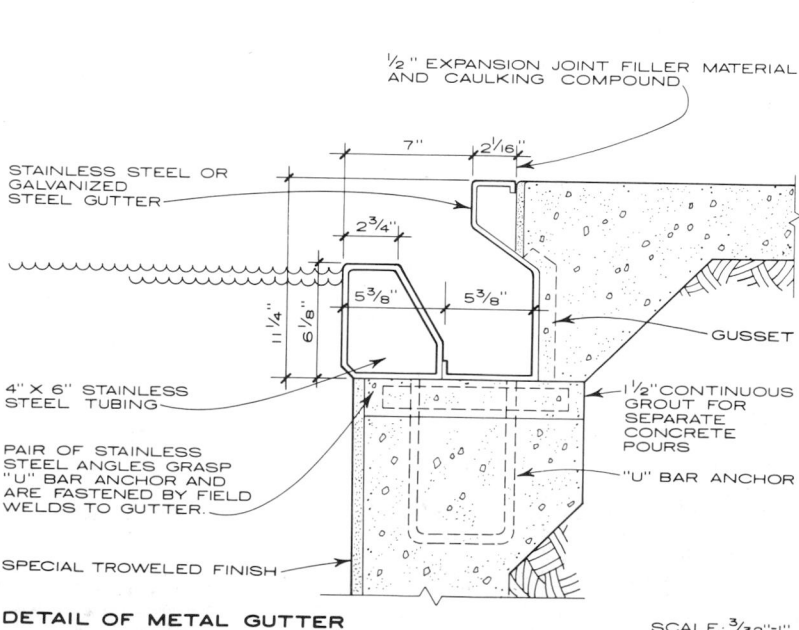

½″ EXPANSION JOINT FILLER MATERIAL AND CAULKING COMPOUND

STAINLESS STEEL OR GALVANIZED STEEL GUTTER

GUSSET

4″ X 6″ STAINLESS STEEL TUBING

PAIR OF STAINLESS STEEL ANGLES GRASP "U" BAR ANCHOR AND ARE FASTENED BY FIELD WELDS TO GUTTER.

1½″ CONTINUOUS GROUT FOR SEPARATE CONCRETE POURS

"U" BAR ANCHOR

SPECIAL TROWELED FINISH

DETAIL OF METAL GUTTER   SCALE: ³/₃₂″=1″

Tube and gutter are 12 gauge metal of types indicated.

Douglas S. Stenhouse, AIA; Washington, D. C.

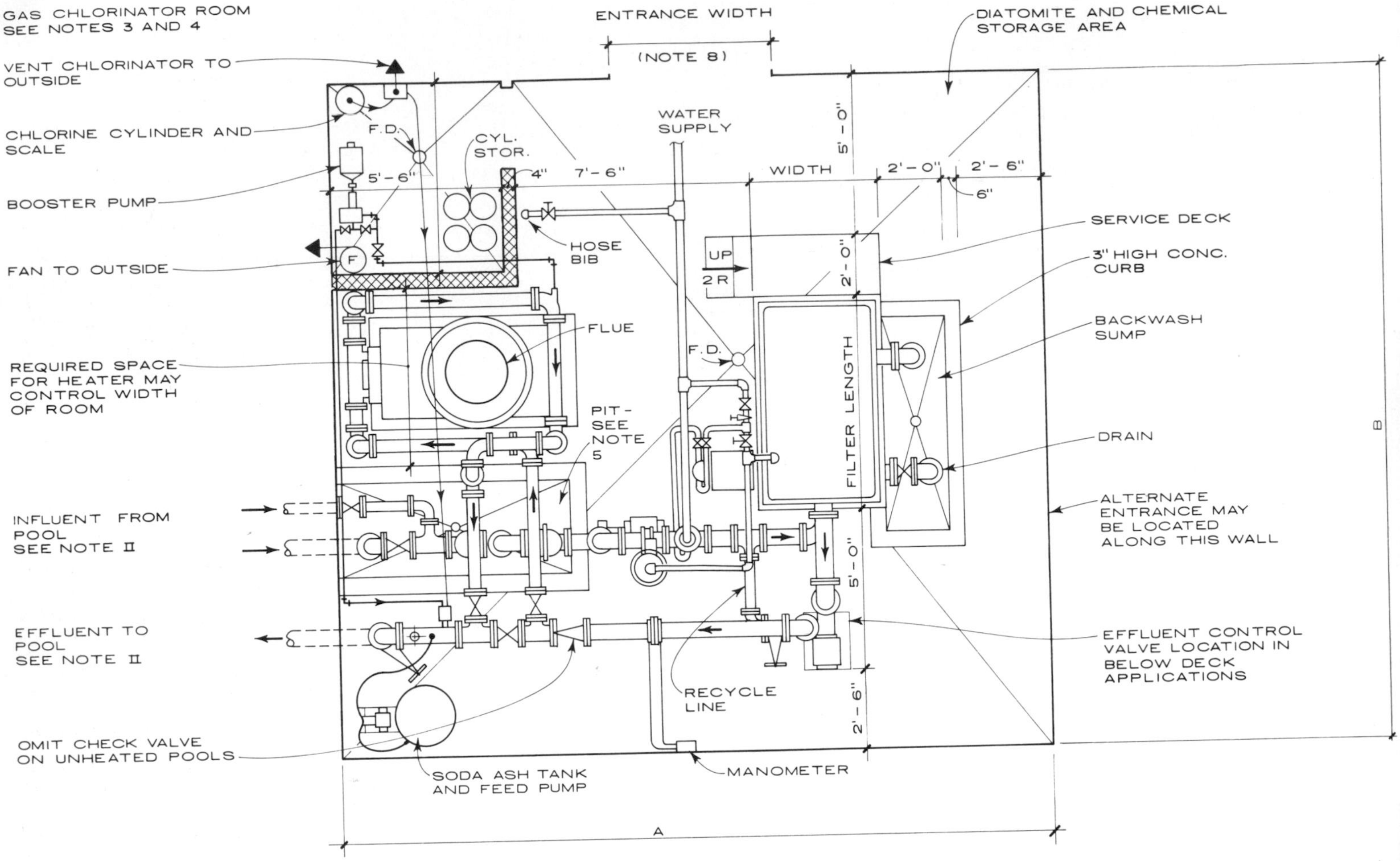

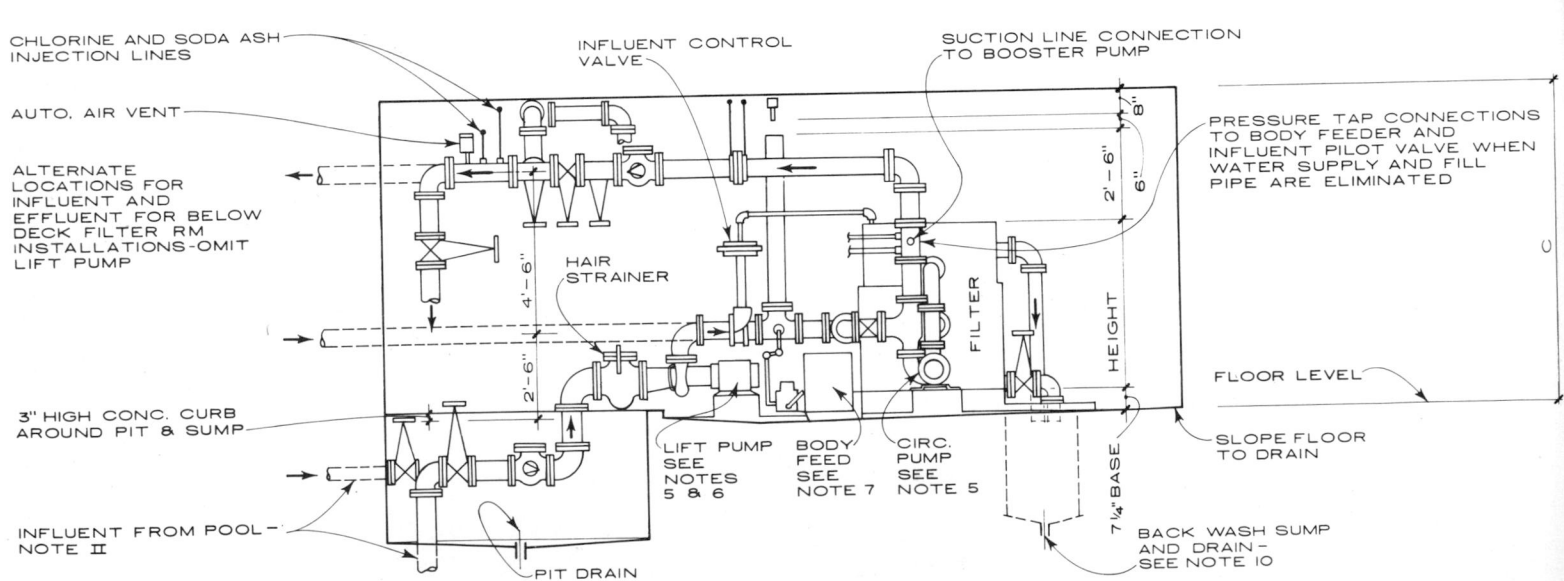

GAS CHLORINATOR ROOM
SEE NOTES 3 AND 4
VENT CHLORINATOR TO OUTSIDE
CHLORINE CYLINDER AND SCALE
BOOSTER PUMP
FAN TO OUTSIDE
REQUIRED SPACE FOR HEATER MAY CONTROL WIDTH OF ROOM
INFLUENT FROM POOL
SEE NOTE II
EFFLUENT TO POOL
SEE NOTE II
OMIT CHECK VALVE ON UNHEATED POOLS
SODA ASH TANK AND FEED PUMP
ENTRANCE WIDTH
(NOTE 8)
F.D.
CYL. STOR.
5'-6"
4"
7'-6"
HOSE BIB
FLUE
PIT - SEE NOTE 5
WATER SUPPLY
UP
2 R
F.D.
WIDTH
2'-0"
2'-6"
6"
5'-0"
2'-0"
FILTER LENGTH
5'-0"
2'-6"
RECYCLE LINE
MANOMETER
DIATOMITE AND CHEMICAL STORAGE AREA
SERVICE DECK
3" HIGH CONC. CURB
BACKWASH SUMP
DRAIN
ALTERNATE ENTRANCE MAY BE LOCATED ALONG THIS WALL
EFFLUENT CONTROL VALVE LOCATION IN BELOW DECK APPLICATIONS
A
B

PLAN
NO SCALE

CHLORINE AND SODA ASH INJECTION LINES
AUTO. AIR VENT
ALTERNATE LOCATIONS FOR INFLUENT AND EFFLUENT FOR BELOW DECK FILTER RM INSTALLATIONS-OMIT LIFT PUMP
3" HIGH CONC. CURB AROUND PIT & SUMP
INFLUENT FROM POOL - NOTE II
PIT DRAIN
INFLUENT CONTROL VALVE
HAIR STRAINER
4'-6"
2'-6"
LIFT PUMP SEE NOTES 5 & 6
BODY FEED SEE NOTE 7
CIRC. PUMP SEE NOTE 5
FILTER
SUCTION LINE CONNECTION TO BOOSTER PUMP
8"
2'-6"
6"
HEIGHT
7 1/4" BASE
PRESSURE TAP CONNECTIONS TO BODY FEEDER AND INFLUENT PILOT VALVE WHEN WATER SUPPLY AND FILL PIPE ARE ELIMINATED
FLOOR LEVEL
SLOPE FLOOR TO DRAIN
BACK WASH SUMP AND DRAIN - SEE NOTE 10
C

LONGITUDINAL SECTION
NO SCALE

TYPICAL DIATOMACEOUS EARTH VACUUM TYPE FILTER EQUIPMENT ROOM LAYOUT

Refer to last page in this series for dimensions of room, equipment and required clearances. See next page for numbered notes.

Douglas S. Stenhouse, AIA; Washington, D. C.

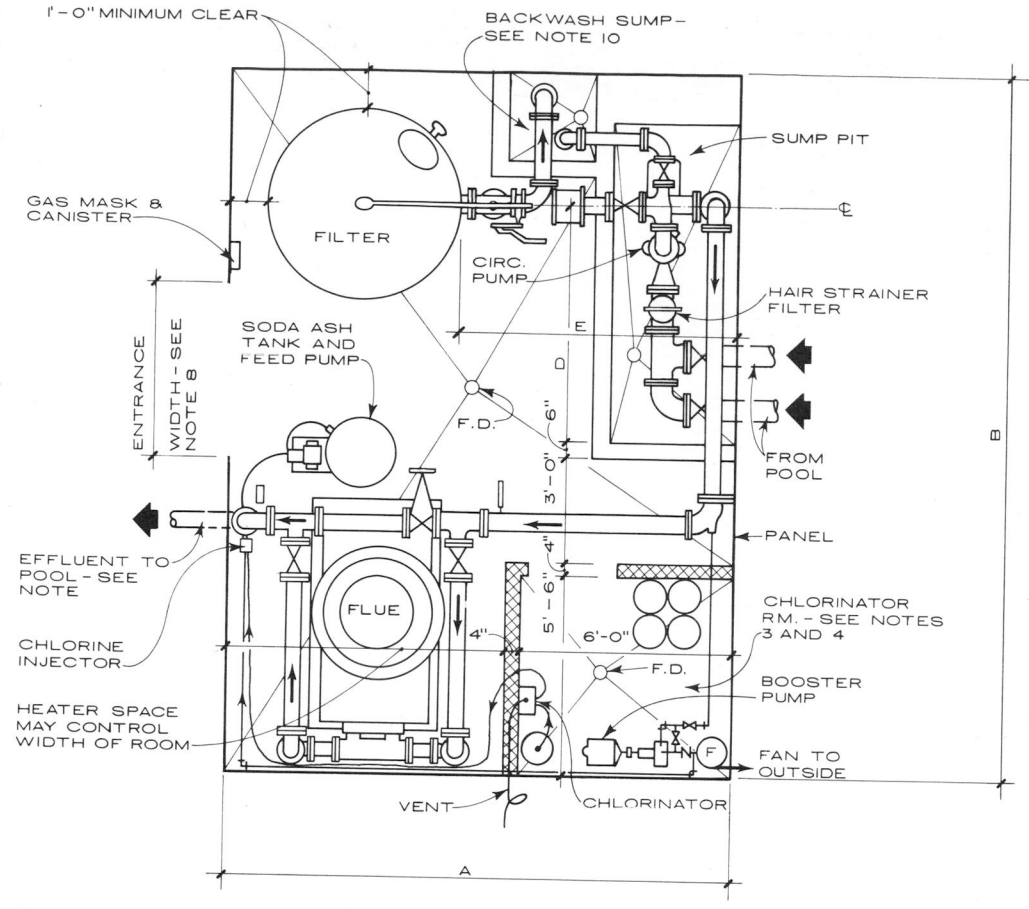

PLAN
NO SCALE

1. Illustrations show heaters for 35° temperature differential. Determine exact space requirements by choosing fueling system, calculating heat loss in BTUs and selecting unit.

2. Water supply and fill pipe required with either system when make-up is added ahead of filter. In skimmer type pool more usual method is to add make-up water directly to pool with fill spout. (see Note 11 below)

3. Gas chlorination system is illustrated. For smaller pools indicated in tables, liquid type sodium hypochloride system is often used. For larger outdoor pools large storage tanks filled with sodium hypochloride may be delivered to a site by tank trucks. A hypochlorinator type diaphragm feed pump is used with muriatic acid in lieu of soda ash for PH control.

4. Provide louvered-type door sized to accommodate equipment. Ceiling light and exhaust fan should be connected to same switch. Consult local code for further information and details.

5. Lift and circulating pumps should be end-suction close-coupled centrifugal types, the former rated at 15 feet total loss of head, the latter at 35, including 20 feet of suction lift for above pool water level applications, 45, below. Pool piping designs, accumulated losses of piping runs, differential filter pressures, additions of special valves or equipment will also affect pump capacity and therefore size required.

6. Lift pump and check valve not shown in high rate permanent media filter room layout. Need for lift pump or even pit depends on relation of pool water level to circulating pump which must be flooded by pool water. One layout shows above deck room with pool water level below the floor of equipment room and circulating pump. High rate system shows above deck room with the pool water level below level of floor of equipment room but above level of circulating pump, thus requiring no lift pump and check valve.

7. Dry type body feeder supplies diatomaceous earth during filter operation to extend length of filter run by keeping filter cake porous.

8. Provide method for replacing equipment, if necessary sizing entrance to accept same.

9. Main line valves to be butterfly, gate, plug type without high head loss characteristics.

10. Consult codes to find size of backwash sump, drain, type of permissible sewer connection.

11. Influent lines shown may originate from main drain at deepest point of pool and from skimmers or scum gutters depending upon pool design. Consult local code to determine if influent from scum gutters may be returned to filters or wasted. If recirculated, a surge tank is required. Locate in filter room. Water make-up is controlled by float valve in surge tank.

12. Effluent lines may run in any direction and are shown as they are for convenience of the illustration only. Piping arrangements and locations of all equipment also may vary. The layouts indicated are for preliminary guidance in design only.

13. Floor, deck and pit drains should not be connected to the filter system but directly or indirectly to sewer.

14. Check local health, plumbing and public safety codes for acceptability of basic systems.

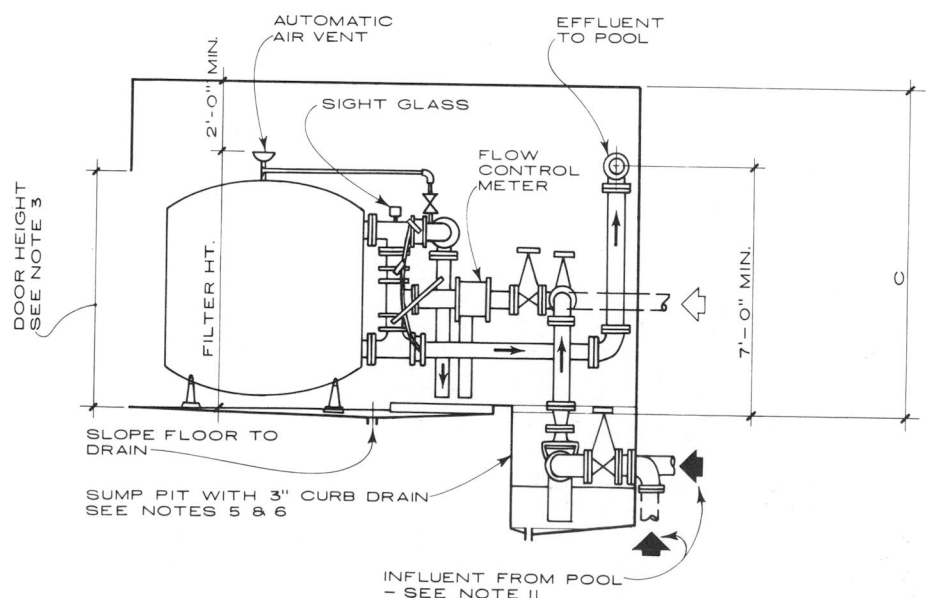

CROSS SECTION
NO SCALE

TYPICAL HIGH RATE PERMANENT MEDIA TYPE FILTER EQUIPMENT ROOM LAYOUT
REFER TO NEXT PAGE FOR DIMENSIONS OF ROOM EQUIPMENT AND REQUIRED CLEARANCES

Douglas S. Stenhouse, AIA; Washington, D. C.

DIMENSIONAL REQUIREMENTS FOR HIGH RATE PERMANENT MEDIA (SWIMMING POOL) WATER FILTRATION SYSTEM

POOL CAPACITY IN KILO GALS.	RATE GPM PER SQ. FT.	FILTER SIZE & CAPACITY				PUMP SIZES IN HP (SEE NOTES BELOW)			FILTER ROOM DIMENSIONS (BASED ON FILTER SIZE. CHECK AGAINST SPACE REQUIREMENTS FOR HEATER)					MAIN PIPING SIZES				POOL CAPACITY IN KILO GALS.
														INFLUENT				
		AREA SQ. FT.	DIAM.	HEIGHT	TOTAL RATE	CIRC. PUMP	FEED PUMP	BOOSTER	A	B	C	D	E	POOL-PUMP	PUMP-FILT'R	EFFLU-ENT	DRAIN	
36	15	4.9	2'– 6"	5'– 1"	74	3			7'– 6"	17'– 7"	7'– 8"	6'– 0"	4'– 0"	2 1/2"	2"	2"	2 1/2"	26
47	20	4.9	2'– 6"	5'– 1"	98	3			8'– 0"	17'– 7"	7'– 8"	6'– 0"	4'– 6"	3"	2 1/2"	2 1/2"	3"	35
51	15	7.1	3'– 0"	5'– 1"	107	3			8'– 6"	17'– 10"	7'– 8"	6'– 0"	4'– 6"	3"	2 1/2"	2 1/2"	3"	38
68	20	7.1	3'– 0"	5'– 1"	142	5			9'– 6"	18'– 3"	7'– 8"	6'– 9"	5'– 6"	4"	3"	3"	4"	51
69	15	9.6	3'– 6"	5'– 1"	144	5			10'– 0"	18'– 10"	7'– 8"	6'– 9"	5'– 6"	4"	3"	3"	4"	52
91	15	12.6	4'– 0"	5'– 11"	189	5			10'– 7"	19'– 1"	7'– 11"	6'– 9"	5'– 7"	4"	4"	4"	4"	68
92	20	9.6	3'– 6"	5'– 1"	192	5			10'– 0"	18'– 10"	7'– 8"	6'– 9"	5'– 6"	4"	3"	3"	4"	69
114	15	15.9	4'– 6"	6'– 4"	238	7 1/2		3/4	11'– 1"	19'– 4"	8'– 4"	6'– 9"	5'– 7"	4"	4"	4"	5"	86
121	20	12.6	4'– 0"	5'– 11"	252	7 1/2		3/4	10'– 7"	19'– 1"	7'– 11"	6'– 9"	5'– 7"	4"	4"	4"	4"	91
141	15	19.6	5'– 0"	7'– 1"	294	10		3/4	12'– 1"	19'– 10"	9'– 4"	7'– 0"	6'– 1"	5"	4"	4"	5"	106
153	20	15.9	4'– 6"	6'– 4"	318	10		3/4	11'– 7"	19'– 7"	8'– 4"	7'– 0"	6'– 1"	4"	4"	4"	5"	114
● 171	15	23.7	5'– 6"	7'– 2"	355	15		3/4	12'– 7"	20'– 1"	9'– 2"	7'– 0"	6'– 1"	5"	4"	4"	5"	128 ●
188	20	19.6	5'– 0"	7'– 1"	392	15		1	12'– 5"	20'– 2"	9'– 1"	7'– 4"	6'– 5"	5"	5"	5"	5"	141
204	15	28.3	6'– 0"	7'– 3"	424	15		1	13'– 5"	20'– 8"	9'– 3"	7'– 4"	6'– 5"	5"	5"	5"	6"	153
228	20	23.7	5'– 6"	7'– 2"	474	15		1	12'– 11"	20'– 5"	9'– 2"	7'– 4"	6'– 5"	5"	5"	5"	6"	170
239	15	33.2	6'– 6"	7'– 4"	498	20		1	14'– 9"	20'– 11"	9'– 4"	7'– 4"	7'– 3"	6"	5"	5"	6"	179
272	20	28.3	6'– 0"	7'– 3"	566	20	1/4	1	14'– 4"	20'– 4"	9'– 4"	7'– 4"	7'– 3"	6"	5"	5"	6"	204
277	15	33.5	7'– 0"	7'– 10"	577	20		1	15'– 3"	21'– 4"	9'– 10"	7'– 4"	7'– 3"	6"	5"	5"	6"	208
319	20	33.2	6'– 6"	7'– 4"	664	20		1	14'– 10"	21'– 4"	9'– 4"	7'– 7"	7'– 4"	6"	6"	6"	6"	239
370	20	38.5	7'– 0"	7'– 10"	770	25		1	15'– 4"	21'– 5"	9'– 10"	7'– 7"	7'– 4"	6"	6"	6"	8"	277

Note (Feed Pump column): 3/4 if gas chlorinator is used. Hypochlorinator is, however, more usual.

● Indicates Filter Room Illustrated — For 8 hour turnover, read from left to right; for 6 hour turnover, read from right to left.

DESCRIPTION OF HIGH RATE PERMANENT MEDIA (SWIMMING POOL) WATER FILTRATION SYSTEM:

The vacuum type filter consists of a permeable surface supporting a layer of diatomateous earth. This layer of filter aid, due to its myriad of microscopic openings, produces a brilliantly clear water and a fresh, sterile media after filter is backwashed. Vacuum type filters are constructed of relatively few elements with an open type tank which permits complete visual inspection and ready access to the filter elements at all times. Pump horsepowers are usually smaller compared to other systems. To prepare the filter for operation, an initial filtering mat of diatomaceous earth known as precoat is manually placed on the elements at the start of the filter run. To maintain porosity—and therefore effectiveness of the filter coat—and to provide longer filter runs at normal rates of flow, additional diatomite, known as body feed, is introduced continuously throughout the filter run. A gas chlorinizer and soda ash or caustic feeder or a hypochlorinator are used to provide water sterilization and to maintain PH control.

Note: Booster pump sizes indicated are generally at their limit of capacity and should be verified to provide necessary 2 1/2 to 1 pressure ratio at injector point and effective chlorination.

DIMENSIONAL REQUIREMENTS FOR DIATOMACEOUS EARTH VACUUM (SWIMMING POOL) WATER FILTRATION SYSTEM

POOL CAPACITY IN KILO GALS.	AREA SQ. FT.	FILTER SIZE & CAPACITY (RATE : 1.6-2.1 GPM/SQ. FT.)				PUMP SIZES IN HP (SEE NOTES ABOVE)				FILTER RM DIMEN. (BASED ON FILTER SIZES CHECK HEATER SPACE REQ.)			MAIN PIPING SIZES					POOL CAPACITY IN KILO GALS.
													INFLUENT					
		L	W	H	TOTAL RATE	CIRC. PUMP	LIFT PUMP	FEED PUMP	BOOSTER	A	B	C	POOL PUMP	PUMP FILT'R	EFFLU-ENT	RECYC.	DRAIN	
30	30	2'– 10"	1'– 5"	4'– 4 1/4"	63	1 1/2	3/4			19'– 9"	17'– 4"	8'– 7 1/2"	3"	2 1/2"	2 1/2"	1 1/4"	2"	22
36	40	2'– 10"	1'– 9"	4'– 4 1/4"	75	1 1/2	3/4			20'– 1"	17'– 4"	8'– 7 1/2"	3"	2 1/2"	2 1/2"	1 1/4"	2"	27
55	60	2'– 10"	2'– 5"	4'– 4 1/4"	115	1 1/2	3/4			20'– 9"	17'– 4"	8'– 7 1/2"	4"	3"	3"	1 1/2"	2"	41
68	80	2'– 10"	3'– 1"	4'– 4 1/4"	145	2		3/4		21'– 5"	17'– 4"	8'– 7 1/2"	4"	4"	3"	1 1/2"	3"	52
80	100	2'– 10"	3'– 9"	4'– 4 1/4"	170	3	1			22'– 5"	17'– 4"	8'– 7 1/2"	4"	4"	4"	2"	3"	61
102	120	6'– 8"	2'– 6"	4'– 8 1/4"	215	3	1 1/2		3/4	20'– 10"	21'– 2"	8'– 11 1/2"	5"	4"	4"	2"	3"	77
120	120	6'– 8"	2'– 6"	4'– 8 1/4"	250	3	1 1/2		3/4	20'– 10"	21'– 2"	8'– 11 1/2"	5"	4"	4"	2"	3"	90
140	150	6'– 8"	2'– 10"	4'– 8 1/4"	295	5	2		3/4	21'– 2"	21'– 2"	8'– 11 1/2"	5"	5"	4"	2"	3"	106
155	180	6'– 8"	3'– 3"	4'– 8 1/4"	325	5	2		3/4	21'– 7"	21'– 2"	8'– 11 1/2"	6"	5"	5"	2 1/2"	3"	117
● 180	240	6'– 8"	4'– 0"	4'– 8 1/4"	380	5	3	1/6	3/4	22'– 4"	21'– 2"	8'– 11 1/2"	6"	5"	5"	2 1/2"	4"	137 ●
207	240	6'– 8"	4'– 0"	4'– 8 1/4"	435	7 1/2	3		1	22'– 4"	21'– 2"	8'– 11 1/2"	6"	5"	5"	2 1/2"	4"	156
248	300	6'– 8"	4'– 9"	4'– 8 1/4"	520	7 1/2	5		1	23'– 1"	21'– 2"	8'– 11 1/2"	6"	6"	5"	2 1/2"	4"	187
280	300	6'– 8"	5'– 6"	4'– 8 1/4"	650	7 1/2	5		1	23'– 10"	21'– 2"	8'– 11 1/2"	6"	6"	6"	3"	4"	210
310	360	6'– 8"	5'– 6"	4'– 8 1/4"	650	10	5		1	23'– 10"	21'– 2"	8'– 11 1/2"	6"	6"	6"	3"	4"	234
370	420	6'– 8"	6'– 3"	4'– 8 1/4"	775	10	7 1/2		1	24'– 7"	21'– 2"	8'– 11 1/2"	8"	6"	6"	3"	4"	279
420	480	6'– 8"	7'– 0"	4'– 8 1/4"	875	15	7 1/2		1	25'– 4"	21'– 2"	8'– 11 1/2"	8"	6"	6"	3"	4"	315

Note (Feed Pump column): 3/4 if gas chlor. used. Hypochlor. more usual.

● Indicates Filter Room Layout Illustrated — For 8 hour turnover, read from left to right; for 6 hour turnover, read from right to left.

DESCRIPTION OF DIATOMACEOUS EARTH VACUUM (SWIMMING POOL) WATER FILTRATION SYSTEM:

Here are some of the basic principles employed in Hi-Rate filtration: (1) Parallel flow, with very close control of velocity and hydraulic balance inside, enables the filter to achieve flow rates up to 20 GPM/sq. ft. of filter area, (2) High backwash rates without loss of media, and (3) The depth of filtration produced in a High Rate enables most of the bed volume to be used to store collected solids. This provides the filter a large dirt holding capacity in spite of its reduced surface area. A single lever control with adjustable linkage insures positive valve operation with complete shutoff. The simplest systems can be automated at an exceptionally low cost because they utilize a simple reverse flow for cleaning. Complicated operations such as draining, sluicing, or precoating are not required before the filter returns to service. The rugged, dependable and effective High Rate filter can be economical, yet simple, manual or fully automated system.

Douglas S. Stenhouse, AIA; Washington, D. C.

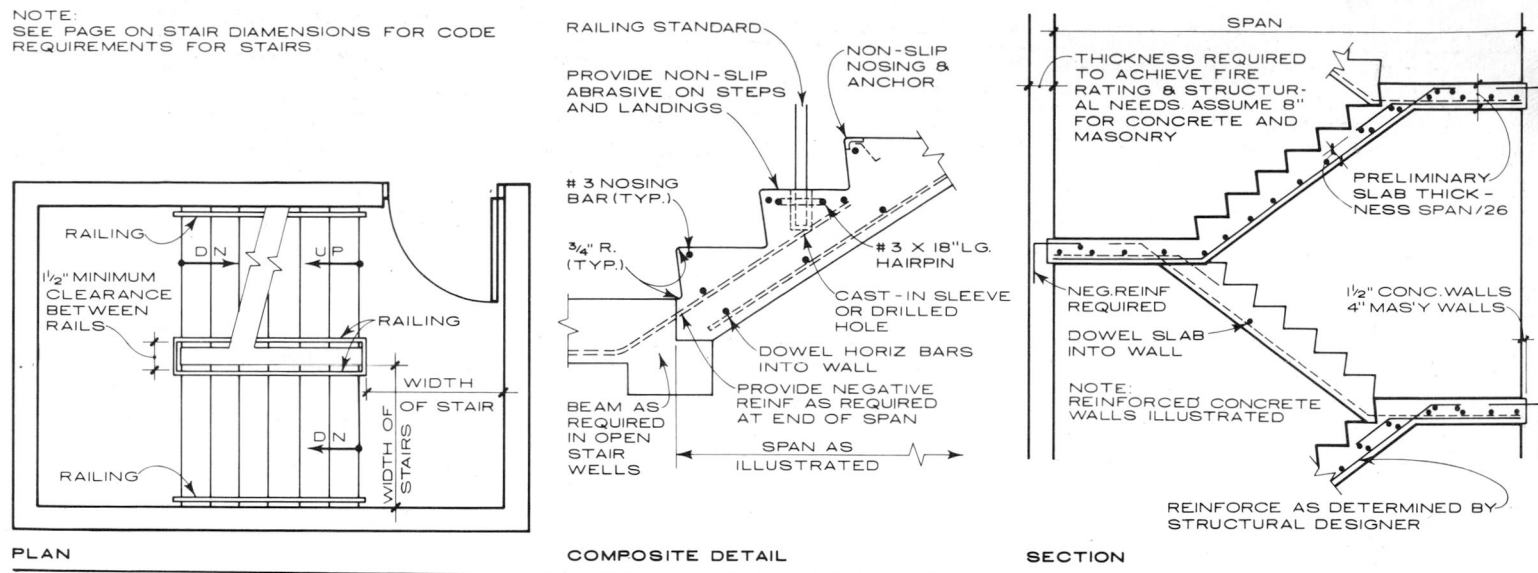

NOTE:
SEE PAGE ON STAIR DIAMENSIONS FOR CODE REQUIREMENTS FOR STAIRS

RAILING STANDARD

PROVIDE NON-SLIP ABRASIVE ON STEPS AND LANDINGS

NON-SLIP NOSING & ANCHOR

THICKNESS REQUIRED TO ACHIEVE FIRE RATING & STRUCTURAL NEEDS ASSUME 8" FOR CONCRETE AND MASONRY

SPAN

PRELIMINARY SLAB THICKNESS SPAN/26

3 NOSING BAR (TYP.)

3/4" R. (TYP.)

3 X 18"LG. HAIRPIN

CAST-IN SLEEVE OR DRILLED HOLE

DOWEL HORIZ BARS INTO WALL

PROVIDE NEGATIVE REINF AS REQUIRED AT END OF SPAN

NEG. REINF REQUIRED

DOWEL SLAB INTO WALL

NOTE: REINFORCED CONCRETE WALLS ILLUSTRATED

1½" CONC. WALLS 4" MAS'Y WALLS

BEAM AS REQUIRED IN OPEN STAIR WELLS

SPAN AS ILLUSTRATED

REINFORCE AS DETERMINED BY STRUCTURAL DESIGNER

RAILING

1½" MINIMUM CLEARANCE BETWEEN RAILS

RAILING

WIDTH OF STAIR

WIDTH OF STAIRS

RAILING

DN   UP

DN

PLAN

COMPOSITE DETAIL

SECTION

"U" TYPE CONCRETE STAIRS

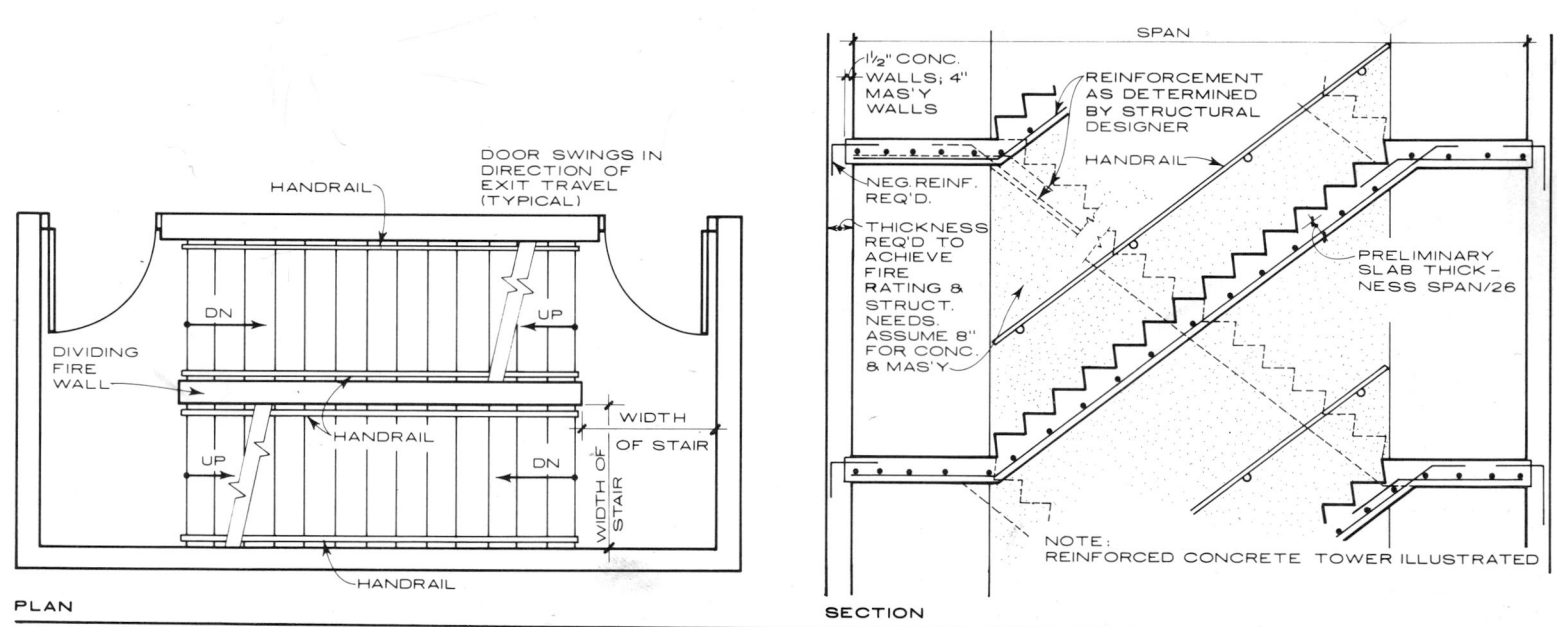

HANDRAIL

DOOR SWINGS IN DIRECTION OF EXIT TRAVEL (TYPICAL)

1½" CONC. WALLS; 4" MAS'Y WALLS

REINFORCEMENT AS DETERMINED BY STRUCTURAL DESIGNER

HANDRAIL

SPAN

DIVIDING FIRE WALL

HANDRAIL

HANDRAIL

WIDTH OF STAIR

WIDTH OF STAIR

DN   UP

UP   DN

NEG. REINF. REQ'D.

THICKNESS REQ'D TO ACHIEVE FIRE RATING & STRUCT. NEEDS. ASSUME 8" FOR CONC. & MAS'Y

PRELIMINARY SLAB THICKNESS SPAN/26

NOTE: REINFORCED CONCRETE TOWER ILLUSTRATED

PLAN

SECTION

SCISSOR TYPE CONCRETE STAIRS

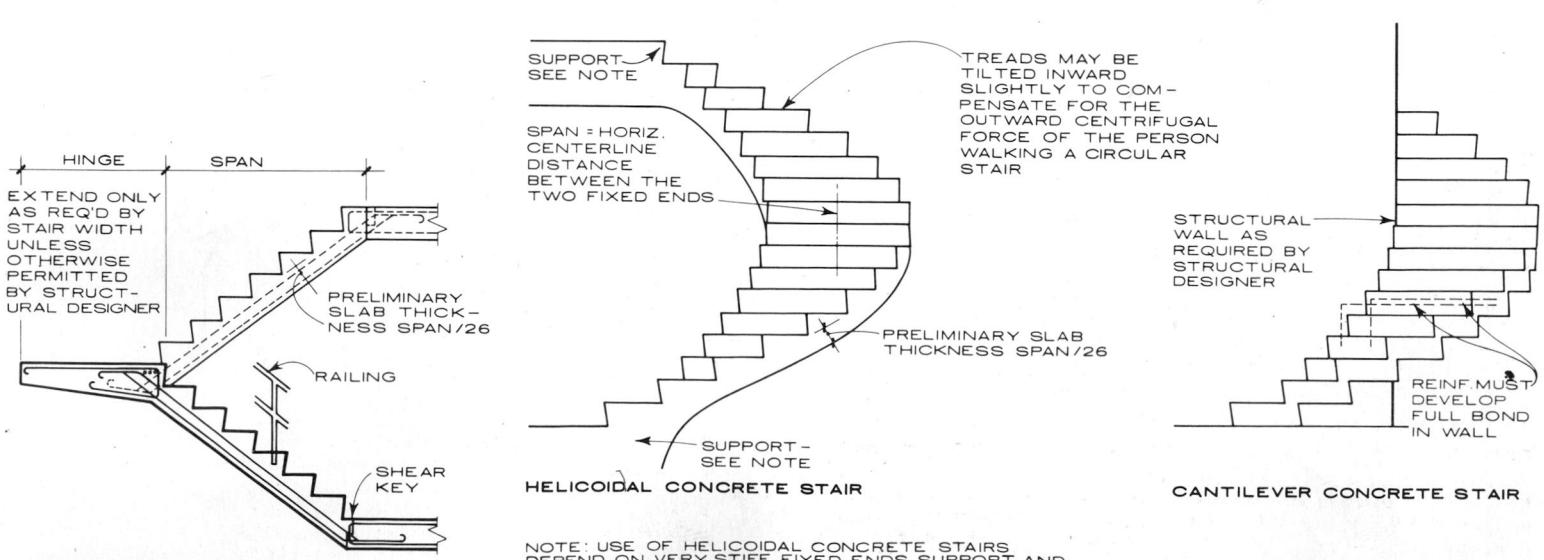

HINGE   SPAN

EXTEND ONLY AS REQ'D BY STAIR WIDTH UNLESS OTHERWISE PERMITTED BY STRUCTURAL DESIGNER

PRELIMINARY SLAB THICKNESS SPAN/26

RAILING

SHEAR KEY

SUPPORT - SEE NOTE

SPAN = HORIZ. CENTERLINE DISTANCE BETWEEN THE TWO FIXED ENDS

TREADS MAY BE TILTED INWARD SLIGHTLY TO COMPENSATE FOR THE OUTWARD CENTRIFUGAL FORCE OF THE PERSON WALKING A CIRCULAR STAIR

PRELIMINARY SLAB THICKNESS SPAN/26

SUPPORT - SEE NOTE

STRUCTURAL WALL AS REQUIRED BY STRUCTURAL DESIGNER

REINF. MUST DEVELOP FULL BOND IN WALL

FREE STANDING CONCRETE STAIR

HELICOIDAL CONCRETE STAIR

NOTE: USE OF HELICOIDAL CONCRETE STAIRS DEPEND ON VERY STIFF FIXED ENDS SUPPORT AND SMALL SUPPORT DEFLECTION

CANTILEVER CONCRETE STAIR

Irvin Bruce Schafer; Peoria, Illinois

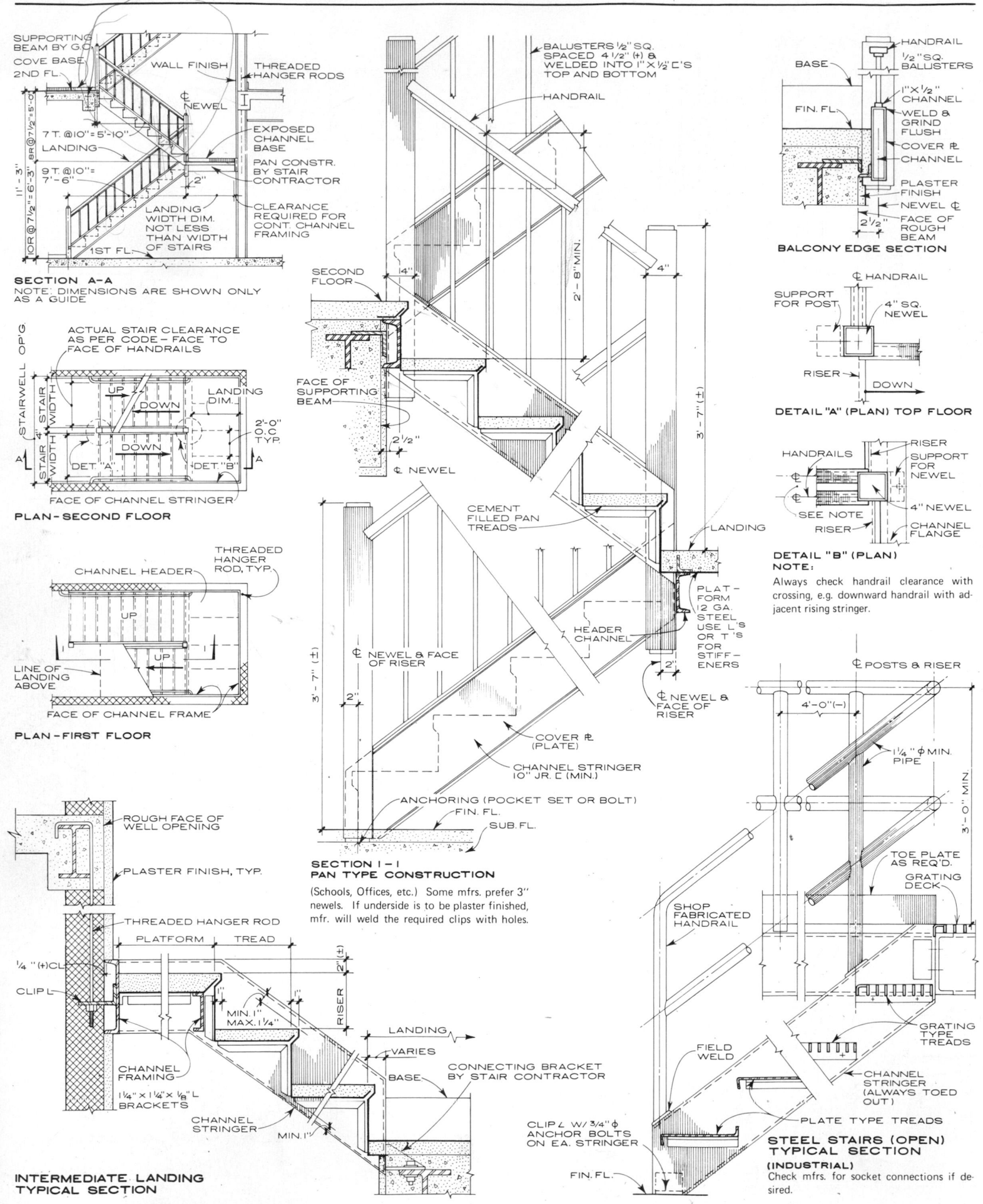

SECTION A-A
NOTE: DIMENSIONS ARE SHOWN ONLY AS A GUIDE

SUPPORTING BEAM BY G.C.
COVE BASE 2ND FL.
WALL FINISH
THREADED HANGER RODS
₵ NEWEL
7 T. @10" = 5'-10"
LANDING
9 T. @10" = 7'-6"
11'-3"
10R @ 7½"=6'-3" OR 8R @ 7½"=5'-0"
EXPOSED CHANNEL BASE
PAN CONSTR. BY STAIR CONTRACTOR
2"
LANDING WIDTH DIM. NOT LESS THAN WIDTH OF STAIRS
CLEARANCE REQUIRED FOR CONT. CHANNEL FRAMING
1ST FL.

PLAN-SECOND FLOOR
STAIRWELL OPG.
STAIR WIDTH
4"
STAIR WIDTH
ACTUAL STAIR CLEARANCE AS PER CODE — FACE TO FACE OF HANDRAILS
UP
DOWN
DOWN
DET. "A"
DET. "B"
LANDING DIM.
2'-0" O.C. TYP.
A — A
FACE OF CHANNEL STRINGER

PLAN-FIRST FLOOR
THREADED HANGER ROD, TYP.
CHANNEL HEADER
UP
UP
UP
LINE OF LANDING ABOVE
FACE OF CHANNEL FRAME

INTERMEDIATE LANDING TYPICAL SECTION
ROUGH FACE OF WELL OPENING
PLASTER FINISH, TYP.
THREADED HANGER ROD
¼" (+)CL.
CLIP L
PLATFORM   TREAD
2" (±)
RISER
MIN. 1"
MAX. 1¼"
1"
CHANNEL FRAMING
1¼" x 1¼" x ⅛" L BRACKETS
CHANNEL STRINGER
MIN. 1"
LANDING
VARIES
BASE
CONNECTING BRACKET BY STAIR CONTRACTOR

BALUSTERS ½" SQ. SPACED 4½" (+) & WELDED INTO 1" X ½" C'S TOP AND BOTTOM
HANDRAIL
SECOND FLOOR
14"
2'-8" MIN.
4"
3'-7" (±)
FACE OF SUPPORTING BEAM
2½"
₵ NEWEL
CEMENT FILLED PAN TREADS
LANDING
3'-7" (±)
₵ NEWEL & FACE OF RISER
2"
₵ NEWEL & FACE OF RISER
2"
PLATFORM 12 GA. STEEL USE L'S OR T'S FOR STIFFENERS
HEADER CHANNEL
COVER PL (PLATE)
CHANNEL STRINGER 10" JR. C (MIN.)
ANCHORING (POCKET SET OR BOLT)
FIN. FL.
SUB. FL.

SECTION I–I
PAN TYPE CONSTRUCTION
(Schools, Offices, etc.) Some mfrs. prefer 3" newels. If underside is to be plaster finished, mfr. will weld the required clips with holes.

CLIP L W/ ¾" φ ANCHOR BOLTS ON EA. STRINGER
FIELD WELD
SHOP FABRICATED HANDRAIL
FIN. FL.

BASE
FIN. FL.
HANDRAIL
½" SQ. BALUSTERS
1" X ½" CHANNEL
WELD & GRIND FLUSH
COVER PL
CHANNEL
PLASTER FINISH
NEWEL ₵
2½"
FACE OF ROUGH BEAM

BALCONY EDGE SECTION

₵ HANDRAIL
SUPPORT FOR POST
4" SQ. NEWEL
RISER
DOWN

DETAIL "A" (PLAN) TOP FLOOR

HANDRAILS
₵
₵
SEE NOTE
RISER
RISER
SUPPORT FOR NEWEL
4" NEWEL
CHANNEL FLANGE

DETAIL "B" (PLAN)
NOTE:
Always check handrail clearance with crossing, e.g. downward handrail with adjacent rising stringer.

₵ POSTS & RISER
4'-0" (−)
1¼" φ MIN. PIPE
3'-0" MIN.
TOE PLATE AS REQ'D.
GRATING DECK
GRATING TYPE TREADS
CHANNEL STRINGER (ALWAYS TOED OUT)
PLATE TYPE TREADS

STEEL STAIRS (OPEN) TYPICAL SECTION
(INDUSTRIAL)
Check mfrs. for socket connections if desired.

Paul R. Schieve, Sr. and Joseph Hornyak; Tippetts, Abbett, McCarthy, Stratton; New York, New York

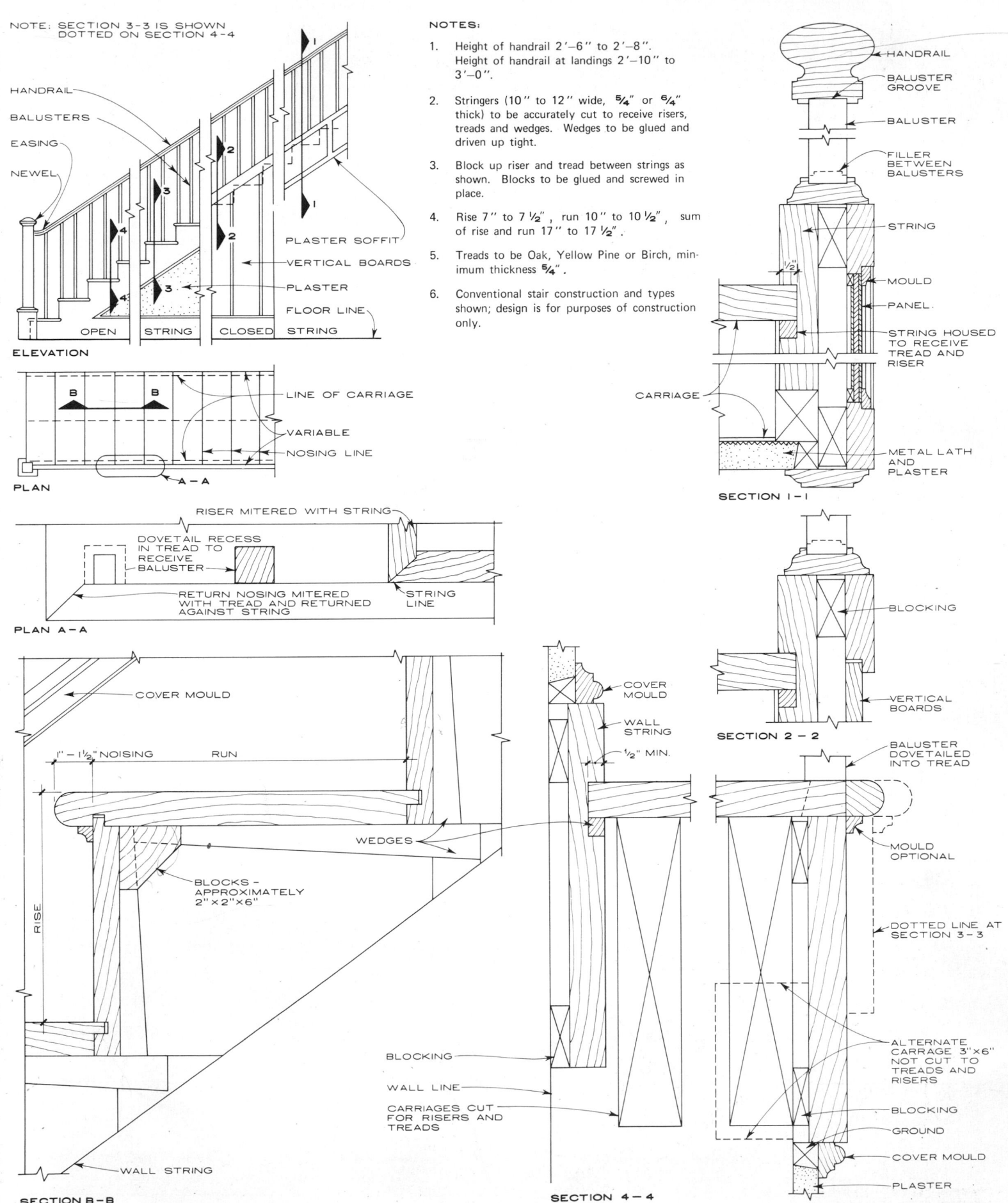

NOTE: SECTION 3-3 IS SHOWN DOTTED ON SECTION 4-4

HANDRAIL
BALUSTERS
EASING
NEWEL
OPEN STRING   CLOSED STRING
PLASTER SOFFIT
VERTICAL BOARDS
PLASTER
FLOOR LINE

ELEVATION

NOTES:

1. Height of handrail 2'–6'' to 2'–8''. Height of handrail at landings 2'–10'' to 3'–0''.

2. Stringers (10'' to 12'' wide, 5/4'' or 6/4'' thick) to be accurately cut to receive risers, treads and wedges. Wedges to be glued and driven up tight.

3. Block up riser and tread between strings as shown. Blocks to be glued and screwed in place.

4. Rise 7'' to 7 1/2'', run 10'' to 10 1/2'', sum of rise and run 17'' to 17 1/2''.

5. Treads to be Oak, Yellow Pine or Birch, minimum thickness 5/4''.

6. Conventional stair construction and types shown; design is for purposes of construction only.

HANDRAIL
BALUSTER GROOVE
BALUSTER
FILLER BETWEEN BALUSTERS
STRING
MOULD
PANEL
STRING HOUSED TO RECEIVE TREAD AND RISER
CARRIAGE
METAL LATH AND PLASTER

SECTION 1–1

B   B
LINE OF CARRIAGE
VARIABLE
NOSING LINE
A – A

PLAN

RISER MITERED WITH STRING
DOVETAIL RECESS IN TREAD TO RECEIVE BALUSTER
RETURN NOSING MITERED WITH TREAD AND RETURNED AGAINST STRING
STRING LINE

PLAN A–A

BLOCKING
VERTICAL BOARDS

SECTION 2 – 2

COVER MOULD
1'' – 1 1/2'' NOISING   RUN
RISE
BLOCKS – APPROXIMATELY 2'' x 2'' x 6''
WEDGES
WALL STRING

SECTION B–B

COVER MOULD
WALL STRING
1/2'' MIN.
BLOCKING
WALL LINE
CARRIAGES CUT FOR RISERS AND TREADS

SECTION 4 – 4

BALUSTER DOVETAILED INTO TREAD
MOULD OPTIONAL
DOTTED LINE AT SECTION 3–3
ALTERNATE CARRIAGE 3'' x 6'' NOT CUT TO TREADS AND RISERS
BLOCKING
GROUND
COVER MOULD
PLASTER

H. E. Heidtmann and R. Paccone; Sargent, Webster, Crenshaw & Folley; Syracuse, New York

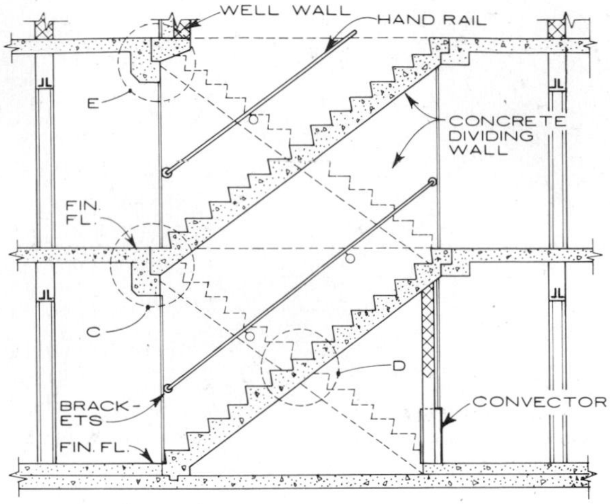

SECTION A-A

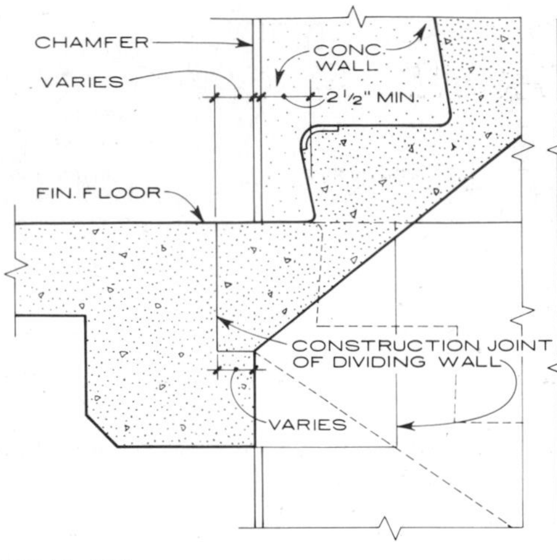

WELL WALL — HAND RAIL — CONCRETE DIVIDING WALL — BRACKETS — FIN. FL. — FIN. FL. — CONVECTOR — E — C — D

DETAIL "C"

CHAMFER VARIES — CONC. WALL — 2½" MIN. — FIN. FLOOR — CONSTRUCTION JOINT OF DIVIDING WALL — VARIES

DETAIL "D"

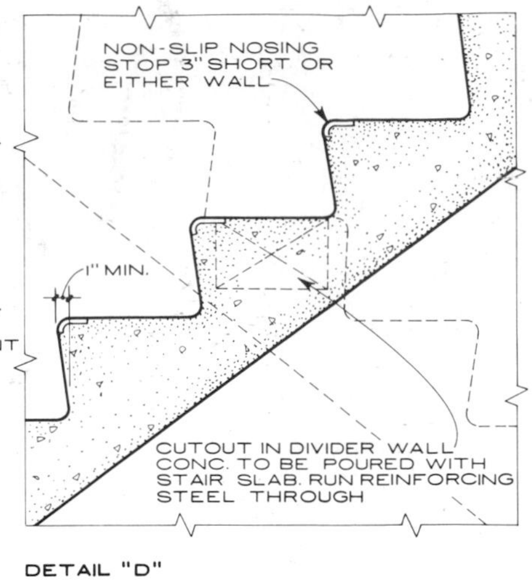

NON-SLIP NOSING STOP 3" SHORT OR EITHER WALL — 1" MIN. — CUTOUT IN DIVIDER WALL CONC. TO BE POURED WITH STAIR SLAB. RUN REINFORCING STEEL THROUGH

FIRST FLOOR PLAN

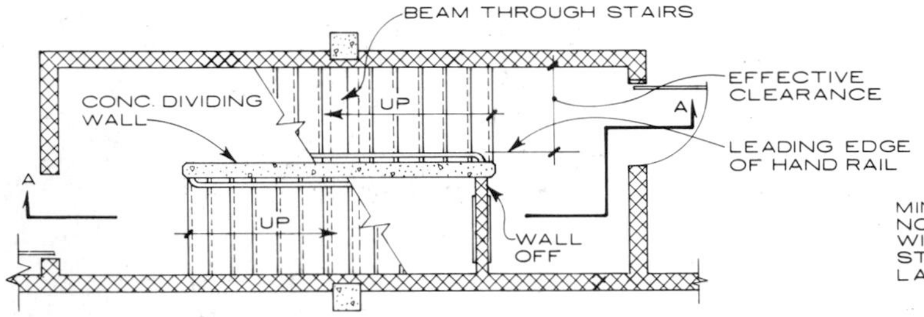

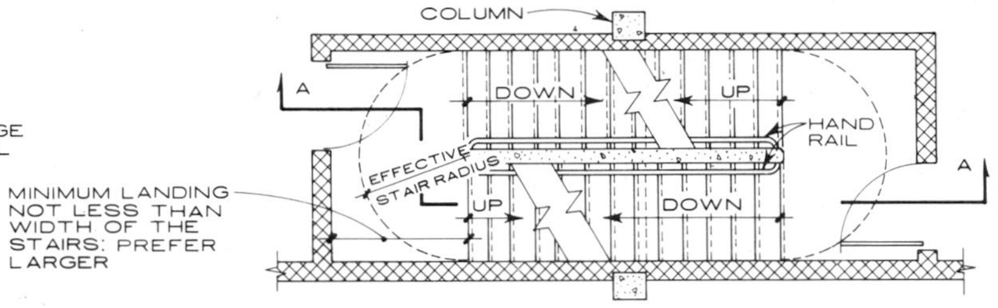

BEAM THROUGH STAIRS — CONC. DIVIDING WALL — UP — EFFECTIVE CLEARANCE — LEADING EDGE OF HAND RAIL — UP — WALL OFF — A — A

SECOND FLOOR PLAN

COLUMN — DOWN — UP — HAND RAIL — EFFECTIVE STAIR RADIUS — UP — DOWN — MINIMUM LANDING NOT LESS THAN WIDTH OF THE STAIRS; PREFER LARGER — A — A

When columns are located as shown, tie in with stair beam reinforcing. Columns are not mandatory. Check governing code for permissible encroachment of door into effective stair radius, usually it is 6″. On upper floors, doors must swing into the well and in the direction of the downward personnel flow. All doors on the first floor must always swing out of the stair well. Check governing codes to determine stair width, number of continuous risers, etc.

SCISSOR STAIRS

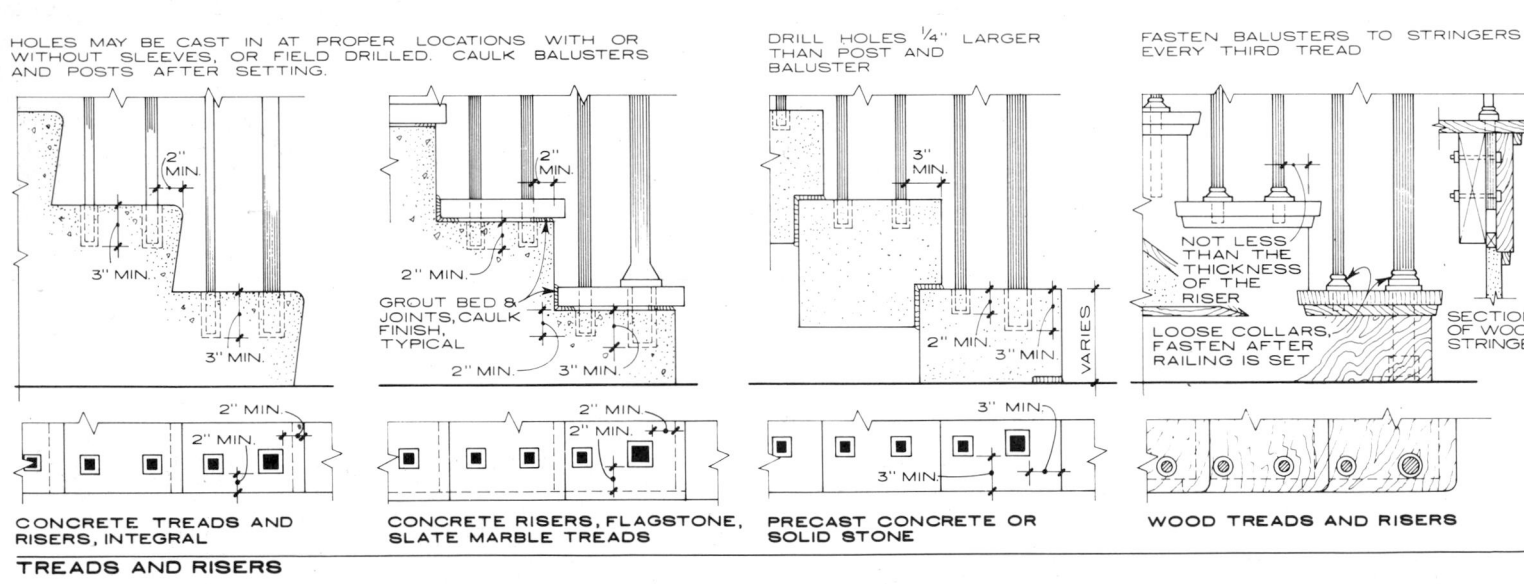

HOLES MAY BE CAST IN AT PROPER LOCATIONS WITH OR WITHOUT SLEEVES, OR FIELD DRILLED. CAULK BALUSTERS AND POSTS AFTER SETTING.

DRILL HOLES ¼" LARGER THAN POST AND BALUSTER

FASTEN BALUSTERS TO STRINGERS EVERY THIRD TREAD

2" MIN. — 3" MIN. — 3" MIN.

2" MIN. — GROUT BED & JOINTS, CAULK FINISH, TYPICAL — 2" MIN. — 2" MIN. — 3" MIN.

3" MIN. — 2" MIN. — 3" MIN. — VARIES

NOT LESS THAN THE THICKNESS OF THE RISER — LOOSE COLLARS, FASTEN AFTER RAILING IS SET — SECTION OF WOOD STRINGER

2" MIN. — 2" MIN.   2" MIN. — 2" MIN.   3" MIN. — 3" MIN.

CONCRETE TREADS AND RISERS, INTEGRAL

CONCRETE RISERS, FLAGSTONE, SLATE MARBLE TREADS

PRECAST CONCRETE OR SOLID STONE

WOOD TREADS AND RISERS

TREADS AND RISERS

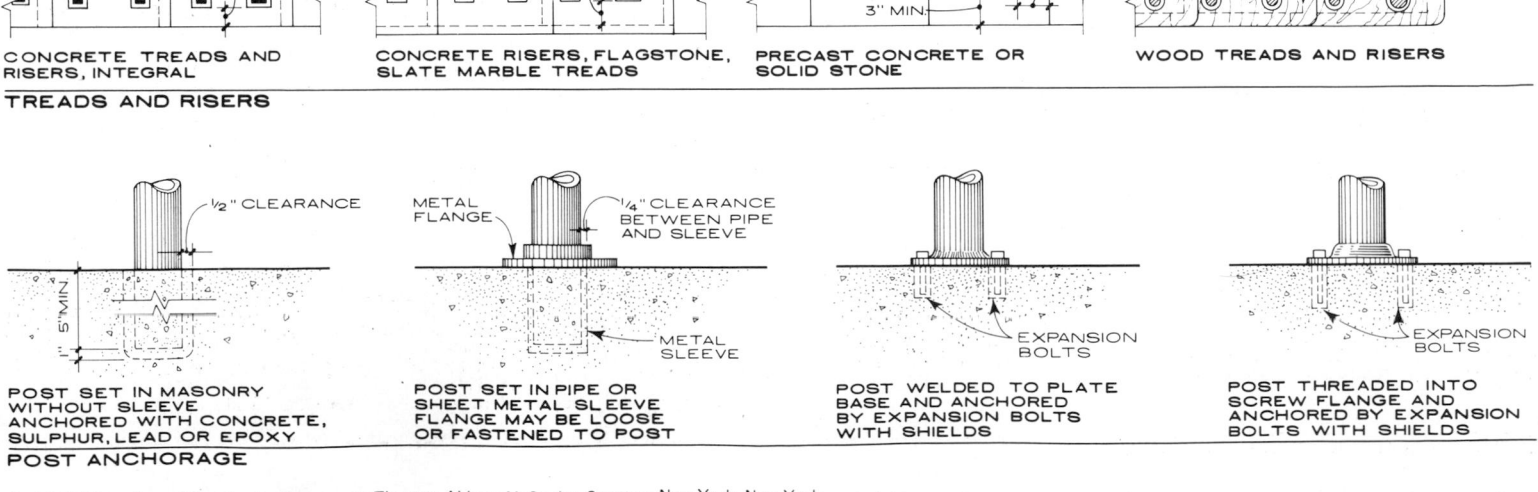

½" CLEARANCE — 5" MIN.

METAL FLANGE — ¼" CLEARANCE BETWEEN PIPE AND SLEEVE — METAL SLEEVE

EXPANSION BOLTS

EXPANSION BOLTS

POST SET IN MASONRY WITHOUT SLEEVE ANCHORED WITH CONCRETE, SULPHUR, LEAD OR EPOXY

POST SET IN PIPE OR SHEET METAL SLEEVE FLANGE MAY BE LOOSE OR FASTENED TO POST

POST WELDED TO PLATE BASE AND ANCHORED BY EXPANSION BOLTS WITH SHIELDS

POST THREADED INTO SCREW FLANGE AND ANCHORED BY EXPANSION BOLTS WITH SHIELDS

POST ANCHORAGE

Paul R. Schieve, Sr. and Constantine Economou; Tippetts, Abbett, McCarthy, Stratton; New York, New York

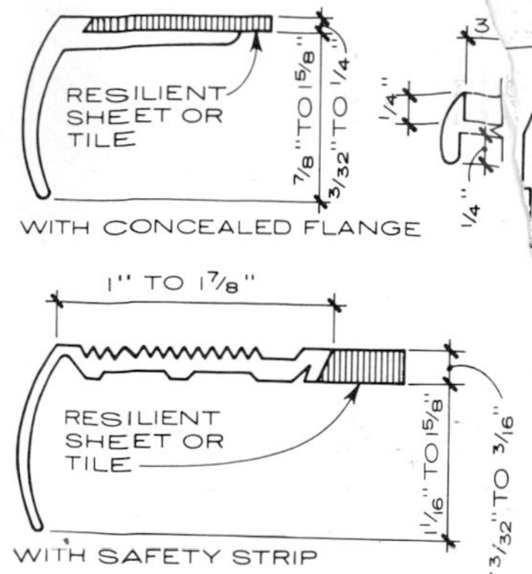

EXTRUDED NOSINGS

RESILIENT SHEET OR TILE
WITH CONCEALED FLANGE

1" TO 1⅞"
RESILIENT SHEET OR TILE
WITH SAFETY STRIP

For use on wood steps with the following finishes: vinyl, cork, rubber, etc. All with saturated felt paper under to align with nosing.

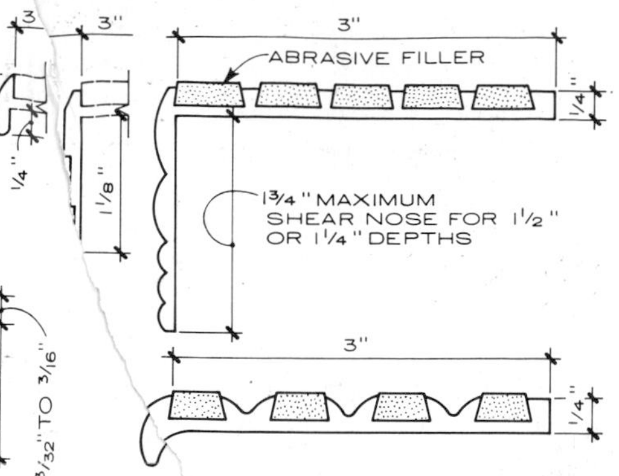

EXTRUDED SAFETY TREADS

ABRASIVE FILLER
3"
1¾" MAXIMUM SHEAR NOSE FOR 1½" OR 1¼" DEPTHS
3"

For use on concrete or wood steps, recessed or surface mounted. Surface mounted type i 7" or 8" deep with beveled back edge.

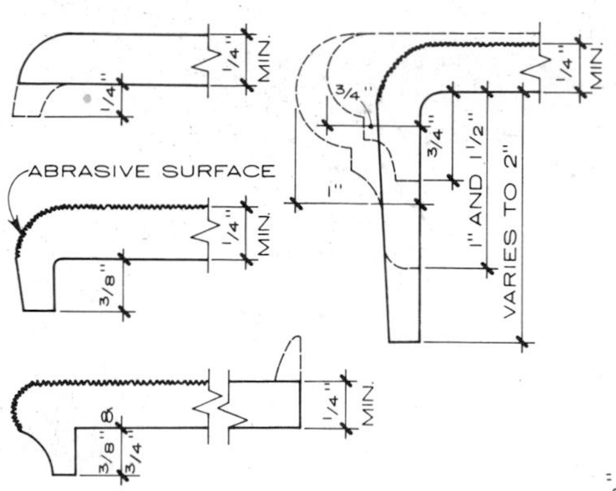

CAST ABRASIVE SAFETY TREADS

ABRASIVE SURFACE

For use on concrete steps applied abrasive tread is at full depth on old work; but can be full depth or recessed at varying depths on new work.

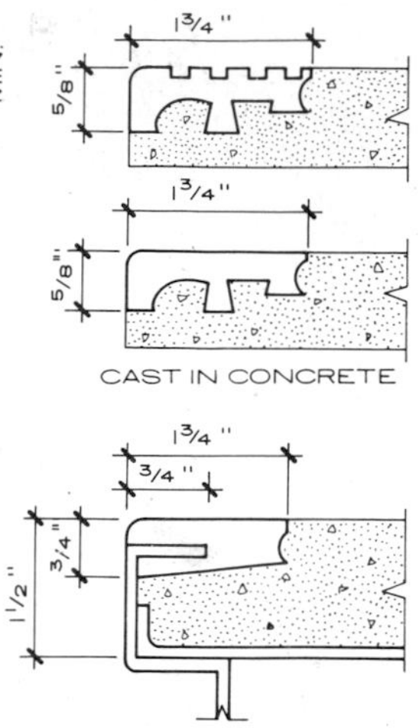

CAST IN CONCRETE

METAL PAN STAIRS

1. Extruded types: Aluminum and aluminum with abrasive filler in lengths; as required up to 12'–0".
2. Cast Types: Iron, aluminum, or bronze, and are made to order to exact size.
3. Types shown are used on new or old work. Old work: Fill worn surfaces to level.
4. Nosings and treads come with factory drilled countersunk holes, or with riveted strap anchors, or with wing type anchors.
5. Wood Application: Secure with wood screws.
6. Concrete Application: Secure with adhesive shields and screws, or with strap or wing anchors.
7. Nosings for concrete stairs: steel, bronze, brass and aluminum rolled, drawn or extruded cast abrasive.

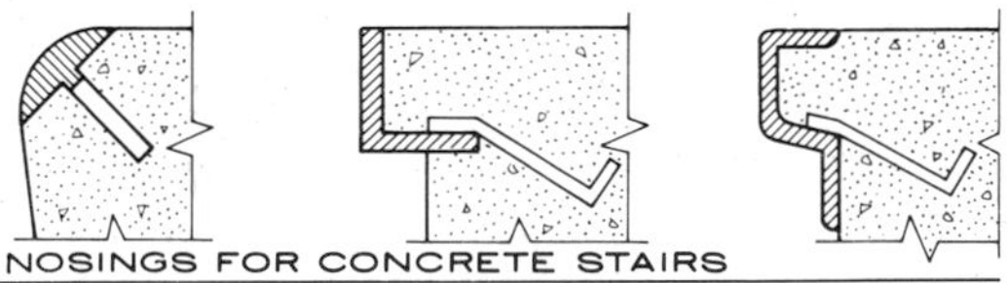

NOSINGS FOR CONCRETE STAIRS

STANDARD EXTRUDED NOSINGS, STANDARD EXTRUDED & CAST ABRASIVE SAFETY TREADS & NOSINGS FOR CONCRETE STAIRS

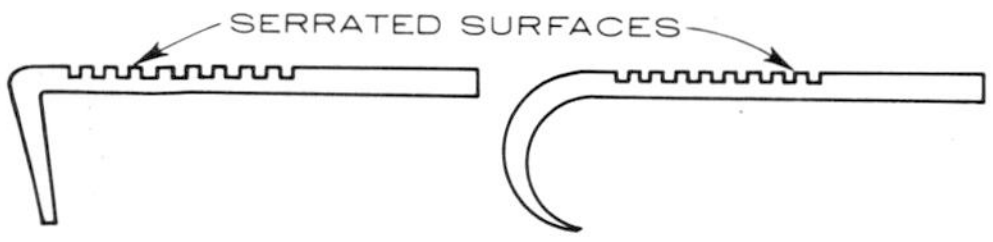

SERRATED SURFACES

RUBBER SAFETY TREADS

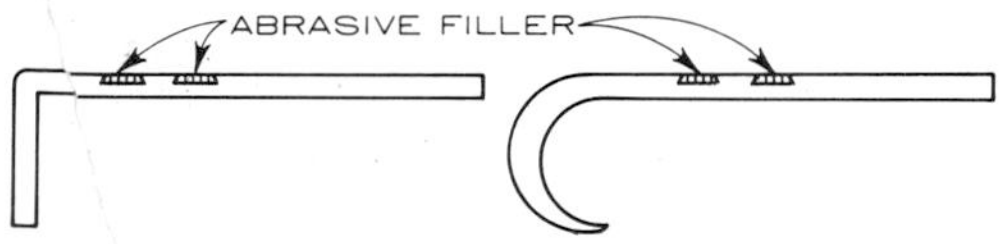

ABRASIVE FILLER

VINYL SAFETY TREADS

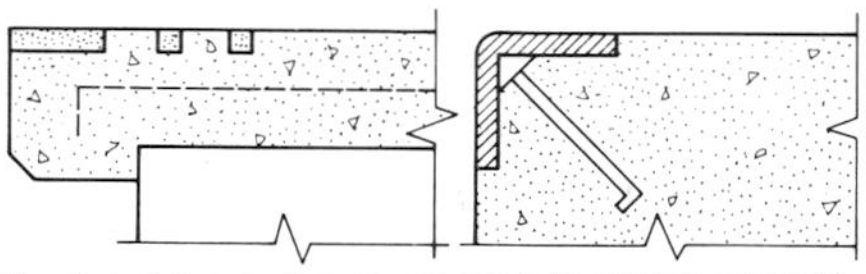

Abrasive strips or shapes are set into precast concrete, terrazzo or stone in various patterns.

NON-SLIP TREADS

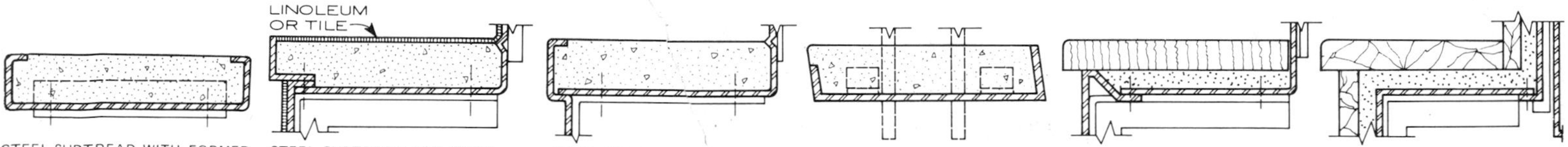

LINOLEUM OR TILE

STEEL SUBTREAD WITH FORMED NOSING, NO RISER

STEEL SUBTREAD AND RISER WITH SANITARY COVE, NOSING OF STEEL ANGLE

STEEL SUBTREAD AND RISER WITH FORMED NOSING AND SANITARY COVE

CURVED STEEL STAIR TREAD

STEEL SUBTREAD AND RISER FORMED TO SUPPORT PRECAST OR MARBLE TREAD

STEEL STAIR WITH MARBLE TREADS

CEMENT FILLED

STONE

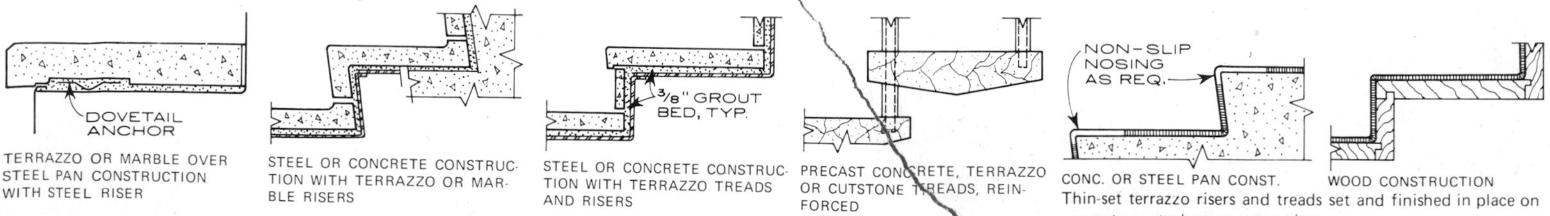

DOVETAIL ANCHOR
TERRAZZO OR MARBLE OVER STEEL PAN CONSTRUCTION WITH STEEL RISER

STEEL OR CONCRETE CONSTRUCTION WITH TERRAZZO OR MARBLE RISERS

⅜" GROUT BED, TYP.
STEEL OR CONCRETE CONSTRUCTION WITH TERRAZZO TREADS AND RISERS

PRECAST CONCRETE, TERRAZZO OR CUTSTONE TREADS, REINFORCED

NON-SLIP NOSING AS REQ.
CONC. OR STEEL PAN CONST.

WOOD CONSTRUCTION
Thin-set terrazzo risers and treads set and finished in place on concrete or steel pan construction.

PRECAST

THIN-SET

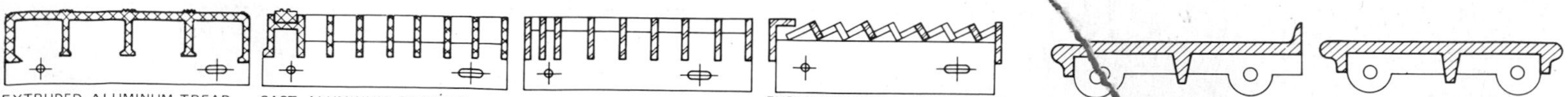

EXTRUDED ALUMINUM TREAD WITH WELDED END BARS BOLTED TO STRING

CAST ALUMINUM GRATING TREAD WITH ABRASIVE NOSING

STEEL GRATING TREAD

EXPANDED METAL TREAD WITH ANGLE NOSING FLAT
Back bars and end bars bolted to string.

ABRASIVE TREADS CAST INTEGRALLY WITH LUGS OR BOLTED TO CLIP ANGLES
Lugs or clips angle bolted to structural member (stronger) on each side.

TYPICAL RISER & TREAD DETAILS

Paul R. Schieve, Sr. and Joseph Hornyak; Tippetts, Abbett, McCarthy, Stratton; New York, New York

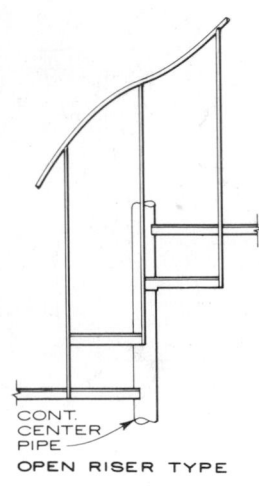

CONT. CENTER PIPE

OPEN RISER TYPE

CONT. CENTER PIPE

CLOSED RISER TYPE

GENERAL NOTES:

1. C.I., stl. or alum. stairs are identified by treads. When al. treads are specified all parts are alum.

2. Center pipe may terminate at platform, or be capped above well rail, or be extended and secured to clg.

3. Balusters: 1 Per tread. 3/4" bar or 3/4" O.D. for stl/al, 15/16" for C.I. At quarter points 1 1/4" O.D. for C.I.

4. Formed steel floor plate tread is welded to steel collar and web for cantilever type, or to steel collar and riser assembly for open riser type.

5. Cantilever treads are secured and held in position by set screws in the hub, or welded.

6. Plated screw and bolt fasteners for stl and C.I. stairs. SST fasteners for al. stairs.

7. Platform sizes are 1" larger than stair radius and anchored to suit well opening construction.

8. Design refence must be made to state or local laws and ordinances.

WELL OPENING

1 1/4" O.D.

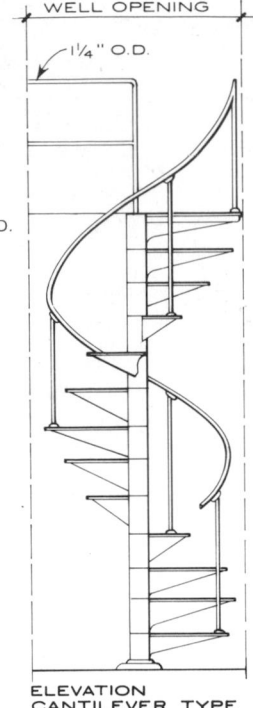

ELEVATION CANTILEVER TYPE

PLATFORM

DN.

PLAN
SQUARE WELL
LEFT HAND STAIR
RAILING ON LEFT
GOING UP

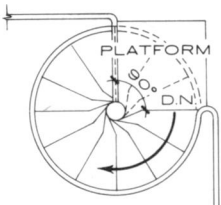

PLATFORM

DN.

PLAN
SQUARE WELL
RIGHT HAND STAIR
RAILING ON RIGHT
GOING UP

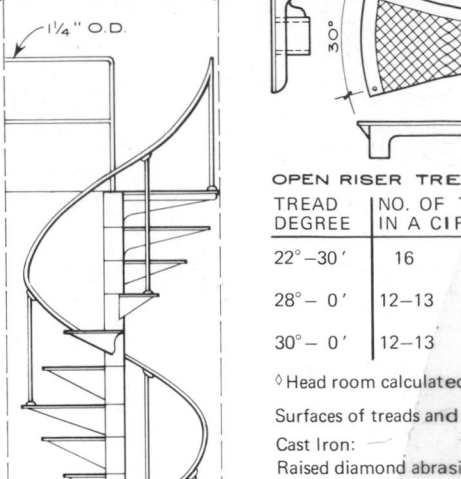

30°   30°

| OPEN RISER TREADS | | | CANTILEVER TREADS | |
TREAD DEGREE	NO. OF TREADS IN A CIRCLE	RISER SIZE	HEAD◊ ROOM	REMARKS
22°–30'	16	7"	7'–0"	Narrowest treads, Lowest riser
28°–0'	12–13	7 5/8"–7 3/4"	6'–9"	
30°–0'	12–13	8 3/8"–9"	6'–9"	Widest treads, Highest riser

◊ Head room calculated on a basis of 3/4 of a circle.

Surfaces of treads and platforms

Cast Iron:
Raised diamond abrasie

Steel:
Checkered plate abrasive,
expanded metal grating,
bar grating

Aluminum:
Checkered plate, abrasive
bar grating

Special:
Wood or rubbe cemented to steel tread,
or plywood treads for carpeting.

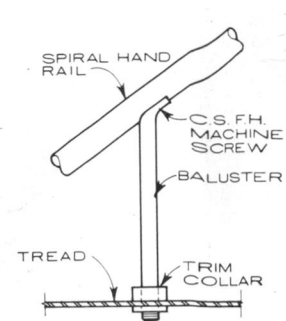

SPIRAL HAND RAIL

C.S.F.H. MACHINE SCREW

BALUSTER

TREAD

TRIM COLLAR

BALUSTER DETAIL

STANDARD SIZES OF STAIRS, PLATFORMS AND WELLS

| *DIA. OF STAIR (IN) | CENTER PIPE, O.D. (IN) | | PLATFORM SIZE (IN) SQ/ 1/4 CIRCLE | WELL OPEN'G (IN) SQ/CIRCULAR |
	C.I.	STL/AL		
42	3 1/2	3 1/2	22	44
48⁺	3 1/2	3 1/2	25	50
54⁺	4 1/2	3 1/2	28	56
60⁺	4 1/2	3 1/2	31	62
66	4 1/2	5	34	68
72	4 1/2	5	37	74

*Also available in 78" 84" 90" & 98" - special sizes.
⁺Most residential stairs - with 28° treads, larger dia.
Residential stairs usually 22°–30'.

SPIRAL STAIRS OF CAST IRON, STEEL OR ALUMINUM

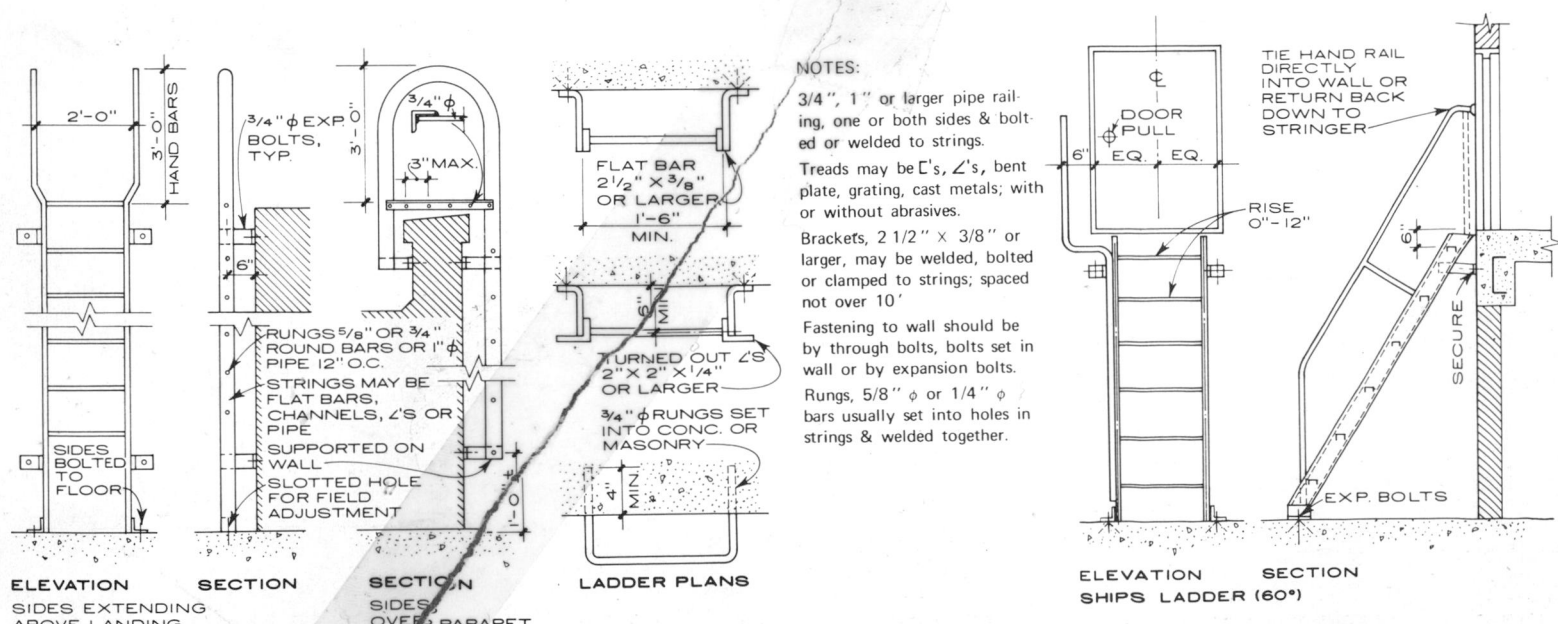

2'-0"

HAND BARS

3/4"φ EXP. BOLTS, TYP.

3"MAX.

3/4"φ

FLAT BAR 2 1/2" X 3/8" OR LARGER 1'-6" MIN.

RUNGS 5/8" OR 3/4" ROUND BARS OR 1" φ PIPE 12" O.C.

STRINGS MAY BE FLAT BARS, CHANNELS, ∠'S OR PIPE SUPPORTED ON WALL

SLOTTED HOLE FOR FIELD ADJUSTMENT

TURNED OUT ∠'S 2" X 2" X 1/4" OR LARGER

3/4" φ RUNGS SET INTO CONC. OR MASONRY

SIDES BOLTED TO FLOOR

NOTES:

3/4", 1" or larger pipe railing, one or both sides & bolted or welded to strings.

Treads may be ['s, ∠'s, bent plate, grating, cast metals; with or without abrasives.

Brackets, 2 1/2" X 3/8" or larger, may be welded, bolted or clamped to strings; spaced not over 10'

Fastening to wall should be by through bolts, bolts set in wall or by expansion bolts.

Rungs, 5/8" φ or 1/4" φ bars usually set into holes in strings & welded together.

TIE HAND RAIL DIRECTLY INTO WALL OR RETURN BACK DOWN TO STRINGER

DOOR PULL

EQ. EQ.

RISE 0"-12"

SECURE

EXP. BOLTS

ELEVATION   **SECTION**
SIDES EXTENDING ABOVE LANDING   SIDES OVER PARAPET

LADDER PLANS

ELEVATION   **SECTION**
SHIPS LADDER (60°)

VERTICAL AND SHIPS LADDERS

Paul R. Schieve, Sr. and Joseph Hornyak; Tippetts, Abbett, McCarthy, Stratton; New York, New York

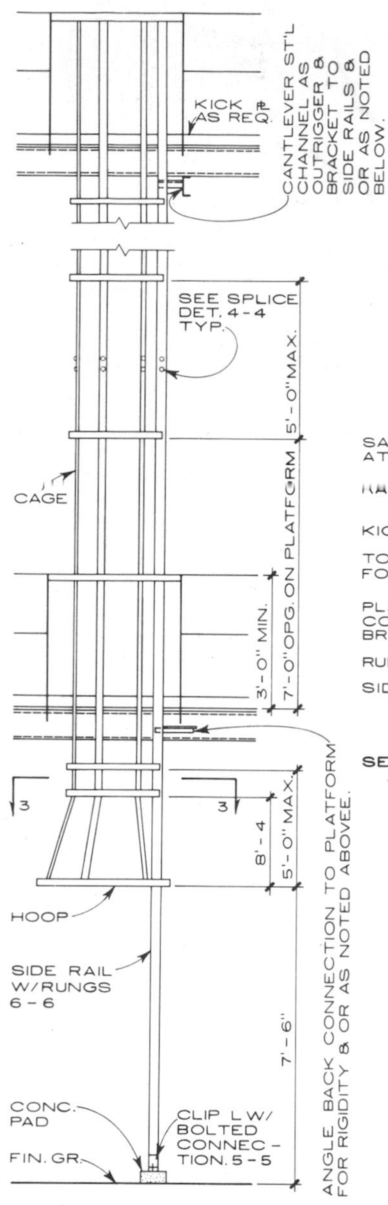

KICK ₤ AS REQ.

CANTILEVER STL CHANNEL AS OUTRIGGER & BRACKET TO SIDE RAILS 8 OR AS NOTED BELOW.

SEE SPLICE DET. 4-4 TYP.

CAGE

5'-0" MAX.

7'-0" OPG. ON PLATFORM

3'-0" MIN.

8'-4 5'-0" MAX.

7'-6"

HOOP

SIDE RAIL W/RUNGS 6-6

CONC. PAD

FIN. GR.

CLIP L W/ BOLTED CONNEC- TION. 5-5

ANGLE BACK CONNECTION TO PLATFORM FOR RIGIDITY & OR AS NOTED ABOVE.

TYPICAL ELEVATION 7 — 7 SIDE MOUNTED

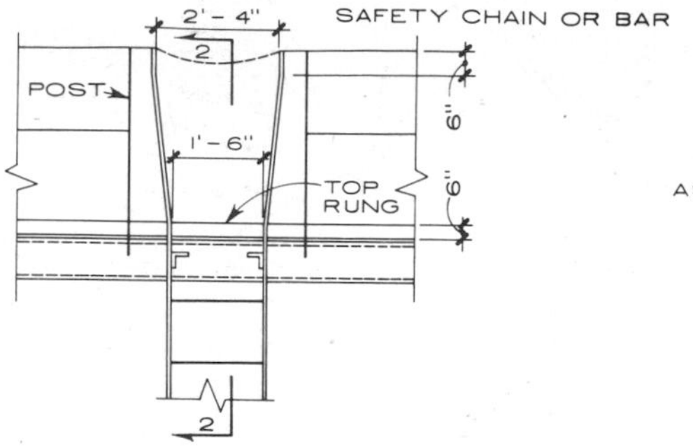

SAFETY CHAIN OR BAR

POST

2'- 4"

1'- 6"

6"

6"

TOP RUNG

SECTION 1-1

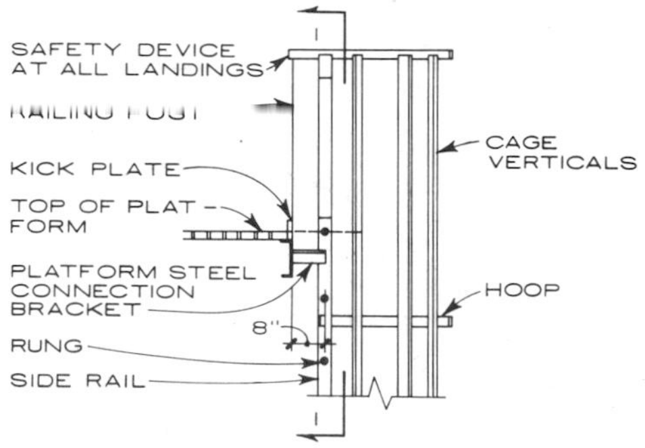

SAFETY DEVICE AT ALL LANDINGS

RAILING POST

KICK PLATE

TOP OF PLAT- FORM

PLATFORM STEEL CONNECTION BRACKET

RUNG

SIDE RAIL

CAGE VERTICALS

HOOP

8"

SECTION 2-2

8" 1'-2" 1'-10"

6" MIN. 8" MAX.

LINE OF SUPPORTING STEEL

48° 48° 60° 48° 60° 48° 48°

1'-6" 1'-2"

CAGE VERTICALS

HOOP

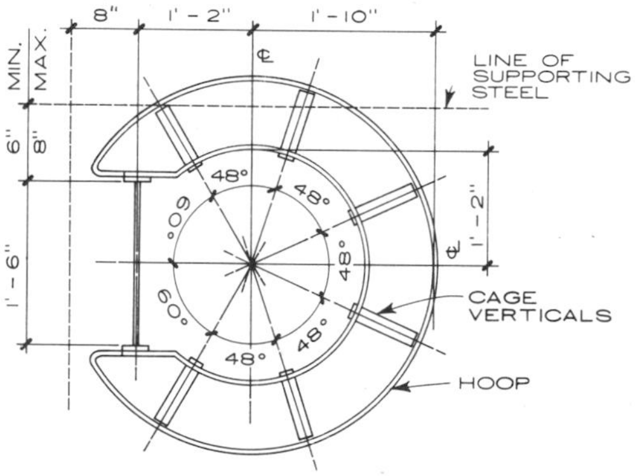

SECTION 3-3 CAGE & HOOP DETAILS

SUGGESTED FRAMING

MEMBER	SIZE	SUPPORT SPACING
LADDER SIDE RAILS	2 1/2" x 3/8"	8'—0" Maximum
	3" x 3/8"	12'—0" Maximum
	3 1/2" x 3/8"	16'—0" Maximum
CAGE HOOP	5" x 3/8"	20'—0" Maximum top & bottom
	2" x 3/8"	All intermediates
CAGE VERTICALS	2" x 3/8"	See section 3—3 above
LADDER RUNGS	3/4" φ Plug welded into side rails.	

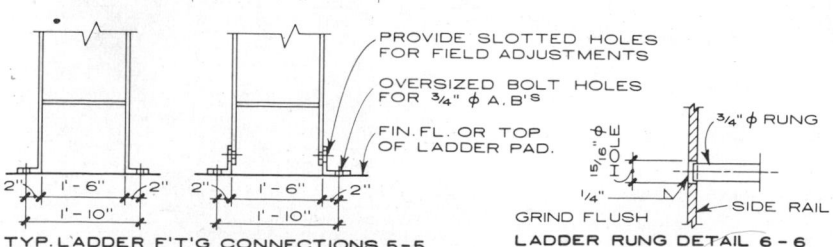

PROVIDE SLOTTED HOLES FOR FIELD ADJUSTMENTS

OVERSIZED BOLT HOLES FOR 3/4" φ A.B'S

FIN.FL. OR TOP OF LADDER PAD.

2" 1'- 6" 2"
1'- 10"

2" 1'- 6" 2"
1'- 10"

φ HOLE

15/16" φ HOLE

1/4"

3/4" φ RUNG

SIDE RAIL

GRIND FLUSH

TYP. LADDER F'T'G CONNECTIONS 5-5

LADDER RUNG DETAIL 6-6

TYPICAL CAGED LADDER DETAILS
CONSULT LOCAL CODE FOR POSSIBLE VARIATIONS

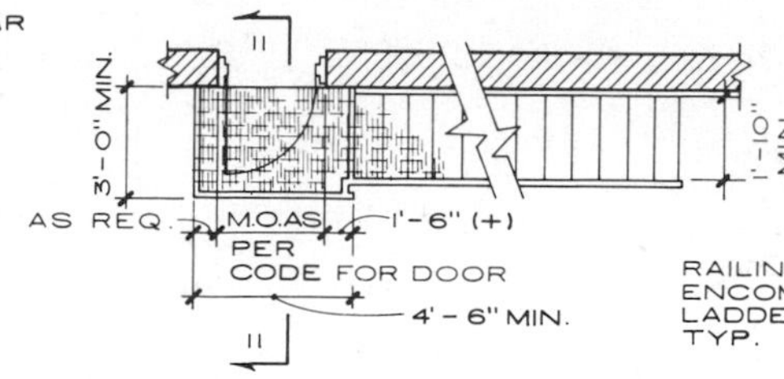

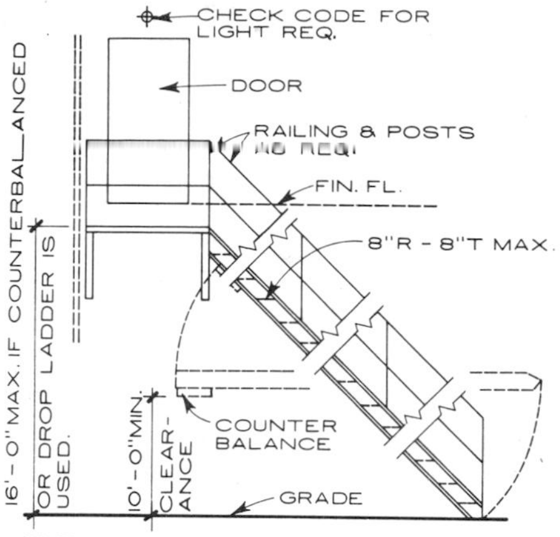

3'-0" MIN. AS REQ.

1'-10" MIN.

M.O. AS PER CODE FOR DOOR

1'-6" (+)

4'-6" MIN.

CHECK CODE FOR LIGHT REQ.

DOOR

RAILING & POSTS NO REQ'

FIN. FL.

8"R - 8"T MAX.

16'-0" MAX. IF COUNTERBALANCED OR DROP LADDER IS USED.

10'-0" MIN. CLEARANCE

COUNTER BALANCE

GRADE

ELEVATION 9-9

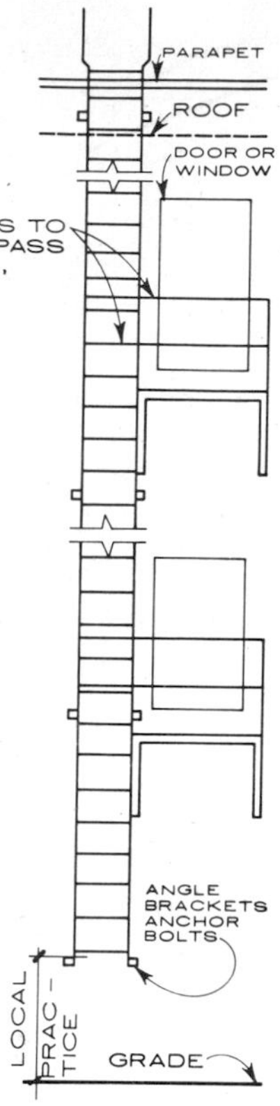

PARAPET

ROOF

DOOR OR WINDOW

RAILINGS TO ENCOMPASS LADDER, TYP.

ANGLE BRACKETS ANCHOR BOLTS

LOCAL PRAC- TICE

GRADE

ELEVATION 8-8

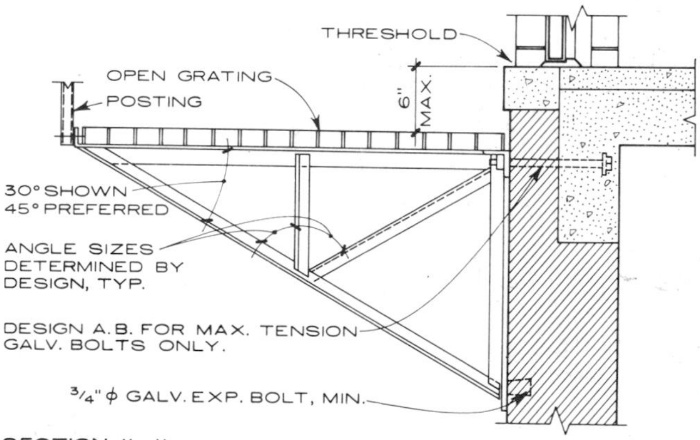

THRESHOLD

OPEN GRATING

POSTING

6" MAX.

30° SHOWN 45° PREFERRED

ANGLE SIZES DETERMINED BY DESIGN, TYP.

DESIGN A.B. FOR MAX. TENSION GALV. BOLTS ONLY.

3/4" φ GALV. EXP. BOLT, MIN.

SECTION 11-11

TYPICAL FIRE ESCAPE DETAILS

GENERAL NOTES: 4 BASIC TYPES

1. Vertical ladders with platforms at exit door & windows. This type used only for industrial buildings of low height.
2. Stairways supported on brackets attached to building walls with platforms at exits. This type used for any height building permitted by code. Lowest section may be counter-balanced or drop ladder. Fire escape stairs may be used as required means of exit only in existing buildings, subject to provisions of occupancy chapter applying....."not more than 50 percent of required exit cpaacity in any case." (NFPA 1.01 Life Safety Code 1966). (5—9111)
3. Free-standing stairways independently supported on steel columns, with platforms & walk-ways at exits. This type used on buildings where the construction cannot be attached to.
4. Chute-fire escapes, used chiefly for buildings where persons are under institutional care.

A—On all fire escapes, design reference must be made to state or local laws & ordinances.

B—Frames for platforms may be angles as shown, or channels bolted to brackets; grating can be bolted, welded to or set in frame loose. Alternate bracket may be round or square steel, usually 1" or 1 1/4".

Paul R. Schieve, Sr. and Joseph Hornyak; Tippetts, Abbett, McCarthy, Stratton; New York, New York

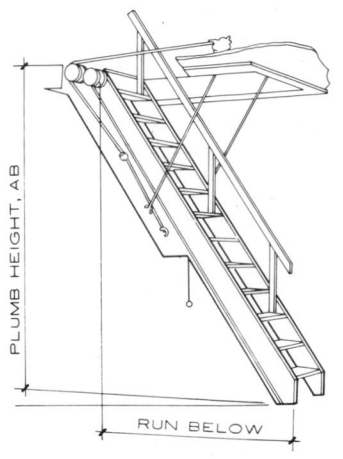

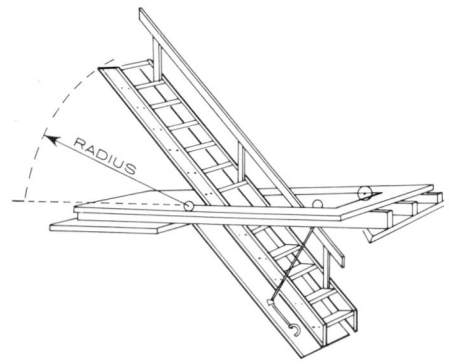

SLIDE UP PIVOT TYPE

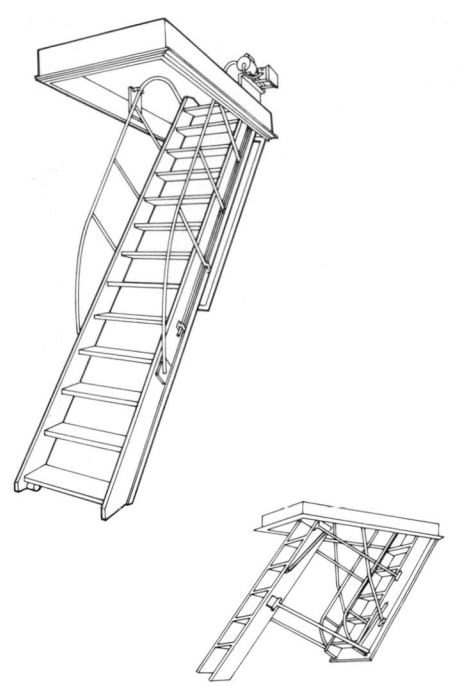

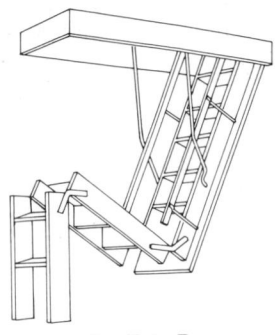

TRIPLE FOLD

MODEL	FL. TO CLG.	ROUGH OPENING
LIGHT	7'-0" TO 8'-9"	2'-1½" × 4'-6 ½" *
WEIGHT	8'-10" TO 9'-9"	2'-6" × 4'-6" *
JUNIOR	7'-6" TO 8'-9"	2'-2" × 4'-6"
MEDIUM	7'-6" TO 8'-8"	2'-1½" × 5'-0 ½" *
WEIGHT	8'-9" TO 9'-10"	2'-6" × 4'-6"

* Available with balanced spring action or activated by counterweights.

DOUBLE FOLD

FLOOR TO CEILING	ROUGH OPENING
7'-0" TO 8'-6"	2'-3" × 4'-10"
8'-0" TO 8'-6"	2'-9" × 5'-4"

TABLE FOR SELECTING SIZE NUMBER

SIZE	FL. TO FL. HT.	SIZE	FL. TO FL. HT.
1	7'-7" TO 7'-10"	12	12'-11" TO 13'-4"
2	7'-11" TO 8'-4"	13	13'-5" TO 13'-10"
3	8'-5" TO 8'-10"	14	13'-11" TO 14'-4"
4	8'-11" TO 9'-4"	15	14'-5" TO 14'-10"
5	9'-5" TO 9'-10"	16	14'-11" TO 15'-4"
6	9'-11" TO 10'-4"	17	15'-5" TO 15'-10"
7	10'-5" TO 10'-10"	18	15'-11" TO 16'-4"
8	10'-11" TO 11'-4"		
9	11'-5" TO 11'-10"	S	7'-7" TO 8'-3"
10	11'-11" TO 12'-4"	M	8'-4" TO 8'-9"
11	12'-5" TO 12'-10"	L	8'-10" TO 9'-3"

AUTOMATIC ELECTRIC

WOOD OR ALUMINUM

FLOOR TO CEILING	EXTEND BEYOND OPENING ABOVE	CLEAR HEIGHT ABOVE OPENING	RUN BELOW
7'-0"	5'-0"	3'-6"	7'-0½"
8'-0"	6'-3"	4'-1"	7'-10"
9'-0"	7'-6"	4'-8"	8'-7½"
10'-0"	8'-9"	5'-3"	9'-5"
11'-0"	10'-0"	5'-10"	10'-2½"
12'-0"	11'-3"	6'-5"	11'-0"
13'-0"	12'-6"	7'-0"	11'-9½"

STAIR WIDTH 17 3/16"
TREADS AND STRINGERS 4"

SIZE	RAD. ABOVE	PLUMB HT. AB.	RUN BELOW	PANEL OPNG.
S	5'-0"	3'-0"	3'-8½"	2'-0" × 4'-0"
M	5'-6"	3'-8"	3'-11"	2'-0" × 4'-0"
L	6'-0"	4'-4"	4'-1¼"	2'-0" × 4'-0"

STAIR WIDTH 17 3/16"
TREADS AND STRINGERS 6"

SIZE	RAD. ABOVE	PLUMB HT. AB.	RUN BELOW	PANEL OPNG.
1	4'-1"	2'-11"	5'-4"	2'-0" × 5'-6"
2	4'-8"	3'-5"	5'-8"	2'-0" × 5'-6"
3	5'-3"	3'-11"	6'-0"	2'-0" × 5'-6"
4	5'-10"	4'-5"	6'-4"	2'-0" × 5'-6"
5	5'-10"	4'-6"	6'-8"	2'-0" × 6'-0"
6	6'-6"	5'-1"	6'-11"	2'-0" × 6'-0"
7	7'-1"	5'-5"	7'-4"	2'-0" × 6'-0"

STAIR WIDTH 19"
TREADS AND STRINGERS 6"

SIZE	RAD. ABOVE	PLUMB HT. AB.	RUN BELOW	PANEL OPNG.
1	4'-1"	2'-11"	5'-4"	2'-6" × 5'-6"
2	4'-8"	3'-5"	5'-8"	2'-6" × 5'-6"
3	5'-3"	3'-11"	6'-0"	2'-6" × 5'-6"
4	5'-10"	4'-5"	6'-4"	2'-6" × 5'-6"
5	5'-10"	4'-6"	6'-8"	2'-6" × 6'-0"
6	6'-6"	5'-1"	6'-11"	2'-6" × 6'-0"
7	7'-4"	5'-5"	7'-4"	2'-6" × 6'-0"

STAIR WIDTH 19"
TREADS AND STRINGERS 8" & 10"

SIZE	RAD. ABOVE	PLUMB HT. AB.	RUN BELOW	PANEL OPNG.
1	4'-4"	3'-2"	6'-5"	2'-6" × 5'-10"
2	4'-11"	3'-8"	6'-10"	2'-6" × 5'-10"
3	5'-7"	4'-1"	7'-3"	2'-6" × 5'-10"
4	6'-2"	4'-6"	7'-7"	2'-6" × 6'-0"
5	6'-4"	4'-9"	8'-0"	2'-6" × 6'-4"
6	6'-8"	5'-0"	8'-4"	2'-6" × 6'-8"
7	7'-1"	5'-3"	8'-9"	2'-6" × 6'-11"
8	7'-6"	5'-5"	9'-2"	2'-6" × 7'-3"
9	7'-9"	5'-10"	9'-6"	2'-6" × 7'-6"
10	8'-1"	6'-1"	9'-10"	2'-6" × 7'-9"
11	8'-5"	6'-4"	10'-3"	2'-6" × 8'-1"
12	8'-9"	6'-6"	10'-8"	2'-6" × 8'-4"
13	9'-1"	6'-9"	11'-0"	2'-6" × 8'-8"
14	9'-5"	7'-0"	11'-5"	2'-6" × 9'-0"
15	9'-8"	7'-3"	11'-9"	2'-6" × 9'-3"
16	10'-3"	7'-7"	12'-3"	2'-6" × 9'-6"
17	10'-9"	8'-1"	12'-10"	2'-6" × 9'-9"
18	11'-1"	8'-4"	13'-1"	2'-6" × 10'-1"

P. M. M.; Ewing Cole Erdman & Eubank; Philadelphia, Pennsylvania

Panel modular 2'-0" x 2'-0"
1 1/4" thick w/1" resin bonded
core—1/8" resilient flooring at top
surface & bottom surface 1/8"
plastic laminate.

Removable floor panels modular
3'-0" or 2'-0", 1" & 3/4" thickness.
Compressed resin bonded core w/
24 ga. zinc coated sheet steel
laminated to top & bottom surfaces.

Panel modular 2'-0" x 2'-0"
1 1/4" thick die-formed steel
grid panel. No structural
stringers required.

Poured conc. w/wire mesh
reinf. to corrugated steel
form.

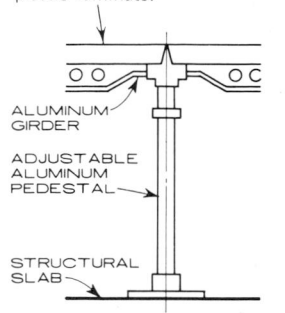

ALUMINUM
GIRDER

ADJUSTABLE
ALUMINUM
PEDESTAL

STRUCTURAL
SLAB

**1. ALUMINUM GIRDER
ASSEMBLY**
(WESTINGHOUSE)

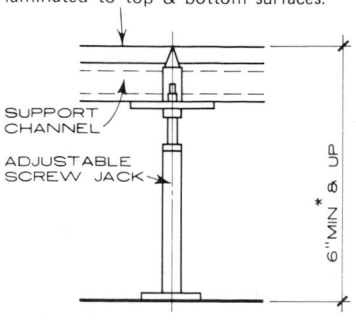

SUPPORT
CHANNEL

ADJUSTABLE
SCREW JACK

6" MIN * & UP

**2. CHANNEL GRID
ASSEMBLY**
(MET-L-STRUCT)

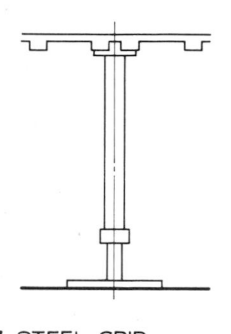

**3. STEEL GRID
PANEL SYSTEM**
(TATE)

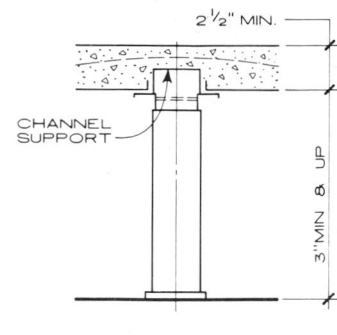

2½" MIN.

CHANNEL
SUPPORT

3" MIN & UP

**4. CORRUGATED
STEEL FORM**
(GRANCO)

* MECHANICAL REQUIREMENTS DICTATE MIN., GENERALLY NOT LESS THAN 6"

TYPES OF PEDESTAL FLOORS

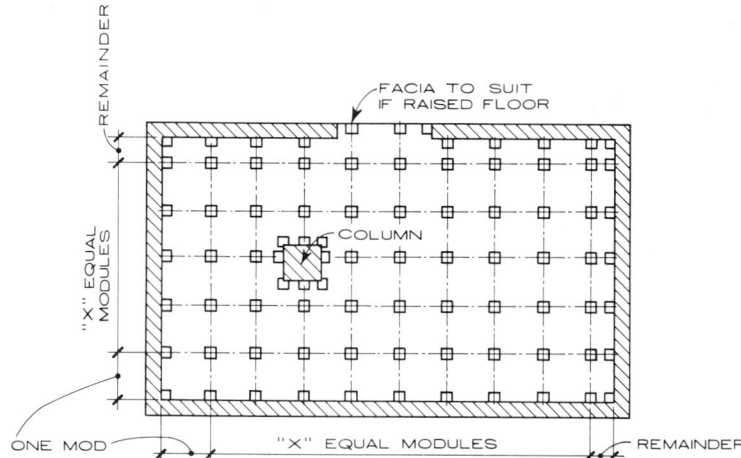

REMAINDER

FACIA TO SUIT
IF RAISED FLOOR

"X" EQUAL MODULES

COLUMN

ONE MOD

"X" EQUAL MODULES

REMAINDER

TYPICAL PEDESTAL ARRANGEMENT
MODULES ; 18" x 18" : 24" x 24" OR 36" x 36"
CAPACITY ; 250 P.S.F ; 5000 #/PEDESTAL

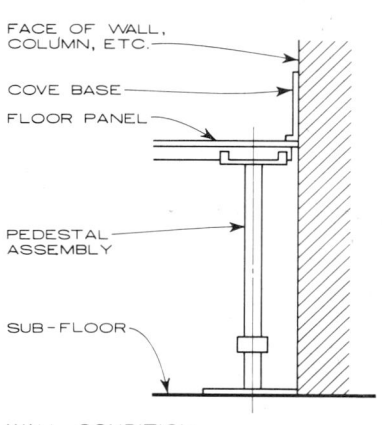

FACE OF WALL,
COLUMN, ETC.

COVE BASE

FLOOR PANEL

PEDESTAL
ASSEMBLY

SUB-FLOOR

WALL CONDITION

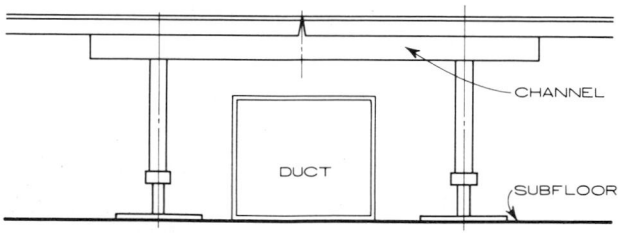

CHANNEL

DUCT

SUBFLOOR

**SPANNING DUCTS
INSTALLATION DETAILS**

PEDESTAL

SUBFLOOR

PLENUM DIVIDER

PLENUM

NOTE:
Pedestal floors are also known by the
following names:
Floating, Infinite Access, Elevated Floors,
Raised Floors.

Damaz, Pokorny, Weigel; New York, New York

Pedestal floors provide high strength for support
of uniform & concentrated loads.
Space below floors serves as plenum, duct spaces,
electrical cables for computers, etc.

First three panel types above have removable
modular panels for easy access to equipment
below floor.

TYPICAL STORAGE	TEMPERATURE
ICE CREAM	-30°
FROZEN FOOD	-10°
MEATS	+33°
POULTRY	+33° TO 34°
DAIRY FOODS	+36°
PRODUCE	+36° TO 38°

GENERAL NOTES
DOORS

Insulation thicknesses vary with the box temperature, the type of insulation and conditions in surrounding areas and outside. In temperate climates cooler boxes at temperatures above 32° usually do not require floor insulation. Penetration of insulation by pipes, conduit, and hangers should be kept to an absolute minimum. Rods or pipes through ceiling insulation should be insulated 3'— 0" above ceiling. Protection of insulation from damage from trucks and abrasion by stored goods is extremely important. Punctures in insulation finish allow moisture penetration with resulting drop in insulating efficiency and destruction of insulation structure.

INSULATION

Refrigerator doors are available in a wide variety of types and finishes including sliding, overhead types and special vestibule doors to minimize refrigeration losses where long periods of opening will prevail. Consult manufacturers for door selection.

VENTILATION

All spaces above suspended ceilings must be well ventilated. Freezers on slab on grade must be vented or heated below the slab.

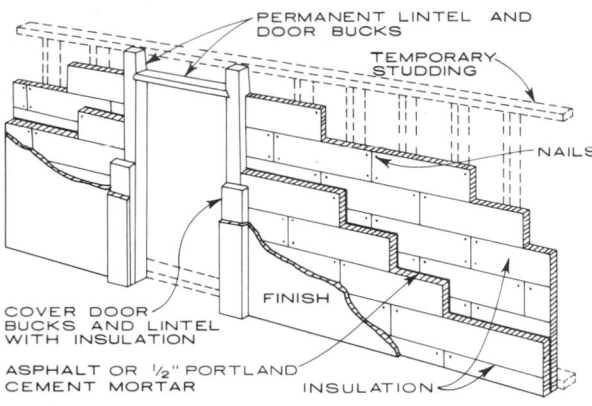

FREE STANDING PARTITION

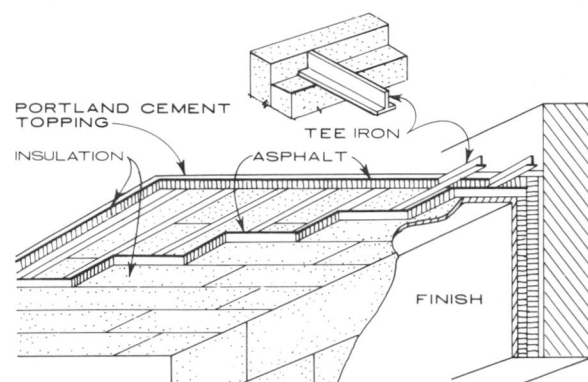

ON SUSPENDED STEEL CONSTRUCTION

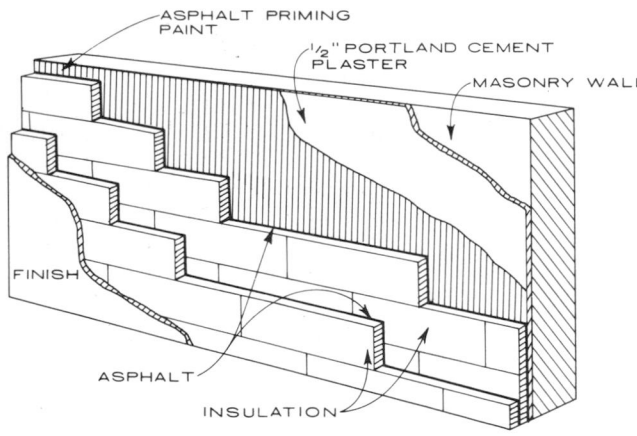

ON MASONRY WALLS

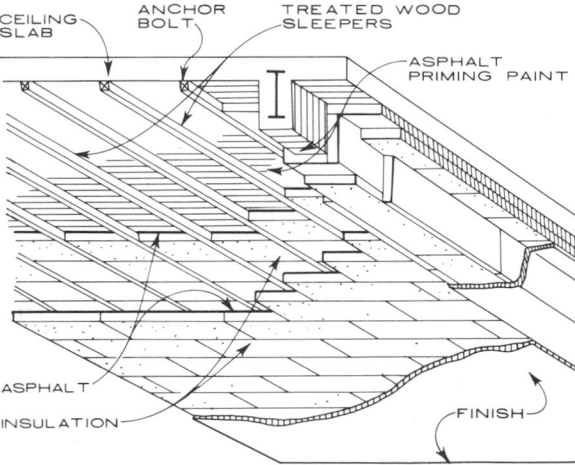

ON CONCRETE CONSTRUCTION

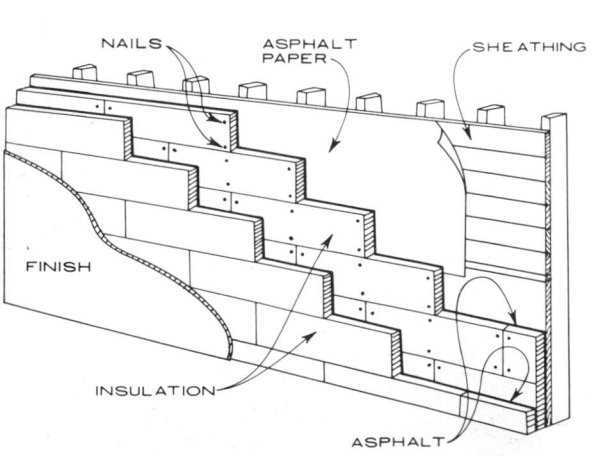

ON WOOD WALLS

TYPICAL WALL DETAILS

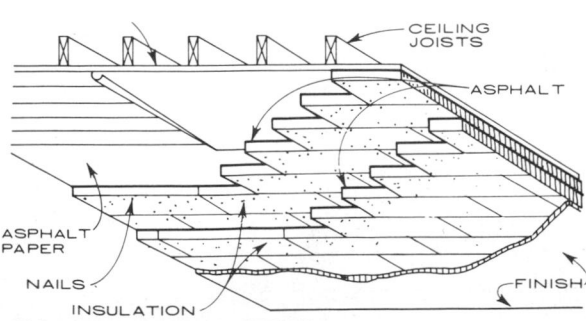

ON WOOD CONSTRUCTION

TYPICAL CEILING DETAILS

Elwood Taylor; The Ballinger Company; Philadelphia, Pennsylvania

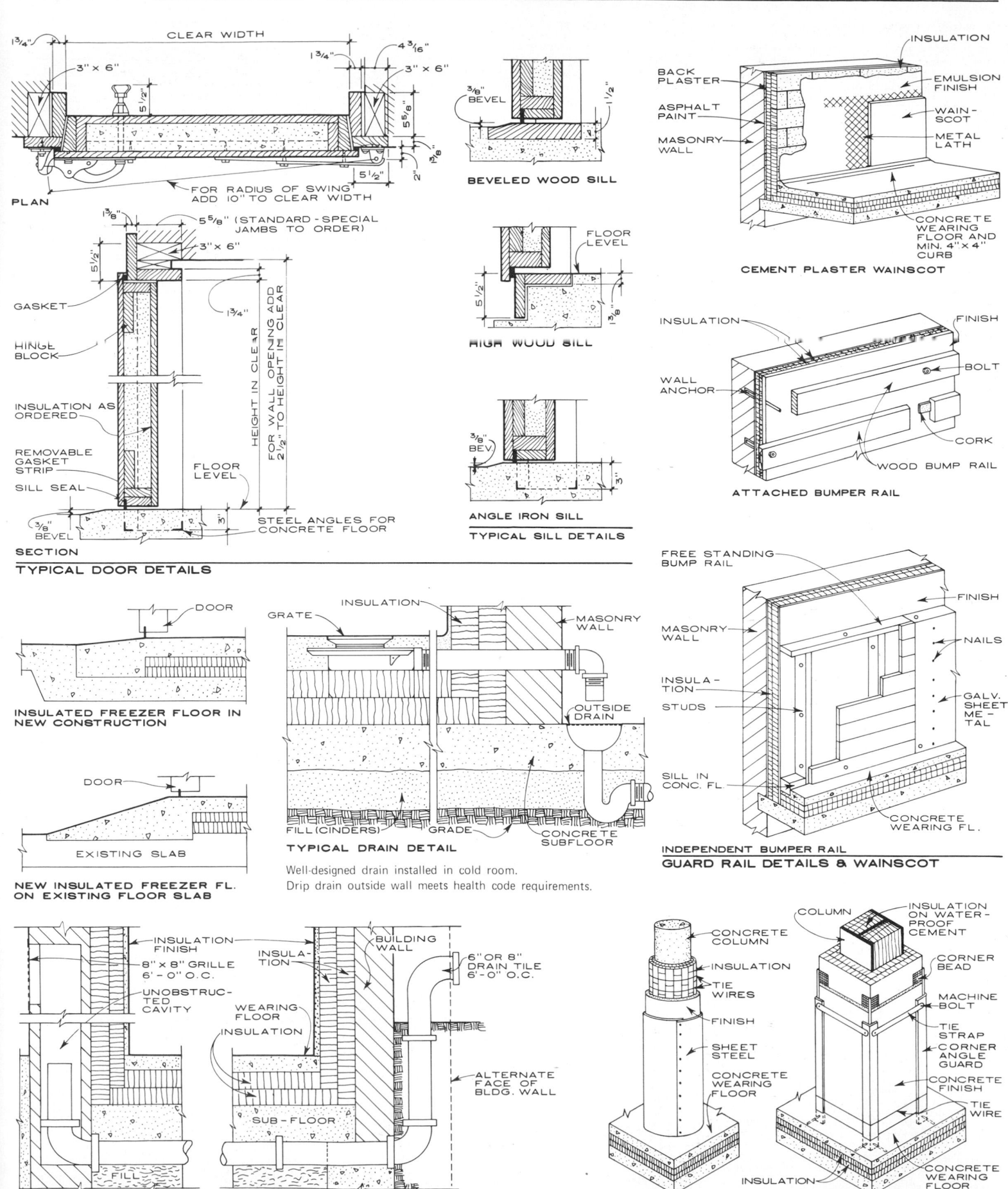

PLAN

CLEAR WIDTH

3" × 6"

5 1/2"

FOR RADIUS OF SWING
ADD 10" TO CLEAR WIDTH

BEVELED WOOD SILL

HIGH WOOD SILL

ANGLE IRON SILL

TYPICAL SILL DETAILS

SECTION

TYPICAL DOOR DETAILS

GASKET

HINGE BLOCK

INSULATION AS ORDERED

REMOVABLE GASKET STRIP

SILL SEAL

3/8" BEVEL

5 5/8" (STANDARD - SPECIAL JAMBS TO ORDER)

3" × 6"

HEIGHT IN CLEAR
FOR WALL OPENING ADD 2 1/2" TO HEIGHT IN CLEAR

FLOOR LEVEL

STEEL ANGLES FOR CONCRETE FLOOR

CEMENT PLASTER WAINSCOT

BACK PLASTER

ASPHALT PAINT

MASONRY WALL

INSULATION

EMULSION FINISH

WAIN-SCOT

METAL LATH

CONCRETE WEARING FLOOR AND MIN. 4" × 4" CURB

ATTACHED BUMPER RAIL

INSULATION

WALL ANCHOR

FINISH

BOLT

CORK

WOOD BUMP RAIL

INSULATED FREEZER FLOOR IN NEW CONSTRUCTION

DOOR

NEW INSULATED FREEZER FL. ON EXISTING FLOOR SLAB

DOOR

EXISTING SLAB

TYPICAL DRAIN DETAIL

Well-designed drain installed in cold room.
Drip drain outside wall meets health code requirements.

INSULATION

GRATE

MASONRY WALL

OUTSIDE DRAIN

FILL (CINDERS)

GRADE

CONCRETE SUBFLOOR

INDEPENDENT BUMPER RAIL

GUARD RAIL DETAILS & WAINSCOT

FREE STANDING BUMP RAIL

MASONRY WALL

INSULA-TION

STUDS

SILL IN CONC. FL.

FINISH

NAILS

GALV. SHEET ME-TAL

CONCRETE WEARING FL.

DETAIL OF SUBFLOOR VENT

INTERIOR WALL

EXTERIOR WALL

INSULATION FINISH

8" × 8" GRILLE 6'-0" O.C.

UNOBSTRUC-TED CAVITY

INSULA-TION

BUILDING WALL

WEARING FLOOR

INSULATION

SUB-FLOOR

FILL

6" OR 8" DRAIN TILE 6'-0" O.C.

ALTERNATE FACE OF BLDG. WALL

TYPICAL COLUMN GUARD DETAILS

CONCRETE COLUMN

INSULATION

TIE WIRES

FINISH

SHEET STEEL

CONCRETE WEARING FLOOR

COLUMN

INSULATION ON WATER-PROOF CEMENT

CORNER BEAD

MACHINE BOLT

TIE STRAP

CORNER ANGLE GUARD

CONCRETE FINISH

TIE WIRE

INSULATION

CONCRETE WEARING FLOOR

Elwood Taylor; The Ballinger Company; Philadelphia, Pennsylvania

ASEISMIC DESIGN CONCEPT

Earthquake forces result from very erratic vertical and horizontal vibratory motion of the ground on which the structure rests. For the most part, the vertical forces are neglected by the codes owing to the combination of safety factors inherent in the vertical framing members. The horizontal forces may vary in direction, intensity and duration and are affected materially by geological conditions.

Seismic forces are assumed to act as static horizontal loads on a structure as a function of the mass multiplied by certain factors for different types of resisting elements. Resisting elements may be moment resisting frames or shear walls or a combination of both.

The configuration of a structure and its fundamental period affects its earthquake resistance considerably. Symmetry in plan is very desirable. Unusual shaped plans result in highstress concentration areas and must be specifically designed for. Structural elements must be tied together to make them respond to earthquake motion as a unit; or structural separations may be required.

Most building materials are adaptable to use as resisting elements. Brittle materials must be avoided, unless properly reinforced. Ductile materials are most desirable. Up-to-date codes require that all buildings over 160 feet high must have "ductile" moment resisting frames.

Earthquake resistant structures can be designed, however, to result in minimum structural damage and maximum safety within economic limits. Aseismic knowledge and design is being steadily improved, and there is no substitute for sound structural engineering experience and judgment.

The data set forth herewith is a very brief resume of "Recommended Lateral Force Requirements and Commentary" prepared by the Seismology Committee of the Structural Engineers Association of California, 1967. These requirements have been adopted by several codes.

DEFINITIONS

SPACE FRAME is a three dimensional structural system composed of interconnected members, other than bearing walls, laterally supported so as to function as a complete self-contained unit with or without the aid of horizontal diaphragms or floor bracing systems.

SPACE FRAME — VERTICAL LOAD-CARRYING: a space frame designed to carry all vertical loads.

SPACE FRAME — MOMENT RESISTING: a vertical load-carrying space frame in which the members and joints are capable of resisting design lateral forces by bending moments.

SPACE FRAME — DUCTILE MOMENT RESISTING: A space frame-moment resisting complying with special requirements for a ductile moment resisting space frame.

BOX SYSTEM is a structural system without a complete vertical load-carrying space frame. In this system, the required lateral forces are resisted by shear walls as hereinafter defined.

SHEAR WALL is a wall designed to resist lateral forces parallel to the wall. Braced frames subjected primarily to axial stresses shall be considered as shear walls for the purpose of this definition.

LATERAL FORCE RESISTING SYSTEM is that part of the structural system to which the lateral forces are assigned.

TOTAL LATERAL FORCE OR BASE SHEAR FORMULA

$$V = ZKCW$$

V = Total lateral force or shear at the base.

Z = Numerical coefficient dependent upon the zone as determined by the seismic zone map.

K = Numerical coefficient set forth in Table A.

C = Numerical coefficient dependent upon the fundamental period of vibration of the structure determined by properly substantiated technical data or by arbitrary code formula.

W = Total dead load. (Plus 25 percent of storage and warehouse live loads.)

TABLE A

HORIZONTAL FORCE FACTOR "K" FOR BUILDINGS OR OTHER STRUCTURES

TYPE OR ARRANGEMENT OF RESISTING ELEMENTS	K
All building framing systems except as hereinafter classified.	1.00
Buildings with a box system as defined	1.33
Buildings with a dual bracing system consisting of a ductile moment resisting space frame and shear walls designed with the following criteria: 1. The frames and shear walls shall resist the total lateral force in accordance with their relative rigidities considering the inraction of the shear walls and frames. 2. The shear walls acting independently of the ductile moment resisting space frame shall resist the total required lateral force. 3. The ductile moment resisting space frame shall have the capacity to resist not less than 25 percent of the required lateral force.	0.80
Buildings with a ductile moment resisting space frame designed in accordance with the following criteria: The ductile moment resisting space frame shall have the capacity to resist the total required lateral force.	0.67
Elevated tanks plus full contents, on four or more cross braced legs and not supported by a building.	3.00
Structures other than buildings.	2.00

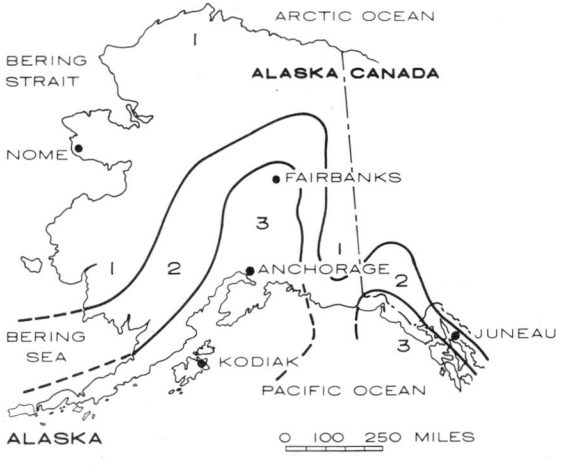

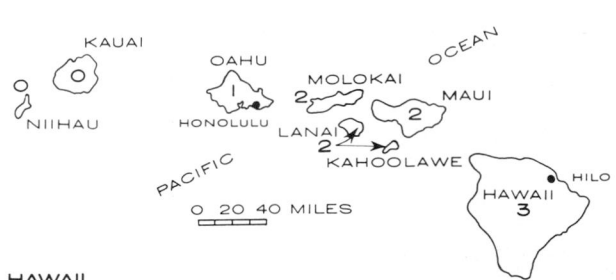

SEISMIC PROBABILITY

ZONE	DAMAGE	"Z"
0	None	0
1	Minor	0.25
2	Moderate	0.50
3	Major	1.00

SEISMIC ZONE MAPS OF THE UNITED STATES

Harold P. King, CEC; King, Benioff, Steinmann, King; Sherman Oaks, California

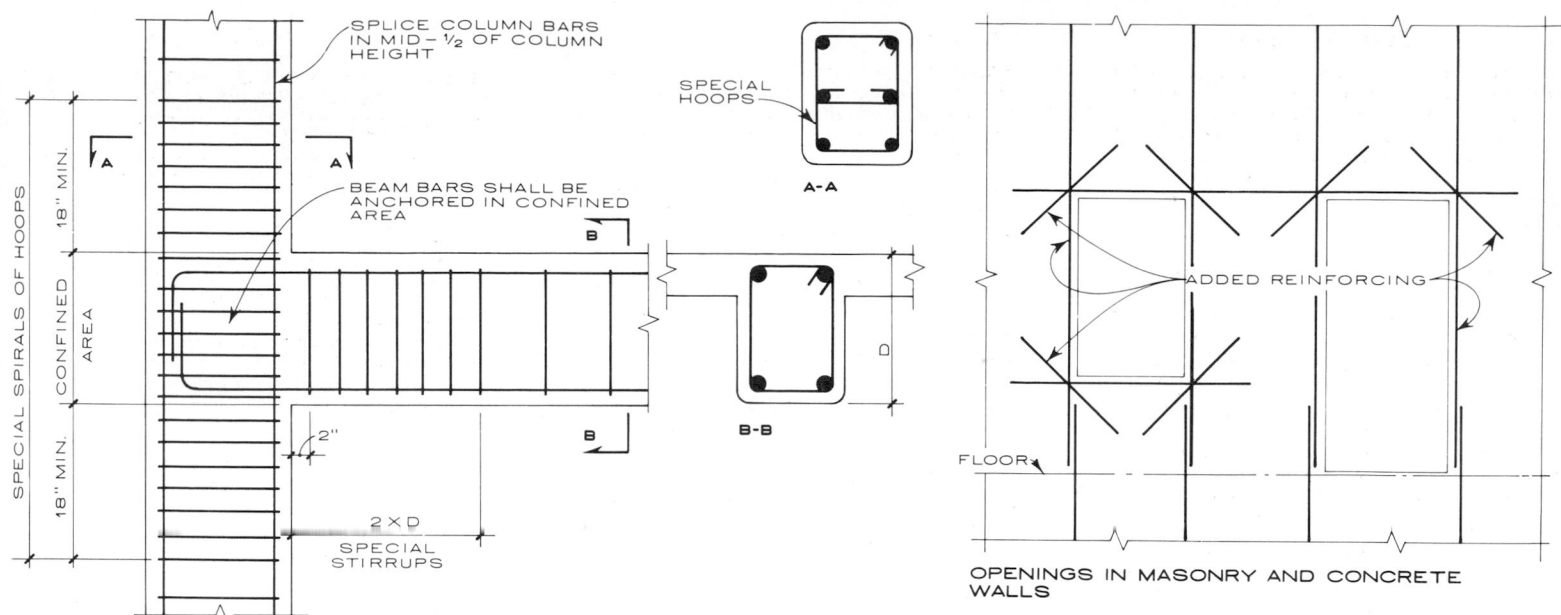

REINFORCING DETAIL FOR DUCTILE MOMENT RESISTING SPACE FRAME

Labels: SPLICE COLUMN BARS IN MID – ½ OF COLUMN HEIGHT; SPECIAL HOOPS; A-A; BEAM BARS SHALL BE ANCHORED IN CONFINED AREA; B-B; SPECIAL SPIRALS OF HOOPS; 18" MIN.; CONFINED AREA; 18" MIN.; 2"; 2 × D SPECIAL STIRRUPS; D

OPENINGS IN MASONRY AND CONCRETE WALLS

Labels: ADDED REINFORCING; FLOOR

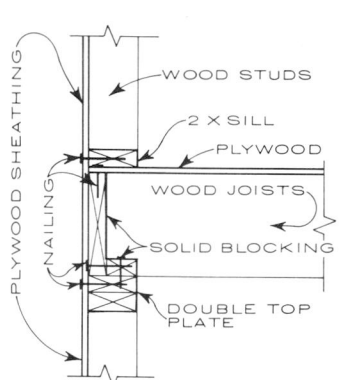

WOOD DIAPHRAGM WITH PLYWOOD SHEAR WALLS

Labels: WOOD STUDS; 2 × SILL; PLYWOOD; WOOD JOISTS; SOLID BLOCKING; DOUBLE TOP PLATE; PLYWOOD SHEATHING; NAILING

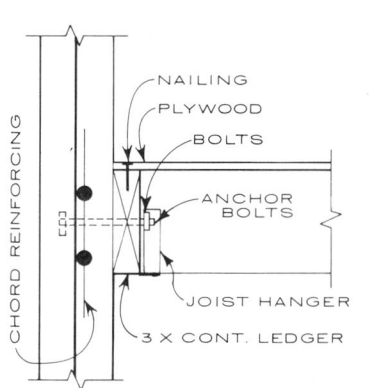

WOOD DIAPHRAGM WITH MASONRY OR CONCRETE SHEAR WALLS

Labels: NAILING; PLYWOOD; BOLTS; ANCHOR BOLTS; JOIST HANGER; 3 × CONT. LEDGER; CHORD REINFORCING

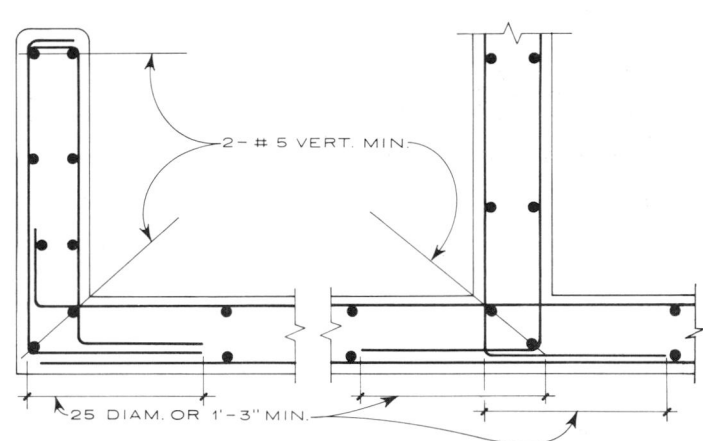

INTERSECTION OF CONCRETE OR REINFORCED MASONRY WALLS

Labels: 2 – #5 VERT. MIN.; 25 DIAM. OR 1'-3" MIN.

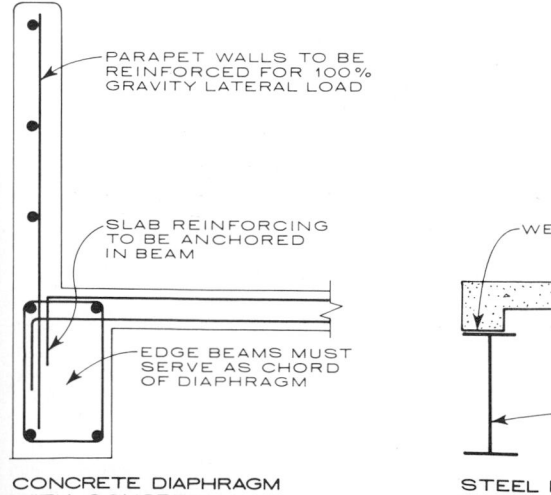

CONCRETE DIAPHRAGM WITH CONCRETE FRAME

Labels: PARAPET WALLS TO BE REINFORCED FOR 100% GRAVITY LATERAL LOAD; SLAB REINFORCING TO BE ANCHORED IN BEAM; EDGE BEAMS MUST SERVE AS CHORD OF DIAPHRAGM

STEEL DECK DIAPHRAGM WITH STEEL FRAME

Labels: WELD; CONC. FILL; STEEL DECK; STEEL BEAM

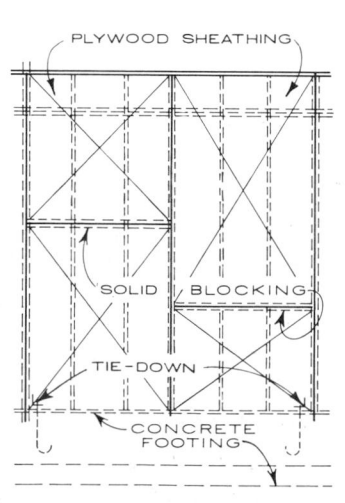

PLYWOOD SHEATHED SHEAR WALL WITH TIE-DOWNS

Labels: PLYWOOD SHEATHING; SOLID BLOCKING; TIE-DOWN; CONCRETE FOOTING

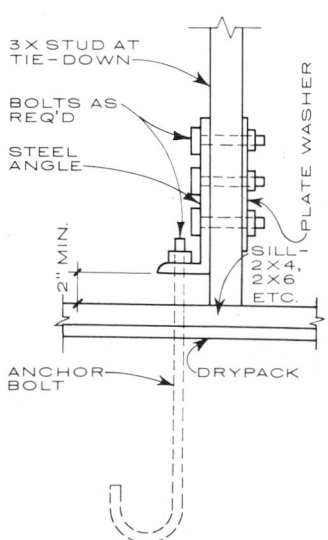

TIE DOWN

Labels: 3 × STUD AT TIE-DOWN; BOLTS AS REQ'D; STEEL ANGLE; PLATE WASHER; SILL– 2×4, 2×6 ETC.; 2" MIN.; ANCHOR BOLT; DRYPACK

Harold P. King, CEC; King, Benioff, Steinmann, King; Sherman Oaks, California

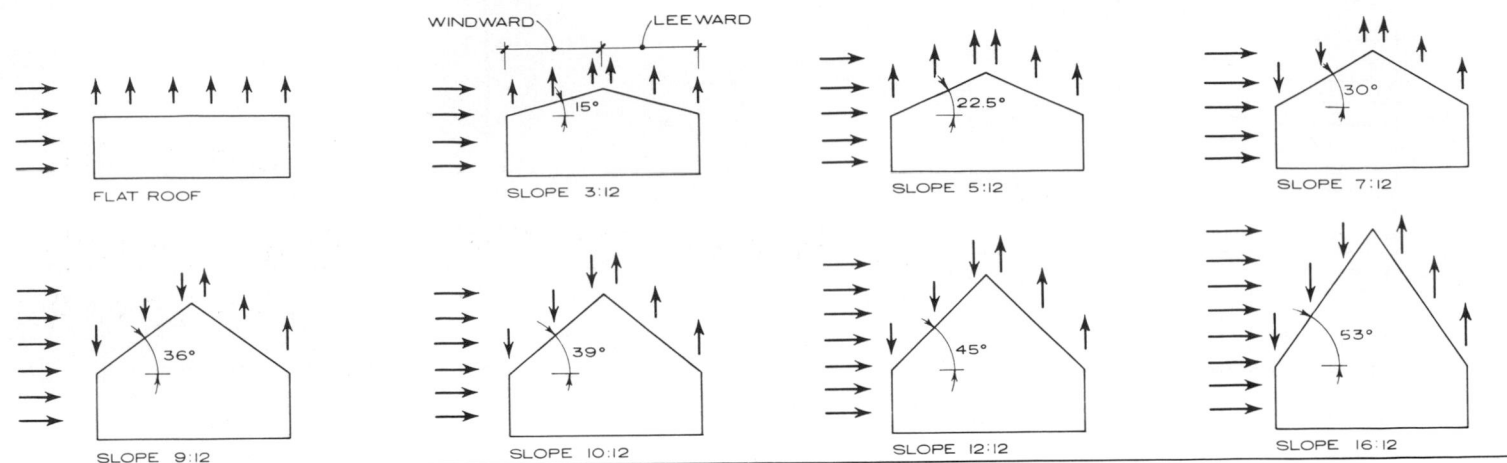

WINDWARD — LEEWARD

FLAT ROOF

SLOPE 3:12 — 15°

SLOPE 5:12 — 22.5°

SLOPE 7:12 — 30°

SLOPE 9:12 — 36°

SLOPE 10:12 — 39°

SLOPE 12:12 — 45°

SLOPE 16:12 — 53°

WIND PRESSURE DISTRIBUTION ON PITCHED, OR GABLE, ROOFS OF VARYING SLOPES

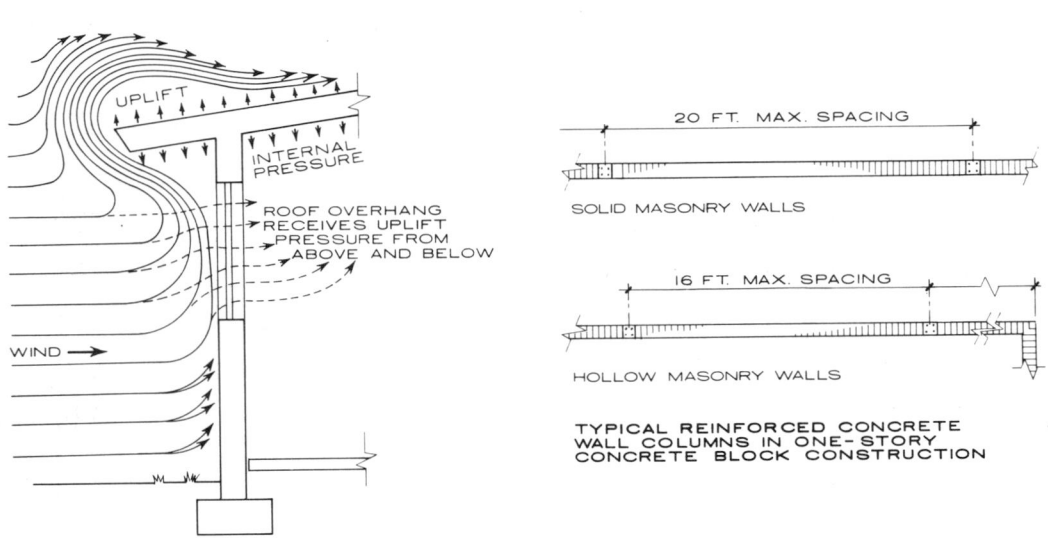

UPLIFT

INTERNAL PRESSURE

ROOF OVERHANG RECEIVES UPLIFT PRESSURE FROM ABOVE AND BELOW

WIND →

WIND PRESSURE DIAGRAM

20 FT. MAX. SPACING

SOLID MASONRY WALLS

16 FT. MAX. SPACING

HOLLOW MASONRY WALLS

TYPICAL REINFORCED CONCRETE WALL COLUMNS IN ONE-STORY CONCRETE BLOCK CONSTRUCTION

TIE-DOWN ANCHORS
8"
12"
4-#5 RODS CONC. TIE BEAM
CONC. BLOCK
4-#5 RODS WITH #2 TIES AT 12" O.C.
8" 12"

ISOMETRIC OF TYP. WALL COLUMN WITH CONTINUOUS TOP TIE BEAM

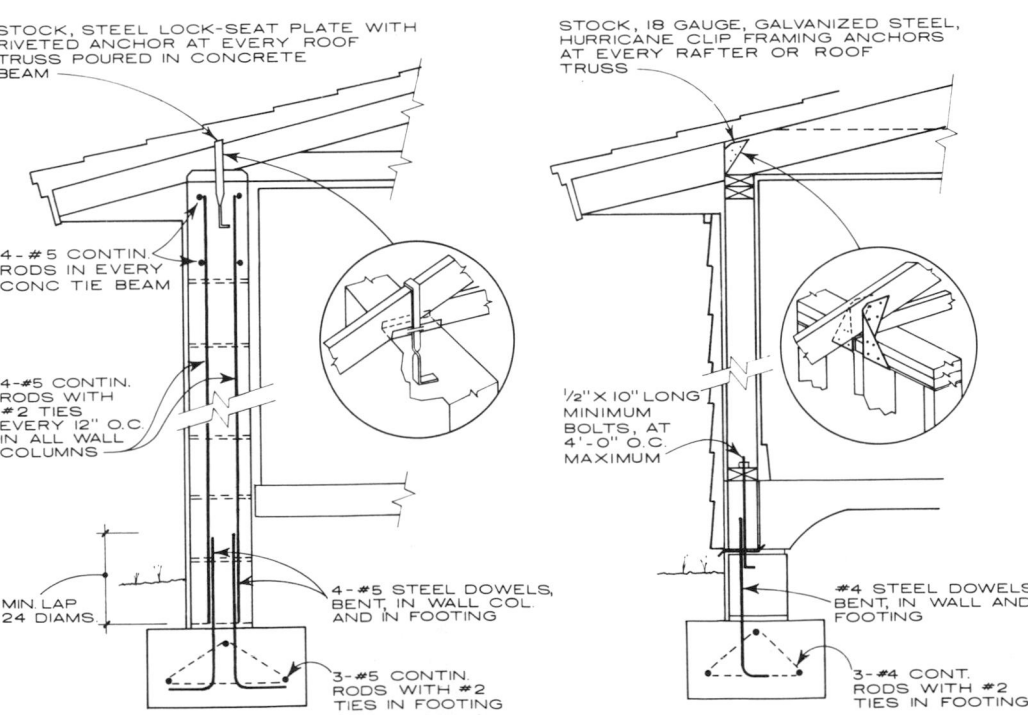

STOCK, STEEL LOCK-SEAT PLATE WITH RIVETED ANCHOR AT EVERY ROOF TRUSS POURED IN CONCRETE BEAM

4-#5 CONTIN. RODS IN EVERY CONC TIE BEAM

4-#5 CONTIN. RODS WITH #2 TIES EVERY 12" O.C. IN ALL WALL COLUMNS

MIN. LAP 24 DIAMS.

4-#5 STEEL DOWELS, BENT, IN WALL COL. AND IN FOOTING

3-#5 CONTIN. RODS WITH #2 TIES IN FOOTING

ONE-STORY CONCRETE BLOCK WALL SECTION
SCALE: ½"=1'-0"

STOCK, 18 GAUGE, GALVANIZED STEEL, HURRICANE CLIP FRAMING ANCHORS AT EVERY RAFTER OR ROOF TRUSS

½" X 10" LONG MINIMUM BOLTS, AT 4'-0" O.C. MAXIMUM

#4 STEEL DOWELS, BENT, IN WALL AND FOOTING

3-#4 CONT. RODS WITH #2 TIES IN FOOTING

ONE-STORY WOOD FRAME WALL SECTION
SCALE: ½"=1'-0"

John Stetson; Stetson—Spina Associates; Palm Beach, Florida

MINIMUM DESIGN WIND LOAD FACTORS FOR VARIOUS HEIGHT ZONES ON VERTICAL PROJECTIONS OF BUILDINGS

Southern Std. Bldg. Code			Uniform Code	
Height Zone	Horizontal Loads		Height Zone	Horizontal Loads
Feet	lbs. per sq.ft.		Feet	lbs/sq.ft.
	inland region	coastal region		
0—30	10	25	0—60	15
31—50	20	35	60 up	20
51—99	24	45		
100—199	28	50	Coastal region is
200—299	30	50	that area lying
300—399	32	50	within 125 miles
over 400	40	50	of the coast.

MINIMUM REQUIRED WIND LOADS ON PITCHED, OR GABLE, ROOFS OF BUILDINGS

1. For roof slopes less than 30° designed to withstand loads acting outward normal to the surface equal to 1 ¼ times the horizontal loads specified for the corresponding height zone in which the roof is located.

2. For roof slopes greater than 30° designed to withstand loads acting inward normal to the surface equal to those specified for zone, load applied to windward slope.

ELEVATORS AND CONVEYING SYSTEMS

ELEVATOR is a hoisting or lowering mechanism which moves in guides in a vertical position.

CONTROL PANEL registers calls and governs response of elevator(s) to them.

MOTOR—GENERATOR supplies direct current to motor. Used with generator-field control.

GENERATOR—FIELD CONTROL uses an individual generator for each elevator, so that the voltage applied to the hoisting motor is adjusted by varying the strength of the generator-field. Allows wide range of speeds, including high speeds, and permits smooth acceleration and retardation of car.

MACHINE BEAMS are structural supports for elevator machines.

GUIDE RAILS, with guide shoes, serve to guide car in vertical direction and prevents sideways or twisting motion.

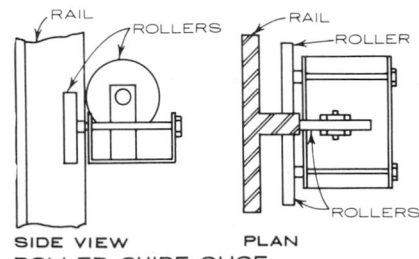

SIDE VIEW   PLAN
ROLLER GUIDE SHOE

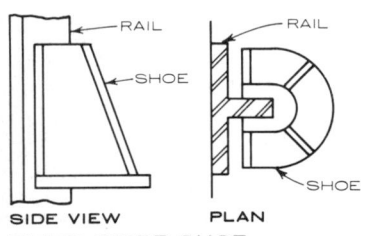

SIDE VIEW   PLAN
FIXED GUIDE SHOE

GUIDE SHOES are fastened to car frame and counterweight at top and bottom. They fit guide rails.

TRAVEL is the vertical distance between the bottom and top terminal landings.

COMPENSATION: ropes or chains hung from bottom of car to bottom of counterweight, to balance the weight of the hoist ropes.

PIT is that portion of a hoistway extending below the level of the bottom landing to provide for over-travel and clearance and for parts which require space below the bottom limit of car travel.

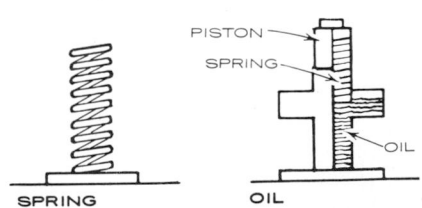

SPRING   OIL
BUFFER is a device to absorb impact of car or counterweight at the lower limits of travel

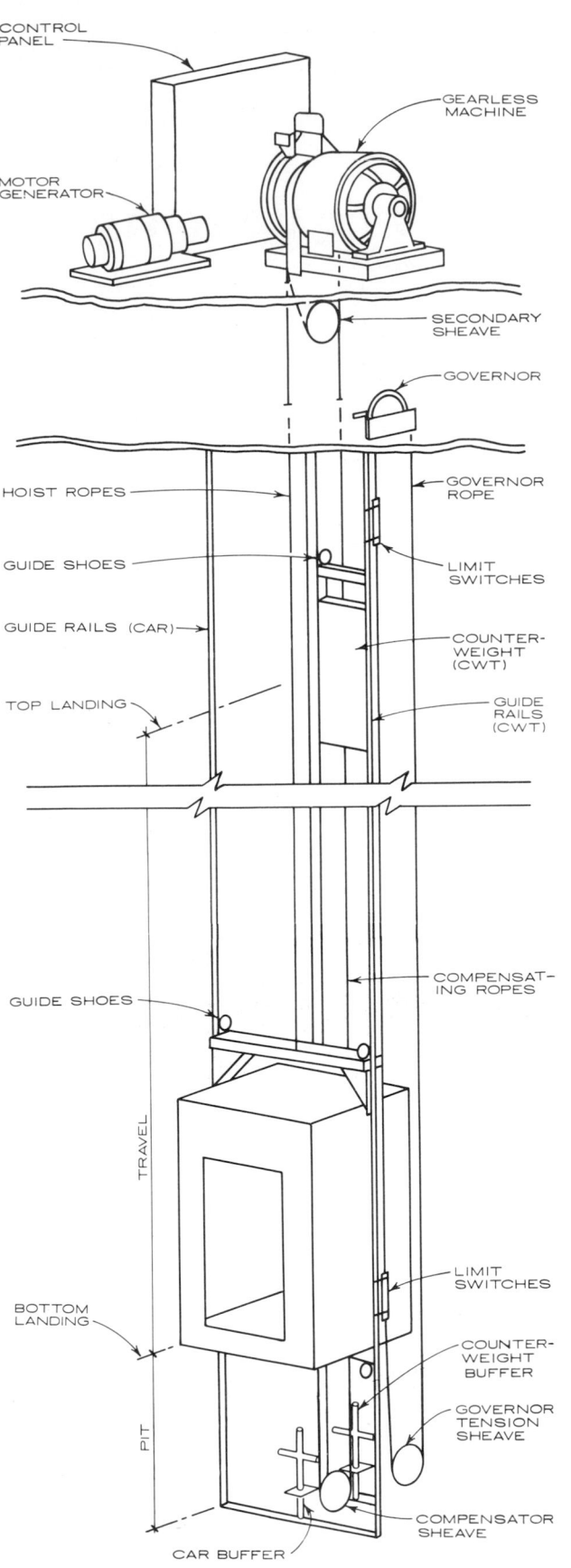

COMPONENTS OF A TYPICAL ELECTRIC ELEVATOR

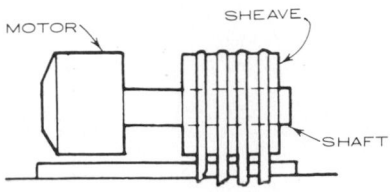

GEARLESS MACHINE is one in which power is transmitted directly to the driving sheave without intermidiate gears or mechanism.

SECONDARY SHEAVE provides double wrap of ropes for traction and leads ropes over to counterweight.

GOVERNOR stops car and (if required) counterweight in case of emergency by actuating the safety.

SAFETY is a device incorporated in the bottom beam of the car frame and counterweight. Exerts retarding force in case of overspeed, by gripping guide rails.

LIMIT SWITCHES are automatic devices which stop the car within the overtravel, independently of the operating device.

OPERATING DEVICE: the car switch, push button. wheel, level, etc. which enables the operator to actuate the control.

HOIST ROPES are steel wire ropes used for suspension of car and counterweight.

TENSION SHEAVE gives stability in governor's ropes.

CAR is the load-carrying unit, including its platform, frame and enclosure.

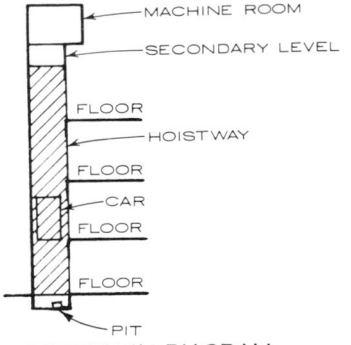

HOISTWAY, DIAGRAM

HOISTWAY is any vertical opening or space in which an elevator or dumbwaiter is designed to operate.

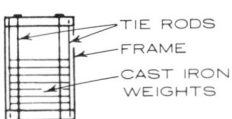

COUNTERWEIGHT balances the weight of the car, and usually equals weight of car plus 40% of car capacity.

CAR—LEVELLING DEVICE is any mechanism or control which will move the car to within a limited zone, and stop it at the landing.

LANDING ZONE is 18 inches above or below a landing.

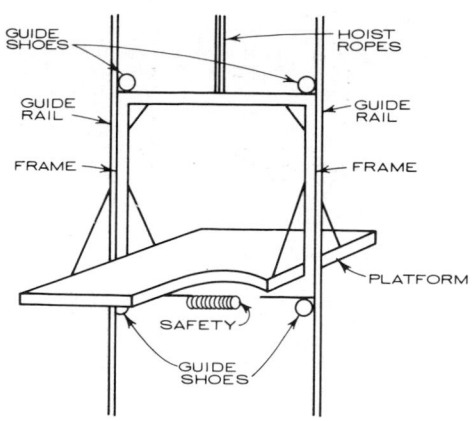

TYPICAL FRAME & PLATFORM

CAR FRAME is the supporting frame to which the platform, upper and lower set of guide shoes and the hoisting cables are usually attached.

CAR PLATFORM is the structure which supports the floor of the car and directly supports the load.

RATED SPEED is that speed at which the elevator is designed to operate with rated load in the car.

RATED LOAD is that load which the elevator is designed to carry dependent on platform area.

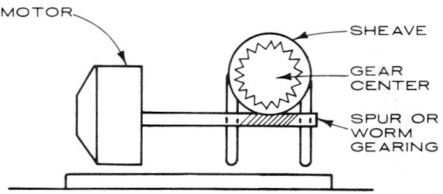

GEARED MACHINE is one in which power is transmitted to the driving sheave or drum through worm or spur gearing. It uses rheostatic as well as generator-field control.

RHEOSTATIC CONTROL is a direct current system of control by varying resistance and reactance in the field circuit of the hoisting motor. Alternating current motors start across the line.

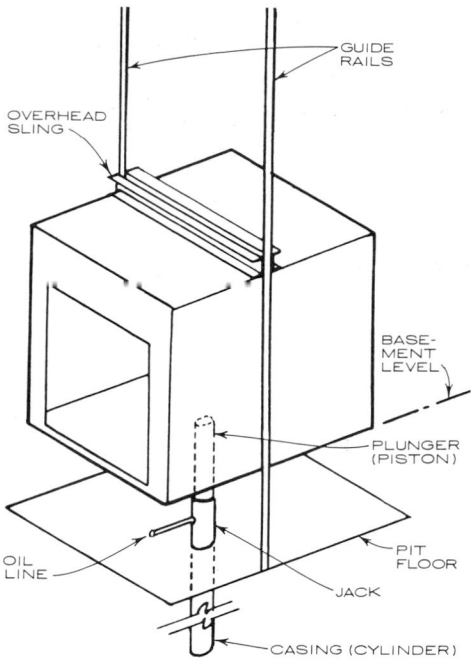

HYDRAULIC ELEVATOR is one in which the motion of the car is obtained from a liquid (usually oil) under pressure. The plunger must extend below basement level a minimum distance equal to travel. Used where travel is short, required speed is low, and where overhead machine room is not desired.

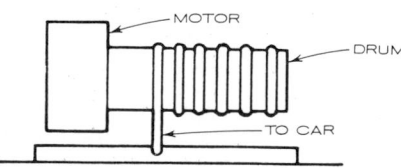

WINDING DRUM MACHINE is one in which the ropes are fastened to and wound on a drum. No counterweight is required, but it is not permitted on passenger elevators.

TRACTION MACHINE is one in which the motion of the car is obtained by means of friction between the traction sheave and the hoisting cables.

HALF-ROUND AND DOUBLE WRAP TRACTION SHEAVE provides least wear and least traction.

UNDERCUT "V" TRACTION SHEAVE produces the highest wear and the best traction.

UNDERCUT HALF-ROUND TRACTION SHEAVE provides high wear and high traction.

PASSENGER ELEVATORS: PRELIMINARY SELECTION.

The data given on this, and the following pages, is to assist in the selection of passenger elevators for office buildings, industrial buildings, hotels, department stores, apartment houses, and hospitals. The results of the calculations will give general information on the economical number, characteristics, and groupings (local or express) of elevator installations. The cost of various installations must also be considered. A competent elevator engineer should be consulted before any decision is made.

The selection of elevators will depend on factual information concerning the particular building, and certain other determinations, as follows:

A. Factual information
   1. building characteristics
      a. number of floors
      b. floor-to-floor heights
      c. travel
      d. location
   2. population characteristics (the temp of the traffic)
B. Determinations
   1. average round-trip time
   2. interval
   3. passenger-carrying capacity of the system.

The total round-trip time depends on the various times involved in the operation of an elevator, such as running time, number of stops, time required in passenger loading and unloading, and so on. Calculations of the times governing round-trip time are expressed in the Round-Trip Time graphs given on a following page.

The interval is the average time a passenger must wait for an elevator. Minimum intervals are given below. The desirable interval depends on the type and location of the building. In large buildings, the maximum interval is 30 seconds. For small buildings, 40 seconds is usually satisfactory. Intervals longer than 40 seconds are permissible only in hospitals, apartment houses, or buildings where one or two elevators will provide more than adequate passenger-carrying capacity.

The passenger-carrying capacity of an elevator is expressed as the percentage of the building population than can be carried one way in a period of time, usually five minutes. Exception: the passenger-carrying capacity of department store elevators is generally expressed as the number of people that can be carried in one hour. Elevator capacities are given in the tables below.

CONT. ON NEXT PAGE

PRELIMINARY SELECTION (CONT.)
SAMPLE PROBLEM

Given: type of building: office
 number of floors: 20 (above ground floor)
 floor-to-floor height: 12 feet
 total population: 2000 (see Speed and Travel Table, a following page)
 maximum interval: 30 seconds

SOLUTION

1. Find the total travel (equal to the number of floors above ground floor times the floor-to-floor height) = 20 x 12 = 240 feet.

2. Find the required passenger-carrying capacity. This equals the maximum number of people expected to arrive or depart in any five minute period. Where this figure is not known, the following assumptions may be made:

TRAFFIC	PERCENT OF POPULATION
light	12
average	13
heavy	14 for first 30 floors, 12 in any tower section. (Requirements for a single occupancy building may vary.)

Assume light traffic. Use 13% of 2000 population, or, 260 people.

3. Use Speed and Travel Table to select an elevator capacity. The table for Office Buildings indicates that the minimum speed for a travel of 240 feet is 700 feet per minute. This speed is available with any capacity from 2500 to 4000 pounds. Select the 3000 capacity for trial.

4. Using the selected capacity and the number of floors (above ground floor), find from the Round-Trip Time graphs the round-trip time in seconds. Graph "C", for a 3000-pound capacity, indicates that the round-trip time for a 700 feet per minute elevator, for 20 floors, is 148 seconds.

5. Find the number of passengers per trip, normal peak, from Elevator Capacities Table below. For 3000-pound capacity, the normal peak is 16 passengers per trip.

6. Find the number of passengers one car can carry in five minutes by using the following formula:

passenger cap. per car, 5 min. $= \dfrac{60 \times 5 \times \text{number passengers per trip}}{\text{round-trip time (seconds)}}$

$$= \dfrac{60 \times 5 \times 16}{148}$$

= 32.5 people for 5 min.

7. Find the number of cars required in the bank elevators (divide the required passenger-carrying capacity by the number of passengers one car can carry in 5 minutes) $\dfrac{260}{32.5} = 8$ cars

8. Check the result by finding the interval. The determined interval should be equal to or more than the minimum given in the Minimum Interval Table below, and should not exceed the given maximum interval:

interval $= \dfrac{\text{round-trip time}}{\text{number of cars in bank}}$

$= \dfrac{148}{8}$

= 18.5 seconds

The minimum interval for a 3000 pound capacity elevator is 18 seconds; the given maximum interval was 30 seconds. Therefore eight 3000-pound, 700 feet per minute elevators is one acceptable solution.

9. Another trial may be made with a larger selected capacity to determine if fewer cars can be used. Using a 4000 pound capacity, the solution would be seven 4000-pound, 700-feet per minute elevators.

It may be determined if the use of local and express cars would result in a better solution by figuring separately the required number of elevators for the local floors and the express floors.

In all cases, the cost of the various types of installations will affect a final decision.

10. When population of the building is unknown, a different approach must be used. From "Office Buildings, etc." on the Speed and Travel Table page, find the appropriate square foot area per person. For example, use 90 sq. ft. per person.

11. The area on which calculations are based is the net usable area. This is roughly 75% of the total floor area and does not include such items as partitions, mechanical equipment rooms, etc. Assume total floor area is 240,000 sq. ft. Then net usable area = 0.75 x 240,000 = 180,000 sq. ft.

12. With 90 sq. ft. per person and a net usable area of 180,000 sq. ft., the population density may be estimated at 2000 persons.

13. Refer to the Capacity and Interval Table below. Assume 14% of the population must be handled in five minutes. Read down under 14% to the figure 2000. To find required car size, read left to car capacity, in this case, 4000 lbs.

14. With this information, return to step 4 to complete the preliminary selection.

ELEVATOR CAPACITIES

WEIGHT CAP POUNDS	PASSENGER CAPACITY	PASSENGERS PER TRIP NORMAL PEAK
1200	7	6
2000	14	10
2500	16	13
3000	19	16
3500	22	18
4000	26	21

MAX. CAPACITY, ONE BANK OF ELEVATORS

CAR CAP.	AVER. PASS./ TRIP	MIN. INT.	PERCENTAGE OF TOTAL POP. HANDLED IN 5 MINUTES					
			12.5	13	13.5	14	14.5	15
2000	10	12	2000	1920	1850	1785	1725	1670
2500	13	15	2080	2000	1935	1855	1800	1735
3000	16	18	2130	2050	1965	1900	1830	1775
3500	18	20	2160	2080	2000	1930	1865	1800
4000	21	23	2220	2140	2065	2000	1940	1885
5000	26	28	2260	2180	2090	2020	1950	1895

NOTES

1. Passenger capacity is generally found by dividing the rated capacity of the elevator by 150.

2. Passengers per trip, average, is assumed to be 80 percent of the elevator passenger capacity.

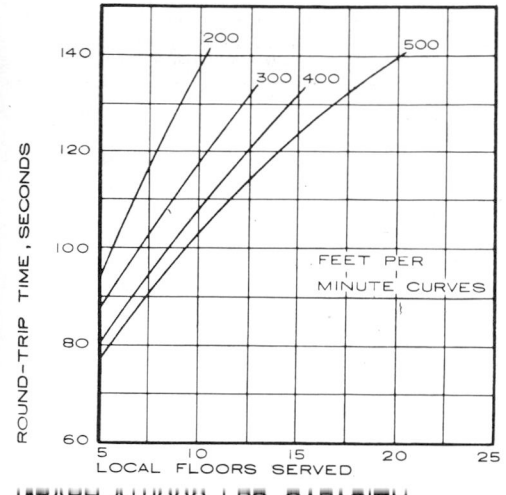

GRAPH A: 2000 LBS. CAPACITY
TYPE "A" CONTROL

GRAPH B: 2500 LBS. CAPACITY
TYPE "A" CONTROL

GRAPH C: 3000 LBS. CAPACITY
TYPE "A" CONTROL

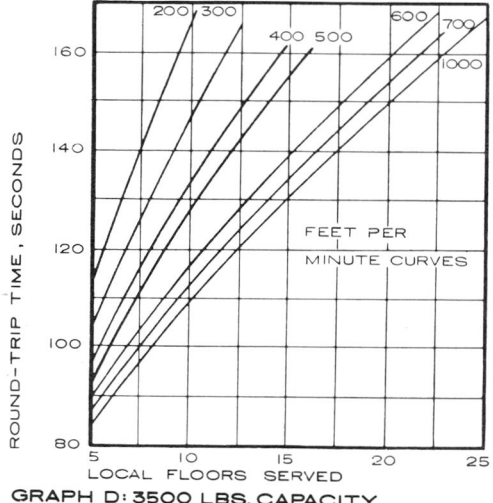

GRAPH D: 3500 LBS. CAPACITY
TYPE "A" CONTROL

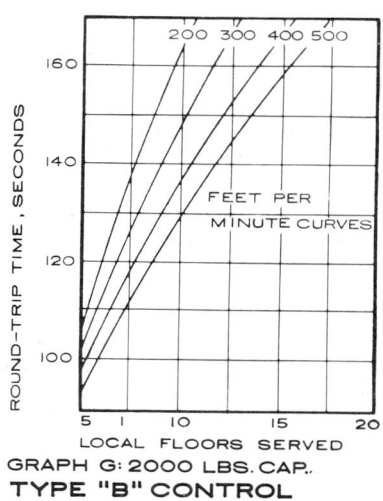

GRAPH G: 2000 LBS. CAP.
TYPE "B" CONTROL

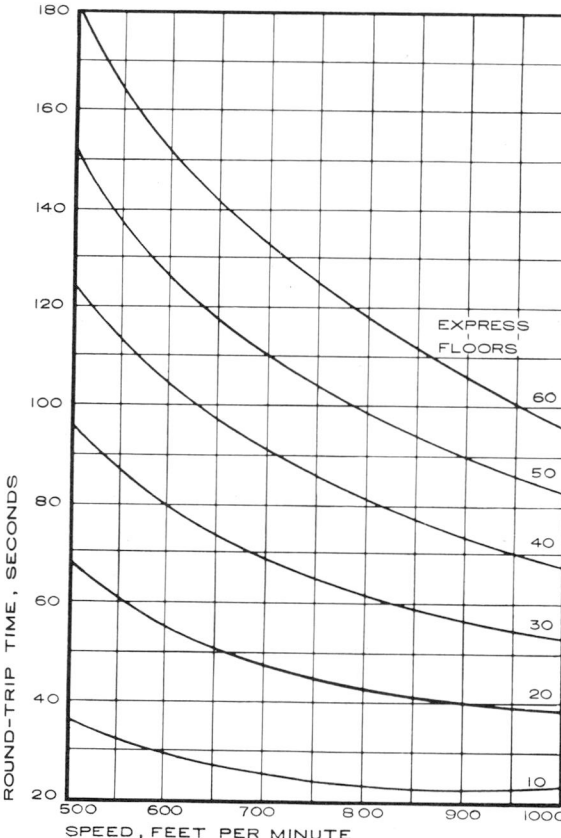

GRAPH F: ALL CAPACITIES
TYPE "A" OR "B" CONTROL

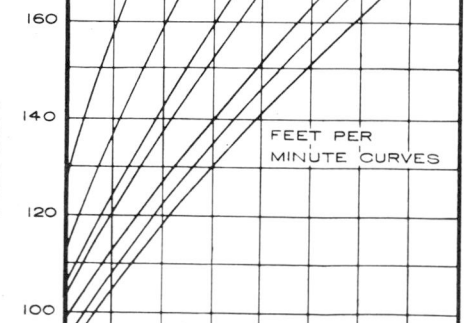

GRAPH E: 4000 LBS. CAPACITY
TYPE "A" CONTROL

NOTES

1. Round-Trip time graphs shown are based on an assumed floor to floor height of 12 feet.

2. Basically, Type "A" and "B" control systems are alike, differing in the use for which they are intended. Type "A", which has a supervisory system with six traffic patterns, is intended for buildings with heavy traffic such as hotels, office buildings, etc.

3. Type "B" is essentially intended for buildings with light or moderate traffic such as apartment houses and small office buildings.

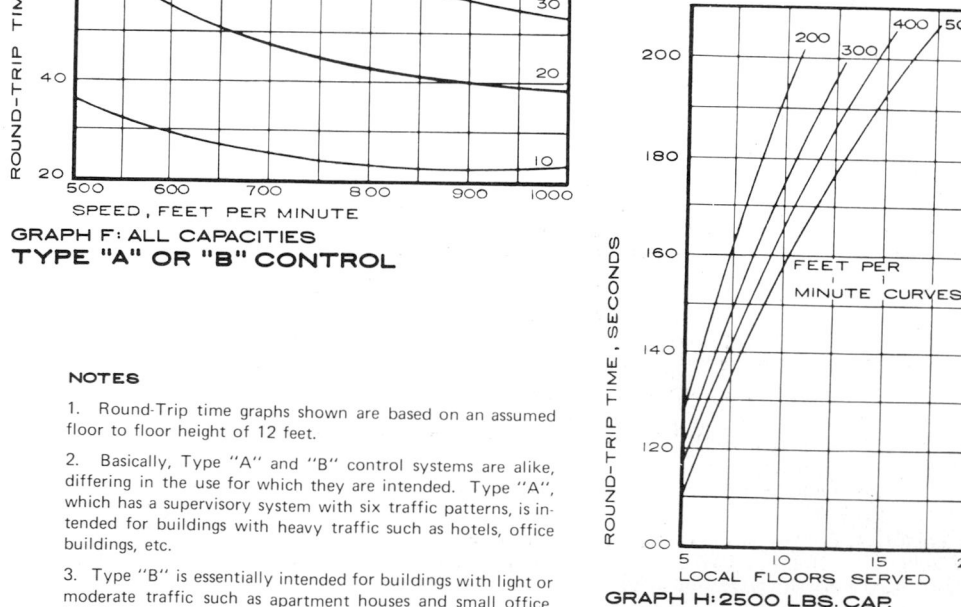

GRAPH H: 2500 LBS. CAP.
TYPE "B" CONTROL

SPEED AND TRAVEL TABLE

TYPE OF BUILDING

OFFICE BUILDINGS, HOTELS AND INDUSTRIAL BUILDINGS

Where expected population or density per floor is unknown, assume one person for each given square foot area, as follows:

SQUARE-FOOT AREA   GOVERNING CONDITIONS

80 (for one person) — for lower floors, single occupancy buildings

90 (for one person) — for lower floors, buildings in congested areas (heavy traffic)

100 (for one person) — for lower floors, buildings in business sections of average cities (average traffic)

110 (for one person) — for lower floors, buildings in business sections of small cities or outlying districts of larger cities (light traffic)

*10 (for one person) — for buildings of over 20 floors, or where upper floors have smaller areas.

*25 (for one person) — for buildings of over 30 floors, in any tower section.

*Add to base figure of Square Foot Area for lower floors.

CAPACITY POUNDS		SPEED FT./MIN.	TRAVEL FEET
		200	up to 100
2000[2]	All given speeds are available with any given capacity	250	up to 125[3]
2500		350	up to 150[3]
3000		500	up to 175
3500		700	up to 250
4000		800	up to 350
		1000	over 350

APARTMENT HOUSES

Elevator selection may be based on the number of bedrooms or on traffic studies.

The traffic depends on the class of tenant and location of the building in relation to the business center and schools. The heaviest traffic peak may be:

1. the morning downpeak (approximately 50 percent of the population must be handled in 1½ to 2 hours).

2. the after school peak (where the number of school children in the building is large).

3. the evening peak (to local amusements).

A passenger-carrying capacity (for five minutes) of 7 percent of the population is satisfactory due to the smaller and more extended peak in an apartment house. For low-cost housing, percent of population varies from 3.6 to 6.2.

CAPACITY POUNDS		SPEED FT./MIN.	TRAVEL FEET
		100	up to 70
		200	up to 100
1200	All given speeds are available with any given capacity	250	up to 125[3]
2000		350	up to 150[3]
2500		400	up to 175
		500	up to 250
		700	up to 350

HOSPITALS

In large hospitals a bank of passenger elevators may be installed separately from the service elevators. If so, select passenger elevators as for office buildings. For selection of elevators for combined passenger and vehicle use, see notes on the "Hospital Elevators" in "Building Planning and Design Standards" by H.R. Sleeper. Intervals should not be longer than one minute. An automatic control system is recommended. It should have an optional feature allowing attendant operation. At least one elevator should be on the emergency electric power system.

CAPACITY POUNDS		SPEED FT./MIN.	TRAVEL FEET
		100	up to 70
		200	up to 100
	All given speeds are available with any given capacity	250	up to 125[3]
3500		350	up to 150[3]
4000		400	up to 175
		500	up to 250
		700	up to 350

DEPARTMENT STORES

Each department store presents a traffic problem because of the use of electric stairways and the distribution of merchandise. Therefore, round-trip time must be separately calculated for each installation.

Electric stairways handle the majority of traffic. Only ten to twenty percent of the population should usually be considered in planning the elevator installation. For approximation figure one person per 25 square feet of merchandising area, above first floor.

CAPACITY POUNDS		SPEED FT./MIN.	TRAVEL FEET
		200	up to 100
	All given speeds are available with any given capacity	350	up to 125[3]
3000		400	up to 175
4000		500	up to 250
5000		700	up to 350

1. Speeds are recommended minimums for indicated travel.

2. The highest recommended speed for this capacity is 500 feet per minute.

3. Gearless elevators, with speeds beginning at 400 to 500 feet per minute, are recommended.

PASSENGER ELEVATORS, GEARLESS

CAPACITY = 2,000 TO 4,000 LBS.   SPEED = 400 TO 500 FEET PER MINUTE   ROPING = 2:1

CAPACITY POUNDS	SPEED FT./MIN.	DIMENSIONS					TRAVEL FEET	OVERHEAD LOAD IN LBS.							
		BG	UB	TB	MB	HB		D	E	F	G	I	O	DD	FF
2000	400 / 500	42"	11'-9"	9"	10"	10"	200 / 250	8800 / 9000	7900 / 8100	6100 / 6300	3800 / 3900	4800 / 5100	4100 / 4300	3200 / 3300	700 / 700
2500	500	42"	11'-9"	10"	12"	12"	250	10300	9000	7300	3800	5000	3800	3600	700
3000	500	42"	11'-0"	12"	12"	10"	200	7700	8600	5400	6100	5900	3400	5900	3400
3500	500	42"	11'-0"	12"	12"	12"	350	8500	10000	6300	7400	7500	4100	7500	4100
4000	500	42"	11'-0"	12"	12"	12"	220	8700	9800	6400	7100	7400	4100	7400	4100

CAPACITY POUNDS	SPEED FT./MIN.	DIMENSIONS														
		A	B	C	J	K	L	M	P	Q	R	S	T	U	W	Y
2000	400 / 500	6'-4"	4'-5"	3'-0"	15'-8"	5'-9½"	5'-10½"	14'-6"	7'-9" / 8'-9"	2'-4"	3¼"	2'-11"	8'-6"	24'-7" / 26'-1"	15'-7¾"	8"
2500	500	7'-0"	5'-0"	3'-6"	17'-0"	6'-4½"	6'-5½"	23'-0"	10'-3"	2'-5"	5⅛"	1'-9⅛"	8'-6"	26'-1"	21'-6"	8"
3000	500	7'-0"	5'-6"	3'-6"	17'-0"	6'-10½"	6'-11½"	23'-0"	10'-3"	2'-6"	6 5/16"	2'-4 15/16"	8'-6"	26'-1"	21'-6"	8"
3500	500	7'-0"	6'-2"	3'-6"	17'-0"	7'-6½"	7'-7½"	23'-0"	10'-3"	2'-6"	6 5/16"	2'-4 15/16"	8'-6"	26'-1"	22'-3"	8"
4000	500	7'-6"	6'-6"	3'-10"	18'-4"	7'-10½"	7'-11½"	23'-0"	10'-3"	2'-8"	6 5/16"	2'-4 15/16"	9'-0"	26'-1"	23'-0"	10"

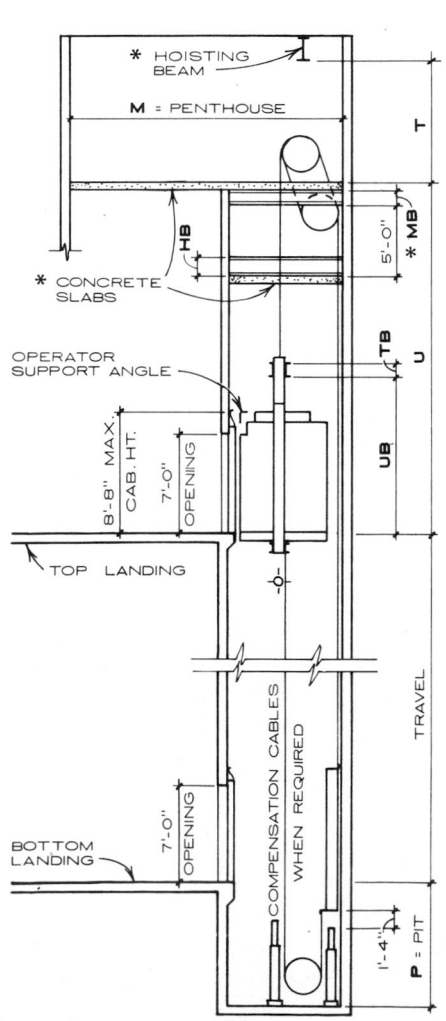

HOISTWAY SECTION

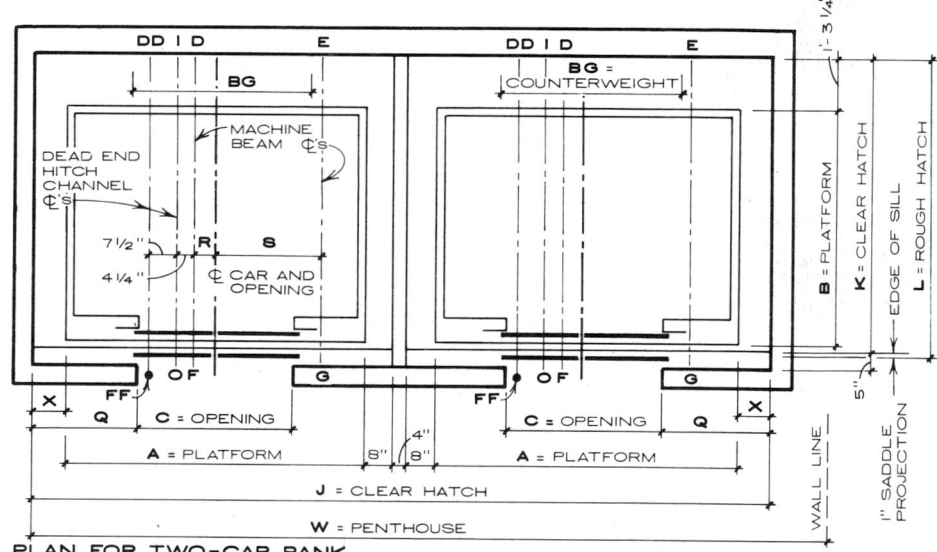

PLAN FOR TWO-CAR BANK

NOTES:

1. If required by local codes, pit depth and penthouse clearances may be increased.

2. Reactions shown for D, E, F, G, I, O, DD and FF include allowance for impact. Weight of concrete slab is not included.

3. The following items by owner; i.e., not normally in elevator contract:

   A. Penthouse access door, windows, light and adequate ventilation.
   B. Light outlet in hoistway located 4'-0" above center of travel.
   C. Other items marked *.

4. Reactions shown are typical. Location and magnitude will vary to some extent with different manufacturers.

PASSENGER ELEVATORS, GEARLESS   CAPACITY = 2,500 TO 4,000 LBS.,   SPEED = 700 TO 1000 FT. PER MIN.   ROPING = 1:1

CAPACITY POUNDS	SPEED FT/MIN.	DIMENSIONS													
		A	B	C	J	K	L	M	P	Q	R	S	T	U	W
2500	700 / 800	7'-0"	5'-0"	3'-6"	17'-2"	6'-4½"	6'-5½"	23'-0"	12'-6"	2'-6"	2'-0-3/16"	1'-1-3/16"	9'-6" / 10'-6"	27'-6" / 29'-10"	21'-6"
3000	700 / 800 / 1000	7'-0"	5'-6"	3'-6"	17'-2"	6'-10½"	6"-11½"	23'-0"	12'-6"	2'-6"	2'-0-3/16" / 1'-3-1/8" / 1'-3-1/8"	1'-1-3/16" / 1'-4-5/8" / 1'-4-5/8"	9'-6" / 10'-6" / 10'-6"	27'-6" / 29'-10" / 29'-10"	21'-6"
3500	700 / 800 / 1000	7'-0"	6'-2"	3'-6"	17'-2"	7'-6½"	7'-7½"	23'-0" / 24'-0" / 24'-0"	13'-0"	2'-6"	1'-3-1/8"	1'-4-5/8"	10'-6"	27'-6" / 29'-10" / 29'-10"	22'-3"
4000	700 / 800 / 1000	7'-6"	6'-6"	3'-10"	18'-4"	7'-10½"	7'-11½"	23'-0" / 24'-0" / 24'-0"	13'-0"	2'-8"	1'-3-1/8"	1-4-5/8"	10'-6"	27'-6" / 29'-10" / 29'-10"	23'-0"

CAPACITY POUNDS	SPEED FT/MIN.	DIMENSIONS						TRAVEL FEET	OVERHEAD LOAD IN LBS.					
		X	Y	N	TB	MB	HH		D	E	F	G	I	O
2500	700 / 800	9"		20"	10"	15"	1-1/16"	350 / 300		13500 / 13700		9000 / 8800	17000 / 17400	16300 / 11200
3000	700 / 800 / 1000	9"	2'-4½" / 2'-4½"	20" / 20" / 22"	10" / 12" / 12"	15" / 14" / 14"	1-1/16" / 1-1/8" / 1-1/8"	275 / 400 / 600	8200 / 8600	14600 / 10300 / 10800	5000 / 5600	9000 / 6200 / 7000	18300 / 21300 / 23300	11200 / 13000 / 15000
3500	700 / 800 / 1000	9"	2'-4½"	39" / 32" / 35"	12"	14" / 14" / 16"	1-1/8"	550 / 450 / 490	8800 / 9100 / 9200	11300 / 11500 / 11550	5200 / 5300 / 5300	6400 / 6700 / 6700	23800 / 24800 / 25950	14100 / 14500 / 14550
4000	700 / 800 / 1000	10"	2'-4½"	32" / 30" / 60"	12"	16"	1-1/8"	450 / 420 / 850	8900 / 8800 / 11600	11250 / 11000 / 13100	5800 / 5900 / 8000	7300 / 7400 / 9000	24600 / 24700 / 28900	15900 / 16100 / 19850

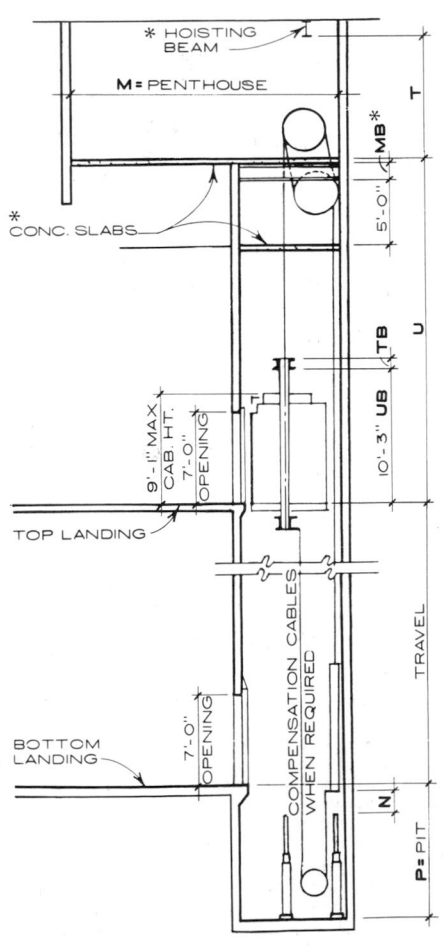

HOISTWAY SECTION

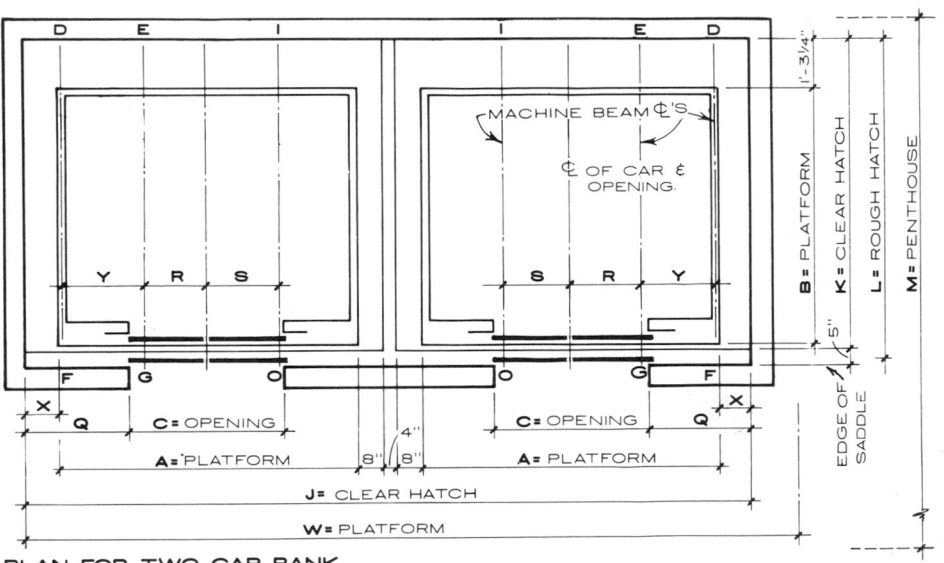

PLAN FOR TWO CAR BANK

NOTES:

1. If required by local codes, pit depth and penthouse clearances may be increased.

2. Reactions shown for D, E, F, G, I, and O include allowance for impact. Weight of concrete slab is not included.

3. The following by owner; i.e., not normally in elevator contract:

   A. Penthouse access door, windows, light and adequate ventilation.
   B. Light outlet in hoistway located 4'—0" above center of travel.
   C. Other items marked *.

4. Reactions shown are typical. Location and magnitude will vary to some extent with different manufacturers.

PASSENGER ELEVATORS, GEARED

CAPACITY = 2,000 TO 4,000 LBS., SPEED = 100 TO 350 FT. PER MIN. ROPING = 1:1
(GENERAL PURPOSE USE IN OFFICE, HOTEL AND INDUSTRIAL BUILDINGS)

CAPACITY POUNDS	SPEED FT. MIN.	DIMENSIONS A	B	C	H	J	K	L	M	N	P	R	S	U	W	MB
2000	*100								11'–0"		4'–6'	8 3/4"		16'–9"		
	200	6'–4"	4'–5"	3'–0"	8'–2"	7'–8"	5'–7 1/4"	5'–8 1/4"	11'–6"	13"	4'–10"	10 3/4"		17'–9"	11'–0"	10"
	250										6'–8"	10 3/4"				
	300											13 3/8"		17'–9"		
2500	*100				8'–2"				11'–0"		4'–7"	10 3/4"		16'–9"		10"
	200	7'–0"	5'–0"	3'–6"	8'–8"	8'–4"	6'–2 1/4"	6'–3 1/4"	11'–6"	13"	5'–2"	10 5/8"		17'–0"	11'–0"	12"
	350										7'–8"	10 1/4"		18'–3"		
3000	*100				8'–2"				11'–0"		4'–9"	10 5/8"		16'–9"		
	200										5'–2"			17'–0"		
	300	7'–0"	5'–6"	3'–6"	8'–8"	8'–4"	6'–9 1/4"	6'–9 1/4"	12'–0"	13"	6'–8"	13 1/4"		17'–6"	11'–0"	12"
	350										7'–8"			18'–3"		
3500	*100								11'–0"		4'–9"	10 5/8"		16'–9"		
	250								12'–0"							
	300	7'–0"	6'–2"	3'–6"	8'–8"	8'–4"	7'–4 1/4"	7'–5 1/4"	13'–6"	13"	6'–9"	13 1/4"		17'–6"	12'–0"	12"
	350										7'–8"	15 1/2"	14 1/2"	18'–3"		
4000	*100								11'–6"		4'–6"			17'–3"		
	200	7'–6"	6'–6"	3'–10"	8'–8"	8'–10"	7'–8"	7'–9"	12'–0"	13"	5'–4"	13 1/4"		17'–6"	12'–0"	12"
	250								13'–6"							
	350								13'–0"		6'–4"	15 1/4"	14 3/4"	19'–6"		15"

CAPACITY POUNDS	SPEED	DIMENSIONS TB	UB	OVERHEAD LOAD IN POUNDS D	E	F	G
2000	*100	8"	9'–6"	7,500	7,000	3,800	3,600
	200			8,700	7,900	4,500	4,200
	250			9,000	8,200	4,600	4,300
	300			9,200	8,500	4,800	4,400
2500	*100	8"	9'–6"	8,000	7,300	5,500	5,000
	200	9"	10'–3"	9,000	8,200	6,200	5,700
	350			10,700	9,800	6,500	5,800
3000	*100	9"	10'–3"	8,700	7,900	6,000	5,600
	200			10,400	9,500	6,600	6,000
	300			11,100	10,100	7,000	6,300
	350			11,300	10,300	7,100	6,400
3500	*100	10"	10'–3"	9,500	8,800	6,900	6,400
	250			11,700	10,700	7,600	7,000
	300			12,300	10,900	8,100	7,200
	350			13,300	12,600	7,600	7,200
4000	*100	12"	10'–3"	11,900	11,100	7,900	7,400
	200			12,600	11,600	8,400	7,700
	250			13,000	11,900	8,400	8,000
	350			15,000	14,000	8,900	8,200

* RHEOSTATIC A-C CONTROL

Reactions shown for D, E, F and G include allowance for impact. Weight of concrete slab is not included.

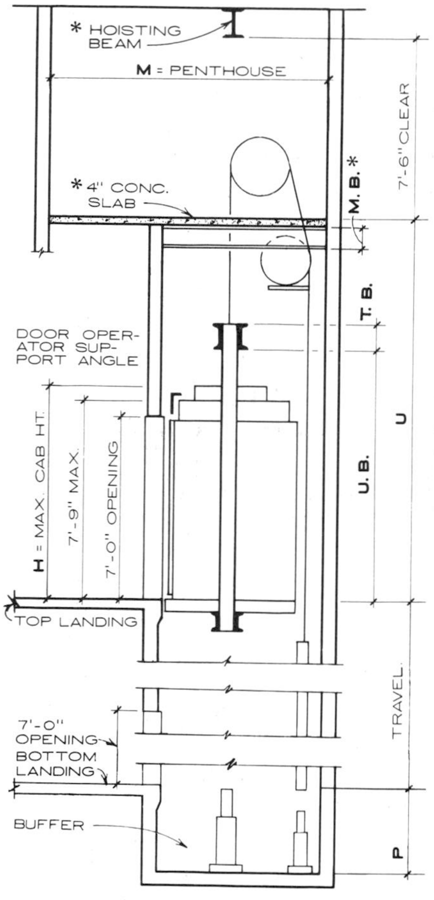

HOISTWAY SECTION

NOTES:

1. If required by local codes, pit depth and penthouse clearances may be increased.
2. The following items by owner; i.e., not normally in elevator contract:
   A. Penthouse access door, windows, light and adequate ventilation.
   B. Light outlet in hoistway located 4'– 0" above center of travel.
   C. Other items marked *.
3. Reactions shown are typical. Location & magnitude will vary to some extent with different mfgrs.
4. Buffer: Spring for speeds to 200 FPM. Oil for speeds over 200 FPM.

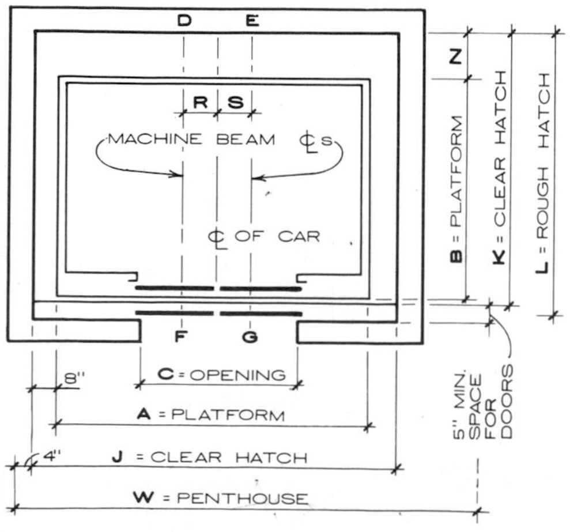

TYPICAL PLAN

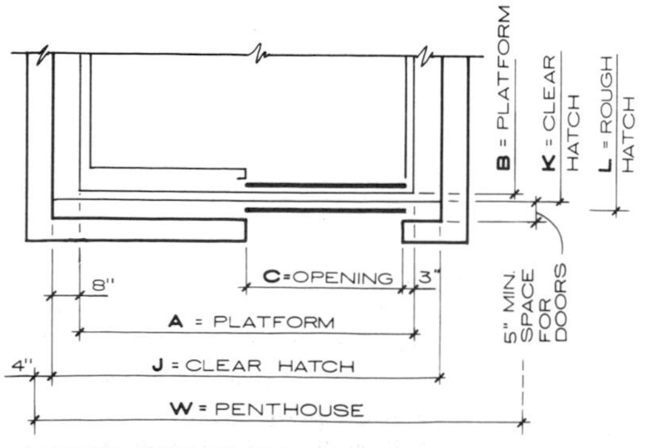

ALTERNATE PLAN SINGLE SPEED FOR 2,000 LB. AND 2,500 LB. CAPACITY ONLY. CENTER OPENING DOORS ALSO AVAILABLE.

APARTMENT HOUSE ELEVATORS, GEARED CAPACITY = 1200 TO 2500, SPEED = 100 TO 350 FEET PER MIN. ROPING = 1:1

CAPACITY POUNDS	SPEED FT. 'MIN.	DIMENSIONS														
		A	B	C	H	J	K	L	M	N	P	R	U	W	Z
1200	*100	5'-0"	4'-0"	3'-0" **	8'-2"	6'-4"	5'-2¼"	5'-4"	9'-6"	13"	4'-6"	9"	16'-9"	7'-0"	18"
2000	*100 250	6'-4"	4'-5"	3'-0"	8'-2"	7'-8"	5'-7¼"	5'-8¼"	11'-0" 11'-6"	13"	4'-6" 6'-8"	8¾" 10¾"	16'-9" 17'-6"	11'-0"	18" 22"
2500	200 350	7'-0"	5'-0"	3'-6"	8'-8"	8'-4"	6'-2¼"	6'-3¼"	11'-6"	13"	5'-2" 7'-8"	10-⅝" 3¼"	17'-0" 18'-3"	11'-0"	20" 26"

*A – C CONTROL **SWINGDOORS ON HATCH 2'-8"

CAPACITY POUNDS	SPEED FT. MIN.	DIMENSIONS					OVERHEAD LOAD IN POUNDS			
		BG	MB	TB	TC	UB	D	E	F	G
1200	*100	36"	8"	7"	5'-8"	9'-6"	6200	5800	3200	3100
2000	*100 250	42"	10"	8"	5'-5" 6'-2"	9'-6"	7500 9000	7000 8200	3800 4600	3600 4300
2500	200 350	42"	12"	9"	4'-8" 5'-11"	10'-3"	9000 10700	8200 9800	6200 6500	5700 5800

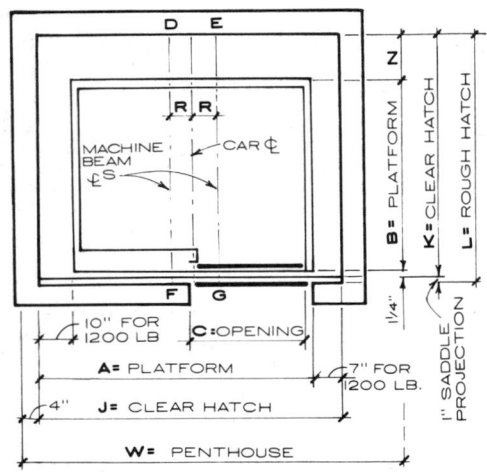

PLAN NO. 1

Single speed car door with swing hatch door for 1,200 and 2,000 pound capacities only.

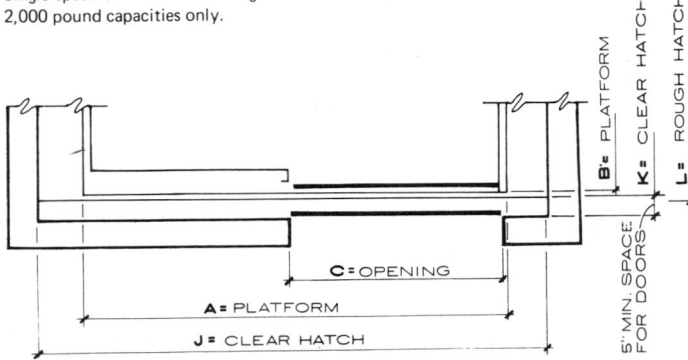

PLAN NO. 2

Single speed doors for 1,200, 2,000, and 2,500 pound capacities. Center opening car and hatch doors for 2,500 pound capacity only. Two speed side opening doors for 1,200 pound capacity only.

NOTES:

1. If required by local codes, pit depth and penthouse clearances may be increased.

2. Reactions shown for D, E, F, and G include allowance for impact. Weight of concrete slab is not included.

3. The following by owner; i.e., not normally in elevator contract:

    A. Penthouse access door, windows, light and adequate ventilation.
    B. Light outlet in hoistway located 4'-0" above center of travel.
    C. Other items marked. *

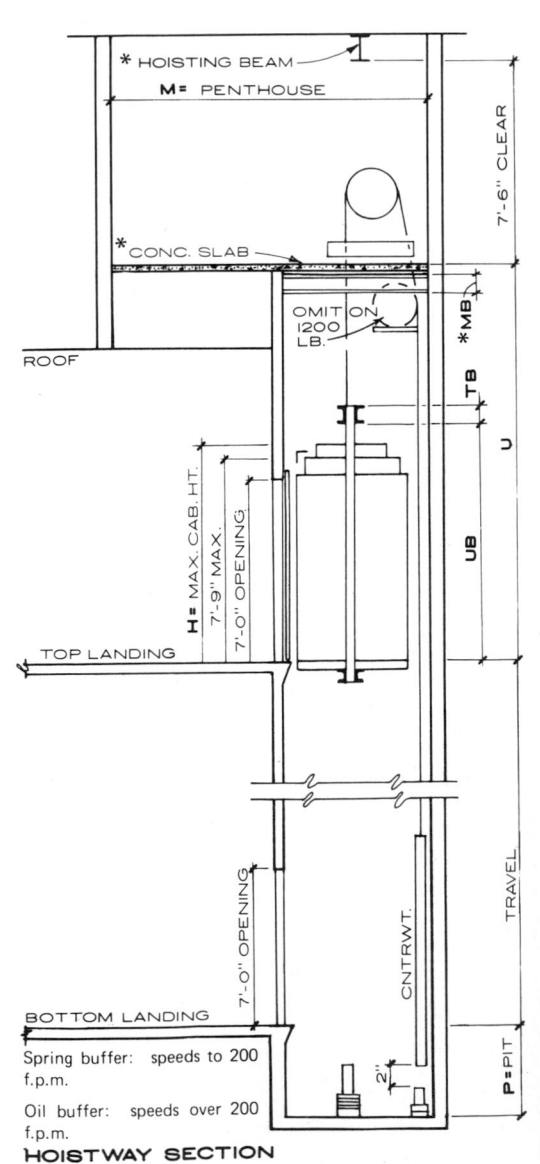

Spring buffer: speeds to 200 f.p.m.

Oil buffer: speeds over 200 f.p.m.

HOISTWAY SECTION

PRELIMINARY SELECTION

The following explanations and examples are to serve as guides in choosing a freight elevator and its carrying capacity for various conditions.

The carrying capacity per hour is determined by the normal load of the elevator and the time required per round trip. The round trip time is made up of the following four elements, as shown below on the Time Curve (All time is in seconds):

1. Running Time: equals the distance travelled divided by the car speed chosen. May be read directly from the Time Curve.

2. Accelerating and Retarding Time: the additional time required to accelerate and retard the car for each stop.

3. Door Time: the time required to operate car gate and hoistway doors for each stop.

4. Loading Time: the time required to load and unload the car. Varies greatly with the type of material handled and the method of handling used.

NOTE:

It is recommended that whenever practical a study be made of the loading and unloading operations of a similar elevator. If local studies on a similar elevator determine more closely the loading time, such figures should be used in preference to those given in the Time Curve.

It is advisable to add 20% to the calculated roundtrip time.

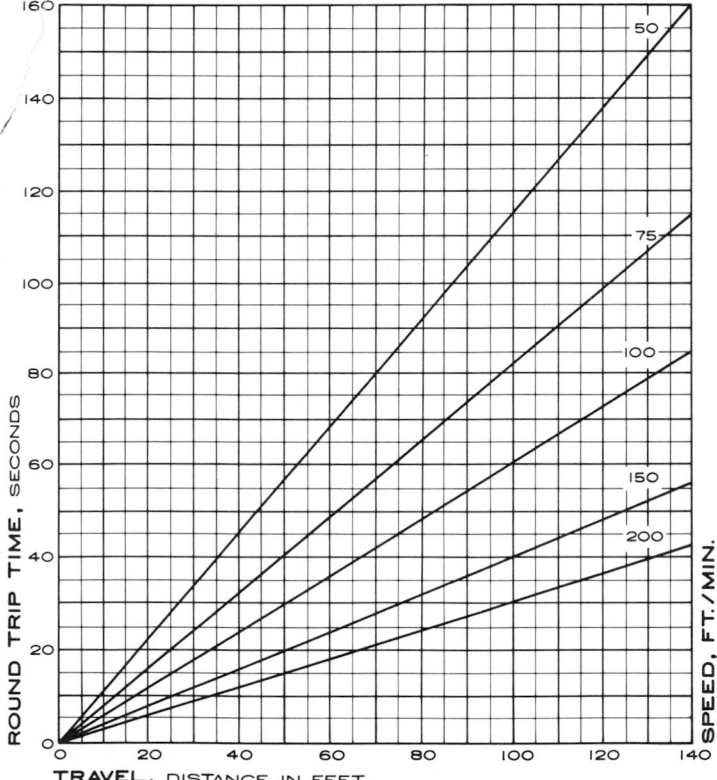

TIME CURVE

NOTES:

Running Time:
Add per stop, acceleration and retardation:
Rheostatic controls = 2 1/4 sec.
Generator field controls = 1 3/4 sec.

Add per stop, door operation:
Manual = 16 sec.
Power =   8 sec.

Add per stop, loading and unloading:
Hand truck = 25 sec.
Power truck = 15 sec.

SAMPLE PROBLEM NO. ONE

Given: a 5-story building

Floor	Height
1 to 2	18 feet
2 to 3	16 "
3 to 4	16 "
4 to 5	16 "

Total travel distances: 66 feet

Material to be handled:

1. 225,000 pounds in pallets between 1st and 4th floors on power trucks. A power truck is 6' − 0" long, 4' − 0" wide, and weighs 3500 pounds empty, 6500 pounds loaded.

2. 75,000 pounds in and out between various floors by hand truck and package.

Total: 300,000 pounds in and out of building per day.

SOLUTION

Capacity and size: The capacity of the elevator depends on the weight of the loaded power truck. A 6000 pound rating could be used if the truck remains on the floor but it provides no reserve. From the General Data table on the following page, the 8'− 4" x 10'− 0" platform size 8000 pound rating would be selected. (It is not necessary, with a 6'− 0" x 4'− 0" power truck, to go to the 8'− 4" x 12'− 0" platform size, which also has an 8000 pound rating.)

Type of equipment: Leveling equipment is desirable to assure accurate landing at the floors to facilitate moving the power truck on and off the car. The weight of material to be moved per day will cause this elevator to be quite active, and thus generator field equipment should be considered.

Door operation: Power operated doors are desirable where elevator is quite active.

Speed selection: See General Data Table, on a following page. The recommended speed for 5 floors (66 feet travel), with generator field controls, is 150 feet per minute.

Calculation of time: For 3/4 service between first and fourth floors:

With loaded power truck on elevator

Running Time	20 sec.
Acceleration and Retardation	1 3/4 "
Door Operation	8 "
Loading and Unloading	15 "

Total time one way . . . . .44 3/4 sec. Use: 45 sec.
Round trip time = 2 x 45 = 90 sec. plus 20% = 108 sec.
225,000 lbs. = 75 trips. 75 trips x 108 sec. = 2 hours 15 min.
3,000 lbs/trip

With power truck remaining on floor (assume 2 pallets per trip)

Running Time	20 sec.
Acceleration and Retardation	1 3/4 "
Door Operation	8 "
Loading and Unloading	90 " (varies widely)

Total time one way . . . . .119 3/4 Use: 120 sec.
Round trip time = 2 x 120 = 240 sec. plus 20% = 288 sec.
225,000 lbs. = 38 trips. 38 trips x 288 sec. = 3 hours 3 min.
6,000 lbs./trip

The balance of the service is moving 75,000 pounds between first and various floors by hand truck and package. Assume an average load of 1500 pounds; average travel first to third floor, 34 feet; and an average of 3 stops per round trip.

Running Time	14 sec.
Acceleration and Retardation (average)	2 5/8 "
Door Operation (average)	12 "
Loading and Unloading (2 hand trucks)	50 "

Total time one way . . . . .78 5/8 sec.
Use 80 sec.
Round-trip time = 2 x 80 = 160 sec. plus 20% =192 sec.
75,000 lbs. (1st to 3rd fl.) = 50 trips. 50 trips x 192 sec.
15,000 lbs./trip   = 2 hours 40 minutes

Total time to move 300,000 pounds in and out of building is:

a. If power truck remains on elevator with load:
2 hrs. 15 min. plus 2 hrs. 40 min. = 4 hrs. 55 min.

b. If power truck remains on floor:
3 hrs. 3 min. plus 2 hrs. 40 min. = 5 hrs. 43 min.

PRELIMINARY SELECTION (CONT.)

SAMPLE PROBLEM NO. TWO

Given: a 3-story building

Floor	Feet
1 to 2	18
2 to 3	16
Total Travel distance	34

material to be handled:
1. miscellaneous freight, some to be moved in hand trucks and some in package form.
2. hand truck size is 4'-6" long, 2'-6" wide; truck weight 250 lbs., load weight 750 lbs.

total: 20,000 lbs. in and out of building per day (8 hrs.)

SOLUTION

Capacity and size: From the General Date Table, the 6'-4" x 8'-0" car would be chosen, to accommodate two hand trucks per trip or 45 square feet for loads of miscellaneous packages. The 3000 pound capacity elevator would be preferable for possible greater loads in the future.

Type of equipment: It is evident that this elevator will not be very active so rheostatic controls will be considered.

Door operation: Because this elevator will not be very active, manually operated doors will be chosen.

Speed selection: See General Data Table. The recommended speed for 3 floors (34 feet travel) with rheostatic control is 75 feet per minute.

Calculation of time: For service from first to third floor without an intermediate stop. Refer to Time Curve on preceding page.

Running Time	27	sec.
Acceleration and Retardation	2 1/4	sec.
Door Operation	16	sec.
Loading and Unloading	50	sec.
Total time one way	95 1/4	sec. Use 95 sec.

Round trip time = 2 x 95 = 190 sec. plus 20% = 228 sec.

$$\frac{20,000 \text{ lbs./day}}{15,000 \text{ lbs./trip}} = 13 \text{ trips} \times 228 \text{ sec.} = 50 \text{ minutes.}$$

If most of the material is carried in package loads, the two types of handling should be figured separately, and the total used. Package loading time will increase the trip times, and will vary greatly.

GENERAL DATA FOR TYPICAL FREIGHT ELEVATORS

TYPES AND USES						CONTROL SYSTEM		
TYPE OF TRAFFIC	METHOD OF LOADING	CAPACI-TY (LBS)	MAX. RISE NO. OF FLOORS	TYPE OF ELEVATOR	GENE-RATOR FIELD FLOORS	RHEO-STATIC FLOORS	ELEVA-TOR SPEED F.T./MIN.
VERY LIGHT	Manual*	2500	3 (or 30') to sidewalk level	Sidewalk		2	50
		2500	3(or 35') inside bldg.	Self sup-porting	2 or 3 (10,000 pound cap.)	3 or 4	75
LIGHT		2500 to 3500	6, 7 or more		2 or 3	5 to 8	100
MEDIUM	Manual* or Automo-bile**	3500 to 8000		General Purpose	4 or 5		150
		8000 to 10,000	Any no. of floors		6 to 10		200
HEAVY	Industrial or Auto Truck	8000 to 20,000 & more		Truck			

*Includes uses of hand trucks and small, slow speed electric pallet trucks.
**Includes passenger cars and light trucks.

NOTE:
1. If one of the floors exceeds 20 feet in height, the next higher speed is desirable.
2. Higher speeds available if needed.

STANDARD CAR SIZES

INSIDE DIMS	PLATFORM DIMS	STANDARD OPENING SIZE	NET AREA SQ.FT.	CAPACITY RATING THOUSANDS OF POUNDS	
5'-0" x 6'-6"	5'-4" x 7'-0"	5'-0" x 8'-0"	32.5	2.5 , 3	(3)
6'-0" x 7'-6"	6'-4" x 8'-0"	6'-0" x 8'-0"	45.0	2.5 , 3, 4	(5)
8'-0" x 9'-6"	8'-4" x 10'-0"	8'-0" x 8'-0"	76.0	4,5, 6, 8	(8)
8'-0" x 11'-6"	8'-4" x 12'-0"	8'-0" x 8'-0"	92.0	5, 6, 8, 10	(10)
10'-0" x 13'-6"	10'-4" x 14'-0"	10'-0" x 8'-0"	135.0	10	(16)
10'-0" x 15'-6"	10'-4" x 16'-0"	Usually deter-mined by load characteristics		12	
10'-0" x 19'-6"	10'-4" x 20'-0"			14	
12'-0" x 15'-6"	12'-4" x 16'-0"			16, 18, 20	
SPECIAL	Usually determined by load characteristics.		24, 30	( ) = Recommended, if also used for passengers.	

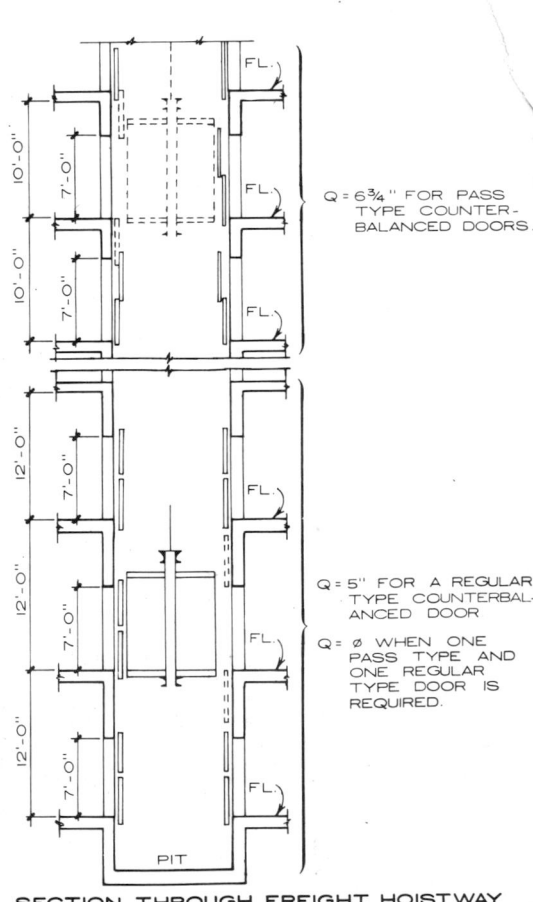

Q = 6¾" FOR PASS TYPE COUNTER-BALANCED DOORS.

Q = 5" FOR A REGULAR TYPE COUNTERBAL-ANCED DOOR

Q = Ø WHEN ONE PASS TYPE AND ONE REGULAR TYPE DOOR IS REQUIRED.

SECTION THROUGH FREIGHT HOISTWAY SHOWING DOOR TYPES

1. For Q values shown above, see following page, "Freight Elevators, Geared. Capacity = 4,000 to 10,000 pounds. Speed = 50 to 200 feet per minute. Roping = 2:1".

2. Pass type doors are required for a 7'-0" high opening when the floor to floor height is less than 11'-0", for an 8'-0" high opening when the floor to floor height is less than 12'-6".

FREIGHT ELEVATORS, GEARED

CAPACITY = 4,000 TO 10,000 LBS., SPEED = 50 TO 200 FT. PER. MINUTE. ROPING = 2:1

CAPACITY (LBS)	SPEED FT/MIN.	A	B	C	J	K = PLAN NO. 2		K = PLAN NO. 1			L	S	N	P	R'	T	V	Z
						Q = 5"	Q = 6¾"	Q = 5"	Q = 6¾"	Q = ∅								
4000	75	6'-4"	8'-0"	6'-0"	8'-5"	8'-7¼"	8'-9"	8'-10"	9'-1½"	8'-11¾"	12"	17"	8"	4'-6"	10⅝"		10"	6¾"
	100	8'-4"	10'-0"	8'-0"	10'-5"	10'-7¼"	10'-9"	10'-10"	11'-1½"	10'-11¾"	12⅝"					9½"		
5000	75		10'-0"			10'-7¼"	10'-9"	10'-10"	11'-1½"	10'-11¾"	12⅜"			4'-9"	10⅝"		10"	
	100	8'-4"	12'-0"	8'-0"	10'-5"	12'-7¼"	10'-9"	12'-10"	13'-1½"	12'-11¾"		18"	8"			9½"		7¾"
	200		10'-0" 12'-0"			10'-7¼" 12'-7¼"	10'-9" 12'-9"	10'-10" 12'-10"	11'-1½" 13'-1½"	10'-11¾" 12'-11¾"	18¾"			5'-3"	13¼"		11"	
6000	50		10'-0" 12'-0"			10'-7¼" 12'-7¼"	10'-9" 12'-9"	10'-10" 12'-10"	11'-1½" 13'-1½"	10'-11¾" 12'-11¾"	12⅜"				10⅝"	9½"	10"	
	75	8'-4"	10'-0"	8'-0"	10'-5"	10'-7¼"	10'-9"	10'-10"	11'-1½"	10'-11¾"		18"	8"	4'-9"				7¾"
	100		12'-0"			12'-7¼"	12'-9"	12'-10"	13'-1½"	12'-11¾"	17¾"				13¼"	10½"	11"	
	200		10'-0" 12'-0"			10'-7¼" 12'-7¼"	10'-9" 10'-9"	10'-10" 12'-10"	11'-1½" 13'-1½"	10'-11¾" 12'-11¾"				5'-3"				
8000	50		10'-0"			10'-7¼"	10'-9"	10'-10"	11'-1½"	10'-11¾"	14⅞"				13"	12½"	12"	8¾"
	100	8'-4"	12'-0"	8'-0"	10'-10"	12'-7¼"	12'-9"	12'-10"	13'-1½"	12'-11¾"	14½"	20"	10"	5'-6"				8½"
	200		10'-0" 12'-0"			10'-7¼" 12'-7¼"	10'-9" 12'-9"	10'-10" 12'-10"	11'-1½" 13'-1½"	10'-11¾" 12'-11¾"	21" 20¾"				14¾" 15¼"	14"	15"	8¾" 8½"
10000	75	8'-4" 10'-4"	12'-0" 14'-0"	8'-0" 10'-0"	10'-11" 12'-11"	12'-7¼" 14'-7¼"	12'-9" 14'-9"	12'-10" 14'-10"	13'-1½" 15'-1½"	12'-11¾" 14'-11¾"	12½"	21"	10"	5'-6"	13"	14½"	12"	9"
	100	8'-4" 10'-4"	12'-0" 14'-0"	8'-0" 10'-0"	10'-11" 12'-11"	12'-7¼" 14'-7¼"	12'-9" 14'-9"	12'-10" 14'-10"	13'-1½" 15'-1½"	12'-11¾" 14'-11¾"	20" 17⅞"			6'-0"	14¾" 15¼"		15"	

CAPACITY (LBS)	SPEED FT/MIN.	DIMENSIONS						MINIMUM		SHEAVES		OVERHEAD LOAD IN POUNDS						
		U	M	W	BG	MB	TB	O.T.	T.C.	CAR	CWT	D	E	F	G	H	X	Y
4000	75	16'-0"	13'- "	11'-1"	30"	10"	9"	2'-1"	4'-0"	24"	24"	8650	5400	4500	3900	3150	5500	6200
	100		10'-3"	12'-3"	36"				4'-2"			10250	6500	4050	3900	4300	6100	6150
5000	75	16'-1"	13'-9"	11'-1"			10"	2'-1"	4'-2"			11000	6600	4800	4900	4850	6700	7050
	100				36"	12"				24"	24"	11350	6900	5500	5100	5050	6950	7550
	200	16'-4"	15'-4"	14'-0"			12"	2'-5"	4'-3"			14250 14400	7400 7700	5300 11500	6250 6400	5250 0	7300 7300	8000 9100
6000	50	15'-10"						2'-11"	3'-11"			11550 11650	7000 7250	5100 5700	5150 5400	5250 5400	7100 7150	7500 7600
	75	16'-1"	13'-9"	11'-1"			10"					12900	6750	10400	5700	0	6650	7300
	100	16'-3"			36"	12"		2'-4"	4'-2"	24"	24"	13150	7050	10600	5900	0	6700	8300
	200	16'-4"	15'-4"	14'-0"			12"	2'-5"	4'-3"			14700 15050	7850 8100	5650 11950	6450 6700	5600 0	7850 7800	8350 9400
8000	50	16'-6"	13'-9"	11'-4"	36"			2'-1"	3'-11"	27"	24"	14650	8050	7450	7250	7300	7300	8650
	100				42"	15"	12"	2'-4"	4'-2"	27"	30"	15200	8350	7700	7500	7500	7500	9000
	200	16'-8"	15'-4"	14'-0"	36"			2'-5"	4'-3"		24" 30"	19450 20150	9900 10200	16400 17000	8200 8500	0 0	8400 8700	7750 8000
10000	75	16'-10"	15'-4"	14'-3"	42"	15"	12"	2'-4"	4'-2"	27"	30"	15310 17350	10200 11400	8900 9200	7800 8000	8350 9400	9760 10850	11000 11200
	100	17'-1"			42" 48"		15"					20950 21000	10600 12500	17700 11900	8800 11050	0 11500	9050 12400	8300 12500

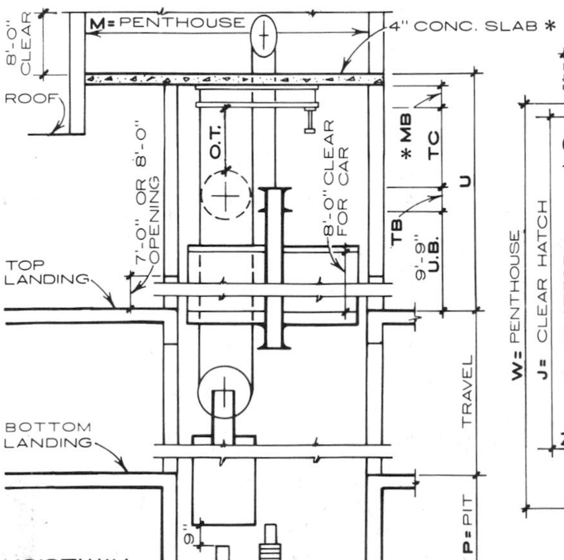

HOISTWAY SECTION

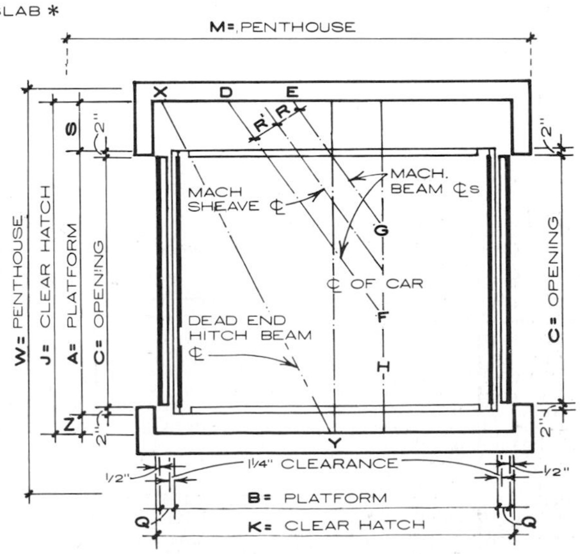

PLAN NO. 1 FRONT AND REAR OPENING

NOTES:

1. If required by local codes, pit depth and penthouse clearances may be increased.
2. Reactions shown for D, E, F, G, H, X and Y include allowance for impact. Weight of concrete slab is not included.
3. The following items by owner; i.e., not normally in elevator contract:
   A. Penthouse access door, windows, light and adequate ventilation.
   B. Light outlet in hoistway located 4'-0" above center of travel.
   C. Other items marked *.

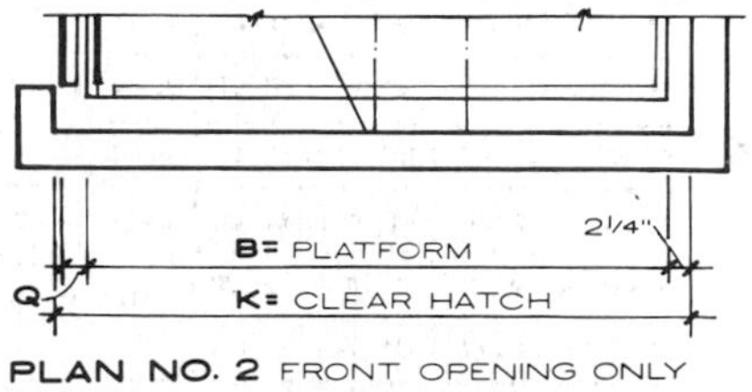

PLAN NO. 2 FRONT OPENING ONLY

DIMENSIONS NOT SHOWN ARE SAME AS PLAN NO. I

FREIGHT ELEVATORS, GEARED.

CAPACITY= 3,000 OR 4,000 LBS.,   SPEED= 50 TO 200 FT. PER. MIN.   ROPING=1:1 (MAX. DISTANCE BETWEEN GUIDE RAIL SUPPORTS= 14'-0". DECREASE IF REQUIRED BY LOCAL CODES. REQUIREMENTS FOR **Q** GIVEN WITH "FREIGHT ELEVATORS, GEARED ROPING= 2:1 ETC.)

CAPACITY (LBS.)	SPEED FT. MIN.	DIMENSIONS											OVERHEAD LOAD IN LBS.					
		A	B	C	J	N	P	R	U	X	M	W	MINIMUM		D	E	F	G
													O.T.	T.C.				
3000	50	5'-4"	7'-0"	5'-0"	7'-3"	15"	4'-6"	10⅝"	15'-6"	6"	9'-9"	10'-2"	2'-1"	3'-1"	8900	6650	4900	5900
	100	6'-4"	8'-0"	6'-0"	8'-3"				16'-0"		10'-3"	11'-0"	2'-4"	3'-11"	9200	7300	5450	6100
4000	200	6'-4"	8'-0"	6'-0"	8'-5"	17"	5'-3"	13¼"	16'-4"	6	9'-6"	13'-0"	2'-5"	4'-3"	14150	10850	7800	9450
		8'-4"	10'-0"	8'-0"	10'-5"										15150	12500	9300	10350

CAPACITY (LBS.)	SPEED FT. MIN.	DIMENSIONS			K-PLAN 1		K-PLAN 2		
		BG	MB	TB	Q=5"	Q=6	Q=5"	Q=6	Q=0
3000	50	27"	12"	8"	7'-7¼"	7'-9"	7'-10"	8'-1½"	7'-11¾"
					8'-7¼"	8'-9"	8'-10"	9'-1½"	8'-11¾"
4000	200	30"	15"	9"	8'-7¼"	8'-9"	8'-10"	9'-1½"	8'-11¾"
		33"		12"	10'-7¼"	10'-9"	10'-10"	11'-1½"	10'-11¾"

NOTES:

1. If required by local codes, pit depth and penthouse clearances may be increased.

2. Reactions shown for D, E, F, and G include allowance for impact. Weight of concrete slab is not included.

3. The following by owner; i.e., not normally in elevator contract:
A. Penthouse access door, windows, light and adequate ventilation.
B. Light outlet in hoistway located 4' − 0" above center of travel.
C. Other items marked.*

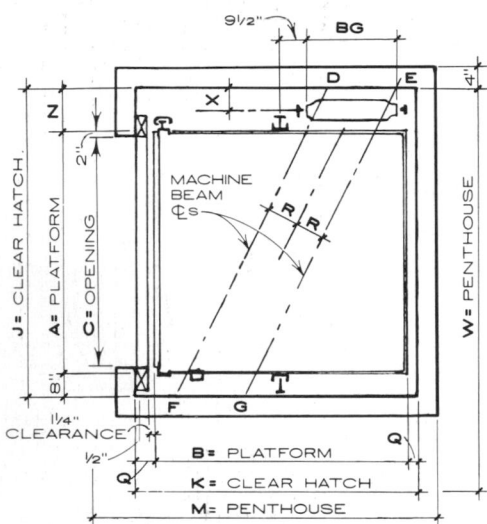

PLAN NO. I FRONT OPENING

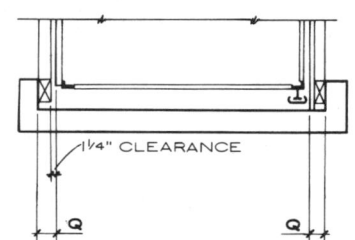

PLAN NO.2 FRONT & REAR OPENING

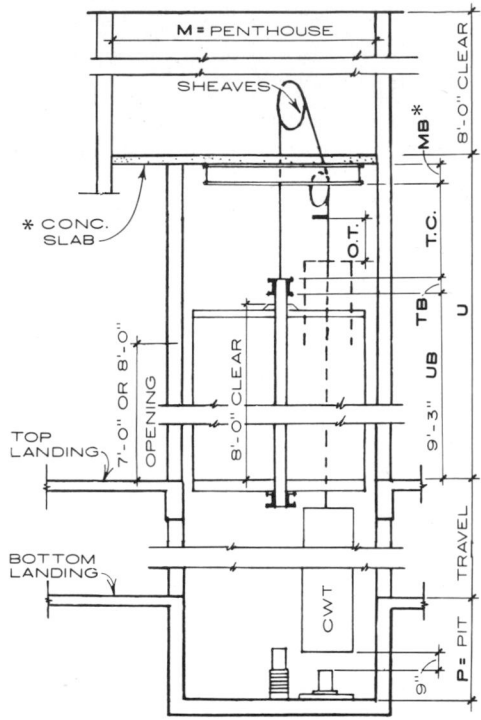

HOISTWAY SECTION

SIDEWALK ELEVATORS

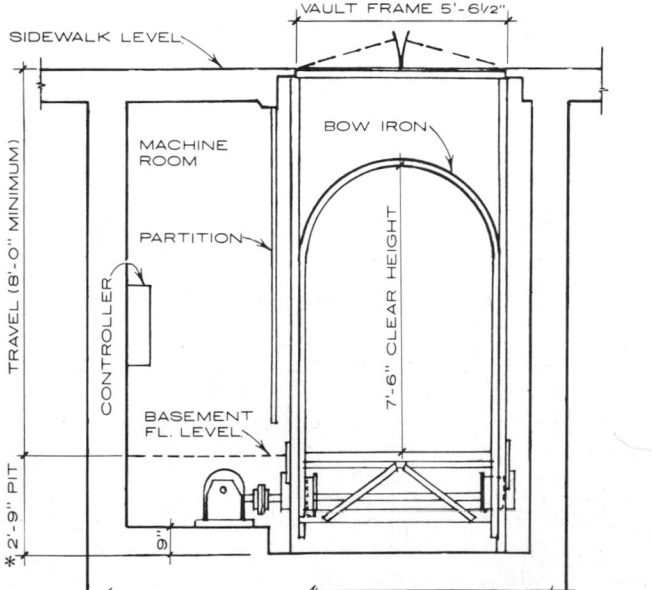

SECTION (INCREASE PIT DEPTH IF TRAVEL IS OVER 15'-0")

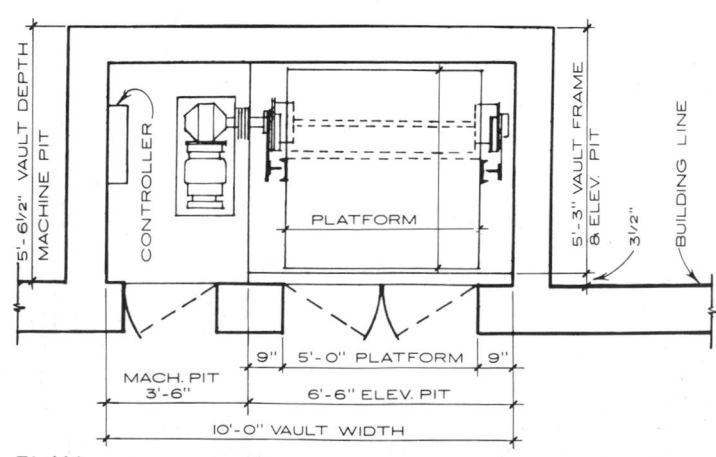

PLAN

Layout is for 15' − 0" travel between sidewalk and basement levels. Standard capacity is usually 2000 lbs. Control is of continuous pressure push button type with Up-Down buttons in each car. Maximum standard platforms are 5' − 0" x 5' − 0" or equivalent, with minimum front-to-back dimension 4' − 0". Where local codes or special conditions of travel and capacity govern, special car sizes and capacities can be provided.

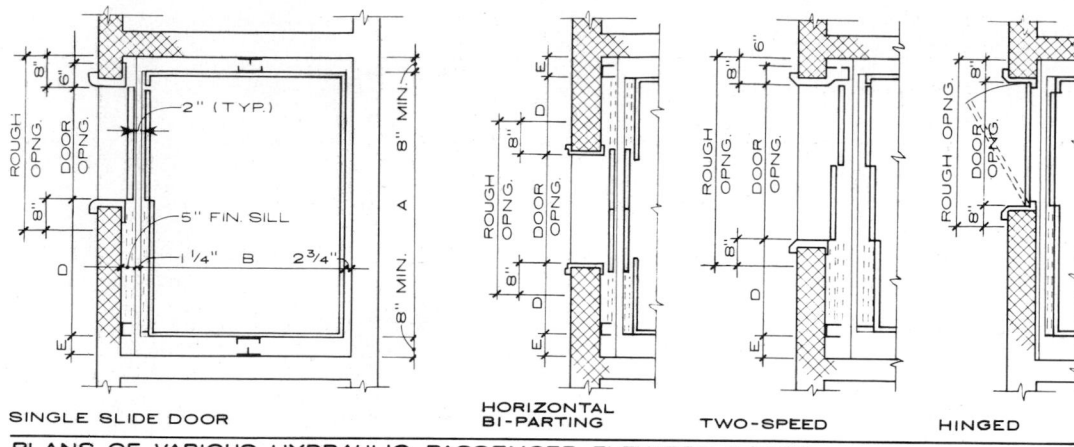

SINGLE SLIDE DOOR | HORIZONTAL BI-PARTING | TWO-SPEED | HINGED

PLANS OF VARIOUS HYDRAULIC PASSENGER ELEVATOR DOORS

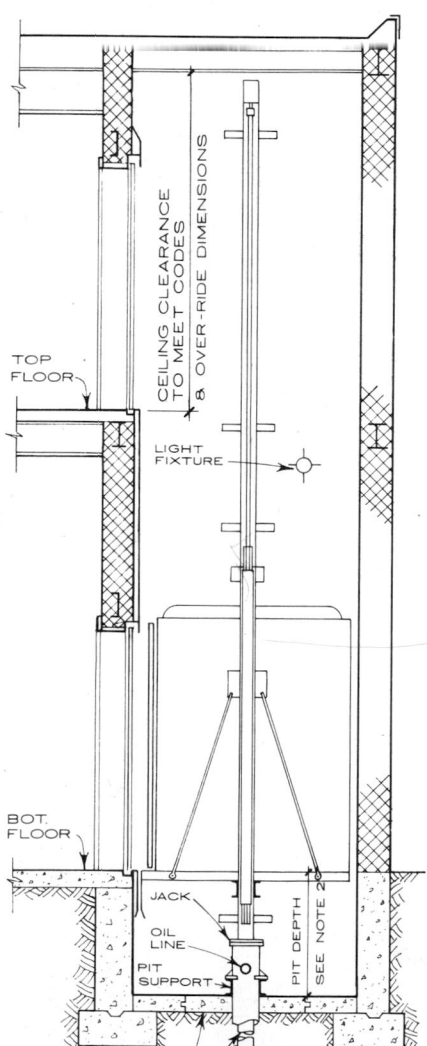

SECTION HYDRAULIC PASSENGER ELEVATOR

NOTE 1.

Minimum ceiling clearance for bi-parting hatchway doors: 13'–6" for single blade doors, 11'–0" for double blade doors, and 11'–6" for fire doors.

NOTE 2.

3'–0" minimum pit depth or to meet local codes. Ladder required if depth exceeds 4'.

PASSENGER ELEVATOR SIZE & DUTY TABLE

CAPACITY (POUNDS)	APPROXIMATE UP-SPEED (FT. PER MIN.)			CAR SIZE	
	2 STOP	3-4 STOP	5-6 STOP	A WIDTH	B WIDTH
1200	100	125	150	5'–0"	4'–0"
1500	100	125	150	5'–0"	4'–6"
2000	100	125	150	6'–4"	4'–5"
2500	100	125	150	7'–0"	5'–0"
3000	100	125	150	7'–0"	5'–6"
3500	100	125	150	7'–0"	6'–2"
4000	100	125	150	8'–0"	6'–0"
3500	100	125	150	5'–4"	8'–0"
4000	100	125	150	5'–8"	8'–4"

E = 5" motorized doors, 3" manually operated.
Speeds up to 200 f.p.m. available.

DESIGN CONSIDERATIONS:

Data shown is general and should be confirmed with manufacturer before beginning final drawings. Car size, speed and capacity can be furnished to meet practically any requirement.

Elevator and hoistway construction shall meet American Standard Safety Code, local and state building codes.

Structure need only support horizontal loadings for guide rail brackets—vertical car loads supported through jack to pit floor.

Provide adjacent space to house power unit and controller. Consider sound installation if adjacent areas occupied.

Hydraulic elevator systems eliminate need of penthouse, load brakes, load supporting columns; provide relatively quiet, smooth, maintenance-free operation for maximum 60 ft. travel. Can be added to existing buildings by segmental drilling in completed shaftway.

FREIGHT ELEVATOR HATCHWAY DOORS:

Vertical bi-parting counterbalanced doors and gates generally used, fire doors where required by code.

Dimensions shown on Section refer to regular vertical bi-parting hatchway doors with 5" clearance. Where floor heights are less than 11'–9" (for 7'–6" opening height), bypass or "pass" type doors are used. These require a minimum spandrel height of 10", clearance of 5 1/2" minimum to 6 3/4" maximum is needed instead of standard 3 1/2" to 5". Clearance varies with manufacturer. "Pass" doors require special fire flap, splay pan and sill.

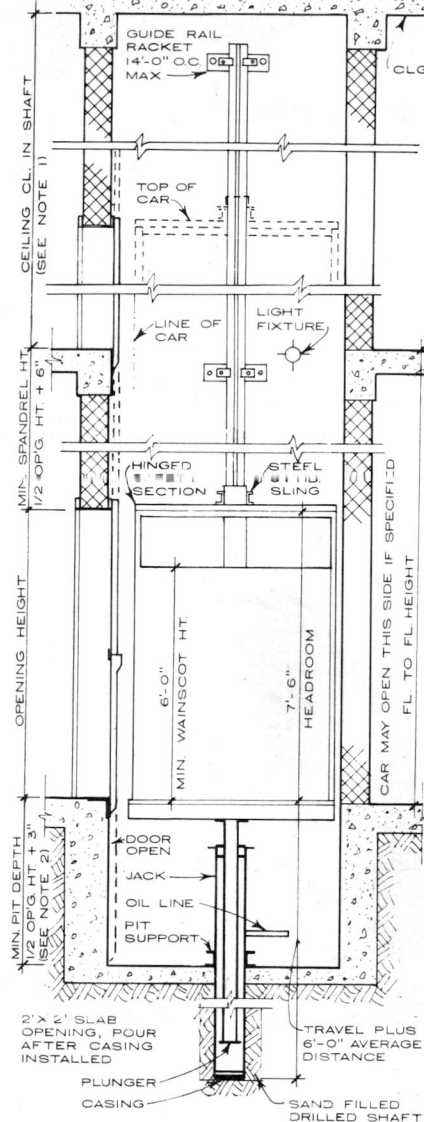

SECTION HATCHWAY DOORS

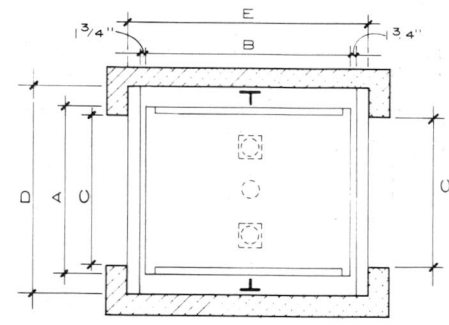

PLAN–HYDRAULIC FREIGHT ELEVATOR

FREIGHT ELEVATOR SIZE & DUTY TABLE

CAPACITY (POUNDS)	APPROXIMATE UP-SPEED (FT. PER MIN.)			CAR SIZE		OPNG. WIDTH	MANUAL GATES, DRS.	MOTORIZED DOORS	MANUAL GATES	BI-PART. DOORS	PASS-TYPE DOORS
	2 STOP	3-4 STOP	5-6 STOP	A	B	C	D	D	E	E	E
(1) 2,000	65	75	100	4'–0"	6'–0"	3'–9"	5'–4"	5'–11"	7'–1 1/2"	6'–10"	7'–1 1/2"
(1) 4,000	50	65	85	5'–0"	7'–0"	4'–9"	6'–4"	6'–11"	8'–1 1/2"	7'–10"	8'–1 1/2"
(1) 5,000	45	60	75	6'–0"	8'–0"	5'–9"	7'–4"	7'–11"	9'–1 1/2"	8'–10"	9'–1 1/2"
(2) 7,500	50	60	75	8'–0"	10'–0"	7'–9"	9'–6"	9'–11"	11'–1 1/2"	10'–10"	11'–1 1/2"
(2)10,000	40	50	70	10'–0"	12'–0"	9'–9"	11'–6"	11'–11"	13'–1 1/2"	12'–10"	13'–1 1/2"
(2)15,000	30	40	45	10'–0"	15'–0"	9'–9"	11'–6"	11'–11"	16'–1 1/2"	15'–10"	16'–1 1/2"
(2)20,000	30	40	45	10'–0"	20'–0"	9'–9"	11'–6"	11'–11"	21'–1 1/2"	20'–10"	21'–1 1/2"

Speeds up to 150 f.p.m. available. (1) Class A Loading: Hand trucks (2) Class C Loading: Power trucks

Warren Anderson; The Perkins and Will Partnership; Chicago, Illinois

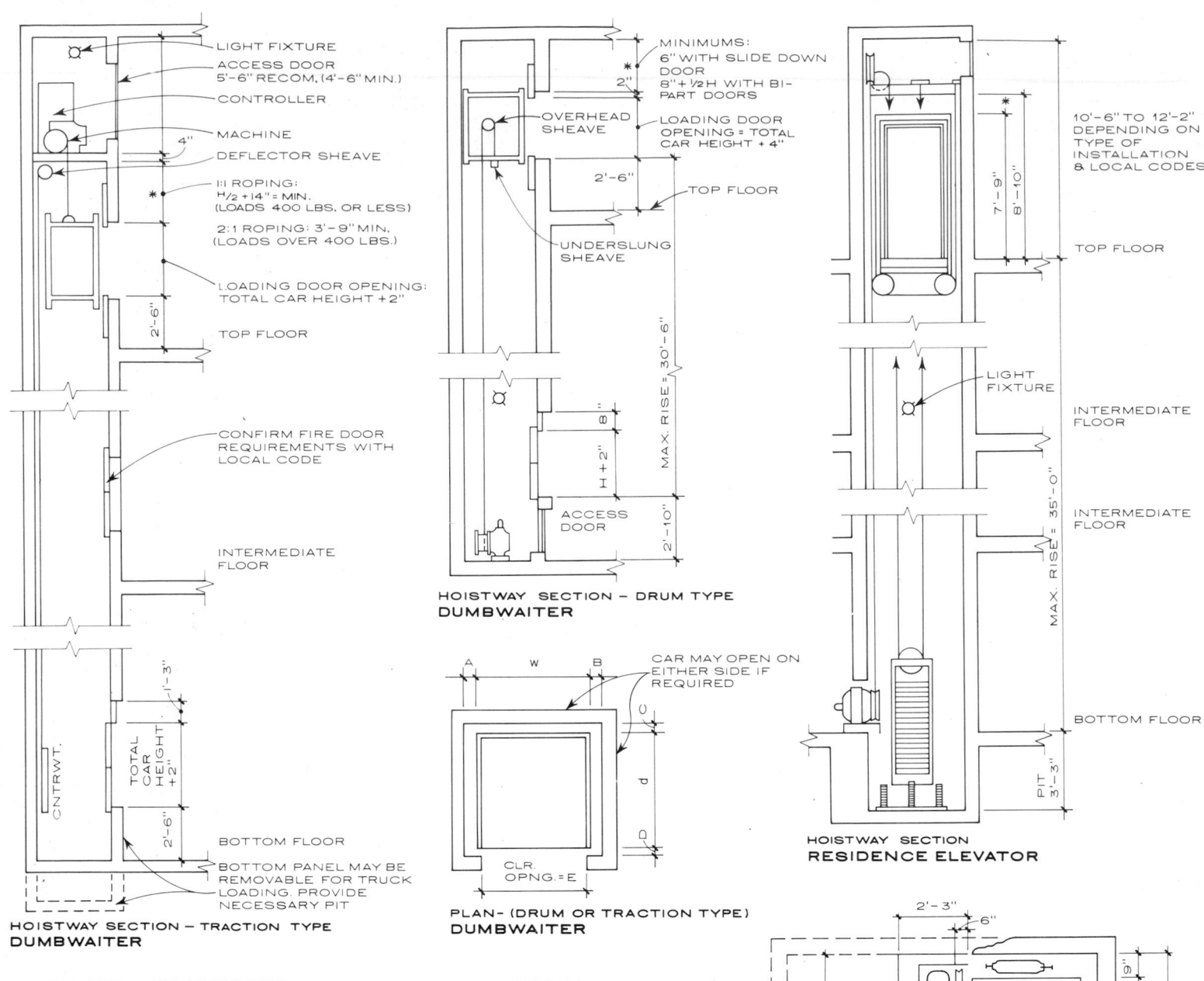

LIGHT FIXTURE

ACCESS DOOR
5'-6" RECOM. (4'-6" MIN.)

CONTROLLER

MACHINE

DEFLECTOR SHEAVE

1:1 ROPING:
H/2 + 14" = MIN.
(LOADS 400 LBS. OR LESS)

2:1 ROPING: 3'-9" MIN.
(LOADS OVER 400 LBS.)

LOADING DOOR OPENING:
TOTAL CAR HEIGHT + 2"

TOP FLOOR

CONFIRM FIRE DOOR
REQUIREMENTS WITH
LOCAL CODE

INTERMEDIATE
FLOOR

CNTRWT.

TOTAL CAR HEIGHT + 2"

BOTTOM FLOOR

BOTTOM PANEL MAY BE
REMOVABLE FOR TRUCK
LOADING. PROVIDE
NECESSARY PIT

HOISTWAY SECTION – TRACTION TYPE
DUMBWAITER

MINIMUMS:
6" WITH SLIDE DOWN DOOR
8" + 1/2H WITH BI-PART DOORS

OVERHEAD SHEAVE

LOADING DOOR OPENING = TOTAL CAR HEIGHT + 4"

2'-6"

TOP FLOOR

UNDERSLUNG SHEAVE

MAX. RISE = 30'-6"

ACCESS DOOR

2'-10"

HOISTWAY SECTION – DRUM TYPE
DUMBWAITER

CAR MAY OPEN ON EITHER SIDE IF REQUIRED

CLR. OPNG. = E

PLAN– (DRUM OR TRACTION TYPE)
DUMBWAITER

10'-6" TO 12'-2" DEPENDING ON TYPE OF INSTALLATION & LOCAL CODES

TOP FLOOR

LIGHT FIXTURE

INTERMEDIATE FLOOR

MAX. RISE = 35'-0"

INTERMEDIATE FLOOR

BOTTOM FLOOR

PIT 3'-3"

HOISTWAY SECTION
RESIDENCE ELEVATOR

2'-3"   6"

COUNTER-WEIGHT

MACHINE SPACE

CLEAR OPNG.

7 1/2"   6 1/2"

3'-0"

PLAN – RESIDENCE ELEVATOR

DUMBWAITER CAR SIZE

w	d
1'-8"	1'-4"
	1'-8"
2'-0"	1'-8"
	2'-0"
	2'-6"
	3'-0"
2'-6"	2'-0"
	2'-6"
	3'-0"
	3'-6"
3'-0"	2'-6"
	3'-0"
3'-6"	2'-6"

DUMBWAITERS (SEE MFRS. CATALOG FOR MAX. LOAD)

CAR HGTS. & CLEARANCE	TRACTION TYPE		DRUM TYPE
	CNTRWT. AT REAR	CNTRWT. AT SIDE **	
Platform clearance in hoistway	A = 6"	A = 8"	A = 6"
	B = 6"	B = 6"	B = 6"
	C = 2"	C = 6"	C = 2"
	† D = 4"	† D = 4"	† D = 4"
Standard car heights	3'-0"	3'-0"	2'-6"
	3'-6"	3'-6"	3'-0"
	4'-0"	4'-0"	4'-0"
Standard under counter car heights			2'-6"
			3'-0"

GENERAL NOTES

All dimensions should be verified with the particular dumbwaiter manufacturer.
Clear opening dimension (E): upper landing same as car width: lower landing (for car removal), car width + 4".
Maximum allowable size for dumbwaiters: 48" height; 9 sq. ft. floor area.
* See local code for minimum override dimension.
** Counterweight can be located at either side of hoistway.
† Dimension D allows clearance for hatchway doors only. Consult manufacturer for additional clearance required for car gates. Hinged hatchway door also available.

Roy F. Deng; The Perkins and Will Partnership; Chicago, Illinois

RESIDENCE ELEVATOR (Speed 35 ft./min.)

Rated Passenger Capacity	Platform		Hoistway		Hoistway door
	w width	d depth	W Width	D Depth	clear opng.
Two	3'-0"	3'-0"	4'-2"	3'-11"	2'-4"
Four or wheel-chair & attend.	3'-4"	4'-4"	4'-6"	5'-3"	2'-8"

Platform sizes available from 2'-3" wide x 2'-7" deep to 3'-5" wide x 4'-4" deep. Standard door 7'-0" high.
* Contingent upon type of safety.

Escalators are the most efficient form of vertical transportation for very heavy traffic and where the number of floors served is limited, normally five to six floors maximum. Escalators are not usually accepted as required exit.

Owner provides and installs: All supports including bearing plates if concrete beams are used, manhole and ladder to pit for basement stairways, lamp receptacles and convenience outlet in machine room and at each access door, light and power supply, vent grilles and various other items described in manufacturers catalogs.

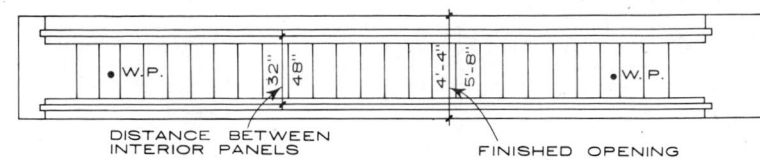

DISTANCE BETWEEN INTERIOR PANELS

FINISHED OPENING

PLAN

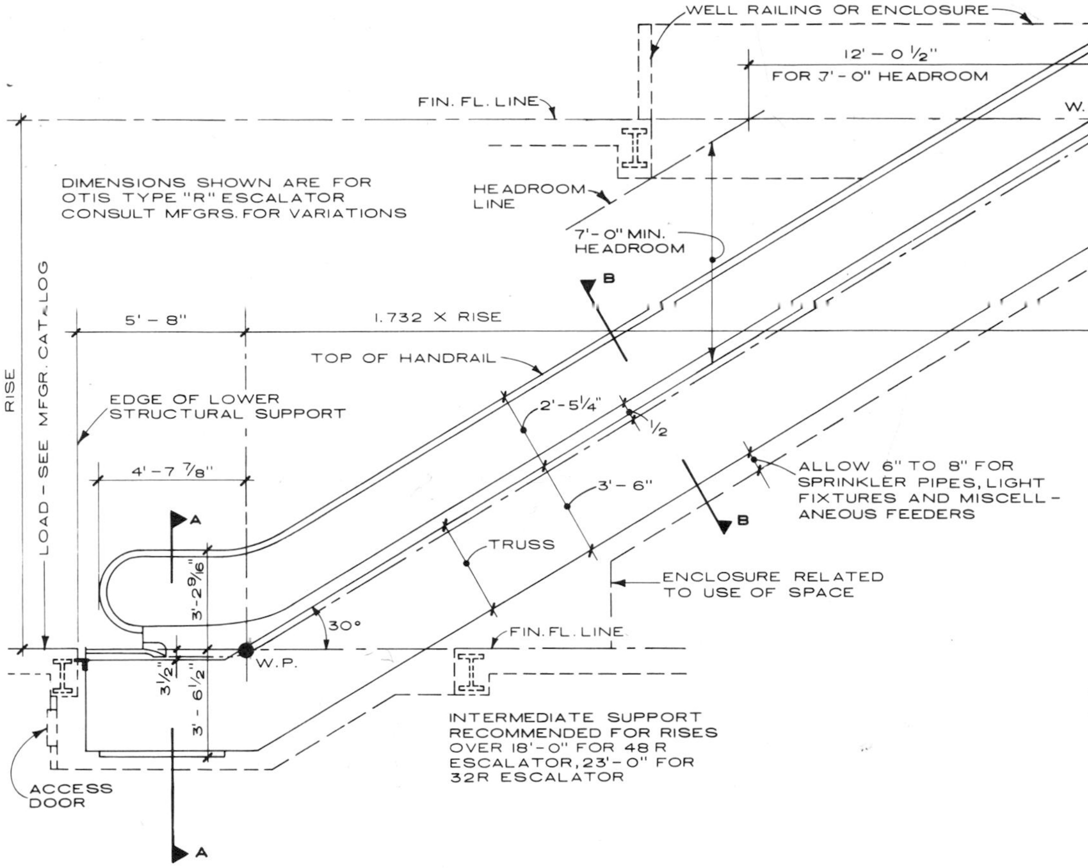

WELL RAILING OR ENCLOSURE

LOAD - SEE MANUFACTURERS' CATALOG

12'-0 1/2"
FOR 7'-0" HEADROOM

5'-5 1/8"

FIN. FL. LINE

W.P.

3'-2 9/16"
3 1/2

MACHINE SPACE

HEADROOM LINE

4'-0 1/4"

DIMENSIONS SHOWN ARE FOR OTIS TYPE "R" ESCALATOR CONSULT MFGRS. FOR VARIATIONS

7'-0" MIN. HEADROOM

VENTILATION FOR MACHINE SPACE

5'-8"

1.732 X RISE

9'-2"

EDGE OF LOWER STRUCTURAL SUPPORT

TOP OF HANDRAIL

EDGE OF UPPER STRUCTURAL SUPPORT

RISE

LOAD - SEE MFGR. CATALOG

4'-7 7/8"

2'-5 1/4"

1/2

3'-6"

ALLOW 6" TO 8" FOR SPRINKLER PIPES, LIGHT FIXTURES AND MISCELLANEOUS FEEDERS

SPEED OF STEPS ALONG INCLINE = 90 FT. PER MIN. OR 120 FT. PER MIN. RATED CAPACITY AT 90 FPM. 5000 PERSONS PER HOUR (32R) 8000 PERSONS PER HOUR (48R)

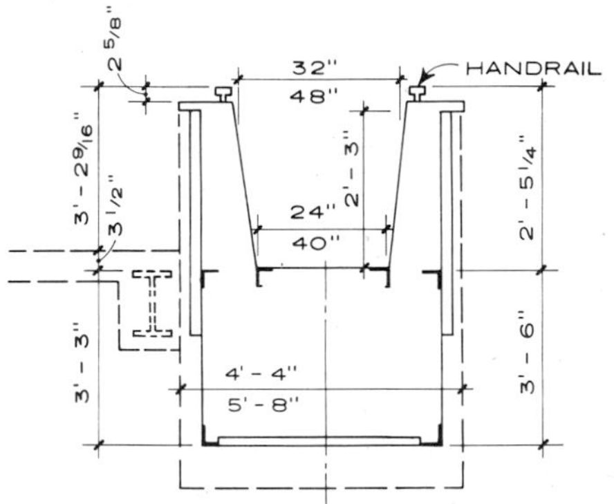

3'-2 9/16"

TRUSS

ENCLOSURE RELATED TO USE OF SPACE

30°

FIN. FL. LINE

W.P.

3 1/2
3'-6 1/2"
3'-6"

INTERMEDIATE SUPPORT RECOMMENDED FOR RISES OVER 18'-0" FOR 48R ESCALATOR, 23'-0" FOR 32R ESCALATOR

32"
48"

HANDRAIL

2 5/8"

3'-2 9/16"
3 1/2

24"
40"

2'-3"

2'-5 1/4"

ACCESS DOOR

3"
3"

4'-4"
5'-8"

3'-6"

ELEVATION

HALF SECT. A - A   HALF SECT. B - B

REVERSIBLE ESCALATOR

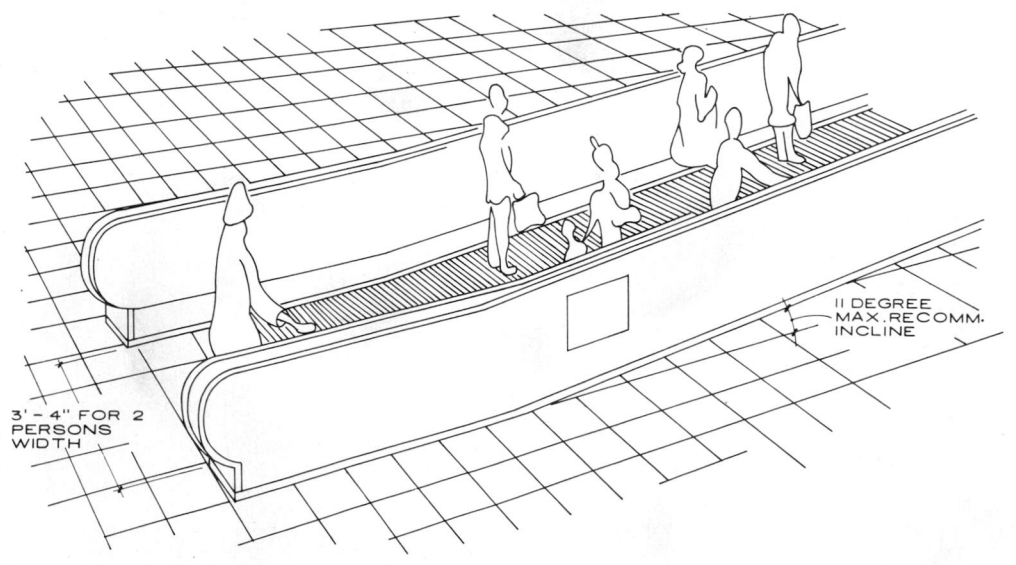

3'-4" FOR 2 PERSONS WIDTH

11 DEGREE MAX. RECOMM. INCLINE

A further step in the development of horizontal and vertical transportation in the extension of the principal lanes of circulation or transportation is the continuous moving passenger conveyor or belt.

The conveyor operates at speeds of either 90 or 120 feet per minute, with 120 feet per minute being the maximum. The safety codes under certain conditions allow a 15 degree incline and speeds up to 180 feet per minute.

Moving passenger conveyors will be found most useful in buildings where large groups of people must move long distances horizontally and go up or down a short rise, such as in air or other transportation terminals, connections between terminals, stadiums, and arenas.

MOVING PASSENGER CONVEYORS

GENERAL NOTES:

Pneumatic Tube Systems: Use of pneumatic tube systems, under vacuum or pressure, allows transmission of paper, small articles and liquids in "carrier" tubes to and from predetermined stations.

Applicable systems are commercial offices and stores; industrial plants, warehouses and air and rail stations;

banks; hospitals and laboratories. Care should be taken in the latter instances to exclude services in areas where centrifuge action in transmitted liquids is undesirable.

Installation of Systems: Systems can be placed anywhere in or about the area served, exposed or furred in structure, outside or underground. Lines exposed to weather or

through refrigerated spaces must be protected and insulated to prevent condensation in the system. Subsurface installations should be placed in corrugated pipe below the frost line, and tubing should be mill wrapped and joints welded and protected with mill wrap tape and pressure tested.

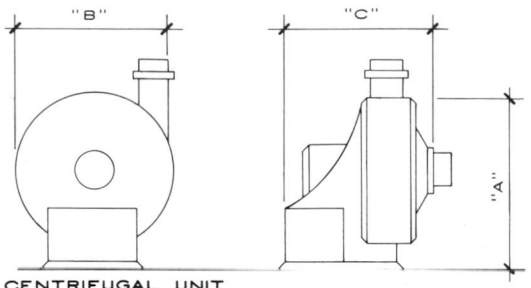

CENTRIFUGAL UNIT

CENTRIFUGAL EXHAUSTERS AND BLOWERS (This chart shows only extremes for each case.)

VACUUM	RPM	HP	A	B	C	VACUUM	RPM	HP	A	B	C
12 oz.	3500	1 min.	30	29	20	20 oz.	3500	1 1/2 min.	36	35	20
		5 max.	36	35	27			15 max.	46	41	42
	1750	7 1/2 min.	54	54	34		1750	7 1/2 min.	54	54	38
		50 max.	93	79	54			60 max.	80	67	60
16 oz.	3500	1 min.	30	29	20	24 oz.	3500	1 1/2 min.	36	35	22
		10 max.	42	42	31			25 max.	59	54	46
	1750	7 1/2 min.	54	54	30		1750	7 1/2 min.	54	54	36
		75 max.	92	80	60			75 max.	80	67	60

Used indoor or outside, centrifugal types operate on vacuum or vacuum and pressure combinations. Quieter than most types, they are recommended except where

long lines are to be used or where reversible action is required. Sizes vary with horsepower of motor, vacuum and r.p.m.

POWER UNITS FOR VACUUM OR PRESSURE

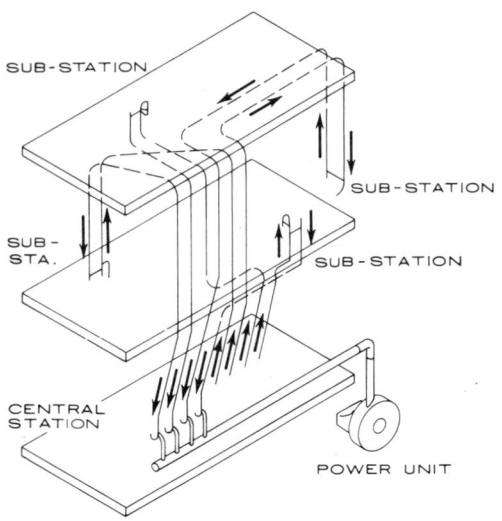

VACUUM TYPE INDEPENDENT TWIN LINE

This system may dispatch carriers from all stations simultaneously with continuous, nearly unlimited transaction. It may have any number of stations since independent lines run to and from all stations. It is considered to be most efficient, low in maintenance cost, and is the quietest system.

VACUUM TYPE COMBINATION LINE

This system may dispatch carriers from the central station to all sub-stations via separate lines, but return lines are common. Where intermittent service is satisfactory, such as in mail order houses and industrial plants, this system may be used to advantage.

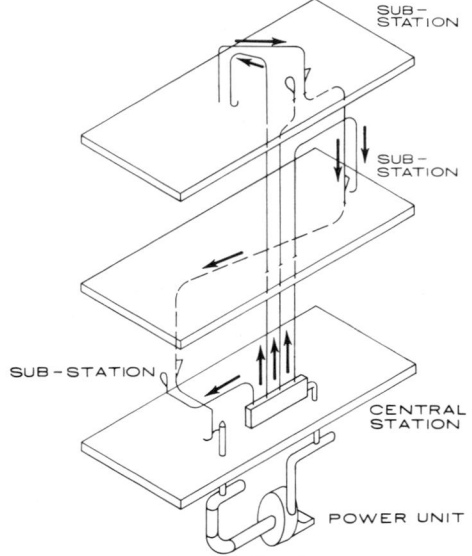

VACUUM-PRESSURE TYPE COMBINATION LINE

This system utilizes both vacuum and pressure. It is economical of power and of length of return lines. It is necessary that the number of open ends be the same for the vacuum as for the pressure lines. Provides quick service. Its use is restricted to mercantile houses, drug, grocery and meat packing plants, and similar types of buildings.

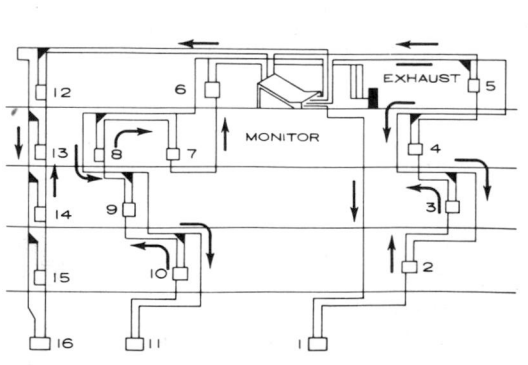

AUTOMATIC SELECTIVE SYSTEM

LWH; King and King; Syracuse, New York

NOTE:

This system operates automatically once the carrier's adjustable ring is set for the proper destination. Within seconds electromechanical switching carries the carrier to the correct station. First, the carrier travels by vacuum to the central station where it is automatically tested to determine the correct line and station. This is done by relays and selectors which establish the path the carrier is to follow to reach its destination. If the carrier is set by mistake for a nonexistent station, it will be discharged into a "reject" tube at the central station. A signal light and bell will indicate an error. This system provides for quicker delivery with less chance of error. It yields economy of length of line. Typical buildings which might find this type suitable are hotels, airline terminals, railroad stations, hospitals, industry.

CARRIER STATISTICS

SIZE	FIGURE	DESCRIPTION	BODY MATERIAL	CLEAR INSIDE LENGTH	CLEAR INSIDE DIMENSIONS	MINIMUM RADIUS BEND
1 1/2"	1	Message	Fiber	5 1/8"	15/16"	15"
	2	Cash	Brass	3 15/16"	1 5/8"	14"
	3	Telegram	Plastic	4 1/4"	1 3/8"	14"
2 1/4" O.D.	4	Message	Plastic	6"	1 3/8"	24"
	4	Message	Plastic	9"	1 3/8"	42"
	4	Message	Plastic	10"	1 3/8"	42"
	6	Utility	Rubber	6"	1 3/8"	24"
	6	Utility	Rubber	9"	1 3/8"	42"
	6	Utility	Rubber	10"	1 3/8"	42"
3" O.D.	5	Message	Plastic	9"	2"	30"
	5	Message	Plastic	10"	2"	48"
	5	Message	Plastic	11"	2"	48"
	6	Utility	Rubber	9"	1 15/16"	30"
	6	Utility	Rubber	10"	1 15/16"	48"
	6	Utility	Rubber	11"	1 15/16"	48"
	7	Test Piece	Steel	9 1/2"	2"	48
	15	Message	Fiberglass	11"	1 3/4"	48"
4" O.D.	5	Message	Plastic	10"	2 3/4"	48"
	5	Message	Plastic	12"	2 3/4"	48"
	5	Message	Plastic	14"	2 3/4"	60"
	6	Message	Rubber	10"	2 11/16"	48"
	6	Message	Rubber	12"	2 11/16"	48"
	6	Message	Rubber	14"	2 11/16"	60"
	7	Test Piece	Steel	Varies	Varies	48"
	8	Punch Card	Alum.	Varies	3 3/8"	48"
	9	Blueprint	Alum.	42"	2 3/8"	SPCL.
	13	Bottle	Leather	Varies	Varies	48"
	16	Message	Plastic	12"	2 13/16"	48"
	16	Message	Plastic	12 1/2"	2 13/16"	60"
	17	X-ray	Plastic	14 1/2"	2"	48"
6" O.D.	11	Utility	Plastic	15 1/2"	4 5/8"	72"
	14	Message	Plastic	14 3/4"	4 1/2"	48"
4" x 7"	12	Message	Plastic	14 5/16"	2 9/16" x 5 9/16"	48"
	18	Message	Plastic	14 5/16"	2 1/2" x 5 9/16"	48"
4" x 12"	10	Utility	Alum.	15"	2 9/16" x 10 7/16"	60"
5" x 13"	10	Utility	Alum.	15 7/8"	3" x 11"	60"

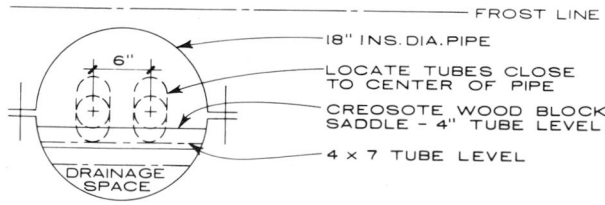

FROST LINE
18" INS. DIA. PIPE
6"
LOCATE TUBES CLOSE TO CENTER OF PIPE
CREOSOTE WOOD BLOCK SADDLE - 4" TUBE LEVEL
4 x 7 TUBE LEVEL
DRAINAGE SPACE

DETAIL OF PIPE BELOW GROUND

TUBE STANDARDS

SIZE TUBE O.D.	MAT.L.	NET WGT. PER FOOT Lbs.	STAND LENGTH	WALL THICKNESS GA.	WALL THICKNESS DIM.
1 1/2"	Steel	.55	15'-0"	20	.035"
2 1/4"	Steel	.85	15'-0"	20	.035"
3"	Steel	1.36	15'-0"	19	.042"
4"	Steel	2.75	15'-0"	16	.065"
6"	Steel	4.00	15'-0"	16	.065"
4" x 7"	Steel	4.54	15'-0"	16	.065"
4" x 12"	Steel	9.00	10'-0"	14	.078"
5" x 13"	Steel	13.15	10'-0"	12	.109"

LWH & RWL; King and King; Syracuse, New York

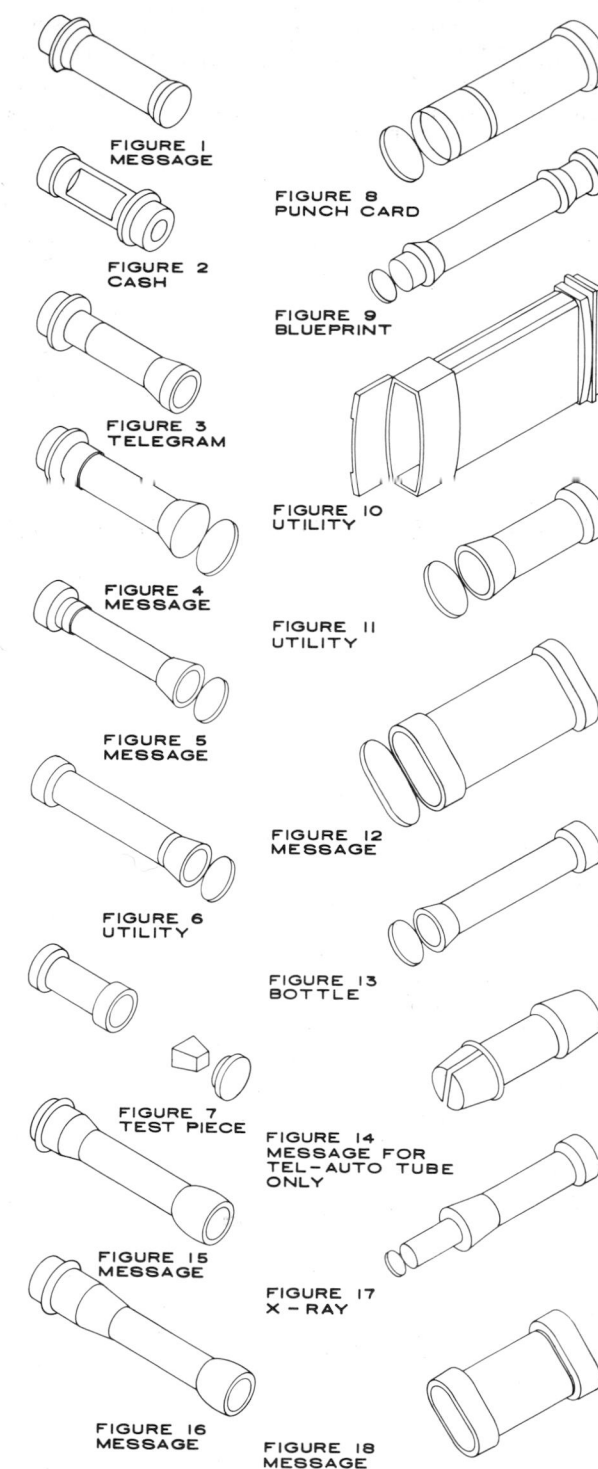

FIGURE 1 MESSAGE
FIGURE 2 CASH
FIGURE 3 TELEGRAM
FIGURE 4 MESSAGE
FIGURE 5 MESSAGE
FIGURE 6 UTILITY
FIGURE 7 TEST PIECE
FIGURE 8 PUNCH CARD
FIGURE 9 BLUEPRINT
FIGURE 10 UTILITY
FIGURE 11 UTILITY
FIGURE 12 MESSAGE
FIGURE 13 BOTTLE
FIGURE 14 MESSAGE FOR TEL-AUTO TUBE ONLY
FIGURE 15 MESSAGE
FIGURE 16 MESSAGE
FIGURE 17 X-RAY
FIGURE 18 MESSAGE

TYPES OF CARRIERS

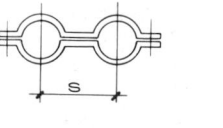

ROUND
S 1 1/2" Size = 2 1/2"
2 1/4 Size = 3" + 3 3/4"
3" Size = 4-1/4"
4" Size = 6"
6" Size = 9"

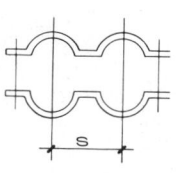

OVAL
S 4" x 7" Size = 6"

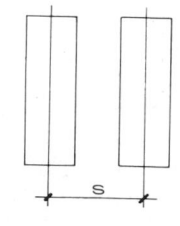

RECTANGLE
S 4" x 12" Size = 6"
5" x 13" Size = 9"

STANDARD TUBE SPACING

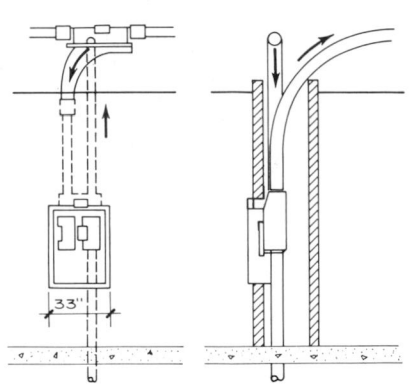

DOWN DISCHARGE TERMINALS

GENERAL NOTES:

A carrier, placed in the sending side of the loop at any one of 16 sending-receiving stations shown at right, will be conveyed swiftly and directly to any one of the other 15. No human element enters to delay or impede the carrier's transit. An Automatic Monitor, in a matter of seconds, transfers the carrier to its correct receiving tube . . . then, an electrically controlled deflector in the receiving tube, delivers the carrier into its ordered station. Such a system has much to recommend it to any user. First, an Automatic System eliminates operating personnel at a Central Station. Not only does this automatic device speed carrier delivery but also permits 24 hour a day communications service, 7 days a week without supervision. Second, by grouping sending-receiving sub-stations along one or more twin-tube loops, 2 airtubes can service all 5 sub-stations as illustrated. The same 2 airtubes could service all 10 sub-stations if that maximum number were located on a given loop. This design effects a tangible saving in space, materials and labor. It also sharply reduces problems encountered when installing a system in existing structures.

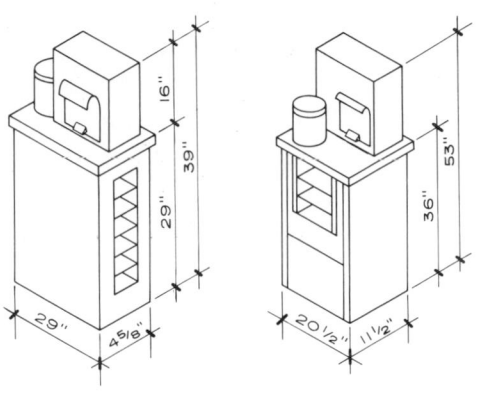

PEDESTALS FOR 2¼" PNEUMATIC TERMINALS

Down Discharge Terminals can be recessed in walls with only dispatching and receiving doors exposed. Can be used for all automatic selective systems.

Pedestal for 2¼" Pneumatic terminals have steel cabinet bases with carrier storage under top. Sending inlet on opposite end.

Pedestals for Down Discharge closed receiver terminals for conventional or sutomatic systems are supplied with base units 20½" wide, 11½" deep, 36" to countertop and an overall height of 53" on 2¼" and 3" systems or an overall height of 56" on 4" systems.
conventional or automatic systems are supplied with base

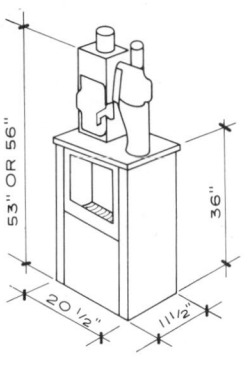

PEDESTAL FOR DOWN DISCHARGE CLOSED RECEIVER TERMINAL

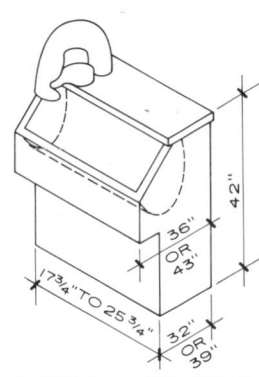

PEDESTAL FOR OVER DELIVERY CARRIER RECEIVING STATION

Pedestal for Over delivery carrier receiving stations have belt sling type pocket sizes available for 2¼", 3" and 4" two station systems. 2¼" and 3" system pedestals are 18" wide and 36" deep; 4" system pedestals are 26" wide by 43" deep.

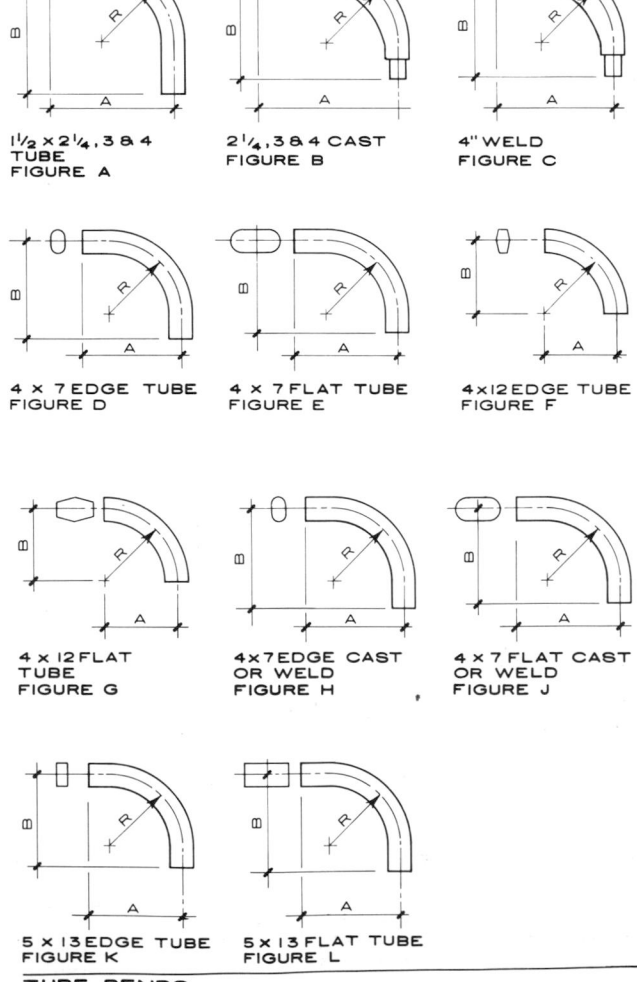

TUBE BENDS

TUBE BENDS: CARRIER LENGTHS AND TYPES

SIZE	FIG.	12	A	B	MAT'L.	GA.	CARRIER LENGTH AND TYPE
1 1/2"	A	15	21	21	Steel	20	5 1/8" Type #1
2 1/4"	A	14	19	20	Steel	20	Varies, Types #2 and 3
	A	18	22	26	Steel	20	Varies, Types #2 and 3
	A	24	30	33	Steel	20	6" Type 4 and 6
	A	42	50	50	Steel	20	10" Type 4 and 6
	B	7 1/2	8 3/8	8 3/8	Cast		Varies, Types #2 and 3
	B	15	17 3/4	17 3/4	Cast		9" Type 4 and 6
3"	A	30	36	36	Steel	19	9" Type 5 and 6
	A	48	54	56	Steel	19	11" Type 5, 6 and 15
	B	24	28	28	Cast		11" Type 5, 6 and 15
4"	A	48	54	86	Steel	16	10" and 12" Types 5, 6, 13
	A	60	65	80	Steel	16	14" Type 5, 6, 13
	B	24	28	28	Cast		14" Type 5, 6, 8, 13 + 16
	C	23	32 1/2	32 1/2	Weld		14" Type 5, 6, 8, 13 + 16
6"	A	48			Steel	16	14 3/4" Type 14
	A	72			Steel	16	15 1/2" Type 11
4 X 7 Edge	D	60	72	74	Steel	16	14 5/16" Type 12 + 18
4 X 7 Flat	E	60	72	74	Steel	16	14 5/16" Type 12 + 18
4 X 7 Edge	H	24	29	29	Cast		14 5/16" Type 12 + 18
4 X 7 Flat	J	24	29	29	Cast		14 5/16" Type 12 + 18
4 X 7 Edge	H	24	32	32	Weld		14 5/16" Type 12 + 18
4 X 7 Flat	J	24	32	32	Weld		14 5/16" Type 12 + 18
4 X 12 Edge	F	60	60	60	Steel	14	15" Type 10
4 X 12 Flat	G	60	60	60	Steel	14	15" Type 10
5 X 13 Edge	K	60	66	66	Steel	12	15 7/8" Type 10
5 X 13 Flat	L	60	66	66	Steel	12	15 7/8" Type 10

LWH; King and King; Syracuse, New York

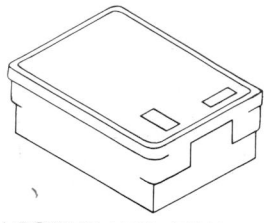

LOCKING MAIL TRAY

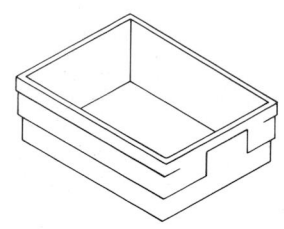

BASIC MODULE TRAY

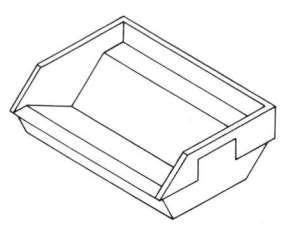

BOOK TRAY

PLASTIC TRAY MODULE TYPES

Fiberglas plastic tray modules are available for all types of services. Standard trays are 16 1/2" long, 12" wide, and 10" high. Also available with locking covers and special compartmental inserts, they can be used for mail distribution in offices as well as in hospital service where special sterilization trays are used. Book trays are available with special sloped bottom form for easy reference stacking, having applications in libraries. Sizes and types are also available for other special services.

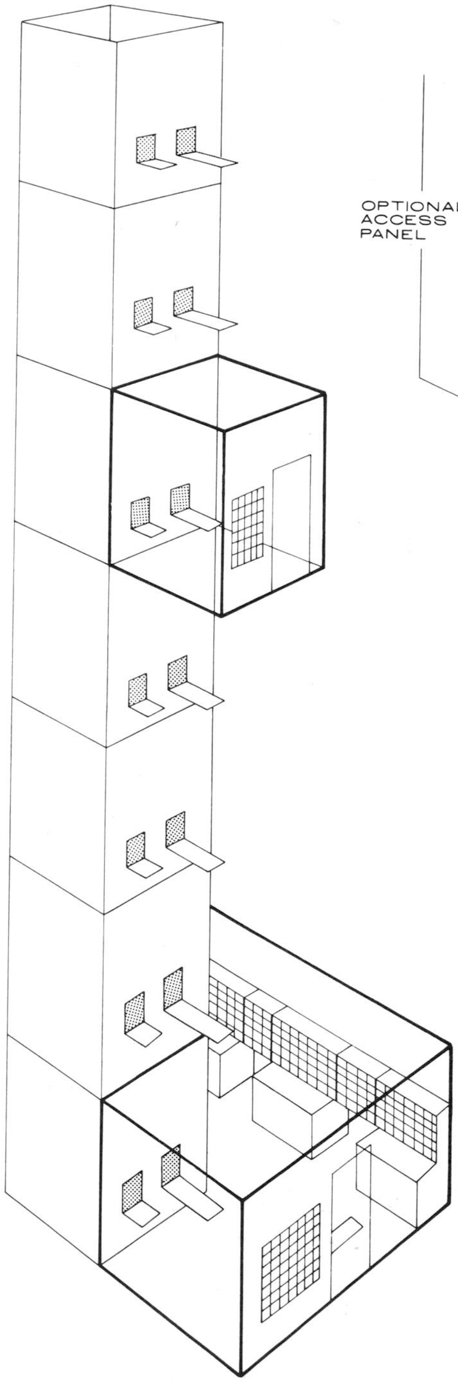

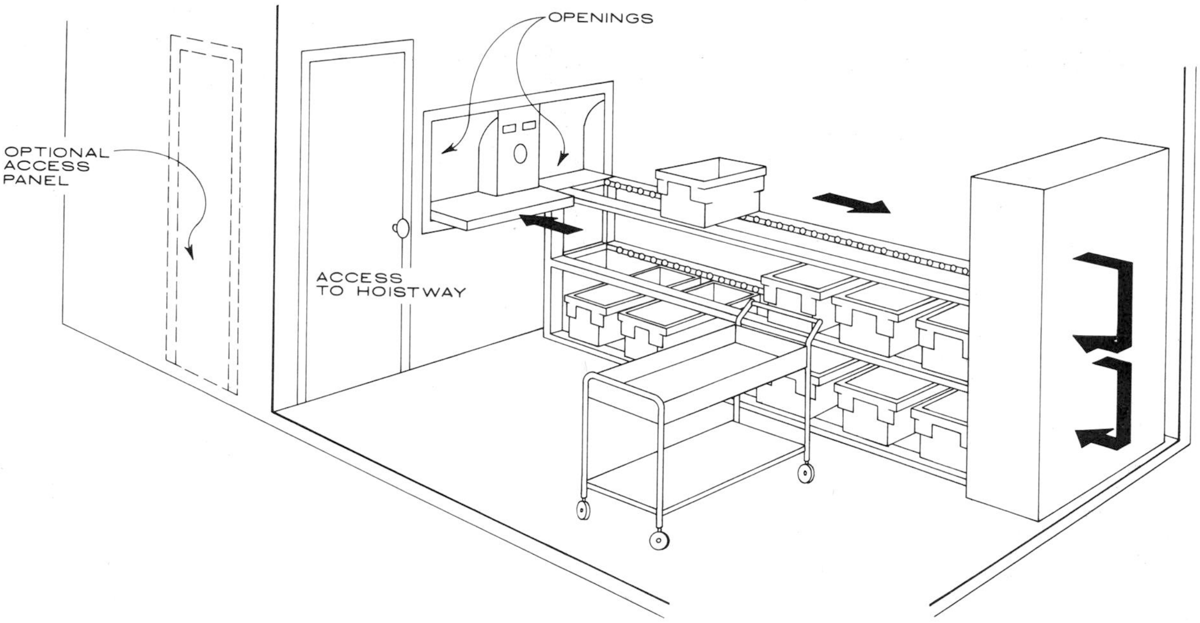

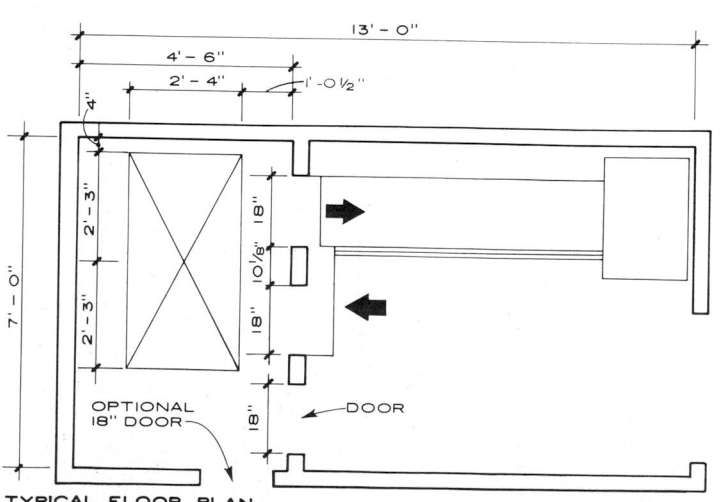

OPENINGS

OPTIONAL ACCESS PANEL

ACCESS TO HOISTWAY

SELECTIVE VERTICAL CONVEYORS

Bulk transmission between vertical and horizontal points in large structures can be accomplished by continuous electric conveyors with automatic loading and unloading at selected substations on any floors. With hourly capacities up to 18 tons, records and mail in office buildings, books in libraries, and bulk packaging and basic patient needs in hospitals can be carried throughout structures.

Several selective verticals can be interconnected with horizontal conveyors to effect a unified three-dimensional conveyor system; carrying modules can be routed automatically from one vertical to another. Remote substations can be connected to the main system by horizontal conveyors in ceiling spaces, with short vertical drops to selected substation work areas.

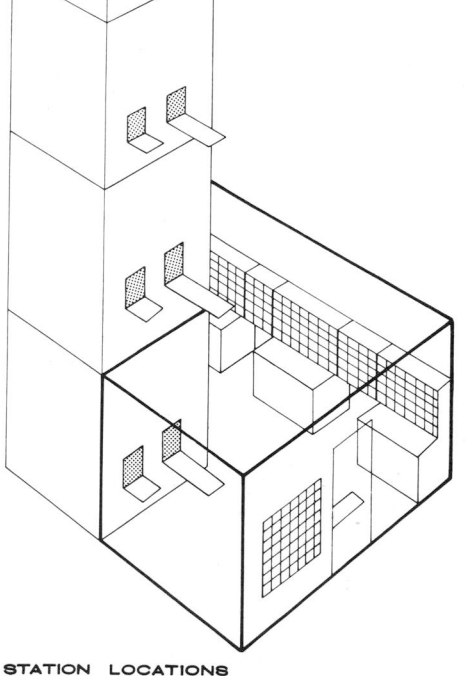

STATION LOCATIONS

Stations can be on any or all floors. Mail systems can be developed thus with central station at grade floor and substations at any upper or lower floors.

LWH & GFL; King and King; Syracuse, New York

TYPICAL FLOOR PLAN

13' - 0"

4' - 6"

2' - 4"

1' - 0 1/2"

4"

2' - 3"

7' - 0"

18"

10 1/8"

18"

2' - 3"

OPTIONAL 18" DOOR

DOOR

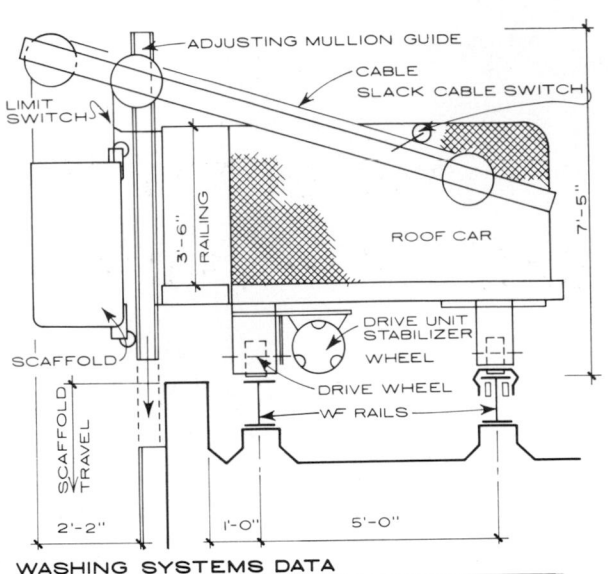

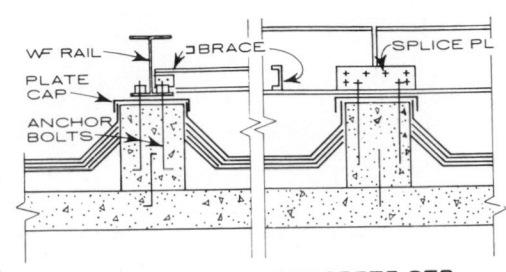

RAIL INSTALLATION-CONCRETE STR.

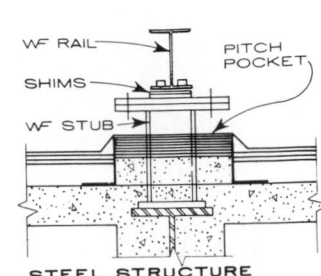

STEEL STRUCTURE

WASHING SYSTEMS DATA

High-rise equipment 400'–450' & over	Speed 60–70 F.P.M.	Suspended scaffold roof hoist	Provide wall guides and intermediate cable stabilizers
Intermediate rise equipt. 130'–150' to 400'–450'	Speed 35 + F.P.M.	Suspended scaffold roof hoist	Provide wall guides
Low rise equipment up to 130'–150'	Speed 35 F.P.M.	Climber scaffold roof davits	Angle cables to hold scaffold against wall face

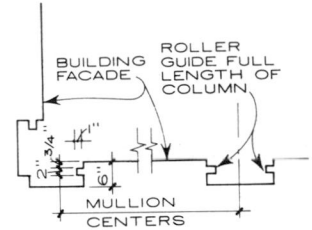

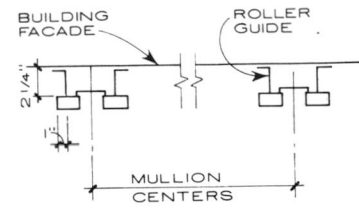

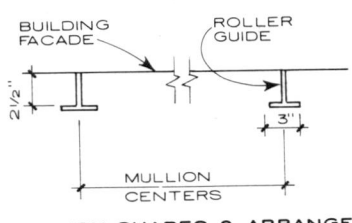

MULLION SHAPES & ARRANGEMENTS

ROOF MOUNTED WINDOW WASHING SYSTEMS

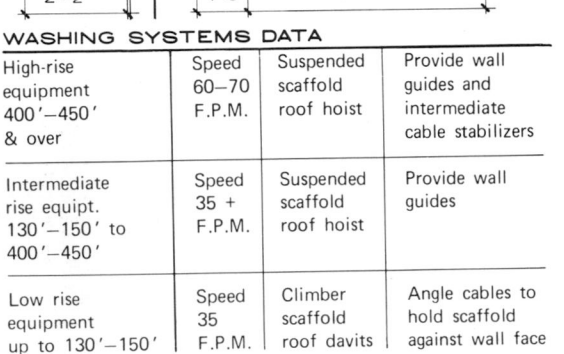

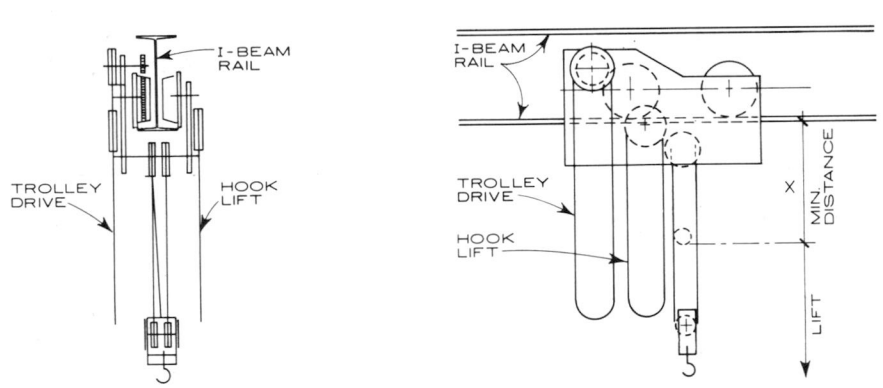

TROLLEY HOISTS (FOR MATERIALS HANDLING ONLY)

PLAN

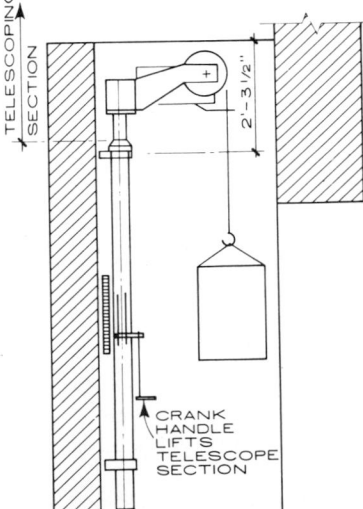

SECTION
ASH HOIST-SIDEWALK LEVEL TYPE

TROLLEY HOIST DATA

Capacity in Tons	Standard Lift–Feet	X	Standard I-Beam	Min. Curve Radius
1/4	8	8 1/2"	5"	3'–6"
1/2	8	8 1/2"	5"	3'–6"
1	8	11 1/4"	6"	3'–6"
1 1/2	8	13"	7"	3'–6"
2	9	15 1/8"	8"	4'–6"
3	10	18 3/4"	10"	5'–0"
4	10	21 3/4"	10"	7'–6"
5	12	25"	12"	7'–6"
6	12	25"	12"	7'–6"
8	12	31 3/8"	15"	8'–0"
10	12	39"	15"	8'–0"

Charles C. Ormsby, AIA; Quinlivan, Pierik & Krause, AIA; Syracuse, New York

MECHANICAL / ELECTRICAL

ARCHITECTURAL GRAPHIC STANDARDS AND THE UNIFORM SYSTEM

Within the limits of Architectural Graphic Standards' fundamental emphasis on graphic presentation of design and construction information, the contents of this edition are arranged in Chapters substantially paralleling the sixteen Divisions of the Uniform System for Construction Specifications, Data Filing & Cost Accounting.

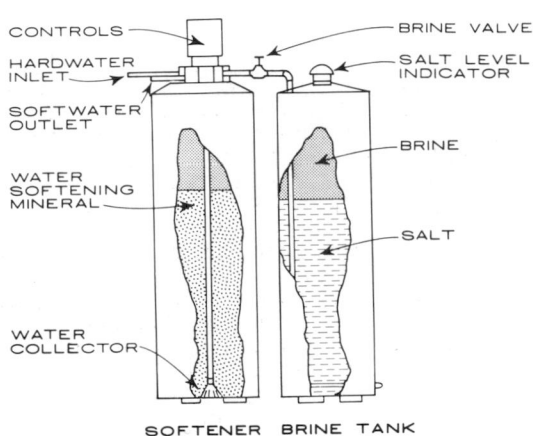

SOFTENER   BRINE TANK

CROSS – SECTION OF TYPICAL TWO TANK WATER SOFTENER SEMI – AUTOMATIC

NOTES:

Water hardness is caused by calcium and magnesium salts and is usually expressed in grains per gallon. For example: New York City 1–5 grains (low); Grand Rapids, Mich. 9 grains (5–9 moderate); Jacksonville, Fla. 18 grains (over 9 high); well water 0–50 grains.

A water softener is typically one tank for manual operation and two adjacent or concentric tanks with automatic controls. To determine the proper size softener for a residence, use this formula:

No. of people x 50 gal. (75 if 3 or more baths) = Gal. of water used/day;
Gal. of water/day x No. of days of service = Gal. of soft water needed;
Gal. of soft water x Hardness (grains/ gal. = Capacity of softener needed.

If the capacity found necessary by this formula is too large, reduce the number of days of service and the softener will need to be regenerated more often. The table given lists data for residential size softeners. If a softener is needed for use in another building type, consult a manufacturer. Rental equipment with service plans are available in some areas, and responsibility for design adequacy should be assumed by the renting company.

When water supplies contain suspended matter, a filter should be placed at the hard water inlet. The softening process often may remove any taste the water can have, but filters can also correct bad taste, acidity, or odor problems which are caused by other salts and minerals.

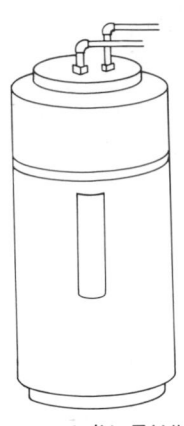

TANK-IN-TANK AUTO. MODEL

TYPICAL MANUFACTURERS' DATA

Characteristics	Expressed In	Models		
Regeneration Method	—	Fully-Auto.[1]	Semi-Auto.[2]	Manual[3]
Capacity	grains	18,000	25,000	50,000
Service flow rate	gallons	10	7.5	8
Rinse flow rate	gallons	.7	.5	1.0
Ion exchanger	cu. ft.	1.0	.85	1.7
Salt per regeneration	pounds	5.5	10	30
Regeneration time	minutes	60	120	90
Service piping	inches	1	3/4	3/4
Waste piping	inches	3/8	3/4	1/2
Pressure range	pounds	25-100	25-100	25-100
Electric current	volts	110-60cy	110-60cy	—
Resin tank diameter	inches	9-3/16	9	12
Bed area	sq. ft.	.442	.44	.78
Shipping weight	pounds	100	116	197
Floor space	inches	22x30	11x15	13x18
Overall height	inches	43-3/4	44-3/4	54

1. Complete regeneration by time clock.
2. Manually operated switch to start regeneration.
3. Complete manual regeneration by adding dry pellet type salt directly into the softener.

WATER SOFTENENERS

Corinne Williams; Ballard Todd Associates; New York, New York

TANK AND CISTERN CAPACITIES IN GALLONS

DEPTH FEET	SQUARE TANKS			ROUND TANKS			
	8'	10'	12'	8'	10'	12'	14'
4	1,920	3,000	4,320	1,500	2,350	3,380	4,610
6	2,880	4,500	6,480	2,250	3,520	5,070	6,920
8	3,840	6,000	8,640	3,000	4,700	6,760	9,220
10	—	7,500	10,800	3,760	5,870	8,460	11,520
12	—	—	12,960	4,510	7,040	10,150	13,830

AVERAGE DAILY HUMAN CONSUMPTION
50 TO 100 GALLONS PER PERSON

AVERAGE DAILY LIVESTOCK CONSUMPTION
EACH MILK COW....................35 GAL.
EACH STEER OR DRY COW..12 GAL.
EACH HORSE..........................12 GAL.
EACH HOG...............................4 GAL.
EACH SHEEP...........................2 GAL.
EACH 100 CHICKENS..............4 GAL.

A = 3" MINIMUM COARSE SAND
B = 3" MINIMUM 1/8" – 3/8" GRAVEL
C = 3" MINIMUM 3/4" – 1 1/4" GRAVEL

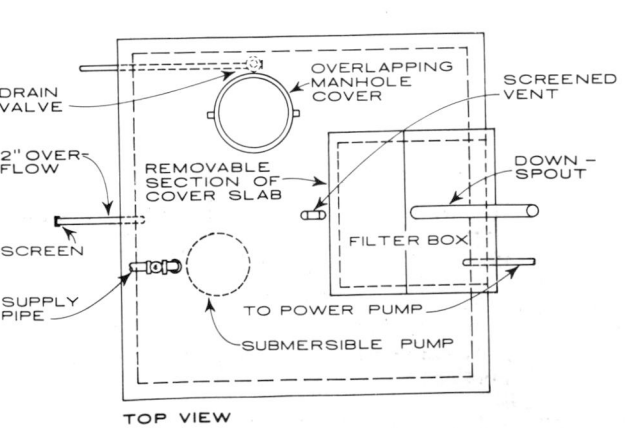

TOP VIEW

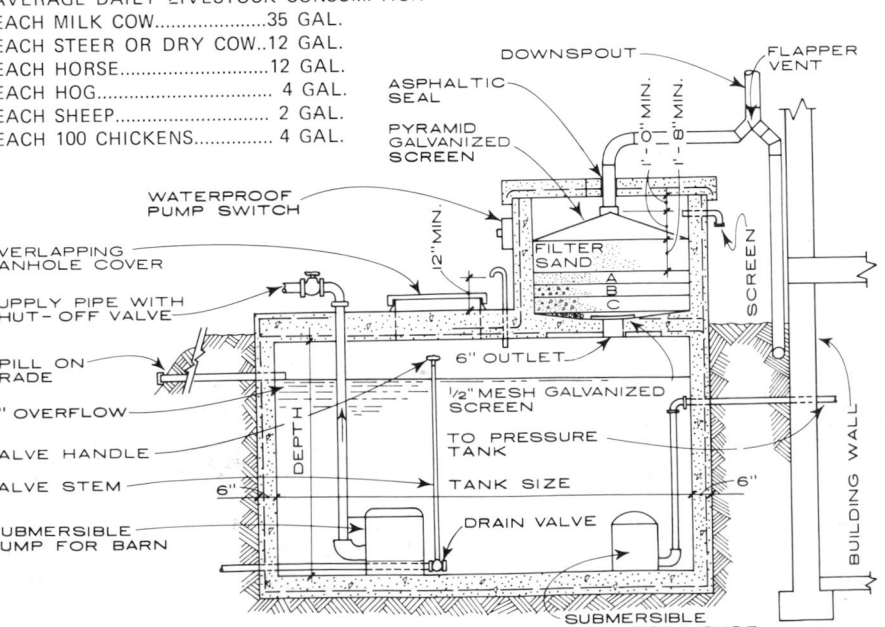

CROSS SECTION

CISTERN FOR RAINWATER STORAGE

Fitzhugh Donnally, Jr.; Frank J. Sullivan Associates; Washington, D. C.

Smith, Hinchman & Grylls Associates, Inc.; Detroit, Michigan

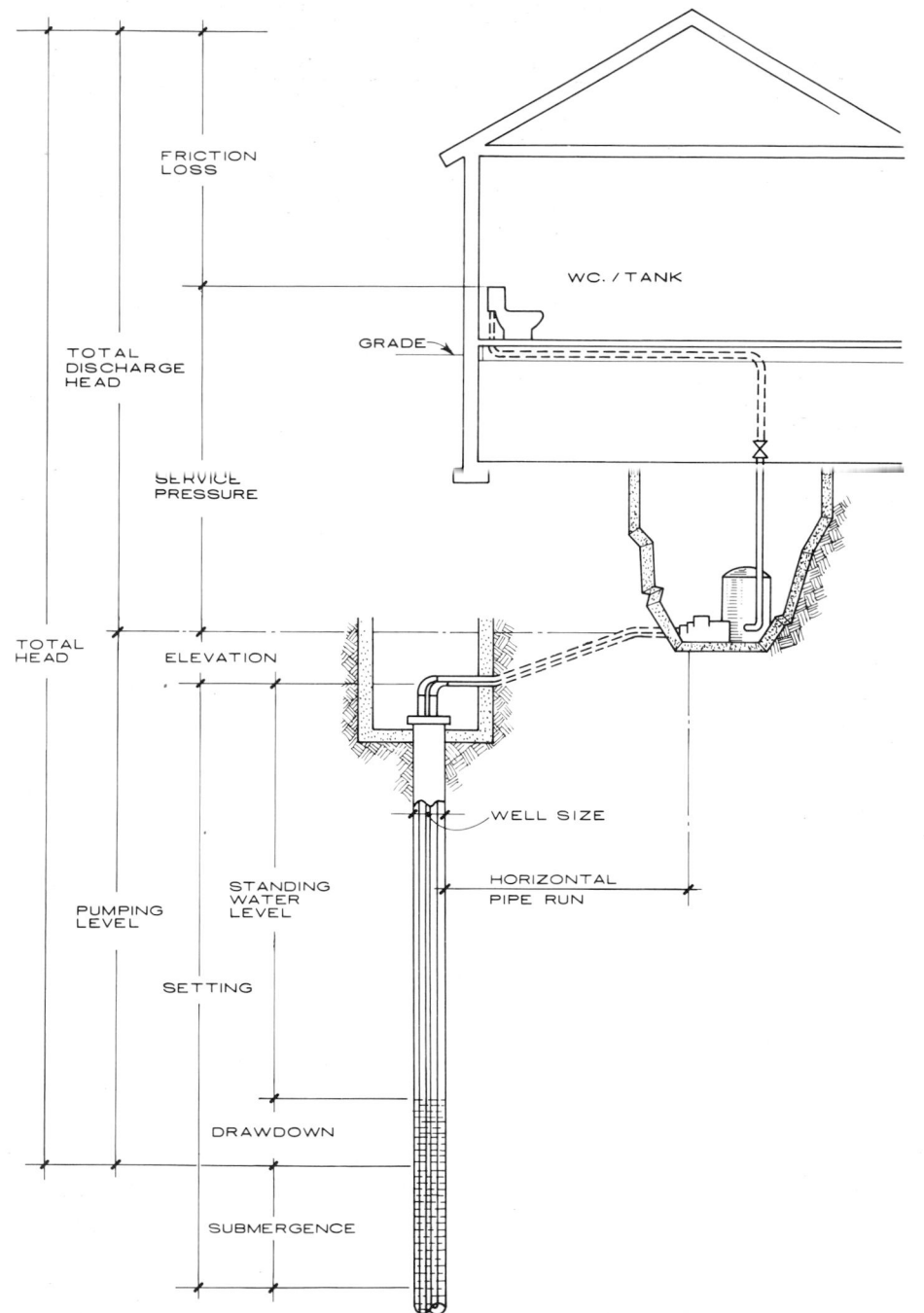

DIAGRAMMATIC SECTION

NOTES:

1. Where connection to a municipal water supply or public water system is not possible, it is essential that certain precautions be taken in the development of individual water supply. Consideration must be given to the geological and bacteriological factors affecting the quantity and quality of available water.

2. The minimum quantity of water to provide for domestic use should be not less than 50 gallons per person per day. Well and pumping equipment should be adequate to provide a minimum quantity of water at the rate of 5 gallons per minute for domestic use.

3. The well should be chlorinated after construction to remove any pathogenic bacteria and other disease-producing organisms. The water should be tested by the State or Local Health Department for possible bacteriological contents.

WELL CONSTRUCTION

TYPE	DEPTH	DIAMETER
DUG	10' to 40'	3' to 20'
BORED	25' to 50'	2'' to 32''
DRIVEN *	10' to 25'	1 1/4 '' to 4''
JETTED	50' to 100'	3'' to 8''
DRILLED	50' to 1500'	3'' to 8''

*Used only in porous soils or where water bearing strata of loose material exists in tight soils.

WELL LOCATION

TYPE OF SYSTEM	MINIMUM DISTANCE
BUILDING SEWER	50' — 0''
SEPTIC TANK	50' — 0''
DISPOSAL FIELD	100' — 0''
SEEPAGE PITS	100' — 0''
CESSPOOLS	150' — 0''

WELL PUMP SELECTION

NOTE: GPH = GALLONS PER HOUR

PUMP CAPACITY	WELL DEPTH: 0 TO 25 FT.	25 TO 60 FT.	60 TO 90 FT.	90 TO 150 FT.	150 FT. AND OVER
300 TO 600 GPH	Submersible Pump Jet Pump Piston Pump	Submersible Pump Jet Pump Deep Well Reciprocating Pump	Submersible Pump Jet Pump Deep Well Reciprocating Pump	Submersible Pump Jet Pump Deep Well Reciprocating Pump	Submersible Pump Jet Pump Deep Well Reciprocating Pump
600 TO 1200 GPH	Submersible Pump Jet Pump Plunger Pump	Submersible Pump Jet Pump	Submersible Pump Jet Pump	Submersible Pump Jet Pump	Submersible Pump
OVER 1200 GPH	Submersible Pump Jet Pump Plunger Pump	Submersible Pump Jet Pump	Submersible Pump Jet Pump	Submersible Pump	Submersible Pump

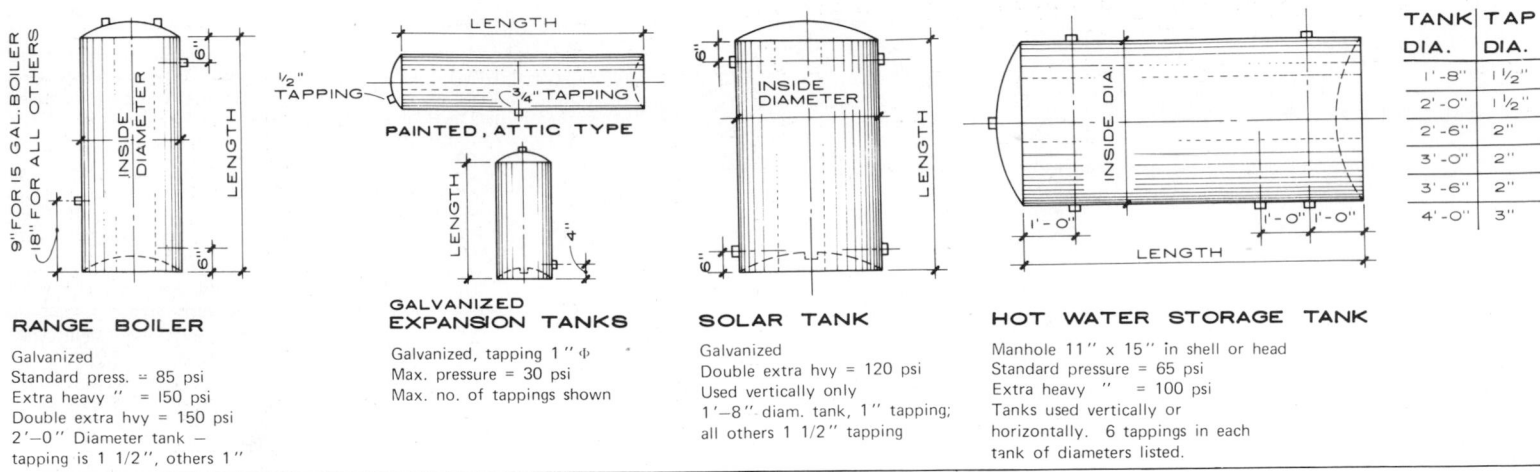

RANGE BOILER

Galvanized
Standard press. = 85 psi
Extra heavy   "   = 150 psi
Double extra hvy = 150 psi
2'-0" Diameter tank —
tapping is 1 1/2", others 1"

GALVANIZED EXPANSION TANKS

Galvanized, tapping 1" Φ
Max. pressure = 30 psi
Max. no. of tappings shown

SOLAR TANK

Galvanized
Double extra hvy = 120 psi
Used vertically only
1'-8" diam. tank, 1" tapping;
all others 1 1/2" tapping

HOT WATER STORAGE TANK

Manhole 11" x 15" in shell or head
Standard pressure = 65 psi
Extra heavy   "   = 100 psi
Tanks used vertically or
horizontally. 6 tappings in each
tank of diameters listed.

TANK DIA.	TAP DIA.
1'-8"	1 1/2"
2'-0"	1 1/2"
2'-6"	2"
3'-0"	2"
3'-6"	2"
4'-0"	3"

TYPES OF TANKS, LOCATIONS OF TAPS AND GENERAL DATA

NOTE: Figures are U.S. Standard Gallons; Length = length of sheets; Hot water tanks are Dept. of Commerce Simplified Practice Recommendation =25, others are =R8-47.

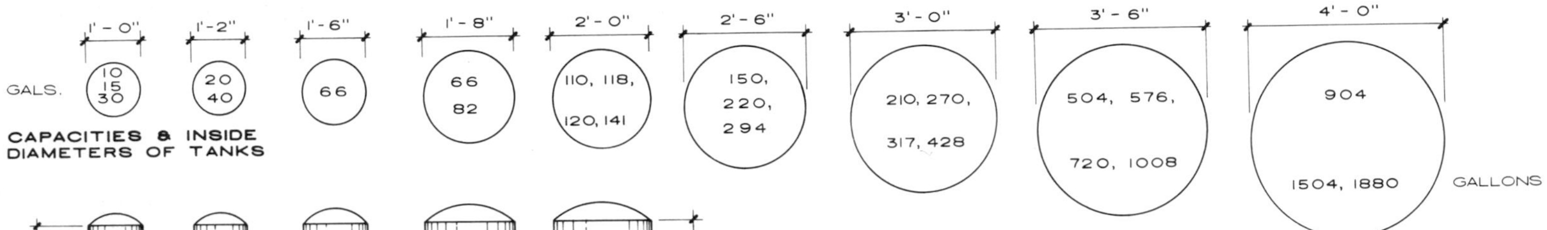

GALS.

I'-0"	I'-2"	I'-6"	I'-8"	2'-0"	2'-6"	3'-0"	3'-6"	4'-0"
10 15 30	20 40	66	66 82	110, 118, 120, 141	150, 220, 294	210, 270, 317, 428	504, 576, 720, 1008	904 1504, 1880

GALLONS

CAPACITIES & INSIDE DIAMETERS OF TANKS

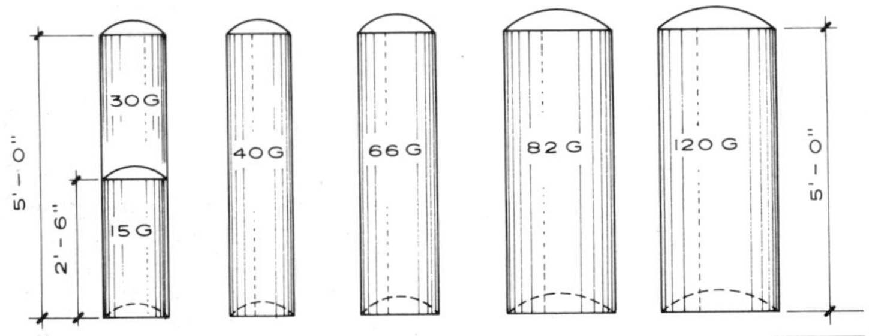

RANGE BOILERS

30 G
15 G
40 G
66 G
82 G
120 G

FORMULAS FOR CAPACITY OF CYLINDRICAL TANKS:

$$DIA.^2 \times 0.7854 \times LENGTH = VOLUME$$

$$CU.FT. \times 7.4805 =$$
OR } CAPACITY IN GALLONS
$$\frac{CU.IN.}{1728} \times 7.4805 =$$

WATER DATA:

1 GALLON = 231 CU.IN.
1 CU. FT. WEIGHS 62.5 LBS.

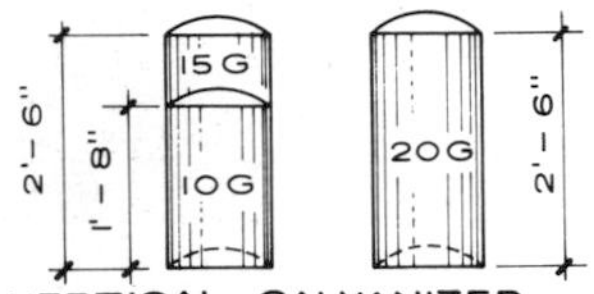

EXPANSION TANKS

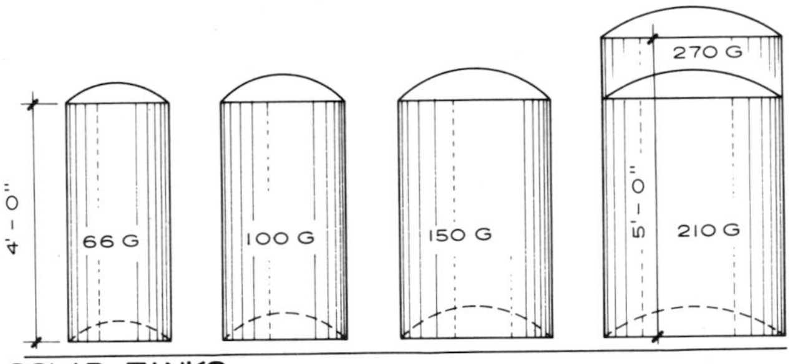

VERTICAL, GALVANIZED

15 G
10 G
20 G

HORIZONTAL, PAINTED

30 G
15 G
40 G

SOLAR TANKS

66 G
100 G
150 G
210 G
270 G

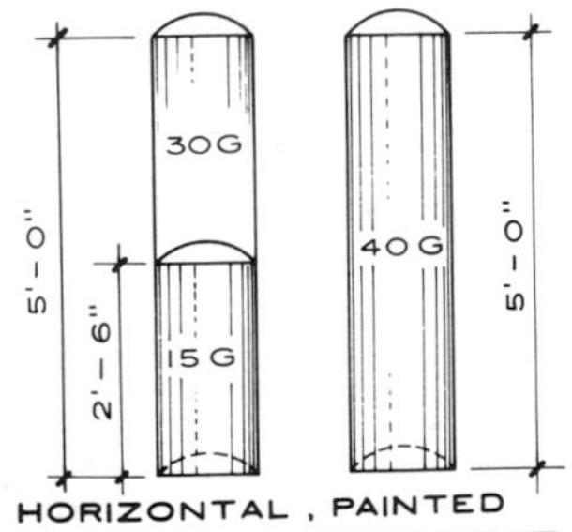

1880 G
1504 G
1008 G
720 G
576 G
504 GAL.
904 G

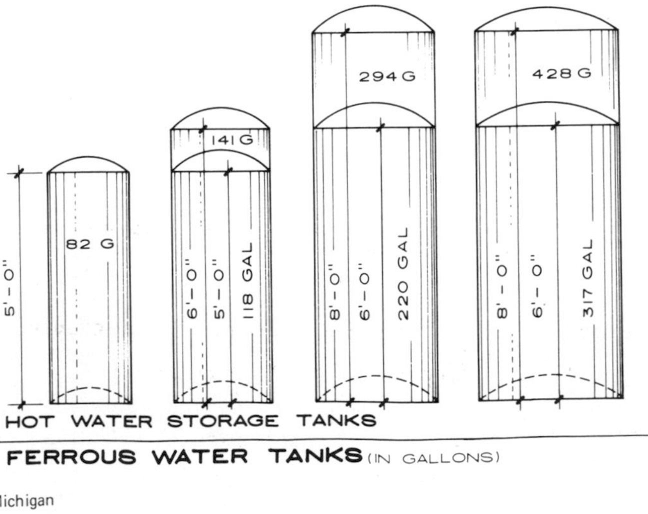

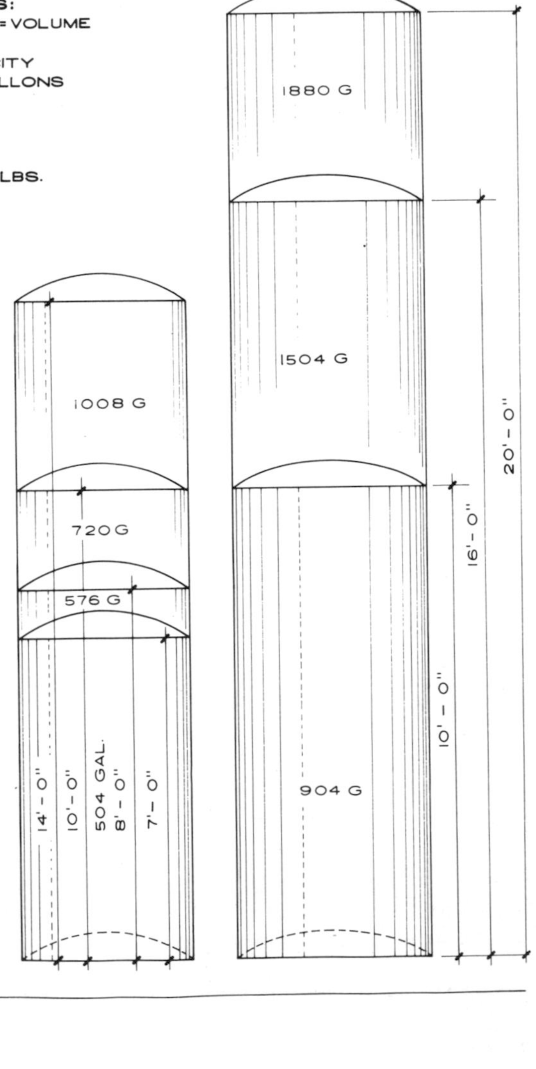

HOT WATER STORAGE TANKS

82 G
141 G
118 GAL
220 GAL
294 G
317 GAL
428 G

SIZE AND CAPACITY OF FERROUS WATER TANKS (IN GALLONS)

B. J. Baldwin; Giffels & Rossetti, Inc.; Detroit, Michigan

CAPACITY OF CYLINDRICAL WATER TANKS — TOTAL GALLONS

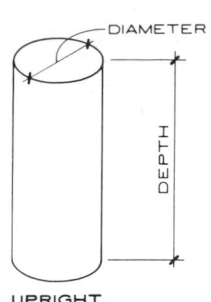

UPRIGHT

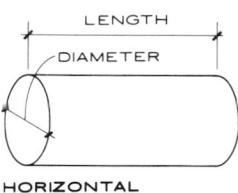

HORIZONTAL

DEPTH OR LENGTH	DIAMETER										
	12"	18"	24"	30"	36"	42"	48"	54"	60"	66"	72"
1"	.49	1.10	1.96	3.06	4.41	5.99	7.83	9.91	12.24	14.81	17.63
1'-0"	5.88	13.22	23.50	36.72	52.88	71.97	94.00	118.97	146.88	177.72	211.51
1'-6"	9	20	35	55.08	79	108	141	179	220	267	317
2'-0"	12	26	47	73	106	144	188	238	294	356	423
2'-6"	15	33	59	92	132	180	235	297	367	444	529
3'-0"	18	40	71	110	159	216	282	357	441	533	635
3'-6"	21	46	82	129	185	252	329	416	514	622	740
4'-0"	24	53	94	147	212	288	376	476	588	711	846
4'-6"	27	60	106	165	238	324	423	535	661	800	952
5'-0"	29	66	118	184	264	360	470	595	734	889	1058
5'-6"	32	73	129	202	291	396	517	654	808	978	1163
6'-0"	35	79	141	220	317	432	564	714	881	1066	1269
7'-0"	41	93	165	257	370	504	658	833	1028	1244	1481
8'-0"	47	106	188	294	423	576	752	952	1175	1422	1692
9'-0"	53	119	212	331	476	648	846	1071	1322	1600	1904
10'-0"	59	137	235	367	529	720	940	1190	1469	1777	2115
12'-0"	71	159	287	441	635	864	1128	1428	1763	2133	2538
14'-0"	82	185	329	514	740	1008	1316	1666	2056	2488	2961
16'-0"	94	212	376	588	846	1152	1504	1904	2350	2844	3384
18'-0"	106	238	423	661	952	1296	1692	2142	2644	3199	3807
20'-0"	118	264	470	734	1058	1439	1880	2380	2938	3555	4230

CAPACITY OF RECTANGULAR WATER TANKS — GALLONS PER FOOT OF HEIGHT

WIDTH OF TANK	LENGTH OF TANK																				
	2'-0"	2'-6"	3'-0"	3'-6"	4'-0"	4'-6"	5'-0"	5'-6"	6'-0"	6'-6"	7'-0"	7'-6"	8'-0"	8'-6"	9'-0"	9'-6"	10'-0"	10'-6"	11'-0"	11'-6"	12'-0"
2'-0"	29.92	37.40	44.88	52.36	59.84	67.32	74.81	82.29	89.77	97.25	104.73	112.21	119.69	127.17	134.65	142.13	149.61	157.09	164.57	172.05	179.53
2'-6"		46.75	56.10	65.45	74.80	84.16	93.51	102.86	112.21	121.56	130.91	140.26	149.61	158.96	168.31	177.66	187.01	196.36	205.71	215.06	224.41
3'-0"			67.32	78.54	89.77	100.99	112.21	123.43	134.65	145.87	157.09	168.31	179.53	190.75	201.97	213.19	224.41	235.63	246.86	258.07	269.30
3'-6"				91.64	104.73	117.82	130.91	144.00	157.09	170.18	183.27	196.36	209.45	222.54	235.63	248.73	261.83	274.90	288.00	301.09	314.18
4'-0"					119.69	134.65	149.61	164.57	179.53	194.49	209.45	224.41	239.37	254.34	269.30	284.26	299.22	314.18	329.14	344.10	359.06
4'-6"						151.48	168.31	185.14	201.97	218.80	235.63	252.47	269.30	286.13	302.96	319.79	336.62	353.45	370.28	387.11	403.94
5'-0"							187.01	205.71	224.41	243.11	261.82	280.52	299.22	317.92	336.62	355.32	374.03	392.72	411.43	430.13	448.83
5'-6"								226.28	246.86	267.43	288.00	308.57	329.14	349.71	370.28	390.85	411.43	432.00	452.57	473.14	493.71
6'-0"									269.30	291.74	314.18	336.62	359.06	381.50	403.94	426.39	448.83	471.27	493.71	516.15	538.59
6'-6"										316.05	340.36	364.67	388.98	413.30	437.60	461.92	486.23	510.54	534.85	559.16	583.47
7'-0"											366.54	392.72	418.91	445.09	471.27	497.45	523.64	549.81	575.99	602.18	628.36
7'-6"												402.78	448.83	476.88	504.93	532.98	561.04	589.06	617.14	645.19	673.24
8'-0"													478.75	508.67	538.59	568.51	598.44	628.36	658.28	688.20	718.12
8'-6"														540.46	572.25	604.05	635.84	667.63	699.42	731.21	763.00
9'-0"															605.92	639.58	673.25	706.90	740.56	774.23	807.89
9'-6"																675.11	710.65	746.17	781.71	817.24	852.77
10'-0"																	748.05	785.45	822.86	860.26	897.66
10'-6"																		824.73	864.00	903.26	942.56
11'-0"																			905.14	946.27	987.43
11'-6"																				989.29	1032.3
12'-0"																					1077.2

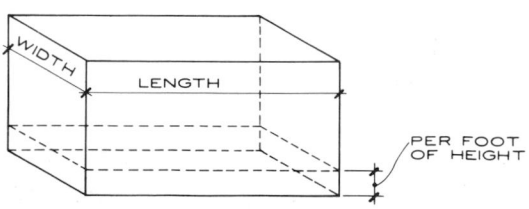

Select a tank of approx. 5000 gals. capacity which must not exceed 8'-0" in width. No limit as to height or length.

8'-0" wide x 12'-0" long = 718 gals. per ft. of height.

$$\frac{5000}{718} = 7 \text{ ft. high — tank required.}$$

EXAMPLE

V. Peruchietti; Giffels & Rossetti, Inc.; Detroit, Michigan

MINIMUM NUMBER OF FIXTURES REQUIRED (SEE GENERAL NOTES)

THE FIGURES SHOWN ARE BASED ON ONE FIXTURE BEING THE MINIMUM REQUIRED FOR THE NUMBER OF PERSONS INDICATED OR ANY FRACTION THEREOF.

TYPE OF BUILDING[1]		WATER CLOSETS		URINALS[5]		LAVATORIES[5]		BATH TUBS OR SHOWERS	DRINKING FOUNTAINS[6]
ELEMENTARY SCHOOLS		One for each 30 males One for each 25 females		One for each 25 males		One for each 35 persons			One for each 40 persons
SECONDARY SCHOOLS		One for each 40 males One for each 30 females		One for each 25 males		One for each 40 persons			One for each 50 persons
GYMNA-SIUMS	HIGH SCHOOLS	One for each 50 males One for each 30 females		One for each 25 males		One for each 20 persons		One for each 2.5 males One for each 3.3 females	
	COLLEGES	One for each 25 males One for each 25 females		One for each 12 males		One for each 25 persons		One for each 4 males One for each 3 females	
OFFICE BUILDINGS OR PUBLIC BUILDINGS		NO. OF PERSONS / CLOSETS Up to 15 — 1 16 to 35 — 2 36 to 55 — 3 56 to 80 — 4 81 to 110 — 5 Add one (1) closet for each additional 40 persons		Whenever urinals are provided for men, one water closet less than the number specified may be provided for each urinal, except that the number of water closets in such cases shall not be reduced to less than 2/3 of the minimum specified.		NO. OF PERSONS / LAVATORIES Up to 15 — 1 16 to 35 — 2 36 to 60 — 3 61 to 90 — 4 91 to 125 — 5 Add one (1) lavatory for each additional 45 persons			One for each 75 persons
MANUFACTURING, WAREHOUSE WORKSHOP & LOFT BUILDINGS MINES, FOUNDRIES ETC.[2]		NO. OF PERSONS / CLOSETS Up to 9 — 1 10 to 24 — 2 25 to 49 — 3 50 to 74 — 4 75 to 100 — 5 Add one (1) closet for each additional 30 persons.		Same as for Office and Public Buildings.		NO. OF PERSONS / LAVATORIES[3] Up to 100 — One for each 10 persons Add one (1) lavatory for each additional 15 persons[4]		One for each 15 persons who may be exposed to excessive heat or to skin contamination with poisonous, infectious or irritating material.	One for each 75 persons
DWELLINGS OR APARTMENT HOUSES		One for each apartment or dwelling unit Laundry Tubs—One single compartment tub for each apartment or dwelling unit or a multiple compartment tub for each 10 apartments. Kitchen Sinks—One for each apartment or dwelling unit.				One for each apartment or dwelling unit		One for each apartment or dwelling unit	
DORMITORIES[7]		Male: 1 for each 10 persons Female: 1 for each 8 persons Over 10 persons add 1 fixture. For each 25 additional males add 1. For each 20 additional females add 1.		1 for each 25 men. Over 150 persons add 1 fixture for each additional 50 males.		1 for each 12 persons (separate Dental Lavatories should be provided in community toilet rooms). Add 1 lavatory for each 20 males and 1 for each 15 females.		1 for each 8 persons. In the case of Women's Dormitories, additional bath tubs should be installed at the ratio of 1 for each 30 females. For over 150 persons, add 1 fixture for each 20 persons.	One for each 75 persons

THEATERS & PLACES OF PUBLIC ASSEMBLY	NO. OF PERSONS	CLOSETS MALE	CLOSETS FEMALE	NO. OF MALES	URINALS	NO. OF PERSONS	LAVATORIES		DRINKING FOUNTAINS
	Up to 100	1	1	Up to 200	1	Up to 200	1		One for each 100 persons
	101 to 200	2	2	201 to 400	2	201 to 400	2		
	201 to 400	3	3	401 to 600	3	401 to 750	3		
	Over 400 add one (1) closet for each 500 additional males and one (1) for each 300 females.			Over 600 add one (1) urinal for each 300 additional males.		Over 750 add one (1) lavatory for each additional 500 persons.			

GENERAL NOTE:

Consult local codes and follow same if their requirements exceed these recommendations.

1. Hospitals, Sanitariums, Hotels and Lodging Houses etc. are not included and must be considered individually.

2. As required by the American Standard Safety Code for industrial sanitation in manufacturing establishments.

3. Where there is exposure to skin contamination with poisonous, infectious, or irritating materials, provide one lavatory for each 5 persons.

4. Twenty four (24) linear inches of wash sink, or eighteen (18) inches of circular basin, when provided with water outlets for such space, shall be considered equivalent to one lavatory.

5. Special requirements applicable to water closets, urinals and lavatories over and above those listed, should be made by the administrative authority concerned with spaces where food or drink is prepared or served.

6. Drinking fountains shall not be installed in toilet rooms.

7. Laundry Trays, 1 for each 50 persons. Slop Sinks, 1 for each 100 persons.

Smith, Hinchman & Grylls Associates, Inc.; Detroit, Michigan

HOT WATER CONSUMPTION

Figures given are in gallons of water per hour per fixture and are based on a final temperature of 140°F (except as noted)

FIXTURES	APARTMENT HOUSE	CLUB	GYMNASIUM	HOSPITAL	HOTEL
PRIVATE LAVATORY	2	2	2	2	2
PUBLIC LAVATORY	4	6	8	6	8
BATH TUBS	20	20	30	20	20
FOOT BASINS	3	3	12	3	3
KITCHEN SINK	10	20		20	30
AUTOMATIC DISH WASHER$_{1,2}$	15	50-150		50-150	50-200
AUTOMATIC CLOTHES WASHER$_1$	75	75		100	150
LAUNDRY TUBS	20	28		28	28
PANTRY SINK	5	10		10	10
SHOWER	30	150	225	75	75
SLOP SINK	20	20		20	30

PERCENT OF WATER LIKELY TO BE DRAWN AT ONE TIME (PROBABLE DEMAND)

	30%	30%	40%	25%	25%

STORAGE CAPACITY IN PERCENT OF MAXIMUM PROBABLE DEMAND PER HOUR

	125%	90%	100%	60%	80%

1. Refer to manufacturers data whenever possible.
2. For dishwashing in public places 180°F water is mandatory.

HOT WATER CONSUMPTION — continued

Figures given are in gallons of water per hour per fixture and are based on a final temperature of 140°F (except as noted)

FIXTURES	INDUSTRIAL PLANT	OFFICE BUILDING	PRIVATE RESIDENCE	SCHOOL	Y.M.C.A.
PRIVATE LAVATORY	2	2	2	2	2
PUBLIC LAVATORY	12	6		15	8
BATH TUBS			20		30
FOOT BASINS	12		3	3	12
KITCHEN SINK	20	20	10	20	20
AUTOMATIC DISH WASHER$_{1,2}$	20-100		15	20-100	20-100
AUTOMATIC CLOTHES WASHER$_1$			75		100
LAUNDRY TUBS			20		28
PANTRY SINK		10	5	10	10
SHOWER	225	30	30	225	225
SLOP SINK	20	20	15	20	20

PERCENT OF WATER LIKELY TO BE DRAWN AT ONE TIME (PROBABLE DEMAND)

	40%	30%	30%	40%	40%

STORAGE CAPACITY IN PERCENT OF MAXIMUM PROBABLE DEMAND PER HOUR

	100%	200%	70%	100%	100%

Note: For notes for subscripts 1 and 2, see top part of table above.

Smith, Hinchman & Grylls Associates, Inc.; Detroit, Michigan

SINGLE BOWL

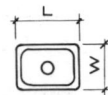

STAINLESS STEEL

	MIN.	MAX.	OTHER
L	11½	33	12½ → 31
W	13	22⅜	14 → 22¼
D	5½	12	6 → 7½

PORCELAIN ENAMELED STEEL

	MIN.	MAX.	OTHER
L	24	30	
W	21		
D	7⅜	8⅛	

ENAMELED CAST IRON

	MIN.	MAX.	OTHER
L	12	30	
W	12	21	18 → 20
D	6	8	6½ → 7½

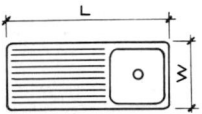

SINGLE BOWL & DRAINBOARD
(RIGHT OR LEFT)

STAINLESS STEEL

	MIN.	MAX.	OTHER
L	39	72	60 → 66
W	21	25	
D	7	7½	

ENAMELED CAST IRON

	MIN.	MAX.	OTHER
L	42	72	
W	20	25	24
D	6	8	6½ → 7½

SINGLE BOWL DOUBLE DRAINBOARD

STAINLESS STEEL

	MIN.	MAX.	OTHER
L	32	72	33 → 42
W	21	25	
D	7	7½	

ENAMELED CAST IRON

	MIN.	MAX.	OTHER
L	54	72	
W	21	25	24
D	6	8	6½ → 7½

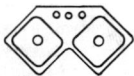

CORNER BOWL

STAINLESS STEEL

	MIN.	MAX.	OTHER
L	31⅞	32½	
W	31⅞	32½	
D	7	7½	

Giffels & Rossetti, Inc.; Detroit, Michigan

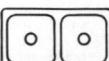

DOUBLE BOWL

STAINLESS STEEL

	MIN.	MAX.	OTHER
L	28	46	30 → 42
W	16	22	17 → 21¼
D	5	10	6½ → 7½

PORCELAIN ENAMELED

	MIN.	MAX.	OTHER
L	32		
W	21		
D	7	8⅛	

ENAMELED CAST IRON STEEL

	MIN.	MAX.	OTHER
L	32	42	
W	20	25	
D	6	8	6½ → 7½

DOUBLE BOWL & DRAINBOARD

STAINLESS STEEL

	MIN.	MAX.	OTHER
L	60	72	66
W	21	25	
D	7	7½	

ENAMELED CAST IRON

	MIN.	MAX.	OTHER
L	54	72	60
W	24	25	
D	6	8	6½ → 7½

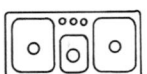

TRIPLE BOWL

STAINLESS STEEL

	MIN.	MAX.	OTHER
L	33	54	37 → 43
W	22		
D	5	7½	

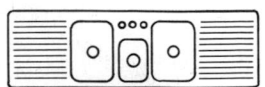

TRIPLE BOWL & DOUBLE DRAINBOARD

STAINLESS STEEL

	MIN.	MAX.	OTHER
L	84		
W	25		
D		7½	

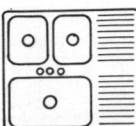
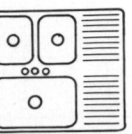

TRIPLE BOWL & DRAIN BOARD (ISLAND)

STAINLESS STEEL

	MIN.	MAX.	OTHER
L	54½	57	
W	40½		
D	4	7½	

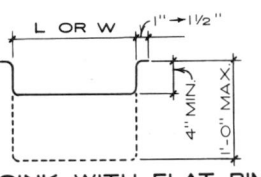

SINK WITH FLAT RIM

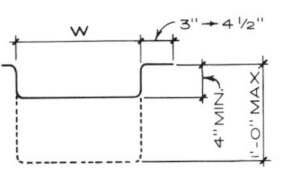

SINK WITH BACK LEDGE

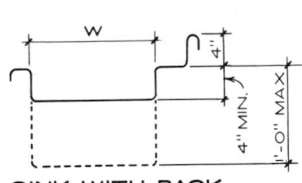

SINK WITH BACK LEDGE & BACKSPLASH

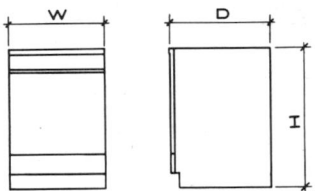

AUTOMATIC DISHWASHERS

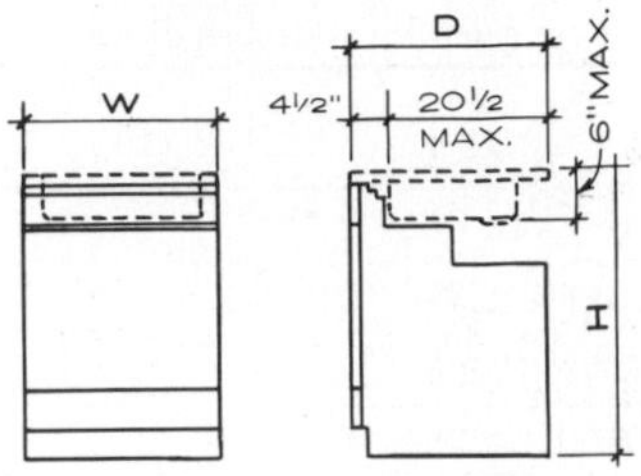

UNDER SINK

	MIN.	MAX.	OTHER
W	24	24¼	
D	25	25½	
H	34¼	34½	

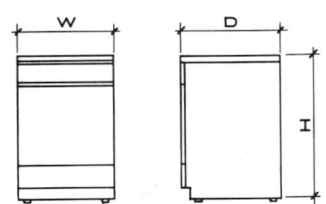

UNDER COUNTER

	MIN.	MAX.	OTHER
W	23	24	23⅞
D	23 11/16	25½	24 → 25¼
H	33½	34½	34⅛ → 34¼

MOBILE (WITH COUNTER TOP)

	MIN.	MAX.	OTHER
W	22½	27	24
D	23 11/16	26½	25½
H	34⅛	39	36

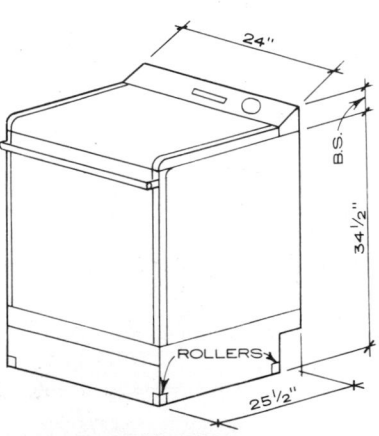

MOBILE DISHWASHER

ALTERNATE FREESTANDING OR ROLLER-TYPE

NOTE:

ALL DIMENSIONS SHOWN ON THIS PAGE ARE IN INCHES

FOR GARBAGE DISPOSERS SEE PAGES ON RESIDENTIAL KITCHEN & LAUNDRY EQUIPMENT, SEE INDEX.

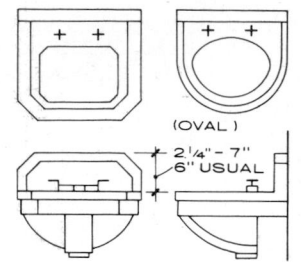

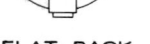

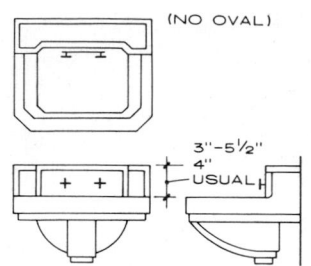

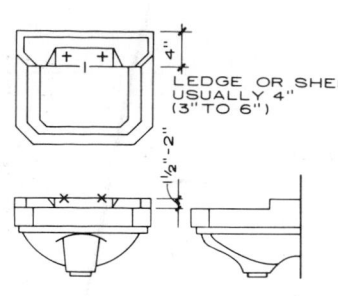

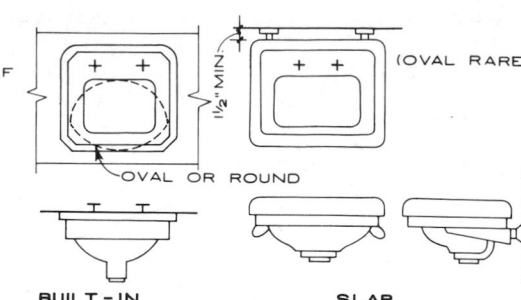

(OVAL)
2 1/4" - 7"
6" USUAL
(NO OVAL)
3"-5 1/2"
4"
USUAL
4"
LEDGE OR SHELF
USUALLY 4"
(3" TO 6")
1 1/2"-2"
1 1/2" MIN.
(OVAL RARE)
OVAL OR ROUND

FLAT BACK

VIT. CH.	EN. C. I.	EN. STEEL
Wall Hung	Wall Hung	Wall Hung, with Legs, or Pedestal
14″x14″*	19″x17″	
18″x15⅞″†	20″x18″tlp	
19″x17″	21″x18″†	
20″x18″†	22″x19″tlp	24″x20″
24″x21″		
Wall Hung or with legs		
20″x18″p		
24″x20″*		
24″x21″*		

SHELF BACK

VIT. CH.	EN. C. I.	EN. STEEL
Wall Hung or with legs	Wall Hung	Wall Hung
	13″x13″†	19″x17″
18″x14″†	16″x14″	20″x18″
19″x17″†	18″x15″	
20″x14″†	20″x14″	
22″x18″lp	Wall Hung or with legs	
24″x20″l		
With legs	19″x11″*	
27″x22″*p	22″x19″†	
26″x22″l		

LEDGE BACK

	VIT. CH.	EN. C. I.	EN. STEEL
	Wall Hung	Wall Hung	Wall Hung or with Legs
	18″x15″	19″x17″	
	19″x17″		
	20″x18″		19″x17″p
Wall or legs	19″x17″		24″x20″p
Wall or legs	20″x18″†		20″x18″
Wall or legs	24″x20″		
Wall or legs	26″x22″		
Legs only	32″x18″		
Legs only	36″x18″		
Legs only	42″x18″		

BUILT-IN

VIT. CH.	EN. C.I.	EN. STEEL
18″x19″rd	18″&19″rd	18″&19″rd
19″x14″	19″x16″	19½″x15¾″†
19″x16″	20″x12″†	20″x18″†
20″x18″†	20″x18″†	20½″x16¾″†
22″x18″	22″x19″†	20″x17″
21″x19″†	26″x18″	
24″x18″†		
24″x20¾″†		
27″x20″		

SLAB

VIT. CH.	EN. STEEL
Wall Hung or with Legs	Wall Hung or with Legs
20″x18″tlp	24″x20″p
24″x20″lp	
24″x21″tlp	
27″x22″p	
With legs	
30″x22″	
36″x22″†	

LAVATORIES—ALL DIMENSIONS IN INCHES

LEGEND & NOTES

Vit. Ch. = Vitreous China
En. C.I. = Enameled Cast Iron
En. Steel = Enameled Steel
p = may have vitreous china leg or pedestal in addition to wall brackets.

* Made in oval rim only
L = may have 2 chrome legs & wall brackets
C = Chair support
Sizes under "with legs" are supported by legs & brackets; they may not be used with bracket support alone.
† = made in rectangular rim only.
Height — finished floor to sink, 2′–6″ to 2′–8″ (Standard 2′–7″).

Lavatories shown with bevelled rect. rims; others have rounded corners or D-shaped (oval) rims. Basins—rectangular or oval, or other shapes (see mfr.). Flat back may have bevelled, rounded or D-shaped corners.

W
1'-10 1/2"
2'-7" TO 2'-10"
3'-4"
4"

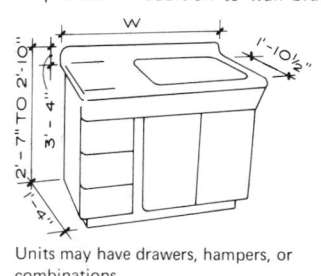

Units may have drawers, hampers, or combinations.

	1 BOWL	2 BOWL
W	2′, 2′–6″, 3′, 3′–6″, 4′, 4′–6″, 5′, 5′–6″, 6′	5′, 5′–6″, 6′

CABINET

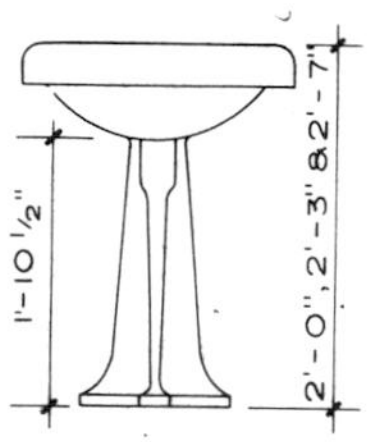

1'-10 1/2"
2'-0", 2'-3" & 2'-7"

WITH WALL BRACKET. VITREOUS CHINA

PEDESTAL

2'-3"

PAIRED LEGS WITH OR WITHOUT TOWEL BARS

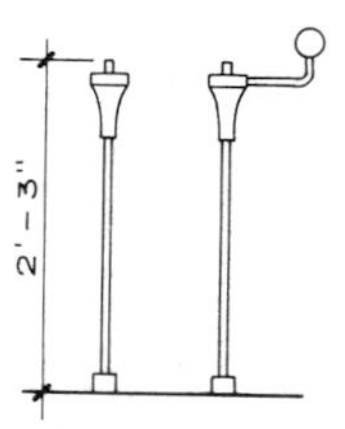

CHROME LEGS

FLOOR SUPPORTED

B
A
2'-7"
2"
USED ON SMALL SINK, WITH LEGS OR PEDESTAL
BOLTS ADJUSTABLE FOR 1 1/4" - 2 1/4" FINISH

SINK:	20″ x 18″	24″ x 20″	27″ x 22″	30″ x 24″
A	13″	13″	17″	17″
B	16″	19″	23″	26″

BRACKET

1 1/2" MIN.
2'-7"
1 1/2" MIN.
A
5"MIN. WALL OTHERWISE IN CORRIDOR BEHIND
F

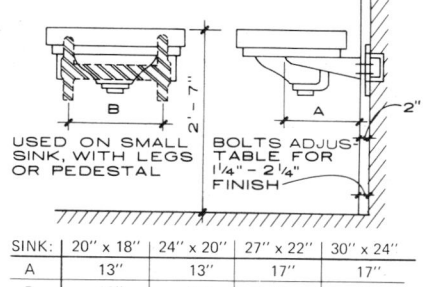

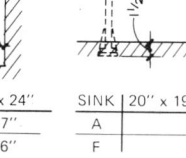

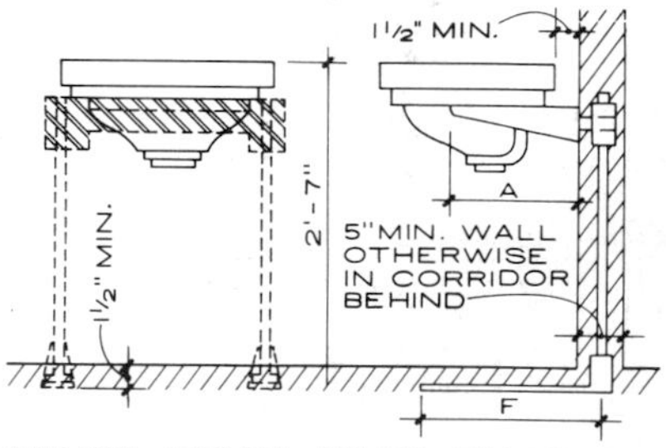

SINK	20″ x 19″ & 24″ x 20″	27″ x 22″ & 30″ x 24″
A	13″	17″
F	15″	18″

CHAIR

WALL HUNG

A
B
6"
2'-7"
FIXTURES ON PANEL OR ON BASIN RIM

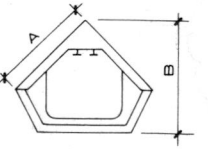

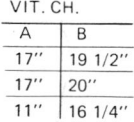

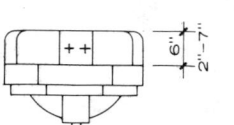

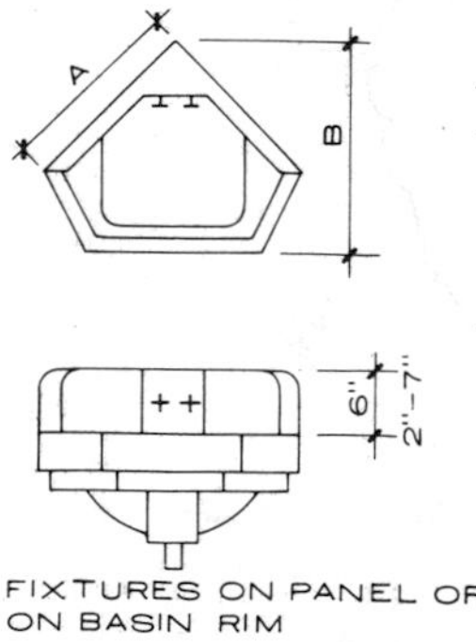

VIT. CH.	
A	B
17″	19 1/2″
17″	20″
11″	16 1/4″
EN. C. I.	
16″	20 1/2″
11″	16″

In flat and shelf back.

CORNER LAVATORY

8 1/2"
3", 5", 6"

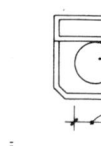

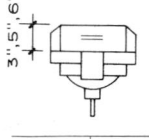

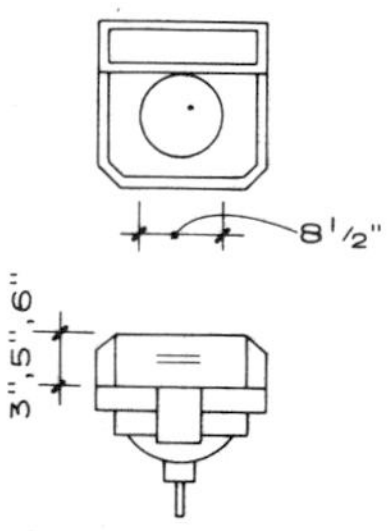

VIT.CH.	14″ x 14″

DENTAL

A
B

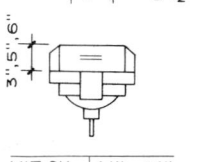

		VIT. CH.	EN. C. I.
SHELF BACK	A	14″	14″
	B	20″	20″
LEDGE BACK	A	13″, 14″, 15″	14″
	B	13″, 16″, 18″	20″
FLAT BACK	A	14″	14″, 16″
	B	16″	16″, 20″
BUILT IN	A		12″
	B		20″

SPACE SAVER

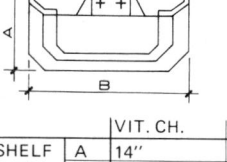

	BACK				NO BACK		
	A	B	C	D	A	B	C
VIT. CH.	20″	16″	10″	8″	20″	22″	18″
	22″	19″	12″	10″	22″	24″	20″
	24″	22″	12″	12″			
C. I. EN.	20″	16″	12″	12″	16″	16″	10″
	22″	18″	12″	12″	20″	14″	12″
	22″	20″	12″	12″	20″	16″	12″
	24″	26″	12″	12″	22″	18″	12″
					24″	20″	12″
					30″	20″	12″
					36″	20″	12″
EARTHEN WARE	20″	18″	12″	8″			
	22″	20″	12″	8″			

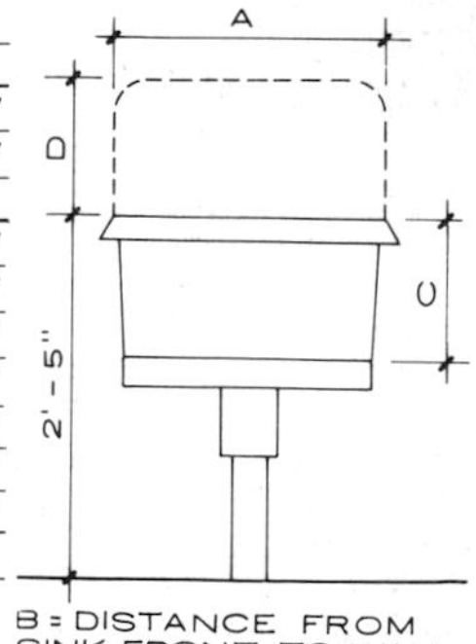

A
D
C
2'-5"

B = DISTANCE FROM SINK FRONT TO WALL

SERVICE SINKS

SINGLE
1'-6" W
L
31"
DOUBLE
2'-6" W
31"

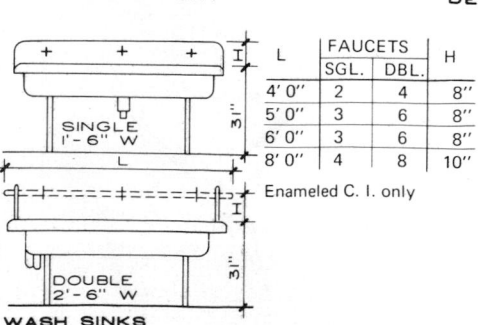

L	FAUCETS		H
	SGL.	DBL.	
4′ 0″	2	4	8″
5′ 0″	3	6	8″
6′ 0″	3	6	8″
8′ 0″	4	8	10″

Enameled C. I. only

WASH SINKS

A
9 1/4" TO 10 1/2"
24" TO 29 1/4"
10"

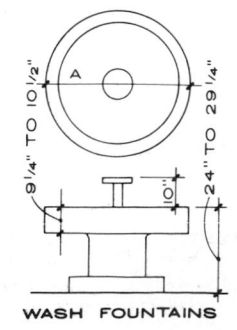

A	SERVES
4′ 6″	8 to 10
4′ 0″*	8
3′ 0″	5 to 6

*Cast Iron only. Others in marble stone, stainless steel, also semicircular

WASH FOUNTAINS

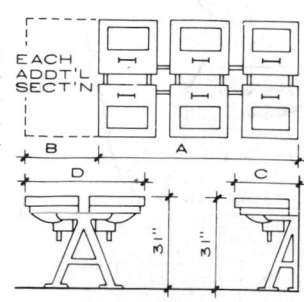

	20″ x 18″ VIT.CH.	24″ x 20″, 21″ VIT.CH.EN.C.I.
A	5′ 8″ or 6′ 2″	6′ 7″ or 7′ 2″
B	2′ 0″	2′ 4″
C	1′ 8″	1′ 10″ to 2′ 0″
D	3′ 2″ to 5′ 4″	3′ 6″ to 3′ 10″

EACH ADDT'L SECT'N
B
A
D
C
31"
31"

BATTERY WASH SINKS

B. J. Baldwin; Giffels & Rossetti, Inc.; Detroit, Michigan

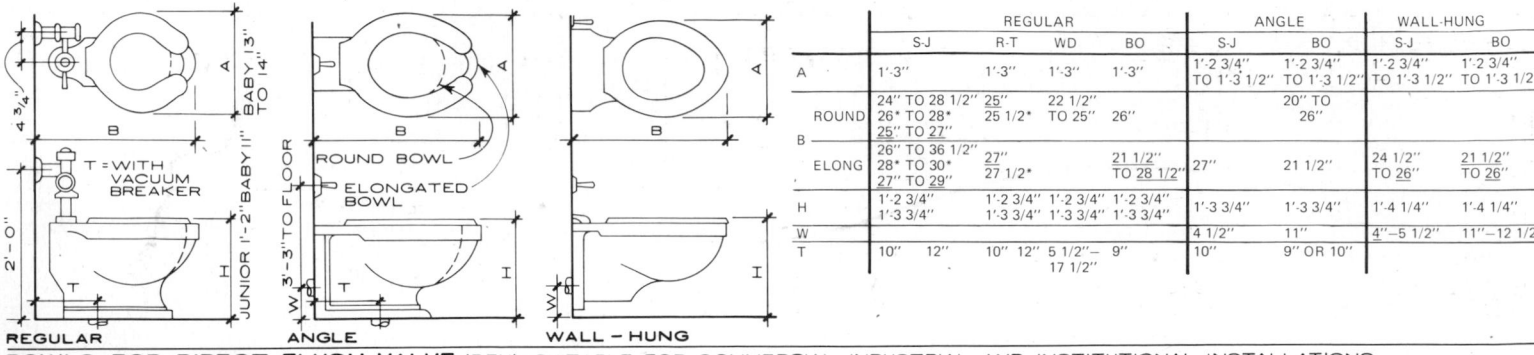

		REGULAR				ANGLE		WALL-HUNG	
		S-J	R-T	WD	BO	S-J	BO	S-J	BO
A		1'-3''	1'-3''	1'-3''	1'-3''	1'-2 3/4'' TO 1'-3 1/2''	1'-2 3/4'' TO 1'-3 1/2''	1'-2 3/4'' TO 1'-3 1/2''	1'-2 3/4'' TO 1'-3 1/2''
B	ROUND	24'' TO 28 1/2'' 26'' TO 28* 25'' TO 27''	25* 25 1/2*	22 1/2'' TO 25''	26''		20'' TO 26''		
	ELONG	26'' TO 36 1/2'' 28* TO 30* 27'' TO 29''	27'' 27 1/2*	21 1/2'' TO 28 1/2''		27''	21 1/2''	24 1/2'' TO 26''	21 1/2'' TO 26''
H		1'-2 3/4'' 1'-3 3/4''	1'-2 3/4'' 1'-3 3/4''	1'-2 3/4'' 1'-3 3/4''	1'-2 3/4'' 1'-3 3/4''	1'-3 3/4''	1'-3 3/4''	1'-4 1/4''	1'-4 1/4''
W						4 1/2''	11''	4''-5 1/2''	11''-12 1/2''
T		10''	12''	10'' 12''	5 1/2''-9'' 17 1/2''	10''	9'' OR 10''		

REGULAR **ANGLE** **WALL-HUNG**

BOWLS FOR DIRECT FLUSH VALVE (DFV)—SUITABLE FOR COMMERCIAL, INDUSTRIAL AND INSTITUTIONAL INSTALLATIONS

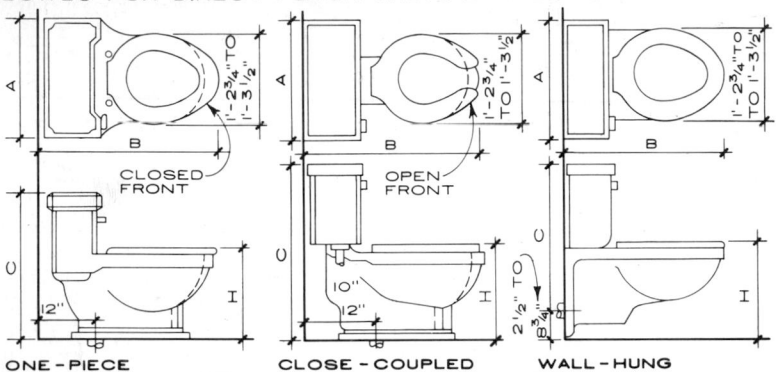

		ONE-PIECE			CLOSE-COUPLED			WALL-HUNG
		S-V	S-J	R-T	S-J	R-T	WD	R-T
A		20 1/2'' TO 22 1/4''	22 1/4''	22 1/4'' TO 23 1/4''	21 1/2''– 23 3/4'' 22''	17'' TO 21 3/4''	20'' TO 21 3/4''	21 7/8''
B	ROUND	26 3/4''		25 1/16''	26 3/4''– 30'' 28''	25''– 28'' 27''	26 1/2'' TO 28 1/2''	
	ELONG	28 1/2'' TO 30 1/2''	28 3/4''	27 5/16'' 29''	28''– 31 3/8'' 29''	30''		27 3/8''
C		24'' OR 18 3/4''	28 3/4''	29'' 20 1/2''	26 1/8'' TO 31''	28'' TO 30''	28 1/2'' TO 30''	30 5/8''
H		14'' TO 15 3/4''	14'' TO 15 3/4''	14'' TO 15 3/4''	14 3/4'' TO 15 3/4''	14 3/4'' TO 15 3/4''	14 3/4'' TO 15 3/4''	15 3/4''

NOTE:
Dimensions include seat
For closed-front seats,
Add 1'' to B. With seat
cover, add 3/4'' to height.
00 = most common.
* – Commercial Standard
CS–20–63 for vitreous
china fixtures (all of
vitreous china except
where noted).
Allow 3 3/4'' to 4 3/4'' behind wall for valve. For concealed carrier for wall-hung,
allow 2 5/8'' min. If foot
(chair) support is necessary,
allow 1'' min. 4'-8'' max.
(usual 2'', 2 1/2'') below
finished floor.

ONE-PIECE **CLOSE-COUPLED** **WALL-HUNG** SUITABLE FOR RESIDENTIAL

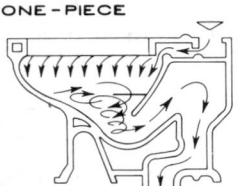 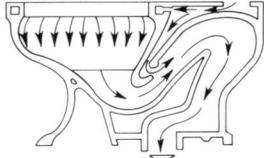 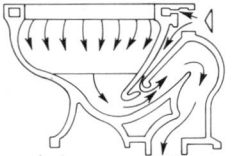 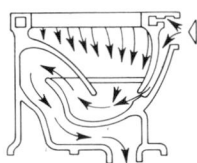 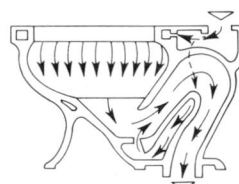

SIPHON - VORTEX (S-V)
Quiet, extremely sanitary.
Water directed thru rim to
create vortex. Scours bowl.
Folds over into jet; siphon.

SIPHON - JET (S-J)
Sanitary, efficient, very quiet.
Water enters thru rim and thru
jets in up-leg of trapway. Jet
acts as siphon in down-leg.

REVERSE - TRAP (R-T)
Same as siphon—jet except
that closet size is smaller.

WASH - DOWN (W-D)
Minimum cost. Simplest design.
With round front bowl and front
trapway only. Head formed in up-
leg overflow, creating siphon.

BLOWOUT (BO)
Noisy but highly efficient and
water-saving. Strong jet into
up-leg forces contents out.
Use with DFV only.

WATER CLOSETS

NOTE: Allow 2 5/8'' min. for concealed carrier for wall hung urinals. If foot (chair) support is used allow 1'' min., 4 1/8'' max. (usually 2'', 2 1/2'') below finished floor.

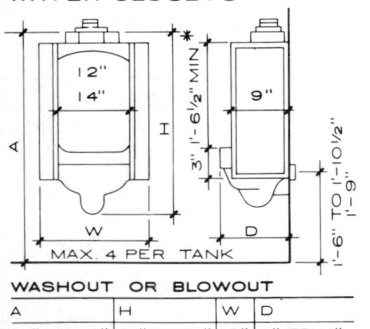 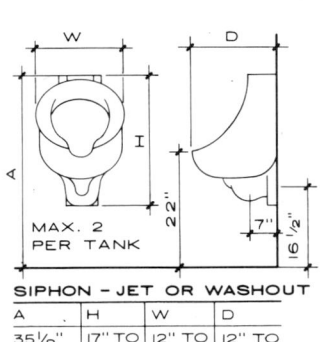 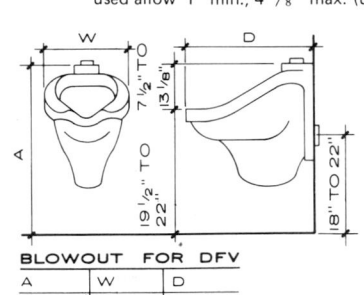 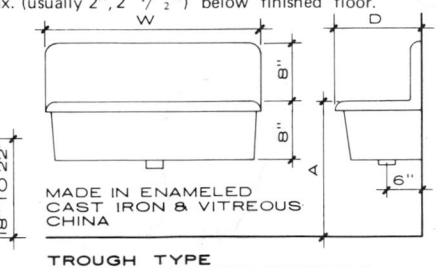

WASHOUT OR BLOWOUT

A	H	W	D
42'' TO 46'' 44 1/2''	25'' TO 30''	18''	11'' TO 14''

SIPHON - JET OR WASHOUT

A	H	W	D
35 1/8'' TO 36''	17'' TO 20''	12'' TO 14 1/4''	12'' TO 14 1/2''

BLOWOUT FOR DFV

A	W	D
27'' TO 25 1/8''	14'' TO 14 1/2''	19'' TO 21''

MADE IN ENAMELED
CAST IRON & VITREOUS
CHINA

TROUGH TYPE

A	W	D
24''	36'', 48'', 60'', 72''	12'' TO 17 1/2''

WALL HUNG URINALS

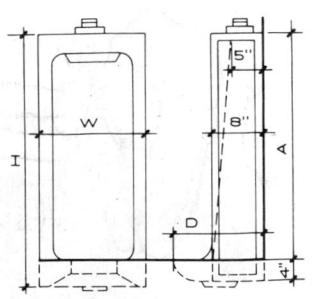 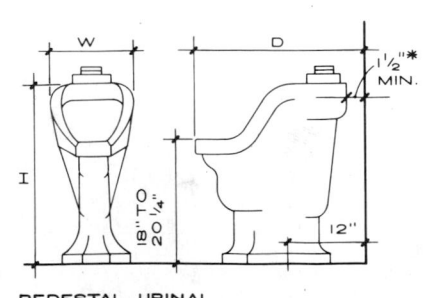 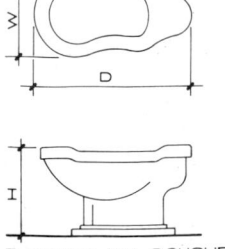 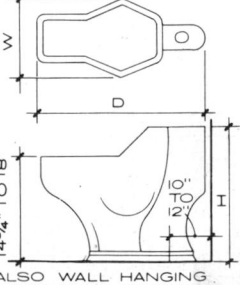

URINAL TANKS
Height: top of tank to finished
floor: 7'–8'' to 7'–10''
Width from 15'' to 26 1/2''
Depth from 7 1/4'' to 14 1/2''
Height from 10'' to 14''
Made in vitreous china or ena-
meled cast iron.

BATTERY STALLS
Stall urinals available with seam
covers for battery installation on
1'–9'' or 2'–0'' centers.

STALL URINAL

A	H	W	D
38''	42''	18''	16''

PEDESTAL URINAL

H	W	D
25 1/4'' TO 28''	14''	21 1/4'' TO 29 1/4''

BIDET
FLUSHING RIM, DOUCHE
POP-UP DRAIN

H	D	W
14'' TO 15''	24 1/2'' TO 25 1/2''	14''

WOMAN'S URINAL
ALSO WALL HANGING
TYPE (S-J)

H	D	W
23''	25 1/2'' TO 29 1/4''	12'' TO 14''

B. J. Baldwin; Giffels & Rossetti, Inc.; Detroit, Michigan

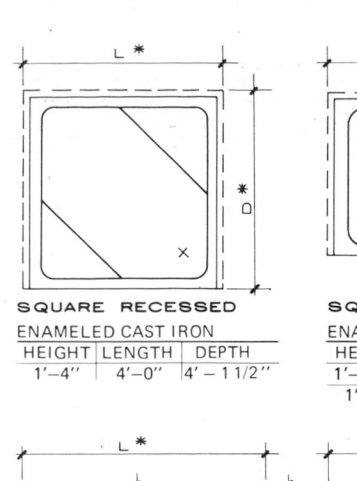

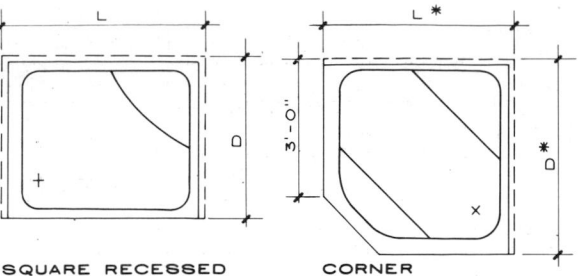

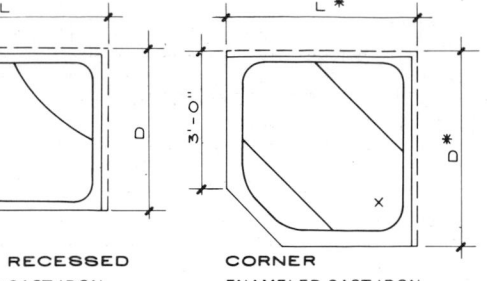

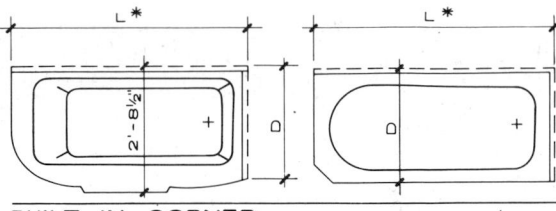

SQUARE RECESSED

ENAMELED CAST IRON

HEIGHT	LENGTH	DEPTH
1'–4''	4'–0''	4' – 1 1/2''

SQUARE RECESSED

ENAMELED CAST IRON

HEIGHT	LENGTH	DEPTH
1'–0'' to	3'–2'' to	3'–1'' to
1'–2''	4'–0''	3'–9''

CORNER

ENAMELED CAST IRON

HEIGHT	LENGTH	DEPTH
1'–4''	4'–0'' to	3'–8'' to
	4'–1 3/4''	4'–1 3/4''

BUILT–IN–CORNER

ENAMELED CAST IRON

HEIGHT	LENGTH	DEPTH
1'–4''	5' – 11/4''	2'–6''

ENAMELED CAST IRON OR ENAMELED STEEL

HEIGHT	LENGTH	DEPTH
1'–3''	4'–6'' to	2'–6 3/4''
1'–4''	5'–6''	to 2'–8''

BUILT–IN RECESS

ENAMELED CAST IRON

HEIGHT	LENGTH	DEPTH
1'–4''	4'–6'' to	2'–6 3/4''
	6'–0''	to 2'–8''

Tile apron: 1'– 4 1/2'' height.

ENAMELED CAST IRON

HEIGHT	LENGTH	DEPTH
1'–6''	5'–6''	2'–6''

1. All dimensions are to rough.

ENAMELED CAST IRON OR ENAMELED STEEL

HEIGHT	LENGTH	DEPTH
1'–0'' to	3'–6'' to	2'–6'' to
1'–4''	5'–6''	2'–8 1/2''

2. Allow 3/4'' to 1'' for finished wall, 1/2'' for finished floor.

FOOT BATH

ENAMELED CAST IRON VITREOUS CHINA OR EARTHENWARE

HEIGHT	LENGTH	DEPTH
1'–3''	1'–2'' &	1'–9'' &
	2'–1''	2'–2 1/2''

FREE–STANDING 1'–2 1/2''

3. * — Standard U.S. Dept. of Commerce for Enameled C.I. Plumbing fixt. (CS77-63)

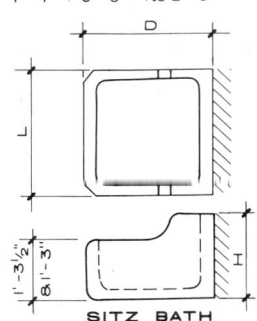

SITZ BATH

ENAMELED CAST IRON VITREOUS CHINA EARTHENWARE

HEIGHT	LENGTH	DEPTH
1'–9'',	2'–6''	2'–3'',
1'–10''	2'–8''	2'–6'', 2'–8''

SQUARE AND RECTANGULAR BATHTUBS

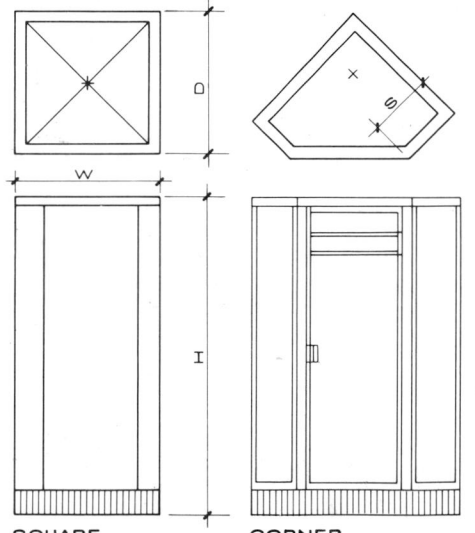

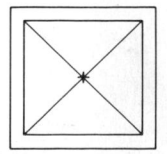

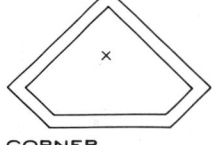

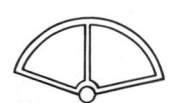

SQUARE **CORNER**

FREE–STANDING SHOWER CABINETS

SIZES OF SQUARE SHOWER CABINETS

W	D	H	WALL MATERIAL	RECEPTOR MATERIAL
2'–6''	2'–6''	6'–3''	Enameled Steel	Enameled St'l. & Terrazzo
2'–8''	2'–8''	6'–4''	Enam. St'l. & Alum.	Enameled St'l. & Terrazzo
2'–8''	2'–8''	6'–8''	Enameled Steel	Terrazzo
3'–0''	3'–0''	6'–4''	Enam. St'l. & Alum.	Enameled St'l. & Terrazzo
3'–0''	3'–0''	6'–8''	Enam. or Stainless St'l.	Terrazzo
3'–0''	3'–0''	6'–10''	Enam. or Stainless St'l.	Terrazzo
3'–0''	3'–0''	7'–0''+	Enameled Steel	Enameled Steel
3'–4''	3'–4''	6'–8''	Enameled Steel	Terrazzo
3'–6''	3'–6''	6'–8''	Enameled Steel	Terrazzo

+ — AVAILABLE TO ORDER 2'–6'', 2'–8'' & 2'–10''

SIZES OF CORNER SHOWER CABINETS

W	D	H	S	WALL MAT'L.	PANEL MAT'L.	RECEPTOR
3'–0''	3'–0''	6'–8''	1'–5''	Enam. St'l.	Enam. St'l.	Terrazzo
3'–4''	3'–4''	6'–8''	1'–7''	Enam. St'l.	Glass	Terrazzo

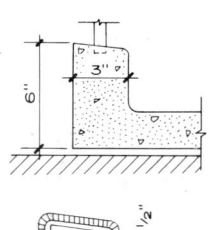

SECTIONS THRU THRESHOLD
WATERPROOFING NOT SHOWN

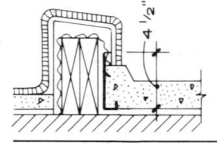

USED WITH MARBLE

SQUARE **CORNER**

SQUARE RECEPTOR — TERRAZZO

W	D	REMARKS
2'–6''	2'–6''	Flat for tile, or with threshold
3'–0''	3'–0''	Flat for tile, or with threshold
3'–4''	3'–4''	Flat for tile, or with threshold
3'–0''	3'–0''	Rabbetted for marble wall
6'–0''	3'–0''	Rabbetted for marble wall

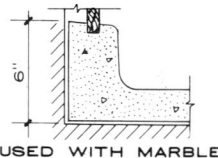

USED WITH TILE, PLASTER

SECTIONS THRU SIDES
WATERPROOFING NOT SHOWN

MULTI–STALL

Wedge Shaped Stalls Grouped in 2's, 3's, 4's, 5's & 6's, with 6'–0'' Standard Ht., 5'–6'' Intermediate Ht. & 5'–0'' Junior Ht.

CORNER RECEPTOR — TERRAZZO

W	D	REMARKS
3'–0''	3'–0''	Flat for tile, or with threshold
3'–4''	3'–4''	Flat for tile, or with threshold

SHOWER RECEPTOR TYPES

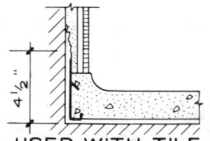

STALL CONSTRUCTION
WATERPROOFING NOTE:

These sections must be adequately waterproofed in order to prevent water seepage from showers to spaces or floors below.

V. Peruchietti; Giffels & Rossetti, Inc.; Detroit, Michigan

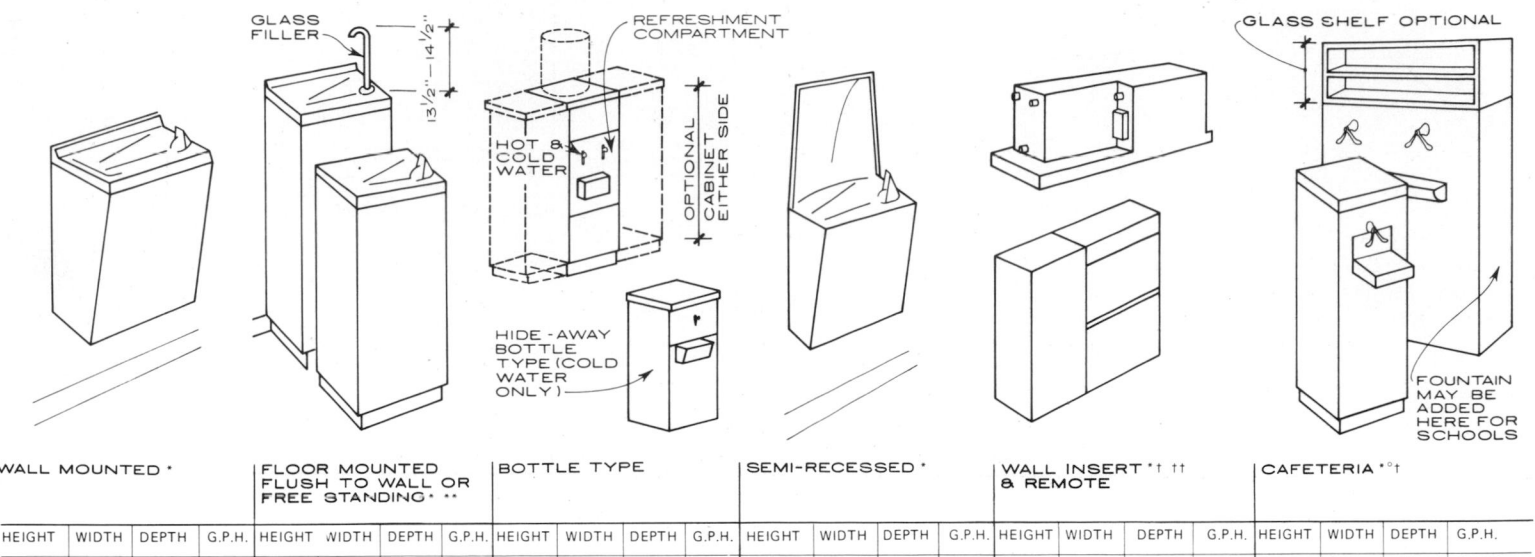

WALL MOUNTED *				FLOOR MOUNTED FLUSH TO WALL OR FREE STANDING * **				BOTTLE TYPE				SEMI-RECESSED *				WALL INSERT * † †† & REMOTE				CAFETERIA * ° †			
HEIGHT	WIDTH	DEPTH	G.P.H.	HEIGHT	WIDTH	DEPTH	G.P.H.	HEIGHT	WIDTH	DEPTH	G.P.H.	HEIGHT	WIDTH	DEPTH	G.P.H.	HEIGHT	WIDTH	DEPTH	G.P.H.	HEIGHT	WIDTH	DEPTH	G.P.H.
25″	17″	14″	5–15	37 1/4″	12″	12″	3	36″	12″	12″	5	21″	17 1/2″	9 1/2″	8–12	25″	22″	7 1/2″	5–10	36″	18″	24″	12–18
24 1/2″	15″	12 1/2″	6–15	40″	14″	14″	3	44″	17″	14″	1					13″	26″	12 1/4″	6	42″	33″	19″	30
				40″	12″	12″	5–10	37″	26″	16 1/2″	1					16″	34″	14 3/4″	13	42″	36″	24″	50
				41″	15″	13″	6–20	42″	14 1/2″	14″	3	WALL RECESS				16″	25″	14 3/4″	16–23	52″	55″	25″	85–125
								40″	14″	14″	2	37 1/4″	15 1/4″	4 1/2″		70″	57″	27″	50–100				
								37 3/4″	14 5/8″	15 1/8″	1	47″	16 1/2″	5 1/2″									

* Air cooled condensers are used for normal room temperatures, water cooled units for high room temperatures and larger capacities. Certain models are available in explosion proof construction.
** Additional fountains can be attached low on the side for use in elementary schools. Some models

are available in 30″ height for primary grades. Some models available with cold and hot water.
°Bubbler fixtures can replace glass fillers on cafeteria models for use in schools.
†Max. water storage for cafeteria types is 40 gals.; for remote types, 300 gals. Cooling capacity is based

on 90° room temperature and 80° inlet water temperature. Power: 110, 115, 230 volts; 50 to 60 cycles, single phase A.C., otherwise transformer is used.
†† For use with multiple fountains shown below.

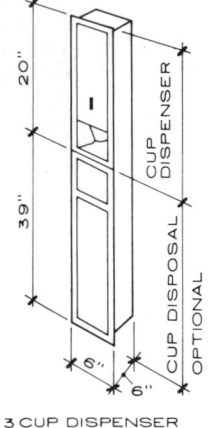

3 CUP DISPENSER AVAILABLE
CUP DISPENSER

Circular bowl 9 1/2″ dia., 2 1/2″ h. Oval 2 1/2″ – 4″ h., 10 1/2″ – 14″ w., 5″ – 10 1/2″ d. All pedestal fountains 30″ & 36″ high.

Oval: 3 1/2″ – 4″ h., 14″ w., 8″ – 10″ d. Rectangular: 3 1/2″ – 11 1/2″ h, 11″ – 14″ w., 11 3/4″ – 13 1/4″ d.

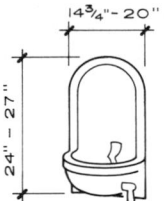

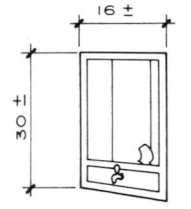

PEDESTAL	WALL HUNG	SEMI-RECESSED	RECESSED	BOTTLES

FOUNTAINS (FOR USE WITH REMOTE STORAGE COOLERS)

CUP DISPENSER, FOUNTAINS AND BOTTLES

DRINKING WATER REQUIREMENTS					COOLERS							
TYPE OF SERVICE	G.P.H. PER PERSON		PERSON PER G.P.H.		TYPE COOLER	RECOMMENDED CAPACITY IN G.P.H.						
	CUP	BUBBLER	CUP	BUBBLER		2	3	5	10	15	20	30
OFFICES, SCHOOLS, CAFETERIAS, HOTELS (PER ROOM) HOSPITALS (PER BED & PER ATTENDANT)	0.033	0.083	30	12		MINIMUM CAPACITY IN G.P.H.						
RESTAURANTS	0.04	0.1	25	10								
LIGHT MANUFACTURING	0.0573	0.143	17.5	7	BOTTLE	1.5	2.7	–	–	–	–	–
HEAVY MANUFACTURING	0.08	0.20	12.5	5	PRESSURE BUBBLER							
HOT, HEAVY MFG.	0.10	0.25	10	4	AIR COOLED CONDENSER	–	2.7	4.5	9	13.5	18	–
THEATERS PER 100 SEATS	0.4GPH/ 100 SEATS	1.0GPH/ 100 SEATS	250 SEATS/ GPH	100 SEATS/ GPH	WATER COOLED CONDENSER	–	–	9	13.5	18	27	
					GLASS FILLER							
DEPARTMENT STORES, LOBBIES, HOTEL & OFFICE BLDGS.	1.6 –2.0 GPH/FOUNT.	4–5 GPH/ FOUNT.	0.5 – 0.625 FOUNT./GPH	0.2 – 0.25 FOUNT./GPH	AIR COOLED CONDENSER	–	–	–	9	–	18	27
					WATER COOLED COND.	–	–	–	9	–	18	27

B. J. Baldwin; Giffels & Rossetti, Inc.; Detroit, Michigan

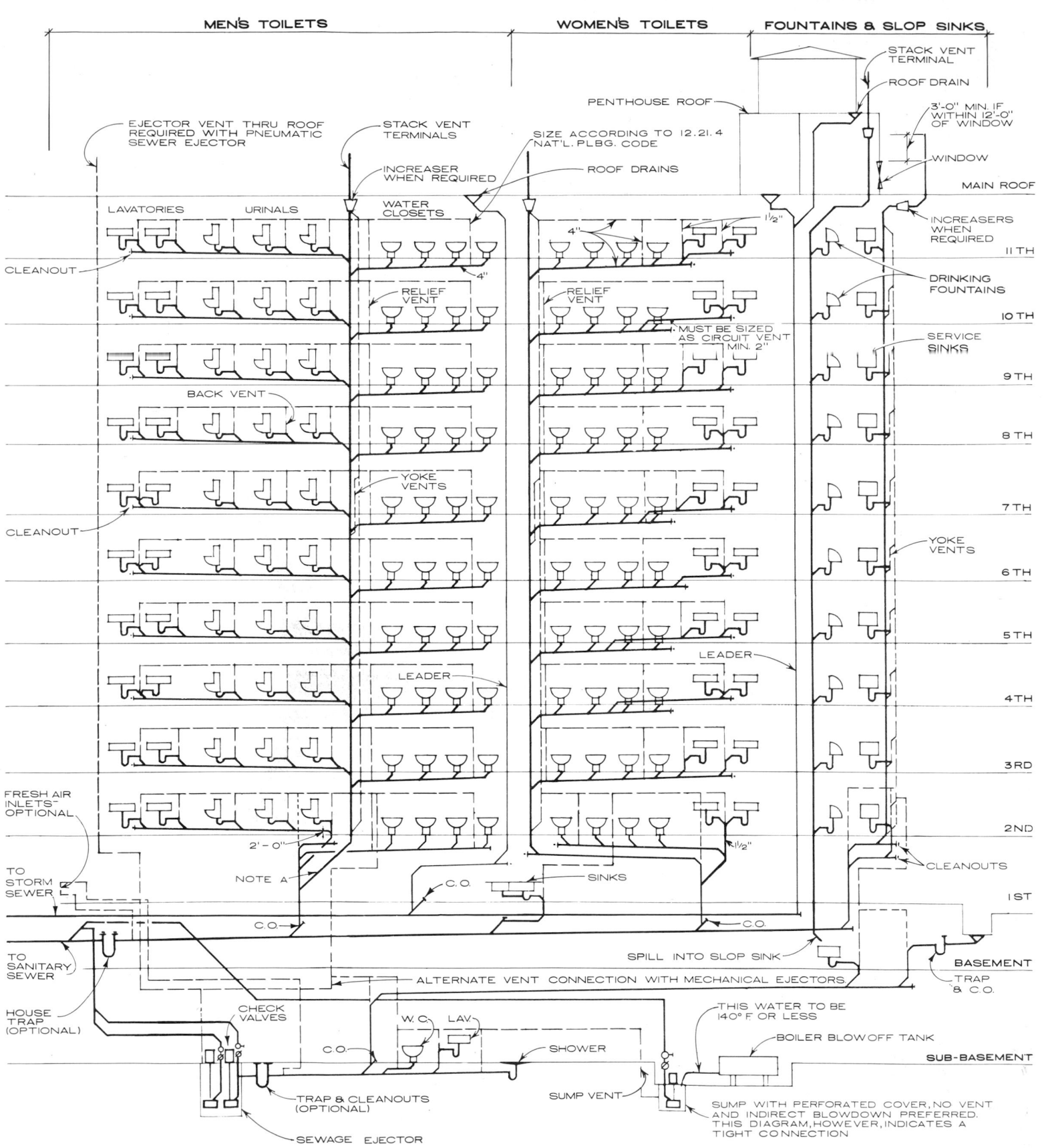

MEN'S TOILETS | WOMEN'S TOILETS | FOUNTAINS & SLOP SINKS

NOTE:
LOCAL CODES SHOULD BE CONSULTED FOR PIPE
SIZES, MATERIALS AND OTHER REQUIREMENTS IN
PLUMBING SYSTEMS.

NOTE A: 45° OR LESS FROM VERTICAL MAY BE
CONSIDERED AS STRAIGHT STOCK IN SIZING EXCEPT
NO FIXTURES OR BRANCHES MAY BE CONNECTED
WITHIN 2'-0" OF OFFSET.

Sargent, Webster, Crenshaw & Folley; Syracuse, New York

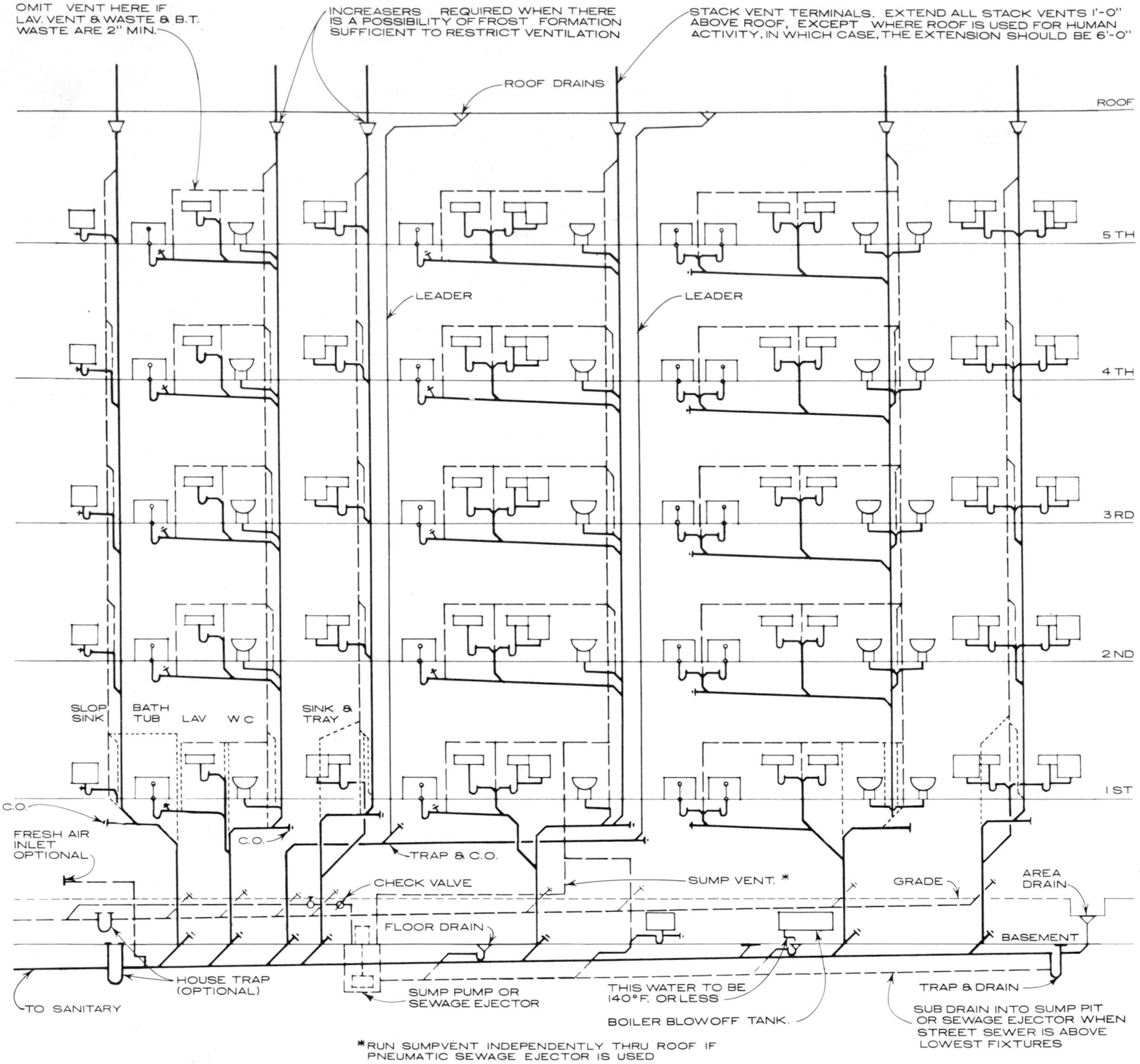

OMIT VENT HERE IF
LAV. VENT & WASTE & B.T.
WASTE ARE 2" MIN.

INCREASERS REQUIRED WHEN THERE
IS A POSSIBILITY OF FROST FORMATION
SUFFICIENT TO RESTRICT VENTILATION

STACK VENT TERMINALS. EXTEND ALL STACK VENTS 1'-0"
ABOVE ROOF, EXCEPT WHERE ROOF IS USED FOR HUMAN
ACTIVITY, IN WHICH CASE, THE EXTENSION SHOULD BE 6'-0"

ROOF DRAINS

ROOF

5 TH

LEADER

LEADER

4 TH

3 RD

2 ND

SLOP
SINK

BATH
TUB   LAV   W C

SINK &
TRAY

1 ST

C.O.

FRESH AIR
INLET
OPTIONAL

C.O.

TRAP & C.O.

CHECK VALVE

SUMP VENT. *

GRADE

AREA
DRAIN

FLOOR DRAIN

BASEMENT

HOUSE TRAP
(OPTIONAL)

TO SANITARY

SUMP PUMP OR
SEWAGE EJECTOR

THIS WATER TO BE
140°F. OR LESS

BOILER BLOWOFF TANK.

TRAP & DRAIN

SUB DRAIN INTO SUMP PIT
OR SEWAGE EJECTOR WHEN
STREET SEWER IS ABOVE
LOWEST FIXTURES

*RUN SUMPVENT INDEPENDENTLY THRU ROOF IF
PNEUMATIC SEWAGE EJECTOR IS USED

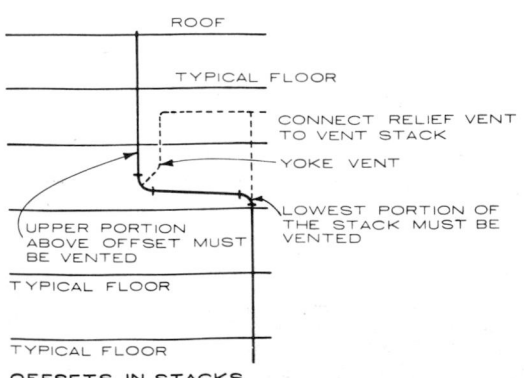

ROOF

TYPICAL FLOOR

CONNECT RELIEF VENT
TO VENT STACK

YOKE VENT

LOWEST PORTION OF
THE STACK MUST BE
VENTED

UPPER PORTION
ABOVE OFFSET MUST
BE VENTED

TYPICAL FLOOR

TYPICAL FLOOR

OFFSETS IN STACKS

NOTE:
Local codes should be consulted for pipe sizes, materials and other requirements in plumbing systems.

Sargent, Webster, Crenshaw & Folley; Syracuse, New York

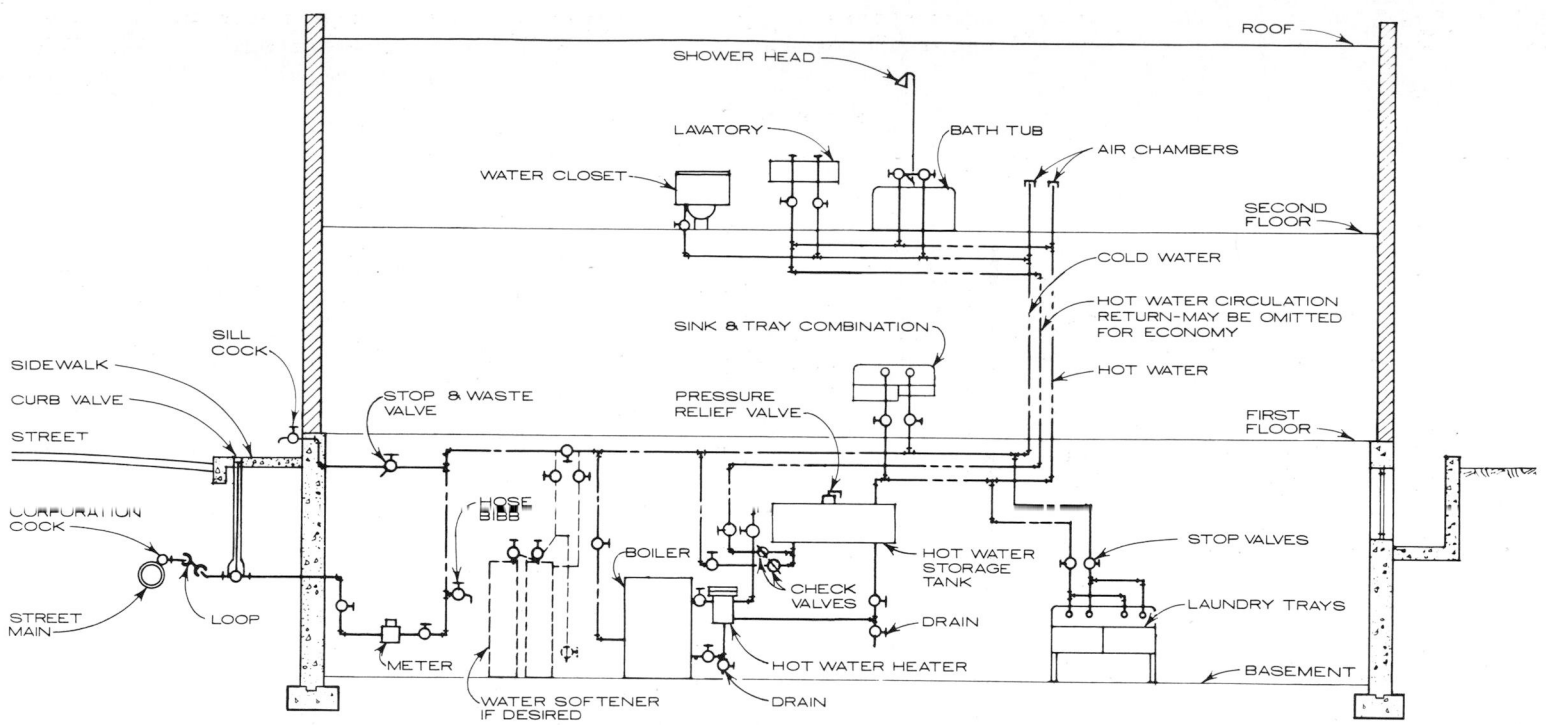

ROOF

SHOWER HEAD

LAVATORY

WATER CLOSET

BATH TUB

AIR CHAMBERS

SECOND FLOOR

COLD WATER

SINK & TRAY COMBINATION

HOT WATER CIRCULATION RETURN-MAY BE OMITTED FOR ECONOMY

HOT WATER

SIDEWALK

SILL COCK

CURB VALVE

STREET

STOP & WASTE VALVE

PRESSURE RELIEF VALVE

FIRST FLOOR

CORPORATION COCK

HOSE BIBB

STOP VALVES

BOILER

HOT WATER STORAGE TANK

STREET MAIN

LOOP

CHECK VALVES

DRAIN

LAUNDRY TRAYS

METER

HOT WATER HEATER

BASEMENT

WATER SOFTENER IF DESIRED

DRAIN

RESIDENTIAL WATER PIPING DIAGRAM

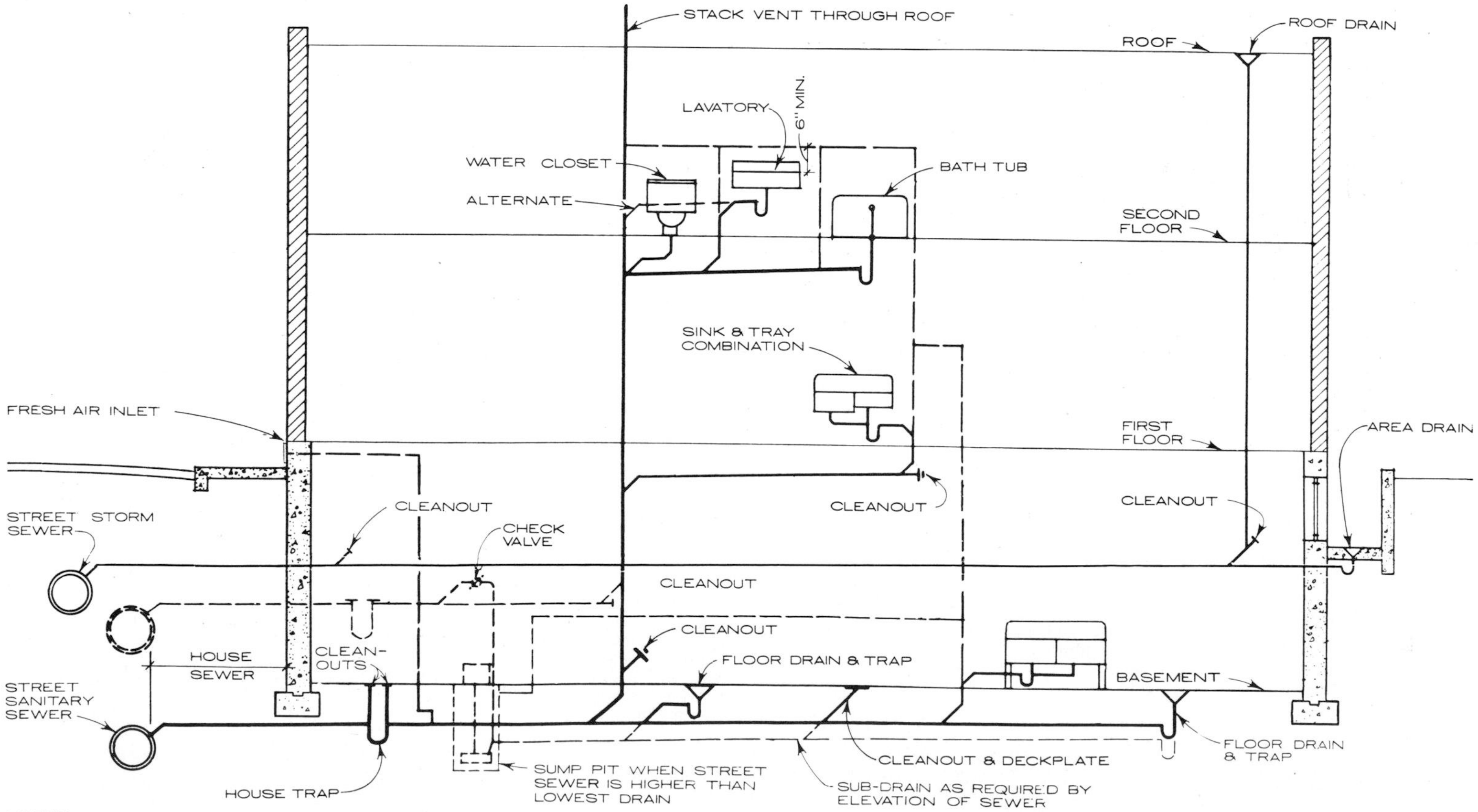

STACK VENT THROUGH ROOF

ROOF

ROOF DRAIN

LAVATORY

6" MIN.

WATER CLOSET

BATH TUB

ALTERNATE

SECOND FLOOR

SINK & TRAY COMBINATION

FRESH AIR INLET

FIRST FLOOR

AREA DRAIN

CLEANOUT

CHECK VALVE

CLEANOUT

CLEANOUT

STREET STORM SEWER

CLEANOUT

CLEANOUT

HOUSE SEWER

CLEAN-OUTS

FLOOR DRAIN & TRAP

BASEMENT

STREET SANITARY SEWER

FLOOR DRAIN & TRAP

HOUSE TRAP

SUMP PIT WHEN STREET SEWER IS HIGHER THAN LOWEST DRAIN

CLEANOUT & DECKPLATE

SUB-DRAIN AS REQUIRED BY ELEVATION OF SEWER

NOTE:
Housetrap is required by some local codes but not recommended by U.S. Dept. of Commerce. Recommended Minimum requirements for Plumbing BH-13.

NOTE:
Local Codes should be consulted for pipe sizes, materials, and other requirements in plumbing systems.

RESIDENTIAL DRAINAGE PIPING DIAGRAM

Sargent, Webster, Crenshaw & Folley; Syracuse, New York

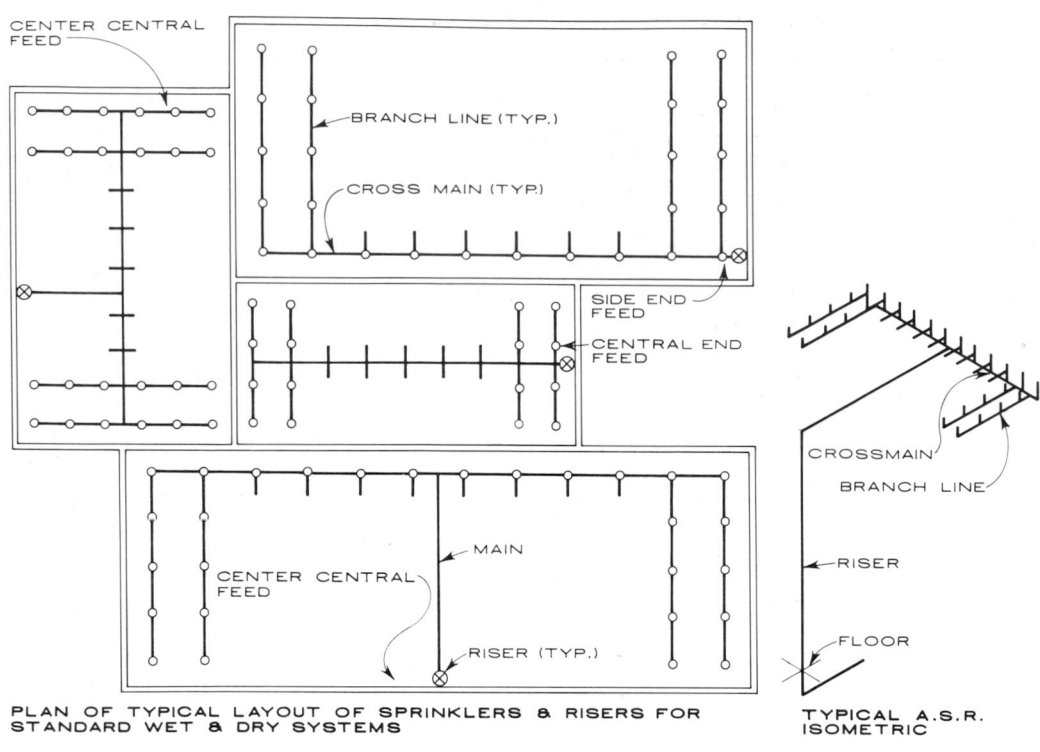

PLAN OF TYPICAL LAYOUT OF SPRINKLERS & RISERS FOR
STANDARD WET & DRY SYSTEMS

TYPICAL A.S.R.
ISOMETRIC

TYPES OF SYSTEMS

A. WET PIPE SYSTEM

A system employing automatic sprinklers attached to a piping system containing water and connected to a water supply so that water discharges immediately from sprinklers opened by a fire.

B. DRY PIPE SYSTEM

A system employing automatic sprinklers attached to a piping system containing air under pressure; the release of which, as from the opening of sprinklers, permits the water pressure to open a valve known as a "dry pipe valve." The water then flows into the piping system and out the open sprinklers.

C. PRE-ACTION SYSTEM

A system employing automatic sprinklers attached to a piping system containing air that may or may not be under pressure, with a supplemental heat responsive system of generally more sensitive characteristics than the automatic sprinklers themselves installed in the same areas as the sprinklers. Actuation of the heat responsive system, as from a fire, opens a valve which permits water to flow into the sprinkler piping system and to be discharged from any sprinklers which may be open.

D. DELUGE SYSTEM

A system employing open sprinklers attached to a piping system connected to a water supply through a valve which is opened by the operation of a heat responsive system installed in the same areas as the sprinklers. When this valve opens, water flows into the piping system and discharges from all sprinklers attached thereto.

E. COMBINED DRY PIPE & PRE-ACTION SPRINKLER SYSTEM

A system employing automatic sprinklers attached to a piping system under air pressure supplemented with a heat responsive system (NAD). N.A.D.S. operate tripping devices and air exhausters, simultaneously allowing valves to open and water to flow into the system.

F. LIMITED WATER SUPPLY SYSTEM

A system employing automatic sprinklers and conforming to these standards but supplied by a pressure tank of limited capacity.

G. FOAM SYSTEMS

The principal use of foam is for the extinguishment of fires involving flammable liquids. Foam is light and has both adhesive and cooling characteristics. This enables it to flow easily across a burning surface, sealing itself if broken and preventing reignition of surfaces already extinguished.

H. CO_2 SYSTEM

I. HOSE STANDPIPE SYSTEMS

Class I for use by fire departments and those trained in handling heavy fire streams. Class II for use by building occupants until the arrival of the fire department and building occupancy.

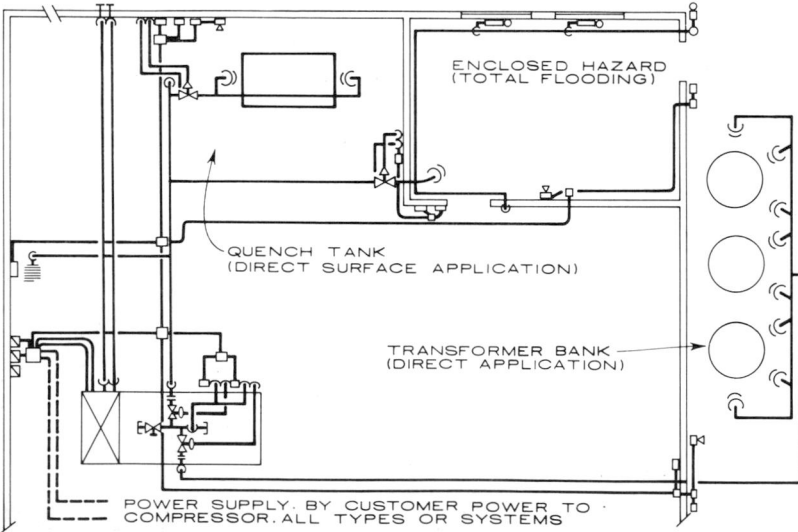

PLAN OF LOW PRESSURE CO_2 SYSTEMS

TYPES OF CO_2 APPLICATIONS

1. TOTAL FLOODING SYSTEM consists of a fixed supply of carbon dioxide normally connected to fixed piping with nozzles arranged to discharge carbon dioxide directly on the burning material.

2. LOCAL APPLICATION SYSTEM consists of a fixed supply of carbon dioxide normally connected to fixed piping with nozzles arranged to discharge carbon dioxide directly on the burning material.

3. HAND HOSE LINE SYSTEM consists of a fixed supply of carbon dioxide supplying hose lines.

4. STANDPIPE SYSTEM & MOBILE SUPPLY consists of a mobile supply of carbon dioxide capable of being quickly moved to position and connected to a system of fixed piping supplying fixed nozzles and/or hose lines that may be used for either total flooding or local application.

Smith, Hinchman & Grylls Associates, Inc.; Detroit, Michigan

PREPARATION FOR FIRE PROTECTION SYSTEM

1. Determine classification of building.

2. Check National, State and Local codes for requirements.

3. Check with authorities having jurisdiction.
   A.   State and Local Fire Marshals.
   B.   Inspection Bureaus.
   C.   Factory Insurance Association or Factory Mutual when they have jurisdiction.

4. Check available water supply.

5. Check space requirements for equipment.

STANDARD MALLEABLE IRON PATTERN

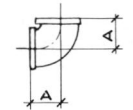 90° ELBOW 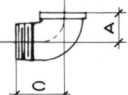 90° STREET ELBOW 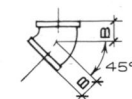 45° ELBOW 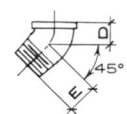 45° STREET ELBOW

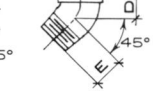 45° Y-BEND 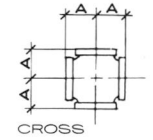 CROSS 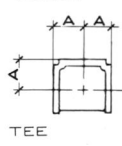 TEE

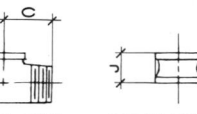 SERVICE TEE 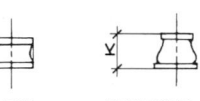 COUPLING REDUCER 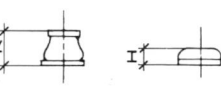 CAP

FITTING DIMENSIONS

SIZE	A	B	C	D	E	F	G	H	J	K
1/8	11/16	1/2	*1		11/16	13/16			9/16	15/16
1/4	13/16	3/4	13/16		3/4	15/16			5/8	1 1/16
3/8	15/16	13/16	1 7/16		11/16	1 1/16	11/16	1 7/16	3/4	1 3/16
1/2	1 1/8	7/8	1 5/8		13/16	1 3/16	3/4	1 11/16	7/8	1 5/16
3/4	15/16	1	1 7/8	15/16	15/16	3/4	2 1/16	1 15/16	1 1/2	1 7/16
1	1 1/2	1 1/8	2 1/8	1 1/8	1 1/2	15/16	2 7/16	1 3/16	1 11/16	1 11/16
1 1/4	1 3/4	1 5/16	2 7/16	1 1/4	1 11/16	1 1/8	2 15/16	1 1/4	1 15/16	2 1/16
1 1/2	1 15/16	1 7/16	2 11/16	1 3/8	1 7/8	1 3/16	3 5/16	1 5/16	2 1/8	2 5/16
2	2 1/4	1 11/16	3 1/4	1 11/16	2 1/4	1 7/16	4	1 7/16	2 1/2	2 13/16
2 1/2	2 11/16	1 15/16	*3 13/16	1 7/8	2 9/16	1 9/16	4 11/16	1 5/8	2 7/8	3 1/4
3	3 1/8	2 3/16	*4 1/2	2 1/8	3	1 11/16	5 9/16	1 3/4	3 3/16	3 11/16
3 1/2	3 7/16	2 3/8	5 1/8	2 3/8	3 3/8			1 15/16	3 7/16	4
4	3 3/4	2 5/8	5 11/16	2 5/8	3 3/4	1 15/16	6 15/16	2 1/16	3 11/16	4 3/8
5	4 1/2	3 1/16	*6 7/8					2 5/16	4 1/4	3 7/8
6	5 1/8	3 7/16	*8					2 9/16	4 3/4	4 3/8

* APPLIES TO STREET ELBOWS ONLY

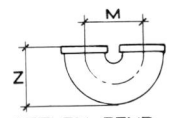

RETURN BEND

RETURN BEND DIMENSIONS

CLOSE PATTERN			OPEN PATTERN		
SIZE	M	N	SIZE	M	N
1/2	1	1 3/4	1/2	1 1/2	1 7/8
3/4	1 1/4	2 3/16	3/4	2	2 1/4
1	1 1/2	2 1/2	1	2 1/2	2 5/8
1 1/4	1 3/4	2 13/16	1 1/4	3	3 3/16
1 1/2	2 3/16	3 3/16	1 1/2	3 1/2	3 5/8
2	2 5/8	3 7/8	2	4	4 3/8
MEDIUM PATTERN			2 1/2	4 1/2	4 15/16
1/2	1 1/4	1 5/8	3	5	5 9/16
3/4	1 1/2	1 15/16	4	6	6 11/16
1	1 7/8	2 1/4			
1 1/4	2 1/4	2 13/16			
1 1/2	2 1/2	3 3/16			
2	3	3 7/8			

SIZES ARE NOMINAL; ALL DIMENSIONS ARE IN INCHES.

FOR REDUCING TEES, CROSSES, ETC. CONSULT MANUFACTURERS CATALOGUES

REDUCERS & REDUCING ELBOWS

SIZE AVAILABLE WHERE MARKED ●

SIZE	MALL. IRON		CAST IRON		
	REDUCING ELBOWS	REDUCERS	REDUCING ELBOWS	REDUCERS	ECCENTRIC REDUCERS
1/4 × 1/8	●	●			
3/8 × 1/4	●	●			
3/8 × 1/8	●	●			
1/2 × 3/8	●	●	●		
1/2 × 1/8	●	●			
1/2 × 1/4	●	●			
3/4 × 1/2	●	●	●	●	
3/4 × 3/8	●	●			
3/4 × 1/4	●	●			
1 × 3/4	●	●	●	●	
1 × 1/2	●	●	●	●	
1 × 1/4	●				
1 × 3/8	●				
1 1/4 × 1	●	●	●	●	●
1 1/4 × 3/4	●	●	●	●	●
1 1/4 × 1/2	●	●			●
1 1/2 × 1 1/4	●	●	●	●	●
1 1/2 × 1	●	●	●	●	●
1 1/2 × 3/4	●	●			●
1 1/2 × 1/2	●	●			●
2 × 1 1/2	●	●	●	●	●
2 × 1 1/4	●	●	●	●	●
2 × 1	●	●	●	●	●
2 × 3/4	●	●			●
2 × 1/2		●			●
2 1/2 × 2	●	●	●	●	●
2 1/2 × 1 1/2	●	●			●
2 1/2 × 1 1/4	●	●			●
2 1/2 × 1		●			●
3 × 2 1/2	●	●	●	●	●
3 × 2	●	●	●	●	●
3 × 1 1/2		●			●
3 × 1 1/4		●			●
3 × 1		●			●
3 1/2 × 3		●	●		●
3 1/2 × 2 1/2		●			●
3 1/2 × 2		●			●
3 1/2 × 1 1/2					●
3 1/2 × 1 1/4					●
3 1/2 × 1					●
4 × 3 1/2		●	●	●	●
4 × 3		●	●	●	●
4 × 2 1/2		●	●	●	●
4 × 2		●	●	●	●
4 × 1 1/2		●			●
4 × 1 1/4					●
4 × 1					●
5 × 4	●	●	●	●	●
5 × 3 1/2			●		●
5 × 3			●		●
5 × 2 1/2			●		●
5 × 2					●
6 × 5	●	●	●	●	●
6 × 4			●	●	●
6 × 3 1/2					●
6 × 3			●		●
6 × 2 1/2					●
6 × 2					●
6 × 6			●	●	●
8 × 8					●
8 × 4					●

STANDARD CAST IRON PATTERN

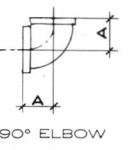 90° ELBOW 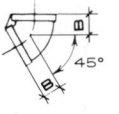 45° ELBOW 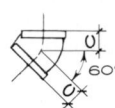 60° ELBOW *

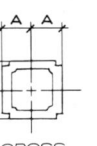 22 1/2° ELBOW * 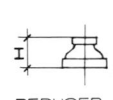 CROSS 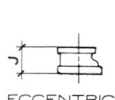 TEE

45° Y-BEND 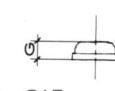 REDUCER ECCENTRIC REDUCER CAP

*60° AND 22 1/2° ELBOWS ARE MADE BY SOME MANUFACTURERS BUT ARE NOT STANDARD.

FITTING DIMENSIONS

SIZE	A	B	C	D	E	F	G	H	J
1/4	13/16	3/4							
3/8	15/16	13/16							
1/2	1 1/8	7/8	1		3/4				1 3/8
3/4	15/16	1	1 1/16	7/8	3/4	2 1/4			1 1/2
1	1 1/2	1 1/8	1 1/4	1	3/4	2 3/4			1 11/16
1 1/4	1 3/4	1 5/16	1 7/16	1 1/8	1	3 1/4		2 1/8	2 1/8
1 1/2	1 15/16	1 7/16	1 5/8	1 1/4	1 1/16	3 13/16		2 1/4	2 1/4
2	2 1/4	1 11/16	1 7/8	1 7/16	1 1/4	4 1/2		2 7/16	2 7/16
2 1/2	2 11/16	1 15/16	2 3/16	1 9/16	1 9/16	5 3/16	1 13/16	2 5/8	2 11/16
3	3 1/8	2 3/16	2 1/2	1 3/4	1 3/4	6 1/8	1 15/16	2 7/8	2 15/16
3 1/2	3 7/16	2 3/8					2 1/16	3 1/8	3 1/8
4	3 3/4	2 5/8	3	2 1/16	2 1/8	7 5/8	2 3/16	3 3/8	3 3/8
5	4 1/2	3 1/16	3 1/2	2 1/4			2 3/8	3 7/8	3 7/8
6	5 1/8	3 7/16	4 1/16	2 7/16			2 5/8	3 13/16	4 3/8
8	6 9/16	4 1/4					2 7/8	5 1/4	5 1/4
10	*8 1/16	5 3/16					3 1/2		
12	*9 1/2	6					3 7/8		

* THIS DIMENSION APPLIES TO ELBOWS AND TEES ONLY.

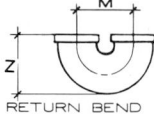

RETURN BEND

RETURN BEND DIMENSIONS

CLOSE PATTERN			OPEN PATTERN			WIDE PATTERN		
SIZE	M	N	SIZE	M	N	SIZE	M	N
1/2	1 1/4	1 23/32	1/2	1 3/4	1 15/16	1	3	3
3/4	1 1/2	2 1/32	3/4	1 7/8	2 7/32	1	4	3 1/2
1	1 3/4	2 3/8	1	2 1/2	2 11/16	1 1/4	4	3 3/4
1 1/4	2 1/4	2 29/32	1 1/4	3	3 9/32	1 1/4	6	4 3/4
1 1/2	2 1/2	3 1/4	1 1/2	3 1/2	3 3/4	1 1/2	6	5
2	3 1/4	3 31/32	2	4 1/2	4 19/32	2	6	5 5/16
2 1/2	3 3/4	4 9/16	2 1/2	5 1/2	5 7/16			
3	4 1/2	5 3/16	3	6 1/2	6 5/16			
4	6	6 13/16	4	7 1/2	7 9/16			

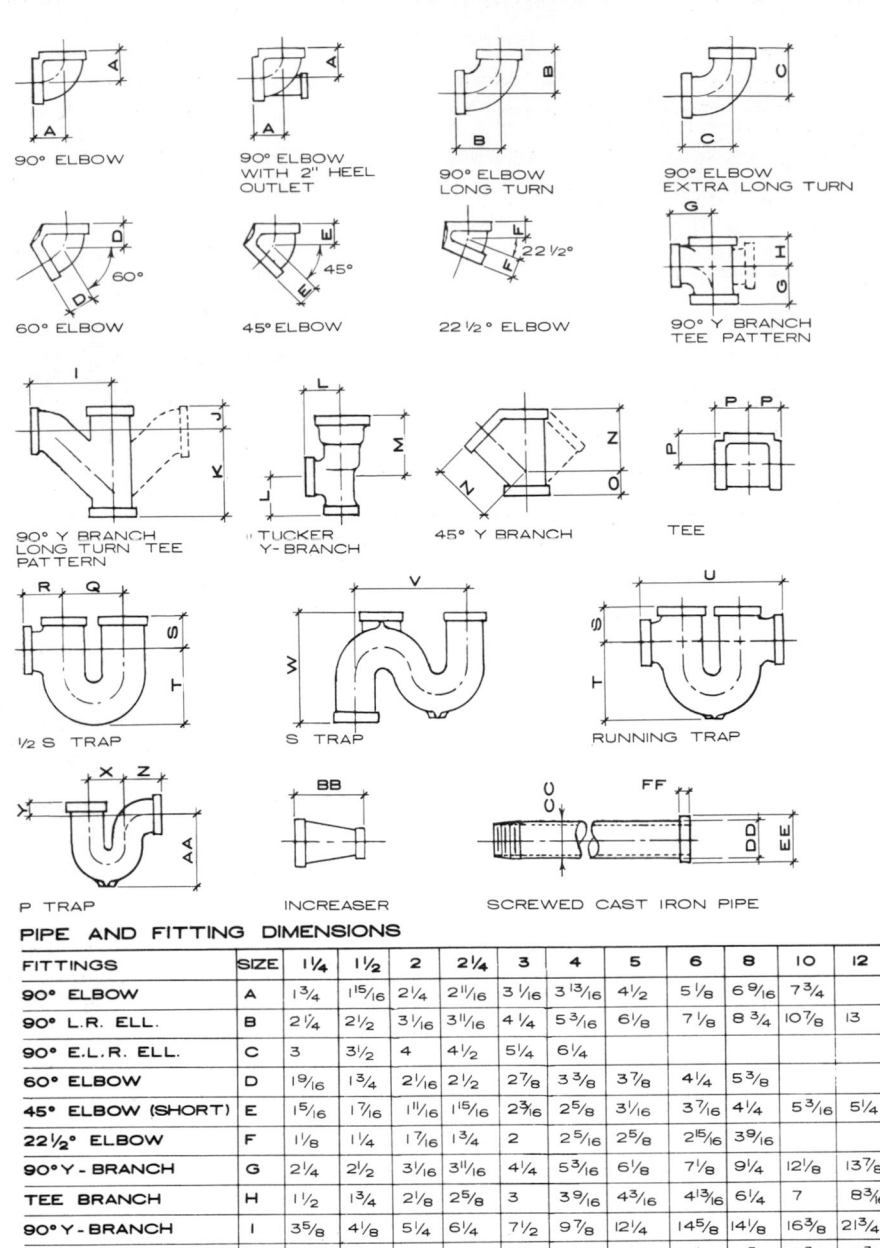

90° ELBOW

90° ELBOW WITH 2" HEEL OUTLET

90° ELBOW LONG TURN

90° ELBOW EXTRA LONG TURN

60° ELBOW

45° ELBOW

22 1/2° ELBOW

90° Y BRANCH TEE PATTERN

90° Y BRANCH LONG TURN TEE PATTERN

TUCKER Y-BRANCH

45° Y BRANCH

TEE

1/2 S TRAP

S TRAP

RUNNING TRAP

P TRAP

INCREASER

SCREWED CAST IRON PIPE

PIPE AND FITTING DIMENSIONS

FITTINGS	SIZE	1 1/4	1 1/2	2	2 1/4	3	4	5	6	8	10	12
90° ELBOW	A	1 3/4	1 15/16	2 1/4	2 11/16	3 1/16	3 13/16	4 1/2	5 1/8	6 9/16	7 3/4	
90° L.R. ELL.	B	2 1/4	2 1/2	3 1/16	3 11/16	4 1/4	5 3/16	6 1/8	7 1/8	8 3/4	10 7/8	13
90° E.L.R. ELL.	C	3	3 1/2	4	4 1/2	5 1/4	6 1/4					
60° ELBOW	D	1 9/16	1 3/4	2 1/16	2 1/2	2 7/8	3 3/8	3 7/8	4 1/4	5 3/8		
45° ELBOW (SHORT)	E	1 5/16	1 7/16	1 11/16	1 15/16	2 3/8	2 5/8	3 1/16	3 7/16	4 1/4	5 3/16	5 1/4
22 1/2° ELBOW	F	1 1/8	1 1/4	1 7/16	1 3/4	2	2 5/16	2 5/8	2 15/16	3 9/16		
90° Y-BRANCH	G	2 1/4	2 1/2	3 1/16	3 11/16	4 1/4	5 3/16	6 1/8	7 1/8	9 1/4	12 1/8	13 7/8
TEE BRANCH	H	1 1/2	1 3/4	2 1/8	2 5/8	3	3 9/16	4 3/16	4 13/16	6 1/4	7	8 3/16
90° Y-BRANCH	I	3 5/8	4 1/8	5 1/4	6 1/4	7 1/2	9 7/8	12 1/4	14 5/8	14 1/8	16 3/8	21 3/4
LONG TURN TEE	J	1 1/8	1 1/4	1 3/4	2	2 3/8	3 1/8	3 1/2	4 1/8	3 3/4	7 3/8	4 3/8
PATTERN	K	3 5/8	4 1/8	5 1/4	6 1/4	7 1/2	9 7/8	12 1/4	14 1/8	13 1/4	15 3/8	21 5/8
TUCKER	L	2 1/4	2 1/2	3 1/16		4 1/4						
Y-BRANCH	M	3 15/16	4 1/4	4 11/16		5 3/8						
45° Y-BRANCH	N	3 1/4	3 5/8	4 7/8	5 5/8	6 3/16	7 11/16	9 3/16	10 3/4	13 9/16	16 1/2	19 5/8
	O	1 3/4	1 7/8	2 1/8	2 1/2	2 13/16	3 3/16	3 3/4	4 1/8	5 1/4	6 1/2	4 5/8
TEE	P	1 3/4	1 15/16	2 1/4	2 11/16	3 1/16	3 13/16	4 1/2	5 1/8	6 1/2	8 1/16	9 1/2
1/2 S-TRAP	Q	3 1/8	3 3/8	4	4 3/4	5 3/8	7	8 3/8	10 1/8	12 3/8	14 3/4	
	R	2 5/16	2 1/2	3 1/16	3 5/8	4 1/8	5 1/8	6 1/16	6 9/16	8 15/16	10 3/4	
	S	2	2 1/4	2 9/16	3 1/4	3 1/2	4 3/16	4 3/4	5 7/16	6 3/4	8 1/4	
RUNNING	T	4 1/2	4 15/16	5 11/16		7 3/8	9 3/8	11 3/8	13 1/2	17 1/4	20 3/4	
TRAP	U	7 3/4	8 3/8	10 1/8		13 3/4	17 1/4	20 1/2	23 1/4	30 1/4	36 3/4	
S-TRAP	V	7 3/4	6 13/16	8		11 3/4	13 1/2					
	W	2	7 1/4	8 3/4		11 1/4	13 7/8					
P-TRAP	X	2	2 1/4	2 3/4		3 3/4	5					
	Y	3/4	7/8	7/8		1 3/16	1 1/2					
	Z	1 15/16	2 1/8	2 9/16		3 3/8	4 1/4					
	AA	4 1/2	5	5 11/16		7 3/4	9 3/16					
INKREASER	BB			9	9	9	9	9	9	9	9	9
SCREWED	CC	1 15/64	1 29/64	1 57/64	2 24/64	2 29/32	3 53/64	4 13/16	5 49/64	7 5/8		
CAST IRON	DD	1 21/32	1 29/32	2 3/8	2 7/8	3 1/2	4 1/2	5 9/16	6 5/8	8 5/8		
PIPE	EE	2 25/64	2 11/16	3 9/32	3 55/64	4 5/8	5 5/8	7 3/64	8 9/32	10 5/8		
	FF	45/64	23/32	49/64	9/64	1 3/64	1 9/64	1 13/32	1 33/64	1 45/64		

REDUCING FITTINGS

NOMINAL SIZES		90° ELBOW	DOUBLE 90° Y-BRANCH TEE PAT.	DOUBLE 90° Y-BRANCH (LG. TR.)	DOUBLE 45° Y-BRANCH	INCREASER
a	b					
1 1/2	1 1/4	●	●	●	●	
2	1 1/2	●	●	●	●	●
2	1 1/4	●	●	●	●	●
2 1/2	2	●	●	●	●	
2 1/2	1 1/2	●	●	●	●	
3	2 1/2				●	
3	2	●	●	●	●	
3	1 1/2	●	●	●	●	
3 1/2	3					
4	3	●	●	●	●	
4	2	●	●	●	●	
4	1 1/2	●	●	●	●	
5	4	●	●	●	●	
5	3	●	●	●	●	
5	2	●	●	●	●	
5	1 1/2					
6	5	●	●	●	●	
6	4	●	●	●	●	
6	3	●	●	●	●	
6	2	●	●	●	●	
8	6	●	●	●	●	
8	5	●	●	●	●	
8	4	●	●	●	●	
8	3	●	●	●	●	
10	8	●	●	●	●	
10	6	●	●	●	●	
10	5	●	●	●	●	
10	4		●	●	●	
12	10					●
12	6					●

REDUCING FITTINGS

NOMINAL SIZES			90° Y-BRANCH TEE PATTERN	90° Y-BRANCH LONG TURN TEE PAT.	45 Y-BRANCH	TEE
a	b	c				
1 1/2	1 1/2	1 1/4	●	●	●	●
1 1/2	1 1/4	1 1/4	●			
2	2	1 1/2	●	●	●	●
2	2	1 1/4	●	●	●	●
2	1 1/2	2	●	●	●	●
2	1 1/2	1 1/2			●	
2 1/2	2 1/2	2	●	●	●	●
2 1/2	2 1/2	1 1/2	●	●	●	●
3	3	2 1/2	●	●	●	●
3	3	2	●	●	●	●
3	3	1 1/2	●	●	●	●
3	3	1 1/4	●	●	●	●
4	4	3	●	●	●	●
4	4	2 1/2	●	●	●	●
4	4	2	●	●	●	●
4	4	1 1/2	●	●	●	●
5	5	4	●	●	●	●
5	5	3	●	●	●	●
5	5	2 1/2				
5	5	2	●	●	●	●
5	5	1 1/2	●	●	●	●
5	5	1 1/4				
6	6	5	●	●	●	●
6	6	4	●	●	●	●
6	6	3	●	●	●	●
6	6	2	●	●	●	●
6	6	1 1/2	●	●	●	●
8	8	6	●	●	●	●
8	8	5	●	●	●	●
8	8	4	●	●	●	●
8	8	3	●	●	●	●
10	10	8		●	●	●
10	10	6		●	●	●
10	10	5		●	●	●
10	10	4		●	●	●
12	12	10				●
12	12	8	●	●	●	●
12	12	6			●	
12	12	4	●			

1/8 BENT OFFSET

SIZE	A	B	SIZE	A	B
2	4	7 1/2	4	10	15 3/4
2	6	9 1/2	4	12	17 3/4
2	8	11 1/2	5	6	12 5/8
2	10	13 1/2	5	8	14 5/8
3	4	8 3/4	5	10	16 5/8
3	6	10 3/4	5	12	18 5/8
3	8	12 3/4	6	6	13 5/8
3	10	14 3/4	6	8	15 5/8
4	4	9 3/4	6	10	17 5/8
4	6	11 3/4	6	12	19 5/8
4	8	13 3/4			

SIZES ARE NOMINAL, ALL DIMENSIONS ARE IN INCHES.

DIMENSIONS OF STANDARD IRON SCREW PIPE (ASA SCHEDULE 40)

NOMINAL INTERNAL DIAMETER	1/8"	1/4"	3/8"	1/2"	3/4"	1"	1 1/4"	1 1/2"	2"	2 1/2"	3"	3 1/2"	4"	5"	6"	8"	10"	12"
ACTUAL INTERNAL DIAMETER	.269	.364	.493	.622	.824	1.049	1.38	1.61	2.067	2.469	3.068	3.548	4.026	5.047	6.065	7.981	10.02	12.00
ACTUAL EXTERNAL DIAMETER	.405	.540	.675	.840	1.05	1.315	1.66	1.90	2.375	2.875	3.50	4.00	4.50	5.563	6.625	8.625	10.75	12.75
INTERNAL AREA	.057	.104	.191	.304	.533	.864	1.496	2.036	3.355	4.788	7.393	9.886	12.73	20.00	28.89	50.02	78.85	113.09

DIAMETERS OF FITTINGS ACROSS OUTSIDE FACE

NOMINAL SIZE	1/8"	1/4"	3/8"	1/2"	3/4"	1"	1/4"	1/2"	2"	2 1/2"	3"	3 1/2"	4"	5"	6"	8"	10"	12"
MALLEABLE 150# SWP	11/16"	7/8"	1"	1 1/4"	1 1/2"	1 13/16"	2 3/16"	2 7/6"	3"	3 9/16"	4 5/16"	4 7/8"	5 7/16"	6 5/8"	7 13/16"			
MALLEABLE 300# SWP		15/16"	1 1/8"	1 3/8"	1 5/8"	1 15/16"	2 3/8"	2 11/16"	3 5/16"	3 7/8"	4 5/8"	5 1/4"	5 13/16"	7 1/16"	8 5/16"			
CAST IRON SCREW 125# SWP		15/16"	1 1/8"	1 3/8"	1 5/8"	1 15/16"	2 3/8"	2 11/16"	3 5/16"	3 7/8"	4 5/8"	5 1/4"	5 13/16"	7 1/16"	8 5/16"	10 5/8"	13 1/8"	15 1/2"
CAST IRON SCREW DRAINAGE							2 3/8"	2 11/16"	3 5/16"	3 7/8"	4 5/8"		5 13/16"	7 1/16"	8 5/16"	10 5/8"		
EXTERNAL DIAMETER OF SOIL PIPE XH									2 3/8"		3 1/2"		4 1/2"	5 1/2"	6 1/2"	8 5/8"	10 3/4"	12 3/4"
EXT. DIA. OF BELL ON SOIL PIPE & FITTING XH									3 15/16"		5 3/16"		6 3/16"	7 3/16"	8 3/16"	10 7/8"	13 1/8"	15 1/4"

Standard lengths of iron soil pipes = 5'–0" laying lengths

150# SWP malleable fittings are used on water and vent piping.

300# SWP malleable fittings are used for severe service.

125# SWP cast iron screw fittings are used for sprinkler and steam piping.

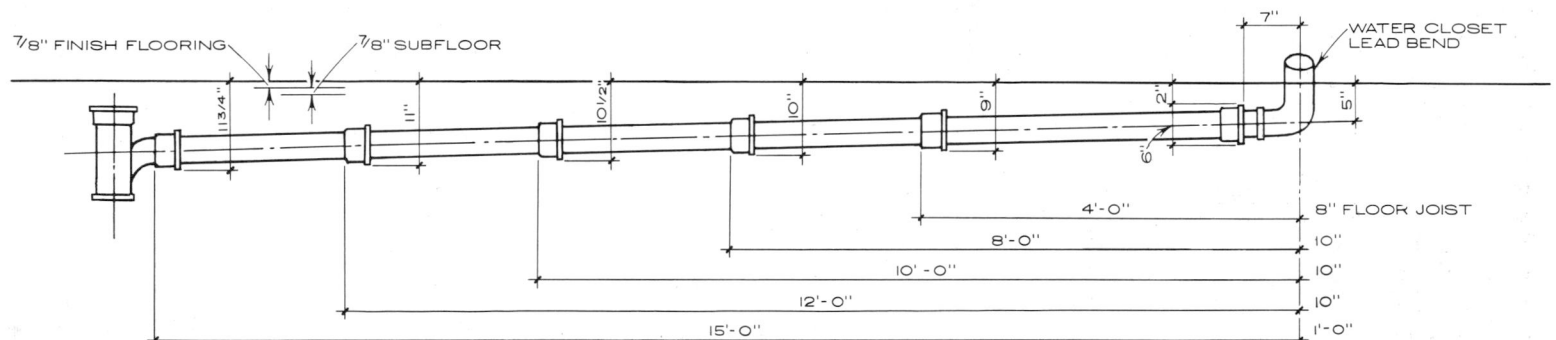

LENGTH OF RUN FROM WATER CLOSET FOR 4" C.I. SOIL LINE (INCLUDING BEND) IN DIFFERENT FLOOR THICKNESSES

DIMENSIONS OF INTERSECTIONS OF VENT WITH SOIL OR WASTE LINE

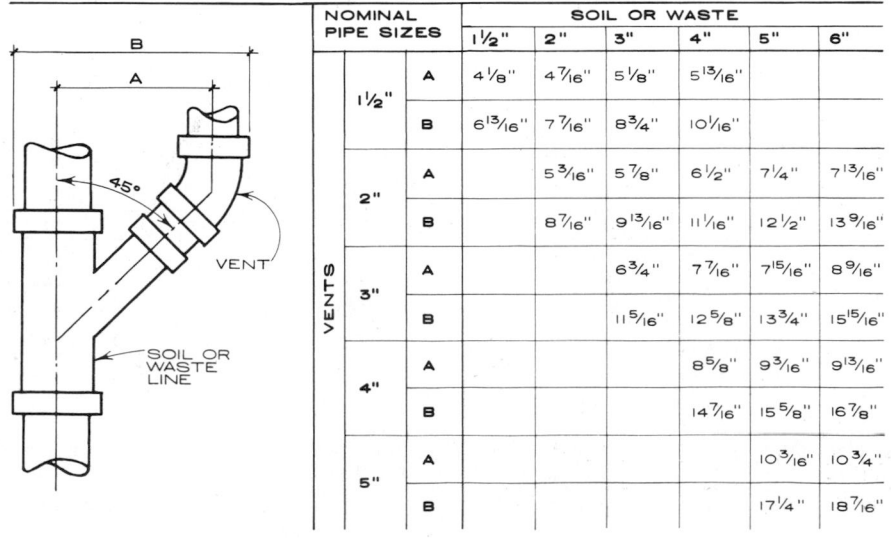

NOMINAL PIPE SIZES		SOIL OR WASTE					
		1 1/2"	2"	3"	4"	5"	6"
1 1/2"	A	4 1/8"	4 7/16"	5 1/8"	5 13/16"		
	B	6 13/16"	7 7/16"	8 3/4"	10 1/16"		
2"	A		5 3/16"	5 7/8"	6 1/2"	7 1/4"	7 13/16"
	B		8 7/16"	9 13/16"	11 1/16"	12 1/2"	13 9/16"
3"	A			6 3/4"	7 7/16"	7 15/16"	8 9/16"
	B			11 5/16"	12 5/8"	13 3/4"	15 15/16"
4"	A				8 5/8"	9 3/16"	9 13/16"
	B				14 7/16"	15 5/8"	16 7/8"
5"	A					10 3/16"	10 3/4"
	B					17 1/4"	18 7/16"

(Left side of table labeled VENTS)

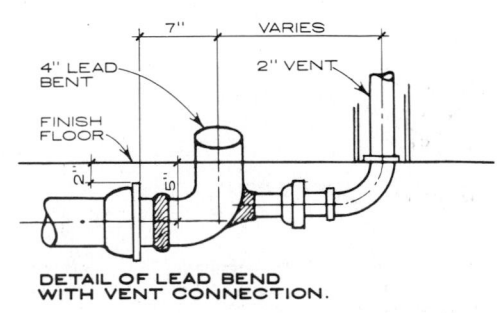

DETAIL OF LEAD BEND WITH VENT CONNECTION.

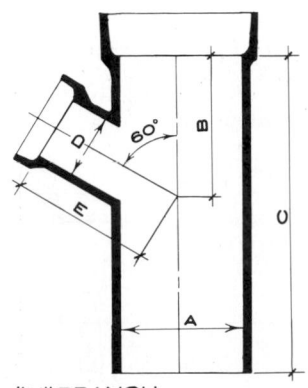

"Y" BRANCH

A	B	C	D	E
4"	8"	1'-0"	4"	6¾"
6"	8¾"	1'-6"	4"	7½"
6"	9¾"	1'-6"	6"	8¾"
8"	9¼"	2'-0"	4"	8¾"
8"	11¼"	&	6"	9¾"
8"	1'-0¼"	3'-0"	8"	11"
10"	11"		4"	10¾"
10"	1'-1"		6"	11¼"
10"	1'-2"		8"	1'-0"
10"	1'-3"		10"	1'-1"
1'-0"	11¼"		4"	1'-0¼"
1'-0"	1'-0¼"		6"	1'-0¾"
1'-0"	1'-2¼"		8"	1'-1½"
1'-0"	1'-3¼"		10"	1'-2¼"
1'-0"	1'-5¼"		1'-0"	1'-3"

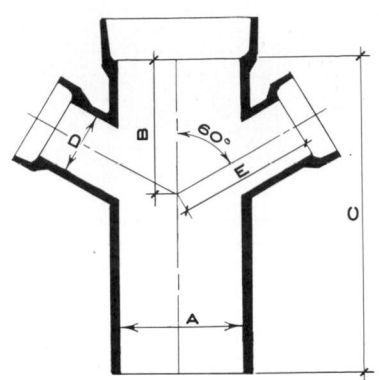

DOUBLE "Y" BRANCH

A	B	C	D	E
4"	8"	1'-0"	4"	6¾"
6"	8¾"	1'-6"	4"	7½"
6	9¾"	1'-6"	6"	8¾"
8"	11¼"	2'-3"	6"	9¾"

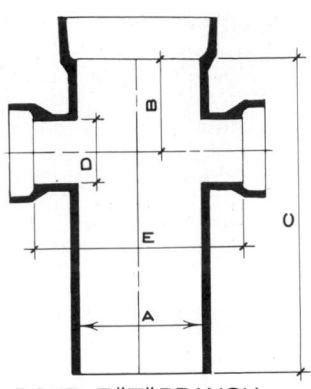

DOUBLE "T" BRANCH

A	B	C	D	E
4"	5"	1'-0"	4"	8½"
6"	5¼"	1'-6"	4"	11"
6"	6¼"	1'-6"	6"	11"
8"	6½"	2'-3"	6"	1'-1½"

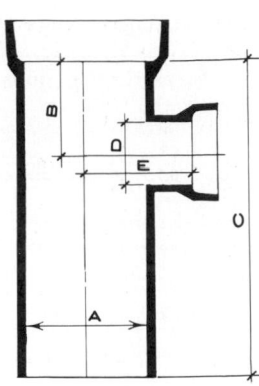

"T" BRANCH

A	B	C	D	E
4"	5"	1'-0"	4"	4¼"
6"	5¼"	1'-6"	4"	5½"
6"	6¼"	1'-6"	6"	5½"
8"	5½"	2'-0"	4"	6½"
8"	6½"	&	6"	6¾"
8"	7¾"	3'-0"	8"	7"
10"	6"		4"	7"
10"	6¾"		6"	7¾"
10"	7¾"		8"	8¼"
10"	9"		10"	8½"
1'-0"	6¼"		4"	8¾"
1'-0"	6¾"		6"	9"
1'-0"	8"		8"	9½"
1'-0"	9¼"		10"	9¾"
1'-0"	10½"		1'-0"	10"

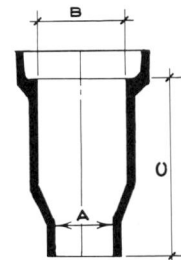

REDUCERS

A	B	C
4"	6"	1'-0"
6"	8"	1'-0"
8"	10"	1'-0"
10"	1'-0"	1'-0"

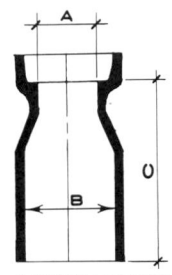

INCREASERS

A	B	C
4"	6"	1'-0"
6"	8"	1'-0"
6"	10"	1'-0"
8"	10"	1'-0"
10"	1'-0"	1'-0"
1'-0"	1'-3"	1'-0"
1'-3"	1'-6"	1'-0"

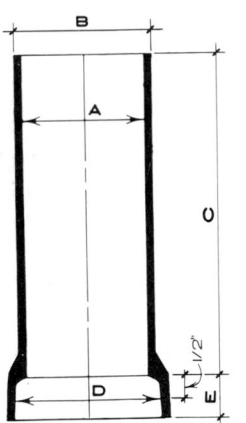

DIAM. IN VARYING INCREMENTS UP TO 3'-0" AVAILABLE

STANDARD STRAIGHT PIPE

A	B	C	D	E
4"	5⅛"	2'-0"	6⅛"	1¾"
6"	7⁷⁄₁₆"	2'-6"	8⅝"	2¼"
8"	9¾"	&	11"	2½"
10"	1'-0"	3'-0"	1-1¼"	2⅝"
1'-0"	1'-2⁵⁄₁₆"		1'-3¾"	2¾"

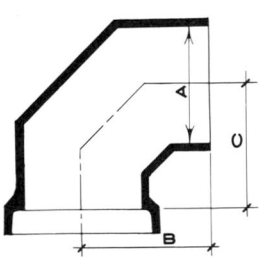

CUT ELBOWS

A	B	C
8"	8"	8"
10"	9½"	9"
1'-0"	10¾"	10¾"

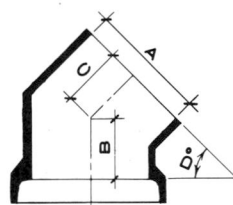

CUT CURVES

A	B	C	D
8"	4½"	4⅝"	30°,
10"	5⅛"	5½"	45°
1'-0"	5⅞"	5⅞"	

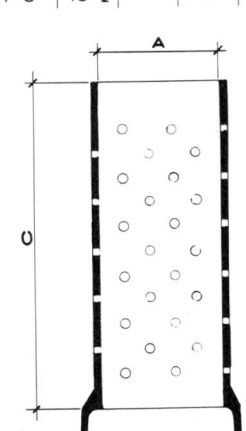

DIAMETERS UP TO 2'-0" AVAILABLE

PERFORATED PIPE

A	C
4"	2'-0"
6"	2'-0"
8"	2'-0"
10"	2'-0"
1'-0"	2'-0"

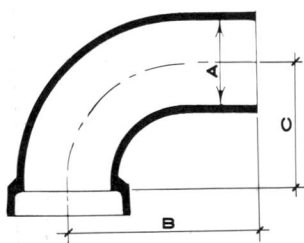

ELBOW (LONG RADIUS) 90°

A	B	C
4"	9¾"	10"
6"	10"	1'-2½"
8"	1'-0"	1'-5"

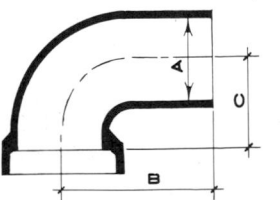

ELBOW (SHORT RADIUS) 90°

A	B	C
4"	7"	4¾"
6"	11"	6½"
8"	1'-2"	8"

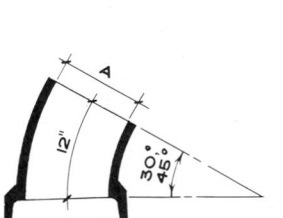

CURVE (SHORT RADIUS)

A
4"
6"

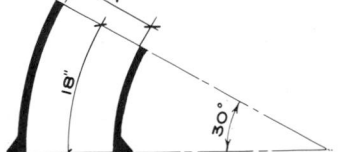

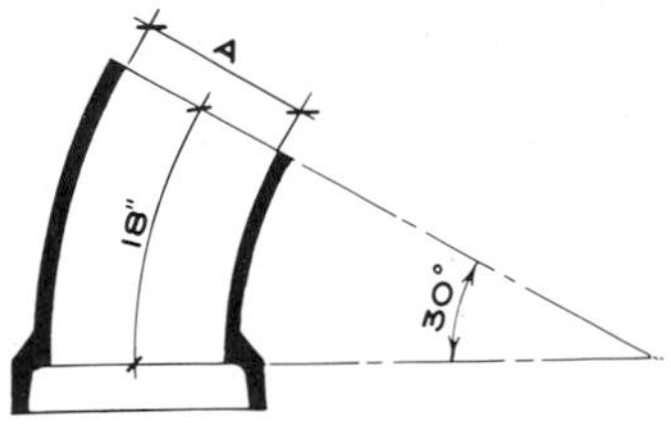

CURVES (LONG RADIUS)

A
4"
6"

DIMENSIONS OF STANDARD PLASTIC PIPE (ASA SCHEDULE 40)

NOMINAL PIPE SIZE	1/4	3/8	1/2	3/4	1	1 1/4	1 1/2	2	2 1/2	3	3 1/2	4	5	6	8
ACTUAL EXTERNAL DIA.	.540	.675	.840	1.050	1.315	1.660	1.900	2.375	2.875	3.500	4.000	4.500	5.563	6.625	8.625
ACTUAL INTERNAL DIA.	.364	.493	.622	.824	1.049	1.380	1.610	2.067	2.469	3.068	3.548	4.026	5.047	6.065	7.981
WALL THICKNESS	.088	.091	.109	.113	.133	.140	.145	.154	.203	.216	.226	.237	.258	.280	.322

DIM. OF ST'D. PLAST. PIPE (ASA SCHED. 40) CONT.

NOMINAL PIPE SIZE	10	12	14	16
ACTUAL EXTERNAL DIA.	10.750	12.750	14.000	16.000
ACTUAL INTERNAL DIA.	10.020	11.938	13.126	15.000
WALL THICKNESS	.365	.406	.437	.500

NOTE: THIS SCHEDULE IS NOT RECOMMENDED FOR THREADED APPLICATIONS.

DIMENSIONS OF STANDARD PLASTIC PIPE (ASA SCHEDULE 80)

NOMINAL PIPE SIZE	1/4	3/8	1/2	3/4	1	1 1/4	1 1/2	2	2 1/2	3	3 1/2	4	5	6	8
ACTUAL EXTERNAL DIA.	.540	.675	.840	1.050	1.315	1.660	1.900	2.375	2.875	3.500	4.000	4.500	5.563	6.625	8.625
ACTUAL INTERNAL DIA.	.302	.432	.546	.742	.957	1.278	1.500	1.939	2.469	3.068	3.548	4.026	5.047	6.065	7.981
WALL THICKNESS	.119	.126	.147	.154	.179	.191	.200	.218	.203	.216	.226	.237	.258	.280	.322

DIM OF ST'D PLAST PIPE CONT

NOMINAL PIPE	10	12
ACTUAL EXTERNAL DIA.	10.750	12.750
ACTUAL INTERNAL DIA.	9.564	11.376
WALL THICKNESS	.593	.687

NOTE: THIS SCHEDULE IS RECOMMENDED FOR THREADED APPLICATIONS.

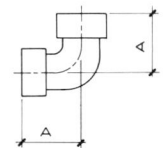

1/4 BEND

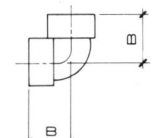

STRAIGHT 90°

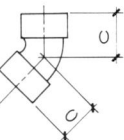

1/8 BEND

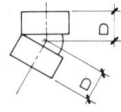

1/16 BEND

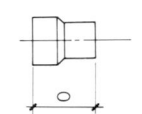

INCREASER

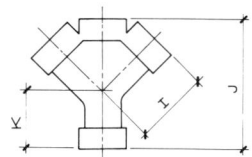

DOUBLE 45° Y-BRANCH

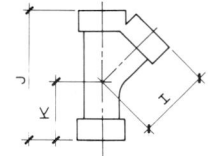

45° Y BRANCH

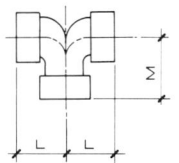

DOUBLE 90° ELBOW

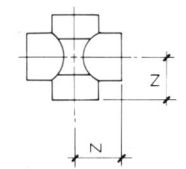

90° CROSS

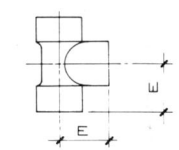

TEE

PLASTIC PIPE

PLASTIC PIPE DRAINAGE FITTINGS

FITTING	SIZE	1 1/2	2	3	4
1/4 BEND	A	2 1/2	3 1/16	4 1/4	5 1/8
STRAIGHT 90°	B	1 15/16	2 1/4	3 1/16	3 11/16
1/8 BEND	C	1 7/8	2 1/4	2 1/8	2 9/16
1/16 BEND	D	1 3/16	1 13/32	1 23/32	2 1/32
STRAIGHT TEE	E	2 1/4	2 25/32	3 1/16	3 21/32
SANITARY TEE AND DOUBLE SANITARY TEE	F	2 15/32	3 1/16	4 9/32	5 1/16
	G	5 7/16	6 1/2	9 1/32	10 5/8
	H	2 15/32	3 1/16	4 9/32	5 1/16
DOUBLE 45° Y-BRANCH AND 45° Y-BRANCH	I	3 19/32	4 3/8	6 7/32	7 3/4
	J	5 7/16	6 1/2	9 1/32	11 1/16
	K	1 27/32	2 1/8	2 13/16	3 5/8
DOUBLE 90° ELBOW	L	1 25/32	2 5/16	3 1/16	4
	M	2 15/32	3 1/16	4 9/16	5 9/32
90° CROSS	N	2 1/4	2 25/32	3 1/2	3 21/32
INCREASER	O	2 9/32	2 61/64	3 3/4	3 15/16
P-TRAP	P	6 1/8	7 1/16		
	Q	4	4		
	R	8 1/4	10 1/2		
	S	8 5/32	8 25/32		
RUNNING P-TRAP	T	8 15/16	10 1/8		
	U	4	4		
	V	6 5/32	6 25/32		

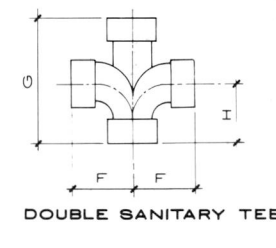

SANITARY TEE

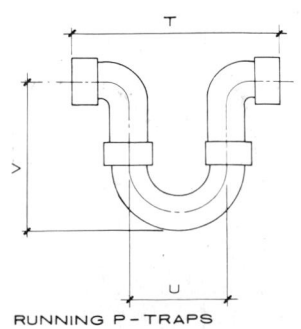

DOUBLE SANITARY TEE

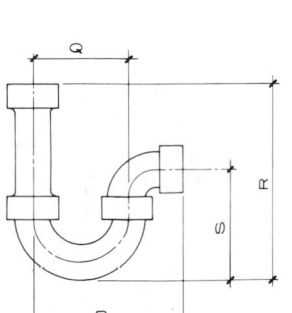

P-TRAP

RUNNING P-TRAPS

V. Peruchietti; Giffels & Rossetti, Inc.; Detroit, Michigan

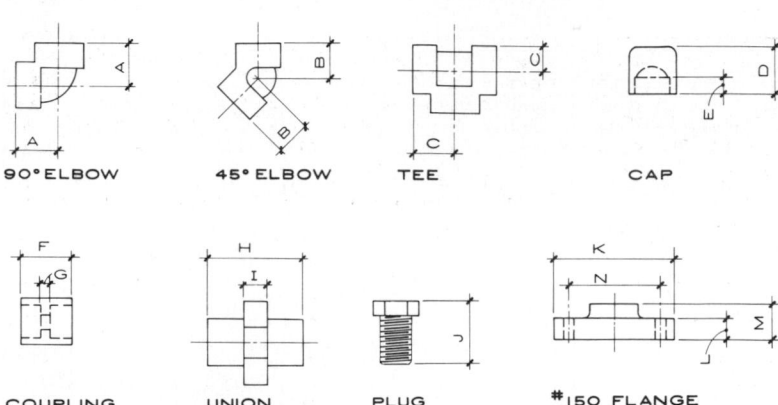

90° ELBOW   45° ELBOW   TEE   CAP

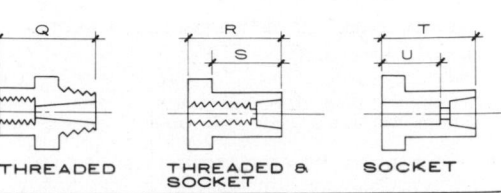

THREADED   THREADED & SOCKET   SOCKET

SCHEDULE 80 PRESSURE FITTINGS REDUCING BUSHINGS

COUPLING   UNION   PLUG   #150 FLANGE

SCHEDULE 80 PRESSURE FITTINGS

SCHEDULE 80 PLASTIC PRESSURE PATTERN

THREADED FITTINGS

NOM. PIPE SIZE	A	B	C	D	E	F	G	H	I	J	K	L	M	N
1/4	7/8	3/4	7/8	3/4		1 3/16	2 3/8		13/16					
3/8	1	13/16	1	13/16		1 1/4	2 5/8		13/16					
1/2	1 1/8	7/8	1 1/8	1		1 3/8	2 5/8		1 1/8		3 1/2	7/16	11/16	2 3/8
3/4	1 5/16	1	1 5/16	1 1/16		1 1/16	3	3			3 7/8	1/2	11/16	2 3/4
1	1 1/2	1 3/16	1 1/2	1 1/4		1 3/4	3	3			4 1/4	9/16	7/8	3 1/8
1 1/4	1 13/16	1 5/16	1 13/16	1 3/8		1 15/16	3 1/4		1 5/16		4 5/8	5/8	7/8	3 1/2
1 1/2	1 15/16	1 7/16	1 15/16	1 5/16		2 1/8	3 11/16		1 5/16		5	11/16	7/8	3 7/8
2	2 1/4	1 11/16	2 1/4	1 9/16		2 1/2	3 15/16		1 3/8		6	3/4	7/8	4 3/4
2 1/2	2 11/16	1 15/16	2 11/16	2 1/2		2 7/8	5		1 7/8		7	15/16	1 1/8	5 1/2
3	3 1/8	2 3/16	3 1/8	3		3 1/8	5		1 15/16		7 1/2	1	1 1/4	6
4	3 3/4	2 5/8	3 3/4	3 5/16		3 3/16			2		9	1 1/8	1 3/8	7 1/2
6											11	1 1/4	1 7/8	9 1/2
8											13 1/2	1 7/16	1 3/4	11 3/4

SOCKET TYPE

NOM. PIPE SIZE	A	B	C	D	E	F	G	H	I	J	K	L	M	N
1/4	1 1/8	1	1 1/8	1 1/16	1/4	1 3/4	1/8	2 3/8	1/2					
3/8	1 3/16	1 1/16	1 3/16	1 1/8	5/16	1 3/4	1/8	2 5/8	1					
1/2	1 3/8	1 1/8	1 3/8	1 5/16	7/16	2	1/4	2 5/8	7/8		3 1/2	7/16	1	2 3/8
3/4	1 5/8	1 5/16	1 5/8	1 1/2	1/2	2 1/4	1/4	3	1		3 7/8	1/2	1 1/8	2 3/4
1	1 7/8	1 1/2	1 7/8	1 9/16	9/16	2 1/2	1/4	3	3/4		4 1/4	9/16	1 1/4	3 1/2
1 1/4	2 3/16	1 11/16	2 3/16	1 7/8	5/8	2 3/4	1/4	3 1/4	3/4		4 5/8	5/8	1 3/8	3 1/2
1 1/2	2 7/16	1 7/8	2 7/16	2	5/8	3	1/4	3 11/16	15/16		5	11/16	1 1/2	3 7/8
2	2 13/16	2 1/8	2 13/16	2 3/16	11/16	3 1/4	1/4	3 15/16	15/16		6	3/4	1 5/8	4 3/4
2 1/2	3 5/16	2 7/16	3	3	1 1/4	3 3/4	1/4	5	1 1/2		7	15/16	1 7/8	5 1/2
3	3 3/4	2 11/16	3 3/4	3 1/8	1 1/4	4	1/4	5	1 1/4		7 1/2	1	2	6
4	4 5/8	3 5/16	4 5/8	3 3/4	1 1/2	4 3/4	1/4				9	1 1/8	2 3/8	7 1/2
6*	6 3/4	4 3/4	6 3/4			6 5/8	5/8				11	1 1/4	3 1/8	9 1/2
8†	7 3/4		7 3/4			9 1/4	1/4				13 1/2	1 7/16	4 5/8	11 3/4

* Available with male ends for makeup with flanges or with grooving for makeup with "Victaulic" couplings.
† Schedule 40 pattern.

NOTE:
1. Flanges available in 10″ and 12″ sizes.
2. Sizes are nominal, all dimensions are given in inches on this sheet.

SCHEDULE 80 PLASTIC PRESSURE PATTERN

NOM. PIPE SIZES	THREADED Q	THREADED SOCKET R	THREADED SOCKET S	SOCKET T	SOCKET U
3/8 x 1/4	1	1	1 3/16	1	1 3/16
1/2 x 3/8	1 1/8	1	7/8	1	1 3/16
1/2 x 3/8	1 1/8	1	7/8	1	1 3/16
3/4 x 3/8	1 1/8	1 1/8	1	1 1/8	1 3/16
3/4 x 1/2	1 13/16	1 1/8	1	1 1/8	7/8
1 x 1/2	2	1 1/4	1 1/8	1 1/4	7/8
1 x 3/4	2	1 1/4	1 1/8	1 1/4	1
1 1/4 x 1/2	1 5/16	1 3/8	1 1/4	1 3/8	7/8
1 1/4 x 3/4	1 5/16	1 3/8	1 1/4	1 3/8	1
1 1/4 x 1	2 3/16	1 3/8	1 1/4	1 3/8	1 1/8
1 1/2 x 1/2	1 5/16	1 1/2	1 3/8	1 1/2	7/8
1 1/2 x 3/4	1 5/16	1 1/2	1 3/8	1 1/2	1
1 1/2 x 1	1 5/16	1 1/2	1 3/8	1 1/2	1 1/8
1 1/2 x 1 1/4	2 3/16	1 1/2	1 3/8	1 1/2	1 1/4
2 x 1/2	1 5/16	1 11/16	1 1/2	1 11/16	7/8
2 x 3/4	1 5/16	1 11/16	1 1/2	1 11/16	
2 x 1	1 5/16	1 11/16	1 1/2	1 11/16	1 1/8
2 x 1 1/4	1 5/16	1 11/16	1 1/2	1 11/16	1 1/4
2 x 1 1/2	2 3/8	1 11/16	1 1/2	1 11/16	1 3/8
2 1/2 x 1/2	2 1/16	2 1/16	1 3/4	2 1/16	7/8
2 1/2 x 3/4	2 1/16	2 1/16	1 3/4	2 1/16	1
2 1/2 x 1	2 1/16	2 1/16	1 3/4	2 1/16	1 1/8
2 1/2 x 1 1/4	2 1/16	2 1/16	1 3/4	2 1/16	1 1/4
2 1/2 x 1 1/2	2 1/16	2 1/16	1 3/4	2 1/16	1 3/8
2 1/2 x 2	2 13/16	2 1/16	1 3/4	2 1/16	1 1/2
3 x 3/4	2	2 3/16	1 7/8	2 3/16	1
3 x 1	2 1/4	2 3/16	1 7/8	2 3/16	1 1/8
3 x 1 1/4	2 1/4	2 3/16	1 7/8	2 3/16	1 1/4
3 x 1 1/2	2 1/4	2 3/16	1 7/8	2 3/16	1 3/8
3 x 2	2	2 3/16	1 7/8	2 3/16	1 1/2
3 x 2 1/2	2	2 3/16	1 7/8	2 3/16	
4 x 2	2	2 9/16	2 1/4	2 9/16	1 1/2
4 x 2 1/2	2 1/2	2 9/16	2 1/4	2 9/16	1 7/8
4 x 3	2 1/2	2 9/16	2 1/4	2 9/16	1 7/8
6 x 3				3	1 7/8
6 x 4				3	2 1/4
8 x 4				4 1/2	2 1/4
8 x 6				4 1/2	3

SCHEDULE 80 PLASTIC PRESSURE PATTERN

NOM. PIPE SIZE	THREADED O	SOCKET TYPE O	SOCKET TYPE P	NOM. PIPE SIZE	THREADED O	SOCKET TYPE O	SOCKET TYPE P
3/4 x 1/2	1 1/2	2 1/8	1	2 x 3/4	2	2 3/4	1 1/2
1 x 1/2	1 5/8	2 1/4	1 1/8	2 x 1	2 3/16	2 7/8	1 1/2
1 x 3/4	1 5/8	2 3/8	1 1/8	2 x 1 1/4	2 3/16	3	1 1/2
1 1/4 x 3/4	1 3/4	2 1/2	1 1/4	2 x 1 1/2	2 1/4	3 1/8	1 1/2
1 1/4 x 1	1 7/8	2 5/8	1 1/4	2 1/2 x 1 1/2	2 1/4	3 3/8	1 3/4
1 1/2 x 3/4	1 13/16	2 5/8	1 3/8	3 x 2	4 1/2	4 1/2	1 7/8
1 1/2 x 1	2	2 3/4	1 3/8	4 x 2	5 11/16	5 11/16	2 1/4
1 1/2 x 1 1/4	2	2 7/8	1 3/8	4 x 3	5 11/16	5 11/16	2 1/4

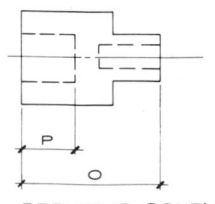

REDUCING COUPLING
SCHEDULE 80 PRESSURE FITTINGS

V. Peruchietti; Giffels & Rossetti, Inc.; Detroit, Michigan

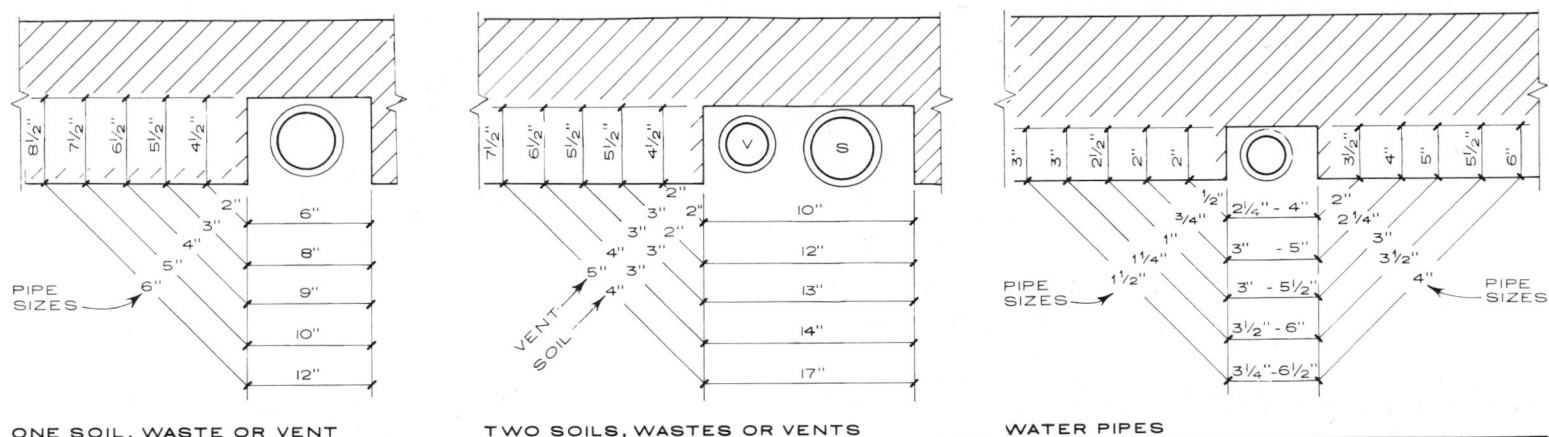

ONE SOIL, WASTE OR VENT   **TWO SOILS, WASTES OR VENTS**   **WATER PIPES**

RECOMENDED CHASE SIZES FOR VARIOUS PIPE SIZES

NOTE: ¾" covering included. For 1" cover add ½" to dimension. For size of chase with several pipes, add width req'd. for each.

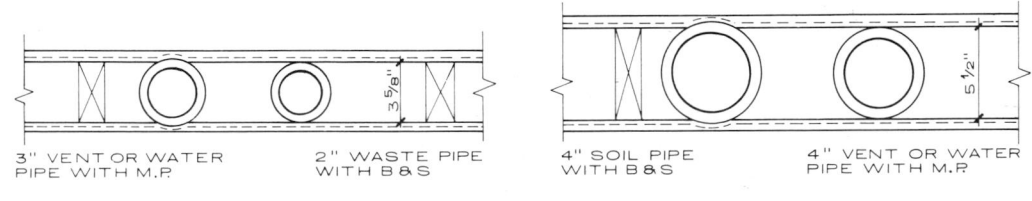

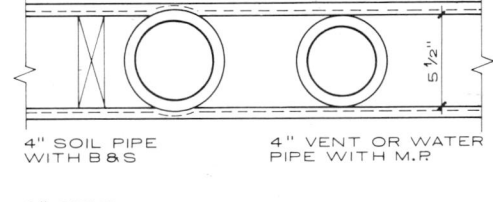

NOTE:

Partitions with ¾" lath & plaster are shown with certain maximum pipes encroaching on the lath & plaster. When rigid board such as gypsum or plaster board is used, the extreme diameter of the bead or bell of the pipe fitting should come within the actual dimension of the wall core.
See "Diameters of Fittings — Across Face Outside."

FITTING ABBREVATIONS

M.P.: malleable pattern

B & S: extra heavy cast iron bell & spigot

3" VENT OR WATER PIPE WITH M.P.   2" WASTE PIPE WITH B & S   4" SOIL PIPE WITH B & S   4" VENT OR WATER PIPE WITH M.P.

4" STUD   **6" STUD**

WOOD STUD PARTITIONS WITH ¾" LATH & PLASTER

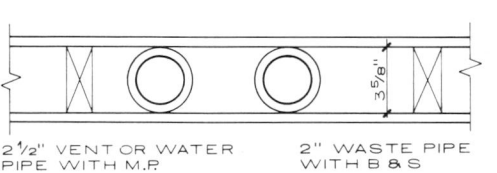

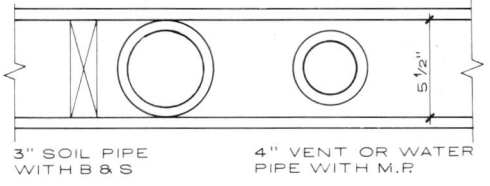

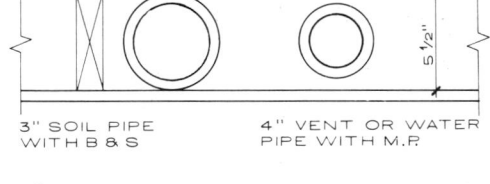

2½" VENT OR WATER PIPE WITH M.P.   2" WASTE PIPE WITH B & S   3" SOIL PIPE WITH B & S   4" VENT OR WATER PIPE WITH M.P.   2" SOIL PIPE WITH B & S   3" VENT OR WATER PIPE WITH M.P.

4" STUD   **6" STUD**   **8" BLOCK OR TILE**

WOOD STUD PARTITIONS WITH RIGID BOARD OR RIGID LATH

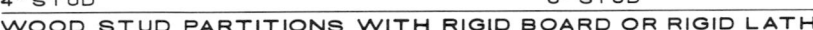

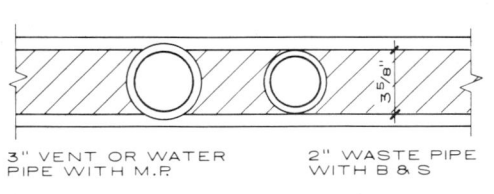

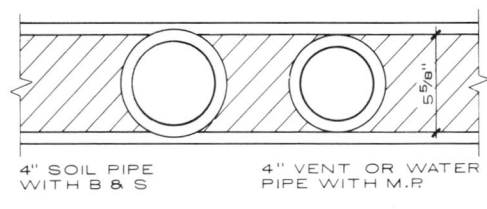

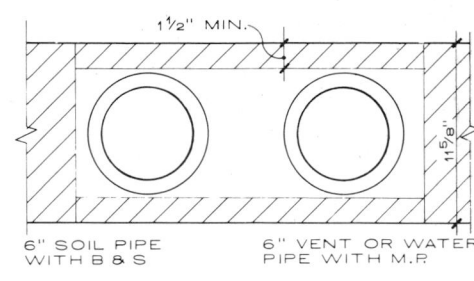

3" VENT OR WATER PIPE WITH M.P.   2" WASTE PIPE WITH B & S   4" SOIL PIPE WITH B & S   4" VENT OR WATER PIPE WITH M.P.   6" SOIL PIPE WITH B & S   6" VENT OR WATER PIPE WITH M.P.

4" BLOCK OR TILE   **6" BLOCK OR TILE**   **12" BLOCK OR TILE**

MASONRY PARTITIONS WITH ⅝" PLASTER   EXPOSED MASONRY

MINIMUM CLEAR CHASE SIZES FOR VARIOUS PARTITIONS

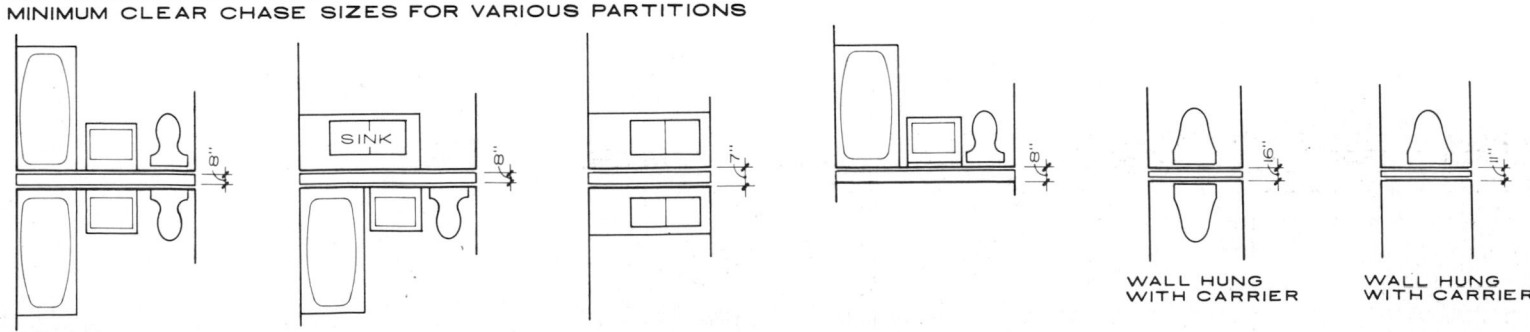

WALL HUNG WITH CARRIER   WALL HUNG WITH CARRIER

MINIMUM CLEAR CHASE SIZES FOR VARIOUS FIXTURE COMBINATIONS

R. C. Armbruster and B. K. Johnson; Grover Dimond Associates, Inc ; St. Paul, Minnesota

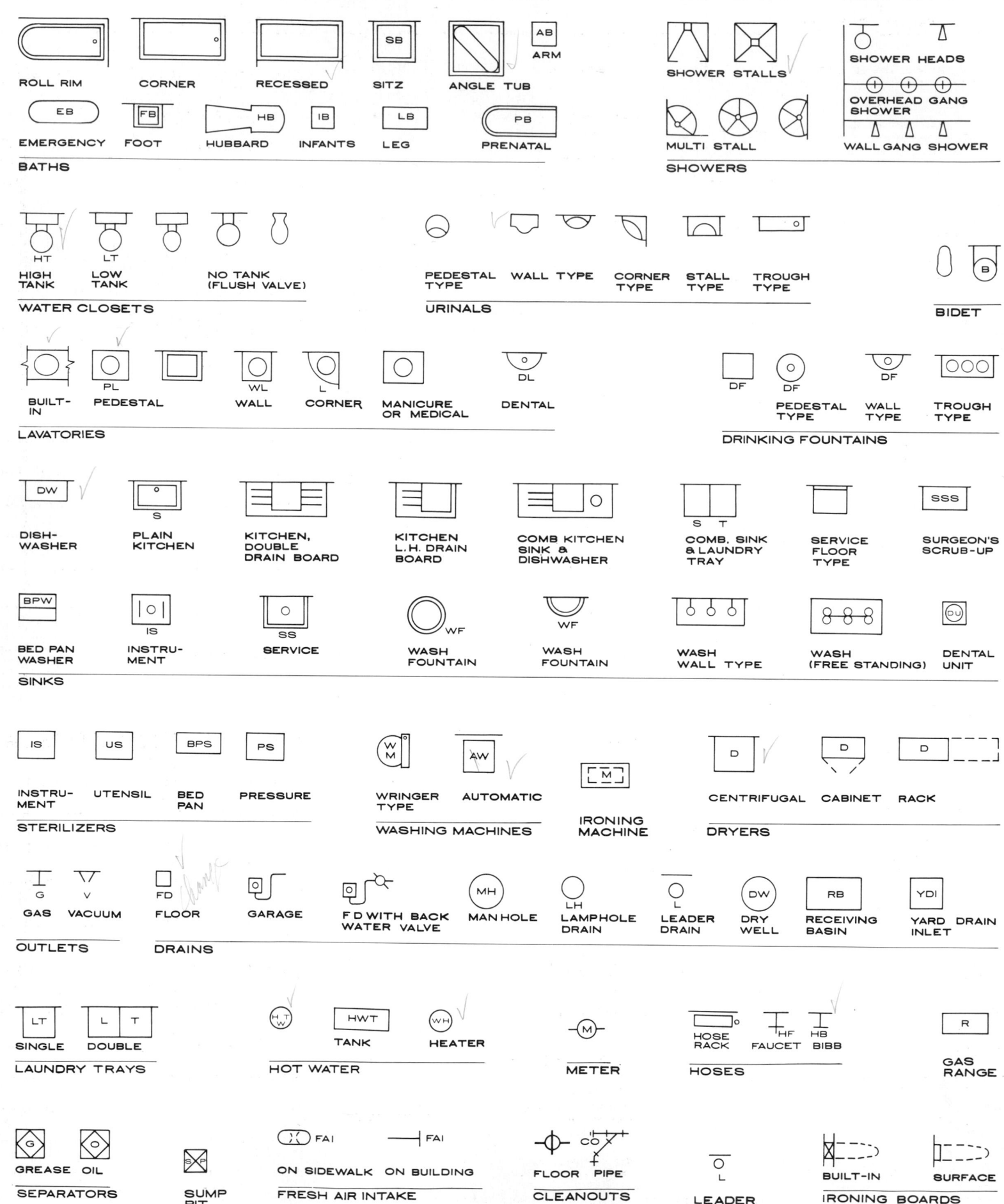

BATHS

ROLL RIM   CORNER   RECESSED   SITZ (SB)   ANGLE TUB (AB ARM)

EMERGENCY (EB)   FOOT (FB)   HUBBARD (HB)   INFANTS (IB)   LEG (LB)   PRENATAL (PB)

SHOWERS

SHOWER STALLS   MULTI STALL

SHOWER HEADS   OVERHEAD GANG SHOWER   WALL GANG SHOWER

WATER CLOSETS

HIGH TANK (HT)   LOW TANK (LT)   NO TANK (FLUSH VALVE)

URINALS

PEDESTAL TYPE   WALL TYPE   CORNER TYPE   STALL TYPE   TROUGH TYPE

BIDET (B)

LAVATORIES

BUILT-IN   PEDESTAL (PL)   WALL (WL L)   CORNER   MANICURE OR MEDICAL   DENTAL (DL)

DRINKING FOUNTAINS

DF   PEDESTAL TYPE (DF)   WALL TYPE (DF)   TROUGH TYPE

SINKS

DISH-WASHER (DW)   PLAIN KITCHEN (S)   KITCHEN, DOUBLE DRAIN BOARD   KITCHEN L.H. DRAIN BOARD   COMB KITCHEN SINK & DISHWASHER   COMB. SINK & LAUNDRY TRAY (S T)   SERVICE FLOOR TYPE   SURGEON'S SCRUB-UP (SSS)

BED PAN WASHER (BPW)   INSTRU-MENT (IS)   SERVICE (SS)   WASH FOUNTAIN (WF)   WASH FOUNTAIN (WF)   WASH WALL TYPE   WASH (FREE STANDING)   DENTAL UNIT (DU)

STERILIZERS

INSTRU-MENT (IS)   UTENSIL (US)   BED PAN (BPS)   PRESSURE (PS)

WASHING MACHINES

WRINGER TYPE (WM)   AUTOMATIC (AW)

IRONING MACHINE (M)

DRYERS

CENTRIFUGAL (D)   CABINET (D)   RACK (D)

OUTLETS

GAS (G)   VACUUM (V)

DRAINS

FLOOR (FD)   GARAGE   F D WITH BACK WATER VALVE   MAN HOLE (MH)   LAMPHOLE DRAIN (LH)   LEADER DRAIN (L)   DRY WELL (DW)   RECEIVING BASIN (RB)   YARD DRAIN INLET (YDI)

LAUNDRY TRAYS

SINGLE (LT)   DOUBLE (L T)

HOT WATER

TANK (H T W) (HWT)   HEATER (W H)

METER (M)

HOSES

HOSE RACK   FAUCET (HF)   BIBB (HB)

GAS RANGE (R)

SEPARATORS

GREASE (G)   OIL

SUMP PIT (S P)

FRESH AIR INTAKE

ON SIDEWALK (FAI)   ON BUILDING (FAI)

CLEANOUTS

FLOOR (CO)   PIPE

LEADER (L)

IRONING BOARDS

BUILT-IN   SURFACE

Amor Halperin, P. E.; Ayres, Cohen and Hayakawa; Consulting Engineers; Los Angeles/San Francisco, California

PLUMBING PIPING

SOIL, WASTE OR LEADER (ABOVE GRADE)	——————
SOIL, WASTE OR LEADER (BELOW GRADE)	— — — — —
VENT	- - - - - - -
COMBINATION WASTE AND VENT	—— CWV ——
ACID WASTE	—— AW ——
ACID VENT	— — — AV — — —
INDIRECT DRAIN	—— D ——
STORM DRAIN	—— SD ——
COLD WATER	— — - — - —
SOFT COLD WATER	—— SW ——
INDUSTRIALIZED COLD WATER	—— ICW ——
CHILLED DRINKING WATER SUPPLY	—— DWS ——
CHILLED DRINKING WATER RETURN	—— DWR ——
HOT WATER	— — ·· — ·· —
HOT WATER RETURN	— — ··· — ··· —
SANITIZING HOT WATER SUPPLY (180°F.)	+ ·· — + ·· +
SANITIZING HOT WATER RETURN (180°F.)	+ ··· — + ··
INDUSTRIALIZED HOT WATER SUPPLY	—— IHW ——
INDUSTRIALIZED HOT WATER RETURN	—— IHR ——
TEMPERED WATER SUPPLY	—— TS ——
TEMPERED WATER RETURN	—— TR ——
FIRE LINE	—— F —— F ——
WET STANDPIPE	—— WSP ——

DRY STANDPIPE	—— DSP ——
COMBINATION STANDPIPE	—— CSP ——
MAIN SUPPLIES SPRINKLER	—— S ——
BRANCH AND HEAD SPRINKLER	——o——o——
GAS - LOW PRESSURE	—— G —— G ——
GAS - MEDIUM PRESSURE	—— MG ——
GAS - HIGH PRESSURE	—— HG ——
COMPRESSED AIR	—— A ——
VACUUM	—— V ——
VACUUM CLEANING	—— VC ——
OXYGEN	—— O ——
LIQUID OXYGEN	—— LOX ——
NITROGEN	—— N ——
LIQUID NITROGEN	—— LN ——
NITROUS OXIDE	—— NO ——
HYDROGEN	—— H ——
HELIUM	—— HE ——
ARGON	—— AR ——
LIQUID PETROLEUM GAS	—— LPG ——
INDUSTRIAL WASTE	—— INW ——
PNEUMATIC TUBES TUBE RUNS	—— PN ——
SEWER - CAST IRON	S - CI
SEWER - CLAY TILE BELL & SPIGOT	S - CT
DRAIN - CLAY TILE BELL & SPIGOT	——————
DRAIN - OPEN TILE OR AGRICULTURAL TILE	— — — — —

HEATING PIPING

HIGH PRESSURE STEAM	—//——//—
MEDIUM PRESSURE STEAM	—/——/——/—
LOW PRESSURE STEAM	——————
HIGH PRESSURE RETURN	—//— — —//—
MEDIUM PRESSURE RETURN	—/— — —/— — —/
LOW PRESSURE RETURN	— — — —
BOILER BLOW OFF	— — —
CONDENSATE OR VACUUM PUMP DISCHARGE	— —o— —o— —
FEEDWATER PUMP DISCHARGE	— —oo— —oo— —
MAKE UP WATER	- — · — · — - -
AIR RELIEF LINE	— — — — —
FUEL OIL SUPPLY	—— FOS ——
FUEL OIL RETURN	—— FOR ——
FUEL OIL TANK VENT	—— FOV ——
COMPRESSED AIR	—— A ——
HOT WATER HEATING SUPPLY	—— HW ——
HOT WATER HEATING RETURN	—— HWR ——

AIR CONDITIONING PIPING

REFRIGERANT LIQUID	—— RL ——
REFRIGERANT DISCHARGE	—— RD ——
REFRIGERANT SUCTION	— — RS — —
CONDENSER WATER SUPPLY	—— C ——
CONDENSER WATER RETURN	—— CR ——
CHILLED WATER SUPPLY	—— CH ——
CHILLED WATER RETURN	—— CHR ——
MAKE UP WATER	—— · — · ——
HUMIDIFICATION LINE	—— ·· H — ·· —
DRAIN	—— D ——
BRINE SUPPLY	—— B ——
BRINE RETURN	—— BR ——

Amor Halperin, P. E.; Ayres, Cohen and Hayakawa; Consulting Engineers; Los Angeles/San Francisco, California

TYPE OF PIPE FITTING OR VALVE	FLANGED	SCREWED	BELL & SPIGOT	WELDED	SOLDERED
ELBOW – 90 DEG.					
ELBOW – 45 DEG.					
ELBOW – TURNED UP					
ELBOW – TURNED DOWN					
ELBOW – LONG RADIUS					
SIDE OUTLET ELBOW – OUTLET DOWN . . .					
SIDE OUTLET ELBOW – OUTLET UP					
BASE ELBOW					
DOUBLE BRANCH ELBOW					
REDUCING ELBOW					
SINGLE SWEEP TEE					
DOUBLE SWEEP TEE					
TEE STRAIGHT SIZE					
TEE – OUTLET UP					
TEE – OUTLET DOWN					
SIDE OUTLET TEE – OUTLET UP					
SIDE OUTLET TEE – OUTLET DOWN					
CROSS STRAIGHT SIZE					
REDUCER – CONCENTRIC					
REDUCER – ECCENTRIC					
JOINT CONECTING PIPE					

Amor Halperin, P. E.; Ayres, Cohen and Hayakawa; Consulting Engineers; Los Angeles/San Francisco, California

TYPE OF PIPE FITTING OR VALVE	FLANGED	SCREWED	BELL & SPIGOT	WELDED	SOLDERED
LATERAL					
GATE VALVE					
GLOBE VALVE					
HOSE GATE VALVE					
HOSE GLOBE VALVE					
ANGLE GATE VALVE, ELEVATION					
ANGLE GATE VALVE, PLAN					
ANGLE GLOBE VALVE, ELEVATION					
ANGLE GLOBE VALVE, PLAN					
CHECK VALVE, STRAIGHT WAY					
ANGLE CHECK VALVE					
COCK VALVE					
SAFETY VALVE					
QUICK OPENING VALVE					
FLOAT VALVE					
MOTOR OPERATED GATE VALVE					
MOTOR OPERATED GLOBE VALVE					
EXPANSION JOINT					
REDUCING FLANGE					
UNION					
SLEEVE					
BUSHING					

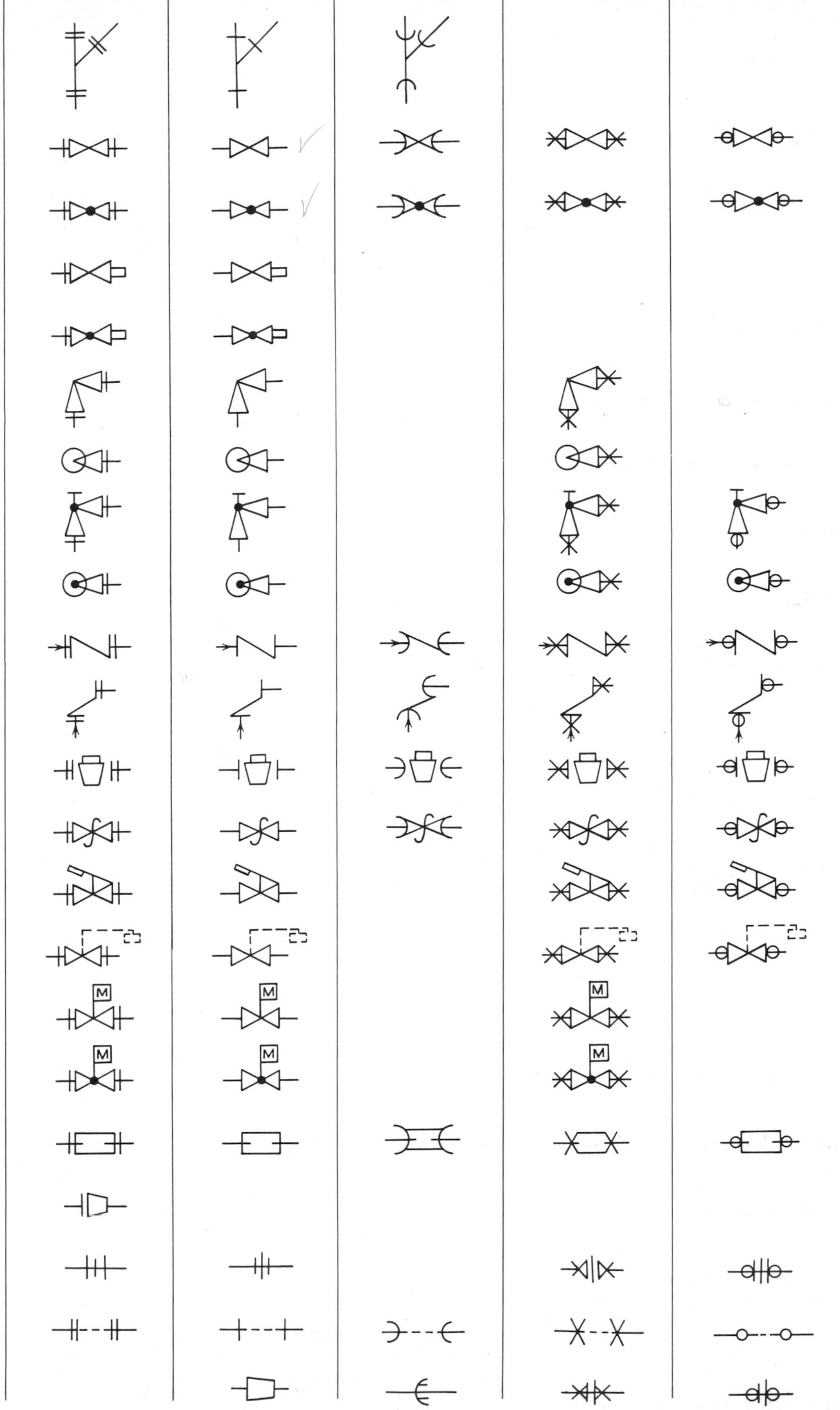

Amor Halperin, P. E.; Ayres, Cohen and Hayakawa; Consulting Engineers; Los Angeles/San Francisco, California

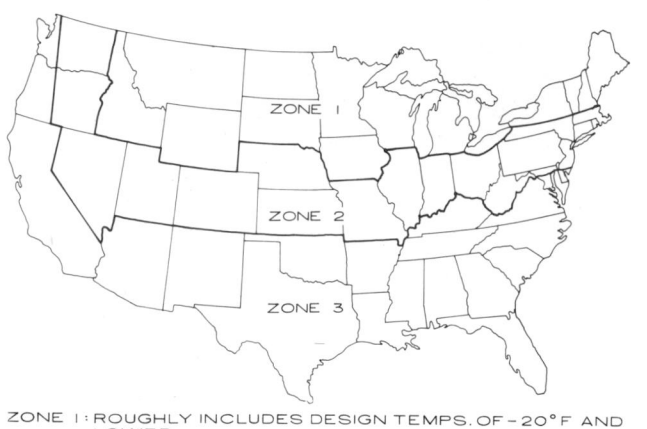

ZONE 1: ROUGHLY INCLUDES DESIGN TEMPS. OF –20°F AND
        LOWER
ZONE 2: FROM 0° TO –10°F
ZONE 3: AREAS WARMER THAN 0°F
CONDENSATION ZONES

ATTIC	TYPE OF ROOF	TOTAL FREE AREA OF VENTILATION*	VAPOR BARRIERS ZONE 1	ZONE 2	ZONE 3
UNHEATED	FLAT ROOF Slope less than: 3/12	1/300 Uniformly distributed at eaves. Free circulation through all spaces required.	Required on warm side in top story ceiling.		
	GABLE ROOF Slope over: 3/12	1/300 At least two louvers on opposite sides near ridge.	Required on warm side in top story ceiling.	Considered unnecessary	
	HIP ROOF	1/300,1/600 Uniformly distributed at eaves and 1/600 at ridge with all interconnected.	Required on warm side in top story ceiling.	Considered unnecessary	
HEATED	GABLE OR HIP ROOF		Recommended on warm side in top story ceiling, dwarf walls, sloping part of roof and attic story ceiling.	Considered necessary if insulation is omitted.	

*The figure given indicates that the clear opening of vents totaled should be 1/300 of the building area at eave line.

**It is recognized that in many areas increased ventilation may be desirable for summer comfort. For winter comfort, insulation is recommended between a living space and a loft or attic ventilated at these rates.

ATTIC SPACE VENTILATION AND VAPOR BARRIER REQUIREMENTS TO PREVENT CONDENSATION

CRAWL SPACE VENTILATION RECOMMENDATIONS:

Crawl spaces under dwellings where the earth is damp and uncovered require a high rate of ventilation. At least four openings, one at each corner as high as possible, should be provided. Their total net area may be calculated by formula, at right:

$$a = \frac{2L}{100} + \frac{A}{300}$$

L = the perimeter of the crawl space in linear feet.

A = the area of the crawl space in square feet.

a = the total net area of all vents (or the gross area if 4-mesh screen is used) in square feet.

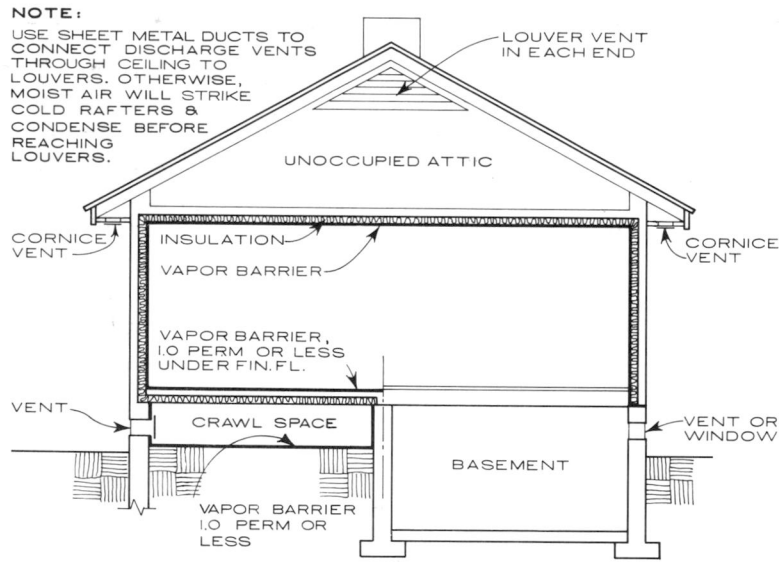

NOTE:
USE SHEET METAL DUCTS TO CONNECT DISCHARGE VENTS THROUGH CEILING TO LOUVERS. OTHERWISE, MOIST AIR WILL STRIKE COLD RAFTERS & CONDENSE BEFORE REACHING LOUVERS.

GABLE ROOF WITH UNOCCUPIED ATTIC
CORNICE VENTS NOT REQUIRED IF AREA IS SMALL

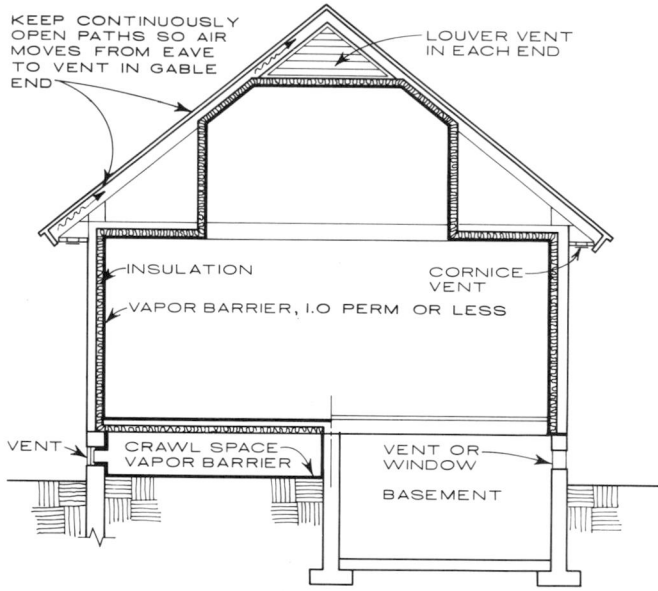

GABLE ROOF WITH OCCUPIED ATTIC –CORNICE VENTS REQUIRED TO CREATE "STACK EFFECT" TO RIDGE

TYPICAL ATTIC AND CRAWL SPACE VENTILATION APPLICATIONS

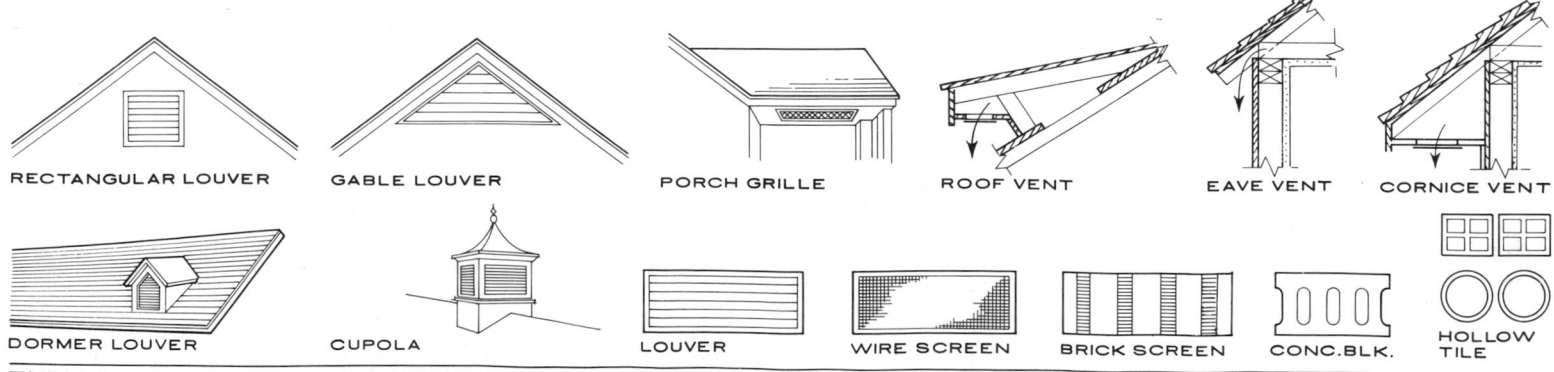

RECTANGULAR LOUVER   GABLE LOUVER   PORCH GRILLE   ROOF VENT   EAVE VENT   CORNICE VENT

DORMER LOUVER   CUPOLA   LOUVER   WIRE SCREEN   BRICK SCREEN   CONC.BLK.   HOLLOW TILE

TYPICAL ATTIC AND CRAWL SPACE VENT OPENINGS

Tseng - Yao Sun, P. E.; Ayres, Cohen and Hayakawa; Consulting Engineers; Los Angeles/San Francisco, California and Lawrence Conde; Frost Associates; New York, New York
E. C. Shuman, P. E.; Consulting Engineer; State College, Pennsylvania

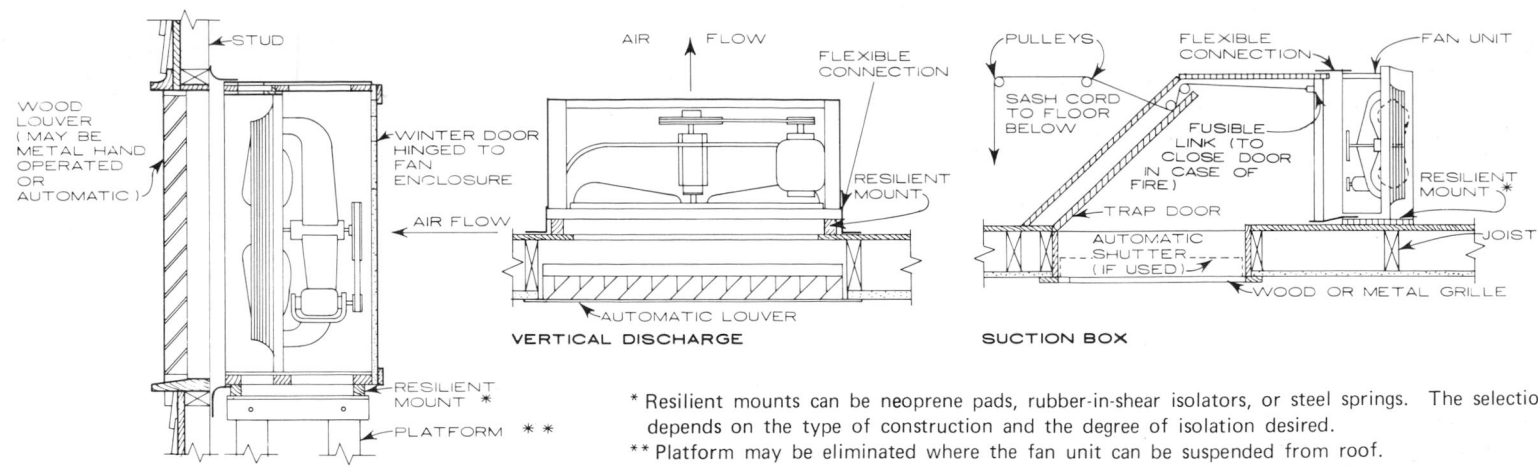

HORIZONTAL DISCHARGE

VERTICAL DISCHARGE

SUCTION BOX

* Resilient mounts can be neoprene pads, rubber-in-shear isolators, or steel springs. The selection depends on the type of construction and the degree of isolation desired.

** Platform may be eliminated where the fan unit can be suspended from roof.

VERTICAL DISCHARGE-LOW ROOF INSTALLATION

SUCTION BOX INSTALLATION

HORIZONTAL DISCHARGE- GABLE INSTALLATION

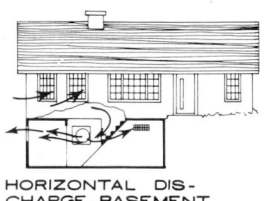

HORIZONTAL DIS- CHARGE-BASEMENT INSTALLATION

TYPICAL VENTILATING INSTALLATIONS AND APPLICATIONS

ZONE - 2

ZONE - 1

| | ZONE I
I MINUTE AIR CHANGE | | ZONE 2
1½ MINUTE AIR CHANGE |

VENTILATION REQUIREMENT ZONES

NOTE:

Air quantity for ventilation in cu. ft. per min. (CFM) can be obtained by dividing building volume with number of minute air change.

MINIMUM GROSS OUTLET AREAS FOR ATTIC FAN DISCHARGE OPENING

TYPE OF OPENING	Gross Area per 1000 CFM Free Air Fan Delivery
Wood louvers with 1/2" hardware cloth. 40% minimum free area.	2.27 sq. ft.
Metal louvers with 1/2" hardware cloth. 50% minimum free area.	1.82 sq. ft.
Plain opening covered with 1/2" hardware cloth. 80% minimum free area.	1.14 sq. ft.
Automatic or manual shutters, 90% minimum free area.	1.01 sq. ft.

Note: If opening is covered with #16 mesh screen, double the gross area of the opening.

FAN SIZES AND CAPACITY RANGES

	FAN DIA.	RANGE	CAPACITY FREE AIR	CFM ◇ 0.1" S.P.	MOTOR HP	DIMENSIONS A IN.	B IN.	FAN WT. LBS.
HORIZONTAL DISCH.	24"	MAX.	8170	7840	1	31 ± 3	21 ± 4	128
		MIN.	4107	3047	1/6			70
	30"	MAX.	13270	12840	2	39 ± 3	23 ± 6	192
		MIN.	6124	4653	1/4			98
	36"	MAX.	19700	19070	3	45 ± 3	24 ± 6	293
		MIN.	9250	5285	1/4			106
	42"	MAX.	29540	28700	5	51 ± 3	25 ± 6	374
		MIN.	12800	8052	1/2			180
	48"	MAX.	40090	39080	7 1/2	57 ± 3	27 ± 7	477
		MIN.	15300	11300	1/3			250
VERTICAL DISCH.	24"	MAX.	5350	4700	1/3	34 ± 2	18 ± 2	128
		MIN.	4800	3800	1/6			69
	30"	MAX.	7300	6000	1/3	38 ± 2	18 ± 2	150
		MIN.	7200	5300	1/4			74
	36"	MAX.	10550	8500	1/2	44 ± 2	19 ± 2	175
		MIN.	8600	6500	1/4			84
	42"	MAX.	16000	12000	1/2	51 ± 2	20 ± 3	275
		MIN.	12100	8600	1/3			170

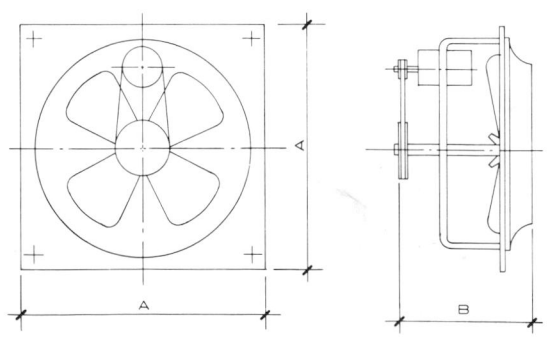

* Belt drive fans are quieter and easier to maintain than direct drive type.

◇ Fan should be selected for minimum static pressure drop (S.P.) of 0.1". Where ductwork is required upstream or downstream from the fan, centrifugal blowers should be used.

Tseng - Yao Sun, P. E.; Ayres, Cohen and Hayakawa; Consulting Engineers; Los Angeles/San Francisco, California

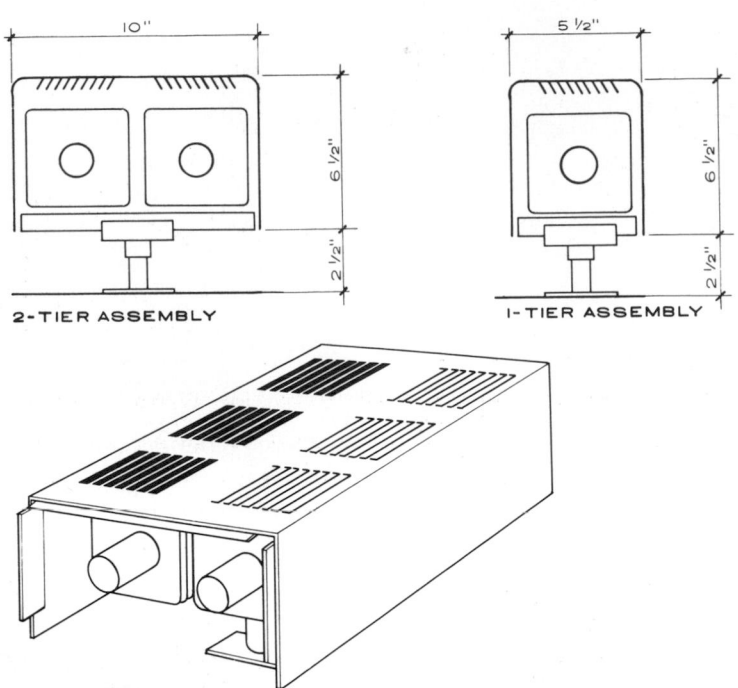

2-TIER ASSEMBLY   **1-TIER ASSEMBLY**

FREE STANDING INSTALLATION

Units are designed for use in areas where exterior walls are glazed from floor to ceiling, and wall hung units cannot be used. They can be installed away from the window and have a low silhouette.

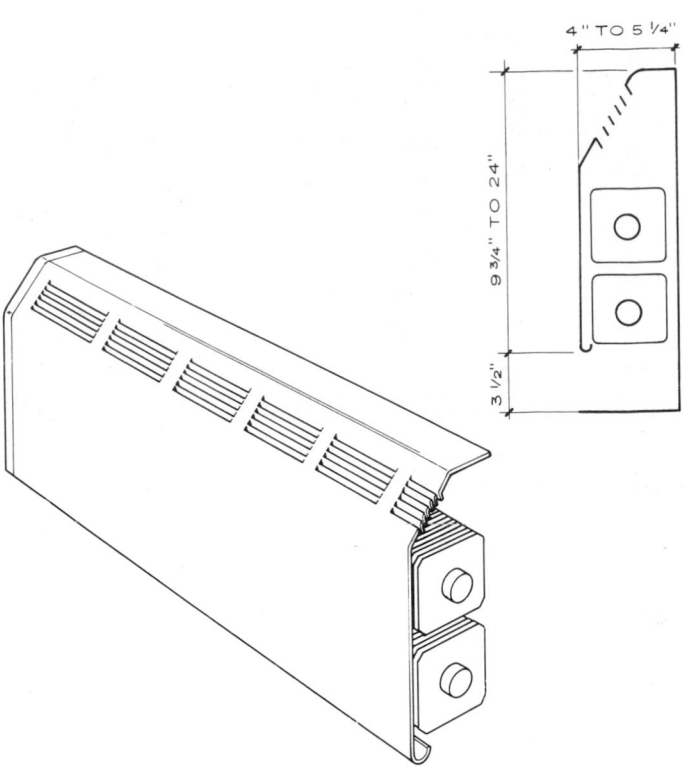

WALL OR SILL INSTALLATION

Units are commonly used in commercial applications where capacity ranges are required. They can be supplied with sloping top enclosures (as shown) or flat top with front grille.

2 tiers of finned-tube shown, 1-tier and 3-tier assemblies are also available.

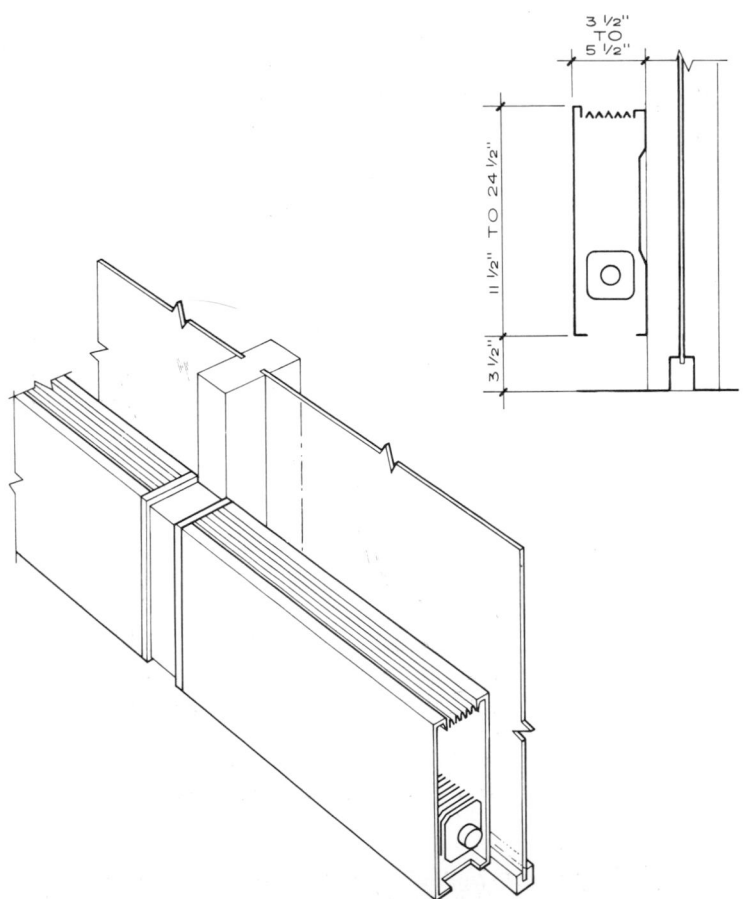

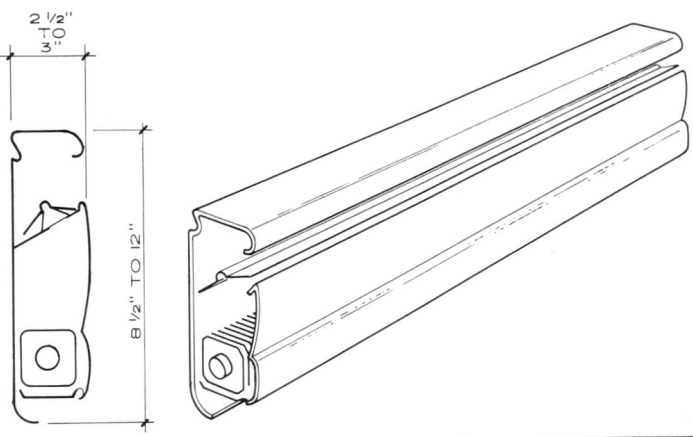

BASEBOARD INSTALLATION

Units are commonly used in residential applications. They are the smallest finned-tube radiation available, have limited capacity ranges, and are available with only one-tier of finned-tube.

WINDOW WALL INSTALLATION

Units can be mullioned or wall mounted. When installed 30″ above the floor, they can also serve as a physical barrier at the glass line.

1 tier of finned-tube shown, 2-tier assemblies are also available.

GENERAL NOTES:

Finned-tube radiation is generally used in the colder climates. Their function is to maintain the desired air temperature in the space by introducing heat to the room via radiation and convection. In general, they should be placed at the areas of the greatest heat loss such as under windows, at exterior walls and near door openings to offset the heat losses.

All units are designed for use in low pressure steam and low temperature hot water heating systems. They can be installed as continuous elements or divided into sections of various lengths.

Tseng - Yao Sun, P. E.; Ayres, Cohen and Hayakawa; Consulting Engineers; Los Angeles/San Francisco, California

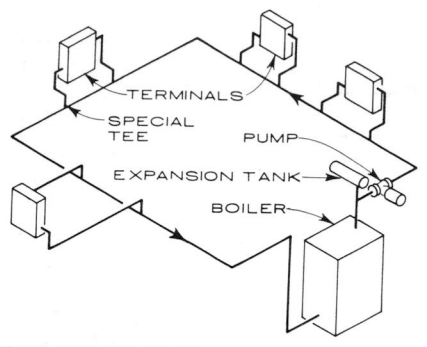

ONE PIPE SYSTEM

Supply and return flow through the same main. Special tee fittings are required to divert water into each terminal.

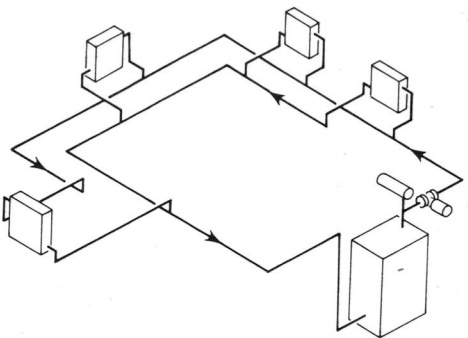

TWO PIPE SYSTEM — REVERSE RETURN

Supply and return flow through separate mains. The pipe length from the boiler through any terminal and back to the boiler is approximately the same.

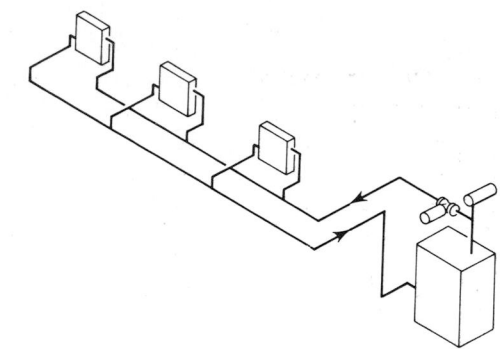

TWO PIPE SYSTEM - DIRECT RETURN

Supply and return flow through separate mains. The pipe length from the boiler through each terminal and back to the boiler varies. Balancing devices must be used to get proper flow through each terminal.

HYDRONIC HEATING SYSTEMS — HOT WATER

NOTE : SEE LOWER PORTION OF THIS PAGE FOR RADIANT PANEL HEATING APPLICATION.

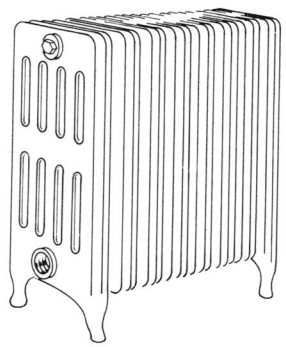

CAST IRON RADIATOR

This type of cast iron radiator is no longer manufactured and is shown here for reference purpose only. A few small tube cast iron radiators designed for recessed installations are available.

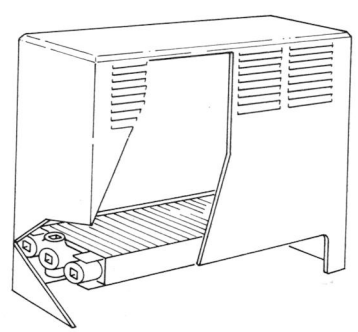

CONVECTOR

Wide variety of enclosures are available. Many are designed for installation in wall recesses or under the window cabinets.

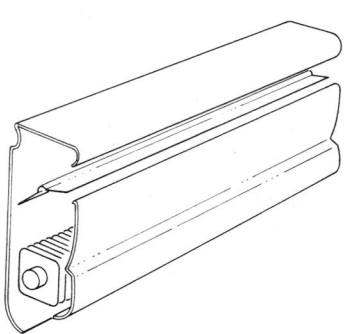

FIN TUBE RADIATION

See page on Fin Tube Radiation for type and applications.

HYDRONIC HEATING TERMINALS — HOT WATER

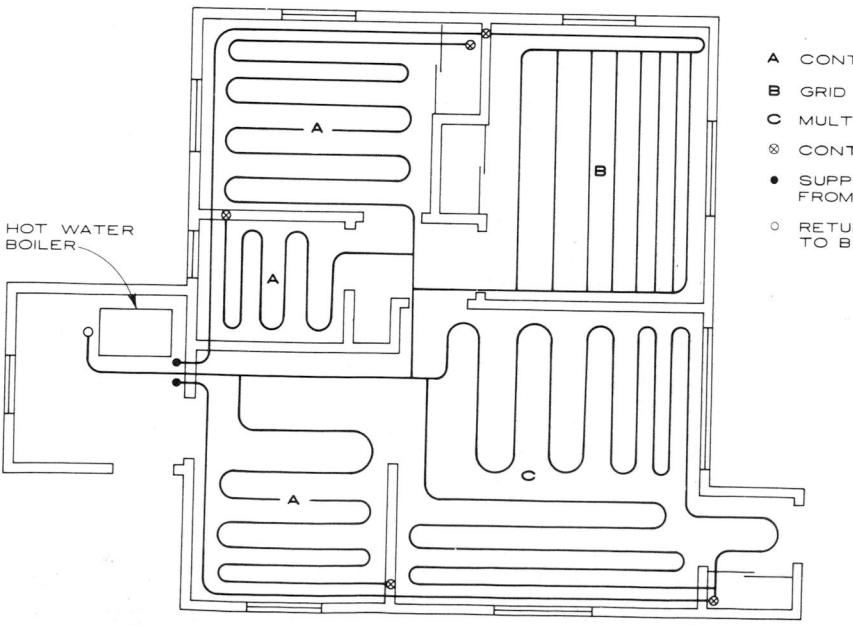

A CONTINUOUS COIL
B GRID
C MULTIPLE COIL
⊗ CONTROL VALVE
● SUPPLY MAINS FROM BOILER
○ RETURN MAIN TO BOILER

TYPICAL RADIANT PANEL LAYOUT WITH VARIOUS COIL PATTERNS

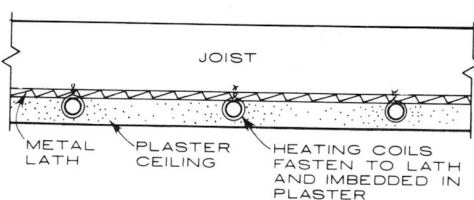

RADIANT CEILING APPLICATION

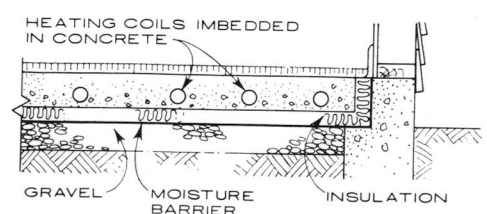

RADIANT FLOOR APPLICATION

NOTE :

The continuous coil pattern (A) is commonly used in residential applications because it is easy to install in small irregular shaped rooms. Its use in large rooms is restricted by the high friction loss in the long coils. The grid pattern (B) offers lower friction loss and excellent thermal distribution. The multiple coil pattern (C) is the combination of A and B.

RADIANT PANEL HEATING APPLICATION

Tseng - Yao Sun, P. E. and Kyoung S. Park, P. E.; Ayres, Cohen and Hayakawa; Consulting Engineers; Los Angeles/San Francisco, California

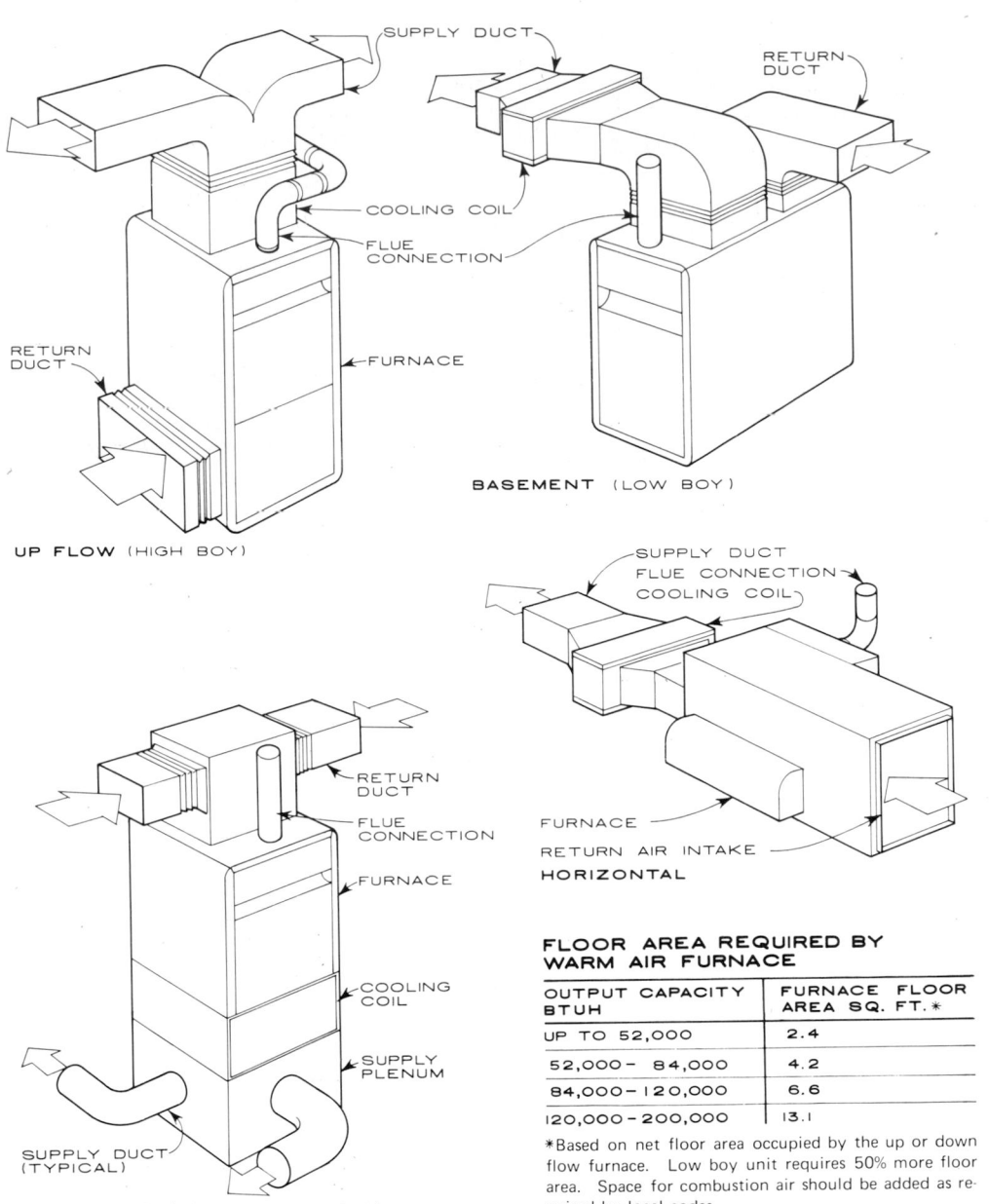

UP FLOW (HIGH BOY)

BASEMENT (LOW BOY)

DOWN FLOW (COUNTER FLOW)

HORIZONTAL

VARIOUS TYPES OF WARM AIR FURNACES

FLOOR AREA REQUIRED BY WARM AIR FURNACE

OUTPUT CAPACITY BTUH	FURNACE FLOOR AREA SQ. FT. *
UP TO 52,000	2.4
52,000 - 84,000	4.2
84,000 - 120,000	6.6
120,000 - 200,000	13.1

*Based on net floor area occupied by the up or down flow furnace. Low boy unit requires 50% more floor area. Space for combustion air should be added as required by local codes.

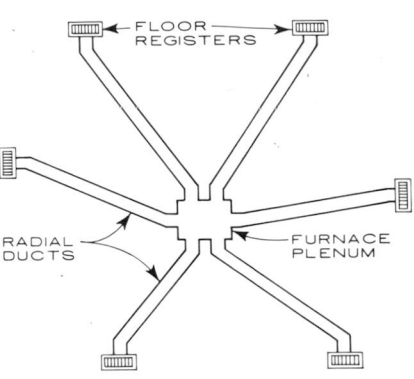

PERIMETER LOOP SYSTEM

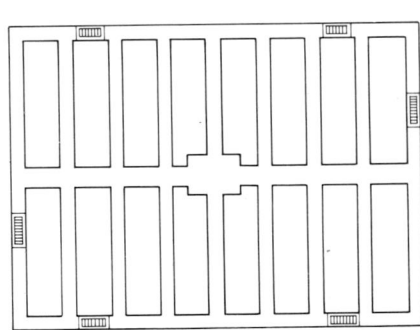

PERIMETER RADIAL SYSTEM

PERIMETER LATERAL SYSTEM

VARIOUS TYPES OF DUCT SYSTEM IN CONCRETE SLAB

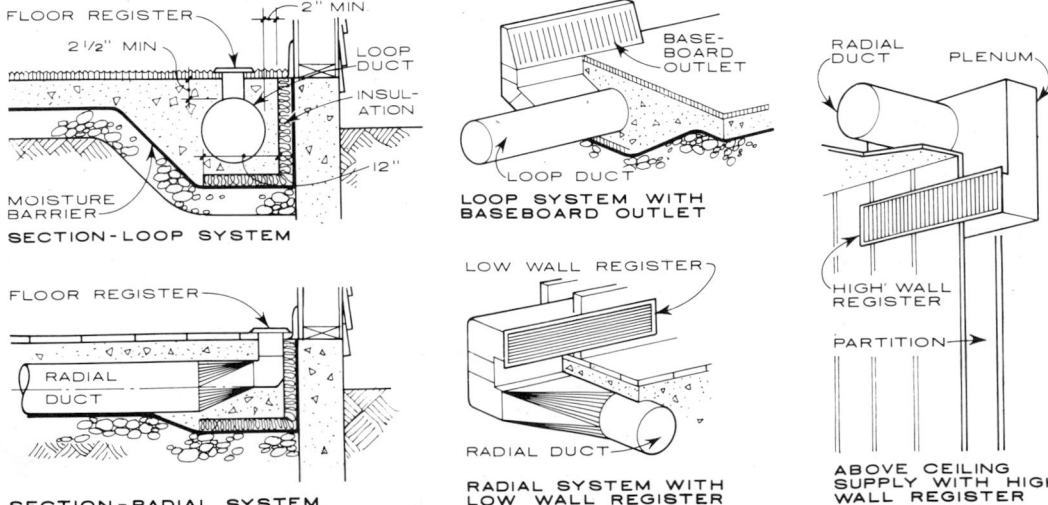

SECTION-LOOP SYSTEM

LOOP SYSTEM WITH BASEBOARD OUTLET

SECTION-RADIAL SYSTEM

RADIAL SYSTEM WITH LOW WALL REGISTER

ABOVE CEILING SUPPLY WITH HIGH WALL REGISTER

VARIOUS TYPES OF AIR OUTLETS

NOTE:

Warm air furnace units are designed primarily for residential, small commercial or classroom heating. Cooling can be added to these units by installing a cooling coil downstream from the furnace with refrigerant compressor and condenser remotely located outside of the building.

Duct system from the furnace unit can be either above the ceiling or in the floor slab. Above ceiling distribution systems are usually the radial type with high wall registers. Perimeter loop and perimeter lateral systems in floor slabs provide good air distribution. There are less temperature variations across the floor with perimeter lateral systems than radial or perimeter loop systems.

Duct systems may also be installed below the living spaces in a crawl space or basement.

Tseng - Yao Sun, P. E.; Ayres, Cohen and Hayakawa; Consulting Engineers; Los Angeles/San Francisco, California

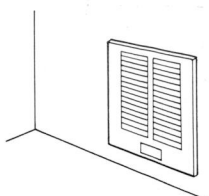

Dimension Range:
    Height: 9'' to 24''   Width: 10'' to 18''
    Depth: 2'' to 6'' (Can be recessed in wall)
Capacity Range: 750 W to 4000 W
Form of Heat Transfer:
    Radiation—convection or forced air.

WALL HEATER

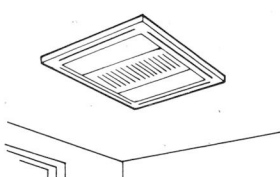

Dimension Range:
    Length: 10'' to 14''. Width: 8'' to 14''
    Depth: 4'' to 8'' recessed
    Circular shape available
Capacity Range: 500 W to 1500 W
Form of Heat Transfer:
    Radiation—Convection or forced air.

CEILING HEATER

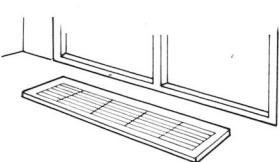

Dimension Range:
    Width: 5'' to 6''   Length: 14'' to 108''
    Depth: 8'' to 10''
Capacity Range: 300 W to 2000 W
Form of Heat Transfer: Convection.

FLOOR HEATER

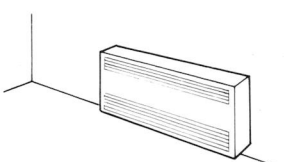

Dimension Range:
    Height: 11'' to 32''   Length: 24'' to 96''
    Depth: 3'' to 7''
Capacity Range: 1000 W to 4000 W
Form of Heat Transfer: Convection.

CONVECTOR

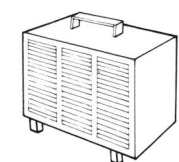

Dimension Range:
    Height: 7'' to 24''   Width: 10'' to 72''
    Depth: 2'' to 12''
Capacity Range: 500 W to 5000 W
Form of Heat Transfer:
    Radiation: Convection or forced air

PORTABLE HEATER

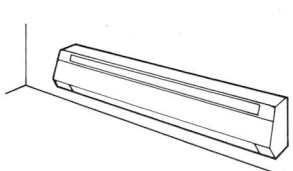

Dimension Range:
    Height: 4'' to 9''.   Length: 24''-120''
    Depth: 2'' to 3''
Capacity Range: 300 W to 3500 W
Form of Heat Transfer:
    Convection.

BASEBOARD HEATER

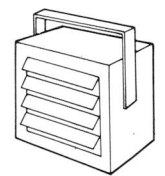

Dimension Range:
    Height: 12'' to 26''.   Width: 12'' to 52''
    Depth: 6'' to 22''
Capacity Range: 1.5 KW to 50 KW
Form of Heat Transfer: Forced air.

UNIT HEATER

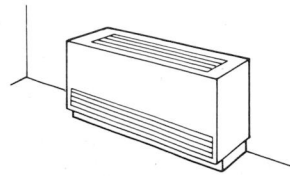

Dimension Range:
    Height: 26'' to 32''.   Width: 48'' to 104''
    Depth: 11'' to 26''.
Capacity Range: 1 KW to 36 KW
Form of Heat Transfer:
    Forced air.

UNIT VENTILATOR

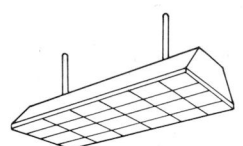

Dimension Range:
    Width: 4'' to 12''.   Length: 14'' to 86''
    Height: 3'' to 16''
    Circular shape available
Capacity Range: 500 W to 7000 W
Form of Heat Transfer: Radiation.

INFRARED HEATER

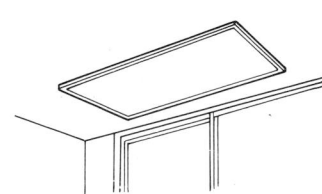

Dimension Range:
    Width: 24'' to 48''. Length: 48'' to 144''
    Depth: 1''
Capacity: 500 W to 1000 W
Form of Heat Transfer: Radiation

RADIANT HEATING PANEL

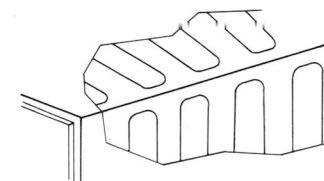

Dimension Range: Not applicable
Capacity Range:
    Varies with coverage.
Form of Heat Transfer:
    Radiation with some convection.

RADIANT HEATING CABLE IN WALL & CEILING

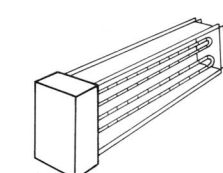

Dimension Range:
    Varies with duct sizes.
Capacity Range: 0.3 KW to 2000 KW
Form of Heat Transfer:
    Forced air.

DUCT INSERT HEATER

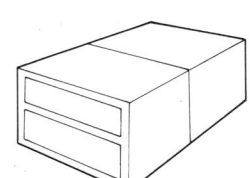

Dimension Range: Varies.
Capacity Range: 2 KW to 100 KW
Form of Heat Transfer:
    Forced air. Heat from refrigeration
    cycle.

HEAT PUMP

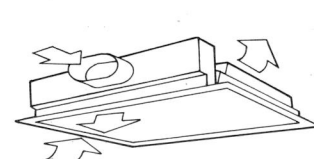

Dimension Range: Not applicable. Shown
    with fluorescent light, can be applied to
    incandescent lights.
Capacity Range: Varies with air velocity
    and shape of the light fixture.
Form of Heat Transfer: Forced air.

HEAT-OF-LIGHT

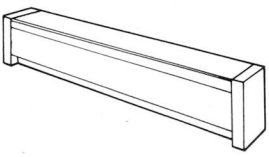

Dimension Range:
    Height: 9'' to 10''.   Length: 23'' to 107''
    Depth: 3'' to 4''
Capacity Range: 300 W to 2000 W
Form of Heat Transfer:
    Convection (Indirect heat)

HYDRONIC BASEBOARD

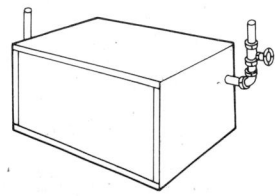

Dimension Range: Varies.
Capacity Range: 6 KW to 40 KW
Form of Heat Transfer:
    Heats water for remote hot water
    heating systems.

ELECTRIC BOILER

Tseng - Yao Sun, P. E. and Kyoung S. Park, P. E.; Ayres, Cohen and Hayakawa; Consulting Engineers; Los Angeles/San Francisco, California

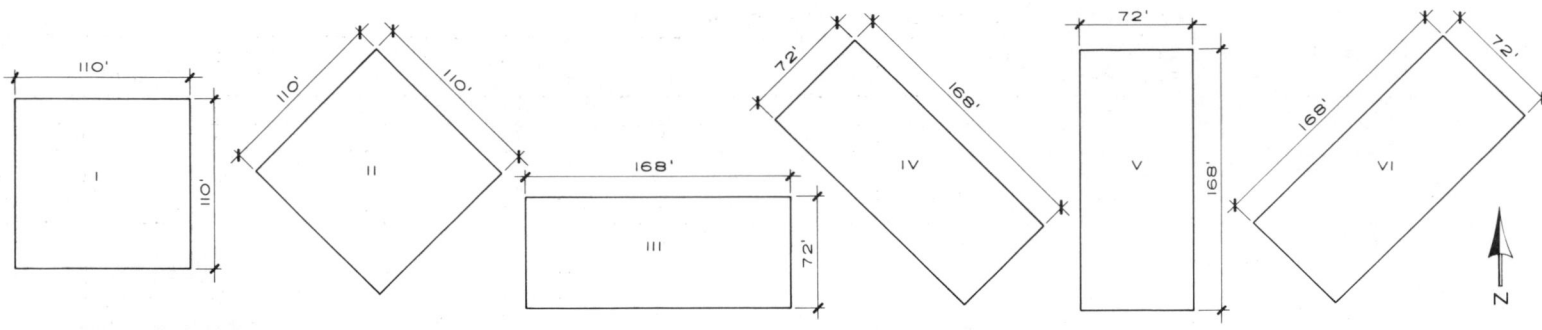

BUILDING SHAPE, SIZE AND ORIENTATION

Tabulated figures are based on calculated* loads for typical floors of office buildings of sizes, shapes and orientations shown. Areas are gross sq. ft. See another page in this series for illustration on use of the tabulated data.

AIR CONDITIONING LOAD AND AIR QUANTITY

	BUILDING SHAPE	GLASS AREA – PERCENT OF GROSS WALL AREA								
		0%	20%		40%		60%		80%	
			INDOOR SHADING DEVICE							
			WITH	WITHOUT	WITH	WITHOUT	WITH	WITHOUT	WITH	WITHOUT
AIR CONDITIONING LOAD (SQ. FT./TON)	I	516	391	343	314	256	262	204	225	170
	II	507	385	337	311	253	260	202	224	168
	III	520	383	344	303	256	251	204	214	169
	IV	511	372	331	292	245	241	194	205	161
	V	510	379	329	301	242	250	192	214	159
	VI	513	375	323	295	236	243	186	207	153
AIR QUANTITY (CFM/SQ. FT.)	I	0.75	1.10	1.35	1.47	1.96	1.83	2.57	2.19	3.18
	II	0.75	1.13	1.40	1.51	2.06	1.89	2.71	2.27	3.36
	III	0.74	1.08	1.31	1.45	1.90	1.81	2.50	2.18	3.09
	IV	0.76	1.18	1.48	1.61	2.21	2.04	2.94	2.47	3.67
	V	0.75	1.17	1.47	1.59	2.19	2.01	2.92	2.43	3.64
	VI	0.75	1.16	1.45	1.57	2.16	1.98	2.87	2.39	3.58

HEATING LOAD (BTU/HR/SQ. FT.)

OUTDOOR TEMPERATURE (°F)	GLASS AREA – PERCENT OF GROSS WALL AREA									
	0%		20%		40%		60%		80%	
	BUILDING SHAPES									
	I II	III IV V VI	I II	III IV V VI	I II	III IV V VI	I II	III IV V VI	I II	III IV V VI
0	13.5	14.6	28.9	33.1	44.6	52.9	60.2	72.7	77.2	92.6
10	12.1	13.1	25.7	29.8	39.6	47.9	53.5	66.0	68.6	84.2
20	10.7	11.6	22.4	26.4	34.5	42.6	46.6	59.0	59.8	75.4
30	9.2	10.0	19.0	22.8	29.3	37.0	39.5	51.5	50.7	66.0
40	7.6	8.2	15.5	18.9	23.8	31.0	32.1	43.3	41.2	55.6
50	5.8	6.4	11.8	14.6	18.1	24.3	24.4	34.1	31.3	44.0

* Basis for load Calculations:

1. Design procedures: American Society of Heating, Refrigeration and Air Conditioning Engineers, 1966 Guide and Data Book.
2. Building location: Sea level, 40° N. Latitude.
3. Building description: 12 feet floor to floor, curtain wall.
4. Design Conditions:
   Outdoor Summer: 93° F. DB, 75° F. WB, 20° F. Daily Range
   Winter: Varies, See above table.
   Indoor Summer: 75° F. DB, 50% RH
   Winter: 75° F. DB, RH Varies.

5. Heat Transmission Coefficients:
   Curtain Wall: U = 0.18
   Glass, 1/4″ Clear Plate:
                     U Summer = 1.06
                     U Winter = 1.13
   Inside shading devices on glass equal to light colored Venetian blind or light colored semi-open weave drapery. Shading Coefficient: 0.55.
6. People: 100 Sq. ft. per person (Sq. ft. = 90% gross area)
7. Lights: 4 Watts per sq. ft. (sq. ft. = 90% gross area) 75% of light load (3 watts per sq. ft.) to occupied space and 25% to ceiling plenum return air.

8. Supply air quantities: Required for the sum of instantaneous peak cooling loads based on 20° F. differential at outlets. Minimum of 0.8 cfm per sq. ft. in interior areas (other than 15 ft. from building perimeter).
9. No internal heat gains (light or people) credited to heating load.
10. Fixed outside air quantity equal to 15% of supply air.
11. Load through roof (2000 sq. ft.◊ per ton, 0.28 cfm per sq. ft.◊ and 0.1 t Btu per hr. per sq. ft.◊) not included.
12. Heat loss through ground floor perimeter (0.81 △t Btu per hr. per linear ft. of perimeter) not included.

   ◊ Roof area.

Tseng - Yao Sun, P. E. and Kyoung S. Park, P. E.; Ayres, Cohen and Hayakawa; Consulting Engineers; Los Angeles/San Francisco, California

SYSTEM	SPACE	NO. OF STORIES ABOVE FAN ROOM	SUPPLY AIR QUANTITIES PER FLOOR (CFM)						
			UP TO 5000	5000 TO 7500	7500 TO 10000	10000 TO 12500	12500 TO 15000	15000 TO 17500	17500 TO 20000
SINGLE DUCT LOW VELOCITY	DUCT SHAFT (SQ. FT.)	1	14	18	22	26	30	33	37
		2	32	40	47	55	63	70	78
		3	40	51	63	74	85	97	108
		4	47	63	78	93	108	123	138
		5	55	74	93	112	131	150	168
	CEILING SPACE (IN.)		19	21	23	25	27	29	31
SINGLE DUCT HIGH VELOCITY	DUCT SHAFT (SQ. FT.)	1	12	15	18	20	23	26	29
		2	28	33	39	45	51	57	63
		3	33	42	51	60	68	77	86
		4	39	51	63	74	86	97	109
		5	45	60	74	89	103	118	132
		6	51	68	86	103	120	138	155
		7	57	77	97	118	138	158	178
		8	63	86	109	132	155	178	201
		9	68	94	120	146	172	198	224
		10	74	103	132	161	189	218	247
	CEILING SPACE (IN.)		15	19	21	23	23	25	25
DOUBLE DUCT LOW VELOCITY	DUCT SHAFT (SQ. FT.)	1	16	21	25	30	35	39	44
		2	35	45	54	63	72	81	90
		3	45	58	72	86	99	113	126
		4	54	72	90	108	126	144	162
		5	63	86	108	130	153	175	197
	CEILING SPACE (IN.)		28	30	32	34	36	38	38
DOUBLE DUCT HIGH VELOCITY	DUCT SHAFT (SQ. FT.)	1	13	16	19	23	26	29	33
		2	29	36	43	49	56	62	69
		3	36	46	56	65	75	85	94
		4	43	56	69	81	94	107	120
		5	49	65	81	97	113	129	145
		6	56	75	94	113	133	152	171
		7	62	85	107	129	152	174	196
		8	69	94	120	145	177	196	222
		9	75	104	133	161	190	219	247
		10	81	113	145	177	209	241	273
	CEILING SPACE (IN.)		26	28	30	32	32	34	36

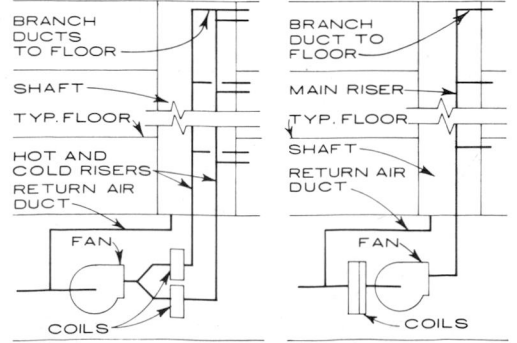

DOUBLE DUCT SYSTEM

BRANCH DUCTS TO FLOOR
SHAFT
TYP. FLOOR
HOT AND COLD RISERS RETURN AIR DUCT
FAN
COILS

SINGLE DUCT SYSTEM

BRANCH DUCT TO FLOOR
MAIN RISER
TYP. FLOOR
SHAFT
RETURN AIR DUCT
FAN
COILS

NOTES:

Space requirements are for schematic studies only and are based on the following assumptions. See related page for illustration on use of tabulated data.

1. All air double duct or single duct up feed systems shown in diagram at left. Shaft around supply ducts used for return air.
2. No exhaust duct in shaft. Shaft areas at each floor include allowances for miscellaneous protrusions (pipe risers, branch duct take-offs, recesses for fire hose cabinets, drinking fountains or electric panel). Single story building, 5 sq. ft.; multistory building, 15 sq. ft.
3. Main riser ducts and shaft sized as follows:

   High Velocity: Round ducts, 3500 fpm average velocity.

   Low Velocity: Rectangular ducts, 1:2 aspect ratio, 1600 fpm average velocity.

   Return Air: 1000 fpm average velocity.
4. All supply riser and branch ducts insulated, 2'' thick.
5. Ceiling space defined as depth required between top of ceiling suspension system (or top of recessed light fixture, if used) and bottom of structural element (including fireproofing, if used). Space base on ceiling plenum return (no return air ducts) and 1:4 aspect ratio rectangular supply air ducts. Depth can be appreciably reduced if duct crossovers can be arranged to utilize the space between beams.

Tseng - Yao Sun, P. E. and Kyoung S. Park, P. E.; Ayres, Cohen and Hayakawa; Consulting Engineers; Los Angeles/San Francisco, California

REFRIGERATION MACHINE ROOM

COOLING LOAD (TONS)	MACHINE ROOM AREA (SQ. FT.) [a]				HEAT REMOVAL EQUIP. [c] DIMENSION (W × L × H)(FT.)		OPERATING WEIGHT (1000 LBS) [d]			
	DIRECT EXPANSION SYSTEM	RECIPRO-CATING CHILLER	GENTRI-FUGAL CHILLER	ABSORP-TION CHILLER	COOLING TOWER	AIRCOOLED CONDENSER	CENTRI-FUGAL CHILLER	ABSORPTION CHILLER	COOLING TOWER	AIR COOLED CONDENSER
Up to 50	160	350	—	—	7 x 6 x 7	7 x 16 x 6	4.3[e]	—	3.6	2.3
50 to 100	160	400	480	420	12 x 8 x 8	8 x 16 x 6	8.8[f]	13.7	10.0	3.5
100 to 250	—	530[b]	620	640	19 x 13 x 9	—	17.9[g]	26.7	23.0	—
250 to 500	—	—	960[b]	1100[b]	26 x 14 x 13	—	35.8	53.4	30.0	—
500 to 750	—	—	1160[b]	1400[b]	26 x 21 x 13	—	39.4	89.2	43.0	—
750 to 1000	—	—	1500[b]	1500[b]	26 x 27 x 13	—	73.3	98.3	60.0	—
1000 to 1500	—	—	1640[b]	1680[b]	26 x 42 x 13	—	101.0	137.0	86.0	—

BOILER ROOM

HEATING LOAD (100 MBH)	ONE BOILER		TWO BOILERS	
	ROOM [h] AREA (SQ. FT.)	BOILER [i] WEIGHT (LBS.)	ROOM [h] AREA (SQ. FT.)	WEIGHT [i] PER BOILER (LBS.)
Up to 5	130	1680	200	2050
5 to 10	170	2740	240	3360
10 to 15	200	4340	260	4580
15 to 20	230	4930	290	5480
20 to 30	260	7140	320	8680
30 to 40	290	8680	380	9860
40 to 50	370	13060	420	11960

FAN ROOM

SUPPLY AIR (1000 CFM)	PACKAGED UNIT		BUILT—UP SYSTEM		
	ROOM [j] AREA (SQ. FT.)	UNIT [k] WEIGHT (LBS)	ROOM AREA (SQ. FT.) [j]		EQUIP. [k] WEIGHT (LBS.)
			SINGLE DUCT	DOUBLE DUCT	
Up to 10	210	3400	290	310	2800
10 to 20	320	5500	350	380	4400
20 to 30	430	9100	470	510	6300
30 to 50	—	—	710	780	10700
50 to 75	—	—	980	1050	15200
75 to 100	—	—	1290	1370	22000
100 to 150	—	—	1510	1600	30000

NOTES :

a. Machine room area includes space for chiller or chillers, 2 chilled water pumps, 2 condensing water pumps, tube pulling space and electric control panels. No space allowed for cooling tower or air cooled condenser.

b. Two chillers each sized for 50% of total load.

c. Net equipment dimensions. Space for architectural screening excluded. Add 3 ft. in height for structural supports under cooling tower. Cooling towers, single cell, sized for 95°/85°F water, 75°FWB. Air cooled condenser sized for 40°F suction/110°F condensing, 100°F outside air.

d. Operating weight includes weight of equipment plus its contents. Add 15% for weight of pipes, expansion tank and pumps. If concrete bases are used, add 2 times the weight of the equipment.

e. Operating weight of reciprocating chiller. Direct expansion machine weighs 2400 lbs.

f. Reciprocating chiller weighs 6500 lbs. and direct expansion machine weighs 3900 lbs.

g. Reciprocating chiller weighs 19400 lbs.

h. Boiler room area includes space for hot water boiler or boilers, tube pulling space, circulating pumps and one tankless domestic hot water generator. Use same data for steam boilers.

i. Add 15% for weight of pipes, expansion tank and pumps.

j. Fan room area includes space for single fan supply system. If return air fan is used, add 30%. If fan room is located on roof or at perimeter of building, areas can be used directly. If fan room is located within building core, additional space is required for outside air, relief or exhaust air shafts.

k. Equipment weight includes fan, coils, filters, plenums and ducts in the fan room.

ILLUSTRATION ON USE OF THE TABULATED DATA IN PAGES OF THIS SERIES TO DETERMINE ROUGH LOADS AND SPACE REQUIREMENTS FOR AIR CONDITIONING SYSTEM

Building Description: 5 story office building, Shape IV, 84 ft x 144 ft, 40% glass with indoor shading device. 20°F winter outdoor temperature.

Gross Area of Building:
84 x 144 x 5 = 60,500 sq. ft.

Roof Area:
84 x 144 = 12,096 sq. ft.

Ground Floor Perimeter:
84 x 2 + 144 x 2 = 456 ft.

Air Conditioning Load and Supply Air Quantities:
From table, preceding page, for building shape IV, 40% glass with indoor shading device: 292 sq. ft/ ton, 1.61 cfm/sq. ft.
Building Cooling Load:
(60500/292) + (12096/2000) = 213 tons
Air Quantities:
Cfm for typical floors:
12096 x 1.61 = 19,500 cfm
Cfm for floor under roof:
19500 + 12096 x 0.28 = 22,900 cfm
Total cfm for building:
(4 x 19500) + 22900 = 100,900 cfm

Heating Load:
From table, preceding pg., for building shape IV, 40% glass at 20°F outdoor temperature:
42.6 Btu/Hr./Sq. ft.
Building Heating Load:
60500 x 42.6 = 257.730 Btu/Hr.
Add roof plus floor slab
(12096 x 0.1* + 456 x 0.81**) (75-20)
= 86500
Total:
257730 + 86500 = 344,320 Btu/Hr. or 344 MBH

Refrigeration Machine Room Size:
From table above, using centrifugal chillers: 620 sq. ft.
Cooling tower size: 19 ft x 13 ft x 9 ft high.

Boiler Room Size:
From table above, using 2 Boilers: 380 sq. ft.

Fan Room Sizes:
Scheme A: One fan room per floor using packaged unit.
From table above, 320 sq. ft. for typical floor and 430 sq. ft. for floor under roof.

Scheme B: One central fan room in basement using double duct system.
From table, 1600 sq. ft.

Duct and shaft space Requirements:
From page titled above, using one central fan room in basement and double duct system.

Scheme A: One shaft, low velocity system.
1st floor: 197 sq. ft.
2nd floor: 162 sq. ft.
3rd floor: 126 sq. ft.
4th floor: 90 sq. ft.
5th floor: 44 sq. ft.
Maximum ceiling space required: 38 in.

Scheme B: Two shafts, high velocity system, each shaft serving half of floor.
1st floor: 81 sq. ft.
2nd floor: 69 sq. ft.
3rd floor: 56 sq. ft.
4th floor: 43 sq. ft.
5th floor: 23 sq. ft.
Maximum ceiling space required: 30 in.

Tseng - Yao Sun, P. E. and Kyoung S. Park, P. E.; Ayres, Cohen and Hayakawa; Consulting Engineers; Los Angeles/San Francisco, California

CLEARANCE IN MECHANICAL EQUIPMENT ROOMS

TYPE OF BUILDING AND TOTAL GROSS FLOOR AREA	PERCENTAGE — FLOOR AREA REQUIRED FOR MECH. SPACE	MIN. CLEAR HEIGHT — AIR HANDLING EQUIPMENT	MIN. CLEAR HEIGHT — HEATING PLANT	MIN. CLEAR HEIGHT — REFRIGERATION PLANT
COMMERCIAL BUILDINGS				
10,000 Sq. Ft.	10%	8'−0"	8'−0"	8'−0"
50,000 Sq. Ft.	8%	9'−0"	10'−0"	9'−0"
100,000 Sq. Ft.	6%	10'−0"	12'−0"	14'−0"
INSTITUTIONAL BUILDINGS				
10,000 Sq. Ft.	12%	8'−0"	10'−0"	8'−0"
50,000 Sq. Ft.	10%	10'−0"	12'−0"	12'−0"
100,000 Sq. Ft.	8%	10'−0"	14'−0"	14'−0"

NOTES:

1. The height clearances indicated above are the recommended minimum for preliminary design. These requirements vary depending on the following:
   a) type of refrigeration plant
   b) type of heating plant
   c) built-up units versus packaged units
   d) main equipment room on roof, main equipment in basement, separate equipment room on each floor, or a combination of all three.

2. When blocking in equipment in mechanical equipment rooms for preliminary layout be sure to allow clearances for the following:
   a) tube removal for fire tube boilers
   b) tube removal for chillers, condensers, converters, etc.
   c) coil removal for air handling systems
   d) adequate access for maintenance of filters, traps, controls, etc.

3. The percentage of total gross floor areas indicated as being required for mechanical space are average and are based upon integral heating and refrigeration plants. If the building is served by an external central plant, the percentages will be reduced.

CLEARANCE IN CEILINGS FOR LOW VELOCITY DUCTWORK

APPROXIMATE AREA SERVED PER SHAFT OR LOCAL EQUIP. ROOM	WITH RETURN AIR DUCTWORK		NO RETURN AIR DUCTWORK (see note five)		DEDUCT IF SYSTEM SERVES INTERIOR AREAS ONLY (NOTE 6)
	WITH LIGHTING BELOW CEILING	RECESSED LIGHTING FLUORESCENT	WITH LIGHTING BELOW CEILING	RECESSED LIGHTING FLUORESCENT	
2500 Sq. Ft.	20" to 30"	24" to 34"	14" to 18"	18" to 22"	4" to 6"
5000 Sq. Ft.	30" to 36"	34" to 40"	18" to 22"	22" to 26"	4" to 7"
10,000 Sq. Ft.	36" to 44"	40" to 48"	22" to 26"	26" to 30"	6" to 8"

NOTES:

1. Clearances given above are between top of ceiling construction and underside of structure for floor above.

2. Variations in required clearances, as indicated depend upon the location of the supply source: if located at the extremity of the area served, greatest clearance should be used: if located at the center of the area served, smallest clearance should be used.

3. It is generally preferable to have upturned beams around a duct shaft, as this permits smoother take-offs.

4. Clearances indicated do not allow for piping. If considerable piping must run in the ceiling, where ducts are largest (such as toilet wastes or rain conductors which must run horizontally at the top floor) clearances must be increased.

5. The clearances listed under "No Return Air Ductwork" are predicated on: a) a central return. This is not feasible for areas larger than 2500 sq. ft., and is not permitted in schools, hospitals, etc. b) utilizing space above ceiling as return air plenum. Building structural system must be suitable. Floor above must be fireproof construction.

6. If low velocity duct system serves interior area only, then the amounts indicated may be deducted from appropriate clearances. These applicable if a separate system serves the perimeter.

Smith, Hinchman & Grylls Associates, Inc.; Detroit, Michigan

COMPARISON OF AIR OUTLETS

CHARACTERISTIC	CEILING DIFFUSERS	SIDEWALL REGISTER	FLOOR REGISTER	LIGHT TROFFER
PERFORMANCE	Excellent	Fair	Good with limited application	Fair with limited capacity
LOCATION	Furred ceiling	Wall or furred soffit	Building perimeter	Furred ceiling
INTERFERENCE WITH INTERIOR DESIGN	Poor	Poor	Fair	No interference
INTERFERENCE WITH FURNITURE PLACEMENT	No interference	No interference	May interfere with furniture. Cannot be placed at doorway	No interference
FLEXIBILITY FOR MOVABLE PARTITIONS	Fair	Poor	Poor	Excellent
OUTLET COST	Low	Low	Medium	Medium
INSTALLATION COST	Low	Low	Medium	High
COORDINATION PROBLEMS	Low	Low	Medium	High
REQUIRES SUPPLEMENTARY OUTLETS OF DIFFERENT TYPE	No	No	Yes, in large areas	Yes, in perimeter areas
MAINTENANCE	Can smudge ceiling	Good	Can collect dirt in supply plenum below floor	Can smudge ceiling

COMPARISON OF AIR OUTLETS - CONTINUED

CHARACTERISTIC	LINEAR CEILING DIFFUSER	LINEAR SIDEWALL REGISTER	LINEAR FLOOR REGISTER	INTEGRATED CEILING AIR BAR
PERFORMANCE	Good with limited capacity	Fair	Good with limited application	Fair with limited capacity
LOCATION	Furred ceiling	Wall or furred soffit	Building perimeter	Furred ceiling
INTERFERENCE WITH INTERIOR DESIGN	Fair	Fair	Fair	No interference
INTERFERENCE WITH FURNITURE PLACEMENT	No interference	No interference	Same as floor register	No interference
FLEXIBILITY FOR MOVABLE PARTITIONS	Fair	Poor	Poor	Good
OUTLET COST	Medium to high, depends on type used	High	High	Medium to high
INSTALLATION COST	High	High	High	High
COORDINATION PROBLEMS	Medium	Medium	Medium	High
REQUIRES SUPPLEMENTARY OUTLETS OF DIFFERENT TYPE	No	No	Yes, in large areas	Yes, in perimeter areas
MAINTENANCE	Can smudge ceiling	Good	Same as floor register	Can smudge ceiling

Tseng - Yao Sun, P. E.; Ayres, Cohen and Hayakawa; Consulting Engineers; Los Angeles/San Francisco, California

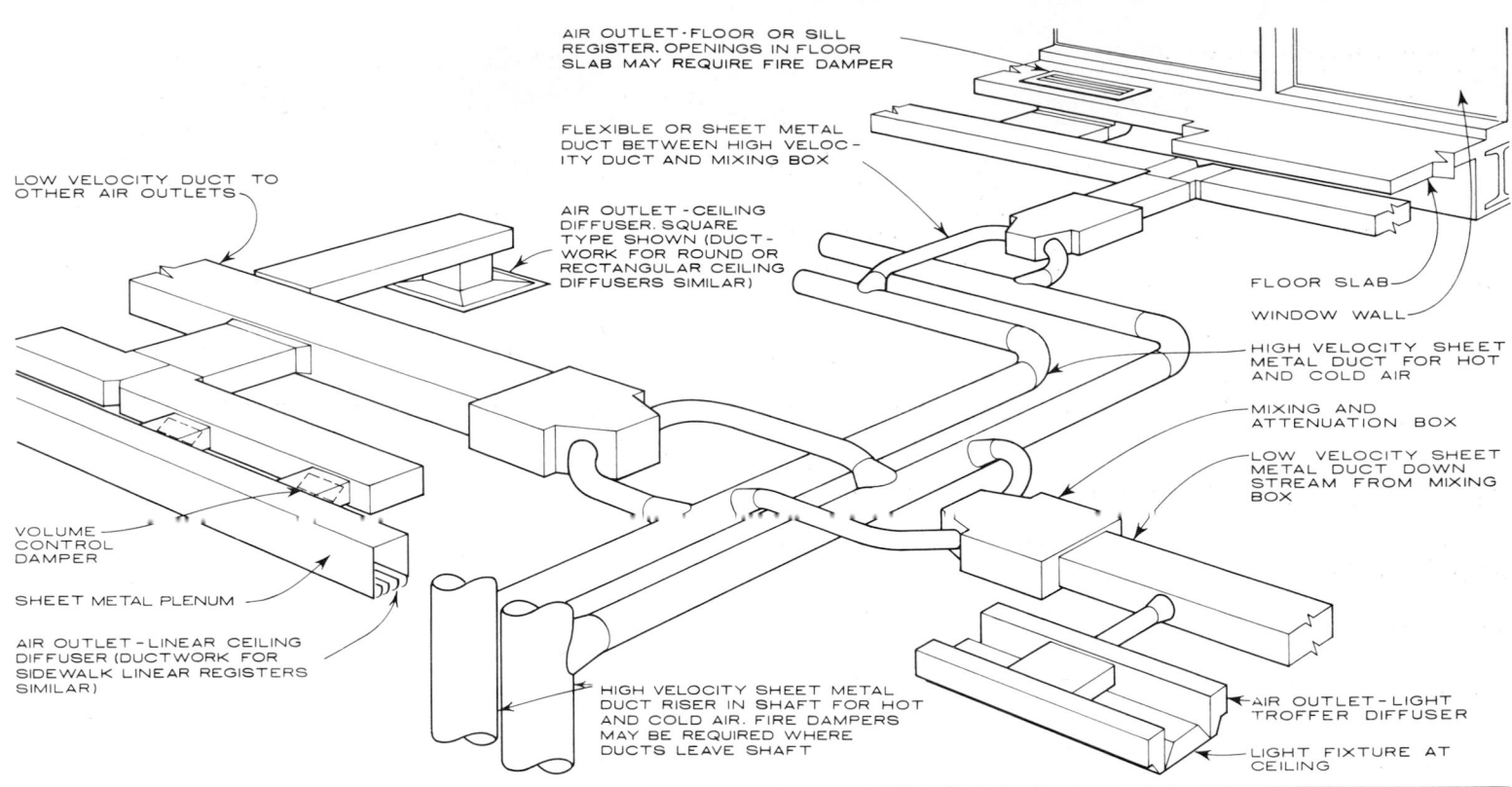

AIR OUTLET·FLOOR OR SILL REGISTER. OPENINGS IN FLOOR SLAB MAY REQUIRE FIRE DAMPER

FLEXIBLE OR SHEET METAL DUCT BETWEEN HIGH VELOCITY DUCT AND MIXING BOX

LOW VELOCITY DUCT TO OTHER AIR OUTLETS

AIR OUTLET·CEILING DIFFUSER. SQUARE TYPE SHOWN (DUCTWORK FOR ROUND OR RECTANGULAR CEILING DIFFUSERS SIMILAR)

FLOOR SLAB

WINDOW WALL

HIGH VELOCITY SHEET METAL DUCT FOR HOT AND COLD AIR

MIXING AND ATTENUATION BOX

LOW VELOCITY SHEET METAL DUCT DOWN STREAM FROM MIXING BOX

VOLUME CONTROL DAMPER

SHEET METAL PLENUM

AIR OUTLET·LINEAR CEILING DIFFUSER (DUCTWORK FOR SIDEWALK LINEAR REGISTERS SIMILAR)

HIGH VELOCITY SHEET METAL DUCT RISER IN SHAFT FOR HOT AND COLD AIR. FIRE DAMPERS MAY BE REQUIRED WHERE DUCTS LEAVE SHAFT

AIR OUTLET·LIGHT TROFFER DIFFUSER

LIGHT FIXTURE AT CEILING

HIGH VELOCITY DOUBLE DUCT WITH VARIOUS AIR OUTLETS

CONDITIONED AIR DISCHARGE GRILLE

DRAPERY

WINDOW

COLUMN

PRIMARY AIR DUCT AND SECONDARY WATER PIPING IN CONCEALED SPACE UP TO OTHER FLOORS

CABINET TYPE INDUCTION UNIT. CAN BE SPECIFIED WITH FACTORY MADE MATCHING CABINET OR SHELVING. UNIT CAN BE CONCEALED BEHIND SPECIALLY DESIGNED ENCLOSURES

PRIMARY AIR DUCT TO INDUCTION UNIT

INDUCED ROOM AIR INTAKE

FLOOR SLAB

SECONDARY WATER PIPES TO INDUCTION UNIT

MATCHING CABINET

ALL AIR INDUCTION UNIT MIXES PRIMARY AIR WITH VARIABLE AMOUNTS OF THE INDUCED ROOM AIR (AIR IN THE CEILING PLENUM) AND DISCHARGES THE CONDITIONED AIR THROUGH LOW VELOCITY DUCTS TO AIR OUTLETS

SECONDARY WATER PIPE LOOP BELOW FLOOR SLAB

PRIMARY AIR MAIN DUCT BELOW FLOOR SLAB

FLEXIBLE OR SHEET METAL DUCT

ALL AIR VARIABLE VOLUME AIR OUTLET VARIES AMOUNT OF CONDITIONED AIR DISCHARGE TO THE SPACE

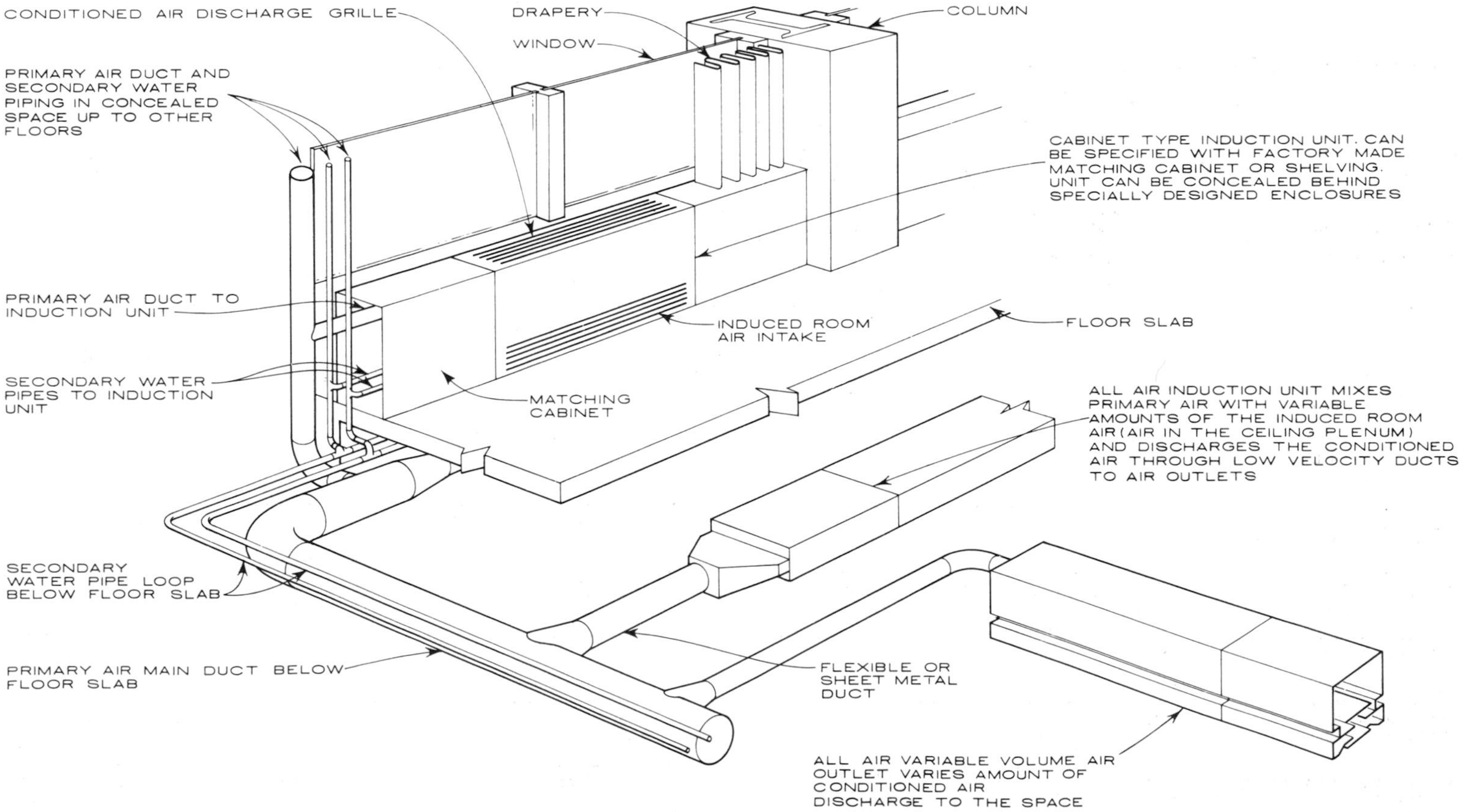

HIGH VELOCITY SINGLE DUCT WITH VARIOUS AIR OUTLETS

Tseng · Yao Sun, P. E.; Ayres, Cohen and Hayakawa; Consulting Engineers; Los Angeles/San Francisco, California

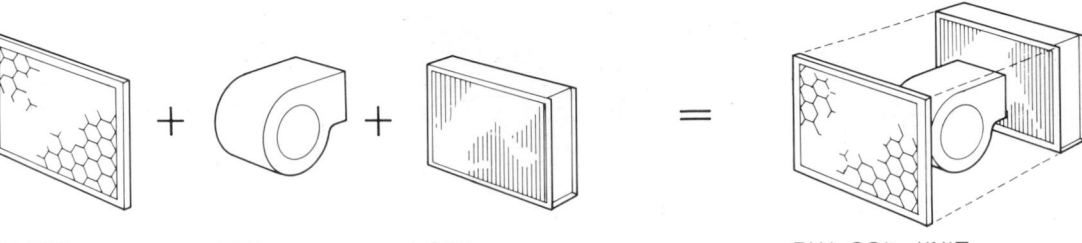

FILTER   FAN   COIL   FAN COIL UNIT

FAN COIL UNIT

Fan coil unit can be placed in horizontal (as shown) or vertical position. It can be located above ceilings, on roofs, in closets or below window sills. Coil can be cooled either by chilled water or by direct expansion refrigeration. The unit is the indoor portion of the unitary air conditioner.

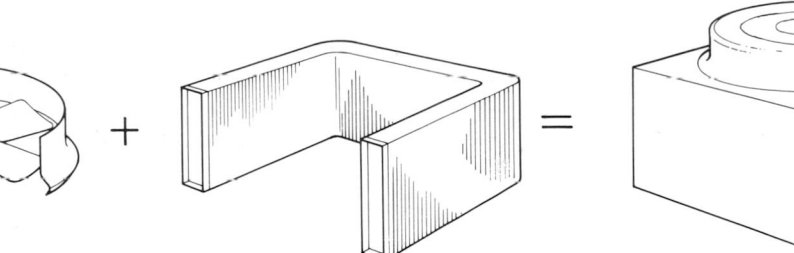

FAN   CONDENSING COIL   AIR COOLED CONDENSER

AIR COOLED CONDENSER

Air cooled condenser is designed to condense the hot refrigerant gas to a liquid by passing air over a condensing coil. The unit is generally placed outdoors, but can be located indoors if air intake and exhaust ducts are extended to the outside. It is available with centrifugal blowers in lieu of propeller fans (as shown) where required to offset the resistance of long duct runs. Water cooled condensers connected to cooling towers and evaporative condensers are also available.

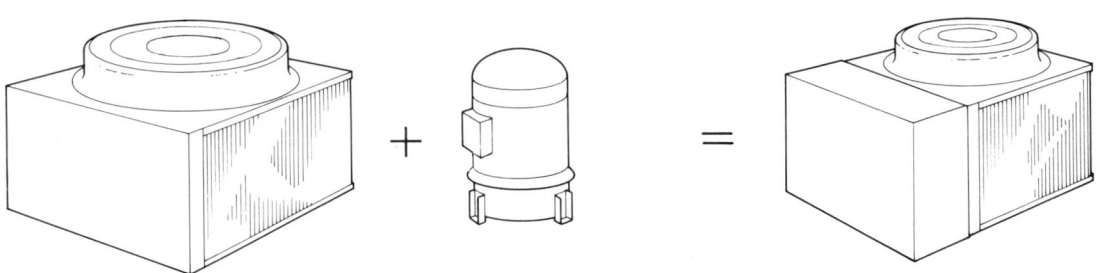

AIR COOLED CONDENSER   COMPRESSOR   AIR COOLED CONDENSING UNIT

AIR COOLED CONDENSING UNIT

Air cooled condensing unit is the complete outdoor portion of a unitary air conditioner. The unit coupled with a fan coil unit using a refrigerant coil becomes a complete unitary air conditioner. Units with centrifugal blower are also available.

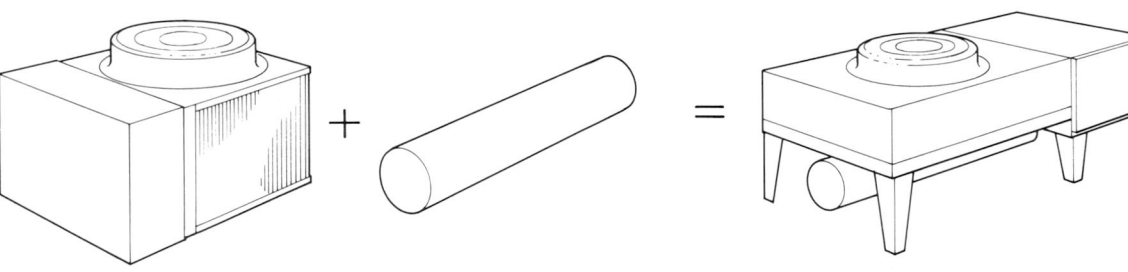

AIR COOLED CONDENSING UNIT   EVAPORATOR   AIR COOLED WATER CHILLER

AIR COOLED WATER CHILLER

Air cooled water chiller is another type of the outdoor portion of a unitary air conditioner. The refrigerant in the evaporator chills water that is then pumped to the coil in the fan coil unit. The fan and coil unit is the indoor portion of the unitary air conditioner.

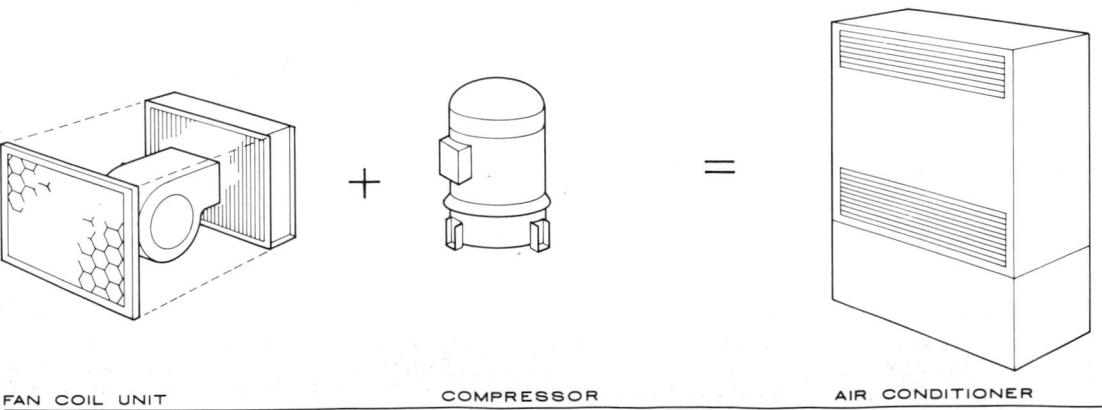

FAN COIL UNIT   COMPRESSOR   AIR CONDITIONER

AIR CONDITIONER

Air conditioner is another arrangement of the indoor portion of the unitary air conditioner. The unit coupled with the air cooled condenser becomes a complete unitary air conditioner. The unit is usually floor mounted.

Tseng - Yao Sun, P. E.; Ayres, Cohen and Hayakawa; Consulting Engineers; Los Angeles/San Francisco, California

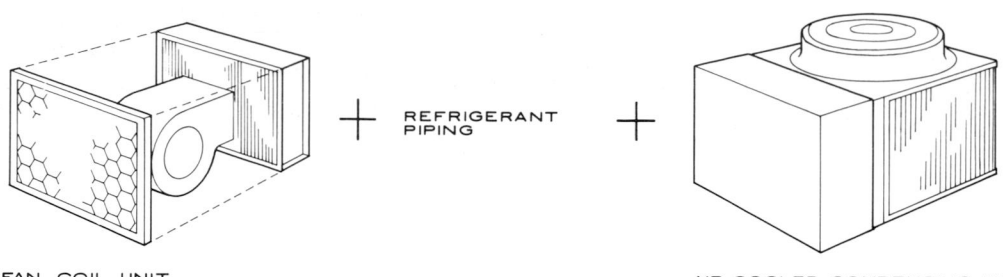

FAN COIL UNIT   +   REFRIGERANT PIPING   +   AIR COOLED CONDENSING UNIT

FAN COIL UNIT PLUS CONDENSING UNIT

Direct expansion refrigeration coil is used in the fan coil unit. Liquid and suction refrigerant piping connect the fan coil unit (indoor portion) to the air cooled condensing unit (outdoor portion). Multiple fan coil units can be served by a single condensing unit.

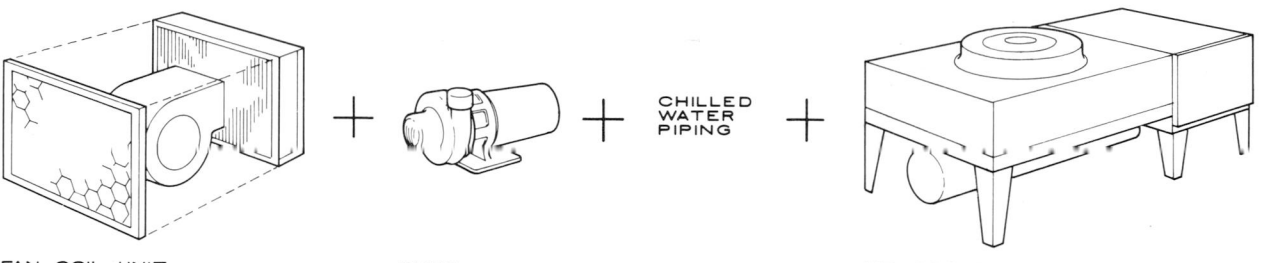

FAN COIL UNIT   +   PUMP   +   CHILLED WATER PIPING   +   AIR COOLED WATER CHILLER

FAN COIL UNIT PLUS WATER CHILLER

Chilled water coil is used in the fan coil unit. A pump is required to circulate chilled water between the fan coil unit (indoor portion) and the water chiller (outdoor portion). This arrangement is generally used where the system requires multiple fan coil units.

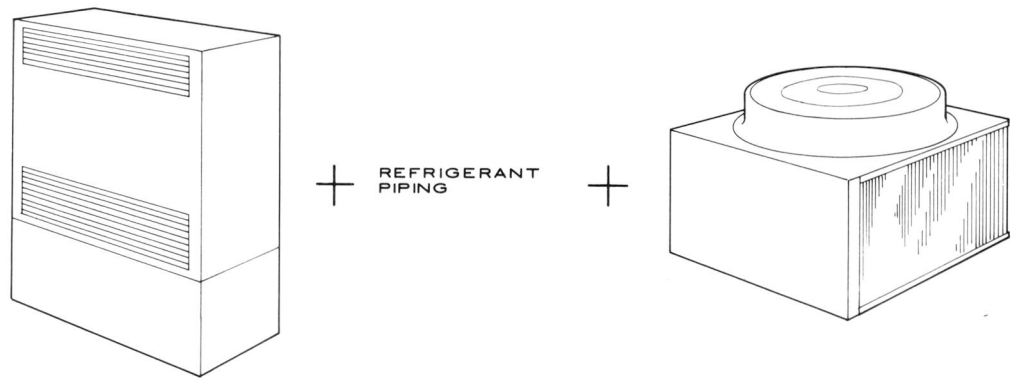

AIR CONDITIONER   +   REFRIGERANT PIPING   +   AIR COOLED CONDENSER

AIR CONDITIONER WITH REMOTE CONDENSER

Hot gas and liquid refrigerant piping connect the air conditioner (indoor portion) to the air cooled condenser (outdoor portion). Each air conditioner must be served by a single condenser.

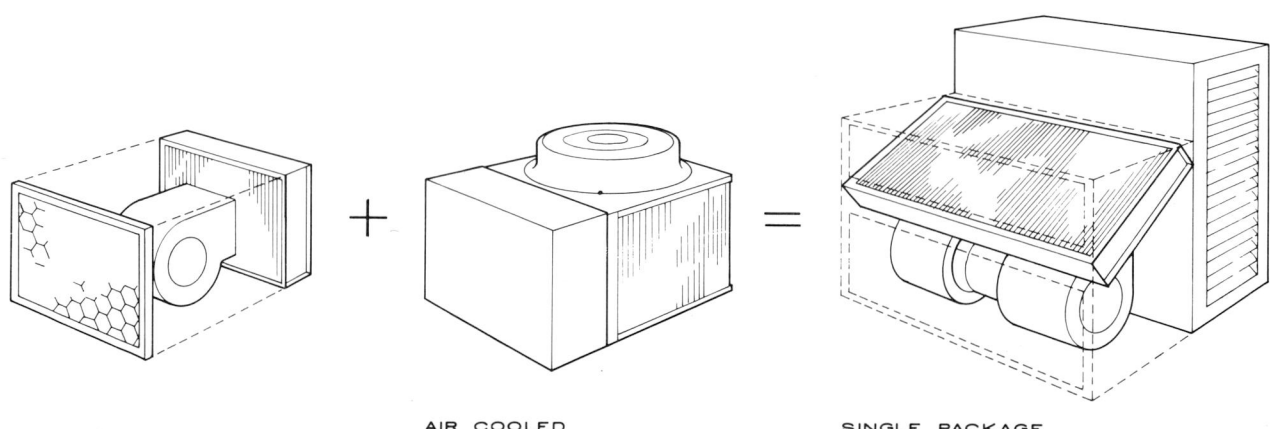

FAN COIL UNIT   +   AIR COOLED CONDENSING UNIT   =   SINGLE PACKAGE AIR CONDITIONER

SINGLE PACKAGE AIR CONDITIONER

No external piping required for the package other than the drip pan drain line. The package is generally installed on a roof or through an exterior wall.

DEFINITION OF THE UNITARY AIR CONDITIONER

A complete, pre-assembled air conditioning system consists of one or more matched factory-made assemblies which normally include an evaporator or cooling coil, a compressor and condenser combination, and may include a heating function* as well.

* The integral heating components of unitary air conditioner can be:

1. Hot water or steam coils using an auxiliary boiler.

2. Electric resistance heaters.

3. Direct-fired furnaces using either gas or oil as fuels.

Heating can also be achieved by making the refrigeration system operate as a heat pump by reversing the function of the evaporator and the condenser during the heating season.

Tseng - Yao Sun, P. E.; Ayres, Cohen and Hayakawa; Consulting Engineers; Los Angeles/San Francisco, California

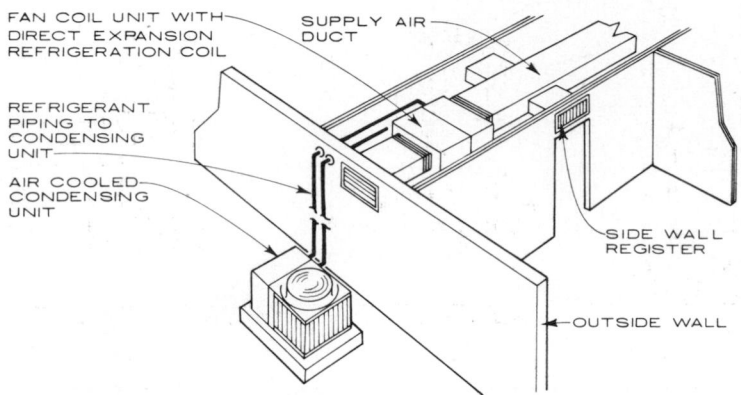

CONDENSING UNIT WITH FAN COIL UNIT ✻

FAN COIL UNIT WITH DIRECT EXPANSION REFRIGERATION COIL

SUPPLY AIR DUCT

REFRIGERANT PIPING TO CONDENSING UNIT

AIR COOLED CONDENSING UNIT

SIDE WALL REGISTER

OUTSIDE WALL

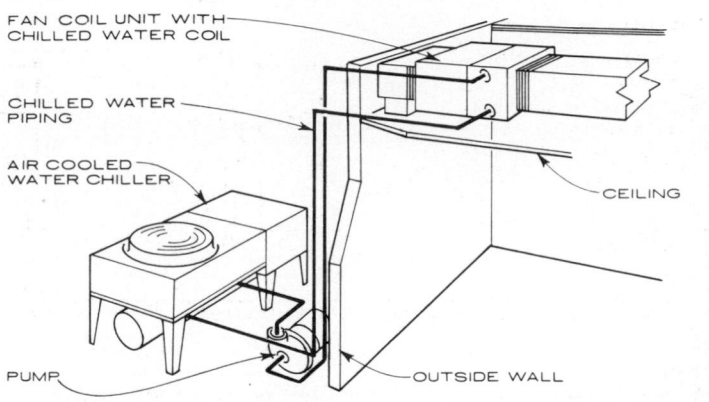

WATER CHILLER WITH FAN COIL UNIT ✻

FAN COIL UNIT WITH CHILLED WATER COIL

CHILLED WATER PIPING

AIR COOLED WATER CHILLER

CEILING

PUMP

OUTSIDE WALL

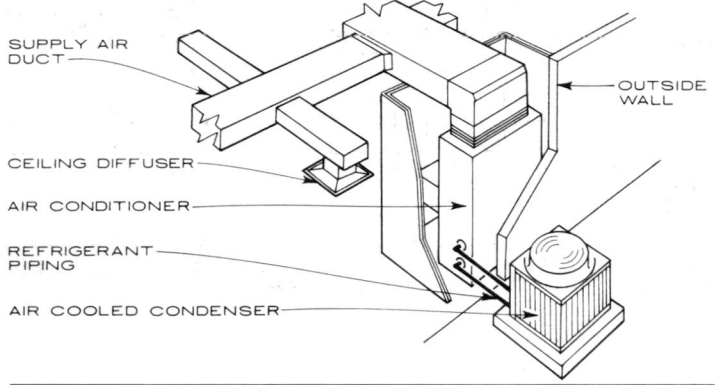

AIR CONDITIONER WITH REMOTE CONDENSER ✻

SUPPLY AIR DUCT

OUTSIDE WALL

CEILING DIFFUSER

AIR CONDITIONER

REFRIGERANT PIPING

AIR COOLED CONDENSER

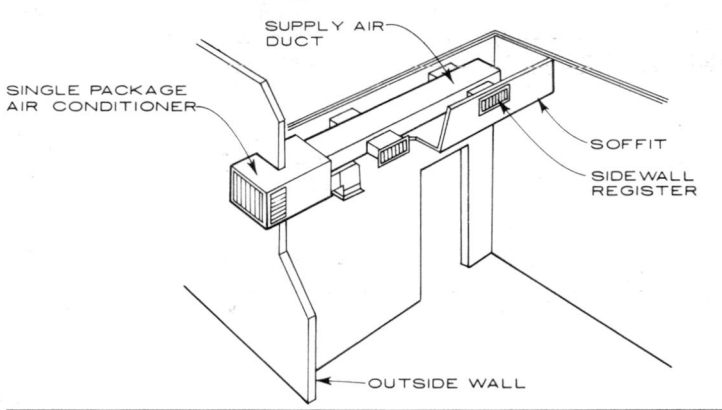

SINGLE PACKAGE AIR CONDITIONER ◊

SUPPLY AIR DUCT

SINGLE PACKAGE AIR CONDITIONER

SOFFIT

SIDEWALL REGISTER

OUTSIDE WALL

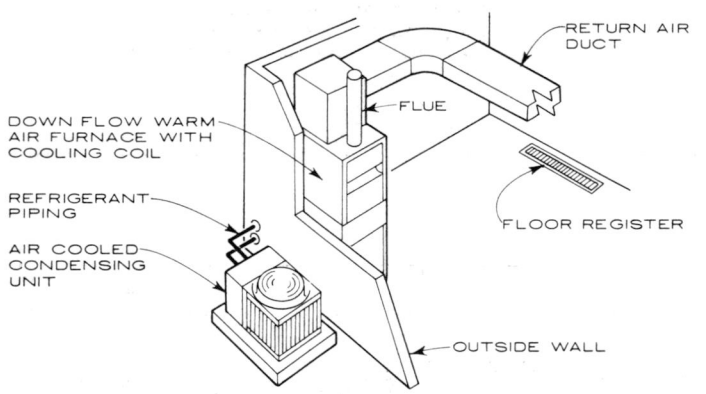

CONDENSING UNIT WITH WARM AIR FURNACE WITH COOLING COIL §

RETURN AIR DUCT

FLUE

DOWN FLOW WARM AIR FURNACE WITH COOLING COIL

REFRIGERANT PIPING

AIR COOLED CONDENSING UNIT

FLOOR REGISTER

OUTSIDE WALL

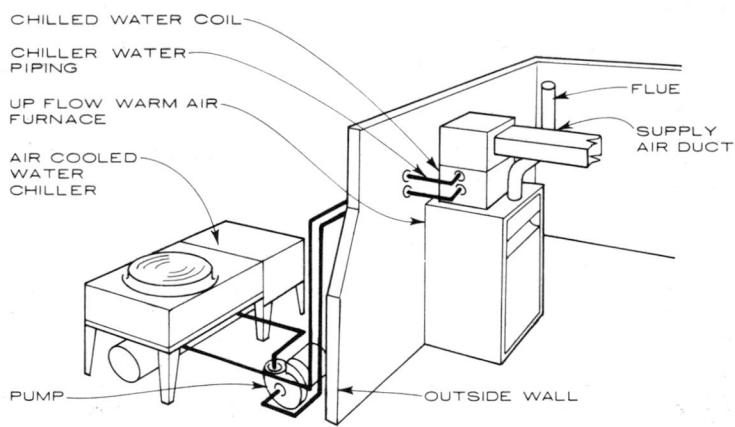

WATER CHILLER WITH WARM AIR FURNACE WITH COOLING COIL §

CHILLED WATER COIL

CHILLER WATER PIPING

UP FLOW WARM AIR FURNACE

AIR COOLED WATER CHILLER

FLUE

SUPPLY AIR DUCT

PUMP

OUTSIDE WALL

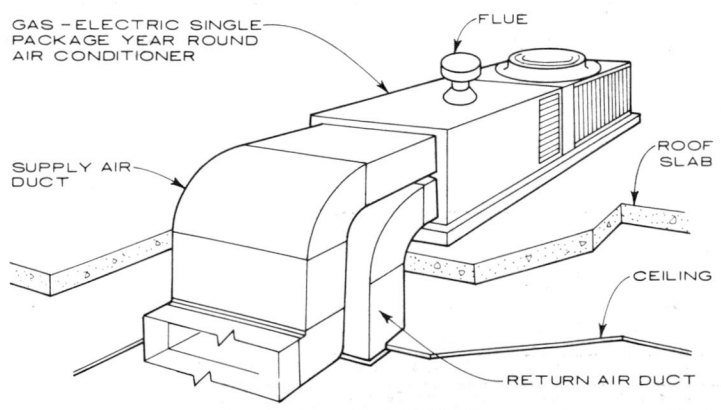

SINGLE PACKAGE YEAR ROUND AIR CONDITIONER
(ROOF TOP UNIT) ✝

GAS - ELECTRIC SINGLE PACKAGE YEAR ROUND AIR CONDITIONER

FLUE

SUPPLY AIR DUCT

ROOF SLAB

CEILING

RETURN AIR DUCT

NOTES APPLY TO VARIOUS SYSTEMS:

✻   These systems furnish cooling only. Heating, if required, must be provided by other means.

◊   Unit provides cooling only unless designed as a heat pump.

§   These systems include a gas fired warm air furnace for heating. They are commonly used in residences and classrooms. See page on Warm Air Heating.

✝   Unit is a single package air conditioner coupled with a gas fired furnace for heating. It is commonly used in single story office, school and industrial buildings. It can also be modified for indoor applications with ducts from condenser extended to the outside.

See pages on Unitary Air Conditioning Components and Systems for components and definition of such systems.

Tseng - Yao Sun, P. E. and Kyoung S. Park, P. E.; Ayres, Cohen and Hayakawa; Consulting Engineers; Los Angeles/San Francisco, California

GENERAL NOTES:

1. All dimensions on this sheet are in inches.

2. Height as required, unit-to-window duct not furnished with unit.

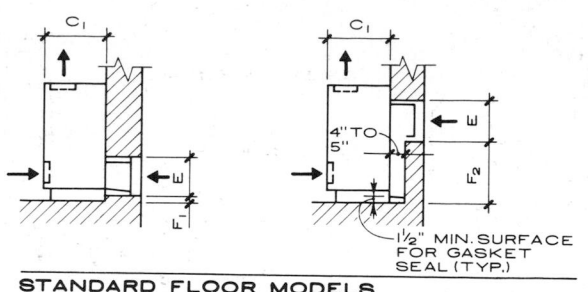

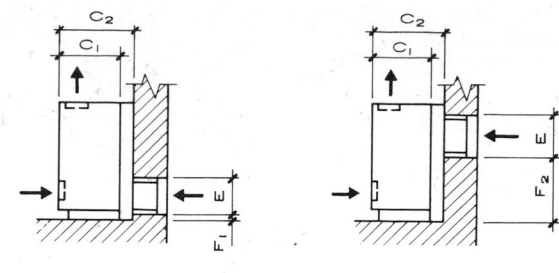

1½" MIN. SURFACE FOR GASKET SEAL (TYP.)

STANDARD FLOOR MODELS   **ADAPTER BACK MODELS**

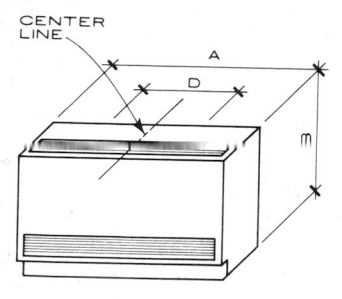

CENTER LINE

TOP AND FRONT VIEW OF VERTICAL MODELS

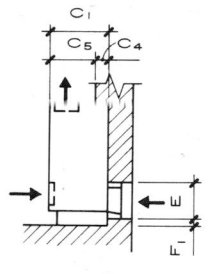

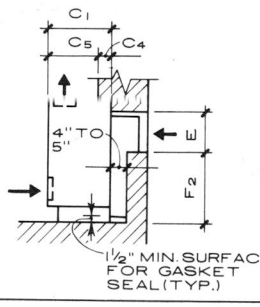

1½" MIN. SURFACE FOR GASKET SEAL (TYP.)

RECESSED MODELS

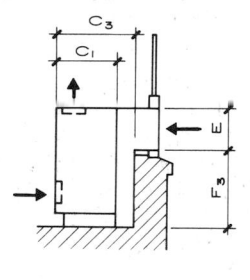

WINDOW INTAKE MODEL

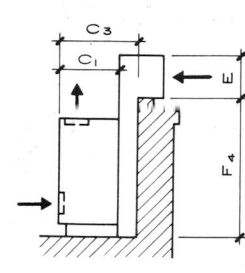

HIGH WALL INTAKE MODEL

VERTICAL MODELS OF CLASSROOM VENTILATORS - WITH VARIATIONS OF SIDE PROFILES FOR ENCLOSURES

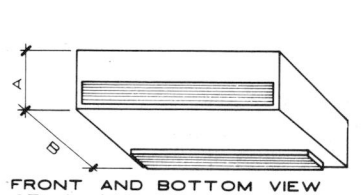

FRONT AND BOTTOM VIEW OF HORIZONTAL MODELS

HORIZONTAL MODEL

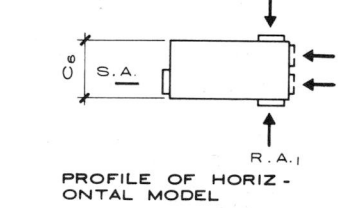

O.A.
S.A.
O.A.
R.A.$_2$
R.A.$_1$

PROFILE OF HORIZONTAL MODEL

O.A. = OUTDOOR AIR, WITH OR WITHOUT COLLAR
R.A.$_1$ = RETURN AIR, GRILLE
R.A.$_2$ = RETURN AIR, COLLAR
S.A. = SUPPLY AIR, COLLAR OR GRILLE

ENCLOSURES

MANUFACTURER	A*					B		C$_1$	C$_2$	C$_3$	C$_4$	C$_5$	C$_6$
	C.F.M. (STD. AIR)					C.F.M. (STD. AIR)		MODELS					
	500	750	1000	1250	1500	500	750-1500	STANDARD FLOOR	ADAPTER BACK	WINDOW INTAKE	RECESSED TYPE		HORIZONTAL
											RECESSED	EXPOSED	
a	50	61	72	83	94	30	30	15	18 & 20¼	20¼	2¾	12¼	15
b		69½	80½	91½	102½		28 OR 32	11⅝	14⅞	14⅞			12
c		68	80	92	104		28 OR 32	15	18½ & 20¼	20¼	4¹⁵⁄₁₆	10¼	15
d	60	72	84	96	108	28 OR 32	28 OR 32	13⅝	18⅛ & 19⅝	19⅝			15

* Add - 1" to manufacturer "d" for ceiling model.
NOTE: a, b, c and d under column headed Manufacturers indicate range of dimensions for several manufacturers.

WALL OPENINGS

MANUFACTURER	D					E	F$_1$ MAX.	F$_2$ MAX.	F$_3$	F$_4$
	C.F.M. (STD. AIR)									
	500	750	1000	1250	1500					
a	25	36	47	58	69	10⅜	O	18	19⅜	60 (MAX.)
b		39	50	61	72	10⅜	O	16 OR 20	19⅜	NOTE # 2
c		41	50	62	74	10⅜	5 (8-32)	16 OR 20	19⅜	NOTE # 2
d	33	45	57	69	81	10⅜	O	16 OR 20	19½	NOTE # 2

V. Peruchietti; Giffels & Rossetti, Inc.; Detroit, Michigan

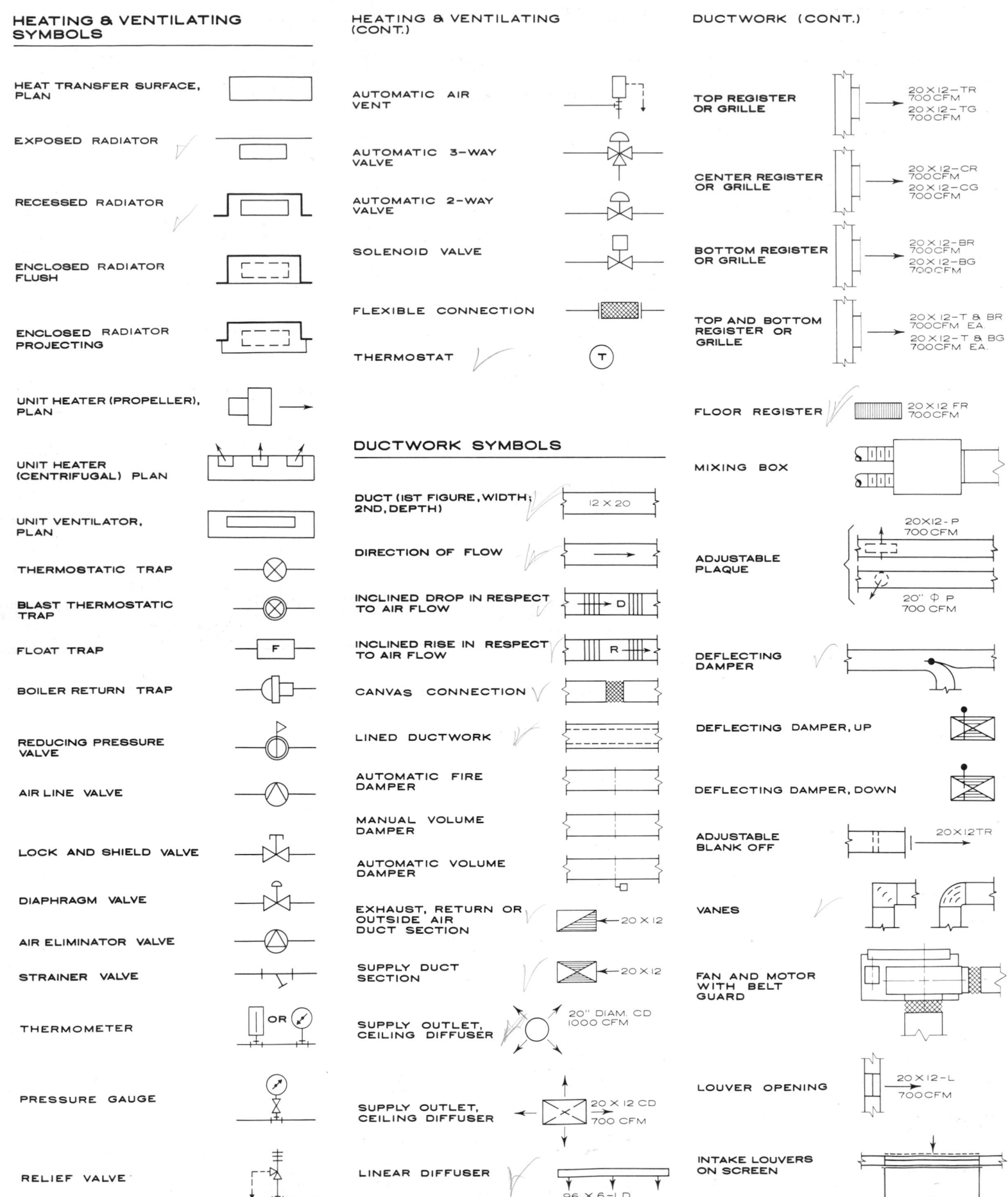

HEATING & VENTILATING SYMBOLS

HEAT TRANSFER SURFACE, PLAN

EXPOSED RADIATOR

RECESSED RADIATOR

ENCLOSED RADIATOR FLUSH

ENCLOSED RADIATOR PROJECTING

UNIT HEATER (PROPELLER), PLAN

UNIT HEATER (CENTRIFUGAL) PLAN

UNIT VENTILATOR, PLAN

THERMOSTATIC TRAP

BLAST THERMOSTATIC TRAP

FLOAT TRAP

BOILER RETURN TRAP

REDUCING PRESSURE VALVE

AIR LINE VALVE

LOCK AND SHIELD VALVE

DIAPHRAGM VALVE

AIR ELIMINATOR VALVE

STRAINER VALVE

THERMOMETER

PRESSURE GAUGE

RELIEF VALVE

HEATING & VENTILATING (CONT.)

AUTOMATIC AIR VENT

AUTOMATIC 3-WAY VALVE

AUTOMATIC 2-WAY VALVE

SOLENOID VALVE

FLEXIBLE CONNECTION

THERMOSTAT

DUCTWORK SYMBOLS

DUCT (1ST FIGURE, WIDTH; 2ND, DEPTH)   12 X 20

DIRECTION OF FLOW

INCLINED DROP IN RESPECT TO AIR FLOW   D

INCLINED RISE IN RESPECT TO AIR FLOW   R

CANVAS CONNECTION

LINED DUCTWORK

AUTOMATIC FIRE DAMPER

MANUAL VOLUME DAMPER

AUTOMATIC VOLUME DAMPER

EXHAUST, RETURN OR OUTSIDE AIR DUCT SECTION   20 X 12

SUPPLY DUCT SECTION   20 X 12

SUPPLY OUTLET, CEILING DIFFUSER   20" DIAM. CD 1000 CFM

SUPPLY OUTLET, CEILING DIFFUSER   20 X 12 CD 700 CFM

LINEAR DIFFUSER   96 X 6-LD 400 CFM

DUCTWORK (CONT.)

TOP REGISTER OR GRILLE   20 X 12-TR 700 CFM / 20 X 12-TG 700 CFM

CENTER REGISTER OR GRILLE   20 X 12-CR 700 CFM / 20 X 12-CG 700 CFM

BOTTOM REGISTER OR GRILLE   20 X 12-BR 700 CFM / 20 X 12-BG 700 CFM

TOP AND BOTTOM REGISTER OR GRILLE   20 X 12-T & BR 700 CFM EA. / 20 X 12-T & BG 700 CFM EA.

FLOOR REGISTER   20 X 12 FR 700 CFM

MIXING BOX

ADJUSTABLE PLAQUE   20X12-P 700 CFM / 20" Φ P 700 CFM

DEFLECTING DAMPER

DEFLECTING DAMPER, UP

DEFLECTING DAMPER, DOWN

ADJUSTABLE BLANK OFF   20X12TR

VANES

FAN AND MOTOR WITH BELT GUARD

LOUVER OPENING   20X12-L 700 CFM

INTAKE LOUVERS ON SCREEN

Amor Halperin, P. E.; Ayres, Cohen and Hayakawa; Consulting Engineers; Los Angeles/San Francisco, California

HEAT-POWER APPARATUS

STEAM GENERATOR (BOILER) .....

FLUE GAS REHEATER
(INTERMEDIATE SUPERHEATER)..

LIVE STEAM SUPERHEATER ......
OR REHEATER

FEED HEATER WITH
AIR OUTLET ....

CONDENSER, SURFACE·········

STEAM TURBINE ....

CONDENSING TURBINE ....

OPEN TANK ....

CLOSED TANK ....

AUTOMATIC REDUCING VALVE ....

AUTOMATIC BY-PASS VALVE ....

AUTOMATIC VALVE
OPERATED BY GOVERNOR ......

BOILER FEED PUMP.............

SERVICE PUMP ....

CONDENSATE PUMP ....

CIRCULATING WATER PUMP ......

AIR PUMP ....

OIL PUMP ....

RECIPROCATING PUMP ....

AIR EJECTOR
(DYNAMIC PUMP)

VACUUM TRAP ....

REFRIGERATION

THERMOSTAT, SELF-CONTAINED

THERMOSTAT, REMOTE BULB ...

PRESSURE SWITCH ....

EXPANSION VALVE, HAND.......

EXPANSION VALVE, AUTOMATIC .

EXPANSION VALVE,
THERMOSTATIC ....

EVAPORATOR PRESSURE
REGULATING VALVE,
THROTTLING TYPE
(EVAPORATOR SIDE)

EVAPORATOR PRESSURE
REGULATING VALVE,
THERMOSTATIC, THROTTLING
TYPE

EVAPORATOR PRESSURE
REGULATING VALVE
SNAP-ACTION

COMPRESSOR SUCTION VALVE,
PRESSURE LIMITING,
THROTTLING TYPE
(COMPRESSOR SIDE)

CONSTANT PRESSURE VALVE,
SUCTION

THERMAL BULB ....

SCALE TRAP ....

DRYER ....

FILTER AND STRAINER ....

COMBINATION STRAINER
AND DRYER

SIGHT GLASS

FLOAT VALVE
HIGH SIDE

FLOAT VALVE
LOW SIDE

GAUGE ....

COOLING TOWER ....

EVAPORATOR,
FINNED TYPE, NATURAL
CONVECTION

EVAPORATOR,
FORCED CONVECTION ....

IMMERSION COOLING UNIT ....

CONDENSER,
AIR-COOLED,
FINNED, FORCED AIR

CONDENSER,
WATER-COOLED,
SHELL AND TUBE

CONDENSER
EVAPORATIVE

HEAT EXCHANGER

CONDENSING UNIT
AIR COOLED

CONDENSING UNIT
WATER COOLED

PRESSURE SWITCH WITH
HIGH PRESSURE CUT-OUT

COMPRESSOR

COMPRESSOR
OPEN CRANKCASE
RECIPROCATING, DIRECT
DRIVE

COMPRESSOR
OPEN CRANKCASE
RECIPROCATING BELTED

COMPRESSOR
ENCLOSED CRANKCASE,
ROTARY, BELTED

Amor Halperin, P. E.; Ayres, Cohen and Hayakawa; Consulting Engineers; Los Angeles/San Francisco, California

EMERGENCY POWER

Basic solutions

1. Battery operated emergency & exit lighting trickle charged.
2. Emergency power & lighting fed from a source ahead of the main secondary circuit breaker or disconnect device.
3. Gasoline, diesel powered or natural gas engine generator sets.

The first two items are usually required for applications in low rise office buildings and retail stores where a minimum of power is required for lighting for egress in the event of power failure and for fire alarm.

The installation of an engine driven generator set is usually recommended for hospitals, experimental laboratories and high rise office buildings and retail stores.

Sets are available in sizes from 3 KILOWATT to 3000 KILOWATTS with the smaller units generally being gasoline fueled and the larger units diesel driven, all larger sizes requiring fuel storage tanks which should be located outside of building.

Essential services only should be fed from the standby power source. In offices and stores these should include power to operate one elevator of a bank, and all down escalators besides emergency and exit lighting. Elevator control should be arranged to operate any one in the group.

In hospitals these services should include mandatory requirements covered by NFPA Bulletin 76 current edition and any critical items requested by the hospital authorities.

An emergency automatic throw-over switch of thoroughly reliable design should be provided, fed from a normal supply source. Both the switch and the generator should be sized for the connected load of the emergency requirements.

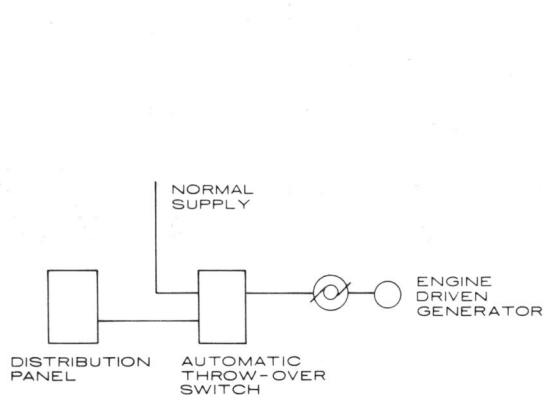

STANDARD EMERGENCY CONNECTIONS

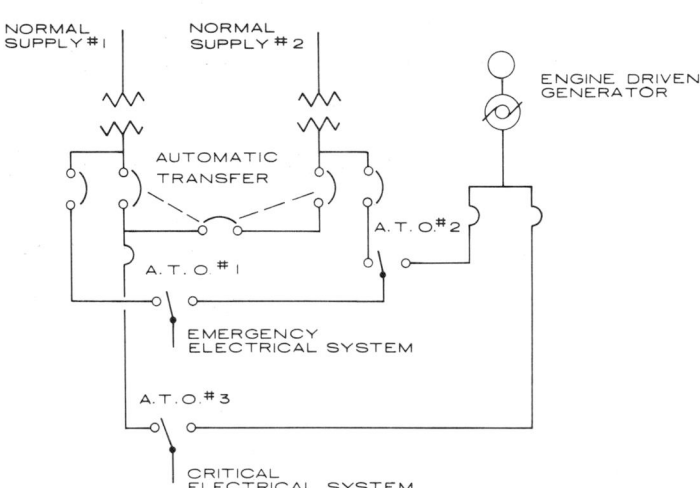

RECOMMENDED HOSPITAL EMERGENCY CONNECTIONS

SITE UTILITIES

In modern practice of supplying electric power to major building sites it is usual for the electric utility company to provide primary service to the project, underground to the primary substation incoming line disconnects or protective devices. These are usually located in the basement and are ideally situated on the outside wall of the building from which the service is to come. This is also true of major telephone service.

The underground duct banks illustrated below are normally supplied as two, three or four ducts wide with as many below as required. Fibre and Poly-vinyl Chloride thin wall duct may be used for concrete encased requirements except under buildings, roadways and rail roads where galvanized iron conduit is preferable.

For low voltage up to 600 volt parking lot and site lighting thick wall direct burial Poly-Vinyl conduit is acceptable.

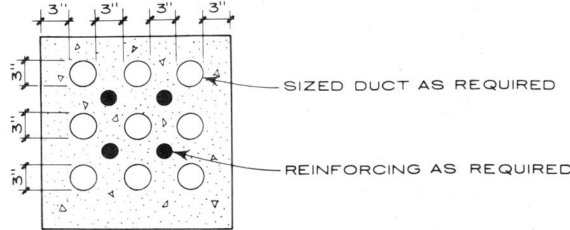

UNDERGROUND DUCT BANK

Smith, Hinchman & Grylls, Associates, Inc.; Detroit, Michigan

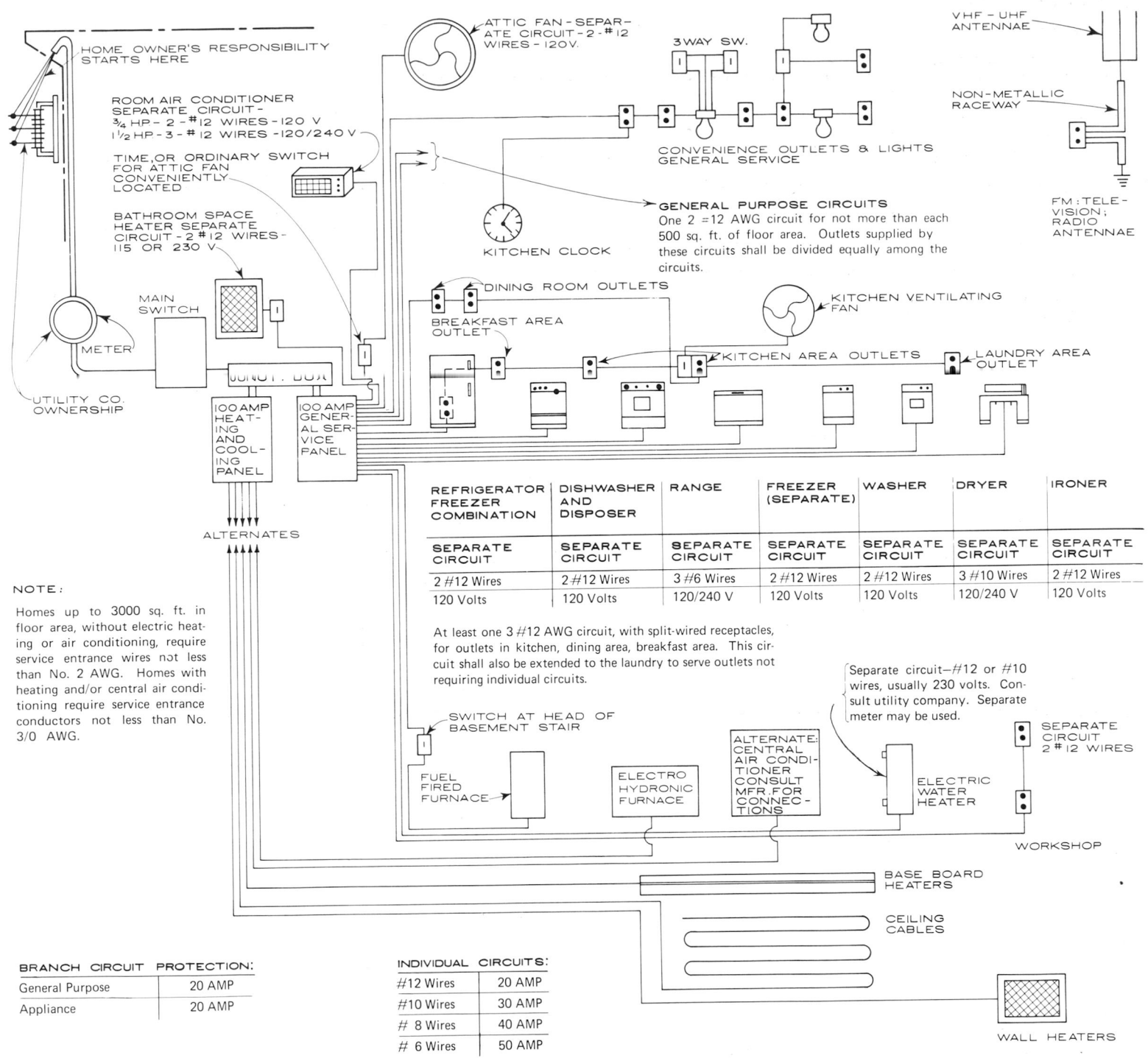

HOME OWNER'S RESPONSIBILITY STARTS HERE

ATTIC FAN-SEPAR-ATE CIRCUIT-2-#12 WIRES-120 V.

3 WAY SW.

VHF - UHF ANTENNAE

ROOM AIR CONDITIONER SEPARATE CIRCUIT - 3/4 HP - 2 - #12 WIRES - 120 V 1 1/2 HP - 3 - #12 WIRES - 120/240 V

NON-METALLIC RACEWAY

CONVENIENCE OUTLETS & LIGHTS GENERAL SERVICE

TIME, OR ORDINARY SWITCH FOR ATTIC FAN CONVENIENTLY LOCATED

GENERAL PURPOSE CIRCUITS
One 2 =12 AWG circuit for not more than each 500 sq. ft. of floor area. Outlets supplied by these circuits shall be divided equally among the circuits.

FM : TELE-VISION; RADIO ANTENNAE

BATHROOM SPACE HEATER SEPARATE CIRCUIT - 2 #12 WIRES - 115 OR 230 V.

KITCHEN CLOCK

DINING ROOM OUTLETS

KITCHEN VENTILATING FAN

MAIN SWITCH

BREAKFAST AREA OUTLET

KITCHEN AREA OUTLETS

LAUNDRY AREA OUTLET

METER

JUNCT. BOX

UTILITY CO. OWNERSHIP

100 AMP HEAT-ING AND COOL-ING PANEL

100 AMP GENER-AL SER-VICE PANEL

ALTERNATES

NOTE:

Homes up to 3000 sq. ft. in floor area, without electric heating or air conditioning, require service entrance wires not less than No. 2 AWG. Homes with heating and/or central air conditioning require service entrance conductors not less than No. 3/0 AWG.

REFRIGERATOR FREEZER COMBINATION	DISHWASHER AND DISPOSER	RANGE	FREEZER (SEPARATE)	WASHER	DRYER	IRONER
SEPARATE CIRCUIT	SEPARATE CIRCUIT	SEPARATE CIRCUIT	SEPARATE CIRCUIT	SEPARATE CIRCUIT	SEPARATE CIRCUIT	SEPARATE CIRCUIT
2 #12 Wires	2 #12 Wires	3 #6 Wires	2 #12 Wires	2 #12 Wires	3 #10 Wires	2 #12 Wires
120 Volts	120 Volts	120/240 V	120 Volts	120 Volts	120/240 V	120 Volts

At least one 3 #12 AWG circuit, with split-wired receptacles, for outlets in kitchen, dining area, breakfast area. This circuit shall also be extended to the laundry to serve outlets not requiring individual circuits.

Separate circuit—#12 or #10 wires, usually 230 volts. Consult utility company. Separate meter may be used.

SWITCH AT HEAD OF BASEMENT STAIR

SEPARATE CIRCUIT 2 #12 WIRES

FUEL FIRED FURNACE

ELECTRO HYDRONIC FURNACE

ALTERNATE: CENTRAL AIR CONDI-TIONER CONSULT MFR. FOR CONNEC-TIONS

ELECTRIC WATER HEATER

WORKSHOP

BASE BOARD HEATERS

CEILING CABLES

BRANCH CIRCUIT PROTECTION:

General Purpose	20 AMP
Appliance	20 AMP

INDIVIDUAL CIRCUITS:

#12 Wires	20 AMP
#10 Wires	30 AMP
# 8 Wires	40 AMP
# 6 Wires	50 AMP

WALL HEATERS

WATTAGE * OF ELECTRICAL OUTLETS FOR RESIDENTIAL WORK: (* AVERAGE)

TYPE	WATTS	TYPE	WATTS	TYPE	WATTS
Air Conditioner	850–1200, 3100	Home Freezer	300–670	Refrigerator	200–670
Attic Fan	500–1500	Hot Plate	600–1000	Roaster	1150–1650
Chafing Dish	660	Infra-Red Lamp	500	Sewing Machine	75
Clothes Dryer	Up to 4500	Iron, Hand	660–1000	Shaver	11
Dishwasher	530–1000	Ironer, Home	1275–1620	Sunlamp	250
Disposer	380–530	Juice Extractor	60–100	Television	200–400
Egg Cooker	660	Mixer	125–150	Toaster	600–1350
Electric Fan	50–300	Motor, 1/4 H.P.	530	Vacuum Cleaner	300
Furnace Blower	380–670	Oil Burner	300–550	Waffle Iron	660–1000
Grill	1000	Percolator	400–600	Washing Machines:	
Hair Dryer	250	Power Tools	Up to 1000	Automatic	350–900
Heater	1000-1650	Radio	50–200	Wringer Type	375–400
Heating Pad	65	Range	7000–14000	Water Heater	750–3000

V. Peruchietti; Giffels & Rossetti, Inc.; Detroit, Michigan

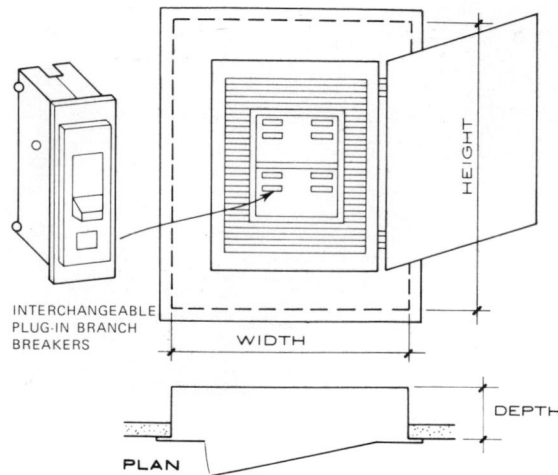

INTERCHANGEABLE
PLUG-IN BRANCH
BREAKERS

PLAN

CIRCUIT BREAKER LIGHTING PANELS - TYPICAL
FOR BETTER RESIDENTIAL & LOWER COST COMMERCIAL WORK

MANUFACTURER	MAX. NO. OF CIRCUITS	BOX SIZES IN INCHES		
		WIDTH	HEIGHT	DEPTH
BULL DOG	12	10 3/4	20	3 3/4
	18	10 3/4	24	3 3/4
SQUARE D	12	9	16	3 3/4
	20	9	20 1/2	3 3/4
	32	12	32	3 3/4
GEN. ELEC. CO.	12	14	18	4
	20		22	
	30		33	
	42		39	
WESTINGHOUSE	12	15	20	4 5/8
	20		24	
	30		30	
	40		34	

Other manufacturers' panels available in similar sizes. Sizes shown are typical of those available.

Automatic circuit breaker — an adjustable time-setting device designed to open a circuit upon any desired degree of overload current.

CIRCUIT BREAKER LIGHTING PANEL

For best quality work.

WIDTH = 20", DEPTH = 5 3/4"
HEIGHT — SEE TABLE BELOW

MAX. NO. OF CIRCUITS	BOX HEIGHT
8	19
16	22
20	24 1/4
24	27 1/2
32	30
36	33
42	35 1/2

Individual circuit breakers may have trip sizes: 15, 20, 30, 40, and 50 amps.

FUSIBLE SWITCH LIGHTING PANEL

Cartridge type fuse used.

WIDTH = 20", DEPTH = 5 3/4"
HEIGHT — SEE TABLE BELOW

MAX. NO. OF CIRCUITS	BOX HEIGHT
8	22
12	24 1/2
16	27
20	32
24	33
28	32 1/2
32	36
36	41
40	44

Smith, Hinchman & Grylls Associates, Inc.; Detroit, Michigan

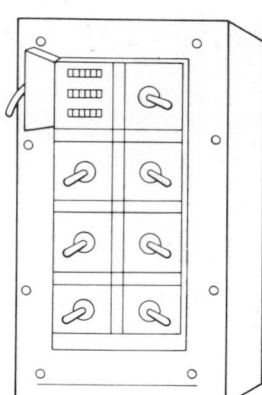

FUSIBLE SWITCH POWER PANELS
CARTRIDGE FUSE USED

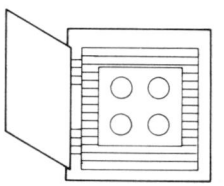

Box dimensions below. For outside dimension add 1 1/4" to height & width.

PLUG FUSE CABINET

PLUG FUSE

BOX DIMENSIONS

BRANCHES	HEIGHT	WIDTH	DEPTH
2	6 5/8	6 5/8	2 3/4
4	6 5/8	6 5/8	2 3/4
6	11 1/8	7 3/8	3 1/8
8	14 1/8	7 3/8	3 1/8

Up to 12 branches same as 8 branches

PLUG FUSE AND PLUG FUSE CABINET
FOR APARTMENTS AND SMALL HOUSES

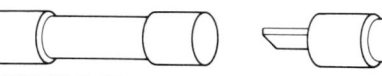

FERRULE TYPE   KNIFE BLADE TYPE
CARTRIDGE FUSES

Ferrule contact 1 to 60 amps.
Knife blade contact 70 to 600 amps.
Ferrule type non-renewable. Knife blade type non-renewable and renewable link.

STANDARD FUSE SIZES

Plug Fuse: 1, 3, 5, 6, 8, 10, 15, 20, 25 and 30 amperes.
Cartridge: 1, 3, 6, 10, 15, 20, 25, 30, 35, 40, 50, 60, 70, 80, 90, 100, 110, 125, 150, 175, 200, 225, 250, 275, 300, 325, 350, 400, 450, 500, & 600 amperes.

Standard knife switches are rated at 30, 60, 100, 200, 400 & 600 amps, and take cartridge fuses up to and including their rating.

Circuit breakers at 50 (trip at 15, 20, 30, 40, 50); 100 (trip at 15, 20, 30, 40, 50, 70, 100); 225 (70 – 225, increment 25); 600 (125 – 350, increment 25 & 400, 500, 600 amp.)

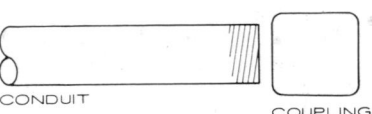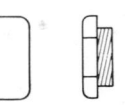

1/2, 3/4, 1, 1 1/4, 1 1/2, 2, 2 1/2, 3, 3 1/2, 4, 4 1/2, 5, 6

CONDUIT   COUPLING   BUSHING   LOCKNUT

RIGID CONDUIT
For fireproof construction.
See page on "conduits" for graphic size & weights.

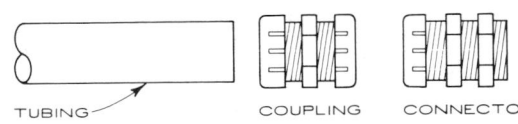

1/2, 3/4, 1, 1 1/4, 1 1/2, 2

TUBING   COUPLING   CONNECTOR

ELECTRICAL METALLIC TUBING
For fireproof construction. Same use as Rigid Conduit above. Walls are thinner, therefore economical.

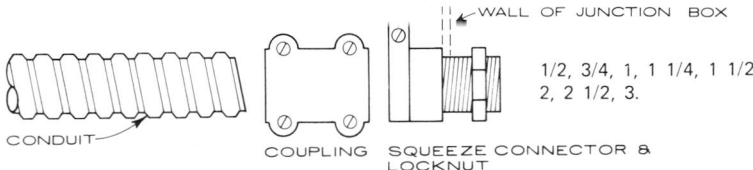

← WALL OF JUNCTION BOX

1/2, 3/4, 1, 1 1/4, 1 1/2, 2, 2 1/2, 3.

CONDUIT   COUPLING   SQUEEZE CONNECTOR & LOCKNUT

FLEXIBLE CONDUIT
For fireproof construction.

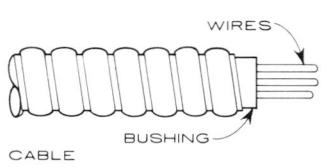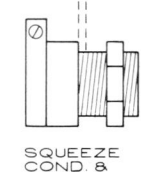

WIRES

BUSHING

CABLE   SQUEEZE COND. & LOCKNUT

2 & 3 Conductor:
#14, 12, 10, 8, 6, 4, 2.
4 Conductor:
#14, 12, 10, 8, 6, 4.
Lead Covered—
2 cond. in #14, 12, 10, 8, & 6; 3 cond. in #14, 12, 10, 8, 6, & 4.

ARMORED CABLE (BX)
For frame construction. Lead covered for wet locations.

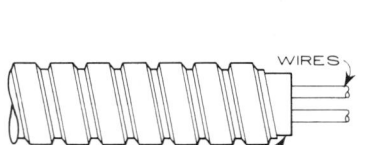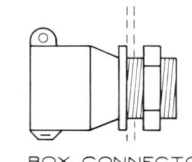

WIRES

BUSHING

CABLE   BOX CONNECTOR

2 Conductor: #14, 12, 10

3 Conductor: #14, 12

FLAT ARMORED CABLE (OVALFLEX)
For plaster extensions

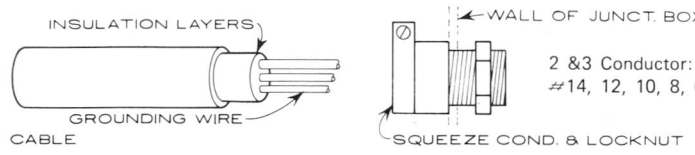

INSULATION LAYERS   ← WALL OF JUNCT. BOX

2 &3 Conductor:
#14, 12, 10, 8, 6 & 4

GROUNDING WIRE

CABLE   SQUEEZE COND. & LOCKNUT

NON-METALLIC SHEATHED CABLE
For frame construction, where permitted, is cheapest.

CABLES, CONDUITS AND TUBING
STANDARD NOMINAL SIZES IN INCHES

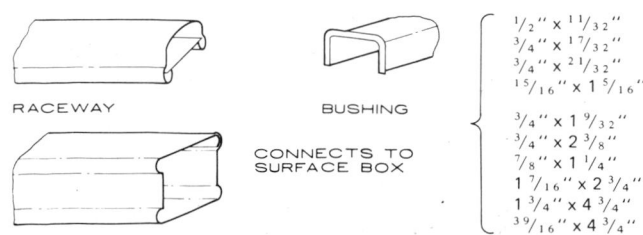

RACEWAY   BUSHING

CONNECTS TO SURFACE BOX

1/2" x 11/32"
3/4" x 17/32"
3/4" x 21/32"
15/16" x 15/16"

3/4" x 1 9/32"
3/4" x 2 3/8"
7/8" x 1 1/4"
1 7/16" x 2 3/4"
1 3/4" x 4 3/4"
3 9/16" x 4 3/4"

SURFACE METAL RACEWAYS

Smith, Hinchman & Grylls Associates, Inc.; Detroit, Michigan

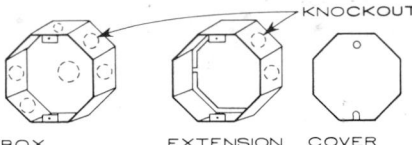

← KNOCKOUTS

WIDTH & DEPTH
3 1/4 x 1 1/2
3 1/2 x 1 1/2
4 x 1 1/2
4 x 2 1/8

BOX   EXTENSION   COVER

OCTAGONAL
Used in ceilings and walls.

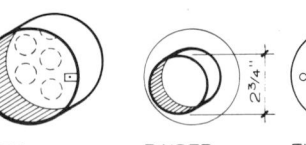

WIDTH & DEPTH
3 1/4 x 3/4, 1 1/2
3 1/2 x 1/2, 1 1/2
4 x 1/2
*4 x 5/8

* Raised Cover

BOX   RAISED COVER   FLAT COVER

ROUND
Used in ceilings.

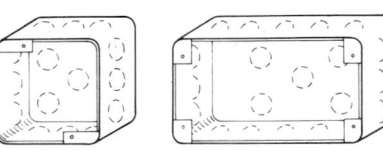

WIDTH & DEPTH
Square box:
4 x 1 1/2, 2 1/8
4 11/16 x 1 1/2, 2 1/8
2 Gang Box
4 1/2 x 1 3/4 x 6 13/16 long

SQUARE   RECTANGULAR

RECTANGULAR
Used in ceilings and walls

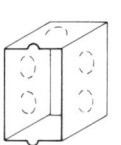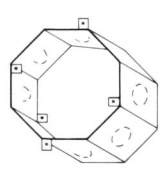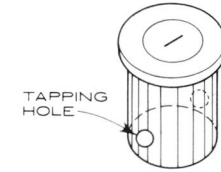

TAPPING HOLE

GEM
for switch or receptacle in narrow location
2" wide x 3" long x 2" or 2 1/2" deep

4" OCTAGONAL
for concrete 1 1/2, 2, 2 1/2, 3, 3 1/2, 4, 5, 6 deep

FLUSH FLOOR BOX
for masonry sizes vary

IN MASONARY

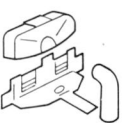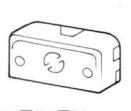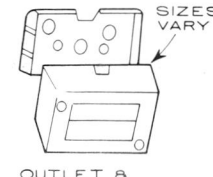

SIZES VARY

ADJUSTABLE JUNCTION BOX   UTILITY BOX   OUTLET & DEVICE BOX

EXPOSED
See manufacturers catalogs for other fittings.

OUTLET AND JUNCTION BOXES
SIZES IN INCHES

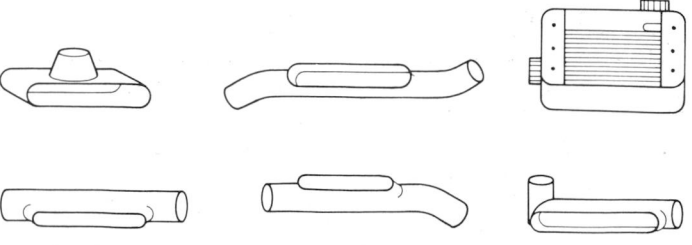

CONDULETS (FOR EXPOSED WORK)
Condulets made in a great many shapes & sizes; consult manufacturers.

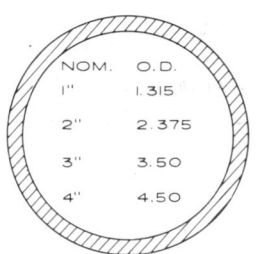

STANDARD ELEC. CONDUITS

NOM.	O.D.
1"	1.315
2"	2.375
3"	3.50
4"	4.50

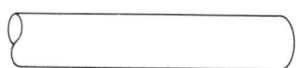

ELECTRIC METALLIC TUBING (EMT)

SIZES IN INCHES	DIAMETER INTERNAL	DIAMETER EXTERNAL	WALL THICKNESS
3/8	0.493	0.577	0.042
1/2	0.622	0.706	0.042
3/4	0.824	0.922	0.049
1	1.049	1.163	0.057
1 1/4	1.380	1.510	0.065
1 1/2	1.610	1.740	0.065
2	2.067	2.197	0.065

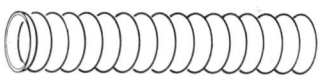

FLEXIBLE CONDUITS

SIZES IN INCHES	APPROXIMATE DIAMETER INSIDE	APPROXIMATE DIAMETER OUTSIDE	THICKNESS OF STEEL STRIP
3/8	0.383	0.610	0.034
1/2	0.638	0.910	0.040
3/4	0.829	1.090	0.040
1	1.020	1.370	0.055
1 1/4	1.275	1.600	0.055
1 1/2	1.530	1.940	0.060
2	2.040	2.420	0.060
2 1/2	2.550	3.000	0.060
3	3.060	3.350	0.060

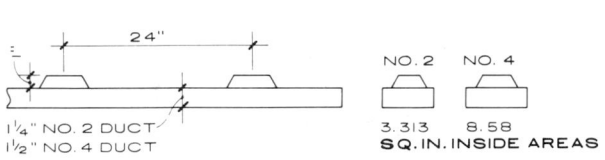

1¼" NO. 2 DUCT
1½" NO. 4 DUCT

NO. 2　NO. 4
3.313　8.58
SQ. IN. INSIDE AREAS

STANDARD UNDERFLOOR DUCT

FLUSH INSERTS

NO. 2　NO. 4
OTHER COMBINATIONS AVAILABLE

FLUSH DUCT

12" TO 36"

6" DIA. ACCESS.
8.58 SQ. IN. INSIDE AREA

HEADER DUCT

REMOVABLE COVER

VARIES
TEL.
POWER　DIVIDER

TRENCH DUCT

NOTE: Same underfloor ducts may be used for telephone service: 1. Headers 50' o.c., 2. Dist. 5' to 6' o.c.

Smith, Hinchman & Grylls Associates, Inc.; Detroit, Michigan

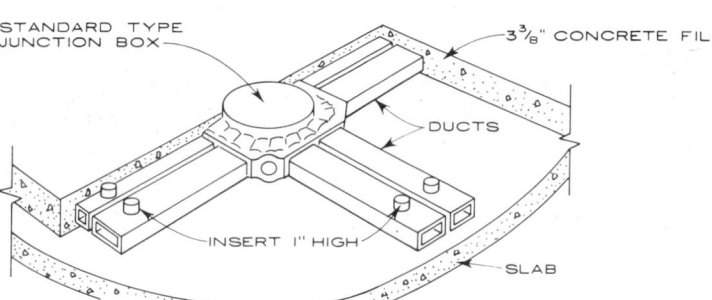

STANDARD TYPE
JUNCTION BOX
3 3/8" CONCRETE FILL
DUCTS
INSERT 1" HIGH
SLAB

STANDARD TYPE DUCT

Placed on top of structural slab. Duct supports are required if the duct is not placed on top of slab.

Junction boxes are available in the following sizes: 3", 2 1/2", flush box and standard heights.

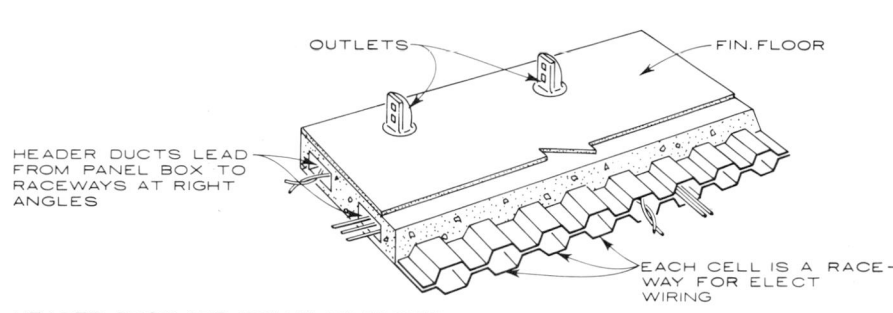

OUTLETS
FIN. FLOOR
HEADER DUCTS LEAD FROM PANEL BOX TO RACEWAYS AT RIGHT ANGLES
EACH CELL IS A RACEWAY FOR ELECT WIRING

HEADER DUCT AND CELLULAR FLOOR

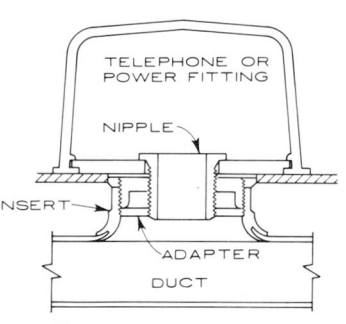

TELEPHONE OR POWER FITTING
NIPPLE
INSERT
ADAPTER
DUCT

TYPICAL UFD FITTING
SEE CATALOGS FOR OTHERS

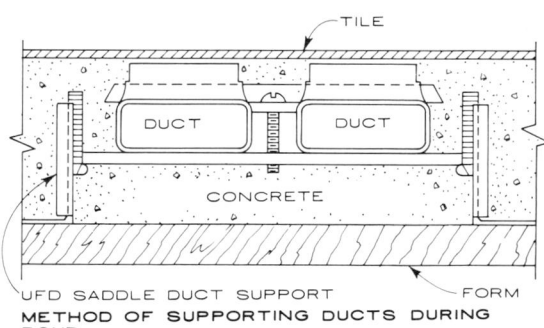

TILE
DUCT　DUCT
CONCRETE
FORM

UFD SADDLE DUCT SUPPORT

METHOD OF SUPPORTING DUCTS DURING POUR

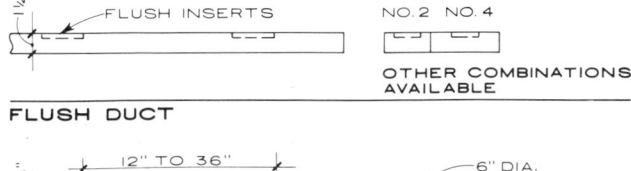

TEL. CAB
TWO COMPT. JUNC. BOX (TYP.)
PANEL BOARD
1¼" C. TO TEL. CAB.
TEL. CAB.
TEL. CAB.
PNL
BLDG. COL. (TYP.)
1¼" C. TO PNL.
1¼" C. TO TEL. CAB.
POWER DUCT
1¼" C. TO TEL. CAB.　PNL.
TELEPHONE DUCT

TYPICAL STANDARD AND FLUSH DUCT LAYOUT

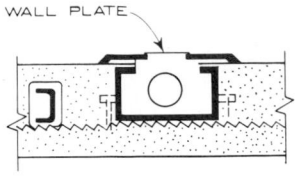
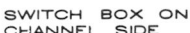
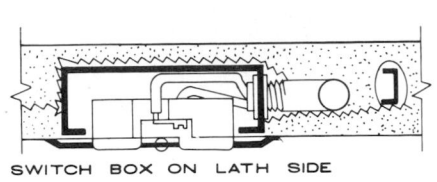
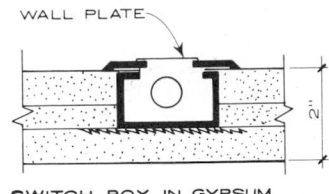

WALL PLATE

SWITCH BOX ON
CHANNEL SIDE

SWITCH BOX ON LATH SIDE

WALL PLATE

SWITCH BOX IN GYPSUM
BOARD & PLASTER WALL

PLANS OF SWITCH BOXES (SWITCH BOXES MAY BE SET HORIZONTALLY OR VERTICALLY)

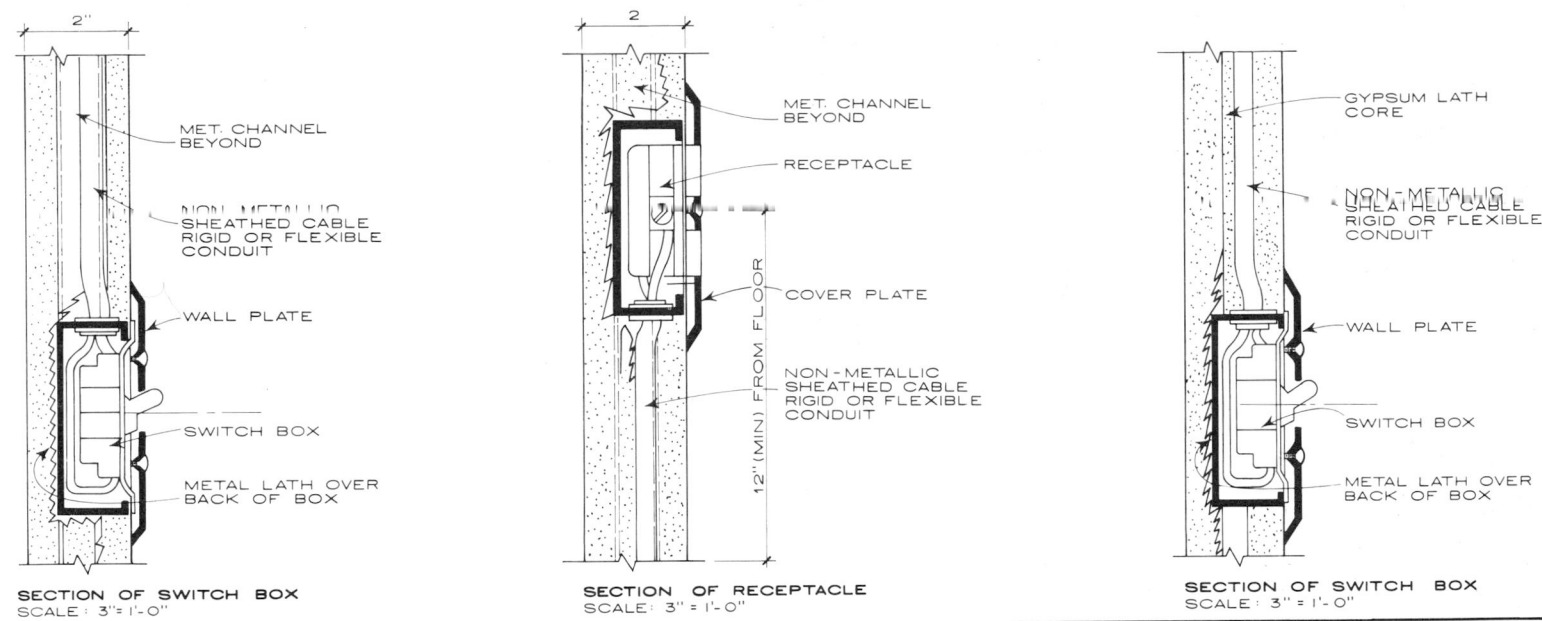

2"

MET. CHANNEL
BEYOND

NON-METALLIC
SHEATHED CABLE
RIGID OR FLEXIBLE
CONDUIT

WALL PLATE

SWITCH BOX

METAL LATH OVER
BACK OF BOX

SECTION OF SWITCH BOX
SCALE: 3"=1'-0"

2"

MET. CHANNEL
BEYOND

RECEPTACLE

COVER PLATE

NON-METALLIC
SHEATHED CABLE
RIGID OR FLEXIBLE
CONDUIT

12" (MIN) FROM FLOOR

SECTION OF RECEPTACLE
SCALE: 3" = 1'-0"

GYPSUM LATH
CORE

NON-METALLIC
SHEATHED CABLE
RIGID OR FLEXIBLE
CONDUIT

WALL PLATE

SWITCH BOX

METAL LATH OVER
BACK OF BOX

SECTION OF SWITCH BOX
SCALE: 3" = 1'-0"

ELECTRICAL WORK IN 2" SOLID LATH & PLASTER PARTITION

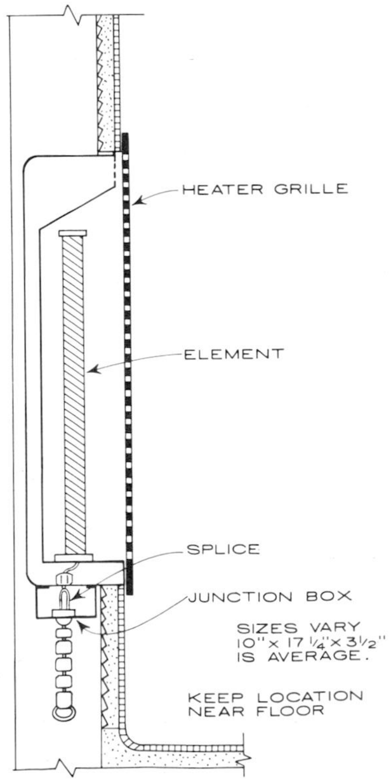

HEATER GRILLE

ELEMENT

SPLICE

JUNCTION BOX

SIZES VARY
10" x 17¼" x 3½"
IS AVERAGE.

KEEP LOCATION
NEAR FLOOR

SECTION OF AUXILIARY HEATER
SCALE: 1½" = 1'-0"

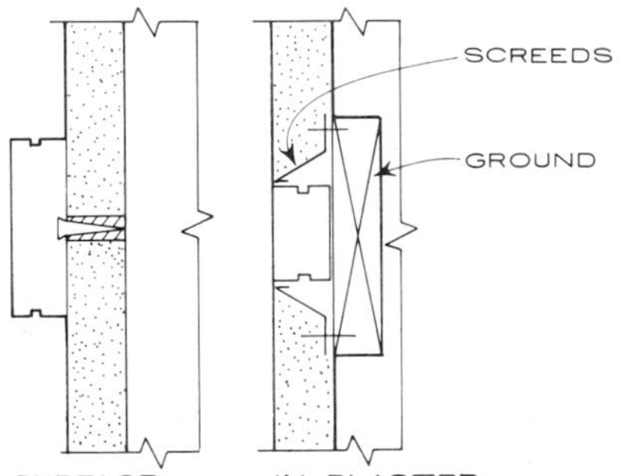

SCREEDS

GROUND

SURFACE
MOUNTED

IN PLASTER

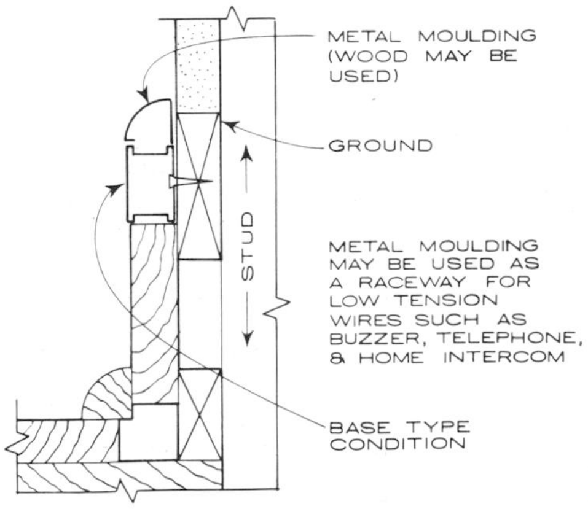

METAL MOULDING
(WOOD MAY BE
USED)

GROUND

STUD

METAL MOULDING
MAY BE USED AS
A RACEWAY FOR
LOW TENSION
WIRES SUCH AS
BUZZER, TELEPHONE,
& HOME INTERCOM

BASE TYPE
CONDITION

SECTION OF "PLUG-IN" STRIP
SCALE: 3" = 1'-0"

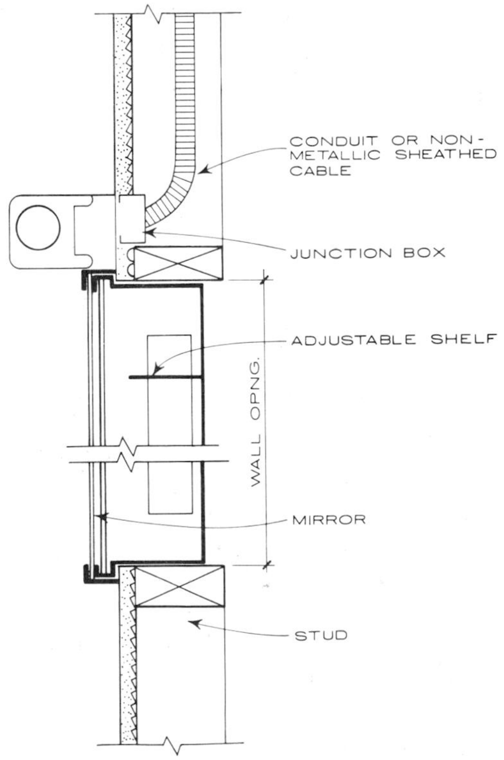

CONDUIT OR NON-
METALLIC SHEATHED
CABLE

JUNCTION BOX

ADJUSTABLE SHELF

WALL OPNG.

MIRROR

STUD

SECTION OF MEDICINE CABINET
SCALE: 1½" = 1'-0"

ELECTRICAL WORK IN BUILT-IN EQUIPMENT

B. J. Baldwin; Giffels & Rossetti, Inc.; Detroit, Michigan

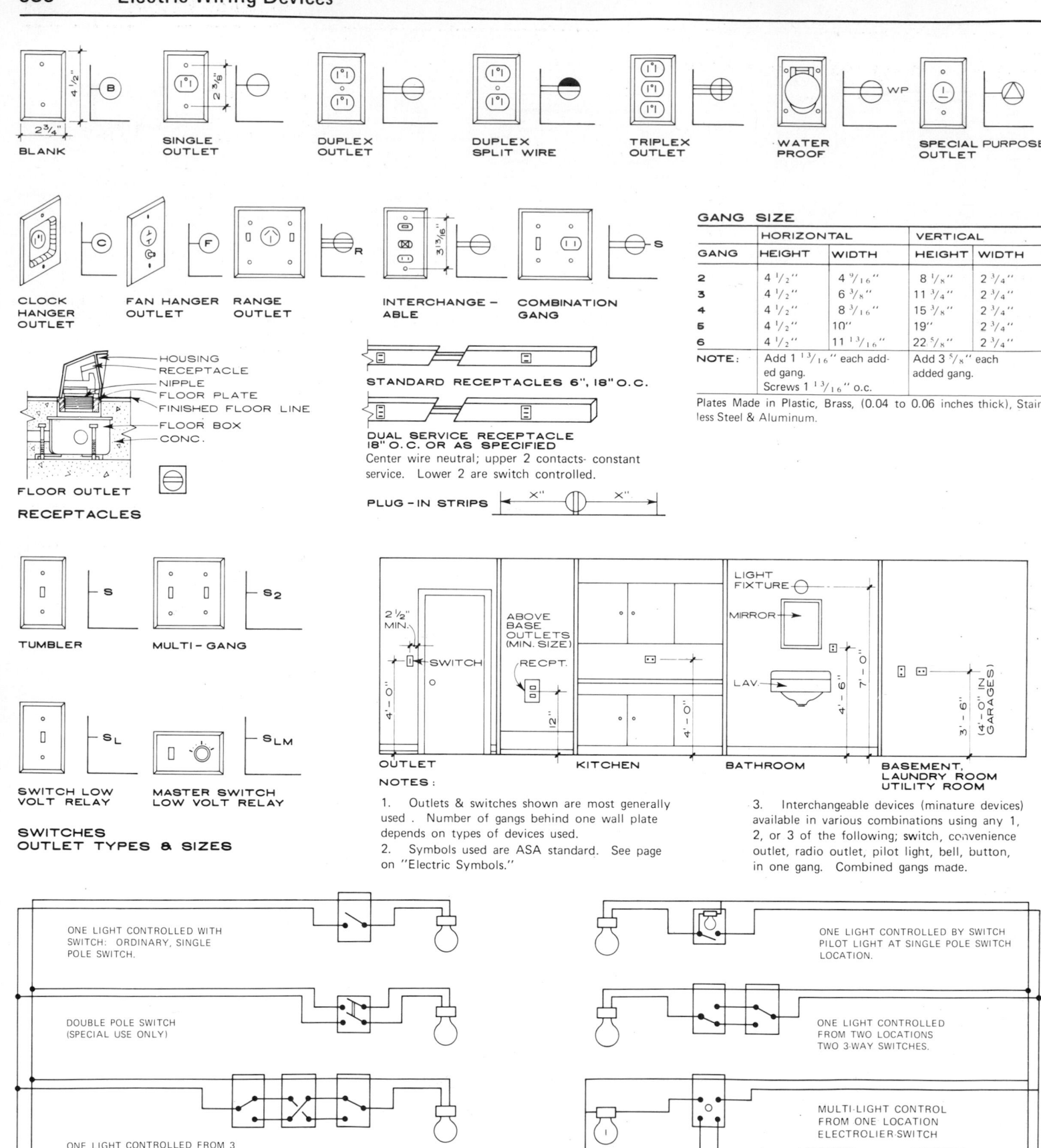

BLANK

SINGLE OUTLET

DUPLEX OUTLET

DUPLEX SPLIT WIRE

TRIPLEX OUTLET

WATER PROOF

SPECIAL PURPOSE OUTLET

CLOCK HANGER OUTLET

FAN HANGER OUTLET

RANGE OUTLET

INTERCHANGE-ABLE

COMBINATION GANG

GANG SIZE

GANG	HORIZONTAL		VERTICAL	
	HEIGHT	WIDTH	HEIGHT	WIDTH
2	4 1/2"	4 9/16"	8 1/8"	2 3/4"
3	4 1/2"	6 3/8"	11 3/4"	2 3/4"
4	4 1/2"	8 3/16"	15 3/8"	2 3/4"
5	4 1/2"	10"	19"	2 3/4"
6	4 1/2"	11 13/16"	22 5/8"	2 3/4"
NOTE:	Add 1 13/16" each added gang. Screws 1 13/16" o.c.		Add 3 5/8" each added gang.	

Plates Made in Plastic, Brass, (0.04 to 0.06 inches thick), Stainless Steel & Aluminum.

HOUSING
RECEPTACLE
NIPPLE
FLOOR PLATE
FINISHED FLOOR LINE
FLOOR BOX
CONC.

FLOOR OUTLET

RECEPTACLES

STANDARD RECEPTACLES 6", 18" O.C.

DUAL SERVICE RECEPTACLE 18" O.C. OR AS SPECIFIED
Center wire neutral; upper 2 contacts- constant service. Lower 2 are switch controlled.

PLUG-IN STRIPS

TUMBLER

MULTI-GANG

SWITCH LOW VOLT RELAY

MASTER SWITCH LOW VOLT RELAY

SWITCHES
OUTLET TYPES & SIZES

OUTLET

KITCHEN

BATHROOM

LIGHT FIXTURE
MIRROR
LAV.

BASEMENT, LAUNDRY ROOM UTILITY ROOM

NOTES:

1. Outlets & switches shown are most generally used. Number of gangs behind one wall plate depends on types of devices used.
2. Symbols used are ASA standard. See page on "Electric Symbols."

3. Interchangeable devices (minature devices) available in various combinations using any 1, 2, or 3 of the following; switch, convenience outlet, radio outlet, pilot light, bell, button, in one gang. Combined gangs made.

ONE LIGHT CONTROLLED WITH SWITCH: ORDINARY, SINGLE POLE SWITCH.

DOUBLE POLE SWITCH (SPECIAL USE ONLY)

ONE LIGHT CONTROLLED FROM 3 LOCATIONS; TWO 3-WAY SWITCHES & ONE 4-WAY SWITCH

ONE LIGHT CONTROLLED BY SWITCH PILOT LIGHT AT SINGLE POLE SWITCH LOCATION.

ONE LIGHT CONTROLLED FROM TWO LOCATIONS TWO 3-WAY SWITCHES.

MULTI-LIGHT CONTROL FROM ONE LOCATION ELECTROLIER SWITCH

1st	POSITION	=	CIRCUIT 1
2	" "	=	" " OFF
3	" "	=	" " 1 & 2
4	" "	=	" " OFF
5	" "	=	" " 1, 2 & 3
6	" "	=	" " OFF

NEUTRAL
PHASE

NEUTRAL
PHASE

SWITCH WIRING DIAGRAM

B. J. Baldwin; Giffels & Rossetti, Inc.; Detroit, Michigan

FOOTCANDLE LEVELS BASED ON I.E.S. RECOMMENDATIONS

5 FC	10 FC	20 FC	30 FC	50 FC	70 FC	100 FC	150 FC	200 FC	500 FC
Parking	Storage	Lobbies	Lavatories	Classrooms	Proof-Reading	Drafting	Fine Drafting	Fine Drafting	Color Identifications
TV viewing	Rough Stock	Auditorium	Corridors	Stores	General Assembly	General Assembly	Fine Assembly	Extra Fine Assembly	Minor Surgery
Construction	Receiving	Corridor	Conference Rooms	Reading Rooms	Testing	Testing	Testing	Testing	Special Inspection
		Stairway	Casual Desk Work	Testing	Inspection	Inspection	Inspection	Severe Office Tasks	Testing
		Dining	Cafeterias	Inspection		Counter Displays	Display Lighting		Very Severe and Prolonged Visual Tasks
				Rough Assembly			Severe and Prolonged Seeing Tasks		
							Medium Severe Office Tasks		

C.U. = Coefficient of Utilization   M.F. = Maintenance Factor

$$\text{NUMBER OF FIXTURES REQUIRED} = \frac{\text{F.C. (Desired) x Room Area}}{\text{C.U. x M.F. x Lamps/Fixture x Lumens/Lamp}} = \frac{\text{Total Lumens}}{\text{Lumens per Fixture}}$$

$$\text{AVERAGE FOOTCANDLES} = \frac{\text{Lamp Lumens x C.U. x M.F.}}{\text{Area Room (Sq. Ft.)}} = \frac{\text{Lumens per Lamp x C.U. x M.F.}}{\text{Area per Lamp (Sq. Ft.)}} = \frac{\text{Lamp Lumens per Fixture x C.U. x M.F.}}{\text{Area per Fixture (Sq. Ft.)}}$$

$$= \text{Total Watts per Sq. Ft. x Overall Lumens per Watt x C.U. x M.F.}$$

$$\text{AREA PER LAMP (SQ. FT.)} = \frac{\text{Lumens per Lamp x C.U. x M.F.}}{\text{Footcandle Level Desired}}$$

$$\text{AREA PER FIXTURE (SQ. FT.)} = \frac{\text{Lumens per Lamp x Number of Lamps per Fixture x C.U. x M.F.}}{\text{Footcandle Level Desired}}$$

$$\text{TOTAL WATTS PER SQ. FT.} = \frac{\text{Footcandle Level Desired}}{\text{Overall Lumens per Watt x C.U. x M.F.}}$$

TYPICAL EXAMPLE

Room Size 25′ x 40′. Ceiling Height 9′. Office Area 70 FC
2′ x 4′ Recessed Troffers With 4 — 40 W. T12 (3100 Lumens) Lamps Each.
From I.E.S. Tables Room Index = E And C.U. = 0.67 (Plastic Lens).

$$\text{NO. OF FIXTURES} = \frac{70 \times 25 \times 40}{0.67 \times 0.7 \times 4 \times 3100} = 8.4 \text{ (Use 8 Fixtures)}$$

$$\text{TOTAL WATTS/SQ. FT.} = \frac{8 \times 200\text{W/Fixture}}{25 \times 40} = 16$$

SOME USEFUL FORMULAS FOR GENERAL LIGHTING DESIGN

* See the Lighting Handbook of the Illuminating Engineering Society and manufacturers' lamp and fixture data for Tables giving values of coefficient of utilization, maintenance factor, lumens per lamp etc.

Smith, Hinchman & Grylls Associates, Inc.; Detroit, Michigan

A TYPE — GENERAL LIGHTING

15–150 WATTS
STANDARD SHAPE

WATTS	DIA.	LENGTH	BASE	BULB
15	1 7/8	3 1/2	Med.	A—15
25	2 3/8	3 15/16	Med.	A—19
40	2 3/8	4 1/4	Med.	A—19
50	2 3/8	4 7/16	Med.	A—19
60	2 3/8	4 7/16	Med.	A—19
60*	2 3/8	4 7/16	Med.	A—19
75	2 3/8	4 7/16	Med.	A—19
100	2 5/8	5 5/16	Med.	A—21
100*	2 7/8	6 1/6	Med.	A—23
150	2 7/8	6 5/16	Med.	A—23
200	2 7/8	6 5/16	Med.	A—23

* Day light type

PS TYPE — GENERAL LIGHTING

150–1500 WATTS
PEAR SHAPE

WATTS	DIA.	LENGTH	BASE	BULB
150	3 1/8	6 15/16	Med.	PS—25
200	3 3/4	8 1/16	Med.	PS—30
300	3 3/4	8 1/16	Med.	PS—30
300	4 3/8	9 3/8	Mog.	PS—35
300	4 3/8	9 7/8	Med. Skt.	PS—35
500	5	9 3/4	Mog.	PS—40
750	6 1/2	13 1/16	Mog.	PS—52
1000	6 1/2	13 1/16	Mog.	PS—52
1500	6 1/2	13 1/16	Mog.	PS—52

REFLECTORS & PROJECTORS

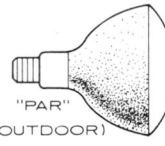 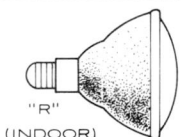

"PAR" (OUTDOOR)   "R" (INDOOR)

WATTS	DIA.	LGTH.	BASE	BULB	TYPE
30	2 1/2	3 15/16	Med.	R—20	Spot
50	2 1/2	3 15/16	Med.	R—20	Spot
75	3 3/4	5 3/16	Med.	R—30	Spot
75	3 3/4	5 3/16	Med.	R—30	Flood
150	5	6 1/2	Med.	R—40	Spot
150	5	6 1/2	Med.	R—40	Flood
150*	4 3/4	5 5/16	Med. Skt.	PAR—38	Spot
150*	4 3/4	5 5/16	Med. Skt.	PAR—38	Flood
300	5	6 1/2	Med.	R—40	Spot
300	5	6 1/2	Med.	R—40	Flood
500*	5	7 1/4	Mog.	R—40	Spot
500*	5	7 1/4	Mog.	R—40	Flood

*OUTDOOR

SCREW BASES

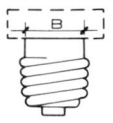

SKIRTED
TYPE BASE

TYPE	SIZE "B"
Candelabra	1/2
Intermediate	5/8
Medium	1
Mogul	1 1/2

Smith, Hinchman & Grylls Associates, Inc.; Detroit, Michigan

FLUORESCENT

RAPID START. STANDARD LIGHTING APPLICATIONS

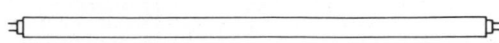

WATTS	MILLI AMPS	LENGTH	DIA.	BASE*	BULB
30	400 MA	36	1 1/2	Med. Bipin	T—12
40	400 MA	48	1 1/2	Med. Bipin	T—12
40	400 MA	60	2 1/8	Mog. Bipin	T—17
60	400 MA	48	1 1/2	Recessed D.C.	T—12
75	800 MA	60	1 1/2	Recessed D.C.	T—12
80	800 MA	64	1 1/2	Recessed D.C.	T—12
85	800 MA	72	1 1/2	Recessed D.C.	T—12
95	800 MA	84	1 1/2	Recessed D.C.	T—12
110	800 MA	96	1 1/2	Recessed D.C.	T—12
110	1500 MA	48	1 1/2	Recessed D.C.	T—12
160	1500 MA	72	1 1/2	Recessed D.C.	T—12
215	1500 MA	96	1 1/2	Recessed D.C.	T—12

D. C. = Double Contact

PREHEAT & TRIGGER START

WATTS	LENGTH	DIA.	BASE	BULB
4	6	5/8	Med. Bipin	T—5
6	9	5/8	Med. Bipin	T—5
8	12	5/8	Med. Bipin	T—5
13	21	5/8	Med. Bipin	T—5
13	12	1	Med. Bipin	T—8
14	12	1	Med. Bipin	T—8
14	15	1	Med. Bipin	T—8
14	15	1 1/2	Med. Bipin	T—12
15	18	1	Med. Bipin	T—8
15	18	1 1/2	Med. Bipin	T—12
20	24	1 1/2	Med. Bipin	T—12
25	28	1 1/2	Med. Bipin	T—12
25	33	1 1/2	Med. Bipin	T—12
30	36	1	Med. Bipin	T—8
90	60	2 1/8	Mog. Bipin	T—17
100	60	2 1/8	Mog. Bipin	T—17

SLIMLINE SPECIAL APPLICATIONS

WATTS	MILLI AMPS	LENGTH	DIA.	BASE	BULB
40	400 MA.	48	1 1/2	Single C	T—12
55	400 MA.	72	1 1/2	Single C	T—12
65	400 MA.	84	1 1/2	Single C	T—12
75	400 MA.	96	1 1/2	Single C	T—12

CIRCLINE

Std. Cool White   Deluxe Cool White
Std. Warm White   Deluxe Warm White
Daylight*

WATTS	BULB DIA.	DIA.	BASE	BULB
22	1 1/8	8 1/4	4–pin	T—9
32	1 1/4	12	4–pin	T—10
40	1 1/4	16	4–pin	T—10

* Available in 32 watt only.

PANEL RECESSED RAPID START

WATTS	
80	Nominal 12" Square Recessed Bipin

DECORATIVE & SPECIAL

"GA"   "C"   "G"   "T"   LUMILINE
"S"   "AF"   "T"

WATTS	DIA.	LENGTH	BASE	BULB
6	1 3/4	3 1/2	Med.	S—14
7	7/8	2 1/8	Cand.	C—7
7 1/2	1 3/8	2 1/4	Med.	S—11
10	1 3/8	2 5/16	Inter.	S 11
10	1 3/4	3 1/2	Med.	S—14
15	1 1/4	3 1/16	Cand.	F—10
15	1 1/4	3 1/8	Inter.	F—10
25	1 7/8	4 1/2	Med.	F—15
25	2 1/16	3	Cand.	G—16 1/2
25	3 1/8	4 7/16	Med.	G—25
25	1 1/4	5 5/8	Med.	T—10
25	13/16	5 1/2	Inter.	T—6 1/2
30	1	17 3/4	Disc.	T—8
40	1 7/8	4 1/2	Med.	F—15
40	3 1/8	4 7/16	Med.	G—25
40	1	11 3/4	Disc.	T—8
40	1	11 7/8	Med.	T—8
40	1 1/4	5 5/8	Med.	T—10
50	2 1/8	4 7/16	Med.	GA—25
60	1	17 3/4	Disc.	T—8
100	3 3/4	66 3/16	Med.	GA—30

THREE — WAY LAMPS

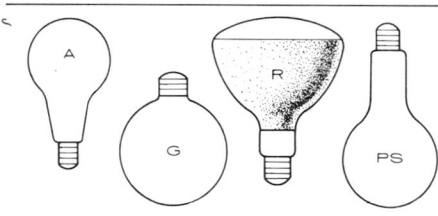

WATTS	DIA.	LGTH.	3—WAY BASE	BULB
30—70—100	2 5/8	5 5/16	Med.	A—21
50—100—150	3 1/8	5 15/16	Med.	PS—25
50—100—150	3 1/8	6 13/16	Mog.	PS—25
50—100—150	5	6 1/8	Med.	R—40
50—200—250	2 7/8	6 5/16	Med.	A—23
100—200—300	3 3/4	6 3/4	Mog.	G—30

GENERAL NOTES :

Sizes given are nominal, in inches. Length = maximum over-all length in inches. Number after lamp shape symbol = number of eighths of an inch in diameter (PS-30). Standard voltage of 115 to 125 is assumed. All fluorescent lamps require auxiliary equipment. Wattages of lamps vary with different manufacturers.

MERCURY DELUXE WHITE

WATTS	DIA.	LENGTH	BASE	BULB
50	2 1/8	5 1/8	Med.	E—17
75	2 5/8	6 1/2	Med.	E—21
100	2 7/8	5 7/16	Med.	A—23
100	2 7/8	7 1/4	Mog.	E—23 1/2
175	3 1/2	8 1/4	Mog.	E—28
250	3 1/2	8 1/4	Mog.	E—28
400	4 5/8	11 7/16	Mog.	E—37
400	4 5/8	11 7/16	Mog.	BT—37
400	6 1/2	11 3/4	Mog.	R—52
700	5 3/4	14 5/16	Mog.	BT—46
1000	7	15 1/16	Mog.	BT—56
1000	10	16 9/16	Mog.	R—80

QUARTZLINE LINEAR
FOR GENERAL LIGHTING

WATTS	VOLTS	DIA.	LENGTH	BASE	BULB
300	120	3/8	4 11/16	RSC	Clear
300	120	3/8	4 11/16	RSC	Frosted
500	120	3/8	4 11/16	RSC	Clear
500	120	3/8	4 11/16	RSC	Frosted
500	120	3/8	4 11/16	RSC	Clear
1000	130	3/8	10 1/16	RSC	Clear
1250	208	3/8	10 1/16	RSC	Clear
1500	240	3/8	10 1/16	RSC	Clear
300	120	1/2	3 1/8	RSC	Clear
300	120	1/2	3 1/8	RSC	Frosted
400	120	1/2	3 1/8	RSC	Clear
400	120	1/2	3 1/8	RSC	Frosted
1000	120	3/4	5 5/8	RSC	Clear
1000	120	3/4	5 5/8	RSC	Frosted
1000	120	3/4	5 5/8	RSC	Clear

QUARTZLINE SINGLE ENDED
FOR GENERAL LIGHTING

WATTS	DIA.	LENGTH	BASE	BULB
250	1/2	3 1/8	M.C.	Frosted
250	1/2	3 1/8	M.C.	Clear
250	1/2	2 13/16	M.C.	Frosted
250	1/2	2 13/16	M.C.	Clear
500	1/2	3 5/8	M.C.	Frosted
500	1/2	3 5/8	M.C.	Clear
500	1/2	3 7/16	M.C.	Frosted
500	1/2	3 7/16	M.C.	Clear
750	3	9 3/16	Med. Bipin	I.F.
1000	3	9 3/16	Med. Bipin	I.F.

QUARTZLINE PAR & REFLECTOR

WATTS	DIA.	LENGTH	BASE	SPREAD	LENS
250	4 3/4	5 5/16	M.S.	24°	Stippled
250	4 3/4	5 5/16	M.S.	60°	Lens
500	7	5	Mep.	15° x 32°	Stippled
500	7	5	Mep.	20° x 42°	Lens
500	7	5	Med.	34° x 66°	Lens
1000	8	6	Emep.	14° x 31°	Stippled
1000	8	6	Emep.	22° x 45°	Lens
1000	8	6	Emep.	45° x 72°	Lens
500	5	7 1/4	Mog.	32°	Light I.F.
500	5	7 1/4	Mog.	110°	I.F.
1000	7 1/2	10 1/8	Mog.	32°	Light I.F.
1000	7 1/2	10 1/8	Mog.	110°	I.F.
1500	7 1/2	10 1/8	Mog.	30°	Light I.F.
1500	7 1/2	10 1/8	Mog.	110°	I.F.

LUCALOX

WATTS	DIA.	LENGTH	BASE	BULB
275	2 1/4	9 3/4	Mog.	Clear
400	2 1/4	9 3/4	Mog.	Clear

LUCALOX

BT

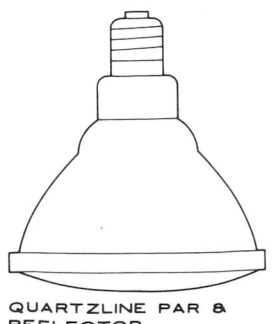
QUARTZLINE PAR & REFLECTOR

TYPICAL SHAPES

Smith, Hinchman & Grylls Associates, Inc.; Detroit, Michigan

ABBREVIATIONS

Med. — Medium
Mog. — Mogul
M.C. — Medium Contact
R.S.C. — Recessed Single Contact
I.F. — Inside Frosted
Mep. — Mogul End Prong
Emep. — Extended Mep.
M.S. — Medium Skirted

NOTE:

Because of their higher efficiency the sources on this page should be considered for all special applications. See manufacturers published data on bulb shapes.

LIGHTING OUTLETS

CEILING, WALL

○ ─○	SURFACE INCANDESCENT
Ⓡ ─Ⓡ	RECESS INCANDESCENT
Ⓑ ─Ⓑ	BLANKED OUTLET
Ⓓ	DROP CORD
Ⓔ ─Ⓔ	ELECTRICAL OUTLET
Ⓕ ─Ⓕ	FAN OUTLET
Ⓙ ─Ⓙ	JUNCTION BOX
Ⓛ$_{PS}$ ─Ⓛ$_{PS}$	LAMP HOLDER WITH PULL SWITCH
Ⓥ ─Ⓥ	OUTLET FOR VAPOR DISCHARGE LAMP
Ⓧ ─Ⓧ	EXIT LIGHT OUTLET
Ⓧ$_R$ ─Ⓧ$_R$	RECESSED EXIT LIGHT OUTLET
Ⓛ ─Ⓛ	OUTLET CONTROLLED BY LOW VOLTAGE SWITCHING WHEN RELAY IS INSTALLED IN OUTLET BOX
▢○▢	SURFACE OR PENDANT INDIVIDUAL FLUORESCENT FIXTURE
▢OR▢	RECESSED INDIVIDUAL FLUORESCENT FIXTURE
▢○▢▢	SURFACE OR PENDANT CONTINUOUS ROW FLUORESCENT FIXTURE
▢OR▢▢	RECESSED CONTINUOUS ROW FLUORESCENT FIXTURE

RECEPTACLE OUTLETS

─⊖	SINGLE RECEPTACLE OUTLET
═⊖	DUPLEX RECEPTACLE OUTLET
≡⊕	TRIPLEX RECEPTACLE OUTLET
═⊕	QUADRUPLEX RECEPTACLE OUTLET
═⊖	DUPLEX RECEPTACLE OUTLET-SPLIT WIRED
≡⊖	TRIPLEX RECEPTACLE OUTLET-SPLIT WIRED
─◁	SINGLE SPECIAL-PURPOSE RECEPTACLE OUTLET
═◁	DUPLEX SPECIAL-PURPOSE RECEPTACLE OUTLET
≡⊖ R	RANGE OUTLET
─▲ DW	SPECIAL PURPOSE CONNECTION
─⊖ X"	MULTI-OUTLET ASSEMBLY
Ⓒ	CLOCK HANGER RECEPTACLE
Ⓕ	FAN HANGER RECEPTACLE
▢⊖▢	FLOOR SINGLE RECEPTACLE OUTLET
▢⊖▢	FLOOR DUPLEX RECEPTACLE OUTLET
△	FLOOR SPECIAL PURPOSE OUTLET
◀	FLOOR TELEPHONE OUTLET-PUBLIC
◁	FLOOR TELEPHONE OUTLET-PRIVATE
▦	UNDERFLOOR DUCT AND JUNCTION BOX FOR TRIPLE, DOUBLE OR SINGLE DUCT SYSTEM AS INDICATED BY NUMBER OF PARALLEL LINES
▦	CELLULAR FLOOR HEADER DUCT

SWITCH OUTLETS

S	SINGLE POLE SWITCH
S$_2$	DOUBLE POLE SWITCH
S$_3$	THREE WAY SWITCH
S$_4$	FOUR WAY SWITCH
S$_D$	AUTOMATIC DOOR SWITCH
S$_K$	KEY OPERATED SWITCH
S$_P$	SWITCH AND PILOT LAMP
S$_{CB}$	CIRCUIT BREAKER
S$_{WCB}$	WEATHERPROOF CIRCUIT BREAKER
S$_{MC}$	MOMENTARY CONTACT SWITCH
S$_{RC}$	REMOTE CONTROL SWITCH
S$_{WP}$	WEATHERPROOF SWITCH
S$_F$	FUSED SWITCH
S$_{WF}$	WEATHERPROOF FUSED SWITCH
S$_L$	SWITCH FOR LOW VOLTAGE SWITCHING SYSTEM
S$_{LM}$	MASTER SWITCH FOR LOW VOLTAGE SWITCHING SYSTEM
S$_T$	TIME SWITCH
Ⓢ	CEILING PULL SWITCH
─⊖$_S$	SWITCH AND SINGLE RECEPTACLE
═⊖$_S$	SWITCH AND DOUBLE RECEPTACLE

○ A,B,C ETC.
═⊖ A,B,C ETC. } SPECIAL OUTLETS
S A,B,C ETC.

Any standard symbol as given above with the addition of lower case subscript lettering may be used to designate some special variation of standard equipment of particular interest in specific set of architectural plans.

When used they must be listed in the schedule of symbols on each drawing and if necessary further described in the specifications.

Frederick R. Brown, P. E.; Ayres, Cohen and Hayakawa; Consulting Engineers; Los Angeles/San Francisco, California

INSTITUTIONAL COMMERCIAL & INDUSTRIAL OCCUPANCIES

NURSES CALL SYSTEM DEVICES. (ANY TYPE)

PAGING SYSTEM DEVICES (ANY TYPE)

FIRE ALARM SYSTEM DEVICES (ANY TYPE)

STAFF REGISTER, SYSTEM (ANY TYPE)

ELECTRICAL CLOCK SYSTEM DEVICES (ANY TYPE)

PUBLIC TELEPHONE SYSTEM DEVICES

PRIVATE TELEPHONE SYSTEM DEVICES

WATCHMAN SYSTEM DEVICES

SOUND SYSTEM

OTHER SIGNAL SYSTEM DEVICES

SC   SIGNAL CENTRAL STATION

INTERCONNECTION BOX

AUXILIARY SYSTEM CIRCUITS

Any line without further designation indicates two-wire system. For a greater number of wires designate with numerals in manner similar to: 12- no. 18W - ³/₄'' C. Designate by numbers corresponding to listing in schedule.

A,B,C, ETC.   SPECIAL AUXILIARY OUTLETS

Subscript lettering refers to notes on drawings or detailed description in specifications.

PANELBOARDS

FLUSH MOUNTED PANELBOARD & CABINET

SURFACE MOUNTED PANELBOARD & CABINET

BUSDUCTS & WIREWAYS

T T T   TROLLEY DUCT

B B B   BUSWAY (SERVICE, FEEDER OR PLUG-IN)

C C C   CABLE THROUGH LADDER OR CHANNEL

W W W   WIREWAY

SIGNALING SYSTEM OUTLETS RESIDENTIAL OCCUPANCIES

PUSH BUTTON

BUZZER

BELL

BELL & BUZZER COMBINATION

ANNUNCIATOR

OUTSIDE TELEPHONE

INTERCONNECTING TELEPHONE

TELEPHONE SWITCHBOARD

BT   BELL RINGING TRANSFORMER

D   ELECTRIC DOOR OPENER

M   MAID'S SIGNAL PLUG

R   RADIO OUTLET

CH   CHIME

TV   TELEVISION OUTLET

T   THERMOSTAT

ELECTRICAL DISTRIBUTION OR LIGHTING SYSTEM, UNDERGROUND

M   MANHOLE

H   HANDHOLE

TM   TRANSFORMER- MANHOLE OR VAULT

TP   TRANSFORMER PAD

UNDERGROUND DIRECT BURIAL CABLE

UNDERGROUND DUCT LINE

STREET LIGHT STANDARD FED FROM UNDERGROUND CIRCUIT

ELECTRICAL DISTRIBUTION OR LIGHTING SYSTEM, AERIAL

POLE

STREET LIGHT & BRACKET

TRANSFORMER

PRIMARY CIRCUIT

SECONDARY CIRCUIT

DOWN GUY

HEAD GUY

SIDEWALK GUY

SERVICE WEATHER

PANELS CIRCUITS & MISCELLANEOUS

LIGHTING PANEL

POWER PANEL

WIRING, CONCEALED IN CEILING OR WALL

WIRING, CONCEALED IN FLOOR

WIRING EXPOSED

HOME RUN TO PANEL BOARD.

Indicate number of circuits by number of arrows. Any circuit without such designation indicates a two-wire circuit. For a greater number of wires indicate as follows: —///— (3 wires) —////— (4 wires), etc.

FEEDERS

Use heavy lines and designate by number corresponding to listing in feeder schedule.

WIRING TURNED UP

WIRING TURNED DOWN

G   GENERATOR

M   MOTOR

I   INSTRUMENT (SPECIFY)

T   TRANSFORMER (OR DRAW TO SCALE)

CONTROLLER

EXTERNALLY OPERATED DISCONNECT SWITCH

Frederick R. Brown, P. E.; Ayres, Cohen and Hayakawa; Consulting Engineers; Los Angeles/San Francisco, California

GENERAL NOTES:

Telephone equipment as shown is typical. A large variety of special equipment is available, and its use is determined by the requirements of the telephone service desired.

Telephone companies provide design and engineering assistance without charge. The local telephone company should be consulted in advance for any type of telephone

installation. Large installations are custom designed to meet many diversified types of service requirements, with space and facilities provides as needed for housing equipment.

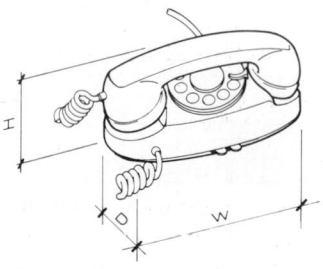

8½"W × 5½"D × 5"H
PRINCESS ®

5½"W × 8½"D × 5"H
PUSH BUTTON

8½"W × 9¼"D × 5⅜"H
I OR 6 BUTTON KEY SET

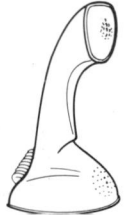

4" × 4½"BASE - 9"H
ERICOFON DIAL

DESK / TABLE TELEPHONE SETS
PLASTIC CASING : IN VARIOUS COLORS

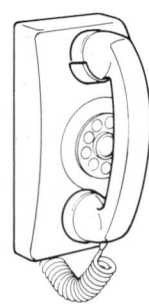

5½"W × 5½"D × 9⅜"H
STANDARD
PLASTIC CASING: IN
VARIOUS COLORS

3½"W × 3½"D × 8½"H
TRIMLINE ®
DESK TYPE ALSO

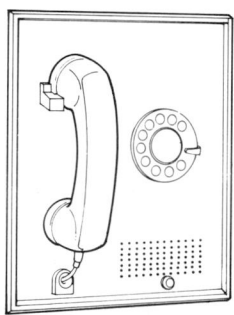

8⅜"W × 1⅝"D × 11 11/16"H(OPENING)
RECESSED PANEL
S.S. COVER PLATE

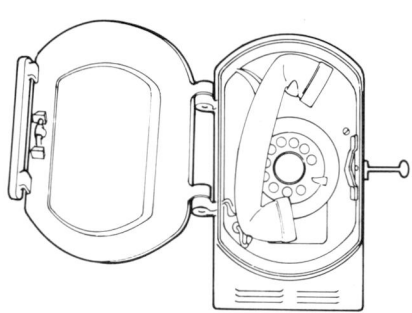

8⅜"W × 6¼"D × 12⅞"H
OUTDOOR / INDOOR PHONE
WEATHERPROOF, STEEL CASING AND
COVER

HANGING OR WALL TELEPHONE SETS

15½" TO 21"W × 7½"D × 5"H, WT. 16 TO 50 LBS.
DESK TYPE CONSOLE
PLASTIC CASING AND FACE PLATE

CONSOLE-DESK TYPE

For intercepting calls in order to direct them to the desired extension, either with hand set as shown, or with head set.

There are many types of consoles.

Types used are as selected by the Telephone Company which best meet customer service requirements.

12½" OR 14⅞"W × 8¼"D × 4¼"H
CALL DIRECTOR ®

A console that completes a call, similar to a 6 button telephone but with 18–30 button capacity.

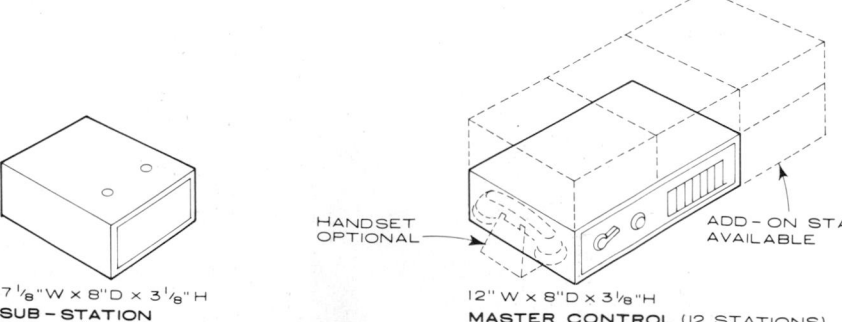

7⅛"W × 8"D × 3⅛"H
SUB - STATION

HANDSET
OPTIONAL

ADD - ON STATIONS
AVAILABLE

12"W × 8"D × 3⅛"H
MASTER CONTROL (12 STATIONS)

OFFICE INTERCOM

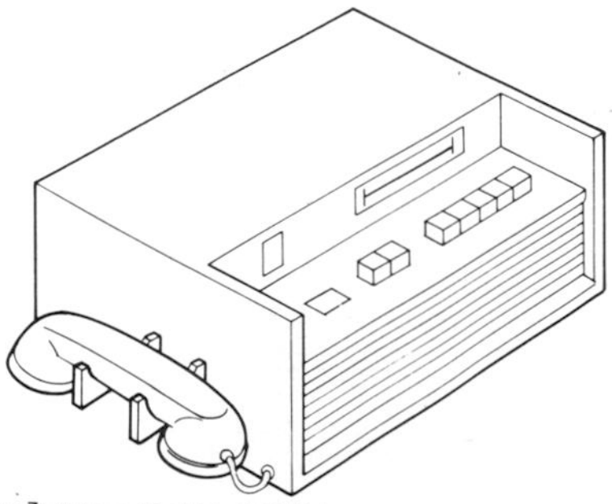

14¾"W × 11¾"D × 5"H
ANSWER & RECORD SET

Robert L. Plumley, AIA; Seibert, Hunter, Shute & Plumley; Medford, Oregon

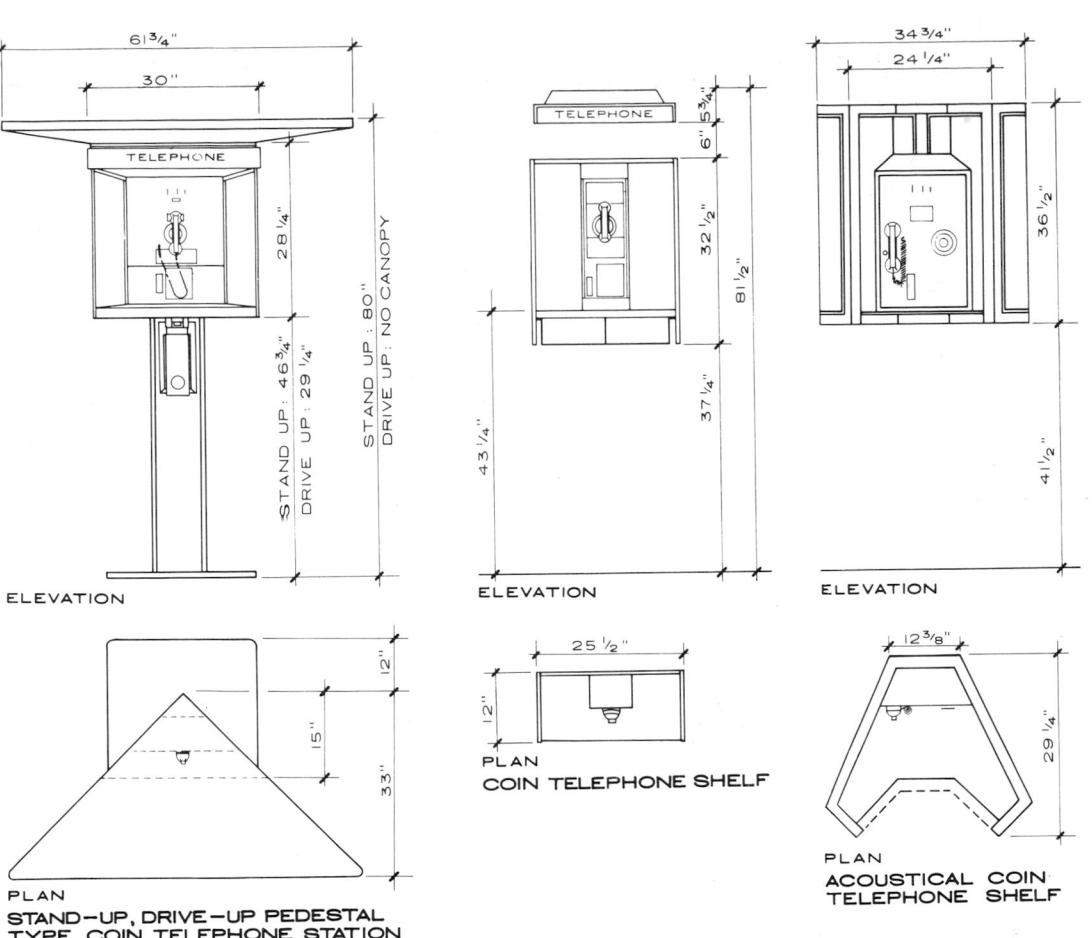

ELEVATION

PLAN
STAND-UP, DRIVE-UP PEDESTAL TYPE COIN TELEPHONE STATION

ELEVATION

PLAN
COIN TELEPHONE SHELF

ELEVATION

PLAN
ACOUSTICAL COIN TELEPHONE SHELF

PEDESTAL TYPE COIN TELEPHONE

Panel type coin telephone set. Steel weather hood and side panels. Built-in fluorescent lighting with sign. S.S. writing ledge. S.S. pedestal with directory holder.

Interior/exterior finishes: porcelain enamel, various colors.

COIN TELEPHONE SHELF

Wall mounted unit. Surface mounted coin telephone set. Steel side and back panels. Fluorescent lighting with sign. S.S. writing ledge with directory holder.

Interior/exterior finishes: Porcelain enamel, various colors or wood finishes.

ACOUSTICAL COIN TELEPHONE SHELF

With any standard surface mount or panel type coin telephone set.

Fabricated with legs, or accessories available for back or side wall mount, shelf mount or pedestal installation.

With built-in fluorescent lighting.

Exterior finish: Steel with porcelain baked enamel finish. Standard color: blue. Other colors available.

Interior finish: Perforated S.S. encasing high-density sound-absorbing fiberglass insulation.

Adaptable to various combinations of multiple assemblies.

Accessories available: Illuminated telephone sign. Directory holder.

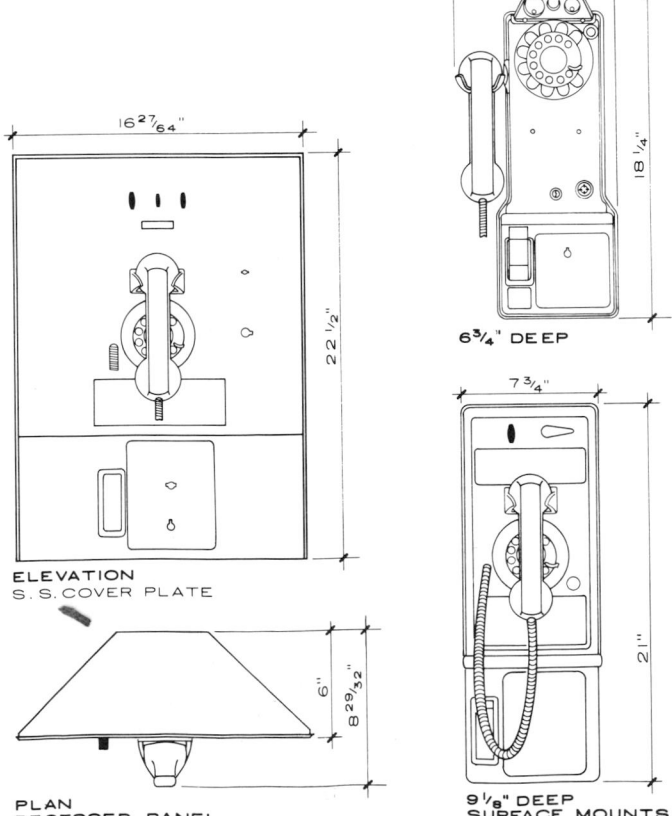

ELEVATION
S.S. COVER PLATE

PLAN
RECESSED PANEL

COIN TELEPHONE SETS

6¾" DEEP

9⅛" DEEP
SURFACE MOUNTS

ELEVATION

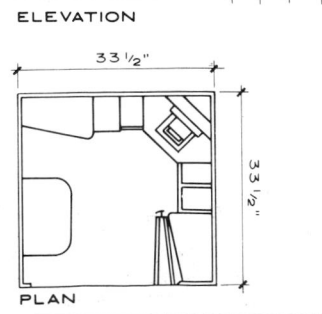

PLAN
AIRLIGHT BOOTH

COIN TELEPHONE BOOTHS

Glass lights = plain tempered glass.

Wooden Booths: Stock woods: Birch, oak, walnut, mahogany. Special woods available for Custom order.

Universal and Airtight booths: Standard indoor/outdoor booths. Metal frame: aluminum, plain or anodized, with bright or matte finish.

Side and back panels: Full or ½ glass, or red, green, or blue porcelain baked enamel or aluminum. Airtight booths available for outdoor installation with panels cut short for easier cleaning.

Other similar standard booths are available.

For multiple installations, booths are fabricated with common panels.

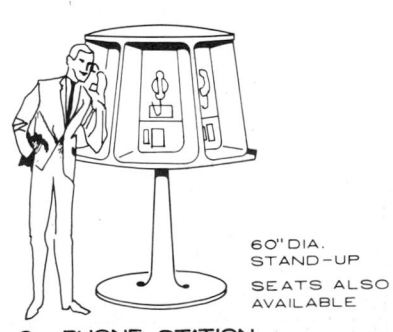

60" DIA.
STAND-UP
SEATS ALSO AVAILABLE

6-PHONE STATION

Robert L. Plumley, AIA; Seibert, Hunter, Shute & Plumley; Medford, Oregon

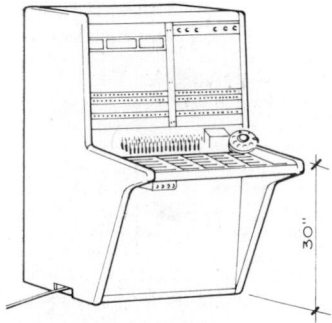

2' – 2⅞" TO 3' – 2" W
2' – 10½" TO 3' – 2½" D
3' – 10 1/16" TO 5' – 0" H
WT. 400 TO 500 LBS.
SWITCHBOARD

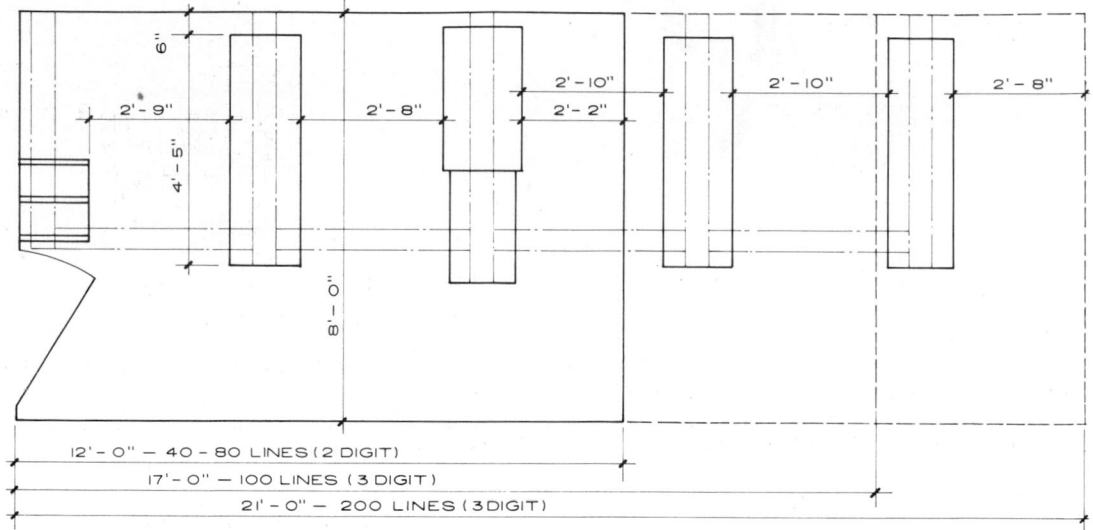

EQUIPMENT ROOM REQUIREMENTS

12' – 0" – 40 – 80 LINES (2 DIGIT)
17' – 0" – 100 LINES (3 DIGIT)
21' – 0" – 200 LINES (3 DIGIT)

Steel casing – various colors and finishes.

There are many types of switchboards.

Selection and trunks and station capacity as required for customer service.

For multiple position installation maximum width is (W) X number of positions.

Removable end panels, or as common panels for multiple installations.

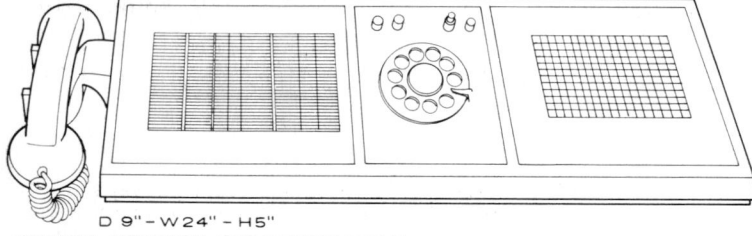

D 9" – W 24" – H 5"
DIRECT STATION SELECTOR (PBX)

9" TO 11" W × 9" TO 14½" D × 4½" TO 5½" H
DATA SET

Plastic casing: various colors.

For transmission of data between computers. Telephone can either be separate or integral as shown.

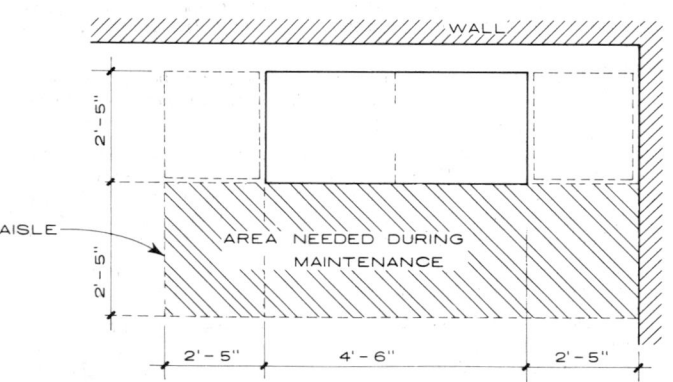

WALL

AISLE

AREA NEEDED DURING MAINTENANCE

2' – 5"   4' – 6"   2' – 5"

21½" W × 18½" D × 33" H   WT = 136 LBS
TELETYPEWRITER ®
AUTOMATIC SEND – RECEIVE SET

EQUIPMENT 5' – 3" HIGH ; PLUS 2' – 6" TO RAISE CABINET LID
WT. 1500 ± LBS.
FLOOR SPACE NEEDED FOR PBX EQUIPMENT

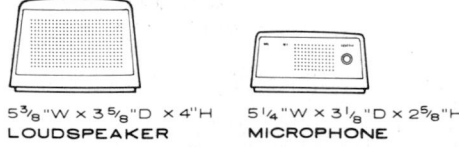

5⅜" W × 3⅝" D × 4" H
LOUDSPEAKER

5¼" W × 3⅛" D × 2⅝" H
MICROPHONE

SPEAKERPHONE

Plastic casing: various colors.

Used with single line or multi-line telephone or call director to permit "hands-free" two-way communication.

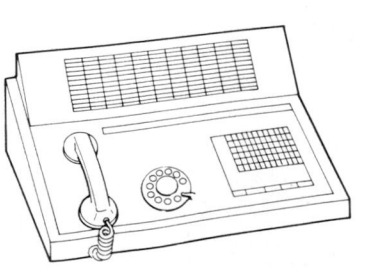

D 17" – W 22" – H 9½"
MOTEL ATTENDANT CONSOLE

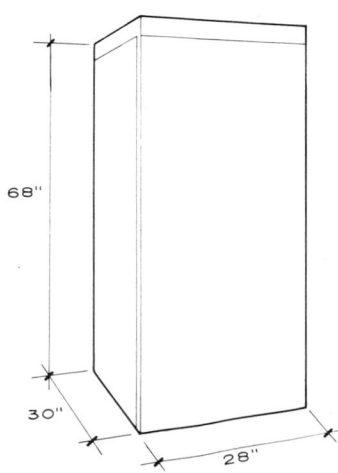

68"

30"

28"

EQUIPMENT CABINET FOR MOTEL CONSOLE
40 UNIT OR SMALLER

Robert L. Plumley, AIA; Seibert, Hunter, Shute & Plumley; Medford, Oregon

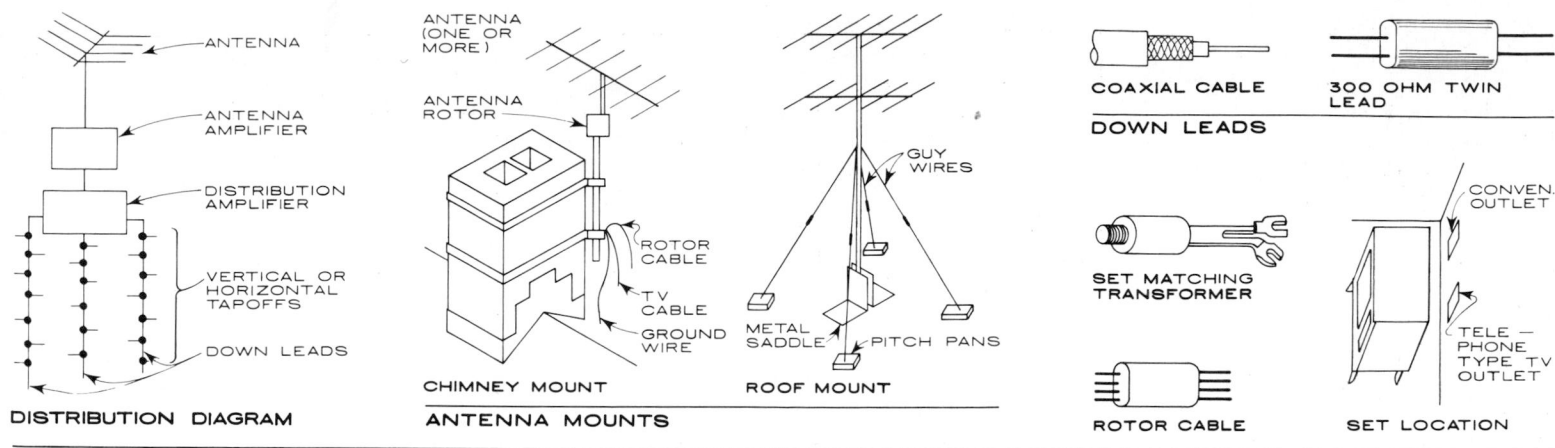

DISTRIBUTION DIAGRAM   ANTENNA MOUNTS   CHIMNEY MOUNT   ROOF MOUNT   DOWN LEADS   ROTOR CABLE   SET LOCATION

ANTENNA SYSTEMS FOR TELEVISION AND FM RADIO

NOTES:

1. Television and FM Radio distribution systems are the same for horizontal, "motel type" and for vertical "hotel type" installations. Summary information shown can be used as a guide for small residential as well as for large systems.

2. TV signals in apartment houses, hotels, institutions and other large buildings go directly from the antenna installation to the amplification and distribution point at roof lever or, after a short cable run, to the basement.

3. For details of Master Antenna Television (MATV) systems, consult a local MATV installer.

4. Locate the amplifiers, power supplies, mixers, filters and related equipment as close to antenna as project conditions permit. Distribution line amplifiers, if necessary, may be located in closets, shafts or similar areas accessible for service.

5. Runs to TV tapoffs are usually 75 ohm coaxial cable and should be in conduit if possibility of stress or accidental cutting exists.

6. Reminder: Roof mounted antennas may need special structural support, and amplifier locations will require access to power.

7. Locate towers, mast and mounts to assure a signal path free of obstructions and of sufficient size to support the antennas required. The number of antennas depends on the number of broadcast stations which can be received.

8. A small tower or guyed mast may be used for either residential or commercial antenna installations. If on a roof top, a base or saddle must be provided to prevent damage to the roof.

9. If a rotor is used (for residential installations only) on the antenna, the down lead is a low voltage cable and may be routed in a manner to comply with low voltage wiring.

10. Adequate ventilation must be provided at TV set location. See TV set manufacturer for details and specifications.

11. A power outlet should be provided near the TV set location. This same power outlet may be used to provide power to the antenna rotor if used.

12. The down lead from the antenna or from the rotor may be terminated in an outlet box at the TV set location.

13. If a coaxial cable is used from the TV antenna to the outlet box, a Set Matching Transformer (illustrated above) will be required at the TV set.

14. For details and specifications see Community Antenna Television (CATV) and MATV suppliers and installers.

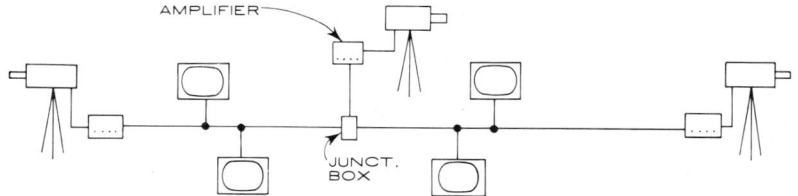

CLOSED CIRCUIT TV:
CAMERA / MONITOR ARRANGEMENT

NOTES:

1. Closed Circuit Television is a system wherein a live pick-up camera signal is fed to a standard television set or a video monitor used as a picture monitor.

2. The pick-up camera signal can be transmitted over coaxial cable by either direct video signals or by modulated (AM) radio frequency signals.

3. Closed Circuit Television cameras are used for observing remote or in accessible locations, for security viewing of restricted areas, or for viewing a hazardous environment.

4. One Closed Circuit Television camera can be called to feed several TV set picture monitors, or several Closed Circuit Television cameras may feed one TV set picture monitor by a switching arrangement.

5. Closed Circuit Television camera or cameras may be added to any Master Antenna system (MATV) or to any Community Antenna Television system. This may be done by considering the camera signal as an additional channel antenna. The Closed Circuit Television camera modulated radio frequency signal is fed into the television distribution system on any unused TV channel.

6. Any number of cameras may be fed into a TV distribution system, depending on the number of TV channels the TV distribution system can accommodate.

7. Video signals from a Closed Circuit Television camera may be fed to a TV picture monitor by coaxial cable up to 2500 feet from the camera. For video cable lengths over 2500 feet, consult your local installer or manufacturer.

8. Video tape (VTR) and film/slide systems may be operated in addition to Closed Circuit Television cameras. The video signal from video tape recorders or from film/slide systems is distributed in the same manner as for Closed Circuit Television.

9. If video tape recorders (VTR) and film/slide equipment are to be operated in conjunction with live Closed Circuit Television cameras, adequate space must be provided for equipment and operators.

10. Power must be provided for the operating equipment and numerous small pieces of associated equipment.

11. For video tape operation, it is desirable to control the dust and humidity, both in the operating area and in the storage area.

12. Adequate lighting must be provided for Closed Circuit Television camera pick-up locations.

13. The audio or sound associated with the Closed Circuit Television system must be treated in the same manner as the television signal when cabled separately, otherwise the audio or sound is transmitted as a part of the television signal.

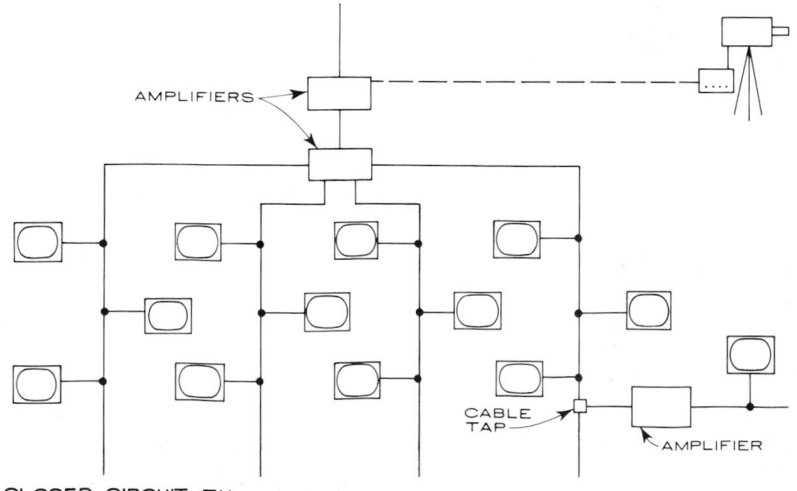

CLOSED CIRCUIT TV
CAMERA AND DISTRIBUTION SYSTEM

Virgil D. Duncan, P. E.; Raleigh, North Carolina
The National Association of Broadcasters; Washington, D. C.

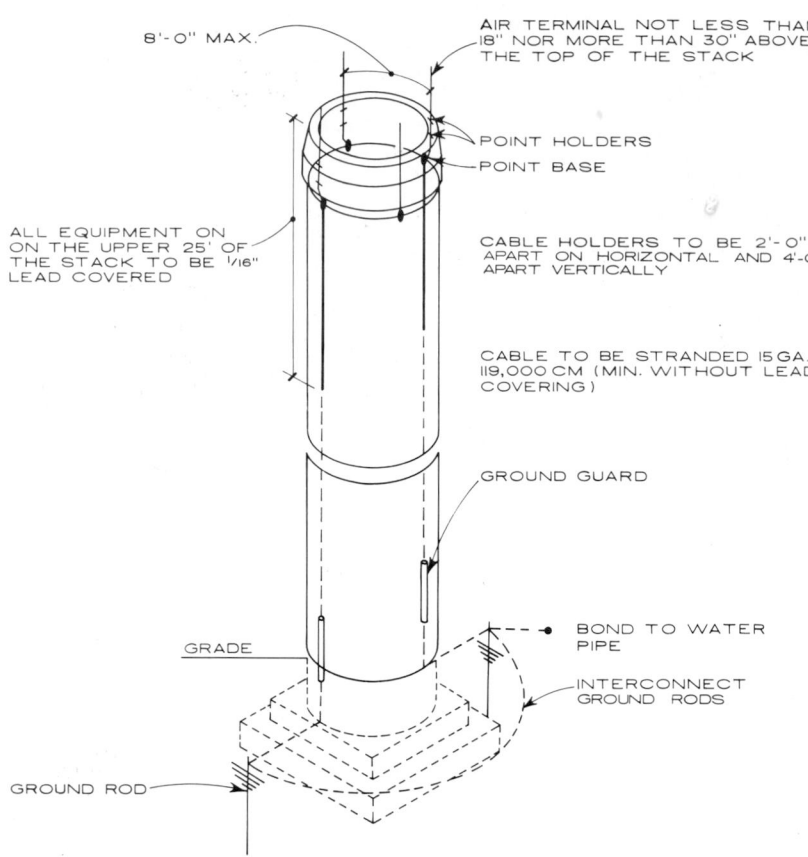

8'-0" MAX.

AIR TERMINAL NOT LESS THAN 18" NOR MORE THAN 30" ABOVE THE TOP OF THE STACK

POINT HOLDERS

POINT BASE

ALL EQUIPMENT ON ON THE UPPER 25' OF THE STACK TO BE 1/16" LEAD COVERED

CABLE HOLDERS TO BE 2'-0" APART ON HORIZONTAL AND 4'-0" APART VERTICALLY

CABLE TO BE STRANDED 15 GA. 119,000 CM (MIN. WITHOUT LEAD COVERING)

GROUND GUARD

BOND TO WATER PIPE

INTERCONNECT GROUND RODS

GRADE

GROUND ROD

TYPICAL SMOKESTACK INSTALLATION

If stack is partly or entirely of reinforced concrete, reinforcing shall be made electrically continuous and bonded to system top and bottom.

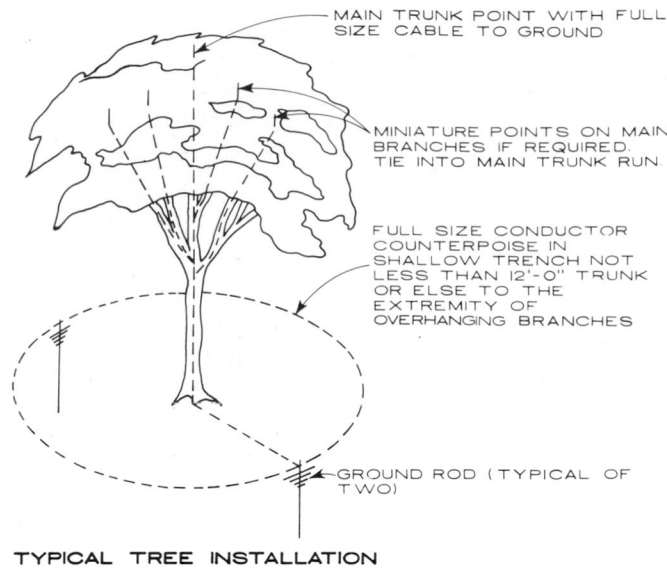

MAIN TRUNK POINT WITH FULL SIZE CABLE TO GROUND

MINIATURE POINTS ON MAIN BRANCHES IF REQUIRED. TIE INTO MAIN TRUNK RUN.

FULL SIZE CONDUCTOR COUNTERPOISE IN SHALLOW TRENCH NOT LESS THAN 12'-0" TRUNK OR ELSE TO THE EXTREMITY OF OVERHANGING BRANCHES

GROUND ROD (TYPICAL OF TWO)

TYPICAL TREE INSTALLATION

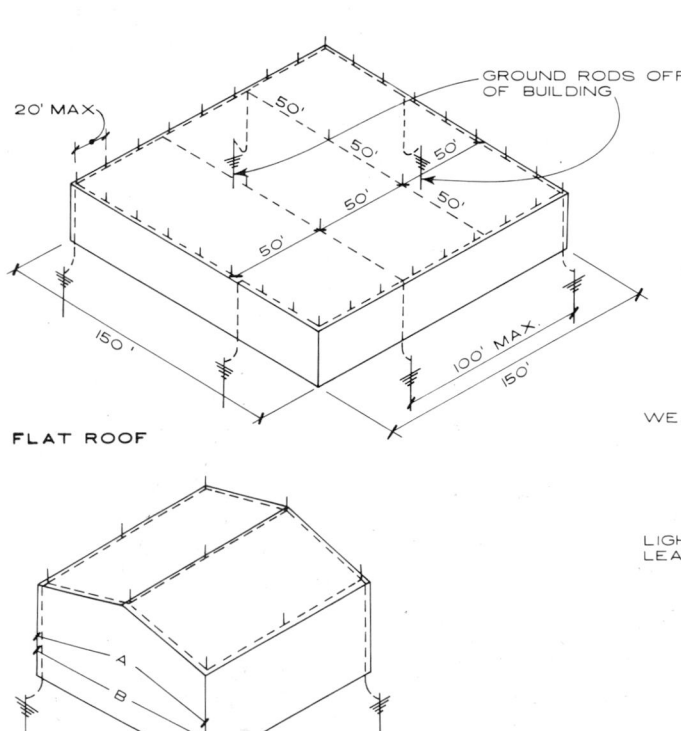

20' MAX.

GROUND RODS OFF SIDES OF BUILDING

50'

50'

50'

50'

50'

50'

150'

100' MAX.

150'

FLAT ROOF

PITCHED ROOF

TYPICAL AIR TERMINAL & CONDUCTOR LAYOUTS

A = 40' or less and 1/8 pitch or less.
B = more than 40' and 1/4 pitch or less.

GROUND ROD OFF REAR CORNER OF BUILDING

TYPICAL DORMER CONNECTIONS

A. No dead ends on main ridge or dormers as high or higher than main ridge.

B. Total conductor less than 16' −0'' (dead end allowable).

C. Conductor exceeds 16' thus requiring continuation to ground.

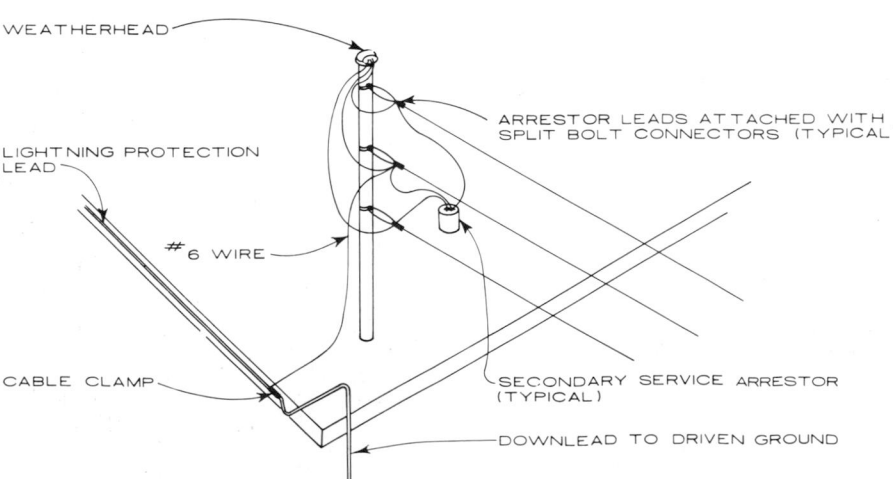

WEATHERHEAD

ARRESTOR LEADS ATTACHED WITH SPLIT BOLT CONNECTORS (TYPICAL

LIGHTNING PROTECTION LEAD

#6 WIRE

CABLE CLAMP

SECONDARY SERVICE ARRESTOR (TYPICAL)

DOWNLEAD TO DRIVEN GROUND

TYPICAL SECONDARY ELECTRICAL SERVICE ARRESTOR

R. W. Lindquist; Thompson Lightning Protection; St. Paul, Minnesota

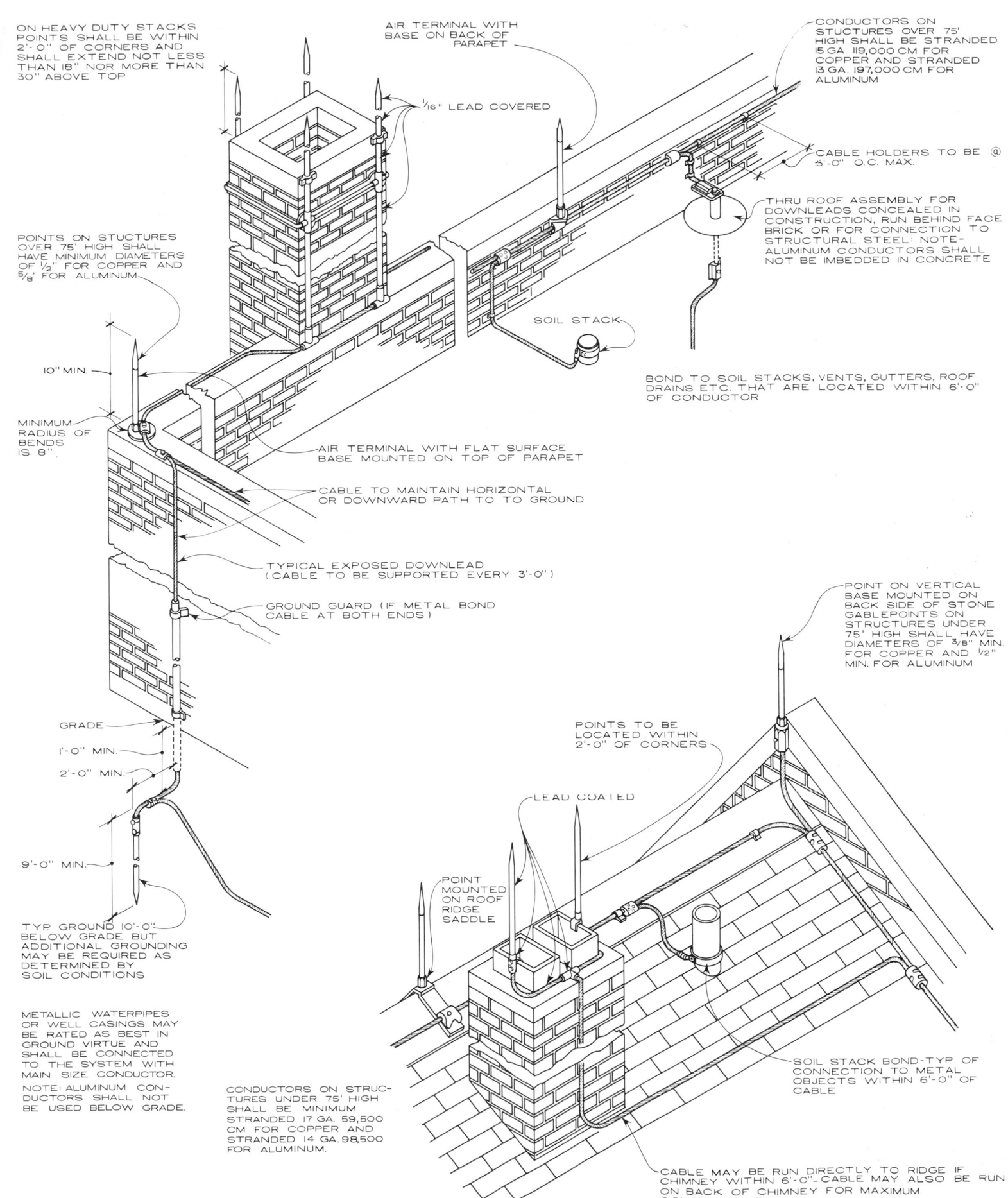

ON HEAVY DUTY STACKS POINTS SHALL BE WITHIN 2'-0" OF CORNERS AND SHALL EXTEND NOT LESS THAN 18" NOR MORE THAN 30" ABOVE TOP

AIR TERMINAL WITH BASE ON BACK OF PARAPET

1/16" LEAD COVERED

CONDUCTORS ON STUCTURES OVER 75' HIGH SHALL BE STRANDED 15 GA. 119,000 CM FOR COPPER AND STRANDED 13 GA. 197,000 CM FOR ALUMINUM

POINTS ON STUCTURES OVER 75' HIGH SHALL HAVE MINIMUM DIAMETERS OF 1/2" FOR COPPER AND 5/8" FOR ALUMINUM

CABLE HOLDERS TO BE @ 3'-0" O.C. MAX.

THRU ROOF ASSEMBLY FOR DOWNLEADS CONCEALED IN CONSTRUCTION, RUN BEHIND FACE BRICK OR FOR CONNECTION TO STRUCTURAL STEEL: NOTE-ALUMINUM CONDUCTORS SHALL NOT BE IMBEDDED IN CONCRETE

SOIL STACK

10" MIN.

BOND TO SOIL STACKS, VENTS, GUTTERS, ROOF DRAINS ETC. THAT ARE LOCATED WITHIN 6'-0" OF CONDUCTOR

MINIMUM RADIUS OF BENDS IS 8"

AIR TERMINAL WITH FLAT SURFACE BASE MOUNTED ON TOP OF PARAPET

CABLE TO MAINTAIN HORIZONTAL OR DOWNWARD PATH TO TO GROUND

TYPICAL EXPOSED DOWNLEAD (CABLE TO BE SUPPORTED EVERY 3'-0")

GROUND GUARD (IF METAL BOND CABLE AT BOTH ENDS)

POINT ON VERTICAL BASE MOUNTED ON BACK SIDE OF STONE GABLEPOINTS ON STRUCTURES UNDER 75' HIGH SHALL HAVE DIAMETERS OF 3/8" MIN. FOR COPPER AND 1/2" MIN. FOR ALUMINUM

POINTS TO BE LOCATED WITHIN 2'-0" OF CORNERS

GRADE

1'-0" MIN.

2'-0" MIN.

LEAD COATED

POINT MOUNTED ON ROOF RIDGE SADDLE

9'-0" MIN.

TYP GROUND 10'-0" BELOW GRADE BUT ADDITIONAL GROUNDING MAY BE REQUIRED AS DETERMINED BY SOIL CONDITIONS

METALLIC WATERPIPES OR WELL CASINGS MAY BE RATED AS BEST IN GROUND VIRTUE AND SHALL BE CONNECTED TO THE SYSTEM WITH MAIN SIZE CONDUCTOR.

NOTE: ALUMINUM CONDUCTORS SHALL NOT BE USED BELOW GRADE.

CONDUCTORS ON STRUCTURES UNDER 75' HIGH SHALL BE MINIMUM STRANDED 17 GA. 59,500 CM FOR COPPER AND STRANDED 14 GA. 98,500 FOR ALUMINUM.

SOIL STACK BOND-TYP OF CONNECTION TO METAL OBJECTS WITHIN 6'-0" OF CABLE

CABLE MAY BE RUN DIRECTLY TO RIDGE IF CHIMNEY WITHIN 6'-0"-CABLE MAY ALSO BE RUN ON BACK OF CHIMNEY FOR MAXIMUM CONCEALMENT

R. W. Lindquist; Thompson Lightning Protection; St. Paul, Minnesota

APPENDIX

CONVENTIONS, GRAPHICAL CONSTRUCTIONS AND MATHEMATICAL DATA

PLAN AND SECTION INDICATIONS

EARTH, ETC.
- EARTH
- ROCK
- STONE FILL

INSULATION
- LOOSE FILL OR BATTS
- BOARDS, OR QUILTS
- SOLID, CORK OR MAGNESIA

CONCRETE
- STRUCTURAL CONCRETE
- LT. WEIGHT CONCRETE
- BLOCK
- TERRAZZO

STRUCTURAL CLAY TILE
- UNGLAZED
- GLAZED

METAL
- ✳ STEEL, IRON
- ALUMINUM
- SHEET METAL & ALL METALS AT SMALL SCALE
- STRUCTURAL STEEL
- REINFORCING BARS
- ✳ BRASS, BRONZE

WOOD
- ✳ FINISH
- ROUGH
- LARGE SCALE PLYWOOD
- SMALL SCALE PLYWOOD
- PLASTIC ON PLYWOOD
- STUD WALL & PARTITION
- WOOD FINISH ON STUD

STONE
- CUT STONE
- RUBBLE
- CAST STONE (CONCRETE)
- MARBLE
- SLATE, BLUESTONE SOAPSTONE

BRICK
- ✳ COMMON
- FACE
- FIRE BRICK ON COMMON

GLASS
- SHEET & PLATE
- STRUCTURAL
- BLOCK

GYPSUM
- PLASTER ON MASONRY
- BLOCK
- SOLID PLASTER PARTITION
- METAL STUD & PLASTER PARTITION
- PLASTER BOARD & PLASTER PARTITION
- PLANK

MISCELLANEOUS
- WATERPROOFING, FELT, FLASHING, ETC.
- RESILIENT TILE
- ✳ PLASTER, SAND & CEMENT
- ACOUSTIC TILE
- CARPET & PAD

ARCHITECTURAL TERRA COTTA
- VENEER
- BLOCK PARTITION

ELEVATION INDICATIONS

- GLASS
- ASHLAR STONE
- ✳ RUBBLE STONE
- SQUARED STONE
- RUNNING BOND MASONRY
- STACK BOND MASONRY
- SHEET METAL

- CONCRETE PLASTER
- SHINGLES SIDING
- BRICK
- CERAMIC TILE

✳ SYMBOLS MARKED ✳ APPROVED AS AMERICAN STANDARD, A.S.A. Y14.2 -1957 BY AMERICAN NATIONAL STANDARDS ASSOCIATION.

NOTE: WHEN SYMBOLS FOR MATERIALS NOT LISTED ABOVE ARE REQUIRED REFER TO A.S.A. Y 142 1957.

PLANS OF EXTERIOR WALLS

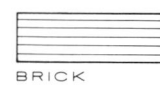

- FACE BRICK / RUBBLE
- BRICK / STRUC. CLAY TILE
- CAST STONE / BRICK
- CUT STONE / STRUC. CONC.
- CUT STONE / CONCRETE BLOCK
- ARCH. T.C. / BRICK
- EXTERIOR OF WALL / INTERIOR

SECTIONS OF FLOOR FINISH

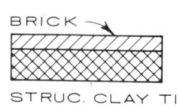
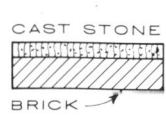
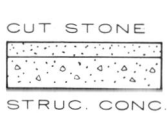
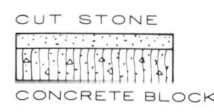
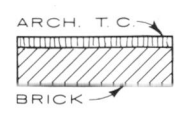
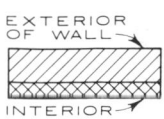

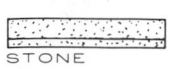
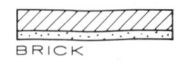

- TILE ON CONCRETE
- MARBLE ON CONCRETE
- WOOD
- TERRAZZO ON CONCRETE
- STONE
- BRICK
- RESILIENT TILE ON CONCRETE

Fred A. Norris; Campbell Aldrich & Nulty; Boston, Massachusetts

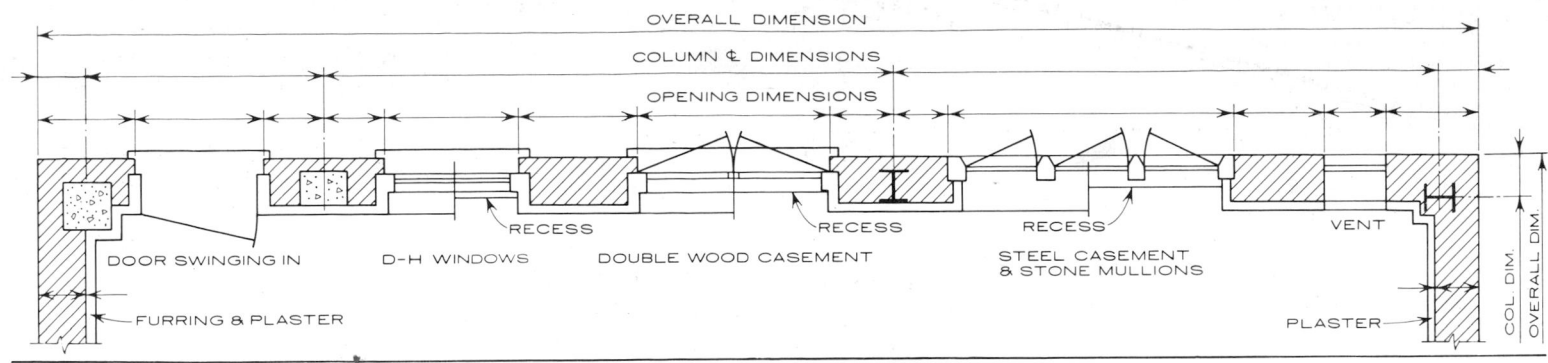

METHOD FOR DIMENSIONING EXTERIOR MASONRY WALLS & OPENINGS

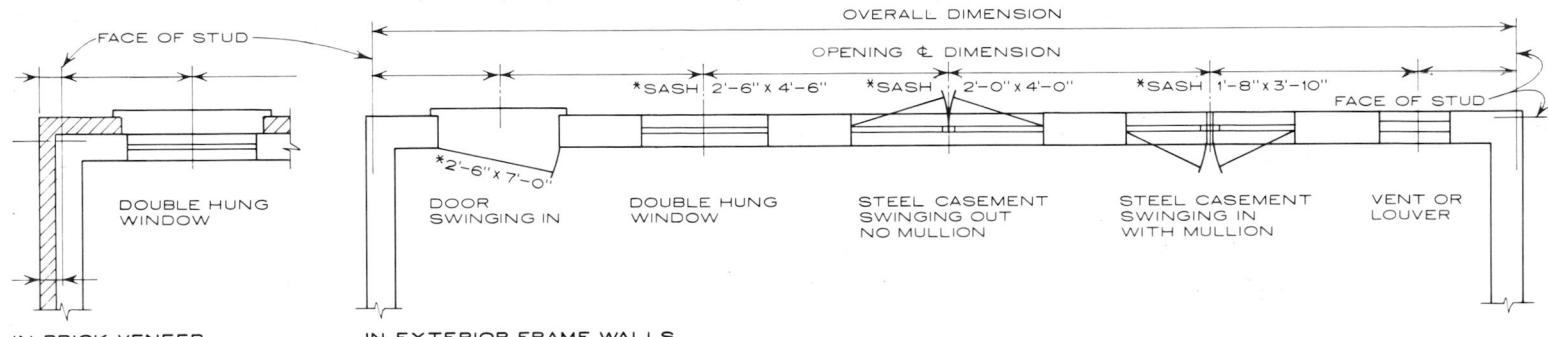

METHOD FOR DIMENSIONING EXTERIOR FRAME WALLS & OPENINGS

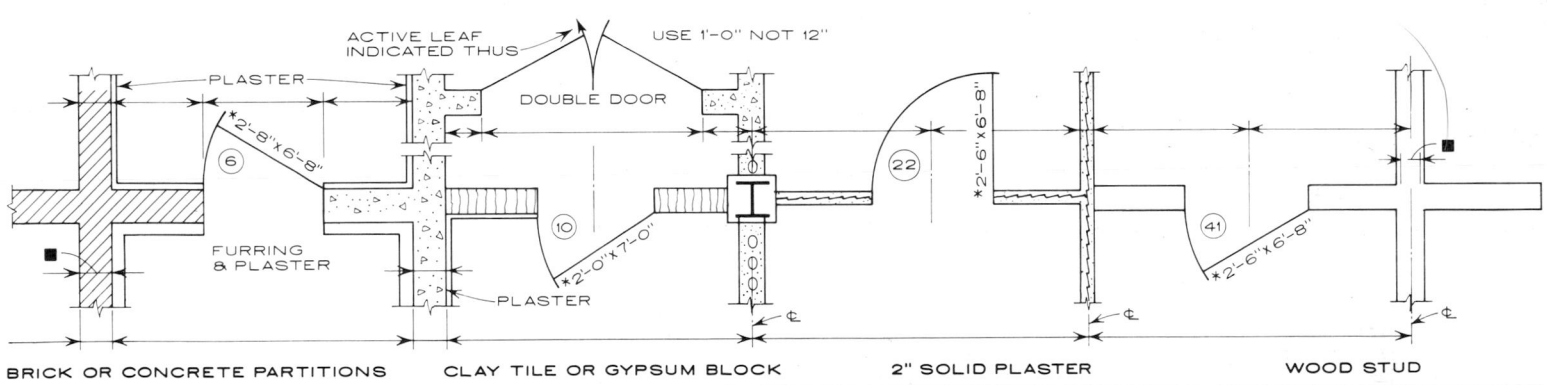

DIMENSIONS & INDICATIONS OF INTERIOR PARTITIONS & DOORS

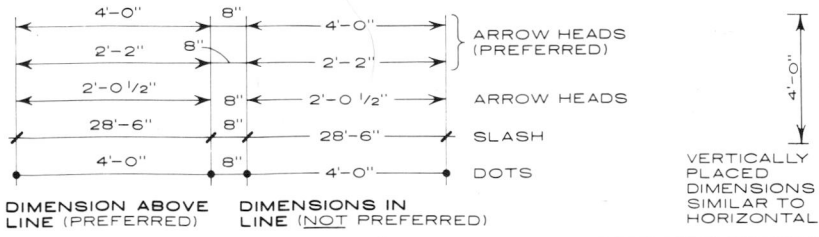

DIMENSIONS (NOT OF THE MODULAR CO-ORDINATION METHOD)

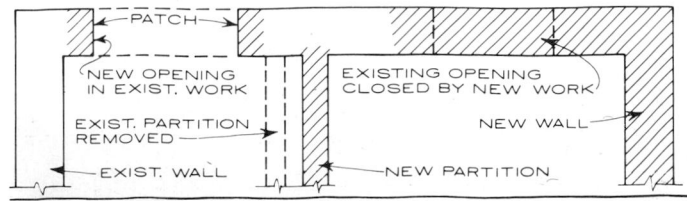

INDICATIONS FOR ALTERATIONS

Fred A. Norris; Campbell Aldrich & Nulty; Boston, Massachusetts

NOTES:

* Show size at doors and windows, only if there is no door or window schedule.

■ Due to regional variations, use local standards when dimensioning thickness of block, brick, tile, lumber, studs, etc.

For vertical dimensioning, see Index for pages where Brick, Wood Frame, Steel, Masonry and Concrete construction are shown.

MODULAR COORDINATION:

Modular Coordination is the term given to the dimensional coordination of building materials and products. Building Industry agreement on American Standards Association standard A62.1 sponsored by the American Institute of Architects, Associated General Contractors of America, National Association of Homebuilders, and the Producers' Council, Inc., established 4 inches as the basic module for U.S. building materials and products. A similar Canadian standard, (A 31) has been adopted. International standards activities have established the 4" basic module for foot—inch countries and 10 cm (almost 4") for metric countries.

Modular Measure is a synonym for Modular Coordination but also implies use of a drafting method (modular drafting or modular dimensioning) as a means of effecting Modular Coordination.

Since adoption of the ASA standard in 1945 and introduction of Modular Drafting in 1946, the drafting system has increased in acceptance and use among architectural offices. Surveys of architectural firms reflect present acceptance of modular construction planning principles, extensive use of the modular drafting system, and a higher-than-average use of modular dimensioning by design award-winning firms.

Modular Construction results from architectural planning based on the use of modular sized building materials and products. The joint-centerline concept of modular products permits accommodation of those materials into buildings designed with planning modules of some multiple of 4" (e.g. 3'—0", 40", 5'—4", etc.) The vast majority of all buildings are currently planned to use materials with modular dimensional characteristics.

DIMENSIONAL CHARACTERISTICS OF MODULAR BUILDING PRODUCTS:

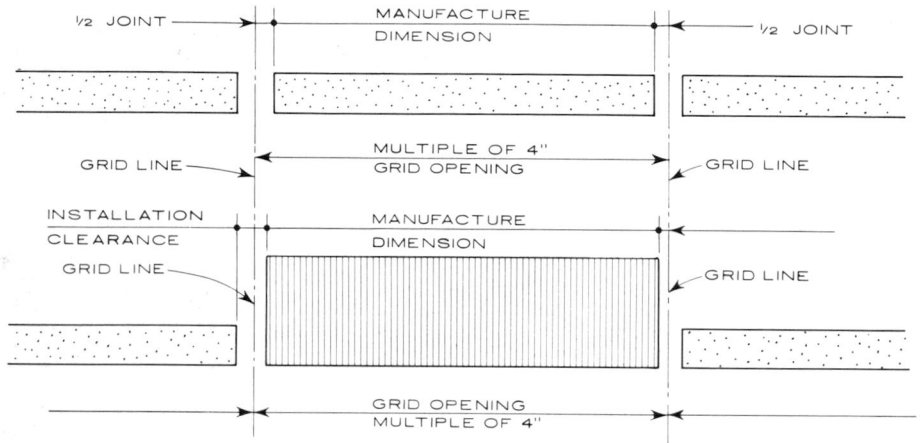

REPEATING ELEMENTS.

(Decking, Masonry Units, Acoustic Tile, etc.) A modular product is measured from centerline of typical installation joint to the centerline of the next joint. When a series of such products are installed, each joint centerline falls on a dimensional increment of four inches. Tables and charts of sizes of modular products are included throughout this issue of Graphic Standards.

ISOLATED COMPONENTS:

(Bathtubs, Unit Air Conditioners, Grilles, etc.) Installation tolerances for isolated components include one-half the minimum joint dimensions of adjacent modular materials plus the prefabricated installation clearance. Most components in this category are sized, or provided with adapters, to adjust to the installation characteristics of anticipated adjacent materials. Integral elements should not extend beyond the "grid opening".

MODULAR DRAFTING CONVENTIONS:

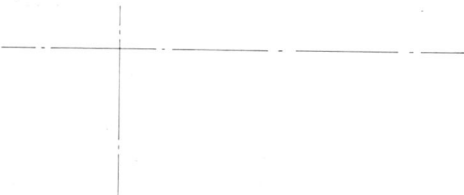

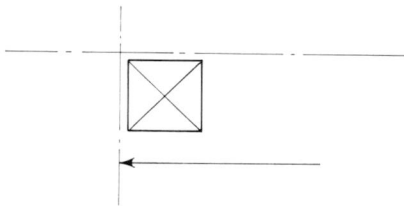

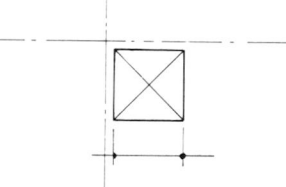

GRID LINES:

Are used to establish reference planes four inches apart in all three dimensions. Grid lines are imaginary and can be thought of as dimensional egg-crates running throughout the structure. The grid lines are partially or entirely shown on large-scale details but will not be shown at all on small scale plans.

ARROW HEADS:

Indicate all dimensions referenced to grid-line locations. This feature of modular drafting is the key to the efficiencies resulting from the use of the system. Preliminary drawings can be fully dimensioned as small scale working drawings knowing that the materials will fit when fully detailed. A number of personnel can proceed with the detailing using the single small scale plan reference without the necessity of frequent checking with each other for dimensional reference points.

DOTS:

Are used to indicate off-grid locations for dimensions. (Half-dots may be used whenever drawing space is limited.) Generally, such dimensional reference points occur when it is critical to show the measured distance to the actual face of a material. Dots are also used for joint centerlines if those points occur off the grid-lines. Column centerlines frequently are located between grid-lines to accommodate more dimensionally critical enclosure and finish materials.

MODULAR DIMENSIONED WORKING DRAWINGS:

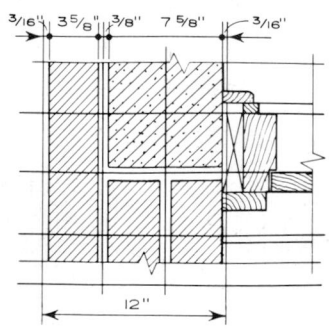

The large-scale detail at the left and the small-scale assembly drawing on the right illustrate modular drafting conventions as used at two different scales.

Large-scale details show the relationship of the components to the grid. Some architects prefer not to draw the entire grid on such details but include only those used as dimensional reference points on the small-scale drawings.

Small-scale assembly drawings such as plans, sections and elevations diagram the relationship of components. Since modular products are normally 4" multiples to joint centerlines, most dimensions are in multiples of 4". Arrowheads indicate dimensions are to grid-lines.

LARGE SCALE RELATIONSHIPS

Byron C. Bloomfield, AIA; Madison, Wisconsin

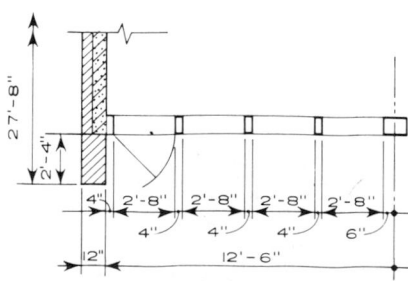

SMALL SCALE ASSEMBLY DRAWING

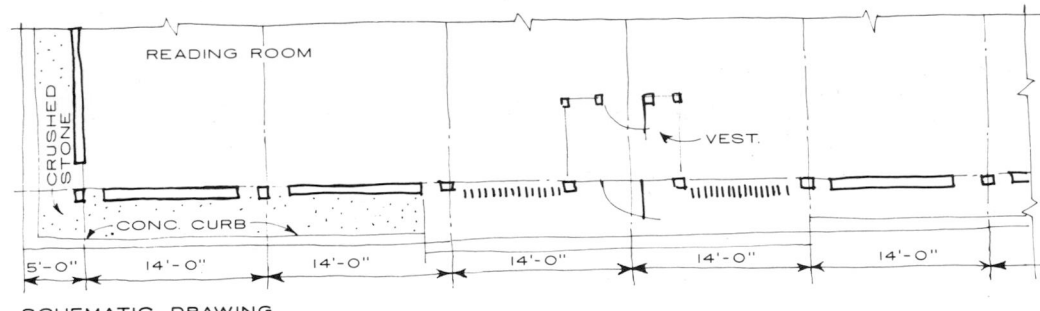

SCHEMATIC DRAWING

SCHEMATIC DESIGN

Modular schematic drawings differ little from conventionally used planning techniques where the structure is reflected in the planning. The structural grid may be derived from design studies which have indicated the best planning grid for the particular building type. Basic dimensions are assumed to be multiples of 4″ making it necessary to indicate only a few dimensions such as column spacing and overall dimensions. Components such as doors, windows, etc., are understood to be modular for easy adjustment in the preliminary and working drawing phases of the project.

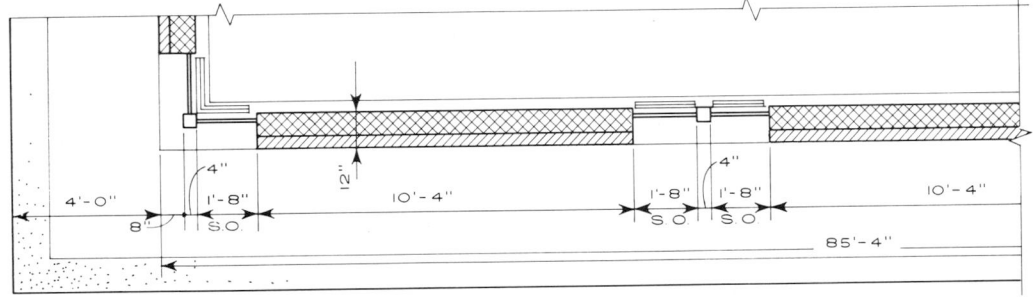

DESIGN DRAWING

DESIGN DEVELOPMENT

Modular design development drawings require few dimensions since all important component dimensions such as door widths, windows, walls, etc., are assumed to be modular and can be easily scaled to 4″ increments during conversion to working drawings. Column and overall dimensions are generally useful for client discussions and area calculations. Absence of excessive dimensions improves the communicative value of the drawings for discussions of plan functions. Ability to scale the drawings enables a number of personnel to develop the working drawings with a minimum of checking with each other.

WORKING DRAWING

Modular working drawings adhere to the principle that the plan should reflect the relationship of assemblies throughout the structure. The plan indicates the materials of each assembly and identifies the basic dimensional relationships among such elements. Arrowheads provide grid-line reference points for large-scale details found on subsequent sheets among the working drawings. Since modular materials and components are normally even increments of 4″ from joint centerline to joint centerline, working drawing dimensioning is grossly simplified and chances of error reduced.

WORKING DRAWING
MODULAR PLAN DRAWINGS

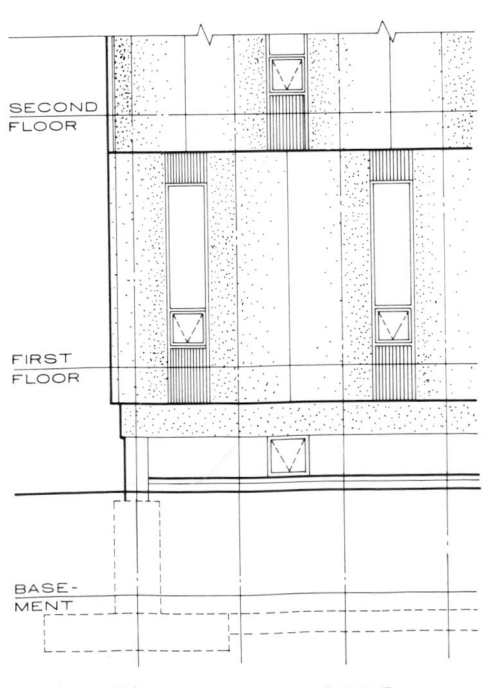

ELEVATION (PARTIAL) NO SCALE

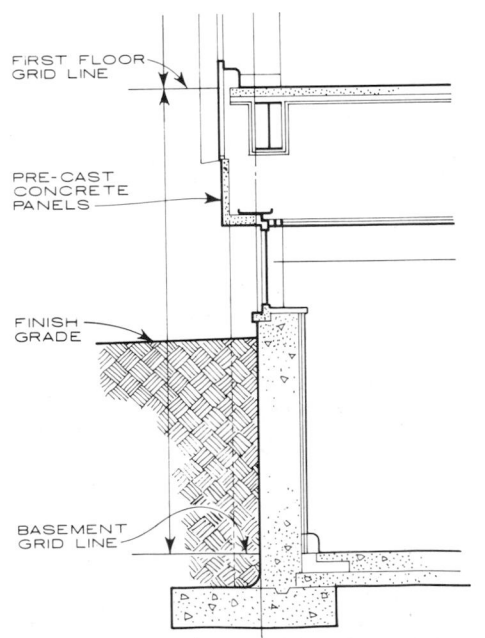

CROSS SECTION (PARTIAL) NO SCALE

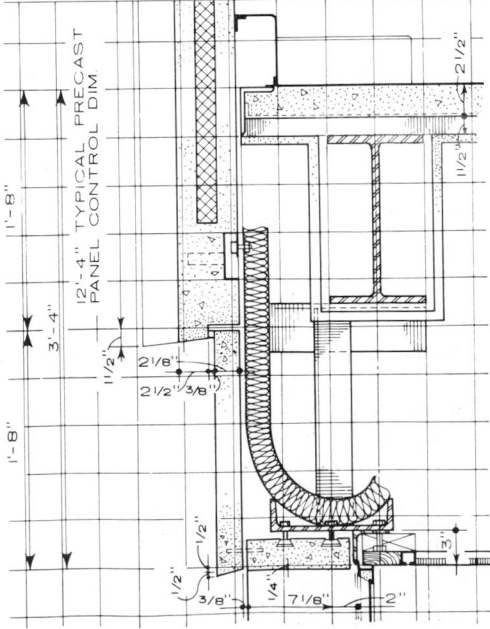

LARGE SCALE DETAIL (PARTIAL)
NO SCALE

Above illustrations from work of Linn Smith & Assoc. and Tarapata-MacMahon Assoc. published in "Modular Practice," John Wiley & Sons.

Byron C. Bloomfield, AIA; Madison, Wisconsin

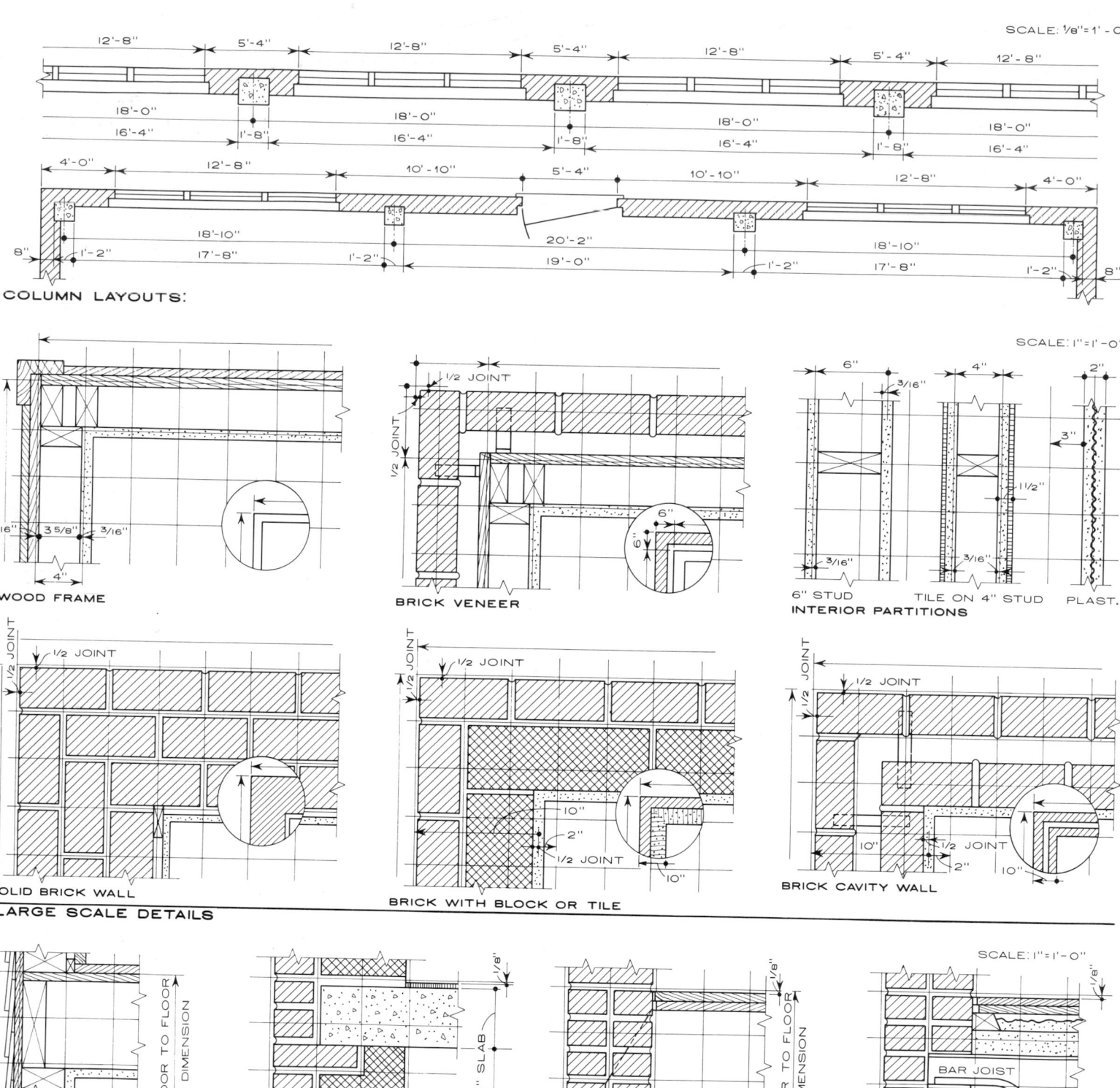

SCALE: 1/8"=1'-0"

COLUMN LAYOUTS:

SCALE: 1"=1'-0"

WOOD FRAME

BRICK VENEER

6" STUD   TILE ON 4" STUD   PLAST.

INTERIOR PARTITIONS

SOLID BRICK WALL

BRICK WITH BLOCK OR TILE

BRICK CAVITY WALL

LARGE SCALE DETAILS

WOOD FRAME   SLAB   WOOD JOIST   BAR JOIST

SCALE: 1"=1'-0"

FLOOR CONSTRUCTION DETAILS

NOTES AND REFERENCES:

Illustration credits——
p. 654 – Dimensional Characteristics of Building Products from Modular Building Standards Assn.
p. 654 – Large Scale Relationships and Small-Scale
Assembly Drawing by S. R. Kent for Canadian Standards
Association.
p. 655 – "Modular Practice," Modular Building Standards Association. John Wiley & Sons, Inc.

Byron C. Bloomfield, AIA; Madison, Wisconsin

p. 656 – "Graphic Standards," 5th Edition. Pages by
Prentice Bradley, AIA. John Wiley & Sons, Inc.

A single comprehensive reference is available on modular
coordination principles and practices. The text covers
use of modular drafting from schematic design through
working drawings with examples drawn from architectural offices using the dimensioning method. American
and Canadian Standards for manufacture of modular materials and products are included along with information
for contractors.

See "Modular Practice," Modular Building Standards
Association, Edited by R. P. Darlington, M. W. Isenberg,
and D. A. Pierce. 198 pages, 8½ x 11, Illustrated. Published by John Wiley & Sons, Inc.

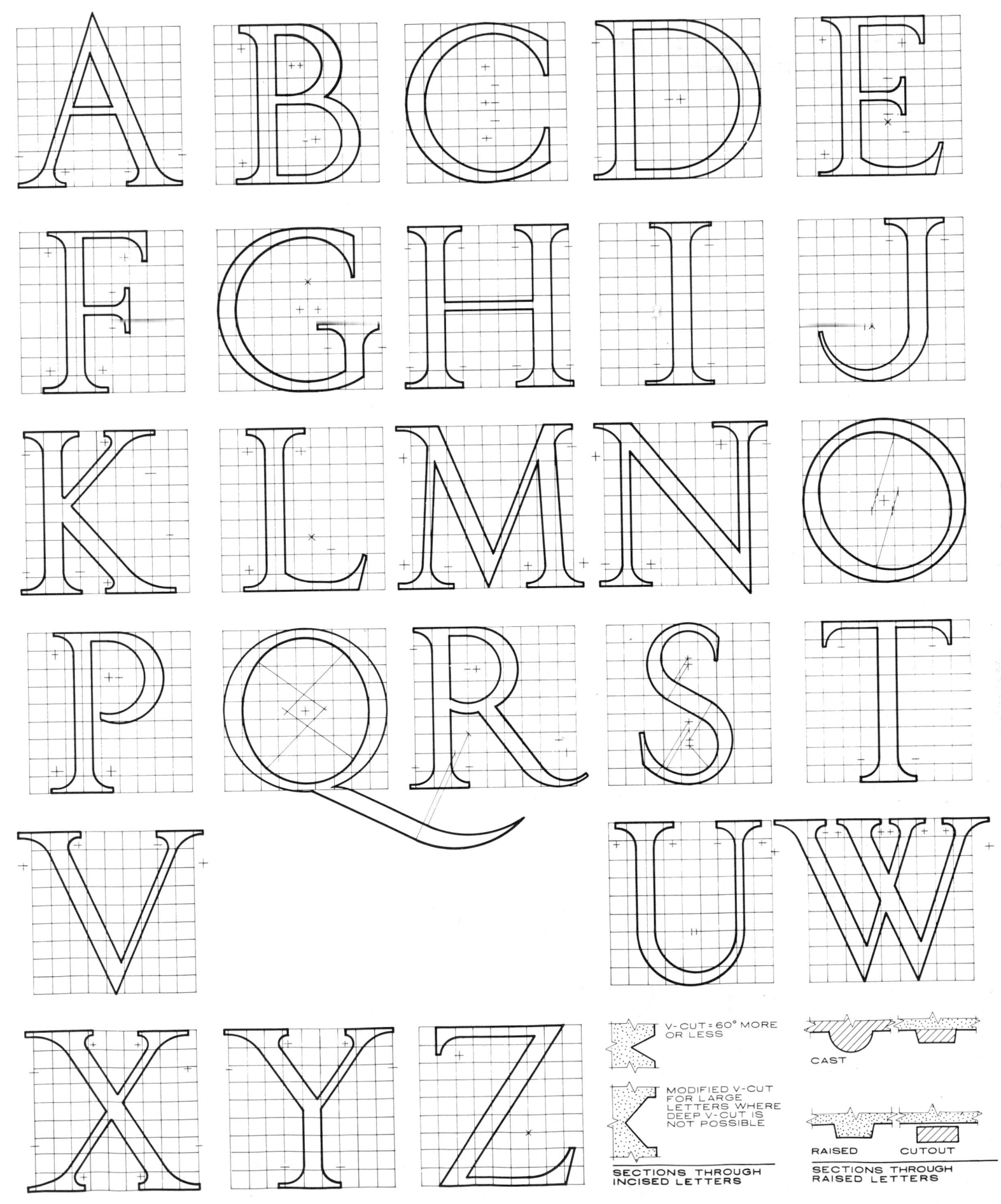

V-CUT = 60° MORE
OR LESS

MODIFIED V-CUT
FOR LARGE
LETTERS WHERE
DEEP V-CUT IS
NOT POSSIBLE

SECTIONS THROUGH
INCISED LETTERS

CAST

RAISED   CUTOUT

SECTIONS THROUGH
RAISED LETTERS

PARALINE DRAWING includes pictorial types in which parallel lines of the object are parallel in the drawing. The most important of these are isometric, dimetric, and oblique drawings.

ORTHOGRAPHIC DRAWING includes all drawing types in which the projectors are perpendicular to the plane of projection. The most common are multi-view, isometric, dimetric, and trimetric.

AXONOMETRIC DRAWING includes paraline types on which measurements can usually be made only on axis direction lines. Widely used axonometric drawings are isometric and dimetric.

OBLIQUE DRAWING has one set of planes parallel to the plane of projection. The parallel projectors are at an oblique angle to show three dimensions of the object. Measurements can be made in any direction on planes parallel to the plane of projection.

AXIS LINES are the three mutually perpendicular lines which meet at the corner of a box shape and all lines parallel to them.

SOME TYPES OF DRAWINGS

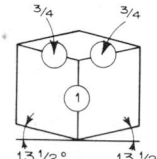 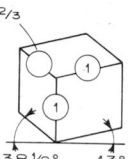 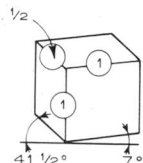

DIMETRIC SCALES—ANGLES FORMULA

$$\cos a = \frac{\sqrt{2H^2 - V^2}}{2H}$$ In this formula:

a = one of two equal angles between the projection of axes. H = one of two equal scales. V = third scale. A = a − 90° = angle with horizontal of two equal axes of symmetrical dimetric. A = one angle with the horizontal of unsymmetrical dimetric. B = 90° − 2A = second angle with horizontal of unsymmetrical dimetric.

THE FORMULA ABOVE can be used to work out the various combinations of scales and angles for dimetric drawing. Three of the most useful of these scales and angles are given on the diagrams of cubes above. The scales are relative ones with the larger scales given as 1 and the smaller ones as fractions.

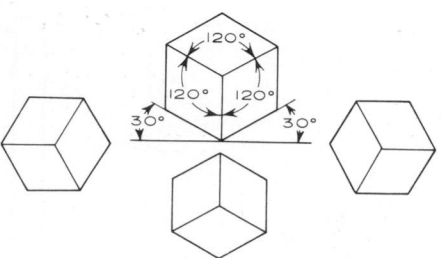

THE THREE ISOMETRIC AXIS must be kept 120° apart since they are required to be at the same angle to the plane of projection in order to be foreshortened equally and to be at the same scale. When one axis is horizontal or vertical the other two axes can be drawn with the 30° x 60° triangle on the T—square. These four positions are illustrated above. The vertical position of one axis is widely used. It allows the top or bottom of the object to be shown. The axes can be at any angle if they are kept 120° apart.

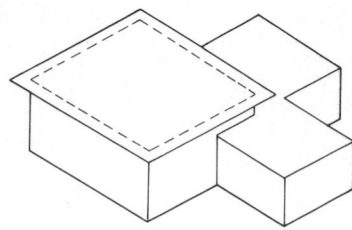

ADVANTAGES of isometric drawing: Use of one scale on the three axes; use of a standard triangle; fairly easy to dimension; and looks neat when dimension lines, arrows, and numerals are kept in isometric forms.

DISADVANTAGES: Equal importance is given to each of the three visible planes. There is no opportunity to emphasize complex and important areas and subordinate blank unimportant ones. Only one picture effect is possible with the three visible planes and unsatisfactory line relations cannot be avoided.

ISOMETRIC DRAWING – MEASURE ON AXES ONLY – ONE SCALE

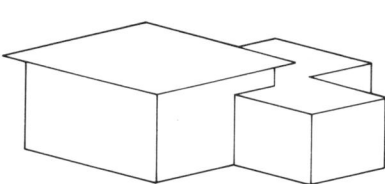

SYMMETRICAL DIMETRIC DRAWING is very useful to reduce the top or bottom area of the object which may be large and blank in an isometric. Only the setup having a common fractional scale relation which can be found on standard scales is illustrated here. When it is desired to make the top or bottom area of a symmetrical dimetric larger than in isometric, it may be found that plan oblique drawing is better for the purpose. Symmetrical dimetric gives equal emphasis to the two wall areas. When one wall area should be emphasized in a paraline drawing, either unsymmetrical dimetric or elevation oblique drawing can be used.

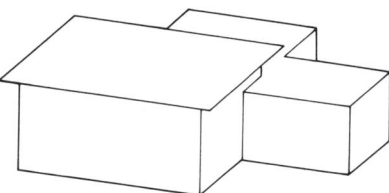

UNSYMMETRICAL DIMETRIC DRAWING allows emphasis on one or two of the three planes represented and subordination of the other two or one. It allows for a great deal of variation in the relative importance of the three sets of areas for best pictorial effect. This type of paraline drawing is for many objects the most natural and best in its pictorial effect. A symmetrical dimetric setup of scales and angles can be turned with one of the two equal axes in a vertical position for unsymmetrical dimetric. When the two equal scale axes are turned to produce equal angles with the horizontal the setup is symmetrical.

DIMETRIC DRAWING – MEASURE ON AXES ONLY – TWO SCALES ARE REQUIRED

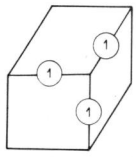  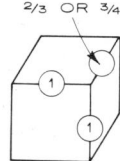 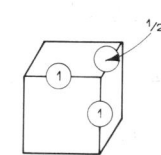

CAVALIER OBLIQUE   **GENERAL OBLIQUE**   **CABINET OBLIQUE**

OBLIQUE DRAWINGS ARE CLASSIFIED according to scale used on the receding lines as Cavalier Oblique Drawings, General Oblique Drawings, and Cabinet Oblique Drawings. Cavalier Oblique is easy to draw since the one scale is used on all axes. However the receding lines appear too long. Cabinet Oblique uses one half scale on receding lines which appear too short. General Oblique drawing uses a scale in between full and half scale to obtain better proportions which give a more satisfactory representation of the appearance of the object. Two thirds and three fourths scale give good proportions and either may be used on the receding lines.

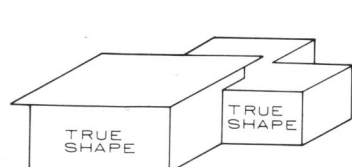

IN ELEVATION OBLIQUE DRAWING a set of vertical planes is parallel to the picture plane and has lines and areas drawn true shape. Any angle can be chosen for the receding lines which are drawn from the true shape areas. It is therefore possible to show top or bottom and either side of the object attached to the front in varying amounts. A low angle of receding lines shows more of the side and less top or bottom while a large angle with the horizontal will show more of the top or bottom and less of the side. Some irregular wall plane shapes are explained better in oblique drawing than in other types of pictorial drawing.

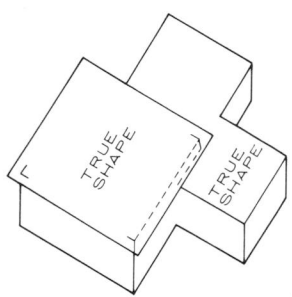

PLAN OBLIQUE DRAWING has plan planes true shape. Turn the plan of the object to a satisfactory angle and then draw verticals, which are the receding lines. The plan can be turned at any angle. Therefore both wall planes can be given equal emphasis, or one can be subordinated.

OBJECTS WITH IRREGULAR or unusual plan shapes sometimes explain more clearly in plan oblique than any other type of pictorial drawing.

OBLIQUE DRAWINGS—MEASURE ON AXES OF RECEDING AREAS—ANY DIRECTION ON TRUE SHAPES

C. Leslie Martin; University of Cincinnati; Cincinnati, Ohio

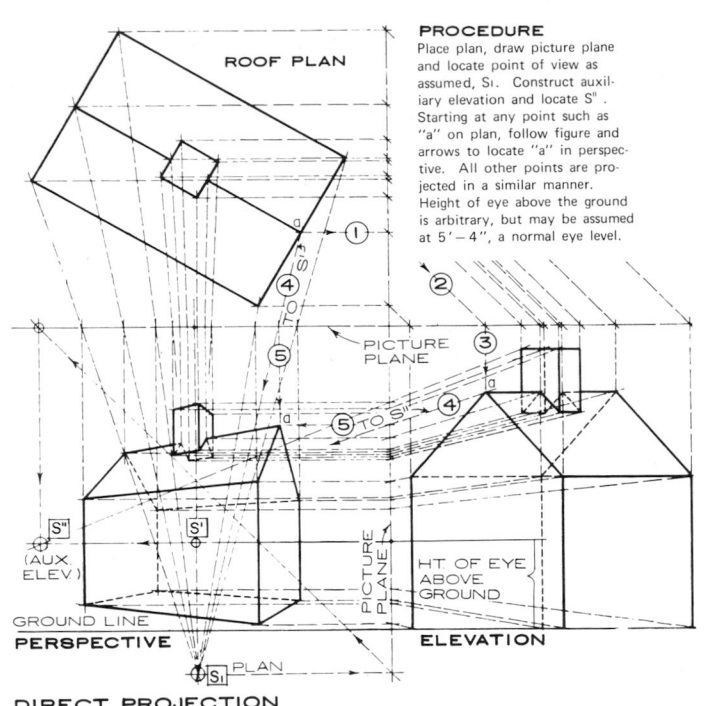

PROCEDURE

Place plan, draw picture plane and locate point of view as assumed, S₁. Construct auxiliary elevation and locate S". Starting at any point such as "a" on plan, follow figure and arrows to locate "a" in perspective. All other points are projected in a similar manner. Height of eye above the ground is arbitrary, but may be assumed at 5'-4", a normal eye level.

ROOF PLAN

PICTURE PLANE

PERSPECTIVE | ELEVATION

S" (AUX ELEV) S' HT OF EYE ABOVE GROUND

GROUND LINE PICTURE PLANE

DIRECT PROJECTION

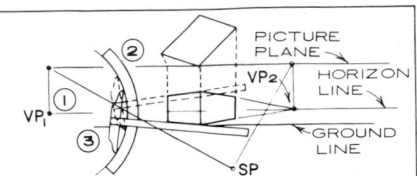

PROCEDURE WHEN VANISHING POINTS ARE OFF BOARD

1. Draw any arc from VP₁.
2. Place a cardboard cutout against curve of circle.
3. Place head of t-square against cutout, making sure both ends of head are always touching cutout, and then draw lines.

PICTURE PLANE
HORIZON LINE
GROUND LINE
VP₁   VP₂
SP

PROCEDURE (ONE POINT)

Draw A.B.C.D., section which is cut by P.P., at any desired scale, and locate S' (point of view in elevation) on line of sight from S₁. Locate the 45° vanishing points VL and VR on either side of S' and as distant as S₁ is from the picture plane. All lines parallel to P.P. will remain parallel and all plane figures parallel to P.P. will show their true shape. Vertical lines will be vertical in perspective. Horizontal lines parallel to P.P. will be horizontal. Horizontal lines perpendicular to P.P. will vanish at S'. Horizontal lines at 45° to F.P. (used to measure distances ⊥ to P.P.) will vanish at 45°VPs.

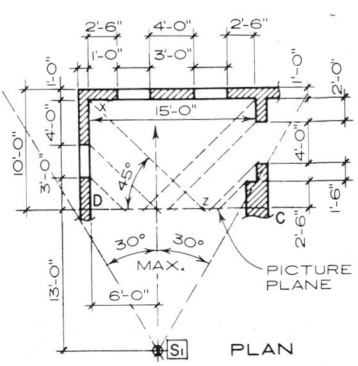

PLAN

HALF SCALE DRAWING OF ASSUMED CONDITIONS

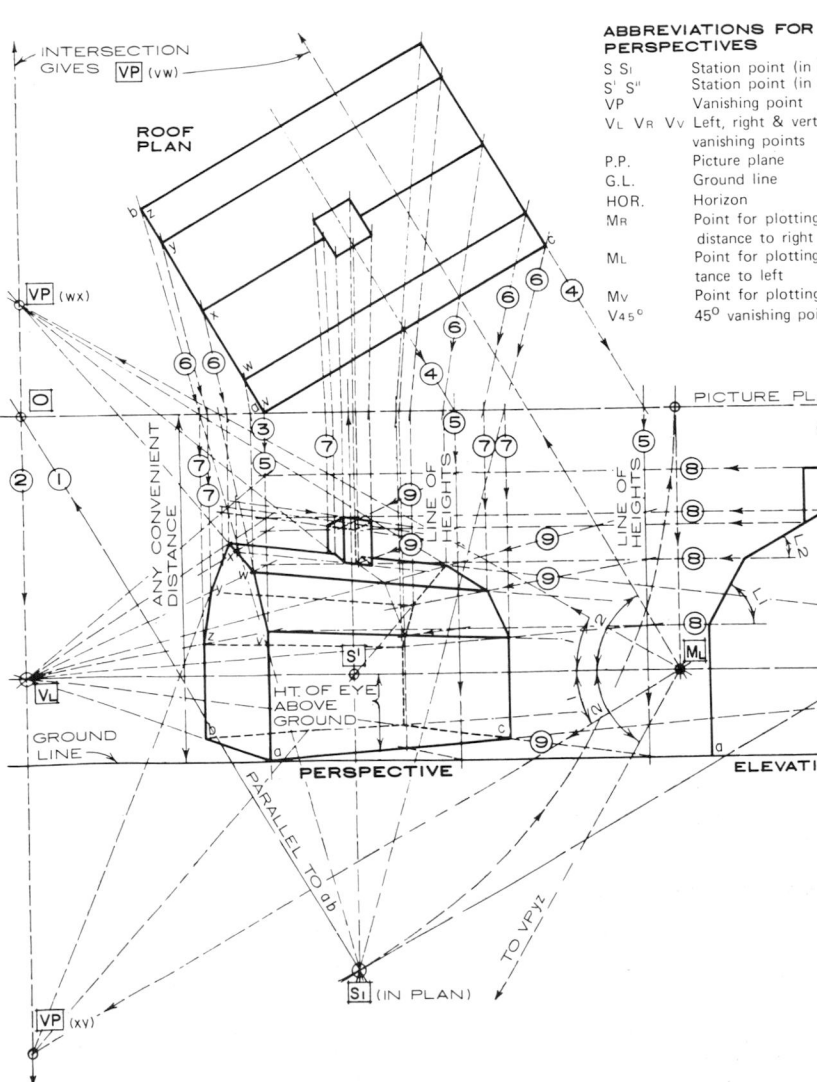

ABBREVIATIONS FOR PERSPECTIVES

S S₁	Station point (in plan)
S' S"	Station point (in elev)
VP	Vanishing point
VL VR Vv	Left, right & vertical vanishing points
P.P.	Picture plane
G.L.	Ground line
HOR.	Horizon
MR	Point for plotting distance to right
ML	Point for plotting distance to left
Mv	Point for plotting hts.
V45°	45° vanishing point

ROOF PLAN

INTERSECTION GIVES VP (vw)

PICTURE PLANE

LINE OF HEIGHTS

HT OF EYE ABOVE GROUND

GROUND LINE

PERSPECTIVE | ELEVATION

PARALLEL TO ab

PARALLEL TO ac

TO VPyz

S₁ (IN PLAN)

VP (xy)

TO VP (yz)

TWO POINT OR ANGULAR PERSPECTIVE ALSO KNOWN AS "OFFICE METHOD"

ACTUAL WIDTHS ACTUAL HTS

VL (45° VP) HOR. VR (45° VP)

GROUND LINE

ACTUAL DEPTHS (⊥ TO P.P.)

VISUAL FIELD WITHIN 60° CONE

"ONE-POINT" OR PARALLEL PERSPECTIVE

PROCEDURE FOR TWO POINT PERSPECTIVE

PLAN: Assume picture plane (P.P.) and locate plan of object as desired. Assume point of view, or station point, S₁. To minimize apparent distortion, this point is commonly taken about opposite the center of the drawing, and far enough away to keep the field of view within about 60° latitude.

ELEVATION: Locate ground line where convenient. Place elevation as indicated, or measure heights directly on any vertical "Line of Heights". Locate S' on vertical through S₁ and at assumed height above ground line.

PERSPECTIVE: Through S' draw horizon. Draw parallel to principal horizontal lines of object through S₁ (in plan), and project intersections with P.P. down to the horizon, giving principal vanishing points VL and VR.

NOTE: To find VPs for inclined lines, swing S₁ about 0 into P.P. and project to horizon at ML. Draw through ML parallel to actual slopes (angles 1 and 2) to intersection with vertically projected line through VL. Vanishing points for inclined lines are not absolutely essential, but are frequently found very useful as is shown in the determination of the inclined lines of the gambrel roof in this perspective. Follow arrows and numbered lines. See figures 4 and 1 on following page.

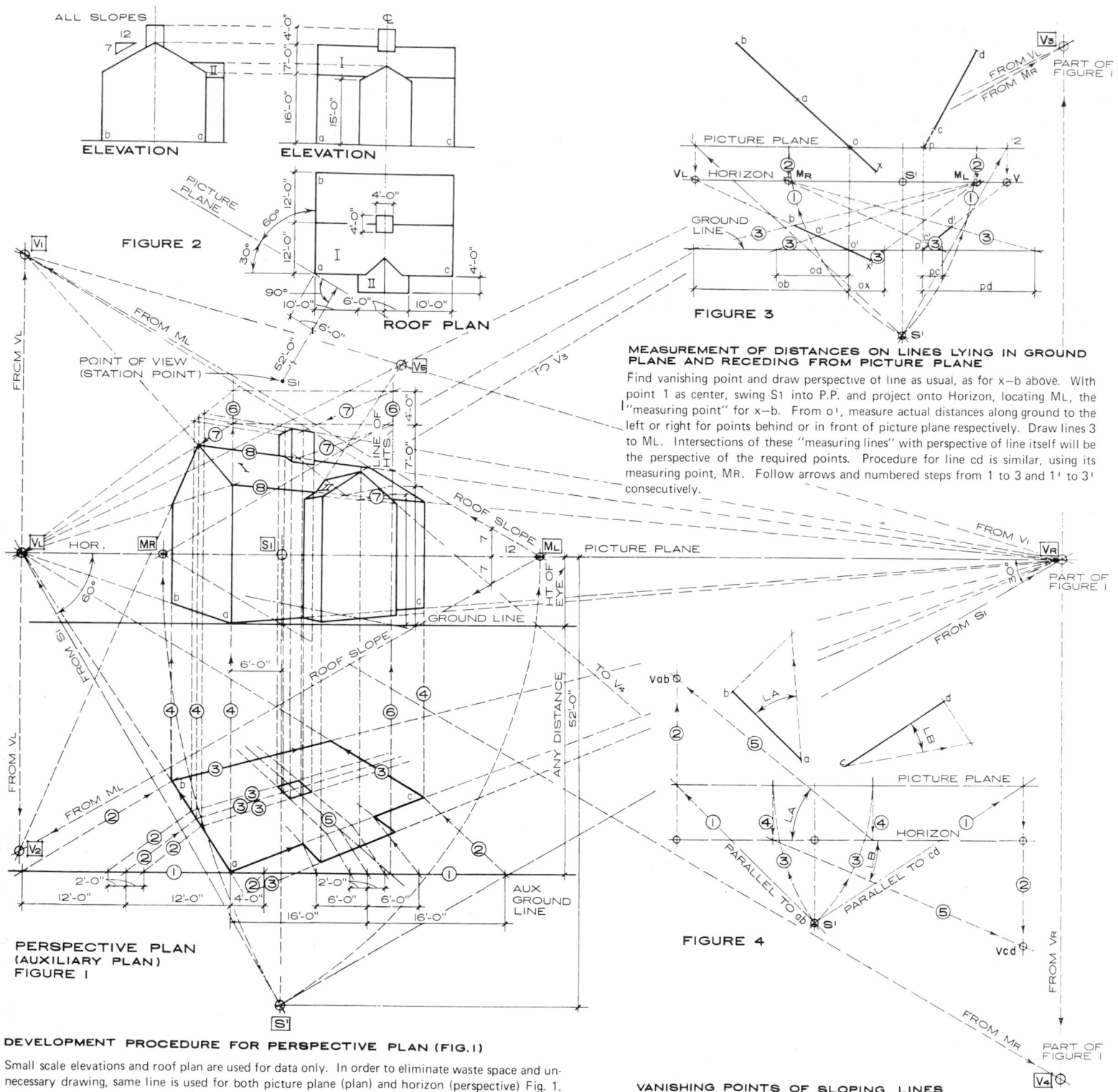

ALL SLOPES
12
7

ELEVATION

ELEVATION

FIGURE 2

ROOF PLAN

PICTURE PLANE

POINT OF VIEW
(STATION POINT)

PERSPECTIVE PLAN
(AUXILIARY PLAN)
FIGURE I

FIGURE 3

MEASUREMENT OF DISTANCES ON LINES LYING IN GROUND PLANE AND RECEDING FROM PICTURE PLANE

Find vanishing point and draw perspective of line as usual, as for x–b above. With point 1 as center, swing S1 into P.P. and project onto Horizon, locating ML, the "measuring point" for x–b. From o', measure actual distances along ground to the left or right for points behind or in front of picture plane respectively. Draw lines 3 to ML. Intersections of these "measuring lines" with perspective of line itself will be the perspective of the required points. Procedure for line cd is similar, using its measuring point, MR. Follow arrows and numbered steps from 1 to 3 and 1' to 3' consecutively.

FIGURE 4

DEVELOPMENT PROCEDURE FOR PERSPECTIVE PLAN (FIG.1)

Small scale elevations and roof plan are used for data only. In order to eliminate waste space and unnecessary drawing, same line is used for both picture plane (plan) and horizon (perspective) Fig. 1.

Locate S1 and draw S1 VL and S1 VR at angles made with P.P. by principal horizontal lines of building, thus locating the vanishing points VL and VR.

Locate ML and MR as shown in Fig. 3 or by laying off the distances VL ML = VL S1 and VR MR = VR S1.

Locate Vanishing points for roof lines V1, V2, V3, V4 as in Fig. 4. Draw V1 VR, the "vanishing trace" of main roof plane I and V3 VL correspondingly for secondary roof plane II. The intersection of these lines, V5, is the vanishing point for the line of intersection of the roof planes (the valley line).

Starting with the corner of the building, point a, draw perspectives of ab and ac. Measure the distances along these lines as described in Fig. 3. (The auxiliary or "sunken" plan gives better intersections and keeps the drawing cleaner).

Complete the plan in perspective by carrying lines to proper vanishing points. Verticals are drawn and heights are measured as usual. (See Two Point or Angular Perspective, known as "Office Method.")

Follow numbers and arrows consecutively from 1 to 8 inclusive.

VANISHING POINTS OF SLOPING LINES

It is frequently very useful to have available the vanishing point for a series of inclined parallel lines; the diagram above shows a procedure for directly locating any such points. Two cases are illustrated.

1. The line ab slopes upward from a to b at the angle A. Starting at S1, follow arrows and numbered steps 1 to 5 inclusive, locating Vab, which is the vanishing point for ab and all the lines parallel to it. Line cd slopes downward from c to d at the angle B.

2. Proceed as above, following arrows and numbered steps 1' to 5' inclusive. Vcd is the required vanishing point. Note that line 5 is drawn upward while 5¹ is downward.

NOTE:

Figures 3 and 4 are for general use, but are shown on this sheet in order to clarify important steps in the construction of Figure 1.

THREE POINT PERSPECTIVE BY DIRECT PROJECTION

SETTING UP THE WORKING LAYOUT – FIG. 1

1. Set Station Point in relation to plan. Its location fully determines the perspective.

2. From S_P in plan, draw the Central Visual Ray CVR_P toward center of interest of the object. Actually S is above (or below) the plan and CVR is at a slope. Line CVR_P is a vertical plane seen on edge; imagine this plan revolved into the paper about line CVR_P.

3. The height of S is laid off in this revolved plane. Choosing proper height is as important as location in plan (and an artistic judgment).

4. CVR_A at true slope is again drawn toward the center of interest (center of Forecourt Fig. 1.)

5. Still in the revolved view, edge view of Picture Plane PP_A is drawn at right angle to CVR_A. Its distance from S_A is arbitrary and determines only the scale of the drawing: as the distance increases the vanishing points spread and the size of the perspective increases.

6. Draw horizontally (i.e. parallel to CVR_P) from S_A to PP_A; this locates the Horizon.

7. Draw vertically (i.e. perpendicular to CVR_P) from S_A to PP_A; this locates the vanishing point of the verticals

8. Back in plan view, draw the Horizon through point (#6 above) at right angles to CVR_P.

9. Draw lines through S_P parallel to lines of building, to locate V_L and V_R on Horizon.

PROJECTING THE PERSPECTIVE – FIG. 2

10. If steps 1–9 are done at reduced scale (as in Fig. 1), transfer Horizon, Station Point, vanishing points to plan drawn at working scale. Mount plan with Horizon horizontal. V_v is located at a distance from Horizon taken from Fig. 1 along PP_A (indic. on drawing).

11. Draw a semi-circle on V_L – V_v as a diameter.

12. Swing S_P onto this with V_L as center, locating S_L. Check: V_R – S_L should be at right angles to V_L – V_v.

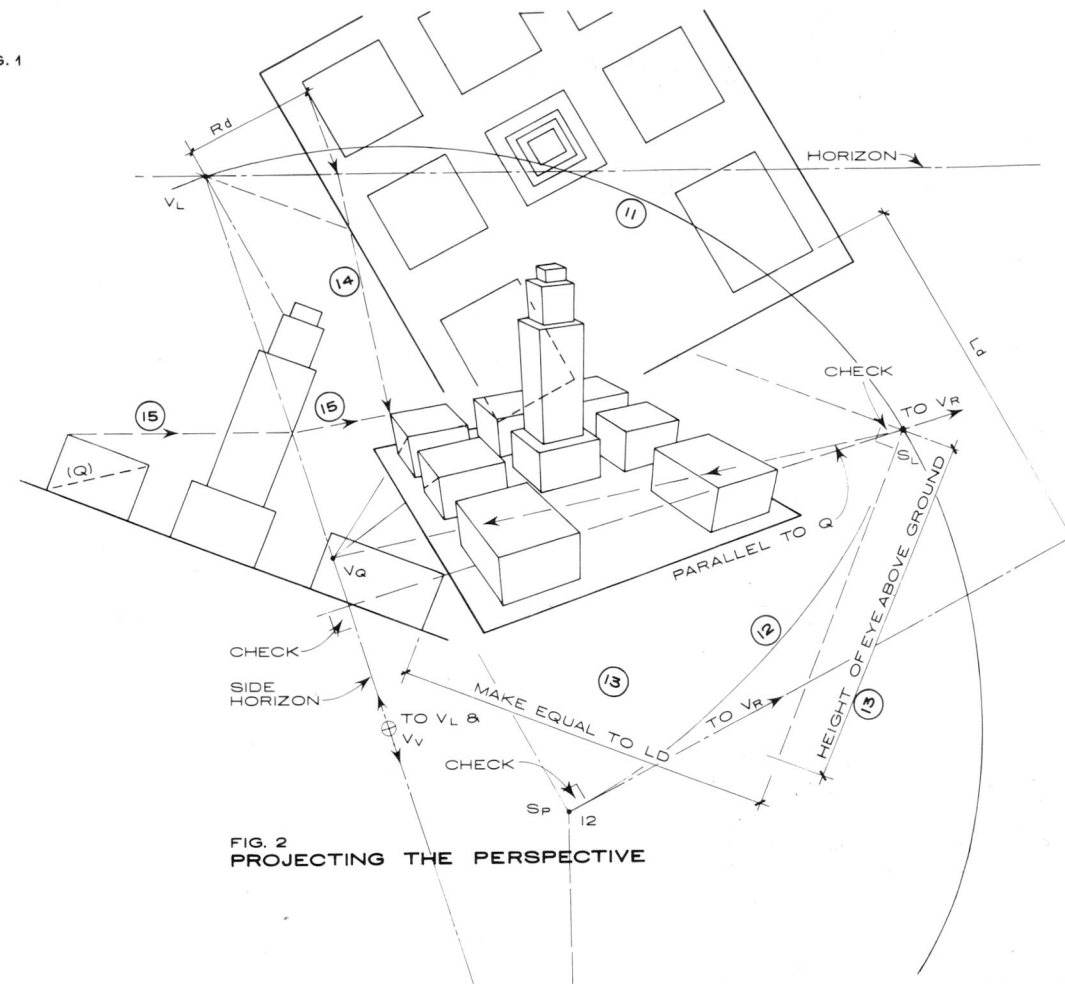
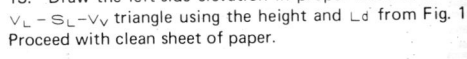

FIG. 2
PROJECTING THE PERSPECTIVE

13. Draw the left-side elevation in proper relation to the V_L – S_L – V_v triangle using the height and L_d from Fig. 1. Proceed with clean sheet of paper.

14. Project points in plan (which represent vertical lines) first to Horizon from S_P and from there to V_v.

15. Project points in side elev. (which represent horiz. lines) first to side Horizon V_L – V_v from S_L, and from there to V_R. Continue until the perspective is finished.

NOTES:

1. Step 13 is critical; the L_d and Horizon ht. must accurately match the corresponding distances in the working layout and in the plan.

2. Accuracy: The method is mathematically true and the perspective will be as accurate as the working layout, and the plan and elevation used.

3. Either the left side or the right side elevation (labeled Front elevation in Fig. 1) may be used or both for a cross-check. The elevation looking from the short leg of the V_L – S_P – V_R triangle, as in Fig. 1, is usually more convenient.

4. Vanishing points of inclined lines are found in same manner as in two-point perspective: see diagonal (Q) in Fig. 2.

5. The experienced delineator may omit steps 1 through 9 and start with an assumed V_L – V_R – V_v triangle. S_P will be found on the vertical through V_v and a semi-circle on V_L – V_R as a diameter; V_v as before. Note 1 above must be carefully observed and CVR must be aimed toward center of interest both in plan and elevation to avoid distortion.

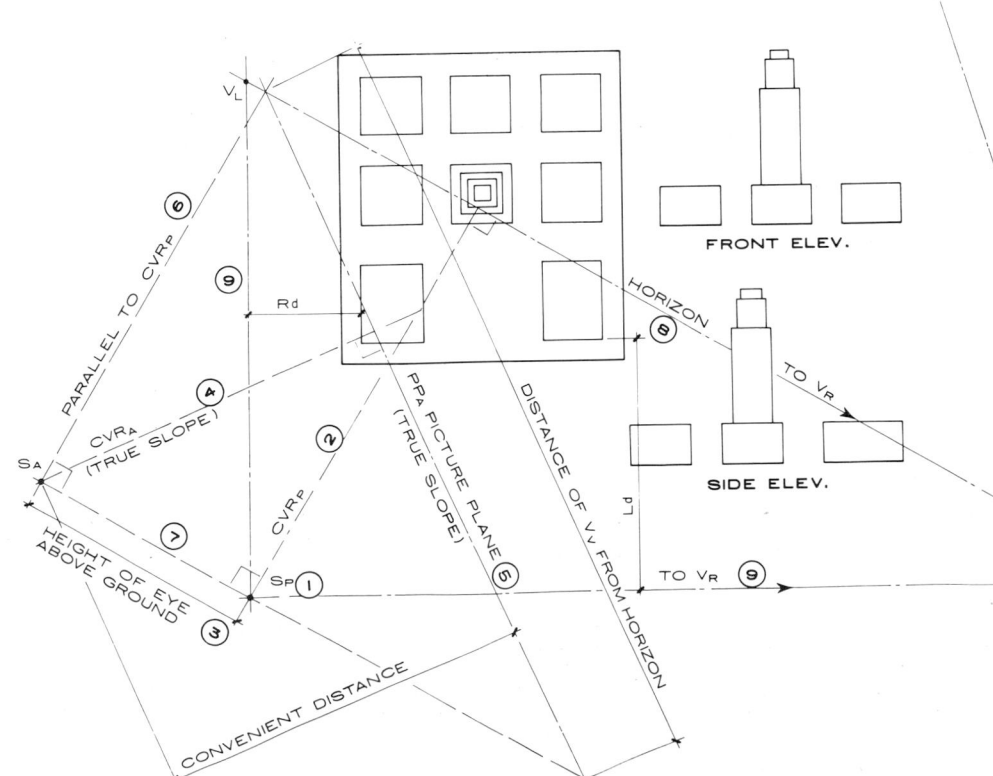

FRONT ELEV.

SIDE ELEV.

FIG. 1 (AT ⅔ SCALE OF PERSPECTIVE)
SETTING UP THE WORKING LAYOUT

The perspective method on this page was developed by Andre Halasz, A.I.A.

Charles L. Clarke; Seibert, Hunter, Shute & Plumley; Medford, Oregon

TO FIND DIRECTIONS OF JOINTS BISECT ANGLE OF FOCI AND EXTEND LINE
TEMPORARY PIN TO FIND STRING LENGTH
RADIUS = 1/2 MAJOR AXIS
AXIS
2
2
MAJOR AXIS
PIN
PIN
MINOR
1
1

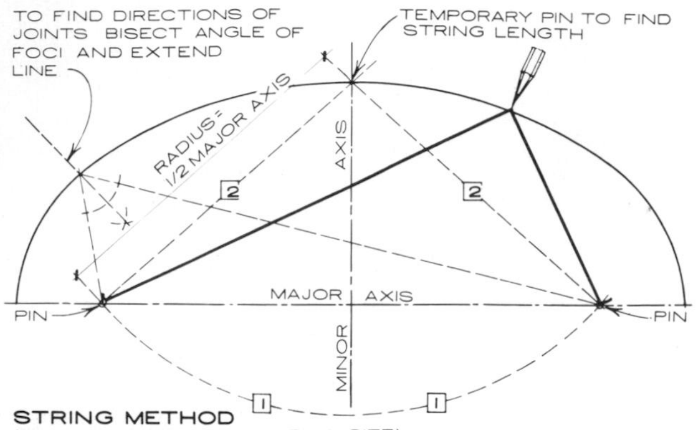

STRING METHOD
(FOR LARGE SCALE AND FULL SIZE)

C
C
HALF MINOR AXIS
HALF MAJOR AXIS
B
B
A
A

CARD METHOD

Move card or straight edge about, keeping B on major axis and A on minor axis. Wherever C falls place a dot.

2
4
2
4
4
3
3
1
3
1
5
5
1/2 MINOR AXIS
MAJOR
AXIS

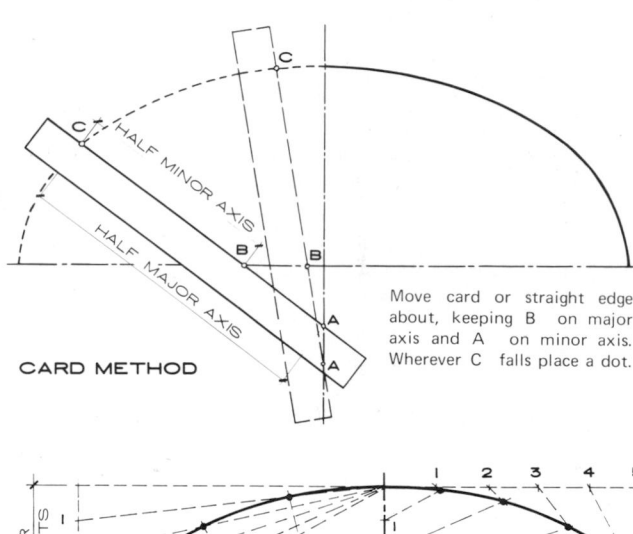

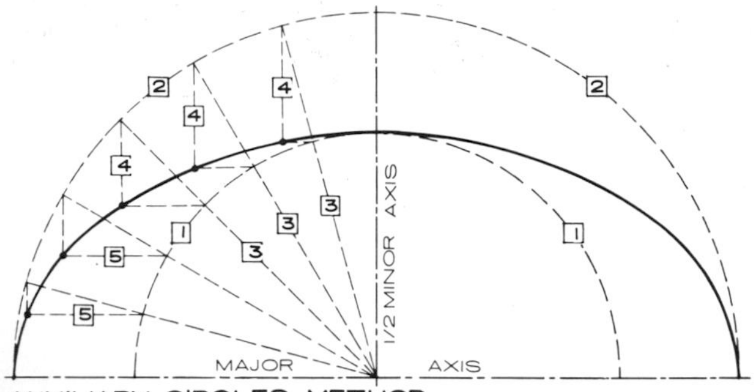

AUXILIARY CIRCLES METHOD

1 2 3 4 5 6
ANY NUMBER OF EQUAL PARTS
1 2 3 4 5 6
1 2 3 4 5
AXIS
MAJOR
AXIS
5 4 3 2 1
SAME NUMBER OF EQUAL PARTS AS HALF MINOR AXIS
MINOR

PARALLELOGRAM METHOD

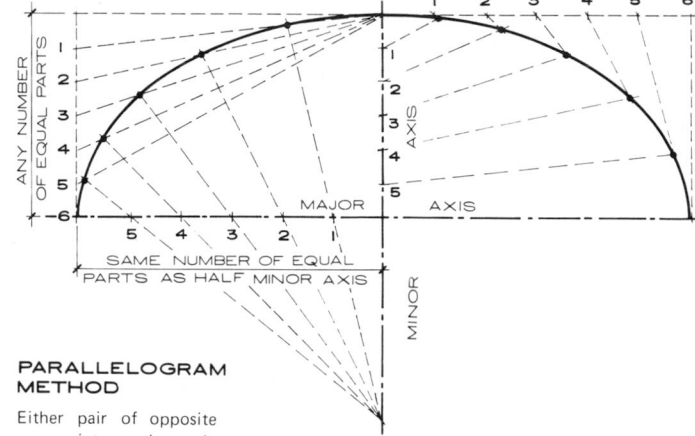

Either pair of opposite apex points may be used.

FROM C2
2
1
3
EQUAL
EQUAL
90°
AXIS
FROM C1
FROM C3
MAJOR AXIS
C1
C3
4
4
MINOR
C2

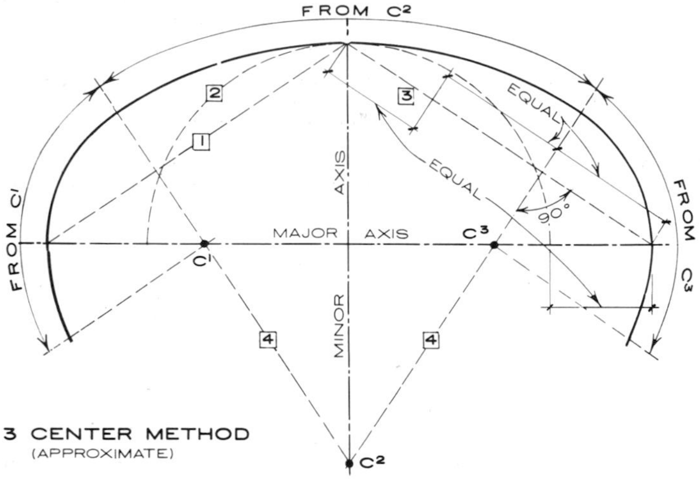

3 CENTER METHOD
(APPROXIMATE)

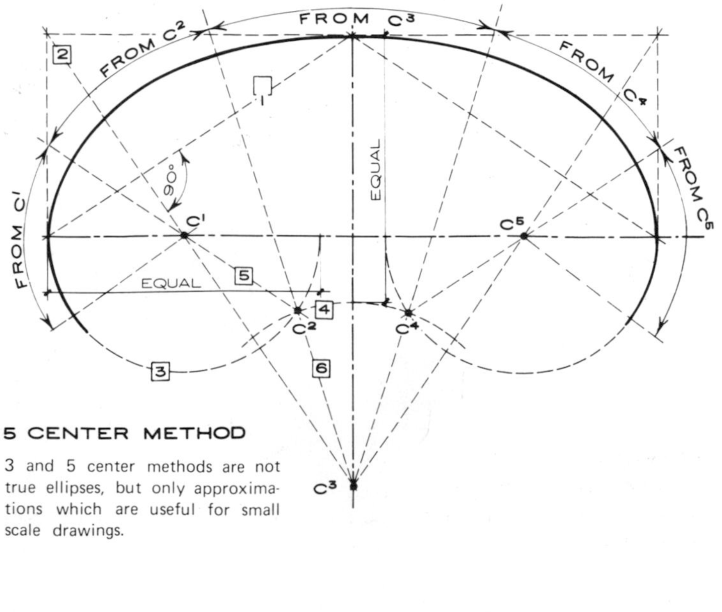

FROM C3
FROM C2
FROM C4
2
1
90°
EQUAL
FROM C1
FROM C5
C1
C5
EQUAL
5
4
C2
C4
3
6
C3

5 CENTER METHOD

3 and 5 center methods are not true ellipses, but only approximations which are useful for small scale drawings.

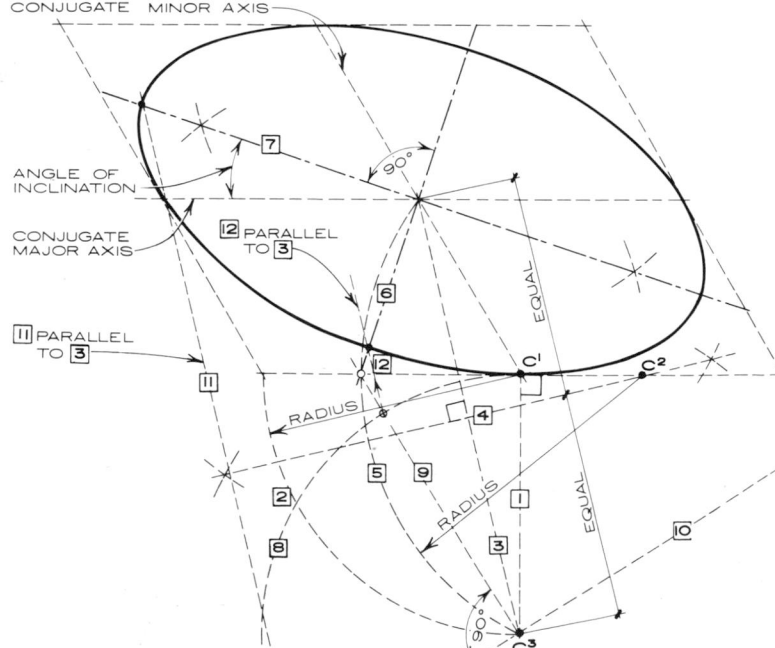

CONJUGATE MINOR AXIS
7
90°
ANGLE OF INCLINATION
CONJUGATE MAJOR AXIS
12 PARALLEL TO 3
6
EQUAL
11 PARALLEL TO 3
11
12
C1
C2
RADIUS
4
5
9
2
RADIUS
1
EQUAL
8
3
10
90°
C3

METHOD FOR FINDING THE ANGLE OF INCLINATION AND THEN THE TRUE LENGTHS OF THE MAJOR & MINOR AXES OF AN ELLIPSE TO BE INSCRIBED WITHIN A PARALLELOGRAM

NOTE:

1. Using the conjugate axes, the ellipse can be drawn directly by using the parallelogram method.
2. Using the true lengths of the axes, the ellipse may be drawn with any one of the methods illustrated on this page.

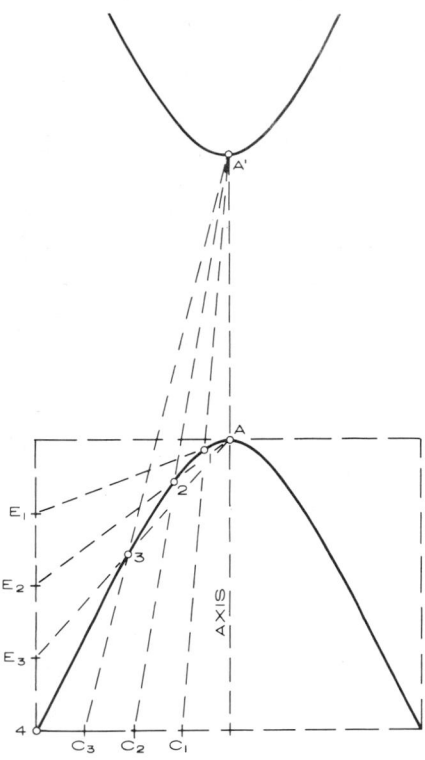

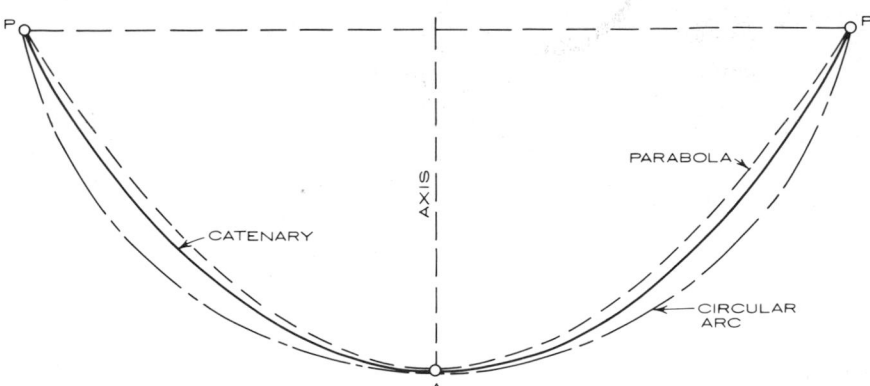

CATENARY

A catenary curve lies between a parabola and a circular arc drawn through the same three points, but is closer to the parabola. The catenary is not a conic section. The easiest method of drawing it is to tilt the drafting board and hang a very fine chain on it, and then prick guide points through the links of the chain.

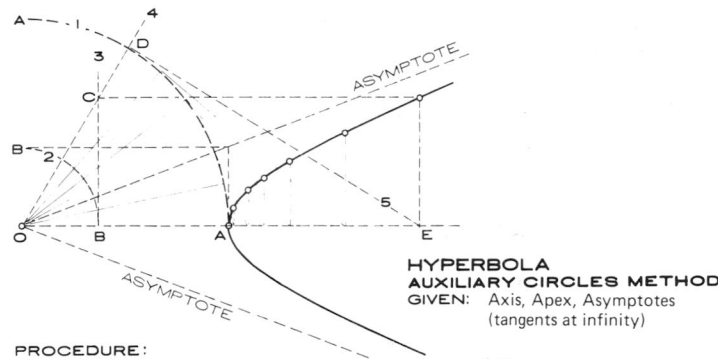

HYPERBOLA
PARALLELOGRAM METHOD
GIVEN:

Axis, two apexes (A and A') and a chord.

1. Draw surrounding parallelogram.
2. Divide chord in whole number of equal spaces (C_1, C_2, C_3, etc.).
3. Divide edge of parallelogram into same integral number of equal spaces (E_1, E_2, E_3, etc.).
4. Join A to points E on edge; join A' to points C on chord. Intersection of these rays are points on curve.

This method can be used equally well for any type of orthogonal or perspective projection, as shown by example of ellipse.

HYPERBOLA
AUXILIARY CIRCLES METHOD
GIVEN: Axis, Apex, Asymptotes
(tangents at infinity)

PROCEDURE:

1. Draw auxiliary circles with OB and OA as radii: note $\frac{OB}{OA}$ = slope of asymptote.
2. Erect perpendicular 3 where circle 2 intersects axis.
3. Draw any line 4 through 0, intersecting circle 1 at B and line 3 at C.
4. Draw line 5 through C parallel to axis.
5. Draw tangent 6 at D, intersecting axis at E.
6. Erect perpendicular 7 at E, intersecting 5 at P, a point on hyperbola.

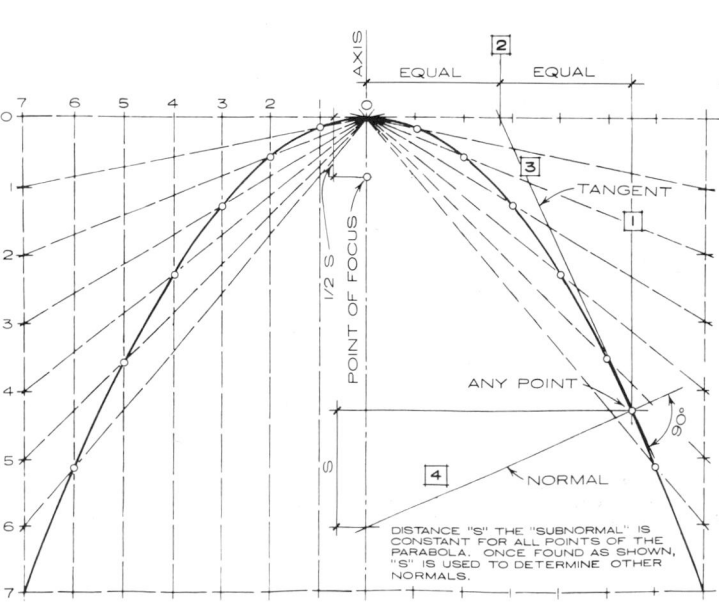

PARABOLA
PARALLELOGRAM METHOD

This method is comparable to the "Parallelogram Method" shown for the hyperbola above and the ellipse on previous page. The other apex 'A' is at infinity.

H. Seymour Howard, Jr., AIA; Oyster Bay, New York

PARABOLA
ENVELOPE OF TANGENTS

This method does not give points on the curve, but a series of tangents within which the parabola can be drawn.

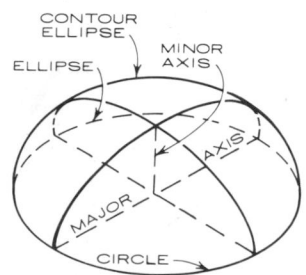

OBLATE SPHEROID

An ellipse rotated about its minor axis.

NOTES:

1. The dome shapes shown above are SURFACES OF POSITIVE CURVATURE, that is, the centers of both principal radii of curvature are on the same side of the surface.

2. SURFACES OF NEGATIVE CURVATURE (saddle shapes) such as those shown below, are surfaces in which the centers of the two principal radii of curvature are on opposite sides of the surface.

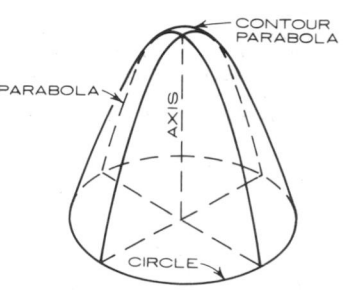

PROLATE SPHEROID

An ellipse rotated about its major axis.

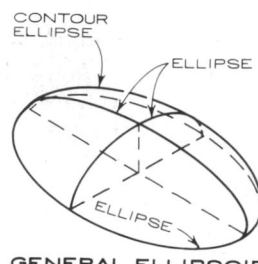

PARABOLOID OF REVOLUTION

A parabola rotated about its axis.

The elliptic paraboloid is similar, but its plan is an ellipse instead of circle, and vertical sections are varying parabolas.

GENERAL ELLIPSOID

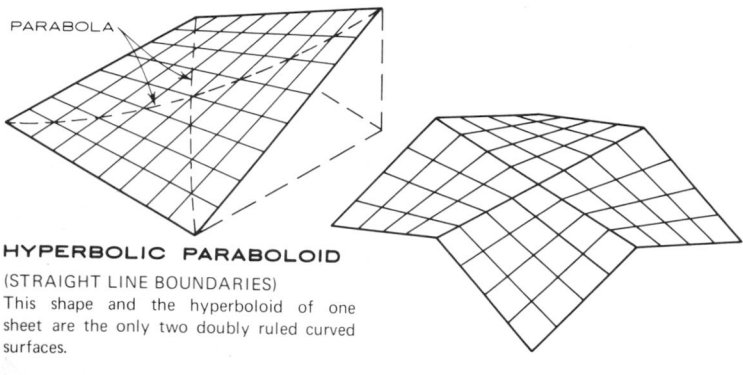

HYPERBOLIC PARABOLOID

(STRAIGHT LINE BOUNDARIES)

This shape and the hyperboloid of one sheet are the only two doubly ruled curved surfaces.

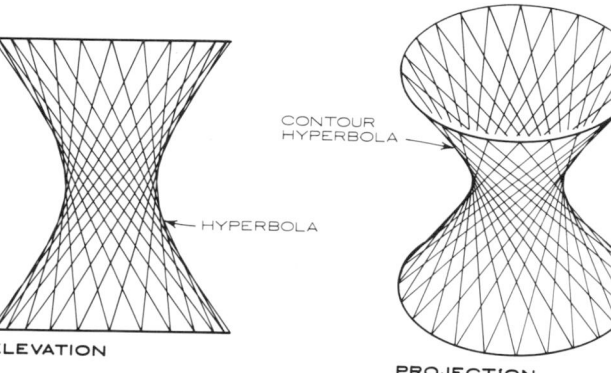

ELEVATION

PROJECTION

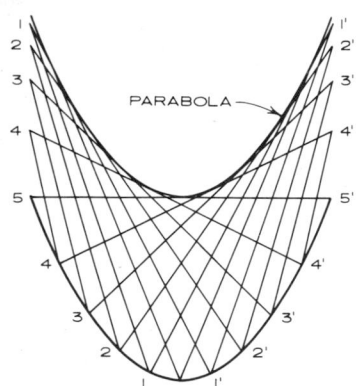

SECTION A-A

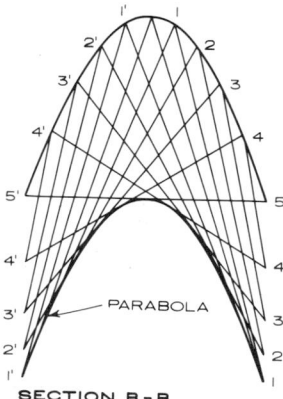

SECTION B-B

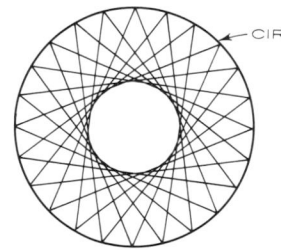

PLAN

HYPERBOLOID OF REVOLUTION
(OR HYPERBOLOID OR ONE SHEET)

NOTE:

This shape is a doubly ruled surface, which can also be drawn with ellipses as plan sections instead of the circles shown.

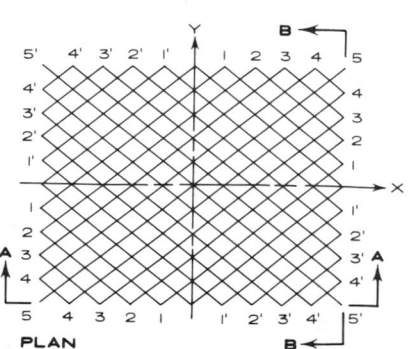

PLAN

HYPERBOLIC PARABOLOID
(PARABOLA BOUNDATIONS)

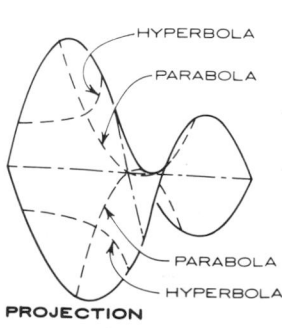

PROJECTION

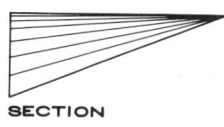

SECTION

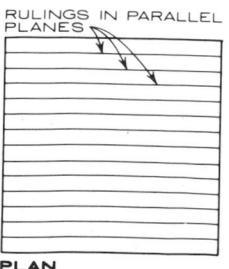

PLAN

CONOID
(SINGLY RULED SURFACE)

ELEVATION

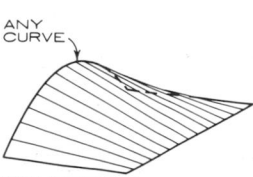

PROJECTION

Divide height into 8 parts and describe circle between 4th and 5th parts as eye of volute; inscribe
square in eye as shown; through the center and parallel to sides of square, draw lines bisecting the latter and divide each line, from center to side of
square, into 3 equal parts. These points are the
centers of arcs required and are taken in order
of succession starting at No. 1 shown on enlarged
drawing of eye. The limits of each separate arc
are obtained by producing the straight line joining two successive central points, starting with
arc No. 1.

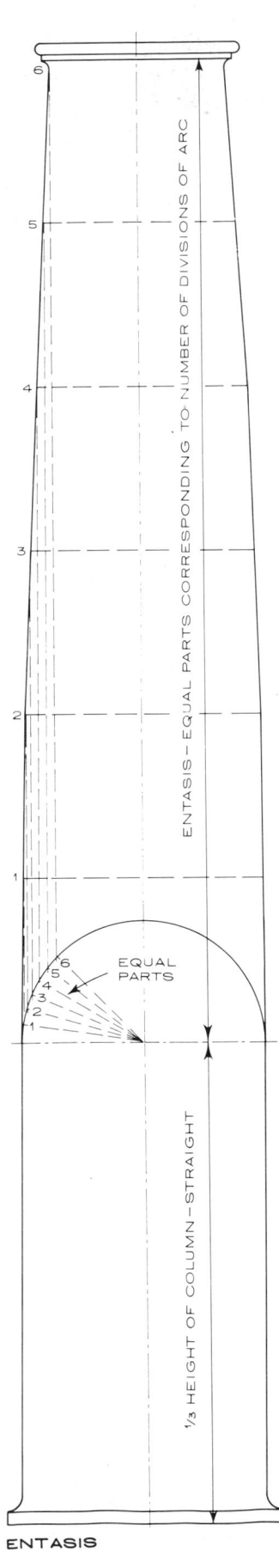

EYE AT LARGE SCALE

METHOD OF DRAWING A VOLUTE

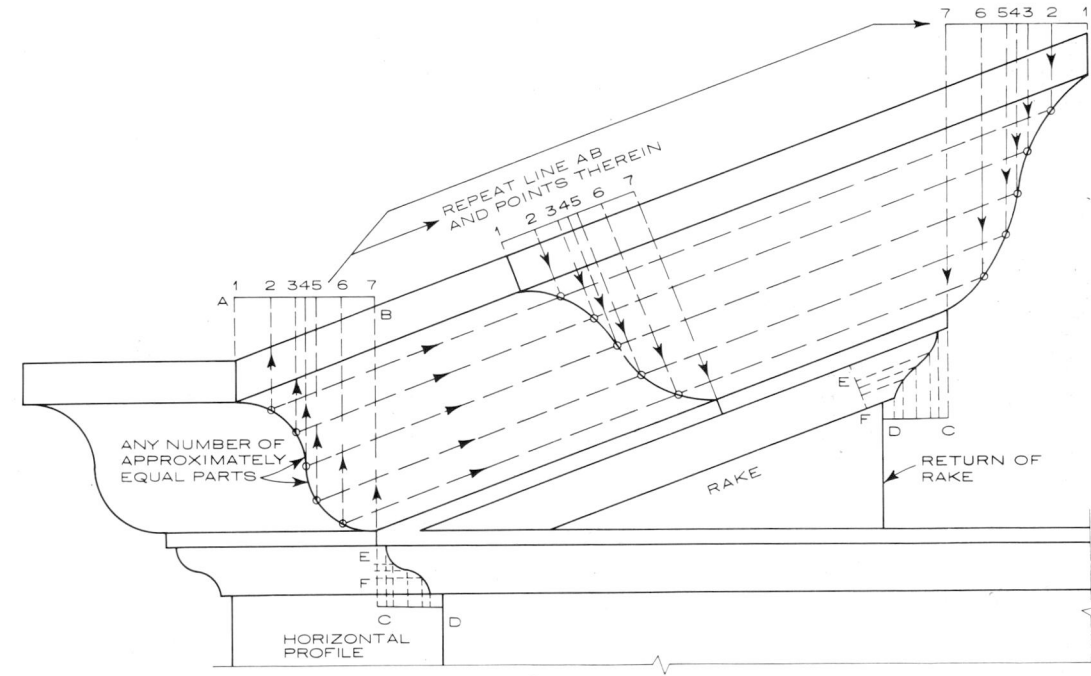

RAKING MOULDINGS

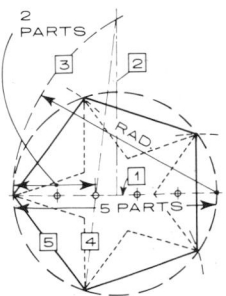

PENTAGON
(IN GIVEN CIRCLE)

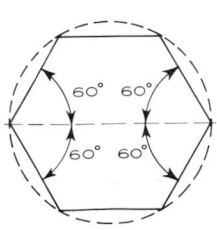

HEXAGON
(IN GIVEN CIRCLE)

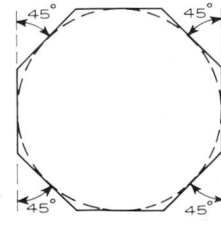

OCTAGON
(AROUND CIRCLE)

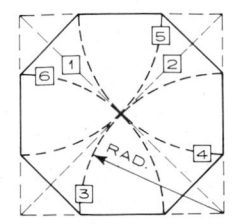

OCTAGON
(AROUND CIRCLE)

ENTASIS

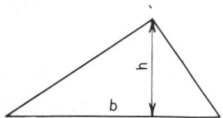

TRIANGLE
AREA = ½ ANY ALTITUDE × ITS BASE (ALTITUDE IS PERPENDICULAR DISTANCE TO OPPOSITE VERTEX OR CORNER.)

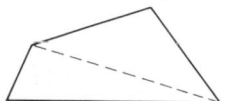

TRAPEZUM
(IRREGULAR QUADRILATERAL)
AREA = DIVIDE FIGURE INTO TWO TRIANGLES AND FIND AREAS AS ABOVE

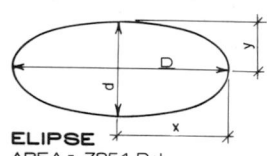

ELIPSE
AREA = .7854 Dd
APPROX. PERIMETER
$= \pi \sqrt{2(x^2+y^2)}$

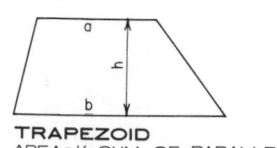

TRAPEZOID
AREA = ½ SUM OF PARALLEL SIDES × ALTITUDE
$A = \dfrac{h(a+b)}{2}$

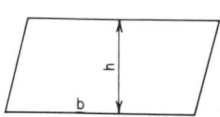

PARALLELOGRAM
AREA = EITHER SIDE × ALTITUDE

PARABOLA
AREA = $\dfrac{4 hb}{3}$

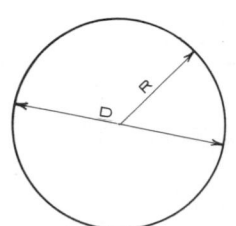

CIRCLE
AREA = $\dfrac{\pi D^2}{4} = \pi R^2$

CIRCUMFERENCE = $2\pi R = \pi D$
(π = 3.14159265359)

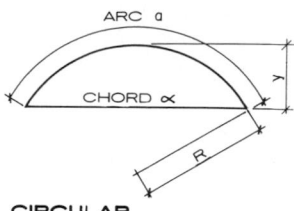

CIRCULAR SEGMENT
AREA = $\dfrac{(\text{LENGTH OF ARC } a \times R - a(R-y))}{2}$

CHORD a = $2\sqrt{2yR - y^2}$
$= \dfrac{2R \sin A°}{2}$

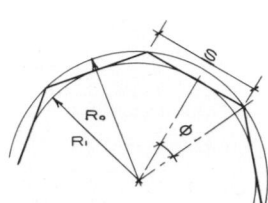

REGULAR POLYGON
AREA = $\dfrac{n S R_i}{2}$
(n = NUMBER OF SIDES)

ANY SIDE S = $2\sqrt{R_o^2 - R_i^2}$

$R_i = \dfrac{S}{2 \tan \emptyset}$ $R_o = \dfrac{S}{2 \sin \emptyset}$

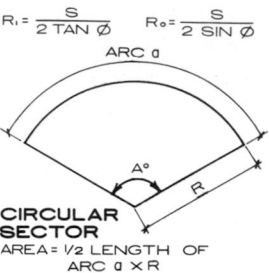

CIRCULAR SECTOR
AREA = ½ LENGTH OF ARC a × R
= AREA OF CIRCLE × $\dfrac{A°}{360}$
= $0.0087 R^2 A°$

ARC a = $\dfrac{\pi R A°}{180°}$ = $0.0175 R A°$

GEOMETRIC PROPERTIES OF PLANE FIGURES

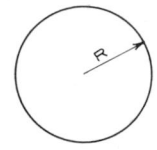

SPHERE
VOLUME = $\dfrac{4\pi R^3}{3}$
= $0.5236 D^3$

SURFACE = $4\pi R^2$
= πD^2

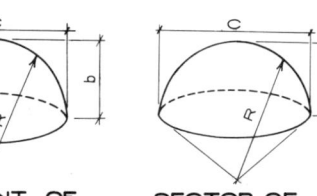

SEGMENT OF SPHERE
VOLUME = $\dfrac{\pi b^2 (3R - b)}{3}$
(OR SECTOR – CONE)

SURFACE = $2\pi R b$
(NOT INCLUDING SURFACE OF CIRCULAR BASE)

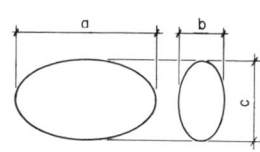

SECTOR OF SPHERE
VOLUME = $\dfrac{2\pi R^2 b}{3}$

SURFACE = $\dfrac{\pi R(4b + c)}{2}$
(OR: SEGMENT + CONE)

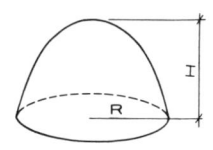

ELIPSOID
VOLUME = $\dfrac{\pi a b c}{6}$

SURFACE: NO SIMPLE RULE

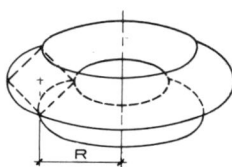

PARABOLOID OF REVOLUTION
VOLUME = AREA OF CIRCULAR BASE × ½ ALTITUDE.

SURFACE: NO SIMPLE RULE

CIRCULAR RING OF ANY SECTION
R = DISTANCE FROM AXIS OF RING TO TRUE CENTER OF SECTION

VOLUME = AREA OF SECTION × $2\pi R$

SURFACE = PERIMETER OF SECTION × $2\pi R$
(CONSIDER THE SECTION ON ONE SIDE OF AXIS ONLY)

VOLUMES AND SURFACES OF DOUBLE-CURVED SOLIDS

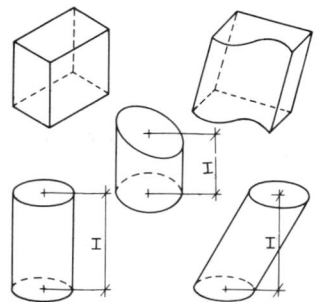

ANY PRISM OR CYLINDER, RIGHT OR OBLIQUE, REGULAR OR IRREGULAR.
Volume = area of base x altitude

Altitude = distance between parallel bases, measured perpendicular to the bases. When bases are not parallel, then Altitude = perpendicular distance from one base to the center of the other.

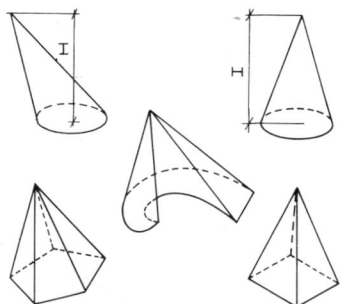

ANY PYRAMID OR CONE, RIGHT OR OBLIQUE, REGULAR OR IRREGULAR.
Volume = area of base x 1/3 altitude

Altitude = distance from base to apex, measured perpendicular to base.

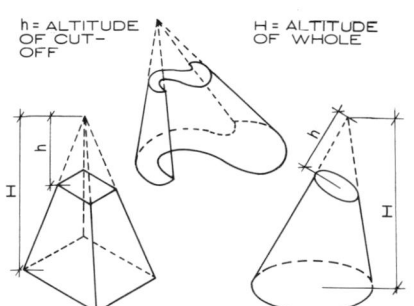

h = ALTITUDE OF CUT-OFF

H = ALTITUDE OF WHOLE

ANY FRUSTUM OR TRUNCATED PORTION OF THE SOLIDS SHOWN
Volume: From the volume of the whole solid, if complete, subtract the volume of the portion cut off.

The altitude of the cut-off part must be measured perpendicular to its own base.

SURFACES OF SOLIDS
The area of the surface is best found by adding together the areas of all the faces.

The area of a right cylindrical surface = perimeter of base x length of elements (average length if other base is oblique).

The area of a right conical surface = perimeter of base x 1/2 length of elements.

There is no simple rule for the area of an oblique conical surface, or for a cylindrical one where neither base is perpendicular to the elements. The best method is to construct a development, as if making a paper model, and measure its area by one of the methods given on the next page.

VOLUMES AND SURFACES OF TYPICAL SOLIDS

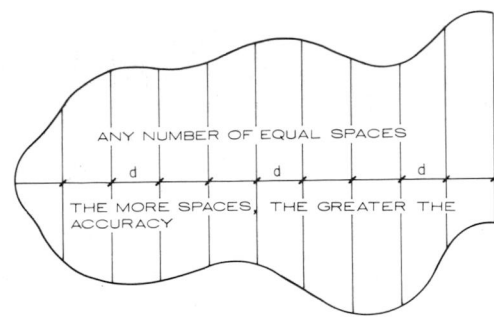

TO FIND THE AREA OF AN IRREGULAR PLANE FIGURE

1. Divide the figure into parallel strips by equally spaced parallel lines.

2. Measure the length of each of the parallel lines.

3. Obtain a summation of the unit areas by one of these 3 "rules".

TRAPEZOID RULE

Add together the length of the parallels, taking the first and last at $1/2$ value, and multiply by the width of the internal "d". This rule is sufficiently accurate for estimating and other ordinary purposes.

SIMPSON'S RULE

Add the parallels, taking the first and last at full value, second the, fourth, sixth, etc. from each end at 4 times full value, and the third, fifth, seventh, etc. from each end at 2 times the value, then multiply by $1/3$ d. This rule works only for an even number of spaces and is accurate for areas bounded by smooth curves.

DURAND'S RULE

Add the parallels taking the first and last at $5/12$ value, the second from each end at $13/12$ value, and all others at full value, then multiply by d. This rule is the most accurate for very irregular shapes.

NOTE

Irregular areas may be directly read off by means of a simple instrument called a Planimeter.

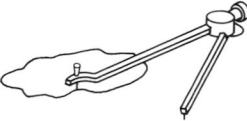

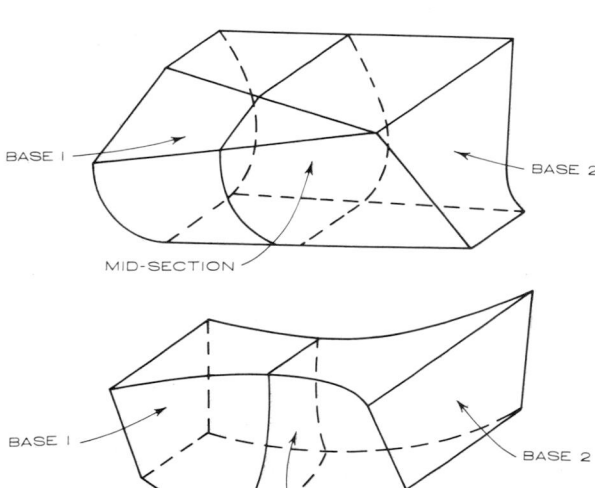

TO FIND THE VOLUME OF AN IRREGULAR FIGURE BY THE PRISMATOID FORMULA

Construct a section midway between the bases. Add 4 to the sum of the areas of the 2 bases and multiply the quantity by the area of the mid-section. Then multiply the total by $1/6$ the perpendicular distance between the bases.

$V = [(\text{area of base}_1 + \text{area of base}_2 + 4) (\text{area of midsection}) \times 1/6$ perpendicular distance between bases.

This formula is quite accurate for any solid with two parallel bases connected by a surface of straight line elements (upper figure), or smooth simple curves (lower figure).

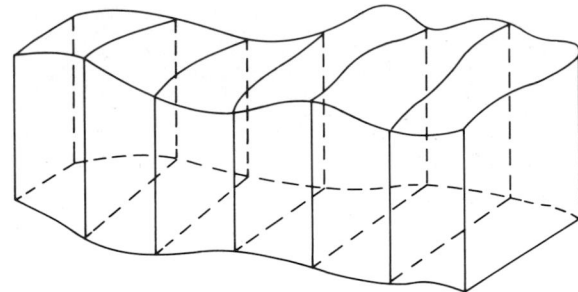

TO FIND THE VOLUME OF A VERY IRREGULAR FIGURE BY THE SECTIONING METHOD

1. Construct a series of equally spaced sections or profiles.

2. Determine the area of each section by any of the methods shown at left (preferably with a Planimeter).

3. Apply any one of the 3 summation "rules" given at left, to determine the total volume.

This method is in general use for estimating quantities of earthwork, etc.

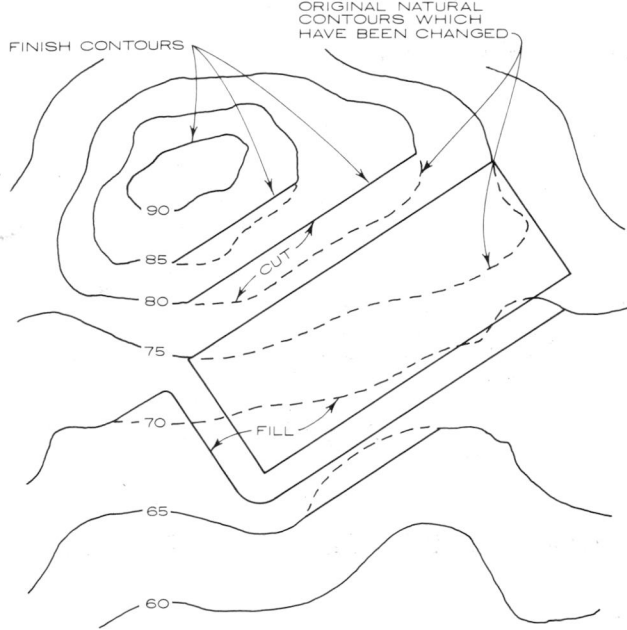

TO FIND THE VOLUME OF CUT AND FILL DIRECTLY FROM THE CONTOUR PLAN

1. Draw "finish" and "original" contours on same contour map.

2. Measure the differential areas between new and old contours of each contour and enter in columns according to whether cut or fill.

3. Add up each column and multiply by the contour interval to determine the volume in cubic feet.

EXAMPLE

CONTOUR	CUT		FILL	
85		300		
80		960		
75	2,460 − 2 =	1,230	3,800 − 2 =	1,900
70		20		2,200
		9,200		6,800
		×5		×5
TOTALS		46,000 cu. ft.		34,000 cu. ft.

NOTE:

1. Where a cut or fill ends directly on a contour level use $1/2$ value.

2. The closer the contour interval, the greater the accuracy.

This method is more rapid than the sectioning method, and is sufficiently accurate for simple estimating purposes and for balancing of cut and fill.

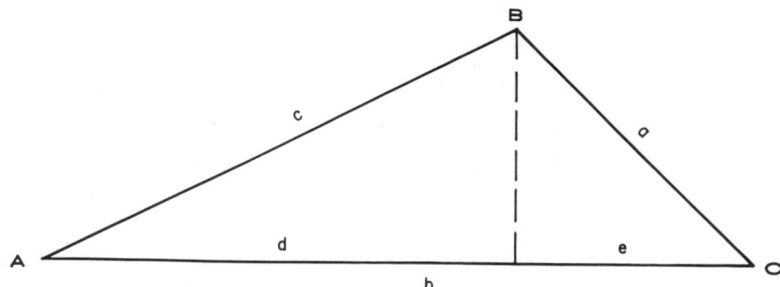

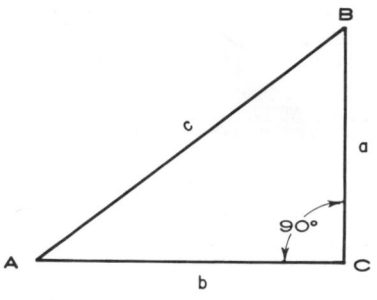

OBLIQUE TRIANGLES

FIND	GIVEN	SOLUTION	FIND	GIVEN	SOLUTION
a	A B b	$b \sin A \div \sin B$		a b c s	$\sin \tfrac{1}{2} A = \sqrt{(s-b)(s-c) \div bc}$
	A B c	$c \sin A \div \sin (A+B)$			$\cos \tfrac{1}{2} A = \sqrt{s(s-a) \div bc}$
	A C b	$b \sin A \div \sin (A+C)$	A		$\tan \tfrac{1}{2} A = \sqrt{(s-b)(s-c) \div s(s-a)}$
	A C c	$c \sin A \div \sin C$		B a b	$\sin A = a \sin B \div b$
	B C b	$b \sin (B+C) \div \sin B$		B a c	$\tfrac{1}{2}(A+C) + \tfrac{1}{2}(A-C)$
	B C c	$c \sin (B+C) \div \sin C$		C a b	$\tfrac{1}{2}(A+B) + \tfrac{1}{2}(A-B)$
	A b c	$\sqrt{b^2 + c^2 - 2bc \cdot \cos A}$		C a c	$\sin A = a \sin C \div c$
b	A B a	$a \sin B \div \sin A$		a b c s	$\sin \tfrac{1}{2} B = \sqrt{(s-a)(s-c) \div s(s-a)}$
	A B c	$c \sin B \div \sin (A+B)$			$\cos \tfrac{1}{2} B = \sqrt{s(s-b) \div ac}$
	A C a	$a \sin (A+C) \div \sin A$			$\tan \tfrac{1}{2} B = \sqrt{(s-a)(s-c) \div s(s-b)}$
	A C c	$c \sin (A+C) \div \sin C$	B	A a b	$\sin B = b \sin A \div a$
	B C a	$a \sin B \div \sin (B+C)$		A b c	$\tfrac{1}{2}(B+C) + \tfrac{1}{2}(B-C)$
	B C c	$c \sin B \div \sin C$		C a b	$\tfrac{1}{2}(A+B) - \tfrac{1}{2}(A-B)$
	B a c	$\sqrt{a^2 + c^2 - 2ac \cdot \cos B}$		C a c	$\sin B = b \sin C \div c$
c	A B a	$a \sin (A+B) \div \sin A$		a b c s	$\sin \tfrac{1}{2} C = \sqrt{(s-a)(s-b) \div ab}$
	A B b	$b \sin (A+B) \div \sin B$			$\cos \tfrac{1}{2} C = \sqrt{s(s-c) \div ab}$
	A C a	$a \sin C \div \sin A$			$\tan \tfrac{1}{2} C = \sqrt{(s-a)(s-b) \div s(s-c)}$
	A C b	$b \sin C \div \sin (A+C)$	C	A a c	$\sin C = c \sin A \div a$
	B C a	$a \sin C \div \sin (B+C)$		A b c	$\tfrac{1}{2}(B+C) - \tfrac{1}{2}(B-C)$
	B C b	$b \sin C \div \sin B$		B a c	$\tfrac{1}{2}(A+C) - \tfrac{1}{2}(A-C)$
	C a b	$\sqrt{a^2 + b^2 - 2ab \cdot \cos C}$		B b c	$\sin C = c \sin B \div b$
$\tfrac{1}{2}(B+C)$	A b c	$90° - \tfrac{1}{2} A$	AREA	a b c	$\sqrt{s(s-a)(s-b)(s-c)}$
$\tfrac{1}{2}(B-C)$		$\tan = [(b-c)\tan(90°-\tfrac{1}{2}A)] \div (b+c)$		C a b	$\tfrac{1}{2} ab \sin C$
$\tfrac{1}{2}(A+C)$	B a c	$90° - \tfrac{1}{2} B$	s	a b c	$a + b + c \div 2$
$\tfrac{1}{2}(A-C)$		$\tan = [(a-c)\tan(90°-\tfrac{1}{2}B)] \div (a+c)$	d	a b c s	$(b^2 + c^2 - a^2) \div 2b$
$\tfrac{1}{2}(A+B)$	C a b	$90° - \tfrac{1}{2} C$	e	a b c s	$(a^2 + b^2 - c^2) \div 2b$
$\tfrac{1}{2}(A-B)$		$\tan = [(a-b)\tan(90°-\tfrac{1}{2}C)] \div (a+b)$			

RIGHT TRIANGLES

FIND	GIVEN	SOLUTION
A	a b	$\tan A = a \div b$
	a c	$\sin A = a \div c$
	b c	$\cos A = b \div c$
B	a b	$\tan B = b \div a$
	a c	$\cos B = a \div c$
	b c	$\sin B = b \div c$
a	A b	$b \tan A$
	A c	$c \sin A$
b	A a	$a \div \tan A$
	A c	$c \cos A$
c	A a	$a \div \sin A$
	A b	$b \div \cos A$
AREA	a b	$ab \div 2$

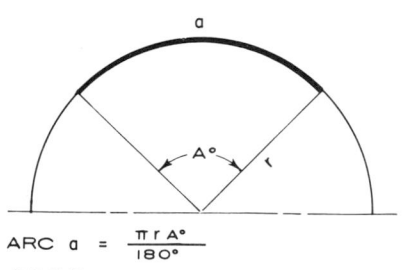

$$\text{ARC } a = \frac{\pi r A°}{180°}$$

ARCS

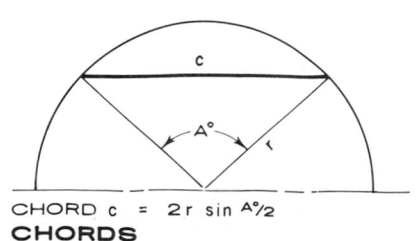

$$\text{CHORD } c = 2r \sin A°/2$$

CHORDS

When estimating the area available for lots on a large site development, it is safe to assume that 20% of the entire site will be streets. To estimate the total number of lots, of a given size, which a site will yield, use the following formula:

$$\text{Number of lots} = \frac{\text{Total site (acres)} \times 34{,}848 \text{ (80\% of an acre in sq. ft.)}}{\text{Width of lot (ft.)} \times \text{Depth of lot (ft.)}}$$

Find the number of 60′– 0″ x 120′– 0″ lots which can be placed on a 50 acre site.

$$\text{Number of lots} = \frac{50 \times 34{,}848}{60 \times 120} = 242 \text{ lots}$$

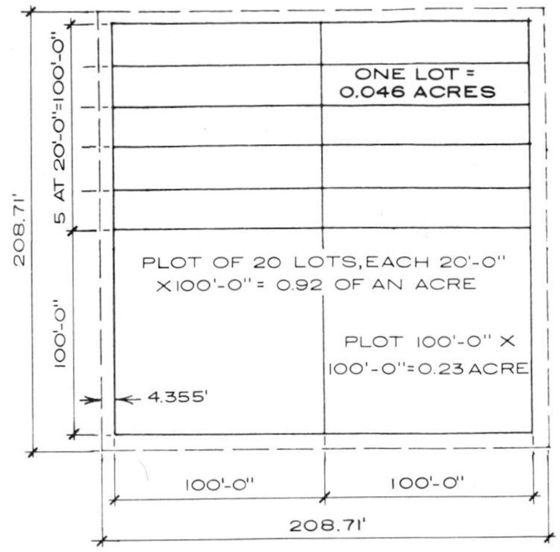

ONE ACRE = 43,560 SQ. FT.
BROKEN LINE ENCLOSES ONE ACRE

PLOT OF 20 LOTS, EACH 20'-0" X 100'-0" SHOWN IN RELATION TO ONE ACRE

USUAL LOT SIZES

A = ACRES; □ = SQ. FT.

DEPTH OF LOT		FRONT OR WIDTH OF LOT 20'	40'	50'	60'	75'	80'	100'
100'	□	2,000	4,000	5,000	6,000	7,500	8,000	10,000
	A	.0459	.0718	.1148	.1377	.1722	.1837	.2296
110'	□	2,200	4,400	5,500	6,600	8,250	8,800	11,000
	A	.0505	.1010	.1263	.1515	.1894	.2021	.2525
120'	□	2,400	4,800	6,000	7,200	9,000	9,600	12,000
	A	.0551	.1102	.1377	.1653	.2066	.2204	.2755
130'	□	2,600	5,200	6,500	7,800	9,750	10,400	13,000
	A	.0597	.1194	.1492	.1791	.2238	.2388	.2984
140'	□	2,800	5,600	7,000	8,400	10,500	11,200	14,000
	A	.0643	.1286	.1607	.1929	.2411	.2571	.3214
150'	□	3,000	6,000	7,500	9,000	11,250	12,000	15,000
	A	.0689	.1377	.1722	.2066	.2582	.2755	.3444

AREA EQUIVALENTS

	SQUARE METERS	SQUARE INCHES	SQUARE FEET	SQUARE YARDS	SQUARE RODS	SQUARE CHAINS	RODS	ACRES	SQ. MILES OR SECTIONS
SQUARE METER	1	1550	10.76	1.196	0.0395	0.002471	0.0009884	0.0002471	0.0000003861
SQUARE INCH	0.0006452	1	0.006944	0.0007716	0.00002551	0.000001594	0.0000006377	0.0000001594	0.0000000002491
SQUARE FOOT	0.09290	144	1	0.1111	0.003673	0.0002296	0.00009184	0.00002296	0.00000003587
SQUARE YARD	0.8361	1296	9	1	0.03306	0.002066	0.0008264	0.0002066	0.0000003228
SQUARE ROD	25.29	39204	272.25	30.25	1	0.0625	0.02500	0.00625	0.000009766
SQUARE CHAIN	404.7	627264	4356	484	16	1	0.4	0.1	0.0001562
ROD	1012	1568160	10890	1210	40	2.5	1	0.25	0.0003096
ACRES	4047	6272640	43560	4840	160	10	4	1	0.001562
SQ. MI. OR SECT.	2589998	....	27878400	3097600	102400	6400	2560	640	1

CONVERSION TABLE - SQ. FT. TO ACRES

SQ. FT.	ACRES	SQ. FT.	ACRES	SQ. FT.	ACRES	SQ. FT.	ACRES	SQ. FT.	ACRES	SQ. FT.	ACRES
10 =	.0002	600 =	.0138	11,000 =	.2525	25,000 =	.5739	39,000 =	.8953	435,600 =	10.0000
20 =	.0005	700 =	.0161	12,000 =	.2755	26,000 =	.5969	40,000 =	.9183	479,160 =	11.0000
30 =	.0007	800 =	.0184	13,000 =	.2984	27,000 =	.6198	41,000 =	.9412	522,720 =	12.0000
40 =	.0009	900 =	.0207	14,000 =	.3214	28,000 =	.6428	42,000 =	.9642	566,280 =	13.0000
50 =	.0011	1,000 =	.0230	15,000 =	.3444	29,000 =	.6657	43,000 =	.9871	609,840 =	14.0000
60 =	.0014	2,000 =	.0459	16,000 =	.3673	30,000 =	.6887	43,560 =	1.00001	653,400 =	15.0000
70 =	.0016	3,000 =	.0689	17,000 =	.3903	31,000 =	.7117	87,120 =	2.0000	696,960 =	16.0000
80 =	.0018	4,000 =	.0918	18,000 =	.4132	32,000 =	.7346	130,680 =	3.0000	740,520 =	17.0000
90 =	.0021	5,000 =	.1148	19,000 =	.4362	33,000 =	.7576	174,240 =	4.0000	784,080 =	18.0000
100 =	.0023	6,000 =	.1377	20,000 =	.4591	34,000 =	.7805	217,800 =	5.0000	827,640 =	19.0000
200 =	.0046	7,000 =	.1607	21,000 =	.4821	35,000 =	.8035	261,360 =	6.0000	871,200 =	20.0000
300 =	.0069	8,000 =	.1837	22,000 =	.5051	36,000 =	.8264	304,920 =	7.0000	914,760 =	21.0000
400 =	.0092	9,000 =	.2066	23,000 =	.5280	37,000 =	.8494	348,480 =	8.0000	958,320 =	22.0000
500 =	.0115	10,000 =	.2296	24,000 =	.5510	38,000 =	.8724	392,040 =	9.0000	1,001,880 =	23.0000

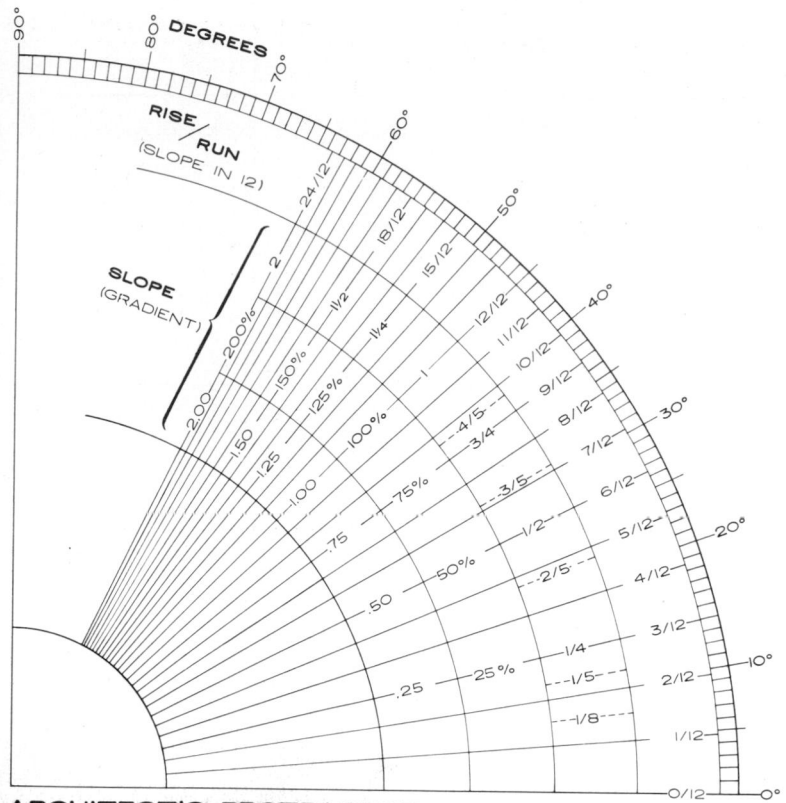

ARCHITECT'S PROTRACTOR

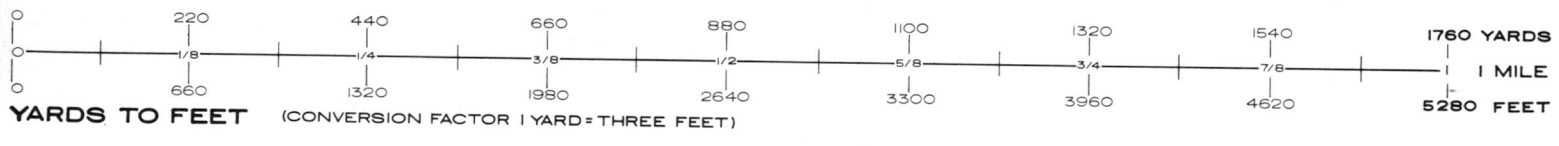

YARDS TO FEET (CONVERSION FACTOR I YARD = THREE FEET)

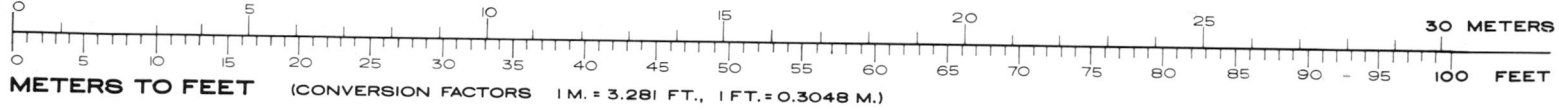

METERS TO FEET (CONVERSION FACTORS I M. = 3.281 FT., I FT. = 0.3048 M.)

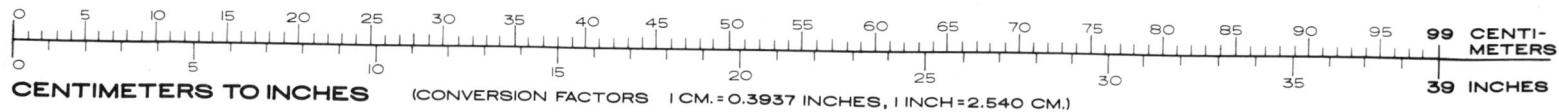

CENTIMETERS TO INCHES (CONVERSION FACTORS I CM. = 0.3937 INCHES, I INCH = 2.540 CM.)

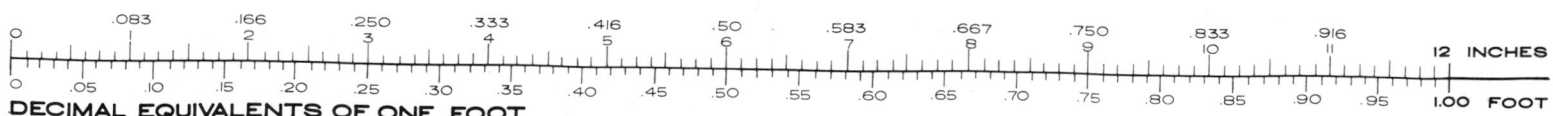

DECIMAL EQUIVALENTS OF ONE FOOT

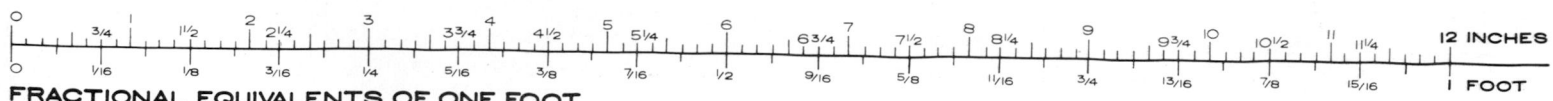

FRACTIONAL EQUIVALENTS OF ONE FOOT

DECIMALS OF A FOOT

FRACTION	DECIMAL	FRACTION	DECIMAL	FRACTION	DECIMAL
1/16	0.0052	4-1/16	0.3385	8-1/16	0.6719
1/8	0.0104	4-1/8	0.3438	8-1/8	0.6771
3/16	0.0156	4-3/16	0.3490	8-3/16	0.6823
1/4	0.0208	4-1/4	0.3542	8-1/4	0.6875
5/16	0.0260	4-5/16	0.3594	8-5/16	0.6927
3/8	0.0313	4-3/8	0.3646	8-3/8	0.6979
7/16	0.0365	4-7/16	0.3698	8-7/16	0.7031
1/2	0.0417	4-1/2	0.3750	8-1/2	0.7083
9/16	0.0469	4-9/16	0.3802	8-9/16	0.7135
5/8	0.0521	4-5/8	0.3854	8-5/8	0.7188
11/16	0.0573	4-11/16	0.3906	8-11/16	0.7240
3/4	0.0625	4-3/4	0.3958	8-3/4	0.7292
13/16	0.0677	4-13/16	0.4010	8-13/16	0.7344
7/8	0.0729	4-7/8	0.4063	8-7/8	0.7396
15/16	0.0781	4-15/16	0.4115	8-1/16	0.7448
1-	0.0833	5-	0.4167	9-	0.7500
1-1/16	0.0885	5-1/16	0.4219	9-1/16	0.7552
1-1/8	0.0938	5-1/8	0.4271	9-1/8	0.7604
1-3/16	0.0990	5-3/16	0.4323	9-3/16	0.7656
1-1/4	0.1042	5-1/4	0.4375	9-1/4	0.7708
1-5/16	0.1094	5-5/16	0.4427	9-5/16	0.7760
1-3/8	0.1146	5-3/8	0.4479	9-3/8	0.7813
1-7/16	0.1198	5-7/16	0.4531	9-7/16	0.7865
1-1/2	0.1250	5-1/2	0.4583	9-1/2	0.7917
1-9/16	0.1302	5-9/16	0.4635	9-9/16	0.7969
1-5/8	0.1354	5-5/8	0.4688	9-5/8	0.8021
1-11/16	0.1406	5-11/16	0.4740	9-11/16	0.8073
1-3/4	0.1458	5-3/4	0.4792	9-3/4	0.8125
1-13/16	0.1510	5-13/16	0.4844	9-13/16	0.8177
1-7/8	0.1563	5-7/8	0.4896	9-7/8	0.8229
1-15/16	0.1615	5-15/16	0.4948	9-15/16	0.8281
2-	0.1667	6-	0.5000	10-	0.8333
2-1/16	0.1719	6-1/16	0.5052	10-1/16	0.8385
2-1/8	0.1771	6-1/8	0.5104	10-1/8	0.8438
2-3/16	0.1823	6-3/16	0.5156	10-3/16	0.8490
2-1/4	0.1875	6-1/4	0.5208	10-1/4	0.8542
2-5/16	0.1927	6-5/16	0.5260	10-5/16	0.8594
2-3/8	0.1979	6-3/8	0.5313	10-3/8	0.8646
2-7/16	0.2031	6-7/16	0.5365	10-7/16	0.8698
2-1/2	0.2083	6-1/2	0.5417	10-1/2	0.8750
2-9/16	0.2135	6-9/16	0.5469	10-9/16	0.8802
2-5/8	0.2188	6-5/8	0.5521	10-5/8	0.8854
2-11/16	0.2240	6-11/16	0.5573	10-11/16	0.8906
2-3/4	0.2292	6-3/4	0.5625	10-3/4	0.8958
2-13/16	0.2344	6-13/16	0.5677	10-13/16	0.9010
2-7/8	0.2396	6-7/8	0.5729	10-7/8	0.9063
2-15/16	0.2448	6-15/16	0.5781	10-15/16	0.9115
3-	0.2500	7-	0.5833	11-	0.9167
3-1/16	0.2552	7-1/16	0.5885	11-1/16	0.9219
3-1/8	0.2604	7-1/8	0.5938	11-1/8	0.9271
3-3/16	0.2656	7-3/16	0.5990	11-3/16	0.9323
3-1/4	0.2708	7-1/4	0.6042	11-1/4	0.9375
3-5/16	0.2760	7-5/16	0.6094	11-5/16	0.9427
3-3/8	0.2813	7-3/8	0.6146	11-3/8	0.9479
3-7/16	0.2865	7-7/16	0.6198	11-7/16	0.9531
3-1/2	0.2917	7-1/2	0.6250	11-1/2	0.9583
3-9/16	0.2969	7-9/16	0.6302	11-9/16	0.9635
3-5/8	0.3021	7-5/8	0.6354	11-5/8	0.9688
3-11/16	0.3073	7-11/16	0.6406	11-11/16	0.9740
3-3/4	0.3125	7-3/4	0.6458	11-3/4	0.9792
3-13/16	0.3177	7-13/16	0.6510	11-13/16	0.9844
3-7/8	0.3229	7-7/8	0.6563	11-7/8	0.9896
3-15/16	0.3281	7-15/16	0.6615	11-15/16	0.9948
4-	0.3333	8-	0.6667	12-	1.0000

DECIMALS OF AN INCH

FRACTION	DECIMAL
1/64	0.015625
1/32	0.03125
3/64	0.046875
1/16	0.0625
5/64	0.078125
3/32	0.09375
7/64	0.109375
1/8	0.125
9/64	0.140625
5/32	0.15625
11/64	0.171875
3/16	0.1875
13/64	0.203125
7/32	0.21875
15/64	0.234375
1/4	0.250
17/64	0.265625
9/32	0.28125
19/64	0.296875
5/16	0.3125
21/64	0.328125
11/32	0.34375
23/64	0.359375
3/8	0.375
25/64	0.390625
13/32	0.40625
27/64	0.421875
7/16	0.4375
29/64	0.453125
15/32	0.46875
31/64	0.484375
1/2	0.500
33/64	0.515625
17/32	0.53125
35/64	0.546875
9/16	0.5625
37/64	0.578125
19/32	0.59375
39/64	0.609375
5/8	0.625
41/64	0.640625
21/32	0.65625
43/64	0.671875
11/16	0.6875
45/64	0.703125
23/32	0.71875
47/64	0.734375
3/4	0.750
49/64	0.765625
25/32	0.78125
51/64	0.796875
13/16	0.8125
53/64	0.828125
27/32	0.84375
55/64	0.859375
7/8	0.875
57/64	0.890625
29/32	0.90625
59/64	0.921875
15/16	0.9375
61/64	0.953125
31/32	0.96875
63/64	0.984375
1"	1.000

AVERAGE WEIGHTS OF MATERIALS :

SOIL, SAND & GRAVEL	LBS. PER CU. FT.
Cinders or Ashes	40—45
Clay, damp & plastic	110
Clay, dry	63
Clay & gravel, dry	100
Earth, dry & loose	76
Earth, dry & packed	95
Earth, moist & loose	78
Earth, moist & packed	96
Earth, mud, packed	115
Sand or gravel, dry & loose	90—105
Sand or gravel, dry & packed	100—120
Sand or gravel, dry & wet	118—120

STONE	LBS. PER CU. FT.
Granite	175
Limestone	165
Marble	165
Sandstone, bluestone	147
Slate	175
(See also stone veneer)	

BRICK & BLOCK MASONRY (INCL. MORTAR)	LBS. PER SQ. FT.
4" brickwork	35
4" concrete block stone or gravel	34
4" concrete block lightwt. aggregate (avg.)	22
6" concrete block stone or gravel	50
6" concrete block lightwt. aggregate (avg.)	31
8" concrete block stone or gravel	58
8" concrete block lightwt. aggregate (avg.)	36
12" concrete block stone or gravel	90
12" concrete block lightwt. aggregate (avg.)	58

CONCRETE	LBS. PER CU. FT.
Stone, reinforced	150
Stone, plain	144
Slag, plain	130
Cinder, reinforced	100—115

METALS	LBS. PER CU. FT.
Aluminum, cast	165
Brass, red	546
Brass, yellow, extruded bronze	528
Bronze, commercial	552
Bronze, statuary	509
Copper, cast or rolled	556
Iron, cast gray	450
Iron, wrought	485
Lead	710
Monel metal	552
Nickel	555
Stainless steel, rolled	492—510
Steel, rolled	490
Zinc, rolled or cast	440

LIGHT WEIGHT CONCRETE	LBS. PER CU. FT.
Concrete, Aerocrete	50—80
Concrete, cinder fill	60
Concrete, Haydite	85—100
Concrete, Nailcode	75
Concrete, Perlite	35—50
Concrete, Pumice	60—90
Concrete, Vermiculite	25—60

TILE—STRUCTURAL CLAY (INCL. MORTAR)	LBS. PER SQ. FT.
4" hollow	23
6" hollow	33
8" hollow, 5" unit ht.	42
8" hollow, 8" unit ht.	38
8" hollow, 12" unit ht.	34
12" hollow, 5" unit ht.	66
12" hollow, 8" unit ht.	55
12" hollow, 12" unit ht.	49

MORTAR & PLASTER	LBS. PER CU. FT.
Mortar, masonry	116
Plaster, gypsum, sand	104—120
Plaster, gypsum, perlite	50—55
Plaster, Portland Cement, sand	104—120
Plaster, Portland Cement, perlite	50—55
Plaster, Portland Cement, vermiculite	50—55

TILE—STRUCTURAL FACING (INCL. MORTAR)	LBS. PER SQ. FT.
2" facing tile	16
4" facing tile	30
6" facing tile	41

WOOD (12% MOISTURE CONTENT)	LBS. PER CU. FT.
Birch, red oak	44
Cedar, northern white	22
Cedar, western red	23
Cypress, southern	32
Douglas Fir (coast region)	34
Fir, commercial, white; Idaho white pine	27
Hemlock	28—29
Maple, hard (black & sugar)	42
Oak, white	47
Pine, northern white sugar	25
Pine, long leaf southern	29
Pine, ponderosa; Spruce: eastern & sitka	28
Pine, short leaf southern	36
Poplar, yellow	28
Redwood	28
Walnut, black	38

FUELS & LIQUIDS	LBS. PER CU. FT.
Coal, piled anthracite	47—58
Coal, piled bituminous	40—54
Gasoline	75
Water at 4°C	62.4
Water, ice	56

STONE VENEER (NO MORTAR)	LBS. PER SQ. FT.
2" granite, 1/2" parging	30
4" granite, 1/2" parging	59
6" limestone facing, 1/2" parging	55
4" sandstone or bluestone, 1/2" parging	49
1" marble	13
1" slate	14

MacKnight, Kirmmse, French & Sizing; Syracuse, New York

AVERAGE WEIGHTS OF MATERIALS:

PARTITIONS	LBS. PER SQ. FT.
2x4 wood stud, lath & plaster 2S	14—16
4″ metal stud, lath & plaster 2S	18
4″ conc. part'n. block lightweight, plaster 2S	34
6″ conc. part'n. block lightweight, plaster 2S	43
3″ gypsum block, plaster 2S	21
4″ gypsum block, plaster 2S	25
6″ gypsum block, plaster 2S	31
2″ solid plaster	18
3″ solid plaster	27
moveable steel (office type)	4—8

FINISH MATERIALS FLOOR, WALL, CEILING	LBS. PER SQ. FT.
Acoustical tile unsupported per 1/2″ thickness	.8
Building board, 1/2″	.8
Cement finish, 1″	12
Gypsum board 1/2″	2.1
Marble & setting bed	25—30
Plaster, 1/2″	4.5
Plaster, suspended w/lath	10
Plywood, 1/2″	1.5
Tile, glazed wall 3/8″	3
Tile, ceramic mosaic 1/4″	2.5
Quarry tile, 1/2″	5.8
Quarry tile, 3/4″	8.6
Terrazzo, 2″	25
Terrazzo, 3″	38
Vinyl asbestos tile, 1/8″	1.33
Hardwood flooring 25/32″	4
Wood block flooring 3″	15

FLOOR & ROOF CONSTRUCTION	LBS. PER SQ. FT.
Flexicore, 6″ pre-cast lightwt. conc.	30
Flexicore, 6″ pre-cast stone concrete	40
Plank, cinder conc. 2″	15
Plank, Durisol roof 3 1/4″ & 4 1/4″	14, 17
Plank, gypsum 2″	12
Concrete, reinforced 1″	
stone	12.5
slag	11.5
lightweight	6—10
Concrete, plain 1″	
stone	12
slag	11
lightweight	3—9

MacKnight, Kirmmse, French & Sizing; Syracuse, New York

ROOFING MATERIALS	LBS. PER SQ. FT.
Built-up	6.5
Cemesto roof deck 1 9/16″	4.8
Copper	1.5—2.5
Corrugated Asbestos	4
Corrugated glass	6.3
Corrugated iron	1.2—1.7
Deck, steel without roofing or insulation	2.2—3.6
Fiberglass panels (2 1/2″ corr.)	5—8 oz.
Galvanized iron	1.2—1.7
Gypsum tile, 3″	17
Lead 1/8″	6—8
Monel metal	1.2—1.5
Plank, cinder conc. 2″	15
Plastic sandwich panel, 2 1/2″ thick	2.6
Shingles, asbestos cement	2.6
Shingles, asphalt	1.7—2.8
Shingles, wood	2—3
Slate, 3/16″ to 1/4″	7—9.5
Slate, 3/8″ to 1/2″	14—18
Stainless steel	2.5
Tile, cement flat	13.0
Tile, cement ribbed	16
Tile, clay mission	13.5
Tile, clay shingle type	8—16
Tile, clay flat with setting bed	15—20

INSULATION	LBS. PER SQ. FT.
Bat, blankets, per 1″ thickness	.1—.4
Boards, vegetable fiber	1.5—2
Cork board per 1″ thickness	.58
Foamed board insulation per 1″ thickness	2.6 oz.

GLASS	LBS. PER SQ. FT.
Polished plate 1/4″	3.28
Polished plate 1/2″	6.56
Double strength 1/8″	26 oz.
Sheet A, B, 1/32″	45 oz.
Sheet A, B, 1/4″	52 oz.
Spandrel glass app. same as window glass	
Insulating glass 1/8″ plate with air space	3.25
1/4″ wire, glass	3.5
Glass block, 4″	20

PORCELAIN ENAMEL PANELS	LBS. PER SQ. FT.
Porcelain on alum. lam to 1/8″ cem. asb. & backed with aluminum foil	2.25—2.5
Porcelain on alum. unbacked "pan-type"	1.0
Porcelain on steel panel, double faced, lam. to 1 1/8″ insulating core	4—6.5
Porcelain on steel panel, unbacked "pan-type"	2.5—3

SUSPENDED CEILING MATERIALS	LBS. PER SQ. FT.
Mineral fiber tile 3/4″, 12″ x 12″	1.2—1.57
Wood fiber tile 3/4″, 12″ x 12″ or 12″ x 24″	.78—1.07
Mineral fiber board 5/8″, 24″ x 24″	1.4
Wood fiber board 5/8″, 24″ x 48″	.87
1″, 24″ x 48″	1.18
Acoustic plaster on gyp. lath base	10—11

LIVE LOADS	LBS. PER SQ. FT.
In general see building codes for specific requirements	
Dwellings, apartments, hotels, clubs, hospitals, prisons	40
Factories, workshops—variable	
Office buildings:	
office space	50
corridors, public space	100
Schools:	
classrooms	40, 50, or 60
corridors	100
Sidewalks	250 & 300
Theater lobbies, gyms, grandstands, stages, places of assembly with no fixed seats	100
Theaters, auditoriums with fixed seats	50—100
Stairs & fire escapes, except private residences	100

LINEAR MEASURE

LENGTH
4 inches = 1 hand
9 inches = 1 span
12 inches = 1 foot
3 feet = 1 yard

5-1/2 yds. = 16-01/2 feet = 1 rod =
1 pole = 1 perch.

40 poles = 220 yds. = 1 furlong

8 furlongs = 1,760 yds. = 5,280
feet = 1 mile

3 miles (U.S. naut.) = 1 league

NAUTICAL
6,080.27 feet = 1 nautical mile
1.15156 statute mi.= 1 nautical mile
1 nautical mi. per hr. = 1 knot
6 feet = 1 fathom
120 fathoms = 1 cable length

SURVEYOR OR GUNTHER
7.92 inches = 1 link
100 links = 66 ft. = 4 rods = 1 chain
80 chains = 1 mile
1 vara (Texas) = 33 1/3 in. =
2-03/4 ft.

EQUIVALENTS

CENTI-METERS	INCHES	FEET	YARDS	METERS	CHAINS	KILO-METERS	MILE
1	0.3937	0.03281	0.01094	0.01	0.0_34971	0.0_41	0.0_56214
2.540	1	0.0833	0.02778	0.0254	0.001263	0.0_4254	0.0_41578
30.48	12	1	0.3333	0.3048	0.01515	0.0_33048	0.0_31894
91.44	36	3	1	0.9144	0.04545	0.0_39144	0.0_35682
100	39.37	3.281	1.0936	1	0.04971	0.001	0.0_36214
2012	732	66	23	20.12	1	0.02012	0.0125
100,000	39,370	3,281	1,093.6	1,000	49.71	1	0.6214
160,935	63,360	5,280	1,760	1,609	80	1.609	1

Subscripts after any figure: 0_2, 0_3, etc. mean that that figure is to be repeated the indicated number of times; i.e.: $0.0_327 = 0.00027$.

CUBIC MEASURE

VOLUME
1 cord of wood

1 perch of masonry
in most localities
Standard is 24-3/4 cubic feet

LIQUID
4 gills = 1 pint = 16 fluid oz.
2 pints = 1 quart = 32 fluid oz.
4 quarts = 1 gallon = 128 fluid oz.

APOTHECARY
1 fluid oz. = 8 drams = 480 minimums
= 2 tablespoons = 6 teaspoons =
1.805 cu. in. = 29.58 cu. cm. =
1/128th gallon.

DRY
2 pints = 1 quart = 67.2 cu.in.
4 quarts = 8 pints = 268.8 cu. in.
1 peck = 16 pints = 537.6 cu. in.
4 pecks = 1 bushel = 2150.42 cu. in.

1 std. barrel (for fruit & veg.) =
7056 cu. in. = 105 dry quarts.
"Struck barrel" is 20" dia.,
28-1/2" high.

EQUIVALENTS

CUBIC INCHES	CUBIC FEET	CUBIC YARDS	U.S. OZ. APOTH.	U.S. QUARTS		U.S. GALLONS		BUSHEL	LITERS
				LIQUID	DRY	LIQUID	DRY		
1	0.0_35787	0.0_42143	0.5541	0.01732	0.01488	0.0_24329	0.0_23720	0.0_34650	0.01639
1728	1	0.03704	957.5	29.92	25.71	7.4805	6.429	0.8036	28.32
46656	27	1	25853	807.9	694.3	202.0	173.6	21.70	764.6
1.805	0.001044	0.0_43868	1	0.03125	0.02686	0.007813	0.006714	0.0_38392	0.02957
57.75	0.03342	0.001238	32	1	0.8594	0.25	0.2148	0.02686	0.9464
67.20	0 03889	0.001440	37.24	1.164	1	0.2909	0.25	0.03125	1.101
231	0.1337	0.004951	128	4	3.437	1	0.8594	0.1074	3.785
268.8	0.1556	0.005761	148.9	4.655	4	1.164	1	0.125	4.405
2150	1.244	0.04609	1192	37.24	32	9.309	8	1	35.25
61.02	0.03531	0.001308	33.81	1.057	0.9081	0.2642	0.2270	0.02838	1

WEIGHT MEASURE

METRIC
10 milligrams = 1 centigram
10 centigrams = 1 decigram
10 decigrams = 1 gram
10 grams = 1 decagram
10 decagrams = 1 hectogram
10 hectograms = 1 kilogram

TROY
24 grains = 1 pennyweight (dwt.)
20 dwts. = 480 grains = 1 ounce
1 assay ton = 29,167 milligrams

1 carat (for weighing diamonds) =
3,086 grains = 200 grams.

AVOIRDUPOIS
16 drams = 437.5 grains = 1 ounce
16 ounces = 7000 grains = 1 pound
100 lbs. = 100 hundred weight = 1 cental
2000 lbs. = 20 hundred weight =
1 short ton
28 lbs. = 2 stones = 1 quarter
4 quarters (long unit) = 112 lbs.
2240 lbs. = 20 hundred wt. = 1 long ton

APOTHECARY
20 grains = 1 scruple 3
3 scruples = 60 grains = 1 dram 3
8 drams (drachms) = 1 ounce 3

NOTE:
Unit of grain is same in all.

EQUIVALENTS

KILO-GRAMS	GRAINS	OUNCES		POUNDS		TONS		
		TR & APOTH	AVOIR.	TR & APOTH	AVOIR.	SHORT	LONG	METRIC
0.0_46480	15,432	32.15	35.27	2.6792	2.205	0.0_21102	0.0_39842	0.001
0.03110	480	0.0_22083	0.0_22286	0.0_31736	0.0_31429	0.0_7143	0.0_76378	0.0_76480
0.02835	437.5	0.9115	1	1.09714	0.08333	0.06857	0.0_43429	0.0_43061	0.0_43110
0.3732	5,760	12	13.17	1	0.8229	0.0_34114	0.0_33673	0.0_33732
0.4536	7,000	14.58	16	1.215	1	0.0005	0.0_34464	0.0_34536
907.2	140_6	29,167	320_3	2,431	2,000	1	0.8929	0.9072
1,016	15680_4	32,667	35,840	2,722	2,240	1.12	1	1.016
1,000		32,151	35,274	2,679	2,205	1.102	0.9842	1

MISCELLANEOUS WEIGHTS & MEASURES

WATER
1 cu. ft. weighs 62.4 lbs.
1 cu. in. weighs .0361 lbs.
1 gallon weighs 8.33 lbs.

LEAD
Sheet lead @ 1/64" thickness =
1 lbs./sq. ft. approx.
Sold by weight in lbs./sq. ft.

BOARD FEET
1 board foot = 144 sq. in. = volume
of board 1 ft. square and 1" thick

No. of board feet in a log:

Board Ft. Vol. $= \dfrac{(D'' - 4)^2 \cdot L}{16}$

D = smaller diameter of log.
L = length of log in feet.
4 = slab deduction allowance.

Above formula appropriate for
rough approximation only

CEMENT
Natural
1 bag = 85 lbs. ASTM-64.
1 barrel = 4 bags = 340 lbs.

Portland
1 bag = 94 lbs. ASTM-65
1 barrel = 4 bags = 376 lbs.

Bag and bulk only.
Barrel is a trade term.

SAND & LIME
Sand — damp or moist, not wet:
105-115 lbs./cu. ft. 110 lbs. average.

Structural lime:
Hydrated — slaked, as dry powder
30-40 lbs./cu. ft. 35 lbs. average.
1 bag = 50 lbs.

Quick — unslacked:
65-75 lbs./cu. ft. 70 lbs. average
1 bag = 80 lbs.

ROMAN NUMERALS

ARABIC:	1	5	10	50	100	500	1000	50,000
ROMAN:	I	V	X	L	C	D	M	$\overline{L}$

RULES:

1. If no letter precedes a letter of greater value, add the number represented by the letters.
Example:
XXX represents 30.
VI represents 6.

2. If a letter precedes a letter of greater value, subtract the smaller from the greater add the remainder or remainders thus obtained to the numbers represented by the other letters.
Example:
IV represents 4.
XL represents 40.
CXLV represents 145.

3. A bar placed over a letter multiplies value by 1000.

OTHER ILLUSTRATIONS:

ARABIC:	9	13	14	42	55	96	1601	4240
ROMAN:	IX	XIII	XIV	XLII	LV	XCVI	MDCI	$\overline{IV}$CCXL

LINEAR MEASURE - EQUIVALENTS

MILLIMETERS	CENTIMETERS	DECIMETERS	METERS	DECAMETERS	HECTOMETERS	KILOMETERS	YARDS
1	.1	.01	.001	.0001	.00001	.000001	
10	1.	.1	.01	.001	.0001	.00001	
100	10	1	.1	.01	.001	.0001	
1,000	100	10	1	.1	.01	.001	1.0936
10,000	1,000	100	10	1	.1	.01	
100,000	10,000	1,000	100	10	1	.1	
1,000,000	100,000	10,000	1,000	100	10	1	
			.9144				1

AREA MEASURE - EQUIVALENTS

SQUARE MILLIMETERS	SQUARE CENTIMETERS	SQUARE DECIMETERS	SQUARE METERS	ARES	HECTARES	SQUARE KILOMETERS	ACRES
1	.01	.0001	.000001				
100	1	.01	.0001	.000001			
10,000	100	1	.01	.0001	.000001		
1,000,000	10,000	100	1	.01	.0001	.000001	
	1,000,000	10,000	100	1	.01	.0001	
		1,000,000	10,000	100	1	.01	2.471
			1,000,000	10,000	100	1	247.1
				40.47	.4047		1

LIQUID AND DRY MEASURE - EQUIVALENTS

CUBIC CENTIMETERS (C.C.) MILLILITERS	CENTILITERS	DECILITERS	LITERS	DECALITERS	HECTOLITERS	CUBIC METERS STERES KILOLITERS	QUARTS (LIQUID)
1	.1	.01	.001	.0001			
10	1	.1	.01	.001	.0001		
100	10	1	.1	.01	.001	.0001	
1,000	100	10	1	.1	.01	.001	1.057
	1,000	100	10	1	.1	.01	
		1,000	100	10	1	.1	
			1,000	100	10	1	
			1.9464				1

WEIGHT MEASURE

See another page in this series titled "Weights and Measures".

TEMPERATURE EQUIVALENTS (MEASURED AT SEA LEVEL AIR PRESSURE)

SCALE	ABSOLUTE ZERO (NO MOLECULAR MOTION)	WATER FREEZING	WATER BOILING	CONVERSION FACTORS
CENTIGRADE (METRIC)	$-273.11°$	$0°$	$+100°$	Degrees C. = (Degrees F. $-$ 32) x $5/9$
FAHRENHEIT	$-459.58°$	$+32°$	$+212°$	Degrees F. = (Degrees C. x 1.8) + 32

One calorie of heat energy is required to raise 1 c.c. of water $1°C$. (As measured between $3°$ and $4°$ C.).

Foster C. Parriott; James M. Hunter & Associates; Boulder, Colorado

DESCRIPTION

CPM (Critical Path Method) is a form of scheduling operations against time periods and resources. Other names for variations of CPM are CPP (Critical Path Planning), PERT (Program Evaluation and Review Technique), PERTCO (Program Evaluation and Review Techniques Cost), PEP (Program Evaluation Procedure), and LESS (Least Cost Estimating and Scheduling). All are somewhat similar and are tools whose purpose it is to assure management that detailed analytic planning and evaluation of complex operations are carried out by those charged with them. Furthermore, it helps to:

   a. flag the critical activities which, if delayed, would delay the final completion of the project. These are called critical operations.

   b. show the number of spare days that the noncritical operations possess, making it possible to adjust their duration to the convenience of the project. These spare days are known as "float".

   c. show the most economical scheduling for each operation in order to vary completion dates ("normal" versus "crash" programs). This, in turn, makes it possible to select a desirable optimum completion date.

   d. assess time and cost effects on a project due to changes in the work, strikes or other forced work stoppages.

   e. provide a salutary effect on a project in that it discourages procrastination, delayed decisions or second-guessing.

OPERATION

It is important to remember that in C.P.M. the planning and the scheduling functions are two distinct and different operations. The first is started by putting all necessary activities down on paper. All activities are then connected in their required sequence of execution with arrows. This is called the network diagram, or the arrow diagram, or the model.

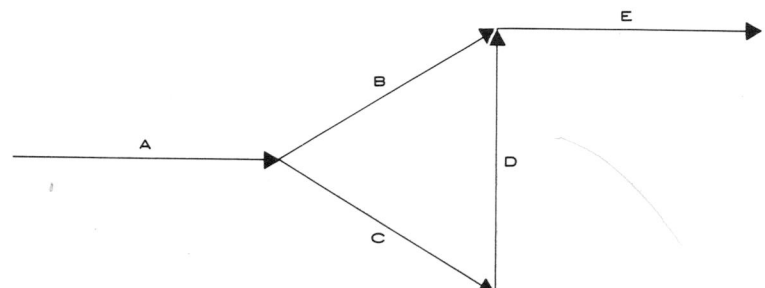

SIMPLIFIED NETWORK MODEL

The length of the arrows have no significance; the point to remember is that time flows from the tail of the arrow to its head, and most important, that no new activity can be started until activities indicated by all previous arrow-heads are completed. With that in mind, the following interpretations of the network can be made:

   a. Operation B and C cannot start until A is completed.

   b. Operation B and C can start simultaneously and can be performed concurrently.

   c. Operation D cannot start until C is completed.

   d. Operation E cannot start until both B and D are completed.

We can now translate this into an actual network.

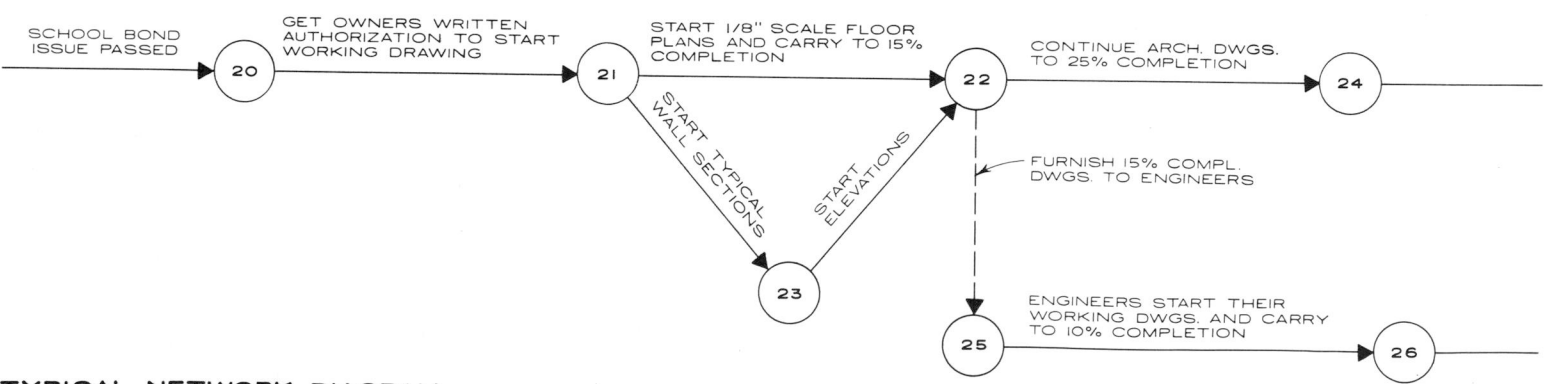

TYPICAL NETWORK DIAGRAM

Note that former operation A is now labeled 20–21, C is labeled 21–23, etc. Numerical sequence of the numbers has no significance whatever. We have essentially the same diagram; its sequential nature is now evident. This is referred to as the logic of arrow diagramming.

The broken line with an arrow which appears at 22–25 is called a Dummy Activity. It has no duration, but is inserted to insure that the activity at its head will not commence until the activity at its tail is completed.

The network model now shows the relationship of sequences of activities, but does not indicate time factors. This is accomplished in the second phase, the "Schedule", which superimposes duration times over the network for each separate activity, and determines which activities are critical and where float occurs.

Gustave R. Keane, FAIA; Eggers and Higgins, Architects–Planners; New York, New York

TYPICAL CPM SCHEDULE

BY ADDING TIME FACTORS TO THE NETWORK DIAGRAM WE COMPLETE THE CPM SCHEDULE

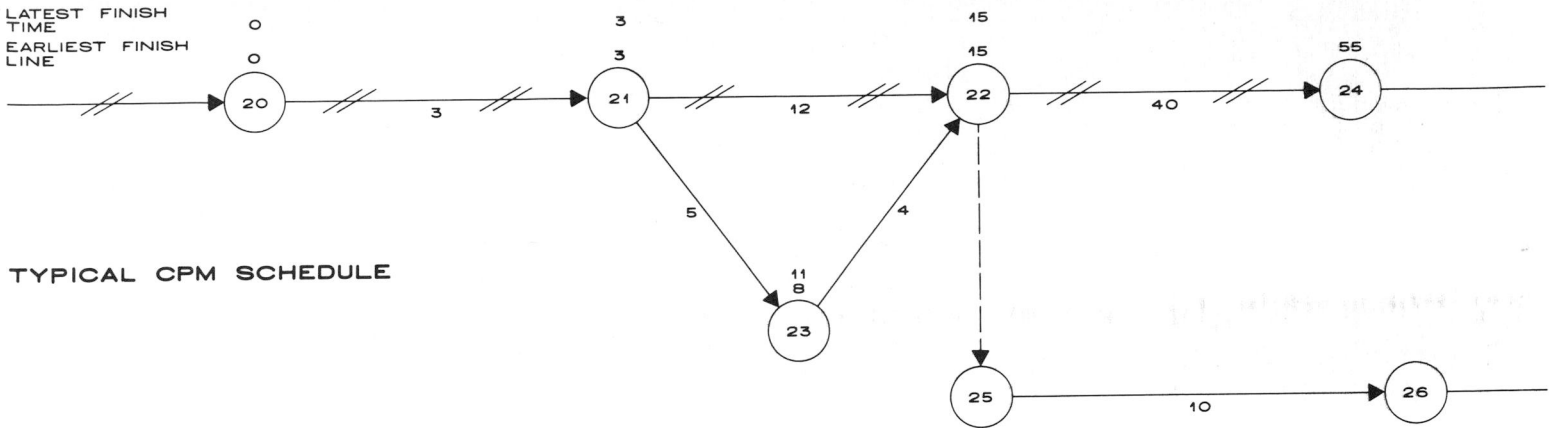

TYPICAL CPM SCHEDULE

1.   Duration time, in working days, for each activity is noted below each arrow line (for instance, 12 days for 21—22).

2.   Duration times are added consecutively for each activity and noted above each nodule. This addition gives us the "earliest finish time" for each activity; i.e. the least number of working days in which all preceding activities can be completed.

3.   After establishing all earliest finish times for all activities, the right hand end is reached. We now go back again and by subtracting duration times from the lesser of the right side totals we establish "latest finish times" for each activity and enter them above the "earliest finish time". The difference is called "Float" and shows permissible flexibility (if any) in scheduling each activity.

   For example, there is a 3 day period of "float" which can be used to adjust either the start of 21—23, or 23—22, or the intensity with which these activities are carried out (man power). If earliest finish and latest starting times are the same, it means that there is no float and that the activity is, therefore, on the critical path.

4.   The critical path is indicated on the arrow line with an appropriate mark or a special color. In this illustration it is marked thusly:
Phase II, the scheduling, is now complete. In many cases, this will be a sufficient excursion into C.P.M., because on comparatively simple projects the influence of lost days on the critical path can be easily ascertained by observation of the network schedule.

COMPUTER UP-DATING; MONITORING

On complicated projects where many parallel activities take place during the construction stage, and where several parties share the responsibility for scheduled completion, the use of Phase III, Computer Up-Dating and subsequent Monitoring is indicated.

The computer input consists of a prescribed form on which all planned, started and completed activities and their time increments are entered. The computer output (print-out) shows "Earliest Finish", "Latest Finish" and "Float" times. "Latest Finish Time" is sometimes called "Latest Starting Time". Depending on the complexity of the project the computer runs are made bi-monthly or even monthly.

Monitoring is accomplished by visually comparing the originally scheduled completion times for each activity with the times shown on the computer print-out. This indicates what effect deviation from the original schedule will have on the completion date. It makes it possible to adjust the original schedule to make up time.

The speed of the computer makes it economical to ascertain the impact of a large number of inputs regarding the speeding up of individual activities on the total completion time. By adding costs of the different alternate solutions to the imput the computer print-out will furnish a clear picture of the influence of each activity decision on the final total cost of the project.

This Up-Dating and Monitoring also allows exact determination of the time changes due to change orders, delays, or other factors. It provides a precise project record with detailed recordings of the job progress at pre-determined time intervals, and may be valuable in settling later conflicts, and in evaluating claims of delay by any of the parties responsible for timely completion of the project.

PORTION OF CPM

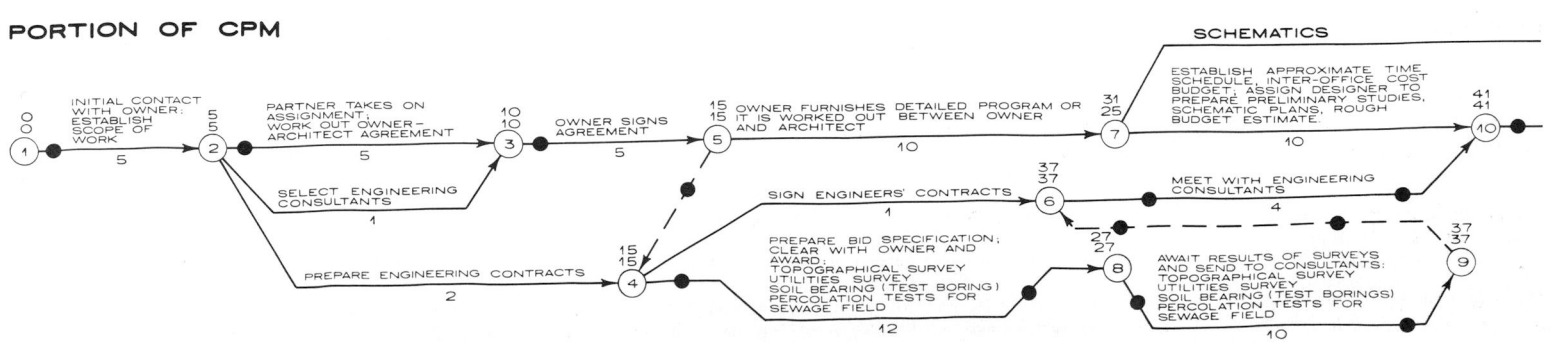

Gustave R. Keane, FAIA; Eggers and Higgins, Architects—Planners; New York, New York

GRAPHIC REPRODUCTION SYSTEMS

PROCESS	IMAGE	SHEET SIZE (INCHES)	MASTER COPY (cost)	FIRST COPY (cost)	ADDITIONAL COPIES (cost)	TRANSLUCENT	OPAQUE	PHOTOGRAPHS	ALL COLORS	MASTER COPY	SPECIAL COPY PAPER	ORDINARY COPY PAPER	SPEED (F.P.M. / C.P.M.)	FIRST COPY (SECONDS)	WIDTH	DEPTH	HEIGHT	REMARKS
BLUEPRINT	Negative	42″ x any			1								32 FPM		69	118	65	Various combinations of size and speed. Chemical spray, immersion, drying in developing process. Production of machines discontinued.
		54″ x any				●		●				●	45 FPM Maximums		81	118	65	
DIAZO MOIST	Positive	11″ x any			1.1	●		●				●	13 FPM		23	30	15	Developer a salt solution in water. Drying required. * 11″ wide for sheets automatically fed. Translucent or opaque copies.
		18″ x any											25 FPM		35	38	48	
		42″ x any											25 FPM		64	36	22	
		42″ x any											65 FPM		74	63	64	
DIAZO DRY	Positive	9″ x any			1.1	●		●				●	10 FPM		16	12	13	Ammonia developer. Translucent or opaque copies.
		18″ x any											60 FPM		44	44	57	
		47″ x any											9 FPM		61	9	9	
		42″ x any											40 FPM		74	63	74	
P.D. DIAZO	Positive	42″ x any			1.1	●		●				●	15 FPM		64	14	16	Metered amounts of activator. No vapors, seals, heat or drying
ELECTROSTATIC	Positive	9″ x 14″	Graduated 4.2 to .7			●	●	●	●		●		6 CPM	26		26	20	Reduction approx. 6%. Usually leased, not sold. (Xerox 813)
		8½″ x 14″	Graduated 2.75 to 1.65 *			●	●	●	●		●			12	26	26	20	1-1 Copy size ratio. * $60 monthly minimum. (Xerox 660)
		9″ x 14″	$25/mo. + 4 /copy			●	●	●	●			●	8 CPM	30	45	46	42	Flat bound material copied. (Xerox 914)
		11″ x 24″		3.5	3.5	●	●	●	●	●				6	15	28	15	Flat bound material copied.
		8½″ x 8½″ to 18″ x 60″				●	●						Sizes to 36″ x 120″					Copies on opaque or translucent stock. Reductions 100%, 95%, 75%, 62%, 50%, 45% of original size. (Xerox 1860) Equipment leased or repro. service at Xerox Service Center. Intermediates from prints or recall tracings of poor quality.
		8½″ x 11″				●	●					●	40 CPM					(Xerox 2400) Used with collator for rapid runs. Leased equipment or service at Xerox Service Center.
IMAGE DRAFTING SYSTEM	Positive	8½″ x 11″				●	●				●	●	2 CPM	60				Copies from a variety of originals on opaque or translucent stock and translucent stick-on film. Title blocks and "scissors drafting" (3M Models 570 and 71)
		11″ x 17″																
PHOTOCOPY — DIFFUSION	Positive / Negative	9″ x any	9.4	9.4	9.4	●	●		●	●	●		5 CPM	10	20	13	8	Flat bound material copied. Anken 950 M.
		14″ x 18″				●	●	●	●	●								Flat bed exposure unit. Carrying case and air pump available.
		11″ x 36″		8.5	8.5	●	●		●		●		7 CPM	10	14	19	8	
PHOTOCOPY — DYE TRANSFER	Positive	8½″ x 14″	7	8	10	●	●	●		●	●		7 CPM	35	18	27	11	Flat bound mat. copied w/flat bed exp. unit.
		11″ x 17″ *	7	8	10	●	●	●		●	●	●	7 CPM	40	15	24	22	Flat bound material copied. *8½″ x 14″ copy.
THERMAL	Positive	8½″ x any		4	4	●				●			12 CPM	4	12	17	5	Primary use - ready reference.
		10¾″ x 16¾″		9	4	●				●			3 CPM	12	26	21	13	
OFFSET	Positive	11″ x 14″		⅓ to ½		●	●	●		●		●	125 CPM		24	35		Masters of paper, plastics, or metal. Some machines make full color reproductions. Based on lithography.
		11″ x 17″					●	●		●		●	108 CPM		28	75		
		20″ x 24″					●	●		●			100 CPM		38	97		
STENCIL		9″ x 15″	7½	½ to 1½						●	●		200 CPM		20	37	19	Typewriter or stylus cut stencils and ink. Color selection.
		14″ x 18″	+labor							●	●		80 CPM		42	27	20	
		5″ x 3″								●	●				4	7	4	Postcard printer hand operated. Stencils same.
SPIRIT PROCESS		9″ x 14″	7½	¾ to 1¾						●	●		Hand crank		19	30	12	Ink transfer by pressure to back of master, to copy contact and chemical. Color selection.
		14″ x 18″	+labor										120 CPM		23	35	37	
STENCIL CUTTING MACHINE		9″ x 15″	28			●	●			●			5 Min.		16	25	9	Electronic stencil cutting from line originals.
SPIRIT MASTER MAKER		9″ x any	6			●	●			●			4 Seconds		18	12	6	Spirit masters from line originals.
MICROFILM																		Processor — camera: 72″ W x 34″ L x 61″ h. Reduces drawings up to 24″ x 36″ to microfilm mounted in aperture cards. Copies $.127 each. Reader — printer: Projects and prints image 18″ x 24″ @ $.03/s.f. Non-reading printers print copies 8½″ x 11″, 11″ x 17″, 18″ x 24″. (With stand)

NOTE:

This is a brief sampling of processes, sizes, and capacities. A variety of automatic folders, trimmers, perforators, stackers, collators, etc. are available with many of the machines.

Foster C. Parriott; James M. Hunter & Associates; Boulder, Colorado

DATA SOURCES AND ACKNOWLEDGMENTS

The list of individuals, partnerships, corporations, professional societies, and trade associations below have directly and indirectly contributed data that have been effectively utilized by plate contributors. Every effort has been made to acknowledge data sources and any omission has been inadvertent. To all we extend our thanks.

CHAPTER 1 GENERAL PLANNING AND DESIGN DATA

Amateur Athletic Union, Young Men's Christian Assn.
Amateur Fencers League of America
Amateur Trapshooting Assn.
American Badminton Assn.
American Fencing Rules and Manual (1965), Amateur Fencers League of America
American Insurance Assn.
Anderson, Warren, Perkins and Will Partnership
Assn. of American Railroads
Automobile Manufacturers Assn.

Basic Building Code, Building Officials and Code Administrators International
Boulder, Colo., Zoning Dept.
Brunswick-Balke-Collander (Brunswick Corp.)
Building Officials Conference of America
Building, Planning and Design Standards, Harold R. Sleeper, Wiley
Building Standards, Physical Plant Dept., University of Illinois

Chrysler Motors Corp.
Cushman Motors

Data Book for Civil Engineers: "Design," Elwyn E. Seelye, Wiley
Division for Girls and Women's Sports Guides (1968), American Assn. for Health, Phys. Ed. and Recreation, A Dept. of the National Education Assn.
Don Graf's Sheets, Reinhold
Downs, Aubrey L., Equestrian Consultant

Eberlin and Eberlin, Engineering Consultant
Eberlin, Ralph, Consultant
Elcona Homes Corp.
Eno Foundation for Highway Traffic Control

Federal Housing Administration, U.S. Dept. of Housing and Urban Development

General Motors Corp.
G. M. Ketcham Manufacturing Co.

Halasz, André, AIA (consultant, Architectural Graphics)
Harley-Davidson Motor Co.

International Conference of Building Officials

Kelley Co., Inc.

Liberty Homes Co., Inc.

Mobile Home Manufacturers Assn.

National Archery Assn.
National Building Code, American Insurance Assn.
National Collegiate Athletic Assn.
National Federation of State High School Athletic Assns.
National Fire Protection Assn.
National Horse Show Assn.
National Rifle Assn.
NCAA College Athletics Publishing Service Guidebook
New York State Council of Park and Outdoor Recreation
Novick, Leo A., Landscape Architect Consultant

Official Railway Equipment Register, Railway Equipment and Publishing Co.
Operations Council, American Trucking Assn., Inc.
Orchard Grove Mobile Home Park
Ostermayer, William H., Ballinger Co.
Outdoor Recreation for Physically Handicapped — A Handbook of Design Standards, New York State Dept. of Conservation

Planning Brunswick Bowling Centers, Brunswick Corp.
Price-Meyers Corp.

Rogers, Richard H.

Sasaki, Dawson, DeMay Assoc., Inc.
Schwinn Bicycle Co.
Sharp, J. Stanley, AIA, Design Data
Wilbur Smith and Assoc., Engineering Consultants
Southern Standard Building Code, Southern Building Code Congress
Sparkman and Stephens, Inc., Naval Architects
State Council of Parks and Outdoor Recreation

Theatres and Auditoriums, Burris-Meyer, H. and Cole, E. G., Reinhold
Time Saver Standards: A Handbook of Architectural Design, 4th ed. John Hancock Callender, Ed. Copyright 1966, McGraw-Hill, Inc. Used by permission of McGraw-Hill Book Co.
Truck Trailer Manufacturers Assn., Inc.

Uniform Building Code, International Conference of Building Officials
U.S. Dept. of Urban Development
U.S. Polo Assn.
U.S. Volleyball Assn.

Vaughan, Paul, AIA, Stair Data Consultant
Vendo Co.
Vermilya, Howard R., AIA; Plate 5. Material reprinted by permission from *Architectural Record,* Dec. 1962. Copyright, 1962 by McGraw-Hill, Inc., with all rights reserved.

Young Men's Christian Assn.
Yurchenco, Basil, AIA, Parking Facilities Consultant

CHAPTER 2 FOUNDATIONS AND SITEWORK

Aluminum Co. of America
American Assn. of Nurserymen, Inc.
American Concrete Institute
American Society for Testing Materials

Brick and Tile Service, Inc.

Civil Engineering Handbook, Urquhart
Concrete Information ST 46, Portland Cement Assn.
Concrete Masonry Retaining Walls, NCMA Tek 4 National Concrete Masonry Assn.
Concrete Reinforcing Steel Institute Design Handbook, Volume 11, Concrete Reinforcing Steel Institute
Coverstone, Dale, Lawn Equipment Consultant
Creative Playthings, Inc.

Decay and Termites, Publ. 448, National Academy of Sciences, National Research Council
Design of Concrete Pavements for City Streets, Portland Cement Assn.

Eberlin, Monroe M., Eberlin and Eberlin, Engineering Consultants
Engineers Collaborative

Form, Inc.

Michigan State Highway Dept.
Minimum Property Standards, Interim Review No. 30, Federal Housing Administration, U.S. Dept. of Housing and Urban Development
Miracle Equipment Co.

National Building Code, American Insurance Assn.

Niedermeyer-Martin Co.

Pile Foundations, Robert D. Chelus. Copyright by McGraw-Hill, Inc. Used by permission of McGraw-Hill Book Co.

Structural Clay Products Institute
Structural Engineering, PBSP 3475 IA, U.S. Government Services Administration

Time Savers Standards: A Handbook of Architectural Design, 4th ed., John Hancock Callender, Ed. Copyright 1966, McGraw-Hill, Inc. Used by permission of McGraw-Hill Book Co.

U.S. Dept. of Agriculture Publication B14
U.S. Dept. of the Navy Manual on Foundations, NavDocks DM-7

Weather Bureau, U.S. Dept. of Commerce

CHAPTER 3 CONCRETE CONSTRUCTION

American Concrete Institute
Architectural Concrete Consultants, Inc.
Architectural Concrete Institute
Architectural Index, Irvin J. Bell, Architectural Index

Concrete Products, Maclean-Hunter Publishing Corp.

"Data Sheets Estimating Guides for Floor Framing Systems," *Reinforced Concrete* Series 22, Portland Cement Assn.

Freyssenite Co. Inc.

Gates and Sons, Inc.

Kaiser Cement and Gypsum Corp.

Marsh, James, H., III, Texas A & M University
McQuarrie, John A., Professional Shoring Equipment Co.

Portland Cement Assn.
Prescon Corp. Publication WL-7-64-ZM

Schafer, Irvin Bruce, Precast Concrete Wall Units Consultant
Schokbeton, Buehner, Schokbeton Products, Inc.
Stressteel Corp. Publication 95-6

U.S. Steel Corp.

Wheeler, Walter, Wheeler and Tillitt, Inc., Consulting Engineers

CHAPTER 4 MASONRY CONSTRUCTION

Architects and Builder's Handbook, Kidder and Parker, Wiley
Architectural Construction, T. Crane, Wiley

BSI Stone Catalog, Building Stone Institute
Brick and Tile Engineering, H. C. Plummer, Ctructural Clay Products Institute

Federal Seaboard Terracotta Corp.

Georgia Marble Co.
Granite, Swenson, John Swenson Granite Co., Inc.

Indiana Limestone Co., Inc.

Marble Institute of America, Inc.
Mason's and Builder's Guide, Audel
Materials and Methods of Construction, Gay, Parker, MacGuire, Wiley
Morse, Richard A., AIA, Adobe Construction Consultant

National Concrete Masonry Assn. Tek 1, 2, 3, 5, and 6

Phillips Drill Co. Inc.
Pittsburgh Corning Corp.

Seelye, Elwyn E., Engineering Consultant
Steinhouse, Douglas S., AIA
Stone in Modular Building, Vickery Stone

Technical Notes on Brick and Tile Construction, Structural Clay Products Institute
"Tectum," ⓣ National Gypsum Co.

U.S. Dept. of Agriculture Bulletin 1720

CHAPTER **5** **METALS**

Aluminum Assn.
American Iron and Steel Institute
Architectural Metal Handbook, National Assn. of Architectural Metal Manufacturers

Fabricated Products Co., Inc.

Idependent Nail and Packing Co.

Jones and Laughlin Steel Corp.

Knape and Vogt Manufacturing Co.

Lawrence Metal Products, Inc.

Making, Shaping, and Treating of Steel, U.S. Steel Corp.
Manual of Steel Construction, American Institute of Steel Construction, Inc.
W. H. Maze Co.
Michel and Pfeffer, Metal Products Consultants

National Fire Protection Assn.

Penn Metal Co., Inc.
Phillips Drill Co.

Ramset Fastening System, Winchester-Western Division, Olin Mathieson Chemical Corp.
Rawlplug Co., Inc.
Ruco Division, Hooker Chemical Corp.
Ryerson, Inc.

Seelye, Elwyn E., Engineering Consultant
Seelye, Stevenson, Value, and Knecht, Engineering Consultants
Simplex Nails, Inc.
David Smith, Inc.

Timber Engineering Co.

Woven Wire Products Assn.

CHAPTER **6** **CARPENTRY**

American Hardboard Assn.
American Institute of Timber Construction
American Lumber Standards Committee, National Forest Products Assn.
American Plywood Assn.
Architectural Woodworking Institute
Arkansas Soft Pine Bureau

"Bestwall," ⓣ Gypsum Division, Georgia-Pacific
Brick and Tile Engineering, H. C. Plummer, Structural Clay Products Institute
Building Products Division, Johns-Manville Sales Corp.

California Redwood Assn.
Casement Details from Anderson Corp.
"Consoweld," ⓣ Consoweld Wood Product Co., Inc.
Copper and Brass Research Assn.

Dodge Cork Co.
Douglas Fir Plywood Assn.

Entec Products

Fay, Albert H., Mineral Fiber Products
Forest Products Division, Koppers Co., Inc.
"Formica," ⓣ Formica Corp.

Guide to Plywood Sheathing for Floors, Walls and Roofs, American Plywood Assn.

Hansen, Carl V., Truss Plate Institute
Hardwood Plywood Manufacturers Assn.

Insulation Board Institute

Line-A-Joist Data, Timber Engineering Co.

Manual for Housing Framing, National Forest Products Assn.
"Marlite" ⓣ Marsh Wall Products Division, Masonite Corp.
"Masonite," ⓣ Masonite Corp.
"Melamite," ⓣ Johns-Manville Corp.
Metal Tile Products
"Micarta," ⓣ Westinghouse Electric Corp.
Millwork, William B. Lloyd. Cahmers Publishing Co., Inc.

Minimum Property Standards, Federal Housing Administration, U.S. Dept. of Housing and Urban Development

National Design Specifications, National Forest Products Assn.
National Gypsum Co.
National Lumber Manufacturers Assn.
National Particle Board Assn.
"Nevamar," ⓣ Enjay Fibers and Laminates Co.
Nordholm, E., Kapp and Nordholm Co., Inc.
Northern Hardwood and Hemlock Manufacturers

Office of Technical Services, U.S. Dept. of Commerce

"Panelyte," ⓣ Thiokol Chemical Corp.
"Pionite," ⓣ Goodyear Tire and Rubber Co.
Pittsburgh Tile Co.
Plank-and-Beam System for Residential Construction, Housing and Home Finance Agency, U.S. Dept. of Housing and Urban Development
Plywood Fabricator Service, Inc.
Porcelain Enamel Products

Reliance Panelyte

Southern Pine Inspection Bureau

Technical Notes on Brick and Tile Construction, Structural Clay Products Institute
Technique of House Nailing, Housing and Home Finance Agency, U.S. Dept. of Housing and Urban Development
"Texolite," ⓣ U.S. Gypsum Co.
Timber Structure, Inc.
"Trip-L-Grip," ⓣ "Ty-Down" ⓣ Anchor, "Du-Al Clip," ⓣ Timber Engineering Co.

Unit Structures, Inc.
U.S. Gypsum Co.
U.S. Plywood Division, U.S. Plywood Champion Papers, Inc.
Upson Co.

Vinyl Plastics, Inc.
Vikon Tile Corp.

West Coast Lumber Inspection Bureau
Western Pine Assn.
Weyerhaeuser Co.
Wilkes, Joseph A., AIA, Wilkes and Faulkner
Wood Construction Data, National Forest Products Assn.
Wood Construction Data 4, National Lumber Manufacturers Assn.
Wood Products Division, Potlatch Forests, Inc.

CHAPTER **7** **THERMAL AND MOISTURE PROTECTION**

Aluminum Co. of America
Anaconda American Brass Co.
American Zinc Institute
Architectural Art Manufacturing Co.
Architectural Record (general reference), McGraw-Hill, Inc.
Architectural Sheet Metal Manual, Sheet Metal and Air Conditioning Contractors' National Assn.
ASHRAE Handbook of Fundamentals, American Society of Heating, Refrigeration and Airconditioning Engineers, Inc.

Berger Brothers Co.
Bilco Co.

Committee of Stainless Steel Producers, American Iron and Steel Institute
Concrete Construction, Concrete Constructions Inc.
Copper and Brass Research Assn.
Copper and Common Sense, Revere Copper and Brass, Inc.

Design of Insulated Buildings for Various Climates, Tyler Stewart Rogers, F. W. Dodge Corp., copyright 1951 by McGraw-Hill, Inc. with all rights reserved.

Enjay Chemical Co.

Fay, Albert H., Mineral Fiber Products
Fisher Skylights
Follansbee Steel Corp.

B. F. Goodrich Co.
Grefco, Inc.

W. P. Hickman Co., Inc.

International Nickel Co., Inc.

Johns-Manville Sales Corp.

Kimmell, G. Franklin, AIA, Roofing and Siding Consultant

Lamont and Riley, Inc.
Lead Industries Assn., Inc.
Lexsuco Inc.
Long Fir Gutter Co.

Loren Cook Co.
Ludowici-Celadon Co.

Manual on Steel Construction, American Institute of Steel Construction, Inc.
Manufacture, Selection and Application of Asphalt Roofing and Siding Products, Asphalt Roofing Manufacturers Assn.
Masbeta Corp.
Minimum Property Standards, Federal Housing Administration, U.S. Dept. of Housing and Urban Development
Minway Co., Inc.
Mississippi Glass Co.

National Bureau of Standards, U.S. Dept. of Commerce
National Gypsum Co.

Overly Manufacturing Co.

Philip Carey Manufacturing Co.
Progressive Architecture, March 1965, Reinhold

Reynolds Metal Co.
H. H. Robertson Co.

Stafford, Robert M., Flashing Consultant
Super Sky Products Inc.

Technical Information, Roof Drainage Manufacturers Institute
Technical Notes on Brick and Tile Construction, Structural Clay Products Institute
Turner Construction Co.

Underwriters Laboratories

Vermont Structural Slate Co., Inc.

Western Waterproofing Co., Inc.
Williams-Bermuda Corp.

CHAPTER **8** **CURTAIN WALLS, DOORS, WINDOWS, GLASS**

Allied Steel Products Division, Maizler Iron Works, Inc.
Aluminum Co. of America
American Abrasive Metals Co.
American Saint Gobain Corp.
Amweld Building Products, American Welding and Manufacturing Co.
Andersen Corp.
Anson and Gilkey Co.
Architectural Aluminum Manufacturers Assn.
Architectural Woodworking Institute
Atlantic Metal Products, Inc.

Bilco Co.
Julius Blum and Co., Inc.

Caradco, Inc.
Ceco Corp.
Commercial Standards 120–58, 171–58, U.S. Dept. of Commerce
Construction Specialties, Inc.
Construction Specification Institute
Corning Glass Works
Crane Fulview Glass Door Co.
Cupples Products Division, H. H. Robertson Co.
Curtis Companies, Inc.

General Bronze Corp.

Himmel Brothers Co.
Hope's Windows, Inc.

International Steel Co.
H. B. Ives Co.

Albert Kahn Associates, Architects and Engineers
Kawneer Co., Inc.
Koppers Co., Inc.
Koppes, Wayne F., AIA, Curtain Wall Consultant

Libbey-Owens-Ford Glass Co.
Lupton Manufacturing Co.

R. C. Mahon Co.
F. H. Maloney Co.
Malta Manufacturing Co.
Metal Curtain Wall Specifications Manual, National Association of Architectural Metal Manufacturers
Millwork, William B. Lloyd. Cahners Publishing Co., Inc.
Mississippi Glass Co.

National Assn. of Architectural Metal Manufacturers
National Builders Hardware Assn.
National Woodwork Manufacturers Assn., Inc.
New York Awning Co., Inc.
Northrop Architectural Systems, Northrop Corp.

Overhead Door Corp.

Overly Manufacturing Co.

Pemko Manufacturing Co.
Pioneer Fireproof Door, Co.
Pittsburgh Plate Glass Co.

Reese Metal Weatherstrip Co.
Republic Steel Manufacturing Division, Republic Steel Corp.
Reynolds Metal Co.
H. H. Robertson Co.
Rolscreen Co.
Rusco Division, Rusco Industries

Schacht Assoc., Inc.
Schwab Jalousie and Awning Co., Inc.
Steel Window Institute
Steelcraft Manufacturing Co.
Superior Fireproof Door and Sash Co. Inc.

Technical Committee, Steel Door Institute
Time Saver Standards, A Handbook of Architectural Design, 4th
  ed., John Hancock Callender, Ed. Copyright 1966 by McGraw-
  Hill, Inc. Used by permission of McGraw-Hill Book Co.
Trussbilt

Walcon Corp.
Williamsburg Steel Products Co.
Woodco Corp.

Zero Weatherstripping Co.

CHAPTER **9 FINISH MATERIALS**

American Terrazzo Strip Co., Inc.

B and T Metals Co.
Building Products Div., Armstrong Cork Co.

Contracting Plasters' and Lathers National Assn.

Diehl, John R., AIA, Plastering Consultant

Englebry, Carl, Plastering Consultant

Fantaci, Antony, Plastering Consultant
Ford, Jeremiah, III. AIA, Plastering Consultant

Gypsum Assn.

Inland-Ryerson Construction Products
Inland Steel Products Co.

Less Noise Better Hearing, The Celotex Corp.

Maple Flooring Manufacturers Assn.
Metal Lath Institute
Mosaic Tile Co.

National Forest Products Assn.
National Gypsum Co.
National Oak Flooring Manufacturers Assn.
National Terrazzo and Mosaic Assn., Inc.

Penn Metal Co., Inc.

Southern Pine Assn.
Walter Selck and Co.
Standard Specifications, Gypsum Wallboard Finishes, Gypsum
  Assn.
Structural Clay Products Institute
Superior Metal Trim, Youngstown Manufacturing, Inc.

Technical Data 1966–67, Floor Division, Armstrong Cork Co.
Tile Council of America, Inc.

U.S. Gypsum Co.

Western Wood Products Assn.

CHAPTERS **10/11 SPECIALTIES AND EQUIPMENT**

A.P.W. Products Co., Inc.
Accessory Specialties, Inc.
Amendola, Anthony J., Food Facilities Planning Consultant
American Insurance Assn.
Auth Electric Co., Inc.

Beneke Corp.
Building, Planning and Design Standards, H. R. Sleeper, Wiley

Canterbury Clocks
Cokesbury, Church Pews Consultant
Construction Products Co.
Cookson Co.
Cutler Mail Chute Co.

L. F. Dettenborn Woodworking Co.
Douglas Crestlyn International, Inc.
Dwyer Products Corp.

Educational Facilities Laboratories, Inc.

General Fire Extinguisher Corp.
Geneva Industries, Inc.
Gothic Craft, Church Pews Consultant
Grade-Aid Corp.

Holcomb & Hoke Manufacturing Co., Inc.
Horn Division, Brunswick Corp.
Hussey Manufacturing Co., Inc.

Jacobsen, Hugh Newell, AIA. Residential Kitchen Equipment
  Consultant

G. M. Ketcham Manufacturing Co.
Keystone Cabinet Co.
Knape and Vogt Manufacturing Co.
Kramer, Justin, Tower Clocks and Bells Consultant

F. H. Lawson Manufacturing Co.
Library Bureau, Remington Office Equipment, Sperry Rand Corp.
Linen Supply Assn. of America

Odell MacConnel Assn., Education Planning Consultants
Maintowoc Church Furniture Co.
Marble Institute of America
Masonite Corp.
Metal Compartments Assn.
Metropolitan Wire Goods Corp.
Miami Carey Division, Philip Carey Manufacturing Co.
Herman Miller, Inc.
Milo Products
Murphy-in-A-Door
Modernfold Doors, Inc.

Nelson Adams Co.
New Holland Church Furniture Co.

Ossit Church Furniture Co.

Charles Parker Co.
Perey Manufacturing Co., Inc.
Perkins and Will Partnership
Physical Planning, C22-6820-7, International Business Machines
  Corp.
Physical Property Division, San Francisco Unified School District
Plaza Towel Holder Co.
Post Office Publications 16, 17 and 55, U.S. Post Office Dept.

Reliable Metal Products Co., Inc.
Reserv-A-Roll Co.
Rothschild, Bernard B., FAIA, Commercial Kitchen Equipment
  Consultant

St. Charles Corp.
L. L. Sams and Sons, Church Pews Consultant
Scott Paper Co.
John E. Sjostrom Co.
C. D. Sparling Co.

Torjesen, Inc.
Turney Wood Products, Inc.

Unistrut Corp.

I. T. Verdin Co.
Voorhis-Trebout Co., Inc.

Wayne Iron Works
Wilkinson Chutes, Inc.
John W. Winterich and Assoc.
World Dryer Corp.

CHAPTER **12 FURNISHINGS**

Admiral Corp.
American Athletic Equipment Co.
American Seating Co.
Architectural Pottery
Art Metal, Inc.
Atelier International, Ltd.

Ward Bennett Designs
Brickel Associates, Inc.

Children's Workbench
C. G. Conn Ltd.
Corry Jamestown Corp.
Cumberland Furniture Corp.

Design Group
A. B. Dick Co.
Dunbar Furniture Corp.

Eastman Kodak Co.
Encyclopedia of Sports, A. S. Barnes Co. (General Reference)

General Fireproofing Co.
General Sportscraft Co., Ltd.
Graber Manufacturing Co.

Habitat, Inc.
Hammond Organ Co.
Hanseatic Furniture Co.
Fritz Hansen, Inc.
Holland Shade Co.
Horn Bostel and Bennett
Howe Folding Furniture, Inc.
Hugh Action Design, Burke Division, Brunswick Corp.

International Contract Furnishings, Inc.
Intrex, Inc.

JG Furniture Co. Inc.

Keuffel and Esser Co.

Georg Jensen, Inc.

Kirsch Co.
Knoll Associates, Inc.
Kreuger Metal Products Co.

Laverne International, Ltd.
Lehigh Furniture Corp.
Lightolier, Inc.
Luggage and Leather Goods Manufacturers of America
Luxo Lamp Corp.

Herman Miller, Inc.
Motorola, Inc.

Nessen Lamps, Inc.

Oriental Rugs in Colour, Preben Liebertrau, Copyright 1962,
  MacMillan and Co.

Peabody Seating Co.
Plan Hold Corp.
Harvey Probber, Inc.

Radiant Corp.
Remington Rand Office System Division, Rand Corp.
Jens Risom Design, Inc.
Roffman Associates, Inc.

Simon Ventilighter Co., Inc.
Sony Corp. of America
System Division, Sperry Rand Corp.
Steelcase, Inc.
Stendig, Inc.
Stow/Davis Furniture Co.

Thonet Industries, Inc.
"Thru-Vu" ™ Vertical Blind Corp.
Vogel-Peterson Co.

Welsh Co.
Wurlitzer Co.

Zenith Sales Corp.
Zographos Designs Ltd.

CHAPTER **13 ASSEMBLED CONSTRUCTION**

AAU and NCAA Guide, 1966, Amateur Athletic Union and National
  Collegiate Athletic Assn.
Acorn Fireplace
Acoustical Materials Assn.
American Institute of Steel Construction, Inc.
American Insurance Assn.
American Plywood Assn.
Architectural Systems Division, Westinghouse Electric Corp.
Armstrong Industrial Insulation, Armstrong Cork Co.

Basics of Sound Control, U.S. Gypsum Co.
Bessler Disappearing Stair Co.
BIF Division, Air Brake Co.
Butcher Boy Refrigerator Door Co.

Caradco Inc.
Celotex Corp.
Chester Swimming Pools
C. Plank Co.

Demarest, William, Fireplaces Consultant
Diebold, Inc.
Donley Brothers Co.
Duvinage Corp.

Elgin Softener Corp.

Federation Internationale de Natation Amateur
"Fire Circle," ™ Fireplace, Hanova, Inc.
"Firemite" ™ Fireplace, Northwest Tube and Metal Fabricators

Flexicore Co.
Florida Hurricane Reports, 1961 and 1965, Army Corps of Engineers, U.S. Dept. of Defense
"Franklyn Heater-Fireplace,"℗ Washington Stove Works

Granco Steel Products, Inc.

"Haydite,"℗ Buffalo Haydite Division, J. P. Burroughs

Inland Steel Co.

Journal of the Acoustical Society of America (Sound Control Reference)

Landon, Inc.

Manual of Burglary Insurance, National Bureau of Casualty Insurance
Merchandise Vaults and Safes, American Insurance Assn.
"Met-L-Strut,"℗ Unistrut Corp.
Morse Boulger Inc.
Mosler Safe Co.

National Assn. of Architectural Metal Manufacturers

Official Handbook Amateur Athletic Union, 1966

Paddock of California, Inc.
Paragon Swimming Pool Co.
"Porex,"℗ Concrete Plank Co.
Portland Cement Assn.
Precision Parts Corp.

George Rackle and Sons
H. H. Robertson Co.
"Rooftite,"℗ (Reference Whitley)
Ruco Division, Hooker Chemical Corp.

Sears, Roebuck and Co.
Scholz, Don, Fireplaces Consultant
T. J. Schultz, Bolt Beranek and Newman
Smith, R. Jackson, AIA, Eggers and Higgins
Structural Clay Products Institute
Swan Manufacturing Co.
Swimquip, Inc.

Tate Architectural Products, Inc.
"Tectum,"℗ National Gypsum Co.
Trends in Swimming Pool Design, Maryland Health Dept.
"Tufcor,"℗ Granco Steel

Underwriters Laboratories
Undilla Co.
U.S. Dept. of the Navy, NavDocks P-355.
U.S. Gypsum Co.

Waegemann, A. E., Swimming Pools Consultant
Washington Stoveworks, Fireplaces Consultants
Wheeling Corrugating Co.
Whitley, Frederic N., Fireplaces Consultant

CHAPTER 14 ELEVATORS AND CONVEYING SYSTEMS

Ball Engineering Co.
Building, Planning and Design Standards, Harold Sleeper, Wiley

Economy Engineering Co.
Elevator Division, Dover Corp.

Fosburg, P. L., Elevator Division, Westinghouse Electric Corp.

Albert Kahn and Assoc., Architects

Lamson Division, Diebold, Inc.

Matot Elevator Co.

Otis Elevator Co.

Potts Ash Hoist Corp.

Robbins and Myers, Inc.

Sedgwick Elevator Co.
Standard Conveyor Co.

U.S. Post Office Dept.

CHAPTER 15/16 MECHANICAL/ELECTRICAL

American Society of Mechanical Engineers
American Standards Assn.
American Standard Plumbing and Heating Division, American Radiator and Standard Sanitary Corp.
American Telephone and Telegraph Co.
Anemostat Corp.
ASHRAE Guide and Data Book, American Society of Heating, Refrigeration and Airconditioning Engineers
ASHRAE Handbook of Fundamentals 1967, American Society of Heating, Refrigeration and Airconditioning Engineers

Barber-Colman Co.
Blonder Tongue Laboratories, Inc.
Bradley Washfountain Co.

Carrier Corp.
Commercial Standard, 88–66, U.S. Dept. of Commerce
Condensation Control in Dwelling Construction, Federal Housing Administration, U.S. Dept. of Housing and Urban Development
Crane Co.

Dunham-Bush, Inc.

Elective Comfort Conditioning Journal, Electric Information Publications, Inc. (General Reference)
Environmental Products Division, International Telephone and Telegraph Corp.

General Electric Co.
General Telephone and Electronics Corp.

Haws Drinking Faucet Co.

The Ideal Fitter, American Radiator and Standard Sanitary Corp.

Kohler of Kohler, Kohler Co.

Lighting Handbook, Illuminating Engineering Society

McGuinness, W. J., Mechanical/Electrical Consultant
Mongitore and Moesel, Consulting Engineers

National Gypsum Co.
National Plumbing Code Illustrated, Manas Publications (Plumbing Symbols)
National Wiring Bureau
N. Electric Co.
J. J. Nesbitt, Inc.

Permutit Corp.
Plastic Piping Handbook, Plastic Division, Cabot Corp.
Plumbing Fixtures for Educational Facilities, Stanford University
Practical Builder Product Data File, Cahmers Publishing Co.

Simplified Practice Recommendations 25 and R8-47, U.S. Dept. of Commerce
Southern Standard Building Code, 1958
Sylvania Electric Products Inc.

Triangle Corp.

USA Standards Institute publications Y 32.9-1962, Z 32.2.3-1949, and A 40.8-1955

Walker-Parkersburg Division, Textron, Inc.
Westinghouse Electric Corp.

APPENDIX CONVENTIONS, GRAPHICAL CONSTRUCTIONS, AND MATHEMATICAL DATA

A. B. Dick Co.
Architects and Builders' Handbook, Kidder-Parker, Wiley
Architectural Metal Handbook, National Assn. of Architectural Metal Manufacturers

Baxter, H. E., Perspective Consultant
Bradley, Prentice, FAIA, Modular Coordination Consultant
Brick Engineering Handbook of Design, Structural Clay Products Institute
Charles Bruning Co.

Design: Data Book for Civil Engineers, Elwyn E. Seelye, Wiley

Eberlin, Monroe, Eberlin and Eberlin, Consulting Engineers
Eugene Dietzgen Co.

Forest Service, Forest Products Laboratory, U.S. Dept. of Agriculture

Gestetner Corp.
Graphic Systems Division, 3M Business Products Sales, Inc.

Halasz, André, AIA, Areas, Volumes and Geometric Constructions Consultant

Manual of Steel Construction, American Institute of Steel Construction, Inc.
Modern Office Procedures, Copyright Industrial Publishing Co.
Modular Building Standards Assn.
Modular Drafting Manual, Division of Building Research, National Research Council, Ottawa, Canada
Modular Practice, Modular Building Standards Assn., Wiley

Partition Handbook, Edwin M. Lurie, Metal Lath Institute
Portland Cement Assn.

Lynn Smith and Assoc.
Standard Duplicating, Moeline Corp.

Tarapata-MacMahon Assoc.
Tile Engineering Handbook of Design, Harry C. Plummer and E. F. Wanner, Structural Clay Products Institute

USA Standards Institute

Wood Structural Design Data, National Forest Products Assn.

Xerox Corp.

INDEX